LIGHTING HANDBOOK

REFERENCE & APPLICATION

Illuminating Engineering Society of North America (IESNA)

IESNA is the recognized technical authority for the illumination field. For over 80 years its objective has been to communicate information on all aspects of good lighting practice to its members and to the lighting community and consumers through a variety of programs, publications and services. The strength of IESNA is its diversified membership: engineers, architects, designers, educators, students, contractors, distributors, utility personnel, manufacturers and scientists, all *contributing to* and *benefiting from* the Society.

IESNA is a forum for exchange of ideas and information and a vehicle for its members' professional development and recognition. Through its technical committees, with hundreds of qualified members from the lighting community, the IES correlates vast amounts of research, investigations and discussions to guide lighting experts and laymen on research- and consensus-based lighting recommendations. Complete lists of current and available recommendations may be obtained by writing to the IESNA Publications Office.

In addition to the IESNA *Lighting Handbook*, the IESNA publishes *Lighting Design + Application (LD + A)* and the *Journal of the Illuminating Engineering Society* (JIES) as the official magazines of the Society. *LD + A* is a popular application-oriented monthly magazine. Every issue contains special feature articles and news of practical and innovative lighting layouts, systems, equipment and economics, and news of the industry and its people. The *Journal*, a more technical publication, contains technically oriented papers, articles, American National Standards, IESNA recommended practices and other committee reports.

The Society also publishes nearly 100 varied publications (including: education courses; educational video tapes; IESNA technical committee reports covering many specific lighting applications; forms and guides used for measuring and reporting lighting values, lighting calculations, performance of light sources and luminaires, energy management, etc; and the *IESNA Ready Reference*, a condensed lighting manual). The *IESNA Lighting Library*, a complete reference package encompassing all essential IESNA documents, is also available along with a yearly updating service.

The Society has two types of membership: individual and sustaining. Applications and current dues schedules are available upon request from the Membership Department. IESNA local, regional and transnational meetings, conferences, symposiums, seminars, workshops and lighting exhibitions provide current information on the latest developments in illumination. IESNA has a strong education program with basic and intermediate level courses offered through its Sections, leading to a Technical Knowledge Examination (TKE) opportunity. Successful examinees are awarded the Society's Certificate of Technical Knowledge (CTK). In addition, there is an introductory general lighting course as well as a fundamental course specifically for roadway lighting interests. The Society also offers academic programs to assist in faculty development and continuing education for teachers through its annual workshops program, fundamental and advanced sessions, for professional educators. Information about these programs may be obtained by contacting the Educational/Technical Department at the IESNA office.

8TH EDITION

LIGHTING HANDBOOK

REFERENCE & APPLICATION

MARK S. REA, Ph.D. FIES
EDITOR-IN-CHIEF
RENSSELAER POLYTECHNIC INSTITUTE

ILLUMINATING ENGINEERING SOCIETY OF NORTH AMERICA
NEW YORK

Managing Editor: Judith Block
Production Manager: Judith Block
Editorial Assistant: John Bullough
Copyeditor: Joseph C. Fineman
Illustrators: Bruce Kaiser and DeWitt Gorman
Indexer: Robert J. Richardson
Typesetting and graphics: Science Typographers, Inc.
Marketing: Beth Bay
Cover design: Tony Picco

LIGHTING HANDBOOK, Eighth Edition

ISBN 0-87995-102-8

Library of Congress Catalog Card Number: 93-78569

Printed in the United States of America.

The Illuminating Engineering Society of North America welcomes your comments. Please send all correspondence to:

Publications Department
IESNA
120 Wall Street, 17th Floor
New York, NY 10005

Contents

Preface

The purpose of any handbook is to provide a specialist in one field, or a specialist in a closely related discipline, with easy access to technical information. Lighting is an unusual field because of the diversity of thought and activities undertaken by the technical specialists within it. Business people, scientists, engineers, architects and designers of all types participate in this special field we call lighting. A handbook on lighting is therefore essential as a bridge from one perspective to the many others that constitute the field of lighting. The purpose of the 1993 *Lighting Handbook*, as well as previous editions, is to serve as that bridge.

Previous editions of the IES *Lighting Handbook* have been edited by IESNA staff. John Kaufman, Technical Director of the IESNA for many years and editor of the most recent editions of the IES *Lighting Handbook*, retired in 1992. In response to this transition, Society President Jerry White, President-elect Russ Churchill, Executive Vice President Bill Hanley, and the remaining members of the IESNA Board of Directors decided in consulation with the Society's Handbook Committee, chaired by Tom Lemons, that this edition of the *Lighting Handbook* should be produced under contract by an outside agency. The Lighting Research Center at Rensselaer Polytechnic Institute responded to their request for proposal and was awarded the contract to produce this edition in one year.

To produce the *Lighting Handbook* in one year, it was necessary to develop and execute a complex plan of action that required expertise from writers, artists, copyeditors, indexers, typesetters and printers, as well as from the various lighting experts that make up the IESNA committees. Further, sophisticated electronic communications techniques as well as old-fashioned, face-to-face diplomacy were required to bring this large project to completion within the specified time frame. This complex plan was handled largely by Judith Block who served as Managing Editor for this edition of the *Lighting Handbook*. Without her experience and personal grace this edition could not have been produced with this quality in the short time frame available.

Four Topic Editors, David DiLaura, Roger Knott, Alan Lewis, and Sandra Stashik, each prominent leaders in the lighting community, were also engaged to assist in bringing this volume to completion. The primary role of the Topic Editors was to work with designated IESNA committee chairs to provide the source materials for the revised chapters. In fact, the various committees were the main sources of technical information, and without their hard work and cooperation with the Topic Editors, the Handbook could not have been produced at all.

In August 1992 the four Topic Editors, along with Beth Bay, John Bullough, Mary Ellen Frier, Rita Harrold, Jerry Irvine, John Kaufman, Rick Mistrick, and Pamela Schemenaur convened with Judith Block and myself in a retreat setting on the shores of Lake George in upstate New York to structure the organization of the new Handbook and to begin to assemble its various chapters. At that retreat and throughout the winter of 1992–1993, the chapters were configured and edited. Many new sections were also written by several members of the retreat. Mary Ellen Frier deserves special mention because of her efforts in preparing several new chapters for this edition. In addition to the IESNA committees and the members of the retreat, Peter Boyce, Christopher Cuttle, Naomi Miller, Janet Moyer, Carl Pechman, Pamela Schemenaur, Steven Treado and Robert Wolsey prepared new text for this edition; their contributions are gratefully acknowledged since they did so largely on their own time. The new materials and those supplied by the IESNA committees evolved into the thirty-four chapters which follow.

Perhaps the greatest pleasure in working on this large project was getting to know the fine people who make up the IESNA. The breadth and depth of of experience in this diverse field called "lighting" is a true marvel. What is more, despite the wide variety of attitudes and personalities, everyone cooperated to the fullest to make this edition of the *Lighting Handbook* a reality for our Society. In particular, Rita Harrold, Director, Educational and Technical Development, was invaluable for her enthusiastic facilitation of the project to completion. It was a true honor to serve as editor-in-chief for this edition, and an experience that makes me proud to be a member of the IESNA.

Mark S. Rea, Ph.D., FIES

Foreword

The Illuminating Engineering Society was founded in 1906, but it was not until 1947 that the First Edition of the Handbook appeared, thus representing the accumulation of 41 years of lighting progress since the Society's founding. It was produced by "a highly qualified group of over 100 contributing specialists—engineers, architects, physicists, decorators, artists and opthamologists—who worked for more than two years under the direction of a special committee of the Society and a full time editorial staff to provide the most complete coverage of the field possible within the limits of a conveniently sized volume." (*Preface, First Edition*).

Since that auspicious beginning with the First Edition, the Society has published Editions two through five, in 1952, 1959, 1966 and 1972, respectively, followed by separate volumes—Application in 1981 and 1987 and Reference in 1981 and 1984, and a return to a single Handbook with this Eighth Edition.

Frequency of publication has provided up-to-date coverage of lighting developments, evaluation and interpretation of technical and research findings and their application guidelines.

Just as was stated in the 1947 First Edition, the 1993 editorial team has taken every precaution to secure broad knowledge of all phases of lighting and has demonstrated the integration of views of specialists in each knowledge area.

In the Eighth Edition there are new chapters on such diverse topics as energy concerns, maintenance, light source technology, environmental issues such as lighting and air pollution and ballast disposal, the lighting design process, and much more.

A new center section, a special reference section, not only provides useful calculation procedures and examples in one place in the book, but also serves to bridge the technical data from the application guidelines to facilitate use of the book.

Over three times the number of contributing specialists were involved in the development of this Handbook compared to the 1947 Edition. Today's subjects are more diverse and complex and our interested, willing volunteers more numerous from among the 10,000 members.

The professional edit team brought talent and discipline to the process, which has been invaluable. Dr. Mark Rea, Judith Block and John Bullough of Rensselaer Polytechnic Institute, together with the four Topic Editors, David DiLaura, Roger Knott, Dr. Alan Lewis and Sandra Stashik, deserve our full appreciation for their contributions in evaluating, editing and, where necessary, developing material.

The Society is successful only because of the contribution of its members. Without the Society's committees and their efforts, this Handbook could not have been published. IESNA is indebted to its committees, who have worked so diligently to develop the content of this Handbook. It has been an exciting and exacting task. The experience has been rewarding for all who have had the opportunity to share in the commitment and enjoyed the opportunity of working with such dedicated professionals. To see the project come to such a successful completion gives a great feeling of accomplishment. The first and final thanks go to each of the Committee contributors, too many to name individually, who made this Handbook possible. Each joins a distinguished list of contributors, who over 46 years, since 1947, have been responsible for all of the Handbooks.

Dissemination of knowledge is what the Society is all about. The Handbook represents the most important vehicle to that end. As a reference tool it is matchless. Contained in one publication is the information that the lighting professional finds useful to provide new knowledge, verify that which is known, or refresh that which has been misplaced in memory. It is our hope that this Eighth Edition will be your, the reader's, principal source of lighting information.

William H. Hanley
Executive Vice President

Rita M. Harrold
Director, Educational and
Technical Development

Acknowledgments

We acknowledge the four Topic Editors

> David DiLaura, Lighting Technologies, Inc.
> Roger Knott, HWH Architects, Engineers, Planners
> Alan Lewis, Ferris State University
> Sandra Stashik, Grenald Associates, Ltd.

who reviewed, edited and developed material for this Eighth Edition of the *Lighting Handbook*. Each oversaw the revision of several chapters and served as the liaison between the editorial staff and the committees.

We acknowledge the following committees and committee chairs for their efforts on behalf of this revision of the Handbook:

Aviation: Michael L. Borta, Chair
Calculation Procedures: Richard G. Mistrick, Chair
Color: Wolfgang Walter, Ph.D., Chair
Computer: Richard V. Heinisch, Chair
Daylighting: Mojtaba Navvab, Chair
Design Process: Tony Novo, Chair
Emergency Lighting: Mary Kim Reitterer, Chair
Energy Management: James M. Yorgey, Chair
Financial Facilities: Hyman M. Kaplan, Chair
Health Care Facilities: Edward J. Sherman, Chair
Hospitality Facilities: Candace M. Kling, Chair
Houses of Worship: Viggo B. Rambusch, Chair
Industrial: Paul F. Lienesch, Chair
Landscape, Interior and Exterior:
    Janet L. Moyer, Chair
Light Control and Luminaire Design:
    Thomas M. Lemons, Chair
Light Sources: William M. Keeffe, Chair
Lighting Economics: M. Clay Belcher, Chair
Maintenance: Norma Frank, Chair

Marine Lighting: Michael J. Leite, Chair
Museum and Art Gallery: Frank A. Florentine, Chair
Nomenclature:
    Robert A. Levin, Ph.D., P.E., FIES, Chair
Office Lighting: Mitchell B. Kohn, Chair
Photobiology: George C. Brainard, Ph.D., Chair
Psychological Aspects of Lighting: Dale K. Tiller, Chair
Quality and Quantity of Illumination:
    Theodore Ake, Chair
Residence: Jane S. Grosslight, Chair
Retail Areas: Allan Ullman, Chair
Roadway: Edward C. Rowsell, Chair
School and College: Shail Mahanti, Chair
Sports and Recreational Areas:
    Robert D. Mosier, Chair
Sports Lighting Handbook Subcommittee:
    William Tao, Chair
Theatre, Television and Film:
    Joseph M. Good, III, Chair

Contributing individuals, in alphabetical order:

Robert Allen, J. Del Armstrong, Helge Austad, Felix Barker, Bernie Bauer, Beth Bay, Richard Beckford, Sam Berman, Peter Boyce, Tom Bullpit, Randy Burkett, Joseph Ceterski, Nancy Clanton, Richard Collins, Christopher Cuttle, Robert G. Davis, Pierrette Dayhaw-Barker, David H. Epley, Larry French, Mary Ellen Frier, Philip Gabriel, Pekka Hakkarainen, Rita M. Harrold, Kevin Heslin, Michael Holick, Jerry Irvine, Mark Jongewaard, John Kaufman, Randall King, Richard Kiss, Stephen Klibansky, Frank LaGiusa, Ian Lewin, Joanne Lindsley, Russ Little, James Love, Catherine Luo, Craig McCarter, James McCormick, Greg McKee, Naomi Johnson Miller, Warwick Morison, Janet Lennox Moyer, Joseph Murdoch, Martin Needleman, C. T. Oakes, Carl Pechman, Patricia A. Pitzer, Robert Prouse, David Ranieri, Alan Robertson, Frederick Ruberg, Daymond Ryer, Robert Saunders, Pamela Schemenaur, Billy Lee Shelby, Greg Shick, Donald Smith, Kendric Smith, Theodore Tibbitts, Steven Treado, William Venable, Rudy Verderber, Rupert Wentz, and Robert Wolsey.

The Science of Lighting

I

Light and Optics

1

FUNDAMENTALS

For illuminating engineering purposes, the Illuminating Engineering Society of North America (IESNA) has defined light as radiant energy that is capable of exciting the human retina and creating a visual sensation.

As a physical quantity, light is defined in terms of its relative efficiency throughout the electromagnetic spectrum lying between 380 and 770 nm. Visually, there is some individual variation in efficiency within these limits.

Theories

Several theories describing light have been advanced.[1-4] They are briefly discussed below.

Corpuscular Theory. The theory advocated by Newton, based on these premises:

1. That luminous bodies emit radiant energy in particles.
2. That these particles are intermittently ejected in straight lines.
3. That the particles act on the retina, stimulating a response that produces a visual sensation.

Wave Theory. The theory advocated by Huygens, based on these premises:

1. That light results from the molecular vibration in the luminous material.
2. That vibrations are transmitted through an "ether" as wavelike movements (comparable to ripples in water).
3. That the vibrations thus transmitted act on the retina, stimulating a response that produces a visual sensation.

Electromagnetic Theory.[5] The theory advanced by Maxwell, based on these premises:

1. That luminous bodies emit light in the form of radiant energy.

2. That this radiant energy is propagated in the form of electromagnetic waves.
3. That the electromagnetic waves act upon the retina, stimulating a response that produces a visual sensation.

Quantum Theory. A modern form of the corpuscular theory advanced by Planck, based on these premises:

1. That energy is emitted and absorbed in discrete quanta (photons).
2. That the magnitude of each quantum is determined by the product of h and ν, where h is 6.626×10^{-34} J · s (Planck's constant), and ν is the frequency of the photon vibration in Hz.

Unified Theory. The theory proposed by De Broglie and Heisenberg and based on these premises:

1. Every moving element of mass has associated with it a wave whose length is given by the equation

$$\nu = h/mv \qquad (1\text{-}1)$$

where

ν = wavelength of the wave motion,
h = Planck's constant,
m = mass of the particle,
v = velocity of the particle.

2. It is impossible to simultaneously determine all of the properties that are distinctive of a wave or a corpuscle.

The quantum and electromagnetic wave theories provide an explanation of those characteristics of radiant energy of concern to the illuminating engineer. Whether light is thought of as wavelike or photonlike in nature, it is radiation that is produced by electronic processes in the most exact sense of the term. It is produced in an incandescent body, a gas discharge or a solid-state device, by excited electrons just having reverted to more stable positions in their atoms, releasing energy.

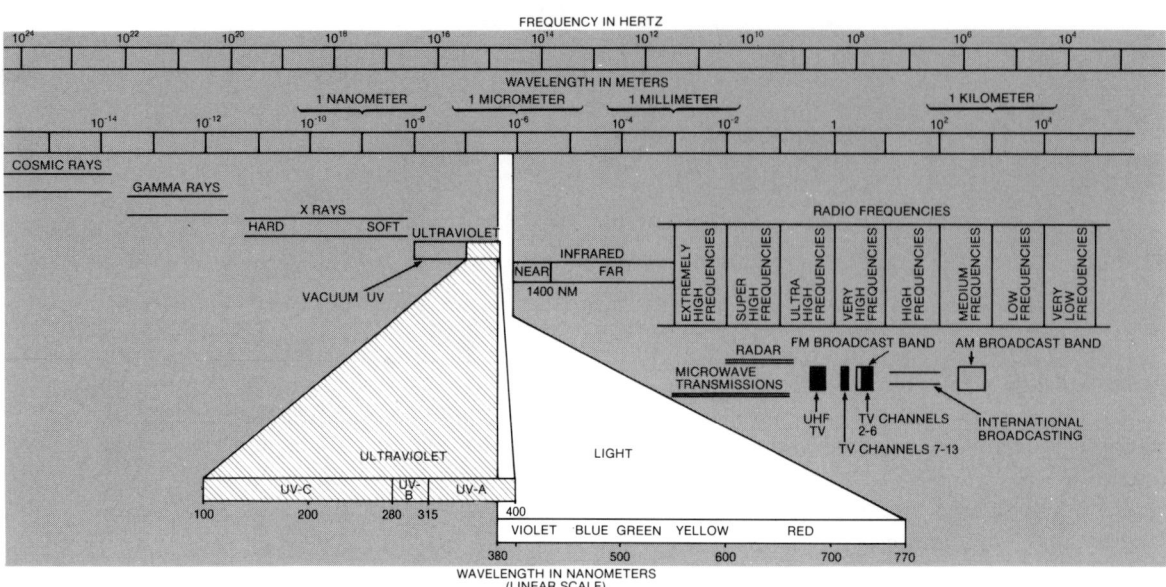

Fig. 1-1. The radiant energy (electromagnetic) spectrum.

Light and the Energy Spectrum[6]

The wave theory permits a convenient graphical representation of radiant energy in an orderly arrangement according to its wavelength or frequency. This arrangement is called a *spectrum* (see figure 1-1). It is useful in indicating the relationship between various radiant energy wavelength regions. Such a graphical representation should not be construed to indicate that each region of the spectrum is divided from the others in any physical way whatsoever. Actually there is a gradual transition from one region to another. The radiant energy spectrum extends over a range of wavelengths from 10^{-16} to 10^5 m. The Angstrom unit (Å), the nanometer (nm) and the micrometer (μm), which are respectively 10^{-10}, 10^{-9} and 10^{-6} m, are commonly used units of length in the visible spectrum region. The nanometer is the preferred unit.

Of particular importance to illuminating engineering are three regions of the electromagnetic spectrum: ultraviolet, visible and infrared. On the basis of practical applications and the effect obtained, the ultraviolet (UV) region is divided into the following bands (for engineering purposes, the "black light" region extends slightly into the visible portion of the spectrum):

Ozone-producing	180–220 nm
Bactericidal (germicidal)	220–300 nm
Erythemal	280–320 nm
"Black light"	300–400 nm

Another division of the ultraviolet spectrum, often used by photobiologists, is given by the Commission

Internationale de l'Éclairage (CIE):

UV-A	315–400 nm
UV-B	280–315 nm
UV-C	100–280 nm

Radiant energy in the visible spectrum lies between 380 and 770 nm. Most of the discussion in this Handbook deals with radiant energy in this portion of the spectrum.

For practical purposes, infrared radiant energy is within the wavelength range of 770 to 10^6 nm. This band is arbitrarily divided as follows:

Near (short wavelength) infrared	770–1,400 nm
Far (long wavelength) infrared	1,400–1,000,000 nm

In general, unlike ultraviolet energy, infrared energy is not evaluated on a wavelength basis but rather in terms of all such energy incident upon a surface. Examples of these applications are industrial heating, drying, baking and photoreproduction. However, some applications, such as infrared viewing devices, involve detectors sensitive to a restricted range of wavelengths; in such cases the spectral characteristics of the source and receiver are of importance.

All forms of radiant energy are transmitted at the same speed in vacuum (299,793 km/s, or 186,282 mi/s). However, each form differs in wavelength and thus in frequency. The wavelength and velocity may be altered by the medium through which it passes, but the frequency remains constant independent of the

Fig. 1-2. Speed of Light for a Wavelength of 589 nm (Na D-lines)

Medium	Speed (meters per second)
Vacuum	2.99793×10^8
Air (760 mm at 0°C)	2.99724×10^8
Crown Glass	1.98223×10^8
Water	2.24915×10^8

medium. Thus, through the equation

$$\text{velocity} = \frac{\lambda \nu}{n} \qquad (1\text{-}2)$$

where

n = index of refraction of the medium,
λ = wavelength in a vacuum,
ν = frequency in Hz,

it is possible to determine the velocity of radiant energy and also to indicate the relationship between frequency and wavelength. Figure 1-2 gives the speed of light in different media for a frequency corresponding to a wavelength of 589 nm in air.

Blackbody Radiation

A blackbody radiator is one whose intensity and spectral properties are dependent solely upon its temperature. In practice a blackbody radiator may be closely approximated by the radiant power emitted from a small aperture in an enclosure, the walls of which are maintained at a uniform temperature (see figure 1-3).

Emitted light from a practical light source, particularly from an incandescent lamp, is often described by comparison with that from a blackbody radiator. In theory, all of the energy emitted by the walls of the blackbody radiator is eventually reabsorbed by the walls; that is, none escapes from the enclosure. Thus, a blackbody will, for the same area, radiate more total power and more power at a given wavelength than any other light source operating at the same temperature.

From 1948 to 1979 the luminance of a blackbody operated at the temperature of freezing platinum was used as an international reference standard for maintaining the unit of luminous intensity. Specifically, it has a luminance of 60 cd/m². Since operating and

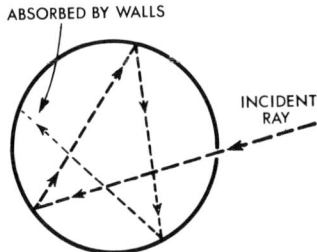

Fig. 1-3. Small aperture in an enclosure exhibits blackbody characteristics.

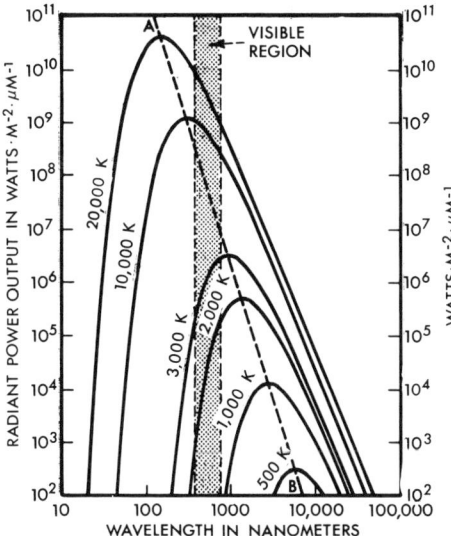

Fig. 1-4. Blackbody radiation curves for operating temperatures between 500 and 20,000 K, showing Wien displacement of peaks. The shaded area is the region of visible wavelengths.

maintaining a blackbody radiator at the freezing point of platinum is a major undertaking, a new definition of the candela was adopted in 1979. The candela is now, essentially, the luminous intensity of a 555.016-nm source whose radiant intensity is $\frac{1}{683}$ W/sr. The new photometric standard is based upon an electrical standard, the watt, which is precisely and easily measurable with an electrically calibrated radiometer. A further advantage of this definition is that the measured candela can now be conveniently linked to the lumen, which is the basic unit for photometry.

Planck Radiation Law. Data describing blackbody radiation curves were obtained by Lummer and Pringsheim using a specially constructed and uniformly heated tube as the source. Planck, introducing the concept of discrete quanta of energy, developed an equation depicting these curves. It gives the spectral radiance of a blackbody as a function of the wavelength and temperature. See the definition of Planck's radiation law in the Glossary.

Figure 1-4 shows the spectral radiance of a blackbody as a function of wavelength for several values of absolute temperature, plotted on a logarithmic scale.

Wien Radiation Law. In the temperature range of incandescent filament lamps (2000–3400 K) and in the visible wavelength region (380–770 nm), a simplification of the Planck equation, known as the Wien radiation law, gives a good representation of the blackbody distribution of spectral radiance. See the Glossary.

Wien Displacement Law. This gives the relation between blackbody distributions for various temperatures. (See line AB in figure 1-4, and the Glossary.)

Stefan-Boltzmann Law. This law, obtained by integrating Planck's expression for L_λ from zero to infinity, states that the total radiant power per unit area of a blackbody varies as the fourth power of the absolute temperature. See the Glossary.

It should be noted that this law applies to the total power, that is, the whole spectrum. It cannot be used to estimate the power in the visible portion of the spectrum alone.

Spectral Emissivity

No known radiator has the same emissive power as a blackbody. The ratio of the output of a radiator at any wavelength to that of a blackbody at the same temperature and the same wavelength is known as the *spectral emissivity*, $\epsilon(\lambda)$, of the radiator.

Graybody Radiation

When the spectral emissivity is constant for all wavelengths, the radiator is known as a graybody. No known radiator has a constant spectral emissivity for all visible, infrared and ultraviolet wavelengths, but in the visible region a carbon filament exhibits very nearly uniform emissivity, that is, it is nearly a graybody.

Selective Radiators

The emissivity of all known material varies with wavelength. Therefore, they are called selective radiators. In figure 1-5 the radiation curves for a blackbody, a graybody and a selective radiator (tungsten), all operating at 3000 K, are plotted on the same logarithmic scale to show the characteristic differences in output.

Radiation Equations. When spectral-total directional emissivity is introduced as a multiplier in the Planck radiation law and the Wien radiation law equations,

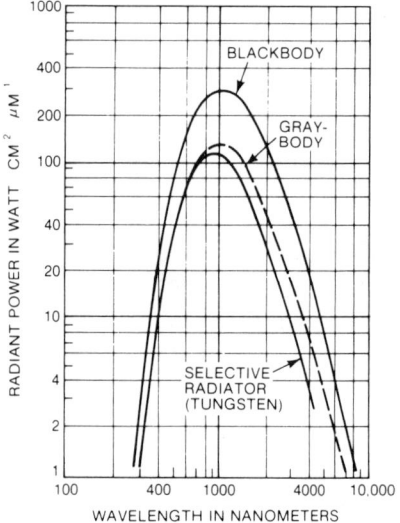

Fig. 1-5. Radiation curves for blackbody, graybody and selective radiators operating at 3000 K.

and spectral-total hemispherical emissivity is used as a multiplier in the Stefan-Boltzman law equation, those equations become applicable to any incandescent source.

Color Temperature

The radiation characteristics of a blackbody of unknown area may be specified with the aid of the above equations by fixing only two quantities: the magnitude of the radiation at any given wavelength and the absolute temperature. The same type of specification may be used with reasonable accuracy in the visible region of the spectrum for tungsten filaments and other incandescent sources. However, the temperature used in the case of selective radiators is not that of the filament but a value called the *color temperature*.

The color temperature of a selective radiator is that temperature at which a blackbody would have to be operated in order for its output to be the closest possible approximation to a perfect color match with the output of the selective radiator (see chapter 4, Color). While the match is never perfect, the small deviations that occur in the case of incandescent filament lamps are not of practical importance.

The apertures between coils of the filaments used in many tungsten lamps act somewhat as a blackbody because of the interreflections which occur at the inner surfaces of the helix formed by the coil. For this reason the distribution from coiled filaments exhibits a combination of the characteristics of the straight filament and of a blackbody operating at the same temperature.

The application of the color temperature method to deduce the spectral distribution from other than incandescent sources even in the visible region of the spectrum will usually result in appreciable error. Color temperature values associated with light sources other than incandescent are *correlated color temperatures* and not true color temperatures (see chapter 5, Color).

Atomic Structure and Radiation

The atomic theories first proposed by Rutherford and Bohr in 1913 have since been expanded upon and confirmed by an overwhelming amount of experimental evidence. They hypothesize that each atom in reality resembles a minute solar system, such as that shown in figure 1-6.

The *atom* consists of a central nucleus possessing a positive charge $+n$, about which revolve n negatively charged electrons. In the normal state these electrons remain in particular orbits, or *energy levels*, and radiation is not emitted by the atom.

The *orbit* described by a particular electron rotating about the nucleus is determined by the energy of that electron. That is to say, there is a particular energy associated with each orbit. The system of orbits or

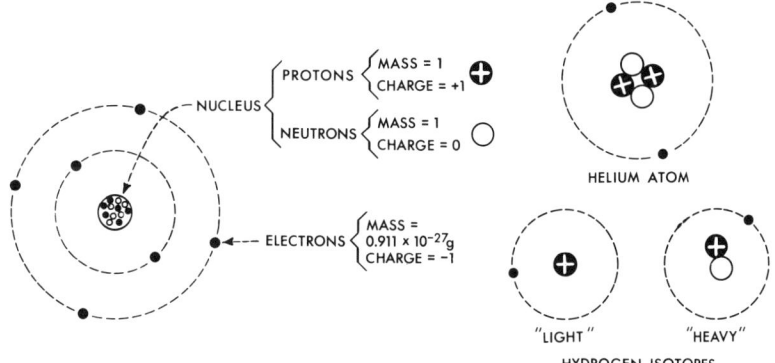

Fig. 1-6. Schematic structure of the atom, showing electron orbits around a central nucleus. Hydrogen and helium atoms are the simplest of all atomic structures.

energy levels is characteristic of each element and remains stable unless disturbed by external forces.

The *electrons* of an atom can be divided into two classes. The first includes the inner shell electrons, which are not readily removed or excited except by high-energy radiation. The second class includes the outer shell (valence) electrons, which cause chemical bonding into molecules. Valence electrons are readily excited by ultraviolet or visible radiation or by electron impact and can be removed completely with relative ease. The valence electrons of an atom in a solid, when removed from their associated nuclei, enter the so-called conduction band and confer on the solid the property of electrical conductivity.

Upon the absorption of sufficient energy by an atom in the gaseous state, the valence electron is pushed to a higher energy level further from the nucleus. Eventually, the electron returns to the normal orbit, or an intermediate one, and in so doing the energy that the atom loses is emitted as a quantum of radiation. The wavelength of the radiation is determined by Planck's formula:

$$E_2 - E_1 = h\nu_{21} \quad (1\text{-}3)$$

where

E_2 = energy associated with the excited orbit,
E_1 = energy associated with the normal orbit,
h = Planck's constant,
ν_{21} = frequency of the emitted radiation as the electron moves from level 2 to level 1.

This formula can be converted to a more usable form:

$$\text{wavelength} = \frac{1239.76}{V_d} \text{ nm} \quad (1\text{-}4)$$

where

V_d = potential difference in volts between two energy levels through which the displaced electron has fallen in one transition.

Luminous Flux and the Lumen[7,8]

Of particular importance to illuminating engineering is the lumen. The goal of this section is to show how electric power of radiant flux (in watts) is converted into luminous flux (in lumens), and to describe the underlying rationale for this process. The lumen is, in fact, a unit relating radiant flux (in watts) to visually effective light for a standard human observer.

Two kinds of radiant power are important to consider, because there are two classes of photoreceptors in the human eye, rods and cones. The *photopic function* V_λ describes the spectral luminous efficiency function for photopic (cone) vision, and the *scotopic function* V_λ' describes the spectral luminous efficiency for scotopic (rod) vision. See figures 1-7 and 1-8.

The photopic luminous efficiency function was established in 1924 by a committee of the Commission Internationale de l'Éclairage (CIE) and is based upon data from several experimenters using different techniques. The two primary techniques used were flicker photometry and step-by-step heterochromatic brightness matching.

Flicker photometry is the least variable technique for determining the photopic spectral efficiency function. With this technique, two lights are seen alternately in rapid succession. The radiance of one light, called the standard, is held constant while the radiance of the other light, which is monochromatic and whose wavelength is called the test wavelength, is varied to the point where minimum flicker is perceived. At this point the luminance of both lights is defined to be the equal. Each test wavelength is compared with the standard light in this way, and the reciprocal of the radiance needed to match the standard light is defined as the unit value of the photopic function ($V_\lambda = 1$).

In heterochromatic brightness matching a standard light of constant radiance is juxtaposed with a test wavelength having variable radiance. The subject simply adjusts the radiance of the test wavelength until it appears to be equal in brightness to the standard. This

Fig. 1-7. Photopic Spectral Luminous Efficiency, $V(\lambda)$. (Unity at wavelength of maximum luminous efficiency)

Wavelength λ (nanometers)	Standard Values	Values Interpolated at Intervals of One Nanometer								
		1	2	3	4	5	6	7	8	9
380	0.00004	0.000045	0.000049	0.000054	0.000058	0.000064	0.000071	0.000080	0.000090	0.000104
390	.00012	.000138	.000155	.000173	.000193	.000215	.000241	.000272	.000308	.000350
400	.0004	.00045	.00049	.00054	.00059	.00064	.00071	.00080	.00090	.00104
410	.0012	.00138	.00156	.00174	.00195	.00218	.00244	.00274	.00310	.00352
420	.0040	.00455	.00515	.00581	.00651	.00726	.00806	.00889	.00976	.01066
430	.0116	.01257	.01358	.01463	.01571	.01684	.01800	.01920	.02043	.02170
440	.023	.0243	.0257	.0270	.0284	.0298	.0313	.0329	.0345	.0362
450	.038	.0399	.0418	.0438	.0459	.0480	.0502	.0525	.0549	.0574
460	.060	.0627	.0654	.0681	.0709	.0739	.0769	.0802	.0836	.0872
470	.091	.0950	.0992	.1035	.1080	.1126	.1175	.1225	.1278	.1333
480	.139	.1448	.1507	.1567	.1629	.1693	.1761	.1833	.1909	.1991
490	.208	.2173	.2270	.2371	.2476	.2586	.2701	.2823	.2951	.3087
500	.323	.3382	.3544	.3714	.3890	.4073	.4259	.4450	.4642	.4836
510	.503	.5229	.5436	.5648	.5865	.6082	.6299	.6511	.6717	.6914
520	.710	.7277	.7449	.7615	.7776	.7932	.8082	.8225	.8363	.8495
530	.862	.8739	.8851	.8956	.9056	.9149	.9238	.9320	.9398	.9471
540	.954	.9604	.9661	.9713	.9760	.9803	.9840	.9873	.9902	.9928
550	.995	.9969	.9983	.9994	1.0000	1.0002	1.0001	.9995	.9984	.9969
560	.995	.9926	.9898	.9865	.9828	.9786	.9741	.9691	.9638	.9581
570	.952	.9455	.9386	.9312	.9235	.9154	.9069	.8981	.8890	.8796
580	.870	.8600	.8496	.8388	.8277	.8163	.8046	.7928	.7809	.7690
590	.757	.7449	.7327	.7202	.7076	.6949	.6822	.6694	.6565	.6437
600	.631	.6182	.6054	.5926	.5797	.5668	.5539	.5410	.5282	.5156
610	.503	.4905	.4781	.4568	.4535	.4412	.4291	.4170	.4049	.3929
620	.381	.3690	.3570	.3449	.3329	.3210	.3092	.2977	.2864	.2755
630	.265	.2548	.2450	.2354	.2261	.2170	.2082	.1996	.1912	.1830
640	.175	.1672	.1596	.1523	.1452	.1382	.1316	.1251	.1188	.1128
650	.107	.1014	.0961	.0910	.0862	.0816	.0771	.0729	.0688	.0648
660	.061	.0574	.0539	.0506	.0475	.0446	.0418	.0391	.0366	.0343
670	.032	.0299	.0280	.0263	.0247	.0232	.0219	.0206	.0194	.0182
680	.017	.01585	.01477	.01376	.01281	.01192	.01108	.01030	.00956	.00886
690	.0082	.00759	.00705	.00656	.00612	.00572	.00536	.00503	.00471	.00440
700	.0041	.00381	.00355	.00332	.00310	.00291	.00273	.00256	.00241	.00225
710	.0021	.001954	.001821	.001699	.001587	.001483	.001387	.001297	.001212	.001130
720	.00105	.000975	.000907	.000845	.000788	.000736	.000688	.000644	.000601	.000560
730	.00052	.000482	.000447	.000415	.000387	.000360	.000335	.000313	.000291	.000270
740	.00025	.000231	.000214	.000198	.000185	.000172	.000160	.000149	.000139	.000130
750	.00012	.000111	.000103	.000096	.000090	.000084	.000078	.000074	.000069	.000064
760	.00006	.000056	.000052	.000048	.000045	.000042	.000039	.000037	.000035	.000032

Fig. 1-8. Scotopic Spectral Luminous Efficiency, $V'(\lambda)$. (Unity at wavelength of maximum luminous efficiency)

Wavelength λ (nanometers)	Relative Value	Wavelength λ (nanometers)	Relative Value
380	0.000589	590	0.0655
390	.002209	600	.03315
400	.00929	610	.01593
410	.03484	620	.00737
420	.0966	630	.003335
430	.1998	640	.001497
440	.3281	650	.000677
450	.455	660	.0003129
460	.567	670	.0001480
470	.676	680	.0000715
480	.793	690	.00003533
490	.904	700	.00001780
500	.982	710	.00000914
510	.997	720	.00000478
520	.935	730	.000002546
530	.811	740	.000001379
540	.650	750	.000000760
550	.481	760	.000000425
560	.3288	770	.0000002413
570	.2076	780	.0000001390
580	.1212		

technique is highly variable and produces results very different from flicker photometry unless the spectral difference between the test wavelength and the standard light is small. To obtain useful results, then, the standard light must be different for different regions of the spectrum. Since the standard test changes across the spectrum, this method is known as the step-by-step heterochromatic brightness matching technique.

Several consistent experimental conditions were used in these early experiments. The test fields were small, usually less than 2° across, the luminance was fairly low due to light source limitations, and a natural pupil was used by the subjects during testing. Gibson and Tyndall[8] pieced together results from several experiments and recommended a particular spectral luminous efficiency function for the photopic (cone) system, which was approved by a committee of the CIE in 1924.

Modification to the CIE 1924 curve followed, based upon work by Judd in 1951. The 1924 curve was shown to be inadequate in describing visual sensitivity in the short-wavelength region of the visible spectrum. Since not all test fields of interest to experimentalists were 2° or less, a standard function for a 10° field was devised in 1964, which shows a still greater influence of the short-wavelength cones on the photopic curve.

In 1951 the CIE also established a scotopic luminous efficiency function based upon the heterochromatic brightness matching technique (not step by step). Each wavelength was compared with a large, approximately 20°, "white" test field with a luminance of approximately 0.00003 cd/m². The field was also viewed by subjects after an extended period in the dark using natural pupils.

It is important to point out that everyone in the previous studies was *color normal*. A small percentage of the population (approximately 8%, and mostly males) do not have all three cone photopigments or do not have the same ones as color-normal people. The photopic spectral luminous efficiency curves will be different for these people, since the cone photopigments determine the shape and amplitudes of these curves.

Luminous Efficacy of Light Sources

The luminous efficacy of a light source is defined as the ratio of the total luminous flux (in lumens) to the total power input (in watts or equivalent).

Rods and cones are not equally sensitive to radiant energy, and it is necessary to establish a scaling factor for the photopic and for the scotopic spectral luminous efficiency functions. Therefore, the number of photopic lumens (F) or of scotopic lumens (F') must be determined from the luminous *efficacy* of the light source:

$$F = 683 \sum_{380}^{770} P_\lambda V_\lambda \, \Delta \lambda \qquad (1\text{-}5)$$

where

P_λ = spectral power, in watts, of the source at the wavelength λ,

V_λ = photopic luminous efficiency function value at λ,

Δ_λ = interval over which values of the spectral power were measured,

and

$$F' = 1700 \sum_{300}^{770} P_\lambda V'_\lambda \, \Delta \lambda \qquad (1\text{-}6)$$

where

V'_λ = scotopic luminous efficiency function value at λ.

The maximum luminous efficacy of an *ideal* white source, defined as a radiator with constant output over

the visible part of the spectrum and no radiation in other parts, is approximately 220 lm/W.

LIGHT GENERATION

Natural Phenomena

Sunlight. Energy of color temperature about 6500 K is received from the sun at the outside of the earth's atmosphere at an average rate of about 1350 W/m².[9] About 75% of this energy reaches the earth's surface at sea level (on the equator) on a clear day.

The average luminance of the sun is approximately 1600 Mcd/m² viewed from sea level. The illuminance on the earth's surface by the sun may exceed 100 klx (10,000 fc); on cloudy days the illuminance drops to less than 10 klx (1000 fc). See chapter 8, Daylighting.

Sky Light. A considerable amount of light is scattered in all directions by the earth's atmosphere. The investigations of Rayleigh first showed that this was a true scattering effect. On theoretical grounds the scattering should vary inversely as the fourth power of the wavelength when the size of the scattering particles is small compared to the wavelength of light, as in the case of the air molecules themselves. The blue color of a clear sky and the reddish appearance of the rising or setting sun are common examples of this scattering effect. If the scattering particles are relatively large (the water droplets in a cloud, for example), scattering is essentially the same for all wavelengths (clouds appear white). The scattered light from parts of the sky is partially polarized, up to 50%.

Moonlight. The moon shines purely by virtue of its ability to reflect sunlight. Since the reflectance of its surface is rather low, its luminance is only about 2500 cd/m². Illumination of the earth's surface by the moon may be as high as 0.1 lx (0.01 fc).

Lightning. Lightning is a meteorological phenomenon arising from the accumulation, in the formation of clouds, of tremendous electrical charges, usually positive, which are suddenly released in a spark discharge. The lightning spectrum corresponds closely to that of an ordinary spark in air, consisting principally of nitrogen bands, though hydrogen lines may sometimes appear owing to dissociation of water vapor.

Aurora Borealis (Northern Lights) and Aurora Australis (Southern Lights). These hazy patches or bands of greenish light, on which white, pink or red streamers sometimes are superposed, appear 100–200 km (60–120 mi) above the earth. They are caused by electron streams spiraling into the atmosphere, primarily at polar latitudes. Some of the lines in their spectra have been identified with transitions of valence electrons from metastable states of oxygen and nitrogen atoms.

Bioluminescence. "Living light" is a form of chemiluminescence in which special compounds manufactured by plants and animals are oxidized, producing light. The light-producing compounds are not always required to be in a living organism. Many bioluminescent compounds can be dried and stored many years, and then upon exposure to oxygen, or some other catalyst, emit light.

Fabricated Sources

Historically, light sources have been divided into two types, incandescent and luminescent. Fundamentally, the cause of light emission is the same, that is, electronic transitions from higher to lower energy states. The mode of electron excitation is different, however, as well as the spectral distribution of the radiation. Incandescent solid substances emit a continuous spectrum, while gaseous discharges radiate mainly in discrete spectral lines. There is some overlap, however. Incandescent rare-earth elements can emit discrete spectra, whereas high-pressure discharges produce a continuous spectrum.

The two classical types, with subdivisions showing associated devices or processes, are listed as follows (see also chapter 6, Light Sources):

1. Incandescence
   (a) Filament lamps
   (b) Pyroluminescence (flames)
   (c) Candoluminescence (gas mantle)
   (d) Carbon arc radiation
2. Luminescence
   (a) Photoluminescence
      (1) Gaseous discharges
      (2) Fluorescence
      (3) Phosphorescence
      (4) Lasers
   (b) Electroluminescence
      (1) Electroluminescent lamps (ac capacitive)
      (2) Light-emitting diodes
      (3) Cathodoluminescence (electron excitation)
   (c) Miscellaneous luminescence phenomena
      (1) Galvanoluminescence (chemical)
      (2) Crystalloluminescence (crystallization)
      (3) Chemiluminescence (oxidation)
      (4) Thermoluminescence (heat)
      (5) Triboluminescence (friction or fracture)
      (6) Sonoluminescence (ultrasonics)
      (7) Radioluminescence (α, β, γ, and X rays)

INCANDESCENCE

Incandescent Filament Lamps

All familiar physical objects are combinations of chemically identifiable molecules, which in turn are made up of atoms. In solid materials the molecules are packed together and the substances hold their shape over a wide range of physical conditions. In contrast, the molecules of a gas are highly mobile and occupy only a small part of the space filled by the gas.

Molecules of both gases and solids are constantly in motion at temperatures above absolute zero (0 K or $-273°C$) and their movement is a function of temperature. If the solid or gas is hot, the molecules move rapidly; if it is cold, they move more slowly.

At temperatures below about 873 K (600°C) only invisible energy of the longer infrared (heat) wavelengths is emitted by any body—a coal stove or an electric iron, for example. Electronic transitions in atoms and molecules at temperatures of about 600°C result in the release of visible radiation along with the heat.

The incandescence of a lamp filament is caused by the heating action of an electric current. This heating action raises the filament temperature substantially above 600°C, producing light.

Pyroluminescence (Flame Luminescence)

A flame is the most often noted visible evidence of combustion. Flame light may be due to recombination of ions to form molecules, reflection from solid particles in the flame, incandescence of carbon or other solid particles, or any combination of these.

The combustion process is a high-temperature energy exchange between highly excited molecules and atoms. The process releases and radiates energy, some of which is in that portion of the electromagnetic spectrum called light. The quality and the amount of light generated depend upon the material undergoing combustion. For example, a flashbulb containing zirconium yields the equivalent of 56 lm/W, whereas an acetylene flame yields 0.2 lm/W.

Candoluminescence (Gas Mantle)

Incandescence is exhibited by heated bodies which give off shorter-wavelength radiation than would be expected according to the radiation laws, because of fluorescence excited by incandescent radiation. Materials producing such emission include zinc oxide, as well as rare-earth elements (cerium, thorium) used in the Welsbach gas mantle.

Carbon Arc Radiation

A carbon arc source radiates because of incandescence of the electrodes and because of luminescence of vaporized electrode material and other constituents of the surrounding gaseous atmosphere. Considerable spread in the luminance, total radiation and spectral power distribution may be achieved by varying the electrode materials.

LUMINESCENCE[10-14]

Radiation from luminescent sources results from the excitation of single valence electrons of an atom, either in a gaseous state, where each atom is free from interference from its neighbors, or in a crystalline solid or organic molecule, where the action of its neighbors exerts a marked effect. In the first case line spectra, such as those of mercury or sodium arcs, result. In the second case narrow emission bands, which cover a portion of the spectrum (usually in the visible region) result. Both of these cases contrast with the radiation from incandescent sources, where the irregular excitation at high temperature of the free electrons of innumerable atoms gives rise to all wavelengths of radiation to form a continuous spectrum of radiation, as discussed in the section on Blackbody Radiation.

Photoluminescence

Gaseous Discharge. Radiation, including light, can be produced by gaseous discharges as discussed above and previously under Atomic Structure and Radiation. A typical mechanism for generating light (photons) from a gaseous discharge (such as in a fluorescent lamp) is described below. See figure 1-9.

1. A free electron emitted from the cathode collides with one of the two valence electrons of a mercury atom and excites it by imparting to it part of the kinetic energy of the moving electron, thus raising the valence electron from its normal energy level to a higher one.

2. The conduction electron loses speed in the impact and changes direction, but continues along the tube to excite or ionize one or more additional atoms before losing its energy stepwise and completing its path. It generally ends at the wall of the tube, where it recombines with an ionized atom. A part of the electron current is collected at the anode.

3. Conduction electrons, either from the cathode or formed by collision processes, gain energy from the electric field, thus maintaining the discharge along the length of the tube.

4. After a short delay the valence electron returns to its normal energy level, either in a single transition or by a series of steps from one excited level to a lower level. At each of these steps a photon (quantum of radiant energy) is emitted. If the electron returns to its normal energy level in a single transition the emitted radiation is called *resonance* radiation. See figure 1-10.

5. In some cases (as in the high-pressure sodium lamp) a portion of the resonance radiation is self-absorbed by the gas of the discharge before it leaves the discharge envelope. The absorbed energy is then reradiated as a continuum on either side of the resonant wavelength, leaving a depressed or dark region at that point in the spectrum.

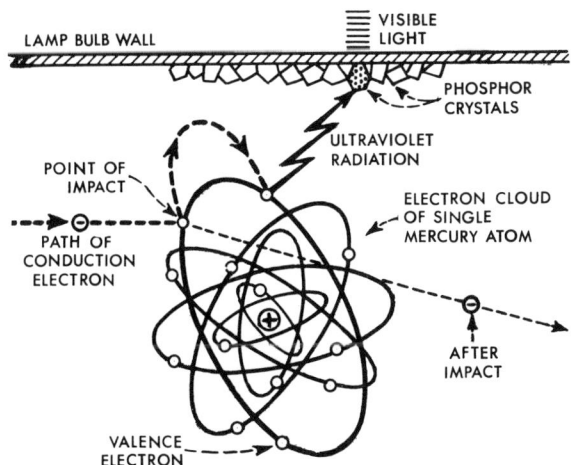

Fig. 1-9. Magnified cross section of a fluorescent lamp, schematically showing progressive steps in the luminescent process which finally result in the release of visible light.

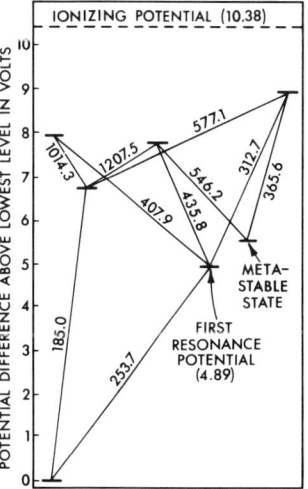

Fig. 1-10. Simplified energy diagram for mercury, showing a few of the characteristic spectral lines.

Fluorescence. In the fluorescent lamp and in the fluorescent mercury lamp, ultraviolet radiation resulting from luminescence of the mercury vapor due to a gas discharge is converted into visible light by a phosphor coating on the inside of the tube or outer jacket. If this emission continues only during the excitation, it is called *fluorescence*. Figure 1-9 shows schematically a greatly magnified section of a part of a fluorescent lamp.

The phosphors used in fluorescent lamps are crystalline inorganic compounds, of exceptionally high chemical purity and of controlled composition, to which small quantities of other substances (the activators) have been added to convert them into efficient fluorescent materials. By choice of the right combination of activator and inorganic compound, the color of the emission can be controlled. A typical schematic model for a phosphor is given in figure 1-11, and an energy diagram for a typical phosphor is shown in figure 1-12. In the normal state the electron oscillates about position *A* on the energy curve in figure 1-12, as the lattice expands and contracts due to thermal vibration. For the phosphor to emit light it must first absorb radiation. In the fluorescent lamp this is chiefly that at 253.7 nm, while in the mercury lamp it may be ultraviolet radiation of this and longer wavelengths generated in the arc. The absorbed energy transfers the electron to an excited state at position *B*. After loss of excess energy to the lattice as vibrational energy (heat), the electron again oscillates around a stable position *C* for a very short time, after which it returns to position *D* on the normal energy curve, with simultaneous emission of a photon of radiation. Stokes' law, stating that the radiation emitted must be of longer wavelength than that absorbed, is readily explained by this model. It then returns to *A* with a further loss of energy as heat and is ready for another cycle of excitation and emission.

Because of the oscillation around both stable positions *A* and *C*, the excitation and emission processes cover ranges of wavelength, commonly referred to as *bands*.

In some phosphors two activators are present. One of these, the primary activator, determines the absorption characteristics and can be used alone, as it also gives emission. The other, the secondary activator,

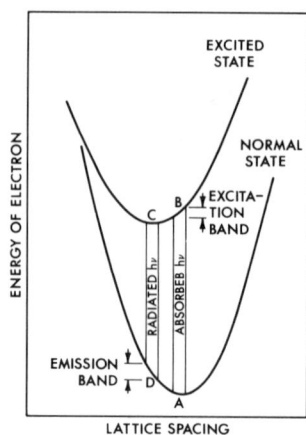

Fig. 1-12. Simplified energy diagram for a typical phosphor.

does not enter into the absorption mechanism but receives its energy by transfer within the crystal from a neighboring primary activator. The emitted light from the secondary activator is longer in wavelength than that from the primary activator. The relative amount of emission from the two activators is determined by the concentration of the secondary activator. The phosphors now used in most "white" fluorescent lamps are doubly activated calcium halophosphate phosphors. However, in the newer high-CRI, high-performance lamps, these phosphors are supplemented by rare-earth-activated phosphors.

Figure 1-13 shows the characteristic colors and uses of phosphors currently employed in the manufacture of fluorescent lamps. Figure 1-14 gives the characteristics of some phosphors useful in fluorescent-mercury lamps.

Impurities other than activators and excessive amounts of activators have a serious deleterious effect on the efficiency of a phosphor.[14]

Phosphorescence.[12-14] In some fluorescent materials, electrons can be trapped in metastable excited states, for a time varying from milliseconds to days. After release from these states they emit light. This phenomenon is called *phosphorescence*. The metastable states lie slightly below the usual excited states responsible for fluorescence, and energy—usually derived from heat—is required to transfer the electron from the metastable state to the emitting state. Since the same emitting state is usually involved, the color of fluorescence and phosphorescence is generally the same for a given phosphor. In doubly activated phosphors the secondary activator phosphoresces longer than the primary activator, so the color changes with time.

Short-duration phosphorescence is important in fluorescent lamps in reducing the stroboscopic effect in alternating-current operation.

Phosphors activated by infrared radiation have an unusual type of phosphorescence. After excitation they show phosphorescence, which becomes invisible in a

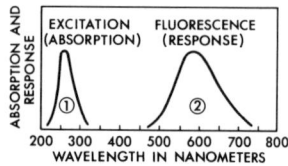

Fig. 1-11. Fluorescence curve of a typical phosphor, showing initial excitation by ultraviolet rays and subsequent release of visible radiation.

Fig. 1-13. Color Characteristics of Important Fluorescent Lamp Phosphors

Material	Activator	Peak of Fluorescent Band*	Color of Fluorescence
Calcium phosphate	Thallium	310	Ultraviolet
Barium disilicate	Lead	355	Pale blue
Barium strontium magnesium silicate	Lead	370	Pale blue
Calcium tungstate	Lead	440	Blue
Strontium chloroapotite	Europium	445	Blue
Barium magnesium aluminate	Europium	450	Blue
Strontium pyrophosphate	Tin	470	Blue
Magnesium tungstate	None	480	Blue white
Calcium halophosphate	Antimony	480	Blue white
Barium titanium phosphate	Titanium	490	Blue green
Zinc silicate	Manganese	520	Green
Cerium terbium magnesium aluminate	Terbium	545	Green
Calcium halophosphate	Antimony and manganese	590	White to yellow
Calcium silicate	Lead and manganese	610	Pink
Yttrium oxide	Europium	612	Orange red
Cadmium borate	Manganese	615	Pink
Strontium magnesium phosphate	Tin	620	Pink
Calcium strontium phosphate	Tin	640	Pink
Magnesium fluorogermanate	Manganese	660	Red
Lithium pentaaluminate	Iron	743	Infrared

* Wavelength in nanometers

few seconds. However, they retain a considerable amount of energy trapped in metastable states, which can be released as visible light by infrared radiation of the proper wavelength.

Solid Laser.[15-17] A *laser* is defined by its component letters as a light source in which there is *l*ight *a*mplification by *s*timulated *e*mission of *r*adiation. However, there are other characteristics of laser light which are of major interest to illuminating engineers. In addition to amplifying light, lasers produce intense, highly monochromatic, well-collimated, coherent light.

Coherent light consists of radiation whose waves are in phase with regard to time and space. Ordinary light, although it may contain a finite proportion of coherent light, is incoherent because the atomic processes that cause its emission occur in a random fashion. In a laser, however, electronic transitions are triggered (stimulated) by a wave of the same frequency as the emitted light instead of occurring at random. As a consequence, a beam of light is emitted, all of whose waves are in phase and of the same frequency.

A prerequisite to laser action is a pumping process whereby an upper and a lower electron level in the active material undergo a population inversion. The pumping source may be a light, as in a ruby laser, or electronic excitation, as in a gas laser.

The choice of laser materials is quite limited. First, it must be possible to highly populate an upper electronic level; second, there must be a light-emitting transition from this upper level with a long lifetime; and third, a lower level must exist which can be depopulated either spontaneously or through pumping.

Laser construction is as important to laser action, as is the source material. Since light wavelengths are too short to allow building a resonant cavity, long multinodal chambers are made with parallel reflectors at each end to feed back radiation until lasing takes place. The effect is to produce well-collimated light that is highly directional.

Consider as an example the pink ruby laser, whose electronic transitions are shown in figure 1-15 and whose mechanical construction is indicated in figure 1-16. This laser is pumped by a flash tube (a), and electrons in the ruby (b) are raised from level E_1 to E_3. The electrons decay rapidly and spontaneously from E_3 to E_2. They can then spontaneously move from E_2 to E_1 and slowly emit fluorescent light, $h\nu_{21}$ (see equation 1-3), or they can be stimulated to emit coherent light, $h\nu_{21}$. The full reflector (c) and the partial reflector (d) channel the coherent radiation, $h\nu_{21}$, until it has built up enough to emit coherent light $h\nu_{21}$ through (d). The fact that this light has been

Fig. 1-14. Color Characteristics of Some Phosphors for Mercury and Metal Halide Lamps

Material	Activator	Peak of Fluorescent Band*	Color of Fluorescence
Strontium chloropatite	Europium	445	Blue
Strontium-magnesium phosphate	Tin	610	Orange red
Strontium-zinc phosphate	Tin	610	Orange red
Yttrium-vanadate	Europium	612	Orange red
Yttrium-vanadate phosphate	Europium	612	Orange red
Magnesium fluorogermanate	Manganese	660	Deep red
Magnesium arsenate	Manganese	660	Deep red

* Wavelength in nanometers

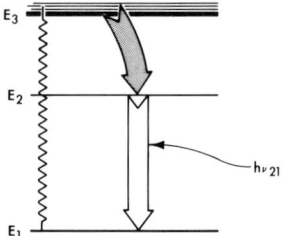

Fig. 1-15. Simplified diagrammatic representation of electronic transitions in a ruby laser.

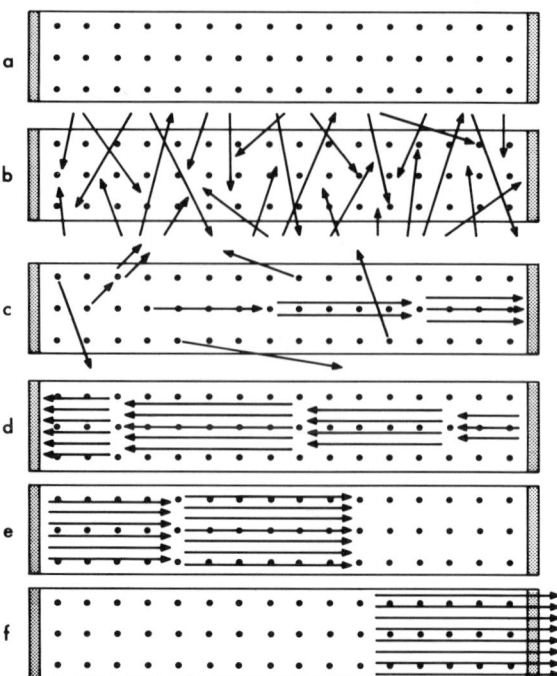

Fig. 1-17. Photon cascade in a solid laser. Before the buildup begins, atoms in the laser crystal are in the ground state (a). Pumping light [arrows in (b)] raises most of the atoms to the excited state. The cascade (c) begins when an excited atom spontaneously emits a photon parallel to the axis of the crystal (photons emitted in other directions pass out of the crystal). The buildup continues in (d) and (e) through thousands of reflections back and forth from the silvered surfaces at the ends of the crystal. When amplification is great enough, light passes out at (f).

reflected many times by parallel mirrors ensures that it is well collimated. The electrons are then available for further pumping. See figure 1-17.

Gas Laser. In a solid laser there are three requirements: a material which reacts energetically to light, a population inversion generated by pumping in energy at the correct level and a growth of the internal energy caused by the reflection of photons within the solid. While the same requirements are met in a gas laser, two other characteristics are available, namely strong, narrow spectral lines and unequal emission at different energy levels. An example of such a gas laser is that containing a mixture of helium and neon. See figure 1-18. Helium is used as the energizing gas because it has a level from which it can lose energy only by collision. This level corresponds to the one at which neon radiates energy in the form of red light. On energizing helium in a gas discharge inside a cavity whose ends are reflecting and that contains both helium and neon, the helium transfers energy by collision with neon. The excited neon emits photons, which begin to amplify by cascading between the two reflecting surfaces until the internal energy is so large that the losses through the partially transmitting mirror become equal to the internal gains and the laser becomes saturated.

Semiconductor Laser. A third type of laser utilizes a semiconducting solid material where the electron current flowing across a junction between p- and n-type material produces extra electrons in the conduction band. These radiate upon their making a transition

back to the valence band or lower-energy states. If the junction current is large enough, there will be more electrons near the edge of the conduction band than there are at the edge of the valence band and a population inversion may occur. To utilize this effect, the semiconductor crystal is polished with two parallel faces perpendicular to the junction plane. The ampli-

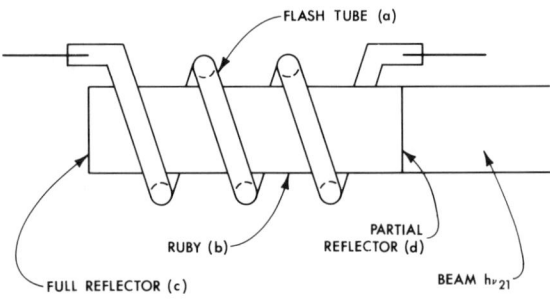

Fig. 1-16. Simplified diagram of a ruby laser.

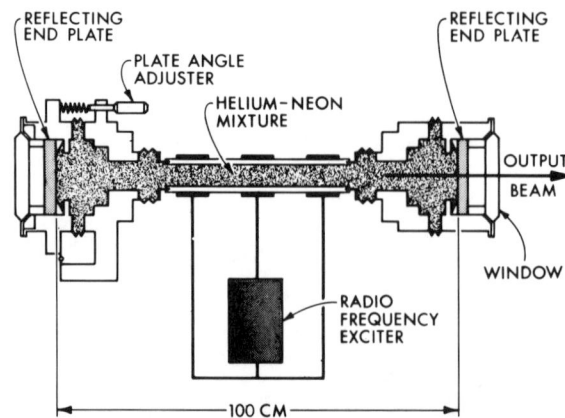

Fig. 1-18. Structure of helium-neon gas laser, showing essential parts. Operation of the laser depends on the right mixture of helium and neon to provide an active medium. A radio-frequency exciter puts energy into the medium. The output beam is built up by repeated passes back and forth between reflecting end plates.

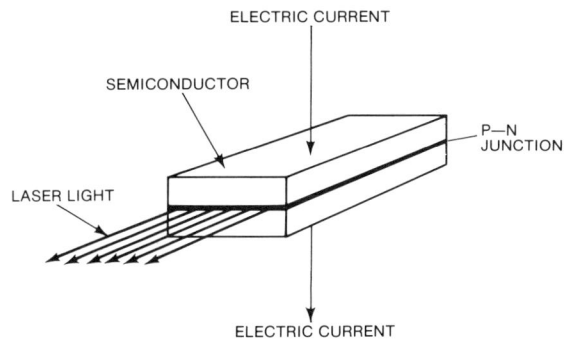

Fig. 1-19. Highly schematic diagram of a semiconductor (gallium arsenide) laser.

fied waves can then propagate along the plane of the junction and are reflected back and forth at the surfaces. See figure 1-19.

Electroluminescence[18]

Certain special phosphors convert alternating-current energy directly into light, without using an intermediate step as in a gas discharge, by utilizing the phenomenon of electroluminescence.

Electroluminescent Lamps (ac Capacitive). An electroluminescent lamp is composed of a two-dimensional area conductor (transparent or opaque) on which a dielectric-phosphor layer is deposited. A second two-dimensional area conductor of transparent material is deposited over the dielectric-phosphor mixture.

An alternating electric field is established between the two conductors with the application of a voltage across the two-dimensional (area) conductors. Under the influence of this field, some electrons in the electroluminescent phosphor are excited. During the return of these electrons to their ground or normal state the excess energy is radiated as visible light.

Figure 1-20 shows a cross-sectional view of an electroluminescent lamp. Figure 1-21 gives the properties of some electroluminescent phosphors.

The color of the light emitted by an electroluminescent lamp is dependent on frequency, while the luminance is dependent on frequency and voltage. These effects vary from phosphor to phosphor.

The efficacy of electroluminescent devices is low compared to incandescent lamps. It is of the order of a few lumens per watt.

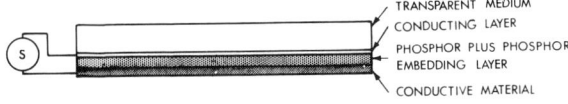

Fig. 1-20. Diagrammatic cross section of an electroluminescent lamp.

Fig. 1-21. Properties of Some Electroluminescent Phosphors

Material	Activators	Color of Light
Cubic zinc sulfide	Copper (low), lead	Blue
Cubic zinc sulfide	Copper (high), lead	Green
Cubic zinc sulfide	Copper (high), lead, manganese	Yellow
Hexagonal zinc sulfide	Copper (very high)	Green
Hexagonal zinc sulfide	Copper (very high), manganese	Yellow
Zinc sulfo selenide	Copper	Green to yellow
Zinc cadmium sulfo selenide	Copper	Yellow to pink

Light-Emitting Diodes. Light-emitting diodes (LED), also called solid-state lamps (SSL), produce light by electroluminescence when low-voltage direct current is applied to a suitably doped crystal containing a p-n junction. The phenomenon was observed as early as 1923 in naturally occurring junctions, but was not considered practical due to its low luminous efficacy in converting electric energy to light. Recently it was discovered that under certain conditions the conversion was of useful magnitude.

The efficacy is dependent upon the visible energy generated at the junction and losses due to reabsorption when light tries to escape through the crystal. Due to the high index of refraction of most semiconductors, light is re-reflected back from the surface into the crystal and highly attenuated before finally exiting. The efficacy expressed in terms of this ultimate measurable visible energy is called the *external* efficacy. The external efficacies are moderate, though the internal efficacies are calculated to be very high. For more information see chapter 6, Light Sources.

Cathodoluminescence. Cathodoluminescence is light emitted when a substance is bombarded by an electron beam from a cathode, as in cathode-ray and television picture tubes.

Miscellaneous Luminescence Phenomena

Galvanoluminescence. Galvanoluminescence is light which appears at either the anode or the cathode when solutions are electrolyzed.

Crystalloluminescence. Crystalloluminescence (lyoluminescence) is observed when solutions crystallize; it is believed to be due to rapid re-formation of molecules from ions. The intensity increases upon stirring, perhaps on account of triboluminescence (see below).

Chemiluminescence. Chemiluminescence (oxyluminescence) is the production of light during a chemical reaction at room temperatures. True chemiluminescences are oxidation reactions involving valence changes.

Thermoluminescence. Thermoluminescence is luminescence exhibited by some materials when slightly heated. In all cases of thermoluminescence the effect is dependent upon some previous illumination or radiation of the crystal. Diamonds, marble apatite, quartz and fluorspar are thermoluminescent.

Triboluminescence. Triboluminescence (piezoluminescence) is light produced by shaking, rubbing or crushing crystals. Triboluminescent light may result from unstable light centers previously exposed to some source or radiation, such as light, X rays, radium emissions and cathode rays; centers not exposed to previous radiation but characteristic of the crystal itself; or electrical discharges from fracturing crystals.

Sonoluminescence. Sonoluminescence is light which is observed when sound waves are passed through fluids. It occurs when the fluids are completely shielded from an electrical field and is always connected with cavitation (the formation of gas or vapor cavities in a liquid). It is believed the minute gas bubbles of cavitated gas develop a considerable charge as their surface increases. When they collapse, their capacitance decreases and their voltage rises until a discharge takes place in the gas, causing a faint luminescence.

Radioluminescence. Radioluminescence is light emitted from a material under bombardment from α rays, β rays, γ rays or X rays.

LIGHT DETECTION

The most universally used detector of light is the human eye (see chapter 3, Vision and Perception). Other common detectors are photovoltaic cells, photoconductor cells, photoelectric tubes, photodiodes, phototransistors and photographic film.

Photovoltaic Cells

Common photovoltaic cells include selenium barrier-layer cells and silicon or gallium arsenide photodiodes operated in the photovoltaic, or unbiased, mode. They depend upon the generation of a voltage as a result of the absorption of a photon. The cell is composed of a metal plate coated with a semiconductor material, for example, iron coated with selenium (p type) or cadmium oxide (semitransparent, n type). Upon exposure to light, electrons liberated from the semiconductor are trapped at the interface unless there is an external circuit provided through which they may escape. They thus convert radiant energy to electric energy, which can be used directly or amplified to drive a microammeter (see figure 1-22). The cells can be filtered to

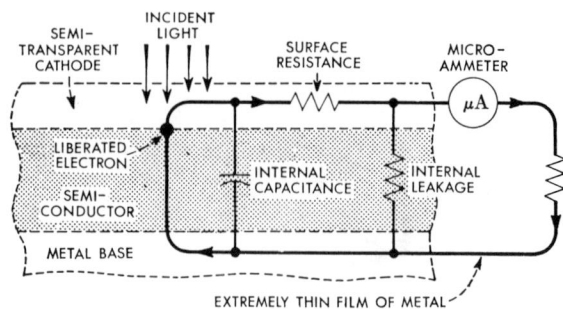

Fig. 1-22. Cross section of a barrier-layer photovoltaic cell, showing the motion of photoelectrons through a microammeter circuit.

correct their spectral response so that the meter can be calibrated in units of illuminance. Factors such as response time, fatigue, temperature effects, linearity, stability, noise and magnitude of current influence the choice of cell and circuit for a given application.

Photoconductor Cells

Photoconductor cells are cells whose resistance changes directly as a result of photon absorption. These detectors use materials such as cadmium sulfide, cadmium selenide and selenium. Cadmium sulfide and cadmium selenide are available in transparent resin or glass envelopes and are suitable for low illuminance levels, less than 10^{-4} lx (10^{-5} fc).

Photoelectric Tubes

The emission of electrons from a surface when bombarded by sufficiently energetic photons is known as the *photoelectric effect*. If the surface is connected as a cathode in an electric field (see figure 1-23), the liberated electrons will flow to the anode, creating a photoelectric current. An arrangement of this sort may be used as an illuminance meter and can be calibrated in lux or footcandles.

The photoelectric current in a vacuum varies directly with the illuminance level over a wide range (spectral distribution, polarization and cathode potential remaining the same). In gas-filled tubes the re-

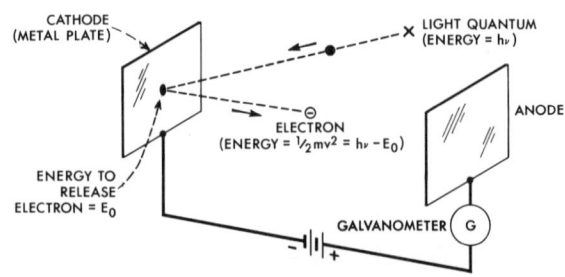

Fig. 1-23. By the photoelectric effect, electrons may be liberated from illuminated metal surfaces. In an electric field these will flow to an anode and create an electric current, which may be detected by means of a galvanometer.

sponse is linear over only a limited range. If the radiant energy is polarized, the photoelectric current will vary as the orientation of the polarization is changed (except at normal incidence).

Photodiodes and Phototransistors

Photodiodes, or junction photocells, are based on solid-state p-n junctions that react to external stimuli such as light. If properly constructed, they can also emit light (see the subsection on Light-Emitting Diodes above). In a photosensitive diode the reverse saturation current of the junction increases in proportion to the illuminance. Such a diode can therefore be used as a sensitive detector of light; it is particularly suitable for indicating extremely short pulses of radiation because of its very fast response.

Phototransistors operate in a manner similar to photodiodes, but because they provide an additional amplifier effect, they are many times more sensitive than simple photodiodes.

OPTICAL CONTROL[19-21]

Optical control may be provided in a number of ways. All are applications of one or more of the following phenomena: reflection, refraction, polarization, interference, diffraction, diffusion and absorption.

Reflection and Reflectors

Reflection is the process by which a part of the light falling on a medium leaves that medium from the incident side. Reflection may be specular, spread, diffuse or compound, and selective or nonselective. Reflection from the front of a transparent plate is called first-surface reflection, and that from the back second-surface reflection. Refraction and absorption by supporting media are avoided in first-surface reflection.

Specular Reflection.
If a surface is polished, it reflects specularly; that is, the angle between the reflected ray and the normal to the surface will equal the angle between the incident ray and the normal, as shown in figure 1-24. If two or more rays are reflected, they may produce a virtual, erect or inverted image of the source.

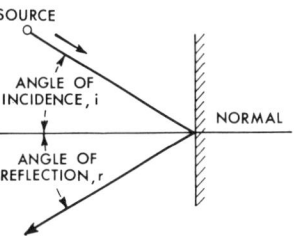

Fig. 1-24. The law of reflection states that the angle of incidence *i* equals the angle of reflection *r*.

Specular Reflectors. Examples of specular reflectors are:

1. Smooth polished metal and aluminized or silvered smooth glass or plastic surfaces. Reflector lamps utilize first-surface reflection when the inside bulb is coated with a thin metal reflecting mirror surface as shown in figure 1-25b. Light reflected from the upper surface of a transparent medium, such as glass plate, as in figure 1-25a and c, also is an example of first-surface reflection. As shown in figure 1-26, less than 5% of the incident light is reflected at the first surface unless it strikes the surface at wide angles from the normal. The sheen of silk and the shine from smooth or coated paper are images of light sources reflected in the first surface.
2. Rear-surface mirrors. Some light, the quantity depending on the incident angle, is reflected by the first surface. The rest goes through the transparent medium to a rear-surface mirror coating, where it is reflected as shown in figure 1-25c.

Reflection from Curved Surfaces. Figure 1-27 shows the reflection of a beam of light by a concave surface and by a convex surface. A ray of light striking the surface at point *T* obeys the law of reflection (see figure 1-24), and by taking each ray separately, the paths of various reflected rays may be constructed.

In the case of parallel rays reflected from a concave surface, all the rays can be directed through a common point *F* by properly designing the curvature of the

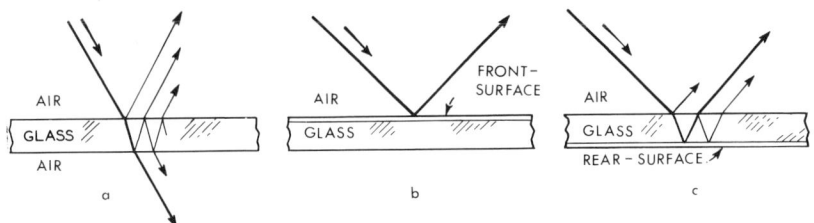

Fig. 1-25. Reflections from (a) a transparent medium, such as clear plate glass, and from (b) front-surface and (c) rear-surface mirrors.

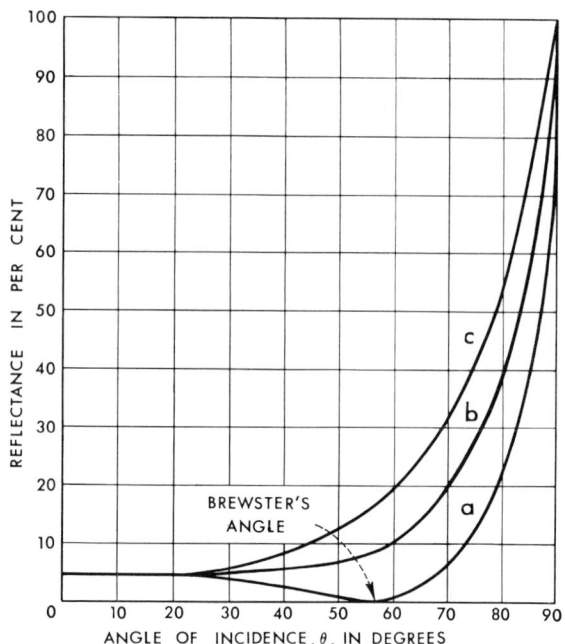

Fig. 1-26. Effect of angle of incidence and state of polarization on the percentage of light reflected at an air-glass surface: (a) Light that is polarized in the plane of incidence. (b) Nonpolarized light. (c) Light that is polarized in a plane perpendicular to the plane of incidence.

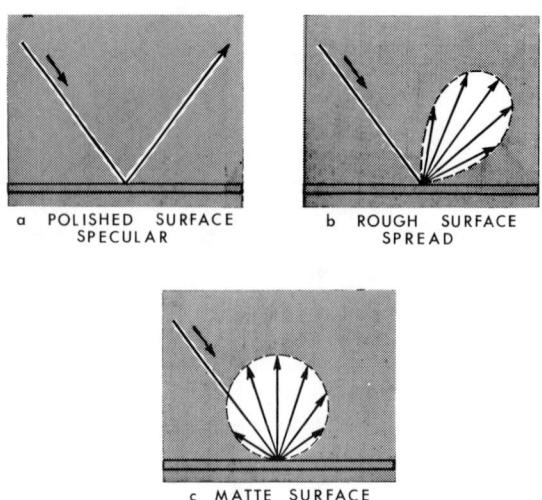

Fig. 1-28. The type of reflection depends on the surface: (a) polished surface (specular); (b) rough surface (spread); (c) matte surface (diffuse).

surface. This is called the *focal point*. The *focal length FA* is denoted by *f*.

Spread Reflection. If a reflecting surface is not smooth—that is, corrugated, etched or hammered, it spreads parallel rays into a cone of reflected rays, as shown in figure 1-28b.

Spread Reflectors. Slightly textured or hammered surfaces reflect individual rays at slightly different angles, but all in the same general direction. These are used to smooth beam irregularities and where moderate control or minimum beam spread is desired.

Corrugated, brushed, dimpled, etched or pebbled surfaces consist of small specular surfaces in irregular planes. Brushing the surface spreads the image at right angles to the brushing. Pebbled, peened or etched surfaces produce a random patch of highlights. These

are used where wide beams free from striations and filament images are required.

The angle through which reflections are spread can be controlled by proper peening, for which equations describing peen radius and depth are available.[23] Shot- or sandblasting and etching may cause serious losses in efficiency as a result of multiple reflections in random directions.

Diffuse Reflection. If a material has a rough surface or is composed of minute crystals or pigment particles, the reflection is diffuse. Each ray falling on an infinitesimal particle obeys the law of reflection, but as the surfaces of the particles are in different planes, they reflect the light at many angles, as shown in figure 1-28c.

Diffuse Reflectors. Flat paints and other matte finishes and materials reflect at all angles and exhibit little directional control. These are used where wide distribution of light is desired.

Compound Reflection. Most common materials are compound reflectors and exhibit all three reflection components (specular, spread and diffuse) to varying degrees. In some, one or two components predominate, as shown in figure 1-29. Specular and narrowly spread reflections (usually surface reflections) cause the sheen on etched aluminum and semigloss paint.

Diffuse-Specular Reflectors. Porcelain enamel, glossy synthetic finishes and other surfaces with a shiny transparent finish over a matte base exhibit no directional control except for a specularly reflected ray as shown in figure 1-29a, with an intensity of approximately 5–15% of the incident light.

Total Reflection. Total reflection of a light ray at a surface of a transmitting medium (see figure 1-30)

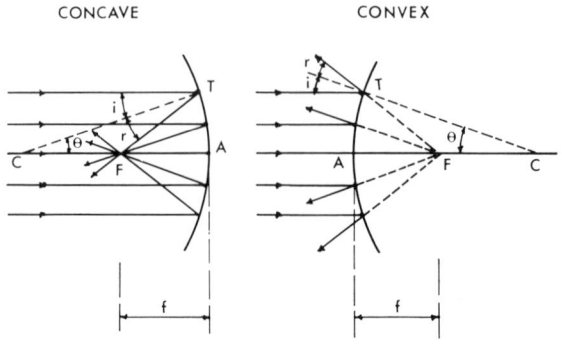

Fig. 1-27. Focal point and focal length of curved surfaces.

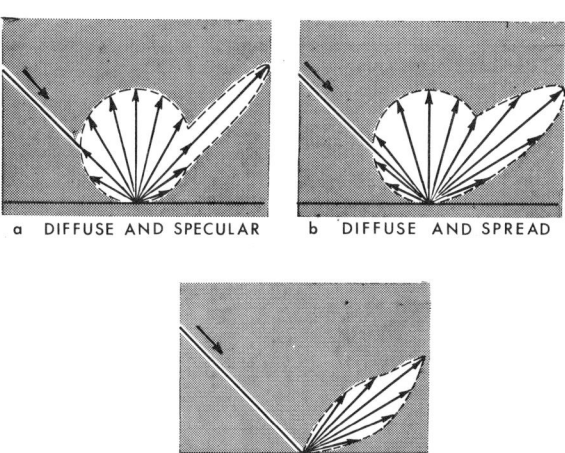

a DIFFUSE AND SPECULAR   b DIFFUSE AND SPREAD

c SPECULAR AND SPREAD

Fig. 1-29. Examples of compound reflection: (a) diffuse and specular; (b) diffuse and spread; (c) specular and spread.

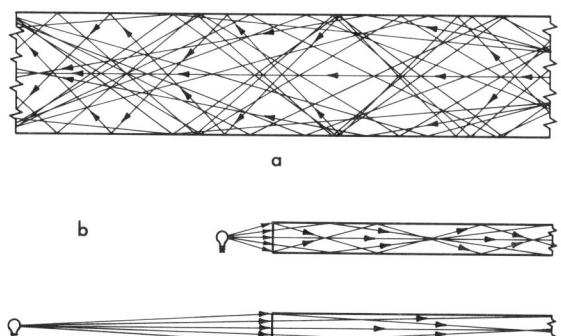

a

b

Fig. 1-31. Representation of light transmission through a single fiber of a fiber-optics system, showing (a) internal reflections and (b) the effect of light source location on collimation of light.

occurs when the angle of incidence (i) exceeds a certain value whose sine equals n_2/n_1, the ratio of indices of refraction. If the index of refraction of the first medium (n_1) is greater than that of the second medium (n_2), $\sin r$ will become unity when $\sin i$ is equal to n_2/n_1. At angles of incidence greater than this critical angle (i_c) the incident rays are reflected totally, as in figure 1-30. In most glass total reflection occurs whenever $\sin i$ is greater than 0.66, that is, for all angles of incidence greater than 41.8° (glass to air). Light piping by edge lighting and light transmission through rods and tubes are examples of total (internal) reflection.

When light, passing through air, strikes a piece of ordinary glass ($n_2/n_1 \approx 1.5$) normal to its surface, about 4.5% is reflected from the upper surface and about 4% from the lower surface. Approximately 90% of the light is transmitted and the rest absorbed. The proportion of reflected light increases as the angle of incidence is increased. See figure 1-26.

Fiber Optics. Fiber optics is the branch of optical science concerned with thin, cylindrical glass or plastic fibers of optical quality. Light entering one end of the fiber is transmitted to the other end through the process of total internal reflection. See figure 1-31. In order to prevent light leaking from a fiber, it is coated with a lower-refractive-index material. Large numbers of fibers (from 100 to 1,000,000) can be clustered together to form a bundle. Fiber bundles are of two major types: coherent and noncoherent. The first are used for transmitting images, and each individual fiber is carefully oriented with respect to its neighbors in the entire bundle. Noncoherent bundles have random fiber locations in the bundle, but are suitable for transmitting light between points.

Refraction and Refractors

A change in the velocity of light (speed of propagation, not frequency) occurs when a ray leaves one material and enters another of greater or lower optical density. The speed will be reduced if the medium entered is more dense, and increased if it is less dense.

Except when light enters at an angle normal to the surface of the new medium, the change in speed always is accompanied by a bending of the light from its original path at the point of entrance, as shown in figure 1-32. This is known as *refraction*. The degree of bending depends on the relative densities of the two substances, on the wavelength of the light and on the angle of incidence, being greater for large differences in density than for small. The light is bent toward the normal to the surface when it enters a more dense medium and away from the normal when it enters a less dense material.

When light is transmitted from one medium to another, each ray follows the law of refraction. When rays strike or enter a new medium, they may also be scattered in many directions because of irregularities of the surface, such as fine cracks, mold marks, scratches or

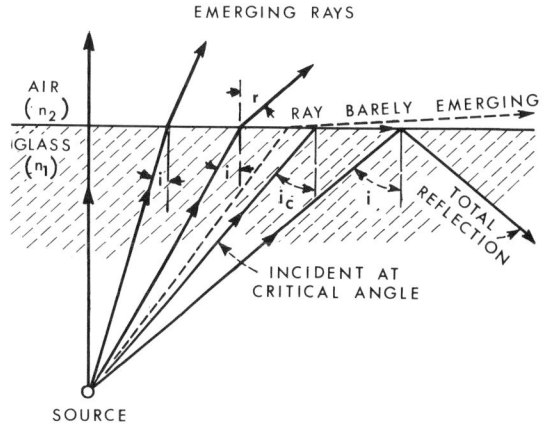

EMERGING RAYS

AIR (n_2)

RAY BARELY EMERGING

GLASS (n_1)

i i i_c i

TOTAL REFLECTION

INCIDENT AT CRITICAL ANGLE

SOURCE

Fig. 1-30. Total reflection occurs when $\sin r = 1$. The critical angle i_c varies with the medium.

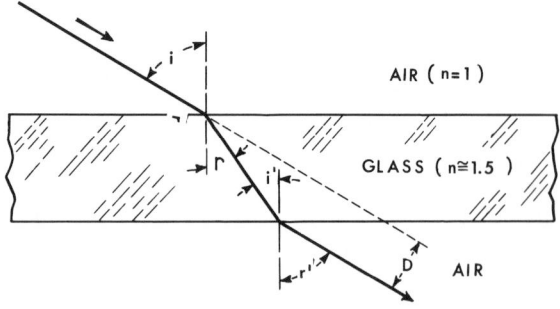

Fig. 1-32. Refraction of light rays at a plane surface causes bending of the incident rays and displacement of the emergent rays. A ray passing from a rare to a denser medium is bent toward the normal to the interface, while a ray passing from a dense to a rarer medium is bent away from the normal.

changes in contour, or because of foreign deposits of dirt, grease or moisture.

Snell's Law. The law of refraction (Snell's law) is expressed as follows:

$$n_1 \sin i = n_2 \sin r \qquad (1\text{-}7)$$

where

n_1 = index of refraction of the first medium,
i = angle the incident light ray forms with the normal to the surface,
n_2 = index of refraction of the second medium,
r = angle the refracted light ray forms with the normal to the surface.

When the first medium is air, of which the index of refraction usually is taken as 1 (the vacuum value; this approximation is correct to three decimal places), the formula becomes

$$\sin i = n_2 \sin r \qquad (1\text{-}8)$$

The two interfaces of the glass plate shown in figure 1-32 are parallel, and therefore the entering and emerging rays also are parallel. The rays are displaced from each other (a distance D) because of refraction.

Examples of Refraction. A common example of refraction is the apparent bending of a straw at the point where it enters the water in a drinking glass. Although the straw is straight, light rays coming from that part of the straw under water are refracted when they pass from the water into the air and appear to come from higher points. These irregularities cause irregular refraction of transmitted rays and distortion of the images of objects at which the rays originate.

Prismatic light directors, such as shown in figure 1-33a and b, may be designed to provide a variety of light distributions using the principles of refraction. Lens systems controlling light by refraction are used in

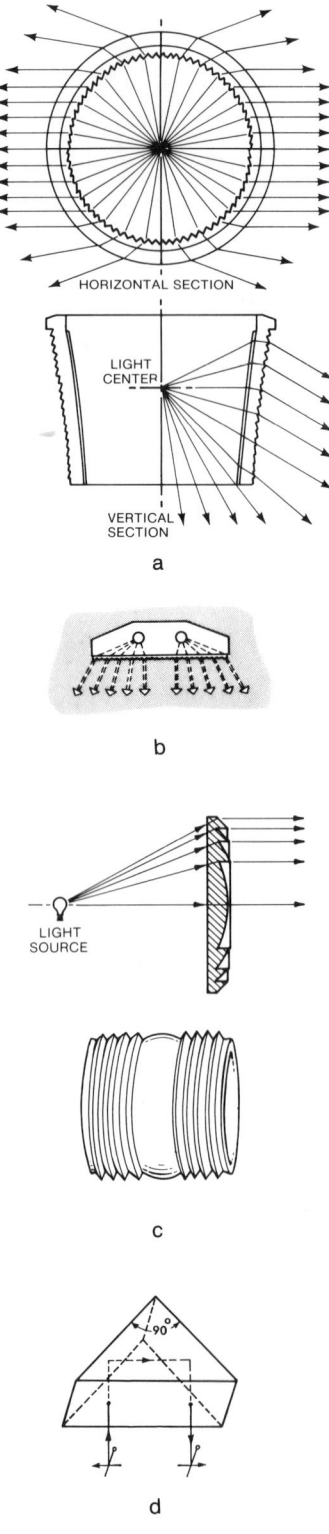

Fig. 1-33. Optical systems utilizing the refractive properties of prisms and lenses: (a) Street lighting unit in which the outer piece controls the light in vertical directions (concentrating the rays into a narrow beam at about 75° from the vertical) and the inner piece redirects the light in the horizontal plane. The result is a "two-way" type of candlepower distribution. (b) Prismatic lens for a fluorescent lamp luminaire intercepts as much light as possible, redirecting part from the glare zone to more useful directions. (c) Cylindrical and flat Fresnel lenses. (d) Reflecting prism.

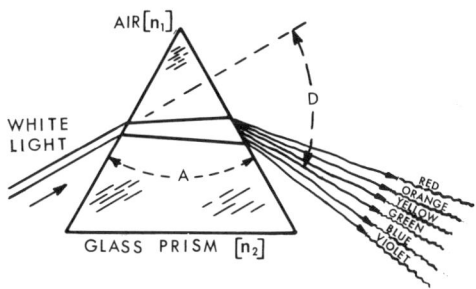

Fig. 1-34. White light is dispersed into its component colors by refraction when passed through a prism. The angle of deviation D (illustrated for green light) varies with wavelength.

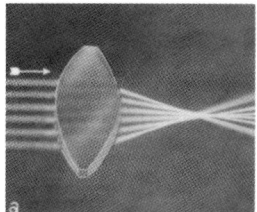 

Fig. 1-35. Ray path traces through lenses: (a) positive; (b) negative.

automobile headlights, and in beacon, floodlight and spotlight Fresnel lenses as shown in figure 1-33.

Prisms. Consider Snell's law:

$$n_2 = \frac{\sin i}{\sin r} = \frac{\text{velocity of light in air}}{\text{velocity of light in a prism}} \quad (1\text{-}9)$$

This equation suggests, since the velocity of light is a function of the index of refraction of the media involved and also of wavelength, that the exit path from a prism will be different for each wavelength of incident light and for each angle of incidence. See figure 1-34. This orderly separation of incident light into its spectrum of component wavelengths is called *dispersion*.

Refracting Prisms. The degree of bending of light at each prism surface is a function of the refractive indices of the media and the prism angle (*A* in figure 1-34). Light can be directed accurately within certain angles by having the proper angle between the prism faces.

Refracting prisms are used in such devices as headlight lenses and refracting luminaires. In the design of refracting equipment, the same general considerations of proper flux distribution hold true as for the design of reflectors. Following Snell's law of refraction, the prism angles can be computed to provide the proper deviation of the light rays from the source. For most commercially available transparent materials like glasses and plastics, the index of refraction lies between 1.4 and 1.6.

Often, by proper placement of the prisms, it is possible to limit the prismatic structure to one surface of the refractor, leaving the other surfaces smooth for easy maintenance. The number and the sizes of prisms used are governed by several considerations. Among them are ease of manufacture and convenient maintenance of lighting equipment in service. Use of a large number of small prisms may magnify the effect of rounding of prisms that occurs in manufacture; on the other hand, small prisms produce greater accuracy of light control.

Ribbed and Prismed Surfaces. These can be designed to spread rays in one plane or scatter them in all directions. Such surfaces are used in lenses, luminous elements, glass blocks, windows and skylights.

Reflecting Prisms. These reflect light internally, as shown in figure 1-33d, and are used in luminaires and retrodirective markers. Their performance quality depends on the flatness of reflecting surfaces, accuracy of prism angles, elimination of dirt in optical contact with the surface and elimination (in manufacturing) of prismatic error.

Lenses. Positive lenses form convergent beams and real inverted images as in figure 1-35a. Negative lenses form divergent beams and virtual, inverted images as in figure 1-35b.

Stepped and Fresnel Lenses. The weight and cost of glass in large lenses used in illumination equipment can be reduced by making cylindrical steps in the flat surface. The hollow, stepped back surface reduces the total quantity of glass used in the lens. In a method developed by Fresnel, as shown in figure 1-33c, the curved face of the stepped lens becomes curved rings and the back is flat. Both the stepped and Fresnel lenses reduce the thickness, and the optical action is approximately the same. Although outside prisms are slightly more efficient, they are likely to collect more dust. Therefore, prismatic faces are often formed on the inside.

Lens Aberrations. There are, in all, seven principal lens aberrations: spherical aberration, coma, axial and lateral chromatism, astigmatism, curvature and distortion. See figure 1-36. Usually they are of little importance in lenses used in common types of lighting equipment. The simpler the lens system, the more difficult is the correction of the aberrations.

Transmission and Transmitting Materials

Transmission is a characteristic of many materials: glass, plastics, textiles, crystals and so forth. The luminous transmittance τ of a material is the ratio of the

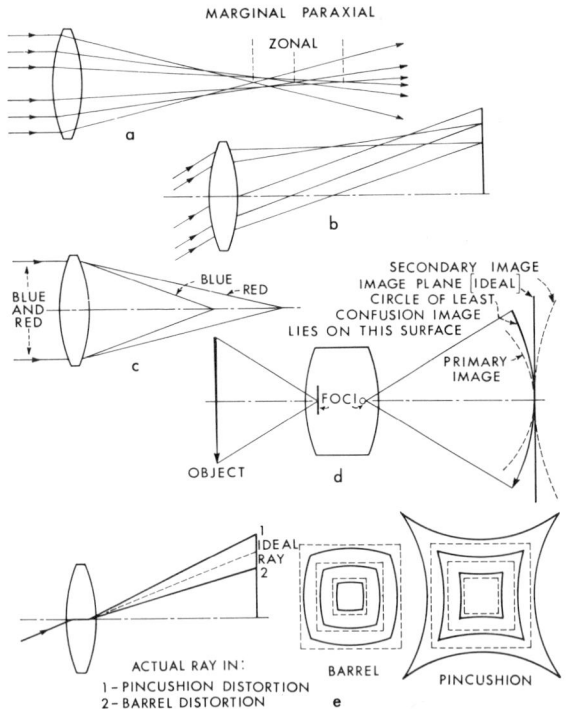

Fig. 1-36. Lens aberrations. (a) Spherical aberration: convergence of parallel rays at different focal points at different distances from the axis of a lens. (b) Coma: difference in the lateral magnification of rays passing through different zones of a lens. (c) Chromatism: a difference in focal length for rays of different wavelengths. (d) Astigmatism and curvature: existence in two parallel planes of two mutually perpendicular line foci and a curved image plane. (e) Distortion: a difference in the magnification of rays passing through a lens at different angles.

total emitted light to the total incident light; it is affected by reflections at each surface of the material, as explained in figure 1-26, and by absorption within the material. Figure 1-37 lists characteristics of several materials.

Bouguer's or Lambert's Law. Absorption in a clear transmitting medium is an exponential function of the thickness of the medium traversed:

$$I = I_0 \tau^x \qquad (1\text{-}10)$$

where

I = intensity of transmitted light,
I_0 = intensity of light entering the medium after surface reflection,
τ = transmittance of a unit thickness,
x = thickness of the sample traversed.

The optical density D is the common logarithm of the reciprocal of the transmittance:

$$D = \log_{10}(1/\tau) \qquad (1\text{-}11)$$

Spread Transmission. Spread transmission materials offer a wide range of textures. They are used for brightness control, as in frosted lamp bulbs, in luminous elements where accents of brilliance and sparkle are desired, and in moderately uniform brightness luminaire-enclosing globes. Care should be used in placing lamps to avoid glare and spotty appearance.

Figure 1-38a shows a beam of light striking the smooth side of a piece of etched glass. In figure 1-38b the frosted side is toward the source, a condition that with many ground or otherwise roughened glasses results in appreciably higher transmittance. For outdoor use the rough surface usually must be enclosed to avoid excessive dirt collection.

Diffuse Transmission. Diffusing materials scatter light in all directions, as shown in figure 1-38c. White, opal and prismatic plastics and glass are widely used where uniform brightness is desired.

Mixed Transmission. Mixed transmission is a result of a spectrally selective diffusion characteristic exhibited by certain materials such as fine opal glass, which permits the regular transmission of certain colors (wavelengths) while diffusing other wavelengths. This characteristic in glass varies greatly, depending on such factors as its heat treatment, composition and thickness and the wavelengths of the incident light.

Polarization

Unpolarized light consists of visible electromagnetic waves having transverse vibrations of equal magnitude in an infinite number of planes, all of which oscillate about the line representing the direction of propagation. See figure 1-39. In explaining the properties of polarized light, it is common to resolve the amplitude of the vibrations of any light ray into components vibrating in two orthogonal planes each containing the light ray. These two principal directions are usually referred to as the horizontal and vertical vibrations. The horizontal component of light is the summation of the horizontal components of the infinite number of vibrations making up the light ray. When the horizontal and vertical components are equal, the light is unpolarized. When these two components are not equal, the light is partially or totally polarized as shown in figure 1-39.

The percentage polarization of light from a source or luminaire at a given angle is defined by the following relation:[22]

$$\text{percent vertical polarization} = \frac{I_v - I_h}{I_v + I_h} \times 100 \quad (1\text{-}12)$$

where I_v and I_h are the intensities of the vertical and horizontal components of light, respectively, at the given angle.

Fig. 1-37. Reflecting and Transmitting Materials

Material	Reflectance* or Trans- mittance† (per cent)	Characteristics
	Reflecting	
Specular		
Mirrored and optical coated glass	80 to 99	Provide directional control of light and brightness at specific viewing
Metallized and optical coated plastic	75 to 97	angles. Effective as efficient reflectors and for special decorative
Processed anodized and optical coated aluminum	75 to 95	lighting effects.
Polished aluminum	60 to 70	
Chromium	60 to 65	
Stainless steel	55 to 65	
Black structural glass	5	
Spread		
Processed aluminum (diffuse)	70 to 80	General diffuse reflection with a high specular surface reflection of
Etched aluminum	70 to 85	from 5 to 10 per cent of the light.
Satin chromium	50 to 55	
Brushed aluminum	55 to 58	
Aluminum paint	60 to 70	
Diffuse		
White plaster	90 to 92	Diffuse reflection results in uniform surface brightness at all viewing
White paint**	75 to 90	angles. Materials of this type are good reflecting backgrounds for
Porcelain enamel**	65 to 90	coves and luminous forms.
White terra-cotta**	65 to 80	
White structural glass	75 to 80	
Limestone	35 to 65	
	Transmitting	
Glass		
Clear and optical coated	80 to 99	Low absorption; no diffusion; high concentrated transmission. Used as protective cover plates for concealed light sources.
Configured, obscure, etched, ground, sandblasted, and frosted	70 to 85	Low absorption; high transmission; poor diffusion. Used only when backed by good diffusing glass or when light sources are placed at edges of panel to light the background.
Opalescent and alabaster	55 to 80	Lower transmission than above glasses; fair diffusion. Used for favorable appearance when indirectly lighted.
Flashed (cased) opal	30 to 65	Low absorption; excellent diffusion. used for panels of uniform brightness with good efficiency.
Solid opal glass	15 to 40	Higher absorption than flashed opal glass; excellent diffusion. Used in place of flashed opal where a white appearance is required.
Plastics		
Clear prismatic lens	70 to 92	Low absorption; no diffusion; high concentrated transmission. Used as shielding for fluorescent luminaires, outdoor signs and luminaires.
White	30 to 70	High absorption; excellent diffusion. Used to diffuse lamp images and provide even appearance in fluorescent luminaires.
Colors	0 to 90	Available in any color for special color rendering lighting requirements or esthetic reasons.
Marble (impregnated)	5 to 30	High absorption; excellent diffusion; used for panels of low brightness. Seldom used in producing general illumination because of the low efficiency.
Alabaster	20 to 50	High absorption; good diffusion. Used for favorable appearance when directly lighted.

* Specular and diffuse reflectance.
† Inasmuch as the amount of light transmitted depends upon the thickness of the material and angle of incidence of light, the figures given are based on thicknesses generally used in lighting applications and on near normal angles of incidence.
** These provide compound diffuse-specular reflection unless matte finished.

Reference to vertically polarized light or horizontally polarized light can be misleading in that it suggests that all light waves vibrate either horizontally or vertically. A better terminology would be to refer to light at a given instant as consisting of one component vibrating in a horizontal plane and another component vibrating in a vertical plane. A general terminology would identify the light components in terms of two reference planes as shown in figure 1-40. One plane is the plane of the task at the point of the incident light ray, and the second plane is the plane of incidence: the plane perpendicular to the plane of the task and containing the incident light ray. Then the two components of light would be referred to as the parallel component, or component in the plane of incidence, and the perpendicular component. This terminology

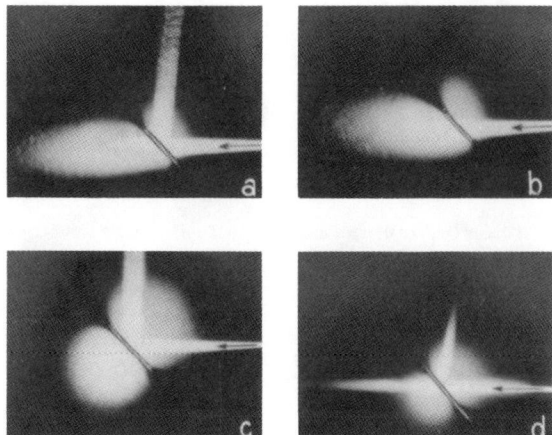

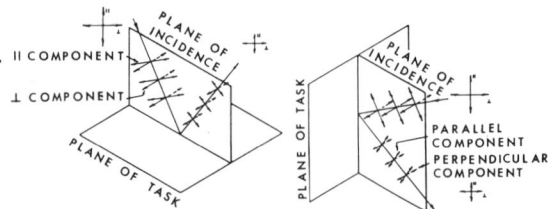

Fig. 1-40. Reference planes of a task.

Fig. 1-38. (a) Spread transmission of light incident on the smooth surface of figured, etched, ground and hammered glass samples. (b) Spread transmission of light incident on the rough surface of the same samples. (c) Diffuse transmission of light incident on solid opal and on flashed opal glass, white plastic or marble sheet. (d) Mixed transmission through opalescent glass.

would apply to any task position and would be free of ambiguity with respect to spatial orientation.

Polarized light can be produced in four ways: (1) scattering, (2) birefringence, (3) absorption and (4) reflection and refraction.

Scattering is the mechanism of polarization in daylighting; that is, light from a clear blue sky is partially polarized due to the scattering of light by particles in the air.

The *birefringence*, or double refraction property, of certain crystals can be utilized to achieve polarization. However, the size of these crystals limits this technique to scientific applications; it is not suitable for general lighting.

Polarization by *absorption* can be achieved by using dichroic polarizers. These polarizers absorb all of the light that is in one particular plane and transmit a high percentage of the light polarized in a perpendicular plane. A high percentage of polarization can be ob-

tained by this method, but with a loss of total luminous transmittance. This type of polarizer is commonly used in sunglasses, where it is oriented to transmit the vertical component of light while suppressing the horizontal (typically reflected) component.

Light may be polarized by utilizing the *reflection* characteristics of dielectric materials. When light is reflected from a glass surface, it is partially polarized; a larger percentage of the horizontal component is reflected than of the vertical component. At approximately 57° (Brewster's angle), the reflected light contains only the horizontal component. See figure 1-26. For this one surface, however, only 15% of the incident horizontal component is reflected. The light transmitted through a plate at this angle is made up of the remaining portion of the horizontal component and all the vertical component of the original beam. The resulting light is partially polarized. See figure 1-41. As additional glass plates are added to the system, more and more of the horizontal component is reflected and the transmitted light is more completely vertically polarized. A stack of glass plates, as shown in figure 1-42, thus becomes a method of producing polarization, and the polarizing effect is greatest at Brewster's angle. The percentage polarization is less at all other angles and is zero for a light ray at normal incidence. Polarization by this method can be obtained by arranging glass or plastic flakes in a suitable material.

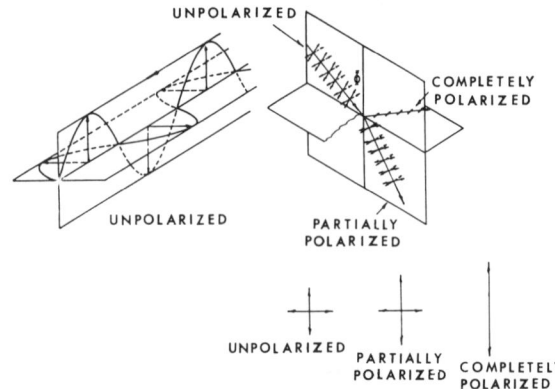

Fig. 1-39. Graphical representations of polarized and unpolarized light.

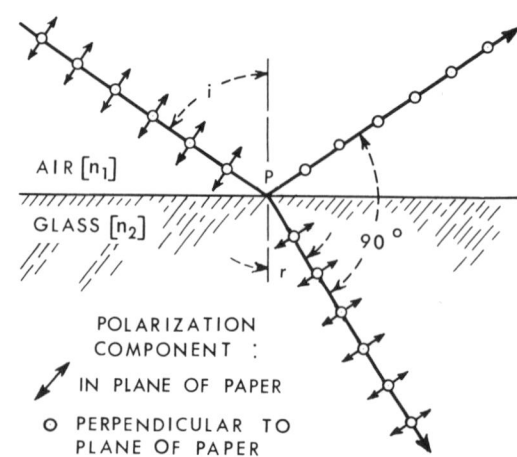

Fig. 1-41. Polarization by reflection at a glass-air surface is at a maximum when the angle of incidence *i* plus the angle of refraction *r* equals 90°.

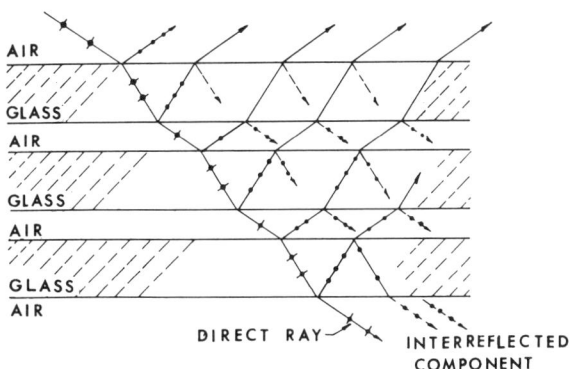

Fig. 1-42. Principle of multilayer polarizers.

Interference

When two light waves of the same wavelength come together at different phases of their vibration, they combine to make up a single wave whose amplitude is between the difference and the sum of the amplitudes of the two, depending on their relative phase. Figure 1-43 shows the resulting interference. Part of the incident light *ab* is first reflected as *bc*. Part is refracted as *bd*, which again reflects as *de*, and finally emerges as *ef*. If waves *bc* and *ef* have wavefronts of appreciable width, they will overlap and interfere. Optical interference coatings have been used for many years in cameras, projectors and other optical instruments, and can reduce reflection from transmitting surfaces, separate heat from light, transmit or reflect light according to color, increase reflections from reflectors, or perform other light control functions. Naturally occurring examples of interference are soap bubbles and oil slicks. Also, many birds, insects and fish get their iridescent colors from interference films. The application of interference coatings can significantly increase the reflectance of reflectors and the transmittance of luminaire glass or plastic enclosures.

Low-Reflectance Films. Dielectric optical interference films are applied to surfaces to reduce reflectance, increase transmittance and consequently improve contrast relationships. Films a quarter wavelength thick with an index of refraction between that of the medium surrounding the glass and that of the glass are used. The hardest and most permanent films are those of magnesium fluoride condensed on the transmitting surface after thermal evaporation in vacuum.

The usual 4% reflection at uncoated air-glass surfaces may be reduced to less than 0.5% at each filmed surface at normal incidence, as a result of the canceling interference between the waves reflected at the air-to-film and film-to-glass surfaces. Dielectric coatings can be made very specific to one reflected wavelength or, by varying the layer's thickness or index of refraction, spread over a wide wavelength interval.

Dichroic (Dielectric) Coating. A multilayer coating which selectively transmits or reflects portions of the spectrum can be added to optical materials. Often called hot or cold mirrors, such coatings are efficient in their selective reflection and transmission, respectively, of infrared (IR) energy. The coatings are typically designed for incident radiation at 45 or 90° to the coated surface. Deviations from the design angle will change the reflected and the transmitted energy. Undesirable results occur when dichroic filters are used in wide beams of light, since the color varies across the resulting beam.

Hot-mirror lamp envelopes which reflect IR back to a filament are used with special tungsten-halogen lamps to increase their efficacy without increasing their wattage and reducing their life.

Diffraction

Due to its wave nature, light will be redirected as it passes by an opaque edge or through a small slit. The wavefront broadens as it passes by an obstruction, producing an indistinct, rather than sharp, shadow of the edge. The intensity and spatial extent of the shadow depends upon the geometric characteristics of the edge, the physical extent (size and shape) of the source and the spectral properties of the light. Light passing through a small slit will produce alternating light and dark bars as the wavefronts created by the two edges of the slit interfere with one another.

Diffusion

Diffusion is the breaking up of a beam of light and the spreading of its rays in many directions by irregular reflection and refraction from microscopic crystalline particles, droplets or bubbles within a transmitting medium, or from microscopic irregularities of a reflecting surface. Perfect diffusion seldom is attained in practice but sometimes is assumed in calculations in

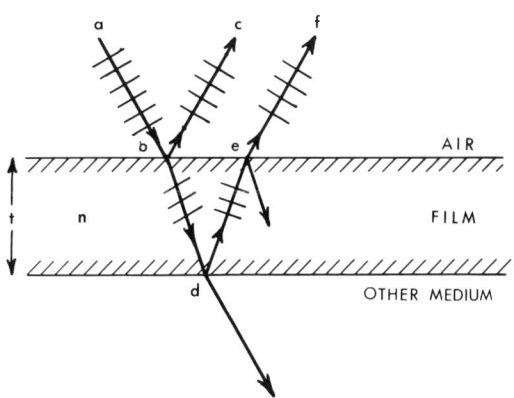

Fig. 1-43. Interference.

order to simplify the mathematics. See figures 1-28c and 1-29.

Absorption

Absorption occurs when a light beam passes through a transparent or translucent medium or meets a dense body such as an opaque reflector surface. If the intensity of all wavelengths of the light passing through a transparent body is reduced by nearly the same amount, the substance is said to show general absorption. The absorption of certain wavelengths of light in preference to others is called selective absorption. Practically all colored objects owe their color to selective absorption in some part of the visible spectrum with resulting reflection and transmission in other selected parts of the spectrum.

REFERENCES

1. Richtmyer, F. K., E. H. Kennard, and J. N. Cooper. 1969. *Introduction to modern physics.* 6th ed. New York: McGraw-Hill.
2. Born, M. 1970. *Atomic physics.* 8th ed., rev. by R. J. Blin-Stoyle and J. M. Radcliffe. Darien, Conn.: Hafner Publishing.
3. Born, M. and E. Wolf. 1970. *Principles of optics: Electromagnetic theory of propagation, interference and diffraction of light.* 4th ed. Oxford and New York: Pergamon Press.
4. Elenbaas, W. 1972. *Light sources.* London and New York: Macmillan and Crane, Russak.
5. Maxwell, C. J. 1954. *A treatise on electricity and magnetism.* 3rd ed. New York: Dover.
6. Forsythe, W. E. 1937. *Measurement of radiant energy.* New York: McGraw-Hill.
7. Goodeve, C. F. 1936. Relative luminosity in the extreme red. *Proc. Roy. Soc. London, Ser. A* 155:664–683.
8. Commission Internationale de L'Éclairage. 1978. *Light as a true visual quantity: Principles of measurement.* CIE publication 41 (TC-1.4). Paris.
9. Forgan, B. W. 1977. Solar constants and radiometric scales. *Appl. Opt.* 16(6):1628–1632.
10. Waymouth, J. F. 1971. *Electric discharge lamps.* Cambridge, Mass.: MIT Press.
11. Fonda, G. R. and F. Seitz, eds. 1948. *Preparation and characteristics of solid luminescent materials.* New York: Wiley.
12. Leverenz, H. W. 1950. *An introduction to luminescence of solids.* New York: Wiley.
13. Harvey, E. N. 1957. *A history of luminescence from the earliest times until 1900.* Philadelphia: American Philosophical Society.
14. Wachtel, A. 1958. The effect of impurities on the plaque brightness of a 3000° K calcium halophosphate phosphor. *J. Electro-Chem. Soc.* 105(5):256–260.
15. Brotherton, M. 1964. *Masers and lasers: How they work, what they do.* New York: McGraw-Hill.
16. Harvey, A. F. 1970. *Coherent light.* London and New York: Wiley-Interscience.
17. Lengyel, B. A. 1966. *Introduction to laser physics.* New York: Wiley.
18. Ivey, H. F. 1963. *Electroluminescence and related effects.* New York: Academic.
19. Illuminating Engineering Society of North America. Committee on Light Control and Equipment Design. 1959. IES guide to design of light control. Part I: Physical principles; Part II: Design of reflector and optical elements. *Illum. Eng.* 54(2):722–727; 54(12):778–786.
20. Resnick, R. and D. Halliday. 1977. *Physics.* 3rd ed. New York: Wiley.
21. Hardy, A. C. and F. H. Perrin. 1932. *The principles of optics.* 1st ed. New York and London: McGraw-Hill.
22. Illuminating Engineering Society of North America. Committee on Testing Procedures for Illumination Characteristics. 1963. Resolution on reporting polarization. *Illum. Eng.* 58(5):386.

Measurement of Light and Other Radiant Energy

2

PRINCIPLES OF PHOTOMETRY AND RADIOMETRY

Introduction

Progress in a branch of science or engineering is very much dependent on the ability to measure the associated quantities. A quotation from Lord Kelvin, the famous British scientist (1824–1907), perhaps expresses this thought best:

> When you can measure what you are speaking about, and express it in numbers, you know something about it; but when you cannot express it in numbers, your knowledge is of a meager and unsatisfactory kind; it may be the beginning of knowledge, but you have scarcely, in your thoughts, advanced to the stage of science, whatever the matter may be.

The earliest instruments for measuring luminous quantities depended on visual appraisal as a means of measurement. Such methods lacked both precision and accuracy, largely because the results were dependent on the individual observers making the measurement. Even for a particular observer, measurement reproducibility was poor because a number of variables influencing the measurements could not be controlled or explained. These visual methods are now rarely used, being restricted to research and experimental work; conventional measurements today are made using physical instruments that utilize the radiant energy incident upon a receiver. The receiver produces measurable electrical quantities that have a defined, mathematical relationship (preferably a linear one) to the luminous quantity being measured.

The human visual response itself is produced only by radiation in a very narrow band of the electromagnetic spectrum. This range of wavelengths is approximately from 380 to 770 nm; these limits are slightly dependent on the individual observer. It should be kept in mind that for any source of illumination, the radiant energy produced is rarely limited to wavelengths within these boundaries. Although the primary concern in this chapter is the measurement of radiation that results in visual sensation, measurements of radiant quantities outside the visible spectrum are also important because of the nonvisual effects that this radiation produces.

Optical radiation generally refers to all radiation that can be measured using certain techniques and equipment (employing mirrors, lenses, filters, diffraction gratings, prisms). Thus visible, ultraviolet (UV) and infrared (IR) radiation are collectively considered as optical radiation. The measurement of optical radiation is called *radiometry*. Radiometry is thus the science of measuring radiant quantities without regard for the visual effects of the radiation. *Light* almost always refers to visible wavelengths, although sometimes invisible radiation is so called, as when discussing the effects of radiation on plants or on skin.

Photometry is the measurement of radiation in terms of human visual response. Light measurements with physical instruments are most useful if they are sensitive to the spectral power distribution of radiant energy in the same way as the human eye. Because there are substantial differences in vision between individual observers in this respect, the Commission Internationale de l'Éclairage (CIE) has established a *standard observer* response curve (also known as the photopic luminous efficiency function), denoted by $V(\lambda)$. See chapter 1, Light and Optics. This standard observer response curve with its peak at about 555 nm is used as a standard weighting function which, when applied to a spectral power distribution of the light being measured, characterizes the perceived brightness of that light. Photometry may thus be considered a special branch of radiometry.

The standardization of the eye sensitivity weighting curve is the key to photometry, removing the influence of the observer from the measurements. However, despite the industry-wide acceptance of this criterion, one should recognize that it represents a compromise in assuming a predictable correlation of physical measurements with visual response, and there are some circumstances where the system works poorly.[1]

Photopic, Mesopic and Scotopic Vision. These categories of vision are defined with reference to the adaptive state of the rod and cone photoreceptors of the retina. At very low luminance levels, below about 0.01 cd/m^2—the *scotopic region*—the light energy is insufficient to energize the cone photoreceptor system, but is adequate to stimulate the rod photoreceptor system. At this level, color vision is absent, and as there are no rod photoreceptors in the central fovea of the retina, objects are best seen at about 10–20° off axis from the point of visual regard, where the rod population in the retina is maximum. The standard luminous efficiency function for scotopic vision is represented by the function $V'(\lambda)$ with its peak at about 507 nm (see chapter 1, Light and Optics).

At luminance levels greater than 3 cd/m²—the *photopic region*—colors can be distinguished, and objects having fine detail can be readily seen in the central visual field, where the density of the cone population of the retina is highest, that is, in the fovea. Strictly speaking, the photopic luminous efficiency function applies to visual fields of size 2° or less. The function $V(\lambda)$ is of fundamental importance for lighting, allowing quantitative comparison of photometric quantities on the basis of a well-defined psychophysical measure of human response.

At intermediate luminance levels, between 0.01 and 3 cd/m²—the *mesopic region*— vision is both peripheral and central, and there is some ability to distinguish colors. In addition, as the luminance increases through the mesopic range there is a stronger increase in brightness perception for large reddish objects than for large bluish objects. These visual experiences suggest that both rod and cone photoreceptors are contributing to the vision process. Because of the methodological difficulties in adequately incorporating the features of mesopic vision, there is presently no standard luminous efficiency function for this level of luminance, although it is of practical importance for roadway, security and other exterior nighttime conditions.

Basic Concepts

Units of Measurement. The International System of Units, abbreviated SI, is accepted worldwide as a practical system of units of measurement. In that system, the fundamental photometric quantity, *luminous intensity*, is expressed in *candelas* (cd). The magnitude of the candela has a historical basis. At one time called the candlepower, it was defined in terms of flame or filament standards. For practical purposes the terms candela and candlepower are equivalent and, though no longer standard, the latter term is still occasionally used. The current definition of the candela is[2]

… the luminous intensity, in a given direction, of a source that emits monochromatic radiation of frequency 540×10^{12} Hz and that has a radiant intensity in that direction of $\frac{1}{683}$ W/sr.

The candela is now formally defined on this radiometric basis because of advances that have been made in

this area of metrology. The definition expresses the candela in terms of the watt and the steradian. The *steradian* is defined as the solid angle subtending an area on the surface of a sphere equal to the square of the sphere's radius. The steradian is an SI supplementary unit. The unit of power, the *watt*, is likewise not a base SI unit but can be defined as 1 J/s (energy per unit time) or, in base units, $1 \text{ m}^2 \cdot \text{kg} \cdot \text{s}^{-3}$. Since the formal definition of the candela is at a single wavelength (at the peak of the photopic luminous efficiency function), $V(\lambda)$ must be applied to measurements of radiant power produced by real sources in order to reduce them to candelas.

In casual discussions, the terms energy and power are often used interchangeably, and in general discussions on measurements of optical radiation, the term radiant energy is most commonly used (as in the title of this chapter). However, it should be kept in mind that it is radiant power (that is, the transfer of energy per unit of time) weighted in terms of an eye sensitivity curve, and not radiant energy, that acts as the visual stimulus. The terms "radiant power" and "radiant flux" are used synonymously. There is no photopic weighting inherent in the concept of radiant flux; it is strictly a radiometric quantity. The unit of radiant flux is the watt.

Two important derived units based on the candela are those of *luminous flux* and *illuminance*. To understand how these two quantities are related to the luminous intensity, consider a hypothetical model, illustrated in figure 2-1. An isotropic point source of radiation (that is, one that radiates energy uniformly in all directions) is located at the geometric center of an ideal sphere of zero reflectance (all incident radiation is absorbed). Any portion of the inner sphere's surface will then receive only direct radiation from the point source itself and not reflected radiation from other parts of the sphere's surface. For a sphere having a radius of one unit, an area on the sphere's surface of one square unit represents a solid angle of one steradian. (The two-dimensional shape of this area is irrelevant; it might be a circle, in which case the steradian would be represented by a cone. This becomes more clear when the strict definition of luminous intensity is given in terms of a limit.) The luminous intensity of the source in this model is the same in all directions and assumed to be 1 cd. The radiant flux falling on a unit area of the sphere's surface can now be defined to be the luminous flux.

The unit of luminous flux is the *lumen* (lm); the quantity of luminous flux falling on one square unit of the sphere's surface is defined as 1 lm. Note that the unit itself is arbitrary, since the total quantity of flux that will be incident on this area is independent of the size of the sphere. For a sphere of unit radius, it can be shown by simple geometry that the area of the sphere's surface is equal to 4π square units; thus the isotropic

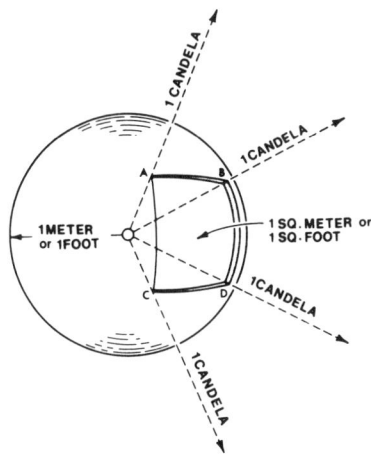

Fig. 2-1. Relationship between candelas, lumens, lux and foot-candles. A point source (luminous intensity = 1 cd) is shown at the center of a sphere of unit radius whose surface has a reflectance of zero. The illuminance at any point on the sphere is 1 lx if the radius is 1 m, or 1 fc if the radius is 1 ft. The solid angle subtended by the area *ABCD* is 1 sr. The flux density is therefore 1 lm / sr, which corresponds to a luminous intensity of 1 cd as originally assumed. The sphere has a total area of 4π m^2 or ft^2, and there is a luminous flux of 1 lm falling on each unit area. Thus the source provides a total of 4π lm.

source having a luminous intensity of 1 cd produces a total luminous flux of 4π lm.

The concentration of luminous flux falling on a surface, that is, the incident flux per unit area, is called *illuminance*. To define a unit of illuminance, the sphere must now be given real dimensions, because the flux density diminishes with increasing distance from the source. If the sphere's radius is 1 m, the illuminance on the sphere's wall is 1 lm/m^2, or 1 *lux* (lx). If the radius is 1 ft, the illuminance is 1 lm/ft^2, or 1 *footcandle* (fc).

Another important luminous quantity is *luminance*. This quantity is more difficult to grasp, and the sphere model is not useful for that purpose. Luminance relates directly to perceived "brightness," that is, the visual effect that illumination produces. Luminance depends not only on the illuminance on an object and its reflective properties, but also on its projected area on a plane perpendicular to the direction of view. There is a direct relationship between the luminance of

a viewed object and the illuminance of the resulting image on the retina of the eye. This is analogous to the exposure requirements in photography. The unit of luminance is the candela per square meter (cd/m^2).

Photometric quantities along with their radiometric counterparts are discussed and defined in the Glossary.

Radiometric and photometric measurements frequently involve a consideration of the inverse square law (which is strictly applicable only for point sources) and the cosine law.

Inverse Square Law. The inverse square law (see figure 2-2a) states that the illumination E at a point on a surface varies directly with the luminous intensity I of the source, and inversely as the square of the distance d between the source and the point. If the surface at the point is normal to the direction of the incident light, the law may be expressed as follows:

$$E = \frac{I}{d^2} \qquad (2\text{-}1)$$

This equation holds true within $\frac{1}{2}\%$ when d is at least five times the maximum dimension of the source (or luminaire) as viewed from the point on the surface. For a further discussion of this "five-times rule," see chapter 9, Lighting Calculations.

Cosine Law. The cosine law (see figure 2-2b), also known as Lambert's law, states that the illuminance on any surface varies as the cosine of the angle of incidence. The angle of incidence, θ, is the angle between the normal to the surface and the direction of the incident light. The inverse square law and the cosine law can be combined as follows:

$$E = \frac{I}{d^2} \cos \theta \qquad (2\text{-}2)$$

Cosine-Cubed Law. A useful extension of the cosine law is the *cosine-cubed equation* (see figure 2-2c). By substituting $h/\cos\theta$ for d, the above equation may be

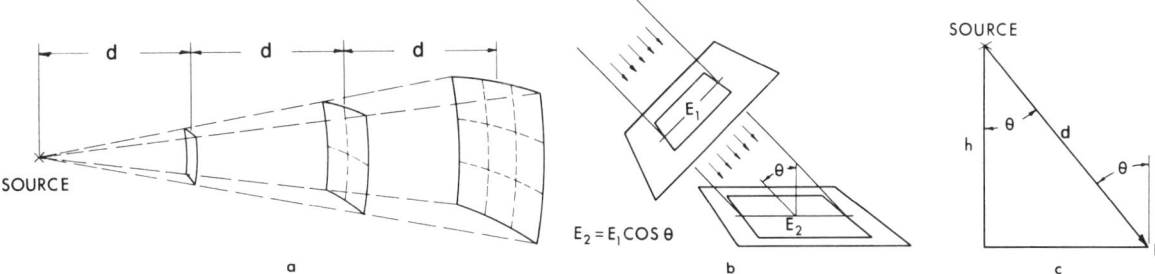

Fig. 2-2. (a) The inverse-square law illustrating how the same quantity of light flux is distributed over a greater area, as the distance from source to surface is increased. (b) The Lambert cosine law showing that light flux striking a surface at angles other than normal is distributed over a greater area. (c) The cosine-cubed law explaining the transformation of the formula.

Fig. 2-3. Some Measurable Characteristics of Light, Light Sources and Lighting Materials

Characteristic	Dimensional Unit	Equipment	Technique
Light			
Wavelength	Nanometer	Spectrometer	Laboratory
Color	None	Spectrophotometer and colorimeter	Laboratory
Flux density (illuminance)	Lumen per unit area (lux and footcandle)	Photometer	Laboratory or field
Orientation of polarization	Degree (angle)	Analyzing Nicol prism	Laboratory
Degree of polarization*	Per cent (dimensionless ratio)	Polarization photometer	Laboratory
Light Sources			
Energy radiated	Joule per square meter	Calibrated radiometer	Laboratory
Color temperature	Kelvin (K)	Colorimeter or filtered photometer	Laboratory or field
Luminous intensity	Candela	Photometer	Laboratory or field
Luminance	Candela per unit area	Photometer or luminance meter	Laboratory or field
Spectral power distribution	Watts per nanometer	Spectroradiometer	Laboratory
Power consumption	Watt	Wattmeter, or voltmeter and ammeter for dc, and unity power factor ac circuits	Laboratory or field
Light output (total flux)	Lumen	Integrating sphere photometer	Laboratory
Zonal distribution	Lumen or candelas	Distribution or goniophotometer	Laboratory
Lighting Materials			
Reflectance	Per cent (dimensionless ratio)	Reflectometer	Laboratory or field
Transmittance	Per cent (dimensionless ratio)	Photometer	Laboratory or field
Spectral reflectance and transmittance	Per cent (at specific wavelengths)	Spectrophotometer	Laboratory
Optical density	Dimensionless number	Densitometer	Laboratory

* Committee on Testing Procedures for Illumination Characteristics of the IES: "Resolution on Reporting Polarization," *Illum. Eng.*, Vol. LVIII, p. 386, May 1963.

written

$$E = \frac{I \cos^3 \theta}{h^2} \qquad (2\text{-}3)$$

Other Measurable Quantities. The principal photometric quantities have been discussed. These and other quantities of interest are summarized in figure 2-3 and in the Glossary.

PHOTOMETRY IN PRACTICE: GENERAL REQUIREMENTS

Standards[3]

Calibration standards are used by photometric laboratories to tie all measurement to a common base. An ideal standard has two principal characteristics: it should be both accessible and invariant. There is no ideal standard for photometric measurements, so in practice, the deployment of a system or hierarchy of standards is required to maintain a usable link to the common base. These standards usually take the form of calibrated light sources.

Primary Standards. Primary standards that define radiometric and photometric quantities are maintained by national standardizing laboratories.[2] They are reproducible only through a specified, usually complex experimental procedure. A primary standard defined from this operational point of view is not normally directly accessible by other laboratories. To link the measurement systems of the standardizing laboratory to other laboratories, it is necessary to utilize some kind of intermediate, or secondary, standard that is traceable in some way to the primary standard.

Secondary Standards. Secondary, or reference, standards are usually derived directly from a primary standard. A secondary standard is usually prepared with precise electrical and radiometric measurement equipment by a national standardizing laboratory. National as well as other photometric laboratories maintain secondary standards. Preservation of the initial rating of a secondary standard is of prime importance. Accordingly, a secondary standard will be used as seldom as possible, usually to calibrate working standards that will be used routinely. Secondary standards should always be handled and stored with special care.

Working Standards. Working standards are used for routine measurements in a laboratory and are usually prepared and calibrated by that same laboratory from its own secondary standard. Many laboratories institute methods for minimizing the use of working standards to prolong the validity of their rating. An example is the use of an auxiliary or monitor lamp for checking the stability of an integrating sphere used for total-flux measurements (see the subsection on the Integrating-Sphere Photometer below).

For reasons of cost, availability and convenience, a laboratory may obtain standards from a *reference laboratory*, a private laboratory that offers calibration standards on a commercial basis. This usually adds another step in the calibration chain and generally increases the uncertainties in the calibration.

The preceding classification of standards has evolved, more or less, from historical usage; it does not represent strict scientific definitions. A given standard may have one designation in the laboratory of origin, and another designation in the user laboratory. For example, the term "primary standard" is often used within a secondary laboratory to designate a standard source that was purchased from the national standardizing laboratory and that is used only to make other working standards for everyday use in that laboratory. Sometimes, in this context, the primary standard is referred to as a "master standard." The term "secondary standard" is also commonly used in private laboratories to distinguish a standard from the one called "primary," and sometimes the terms "secondary standard" and "working standard" are used interchangeably. The term "tertiary standard" is used if there are three levels of standards deployed.

Regardless of the nomenclature for standards, it is most important to document the lineage of all standards to the primary standard maintained at the national standardizing laboratory. The uncertainties in calibrating each standard should also be specified.

Types of Standards. The most commonly used standards are (1) calibrated light sources of various types and (2) detectors. In the United States, lamp and detector standards may be purchased from the National Institute of Standards and Technology (NIST). In Canada, consult the National Research Council of Canada (NRCC). What is available is subject to change resulting from technical developments. Personnel at NIST or NRCC should be consulted at the time the standard is purchased.

Standards for luminous flux are usually incandescent lamps of various wattages. As an alternative to using a calibrated source for luminous intensity calibrations, standard detectors are available from which sources themselves can be calibrated. These detectors can also be used to calibrate other detectors used to measure illuminance.

Corrections in calibration are usually required for measurements involving sources that are dissimilar in size, wattage, shape and spectral composition. Considerable effort is required to minimize errors when applying these corrections. Typically, special measurements have to be taken or new secondary sources have to be prepared by the standardizing laboratories. In some cases these procedures may not be straightforward. To avoid errors then, it is always desirable to use the same type of light source for the secondary or working standards as is available from the standardizing laboratory.

Other Radiometric Standards. *Spectral standards* are calibrated in terms of intensity per unit wavelength. These are usually tungsten-halogen lamps, ANSI code FEL, most often calibrated for total spectral flux. The calibration typically includes portions of the UV and IR regions of the spectrum. Deuterium standards provide greater intensity than FEL lamps in the UV and extend the calibration range to below 250 nm. Ribbon filament lamps are used for radiance calibrations.

There are other types of standards for special purposes.

General Methods

Photometric measurements, in general, make use of the basic laws of photometry previously desribed. Three types of photometric measurement procedures are:

Direct Photometry. Direct photometry consists of the simultaneous comparison of a standard lamp and an unknown light source.

Substitution Photometry. Substitution photometry consists in the sequential evaluation of the desired photometric characteristics of a standard lamp and an unknown light source in terms of an arbitrary reference.

Relative Photometry. To avoid the use of standard lamps, the relative method is widely applied. It consists in the evaluation of the photometric characteristic of a lamp by comparison with the assumed lumen or spectral output of a test lamp.

MEASURING EQUIPMENT

Radiometric measurement instrumentation consists of a detector, a means of conditioning or amplifying the output of the detector, a method of displaying or of storing the measurement, and possibly an optical element or system of elements to collect the radiant power to be measured. Depending on the geometric relationship between the source and detector, the quantity measured is radiance, irradiance or radiant intensity (or the corresponding photometric quantity: luminance, illuminance or luminous intensity).

A *radiometer* measures radiant power over a wide range of wavelengths which may include the ultraviolet, visible or infrared regions of the spectrum. It may employ a detector which is nonselective in wavelength response or one which gives adequate response in a specific wavelength band. Optical filtering may be used to level (flatten) the radiometer's response over a particular range of wavelengths or to approximate some desired function. For example, a number of useful *action functions* have been defined in the ultraviolet range, to which detector responses can be matched. Examples are industrial polymerization functions used for photoresist exposures and for UV curing. Another example is the erythemal effectiveness function (chapter 5, Nonvisual Effects of Radiant Energy). The filtering must compensate not only for the spectral selectivity of the detector, but also for the transmission characteristics of any optical components incorporated into the radiometer. Filtering may also be used to suppress the detector's response to radiant power outside the desired range.

A radiometer which has been optically or electronically filtered to approximate a spectral sensitivity function of the eye is called a *photometer*. The spectral response characteristic of a photometer is typically designed to match the CIE photopic standard observer. Photometers can also be filtered to provide a response similar to the CIE scotopic standard observer.

A more elaborate radiometer, really a photometric measurement system, is the *colorimeter*, which incorporates multiple detectors corrected to respond according to the CIE tristimulus functions. Filter colorimeters are used extensively to measure the color characteristics of visible radiation.

Detectors

Thermal Detectors. Thermal detectors include thermopiles, bolometers and pyroelectric detectors. They produce a voltage proportional to the absorbed radiant power. The absorbing surface of the detector is usually blackened, making it nonselective over a wide range of wavelengths. The signal levels of these detectors are very low, and they are very sensitive to ambient temperature changes. Once used extensively, they are now largely confined to laser light measurements.

Phototubes. A phototube is a vacuum or gas-filled glass tube containing a photoemissive surface as the source of electrical current. Radiant power striking the photoemissive surface releases electrons by the photoelectric effect, which are collected by an anode having a higher voltage. The smallness of the resulting current limits the usefulness of vacuum phototubes to applications with high levels of radiant power.

Adding a gas to a phototube and impressing a high voltage on the anode produces an avalanche amplification of the current. Gas-filled phototubes can measure lower levels of radiant power; however, their nonlinear response to power makes them a poor choice for measurement purposes.

The most useful form of phototube is the photomultiplier tube (PMT). Photomultiplier tubes employ a photoemissive cathode which emits electrons when irradiated. Their spectral sensitivity depends on the cathode material, for which many choices are available. When photons strike the photocathode, electrons are emitted, which are accelerated through a series of electron multipliers (dynodes), where the signal is greatly multiplied. The electrons are collected by an anode, where the output current is measured. A voltage divider chain connects the elements in the PMT in such a way that electrons are accelerated from one stage to the next. Typical PMT designs employ 9–11 stages of electron multiplication and produce signal gains from several thousand to several million. The voltage required to operate the PMT may vary from 500 to 2000 V, depending on the tube construction and number of dynodes. The overall gain of the PMT is controlled by the voltage applied between elements, and a high degree of voltage regulation is required for accurate operation.

PMT detectors differ from solid-state devices in that they produce an output signal (dark current) in the absence of light, due to thermionic emission. The dark current can be reduced by lowering the temperature of the PMT. Most PMTs exhibit gain differences when exposed to magnetic fields or when their orientation in the earth's magnetic field is changed. Magnetic shielding is required in most applications where calibration stability is important. Most PMTs are shock sensitive, and rough handling may cause failure or loss of previous calibration. All phototubes have highly selective spectral response characteristics. Depending upon the photoemissive cathode material used, a phototube may be used for UV, visible or near-IR measurement; however, a single phototube cannot cover this entire spectral range.

Solid-State Detectors. This is a very large category of detectors incorporating semiconducting materials. All exhibit similar spectral response characteristics: their sensitivity to longer wavelengths increases up to a photon energy limit, where the detector response drops to zero. The useful spectral ranges of solid-state detectors extend from the UV to the far IR region. Some detectors are used in the *photovoltaic* mode, where the short-circuit current is measured; others are used as *photoconductors*, that is, a reverse bias voltage is applied and the device is treated as a radiation-sensitive variable resistor. Examples of photoconductive detectors include cadmium sulfide and cadmium selenide cells.

The photovoltaic mode is most frequently used for radiant power measurements because of its inherent linearity of current as a function of radiant power level. The quantum nature of photovoltaic detectors makes them ideal for instruments which must perform over a wide range of radiation levels. The selenium *barrier-layer cell*, an early type of photovoltaic solid-state detector, became widely used in laboratory photometers and in photographic exposure meters. The spectral response of selenium photovoltaic cells is shown in figure 2-4. Selenium cells, however, have been largely

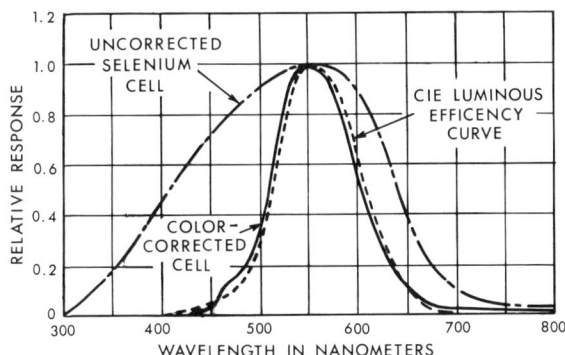

Fig. 2-4. Average spectral sensitivity characteristics of selenium photovoltaic cells, compared with the CIE photopic spectral luminous efficiency curve.

replaced by *silicon photovoltaic cells*, which offer a wider spectral range and the ability to measure lower levels of radiant power. Silicon detectors are also used in self-scanning linear arrays, facsimile (fax) machines, some spectral measuring instruments, and two-dimensional charge-coupled devices (CCDs) used in television cameras. See the subsection on Video-Based Photometers below.

Photodiodes perform best when operated as current sources into "zero-impedance" amplifier circuitry. The linearity of silicon photodiodes has been shown to extend over 10 decades with appropriate amplification. Because very small currents are involved (typically $10^{-13}-10^{-3}$ A), proper amplifier design is essential for the performance of these photometric instruments.

CIE Publication 69[6] outlines test methods, classes and performance characteristics of photometers for luminance and incident-light measurement. Digital instrumentation for display and computer data acquisition further enhance the utility of modern photometric detectors.

General Considerations

Spectral Response. The detector is the principal component affecting spectral response in a radiant-power-measuring instrument. Photomultiplier tubes (PMTs) and silicon photovoltaic detectors are most commonly used in radiometers and photometers. As previously noted, these detectors respond differently to different regions of the spectrum. It is recommended that the spectral range of the detector be matched to the spectral region to be measured. This can significantly improve sensitivity or relieve the burden on filtering. Photometers require good suppression of both ultraviolet and infrared and careful correction to a photopic spectral sensitivity.

Transient Effects. The output of selenium photovoltaic cells, when they are suddenly exposed to constant illumination, will require a short rise time to reach a stable output and thereafter may decrease slightly over a longer time due to fatigue. By contrast,

silicon photovoltaic cells typically exhibit microsecond rise times and no fatigue. The rise and fall times for most photometers employing silicon photodiodes are usually limited by the amplification circuitry. PMTs have nanosecond rise times but exhibit hysteresis, requiring from seconds to minutes to adapt to light-level changes. Precision radiometers and photometers usually employ PMTs with minimum hysteresis.

Temperature Effects. Temperature variations affect the performance of all photodetectors. Selenium photovoltaic cells exhibit significant changes in shunt resistance with temperature which can interact with external circuit impedance and produce gain changes. In addition, selenium cells can be permanently damaged by temperatures above 50°C (120°F). Silicon cells are considerably less affected by temperature; however, problems can arise from the effects of temperature on detector response. The transmission of the spectral correction filters may also be affected by temperature. Correction factors may be employed when using photovoltaic detectors at other than their calibrated temperature (typically 23°C), or means may be provided to maintain the instrument temperature near the calibration temperature. Hermetically sealed detectors provide protection against the effects of humidity and some insulation against temperature cycling. Care should be taken that the effects of high temperature or temperature cycling do not damage cemented layers of the detector filter.

PMTs are quite temperature sensitive. Both dark current and noise increase at higher temperatures. Also, the spectral response can vary significantly with temperature changes. Thermoelectric temperature control is frequently used to control the dark current, noise and spectral characteristics of PMTs.

Effect of Pulsed or Cyclical Variation of Light.[7] Electric discharge sources flicker when operated on alternating-current (ac) power supplies. Precautions should be taken with regard to the effects of frequency, pulse rate and pulse width when measuring the luminous properties of lamp sources.[8] It cannot be assumed that an instrument will treat modulation of a light source in the same way as the human eye. The internal capacitance of the detector, the response time of the amplifier and the response of the readout device (whether analog or digital) to pulsating signals must be considered. Special metering circuitry for the integration of pulsed light is available for the measurement of flashing incandescent and pulsed xenon sources. See the IES Guide to Calculating the Effective Intensity of Flashing Signal Lights.

Instrument Zeroing. It is important to check the photometer or radiometer zeroing prior to taking measurements. For any type of equipment using an amplifier, it may be necessary to zero both the amplifier and the dark current. Where possible, it should be verified that the instrument remains correctly zeroed when the range is changed. Alternatively, any deviation from zero under dark current conditions may be measured and subtracted from the test readings.

Electrical Interference. With electronic instrumentation, electrical interference may be induced in the leads between the detector and the instrumentation. This effect may be minimized by using filter networks, shielding, grounding or combinations of the above.

Means of Attenuation. Modern detectors have a linear response over many orders of magnitude, and the accompanying electronics are capable of maintaining a wide dynamic measuring range for the radiometric measurement device. Other means of attenuation for this purpose may also be employed in some photometric measurements:

- A rotating sector disk, or *chopper*, with one or more angular apertures is placed between a source and the detector, and rotated at such speed that the cyclical variations in the light source do not interact with the frequency of the disk rotation.[5] The luminous attenuation is by a factor of $\theta/360°$, where θ is the total angular aperture size in degrees. The sector disk has advantages over many other filters. The light attenuation characteristics of the chopper do not change over time, and it reduces the luminous flux without changing the spectral composition of the light.

- Various types of neutral-density filters made of glass or gelatin are often used for attenuation, but they are seldom in fact spectrally neutral, and their transmission characteristics should be determined before use. Further, filters can vary in transmittance with ambient temperature and over time. Stacked filters can cause additional errors from interference between surfaces. Wire mesh or perforated metal filters are spectrally neutral, but have a limited range of attenuation. Partially silvered mirrors can also be used, but reflected light must be controlled to avoid photometric errors.

Magnetic Fields. As previously noted, radiometers and photometers containing PMTs may be sensitive to strong magnetic fields which can alter their calibration. Commercial instruments containing PMTs use magnetic shielding adequate to protect them from most ambient magnetic fields; however, it is advisable to keep them away from heavy-duty electrical machinery.

Signal Conditioning. The current produced by photovoltaic detectors usually requires amplification and other kinds of signal conditioning. The most common signal conditioning method uses an operational amplifier in a current follower configuration. This configuration provides low input impedance, and the output

voltage is the product of the detector current and the feedback resistance. Although PMTs provide much higher signal currents, they are frequently used with a similar circuit to assure linearity. The output of the operational amplifier can drive most displays, whether analog or digital. Frequently, commercial instrumentation provides other kinds of signal conditioning. If signal currents are very low, integration may be used to increase the signal level and to improve the signal-to-noise ratio. Analog-to-digital conversion may be introduced in order to provide an interface to digital computing or a means of signal averaging. Memory may also be provided for data logging. Computing may be done inside the instrument by a microprocessor or fed to an external computer by means of a data link.

Measuring Instruments

Instruments for photometric measurement come in a wide variety of shapes and sizes, from hand-held to stationary. Various instruments are shown in figure 2-5.

Illuminance Photometers

Typical Configurations. The simplest illuminance photometer consists of a photovoltaic detector with a photopic correction filter, connected to an operational amplifier with a display. These can be enclosed in one case, or, as is more common with laboratory photometers, the detector and filter can be in one module that is connected by a cable to a console, at a convenient distance, containing the amplifier and display. Illuminance photometers of this type detect light over a large angle.

Effect of Angle of Incidence (Cosine Effect). Illuminance photometers are frequently used to measure the total luminous flux density incident on a surface such as a table top, a wall or a road surface. Part of the light reaching the detector at high angles of incidence is reflected by the cell surface or the filter or cover glass in front of it, and some may be obstructed by the rim of the case surrounding the detector. The resultant error increases with angle of incidence; where an appreciable portion of the flux comes at large angles, values as much as 25% below the true illuminance value can be obtained.

The component of illuminance contributed by single sources at large angles of incidence may be determined by orienting the plane of the detector perpendicular to the direction of the light, and multiplying the reading thus obtained by the cosine of the angle of incidence. Detectors used in most illuminance photometers now have diffusing covers or some means of correcting the readings to a true cosine response. A frequently used solution to the cosine problem consists in placing a flashed opal glass or diffusing acrylic disk over the detector. At high angles of incidence, however, light is

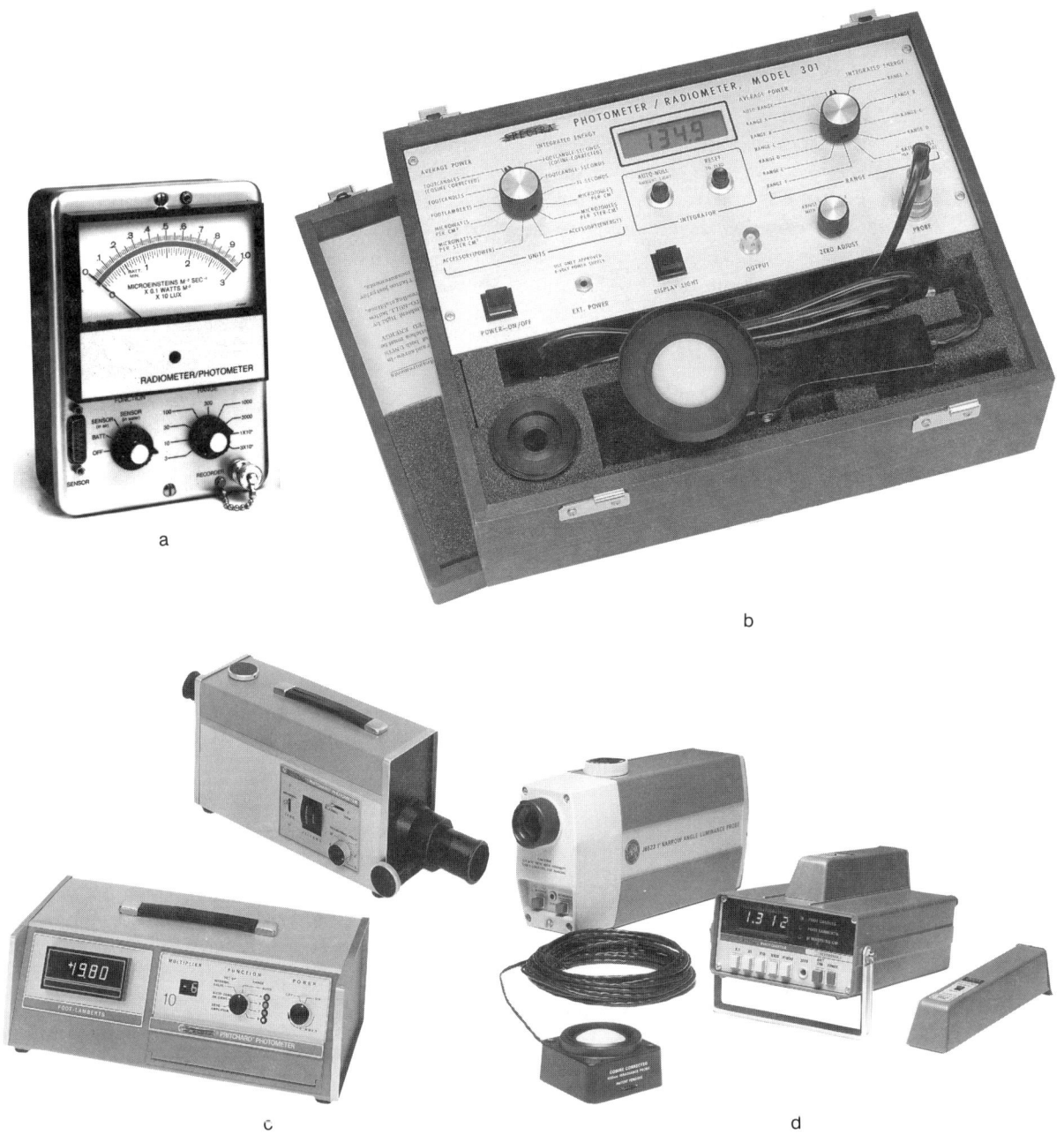

Fig. 2-5. Various photometric measurement devices. (a) portable meter for radiometric and photometric measurements; (b) a paddle-type illuminance meter; (c) Pritchard luminance photometer; (d) combined illuminance, luminance and irradiance system.

reflected specularly, so that the readings are still too low. This can be compensated by allowing light to enter through the edges of the diffuser. The readings at very high angles will then be too high, but can be corrected by using a screening ring.

Leveling. Particularly during photometry of lighting systems where light is received from one or a small number of discrete sources, such as in roadway lighting, accurate leveling of the illuminance photometer is important. Instruments are available where the detector is gimbal mounted and self-leveling. This removes

problems when trying to measure horizontal illuminance on surfaces which may be uneven or sloping.

Luminance Photometers (Telephotometers)

Luminance photometers consist essentially of the same elements as illuminance photometers but with the addition of suitable optics to image an object onto the detector. A means of viewing the object is usually provided, so that the user is able to see the area that is being measured as well as the surrounding field. Because of the similarity of this optical system to a telescope, these instruments are frequently referred to as telephotometers.

Changing the focal length of the objective lens will change the field of view and thus the size of the measurement field. Apertures of various sizes can further define the measured area. Angular measurement fields from seconds of arc to several degrees may be selected.

Typically, modern luminance photometers will use silicon photovoltaic detectors or photomultiplier tubes. The amplifier sensitivity may be either manually selected or automatic. Color filters may be incorporated for color measurements, and neutral-density filters to extend the measurement range.

Photodetectors are typically silicon for portable and low-sensitivity instruments, and photomultiplier tubes for high-sensitivity instruments. Most instruments have at least four electrical ranges, and many incorporate attenuation screens or neutral-density filters for additional range. Most instruments in current manufacture incorporate digital displays. The electrical scheme may be anything from a simple amplifier with manual controls to a programmed microprocessor with routines for calibration, measurement and conversion of display units.

Beamsplitter Spot Meters. This type of photometer employs a beamsplitter behind the objective lens, which divides the incoming radiation into two paths. Approximately half of the radiation passes through the beamsplitter and is focused on an aperture defining the measurement field. The radiation passing through the aperture can be measured with either a PMT or a solid-state detector. The radiation reflected from the beamsplitter is focused on a reticle having an etched pattern with the same dimensions as the measurement aperture. A viewing system with an eyepiece allows the user to see the field of view and an outline of the area being measured. The reticle must be carefully aligned with the measuring field. Readings may be in cd/m^2 or cd/ft^2. Some instruments may include colorimetric filter options. Field-of-view capabilities may range from 0.25 to 10°, with sensitivity ranging from 10^{-2} to 10^6 cd/m^2.

Although good measurements can be made with this type of instrument, it does have some noteworthy disadvantages. Among these are loss of illumination to both the detector and the viewer, introduction of polarization which will affect the measurement of polarized sources, and the difficulty of changing apertures and reticles for different measurement fields. In general, a low-cost instrument using a beamsplitter will provide adequate but not precise location of the measured spot. In addition, instruments in this category have less than precise correction to the photopic function. The accuracy for this class of instrument is usually no better than 5%.

Aperture Mirror Photometers. Most of the problems of the beamsplitter spot meter are addressed by the aperture mirror photometer. There is no beamsplitter to introduce polarization error or reduce the brightness at either the measuring aperture or the viewed image. The image formed by the objective lens falls on an angled first surface mirror with a through hole for the measuring aperture. The viewing optics are focused on the aperture, which appears as a black hole. The field around the measurement aperture is clearly seen in the eyepiece. This arrangement allows apertures to be changed without the need to also change precisely aligned reticles. A disadvantage of the aperture mirror photometer is that if a small source is imaged within the measuring aperture, it cannot be seen in the viewing optics. Instruments of this class usually employ high-quality detectors, one or more neutral-density range-multiplying filters, lens options and some degree of colorimetric capability. They are available with internal microprocessor control and direct reading capability for luminance in several units, for color chromaticity coordinates and for color temperature. The full-scale sensitivity for the best laboratory instruments ranges from 10^{-4} to 10^8 cd/m^2 with an accuracy of about 2%.

Video-Based Photometers. New systems of photometry have recently been developed which use video cameras incorporating *charge-coupled devices* (CCDs).[14, 15] The system consists typically of the camera, an image acquisition board and a microcomputer. On instruction from the software, the image board freezes and digitizes the luminance pattern viewed by the camera. The digitized signal may consist of many thousands of individual bit values, corresponding to the pixels of the camera's CCD array. By suitable calibration, the bit values can be processed by the microcomputer to provide the luminance values at corresponding points in the camera's field of view.

This system is fast and convenient where it is necessary to obtain a large number of luminance values. As the information is provided in digital form, complicated functions of the luminance can be calculated.

One disadvantage of the system is the extensive work required to provide calibration for all the possible camera settings and gains, although automated procedures are being developed for this purpose. The effects of temperature must also be considered, but techniques are also available to overcome this problem.

Reflectometers

Reflectometers are photometers used to measure the reflectances of materials or surfaces in special ways.

The design of the reflectometer and the method of measurement depend upon the reflectance properties of the sample and what part of the reflectance one desires to measure.

Two types of reflection are of general interest. One, reflection from the interface between a specimen and the surrounding medium, is called *first-surface reflection*. All reflection from metallic specimens is first-surface reflection, with as much as 90% of the incident light being returned; dielectric specimens reflect from 4 to 5% of the incoming light in this way. With a few exceptions such as the metals gold and copper, first-surface reflected light has approximately the same spectral characteristics as the source of illumination. The spatial distribution of first-surface reflected light depends upon the surface texture. A highly polished surface produces a specular (mirrorlike) reflection; rough surfaces produce a highly diffused distribution of reflected light. Most commonly encountered surfaces fall between these extremes.

The second type of reflection is called *body reflection*. In this case, the light that penetrates the first surface in a dielectric specimen is diffusely reflected many times by small inclusions such as pigment particles or air bubbles beneath the surface before it reemerges. Light returned by body reflection is always highly diffused with respect to direction and can have its spectral distribution strongly modified by absorption in the specimen, giving rise to the sensation of color. Most objects in everyday life are seen by body-reflected light. First-surface reflection and body reflection combine to give the total reflection from a specimen.

Reflectance, the ratio of reflected light to incident light, is not an intrinsic property of a material, but rather depends upon the measurement geometry, that is, the spatial characteristics of both the source and the detector. If the specimen to be considered is large, several measurements should be taken at different points on it and averaged to obtain a representative value.

The fraction of the incident light reflected is very difficult to determine directly, particularly for diffuse reflection. To bring some order into what could be a chaotic measurement situation, reflectance is usually expressed as a *reflectance factor*, the ratio of the reflectance of a specimen to that of an idealized standard specimen under the same measurement geometry. Three commonly considered idealized specimens are a totally reflecting perfect mirror, a perfectly polished black glass having a specified index of refraction, and a totally reflecting perfect diffuser.

In one method commonly used for measuring total reflectance, the specimen is illuminated by a narrow cone of light from a given angle, typically 10° from the normal to the specimen surface, and the reflected light

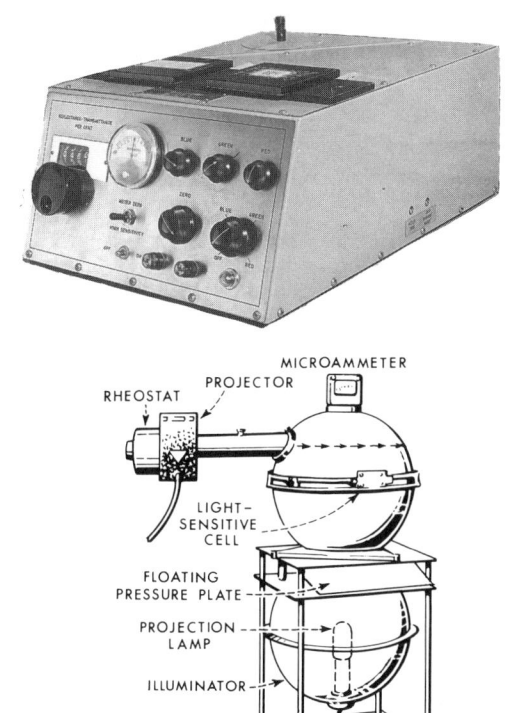

Fig. 2-6. (a) A 45 / 0 reflectometer. (b) A Baumgartner light cell reflectometer showing arrangement for transmittance measurement.

is collected over the entire hemisphere surrounding the specimen. Instruments of this type are said to employ a *conical-hemispherical* geometry. The hemispherical flux collection is often done by means of an integrating sphere with a detector, arranged so that it does not receive light from the specimen directly, but rather views the sphere wall. In this way the signal is proportional to the total flux reflected from the sample.

The same type of instrument can also be used to measure only that part of the light which is diffusely reflected. One example of a specimen which one might measure in this way is one with a very smooth dielectric surface which reflects strongly by scattering from pigments or other inclusions beneath the surface. In this case light specularly reflected from the specimen is allowed to escape through an appropriately located hole in the sphere wall, where a light trap can be positioned to absorb it.

For measuring color, a 45/0 reflectometer such as the one illustrated in figure 2-6a is often used to evaluate the spectral character of diffusely reflected light. The source and the detector are mounted in a fixed relationship in the same housing. Light is incident on the surface from an angle of 45°, and the detector is positioned above and normal to the specimen surface.

Reflectances from plane specimens can be measured in several ways. One method employs a reflectometer that compares, with the aid of an auxiliary mirror, the incident flux with the flux after two reflections from the specimen. Such a reflectometer is often available as an accessory to commercial spectrophotometers. Another method employs a reflectometer that, by repositioning the detector, compares the incident flux of a collimated beam with that reflected by the specimen. In this case, the reflectance value is given directly by the ratio of the two readings. In other instruments of this type, the photocell is fixed to receive the reflected light only, and measurements are made relative to a reflectance standard.

Another type[16] of instrument, a *Baumgartner reflectometer*, shown in figure 2-6b, measures both total reflectance and diffuse transmittance. It consists of two spheres, two light sources and a detector in the upper sphere. The upper sphere is used alone for the measurement of reflectance. The specimen to be measured is placed over an opening at the bottom of the sphere, a collimated beam of light is directed on it from about 30° to the normal, and the total reflected light, integrated by the sphere, is measured by two cells mounted in the sphere wall. The tube holding the light source and the collimating lenses is then rotated so that the light is incident on the sphere wall, and a second reading is taken. The specimen is in place during both measurements, so that the effect on both readings of the small area of the sphere surface it occupies is the same.[17] The ratio of the first reading to the second is the reflectance of the sample for the conditions of the test. Test specimens of translucent materials should be backed by a nonreflecting diffuse material.

Transmittance for diffuse incident light is measured by using the light source in the lower sphere, and taking readings with and without the sample in the opening between the two spheres. The introduction of the sample will change the characteristics of the upper sphere. Correction must be made to compensate for the error thus introduced.[18, 19]

Various other instruments are available for measuring reflectance characteristics of materials.[20] For any reflectance measurements, the reflectometer geometry employed should be specified, and for reflectance factor measurements the ideal reflector should also be specified.

Spectral Measuring Systems

General Principles

The spectral response of a particular detector can be modified using optical or electronic filters to approximate some desired spectral response function (such as photopic correction). The detector itself, of course, must have adequate sensitivity over the spectral range being measured. Measurements with instruments that utilize corrected detectors are often called broad-band or heterochromatic radiometric measurements.

Good-quality detectors are stable over time, and once they are calibrated, accurate measurements can be made without frequent corrections. Broad-band measurements are very practical because they are inexpensive and simple to use.

A disadvantage to broad-band measurement is that it is difficult to design a filter correction to fit a desired function exactly, and although corrections can be applied, these corrections are usually themselves approximations. This can be a problem for the most critical measurements that demand the highest accuracy. In some circumstances, measurement errors can be very large if the corrections are not appropriately applied or if there is a wide departure in filter correction from the ideal response function at wavelengths where a test source produces significant energy. Sometimes, as in the case of a photopically corrected detector, a very accurate fit can be achieved only at substantial cost, and even if the fit is initially satisfactory, the response of the detector or the filter can, at least theoretically, change over time. Commercial instruments usually provide an approximate correction, stating in their specification how closely their detector conforms to an ideal function.

Methods have been developed for correcting measurement errors due to imperfect filter design. For measurements on light sources, errors can be minimized by calibrating a detector with sources that have a known output and a spectral power distribution similar to that of the test source being measured. There are also methods for characterizing a given detector and providing an analytical correction to the measurements.

Perhaps the most important disadvantage of broad-band measurement is the loss of specific wavelength information which results from the integration of radiation by the detector. Although detailed spectral information is not always needed, for some purposes the complete spectral power distribution (SPD) of a source, that is, the radiant power per unit wavelength as a function of wavelength, must be known.

Spectral measurement systems are capable of determining the SPD in a very small band of wavelengths. The measurement of an SPD is considered fundamental; from these data, absolute radiometric, photometric and colorimetric properties of a source can be determined.

In comparison with broad-band measuring systems, spectral measuring systems are inherently complex and costly. The measurements are also generally more difficult and time consuming to make, often requiring a trained operator.

There are different types of spectral measuring systems to suit specific applications, but they all generally incorporate the following elements: collection optics to receive and limit the radiation to be measured, a monochromator, a detector, electronics to process the detector signal and some kind of readout or display. The monochromator separates or disperses the various wavelengths of the spectrum by means of prisms or diffraction gratings. It has an entrance aperture, usually in the form of a rectangular slit, through which the collected radiation enters; some optical elements which image the entrance slit onto the dispersing element(s); and an exit slit through which selected wavelengths of the dispersed radiation pass. A suitable detector is positioned at the exit slit to measure the SPD at the source. To make the many measurements necessary for a complete SPD, the process must be automated. There are many variations on the automation scheme, but typically it incorporates a drive system to scan through a range of wavelengths (such as a means of rotating the monochromator grating) and a means of reading and storing the detector output for each sample, performing the necessary calculations and reporting the results (in printouts or graphs). This entire process is usually carried out using computers.

Types of Systems. A *spectroradiometer* is used to measure the SPD of light sources. The collection optics of a spectroradiometer system typically directs the radiation into a small integrating sphere positioned in front of the entrance slit of the monochromator. The integrating sphere minimizes polarization and spatial measurement errors. A detector, designed for the wavelengths and intensities being measured, receives radiation leaving the exit slit.

A *spectrophotometer* is used to determine spectral reflectance and transmittance properties of materials. It provides a means of examining the color of a material for analysis, standardization and specification. In addition, it is the only means of color standardization that is independent of material color standards (always of questionable permanence) and independent of the differences in color vision existing among even so-called normal observers. Although called a spectrophotometer because of its principal application to measurements in the visible spectrum, this type of instrument is often designed for measuring UV and near-IR radiation. Some spectrophotometers are, in fact, designed especially for UV or IR measurements.

Spectroradiometers and spectrophotometers are closely related instruments in that they involve similar dispersion methods, detectors and automation requirements. The principal difference is that a spectroradiometer measures sources external to the system itself, while a spectrophotometer incorporates internal sources and a housing or chamber in which test samples are placed. It should be kept in mind that in using spectrophotometers for color standardization, it is re-

ally the reflectance properties of the test sample that are being measured and that the actual color appearance is dependent on the SPD of the source being used to evaluate the sample.

Both of these instruments can be used in a configuration called a *spectrograph*. In this type of instrument, the exit slit is replaced by photographic film. Because there is no restrictive aperture, the dispersed radiation falls on the film plane and the various wavelengths are thereby spread out simultaneously. The exposed film provides a qualitative "picture" of the spectral components present. This is particularly useful in studying line emission sources, where the lines provide a "signature" of the source or material present. A means of measuring the optical density of the photographic emulsion where the various lines appear can provide quantitative information as to the intensity of the lines. An advantage of this type of system is the elimination of the need for mechanically scanning through the spectrum. In the form of a spectroradiometer, the instrument is used as an astronomical tool to evaluate the chemical composition of stellar objects. In the form of a spectrophotometer, it can be used for quantitative analysis of materials.

In modern instruments, the spectrograph employs diode arrays in the place of a photographic emulsion. Each diode detects the intensity of incident radiation in a narrow wavelength band. Many modern spectroradiometers and spectrophotometers use this approach. Electronically scanned silicon photodiode arrays provide nearly instantaneous determination of a spectral power distribution. For many applications, array radiometry has replaced scanning systems, with the advantage of much greater measurement speed and the elimination of complex moving parts. For routine work, this reduced measurement time allows many more measurements to be taken, and changes in the SPD of a nonstable test source over time can be monitored. The disadvantage of array systems is that they inherently have more stray-light problems and they do not have the absolute accuracy and sensitivity of the best scanning systems.

Another very simple spectral measuring instrument, used to examine a spectrum visually rather than with a photodetector, is a *spectroscope*.

For a more complete discussion on spectroradiometers, including diode array types, see the IES Guide to Spectroradiometric Measurements.[48]

Special Considerations. The ranges of spectral response in spectral measurement systems generally depend on the nature of the detector. Scanning spectroradiometers usually utilize PMTs because of their high sensitivity. The response of PMTs extends from 125 to 1100 nm.[21] Various types of silicon photodiodes cover the range from 200 to 1200 nm.[21] For IR measurements several compounds can be used: intrinsic germanium (900–1500 nm), lead sulfide (1000–4000 nm), indium arsenide (1000–3600 nm), indium antinomide (2000–5400 nm), various types of doped germanium (zinc-doped, 2000–40,000 nm), and mercury cadmium telluride (1000–13,000 nm).[22] The response of nonselective detectors spans a range from the near ultraviolet to beyond 30,000 nm.[22] Where monochromators utilize diffraction gratings, the grating itself also influences the system response, so gratings must be carefully selected for the range of wavelengths being measured.

For accurate quantitative measurements, the electrical output of the detector as a function of the input radiation to a spectral measuring system must be known. Thus, for processing the electrical output of detectors (voltage, current or charge), the instrumentation and the measurement method must be carefully selected with regard to a number of parameters, such as signal level (saturation), signal-to-noise ratios, fatigue, linearity and response times (for rapidly varying signals). Photon counting and charge integration techniques are sometimes used for extremely low radiation levels.[23]

The influence of stray radiation on the measurement results must be minimized. This can be accomplished by designing an optical system to prevent unwanted wavelengths from reaching the detector. In all radiometric work there are two types of unwanted radiation: out-of-band radiation (radiation that is not completely dispersed) and higher-order radiation coming from diffraction gratings. Out-of-band radiation can usually be minimized by using a double monochromator (dispersing the radiation twice) or using a single monochromator with appropriate filters. This type of unwanted radiation limits the use of diode array spectroradiometers. It arises primarily from the properties of diffraction, so it cannot be eliminated entirely. Higher-order radiation can also be effectively limited by appropriate filters or by using a double monochromator employing a prism as one of the dispersing elements.

Radiated flux of some wavelengths (mainly UV below 200 nm) is dispersed or absorbed by a layer of air between the radiator and the detector. In this case consideration must be given to the placement of the source and the detector, and to the surrounding medium.

All observed spectroradiometric data (sometimes called raw data) are a function not only of the SPD of the light source, but also of the spectral transmission of the optical system, the spectral band-width of the monochromator and the spectral responsivity of the detector. Collectively, these define the *system responsivity*, which is determined by measuring, at each wavelength, the output of a calibration or standard source

having a known output. Once this function is known, the test-source observed data can be corrected by multiplying each value by the known output of the standard source divided by its observed value at that wavelength.

Photometric Measuring Systems — Basic Equipment Types

Different types of photometric instrumentation have been discussed. These instruments can be incorporated into measuring systems, for example when certain measurements are repetitive or where measurements are taken in a number of positions or from a number of directions with respect to a source being measured.

Optical Bench Photometers. Optical bench photometers are used for the calibration of instruments for illuminance measurement. They provide a means for mounting sources and detectors in proper alignment and a means for easily determining the distances between them. If the source is of known luminous intensity in a specified direction, and is distant enough from the detector so its radiation can be treated spatially as if it were emanating from a point, the inverse square law can be used to compute illuminance.

Distribution Photometers. For characterizing the spatial distribution of illumination from a source, a series of luminous intensity measurements are made on a distribution photometer, which may be one of the following types:

- Goniometer and single detector
- Fixed multiple detector
- Moving detector
- Moving mirror

All types of distribution photometers have advantages and disadvantages. The significance attached to each advantage or disadvantage is very dependent on other factors, such as available space and facilities, polarization requirements and economic considerations.

Goniometer and Single Detector. The light source is mounted on a goniometer which allows it to be rotated about both horizontal and vertical axes. The luminous intensity is measured by a single fixed detector.

There are several different versions of goniometers. Each is related to the type of source or luminaire being measured and the facilities in which it is located. With the use of computers the coordinate system of a goniometer system can be easily transformed to another coordinate system[24]; thus universality of data reporting becomes more practical. Figure 2-7 shows two types of goniometer systems, known as Type A and Type B.

Fixed-Multiple-Detector Photometer. Numerous individual detectors are positioned at various angles around

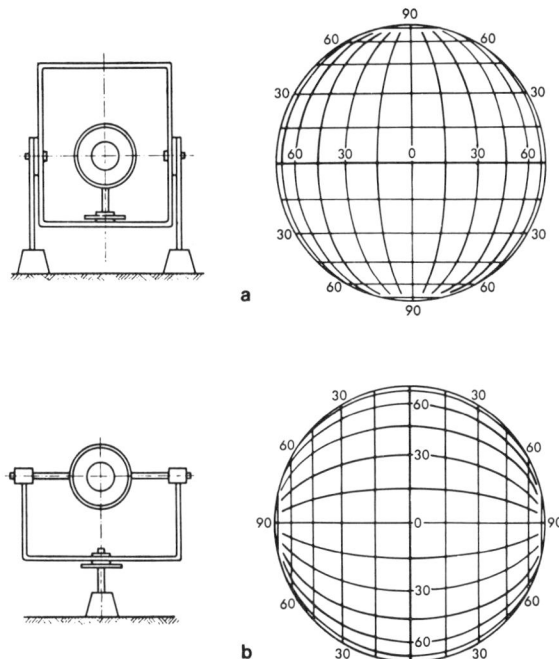

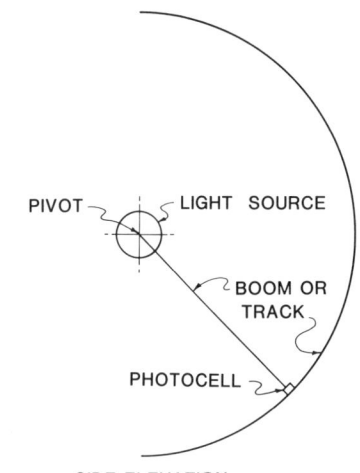

Fig. 2-9. Schematic side elevation of a moving cell photometer.

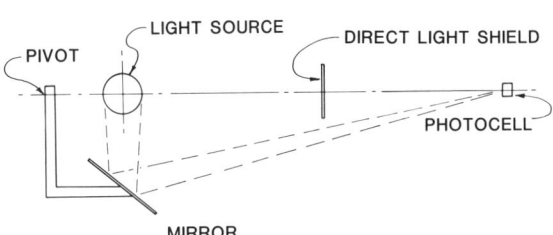

Fig. 2-10. Schematic diagram of a moving mirror photometer.

Fig. 2-7. (a) Type A goniometer where the projector turns about a fixed horizontal axis and also about an axis which, in the position of rest, is vertical, and upon rotation follows the movement of the horizontal axis. (b) Type B goniometer where the light source turns about a fixed vertical axis and also about a horizontal axis following the movement of the vertical axis. The grid lines shown represent the loci traced by the photocell as the goniometer axes are rotated.

the light source under test. Readings are taken on each detector to determine the intensity distribution. See figure 2-8.

Moving-Detector Photometer. This device consists of a detector which rides on a rotating boom or arc-shaped track; the light source is centered in the arc traced by the detector. Readings are collected with the detector positioned at the desired angular settings. Sometimes a mirror is placed on a boom to extend the test distance. See figure 2-9.

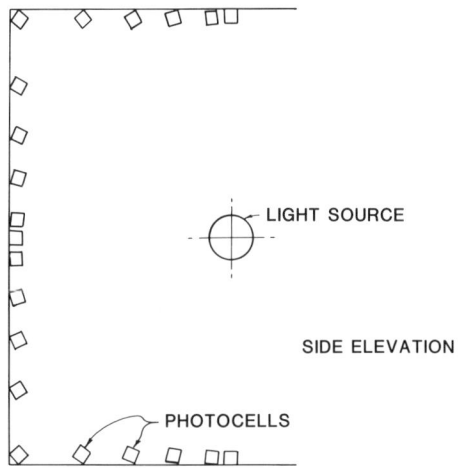

Fig. 2-8. Schematic side elevation of a fixed multiple cell photometer.

Moving-Mirror Photometer. In this type of photometer the mirror rotates around the light source, reflecting the intensity to a single detector. Readings are taken at each desired angle as the mirror moves to that location. See figure 2-10.

Integrating-Sphere Photometer. The integrating-sphere photometer is used to measure the total luminous flux from a source (lamp or luminaire). The most common type is the Ulbricht[25] sphere. See figure 2-11. Other geometric forms are sometimes used.[26] The theory of the integrating sphere assumes an empty sphere whose inner surface is perfectly diffusing and of uniform nonselective reflectance. Every point on the inner surface then reflects to every other point, and the illuminance at any point is therefore made up of two components: the flux coming directly from the source and that reflected from other parts of the sphere wall. With these assumptions, it follows that the illuminance, and hence the luminance, of any part of the wall due to reflected light only is proportional to the total flux from the source, regardless of its distribution. The luminance of a small area of the wall, or the luminance of the outer surface of a diffusely transmitting window in the wall, carefully screened from direct light from the source, but receiving light from other portions of the sphere, is therefore a relative measurement of the flux output of the source. If a source of known output

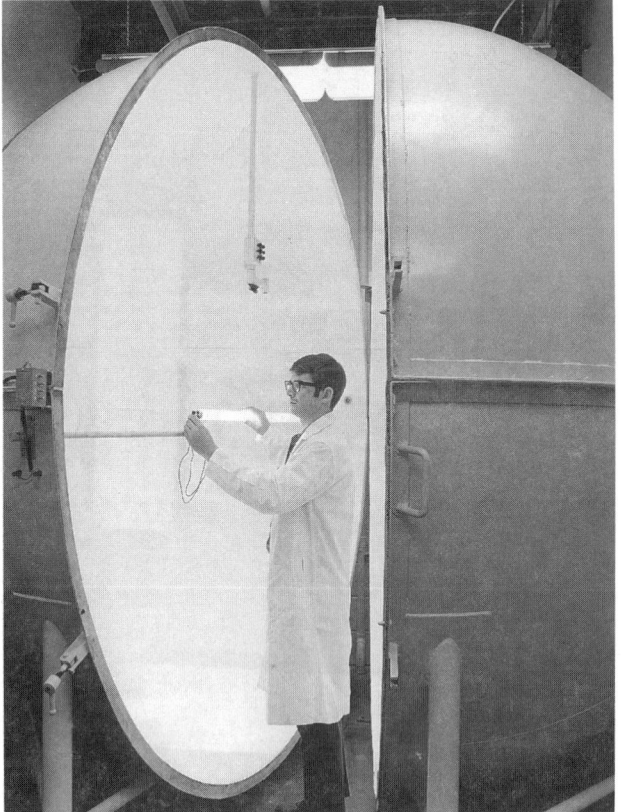

Fig. 2-11. Integrating (Ulbricht) sphere used at the Canadian Standards Association. It is used for directly obtaining total light output of lamps and luminaires.

(in terms of luminous flux) is measured in the sphere, a calibration constant can be determined and thus the luminous flux of a source of unknown output can be determined.

The presence of a source having finite dimensions, its supports and electrical connections, the necessary baffle or shield, and the exit window or port are all departures from the basic assumptions of the integrating-sphere theory. Also, none of the practical coatings used for the sphere interior exhibit the ideal properties of perfect diffusivity and spectral nonselectivity. Despite these limitations, however, if the calibration source and the source to be tested are similar in shape, size and surface reflectance characteristics and their light distribution patterns are similar, the errors introduced by a nonideal integrator can be minimized. In cases where the calibration and test source are substantially different in the above respects, corrections must be determined and applied.[27, 28]

Despite its shortcomings, the integrating sphere is an important tool for photometric measurements, and it has served the lighting industry well for many years. It can produce measurement results quickly with a single measurement, and high accuracy can be achieved if good instrumentation and proper procedures are employed.

LABORATORY MEASUREMENTS[29-32]

Precision and accuracy of laboratory measurements are consistently attained by correctly following a set of standard procedures and using good equipment. Such procedures are prepared and published by standardizing committees or consensus organizations to serve as a common basis for measurements. IES guides provide detailed procedures for the many required electrical and photometric tests for different lamp types. These should be consulted when actual testing is being performed. The information presented in this chapter is intended to be a general overview of good laboratory practices.

Important elements that standard procedures embody are:

- Controlling the electrical supply characteristics
- Ensuring electrical stability of test sources when they are to be used as calibration standards
- Securely mounting the test source or luminaire
- Minimizing the influence of stray light
- Frequently checking instrument readings
- Stabilizing sources and auxiliaries by operating them for a sufficient period of time before measurements are taken
- Compensating for the inherent nonsymmetry of sources and luminaires[32]
- Using instruments that have adequate precision and rated accuracy to meet the requirements of the test
- Understanding the limitations of instruments used with respect to sensitivity, linearity and dynamic range
- Ensuring that the instruments used are in calibration

The laboratory must provide an adequate test distance for sealed beam, floodlight and projector lamp measurements. Space can be conserved by the use of mirrors to permit the folding of the effective test distance. Large integrating spheres may require extending the ceiling height. For testing the different sizes of lamps, there must be adequate space surrounding the sphere to gain access to the sphere interior. Temperature and air circulation control are critical requirements for discharge lamp photometry. Cleanliness, provision for suitable electric power, and storage space for lamps, luminaires and instruments are also important requirements in any photometric laboratory.

Electrical Measurements

Photometry measurement results depend on the electrical operating characteristics of a light source being tested. For this reason, electrical and photometric measurements are almost always done concurrently and the measurement data from both are included in one report.

Electrical measuring instruments should be selected to have current and voltage ratings corresponding to the circuit conditions to be encountered and should give indications of the desired precision. High-accuracy digital instrumentation has replaced analog instruments in most cases, and their use is highly recommended. A comprehensive discussion on instrumentation requirements is given in the IES guide "Selection, Care, and Use of Electrical Instruments in the Photometric Laboratory."[33] If analog instruments are used, it is especially important to consult this reference so that appropriate instrument corrections can be applied for the type of measurement being performed.

Test lamps must be known to be stable before attempting any accurate electrical measurement. To accomplish this it is necessary to season (burn) them in accordance with established procedures.[34]

Instrumentation

Direct-Current Circuits

CURRENT. Current-measuring instruments, or *ammeters*, are inserted in series with the source and have fairly low impedances, thus adding little to the load on the power supply. They may be self-contained, but this type of instrument may not have sufficient range to directly measure the current through high-wattage sources. When it exceeds several amperes, current is usually determined using an accurate digital voltmeter (DVM) in combination with a calibrated current shunt. The shunt resistance should be sufficient to produce a voltage drop that can be measured accurately, but too high a resistance will lower the current appreciably. For most lamp types an appropriate shunt resistance is between 0.1 and 1 Ω.

VOLTAGE. The voltage applied to the light source is measured by means of a voltmeter connected in parallel with the source. It should have the highest impedance possible so as not to disturb the circuit. To avoid corrections to compensate for a voltage drop in the ammeter or across the current shunt, the voltmeter is usually connected directly across the load. Often, separate voltage leads are connected to the base of the lamp through special lamp holders to avoid voltage drop errors resulting from socket-to-lamp connections.

POWER. Power may be computed by multiplying together the observed values of current and voltage.

Alternating-Current Circuits. Ac measuring instruments must be compatible with the waveform and frequency of the voltage or current being measured. They should have a frequency response at least up to the supply frequency. For measurements of sinusoidal waveforms, average-sensing instruments that indicate rms values are satisfactory. For accurate measurements of distorted waveforms that contain harmonics, true rms instruments with a frequency response well above that fundamental are required.

In some ac circuits, a dc component may also be present. In this case a true rms instrument which measures ac + dc must be used; otherwise a separate dc measurement is necessary to determine the true rms value of the voltage or current. Many "true rms" measuring instruments do not include the dc component in the measurement.

Ac instruments are connected to the test circuit in the same manner as described for dc instruments, and the same impedance considerations apply.

In electrical measurements on high-intensity discharge lamps, some instruments require protection from transient voltages (on the order of 1500–4500 V) that occur when lamps are turned on and off. This is usually accomplished by providing switches to connect the instruments into the circuit only after the lamp is operating.

CURRENT. Ammeters for use in ac circuits may be self-contained; however, as with dc circuits, the rating of such meters may be too low. A transformer or current shunt may be used in combination with a digital meter to achieve a more extensive measuring range.

VOLTAGE. As with dc circuits, voltage can be measured directly across the load using an ac voltmeter. The measuring range can be extended using a potential transformer or voltage divider.

POWER. In a resistive circuit (e.g., an incandescent filament lamp) the ac power consumed can be computed as the volt-ampere product or measured directly with a wattmeter. In reactive circuits or where distorted waveforms are present, power is measured with a wattmeter which measures or computes the real power by averaging all the instantaneous volt-ampere products over one cycle of lamp operation. Such an instrument should be capable of responding to harmonics well above that of the fundamental. Older analog wattmeters require corrections to achieve high accuracy. Modern digital power-measuring instruments are often capable of performing all the necessary electrical measurements and seldom require corrections.

Electrical Measurements on Incandescent Lamp Circuits

Incandescent filament lamps are usually measured on a dc circuit where accurate measurement results can be obtained using inexpensive dc power sources and measuring instruments. High-accuracy electrical measurements on incandescent lamps are especially desirable because their light output is very sensitive to small changes in electrical settings. For example, a 1% change in current through a typical filament lamp results in a 5–7% change in light output.

Some incandescent sources have integral electronic components such as diodes and are designed to operate only on ac circuits. True rms instruments that also measure the dc component of a waveform should be used for measurments on this type of source.

Electrical Measurements on Discharge Lamp Circuits. All electric discharge lamps have negative volt-ampere characteristics and must therefore be operated in conjunction with internal or external current-limiting devices, such as resistors or reactors. These are described in chapter 6, Light sources. Because of the presence of distorted waveforms, true rms measuring instruments must be used for any measurements on discharge lamp circuits.

Such measurements may involve lamps or ballasts. In some cases the two are inseparable and measurements are made on the combination as if it were a single device. Because of normal manufacturing tolerances, commercial ballasts supply lamps with some variation in voltage and current characteristics, which affect the electrical input and the light output of lamps. To promote uniformity of testing, the International Electrotechnical Commission (IEC), working through the American National Standards Institute (ANSI), the Canadian Standards Association (CSA) and similar national standardizing bodies throughout the world, has established or is establishing standardized testing procedures for determining the electrical characteristics for most of the common types of discharge lamps. These standard tests are performed using reference circuits and reference ballasts that comply with specified electrical requirements.

Where international standards have not been established, national standards are used.

Lamp Testing. Lamp parameters are influenced by many factors. Detailed, accepted testing procedures where these factors are controlled or specified are described in the appropriate IESNA guides.[35–37] Some of the more important conditions affecting lamp test results are listed below:

- Ambient temperature
- Drafts
- Lamp position
- Lamp connections
- Lamp stabilization
- Power-supply characteristics
- Ballast characteristics
- Lamp circuit characteristics

Ballast Testing. Ballast parameters are influenced by many factors. Detailed accepted testing procedures are described in the appropriate ANSI standards.[38] Ballast testing requires consideration of some or all of the following:

VOLTAGE RANGE. For most tests, ballasts should be operated at their rated primary voltage.

REFERENCE LAMPS. Some tests on ballasts specify that the ballast shall be operating a *reference lamp*. Reference lamps are seasoned lamps which, when operated under stated conditions with the specified reference ballast, operate within specified tolerances of electrical values established by the appropriate existing or proposed specifications.

OPEN-CIRCUIT VOLTAGE. This measurement is necessary only for ballasts containing a transformer.

ELECTRODE HEATING VOLTAGE. On ballasts for use with lamps having continuously heated electrodes, the electrode heating voltages are measured with the electrode windings loaded with the specified dummy load.

SHORT-CIRCUIT CURRENT (HID BALLASTS). An ammeter is inserted in the circuit in place of the lamp, and the short-circuit current of the ballast is measured.

STARTING CURRENT. For fluorescent instant-start ballasts, a resistor and ammeter, in series, with a total resistance equivalent to the value specified in the appropriate standard,[38, 39] is used instead of the lamp. For high-intensity discharge ballasts, the secondary circuit is short-circuited.

ELECTRODE PREHEATING CURRENT (FLUORESCENT PREHEAT BALLASTS). This measurement is made with an ammeter connected in series with the lamp electrodes while the lamp is maintained in the preheat condition.

FLUORESCENT BALLAST OUTPUT. For preheat and instant start ballasts, specifications are in terms of the power delivered to a reference lamp operated by the ballast under test, as compared with the power delivered to the same lamp by the appropriate reference ballast.

With continuously heated electrodes, specifications are in terms of the light output of a reference lamp operated with the ballast under test, as compared with the light output of the same reference lamp when operated with the appropriate reference ballast.

FLUORESCENT BALLAST REGULATION. This measurement involves the relative lamp power input and light output at 90% and 110% of rated ballast input voltage.

FLUORESCENT LAMP CURRENT. The current of a reference lamp should be measured on both the ballast under test and the reference ballast.

For lamps with continuously heated electrodes,[39] unless the internal connections of the ballasts are accessible, measurement of lamp current requires special instrumentation to supply the vector summation of currents in the two leads to an electrode.

Photometric Measurements

Incandescent Filament Lamps[40]. In determining the photometric characteristics of bare incandescent filament lamps, the requirements for electrical measurements previously described should be observed. Test lamps (except series types) are usually measured at rated voltage.

Reference standard lamps[41] may be purchased from or recalibrated by NIST, NRCC or other established laboratories. Lamp standards are usually rated for lumens at a current or voltage a little below their nominal rating, in order to extend the burning time within which the assignment is still valid. The correct color temperature and lamp filament temperature should be maintained. Nickel-plated bases are used on these standards to reduce corrosion and high-resistance problems over their long life.

Working standards are usually made by comparison with reference standards. They should have the loops of filament supports closed firmly around the filament to avoid the possibility of random short-circuiting of a portion of the filament by the support. They should be adequately seasoned and selected by successive comparisons with reference standards for stability. All standards should be handled carefully to avoid exposure to electrical and mechanical shocks. Exposure to current or voltage above the standard value may alter lamp ratings. It is recommended that the voltage applied to the test lamp be ramped up slowly to its final setting.

Intensity Measurements. Sources may be measured on an optical bench photometer if the luminous intensity in a particular direction, or a mean horizontal luminous intensity, is desired. Lamps standardized for unidirectional measurements are usually marked to indicate the orientation. A common practice is to inscribe a circle and a vertical line on opposite sides of the bulb. The standardized direction is from the circle toward the line, when they are centered on each other, looking toward the receiver.

Total Flux Measurements. Most routine photometric measurments on incandescent filament lamps require total light output or total luminous flux and are made in a sphere (see figure 2-11 and the discussion on Integrating-Sphere Photometers above). Strict substitution procedures should be followed, or necessary corrections made. A standard should be selected of about the same physical size, lumen output and color temperature as the lamp under test. The unknown lamp should be measured at the same position in the sphere as the standard.

Readings to determine lamp depreciation are usually takcn at 70% of ratcd lamp life. By this time, some blackening of the bulb is likely. This blackening may lead to errors in photometric measurements taken with an integrating sphere because the blackened area of the lamp will absorb some of the interreflected light. To overcome these errors, a third lamp, commonly called the "absorption," "comparison" or "auxiliary" lamp, should be installed in the sphere so that it is shielded from both the integrating sphere detector and

the test lamps. Successive readings should be taken with the absorption lamp operating: first with the reference (known) lamp installed but not operating, then with the blackened (aged) lamp installed but not operating. The difference between these readings represents the light absorbed by the blackened lamp and can be used to correct the values given by the integrating sphere. The same general procedure can be followed in most cases where the characteristics of the integrator are altered during the test by the introduction of light-absorbing elements (see the discussion on Integrating-Sphere Photometers above).

Photometry of Discharge Lamps.[42] As with incandescent lamp measurements, the photometric characteristics of discharge lamps are usually determined in conjunction with electrical measurements, whose general requirements have been given. The substitution method is normally employed for photometric measurements. Complete, detailed photometry procedures will be found in the appropriate IESNA test guides.[35-37]

Equipment.

BALLASTS. When a lamp is being measured for rating purposes, it should be operating on the appropriate reference ballast. If no standard exists, the ballast used should comply with the general lamp requirements. In general practice, photometric measurements on fluorescent lamps burning on commercial ballasts should be made with the ballast operating at rated input voltage, and measurements on high-intensity discharge lamps should be made with the lamp operating at rated wattage. The ballast should be operated long enough to reach thermal equilibrium. The use of commercial ballasts should conform to the procedures given in the appropriate standards.[30]

DETECTORS. Detectors should be selected according to the criterion given in the subsection on Illuminance Photometers above. Additional corrections may have to be applied to the measured data.

STANDARD LAMPS. These should have characteristics similar to the lamp under test with respect to light output, physical size, shape and spectral distribution.

INTEGRATING SPHERES.[25,26] The integrating sphere to be used should comply with the requirements described in the discussion on Integrating-Sphere Photometers above. To provide acceptable performance, integrating spheres should be of adequate size for the lamp being tested. Direct substitution is not always possible, and generally the larger the integrator with respect to the test lamp dimensions, the smaller any necessary corrections will be. Also, the ambient temperature in a larger sphere will be less affected by heat generated by the test lamp. It is recommended that the sphere diameter be at least 1.5 m for high-intensity discharge lamps and at least 1.2 times the length of the lamp for straight lamps; the area of the light source should not exceed 2% of the interior surface of the sphere. If direct substitution is used, these requirements are less stringent.

DISTRIBUTION PHOTOMETER.[43, 44] The lamp is mounted in open air with the distance between receiver and lamp at least 5 times the lamp length or 3 m, whichever is greater. Except as stipulated below, the lamp should be operated in the same burning position as associated with the luminaire for which it is intended, and it should be held stationary during measurement, since any movement may disturb its stabilization.[35–37] The total light output can be computed if the lumen-candlepower ratio is known, or if strict substitution is practiced. The measured luminous intensity values for a lamp are established by multiplying the test readings by the photometric calibration constant. The total light output is the sum of products of these values with the appropriate zonal lumen constants. Measures should be taken to exclude stray light, to control ambient temperature and drafts and to reduce the effects of light-absorbing or -reflecting materials. For fluorescent lamp measurements the lamp is mounted in a horizontal position and measurements taken normal to the axis of the lamp. To provide the greatest accuracy these measurements must be taken at several angular positions by rotating the lamp around its axis between sets of measurements. For measurements of high-intensity discharge lamps, especially metal halide lamps, the lamp should be placed in its designed operating position. If this is vertical, measurements may be made while the lamp is rotating slowly on its longitudinal axis. Holding the lamp stationary is desirable for stabilization and accuracy. If the lamp is to be operated in any other position, it must be held stationary during measurement, since the light distribution from a high-intensity discharge lamp is a function of arc position, which is influenced by gravity.

Reflector-Type Lamps.[45] For purposes of identification, a reflector-type lamp is defined as a lamp having a reflective coating applied to part of the bulb, this *reflector* being specifically contoured for control of the luminous distribution. Included are pressed or blown lamps such as PAR and ER lamps, as well as other lamps with optically contoured reflectors. Excluded are lamps of standard bulb shape to which an integral reflector is added, such as silvered-bowl and silvered-neck lamps; lamps designated for special applications, such as automotive headlamps and picture projection lamps, for which special test procedures are already established; lamps having translucent coatings, such as partially phosphor-coated mercury lamps; and reflector fluorescent lamps.

Intensity Distribution. Several different methods of making intensity distribution measurements may be used, depending on the type of lamp and the purpose of the test. The photometric center of the lamp nor-

mally should be taken as the center of the bulb face, disregarding any protuberances or recesses in the face, and the test distance should be great enough so that the inverse square law applies.

The intensity distribution of a circular beam is commonly represented by an average curve in a plane along the beam axis. (The beam axis is that axis around which the average distribution is substantially symmetrical; the beam axis and photometric axis are adjusted to coincide.) The curve is obtained either by taking measurements with the lamp rotating about the beam axis, or by averaging a number of curves (at least eight) taken in planes at equally spaced azimuthal intervals about the axis.

The intensity distribution of a lamp whose beam is oval or rectangular in cross section is not adequately represented by one average curve. For some lamps two curves through the beam axis, one in the plane of each axis of symmetry, may supply sufficient information. The necessary number of traverses, their distribution within the beam, and the intervals between individual readings vary considerably with the type of lamp; sufficient measurements should be made to describe the average distribution pattern adequately.

When reflector-type lamps are considered for a specific application, test results will be most readily comparable when in the same form as that for equipment used for the same application. For example, when a direct performance comparison of a reflector lamp with floodlighting luminaires is desired, the lamp should be tested according to approved floodlight testing procedures.[46] The same is true for indoor luminaire applications.

Total Flux Measurements.[47] The total flux may be obtained by direct measurement in an integrating sphere or by calculation from intensity distribution data. Because of the high-intensity spot produced by most reflector-type lamps, special precautions should be taken when using an integrating sphere. One possible position for the test lamp in the sphere is with its base close to the sphere wall and the beam aimed through the sphere center, thus distributing the flux over as large an area of the sphere as possible. An appropriate baffle should be placed between the light source and the detector.

When reflector-type standards are available, the calibration of the sphere follows the usual substitution procedure, and for maximum accuracy the standard lamp should be of the same type as the test lamps.

Beam and Field Flux. The beam and field flux may be calculated from an average intensity distribution curve or from an isocandela diagram. Of particular interest is the flux contained within the limits of 50% and 10%, respectively, of the maximum intensity. The beam angle is defined as the total angular spread of the cone intercepting the 50%-of-maximum intensity.

The field angle is defined as the total angular spread of the cone intercepting the 10%-of-maximum intensity.

Spectroradiometric Measurements[48,49]

Spectroradiometric measurements on light sources can be reported in relative terms or as absolute values. The units of the latter are generally watts per unit area as a function of specified wavelength bands for spectral irradiance and watts within the wavelength bands for spectral flux.

Spectroradiometric measurements provide the fundamental data for the determination of radiant quantities; all other quantities can be computed from measurements taken in this way. To give meaningful results, the measuring setup, the equipment used and the technique employed must satisfy strict requirements.

Measurement Methods. Spectroradiometric measurement involves the comparison of two light sources: a reference source of known SPD and a test source whose SPD is to be determined. The two sources can be compared wavelength by wavelength, or they can be measured sequentially by completely scanning each source throughout the spectrum.

When the sources are compared wavelength by wavelength, the two sources are operated simultaneously. This approach necessitates discontinuous wavelength scanning, pausing at each measurement point. It also requires that the reference and test source not drift over the lengthy measurement period. The advantage of this method is the minimizing of errors due to short-term drift in the instrument's response function.

When the sources are measured sequentially, either continuous or discontinuous wavelength scanning may be adopted. When this method is used, the spectral response of the measuring system must remain constant throughout the measurement period. Instrument drift can be checked by remeasuring the standard source.

With discontinuous measurements, several readings at each wavelength can be taken and averaged, or other filtering methods can be employed to minimize the effect of electrical noise on the measurement.

With continuous measurements, the spectrum is scanned from one end to the other at a uniform rate and the signal from the detector is integrated over discrete intervals within the scanning period. This approach effectively converts the spectral power distribution into a histogram, the height of a segment being proportional to the power emitted by the source over that interval. In principle, this method does not require that the scanning intervals and the monochromator bandwidths be perfectly correlated, but the best resolution is obtained when they are. An advantage of this method is excellent rejection of electrical noise, which is integrated out of the measurement in the signal

averaging that takes place over each interval. It is also efficient, as there is no stopping and starting of the wavelength drive. When this method is adopted, the timing requirements are critical and the system response time must be adequate to capture the rapidly changing signal levels encountered during the scanning process. This is especially important when strong spectral lines are present.

These sampling methods can be used effectively if good equipment and procedures are utilized and the limitations of the equipment are understood.

Modern spectroradiometers incorporate a means of automating both the operation of the system and the data collection process.[50,51] Some form of immediate presentation of the data, such as a graph on a chart recorder, is desirable to aid in the recognition of malfunctions in the measurement system or instability in the test source.

The final presentation of the data is usually in the form of a series of values which describe the SPD of the light source over a particular spectral range. Typically an SPD curve accompanies the report of numerical data on output versus wavelength. Such a curve can be smooth and continuous (figure 2-12) or be in the form of a histogram representing discrete measured values (figure 2-13).

A suitable wavelength interval for a particular test is chosen by considering the type of spectra being measured. Using too small an interval will be wasteful, requiring the collection of unnecessary data, and using too large an interval can result in missed information. For optimum results, the sample interval and the bandwidth of an instrument are usually set to be the same. The spectral power distribution from an incandescent lamp can be adequately represented by a series of measurements at 10 nm intervals across the spectrum, since the intensity changes gradually with respect to

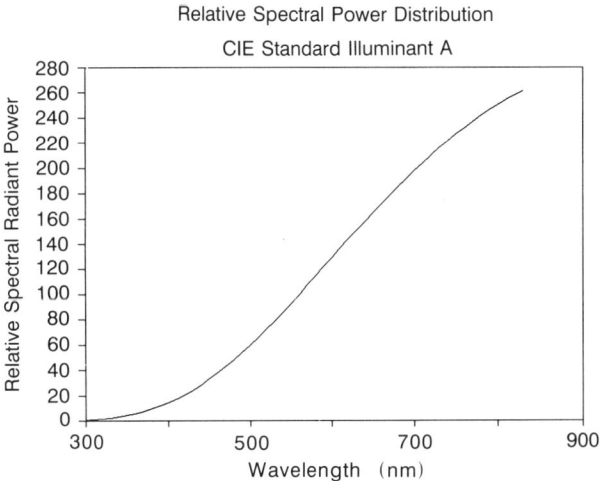

Fig. 2-12. Continuous spectral power distribution (SPD) curve for CIE standard illuminant A.

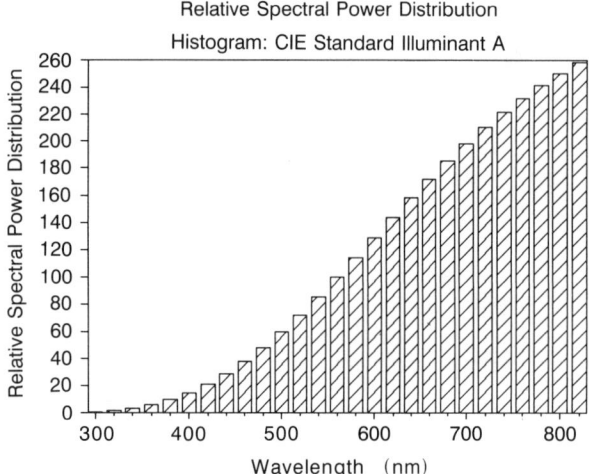

Relative Spectral Power Distribution
Histogram: CIE Standard Illuminant A

Fig. 2-13. Histogram of the relative spectral power distribution of CIE standard illuminant A.

wavelength. For measurements on discharge lamps, whose spectra include a number of emission lines, a smaller interval is required. For the calculation of chromaticity, which is one of the most important applications of spectroradiometric data, a 2 nm sample interval and bandwidth will give values of the chromaticity coordinates x and y accurate to ± 0.001 for almost any type of source, and this is adequate for most purposes.

Color Appearance of Light Sources

For measurement of the color appearance of a light source, see chapter 5, Color.

Life Performance Testing of Lamps

Life tests are performed on a very small portion of the product under consideration. Under such conditions test program planning, sampling techniques and data evaluation become especially important.[52]

It is recognized that it is not practical to test lamps under all of the many variables that occur in service; hence specific reproducible procedures must be included in the test experiment plan.

Incandescent Lamp Life Testing.[53,54] Life tests of incandescent filament lamps may be divided into two classes: *rated-voltage* and *overvoltage* tests.

Rated Voltage. Lamps are operated in the specified burning position at a voltage or current held within $\pm 0.25\%$ of rated value. Sockets should be designed to assure good contact with lamp bases, and the racks should not be subjected to excessive shocks or vibration. If lamps are removed for interim photometric readings, great care should be taken to avoid acciden-

tal filament breakage. Sockets should be lubricated, because the vibration of a squeak as the lamp is removed or replaced may be sufficient to break a filament which has been rendered brittle by burning.

Overvoltage (Accelerated) Tests. Lamp life is shortened by voltages in excess of rated. Extreme overvoltage life testing, sometimes called "high forced testing," will exponentially shorten lamp life, so that an evaluation of lamps may be obtained in a shortened period of time. The exponents are empirical and require many comparison tests at rated voltages to determine them.

Electric Discharge Lamp Life Testing.[55-57] Tests are generally made on ac. The power supply should have a voltage waveform in which the harmonic content does not exceed 3% of the fundamental. The line voltage should be regulated. There is no generally accepted method of accelerated life testing of discharge lamps.

Auxiliaries. Since an electric discharge lamp must be operated with auxiliaries, which often affect lamp life, they must be selected to conform with the requirements of the appropriate guides, test methods and specifications.

Test Cycles. An on-off cycle is normally employed to simulate field conditions. The commonly accepted cycles are 3 h on and 20 min off for fluorescent lamps, and 11 h on and 1 h off for high-intensity discharge lamps, although others are in use. It is known that increasing the rapidity of this cycling (that is, burning lamps for a shorter period of time between outages) will materially shorten lamp life, but the correlation with the standard cycle is not sufficiently accurate to predict the life on the standard cycle.

Environment. Vibration, shock, room temperature and drafts should be controlled to minimize their effect on measurement results.

Orientation. Lamps should be tested in an orientation recommended by the lamp manufacturer. See the IESNA guides for testing specific lamp types.

Luminaire Photometry

The purpose of making photometric measurements of a luminaire is to accurately determine and report its light distribution and characteristics in a way that will most adequately describe its performance. Characteristics such as intensity distribution, zonal lumens, efficiency, luminances, beam widths and typing are necessary in designing, specifying and selecting lighting equipment. Photometric data are essential in deriving and developing additional application information.

The information that follows is only a rudimentary guide to the photometry of luminaires. Specific photometric guides and practices are referenced below and should be consulted to obtain the detailed testing procedure for each type of luminaire. The IES Practical

Guide to Photometry[30] provides information covering general photometric practices, equipment and related matters. Each specific type of luminaire (indoor lighting, task lighting, floodlighting, or streetlighting) requires different testing procedures. However, there are several general requirements that should be met in all tests. The luminaire to be tested should be (1) typical of the unit it is to represent, (2) clean and free of defects (unless it is the purpose of the test to determine the effects of such conditions), (3) equipped with lamps of the size and type recommended for use in service and (4) installed with the light source in the recommended operating position for service. If the location of the source in a beam-producing luminaire is adjustable, it should be positioned as recommended to obtain such a beam as is desired in service.

To provide an accurate description of the characteristics of the materials used in the manufacture of a luminaire, measurements should be made of the reflectances of reflecting surfaces where applicable.

Luminaires should be tested in a controlled environment under controlled conditions. The photometric laboratory temperature should be held steady. Typically, for fluorescent photometry, where lamps are sensitive to temperature variations, the room temperature should be held to $25 \pm 1°C$. Power supplies should be regulated and free of distortion to minimize any effects of line voltage variations. Test rooms should be painted black or provided with sufficient baffling to minimize or eliminate extraneous and reflected light during testing.

For accurate measurements, the distance between the luminaire and the light sensor should be great enough that the inverse square law applies. The minimum test distance is governed by the dimensions of the luminaire. This distance should not be less than 3 m (10 ft), and at least five times the maximum dimension of the luminous area of the luminaire. For maximum precision the test distance should be measured from the center of the apparent source to the surface of the detector. However, from a practical standpoint, the following rules should suffice: (1) for recessed, coffered and totally direct luminaires, the test distance should be measured to the plane of the light opening (plane of the ceiling); (2) for luminous-sided luminaires the test distance should be measured to the geometric center of the lamps; (3) for suspended luminaires, (a) if the light center of the lamp(s) is within the bounds of the reflector and there is no refractor, the test distance should be measured to the plane of the light opening, (b) if the light center of the lamp(s) does not fall within the bounds of the reflector and there is no refractor, the test distance should be measured to the light center of the lamp(s), and (c) if a refractor is attached, then the test distance should be measured to the geometric center of the refractor.

General-Lighting Luminaires

Intensity Distribution. For specific information on testing general-lighting luminaires, the following IESNA guides should be consulted: Photometric Testing of Indoor Fluorescent Luminaires,[58] Photometric Testing of Indoor Luminaires Using High Intensity Discharge or Incandescent Filament Lamps[59] and Reporting General Lighting Equipment Engineering Data.[60]

The basic measurement made in a photometric test of a luminaire is the luminous intensity in specified planes and angles. The resulting intensity distribution is used to determine zonal lumens, efficiency and average luminances. It is therefore essential that sufficient data be taken to adequately describe the intensity distribution and the luminaire's total light output.

Luminaires having a symmetric distribution can be measured in five to twelve equally spaced planes and the results averaged. Most fluorescent luminaires are measured in five planes per quadrant in opposite quadrants, and the results for the two quadrants averaged to give the five-plane data. To adequately describe a highly asymmetric luminaire it may be necessary to measure in planes at 10° (or smaller) intervals.

The distribution in each vertical plane is determined by taking readings at 10° (or smaller) intervals. If the luminaire is of the beam-forming type, the intensity measurements should be made at smaller intervals in the beam-forming area. If visual comfort probability calculations are to be made, it is recommended that intensity measurements be made at least at every 5° in the vertical plane, and preferably every $2\frac{1}{2}°$.

Most luminaires are measured using the relative method, similar to that for lamps. From these readings a total quasi-lumen value can be calculated using the zonal lumen method. The lumen rating of the lamp is divided by this value to give the constant factor for that lamp on that photometer. By multiplying by that constant, the readings taken on the luminaire can be converted to candlepower values that would be obtained at that point if the lamp were furnishing rated lumens.

The intensity distribution data are generally presented in tabular form on the test report sheet. Data for a lens or indoor luminaire are given in five planes. Three distributions (parallel to the lamps; 45° to parallel; perpendicular to the lamps) are usually presented in the form of polar distribution curves.

Luminance. Either before or after the photometric test, while the lamps are still installed and stabilized, the maximum luminance of the luminaire should be measured at the angles specified in the appropriate guide and at the shielding angles. The measurements may be in candelas per square meter, candelas per square inch or footlamberts. The readings should be taken both crosswise and lengthwise in the case of

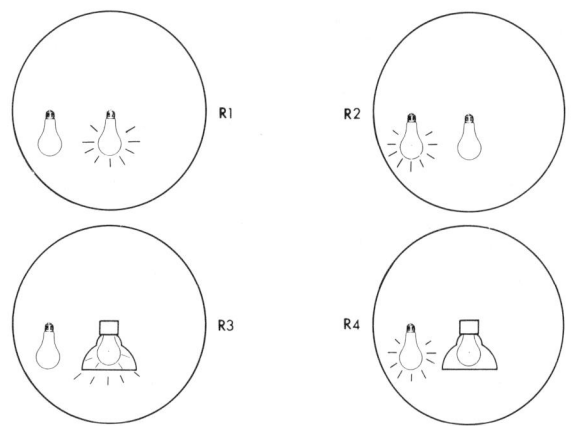

Fig. 2-14. Luminaire and lamp positions within an integrating sphere for the relative method of determining luminaire efficiency. The diameter of the sphere should be at least twice the maximum dimension of the luminaire to be measured.

fluorescent luminaires or luminaires with an asymmetric distribution. The projection of the measurement field should be circular and of 6.45 cm² (1 in²) area. Care must be taken that luminance measurements are related to the lumen output of the lamps, and thus luminance measuring instruments must be calibrated against the test lamps, employing the principles of the techniques described above.

If average luminance values are desired, they can be calculated by using the candlepower measurements obtained from the test data. By definition, luminance is the luminous intensity (candlepower) of any surface in a given direction per unit of projected area of the surface viewed from that direction. See reference 61.

Total Lumen Output. The total light output of the luminaire, needed to establish its efficiency in terms of the lumen output of lamp(s) with which it is equipped,

can be determined in an integrating-sphere photometer or by computations from the candlepower distribution data.

If it is to be measured in a sphere, the efficiency can be determined by the relative method. See figure 2-14. First, lamps are mounted at the center of the sphere and a reading taken. A reading is then taken on an auxiliary lamp mounted at some other point in the sphere. The luminaire is then mounted at the center of the sphere, and a reading is taken. Then another reading is taken on the auxiliary lamp mounted in the sphere. The efficiency is then calculated as follows:

$$\text{efficiency} = \frac{R_3 R_2}{R_1 R_4} \times 100\% \qquad (2\text{-}4)$$

where

R_1 = reading of lamp(s) at the center of the sphere,
R_2 = auxiliary lamp reading,
R_3 = luminaire reading,
R_4 = auxiliary lamp reading with luminaire in the sphere.

It is understood that while a reading is being taken only one lamp (or one luminaire) is operated. The sphere method is not considered to be as accurate as the method using luminous intensity distribution data.

Intensity distribution data are used to compute the luminous flux in any angular zone from nadir to 180°. The product of the mid-zone intensity and the zonal constant gives the zonal lumens. The summation of the zonal lumens multiplied by 100 and divided by the nominal lamp lumens gives the efficiency in percent.

Constants useful in calculating luminous flux from intensity data are given in figures 2-15 and 2-16. For

Fig. 2-15. Constants for Use in the Zonal Method of Computing Luminous Flux from Intensity Data
(1°, 2°, 5° and 10° Zones)

1 Degree Zones		2 Degree Zones		5 Degree Zones		10 Degree Zones	
Zone Limits (degrees)	Zonal Constant	Zone Limits (degrees)	Zonal Constant	Zone Limits (degrees)	Zonal Constant	Zone Limits (degrees)	Zonal Constant
0–1	0.0009	0–2	0.0038	0–5	0.0239	0–10	0.095
1–2	.0029	2–4	.0115	5–10	.0715	10–20	.283
2–3	.0048	4–6	.0191	10–15	.1186	20–30	.463
3–4	.0067	6–8	.0267	15–20	.1649	30–40	.628
4–5	.0086	8–10	.0343	20–25	.2097	40–50	.774
5–6	.0105	10–12	.0418	25–30	.2531	50–60	.897
6–7	.0124	12–14	.0493	30–35	.2946	60–70	.993
7–8	.0143	14–16	.0568	35–40	.3337	70–80	1.058
8–9	.0162	16–18	.0641	40–45	.3703	80–90	1.091
9–10	.0181	18–20	.0714	45–50	.4041		
				50–55	.4349		
				55–60	.4623		
				60–65	.4862		
				65–70	.5064		
				70–75	.5228		
				75–80	.5351		
				80–85	.5434		
				85–90	.5476		

Fig. 2-16. Constants* (K) for Converting Beam Intensity of Projector-Type Luminaires (Searchlights, Floodlights and Spotlights) into Luminous Flux

Spacing 0.1° Vertical

0.1° Horizontal

Horizontal Angle and Setting	K	Horizontal Angle and Setting	K	Horizontal Angle and Setting	K
0.05	$0.^{5}3046$	2.75	$0.^{5}3043$	5.45	$0.^{5}3032$
0.15	3046	2.85	3042	5.55	3032
0.25	3046	2.95	3042	5.65	3031
0.35	3046	3.05	3042	5.75	3031
0.45	3046	3.15	3042	5.85	3030
0.55	3046	3.25	3041	5.95	3030
0.65	3046	3.35	3041	6.05	3029
0.75	3046	3.45	3041	6.15	3029
0.85	3046	3.55	3040	6.25	3028
0.95	3046	3.65	3040	6.35	3028
1.05	3046	3.75	3040	6.45	3027
1.15	3045	3.85	3039	6.55	3026
1.25	3045	3.95	3039	6.65	3026
1.35	3045	4.05	3039	6.75	3025
1.45	3045	4.15	3038	6.85	3024
1.55	3045	4.25	3038	6.95	3024
1.65	3045	4.35	3037	7.05	3023
1.75	3045	4.45	3037	7.15	3023
1.85	3045	4.55	3037	7.25	3022
1.95	3044	4.65	3036	7.35	3021
2.05	3044	4.75	3036	7.45	3021
2.15	3044	4.85	3035	7.55	3020
2.25	3044	4.95	3035	7.65	3019
2.35	3044	5.05	3034	7.75	3018
2.45	3043	5.15	3034	7.85	3018
2.55	3043	5.25	3033	7.95	3017
2.65	3043	5.35	3033		

0.2° Horizontal

Horizontal Angle and Setting	K
0.1	$0.^{6}6092$
0.3	6092
0.5	6092
0.7	6092
0.9	6091

Spacing 0.1° Vertical Continued

0.2° Horizontal Continued

Horizontal Angle and Setting	K	Horizontal Angle and Setting	K	Horizontal Angle and Setting	K
1.1	6091	6.5	6079	6.5	6054
1.3	6091	6.7	6077	6.7	6051
1.5	6090	6.9	6076	6.9	6049
1.7	6089	7.1	6074	7.1	6046
1.9	6089	7.3	6073	7.3	6044
2.1	6088	7.5	6071	7.5	6041
2.3	6087	7.7	6069	7.7	6038
2.5	6087	7.9	6067	7.9	6035
2.7	6086				

0.4° Horizontal

Horizontal Angle and Setting	K	Horizontal Angle and Setting	K
0.2	$0.^{4}1219$	5.8	$0.^{4}1217$
0.6	1218	6.2	1216
1.0	1218	6.6	1216
1.4	1218	7.0	1215
1.8	1218	7.4	1215
2.2	1217	7.8	1214
2.6	1217		1213
		7.8	1207

0.6° Horizontal

Horizontal Angle and Setting	K	Horizontal Angle and Setting	K	Horizontal Angle and Setting	K
0.3	$0.^{4}1827$	5.7	$0.^{4}1825$		$0.^{4}1819$
0.9	1827	6.3	1824		1816
1.5	1827	6.9	1822		1814
2.1	1826	7.5	1821	7.8	1810

0.8° Horizontal

Horizontal Angle and Setting	K	Horizontal Angle and Setting	K	Horizontal Angle and Setting	K
0.4	$0.^{4}2437$	3.6	$0.^{4}2432$	6.0	$0.^{4}2424$
1.2	2436	4.4	2429	6.8	2420
2.0	2435	5.2	2427	7.6	2416
2.8	2434				

1.0° Horizontal

Horizontal Angle and Setting	K	Horizontal Angle and Setting	K	Horizontal Angle and Setting	K
0.5	$0.^{3}3046$	3.5	$0.^{3}3041$	6.5	$0.^{3}3027$
1.5	3045	4.5	3037	7.5	3020
2.5	3043	5.5	3032		

Spacing 0.2° Vertical

0.2° Horizontal

Horizontal Angle and Setting	K	Horizontal Angle and Setting	K	Horizontal Angle and Setting	K
0.1	$0.^{4}1219$	2.9	$0.^{4}1217$	5.5	$0.^{4}1213$
0.3	1219	3.1	1217	5.7	1212
0.5	1218	3.3	1217	5.9	1212
0.7	1218	3.5	1216	6.1	1212
0.9	1218	3.7	1216	6.3	1211
1.1	1218	3.9	1216	6.5	1211
1.3	1218	4.1	1215	6.7	1210
1.5	1218	4.3	1215	6.9	1210
1.7	1218	4.5	1215	7.1	1209
1.9	1218	4.7	1214	7.3	1209
2.1	1218	4.9	1214	7.5	1208
2.3	1218	5.1	1214	7.7	1208
2.5	1217	5.3	1213	7.9	1207
2.7	1217				

0.4° Horizontal

Horizontal Angle and Setting	K	Horizontal Angle and Setting	K	Horizontal Angle and Setting	K
0.2	$0.^{4}2437$	3.0	$0.^{4}2434$	5.8	$0.^{4}2425$
0.6	2437	3.4	2433	6.2	2423
1.0	2437	3.8	2432	6.6	2421
1.4	2436	4.2	2430	7.0	2419
1.8	2436	4.6	2429	7.4	2417
2.2	2435	5.0	2428	7.8	2414
2.6	2434	5.4	2426		

0.6° Horizontal

Horizontal Angle and Setting	K	Horizontal Angle and Setting	K	Horizontal Angle and Setting	K
0.3	$0.^{4}3655$	3.3	$0.^{4}3649$	5.7	$0.^{4}3637$
0.9	3655	3.9	3647	6.3	3633
1.5	3654	4.5	3644	6.9	3629
2.1	3653	5.1	3641	7.5	3624
2.7	3651				

0.8° Horizontal

Horizontal Angle and Setting	K	Horizontal Angle and Setting	K	Horizontal Angle and Setting	K
0.4	$0.^{4}4874$	3.6	$0.^{4}4864$	6.0	$0.^{4}4848$
1.2	4872	4.4	4858	6.8	4840
2.0	4870	5.2	4854	7.6	4832
2.8	4868				

Fig. 2-16 *Continued*

Note: the exponent printed as a superscript digit before the significant figures indicates the number of zeros following the decimal point, e.g. $0.^{6}6092 = 0.0000006092$.

Spacing 0.2° Vertical (Continued)

1.0° HORIZONTAL

Horizontal Angle and Setting	K
0.5	$0.^{6}6092$
1.5	6090
2.5	6086
3.5	$0.^{6}6082$
4.5	6074
5.5	6064
6.5	$0.^{6}6054$
7.5	6040

Spacing 0.4° Vertical

0.2° HORIZONTAL

Horizontal Angle and Setting	K		Horizontal Angle and Setting	K
0.1	$0.^{4}2437$		4.1	2431
0.3	2437		4.3	2430
0.5	2437		4.5	2430
0.7	2437		4.7	2429
0.9	2437		4.9	2428
1.1	2437		5.1	2427
1.3	2436		5.3	2426
1.5	2436		5.5	$0.^{4}2426$
1.7	2436		5.7	2425
1.9	2436		5.9	2424
2.1	2435		6.1	2423
2.3	2435		6.3	2422
2.5	2434		6.5	2421
2.7	2434		6.7	2420
2.9	$0.^{4}2434$		6.9	2419
3.1	2434		7.1	2418
3.3	2433		7.3	2417
3.5	2432		7.5	2416
3.7	2432		7.7	2415
3.9	2431		7.9	2414

0.4° HORIZONTAL

Horizontal Angle and Setting	K
0.2	$0.^{4}4874$
0.6	4874
1.0	4874
1.4	4872
1.8	4872
2.2	4870
2.6	4869
3.0	$0.^{4}4867$
3.4	4865
3.8	4863
4.2	4861
4.6	4858
5.0	4855
5.4	4852
5.8	$0.^{4}4849$
6.2	4846
6.6	4842
7.0	4838
7.4	4834
7.8	4829

0.6° HORIZONTAL

Horizontal Angle and Setting	K
0.3	$0.^{7}7310$
0.9	7310
1.5	7308
2.1	7306
2.7	7302
3.3	$0.^{7}7299$
3.9	7294
4.5	7288
5.1	7282
5.7	$0.^{7}7274$
6.3	7267
6.9	7258
7.5	7248

0.8° HORIZONTAL

Horizontal Angle and Setting	K
0.4	$0.^{9}9747$
1.2	9746
2.0	9742
2.8	9736
3.6	$0.^{9}9728$
4.4	9719
5.2	9707
6.0	$0.^{9}9694$
6.8	9679
7.6	9662

1.0° HORIZONTAL

Horizontal Angle and Setting	K
0.5	$0.^{3}1218$
1.5	1218
2.5	1217
3.5	$0.^{3}1216$
4.5	1215
5.5	1212
6.5	$0.^{3}1211$
7.5	1208

Spacing 0.6° Vertical

0.2° HORIZONTAL

Horizontal Angle and Setting	K		Horizontal Angle and Setting	K
0.1	$0.^{4}3655$		4.1	3646
0.3	3655		4.3	3645
0.5	3655		4.5	3644
0.7	3655		4.7	3643
0.9	3655		4.9	3642
1.1	3655		5.1	3641
1.3	3654		5.3	3640
1.5	3654		5.5	$0.^{4}3637$
1.7	3654		5.7	3636
1.9	3653		5.9	3636
2.1	3653		6.1	3635
2.3	3653		6.3	3634
2.5	3652		6.5	3632
2.7	3652		6.7	3631
2.9	$0.^{4}3650$		6.9	3629
3.1	3650		7.1	3628
3.3	3649		7.3	3626
3.5	3649		7.5	3625
3.7	3648		7.7	3622
3.9	3647		7.9	3621

0.4° HORIZONTAL

Horizontal Angle and Setting	K
3.0	$0.^{7}7301$
3.4	7299
3.8	7295
4.2	7292
4.6	7288
5.0	7283
5.4	7278
5.8	$0.^{7}7273$
6.2	7268
6.6	7262
7.0	7256
7.4	7250
7.8	7243

0.6° HORIZONTAL

Horizontal Angle and Setting	K
0.3	$0.^{3}1097$
0.9	1097
1.5	1096
2.1	1096
2.7	1095
3.3	$0.^{3}1095$
3.9	1094
4.5	1093
5.1	1092
5.7	$0.^{3}1091$
6.3	1090
6.9	1089
7.5	1087

0.8° HORIZONTAL

Horizontal Angle and Setting	K
0.4	$0.^{3}1462$
1.2	1462
2.0	1461
2.8	1460
3.6	$0.^{3}1459$
4.4	1458
5.2	1456
6.0	$0.^{3}1454$
6.8	1452
7.6	1449

1.0° HORIZONTAL

Horizontal Angle and Setting	K
0.5	$0.^{3}1828$
1.5	1827
2.5	1826
3.5	$0.^{3}1824$
4.5	1822
5.5	1819
6.5	$0.^{3}1816$
7.5	1812

Spacing 0.8° Vertical

0.2° HORIZONTAL

Horizontal Angle and Setting	K		Horizontal Angle and Setting	K
0.1	$0.^{4}4874$		4.1	4862
0.3	4874		4.3	4860
0.5	4874		4.5	4859
0.7	4874		4.7	4858
0.9	4874		4.9	4856
1.1	4874		5.1	4854
1.3	4872		5.3	4853
1.5	4872		5.5	$0.^{4}4851$
1.7	4872		5.7	4850
1.9	4871		5.9	4848
2.1	4870		6.1	4846
2.3	4870		6.3	4845
2.5	4869		6.5	4842
2.7	4869		6.7	4841
2.9	$0.^{4}4867$		6.9	4838
3.1	4867		7.1	4837
3.3	4866		7.3	4834
3.5	4865		7.5	4833
3.7	4864		7.7	4830
3.9	4862		7.9	4828

0.4° HORIZONTAL

Horizontal Angle and Setting	K
0.2	$0.^{9}9747$
0.6	9734
3.0	$0.^{9}9734$
3.4	9730
5.8	$0.^{9}9698$
6.2	9691

Fig. 2-16. *Continued*

Spacing 0.8° Vertical Continued

0.4° HORIZONTAL Continued

Horizontal Angle and Setting	K	Horizontal Angle and Setting	K	Horizontal Angle and Setting	K
1.0	9747	3.8	9726	6.6	9683
1.4	9744	4.2	9722	7.0	9675
1.8	9743	4.6	9717	7.4	9667
2.2	9741	5.0	9710	7.8	9658
2.6	9738	5.4	9704		

0.6° HORIZONTAL

Horizontal Angle and Setting	K	Horizontal Angle and Setting	K	Horizontal Angle and Setting	K
0.3	$0.^{3}1462$	3.3	$0.^{3}1460$	5.7	$0.^{3}1455$
0.9	1462	3.9	1459	6.3	1453
1.5	1462	4.5	1458	6.9	1452
2.1	1461	5.1	1456	7.5	1450
2.7	1460				

0.8° HORIZONTAL

Horizontal Angle and Setting	K	Horizontal Angle and Setting	K	Horizontal Angle and Setting	K
0.4	$0.^{3}1949$	3.6	$0.^{3}1946$	6.0	$0.^{3}1939$
1.2	1949	4.4	1944	6.8	1936
2.0	1948	5.2	1941	7.6	1932
2.8	1947				

1.0° HORIZONTAL

Horizontal Angle and Setting	K	Horizontal Angle and Setting	K	Horizontal Angle and Setting	K
0.5	$0.^{2}2437$	3.5	$0.^{2}2432$	6.5	$0.^{2}2421$
1.5	2436	4.5	2429	7.5	2416
2.5	2435	5.5	2426		

Spacing 1.0° Vertical

0.1° HORIZONTAL

Horizontal Angle and Setting	K	Horizontal Angle and Setting	K	Horizontal Angle and Setting	K
0.05	$0.^{4}3046$	2.75	$0.^{4}3043$	5.45	$0.^{4}3032$
0.15	3046	2.85	3042	5.55	3031
0.25	3046	2.95	3042	5.65	3031
0.35	3046	3.05	3042	5.75	3031
0.45	3046	3.15	3042	5.85	3030
0.55	3046	3.25	3041	5.95	3030

Spacing 1.0° Vertical Continued

0.1° HORIZONTAL Continued

Horizontal Angle and Setting	K	Horizontal Angle and Setting	K	Horizontal Angle and Setting	K
0.65	3046	3.35	3041	6.05	3029
0.75	3046	3.45	3041	6.15	3029
0.85	3046	3.55	3040	6.25	3028
0.95	3046	3.65	3040	6.35	3028
1.05	3046	3.75	3040	6.45	3027
1.15	3046	3.85	3039	6.55	3026
1.25	3045	3.95	3039	6.65	3026
1.35	3045	4.05	3039	6.75	3025
1.45	3045	4.15	3038	6.85	3024
1.55	3045	4.25	3038	6.95	3024
1.65	3045	4.35	3037	7.05	3023
1.75	3045	4.45	3037	7.15	3023
1.85	3045	4.55	3037	7.25	3022
1.95	3044	4.65	3036	7.35	3021
2.05	3044	4.75	3036	7.45	3021
2.15	3044	4.85	3035	7.55	3020
2.25	3044	4.95	3035	7.65	3019
2.35	3044	5.05	3034	7.75	3018
2.45	3043	5.15	3034	7.85	3018
2.55	3043	5.25	3033	7.95	3017
2.65	3043	5.35	3033		

0.2° HORIZONTAL

Horizontal Angle and Setting	K	Horizontal Angle and Setting	K	Horizontal Angle and Setting	K
0.1	$0.^{4}6092$	2.9	$0.^{4}6085$	5.5	$0.^{4}6065$
0.3	6092	3.1	6084	5.7	6063
0.5	6092	3.3	6083	5.9	6061
0.7	6092	3.5	6081	6.1	6058
0.9	6092	3.7	6080	6.3	6056
1.1	6092	3.9	6079	6.5	6054
1.3	6090	4.1	6077	6.7	6051
1.5	6090	4.3	6076	6.9	6049
1.7	6089	4.5	6074	7.1	6046
1.9	6089	4.7	6073	7.3	6044

0.2° HORIZONTAL Continued

Horizontal Angle and Setting	K	Horizontal Angle and Setting	K	Horizontal Angle and Setting	K
2.1	6088	4.9	6071	7.5	6041
2.3	6087	5.1	6069	7.7	6038
2.5	6087	5.3	6067	7.9	6035
2.7	6086				

0.4° HORIZONTAL

Horizontal Angle and Setting	K	Horizontal Angle and Setting	K	Horizontal Angle and Setting	K
0.2	$0.^{3}1219$	3.0	$0.^{3}1217$	5.8	$0.^{3}1212$
0.6	1218	3.4	1216	6.2	1211
1.0	1218	3.8	1216	6.6	1210
1.4	1218	4.2	1215	7.0	1210
1.8	1218	4.6	1215	7.4	1208
2.2	1217	5.0	1214	7.8	1207
2.6	1217	5.4	1213		

0.6° HORIZONTAL

Horizontal Angle and Setting	K	Horizontal Angle and Setting	K	Horizontal Angle and Setting	K
0.3	$0.^{3}1828$	3.3	$0.^{3}1825$	5.7	$0.^{3}1819$
0.9	1828	3.9	1824	6.3	1816
1.5	1827	4.5	1822	6.9	1814
2.1	1827	5.1	1821	7.5	1810
2.7	1826				

0.8° HORIZONTAL

Horizontal Angle and Setting	K	Horizontal Angle and Setting	K	Horizontal Angle and Setting	K
0.4	$0.^{3}2437$	3.6	$0.^{3}2432$	6.0	$0.^{3}2424$
1.2	2436	4.4	2430	6.8	2420
2.0	2436	5.2	2427	7.6	2416
2.8	2434				

1.0° HORIZONTAL

Horizontal Angle and Setting	K	Horizontal Angle and Setting	K	Horizontal Angle and Setting	K
0.5	$0.^{3}3046$	3.5	$0.^{3}3041$	6.5	$0.^{3}3027$
1.5	3045	4.5	3037	7.5	3020
2.5	3043	5.5	3032		

Spacing 2° Vertical

2° HORIZONTAL

Horizontal Angle and Setting	K	Horizontal Angle and Setting	K	Horizontal Angle and Setting	K
1	$0.^{2}2122$	31	$0.^{2}2104$	61	$0.^{2}59$

Fig. 2-16. *Continued*

Spacing 0.2° Vertical Continued

0.2° HORIZONTAL Continued

Horizontal Angle and Setting	K	Horizontal Angle and Setting	K	Horizontal Angle and Setting	K
3	122	33	102	63	55
5	121	35	100	65	51
7	121	37	097	67	48
9	120	39	095	69	44
11	120	41	092	71	40
13	119	43	089	73	36
15	118	45	086	75	32
17	116	47	083	77	27
19	115	49	080	79	23
21	114	51	077	81	19
23	112	53	073	83	15
25	110	55	070	85	11
27	108	57	066	87	06
29	107	59	063	89	02

5° HORIZONTAL

Horizontal Angle and Setting	K	Horizontal Angle and Setting	K	Horizontal Angle and Setting	K
2.5	$0.^{3}3046$	32.5	$0.^{2}2570$	62.5	$0.^{2}1406$

Spacing 2° Vertical Continued

5° HORIZONTAL Continued

Horizontal Angle and Setting	K	Horizontal Angle and Setting	K	Horizontal Angle and Setting	K
7.5	3020	37.5	2416	7.5	1166
12.5	2970	42.5	2246	12.5	0918
17.5	2906	47.5	2060	17.5	658
22.5	2814	52.5	1856	22.5	396
27.5	2702	57.5	1638	27.5	134

10° HORIZONTAL

Horizontal Angle and Setting	K	Horizontal Angle and Setting	K	Horizontal Angle and Setting	K
5	$0.^{2}6066$	65	$0.^{2}4986$	5	$0.^{2}2572$
15	5876	75	4306	15	1576
25	5576	85	3494	25	0530

Spacing 5° Vertical

5° HORIZONTAL

Horizontal Angle and Setting	K	Horizontal Angle and Setting	K	Horizontal Angle and Setting	K
2.5	$0.^{2}760$	32.5	$0.^{2}642$	62.5	$0.^{2}352$

Spacing 5° Vertical Continued

5° HORIZONTAL Continued

Horizontal Angle and Setting	K	Horizontal Angle and Setting	K	Horizontal Angle and Setting	K
7.5	755	37.5	604	67.5	291
12.5	744	42.5	562	72.5	229
17.5	726	47.5	514	77.5	165
22.5	704	52.5	463	82.5	099
27.5	676	57.5	409	87.5	033

10° HORIZONTAL

Horizontal Angle and Setting	K	Horizontal Angle and Setting	K	Horizontal Angle and Setting	K
5	0.015165	35	0.012465	65	$0.^{2}6430$
15	14690	45	10765	75	3940
25	13790	55	08735	85	1325
5	0.0304	35	0.0249	65	0.0129
15	294	45	214	75	076
25	276	55	174	85	026

* Note: Small numbers following the decimal point indicate number of zeros following the decimal point but before the numbers shown.

computing the luminous flux, the average luminous intensity at the center of each zone should be multiplied by the zonal constant (figure 2-15) equal to $2\pi(\cos\theta_1 - \cos\theta_2)$. In figure 2-14, the zone limits represent θ_1 and θ_2. The measurements should be made at the midpoint of this interval.

The constants in figure 2-16 are computed for intensity measurments on projector-type luminaires made on a goniometer of the type shown in figure 2-7b. In this figure, the vertical spacing is ϕ and the horizontal angle and setting represents the midpoint between θ_1 and θ_2. If the measurements have been made with the type shown in figure 2-7a, the same constants may be used by interchanging the vertical and horizontal angular arguments, that is, by substituting the word "vertical" wherever "horizontal" appears, and vice versa. The zonal constants for figure 2-16 were computed as $\phi\pi(\sin\theta_2 - \sin\theta_1)/180$, where ϕ is the vertical interval and θ_1 and θ_2 are the limits of the horizontal interval. If a goniometer of the type in figure 2-7a is used, the constant is equal to $\theta\pi(\sin\phi_2 - \sin\phi_1)/180$, where θ is the horizontal interval and ϕ_1 and ϕ_2 are the limits of the vertical interval. See reference 62 for additional zonal constants.

If a number of constants are to be calculated for the same interval, the following shortcut method is a timesaver and is completely accurate. For the first formula above, let θ_m be the mid-zone angle and let P equal one-half the zone interval. The formula becomes

$$4\pi \sin P \sin\theta_m \qquad (2\text{-}5)$$

The zone width is often the same for a series of constants, and then the first factor will simply be multiplied successively by the sines of the mid-zone angles.

For the second formula above, let θ_m be the median angle on the horizontal interval. The formula then becomes

$$2\pi\frac{\theta}{180}\sin P \cos\theta_m \qquad (2\text{-}6)$$

It is commonly assumed that a ballast operated at its rated input voltage delivers rated wattage to a lamp and that a lamp operated at its rated wattage delivers its rated lumen output. In many instances this may not be true. Therefore, a procedure has been developed[62] to provide a factor called the *equipment operating factor* to be applied to photometric data on high-intensity discharge luminaires to adjust them to the specific combination of luminaire, lamp type and ballast used in a system. By repetitive tests, this procedure may be used to determine variations of system performance exclusive of lamp variations. Such a factor can be applied specifically to lumens, candelas and illuminances as they appear on photometric data sheets.

Two possibilities are recognized: the first (LLB1) in which the lamp is used in the operating position for which it is rated, and the second (LLB2) in which the lamp is operated in a position other than the one for which it is rated. The factors determined are equipment (luminaire-lamp-ballast combination) specific under initial conditions unless otherwise specified.

The procedures essentially involve a relative light output measurement. The test luminaire is operated at the rated supply voltage, after operating conditions have stabilized. Relative light output measurements are obtained with the test ballast and, without extinguishing the lamp, with the reference ballast operated at its rated input voltage. The equipment operating factor is the ratio of the light output measurements made in the first measurement to that made in the second.

Floodlight-Type Luminaires. The following applies to floodlighting equipment having a total beam spread (divergence) of more than 10°. For specific information on testing this type of equipment, consult the IES Approved Method for Photometric Testing of Floodlights Using Incandescent Filament or Discharge Lamps.[46] For equipment having a beam spread less than 10°, see the IES Guide for Photometric Testing of Searchlights.[63]

The classification of floodlights is based upon their beam width on their horizontal and vertical axes. The classification is designated by NEMA type numbers.[64] For symmetrical beams the floodlight type is defined by the average of the horizontal and vertical beam spreads. For asymmetrical beams it is defined by the horizontal and vertical beam spreads in that order; for example, a floodlight with a horizontal beam spread of 75° (Type 5) and a vertical beam spread of 35° (Type 3) would be designated as a Type 5 × 3 floodlight.

Stray light may be defined as light emitted by the floodlight which is outside the floodlight beam as defined by the beam classification. In some instances stray light may be useful in illumination, or it may be detrimental to vision, depending upon its magnitude and direction. When it is desired to determine the amount and direction of stray light, it is necessary to make measurements as far horizontally and vertically as the readings have significant values in relation to the measuring system.

If the light center of the test lamp, or if more than one lamp, the geometric center of lamp light centers, is not enclosed by the reflector, the floodlight should be mounted on the goniometer so that the light center of the lamp is at the goniometer center. If the lamp light center is within the reflector, the floodlight should be positioned so that the center of the reflector opening coincides with the goniometer center.

Either the direct or the relative method of photometry may be used for floodlights, but the relative method has an advantage in that cumulative errors may be reduced and maintenance of standards of luminous intensity and flux is not necessary. In the latter method, relative intensity readings for the test lamp alone made with a distribution photometer, and for the lamp-floodlight combination made with a floodlight photometer, are taken with the lamp operating under identical electrical conditions in both tests.

The method of taking intensity readings is to traverse the beam with such angular spacings as to give approximately 100 reading stations uniformly spaced throughout the beam. For the definition of the beam limit see reference 65. By interpolating between these readings an isocandela diagram may be plotted on rectangular coordinates (see chapter 9, Lighting Calculations). The lumens in the beam may be computed using the constants in figure 2-16.

The information usually reported for floodlights includes the following: NEMA type, horizontal and vertical beam distribution curves, maximum beam luminous intensity, average maximum beam luminous intensity, beam spread in both horizontal and vertical directions, beam flux, beam efficiency, total floodlight flux and total efficiency. In addition, the report should indicate whether the data were obtained on a Type A or a Type B goniometer.[65]

Roadway Luminaires. A guide has been prepared to provide test procedures and methods of reporting data to promote the uniform evaluation of the optimal performance of roadway luminaires using incandescent filament and high-intensity discharge lamps.[66]

Luminaires selected for test should be representative of the manufacturer's product. A test distance of 8–10 m (25–30 ft) should be sufficient for most beam-forming luminaires. The photometric test distance is in general defined as the distance from the goniometer center to the surface of the detector, taking into account the distances to and from any mirrors that may be used.

The number of planes explored during photometric measurements should be determined by the symmetry or irregularity of the distribution and by the purpose of the test. The number of vertical angles at which readings are taken will depend on how the readings are to be used. If an isocandela diagram is to be plotted, readings may have to be taken at close intervals, especially if the values are changing rapidly. If, as is becoming usual, a computer is used to provide comprehensive evaluation of luminaires and lighting application de-

signs, readings must be taken at vertical angle intervals through the beam section not exceeding $2\frac{1}{2}°$.

For luminaires having a distribution that is symmetrical about a vertical axis (IES Type V), readings may be taken in ten or more vertical planes and averaged.

For luminaires having a distribution that is symmetrical about a single vertical plane (IES Types II, III, IV and II four-way), readings may be taken in vertical planes that are 10° apart. Due to the method used in data processing, it may be advantageous to divide the beam section laterally into 10° zones and measure at the mid-zone angle. Averages may be taken of the readings at corresponding angles on the opposite sides of the plane of symmetry. Any computations that are to be performed may then be done on one side of the plane of symmetry, using the averaged data.

For luminaires having a distribution that is symmetric about two vertical planes (IES Type I), readings may be taken as above, but the computations may be performed in one quadrant of the sphere.

For luminaires having a distribution that is symmetric about four vertical planes (IES Type I four-way), readings may be taken as above, but the computations may be performed in one octant of the sphere.

For luminaires having an asymmetric distribution, readings may be taken in vertical planes that are 10° apart. Since there is no symmetry, any computations performed should be done without averaging.

Sufficient data should be obtained to allow classification of the light distribution in accordance with recommended practice (see chapter 24, Roadway Lighting) as well as to provide an isolux (isofootcandle) diagram, the utilization efficiency, and the total and four quadrant efficiencies.

Projector Luminaires.[67] The equipment required for photometric measurements of projectors, searchlights and beacons is similar in most respects to that required for other types of photometry.

Automatic recording photometers are frequently employed in order to obtain rapid measurements or to obtain statistically valid quantities of data. Multielement oscillographs are particularly valuable, since they facilitate simultaneous recording of electrical parameters, such as voltage and current, along with the basic photometric data.

The usual method for measuring angles in intensity distribution measurements is to mount the test equipment on a goniometer, keeping the photometric equipment fixed.[69] Basically, goniometers provide means for mounting the equipment, for rotating it around two axes (horizontal and vertical) and for measuring the angles of rotation. (See figures 2-7 and 2-17.)

When the projector luminaire is of unusual size and weight, it may be necessary to utilize its own mounting

Fig. 2-17. Typical goniometer for indoor photometric range. Two rotary tables of the type used in large machine tools are incorporated into the goniometer to provide two of the three rotations available. For horizontal distributions either the rotary table on which the outer frame is mounted or the inner table on which the test equipment is mounted may be used. This makes for flexibility and is especially useful for obtaining polar angle distributions. The pinion gear in the vertical drive may be disengaged readily and the inner frame with the test unit mounted can then be balanced with the adjustable counterweights. After balancing, a small constant torque is applied to the inner frame through the use of the pulley and weight at the side, thus eliminating backlash.

and goniometric facilities for the photometric work or to hold the luminaire fixed and traverse the beam by moving the photometric receptor.

Since projector luminaires may have a total beam spread of less than 1° and may furthermore be of great weight, the mechanical requirements on the goniometer are severe. Rigidity, freedom from backlash, and accuracy of angular measurements are prime requirements. There should be provision for accurate angular settings of the order of 0.1°. In special cases higher accuracy may be required.

Indoor photometric measurements are in general preferable, but are frequently impracticable because of the lengths required. For photometry on the relatively short indoor ranges, proper photometric procedures must be followed. See references 27, 62 and 70. Outdoor ranges require much more attention to methods of reducing stray light, minimizing atmospheric disturbances and correcting for atmospheric transmission. Range sites should be selected where the terrain is flat and uniform. The range should be as high off the ground as practicable. Stray light should be minimized by a suitable system of diaphragms. Any remaining

stray light should be measured and subtracted from all readings.

Ranges should not be located where atmospheric disturbances occur regularly or where dust or moisture are prevalent, and corrections must be made for other than perfect atmospheric transmission. The absorption of light by moisture, smoke and dust particles, even in an apparently clear atmosphere, may introduce considerable errors in measurements.[71] Therefore, it is desirable to measure the atmospheric transmittance before and after the test has been made. A standard reference projector is frequently employed, and is calibrated either by repeated observations in the clearest weather, when the atmospheric transmittance may be accurately estimated or independently measured, or by laboratory measurement methods.

The illuminance from searchlights, beacons or other highly collimating luminaires, if measured at distances greater than a certain minimum, obeys the inverse square law. This minimum distance is a function of the focal length of the reflector, the diameter of the reflector aperture and the diameter of the smallest element of the light source (arc stream or filament). This minimum distance is called the *beam crossover point* and is the distance where the optic is seen to be completely flashed, that is, the minimum distance where the refracting lens or the reflector is seen as completely luminous. Only at distances greater than this does the inverse square law apply. This minimum distance may be calculated by using the following general formula:

$$L_0 = \frac{ad}{Ks} \qquad (2\text{-}7)$$

where (see figure 2-18)

L_0 = minimum distance for optic under consideration,
 a = distance from the optical axis to the outermost flashed point when viewed from a distance point on the optical axis,
 d = distance from the centroid of the light source to the same outermost flashed point as used to determine a,

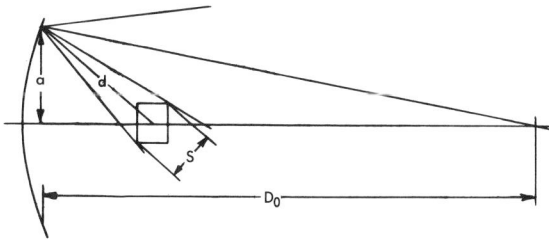

Fig. 2-18. Diagram showing distances and dimensions used to determine minimum inverse-square distance.

s = diameter of the smallest element of the light source (for example, the arc stream width of an arc source, or one coil of a multicoil filament lamp),

K = constant equal to 500 when a, d and s are in mm and L_0 is in m, and 6 when a, d and s are in in. and L_0 is in ft.

The above calculation determines the minimum inverse square distance based on ideal light sources and axial measurements, and therefore should be considered approximate. In practice, the range used should be much larger than this calculated distance to ensure conformance. Methods for using shorter ranges and "zero-length photometry" have been devised; however, the full length range is preferable for highest accuracy. These methods and a fuller discussion of minimum-inverse-square-distance calculations may be found in references 62, 67 and 68.

Luminance Measurements[72]

Luminance measurements on lamps and luminaires should be made by either the absolute or the relative method. With the absolute method, reference standards must be available for equipment calibration. In practice the relative method is generally used.

The published luminances of nonasymmetric fluorescent lamps are computed from the rated lumen output of the lamp according to the following formula:[73]

$$L_{avg} = \frac{K \times (\text{total lamp lumens})}{(\text{lamp diameter}) \times (\text{lamp luminous length})}$$

(2-8)

where L_{avg} is the average luminance of the full width of the lamp at its center, in candelas per square meter or per square inch. The diameter and length are expressed in meters or inches, and K for T-12 lamps is as follows:

Size		
(m)	(in.)	K
1.22	48	0.118
1.83	72	0.115
2.44	96	0.113

To compute the approximate luminance L_θ of a fluorescent lamp at any angle to the lamp axis, the following formula is used:

$$L_\theta = \frac{\text{total lamp lumens}}{K_\theta \times (\text{lamp diameter}) \times (\text{lamp luminous length}) \times \sin\theta}$$

where K_θ is as shown in figure 2-19.

In the laboratory, an accurate means of establishing lamp luminance is secured by constructing a baffled collimating tube 0.6–1.0 m (2–3 ft) long, with a detector at one end, and at the other end a rectangular aperture having one dimension equal to the lamp diameter, and the second dimension such that the product of the two dimensions equals 645 mm² (1 in²).[74] This is placed against the lamp near its midpoint so that the entire diameter of the lamp fills the aperture. The output of the detector should be directly proportional to L_{avg}. The instrument is thus calibrated when a lamp of known lumen output is viewed, and direct comparisons can be made with lamps of similar diameters. If the lumen output is known to be a given value, the instrument is calibrated for the relative method so that all subsequent luminance measurements are related to the known lumen output. Techniques also are available for the relative method of calibration for incandescent and high-intensity discharge sources.

For measuring the luminance of a luminaire, an instrument having a circular aperture is preferable, so that rotation of the instrument or change in the angular position of the luminaire will not affect readings. It is convenient, therefore, to use another collimating tube with an aperture 29 mm ($1\frac{1}{8}$ in) in diameter, or luminance meters with circular fields of view, encompassing 645 mm² (1 in²) at the measuring distance, and calibrated against a working standard which can be similar to the device shown in figure 2-20. In use, the luminance of the device's diffusing face is adjusted so that the response of the photometer used with the collimating tube equipped with a rectangular aperture is the same as when the same aperture is placed against the reference fluorescent lamp. The collimator with circular aperture is then substituted and the response noted; this then will be the measured lamp luminance. All luminaire luminance readings made with this circular aperture are then directly related to the lamp luminance.

Fig. 2-19. Values at Various Angles of the Lamp: Intensity Ratio K_θ for Preheat-Starting Types of Fluorescent Lamps (Average for 15, 20, 30, 40 and 100 W Lamps)

Angle (degrees)	0	10	20	30	40	50	60	70	80	90
K_θ	—	172.0	46.0	24.7	17.1	13.3	11.3	10.1	9.5	9.25

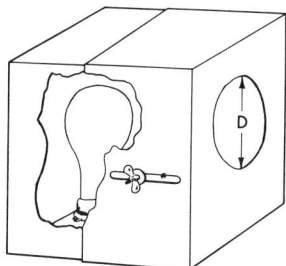

Fig. 2-20. An adjustable source of luminance, useful when calibrating luminance measuring devices having apertures of different shapes. *D* is about 76 mm (3 in).

An alternative method is to use a luminance meter to make direct measurements of the luminaire luminance. The characteristics of the luminance meter should be such that the field of measurement corresponds to a projected area of 645 mm² (1 in²) normal to its axis at the distance of measurement. This may be achieved with an appropriate lens system and a measurement distance which may be determined from the manufacturer's specifications. This technique has the advantage of the observer being able to view the exact area being measured through the luminance photometer. It also avoids another disadvantage of the collimating tube in that the tube can cast a shadow on the area whose luminance is being measured.

Where luminance photometers are calibrated by means of a diffusing test plate with a known illuminance, the characteristics of the test plate for specific conditions of incidence, spectral power distribution of the source and angle of view must be known. For a perfectly diffusing reflecting test plate the luminance is uniform at all angles, since no surface is perfectly diffusing, serious error can result from this assumption. It is essential that the directional reflectance characteristic of the test plate be known and taken into consideration in the luminance photometer calibration.

Calorimetry of Luminaires

A thermal testing method has been developed for compiling data on air-cooled heat transfer luminaires.[75] The method uses a calorimeter to measure the thermal energy distribution of the luminaires. The entire laboratory room in which the calorimeter is located becomes a part of the calorimetric system. The room must be controlled closely with respect to temperature, air motion and relative humidity. Varying conditions can materially affect the results of the calorimetric measurements. The room conditions should be as follows: the temperature should be controlled at 25 ± 0.3°C; the velocity of the air in the space containing the calorimeter should be held constant and not exceed 0.15 m/s (30 ft/min); the relative humidity should be held constant at any convenient value between 20 and 50%; and the room should not be affected by external conditions.

The selection of a calorimeter type is determined by the purpose of the device and the degree to which its conditions can be controlled. Three types of calorimeters are: the zero-heat-loss calorimeter, a calorimeter constructed to compensate for the heat transfer through its walls; the calibrated-heat-loss calorimeter (the approved IESNA type), a box in which the heat loss can be determined by dissipating a measured quantity of energy in the plenum; and the continuous-fluid-flow calorimeter, a modification of the zero-heat-loss calorimeter consisting of a heavily insulated heat exchanger installed over the luminaire.

Precision instrumentation is needed to measure temperature (thermometers, thermocouples, thermistors and resistance elements), pressure (manometers, micromanometers, draft gages and swinging-vane gages), mass flow rate of air and water, electrical quantities and light output.

Each luminaire that is to be tested for energy distribution should first be measured photometrically in accordance with accepted procedures. During calorimetry, the photometer should be installed at luminaire nadir, not less than 300 mm (1 ft) from the bottom of the enclosure. The distance at which the detector should be mounted below the luminaire is limited by the distance required for the cell to integrate flux over the entire luminous area of the luminaire. It is necessary that precautions be taken to prevent the detector from responding to luminous flux other than that transmitted by the luminaire under test. Its position must not be changed during the test.

The data to be recorded and reported should include the description and size of the luminaire, mode of operation, test conditions (space and plenum temperatures), relative light output from a 25°C base with the luminaire operated in free air outside the calorimeter, energy to space, energy removed by the exhaust air stream, and exhaust air temperature, all as functions of the exhaust flow rate. Energy and relative light output values should be reported as a function of the air volume flow rate.

FIELD MEASUREMENTS

In evaluating an actual lighting installation in the field it is necessary to measure or survey the quality and quantity of lighting in the particular environment.

Field measurements apply only to the conditions that exist during the survey. Recognizing this, it is very important to record a complete detailed description of the surveyed area and all factors that might affect results, such as interior surface reflectances, lamp type and age, voltage, and instruments used in the survey.

In measuring illuminance, detectors should be cosine and color corrected. They should be used at a temperature above 15°C (60°F) and below 50°C (120°F), if possible. Care should be exercised while taking readings to avoid casting shadows on the detector of the measuring instrument, and also by standing far enough away from the detector, especially when wearing light-colored clothes, to prevent light from the source from being reflected onto it. A high-intensity discharge or fluorescent system must be lighted for at least 1 h before measurements are taken to be sure that normal operating output has been attained. In new lamp installations, at least 100 h of operation of a gaseous source should elapse before measurements are taken. With incandescent lamps, seasoning is accomplished in a shorter time (20 h or less for common sizes).

The IESNA has developed a uniform survey method for measuring and reporting the necessary data for interior applications.[76] The results of the uniform surveys can be used alone or with those of other surveys for comparison purposes, to determine compliance with specifications, and to reveal the need for maintenance, modification or replacement.

Interior Measurements

Illuminance Measurements — Average

Determination of Average Illuminance on a Horizontal Plane from General Lighting Only. The measuring instrument should be positioned so that when readings are taken, the surface of the detector is in a horizontal plane and 760 mm (30 in.) above the floor. This can be facilitated by means of a small portable stand to support the detector. The area should be divided into 0.6 m (2 ft) squares, taking a reading in each square and averaging. Daylight may be excluded during illuminance measurements, by taking the readings either at night or with shades, blinds or other opaque covering on the fenestration. This should result in values of average illuminance within 10% of the calculated values using the zonal cavity method.

Regular Area with Symmetrically Spaced Luminaires in Two or More Rows. See figure 2-21a.

1. Take readings at stations r-1, r-2, r-3 and r-4 for a typical inner bay. Repeat at stations r-5, r-6, r-7 and r-8 for a typical centrally located bay. Average the eight readings. This is R in equation 2-8.
2. Take readings at stations q-1, q-2, q-3 and q-4 in two typical half bays on each side of the room. Average the four readings. This is Q in equation 2-8.

3. Take readings at stations t-1, t-2, t-3 and t-4 in two typical half bays at each end of the room. Average the four readings. This is T in equation 2-8.
4. Take readings at stations p-1 and p-2 in two typical corner quarter bays. Average the two readings. This is P in equation 2-8.
5. Determine the average illuminance in the area by using the equation

average illuminance

$$= \frac{R(N-1)(M-1) + Q(N-1) + T(M-1) + P}{NM}$$

$$(2\text{-}8)$$

where

N = number of luminaires per row,
M = number of rows.

Regular Area with Symmetrically Located Single Luminaire. See figure 2-21b. Take readings at stations p-1, p-2, p-3 and p-4 in all four quarter bays. Average the four readings. This is P, the average illuminance in the area.

Regular Area with Single Row of Individual Luminaires. See figure 2-21c.

1. Take readings at stations q-1 through q-8 in four typical half bays located two on each side of the area. Average the eight readings. This is Q in equation 2-9.
2. Take readings at stations p-1 and p-2 for two typical corner quarter bays. Average the two readings. This is P in equation 2-9.
3. Determine the average illuminance in the area by using the equation

$$\text{average illuminance} = \frac{Q(N-1) + P}{N} \quad (2\text{-}9)$$

where

N = number of luminaires.

Regular Area with Two or More Continuous Rows of Luminaires. See figure 2-21d.

1. Take readings at stations r-1 through r-4 located near the center of the area. Average the four readings. This is R in equation 2-10.
2. Take readings at stations q-1 and q-2 located at each midside of the room and midway between the outside row of luminaires and the wall. Average the two readings. This is Q in equation 2-10.

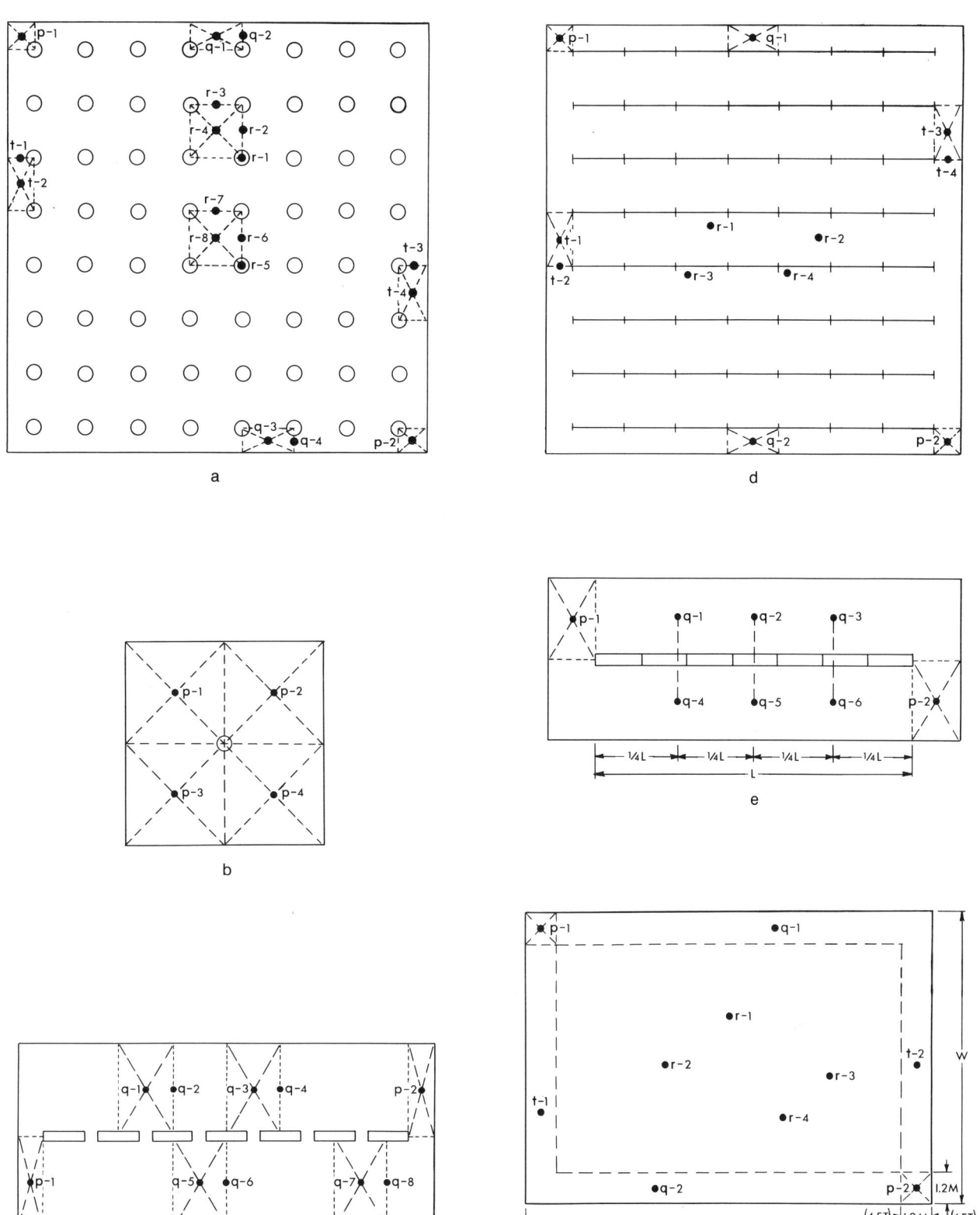

Fig. 2-21. Location of illuminance measurement stations in (a) regular area with symmetrically located single luminaire; (b) regular area with symmetrically located single luminaire; (c) regular area with single row of continuous luminaires; (d) regular area with 2 or more continuous rows of luminaires; (e) regular area with single row of continuous luminaires; (f) regular area with luminous or louverall ceiling.

3. Take readings at stations t-1 through t-4 at each end of the room. Average the four readings. This is T in equation 2-10.
4. Take readings at stations p-1 and p-2 in two typical corners. Average the two readings. This is P.
5. Determine the average illuminance in the area by using the equation

average illuminance

$$= \frac{RN(M-1) + QN + T(M-1) + P}{M(N+1)}$$

(2-10)

where

N = number of luminaires per row,
M = number of rows.

Regular Area with Single Row of Continuous Luminaires. See figure 2-21e.

1. Take readings at stations q-1 through q-6. Average the six readings. This is Q in equation 2-11.
2. Take readings at stations p-1 and p-2 in typical corners. Average the two readings. This is P in equation 2-11.
3. Determine the average illuminance in the area by using the equation

$$\text{average illuminance} = \frac{QN + P}{N + 1} \quad (2\text{-}11)$$

where

N = number of luminaires.

Regular Area with Luminous or Louvered Ceiling. See figure 2-21f.

1. Take readings at stations r-1 through r-4 located at random in the central portion of the area. Average the four readings. This is R in the equation directly below.
2. Take readings at stations q-1 and q-2 located 0.6 m (2 ft) from the long walls, at random lengthwise of the room. Average the two readings. This is Q in the equation below.
3. Take readings at stations t-1 and t-2 located 0.6 m (2 ft) from the short walls, at random crosswise of the room. Average the two readings. This is T in the equation below.
4. Take readings at stations p-1 and p-2 located at diagonally opposite corners 0.6 m (2 ft) from

Fig. 2-22. Form for Tabulation of Point Illuminance Measurements

Work Point	Description of Work Point	Height Above Floor	Plane (horizontal, vertical, or inclined)	Illuminance	
				Total (general + supplementary)	General Only
1—(max.)					
2—(min.)					
3—					
4—					
5—					

each wall. Average the two readings. This is P in the equation.
5. Determine the average illuminance in the area by using the equation

average illuminance

$$= \frac{R(L-8)(W-8) + 8Q(L-8) + 8T(W-8) + 64P}{WL}$$

(2-12)

where

W = number of luminaires per row,
L = number of rows.

Illuminance Measurements — Point

With task, general and supplementary lighting in use, the illuminance at the point of work should be measured with the worker in his or her normal working position. The measuring instrument should be located so that when readings are taken, the surface of the light-sensitive cell is in the plane of the work or of that portion of the work on which the critical visual task is performed—horizontal, vertical or inclined. Readings should be recorded as shown in figure 2-22.

Luminance Measurements

Luminance surveys may be made under actual working conditions and from a specified work point location with the combinations of daylight and electric lighting facilities available. Consideration should be given to sun position and weather conditions, both of which may have a marked effect on the luminance distribution. All lighting in the area—task, general and supplementary—should be in normal use. Work areas used only in the daytime should be surveyed in the daytime; work areas used both day and night should preferably have two luminance surveys made under the two sets of conditions, as the luminance distribution and the possibilities of comfort and discomfort will differ markedly between them. Nighttime surveys should be made with

Fig. 2-23. Form for Tabulation of Luminance Measurements

Work Point Location*	Luminance					
	A	B	C	D	E	F
Luminaire at 45° above eye level						
Luminaire at 30° above eye level						
Luminaire at 15° above eye level						
Ceiling, above luminaire						
Ceiling, between luminaires						
Upper wall or ceiling adjacent to a luminaire						
Upper wall between two luminaires						
Wall at eye level						
Dado						
Floor						
Shades and blinds						
Windows						
Task						
Immediate surroundings of task						
Peripheral surroundings of task						
Highest luminance in field of view						

* Describe locations A thru F.

shades drawn. Daytime surveys should be made with shades adjusted for best control of daylight.

On a floor plan sketch of the area, an indication should be made of which exterior wall or walls, if any, were exposed to direct sunlight during the time of the survey by writing the word "Sun" in the appropriate location. Readings should be taken, successively, from the worker's position at each work point location *A*, *B*, *C*, etc., and luminance readings from each location recorded as shown in figure 2-23.

Outdoor Measurements

In roadway and many floodlight installations light is projected to the surface to be lighted, and each luminaire must be adjusted carefully to produce the best utilization and quality of illumination. For an accurate evaluation of this type of installation, special care must be taken in the measurement of the resultant illumination. A summary of appropriate IESNA guides follows, but the full guides should be consulted before making an actual survey.[77–79]

Preparation for the Survey

1. Inspect and record the condition of the luminaires (globes, reflectors, refractors, lamp positioning, etc.). In the case of roadway lighting, make sure luminaires are level and their vertical and lateral placement is as designed. Unless the purpose of the test is to check depreciation or actual in-service performance, all units should be cleaned and new lamps installed. New lamps should be seasoned properly.[65] While inoperative lamps are readily noticed in roadway installations, they can easily be overlooked in large floodlighting systems. If these lamps are not replaced for the field survey, proper consideration must be given when evaluating the test.

2. Measure and record the mounting heights of the luminaires.

3. Measure and record the locations of the poles, the number of luminaires per pole, the wattage of the lamps and other pertinent data. Check these data against the recommended layout; a small change in the location or adjustment of the luminaires can make a considerable difference in the resultant illuminance.

4. Determine and record the burning hours of the installed lamps.

5. Consider the impact of stray light on the measurements. The survey should be made only when the atmosphere is reasonably clear. Extraneous light produced by a store, a service station or other lights in the vicinity requires careful attention in street lighting tests.

6. Because of the influence of the electrical circuit operating conditions on lamp light output, it is usually necessary to know precisely the operating conditions of the luminaires at the time of the photometric measurements. At night, during the hours when the luminaires will normally be used, record the voltage at the lamp socket with all of the lamps operating. The voltage at the main switch may be used instead, provided allowance is made for the voltage drop to the individual luminaires. If discharge lamps are being used, record the input voltage to the ballast at the ballast terminals. Discharge lamps should be operated at least 60 min to reach normal operating conditions before measurements are made.

Survey Procedures. Measurements should be made with a recently calibrated, color- and cosine-corrected photometer capable of being leveled for horizontal measurements or positioned accurately for other measurement planes as required. The photometer should be selected for its portability, repeatability and measurement range. If required by the spectral characteristics of the light source in the system being measured, appropriate corrections should be made to each reading.

1. For roadway lighting systems, at least one traffic lane must be closed for substantial periods of time. Because of this difficulty and expense of making field measurements of pavement luminance, it is common to utilize a computerized design procedure using point calculations, which can easily generate the horizontal illuminance level at each of the pavement lumi-

nance measurement points recommended. As a check on the performance of the lighting system, it is only necessary to measure the illuminance at these points thus simplifying the survey procedures.[77]

2. For roadway signs, the minimum and maximum illuminance levels are determined by scanning the sign face. Additional illuminance measurements are taken at specific locations according to the sign size. Luminance measurements are also made for both externally and internally illuminated signs.[79]

3. For sports installations,[78] the sports area, or that portion of the area under immediate consideration, should be divided into test areas of approximately 5% of the total area, and readings should be taken at the center of each area. Where lighting for color television is involved,[80] horizontal illuminance readings need to be taken at each station. Another set of readings should be made with the detector tilted 15° from vertical in the direction of each camera location and 0.9 m (36 in) above ground level (unless otherwise specified for the particular activity). This will help ensure adequate illumination for the color television cameras.

4. Readings should be made at each test station, with repeat measurements at the first station frequently enough to assure stability of the system and repeatability of results. Readings should be reproducible within 5%. Enough readings should be taken so that additional readings in similar locations will not change the average results significantly.

REFERENCES

1. Commission Internationale de l'Éclairage. 1983. *The basis of physical photometry*. CIE Publication No. 18.2. Paris: Bureau Central de la CIE.

2. U.S. Department of Commerce. National Bureau of Standards. 1986. *The International System of Units (SI)*. NBS Special Publication 330. Prepared by D. T. Goldman and D. T. Bell. Gaithersburg, MD: National Bureau of Standards.

3. Walsh, J. W. T. 1958. *Photometry*, 174. 3rd ed. London: Constable.

4. U.S. Department of Commerce. National Bureau of Standards. 1987. *NBS measurement services: Photometric calibrations*. NBS Special Publication No. 250-15. Prepared by R. L. Booker and D. A. McSparron. Gaithersburg, MD: National Bureau of Standards.

5. Walsh, J. W. T. 1958. *Photometry*, 223. 3rd ed. London: Constable. Lewin, I., G. A. Baker, and M. T. Baker. 1979. Developments in high speed photometry and spectroradiometry. *J. Illum. Eng. Soc.* 8(4):214–219.

6. Commission Internationale de l'Éclairage. 1987. *Methods of characterizing illuminance meters and luminance me-*
ters: Performance, characteristics and specifications. CIE Publication No. 69. Vienna: Bureau Central de la CIE.

7. Walsh, J. W. T. 1958. *Photometry*, 235–237. 3rd ed. London: Constable. Projector, T. E. 1957. Effective intensity of flashing lights. *Illum. Eng.* 52(12):630–640. Douglas, C. A. 1957. Computation of the effective intensity of flashing lights. *Illum. Eng.* 52(12):641–646. Lash, J. D., and G. F. Prideaux. 1943. Visibility of signal lights. *Illum. Eng.* 38(9):481–492. Preston, J. S. 1941. Note on the photoelectric measurement of the average intensity of fluctuating light sources. *J. Sci. Inst.* 18(4):57–59. Schuil, A. E. 1940. The effect of flash frequency on the apparent intensity of flashing lights having constant flash duration. *Trans. Illum. Eng. Soc. (London)* 35:117. Neeland, G. K., M. K. Laufer, and W. R. Schaub. 1938. Measurement of the equivalent luminous intensity of rotating beacons. *J. Opt. Soc. Am.* 28(8):280–285. Blondel, A., and J. Rey. 1912. The perception of lights of short duration at their range limits. *Trans. Illum. Eng. Soc.* 7(8):625–662.

8. MacGregor-Morris, J. T., and R. M. Billington. 1936. The selenium rectifier photo-electric cell: Its characteristics and response to intermittent illumination. *J. Inst. Elec. Eng. (London)* 77(478):435–438. Zworykin, V. K., and E. G. Ramberg. 1949. *Photoelectricity and its application*, 211. New York: Wiley. Gleason, P. R. 1934. Failure of Talbot's Law for barrier-layer photocells [abstract]. *Phys. Rev.*, 2nd series, 45(10):745. Walsh, J. W. T. 1958. *Photometry*, 98, 107. 3rd ed. London: Constable. Lange, B. 1938. *Photoelements and their application*, 151. A. St. John, trans. New York: Reinhold.

9. Blackwell, H. R., R. N. Helms, and D. L. DiLaura. 1973. Application procedures for evaluation of veiling reflections in terms of ESI: III. Validation of a predetermination method for luminaire installations. *J. Illum. Eng. Soc.* 2(3):284–298.

10. Ngai, P. Y., R. D. Zeller, and J. W. Griffith. 1975. The ESI meter: Theory and practical embodiment. *J. Illum. Eng. Soc.* 5(1):58–65.

11. DiLaura, D. L., and S. M. Stannard. 1978. An instrument for the measurement of equivalent sphere illumination. *J. Illum. Eng. Soc.* 7(3):183–189.

12. Green, J. 1980. A practical direct reading ESI meter for field use. *J. Illum. Eng. Soc.* 9(4):247–251.

13. Blackwell, H. R., and D. L. DiLaura. 1973. Application procedures for evaluation of veiling reflections in terms of ESI: II. Gonio data for the standard pencil task. *J. Illum. Eng. Soc.* 2(3):254–283.

14. Rea, M. S., and I. G. Jeffrey. 1990. A new luminance and image analysis system for lighting and vision: I. Equipment and calibration. *J. Illum. Eng. Soc.* 19(1):64–72.

15. Lewin, I., R. Laird, and J. Young. 1992. Video photometry for quality control. *Light. Des. Appl.* 22(1):16–20.

16. IES. Committee on Testing Procedures. Subcommittee on General Photometry. 1974. IES approved method of reflectometry. *J. Illum. Eng. Soc.* 3(2):167–169. Baumgartner, G. R. 1937. A light-sensitive cell reflectometer. *Gen. Elec. Rev.* 40(11):525–527.

17. Taylor, A. H. 1935. Errors in reflectometry. *J. Opt. Soc. Am.* 25(2):51–56.

18. McNichols, H. J. 1928. Absolute methods in reflectometry [Paper No. 3]. *J. Res. Natl. Bur. Stand.* 1(1):29–73.

Hunter, R. S. 1940. A multipurpose photoelectric reflectometer [Paper RP 1345]. *J. Res. Natl. Bur. Stand.* 25(5):581–618. McNicholas, H. J. 1934. Equipment for measuring the reflective and transmissive properties of diffusing media [Paper RP 704]. *J. Res. Natl. Bur. Stand.* 13(2):211–236. Sharp, C. H., and W. F. Little. 1920. Measurement of reflection factors. *Trans. Illum. Eng. Soc.* 15(9):802–810.

19. Taylor, A. H. 1920. A simple portable instrument for the absolute measurement of reflection and transmission factors [Paper No. 405]. *Sci. Pap. Bur. Stand.* 17:1–6.

20. Dows, C. L., and G. R. Baumgartner. 1935. Two photovoltaic cell photometers for measurement of light distribution. *Trans. Illum. Eng. Soc.* 30(6):476–491. Permanent gloss standards. 1950. *Illum. Eng.* 45(2):101. Spencer, D. E., and S. M. Gray. 1960. On the foundations of goniophotometry. *Illum. Eng.* 55(4):228–234. Nimeroff, I. 1952. Analysis of goniophotometric reflection curves. *J. Res. Natl. Bur. Stand.* 48(6):441–448. American Society for Testing and Materials. 1977. *American national standard practice for goniophotometry of objects and materials, ANSI/ASTM E167-77.* Philadelphia: American Society for Testing and Materials.

21. Cunningham, R. C. 1974. Silicon photodiode or photomultiplier tube? *Electro-Opt. Sys. Des.* 6(8):21–26.

22. Bode, D. E. 1971. Optical detectors. In *Handbook of Lasers.* R. J. Pressley, ed., Chapter 5. Cleveland, OH: Chemical Rubber Company. Bode, D. E. 1980. Infrared detectors. In *Applied optics and optical engineering,* vol. 6. R. Kingslake and B. J. Thompson, eds. New York: Academic Press.

23. Weekes, F. 1977. Photon counting: Notes on a basic system. *Electro-Opt. Sys. Des.* 9(6):30–34. Morton, G. A. 1968. Photon counting. *Appl. Opt.* 7(1):1–10.

24. McCulloch, J. H., and H. McCulloch. 1967. Floodlight photometry without special photometer and without tipping luminaire: A computer application. *Illum. Eng.* 42(4):243–245.

25. Rosa, E. B., and A. H. Taylor. 1922. Theory, construction, and use of the photometric integrating sphere: Paper No. 447. *Sci. Pap. Bur. Stand.* 18:281–325. Walsh, J. W. T. 1958. *Photometry,* 257. 3rd ed. London: Constable. Buckley, H. 1946. The effect of non-uniform reflectance of the interior surface of spherical photometric integrators. *Trans. Illum. Eng. Soc. (London)* 41:167. Hardy, A. C., and O. W. Pineo. 1931. The errors due to the finite size of holes and sample in integrating spheres. *J. Opt. Soc. Am.* 21(8):502–506. Gabriel, M. H., C. F. Koenig, and E. S. Steeb. 1951. Photometry: Parts I and II. *Gen. Elec. Rev.* 54(9):30–37, 54(10):23–29.

26. Weaver, K. S., and B. E. Shackleford. 1923. The regular icosahedron as a substitute for the Ulbricht sphere. *Trans. Illum. Eng. Soc.* 18(3):290–304.

27. Commission Internationale de l'Éclairage. 1973. *Procedures for the measurement of luminaire flux of discharge lamps and for their calibration as working standards.* CIE Publication No. 25. Paris: Bureau Central de la CIE.

28. Walsh, J. W. T. 1958. *Photometry,* 265. 3rd ed. London: Constable.

29. IES. Committee on Testing Procedures for Illumination Characteristics. 1955. IES general guide to photometry. *Illum. Eng.* 50(4):201–210. Stephenson, H. F. 1952. The equipment and functions of an illumination laboratory. *Trans. Illum. Eng. Soc. (London)* 17(1):1–29.

30. IES. Committee on Testing Procedures. Subcommittee on Practical Guide to Photometry. 1971. IES practical guide to photometry. *J. Illum. Eng. Soc.* 1(1):73–96.

31. Walsh, J. W. T. 1958. *Photometry,* 486. 3rd ed. London: Constable.

32. Levin, R. E. 1982. The photometric connection: Parts 1–4. *Light. Des. Appl.* 12(9):28–35, 12(10):60–63, 12(11):42–47, 12(12):16–18.

33. IES. Committee on Testing Procedures. Subcommittee of Outdoor Luminaires. 1989. *IES guide for the selection, care and use of electrical instruments in the photometric laboratory.* IES LM-28-1989. New York: Illuminating Engineering Society of North America.

34. IES. Committee on Testing Procedures. Subcommittee on Photometry of Light Sources. 1991. *IES guide to lamp seasoning.* IES LM-54-1991. New York: Illuminating Engineering Society of North America.

35. IES. Committee on Testing Procedures. Subcommittee on Photometry of Light Sources. 1988. *IES approved method for the electrical and photometric measurements of fluorescent lamps.* IES LM-9-1988. New York: Illuminating Engineering Society of North America.

36. IES. Committee on Testing Procedures. Photometry of Light Sources Subcommittee. 1984. *IES approved method for the electrical and photometric measurements of high intensity discharge.* IES LM-51-1984. New York: Illuminating Engineering Society of North America.

37. IES. Committee on Testing Procedures. Subcommittee on Photometry of Light Sources. 1991. *IES approved method of life testing of low pressure sodium lamps.* IES LM-60-1991. New York: Illuminating Engineering Society of North America.

38. American National Standards Institute. 1977. *American national standard specifications for fluorescent lamp ballasts, ANSI C82.1-1977.* New York: American National Standards Institute. American National Standards Institute. 1983. *American national standard for reference ballasts for fluorescent lamps, ANSI C82.3-1983.* New York: American National Standards Institute. American National Standards Institute. 1978. *American national standard specifications for high-intensity-discharge lamp ballasts (multiple-supply type), ANSI C82.4-1978.* New York: American National Standards Institute. American National Standards Institute. 1983. *American national standard reference ballasts for high-intensity-discharge lamps, ANSI C82.5-1983.* New York: American National Standards Institute. American National Standards Institute. 1980. *American national standard methods of measurement of high-intensity-discharge-lamp ballasts, ANSI C82.6-1980.* New York: American National Standards Institute.

39. American National Standards Institute. 1983. *American national standard for fluorescent lamp ballasts: Methods of measurement, ANSI C82.2-1984.* New York: American National Standards Institute.

40. IES. Committee on Testing Procedures. Subcommittee on Photometry of Light Sources. 1990. *IES approved method for electrical and photometric measurements of general service incandescent filament lamps, IES LM-45-91.* New York: Illuminating Engineering Society.

41. Teele, R. P. 1930. Gas-filled lamps as photometric standards. *Trans. Illum. Eng. Soc.* 25(1):78–96. Knowles-Middleton, W. E., and E. G. Mayo. 1951. Variation in the horizontal distribution of light from candlepower standards. *J. Opt. Soc. Am.* 41(8):513–516. Winch, G. T. 1956. Recent developments in photometry and colorimetry. *Trans. Illum. Eng. Soc. (London)* 21(5):91–116. Also see reference 3.

42. Winch, G. T. 1946. Photometry and colorimetry of fluorescent and other discharge lamps. *Trans. Illum. Eng. Soc. (London)* 21:107. Voogd, J. 1939. Physical photometry. *Philips Tech. Rev.* 4(9):260–266. Winch, G. T. 1949. The measurement of light and colour. *Proc. Inst. Elec. Eng. (London)* 96(2):452–470.

43. Franck, K., and R. L. Smith. 1954. A photometric laboratory for today's light sources. *Illum. Eng.* 49(6):287–291. Baumgartner, G. R. 1950. New semi-automatic distribution photometer and simplified calculation of light flux. *Illum. Eng.* 45(4):253–261.

44. Baumgartner, G. R. 1941. Practical photometry of fluorescent lamps and reflectors. *Illum. Eng.* 36(10): 1340–1353.

45. IES. Committee on Testing Procedures. Subcommittee on Photometry of Light Sources. 1982. IES approved method for photometric measuring and reporting tests on reflector type lamps. *J. Illum. Eng. Soc.* 11(3):130–134.

46. IES. Committee on Testing Procedures. Subcommittee on Photometry of Outdoor Luminaires. 1989. *IES approved method for photometric testing of floodlights using incandescent filament or discharge lamps, IES LM-35-1989.* New York: Illuminating Engineering Society of North America.

47. Walsh, J. W. T. 1958. *Photometry*, 257. 3rd ed. London: Constable.

48. IES. Committee on Testing Procedures. Photometry of Light Sources Subcommittee. 1983. IES guide to spectroradiometric measurements. *J. Illum. Eng. Soc.* 12(3): 136–140.

49. Spears, G. R. 1974. Spectroradiometry photometry. *J. Illum. Eng. Soc.* 3(3):229–233.

50. Elby, J. E. 1970. A computer based spectroradiometer system. *Appl. Opt.* 9(4):888–894.

51. Lewin, I., G. A. Baker, and M. T. Baker. 1979. Developments in high speed photometry and spectroradiometry. *J. Illum. Eng. Soc.* 8(4):214–219.

52. U.S. National Bureau of Standards. 1963. Comparing materials or products with respect to average performance. In *Experimental statistics*, Chapter 3. M. Gibbons, ed. NBS Handbook, 91. Washington: U.S. Government Printing Office. American Society for Testing Materials. 1958. *Standard practice for probability sampling of materials, ASTM E105-58.* Philadelphia: American Society for Testing Materials. U.S. National Bureau of Standards. 1963. Characterizing the measured performance of a material, product or process. In *Experimental statistics*, Chapter 2. M. Gibbons, ed. NBS Handbook, 91. Washington: U.S. Government Printing Office.

53. Lewinson, L. J. 1916. The interpretation of forced life tests of incandescent electric lamps. *Trans. Illum. Eng. Soc.* 11(8):815–835. Millar, P. S., and L. J. Lewinson. 1911. The evaluation of lamp life. *Trans. Illum. Eng. Soc.*

6(8):774–781. Purcell, W. R. 1949. Saving time in testing life. *Elec. Eng.* 68(7):617–620.

54. IES. Committee on Testing Procedures. 1979. IES approved method for life testing of general lighting incandescent filament lamps. *J. Illum. Eng. Soc.* 8(3):152–154.

55. IES. Committee on Testing Procedures. Subcommittee on Photometry of Light Sources. 1987. *IES approved method for life performance testing of fluorescent lamps, IES LM-40-1987.* New York: Illuminating Engineering Society of North America.

56. IES. Committee on Testing Procedures. Subcommittee on Photometry of Light Sources. 1987. *IES approved method for life testing of high intensity discharge (HID) lamps, IES LM-47-1987.* New York: Illuminating Engineering Society of North America.

57. IES. Committee on Testing Procedures. Subcommittee on Photometry of Light Sources. 1991. *IES approved method for the electrical and photometric measurements of low pressure sodium lamps, IES LM-59-1991.* New York: Illuminating Engineering Society of North America.

58. IES. Committee on Testing Procedures. Subcommittee on Photometry of Indoor Luminaires. 1985. *IES approved method for photometric testing of indoor fluorescent luminaires, IES LM-41-1985.* New York: Illuminating Engineering Society of North America.

59. IES. Committee on Testing Procedures. Subcommittee on Photometry of Indoor Luminaires. 1985. *IES approved method for photometric testing of indoor luminaires using high intensity discharge or incandescent filament lamps, IES LM-46-1985.* New York: Illuminating Engineering Society of North America.

60. IES. Committee on Testing Procedures. 1972. IES guide for reporting general lighting equipment engineering data. *J. Illum. Eng. Soc.* 1(2):175–180. IES. Committee on Testing Procedures. 1976. Addendum to IES guide for reporting general lighting equipment engineering data. *J. Illum. Eng. Soc.* 5(4):243.

61. IES. Committee on Testing Procedures. Subcommittee on Photometry of Indoor Luminaires. 1972. Determination of average luminance of luminaires. *J. Illum. Eng. Soc.* 1(2):181–184.

62. IES. Committee on Testing Procedures. Subcommittee on Photometry of Outdoor Luminaires. 1986. *IES approved guide for identifying operating factors for installed high intensity discharge (HID) luminaires, IES LM-61-1986.* New York: Illuminating Engineering Society of North America.

63. IES. Committee on Testing Procedures. Subcommittee on Photometry of Outdoor Luminaires. 1984. IES guide for photometric testing of searchlights. *J. Illum. Eng. Soc.* 13(4):372–380.

64. National Electrical Manufacturers Association. 1973. *Outdoor floodlighting equipment, NEMA FA1-1973 (R1979).* Washington: National Electrical Manufacturers Association.

65. IES. Committee on Testing Procedures. Subcommittee on Photometry of Outdoor Luminaires. 1989. *IES approved method for photometric testing of floodlights using incandescent filament or discharge lamps, IES LM-35-1989.* New York: Illuminating Engineering Society of North America. Joint IES-SMPTE Committee on Equipment

Performance Ratings. 1958. Recommended practice for reporting photometric performance of incandescent filament lighting units used in theatre and television production. *Illum. Eng.* 53(9):516–520. Commission Internationale de l'Éclairage. 1979. *Photometry of floodlights.* CIE Publication No. 43. Prepared by CIE Technical Committee TC 2.4. Paris: Bureau Central de la CIE.

66. IES. Committee on Testing Procedures. Subcommittee on Photometry of Outdoor Luminaires. 1988. *IES approved method for photometric testing of roadway luminaires using incandescent filament and high intensity discharge lamps, IES LM-31-1988.* New York: Illuminating Engineering Society of North America.

67. U.S. Department of Commerce. National Bureau of Standards. 1963. *Photometry of projectors at the National Bureau of Standards.* NBS Tech. Note 198. Prepared by L. Chernoff. Gaithersburg, MD: National Bureau of Standards. Johnson, J. 1962. Zero-length searchlight photometry system. *Illum. Eng.* 57(3):187–194.

68. Frederiksen, E. 1967. Unidirectional-sensitive photometer. *Light.* 60(2):46–48.

69. U.S. Civil Aeronautics Authority. 1944. *Construction of a goniometer for use in determining the candlepower characteristics of beacons.* CAA Technical Development Report No. 39. Prepared by F. C. Breckenridge and T. H. Projector. Washington: U.S. Government Printing Office. Projector, T. H. 1953. Versatile goniometer for projection photometry. *Illum. Eng.* 48(4):192–196.

70. IES. Committee on Testing Procedures for Illumination Characteristics. 1955. IES general guide to photometry. *Illum. Eng.* 50(4):201–210. Stephenson, H. F. 1952. The equipment and functions of an illumination laboratory. *Trans. Illum. Eng. Soc. (London)* 17(1):1–29.

71. U.S. Civil Aeronautics Administration. 1945. *Development of a transmissiometer for determining visual range.* CAA Technical Development Report No. 47. Prepared by C. A. Douglas and L. L. Young. Washington: U.S. Government Printing Office. Knowles-Middleton, W. E. 1952. *Vision through the atmosphere.* Toronto: University of Toronto Press. IES. Committee on Instruments and Measurements. 1943. Annual report of Committee on Instruments and Measurements. Part II: Description of method for measuring atmospheric transmission. *Illum. Eng.* 38(9):515–517.

72. IES. Committee on Testing Procedures. Subcommittee on Guide for Measurement of Photometric Brightness. 1961. IES guide for measurement of photometric brightness (luminance). *Illum. Eng.* 56(7):457–462.

73. Lindsay, E. A. 1944. Brightness of cylindrical fluorescent sources. *Illum. Eng.* 39(1):23–30.

74. Horton, G. A. 1950. Modern photometry of fluorescent luminaires. *Illum. Eng.* 45(7):458–467.

75. IES. Committee on Testing Procedures. Subcommittee on Photometry of Indoor Luminaires. 1978. IES approved guide for the photometric and thermal testing of air cooled heat transfer luminaires. *J. Illum. Eng. Soc.* 8(1):57–62.

76. Joint Lighting Survey Committee of the Illuminating Engineering Society and the U.S. Public Health Service. 1963. How to make a lighting survey. *Illum. Eng.* 57(2):87–100.

77. IES. Committee on Testing Procedures. Subcommittee on Photometry of Outdoor Luminaires. 1991. *IES guide for photometric measurement of roadway lighting installations, IES LM-50-1991.* New York: Illuminating Engineering Society of North America.

78. IES. Committee on Testing Procedures. Subcommittee on Photometry of Outdoor Luminaires. 1974. IES guide for photometric measurements of area and sports lighting installations. *J. Illum. Eng. Soc.* 4(1):60–69.

79. IES. Committee on Testing Procedures. Subcommittee on Photometry for Outdoor Luminaires. 1990. *IES guide for photometric measurements of roadway sign installations, IES LM-52-1990.* New York: Illuminating Engineering Society of North America.

80. IES. Committee on Sports and Recreational Areas, and Committee on Theatre, Television and Film Lighting. 1969. Interim Report: Design criteria for lighting of sports events for color television broadcasting. *Illum. Eng.* 64(3):191–195.

Vision and Perception *3*

Vision depends on light. It is the role of those responsible for lighting design to provide an environment in which people, through the sense of vision, can function effectively, efficiently and comfortably. To have the ability to predict human behavior as a function of the lighting conditions, however restricted that behavior may be, it is necessary to know the physical, physiological and psychological components of the behavior and how lighting affects each. Although a great deal is known about how simple visual stimuli produce simple visual behaviors, little is known about human response to even moderately complex scenarios.

Optometrists and ophthalmologists are responsible for maximizing the capabilities of the human visual system; lighting designers are responsible for optimizing the visual environment, considering cost, energy, visual performance, comfort and appearance. Both groups are dependent on data from basic and applied research studies from many disciplines that are supported by a variety of funding agencies. Together, they work toward the development of better lighting practice based on a solid foundation of knowledge.

This chapter attempts to highlight some of the basic interactions between light and vision. It is intended to provide some fundamental data which the designer may find useful, and to call attention to the types of considerations that may be necessary if one is to design lighting for optimal visual performance and comfort.

THE STRUCTURE AND FUNCTION OF THE EYE

The eye is a complex sensory organ which maintains the spatial and temporal relationships of objects in visual space and converts the light energy it receives into electrical signals for processing by the brain. The eye can be divided into optical components (the cornea, crystalline lens, pupil and intraocular humors) and neurological components (the retina and optic nerve). See figure 3-1.

Optical Components

A thin film of *tears* is the first optical component of the eye. This film is important because it cleans the surface of the eye, starts the optical refraction (light bending) process necessary for focusing objects, and smoothes out small imperfections in the surface of the subsequent refracting medium, the cornea. The *cornea* covers the transparent anterior one-fifth of the eyeball. With the tear layer, it forms the major refracting component of the eye and gives the eye about 70% of its power. The *crystalline lens* provides most of the remaining 30% of the refracting power. The *ciliary muscles* have the ability to change the curvature of the lens and thereby adjust the power of the eye, when needed, in response to changing object distances or certain types of refractive errors; this change in power is called *accommodation*.

The aqueous humor and vitreous humor help maintain the shape of the globe and provide nutrients to the nonvascular structures within the eye.

The transmittance of the eye varies with wavelength and with age.[1] In young eyes, the cornea absorbs most of the incident radiation shorter than 300 nm while the crystalline lens effectively filters out wavelengths shorter than 380 nm (see figure 3-2). Accordingly, the retina receives radiation in the range from 380 to 950 nm with little attenuation. Beyond 950 nm, transmittance is variable, with major absorptance in the infrared water bands. There is very little infrared radiation passed beyond 1400 nm.

Because of the excellent transmittance of the eye to infrared, such radiation can be dangerous to the retina, and sources with a substantial infrared radiance should not be viewed directly.

In the visible range of the spectrum, the optics of the eye transmit more light at long wavelengths (the red end) than at short wavelengths (the blue end). On average, some 70–85% of the visible spectrum reaches the retina in young eyes.[2] As one ages, there is a general reduction in the transmittance at all wavelengths combined with a marked reduction (greater

69

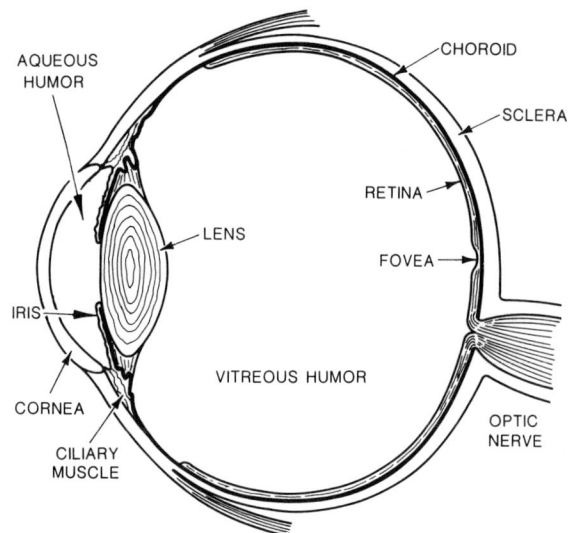

Fig. 3-1. A horizontal cross-section of the human eye. Approximate length from cornea to cone layer of retina is 24 mm. Thickness of choroid is about 0.05 mm and the sclera 1.0 mm.

than 4 times) in short-wavelength transmittance, due primarily to thickening and perhaps further yellowing of the crystalline lens (see figure 3-3).[3]

In addition to the absorption of light by the optical media, the efficiency of light for visual perception can be reduced by reflection from the tear-cornea surface and by scattering within the eye.[4] The eye suffers primarily from large-particle scattering, which is not wavelength dependent; therefore, the amount of scattered light within the eye decreases only slightly with increasing wavelength. In young eyes, some 25% of the scattered light is produced by the cornea,[5] another 25% by the fundus[6-8] and the rest by the lens and the vitreous humor. The aqueous humor produces little, if any, scattered light. The amount of scattered light in the eye increases with age. Almost all of this increase is due to changes in the lens.[4]

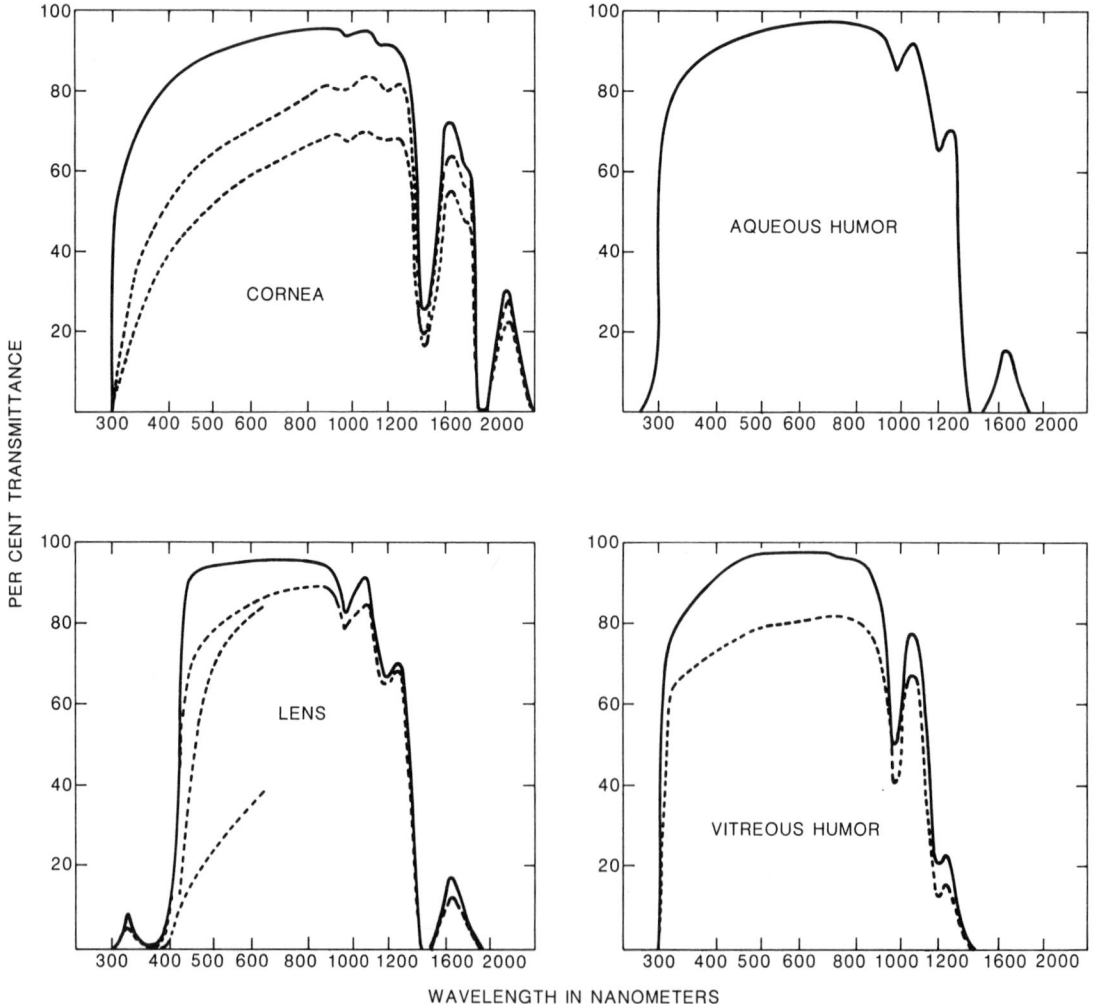

Fig. 3-2. Transmission properties of human ocular media. The solid curves refer to the total light transmitted through the media. The dashed curves refer to the direct, unscattered components only. Where more than one dashed curve is shown, the lower are for older eyes.

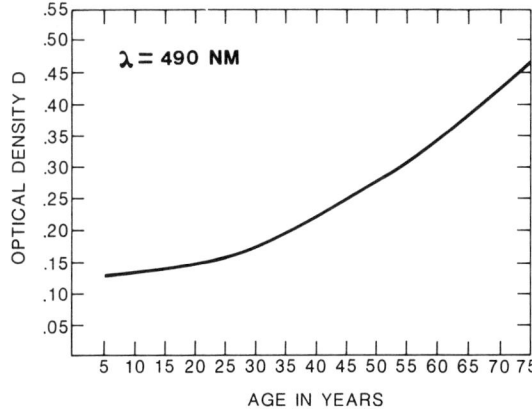

Fig. 3-3. The optical density of the human lens as a function of age. $D = \log 1/t$ where t = total internal transmittance.

Neurological Components

The posterior 80% of the eyeball is enclosed by three layers of tissue:

1. The *sclera*—the outermost covering of the globe, which is continuous with the cornea and which protects the eye's contents.
2. The *choroid*—a highly vascular tissue that contains the blood supply to much of the eye.
3. The *retina*—the innermost layer of the eyeball, which converts radiant energy into electrical signals that are sent to the brain.

Radiation which reaches the retina can be absorbed by photopigments located in the outer segments of the retinal receptors: the rods and cones. This absorbed energy is then converted electrochemically into neural signals, which are then communicated to subsequent neurons in the retina.

Receptive Fields

Receptors do not send their information directly to the brain, but rather to several other cells in the retina, which in turn send them to ganglion cells, whose terminal axons constitute the optic nerve (figure 3-4). In this way, light received by a number of receptors is "pooled" to provide the stronger signal necessary to stimulate a ganglion cell. The area of retina that stimulates a ganglion cell is called a *receptive field*. Although receptors are the primary transducers of light into electrical signals, it is the receptive fields that begin to make the light useful by providing information about the visual environment.

Receptive fields are the primary neural units of the human visual system. They represent areas of the retina within which spatial differences cannot be discriminated (see figure 3-5). A given receptive field always represents the activity of a number of receptors, and often may reflect input from different classes of cones

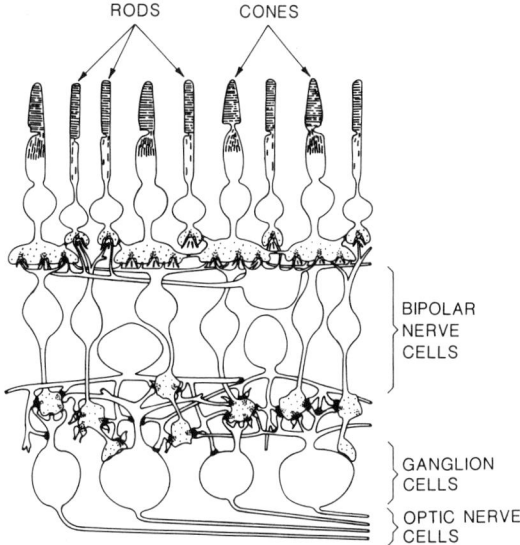

Fig. 3-4. Simplified diagram of the connections among neural elements in the retina. The regions where the cells are contiguous are synapses. The direction of the light is from the bottom up in this diagram.

as well as from rods. The characteristics of a receptive field mostly depends on:

- The amount of light incident on the retina
- The location of the visual stimulus on the retina

The sensitivity of a receptive field to light is primarily determined by its area. Because all ganglion cells require some finite minimum electrical input to be stimulated, a receptive field which receives input from a large number of receptors can be stimulated by a lower illuminance than can a receptive field which receives input from only a few receptors. Furthermore, the general size of a receptive field will reflect the number of receptors that provide input to it: a small receptive field will collect information from a few receptors, and a large receptive field from many. Hence the sensitivity

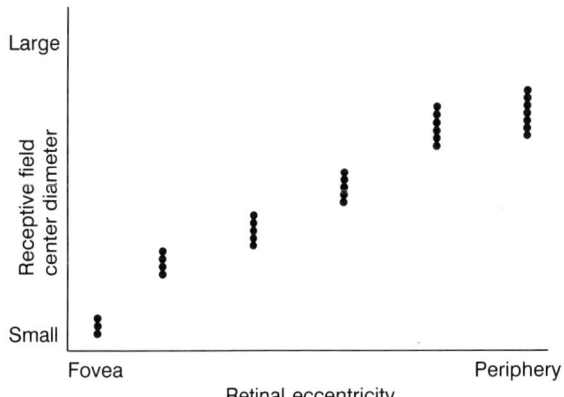

Fig. 3-5. The sizes of receptive field centers on the retina increase as a function of the distance from the fovea.

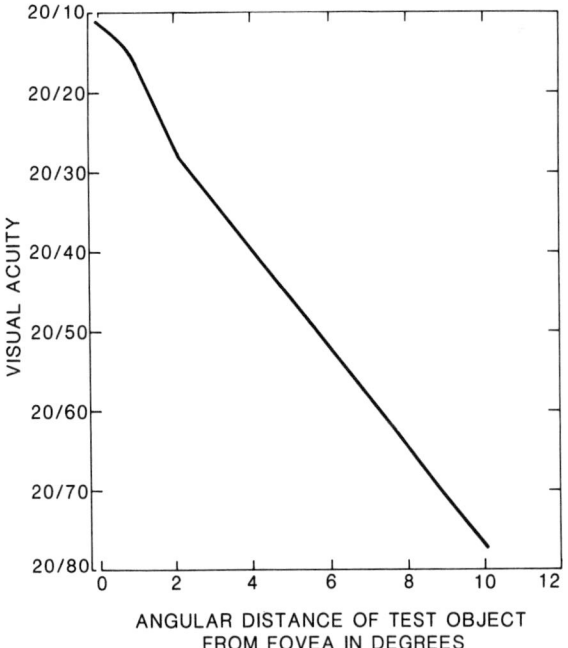

Fig. 3-6. Relation of visual acuity to angular distance of the test object from the fovea.

While sensitivity is gained from large receptive fields, resolution or acuity (the ability to discriminate fine details) requires small receptive fields. Consequently, there is a trade-off between the ability to see at low luminances and the ability to see small objects clearly or read fine print. In addition, the anatomy of the retina is such that the smallest receptive fields are concentrated in one part, known as the fovea, which is populated almost exclusively by cone receptors. At the fovea, there are nearly as many optic nerve fibers relaying information to the brain as there are receptors, and the receptive fields project to less than 1 minute of arc of visual space; this accounts for the normal visual acuity of about 20/20 (usually somewhat better). Receptive fields get progressively larger away from the fovea, increasing to over 10 minutes of arc in diameter toward the retinal periphery and limiting acuity there to less than 20/400. Figure 3-6 gives the maximum visual acuities to be found at various retinal eccentricities.

Receptors

The human eye contains two main classes of light-sensitive receptors which are differentiated by their morphology and by the spectral sensitivity of the photopigments which they contain.

Rods, which are absent in the fovea, increase in number to a maximum at about 20° of eccentricity and then gradually decrease towards the edges of the retina (figure 3-7). All rods contain the same photopigment (rhodopsin) and are organized into relatively large receptive fields. The combination of large receptive fields and relatively low spontaneous neural activity (noise) levels makes the rod system extremely sensitive to light. The rod photopigment, rhodopsin, has a peak spectral sensitivity at about 507 nm (see figure 3-8).

to light of small receptive fields is usually significantly less than that of larger fields. Indeed, there is a reciprocal relationship between receptive field size and sensitivity to light, which is expressed as

$$LA = \text{constant} \qquad (3\text{-}1)$$

where

L = luminance of the stimulus,
A = projected area of the stimulus.

This relationship is known as *Ricco's law*.

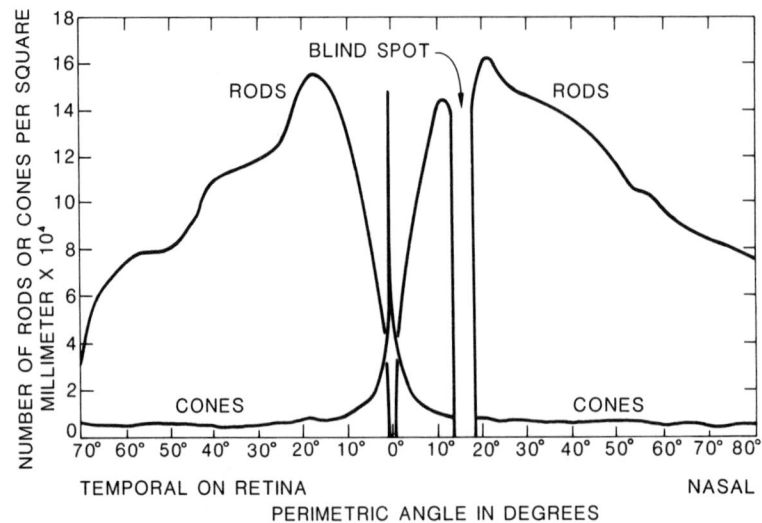

Fig. 3-7. The distribution of rods and cones in the retina. The 0° point represents the *fovea centralis*.

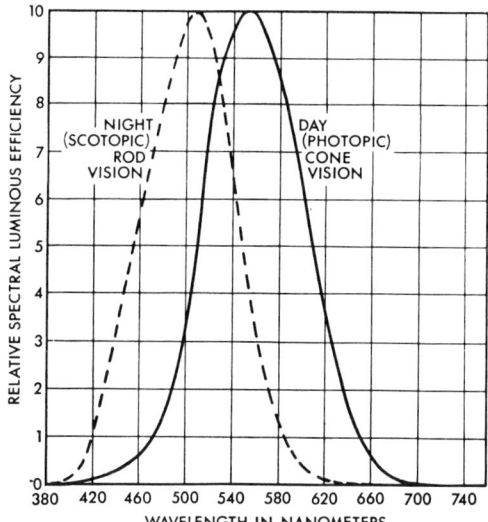

Fig. 3-8. The relative spectral sensitivity for photopic (cone) and scotopic (rod) vision.

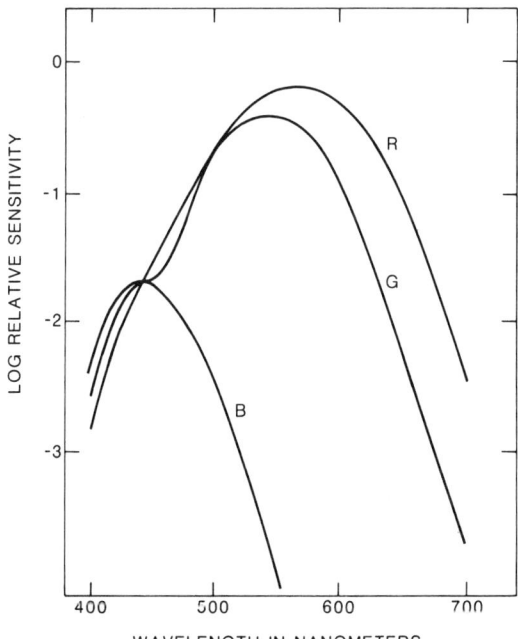

Fig. 3-9. The relative spectral sensitivity curves of the three cone types: long (R), middle, (G) and short (B).

Cones are divided into three known classes, each characterized by the photopigment which it contains: erythrolabe, chlorolabe or cyanolabe (see figure 3-9). Of approximately 6 million cones in the retina, over 1 million are located in the central 1°. It is the different photopigments in the cones which make possible color discrimination (see the subsection on Color Vision below).

Adaptation

Although receptive field sizes account for some of the differences in visual sensitivity across the retina, the sensitivity at a given retinal location also can vary. The human eye can process information over an enormous range of luminances (about 12 log units). The visual system changes its sensitivity to light, a process called adaptation, so that it may detect the faintest signal on a dark night and yet not be overloaded by the high brightnesses of a summer beach scene. Adaptation involves four major processes:

1. *Change in Pupil Size.* The iris constricts and dilates in response to increased and decreased levels of retinal illumination. Iris constriction has a shorter latency and is faster (about 0.3 s) than dilation (about 1.5 s).[9] There are wide variations in pupil sizes among individuals and for a particular individual at different times. Thus, for a given luminous stimulus, some uncertainty is associated with an individual's pupil size unless it is measured. In general, however, the range in pupil diameter for young people may be considered to be from 2 mm for high levels to 8 mm for low levels of retinal illumination. This change in pupil size in response to retinal illumination can only account for a 1.2 log unit change in sensitivity to light. Older people tend to have smaller pupils under comparable conditions.

2. *Neural Adaptation.* This is a fast (less than 1 s) change in sensitivity produced by synaptic interactions in the visual system.[10] Neural processes account for virtually all the transitory changes in sensitivity of the eye where cone photopigment bleaching has not yet taken place (discussed below)—in other words, at luminance values commonly encountered in electrically lighted environments, below about 600 cd/m². Because neural adaptation is so fast and is operative at moderate light levels, the sensitivity of the visual system is typically well adjusted to the interior scene. Only under special circumstances in interiors, such as glancing out a window or directly at a bright light source before looking back at a task, will the capabilities of rapid neural adaptation be exceeded. Under these conditions, and in situations associated with exteriors, neural adaptation will not be completely able to handle the changes in luminance necessary for efficient visual function.

3. *Photochemical Adaptation.* The retinal receptors (rods and cones) contain pigments which, upon absorbing light energy, change composition and release ions which provide, after processing, an electrical signal to the brain. As previously stated, there are believed to be four photopigments in the human eye, one in the rods and one each in the three cone types. When light is absorbed, the pigment breaks down into an unstable aldehyde of vitamin A and a protein (opsin) and gives off energy that generates signals that are relayed to the brain and interpreted as light. In the dark, the pigment is regenerated and is again available to receive light.

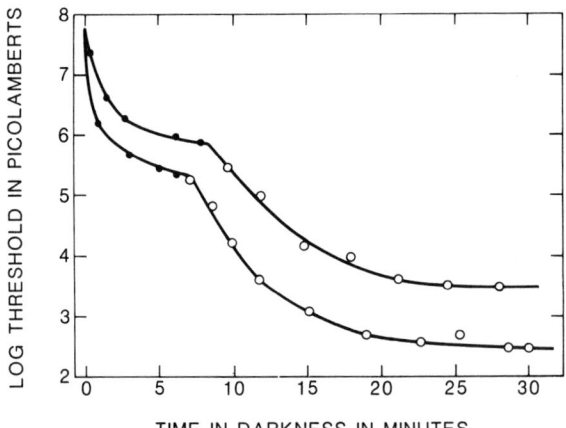

Fig. 3-10. The increase in sensitivity to light (decrease in threshold) as a function of time in the dark after exposure to a bright light. Sensitivity is measured at a point 7° from the line of sight. The two curves represent the extremes of the normal range of observers. 1 picolambert = 3.2×10^{-9} cd / m^2.

The sensitivity of the eye to light is largely a function of the percentage of unbleached pigment. Under conditions of steady brightness, the concentration of photopigment is in equilibrium; when the brightness is changed, pigment is either bleached or regenerated to reestablish equilibrium. Because the time required to accomplish the photochemical reactions is finite, changes in the sensitivity lag behind the stimulus changes. The cone system adapts much more rapidly than does the rod system; even after exposure to high levels of brightness, the cones will regain nearly complete sensitivity in 10–12 min, while the rods will require 60 min (or longer) to fully dark-adapt (see figure 3-10).[11]

4. *Transient Adaptation.* Transient adaptation is a phenomenon associated with reduced visibility after viewing a higher or lower luminance than that of the task.[12–14] If recovery from transient adaptation is fast (less than 1 s), neural processes are causing the change. If recovery is slow (longer than 1 s), some changes in the photopigments have taken place. Transient adaptation is usually insignificant in interiors, but can be a problem in brightly lighted exteriors where photopigment bleaching has taken place. The reduced visibility after entering a dark movie theater from the outside on a sunny day is an illustration of this latter effect.

Eye Movements

It is the function of the oculomotor systems of the eye to position the lines of sight of the two eyes so that they are pointed at the object of regard. If the image of a target does not fall on the fovea, acuity for that target may be reduced. Additionally, if both lines of sight are not aimed at the object, the target may be seen as double (diplopia).

Eye movements can be classified into the following general categories:

1. *Micronystagmus.* Very small movements (10–60 minutes of arc) of the eyes that occur when observers consider themselves to be fixating steadily in a given direction. The movements consist of high-frequency tremors, drifts and flicks.

2. *Saccades.* High-velocity movements, usually generated to move the line of sight from one target to another, or to make it join up with a moving target. Velocities may range up to 1000°/s, depending upon the distance moved. Saccadic eye movements have a latency of 150–200 ms, which limits the number of fixations that can be made in a given time period; four or five fixations per second is the maximum. Visual functions are substantially limited during saccadic movements. Saccades are also referred to as fixational jump movements.

3. *Pursuits.* Smooth eye movements used to follow a moving target after a saccade has been used to make the line of sight join up with it. The pursuit system cannot follow targets at high velocities. This may cause the eyes to lag behind a rapidly moving object. When speeds exceed 20–30°/s, detection and acuity abilities decrease (see figure 3-11).[15] Binocular pursuit and jump movements, which involve objects in a frontal plane, are referred to as *versions*, because when both eyes are involved, the two eyes make equal movements in the same direction; there is no change in the angle of convergence. See figure 3-12.

4. *Compensatory movements.* Movements of the eyes to compensate for the movement of the head so that eyes continue to fixate the same target while the head is turning.

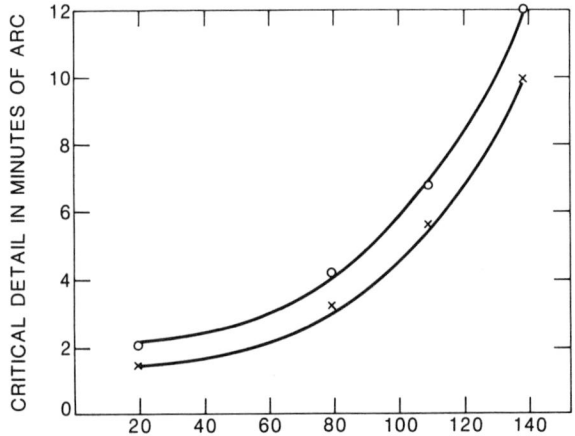

Fig. 3-11. The mean dynamic visual acuity threshold values of nine subjects obtained in the horizontal (○) and vertical (×) planes of pursuit.

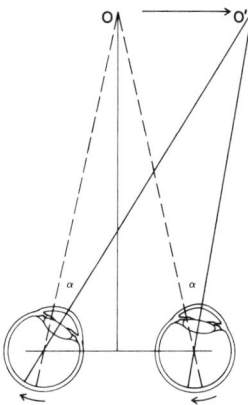

Fig. 3-12. In a version movement, as the target moves from point O to point O', the angle (α) between the eyes remains constant.

5. *Binocular movements.* Although the movements described above can be observed in a single eye while the other eye is covered, the covered eye will generally mimic the uncovered eye so that most of the movements of the fixing eye are correlated with conjugate or corresponding movements in the covered eye.

6. *Vergence movements.* Movements of the two eyes which keep the primary lines of sight converged on a target or which may be used to switch fixation from a target at one distance to a new target at a different distance (see figure 3-13). Vergences can occur as a jump movement or can smoothly follow a target moving in a fore-and-aft direction. When the primary lines of sight drift apart so that they fail to converge at the intended point of fixation, vergence movements play a major role in making the eyes converge on the target. These movements include also cyclovergence movements of the eyes around their primary lines of sight.

Accommodation

As the distance between the viewer and the target is decreased, the refracting power of the eyes must be

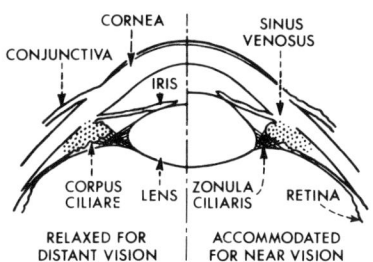

Fig. 3-14. Change in the form and position of the lens during accommodation.

increased to maintain a clear image on the retina. Such a change is called accommodation and is accomplished by a change in the shape and position of the crystalline lens within the eye (see figure 3-14).

Accommodation is always a response to an image of the target located on or near the fovea. It is used to bring a defocused target image into focus or to change focus from one target to another at a different distance. It may be gradually changed to keep a target which is moving in a fore-and-aft direction in focus. Any condition, either physical or physiological, that handicaps the fovea, such as a low retinal illuminance, will adversely affect accommodative ability.

Accommodative function decreases rapidly with age, so that by the mid-forties most persons can no longer see clearly at normal near-working distances and may need optical assistance. By age 60, there is very little accommodative ability remaining in most of the population (see figure 3-15), resulting in a fixed-focus optical system. This lack of focusing ability is compensated somewhat by physiologically smaller pupils in the elderly (which increase the depth of focus of the eye), but the smaller pupils in turn increase the requirement for task luminance to maintain the same retinal illuminance as when the pupils were larger. Even when the

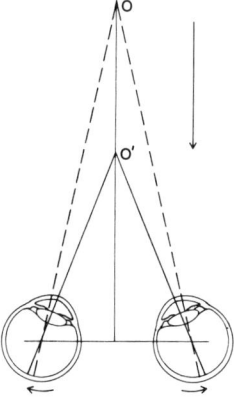

Fig. 3-13. In a vergence movement, as the target moves from point O to point O', the angle between the eyes changes.

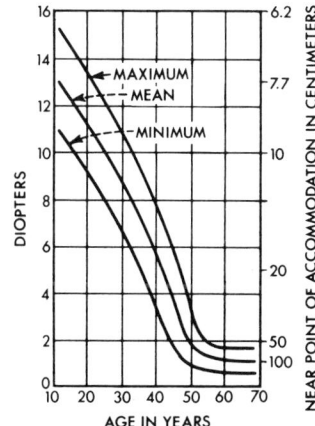

Fig. 3-15. The decrease of the amplitude of accommodation with age.

eyes are properly corrected for near viewing, the range of vision can be extended with good lighting.

Color Vision

The ability to discriminate among wavelengths of light is due to a combination of photochemical and neurological processes. Signals from the three cone types are coded in the retina and the lateral geniculate body (in the brain) into chromatic and achromatic information. As a first-order model of color and brightness, chromatic information is a result of a subtraction of receptor signals, while achromatic information is a result of the addition of receptor signals. However, many experiments using various testing procedures and stimuli demonstrate that this is an oversimplification of how the visual system processes light. Chromatic, achromatic, spatial and temporal information are combined nonlinearly to give final perceptions of light and color. For example, equal-luminance colored lamps may have

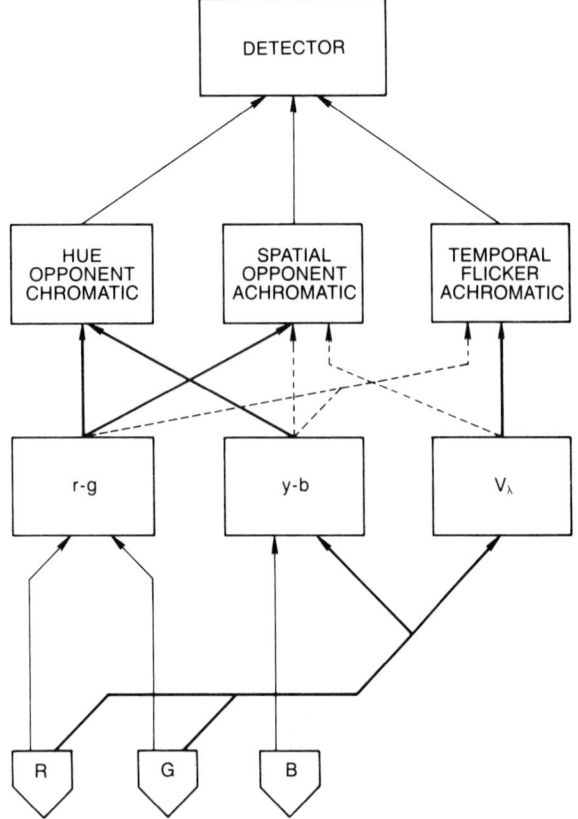

Fig. 3-16. A proposed model for connections in the visual system. Information from the first-stage photoreceptors (*R*, *G* and *B*) goes to mechanisms that sum or subtract input to give achromatic and chromatic information, respectively. Subsequent "cortical analysis" mechanisms receive multiple inputs from the second stage. Such a model attempts to qualitatively describe some of the nonlinearities in the visual system that have been discovered using stimuli that vary in several dimensions (spatial, temporal, chromatic and achromatic).

different apparent brightnesses because of the interaction between achromatic and chromatic channels.[16] Figure 3-16 is a proposed model of how the visual system combines the information from these various channels to produce human perceptions.

The normal visual system varies in its ability to discriminate among wavelengths. There are three peaks of maximum wavelength discrimination in the middle of the visible spectrum; discrimination falls off rapidly at the spectral extremes.[17] Likewise, the ability to discriminate hue from white is wavelength dependent. Monochromatic colors from the ends of the visual spectrum are more easily discriminated from white because they are more saturated than colors in the middle of the spectrum.[18] The ability to discriminate nonspectral colors is also related to their chromaticities.[19]

Generally, color discrimination is best in the fovea and decreases toward the periphery, where there are fewer cones. However, color discrimination for small fields (20 minutes of arc or less) presented to the fovea will not be good, because there are very few short-wavelength (blue) cones in the middle of the fovea. This effect is known as small-field tritanopia.[19]

About 8% of the male population is color deficient to some degree and may be limited in ability to perform certain tasks requiring color discrimination. Additionally, certain types of color deficiencies modify the achromatic sensitivity of the eye and reduce the effective brightness of middle- and long-wavelength lights; the long-wavelength loss in sensitivity often can be severe.

The Field of View

The extent of the visual field seen by a person when looking straight ahead must be divided into monocular and binocular portions. The monocular field is generally considered to be approximately 90° temporally, 60° nasally (depending on the prominence of the nose), 70° inferiorly (restricted by the cheek), and 50° superiorly (restricted by the brow). In addition, the field of each eye contains a blind spot (scotoma) corresponding to the area of the retina where the optic nerve and retinal blood vessels leave the globe and where there are no photoreceptors. The blind spot is located approximately 16° temporal to the line of sight and is elliptically shaped, 8° high by 5° wide.

The monocular visual fields overlap to form a combined binocular field, the central 120° of which is seen by both eyes (see figure 3-17). Under binocular conditions it is difficult to detect the blind spots because of the retinal overlap from the opposite eye. It is interesting to note that people are usually unaware of the blind spots, even under monocular conditions, because neurological processes "fill in" the blind spot. Even

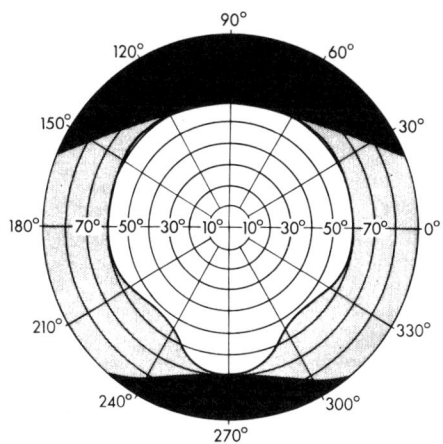

Fig. 3-17. The normal field of view of a pair of human eyes. The white central portion represents the region seen by both eyes. The gray portions represent the regions seen only by the left and right eyes. The cutoff by the eyebrows, cheeks and nose is shown by the dark areas.

cortical scotomas resulting from stroke or insult to the cortex may go unnoticed because of this neurological phenomenon.

The visual field will vary considerably depending upon the facial anatomy, state of adaptation, stimulus size used to measure it, and stimulus duration and color.

RETINAL IMAGE

Retinal Illuminance

The retina is sensitive to the flux density (illuminance) of light falling on it. In daylight conditions, and for all but very small or briefly presented objects, the brightness sensation is monotonically related to the retinal illuminance produced by that object. However, flux density by itself does not determine the perception of brightness. Rather, it is the *relative* flux density, or *contrast*, between adjacent areas of the retina that determines these impressions. A patch of retina with an invariant retinal illuminance may appear bright or dark depending upon the illuminance falling on adjacent areas.

Luminances in object space can be related to illuminance at the retina by the following function:

$$E_r = e_r T \frac{\cos \theta}{k^2} \qquad (3\text{-}2)$$

where

E_r = retinal illuminance in lm/m^2,
T = ocular transmittance,
θ = angular displacement from the line of sight,
k = a constant whose value is 15,
e_r = amount of light entering the eye, in trolands (T).

The value e_r, in trolands, is calculated by

$$e_r = Lp \qquad (3\text{-}3)$$

where

L = surface luminance in cd/m^2,
p = pupil area in mm^2.

It can be seen that persons with different pupil sizes or different transmission characteristics may receive significantly different visual effects from identical objects. These individual variations must be considered when predictions of visual behavior are made solely from luminance descriptions of the scene.

Blur

An object can be thought of as an array of points, each of which radiates light toward the eye. If that object is imaged on the retina by a theoretically perfect optical system, the rays from each point in object space will focus at a point in image space (see figure 3-18a). However, if the optical system of the eye does not focus the object's rays at the retina, the image of each object point will no longer be a point, but rather will form a patch of light (see figure 3-18b). Blurring of the image will result in a defocused image of each point, an overlap of the images of adjacent points and consequently a reduction in perceived contrast when the objects are small.

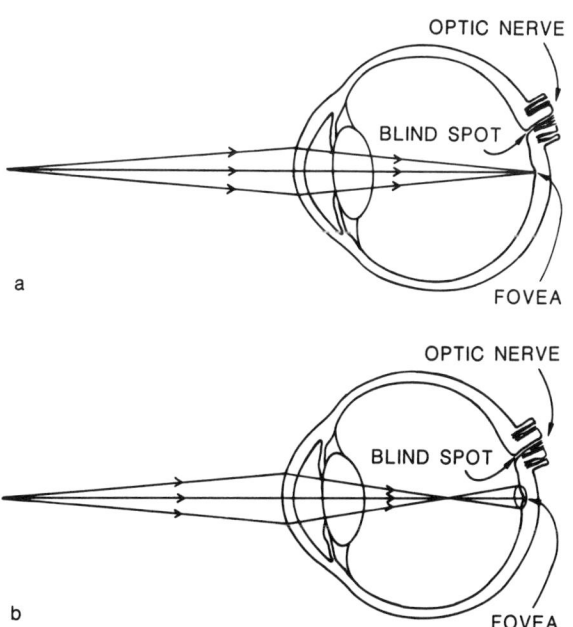

Fig. 3-18. (a) In a perfectly focused optical system, a point source or object is imaged as a point on the retina. (b) The retinal image of a point source or object in an eye with too much power for its length is no longer a point. Such an eye is called *myopic* or "near-sighted."

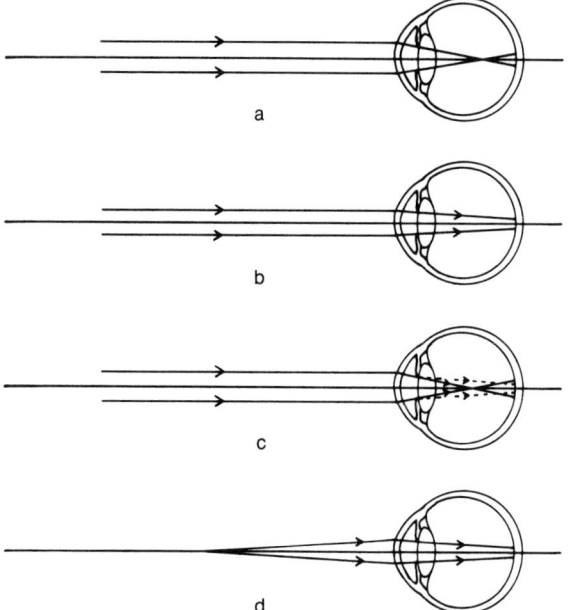

Fig. 3-19. The relationship between the image of a point object and the retina in the common refractive errors. (a) In myopia, the image forms in front of the retina. (b) In hyperopia, the image forms behind the retina. (c) In astigmatism, multiple foci are formed due to different powers in the various meridians of the eye. (d) In presbyopia, accommodation is sufficiently limited so that near objects focus behind the retina.

Blur can be caused by several factors in the human eye:

1. *Uncorrected refractive errors.* The eyes do not focus a sharp image on the retina (see figure 3-19).
   a. *Myopia.* Object points at a distance are focused in front of the retina (see figure 3-19a).
   b. *Hyperopia.* Object points at a distance are focused behind the retina (see figure 3-19b).
   c. *Astigmatism.* Object points are not focused at a point in any plane (see figure 3-19c). This condition is caused by different powers in the various meridians of the eye.
   d. *Presbyopia.* Near objects focus behind the retina (see figure 3-19d). Caused by a loss of accommodative ability, usually as one ages.
2. *Aberrations.* Even when the eye is perfectly corrected for refractive errors, a residual blur remains due to the existence of spherical and chromatic aberrations.
   a. *Spherical aberration.* Light rays which enter the periphery of the cornea are refracted more than those which enter through the central zones (see figure 3-20a). Thus, light in the retinal image is partially redistributed over a larger retinal area than

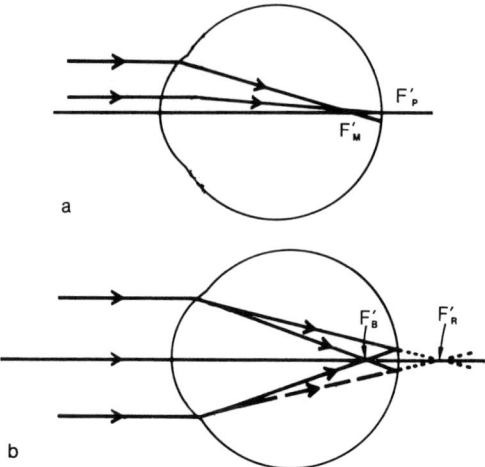

Fig. 3-20. (a) Spherical aberration: peripheral rays are focused in front of rays entering the eye near the center of the pupil. (b) Longitudinal chromatic aberration: because the eye's index of refraction is greater for short wavelengths (from blue objects) than for long wavelengths (from orange and red obejcts), the eye focuses short wavelengths in front of long wavelengths.

would be the case in an aberration-free system. The amount and type of spherical aberration varies with the state of accommodation (see figure 3-21).[20]

   b. *Chromatic aberration.* Shorter wavelengths are refracted more than longer wavelengths (see figure 3-22). As in spherical aberration, the results of the different foci cause blur (see figure 3-20b).

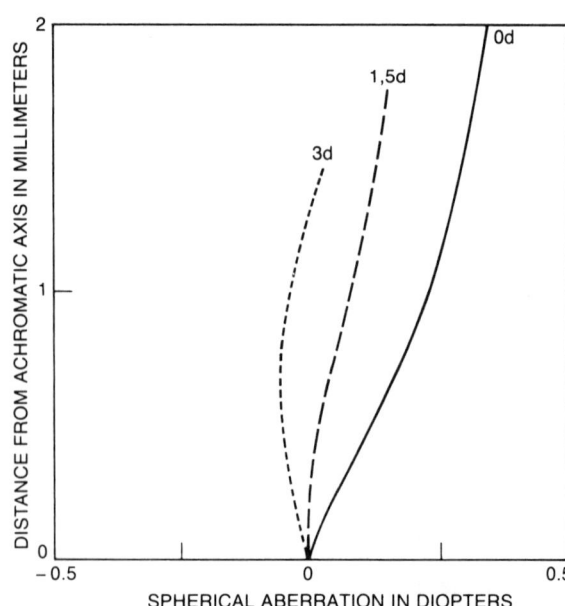

Fig. 3-21. Spherical aberration of the human eye based upon the average of ten observers. The amount of spherical aberration (in diopters) is on the abscissa (positive when undercorrected), and the distance from the achromatic axis is on the ordinate. The solid line corresponds to the unaccommodated eye; the dashed line corresponds to the average eye with 1.5 diopters accommodation; and the dotted line to 3.0 diopters accommodation.

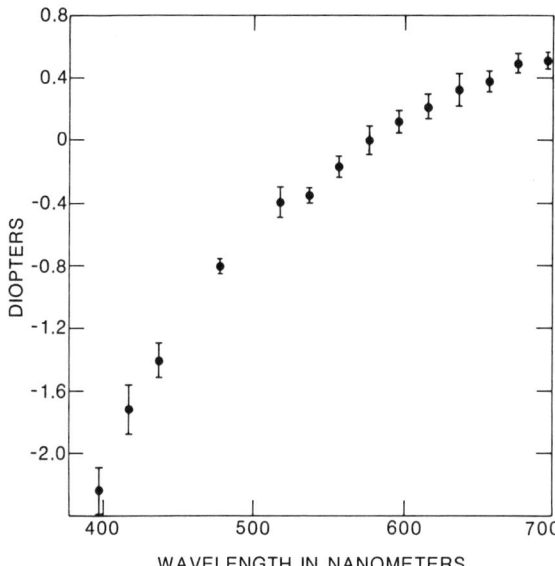

Fig. 3-22. The power necessary to correct an eye for the difference in refraction of wavelengths between 400 and 700 nm (zero is arbitrarily set at 589 nm).

While these aberrations (and others) are of theoretical interest to the lighting designer, they are partially compensated by the structure of the eye and can usually be neglected in practical lighting design. They may, however, be important in certain specialized applications, such as work under reduced illuminances where pupil sizes may be large.

3. *Diffraction.* Regardless of whether rays are in focus or not, there is always a certain amount of blur due to the diffraction of light. This determines the ultimate resolving power when the eye is in best focus, but the blur due to diffraction is not large enough to be perceived unless the pupil size is artificially fixed at less than about 2 mm in diameter.

Veiling Luminance (Disability Glare)

If the eye were a perfect optical system, image blur could be substantially accounted for by the degree to which the image on the retina was out of focus. In reality, however, the ocular media contain many inhomogeneities which scatter the incident light, and accordingly they reduce the contrast of even a perfectly focused retinal image. This reduction in contrast occurs because light intended for the primary image is scattered to adjacent retinal areas while light intended for the adjacent areas is scattered onto the primary image.

Because the reduction in contrast of an image from scattered light can be mimicked by adding a uniform "veil" of luminance to the object, the effect is considered to be equivalent to a *veiling luminance*; it is also called *disability glare*. This phenomenon is different

from veiling *reflections*, which are associated with geometric and specular properties of the light source and the task.

Although veiling luminance is most commonly thought of as coming from discrete sources of glare, such as that from oncoming automobile headlamps, every luminous point in space acts as a source of stray light for nearby points, lines, and borders and reduces their contrast.

Because the visibility of objects on or near the line of sight is usually of concern, it is useful to understand the effect of surrounding areas on the appearance of objects which are viewed foveally. Several investigators[21–24] have analyzed the role of glare-source luminance and distance from the primary object of regard as producers of disability glare; they have each derived slightly different functions, which however generally take the form

$$L_v = \frac{kE_0}{f(\theta)} \qquad (3\text{-}4a)$$

where

L_v = equivalent veiling luminance in cd/m^2,
E_0 = illuminance from the glare source at the eye in lx (this term is essential for integrating the effects at a given point produced by stray light from all other points),
k = a constant dependent upon the experimental conditions and the photometric units,
θ = angle between the primary object and the glare source in degrees.

Although the constants and the form of the function vary from observer to observer, a commonly used expression is[21]

$$L_v = \frac{9.2E_0}{\theta(\theta + 1.5)} \qquad (3\text{-}4b)$$

DISCOMFORT GLARE

Discomfort glare is a sensation of annoyance or pain caused by high or nonuniform distributions of brightness in the field of view. Discomfort may be caused by viewing a light source directly (sometimes called direct glare) or by viewing a reflection of the light source from a specular or semispecular surface (so-called reflected glare). Discomfort glare can be reduced by:

- Decreasing the luminance of the light source (windows, skylights, luminaires)
- Diminishing the area of the light source
- Increasing the background luminance around the source

Discomfort glare may be accompanied by disability

glare (see above), but is a distinctly different phenomenon.

While the cause of disability glare is well known (intraocular light scattering), that of discomfort glare is less well understood. Laboratory studies[25, 26] have related discomfort glare to pupillary activity, but such data are as yet insufficient to be applied in engineering practice. Consequently, most of the assessments of discomfort glare are based on consideration of the size, luminance and number of glare sources, their locations in the field of view, and the background luminance. Most measurements of discomfort produced by single glare sources have been performed by determining the luminance L just necessary to cause discomfort, a threshold criterion termed the *borderline between comfort and discomfort* (BCD).[27] These investigations have included the effect of adaptation luminance F on the BCD at the moderate levels of luminance likely to be encountered in interior spaces. Figure 3-23 shows the results for a source subtending 0.0011 sr (approximately 2° square) on the line of sight. Data from another investigation, performed as a parallel study at low adaptation luminances, are presented in figure 3-24. Both sets of data fit the function

$$L = cF^{0.44}$$

where $c = 302$ in one study[27] and 529 in the other.[28] The difference in the value of the constant is significant and may be due both to the different levels of background luminance at which the experiments were performed and to the differences among the subject populations. Care must be taken to utilize the appropriate function for the application conditions; the data from figure 3-23 are appropriate for interior applications, while those from figure 3-24 apply to night driving.

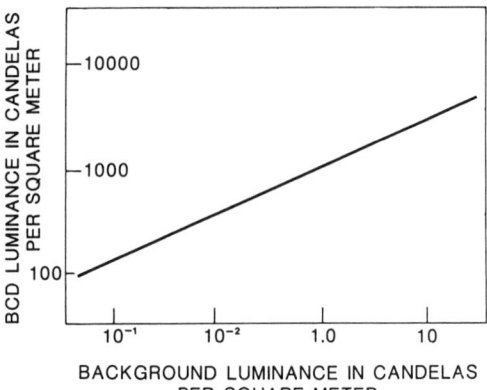

Fig. 3-24. The luminance of a glare source at discomfort threshold (BCD) as a function of the background luminance (light to which the eyes are adapted): low background luminances. $L_b = 529F^{0.44}$.

Figures 3-25 and 3-26 show the effect of glare source size on BCD luminance. Once again, it is clear that there are differences between the higher- and lower-luminance conditions and that caution must be used in applying the results.

As the glare source is moved away from the primary line of sight, the BCD luminance increases. Data for locations at various eccentricities and along several meridians are presented in figure 3-27 for a background luminance of 34.3 cd/m².[27]

The data taken at moderate luminances, combined with considerations such as the effect of multiple sources, have been used to develop the *visual comfort probability* (VCP) system. This system evaluates lighting systems in terms of the fraction of the observer population which will accept the lighting system and its

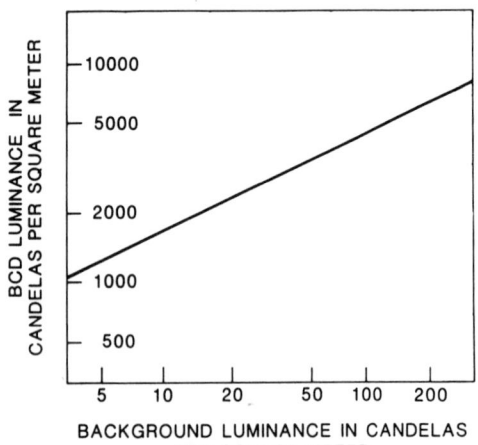

Fig. 3-23. The luminance of a glare source at discomfort threshold (BCD) as a function of the background luminance (light to which the eyes are adapted): moderate background luminances. $L_b = 302F^{0.44}$.

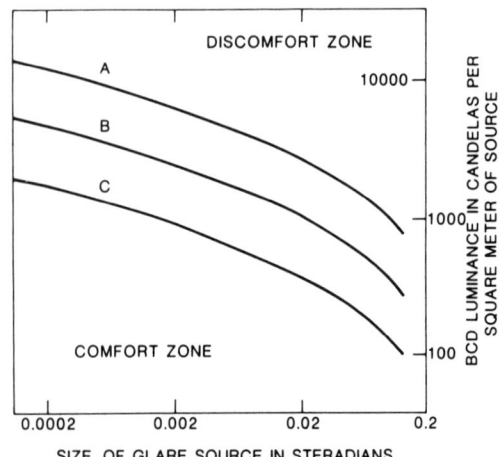

Fig. 3-25. The effect of glare source on the BCD at three levels of background luminance (L_b). $A = 343$ cd/m², $B = 34.3$ cd/m², and $C = 3.43$ cd/m². Larger sources result in a lower BCD. Sources are located on the primary line of sight—moderate background luminance.

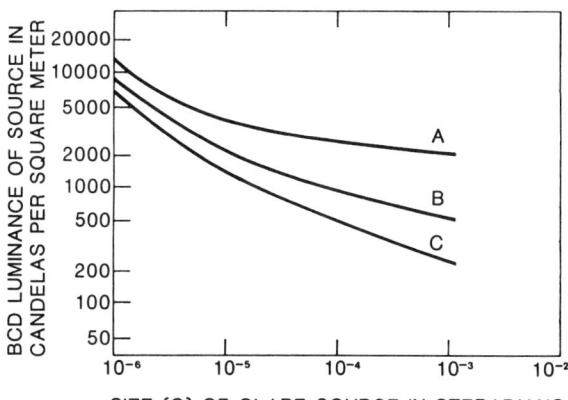

Fig. 3-26. The effect of glare source on the BCD at three levels of background luminance (L_b). $A = 0.34$ cd / m², $B = 0.034$ cd / m², and, $C = 0.0034$ cd / m². Larger sources result in a lower BCD. Sources are located on the primary line of sight — low luminance background.

environment as being comfortable, using the perception of glare due to direct light from luminaires to the observer as a criterion.

The following factors influence subjective judgments of visual comfort:

- Room size and shape
- Room surface reflectances
- Illuminance levels
- Luminaire characteristics
- Number and location of luminaires
- Luminance of the entire field of view
- Observer location and line of sight
- Differences in individual glare sensitivity

The VCP can be calculated for specific lighting systems and given observer lines of sight (see chapter 9, Lighting Calculations). However, in order to systematize the calculations to aid in the development of VCP tables

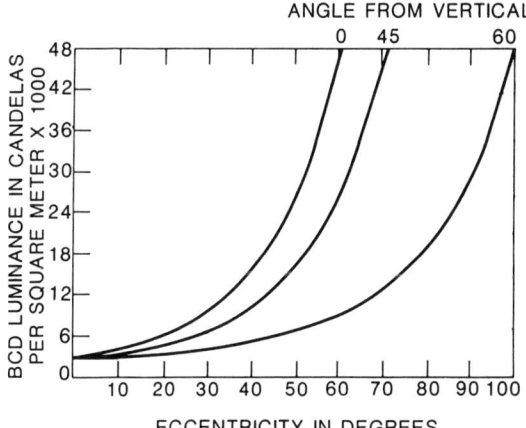

Fig. 3-27. BCD luminance for glare sources at various angular distances from the line of sight along several meridians. Background luminance was 34.3 cd/m².

and to permit comparison of luminaires, standard conditions have been adopted:[29]

- An initial illuminance of 1000 lx (100 fc)
- Room surfaces with 80% for the effective ceiling cavity reflectance, 50% for the wall reflectance and 20% for the effective floor cavity reflectance
- Mounting heights above the floor of 2.6, 3, 4 and 4.9 m (8.5, 10, 13 and 16 ft)
- A range of room dimensions to include square, long narrow and short wide rooms
- A standard layout involving luminaires uniformly distributed throughout the space
- An observation point 1.2 m (4 ft) in front of the center of the rear wall and 1.2 m (4 ft) above the floor
- A horizontal line of sight directly forward
- A limit to the field of view corresponding to an angle of 53° above and directly forward from the observer

By consensus, discomfort glare will not be a problem in lighting installations if all three of the following conditions are satisfied:[29]

- The VCP is 70 or more
- The ratio of the maximum luminance (luminance of the brightest 6.5-cm² [1-in²] area) to the average luminaire luminance does not exceed 5 : 1 at 45, 55, 65, 75 and 85° from nadir, crosswise and lengthwise
- Maximum luminances of the luminaire crosswise and lengthwise do not exceed the following values:

Angle above nadir (degrees)	Maximum luminance (cd/m²)
45	7710
55	5500
65	3860
75	2570
85	1695

The principal research used to establish the VCP system involved luminances of magnitude comparable to those produced by fluorescent lamps.[27,30–36] Further, the most extensive field validation utilized lighting systems containing fluorescent luminaires. Although VCP can be applied to virtually any situation, extrapolation to significantly different visual fields has not been validated.

The VCP system is based on empirical relations derived from a variety of experiments. It has been concluded that differences of 5 percentage points or less are not significant. In other words, if two lighting systems do not differ in VCP rating by more than 5 units, there is no basis for judging that there is a difference in visual comfort between the two systems. Artifacts introduced by using different computational procedures for two lighting systems can further spread the VCP values for two systems that are not reliably different.[37]

An alternative, simplified method of providing an acceptable degree of comfort has been derived from the formulas for discomfort glare. This method is based on the premise that luminaire designers do not design different units for rooms of different sizes, but consider the probable range of room sizes and design for the "commonly found more difficult" potential glare situation (in rooms less than 6 m [20 ft] in length and width, the luminaires are largely out of the field of view). This simplified method is only applicable to flat-bottom luminaires and is found in chapter 9, Lighting Calculations.[38–40]

DESCRIPTION OF THE VISUAL DISPLAY

Visual displays (visual stimuli, visual tasks) can be specified in terms of quantities that are measurable in object space. Some of these quantities are:

- Luminance of the object
- Luminance of the background
- Contrast (calculated from eqs. 3-6, 3-7, and 3-8 below)
- Spectral distributions of the object and background

- Size (in units of linear measure, visual angle or solid angle)
- Duration
- Temporal frequency characteristics
- Location relative to the line of sight
- Movement in the field of view
- Nonuniformities of luminance in the object and the background

The visibility of any target is a function of all of the above parameters; additionally, cognitive factors such as attention, expectation and habituation will greatly affect the detectability and recognition of objects.

The designer can exert the most direct effect on the first four parameters listed above, and has opportunities to affect the remainder in many cases.

An object may be differentiated from its background because it differs either in luminance or in color; that is, there may be either a luminance contrast or a chromatic contrast (the term "luminance" is used instead of "brightness" because most objects are measured with photoelectric photometers today). Except in the case of self-luminous objects, both types of contrast are a function of the reflectance properties of the scene and of the incident illumination.

The apparent size of a target depends on several factors: the physical dimensions of the object itself, the viewing angle (from the normal to the line of sight) and the distance from the viewer. Size can be measured in terms of visual angle, as shown in figure 3-28a. Given the length d, a viewing angle θ and a distance l, the visual angle $\angle$ can be approximated by the following equation:

$$\angle \cong \arcsin\left(\frac{d\cos\theta}{l}\right) \qquad (3\text{-}5a)$$

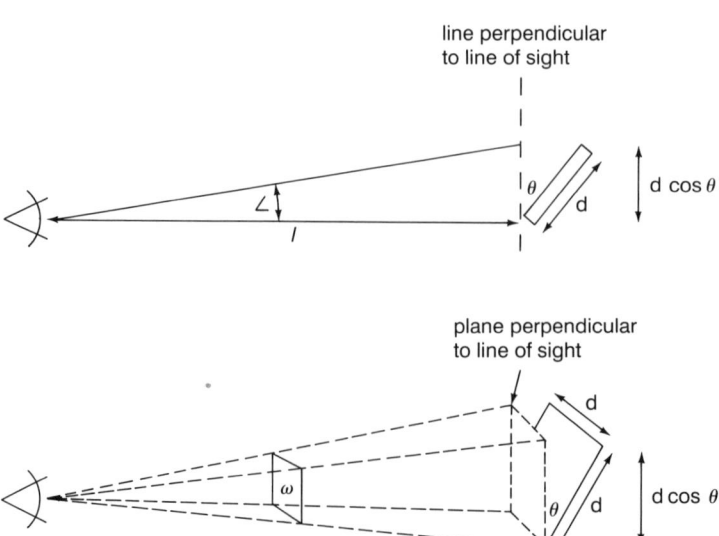

Fig. 3-28. (a) Approximation of visual angle $\angle$. $\angle \cong \arcsin\left[(d\cos\theta)/l\right]$. (b) Calculation of solid angle ω. $\omega = (d^2\cos\theta)/l^2$.

Many times, $\angle$ will be small and can be measured in minutes of arc (60 minutes equals 1 degree). The target size also can be expressed in terms of solid angle. Extending figure 3-28a into three dimensions as in figure 3-28b, the solid angle is seen to be a function of the surface area of the target, the viewing angle and the distance. Given a square target of dimension d, viewing angle θ and distance l, the solid angle ω is given by the following equation:

$$\omega = \frac{d^2 \cos \theta}{l^2} \quad (3\text{-}5b)$$

Luminance Contrast

Luminance contrast is defined in several ways:

$$C = \left| \frac{L_d - L_b}{L_b} \right| \quad (3\text{-}6)$$

where

L_d = luminance of the detail,
L_b = luminance of the background;

or

$$C = \frac{L_g - L_t}{L_g} \quad (3\text{-}7)$$

where

L_g = greater luminance,
L_t = lesser luminance;

or

$$C_{mod} = \frac{L_{max} - L_{min}}{L_{max} + L_{min}} \quad (3\text{-}8)$$

where

L_{max} = maximum luminance,
L_{min} = minimum luminance.

Equation 3-6 will result in contrasts that range between 0 and 1 for objects that are darker than their backgrounds, and between 0 and ∞ for objects that are brighter than their backgrounds. This equation is used more often in the former case, where the background is brighter than the target.

Equation 3-7 results in contrasts between 0 and 1 for all objects, whether brighter or darker than their backgrounds. It is especially applicable in a situation like a bipartite pattern in which neither of the areas on the two sides of the border can be identified as object or background.

The quantity defined by eq. 3-8 is often called contrast but is usually, and more properly, called modulation. It applies to periodic patterns, such as gratings, which have one maximum and one minimum in each cycle.

Because of the several different definitions of contrast, it is important for the designer to know which definition is being used when the contrast of an object is specified.

When an object and its background are illuminated by a single source and the luminances are dependent on their reflectances, the contrast is not affected by changing the intensity of the source. For example, a target that consists of a disk (reflectance = 0.5) on a background (reflectance = 0.9) will have a contrast (eq. 3-6) of 0.44 regardless of the illuminance on the scene:

$$C = \left| \frac{L_d - L_b}{L_b} \right| = \left| \frac{E(\rho_d) - E(\rho_b)}{E(\rho_b)} \right|$$

$$= \left| \frac{\rho_d - \rho_b}{\rho_b} \right| = \left| \frac{0.5 - 0.9}{0.9} \right| = 0.44$$

It is important to note, however, that the values of the reflectance ρ are dependent upon the geometric relationship between the directions of measurement and of illumination. Thus, if the position of the source changes, or if other sources of illumination are added, the contrast will change.

Reflections

Veiling reflections are luminous reflections from specular or semimatte surfaces that physically reduce the contrast of the visual task. This phenomenon is different from veiling luminance, or disability glare, described previously, wherein the contrast of the visual task has been reduced by scattered light within the eye.

The effect of veiling reflections on contrast may be quantified by modifications to the previous contrast equations based on luminance. From these contrast values the impact of veiling reflections on visual performance can be computed. In this simplest treatment, the luminous veil V is added to the luminance of the target and the luminance of the background. Modifying eq. 3-8, for example, to include the veiling luminance results in

$$C_{mod} = \frac{(L_{max} + V) - (L_{min} + V)}{(L_{max} + V) + (L_{min} + V)} \quad (3\text{-}9)$$

By rearranging,

$$C_{mod} = \frac{L_{max} - L_{min}}{L_{max} + L_{min} + 2V} \quad (3\text{-}10)$$

where

C_{mod} = modulation contrast,
L_{max} = maximum luminance,
L_{min} = minimum luminance,
V = luminance of the veiling reflection superimposed on the image.

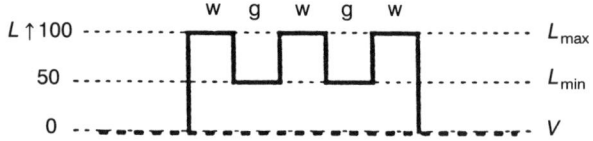

$$\text{CONTRAST} = \frac{(100 - 50)}{100 + 50 + 2(0)} = 0.33$$

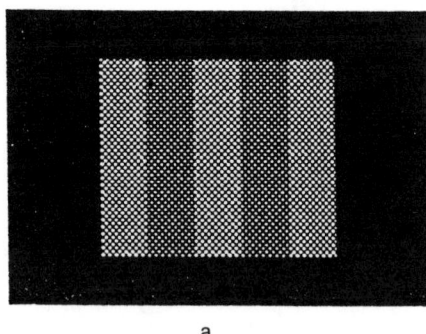

a

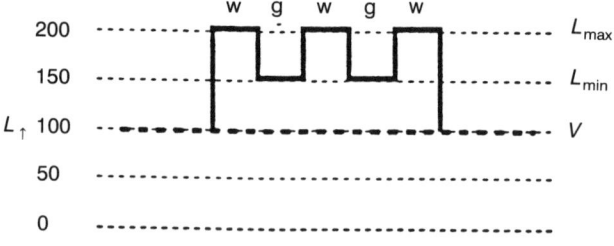

$$\text{CONTRAST} = \frac{(100 - 50)}{100 + 50 + 2(100)} = 0.14$$

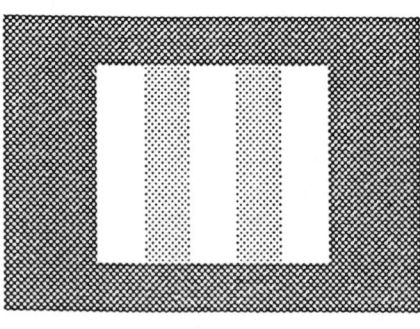

b

Fig. 3-29. (a) Representation of alternating gray and white bars on a VDT screen with no veiling reflection ($V = 0$ cd/m^2). Modulation contrast is 0.33. (b) The same alternating bars on a VDT screen with a veiling reflection ($V = 100$ cd/m^2). Modulation contrast becomes 0.14.

In figure 3-29, for example, the solid lines represent the luminance profile of white (w) and gray (g) bars on a black VDT screen (screen luminance is 0). For this example, with no veiling reflections, the luminance of the white bars (L$_{max}$) is 100 cd/m^2, and the luminance of the gray bars is 50 cd/m^2, thus producing a contrast of 0.33. If the same image were seen so that reflections from the ceiling were visible in the screen and produced a veiling luminance of 100 cd/m^2, the contrast between the gray and white bars would become 0.14.

In the situation where the directional reflectances of the detail and the background are anisotropic (that is, sensitive to the direction and polarization of the illumination), as, for example, with the steel rule of a carpenter's square, the contrast equations based upon luminance are not appropriate in determining the contrast; an equation based on reflectance (ρ) should be used, where the values of ρ are specific to the direction of illumination and to its degree and plane of polarization.

Additionally, for anisotropic materials, a reflected image of the light source can be formed by the surface. This image will not only reduce the contrast of the task detail, but also constitutes a visual object at a different focal distance than that of the surface. This *reflected glare* can cause discomfort. Perhaps more importantly, reflected images in the visual field can compete for the attention of the worker. This latter effect can be a serious problem, particularly for VDT applications, where two bright images of the luminaire, one for each eye, are reflected from a surface. Since the reflected images are at a different focal distance than the surface, fluctuations in accommodation and vergence may cause fatigue and discomfort to the worker during prolonged viewing. It is therefore quite important to limit brightness in the so-called "offending zone" (see chapter 15, Office Lighting). To do so will reduce the nuisance of veiling reflections, reflected glare and multiple images in the field of view.

Chromatic Contrast

Visual targets that have the same luminance as the background may still be discerned by color information. These equal-luminance chromatic contrasts are generally less distinct than achromatic contrasts,[41, 42] but under some conditions they can be quite visible. This is especially true if there is a sharp spatial discontinuity between the two colors. The distinctness of such a chromatic border can be estimated by matching it to the contrast of an achromatic border. Compared in this way, chromatic contrasts range from below the achromatic contrast threshold to about 0.30. A model for chromatic contrast has been developed using the responses of the long- and middle-wavelength-sensitive cones.[43]

Brightness Perception

Brightness is the perceptual counterpart to the photometric quantity luminance, but brightness and luminance are not always proportional to one another. Because color contributes to the perceptions of scenes, predictions of visibility based only upon achromatic luminances can be wrong.[44] These errors can arise not only because of chromatic contrast (as discussed above), but also because perceived brightness is modified by color information. As described previously, brightness is not based only upon achromatic luminance. The input from the color channels can also modulate luminance information to make borders more or less distinct. Roughly, the larger the difference in saturation between the target and the background, the larger the discrepancy between the perceived contrast and the estimated contrast based only on achromatic luminance.

Human brightness perception at photopic luminance levels has long been believed to depend solely on the cone system. The question of whether or not the rod system contributes to the perception of brightness at photopic luminance levels is currently an unresolved issue. In 1924 the Commission Internationale de L'Éclairage (CIE) defined the relative spectral sensitivity of the visual system $V(\lambda)$, using data obtained from several studies and different psychophysical techniques.[7] The underlying assumption was that human sensitivity to light, at photopic levels, was governed by mechanisms which were mediated by activity in the three cone receptor systems; rods were considered to play no role at photopic levels of adaptation. The 1924 Standard Observer, and its 1931 colorimetric counterpart, also assumed that luminances were additive, at least for small (2°), foveally fixated fields. Indeed, even the 1964 Standard Observer for large fields (10°) still assumed that cones were the only mechanisms that contributed to the sensitivity of the eye at photopic luminance levels. Nonetheless, from the time of the adoption of the Standard Observers, it was known that luminance additivity held true for only a very restricted range of viewing conditions and that luminance did not predict subjective brightness under most viewing conditions.[45-47] A number of models have been proposed to account for these differences, but, with few exceptions, all have denied rod contributions to the brightness sensation under real-life viewing conditions.

More recently, with the opponent-color vision models, brightness perception has been understood more completely, but these models still deal only with the cone systems. The opponent-color vision models[47-53] suggest the existence of two types of neural encoding channels which combine the outputs of the three cone types. One is the achromatic system or luminance channel, wherein the signals from middle- and long-wavelength cones (and, in some models, short-wavelength cones) are summed. The other is the chromatic system or opponent system, in which the output of one type of cone is subtracted from that of another type of cone, leading to the r-g and b-y opponent visual pathways.

Crucial to the understanding of brightness perception is the assumption, made in the opponent-color vision models, that differences in sensitivity between brightness perception and luminance appear because brightness is mediated by both chromatic and achromatic channels, whereas luminance depends solely on the achromatic channel.[47] Large contributions to brightness perception by the chromatic channels are shown clearly for small (2°) fields of view.[54,55] With a larger field of view (10°), different values for the relation between brightness perception and luminance were obtained. Some comprehensive experiments have been conducted to measure brightness perception for larger fields of view and to explain the different values. A role for rods in brightness perception has been proposed.

For large photopic viewing fields, pupil size is better predicted by a rod-dominated spectral response than by a cone-dominated one.[56] It has been found that significant differences in pupil size occur when subjects are adapted to indirect high-pressure sodium lighting as compared with indirect incandescent lighting, even when the luminances are photopically matched. The observed differences in pupil size are attributed to the differences in spectral power distribution of the two lighting systems. Pupil size is smaller when the eye is stimulated by sources which have more radiant energy at the short-wavelength end of the spectrum, where the rods are more sensitive than are the cones. This effect is present even when the light sources are visually indistinguishable (metameric).

Under some viewing conditions, the brightness perception of photopically equated fields with different spectral power distributions can paradoxically be opposite to their relative photopic luminance.[57] This effect is incompatible with the opponent-color vision model, which states that brightness depends solely on cone contributions. Apparently, scotopic luminance is the predominant factor in brightness judgments, but it does not fully account for them. Neither the scotopic nor the photopic luminance alone accounts for perceived brightness. Brightness is better predicted by a sensitivity function (or more precisely, sensation function) weighted somewhere between the normally assumed cone response function and the scotopic response of the eye.

In related research, a subjective increase in perceived brightness while viewing a scene through yellow filters has also suggested that the signals from the rod system are involved in brightness perception. This research has hypothesized that the tasks mediated by the chromatic pathway may be enhanced by yellow filters because the elimination of short wavelengths might reduce the opponent components and increase the outputs of the opponent channels, and thereby increase the brightness.[58] When comparing small and large targets viewed through yellow filters and luminance-matched neutral filters, brightness perception is enhanced by up to 40% with yellow filters when the spatial extent of the stimulus exceeds that of the fovea.[59] The brightness enhancement effect is negligible when the rods are desensitized by bleaching during the cone plateau of the dark adaptation curve. Because this effect is present only for large fields and at adaptation levels below which rods saturate, the increase in brightness is likely mediated not by the cone system, but rather by the rod system. The contribution of rod signals to chromatic channels could be largely responsible for the brightness enhancement.

VISUAL ABILITY

Contrast Detection

Contrast detection is a basic visual task from which many other visual behaviors are derived. The visual system gives virtually no useful information when the retina is uniformly illuminated, but is highly specialized to gather information about luminous discontinuities and gradients in the visual field.

One of the simplest visual tasks is to detect a small difference in luminance between a region and an otherwise uniform surround. This function has been studied in great detail[60, 61] and has, for example, been used to relate the probability of detecting a small disk test object on a uniform background to the contrast and the luminance of the background (see figure 3-30).

As the contrast (defined as in eq. 3-5) of the test disk is raised, the probability of seeing increases until,

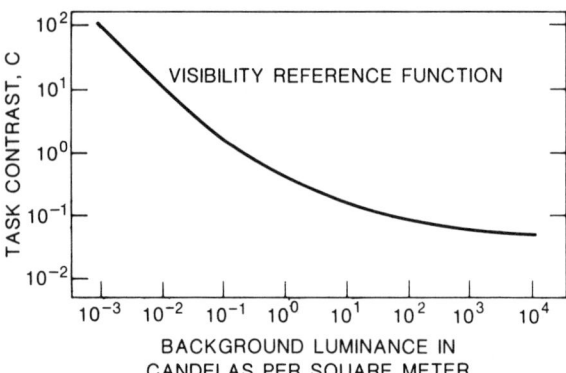

Fig. 3-31. Plot of the Visibility Reference Function (VL1) representing task contrast required at different levels of task background luminance to achieve threshold visibility for a 4 min luminous disk exposed for 0.2 s.

at a certain contrast, it can be detected 100% of the time. The contrast at which the object can be detected 50% of the time is called the *threshold contrast*. It varies among individuals, with the duration of exposure of the test object, with the size and shape of the object and with the luminance of the background.

The change in threshold contrast for the test disk as a function of background luminance is shown in figure 3-31. It represents a specific group of observers and a particular test object on a uniform background. This curve has been used by the IESNA to illustrate the fundamental relationship between object detection and the luminances of the background. It is called the *visibility reference function* (VL1). Because so many factors affect the contrast necessary to detect a particu-

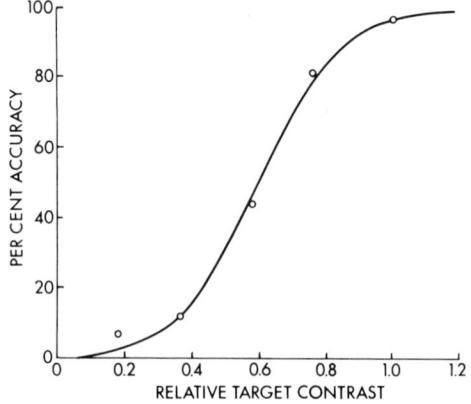

Fig. 3-30. A frequency of seeing function. As contrast is increased, the number of times it is seen relative to the number of times it is presented increases to a maximum of 100%.

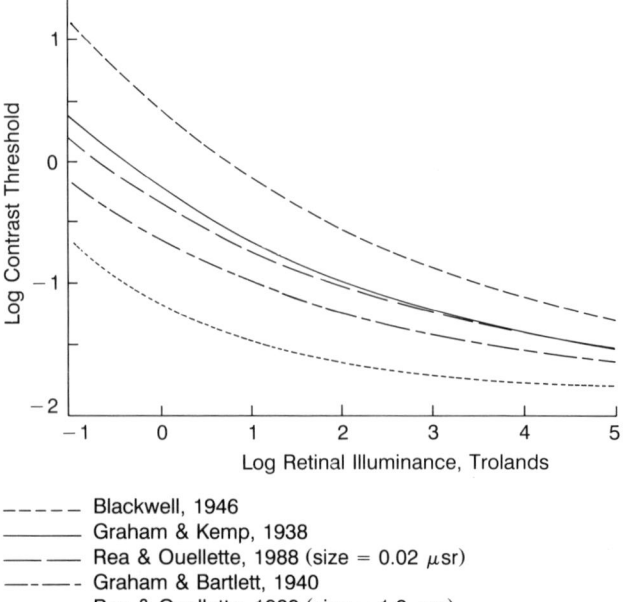

----- Blackwell, 1946
——— Graham & Kemp, 1938
— — Rea & Ouellette, 1988 (size = 0.02 μsr)
—·—· Graham & Bartlett, 1940
········ Rea & Ouellette, 1988 (size = 1.3 μsr)

Fig. 3-32. Threshold contrast as a function of retinal illuminance, based on data from several researchers. Note the similar shapes of each of the five curves.

lar target, however, no one function can be considered fundamental in any way.

Nevertheless, the shapes of the contrast threshold curves for simple detection tasks in controlled environments (see figure 3-32) are relatively invariant. Every contrast threshold function in figure 3-32 shows the same trend: as the background luminance (and therefore the retinal illuminance) increases, the contrast threshold decreases, rapidly at first and then more slowly.

Visual Acuity

The word "acuity" is often used to describe the visibility of fine details involved in various kinds of displays. Several different kinds of acuity are recognized; in particular:

1. *Resolution acuity*, the ability to detect that there are two stimuli, rather than one, in the visual field. It is measured in terms of the smallest angular separation between two stimuli that can still be seen as separate.
2. *Recognition acuity*, the ability to correctly identify a visual target, as in differentiating between a "G" and a "C." Usually, but not always, it is measured in terms of the angular dimension of the smallest target that can be discriminated. Visual acuity testing performed using letters, as is done clinically, is a form of recognition acuity testing.

Recognition acuity can involve very complex perceptual processing and often cannot be simply related to resolution acuity. Although detecting the difference between an "O" and a "C" may be identical to resolution acuity, differentiating between a circle and an octagon is a more complex task. Furthermore, the polarity (bright on dark versus dark on bright) can affect the result. For example, dark-on-bright discriminations are often more appropriately considered contrast detection tasks than visual acuity tasks.

Several examples of acuity test objects are shown in figure 3-33. Gratings, letters and Landolt rings all have been used as acuity test objects. Also, several measures of acuity may be used. The angular size of the critical detail (*d* in figure 3-33) or the overall width and height

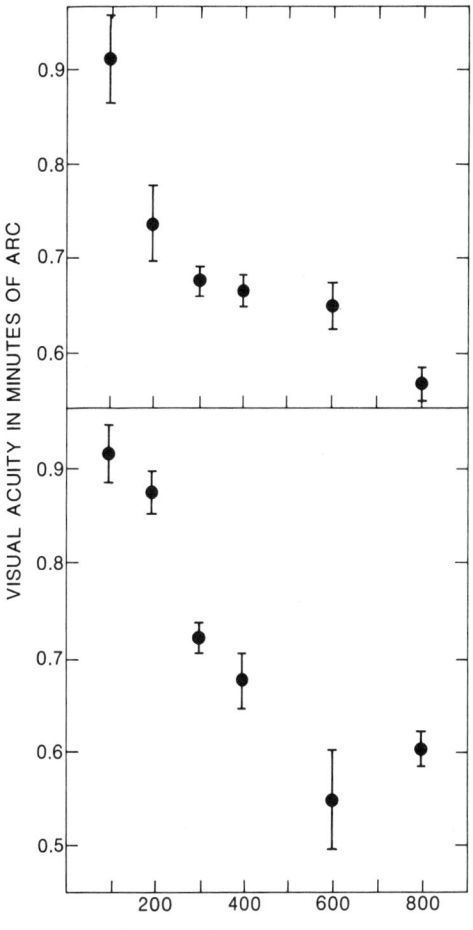

Fig. 3-34. The minimum angle of resolution versus exposure duration for two different subjects. Visual acuity is found to improve with exposure durations out to about 400 ms and then reaches a plateau. The vertical bars indicate the 50 fiducial limits of the means of the fitted frequency-of-seeing curves.

of the target can be measured as a planar angle (in degrees).

Visual acuity, like detection, varies with exposure duration and luminance (retinal illuminance). See figures 3-34 and 3-35. In general, visual acuity continues to improve as the duration increases. It has also been seen that acuity increases and then begins to decrease as the background luminance increases. This phenomenon appears to be related to the size of the background field; Lythgoe[62] has shown that acuity will continue to improve with background luminance as long as the background is large (see figure 3-35).

Temporal Resolution

Just as the visual system responds to contrasts in space, it also responds to contrasts in time. Because of the movement of targets across the retina, due either to eye movements or to motion of the object itself, virtually all spatial contrasts can also involve temporal contrasts.

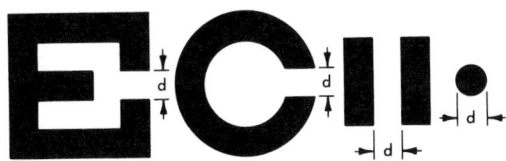

Fig. 3-33. Commonly used test objects for determining size discrimination and visual acuity. The critical detail size is represented by *d*.

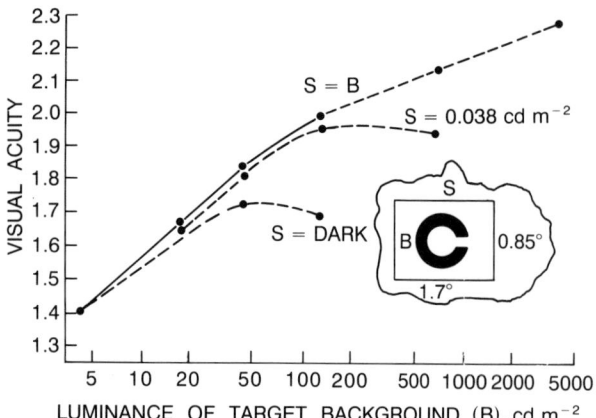

Fig. 3-35. Effect of background luminance on visual acuity. The targets are Landolt rings on a background field measuring 0.85° by 1.7°. When the luminance of the background field equals the luminance of the surrounding area, visual acuity continues to improve as background luminance increases.

At detection threshold, the visual system sums flashes of light over brief periods of time. For brief flashes (less than 100 ms—see figure 3-36), luminance (L) can be traded for duration (t), a relationship known as Bloch's law:

$$Lt = \text{constant} \qquad (3\text{-}11)$$

For flashes longer than 100–200 ms, the threshold becomes independent of time. That is, it is solely a function of stimulus luminance.

Repetitive square-wave flashes at frequencies between 2 and 20 Hz may have suprathreshold brightnesses greater than that of the same stimulus presented continuously.[63,64] This is known as *brightness enhancement*. Even single pulses of light may, under the proper stimulus conditions, appear brighter than a steady light.[65]

As a flashing stimulus is increased in frequency, it will eventually reach a point where it will be perceived as steady rather than as intermittent; this is the *critical*

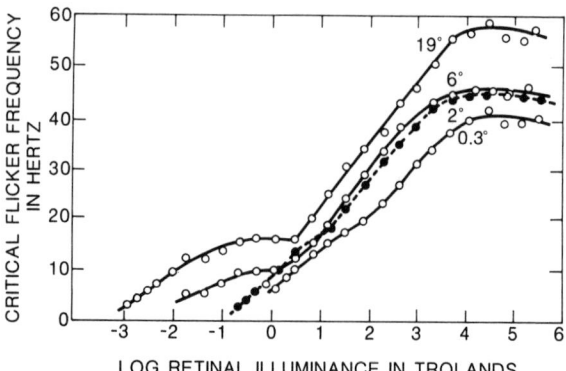

Fig. 3-37. Critical flicker frequency (CFF) as a function of source area and retinal illuminance.

flicker (or *fusion*) *frequency* (CFF). The frequency at which the fusion occurs will vary with stimulus size, shape, retinal location, spectral distribution, luminance, modulation depth and state of adaptation. Figure 3-37 shows the relationship of CFF to adaptation luminance for centrally fixated test objects of several different sizes. The CFF rarely exceeds 60 Hz even under optimal conditions.

For an intermittent stimulus, the modulation necessary to just detect the flicker varies with the temporal frequency of the stimulus[66] (see figure 3-38), so that stimuli presented at frequencies in the midrange (6–10 Hz) are easier to detect than are stimuli presented at either a lower or a higher rate. Functions such as in

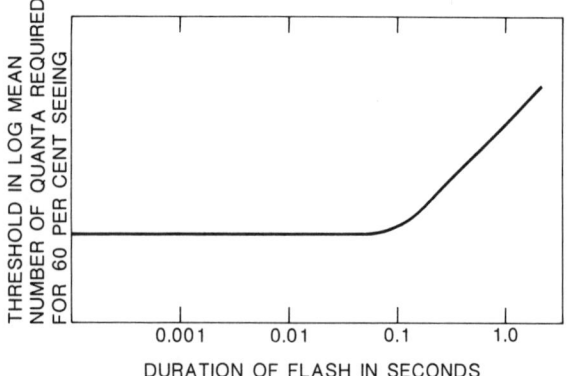

Fig. 3-36. Total light required for seeing a flash as a function of the duration of the flash.

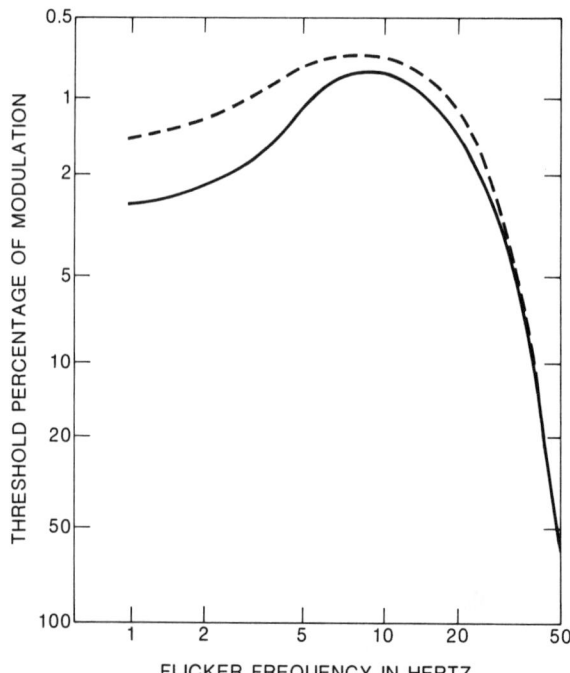

Fig. 3-38. Temporal modulation transfer functions for small flickering fields against a nonflickering background whose luminance is the same as the average of the flickering field. The dashed curve is for a field with sharp edges and the solid one for a field with blurred edges.

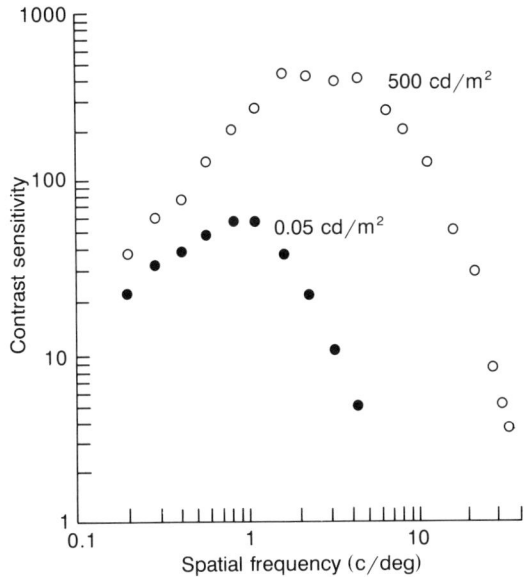

Fig. 3-39. Contrast sensitivity for sine-wave gratings at two different luminances. The higher curve is at an average luminance of 500 cd / m²; the lower is at 0.05 cd / m².

figure 3-38 are known as De Lange curves and may be called *temporal modulation transfer functions* in analogy with the spatial modulation transfer functions (see figure 3-39 for comparison). To be just detectable, the rate of change of a flash whose luminance increases with time must be greater for a short flash than for a long flash (see figure 3-40).[67]

Sensitivity to flicker differs across the retina. The fovea can follow flicker rates up to about 60 Hz at moderate luminances, but is relatively insensitive to low flicker modulations. The peripheral retina, on the

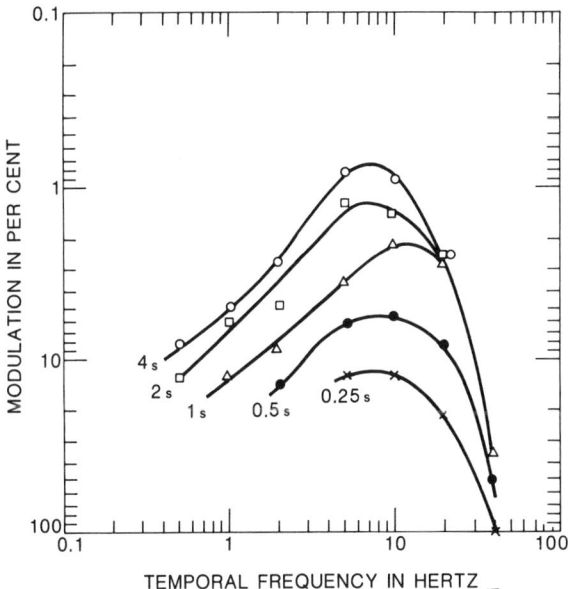

Fig. 3-40. Flicker thresholds plotted as a function of the frequency (*De Lange* curves) for various stimulus durations, in s.

other hand, can detect flicker rates only to about 15 Hz, but is very sensitive to small flicker amplitudes. This is why flicker is often detected in the peripheral field but disappears when the light is viewed directly.

It is generally believed that flicker must be perceived in order to cause visual discomfort or annoyance. Recently, however, statistically significant increases in subjects' comfort have been reported when fluorescent lamps were operated on high-frequency electronic ballasts as compared to when they were operated on conventional (British) 50-Hz magnetic ballasts, even though no flicker was perceived with either system. This implies that flicker may have subliminal effects on the visual system.[68] These results need to be replicated and extended before major changes in lamp ballasting are considered beneficial.

Knowledge of flicker effects is most helpful when considering signal detection, animated signs, and reported problems with fluorescent lamp flicker.

Visual Performance and Illuminance Selection

The Illuminating Engineering Society of North America (IESNA) has recommended illuminance levels for interior tasks for over eighty years. In general, the visual system performs better at higher illuminance levels. However, visual performance depends upon other factors, such as the size and the contrast of the retinal image, that confound a simple understanding of the relationship between illuminance levels and visual performance. The principle behind the illuminance recommendations of the IESNA has always been to maximize productivity in terms of greater speed and fewer errors, while limiting the cost of lighting equipment and electric energy. This subsection briefly discusses the current and past thinking about the relationship between visual performance and illuminance selection.

The Floor of Visual Response. To see a task at all, it must receive (or generate) some minimal amount of illumination. Likewise, it must have a minimal size and also a minimal amount of luminous contrast with its background. It is convenient to think of the lowest level of visual response as a floor whose two dimensions are *contrast* and *size*. The visual system's state of light adaptation, which is largely governed by the illuminance level in the visual scene, sets the height and the shape of the floor of visual response.

Historically, researchers have studied one dimension of the floor at a time. Studies have been conducted to determine the smallest size (acuity)[62, 69-74] or the lowest contrast (threshold contrast) that can be seen at different adaptation levels (see above discussion). It has only been recently that the two dimensions have been systematically studied together to describe the floor of visual response.

The Contrast Sensitivity Function. Since the platform of visual response is two dimensional, it is appropriate that both contrast and size be systematically studied together. Although a variety of targets could be used to define the floor of visual response,[75] sine-wave gratings of different spatial frequency have been used most often.

Figure 3-39 shows typical *contrast sensitivity functions*, which represent the contrast necessary to just see gratings of different spatial frequencies.[76] The horizontal dimension of the contrast sensitivity function is size, measured in terms of spatial frequency. Spatial frequency increases from left (low spatial frequencies, corresponding to large objects) to right (high spatial frequencies, corresponding to small objects). The vertical dimension is the reciprocal of the *threshold contrast*, that is, the contrast necessary to just detect a sine-wave grating.

The contrast sensitivity function has an optimal spatial frequency. In other words, the visual system is less sensitive to (has a higher threshold for) gratings of higher or lower spatial frequency. The highest spatial frequency that can be resolved will be associated with the highest grating contrast possible (that is, 1.0). This spatial frequency is known as the *high-frequency cutoff* or *acuity limit*.

The contrast sensitivity functions in figure 3-39 show two adaptation levels, which again are determined by the overall luminance of the grating. The height and the shape of the contrast sensitivity functions depend upon the overall luminance level. In general, as the adaptation level increases there is an increase in sensitivity at all spatial frequencies; further, the optimum contrast sensitivity becomes more prominent and shifts to higher spatial frequencies. Also, the high-frequency cutoff shifts to higher spatial frequencies.

As with acuity,[62] the size of the viewing field affects contrast sensitivity. The sensitivity at low spatial frequencies increases with field size (figure 3-41).[77]

Suprathreshold Tasks. The previous discussion focused on the lowest level, or floor, of visual response. Most visual tasks of interest to illuminating engineering are well above this threshold level. Thus it is necessary to characterize the visual system's response at suprathreshold (above the threshold) levels.

One approach is to study performance for a variety of realistic tasks. Several studies have been conducted mimicking realistic tasks to determine how illumination affects performance.[78-82] This approach allows the experimenter to assess performance at suprathreshold conditions, but it is much more difficult to separate visual from nonvisual components of performance, such as comprehension in a reading task.

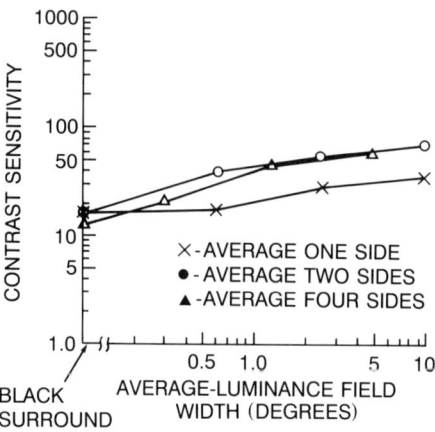

Fig. 3-41. The effect of average-luminance field size on contrast sensitivity.

As early as 1935, Weston[83, 84] recognized the importance of a carefully controlled, analytic study of suprathreshold performance that utilized the same stimulus conditions important to threshold vision, target size and target contrast seen at different background luminance levels. The curves in figure 3-42 demonstrate the effects of illuminance level on search performance for Landolt rings of different orientations and printed in different contrasts and sizes.[84] Search performance was defined, in these studies, as an aggregate score based on speed and accuracy.

An analysis of Weston's work[85] identified several design and analysis flaws, including a lack of documentation about specific visual characteristics, and the use of a scoring system which failed to include correct rejections as part of the accuracy metric. Nevertheless, Weston's performance data in figure 3-42 provide general trends in suprathreshold response that cannot be gleaned from a knowledge of threshold vision (the floor of visual response).

In general, Weston showed that as background luminance increased, performance, measured in terms of speed and accuracy, increased at a lower and lower rate until a point was reached where very large changes in background luminance were required to make very small changes in performance. This trend of diminishing returns was more pronounced for high-contrast, large targets than for low-contrast, small targets.

In contrast to the wealth of data on the threshold of visual response, there are surprisingly few analytic studies of suprathreshold visual response that followed Weston's work. Several studies of suprathreshold performance have extended Weston's approach while attempting to avoid its many methodological problems.[78-82, 86-90] In general, a more complete and detailed picture of suprathreshold performance has emerged from this work. Figure 3-43 is a graphic representation of the relationship of visual performance to contrast, size and adaptation luminance.[89] In

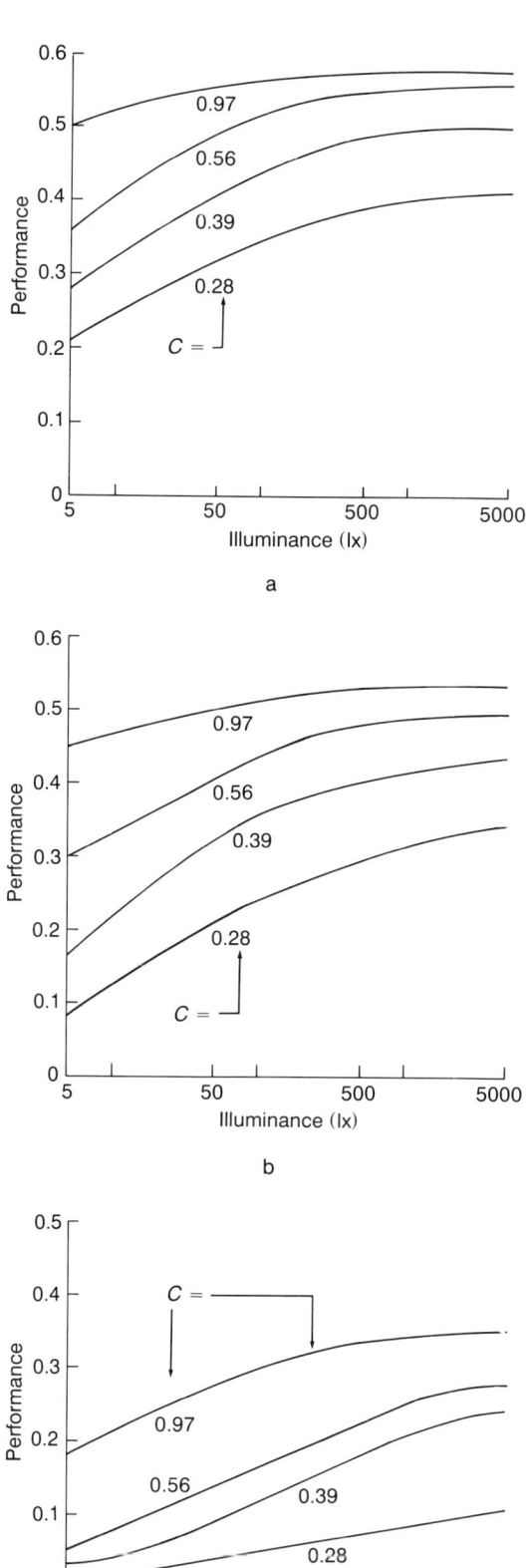

Fig. 3-42. Performance as a function of illuminance, target size, and task contrast *C* in Weston's Landolt ring search task. (a) Nominal apparent size = 4.5 min. (b) Nominal apparent size = 3.0 min. (c) Nominal apparent size = 1.5 min.

general, such surfaces give a precise picture of the "plateau and escarpment" of suprathreshold visual performance.[88]

Relationship to Illuminance Selection. The Illuminating Engineering Society of North America has, for many years, utilized information from studies of visual performance to construct a framework for the selection of illuminance levels. The first recommendations from the Society reflected the importance of providing more illuminance on tasks of smaller size and lower contrast. The work of Luckiesh had a strong impact on lighting for schools.[91, 92] Blackwell's research has also had a significant impact on illuminance levels in the United States[60, 61, 93, 94] as has Weston's work in Great Britain.[83, 84]

Illuminance levels have almost always been set by consensus. Committee members make judgments about the significance of illuminance for productivity, in terms of greater speed and fewer errors, relative to the cost of lighting equipment and electric energy. Although the committee members have a general qualitative appreciation of the relationship between contrast, size and luminance, the conceptual "model" of visual performance used has often been imprecise and undeclared.

In 1978 the IESNA Committee for Recommendations of the Quality and Quantity of Illumination, or RQQ committee, developed a more specific model of visual performance as it relates to illuminance selection, although one still based on consensus. This model gives the illuminating engineer a method whereby visual factors such as contrast and size have a defined influence on the illuminance level recommended. In general, as task contrast and size become smaller, higher levels of illuminance are recommended. This model is discussed more completely in Chapter 11, Illuminance Selection. Although the illuminance selection model is imperfect,[95] it has served the Society for over a decade and will probably be recommended by the Society for several years to come.

Two serious attempts have been made by the Society to develop a more precise quantitative model of illuminance selection based upon knowledge of visual performance. The first one is known as *equivalent sphere illuminance* (ESI). As the name implies, ESI characterizes a lighting system in terms of its ability to illuminate a task and produce a visual effect equivalent to that produced under *reference* diffuse (hemi)sphere illumination.

Lighting systems affect both task background luminance and task contrast. Underlying ESI is the assumption that two lighting systems can produce the same visual performance effect by different means. Thus, a lighting system that produces high background luminance but low task contrast can have the same visual

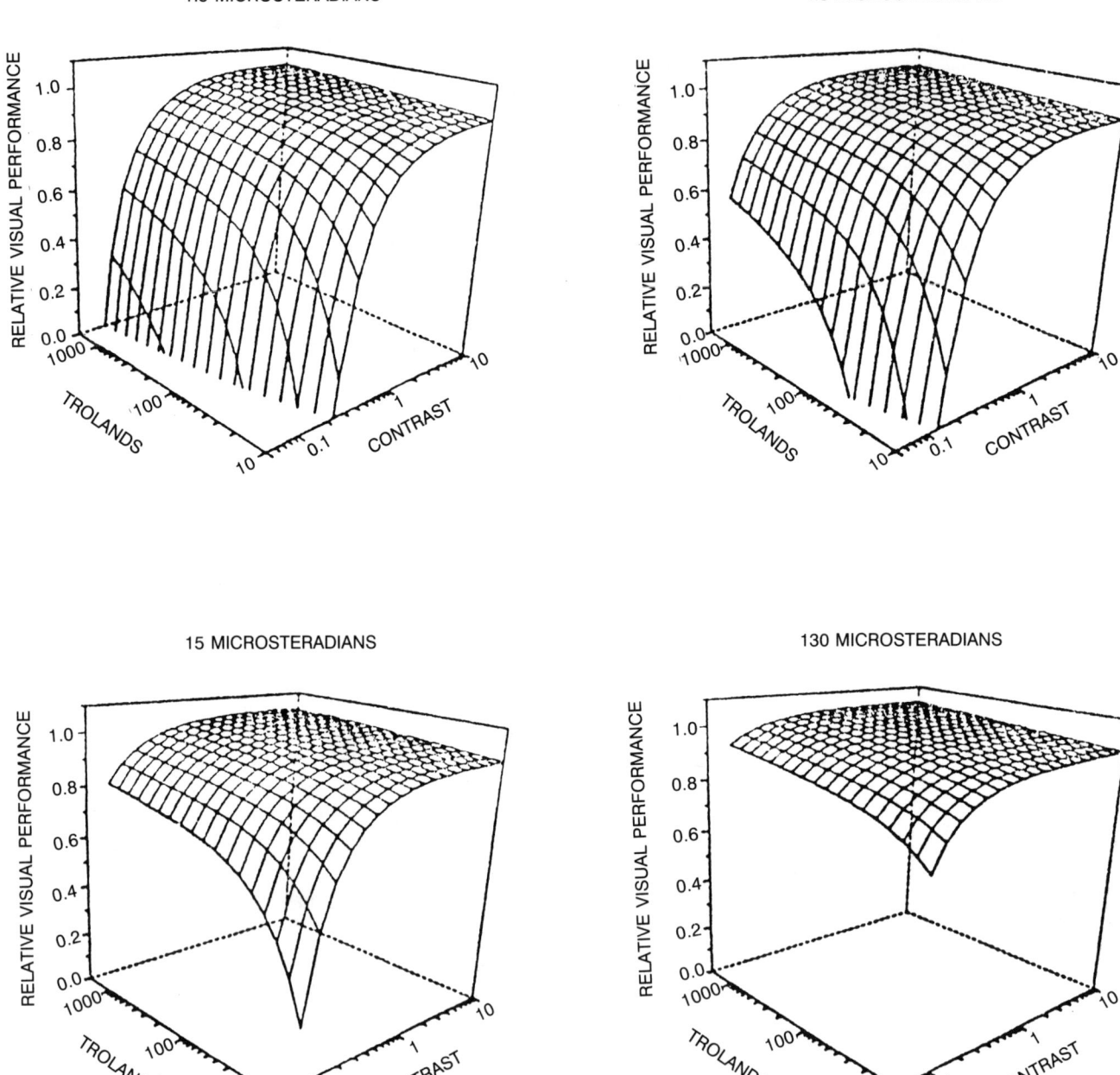

Fig. 3-43. Relative Visual Performance (RVP) plotted as a function of task contrast and retinal illuminance for several different target sizes. Note the plateau shape of each of the surfaces.

performance effect as another one that produces low background luminance but high task contrast. In terms of illuminance selection, then, the attractive assumption underlying ESI is that by providing a recommended equivalent sphere illuminance, one can produce the same visual effect for any type of lighting system.[92, 93, 96–98]

To employ ESI, one needs to know how much task contrast is gained or lost by the geometry of the lighting system relative to the task contrast obtained in a hemisphere, the reference lighting system; this is represented by the *contrast rendering factor* (CRF). One also needs to know the reflectance of the task background material; this is known as the *luminance factor* (LF). Using the CRF, the LF and VL1, the visibility reference function (figure 3-31)[60, 61] to trade off background luminance against task contrast, a value of diffuse illuminance (ESI) can be found that will produce a visual effect equivalent to that of the lighting system being evaluated.[99]

Limiting the effectiveness of ESI is the assumption that the visibility reference function is fundamental in trading off task background luminance and task contrast. Although all threshold functions of this type are of the same general shape (figure 3-32), other visual factors (target size, shape, exposure duration and location in the visual field) affect the exact relationship between target contrast and background luminance. Individual differences, such as age or disease, also affect this relationship. Finally, suprathreshold conditions and functions are of more interest to illuminating engineering because they are much more common. Because the visibility reference function is arbitrary and is applicable only to certain limited experimental conditions, ESI has limited utility in illuminance selection.

A more complete but also more complex formulation of suprathreshold visual responses, known as *relative visual performance* (RVP), has recently been developed. Like the current model of illuminance selection, RVP is based on the assumption that target size, contrast and background luminance are fundamentally important to visual performance. Several independent lines of research confirm that the RVP formulation characterizes suprathreshold visual response for these three visual factors.[86, 87, 89, 100, 101] To utilize RVP it is necessary to make measurements of task contrast, task size and background luminance. From these measurements a value of RVP is obtained. RVP cannot be easily calculated by hand; a computer or programmable calculator is recommended.

It remains to be determined whether the added accuracy in predicting visual performance will be utilized in the illuminance selection procedure. A model of visual performance, no matter how accurate, is only part of illuminance selection. The cost of equipment and energy will always be an important part of the Society's decision. If electric energy prices were to double, recommended illuminance levels would certainly become lower. Further, there are other, perhaps more important, lighting design factors that the practicing illuminating engineer must consider in setting illuminance levels. Visual performance is relatively unimportant in restaurant or retail lighting, so a model of visual performance will have, and should have, little influence on illuminance levels in these applications.

VISUAL RANGE OF LUMINOUS SIGNALS

Basic Principles

Some of the principles discussed above have been incorporated into empirical methods for evaluating signal lights. By these methods, the measured illuminance at an observer's eye, produced by a light, can be used to predict whether the light will be seen. The illumi-

nance E produced at a distance x by a source of luminous intensity I in an atmosphere having a transmissivity (transmittance per unit distance) τ is

$$E = \frac{I\tau^x}{x^2} \qquad (3\text{-}12)$$

If the illuminance E at the eye is greater than E_m, the minimum perceptible (or threshold) illuminance, then the light will be visible. If the distance at which E is equal to E_m is designated as V, the visual range of the light, then[102]

$$E_m = \frac{I\tau^V}{V^2} \qquad (3\text{-}13)$$

This equation is generally known as *Allard's law*.[103, 104]

Equations 3-12 and 3-13 above are strictly applicable only when the luminance of the background is small compared to the average luminance of the light.[103, 105] Otherwise eq. 3-12 becomes

$$E = \frac{[I - (L - L')A]\tau^x}{x^2} \qquad (3\text{-}14)$$

where

L = luminance of the background of the light in cd/m^2,
L' = average luminance of the unlighted source in cd/m^2,
A = area of the entire source projected on a plane normal to the line of sight.

Both L and L' are measured in the direction of the line of sight. The quantity $(L - L')A$ is the intensity required of the source to make its average luminance equal to that of its background. The visual range of the light is determined by the net intensity, that is, the difference between the measured intensity of the source and that intensity. Typically, the term $(L - L')A$ has a significant effect on the visual range of a signal light only under daylight conditions when the source is dimmed or when it has a low average luminance in the direction of view.

Effects of the Atmosphere. The atmosphere is never perfectly transparent. Hence, unless the viewing distance is short, atmospheric losses may have a significant effect upon the illuminance at the observer's eye. In fog, the law of diminishing returns takes effect at relatively short distances. For example, if the transmissivity is 0.01/mi (light fog), a light with an intensity of 100 cd will produce an illuminance of one *milecandle* (lm/mi^2) at a distance of 1 mi; an intensity of 40,000 cd is required to produce that illuminance at 2 mi, and 9,000,000 cd is required at 3 mi.

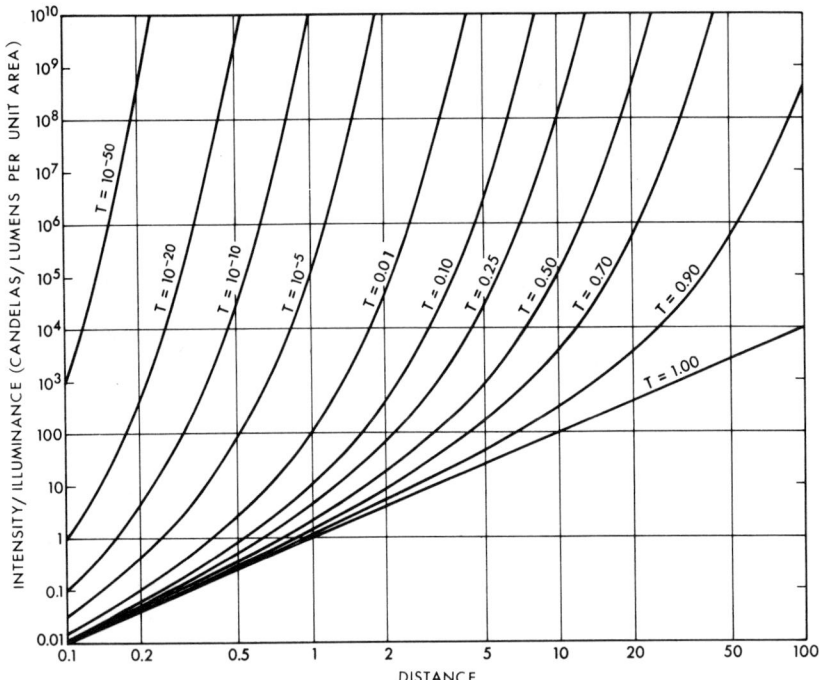

Fig. 3-44. Curves for solving Allard's law for several atmospheric transmissivities. Illuminance, distance, and transmissivity must be in consistent units, such as lx, m, and m^{-1}.

Equations 3-12, 3-13 and 3-14 can be best solved by using an iterative process with a computer or programmable hand calculator or by graphical methods. In figure 3-44 curves relating distance and the ratio of intensity to illuminance are shown for several values of the atmospheric transmissivity. These curves may be used with any consistent set of units; for example, I in candelas, D in miles, E in lumens per square mile and τ as the transmittance per mile.

The clarity of the atmosphere may be conveniently expressed by a distance defined as the meteorological optical range. This is the distance at which the trans-

mittance of light from a full body radiator having a color temperature of 2700 K is equal to 0.05. This distance corresponds closely with the maximum distance at which dark objects may be observed through such an atmosphere in the daytime.[106, 107]

The distance V_0 at which a large black object can be seen against the horizon sky is given by the relation[103, 108, 109]

$$\epsilon = e^{-\sigma V_0} \tag{3-15a}$$

or

$$\epsilon = \tau^{V_0} \tag{3-15b}$$

Fig. 3-45. Transmissivities and Extinction Coefficients for Various Weather Conditions

Code Number	Weather	Maximum Meteorological Optical Range (kilometers)	Minimum Extinction Coefficient (per meter)	Maximum Transmissivity		
				(per kilometer)	(per statute mile)	(per nautical mile)
9	Exceptionally clear	50+	0.00006−	0.94+	0.91+	0.89+
8	Very clear	50	0.00006	0.94	0.91	0.89
7	Clear	20	0.00015	0.86	0.79	0.76
6	Light haze	10	0.00030	0.74	0.62	0.57
5	Haze	4	0.00075	0.47	0.30	0.25
4	Thin fog	2	0.0015	0.22	0.090	0.062
3	Light fog	1	0.0030	0.050	0.0081	0.0039
2	Moderate fog	0.5	0.0060	0.0025	0.000065	0.000015
1	Thick fog	0.2	0.015	3.1×10^{-7}	3.4×10^{-11}	9.0×10^{-13}
0	Dense fog	0.05	0.060	9.5×10^{-27}	1.3×10^{-42}	6.5×10^{-49}
	Very dense fog	0.03	0.10	4.3×10^{-44}	1.6×10^{-70}	4.8×10^{-81}
	Exceptionally dense fog	0.015	0.20	1.8×10^{-87}	2.6×10^{-140}	2.3×10^{-161}

where

σ = extinction coefficient,
τ = transmissivity,
ϵ = minimum perceptible contrast, or threshold contrast, of the observer.

A value of 0.05 is considered representative for the daylight contrast threshold of a meteorological observer.[104] Values of meteorological optical ranges, extinction coefficient and transmissivity for various descriptors are given in figure 3-45.

Equation 3-15 is a particular case of *Koschmieder's law*.[103, 108–110] If the object is not black, eq. 3-15 becomes

$$\epsilon = \frac{L_0 - L_H}{L_H}\tau^V \qquad (3\text{-}16a)$$

or

$$\epsilon = C_0 \tau^V \qquad (3\text{-}16b)$$

where

L_0 = luminance of the object,
L_H = luminance of the horizon sky,
V = visual range of the object,
C_0 = inherent contrast between the object and the sky.

Note that ϵ may be either positive or negative, having the same sign as $L_0 - L_H$. Equation 3-16 applies to electrically lighted as well as daylighted objects.

If the object, or area, is viewed against a background other than the horizon sky, eq. 3-16 becomes[103]

$$\epsilon = \frac{\left[L_0 - L_H - (L_b - L_H)\tau^d\right]\tau^V}{(L_b - L_H)\tau^{d+V} + L_H} \qquad (3\text{-}17)$$

where L_0 is the inherent luminance of the background and L_H is the distance between the object and its background.

Equations 3-15 and 3-16 may be used without significant error in computing the visual range of objects, or area sources, viewed against a terrestrial background if the distance d between the object and its background exceeds one-half of V_0 from eq. 3-15.

Equations 3-12 through 3-17 are based upon the assumption that the transmittance of the atmosphere is independent of wavelength throughout the visible portion of the spectrum. In clean fogs and in rain this assumption is usually valid. However, in smoke or dust there may, on occasion, be significant differences, with the transmittance of long-wavelength (red) light being greater than that of short-wavelength (blue) light; then these equations must be applied wavelength by wave-

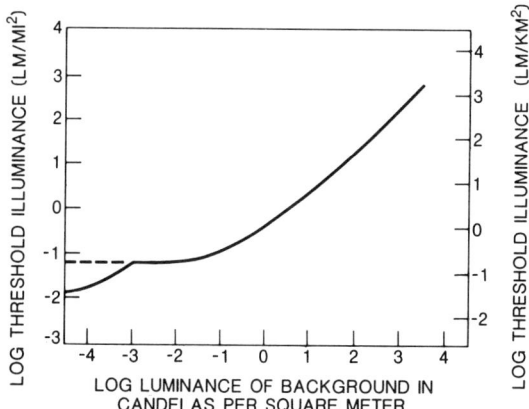

Fig. 3-46. Threshold illuminance at the eye from an achromatic (white) point source for about 98% probability of detection as a function of background luminance.

length.[111] For example, eq. 3-12 takes the form

$$E_m = \frac{\sum_{380}^{830} I_\lambda V(\lambda)\left[\tau(\lambda)\right]^x \Delta\lambda}{x^2} \qquad (3\text{-}18)$$

where I_λ is the spectral radiant intensity of the source.

Threshold Illuminance. As previously discussed, the threshold for visual response depends upon many factors. Figure 3-46 shows a relation between threshold illuminance and background luminance used for determining the detection of luminous signals. The threshold illuminance values shown are applicable only when the observer knows precisely where to look for the light. Even if the illuminance is twice the values shown, the light will be hard to find. The illuminance values must be increased by a factor of 5–10 if the light is to be easy to find.[112]

These increases in illuminance are applicable only when the observer is looking for the light signal. Much greater increases are needed if the light signal is to attract the attention of an observer who is not searching for it. Factors of 100–1000 are not excessive.[113]

The break in the curve represents the change from cone to rod vision. At low background luminances, the threshold illuminance for cone vision remains essentially unchanged, as indicated by the broken line at the left. The horizontal portion of the curve represents most night seeing conditions, since a light used as a signal is usually observed by looking directly at it; hence cone, not rod, vision is used. Moreover, it is doubtful whether those engaged in transport, with the possible exception of lookouts on ships, ever reach the state of dark adaptation required for rod vision.

Representative background luminances are given in figure 3-47. It should be noted that the luminance of the night sky in the vicinity of cities and airports seldom falls below 0.003 cd/m² because of the effects of electric light sources. Note also that, unless there are glare sources in the field of view, it is probably

Fig. 3-47. Representative Luminance Values of Various Backgrounds Against which Luminous Signals are Viewed

Background	Representative Luminance
	Candelas per Square Meter
Horizon sky	
Overcast, no moon	0.00003
Clear, no moon	.0003
Overcast, moon	.003
Clear, moonlight	.03
Deep twilight	.3
Twilight	3
Very dark day	30
Overcast day	300
Clear day	3000
Clouds, sun-lighted	30000
Daylight fog	
Dull	300–1000
Typical	1000–3000
Bright	3000–16000
Ground	
On overcast day	30–100
On sunny day	300
Snow, full sunlight	16000

Fig. 3-49. Size Factors for Sources Other than Point Sources

Ratio of Source Diameter to Viewing Distance	Size Factor	
	Night	Day
0.0005	1.0	1.0
0.001	1.0	1.2
0.003	1.1	2.5
0.005	1.4	4.9
0.01	2.5	20.0

necessary to consider only the background in the immediate vicinity of the light.[114]

Source Size. The threshold illuminance values shown in figure 3-46 are applicable to sources which are in effect point sources. Figure 3-48 shows the maximum diameter of a source which may be considered a point source.[60] Most signal lights behave as point sources. Approximate thresholds for sources which are too large to be considered point sources may be obtained by multiplying the threshold values obtained from figure 3-46 by the size factors given in figure 3-49.[115]

Figures 3-48 and 3-49 apply only to threshold and near-threshold viewing. Recent work has shown that the intensity of a red traffic signal light required to produce optimum recognition under bright daylight

conditions is independent of source size for sources subtending up to 16.5 minutes of arc.[116]

Colored Light Signals

The threshold for the identification of the color of a light signal is about the same as the cone threshold for detection of that light. At the spectral extremes these threshold values are nearly identical, but at the center of the visible spectrum the cone threshold for detection may be as much as a half a log unit lower than it is for color. In the luminance range between the absolute rod threshold and the cone threshold for identification of color (about three log units), no perception of hue can be made. This luminance range is known as the *photochromatic interval*.[117-119] Color discrimination should not be required when signal light luminances are in this interval.

As noted before, color perception of very small lights may not be good, due to small-field tritanopia. For this reason, color identification is rarely required for signal lights that have to be seen at great distances. Lights of larger areal extent should be used when color discrimination is necessary. Traffic lights, for example, are usually of sufficient areal extent when color judgments are required (near a road intersection). Similarly, atmospheric pollutants may selectively attenuate certain regions of the spectrum. In such circumstances the apparent hue of the signal light may change, and color discrimination may be impaired.

Flashing Light Signals

The luminance of a steady light at threshold will be less than the peak luminance of a brief light flash at threshold.[120,121] It is convenient to evaluate light flashes in terms of the intensity of a steady light of the same color, size and shape that will produce the same criterion response. This intensity is known as the *effective luminous intensity* of the flash. Although alternative equations are available, the effective intensity may be computed from the relation[122,123]

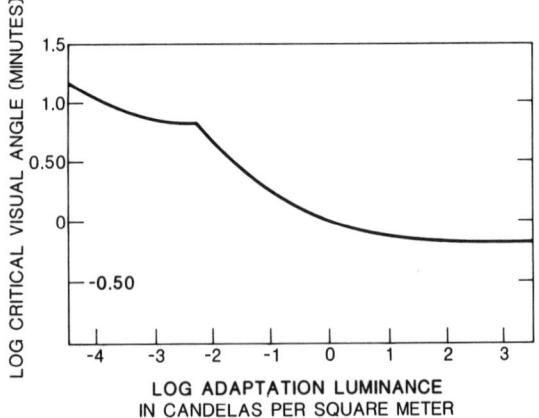

Fig. 3-48. Maximum angular diameter of a circular source which can be considered strictly as a point source.

$$I_e = \frac{\int_{t_1}^{t_2} I \, dt}{a + t_1 + t_2} \qquad (3-19)$$

where

I_e = effective intensity,
I = instantaneous intensity,
t_1, t_2 = times, in s, of the beginning and end of that part of the flash when the value of I exceeds I_e (this choice of times maximizes the value of I_e),
a = a constant which corresponds to a night-time threshold value and has a value of 0.2.

Methods have been developed whereby the maximum value of I_e can be obtained in two or three steps.[122, 123]

The term a is a function of the effective illuminance produced by the flashing source at the eye. The value of a decreases as the illuminance increases above threshold. Various values of a have been suggested from time to time as the most applicable to a particular signal problem. In the United States a value of 0.2 is usually used for specification purposes corresponding to nighttime.[122, 123] This was chosen as an interim value until a value appropriate to the search situation is determined by definitive experimental work.

If the duration of the flash is less than about 1 ms, the effective intensity is given by

$$I_e = 5 \int_{t_s}^{t_e} I \, dt \qquad (3\text{-}20)$$

where the integration is performed over the entire flash cycle, start (t_s) to end (t_e). The effective intensity can then be measured directly, using simple electronic integration.

As noted previously, repetitive flashes may appear brighter than comparable steady lights of the same luminance, on account of brightness enhancement. Consequently, flickering is often used to increase the conspicuity of signal lights.

PSYCHOLOGICAL CONSIDERATIONS

There is growing evidence that light can make an identifiable contribution to the perceived quality of a room, and this contribution clearly goes beyond simple task visibility.

Illuminance

The acceptability of different illuminance levels in offices and other areas has been examined to try to determine the effect of illuminance on observer preference.[124] Figure 3-50 shows the results on subjects' ratings of rooms with systematically varied room surface luminances up to 150 cd/m². Independently of

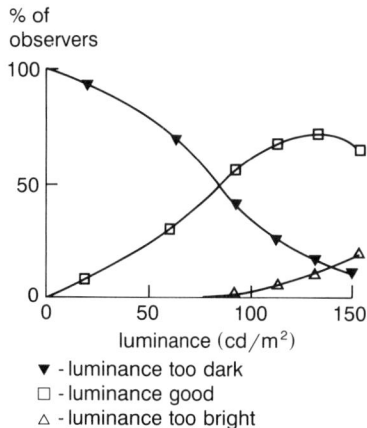

▼ - luminance too dark
□ - luminance good
△ - luminance too bright

Fig. 3-50. The percentages of observers rating the luminance of their desks as too dark, good, or too bright.

the wall and ceiling luminances, as figure 3-50 demonstrates, the maximum proportion of "good" appraisals occurred when the luminance of the working plane was 130 cd/m².

These findings were further verified and extended over a wider range of illuminance.[125-127] Test conditions were created; for example, in one experiment,[125] the task of searching a test sheet of random numbers for a particular number was carried out under a range of illuminance from 50 to 10,000 lx, and with varying contrast (black numbers on white and gray paper). Each subject gave an opinion of the lighting, indicating whether it was "too dark," "good" or "too bright." Judgments of optimum illuminance increased with age and task contrast. Most subjects preferred 1000 lx when searching the higher-contrast number lists, but preferred 1800 lx when searching the lower-contrast materials. On average, for both contrast levels, the younger subjects (less than 50 years of age) indicated that 2000 lx was preferable, while the older subjects required 5000 lx to achieve comparable satisfaction. At the highest illuminances (5000–10,000 lx), rated acceptability decreased, even though performance of the task continued to increase.

This general trend of increased satisfaction with higher illuminance, followed by a decrease in satisfaction at the highest illuminance, was replicated by subsequent investigators using a variety of tasks and subjective scaling techniques.[80, 128-131] Ranges of preferred illuminances identified in these studies are presented in figure 3-51.[124-126, 130-132] Although an initial inspection of this table suggests that these ranges are so wide as to be of little practical use, the illuminance chosen as most satisfactory depends on the task being performed and the age of the observer; preferred illuminances were higher when performing a specific visual task[125-127] than they were for simple judgments of preferred workplane illuminance.[124, 130, 131]

Fig. 3-51. Preferred Light Levels

Experimenter	Preferred Average Light Level at Working Plane	
	Illuminance (lux)	Luminance (cd / m²)
Balder, 1957		130
Bodmann, 1962–7	700–3000	90–380
Saunders, 1969	800–1000	
Bean & Hopkins, 1980	> 200	
Nemecek & Grandjean, 1973	400–850	

Fig. 3.52. Preferred Luminance Ratios

Experimenter	Area					
	Immediate Surround	Front Wall	Rear Wall	Right Wall	Left Wall	Ceiling
Touw, 1951	.3					
Bean & Hopkins, 1980	1					
Tregenza et al., 1974		.52	.64	.51	.55	.85
van Ooyen et al., 1987	.4		.3	(All Walls)		
Roll & Hentschell, 1987	.1 – .6					.1 – 3

Note: All entries are relative to the task background luminances.

Satisfaction with illuminances was also found to depend on light source color and on the spatial distribution of light.

Spatial Distribution of Light

Reports that changing the spatial distribution of light affects vision have been known since the mid nineteenth century.[62] A good deal of research directed at identifying the effects of different spatial distributions of light on visual performance and preference has been conducted. Many studies have focused on performance effects.[62, 133–142] In general, the more uniform the light distribution in the visual field, the better one sees the visual task.

Some investigators have also considered the psychological effects of different spatial distributions of light. In one attempt to determine the preferred ratio of task to desktop luminances under different levels of ambient illumination, subjects were asked to sit at each of six desks (different unspecified reflectance of each desk top) under four illuminances (50, 100, 500, 1000 lx) and copy figures from one white sheet of paper onto another.[143] They were then asked to indicate at which desk they preferred to perform this task under the different illuminances. As the illuminance increased, the subjects preferred lower-reflectance desk tops. For higher illuminances (500 lx) the preferred ratio was 3 : 1, whereas for lower illuminances 2 : 1 was preferred.

Subsequent investigators broadened the scope of this work, examining the effects on preferences of varying the luminances of surfaces other than the immediate surround, such as walls and ceilings. Figure 3-52 summarizes the results of these studies.[132, 143–146] Inspection of this table suggests that although some consensus on preferred ratios of task to immediate surround luminances can be identified, less agreement exists about preferences for luminances of more remote surfaces. Obviously, more systematic research is required before a complete specification of preferred luminance ratios throughout the visual environment can be identified.

As a guide for design purposes, luminance ratio limits have been recommended for various applications, such as offices, educational facilities, institutions, industrial areas and residences (see chapters 15 through

20). For additional guidance, recommended limits on reflectances (both upper and lower) of large surfaces are given for the same applications. The use of these reflectance limits, along with a selection of appropriate colors, should help to control luminances and keep within the ratio limits without creating a bland and uninteresting environment.

Light Source Color

The color of light sources can be described by two independent properties: chromaticity or color temperature (actually correlated color temperature for practical light sources) and color rendering index. There is often confusion between chromaticity and color rendering of light sources. In simple terms, chromaticity refers to the color appearance of a light source, or its color temperature. Color rendering refers to the ability of a light source, with its particular chromaticity, to render colors of objects as one would expect them to appear at the same color temperature. See chapter 4, Color, and chapter 6, Light Sources, for more information.

Color Temperature

Experiments examining the psychological effects of varying lamp color temperature and illuminance have suggested that using lamps with high color temperatures at low illuminances will make a space appear cold and dim. Conversely, using lamps with low color temperatures at high levels of illumination will make a space appear artificial and overly colorful. Figure 3-53 illustrates the so-called *Kruithof effect*.[147] Although these findings were subsequently replicated,[127, 148] some recent investigators have failed to find similar effects of color temperature and illuminance.[149–151] Thus, current recommendations regarding pleasant combinations of lamp color temperature and illuminance should be regarded as tentative.

Color Rendering

More agreement exists concerning the psychological effects of variations in lamp color rendering. Lower illuminances are required from lamps with good color rendering properties to achieve judgments of equiva-

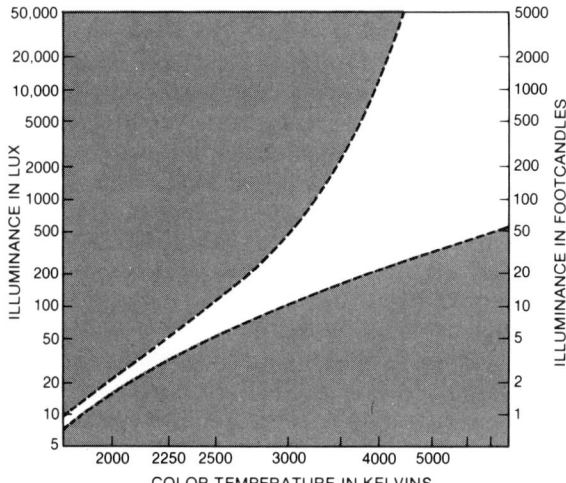

Fig. 3-53. Experiments have shown the preferred color temperature of light sources at various illuminance levels (the unshaded area). Color temperatures—illuminance combinations in the lower shaded area produce cold, drab environments, while those in the upper shaded area can produce overly colorful and unnatural appearances.

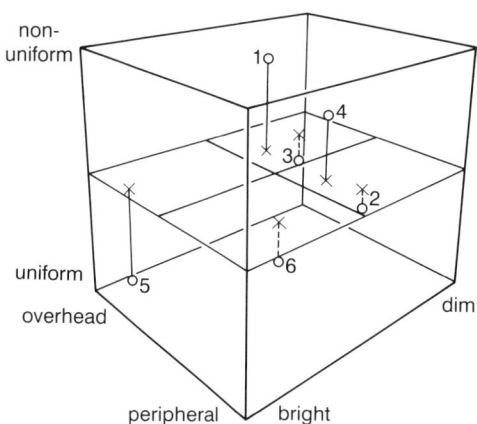

Fig. 3-54. Light structure model indicating lighting design decision for affecting impressions of relaxation and tension.

lent brightness,[151] visual clarity[152, 153] and visual satisfaction[154] than from lamps with poorer color rendering properties. For example, lamps with color rendering indices (CRI) of 70, 85 and 100 require about 10, 25 and 40% lower illuminances than illuminants with a color rendering index of 60, respectively, to achieve impressions of equivalent brightness.[151]

These effects may be mediated by differences in the gamut areas for reference colors when viewed under different sources.[154] Perceived color saturation is less under lamps with poorer color rendering and smaller gamut areas than under lamps having better color rendering and larger gamut areas. Higher illuminances are therefore required from lamps with poorer color rendering to achieve a saturation match to colors lit by lamps with better color rendering properties and larger gamut areas.

Light Structure Models

Much of the work cited above can be termed "correlation studies" in that a relationship can be found between subjective responses and lighting factors such as illuminance and color temperature. Other psychological techniques have been used in lighting research, such as semantic differential rating scales, multidimensional scaling and factor analysis. These techniques have been used to develop *light structure* models for use by designers.

The concept of light structure is based on the notion that the experience of room lighting is, in part, an experience of recognizing and assimilating complex light patterns. It contains the suggestion that different

pattern aspects of light interact and convey information about the visual world. The brain constructs an impression of the phenomenal world from this information. This concept of information content and "meaning" further suggests that lighting should be considered not merely as a stimulus but also as a "structure."

An example of a light structure model is shown in figure 3-54. Models have been developed to serve as a partial guide for the use of lighting effects appropriate for various task and nontask applications. Figure 3-55 shows a lighting design guide that may help the designer achieve specific subjective impressions with different lighting design strategies.[155] Some designers have found the following categories of impression particularly useful in their design work.

Fig. 3-55. Lighting Reinforcement of Subjective Effects

Subjective Impression	Reinforcing Lighting Modes
Impression of *Visual Clarity*	• Bright, uniform lighting mode • Some peripheral emphasis, such as with high reflectance walls or wall lighting
Impression of *Spaciousness*	• Uniform, peripheral (wall) lighting • Brightness is a reinforcing factor, but not a decisive one
Impression of *Relaxation*	• Non-uniform lighting mode • Peripheral (wall) emphasis, rather than overhead lighting
Impressions of *Privacy* or *Intimacy*	• Non-uniform lighting mode • Tendency toward low light intensities in the immediate locale of the user, with higher brightness remote from the user • Peripheral (wall) emphasis is a reinforcing factor, but not a decisive one
Impressions of *Pleasantness* and *Preference*	• Non-uniform lighting mode • Peripheral (wall) emphasis

Impressions of Relaxation. Impressions of relaxation are an important subjective factor to be considered in the design of more casual areas, such as waiting rooms, lounges and some restaurants. Such impressions are reinforced by the following lighting factors:

1. *Uniformity.* Relaxation is reinforced by non-uniform lighting.
2. *Distribution.* Relaxation is reinforced, more specifically, by nonuniform wall lighting.
3. *Color.* Relaxation is reinforced by warm, white light.

Impressions of Perceptual Clarity. Impressions of perceptual clarity are important subjective factors to be considered in the design of work spaces. Such impressions appear to be reinforced by four lighting factors:

1. *Luminance.* Clarity is reinforced by high luminance of the horizontal plane.
2. *Location.* Clarity is reinforced by high luminance in the central part of the room.
3. *Color.* Clarity is reinforced by cool tones created by lamps with a broad spectral power distribution.
4. *Distribution.* Clarity is reinforced by peripheral wall brightness.

Impressions of Spaciousness. Impressions of spaciousness are important in the design of circulation and assembly spaces, such as corridors, lobbies and assembly halls. This impression is reinforced by the following factors:

1. *Uniformity.* Spaciousness is reinforced by evenly distributed brightness throughout the space.
2. *Distribution.* Spaciousness is reinforced by wall brightness.

The color of the light (warm or cool) appears to be a negligible subjective factor of spaciousness.

Behavioral Studies[156–163]

Research has also been devoted to the influence of lighting on overt behavior. Although this research supports the notion that lighting can be used to cue orientation and circulation in humans and that it increases activity, the results discussed below should be interpreted with caution, for at least two reasons. First, the range of illuminances studied has been small. In many experiments the effects of only two or three levels are studied. More importantly, the effects of illuminance have been shown to interact with other independent variables.[161, 162] Simple linear relationships are often insufficient for describing relationships

among different environmental variables; effects may be facilitated or inhibited depending on the presence of other moderating factors.[163] Hence, further studies using a wider range of lighting conditions and additional independent variables will be required before firm conclusions about the effects of illuminance on orientation, wayfinding, activity and attention can be drawn.

Spatial Orientation and Wayfinding. Light clearly affects spatial orientation and wayfinding. For example, when navigating around a barrier, people will tend to follow the direction of higher illuminance.[156] These results support the notion that the distribution of light in a space might be used to direct circulation, and as an aid to wayfinding.

Similar findings have been reported in another context. An investigation of the effects of spatial distribution of light on seat choice and orientation in a cafeteria showed that people selected seats facing bright areas. When the lighting was changed to highlight a different surface, patterns of seat selection and orientation changed to face the new bright area.[157] The effects of wall lighting on desk selection have also been observed. Subjects entered a room, and sat at one of three desks to complete a series of questionnaires. Desks were located next to the door, in the middle of the room and at the far side of the room opposite the door. When the wall opposite the door was illuminated, most subjects crossed the room and sat at the desk located next to that wall. When that wall was not illuminated, most subjects sat at the desk located next to the door.[158]

Activity Level and Attention. Lighting also can affect activities not directly related to seeing and vision. A significant reduction in sound level in a school hallway was found when the illuminance was low.[159] Other researchers extended these findings by examining possible interactions between illuminances and other variables in their effects on human performance. An interaction was found between light and sound levels in their effects on the performance of a reaction time task. The presence of a white-noise sound increased reaction times under higher illuminances and had no effect in the dark.[161]

The effects of illuminance and gender on the estimation of the length of 15 s time intervals has also been studied, and an interaction of gender and light level found.[162] Females gave shorter time estimates with increasing illuminance. In contrast, males gave shorter estimates in the dark than females, nearly the same estimates as the females under low illumination, and longer estimates than females under the highest illuminances. These gender differences may be due to different levels of physiological arousal in the two sexes. Relationships between arousal and performance are often characterized by initial performance increases, followed by performance decrements at the highest levels of arousal.[162] The illuminances studied may produce more arousal in males than in females, although there are no physiological data to support the supposed link between illuminance and physiological arousal, and the observed differences could reflect cultural effects.

The effectiveness of supplementary classroom lighting in improving attentiveness in primary school children has also been studied. Lists of words used in spelling tests were displayed at the front of classrooms. Supplementary lighting was used to highlight the word lists in one condition of the experiment, but not in the control condition. Significantly more inattentive behaviors were coded in the control condition than when the word lists were highlighted.

REFERENCES

1. Boettner, E. A., and J. R. Wolter. 1962. Transmission of the ocular media. *Invest. Ophthalmol.* 1:776.
2. Said, F. S., and R. A. Weale. 1959. The variation with age of the spectral transmissivity of the living human crystalline lens. *Gerontologia* 3(4):213.
3. Coren, S., and J. S. Girgus. 1972. Density of human lens pigmentation: In vivo measures over an extended age range [Letter]. *Vision Res.* 12(2):343–346.
4. Wolf, E., and J. S. Gardiner. 1965. Studies on the scatter of light in the dioptric media of the eye as a basis of visual glare. *Arch. Ophthalmol.* 74(3):338–345.
5. Vos, J. J., and J. Boogaard. 1963. Contribution of the cornea to entoptic scatter. *J. Opt. Soc. Am.* 53(7):869–873.
6. Boynton, R. M., and F. J. J. Clarke. 1964. Sources of entoptic scatter in the human eye. *J. Opt. Soc. Am.* 54(1):110–119.
7. Wyszecki, G., and W. S. Stiles. 1982. *Color science: Concepts and methods, quantitative data and formulae.* 2nd ed. New York: Wiley.
8. Vos, J. J. 1963. Contribution of the fundus oculi to entoptic scatter [Letter]. *J. Opt. Soc. Am.* 53(12): 1449–1451.
9. Bouma, H. 1965. *Receptive systems mediating certain light reactions of the pupil of the human eye.* Philips Research Report Supplements, No. 5. Eindhoven, The Netherlands: Philips Research Laboratories.
10. Dowling, J. A. 1967. The site of visual adaptation. *Science* 155:273–279.
11. Hecht, S., and J. Mandelbaum. 1939. The relation between vitamin A and dark adaptation. *JAMA* 112(19):1910–1916.
12. Boynton, R. M., and N. D. Miller. 1963. Visual performance under conditions of transient adaptation. *Illum. Eng.* 58(8):541–550.
13. Boynton, R. M., E. J. Rinalducci, and C. Sternheim. 1969. Visibility losses produced by transient adaptational changes in the range from 0.4 to 4000 footlamberts. *Illum. Eng.* 64(4):217–227.
14. Boynton, R. M., T. R. Corwin, and C. Sternheim. 1970. Visibility losses produced by flash adaptation. *Illum. Eng.* 65(3):259–266.
15. Miller, J. W. 1958. Study of visual acuity during the ocular pursuit of moving test objects. II. Effects of direction of movement, relative movement, and illumination. *J. Opt. Soc. Am.* 48(11):803–808.
16. Alman, D. H. 1977. Errors of the standard photometric system when measuring the brightness of general illumination light sources. *J. Illum. Eng. Soc.* 7(1):55–62.
17. Bedford, R. E., and G. W. Wyszecki. 1958. Wavelength discrimination for point sources. *J. Opt. Soc. Am.* 48(2):129–135.
18. Wright, W. D. 1946. *Researches on normal and defective color vision.* London: Henry Kimpton.
19. Robertson, A. R. 1981. Color differences. *Die Farbe* 29:273.
20. Ivanoff, A. 1956. About spherical aberration of the eye [Letter]. *J. Opt. Soc. Am.* 46(10):901–903.
21. Fry, G. A. 1954. A re-evaluation of the scattering theory of glare. *Illum. Eng.* 49(2):98–102.
22. Holladay, L. L. 1926. The fundamentals of glare and visibility. *J. Opt. Soc. Am.* 12(4):271–319.
23. Holladay, L. L. 1927. Action of a light source in the field of view on lowering visibility. *J. Opt. Soc. Am.* 14(1):1–15.
24. Stiles, W. S. 1929. The effect of glare on the brightness difference threshold. *Proc. R. Soc. Lond. Ser. B* 104:322–351.
25. Fugate, J. M., and G. A. Fry. 1956. Relation of changes in pupil size to visual discomfort. *Illum. Eng.* 51(7):537–549.
26. Fry, G. A., and V. M. King. 1975. The pupillary response and discomfort glare. *J. Illum. Eng. Soc.* 4(4):307–324.
27. Luckiesh, M., and S. K. Guth. 1949. Brightness in visual field at borderline between comfort and discomfort (BCD). *Illum. Eng.* 44(11):650–670.
28. Putman, R. C., and R. E. Faucett. 1951. The threshold of discomfort glare at low adaptation levels. *Illum. Eng.* 46(10):505–510.
29. IES. Committee on Recommendations for Quality and Quantity of Illumination. Subcommittee on Direct Glare. 1966. Outline of a standard procedure for computing visual comfort ratings for interior lighting: Report No. 2. *Illum. Eng.* 61(10):643–666.
30. Hopkinson, R. G. 1957. Evaluation of glare. *Illum. Eng.* 52(6):305–316.
31. Guth, S. K., and J. F. McNelis. 1959. A discomfort glare evaluator. *Illum. Eng.* 54(6):398–406.
32. Guth, S. K., and J. F. McNelis. 1961. Further data on discomfort glare from multiple sources. *Illum. Eng.* 56(1):46–57.
33. Bradley, R. D., and H. L. Logan. 1964. A uniform method for computing the probability of comfort response in a visual field. *Illum. Eng.* 59(3):189–206.
34. Guth, S. K. 1963. A method for the evaluation of discomfort glare. *Illum. Eng.* 57(5):351–364.
35. Allphin, W. 1966. Influence of sight line on BCD judgments of direct discomfort glare. *Illum. Eng.* 61(10):629–633.

36. Allphin, W. 1968. Further studies of sight line and direct discomfort glare. *Illum. Eng.* 63(1):26–31.

37. Levin, R. E. 1973. An evaluation of VCP calculations. *J. Illum. Eng. Soc.* 2(4):355–361.

38. IES. Committee on Recommendations for Quality and Quantity of Illumination. 1972. An alternate simplified method for determining the acceptability of a luminaire from the VCP standpoint for use in large rooms: RQQ Report No. 3. *J. Illum. Eng. Soc.* 1(3):256–260.

39. Fry, G. A. 1976. A simplified formula for discomfort glare. *J. Illum. Eng. Soc.* 6(1):10–20.

40. Goodbar, I. 1976. A simplified method for determining the acceptability of a luminaire from the VCP standpoint. *J. Illum. Eng. Soc.* 6(1):21–28.

41. Kaiser, P. K., P. A. Herzberg, and R. M. Boynton. 1971. Chromatic border distinctness and its relation to saturation. *Vision Res.* 11(9):953–968.

42. Boynton, R. M., and P. K. Kaiser. 1968. Vision: The additivity law made to work for heterochromatic photometry with bipartite fields. *Science* 161:366–368.

43. Tansley, B. W., and R. M. Boynton. 1978. Chromatic border perception: The role of red- and green-sensitive cones. *Vision Res.* 18(6):683–697.

44. Kaiser, P. K. 1971. Luminance and brightness [Letter]. *Appl. Opt.* 10(12):2768–2770.

45. Kaiser, P. K., and G. Wyszecki. 1978. Additivity failures in heterochromatic brightness matching. *Color Res. Appl.* 3(4):177–182.

46. Wagner, G., and R. M. Boynton. 1972. Comparison of four methods of heterochromatic photometry. *J. Opt. Soc. Am.* 62(12):1508–1515.

47. Guth, S. L., and H. R. Lodge. 1973. Heterochromatic additivity, foveal spectral sensitivity, and a new color model. *J. Opt. Soc. Am.* 63(4):450–462.

48. Hurvich, L. M., and D. Jameson. 1955. Some quantitative aspects of an opponent-colors theory. II. Brightness, saturation, and hue in normal and dichromatic vision. *J. Opt. Soc. Am.* 45(8):602–616.

49. Hurvich, L. M., and D. Jameson. 1957. Further development of a quantified opponent-colours theory. In *Visual Problems of Color Symposium*, vol. 2, Paper 22. New York: Chemical Publishing Co.

50. Jameson, D., and L. M. Hurvich. 1961. Opponent chromatic induction: Experimental evaluation and theoretical account. *J. Opt. Soc. Am.* 51(1):46–53.

51. Ingling, C. R., Jr. 1977. The spectral sensitivity of the opponent-color channels. *Vision Res.* 17(9):1083–1089.

52. Ingling, C. R., Jr., and B. A. Drum. 1973. How neural adaptation changes chromaticity coordinates. *J. Opt. Soc. Am.* 63(3):369–373.

53. Guth, S. L., R. W. Massof, and T. Benzschawel. 1980. Vector model for normal and dichromatic color vision. *J. Opt. Soc. Am.* 70(2):197–212.

54. Burns, S. A., V. C. Smith, J. Pokorny, and A. E. Elsner. 1982. Brightness of equal-luminance lights. *J. Opt. Soc. Am.* 72(9):1225–1231.

55. Alman, D. H., M. E. Breton, and J. Barbour. 1983. New results on the brightness matching of heterochromatic stimuli. *J. Illum. Eng. Soc.* 12(4):268–274.

56. Berman, S. M., D. L. Jewett, L. R. Bingham, R. M. Nahass, F. Perry, and G. Fein. 1987. Pupillary size differences under incandescent and high pressure sodium lamps. *J. Illum. Eng. Soc.* 16(1):3–20.

57. Berman, S. M., D. L. Jewett, G. Fein, G. Saika, and F. Ashford. 1990. Photopic luminance does not always predict perceived room brightness. *Light. Res. Tech.* 22(1):37–41.

58. Kinney, J., C. L. Schlichting, D. Neri, and S. W. Kindness. 1983. Reaction time to spatial frequencies using yellow and luminance-matched neutral goggles. *Am. J. Opt. Phys. Optics* 60(2):132–138.

59. Kelly, S. A. 1990. Effect of yellow-tinted lenses on brightness. *J. Opt. Soc. Am. A* 7(10):1905–1911.

60. Blackwell, H. R. 1946. Contrast thresholds of the human eye. *J. Opt. Soc. Am.* 36(11):624–643.

61. Blackwell, H. R. 1959. Development and use of a quantitative method for specification of interior illumination levels on the basis performance data. *Illum. Eng.* 54(6):317–353.

62. Lythgoe, R. J. 1932. *The measurement of visual acuity.* Medical Research Council Special Report, No. 173. London: H.M. Stationary Office.

63. Bartley, S. H. 1951. Intermittent photic stimulation at marginal intensity levels. *J. Psychol.* 32(3):217–223.

64. Bartley, S. H. 1938. Subjective brightness in relation to flash rate and the light-dark ratio. *J. Exp. Psychol.* 23(3):313–319.

65. Katz, M. A. 1964. Brief flash brightness. *Vision Res.* 4(7/8):361–373.

66. Kelly, D. H. 1969. Flickering patterns and lateral inhibition. *J. Opt. Soc. Am.* 59(10):1361–1370.

67. van der Wildt, G. J., and J. P. Rijsdijk. 1979. Flicker sensitivity measured with intermittent stimuli: I. Influence of the stimulus duration on the flicker threshold. *J. Opt. Soc. Am.* 69(5):660–665.

68. Wilkins, A. J. 1993. Health and efficiency in lighting practice. *Energy* 18(2):123–129.

69. König, A. 1897. Die Abhängigkeit der Sehschärfe von der Beleuchtungsintensität. *Sitzber. Akad. Wiss. (Berlin)* 33:559.

70. Hecht, S. 1934. Vision: II. The nature of the photoreceptor process. In *A handbook of general experimental psychology.* C. Murchison, ed. Worcester, MA: Clark Univ. Press.

71. Hecht, S., and E. U. Mintz. 1939. The visibility of single lines at various illuminations and the retinal basis of visual resolution. *J. Gen. Physiol.* 22(5):593–612.

72. Shlaer, S. 1937. The relation between visual acuity and illumination. *J. Gen. Physiol.* 21(2):165–188.

73. Richards, O. W. 1977. Effects of luminance and contrast on visual acuity, ages 16 to 90 years. *Am. J. Opt. Phys. Optics* 54(3):178–184.

74. Julian, W. G. 1984. Variation in near visual acuity with illuminance for a group of 27 partially-sighted people. *Light. Res. Tech.* 16(1):34–41.

75. Pelli, D. G., J. G. Robson, and A. J. Wilkins. 1988. The Design of a New Letter Chart for Measuring Contrast Sensitivity. *Clin. Vis. Sci.* 2(3):187.

76. Campbell, F. W., and J. G. Robson. 1968. Application of Fourier analysis to the visibility of gratings. *J. Physiol.* 197(3):551–566.

77. McCann, J. J., and J. A. Hall Jr. 1980. Effects of average-luminance surrounds on the visibility of sine-wave gratings. *J. Opt. Soc. Am.* 70(2):212–219.

78. Roethlisberger, F. J., and W. J. Dickson. 1934. *Management and the worker: Technical vs. social organization in an industrial plant.* Boston: Harvard Univ. Press.

79. Smith, S. W., and M. S. Rea. 1978. Proofreading under different levels of illumination. *J. Illum. Eng. Soc.* 8(1):47–52.

80. Smith, S. W., and M. S. Rea. 1980. Relationships between office task performance and ratings of feelings and task evaluations under different light sources and levels. In *Proceedings: 19th session. Commission Internationale de l'Éclairage, Kyoto, 1979.* Paris: Bureau Central de la CIE.

81. Smith, S. W., and M. S. Rea. 1982. Performance of a reading test under different levels of illumination. *J. Illum. Eng. Soc.* 12(1):29–33.

82. Smith, S. W., and M. S. Rea. 1987. Check value verification under different levels of illumination. *J. Illum. Eng. Soc.* 16(1):143–149.

83. Weston, H. C. 1935. *The relation between illumination and visual efficiency: The effect of size of work.* Prepared for Industrial Health Research Board (Great Britain) and Medical Research Council (London). London: H.M. Stationery Office.

84. Weston, H. C. 1945. *The relation between illumination and visual efficiency: The effect of brightness contrast.* Report No. 87. Prepared for Industrial Health Research Board (Great Britain) and Medical Research Council (London). London: H.M. Stationery Office.

85. Rea, M. S. 1987. Toward a model of visual performance: A review of methodologies. *J. Illum. Eng. Soc.* 16(1):128–142.

86. Rea, M. S. 1981. Visual performance with realistic methods of changing contrast. *J. Illum. Eng. Soc.* 10(3):164–177.

87. Rea, M. S. 1986. Toward a model of visual performance: Foundations and data. *J. Illum. Eng. Soc.* 15(2):41–57.

88. Boyce, P. R., and M. S. Rea. 1987. Plateau and escarpment: The shape of visual performance. In *Proceedings: 21st session. Commission Internationale de l'Éclairage, Venice, June 17–25, 1987.* Paris: Bureau Central de la CIE.

89. Rea, M. S., and M. J. Ouellette. 1988. Visual performance using reaction times. *Light. Res. Tech.* 20(4):139–153.

90. Rea, M. S., and M. J. Ouellette. 1991. Relative visual performance: A basis for application. *Light. Res. Tech.* 23(3):135–144.

91. Luckiesh, M., and F. M. Moss. 1937. *The science of seeing.* New York: Van Nostrand.

92. Luckiesh, M., and F. K. Moss. 1934. A visual thresholdometer. *J. Opt. Soc. Am.* 24(11):305–307.

93. Blackwell, H. R. 1970. Development of procedures and instruments for visual task evaluation. *Illum. Eng.* 65(4):267–291.

94. Blackwell, O. M., and H. R. Blackwell. 1971. Visual performance data for 156 normal observers of various ages. *J. Illum. Eng. Soc.* 1(1):3–13.

95. Rea, M. S. 1988. Proposed revision of the IESNA illuminance selection procedure. *J. Illum. Eng. Soc.* 17(1):20–28.

96. Rea, M. S. and M. J. Ouellette. 1984. *An assessment of the Blackwell Visual Task Evaluator, Model 3X, NRCC 22960.* Ottawa: National Research Council Canada. Division of Building Research.

97. Eastman, A. A. 1968. A new contrast threshold visibility meter. *Illum. Eng.* 63(1):37–40.

98. Slater, A. I. 1975. A simple contrast reducing visibility meter. *Light. Res. Tech.* 7(1):52–55.

99. Rea, M. S. 1984. What's happening to ESI. *Light. Des. Appl.* 14(6):46–50.

100. Ross, D. K. 1978. Task lighting: Yet another view. *Light. Des. Appl.* 8(5):37–43.

101. Rea, M. 1989. Psychological aspects of lighting. *Elec. Des.* 4(3):13.

102. Reynaud, M. L. 1876. *Memoir upon the illumination and beaconage of the coasts of France.* P. C. Hains, trans. Washington: U.S. Government Printing Office.

103. Knowles-Middleton, W. E. 1952. *Vision through the atmosphere.* Toronto: Univ. of Toronto Press.

104. Douglas, C. A., and R. L. Booker. 1977. *Visual range: Concepts, instrumental determination, and aviation applications.* National Bureau of Standards Monograph, 159. Washington: U.S. National Bureau of Standards.

105. Kevern, G. M. 1950. Effect of source size upon approach light performance. *Illum. Eng.* 45(2):96–98.

106. U.S. Civil Aeronautics Administration. 1945. *Development of transmissiometer for determining visual range.* CAA Technical Development Report No. 47. Prepared by C. A. Douglas and L. L. Young. Washington: U.S. Government Printing Office.

107. World Meteorological Organization. 1971. *Guide to meteorological instrument and observing practices.* World Meteorological Organization.

108. Tricker, R. A. R. 1970. *Introduction to meterological optics.* New York: American Elsevier Publishing Co.

109. Duntley, S. Q. 1948. The reduction of apparent contrast by the atmosphere. *J. Opt. Soc. Am.* 38(2):179–191.

110. Duntley, S. Q., J. I. Gordon, J. H. Taylor, C. T. White, A. R. Boileau, J. E. Tyler, R. W. Austin, and J. L. Harris. 1964. Visibility. *Appl. Opt.* 3(5):549–598.

111. Zuev, V. E. 1970. *Atmospheric transparency in the visible and the infrared (Prozrachnost' atmosfery dlya vidimykh i infrakrasnykh luchei).* Israel Program for Translations: Jerusalem. Available from National Technical Information Service, Springfield, Virginia 22151 as TT69-55102.

112. Tousey, R., and M. J. Koomen. 1953. The visibility of stars and planets during twilight. *J. Opt. Soc. Am.* 43(3):177–183.

113. Breckenridge, F. C., and C. A. Douglas. 1945. Development of approach- and contact-light systems. *Illum. Eng.* 40(9):785–829.

114. Knoll, H. A., R. Tousey, and E. O. Hulbert. 1946. Visual thresholds of steady point sources of light in fields of brightness from dark to daylight. *J. Opt. Soc. Am.* 36(8):480–482.

115. de Boer, J. B. 1951. Visibility of approach and runway lights. *Philips Res. Repts.* 6(3):224–239.

116. Fisher, A. J., and B. L. Cole. 1974. The photometric requirements of vehicle traffic signal lanterns. *Proc. Austral. Road Res. Board* 7(5).

117. Stiles, W. S., M. G. Bennett, and H. N. Green. 1937. *Visibility of light signals with special reference to aviation lights.* Aeronautical Research Committee Reports and Memoranda, No. 1793. London: H.M. Stationery Office.

118. Hill, N. E. G. 1947. The recognition of coloured light signals which are near the limit of visibility. *Proc. Phys. Soc. (London)* 59(4):560–574.

119. Hill, N. E. G. 1947. The measurement of the chromatic and achromatic thresholds of colored point sources against a white background. *Proc. Phys. Soc. (London)* 59(4):574–585.

120. Blondel, A., and J. Rey. 1912. The perception of lights of short duration at their range limits. *Trans. Illum. Eng. Soc.* 7(8):625–662.

121. Projector, T. E. 1957. Effective intensity of flashing lights. *Illum. Eng.* 52(12):630–640.

122. IES. Aviation Committee. 1964. IES guide for calculating the effective intensity of flashing signal lights. *Illum. Eng.* 59(11):747–753.

123. Douglas, C. A. 1957. Computation of the effective intensity of flashing lights. *Illum. Eng.* 52(12):641–646.

124. Balder, J. J. 1957. Erwünschte Leuchtdichten in Büroräumen. *Lichttechnik* 9(9):455–461.

125. Bodmann, H. W. 1967. Quality of interior lighting based on luminance. *Trans. Illum. Eng. Soc. (London)* 32(1):22–40.

126. Bodmann, H. W. 1962. Illumination levels and visual performance. *Int. Light. Rev.* 13(2):41–47.

127. Bodmann, H. W., Sollner G., and E. Voit. 1963. Bewertung von Beleuchtungsniveaus bei Verschiedenen Lichtarten. In *Proceedings. Commission Internationale de l'Éclairage 15th Session, Vienna.*

128. Boyce, P. R. 1973. Age, illuminance, visual performance and preference. *Light. Res. Tech.* 5(3):125–145.

129. Hughes, P. C., and J. F. McNelis. 1978. Lighting, productivity, and the work environment. *Light. Des. Appl.* 8(12):32-40.

130. Nemecek, J., and E. Grandjean. 1973. Results of an ergonomic investigation of large-space offices. *Hum. Factors* 15(2):111–124.

131. Saunders, J. E. 1969. The role of the level and diversity of horizontal illumination in an appraisal of a simple office task. *Light. Res. Tech.* 1(1):37–46.

132. Bean, A. R., and A. G. Hopkins. 1980. Task and background lighting. *Light. Res. Tech.* 12(3):135–139.

133. Adrian, W., and K. Eberbach. 1969. On the relationship between the visual threshold and the size of the surrounding field. *Light. Res. Tech.* 1(4):251–258.

134. Bisele, R. L. J. 1950. Effect of task-to-surround luminance ratios on visual performance. *Illum. Eng.* 45(12):733–740.

135. Cobb, P. W. 1914. The effect on foveal vision of bright surroundings. *Psychol. Rev.* 21(1):23–32.

136. Cobb Percy W. 1916. The effect on foveal vision of bright surroundings IV. *J. Exp. Psychol.* 1(6):540–566.

137. Cobb, P. W., and L. R. Geissler. 1913. The effect on foveal vision of bright surroundings. *Psychol. Rev.* 20(6):425–447.

138. Cobb, P. W., and F. K. Moss. 1928. The effect of dark surroundings upon vision. *J. Franklin Inst.* 206(6):827–840.

139. Johnson, H. M. 1924. Speed, accuracy, and constancy of response to visual stimuli as related to the distribution of brightnesses over the visual field. *J. Exp. Psychol.* 7(1):1–44.

140. Luckiesh, M. 1944. Brightness engineering. *Illum. Eng.* 39(2):75–92.

141. Rea, M. S., M. J. Ouellette, and D. K. Tiller. 1990. The effects of luminous surroundings on visual performance, pupil size, and human preference. *J. Illum. Eng. Soc.* 19(2):45–58.

142. Wilson, A. J., and A. Lit. 1981. Effects of photopic annulus luminance level on reaction time and on the latency of evoked cortical potential responses to target flashes. *J. Opt. Soc. Am.* 71(12):1481–1486.

143. Tuow, L. M. C. 1951. Preferred brightness ratio of task and its immediate surroundings. In *Proceedings. Commission Internationale de l'Éclairage 12th Session, Stockholm.*

144. Tregenza, P. R., S. M. Romaya, S. P. Dawe, L. J. Heap, and B. Tuck. 1974 Consistency and variation in preferences for office lighting. *Light. Res. Tech.* 6(4):205–211.

145. van Ooyen, M. H. F., J. A. C. van de Weijgert, and S. H. A. Begemann. 1987. Preferred luminances in offices. *J. Illum. Eng. Soc.* 16(2):152–156.

146. Roll, K. F., and H. J. Hentschell. 1987. Luminance patterns in interiors and balanced perception. In *Proceedings: 21st session. Commission Internationale de l'Éclairage, Venice, June 17–25, 1987.* Paris: Bureau Central de la CIE.

147. Kruithof, A. A. 1941. Tubular luminescence lamps for general illumination. *Philips Tech. Rev.* 6(3):65–73.

148. Baron, R. A., M. S. Rea, and S. G. Daniels. 1992. Effects of indoor lighting (illuminance and spectral distribution) on the performance of cognitive tasks and interpersonal behaviors: The potential mediating role of positive affect. *Motiv. Emot.* 16(1):1–33.

149. Cuttle, C., and P. R. Boyce. 1988. Kruithof revisited: A study of people's responses to illuminance and colour temperature of lighting. *Light. Aust.* 8(6):17–27.

150. Davis, R. G., and D. N. Ginthner. 1990. Correlated color temperature, illuminance level, and the Kruithof curve. *J. Illum. Eng. Soc.* 19(1):27–38.

151. Kanaya, S., Hashimoto K., and Kichize E. 1979. Subjective balance between general colour rendering index, colour temperature, and illuminance of interior lighting. In *Proceedings: 19th session. Commission Internationale de l'Éclairage, Kyoto, 1979.* Paris: Bureau Central de la CIE.

152. Adrian, W., and K. Eberbach. 1969. On the relationship between the visual threshold and the size of the surrounding field. *Light. Res. Tech.* 1(4):251–258.

153. Bellchambers, H. E., and A. C. Godby. 1972. Illumination, color rendering and visual clarity. *Light. Res. Tech.* 4(2):104–106.

154. Boyce, P. R. 1977. Investigations of the subjective balance between illuminance and lamp colour properties. *Light. Res. Tech.* 9(1):11–24.

155. Flynn, J. E. 1977. A study of subjective responses to low energy and nonuniform lighting systems. *Light. Des. Appl.* 7(2):6–15.

156. Taylor, L. H., and E. W. Socov. 1974. The movement of people toward lights. *J. Illum. Eng. Soc.* 3(3):237–241.

157. Flynn, J. E., and G. J. Subisak. 1978. A procedure for qualitative study of light level variations and system performance. *J. Illum. Eng. Soc.* 8(1):28–35.

158. Yorks, P., and D. Ginthner. 1987. Wall lighting placement: Effect on behavior in the work environment. *Light. Des. Appl.* 17(7):30–37.

159. LaGiusa, F. F., and L. R. Perney. 1974. Further studies on the effects of brightness variations on attention span in a learning environment. *J. Illum. Eng. Soc.* 3(3):249–252.

160. Sanders, M., J. Gustanski, and M. Lawton. 1974. Effect of ambient illumination on noise level of groups. *J. Appl. Psychol.* 59(4):527–528.

161. Kallman, W. M., and W. Isaac. 1977. Altering arousal in humans by varying ambient sensory conditions. *Percept. Mot. Skills* 44(1):19–22.

162. Delay, E. R., and M. A. Richardson. 1981. Time estimation in humans: Effects of ambient illumination and sex. *Percept. Mot. Skills* 53(3):747–750.

163. Wilkinson, R. 1969. Some factors influencing the effect of environmental stressors upon performance. *Psychol. Bul.* 72(4):260–272.

Color

4

Architects, engineers, interior and industrial designers, colorists and color stylists, and lighting designers all have a need to understand color. To satisfy this need, this chapter has been prepared to increase mutual understanding among those responsible for creating the environment and making it visible and visually functional.

Electromagnetic radiant energy provides a physical stimulus that enters the eye and causes the sensation of color. The spectral characteristics of the stimulus are integrated by the visual system and cannot be differentiated without the use of an instrument. Because the color and the color rendering properties of light sources are becoming increasingly important in the design of an illuminated environment, today's designer of lighting needs a good working knowledge of the vocabulary and practices of modern color science.

The esthetic use of color to produce a pleasing interior requires coordination between the interior designer and the person designing the lighting. Each needs to know how to use color to help provide the desired brightness levels and distributions. Today's lighting designer is faced not only with a choice of color in light sources, but with wide variations in color rendering properties of light sources that may be identical in color.[1]

To provide lighting designers with a basis for their studies in color, the IESNA committees have developed several reports[2-5] that provide useful background material for this section. In addition, the section concludes with examples of several fields of special applications. A few other sections contain brief discussions of color, with specialized applications. Information on colorimetry of light sources is not contained in this chapter and is found in *IES LM-16-1984*.[2]

BASIC CONCEPTS OF COLOR

Color Terms

In the Glossary, color terms are carefully defined to provide a way of distinguishing between several commonly confused meanings of the word "color." Whether one makes strict use of the definitions or not, an understanding of the purpose and need for the differentiations that are made is basic to an understanding of the subject.

The *perceived color*, the color perceived as belonging to an object or light source, is something perceived instantaneously. It is so common an experience that many persons find it hard to understand why color is not simple to explain in a few easy lessons. But a color perception results from the interaction of many highly complex factors, such as the characteristics of the object or light source, the light incident on an object, the surround, the viewing direction, observer characteristics, and the observer's adaptation. Characteristics of object, light, surround and observer may vary both spectrally and directionally, each in a different manner. The observer may vary in regard to time of seeing, what was seen last, or how attention was focused in relation to the time of seeing. Unless the circumstances of a former situation with which the layperson, interior designer or lighting designer may be familiar are similar enough in all important respects, a new situation cannot be responded to by reference to past experience alone. Laypersons may cope with a new situation by making certain assumptions or by limiting themselves to the use of conditions with which they are familiar. But lighting designers may not do this if they are to deal with all types of architectural situations, with all types of light sources and with requirements that will fit new or specialized situations.

Color (sometimes called *psychophysical color*) is defined as the characteristic of light by which an observer may distinguish between patches of light of the same size, shape and structure. It reduces itself to a basic description of light in terms of amounts of radiant power at the different wavelengths of the visually effective spectrum, which for most practical purposes is considered to extend from 380 to 780 nm. (To identify colors due in part to fluorescent dyes activated by energy in the ultraviolet (UV) region, it is necessary in specifying the spectral distribution of a light source to extend the wavelength range beyond that which is visually effective, down to 300 nm in the UV region, particularly for sources that are intended to reproduce daylight.) Identical colors are produced not only by identical spectral power distributions but also by many different spectral power distributions. Such different spectral distributions are called metamers.

The color of an object, or *object color*, is defined as the color of light reflected or transmitted by an object when it is illuminated by a standard light source. For this purpose, a Commission Internationale de l'Éclairage (CIE) standard observer, using standardized conditions of observation, must be assumed.

The word "color" often is used to cover all three meanings discussed above. When the assumed standard conditions are satisfied, then there is little need for distinguishing between the perceived color, the psychophysical color, and the object color. However, if designers are to handle new problems in color, including new light sources that may vary widely in spectral distributions, they must know the differences between the meanings of color, and keep these distinctions in mind even when using the one term to cover all three.

The term "color temperature" is widely used, and often misused, in illumination work. It relates to the color of a completely radiating (blackbody) source at a particular temperature and of light sources that color-match such a body. The *color temperature* of a light source is the absolute temperature of a blackbody radiator having a color equal to that of the light source. Its *correlated color temperature* is the absolute temperature of a blackbody whose color most nearly resembles that of the light source.

Defective Color Vision

About 8% of males and 0.5% of females have color vision that differs from that of the majority of the population. These people are usually called "color blind," although very few (about 0.003% of the total population) can see no color at all.[6] Most color-blind people can distinguish yellows from blues, but confuse reds and greens. Their data should be excluded from any color measurements or color evaluation procedures that are to be used for application to the general population.

Color Rendering

Color rendering is a general expression for the effect of a light source on the color appearance of objects in conscious or subconscious comparison with their color appearance under another, reference, light source.

The color rendering properties of a light source cannot be assessed by visual inspection of the source, or by a knowledge of its color.[7] For this purpose, full knowledge of its spectral power distribution (SPD) is required. Viewed in succession under lamps that look quite alike but are different in spectral distribution, objects may look entirely different in color. An extreme case is a pair of color-matched low-pressure sodium

and yellow fluorescent lamps. Most objects, which in daylight may look red, yellow, green, blue or purple, will appear quite different under these two lamps. Under the sodium lamp objects will lose their daylight appearance, appearing more or less as one hue, from light to very dark (near-black). Under the yellow fluorescent lamp, more hues can be recognized, but the color of objects will still differ considerably from their daylight color.

Methods of measuring and specifying color rendering properties of light sources depend on the color appearance of objects under a reference, or standard, light source compared with the appearance of the same objects under the test source.

Basis for Measurements

Because color is the characteristic by which a human observer distinguishes patches of light, and light is visually evaluated radiant energy, color may be computed by combining physical measurements of radiant power, wavelength by wavelength, with data on how an observer matches colors. The color matching characteristics of the internationally adopted CIE standard observers, defined by the tristimulus values of an equal-power spectrum, are provided in figures 4-1 and 4-2. These *spectral tristimulus values* are called *color matching functions*. With data for a standard observer and the spectroradiometric measurement of a light source, the color of that light source can be calculated. Thus spectroradiometry becomes a tool for color measurement. Measurements of radiant power are physical, while evaluation of radiant power by a human observer, based solely on perception, is psychological. Visual evaluations, quantified through measurements made for standardized conditions of test, provide psychophysical methods of measurement.

Visual evaluation of the appearance of objects and light sources may be in terms derived wholly from one's perceptions. One convenient and useful set of terms describing these perceptions for light sources is hue, brightness and saturation.[8] *Hue* is the attribute according to which an area appears to be similar to one, or to proportions of two, of the perceived colors red, yellow, green and blue. *Brightness* is the attribute according to which an area appears to be emitting more or less light. *Saturation* is the attribute by which an area appears to exhibit more or less chromatic color (that is, departure from gray), judged in proportion to its brightness.

Many widely used psychophysical methods for describing and specifying color show poor correlation with perceptual factors, and often these are converted to more meaningful visual terms, usually to a more uniform color spacing, of which the Munsell system[9] and the CIE 1976 Uniform Color Spaces[10, 11] are prime examples.

Fig. 4-1. Color Matching Functions. (a) CIE 1931 Standard Observer (2°). (b) CIE 1964 Standard Observer (10°)

Wavelength (nanometer)	$\bar{x}(\lambda)$	$\bar{y}(\lambda)$	$\bar{z}(\lambda)$	Wavelength (nanometer)	$\bar{x}(\lambda)$	$\bar{y}(\lambda)$	$\bar{z}(\lambda)$
380	0.0014	0.0000	0.0065	580	0.9163	0.8700	0.0017
385	0.0022	0.0001	0.0105	585	0.9786	0.8163	0.0014
390	0.0042	0.0001	0.0201	590	1.0263	0.7570	0.0011
395	0.0076	0.0002	0.0362	595	1.0567	0.6949	0.0010
400	0.0143	0.0004	0.0679	600	1.0622	0.6310	0.0008
405	0.0232	0.0006	0.1102	605	1.0456	0.5668	0.0006
410	0.0435	0.0012	0.2074	610	1.0026	0.5030	0.0003
415	0.0776	0.0022	0.3713	615	0.9384	0.4412	0.0002
420	0.1344	0.0040	0.6456	620	0.8544	0.3810	0.0002
425	0.2148	0.0073	1.0391	625	0.7514	0.3210	0.0001
430	0.2839	0.0116	1.3856	630	0.6424	0.2650	0.0000
435	0.3285	0.0168	1.6230	635	0.5419	0.2170	0.0000
440	0.3483	0.0230	1.7471	640	0.4479	0.1750	0.0000
445	0.3481	0.0298	1.7826	645	0.3608	0.1382	0.0000
450	0.3362	0.0380	1.7721	650	0.2835	0.1070	0.0000
455	0.3187	0.0480	1.7441	655	0.2187	0.0816	0.0000
460	0.2908	0.0600	1.6692	660	0.1649	0.0610	0.0000
465	0.2511	0.0739	1.5281	665	0.1212	0.0446	0.0000
470	0.1954	0.0910	1.2876	670	0.0874	0.0320	0.0000
475	0.1421	0.1126	1.0419	675	0.0636	0.0232	0.0000
480	0.0956	0.1390	0.8130	680	0.0468	0.0170	0.0000
485	0.0580	0.1693	0.6162	685	0.0329	0.0119	0.0000
490	0.0320	0.2080	0.4652	690	0.0227	0.0082	0.0000
495	0.0147	0.2586	0.3533	695	0.0158	0.0057	0.0000
500	0.0049	0.3230	0.2720	700	0.0114	0.0041	0.0000
505	0.0024	0.4073	0.2123	705	0.0081	0.0029	0.0000
510	0.0093	0.5030	0.1582	710	0.0058	0.0021	0.0000
515	0.0291	0.6082	0.1117	715	0.0041	0.0015	0.0000
520	0.0633	0.7100	0.0782	720	0.0029	0.0010	0.0000
525	0.1096	0.7932	0.0573	725	0.0020	0.0007	0.0000
530	0.1655	0.8620	0.0422	730	0.0014	0.0005	0.0000
535	0.2257	0.9149	0.0298	735	0.0010	0.0004	0.0000
540	0.2904	0.9540	0.0203	740	0.0007	0.0002	0.0000
545	0.3597	0.9803	0.0134	745	0.0005	0.0002	0.0000
550	0.4334	0.9950	0.0087	750	0.0003	0.0001	0.0000
555	0.5121	1.0000	0.0057	755	0.0002	0.0001	0.0000
560	0.5945	0.9950	0.0039	760	0.0002	0.0001	0.0000
565	0.6784	0.9786	0.0027	765	0.0001	0.0000	0.0000
570	0.7621	0.9520	0.0021	770	0.0001	0.0000	0.0000
575	0.8425	0.9154	0.0018	775	0.0001	0.0000	0.0000
580	0.9163	0.8700	0.0017	780	0.0000	0.0000	0.0000
Totals					21.3714	21.3711	21.3715

Wavelength (nanometer)	$\bar{x}_{10}(\lambda)$	$\bar{y}_{10}(\lambda)$	$\bar{z}_{10}(\lambda)$	Wavelength (nanometer)	$\bar{x}_{10}(\lambda)$	$\bar{y}_{10}(\lambda)$	$\bar{z}_{10}(\lambda)$
380	0.0002	0.0000	0.0007	580	1.0142	0.8689	0.0000
385	0.0007	0.0001	0.0029	585	1.0743	0.8256	0.0000
390	0.0024	0.0003	0.0105	590	1.1185	0.7774	0.0000
395	0.0072	0.0008	0.0323	595	1.1343	0.7204	0.0000
400	0.0191	0.0020	0.0860	600	1.1240	0.6583	0.0000
405	0.0434	0.0045	0.1971	605	1.0891	0.5939	0.0000
410	0.0847	0.0088	0.3894	610	1.0305	0.5280	0.0000
415	0.1406	0.0145	0.6568	615	0.9507	0.4618	0.0000
420	0.2045	0.0214	0.9725	620	0.8563	0.3981	0.0000
425	0.2647	0.0295	1.2825	625	0.7549	0.3396	0.0000
430	0.3147	0.0387	1.5535	630	0.6475	0.2835	0.0000
435	0.3577	0.0496	1.7985	635	0.5351	0.2283	0.0000
440	0.3837	0.0621	1.9673	640	0.4316	0.1798	0.0000
445	0.3867	0.0747	2.0273	645	0.3437	0.1402	0.0000
450	0.3707	0.0895	1.9948	650	0.2683	0.1076	0.0000
455	0.3430	0.1063	1.9007	655	0.2043	0.0812	0.0000
460	0.3023	0.1282	1.7454	660	0.1526	0.0603	0.0000
465	0.2541	0.1528	1.5549	665	0.1122	0.0441	0.0000
470	0.1956	0.1852	1.3176	670	0.0813	0.0318	0.0000
475	0.1323	0.2199	1.0302	675	0.0579	0.0226	0.0000
480	0.0805	0.2536	0.7721	680	0.0409	0.0159	0.0000
485	0.0411	0.2977	0.5701	685	0.0286	0.0111	0.0000
490	0.0162	0.3391	0.4153	690	0.0199	0.0077	0.0000
495	0.0051	0.3954	0.3024	695	0.0138	0.0054	0.0000
500	0.0038	0.4608	0.2185	700	0.0096	0.0037	0.0000
505	0.0154	0.5314	0.1592	705	0.0066	0.0026	0.0000
510	0.0375	0.6067	0.1120	710	0.0046	0.0018	0.0000
515	0.0714	0.6857	0.0822	715	0.0031	0.0012	0.0000
520	0.1177	0.7618	0.0607	720	0.0022	0.0008	0.0000
525	0.1730	0.8233	0.0431	725	0.0015	0.0006	0.0000
530	0.2365	0.8752	0.0305	730	0.0010	0.0004	0.0000
535	0.3042	0.9238	0.0206	735	0.0007	0.0003	0.0000
540	0.3768	0.9620	0.0137	740	0.0005	0.0002	0.0000
545	0.4516	0.9822	0.0079	745	0.0004	0.0001	0.0000
550	0.5298	0.9918	0.0040	750	0.0003	0.0001	0.0000
555	0.6161	0.9991	0.0011	755	0.0002	0.0001	0.0000
560	0.7052	0.9973	0.0000	760	0.0001	0.0000	0.0000
565	0.7938	0.9824	0.0000	765	0.0001	0.0000	0.0000
570	0.8787	0.9556	0.0000	770	0.0001	0.0000	0.0000
575	0.9512	0.9152	0.0000	775	0.0000	0.0000	0.0000
580	1.0142	0.8689	0.0000	780	0.0000	0.0000	0.0000
Totals					23.3294	23.3324	23.3343

CIE Method of Color Specification

Basic CIE Method.[12] This is a method originally recommended in 1931 by the CIE to define all metameric pairs by giving the amounts X, Y, Z of three imaginary primary colors required by a standard observer to match the color being specified. These amounts may be calculated as a summation of the spectral compositions of the radiant power of the source or the illuminated color specimen, times the spectral tristimulus values for an equal-power source (see figure 4-1). For example,

$$X = k \sum_{\lambda = 380\ nm}^{780\ nm} S(\lambda)\rho(\lambda)\bar{x}(\lambda)\ \Delta\lambda \quad (4\text{-}1a)$$

where

$S(\lambda)$ = spectral irradiance distribution of the source (see figure 4-3),
$\rho(\lambda)$ = spectral reflectance of the specimen,
k = a normalizing factor,
$\bar{x}(\lambda)$ = spectral tristimulus value from figure 4-1,

with similar expressions for Y and Z, wherein $\bar{y}(\lambda)$ and $\bar{z}(\lambda)$ respectively are substituted for $\bar{x}(\lambda)$.

The normalizing factor k may be assigned any arbitrary value provided it is kept constant throughout any particular application. Where only the relative values of X, Y, and Z are required, the value of k is usually chosen so that Y has the value 100.0. In the special case where the absolute values of $S(\lambda)\ \Delta\lambda$ are given (for example, in watts), it is convenient to take $k = K_m$ = 683 lm/W, whereby the value of Y gives the equivalent luminous quantity in lumens. Here, the accepted symbol for $S(\lambda)$ is $\Phi_{e,\lambda}$ (see Glossary under luminous flux).

For colors of reflecting objects, the reflectance factor, $R(\lambda)$, must be introduced, so that

$$X = k \sum_{\lambda = 380\ nm}^{780\ nm} S(\lambda)R(\lambda)\bar{x}(\lambda)\ \Delta\lambda \quad (4\text{-}1b)$$

In this case, the normalizing factor k is usually given

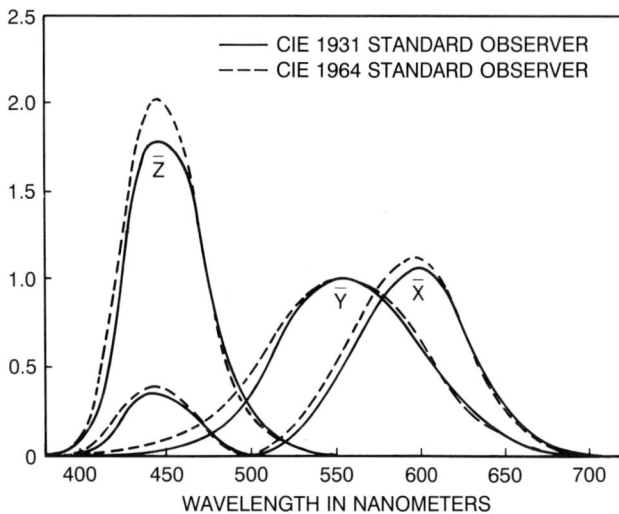

Fig. 4-2. Graph of CIE 1931 and 1964 color matching functions.

the value

$$k = \frac{100}{\sum S(\lambda)\,\bar{y}(\lambda)\,\Delta\lambda} \qquad (4\text{-}2)$$

With this normalization, the value of Y is the luminous reflectance factor expressed in percent.

Use of the *reflectance factor*, $R(\lambda)$, is appropriate for calculating tristimulus values that relate to the appearance of objects. For other applications, such as calculations of light flux in a space, the *reflectance*, $\rho(\lambda)$, may be more appropriate. Precise definitions of $R(\lambda)$ and $\rho(\lambda)$ are given in the Glossary under reflectance and reflectance factor. The essential difference between the two quantities is that the reflectance factor is directional and is measured relative to a perfect diffuser. Consequently it may be greater than 1 in certain directions as long as this is compensated by values less than 1 in other directions.

For transmitting objects, the transmittance or transmittance factor must be used in place of the reflectance or reflectance factor.

The CIE has recommended two sets of standard color matching functions. The first is known as the CIE 1931 Standard Observer (figure 4-1a) and is intended for use when the angular subtense of the field of view is between 1 and 4°. The second is the CIE 1964 Standard Observer (figure 4-1b), intended for use with angular subtenses greater than 4°.

The CIE has also recommended several standard illuminants (spectral power distributions) for use in computing object colors. The most commonly used are listed in figure 4-3. They include Standard Illuminant A (representing tungsten at a color temperature of 2856 K), Standard Illuminant C (based on a laboratory simulation of average daylight) and Standard Illuminant D_{65} (a more modern and preferred representation

of a phase of daylight at a correlated color temperature of approximately 6500 K). In addition, the CIE recommends a calculation method for standard illuminants representing phases of daylight at any correlated color temperature between 4000 and 25,000 K. In its recommendation, the CIE distinguishes between *illuminant* and *source*. The term *source* refers to a physical emitter of light, such as a lamp or the sun and sky. The term *illuminant* refers to a specific spectral power distribution.

The most accurate calculation method recommended by the CIE is summation at 1-nm intervals from 360 to 830 nm. However, the color matching functions have relatively small values at the ends of the spectrum, and furthermore, many sources and objects have fairly smooth spectral distributions, so that summation from 380 to 780 nm at 5-nm intervals will suffice for many practical purposes, allowing the use of simpler instrumentation and computation. If data are available only for a restricted wavelength range (for example 400–700 nm) or for a wider wavelength interval (for example 10 or 20 nm), the appropriate values may be selected from figures 4-1 and 4-3. An accurate method for dealing with incomplete data is to use special tables given in ASTM Standard Method E 308, *Computing Colors of Objects by Using the CIE System*.

An important practical consideration for sources such as discharge lamps that do not have a smooth spectral power distribution is that the measurement bandwidth should be an integer multiple of the wavelength interval.

The fractions $X/(X + Y + Z)$, $Y/(X + Y + Z)$, and $Z/(X + Y + Z)$ are known as the *chromaticity coordinates*, x, y, z respectively. Note that $x + y + z = 1$, and specification of any two fixes the third. By convention, chromaticity usually is stated in terms of x and y and plotted in a rectangular coordinate system as shown in figure 4-4. In this *chromaticity diagram*, the points representing light of single wavelengths plot along a horseshoe-shaped curve called the *spectrum locus*. The line joining the extremities of the spectrum locus is known as the *purple boundary* and is the locus of the most saturated purples obtainable.

A sample calculation for determining the CIE coordinates x, y and Y is shown in figure 4-5 for a deep-red surface when illuminated by CIE illuminant D_{65}. In figure 4-5, column I is a listing of wavelengths in 5-nm steps, column II is a tabulation of spectral reflectance values for the deep-red surface at each wavelength in column I, and column III lists the CIE tristimulus computational data for CIE illuminant D_{65}. By multiplying the row entry in column II by the corresponding one in column III and summing the products given in column IV, the values of X, Y and Z are determined. Then by using the three fractions above, the chromaticity coordinates are determined.

Fig. 4-3. Spectral Power Distributions of CIE Standard Illuminants

λ (nm)	Standard Illuminant						λ (nm)	Standard Illuminant					
	A	C	D₅₀	D₅₅	D₆₅	D₇₅		A	C	D₅₀	D₅₅	D₆₅	D₇₅
300	0.93		0.02	0.02	0.03	0.04	570	107.2	102.3	97.74	97.22	96.33	95.62
305	1.13		1.03	1.05	1.66	2.59	575	110.8	100.2	98.33	97.48	96.06	94.91
310	1.36		2.05	2.07	3.29	5.13	580	114.4	97.80	98.92	97.75	95.79	94.21
315	1.62		4.91	6.65	11.77	17.47	585	118.1	95.43	96.21	94.59	92.24	90.60
320	1.93	0.01	7.78	11.22	20.24	29.81	590	121.7	93.20	93.50	91.43	88.69	87.00
325	2.27	0.20	11.26	15.94	28.64	42.37	595	125.4	91.22	95.59	92.93	89.35	87.11
330	2.66	0.40	14.75	20.65	37.05	54.93	600	129.0	89.70	97.69	94.42	90.01	87.23
335	3.10	1.55	16.35	22.27	38.50	56.09	605	132.7	88.83	98.48	94.78	89.80	86.68
340	3.59	2.70	17.95	23.88	39.95	57.26	610	136.3	88.40	99.27	95.14	89.60	86.14
345	4.14	4.85	19.48	25.85	42.43	60.00	615	140.0	88.19	99.16	94.68	88.65	84.86
350	4.74	7.00	21.01	27.82	44.91	62.74	620	143.6	88.10	99.04	94.22	87.70	83.58
355	5.41	9.95	22.48	29.22	45.78	62.86	625	147.2	88.06	97.38	92.33	85.49	81.16
360	6.14	12.90	23.94	30.62	46.64	62.98	630	150.8	88.00	95.72	90.45	83.29	78.75
365	6.95	17.20	25.45	32.46	49.36	66.65	635	154.4	87.86	97.29	91.39	83.49	78.59
370	7.82	21.40	26.96	34.31	52.09	70.31	640	158.0	87.80	98.86	92.33	83.70	78.43
375	8.77	27.50	25.72	33.45	51.03	68.51	645	161.5	87.99	97.26	90.59	81.86	76.61
380	9.80	33.00	24.49	32.58	49.98	66.70	650	165.0	88.20	95.67	88.85	80.03	74.80
385	10.90	39.92	27.18	35.34	52.31	68.33	655	168.5	88.20	96.93	89.59	80.12	74.56
390	12.09	47.40	29.87	38.09	54.65	69.96	660	172.0	87.90	98.19	90.32	80.21	74.32
395	13.35	55.17	39.59	49.52	68.70	85.95	665	175.4	87.22	100.6	92.13	81.25	74.87
400	14.71	63.30	49.31	60.95	82.75	101.9	670	178.8	86.30	103.0	93.95	82.28	75.42
405	16.15	71.81	52.91	64.75	87.12	106.9	675	182.1	85.30	101.1	91.95	80.28	73.50
410	17.68	80.60	56.51	68.55	91.49	111.9	680	185.4	84.00	99.13	89.96	78.28	71.58
415	19.29	89.53	58.27	70.07	92.46	112.4	685	188.7	82.21	93.26	94.82	74.00	67.71
420	20.99	98.10	60.03	71.58	93.43	112.8	690	191.9	80.20	87.38	79.86	69.72	63.85
425	22.79	105.8	58.93	69.75	90.06	107.9	695	195.1	78.24	89.49	81.26	70.67	64.46
430	24.67	112.4	57.82	67.91	86.68	103.1	700	198.3	76.30	91.60	82.84	71.61	65.08
435	26.64	117.8	66.32	76.76	95.77	112.1	705	201.4	74.36	92.25	83.84	72.98	66.57
440	28.70	121.5	74.82	85.61	104.9	121.2	710	204.4	72.40	92.89	84.84	74.35	68.07
445	30.85	123.4	81.04	91.80	110.9	127.1	715	207.4	70.40	84.87	77.54	67.98	62.26
450	33.09	124.0	87.25	97.99	117.0	133.0	720	210.4	68.30	76.85	70.24	61.60	56.44
455	35.41	123.6	88.93	99.23	117.4	132.7	725	213.3	66.30	81.68	74.77	65.74	60.34
460	37.81	123.1	90.61	100.5	117.8	132.4	730	216.1	64.40	86.51	79.30	69.89	64.24
465	40.30	123.3	90.9	100.2	116.3	129.8	735	218.9	62.80	89.55	82.15	72.49	66.70
470	42.87	123.8	91.37	99.91	114.5	127.3	740	221.7	91.50	92.58	84.99	75.09	69.15
475	45.52	124.1	93.24	101.3	115.4	127.1	745	224.4	60.20	85.40	78.44	69.34	63.89
480	48.54	123.9	95.11	102.7	115.9	126.8	750	227.0	59.20	78.23	71.88	63.59	58.63
485	51.04	122.9	93.54	100.4	112.4	122.3	755	229.6	58.50	67.96	62.34	55.01	50.62
490	53.91	120.7	91.96	98.08	108.8	117.8	760	232.1	58.10	57.69	52.79	46.42	42.62
495	56.95	116.9	93.84	99.38	109.1	117.2	765	234.6	58.00	70.31	64.36	56.61	51.98
500	59.86	112.1	95.72	100.7	109.4	116.6	770	237.0	58.20	82.92	75.93	66.81	61.35
505	62.93	107.0	96.17	100.7	108.6	115.2	775	239.4	58.50	80.60	73.87	65.09	59.84
510	66.06	102.3	96.61	100.7	107.8	113.7	780	241.7	59.10	78.27	71.82	63.38	58.32
515	69.25	98.81	96.87	100.3	106.3	111.2	785	243.9		78.91	72.38	63.84	58.73
520	72.50	96.90	97.13	100.0	104.8	108.7	790	246.1		79.55	72.94	64.30	59.14
525	75.79	96.78	99.61	102.1	106.2	109.6	795	248.2		76.48	70.14	61.88	56.94
530	79.13	98.00	102.1	104.2	107.7	110.4	800	250.3		73.40	67.35	59.45	54.73
535	82.52	99.94	101.4	103.2	106.0	108.4	805	252.4		68.66	63.04	55.71	51.32
540	85.95	102.1	100.8	102.1	104.4	106.3	810	254.3		63.92	58.73	51.96	47.92
545	89.41	104.0	101.5	102.5	104.2	105.6	815	256.2		97.35	61.86	54.70	50.42
550	92.91	105.2	102.3	103.0	104.0	104.9	820	258.1		70.78	64.99	57.44	52.92
555	96.44	105.7	101.2	101.5	102.0	102.4	825	259.9		72.61	66.65	58.88	54.23
560	100.0	105.3	100.0	100.0	100.0	100.0	830	261.6		74.44	68.31	60.31	55.54
565	103.6	104.1	98.87	98.61	98.17	97.81							

Chromaticity coordinates (CIE 1931 System)

x:	0.448	0.310	0.346	0.332	0.313	0.299	y:	0.407	0.316	0.358	0.347	0.329	0.315

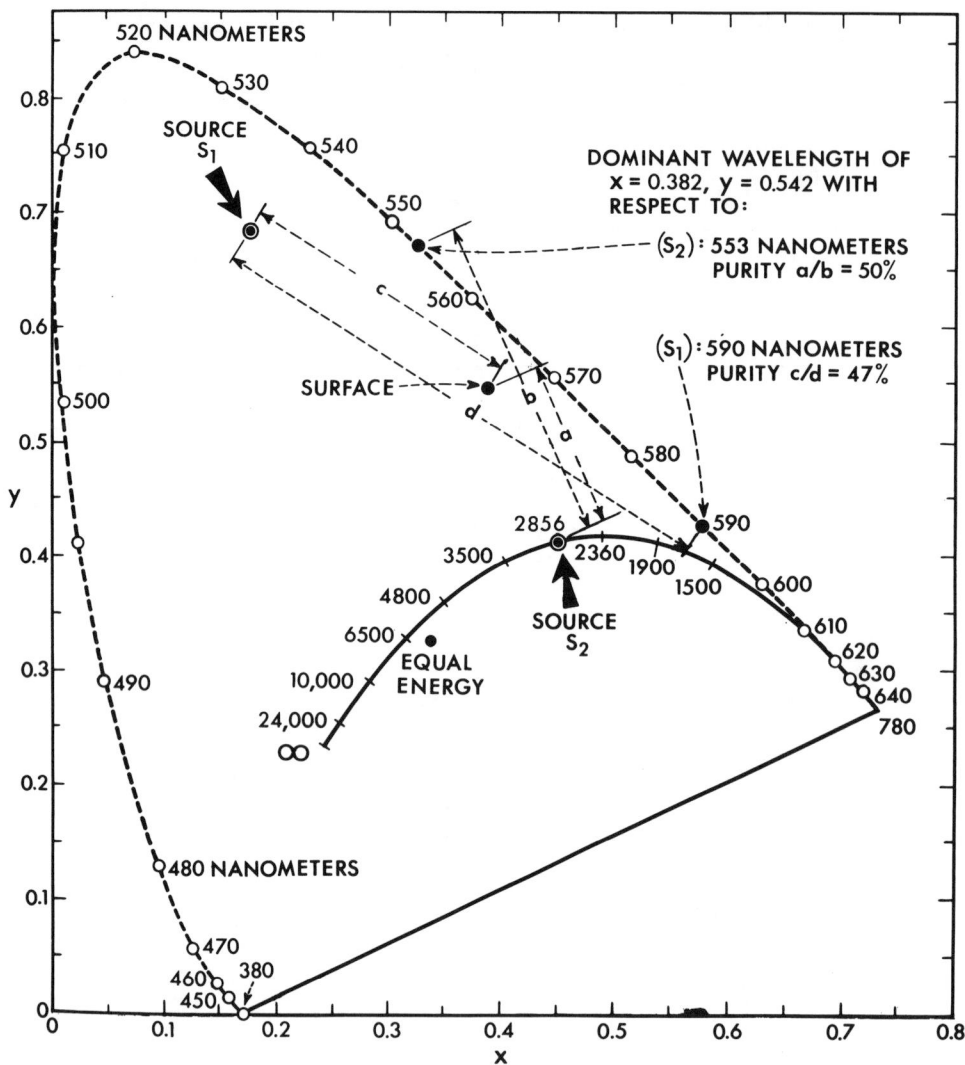

Fig. 4-4. The 1931 CIE chromaticity diagram showing method of obtaining dominant wavelength and purity for different samples under different light sources.

The percentage luminous reflectance is determined by multiplying the Y value by the normalizing factor $k = 100/\Sigma S(\lambda)\bar{y}(\lambda)\,\Delta\lambda = \frac{1}{1000}$.

A final recommendation of the CIE concerns geometrical arrangements for measuring colors of reflecting objects. Four alternative conditions for illuminating/viewing a test sample are specified: (1) 45°/normal, (2) normal/45°, (3) diffuse/normal and (4) normal/diffuse (diffuse illuminating or viewing is usually achieved by placing a sample in an integrating sphere). Consult Wyszecki and Stiles's *Color Science*[13] for an extended discussion of the calculation and application of CIE data, including extensive tables of quantitative data and methods of colorimetry.

Dominant Wavelength and Excitation Purity. Dominant wavelength and excitation purity are quantities more suggestive of the color appearance of objects than a CIE x, y specification, and may be determined on an x, y diagram in relation to the spectrum locus and an assumed achromatic point (for object colors this is usually the point for the light source). See figure 4-4. The dominant wavelength of all colors whose x, y coordinates fall on a straight line connecting the achromatic point with a point on the spectrum locus is the wavelength indicated at the intersection of that line with the spectrum locus. For some colors, the straight line from the achromatic point though the test chromaticity will strike the purple boundary rather than the spectrum locus. For these colors the line must be extended backwards from the achromatic point. The point where the extended line strikes the spectrum locus determines the *complementary wavelength* of such a color. The *excitation purity* is defined as the distance from the achromatic point to (x, y) divided by the total distance in the same direction from the achromatic point to the spectrum locus or the purple boundary, as the case may be.

Fig. 4-5. Determination of CIE Chromaticity Coordinates from the Spectrophotometric Curve for a Surface Illuminated by Standard Illuminant D_{65}

I Wavelength λ (nm)	II Reflectance $\rho(\lambda)$	III CIE Data for Illuminant D_{65}			IV (II × III)		
		$\bar{x}(\lambda)S(\lambda)$	$\bar{y}(\lambda)S(\lambda)$	$\bar{z}(\lambda)S(\lambda)$	$\rho(\lambda)\bar{x}(\lambda)S(\lambda)$	$\rho(\lambda)\bar{y}(\lambda)S(\lambda)$	$\rho(\lambda)\bar{z}(\lambda)S(\lambda)$
380	0.051	0.06	0.00	0.29	0.00	0.00	0.01
385	0.051	0.10	0.00	0.49	0.01	0.00	0.03
390	0.051	0.21	0.01	0.97	0.01	0.00	0.05
395	0.051	0.46	0.01	2.19	0.02	0.00	0.11
400	0.051	1.06	0.03	5.05	0.05	0.00	0.26
405	0.051	1.81	0.05	8.58	0.09	0.00	0.44
410	0.051	3.52	0.10	16.77	0.18	0.00	0.86
415	0.051	6.40	0.18	30.59	0.33	0.01	1.56
420	0.050	11.28	0.33	54.15	0.56	0.02	2.71
425	0.050	17.89	0.59	86.14	0.89	0.03	4.32
430	0.050	23.56	0.92	114.76	1.18	0.05	5.74
435	0.050	30.80	1.51	151.78	1.54	0.08	7.59
440	0.050	36.30	2.28	181.45	1.81	0.11	9.07
445	0.049	38.75	3.15	197.52	1.90	0.15	9.68
450	0.047	39.68	4.24	207.79	1.86	0.20	9.77
455	0.046	37.91	5.38	205.76	1.74	0.25	9.46
460	0.045	35.02	6.77	198.95	1.58	0.30	8.95
465	0.045	30.30	8.25	182.02	1.36	0.37	8.19
470	0.044	23.75	10.02	153.77	1.05	0.44	6.77
475	0.044	17.57	12.45	126.79	0.77	0.55	5.53
480	0.043	12.09	15.47	99.30	0.52	0.67	4.27
485	0.042	7.26	18.28	73.29	0.30	0.77	3.08
490	0.041	3.96	21.70	53.53	0.16	0.89	2.19
495	0.041	1.91	27.00	40.68	0.08	1.11	1.67
500	0.041	0.69	33.74	31.29	0.03	1.38	1.28
505	0.041	0.24	42.27	24.26	0.01	1.73	0.99
510	0.041	0.75	52.06	18.17	0.03	2.13	0.75
515	0.041	2.55	62.39	12.76	0.10	2.56	0.52
520	0.041	5.80	72.39	8.79	0.24	2.97	0.36
525	0.041	10.57	82.64	6.46	0.43	3.39	0.26
530	0.041	16.57	91.48	4.84	0.68	3.75	0.20
535	0.041	22.63	96.02	3.40	0.93	3.94	0.14
540	0.041	28.93	98.90	2.30	1.19	4.05	0.09
545	0.042	36.01	101.73	1.52	1.51	4.27	0.06
550	0.042	43.53	103.30	0.99	1.83	4.34	0.04
555	0.043	50.60	101.99	0.64	2.18	4.39	0.03
560	0.043	57.78	99.69	0.42	2.48	4.29	0.02
565	0.046	64.95	96.47	0.29	2.99	4.44	0.01
570	0.050	71.82	92.30	0.21	3.59	4.61	0.01
575	0.062	79.42	88.71	0.18	4.92	5.50	0.01
580	0.075	86.43	84.27	0.16	6.48	6.32	0.01
585	0.110	89.22	76.34	0.13	9.81	8.40	0.01
590	0.145	90.29	68.22	0.10	13.09	9.89	0.01
595	0.218	94.04	63.21	0.09	20.50	13.78	0.02
600	0.290	95.67	57.95	0.08	27.76	16.81	0.02
605	0.378	94.38	52.05	0.06	35.67	19.68	0.02
610	0.465	90.77	46.20	0.03	42.21	21.48	0.02
615	0.520	84.47	40.19	0.02	43.92	20.90	0.01
620	0.575	76.56	34.47	0.02	44.02	19.82	0.01
625	0.599	66.08	28.45	0.01	39.58	17.04	0.01
630	0.623	55.29	22.96	0.00	34.44	14.30	0.00
635	0.636	46.87	18.87	0.00	29.81	12.00	0.00
640	0.648	39.02	15.31	0.00	25.29	9.92	0.00
645	0.656	30.90	11.88	0.00	20.27	7.79	0.00
650	0.667	23.85	9.02	0.00	15.91	6.02	0.00
655	0.675	18.49	6.91	0.00	12.48	4.67	0.00
660	0.683	14.02	5.20	0.00	9.58	3.55	0.00
665	0.691	10.49	3.86	0.00	7.25	2.67	0.00
670	0.699	7.68	2.81	0.00	5.37	1.97	0.00
675	0.706	5.43	1.98	0.00	3.84	1.40	0.00
680	0.713	3.90	1.42	0.00	2.78	1.01	0.00
685	0.719	2.62	0.95	0.00	1.88	0.68	0.00
690	0.725	1.70	0.62	0.00	1.24	0.45	0.00
695	0.732	1.20	0.43	0.00	0.88	0.32	0.00
700	0.739	0.87	0.31	0.00	0.64	0.23	0.00
705	0.744	0.63	0.23	0.00	0.47	0.17	0.00
710	0.749	0.46	0.17	0.00	0.35	0.12	0.00
715	0.755	0.30	0.11	0.00	0.23	0.08	0.00
720	0.762	0.19	0.07	0.00	0.15	0.05	0.00
725	0.768	0.14	0.05	0.00	0.11	0.04	0.00
730	0.775	0.11	0.04	0.00	0.08	0.03	0.00
735	0.780	0.08	0.03	0.00	0.06	0.02	0.00
740	0.785	0.06	0.02	0.00	0.04	0.02	0.00
745	0.788	0.04	0.01	0.00	0.03	0.01	0.00
750	0.791	0.02	0.01	0.00	0.02	0.01	0.00
755	0.793	0.01	0.00	0.00	0.01	0.00	0.00
760	0.795	0.01	0.00	0.00	0.01	0.00	0.00
765	0.796	0.01	0.00	0.00	0.01	0.00	0.00
770	0.797	0.01	0.00	0.00	0.00	0.00	0.00
775	0.798	0.00	0.00	0.00	0.00	0.00	0.00
780	0.798	0.00	0.00	0.00	0.00	0.00	0.00
Sums		2006.81	2109.47	2309.09	X = 497.42	Y = 285.41	Z = 107.25

x = 0.559, y = 0.321, z = 0.120   Luminous reflectance = 13.5%

An x, y specification of any object color relates it only to the light source for which the object color is calculated; consequently, the dominant wavelength and excitation purity of any object depend on the spectral composition of its illumination.

CIE Uniform Color Spaces. Distances in the CIE x, y diagram or X, Y, Z space do not correlate well with the perceived magnitudes of color differences. For this reason various transformations have been suggested that provide more uniform spacing.

In 1960 the CIE provisionally recommended that whenever a diagram is desired to yield chromaticity spacing more uniform than the CIE x, y diagram, a uniform chromaticity-scale diagram based on that described in 1937 by MacAdam[14] be used. The ordinate and abscissa of this u, v *diagram* are defined as

$$u = \frac{4X}{X + 15Y + 3Z} = \frac{4x}{-2x + 12y + 3} \quad (4\text{-}3)$$

$$v = \frac{6Y}{X + 15Y + 3Z} = \frac{6y}{-2x + 12y + 3} \quad (4\text{-}4)$$

To convert this to a three-dimensional system that is useful in studying color differences, the CIE, in 1964, added a recommendation developed for the purpose by Wyszecki[15] that converts Y to a lightness index, W^*, by the relationship

$$W^* = 25Y^{1/3} - 17 \quad (1 \leqslant Y \leqslant 100) \quad (4\text{-}5)$$

and converts the chromaticity coordinates u, v to chromaticness indices U^*, V^* by the relationships

$$U^* = 13W^*(u - u_n) \quad (4\text{-}6)$$

$$V^* = 13W^*(v - v_n) \quad (4\text{-}7)$$

The lightness index W^* approximates the Munsell value function in the range of Y from 1 to 100%. The chromaticity coordinates u_n, v_n refer to the nominally achromatic (or *neutral*) color (usually that of the source) placed at the origin of the U^*, V^* system.

In 1976 the CIE[10, 11] recommended two new uniform color spaces, known as CIELUV and CIELAB. Although these give a more uniform representation of color differences and therefore supersede the U^*, V^*, W^* space for most purposes, the earlier system is still used for the calculation of CIE color rendering indices. Two spaces were recommended, rather than one, because experimental evidence was insufficient to select a single space that would be satisfactory for most industrial applications.

The three coordinates of CIELUV are L^*, u^* and v^*, defined by

$$L^* = 116\left(\frac{Y}{Y_n}\right)^{1/3} - 16 \quad \text{for} \quad \frac{Y}{Y_n} > 0.008856 \quad (4\text{-}8)$$

$$L^* = 903.29\frac{Y}{Y_n} \quad \text{for} \quad \frac{Y}{Y_n} \leqslant 0.008856 \quad (4\text{-}9)$$

$$u^* = 13L^*(u' - u'_n) \quad (4\text{-}10)$$

$$v^* = 13L^*(v' - v'_n) \quad (4\text{-}11)$$

where

$$u' = 4X/(X + 15Y + 3Z),$$
$$v' = 9Y/(X + 15Y + 3Z),$$
u'_n, v'_n, Y_n = values of u', v' and Y for the nominally achromatic color (usually that of the source with $Y_n = 100$).

The major change from the U^*, V^*, W^* system is that $v' = 1.5v$. The quantity L^* is a minor modification of W^*, and u' is the same as u.

The three coordinates of CIELAB are L^*, a^* and b^*, defined by

$$L^* = 116f(Y/Y_n) - 16 \quad (4\text{-}12)$$

$$a^* = 500[f(X/X_n) - f(Y/Y_n)] \quad (4\text{-}13)$$

$$b^* = 200[f(Y/Y_n) - f(Z/Z_n)] \quad (4\text{-}14)$$

where

$$f(q) = \begin{cases} q^{1/3} & \text{for} \quad q > 0.008856 \\ 7.787q + \frac{4}{29} & \text{for} \quad q \leqslant 0.008856 \end{cases}$$

(with $q = X/X_n$, Y/Y_n or Z/Z_n). Here X_n, Y_n and Z_n are the values of X, Y and Z for the nominally achromatic color (usually that of the source with $Y_n = 100$). The lightness index L^* is the same for both CIELUV and CIELAB.

Loci of constant Munsell hue and chroma for value 5/ (see discussion of Munsell Color System below) are plotted in u^*, v^* and a^*, b^* diagrams[16] in figure 4-6.

These two uniform color spaces each have associated with them a color-difference formula by which a measure of the total difference between two object colors may be calculated. In the CIELUV system, the color difference is measured by

$$\Delta E^*_{uv} = \left[(\Delta L^*)^2 + (\Delta u^*)^2 + (\Delta v^*)^2\right]^{1/2} \quad (4\text{-}15)$$

In the CIELAB system it is measured by

$$\Delta E^*_{ab} = \left[(\Delta L^*)^2 + (\Delta a^*)^2 + (\Delta b^*)^2\right]^{1/2} \quad (4\text{-}16)$$

These two formulas are useful for setting color tolerances in industrial situations. They are recommended

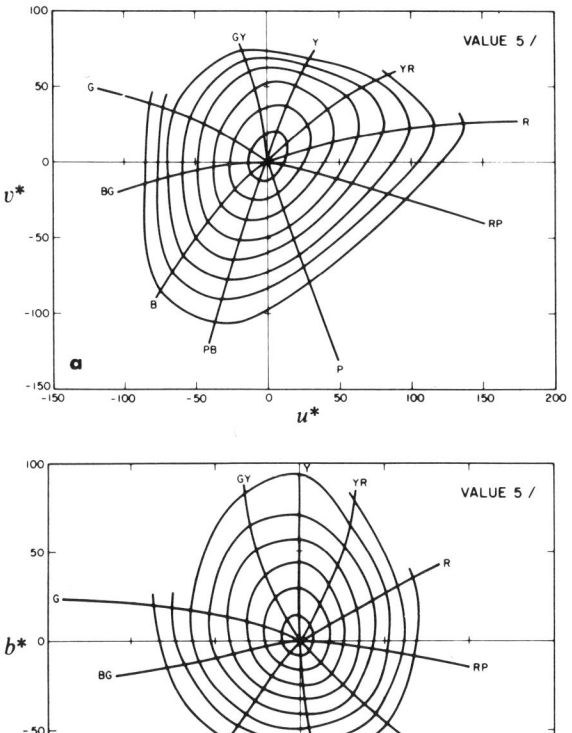

Fig. 4-6. Loci of constant Munsell hue and chroma plotted in the CIE 1976 u^*v^* diagram (a), and the CIE 1976 a^*b^* diagram (b).

by the CIE to unify practice, which in the past has involved the use of 10 or 20 different color-difference formulas.

Correlates of the subjective attributes lightness, perceived chroma and hue can be derived from either CIELUV or CIELAB as follows:

$$\text{CIE 1976 lightness} = L^* \quad (4\text{-}17a)$$

$$\text{CIE 1976 } u,v \text{ chroma} = C^*_{uv} = (u^{*2} + v^{*2})^{1/2} \quad (4\text{-}17b)$$

or

$$\text{CIE 1976 } a,b \text{ chroma} = C^*_{ab} = (a^{*2} + b^{*2})^{1/2} \quad (4\text{-}17c)$$

and

$$\text{CIE 1976 } u,v \text{ hue angle} = h_{uv} = \arctan\left(\frac{v^*}{u^*}\right) \quad (4\text{-}17d)$$

or

$$\text{CIE 1976 } a,b \text{ hue angle} = h_{ab} = \arctan\left(\frac{b^*}{a^*}\right) \quad (4\text{-}17e)$$

Although these quantities are approximate correlates of the respective subjective attributes, the actual perceived color depends significantly on the viewing conditions such as the nature of the surround. The exact degree of agreement of these measures with the corresponding subjective attributes, even for standard daylight viewing conditions, has not been determined. In commercial situations involving small color differences, tolerances are often set differently for L^*, C^*, and h because the acceptability may be different for the three components.

The geometrical relationships among CIELAB coordinates are illustrated in figure 4-7. The relationships in CIELUV are similar.

The 1976 CIELAB-CIELUV recommendation has been much more successful than the 1964 (U^*, V^*, W^*) convention. Both formulas are in widespread use, the choice between them being based mainly on practical considerations other than uniformity of spacing. In industries concerned with self-luminous colors such as television screens and video displays, CIELUV has been used more than has CIELAB, but not exclusively so. The reverse has been true of industries concerned with object colors. Indeed, some formulas, such as the CMC formula,[17-19] developed since 1976, continue to use CIELAB as a base and add extra complexity to improve the fit to visual acceptability data.

Other Systems of Color Specification

Munsell System. This is a system of specifying color on scales of hue, value and chroma. The hue scale consists of 100 steps in a circle containing five principal and five intermediate hues. The value scale contains ten steps from black to white, 0 to 10. The chroma scale may contain 20 or more steps from neutral gray to highly saturated. Each of the three scales is intended to represent equal visual intervals for a normal observer fully adapted to daylight viewing conditions (CIE source C) with gray to white surroundings. Under these conditions the Munsell hue, value and chroma of a color correlate closely with the hue, lightness and perceived chroma of color perception; under other conditions the correlation is lost. It is only for daylight conditions that Munsell samples are expected to appear equally spaced. When problems of color adaptation are fully solved, it may be possible to calculate the change in appearance and spacing that takes place when samples are viewed under a light source of different spectral power distribution.

Munsell notation is useful whether or not reference is made to Munsell samples. It has the form [hue] [value]/[chroma], for example, 5R 4/10. This is read "5 red, 4 over 10" or "5 red, 4 slash 10." Colors of zero chroma, which are known as neutral colors, are written N1/, N2/, etc., as shown in figure 4-8. One widely used approximation of equivalence between hue, value

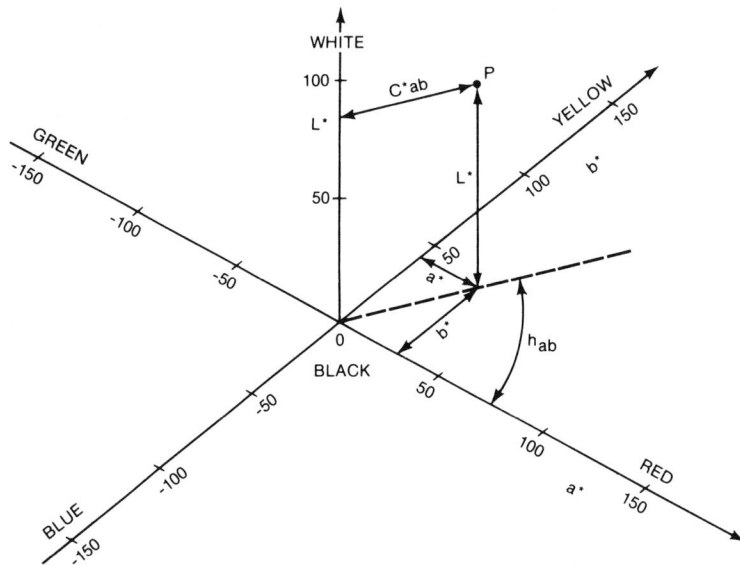

Fig. 4-7. CIE 1976 ($L^*a^*b^*$) uniform color space. The color represented by point P has CIE 1976 a,b lightness $=L^*$, CIE 1976 a,b chroma $=C^*_{ab}$ and CIE 1976 a,b hue angle $=h_{ab}$. The geometrical arrangement of the CIE 1976 ($L^*u^*v^*$) uniform color space is similar.

and chroma units is 1 value step = 2 chroma steps = 3 hue steps (when the hue is at chroma 5).

The Munsell scales are exemplified by a collection of color chips forming an atlas of charts that show linear series for which two of the three variables are constant (figure 4-8). For use as standards or in technical color control, collections of carefully standardized color chips in matte or glossy surface may be obtained from Munsell Color Company, c/o Macbeth, P.O. Box 230, Newburgh, NY 12550, in several different forms. Since 1943 the smoothed renotation for the system, recommended by the Optical Society of America's Colorimetry Committee, has been recognized as the primary standard for these papers. Instructions for obtain-

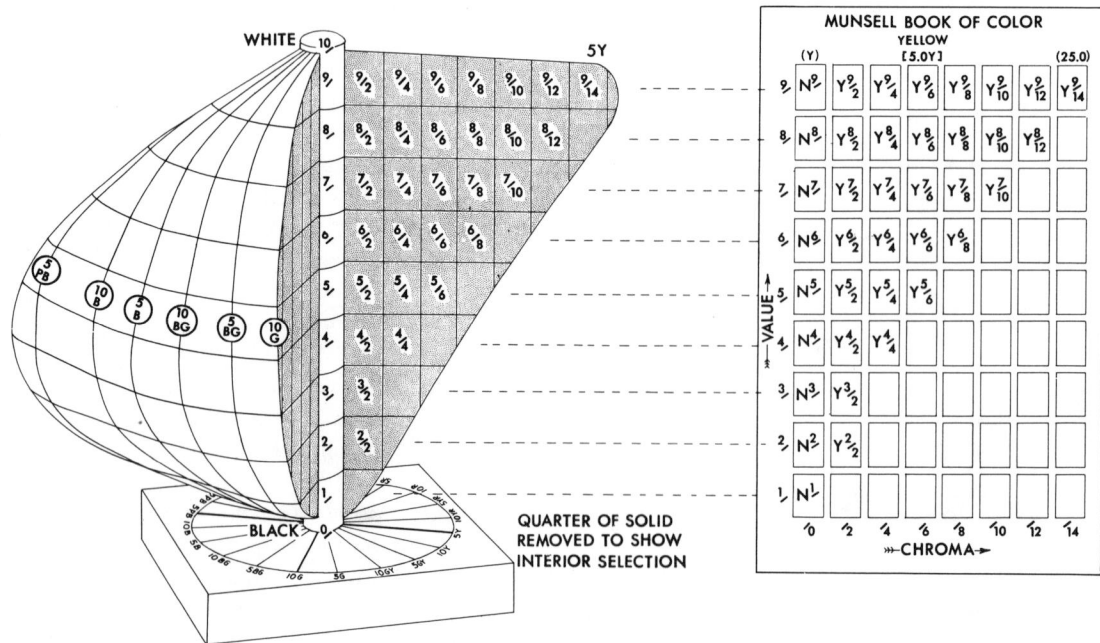

Fig. 4-8. Cut-away view of the Munsell color solid showing notation scales of hue, value and chroma (for example, 5Y 5/4), and the relation of constant hue charts to the three-dimensional representation.

Fig. 4-9. Relationship between Munsell Value and Luminous Reflectance Factor

Munsell Value	Luminous Reflectance Factor (percent)
10.0	100.0
9.5	87.8
9.0	76.7
8.5	66.7
8.0	57.6
7.5	49.4
7.0	42.0
6.5	35.3
6.0	29.3
5.5	24.0
5.0	19.3
4.5	15.2
4.0	11.7
3.5	8.8
3.0	6.4
2.5	4.5
2.0	3.0
1.5	2.0
1.0	1.2
0	0

Fig. 4-10. ISCC-NBS Standard Hue Names and Modifiers

Hue Name	Abbreviation	Hue Name	Abbreviation
red	R	purple	P
reddish orange	rO	reddish purple	rP
orange	O	purplish red	pR
orange yellow	OY	purplish pink	pPk
yellow	Y	pink	Pk
greenish yellow	gY	yellowish pink	yPk
yellow green	YG	brownish pink	brPk
yellowish green	yG	brownish orange	brO
green	G	reddish brown	rBr
bluish green	bG	brown	Br
greenish blue	gB	yellowish brown	yBr
blue	B	olive brown	OlBr
purplish blue	pB	olive	Ol
violet	.V	olive green	OlG

Hue Modifier	Abbreviation	Hue Modifier	Abbreviation
very pale	v.p.	moderate	m.
pale	p.	dark	d.
light grayish	l.gy.	very dark	v.d.
grayish	gy.	brilliant	brill.
dark grayish	d.gy.	strong	s.
blackish	bk.	deep	deep
very light	v.l.	very deep	v.deep
light	l.	vivid	v.

ing Munsell values by calculation, or by conversion through CIE are contained in several publications.[6, 9, 20] The relationship between Munsell value and CIE luminous reflectance factor is summarized in figure 4-9.

ISCC-NBS Method of Designating Colors. The Inter-Society Color Council–National Bureau of Standards method of designating colors appeared in its original form in 1939 as NBS Research Paper RP 1239. The second edition appeared in book form in 1955 as NBS Circular 553, usually called the *Color Names Dictionary* (CND). The first Supplement to the CND, called the *Centroid Color Charts* (1965),[21] provides useful low-cost color charts that illustrate, with 1-in.² samples, the centroid color for as many (251) of the 267 color names in the system as could be matched at that time. Each of the names defines a block in color space. This method is distinguished from all others in that the boundaries of each name are given, rather than points. These boundaries are defined in Munsell notation. A method for pinpointing colors is not provided, but the system does give an understandable color description. When close distinctions must be made between samples that might bear the same ISCC-NBS designation, other specifications such as CIE or Munsell should be used.

The method is simple in principle: terms *light*, *medium* and *dark* designate decreasing degrees of lightness, and the adverb *very* extends the scale to *very light* and *very dark*; adjectives *grayish*, *moderate*, *strong* and *vivid* designate increasing degrees of saturation. These and a series of hue names, used in both noun and adjective forms, are combined to form names for describing color in terms of its three perceptual attributes: hue, lightness and perceived chroma. A few adjectives are added to cover combinations of lightness and perceived chroma: *brilliant* for light and strong, *pale* for light and grayish, and *deep* for dark and strong. The hue names and modifiers are listed in figure 4-10.

The second supplement to the CND, entitled *The Universal Color Language* (UCL), was published also in 1965.[22] The UCL serves as the means of updating the CND. It brings together all the well-known color-order systems and methods of designating colors, and interrelates them in six correlated levels of fineness of color designation, each higher level indicating a finer division of the color solid. It follows closely and extends the original requirements of the ISCC-NBS method of designating colors in the CND. The CND and the UCL have been published together as NBS Special Publication SP 440, with the UCL illustrated in color.[23]

OSA UCS System. The Optical Society of America (OSA) has produced a set of 558 color chips to illustrate uniform visual spacing on a regular rhombohedral lattice.[24] Each chip is intended to be equally different from its 12 nearest neighbors in the lattice. Because of the noneuclidean nature of color space, perfectly uniform spacing is impossible to achieve in a three-dimensional lattice. Thus, the OSA Committee on Uniform Color Scales was forced to make some compromises in specifying the colors. These compromises are not evident on casual study, although they can be seen in more careful analyses. The set is sold by the Optical Society of America, 2010 Massachusetts Avenue NW, Washington, DC 20036, and has generated much interest, especially among artists, designers and color scientists.

Natural Color System (NCS). The NCS[25] is based on an entirely different principle from that of the Munsell or the OSA system. The principle is that of resemblances to six elementary perceived colors: red, yellow, blue, green, black and white. Of these, the four chromatic colors are those in which no trace of the others can be seen. In a geometric representation, they are placed 90° apart on a hue circle. Black and white are perceived colors that contain no trace of each other or of any of the four chromatic colors. They are placed at the apexes of two opposite cones with their bases on the hue circle. Any color resembles at most two of the chromatic elementary colors plus black and white. It is claimed that the degree of resemblance can be estimated to within about 5%, even by naive observers.

DIN System. The DIN color system[26] is the official German standard. It is organized in terms of hue (*Färbton*), saturation (*Sattigung*) and darkness (*Dunkelstufe*). The system is defined in terms of CIE chromaticity and luminance factors with certain compromises made to keep the relationships as simple as possible. It attempts to show uniform steps of color difference and uses CIE colorimetry extensively for interpolation and extrapolation.

Correlation Among Methods. Frequently it is desirable to convert from one system of specification to another, or to convert or identify the color of samples on a chart or color card to terms of another. If the coordinates or samples of one system are given in CIE or Munsell terms, they may be converted or compared to any other system for which a similar conversion is available. Color charts of the German standard 6164 DIN system are provided with both CIE and Munsell equivalents. The Japanese standard system of color specification, JIS Z 8721-1958, is in terms of hue, value and chroma of the Munsell renotation system, according to the CIE x, y coordinates recommended by the Optical Society of America's 1943 subcommittee report.[9] The name blocks of the ISCC-NBS method are in terms of the Munsell renotation system with samples measured in CIE terms. Having a common conversion language helps promote international cooperation and understanding of the subject. Complete sets of CIE-Munsell conversion charts are contained in ASTM Test Method D1535.[20] Many of the available conversions are referenced in a 1957 paper by Nickerson.[27] For more detailed descriptions of color systems or conversions, consult *Color in Business, Science and Industry*.[6] For a useful survey of color order systems, consult reference 28.

Color Temperature

Blackbody characteristics at different temperatures are defined by Planck's radiation law; see chapter 1, Light and Optics. The perceived colors of blackbody radia-tors at different temperatures depend on the state of adaptation of the observer. Figure 4-21 gives an approximate illustration of the perceived colors at various color temperatures for various states of adaptation; it shows that, as the temperature rises, the color changes from red to orange to yellow to white to blue.

The locus of blackbody chromaticities on the x, y diagram is known as the *planckian locus*. Any chromaticity represented by a point on this locus may be specified by color temperature. Strictly speaking, color temperature should not be used to specify a chromaticity that does not lie on the Planckian locus. However, what is called the *correlated* color temperature (the temperature of the blackbody whose chromaticity most resembles that of the light source) is sometimes of interest. The correlated color temperature can be determined from diagrams[29] similar to the one shown in figure 4-11, either by graphical interpolation or by a computer program.[30] It should be noted that the concept becomes less meaningful as the distance from the planckian locus increases.

Equal color differences on the planckian locus are more nearly expressed by equal steps of reciprocal color temperature than by equal steps of color temperature itself. The usual unit is the reciprocal megakelvin (MK^{-1}), so that the reciprocal color temperature is 10^6 divided by the color temperature in kelvins (K). The term "mired" (pronounced mī′rĕd), an abbreviation for "micro-reciprocal-degree," was formerly used for the unit. A difference of one reciprocal megakelvin indicates approximately the same color difference anywhere on the color temperature scale above 1800 K; yet it corresponds to a temperature difference that varies from about 4 K at 2000 K to 100 K at 10,000 K.

Color temperature is a specification of chromaticity only. It does not represent the spectral power distribution of a light source. Chromaticities of many "daylight" lamps plot very close to the planckian locus, and their colors may be specified in terms of correlated color temperature. However, this specification gives no information about their spectral power distributions, which can, and often do, depart widely from that of daylight. In particular, the addition of light from two sources each having blackbody distribution but different color temperatures does not produce a blackbody mixture. Figure 4-12 shows spectral curves for planckian distributions for different color temperatures. Distributions based on daylight[31] are also available for several correlated color temperatures (see chapter 8, Daylighting).

Most tungsten filament lamps approach the relative spectral power distribution of a blackbody quite closely. The color temperature of such lamps varies with the current passing through them. By varying the voltage across such a lamp a series of color temperatures can be obtained covering a very wide range up to about 3600 K.

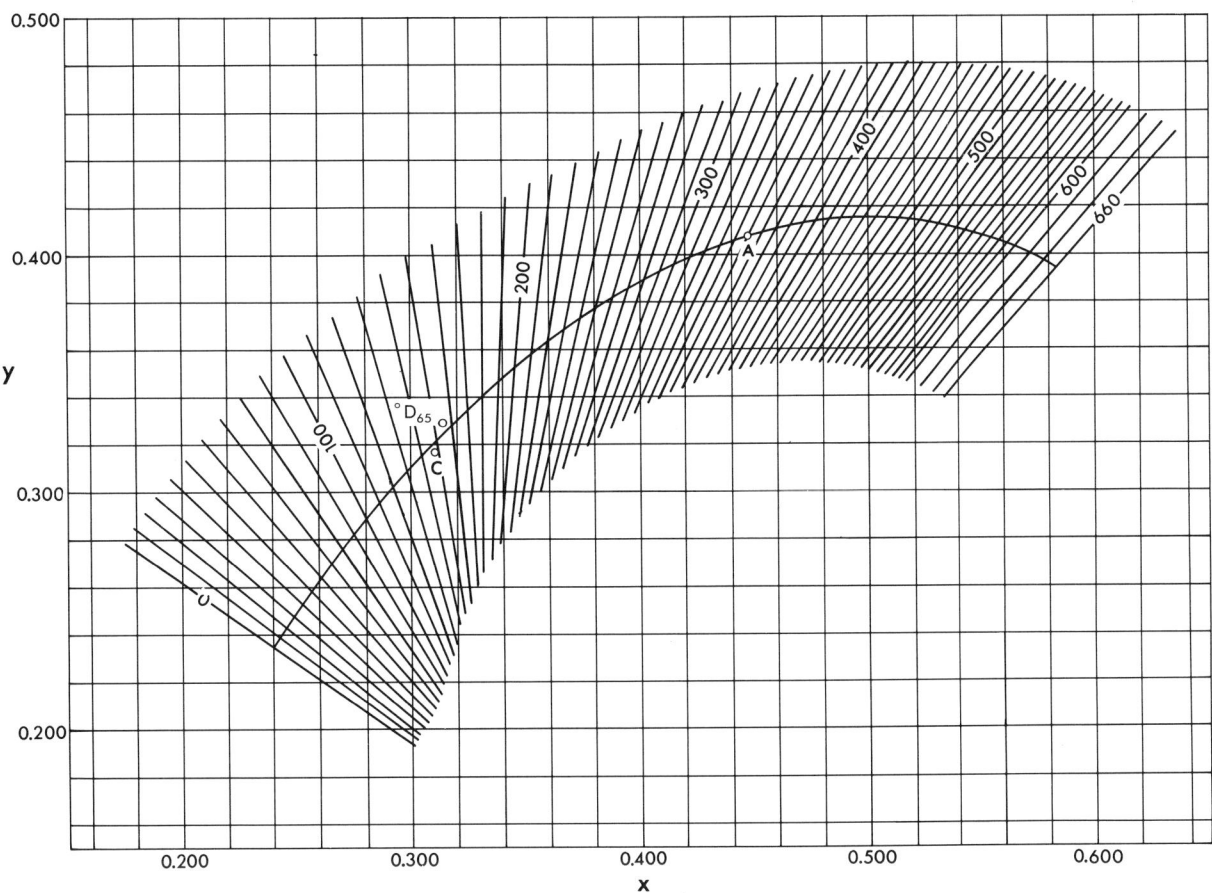

Fig. 4-11. CIE 1931 (x, y) chromaticity diagram showing isotemperature lines. Lines of constant correlated color temperature are given at every 10 reciprocal MK.

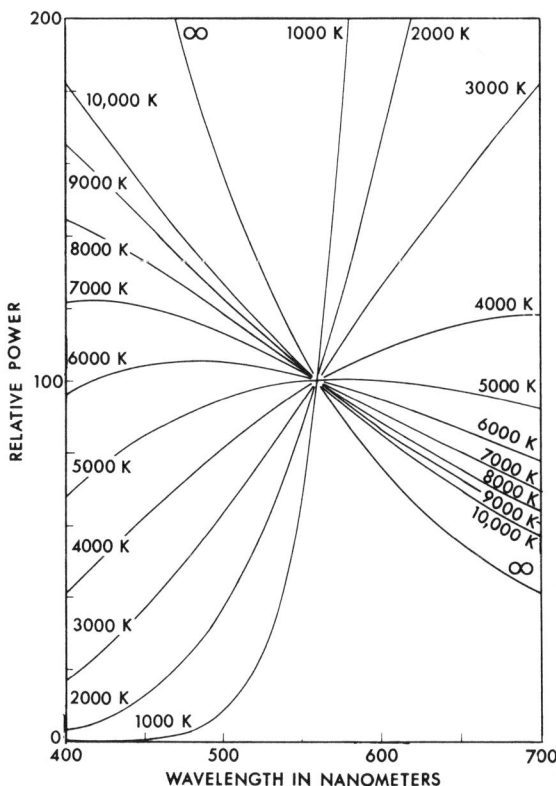

Fig. 4-12. Family of Planckian distribution curves.

Color Constancy and Adaptation[4, 32, 33]

A nonluminous colored object contributes to observed color by modifying the spectral power distribution of the light radiated to the eye. The color of the light reflected or transmitted by the object when it is illuminated by a standard light source is known as the *object color* and can be calculated by assuming certain conventions (as in the CIE system). The color seen when the object is viewed normally in daylight is a perceptual phenomenon, and is referred to as the *perceived color* of the object. While there are exceptions, the perceived colors of objects, when illuminated by various sources, do not change as much as might be expected from the calculated difference in chromaticities. This phenomenon is known as *color constancy*. Objects whose perceived colors change greatly when there is a wide change in illumination, as for example from daylight to incandescent filament light, are said to have *unstable* colors. It is important to remember that whereas the perceived color of an object may not change much with a change of light source color, the object color (as specified for example by CIE chromaticity coordinates) will change. For example, a piece of white paper will appear white under both incandescent light and daylight, but the object color will be quite different in the two cases because the paper, being spectrally neutral, will have almost the same chromaticity as the source in each case.

The impression that the perceived colors of most objects do not change greatly with the spectral power distribution of the light source is due primarily to a low degree of spectral selectivity in daylight and incandescent sources. Color constancy is affected by such factors as awareness of the illuminant, persistence of memory of colors, consistency of attitude toward the object, and adaptation of the visual mechanism. Adaptation is, in effect, a rebalancing of the color response of the visual system as the spectral composition of the visual scene changes. Thus, adaptation tends to counteract the shift in chromaticity of the source, and thereby preserves the appearance of object colors. There are, however, cases where even slight residual shifts may be noticeable and annoying or even intolerable. Such cases may be encountered with foodstuffs, with displayed merchandise or in the grading of various commercial products.

The facts of color constancy and adaptation are not yet known well enough to make possible the computation of color rendering properties of a lamp with sufficient accuracy except when the reference or standard lamp is required to have the same correlated color temperature as the test lamp. When it becomes possible to compute the effects of constancy and adaptation so that the results agree with the subjective experience, then it will be possible to calculate the color rendering properties of a lamp irrespective of its spectral power distribution. In the meantime, as will be seen later, the CIE color rendering index does make an allowance for chromatic adaptation, even though the allowance is not perfectly accurate.

Color Appearance Models

In 1983 the CIE established a committee to develop a mathematical model for color appearance. It is anticipated that the model will eventually have applications such as color rendering indices and the appearance of self-luminous displays. Thus far, two different models have been proposed—one by Hunt[34] and the other by Nayatani et al.[35] In July 1991, neither model had been accepted over the other by the CIE.

Color Contrast

Color appearance is affected markedly by the color of adjacent areas, particularly if one surrounds the other. For example, a color patch appears brighter (less gray) if it is surrounded by a large dark area. It appears dimmer (more gray) if it is surrounded by a similar light area. Juxtaposed areas also induce shifts in hue and saturation in one another. Hues shift in opposite directions in color space, tending to induce complementary hues. Similarly, saturation interacts, magnify-

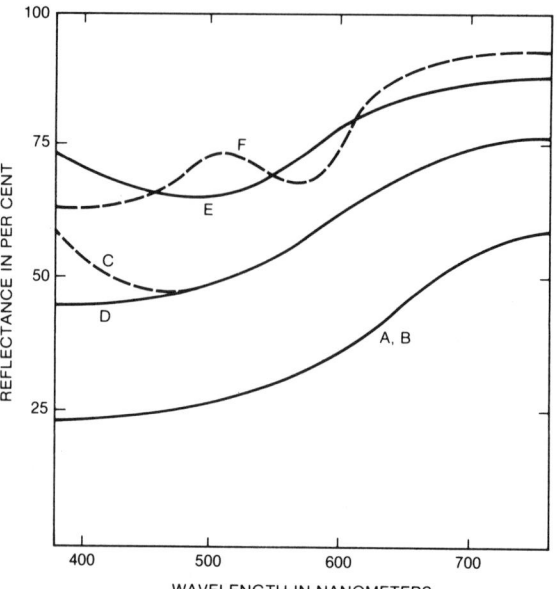

Fig. 4-13. Color matches. A and B are nonmetameric matches and will match for any observer under any light source. C and D will match for any observer under a source with no power at wavelengths less than 500 nm, but will not match for some observers under a source that does have some power in the wavelength region from 380 to 480 nm. C and D produce a source-conditional match, but they do not form a metameric pair, any more than A and B do, because the matching beams do not have different spectral compositions. E and F may form a metameric pair for some source-observer combinations.

ing saturation differences in juxtaposed palates of color. In general, there tends to be a simultaneous and complex shift in all three attributes when colors are placed side by side.

Metameric and Conditional Color Matches

If two lights are visually indistinguishable because they have the same spectral compositions, they are said to form a spectral match. Two lights may, however, be visually indistinguishable in spite of having quite different spectral power distributions. Such a color match is said to be *metameric*, and the lights to be *metameres*. In the CIE system, the computed match is identified by application of color matching functions which show that the tristimulus values for one light are identical to those for the other. If the lights are viewed by an observer characterized by different color matching functions, they may no longer match. All metameric matches are therefore conditional matches. The metameric character of a match sometimes will be revealed by looking at a spectrally selective object and noting that the object is of different color when illuminated by the two lights. This is illustrated in figure 4-22 at the end of the chapter.

Objects with identical spectral reflectance distributions (see samples A and B, figure 4-13) are said to produce an *unconditional* match. They match to everyone, no matter what source illuminates it. If, however, the color-matched reflected light comes from identically illuminated objects that have different spectral reflectances (see samples E and F, figure 4-13), the match is metameric. Substitution of another light source, or another observer, may upset the match; so objects that can produce a metameric match, though identically illuminated, may be said to produce a match that is both observer conditional and source conditional. Such a match is illustrated in figure 4-23.

It has sometimes been wrongly argued that, because the presence of metamerism always corresponds to a conditional match, a metameric match is the same as a conditional match. Not all conditional matches, however, are metameric. Figure 4-13 shows the reflectance curves of two samples, C and D, that have different colors if the light source contains a significant amount of radiant power between 380 and 480 nm, but produce a match if the power of the source is confined to wavelengths greater than 500 nm. Samples C and D thus form a source-conditional match; but no metamerism is involved, because there is no source for which the spectral power distributions reflected from C and D have the same color but are spectrally different.

There is a necessary, though not sufficient, condition that must be satisfied by the spectral reflectances of objects that, identically illuminated, may produce metameric reflected lights. First, the two reflectance curves must be different in some part of the visible spectrum, or the reflected lights will be a spectral rather than a metameric match. Second, to be a color match the two objects must reflect equal amounts of the incident light, and this means that the curves must cross at least once within the visible spectrum. Third, the two objects must not differ in the yellow-blue sense (if the curves cross at only one wavelength within the visible spectrum, a yellow-blue difference is implied; therefore, the curves must cross at least at two wavelengths). Finally, the two objects must not differ in the purple-green sense; (if the curves cross at only two wavelengths, a purple-green difference is implied). Therefore, the reflectance curves of objects capable of producing a metameric match for some combination of trichromatic observer and source must cross at at least three wavelengths in the visible spectrum. Samples E and F, figure 4-13, have this property, and so for some source-observer combination might produce a metameric pair of reflected lights, that is, they may match. For a discussion of the exact conditions under which a certain number of intersections is required, see Stiles and Wyszecki.[36]

USE OF COLOR

Reflectance

Every object reflects some fraction of the light incident upon it. The larger the fraction reflected, the "lighter"

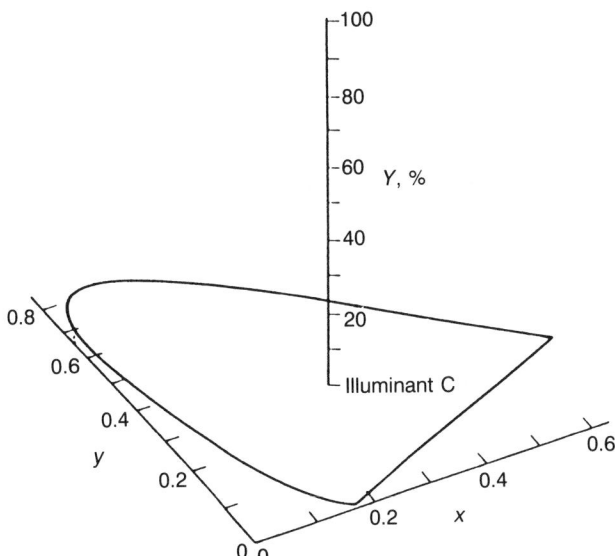

Fig. 4-14. The chromaticity diagram can be extended by adding a third axis for luminance factor. Lighter colors then appear directly above the points representing their chromaticity at a height representing their lightness.

is the color of the object and the higher is the assigned Munsell value. In the Munsell color solid of figure 4-8, the lightness dimension is in the vertical direction, along the scale of Munsell value, and ranges from black at the bottom to perfectly reflecting at the top. In the two-dimensional CIE chromaticity diagram of figure 4-4 are plotted the two CIE coordinates which are related to Munsell perceived hue and to Munsell perceived chroma or saturation, constituting a horizontal plane in the color solid of figure 4-8.

Figure 4-14 shows how the lightness dimension relates to the chromaticity diagram. In the CIE system, the Y tristimulus value of the light reflected from an object represents the luminous reflectance factor expressed as the percentage of the light that would be reflected by a perfectly reflecting diffuser. Computation of the percentage luminous reflectance is demonstrated in figure 4-5, and its relation to Munsell value is shown in figure 4-9.

The luminous reflectance scale is not visually uniform between 0 and 100%, black and white. An object that reflects 50% does not look halfway between black and white, but looks much nearer to white. On the other hand, the purpose of the Munsell value scale is to illustrate equal visual steps for a given set of standard conditions. In figure 4-9 (a condensed table), reflectance and Munsell value units are related. Thus, under daylight conditions, and for a light gray surround, a Munsell value of 5 should look about halfway in lightness between the black and white endpoints of the scale. Yet the luminance factor of a value-5 sample is only about 20%. A color with Munsell value 7 is called a light color, yet it reflects less than half (only 42%) of the light it receives. This is an important point for lighting designers to consider, for unless all the colors in the color scheme of a room layout are very light, well over 50% of the light is absorbed. If value-5 colors are used, as much as 80% of the incident light may be absorbed. With practice in the use of a Munsell value scale, particularly, the special set of Munsell scales developed for lighting and interior designers, one may learn to estimate Munsell values rather accurately, and convert them to luminous reflectance by means of figure 4-9. Value-reflectance conversion tables for every Munsell value in steps of 0.1 are available in several publications[6,9,20] or may be calculated as follows:[6]

for $Y > 0.9$,

$$V = UY^W \qquad (4\text{-}18a)$$

for $Y \geqslant 0.9$,

$$V = AY^{1/3} - B - \frac{C}{(DY - E)^2 + F}$$
$$+ \frac{G}{Y^H} + J\sin(KY^{1/3} + 1)$$
$$+ \frac{M}{Y}\sin[N(Y - 2)]$$
$$- \frac{P}{QY}\sin[S(Y - T)] \qquad (4\text{-}18b)$$

where

$A = 2.49268$,	$G = 0.0133$,	$P = 0.0037$,
$B = 1.5614$,	$H = 2.3$,	$Q = 0.44$,
$C = 0.985$,	$J = 0.0084$,	$S = 1.28$,
$D = 0.1073$,	$K = 4.1$,	$T = 0.53$,
$E = 3.084$,	$M = 0.0221$,	$U = 0.87445$,
$F = 7.54$,	$N = 0.39$,	$W = 0.9967$,

Y = luminous reflectance relative to a perfect diffuser, in %,
V = Munsell value.

Multiply Y by 1.0257 to convert it to the formerly used scale on which smoked magnesium oxide had the value of 100.

The luminous reflectance of spectrally nonselective white, gray and black objects remains constant for all light sources, but the luminous reflectances of colored objects will differ in accordance with the spectral power distribution of the light source. For example, with illumination from incandescent sources, which have relatively high radiant power in the middle and long-wavelength portions of the visible spectrum and low power at the short-wavelength end, yellow objects appear lighter and blue objects darker than they do under daylight illumination; under blue sky the reverse will be true. On many sets of Munsell scales for judging reflectance, reflectances of each sample are given for three light sources: CIE A at 2856 K, CIE D_{65} at 6500 K and cool white fluorescent at 4300 K.

Light walls and ceilings, whether neutral or chromatic, are much more efficient than dark walls in distributing light uniformly. Step-by-step changes studied by Brainerd and Massey in 1942[37] have been reported in terms of illuminance and coefficients of utilization and are shown in figure 4-15. Mathematical analyses by Moon[38] on the effect of wall colors on illuminance and luminance ratios in cubical rooms show that an increase of wall reflectance by a factor of 9 can result in an increase in illuminance by a factor of about 3. Moon[38] has also published much information concerning spectral and colorimetric characteristics of materials used in room interiors.

When neutral and chromatic surfaces of equal reflectance are uniformly and directly illuminated, they will have equal luminances. But by interreflections in a room, the light reaching a working surface will have undergone several reflections from ceiling and walls, and the perceived colors of ceiling and walls, as well the light reaching the working surface, will have become more saturated. Figure 4-16 shows the measured spectral reflectance (dashed curve) of a pale pink surface. The spectral power distribution of incoming sunlight is represented by the topmost solid curve. The

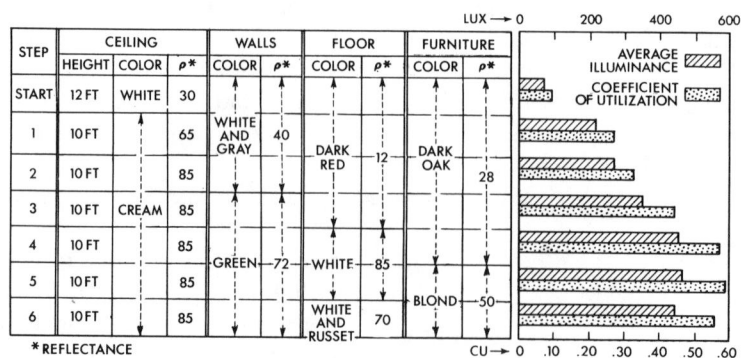

Fig. 4-15. Variation of illuminance and utilization coefficient with color scheme. The luminaire used for these results had a general diffuse distribution.

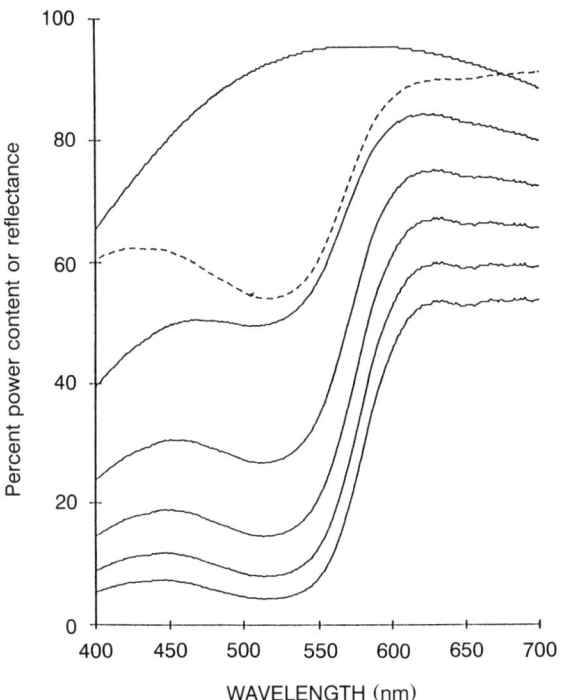

Fig. 4-16. Graph showing how the spectral power distribution of sunlight when interreflected on a surface (spectral reflectance shown by the dashed line) changes with successive reflections in distribution and overall intensity. The top curve is the original source and the bottom the light after 5 reflections.

finite rectangular room, and O'Brien has developed and used computer methods and results to provide charts and tables to aid designers in making detailed predictions of illuminance and luminance distributions in rooms, a prerequisite for solving the problem for color interreflections. In France, Barthès has published experimental measurements for a model room.[42] In Japan, Krossawa[43] has computed data on a closed surface painted with a uniform color and derived a general empirical formula for the color shift due to interreflections for different colors. Yamanaka and Nayatani[44] have compared results for computed and actual rooms, and consider the agreements to be quite satisfactory under the model conditions. Gradually the data based on such studies will reach a form in which the practicing designer can use them. Meanwhile designers should understand the general principles so that color change by room interreflections can be taken into consideration in planning a lighting layout.

Color Schemes: Choosing Suitable Colors

No set of simple rules can allow for tastes of different people, or for different conditions and changing fashions. However, the following suggestions provide a place to start:

lower curves are the result, respectively, of one to five reflections from the pale pink surface. The remaining light deepens in color progressively. Figure 4-17 lists, for the six SPDs, the computed chromaticity, remaining power content, remaining lumen content and perceived color of the light. It is clear that multiple reflections are costly in lumen content of the illumination and can cause unpleasant intensification of its color.

Spencer and Sanborn,[39] O'Brien,[40] and Jones and Jones[41] have published basic studies in this field. Spencer and Sanborn have analytically found the color shift due to interreflection in an infinite room and in a

1. Ceilings are assumed to be white, or slightly tinted. (Note: Some hospital ceilings can be treated as a fifth wall for the supine patient.)
2. Walls, floors and other structural elements, which will be changed infrequently, must be considered first in the color scheme.
3. Smaller areas, such as machinery or furniture, need only blend or contrast with walls and floors.
4. Color schemes, represented by material, surfacing or paint (coating) samples, should be assembled and evaluated under lighting conditions closely duplicating those under which the

Fig. 4-17. Characteristics of Illumination as it Enters a Space and After Successive Reflections

Number of Reflections	Computed Chromaticity		Remaining Radiant Flux (%)	Remaining Luminous Flux (%)	Perceived Color
	x	y			
0	0.345	0.352	100	100	white
1	0.386	0.350	71	69	pinkish white
2	0.428	0.350	54	50	orange-pink
3	0.469	0.350	42	37	deep orange pink
4	0.507	0.350	34	28	deep orange pink
5	0.540	0.350	28	22	reddish-orange

scheme will be used. This will help avoid the problem of significant color shifts and of failures in metameric matches.

5. Because major surfaces can contribute considerably to the distribution of light by reflection and interreflection, the luminous reflectance (Munsell value) should be high where high task luminances are important.

6. The prime purpose of the color scheme needs consideration. Seeing may be most important in a schoolroom, dignity in a church, a sense of well being in a factory, an atmosphere of excitement in a circus, and quiet in an office.

7. Limitations may exist for redecoration schemes that must be built around existing colors of carpeting or other flooring, draperies or furniture.

The 1962 report of the Color Committee[3] has three useful color charts. The first provides scales of hue, value and chroma to help in understanding color terminology used in interior design. The second provides a series of 66 color chips arranged to show strong versus weak chromas, and warm versus cool colors, with reflectances and Munsell notation for each sample, for colors used for interior surfaces. The third shows a 10-sample hue circle of typical wall colors at 60% reflectance, and three sample color scheme selections.

To assist the designer, the following narrative describes current thinking on color schemes. Only limited research data support these conclusions, however. Color schemes usually are variations of basic plans classified as monochromatic (single-hued), complementary, adjacent or analogous, split complementary, or triads. The dominant character usually is determined by the largest area, and in three-hued schemes this usually is the least saturated. A large pattern, strong in value contrast, makes a room seem smaller; a small pattern, in gentle contrast and high reflectance, can make it seem larger. The absence of pattern can provide the illusion of maximum space. The effects of strong contrasts of color or pattern are similar to each other, that is, they both are stimulating, make people restless and make time seem longer. They are effective for corridors, places of entertainment, entrance halls, public washrooms, quick lunch counters and other locations where it is desired that people spend a short time; but they are undesirable in hospitals, for example. Gentle contrast is restful and makes time seem shorter. The play of molded form and texture can add interest; contrasts of natural wood, brick, stone and woven materials add interest to smooth painted walls.

Although personal tastes in color vary with climate, nationality, age, gender and personality, there is almost universal agreement to call yellows, yellow-reds, reds, and red-purples warm colors, and to call greens, blue-greens, blues, and purple-blues cool colors. All grays approach neutral.

The apparent size and position of objects are affected by color. High-chroma, warm colors usually are the most advancing, and cool colors the most receding. Lowering the chroma reduces the effect on apparent position. Light colors make objects appear larger; dark colors make objects appear smaller.

Selection Guide

By considering factors such as warmth, spaciousness and excitement level, it is possible to determine a suitable dominant color and degree of contrast. These considerations may be dealt with in four steps[3] to help decide on values, hues, chromas and contrasts in the Munsell system.

Step 1. This step helps decide the *value*, that is, how light or dark a color scheme should be. If a high level is necessary, colors with a high reflectance should be used. Dark colors tend to reduce luminance and contrast, and produce luminance ratios that are unsatisfactory for efficient seeing. For areas in which illuminances of 750 lx (75 fc) or higher are recommended, the dominant values should be kept high, with reflectances of 40–60% or higher where the task is critical. Where lower illuminances are recommended, around 300 lx (30 fc), lower values may be introduced, at reflectances of 35–60%. For still lower levels, the dominant values may be even lower, with reflectances for large areas down to 15–35%. Where the best feasible visibility at low illuminances must be the goal, as for example in a parking garage, light colored (high-value) walls and ceilings are recommended.

Step 2. This step helps decide the *hue*. Use warm, exciting, advancing colors where rooms have northern exposure, cool temperatures and low noise element; where the room is too large and has smooth textures; where there is light physical exertion, time exposure is short, and a stimulating atmosphere is required; and where lamps are cool fluorescent. Use cool, restful, receding colors for rooms with southern exposure, warm temperatures and high noise element; for small rooms with rough texture; where physical exertion is heavy, time exposure is long, and a restful atmosphere is desired; and where lamps are incandescent or warm fluorescent.

Step 3. This step helps decide the *chroma*. Strong chromas are used primarily for advertising, display, accents and food merchandising; achromatic colors are primarily used for fashion areas, general interiors and other merchandising. Use strong chromas if the time of occupant exposure is short, general level of responsibility low, lively atmosphere desired, noise level low, and sense of taste or smell unimportant. Use gray, low-chroma colors if the time exposure is long, responsibility high, atmosphere of dignity desired, noise level high, or sense of taste or smell important.

Step 4. This step helps decide the amount of *contrast*. Contrast is obtained by using light with dark, low and high chromas, and hues that are complementary. Little or no contrast should be used if the time of occupant exposure is long, the room size is small, a dignified atmosphere is required or the wall surfaces are textured. Strong contrast should be used if the time of occupant exposure is short, the room size is large, a lively or exciting atmosphere is desired or the wall surfaces are flat.

These recommendations represent a consensus from working knowledge of designers and architects, based on field experience. Inasmuch as results from scientific investigations do not contradict them, they remain generally accepted. The designer must realize that in some cases a new or different approach may overrule common practice for a number of reasons.

Color Preference

Research by Helson[45-48] and others[49,50] have added to our understanding of color preference in lighting. In his reports, Helson states the pleasantness of object colors depends on the interaction of the light source with the background color and with the hue, lightness and saturation of the object color. The best background colors for enhancing the pleasantness of object colors were found to have either very high Munsell values (8/ or 9/) or very low values (2/ or 1/), and, with only one exception, very low or zero chroma. The background color was found to be more important than the spectral power distribution of the light source. Neutrals rank high as background colors, but very low for object colors. High chromas are preferred over low for object colors.

The chief single factor responsible for pleasant color harmonies was found to be lightness contrast between object and background colors. The greater the lightness contrast, the greater are the chances of pleasant color combinations; this may be because lightness contrast is also most important for pattern vision. The influences of hue and saturation difference cannot be stated simply. A certain amount of variety, change, differentiation or contrast is pleasant; sameness, monotony and repetition tend to be unpleasant. Configurations of colors should contain some variations in hue, lightness and saturation, and over a period of time different configurations of colors should be employed to prevent satiation by overly familiar patterns of stimulation. Color preferences may differ due to such factors as function, size, configuration, climate and socio-cultural background.

Safety Colors

Safety colors are used to indicate the presence of a hazard or safety facility such as an explosive hazard or a first aid station. These are carefully developed colors that are specified in American National Standard Z53.1-1979.[51] The background around these safety colors should be kept as free of competing colors as possible, and the number of other colors in the area should be kept to a minimum. These colors should be illuminated by a light source to levels which will permit positive identification of the color and the hazard or situation which it identifies, but which will not distort it and thereby obscure the message it conveys.

The specification of these colors is given in figure 4-24. Designers must be aware that these color specifications are based on illuminant C. The colors will be recognizable under daylight and conventional incandescent and fluorescent light sources, which have a broad spectrum, but high-intensity discharge light sources, which have come into use in industry and may be widely used in the future, render some colors differently than the sources mentioned above. They may cause some confusion, especially at illuminances of 5 lx (0.5 fc) and lower, which are not uncommon in industrial spaces. Possible solutions are given in references 52 and 53.

Color tolerance charts showing the safety colors and their tolerance limits are available from Hale Color Consultants.

Chromaticity and Illuminance

The chromaticity of the light source should be matched to the illuminances.[54] From experience it has been found that at low illuminances a "warm light" (less than 3300 K) is usually preferred, but the color temperature of the light source should increase as the illuminance increases.[55] Recent data, however, both support and contradict this assertion, so these statements cannot be taken as conclusive.

COLOR RENDERING

As previously discussed, lamps cannot be assessed for color rendering properties by visual inspection of the lamps themselves. To provide a color rendering index (CRI), it is necessary to have accurate and precise spectroradiometric measurements of light sources (see chapter 2, Measurement of Light and other Radiant Energy). It is also necessary to understand the mechanisms of color vision, particularly chromatic adaptation. Knowledge in this area is still incomplete. However, in most cases it is possible to provide a useful answer. The recommendations below are based on the following assumptions.

The color shift that occurs when an object is observed under different light sources may be classified in three ways: as a colorimetric shift, an adaptive shift, or a resultant color shift in which the first two are combined. To understand the subject it is extremely important that the three concepts be understood:

1. *Colorimetric shift* is the difference between the color (luminance and chromaticity) of an object illuminated by a nonstandard source and the color of the same object illuminated by the standard source, usually measured on a scale appropriate for assessing color differences.
2. *Adaptive color shift* is the difference in the perceived color of an object caused solely by chromatic adaptation.
3. *Resultant color shift* is the difference between the perceived color of an object illuminated by a nonstandard source and that of the same object illuminated by the standard source for specified viewing conditions. The conditions usually are that the observer shall have normal color vision and be adapted to the environment illuminated by each source in turn. The color shift is the resultant of the colorimetric and adaptive color shifts.

The colorimetric shift can be determined using standard CIE conventions, but determination of the adaptive shift requires some assumptions about the effects of chromatic adaptation.

CIE Test-Color Method

The CIE recommends a test-color method for measuring and specifying the color rendering properties of light sources.[1] It rates lamps in terms of a color rendering index (CRI) that represents the degree of resultant color shift of a test object under a test lamp in comparison with its color under a standard lamp of the same correlated color temperature. The indices are based on a general comparison of the lengths of chromaticity-difference vectors in the 1964 uniform color space. The rating consists of a *general index*, R_a, which is the mean of the *special indices*, R_i, for a set of eight test-color samples that have been found adequate to cover the hue circuit (see figure 4-25). This may be supplemented by special indices based on special-pur-

pose test samples, such as CIE colors 9–14. Unless otherwise specified, the reference light source for sources with a correlated color temperature below 5000 K is a planckian radiator of the same correlated color temperature (see figure 4-12). For 5000 K and above the reference source is one of a series of spectral energy distributions of daylight based on reconstituted daylight data[31] developed from daylight measurements made in Enfield, England; Rochester, N.Y.; and Ottawa, Canada (see chapter 8, Daylighting). Tables of colorimetric data are included in the CIE recommendations for planckian radiators up to 5000 K, and on these reconstituted daylight curves from 5000 K to infinity, for eight general and six special test-color samples.

The current version of the CIE method is basically the same as an earlier version but with a better correction for the adaptive color shift. A paper by Nickerson and Jerome[56] on the earlier version provides a working text and formulas, discusses the meaning of the index and shows applications to a number of lamps. A 1962 IES report[4] discusses in more detail the problems involved in the more than ten year study of the subject. It indicates some of the problems, particularly those of chromatic adaptation, that remain to be solved before an all-purpose, completely satisfactory method can be established for rating a lamp, regardless of its color, against a single standard (probably daylight). Because of these problems, the index is not an absolute figure. For example, a 6500-K daylight lamp and a 3000-K warm white lamp having equal values on the general color rendering index will differ from their respective reference illuminants, the CIE phase of daylight D_{65} and the 3000-K planckian radiator, by about the same amount. These reference illuminants differ from one another in their color rendering, and so will the two lamps tested, even though they have the same general color rendering index.[1] Figure 4-18 shows the basis for the CIE index where the test and reference lamp have the same chromaticity.

CIE ratings are in terms of a single index, R_a, but to provide more information on the color rendering properties of a lamp, it is recommended that this be accompanied by a listing of the eight special index values on which the rating is based. Since the eight test samples cover the hue circuit, this makes it possible to obtain a record of the relative colorimetric shift in the different hues under the test lamp. Plotting the chromaticity difference vectors provides even more information, for this indicates the direction, as well as the degree, of colorimetric shift that is involved.

If two lamps differ in R_i by about 5 units, the colors of test sample i rendered by the two lamps will be just perceptibly different under the best conditions, provided that the directions of the color shifts are nearly

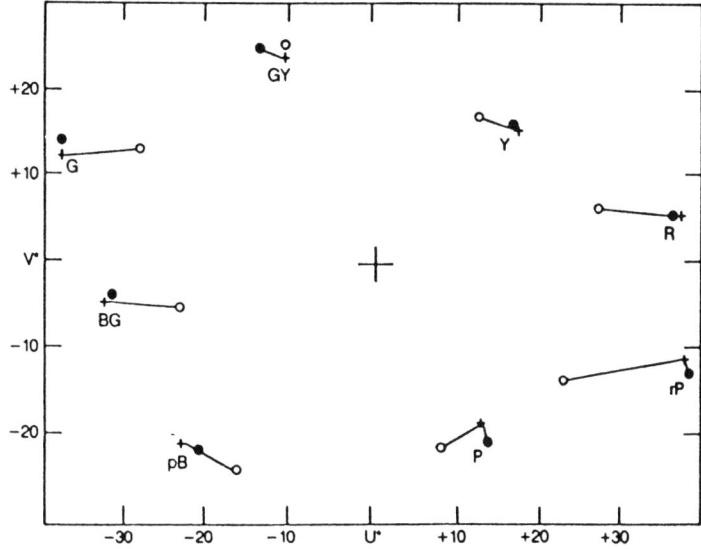

Fig. 4-18. Graphic basis for color rendering index.

the same. No such simple rule can be given for R_a. It is obtained as the mean of eight R_i values, and even when two lamps have exactly the same R_a, differences of about 5 units or more in one or more of the R_i values may still be possible, so that their color rendering properties will be different for the object colors in question. Where the R_a values are close to 100, the R_i values are unlikely to show variations large enough to result in noticeable color differences. But as the value of R_a decreases from 100, the corresponding special indices R_i show increasing spread. Ratings are illustrated in figure 4-19 for a number of typical lamps. The best color rendering lamps not only have a high index, but also have the least variation in special indices for the different hues that are used as test samples. The closer one comes to a perfect color matching lamp, the tighter must be these tolerances.

It makes sense to compare color rendering indices only of lamps with chromaticities close to each other. The standard illuminants A and D_{65} both have CRIs of 100 yet render colors quite differently. Likewise, commercial daylight and warm white lamps will render colors differently even if their CRI values match.

The CIE may change its recommendations for computing CRI in the future. The present method is based on the CIE 1964 uniform color space, which is now obsolete. In any case, it will eventually be more appropriate to change the basis of color rendering to a color appearance model.

Visual Clarity

The concept of "visual clarity" has been used in several studies[57,58] to indicate a preferred appearance of scenes containing colored objects when illuminated by certain sources. "Visual clarity" seems to be a combination of various factors, such as perceived color and contrast, color rendering, color discrimination, color preference and border sharpness, but it is not as yet a well-understood notion.

LIGHT SOURCES FOR COLOR APPRAISAL, COLOR MATCHING AND COLOR REPRODUCTION

General Principles

General lighting may be unsatisfactory for the precise appraisal of the colors of objects, including matching and reproducing colors. Such tasks are necessary in industries that make and market colorants, such as pigments and dyes, and in arts and industries involving color production, such as painting, textile dyeing, photography and color printing. These tasks are also necessary in commercial evaluation of naturally colored objects such as fibers, foods, minerals and gemstones. Although color processes are often controlled by means of instrumentation, the ultimate approval of colored products is based on visual judgment, generally the comparison of the product with a colored standard. The grade of a natural material may be based on a visual judgment of the correspondence of its colors to a series of standards.

Since two objects may match under one kind of illumination, but not match under another, the kind of illumination used for inspection is crucial. The specification of the illuminant must be expressed in any written or oral contract or other commitment involving color production. Very often, the intention is to have

Fig. 4-19. Color and Color Rendering Characteristics of Common Light Sources

Lamp	x	y	CCT	R_a	R_1	R_2	R_3	R_4	R_5	R_6	R_7	R_8	R_9	R_{10}	R_{11}	R_{12}	R_{13}	R_{14}
Fluorescent																		
CIE F1, Daylight	0.313	0.337	6430	76	69	84	92	73	74	80	82	53	-47	61	67	75	73	95
CIE F2, Cool white	0.372	0.375	4230	64	56	77	90	57	59	67	74	33	-84	45	46	54	60	94
CIE F3, White	0.409	0.394	3450	57	48	72	90	46	49	59	69	21	-102	36	31	38	52	94
CIE F4, Warm white	0.440	0.403	2940	51	42	70	90	38	41	54	65	11	-111	31	18	25	47	94
CIE F5	0.314	0.345	6350	72	63	80	91	67	68	75	81	48	-68	54	61	68	67	94
CIE F6	0.378	0.388	4150	59	49	72	88	51	52	60	73	27	-105	35	38	42	54	93
CIE F7, Broad-band	0.313	0.329	6500	90	89	92	91	91	90	89	93	87	61	78	89	87	90	94
CIE F8, Broad-band	0.346	0.359	5000	95	97	96	91	97	96	93	96	97	98	88	95	90	97	95
CIE F9, Broad-band	0.374	0.373	4150	90	90	93	90	90	89	88	94	89	70	79	87	83	90	94
CIE F10, 3 narrow bands	0.346	0.359	5000	81	93	90	53	86	83	74	89	80	27	42	66	51	93	69
CIE F11, 3 narrow bands	0.380	0.377	4000	83	98	93	50	88	87	77	88	79	25	47	72	53	97	67
CIE F12, 3 narrow bands	0.437	0.404	3000	83	99	95	54	89	88	83	89	68	1	53	77	53	96	68
Cool white deluxe	0.375	0.367	4080	89	92	91	84	89	90	86	89	89	73	74	90	78	92	90
Warm white deluxe	0.440	0.403	2940	73	72	80	81	71	69	67	83	65	15	49	80	43	73	88
HID																		
Metal halide	0.374	0.383	4220	67	59	84	88	63	67	84	67	21	-113	69	63	78	67	92
Metal halide, coated	0.388	0.379	3800	70	64	88	86	66	71	89	67	25	-88	78	67	84	72	91
Mercury, clear	0.308	0.377	6410	18	-9	32	51	7	8	8	47	-4	-299	-58	-17	-21	1	70
Mercury, coated	0.405	0.402	3600	49	44	60	59	45	40	36	69	41	-68	-5	20	-9	46	75
High pressure sodium	0.519	0.417	2100	24	15	66	55	-5	14	56	37	-45	-197	46	-29	34	21	71
Xenon	0.324	0.324	5920	94	94	91	90	96	95	92	95	96	81	81	97	93	92	95
Other																		
Low pressure sodium	0.569	0.421	1740	-44	-68	44	-2	-101	-67	29	-23	-165	-492	20	-128	-21	-39	31
Tungsten halogen	0.424	0.399	3190	100	100	100	100	100	100	100	100	100	100	99	100	100	100	100

the product match the standard satisfactorily under any kind of illumination likely to be encountered. This requires that the product be compared with the standard under several kinds of illumination, typically two phases of daylight of widely different correlated color temperature, as well as fluorescent and incandescent light. Natural daylight is highly variable, not available at night, and not easily available in interior spaces, so a source of electric light that simulates daylight is usually used.

Clearly, lighting for these purposes must meet specifications far more stringent than those that are applied to general interior and exterior lighting, and these specifications have been agreed to by national and international standardizing bodies. Fortunately for the practicing illuminating engineer, the specifications are easily met, because viewing booths that exclude extraneous light and provide several kinds of illumination meeting these standards are commercially available and are customarily used in these applications.

Light used for these purposes must have a specified spectral power distribution. Because of the widespread natural occurrence and deliberate use of fluorescence, the ultraviolet spectrum must be specified as well as the visible spectrum. Other, less restrictive means of specifying light are not satisfactory. A given correlated color temperature permits an infinite variety of chromaticities and a given chromaticity permits an infinite variety of spectra. The spectral quality of light sources that simulate standard daylight for judging colors is assessed by a method adopted by the CIE.[59] The basic premise of this method is that the best of several available sources is the one that causes the least average color difference for specified pairs of hypothetical colored surfaces which match metamerically in daylight.

In some cases, especially in the grading of natural materials, the color difference between grades may be accentuated and made more readily apparent by a well-chosen light source. For example, if materials yellow with age, yellowness may be regarded as undesirable. Slight differences in yellowness can be more readily perceived with a light source that appears white but is rich in the short-wavelength end of the spectrum.

Illuminance affects color judgment and must be specified. Dark colors require more illuminance than light colors.

Some materials, notably wood and textiles as well as metallic and pearlescent paints, may match under certain angular conditions of illumination and viewing, but not under others. For this reason, the geometry of illumination and viewing must be specified. In most specifications, opaque surfaces are illuminated at 45° to their normal and viewed on the normal, or the reverse of this arrangement.

The background or surround color influences color judgments, so it must be specified. Small color differences are best perceived if the surround is of a color between the two colors being compared. This ideal is usually approximated by the use of a neutral (black, gray or white) surround of about the same lightness as the specimens. A neutral surround does not influence the appearance of hue.

When glossy specimens are viewed at 45° to their normal, something on the opposite side of the normal may be seen reflected in the surfaces. That specularly reflected light is added to the diffusely reflected light, interfering with color judgment. It is standard practice to minimize this effect by placing black velvet on the opposite side.

Color differences are usually controlled through the use of a set of seven colors which constitute a color tolerance standard. The set utilizes an ideal color, the lightest and darkest acceptable colors of the same hue and chroma, the two extremes of acceptable hue variation with the same lightness and chroma, and the weak and strong (chroma) limits with the same lightness and hue. The colors are arranged on a card with slots permitting the direct comparison of the underlying surface with each of the standard colors.

Standard Viewing Conditions

The grading of raw cotton, on the basis of its color, is a visual task of great commercial importance. Studies in the U.S. Department of Agriculture, reported as early as 1939, provided the basis for specifying 600–800 lx (60–80 fc) and a spectral power distribution closely simulating daylight, with a correlated color temperature of 7500 K, for this task. To minimize glare, the geometric relationship of the luminaires to the work surface is also specified.[60]

Recommendations for viewing textiles have been made by the American Association of Textile Chemists and Colorists, and for judging diamonds by the Gemological Institute of America. The results of experiments coordinated by a committee of the Inter-Society Color Council indicated that textile color matchers prefer a range of correlated color temperatures that depends on the illuminance, as shown in figure 4-20.[61]

Conditions for comparison of opaque specimens, in general, have been standardized by the American Society for Testing and Materials (ASTM).[62] Several different spectral power distributions are specified, so proposed color matches can be examined under various lights to test for or optimize metamerism. In addition to daylight, a light simulating sunlight, a typical tungsten source, and cool white fluorescent lamps are specified. For materials of medium lightness, an illuminance of 1000–1250 lx (100–125 fc) is recommended

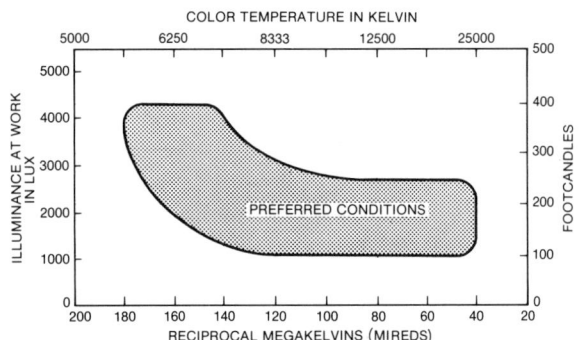

Fig. 4-20. Tests conducted under the direction of the Inter-Society Color Council show the characteristics of preferred daylight illumination conditions for color matching, grading and classing.

for critical evaluation, and 750–1750 lx (75–175 fc) for general evaluation. For very light materials, 500 lx (50 fc) is adequate, and for very dark materials, the illuminance may be increased to as much as 2000 lx (200 fc).

Specifications for viewing conditions in photography and graphic arts have been standardized by the American National Standards Institute (ANSI).[63] In these applications, it is standard practice to use illumination simulating a phase of daylight having a correlated color temperature of 5000 K. Large transparencies are viewed against a luminous surface of standard luminance and spectral distribution, and small transparencies are viewed by means of a standardized projection system. Both methods permit direct comparison of transparencies and opaque prints.

In the United States, standards other than those for photography and color printing specify a phase of daylight having a correlated color temperature of 7500 K, typical of light from a slightly overcast north sky (south sky in the southern hemisphere). Most of the rest of the world follows a recommendation of the CIE to use 6500 K, which corresponds to average daylight. Viewing booths of both kinds are commercially available.

Color Reproduction in Photography, Television and Printing

Color photography is based on the same general principle as color vision: the eye employs three kinds of cones, and color film has three photosensitive layers, each maximally sensitive to a different part of the visible spectrum. Films designed for making transparencies are very different from those designed for making opaque prints, but the same three-layer principle is used. The spectral sensitivities of the three film layers differ considerably from those of the human visual system, and the dye images are at best metameric matches to the objects photographed. Objects that match when viewed directly may not match in the photograph, and objects that do not match when viewed directly may match in the photograph. Color films are designed to give satisfactory color rendition when the subject is illuminated with a specific kind of source. Flash lamps, for example, are designed to simulate daylight. ANSI and the International Organization for Standardization (ISO) have adopted standards specifying light sources for testing films, the color contribution of camera lenses and methods for testing flash equipment, as well as conditions for viewing prints and transparencies.[64–68]

Television images are mediated through the spectral sensitivities of the camera, the electronic processing of the image and the three color phosphors on the face of the display tube. The problems associated with color reproduction in photography are also experienced in television, with the added burden of a far greater variety in the characteristics of the final display medium. The quality of the color reproduction depends, of course, on the spectral quality of the illumination of the scene to be televised, as well as the characteristics of the equipment.

In color printing, various kinds of plates are used to apply colored inks to paper. The inks are usually yellow, magenta, cyan and black. The plates are made by photoengraving or by electronic scanners. Like color photography, color printing may also suffer from discrepancies in color appearance with the actual objects.

The color rendition of color reproduction processes can be evaluated by the use of a commercially available colored test chart designed for this purpose.[69] The chart is photographed, viewed by television equipment or printed, and the resulting image is compared with the original chart or a second chart of the same kind, under standardized viewing conditions. The comparison can be made quantitative by performing color difference measurements. These charts may also be used to make simple direct visual appraisals of the color rendering of light sources.

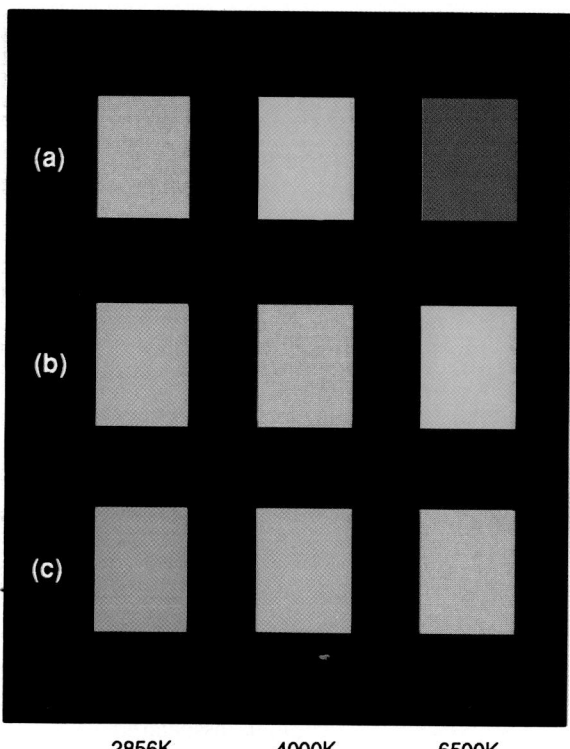

Fig. 4-21. Illustration of appearance of sources of different color temperatures after different chromatic adaptations. (a) After adaptation to 2856 K; (b) after adaptation to 4000 K; (c) after adaptation to 6500 K. Colors shown are only approximate representations.

2856K   4000K   6500K

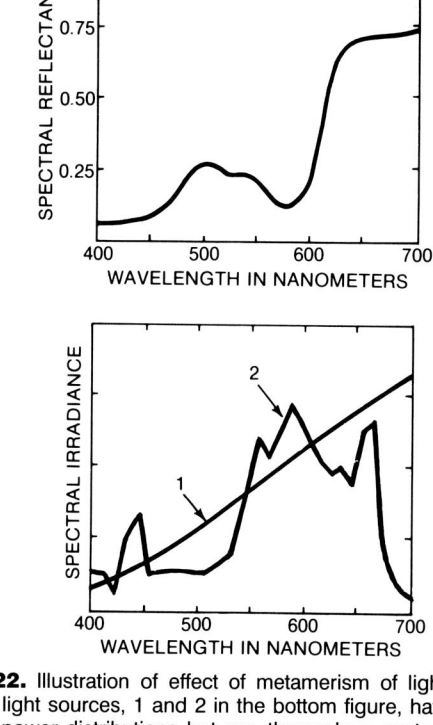

Fig. 4-22. Illustration of effect of metamerism of light sources. The two light sources, 1 and 2 in the bottom figure, have different spectral power distributions but are, themselves, metamers when illuminating a spectrally flat object. An object, such as the one whose spectral reflectance curve is shown in the top figure, may have different color appearances when illuminated by each of the two sources.

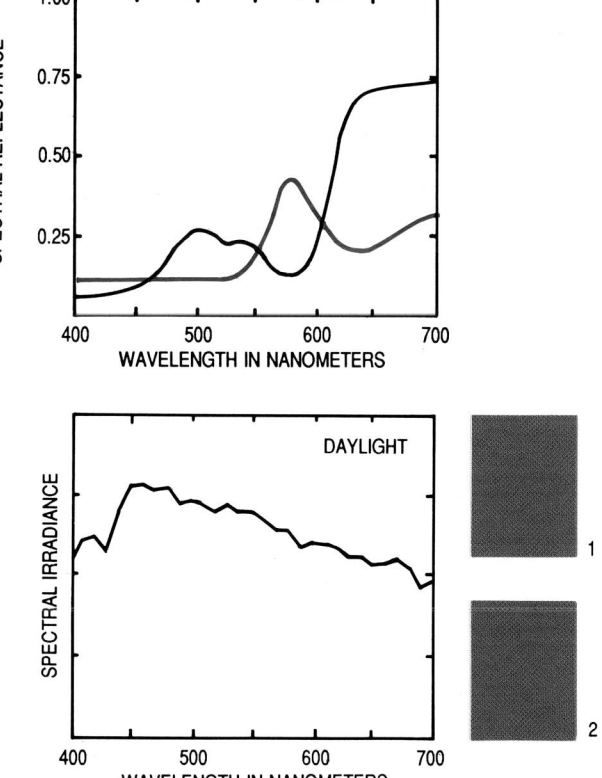

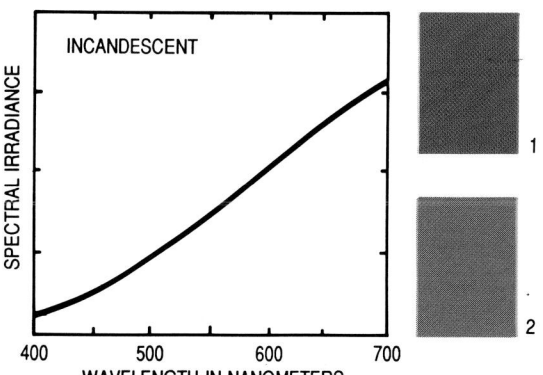

Fig. 4-23. Illustration of metamerism of reflecting objects. The objects whose spectral reflectance curves are shown here have the same color when illuminated by daylight but are quite different in color when illuminated by an incandescent source. The actual colors shown are for illustration purposes only and are not accurate representations of the color appearance.

Fig. 4-24. Specification of ANSI Safety Colors Viewed Under CiE Standard Illuminant C

Color Name	Munsell Notation	CIE Specification			ISCC-NBS Name
		x	y	Y	
Safety Red	7.5R 4.0/14	0.5959	0.3269	12.00	Vivid Red
Safety Orange	5.0YR 6.0/15	0.5510	0.4214	30.05	Vivid Orange
Highway Brown	5.0YR 2.75/5	0.4766	0.3816	5.52	Moderate Brown
Safety Yellow	5.0Y 8.0/12	0.4562	0.4788	59.10	Vivid Yellow
Safety Green	7.5G 4.0/9	0.2110	0.4120	12.00	Strong Green
Safety Blue	2.5PB 3.5/10	0.1690	0.1744	9.00	Strong Blue
Safety Purple	10.0P 4.5/10	0.3307	0.2245	15.57	Strong Reddish Purple
Safety White	N9.0/	0.3101	0.3162	78.70	White
Safety Gray	N5.0/	0.3101	0.3162	19.80	Medium Gray
Safety Black	N1.5/	0.3101	0.3162	2.02	Black

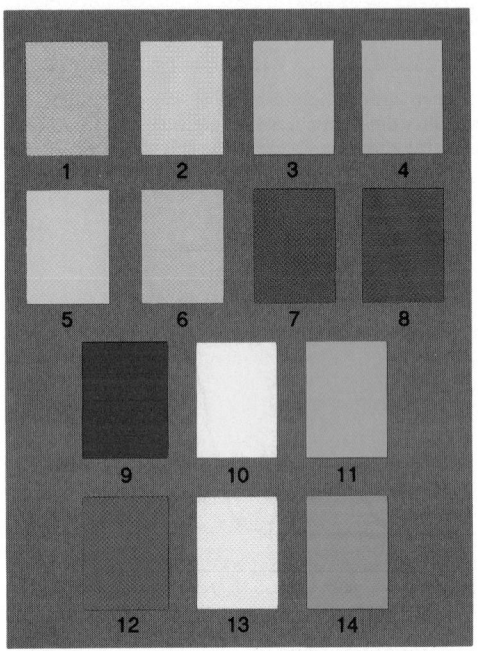

Test Color Number	Munsell Notation	CIE Specification			ISCC-NBS Name
		x	y	Y	
1.	7.5 R 6/4	0.375	0.331	29.9	Light grayish red
2.	5 Y 6/4	0.385	0.395	28.9	Dark grayish yellow
3.	5 GY 6/8	0.373	0.464	30.4	Strong yellow green
4.	2.5G 6/6	0.287	0.400	29.2	Moderate yellowish green
5.	10 BG 6/4	0.258	0.306	30.7	Light bluish green
6.	5 PB 6/8	0.241	0.243	29.7	Light blue
7.	2.5 P 6/8	0.284	0.241	29.5	Light violet
8.	10 P 6/8	0.325	0.262	31.5	Light reddish purple
9.	4.5 R 4/13	0.567	0.306	11.4	Strong red
10.	5 Y 8/10	0.438	0.462	59.1	Strong yellow
11.	4.5 G 5/8	0.254	0.410	20.0	Strong green
12.	3 PB 3/11	0.155	0.150	6.4	Strong blue
13.	5 YR 8.4	0.372	0.352	57.3	Light yellowish pink (Caucasian complexion)
14.	5 GY 4/4	0.353	0.432	11.7	Moderate olive green (leaf green)

Fig. 4-25. Specifications of test colors used in calculating the CIE color rendering index (calculated for CIE standard illuminant C). The definitive specifications are in terms of spectral radiance factor. The colors shown are approximations and should not be used in place of the actual samples.

REFERENCES

1. Commission Internationale de l'Éclairage. 1974. *Method of measuring and specifying colour rendering properties of light sources.* CIE Publication No. 13.2. Prepared by CIE Committee TC-3.2. Paris: Bureau Central de la CIE.

2. IES. Testing Procedures Committee. Photometry of Light Sources Subcommittee. 1989. IES practical guide to colorimetry of light sources, IES LM-16-1984. *J. Illum. Eng. Soc.* 18(2):122–127.

3. IES. Color Committee. 1962. Color and the use of color by the illuminating engineer. *Illum. Eng.* 57(12):764–776.

4. IES. Light Sources Committee. Subcommittee on Color Rendering. 1962. Interim method of measuring and specifying color rendering of light sources. *Illum. Eng.* 57(7):471–495.

5. IES. Color Committee. 1992. *Color and illumination.* New York: Illuminating Engineering Society of North America.

6. Judd, D. B., and G. Wyszecki. 1975. *Color in business, science and industry.* 3rd ed. New York: Wiley.

7. Nickerson, D. 1960. Light sources and color rendering. *J. Opt. Soc. Am.* 50(1):57–69.

8. Hunt, R. W. G. 1978. Colour terminology. *Color Res. Appl.* 3(2):79–87.

9. Newhall, S. M., D. Nickerson, and D. B. Judd. 1943. Final report of the OSA Subcommittee on the Spacing of the Munsell Colors. *J. Opt. Soc. Am.* 33(7):385–418.

10. Commission Internationale de l'Éclairage. 1978. *Recommendations on uniform color spaces, color-difference equations and psychometric color terms.* CIE Publication No. 15, Supp. 2. Paris: Bureau Central de la CIE.

11. Robertson, A. R. 1977. The CIE 1976 color-difference formulae. *Color Res. Appl.* 2(1):7–11.

12. Commission Internationale de l'Éclairage. 1971. *Colorimetry.* CIE Publication No. 15. Paris: Bureau Central de la CIE.

13. Wyszecki, G., and W. S. Stiles. 1982. *Color science: Concepts and methods quantitative data and formulae.* 2nd ed. New York: Wiley.

14. MacAdam, D. L. 1937. Projective transformations of ICI color specifications. *J. Opt. Soc. Am.* 27(8):294–299.

15. Wyszecki, G. 1963. Proposal for a new color-difference formula [Letter]. *J. Opt. Soc. Am.* 53(11):1318–1319.

16. Recommendations on uniform color spaces, color-difference equations, and metric color terms [Editorial]. 1977. *Color Res. Appl.* 2(1):5–6.

17. Clarke, F. J. J., R. McDonald, and B. Rigg. 1984. Modification to the JPC79 colour difference formula. *J. Soc. Dyers Col.* 100(4):128–132.

18. Clarke, F. J. J., R. McDonald, and B. Rigg. 1984. Modification to the JPC79 colour difference formula [Letter]. *J. Soc. Dyers Col.* 100(9):281–282.

19. American Association of Textile Chemists and Colorists. *CMC: Calculation of small color differences for acceptability, Test Method 173-1989.* Research Triangle Park, NC: American Association of Textile Chemists and Colorists.

20. American Society for Testing and Materials. 1980. *Standard test method for specifying color by the Munsell system, D 1535-80.* Philadelphia: American Society for Testing and Materials.

21. Kelly, K. L., and D. B. Judd. 1965. *The ISCC-NBS centroid color charts, SRM #2106.* Washington DC: The Office of Standard Reference Materials, National Bureau of Standards.

22. Kelly, K. L. 1965. The universal color language. *Color Eng.* 3(2):16–21.

23. United States. Department of Commerce. National Bureau of Standards. 1978. *Color: Universal language and dictionary of names.* NBS Special Publication 440. Prepared by K. L. Kelly and D. B. Judd. Washington: U.S. Government Printing Office.

24. MacAdam, D. L. 1974. Uniform color scales. *J. Opt. Soc. Am.* 64(12):1691–1702.

25. Hård, A., and L. Sivik. 1981. NCS—Natural Color System: A Swedish standard for color notation. *Color Res. Appl.* 6(3):127–138.

26. Richter, M., and K. Witt. 1986. The story of the DIN color system. *Color Res. Appl.* 11(2):138–145.

27. Nickerson, D. 1957. Horticultural color chart names with Munsell key. *J. Opt. Soc. Am.* 47(7):619–621.

28. Billmeyer, F. W., Jr. 1987. Survey of color order systems. *Color Res. Appl.* 12(4):173–186.

29. Kelly, K. L. 1963. Lines of constant correlated color temperature based on MacAdam's (u, v) uniform chromaticity transformation of the CIE diagram. *J. Opt. Soc. Am.* 53(8):999–1002.

30. Robertson, A. R. 1968. Computation of correlated color temperature and distribution temperature. *J. Opt. Soc. Am.* 58(11):1528–1535.

31. Judd, D. B., D. L. MacAdam, and G. Wyszecki. 1964. Spectral distribution of typical daylight as a function of correlated color temperature. *J. Opt. Soc. Am.* 54(8):1031–1040. Summary in *Illum. Eng.* 60(4):272–278.

32. Evans, R. M. 1948. *An introduction to color.* New York: Wiley.

33. Burnham, R. W., R. M. Hanes, and C. J. Bartleson. 1963. *Color: A guide to basic facts and concepts.* New York: Wiley.

34. Hunt, R. W. G. 1991. A revised colour appearance model for related and unrelated colours. *Color Res. Appl.* 16(3):146–165.

35. Nayatani, Y., K. Takhama, H. Sobagaki, and K. Hashimoto. 1990. Color-appearance model and chromatic adaptation transform. *Color Res. Appl.* 15(4):210–221.

36. Stiles, W. S., and G. Wyszecki. 1968. Intersections of the spectral reflectance curves of metameric object colors. *J. Opt. Soc. Am.* 58(1):32–40.

37. Brainerd, A. A., and R. A. Massey. 1942. Salvaging waste light for victory. *Illum. Eng.* 37(10):738–757.

38. Moon, P. 1941. Wall materials and lighting. *J. Opt. Soc. Am.* 31(12):723–729.

39. Spencer, D. E., and S. E. Sanborn. 1961. Interflections and color. *J. Franklin Inst.* 252(5):413–426.

40. O'Brien, P. F. 1960. Lighting calculations for thirty-five thousand rooms. *Illum. Eng.* 55(4):215–226.

41. Jones, B. F., and J. R. Jones. 1959. A versatile method of calculating illumination and brightness. *Illum. Eng.* 54(2):113–121.

42. Barthès, E. 1957. Etudes expérimental de calcul de point de couleur de la lumière reçue par le plan utile dans un local a parois colorées. *Bull. Soc. Franc. Elec.* 7(81):546.

43. Krossawa, R. 1963. Color shift of room interior surfaces due to interreflection. *Die Farbe* 12:117.

44. Yamanaka, T., and Y. Nayatani. 1964. A note on predetermination of color shift due to interreflection in a colored room. *Acta Chromatica* 1:111.

45. Helson, H. 1954. Color and vision. *Illum. Eng.* 49(2):92–93.

46. Helson, H. 1955. Color and seeing. *Illum. Eng.* 50(6):271–278.

47. Helson, H., D. B. Judd, and M. Wilson. 1956. Color rendition with fluorescent sources of illumination. *Illum. Eng.* 51(4):329–346.

48. Helson, H. 1965. *Role of sources and backgrounds on pleasantness of object colors.* Paper presented at the IES National Technical Conference, New York, September 1965.

49. Judd, D. B. 1971. Choosing pleasant color combinations. *Light. Des. Appl.* 1(2):31–41.

50. Helson, H., and T. Lansford. 1970. The role of spectral energy of source and background color in the pleasantness of object colors. *Appl. Opt.* 9(7):1513–1562.

51. American National Standards Institute. 1979. *American national standard safety color code for marking physical hazards, ANSI Z53.1-1979.* New York: American National Standards Institute.

52. IES. Color Committee. 1980. Potential misidentification of industrial safety colors with certain lighting. *Light. Des. Appl.* 10(11):20.

53. U.S. National Bureau of Standards. 1983. *Some criteria for colors and signs in workplaces, NBSIR 83-2694.* Prepared by R. A. Glass, G. L. Howett, K. Lister, and B. L. Collins. Washington: National Bureau of Standards.

54. Commission Internationale de l'Éclairage. 1975. *Guide on interior lighting.* CIE Publication No. 29. Prepared by CIE Committee TC-4.1. Paris: Bureau Central de la CIE.

55. Kruithof, A. A. 1941. Tubular luminescence lamps for general illumination. *Philips Tech. Rev.* 6(3):65–73.

56. Nickerson, D., and C. W. Jerome. 1965. Color rendering of light sources: CIE method of specification and its application. *Illum. Eng.* 60(4):262–271.

57. Aston, S. M., and H. E. Bellchambers. 1969. Illumination, colour rendering and visual clarity. *Light. Res. Tech.* 1(4):259–261.

58. Thornton, W. A., and E. Chen. 1978. What is visual clarity? *J. Illum. Eng. Soc.* 7(2):85–94.

59. Commission Internationale de l'Éclairage. 1981. *A method for assessing the quality of daylight simulators for colorimetry.* CIE Publication No. 51. Vienna: Bureau Central de la CIE.

60. American Society for Testing and Materials. 1981. *Standard practice for lighting cotton classing rooms for color grading, ASTM D1684-81.* Philadelphia: American Society for Testing and Materials.

61. Nickerson, D. 1948. The illuminant in textile color matching. *Illum. Eng.* 43(4):416–467.

62. American Society for Testing and Materials. 1989. *Standard practice for visual evaluation of color differences of opaque materials, D 1729-89.* Philadelphia: American Society for Testing and Materials.

63. American National Standards Institute. 1981. *American national standard viewing conditions for the appraisal of color quality and color uniformity in the graphic arts, ANSI PH2.32-1972 (R1981).* New York: American National Standards Institute.

64. Amphoto. 1978. *Lighting.* Vol. 9 in Encyclopedia of practical photography. Garden City, NJ: American Photographic Book Publishing Co.

65. Society of Photographic Scientists and Engineers. 1973. *SPSE handbook for photographic science and engineering.* T. Woodlief, ed. New York: Wiley.

66. Spencer, D. A. 1966. *Colour photography in practice.* Rev. ed. London, New York: Focal Press.

67. Hunt, R. W. G. 1967. *The reproduction of colour.* 2nd ed. London: Fountain Press.

68. McCamy, C. S. 1959. A nomograph for selecting light balancing filters for camera exposure of color films. *Photogr. Sci. Eng.* 3(6):302–304.

69. McCamy, C. S., H. Marcus, and J. G. Davidson. 1976. A color-rendition chart. *J. Appl. Photo. Eng.* 2(3):95–99.

Nonvisual Effects of Radiant Energy

5

Life has evolved under the influence of radiation from the sun, and as a result, humans, animals and plants have developed complex physiological responses for a variety of biological functions to the daily and seasonal variations in solar radiation. The spectral power distribution of solar radiation at sea level is shown in figure 5-1.

The study of the interaction of biological systems with nonionizing radiant energy in the ultraviolet, visible and infrared portions of the electromagnetic spectrum is known as *photobiology*. Photobiological responses result from chemical and physical changes induced by the quantal absorption of radiation by specific molecules in the living organism. The absorbed radiation produces excited electronic states in these molecules which may lead to photochemical reactions of biological consequence. The distinguishing feature of photochemical reactions is that the energy of activation is provided by the quantum absorption of nonionizing photons which cause reactions to occur at low (physiological) temperatures.

The human visual system is discussed in chapter 3, Vision and Perception. Extravisual photobiological effects occurring in humans, animals, microorganisms and plants, as well as nonbiological effects on matter, are covered in this section.

EFFECTS ON HUMANS AND ANIMALS (PHOTOBIOLOGY)

The effects of solar radiation on humans and animals include wide-ranging phenomena such as damage to ocular tissues, skin effects, tumor formation and the synchronization of biological rhythms. A variety of diseases have been treated with visible or ultraviolet energy, alone or in combination with sensitizing drugs. Since the beginning of recorded history, psoralens, an ultraviolet-activated drug, combined with exposure to solar ultraviolet radiation has been the therapy for vitiligo, a skin condition marked by an absence of normal pigment. By the turn of the century, lupus vulgaris, a condition where skin nodules are present,

was shown to be cured with ultraviolet either from sunlight or from carbon arcs. Psoriasis, a skin condition where lesions are covered with scales, is now being alleviated with the same therapy that has been applied to vitiligo, using artificial energy sources of more constant ultraviolet output than from the sun. Visible light, particularly the short wavelengths (400–500 nm), is used in the phototherapy of jaundiced infants. Other extravisual effects of light include the regulation of biological rhythm and neuroendocrine responses.

Effects on the Eye[1-24]

For the purposes of this discussion, the radiant energy spectrum is divided into three components: ultraviolet, 100–380 nm; visible and near-infrared, 380–1400 nm; and infrared, 1400 nm to 1 mm. Figure 5-2 summarizes in abbreviated form the overall effects of radiation as a function of wavelength, and indicates that ultraviolet bands in particular induce adverse effects such as erythema (reddening of the skin), photokeratitis (an inflammation of the cornea, also commonly known as "flash blindness" or "welder's burn") and photosensitized skin damage, as well as some beneficial effects, as in phototherapy. The harmful effects of any given wavelength upon the eye can be determined by evaluating the accessibility of that wavelength to the tissue in question, the absorbency of that wavelength in the tissue, and the effectiveness of the tissue in dealing with the insult that the absorption of energy represents.

Ultraviolet Radiation Effects. The biological effects of ultraviolet radiation depend upon the spectral absorption by and the radiation of the various components of the ocular media and upon the photochemical sensitivity of the tissue. The ultraviolet region of the electromagnetic spectrum is subdivided by international convention (CIE) into near ultraviolet (UV-A, 380–315 nm), middle ultraviolet (UV-B, 315–280 nm) and far ultraviolet (280–100 nm). Figure 5-3 shows that for wavelengths less than 320 nm, nearly all of the radiation is absorbed by the cornea. Between 320 and

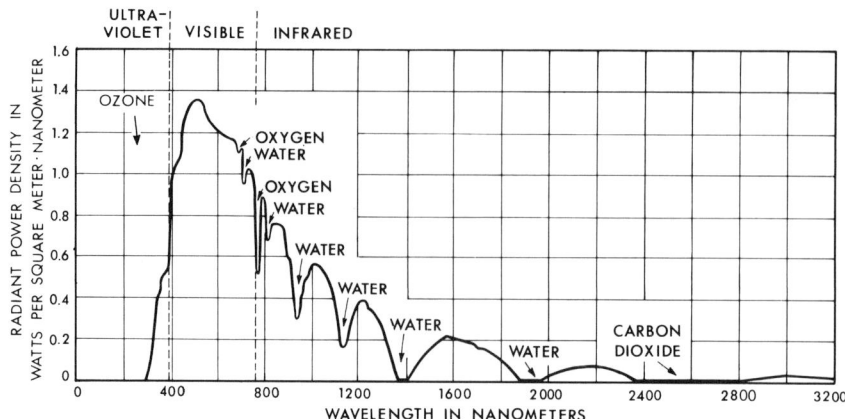

Fig. 5-1. Spectral distribution of solar radiant power density at sea level, showing the ozone, oxygen, water and carbon dioxide absorption bands.

400 nm, much of the ultraviolet radiation is absorbed by the lens; the proportion is directly dependent upon age (see figure 5-4). Analyses of human lenses across different age groups have concluded that the human eye, until about 30 years of age, transmits a small percentage of UV light, resulting in a visual perceptive response down to a wavelength of 300 nm.

Photokeratitis is a painful, but not necessarily serious, inflammation of the epithelial (outermost) layer of the cornea. The period of latency between exposure and the onset of effects varies from 2 to 8 hours, depending upon the amount of radiation received. For moderate exposures, the effects are more frightening than serious. The symptoms include inflammation of the conjunctiva accompanied by a reddening of the surrounding skin and eyelids. There is a sensation of "sand" in the eyes, tearing, sensitivity to light and twitching of the eyelids. Recovery is rapid and usually

Fig. 5-2. Physiological Effects or Applications of Ultraviolet, Visible and Near-Infrared, and Infrared Radiation

Effects or Applications	Ultraviolet (100-400 nm)	Visible, Near-Infrared (380-1400 nm)	Infrared (over 1400 nm)
Skin	Erythema Carcinogenesis Aging Drug Photosensitivity Melanoma*	Burns Drug Photosensitivity	Burns
Eye			
Cornea	Photokeratitis		Burns, Shocks
Lens	Cataracts (Immediate and long term) Coloration Sclerosis	Near-Infrared Cataracts	Infrared Cataracts
Retina	Retinal Changes†	Thermal Lesion Photochemical Lesion Shock Lesion Solar Retinitis Macula Degeneration* Loss of Visual Acuity*	

Phototherapy	Psoriasis
	Herpes Simplex
	Dentistry
	
	Vitiligo, Photochemotherapy, Eczyma, and Mycosis fungoides.
		Retinal Detachment
		Diabetic Retinopathy
		Bilirubinemia
		Glaucoma
		Removal of Port Wine Stains and Tattoos
		Surgery
		Winter Depression (SAD),
		  Shift Work, Jet Lag,
		  Sustained Performance,
		  Low Level Laser Therapy	

Benefits	Vitamin D Protective Pigmentation	Biological Rhythms Hormonal Activity Behavior*	Radiant Heating

* Extent of effects unknown at this time.

† Susceptibility to light induced retinal degeration increases with aphakia (*i.e.*, with surgical removal of the lens.)

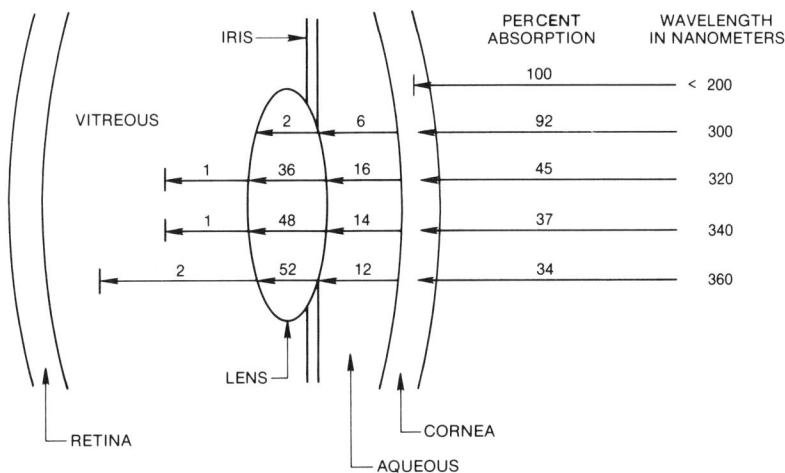

Fig. 5-3. Percentage of energy on the surface of the cornea absorbed by various layers, after data by E. A. Boettner and J. R. Walter, MRL-TDR-62.31.

complete within 48 hours except for severe cases. The action spectrum, similar to that for skin erythema, peaks at 270–280 nm (with recent research suggesting that it is closer to 270 nm), falling off to negligible values at 320 nm (see figure 5-5).

Lenticular effects of UV radiation have recently been undergoing extensive investigation. The lens shows a number of changes with aging, including a yellowing coloration, an increasing proportion of insoluble proteins, sclerosis with loss of accommodation, and

cataract. There is a growing body of evidence, mostly epidemiological, to implicate ultraviolet radiation in these changes. For example, cataract extractions are significantly more frequent in India than in western Europe. Part of the difference may be due to diet and genetic factors, but most authorities believe that exposure to sunlight plays an important role. While many of the early epidemiological studies of cataract have been inconclusive, more recent attempts have shown statistical significance in the relationship between cortical

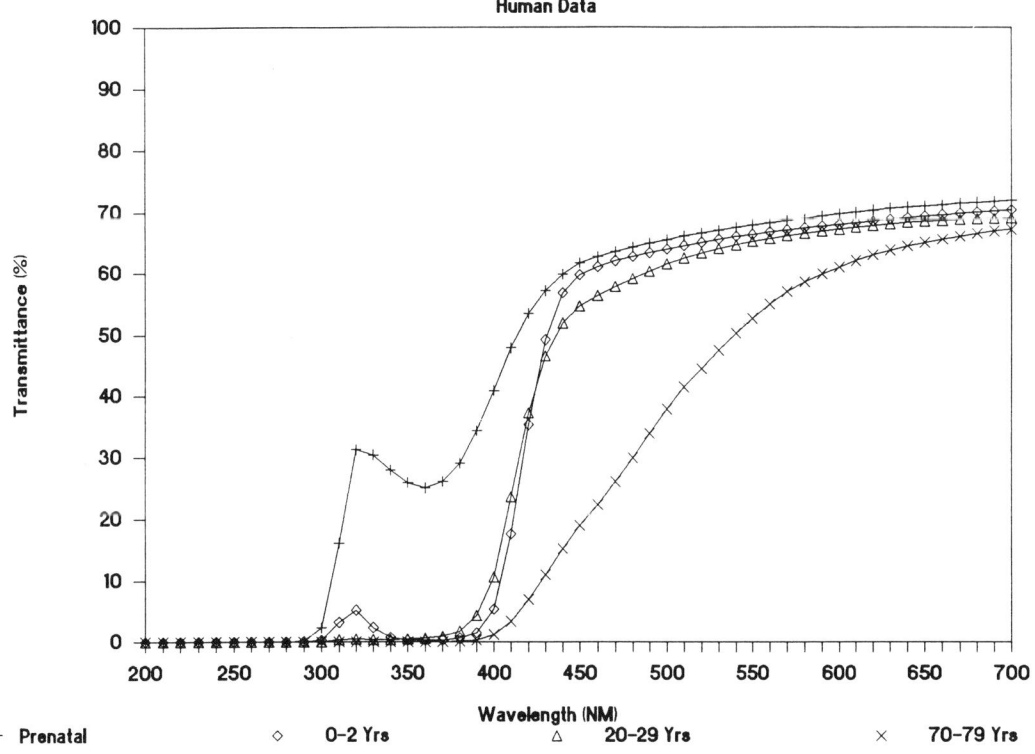

Fig. 5-4. Age related lens transmittance.

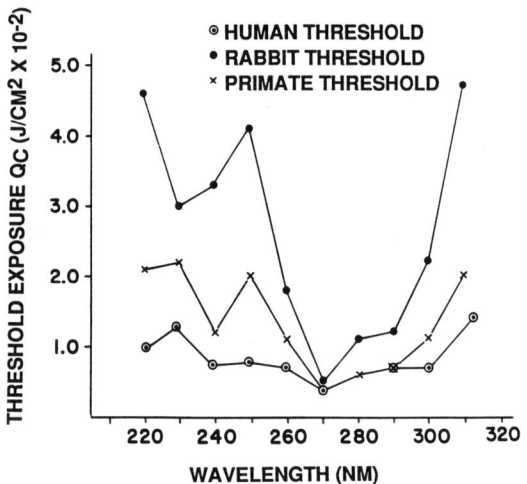

Fig. 5-5. Comparison of the radiant exposure thresholds for injuring the cornea Q_C of the human, the primate and the rabbit. The data were established by exposing 238 rabbit eyes, 83 primate eyes, and 39 human eyes to ultraviolet radiation.

lens opacities and lifelong UV-B (290–315 nm) exposure in persons living and working in high levels of solar energy. The relationship to UV-A (315–400 nm) is also suspected to have a role in cataract formation and may prove to be significant as well.

Retinal effects of ultraviolet radiation are difficult to categorize generally, for they depend on the individual filtering capabilities of the preretinal ocular media. In the adult, the crystalline lens, which typically absorbs wavelengths below about 400 nm, effectively shields the retina from UV. Studies have shown, however, that a small percentage of UV radiation can reach the retina in human adults up to 30 years of age. Removal of the lens in cataract surgery renders the retina more susceptible to damage from wavelengths down to 300 nm. If a modern, UV-blocking intraocular lens (IOL) is surgically implanted, however, then the UV block is restored.

UV shielding in contact lenses of the rigid gas-permeable (RGP) and hydrogel varieties has recently been introduced, making such lenses suitable for use by aphakics for whom intraocular lens implants are not possible.

Visible and Near-Infrared Radiation Effects. The infrared region of the electromagnetic spectrum falls between wavelengths of 780 nm and 1 mm. Like UV, it has been divided into three subregions: IR-A (near-infrared, 780–1400 nm), IR-B (middle-infrared, 1400–3000 nm), and IR-C (far-infrared, 3000 nm–1 mm). Visible light occupies the wavelength region bounded by UV and IR, falling between 400 and 780 nm.

While the sun radiates at all wavelengths across the electromagnetic spectrum, only UV, IR and visible light reach the earth's surface. Retinal injury resulting

in a loss of vision (scotoma) following observation of the sun has been described throughout history. The incidence of chorioretinal injuries from man-made sources is extremely small and is no doubt far less than the incidence of eclipse blindness. Until recently it was believed that chorioretinal burns would not occur from exposure to light resulting from industrial operations. Indeed, this is still largely true, since the normal aversion to high-brightness light sources (the blink reflex and movement of the eyes away from the source) provides adequate protection unless the exposure is hazardous within the duration of the blink reflex. The recent revolution in optical technology, however, forged principally by the invention of the laser, has meant a great increase in the use of high-intensity, high-radiance sources. Many such sources have output parameters significantly different from those encountered in the past and may present serious chorioretinal burn hazards. In addition to lasers, one may encounter the following sources of continuous optical radiation in industry: compact arc lamps (as in solar simulators), tungsten-halogen lamps, gas and vapor discharge tubes, electric welding units, and sources of pulsed optical radiation, such as flash lamps and exploding wires. Infrared irradiance levels in the workplace can reach 600 mW/cm² in the glass industry and 1000 mW/cm² in the steel industry. The intensities of these sources may be of concern if adequate protective measures are not taken. Extreme IR irradiances have been linked to corneal, lenticular and retinal damage; although the ocular structures can adequately dissipate the heat from low-power diffuse IR exposures, the same amount of energy delivered in pulses to very small areas of tissue can cause damage. Coherent light generated by YAG and argon lasers can penetrate to intraocular structures.

Light from krypton, HeNe, and ruby lasers will reach the retina. Such sources have been used therapeutically in retinal photocoagulation procedures.

To place chorioretinal injury data in perspective, figure 5-6 shows the retinal irradiance for many continuous wave sources. It is reemphasized that several orders of magnitude in radiance or luminance exist between sources which cause chorioretinal burns and those levels to which individuals are continuously exposed. The retinal irradiances shown are only approximate and assume minimal pupil sizes and some squinting for all the very high luminance sources (except the xenon searchlight, for which a 7-mm-diameter pupil was assumed so as to apply to nighttime illumination).

Light entering the cornea passes through the anterior chamber (which contains the aqueous humor), the lens and the vitreous humor and impinges upon the retina (see figure 3-1). Examination of those curves shows that between 400 and 1400 nm the retina is vulnerable to radiation effects. Between these wave-

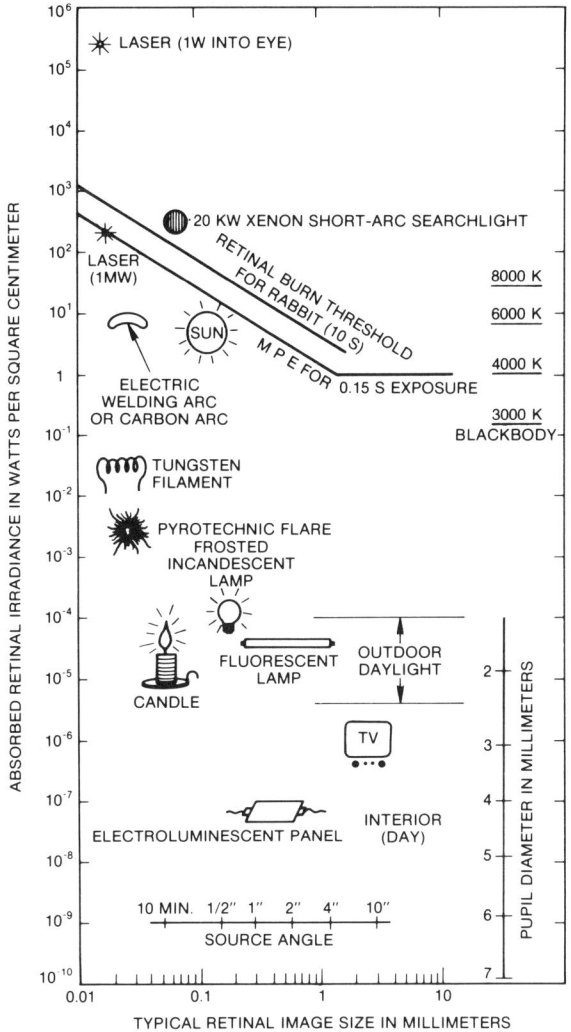

Fig. 5-6. The eye is exposed to light sources having radiances varying from about 10^4 to 10^6 W / (cm$^{-2} \cdot$ sr) or less. The resulting retinal irradiances vary from about 200 down to 10^{-7} W / cm^{-2} and even lower; retinal irradiances are shown for typical image sizes for several sources. A minimal pupil size was assumed for intense sources, except for the searchlight. The retinal burn threshold for a 10-s exposure of the rabbit retina is shown as the upper solid line. The maximum permissible exposure (MPE) applied by the U.S. Army Environmental Hygiene Agency in evaluating momentary viewing of continuous-wave light sources is shown as the lower solid line. Approximate pupil sizes are shown at the lower left, based upon exposure of most of the retina to light of the given irradiance.

lengths the retina is by far the most sensitive tissue of the body.

In the retina, light passes through multiple layers of neural cells before encountering the photoreceptor cells (the rods and cones). Photoreceptors are neural transducers, converting absorbed photons of light into electrical impulses sent to the brain via the optic tract. Just behind the rods and cones is a single layer of heavily pigmented cells (the pigment epithelium) which absorbs a large portion of the light passing through the neural retina. The pigment epithelium acts like a dark curtain to absorb and prevent backscatter from those

photons which are not absorbed in the outer segments of the rods and cones. The neural retina itself is almost transparent to light. The pigment epithelium is about 10 μm in thickness, while the choroid—a layer of blood vessels behind it—ranges from 100 to 200 μm. Most of the energy in the form of light which reaches the retina is converted to heat by the pigment epithelium and the choroid. Sufficiently large quantities of light can generate heat sufficient to cause thermal damage to the retina.

Research over the past decade has demonstrated that in the range of wavelengths between 400 and 1400 nm, there are at least three different mechanisms leading to retinal damage. These are:

1. Mechanical (shock-wave) damage from picosecond and nanosecond pulses of mode-locked or *Q*-switched lasers.
2. Thermal damage from pulse durations extending from microseconds to seconds. Except for minor variations in transmittance through the ocular media and variations of absorbance in the pigmented epithelium and choroid, thermal damage is not wavelength dependent.
3. Photochemical damage from exposure to short wavelengths in the visible spectrum for time durations and power densities on the retina which preclude thermal effects. Photochemical damage is wavelength dependent.

In terms of exposure time and wavelength there is no abrupt transition from one type of damage to the other. For example, a YAG laser emitting a pulse train of *Q*-switched pulses (several nanoseconds in duration) at 1064 nm may produce a combination of shock-wave and thermal damage depending on the pulse width and the time interval between pulses, whereas an acoustically modulated pulse train from an argon ion laser emitting 10-μs pulses of 488-nm radiation might produce a combination of thermal and photochemical damage.

A number of researchers have shown that long-term exposure to visible light can cause retinal damage in some animals. For example, when rats and mice are subjected to cool white fluorescent lighting for extended periods of time (weeks to months), they become blind. Histological examination reveals that the photoreceptors in the retinae of these animals have degenerated. Although rodent retinal photoreceptors can be damaged with long exposures to relatively low levels of white light, such damage in primates has been demonstrated only with the eyes dilated and at a continuous exposure of 10,800 lux for 12 hours. Exposure of the undilated monkey eye at that illuminance for 12 hours per day for 4 weeks did not produce photoreceptor damage.

Far-Infrared Radiation Effects. Wavelengths greater than 1400 nm do not reach the retina, but can produce ocular effects leading to corneal and lenticular damage. Cataracts from exposure to infrared radiation have been reported in the literature for a long time, but there are few or no recent quantitative data to substantiate the clinical observations. It was previously thought that long-term exposure to infrared radiation produces an elevated temperature in the lens which, over a period of years, leads to denaturation of the lens proteins with consequent opacification. Recently, however, authorities have come to believe that infrared radiation is absorbed by the pigmented iris and converted to heat which is conducted to the lens, rather than by direct absorption of radiation in the lens. Infrared cataractogenesis has been reported to occur among glassblowers, steel puddlers and others who undergo long-term occupational exposure to infrared radiation. Present industrial safety practices have virtually eliminated this effect in workers of today.

Photosensitization. Retinal and other ocular effects can also be increased or decreased in their severity by the presence of endogenously or exogenously supplied photoactive compounds. Psoralens, hematoporphyrin derivatives and other phototherapeutic agents can enhance the damaging effects of various wavelengths upon the eye and other tissues. In contrast, quenchers of excited-state species such as vitamin E have been hypothesized to increase the threshold for light-induced damage. Many new pharmaceutical agents contain conjugated bond and ring structures which may also increase the potential for phototoxic effects.

Effects of Ultraviolet Radiation Upon the Skin[25–39]

There are at least two known benefits of ultraviolet radiation exposure upon skin: the production of vitamin D from precursor chemicals which are formed in the skin (see below) and the induction of protective pigmentation. Known harmful effects include sunburn, skin cancer and morphologic alterations (wrinkling, irregularity, altered pigmentation, thinning and thickening of skin) which appear as "premature aging." Delayed tanning and increased thickening of skin is a protective response initiated by ultraviolet radiation. The function of immediate tanning is uncertain.

Optical Properties of the Skin. The reflectance of skin for wavelengths shorter than 320 nm is low, regardless of skin color; however, from 320 to 750 nm the reflectance is dependent upon skin pigmentation. The transmission of ultraviolet radiation through the skin depends on wavelength, skin color (melanin content) and skin thickness. In general, transmission increases with increasing wavelength from 280 to 1200 nm. Typi-

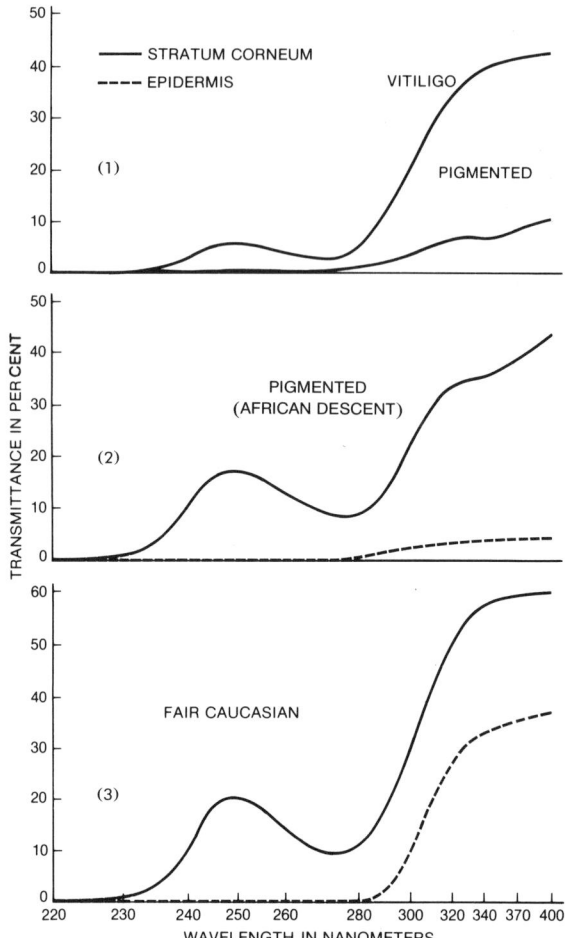

Fig. 5-7. Light-transmission spectra of stratum corneum and epidermis from the scapular region of three subjects: (1) a pigmented person of African descent with vitiligo (pigmented and nonpigmented stratum corneum); and (2) pigmented stratum corneum and whole epidermis; and (3) a fair-skinned Caucasian.

cally, for Europeans, the transmittance at the base of the top layer of skin (stratum corneum) is 34% at 300 nm and 60% at 400 nm. In persons of African descent, the transmittance of the stratum corneum is about 22% at 300 nm and 42% at 400 nm. Transmission decreases with increasing melanin content of the skin and with increasing skin thickness. See figures 5-7 and 5-8.

While skin color is the genetically determined result of a number of factors, the primary factor is melanin. Its quantity, granule size and distribution all affect skin color. The immediate tanning that occurs with exposure to ultraviolet radiation of wavelengths longer than 300 nm and extending into the visible blue region is the darkening of existing melanin. Delayed tanning results from ultraviolet stimulation of the melanin-producing cells (the melanocytes) to produce additional melanin. Pigmentation from this process begins immediately at the subcellular level. Gross changes in skin color can be observed three days after ultraviolet irradiation and

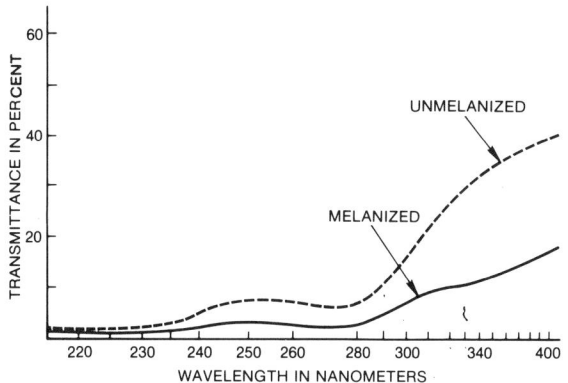

Fig. 5-8. Light-transmission spectra of human epidermis of equal thickness (12 μm) obtained from the infrascapular region of two subjects: a fair-skinned Caucausian and a pigmented African.

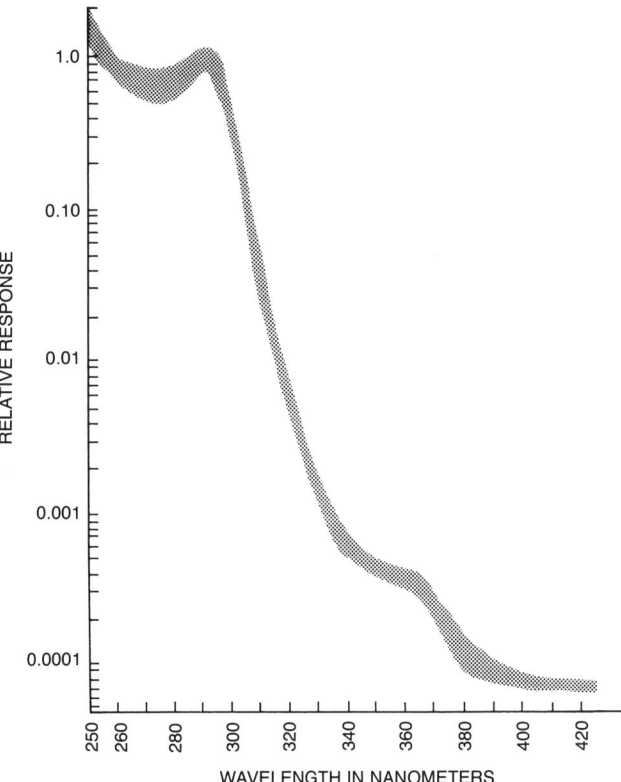

Fig. 5-9. Erythema action spectrum for human skin. Note logarithmic vertical axis.

reach a peak about 1–3 weeks later. Fading requires months, as melanin is lost during the normal shedding process.

Melanin protects against ultraviolet damage by reducing transmission through absorption and scattering, both of which serve to increase the effective path length.

Erythema. The delayed reddening (erythema) of the skin caused by exposure to ultraviolet radiation is a widely observed phenomenon. The spectral efficiency of this process, particularly for sunlight wavelengths from 290 to 320 nm, has been well studied.

The reported erythema action spectrum for wavelengths shorter than 300 nm varies considerably among observers because of differences in the degree of erythema taken as the endpoint criterion and differences in the time of observation after irradiation.

Erythema is a component of skin inflammation and results from increased blood volume in superficial cutaneous vessels. The skin may also be warm and tender.

Approximately 18 mJ/cm^2 of energy at the most effective wavelength (297 nm) will cause a barely perceptible reddening in 50% of all Europeans. This amount of effective energy can be experienced in about a 12-min exposure under overhead sun in the tropics (because the stratospheric ozone layer is thin there). When the sun is 20° from its zenith and the ozone layer thickness is about 3.2 mm, an exposure of 20 min is typically required for the same degree of reddening.

Exposure to ultraviolet radiation (particularly at high irradiance levels) may result in an immediate erythema. This may fade a few minutes after irradiation ceases, and may reappear after 1–3 hours. The greater the dose, the faster the reappearance, and the longer the persistence of erythema.

If the erythema is severe enough, skin peeling (desquamation) will begin about 10 days after irradiation. This rapid sloughing off of the top skin layer results from the increased proliferation of skin cells during recovery after ultraviolet damage. Desquamation carries away some of the melanin granules stimulated by the ultraviolet radiation.

Photoprotection, in its common usage, refers to the protection against the detrimental effects of light afforded by sunscreens topically applied to the skin. These sunscreens reduce the effect of ultraviolet exposure primarily by absorption, although reflection may be of some consequence. Considerable progress has been recently achieved in the development of sunscreens which are effective and relatively resistant to being washed away by sweating or swimming. Paraaminobenzoic acid (PABA) in an alcohol base has proven quite effective in preventing sunburn. Other materials in use include benzophenones, cinnamates and salicylates.

Effects of Dermal Illumination Upon the Immune System. Photoimmunology is a term used to describe the study of interactions of nonionizing radiation, predominantly in the ultraviolet (UV) portion of the spectrum, and the immune system. The photoimmunologic effects of UV radiation are very selective: only a few immune responses are affected. The alterations studied in greatest detail are the induction of susceptibility to UV-induced neoplasia and systemic and local suppression of contact hypersensitivity. Most observations have been made in experimental animal systems, but recently, photoimmunologic effects have been observed in humans.

An important feature of the effect of UV radiation on immunity is that it can be a systemic effect. For example, exposure of the skin to UV at one place on the body can reduce the sensitivity to UV at a site that has not been exposed. This probably occurs through the release of mediators from the skin at the exposure site, which in turn results in the formation of antigen-specific T suppressor lymphocytes (white blood cells); such cells have been found in the spleens of animals.

Skin Cancer. The three varieties of skin cancer are basal cell, squamous cell and malignant melanoma. The frequency of occurrence is in the order stated, basal cell cancer being the most common. The prevalence of basal cell carcinoma increases with latitude. The prevalence of both basal and squamous cell cancer correlates positively with solar UV exposure. Both have a very high cure rate if treated promptly. Melanomas are considerably rarer, have a poorer cure rate, and show a poorer correlation with ultraviolet exposure.

Whether commonly used electric light sources provide enough ultraviolet radiation to increase carcinogenic risk is not certain. The newer, unfiltered quartz lamps may emit enough ultraviolet radiation to induce erythema in people who work under them for extended periods.

Effects of Light Upon Vitamin D and Calcium Metabolism[40-44]

Ultraviolet radiation plays an important role in the production of vitamin D in the skin. This vitamin is essential for normal intestinal absorption of calcium and phosphorus from the diet and for the normal mineralization of bone. Vitamin D deficiency causes a deficiency of calcium and phosphorus in the bones (such that they bend, fracture or become painful) and causes bone-softening diseases, such as rickets, in children and osteomalacia in adults. Vitamin D poisoning, on the other hand, leads to excessive absorption of calcium and phosphorus from the diet, and consequently, a toxic effect on the skeleton. There is also a resultant increase in the blood calcium concentration and a precipitation of calcium phosphate deposits in vital organs, causing permanent damage or even death. Vitamin D poisoning also causes increased excretion of calcium in the urine, which can produce kidney stones or bladder stones. When vitamin D poisoning is very mild, the increased urinary calcium excretion may be the only medically important abnormality.

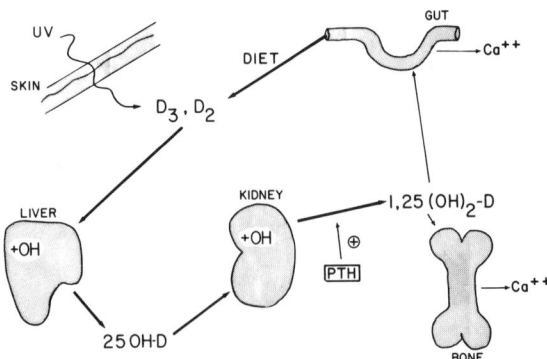

Fig. 5-10. Activation sequence for vitamin D. After synthesis in the skin or absorption from the diet, vitamin D is first converted to 25-hydroxyvitamin D (25-OHD) in the liver and then converted in the kidneys to 1,25-dihydroxyvitamin D [1,25(OH)$_2$D], the active D metabolite which influences intestinal calcium absorption and bone calcium release. The amount of 1,25(OH)$_2$D formed in the kidneys is metabolically regulated by parathyroid hormone (PTH) and a variety of other factors to meet the body's varying needs for calcium and/or phosphorus.

Vitamin D Metabolism. Vitamin D formed in the skin (or absorbed from the diet) is inert until carried by the blood to other organs for activation. Activation involves two sequential chemical changes in the vitamin D molecule (see figure 5-10). Only then is the vitamin D fully activated to 1,25-dihydroxyvitamin D [1,25(OH)$_2$,D, or 25-OHD for short] and able to exert its characteristic effects on the intestines and bones.

The activation of vitamin D is regulated to meet the body's needs for calcium and phosphorus. A deficiency of calcium or phosphorus leads to increased production of 1,25(OH)$_2$D. A surfeit of calcium leads to decreased production of 25-OHD (see figure 5-10). This controlled activation also smooths out the effects of variations in dietary vitamin D intake or variations in vitamin D synthesis in the skin. If the supply of 25-OHD (figure 5-10) or its parent vitamin D becomes low, so that calcium or phosphorus deficiency begins to develop, the body increases the efficiency of vitamin D activation, assuring maximal effectiveness of whatever vitamin D or 25-OHD is available. On the other hand, when there is an excess of vitamin D, the increasing accumulation of calcium rapidly halts further activation of the vitamin.

Vitamin D Photoproduction in Skin. Vitamin D is produced photochemically in the skin from 7-dehydrocholesterol, an intermediate in cholesterol biosynthesis. Absorption of ultraviolet radiation by the 7-dehydrocholesterol molecule rapidly causes its conversion to previtamin D (see figure 5-11), which, in turn, isomerizes to vitamin D. This second step does not involve light absorption and occurs slowly over several hours. Thus, even though the initial photochemical reaction is rapid, vitamin D is formed and released into the blood

Fig. 5-11. Steps in the photoproduction of vitamin D in the skin.

slowly. The biochemistry of these reactions is currently being investigated.

Studies in animals and humans clearly show that ultraviolet radiation in the range 250–315 nm is effective in producing vitamin D in the skin. The action spectrum for this effect has been directly determined in human skin, with a peak of effectiveness near 297 nm. Most of the previtamin D_3 synthesis occurs in the inviable epidermis, and about 10% is made in the dermis. Melanin content in the skin, sunscreen use and aging decrease the capacity of the skin to produce vitamin D. Furthermore, environmental factors such as changes in latitude, season and time of day also greatly influence the cutaneous production of vitamin D. The concentration of 7-dehydroxycholesterol in the skin is about 0.5–1.5 μg/cm^2. Increased exposure to sunlight results in an increased production of vitamin D, which can be detected in the blood as increased concentrations of 25-OHD. The 25-OHD concentrations in healthy humans are greater in summer than in winter, greater at higher altitudes and more tropical latitudes, and greater in people who work outdoors than in those who work indoors. For children and adults, most of the vitamin D requirement (upwards of 90%) comes from casual exposure to sunlight. Elderly persons who are infirm and consequently may not be exposed to normal environmental levels of ultraviolet depend on dietary sources and supplements for their vitamin D requirement.

Light Versus Diet as Sources of Vitamin D. Natural foods contain little vitamin D, with the exception of certain fatty fish and fish liver oils. To reduce the dependence on environmental radiation, dairy products, cereals and certain other foods are fortified with vitamin D in North America and some European countries. In some areas, the fortification of dairy products is accomplished with vitamin D_2, which is biologically similar to but chemically distinct from the vitamin D_3 produced in the skin.

The incremental vitamin D provided by diet fortification has virtually eliminated childhood vitamin D deficiency in areas where it was formerly a common and serious public health problem, such as countries in high latitudes. Since many adults do not eat vitamin-D-fortified foods, they remain relatively dependent on

cutaneous synthesis to meet their requirements for vitamin D. The current recommended dietary allowance for vitamin D in adults in the United States is 10 μg/day, or 400 international units. Excessive exposure to sunlight will not cause vitamin D intoxication; however, excessive vitamin D intake can occur, although this usually requires ingestion of over 1000 μg (40,000 international units) of vitamin D daily for some time.

Biological Rhythms[3, 45–72]

Cyclic changes in biological parameters have been observed across species throughout both the plant and animal kingdoms. These rhythmic alterations are loosely termed *biological rhythms*. Biological rhythms manifest themselves at both the macroscopic (multicellular) and microscopic (unicellular and subcellular) levels. Each rhythm has a characteristic amplitude, or magnitude of periodic change, and a characteristic period τ, or frequency f, of oscillation.

The timing of all biological rhythms involves the coordination, or *entrainment*, of external time cues (called *exogenous zeitgebers*) with an internal, or *endogenous*, pacemaker. External cues are for the most part derived from one or more of four geophysical cycles occurring in the natural environment: the tidal cycle, day-night cycle, lunar cycle and seasonal cycle. Each natural cycle causes the synchronization of a particular rhythm (called a *circarhythm*). For example, circa*dian* rhythms (entrained to the day-night cycle) are manifest in almost every plant (the raising and lowering of plant leaves throughout the day) and animal (the sleep-wake cycle). Seasonal rhythms, or circ*annual* rhythms, are also widely manifest, as in plant seed germination and the seasonal breeding of many mammalian species. In addition to circarhythms, many cyclic patterns have been observed that cannot be directly linked to an external environmental synchronization. These rhythms tend to be shorter than one day (*ultradian*) as in the 90-min sleep cycle, or longer than one day (*infradian*), as in the female estrous or menstrual rhythm. In short, the timing of all biological rhythms, irrespective of period length, is dependent upon both exogenous and endogenous entrainment cues.

Circadian Rhythms. Rhythms which occur on an approximate 24-h schedule are termed circadian rhythms. Circadian rhythms are of particular interest, for they characterize the pattern of variation observed in the majority of human physiologic rhythms, including body temperature, sleep pattern, hormone secretion and blood pressure. Environmental light is the primary stimulus which mediates entrainment in the nonhuman mammalian circadian system. Recent studies have clearly demonstrated that light is an entraining stimulus in humans as well; however, there is some evidence which suggests that behavioral cues (social interaction) and artificial cues (alarm clocks) can also serve as entraining factors in humans.

Evidence for an internal timing mechanism (or *biological clock*) can be produced by placing an organism under constant conditions (constant light or darkness), thereby denying it access to exogenous time cues. Organisms placed under such conditions continue to manifest circadian rhythms, but at a period characteristic of their own internal clocks. Such rhythms, which vary in period among species, are said to be *free-running*. In mammals, for example, nocturnal (night-active) species tend to have "faster" internal clocks with periods less than 24 h, while diurnal (day-active) species tend to have "slower" clocks with periods greater than 24 h. The average human free-running period is approximately 25 h.

Retinal Physiology. In the mammalian circadian system, photic information is processed by the retina and relayed to the hypothalamus of the brain via a neural pathway called the retinohypothalamic tract (RHT). The retinal photoreceptors and photopigments employed in the visual system are discussed in chapter 3, Vision and Perception. It remains, however, to be determined which photoreceptors and photopigments are responsible for signal transduction in the circadian system. In examining studies from many laboratories, some data have indicated that the peak sensitivity of the circadian and neuroendocrine system is around 500 nm, thus supporting the hypothesis that rhodopsin or a rhodopsin-based molecule is the primary receptor for circadian and neuroendocrine regulation, although other data have suggested that one or more cone photopigments may be involved in these regulatory effects. For example, in rodents, short wavelengths of sufficient intensity in the ultraviolet region of the spectrum as well as long wavelengths in the visible region are capable of suppressing melatonin (a hormone secreted by the pineal gland which follows a circadian pattern), entraining circadian rhythms and influencing reproductive responses. Further studies are required to identify conclusively which specific photoreceptors and photopigments are involved in regulating the circadian and neuroendocrine systems among different animals.

Neural Pathway. After the retinal detection of photic information, the RHT projects directly to a bilateral structure known as the suprachiasmatic nucleus (SCN), which is believed to be the biological clock in humans and other mammals. Ablation of the SCN in rats and hamsters causes arrhythmia (loss of circadian rhythmicity). Neural projections from the SCN travel to many diverse control centers in the nervous system, including other areas of the hypothalamus as well as the thalamus, midbrain, brain stem and spinal cord. One nerve pathway that carries nonvisual photic information extends from the SCN to the pineal gland (located in the brain itself) via a multisynaptic pathway, with connections being made sequentially in the paraventricular hypothalamus, the upper thoracic intermediolateral cell column and the superior cervical ganglion (see figure 5-12). Cycles of light and darkness relayed by the retina entrain SCN neural activity, which in turn entrains the rhythmic production and secretion of melatonin from the pineal gland. In all vertebrate species studied to date, including humans, high levels of melatonin are secreted during the night and low levels are secreted during the day.

In addition to entraining melatonin secretion from the pineal gland, light can have an acute suppressive effect on melatonin. Specifically, exposure of the eyes to light during the night can cause a rapid decrease in the high nocturnal synthesis and secretion of melatonin. Numerous studies have examined how the photic parameters of light intensity, wavelength, exposure duration and timing interact with melatonin regulation.

Human Biological Rhythms and the Circadian System. There are a myriad of measurable human physiological quantities which vary cyclically on a 24-h schedule. The core body temperature reaches its peak during midday, dropping about $1°$C to a nadir during sleep. Concentrations of various hormones (for example, melatonin) change regularly with the time of day. Other measurable quantities, including blood pressure, hand grip strength, alertness, cognitive performance and visual sensitivity, also show circadian rhythmicity.

The effects of drugs upon the body vary with a circadian rhythmicity as well. *Chronopharmacology* examines rhythmic sensitivity to drugs—that is, how a certain dosage may elicit a response at one time of day, but prove to be ineffective after another administration that same day. Drug prescription and administration should be considerate of this circadian variation in threshold response sensitivity.

Desynchronization of Rhythms. The various circadian rhythms detailed above are all synchronized by the internal clock, which is in turn entrained to the external 24-h light schedule. Sleep deprivation, placement in constant conditions or exposure to light during the night hours causes a loss of entrainment to the envi-

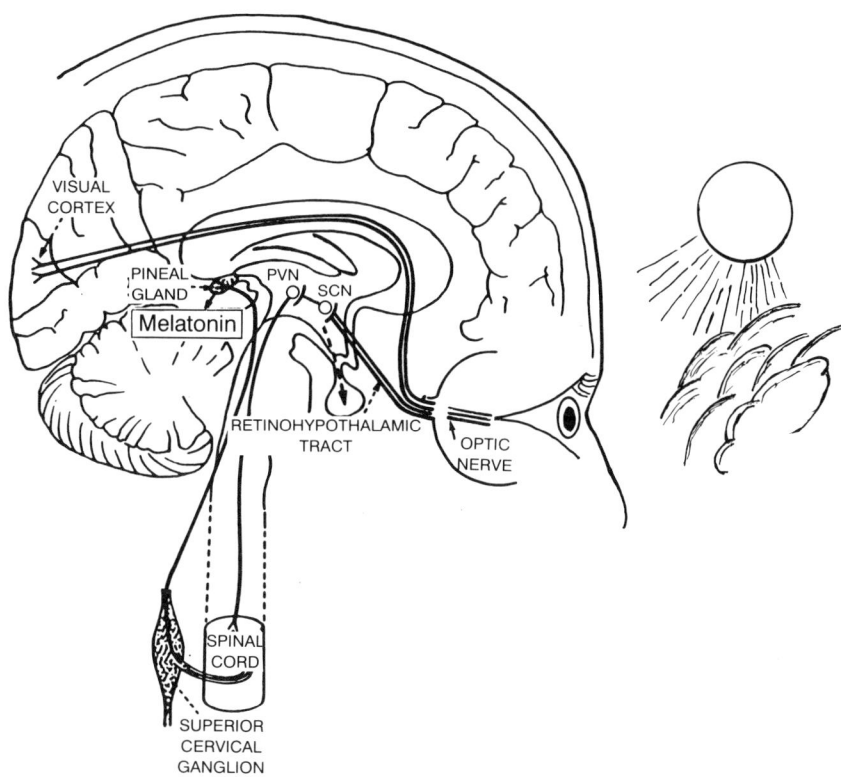

Fig. 5-12. Simplified illustration of pathway from the retina to the suprachiasmatic nucleus (SCN) or the hypothalamic "clock" and its long multisynaptic projection to the pineal gland by way of the paraventricular nucleus (PVN) in the hypothalamus. Note this pathway is anatomically separate from the pathway to the visual cortex which serves the sensory capacity of vision.

ronment. Thus, the internal clock can become *phase shifted*, or out of synchrony with the external world. This desynchronization often contributes to feelings of discomfort, as commonly manifested in the jet-lag syndrome. Symptoms of jet lag can include a disturbance in sleep and wakefulness, digestive difficulties, physical fatigue, menstrual irregularity, confusion and irritability, and reduced cognitive performance.

Certain occupational hazards often involve mandatory phase shifting of the internal clock. Perhaps the most common of these is shift work. By the broadest definition, shift workers are persons who do not work a standard daytime schedule. Instead, they work nights, evenings, rotating shifts, split shifts or extended shifts. In a recent report from the U.S. Congress, it was estimated that one out of five full-time workers in the United States is a shift worker. In agreement with many investigators, that report indicated that the two most common and destructive problems associated with shift work are a reduced quality of sleep following night work and a reduced capacity to maintain alertness while at work. These side effects translate into increased accidents, decreased production, and performance deficits among those who are working at night. Furthermore, evidence indicates that shift workers have increased health problems, including a higher risk of cardiovascular disease, gastrointestinal distress, and

cognitive and emotional problems. They are also likely to experience one or more of the symptoms attributed above to jet lag. In both conditions, chronic desynchronization of internal biological rhythms is thought to be a cause of such symptoms. Despite these deleterious effects on worker health and efficiency, the number of people involved in shift work is likely to increase.

Researchers believe that poor chronobiological adjustment to a permanent or rotating schedule causes some of these ailments. Not all of them, however, are solely due to a maladapted biological clock. In addition to a desynchronized circadian system, shift workers generally tend to be chronically sleep deprived and experience domestic stresses that are more or less independent of circadian adaptation.

On the frontiers of shift-work research, some investigators are attempting to develop strategies of light stimulation in an effort to improve circadian entrainment and to enhance performance and alertness in night workers. This new form of light therapy will be discussed below.

Phototherapy[3, 63, 71, 73–136]

Phototherapy, or the use of light as the primary or supplementary source of treatment for a disorder, is an established yet burgeoning field. Light has been used therapeutically in a wide variety of applications, including dermatology, photochemistry, psychiatry and oncology. Some forms of treatment, such as photochemotherapy, are established and have been practiced for decades, while others, such as low-level laser therapy, remain experimental.

Retinal Photocoagulation. A therapeutic effect of both incoherent and coherent (laser) radiation in the 400–1400-nm wavelength bands involves photocoagulation techniques used to repair retinal detachment. The original coagulation process, involving the "welding" of the detached retina to the sclera, was accomplished with incoherent white light from a xenon lamp coagulator. The lamp has been superseded in most ophthalmological clinics by ruby, argon and diode laser coagulators. Today, the photocoagulation technique in ophthalmology has been applied to the treatment of diabetic retinopathy, age-related maculopathy and many other pathologies involving the eye.

Phototherapy of Neonatal Hyperbilirubinemia.[73-77] Hyperbilirubinemia in neonates is more commonly known as jaundice of the newborn. It is estimated that 50% of all infants develop at least mild jaundice during the first week of life and that about 7–10% of neonates have hyperbilirubinemia of sufficient severity to require medical attention.

Jaundice is the symptom and not the disease. It results from the accumulation of a yellow pigment, bilirubin, as a result of the infant's inability to rid itself of bilirubin as rapidly as it is produced. Bilirubin is chemically a tetrapyrrole and is derived principally from the degradation of hemoglobin. At normal concentrations, bilirubin is transported in the blood by binding to albumin. When the bound bilirubin reaches the liver, it is conjugated from a lipophilic to a hydrophilic substance which can be excreted in the urine. Infants with hyperbilirubinemia lack the ability to bind and excrete bilirubin in the normal manner.

In neonates, increased amounts of unconjugated bilirubin circulate in the blood. This is a result of normal red corpuscle degradation coupled with the functional immaturity of the neonatal liver. Normal unconjugated plasma bilirubin concentrations in newborns rarely exceed 1.5–2.0 mg/dl; however, when concentrations rise to 5.0–6.0 mg/dl, a quantity of the pigment is transferred to the skin to produce the yellowish skin color known as jaundice. After detection, the condition can be monitored by measurement of the blood plasma bilirubin level.

As the plasma concentration of bilirubin increases, there is a danger of exceeding the body's albumin-binding capacity, allowing free bilirubin to circulate. If unconjugated bilirubin levels reach 10–15 mg/dl in a newborn, the pigment can penetrate the blood-brain barrier and accumulate in the brain, thus producing bilirubin encephalopathy and irreversible damage from toxic injury to brain cells, a condition known as *kernicterus*. Kernicterus often leads to the development of neurological injuries, including learning impairment, cerebral palsy, deafness and, in extreme cases, death. Phototherapy is used to prevent the dangerous rise in plasma bilirubin.

Phototherapy of neonatal jaundice is a therapeutic alternative to exchange plasma transfusion. It is administered as a whole-body, commonly ventral, irradiation, usually by banked 20-W fluorescent lamps, with some portion of lamp emission falling in the visible spectral region of 400–450 nm. An infant is placed beneath the phototherapy light unit at a distance of 40–50 cm and is kept unclothed (undiapered) with both eyes shielded by an opaque eye mask to protect the retina.

Originally, in vitro studies employing light between 450 and 500 nm caused the photodegradation of bilirubin. The concentration of free bilirubin was also drastically reduced by irradiation of this sort. These findings led to the conclusion that the degradation of bilirubin was necessary for benificial biological effects. Recently, however, in vitro studies employing short-wavelength visible light have resulted in the photooxidation of bilirubin, with the products of exposure lacking the toxicity of unconjugated bilirubin. These bilirubin derivatives are also more readily excreted in vivo and are similarly less likely to accumulate in neural tissue. The excreted products are isomers of bilirubin and not products of a degradation reaction. Hence, the present understanding of the efficacy of phototherapy for hyperbilirubinemia is via a photoisomerization mechanism rather than one hypothesizing photodegradation.

Most clinical phototherapy regimens are conducted by constant exposure. Exposure at an irradiance of 0.9 μW/cm^2 in the 450–500-nm range will cause a visual fading of the yellow skin color within 2–3 h, accompanied by a reduction of unconjugated bilirubin in plasma. The irradiance used can range up to 2.1 mW/cm^2 in the 420–490-nm region. There does not seem to be a linear relationship between irradiance and bilirubin reduction. The effect of phototherapy on plasma-free bilirubin concentration is shown in figure 5-13.

Phototherapy is an effective modality for correcting hyperbilirubinemia in the newborn. In contrast to the alternative therapy, exchange transfusion, it is noninvasive and poses less risk of mortality. Nevertheless, several side effects have been observed (see figure 5-14).

Equipment Design and Measurement. Some essentials for phototherapy light unit design and radiation measurement are listed below.

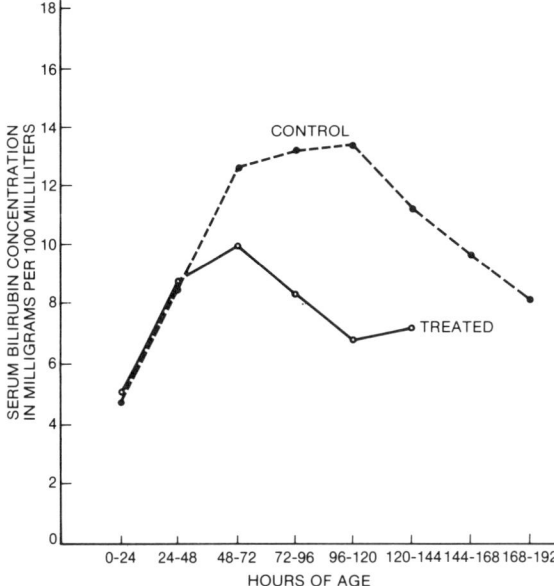

Fig. 5-13. The effect of phototherapy of neonatal hyperbilirubinemia upon the mean serum bilirubin concentrations of 32 infants compared with that of 33 hyperbilirubinemic infants who received no treatment.

Fig. 5-14. Side Effects of Phototherapy

Determined *in vitro*
  1. Albumin denaturation
  2. Diminished riboflavin levels
  3. G-6-PD activity loss
  4. Glutathione reductase activity loss
  5. Mutagenesis in cell cultures
Determined *in vivo* (animals)
  1. Retinal damage
  2. Increased liver glycogen in rats
  3. Retarded gonadal growth (not function) in rats
Determined *in vivo* (human infants)
  1. Excess body heat from thermal output of lamps
  2. Temporary growth retardation
  3. Increased insensible water loss
  4. Transient hemolysis (uncommon)
  5. Loose, discolored stools
  6. Transient skin rash
  7. Reduction of whole blood riboflavine
  8. Alteration of tryptophan—kynurenine metabolism
  9. Alteration of biologic rhythms
  10. Physical hazards from inappropriate phototherapy—unit construction
  11. Increase in gut transit time
  12. Increase in respiration
  13. Increase in peripheral blood flow
  14. Decrease in circulating platelets

Lamp Requirements

1. Deliver sufficient irradiance, between 400 and 500 nm, on the infant's skin to lower plasma bilirubin levels.
2. Provide illuminance and color rendering sufficient for monitoring and detecting changes in skin color.

3. Limit infrared irradiation to a level that prevents excessive water loss from the infant.

Phototherapy Light Unit Requirements

1. Place a protective acrylic shield between the lamps and the infant to absorb ultraviolet radiation from the lamps and to protect the infant from improperly installed lamps that may fall on the infant.
2. Use a heat mirror with lamps producing a large proportion of infrared radiation to reduce heat load, stress and water loss from the infant.
3. Provide adequate ventilation to prevent heat buildup due to radiation, conduction and convection and to maintain the required operative temperature for adequate life and output of fluorescent lamps.
4. Distribute visible light from lamps uniformly over the infant's skin.

Radiation Measurement Requirements

1. Employ instruments that accurately measure irradiance (mW/cm^2 or $\mu W/cm^2$) only in the 400–490-nm region with optical blocking of all other spectral regions.
2. If an accurate spectral power distribution of the light source is available, an alternative method may be used to estimate the irradiance. Illuminance can be measured and converted to irradiance by a mathematical algorithm. This method is not as precise as the one above, and the conversion factor will differ with each light source having a different spectral power distribution; however, it is a practical method that can be used to determine the level and uniformity of irradiance and to determine when lamps need replacing.

Phototherapy of Skin Disease.[78-80] UV radiation is used for the treatment of various skin diseases such as psoriasis and eczema. The most effective wavelengths appear to be in the UV-B (280–320-nm) portion of the spectrum. Patients are usually given a small, whole-body exposure to a suberythemogenic or minimally erythemogenic dose of radiation three to five times a week. Twenty to forty such treatments are usually required to clear the skin. Maintenance treatments are then necessary at weekly intervals to control the condition until remission occurs. Various sources of radiation have been used, but at this time, fluorescent and metal halide lamps are preferred. Adverse effects from this treatment are uncommon except for the short-term problem of erythema. Photoaging of the skin and presumably skin cancer are potential long-term problems, although the risk of the latter effect has not been fully evaluated.

Photochemotherapy of Skin Disorders.[81-93] Photochemotherapy is defined as the combination of non-ionizing electromagnetic radiation and a drug to bring about a beneficial effect. Usually, in the doses used, neither the drug alone nor the radiation alone has any significant biologic activity; it is only the combination of drug and radiation that is therapeutic. PUVA (psoralen and UV-A) is a term used to describe oral administration of psoralen and subsequent exposure to UV-A (long-wave ultraviolet, 320–400 nm). PUVA has proven to be effective in treating psoriasis, vitiligo (a skin disorder consisting in absent pigment cells), certain forms of severe eczema, a malignant disorder called mycosis fungoides and a growing list of other skin disorders.

Psoralens are naturally occurring tricyclic, furocoumarin-like chemicals, some of which can be photoactivated by UV-A. In living cell systems, absorption of energy from photons within the 320–400-nm waveband (with a broad peak at 340–360 nm) results in thymine-psoralen photoproducts and the transient inhibition of DNA synthesis. When certain psoralens are delivered to the skin either by direct application or by oral route, subsequent exposure to UV-A may result in redness and tanning, which are delayed in onset, occurring hours to days after exposure.

The redness, or skin inflammation, from PUVA can be severe and is the limiting factor during treatment. The occurrence and degree of redness, however, is predictable and related to the doses of both the drug and UV-A irradiance. The redness which results from PUVA differs from sunburn in its time course. PUVA redness may be absent or just beginning at 12–24 h after ultraviolet exposure (when sunburn redness is normally at its peak) and peaks at 48–72 h or later. Because skin diseases can be treated at PUVA dose exposures which are less than those causing severe redness, careful dosimetry permits safe PUVA treatments. The pigmentation which results from PUVA appears histologically and morphologically similar to true melanogenesis (delayed tanning). Pigmentation reaches a maximum at about 5–10 days after PUVA exposure and lasts weeks to months.

Psoriasis is a genetically determined hyperproliferative epidermal disorder. Until its cause or basic mediators are known, the most effective therapeutic agents must be those which have cytotoxic effects. Many such agents are effective but have potential cytotoxic effects on other than cutaneous organ systems. Since PUVA effects require UV-A, which penetrates into the skin but does not reach internal organs, PUVA offers the potential for combining the ease of systemic administration with the relative safety of limiting the biologic effects to the irradiated skin.

Repeated PUVA exposures cause the disappearance of lesions of psoriasis in most patients. Ten to thirty treatments, given twice weekly, are usually adequate to achieve clearing. Weekly maintenance treatments keep most psoriatics free of evidence of their disease. Although no rebound exacerbation of psoriasis lesions has been seen after discontinuation of therapy, psoriasis recurs weeks to months after PUVA therapy ceases. Patients with recurrent psoriasis respond to repeated PUVA therapy. The scalp, body folds and other areas not exposed to UV-A do not respond to the therapy.

Two hours after ingestion of 0.6 mg/kg body weight of 8-methoxypsoralen, patients are exposed to UV-A. The initial UV-A exposure ($1.0-5.0$ J/cm^2) depends on the degree of melanization and on the sunburn history. The exposure must be increased as tanning occurs, because the pigmented skin diminishes UV-A penetration to the deeper levels of skin. Ideal radiation sources are those which have high radiant output of UV-A, the capability to irradiate the entire body surface, little UV-B and infrared output, and uniform irradiance at all sites within the radiation chamber. Safety devices and reliable methods of measuring and delivering exact exposures are essential.

The sun can be used as a PUVA radiation source, but carries the disadvantage of varying and unpredictable ultraviolet irradiance and spectral distribution at the earth's surface. In tanned or pigmented patients, long exposure times may be required. For example, the exposure duration for both front and back of the body may be two to three times that needed for a single total-body treatment in an experimental photochemotherapy system. Some patients, however, are willing to tolerate the heat and boredom of sun exposure in order to have the advantage of home treatment. Intense sun, clear skies, metering devices, careful instruction, and intelligent, cooperative and motivated patients are required to make sun PUVA therapy a reasonable alternative to hospital or office treatment.

Exposure to high irradiances of UV-A for prolonged periods of time causes cataract and skin cancer in laboratory animals. These effects are enhanced by psoralens. The exposures used in these studies are much greater than therapeutic exposures. Observations in animal systems indicate that the extent of skin cancer induction varies with dose and route of psoralen administration and UV exposure. Both basal cell and squamous cell carcinomas have been observed in patients treated with PUVA. The incidence of these tumors is highest in patients with a prior history of exposure to ionizing radiation or a previous cutaneous carcinoma. These findings suggest that the potential risk of PUVA-related cutaneous carcinogenesis should be carefully weighed against the potential benefit of this therapy. Special care must be taken in treating patients with prior histories of cutaneous carcinoma or exposure to ionizing radiation.

Experimental animal studies indicate that 8-methoxypsoralen also sensitizes the cornea and lens of certain species to UV-A exposure. It is not yet known how this sensitization relates to the use of psoralens in photochemotherapy of humans. Although humans have used 8-methoxypsoralen therapeutically for decades, no cataracts attributable to PUVA have been reported. It seems wise, however, to limit the use of psoralen photochemotherapy to those with significant skin disease and to use adequate UV-A eye protection during the course of therapy. After ingesting psoralens, patients should protect their eyes for at least the remainder of that day.

Physicians must be aware of these theoretical concerns and must carefully observe patients for signs of accelerated actinic damage. Glasses which are opaque to UV-A decrease total UV-A exposure to the lens and should be worn on treatment days.

Photochemotherapy of Tumors.[94-98] The photochemotherapy of tumors (also known as photodynamic therapy) employs visible light of a particular wavelength band as a catalyst in a photodegradation reaction. The products of this reaction are cytotoxic and effectively destroy tumor cells. The chemical hematoporphyrin derivative (HpD), when introduced into the blood, locates and binds to tumor cells. Exposure of the tumor to visible light at 630 nm causes the production of singlet oxygen from its previously bound triplet state in HpD. Singlet oxygen is highly cytotoxic and consequently causes tumor cell degradation.

Filtered xenon and tungsten lamps can be used to treat cutaneous lesions. A pumped dye argon laser radiating at 630 nm, connected to an optical delivery system such as fiber optics, can be used with an endoscope or similar device to reach internal cavities. Photodynamic therapy has achieved partial or complete response in 85% of patients with lung, esophageal, bladder, ocular, head and neck, neurological and gynecological tumors. Despite this success, treatment has generally been limited to cutaneous and subcutaneous tumors (including breast cancers, melanomas and basal cell carcinomas.) The photoreactivity of HpD can also be employed in tumor localization and detection, as light of 400 nm causes HpD to fluoresce. HpD is not toxic in the absence of light; however, as the substance is retained in the skin, it can cause photosensitivity that may persist for 3–4 weeks after infusion.

Phototherapy for Seasonal Affective Disorder (SAD).[99-116] During the past decade, the specific condition of fall and winter depression, or *seasonal affective disorder* (SAD), has been formally described in the scientific literature and included in the latest edition of the American Psychiatric Association's diagnostic manual, DSM-III-R. Although this syndrome is newly identified, several independent studies in the United States and Europe suggest that winter depression is a widespread syndrome. A study of the frequency of SAD manifestation on the east coast of the United States estimated that SAD occurs in less than 2% of the population in Florida, but in New Hampshire nearly 10% of the population show symptoms. From this study, it has been projected that as many as 10 million Americans have SAD and possibly an additional 25 million have some susceptibility to SAD.

People affected with this malady experience a dramatic decrease in their physical energy and stamina during the fall and winter months. As days become shorter and cooler, persons with SAD often find it increasingly difficult to meet the routine demands at work and at home. In addition to this general decrease in energy, SAD sufferers experience emotional depression, feelings of hopelessness, and despair. Other symptoms of winter depression or SAD may include increased sleepiness and need for sleep, increased appetite (particularly for sweets and other carbohydrates), and a general desire to withdraw from society. Fortunately, daily light therapy has been found to effectively reduce symptoms in many patients.

There are now numerous clinics across North America that offer light therapy for people who are afflicted with winter depression. Specific treatment protocols vary somewhat among clinics. One frequently used procedure involves having a patient sit at a specific distance from a fluorescent light panel which provides a 2500 lx illuminance to the face. The patient is told not to gaze steadily at the bright light, but rather to glance directly at the unit for a few seconds each minute over a two-hour period. During the therapy period, a patient may read, watch television, work at a computer or do other hand work. Response to this therapy is often noted after two to seven days of light treatment. Benefits continue as long as the treatment is repeated regularly throughout the months that the individual experiences winter depression.

Considerable research has been directed at determining the optimum illuminance, exposure and time of day for the light treatment of winter depression. Most studies indicate that illuminances below 500 lx are not effective for treating SAD, while levels from 2500 to 10,000 lx produce strong therapeutic results. In determining the best dosage of light, the intensity and exposure duration must be considered together. To date, no genuine dose-response functions have been established for light therapy, but exposure durations ranging from 30 min to 6 h in single or split sessions have been tested. The strongest therapeutic responses have been documented with a 2500-lx exposure over 2–4 h and with a 10,000-lx exposure over 30 min. Considerable data suggest that morning light treatment is superior, but not all investigators agree on this point.

Current evidence supports the hypothesis that light therapy works by way of an ocular pathway as opposed to a dermal or transdermal mechanism. To date, only three studies have investigated the action spectrum for SAD light therapy. Ultimately, a thoroughly defined action spectrum can both guide the development of light treatment devices and yield important information about the photosensory mechanism responsible for the beneficial effects of light therapy. Currently, it is premature to predict which photopigments or photoreceptors mediate the antidepressant effects of light.

A practical issue debated among researchers concerns the role of UV in light therapy. Most of the early studies on SAD therapy utilized fluorescent lamps that emitted "white" light containing a portion of UV wavelengths. Those early findings erroneously led to the suggestion that UV wavelengths are necessary for successful therapy. The current literature, however, clearly shows that SAD symptoms can be reduced by lamps which emit little or no UV. Hence, UV radiation does not appear to be necessary for eliciting positive therapeutic results.

Most of the clinical trials treating winter depression have employed "white" light emitted by commercially available lamps. The white light used for treating SAD can be provided by a range of lamp types, including incandescent, cool white fluorescent, and "sunlight-simulating" fluorescent. There is an assortment of light devices specifically designed for the treatment of SAD. Light therapy instruments come in a variety of shapes and configurations, including workstations, head-mounted light visors, and automatic dawn simulators. These devices are configured to shorten therapeutic time, increase patient mobility or permit therapy during the sleep period. Because dose-response comparisons have not been performed among different lamp types and light devices, it is not possible to distinguish which, if any, type of light is superior for treating depression.

Light Therapy for Jet Lag, Shift Work and Sustained Performance.[71, 117–126] As scientists have explored the physiology of the human biological clock under normal conditions, they have also examined how that clock functions or dysfunctions under more unusual situations. Jet lag is a condition that results from rapidly moving across time zones. Although the human biolog-

ical clock adjusts within three to seven days after such an event, during the adjustment period many people experience uncomfortable symptoms, which may include sleep and wake disruptions, gastric distress, irritability, depression and confusion. Such symptoms can pose serious problems for the business traveler and can diminish the enjoyment of a vacation for the leisure traveler. Some preliminary studies have tested the use of light exposure to prevent or ameliorate jet-lag symptoms. Investigators are optimistic that light may be a useful tool for the immediate resetting of the traveler's biological clock and can help overcome some of the problems associated with jet travel. There is a consensus among scientists, however, that there currently are insufficient data for a set prescription on how to best use light for this modern malady.[71, 125]

Shift work poses a problem analogous to that found in jet lag. Instead of rapidly flying to distant places, shiftworkers may just as suddenly change the time period that they are awake or asleep. These individuals are awake and working during the night and attempting to sleep during the daylight hours. Although some individuals prefer night work over day work and are well adapted to shift schedules, shift work is often associated with decreased production, performance deficits and increased health complaints. Some investigators are attempting to develop strategies of light stimulation to enhance performance and alertness in night workers. Studying simulated shift work over a 2–5-day period, different groups of investigators have shown that night workers had better circadian adaptation and improved alertness and cognitive performance when they worked under bright light (1,000–12,000 lx) than under dim light (100–150 lx). Other studies on simulated shift work have shown that exposure to bright white fluorescent light at specific times can improve sleep quality, enhance performance and speed the adjustment of the circadian system.

The U.S. military currently has a triservice research program aimed at finding ways of enhancing physical and mental performance in personnel who are on continuous duty for prolonged periods of time. A major focus of this program has been to study pharmacological agents which can help sustain alertness without degrading performance. Recently, however, sustained performance studies have shown that workers exposed to bright light (3000 or 5000 lx) exhibited significantly improved behavioral and cognitive performance on selected tasks compared to their own performance on a separate occasion under 100 lx. In addition to these behavioral effects, there were significant differences in the body temperatures, plasma cortisol levels and plasma melatonin levels associated with light stimuli. In these acute studies, it is not clear how light is influencing performance. However, there is a consensus among scientists that it is still premature to formulate a prescription on how to best use light for both short-term and long-term work applications.[71, 125]

Potential Placebo Responses in Light Therapy, Mood, and Performance Effects.[127-128] In considering the newer uses of light for therapeutically reducing the symptoms of winter depression, jet lag and shift work, it is important to examine whether the observed effects are due to specific light therapy or to a nonspecific or placebo response. When using light experimentally on humans, either for therapeutic purposes or for work or travel applications, investigators are confronted with a dilemma. Simply put, when volunteers can readily see that a manipulation of light is part of an experiment, there is a distinct risk of finding a placebo reaction to the specific light treatments.

In the medical literature it has been well documented that patients with a wide range of disorders—depression, schizophrenia and anxiety as well as cancer, diabetes and ulcers—can successfully respond to inactive (placebo) treatments. Hence it is likely that SAD patients, world travelers and shift workers will show some level of placebo response to light therapy. The degree to which the patients' response to light therapy is due to a nonspecific placebo response or to a genuine clinical response remains an open question.

Some experimental strategies can help address the placebo problem.

Low-Level Laser Therapy.[129-130] Although not yet approved for routine medical use in the United States, low-level lasers at 633, 830 and 904 nm are used widely throughout the world in sports medicine clinics and by veterinarians to accelerate wound healing, treat sprains and control certain types of pain. Unfortunately, low-level lasers are also used to treat other conditions for which there is little hard evidence for benefit. The scientific community should encourage this fledgling field to establish proper controls and to learn more photobiology in order to establish unequivocally which clinical conditions are improved by this type of therapy and which are not. Attempts have been made to explain the photobiological basis of how visible and infrared radiation can produce similar clinical and cellular responses.

Environmental Lighting Safety Criteria.[131-136] Many exposure limits for optical radiation have been proposed in the literature; however, the only widely accepted standards are for the ultraviolet spectral region. Even these standards have provoked controversy. At present there is movement toward the development of both human exposure limits and product performance standards. For further information refer to such agen-

cies and organizations as the Army Environmental Hygiene Agency, American Conference of Governmental Industrial Hygienists (ACGIH), National Institute of Occupational Safety and Health (NIOSH), Center for Devices and Radiation Health (CDRH) of the Food and Drug Administration, and American National Standards Institute (ANSI).

EFFECTS ON MICROORGANISMS

Germicidal (Bactericidal) Ultraviolet Irradiance[137-143]

Electromagnetic radiation in the wavelength range between 180 and 700 nm is capable of killing many species of bacteria, molds, yeasts and viruses. The germicidal effectiveness of the different wavelength regions may vary by several orders of magnitude, but the wavelengths falling in the far ultraviolet and UV-B part of the spectrum are generally the most effective for bactericidal purposes.

The bacterium most widely used for the study of bactericidal effects is *Escherichia coli*. Studies have shown the most effective wavelength range to be between 220 and 300 nm, corresponding to the peak of photic absorption by bacterial deoxyribonucleic acid (DNA). The absorption of the ultraviolet radiation by the DNA molecule produces mutations and/or cell death. The relative effectiveness of different wavelengths of radiation in killing a common strain of *E. coli* is shown in figure 5-15.

Germicidal (Bactericidal) Lamps. The most practical method of generating germicidal radiation is by passage of an electric discharge through low-pressure mercury vapor enclosed in a special glass tube which transmits shortwave ultraviolet radiation. About 95% of the energy from such a device is radiated in the 253.7-nm band, which is very close to the wavelength corresponding to the greatest lethal effectiveness. See chapter 6, Light Sources, for the germicidal output of various commercial lamps.

Hot-cathode germicidal lamps are similar in physical dimensions and electrical characteristics to the standard preheat 8-, 15- and 30-W fluorescent lamps. While both types of lamps operate on the same auxiliaries, germicidal lamps contain no phosphor and are enclosed by glass which permits the maximum emission of UV wavelengths. Slimline germicidal lamps are instant-start lamps capable of operating at several current densities within their design range, 120–420 mA, depending upon the ballast with which they are used. Cold-cathode germicidal lamps are instant-start lamps with a cylindrical cathode. They are made in many sizes and operate from a transformer.

Fig. 5-15. Erythemal and Germicidal (Bactericidal) Efficiency of Ultraviolet Radiation.

Wavelength (nanometers)	Erythemal Efficiency	Tentative Bactericidal Efficiency
*235.3	....	0.35
240.0	0.56	....
*244.6	0.57	0.58
*248.2	0.57	0.70
250.0	0.57	....
*253.7	0.55	0.85
*257.6	0.49	0.94
260.0	0.42	....
265.0	....	1.00
*265.4	0.25	0.99
*267.5	0.20	0.98
*270.0	0.14	0.95
*275.3	0.07	0.81
*280.4	0.06	0.68
285.0	0.09	....
*285.7	0.10	0.55
*289.4	0.25	0.46
290.0	0.31	....
*292.5	0.70	0.38
295.0	0.98	....
*296.7	1.00	0.27
300.0	0.83	....
*302.2	0.55	0.13
305.0	0.33	....
310.0	0.11	....
*313.0	0.03	0.01
315.0	0.01	....
320.0	0.005	....
325.0	0.003	....
330.0	0.000	....

* Emission lines in the mercury spectrum; other values interpolated.

The life of the hot-cathode and slimline germicidal lamps is governed by the electrode life and frequency of starts. (Their effective life is sometimes limited by the transmission of the bulb, particularly when operated at low temperatures.) The electrodes of cold-cathode lamps are not affected by the number of starts, and their useful life is determined entirely by the transmission of the bulb. All types of germicidal lamps experience a decrement in UV emission as the time of constant illumination increases. Lamps should be checked periodically for ultraviolet output to ensure that their germicidal effectiveness is being maintained.

The majority of germicidal lamps operate most efficiently in still air at room temperature. For lamp efficiency measurements, ultraviolet output is standardized at an ambient temperature of 25° C. Temperatures either higher or lower than this optimum value decrease the output of the lamp. Lamps operating in a room at 4° C produce only about two-thirds to three-fourths as much ultraviolet as at 25° C. Cooling the

lamp by passing air currents over it or by submerging it in liquid likewise lowers its output.

Slimline germicidal lamps operated at currents ranging from 300 to 420 mA and certain preheat germicidal lamps operated at 600 mA are designed exceptions to this general rule. At these high current loadings, the lamp temperature is above the normal value for optimum operation; therefore, cooling of the bulb does not have the same adverse effect as with other lamps. Thus, these lamps are well suited for use in air conditioning ducts.

In addition to emissions in the 253.7-nm bandwidth, some germicidal lamps generate a controlled amount of 184.9-nm radiation, which produces ozone in the air (see figure 5-16). Since ozone is highly toxic, its environmental concentrations have been limited by an Occupational Safety and Health Administration (OSHA) regulatory mandate to 0.1 ppm, or 0.2 mg/m^3. Care should be taken when choosing germicidal lamps to meet the requirements of these regulations.

Photoreactivation. It has been observed that the survival of ultraviolet-irradiated bacteria could be greatly enhanced if the cells were subsequently exposed to an intense source of blue light. Researchers have demonstrated the existence of a photoreactivating enzyme and established its basic properties in repair of damaged DNA.

The enzyme combines in the dark with cyclobutyl pyrimidine dimers in ultraviolet-irradiated DNA to form an enzyme-substrate complex. When the complex is activated by the absorption of energy between 320 and 410 nm, the cyclobutyl pyrimidine dimers are converted to monomeric pyrimidines and the enzyme is released.

Under certain experimental conditions, as much as 80% of the lethal damage induced in bacteria by low-energy ultraviolet radiation at 254 nm can be photoreactivated, thus indicating the importance of cyclobutyl pyrimidine dimers as lethal lesions. Photoreactivating enzymes have been found in a wide range of species, from the simplest living cells to the skin and white blood cells of man.

Germicidal Effectiveness. The effectiveness of germicidal radiation is dependent on many parameters, including the specific susceptibility of the organism, the wavelength of radiation emitted, the radiant flux and the time of exposure. Figure 5-17 lists the exposure intensity (joules per square meter) of the 253.7-nm ultraviolet radiation necessary for the inhibition of colony formation (a 90% reduction in population) in a wide variety of microorganisms.

Germicidal effectiveness is proportional to the product of intensity and time (from one microsecond to a few hours). A nonlinear relationship exists between

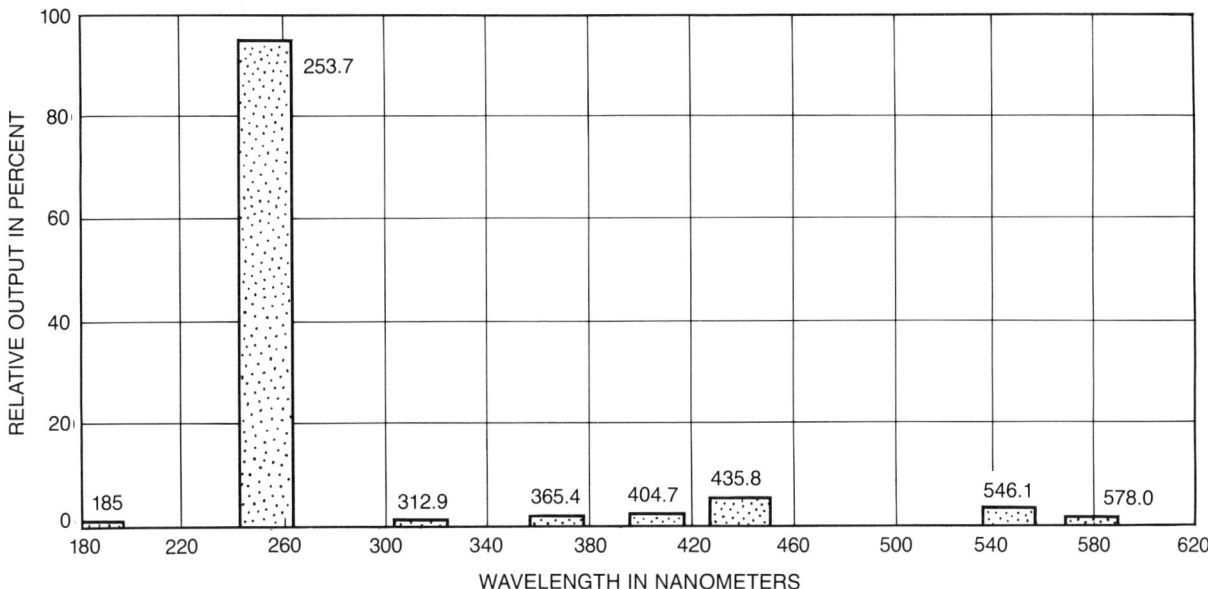

Fig. 5-16. Relative spectral distribution of energy emitted by ozone-producing germicidal lamps.

ultraviolet exposure and germicidal efficacy. For example, if a certain ultraviolet exposure produces a 90% kill of a bacterial population, doubling the exposure intensity can only produce a 90% kill of the residual 10%, for an overall 99%. Likewise, a 50% decrease in intensity or exposure only results in a decrease in germicidal efficacy from 99% to 90%.

Precautions. Exposure to germicidal ultraviolet radiation can produce eye injury and skin erythema, and has produced skin cancer in laboratory animals. The ACGIH has set a limit of 0.2 μW/cm^2 for an 8-h continuous exposure and 0.4 μW/cm^2 for a 4-h exposure. This conservative limitation can be extrapolated to 10 μW/cm^2 for a 10-min exposure, and to a maximum time of only 1 min for the 100 μW/cm^2 emitted by an unshielded Sylvania G30T8 lamp at 0.75 m. See chapter 6, Light Sources.

Based on the potential for producing threshold keratitis, the NIOSH has proposed a value of half of the above restrictions as a safe industrial exposure for the eye. Eye protection is essential for all who are exposed to the direct or reflected radiation from lamps emitting UV wavelengths, especially those germicidal lamps emitting shortwave UV radiation. Ordinary window or plate glass or goggles that shield the eyes from wavelengths shorter than 340 nm are usually sufficient protection. However, if the radiation is intense or is to be stared at for some time, special goggles should be used. Failure to wear proper eye protection can result in temporary but painful inflammations of the conjunctiva, cornea and iris, photophobia, blepharospasm and/or ciliary neuralgia. Skin protection, achieved by wearing clothing and gloves that are opaque to germici-

dal radiation, is advised if the radiant intensity of UV is especially high or if the exposure duration is unusually long.

Applications

Air Disinfection in Rooms. In occupied rooms, irradiation by an open-fixture germicidal lamp should be confined to the area above the heads of occupants as shown in figure 5-18. The ceiling of the room to be disinfected should be higher than 2.9 m, and occupants should not remain in the room for more than 8 h at a time. If either of the above conditions does not meet the requirements of the workspace, louvered equipment should be used to avoid localized high concentration of flux which may be reflected down upon room occupants. An average irradiation of 20–25 μW/cm^2 is effective for a slow circulation of upper air and will maintain freedom from respiratory disease organisms comparable to outdoor air.

Upper-air disinfection as practiced in hospitals, schools and offices is effective in providing air relatively free of bacteria at the breathing level of room occupants. Personnel movement, body heat and winter heating methods create convection currents through cross sections of a room sufficient to provide "sanitary ventilation" of 1 to 2 air changes per minute. All surfaces irradiated by UV germicidal radiation (including ceilings and upper walls) should have an ultraviolet reflectance as low as 5% (characteristic of most oil and some waterbase paints). See figure 5-19. "White coat" plaster or gypsum-product surfaced wallboard and acoustical tile may have higher germicidal reflectance and should always be painted with a less reflective

Fig. 5-17. Incident Radiation at 253.7 nm Necessary to Inhibit Colony Formation in 90% of the Organisms

Organism		Exposure (joules per square meter)
Bacillus anthracis		45.2
S. enteritidis		40.0
B. megatherium sp. (veg.)		13.0
B. megatherium sp. (spores)		27.3
B. paratyphosus		32.0
B. subtilis		71.0
B. subtilis spores		120.0
Corynebacterium diphtheriae		33.7
Eberthella typhosa		21.4
Escherichia coli		30.0
Micrococcus candidus		60.5
Micrococcus sphaeroides		100.0
Neisseria catarrhalis		44.0
Phytomonas tumefaciens		44.0
Proteus vulgaris		26.4
Pseudomonas aeruginosa		55.0
Pseudomonas fluorescens		35.0
S. typhimurium		80.0
Sarcina lutea		197.0
Seratia marcescens		24.2
Dysentery bacilli		22.0
Shigella paradysenteriae		16.3
Spirillum rubrum		44.0
Staphylococcus albus		18.4
Staphylococcus aureus		26.0
Streptococcus hemolyticus		21.6
Streptococcus lactis		61.5
Streptococcus viridans		20.0
Yeast		
Saccharomyces ellipsoideus		60.0
Saccharomyces sp.		80.0
Saccharomyces cerevisiae		60.0
Brewers' yeast		33.0
Bakers' yeast		39.0
Common yeast cake		60.0
Mold Spores	**Color**	
Penicillium roqueforti	Green	130.0
Penicillium expansum	Olive	130.0
Penicillium digitatum	Olive	440.0
Aspergillus glaucus	Bluish green	440.0
Aspergillus flavus	Yellowish green	600.0
Aspergillus niger	Black	1320.0
Rhizopus nigricans	Black	1110.0
Mucor racemosus A	White gray	170.0
Mucor racemosus B	White gray	170.0
Oospora lactis	White	50.0

substance such as the above types of paint. Unpainted white plaster walls and ceilings can limit safe exposure to only 2–3 h even with louvered fixtures (see figure 5-20.) These precautions are especially important in the hospital infants' ward, as children are more sensitive to UV than adults.

In hospital operating rooms, especially where such prolonged surgery as heart, brain and lung operations is performed, a combination of upper-air disinfection and vertical barriers at 25 μW/cm^2 is used, with head, eye and ear protection in addition to the usual face mask.

Air Duct Installations. It is possible to provide a sufficiently high level of ultraviolet radiation for a 90–99% kill of most bacteria in the very short exposure times of duct air at usual air velocities. The limitation of the method is that it can only make the duct air equivalent to good outdoor air. Its value is in the treatment of recirculated air and contaminated outdoor air in hospitals, pharmaceutical facilities and food processing plants. Duct installations are especially valuable where central air heating and ventilating systems recirculate air through all of the otherwise isolated areas of an institution. Slimline germicidal lamps, especially designed for satisfactory ultraviolet output even when cooled by high-velocity duct air, are installed on doors in the sides of ducts, or inserted across their axis, depending upon the size and shape of the duct and access for servicing. Where possible, the best placement for lamps is across the duct to secure longer travel of the energy before absorption by the duct walls and to promote turbulence to offset the variation in ultraviolet level throughout the irradiated part of the duct. Upon installation, care must be taken to ensure that the lamps are accessible for periodic cleaning, as dust buildup lowers overall UV emission.

Sanitization Techniques. Three general methods of germicidal lamp placement may be employed to establish a sanitary environment: upper-air irradiation, barrier-type irradiation and direct irradiation. As previously outlined, upper-air irradiation maintains purified air at the normal breathing level of room occupants. It also permits safe continuous occupancy. Barrier irradiation techniques employ a narrow beam of UV directed across an opening, effectively preventing live organisms from passing from one place to another. Direct irradiation exposes whole surfaces to germicidal radiation. While the most effective and efficient form of sanitization, direct irradiation is also hazardous to room occupants. In such conditions, proper eye and skin protection must be worn while germicidal lamps are illuminated.

Liquid Disinfection. Ultraviolet disinfection of water is used when it is essential that no residual substance or taste remain in the liquid. Water disinfection methods require that allowances be made for some ultraviolet absorption by traces of natural chemical contaminants, such as iron-based and organic compounds. In addition, one must compensate for the decrease in UV intensity due to absorption by the DNA of water-dwelling organisms. Hence, disinfection of water often involves exposure intensities 40–50 times greater than those used in air sanitation. Such exposures are secured by slow gravity flow of water through shallow tanks under banks of lamps, or by immersing lamps enclosed in quartz tubes directly into the water.

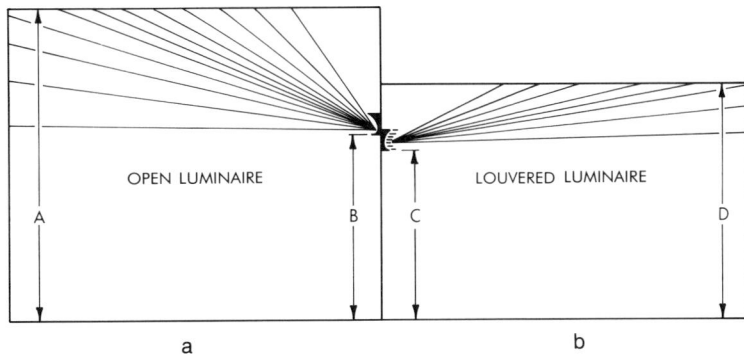

Fig. 5-18. Germicidal lamps for air disinfection in occupied rooms: (a) open unit used in rooms over 2.7 m (9 ft) in height; (b) louvered unit used where ceilings are lower than 2.7 m (9 ft). Dimensions: *A*, 3.7 m (12 ft); *B*, 2.1 m (7 ft); *C*, 2 m (6.5 ft); *D*, 2.7 m (9 ft).

Liquids of high absorbance, such as fruit juices, milk, blood, serums and vaccines, are disinfected with various *film spreaders*. These range from high-speed centrifugal devices and surface-adhering rotating cylinders to gravity-flow-down screens and inclined planes. Such devices spread a film of liquid nearly to the thickness of its molecular size.

Disinfection of Granular Material. The surfaces of granular materials (such as sugar) are disinfected on traveling belts of vibrating conveyors designed to agitate the material during travel under banks of closely spaced germicidal lamps. During a transit, which defines the exposure time, all the particles are brought to the top frequently and long enough to provide an effective exposure of their surface to the radiation. In the case of sugar, for example, thermoduric bacteria survive the vacuum evaporator temperatures of a sugar-syrup concentration and, forced out of the sugar crystals during lattice formation, remain in the final film of dilute syrup left on the crystal surface. Ordinarily harmless, these bacteria may cause serious spoilage in canned foods and beverages.

Fig. 5-19. Reflectance of Various Materials for Energy of Wavelengths in the Region of 253.7 nm

Material	Reflectance (per cent)
Aluminum	
Untreated surface	40–60
Treated surface	60–89
Sputtered on glass	75–85
Paints	55–75
Stainless steel	25–30
Tin plate	25–30
Magnesium oxide	75–88
Calcium carbonate	70–80
New plaster	55–60
White baked enamels	5–10
White oil paints	5–10
White water paints	10–35
Zinc oxide paints	4–5

Product Protection and Sanitation. Product protection and sanitation are achieved by both air disinfection and surface irradiation (as with sugar). In this field, however, the usefulness of germicidal ultraviolet radiation is generally limited to the prevention of contamination during processing rather than the disinfection of an otherwise final product. For example, where sufficient irradiation to kill mold spores may be impractical, the vegetative growth of mold itself can be prevented by continuous irradiation at levels lethal to ordinary bacteria. Germicidal lamps installed in concentrating reflectors are used to disinfect any air which might contaminate a product during processing and packaging, as in the travel of bottles from washing to filling to capping. Lamps serve to replace or supplement heat in processes where sterilization by heat might be destructive. Intensive irradiation of container surfaces can also supplement or replace washing between uses. Ultraviolet sanitization techniques are used in bakeries, in breweries and in packaging plants for liquid sugar, syrup, fruit juices and beverages.

EFFECTS ON INSECTS

Insect Responses[144–150]

The increasing popularity of outdoor living, drive-in businesses, and outdoor recreational establishments has been accompanied by intensified insect problems caused particularly by nocturnal insects attracted to light. Similar problems are encountered at lighted farmsteads, animal pens, feedlots, processing plants and industries operating at night in lighted facilities. Many of these problems can be prevented, or greatly reduced, if the responses of the insect pests involved are considered when designing and planning the use of facilities.

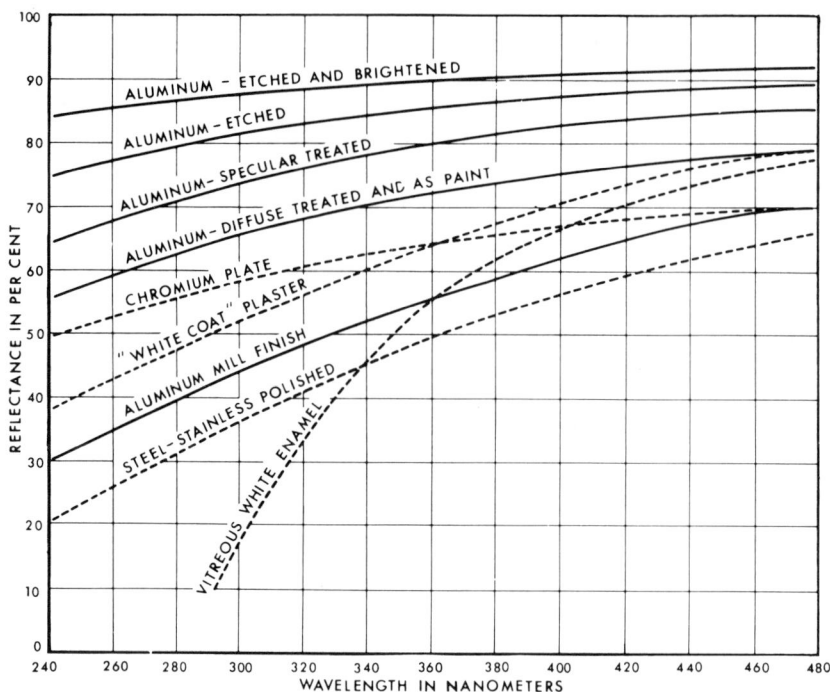

Fig. 5-20. Spectral reflectance characteristics of various materials in the short wavelength visible and the UV spectral regions.

The insect nuisance problems associated with lighting have four distinct but related aspects:

- the existing insect population in the surrounding vicinity
- the attractiveness to insects of the activity carried on in the lighted area
- the attractiveness of the lighting system used
- the suitability of the desired insect-free area for sustaining insect life.

The circumstances of each situation are different, and usually little can be done about the insect population in the vicinity.

A knowledge of the insects in relation to their normal habitats and of the activities to be carried on in the desired insect-free areas usually helps to anticipate problems. Preventive maintenance can be based on the known behavioral patterns of the expected insects. Insects likely to cause problems can be broadly categorized as follows:

Insects Not Attracted by Light. Insects not necessarily attracted to light are indigenous to enclosures and buildings, and most live continuously within the desired insect-free area. Included are cockroaches, ants and flour beetles.

Diurnal Insects. These insects normally live outside the desired insect-free area and are active during the day. They are attracted to the area for food, shelter and/or breeding sites. Examples are houseflies, pomance or fruit flies, and honey bees.

Nocturnal Insects. This group usually feeds and lives beyond the desired insect-free area and is attracted there by electromagnetic radiation. These insects are the true problem associated with lighting systems. Most nocturnal insects, such as moths, leafhoppers, mayflies, caddisflies, and various beetles, midges and mosquitoes, are capable of flight and are active primarily at night.

Phototaxis is the term applied to the visual response which causes the insect to be attracted to a source of electromagnetic radiation. Insects which are attracted to a radiation source are said to be photopositive or to exhibit positive phototaxis.

The spectral region most attractive to a wide range of insect species, especially nocturnal species, is in the near-ultraviolet (310–380-nm) range. Other species are known to respond to energy in the visible and infrared as well.

Research and experience have shown that light-caused insect problems can be greatly reduced with properly designed lighting systems and with proper management of the area.

Lighting System Attraction

One means of reducing the insect nuisance is to select light sources having low insect attractiveness. In practice, this involves maximum use of yellow-red light and the reduction of ultraviolet and blue wavelengths.

Mercury lamps which generate ultraviolet radiation can be filtered to remove the ultraviolet, either by the lamp envelope or by a refractor, but this may also reduce the light output. If filtering is extended to remove some visible wavelengths, to reduce attraction further, the loss will be even greater.

High-pressure sodium lamps have a higher lumen-per-watt output than mercury lamps, yet have about one-third as much associated insect nuisance as a comparable mercury lamp system. Thus, mercury lamps should be avoided for area lighting either inside or outside buildings where night-flying insects are a potential problem.

If, for example, insect-attractive lamps must be used for color rendition reasons, they can be shaded so that all their radiant output is confined to the area to be illuminated. If lamps must remain visible from the outside, consideration should be given to the use of refractors, filters and shields made of glass or plastic material to filter out the ultraviolet radiation. If lamps emitting blue light and near-ultraviolet energy are used for lighting, they should not be directly visible at distances beyond a few meters from the illuminated area.

Highly attracting small mercury lamps and exposed incandescent lamps should not be located directly over entrances or outside of buildings, for insects will be attracted and annoy people using the entrances. Furthermore, they will gain access to the interior when a door is opened. This problem can be greatly reduced by using yellow incandescent or sodium lamps. If fluorescent lamps are to be used, gold ones will be less attracting than the "white" type. At the least, an attracting lamp can be shaded so that its radiant output is directed downward and confined to the immediate area. Any type of lamp used to light an entrance or work area should be located a short distance away, with the light directed toward the area to be illuminated.

As insects are also attracted to reflected radiant energy, care should be taken to avoid using a surface or a paint with a high reflectance for blue visible or ultraviolet radiation.

Decoy Lamps and Insect Traps

In addition to careful lamp selection and shielding designs, the number of night-flying insects within a desired insect-free area also can be reduced by placing attracting "black light" (BL) fluorescent or mercury decoy lamps at 30–60-m distances around the perimeter of the area to intercept those insects trying to enter. The location, number and design of the decoys will depend upon the area to be protected. In addition, collecting-killing devices (traps) can be used to capture those insects attempting to enter or those having already gained entrance to the lighted area.

Insect traps commonly contain "black light" lamps to attract photopositive insects as a means for killing or trapping them. One of the common killing mechanisms is an electric grid which electrocutes the insects attracted to the trap. Various designs are available for commercial, industrial and residential use. The placement and number of traps should vary with the individual situation and the species of insects involved. Specialists in this field are usually required to determine the best placement of traps for solving specific insect problems.

If grid traps are used, they should not be placed so that electrocuted insects fall or are blown into working and food processing areas. System designs and installations should be in compliance with the National Electrical Code.

In agriculture, insect traps of various designs have been used for survey purposes to detect insects in a crop area, to predict the need for pesticide application and to evaluate effects of insecticide measures. Survey traps used over large areas can be used to determine migration of insects and to predict potential infestation. The trap designs usually include a "black light" or other fluorescent lamp and a means of trapping insects. Designs are altered for specific insect species.

Studies with "black light" insect traps in large tobacco- or tomato-growing areas of over 293 km^2 have shown that one or more traps per square kilometer reduce tobacco and tomato hornworm populations. Indications are that insect traps are best used in conjunction with insecticides. The use of such traps would generally reduce the number of insecticide applications in a growing season.

EFFECTS ON PLANTS[151–174]

Because plants and humans share the same terrestrial environment, daylight has been important to the evolution of their respective spectral sensitivities. Most of the energy incident on earth from the sun is in the visible portion of the electromagnetic spectrum (see figure 5-1). However, plants and the human visual system have evolved very different spectral sensitivities. Strictly speaking, the term "light" is reserved for humans as visually effective radiant energy. Nevertheless, "light" is also used loosely to describe all radiant energy within the visible portion of the electromagnetic spectrum and, for the purposes of discussion in this section, the term "light" will be used in that sense.

Plant Responses

Photosynthesis. Plants respond to light in many ways (Fig. 5-21). Light provides the energy necessary for the conversion of carbon dioxide and water by chlorophyll-containing plants into carbohydrates in the process known as photosynthesis. These carbohydrates are essential foods and are the substrate for proteins, fats and vitamins required for the survival of all other living organisms. Oxygen, formed as a by-product, is the major source of atmospheric oxygen. Most fossil fuel resources are derived from photosynthetic processes of a past geological period.

Light is also essential for the formation of such important plant pigments as chlorophyll, carotenoids, xanthophylls, anthocyanins and phytochrome. Light is effective in the opening of stomates, the setting of internal biological clocks, and the modification of such factors as plant size and shape; leaf size, movement, shape and color; internodal length; flower production, size and shape; petal movement; and fruit yield, size, shape and color.

Respiration. The reverse of photosynthesis is respiration, whereby the carbohydrates formed in photosynthesis are oxidized to carbon dioxide, water and energy. Respiration does not require either light or chlorophyll, but does require food, enzymes and oxygen. Respiration is continuous, whereas photosynthesis occurs only in light under normal conditions.

At moderate to high irradiances, photosynthesis in plants exceeds respiration, so the net effect is the production of oxygen from leaves during the light period. If the irradiance is diminished to the point where the carbohydrate produced is equal to that used in respiration, the apparent photosynthetic rate is zero and there is no diffusion of gas from the leaf pores (stomata). This phenomenon is called the compensation point. Plants lighted at the compensation point cannot survive long, because stored carbohydrate is used during the dark period. When the carbohydrate reserves are gone, the plant will succumb. This is an important fact in the maintenance of plants in interior environments.

Many plant species under high light levels experience an increase in respiration. This phenomenon, called photorespiration, results in a decrease in the apparent photosynthetic rate.

Other Photoresponses. In addition to photosynthesis, there are two other major photoresponses of plants: phototropism and photomorphogenesis. Phototropism is a light-induced growth movement of a plant organ, controlled by a short-wavelength-absorbing photoreceptor. Photomorphogenesis is light-controlled enlargement, development and differentiation of a plant due to responses initiated by the short-wavelength-absorbing photoreceptor and by phytochrome.

The spectral responses of the major photoreceptors are shown in comparison with that of human vision in figure 5-21. The spectral responses of the plants were obtained under monochromatic irradiation.

The short-wavelength-absorbing photoreceptor appears to be a flavin, but may differ among species of plants. Phytochrome is a blue-green biliprotein; it has a chromophore that absorbs radiant energy and undergoes excitation, which is used to change its molecular structure.

The photomorphogenic responses include flowering, seed germination, stem elongation and anthocyanin pigment formation.

Light-induced movements of plants are phototropism, photonasty and phototaxis. Phototropism is the bending of an organ toward or away from the direction of the source of light. Photonasty is the movement of plant organs, such as the closing of flowers at night and opening during the day, due to changes in irradiance. Phototaxis is the movement of the whole organism in response to light and is restricted to sex cells of aquatic plants and unicellular aquatic plants.

Limiting Factors for Growth

In addition to light, which provides the energy for plants, other requirements must be available in optimum amounts for rapid photosynthesis and growth. These requirements are water, nutrients (inorganic

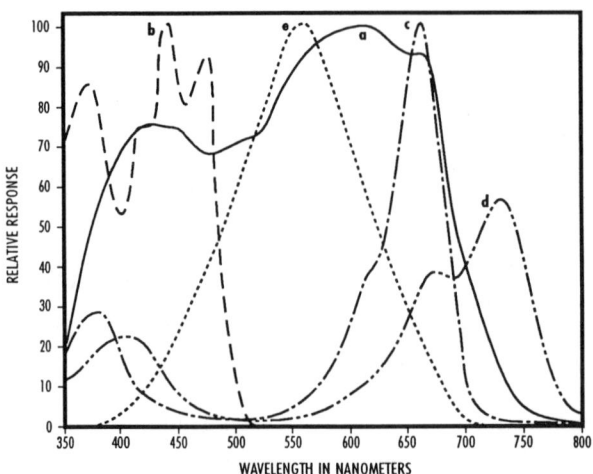

Fig. 5-21. Relative quantum yield for photosynthesis. (a) The action spectra for the short wavelength absorbing photoreceptor (b) and for the phytochrome in its long wavelength induced form (c) and infrared induced form (d) compared to human photopic vision (e).

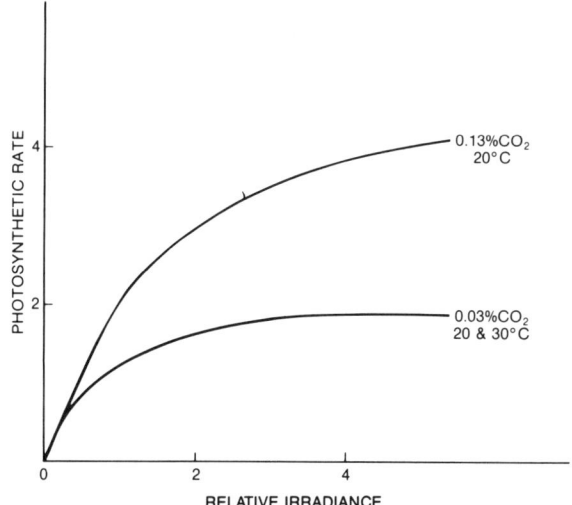

Fig. 5-22. Relative photosynthetic rate in relation to irradiance and carbon dioxide concentration.

salts), suitable temperature and carbon dioxide. Lack of any one of these requirements will place the plant in stress and will limit or halt growth. The relationship between carbon dioxide and irradiance is shown in figure 5-22, where it can be seen that the photosynthetic rate is accelerated by an increase in irradiance or in the carbon dioxide level. These principles are important in the application of light to accelerate plant growth.

PLANT LIGHTING

Plant lighting is the application of light sources for the control of growth, flowering or maintenance of plants in interior and outdoor environments. Light sources may be used to simulate or duplicate the spectral power and photoperiod of daylight for research in a controlled environment. Xenon or metal halide lamps are used as solar simulators. However, it is more common to use light sources to provide a lower, but sufficient, level of irradiance and to manipulate the photoperiod in controlled environmental chambers, greenhouses and other interiors.

Light Sources

Electric lamps which emit sufficient energy over the entire 300–800-nm spectral region are effective in photosynthesis and other photoresponses of plants. Experimental work in plant science uses many types of light sources, including incandescent (for example, tungsten-halogen), fluorescent, xenon, low- and high-pressure sodium, and metal halide lamps. Various combinations of lamp types are sometimes used, the most common combinations being incandescent and fluorescent. Other combinations include high-pressure sodium plus metal halide and metal halide plus incandescent.

Generally, the most efficacious lamps for plant growth provide the greatest portion of their energy between 580 and 700 nm. Of the various fluorescent lamps, the cool white lamp has been found to be most efficient in the synthesis of dry matter in plants. Incandescent lamps, which emit a high percentage of their output in the far red region, have found wide usage in the control of flowering horticultural crops.

Special fluorescent lamps, termed "plant growth lamps," have been developed with phosphors providing emissions that match the absorption maxima of chlorophyll. See figure 5-23. These lamps have found some use in residential lighting for the growth and color enhancement of house plants requiring low energy levels, especially African violets and gloxinias. However, they are expensive and have not been found to be superior to cool white fluorescent lamps for providing photosynthetic requirements of plants; thus they are not in general use.

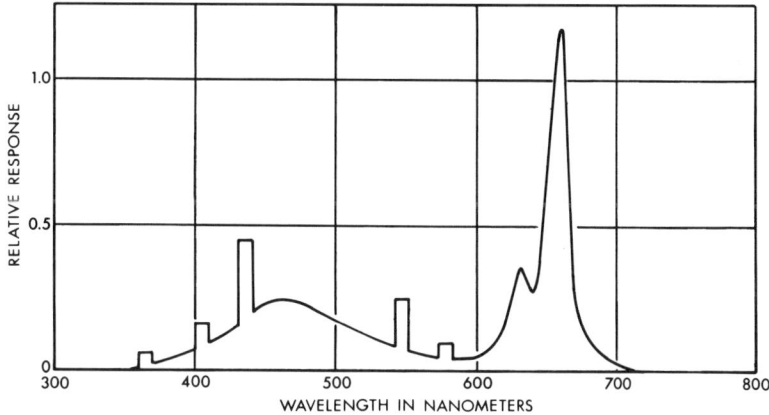

Fig. 5-23. Fluorescent plant growth lamps have been designed with emission spectra that closely match the absorption spectra of chlorophyll (a in Fig. 5-21).

Radiant-Energy Measurement

As previously noted, plants respond to radiant energy quite differently from the human eye. Therefore, it is not accurate to measure plant irradiance in terms of illuminance. This is especially important when comparing the effects on plants of lamps with different spectral power distributions.

Quantum meters are used for plant growth measurements, because photon (quantum) flux is better than radiant energy flux as a measure of photosynthetically active radiation. These meters are filtered to provide a photon flux measurement between 400 and 700 nm in micromoles per second per square meter (μmol $\cdot$ s^{-1} $\cdot$ m^{-2}). The conversion from energy flux to quantum flux varies with spectral power distribution; it has been found to be between 4.5 and 5.0 μmol $\cdot$ s^{-1} $\cdot$ m^{-2} for each watt per second per square meter of sunlight or of light emitted from lamps commonly used to grow plants. The conversion from light flux to quantum flux has been found to be between 0.010 and 0.020 μmol $\cdot$ s^{-1} $\cdot$ m^{-2} for each lux.

PLANT APPLICATIONS

In plant science there are two typical uses for lighting: photosynthesis and photoperiodism. In lighting for photosynthesis, light is applied to plants to sustain, partly or wholly, the photosynthetic processes necessary for desired growth. In lighting for photoperiodism, light is applied to plants to sustain, partly or wholly, the photoperiod necessary to produce a desired flowering response. For many plants, the quantity of light required for photosynthesis can be from 10 to more than 100 times greater than that required for photoperiodism.

Photosynthetic Lighting in Greenhouses

Photosynthetic lighting is used in the greenhouse during periods of diminished sunlight in winter months for the growth of out-of-season crops. See figure 5-24. This supplementary lighting can be much less than full sunlight, the level being determined by the requirements of the particular plant species.

The different applications of lighting for photosynthesis are as follows:

- *Day length extension*—lighting in the greenhouse before sunrise or after sunset to extend the light period
- *Dark day*—lighting in the greenhouse on dark, overcast days for the whole light period
- *Night*—lighting in the middle of the dark period

Fig. 5-24. Photosynthetic lighting in the greenhouse is a means of increasing crop production efficiency and of timing crops for a market advantage. Luminaires should provide maximum incident light on plants, minimum shading of sunlight and minimum interference with greenhouse routine. Such luminaires, using high-pressure sodium lamps, are shown for lighting roses.

Photosynthetic Lighting — Growth Rooms

Photosynthetic lighting in these areas includes lighting provided totally by lamps within commercial growth facilities or research chambers. It also includes lighting for plants used for esthetic purposes in any interior space, including commercial and residential gardening.

Considerable attention has been given to the development of commercial production of salad crops, particularly lettuce, in growth rooms to compete with conventional crop production. Such production of crops is called controlled environment agriculture. Hydroponic (soilless) culture of plants is used in these ventures.

Plant growth rooms and chambers are now used extensively for research in agricultural experimental stations, educational institutions and industrial research laboratories for the growth of plants under controlled environmental conditions (see figure 5-25). The environmental conditions which are controlled and monitored include light, temperature, humidity and carbon dioxide. A research facility which consists of several plant growth chambers (controlled environment rooms) is called a *phytotron* or, when combined with rooms for animals, a *biotron*.

To obtain a photon flux of about 400 μmol s^{-1} $\cdot$ m^{-2}, 1500-mA, 2.4-m (8-ft) T-12 cool white fluorescent lamps are closely spaced and mounted under a white perforated ceiling through which lamp heat is exhausted. Spaced at uniform intervals between the fluorescent lamps are 60- or 100-W incandescent lamps which provide the long-wavelength and near-infrared component desired for some plants. For higher irradiances, reflector-type 1500-mA fluorescent lamps permit closer spacing, or high-intensity discharge (HID) lamps can be used.

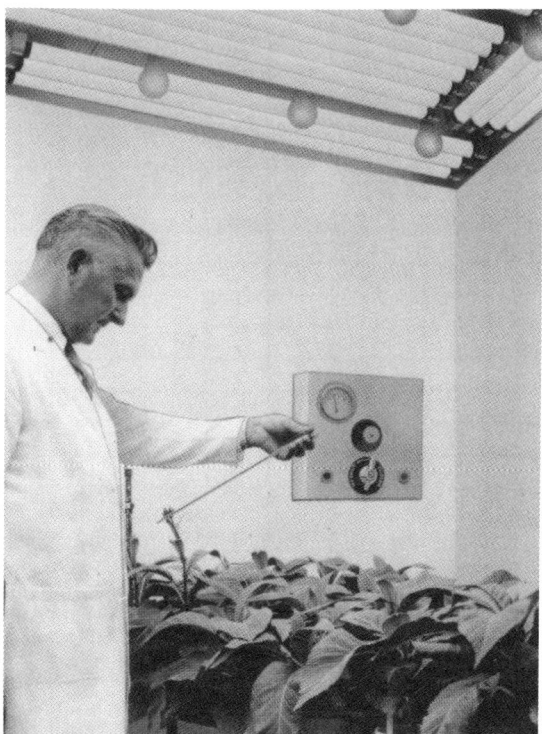

Fig. 5-25. Plant growth chamber 1.5 × 3 × 2.4 m (5 × 10 × 8 ft), equipped with closely spaced 1500-mA fluorescent lamps mounted on a perforated white ceiling through which lamp heat is exhausted. Also, 100-W, 2500-h-life incandescent lamps at uniform spacings provide a far-red component. Glossy-white thermally fabricated walls absorb radiant heat from lamps and reflect light downward to the plant area.

For photon levels of 1000 μmol s^{-1} m^{-2} or higher, HID or xenon lamps must be used. Most growth rooms have been fitted with HID lamps because the cost is less and the lamps have much longer lives. Rooms are fitted either with metal halide lamps alone or with a combination of metal halide and high-pressure sodium lamps. The former scheme ensures a more uniform spectral distribution in the room, but has fewer photosynthetically active photons, and metal halide lamps degrade faster over time than do high-pressure sodium lamps. Both of these HID lamps, as well as xenon lamps, have much higher output of radiant heat than sunlight, and serious leaf and soil heating problems result at high photon fluxes unless special precautions are taken to absorb the radiant heat before it reaches the plant canopy.

For closer control, some growth chamber walls are made of glossy-white, thermally fabricated material, which absorbs the infrared energy received from the lamps, or of specular material that reflects a high percentage of the light downward to plant growth areas. Uniformly spaced groups of lamps are separately circuited to provide several steps of irradiance while maintaining a uniform light distribution. To compensate for early light output depreciation of fluorescent lamps, the system should be designed to produce initially 25% higher photon flux than the maximum level. Circuitry control is used to regulate levels as lamps age. Quantum meters are used to check levels periodically.

Most growth chamber fluorescent or HID lighting systems are operated with ballasts located remotely outside the growing area. This arrangement reduces the air-conditioning load.

Photoperiodic Lighting

In the United States the greatest use of lighting in plant reproduction is that of photoperiodism to control the out-of-season flowering of certain species of plants which require specific ratios of light to dark periods for flowering. Such plants will remain vegetative rather than flower until these requirements are met. Therefore, plants are classified as to the relative length of light period to dark period needed to set flower buds and to bloom. This knowledge is used to bring plants into bloom when there is a particular market advantage. In Florida and California the flowering of several hundred acres of chrysanthemums in the field is controlled by this type of lighting. See figure 5-26.

During winter months it is essential to extend the day length to promote the flowering of long-day (short-night) plants and to inhibit the flowering of short-day (long-night) plants. It is also essential that the grower be able to shorten the day length to promote the flowering of short-day plants and to inhibit the flowering of long-day plants. During summer months, the grower must apply an opaque cloth or plastic covering over the plants for part of the day to simulate a short day. It is essential that the material used be opaque and that the plants be exposed to no light during this time, because very low levels are

Fig. 5-26. Photoperiodic lighting enables the grower in southern climates to control the flowering of chrysanthemums in the field. This installation utilized 150-W neck-reflector incandescent lamps on 3.7 × 4.3-m (12 × 14-ft) centers.

Fig. 5-27. Over-bed or over-bench photoperiodic lighting in the greenhouse, used in conjunction with opaque coverings, enables the grower to grow both short-day and long-day plants the year round and to time flowering for the best market period.

Fig. 5-28. Attractive equipment for the home has changed the culture and types of plants grown. Such lighting has replaced window sill culture and enables the grower to display and grow plants anywhere in the house.

effective in this response. The use of lighting and opaque covering permits the growth and flowering of both long-day and short-day plants the year round.

Long-day responses for both short-day and long-day plants are usually obtained by irradiating plants 4–8 h before sunrise or after sunset or by the more effective 2–5-h light period in the middle of the dark period (called a *night break*).

The commercially most important group of photoperiodic plants are short-day plants: chrysanthemums and poinsettias. Such plants remain vegetative with a continuous light period greater than 12 h or with a night break. When flowering is desired, the photoperiod is shortened to about 10 h and the night break is discontinued. By providing long-day plants such as China aster and Shasta daisy with a continuous 16–18-h day as well as supplementary light, they can be brought into flower, whereas continuous short days will cause them to remain in the nonflowering or vegetative state.

Incandescent and fluorescent lamps are used for photoperiodic lighting. Clear incandescent lamps in industrial reflector luminaires or reflector incandescent lamps are commonly used in the field (see figure 5-26) or in the greenhouse (see figure 5-27). Incandescent lamps may produce greater internodal elongation in some plants, and this may be undesirable.

The use of HID lamps is not practical for this purpose, because their life is reduced by frequent starts.

Home Hobby Applications

With available lighting equipment for indoor plant culture (see figures 5-28 and 5-29), flowering and foliage plants can be taken off the window sill to a place in the room where they can be grown and displayed to best advantage. Some luminaires are equipped with trays to hold moisture to raise the humidity about

plants and with timers to turn lights on and off automatically.

Some amateurs, unsatisfied with the number and types of plants which can be grown for decorative purposes, have set up basement gardens of varying sizes in which plants are grown from seed, cuttings and bulbs as shown in figure 5-30. A wide variety of flowering and foliage plants, including all plants of the house plant category, have been successfully grown under lights. Fluorescent lamps in T-8 and T-12 sizes and with ordinary loadings have been accepted for this type

Fig. 5-29. Portable carts made of tubing, with two 40-W fluorescent lamps in a special reflector mounted over each tray, make convenient racks for growth of African violets, gloxinias and similar house plants.

Fig. 5-30. Both amateur and professional growers have found value in basement gardens. They allow the amateur to increase the size of his or her hobby and enable the professional grower to utilize unproductive space for rooting of cuttings and growth of seedlings.

of horticulture. Ordinary loading lamps (400 mA) can be used to grow seedlings and short plants (< 6 inches) but high output lamps (800 mA) and very high output lamps (1500 mA) are needed for taller plants.

Commercial and Industrial Applications

Interior spaces with live plants and trees are now commonplace in lobbies, offices, shopping malls, airport waiting rooms, banks, country clubs, restaurants, entryways of condominiums and apartments, and atria of large hotels and of government, commercial and industrial buildings. Before any plants are chosen or plans are made for their use, the designer, plant specialist or architect must first determine if the environment is suitable. Lighting in these spaces serves a dual purpose–lighting for people and for plants. Therefore, illuminance is specified rather than irradiance.

- Is there sufficient light (250 lx minimum, specified in illuminance, rather than irradiance)?
- Is the temperature range tolerable (day, 18–35° C; night, 10–18° C)?
- Is the humidity range tolerable (25–50%)?
- Is the light period sufficient (12–16 h)?

If the illuminance is below 250 lx and the building owner is unwilling to provide additional light, it is best not to use live plants. If the temperature, humidity and

light period are below the minimum requirements listed above for any extended period, live plants will not survive. When the environment is not suitable for even plant maintenance, then plants will have to be replaced as they succumb.

Photon Flux Needed

The photon flux in the space will determine the species of plants that will survive. If the photon flux due to daylight is not sufficient for live plants, then supplemental lighting should be used, provided that other factors are favorable. The amount of supplemental light is determined by the plant species having the greatest light requirement.

Professional plant specialists who work with the plants for interiorscaping make a special effort to use acclimatized plants. Acclimatized plants are those that have been conditioned for use in the low-humidity and low-illuminance indoor environments. These plants are taken from greenhouses that often receive full sunlight to a greenhouse with heavy shade. Here they remain for two months or more before being used for interiorscaping. Also, the watering frequency is reduced to condition the plants for indoor use. Such acclimatization prevents the shock that frequently results in rapid defoliation when plants are taken without conditioning from the bright greenhouse to the interiorscape.

COMMON PLANTS AND ILLUMINANCES

Recommended illuminances for common plants are shown in figure 5-31. Plants are categorized as trees, floor plants and table or desk plants. The lowest illuminances in this figure are the minimum for maintenance. Higher values are more satisfactory for good plant condition. The recommendations are for acclimatized plants receiving 14 h of light per day.

AQUARIUM AND TERRARIUM LIGHTING

Aquaria and terraria are also found in the home, office and school for hobby, decorative and educational purposes.

Aquarium lighting serves both a functional and an ornamental purpose when plants are part of the aquarium environment. Through the process of photosynthesis, lighted aquarium plants increase the oxygen level essential for fish respiration and at the same time reduce the carbon dioxide level, preventing the buildup of carbonic acid, which can be harmful to fish. The light also illuminates both the fish and the aquarium. Dramatic colors of both fish and plants are observed when special fluorescent plant growth lamps are used,

Fig. 5-31. Recommended Illuminances* for Acclimatized Plants (14 h of Light Per Day)

A. Trees 1.5 to 3 Meters (5 to 10 Feet) Tall

Tree	Illuminances	
	Lux	Footcandles
Araucaria excelsa (Norfolk Island Pine)	above 2000	above 200
Eriobotrya japonica (Chinese Loquator, Japan Plum)	above 2000	above 200
Ficus benjamina 'Exotica' (Weeping Java Fig)	750–2000	75–200
Ficus lyrata (Fiddleleaf Fig)	750–2000	75–200
Ficus retusa nitida (Indian Laurel)	750–2000	75–200
Ligustrum lucidum (Waxleaf)	750–2000	75–200

B. Floor plants 0.6 to 1.8 Meters (2 to 6 Feet) Tall

Plant	Illuminances	
	Lux	Footcandles
Brassaia actinophylla (Schefflera)	750–2000	75–200
Chamaedorea elegans 'bella' (Neanthe Bella Palm)	250–750	25–75
Chamaedorea erumpens (Bamboo Palm)	250–750	25–75
Chamaerops humilis (European Fanpalm)	above 2000	above 200
Dieffenbachia amoena (Giant Dumb Cane)	750–2000	75–200
Dizygotheca elegantissima (False Aralia)	above 2000	above 200
Dracaena deremensis 'Janet Craig' (Green Drasena)	750–200	75–200
Dracaena fragrans massangeana (Corn Plant)	250–750	25–75
Dracaena marginata (Dwarf Dragon Tree)	750–2000	75–200
Ficus elastica 'Decora' (Rubber Plant)	750–2000	75–200
Ficus philippinensis (Philippine Fig)	750–2000	75–200
Howeia forsteriana (Kentia Palm)	250–750	25–75
Philodendron x evansii (Selfheading Philodendron)	750–2000	75–200
Phoenix roebelenii (Pigmy Date Palm)	750–2000	75–200
Pittosporum tobira (Mock Orange)	above 2000	above 200
Podocarpus macrophylla Maki (Podocarpus)	above 2000	above 200
Polyscias guilfoylei (Parsley Aralia)	750–2000	75–200
Rhapis exclesa (Lady Palm)	750–2000	75–200
Yucca elephantipes (Palm-Lily)	above 2000	above 200

C. Table or desk plants

Plant	Illuminances	
	Lux	Footcandles
Aechmea fasciata (Bromeliad)	750–2000	75–200
Aglaonema commutatum (Variegated Chinese Evergreen)	250–750	25–75
Agalonema 'Pseudobacteatum' (Golden Aglaonema)	250–750	25–75
Aglaonema roebelinii (Peuter Plant)	250–750	25–75
Asparagus sprengeri (Asparagus Fern)	750–2000	75–200
Ciccus antarctiva (Kangaroo Vine)	above 2000	above 200
Cissus rhombifolia (Grape Ivy)	750–2000	75–200
Citrus mitis (Calamondin)	above 2000	above 200
Dieffenbachia 'Exoctica' (Dumb Cane)	750–2000	75–200
Dracaena deremensis 'Warneckei' (White Striped Dracaena)	750–2000	75–200
Dracaena fragrans massangeana (Corn Plant)	250–750	25–75
Hoya carnosa (Wax plant)	750–2000	75–200
Maranta leuconeura (Prayer Plant)	750–2000	75–200
Nephrolepsis exaltata bostoniensis (Boston Fern)	750–2000	75–200
Peperomia caperata (Emerald Ripple)	250–750	25–75
Philodendron oxycardium (cordatum) (Common Philodendron)	250–750	25–75
Spathiphyllum 'Mauna Loa' (White Flag)	750–2000	75–200

*For cool white fluorescent lamps, 100 lx ≈ 13 μmol s^{-1} m^{-2}.

because of the high red and blue emission of such lamps. Colors are more natural with cool white or daylight fluorescent lamps.

Both fluorescent and incandescent lamps are used, with a preference for fluorescent because they produce more light and less heat per watt. Lighting requirements for aquaria usually range from 0.25 to 0.50 lamp watt per liter (1 to 2 lamp watts per gallon) of tank capacity.

Terrarium lighting usually requires both fluorescent and incandescent lighting. Fluorescent light is applied at about 200 lamp watts per square meter for the plant life while an incandescent lamp is used to light a portion of the terrarium to simulate the infrared of sunlight for the animal life (lizards, frogs, etc.) usually found in such environments.

EFFECTS ON MATERIALS

Fading and Bleaching[175-192]

Fading and bleaching of colored textiles and other materials upon exposure to light and other radiant energy is of special interest because of the high illuminances now employed in merchandising. Consequently, a knowledge of some of the factors involved is important. Some of these (not necessarily in order of importance) are as follows:

- Illuminance
- Duration of exposure
- Spectral distribution of the radiation
- Moisture
- Temperature of the material
- Chemical composition of the dye or other colorant
- Saturation of the dye (tints versus saturated colors)
- Composition and weave of fabric
- Intermittency of exposure
- Chemical fumes in the atmosphere

While many studies of fading and colorfastness have been published, especially in textile journals, most of them are deficient in data on the illuminances involved. In general, these articles have dealt primarily with improvements in dyes and dyeing methods. Such tests have involved exposures to daylight in various geographical regions and to standardized types of arc lamps, called "fading lamps." The National Institute of Standards and Technology has developed standardized methods and lamps for conducting such tests.

A long review of research in this field,[175] with extensive bibliography, summarizes the subject as follows. The rate at which a dye fades is governed by seven factors:

- Photochemistry of the dye molecule
- Physical state of the dye
- Chemistry of the substrate
- Fine structure of the substrate
- Presence of foreign substances
- Atmosphere
- Illumination

Certain general conclusions have been derived from studies of several hundred specimens of colored textiles. In view of the fact that the tests have been limited to an infinitesimal percentage of the dyes and textiles in general use, it must be realized that such conclusions are not definitive and many exceptions may be found.

The illuminance and duration of exposure to the light source are two of the most important factors. Two studies[179, 180] indicate an approximate reciprocal relationship between time and illuminance in the production of fading; that is, the fading is dependent upon the product of these two factors and is substantially unaffected by variations in both as long as the product is unchanged. A third study[181] disagrees with this conclusion, indicating that at higher illuminances this relationship breaks down.

The spectral power distribution of the incident radiation used affects the rate of fading. It has been found[177] that ultraviolet energy of wavelengths shorter than 300 nm (a small component in most practical light sources) may cause very rapid fading and other forms of product deterioration in some cases. Energy in the region from 300 to 400 nm is emitted from most electric light sources, but in a much smaller amount per lumen than it is in daylight. This spectral region apparently produces more fading per unit of energy than an equal amount in the visible spectrum. Filters which absorb much of the near ultraviolet, but very little visible light, have been found to reduce fading somewhat,[178] but not as much as is sometimes suggested. In sunlight it has been found that fading is produced by energy through the whole region shorter in wavelength than the orange-red (approximately 600 nm). Daylight produces more fading than tungsten and fluorescent sources for the same number of lumens because daylight has more energy in the short-wavelength region of the spectrum than those two sources.[176]

Figure 5-32 shows spectral reflectance curves for new and slightly faded specimens of pink silk cloth. It will be noted that the spectral changes indicate bleaching in regions of maximum absorption and darkening in regions of minimum absorption. These changes are typical of many specimens tested.

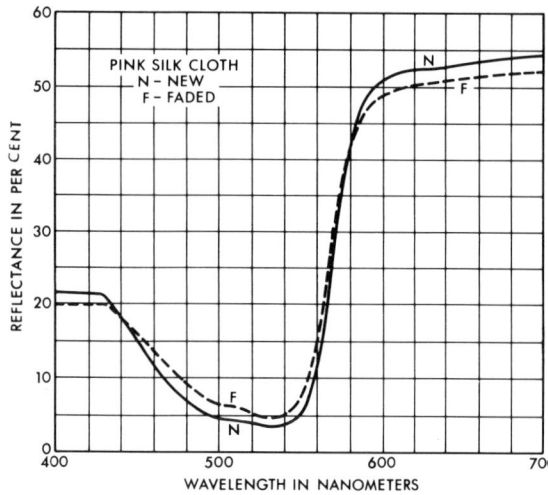

Fig. 5-32. Spectral reflectance of a specimen of pink silk before and after exposure sufficient to cause moderate fading.

Fading appears to be a photochemical process requiring oxygen and is inhibited or greatly reduced in a vacuum. An increase in moisture content can also produce greater fading. Cellulose is particularly affected by moisture, and wool is less affected, for example.[175]

Temperature appears to have little effect on the fading rate of silk and cotton at temperatures below 50°C (120°F), but the rate is approximately twice as great at 65°C (150°F) as at 30°C (85°F). It is often found that a light tint is more fugitive than a higher concentration of the same dye.

Fading is of major importance to the merchandising field. Tests of approximately 100 textile specimens performed about 1940 showed that about half of the samples faded to some degree after 500 klx·h (50,000 fc·h) of incandescent illumination. A more recent study[97] of 100 commercial fabrics showed that approximately 10 times that exposure was required to produce a minimum perceptible fading with incandescent and fluorescent lamps. Obviously, dyes have greatly improved in light-fastness, and fading is not as critical a problem as it was when the fluorescent lamp first became an important light source.

Fading of merchandise is most readily apparent where one area has received a high level of exposure and an adjacent area has not. Typical examples are folded neckties and socks stacked on shelves in display cases. To reduce perceptible fading, displayed goods should be rotated on a 7–10-day cycle.

Modern grocery stores display packaged meats in refrigerated cases under high illuminances. Fresh meats show no appreciable color change due to light within any reasonable display period, though unwrapped meats may show color changes due to dehydration. However, many processed meats, such as bologna, receive their red color from a curing process using salt or

sodium nitrate. Through a reaction with light and air, such meats will return to their original gray color, and this fading takes place very rapidly in some meats. Some, especially veal loaf and bologna, will show perceptible color change in 1500–2000 lx·h (150–200 fc·h). Since the illuminance in some of these cases may be as high as 1000 lx (100 fc), it is found that undesirable changes may occur in $1\frac{1}{2}$–2 h. The most susceptible meats should be placed as far away from the lamps as possible.

Depending on the degree of original muscle pigmentation, frozen meat is considered salable for 3–6 days under illuminances between 500 and 2000 lx (50 and 200 fc).[182] Above 2000 lx (200 fc), shelf life is considerably reduced. Differences in the spectral power distribution of the light sources result in no apparent or statistically significant differences in the rate of color degradation.

Cigars may bleach to some degree in cases illuminated by fluorescent lamps, but the exposures must be quite high. In a test using seven brands of cigars it was found that an exposure of approximately 400 klx·h (40,000 fc·h) produced a just-noticeable change, and that this exposure could be doubled before the color change reached an objectionable degree. Exposures of this magnitude are greater than typical for the merchandising of cigars.

The germicidal (bactericidal) lamp, producing high energy at 253.7 nm, has been used as a potent source for accelerated fading.[177] However, these lamps should not be used for accelerated-fading tests, because no relationship has been found between fading by germicidal lamps and fading by sunlight or commonly used electric light sources.

Luminescence and Luminescent Materials

Photoluminescence occurs in many hundreds of materials when they are exposed to radiation. The most important practical application of photoluminescent materials is in fluorescent light sources, where ultraviolet radiation excites the lamp phosphors. These phosphors are oxygen-dominated inorganic crystalline materials. Other materials, such as the zinc and cadmium sulfides and a wide variety of organic compounds excited by the near ultraviolet (approximately 360 nm), are used extensively to achieve spectacular theatrical effects and in various signs and instrument dials. So-called "optical bleaches" are fluorescent organics used as whiteners in laundered items such as shirts and sheets; they are excited by the near-ultraviolet and short-wavelength visible radiation to fluoresce a bright blue. This balances for the natural yellow-white appearance of the unimpregnated cloth. Superbright orange and red organic dyes which are fluorescent under near-ultraviolet excitation are widely used as identification and warning markers, for example, in high-speed aircraft to aid in rapid visual acquisition to avoid collision. Fluorescent paint, ink and dyed fabrics are available in many colors, including red, orange, yellow, blue and a white that appears blue under ultraviolet radiation. Because these materials transform ultraviolet and short-wavelength visible energy into light, as well as reflect incident light, their brightness under daylight is conspicuously high. Some fluorescent materials have an apparent reflectance (under daylight) of over 100%; that is, they send back more visible light than strikes them.

These colored fluorescent materials are especially useful on signal flags and signal panels, since they can be identified more easily and at greater distances than nonfluorescent surfaces. The increased range over which the fluorescent flags can be identified is most apparent during the half-light conditions of dawn and twilight. Organic fluorescent dyed materials are at times used to produce spectacular signs, such as used on streetcars or buses, and very colorful clothing.

Other photoluminescence applications include X-ray- and γ-ray-stimulable crystals, which find extensive use in scintillation counters, used for detecting the exciting radiation itself. Chemical analyses are often based upon the use of the characteristic luminescence of certain activator ions in known host media.

Cathodoluminescent materials find their most important application in television screens and in scientific instruments such as oscilloscopes, electron microscopes, image intensifiers and radar screens. Here zinc and cadmium sulfides and oxygen-dominated phosphors such as the silicates, phosphates and tungstates are used. An improvement in color television screens has resulted from the development of a rare-earth (europium) activated deep-red phosphate phosphor.

Luminescence attending chemical reactions has been observed widely in both organic and inorganic systems. One of the most interesting is the reaction between the naturally occurring chemicals luciferin, luciferase and adenosine triphosphate (ATP) as it takes place in the firefly.

Ion, sound, friction and electric field excitation of phosphors are phenomena of relatively little practical application, except that the last has found use in read-out devices.

Phosphorescent Materials. Phosphorescent materials, excited by ultraviolet energy, daylight or light from electric lamps, have been shown to have a high brightness of afterglow for periods of 6–9 h, and some of them have a noticeable brightness for as long as 24 h after the exciting source has been removed.

Certain phosphorescent materials, generally combinations of zinc, calcium, cadmium and strontium sulfides, can be incorporated into adhesive tapes (plastic overcoatings), paints and certain molded plastics. Because of the tendency of many plastics either to transmit moisture which decomposes the sulfide, or to react directly with the phosphor, care should be exercised in the choice of a plastic to carry the phosphorescent powders. Both vinyl and polystyrene plastics have been found well suited to this application.

Phosphorescent materials are suitable only for applications where it is possible to light them before they are needed. While some materials can be used in spots where a visible brightness is necessary for about 6–9 h, only a few of the many phosphorescent compounds have this degree of persistence. Those manufactured from zinc sulfide have high initial brightness after extinguishing the light source, but their useful brightness period does not extend beyond 20–30 minutes. Before refinements in the processing of calcium and strontium phosphors were made in 1944, the useful brightness of these types did not extend beyond 2–3 h after activation. However, now that long-persistence phosphors are available, phosphorescent materials are suitable, in many applications, for night-long use.

Brightness reduction (decay) rates are hastened by high temperatures. At very low temperatures (60 K) luminescence may be completely arrested, to recur later upon warming.

Radioactive Excitation. This is simply excitation by electrons, ions (atoms, nuclear fragments), or γ rays, singly or in combination, resulting from the fission or radioactive decay of certain elements. For example, radium emits α particles which can excite luminescence when they strike a suitable phosphor. Krypton-85 excites by emission of β rays or high-energy electrons. The sulfide phosphors emit light not only when exposed to ultraviolet energy or light, but also under bombardment by the rays from radioactive materials. Thus, by compounding a mixture of such a radioluminescent material such as zinc sulfide and a small amount of radioactive material, a self-luminous mixture can be produced. Such a radioactive luminous compound will continue to emit light without the help of external excitation for a very long time (several years) in practical applications. Radioactive-luminous materials have been used for many years on watch and clock dials and on the faces of other instruments that must be read in the dark. They are the only type of commercially available luminous materials that maintain self-luminosity over long periods of time. The power source was formerly some salt of radium or more frequently the lower-priced mesothorium. These were displaced by strontium-90, and more recently polonium, which has certain advantages with regard to cost and safety.

The bombardment of the fluorescent materials by radiation causes them to decompose, which limits the life of the combination. A good-quality material will be useful for a few years and will maintain a fairly constant brightness during this period. The life of radioactive-luminous paint is controlled to a great extent by the concentration of radioactive material in the mixture, as is the brightness. Increased radioactive content means increased brightness, but more rapid decomposition of the glowing salt.

Because of the expense of the radioactive substances used to activate this material, radioactive-luminous paint seldom is used in large quantities or to cover large areas.

EFFECTS OF INFRARED ENERGY[184–192]

Heat may be transferred from one body to another by conduction, convection or radiation, or by a combination of these processes. Infrared heating involves energy transfer primarily by radiation, although some convection heating may exist simultaneously due to natural or forced air movement.

Transfer of energy or heat occurs whenever any amount of radiant energy emitted by one body is absorbed by another. However, it is the wavelengths longer than those of visible energy and shorter than those of radar waves that are utilized for radiant heating (770–100,000 nm). Energy absorption of white, pastel-colored and translucent materials is best obtained by using wavelength emissions longer than 2500 nm, whereas the majority of dark-pigmented and oxide-coated materials will readily absorb the full range of emissions, visible as well as infrared. Water vapor, steam and other gases absorb infrared energy in specific, characteristic bands throughout the spectrum.

Glass and quartz materials effectively transmit infrared energy only out to about 5000 nm.

Sources of Infrared Energy

Many sources for producing infrared energy are now available. These can be classified generally as point, line and area sources. Their temperatures, spectral power distribution and life characteristics vary widely, although source selection generally is not critical unless the products to be heated are selective as to wavelength penetration or absorption, as in the case of many translucent plastics.

Maximum design flexibility and economy for industrial installations are generally obtained by using tungsten-filament quartz lamps, alloy-resistor quartz tubes, or rod-type metal-sheath heaters in air- or water-cooled external reflectors. These are available in power ratings up to 24 W/mm (600 W/in.) of length, and in sizes from 9.5 mm (0.375 in.) diameter by 200 mm (8 in.) long to 19 mm (0.75 in.) diameter by 1600 mm

(63 in.) long. Additionally, a variety of screw-base lamps, with and without internal reflectors, is available for special applications. All are listed in chapter 6, Light Sources. Precise voltage ratings as used for lighting service lamps need not be followed in using these infrared sources, often employed at voltages as low as 50% of manufacturers' rating. Most of the tungsten-filament heaters are designed for a color temperature of 2500 K and a life rating of 5000 h when operated at rated voltage. Metal rod heaters and quartz tubes using coiled alloy resistors are usually designed for 790°C (1450°F) operating temperature and a life span of approximately 10,000 h.

Tungsten-filament heaters provide instant on-off response from a power source, and their radiant energy efficiency, 86% of power input, makes them a preferred infrared source. Other heaters have thermal inertia varying from about 1 minute for quartz tubes to 4–5 min for metal-sheath heaters. Operating efficiencies are substantially influenced by the design and maintenance of external reflector systems and to a lesser extent by the air temperature and velocity within the heating zone. Overall efficiencies of 35–60% are readily obtained in well-designed systems where a long holding time at the designed product temperature is not required. All of the quartz heat sources can accept high thermal shock. However, metal heaters are best qualified for applications subject to mechanical shock and vibration. A variety of porcelain holders and terminals is available for these sources. Specular reflectors of anodized aluminum, gold or rhodium are recommended for directing the radiant energy to product surfaces.

By comparison, gas infrared systems require far heavier and more costly construction to comply with insurance safety standards. In calculating their operating efficiencies one must take into account energy loss in the combustion flue products as well as other design factors affecting the ultimate energy utilization.

Advantages

The ease with which electric infrared heating can be controlled quickly and reliably with modern radiation detectors and power control devices has greatly advanced its acceptance and range of use. The ability to focus heat energy on the object to be heated and the ability to turn the source on and off quickly minimize the heating of the surrounding atmosphere and structure and can reduce the total energy needed. Heating the object directly eliminates the need for a closed oven, preheating, heavy insulating structures, and the high heat losses to the structure and to the air when the oven is opened. Electric infrared can be used outdoors, in a vacuum, or in other hostile environments when conventional heating systems cannot.

Designed and applied with reasonable care and proper controls, electric infrared can reduce heating energy requirements and costs.

Processes that once required great quantities of fossil fuels and hours in convection ovens, or periods of several minutes in early infrared systems, are often handled in seconds with present-day coordination of materials, chemistry and infrared application. The absence of combustion hazard and of the need for handling large volumes of air, the saving of space, and the capability for high-volume, clean processing keep this form of electric heat in the foreground of manufacturing technology.

Product Heating with Infrared

Infrared radiant energy may be used for any heating application where the principal product surfaces can be arranged for exposure to the heat sources.[184] Modern methods of conveying materials have greatly accelerated the use of heat sources arranged in banks or tunnels. Typical applications include:

- Drying and baking of paints, varnishes, enamels, adhesives, printer's ink and other coatings
- Preheating of thermoplastic materials for forming and tacking
- Heating of metal parts for shrink fit assembly, forming, thermal aging, brazing, radiation testing, and conditioning surfaces for application of adhesives and welding
- Dehydrating of textiles, paper, leather, meat, vegetables, pottery ware and sand molds
- Spot and localized heating for any desired objective

Rapid rates of heating can be provided in relatively cold surroundings by controlling the amount of radiant energy, absorption characteristics of the exposed surfaces, and rate of heat loss to the surroundings.[185] Highly reflective enclosures, with or without thermal insulation, are commonly employed to assure maximum energy utilization. Limited amounts of air movement are often essential in portions or all of the heating cycle, to avoid temperature stratification and assure removal of water or solvent vapors.[186] Product temperature control is normally provided by varying the exposure time to infrared energy, or the heater wattage per unit area of facing tunnel area. With modern linear heaters, power densities of 5–130 kW/m^2 (0.5–12 kW/ft^2) can accommodate high automation speeds.

Where precise temperatures are needed, the design condition may then be modified by voltage or current input controls to add flexibility for a variety of product conditions, handling speeds or chemical formulations. The temperature of moving parts can be accurately measured by scanning with a radiation pyrometer to provide indication or full automatic control of the heating cycle. Where small variations in temperature are compatible with quality standards, an initial installation test may be made with portable instrumentation, and thereafter the cycle will repeat itself with a degree of reliability consistent with the power supply voltage, thus avoiding the need for the usual controls required for other types of process heating.

Spot heating of a portion of an object can eliminate the need for energy formerly required to preheat the whole object. Appropriate applications of infrared heating can lead to more efficient use of all energy forms in today's modern production facility.

Comfort Heating with Infrared

In recent years, the use of infrared radiation for heating in commercial and industrial areas has become quite popular. The T-3 quartz lamp as a semiluminous infrared source has distinguished itself for a wide variety of applications in commercial buildings, marquee areas, industrial plants, warehouses, stadiums, pavilions and other public areas. Units are usually of the pendant or recessed type, with reflector control for the combined visible and infrared radiation, using the quartz tube and quartz lamp sources listed in chapter 6, Light Sources. In contrast, residential use (except for bathroom areas) is mostly confined to low-temperature sources such as electric baseboards and plastered radiant ceilings.

By supplying heat only when and where needed, infrared heating allows thermostats of the conventional heating systems to be lowered while comfort is maintained locally and energy conserved overall.

Applications. Radiant comfort heating applications fall into two broad classifications, general heating and spot heating.[187] General heating installations irradiate complete room areas. High levels of building insulation are generally recommended. The installation in this case often provides a uniform radiant wattage density in the range of 100–320 W/m^2 (10–30 W/ft^2) incident on the floor surface. However, some system designers prefer equipment layouts using asymmetric units to provide a somewhat higher density in the areas adjacent to outside walls to help offset the wall thermal loss. To date, like convection heating systems, overall radiant systems have had an installed capacity sufficient to hold the desired indoor temperature and overcome the building heat loss at the specified outdoor design temperature; but performance data on some installations indicate a capacity 70–90% of the building thermal loss is adequate.[188] This reduction is probably due to the direct personnel heating and an improved mean radiant temperature in the space.

Infrared energy passes through air with little absorption, and this is particularly true of the near infrared. Therefore, installations involving quartz infrared lamps may be mounted at much greater heights than those with far-infrared sources. One may choose equipment of narrow beam spread so the radiation can be confined primarily to the floor, where it will be most beneficial, and losses through the walls will be limited. By this means, the mounting height may be increased without requiring a greater installed capacity. It is good practice to keep the radiation from striking the walls at heights more than 2.4 m (8 ft) above the floor.

Although infrared heating of the air is minimal, air in radiation-heated areas is warmed from energy absorption by the floor and other solid surfaces. This causes upward gravitational movement, permitting conventional control with air thermostats[188] which are shielded from the infrared sources.

In the case of quartz tubes, metal-sheath heaters and gas-fired infrared units, on-off cycling of the equipment is permissible. When lamps are used, unless the visible energy (about 7–8 lm/W) is reduced by filtering, the cycling should be from full to half voltage to prevent a severe change in illumination. Operation of this sort not only gives some lighting but also provides some radiant heat at all times.

Infrared heating systems have an advantage over convection air heating systems for spaces that are subject to high rates of air change (for example, where overhead doors are opened frequently). In these areas, the warm air is lost immediately and air temperature recovery can be lengthy with convection heating. With a radiant system, most objects are warmer than the air, so the air in the space recovers temperature faster.

Spot Heating. The greatest potential use for high-intensity radiant heating lies in spot or zone heating in exposed areas where conventional heating is impractical, such as marquees, waiting platforms and loading docks, and in infrequently used areas such as stadiums, arenas, viewing stands, churches and assembly halls.

The radiation intensity needed for spot heating varies with a number of factors. The major ones are:

1. The degree of body activity as dictated by the task. The more physical effort expended by the worker, the lower the temperature at which heat is needed. Type of clothing also influences this temperature.
2. The lowest temperature which is apt to exist in the space (or the lowest temperature at which the owner wants to provide comfort).
3. The amount of air movement at the location. Indoor drafts and slight air movements out-

doors can be overcome by higher energy densities, but compensation for wind velocities of more than 2.2–4.5 m/s (5–10 mph) at temperatures below −1°C (30°F) will not be sufficient. Wind screens are far more beneficial than increased radiation levels. For spot heating, units should be positioned to supply radiation from at least two directions,[187] preferably above and to the side of the area to be heated. Care should be taken to avoid locating equipment directly over a person's head.[188] In practice, levels for spot heating vary from 100 W/m² (10 W/ft²) at waist level for an indoor installation supplementing an inadequate convection system to more than 1 kW/m² (100 W/ft²) for a marquee or sidewalk people-heating system.

At the higher radiation levels, ice and snow are melted[189] and water on the floor is evaporated. This can reduce the safety hazard of a slippery floor and improve housekeeping by minimizing the tracking in of snow and water in inclement weather. Where snow melting is desirable, the heating units should be energized as soon as snow starts to fall to avoid any accumulation and consequent high reflection of infrared energy.

Infrared heating installations in infrequently used areas can often be turned on before an event to preheat the room surfaces, then turned off before the event is over, with the heat stored in the surfaces and body heat maintaining the comfort level.

REFERENCES

1. Boettner, E. A., and J. R. Wolter. 1962. Transmission of the ocular media. *Invest. Ophthalmol.* 1:176.
2. Berler, D. K. 1989. Muller cell alterations from long-term ambient fluorescent light exposure in monkeys: Ling and electron microscopic fluorescein and lipofuscin study. *Trans. Am. Ophthal. Soc.* 87:515–576.
3. Brainard, G. C., S. Beacham, J. P. Hanifin, D. Sliney, and L. Streletz. 1992. Ultraviolet regulation of neuroendocrine physiology in rodents and the visual evoked response in children. In *Biological responses to UV-A radiation.* F. Urbach, ed. Overland Park, KS: Valdenmar Publishing.
4. Chou, B. R., A. P. Cullen, and K. A. Dumbleton. 1988. Protection factors of ultraviolet-blocking contact lenses. *Int. Contact Lens Clin.* 15:244–250.
5. Clayman, H. M. 1984. Ultraviolet-absorbing intraocular lenses. *Am. Intra-Oc. Imp. Soc. J.* 10(4):429–432.
6. Cullen, A. P., K. A. Dumbleton, and B. R. Chou. 1989. Contact lenses and acute exposure to ultraviolet radiation. *Opt. Vis. Sci.* 66(6):407–411.

7. Dayshaw-Barker, P. 1987. Ocular photosensitization. *Photochem. Photobiol.* 46(6):1051–1055.

8. Gies, H. P., C. R. Roy, and G. Elliott. 1990. A proposed UVR protection factor for sunglasses. *Clin. Exp. Optom.* 73(6):184–189.

9. Goldman, A. I., W. T. Ham Jr., and H. A. Mueller. 1975. Mechanisms of retinal damage resulting from the exposure of rhesus monkeys to ultrashort laser pulses. *Exp. Eye Res.* 21(5):457–469.

10. Goldman, A. I., W. T. Ham Jr., and H. A. Mueller. 1977. Ocular damage thresholds and mechanisms for ultrashort pulses of both visible and infrared laser radiation in the rhesus monkey. *Exp. Eye Res.* 24(1):45–56.

11. Goldmann. 1933. Genesis of heat cataract. *Arch. Ophthalmol.* 9(2):314.

12. Ham, W. T., Jr., R. C. Williams, H. A. Mueller, D. Guerry, A. M. Clarke, and W. J. Geeraets. 1966. Effects of laser radiation on the mammalian eye. *Trans. N.Y. Acad. Sci.* 28(4):517–526.

13. Lydahl, E. 1984. Infrared radiation and cataract. *Acta Ophthalmol.*, Suppl. 166.

14. Marshall, J. H. 1991. *The susceptible visual apparatus.* London: MacMillan.

15. McCanna, P., S. R. Chandra, T. S. Stevens, F. L. Myers, G. de Venecia, and G. H. Bresnick. 1982. Argon laser–induced cataract as a complication of retinal photocoagulation. *Arch. Ophthalmol.* 100(7):1071–1073.

16. U.S. National Institute for Occupational Safety and Health. 1977. *Ocular ultraviolet effects from 295 nm to 335 nm in the rabbit eye.* NIOSH 77-1977. Principal investigators D. G. Pitts and A. P. Cullen. Washington DC: National Institute for Occupational Safety and Health.

17. Pitts, D. G., and A. P. Cullen. 1981. Determination of IR radiation levels for acute ocular cataractogenesis. *Grafes Arch. Clin. Exp. Ophthalmol.* 217(4):285–297.

18. Pitts, D. G., and M. R. Lattimore. 1987. Protection against UVR using the Vistakon UV-Block soft contact lens. *Int. Contact Lens Clin.* 14:22–29.

19. Pitts, D. G., A. P. Cullen, and P. Dayshaw-Barker. 1980. *Determination of ocular threshold levels for infrared radiation cataractogenesis.* NIOSH 77-0042-7701. Cincinnati, OH: National Institute for Occupational Safety and Health.

20. Sanford, B., G. C. Brainard, S. Beacham, J. P. Hanifin, J. Markoff, and L. Streletz. Dose dependent effects of UV-A on visual evoked potentials in humans. In *Biological effects of light.* M. Houck and A. Klieman, eds. New York: Walter de Gruyter.

21. Sliney, D., and M. Wolbarsht. 1980. *Safety with lasers and other optical sources.* New York: Plenum.

22. Sykes, S. M., W. G. Robinson, M. Waxler, and T. Kuwabara. 1981. Damage to the monkey retina by broad-spectrum fluorescent light. *Invest. Ophthalmol. Vis. Sci.* 20(4):425–434.

23. Taylor, H. R., S. K. West, F. S. Rosenthal, B. Muñoz, H. S. Newland, H. Abbey, and E. A. Emmett. 1988. Effect of ultraviolet radiation on cataract formation. *New Engl. J. Med.* 319(22):1429–1433.

24. Waxler, M. 1988. Long-term visual health risks from solar ultraviolet radiation. *Ophthalmic Res.* 20(3):179–182.

25. Baadsgaard, O. 1991. In vivo ultraviolet irradiation of human skin results in profound perturbation of the immune system. *Arch. Dermatol.* 127(1):99–109.

26. Bachem, A., and C. I. Reed. 1930. The penetration of ultraviolet light through the human skin. *Arch. Phys. Ther.* 11(2):49–56.

27. Berger, D. 1968. Action spectrum of erythema. In *XIII Congressus Internationalis Dermatologiae, Munich, 1967.* W. Jadassohn, and C. G. Schirren, eds. Berlin: Springer-Verlag.

28. Coblentz, W. W., and R. Stair. 1934. Data on the spectral erythemic reaction of the untanned human skin to ultraviolet radiation. *Bur. Stand. (U.S.) J. Res.* 12(1):13–14.

29. Cole, C., P. D. Forbes, R. E. Davies, and F. Urbach. 1985. Effect of indoor lighting on normal skin. In *The medical and biological effects of light.* R. J. Wurtman, M. J. Baum, and J. T. Potts, eds. Annals of the New York Academy of Sciences, vol. 453. New York: New York Academy of Sciences.

30. U.S. Federal Aviation Administration. 1978. *On the linkage of solar ultraviolet radiation to skin cancer.* FAA EQ-78-19. Prepared by P. Cutchis. Springfield, VA: Federal Aviation Administration.

31. Daniels, F., Jr., and B. E. Johnson. 1974. Normal, physiologic and pathologic effects of solar radiation on the skin. In *Sunlight and man: Normal and abnormal photobiologic responses.* T. B. Fitzpatrick, ed. Tokyo: Univ. of Tokyo Press.

32. Everett, M. A., R. M. Sayre, and R. L. Olson. 1969. Physiologic response of human skin to ultraviolet light. In *Biologic effects of ultraviolet radiation.* F. Urbach, ed. Oxford: Pergamon.

33. Freeman, R., D. W. Owens, J. M. Knox, and H. T. Hudson. 1966. Relative energy requirements for an erythemal response of skin to monochromatic wave lengths of ultraviolet present in the solar spectrum. *J. Invest. Dermatol.* 47(6):586–592.

34. Kripke, M. L. 1986. Immunology and photocarcinogenesis. *J. Am. Acad. Dermatol.* 14(1):149–155.

35. Krutmann, J., and C. A. Elmets. 1988. Recent studies on mechanisms in photoimmunology. *Photochem. Photobiol.* 48(6):787–798.

36. Morrison, W. L. 1989. Effects of ultraviolet radiation on the immune system in humans. *Photochem. Photobiol.* 50(5):515–524.

37. Pathak, M., and K. Stratton. 1969. Effects of ultraviolet and visible radiation and the production of free radicals in skin. In *Biologic effects of ultraviolet radiation.* F. Urbach, ed. Oxford: Pergamon.

38. Quevedo, W., Jr. 1974. Light and skin color. In *Sunlight and man: Normal and abnormal photobiologic responses.* T. B. Fitzpatrick, ed. Tokyo: Univ. of Tokyo Press.

39. Sams, W. M. 1974. Inflammatory mediators in ultraviolet erythema. In *Sunlight and man: Normal and abnormal photobiologic responses.* T. B. Fitzpatrick, ed. Tokyo: Univ. of Tokyo Press.

40. Holick, M. F. 1989. 1,25-Dihydroxyvitamin D3 and the skin: A unique application for the treatment of psoriasis. *Prod. Soc. Exp. Biol. Med.* 191(3):246–257.

41. Holick, M. F. 1989. Vitamin D: Biosynthesis, metabolism, and mode of action. In *Endocrinology*, vol. 2, chapter 56. L. J. DeGroot, ed. New York: W. B. Saunders.

42. Maclaughlin, J. A., R. R. Anderson, and M. F. Holick. 1982. Spectral character of sunlight modulates photosynthesis of previtamin D3 and its photoisomers in human skin. *Science* 216:1001–1003.

43. Webb, A. R., L. Kline, and M. F. Holik. 1988. Influence of season and latitude on the cutaneous synthesis of vitamin D3: Exposure to winter sunlight in Boston and Edmonton will not promote vitamin D3 synthesis in human skin. *J. Clin. Endocrinol. Metab.* 67(2):373–378.

44. Webb, A. R., C. Pilbeam, N. Hanafin, and M. F. Holick. 1990. An evaluation of the relative contributions of exposure to sunlight and of diet to the circulating concentrations of 25-hydroxyvitamin D in an elderly population in Boston. *J. Clin. Nutr.* 51(6):1075–1081.

45. Akerstedt, T., A. Knuttson, L. Alfredsson, and T. Theorell. 1984. Shiftwork and cardiovascular disease. *Scandinavian J. Work and Environmental Health* 10:409.

46. Aschoff, J., and R. Wever. 1981. The circadian system of man. In *Biological rhythms*, chapter 17. J. Aschoff, ed. Handbook of Behavioral Neurobiology, Vol. 4. New York: Plenum.

47. Aschoff, J. 1981. A survey on biological rhythms. In *Biological rhythms*. J. Aschoff, ed. Handbook of behavioral neurobiology, Volume 4. New York, London: Plenum.

48. Aschoff, J. 1981. Freerunning and entrained circadian rhythms. In *Biological rhythms*, chapter 6. J. Aschoff, ed. Handbook of Behavioral Neurobiology, Vol. 4. New York: Plenum.

49. Menanker, M., and S. Binkley. 1981. Neural and endocrine control of circadian rhythms in the vertebrates. In *Biological rhythms*, chapter 13. J. Aschoff, ed. Handbook of Behavioral Neurobiology, Vol. 4. New York: Plenum.

50. Binkley, S. 1990. *The clockwork sparrow: Time, clocks, and calendars in biological organisms.* Englewood Cliffs, NJ: Prentice-Hall.

51. Brainard, G. C., A. J. Lewy, M. Menaker, R. H. Fredrickson, L. S. Miller, R. G. Weleber, V. Cassone, and D. Hudson. 1988. Dose-response relationship between light irradiance and the suppression of plasma melatonin in human volunteers. *Brain Res.* 454(1/2):212–218.

52. Brainard, G. C., B. A. Richardson, T. S. King, and R. J. Reiter. 1984. The influence of different light spectra on the suppression of pineal melatonin content in the Syrian hamster. *Brain Res.* 294(2):333–339.

53. Bronstein, D. M., G. H. Jacobs, K. A. Haak, J. Neitz, and L. D. Lytle. 1987. Action spectrum of the retinal mechanism mediating nocturnal light-induced suppression of rat pineal gland *N*-acetyltransferase. *Brain Res.* 406(1/2):352–356.

54. Cardinali, D. P., F. Larin, and R. J. Wurtman. 1972. Control of the rat pineal gland by light spectra. *Proc. Natl. Acad. Sci. (U.S.)* 69(8):2003–2005.

55. Czeisler, C. A., J. S. Allan, S. H. Strogatz, J. M. Ronda, R. S nchez, C. D. R!os, W. O. Freitag, G. S. Richardson, and R. E. Kronauer. 1986. Bright light resets the human circadian pacemaker independent of the timing of the sleep-wake cycle. *Science* 233:667–671.

56. Czeisler, C. A., M. C. Moore-Ede, and R. M. Coleman. 1982. Rotating shift work schedules that disrupt sleep are improved by applying circadian principles. *Science* 217:460–463.

57. Folkard, S., and T. H. Monk. 1985. *Hours of work: Temporal factors in work scheduling.* New York: Wiley.

58. Halberg, F., E. A. Johnson, B. W. Broun, and J. J. Bittner. 1960. Susceptibility rhythm to *E. coli* endotoxin and bioassay. *Proc. Soc. Exp. Biol. Med.* 103(1):142–144.

59. Klein, D. C., R. Smoot, J. L. Weller, S. Higa, S. P. Markey, G. J. Creed, and D. M. Jacobowitz. 1983. Lesions of the paraventricular nucleus area of the hypothalamus disrupt the suprachiasmatic spinal cord circuit in the melatonin rhythm generating system. *Brain Res. Bul.* 10(5):647–652.

60. Lewy, A. J., T. A. Wehr, F. K. Goodwin, D. A. Newsome, and S. P. Markey. 1980. Light suppresses melatonin secretion in humans. *Science* 210:1267–1269.

61. Moore, R. Y. 1983. Organization and function of a central nervous system circadian oscillator: The suprachiasmatic hypothalmic nucleus. *Federation Proc.* 42(11):2783–2789.

62. Moore, R. Y. 1991. The suprachiasmatic nucleus and the circadian timing system. In *Suprachiasmatic nucleus*, Introduction to Part 2. D. C. Klein, R. Y. Moore, and S. M. Reppert, eds. New York: Oxford Univ. Press.

63. Moore-Ede, M. C., C. A. Czeisler, and G. S. Richardson. 1983. Circadian timekeeping in health and disease. *New Engl. J. Med.* 309(9):530–536.

64. Moore-Ede, M. C., F. M. Sulzman, and C. A. Fuller. 1982. *The clocks that time us: Physiology of the circadian timing system.* Cambridge, MA: Harvard Univ. Press.

65. Nelson, D. E., and J. S. Takahashi. 1991. Comparison of visual sensitivity for suppression of pineal melatonin and circadian phase-shifting in the golden hamster. *Brain Res.* 554(1/2):272–277.

66. Nelson, D. E., and J. S. Takahashi. 1991. Sensitivity and integration in a visual pathway for circadian entrainment in the hamster (*Mesocricetus auratus*). *J. Physiol.* 439:115–145.

67. Pickard, G. E., and A. J. Silverman. 1981. Direct retinal projections to the hypothalamus, piriform cortex, and accessory optic nuclei in the golden hamster as demonstrated by a sensitive anterograde horseradish peroxidase technique. *J. Comp. Neurol.* 196(1):155–172.

68. Podolin, P. C., M. D. Rollag, and G. C. Brainard. 1987. The suppression of nocturnal pineal melatonin in the Syrian hamster: Dose-response curves at 500 and 360 nm. *Endocrinology* 121(1):266–270.

69. Reiter, R. 1991. Pineal gland: Interface between the photoperiodic environment and the endocrine system. *Trends Endocrin. Metab.* 2(1):13–19.

70. Takahashi, J. S., P. J. DeCoursey, L. Bauman, and M. Menaker. 1984. Spectral sensitivity of a novel photo-receptive system mediating entrainment of mammalian circadian rhythms. *Nature* 308:186–188.

71. U.S. Congress. Office of Technology Assessment. 1991. *Biological rhythms: Implications for the worker* OTA-BA-463. Washington: Office of Technology Assessment.

72. Wever, R. A. 1985. Use of light to treat jet lag: Differential effects of normal and bright artificial light on human circadian rhythms. In *The medical and biological effects of light.* R. J. Wurtman, M. J. Baum, and J. T. Potts, eds. Annals of the New York Academy of Science, 453. New York: New York Academy of Sciences.

73. Epstein, J. H. 1989. Photomedicine. In *The science of photobiology*, chapter 6. 2nd ed. K. C. Smith, ed. New York: Plenum.

74. Fitzpatrick, T. B., M. A. Pathak, L. C. Herber, M. Seiji, and A. Kukita. 1974. *Sunlight and man: Normal and abnormal photobiologic responses.* Tokyo: Univ. of Tokyo Press.

75. Assembly of Life Sciences. Committee on Phototherapy in the Newborn. 1974. *Phototherapy in the newborn: An overview.* G. B. Odell, R. Schaffer, and A. P. Simopoulos, eds. Washington: National Academy of Sciences.

76. Regan, J. D., and J. A. Parrish, eds. 1978. *The science of photomedicine.* New York: Plenum.

77. Sisson, T. R. C. 1976. Visible light therapy of neonatal hyperbilirubinemia. In *Photochemical and photobiological reviews*, vol. 1, chapter 6. K. C. Smith, ed. New York: Plenum.

78. Adrian, R. M., J. A. Parrish, T. K. Momtaz, and M. J. Karlin. 1981. Outpatient phototherapy for psoriasis. *Arch. Dermatol.* 117(10):623–626.

79. Anderson, T. F., T. P. Waldinger, and J. J. Voorhees. 1984. UV-B phototherapy. *Arch. Dermatol.* 120(11):1502–1507.

80. Parrish, J. A., and K. F. Jaenicke. 1981. Action spectrum for phototherapy of psoriasis. *J. Invest. Dermatol.* 76(5):359–362.

81. Bruynzeel, I., W. Bergman, H. M. Hartevelt, C. C. Kenter, E. A. Van de Velde, A. A. Schothorst, and D. Suurmond. 1991. "High single-dose" European PUVA regimen also causes an excess of non melanoma skin cancer. *Brit. J. Dermatol.* 124(1):49–55.

82. Gilchrest, B. A., J. A. Parrish, L. Tanenbaum, H. A. Haynes, and T. B. Fitzpatrick. 1976. Oral methoxsalen photochemotherapy of mycosis fungoides. *Cancer* 38(2):683–689.

83. Lerman, S., M. Jocoy, and R. F. Borkman. 1977. Photosensitization of the lens by 8-methoxypsoralen. *Invest. Ophthalmol. Vis. Sci.* 16(8):1065–1068.

84. Lerman, S., and R. F. Borkman. 1977. A method for detecting 8-methoxypsoralen in the ocular lens. *Science* 197:1287–1288.

85. Morison, W. L., J. A. Parrish, and T. B. Fitzpatrick. 1978. Oral psoralen photochemotherapy of atopic eczema. *Brit. J. Dermatol.* 98(1):25–30.

86. Parrish, J. A., T. B. Fitzpatrick, M. A. Pathak, and C. Shea. 1976. Photochemotherapy of vitiligo: Oral psoralen and a new high-intensity long-wave ultraviolet light system. *Arch. Dermatol.* 112(11):1531–1534.

87. Parrish, J. A., T. B. Fitzpatrick, L. Tanenbaum, and M. A. Pathak. 1974. Photochemotherapy of psoriasis with oral methoxsalen and longwave ultraviolet light. *New Engl. J. Med.* 291(23):1207–1211.

88. Parrish, J. A., M. J. LeVine, W. L. Morison, E. Gonzalez, and T. B. Fitzpatrick. 1979. Comparison of PUVA and beta-carotene in the treatment of polymorphous light eruption. *Brit. J. Dermatol.* 100(2):187–191.

89. Pathak, M. A., D. M. Kramer, and T. B. Fitzpatrick. 1974. Photobiology and photochemistry of furocoumarins (psoralens). In *Sunlight and man: Normal and abnormal photobiologic responses.* T. B. Fitzpatrick, ed. Tokyo: Univ. of Tokyo Press.

90. IES. Photobiology Committee. 1979. Risks associated with use of UV-A irradiators being used in treating psoriasis and other conditions. *Light. Des. Appl.* 9(3):56–60.

91. Stern, R. S., and R. Lange. 1988. Members of the Photochemotherapy Follow-up Study. Non-melanoma skin cancer occurring in patients treated with PUVA five to ten years after first treatment. *J. Invest. Dermatol.* 91(2):120–124.

92. Stern, R. S. 1990. Members of the photochemotherapy follow-up study. Genital tumors among men with psoriasis exposed to psoralens and ultraviolet A radiation (PUVA) and ultraviolet B radiation. *New Engl. J. Med.* 322(16):1093–1097.

93. Stern, R. S., L. A. Thibodeau, R. A. Kleinerman, J. A. Parrish, T. B. Fitzpatrick, and 22 participating investigators. 1979. Risk of cutaneous carcinoma in patients treated with oral methoxsalen photochemotherapy for psoriasis. *New Engl. J. Med.* 300(15):809–813.

94. Doiron, D. R., and G. S. Keller. 1986. Porphyrin photodynamic therapy: Principles and clinical applications. In *Therapeutic photomedicine.* H. Hönigsmann, and G. Stengl, eds. Basel: Karger.

95. Doiron, D. R., L. O. Svaasand, and A. E. Profio. 1983. Light dosimetry in tissue: Application to photoradiation therapy. In *Porphyrin photosensitization.* D. Kessel, and T. J. Dougherty, eds. Advances in Experimental Medicine and Biology, vol. 160. New York: Plenum.

96. Dougherty, T. J., W. R. Potter, and K. R. Weishaupt. 1984. The structure of the active component of hematoporphyrin derivative. In *Porphyrin Localization and Treatment of Tumors.* D. R. Doiron and C. J. Gomer, eds. Progress in Clinical and Biological Research, vol. 170. New York: Alan R. Liss.

97. Epstein, J. H. 1989. Photomedicine. In *The science of photobiology,* chapter 6. 2nd ed. K. C. Smith, ed. New York: Plenum.

98. Regan, J. D., and J. A. Parrish, eds. 1978. *The science of photomedicine.* New York: Plenum.

99. American Psychiatric Association. 1987. *Diagnostic and statistical manual of mental disorders.* 3rd. ed. rev. Washington: American Psychiatric Association.

100. Avery, D., M. A. Bolte, S. R. Dager, L. G. Wilson, M. Weyer, G. B. Cox, and D. L. Dunner. 1993. Dawn simulation treatment of winter depression: A controlled study. *Am. J. Psychiatry* 150(1):113–117.

101. Brainard, G. C., D. Sherry, R. G. Skwerer, M. Waxler, K. Kelly, and N. E. Rosenthal. 1990. Effects of different

wavelengths in seasonal affective disorder. *J. Affect. Disord.* 20(4):209–216.

102. Lewy, A. J., R. L. Sack, L. S. Miller, and T. M. Hoban. 1987. Antidepressant and circadian phase-shifting effects of light. *Science* 235:352–354.

103. Lewy, A. J., H. A. Kern, N. E. Rosenthal, and T. A. Wehr. 1982. Bright artificial light treatment of a manic-depressive patient with a seasonal mood cycle. *Am. J. Psychiatry* 139(11):1496–1498.

104. Oren, D. A., G. C. Brainard, S. H. Johnston, J. R. Joseph-Vanderpool, E Sorek, and N. E. Rosenthal. 1991. Treatment of seasonal affective disorder with green light versus red light. *Am. J. Psychiatry* 148(4):509–511.

105. Rosen, L. N., S. D. Targum, M. Terman, M. J. Bryant, H. Hoffman, S. F. Kasper, J. R. Hamovit, J. P. Docerty, B. Welch, and N. E. Rosenthal. 1990. Prevalence of seasonal affective disorder at four latitudes. *Psychiatry Res.* 31(2):131–144.

106. Rosenthal, N. E., D. A. Sack, J. C. Gillin, A. J. Lewy, F. K. Goodwin, Y. Davenport, P. S. Mueller, D. A. Newsome, and T. A. Wehr. 1984. Seasonal affective disorder: A description of the syndrome and preliminary findings with light therapy. *Arch. Gen. Psychiatry* 41(1):72–80.

107. Rosenthal, N. E., D. A. Sack, R. G. Skwerer, F. M. Jacobsen, and T. A. Wehr. 1988. Phototherapy for Seasonal Affective Disorder. *J. Biol. Rhythms* 3(2):101–120.

108. Rosenthal, N. E., D. E. Moul, C. J. Hellekson, D. A. Oren, A. Frank, G. C. Brainard, M. G. Murray, and T. A. Wehr. 1993. A multicenter study of the light visor for seasonal affective disorder: No difference in efficacy found between two different intensities. *Neuropsychopharmacology* 8(2):151.

109. Society for Light Treatment and Biological Rhythms. 1991. *1991 membership directory.* Wilsonville, OR: Society for Light Treatment and Biological Rhythms.

110. Stewart, K. T., J. R. Gaddy, B. Byrne, S. Miller, and G. C. Brainard. 1991. Effects of green or white light for treatment of seasonal depression. *Psychiatry Res.* 38(3):261–270.

111. Stewart, K. T., J. R. Gaddy, D. M. Benson, B. Byrne, K. Doghramji, and G. C. Brainard. 1990. Treatment of winter depression with a portable, head-mounted phototherapy device. *Prog. Neuropsychopharmacol. Biol. Psychiatry* 14(4):569–578.

112. Terman, J. S., M. Terman, D. Schlager, B. Rafferty, M. Rosofsky, M. J. Link, P. F. Gallin, and F. M. Quitkin. 1990. Efficacy of brief intense light exposure for treatment of winter depression. *Psychopharmacol. Bul.* 26(1):3–11.

113. Terman, M., J. S. Terman, F. M. Quitkin, and P. J. McGrath. 1989. Light therapy for seasonal affective disorder: A review of efficacy. *Neuropsychopharmacology* 2(1):1–22.

114. Terman, M., D. Schlager, S. Fairhurst, and B. Perlman. 1989. Dawn and dusk simulation as a therapeutic intervention. *Biol. Psychiatry* 25(7):966–970.

115. Wehr, T. A., R. G. Skwerer, F. M. Jacobsen, D. A. Sack, and N. E. Rosenthal. 1987. Eye versus skin phototherapy of seasonal affective disorder. *Am. J. Psychiatry* 144(6):753–757.

116. Yerevanian, B. I., J. L. Anderson, L. J. Grota, and M. Bray. 1986. Effects of bright incandescent light on seasonal and nonseasonal major depressive disorder. *Psychiatry Res.* 18(4):355–364.

117. Brainard, G. C., J. French, P. R. Hannon, M. D. Rollag, J. P. Hanifin, and W. Storm. 1991. The influence of bright illumination on plasma melatonin, prolactin and cortisol rhythms in normal subjects during sustained wakefulness. *Sleep Res.* 20:444.

118. Campbell, S. S., and W. A. Dawson. [In press.] Bright light effects on human sleep and alertness during simulated night shift work. *In Biological effects of light.* M. Holick, and A. Kligman, eds. Berlin: Walter de Gruyter.

119. Czeisler, C. A., M. P. Johnson, J. F. Duffy, E. N. Brown, J. M. Ronda, and R. E. Kronauer. 1990. Exposure to bright light and darkness to treat physiologic maladaptation to night work. *New Engl. J. Med.* 322(18):1253–1259.

120. Daan, S., and A. J. Lewy. 1984. Scheduled exposure to daylight: A potential strategy to reduce "jet lag" following transmeridian flight. *Psychopharmacol. Bul.* 20(3):566–568.

121. Eastman, C. I. 1990. Circadian rhythms and bright light: Recommendations for shift work. *Work and Stress* 4(3):245–260.

122. Eastman, C. I. 1991. Squashing versus nudging circadian rhythms with artificial bright light: Solutions for shift work? *Perspect. Biol. Med.* 34(2):181–195.

123. French, J., P. R. Hannon, and G. C. Brainard. 1990. Effects of bright illuminance on body temperature and human performance. In *Ann. Rev. Chronopharmacol.,* Vol. 7. Oxford: Pergamon.

124. Monk, T. H., M. L. Moline, and R. C. Graeber. 1988. Inducing jet lag in the laboratory: Patterns of adjustment to an active shift routine. *Aviat. Space Environ. Med.* 59(8):703–710.

125. Society for Light Treatment and Biological Rhythms. 1991. Consensus statements on the safety and effectiveness of light therapy of depression and disorders of biological rhythms. *Light Treat. Biol. Rhythms* 3:4–9.

126. Wever, R. A. 1985. Use of light to treat jet lag: Differential effects of normal and bright artificial light on human circadian rhythms. In *The medical and biological effects of light.* R. J. Wurtman, M. J. Baum, and J. T. Potts, eds. Annals of the New York Academy of Science, 453. New York: New York Academy of Sciences.

127. Eastman, C. I. 1990. What the placebo literature can tell us about light therapy for SAD. *Psychopharmacol. Bul.* 26(4):495–504.

128. Ross, M., and J. M. Olson. 1981. An expectancy-attribution model of the effects of placebos. *Psychol. Rev.* 88(5):408–437.

129. Karn, T. 1988. Molecular mechanisms of therapeutic effects of low-intensity laser radiation. *Lasers Life Sci.* 2:53–74.

130. Smith, K. C. 1991. The photobiological basis of low level laser radiation therapy. *Laser Therapy* 3:19–24.

REFERENCES

175

131. Bickford, E. D., G. W. Clark, and G. R. Spears. 1974. Measurement of ultraviolet irradiance from illuminants in terms of proposed public health standards. *J. Illum. Eng. Soc.* 4(1):43–48.

132. American National Standards Institute. 1976. *American national standard for the safe use of lasers, ANSI Z136.1-1976.* New York: American National Standards Institute.

133. Sliney, D., and M. Wolbarsht. 1980. *Safety with lasers and other optical sources.* New York: Plenum.

134. United States. Army Environmental Hygiene Agency. 1979. *Laser hazards bibliography.* Prepared by D. H. Sliney, N. Krial, D. W. Griffis, and L. L. Ryan. Aberdeen Proving Ground, MD: Army Environmental Hygiene Agency.

135. Sliney, D. H. 1972. The merits of an envelope action spectrum for ultraviolet radiation exposure criteria. *Am. Industr. Hyg. Assoc. J.* 33(10):644–653.

136. American Conference of Governmental Industrial Hygienists. 1979. *Threshold limit values and for physical agents.* Cincinnati, OH: American Conference of Governmental Industrial Hygienists.

137. Friedberg, E. C., K. H. Cook, J. Duncan, and K. Mortelmans. 1977. DNA repair enzymes in mammalian cells. In *Photochemical and photobiological reviews*, vol. 2, chapter 5. K. C. Smith, ed. New York: Plenum.

138. Harm, W., C. S. Rupert, and H. Harm. 1971. The study of photoenzymatic repair of UV lesions in DNA by flash photolysis. In *Photophysiology: Current topics in photobiology and photochemistry*, vol. 6, chapter 7. A. C. Giese, ed. New York: Academic Press.

139. Kelner, A. 1949. Effect of visible light on the recovery of *Streptomyces griseus* conidia from ultra-violet irradiation injury. *Proc. Natl. Acad. Sci. (U.S.)* 35(2):73–79.

140. GTE. Sylvania. *Germicidal and short wave radiation.* Sylvania Engineering Bulletin 0-342. Prepared by C. C. Mpelkas. Danvers, MA: Sylvania.

141. Setlow, J. K. 1966. The molecular bases of biological effects of ultraviolet radiation and photoreactivation. In *Current topics in radiation research*, vol. 2, chapter 4. M. Ebert, and A. Howard, eds. Amsterdam: North-Holland.

142. Smith, K. C. 1978. Multiple pathways of DNA repair in bacteria and their roles in mutagenesis. *Photochem. Photobiol.* 28(2):121–129.

143. Snapka, R. M., and C. O. Fuselier. 1977. Photoreactivating enzyme from *Escherichia coli. Photochem. Photobiol.* 25(5):415–420.

144. Baker, H., and T. E. Hienton. 1952. Traps have some value. In *Insects: Yearbook of agriculture 1952.* U.S. Department of Agriculture. Washington: U.S. Government Printing Office.

145. Barrett, J. R., Jr., R. T. Huber, and F. W. Harwood. 1973. Selection of lamps for minimal insect attraction. *Trans. Am. Soc. Ag. Eng.* 17(4):710–711.

146. Barrett, J. R., Jr., R. A. Killough, and J. G. Hartsock. 1974. Reducing insect problems in lighted areas. *Trans. Am. Soc. Ag. Eng.* 17(2):329–330, 338.

147. Goldsmith, T. H. 1961. The color vision of insects. In *A symposium on light and life.* W. D. McElroy, and B. Glass, eds. Baltimore, MD: John Hopkins Univ. Press.

148. Hollingsworth, J. P., and A. W. J. Hartstack. 1971. *Recent research on light trap design.* American Society of Agriculture Engineering Paper, 71-803.

149. U.S. Department of Agriculture. Agricultural Research Service. 1963. *Electric insect traps for survey purposes.* ARS 42-3-1. Prepared by J. P. Hollingsworth, J. G. Hartsock, and J. M. Stanley. Washington: Agricultural Research Service.

150. U.S. Department of Agriculture. Agricultural Research Service. 1961. *Response of insects to induced light: Presentation papers.* ARS 20-10. Washington: Agricultural Research Service.

151. Bickford, E. D. and S. Dunn. 1972. *Lighting For Plant Growth.* 1st ed. Kent, OH: Kent State University Press.

152. Bickford, E. D. 1977. Interiorscape lighting. *Light Des. Appl.* 7(10):22–25.

153. Langhans, R. W., ed. 1978. *Growth chamber manual: Enviromental control for plants.* Ithaca, NY: Comstock.

154. Cathey, H. M. 1969. Guidelines for the germination of annual, pot plant and ornamental herb seeds. Part 3. *Florists' Rev.* 144(3744):26, 29, 75–77.

155. Williams, T. J., W. J. Doty and A. C. Sinnes. 1982. *Gardening under glass and lights.* Mount Vernon, VA: American Horticultural Society.

156. Hart, J. W. 1988. *Light and plant growth.* London: Unwin Hyman.

157. Cathey, H. M. and L. E. Campbell. 1974. Lamps and lighting: A horticultural view. *Light Des. Appl.* 4(11):41–52.

158. Downs, R. J. 1975. *Controlled environments for plant research.* New York: Columbia University Press.

159. McCree, K. J. 1972. Test of current definitions of photosynthetically active radiation against leaf photosynthesis data. *Agric. Meteorol.* 10(6):443–453.

160. Cathey, H. M., L. E. Campbell and R. W. Thimijan. 1978. Plant growth under fluorescent lamps: Comparative development of 11 species. *Florists' Rev.* 163(4213):26–29, 67–69.

161. Elbert, G. and Elbert, V. F. 1974. *Plants that really bloom indoors.* New York: Simon and Schuster.

162. Fitch, C. M. 1972. *The complete book of house plants.* New York, Hawthorn.

163. Gaines, R. L. 1977. *Interior plantscaping: Building design for interior foliage plants.* 1st ed. New York: Architectural Record Books.

164. Associated Landscape Contractors of America. Interior Plantscape Division. 1988. *Guide to interior landscape specifications.* Falls Church, VA: Associated Landscape Contractors of America.

165. Kranz, F. H. and J. L. Kranz. 1971. *Gardening indoors under lights.* New rev. ed. New York: Viking.

166. Whately, J. M. and F. R. Whately. 1980. *Light and plant life.* London: E. Arnold.

167. Orans, M. 1984. *Houseplants and indoor landscaping.* Clearwater, FL: A. B. Morse.

168. Scrivens, S. and L. Pemberton. 1980. *Interior planting in large buildings.* New York: Wiley.

169. Withrow, R. B., ed. 1959. *Photoperiodism and related phenomena in plants and animals*, Publication 55. Washington, DC: American Association for the Advancement of Science.

170. Rabinowitch, E. and Govindjee. 1969. *Photosynthesis*. New York: Wiley.

171. Austin, R. L. 1985. *Designing the interior landscape*. New York: Van Nostrand Reinhold.

172. Shibles, R. 1976. Terminology pertaining to photosynthesis: Report by the Crop Science Committee on Crop Terminology. *Crop Sci*. 16(3):437–439.

173. Sager, J. C., O. W. Smith, J. L. Edwards and K. L. Cyr. 1988. Photosynthetic efficiency and phytochrome photoequilibria determination using spectral data. *Trans. ASAE* 31(6):1882–1889.

174. McCree, K. J. 1972. The action spectrum, absorptance and quantum yield of photosynthesis in crop plants. *Agric. Meteorol*. 9(3/4):191–216.

175. Giles, C. A., and R. B. McKay. 1963. The light-fastness of dyes, a review. *Textile Res. J*. 33(7):527–577.

176. Luckiesh, M., and A. H. Taylor. 1940. Fading of dyed textiles by radiant energy. *Am. Dyest. Rep*. 29(21): 543–546, 548.

177. Taylor, A. H. 1946. Fading of colored textiles. *Illum. Eng*. 41(1):35–38.

178. Taylor, A. H., and W. G. Pracejus. 1950. Fading of colored materials by light and radiant energy. *Illum. Eng*. 45(3):149-151.

179. Luckiesh, M., and A. H. Taylor. 1925. Fading of colored materials by daylight and artificial light. *Trans. Illum. Eng. Soc*. 20(10):1078–1099.

180. American Association of Textile Chemists and Colorists. Committee on Color-Fastness to Light. 1957. A study of the variables in natural light fading. *Am. Dyest. Rep*. 46(23):861–883.

181. DeLaney, W. B., and A. Makulec. 1963. A review of the fading effects of modern light sources on modern fabrics. *Illum. Eng*. 58(11):676–684.

182. Hansen, L. J., and H. E. Sereika. 1969. Factors affecting color stability of prepackaged frozen fresh beef in display cases. *Illum. Eng*. 64(10):620–624.

183. Little, A. H. 1964. The effect of light on textiles. *J. Soc. Dyers Col*. 80(10):527–534.

184. Hall, J. D. 1947. *Industrial applications of infrared*. 1st ed. New York: McGraw-Hill.

185. Tiller, F. M., and H. J. Garber. 1942. Infrared radiant heating. *Ind. Eng. Chem*. 34(7):773–781. Garber, H. J., and F. M. Tiller. 1950. Infrared radiant heating. *Ind. Eng. Chem*. 42(3):456–463.

186. National Fire Protection Association. 1969. *Standards for Class A ovens and furnaces (including industrial infrared heating systems)*. NFPA 86A. Boston: National Fire Protection Association.

187. Frier, J. P., and W. R. Stephens. 1962. Design fundamentals for space heating with infrared lamps. *Illum. Eng*. 42(12):779–784.

188. 1962. Heating with infrared. *Elec. Constr. Maint*. 61(8):92–95, 61(10):133–135.

189. Frier, J. P. 1964. Design requirements for infrared snow melting systems. *Illum. Eng*. 59(10):686–693.

190. Goodell, P. H. 1941. Radiant heat: A full-fledged industrial tool. *Trans. Am. Inst. Elec. Eng*. 60:464–470.

191. Bennett, H. J., and H. Haynes. 1940. Paint baking with near infra-red. *Chem. Metal. Eng*. 47(2):106–108.

192. Haynes, H. 1941. The use of radiant energy for the application of heat. *Illum. Eng*. 36(1):61–78.

Lighting
Engineering

II

Light Sources

6

This chapter is devoted almost exclusively to a detailed description of the various light sources now available. Fundamental information concerning the generation of light and the operating principles of electric light sources is given in chapter 1 and in other sources.[1] Applications of lighting control equipment are given in chapter 31. The sun and sky as light sources are covered in chapter 8. For information about the development of electric light sources since the nineteenth century, a number of books and articles may be consulted.[2-6]

INCANDESCENT FILAMENT LAMPS

The primary consideration of lamp design is that the lamp will produce the spectral radiation desired (light, infrared, ultraviolet) most economically for the application intended, or, in other words, yield the best balance of overall lighting cost and lighting results. Realization of this objective in an incandescent filament lamp requires the specification of the following: filament material, length, diameter, form, coil spacing and mandrel size (the mandrel is the form on which the filament is wound); lead-in wires; number of filament supports; filament mounting method; vacuum or filling gas; gas pressure; gas composition; and bulb size, shape, glass composition and finish. The manufacture of good lamps requires adherence to these specifications and necessitates careful process controls.[7, 8]

Filaments

The efficacy of light production by incandescent filament lamps depends upon the temperature of the filament. The higher the temperature of the filament, the greater the portion of the radiated energy that falls in the visible region; for this reason it is important in the design of a lamp to keep the filament temperature as high as is consistent with satisfactory life. An iron rod heated in a furnace will first glow a dull red, becoming brighter and whiter as its temperature increases. Iron, however, melts at about 1800 K and so cannot be an efficient light producer as a solid. A variety of materials have been investigated in order to find a suitable filament. The desirable properties of filament materials are high melting point, low vapor

pressure, high strength, high ductility, and suitable radiation and electrical resistance.

Tungsten for Filaments. Early incandescent lamps utilized carbon, osmium and tantalum filaments, but tungsten has many desirable properties for use as an incandescent light source. Its low vapor pressure and high melting point (3655 K) permit high operating temperatures and consequently high efficacies. Drawn tungsten wire has high strength and ductility, allowing the high degree of uniformity necessary for the exacting specifications of present-day lamps. Alloys of tungsten with other metals such as rhenium are useful in some lamp designs. Thoriated tungsten wire is used in filaments for rough service applications.

Radiating Characteristics of Tungsten.[9-12] The ratio of the radiant exitance of a thermal radiator to that of a blackbody radiator is called the emissivity, and thus the emissivity of a blackbody is 1.0 for all wavelengths (see chapter 1). The emissivity of tungsten, however, is a function of the wavelength: tungsten is a *selective radiator*. Figure 6-1 illustrates the radiation characteristics of tungsten and of a blackbody. This figure illustrates that for the same amount of visible radiation, tungsten radiates only a fraction (76%) of the total radiation from a blackbody at the same temperature.

Only a small percentage of the total radiation from an incandescent source is in the visible region of the spectrum. As the temperature of a tungsten filament is raised, the radiation in the visible region (see figure 6-2) increases more rapidly than the radiation in the infrared region, and thus the luminous efficacy increases. The luminous efficacy of an uncoiled tungsten wire at its melting point (3655 K) is approximately 53 lm/W. In order to obtain long life, it is necessary to operate a filament at a temperature well below the melting point and consequently at a loss in efficacy.

Resistance Characteristics of Tungsten. Tungsten has a positive resistance characteristic, so that its resistance at operating temperature is much greater than its cold resistance. In general-service lamps, the hot resistance is 12–16 times the cold resistance. Figure 6-3 illustrates the change in resistance of the tungsten filament with temperature for various lamps. The low cold resistance

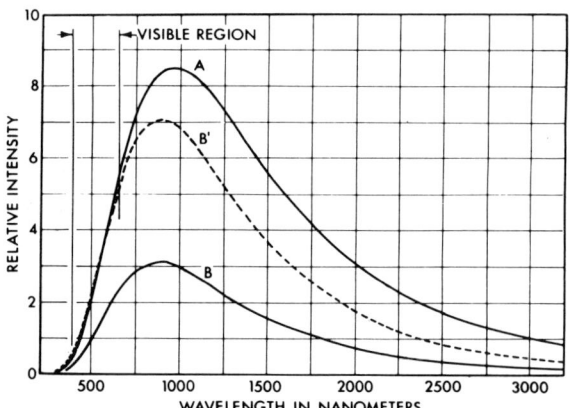

Fig. 6-1. Radiating characteristics of tungsten. Curve A: radiant flux from one square centimeter of a blackbody at 3000 K. Curve B: radiant flux from one square centimeter of tungsten at 3000 K. Curve B': radiant flux from 2.27 square centimeters of tungsten at 3000 K (equal to curve A in visible region). (The 500 watt 120-volt general service lamp operates at about 3000 K.)

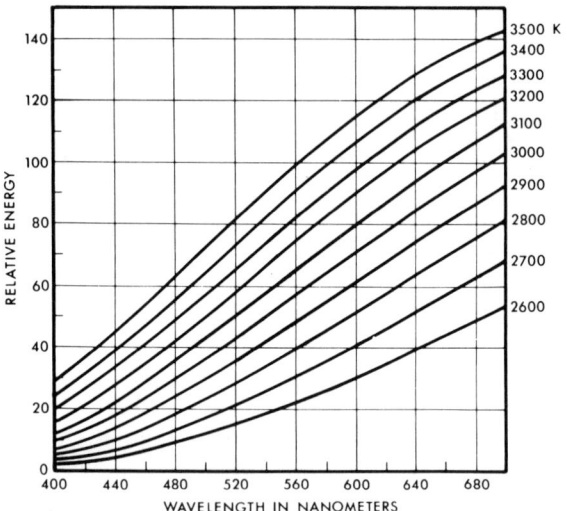

Fig. 6-2. Spectral power distribution in the visible region from tungsten filaments of equal wattage but different temperatures.

of tungsten filaments results in an initial inrush of current which, because of the reactive impedance characteristic of the circuit, does not reach the theoretical value indicated by the ratio of the hot to cold resistance. Figure 6-79 at the end of the chapter gives the effect of the change in resistance on the current in incandescent filament lamps. The inrush current due to incandescent filament loads is important in the design and adjustment of circuit breakers, in circuit fusing, in the design of lighting-circuit switch contacts and in dimmer designs.

Color Temperature. In many applications, it is important to know the apparent color temperature of an incandescent lamp. Figure 6-4 expresses the approximate relationship between color temperature and luminous efficacy for a fairly wide wattage range of gas-filled

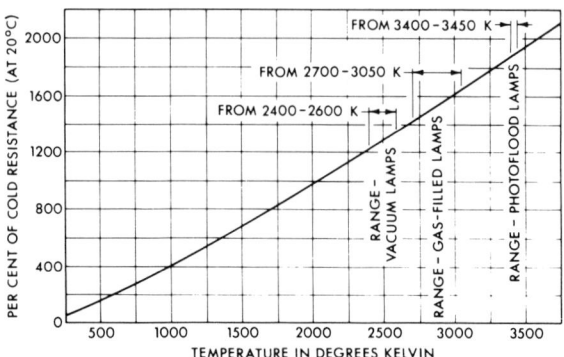

Fig. 6-3. Variation of tungsten filament hot resistance with temperature.

lamps. The value of the efficacy may often be found in the literature, or it may be calculated from published lumen and wattage data. From this value it is possible to approximate the average color temperature of the filament.

Construction and Assembly. Figure 6-5 shows the basic parts and steps in the assembly of a typical incandescent, general-service filament lamp. In miniature lamps three methods of construction are typically used: flange seal, butt seal and pinch seal (see figure 6-6).

The *flange seal* is generally used with lamps 20 mm ($\frac{3}{4}$ in.) and larger in bulb diameter. This construction features a glass stem with a flange at the bottom which is sealed to the neck of the bulb. When used with bayonet bases the plane of the filament and lead wires is normally at right angles to the plane of the base pins. However, a tolerance of 15° is generally permitted. The advantages of this construction are: (1) heavy lead-in wires can be used for lamp currents up to 12 A; (2) the filament can be accurately positioned; and (3) sturdy stem construction resists filament displacement and damage from shock and vibration.

The *butt seal* is constructed as follows: A mount consisting of lead-in wires, bead and filament is

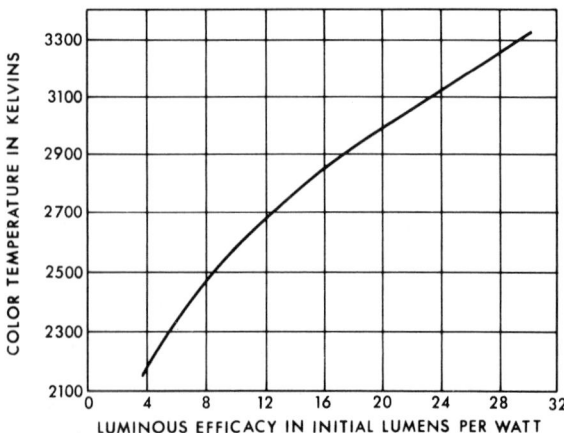

Fig. 6-4. Variation of color temperature with lamp efficacy.

ASSEMBLY OF INNER STRUCTURE (MOUNT)

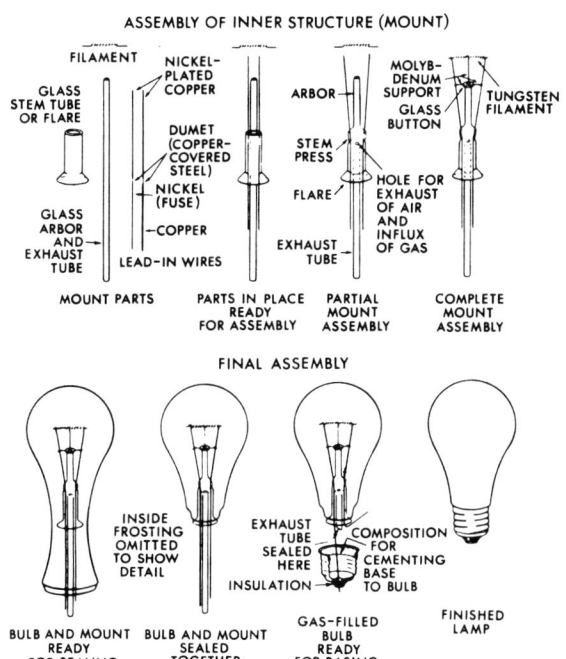

Fig. 6-5. Steps in the manufacture of a typical incandescent filament lamp.

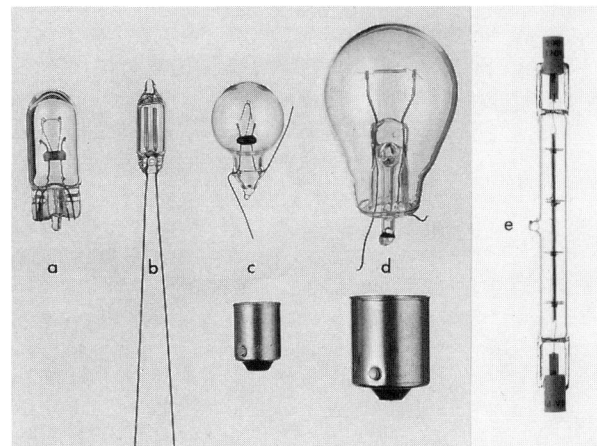

Fig. 6-6. Primary type of bulb construction: a. pinch seal with wedge base, b. pinch seal with lead-in wire terminals, c. butt seal, d. flange seal, e. molybdenum ribbon pinch seal.

dropped into the open end of the bulb. The lead-in wires are bent to locate the filament at the desired distance from the bulb end. An exhaust tube is then dropped down and butted against the lead-in wire and glass bulb just prior to sealing and exhausting. The base, applied later, together with the basing cement, must not only provide the lamp contacts but also protect the delicate seal. Because of seal limitations, butt seal lamps are restricted to small wire sizes with a current limit of about 1.0 A. The filament position varies considerably more than in flange seal lamps, since there is no definite relationship between the planes of the filament and base pins. Occasionally butt seal lamps are used without bases; these lamps should be handled carefully. When used with a base, the advantages of butt seal construction are (1) low cost and (2) small size (usually 20 mm [0.75 in.] and below).

The *pinch seal* is so named because glass is pinched, or formed, around the lead-in wires. Two forms are used: wire terminals and wedge base construction. For the smaller types of glow lamps, the bulb is exhausted and tipped off at the end opposite the lead-in wires. With the newer wedge base lamps, the exhaust tip is at the bottom rather than the top. Pinch seal construction eliminates the need for a conventional base. The advantages are: (1) low cost; (2) small size; (3) with filament lamps, the elimination of solder and cement, which allows operation up to 300°C; and (4) small space required for wedge base lamps.

The *molybdenum seal* is used in tungsten-halogen lamps, where wire seals cannot be employed, due to

their thermal expansion mismatch with the fused silica envelope material. Molybdenum seals consist of thin ribbons or foils of molybdenum which are pinched in the base of the lamps to provide the required electrical lead-in. The ribbons can provide a reliable seal as long as the base temperature is kept below the molybdenum oxidation temperature of 350°C.

Filament Forms and Designations. Filament design represents a careful balance between light output and life. Filament forms, sizes and support constructions vary widely with different types of lamps. See figure 6-7. Their designs are determined largely by service requirements. Filament forms are designated by a letter or letters followed by an arbitrary number. The most commonly used letters are: S (straight), meaning the wire is uncoiled; C (coiled), meaning the wire is wound into a helical coil; and CC (coiled coil), meaning the coil is itself wound into a helical coil. Coiling the filament increases its luminous efficacy; forming a coiled coil further increases efficacy. More filament supports are required in lamps designed for rough service and vibration service than for general-service lamps.

Bulbs

Shapes and Sizes. Common bulb shapes are shown in figure 6-8. Bulbs are designated by a letter referring to the shape classification, and a number indicating the maximum diameter in multiples of eighths of an inch (3.2 mm). Thus, R-40 designates a bulb of the R shape which is 40/8 = 5 in. (127 mm) in diameter.

Types of Glass. Most bulbs are made of regular lead or soda lime ("soft") glass, but some types are made of borosilicate heat-resisting ("hard") glass. The latter withstand higher temperatures and are used for highly loaded lamps. Under most circumstances they will bet-

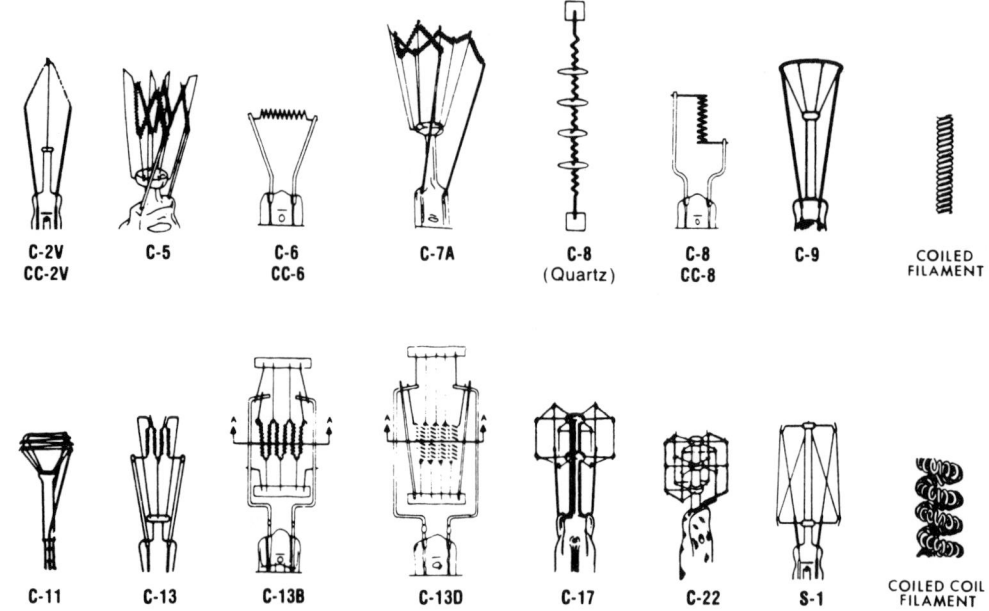

| C-2V CC-2V | C-5 | C-6 CC-6 | C-7A | C-8 (Quartz) | C-8 CC-8 | C-9 | COILED FILAMENT |

| C-11 | C-13 | C-13B | C-13D | C-17 | C-22 | S-1 | COILED COIL FILAMENT |

Fig. 6-7. Typical incandescent lamp filament constructions (not to scale).

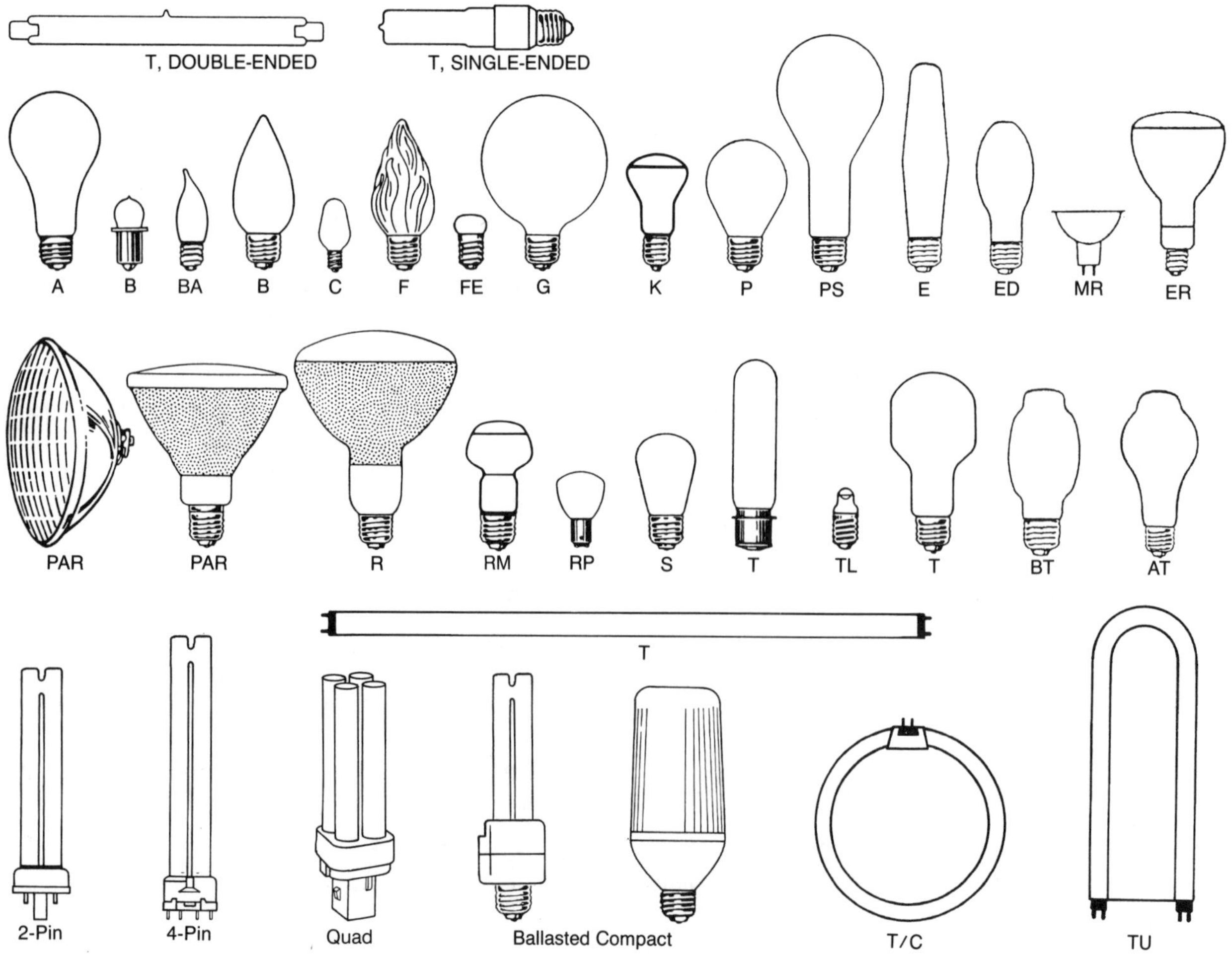

T, DOUBLE-ENDED   T, SINGLE-ENDED

A B BA B C F FE G K P PS E ED MR ER

PAR PAR R RM RP S T TL T BT AT

T

2-Pin 4-Pin Quad Ballasted Compact T/C TU

Fig. 6-8. Typical bulb shapes and designations (not to scale).

ter withstand exposure to moisture or luminaire parts touching the bulb. (See Bulb and Socket Temperatures, below.) Three specialized forms of glass are also used as lamp envelopes: fused silica, high-silica and aluminosilicate glass. These materials can withstand still higher temperatures.

Bulb Finishes and Colors. Inside frosting is applied to many types and sizes of bulbs. It produces moderate diffusion of the light with less than 2% reduction in output. The extremely high filament luminance of clear lamps is reduced, and striations and shadows are practically eliminated with the use of frosting. White lamps having an inside coating of finely powdered white silica provide a substantially greater degree of diffusion with very little absorption of light.

Daylight lamps have bluish glass bulbs which absorb some of the red and yellow light produced by the filament. The resulting light output is of a higher correlated color temperature. This color, achieved at the expense of about 35% reduction in light output through absorption, varies between 3500 and 4000 K. This is about midway between tungsten filament light and natural daylight.

General-service incandescent colored lamps are available with inside- and outside-spray-coated, outside-ceramic, transparent-plastic-coated, and natural-colored bulbs. Outside-spray-coated lamps are generally used for indoor use where not exposed to the weather. Their surfaces collect dirt readily and are not easily cleaned. Inside-coated bulbs have smooth outside surfaces which are easily cleaned; the pigments are not exposed to weather and therefore have the advantage in permanence of color. Ceramic-coated bulbs have the colored pigments fused onto the glass, providing a permanent finish. They are suitable for indoor or outdoor use. Most transparent-plastic-coated bulbs also can be used both indoors and outside. The coating permits the filament to be observed directly. "Natural-colored" bulbs are made of colored glass. Colored reflector lamps utilize ceramic-coated bulbs, stained bulbs, plastic-coated bulbs, and dichroic interference filters to obtain the desired color characteristics.

Bases

Figure 6-9 shows the most common types of lamp bases. Most lamps for general lighting purposes employ one of the various types of screw bases. Where a high degree of accuracy in positioning of light sources with relation to optical elements is important, as in the case of projection systems, bipost and prefocus bases ensure proper filament location. Lamp wattage is often a factor in determining the base type.

Most bases are secured to the bulbs by cement and are cured by heat when the lamp is manufactured. Since this cement becomes weaker with age, particularly if exposed to excessive heat, some lamps intended for high-temperature service use a special heat-tolerant basing cement, or bases that are mechanically fastened without the use of cement.

Gas Fill

Around 1911, attempts were made to reduce the rate of evaporation of the filament by the use of gas-filled bulbs. Although the fill gas successfully reduced bulb wall blackening, it increased heat loss, leading to even greater light loss. An incandescent filament operating in an inert gas is surrounded by a thin sheath of heated gas, to which some of the input energy is lost; the proportion lost decreases as the filament diameter is

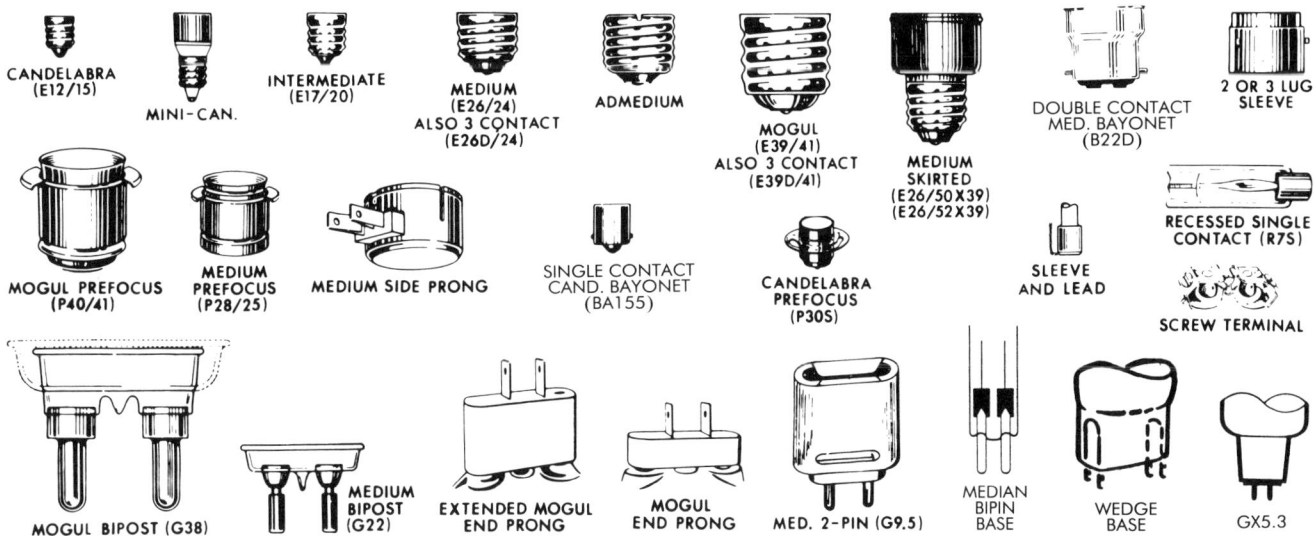

Fig. 6-9. Common lamp bases (not to scale). International Electrotechnical Commission (IEC) designations are shown, where available.

increased. When the filament is coiled in a tight helix, the sheath surrounds the entire coil, so that the heat loss is no longer determined by the diameter of the wire but by the diameter of the coil, thus greatly reducing this energy loss. A coiled-coil filament has even less length for a given power rating, thus further reducing the area available for convective cooling. The use of coiled-coil filaments and gas-filled bulbs has yielded major improvement in incandescent lamp efficacies. However, general-service 120-V lamps below 25 W are usually of the vacuum type, since gas filling does not improve the luminous efficacy in this wattage range.

Inert gases are chosen because they do not react with the internal parts of the lamp. Nitrogen was first used for this purpose.[13] It was known that argon, due to its lower heat conductivity, was superior to nitrogen, but it was some years after the development of the gas-filled lamps before argon became available in sufficient quantity and purity, and at reasonable cost. Most lamps are now filled with argon and a small percentage of nitrogen; some nitrogen is necessary to suppress the tendency for arcing to occur between the lead-in wires.

The proportion of argon and nitrogen depends on the voltage rating, the filament construction and temperature, and the lead-tip spacing. Typical amounts of argon in use are: 99.6% for 6-V lamps, 95% for 120-V general-service coiled-coil lamps, 90% for 230-V lamps having fused lead wires, and 50% or less for 230-V lamps when no fuses are used in the leads. Some projection lamps are 100% nitrogen filled.

Krypton, though expensive, is used in some lamps where the increase in cost is justified by the increased efficacy or increased life. Krypton gas has lower heat conductivity than argon. Also, the krypton molecule is larger than that of argon, and therefore further retards the evaporation of the filament. Depending upon the filament form, bulb size, and mixture of nitrogen and argon, conversion to krypton fill may increase efficacy by 7–20%.[14, 15] Krypton is used in some special lamps such as marine signal and miner's cap lamps, because the resulting high efficacy means less drain on the power source for a given amount of light produced.

Hydrogen gas has a high heat conductivity and is therefore useful for filling signaling lamps where quick flashing is desired.[16]

Tungsten-halogen lamps, a variation of incandescent filament lamps, utilize a halogen regenerative cycle to provide excellent lumen maintenance, together with lamp compactness. Halogen is the name given to a family of electronegative elements, including bromine, chlorine, fluorine and iodine. Although the tungsten-halogen regenerative cycle has been known for many years, no practical method of using it was established until the development of small-diameter fused quartz envelopes for filament lamps provided the proper tem-

perature parameters. Iodine was the halogen used in the first tungsten-halogen lamp; today, other halogens are being used.[17]

It is generally accepted that the regenerative cycle starts with the tungsten filament operating at incandescence, evaporating tungsten off the filament. Normally the tungsten particles would collect on the bulb wall, resulting in bulb blackening, common with incandescent lamps, and most evident near the end of their life. However, in halogen lamps the temperature of the bulb is high enough so that the tungsten combines with the halogen. (The correlated minimum temperature of the bulb has to be approximately 260°C.) The resulting tungsten-halogen compound is also gaseous, and continues to circulate inside the lamp until it comes in contact with the incandescent filament. Here, the heat is sufficient to break down the compound into tungsten, which is redeposited on the filament, and halogen, which is freed to continue its role in the regenerative cycle. It should be noted, however, that since the tungsten does not necessarily redeposit exactly where it came from, the tungsten-halogen lamp still has a finite life. When dimming tungsten-halogen lamps, it is recommended to periodically run the lamps at full power, inducing the tungsten-halogen cycle to clean the tungsten off the bulb wall, and enhancing lamp efficacy over time.

Energy Characteristics

The manner in which the energy input to a lamp is dissipated can be seen by reference to figure 6-83 below for typical general-service lamps. The radiation in the visible spectrum (column 2) is the percentage of the input power actually converted to visible radiation. The gas loss (column 4) indicates the amount of heat lost by the filament due to the conduction through and convection by the surrounding gas in gas-filled lamps. The end loss (column 6) is the heat lost from the filament by the lead-in wires and support hooks which conduct heat from the filament. Column 3 shows the total radiation beyond the bulb, which is less than the actual filament radiation on account of absorption by the glass bulb and the lamp base.

Bulb and Socket Temperatures. Incandescent filament lamp operating temperatures are important for several reasons. Excessive lamp temperatures may affect the performance of the lamp itself. They may shorten the life of the luminaire or of the electrical supply circuit. They may also result in unsafe temperatures of combustible materials that form a part of the luminaire or of the material adjacent to the luminaire. Under certain atmosphere or dust conditions, high bulb temperatures (above 160°C) may induce explosion or fire. Bulb and socket temperatures for a 100-W

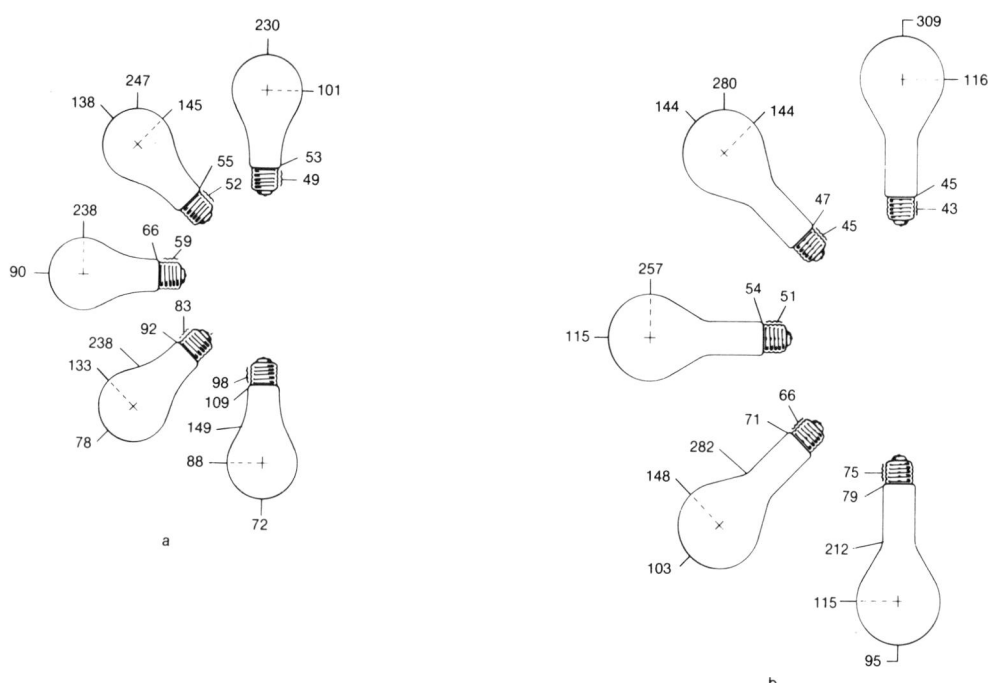

Fig. 6-10. Incandescent filament lamp operating temperatures in still air at 25°C ambient: (a) 100 watt CC-8, A-19 lamp; (b) 500 watt CC-8, PS-35 lamp. All temperatures shown are in degrees Celsius.

A-19 lamp and a 500-W PS-35 lamp for different operating positions are shown in figure 6-10.

General-service incandescent filament lamps are made of regular lead or lime "soft" glass, the maximum safe operating temperature of which is 370°C. Some lamps for special application, such as outdoor floodlighting lamps, have "hard" glass bulbs which have a safe temperature limit of 470°C. Lamps with "still harder" glass bulbs can be operated up to 520°C. For thermal shock conditions, such as rain, safe operating temperatures would be substantially lower. Many low-wattage lamps have inner parts that will not operate at high bulb temperatures.

From a lamp performance standpoint, the maximum safe base temperature for general-service lamps is 170°C, measured at the junction of the base and the bulb. In all cases excessive temperature may cause failure of the basing cement, as well as softening of the solder used to connect the lead wires to the base. Silicone cement and high-melting-point solder permit base temperatures to approach 260°C. Mechanical bases, which are used in some lamps without basing cement, generally should not be operated above 200°C. There are some incandescent filament lamps which have internal parts which will withstand operation of the mechanical base up to 210°C. Care must always be exercised to ensure that allowable luminaire socket temperatures are not exceeded. Bipost bases carry considerable heat to the socket through the base pins, and the parts of the socket in contact with the base pins should be capable of withstanding a temperature

of 290°C. Tubular fused quartz infrared and tungsten-halogen cycle lamps generally have a maximum seal temperature of 350°C to prevent oxidation. In addition, tungsten-halogen lamps have a minimum bulb temperature of 260°C to ensure proper functioning of the regenerative cycle.

Some of the factors affecting base temperature are filament type, light center length, heat shields, bulb shape and size, and gas fill. Base temperature may not parallel wattage ratings; that is, lamps of lower wattage do not necessarily have lower base temperatures. Medium-base luminaires should be capable of accepting lamp base temperatures on the order of 135–150°C. These limits are consistent with Canadian Standards Association (CSA), American National Standards Institute (ANSI), and International Electrotechnical Commission (IEC) standards for base temperature for A-type lamps. Measurements should be made in accordance with ANSI C78.25, "Lamp-Base Temperature Rise—Method of Measurements." If the luminaire will accept R and PAR lamps, then the temperature capability of the luminaire should be 170–185°C if reasonable electrical insulation life is desired for the luminaire. Heat-transmitting dichroic-reflector lamps should be placed only in luminaires specifically designed for them; this is normally indicated on the luminaire.

For base-up burning, and where only slight enclosing of the lamp is provided by the luminaire, base temperature is the major factor affecting luminaire temperatures, with lamp wattage being a minor consid-

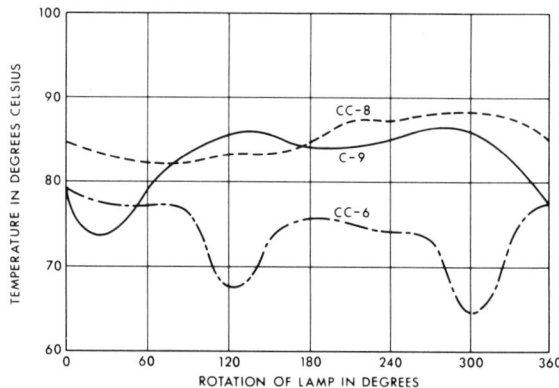

Fig. 6-11. Profile temperatures vary with rotation of lamp filament; three types shown.

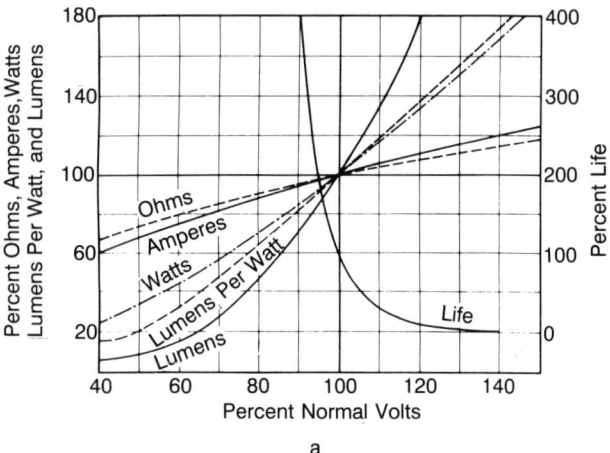

a

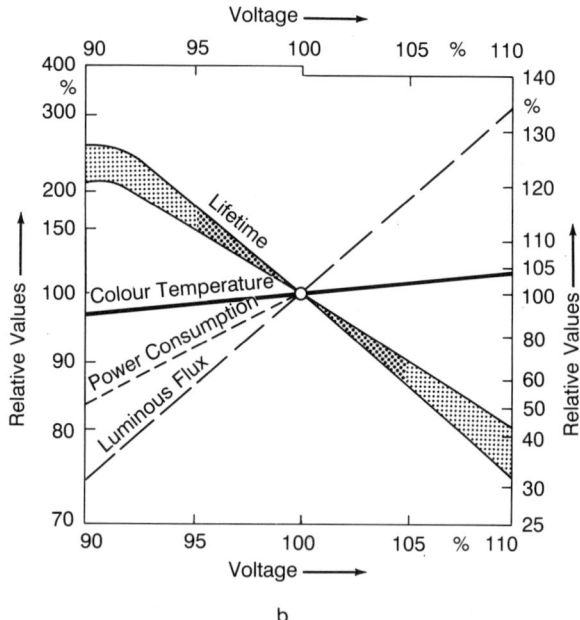

b

Fig. 6-12. Effect of voltage and current variation on the operating characteristics of: (a) incandescent filament lamps in general lighting (multiple) circuits and (b) incandescent filament lamps in series street lighting circuits.

eration. As the luminaire provides more and more enclosing of the lamp, base temperatures have a lesser effect, and wattage assumes more importance.

High temperatures reduce the life of electrical insulation for lamp and luminaire parts. Figure 6-11 shows how the position of the filament affects the temperature of the bulb. This variation in temperature with position is sufficiently large to affect the life of wire insulation and other luminaire components.

Lamp Characteristics

Life, Efficacy, Color Temperature and Voltage Relationships. If the voltage applied to an incandescent filament lamp is varied, there is a resulting change in the filament resistance and temperature, current, power, light output, efficacy, and life. These characteristics are interrelated, and no one of them can be changed without affecting the others. The following equations can be used to calculate the effect of a change from the design conditions on lamp performance (capital letters represent normal rated values, lowercase letters represent changed values):

$$\frac{\text{life}}{\text{LIFE}} = \left(\frac{\text{VOLTS}}{\text{volts}}\right)^d$$

$$\frac{\text{lumens}}{\text{LUMENS}} = \left(\frac{\text{VOLTS}}{\text{volts}}\right)^k$$

$$\frac{\text{LPW}}{\text{lpw}} = \left(\frac{\text{VOLTS}}{\text{volts}}\right)^g$$

$$\frac{\text{watts}}{\text{WATTS}} = \left(\frac{\text{volts}}{\text{VOLTS}}\right)^m$$

$$\frac{\text{color temperature}}{\text{COLOR TEMPERATURE}} = \left(\frac{\text{volts}}{\text{VOLTS}}\right)^m$$

For approximate calculations, the following exponents may be used in the above equations: $d = 13$, $g = 1.9$,

$k = 3.4$, $n = 1.6$ and $m = 0.42$. For more accuracy, the exponents must be determined by each lamp manufacturer from a comparison of normal-voltage and over- or undervoltage tests of many lamp groups. Exponents will vary for different lamp types, lamp wattages, and ranges of percentage voltage variation. The values given above are roughly applicable to vacuum lamps of about 10 lm/W and gas-filled lamps of about 16 lm/W in a voltage range of 90–110% of rated voltage. For information outside this range, refer to figure 6-12.

The curves of figure 6-12a show the effect of voltage variations[18, 19] on the characteristics of lamps in general lighting (multiple) circuits. The effect of voltage variation on the characteristics of tungsten-halogen lamps cannot be accurately predicted outside of the voltage range of 90–110% of the rated voltage. (See below for further discussion of multiple circuits in street lighting.)

Filament Notching. Ordinarily, for laboratory test operation, normal tungsten filament evaporation controls incandescent lamp life. Where that is so, lamps should reach their design-predicted life. In recent years, another factor influencing filament life, known as "filament notching," has become prominent. Filament notching is the appearance of steplike or sawtooth irregularities on all or part of the tungsten filament surface after long use. These notches reduce the filament wire diameter at random points. In some cases, especially for fine-wire filaments, the notching is so deep as to almost sever the wire. Thus, faster spot evaporation due to this notching and reduced filament strength become the dominant factors influencing lamp life. Predicted lamp life may be reduced by as much as one-half from this cause.

Filament notching is associated with at least three factors (primarily occurring in fine-wire filament lamps): (1) low-temperature filament operation, as in long-life lamp types such as 10,000–100,000-h designs; (2) small filament wire sizes, typically less than 0.025 mm (0.001 in.) in diameter; and (3) use of direct current.

Depreciation During Life. Over a period of time, incandescent filaments evaporate and become smaller, which increases their resistance. In multiple circuits, the increase in filament resistance causes a reduction in amperes, watts and lumens. A further reduction in lumen output is caused by the absorption of light by the deposit of the evaporated tungsten particles on the bulb. Figure 6-13a shows the change in watts, lumens and lumens per watt for a 200-W lamp.

In series circuits having constant-current regulators, the increase in filament resistance during life causes an increase in the voltage across the lamp and a consequent increase in wattage and generated lumens. This increase in lumens is offset to varying degrees by the absorption of light by the tungsten deposit on the bulb. In low-current lamps the net depreciation in light output during life is very small, or in the smaller sizes there may be an actual increase. In lamps of 15- and 20-A ratings, the bulb blackening is much greater and more than offsets throughout life the increase in lumens due to the increased wattage.

The blackening in vacuum lamps is uniform over the bulb. In gas-filled lamps the evaporated tungsten particles are carried by convection currents to the upper part of the bulb. When gas-filled lamps are burned base up, most of the blackening occurs on the neck area, where some of the light is normally intercepted by the base. Consequently, the lumen maintenance for base-up burning is better than for base-down or horizontal burning with gas-filled lamps.

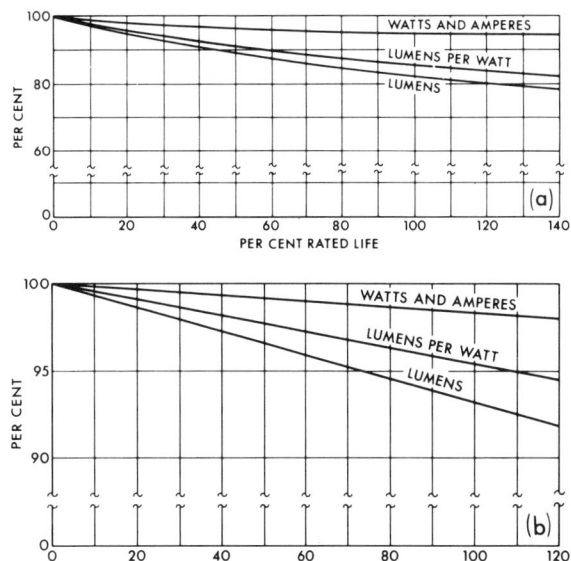

Fig. 6-13. Typical operating characteristics of lamps as a function of burning time: (a) general-service lamps and (b) tungsten-halogen lamps. (*Note differences in scales.*)

In a base-up burning lamp, an appreciable gain in lumen maintenance can be obtained through the use of a coiled-coil filament located on or parallel to the bulb axis.

To reduce blackening from traces of oxygen or water vapor in the gas filling, an active chemical, known as a *getter*, is used inside the bulb to combine with and absorb any such impurities remaining in the bulb.

Tungsten-halogen cycle lamps generally have significantly less depreciation during life, due to the regenerative cycle which removes the evaporated tungsten from the bulb and redeposits it on the filament. Figure 6-13b shows the change in lumens, watts and lumens per watt for a 500-W tungsten-halogen lamp.

Lamp Mortality. Many factors inherent in lamp manufacturing and materials make it impossible for every lamp to achieve the rated life for which it was designed. For this reason, lamp life is rated as the average of a large group. A typical mortality curve for a large group of lamps is illustrated in figure 6-14 and is representative of the performance of high-quality lamps.

Flicker and Stroboscopic Effect. All light sources operated on alternating current will flicker. The degree to which flicker is perceived depends upon the frequency of the alternating current, the persistence of light generated by the source and the viewing conditions.

Flicker has special significance for objects moving within the field of view. Objects may appear to move discretely rather than continuously under flickering illumination; this is known as the stroboscopic effect. The magnitude of the effect depends upon the rate

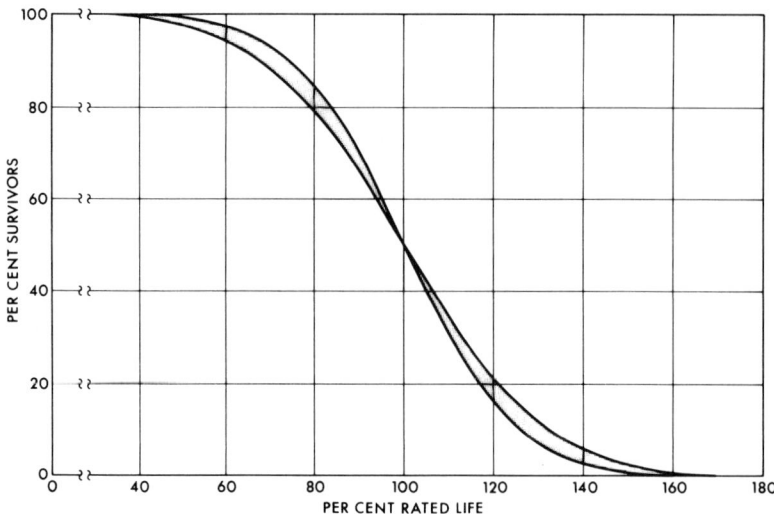

Fig. 6-14. Range of typical mortality curves (average for a statistically large group of incandescent filament lamps).

and amplitude of the flicker, the rate of object motion and the viewing conditions.

The *flicker index*[41] has been established as a reliable relative measure of the cyclic variation in output of various sources at a given power frequency. It takes into account the waveform of the light output as well as its amplitude. It is calculated by dividing the area above the line of average light output by the total area under the light output curve for a single cycle (see figure 6-15). Area 2 in figure 6-15 may be close to zero if light output varies as periodic spikes.

The flicker index assumes values from 0 to 1.0, with 0 for steady light output. Higher values indicate an increased possibility of noticeable stroboscopic effect, as well as lamp flicker.

Incandescent lamps operated below 25 Hz will produce perceptible flicker and can create a stroboscopic effect. Flicker will be less from an incandescent source if it has a larger filament, is operated at a higher wattage and at a higher supply frequency. Modern incandescent light sources operated at 60 Hz do not produce noticeable flicker nor a stroboscopic effect.

The UV energy generated by an arc discharge is a function of the instantaneous power input. As a consequence, the generated UV energy shows cyclic changes similar to those in the power input. The frequency of this variation is twice the input frequency, and it ranges from 0 to maximum. The cyclic variation of the UV energy is transferred to the phosphors, which show both fluorescence and phosphorescence. Flicker is produced, but since the response of the phosphors is not instantaneous, some persistence of the light output occurs. With a 60-Hz input frequency, the resulting 120-Hz variation is too rapid to be perceived. Operation of fluorescent lamps on most high-frequency electronic ballasts minimizes flicker and stroboscopic effect by excluding a significant portion of the 60-Hz light variation. In figure 6-16 the flicker index is listed for a

variety of fluorescent lamps when operated from typical circuits.

The light output of all HID lamps varies to some degree with the cyclic changes of the line voltage. This *flicker* is a function of both the lamp type and the ballast circuit.

Figure 6-17 illustrates the variation in flicker index for mercury, metal halide and high-pressure sodium lamps for several ballast types operated at 60 Hz.[71] The flicker index is considerbly higher in 50-Hz power systems. The flicker effect can be eliminated by using electronic ballasts having high-frequency or rectangular current wave characteristics.

Flicker is an important consideration for HID lamps. In many lighting applications the stroboscopic effect from HID sources is not a problem. It can, however, be annoying to spectators in some ball games such as tennis and ping-pong. Occasionally it can be a nuisance or distraction with rotating machinery such as a lathe.

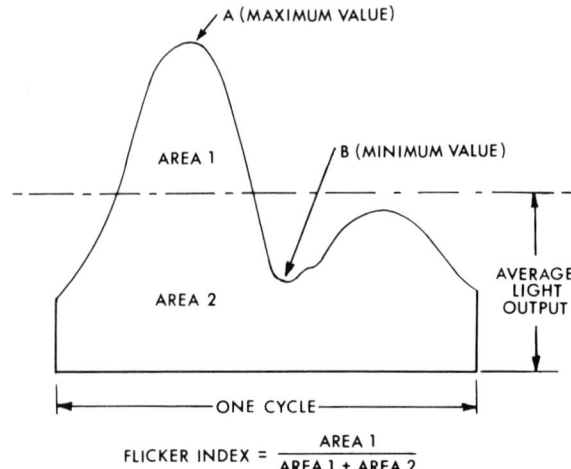

Fig. 6-15. Curve of the light output variation from a fluorescent lamp during each cycle, showing the method of calculating the Flicker Index.

Fig. 6-16. Flicker Index for Typical Fluorescent
Lamp Types

LAMP TYPE	BALLAST	FLICKER INDEX
35W Regal White	Reactor	.042
35W Lite White	Reactor	.016
40W Warm White	Reactor	.020
40W Cool White	Reactor	.038
40W White	Reactor	.028
40W Daylight	Reactor	.056
40W Natural	Reactor	.089
40W Soft White	Reactor	.087
40W Optima 32	Reactor	.089
40W Kolorite	Reactor	.106
40W IncandescentFluor.	Reactor	.101
40W Royal / Regal White	Reactor	.042
40W Chroma 50	Reactor	.111
40W Chroma 70	Reactor	.123
40W Verilux	Reactor	.084
40W Cool White Deluxe	Reactor	.107
40W Ultralume 3000	Reactor	.057
40W Ultralume 4100	Reactor	.046
35W Regal White	Series-Sequence	.035
35W Lite White	Series-Sequence	.016
40W Warm White	Series-Sequence	.018
40W Cool White	Series-Sequence	.037
40W White	Series-Sequence	.026
40W Daylight	Series-Sequence	.047
40W Cool White Deluxe	Series-Sequence	.097
40W Optima 32	Series-Sequence	.084
40W Chroma 50	Series-Sequence	.095
40W Chroma 70	Series-Sequence	.102
40W Verilux	Series-Sequence	.055
1500mA Cool White	Series-Sequence	.040
HO Warm White	Series-Sequence	.036
Slimline Cool White	Series-Sequence	.043
Slimline Lite White	Series-Sequence	.029
22W Circline Cool White	Reactor	.043
SL-18W (2900K)	Reactor	.045

Fig. 6-17. Flicker Index for HID Lamps Operated
on Different Ballast Types

LAMP TYPE	BALLAST	FLICKER INDEX
MERCURY		
250W Warm Deluxe	Reactor	.127
250W Cool Deluxe	Reactor	.137
250W Deluxe White	Reactor	.131
250W Deluxe White	CWA (M-H type)	.172
100W Deluxe White	CW-Premium	.142
100W Deluxe White	CW	.183
400W Deluxe White	Reactor	.121
400W Deluxe White	CWA (M-H type)	.144
HIGH PRESSURE SODIUM		
250W Deluxe	Reactor of CWA	.131
250W Standard	Reactor or CWA	.200
METAL HALIDE		
250W High Color Quality	Reactor	.080
250W High Color Quality	HPS-CWA	.102
175W Coated	CWA	.083
175W Clear-Vertical	CWA	.078
175W Clear-Horizontal		.092
250W Coated (A)	CWA	.070
250W Clear-Vertical	CWA	.102
250W Clear-Horizontal		.121
250W Coated (B)	CWA	.092
250W Clear-Vertical	CWA-Premium	.088
250W Clear-Horizontal		.097
400W Clear-Vertical	CWA	.086
400W Clear-Horizontal		.095
1000W Clear (vert)	CWA	.067
175W (3200K)	CWA	.090

To minimize stroboscopic effect, systems with a flicker index of 0.1 or less are suggested, or luminaries should be alternately wired on three-phase systems.

Some flicker may be seen from the ends of a lamp when viewed on the periphery of the retina (out of the "corner of one's eye"). This is due to the arc being initiated at alternate electrodes.

Classes of Lamps

Incandescent filament lamps are divided into three major groups: large lamps, miniature lamps and specialty lamps. These are cataloged separately by lamp manufacturers. There is no sharp dividing line between the groups. The large lamp classification generally refers to those with larger bulbs, with medium or mogul bases and for operating circuits of 30 V or higher. The miniature classification generally includes such types as automotive, aircraft, flashlight, holiday, radio panel, telephone switchboard, bicycle, toy train, and many other small lamps generally operated from circuits of less than 50 V. The specialty classification includes lamps designed for photographic or projection service. The following gives a brief description of a few of the many types of lamps that are regularly manufac-

tured. More complete details are available in manufacturers' catalogs.

General Service. These are large lamps made for general lighting use on 120-V circuits. General-service lamps range from 10 to 1500 W and satisfy the majority of lighting applications. All sizes are made in both clear and inside-frosted bulbs. Below 200 W, inside-white-coated finishes are also available. Performance data are shown in figure 6-78.

High Voltage. This voltage class refers to lamps designed to operate directly on circuits of 220–300 V, and represents a very small portion of the lamp demand in North America. Lampholders should be UL or CSA approved for a voltage level appropriate to the voltage rating of the lamps being used, *i.e.*, 250 V for lamps up to 250 V, 600 V for lamps above 250 V.

High-voltage lamps have filaments of small diameter and longer length, and the filaments require more supports than corresponding 120-V lamps. Therefore, they are less rugged and produce 25–30% fewer lumens per watt because of greater heat losses. Due to the higher operating voltage, these lamps require less current for the same power, permitting some wiring economy.[20] Operating characteristics and physical data are shown in figure 6-82.

Extended Service. Extended-service lamps are intended for use in applications where a lamp failure causes great inconvenience, a nuisance or a hazard, or where replacement labor cost is high or power cost is unusually low. For such applications, where long life is most important and a reduction of light output is acceptable, lamps with 2500-h or longer rated life are available. Longer life is obtained by operating the lamp's filament at lower temperatures than normal. This, however, lowers the lamp's luminous efficacy. In most general-service use the cost of power used during the lamp life runs many times the lamp life, and therefore efficacy is important. Where replacement of burned-out lamps is an easy, convenient operation, as in residential use, long-life lamps are not usually recommended.[21] For such use, incandescent lamps with the usual 750- or 1000-h design life give a lower cost of light than extended-service lamps. See figure 6-84.

General-Lighting Tungsten-Halogen Lamps. These lamps improve on the regular incandescent sources. Their advantages over regular incandescent lamps include excellent lumen maintenance and compactness. They also provide whiter light (higher color temperature) and longer life at a given light output. The lamps shown in figure 6-88 are tungsten-halogen lamps intended for general and specialty use.

There is more ultraviolet (UV) radiation generated from tungsten-halogen lamps than from regular incandescent lamps, due to the higher filament temperature. The amount of ultraviolet radiation emitted is determined by the envelope material. Fused quartz and high-silica glass transmit most of the UV radiated by the filament, while special high-silica glass and aluminosilicate glasses absorb UV radiation. In general lighting applications, it is recommended that luminaires for tungsten-halogen lamps have a lens or cover glass which will, in addition to providing the required safety protection, filter out most of the UV radiation. In applications where the reduction of UV radiation is critical, additional filtering may be required. Special care should be taken when applying lamps operating at correlated color temperatures above 3100 K, since both ultraviolet and short-wavelength visible radiation increase with color temperature,[22] creating potential hazard for both people and objects.

Tungsten-halogen lamps are very temperature sensitive. Operating lamps at voltages above or below manufacturer's recommendations may have adverse effects on the internal chemical processes, because the temperature will differ from the design value. It is also important to follow manufacturer's recommendations as to burning position, bulb handling and luminaire temperatures.

The halogen cycle allows tungsten-halogen lamps to be designed for higher efficacy and longer life than normal incandescent lamps of the same wattage. For example, the 500-W nonregenerative cycle lamp is rated

at 10,600 lm for 1000 h, while the 500-W T-3 tungsten-halogen lamp is rated at 10,950 lm for 2000 h.

Multilayer interference film (dichroic) coating technology has been applied to tungsten-halogen lamps to increase their efficacy by 30–50%. The transparent, slightly iridescent external coating transmits visible light and reflects infrared energy back to the filament, thereby reducing the input power required to reach a given filament temperature. Luminous efficacies of 27.0–35.6 lm/W are obtained with this technique without reducing life.

Spotlight and Floodlight. Lamps used in spotlights, floodlights and other specialized luminaires for lighting theater stages, motion picture studios and television studios have concentrated filaments accurately positioned with respect to the base. When the filament is placed at the focal point of a reflector or lens system, a precisely controlled beam is obtained. These lamps, listed in figure 6-95, are intended for use with external reflector systems. Because of their construction, these lamps must be burned in positions for which they are designed, to avoid premature failures.

Reflector. These lamps include those made in standard and special bulb shapes and which have a reflecting coating directly applied to part of the bulb surface. Both silver and aluminum coatings are used.[23] Silver coatings may be applied internally or externally, and in the latter case the coating is protected by an electrolytically applied copper coating and sprayed aluminum finish. Aluminum coatings are applied internally by condensation of vaporized aluminum on the bulb surface. The following reflector lamps are readily available: *bowl reflector lamps*, data for which are given in figure 6-96; *neck reflector lamps*; *reflector spot* and *reflector flood lamps* in R-type bulbs (certain sizes of reflector lamps are available with heat-resisting glass bulbs; performance data are given in figure 6-97); *ellipsoidal reflector lamps* (ER types), which allow substantially improved energy utilization in deep, well-shielded downlights.[24] *PAR spot* and *PAR flood lamps* contain PAR bulbs, typically constructed from two molded glass parts, the reflector and the lens, which are fused together; see figure 6-97 for performance data, and figure 6-18 for typical candlepower distribution curves. Colored R and PAR lamps are available. "Cool beam" PAR lamps with heat-transmitting dichroic reflectors are available for applications where it is desirable to reduce the infrared energy in the beam. General-lighting PAR lamps utilizing tungsten-halogen cycle filament tubes are included in figure 6-97. Long-neck halogen PAR-30 lamps are available for retrofitting standard R-30 fixtures without the use of socket extenders. *Multifaceted pressed glass reflector lamps* using quartz tungsten-halogen filament tubes

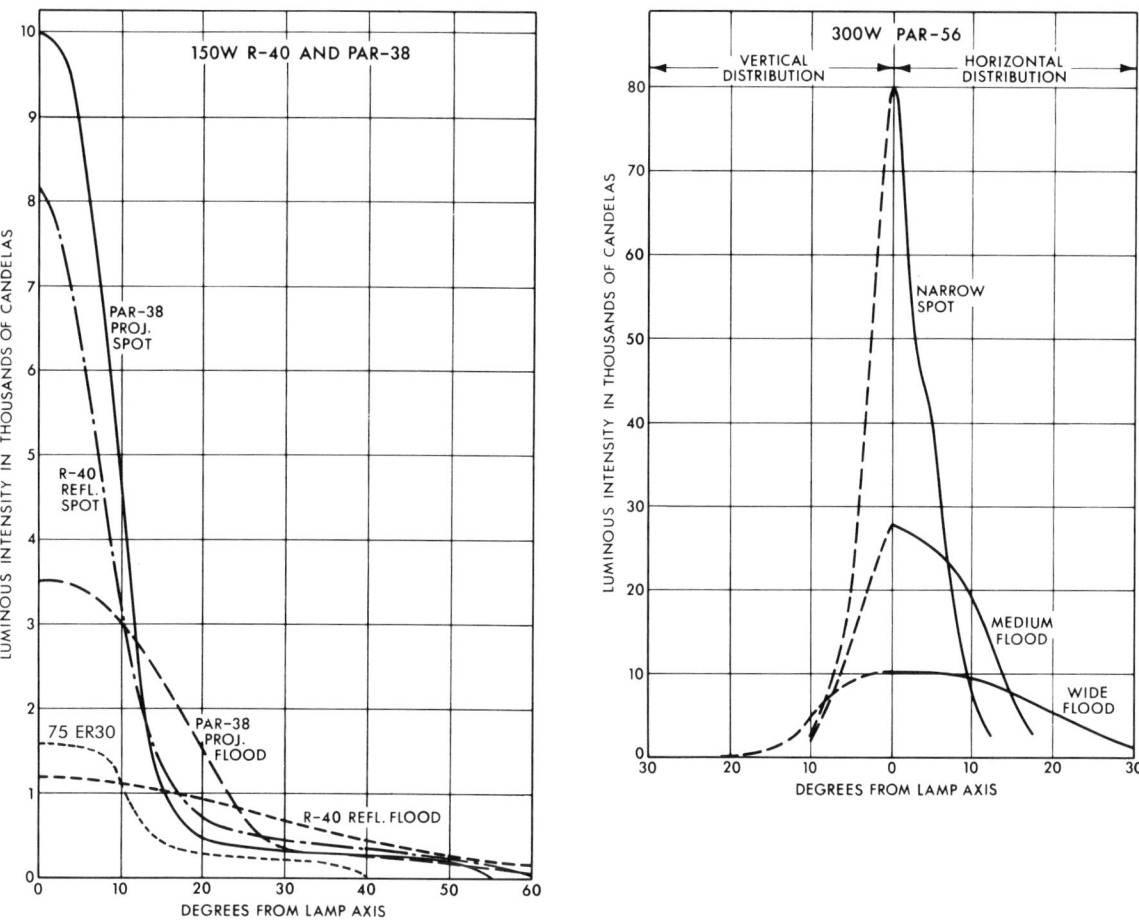

Fig. 6-18. Typical candlepower distribution characteristics of representative types of reflector and PAR lamps.

and infrared-transmitting dichroic reflectors have been adapted from projection lamp designs (see section 18, Lighting for Merchandise Areas) for display lighting applications. See figure 6-92.

High-Temperature Appliance. These lamps are specially constructed for high-temperature service. The most common types are clear, medium-base, 40-W, A-15 appliance and oven lamps; 50-W, A-19 lamps; and 100-W, A-23 bake oven lamps. Range oven lamps are designed to withstand oven temperatures up to 245°C (475°F), and bake oven up to 315°C (600°F).

Rough Service. To provide the resistance to filament breakage required for, say, portable extension cords, rough-service lamps employ special, multiple-filament-support construction. See figure 6-7, C-22. Because of the number of supports, the heat loss is higher and the efficacy lower than for general-service lamps. Performance data are given in figure 6-83.

In using miniature lamps where rough-service conditions are encountered, bayonet and wedge base lamps should be chosen instead of screw base lamps. Bayonet and wedge base lamps lock in the socket, whereas screw base lamps tend to work loose.

Vibration Service. Most lamps have coiled filaments made of tungsten having high sag resistance. Vibration lamps, designed for use where high-frequency vibrations would cause early failure of general-service lamps, are made with a more flexible tungsten filament. The sagging of the wire used allows the coils to open up under vibration, thus preventing short circuits between coils. See figure 6-86 for data.

To withstand shock and vibration, miniature radio panel lamps of 6.3 V and under incorporate mounts whose resonant frequency has been synchronized with that of the coiled filament.

Sometimes only experiment will determine the best lamp to resist shock and vibration. Vibration-resistant sockets or equipment, utilizing a coiled spring or other flexible material to deaden vibration, have been employed where general-service lamps are used under conditions of severe vibration.

Linear Incandescent. The lumiline lamp has a tubular bulb diameter of 26 mm (1 in.) and two metal disk bases, one at each end of the lamp, with the filament connected between them. A more recent version has adjustable insert tabs attached to the bases, thereby simplifying insertion into their sockets. The filament, in the form of a stretched coil, is supported on glass insulating beads along a small metal channel within the bulb. The 30- and 60-W sizes are available in the 450-mm (17-in.) length. The 40-W lamp is made in a 300-mm (11-in.) length. All sizes are available in either clear or inside-frosted tubes as well as white and various color coatings. See figure 6-93 for data.

Another style of linear incandescent lamp, using the S14 base, is available in 35-, 60-, and 150-W versions.

Showcase. Showcases use tubular bulbs with conventional screw bases. The longer lamps have elongated filaments with supports similar to lumiline lamps. The common sizes are 25 and 40 W, but sizes up to 75 W are available. See figure 6-89.

Three-Lite. These lamps employ two filaments, operated separately or in combination, to provide three illuminance levels. The common lead-in wire is connected to the shell of the base; the other end of one filament is connected to a ring contact, and the end of the other filament to a center contact. Three-lite lamps are available in different wattage combinations. See figure 6-81.

Sign. While large numbers of gas-filled lamps are used in enclosed and other types of electric signs, those designated particularly as "sign" lamps are mostly of the vacuum type. These lamps are best adapted for exposed sign and festoon service because the lower bulb temperature of vacuum lamps minimizes the occurrence of thermal cracks resulting from rain and snow. Some low-wattage lamps, however, are gas filled for use in flashing signs. Bulb temperatures of these low-wattage, gas-filled lamps are sufficiently low to permit exposed outdoor use on high-speed flashing circuits.

Decorative. A wide variety of lamps for decorative application is available. Different bulb shapes, together with numerous colors and finishes, are used to achieve the desired appearance. Lamp manufacturers' catalogs should be consulted for information on the many decorative types.

Multiple Street Lighting. Multiple street lighting lamps are designed so that their mean lumens correspond approximately to the mean lumens of the now obsolete series lamps of the same initial lumen rating. Since the lamp voltage is established by a multiple circuit and the design goal is to obtain desired nominal lumen ratings, the resulting wattages seem unusual, compared with general-service lamps. See figure 6-100 for performance data.

Traffic Signal Lamps. Lamps used in traffic signals are subjected to more severe service requirements than in most applications of incandescent lamps. In order to provide uniformity of application, lamps must be compatible with the design requirements of optical systems of standard traffic signals. Data on typical traffic signal lamps are shown in figure 6-98.

Train and Locomotive. Lamps designated as train and locomotive service are designed for several classes of low-voltage (75 V or lower) service. The power is usually provided by generators, with a battery connected in parallel so that both supply power to the lamps. Data for these lamps are shown in figure 6-94. Low-voltage lamps have shorter and heavier filaments than 120-V lamps of the same wattage; consequently they are more rugged and generally produce more lumens per watt.

DC Series. Transit system voltages and some railway shop and yard voltages range from 525 to 625 V. Lamps for this service (see figure 6-99) are operated with five to twenty lamps in series. The design voltages of individual lamps operated five in series are nominally 115, 120 and 125 V. To identify dc series lamps, they are rated in unusual wattages (36, 56, 94 or 101 W).

Gas-filled, 30-V lamps are used for car lighting. The trolley voltage divided by 30 determines the number of lamps connected in series across the line. These lamps are equipped with short-circuiting cutouts which short-circuit the lamps on burnout, thus preventing arcing and leaving the remainder of the lamps in a given circuit operating. These 30-V lamps are rated in amperes, instead of the usual watt rating.

Aviation. Lighting for aviation is divided into two classes: lighting on and around airports, and lighting on aircraft.

In airport lighting, both multiple and series type lamps are used. Most systems being installed use series lamps of 6.6- and 20-A designs for airport approach, runway and taxiway lighting, whereas multiple lamps are used for obstruction, hazard beacon and airport identification beacon lighting. On aircraft, small and miniature lamps are used for both interior and exterior lighting.

Most of the lamps used in airport lighting are designed to be used in precise projection-type equipment to produce a controlled beam of light complying with required standards.

Hazard beacons and airport identification beacons, signaling the presence of high obstructions or the whereabouts of the airport, use lamps of wattages ranging from 500 to 1200 W. Lamps used on the airport proper range in size from 10 to 500 W. Lamps used for aircraft lighting are in the miniature classification, although landing lamps as large as 1000 W are used.

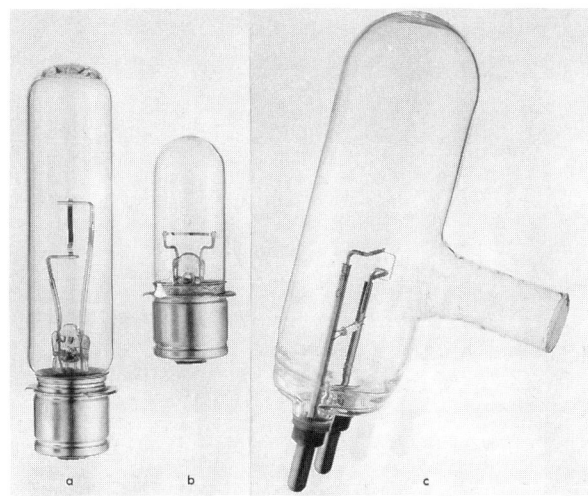

Fig. 6-19. Typical ribbon filament lamps: (a) 6-volt, 18-ampere, T-10, 2-mm., 3000 K microscope illuminator; (b) 6 volt, 9-ampere, T-8½, 1 mm., 3000 K optical source; and (c) 3.5 volt, 30-ampere, T-24 with quartz window, 3 mm., U-shaped filament, 2300 K pyrometer and spectroscope source.

Lamps widely used for aviation service are listed in figures 6-101 and 6-102. These tabulations include those lamps currently recommended for use in aircraft and airport lighting. In addition, tungsten-halogen lamps can be provided in place of many regular incandescent types. Tungsten-halogen lamps have the advantage of better lumen maintenance and longer life. Many of the types of lamps available but seldom used are not shown. Refer to chapter 25 for information on the application of lamps in the airport and aircraft lighting fields.

Ribbon Filament Lamps. Incandescent lamps made with ribbons or strips of tungsten for the filaments have been used in special applications where it is desirable to have a substantial area of fairly uniform luminance.[25] Ribbon dimensions vary from 0.7 to 4 mm in width and up to 50 mm in length. The 5–20-A ribbon filament lamps are usually employed in recorders, instruments, oscillographs and microscope illuminators. The 30–75-A lamps are used for pyrometer calibration standards and for spectrographic work. Figure 6-19 shows typical lamps.

Miniature and Sealed Beam Lamps

The term "miniature" applied to light sources is a lamp manufacturer's designation determined by the trade channels through which these lamps are distributed, rather than by the size or characteristics of the lamps. In general, however, it is true that most miniature lamps are small and require relatively little power. The most notable exceptions to this generalization are the sealed beam lamps, such as automotive headlamps and aircraft landing lamps, some of which are classed as miniature lamps, even though they may

be as large as 200 mm (8 in.) in diameter and dissipate up to 1000 W.

The great majority of miniature lamps are either incandescent filament lamps or glow lamps; the latter are discussed under Miscellaneous Discharge Lamps below. Some low-wattage and medium-low-voltage fluorescent lamps are listed as miniature types by at least one lamp manufacturer. Also, electroluminescent lamps and light-emitting diodes (see sections below) are included in the miniature lamp family. Incandescent miniature lamps[26] and glow lamps[27] are specified completely by numbers standardized and issued by the American National Standards Institute (ANSI).

With the notable exception of multiple holiday lamps, miniature incandescent lamps are designed to operate below 50 V. These voltages may be obtained from batteries, generators or circuits with low-voltage transformers.

Miniature lamps are used chiefly when conditions require a light source to be of small size or little power. They have many uses, principally in automobiles, aircraft, and decoration. Glow lamps are also used as components in electronic circuitry.

Subminiature lamps have increased in popularity. They range in size from T-2 to T-⅛. Since early in World War II, the T-1¾ has been used extensively for instruments and indicators. The T-1 size has become popular for aircraft instruments and indicators. The T-⅝ and smaller sizes down to T-⅛ are used chiefly in novelty applications such as tiny flashlights, jewelry and medical instruments. Examples of variations in their range and specifications are given in figure 6-109.

Replaceable Automotive Halogen Head Lamps. Recent changes in automotive front end styling have led to the creation of replaceable halogen head lamps. These lamps meet the current Society for Automotive Engineers (SAE) standards while allowing the designer to use various shapes of head lamps which otherwise would not be possible. Special automotive bases have the advantage that the lamp, rather than the entire luminaire, can be replaced when necessary.

Power Sources. Most miniature incandescent filament lamps operate below 50 V. However, miniature lamps may be used on 120-V circuits when transformers, rectifiers or resistors are used to reduce the voltage.

The mean effective voltage delivered by the battery or circuit is generally higher than the mean voltage and should be the design voltage of the lamp. Design voltages for flashlight lamps have been determined by extensive tests. Proper lamp and battery combinations are shown in manufacturers' catalogs.

With transformers or resistors, delivered rather than rated voltage must be precisely known in order to obtain proper lamp life and output. On resistor operation, because the voltage increases as the filament evaporates, the lamp life will generally be half that found with transformer operation.

Where space permits, larger rather than smaller dry cells should be chosen to reduce power costs. Refer to the ANSI dry cell specification.

Flashlight, Handlantern and Bicycle. These lamps are commonly operated by dry cell batteries having an open-circuit voltage of 1.5 V per cell for new batteries, dropping to approximately 0.9 V per cell at the end of battery life. This voltage drop results in a reduction in light output. Typical lamps of this group are listed in figure 6-105.

Automotive. Lamps for most passenger vehicles, trucks and coaches presently operate at 12 V. The power source is a storage battery–rectified alternator system. Performance data for 12-V lamps are given in figure 6-106.

Sealed Beam and Tungsten-Halogen Sealed Beam Bonded. These lamps contain filaments, lens and reflectors in a precise, rugged optical package available in a wide variety of sizes and voltages ranging from 6 to 28 V. Sealed beam lamp lenses are made of borosilicate "hard" glass. The reflector is vaporized aluminum on glass, hermetically sealed to the lens cover. The advantages are: (1) accurate reflector contour for accurate beam control; (2) precise filament positioning on rugged filament supports; and (3) high efficacy and excellent luminous intensity maintenance. Vaporized aluminum on glass is an excellent reflector, it does not deteriorate, and the normal bulb blackening has little effect on output throughout lamp life. The sealed beam lamp is particularly suitable where a large amount of concentrated light at low voltage is required. Tungsten-halogen sealed beam bonded lamps contain a very small bulb of quartz, made of 96% silica or aluminosilicate glass, surrounding the filament. The bulb also contains a high-pressure, rare-gas atmosphere with small additions of halogen compounds as required for operation of the tungsten-halogen cycle. Figure 6-107 gives data on typical sealed beam lamps for automotive use.

Indicator and Other Service. Lamps for indicator, radio and television service are usually operated from low-voltage transformers. Performance data on typical lamps are given in figure 6-103.

Flasher Lamps. Incandescent lamps which flash automatically (see figure 6-20), because of a built-in bimetal strip similar to those used in thermostats, are available in several sizes. When the lamp lights, heat from the filament causes the bimetal strip to bend away from the lead-in wire. This breaks the circuit and the lamp goes out. As the bimetal strip cools, it bends back to its

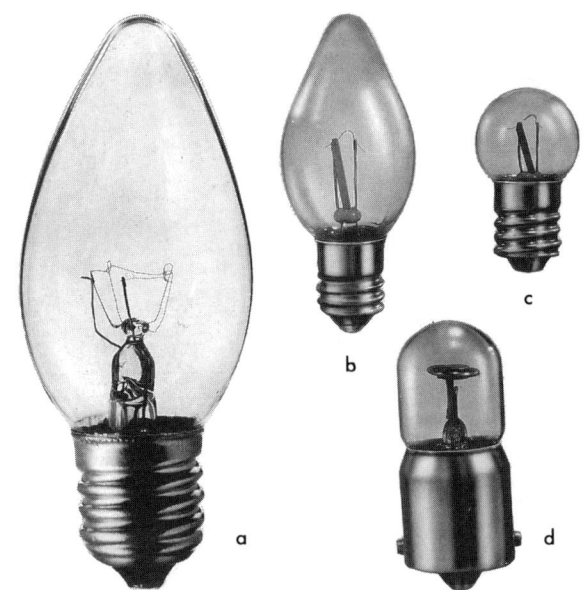

Fig. 6-20. Typical lamps for flashing: a. D27, b. 405, c. 407 (incandescent lamps with integral flasher): d. B6A (NE-21) (a glow lamp). (Shown here at nearly full size.)

original position against the lead-in wire and lights the lamp. This alternating cooling and heating keeps the lamp flashing. An exception to this is found in certain miniature screw base lamps. Some operate as described above; however, a few are of the "shorting" type. The bimetal in the shorting type is so mounted that when it heats up it shorts across the lead-in wire. If these lamps, which are difficult to distinguish from the "opening" type, are inserted in sockets intended for the normal flasher lamps, they may run down batteries, blow fuses, overheat wires, or burn out transformers.

Some of the lamps listed in figure 6-104 (120-V D26 and D27) are available also in translucent colors. These are used primarily for holiday and decorative effects.

Typical Uses. Indicator lamps provide a visual indication of existing circuit conditions. They are widely used in fire and police signaling systems, power plant switchboards, production machinery, motor switches, furnaces and other devices requiring warning or pilot lights.

Miniature lamps may be wired in various ways with motor or heating elements and are used in many appliances to indicate that the current is flowing to the appliance or that it is functioning properly. They are used in many ways in instrumentation and in connection with photocells and relays, and play a vital part in computers and automation in general. Flashlights, radios, clocks, bicycles and toys account for more uses.

Other applications include the use of miniature lamps for holiday and other festive occasions, and for colorful patio and garden lighting. For garden lighting low-voltage miniature equipment is available.

Incandescent Filament Lamps for Photography

Lamps used specifically for photographic service are adapted to the response or sensitivity of several classes of film emulsions. Some lamps are specified in terms of color temperature, which serves as a basic rating for film exposure data. Thus, several lines of lamps are made available for the requirements of commercial studios as well as for home movies and still hobby photography. Photographic efficiency and unvarying spectral quality are of major concern to the photographer. Lamp life is less important. Lamps of various sizes are often matched for color temperature, and rated life varies as necessary with wattage to achieve the specified color temperature.

Lamps with Color Temperature Ratings. Lamps rated at 3200 K are used primarily in professional photography, with both black-and-white films and many types of color films. Another group of lamps, rated at 3350 K, is used primarily in professional color motion picture work, sometimes in conjunction with blue filters to simulate daylight color quality. Lamps rated at 3400 K are widely used with color film by hobbyists and some professional photographers. So-called "daylight blue" photoflood lamps provide light of approximately 5000 K. Their blue bulbs absorb longer wavelengths and produce a whiter light. The "photographic blue" lamps approximate sunlight at approximately 5500 K.

Maintenance of color temperature throughout lamp life is important in color photography. Typical color-temperature-rated lamps of conventional construction may drop about 100 K through life. There is negligible change in the color temperature of tungsten-halogen lamps during their life.

Photoflood. These are high-efficacy sources of the same character as other incandescent filament lamps for picture taking, with color temperatures ranging from 3200 to 3400 K. Because of their high filament temperature, these lamps generally produce about twice the lumens and three times the photographic effectiveness of similar wattages of general-service lamps. Relatively small bulb sizes are employed. The 250-W No. 1 photoflood, for example, has the same size bulb as the 60-W general-service lamp. These lamps may be conveniently used in less bulky reflecting equipment or for certain effects in ordinary residential or commercial luminaires.

The photoflood family includes reflector (R) and projector (PAR) lamps with various beam spreads. Some of these have tungsten-halogen light sources;

some have built-in 5000-K daylight filters. In addition, tungsten-halogen lamps in several sizes and color temperatures are classed as photofloods and used in specially designed reflectors. See figure 6-95.

Photoflash. These are patterned after standard incandescent filament lamps but are actually combustion sources. The lamp bulb is simply a container for the flammable material (usually metallic aluminum or zirconium or a metallic compound), a tungsten filament with a small amount of chemical applied or a pressure-sensitive chemical ignitor, and oxygen. The bulbs are coated with lacquer to safeguard against shattering the glass. These lamps are designed to function over specified voltage ranges or within fixed force and energy limits (pressure-sensitive ignitors).

Photoflash lamps have a burning life of only a few hundredths of a second, and the design is predicated on the service, the type of camera and the necessary synchronism of flash and shutter opening.

The use of more efficient flammable materials such as zirconium has made possible the popular reflector lamp cube and the *flashbar*. These lamps may be ignited either electrically or mechanically.

Photoflash lamps are rated in lumen-seconds, while reflector units are rated in beam-candela-seconds, which is a measure of their photographic effectiveness. Color-corrected or blue-bulb photoflash lamps and cubes are used to simulate daylight at approximately 5500 K. This correction reduces the light output by about one-fourth; see figure 6-111 for lamp data. Deep-red-purple bulbs are used to filter out all visible light for taking pictures with infrared film.

Photoenlarger. Most equipment used in the process of enlarging requires a highly diffused light source. For this service incandescent filament enlarger lamps in diffuse-white glass bulbs are available. These lamps are designed for high efficacy and short life. See figure 6-113.

Projection. Lamps for projectors have carefully positioned filaments and prefocus-type bases so the filament will be properly aligned with the optical system. The filaments are very compact and operate at high temperatures. Their efficacy, therefore, is high but their life is short. Forced-air cooling is frequently required because of the high lamp temperatures.

The four-pin base is widely used, because it provides accurate light source positioning, allows minimum bulb height in low-profile projectors, and facilitates the use of internal reflectors. Internal proximity reflectors, usually made of metal, eliminate the need for the spherical mirrors formerly used behind the lamp in conventional projectors. Internal ellipsoidal or parabolic reflectors, made from metal or from glass with dichroic heat-transmitting mirror coating, focus light through the film aperture into the projection lens, replacing both the conventional external heat-transmitting dichroic mirror and condenser lenses. For projection lamp data, see figure 6-108.

Tungsten-halogen lamps have nearly replaced conventional incandescent lamps for projection. Halogen lamps are available for direct replacement of many existing incandescent projection lamps. In addition, special lamps and sockets have been devised to take advantage of the compact size and greater efficacy of halogen lamps.

One of the principal developments has been the adoption of halogen lamp types with integrated external dichroic mirrors. By carefully positioning the lamp filament in ellipsoidal or parabolic dichroic reflectors, precise beam control is possible. This obviates bulky and expensive external condensers and reflectors. The dichroic mirror is constructed to transmit nearly all of the infrared radiation and reflect light through the film plane. This results in a lower film gate temperature and longer film life.

Infrared Heat Lamps

Any incandescent filament lamp is a very effective generator of infrared radiation. From 75 to 80% of the incandescent filament lamp watts are radiated as infrared energy. Wavelengths longer than 5000 nm are absorbed to a large extent by the glass or fused quartz envelope. Lamps for heating applications are specially designed for low light output and long life. Tubular fused quartz lamps are also available with a ceramic reflector which increases heat by approximately 50% directly below the center line of lamp.

Tungsten filament infrared lamps are available with ratings up to 5000 W. Generally speaking, tungsten filament lamps for industrial, commercial and residential service operate at a filament color temperature of 2500 K. At this low operating temperature compared to lighting lamp filament temperatures, the service life is well in excess of 5000 h. Frequently, lamps using tungsten filaments have provided many years of operation because the service life is generally determined by mechanical breakage or rupture of the filament due to vibration or handling, rather than the rate of evaporation of tungsten, as is the case with lamps used for light. Lamps having heat-resisting glass bulbs or tubular fused quartz envelopes are recommended where liquids may come in contact with the bulb.

The distribution of power radiated by various infrared sources is shown in figure 6-21, while figure 6-110 tabulates the most popular types of infrared lamps and metal-sheathed heaters. For application information, see chapter 5, Nonvisual Effects of Radiant Energy.

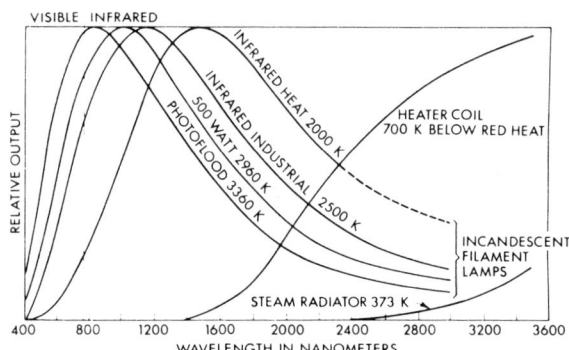

Fig. 6-21. Spectral power distribution from various infrared sources.

Energy-Saving Lamps

Most general and extended service lamps are now available in reduced wattages, which also have slightly lower lumen output. The use of reflector lamps to improve directional lighting has also become popular for energy-saving lamps. Better optical control places the same illuminance on a specific area for fewer watts. A variety of reflector lamps is now available, including lower-wattage R-30 and R-40, reduced-wattage halogen PAR lamps, and new shapes such as the BR (double reflector) bulb and K (semireflector) bulb. In the traffic signal category, lamps are now being marketed with a ring mirror so as to "capture lost light" and redirect it through the lens.

Dimming of Incandescent Lamps

Dimmers today have a dual purpose: energy conservation and esthetic lighting effects. Incandescent lamps can be dimmed simply by lowering the rms voltage across the lamp filament. When the voltage is lowered, less power is dissipated and less light is produced with a lower color temperature.

In the 1950s, rheostats were used for regulating the lamp current in an incandescent lamp. These rheostats were large and very inefficient. Today, most dimmers are electronic, using thyristor and transistor circuits that have low power dissipation. Modern dimmers are efficient and reduce power as the source is dimmed.

Thyristors operate as high-speed switches that rapidly turn the voltage to the lamp on and off. This switching may cause electromagnetic interference with other electrical equipment as well as audible buzzing in the lamp filament. Magnetic coils known as chokes are usually used as filters to bring these effects to acceptable levels. With many wall-box dimmers, however, lamp buzzing cannot be completely eliminated because a larger choke is needed than space allows. For these cases, remotely mounted properly sized *lamp debuzzing coils* are recommended.

FLUORESCENT LAMPS

The fluorescent lamp is a low-pressure gas discharge source, in which light is produced predominantly by fluorescent powders activated by UV energy generated by a mercury arc. The lamp, usually in the form of a long tubular bulb with an electrode sealed into each end, contains mercury vapor at low pressure with a small amount of inert gas for starting. The inner walls of the bulb are coated with fluorescent powders commonly called phosphors (see figure 6-22). When the proper voltage is applied, an *arc* is produced by current flowing between the electrodes through the mercury vapor. This discharge generates some visible radiation, but mostly invisible UV radiation. The UV in turn excites the phosphors to emit light. See the discussion of fluorescence in chapter 1.

The phosphors in general use have been selected and blended to respond most efficiently to UV energy at a wavelength of 253.7 nm,[28, 29] the primary wavelength generated in a mercury low-pressure discharge.

Like most gas discharge lamps, fluorescent lamps must be operated in series with a current-limiting device. This auxiliary, commonly called a *ballast*, limits the current to the value for which each lamp is designed. It also provides the required starting and operating lamp voltages.

Lamp Construction

Bulbs. Fluorescent lamps are most commonly made with straight, tubular bulbs varying in diameter from approximately 12 mm (0.5-in. T-4) to 54-mm. (2.125 in T-17) and in overall length from a nominal 100 to 2440 mm (4 to 96 in.). The bulb is historically designated by a letter indicating the shape, followed by a number indicating the maximum diameter in eighths of an inch. Hence "T-17" indicates a tubular bulb $\frac{17}{8}$, or $2\frac{1}{8}$ in. (54 mm) in diameter. The nominal length of the lamp includes the thickness of the standard lampholders, and is the back-to-back dimension of the lampholders with a seated lamp.

Fluorescent lamps come in shapes other than straight tubes. Circular (circline) lamps are tubes bent in a circle with the two ends adjacent to each other. A helicoid lamp is a straight tube with a spiral groove running its length. Intermittently grooved tubes are also available, as well as a U-shaped tube, which is bent back upon itself.

In addition, there are smaller-diameter, single-ended, twin or quad parallel-tube lamps, commonly known as compact fluorescent lamps.[30] These lamps are formed by U shapes or have small connecting tubes near the closed ends of the parallel tubes.

Electrodes. Two electrodes are hermetically sealed into the bulb, one at each end. These electrodes are designed for operation as either "cold" or "hot" cathodes, more correctly called glow or arc modes of discharge operation.

Electrodes for *glow*, or cold cathode, operation may consist of closed-end metal cylinders, generally coated on the inside with an emissive material. Cold cathode lamps operate at a current on the order of a few hundred milliamperes, with a high value of the *cathode fall* (the voltage required to create ion and electron current flow), something in excess of 50 V.

The *arc* mode, or hot cathode, electrode is generally constructed from a single tungsten wire, or a tungsten wire around which another very fine tungsten wire has been uniformly wound. The larger tungsten wire is coiled, producing a triple-coil electrode. When the fine wire is absent, the electrode is referred to as a coiled-coil electrode. The coiled-coil or triple-coil tungsten wire is coated with a mixture of alkaline earth oxides to enhance electron emission. During lamp operation, the coil and coating reach temperatures of about 1100°C, at which point the coil-and-coating combination thermally emits large quantities of electrons at a low cathode fall, in the range of 10–12 V. The normal operating current of arc mode lamps is approximately 1.5 A. As a consequence of the lower cathode fall associated with the "hot" cathode, more efficient lamp operation is obtained, and therefore most fluorescent lamps are designed for such operation.

Gas Fill. The operation of the fluorescent lamp depends upon the development of a discharge between the two electrodes sealed at the extremities of the lamp bulb. This discharge is developed by ionization of mercury gas contained in the bulb. The mercury gas is typically maintained at a pressure of approximately 1.07 Pa (0.00016 lb/in.²), which is the vapor pressure of liquid mercury at 40°C (104°F), the optimum bulb wall temperature of operation for which most lamps are designed (see subsection on Temperature Effect on Operation, below). In addition to the mercury, a rare gas or a combination of gases at low pressure, from 100–400 Pa (0.015–0.058 lb/in.²), is added to the lamp to facilitate ignition of the discharge. Standard lamps employ argon gas; energy-saving types, a mixture of krypton and argon; others, a combination of neon and argon or neon, xenon, and argon. As a consequence of ionization and mercury atom excitation, UV and visible radiation is generated, the principle lines being approximately 254, 313, 365, 405, 436, 546 and 578 nm.

Phosphors. The color produced by a fluorescent lamp depends upon the blend of fluorescent chemicals (phosphors) used to coat the wall of the tube. (See figure 1-11 for a list of important phosphors.) There are different "white" and colored fluorescent lamps available, each having its own characteristic spectral

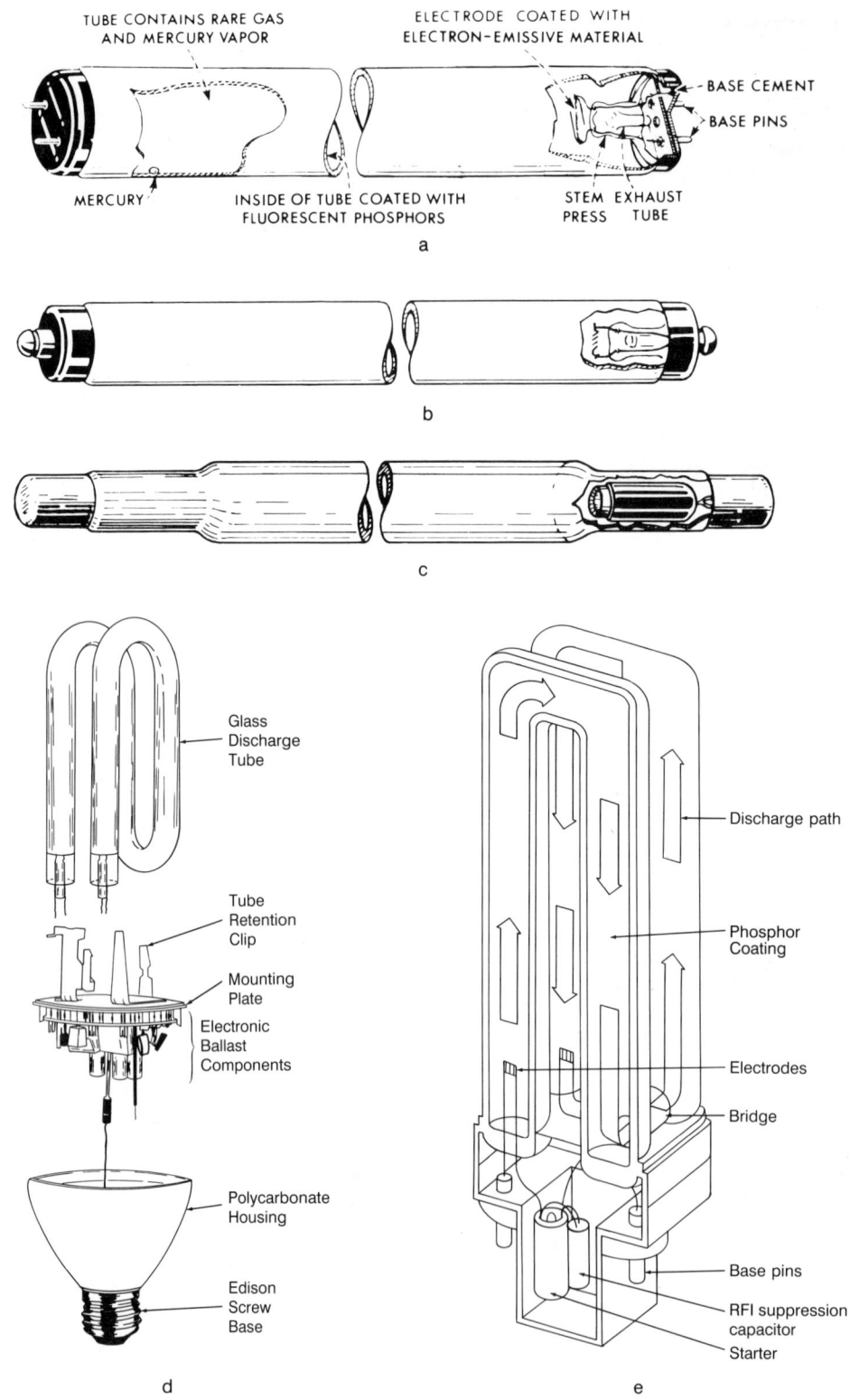

Fig. 6-22. Cutaway view of fluorescent lamps showing typical electrodes: (a) hot cathode (filamentary) rapid-starting or preheat-starting; (b) hot cathode (filamentary) instant-starting; (c) cold-cathode (cylindrical) instant-starting; (d) compact fluorescent with built in ballast; (e) quad tube compact fluorescent with built-in starter.

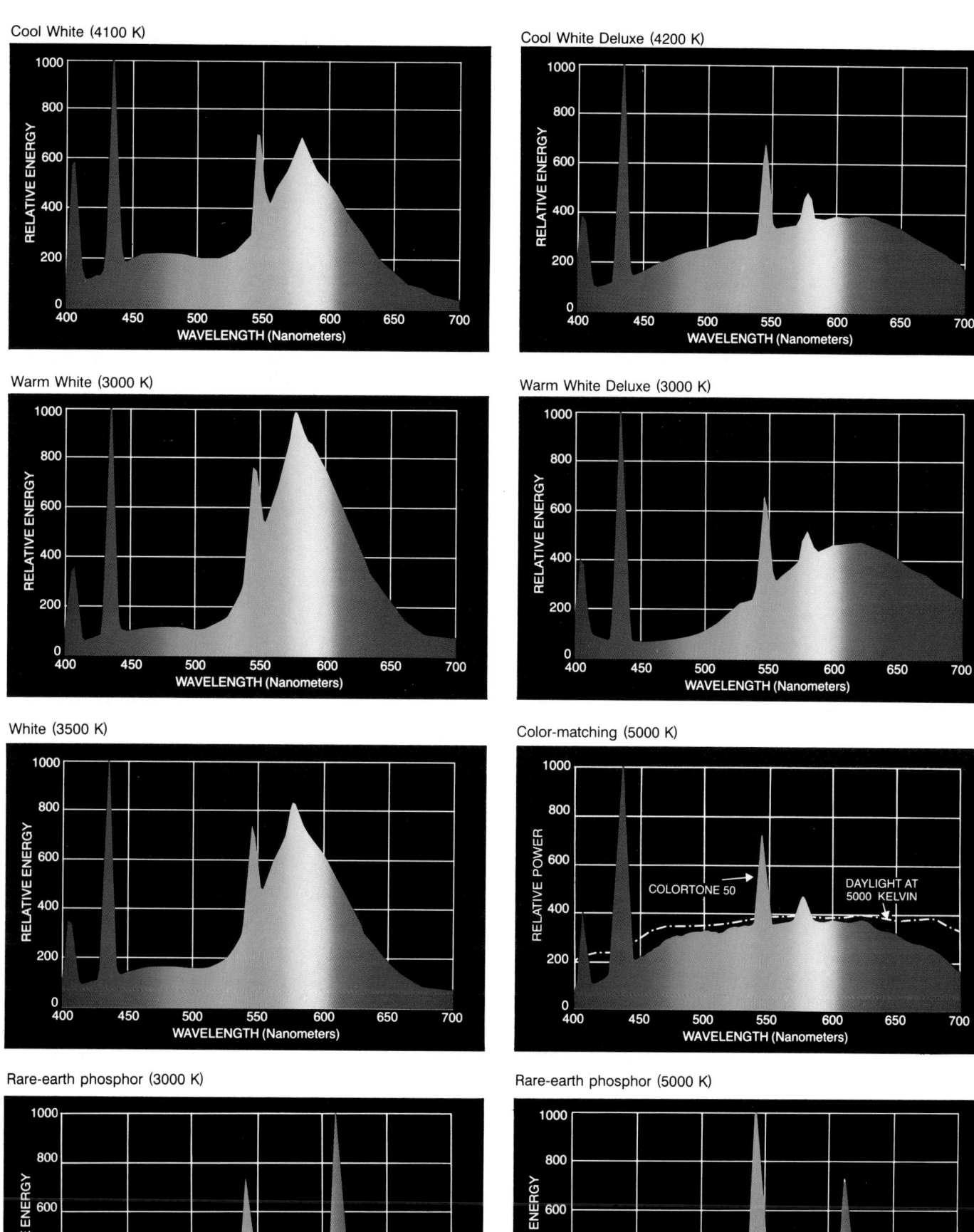

Fig. 6-23. Approximate spectral distribution charts for various types of fluorescent lamps.

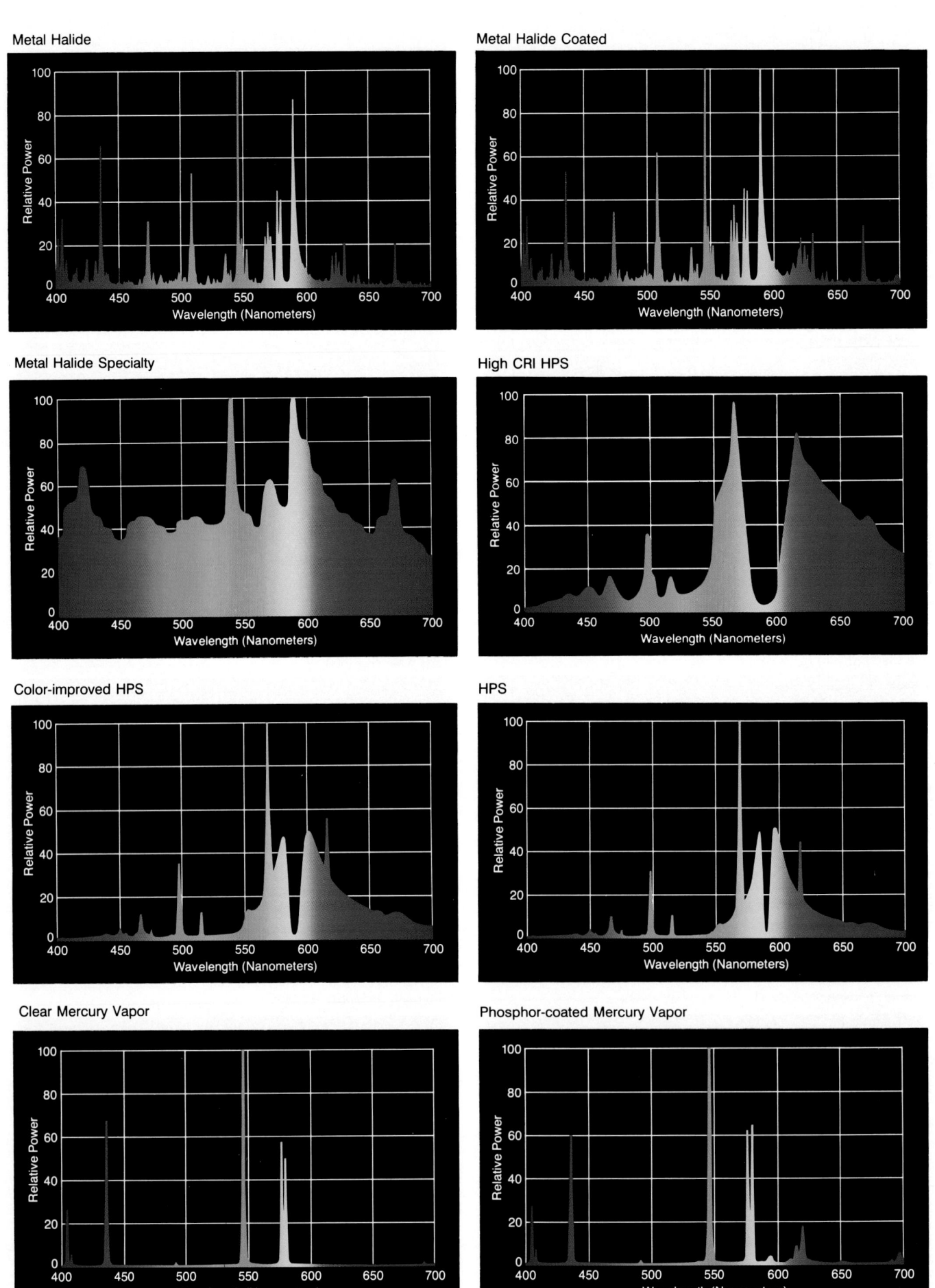

Fig. 6-23. *Continued*. Approximate spectral distribution charts for various types of HID lamps.

power distribution. The most commonly used lamps have been the halophosphate cool white and warm white lamps; their spectral power distributions are shown in figure 6-23. These types have a combination of continuous and line spectra.

An increasingly popular approach to blending of phosphors for fluorescent lamps is the triphosphor system. Three highly efficient narrow-band rare-earth activated phosphors have been developed which show emission peaks in the short-, middle- and long-wave regions of the visible spectrum. By using a mixture of these prime color phosphors, a lamp can be obtained with both high color rendering and good efficacy. The correlated color temperature can be varied between 2500 and 6000 K by changing the concentration of the phosphor components.[31, 32]

In addition, these relatively new phosphors are very stable under intense UV radiation, allowing for the construction of fluorescent and compact fluorescent lamps with high efficacy and good lumen maintenance.

Since the new phosphors are expensive, the longer T-8, T-10 and T-12 triphosphor lamps typically employ a two-coat system consisting of the traditional halophosphate type and new rare-earth activated type. The rare-earth activated phosphor is applied closest to the mercury discharge and, as a result, the spectral power distribution of the lamp is more influenced by these phosphors. Common commercial types have correlated color temperatures of 3000, 3500 and 4100 K.

Another type of lamp has a continuous spectral power distribution which includes a small quantity of UV radiation. These lamps are designed with the objective of duplicating the daylight spectrum, including its content of near UV radiation.[33, 34]

Also, a variety of lamp types are available which generate radiation in particular wavelength regions for specific purposes, such as plant growth, merchandise enhancement and medical therapy.

Most fluorescent phosphors appear as a matte white, translucent coating when the lamp is not operating. Various colored lamps, such as red, green and gold, are obtained by phosphor selection and filtration through pigments.

Bases. For satisfactory performance, each fluorescent lamp must be connected to a ballasted electrical circuit with proper voltage and current characteristics for its type. A number of different fluorescent lamp base designs are used. The bases physically support the lamp in most cases, and provide a means of electrical connection (see figure 6-22).

The design of the base is dependent upon the lamp type. Straight tube lamps designed for instant-start operation (see sub-subsection on Instant-Start Lamp and Ballast Operation, below) generally have a single connection at each end. As a consequence, a single-pin base is satisfactory.

Preheat and rapid-start lamps (see section on lamp starting below) have four electrical connections, two at each end of the tube, therefore requiring dual-contact bases. In the case of the circline lamp, a single four-pin connector is required. Examples of such bases are shown in figure 6-24. The base numbered 1 is designed for use in a circline lamp, the bipin bases from 4 through 7 for use in low-current applications (less than about 0.5 A), 11 and 12 for use in higher-current applications, and 13 and 14 for use in high-current (0.8- to 1.5-A) rapid-start lamp applications.

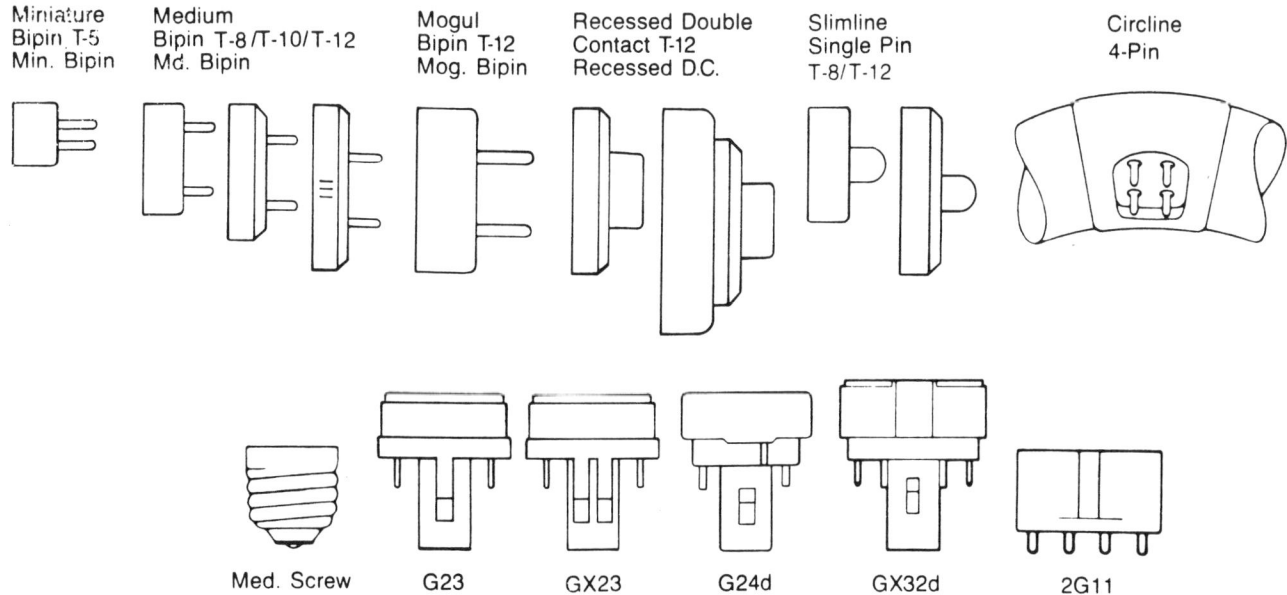

Fig. 6-24. Typical bases for fluorescent lamps.

Single-ended compact fluorescent lamps with integral starters have plastic bases containing a glow switch and a noise reduction filter capacitor. These bases have two connection pins. Some lamp wattages are available without the starting components mounted within the bases, and have four connection pins (see figure 8-22). For incandescent lamp retrofit applications, self-ballasted compact fluorescent lamps have medium screw bases.

Common Fluorescent Lamp Families

T-12 Fluorescent Lamps. The T-12, 40-W, 4-ft, rapid-start lamp is still the most commonly applied fluorescent lamp in the United States. The large demand for this lamp in the last 40 years has resulted in mass production and consequent low cost. The lamp type is typically used in the office or commercial environment, where improvement in life and efficacy over the incandescent lamp has resulted in widespread acceptance. Typically, the lamps employ cool white and warm white halophosphate phosphors and have lamp efficacies of approximately 80 lm/W with a color rendering index between 50 and 60. Other commonly used members of the T-12 lamp family include 2-ft preheat, 3-ft rapid-start, and 8-ft instant-start types.

T-8 Fluorescent Lamps.[35, 36] T-8 fluorescent lamps are a family of 1-in.-diameter straight tube lamps manufactured in some of the same lengths as conventional lamps. The 4-ft version of the lamp is designed to consume approximately 32 W. They are also available in 2-, 3-, 5- and 8-ft lengths. The smaller diameter makes it economical to use the more efficient and more expensive rare-earth phosphors. Although the T-8 and T-12 lamps are physically interchangeable, they cannot operate on the same ballast. T-8 lamps are designed to operate on line-frequency rapid-start ballasting systems at approximately 265 mA, or on high-frequency electronic ballasts at slightly less current. Due to the higher efficacies which can be reached with T-8 systems, they are replacing the conventional T-12 lamps in many applications.

Compact Fluorescent Lamps. The new rare-earth activated phosphor technology has led to the development of a growing variety of multitube single-ended lamps known as compact fluorescent lamps. The lamps were originally designed to be interchangeable with conventional 25–100-W incandescent lamps, but now this lamp type includes sizes and colors to replace conventional fluorescent lamps in smaller luminaires.

T-4 (13 mm) and T-5 (16 mm) tubes are used in compact fluorescent lamps. They are assembled in the two tube, twin, and the four tube, quad, designs. By using quad construction, the lumen output is increased without increasing the overall length of the lamp. The

tube portion of the lamp is sometimes enclosed in a cylindrical or spherical outer translucent jacket made of glass or plastic. Some lamps contain the lamp starter, while others contain both the starter and the ballast, which can take the form of a simple magnetic choke or an electronic ballast.

Present compact lamp wattages vary from 5 to 55 W, and rated lumen output ranges from 250 to 4800 lm. Overall lamp length varies from 100 to 570 mm, depending on lamp wattage and construction. Some designs with self-contained ballasts are equipped with Edison-type screw-in bases for adaptation to incandescent sockets, while other designs use special pin-type bases for dedicated use with mating sockets designed for lamps of a particular wattage. Because of the high power density in these lamps, high-performance phosphors are used extensively in order to enhance brightness, maintenance and color rendering ability.

Energy-Saving Fluorescent Lamps

In response to the energy crisis of the 1970s, lamp companies introduced halophosphate T-12 lamps filled with an argon-krypton gas mixture, rather than argon only. The 4-ft lamps may be operated suitably on a ballast designed for 4-ft 40-W lamps, but because of the different gas mixture, they dissipate about 34 W per lamp. Also, any of the energy-saving ballasts which operate standard lamps at full light output can be used, provided the ballast is listed for use with the lamps and this is stated on the ballast label. These lamps may not be used with any ballast which provides reduced wattage and thus reduced light output in a standard lamp, nor with any ballast which does not list the lamp on its label. A transparent conductive coating is applied to these energy-saving lamps, resulting in a lower required starting voltage and less lumen output. By using these lamps as a retrofit in overilluminated spaces, a saving of 5–6 W per lamp can be achieved.

Whether operated on standard or energy-efficient magnetic ballasts, energy-saving fluorescent lamps generate about 87% of the light generated by a standard (40-W T-12) lamp at 25°C. This lamp-ballast system is less energy efficient than the standard argon gas lamp-ballast system, since it generates fewer lumens per watt. This is due to increased ballast losses. In addition, these lamps cannot be dimmed as easily as standard T-12 lamps, and they are more sensitive to temperature.

Additional energy savings (approximately 3 W per lamp) can be achieved by disconnecting the 3.5-V electrode heating circuit of typical rapid-start ballasts. This is accomplished inside the lamp with a bimetal switch in series with each electrode. If lamps are turned off for several seconds, there may be a delay of up to 60 s before relighting. Instant relight should occur after a momentary power interruption. Another form of reduced wattage lamp is one which includes a reactive impedance built into its end. These lamps are used to replace one of the two lamps operating on a two-lamp series rapid-start circuit. They reduce the wattage and output of the total system by approximately 33 or 50%, depending upon the lamp type chosen.

Special Fluorescent Lamps: Subminiature, Reflector, Cold Cathode

In addition to the lamps described above, there are three families of lamps which are designed and constructed for special applications. They are subminiature, reflector, and cold cathode fluorescent.

First in this group is a family of lamps with extremely small dimensions called subminiature fluorescent lamps. This family first saw application in the backlighting of liquid crystal displays because there was a need for very small diameter lamps. It developed into two basic types: a hot cathode and a cold cathode design. The lamps all have bulb diameters of 7 mm (approximately T-2$\frac{1}{2}$).

The cold cathode series ranges from 1 to 3 W, having an output of 15–130 lm, respectively. Standard lamp lengths range from 10 to 50 mm (4 to 20 in.). These low-power light sources have a low bulb wall temperature, which is important when backlighting displays where space is limited and components must be kept cool. The lamps have a rated life of 20,000 h based on 3 h per start.

The hot cathode family of subminiature fluorescent lamps ranges from 4 to 13 W, with lumen output packages ranging from 95 to 860 lm, respectively. The lumen output is similar to comparable-length T-5 preheat fluorescent lamps. The hot cathode lamps have a rated life of 10,000 h at 3 h per start. Their high lumen output lends them to such general lighting applications as display lighting, valance lighting, furniture-mounted task lighting, and other applications calling for small-diameter, linear light sources.

The triphosphor blends in both hot and cold cathode products provide for improved efficacy at the higher wattages. The lamps also provide good color rendering characteristics, having a CRI of about 80.

Lamps in the next special family, called reflector fluorescent lamps, have a white powder layer between the phosphor and the bulb. This coating, which covers a major angular portion of the envelope wall, reflects a high percentage of the visible radiation striking it. The major portion of the light is emitted through the strip coated with just the fluorescent phosphor. A cross-sectional diagram and relative candlepower distribution for a 235° reflector lamp are shown in figure 6-25. Reflector lamps whose reflectors have other angular widths are available. As a consequence of the reflector

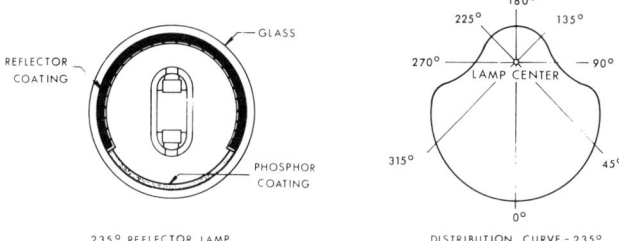

Fig. 6-25. Cross-section diagrams and relative candlepower distribution curves for 235-degree reflector lamp.

layer, absorption of generated light is somewhat higher than in standard fluorescent lamps, producing a somewhat reduced total lumen output. However, these lamps are designed for applications which can effectively utilize the resulting light output distribution pattern.

Cold cathode fluorescent lamps are finding greater use in decorative, sign lighting, and other architectural applications. Due to high electrode losses associated with cold cathode operation, they are not as efficient as the more widespread hot cathode types for lengths up to 8 ft; for longer lengths, however, where the electrode losses contribute a smaller fraction of the total losses, the lamps can be economical. The lamps are usually custom manufactured in special shapes and sizes to fit the application. Cold cathode lamps with color phosphors are replacing neon tubes in many applications where exposed sources are convenient. Other advantages of cold cathode lamps include long life, immediate start (even under cold conditions) and a life that is unaffected by the number of starts.

Other special lamps are available for unusual ambient temperatures. One family, designed for low temperatures, incorporates a jacket to conserve heat. Another, for high temperatures, incorporates a mercury amalgam. In both cases, these lamps are designed for optimization of the mercury vapor pressures at unusual temperatures.

Performance Parameters

To fully describe a light source, the performance parameters of the device need to be defined. Some of the more important parameters are:

- Luminous efficacy
- Lamp life
- Lumen maintenance
- Color (spectral power distribution, CRI and chromaticity)
- Candela distribution
- Temperature effect on operation
- Flicker and stroboscopic effect
- High-frequency operation
- Radio interference

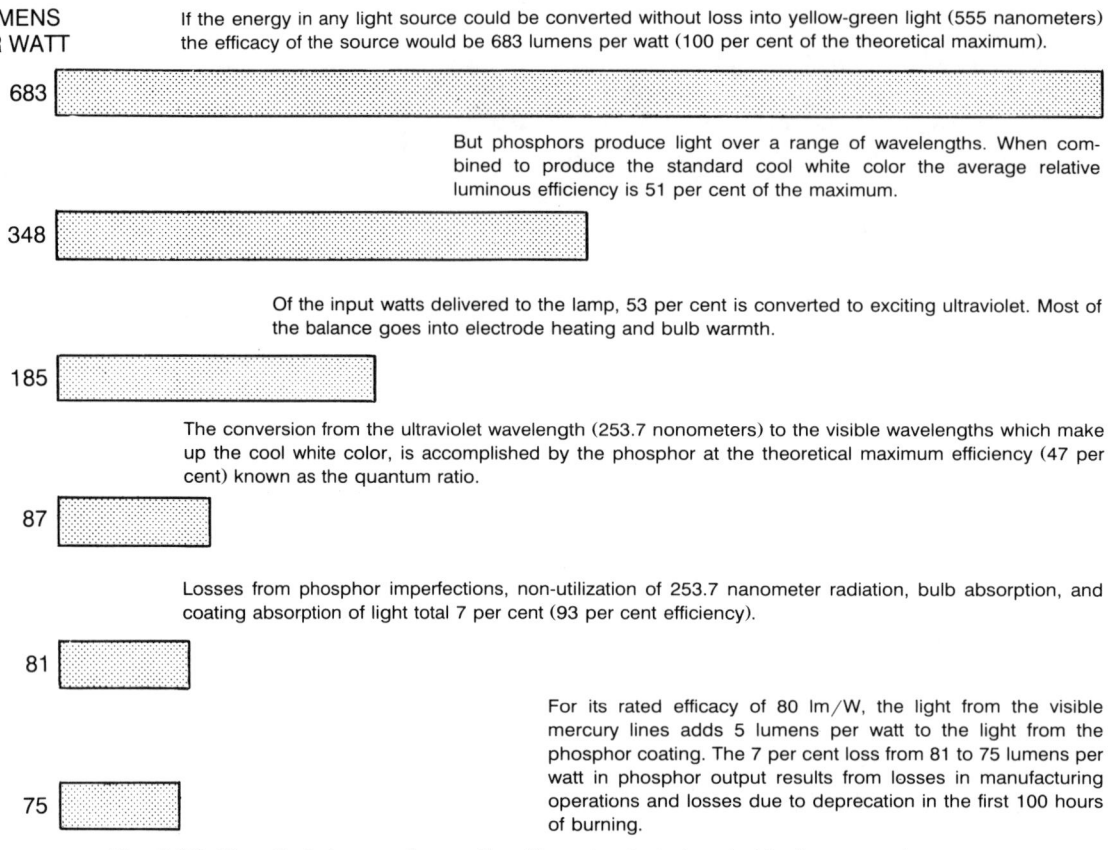

LUMENS
PER WATT

If the energy in any light source could be converted without loss into yellow-green light (555 nanometers) the efficacy of the source would be 683 lumens per watt (100 per cent of the theoretical maximum).

683

But phosphors produce light over a range of wavelengths. When combined to produce the standard cool white color the average relative luminous efficiency is 51 per cent of the maximum.

348

Of the input watts delivered to the lamp, 53 per cent is converted to exciting ultraviolet. Most of the balance goes into electrode heating and bulb warmth.

185

The conversion from the ultraviolet wavelength (253.7 nonometers) to the visible wavelengths which make up the cool white color, is accomplished by the phosphor at the theoretical maximum efficiency (47 per cent) known as the quantum ratio.

87

Losses from phosphor imperfections, non-utilization of 253.7 nanometer radiation, bulb absorption, and coating absorption of light total 7 per cent (93 per cent efficiency).

81

For its rated efficacy of 80 lm/W, the light from the visible mercury lines adds 5 lumens per watt to the light from the phosphor coating. The 7 per cent loss from 81 to 75 lumens per watt in phosphor output results from losses in manufacturing operations and losses due to deprecation in the first 100 hours of burning.

75

Fig. 6-26. The effect of energy loss on the efficacy in a typical cool white fluorescent lamp.

Luminous Efficacy: Light Output. Three main energy conversions occur during the process of generating light by a fluorescent lamp. Initially, electrical energy is converted into kinetic energy by accelerating charged particles. These in turn yield their energy during particle collision to electromagnetic radiation, particularly UV. This UV energy in turn is converted to visible energy by the lamp phosphor. During each of these conversions some energy is lost, so that only a small percentage of the input is converted into visible radia-

tion, as shown in figure 6-26. Figure 6-27 shows the approximate distribution of energy in a typical cool white fluorescent lamp.

The geometric design and operating conditions of a lamp influence the efficacy with which energy conversions take place. Figures 6-28 through 6-32 present data depicting the effect of bulb design on efficacy.

Figures 6-28 and 6-29 show the effect of the bulb design on lamp operation. As seen in figure 6-28, at a

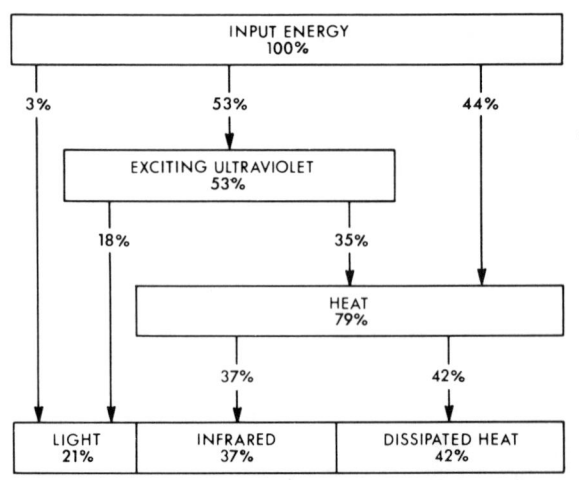

Fig. 6-27. Energy distribution in a typical cool white fluorescent lamp.

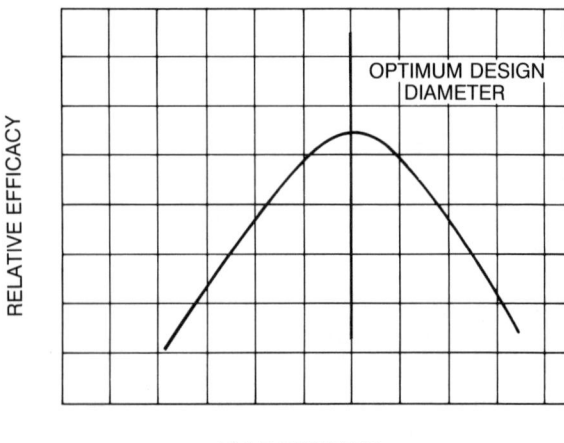

Fig. 6-28. Efficacy of typical argon-filled fluorescent lamps as a function of bulb diameter.

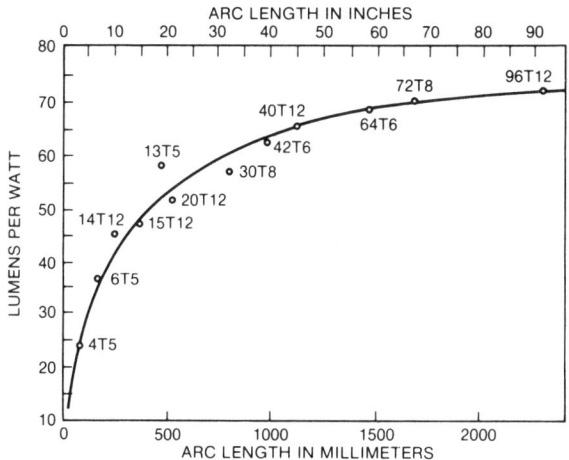

Fig. 6-29. Efficacy of a typical fluorescent lamp as a function of lamp length.

constant current, as the lamp diameter increases, the efficacy increases, passes through a maximum and decreases.[37] There are at least two important reasons for this phenomenon. In lamps of small diameter, an excessive amount of energy is lost by recombinations of electrons with ions at the bulb wall. As the bulb diameter is increased, this loss becomes progressively smaller, but losses due to "imprisonment of radiation" become correspondingly larger.

As shown in figures 6-29 and 6-30, the length of a lamp influences its efficacy; the greater the length, the higher the efficacy. This is based on two separate energy losses within the lamp: the energy absorbed by the electrodes, which do not generate any appreciable light, and the energy loss directly associated with the

generation of light. The electrode loss is essentially a constant, whereas the loss associated with light generation is a function of lamp length. As the lamp length increases, the effect of the electrode loss becomes less in comparison with the total losses.

The operating voltage of a lamp, like its efficacy, is a function of its length. This effect is shown in figures 6-31 and 6-32. Figure 6-31 presents data for hot cathode T-12 operation at four different lamp operating current levels. Figure 6-32 presents similar data for both hot and cold cathode T-8 lamp operation. The characteristic electrode drop for the two types of cathodes is indicated by the intersection of the curves with the ordinate corresponding to zero length.[38]

Figures 6-114 through 6-121 show the light output data on typical fluorescent lamps. So far as possible, data presented on types produced by several manufacturers represent industry averages. Since these data are likely to differ slightly from specific figures for one manufacturer's product, it is advisable to check the manufacturers' sheets for detailed information on current production.

Lamp Life. The lamp life of hot cathode lamps is determined by the rate of loss of the emissive coating on the electrodes. Some of the coating is eroded from the filaments each time the lamp is started. Also, during lamp operation there is evaporation of emissive material. Electrodes are designed to minimize both of these effects. The end of lamp life is reached when either the coating is completely removed from one or both electrodes, or the remaining coating becomes nonemissive.

Fig. 6-30. Relationship of Arc Length and Lumens per Watt for Typical Cool White Fluorescent Lamps

Approximate Arc Length		Approximate Efficacy (lumens per watt)	Hot Cathode			Low Pressure T-8 Cold Cathode
			Approximate Lamp and Auxiliary Efficacy (lumens per watt)			
(millimeters)	(inches)		Preheat Start	Instant Start	Rapid Start	Approximate Efficacy (lumens per watt)
130	5	33	22			
250	10	45	34			
380	15	53	42			
500	20	59	48			
630	25	63	53			
760	30	66	57			
890	35	68	59			
1010	40	69	61	52	60	38
1140	45	70	62			
1270	50	71	63	54	63	41
1400	55	72				
1520	60	73		56	65	44
1650	65	73				
1780	70	74		59	67	47
1900	75	75				
2030	80	76		61	69	50
2160	85	77				
2290	90	77		63	71	52

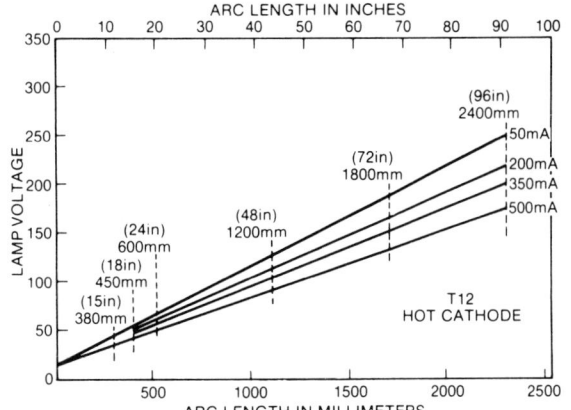

Fig. 6-31. Operating voltage of typical 38-mm (T-12) hot-cathode fluorescent lamps as a function of arc length.

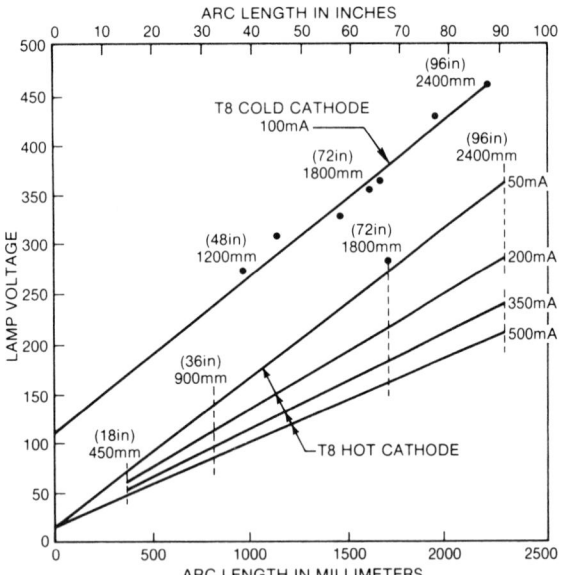

Fig. 6-32. Operating voltage of typical hot and cold-cathode 25-millimeter (T-8) fluorescent lamps as a function of arc length.

Because some of the emissive coating is lost from the electrodes during each start, the frequency of starting hot cathode lamps influences lamp life. The rated average life of fluorescent lamps is usually based on three hours of operation per start. The effect of starting frequency on life is presented in figure 6-33. These data have been normalized to 100% for life at three hours per start. Cold cathode lamps are not appreciably affected by starting frequency because of the type of electrode used.

Electronic ballasts have been designed to instant start rapid-start T-8 and T-12 lamps. Typically there is a 25% reduction in lamp life based upon 3 h per start. For applications where the number of hours per start is considerably less than 3 h, the instant-start operation should be avoided.

There are many other variable conditions that affect lamp life in actual use. Ballast characteristics and starter design are key factors in the case of preheat circuits. Ballasts which do not provide specified starting requirements or which do not operate lamps at proper voltage levels can greatly affect lamp life. For preheat circuits, starters must also be designed to meet specified characteristics.

The electrode heating current in rapid-start lamps is critical and is affected not only by ballasts, but also by poor lamp-to-lampholder contact or improper circuit wiring. Improper seating of a lamp in a lampholder may result in no electrode heating. Lamps operating in this mode will fail within a short time, typically 50–500 h. Another factor in lamp life is line voltage. If the line voltage is too high, it may cause instant starting of lamps in preheat and rapid-start circuits. If it is low, slow starting of rapid-start or instant-start lamps, or recycling of starters in preheat circuits, may result. All of these conditions adversely affect lamp life. A typical mortality curve for a large group of good-quality fluorescent lamps is given in figure 6-34.

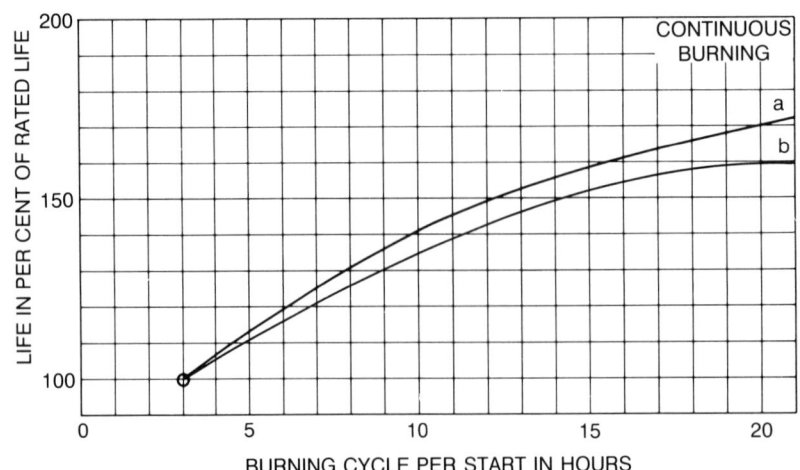

Fig. 6-33. Life of typical preheat (a) and rapid-start (b) fluorescent lamp as a function of burning cycle. Variations from these curves can be expected with lamp loading.

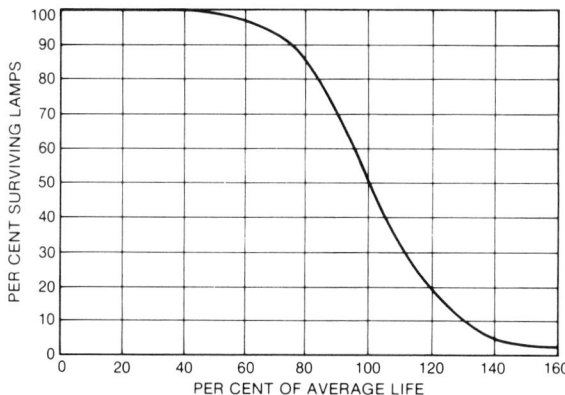

Fig. 6-34. Typical mortality curve for a statistically large group of fluorescent lamps (at 3 operating hours per start).

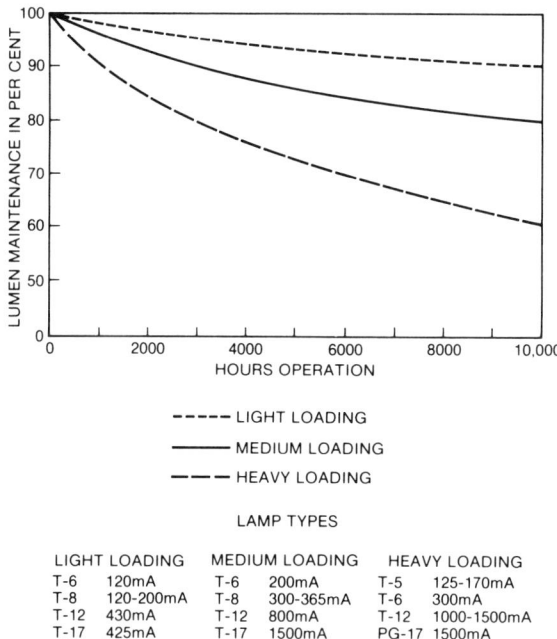

----- LIGHT LOADING

——— MEDIUM LOADING

— — — HEAVY LOADING

LAMP TYPES

LIGHT LOADING		MEDIUM LOADING		HEAVY LOADING	
T-6	120mA	T-6	200mA	T-5	125-170mA
T-8	120-200mA	T-8	300-365mA	T-6	300mA
T-12	430mA	T-12	800mA	T-12	1000-1500mA
T-17	425mA	T-17	1500mA	PG-17	1500mA

a

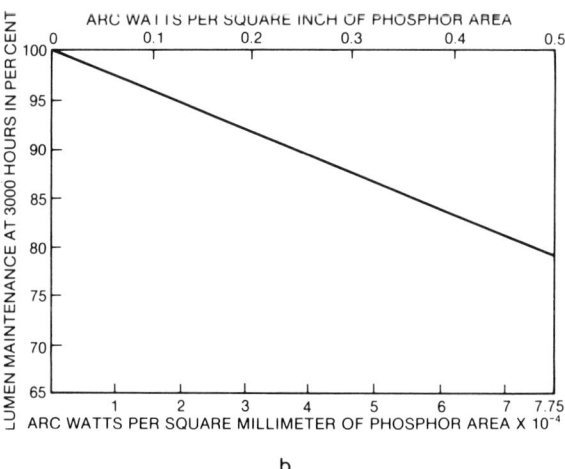

b

Fig. 6-35. Lumen maintenance curves for typical fluorescent lamps as a function of: (a) hours operation and (b) incident radiation power density on the phosphor surface.

Ballasts are available for low-temperature starting of rapid-start lamps. At the higher temperatures encountered during the summer months, lamps operating on these ballasts will start before the electrodes are properly heated. This has an adverse effect on lamp life. Time delay relays are available to ensure proper electrode heating prior to application of ignition voltage to the lamp.

Lumen Maintenance. The lumen output of fluorescent lamps decreases with accumulated burning time, owing to photochemical degradation of the phosphor coating and glass tube and to the accumulation of light-absorbing deposits within the lamp. The rate of phosphor degradation increases with arc power and decreases with increasing the coated area of the phosphor. The lumen maintenance curves for lamps with different ratios of arc power to phosphor area are shown in figure 6-35a, and the effect of lamp loading on lumen maintenance is presented in figure 6-35b.[39,40] Protective coatings are sometimes used to reduce the phosphor degradation. The newer triphosphors are more stable and allow higher loading levels, as for example in T-8, compact, and subminiature lamps.

Glass solarization is a photochemical degradation of the glass tube which reduces its transmission and leads to a reduction of light output with time.

The deposit of cathode coating material evaporated during lamp operation causes end darkening, which reduces the transmission of UV radiation into the phosphor, thereby reducing the phosphor light output as the lamp ages.

Spectral Power Distribution and Chromaticity. Spectral power distribution data for typical colors of fluorescent lamps are shown in figure 6-23. For a discussion of color and color rendering index, see chapter 4.

Temperature Effect on Operation. The characteristics of a fluorescent lamp are very much dependent upon the concentration of mercury vapor, that is to say, the mercury vapor pressure within the lamp, which depends upon temperature.

A fluorescent lamp contains a larger quantity of liquid mercury than will become vaporized at any one time. The excess liquid mercury tends to condense at the coolest point or points on the lamp. If any one location is significantly cooler than the rest of the lamp, all the liquid mercury will collect there. The mercury pressure within the lamp will depend upon the temperature of the coolest point or points, which in turn depends upon the lamp construction, lamp wattage, ambient temperature, luminaire design and wind or draft conditions.

The effect of temperature on mercury vapor pressure manifests itself as variations in light output and color.

Lamps using mercury amalgams are available for extending the usable ambient temperatures to higher values. The amalgam functions to stabilize and control the mercury pressure.

The internal temperature of a luminaire can adversely affect the life of some types of fluorescent lamps. High ambient temperatures not only lower the lamp's lumen output but can also change its electrical characteristics, bring it outside the design range of the ballast and therefore allow more than rated current to flow. Long-term operation at higher currents will shorten the life of the lamp.

As the temperature of a fluorescent bulb increases, both the light output and the active power consumption also increase. However, as the temperature rises above 32°C, the power consumption gradually begins to decrease. The light output continues to increase until the temperature reaches approximately 38°C, at which point it begins to drop dramatically. The system efficacy, defined as light output divided by active power, is therefore maximized at approximately 40°C. Typical characteristics of a lamp operated at constant current are shown in figure 6-36. The exact shape of the curves depends upon the lamp cross section, loading and type of ballasting. However, all fluorescent lamps have essentially the same relation between light output and minimum bulb wall temperature.

Most T-8 and T-12 lamps, which are intended primarily for indoor use, have been designed for their light output and luminous efficacy to reach optimum values at a minimum bulb wall temperature of 38°C. In well-designed luminaires, this temperature is typically reached when the lamps are operated at rated power under usual indoor temperatures.

Compact fluorescent lamps characteristically are more sensitive to the temperature of the operating

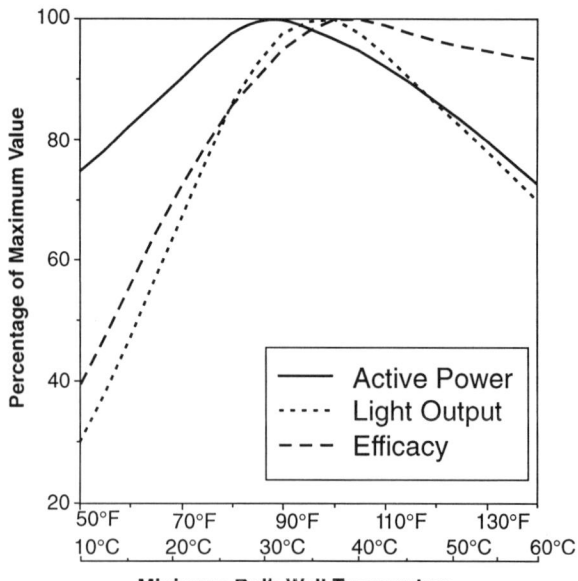

Fig. 6-36. Typical fluorescent lamp temperature characteristics. Exact shape of curves will depend upon lamp and ballast type; however, all fluorescent lamps have curves of the same general shape, since this depends upon mercury vapor pressure.

environment than the standard straight-tube lamps. In some cases the increased temperature inside the luminaire results in lower than rated light output.

Curves for an 800-mA high-output fluorescent lamp are shown in figure 6-37 (left). As these curves indicate, the light output falls to very low values at temperatures below freezing. Lamps intended for indoor operation will display poor low-temperature performance unless protected by suitable enclosures. Figure 6-37 (right) shows the relationship between ambient temperature and light output for a typical outdoor floodlight using 800-mA high-output lamps. While con-

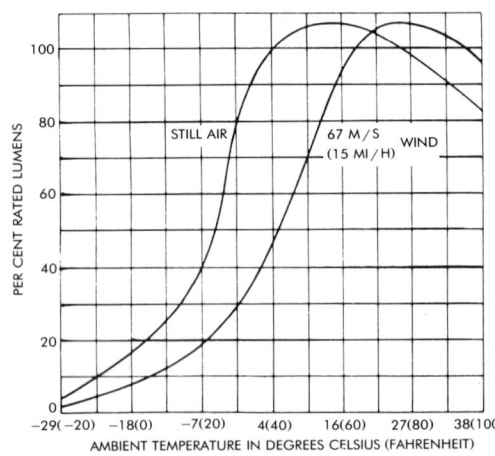
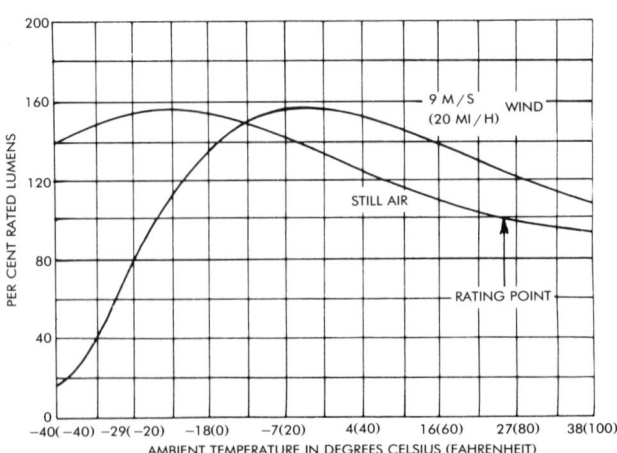

Fig. 6-37. Light output versus ambient temperature. (*Left*) F96T12/HO fluorescent lamp. Light output falls to low values at temperatures below freezing. Loss in light at high ambient temperatures is much less. (*Right*) Typical outdoor floodlight with two F72T12/HO. By a suitable enclosure, the lamp is warmed to a high enough temperature to produce good light output under cold windy conditions.

siderable variation occurs with temperature change, satisfactory illumination is obtained for temperatures commonly encountered in most areas of the United States and Canada.

Each lamp-luminaire combination has its own distinctive characteristic of light output as a function of ambient temperature. In general, the shape of the curve will be quite similar for all luminaires, but the temperature at which the highest light output will be reached may be different.

Figure 6-36 shows that the loss in light as the lamp is heated beyond the optimum temperature is nearly linear. From this fact an estimating rule can be derived which enables the designer to compensate for high ambient temperature. There will be a 1% loss in light for every 1.1°C (2°F) by which the ambient temperature around the lamp exceeds 25°C (77°F).

Effects of Temperature on Color. The temperature affects not only the light output of a lamp, but also the color of the light produced. The color of light from the traditional halophosphate fluorescent lamp has two components, one from the phosphor coating and the other from the mercury arc discharge itself. Each of these components reacts independently to temperature changes. In general, the lamp color shifts toward the blue-green with increasing temperature due to the increasing contribution from the mercury arc visible spectrum. The same type of shift occurs in lamps which employ the triphosphor coating system.

Figure 6-38 shows a typical color shift characteristic of a fluorescent lamp employing a halophosphate. In addition, the MacAdam four-step ovals are noted for

each color. These ovals depict the color tolerance limits for lamps operated at 25°C (77°F). Variations are due to manufacturing and color changes through life. In a new interior lighting installation, the color is much more uniform than this, since all lamps are typically of the same manufacture and age.

Color shift becomes a concern to the lighting designer chiefly in cases where substantial differences in internal temperature may exist between adjacent luminaires. This may arise from the proximity of certain luminaires to air diffusers or open windows; differences in ceiling cavity conditions or ceiling material with surface and recessed equipment; differences in the tightness of enclosures with enclosed equipment; differences in lamp loading or number of lamps in identical luminaires; and use of some of the luminaires as air diffusers in the air-conditioning system.

High-Frequency Operation of Fluorescent Lamps. The fluorescent lighting industry is rapidly progressing towards high-frequency operation of fluorescent lamps with the advent of highly efficient electronic ballasts. High-frequency electronic ballasts generally provide power to the fluorescent lamp in the range of 10–50 kHz from a 50–60-Hz supply. The primary advantages of high-frequency fluorescent lighting are the reduction in ballast losses and the improvement in lamp lumen efficacy relative to lighting systems with 60-Hz magnetic ballasts.

As shown in figure 6-39, a 10% gain in lamp efficacy can be obtained by operating the lamp above 10 kHz. In the range from 10 to 100 kHz, the efficacy is constant. The improved performance of the fluorescent lamp at high frequencies has been attributed to two factors. A reduction in end losses is achieved by elimination of the oscillation on the anode half of the operating cycle. An increase in efficiency of the lamp's positive column (major portion of the arc stream) is

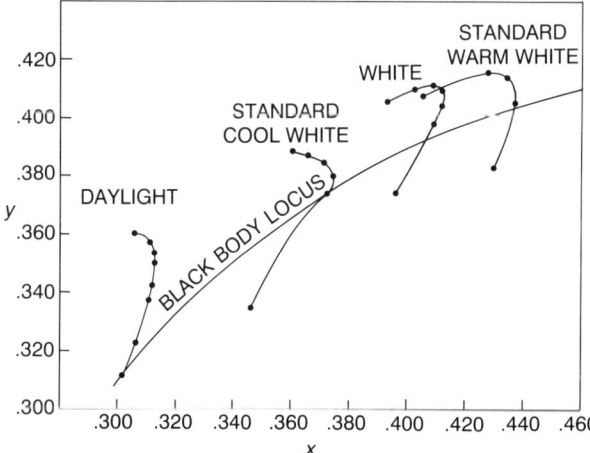

Fig. 6-38. Typical color shift characteristic of a fluorescent lamp with changes in ambient temperature. Color shift over a normal temperature range is in the same order of magnitude as that which may be experienced between lamps of the same nominal color due to manufacturing variations, depreciation through life, etc. (The lowest point on each curve is at −20°C [-4°F], the furthest point on the curve is at 120°C [248°F], intermediate points are 20°C [36°F] apart.)

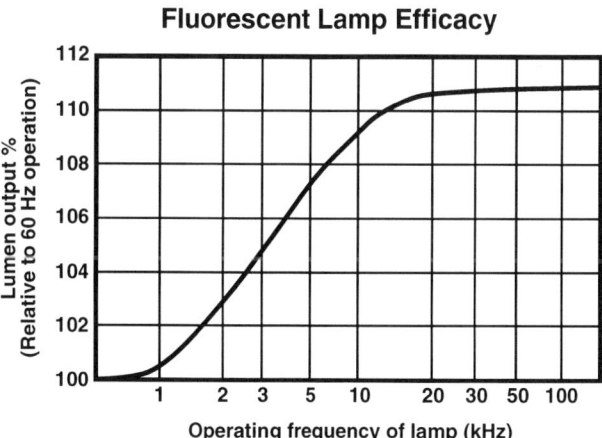

Fig. 6-39. Lamp efficacy gain at constant lumen output vs operating frequency for a 40-watt, T-12 rapid-start lamp.

achieved by operating at lower wattage. In order to save energy, fluorescent lamps are normally operated at lower than rated wattage with high-frequency electronic ballasts while maintaining the lamp's rated lumen output.

In order to avoid audible noise problems, most electronic ballasts operate the lamp in the 20–30-kHz range. A major consideration in high-frequency operation of fluorescent lamps is radiated and conducted radio-frequency (RF) noise. The electronic ballast must have filter circuitry to reduce the conducted RF below government regulations. In addition, the lamp current waveform must be chosen to limit the amount of radiated RF noise.

Radio Interference. The mercury arc in a fluorescent lamp emits electromagnetic radiation. This radiation may be picked up by nearby radios, causing an audible sound. Because of the frequencies generated by the fluorescent lamp, interference is ordinarily limited to the AM broadcast band and nearby amateur and communications bands. FM, television and higher frequencies are very rarely affected by radiated interference but may be affected by conducted interference. Most instant-start ballasts and starters for preheat circuits have capacitors for reduction of radio interference.

Radio noise reaches the receiver either by radiation to the antenna or by conduction over the power lines. Radiated interference may be eliminated by moving the antenna farther from the lamp. A distance of 3 m (10 ft) is usually sufficient. Where this is not practical, shielding media, such as electrically conducting glass or certain louver materials, will suppress the noise below the interference level. Conducted interference may be suppressed by an electric filter in the line at the luminaire. Figure 6-40 shows a typical design. Luminaires with this type of filtering and appropriate shielding material have been qualified under pertinent military specifications for sensitive areas.

Lamp Circuits and Auxiliary Equipment

Like most arc discharge lamps, fluorescent lamps have a negative volt-ampere characteristic and therefore re-

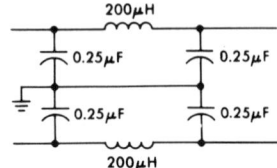

Fig. 6-40. Typical radio interference filter.

quire an auxiliary device to limit current flow. This device, called a ballast, may incorporate an added function which provides a voltage sufficient to ensure ignition of the arc discharge. This voltage may vary between 1.5 to 4 times the normal lamp operating voltage.

The life and light output ratings of fluorescent lamps are based on their use with ballasts providing proper operating characteristics, which have been established in the American National Standards for Dimensional and Electrical Characteristics of Fluorescent Lamps (C78 Series). Ballasts that do not provide proper electrical values may reduce either lamp life or light output or both. This auxiliary equipment consumes power and therefore reduces the overall lm/W rating below that based on the power consumed by the lamp. Typical data are presented in figure 6-120.

Lamp Starting

The starting of a fluorescent lamp occurs in two stages. First, the electrodes must be heated to their emission temperatures. Secondly, a sufficient voltage must exist across the lamp to initiate ionization of the gas in the lamp and develop the arc. In some starting systems, a voltage is applied between one of the electrodes and ground to help the ionization of the gas.

As the ambient temperature is reduced, starting of all fluorescent lamps becomes more difficult. For reliable starting at low temperatures higher available output voltages are required. For more efficient lamp and ballast operation, ballasts are available for each of the following temperature ranges:

- Above 10°C (50°F) for indoor applications
- Above −18°C (0°F) for outdoor temperature applications
- Above −29°C (−20°F) for outdoor temperature applications

A number of different means of lamp starting have been developed since the advent of the fluorescent lamp. The first was preheat starting, which required an automatic or manual starting switch. Although not commonly used in North America for the starting of conventional and T-8 fluorescent lamps, preheat starting is employed extensively to start compact fluorescent lamps. The next development in lamp starting was instant starting, which requires a higher ballast open-circuit voltage. In conjunction with magnetic ballast circuits, specially constructed instant-start lamps are required. Recently electronic ballasts have been developed that can instant-start most types of fluorescent lamps. The most commonly used starting circuit is

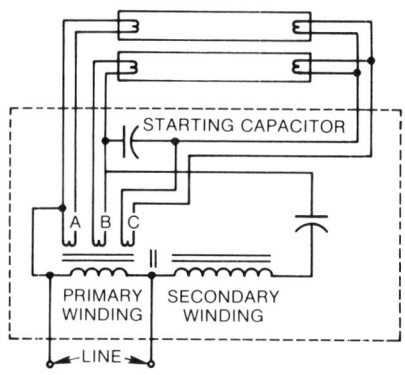

(a) Two-lamp rapid-start high power factor. Used for rapid-start, high output and extra high output lamps, for both indoor and low temperature applications. The small capacitor shunted across one lamp momentarily applies nearly all of the ballast secondary voltage across the other lamp. The lamp cathodes are continuously heated by the cathode heating windings (A, B, and C) in the ballast.

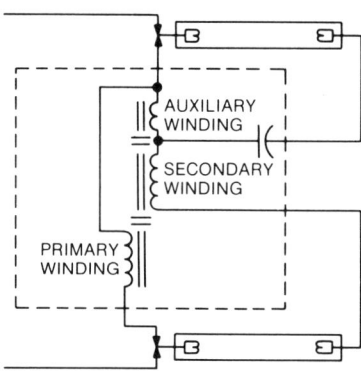

(b) Two-lamp series-sequence instant-start high power factor. Used in instant-start (slimline) indoor units. Lamps start in sequence with auxiliary winding helping to start first lamp. Note disconnect lampholder connection which removes power from the ballast primary when lamps are being changed, thus preventing electric shock.

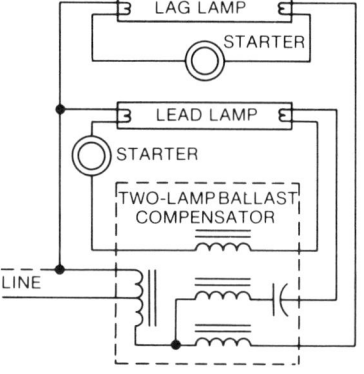

(c) Two-lamp lead-lag preheat, high power factor. Used in 40-watt and 90-watt preheat-type general luminaires. Note compensator winding, which is needed to produce sufficient preheat current in the lead circuit.

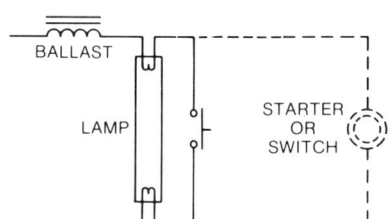

(d) Simple preheat circuit low power factor. Used for appliances, desk lamps, etc.

Fig. 6-41. Typical fluorescent lamp circuits.

rapid starting, where the use of continuously heated electrodes resulted in lamp starting without high voltages or starting switches. Several circuits for operating lamps are shown in figure 6-41.

Preheat Lamp and Ballast Operation. In preheat circuits, the lamp electrodes are heated before application of the high voltage across the lamp. Lamps designed for such operation have bipin bases to facilitate electrode heating. Many preheat-starting compact fluorescent lamps have the starting devices built into the lamp base.

The preheating requires a few seconds, and the necessary delay is usually accomplished by an automatic switch which places the lamp electrodes in series across the output of the ballast. Current flows through both electrode filaments, heating them. Subsequently, the switch opens, applying the voltage across the lamp. Due to the opening of the switch under load, a transient voltage (an inductive spike) is developed in the circuit, which aids in ignition of the lamp. If the lamp does not ignite, the switch will reclose and reheat the filaments. In some applications preheating is accomplished by a manual switch.

The automatic switch is commonly called a *starter*. It may incorporate a small capacitor (0.006 μF) across the switch contacts to shunt high-frequency oscillations which may cause radio interference.

Ballasts are available to operate some preheat lamps without the use of starters. These ballasts use the rapid-start principle of lamp starting and operation and are popularly called trigger start ballasts.

Starters for Preheat Circuits. The operation of a preheat circuit requires heating of the electrodes prior to application of voltage across the lamp. Preheating can be effected by use of a manual switch or one which is activated by application of voltage to the ballast circuit. A number of designs of automatic switches are commercially available. Circuit diagrams of designs are presented in figure 6-42 below.

Thermal Switch Starter. A circuit diagram of this starter type is presented in figure 6-42. Initially the silver-carbon contact of the thermal starter is closed, placing the electrodes in series with the parallel combination of the bimetal and the carbon resistor. Upon closing the ballast supply circuit, the output voltage of the ballast is applied to this series-parallel wiring combination. The current heats the bimetallic strip in the starter, causing it to open the silver-carbon contact. The time of opening is sufficient to raise the temperature of the electrodes to approximately its normal operating value. Upon opening the circuit, the ballast output voltage in series with an inductive spike (kick) voltage is applied to the lamp. If the lamp ignites, its normal operating voltage maintains a low current through the carbon resistor, developing and transferring sufficient heat to the bimetal to hold its contact open thereafter.

Should the lamp fail to start on the first attempt, the ballast open-circuit voltage applied to the carbon resistor heats the bimetal sufficiently to cause the silver contact to move against the third contact. This short-circuits the carbon resistor, permitting preheating current to flow through the electrodes. As the bimetal cools, the circuit through the third contact is opened, resulting in the application of the circuit voltage to the lamp again. This making and breaking of the circuit through the third contact continues until the lamp ignites. The bimetal circuit is held open thereafter as noted above. The carbon contact circuit functions only when the line voltage is initially applied to the ballast.

Thermal-switch starters consume some power (0.5–1.5 W) during lamp operation, but their design

ensures positive starting by providing an adequate preheating period, a high induced starting voltage, and characteristics inherently less susceptible to line voltage variations. For these reasons they give good all-around performance under adverse conditions, such as direct-current operation, low ambient temperature and varying voltage.

Glow-Switch Starter. The circuit for this starter is presented in figure 6-42 below. The bulb is filled with an inert gas chosen for the voltage characteristics desired. On starting, the line switch is closed. There is practically no voltage drop in the ballast, and the voltage at the starter is sufficient to produce a glow discharge between the contacts. The heat from the glow distorts the bimetallic strip, the contacts close, and electrode preheating begins. This short-circuits the glow discharge so that the bimetal cools, and in a short time the contacts open. The open-circuit voltage in series with an inductive spike voltage is applied to the lamp. If the lamp fails to ignite, the ballast open-circuit voltage again develops a glow in the bulb and the sequence of events is repeated. This continues until the lamp ignites. During normal operation, there is not enough voltage across the lamp to produce further starter glow, so the contacts remain open and the starter consumes no power.

Cutout Starter. This starter may be made to reset either manually or automatically. It is designed to prevent repeated blinking or attempts to start a deactivated lamp. This type of starter should be good for at least ten or more renewals.

Lamp Failure in Preheat Circuit. Starters which provide no means for deactivation when a lamp fails will continue to function and attempt to start the lamp. The lamp may blink, and the ballast or starter may eventually fail. Thus it is important to remove a failed preheat lamp without delay.

Instant-Start Lamp and Ballast Operation. Arc initiation in instant-start lamps depends solely on the application of a high voltage across the lamp. This voltage (400–1000 V) ejects electrons from the electrodes by field emission. These electrons flow through the tube, ionizing the gas and initiating an arc discharge. Thereafter, the arc current provides electrode heating. Because no preheating of electrodes is required, instant-start lamps need only a single contact at each end. Thus, a single pin is used on most instant-start lamps. These are commonly called *slimline* lamps. A few instant-start lamps use bipin bases with the pins connected internally. In the case of lamps designed for instant starting at 400–1000 V open circuit, it is necessary to provide some means of counteracting the effect

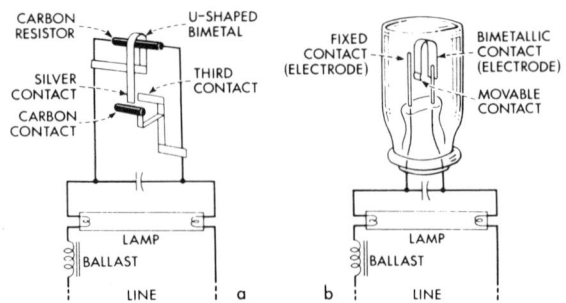

Fig. 6-42. Starter switches for preheat cathode circuits: (a) thermal type; (b) glow switch type.

of humidity on the capacitive lamp-ground current which initiates the necessary glow discharge. Most manufacturers coat the outside of bulbs of this type of lamp with a transparent, nonwetting material; others apply a narrow conducting strip along the bulb. A grounded conducting plate, such as a metal reflector near the lamp, commonly known as a *starting aid*, is necessary to obtain the lowest lamp starting voltage.[42]

Rapid-Start Lamp and Ballast Operation.[43-46] Lamps designed for rapid-start operation typically have low-resistance cathodes. Normally, the cathodes are heated continuously by the application of cathode voltage while the lamps are in operation. In some energy-saving circuits, the cathode voltage is reduced or disconnected after the starting of the lamps. Heating is accomplished through low-voltage windings built into the ballast or through separate low-voltage transformers designed for this purpose. This results in a starting-voltage requirement similar to that of preheat lamps. Lamps usually start in one second, the time required to bring the filaments up to proper temperature.

A starting aid, consisting of a grounded conducting plate extending the length of and adjacent to the lamp, is a prerequisite to reliable starting. For lamps operating at 500 mA or less the nominal distance between the lamp and a 25-mm (1-in.) wide conducting plate is 13 mm (0.5 in.); for lamps operating at currents greater than 500 mA the nominal distance to the conducting strip is 25 mm (1 in.). Peak voltage recommendations for lamp ignition using starting aids other than the nominal are listed in figure 6-43.

Rapid-start lamps are coated with a transparent nonwetting material to counteract the adverse effect of

humidity in lamp starting. All 800-mA and most 1500-mA lamp types operate on the rapid-start principle. Forty-watt and circline lamps designed for rapid-start service can also be used in comparable preheat circuits.

Electronic Ballast Starting. All three starting methods are employed in electronic ballast designs on the market today. When applied to electronic ballasts, the differences between the rapid-start and the preheat technique become less significant. The preheat designs use internal timing components which delay the full open-circuit voltage while applying power to the electrodes for preheating. After starting, the power to the electrodes is reduced to almost zero. Most of the rapid-starting systems do not rely on a potential to ground to aid the start as with the magnetic ballast. The starting method is similar to the preheat technique except that the electrode voltage usually remains after the lamp starts. Electronic ballasts have been designed to "instant-start" rapid-start fluorescent lamps. Typically there is a reduction in expected life when operated in this manner.

Ballast Construction. The construction of a typical thermally protected rapid-start ballast is shown in figure 6-44. The components consist of a transformer-type core and coil. Depending upon the circuit, a capacitor may be part of the ballast. These components are the heart of the ballast, providing sufficient voltage for lamp ignition and lamp current regulation through their reactance.

The core-and-coil assembly is made of laminated transformer steel wound with copper or aluminum magnet wire. The assembly is impregnated with a non-

Fig. 6-43. Effect of Starting Aid Dimensions on Peak Voltage Requirements for Reliable Starting of T-12 Argon-Filled Rapid-Start Lamps

Distance to Lamp (millimeters)	Distance to Lamp (inches)	Width of Aid (millimeters)	Width of Aid (inches)	Per Cent Change, Current ≤ 500 mA	Per Cent Change, Current > 500 mA
	Nominal*	200	8 or greater	−8	−8
	"	50	2	−4	−4
	"	25	1	−0	0
	"	13	1/2	+4	+4
	"	6	1/4	+8	+8
	"	3	1/8	+12	+12
	"	1.5	1/16	+20	+20
75	3	25	1	+32	+25
50	2	25	1	+22	+15
38	1-1/2	25	1	+15	+8
25	1	25	1	+7	0
13	1/2	25	1	0	−7
6	1/4	25	1	−8	−15
3	1/8 or less	25	1	−12	−20

* Nominal distance from starting aid to lamp is 13 millimeters (1/2 inch) for operating lamp current of 500 mA or less and 25 millimeters (1 inch) for operating lamp current of greater than 500 mA.

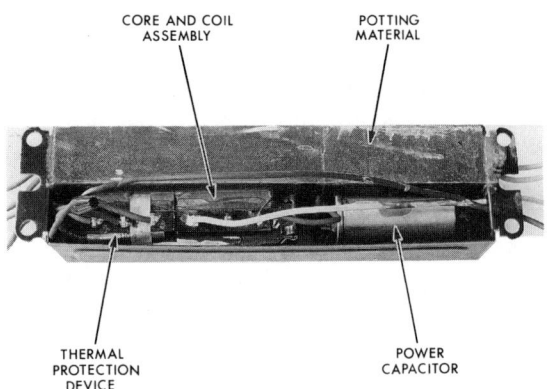

Fig. 6-44. Construction of typical rapid-start ballast.

electrical insulation to aid in heat dissipation and, with leads attached, is placed in a case. The case is filled with a potting material (hot asphalt, for example) containing a filler such as silica. This compound completely fills the case, encapsulating the core and coil and the capacitor. The base is then attached.

The average ballast life at a 50% duty cycle and a proper ballast operating temperature is normally estimated at about twelve years. Shorter ballast life will result at higher ballast temperature or longer duty cycle.

Most fluorescent lamp ballasts used indoors should be thermally protected internally. This is done to prevent misapplication of the ballast as well as to protect against failure and undesirable conditions which can occur at end of ballast life. In the United States the thermally protected ballast approved by Underwriters Laboratories is known and marked or labeled as "Class P."

Because of the magnetic elements in a ballast, vibrations are set up in the luminaire depending on the input power frequency. This may produce an audible hum which is undesirable. The sound level produced will depend upon the ballast and luminaire construction and mounting. The acoustical characteristics of the space and the number of luminaires will also have an effect on ballast noise. Ballast manufacturers publish *sound ratings* which indicate the relative sound-producing potential of their different models:

Sound ratings	Average noise rating (dB)
A	20–24
B	25–30
C	31–36
D	37–42
E	43–48
F	49 and higher

Some luminaire manufacturers also publish sound ratings for their units (see chapter 7, Luminaires).

Electronic Ballasts.[47] With improvements in solid-state devices and the availability of sophisticated integrated circuit functions, there now are commercially available electronic ballasts that provide 50–60-Hz ac input to the ballast and operate the lamps at 20–50 kHz, with resulting improvements in ballast efficiency and lamp efficacy.

The operating frequency is chosen to be high enough to increase the lamp efficacy and to shift the ballast noise to the inaudible range of the noise spectrum, but not so high as to cause electromagnetic interference (EMI) problems. Designs are available for the rapid and instant start of lamps. Typically, lamp life is better on the rapid-start units, but the instant-start units are more efficient. In order to offset the higher costs of electronic ballasts, some are designed to operate up to four lamps each. Many are made in the same size and shape as magnetic units in order to ease direct replacement. The better designs have circuits which keep the line-current harmonic distortion below 20% and provide a power factor in excess of 90%.

Electronic control affords a level of light output regulation which was previously unavailable in totally passive ballast design. With electronic lamp-current regulation, the effect of the lighting design variables of line voltage, ambient temperature and individual ballast differences can be minimized.

Electronic ballasts can also be designed to operate off dc and low-voltage systems for applications in buses, airplanes, trailers and battery-operated emergency systems.

Reduced-Wattage Ballasts. Ballasts are available which operate standard lamps at 50–80% of their rated wattage. Energy-saving lamps should not be used in combination with these ballasts, since the arc will tend to waver.

Energy-Saving Ballasts. Energy-saving ballasts have lower losses than standard ballasts. These may be rated by Certified Ballast Manufacturers (CBM) and may be used either with standard lamps or with reduced-wattage lamps. For example, losses in two-lamp 40-W rapid-start ballasts have been reduced by 4–5 W per lamp over standard ballasts. A typical two-lamp 40-W unit with a low-loss energy-saving ballast will dissipate approximately 86 W, compared with approximately 95 W for normal ballasts.

Energy-Saving Systems. Specialized lamp-and-ballast combinations are available to achieve even greater energy savings. These include a 32-W T-8 (4-ft) lamp with a high-efficiency ballast, and a 28-W T-12 lamp, also with a high-efficiency ballast, having internal solid-state switches which turn off the usual rapid-start cathode heater voltage. The latter ballast will also operate a 34-W reduced-wattage lamp. Power reducers are also available for energy saving. These solid-state electronic devices are wired in series with the lamp ballast to reduce operating wattage. Note that a reduction in light output results.

Ballast Power Factor. The power factor is defined as the ratio of input wattage to the product of rms voltage and rms current. It represents the amount of current and voltage which the customer is actually using as a fraction of what the utility must supply. High power factor is defined as being above 90%. A lower-power-factor ballast draws more current from the power supply, and therefore, larger supply conductors can be necessary. Low-power-factor types are more common with compact fluorescent systems than for larger, standard fluorescent systems. Some public utilities have established penalty clauses in their rate schedule for low-power-factor installations. In some localities utilities require the use of equipment providing a high power factor.

Ballast Factor and Ballast Efficacy Factor. The *ballast factor* is defined by ANSI (ANSI C82.2—1984) as the relative luminous output of a lamp operated on the ballast with respect to the same lamp on a "reference ballast," usually expressed in percent. The reference ballasts are discussed in detail for each fluorescent lamp type in the applicable ANSI lamp standards. The *ballast efficacy factor* (BEF), in turn, is defined as the ballast factor in percent, divided by the total input power in watts. Federal regulation sets limits on the BEF of some ballasts for 4-ft and 8-ft fluorescent lamps, summarized in the table below:

	Voltage	Nominal lamp power (W)	Minimum BEF
One F40T12	120, 277	40	1.805
Two F40T12	120	80	1.060
	277	80	1.050
Two F96T12	120, 277	150	0.570
Two F96T12/HO	120, 277	220	0.390

In addition to the federal regulation, some states may impose additional restrictions on the above or on additional lamp types. Specifically excluded are dimming ballasts, ballasts intended for use in ambient temperatures of 0°F or lower and ballasts with power factor less than 90% that are designed for residential use (in buildings up to three stories). Moreover, some utility companies have specified a minimum BEF and ballast factor in their rebate programs for energy-effi-

cient equipment. They generally pertain to the same lamps as the federal regulation.

Harmonics. Line-current harmonics are those components of the line current that oscillate at low integer multiples of the fundamental frequency of the power supply. For instance, in North America, the fundamental frequency is 60 Hz, the second harmonic is 120 Hz, the third harmonic is 180 Hz, and so forth. Switching in modern solid-state electronic ballasts can cause substantial line-current harmonics when corrections are not implemented in the ballast. This can be especially harmful in three-phase installations if the third-harmonic current is large. The third harmonic and its multiples add in the neutral wire, while the fundamental currents tend to cancel one another there. If the third harmonic is 33.3% of the fundamental, then the total third harmonic in the neutral wire is equal to the fundamental in the hot wires. This can cause problems if the neutral wire is not properly sized.

For these reasons, regulations limit harmonic content in the line current, and these regulations are typically more stringent for fluorescent lamp-ballast systems than they are for incandescent systems. Internationally, the International Electrotechnical Commission (IEC) Standard 555-2 limits line-current harmonics in commercial and residential lighting. However, the exact limits have not been agreed upon at the time of this writing. In the United States, several utility companies have included harmonics as an issue in their rebate programs intended for customers who purchase energy-efficient equipment. They typically limit the total harmonic distortion (THD) caused by the equipment. THD is defined as the rms of all the harmonic components divided by the total fundamental current. In the case of fluorescent lamp ballasts, THD is typically limited to a maximum of 20–30%, depending on the utility company, with 20% THD being the most common limit.

Fluorescent Lampholders

Lampholders are designed for each lamp base style. Several versions of each are typically available, to allow various spacings and mounting methods in luminaires. See figure 6-45. It is important that proper spacing be maintained between lampholders in luminaires to ensure satisfactory electrical contact. Manufacturers' catalogs should be consulted for dimension and spacing information on any particular lampholder type.

When fluorescent lamps are used in circuits providing an open-circuit voltage in excess of 300 V, or in circuits which may permit a lamp to ionize and conduct current with only one end inserted in the lampholder, electrical codes usually require some automatic means

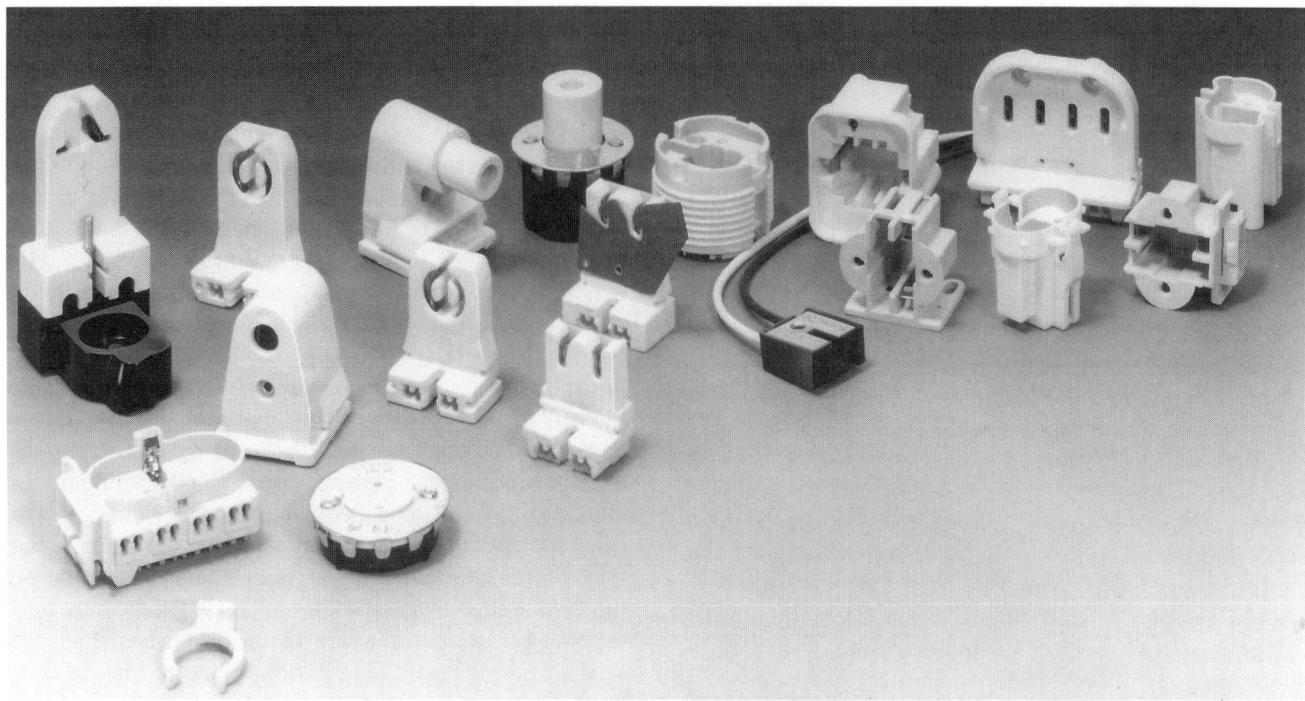

Fig. 6-45. Typical lampholder designs.

for deenergizing the circuit when the lamp is removed. This is usually accomplished by the lampholder so that upon lamp removal, the ballast primary circuit is opened. The use of recessed contact bases on 800- and 1500-mA fluorescent lamps has eliminated the need for this disconnect feature in lampholders for these lamps.

Lamp bases for compact fluorescent lamps are constructed with unique pin-and-keyway systems to prevent the wrong lamp from being installed. Lampholders should be designed to maintain the integrity of the system. Universal lampholders which allow lamps of any wattage to fit should be avoided.

Dimming of Fluorescent Lamps[48–50]

Many types of fluorescent lamps are suitable for dimming applications. It is also now economical to dim fluorescent lamps, particularly when it is possible to eliminate incandescent downlights as a result. Dimming fluorescent lamps differs from dimming incandescent lamps in two key ways. First, fluorescent dimmers do not provide dimming to zero light as do incandescent dimmers. However, commercially available products are available to dim as low as 0.5–25% of maximum luminous output. Second, when dimming fluorescent lamps, the color temperature does not vary substantially over the dimming range. This is quite unlike incandescent lamps, which tend to turn yellower when dimmed.

Dimming is achieved by reducing the effective lamp current. When doing so, it is necessary to supply the full starting voltage, and to maintain the restriking voltage necessary at each 60-Hz half cycle. This is especially true when operating the lamp at low luminous output. It is also necessary to provide filament heating for all except cold cathode lamps in order to maintain the required electron emissions from the hot cathode at all intensities.

The early magnetic dimming ballasts achieved dimming by lowering the primary voltage to the ballast transformer. Such a dimming system can be used with two-pin cold cathode fluorescent lamps in a series circuit as shown in figure 6-46a. With this arrangement, it is possible to reduce the luminous intensity to about 10% of rated light output. The performance of magnetic dimming ballasts can be improved by adding one or more of the following features: filament transformers to provide filament heat, pulse networks to provide the required restriking voltage at low intensities, and high-frequency keep-alive current to maintain the discharge when the line current is cut off during part of the 60-Hz cycle. These components can be packaged together with the magnetic ballast, or be separately installed in the luminaires as dimming adapters.

The vast majority of available fluorescent dimming ballasts are of the solid-state (electronic) type. They are designed to be used with four-pin, rapid-start and compact fluorescent lamps, and are available for several lamp diameters and lengths. Electronic dimming

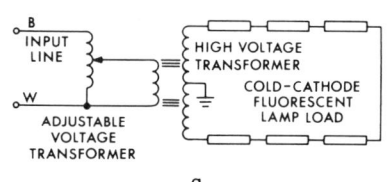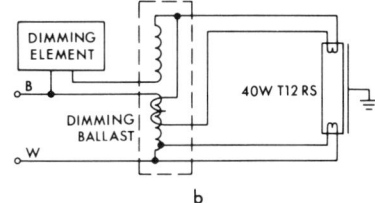

Fig. 6-46. Typical dimming circuits for: (a) series-connected cold-cathode lamps; (b) hot-cathode rapid-start lamps.

ballasts are generally more efficient and less bulky than their autotransformer predecessors. The useful dimming range is also comparable to that of the autotransformer type. Furthermore, lamp flicker can be substantially reduced when using electronic dimming ballasts. Finally, the tracking between lamps in a two-lamp fixture is often better when using electronic ballasts than with magnetic dimming ballasts. All electronic ballasts operate using high-frequency (typically 20–50 kHz) switching. The lamp or arc current is lowered by shortening the time that the current flows during each cycle.

Controls for the magnetic dimming ballasts are available in *two-wire* and *three-wire* configurations. The two-wire systems have a limited dimming range, typically about 25% light output at the low end, but can be retrofitted with existing wiring in most cases. The three-wire configurations bring a control wire to an external control, such as a wall station (see figure 6-45b). This flexibility allows for a substantial improvement in the dimming performance. For electronic dimming ballasts, there are several control schemes available. Some manufacturers use a three-wire scheme as described above, so that electronic dimming ballasts can directly replace magnetic dimming ballasts without affecting the control unit. Other three-wire implementations also require the control to be changed. Yet other manufacturers use four-wire systems where two of the wires are used for the dimming signal and the other two to carry the main lamp current.

Most electronic ballasts offer energy savings proportional to the reduction in light output (figure 6-47). This is particularly true at dimmer settings above 25–50% luminous output. Furthermore, four-pin construction allows cathode heating when dimming. This is important, since it extends lamp life and eliminates flicker when properly implemented. It is also advisable to select premium-quality knife-edge sockets rather than leaf-spring contacts. This ensures that cathode heating is reliably supplied. Finally, solid-state dimmers are substantially quieter than their magnetic predecessors.

The performance of a fluorescent dimming system may not be satisfactory if the lamp is not correctly matched with the dimming ballast and the controller.

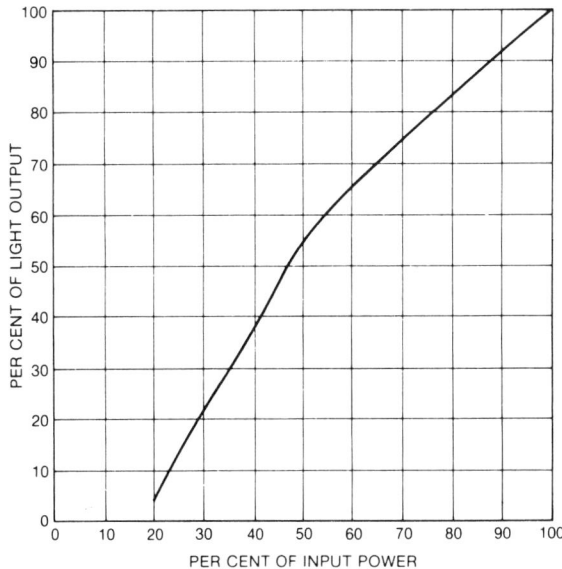

Fig. 6-47. Light output vs. input power for a typical 40-watt 120-volt rapid-start fluorescent dimming system.

In particular, reduced wattage, energy-saving, retrofit lamps should not be used in dimming systems, unless so recommended by the dimmer manufacturer. Doing so may shorten the life of the lamp and ballast.

Flashing of Fluorescent Lamps[51,52]

Cold cathode and rapid-start or preheat-start hot cathode fluorescent lamps can be flashed and still maintain good performance. Cold cathode lamps are flashed through control of either the transformer primary or secondary voltage. Hot cathode lamps can be flashed by means of a special single-lamp arc current while retaining cathode circuit voltage. An external flashing device is required with either system. This unit must be rated for the voltage and current involved, and it is recommended that separate contacts be used for each ballast to prevent circulating currents between ballasts. The single-lamp circuit is similar to the single-lamp dimming circuit shown in figure 6-46b, except that a flashing device is required in place of the dimming element. Flashing of fluorescent lamps has had application in electrical advertising.

HIGH-INTENSITY DISCHARGE LAMPS

High-intensity discharge (HID) lamps include the groups of lamps commonly known as mercury, metal halide and high-pressure sodium. The light-producing element of these lamp types is a wall-stabilized arc discharge contained within a refractory envelope (arc tube) with wall loading in excess of 3 W/cm^2.

Lamp Construction and Operation

Mercury Lamps.[53-57] In mercury lamps, light is produced by the passage of an electric current through mercury vapor. Since mercury has a low vapor pressure at room temperature, and even lower when it is cold, a small amount of more readily ionized argon gas is introduced to facilitate starting. The original arc is struck through the ionization of this argon. Once the arc strikes, its heat begins to vaporize the mercury, and this process continues until all of the mercury is evaporated. The amount of mercury in the lamp essentially determines the final operating pressure, which is 200–400 kPa (30–60 lb/in.^{2}) in the majority of lamps.

The operating electrodes used in mercury lamps are usually of the metal oxide type, in which the emission material, composed of several metallic oxides, is embedded within the turns of a tungsten coil protected by an outer tungsten coil. The electrodes are heated to the proper electron-emissive temperature by bombardment energy received from the arc.

Most mercury lamps are constructed with two envelopes: an inner envelope (arc tube) which contains the arc, and an outer envelope which (1) shields the arc tube from outside drafts and changes in temperature, (2) usually contains an inert gas (generally nitrogen) which prevents oxidation of internal parts and also increases the breakdown voltage across the outer bulb parts, (3) provides an inner surface for coating of phosphors, and (4) normally acts as a filter to remove certain wavelengths of arc radiation (UV-B and UV-C). In most cases the arc tube is made of fused silica with thin molybdenum ribbons sealed into the ends as current conductors. The outer bulb is usually made of "hard" (borosilicate) glass, but may also be of other glasses for special transmission or where thermal shock or pollution attack is not a problem.

The essential construction details shown in figure 6-48 are typical of lamps with fused silica inner arc tubes within an outer envelope. Other lamps, such as those for special photochemical application and self-ballasted types, have different constructions.

The pressure at which a mercury lamp operates accounts in large measure for its characteristic spectral power distribution. In general, higher operating pressure tends to shift a larger proportion of emitted radiation into longer wavelengths. At extremely high

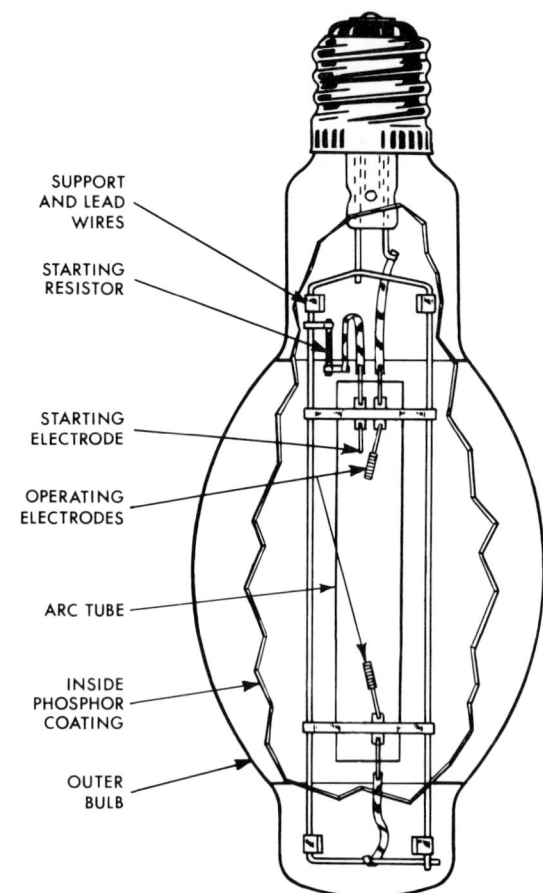

Fig. 6-48. A 400-watt phosphor-coated mercury lamp. Lamps of other sizes are constructed similarly.

pressure there is also a tendency to spread the line spectrum into wider bands. Within the visible region the mercury spectrum consists of five principal lines (404.7, 435.8, 546.1, 577 and 579 nm) which result in greenish-blue light at efficacies of 30 to 65 lm/W, excluding ballast losses. While the light source itself appears to be bluish-white, there is a deficiency of long-wavelength radiation, especially in low- and medium-pressure lamps, and most objects appear to have distorted colors. Blue, green and yellow are emphasized; orange and red appear brownish.

A significant portion of the energy radiated by the mercury arc is in the ultraviolet region. Through the use of phosphor coatings on the inside surface of the outer envelope, some of this ultraviolet energy is converted to visible light by the same mechanism employed in fluorescent lamps. The most widely used lamps of this type are coated with a vanadate phosphor (4000 K, designation DX) which emits long-wavelength radiation (orange-red); this improves efficacy and color rendering. This phosphor is also blended with others to produce "cooler" or "warmer" colors. Figure 6-23 shows the spectral distribution of a clear lamp and lamps using these phosphors. Special lamp types are also available for those applications where it is desirable to extinguish the arc if the outer bulb is punctured or broken; thereby potential exposure to ultraviolet energy and fire hazard are minimized.[58]

Metal Halide Lamps.[59-64] Metal halide lamps are very similar in construction to mercury lamps, the major difference being that the metal halide arc tube contains various metallic halides in addition to mercury and argon. When the lamp has attained full operating temperature, the metal halides in the arc tube are partially vaporized. When the halide vapors approach the high-temperature central core of the discharge, they are dissociated into the halogen and the metals, with the metals radiating their spectrum. As the halogen and metal atoms move near the cooler arc tube wall by diffusion and convection, they recombine, and the cycle begins again.

This cycle provides two advantages. First, some metals are vaporized at the temperatures attained, which are higher than those possible with a fused silica arc tube. These metals can be introduced into the discharge by dissociation of their halides, which vaporize at much lower temperatures. Secondly, some metals, which react chemically with the arc tube, can be used in the form of a halide which does not readily react with fused silica.

Compared with mercury lamps, the efficacy of metal halide lamps is greatly improved. Commercially available metal halide lamps have efficacies of 75–125 lm/W (excluding ballast losses). Almost all varieties of available "white"-light metal halide lamps produce color rendering which is as good as or superior to the presently available phosphor-coated mercury lamps.

The radiating metals introduced as halides in these lamps have characteristic emissions which are spectrally selective. Some metals principally produce visible radiation at a single wavelength, while others produce a multitude of discrete wavelengths. Still others provide a continuous spectrum of radiation. In order to obtain a complete balanced spectrum, blends of metal halides are used. Two typical combinations of halides used in these lamps are: (1) scandium and sodium iodides and, (2) dysprosium, holmium and thulium rare-earth (RE) iodides. Their spectral power distributions are shown in figure 6-23. Scandium is a multiple-line emitter and the REs are dense line emitters. Other metals, such as tin, when introduced as halides, radiate as molecules, producing a continuous band spectra across the visible spectrum. Color is balanced to obtain the desired correlated color temperature (CCT) by metal halide species selection and quantity. The scandium-sodium chemical system, for example, can be tuned over the CCT range of 2500–5000 K by varying the blend ratio and arc tube operating temperature. The RE system, on the other hand, has a characteristic CCT of about 5400 K, which, when augmented by the inclusion of sodium iodide, may be lowered to 4300 K. Recent developments indicate that a RE system augmented with cerium and sodium iodides achieves a CCT of 3000 K. The RE system provides a somewhat higher general color rendering index than the scandium-sodium system; however, recent developments show lithium iodide additions enhance the color rendering properties of the scandium-sodium chemistry. Selected colors can also be produced using the metal halide technique: sodium for orange, thallium for green, indium for blue and iron for UV. Luminous efficacy and lamp life tend to be greater for scandium-sodium lamps, but thallium can be used to improve the efficacy of RE lamps. These trade-offs should be considered in selecting a lamp type for each particular application. Metal halide lamps are also available with phosphors applied to the outer envelopes to further modify the color and generally to lower the color temperature of the lamp.

A close look at a metal halide lamp will reveal several construction features which differ from those of mercury lamps:

1. The arc tubes are usually smaller for equivalent wattage, and may be specially shaped, with a white coating at one or both ends of the arc tube. The end coating and small arc tube size serves to increase the temperature at the end of the arc tube to assure vaporization of the halides.
2. Some lamps include a system for either shorting the starting electrode to the operating electrode or opening the starting-electrode circuit. This is required to prevent electrolysis in the fused silica between the starting and operating electrodes, especially when a halide such as sodium iodide is used in the lamp. The type and location of the bimetal switch may or may not restrict the lamp burning position.
3. In some lamps the electrical connection to the electrode at the dome of the lamp is made by means of a small nonmagnetic wire remote from the tube. This is to prevent diffusion of sodium through the arc tube by electrolysis caused by a photoelectric effect when the current lead is close to the arc tube. Most metal halide lamps above 150 W require a higher open-circuit voltage to start than mercury lamps of corresponding wattage. Therefore, they require specifically designed ballasts. Certain metal halide lamp designs, however, can be operated on some types of mercury ballasts in retrofit situations.

In the metal halide lamp family special types are also available where the arc is automatically extinguished if the outer envelope is broken or punctured. They may be required in locations where exposure to UV radiation should be avoided.[58]

Low-wattage metal halide lamps[65-67] (below 175 W) come in many varieties for different applications, such as displays, recessed lighting and track lighting. They produce brilliant white light in a small arc capsule, enclosed in a small outer jacket. Current lamps include:

- Single-ended with medium bases (32–175 W)
- Single-ended with bipin bases (35–150 W)
- Double-ended with recessed single contact bases (70–150 W)

Some single-ended lamps have a transparent sleeve surrounding the arc capsule, which serves as a heat shield to achieve uniform capsule temperatures and retard sodium loss, thereby improving color uniformity and stability over life. Some lamp designs use heavier sleeves and jackets to capture any arc tube fragments in the event of capsule rupture.

Some metal halide lamps must be operated only in fixtures which provide suitable enclosures designed to contain any hot quartz fragments that might result from an arc tube rupture. In addition, there are metal halide lamps which do not have an outer jacket. These lamps must be operated only in fixtures which provide proper UV filtering.

High-Pressure Sodium Lamps.[68] In high-pressure sodium lamps, light is produced by electric current passing through sodium vapor. These lamps are constructed with two envelopes, the inner arc tube being polycrystalline alumina, which is resistant to sodium attack at high temperatures and has a high melting point. Although translucent, this material provides good light transmission (more than 90%). The construction of a typical high-pressure sodium lamp is shown in figure 6-49.

Polycrystalline alumina cannot be fused to metal by melting the alumina without causing the material to crack. Therefore, an intermediate seal is used. Either solder glass or metal can be used. These materials adhere to both the alumina and the niobium, and are sufficiently impervious to high-temperature sodium. Ceramic plugs can also be used to form the intermediate seal. The arc tube contains xenon as a starting gas, and a small quantity of sodium-mercury amalgam which is partially vaporized when the lamp attains operating temperature. The mercury acts as a buffer gas to raise the gas pressure and operating voltage of the lamp.

The outer borosilicate glass envelope is evacuated and serves to prevent chemical attack of the arc tube metal parts as well as maintaining the arc tube temper-

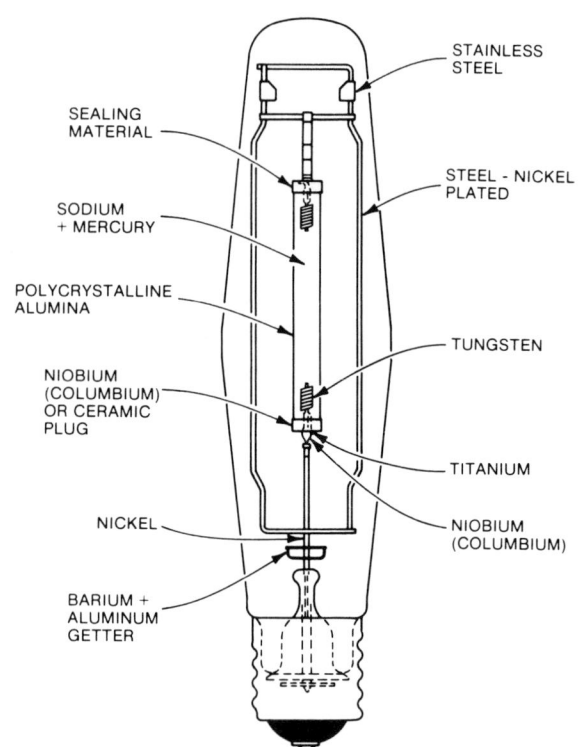

Fig. 6-49. Construction of a typical high pressure sodium lamp.

ature by isolating it from ambient temperature effects and drafts.

Most high-pressure sodium lamps can operate in any position. The burning position has no significant effect on light output. Lamp types are also available with diffuse coatings on the inside of the outer bulb to increase source luminous size or reduce source luminance, if required.

High-pressure sodium lamps radiate energy across the visible spectrum. This is in contrast to low-pressure sodium lamps, which radiate principally the doublet D lines of sodium at 589 nm. Standard high-pressure sodium lamps, with sodium pressures in the 5–10-kPa (40–70-Torr) range, typically exhibit color temperatures of 1900–2200 K and have a CRI of about 22. At higher sodium pressures, above about 27 kPa (200 Torr), sodium radiation of the D line is self-absorbed by the gas and is radiated as a continuum spectrum on both sides of the D line. This results in the "dark" region at 589 nm as shown in the typical spectrum in figure 6-23. Increasing the sodium pressure particularly increases the percentage of long-wavelength radiation and thus improves the CRI to at least 65 at somewhat higher color temperatures; however, life and efficacy are reduced. "White" high-pressure sodium lamps have been developed with correlated color temperatures of 2700–2800 K and a CRI between 70 and 80. Higher-frequency operation is one method of providing "white" light at reduced sodium pressure. High-pressure sodium lamps have efficacies of 45–150 lm/W, depending on the lamp wattage and desired color rendering properties.

Because of the small diameter of a high-pressure sodium lamp arc tube, no starting electrode is included as in the mercury lamp. Instead, a high-voltage, high-frequency pulse is provided by an ignitor to start these lamps. Some special high-pressure sodium lamps use a specific starting-gas mixture (a combination of argon and neon which requires a lower starting voltage than either gas alone) and a starting aid inside the outer bulb. These lamps will start and operate on many mercury lamp ballasts. Consult the lamp manufacturers' literature for suitable ballast types. These lamps are useful retrofit devices to upgrade mercury lamp systems, but are not as efficient as the standard combination of high-pressure sodium lamp and ballast.

Lamp Designations

The current identifying designations of high-intensity discharge lamps generally follow a system which is authorized and administered by the American National Standards Institute (ANSI). All designations start with a letter (H for mercury, M for metal halide, S for high-pressure sodium). This is followed by an ANSI assigned number which identifies the electrical characteristics of the lamp and consequently the ballast. After the number there are two arbitrary letters which identify the size, shape and finish of the bulb, but not its color. After this sequence, the manufacturer may add special letters or numbers to indicate information not covered by the standard sequence of the designation, such as lamp wattage or color.

Lamp Starting

Mercury Lamps. Some special two-electrode mercury lamps, and many photochemical types, require a high open-circuit voltage to ionize the argon gas and permit the arc to strike. In the more common three-electrode lamps an auxiliary starting electrode placed close to one of the main electrodes makes it possible to start the lamp at a lower voltage. Here an electric field is first set up between the starting electrode, which is connected to the opposite main electrode through a current limiting resistor, and the adjacent main electrode. This causes an emission of electrons, which develops a local glow discharge and ionizes the starting gas. The arc then starts between the main electrodes. The mercury gradually becomes vaporized from the heat of the arc and carries an increasing portion of the current. During this process the arc stream changes from the diffuse bluish glow characteristic of the argon arc to the blue-green of mercury, increasing greatly in luminance and becoming concentrated along the axis of the tube. At the instant the arc strikes, the lamp voltage is low. Normal operating values are reached

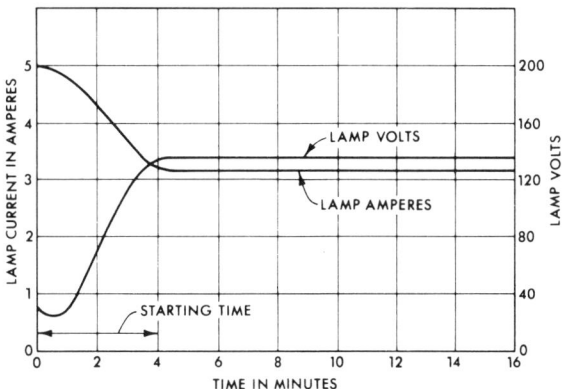

Fig. 6-50. Warm-up characteristics for 400-watt mercury lamp on a lag type ballast. This is typical of most mercury lamp types.

after a warmup period of several minutes, during which the voltage rises until the arc attains a stabilization vapor pressure; the mercury is then entirely evaporated (see figure 6-50).

If the arc is extinguished, the lamp will not relight until it is cooled sufficiently to lower the vapor pressure to a point where the arc will restrike with the voltage available. The time from initial starting to full light output at ordinary room temperatures, with no enclosing lighting unit, and also the restriking time (the cooling time required before the lamp will restart), vary between 3 and 7 min, depending upon the lamp type.

Metal Halide Lamps. The method of starting most metal halide lamps above 150 W is the same as for mercury lamps. However, because of the presence of the halide, the starting voltage required for some types is higher than for mercury lamps. Due to the extremely small physical size of their arc tubes, metal halide lamps below 175 W do not contain starting electrodes. These lamps require ballasting circuits which include an electronic starting device generating high-voltage pulses to start the lamp. As the lamp warms up, it may go through several color changes as the various halides begin to vaporize, until it reaches its equilibrium color and electrical characteristics after 2–10 min, depending on the lamp type.

Since a metal halide arc tube operates at higher temperatures than a mercury lamp arc tube, the time to cool and lower the vapor pressure is generally longer than for the mercury lamp; consequently the restrike time may be as long as 15 min.

High-Pressure Sodium Lamps. Since the high-pressure sodium lamp does not contain a starting electrode, a high-voltage, high-frequency pulse is used to ionize the xenon starting gas. Once started, the lamp warms up to full light output in approximately 10 min, during which time the color changes.

Because the operating pressure of a high-pressure sodium lamp is lower than that of a mercury lamp, the restrike time is shorter. It will usually restrike in less than 1 min and warm up in 3–4 min.

Lamp Operating Position

Mercury Lamps. When a mercury lamp is operated horizontally, the arc tends to bow upward because of the convection currents in the gas. This bowing will generally cause a small change in the electrical characteristics of the lamp as well as a small reduction of lamp output due to a reduction in lamp wattage and efficacy. Many ballasts designed for horizontally operating lamps compensate for this wattage decrease by increasing the current through the lamp, but do not compensate for the loss in efficacy.

Metal Halide Lamps. When a metal halide lamp is operated horizontally, the arc also bows upward, but the effect of a change of operating position can be much greater than in the case of the mercury lamp, especially with regard to color. Because a portion of the halides in metal halide lamps is not vaporized during lamp operation, any change in the cold-spot temperature of the lamp will change the pressure of the halide and therefore the lamp color. Generally, the color temperature of these lamps may vary with operating position. When the burning position of a metal halide lamp is changed, as much as six hours may be required before the lamp characteristics, color, electrical characteristics and efficacy are stabilized. Some lamps have restricted burning positions. These should be observed if optimum performance is to be obtained.

Special shapes of arc tubes are used in certain lamps to increase initial lumens in specific burning positions. These include an arc tube designed for horizontal operation and curved to compensate for the tendency of the arc to rise toward the tube wall in the middle.

High-Pressure Sodium Lamps. High-pressure sodium lamps, since they have small arc tube diameters and so permit only a very small arc bow, exhibit very little change in efficacy or electrical characteristics when operated in a horizontal compared to a vertical position.

Lamp Life and Lumen Maintenance

According to IES testing procedure LM-47, the *average rated lamp life* is defined as that time after which 50% of a large group of lamps are still in operation. The procedure prescribes burning cycles of 11 h on, 1 h off, when doing HID lamp life testing. For certain lamp types and applications, criteria other than failure to light may be considered, such as cycling, drastic color change or significant reduction in lumen output.

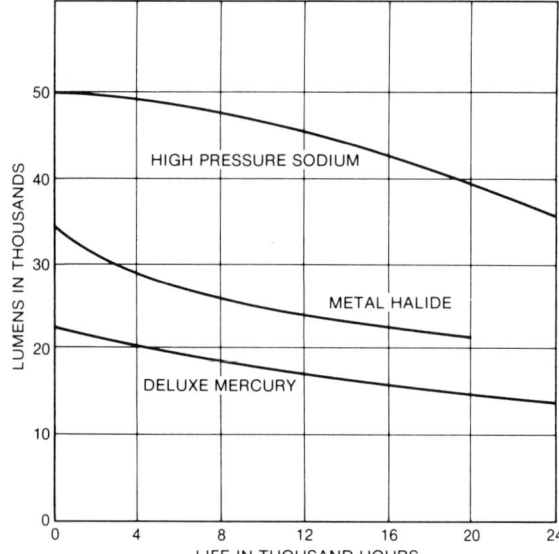

Fig. 6-51. Typical lumen maintenance curves for 400-watt high intensity discharge lamps.

HID lamps are usually rated for "initial" lumens after 100 h of burning. Initial lumens for the various lamp types are given in figure 6-122. Figure 6-51 illustrates a typical lumen maintenance curve.

Mercury Lamps. General-service mercury lamps have a long average rated life. These lamps usually employ an electrode with a mixture of metal oxides embedded in the turns of tungsten coils from which the electrode is assembled. During the life of the lamp, this emission material is very slowly evaporated, or *sputtered*, from the electrode and is deposited on the inner surface of the arc tube. This process results first in a white deposit on the inner surface of the arc tube, eventually in a blackening of the arc tube, and ultimately in the exhaustion of the emission material in the electrodes and the end of lamp life, when the starting voltage exceeds the open-circuit voltage.

Metal Halide Lamps. Chemical reaction between the iodine in a metal halide lamp and the emission materials included in mercury lamp electrodes prevents the use of mercury electrodes in a metal halide lamp. Because the electrodes used with metal halide lamps evaporate more rapidly than mercury lamp electrodes, they generally have shorter life ratings. In addition, some metal halide lamps typically experience strong color changes toward the end of normal life. In applications where the color appearance of the lamps is critical, the useful life of the lamps ends when the color shift becomes objectionable. Life and lumen maintenance are affected by changes in the burning cycle.

High-Pressure Sodium Lamps. High-pressure sodium lamps employ electrodes very similar to those used in mercury lamps. This fact, combined with the smaller diameter of the arc tube, gives high-pressure sodium lamps excellent lumen maintenance.

The life of a high-pressure sodium lamp is limited by a slow rise in operating voltage which occurs over the life of the lamp. This rise is principally caused by arc tube end blackening from electrode sputtering. The blackening absorbs radiation, which heats up the arc tube ends and vaporizes additional sodium amalgam. This increases the arc tube pressure and consequently the arc voltage. Other reasons for arc tube voltage rise are the diffusion of sodium through the arc tube end seals and the removal of sodium from the arc stream by combination with impurities in the arc tube.

When the ballast can no longer supply enough voltage to reignite the arc during each electrical half-cycle, the lamp will extinguish. When it cools down, the lamp will again ignite and warm up until the arc voltage rises so that the ballast cannot support the arc. This cycling process will occur until the lamp is removed.

Life ratings for high-pressure sodium lamps are up to 24,000 h, depending upon lamp design.

Effect of Ambient Temperature

The light output of the typical double-envelope HID arc tube is little affected by the ambient temperature. Experience has shown that these lamps are satisfactory for temperatures down to $-29°C$ ($-20°F$) or lower. On the other hand, single-envelope lamps, intended primarily for use as UV sources, are critically affected by low temperatures, particularly if the surrounding air is moving. They are not considered suitable for use below $0°C$ ($32°F$) without special protection, since they may not warm up to full output. Ambient temperature affects the striking voltage of all discharge lamps, and in some cases higher starting voltages than those listed in figure 6-123 for indoor use are recommended for roadway and floodlighting installations in cold climates. Ballasts for roadway lighting service and other low-temperature applications are designed to provide the necessary voltage to start and operate each particular lamp at temperatures as low as $-29°C$ ($-20°F$). Recommendations for starting voltages have been developed by ANSI.

Lamp Operating Temperature

Excessive envelope and base temperatures may cause failures or unsatisfactory performance due to softening of the glass, damage to the arc tube by moisture driven out of the outer envelope, softening of the basing cement or solder, or corrosion of the base, socket or lead-in wires. Maximum bulb and base temperatures are prescribed by various standards associations. The use of reflecting equipment which concentrates heat and energy on either the inner arc tube or the outer envelope should be avoided.

In the case of metal halide and high-pressure sodium lamps in which all the material is not vaporized, concentrated heat on the arc tube can materially affect their color as well as their electrical characteristics and shorten lamp life.

Auxiliary Equipment

HID lamps have negative volt-ampere characteristics, and therefore some current-limiting device, usually in the form of a transformer and reactor ballast, must be provided to prevent excessive lamp and line currents. The lamps are operated on either multiple or series circuits. Figure 6-52 gives schematic diagrams of several typical ballast types.

A distinction must be made between *lag circuit* and *lead circuit* ballasts. The lamp current control element of a lag circuit ballast consists of an inductive reactance in series with the lamp. The current control element in lead circuit ballasts consists of both inductive and capacitive reactances in series with the lamp; however, the net reactance of such a circuit is capacitive in mercury and metal halide ballasts, and inductive in high-pressure sodium ballasts.

Mercury Lamps. There are a number of lamp ballasts in use for operating mercury lamps. Wattage losses in ballasts are usually in the order of 5–15% of lamp wattage, depending upon ballast and lamp type.

Lag Reactor. The simplest lag circuit ballast is a reactor consisting of a single coil wound on an iron core placed in series with the lamp. The only function of the reactor is to limit the current delivered to the lamp. Such a reactor can only be used when the line voltage is within the specified lamp starting voltage range. Inherently the power factor of this circuit is about 50% lagging; this is commonly referred to as normal or low power factor. The line current under starting conditions is approximately 50% higher than normal operating current; therefore, it is recommended that supply wiring be sized for approximately twice the normal operating current.

High-power-factor versions are available where a capacitor is installed in the circuit to increase the power factor of the system to better than 90%. This is generally the preferred system, since it also reduces the input current under starting and operating conditions almost 50% below that of the low-power-factor system, allowing full utilization of the circuit.

Since a lag reactor performs only the function of current control, it is the most economical, smallest and most efficient ballast. However, it has shortcomings which should be considered in application. The reactor provides little regulation for fluctuations in line voltage; for example, a 3% change in line voltage will cause a 6% change in lamp wattage. Therefore, the

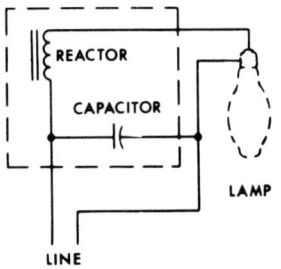

(a) High power factor reactor mercury lamp ballast

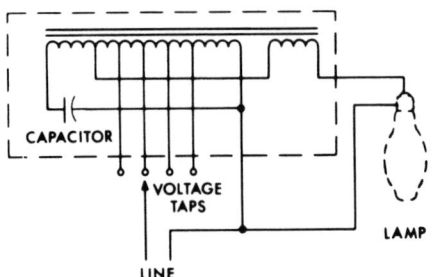

(b) High power factor autotransformer mercury lamp ballast

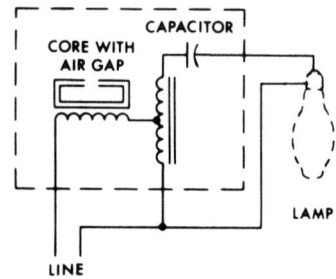

(c) Constant wattage autotransformer ballast for mercury lamps or peak-lead ballast for metal halide lamps

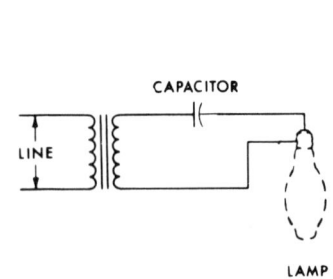

(d) Constant wattage (isolated circuit) ballast for mercury lamps

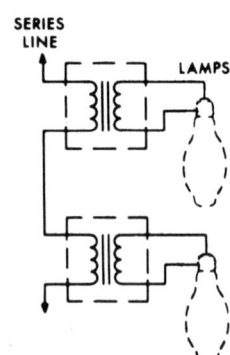

(e) Constant current series regulator ballast for mercury lamps

Fig. 6-52. Typical circuits for operating high intensity discharge lamps.

reactor is not recommended where line fluctuations exceed 5%.

High-Reactance Autotransformer. Where the line voltage is below or above the specified lamp starting voltage range, a transformer is used in conjunction with the reactor to provide proper starting voltage. This is normally accomplished with the combination of primary and secondary coils forming a one-piece single high-reactance autotransformer. The power factor of this circuit is about 50% lagging and has the same advantages and shortcomings as the normal power factor of a reactor lag circuit. High-power-factor versions are available in which a capacitor is installed in the circuit to increase the power factor of the system to better than 90%. The effect on input current is the same as in the high-power-factor reactor. Regulation and lamp performance are unchanged.

Constant-Wattage Autotransformer (CWA). This type of lead circuit ballast is the most widely used in modern mercury lighting systems. It consists of a high-reactance autotransformer with a capacitor in series with the lamp. Use of the capacitor allows the lamp to operate with better wattage stability when the voltage on the branch circuit fluctuates. This ballast is used when line voltage is expected to vary by more than 5%. For example, a 10% change in line voltage would result in only a 5% change in lamp wattage. Other advantages with the CWA ballast are high power factor, low line extinguishing voltage, and line starting currents that are lower than normal line currents. The CWA ballasts allow for maximum loading on branch circuits and provide an economical and efficient mercury lighting system.

The capacitor used with the CWA ballast performs an important ballasting function, as in all lead-type circuits. The capacitor used in lag-type high-power-factor reactor and high-power-factor autotransformer ballasts is purely a power factor correction component and has no ballasting function.

Constant Wattage (CW). This type of ballast, also referred to as regulated or stabilized, has operating characteristics similar to the CWA. The light output and wattage will vary less than 2% with up to a 13% change in line voltage. The CW ballast, like the CWA ballast, uses a lead circuit; it differs in that the lamp circuit is completely isolated from the primary winding. It also has the same advantages as the CWA ballast, such as high power factor, low line extinguishing voltage and low line starting currents.

Two-Lamp Lead-Lag Circuit. The lead-lag ballast design approach is commonly used to operate two 250-, 400-, or 1000-W mercury or metal halide lamps in two independent circuits. A current-limiting reactor operates one lamp, and a combination reactor and capacitor connected in series operates the second. The lamps operate independently, so that a failure of one has no effect on the other. The input current of the combination of capacitors and reactors is lower than the sum of the two individual operating currents. These elements provide a high power factor and reduce the stroboscopic effect. This circuit can only be used when the line voltage is within the specified lamp starting voltage range. It is the most economical two-lamp system with regulation similar to the normal-power-factor reactor and autotransformer ballasts. A lag reactor may be used in one luminaire and a lead reactor in the next luminaire. An equal number of each in a branch circuit will result in a high branch circuit power factor.

Two-Lamp Series (Isolated) Constant Wattage. This circuit is essentially the same as single-lamp constant wattage, except that it operates two lamps in series. The most effective use of this circuit is in applications where the ambient temperature is −18°C (0°F) or above. It is most popular for indoor 400-W applications.

Constant-Current Series Regulators. Mercury lamps are also operated in series on constant-current series regulators. The most commonly used method employs a current transformer for each lamp (figure 6-52e). It differs in design from the more common multiple type of ballast. The usual design is a two-winding transformer as illustrated in figure 6-52e. Since the series circuit regulator reactance limits the current in the circuit, the individual lamp current transformer is not designed to limit current, but rather to transform it from the regulator secondary current to the rated lamp current. In addition, the transformer is made to limit the secondary open-circuit voltage so that no cutout is necessary in case of a lamp failure. Series transformers are available for the more popular lamps to operate from either 6.6-, 7.5- or 20-A series circuits and can be operated on all types of constant-current transformers. These circuits will normally be satisfactory for metal halide lamps and high-pressure sodium lamps designed for operation on reactor-type mercury ballasts.

Two-Level Mercury Ballasts. Two-level operation of mercury lamps can be accomplished by switching capacitors on lead circuit ballasts. Such ballasts are available which will operate 125-, 250- and 400-W mercury lamps at two levels. For example, a 400-W mercury lamp may be operated at either 400 or 300 W by switching leads at the ballast. These two-level mercury ballasts are used for energy saving. Similar designs are available for high-pressure sodium and metal halide lamps. Both lamp manufacturer and ballast manufacturer should be contacted for specific information.

This control technique is presently limited to horizontal operation above 10°C (50°F), and the warmup time is 50% longer on low level.

Metal Halide Lamps. To ensure proper starting and operating, a lead-peaked autotransformer ballast circuit specially designed to accommodate all commercially available metal halide lamps above 150 W is normally used. The regulation of such a ballast is reasonably good, yielding a change in lamp wattage of 7–10% for a line voltage change of 10%. Aside from regulation, the lead-peaked autotransformer ballast performs much like the CWA ballast, having similar operating features. Standard mercury lamps may be operated on this ballast. Certain metal halide lamp types can be operated on mercury-lamp-type ballasts. For operation under these conditions manufacturers' instructions should be consulted.

Metal halide lamps below 175 W are commonly operated on a lag-reactor or high-reactance autotransformer ballast. Power-factor-correcting capacitors are typically employed. The lamp wattage regulation with respect to line voltage variation is poor. A 5% change in line voltage can result in a 12% change in lamp wattage. Long-term operation of lamps under "high-line" conditions will shorten the life of the lamps. For starting, a separate electronic circuit providing high-frequency pulses between 3 and 5 kV is required. These circuits normally use a winding of the ballast as the starter's pulse transformer.

High-Pressure Sodium Lamps. Unlike mercury and metal halide lamps, which exhibit relatively constant lamp voltage with changes in lamp wattage, the high-pressure sodium lamp has a voltage that varies with the lamp wattage. Operating parameters for maximum and minimum permissible lamp wattage and voltage have therefore been established. Figure 6-53 shows the lamp voltage and wattage limits for 400-W high-pressure sodium lamps. These limits form a trapezoid in the voltage-wattage coordinate system. Four basic circuits have evolved which are designed to operate the lamps within the trapezoid. In order to initiate the arc, an electronic starting circuit provides a pulse voltage which generates approximately 4000 V peak for a 1000-W lamp, and 2500 V peak for the other wattages, at least once per 60-Hz cycle until the lamp is started.

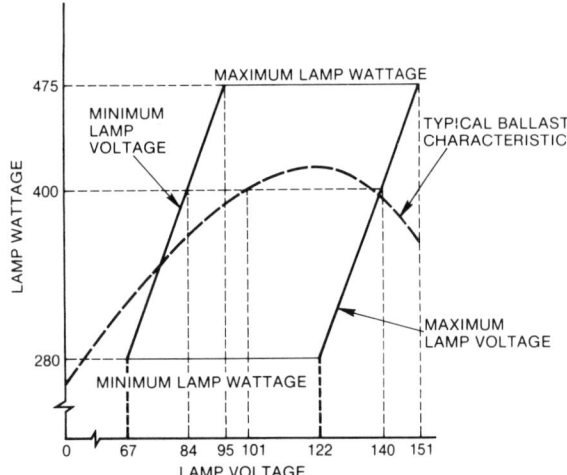

Fig. 6-53. Wattage and voltage limits for 400-watt high pressure sodium lamps.

Lag or Reactor Ballast. This ballast type is similar to the mercury lamp reactor ballast. It is a simple reactor in series with the lamp, designed to keep the operating characteristics within the trapezoid. A starting circuit is incorporated to provide the starting pulse. Step-up or step-down transformers are provided where necessary to match the line voltage. In most cases, a power-factor-correcting capacitor is placed across the line or across a capacitor winding on the ballast primary. This type of ballast usually provides good wattage regulation for variations in lamp voltage, but rather poor regulation for variations in line voltage. It is the least costly ballast with the lowest power loss among ballasts for high-pressure sodium lamps.

Magnetic Regulator or Constant-Wattage Ballast. This ballast consists essentially of a voltage-regulating section which feeds a current-limiting reactor and the pulse starting circuit. It provides good wattage regulation for changes in line voltage, as a result of the voltage-regulating section, and good regulation for changes in lamp voltage, which is the main characteristic of the reactor ballast.

It is a high-cost ballast, having the greatest power losses, but it generally provides good wattage regulation under all conditions of line and lamp voltage. A power-factor-correcting capacitor is usually included. It should be noted that this circuit differs from constant-wattage mercury ballast circuits.

Lead Circuit Ballast. This circuit is similar in circuit configuration to the CWA mercury-lamp ballast. It operates with a combination of inductance and capacitance in series with the lamp. It differs in design from the CWA mercury-lamp ballast in that rather than maintaining a constant current through the lamp, it decreases the current as the lamp voltage increases so as to keep the lamp operating wattage within the

trapezoid limits. This ballast type provides wattage regulation for changes in both line voltage and lamp wattage. For a change of no greater than 10% in line voltage it maintains the lamp wattage within the trapezoid. It is intermediate in cost and power losses.

Ignitors. Ignitors are used in the ballast circuit for most high-pressure sodium lamps, some metal halide lamps and some specialty arc lamps. The ignitor starts cold lamps by first providing a high enough voltage for ionization of the gas to produce a glow discharge. To complete the starting process, enough power must then be provided by the starting pulses to sustain an arc through a glow-to-arc transition. The range of pulse voltages to start cold lamps is 1–5 kV, usually provided by an electronic resonant circuit which applies multiple pulses to the lamp when the circuit is energized. The circuit turns itself off after the lamp starts by sensing the reduction in open-circuit voltage or, with some ignitors, after a fixed period of time.

Instant restarting of hot lamps is accomplished by increased ignition voltage. Voltage pulses of 10–70 kV are required by the range of available HID lamps, and these are again provided by resonant circuits. To reduce the voltage to ground to half these values, ignitor circuits are available to apply opposing pulses simultaneously to the ends of the lamp. Most instant restart lamps are of double-ended construction to minimize arc-over between lead wires, internal supports or base contacts. These high-voltage starting pulses are normally applied in one or several short bursts, using the open-circuit voltage reduction upon restart to turn off the ignitor.

Dimming of High-Intensity Discharge Lamps

Although HID lamps are optimized to operate at full power, some energy savings can be obtained through dimming.

In energy management applications, savings of 50% or more can be obtained where available daylight is used with a photosensor and dimming control system. Daylight also will tend to compensate for the color changes of HID lamps at low lumen output. Additional controls for HID lighting can be employed for lumen maintenance and with time-of-day and demand reduction programs as administered by a computer or a simple time clock. Simple manual control for an HID dimming system can provide flexibility in multipurpose room applications and improved efficiency by tuning the light output for a specific task. The possible energy savings are summarized in figure 6-54.

Some light sources are more suitable for dimming than others. Therefore, when considering a particular HID light source for dimming, it is suggested that the manufacturers of the lamp and the dimming system be

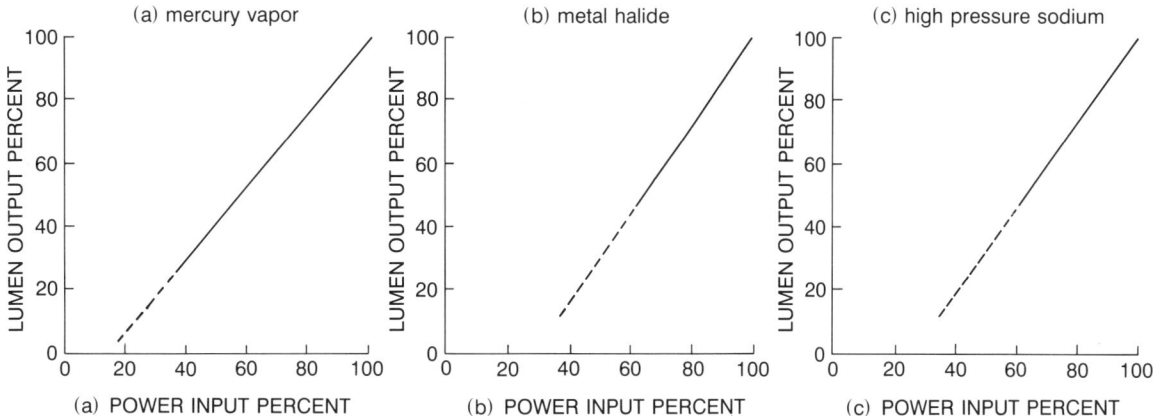

Fig. 6-54. Lumen output vs power input for high intensity discharge lamps: (a) mercury vapor, (b) metal halide, and (c) high pressure sodium. The dotted lines represent significant color changes in the lamp.

contacted to confirm that the source can be dimmed and for information or performance characteristics in the dimmed state. In some cases, the lamp manufacturer's warranty may be limited when dimming. In a properly designed dimming system, however, the lamp life may be equal to that of undimmed lamps.

The slow warmup and hot restrike delay which are characteristic of HID sources also apply to dimming. HID lamps respond to changes in dimmer settings much more slowly than incandescent or fluorescent sources, and typical times required to vary between minimum and maximum light output are about 3–10 min. However, instantaneous dimming can be obtained, over a limited range, for some types of lamps.

For HID lamps, it is recommended that the lamps be started at full power and the dimming be delayed until the lamp is fully warmed up. A properly designed dimming system will make sure this occurs.

In addition to speed, the range of response is not comparable to that of incandescent or fluorescent dimming; however, in most cases the lamp efficacy and color are reasonably good down to 50% lumen output or less. These characteristics are not well suited to dramatic lighting or theatrical effects, but are quite satisfactory for many energy management applications. In energy management applications, the slow response of HID lamps provides additional system stability and minimal occupant distraction.

Characteristic curves of lumen output versus input power are shown in figure 6-54. These curves describe general trends; the dimmer system manufacturer should be consulted for more specific details.

Clear mercury lamps change very little in color from 100 to 25% lumen output; the blue-green color which is characteristic of clear mercury sources is present at all dimmer settings. Color-improved mercury lamps will generally perform well down to about 30% lumen output.

The color appearance, color consistency from lamp to lamp and color rendering of some clear, low-wattage metal halide lamps can begin to change at 80% lumen output. For higher wattages, the color of the clear lamps begins to change at about 60% lumen output, where a blue-green color (characteristic of mercury vapor) starts to appear. The effect will be somewhat less with phosphor-coated lamps.

The color appearance of typical high-pressure sodium lamps does not appreciably change until about 50% lumen output. Below 50%, a strong yellow color, characteristic of low-pressure sodium, begins to prevail. In the case of the higher-color-rendering high-pressure lamps, the lamp manufacturer should be consulted as to dimming performance.

Self-Ballasted Lamps

Self-ballasted mercury lamps are available in various wattages. These lamps have a mercury vapor arc tube in series with a current-limiting tungsten filament. In some types, phosphors coated on the outer envelope are used to provide additional color improvement. The overall efficacy is lower than that of other mercury lamps because of the resistive losses of the tungsten filament. As the name denotes, these lamps do not require an auxiliary ballast as do standard mercury lamps. Typical self-ballasted mercury lamps are shown in figure 6-123.

SHORT-ARC LAMPS

Short-arc, or compact-arc, lamps characteristically provide a source of very high luminance. They are primarily used in searchlights, projectors, display systems and optical instruments (such as spectrophotometers and recording instruments) and for simulation of solar radi-

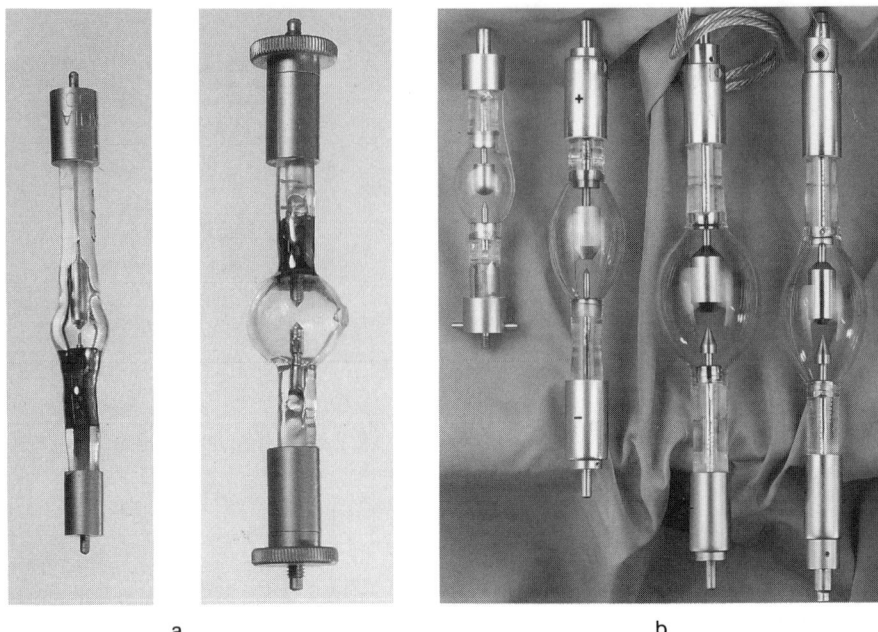

a   b

Fig. 6-55. Typical short-arc lamps. (a) Low wattage mercury-argon lamps (100-watt at left, 200-watt at right). (b) Medium wattage xenon lamps. From left: 1.6; 2.2; 4.2; 3.0-kilowatt.

ation. They also can be used as sources of modulated light, generated through current modulation.

Short-arc lamps are high-pressure gas discharge lamps characterized by an electrode-stabilized arc which is short compared with the diameter of the envelope. Depending on rated wattage and intended application, their arc length may be from about 0.3 to 12 mm. These arcs have the highest luminance and radiance of any continuously operating light source and are the closest to being a true point source.[72-85]

Some typical short-arc lamps are shown in figures 6-55 and 6-56. These lamps have optically clear fused

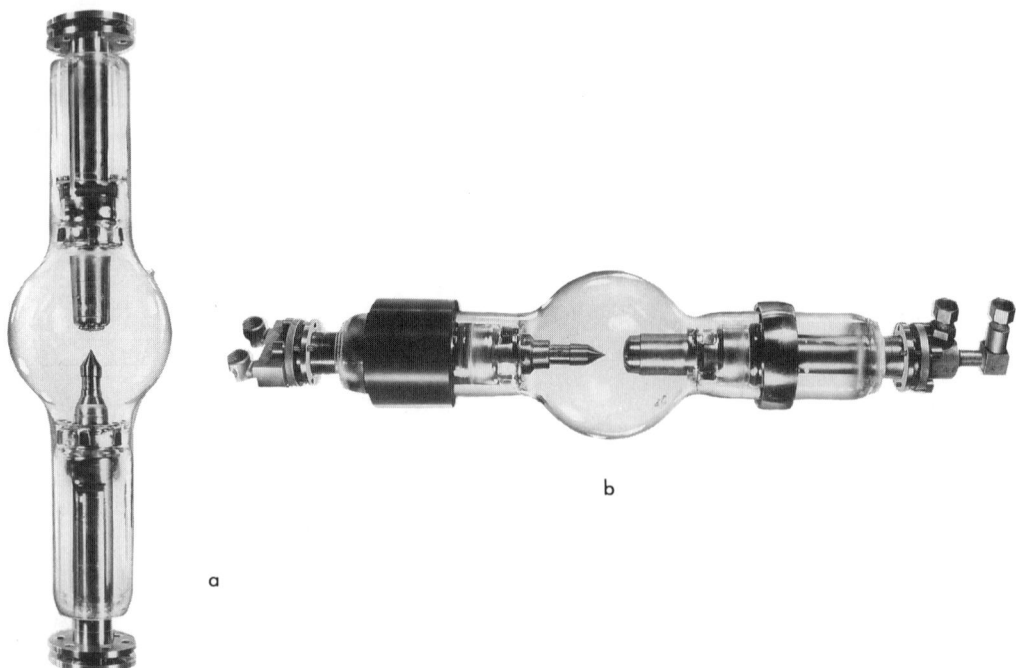

b

a

Fig. 6-56. Typical high power xenon compact arc lamps with liquid-cooled electrodes. (a) 30-kilowatt lamp for solar simulators (principal operating position is vertical) and (b) 20-killowatt lamp for military searchlights (principal operating position is horizontal).

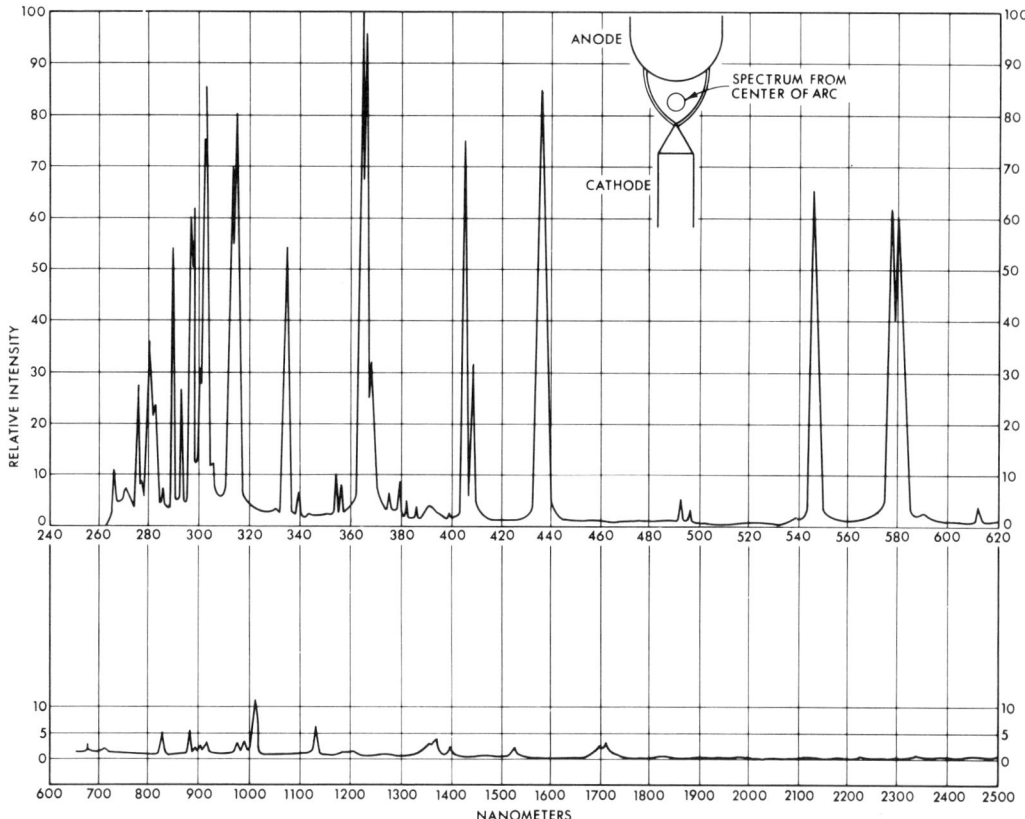

Fig. 6-57. Spectral power distribution of a 2.5 kW mercury-xenon lamp.

silica (fused quartz) bulbs of spherical or ellipsoidal shape with two diametrically opposite seals. Four types of seals are used in short-arc lamps. The graded seal and the molybdenum foil seal are current-carrying seals, while the molybdenum-and-Kovar cup seal and the elastomer (mechanical) seal are separated from the current conductor by a cup or a flange.

Most short-arc lamps are designed for dc operation. The better arc stability and substantially longer life of the dc lamps have limited the use of ac short-arc lamps to special applications.

For applications requiring ozone-free operation, the lamp envelopes are fabricated from quartz, which does not transmit wavelengths below 210 nm.

Mercury and Mercury-Xenon Lamps[72, 73, 75, 79]

To facilitate lamp starting, short-arc mercury lamps contain argon or another rare gas at a pressure of several kilopascals (10–30 Torr), the same as standard mercury lamps. After the initial arc is struck, the lamp gradually warms up, and the voltage increases and stabilizes as the mercury is completely vaporized. A mercury lamp requires several minutes to warm up to full operating pressure and light output. This warmup time is reduced by about 50% if xenon at greater than atmospheric pressure is added to the mercury. Lamps with this type of filling are known as mercury-xenon

short-arc or compact-arc lamps. The spectral power distribution in the visible region is essentially the same for both types, consisting mainly of the five mercury lines and some continuum due to the high operating pressure. The luminous efficacy for these lamps is approximately 50 lm/W at 1000 W and about 55 lm/W at 5000 W.

Mercury and mercury-xenon lamps are available for wattages from 30 to 7000 W and are to be primarily operated in a vertical position. The spectrum of a typical mercury xenon lamp is shown in figure 6-57.

Xenon Lamps[74, 77–85]

Xenon short-arc lamps are filled with several atmospheres of xenon gas. They reach 80% of the final output immediately after the start. The arc color very closely approximates daylight (correlated color temperature of approximately 5000 K). The spectrum is continuous from the UV through the visible into the infrared. Xenon lamps also exhibit strong emission lines in the near infrared between 800 and 1000 nm and some weak lines in the short-wavelength visible region. A spectral power distribution curve is shown in figure 6-58.

Xenon short-arc lamps are made with rated wattages from 5 to 32,000 W and are available for operation in vertical or horizontal positions. Lamps designed to be

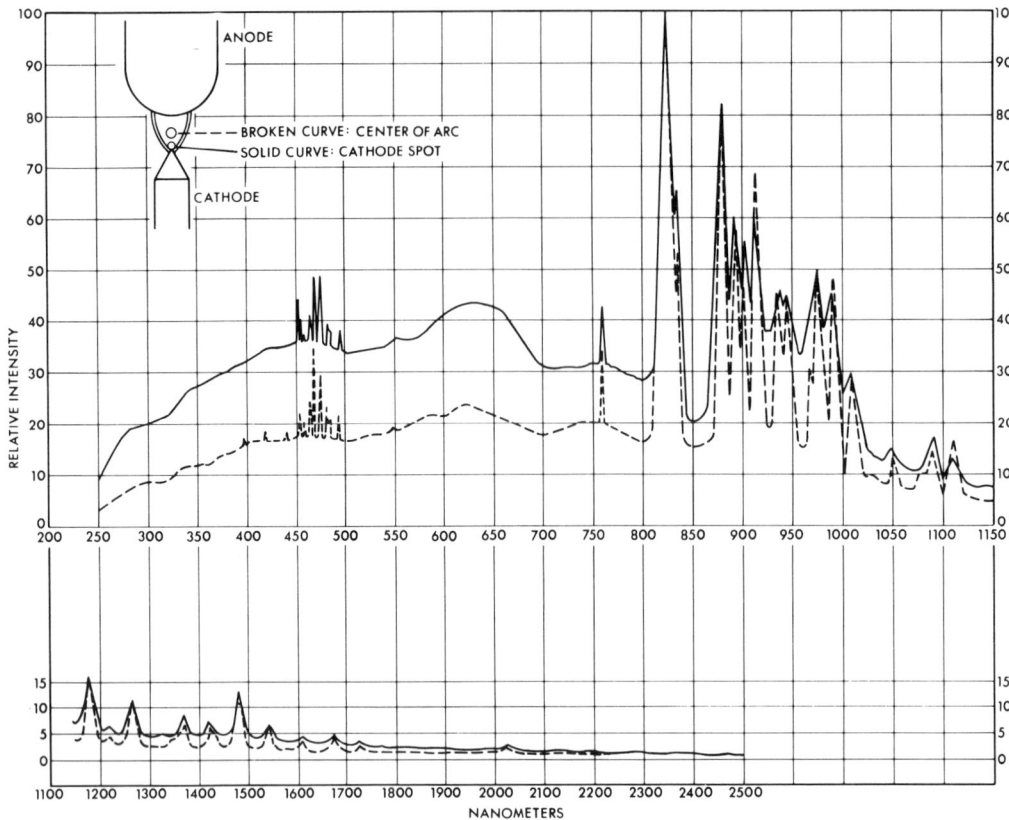

Fig. 6-58. Spectral power distribution of a 2.2 kW xenon lamp.

operated at above 10 kW typically require liquid cooling of the electrodes.

The luminous efficacy of the xenon short-arc lamp is approximately 30 lm/W at 1000 W, 45 lm/W at 5000 W and over 50 lm/W at 20 kW and higher input.

Ceramic Reflector Short-Arc Xenon Lamps

Ceramic reflector xenon (CRX) lamps combine the basic technology of short-arc lamps and an internal reflector that focuses the arc's energy through a sapphire window in the ceramic-to-metal housing. The window transmits energy in both the IR and UV regions of the spectrum. These devices have the advantages of increased output, safety and ease of handling and installation. They also obviate some peripheral equipment needed in many applications where short-arc lamps are used. CRX lamps are available with inputs from 175 to 1000 W. Their spectral power distributions can be varied for special applications by altering the reflector material or its coating.

Lamp Operating Enclosure

Short-arc mercury, mercury-xenon and xenon lamps are under considerable pressure during operation (up to 5 MPa [50 atm] for small lamps and about 1 MPa [10 atm] for large ones) and therefore must be operated in

an enclosure at all times. In addition, precaution must be taken to ensure protection from the powerful UV radiation emitted from these lamps.

In general, short-arc lamps up to about 1 kW are designed to operate with convection cooling. No special ventilation is required unless critical components of the lamps are subjected to excessive temperatures, caused by closely confined enclosures, excessive ambient temperatures or infrared radiation.

For safety during shipment, storage, or handling of xenon or mercury-xenon lamps, special protection cases are provided. These cases are made of metal or plastic and are so arranged around the bulb that the lamp can be electrically connected without removing the case. The case should not be removed until immediately before the lamp is energized.

Like most vapor discharge lamps, short-arc lamps require auxiliary devices to start the arc and limit the current. For ac lamps either resistive or inductive ballasts may be used. Direct-current lamps are best operated from specifically designed power systems which provide, with good efficiency, the high-voltage pulses (up to 50 kV) required to break down the gap between the electrodes, ionize the gas and heat the cathode tip to thermionic emitting temperatures. Further, they provide enough open-circuit dc voltage to assure the transition from the low-current, high-voltage spark discharge initiated by the starter to the high-current, low-voltage arc. With a properly designed system, a short-arc lamp will start within a fraction of a second. Many power supplies are regulated so that lamp operation is independent of line voltage fluctuation. Four basic types of sensors for power regulation are presently in use: current, voltage, power and optical regulators. The type of power system used depends on the specifics of the application.

Compact-Source Metal Halide Lamps

Compact-source, or medium-arc, metal halide lamps[86, 87] are based on a combination of the short-arc lamp and the metal halide lamp technology. Their arc discharge is predominantly electrode stabilized and operates between tungsten electrodes spaced 2.5–35 mm apart in ellipsoidal or almost spherical quartz bulbs. They are filled with mercury and argon as basic elements for starting the arc, and, as in some standard metal halide lamps, rare-earth metal iodides and bromides are added in order to obtain a full spectrum. Both a high luminous efficacy and excellent color rendering with a correlated color temperature close to that of daylight are achieved, together with a high degree of source concentration.

These lamps are available in various single-ended and double-ended constructions from 150 to 24,000 W. They are typically designed to operate on alternating current and require unique power supplies or ballasting equipment with high-voltage starting devices. Most such lamps can be instantly restarted when hot.

Some lamps are available with the arc tubes mounted in integral ellipsoidal reflectors which focus the light through small apertures or fiber-optic bundles. Other lamps are available in PAR configurations for applications that require concentrated beams.

The main fields of application of compact-source lamps are motion picture and television lighting, outdoor location lighting, theatrical lighting, sports lighting, fiber-optic illuminators, liquid crystal displays (LCD) and video projectors.

MISCELLANEOUS DISCHARGE LAMPS

Low-Pressure Sodium Lamps

In low-pressure sodium discharge lamps, the arc is carried through vaporized sodium. The light produced by the low-pressure sodium arc is almost monochromatic, consisting of a double line near the center of the visible spectrum at 589.0 and 589.6 nm. The starting gas is neon with small additions of argon, xenon or helium. In order to obtain the maximum efficacy of the conversion of the electrical input to the arc discharge into light, the vapor pressure of the sodium must be on

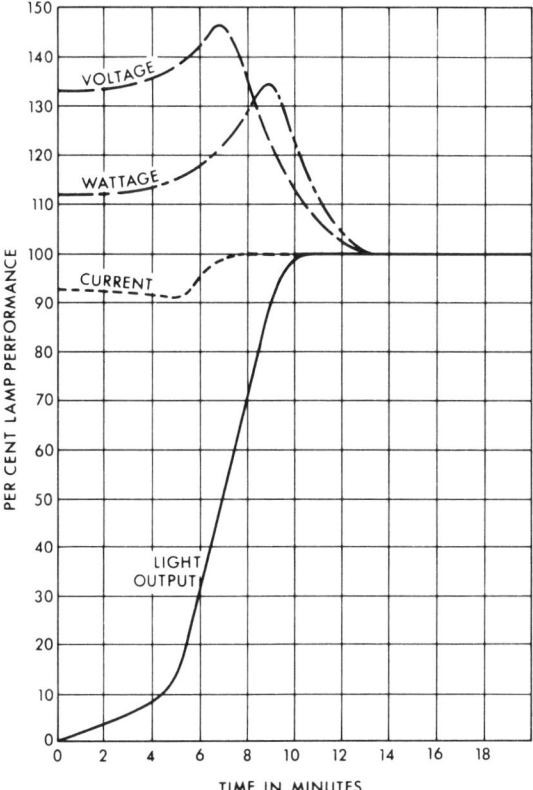

Fig. 6-59. Low pressure sodium lamp performance during starting.

the order of 0.7 Pa (5×10^{-3} Torr), which corresponds to an arc tube bulb wall temperature of approximately 260°C. Any appreciable deviation from this pressure degrades the lamp efficacy. To maintain the operating temperature for this pressure, the arc tube is normally enclosed in a vacuum flask or in an outer bulb at high vacuum.

The run-up time to full light output is 7–15 min. When first started, the light output is the characteristic red of the neon discharge, and this gradually gives way to the characteristic yellow as the sodium is vaporized. The hot reignition is good, and most low-pressure sodium lamps will restart immediately after interruption of the power supply. The lamp performance during starting is shown in figure 6-59.

Efficacy. Low current density is vital to efficient generation of light. High densities result in excitation of atoms to higher energy levels and thus a loss of efficacy in converting electricity to light.[88] It is in the field of thermal insulation that the greatest strides have been made in recent years, resulting in present-day efficacies in excess of 180 lm/W for the 180-W U-type low-pressure sodium lamp, or approximately 150 lm/W if ballast losses are added to lamp wattage. The thermal insulation consists of a light-transparent, IR-reflecting layer on the inside of the outer envelope. In modern designs, it is made of indium oxide; previously it was

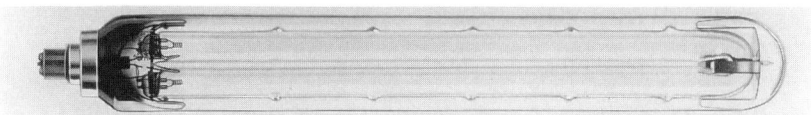

Fig. 6-60. Construction of low pressure sodium lamps (U-tube or hairpin type).

tin oxide, and still earlier, internal glass sleeves were used.

Construction. There are two types of low-pressure sodium lamps: the linear and the hairpin, or U tube. The linear lamp has a double-ended arc tube, similar to a fluorescent lamp, with preheat electrodes sealed into each end. Its arc tube, made of a special sodium-resistant glass, is sealed in turn into an outer vacuum jacket and completed by a medium bipin base at each end. The hairpin type has the arc tube double back on itself, with its limbs very close together.

Two versions of the hairpin lamp are available, based on differing approaches to maintaining even distribution of sodium in the arc tube throughout life. Since low-pressure sodium lamps contain excess metallic sodium, the metal will tend to condense at the coolest part of the lamp. This occurs generally at the bend of the arc tube. If not controlled, sodium migration to the cool point will eventually result in the lamp "burning bare," that is, a return to a neon-argon arc in sections of the lamp.

One form of control is to provide dimples in the outer surface of the arc tube to present alternative cool points as reservoirs for the metallic sodium. The dimples also inhibit migration of sodium due to vibration or gravitational effects. This design ensures even distribution of sodium throughout the arc tube at the time of manufacture, as well as control of the vapor pressure.

The alternative version uses a graded heat-reflecting film along the inside of the outer envelope, progressively increasing the amount of reflected heat as the natural cool point at the bend is approached. In this version no dimples are used. The electrodes are sealed in at the pinches of the arc tube. The lamp is completed by a two-pin bayonet base. A low-pressure sodium lamp is shown in figure 6-60. The electrodes in this lamp are of a metal oxide type and are heated to electron-emissive temperature by ion bombardment.

Auxiliary Equipment. The low-pressure sodium arc, in common with all discharge lamps, has a negative volt-ampere characteristic, and a current-limiting device, usually a transformer and reactor ballast, must be provided to prevent excessive lamp and line currents.

High-power-factor autotransformer ballasts are most commonly used, the required lamp starting voltages ranging between 400 and 550 V. A capacitor wired in parallel on the primary side increases the power factor

to 90% or better. On this type of ballast, lamp regulation is excellent: lamp wattage and lumen output remain within 5% for a varying line voltage range of 20%. Recently, constant-wattage designs have been introduced.

Glow Lamps

These are low-wattage, long-life lamps designed primarily for use as indicator or pilot lamps, night lights, location markers and circuit elements. They range from 0.06 to 3 W and have an efficacy of approximately 0.3 lm/W. A group of typical glow lamps is shown in figure 6-61. These emit light having the spectral character of the gas with which they are filled. The most commonly used gas is neon, having a characteristic orange color. The glow is confined to the negative electrode. Glow lamps have a critical starting voltage, below which they are, in effect, an open circuit.

Like other discharge lamps, glow lamps require a current-limiting resistance in series. Glow lamps with screw bases have this resistor built into the base, while for unbased lamps or lamps with bayonet bases a resistor of the proper value must be employed external to the lamps.

Glow lamps filled with an argon mixture rather than neon radiate chiefly in the near UV region around 360 nm and are therefore used mainly to excite fluorescence in minerals and other materials as well as for some photographic applications.

Electrodeless Lamps

Electrodeless lamps are sources excited by means of electromagnetic energy which passes through the glass lamp envelope without the use of conducting electrodes. These lamps have been developed to eliminate the deleterious effects of electrodes. They take advantage of unique plasma characteristics which can be obtained by coupling energy into a lamp at high frequencies. Advantages include long life and essentially no bulb wall deposits of electrode material. A disadvantage is the cost associated with generating and containing the radio-frequency (RF) or microwave energy.

High-Frequency Powered Fluorescent Lamp. If the lamp bulb is surrounded by a coil of wire electrically energized at a high frequency, the resulting magnetic field will induce a current flow in the lamp's gases,

J5A(NE-30)
J9A(NE-56)

L5A(NE-32)

R2A(NE-34)

R6A(NE-40)

A9A
(NE-2E)

B1A(NE-51)
B2A(NE-51H)

B9A
(NE-48)

B7A(NE-45)
F4A(NE-58)

B5A
(NE-17)

F3A
(NE-57)

Fig. 6-61. Typical glow lamps with American National Standard Institute numbers (old trade numbers).

sustaining a discharge. The result is energy inductively coupled into the discharge. This is similar to the operation of a transformer with the discharge playing the role of the secondary winding. In one configuration a low-pressure discharge is excited by a wire coil with an iron core located at the center of a mercury vapor discharge. As in conventional fluorescent lamps, the excited mercury vapor radiates UV energy, which is then converted to visible light by the phosphor coating. A lamp life of 60,000 h has been claimed for one design, with efficacies of 65 lm/W. These lamps are used where long life offsets the high cost of the system.

Microwave-Powered Lamps. High-power microwave (2.45-gHz) lamps have been commercialized primarily as UV sources for industrial processes. They exist in two forms: linear sources in which microwave energy is coupled into the end of the bulb and propagates along the bulb, and spherical sources contained within a microwave resonant cavity. In both cases, microwave energy is supplied by magnetron electron tubes which are connected to an optical reflector and microwave cavity with a waveguide. The magnetron generators are essentially the same tubes used in home microwave ovens and last from 3000 to 10,000 h.

RF Energy Containment. Microwave- and high-frequency-powered lamps must be certified to pass Federal Communications Commission regulations regarding electromagnetic interference (EMI). Microwave-powered lamps accomplish this by using one or more metallic mesh screens having 85–96% transmission of visible light, which effectively reflect all microwave energy back into the lamp cavity. Some systems use small RF detectors to ensure that these screens are intact.

Zirconium Concentrated Arc Lamps, Enclosed Type

These lamps utilize a direct-current arc constituting a concentrated point source of light of high intrinsic luminance, up to 45 million cd/m^2. They are made with permanently fixed electrodes sealed into an argon-filled glass bulb. The light source is a small spot, 0.13–2.8 mm in diameter (depending on the lamp wattage), which forms on the end of a zirconium oxide–filled tantalum tube which serves as the cathode.

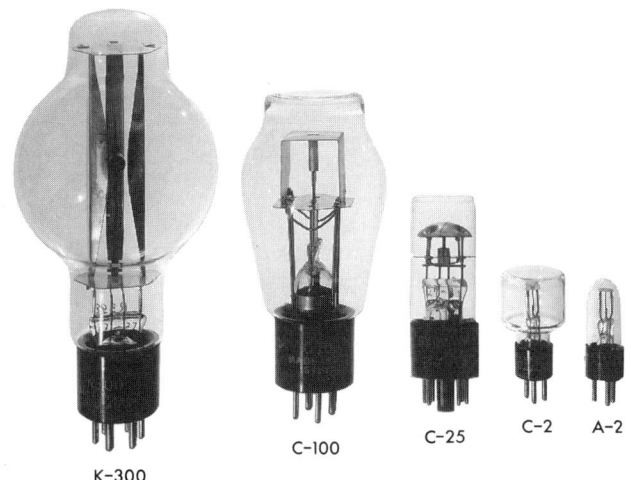

K-300

C-100

C-25

C-2

A-2

Fig. 6-62. Side and end-emission concentrated arc lamps.

The spectral power distribution is similar to that of a blackbody with a correlated color temperature of 3200 K. These lamps produce a candela distribution characterized by the cosine law.

They require special circuits which generate a high-voltage pulse for starting and a well filtered and ballasted operating current. Suitable power supplies are recommended by the manufacturer.

Figure 6-62 illustrates various examples of side- and end-emission lamps.

Pulsed Xenon Arc (PXA) Lamps

These are ac xenon lamps with two active electrodes (a polarized xenon lamp has current flowing in only one direction and one active electrode). A switching reactor in series with the low-pressure lamp forces 50–100 peak amperes (120 pulses per second) through the lamp. The reactor also supplies a continuous current of 2–3 A to keep the lamp operating between pulses. The daylight spectrum produced is characteristic of xenon, typically 6000 K. PXA lamps are available in linear and helical types.

The efficacy of these sources is about 35–40 lm/W. Available lamp wattages range from 300 to 8000 W, and forced-air cooling is required during operation.

PXA lamps are used in the graphic arts industry for applications requiring instant start; high-intensity, stable light output; and daylight-quality color temperature.

Flashtubes

These light sources are designed to produce high-intensity flashes of extremely short duration. They are primarily used for photography; viewing and timing of reciprocating and rotating machinery; airport approach lighting systems, including navigation aids, obstruction marking, and warning and emergency lights; and laser pumping.

A conventional flashtube consists of a transparent tubular envelope of glass or fused silica (quartz) which has its main discharge electrodes internally located near the extremities and usually has an external electrode of wrapped wire for triggering. It generally contains very pure xenon gas at a pressure below atmospheric, usually in the range of 25–80 kPa (200–600 Torr). Sometimes other gases such as argon, hydrogen and krypton are added to the xenon to obtain different spectral power distributions or different electrical, thermal and deionization characteristics. With a voltage applied across its main electrodes, the tube appears as a high impedance or open circuit until a trigger pulse ionizes the gas within the tube. The trigger pulse, usually applied to an external electrode, induces ionization and thereby causes the xenon gas to become conductive. A discharge then occurs between

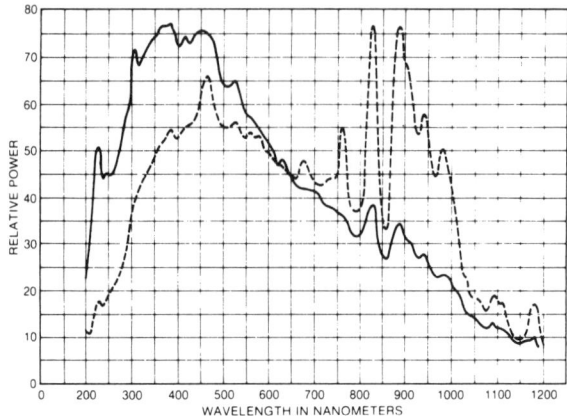

Fig. 6-63. Spectral power distribution of a typical xenon-filled flashtube for two different discharge conditions: (a) high voltage, low capacitance (solid line) and (b) low voltage, high capacitance (dashed line).

the main electrodes, whereupon the gas becomes highly luminescent. In some cases the trigger pulse is added to the voltage across the main electrodes and an external electrode is not required.

A xenon flashtube converts upward of 35% of the input energy to light. The luminous efficacy ranges from 30 to 60 lm · s/J. The spectral quality is close to that of daylight, having a correlated color temperature of approximately 6000 K, so that the radiation encompasses the entire visible spectrum and extends into the UV and near IR. See figure 6-63. Flashtubes are available in all sizes and shapes to suit the user and the type of optical system employed. The most common types are straight (linear), wound (helix) and U shape. Other configurations are available for special applications. Figure 6-64 shows some typical commercially available flashtubes.

Energy and Life. For single-flash operation the limit to the amount of energy which can be consumed depends upon the desired tube life measured in useful flashes. This life is affected by the rate of envelope wall blackening and destruction of the tube or its parts. Flashtubes designed for very high loading have envelopes made of fused silica, which can withstand high thermal shock. The peak power encountered during a discharge produces a thermal shock which may be of sufficient magnitude to shatter the envelope; hence, to maximize the energy per flash the thermal shock must be limited. This can be done by reducing the peak current, which also lengthens the flash duration. To limit peak current and thermal shock as well as control the pulse duration, inductance may be added in series within the discharge loop.

Normally, the life expectancy of a flashtube can be related to the percentage of "explosion energy" expended by a flash in a particular application. The explosion energy is defined by manufacturers as the

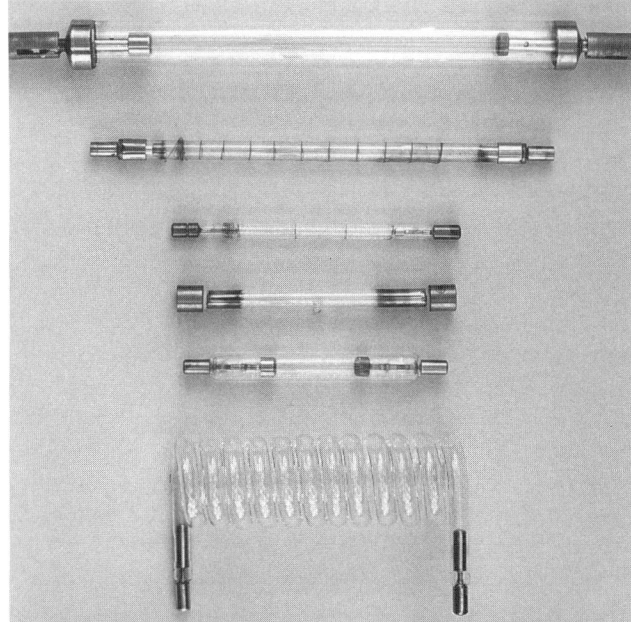

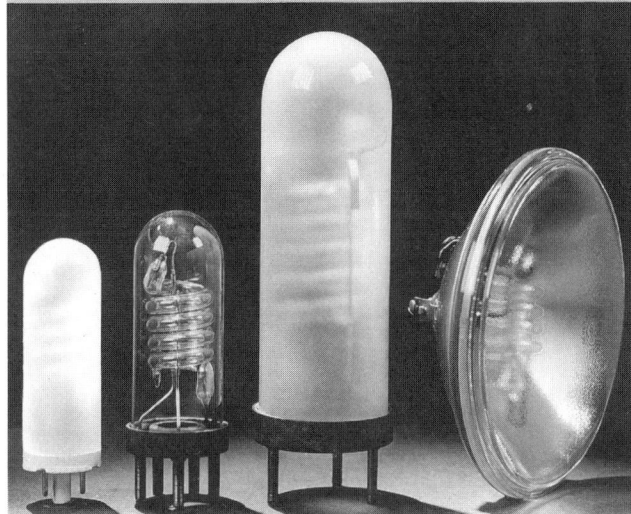

Fig. 6-64. Typical flashtubes.

Limits of Power Input. The average power input is a product of the energy per flash and the flash rate. The maximum power that any flashtube can dissipate is determined by the envelope area, the type of envelope material and the method of cooling, such as free air convection, forced air convection or use of a liquid coolant. For fused silica envelopes the maximum input power can be approximated as follows:

- Free air convection, 5 W/cm^2
- Forced air convection, 40 W/cm^2
- Liquid cooling, 200 W/cm^2

Energy Storage Banks. The electrical energy which subsequently is discharged through the flashtube to produce light is stored in a capacitor bank. This bank must be capable of rapid discharge into a very low impedance load. Therefore, it must have a rather low inductance as well as a very low equivalent series resistance. It must also be capable of storing energy at a high voltage without significant leakage. Typical voltages vary from about 300 to 4000 V. Modern banks use aluminum electrolytic, paper-oil or metalized paper capacitors designed specifically for energy storage applications. All these types are highly efficient in delivering energy to the flashtube. The type selected depends upon the voltage, temperature and life, as well as size and weight limitations.

Electronic Circuitry. In addition to discharge circuitry there are two other basic sections to the circuitry for a conventional xenon flash system: a charging circuit and a trigger circuit. See figure 6-65.

The charging circuit accepts primary electrical power at low voltage, transforms and rectifies it to higher voltage and applies it to the capacitor bank, where it is stored as potential energy. The amount of light generated by the flashtube depends upon its loading, which in turn depends upon the capacitance of the energy storage capacitor and the voltage across it, in accordance with the formula

$$\text{loading in joules} = \frac{CV^2}{2}$$

where
C = capacitance in μF,
V = voltage across the tube (and capacitor) in kV.

energy level at a given flash duration that will cause the tube to fail within ten flashes, usually by disintegration of the envelope. The life can be approximated as follows:

Flash Energy (% of explosion energy)	Flashtube Life (no. of flashes)
100	0–10
70	10–100
50	100–1000
40	1,000–10,000
30	10,000–100,000
20	100,000–1,000,000
5	> 1,000,000

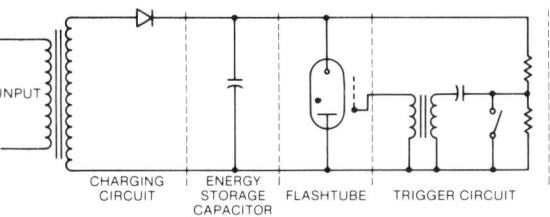

Fig. 6-65. Basic elements of a typical flashtube power supply.

The trigger circuit used for producing the high-voltage ionizing pulse consists of a low-energy capacitor discharge system driving a pulse transformer. The output of the pulse transformer sets up an electric field which starts the ionization process and causes the gas to conduct. This puise is usually applied to the external trigger wire (external electrode), but in some applications it may be applied across the main discharge electrodes by means of a pulse transformer with a very low secondary impedance connected in series with the flashtube discharge circuit.

By varying the voltage to which the capacitor bank is charged as well as its capacitance, and by the insertion of inductance in the discharge circuit, it is possible to vary both the light output and the flash duration of the system. The flash duration is dependent upon the value of the capacitor, the inductance of the discharge circuit and the effective impedance of the flashtube. Although the flashtube is a nonlinear circuit element, its effective impedance can be approximated according to the formula

$$\text{flashtube impedance} = \frac{\rho L}{A}$$

where

ρ = plasma impedance in $\Omega \cdot$ cm,
L = arc length in cm,
A = cross-section area in cm^2.

At current densities encountered in usual practice, ρ has a value of approximately 0.02 $\Omega \cdot$ cm.

Flashtubes with their associated circuitry can be designed to operate with flash energies from fractional watt-seconds to 20,000 watt-seconds, with durations from approximately one microsecond to many milliseconds and with repetition rates from a single flash up to 1000 flashes per second. Even higher repetition rates can be attained with special circuitry and flashtube design.

Linear-Arc Lamps

Linear-arc quartz envelope lamps are available for both continuous wave and pulsed operation. Lamps operated in the pulsed mode are discussed above under flashtubes. Forced-air-cooled long-arc xenon lamps are made with arc lengths up to 1.2 m (4 ft), bore diameters up to 12 mm (0.47 in.) and wattages up to 6 kW. These lamps are used for special illumination requirements and solar simulation. Because of their low efficacy, 30 lm/W, they cannot compete with high-intensity discharge lamps for general illumination usage.

Water-cooled long-arc xenon and krypton lamps are made with arc lengths up to 0.3 m (1 ft), bore diameters up to 10 mm (0.39 in.) and wattages up to 12 kW. Their main application is for laser pumping; krypton arc lamps are especially suitable for pumping neodymium-doped yttrium-aluminum garnet (Nd:YAG) lasers.

Forced-air-cooled mercury and halide-doped long-arc lamps are available in lengths up to 1.2 m (4 ft), bore diameters up to 10 mm (0.39 in.) and wattages up to 5 kW. They are used for UV photochemical applications, including the curing of paints, varnishes and coatings.

Mercury capillary lamps are made with arc lengths up to 150 mm (6 in.), bore diameters from 2 mm (0.08 in.) and wattages up to 6 kW. They are used for UV photoexposure in the semiconductor and other industries. They are also finding use in the rapid thermal processing of silicon wafers.

All linear arc lamps use special ballasts and high-voltage starting devices. Manufacturers' recommendations for operation should be carefully followed.

ELECTROLUMINESCENT LAMPS[89-92]

An electroluminescent lamp is a thin (typically less than 1.2 mm), flat area source in which light is produced by a phosphor excited by a pulsating electric field. In essence, the lamp is a plate capacitor with a phosphor embedded in its dielectric and with one or both of the electrode plates translucent or transparent. Green, blue, amber, yellow or white light may be produced by choice of phosphor. The green phosphor has the highest luminance. Lamps are available in rigid ceramic or flexible plastic and are easily fabricated into simple solid or complex multisegmented shapes. Their thin profile, light weight, solid-state reliability and negligible heat generation make them an ideal low-level light source. Electroluminescent lamps are used in decorative lighting, instrument panels, switches, emergency lighting and signs, and for backlighting liquid crystal displays (LCDs).

Their luminance varies with applied voltage, frequency and temperature as well as with the type of phosphor and lamp construction. The relationship between voltage and luminance for ceramic and plastic electroluminescent lamps is shown in figure 6-66. Unlike that of some light sources, the color does not change as the voltage is increased or decreased. At 120 V, 60 Hz, the luminance of the ceramic form with the green phosphor is approximately 3.5 cd/m^2 (0.4 cd/ft^2); the luminance of the plastic form may be as high as 27 cd/m^2 (2.5 cd/ft^2) under these conditions,

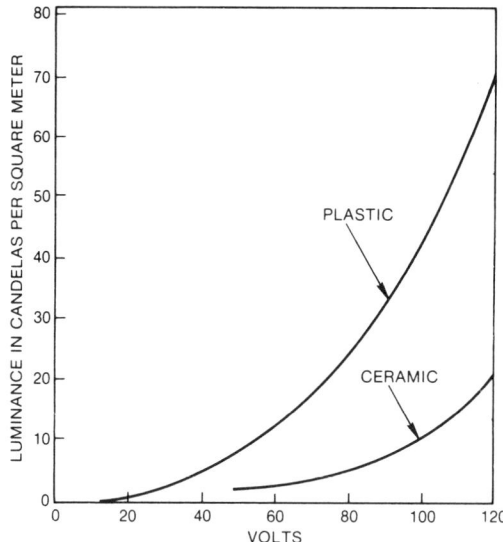

Fig. 6-66. Luminances of green ceramic and plastic electroluminescent lamps operated at 400 hertz as a function of voltage.

or up to 125 cd/m² (12 cd/ft²) at 120 V, 400 Hz. With the ceramic form at 600 V, 400 Hz, a luminance of 70 cd/m² (7 cd/ft²) has been achieved.

The life of electroluminescent lamps is long, and their power consumption is low. There is no abrupt point at which the lamp fails. Because of this, the useful life is taken as the number of operating hours after which the luminance falls below a specified level for a given application. Some electroluminescent lamps utilizing long-life phosphor have operated continuously for more than ten years while powered at 115 V, 400 Hz. The number of operating hours after which the luminance falls to 50% of initial has been used for comparing lamp performance, but this can vary greatly depending on the drive voltage and frequency and the

type of phosphor used. See figure 6-67. The value of the time to half luminance for flexible-type lamps operated at 115 V, 400 Hz can vary from 1000 to 30,000 h, depending upon the type of phosphor. Typical initial current and power at these parameters are 1.2 mA and 40 mW/in².

LIGHT-EMITTING DIODES[93]

The light emitting diode (LED) is a p-n junction semiconductor lamp. LEDs emit radiation when forward biased. The emitted radiation can be either infrared or visible. Semiconductor light sources are available in a wide range of wavelengths, extending from the short-wavelength region of the visible spectrum to the far infrared. Multiple-color lamps are created by combining the light from materials emitting different wavelengths. For example, white LEDs are made by combining red, green and blue emitters on a single substrate.

The light-producing material in an LED is a specially prepared semiconductor material of high purity, with small amounts of other elements added in controlled quantities. Two classes of additives are used. One produces *n-type* material having localized excess electrons. The other produces *p-type* material having localized shortages of electrons, or *holes*, which act as positive charges. These impurities are diffused into the same piece of semiconductor material to create an interface between the p-type and the n-type materials. This interface is called a *junction*. See figure 6-68a.

The size of the semiconducting piece, or *chip*, is typically 0.25 mm² (0.01 in²). This allows LED lamps and arrays of lamps to be made very small and thin.

Typical lamp package construction for plastic encapsulated LEDs is shown in figure 6-68b. The n-type material is glued to the reflector cup located on the cathode lead. A wire bond connects the p-type material to the anode lead. A lens cast onto the chip is used to distribute the radiated energy. Viewing angles of 4 to 180° are possible. Viewing angles are affected by three parameters: the leadframe insertion depth, the amount of diffusant used and the package lens design. Common LED packages are subminiature, T-1, and T-1¾ (see figure 6-69), but a variety of other shapes and sizes are available.

Hermetically sealed LED packaging is also available. The lamp is constructed by having an LED mounted on a header and hermetically sealed in a metal can with a glass window. A plastic lens is glued to the glass window. Such lamps are typically used for military applications.

Certain specialized LEDs are also available. One type combines two semiconductor devices in a common package. The LEDs are mounted on the middle lead of

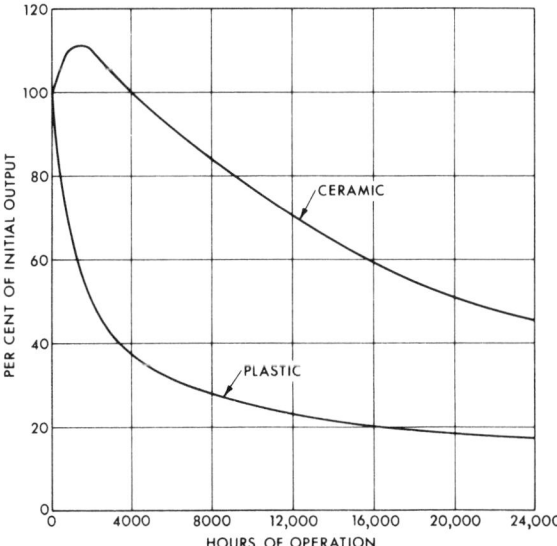

Fig. 6-67. Light output versus hours of operation for green ceramic and plastic electroluminescent lamps.

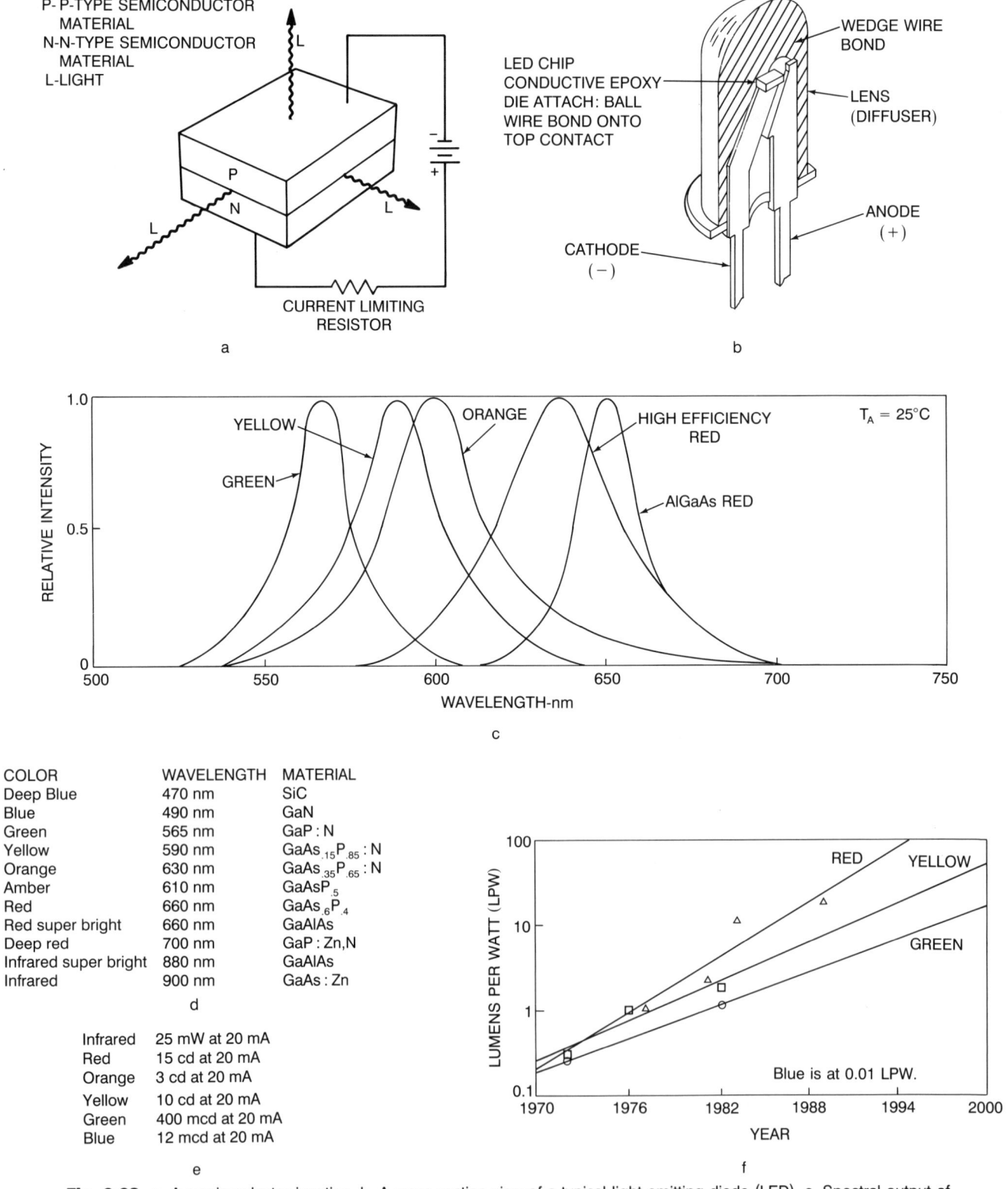

P- P-TYPE SEMICONDUCTOR
     MATERIAL
N-N-TYPE SEMICONDUCTOR
     MATERIAL
L-LIGHT

CURRENT LIMITING
RESISTOR

a

LED CHIP
CONDUCTIVE EPOXY
DIE ATTACH: BALL
WIRE BOND ONTO
TOP CONTACT

WEDGE WIRE
BOND

LENS
(DIFFUSER)

ANODE
(+)

CATHODE
(−)

b

$T_A = 25°C$

YELLOW
GREEN
ORANGE
HIGH EFFICIENCY
RED
AlGaAs RED

RELATIVE INTENSITY

WAVELENGTH-nm

c

COLOR	WAVELENGTH	MATERIAL
Deep Blue	470 nm	SiC
Blue	490 nm	GaN
Green	565 nm	GaP : N
Yellow	590 nm	$GaAs_{.15}P_{.85}$: N
Orange	630 nm	$GaAs_{.35}P_{.65}$: N
Amber	610 nm	$GaAsP_{.5}$
Red	660 nm	$GaAs_{.6}P_{.4}$
Red super bright	660 nm	GaAlAs
Deep red	700 nm	GaP : Zn,N
Infrared super bright	880 nm	GaAlAs
Infrared	900 nm	GaAs : Zn

d

Infrared	25 mW at 20 mA
Red	15 cd at 20 mA
Orange	3 cd at 20 mA
Yellow	10 cd at 20 mA
Green	400 mcd at 20 mA
Blue	12 mcd at 20 mA

e

LUMENS PER WATT (LPW)

RED
YELLOW
GREEN

Blue is at 0.01 LPW.

YEAR

f

Fig. 6-68. a. A semiconductor junction. b. A cross-section view of a typical light emitting diode (LED). c. Spectral output of several LED semiconductor materials. d. Examples of LED materials with peak wavelength and apparent color. e. Maximum intensities of LEDs of various colors. f. LED performance history.

Fig. 6-69. Light Produced by Various Types of Light Emitting Diodes (LED)

Type of LED	Typical Light Output (in millicandelas)*
T-1 Package:	
Red	0.7–2.5
Green	1.8–6.0
Yellow	1.8–4.0
Red (high efficiency)	1.5–2.5
T-1-3/4 Package:	
Red	0.5–2.0
Green	1.0–16.0
Yellow	1.0–16.0
Red (high efficiency)	2.0–24.0

* Light output as measured at design center of lens for recommended operating currents.

a three-leaded leadframe. The middle lead is a common cathode, and the other two leads are separate anodes for the two LEDs. This allows multiple color without having to reverse the polarity. Red, blue and green chips can be combined to produce white light.

An LED is said to be *forward biased* when the positive supply terminal is connected to the anode lead and the negative supply terminal is connected to the cathode lead. This causes the electrons and holes to meet at the junction, where they combine to produce photons. When the LED is forward biased, the model looks like a resistor in series with a battery. The voltage of this battery is called the LED turn-on voltage. Typical turn-on voltages are from 1 to 3 V. The turn-on voltage varies with the LED material used. Infrared LEDs have a lower turn-on voltage than visible-region LEDs. Thus, the turn-on voltage increases as the wavelength decreases. A current-limiting resistor is used to prevent excessive current from flowing through the LED junction. LEDs operate in the range of 1–3 V at currents of 1–100 mA continuous. The operating current is dependent on the maximum LED junction temperature. Operating LEDs in high-temperature environments requires cooling or pulsed operation to avoid degradation of light output.

An LED is said to be *reversed biased* when the connections are reversed from the forward condition. When the LED is reversed biased, the model looks like an open circuit, and in fact only a very small current will flow in the reverse direction.

The spectral characteristic of the emitted light depends upon the semiconductor material and the added impurities. The output spectral characteristics of five solid-state lamp semiconductor materials are shown in figure 6-68c. Figure 6-68d shows some of the many semiconductor emitting materials that are available and their peak emitted wavelengths.

The light output of LEDs depends on the packaging. LEDs are measured and categorized by on-axis

intensity. The total amount of energy emitted by an LED typically falls within a 2:1 range for a given material. However, using different packages can significantly change the on-axis intensity. In particular, LEDs with high on-axis intensity values have to have narrow viewing angles. Figure 6-68e shows the maximum intensity levels achieved for different colors. These values were achieved using narrow-viewing-angle devices.

Varying the LED drive current will change the intensity. The generated light increases with increased current. Pulsing LEDs can also produce higher brightnesses. The generated light is proportional to the time-averaged current and inversely proportional to the temperature. LEDs can be dimmed by either varying the dc current or pulse-width-modulating the current. The former will produce acceptable results over a range of 3:1; the latter, 2000:1. Neither ac nor frequency dimming is recommended.

Solid-state lamps are used because of their long life and rugged packaging. LEDs can be subjected to mechanical shock and vibration with very low failure rates. They are expected to operate from tens of thousands of hours to millions of hours, depending on the device and the operating conditions. Typically, early failures are mechanical in nature. The light output may increase for the first thousand hours, but will fall after that.

Figure 6-68f shows the performance history of visible-light LEDs.

Periodically new materials are introduced. A promising one is aluminum indium gallium phosphide, which is a significantly brighter emitter than commercially available yellow LEDs.

Historically, LEDs have been used as indicators and displays. Recent developments in LED materials have allowed LEDs to be used for exterior light sources, such as stop lamps for automobiles and pedestrian crosswalk signs in Europe. Large arrays of visible-region LEDs have seen limited use as illumination sources.

Infrared LEDs have spectral outputs closely matched to the response of silicon detectors. They are used with receivers for counting, sorting, sensing and positioning in applications as diverse as computer equipment, optical radar and burglar alarms. Infrared LED arrays have also been used as sources of illumination in security lighting applications.

LEDs are available in seven-segment and alphanumeric packages. Such devices are used to display character information.

For exterior lighting, the best LED materials to use are transparent-substrate aluminum gallium arsenide and aluminum indium gallium phosphide. These materials produce enough light to be used as alternatives to colored incandescent lamps. Bright light sources are made by building arrays of LEDs and combining their emitted light output.

NUCLEAR LIGHT SOURCES

Nuclear light sources are self-contained light sources requiring no power supply. They can be easily seen even by a person whose eyes are not dark adapted, and some forms are visible at considerable distances. They typically provide illumination for instrument panels, controls and clocks.

These sources consist of a sealed glass tube or bulb internally coated with a phosphor and filled with tritium gas. Low-energy beta particles (electrons) from the tritium, an isotope of hydrogen, strike the phosphor, which in turn emits light of a color characteristic of the type of phosphor used. Thus, the mechanism of light production is very similar to that in a conventional television tube. The higher the ratio of the quantity of tritium to the phosphor area, the greater the luminance. The luminance can range up to 7 cd/m^2, with a typical average of 1.7 cd/m^2 (this level is approximately that of an illuminated car instrument panel), and the sources can be supplied in a variety of colors. Highest brightness is obtained in the green and yellow phosphors, and green is the usual color supplied. Since tritium has a half-life of 12.3 yr, one might expect the brightness of the source to decay likewise. In reality, the time when half luminance is reached is about 6–7 yr, and the useful life of these lamps is currently about 15 yr. These light sources can be supplied in very small sizes, down to 5 mm in diameter by 2 mm in length.

The glass wall is impervious to tritium and completely absorbs any beta radiation not already absorbed by the phosphor. The unit is thus a completely sealed source and does not present any radiation hazard. Glass capsules can be produced in a wide variety of shapes and sizes and are usually made to normal glassworking tolerances.

All applications of these lamps are monitored by the Nuclear Regulatory Commission.

CARBON ARC LAMPS

Carbon arc lamps were the first commercially practical electric light sources. They were used for many years in applications where extremely high luminance, high correlated color temperature and/or high color rendering was necessary such as motion picture projection lamphouses, theatrical followspots, searchlights and film production "daylight" supplemental lighting. In most of those applications, xenon short arc and metal halide light sources have replaced carbon arc.

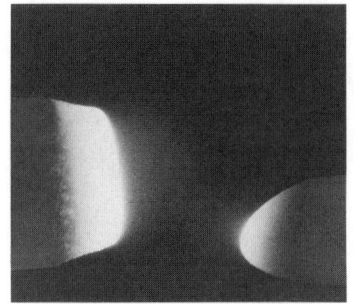
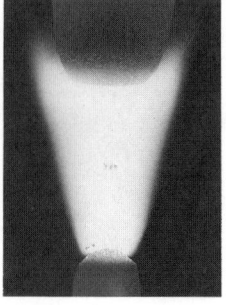

LOW-INTENSITY ARC   FLAME TYPE CARBON ARC

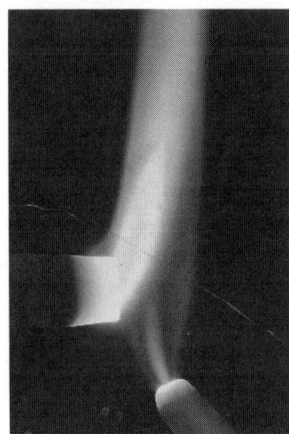
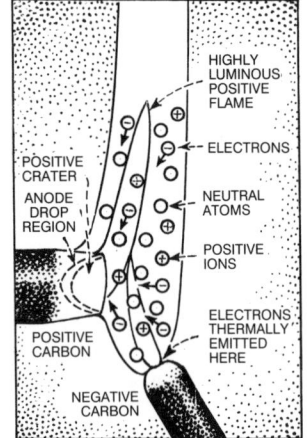

HIGH-INTENSITY ARC

Fig. 6-70. Low-intensity arc, 30 amperes, 55 volts, direct current. Flame arc, 60 amperes, 50 volts, alternating current. (Direct current flame arcs are very similar.) High-intensity arc, 125 amperes, 70 volts, direct current (rotating positive carbon).

Types of Carbon Arcs

Low-Intensity Arcs. Of the three principal types of carbon arcs in commercial use, the low-intensity arc is the simplest. In this arc, the light source is the white-hot tip of the carbon anode. This tip is heated to a temperature near its sublimation point (3700°C) by the concentration of a large part of the electrical energy of the discharge in a narrow region close to the anode surface. See figure 6-70.

Figure 6-71 shows the characteristics of a typical low-intensity carbon arc used for microscope illumination and projection. The light from a low-intensity carbon arc has a luminance of $15–18 \times 10^{-6}$ cd/m^2 and a correlated color temperature of 3600–3800 K. When operated under prescribed conditions,[94] the low-intensity carbon arc produces radiation which closely approximates that from a blackbody at 3800 K and is widely used as a radiation standard.

High Intensity Arcs. The high-intensity arc is obtained from the flame arc by increasing the size and the flame material content of the core of the anode, and at the same time greatly increasing the current density, to a

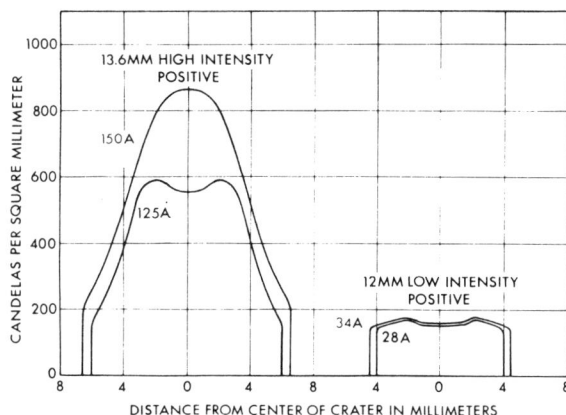

Fig. 6-71. Crater luminance distribution in forward direction for typical low and high intensity carbons.

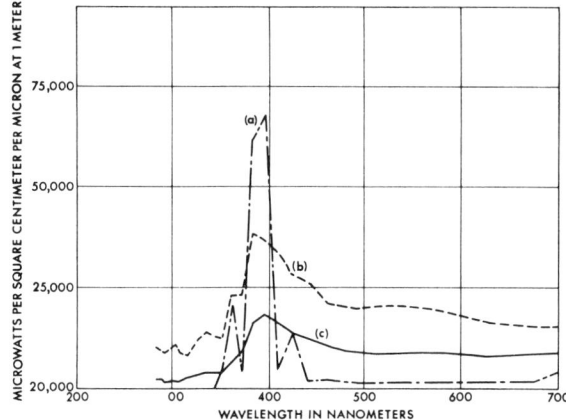

Fig. 6-72. Spectral power distribution of arcs used for graphic arts. (a) Half-inch enclosed arc carbons, 16 amperes, 138 volts. (b) Nine millimeter high-intensity photo carbons, 95 amperes, 30 volts. (c) Half-inch photographic white flame carbons, 38 amperes, 50 volts.

point where the anode spot spreads over the entire tip of the carbon. This results in a rapid evaporation of flame material and carbon from the core, so that a crater is formed. The principal source of light is the crater surface and the gaseous region immediately in front of it. See figure 6-70. Since the flame material is more easily ionized than the carbon, a lower anode drop exists at the core area than at the shell of the carbon. This tends to concentrate the current at the core surface, and so encourages the formation of the crater.

The characteristics of a variety of typical high-intensity carbon arcs range in power input from 2 to 30 kW, in crater luminous intensity from 10,500 to 185,000 cd, and in crater luminance from 55 to 145×10^{-7} cd/m^2. The correlated color temperature ranges from 2900 to 6500 K. These values will be further modified by the characteristics of the optical system used.

Figure 6-71 shows the luminance distribution across the crater for typical low- and high-intensity carbons and illustrates two basic differences in their luminance characteristics. First, the luminance of a low-intensity arc is lower than that for a high-intensity arc. Second, luminance depends more on current for a high-intensity arc than for a low-intensity arc.

Flame Arcs. A flame arc (see figure 6-70) is obtained by enlarging the core in the electrodes of a low-intensity arc and replacing part of the carbon with chemical compounds known as flame materials, capable of radiating efficiently in a highly heated gaseous form. These compounds are vaporized along with the carbon and diffuse throughout the arc stream, producing a flame of a color determined by the compounds used. Typical flame materials are iron for the UV, rare earths of the cerium group for white light, calcium compounds for yellow, and strontium for red.

Figure 6-72 gives characteristics of typical flame arcs. This compilation covers arcs with power input

ranging from 1 to 4 kW and shows the effect of different currents, voltages and flame materials. With one exception, all arcs shown operate on alternating current. The wavelength intervals shown have been chosen to coincide with those important to various applications. The radiation in the indicated wavelength intervals is shown in two ways: first, as radiant intensity, expressed as microwatts incident on one square centimeter of area one meter from the arc, and second, as a percentage of the power input to the arc radiated over the entire sphere.

Carbon Arc Lamps and Power Sources

Carbon arcs are operated in lamphouses which shield the outside from stray radiation. These lamphouses may incorporate optical components, such as lenses, reflectors and filters for eliminating undesired parts of the spectrum. They provide means to conduct the electrical current to the carbon electrodes and to feed the electrodes together to compensate for the portions consumed. They also provide for removal of the products of combustion. Some lamps employ directed streams of air to control the position of the flame with respect to the positive electrode and to remove the combustion products.

Arcs for projection of motion pictures generally operate on direct current to prevent disturbing stroboscopic effects of the projector shutter. Both motor generators and rectifiers are employed. Flame arcs are widely used on both direct and alternating current. In some cases, ac arcs are operated directly from power lines, and in others, from special transformers. Low-current arcs have a negative volt-ampere characteristic and therefore must be operated from circuits which include ballast resistances or reactances, either in the generating or rectifying equipment or as separate units in the arc circuits. High-intensity carbon arcs have positive volt-ampere characteristics and may be operated without ballasts. Suitable power supply equipment is available for all principal types of carbon arc lamps.

GASLIGHTS

Gaslights are devices which use gaseous fuels for light and decorative purposes. They use open gas flames or incandescent mantles of the upright and inverted types (see figure 6-73).

Mantle Construction

Mantles consist of a fabric such as rayon, silk, cotton ramie or viscose woven into fabric tubing of the desired stitch and impregnated with a mixed solution of the nitrates of cerium, thorium, aluminum and magnesium. Rayon is the primary material in use today. After impregnation, the knitted tubing is denitrated and cut into short lengths and attached to individual rings and mountings.

Mantles are available in soft and hard forms. Soft mantles are sold unburned and must be shaped on the burner, a familiar task for those who own gasoline lanterns. Hard mantles are preshaped and preshrunk by burning out the fabric during manufacture. The remaining ash consists of oxides of the impregnating metals. A collodion coating is then applied to strengthen the burned mantle for handling and shipping; the coating, in turn, burns out when the mantle is first put to use.

Fig. 6-73. Portable high intensity gaslight.

Fig. 6-74. Light Output and Efficacies of Various Mantle Arrangements

Arrangement and Type of Mantle(s)	Total Input (watts)	Total Light Output (lumens)	Luminous Efficacy (lumens per watt)	Candelas Per 19 Watts*
One A† upright	645	434	0.67	1.0
Two No. 222‡ inverted	645	851	1.32	2.0
Three No. 222‡ inverted	967	1090	1.31	1.7

* 1.0 is minimum, per ANSI Z21.42-1971.
† Has a coated single wire top support and a single stitch weave.
‡ Representative of most inverted mantles.

Mantle Performance

The incandescence of a gas mantle is mainly dependent on the exact value of the cerium content, as well as on flame temperature and flame velocity. The type of gas, injection pressure and burner design may contribute to the candlepower obtained. The weave of the mantle is well established for each type of gas and is not a factor in mantle life. The single-stitch weave gives the same light output as the double-stitch; however, light from a double-stitch mantle may appear more yellow.

Light Output and Life. The light output, within design limits, is a direct function of the energy consumed in the mantle, and consequently of the mantle temperature. Gaslights are built so that a change in orifice size or the use of a properly adjusted pressure regulator is all that is required to accommodate the available gas pressures.

According to an ANSI standard which covers requirements for gas-fired illuminating appliances,[95] units incorporating a mantle should produce an average light output of at least 1 cd for each 19 W (65 Btu/h) of input rating. Figure 6-74 gives performance data for three mantle arrangements. As can be seen, the light output of a gaslight with a type A upright mantle (434 lm) is about the same as that of a 40-W incandescent lamp; the arrangement of two no. 222 inverted mantles gives out about the same light (851 lm) as a 60-W lamp. Figure 6-75 gives the candlepower distribution for a single upright mantle and a two-cluster inverted mantle. In the span of normal operating temperatures, light output varies as the tenth power of the mantle temperature in degrees Fahrenheit. The luminous efficacy of a gas mantle is the equivalent of 0.67–1.32 lm/W.

Inverted mantles are generally more efficient than upright mantles because of superheating of the gas-air mixture in the mantle. The flame burns back on itself, concentrating more heat on the mantle fabric, and thus more light is generated.

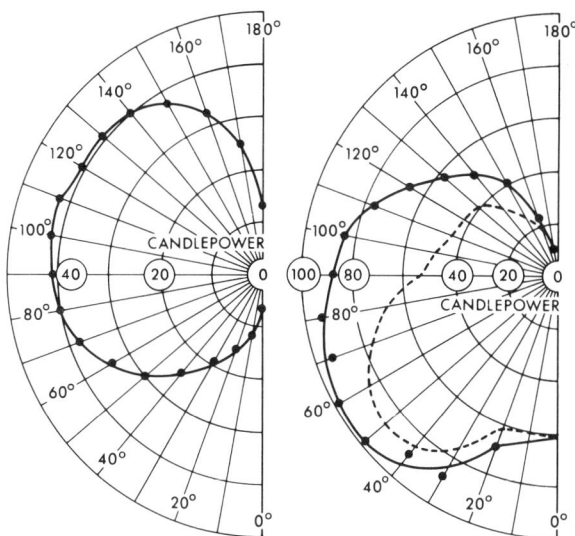

Fig. 6-75. Vertical candlepower distribution, in candelas, for mantles operated with optimum adjustment at total gas inputs of 645 watts: (*left*) a single type A upright mantle — view unobstructed by mantle support bracket; (*right*) a two-cluster No. 222 inverted mantle (solid line — both mantles foremost, dotted line — one mantle foremost). Note difference in scale: 180 degrees shown — the other 180 degrees are symmetrical.

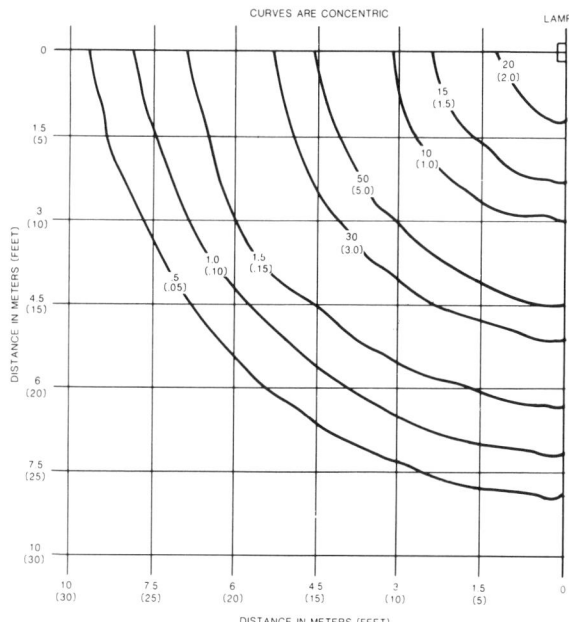

Fig. 6-76. Isofootcandle diagram (calculated) for a 14 kilopascal (2 pounds per square inch) gaslight consisting of 4 inverted mantles 2.5 meters (8 feet 4 inches) above ground.

A properly designed clear glass chimney of about 75-mm (3-in.) diameter, surrounding an upright mantle, will aid in directing the hot gases and improve efficacy as much as 354% above that of a bare mantle with no chimney. Opal domes may be used to produce a low-intensity upward light.

Unless mechanically abused, mantles have an indefinite life.

High-Intensity Gaslights

Advances in gas light technology make it possible to get brighter light from inverted gas mantles for a small increase in natural gas consumed in the mantle. The innovation is higher natural gas pressure, 14–135 kPa (2–20 lb/in.^{2}), rather than the usual pressure of a few hundred pascals. Gas at increased pressure aspirates more primary air and combines more thoroughly with it. The resultant higher-intensity flame, if matched to a suitable mantle, has an appreciably higher luminance. Typical photometric data for a 14 kPa (2 lb/in.^{2}) gaslight are shown in figure 6-76.

Liquefied petroleum gas (propane and butane) at medium pressure (up to 100 kPa, or 15 lb/in^2) has been used for many years in floodlights which use incandescent mantles.

Automatic Controls

When desired, gaslights may be turned down or off by clock- or photocell-actuated devices. However, most gaslights in use burn continuously at full light output.

Open-Flame Gaslights

Open-flame gaslights have no mantles and use nonprimary aerated burners. They are used mainly for ornamental effects rather than for their lighting ability.

Fishtail Burners. These nonprimary aerated burners yield a fan-shaped or fishtail-shaped flame. The head can either be slotted or have two ports angled so that their gas streams impinge. Such burners may be installed in gaslight assemblies if the maximum height of the flame is controlled and flame impingement is avoided (to minimize carbon deposits).

Gas Torches and Torch Lights. Also known as luau torches, these units are often shaped like frustums of cones. Targets or flame spreaders, vanes to redirect drafts, and wire screens or porous plugs to coalesce and harden flames are used to improve the flame stability and wind resistance of these torches.

Portable Candle Lights. Another type of contemporary yellow-flame burner is designed to operate with small portable cans of liquefied petroleum fuel and is meant to simulate a candle flame. A yellow flame about 25 mm (1 in.) high usually is adequate to create the desired effect. The light is normally operated in small lamp assemblies, which are basically miniature models of outdoor gaslight assemblies, and is therefore afforded some protection from drafts.

REFERENCES

1. Elenbaas, W. *Light Sources*. London: Macmillan, and New York: Crane, Russak & Co., 1972.

2. Hammer, W.J. "The William J. Hammer Historical Collection of Incandescent Electric Lamps," Trans. New York Elec. Soc., New Series, No. 4, 1913.

3. Schroeder, H. "History of Electric Light," Smithsonian Miscellaneous Collections, Vol. 76, No. 2, August 15, 1923.

4. Howell, J.W. and Schroeder, H. "History of the Incandescent Lamp," The Maqua Company, 1927.

5. "The Development of the Incandescent Electric Lamp Up to 1879," Trans. Illum. Eng., Vol XXIV, p. 717, October 1929.

6. "The Lamp Makers' Story," Illum. Eng., Vol. LI, p. 1, January 1956.

7. Hall, J.D.: "The Manufacture of Incandescent Lamps, " Elect. Eng., Vol. 60, p. 575, December, 1941.

8. Millar, P.S.: "Safeguarding the Quality of Incandescent Lamps," Trans. Illum. Eng. Soc., Vol. XXVI, p. 948, November, 1931.

9. Coolidge, W.D.: "Ductile Tungsten," Trans. Am. Inst. Elect. Engrs., Vol. XXIX, p. 961, May, 1910.

10. Forsythe, W.E., and Adams, E.Q.: "The Tungsten Filament Incandescent Lamp," J. Sci. Lab., Denison University, June, 1937.

11. Smithells, C.J.: Tungsten, Chemical Publishing Co., New York, 1953.

12. Rieck, G.D.: Tungsten and Its Compounds, Pergamon Press Ltd., London and New York, 1967.

13. Langmuir, I.: "Convection and Conduction of Heat in Gases," Phys. Review, Vol. XXXIV, No. 6, p. 401, June, 1912; Proc. Am. Inst. Elect. Engrs., Vol. XXXI, p. 1229, 1912.

14. Thouret, W.E., Anderson, H.A. and Kaufman, R.: "Krypton Filled Large Incandescent Lamps," Illum. Eng., Vol. 65, p. 231, April, 1970.

15. Thouret, W.E., Kaufman, R. and Orlando, J.W.: "Energy and Cost Saving Krypton Filled Incandescent Lamps," J. Illum. Eng. Soc., Vol. 4, p. 188, April, 1975.

16. Morris, R.W.: "Consideration Affecting the Design of Flashing Signal Filament Lamps," Illum. Eng., Vol. XLII, p. 625, June, 1947.

17. Zubler, E.G. and Mosby, F.A.: "An Iodine Incandescent Lamp with Virtually 100 Per Cent Lumen Maintenance," Illum. Eng., Vol. LIV, p.734, December, 1959.

18. Forsythe, W.E., Adams, E.Q., and Cargill, P.D.: "Some Factors Affecting the Operation of Incandescent Lamps," J. Sci. Lab., Denison University, June, 1939.

19. Merrill, G.S.: "Voltage and Incandescent Electric Lighting," Proc. Intern. Illum. Congr., Vol. II, 1931.

20. The Industry Committee on Interior Wiring Design, Handbook of Interior Wiring Design, 420 Lexington Ave., New York, 1941.

21. Potter, W.M. and Reid, K.M.: "Incandescent Lamp Design Life for Residential Lighting," Illum. Eng. Vol. LIV, p. 751, December, 1959.

22. "Questions and Answers on Light Sources," Illum. Eng., Vol. LXII, p. 139, March, 1967.

23. Whittaker, J.D.: "Applications of Silver Processed Incandescent Lamps with Technical Data," Trans. Illum. Eng. Soc., vol. XXVIII, p. 418, May, 1933.

24. Evans, M.W., LaGuisa, F.F. and Putz, J.M.: "An Evaluation of a New Ellipsoidal Incandescent Reflector Lamp," Light. Des. Appl., p. 22, March, 1977.

25. Leighton, L.G.: "Characteristics of Ribbon Filament Lamps," Illum. Eng., Vol. LVII, p. 121, March, 1962.

26. Method for the Designation of Miniature Incandescent Lamps, C78.390-1983, American National Standards Institute, New York.

27. Method for the Designation of Glow Lamps, C78.381-1961, American National Standards Institute, New York.

28. Waymouth, J.F.: Electric Discharge Lamps, The M.I.T. Press, Cambridge, MA 1971.

29. Townsend, M.A.: "Electronics of the Fluorescent Lamp," Trans. Am. Inst. Elect. Engrs., Vol. 61, p. 607, August, 1942.

30. Bouwknegt, A.: "Compact Fluorescent Lamps," J. Illum. Eng. Soc., Vol. 11, No. 4, p. 204, July, 1982.

31. Haft, H.H. and Thornton, W.A.: "High Performance Fluorescent Lamps," J. Illum. Eng. Soc., Vol. 2, p. 29, October, 1972.

32. Verstegen, J.M.P.J., Radielovic, D. and Vrenken, L.E.: "A New Generation Deluxe Fluorescent Lamp," J. Illum. Eng. Soc., vol. 4, p. 90, January, 1975.

33. Thorington, L., Schiazzano, G. and Parascandola, L.: "Spectral Design of the 40-Watt Fluorescent Lamp," Illum. Eng., Vol. LXI, p. 381, May, 1966.

34. Thorington, L., Parcscandola, L and Cunningham, L.: "Visual and Biologic Aspects of an Artificial Sunlight Illuminant," J. Illum. Eng. Soc., vol. 1, p. 33, October, 1971.

35. Denneman, J.W., de Groot, J.J., Jack, A.G. and Ligthart, F.A.S.: "Insights into the 26mm Diameter Fluorescent Lamp," J. Ilum. Eng. Soc., Vol. 10, No. 1, p. 2, October, 1980.

36. Bessone, C.S. and Citino, R.J.: "Optimum System and Lamp Parameters for Efficient T8 Fluorescent Systems," J. Illum. Eng. Soc., Vol. 11, No. 1, p. 2, October 1981.

37. Lowry, E.F., Gungle, W.C., and Jerome, C.W.: "Some Problems Involved in the Design of Fluorescent Lamps," Illum. Eng., Vol. XLIX, p. 545, November, 1954.

38. Lowry, E.F., Frohock, W.S., and Meyers, G.A.: "Some Fluorescent Lamp Parameters and Their Effect on Lamp Performances," Illum. Eng., Vol. XLI, p. 859, December, 1946.

39. Lowry, E.F.: "The Physical Basis for Some Aspects of Fluorescent Lamp Behavior," Illum. Eng., Vol. XLIII, p. 141, February, 1948.

40. Lowry, E.F. and Mager, E.L.: "Some Factors Affecting the Life and Lumen Maintenance of Fluorescent Lamps," Illum. Eng., Vol XLIV, p. 98, February, 1949

41. Eastman, A.A., and Campbell, J.H.: "Stroboscopic and Flicker Effects from Fluorescent Lamps," Illum. Eng., vol. XLVII, p. 27, January, 1952.

42. McFarland, R.H., and Sargent, T.C.: "Humidity Effect on Instant Starting of Fluorescent Lamps," Illum. Eng., Vol. XLV, p. 423, July, 1950.

43. Hammer, E.E.: "Peak and RMS Starting Voltage Procedure for Standard/Low Energy Fluorescent Lamps," J.

Illum. Eng. Soc., Vol. 10, No. 4, p. 204, July, 1981.

44. Hammer, E.E.: "Fluorescent Lamp Starting Voltage Relationships at 60 Hz and High Frequency," J. Illum. Eng. Soc., Vol. 13, No. 1, p. 36, October, 1983.

45. Hammer, E.E. "Fluorescent System Interactions with Electronic Ballasts," J. Illum.. Eng. Soc., Vol. 20, No. 1, p. 56, Winter, 1991.

46. Hammer, E.E.: "Fluorescent Lamp Operating Characteritics at High Frequency," J. Illum. Eng. Soc., Vol. 14, No. 1, p. 211, October, 1984.

47. Aoike, N., Yuhara, K. and Nobuhara, Y.: "Electronic Ballast for Fluorescent Lamp Lighting System of 100 lm/W Overall Efficiency," J. Ellum. Eng. Soc., Vol. 14, No. 1, p. 225, October, 1984.

48. Carpenter, W.P.: "Application Data for Proper Dimming of Cold Cathode Fluorescent Lamp," Illum. Eng., vol. XLVI, p. 306, June, 1951.

49. Campbell, J.H., Schultz, H.E., and Abbott, W.H.: "Dimming Hot Cathode Fluorescent Lamps," Illum. Eng., Vol. XLIX, p. 7, January, 1954.

50. Von Zastrow, E.E.: "Fluorescent Lamp Dimming with Semiconductors," Illum. Eng., Vol. LVIII, p. 312, April, 1963.

51. Campbell, J.H., and Kershaw, D.C.: "Flashing Characteristics of Fluorescent Lamps," Illum. Eng., Vol. LI, p. 755, November, 1956.

52. Bunner, R.W., and Dorsey, R.T.: "Flashing Applications of Fluorescent Lamps," Illum. Eng., Vol. LI, p. 761, November, 1956.

53. Elenbaas, W.: The High Pressure Mercury Discharge, Interscience Publishers, Inc., New York, 1951.

54. Elenbaas, W.: High-Pressure Mercury-Vapor Lamps and Their Applications, Philips Technical Library, Eindhoven, 1965.

55. Till, W.S., and Pisciotta, M.: "New Designations for Mercury Lamps," Illum. Eng., Vol. LIV, p. 594, September, 1959.

56. Till, W.S. and Unglert, M.C.: "New Designs for Mercury Lamps Increase Their Usefulness," Illum. Eng., Vol. LV, p. 269, May 1960.

57. Jerome, C.W.: "Color of High Pressure Mercury Lamps," Illum. Eng., Vol. LVI, p. 209, March, 1961.

58. U.S. Food and Drug Administration. [Latest issue]. *Performance standards for light-emitting products: Mercury vapor discharge lamps*, 21 CFR 1040.30. Washington, DC: U.S. Government Printing Office.

59. Larson, D.A., Fraser, H.D., Cushing, W.V., and Ungler, M. C.: "Higher Efficiency Light Source Through Use of Additives to Mercury Discharge," Illum. Eng., Vol. LVIII, p. 434, June, 1963.

60. Martt, E.C., Simialek, L.J., and Green, A.C.: "Iodides in Mercury Arcs—For Improved Color and Efficacy," Illum. Eng., Vol. LIX, p. 34, January, 1964.

61. Waymouth, J.F., Gungle, W.C., Harris, J.M., and Koury, F.: "A New Metal Halide Arc Lamp." Illum. Eng., Vol LX, p. 85, February, 1965.

62. Reiling, G.H.: "Characteristics of Mercury Vapor-Metallic Iodide Arc Lamps," J. Opt. Soc. Am., Vol. LIV, p. 532, April, 1964.

63. Kühl, B. 1964. High pressure mercury lamps with iodide additives. Lichttechnik 16(2):68–71.

64. Fromm, O.C., Seehawer, J. and Wagner, W.J.: "A Metal Halide High Pressure Discharge Lamp with Warm White Colour and High Efficacy," Light. Res. Technol., Vol. II, No. 1, p. 1, 1979.

65. Keeffe, W.M., Krasko, Z.K., Morris, J.C., and White, P.J.: "Improved Low Wattage Metal Halide Lamp," J. Illum. Eng. Soc., Vol. 17, No. 2, p. 39, Summer, 1988.

66. Krasko, Z.K. and Keeffe, W.M.: "A New M100 Metal Halide Lamp with Improved Color Rendering Properties," J. Illum. Eng. Soc., Vol. 19, No. 1, p. 118, Winter 1990.

67. Fromm, D.C. and Heider, J.: "Color Rendering, Color Shift, and Lumen Maintenance of Low-Wattage Metal Halide Lamps," J. Illum. Eng. Soc., Vol. 20, No. 1, p. 77, Winter, 1991.

68. American National Standard Specification for 400-Watt High-Pressure Sodium Lamp S51, NASI C78, 1350-1976, American National Standards Institute, New York.

69. Lemons, et. al, "HID Lamp Starters and Ignitors" LD & A, Vol. 15, No. 11, Nov. 1985, p. 54.

70. Pabst, W. and Klein, D., "Igniting High Pressure Lamps with Electronic Ballasts", J. Illum. Eng. Soc., Summer 1992, p. 14.

71. Frier, J.P. and Henderson, A.J.: "Stroboscopic Effect of High Intensity Discharge Lamps," J. Illum. Eng. Soc., Vol. 3, p. 83, October, 1973.

72. Rompe, R. and Thouret, W.E.: "Mercury Vapor Lamps of High Brightness," Zeitsch. Tech. Physik, vol. XIX, p. 352, 1938.

73. Rompe, R., Rhouret, W.E. and Weizel, W.: "The Problem of Stabilisation of Free Burning Arcs," Zeitsch. Physik, Vol. CXXII, p. 1, 1944.

74. Schulz, P.: "Xenon Short Arc Lamps," Ann. Phys., Vol. 1, p. 95, 1947.

75. Bourne, H.K.: Discharge Lamps for Photography and Projection, Chapman A. Hall, Ltd., London, 1948.

76. Thouret, W.E.: "New Designs of Quartz Lamps," Lichttechnik, Vol. II, p. 73, 1950.

77. Thouret, W.E. and Gerung, G.W.: "Xenon Short Arc Lamps and Their Application," Illum. Eng., Vol. XLIX, p. 520, November, 1954.

78. Anderson, W.T.: "Xenon Short Arc Lamps," J. Soc. Mot. Pict. Telev. Eng., Vol. LXIII, p. 96, 1954.

79. Thouret, W.E.: "Tensile and Thermal Stresses in the Envelope of High Brightness High Pressure Discharge Lamps," Illum. Eng., Vol. LV, p. 295, May, 1960.

80. Retzer, T.C.: "Circuits for Short-Arc Lamps," Illum. Eng., Vol. LIII, p. 606, November, 1958.

81. Thouret, W.E., and Strauss, H.S.: "New Designs Demonstrate Versatility of Xenon High-Pressure Lamps," Illum. Eng., Vol. LVII, p. 150, March, 1962.

82. Lienhard, O.E., and McInally, J.A.: "New Compact-Arc Lamps of High Power and High Brightness," Illum. Eng., Vol. LVII, p. 173, March, 1962.

83. Thouret, W.E., Strausse, H.S., Cortorillo, S.F., and Kee, H.: "High Brightness Xenon Lamps with Liquid-Cooled Electrodes," Illum. Eng., Vol. LX, p. 339, May, 1965.

84. Lienhard, O.E.: "Xenon Compact-Arc Lamps with Liq-

uid-Cooled Electrodes," Illum. Eng., Vol. LX, p. 348, May, 1965.

85. Thouret, W.E., Strauss, H.S., Leyden, J., Kee, H. and Shaffer, G.: "20 to 30 KW Xenon Compact Arc Lamps for searchlights and Solar Simulators," J. Illum. Eng. Soc., Vol. 2, p. 8, October 1972.

86. Lemons, T.M.: "HMI Lamps," Light. Des. Appl., Vol. 8, p. 32, August, 1978.

87. Hall, R. and Preston, B.: "High-Power Single-Ended Discharge Lamps for Film Lighting," J. Soc. Mot. Pict. Tel. Eng., Vol. 90, pp. 678–685, August, 1981.

88. Wyszecki, G. and Stiles, W.S. Color Science, John Wiley and Sons, Inc., New York, 1982.

89. Payne, E.C., Mager, E.L., and Jerome, C.W.: "Electro-luminescence—A New Method of Producing Lighting," Illum. Eng., Vol. XLV, p. 688, November, 1950.

90. Ivey, H.F.: "Problems and Progress in Electroluminescent Lamps," Illum. Eng., Vol. LV, p. 13, January 1960.

91. Blazek, R.J.: "High Brightness Electroluminescent Lamps of Improved Maintenance," Illum. Eng., Vol. LVII, p. 726, November, 1962.

92. Weber, K.H.; "Electroluminescence—An Appraisal of Its Short-Term Potential," Illum. Eng., Vol. LIX, p. 329, May, 1964.

93. Hall II, J.W.: "Solid State Lamps—How They Work and Some of Their Applications," Illum. Eng., Vol. LXIV, p. 88, February, 1969.

94. Null, M.R. and Lozier, W.W.: "Carbon Arc as a Radiation Standard," J. Opt. Soc. Amer., Vol. 52, p. 1156, October, 1962.

95. American National Standard for Gas-Fired Illuminating Appliances, Z-21.42-1971, American National Standards Institute, New York.

LIGHT SOURCE TABLES

The light source tables that follow represent an updating of and addition to the tables in the 1984 Reference Volume. The changes and additions are based on material received from light source manufacturers as of January 1992.

These tables are intended to provide the reader with a comprehensive listing of most light sources available in North America. They should be useful in preliminary design by helping find lamps that are appropriate both physically and photometrically. Often, where there are more than one manufacturer for a particular lamp type, average photometric values are provided. For this reason, as well as to get the latest data for a particular lamp, it is recommended that the lamp manufacturers be consulted. The following is an abbreviated index for the tables:

- Airport, airway and aircraft lamps: 6-101 and 6-102.
- Automotive lamps: 6-106.
- Fluorescent lamps: 6-114 to 6-120.
- General-service incandescent lamps: 6-78.
- High-pressure sodium lamps: 6-122.
- Incandescent filament lamps: 6-78 to 6-91.
- Infrared lamps: 6-110.
- Light source luminances: 6-77.
- Mercury lamps: 6-123 and 6-124.
- Metal halide lamps: 6-122.
- Reflectorized incandescent lamps: 6-97.
- Stage, television and photographic lamps: 6-95.
- Street lamps: 6-100.
- Tungsten-halogen lamps: 6-92 and 6-97.
- Ultraviolet sources: 6-124.

Please refer to figure 6-8 for bulb classifications and figure 6-9 for base designations.

Fig. 6-77 Approximate Luminance of Various Light Sources

Light Source		Approximate average luminance (cd / m^2)
Natural light sources:		
Sun (at its surface)		2.3×10^9
Sun (as observed from earth's surface)	At meridian	1.6×10^9
Sun (as observed from earth's surface)	Near horizon	6×10^6
Moon (as observed from earth's surface)	Bright spot	2.5×10^3
Clear sky	Average brightness	8×10^3
Overcast sky		2×10^3
Lightning flash		8×10^{10}
Combustion sources:		
Candle flame (sperm)	Bright spot	1×10^4
Kerosene flame (flat wick)	Bright spot	1.2×10^4
Illuminating gas flame	Fish-tail burner	4×10^3
Welsbach mantle	Bright spot	6.2×10^4
Acetylene flame	Mees burner	1.1×10^5
Photoflash lamps		1.6×10^8 to 4×10^8 peak
Electronic flash		—
Nuclear sources:		
Atomic fusion bomb	0.1 msec after firing — 30-m dia. ball	2×10^{12}
Self-luminous paints		0.2 to 0.3
Incandescent lamps:		
Carbon filament	3.15 lm/W	5.2×10^5
Tantalum filament	6.30 lm/W	7×10^5
Tungsten filament	Vacuum lamp 10 lm/W	2×10^6
Tungsten filament	Gas-filled lamp 20 lm/W	1.2×10^7
Tungsten filament	750-W Projection lamp 26 lm / W	2.4×10^7
Tungsten filament	1200-W Projection lamp 31.5 lm / W	3.3×10^7
RF (radio frequency) lamp	24 mm diameter disk	6.2×10^7
Blackbody at 6500 K		3×10^9
Blackbody at 4000 K		2.5×10^8
Blackbody at 2042 K		6×10^5
60-W inside frosted bulb		1.2×10^5
10-W inside frosted bulb		2×10^4
Tungsten Halogen sources:		
3000 K CCT	—	1.3×10^7
3200 K CCT	—	2.3×10^7
3400 K CCT	—	3.9×10^7
Fluorescent sources:		
T-8 bulb	cool white 265 mA	1.1×10^4
T-12 bulb	cool white 430 mA	8.2×10^3
T-12 bulb 800 mA	cool white 800 mA	1.1×10^4
T-12 bulb 1500 mA	cool white 1500 mA	1.7×10^4
T-17 grooved bulb 1500 mA	cool white 1500 mA	1.5×10^4
Electroluminescent sources:		
Green color at 120 V 60 Hz		27
Green color at 600 V 400 Hz		68
Carbon Arc sources:		
Plain Carbon Arc	positive crater	1.5×10^8
High Intensity Carbon Arc	13.6 rotating positive carbon	1.0×10^9
Enclosed electric arc source:		
High pressure mercury	Type H33 2.5 atm	1.5×10^6
High pressure mercury	Type H38 10 atm	1.8×10^6
High intensity short arc mercury	30 atm	2.4×10^8 (4.3×10^9 peak)
Xenon short arc	900 W dc	1.8×10^8
Electronic flash tubes	900 W dc	1×10^9 to 3×10^9
Photographic flash units	In beam candlepower seconds	400 − 16,000 +
Photographic flash units	(BCPS)	400 − 16,000 +
Clear glass neon tube	15 mm 60 mA	1.6×10^3
Clear glass neon tube	15 mm 60 mA	8×10^2
Clear glass blue tube	15 mm 60 mA	8×10^2
Fluorescent tube		
daylight and white	15 mm 60 mA	5×10^3
green	15 mm 60 mA	9.5×10^3
blue and gold	15 mm 60 mA	3×10^3
pink and coral	15 mm 60 mA	2×10^3

Fig. 6-78. Incandescent General-Service Lamps for 120-, 125-, and 130-Volt Circuits (Will Operate in any Position but Lumen Maintenance is Best for 40 to 1500 Watts when Burned Base Up)

Watts	Bulb and other description	Base	Filament	Rated average life (h)	Maximum Overall length (mm)	(in.)	Average light center length (mm)	(in.)	Approximate color temperature (K)	Maximum bare bulb temperature (°C)*	Base temperature (°C)†	Approximate initial lumens	Initial lumens per watt‡	Lamp lumen depreciation (%)§
10	S-14 inside frosted	Medium	C-9	1500	89	$3\frac{1}{2}$	64	$2\frac{1}{2}$	2420	46.75	41	80	8.0	89
15	A-15 inside frosted	Medium	C-9	2500	89	$3\frac{1}{2}$	60	$2\frac{3}{8}$	—	—	—	126	8.4	83
25	A-19 inside frosted	Medium	C-9	2500	98	$4\frac{7}{8}$	64	$2\frac{1}{2}$	2550	43	42	230	9.2	79
25[d]	T-19 white ‖	Medium	CC-6	2500	113	$4\frac{7}{16}$	79	$3\frac{1}{8}$	—	—	—	235	9.2	80
34[a,b]	A-19 inside frosted	Medium	CC-6 or CC-8	1500	113	$4\frac{7}{16}$	79	$3\frac{1}{8}$	2550	—	—	410	12.1	—
40	A-19 inside frosted or white ‖	Medium	C-9	1500	113	$4\frac{7}{16}$	79	$3\frac{1}{8}$	2650	127	105	474	11.9	88
40[d]	T-19 white ‖	Medium	CC-6	1000	113	$4\frac{7}{16}$	79	$3\frac{1}{8}$	—	—	—	430	12.3	88
50	A-19 inside frosted	Medium	CC-6	1000	113	$4\frac{7}{16}$	79	$3\frac{1}{8}$	—	—	—	680	13.6	—
52[a,c]	A-19 inside frosted or clear	Medium	CC-8	1000	113	$4\frac{7}{16}$	79	$3\frac{1}{8}$	—	—	—	800	15.4	—
55[a]	A-19 clear or white ‖	Medium	CC-8	750	113	$4\frac{7}{16}$	79	$3\frac{1}{8}$	—	—	—	638	11.6	—
60	A-19 inside frosted or white ‖	Medium	CC-6	1000	113	$4\frac{7}{16}$	79	$3\frac{1}{8}$	2790	124	93	1060	14.4	93
60[d]	T-19 white ‖	Medium	CC-8	1000	113	$4\frac{7}{16}$	79	$3\frac{1}{8}$	—	—	—	860	14.3	92
67[a,d]	A-19 inside frosted or clear	Medium	CC-8	750	113	$4\frac{7}{16}$	79	$3\frac{1}{8}$	—	—	—	1130	16.9	—
70[a]	A-19 clear or white ‖	Medium	CC-8	750	113	$4\frac{7}{16}$	79	$3\frac{1}{8}$	—	—	—	1173	16.8	—
75	A-19 inside frosted or white ‖	Medium	CC-6	750	113	$4\frac{7}{16}$	79	$3\frac{1}{8}$	2840	135	96	1190	15.8	92
90[a]	A-19 inside frosted or clear	Medium	CC-8	750	113	$4\frac{7}{16}$	79	$3\frac{1}{8}$	—	—	—	1620	18.0	—
100	A-19 inside frosted or white ‖	Medium	CC-8	750	113	$4\frac{7}{16}$	79	$3\frac{1}{8}$	2905	149	98	1740	17.4	91
95[d]	A-19 inside frosted or white ‖	Medium	CC-8		113	$4\frac{7}{16}$	79	$3\frac{1}{8}$	—	—	—	1710	18.0	90
100	A-19 inside frosted or white ‖	Medium	CC-8	750	113	$4\frac{7}{16}$	79	$3\frac{1}{8}$	—	—	—	1683	16.8	—
100[d]	T-19 white ‖	Medium	CC-8	750	113	$4\frac{7}{16}$	79	$3\frac{1}{8}$	—	—	—	1710	17.1	91
100	A-21 inside frosted	Medium	CC-6	750	133	$5\frac{1}{4}$	98	$3\frac{7}{8}$	2880	127	90	1688	16.9	90
135[a]	A-21 inside frosted or clear	Medium	CC-87	750	139	$5\frac{1}{2}$	103	$4\frac{1}{16}$	—	—	—	2580	19.1	—
150[d]	T-19 white ‖	Medium	CC-8	1000	135	$5\frac{5}{16}$	98	$3\frac{7}{8}$	—	—	—	2650	17.7	87
150	A-21 inside frosted	Medium	CC-8	750	139	$5\frac{1}{2}$	103	$4\frac{1}{16}$	2960	—	—	2873	19.2	89

Watts	Description	Base	Bulb	Rated Life										
150	A-21 white ||	Medium	CC-8	750	139	$5\frac{1}{2}$	103	$4\frac{1}{16}$	2930	—	—	2787	18.5	89
150	A-23 inside frosted, clear, or white ||	Medium	CC-6	750	160	$6\frac{5}{16}$	117	$4\frac{5}{8}$	—	—	—	2780	18.5	89
150	PS-25 inside frosted or clear	Medium	C-9	750	176	$6\frac{15}{16}$	133	$5\frac{1}{4}$	2910	143	99	2663	17.8	88
200^d	T-21 white	Medium	CC-8	1000	156	$6\frac{1}{8}$	117	$4\frac{5}{8}$	—	—	—	3600	18.0	90
200	A-23 inside frosted	Medium	CC-8	750	160	$6\frac{5}{16}$	117	$4\frac{5}{8}$	2980	174	107	4003	20.0	89
200	PS-25 inside frosted	Medium	CC-6	750	176	$6\frac{15}{16}$	133	$5\frac{1}{4}$	—	—	—	3800	19.5	—
200	PS-30 inside frosted or clear	Medium	C-9	750	204	$8\frac{1}{16}$	152	6	2925	152	99	3703	18.5	85
300	PS-25 inside frosted or clear	Medium	CC-8	750	176	$6\frac{15}{16}$	131	$5\frac{3}{16}$	3015	205	112	6340	21.1	88
300	PS-30 inside frosted or clear	Medium	C-9	750	204	$8\frac{1}{16}$	152	6	3000	135	79	6103	20.3	83
300	PS-30 insider frosted or clear	Mogul	CC-8	1000	224	$8\frac{13}{16}$	178	7	—	—	—	5973	19.8	—
300	PS-35 inside frosted or clear	Mogul	C-9	1000	238	$9\frac{3}{8}$	178	7	2980	166	102	5810	19.4	86
500	PS-35 inside frosted or clear	Mogul	CC-8	1000	238	$9\frac{3}{8}$	178	7	3050	213	79	10675	21.3	89
500	PS-40 inside frosted or clear	Mogul	C-9	1000	248	$9\frac{3}{4}$	178	7	2945	199	102	16035	20.2	89
750	PS-52 inside frosted or clear	Mogul	C-7A	1000	332	$13\frac{1}{16}$	241	$9\frac{1}{2}$	2990	—	—	15660	20.7	—
750	PS-52 inside frosted or clear	Mogul	CC-8 or 2CC-8	1000	332	$13\frac{1}{16}$	241	$9\frac{1}{2}$	3090	—	—	16935	22.5	89
1000	PS-52 inside frosted or clear	Mogul	C-7A or 2CC-8	1000	332	$13\frac{1}{16}$	241	$9\frac{1}{2}$	2995	249	113	21800	22.7	89
1000	PS-52 inside frosted or clear	Mogul	CC-8 or 2CC-8	1000	332	$13\frac{1}{16}$	241	$9\frac{1}{2}$	3110	—	—	23510	23.5	89
1500	PS-52 inside frosted or clear	Mogul	C-7A or 2CC-8	1000	332	$13\frac{1}{16}$	241	$9\frac{1}{2}$	3095	266	129	33850	22.5	78

*These valued or clear.
†Used mainly in Canada.
‡For 120 volt lamps.
§Percent initial light output at 70 percent rated life.
\|\| Lamp and lumen per watt value of white lamps are generally lower than for inside frosted.
^{a}General Electric.
^{b}Sylvania.
^{c}Philips.
^{d}OSRAM.

Fig. 6-79. Effect of Hot-Cold Resistance on Current in an Incandescent Filament (Laboratory Conditions)

Lamp wattage	voltage	Normal current (A)	Theoretical inrush: Basis, hot-to-cold resistance (A)*	Time for current to fall to normal value (s)
General-service incandescent					
15	120	0.125	2.30	0.05
25	120	0.208	3.98	0.06
40	120	0.333	7.00	0.07
50	120	0.417	8.34	0.07
60	120	0.500	10.20	0.08
75	120	0.625	13.10	0.09
100	120	0.835	17.90	0.10
150	120	1.25	26.10	0.12
200	120	1.67	39.50	0.13
300	120	2.50	53.00	0.13
500	120	4.17	89.50	0.15
750	120	6.25	113.00	0.17
1000	120	8.30	195.00	0.18
1500	120	12.50	290.00	0.20
2000	120	16.70	378.00	0.23
Tungsten-halogen lamps (C-8 filament)					
300	120	2.50	62.00	†
500	120	4.17	102.00	†
1000	240	4.17	100.00	†
1500	240	6.24	147.00	†
1500	277	5.42	129.00	†

*The current will reach the peak value within the first peak of the supplied voltage. Thus the time approaches zero if the instantaneous supplied voltage is at peak, or it could be as much as 0.006 second.

†Not established. Estimated time is 5 to 20 cycles.

Fig. 6-80. Luminous and Thermal Characteristics of Typical Gas-Filled Incandescent Filament Lamps

Watts	Radiated in visible spectrum (percent of input wattage)	Total filament radiation beyond bulb percent of input wattage	Gas loss (percent of input wattage)	Base and bulb loss (percent of input wattage)	End loss (loss by conduction at filament ends in percent of input wattage)	Filament heat current (J)	Heating time to 90 percent lumens (s)	Cooling time to 10 percent lumens (s)	Percent flicker 60 Hz	Percent flicker 25 Hz
6*	6	93.0	—	5.5	1.5	0.25	0.04	0.01	29	69
10*	7.1	93.5	—	5.0	1.5	0.62	0.06	0.02	17	40
25*	8.7	94.0	—	4.5	1.5	2.8	0.10	0.03	10	28
40†	7.4	71.3	20.0	7.1	1.6	2.5	0.07	0.03	13	29
60‡	7.5	80.8	13.5	4.5	1.2	5.5	0.10	0.04	8	19
100‡	10.0	82.0	11.5	5.2	1.3	14.1	0.13	0.06	5	14
200†	10.2	77.4	13.7	7.2	1.7	39.5	0.22	0.09	4	11
300†	11.1	79.8	11.6	6.8	1.8	80.0	0.27	0.13	3	8
500†	12.0	82.3	8.8	7.1	1.8	182.0	0.38	0.19	2	6
1000†	12.1	87.4	6.0	4.7	1.9	568.0	0.67	0.30	1	4

*Vacuum.
†Coiled — coil filament.
‡Gas-filled.

Fig. 6-81. Three-lite Incandescent Lamps for 120- and 125-Volt Circuits (for base-down burning only)*

Watts	Bulb and other description	Base	Filament	Rated life (h)	Maximum overall length (mm)	(in.)	Average light center length (mm)	(in.)	Initial Lumens	Initial lumens per watt	Lamp lumen depreciation (%)†
15	A-21	3 contact medium	C-2R/CC-8	1500	135	$5\frac{5}{16}$	99	$3\frac{7}{8}$	85	3.7	—
135				1200					2300	17.0	—
150				1200					2385	15.9	—
30	A-21 or	3 contact medium	C-8 or 2CC-6	1300	135	$5\frac{5}{16}$	98	$3\frac{7}{8}$	290	9.7	—
70	T-19		or 2CC-8 or	1200					1028	14.7	—
100	white		C-2R/CC-8	1200					1315	13.2	86
30[b]	T-19	3 contact medium	2CC-6	1600	135	$5\frac{5}{16}$	95	$3\frac{3}{4}$	310	10.3	—
70	white								940	14.0	—
100									1240	12.4	—
50	A-23 or	3 contact medium	2CC-6	1300	148	$5\frac{27}{32}$	99	$3\frac{7}{8}$	607	12.1	—
100	A-21			1200					1607	16.1	—
150	white			1200					2213	14.8	85
50	PS-25 or	3 contact medium	2C-2R or	1200	151	$5\frac{15}{16}$	99	$3\frac{7}{8}$	405	8.1	—
100	T-19		2CC-6 or						967	9.7	—
150	white		2CC-8						1350	9.0	—
50[c]	T-19	3 contact medium	2CC-8	1600	135	$5\frac{5}{16}$	95	$3\frac{3}{4}$	575	11.5	—
100	white								1450	14.5	—
150	(ext. life)								2025	13.5	85
50	PS-25	3 contact mogul	2C-2R or	1200	173	$6\frac{13}{16}$	127	5	640	12.8	—
100	inside		2CC-8						1630	16.3	—
150	frosted								2270	15.1	—
50	A-21	3 contact medium	C-2R/CC-8	1500	113	$4\frac{7}{16}$	79	$3\frac{1}{8}$	580	11.6	—
135				1200					2330	17.3	—
185				1200					2910	15.7	—
100	PS-25	3 contact mogul	2CC-6 or	1300	173	$6\frac{13}{16}$	113	$4\frac{7}{16}$	1350	13.5	—
200	white		2CC-8 or						3350	16.8	—
300			C-2R/CC-8						4700	15.7	72
50	PS-25	3 contact medium	2C-2R or	1200	151	$5\frac{15}{16}$	99	$3\frac{7}{8}$	573	11.5	—
200	A-23 or		2CC-6 or						3640	18.2	—
250	T-21 white		C-2R/CC-8						4230	16.9	72
50	T-21	3 contact medium	2CC-6	1600	135	$5\frac{5}{16}$	98	$3\frac{7}{8}$	575	11.5	—
200	white								3250	16.3	—
250									3825	15.3	72
80[a]	A-23	3 contact medium	C-2R/CC-8	1000	151	$5\frac{15}{16}$	125	$4\frac{15}{16}$	1100	13.8	—
170	white								2800	16.5	—
250									3900	15.6	—

*These values are the average of several manufacturers' data.
†Percent initial light output at 70% rated life.
[a]General Electric.
[b]Philips.
[c]Sylvania.

Fig. 6-82. Incandescent Lamps for High Voltage Service (May be Burned in Any Position)*

Watts	Bulb and other description	Base	Filament	Rated average life (h)	Maximum overall length		Light center length		230 – 250 volts			277 volts		
					(mm)	(in.)	(mm)	(in.)	Initial lumens†	Initial lumens per watt	Lamp lumen depreciation (%)‡	Initial lumens	Initial lumens per watt	Lamp lumen depreciation (%)‡
25	A-19 inside frosted	Medium	C-17 or C-17A	1000	98	$3\frac{7}{8}$	65	$2\frac{9}{16}$	220	8.8	86	210	8.4	—
50	A-19 inside frosted	Medium	C-17 or C-17A	1000	98	$3\frac{7}{8}$	65	$2\frac{9}{16}$	490	9.8	79	490	9.8	—
100	A-21 inside frosted	Medium	C-7A or C-9	817	133	$5\frac{1}{4}$	97	$3\frac{13}{16}$	1280	12.8	90	1280	12.8	—
150	PS-25 inside frosted or clear	Medium	C-7A or C-9	1000	176	$6\frac{15}{16}$	132	$5\frac{3}{16}$	2080	13.9	—	1950	13.0	—
200	PS-30 inside frosted or clear§	Medium	C-9	1000	205	$8\frac{5}{32}$	153	6	3040	15.2	90	2890	14.5	—
300	PS-30 clear	Medium	C-7A	1000	205	$8\frac{5}{32}$	153	6	4735	15.8	—	4450	14.8	—
300	PS-35 inside frosted or clear§	Mogul	C-7A	1000	238	$9\frac{3}{8}$	178	7	4845	16.2	89	4890	16.3	—
500	PS-40 inside frosted or clear§	Mogul	C-7A	1000	248	$9\frac{3}{4}$	178	7	9213	18.5	87	8900	17.8	—
750¶	PS-52 inside frosted or clear§	Mogul	C-7A	1000	330	13	241	$9\frac{1}{2}$	13,600	18.1	—	13,600	18.0	—
1000¶	PS-52 inside frosted or clear§	Mogul	C-7A	1000	330	13	241	$9\frac{1}{2}$	17,800	17.9	82	18,000	1.8	—
1500¶	PS-52 inside frosted or clear§	Mogul	C-7A	1000	330	13	241	$9\frac{1}{2}$	27,000	18	—	26,000	17.3	—

*These values are the average of several manufacturers' data.
†For 230-V lamps
‡Percent initial light at 70% of rated life.
§Clear only for 277-V lamps
¶1000 hour life for 277-V lamps.

Fig. 6-83. Rough Service Incandescent Lamps for 120 and 125/130 Volt Circuits
(May be Burned in any Position)

Watts	Bulb and other description	Base	Filament	Rated life (h)	Max. overall length		Light center length		Initial lumens	Initial lumens per watt	Lamp lumens depreciation (%)†
					(mm)	(in.)	(mm)	(in.)			
25*	A-19 inside frosted	Medium	C-17	1000	100	$3\frac{15}{16}$	65	$2\frac{9}{16}$	217	8.7	—
50	A-19 inside frosted	Medium	C-22 or C-17A	1000	100	$3\frac{15}{16}$	65	$2\frac{9}{16}$	475	9.5	76
75ᵈ	A-19 inside frosted	Medium	C-17A	1000	100	$3\frac{15}{16}$	64	$2\frac{1}{2}$	750	10.0	—
75	A-21 inside frosted	Medium	C-22 or C-17	1000	135	$5\frac{5}{16}$	98	$3\frac{7}{8}$	750	10.0	—
100	A-21 inside frosted	Medium	C-17	1000	135	$5\frac{5}{16}$	98	$3\frac{7}{8}$	1247	12.5	79
150	A-21 inside frosted	Medium	C-17	1000	133	$5\frac{1}{4}$	97	$3\frac{13}{16}$	—	—	—
150	A-23 inside frosted	Medium	C-17	1000	154	$6\frac{1}{16}$	111	$4\frac{3}{8}$	2115	14.1	—
150	PS-25 inside frosted	Medium	C-17	1000	176	$6\frac{15}{16}$	133	$5\frac{1}{4}$	2145	14.3	80
200	PS-30 inside frosted or clear	Medium	C-17	1000	205	$8\frac{1}{16}$	152	6	3387	16.9	82.5
200	A-23 inside frosted or clear	Medium	C-9	1000	154	$6\frac{1}{16}$	111	$4\frac{3}{8}$	3380	16.9	—
300	PS-35 inside frosted	Mogul	C-9	1000	238	$9\frac{3}{8}$	178	7	5295	17.7	—
500	PS-40 clear	Mogul	C-9	1000	248	$9\frac{3}{4}$	178	7	9500	19.0	—

*115 volt not available.
†Percent initial light output at 70% rated life.

Fig. 6-84. Extended Service (2500 Hours Rated Life) Incandescent Filament Lamps*

Watts	Bulb and other description	Base	Filament	Rated average life (h)	Maximum overall length (mm)	Maximum overall length (in.)	Light center length (mm)	Light center length (in.)	Initial lumens	Initial lumens per watt	Lamp lumen depreciation (%)‡
				For 120, 125, and 130 volts†							
15	A-15 inside frosted	Medium	C-9	2500	89	$3\frac{1}{2}$	60	$2\frac{3}{8}$	124	8.3	83
25	A-19 inside frosted	Medium	C-9	2500	100	$3\frac{7}{8}$	64	$2\frac{1}{2}$	227	9.1	79
34§	A-17 or A-19 inside frosted	Medium	CC-6 or CC-8	2500	113	$4\frac{3}{8}$	76	3	373	11.0	—
40	A-17 or A-19 inside frosted	Medium	C-9	2500	108	$4\frac{5}{16}$	73	$2\frac{7}{8}$	418	10.5	88
52§	A-17 or A-19 inside frosted	Medium	CC-8	2500	113	$4\frac{3}{8}$	79	$3\frac{1}{8}$	715	13.4	—
60	A-17 or A-19 inside frosted	Medium	CC-6	2500	113	$4\frac{3}{8}$	79	$3\frac{1}{8}$	763	12.7	92
67§	A-17 or A-19 inside frosted	Medium	CC-8	2500	113	$4\frac{3}{8}$	79	$3\frac{1}{8}$	942	14.1	—
75	A-19 inside frosted	Medium	CC-8	2500	113	$4\frac{3}{8}$	79	$3\frac{1}{8}$	1000	13.3	91
90§	A-17 or A-19 inside frosted	Medium	CC-8	2500	113	$4\frac{3}{8}$	79	$3\frac{1}{8}$	1353	15.4	—
100	A-17 or A-19 inside frosted	Medium	CC-8	2500	113	$4\frac{3}{8}$	79	$3\frac{1}{8}$	1490	14.9	93
100	A-21 inside frosted	Medium	CC-6	2500	134	$5\frac{5}{16}$	98	$3\frac{7}{8}$	1437	14.4	—
135§	A-19 inside frosted and clear	Medium	CC-8	2500	137	$5\frac{3}{8}$	102	4	2150	15.9	—
150	A-21 inside frosted and clear	Medium	CC-8	2500	135	$5\frac{5}{16}$	98	$3\frac{7}{8}$	2350	15.7	90
150	A-23 inside frosted and clear	Medium	CC-6	2500	159	$6\frac{5}{16}$	117	$4\frac{5}{8}$	2337	15.6	89
150	PS-25 inside frosted and clear	Medium	C-9	2500	176	$6\frac{7}{8}$	133	$5\frac{5}{16}$	2300	15.3	86
200	A-23 inside frosted and clear	Medium	CC-8	2500	157	$6\frac{3}{16}$	117	$4\frac{5}{8}$	3353	16.7	88
200	A-25 inside frosted and clear	Medium	CC-6	2500	176	$6\frac{7}{8}$	133	$5\frac{5}{16}$	3250	5.4	—
200	PS-25 inside frosted and clear	Medium	CC-6	2500	176	$6\frac{7}{8}$	133	$5\frac{5}{16}$	3220	16.1	—
200	PS-30 inside frosted and clear	Medium	C-9	2500	205	$8\frac{1}{8}$	152	6	3240	16.2	81
300	PS-25 inside frosted and clear	Medium	CC-8	2500	176	$6\frac{7}{8}$	133	$5\frac{5}{16}$	5060	16.9	81
300	PS-30 inside frosted and clear	Medium	C-9	2500	205	$8\frac{1}{8}$	152	6	3460	17.3	79
300	PS-35 inside frosted and clear	Mogul	C-9	2500	238	$9\frac{3}{8}$	178	7	5190	17.3	84
500	PS-35 inside frosted and clear	Mogul	C-9	2500	238	$9\frac{3}{8}$	178	7	8750	17.5	80
500	PS-40 inside frosted and clear	Mogul	C-9	2500	248	$9\frac{3}{4}$	178	7	9070	18.1	80
750	PS-52 clear	Mogul	C-7A	2500	332	$13\frac{1}{16}$	241	$9\frac{1}{2}$	14,200	18.9	83
1000	PS-52 clear	Mogul	C-7A	2500	332	$13\frac{1}{16}$	241	$9\frac{1}{2}$	19,800	19.8	78
1500	PS-52 clear	Mogul	C-7A	2500	332	$13\frac{1}{16}$	241	$9\frac{1}{2}$	30,000	20.0	—

Fig. 6-84. *Continued*

Watts	Bulb and other description	Base	Filament	Rated average life (h)	Maximum overall length (mm)	(in.)	Light center length (mm)	(in.)	Initial lumens	Initial lumens per watt	Lamp lumen depreciation (%)‡
					For 230, 240, and 250 volts						
100	A-21 inside frosted	Medium	C-7A or C-9	2500	133	$5\frac{1}{4}$	98	$3\frac{7}{8}$	1070	10.7	—
150	PS-25 inside frosted and clear	Medium	C-7A or C-9	2500	176	$5\frac{15}{16}$	133	$5\frac{1}{4}$	1380	9.2	—
200	PS-30 inside frosted and clear	Medium	C-7A or C-9	2500	205	$8\frac{1}{16}$	152	6	2590	9.2	—
300	PS-35 inside frosted and clear	Mogul	C-7A	2500	238	$9\frac{3}{8}$	178	7	4290	10.7	—
500	PS-40 inside frosted and clear	Mogul	C-7A	2500	248	$9\frac{7}{8}$	178	7	7930	15.9	—
750¶	PS-52 clear	Mogul	C-7A	2000	332	$13\frac{1}{16}$	241	$9\frac{1}{2}$	13,600	18.2	—
1000¶	PS-52 clear	Mogul	C-7A	2000	332	$13\frac{1}{16}$	241	$9\frac{1}{2}$	18,600	18.6	78
1500¶	PS-52 clear	Mogul	C-7A	2000	332	$13\frac{1}{16}$	241	$9\frac{1}{2}$	20,250	18.0	—

*Average values for several manufacturers.
†GE has no 125 volt rating.
‡Percent initial light output at 70% of rated life.
§Reduced wattage, high efficacy.
¶Life is 2000 hours.

Fig. 6-85. Industrial Service Incandescent Lamps (3000 – 4000 Hours) for 120-, 125-, and 130-Volt Service.*

Watts	Bulb and other description[a,b]	Base†	Filament	Rated average life (h)	Maximum overall length (mm)	(in.)	Light center length (mm)	(in.)	Initial lumens	Initial lumens per watt[1]	Lamp lumen depreciation (%)
15	A-15 inside frosted	Medium brass base	C-9	3250	89	$3\frac{1}{2}$	60	$2\frac{3}{8}$	123	8.2	80
25	A-19 inside frosted	Medium brass base	C-9	3250	100	$3\frac{15}{16}$	64	$2\frac{1}{2}$	215	8.6	80
40	A-19 inside frosted or diffuse	Medium brass base	C-9	3167	113	$4\frac{7}{16}$	79	$3\frac{1}{8}$	377	9.4	80
60	A-19 inside frosted or diffuse	Medium brass base	C-9	3250	113	$4\frac{7}{16}$	79	$3\frac{1}{8}$	660	11	80
75	A-19 inside frosted or diffuse	Medium brass base	C-9	3000	113	$4\frac{7}{16}$	79	$3\frac{1}{8}$	850	11.3	80
100	A-21 inside frosted or diffuse	Medium brass base	C-9	3250	113	$4\frac{7}{16}$	79	$3\frac{1}{8}$	1220	12.2	80
150	A-19 inside frosted or diffuse	Medium brass base	C-9	3250	125	$4\frac{15}{16}$	86	$3\frac{3}{8}$	2125	14.2	80
200	PS-30 inside frosted	Medium brass base	C-9	3500	160	$6\frac{15}{16}$	133	$5\frac{1}{4}$	2890	14.5	80
300	PS-35 inside frosted	Medium brass base	C-9	3500	205	$8\frac{1}{16}$	152	6	4880	16.3	80
300	PS-35 inside frosted	Mogul brass base	C-9	3500	238	$9\frac{3}{8}$	178	7	4930	16.4	80
500	PS-40 clear	Mogul brass base	C-9	3500	248	$9\frac{3}{4}$	178	7	8480	16.9	80

Note: Values are averaged for several manufacturers' products. Industrial rough service lamps, 60 to 200 watts, are also available with silicon coating.
*Lamps listed at 120 volts are also available in 130 volts.
†All lamps have brass base.
[a]Cataloged by General Electric as "Survivor."
[b]Cataloged by Philips as "Industrial Rough Service."

Fig. 6-86. Incandescent Vibration Service Lamps for 120 and 130 Volt Service

Watts	Bulb and other description*	Base	Filament	Rated average life (h)	Maximum overall length (mm)	Maximum overall length (in.)	Light center length (mm)	Light center length (in.)	Initial lumens	Initial lumens per watt†	Lamp lumen depreciation (%)‡
25	A-19 inside frosted or clear	Medium	C-9	1000	100	$3\frac{15}{16}$	64	$2\frac{1}{2}$	244	9.8	—
50	A-19 inside frosted or clear§	Medium	C-9	1000	100	$3\frac{15}{16}$	64	$2\frac{1}{2}$	555	11.1	72
75	A-21 inside frosted§	Medium	C-9	1000	133	$5\frac{1}{4}$	98	$3\frac{7}{8}$	935	12.5	—
100	A-21 inside frosted or clear§	Medium	C-9	1000	135	$5\frac{5}{16}$	98	$3\frac{7}{8}$	1400	14	83
100	A-23 inside frosted or clear	Medium	C-9	1000	151	$5\frac{15}{16}$	113	$4\frac{7}{16}$	1362	13.6	—
150	PS-25 inside frosted	Medium	C-9	1000	176	$6\frac{15}{16}$	133	$5\frac{1}{4}$	2350	15.7	—

*Burning position, any, except as noted.
†These values are average of several manufacturers' data.
‡Percent initial light output at 70% of rated life except as noted.
§Not horizontal.

Fig. 6-87. Protective Coated Incandescent Lamps for 120 and 125 Volt Service*

Watts	Bulb and other description	Base	Filament	Rated life (h)	Maximum overall length (mm)	Maximum overall length (in.)	Service	Initial lumens	Initial lumens per watt	Lamp lumen depreciation (%)
25	A-19 inside frosted	Medium brass base	C-9	2500	100	$3\frac{15}{16}$	Standard	218	8.7	90
30[a]	R-20 frost coated	Medium brass base	C-9	6000	100	$3\frac{15}{16}$	Sign	—	—	—
40	A-15 inside frosted	Medium brass base	C-9	1000	89	$3\frac{1}{2}$	Appliance	450	11.0	88
40[c]	A-19 inside frosted	Medium brass base	CC-6	1500	113	$4\frac{7}{16}$	Standard	480	12.0	—
50	A-19 inside frosted	Medium brass base	C-17a	1000	98	$3\frac{7}{8}$	Rough service	483	9.7	79.5
60	A-19 inside frosted	Medium brass base	CC-6	1000	113	$4\frac{7}{16}$	Standard	863	14.4	79.5
60[a]	A-19 inside frosted	Medium brass base	C-9	3500	108	$4\frac{1}{4}$	Industrial	650	10.8	88
75	A-21 inside frosted	Medium brass base	C-17	1000	133	$5\frac{1}{4}$	Rough service	750	10.0	79.5
75	R-30 flood frost coated	Medium brass base	CC-6	2000	137	$5\frac{3}{8}$	Flood	835	11.1	80
100	A-21 inside frosted	Medium brass base	CC-6	750	133	$5\frac{1}{4}$	Standard	1625	16.3	91
100[a]	A-21 inside frosted	Medium brass base	C-9	3500	135	$5\frac{5}{16}$	Industrial	1210	12.1	88
100	A-21 inside frosted	Medium brass base	C-17	1000	133	$5\frac{1}{4}$	Rough service	1208	12.1	79.5
150[a]	A-21 inside frosted	Medium brass base	C-17A	1000	135	$5\frac{5}{16}$	Rough service	1850	13.0	89

Fig 6-87. *Continued*

Watts	Bulb and other description	Base	Filament	Rated life (h)	Maximum overall length (mm)	Maximum overall length (in.)	Service	Initial lumens	Initial lumens per watt	Lamp lumen depreciation (%)
150	PS-25 inside frosted	Medium brass base	C-9	1000	176	$6\frac{15}{16}$	Standard	2425	16.2	70
150[a]	A-25 inside frosted	Medium brass base	C-9	1000	176	$6\frac{15}{16}$	Standard	1680	11.2	88
150	PS-25 inside frosted	Medium brass base	C-17	1000	176	$6\frac{15}{16}$	Rough service	2123	14.1	80
150	R-40 frosted face	Medium brass base	CC-6	2000	167	$6\frac{9}{16}$	Flood	1860	12.4	—
200[a]	PS-25 frost	Medium brass base	C-9	750	205	$8\frac{1}{16}$	General	—	—	—
200	PS-30 inside frosted	Medium brass base	C-9	1000	205	$8\frac{1}{16}$	Standard	3480	17.4	
200[a,b]	PS-30 inside frosted	Medium brass base	C-9	3500	205	$8\frac{1}{16}$	Industrial	—	—	—
200	PS-30 inside frosted	Medium brass base	C-9	1000	205	$8\frac{1}{16}$	Rough service	3330	16.6	—

*These values are the average of several manufacturers' data.
[a]Philips.
[b]Operates base up.
[c]General Electric.

Fig. 6-88. Tungsten-Halogen Lamps for General Lighting (Any Burning Position, Except as Noted)

Watts	Volts	Bulb and other description	Base	Filament	Rated life (h)	Maximum Overall length (mm)	Maximum Overall length (in.)	Light center length (mm)	Light center length (in.)	Approximate color temperature (K)	Initial lumens*	Initial lumens per watt	Lamp lumen depreciation (%)†
								Double-Ended Type					
200	120	T-3 frosted	RSC‡	CC-8	1500	79	$3\frac{1}{8}$	24	$\frac{7}{8}$	2850	3350	16.7	96
200	120	T-3 clear	RSC	CC-8	1500	79	$3\frac{1}{8}$	24	$\frac{7}{8}$	2875	3460	16.7	96
225	120	T-3 IR reflector	RSC	C-8	3000	119	$4\frac{11}{16}$	59	$2\frac{5}{16}$	3000	5700	25.3	—
250	120	T-3 clear	RSC	C-8	2000	83	$3\frac{5}{16}$	—	—	—	4000	16.0	—
300	120	T-3 clear	RSC	C-8	2000	119	$4\frac{11}{16}$	59	$2\frac{5}{16}$	2950	5950	19.9	96
300	120	T-3 frosted	RSC	C-8	2000	119	$4\frac{11}{16}$	—	—	2950	4425	19.3	96
300	120	T-3 clear	RSC	CC-8	2000	79	$3\frac{1}{8}$	—	—	2900	2825	18.5	—
300	120	T-4 clear	RSC	CC-8	2000	79	$3\frac{1}{8}$	17	$\frac{11}{16}$	2950	5650	18.9	96
300	130	T-4 clear	RSC	CC-8	2000	79	$3\frac{1}{8}$	—	—	3000	2825	18.9	—
300	120	T-4 frosted	RSC	CC-8	2000	79	$3\frac{1}{8}$	—	—	3000	2650	17.7	—
350	a	T-3 IR reflector	RSC	C-8	2000	119	$4\frac{11}{16}$	60	$2\frac{3}{8}$	3000	7400	28.0	95
400	a	T-3 clear	RSC	CC-8	2000	119	$4\frac{11}{16}$	—	—	—	6750	22.5	—
400	120	T-4 clear	RSC	CC-8	2000	79	$3\frac{1}{8}$	21	$\frac{13}{16}$	2950	7750	21.0	96
400	125	T-4 clear	RSC	CC-8	2000	79	$3\frac{1}{8}$	—	—	3000	3750	18.7	—
400	130	T-4 clear	RSC	CC-8	2000	79	$3\frac{1}{8}$	—	—	3000	3900	19.5	—
425	120	T-3 clear	RSC	C-8	2000	119	$4\frac{11}{16}$	56	$2\frac{3}{16}$	2950	2225	20.9	—
500	120	T-3 clear	RSC	C-8§	1500	119	$4\frac{11}{16}$	60	$2\frac{3}{8}$	2950	10,650	21.4	96
500	120	T-3 clear	RSC	C-8	2000	119	$4\frac{11}{16}$	57	$2\frac{5}{16}$	3000	11,000	22.2	96
500	120	T-3 frosted	RSC	C-8	2000	119	$4\frac{11}{16}$	57	$2\frac{5}{16}$	3000	10,725	21.5	96
500	125	T-3 clear	RSC	C-8	2000	119	$4\frac{11}{16}$	—	—	3000	10,500	21.0	—
500	130	T-3 clear	RSC	C-8	2000	119	$4\frac{11}{16}$	62	$2\frac{3}{8}$	3000	10,750	21.5	96

Fig. 6-88. *Continued*

Watts	Volts	Bulb and other description	Base	Filament	Rated life (h)	Maximum Overall length (mm)	(in.)	Light center length (mm)	(in.)	Approximate color temperature (K)	Initial lumens*	Initial lumens per watt	Lamp lumen depreciation (%)†
Double-Ended Type													
900	b	T-3 IR reflector	RSC	C-8	2000	256	$10\frac{1}{8}$	155	$6\frac{1}{8}$	3160	24,000	35.6	95
900	277	T-3 IR reflector	RSC	C-8	2000	256	$10\frac{1}{8}$	155	$6\frac{1}{8}$	3160	31,000	34.4	95
1000	120	T-6 clear	RSC	CC-8	2000	143	$5\frac{5}{8}$	25	1	3000	23,400	23.4	96
1000	120	T-6 clear	RSC	CC-8	4000	143	$5\frac{5}{8}$	—	—	2950	19,800	19.8	93
1000	120	T-6 frosted	RSC	CC-8	2000	143	$5\frac{5}{8}$	—	—	3000	11,700	22.7	96
1000	120	T-6 clear	RSC	CC-8	500	143	$5\frac{5}{8}$	—	—	3100	24,500	24.5	
1000	220	T-3 clear	RSC	C-8	2000	256	$10\frac{1}{8}$	155	$6\frac{1}{8}$	3000	21,450	21.5	96
1000	240	T-3 clear	RSC	C-8	2000	256	$10\frac{1}{8}$	163	—	3000	21,425	21.4	96
1200	b	T-3 clear	RSC	C-8	2000	256	$10\frac{1}{8}$	—	—	—	29,000	24.2	—
1250	208	T-3 clear	RSC	C-8	2000	256	$10\frac{1}{8}$	—	—	3050	28,000	22.4	96
1500	208	T-3 clear	RSC	C-8	2000	256	$10\frac{1}{8}$	167	$6\frac{5}{8}$	3050	35,800	23.9	96
1500	220	T-3 clear	RSC	C-8	2000	256	$10\frac{1}{8}$	173	$6\frac{13}{16}$	3050	35,800	23.9	96
1500	240	T-3 clear	RSC	C-8	2000	256	$10\frac{1}{8}$	160	$6\frac{5}{16}$	3050	35,800	23.6	96
1500	240	T-3 frosted	RSC	C-8	2000	256	$10\frac{1}{8}$	—	—	3050	32,000	21.3	—
1500	240	T-3 clear RS	RSC	C-8	2000	256	$10\frac{1}{8}$	167	$6\frac{5}{8}$	2900	34,400	22.9	—
1500	277	T-3 clear	RSC	C-8	2000	256	$10\frac{1}{8}$	167	$6\frac{5}{8}$	3050	33,900	22.7	96
1500	277	T-3 frosted	RSC	C-8	2000	256	$10\frac{1}{8}$	—	—	3050	31,600	21.0	—
Single-Ended Types													
5	12	T-3 clear	G4	C-6	2000	31	$1\frac{3}{16}$	—	—	—	60	12.0	—
10	6	T-3 clear	G4	C-6	2000	31	$1\frac{3}{16}$	—	—	—	120	12.0	—
10	12	T-3 clear	G4	C-6	2000	31	$1\frac{3}{16}$	—	—	—	140	14.0	—
20	c	T-3 clear	G4	C-6	2000	31	$1\frac{3}{16}$	—	—	—	350	17.5	—
20	24	T-3 clear	G4	C-6	1000	32	$1\frac{3}{16}$	—	—	—	260	13.0	—
50	12	T-4 clear	GY 6.35	C-6	2000	44	$1\frac{11}{16}$	—	—	—	950	19.0	—
50	24	T-4 clear	GY-6.35	C-6	2000	44	$1\frac{11}{16}$	—	—	—	900	18.0	—
75	28	T-3 clear	Minican	CC-6	2000	63	$2\frac{1}{2}$	30	$1\frac{3}{16}$	—	1400	18.7	—
100	12	T-$3\frac{1}{2}$ clear	Minican	—	1000	57	$2\frac{5}{16}$	—	—	—	2500	25.0	—
100	12	T-4 clear	GY 6.35	C-6	2000	44	$1\frac{11}{16}$	—	—	—	2500	25.0	—
100	24	T-4 clear	GY 6.35	C-6	2000	44	$1\frac{11}{16}$	—	—	—	2000	20.0	—
100	120	T-4 clear	Minican	CC-8	1300	71	$2\frac{13}{16}$	35	$1\frac{3}{8}$	—	1800	18.0	—
100	120	T-4 frosted	Minican	CC-8	1000	71	$2\frac{13}{16}$	35	$1\frac{3}{8}$	—	1750	17.5	—
100	120	T-4 clear	D.C. Bay.	CC-8	1300	62	$2\frac{3}{8}$	35	$1\frac{3}{8}$	—	1800	18.0	—
100	120	T-4 frosted	D.C. Bay.	CC-8	1000	62	$2\frac{3}{8}$	35	$1\frac{3}{8}$	—	1750	17.5	—
150	120	T-4 clear	Minican	CC-8	1750	71	$2\frac{13}{16}$	35	$1\frac{3}{8}$	—	2900	19.3	—
150	120	T-4 clear	Minican	CC-8	2000	71	$2\frac{13}{16}$	35	$1\frac{3}{8}$	2900	—	—	—
150	120	T-4 clear	D.C. Bay.	CC-8	1750	62	$2\frac{3}{8}$	35	$1\frac{3}{8}$	—	2900	19.3	—
150	120	T-4 frosted	D.C. Bay.	CC-8	1000	62	$2\frac{3}{8}$	35	$1\frac{3}{8}$	—	2700	18.0	—
150	120	T-4 clear	Minican	CC-8	2000	76	3	36	$1\frac{1}{2}$	3000	—	—	—
150	120	T-4 frosted	Minican	CC-8	2000	76	3	38	$1\frac{1}{2}$	3000	—	—	—
150	120	T-10 clear or frosted	Med.	C-8	2000	105	$4\frac{1}{8}$	75	$2\frac{7}{8}$	—	2500	16.7	—
150	120	T-5 clear or frosted	D.C. Bay.	C-6	2000	95	$3\frac{13}{16}$	—	—	—	2000	13.3	—

Fig. 6-88. *Continued*

Single-Ended Type

Watts	Volts	Bulb and other description	Base	Filament	Rated life (h)	Maximum Overall length (mm)	(in.)	Light center length (mm)	(in.)	Approximate color temperature (K)	Initial lumens*	Initial lumens per watt	Lamp lumen depreciation (%)†
250	120	T-10 clear or frosted	Med.	C-6	2000	105	$4\frac{1}{8}$	75	$2\frac{7}{8}$	—	4200	16.8	—
250	120	T-5 clear or frosted	D.C. Bay.	C-6	2000	95	$3\frac{13}{16}$	—	—	—	4200	16.8	—
250	120	T-4 clear	Minican	CC-8	2000	80	$3\frac{3}{16}$	41	$1\frac{5}{8}$	—	4850	19.4	96
250	120	T-4 frosted	Minican	CC-8	2000	80	$3\frac{3}{16}$	41	$1\frac{5}{8}$	—	4700	18.8	96
250	120	T-4 clear	D.C. Bay.	CC-8	2000	76	3	41	$1\frac{5}{8}$	2950	—	—	96
250	120	T-4 clear	D.C. Bay.	CC-8	2000	76	3	41	$1\frac{5}{8}$	—	4850	19.4	96
250	120	T-4 frosted	D.C. Bay.	CC-8	2000	76	3	41	$1\frac{5}{8}$	—	4700	18.8	96
250	130	T-4 clear	Minican	CC-8	2000	80	$3\frac{3}{16}$	41	$1\frac{5}{8}$	—	4850	19.4	—
400	120	T-4 frosted	Minican	CC-8	2000	92	$3\frac{5}{8}$	51	2	—	8550	21.4	96
400	120	T-4 clear	Minican	CC-8	2000	92	$3\frac{5}{8}$	51	2	—	8800	22.0	96
500	120	T-4 clear	Minican	CC-8	2000	95	$3\frac{3}{4}$	51	2	—	11,500	23.0	—
500	120	T-4 frosted	Minican	CC-8	2000	95	$3\frac{3}{4}$	51	2	—	10,000	20.0	—
500	120	T-4 frosted	D.C. Bay.	CC-8	2000	87	$3\frac{7}{16}$	54	$2\frac{1}{8}$	—	10,100	20.2	96
500	120	T-4 clear	D.C. Bay.	CC-8	2000	87	$3\frac{7}{16}$	54	$2\frac{1}{8}$	—	10,450	20.9	96
500	130	T-4 clear	Minican	CC-8	2000	95	$3\frac{3}{4}$	51	2	—	11,500	23.0	—
1000	120	T-20 clear	Mog. Bipst.	CC-8	2000	233	$9\frac{1}{2}$	102	4	—	22,400	22.4	93

*These values are the average of several manufacturers' data.
†Percent initial light output at 70% rated life.
‡RSC = recessed single contact; RSC (rect) = rectangular recessed single contact.
§Lamp maintains maximum filament straightness under severe operating conditions.
a120, 130 volts.
b208, 220, 240 volts.
c12 and 24 volts.

Fig. 6-89. Showcase Lamps for 120 and 130 Volt Circuits*

Watts	Bulb and other description	Base	Filament	Rated average life (h)	Maximum Overall Length (mm)	(in.)	Initial Lumens	Lumens per watt†	Lamp lumen depreciation (%)‡
25	T-$6\frac{1}{2}$ clear or inside frosted	Intermed.	C-8	1000	140	$5\frac{1}{2}$	248	9.9	76
25	T-10 clear or inside frosted	Medium	C-8	1000	143	$5\frac{5}{8}$	253	10.1	79
40	T-8 clear or inside frosted	Medium	C-23 or C-8	1000	302	$11\frac{7}{8}$	420	10.5	77
40	T-10 clear or inside frosted	Medium	C-8	1000	143	$5\frac{5}{8}$	435	10.9	77
60§	T-10 clear	Medium	C-8	1000	143	$5\frac{5}{8}$	745	12.4	0
75	T-10 clear	Medium	C-23 or C-8	1000	302	$11\frac{7}{8}$	800	10.7	0

Note: May be burned in any position except as noted.
*These values are the average of several manufacturers' data.
†For 120 volt lamps.
‡Percent of initial lumens at 70% of rated life.
§Must be burned between base-down and horizontal.

Fig. 6-90. Sign Lamps

Watts	Bulb and other description	Base	Filament	Rated life (h)	Maximum Overall Length (mm)	Maximum Overall Length (in.)	Light center length (mm)	Light center length (in.)	Approx. total lumens*	Initial lumens per watt
7.5[b]	S-11 clear	Medium	C-9	1400	41	$1\frac{5}{8}$	3	$1\frac{9}{16}$	49	6.53
10	S-14 clear†	Medium	C-9	1500	89	$3\frac{1}{2}$	64	$2\frac{1}{2}$	89	8.90
10	S-11 clear†	Intermed.	C-7A	1500	59	$2\frac{5}{16}$	41	$1\frac{5}{8}$	80	8.00
10	S-11 high brilliance‡	Intermed. brass base	C-7A	1500	59	$2\frac{5}{16}$	41	$1\frac{5}{8}$	—	—
11	S-14 clear§	Medium	C-9	3000	89	$3\frac{1}{2}$	64	$2\frac{1}{2}$	75	6.82
11	S-11 high brilliance‡	Intermed. brass base	C-9	3000	89	$3\frac{1}{2}$	64	$2\frac{1}{2}$	—	—
15[a]	S-14 clear	Medium brass base	C-9	3000	89	$3\frac{1}{2}$	64	$2\frac{1}{2}$	110	7.33
15	A-15 clear	Medium brass base	C-9	3000	89	$3\frac{1}{2}$	60	$2\frac{3}{8}$	125	8.33
17[d]	A-15 clear and frosted	Medium	C-9	8000	89	$3\frac{1}{2}$	—	—	111	6.53
25[a]	A-15 reflector I.F.	Medium brass base	C-9	3000	89	$3\frac{1}{2}$	60	$2\frac{3}{8}$	—	—
25	A-19 clear§	Medium brass base ‖	C-9	3000	100	$3\frac{15}{16}$	64	$2\frac{1}{2}$	205	8.20
25[a]	A-19 high brilliance‡	Medium brass base	C-9	3000	99	$3\frac{7}{8}$	60	$2\frac{3}{8}$	—	—
30[a]	A-15 I.F.	Medium brass base	C-9	8000	89	$3\frac{1}{2}$	60	$2\frac{3}{8}$	180	6.00
30	R-20 I.F. reflector	Medium brass base	C-9	2000	100	$3\frac{15}{16}$	—	—	210	7.00
32	A-19 clear	Medium	C-9	3000	108	$4\frac{1}{4}$	73	$2\frac{7}{8}$	255	7.03
33	A-19 clear	Medium	C-9	3000	100	$3\frac{15}{16}$	—	—	260	7.88
33	R-17 reflector (frosted)	Medium	C-9	2500	70	$2\frac{3}{4}$	—	—	225	6.82
40	A-21 I.F.§	Medium	C-9	3000	113	$4\frac{7}{16}$	74	$2\frac{29}{32}$	326	8.15
40[b, d]	A-21†§	Medium	C-9	1500	113	$4\frac{7}{16}$	—	—	—	—
40[a, #]	A-21 high brilliance‡	Medium brass base	C-9	1500	111	$4\frac{3}{8}$	75	$2\frac{15}{16}$	—	—
50[c]	R-30 reflector I.F.	Medium	—	5000	132	$5\frac{3}{16}$	—	—	—	—
60[c]	R-20 reflector (blue)	Medium	C-9	6000	100	$3\frac{15}{16}$	—	—	—	—
65[c]	R-30 reflector (frosted)	Medium	C-17A	5000	132	$5\frac{3}{16}$	—	—	—	—

*Ratings are for clear lamps.
†Also available: inside front and ceramic colors; blue, green, orange, red, and yellow.
‡Transparent colors, blue, green, red, yellow; outdoor use.
§Duro–Test product; also available in frost and red, blue, green, yellow, orange–amber.
‖ General Electric is available with brass base.
#130 volts.
[a]General Electric.
[b]Sylvania.
[c]Philips.
[d]Duro–Test.

Fig. 6-91. Common 120 Volt Decorative Incandescent Filament Lamps

Watts	Bulb and Other Description	Base	Filament	Rated Life (h)	Maximum Overall length (mm)	Maximum Overall length (in.)	Light center length (mm)	Light center length (in.)‡	Operating position	Rated initial lumens*	Initial lumens per watt*
2	B-10 clear, flicker	Candelabra brass base	—	2500	98	$3\frac{7}{8}$	—	—	—	—	—
2	CA-8 clear, flicker	Candelabra	—	3000	89	$3\frac{1}{2}$	—	—	—	—	—
2	CA-10 clear, flicker	Medium	—	3000	105	$4\frac{1}{8}$	—	—	—	—	—
5#	C-9$\frac{1}{2}$ flame	Candelabra	C-7A	9000	89	$3\frac{1}{2}$	—	—	—	—	—
8$\frac{1}{2}$#	C-9$\frac{1}{2}$ clear Sparklelite	Candelabra	C-7A	9000	—	—	—	—	—	—	—
10†	B-12 white	Candelabra	CC-2R	1500	65	$2\frac{9}{16}$	—	—	BDTH	—	—
10§	G-16$\frac{1}{2}$ white	Candelabra	C-7A	1500	76	3	—	—	—	66	6.6
12‡	B-10 clear	Candelabra	C-7A	4000	110	$4\frac{5}{16}$	—	—	BD	—	—
15	B-10 clear	Candelabra	C-7A	1500	110	$4\frac{5}{16}$	41	$1\frac{5}{8}$	—	136	9.1
15†	BA-9 clear	Candelabra	CC-2R	1500	95	$3\frac{3}{4}$	—	—	BDTH	—	—
15§	C-9$\frac{1}{2}$ Spunglo	Candelabra	C-7A	4000	92	$3\frac{5}{8}$	—	—	BD	—	—
15#	C-9$\frac{1}{2}$ Sparklelite	Candelabra	C-7A	9000	—	—	—	—	—	—	—
15 ‖	CA-8 clear, bent tip	Candelabra	C-7A	1500	90	$3\frac{9}{16}$	40	$1\frac{9}{16}$	—	—	—
15	F-10 clear	Candelabra	C-7A, CC-2R	1500	79	$3\frac{1}{8}$	—	—	BDTH	136	9.1
15	G-16$\frac{1}{2}$ clear	Candelabra	C-7A, CC-2R	1500	178	7	—	—	BDTH	120	8.0
15#	G-40 clear	Medium	C-9	9000	—	—	—	—	—	50	3.3
20‡	B-10 clear	Candelabra	C-7A	4000	110	$4\frac{5}{16}$	—	—	—	—	—
25	B-10 clear	Candelabra	C-7A	1500	110	$4\frac{5}{16}$	41	$1\frac{5}{8}$	BDTH	—	—
25§	B-10 clear	Medium	C-7A	1500	102	4	—	—	BD	—	—
25†	B-10$\frac{1}{2}$ clear, blunt tip	Candelabra	CC-2R	1500	103	$4\frac{1}{16}$	—	—	BDTH	—	—
25†	BA-9 clear, bent tip	Candelabra	CC-2R	1500	106	$4\frac{3}{16}$	—	—	BDTH	—	—
25†	BA-9$\frac{1}{2}$ clear bent tip	Medium	CC-2R	1500	103	$4\frac{1}{16}$	—	—	BDTH	—	—
25	B-13 clear, blunt tip	Medium	C-7A, C-9	1500	117	$4\frac{5}{8}$	—	—	—	—	—
25#	C-9$\frac{1}{2}$ clear	Candelabra	C-7A	9000	92	$3\frac{5}{8}$	—	—	—	—	—
25#	C-9$\frac{1}{2}$B Sparkletip	Candelabra	C-7A	9000	105	$4\frac{1}{8}$	—	—	BD	—	—
25#	C-11 clear, Sparklelite	Candelabra	C-7A	9000	—	—	—	—	—	—	—
25	C-11 clear, Spunglo	Candelabra	C-7A	2750	114	$4\frac{1}{2}$	54	$2\frac{1}{8}$	BDTH	175	7.0
25#	C-15 clear, Sparklelite	Medium	C-9	9000	—	—	—	—	—	—	—
25§	C-15 clear, Spunglo	Medium	C-9	4000	114	$4\frac{1}{2}$	—	—	BD	—	—
25 ‖	CA-9 clear, bent tip	Medium	CC-2V	4000	116	$4\frac{9}{16}$	54	$2\frac{1}{8}$	—	—	—
25 ‖	CA-10 clear, bent tip	Candelabra	CC-2V	1500	110	$4\frac{5}{16}$	54	$2\frac{1}{8}$	BDTH	—	—
25	F-10 clear,	Candelabra	C-7A, CC-2R	1500	114	$4\frac{1}{2}$	—	—	BD	205	8.2
25	F-15 clear	Medium	CC-2V, C-9	1500	114	$4\frac{1}{2}$	—	—	BDTH	215	8.6
25	G-16$\frac{1}{2}$ white	Candelabra	C-7A, CC-2R	1500	90	$3\frac{9}{16}$	—	—	BDTH	200	8.0
25	G-18$\frac{1}{2}$ clear	Medium	C-9	1500	114	$4\frac{1}{2}$	—	—	—	224	9.0
25	G-25 clear	Medium	C-9	1500	114	$4\frac{1}{2}$	—	—	—	215	8.6
25§	G-30 white	Medium	C-9	2500	178	7	—	—	—	190	7.6
25	G-40 white	Medium	C-9, CC-9	2500	176	$6\frac{15}{16}$	—	—	—	180	7.2
25#	H-19 Chimneylite	Medium	C-9	9000	—	—	—	—	—	—	—
25 ‖	HX-10$\frac{1}{2}$ clear	Candelabra	C-7A	1500	117	$4\frac{5}{8}$	48	$1\frac{7}{8}$	—	175	7.0
25 ‖	ST-9$\frac{1}{2}$ clear	Candelabra	CC-2V	1500	102	4	44	$1\frac{3}{4}$	—	—	—
32§	B-10 clear	Candelabra	C-7A	4000	110	$4\frac{5}{16}$	—	—	—	—	—
32§	B-10 white	Medium	C-7A	4000	102	4	—	—	—	—	—
40	B-10 clear	Candelabra	C-7A, CC-2V	1500	110	$4\frac{5}{16}$	48	$1\frac{7}{8}$	BDTH	—	—
40	†B-10$\frac{1}{2}$ clear, blunt tip	Candelabra	CC-2R	1500	103	$4\frac{1}{16}$	—	—	BDTH	—	—

Fig. 6-91. *Continued*

Watts	Bulb and Other Description	Base	Filament	Rated Life (h)	Maximum Overall length (mm)	(in.)	Light center length (mm)	(in.)	Operating position	Rated initial lumens*	Initial lumens per watt*
40†	BA-9 clear, bent tip	Candelabra	CC-2R	1500	106	$4\frac{3}{16}$	—	—	BDTH	—	—
40†	BA-9$\frac{1}{2}$ clear, bent tip	Medium	CC-2R	1500	103	$4\frac{1}{16}$	—	—	BD	—	—
40	B-13 clear blunt tip	Medium	C-7A, C-9	1500	124	$4\frac{7}{8}$	60	$2\frac{3}{8}$	BD	455	11.4
40#	C-9$\frac{1}{2}$B clear, Sparkletip	Candelabra	C-7A	9000	105	$4\frac{1}{8}$	—	—	BD	—	—
40	C-11 clear, Spunglo	Candelabra	C-7A	2750	114	$4\frac{1}{2}$	54	$2\frac{1}{8}$	BD	360	9.0
40	C-15 clear, Spunglo	Medium	C-9	4000	114	$4\frac{1}{2}$	—	—	BD	—	—
40§	CA-9 clear, bent tip	Medium	CC-2V	1500	116	$4\frac{9}{16}$	54	$2\frac{1}{8}$	—	—	—
40§	CA-10 clear, bent tip	Candelabra	CC-2V	1500	110	$4\frac{5}{16}$	48	$1\frac{7}{8}$	—	—	—
40	F-15 clear	Medium	C-7A, C-9, CC-2V	1500	114	$4\frac{1}{2}$	—	—	BDTH	444	11.1
40	G-16$\frac{1}{2}$ clear	Candelabra	C-7A, CC-2R, C-9	1500	114	$4\frac{1}{2}$	41	$1\frac{5}{8}$	BDTH	302	7.5
40	G-25 white	Medium	C-9	1500	114	$4\frac{1}{2}$	—	—	—	390	9.8
40	G-30 white	Medium	C-9	3250	178	7	—	—	—	340	8.5
40	G-40 white	Medium	C-9, CC-6	2500	176	$6\frac{15}{16}$	—	—	—	357	8.9
40#	H-13 chimney	Medium	C-9	9000	158	6	—	—	—	—	—
40#	H-19 chimney	Medium	C-9	9000	—	—	—	—	—	—	—
48‡	B-10 clear	Candelabra	C-7A	4000	110	$4\frac{5}{16}$	—	—	—	—	—
48‡	B-10 white	Medium	C-7A	4000	102	4	—	—	BD	—	—
60	B-10 clear	Candelabra	C-7A, CC-2V	1500	110	$4\frac{5}{16}$	—	—	—	—	—
60‡	B-10 white	Medium	C-7A	1500	102	4	—	—	BD	—	—
60†	B-10$\frac{1}{2}$ clear, blunt tip	Candelabra	CC-2R	1500	103	$4\frac{1}{16}$	—	—	BDTH	—	—
60†	BA-9 clear, bent tip	Candelabra	CC-2R	1500	106	$4\frac{3}{16}$	—	—	BDTH	—	—
60†	BA-9$\frac{1}{2}$ clear, bent tip	Medium	CC-2R	1500	103	$4\frac{1}{16}$	—	—	BD	—	—
60†	B-13 clear, blunt tip	Medium	C-7A	1500	105	$4\frac{1}{8}$	—	—	BD	—	—
60	C-11 clear, Spunglo	Candelabra	C-7A	4000	105	$4\frac{1}{8}$	—	—	BD	—	—
60#	C-11B clear, Sparkletip	Candelabra	C-7A	9000	114	$4\frac{1}{2}$	—	—	—	—	—
60	C-15 clear, Spunglo	Medium	C-9	4000	114	$4\frac{1}{2}$	—	—	BD	—	—
60§	CA-9 clear, bent tip	Candelabra	CC-2V	1500	116	$4\frac{9}{16}$	54	$2\frac{1}{8}$	—	—	—
60§	CA-19 clear, bent tip	Candelabra	CC-2V	1500	110	$4\frac{5}{16}$	48	$1\frac{7}{8}$	—	—	—
60	F-15 clear	Medium	C-7A, C-9	1500	114	$4\frac{1}{2}$	—	—	—	690	11.5
60	G-25 clear	Medium	C-9, CC-9	1500	113	$4\frac{7}{16}$	71	$2\frac{13}{16}$	—	715	11.9
60	G-30 white	Medium	C-9, CC-9	2500	178	7	79	$3\frac{1}{8}$	—	684	11.4
60	G-40 white	Medium	C-9, CC-6	2500	176	$6\frac{15}{16}$	111	$4\frac{3}{8}$	—	582	9.7
60‡	GT-19 smoke chimney	Medium	C-9	1500	148	$5\frac{13}{16}$	—	—	BD	675	11.3
60‡	GT-24 chimney	Medium Skt.	C-9	3000	208	$8\frac{3}{16}$	—	—	BD	585	9.8
75§	G-40 white	Medium	CC-6	2500	176	$6\frac{15}{16}$	—	—	—	1000	13.3
75#	H-19 chimney	Medium	C-9	2250	—	—	—	—	—	—	—
100‡	F-20 clear, Postlight	Medium	C-9	3500	127	5	—	—	—	—	—
100‡	G-30 white	Medium	C-9	4000	140	7	—	—	—	—	—
100	G-40 white	Medium	C-9, CC-6	3500	225	$8\frac{7}{8}$	111	$4\frac{3}{8}$	—	1167	11.7
100#	G-48 white	Medium Skt.	C-9	9000	225	$8\frac{7}{8}$	—	—	—	1040	10.4
100‡	GT-24 chimney	Medium Skt.	C-9	3000	208	$8\frac{3}{16}$	—	—	BD	1080	10.8
150	G-40 white	Medium	C-9, CC-6	2500	225	$8\frac{7}{8}$	111	$4\frac{3}{8}$	—	1843	12.3
200#	G-48 white	Medium Skt.	C-9	9000	225	$8\frac{7}{8}$	—	—	—	2450	12.3

*These values are average of several manufacturers' data.
†Philips.
‡BD = base down. BDTH = base down to horizontal.
§Sylvania.
‖ General Electric.
#Duro-Test. Note: Since Duro-Test life ratings are based on a different premise than other manufacturers, these ratings are used only with Duro-Test products.

Fig. 6-92. Tungsten-Halogen Low Voltage Lamps with Integral Reflectors

Watts	Manufacturer's ordering code*	Bulb and reflector shape diameter	Base	Rated life (h)	Maximum overall length (m)	(in.)	Bare bulb temperature (°C)	Approximate color temperature (K)	Coated mirror type	Maximum center beam intensity (cd)	Initial lumens	Approx. beam angle (degrees)†	ANSI code
MR-11													
20	20 MRC-11 / SP10^c	MR-11	G4	2333	41	1 5/8	—	2938	Dichroic	4967	260	10.0	FTB
20	20 MRC-11 / FL30^c	MR-11	G4	2333	41	1 5/8	—	2938	Dichroic	1600	260	19.0	FTC
20	41890FL	MR-11	GZ4	2500	37	1 15/32	—	2950	Dichroic	3800	260	30.0	FTD
35	Q35MR11 / NSP	MR-11	G4	2500	37	1 15/32	—	2950	Dichroic	7175	460	10.0	FTE
35	Q35MR-11 / SP	MR-11	G4	2500	37	1 15/32	—	2950	Dichroic	2875	460	20.0	FTF
35	Q35MR11 / NFL	MR-11	G4	2500	37	1 15/32	—	2950	Dichroic	1400	460	30.0	FTH
50	Q50MR11 / SP	MR-11	G4	2500	37	1 15/32	—	3000	Dichroic	11,000	—	20.0	—
50	Q50MR11 / NFL	MR-11	G4	2500	37	1 15/32	—	3000	Dichroic	2600	—	25.0	—
MR-16 and others													
10‡	41960SP^c	AR 48 mm	G4	2000	48	1 15/16	—		Silver	2000	—	10.0	—
20	Accent 1200 display	MR-16	RM2P	2750	44	1 3/4	249 min.	2925	—	574	—	36.0	BAB
20	Accent 1200 display	MR-16	RM2P	2500	44	1 3/4	249 min.	2925	—	4100	—	12.0	ESX
20	41900 Sp^c	AR 48 mm	G4	2000	36	1 13/32	—	3000	Silver	5000	—	10.0	—
20	41900FL^c	AR 48 mm	G4	2000	36	1 13/32	—	3000	Silver	2000	—	15.0	—
20	20MR-16 / ML / SP12	MR-16	GX5.3	3000	44	1 3/4	—	3000		3800	—	12.0	—
20	20MR-16 / ML / FL36	MR-16	GX5.3	3000	44	1 3/4	—	3000		600	—	36.0	—
20	41905SP^c	AR 48 mm	G4	2000	36	1 15/32	—	2600	Gold	4500	—	10.0	—
20	41905FL^c	AR 48 mm	G4	2000	36	1 13/32	—	2600	Gold	1500	—	15.0	—
20§	41930SP^c	AR 48 mm	G4	2000	36	1 13/32	—	3000	Silver	4500	—	10.0	—
20	41970SP^c	AR 48 mm	D.C. Bay.	2000	50	2	—	3000	Silver	7000	—	10.0	—
20	41970FL^c	AR 48 mm	D.C. Bay.	2000	50	2	—	3000	Silver	1000	—	30.0	—
20	20MRC-16 / SP7	MR-16	RM2P	2000	49	1 15/16	—	2925		9060	—	6.5	EZX
25	Accent 1200	MR-16	GX5.3	2000	44	1 3/4	—	3050		8500	—	6.0	FJX
35‡	41830SSP^c	PAR-36	G53 + M4	2000	45	1 3/4	—	3000	Silver	45,000	—	3.0	—
35	Q35MR16 / SP	MR-16	GX5.3	4000	44	1 3/4	—	3000		7900	—	20.0	FRA
35	Q35MR16 / FL	MR-16	GX5.3	1750	44	1 3/4	—	3000		1050	—	40.0	FMW
35	Q35MR16 / NSP	MR-16	GX5.3	1000	44	1 3/4	—	3000		7900	—	12.0	FRB
35	Hal. Alum. Ref.	Rnd. 56 mm	B15d	3000	59	2 5/16	—	—		15,500	—	6.0	GBG
35	35MR16 / Q / NSP / P	MR-16	—	4000	—	—	—	—	Alum./ Lens	8000	—	10.0	—
35	35MR16 / Q / NFL / P	MR-16	—	4000	—	—	—	3000	Alum./ Lens	1800	—	25.0	—

MR-16 and other

Watts	Code	Bulb	Base										ANSI
36[b]	36PAR36CAp / VNSP	PAR-36	Screw / Spd.	4000	70	2 3/4	—	—	—	23,000	—	5.0	—
36[b]	36PAR36CAp / NSP	PAR-36	Screw / Spd.	4000	70	2 3/4	—	—	—	5100	—	10.0	—
36[b]	36PAR36CAp / WFL	PAR-36	Screw / Spd.	4000	70	2 3/4	—	—	—	1175	—	30.0	—
42	42MR16 / Q / FL[b]	MR-16	RM2P	2500	44	1 3/4	—	3050	—	991	—	36.0	EYP[b]
42	42MR16 / Q / FL	MR-16	FM2P	4000	44	1 3/4	—	3000	—	7077	—	11.5	EYR[b]
42	42MR16 / Q / NSP	MR-16	FM2P	1000	44	1 3/4	—	3000	—	2450	—	23.5	EYS[b]
42	42MR16 / Q / SP	MR-16	FM2P	1875	44	1 3/4	—	3000	—	13,300	—	8.0	EZY
50	50MRC-16 / FL38	MR-16	FM2P	3500	49	1 15/16	—	2288	—	1806	895	39.5	EXN
50	50MRC-16 / SP13	MR-16	FM2P	3500	49	1 15/16	—	2288	—	10,250	895	13.0	EXT
50	50MRC-16 / FL24	MR-16	FM2P	3500	49	1 15/16	—	2294	—	3325	895	25.5	EXZ
50	50MR16 / Q / NSP / P	MR-16	GX5.3	3750	44	1 3/4	—	1513	—	9700	—	5.5	—
50	50MR16 / Q / NFL / P	MR-16	GX5.3	3750	44	1 3/4	—	3025	—	3400	12.3	—	—
50	50MR16 / Q / FL / P	MR-16	GX5.3	3750	44	1 3/4	—	3025	—	1450	—	20.8	—
50	50MR-16 / ML / SP12	MR-16	GX5.3	2000	50	2	—	3000	—	2500	—	10.0	—
50	50MR-16 / ML / FL24	MR-16	GX5.3	2000	50	2	—	3000	—	1100	—	30.0	—
50	50MR-16 / ML / FL38	MR-16	GX5.3	2000	50	2	—	2600	Gold	2250	—	10.0	—
50	41995FL[c]	AR-70	D.C. Bay.	2000	50	2	—	2600	—	950	—	30.0	—
65	65MR16 / Q / NSP	MR-16	RM2P	4000	—	—	—	3050	—	11,500	—	14.0	FPA(EYF) ‖
65	65MR16 / Q / NFL	MR-16	RM2P	4000	—	—	—	3050	—	4000	—	23.0	FPC
65	65MR16 / Q / FL	MR-16	RM2P	4000	—	—	—	3050	—	2000	—	38.0	PFB(EYC) ‖
75	41880WFL	MR-16	GX5.3	2000	44	1 3/4	—	3050	—	2400	1300	38.0	EYC
75	41880SP	MR-16	GX5.3	2000	44	1 3/4	—	3050	Dichroic	12,100	1300	14.0	EYF
75	41880FL[c]	MR-16	RM2P	2000	44	1 3/4	—	3050	Dichroic	4400	1300	24.5	EYJ
75	41840SP[c]	PAR-36	M4 Screw	2000	45	1 3/4	—	3000	—	25,000	—	10.0	—
75	41840FL[c]	PAR-36	M4 Screw	2000	50	1 15/16	—	3000	Silver	4000	—	30.0	—
75	41840WF[c]	PAR-36	M4 Screw	2000	48	1 7/8	—	3000	Silver	1300	—	60.0	—
100	41850SP[c]	PAR-36	M4 Screw	2000	45	1 3/4	—	3000	Silver	45,000	—	10.0	—
100	41850FL	PAR-36	M4 Screw	2000	50	1 15/16	—	3000	Silver	6000	—	30.0	—
100	41850WFL	PAR-36	M4 Screw	2000	48	1 7/8	—	3000	Silver	1200	—	60.0	—

Note: GE offers "constant color" versions of the above listings in a 5000 hour rating.

*The FPA and FPB lamps have comparable performance and can directly replace the EYF and EYC lamps. Reflectors are available in glass, ceramic, and aluminum; with or without dichroic action; with silver, gold, and colored surfaces. This table does not attempt to list all available lamps but is representative.

†Measured at 50% maximum candlepower.

‡6 volts.

§24 volts.

‖ If other than ANSI code.

a General Electric.

b Sylvania.

c Osram.

d Philips.

Fig. 6-93. Double-ended Linear Lamps* for 120- and 125-Volt Circuits

Watts	Bulb and other description	Base	Filament	Rated life (h)	Maximum overall length (mm)	(in.)	Initial Lumens	Initial lumens per watt
30	T-8 clear	Disk	C-8	1500	459	$18\frac{1}{16}$	245	8.50
30	T-8 inside frosted	Disk	C-8	1500	459	$18\frac{1}{16}$	240	8.50
30	T-8 white	Disk	C-8	1500	451	$17\frac{3}{4}$	210	7.00
35	T-$9\frac{1}{2}$ opal or inside white	2-S14s	—	2000	300	$11\frac{13}{16}$	—	—
35	T-8 inside white	2xS14s	C-8	1500	300	$11\frac{13}{16}$	230	—
40	T-8 clear	Disk	C-8	1500	306	$12\frac{1}{16}$	357	8.75
40	T-8 inside frosted	Disk	C-8	1500	306	$12\frac{1}{16}$	365	9.00
40	T-8 inside white	Disk	C-8	1500	298	$11\frac{3}{4}$	295	7.40
60	T-8 clear	Disk	C-8	1500	459	$18\frac{1}{16}$	540	9.05
60	T-8 inside frosted	Disk	C-8	1500	459	$18\frac{1}{16}$	543	9.20
60	T-8 inside white	Disk	C-8	1500	451	$17\frac{3}{4}$	450	7.50
60	T-$9\frac{1}{2}$ opal or inside white	2-S14s	C-8	1750	500	$19\frac{11}{16}$	430	7.16
120	T-8 inside white	2-S14s	C-8	1500	1000	$39\frac{3}{8}$	780	6.50
150	T-$9\frac{1}{2}$ opal	2-S14s	C-8	2000	1000	$39\frac{3}{8}$	930	6.20

*Trade designations: Philips, Philinea; General Electric, Lumiline; and OSRAM, Linestra.

Fig. 6-94. Lamps for Train and Locomotive Service*

Watts	Volts	Bulb and other description	Base	Filament	Rate life (h)	Maximum overall length (mm)	(in.)	Light center length (mm)	(in.)	Initial lumens	Initial lumens per watt
					Train						
6	30	S-6 indicator†	Candelbra	C-2V	1500	48	$1\frac{7}{8}$	33	$1\frac{5}{16}$	50	8.3
	60		Screw	C-7A	1500	48	$1\frac{7}{8}$	33	$1\frac{5}{16}$	47	7.8
6	30	S-6 Blue night light†	Candelabra	C-2V	—	47	$1\frac{7}{8}$	—	—	—	—
	60		Screw	C-7A	—	47	$1\frac{7}{8}$	—	—	—	—
6	75	S-6 glossy blue	Candelabra	C-7A	500	47	$1\frac{7}{8}$	33	$1\frac{5}{16}$	—	—
	75	S-6 clear	Screw	C-7A	1000	47	$1\frac{7}{8}$	33	$1\frac{5}{16}$	47	7.8
15	30	A-17 inside									
	34	frosted†	Medium	C-9	1000	92	$3\frac{5}{8}$	60	$2\frac{3}{8}$	179	11.9
	60	A-17 inside frosted†									
	75	A-15 inside frosted	Medium	C-9	1000	92	$3\frac{5}{8}$	60	$2\frac{3}{8}$	147	9.8
25	30	A-19 inside frosted	Medium	C-9	1000	108	$4\frac{15}{16}$	65	$2\frac{5}{8}$	336	13.5
	60	A-19 inside frosted	Medium	C-6	1000	108	$4\frac{15}{16}$	63	$2\frac{1}{2}$	280	11.2
25	30	T-$8\frac{1}{2}$ Inside								325	13.0
	60	frosted	Medium	C-8	1000	139	$5\frac{1}{2}$	—	—	280	11.2
40	30	A-19 Inside								590	14.8
	60	frosted	Medium	C-9	1000	107	$4\frac{1}{4}$	73	$2\frac{7}{8}$	525	13.1
50	30	A-21 Inside	Medium	C-9	1000	125	$4\frac{7}{8}$	87	$3\frac{7}{16}$	820	13.7
	60	frosted	Medium	C-9	1000	125	$4\frac{7}{8}$	86	$3\frac{7}{16}$	698	14.0
	75	A-19 inside frosted RS	Medium	C-9	1000	100	$3\frac{7}{8}$	65	$2\frac{5}{8}$	523	8.6
60	38	PAR-46 (red warning)	Screw Term.	CC-2V	800	—	—	95	$3\frac{3}{4}$	—	—
75	30	A-23	Medium	C-9	1000	154	$6\frac{1}{8}$	111	$4\frac{3}{8}$	1230	16.4
	30	PAR-38 train flood	Med. Skt.	C-6	1000	135	$5\frac{5}{16}$	—	—	975	11.7
	34	A-21 inside frosted	Medium	C-6	500	135	$5\frac{5}{16}$	—	—	1100	14.7
	60	A-23	Medium								
100	30	A-23	Medium	C-9	1000	154	$6\frac{1}{16}$	121	$4\frac{13}{16}$	1800	18.0
	32	A-23 inside frosted LHT	Medium	C-6	1000	154	$6\frac{1}{16}$	111	$4\frac{3}{8}$	1810	18.1
	34	A-23	Medium	C-9	1000	154	$6\frac{1}{16}$	113	$4\frac{7}{16}$	1980	19.8
	34	A-21 inside frosted	Medium	C-6	1000	135	$5\frac{5}{16}$	—	—	1940	19.4
	60	A-23	Medium								

Fig. 6-94. *Continued*

Watts	Volts	Bulb and other description	Base	Filament	Rate life (h)	Maximum overall length (mm)	Maximum overall length (in.)	Light center length (mm)	Light center length (in.)	Initial lumens	Initial lumens per watt
					Locomotive						
6	30	S-6 clear	D.C. Bay.	C-7A	1000	46	$1\frac{13}{16}$	27	$1\frac{1}{8}$	50	8.3
	60	S-6 indicator†	S.C. Bay.	C-7A	1500	46	$1\frac{13}{16}$	26	$1\frac{1}{16}$	48	8.0
	75	S-6 clear	D.C. Bay.	C-7A	1000	46	$1\frac{13}{16}$	—	—	47	7.8
15	75	S-11 Marker†	D.C.	C-9	1000	60	$2\frac{3}{8}$	32	$1\frac{1}{4}$	139	9.3
15	34	S-14 inside frosted Cab†	Medium	C-9	1000	89	$3\frac{1}{2}$	63	$2\frac{1}{2}$	142	9.5
25	60	A-19 inside	Medium	C-9	1000	108	$4\frac{5}{16}$	65	$2\frac{9}{16}$	282	11.3
	75	A-19 inside frost RS	Medium	C-17	1000	100	$3\frac{15}{16}$	—	—	240	9.6
		A-17 RS cab†	Medium	C-9	1000	92	$3\frac{5}{8}$	63	$2\frac{1}{2}$	239	9.6
30	32	S-11 clear	D.C. Bay.	C-9	500	60	$2\frac{3}{8}$	32	$1\frac{1}{4}$	413	13.8
	64	S-11 marker	D.C. Bay.	C-7A	500	60	$2\frac{3}{8}$	49	$1\frac{7}{16}$	345	11.5
	64	S-11 Marker	S.C. Bay.	C-7A							
	75	S-11 clear (BDTH)	D.C. Bay.	C-7A	500	60	$2\frac{3}{8}$	49	$1\frac{7}{16}$	346	11.5
50	60	A-21 inside frosted	Medium	C-9	1000	125	$4\frac{7}{8}$	86	$3\frac{3}{8}$	698	14.0
	75	A-19 RS cab engine	Medium	C-9	1000	100	$3\frac{15}{16}$	65	$2\frac{9}{16}$	517	10.3
75	48	PAR-46 mine locomotive	Screw Term.	CC-2V	800	95	$3\frac{13}{16}$	—	—	—	—
	75	PAR-36 RS train warning		CC-6	500	70	$2\frac{13}{16}$	—	—	—	—
100	32	A-21 headlight	Medium BB	C-5	500	117	$4\frac{5}{8}$	76	3	1587	15.9
	60	PAR-46 mine locomotive	Scr. Term	CC-2V	800	98	$3\frac{7}{8}$	—	—	1240	12.4
200	12	PAR-56 headlight	Screw Term.	CC-8	500					180,000‡	—
	30			CC-8	500	114	$4\frac{1}{2}$	—	—	260,000	—
250	32	P-25 headlight	Medium Pref.								
			Medium	C-5A	500	121	$4\frac{13}{16}$	76	3	4575	18.3
	120	P-25 headlight	Medium (BB)	C-5	500	121	$4\frac{13}{16}$	76	3	3700	14.8
350	75	PAR-56	Screw Term.	CC-8	500	114	$4\frac{1}{2}$	—	—	—	—

*Lamps may be burned in any position except for headlight lamps, which can be burned in any position except within 45° of vertical baseup.
†Vacuum.
‡Max. candlepower.

Fig. 6-95. Frequently Used Incandescent and Tungsten-Halogen Lamps for Theatre Stages, Motion Picture and Television Production, and Still Photography
(All Data for 120 Volt Lamps Except as noted)

I. Tungsten-Halogen Double-Ended Lamps

Watts	Bulb and other description	ANSI code	Filament	Average life (h)	Maximum overall length (mm)	(in.)	Lighted length (mm)	(in.)	Approximate color temperature (K)	Maximum bare bulb temperature (°C)*	Base temperature (°C)†	Recommended operating position	Initial lumens	Initial lumens per watt
(A) T-3 or T-4 bulb; compact CC-8 filament;‡ RSC bases: maximum over-all length 79 mm (3 1/8 in.); burning position: any.														
120	FGY (20V.) clear	FGY	CC-8	2500	79	3 1/8	16	5/8	2900	—	—	Any	1900	15.8
300§	Q300T4/CL clear	EHP	CC-8	2000	79	3 1/8	17	21/32	2900	—	—	Any	5650	18.8
300‖	EHX frosted	EHX	CC-8	2000	79	3 1/8	—	—	2950	—	—	Any	5600	18.7
375	DWZ (30V.) clear	DWZ	CC-8	1750	79	3 1/8	12	15/32	3000	—	—	Any	7500	20.0
400	FDA clear	FDA	CC-8	250	79	3 1/8	16	5/8	3200	—	—	Any	10,400	26.0
400§	EHR clear	EHR	CC-8	2000	79	3 1/8	16	9/16	3000	—	—	Any	7,800	19.5
650	FCA frosted	FCA	CC-8	25	79	3 1/8	—	—	3400	—	—	Any	19,000	29.2
650	FAD clear	FAD	CC-8	100	79	3 1/8	16	5/8	3200	—	—	Any	16,500	25.4
650§	FBX-Q650T4/4 frosted	FBX	CC-8	100	79	3 1/8	16	5/8	3200	—	—	Any	16,500	25.4
650	DWY clear§	DWY	CC-8	25	79	3 1/8	16	5/8	3400	—	—	Any	20,000	30.8
800	DXX (230, 240V.) clear§	DXX	CC-8	75	79	3 1/8	25	1	3200	—	—	Any	20,500	25.6
(B) T-4 or T-5 bulb; compact CC-8 filament; RSC base; maximum overall length: 95 mm														
600§	FCB clear	FCB	CC-8	75	95	3 3/4	18	11/16	3250	—	—	Any	17,000	28.3
1000	BRH clear	BRH	CC-8	75	95	3 3/4	19	3/4	3200	—	—	Any	30,550	30.6
1000	FBZ frosted	FBZ	CC-8	30	95	3 3/4	—	—	3400	—	—	Any	31,500	31.5
1000	DXW clear	DXW	CC-8	150	95	3 3/4	22	7/8	3200	—	—	Any	28,000	28.0
1000	FBY frosted	FBY	CC-8	150	95	3 3/4	—	—	3200	—	—	Any	26,000	26.0
1000	DXN clear§	DXN	CC-8	50	95	3 3/4	19	3/4	3400	—	—	Any	33,500	33.5
(C) T-5 bulb; compact CC-8 filament;‡ RSC base; maximum overall length 111 mm														
1000	DYA-Q1000T5/1CL	DYA	CC-8	150	111	4 3/8	22	7/8	3200	—	—	Any	28,000	28.0
1000	DYN frosted	DYN	CC-8	150	111	4 3/8	—	—	3200	—	—	Any	28,000	28.0
(D) T-3 or T-5 bulb; linear C-8 filament;‡ RSC base; max. overall length: 119 mm (4 11/16 in); burning position: horizontal ± 4°														
300	EHM clear	EHM	C-8	2000	119	4 11/16	51	2	3000	—	—	Horizontal	6000	20.0
300	EHZ frosted	EHZ	C-8	2000	119	4 11/16	—	—	2950	—	—	Horizontal	6000	20.0
500	FCL clear	FCL	C-8	2600	119	4 11/16	51	2	3000	—	—	Horizontal	10,500	21.0
500	FCZ frosted	FCZ	C-8	—	119	4 11/16	—	—	3000	—	—	Horizontal	—	—
500	FDF-Q500T3/4CL clear	FDF	C-8	400	119	4 11/16	60	2 3/8	3200	—	—	Horizontal	13,250	26.5
500	Q500T3/4 frosted	FDN	C-8	400	119	4 11/16	—	—	3200	—	—	Horizontal	12,800	25.6
515§	EJG/HIR-Q515T3/4 clear#	EJG	C-8		119	4 11/16				—	—	Horizontal	—	—
650	Q1000/650T3/4WM clear#	FWM	C-8		119	4 11/16				—	—	Horizontal	—	—

Watts	Designation	Code	Bulb	Life	MOL (mm)	MOL (in)	LCL (mm)	LCL (in)	K	—	—	Burning Position	Lumens	LPW
750	Q750T3/4CL clear	EJG	C-8	400	119	4 11/16	60	2 3/8	3200	—	—	Horizontal	20,600	27.5
750	Q750T3/4 frosted	EMD	C-8	400	119	4 11/16	—	—	3200	—	—	Horizontal	20,600	27.5
800	Q800T3/4CL(240V) clear#	EME	C-8	250	119	4 11/16	70	2 3/4	3200	—	—	Horizontal	22,000	27.5
800	Q800T3/4(240V) frosted	EMF	C-8	250	119	4 11/16	—	—	3200	—	—	Horizontal	21,400	26.8
1000	Q1000T3/3CL(185V) clear	EJD	C-8	100	119	4 11/16	67	2 11/16	3350	—	—	Horizontal	33,600	33.6
1000	Q1000T3/4CL clear	FCM	C-8	300	119	4 11/16	65	2 9/16	3200	—	—	Horizontal	28,000	28.0
1000	Q1000T3/4 frosted	FHM	C-8	500	119	4 11/16	—	—	3200	—	—	Horizontal	28,000	28.0
1050	ELJ clear	ELJ	C-8	75	119	4 11/16	22	7/8	3200	—	—	Horizontal	30,000	28.6

(E) T-6 or T-8 bulb; compact CC-8 filament‡, RSC base; maximum overall length: 143 mm

Watts	Designation	Code	Bulb	Life	MOL (mm)	MOL (in)	LCL (mm)	LCL (in)	K	—	—	Burning Position	Lumens	LPW
1000	Q1000T6/4CL clear	FER	CC-8	500	143	5 5/8	19	3/4	3200	—	—	Any	27,500	27.5
1000	EHS clear	EHS	CC-8	500	143	5 5/8	29	1 1/8	3100	—	—	Any	27,500	27.5
1000	DWT clear	DWT	CC-8	2000	143	5 5/8	29	1 1/8	3000	—	—	Any	23,400	23.4
2000	FEX (240V) clear	FEX	CC-8	300	143	5 5/8	35	1 3/8	3200	—	—	Any	50,000	25
2000	Q2000T8/4CL clear	FEY	CC-8	400	143	5 5/8	43	1 11/16	3200	—	—	Any	57,000	28.5

(F) T-3 or T-4 bulb; linear C-8 filament; recessed single contact bases; maximum overall length: 167 mm (6 9/16 inches); burning position: horizontal ±4° except as noted.

Watts	Designation	Code	Bulb	Life	MOL (mm)	MOL (in)	LCL (mm)	LCL (in)	K	—	—	Burning Position	Lumens	LPW
660	FFT/HIR-Q660T3/4 clear#	—	C-8	—	167	6 9/16	—	—	—	—	—	Horizontal	—	—
1000	Q1000t3/1CL clear	FFT	C-8	300	167	6 9/16	65	2 9/16	3200	—	—	Horizontal	27,000	27.0
1500	Q1500T4/4CL clear	FDB	C-8	400	167	6 9/16	57	2 1/4	3200	—	—	Horizontal	41,200	27.5
1500	Q1500T4/4 frosted	FGT	C-8	400	167	6 9/16	—	—	3200	—	—	Horizontal	40,200	26.8
2000	FFW	FFW	C-8	125	167	6 9/16	79	3 1/8	3200	—	—	Horizontal	57,000	28.5

II. Halogen Single-Ended Lamps

(A) Medium 2-pin base; light center length: 60 mm (2 3/8 in.); burning position: any.

Watts	Designation	Code	Bulb	Life	MOL (mm)	MOL (in)	LCL (mm)	LCL (in)	K	—	—	Burning Position	Lumens	LPW
500	Q500/5CL T-4 clear	EHC/EHB	C-8‡	300	95	3 3/4	60	2 3/8	3200	—	—	Any	13,000	26.0
500	Q500CL/TP T-4 clear	EHD	CC-8‡	2000	95	3 3/4	60	2 3/8	3000	—	—	Any	10,600	21.2
750§	Q750/4CL T-6 clear	EHF	CC-8	300	102	4	60	2 3/8	3200	—	—	Any	20,400	27.2
750	Q750CL/TP T-6 clear	EHG	CC-8‡	2000	105	4 1/8	60	2 3/8	3000	—	—	Any	15,000	20.0
1000	Q1000/4CL T-6 clear	FEL	CC-8‡	300	102	4	60	2 3/8	3200	—	—	Any	27,500	27.5
1000	Q1000/4 T-6 frosted	FCV	CC-8	300	105	4 1/8	60	2 3/8	3200	—	—	Any	26,500	26.5
1000	FEP (240V) T-4 clear	FEP	CC-8	250	105	4 1/8	60	2 3/8	3200	—	—	Any	26,500	26.5

(B) Miniature 2-pin base; light center length: 43 mm (1 11/16 in.);

Watts	Designation	Code	Bulb	Life	MOL (mm)	MOL (in)	LCL (mm)	LCL (in)	K	—	—	Burning Position	Lumens	LPW
600	DYH G-7 clear	DYH	CC-6	75	64	2 1/2	43	1 11/16	3200	—	—	BDTH	17,000	28.3
650§	DVY G-6 clear	DVY	CC-6	25	57	2 1/4	43	1 11/16	3400	—	—	BDTH	20,000	30.8
650	DYJ (230V) G-7 clear	DYJ	CC-2P	20	64	2 1/2	43	1 11/16	3400	—	—	BDTH	20,000	30.8

(C) 2-Pin prefocus base; light center length: 37 mm (1 7/16 in.); burn with coil horizontal

Watts	Designation	Code	Bulb	Life	MOL (mm)	MOL (in)	LCL (mm)	LCL (in)	K	—	—	Burning Position	Lumens	LPW
250§	DYG-Q250/5CL/2PP G-6 clear	DYG	CC-6	15	64	2 1/2	37	1 7/16	3400	—	—	—	8000	32.00
420	EKB-Q420/4CL/2PP G-7 clear	EKB	CC-6	75	64	2 1/2	37	1 7/16	3200	—	—	—	11,000	26.2
600	DYS/DYV/BHC G-7 clear	DYS	CC-6	75	64	2 1/2	37	1 7/16	3200	—	—	—	17,000	28.3

Fig. 6-95. *Continued*

II. Halogen Single-Ended Lamps

(C) 2-pin prefocus base; light center length: 37mm (1 $\frac{7}{16}$ in.);

Watts	Bulb and other description	ANSI code	Filament	Maximum overall length (mm)	(in.)	Lighted length (mm)	(in.)	Approximate color temperature (K)	Maximum bare bulb temperature (°C)*	Base temperature (°C)†	Recommended operating Position	Initial lumens	Initial lumens per watt
650§	EKD-Q650/3CL/2PP G-6 clear	EKD	CC-6	64	2 $\frac{1}{2}$	37	1 $\frac{7}{16}$	3400	—	—	—	20,000	30.8
650§	DYR (220, 240V) G-7 G-7 clear	DYR	2CC-8	64	2 $\frac{1}{2}$	37	1 $\frac{7}{16}$	3200	—	—	—	16,500	25.4

III. Tungsten-Halogen and Incandescent Lamps

(A) PAR-36 bulb; bases: ferrule contacts^FC or screw terminals^ST or 2 prong[j]; "Q" after "WATTS" indicates tungsten-halogen types.

Watts	Bulb and other description	ANSI code	Filament	Average life (h)	Field angle (degrees)**	Beam angle (degrees) ‖	Approximate center beam candlepower	Approximate color temperature (K)	Maximum bare bulb temperature (°C)*	Base temperature (°C)†	Beam pattern	Initial lumens	Initial lumens per watt
250	FGS/DWA^FC	FGS/DWA	—	4	—	30 × 20	18,000	3400	—	—	NFL	—	—
650Q	DWE-Q650PAR36/1ST	DWE	—	100	—	40 × 30	24,000	3200	—	—	WFL	—	—
650Q	DXK-Q650PAR36/2^FC	DXK	—	35	—	40 × 30	30,000	3400	—	—	MFL	—	—
650Q	FAY-Q650PAR36/SD^FC	FAY	—	35	—	25 × 15	35,000	5000§§	—	—	SP	—	—
650Q	FBE-Q650PAR36/5D^ST	FBE	—	35	—	25 × 15	35,000	5000§§	—	—	SP	—	—
650Q	FBJ-Q650PAR36/3^FC	FBJ	—	30	—	25 × 15	75,000	3400	—	—	SP	—	—
250	FGR/FBM |||	FGR/FBM |||	—		—	—	—	—	—	—	—	—	—
650Q	FBOQ650PAR36/5ST	FBO	—	30	—	25 × 15	75,000	3400	—	—	SP	—	—
650Q	FCW-Q650PAR36/6^FC	FCW	—	100	—	50 × 55	9,000	3200	—	—	FL	—	—
650Q	FCX-Q650PAR36/7^FC	FCX	—	100	—	40 × 30	24,000	3200	—	—	MFL	—	—
650Q	FGX-Q650PAR36/8D^ST	FGK	—	35	—	—	24,000	5000§§	—	—	NFL	—	—

(A-1) PAR-46 bulb; medium side-prong^MSP or screw terminal base^ST

Watts	Bulb and other description	ANSI code	Filament	Average life (h)	Field angle (degrees)**	Beam angle (degrees) ‖	Approximate center beam candlepower	Approximate color temperature (K)	Maximum bare bulb temperature (°C)*	Base temperature (°C)†	Beam pattern	Initial lumens	Initial lumens per watt
25	25PAR46## (5.5 V)^ST	—	C-6	1000	5 $\frac{1}{2}$ × 4 $\frac{1}{2}$	—	55,000	—	—	—	VNSP	—	—
52	H7635## (12.8 V)^ST	—	—	100	6 $\frac{1}{2}$ × 4	—	160,000	—	—	—	VNSP	—	—
150	150PAR46/1 (32 V)^ST	—	CC-8	800	9 × 9	—	100,000	—	—	—	VNSP	—	—
200	200PAR46/NSP (120 V)^MSP	—	CC-13	2000	23 × 19	12 × 8	31,000	2750	—	—	NSP	—	—
250	4553ST (28 V)	—	—	25	11 × 12	—	300,000	—	—	—	VNSP	—	—

(A-2) PAR-56 bulb; mogul end-prong^MEP, extended mogul end-prong^EMEP or screw terminals^ST

Watts	Bulb and other description	ANSI code	Filament	Average life (h)	Field angle (degrees)**	Beam angle (degrees) ‖	Approximate center beam candlepower	Approximate color temperature (K)	Maximum bare bulb temperature (°C)*	Base temperature (°C)†	Beam pattern	Initial lumens	Initial lumens per watt
100	4545##^ST (12 V)	—	—	100	9 × 5	—	225,000	—	—	—	VNSP	—	—
240	240PAR56/WFL (12 V)^ST	—	C-6	2000	50 × 27	35 × 18	13,000	—	—	—	WFL	—	—
300	300PAR56/NSP^MEP	—	CC-13	2000	20 × 14	10 × 8	68,000	2750	—	—	WFL	1,800	6
300	300PAR56/2NSP^p. EMEP	—	CC-13	2000	22 × 14	11 × 8	78,000	2750	—	—	NSP	1,800	6
450	4541†††^ST (28 V)	—	—	25	15 × 11	—	470,000	—	—	—	NSP	—	—
500	Q500PAR56NSP^MEP	—	CC-6	4,000	32 × 15	13 × 8	96,000	2950	—	—	NSP	4000	8
500	Q500PAR56WF^MEP	—	CC-6	4000	66C × 34	44 × 20	19,000	2950	—	—	WFL	6,400	12.8

(B) PAR-64 bulb; extended mogul end-prongs^EMEP or screw terminals^ST; burning position: any except as noted

Watts	Bulb and other description	ANSI code	Filament	Average life (h)	(mm)	(mm)	Center beam candlepower	Approximate color temperature (K)	Beam
1000	Q1000PAR64/1^EMEP	FFN	CC-6	800	24 × 10	12 × 6	400,000	3200	VNSP
1000	Q1000PAR64/2^EMEP	FFP	CC-6	800	26 × 14	14 × 7	330,000	3200	NSP
1000	Q1000PAR64/5^EMEP	FFR	CC-6	800	44 × 21	28 × 12	125,000	3200	MFL
1000	Q1000PAR64/6^EMEP	FFS	CC-6	800	71 × 45	48 × 24	40,000	3200	WFL
1000§	Q1000PAR64/3D‡‡‡^EMEP	FGM	CC-6	200	24 × 12	13 × 6	200,000	3200	NSP
1000§	Q1000PAR64/7D##^EMEP	FGN	CC-6	200	43 × 20	27 × 11	70,000	3200	MFL

(B-1) R-14 bulb: D.C. bayonet base; burn horizontal

Watts	Bulb and other description	ANSI code	Filament	Average life (h)	Beam spread (°)	Center beam candlepower	Approximate color temperature (K)	Beam
100§	R-14 BDK	BDK	—	4	30	—	3200	MFL

(C) R-30 bulb; medium screw base; burning position: any

Watts	Bulb and other description	ANSI code	Filament	Average life (h)	Beam spread (°)	Center beam candlepower	Approximate color temperature (K)	Beam
400§	R-30 BEP	BEP	—	4	30	11,000	3400	MFL
375§	R-30 EBR	EBR	—	4	40	14,000	3400	MFL

(D) R-40 bulb; medium screw base; burning position: any

Watts	Bulb and other description	ANSI code	Filament	Average life (h)	Beam spread (°)	Center beam candlepower	Approximate color temperature (K)	Beam
375§	Med. Beam I.F. (375R34/4)	BFA	C-7A	4	35	12,000	3400	MFL
500§	Med. Beam I.F.	EAL	CC-2V	15	60	6,800	3200	MFL
500§	Spot Beam I.F. (RSP-2)	DXB	CC-2V	6	15	45,000	3300	SP
500§	Flood Beam I.F. (RFL-2)	DXC	C-9	6	90	5,500	3300	FL
500§	Flood-Beam I.F. 200-240V	EAH	C-9	6	90	4,500	3200	FL

IV. Bipost Based Lamps — Tungsten-Halogen and Incandescent

(A) Medium bipost base; light center length: 64 mm (2½ in.)

Watts	Bulb and other description	ANSI code	Filament	Average life (h)	Maximum overall length (mm)	Maximum overall length (in.)	Lighted length (mm)	Lighted length (in.)	Approximate color temperature (K)	Maximum bare bulb temperature (°C)*	Base temperature (°C)†	Recommended operating Position	Initial lumens	Initial lumens per watt
500§	T-20 500T20/63	DVG	C-13	50	165	6½	64	2½	3200	—	—	BD45	14,500	29.0
750§	T-24 750T24/16	DVH	C-13	50	165	6½	64	2½	3200	—	—	BD45	22,000	29.3
750	T-24 750T24/13	EDH	C-13	12	165	6½	64	2½	3350	—	—	BD45	25,000	33.3
1000	T-24 1MT24/13	EBB	C-13	12	165	6½	64	2½	3350	—	—	BD45	33,500	33.5
500	T-6 EGN	EGN	C-13D	100	117	4⅝	64	2½	3200	—	—	BD45	13,000	26.0
750	T-7 Q750T7/4CL	EGR	C-13D	150	127	5	64	2½	3200	—	—	BD45	21,000	28.0
1000	T-7 EGT clear	EGT	C-13D	250	127	5	64	2½	3200	—	—	BD45	28,500	28.5

(B) Mogul bipost base; light center length: 127 mm (5 in.)

Watts	Bulb and other description	ANSI code	Filament	Average life (h)	Maximum overall length (mm)	Maximum overall length (in.)	Lighted length (mm)	Lighted length (in.)	Approximate color temperature (K)	Maximum bare bulb temperature (°C)*	Base temperature (°C)†	Recommended operating Position	Initial lumens	Initial lumens per watt
2000	G-48 2M/G48/18	DVF	C-13	100	238	9⅜	127	5	3200	—	—	BD45	61,000	30.5
2000	G-48 2M/G48/14	ECK	C-13	25	238	9⅜	127	5	3350	—	—	BD45	65,000	32.5
2000	T-48 2M/T48/4	EDL	C-13	25	264	10⅜	127	5	3350	—	—	BD45	65,000	32.5
1000	T-7 Q1000T7/4CL/BP	CYV	C-13D	200	203	8	127	5	3200	—	—	BDTH	28,500	28.5
1500	T-11 Q1500T11/4CL	CXZ	C-13	325	216	8½	127	5	3200	—	—	BDTH	44,500	29.7
2000§	T-8 Q2000/4CL/BP	BWA	CC-8	500	203	8	127	5	3200	—	—	BDTH	54,000	27.0
2000	T-10 Q1500T10/4CL	CYX	C-13	300	216	8½	127	5	3200	—	—	BDTH	59,000	29.5
2000	T-11 DCT	DCT	C-13D	900	216	8½	127	5	3050	—	—	BDTH	47,000	23.5

Fig. 6-95. *Continued*

Watts	Bulb and other description	ANSI code	Filament	Average life (h)	Maximum overall length (mm)	(in.)	Lighted length (mm)	(in.)	Approximate color temperature (K)	Maximum bare bulb temperature (°C)*	Base temperature (°C)†	Recommended operating Position	Initial lumens	Initial lumens per watt
(C) Mogul bipost base; light center length: 165 mm ($6\frac{1}{2}$ in.)														
5000§	G-64 5M/G64/7	ECN	C-13	150	302	$11\frac{7}{8}$	165	$6\frac{1}{2}$	3200	—	—	BD45	145,000	29.0
5000	T-64 5M/T64/1	EDN	C-13	75	340	$13\frac{3}{8}$	165	$6\frac{1}{2}$	3350	—	—	BD45	161,500	32.3
5000	T-20 Q5000T20/4CL	DPY	C-13	525	279	11	165	$6\frac{1}{2}$	3200	—	—	BDTH	143,000	28.6
(D) Mogul bipost base; light center length: 254 mm (10 in.)														
1000	G-96 10K/G96/1	EBA	C-13	150	443	$17\frac{7}{16}$	254	10	3200	—	—	BD45	295,000	29.5
1000	G-96 10K/G96	ECP	C-13	75	443	$17\frac{7}{16}$	254	10	3350	—	—	BD45	335,000	33.5
1000	T-24 Q10M/T24/4CL	DTY	C-13	300	391	$15\frac{5}{8}$	254	10	3200	—	—	BD45	287,750	28.8
V. Incandescent Prefocus-Base Lamps														
(A) Medium prefocus base lamps; light center length: 56 mm ($2\frac{3}{16}$ in.)														
250§	T-20 250T20/47 clear	—	C-13	200	146	$5\frac{3}{4}$	56	$2\frac{3}{16}$	2900	—	—	BDTH	4,600	18.4
300	T-6 EEX clear	EEX	C-13	50	121	$4\frac{3}{4}$	56	$2\frac{3}{16}$	3200	—	—	—	7,200	24.0
500§	T-20 500T20' 64 clear	DNW	C-13	500	146	$5\frac{3}{4}$	56	$2\frac{3}{16}$	2900	—	—	—	10,000	20.0
500	T-20 500T20/48 clear	—	C-13	200	146	$5\frac{3}{4}$	56	$2\frac{3}{16}$	3000	—	—	BDTH	11,000	22.0
500§	T-20 DMX-500T20P clear	DMX	C-13	50	146	$5\frac{3}{4}$	56	$2\frac{3}{16}$	3200	—	—	BD30	13,200	26.4
500	T-6 BTL-Q500T6/CL/P clear	BTL	C-13D	500	114	$4\frac{1}{2}$	56	$2\frac{3}{16}$	3050	—	—	BDTH	11,000	22.0
500	T-6 BTM-Q500T6/4CL/2P clear	BTM	C-13D	100	114	$4\frac{1}{2}$	56	$2\frac{3}{16}$	3200	—	—	BDTH	12,000	24.0
750	T-20 750T20P/SP clear	BFE	C-13	200	146	$5\frac{3}{4}$	56	$2\frac{3}{16}$	3000	—	—	BD45	17,000	22.7
750	T-20 BFL/BFK clear	BFL	C-13	200	146	$5\frac{3}{4}$	56	$2\frac{3}{16}$	3050	—	—	BD30	13,500	18.0
750	T-20 DPJ clear	DPJ	C-13D	25	146	$5\frac{3}{4}$	56	$2\frac{3}{16}$	3250	—	—	BD30	19,000	25.3
750	T-7 BTN clear	BTN	C-13D	500	111	$4\frac{3}{8}$	56	$2\frac{3}{16}$	3050	—	—	BDTH	17,000	23.0
750	T-7 BTP-Q750T7/4CL/2P clear	BTP	C-13D	200	111	$4\frac{3}{8}$	56	$2\frac{3}{16}$	3200	—	—	BDTH	21,000	28.0
1000	T-20 1M/T20P/SP clear	—	C-13D	200	146	$5\frac{3}{4}$	56	$2\frac{3}{16}$	3050	—	—	BD45	23,400	23.4
1000§	T-20 DRC clear	DRC	C-13	50	146	$5\frac{3}{4}$	56	$2\frac{3}{16}$	3250	—	—	BD30	30,000	30.0
1000§	T-20 DRS clear	DRS	C-13D	25	146	$5\frac{3}{4}$	56	$2\frac{3}{16}$	3325	—	—	BD30	28,500	28.5
1000§	T-20 DRB clear	DRB	C-13	25	146	$5\frac{3}{4}$	56	$2\frac{3}{16}$	3350	—	—	BD30	32,000	32.0
1000§	T-20 DWK(230V) clear	DWK	CC-13	50	146	$5\frac{3}{4}$	56	$2\frac{3}{16}$	3100	—	—	BD30	23,500	23.5
1000	T-7 BTR-Q1000T7/4CL/2P clear	BTR	C-13D	250	121	$4\frac{3}{4}$	56	$2\frac{3}{16}$	3200	—	—	BDTH	28,500	28.5

VI. Prefocus and Screw-Base Lamps — Tungsten-Halogen and Incandescent

(A) Mogul prefocus base; light center length: 100 mm (3 15/16 in.)

Watts	Lamp	Filament	ANSI	Life (hr)	MOL (mm)	MOL (in)	LCL (mm)	LCL (in)	Color Temp (K)			Base	Lumens	Lm/W
1000	G-40 1M/G40/23 clear	C-13		200	214	$8\frac{7}{16}$	100	$3\frac{15}{16}$	3050	—	—	BDTH	24,000	24.0
1000	G-40 1M/G40PSP clear	C-5		200	214	$8\frac{7}{16}$	100	$3\frac{15}{16}$	3050	—	—	BDTH	22,500	22.5
1000	T-7 BVT-Q1000T7/CL/MP clear	C-13D	BVT	500	184	$7\frac{1}{4}$	100	$3\frac{15}{16}$	3050	—	—	Any	24,500	24.5
1000	T-7 BVV-Q1000T7/4CL/MP clear	C-13D	BVV	250	184	$7\frac{1}{4}$	100	$3\frac{15}{16}$	3200	—	—	Any	28,500	28.5
1500	G-40 1500G40/21 clear	C-13D		200	214	$8\frac{7}{16}$	100	$3\frac{15}{16}$	3000	—	—	BD30	35,500	23.7
1500	T-8 CWZ clear	C-13D	CWZ	325	191	$7\frac{1}{2}$	100	$3\frac{15}{16}$	3200		—	Any	38,500	25.7
2000§	T-10 BVW-Q2000T10/4CL/MP clear	C-13	BVW	300	203	8	100	$3\frac{15}{16}$	3200	—	—	BDTH	59,000	29.5

(B) Medium screw base; light center length: 76 mm (3 in.)

Watts	Lamp	Filament	ANSI	Life (hr)	MOL (mm)	MOL (in)	LCL (mm)	LCL (in)	Color Temp (K)			Base	Lumens	Lm/W
100§	A-21 100A21/SP clear	C-5		200	111	$4\frac{3}{8}$	76	3	2750	—	—	Any	1,340	13.4
250§	G-30 250G/FL clear	C-5		800	130	$5\frac{1}{8}$	76	3	2800	—	—	BDTH	3,650	14.6
250§	G-30 250G/SP clear	C-5		200	130	$5\frac{1}{8}$	76	3	2900	—	—	BDTH	4,500	18.0
400	G-30 400G/FL clear	C-5, C-7A		800	130	$5\frac{1}{8}$	76	3	2850	—	—	BDTH	6,760	16.9
400§	G-30 400G/SP clear	C-5		200	130	$5\frac{1}{8}$	76	3	2950	—	—	BDTH	8,400	21.0
500§	T-20 DMS clear	C-13	DMS	50	140	$5\frac{1}{2}$	76	3	3200	—	—	BD30	13,200	26.4

(C) Mogul screw base; light center length: 108 mm (4 1/4 in.)

Watts	Lamp	Filament	ANSI	Life (hr)	MOL (mm)	MOL (in)	LCL (mm)	LCL (in)	Color Temp (K)			Base	Lumens	Lm/W
500§	G-40 500G/FL clear	C-5		800	179	$7\frac{1}{16}$	108	$4\frac{1}{4}$	—	—	—	BDTH	9,300	18.7

(D) Mogul screw base; light center length: 133 mm (5 1/4 in.)

Watts	Lamp	Filament	ANSI	Life (hr)	MOL (mm)	MOL (in)	LCL (mm)	LCL (in)	Color Temp (K)			Base	Lumens	Lm/W
1000§	G-40 1M/G40FL clear	C-5		800	200	$7\frac{7}{8}$	133	$5\frac{1}{4}$	2950	—	—	BDTH	20,000	20.0
1500 ‖	G-48 1500G48/6 clear	C-5		800	217	$8\frac{9}{16}$	133	$5\frac{1}{4}$	2950	—	—	BDTH	30,000	20.0
2000§	T-8 BWF-Q2000/4CL clear	CC-8	BWF	500	191	$7\frac{1}{2}$	133	$5\frac{1}{4}$	3200	—	—	Any	54,000	27.0
2000	T-8 BWG clear	CC-8	BWG	400	191	$7\frac{1}{2}$	133	$5\frac{1}{4}$	3200	—	—	Any	55,000	27.5

VII. Lamps for Ellipsoidal Reflector Spotlights — Tungsten-Halogen and Incandescent

(A) Medium prefocus base; light center length: 89 mm (3 1/2 in.)

Watts	Lamp	Filament	ANSI	Life (hr)	MOL (mm)	MOL (in)	LCL (mm)	LCL (in)	Color Temp (K)			Base	Lumens	Lm/W
500	T-12 500 & 12/8 clear	C-13D	DEB	800	156	$6\frac{1}{8}$	89	$3\frac{1}{2}$	2850	—	—	BU30	9,000	18.0
500§	T-12 500T12/8 clear	C-13D	DNS	200	156	$6\frac{1}{8}$	89	$3\frac{1}{2}$	2950	—	—	BD30	11,000	22.0
500	T-4 Q500CL/P clear	CC-8	EGE	2000	152	6	89	$3\frac{1}{2}$	3000	—	—	Any	10,000	20.0
500§	T-4 Q500/5CL/P clear	CC-8	EGC	500	152	6	89	$3\frac{1}{2}$	3150	—	—	Any	12,700	25.4
750§	T-12 750T12/9 clear	C-13D	DNT	200	156	$6\frac{1}{8}$	89	$3\frac{1}{2}$	3000	—	—	BD30	17,000	22.7
750	T-6 Q750CL/P clear	CC-8	EGG	2000	152	6	89	$3\frac{1}{2}$	3000	—	—	Any	15,000	20.0
750§	T-6 Q750/4CL/P clear	CC-8	EGF	500	152	6	89	$3\frac{1}{2}$	3200	—	—	Any	20,400	27.2
1000§	T-12 1M/T12/2 clear	C-13D	DNY	200	156	$6\frac{1}{8}$	89	$3\frac{1}{2}$	3050	—	—	BU30	23,400	23.4
1000	T-6 Q1000/4CL/P clear	CC-8	EGJ	400	152	6	89	$3\frac{1}{2}$	3200	—	—	Any	27,500	27.5
1000	T-6 Q1000/4/P frost	CC-8	EGK	400	152	6	89	$3\frac{1}{2}$	3200	—	—	Any	26,500	26.5
1000§	T-6 Q1000CL/P clear	CC-8	EGM	2000	152	6	89	$3\frac{1}{2}$	3000	—	—	Any	21,500	21.5

(B) Medium bipost base; light center length: 102 mm (4 in.)

Watts	Bulb and other description	ANSI code	Filament	Average life (h)	Maximum overall length (mm)	Maximum overall length (in.)	Lighted length (mm)	Lighted length (in.)	Approximate color temperature (K)	Maximum bare bulb temperature (°C)*	Base temperature (°C)†	Recommended operating Position	Initial lumens	Initial lumens per watt
500§	T-14 500T14/7 clear	—	C-13D	800	164	$6\frac{7}{16}$	102	4	2850	—	—	BD30	9,000	18.0
500§	T-5 EFX clear	EFX	CC-8	2000	165	$6\frac{1}{2}$	102	4	3000	—	—	Any	10,000	20.0
750§	T-14 750T14° clear	—	C-13D	200	164	$6\frac{7}{16}$	102	4	3000	—	—	BD30	17,000	22.7
750	T-5 BSC clear	BSC	CC-8	250	165	$6\frac{1}{2}$	102	4	3200	—	—	Any	20,000	26.7
750	T-5 BSD clear	BSD	CC-8	2000	165	$6\frac{1}{2}$	102	4	3000	—	—	Any	15,000	20.0
1000	T-5 DZD clear	DZD	CC-8	400	165	$6\frac{1}{2}$	102	4	3200	—	—	Any	25,500	25.5

(C) Mogul bipost base; light center length: 165 mm ($6\frac{1}{2}$ in.)

Watts	Bulb and other description	ANSI code	Filament	Average life (h)	Maximum overall length (mm)	Maximum overall length (in.)	Lighted length (mm)	Lighted length (in.)	Approximate color temperature (K)	Maximum bare bulb temperature (°C)*	Base temperature (°C)†	Recommended operating Position	Initial lumens	Initial lumens per watt
1500§	T-24 1500T24/6 clear	—	C-13D	200	254	10	165	$6\frac{1}{2}$	3000	—	—	BU30	33,700	22.5
2000	T-30 2M/T30/1 clear	—	C-13D	200	254	10	165	$6\frac{1}{2}$	3050	—	—	BU30	48,000	24.0
2100	T-24 2100T24/9 (60V.)	—	C-13D	50	267	$10\frac{1}{2}$	165	$6\frac{1}{2}$	3100	—	—	BU30	54,100	25.8

(D) Mogul bipost base; light center length: 191 mm ($7\frac{1}{2}$ in.)

Watts	Bulb and other description	ANSI code	Filament	Average life (h)	Maximum overall length (mm)	Maximum overall length (in.)	Lighted length (mm)	Lighted length (in.)	Approximate color temperature (K)	Maximum bare bulb temperature (°C)*	Base temperature (°C)†	Recommended operating Position	Initial lumens	Initial lumens per watt
3000§	T-32 3MT32/2 clear	—	C-13D	100	289	$11\frac{3}{8}$	191	$7\frac{1}{2}$	3150	—	—	BU30	81,000	27.0

VIII. Low-Wattage Lamps for spotlights and projectors

(A) Single-contact bayonet candelabra base; light center length: 35 mm ($1\frac{3}{8}$ in.)

Watts	Bulb and other description	ANSI code	Filament	Average life (h)	Maximum overall length (mm)	Maximum overall length (in.)	Lighted length (mm)	Lighted length (in.)	Approximate color temperature (K)	Maximum bare bulb temperature (°C)*	Base temperature (°C)†	Recommended operating Position	Initial lumens	Initial lumens per watt
100	G-16$\frac{1}{2}$ 100G16$\frac{1}{2}$/29SC clear		CC-13	200	76	3	35	$1\frac{3}{8}$	2850			BDTH	1660	16.6

(B) Double-contact bayonet candelabra base; light center length 35 mm ($1\frac{3}{8}$ in.)

Watts	Bulb and other description	ANSI code	Filament	Average life (h)	Maximum overall length (mm)	Maximum overall length (in.)	Lighted length (mm)	Lighted length (in.)	Approximate color temperature (K)	Maximum bare bulb temperature (°C)*	Base temperature (°C)†	Recommended operating Position	Initial lumens	Initial lumens per watt
50§	T-8 CHY (230V.) clear	CHY	CC-13	50	79	$3\frac{1}{8}$	35	$1\frac{3}{8}$	2550	—	—	BD	650	13.0
100	G-16$\frac{1}{2}$ 100G16$\frac{1}{2}$/29 DC clear	—	CC-2V, CC-	200	76	3	35	$1\frac{3}{8}$	2850	—	—	BDTH	1660	16.6
100§	T-4 Q100CL/DC/2V clear	ESR	CC-2V	750	62	$2\frac{7}{16}$	35	$1\frac{3}{8}$	2850	—	—	Any	1800	18.0
100§	T-8 CJX (230V) clear	CJX	CC-13	50	79	$3\frac{1}{8}$	35	$1\frac{3}{8}$	2850	—	—	BD30	1650	16.5
100§	T-4 Q100DC/2V frosted	ETD	CC-2V	750	62	$2\frac{7}{16}$	35	$1\frac{3}{8}$	2850	—	—	Any	1750	17.5
150§	T-4 Q150CL/DC2V clear	ESP	CC-2V	1000	62	$2\frac{7}{16}$	35	$1\frac{3}{8}$	2850	—	—	Any	2800	18.7
200§	B-12 BDJ clear	BDJ	2CC-8	20	67	$2\frac{5}{8}$	35	$1\frac{3}{8}$	3200	—	—	BD	5000	25.0
200	T-4 FEV Q200/4CL/DC clear	FEV	CC-2V	50	62	$2\frac{7}{16}$	35	$1\frac{3}{8}$	3200	—	—	Any	5500	27.5

IX. Screw-based lamps for floodlights and miscellaneous special effects — Tungsten-Halogen and Incandescent

(A) Medium screw base

Watts	Lamp	Code	Filament	mm	in.	mm	in.	Color temp.			Burning position	Lumens	LPW
250	A-21 BBA I.F.	BBA	C-9	3	125	4 15/16	—	—	3400	—	—	Any	8000	32.0
250§	A-21 BCA I.F. (blue)	BCA	C-9	3	125	4 15/16	—	—	4800	—	—	Any	5000	20.0
250§	A-23 ECA I.F.	ECA	C-9	20	152	6	—	—	3200	—	—	Any	6500	26.0
400§	G-30 400G/FL	—	C-5	800	130	5 1/8	76	3	2850	—	—	BDTH	6800	17.0
500	PS-25 EBV I.F.	EBV	C-9	6	176	6 15/16	—	—	3400	—	—	Any	17,000	34.0
500	PS-25 EBW I.F. (blue)	EBW	C-9	6	176	6 15/16	—	—	4800	—	—	Any	10,500	21.0
500	PS-25 ECT I.F.	ECT	C-9	60	176	6 15/16	—	—	3200	—	—	Any	13,650	27.3
(B) Mogul screw base; light center length: 241 mm (9½ in.)													
1000	PS-52 Q1000PS52/4 I.F.	DKZ/DSE	CC-8	750	330	13	—	—	3200	—	—	Any	28,000	28.0
1500	PS-52 Q1500PS52/4 I.F.	DKX/DSF	C-8	1000	330	13	—	—	3200	—	—	Any	41,000	21.3
2000	T-8 Q2000/4/95 I.F.	BWL	CC-8	5	298	11 3/4	—	—	3200	—	—	Any	57,200	28.6
2000§	T-8 Q2000/4CL	BWF	CC-8	500	191	7 1/2	133	5 1/4	3200	—	—	Any	54,000	27.0
(C) Mogul screw base													
1000§	PS-40 ECV I.F.	ECV§§§	C-7A	60	248	9 3/4	—	—	3200	—	—	Any	26,500	26.5
1000	PS-35 DXR/DXS I.F.	DXR	C-9	10	238	9 3/8	—	—	3400	—	—	Any	31,000	31.0
1000	PS-35 DXT I.F. (blue)	DXT	C-9	10	238	9 3/8	—	—	4800	—	—	Any	19,200	19.2

(X) Incandescent lamps for follow spots, effects projectors

(A) Mogul prefocus base; light center length: 87 mm (3 7/16 in.)

Watts	Lamp	Code	Filament	mm	in.	mm	in.	Color temp.			Burning position	Lumens	LPW
1000	T-20 Clear DPW	DPW	C-13	50	241	9 1/2	87	3 7/16	3200	—	—	BU30	28,000	28.0
1000	T-20 Clear DSB	DSB	C-13D	25	241	9 1/2	87	3 7/16	3225	—	—	BU30	28,500	28.5
1500	T-20 Clear DTJ	DTJ	C-13D	25	241	9 1/2	87	3 7/16	3225	—	—	BU30	42,500	28.3
1500	T-8 Clear DTA	DTA	C-13D	100	168	6 5/8	87	3 7/16	3200	—	—	BDTH	39,000	26.0
2000	T-10 Q2000T10/4CL (220 V.) clear	—	C-13	500	200	7 7/8	87	3 7/16	3200	—	—	BDTH	54,000	27.0
(B) Mogul bipost base; light center length: 102 mm (4 in.)													
2100	T-24 clear 2100T24/8 (60V)	—	C-13D	50	267	10 1/2	102	4	3100	—	—	BD30	54,100	25.8

Fig. 6-95. *Continued*

Watts	Bulb and other description	ANSI code	Nominal lamp supply volts	Nominal lamp amperes	Rated life (h)	Maximum overall length (mm)	(in.)	Lighted length (mm)	(in.)	Approximate color temperature (K)	Maximum bare bulb temperature (°C)*	Recommended operation postion	Base type	Initial lumens
(XI) Metal halide arc in quartz envelope (separate power supply)														
300	GEMINI-300 rim mount glass reflector	EZG	35	—	50	—	—	51	2	6000	—	—	—	—
300	MARC-300/16 rim mount glass reflector	EZM	37.5	—	26	—	—	76	3	5500	—	—	—	—
350	MARC-350/16T rim mount glass reflector	EZT	45	—	50	—	—	76	3	5000	—	—	—	—
(XII) HMI compact double-ended arc lamps in quartz envelopes (separate power supply). CRI = 90 + .														
200	MSI 200		200	3.1	300	75	$2\frac{15}{16}$	—	—	5600	—	—	X515	16,000
575	MSI 575		200	7	750	145	$5\frac{23}{32}$	—	—	5600	—	—	SFc 10-4	49,000
1200	MSI 1200		200	13.8	750	220	$8\frac{21}{32}$	—	—	5600	—	—	Fc 15.5-6	110,000
2500	MSI 2500		210	25.6	500	355	$13\frac{31}{32}$	—	—	5600	—	—	SFa21-12	240,000
4000	MSI 4000		360	24	500	405	$15\frac{15}{16}$	—	—	6000	—	—	SFa21-12	410,000
6000	MSI 6000		200	55	350	450	$17\frac{23}{32}$	—	—	6000	—	—	S25.5 × 60	570,000
12000	GEMI-12000 (160 V)		360	65	250	470	$18\frac{1}{2}$	—	—	6000	—	—	S25.5 × 60	1,100,000
(XIII) MSR single ended gas discharge lamps. burning position: any. color temperature = 5600K.														
(A) Standard (life cycle based on 3 hours on, 1 hour off).														
400	MSR 400	GX 9 $\frac{1}{2}$	67	6.9	500	112	$4\frac{13}{32}$	62	$2\frac{7}{16}$			Any	GX 9.5	30,000
700	MSR 700	Med. Bipost	72	11	750	155	$6\frac{3}{32}$	75	$2\frac{15}{16}$			Any	Med. Bipost	56,000
1200	MSR 1200	Med. Bipost	100	13.8	750	175	$6\frac{7}{8}$	85	$3\frac{11}{32}$			Any	Med. Bipost	110,000
(B) Hot restrike (life cycle based on 3 hours on, 1 hour off. Can be hot-restruck every 15 min). Use only with fixtures designed for hot-restrike.														
575	MSR 575/HR	Med. Bipost	95	6.95	750	145	$5\frac{23}{32}$	70	$2\frac{3}{4}$			Any	Med. Bipost	49,000
1200	MSR 1200/HR	Mog. Bipost	115	13.8	750	200	$7\frac{7}{8}$	107	$4\frac{7}{32}$			Any	Mog. Bipost	110,000
2500	MSR 2500/HR	Mog. Bipost	115	25.6	500	240	$9\frac{7}{16}$	127	5			Any	Mog. Bipost	240,000

‡‡DICHRO LAMP
§Ultraviolet-absorbing bulb.
‡Low noise construction.
|| Beam spread to 50% peak candlepower.
** Beam spread to 10% peak candlepower.
††Candlepower average in central 5° cone for "spot" beam lamps; average in central 10° cone "flood" beam lamps.
‡‡Measured within field angle.
†††Candlepower average in central 5° cone.
¶Tungsten powder cleaner in bulb. Useful lamp life and maintenance of output depend upon removal from socke and scouring of bulb wall with tungsten powder to remove dark film that normally accumulates.
ʳApparent lighted length slightly longer than corresponding clear lamp.
|| || 2 prong base.
§§Blue glass bulb. Apparent color temperature may vary among lamps.
ᶦTop end of bulb is opaque-coated.
ᵐCC-8 filament.
#Infrared reflecting coating.
##Hemispherical shield in front of filament.
***COOL BEAM™
§§§Photo-flood

Fig. 6-96. Silver Bowl Lamps for 120 and 125 Volt Circuits

Watts	Bulb and other description	Base	Filament	Rated life (h)	Maximum overall length (mm)	(in.)	Light center length (mm)	(in.)	Initial lumens	Initial lumens per watt
60	A-19 I.F.	Medium	CC-6 or CC-8	1000	113	$4\frac{7}{16}$	79	$3\frac{1}{8}$	767	12.8
75	A-19 I.F.	Medium	CC-6	1000	135	$5\frac{5}{16}$	—	—	1000	6.7
100*	A-21 I.F.	Medium	CC-6	1000	135	$5\frac{5}{16}$	—	—	1385	13.5
100*	A-23 I.F.	Medium	CC-6	750	151	$5\frac{15}{16}$	113	$4\frac{7}{16}$	1470	14.7
150*	PS-25 I.F.	Mogul	C-9	1000	176	$6\frac{15}{16}$	132	$5\frac{3}{16}$	2320	15.5
200*	PS-30 I.F.	Mogul	C-9	1000	205	$8\frac{1}{16}$	152	6	3320	16.6
300*	PS-35 I.F.	Mogul	C-9	1000	238	$9\frac{3}{8}$	178	7	5403	18.0
500*	PS-40 I.F.	Mogul	C-9	1000	248	$9\frac{3}{4}$	178	7	9477	19.0
750*	PS-52 I.F.	Mogul	C-7A	1000	330	13	241	$9\frac{1}{2}$	15,000	20.0
1000*	PS-52 I.F.	Mogul	C-7A	1000	330	13	241	$9\frac{1}{2}$	20,400	20.4

*Base-up burning only. Use only high-temperature sockets.

Fig. 6-97. Incandescent and Tungsten–Halogen Lamps for 120 V Circuits.

Watts	Bulb and other description	Base	Filament	Rated average life (h)	Maximum Overall Length (mm)	(in.)	Max. Center Beam intensity (cd)	Approximate total lumens	Approximate beam lumens	Approximate beam spread (degrees)*
				R lamps for spotlighting and floodlighting (parabolic reflector)						
27	R-20 Clear	Medium	C-9	2000	100	$3\frac{15}{16}$	270	210	—	43.0
30	R-20 Flood	Medium	C-7A	2000	100	$3\frac{15}{16}$	270	205	50	55.3
45[1]	R-20 Spot	Medium	C-9	2000	100	$3\frac{15}{16}$	530	440	—	43.0
50	R-20 Flood	Medium	C-7A	2000	100	$3\frac{15}{16}$	537	415	143	57.0
65	R-30 Spot	Medium	CC-6	2000	137	$5\frac{3}{8}$	1600	770	—	40.0
65	R-30 Flood	Medium	CC-6	2000	137	$5\frac{3}{8}$	490	770	—	97.0
75	R-30 Spot	Medium	CC-6	2000	137	$5\frac{3}{8}$	1560	865	133	60.0
75	R-30 Flood	Medium	CC-6	2000	137	$5\frac{3}{8}$	457	865	203	110.7
120	R-40 Spot	Medium	CC-6	2000	167	$6\frac{9}{16}$	6700	1600	—	55.0
120	R-40 Flood	Medium	CC-6	2000	167	$6\frac{9}{16}$	1450	1600	—	62.0
150	R-40 Spot	Medium	CC-6	2000	167	$6\frac{9}{16}$	6200	1900	278	33.0
150	R-40 Flood	Medium	CC-6	2000	167	$6\frac{9}{16}$	1297	1900	517	93.0
300	R-40 Spot	Medium	CC-2V	2000	167	$6\frac{9}{16}$	12,167	2450	600	33.33
300	R-40 Flood	Medium	CC-2V	2000	167	$6\frac{9}{16}$	2633	2450	1000	100.7
300	R-40† Spot	Mogul	CC-2V	2000	184	$7\frac{1}{4}$	14,000	—	—	40.0
300	R-40† Flood	Mogul	CC-2V	2000	184	$7\frac{1}{4}$	2600	2450	1000	101.3
500	R-40† Spot	Mogul	CC-2V	2000	167	$6\frac{9}{16}$	21,000	6500	1567	21.0
500	R-40† Flood	Mogul	CC-2V	2000	184	$7\frac{1}{4}$	4550	6500	3900	102.3
1000	R-60†, ‡ Spot	Mogul	C-7A	2000	264	$10\frac{3}{8}$	36,000	—	—	54.0
1000	R-60†, ‡ Flood	Mogul	C-7A	2000	264	$10\frac{3}{8}$	30,000	—	—	80.0
				ER lamps for spotlighting or floodlighting (ellipsoidal reflector)						
50	ER-30 Light inside frost	Medium	CC-6	2000	162	$6\frac{3}{8}$	630	525	—	39.5
75	ER-30 Light inside frost	Medium	CC-6	2000	162	$6\frac{3}{8}$	900	850	—	40.0
120	ER-40 Light inside frost	Medium	CC-6	2000	187	$7\frac{3}{8}$	2025	1475	—	38.5

Fig. 6-97. *Continued*

Watts	Bulb and other description	Base	Filament	Rated average life (h)	Maximum Overall Length (mm)	(in.)	Max. Center Beam intensity (cd)	Approximate total lumens	Approximate beam lumens	Approximate beam spread (degrees)*
BR lamps for spotlighting or floodlighting (proprietary reflector)[2]										
30	BR-19 Light inside frost	Medium	CC-11	2000	102	$4\frac{1}{8}$	380	—	—	25.0
50	BR-19 Light inside frost	Medium	CC-11	2000	102	$4\frac{1}{8}$	700	—	—	25.0
75	BR-19 Light inside frost	Medium	CC-11	2000	102	$4\frac{1}{8}$	1300	—	—	25.0
100	BR-25 Light inside frost	Medium	CC-11	2000	115	$4\frac{5}{8}$	2100	—	—	25.0
R lamps for general lighting‖ (reflector)										
500	R-52 Wide beam	Mogul	C-7A	2000	300	$11\frac{3}{4}$	3545	7725	—	85.7
750	R-52 Wide beam	Mogul	C-7A	2000	300	$11\frac{3}{4}$	5515	7700	—	93.3
1000	R-60 Flood	Mogul	C-7A	2000	264	$10\frac{3}{8}$	—	—	—	0.0
PAR lamps for spotlighting and floodlighting# (parabolic reflector)										
45†	PAR-38 Narrow spot	Med. Skt.	CC-8	2000	135	$5\frac{5}{16}$	11,500	540	—	9.0
45†	PAR-38 Flood	Med. Skt.	CC-8	2000	135	$5\frac{5}{16}$	1750	540	—	32.0
50	PAR-20NSP	Medium	CC-8	2000	89	$3\frac{1}{2}$	5600	560	—	10.3
50	PAR-20NFL	Medium	CC-8	2000	89	$3\frac{1}{2}$	1500	560	—	29.3
50	PAR-30NSP	Medium	CC-8	2000	114	$4\frac{1}{2}$	8967	670	—	10.7
50	PAR-30NFL	Medium	CC-8	2000	114	$4\frac{1}{2}$	2883	670	—	28.7
50	PAR-30FL	Medium	CC-8	2000	114	$4\frac{1}{2}$	1317	670	—	39.3
55	PAR-16NSP	Medium	CC-8	2000	73	$2\frac{7}{8}$	5000	—	—	12.0
55	PAR-16NFL	Medium	CC-8	2000	73	$2\frac{7}{8}$	1300	—	—	30.0
55**	PAR-38 Spot	Med. Skt.	CC-6	2000	135	$5\frac{5}{16}$	4000	520	—	14.0
55**	PAR-38 Flood	Med. Skt.	CC-6	3000	135	$5\frac{5}{16}$	1450	540	—	27.5
60[2]	PAR-38 IR Spot	Med. Skt.	CC-8	2500	135	$5\frac{5}{16}$	18,500	1150	—	10.0
60[2]	PAR-38 IR Wide flood	Med. Skt.	CC-8	2500	135	$5\frac{5}{16}$	1250	1150	—	53.0
65**	PAR-38 Spot	Med. Skt.	CC-6	2000	135	$5\frac{5}{16}$	5500	675	—	13.5
65**	PAR-38 Flood	Med. Skt.	CC-6	2000	135	$5\frac{5}{16}$	1800	675	—	26.0
65**	PAR-38 Spot	Med. S. Pg.	CC-6	2000	110	$4\frac{5}{16}$	5900	675	—	14.0
65**	PAR-38 Flood	Med. S. Pg.	CC-6	2000	110	$4\frac{5}{16}$	1750	225	—	30.0
75	PAR-16NSP	Medium	CC-8	2000	73	$2\frac{7}{8}$	2500	—	—	12.0
75	PAR-NFL	Medium	CC-8	2000	73	$2\frac{7}{8}$	2000	—	—	30.0
75†	PAR-30NSP	Medium	CC-8	2200	114	$4\frac{1}{2}$	13,667	1150	—	11.3
75†	PAR-30SP	Medium	CC-8	2000	114	$4\frac{1}{2}$	6700	—	—	16.0
75†	PAR-30NFL	Medium	CC-8	2200	114	$4\frac{1}{2}$	3300	1150	—	30.0
75	PAR-30FL	Medium	CC-8	2200	114	$4\frac{1}{2}$	2133	1150	—	40.0
75[1]	PAR-38 Spot	Med. Skt.	CC-6	2250	135	$5\frac{5}{16}$	4550	900	—	17.0

Fig. 6-97. Continued

Watts	Bulb and other description	Base	Filament	Rated average life (h)	Maximum Overall Length (mm)	Maximum Overall Length (in.)	Max. Center Beam intensity (cd)	Approximate total lumens	Approximate beam lumens	Approximate beam spread (degrees)*
PAR lamps for general lighting ‖ (parabolic reflector)										
75	PAR-38 Comp. spot	Med. S. Pg.	CC-6	2000	110	$4\frac{5}{16}$	4500	—	—	15.0
75	PAR-38 Comp. flood	Med. S. Pg.	CC-6	2000	110	$4\frac{5}{16}$	1800	—	—	30.0
75[1]	PAR-38 Flood	Med. Skt.	CC-6	2000	135	$5\frac{5}{16}$	1775	900	—	31.5
75	PAR-38 Spot	Med. Skt.	CC-6	2000	135	$5\frac{5}{16}$	5050	765	—	14.5
75	PAR-38 Flood	Med. Skt.	CC-6	2000	135	$5\frac{5}{16}$	1775	765	—	31.5
80**	PAR-38 Spot	Med. Skt.	CC-6	2000	135	$5\frac{5}{16}$	7000	—	—	14.0
80**	PAR-38 Flood	Med. Skt.	CC-6	2000	135	$5\frac{5}{16}$	2700	—	—	22.0
85**	PAR-38 Spot	Med. Skt.	CC-6	2000	135	$5\frac{5}{16}$	15,900	930	—	15.0
85**	PAR-38 Flood	Med. Skt.	CC-6	2000	135	$5\frac{5}{16}$	2000	930	—	37.0
90†	PAR-38 Spot	Med. Skt.	CC-8	2166	135	$5\frac{5}{16}$	22,750	1270	—	8.5
90†	PAR-38 Flood	Med. Skt.	CC-8	2166	135	$5\frac{5}{16}$	3250	1270	—	42.5
100	PAR-38 Spot	Med. Skt.	CC-6	2000	135	$5\frac{5}{16}$	6600	1250	—	15.0
100	PAR-38 Flood	Med. Skt.	CC-6	2000	135	$5\frac{5}{16}$	2400	1250	—	30.0
100†	PAR-38 IR spot	Med. Skt.	CC-8	3000	135	$5\frac{5}{16}$	30,000	2000	—	10.0
100†	PAR-38 IR flood	Med. Skt.	CC-8	3000	135	$5\frac{5}{16}$	5500	2000	—	33.0
120*	PAR-38 Spot	Med. Skt.	CC-6	2000	135	$5\frac{5}{16}$	10,625	1370	—	16.0
120**	PAR-38 Flood	Med. Skt.	CC-6	2000	135	$5\frac{5}{16}$	3800	1410	—	28.5
120**	PAR-38 Spot	Med. S. Pg.	CC-6	2000	110	$4\frac{5}{16}$	10,600	1370	—	16.0
120**	PAR-38 Flood	Med. S. Pg.	CC-6	2000	110	$4\frac{5}{16}$	3800	1370	—	28.5
150††	PAR-38 Spot	Med. Skt.	CC-6	2000	135	$5\frac{5}{16}$	11,750	1735	—	15.5
150††	PAR-38 Flood	Med. Skt.	CC-6	2000	135	$5\frac{5}{16}$	3550	1735	—	38.0
150	PAR-38 Spot	Med. S. Pg.	CC-6	2000	110	$4\frac{5}{16}$	14,750	1735	—	8.0
150	PAR-38 Flood	Med. S. Pg.	CC-6	2000	110	$4\frac{5}{16}$	3100	1735	—	36.0
200	PAR-46 Narrow Spot	Med. S. Pg.	CC-13	2000	102	4	26,850	2260	—	9.0
200	PAR-46 Med. Flood	Med. S. Pg.	CC-13	2000	102	4	6590	2260	—	11 × 26
250†	PAR-38 Spot	Med. Skt.	CC-8	5000	135	$5\frac{5}{16}$	52,000	3200	—	10.0
250†	PAR-38 Flood	Med. Skt. C	CC-8	5000	135	$5\frac{5}{16}$	12,000	3200	—	22.0
300††	PAR-56 Narrow Spot	Mog. E.Pg.	CC-13	2000	127	5	62,000	3780	—	10 × 30
300††	PAR-56 Med. Flood	Mog. E.Pg.	CC-13	2000	127	5	25,050	3780	—	14 × 24
300††	PAR-56 Wide Flood	Mog. E.Pg.	CC-13	2000	127	5	8680	3780	—	25 × 43
500	PAR-64 Narrow Spot	Extended	CC-13	2000	153	6	107,000	6500	—	9 × 13
500	PAR-64 Med. Flood	Mog. End	CC-13	2000	153	6	39,050	6500	—	15 × 28
500	PAR-64 Wide Flood	Prong	CC-13	2000	153	6	13,100	6500	—	21 × 40
500†	PAR-56 Narrow Spot	Mog. E.Pg.	CC-6	4000	127	5	96,100	7150	—	9 × 17
500†	PAR-56 Med. Flood	Mog. E.Pg.	CC-6	4000	127	5	47,200	7217	—	14 × 19
500†	PAR-56 Wide Flood	Mog. E.Pg.	CC-6	4000	127	5	14,700	7217	—	25 × 47
1000†	PAR-64 Narrow Spot	Extended	CC-8	4000	153	6	165,700	17,700	—	10 × 19
1000†	PAR-64 Med. Flood	Mog. E. Pg.	CC-8	4000	153	6	82,000	17,700	—	14 × 32
1000†	PAR-64 Wide flood	Mog. E. Pg.	CC-8	4000	153	6	37,600	17.700	—	24 × 44

*Beam lumens are calculated at 10% of maximum intensity.
†Heat-resistant glass bulb.
‡Halogen cycle lamps
§Krypton filled
‖ Some of these types are also available for 230 to 260 volt circuits.
#All PAR lamps have bulbs of moulded heat-resistant glass.
**High efficacy, reduced wattage
††Also available with an interference (dichroic) reflector.
[1]General Electric
[2]Philips

Fig. 6-98. Clear Traffic Lamps (Medium Screw Base—Voltage as Specified by User)

Watts	Bulb and other description	Wattage group	Base	Filament	Rated average life (h)	Maximum overall Length (mm)	(in.)	Light Center Length (mm)	(in.)	Initial lumens	Initial lumens per watt
	Nominal signal diameter 200 mm (8 in.)										
40	A-21	40	Medium	C-9	2000	113	$4\frac{7}{16}$	62	$2\frac{7}{16}$	374	8.1
40	A-19		Medium	—	6000	—	—	62	$2\frac{7}{16}$	320	8
51	A-19 RR[c]		Medium	C-7A	8000	102	4	62	$2\frac{7}{16}$	—	—
54*	A-19	60	Medium	C-11V, C-9	8000	111	$4\frac{3}{8}$	62	$2\frac{7}{16}$	530	9.8
54	A-21		Medium	C-11V	8000	111	$4\frac{3}{8}$	62	$2\frac{7}{16}$	530	9.8
60*	A-19		Medium	C-11V	8000	111	$4\frac{3}{8}$	62	$2\frac{7}{16}$	610	10.2
60*	A-21		Med. BB	C-11V	8000	111	$4\frac{3}{8}$	62	$2\frac{7}{16}$	610	10.2
60	A-21		Medium	C-11V, C-9	2000	113	$4\frac{7}{16}$	62	$2\frac{7}{16}$	675	11.3
60	A-21		Medium	C-9	4000	113	$4\frac{7}{16}$	62	$2\frac{7}{16}$	585	9.8
64	A-21		Medium	C-9	3000	113	$4\frac{7}{16}$	62	$2\frac{7}{16}$	691	10.8
64*[b]	A-21		Medium	C-9	8000	113	$4\frac{7}{16}$	62	$2\frac{7}{16}$	665	10.4
67	A-19		Medium	—	8000	—	—	62	$2\frac{7}{16}$	610	9.1
67	A-21		Medium	C-9	3000	113	$4\frac{7}{16}$	62	$2\frac{7}{16}$	665	9.9
67	A-21		Medium	C-11V, C-9	8000	113	$4\frac{7}{16}$	62	$2\frac{7}{16}$	618	9.2
69	A-19		Medium	—	8000	—	—	62	$2\frac{7}{16}$	630	9.1
69	A-21		Medium	C-9	8000	113	$4\frac{7}{16}$	62	$2\frac{7}{16}$	678	9.9
75 BH[a]	PAR-46		3 prong	CC-6	6000	98	$3\frac{7}{8}$	—	—	—	—
90*	A-19	100	Medium	C-11V, C-9	8000	111	$4\frac{3}{8}$	62	$2\frac{7}{16}$	1040	11.6
90	A-21		Medium	C-11V	8000	111	$4\frac{3}{8}$	62	$2\frac{7}{16}$	1040	0.0
100	A-21		Medium	C-9	2000	113	$4\frac{7}{16}$	62	$2\frac{7}{16}$	1268	12.7
100	A-21		Medium	C-9	3000	111	$4\frac{3}{8}$	62	$2\frac{7}{16}$	1280	12.8
107	A-21		Medium	C-9	3000	113	$4\frac{7}{16}$	37	$1\frac{7}{16}$	1287	12.0
116	A-21		Medium	C-9	8000	113	$4\frac{7}{16}$	62	$2\frac{7}{16}$	1272	11.0
	Nominal signal diameter 300 mm (12 in.)										
124	A-21 RR[c]	150	Medium	—	8000	—	—	76	3	—	—
135*	A-21		Medium	C-11V, C-9	6333	119	$4\frac{11}{16}$	76	3	1750	13.0
150 BH[a]	PAR-46		3 prong	CC-6	6000	102	4	—	—	—	—
165	P-25		Medium	C-9	8000	121	$4\frac{3}{4}$	77	3	1950	11.8

Note: BH = Burn horizontal.
*Krypton-filled lamps.
[a]General Electric.
[b]Sylvania.
[c]Ring Reflector Philips.

Fig. 6-99. Incandescent Filament Lamps for Series Operation on 600-Volt dc Circuits

Amperes or watts	Volts	Bulb and other description	Base	Filament	Rated life (h)	Maximum overall length (mm)	(in.)	Light center length (mm)	(in.)	Initial lumens	Initial lumens per watt
	These lamps are used chiefly in light rail vehicles, trolley bus and subway car lighting operated 20 in series.										
	Amperes										
1.0	30	A-19 inside frosted	Medium	C-2	2000	100	$3\frac{15}{16}$	64	$2\frac{1}{2}$	365	—
1.6	30	A-21 inside frosted	Medium	C-2	2000	113	$4\frac{7}{16}$	73	$2\frac{7}{8}$	650	—
2.5	30	A-19 inside frosted and white	Medium	C-9	1000	154	$6\frac{1}{16}$	111	$4\frac{3}{8}$	1230	—
	These lamps are used chiefly in light rail vehicles, trolley bus, and subway car lighting operated 5 in series.										
	Watts†										
36[a]	120‡	A-21 inside frosted§	Medium	C-5	1500	111	$4\frac{3}{8}$	75	$2\frac{15}{16}$	380	10.6
56[b]	120‡	A-21 inside frosted§	Medium	C-9	2000	113	$4\frac{7}{16}$	75	$2\frac{15}{16}$	625	11.2
94[c]	120‡	P-25 St. Railway Headlight‡	Medium	C-5	1000	121	$4\frac{3}{4}$	52	$2\frac{1}{16}$	440	4.7
101	120‡	A-23 inside frosted	Medium	C-9	1500	154	$6\frac{1}{16}$	113	$4\frac{7}{16}$	1160	11.5

Note: Several of these lamps are available on special order with an internal film cutout, also with left-hand thread.
†Nominal watts.
‡Also available in 115 and 125-volt designs.
§Vacuum lamp.
[a]Design current 0.342 A.
[b]Design current 0.519 A.
[c]Design current 0.863 A.

Fig. 6-100. Incandescent Multiple Street Lighting Lamps (Any Burning Position)*

Watts	Bulb and other description (all clear)	Nominal lumens	Base	Filament	Rated life (h)	Maximum overall length		Light center length		Initial lumens†	Initial lumens per watt
						(mm)	(in.)	(mm)	(in.)		
A. 1500 hour life											
85	A-23	1000	Medium	C-9	1500	153	6	113	$4\frac{7}{16}$	1140	13.4
175	PS-25	2500	Medium	C-9	1500	176	$6\frac{15}{16}$	133	$5\frac{1}{4}$	2800	16
268	PS-35	4000	Mogul	C-9	1500	238	$9\frac{3}{8}$	178	7	4700	17.5
370	PS-40	6000	Mogul	C-9	1500	248	$9\frac{3}{4}$	178	7	6700	18.1
575	PS-40	10,000	Mogul	C-7A	1500	248	$9\frac{3}{4}$	178	7	11,000	19.1
B. 3000 Hour life											
58	A-19	600	Medium	C-9	3000	108	$4\frac{1}{4}$	73	$2\frac{7}{8}$	656	11.3
92	A-23	1000	Medium	C-9	3000	152	6	113	$4\frac{7}{16}$	1200	13.0
133	A-23	—	Medium	C-9	3000	152	6	111	$4\frac{3}{8}$	1790	13.4
189	PS-25	2500	Medium	C-9	3000	176	$6\frac{15}{16}$	133	$5\frac{1}{4}$	2910	15.3
189	PS-25	2500	Mogul	C-9	3000	181	$7\frac{1}{8}$	137	$5\frac{3}{8}$	2900	15.3
295	PS-35	4000	Mogul	C-9	3000	238	$9\frac{3}{8}$	178	7	4950	16.7
340	PS-35	—	Mogul	C-9	3000	238	$9\frac{3}{8}$	178	7	5600	16.4
405	PS-40	6000	Mogul	C-9	3000	248	$9\frac{3}{4}$	178	7	6850	16.9
620	PS-40	10,000	Mogul	C-7A	3000	248	$9\frac{3}{4}$	178	7	11,000	17.7
860	PS-52	15,000	Mogul	C-7A	3000	332	$13\frac{1}{16}$	241	$9\frac{1}{2}$	15,700	18.3
C. 6000 hour life											
103	A-23	1000	Medium	C-9	6000	154	$6\frac{1}{16}$	111	$4\frac{3}{8}$	1150	11.2
202	PS-25	2500	Medium	C-9	6000	176	$6\frac{15}{16}$	133	$5\frac{1}{4}$	2800	13.9
202	PS-25	2500	Mogul	C-9	6000	181	$7\frac{1}{8}$	137	$5\frac{3}{8}$	2800	13.9
327	PS-35	4000	Mogul	C-9	6000	238	$9\frac{3}{8}$	178	7	4850	14.8
448	PS-40	6000	Mogul	C-9	6000	248	$9\frac{3}{4}$	178	7	8820	15.2
690	PS-40	10,000	Mogul	C-7A	6000	248	$9\frac{3}{4}$	178	7	11,000	15.9
D. 12,000 hour life											
105‡	A-23	1000	Medium	C-9	12,000	151	$5\frac{15}{16}$	68	$4\frac{7}{16}$	1120	10.7
205‡	PS-25	2500	Medium	C-9	12,000	176	$6\frac{15}{16}$	133	$5\frac{1}{4}$	2750	13.4

*120 volt operation. For HID lamps see Fig. 6-122.
†Values apply to vertical base up burning only.
‡Krypton-filled.

Fig. 6-101. Lamps for Airport and Airway Lighting
A. Incandescent filament types

Watts or amperes	Bulb[a]	Amperes or volts	Base	Filament	Rated average life[b] (h)	Maximum overall length (mm)	(in.)	Average light center length (mm)	(in.)	Beamspread to 10% Maximum Luminous Intensity (degrees) Horizontal	Vertical	Initial lumens	Initial luminous intensity (cd)	Federal stock no. (FSN 6240)	MIL Standards (MS)	FAA	MIL specifications	Users†
100	PAR-36	20A	Scr. Term	C-6	100	70	2¾	—	—	9	7	—	80,000	926-4342	21999	—	L-26202	A, C
300	PAR-56[c]	20A	Mog. E. Pg.	C-6[k]	500	127	5	—	—	50	20	—	27,000	929-8003	—	L-982 and E-2048	L-26764	A, C
300	PAR-56[i]	20A	Scr. Term.	C-6[k]	500	114	4½	—	—	18	10	—	200,000	823-3179	—	CAN-1199 L-838	L-26202	A, C
499	PAR-56	20A	Scr. Term.	CC-6[k]	500	114	4½	—	—	16	11	—	330,000	869-5077	24488-7	—	L-26202	A, N, C
500	PAR-56[c]	20A	Mog. E. Pg.	CC-6[k]	375	127	5	—	—	50	25	—	48,000	869-5079	24346-3	—	L-26764	A, N, C
503	T-20	20A	Med. Bipost	C-13	500	165	6½	67	2 21/32	—	—	11,300	—	914-2549	24321-4	—	L-22252 L-26990	A, N
30	T-10	6.6A	Med. Pref.	C-2V	1000	100	3 15/16	38	1½	60	60	435	—	196-4470	25012-1	L-7082	L-7082	A, N, C
45	PAR-38[c]	6.6A	Med. Skt.	C-6	800	135	5 5/16	—	—	—	—	—	1340	889-1777	24479-1	—	—	A
45	PAR-56	6.6A	Scr. Term.	C-8	1000	114	4½	—	—	8	8	—	65,000	914-2546	24488-4	—	L-26202	A, N
45	T-2½	6.6A	RSC	C-8	1000	52	2 1/16	10	13/32	—	—	680	—	889-1801	—	L-842	—	A, N, C
45	T-2½	6.6A	Leads	C-8	1000	44	1 3/4	10	13/32	—	—	680	—	—	—	—	—	A, N, C
45	T-4	6.6A	2 Pin Pref.	C-6	500	64	2½	39	1½	—	—	835	—	—	—	—	—	
45	T-10	6.6A	Med. Pref.	C-2V	1000	100	3 15/16	38	1½	—	—	684	—	196-4472	25012-2	L-802 L-820 L-822	L-7082	A, N, C
100	T-3	6.6A	RSC	C-8	1000	59	2 5/16	6	¼	Filament behind reflector focus		2080	—	196-6408	—	—	—	N
65	T-2½	6.6A	Leads	C-8	1000	44	1 3/4	3	⅛			1060	—	—	—	L-852	—	C
100	T-4	6.6A	2 Pin Pref.	C-6	500	64	2½	39	1½			1620	—	—	—	—	—	
115	T-4	6.6A	2 Pin Pref.	C-6 Flat	500	64	2½	39	1½			2760	—	—	—	—	—	
150	T-4	6.6A	2 Pin Pref.	C-6 Flat	500	64	2½	39	1½			3600	—	—	—	—	—	
200	T-4	6.6A	2 Pin Pref.	CC-6	500	64	2½	39	1½			4800	—	—	—	—	—	
200	T-4	6.6A	D.C. Ring	CC-6	500	60	2 3/8	27	1 1/16			5100	—	—	—	L-850	—	C
200	PAR-46	6.6A	Scr. Term.	CC-6	500	95	3¾	—	—	12	8	—	200,000	752-2423	17994-1	—	L-26202	N
200	PAR-56[i]	6.6A	Scr. Term.	CC-6[k]	1000	114	4½	—	—	50	20	—	16,000	935-6994	24488-6	L-838	26764	A, N, C
200	PAR-56[c]	6.6A	Mog. E. Pg.	CC-6	1000	127	5	—	—	—	—	—	—	538-8853	24348-1	L-850	—	A, N
200	T-4	6.6A	RSC	CC-8	500	65	2 9/16	30	1 3/16	—	—	4500	—	892-1580	L-843	—	—	A, N, C
200	T-4	6.6A	Leads	CC-8	500	54	2 1/8	10	13/32	—	—	4500	—	—	—	—	L-5004	A, N, C
200	T-14	6.6A	Med. Pref.	C-13	75	146	5¾	60	2 3/8	—	—	4900	—	—	—	L-819	L-5004	C
210	T-14	6.6A	Med. Pref.	C-13	375	146	5¾	56	2 3/16	—	—	4500	—	299-6753	25013-3	—	L-5004	A, N
204	T-14	6.6A	Med. Pref.	C-13	500	146	5¾	56	2 3/16	—	—	4200	—	—	25013-2	—	—	
500	PAR-56	20A	Scr. Term.	C-6[k]	500	114	4½	—	—	Filament behind reflector focus		—	—	—	—	E-1328 and E-2351	—	N
200	PAR-64	6.6A	Mog. E. Pg.	CC-6[k]	1500	114	4½	—	—	Filament behind reflector focus		—	—	—	—	—	—	C
300	PAR-64	6.6A	Mog. E. Pg.	CC-6[k]	1500	114	4½	—	—	Filament behind reflector focus		—	—	901-8612	—	E-1328 and E-2351	L-27504	A, N, C
3.04A	RP-11	12.5V.	D.C. Bay.	C-2V	300	57	2¼	32	1¼	—	—	—	130,000	155-7940	15564-6	—	—	N
5.3A	PAR-46	26V	Scr. Term.	4CC-8[d]	50	95	3¾	—	—	10	10	500	—	155-7780	25240	—	—	N

A. Incandescent filament types

Watts or amperes	Bulb[a]	Amperes or volts	Base	Lamp type	Rated average life[b] (h)	Maximum overall length (mm)	(in.)	Average light center length (mm)	(in.)	Beamspread Horizontal	Beamspread Vertical	Initial lumens	Initial luminous intensity (cd)	Federal stock no. (FSN 6240)	MIL Standards (MS)	FAA	MIL specifications	Users†
15	T-7	115/125V	Intermed.	C-7A	1000	57	2 1/4	38	1 1/2	—	—	115	—	617-1720	—	L-840	—	C
40	T-10	120V	Med. Pref.	CC-2V	1000	100	3 15/16	—	—	—	—	425	—	295-2862	—	L-802, L-822	—	C
75	PAR-38[c]	75V.	Med. Scr.	CC-6	1000	135	5 5/16	—	—	60	60	—	1700	—	—	—	L-7802	N
100	T-10	90, 120V.	Med. Pref.	CC-2V	1000	100	3 15/16	38	1 1/2	—	—	1120	—	143-7427	—	L-810	—	N, C
100	A-21	120V.	Med. Scr.	C-9	2000	113	4 7/16	62	2 7/16	—	—	1260	—	617-1824	—	L-810	—	C
107	A-21	120V.	Med. Scr.	C-9	3000	111	4 3/16	62	2 7/16	—	—	1260	—	842-2887	—	L-810	—	C
116	A-21	120V.	Med. Scr.	C-9	6000	111	4 3/16	62	2 7/16	—	—	1260	—	—	—	—	L-7830	N, C
100	PAR-64	6V	Scr. Term.	—	50	102	4	—	—	—	—	—	180,000	299-6769	—	—	—	A, N, C
120	PAR-64	6V.	Scr. Term.	C-6[d]	3000	102	4	—	—	—	5	—	30,000	299-4740	—	—	T-4663	N
399	PAR-56[c]	115V.	Mog. E. Pg.	CC-13	100	127	5	—	—	9	20	—	—	—	24348-4	—	—	A, N, C
420	T-20	12V.	Med. Bipost	C-8	1000	165	6 1/2	64	2 1/2	—	—	7560	—	269-0948	28933-1	—	—	A, N, C
500	PS-40	120V.	Mog. Pref.	C-9	1000	255	10 1/16	144	5 11/16	—	—	9900	—	244-5364	—	—	—	C
500	T-20	120V.	Med. Bipost	C-13B	500	190	7 1/2	76	3	—	—	10,300	—	295-0901	—	—	L-6273	A, N, C
620	PS-40	120V.	Mog. Pref.	C-7A	3000	255	10 1/16	144	5 11/16	—	—	11,200	—	—	27269	L-606	L-6273	A, N, C
700	PS-40[i]	120V.	Mog. Pref.	C-7A	6000	255	10 1/16	144	5 11/16	—	—	11,200	—	—	27268	—	L-6273	A, N, C
1000	T-20[i]	120V.	Mog. Bipost	C-13	500	241	9 1/2	102	4	—	—	22,000	—	250-6435	25015-1	L-291	—	A, N, C
1200	T-20[i]	115V.	Mog. Bipost	CC-8	750	241	9 1/2	102	4	—	—	29,600	—	556-8012	25015-2	—	L-7148	A, N

B. Gaseous discharge type

Watts or amperes	Bulb[a]	Amperes or volts	Base	Lamp type	Rated average life[b] (h)	Maximum overall length (mm)	(in.)	Average light center length (mm)	(in.)	Beamspread Horizontal	Beamspread Vertical	Initial lumens	Initial luminous intensity (cd)	Federal stock no. (FSN 6240)	MIL Standards (MS)	FAA	MIL specifications	Users†
900W[k]	T-2	—	Sleeve	Mercury	100	83	3 1/4	—	—	—	—	65,000	—	—	—	—	—	A, N, C
60 WS FL	Helix[k]	2000	Giant 5 pin	Xenon	500	152	6	102	4	—	—	65,000	—	—	—	L-1106	L-26311	A, N, C
60 WS FL	U shaped	430	Octal	—	—	—	—	—	—	—	—	—	—	—	—	—	—	—
40 WS FL	Helix	450	Octal	Xenon	600	64	2 1/2	41	1 5/8	—	—	—	—	—	—	L-859	—	C
60 WS FL	PAR-56[h]	2000	Screw term.	Xenon	500	114	4 1/2	—	—	70	70	13,700	13,700	—	—	L-847	—	N, C

[a] Clear bulb unless otherwise specified.
[b] Under specified test conditions.
[c] Lens cover, prismatic.
[d] Shielded filament.
[e] Lamp to be used with auxiliary of proper design.
[f] Life based on 3 hours per start.
[g] Nominal length.
[h] Life based on 2 flashes per second.
[i] Stippled cover.
[j] Heat-resistant glass.
[k] Tungsten–halogen lamp within an outer bulb.
[l] Effective candlepower (cd).
* Lamps now in use but not recommended for new design.
†Users:
A — United States Air Force or Army bases.
N — United States Navy Air bases.
C — Civil Airports.

Fig. 6-102. Lamps for Aircraft

Watts or amperes	Bulb	Amperes or volts	Base	Filament	Rated average life (h)†	Max. overall length (mm)	(in.)	Average light center length (mm)	(in.)	Beamspread to 10% maximum luminous intensity (degrees) Horizontal	Vertical	Mean spherical candle power (MSCD)	Initial luminous intensity (cd)	Federal stock (FSN 6240)	MIL Standards
Landing															
100W	PAR-36	13.0	Sc. Term.	C-6	25	70	2 3/4	—	—	11.5	6	—	110,000	237-7867	25243-4509
100W	PAR-46	13.0	Sc. Term.	C-6	25	79	3 1/8	—	—	11	6	—	200,000	946-9636	00000-4537
250W	PAR-36	13.0	Sc. Term	C-6	25	70	2 3/4	—	—	16	7	—	70,000	946-4807	00000-4313
250W	PAR-46	13.0	Sc. Term.	C-2	25	79	3 1/8	—	—	12	10	—	290,000	155-7920	25241-4522
250W	PAR-46	28.0	Sc. Term.	CC-8	25	79	3 1/8	—	—	11	12	—	150,000	816-4808	25241-4553
600W	PAR-64	28.0	Sc. Term.	CC-8	100	122	4 13/16	—	—	12	7	—	620,000	145-1161	25242-Q4559
450W	PAR-46	28.0	Sc. Term.	CC-8	10	102	4	—	—	13	14	—	400,000	557-3065	25241-4581
Taxiing															
250W	PAR-46	28.0	Sc. Term.	CC-6	25	98	3 7/8	—	—	50	10	—	75,000	583-3334	24517-4551
150W	PAR-46	28.0	Sc. Term.	CC-6	30	98	3 7/8	—	—	50	9	—	32,000	132-5328	28926-4570
Navigation															
4.1A	S-8	6.0	S.C. Bay.	C-6	200	51	2	32	1 1/4	—	—	32	—	870-7778	35478-1680
26W	GG-10	6.2	S.C. Index	—	—	—	—	—	—	—	—	—	—	—	25309-600
40W	GG-12	6.2	S.C. Index	—	—	—	—	—	—	—	—	—	—	—	24513-1163
40W	GG-12	6.2	S.C. Index	—	—	—	—	—	—	—	—	—	—	870-0799	25338-1687
100W	T-3	10.0	Spec.	C-8	1000	50	2	29	1 1/8	—	—	130	—	—	00000-1978X
1.52A	S-8	12.8	S.C. Bay.	C-2R	400	51	2	29	1 1/8	—	—	26	—	941-2701	00000-1777
26W	GG-10	13.0	S.C. Index	—	—	—	—	—	—	—	—	—	—	—	—
40W	GG-12	14.0	S.C. Index	—	—	—	—	—	—	—	—	—	—	—	
40W	GG-12	14.0	S.C. Index	—	—	—	—	—	—	—	—	—	—	—	
40W	GG-12	28.0	S.C. Index	—	—	—	—	—	—	—	—	—	—	789-2260	25338-7079
26W	GG-10	28.0	S.C. Index	—	—	—	—	—	—	—	—	—	—	504-2090	25309-7512
40W	GG-12	28.0	S.C. Index	—	—	—	—	—	—	—	—	—	—	519-0854	24513-417A
1.02A	S-8	28.0	S.C. Bay.	2-C6, 2C-2R	500	51	2	32	1 1/4	—	—	32	—	044-6914	35478-1683
100W	T-3	28.0	Spec.	CC-8	1000	57	2 1/4	29	1 1/8	—	—	145	—	—	00000-1970X
150W	T-3	28.0	Spec.	CC-8	1000	57	2 1/4	29	1 1/8	—	—	210	—	045-7173	00000-1967
Wing inspection															
250W	PAR-36	13.0	Scr. Term.	C-6	500	70	2 3/4	—	—	13	12	—	80,000	196-4518	00000-Q4631
50W	PAR-36	28.0	Scr. Term.	CC-6	400	—	—	—	—	40	7	—	10,000	—	25243-4502
Interior incandescent															
1.44A	S-8	12.8	S.C. Bay.	C-6	1000	51	2	32	1 1/4	—	—	21	—	155-7799	35178-1141
0.58A	G-6	13.0	S.C.Bay.	C-2R	750	37	1 7/16	19	3/4	—	—	6	—	143-3159	15570-89
0.17A	G-4 1/2	28.0	Min. Bay.	C-2F	5000	27	1 1/16	14	9/16	—	—	2	—	941-6479	00000-456
0.17A	G-5	28.0	S.C. Bay.	C-2F	500	35	1 3/8	18	11/16	—	—	2	—	155-7947	25238-301
0.30A	G-6	28.0	S.C. Bay.	C-2F	500	37	1 7/16	19	3/4	—	—	5	—	155-7848	15570-303
0.52A	B-6	28.0	S.C. Bay.	2C-2R	300	45	1 3/4	27	1 1/16	—	—	15	—	060-4707	00000-1309
0.51A	S-8	28.0	S.C. Bay.	C-2V	200	51	2	29	1 1/8	—	—	10	—	155-7791	15569-305
0.61A	S-8	28.0	S.C. Bay.	2C-2R	1000	51	2	29	1 1/8	—	—	15	—	295-2668	35478-1691
0.51A	S-81F	28.0	S.C. Bay.	C-2V	200	51	2	—	—	—	—	—	—	295-1680	00000-305IF
0.61A	S-81F	28.0	S.C. Bay.	2C-2R	1000	51	2	29	1 1/8	—	—	—	—	941-2708	00000-1691AF
0.643A	S-8	28.0	S.C.Bay.	CC-8	2000	51	2	30	1 3/16	—	—	18	—	—	35478-2232

Group	Amps / W	Bulb	Volts	Base	Filament	Life (hr)	MOL (mm)	MOL (in)	LCL (mm)	LCL (in)			Candela		Part No.	Part No.
Interior incandescent	0.67A	S-8	28.0	S.C. Bay.	(c03C-2V	300	51	2	29	1 1/8	—	—	21	—	155-7784	35478-307
	0.67A	S-81F	28.0	S.C. Bay.	C-2V	200	51	2	—	—	—	—	—	—	222-0264	00000-307AF
	0.80A	S-8	28.0	S.C. Bay.	C-2V	1000	51	2	29	1 1/8	—	—	21	—	241-9703	00000-1665
	0.80A	S-81F	28.0	S.C. Bay.	C-2V	1000	51	2	—	—	—	—	—	—	941-2709	35478-1665AF
	0.766A	S-8	28.0	S.C. Bay.	CC-8	2000	51	2	30	1 3/16	—	—	14	—	01-015-6	35478-2233
	1.29A	S-11	28.0	S.C. Bay.	C-2V	1000	66	2 3/8	32	1 1/4	—	—	44	—	353-5753	25235-3011
Interior fluorescent	4W	T-5	‡	Min. Pinless	—	5750	152	6	—	—	—	—	140	—	053-8273	00000-5004WW
	8W	T-5	‡	Min. Pinless	—	6750	305	12	—	—	—	—	435	—	955-9174	00000-5008WW
	13W	T-5	‡	Min. Pinless	—	6750	533	21	—	—	—	—	790	—	880-7800	00000-501BWW
	4W	T-5	‡	Min. Bipin	—	5750	152	6	—	—	—	—	140	—	916-8196	00000-5104WW
	6W	T-5	‡	Min. Nipin	—	3750	229	9	—	—	—	—	300	—	691-1397	00000-5106WW
	8W	T-5	‡	Min. Bipin	—	6750	305	12	—	—	—	—	435	—	955-9173	00000-5108WW
	13W	T-5	‡	Min. Bipin	—	6750	533	21	—	—	—	—	790	—	955-9164	00000-5113WW
	4W	T-5	‡	Min. Pinless	—	5750	152	6	—	—	—	—	150	—	—	00000-5004CW
	8W	T-5	‡	Min. Pinless	—	6750	305	12	—	—	—	—	445	—	—	00000-5008CW
	13W	T-5	‡	Min. Pinless	—	6750	533	21	—	—	—	—	820	—	—	00000-5013CW
Indicator or instrument	0.06A	T-1	5.0	Wire Term.	C-2R	60,000	6	1/4	—	—	—	—	0.03 ± 25%	—	878-1965	24367-680
	0.06A	T-1	5.0	Sub-mid FL.	C-2R	60,000	10	3/8	5	3/16	—	—	—	—	879-4980	24515-682AS25
	0.06A	T-1	5.0	Wire Term.	C-2R	32,500	6	1/4	—	—	—	—	0.05 ± 25%	—	060-2941	24367-683
	0.115A	T-1	5.0	Sub-mid FL.	C-2R	32,500	10	3/8	5	3/16	—	—	0.05 ± 25%	—	752-2581	24515-685
	0.115A	T-1	5.0	Wire Term.	C-2R	40,000	6	1/4	—	—	—	—	0.15 ± 25%	—	080-4508	24367-715
	0.115A	T-1 5/8	5.0	Sub-mid FL.	C-2R	20,000	10	3/8	5	3/16	—	—	0.15 ± 25%	—	764-8237	24515-718
	0.7A	T-3 1/4	6.0	Min. Bay.	C-2R	40,000	10	3/8	16	5/8	—	—	0.15 ± 15%	—	954-0124	24367-718S15
	0.2A	T-1 3/4	6.0	S.C. Mid. FL.	C-2R	500	30	1 3/16	10	3/8	—	—	3.4	—	807-9803	25231-316
	0.58A	G-6	13.0	S.C. Bay.	C-2R	1000	37	1 7/16	19	3/4	—	—	0.34	—	155-7857	25237-328
	0.33A	T-3 1/4	13.0	Min. Bay.	C-2V	750	30	1 3/16	16	5/8	—	—	6	—	—	00000-89
	0.08A	T-1 3/4	14.0	S.C. Mid. FL.	C-2F	1000	33	1 5/16	18	11/16	—	—	3	—	155-7949	00000-1816
	0.17A	G-5	28.0	S.C. Bay.	C-2F	1500	35	1 3/8	19	3/4	—	—	0.5	—	851-4352	25237-330
	0.30A	G-6	28.0	S.C. Bay.	C-2F	500	37	1 7/16	16	5/8	—	—	3	—	155-7947	25238-301
	0.17A	T-3 1/4	28.0	Min. Bay.	C-2F	500	30	1 3/16	16	5/8	—	—	6	—	155-7848	15570-303
	0.17A	T-3 3/4	28.0	Min. Bay.	C-2F	500	30	1 3/16	16	5/8	—	—	3.5	—	155-8714	25231-313
	0.04A	T-1 3/4	28.0	S.C. Mid. FL.	C-2F	1500	16	5/8	10	3/8	—	—	3	—	765-8443	00000-1864
	0.04A	T-1 3/4	28.0	S.C. Mid. FL.	C-2F	7000	16	5/8	10	3/8	—	—	0.3	—	763-7744	18209-387
	0.04A	T-1 1/4	28.0	S.C. Mid. FL.	C-2F	4000	10	3/8	16	5/8	—	—	0.34	—	155-7836	25237-327
	0.30A	T-4 1/2	28.0	Min. Bay.	C-2F	500	35	1 3/8	16	5/8	—	—	6	—	299-4742	25069-1495

*For purposes of wiring design maximum amperes at design volts may be approximately 10% greater than design amperes.

†Consult lamp manufacturer before using.

‡Actual life depends on use and environment; theoretical design average life is 40,000 + hours.

§Lamp is aged and selected to ±15% MSCD tolerance.

Fig. 6-103. Lamps for Indicator, LEDs, and Other Services

Lamp number	Bulb	Base	Filament	Rated life (h)	Maximum over-all length (mm)	(in.)	Light center length (mm)	(in.)	Design amperes or watts	Design volts	Luminous intensity (cd) MSCP	Primary application
6RC*	—	Candelabra screw	—	20,000	31	1 7/32	—	—	0.14	6	—	Annunciator (reflector)
120RC*	—	Candelabra screw	—	7500	31	1 7/32	—	—	0.025	120	—	Annunciator (reflector)
49	T-3 1/4	Min. Bay.	S-2	1000	30	1 3/16	—	—	0.06	2	0.04	Radio/TV
253	TL-1 3/4	Midget Grooved	C-2R	10,000	18	1 11/16	—	—	0.35	2.5	—	Instrument, lens end
41	T-3 1/4	Min. Screw	C-2R	3000	31	1 7/32	25	31/32	0.5	2.5	0.5	Radio, indicator
2158-2158D	T-1 3/4	Wire Term.	C-6	20,000	13	1/2	—	—	0.015	3	—	Indicator
1490	T-3 1/4	Min. Bay.	C-2R	3000	30	1 3/16	20	25/32	0.16	3.2	0.2	Radio
680	T-1	Wire Term.	C-2R	60,000	6	1/4	—	—	0.06	5	0.03	Aircraft, 1" tinned leads
680AS15†	T-1	Wire Term.	C-2R	60,000	6	1/4	—	—	0.06	5	0.03	Aircraft, aged and selected ±15% cp
682	T-1	Sub-Midget Flanged	C-2R	60,000	10	3/8	5	3/16	0.06	5	0.03	Aircraft, aged and selected ±15% cp
682AS15†	T-1	Sub-Midget Flanged	C-2R	60,000	10	3/8	5	3/16	0.06	5	0.03	Aircraft, aged and selected ±15% cp
683	T-1	Wire Term.	C-2R	45,000	6	1/4	—	—	0.06	5	0.05	Aircraft, 1" tinned leads
683AS15†	T-1	Wire Term.		25,000	6	1/4	—	—	0.06	5	0.05	Aircraft, aged and selected ±15% cp
685	T-1	Sub-Midget Flanged	C-2R	45,000	10	3/8	5	3/16	0.06	5	0.05	Aircraft
685AS15†	T-1	Sub-Midget Flanged	C-2R	25,000	10	3/8	5	3/16	0.06	5	0.05	Aircraft, aged and selected ±15% cp
1850	T-3 1/4	Min. Bay.	C-2R	1500	31	1 7/32	16	5/8	0.09	5	0.25	Signal
715	T-1	Wire Term.	C-2R	40,000	6	1/4	—	—	0.115	5	0.15	Aircraft, 1" tinned leads
715AS15†	T-1	Wire Term.	C-2R	40,000	6	1/4	—	—	0.115	5	0.15	Aircraft, aged and selected ±15% cp
718	T-1	Sub-Midget Flanged	C-2R	40,000	10	3/8	5	3/16	0.115	5	0.15	Aircraft, aged and selected ±15% cp
718AS-15†	T-1	Sub-Midget Flanged	C-2R	40,000	10	3/8	5	3/16	0.115	5	0.15	Aircraft, aged and selected ±15% cp
328	T-1 3/4	S.C. Midget Flanged	C-2R	1000	16	5/8	10	3/8	0.2	6	0.34	Aircraft
328 AS-10*	T-1 3/4	S.C. Midget Flanged	C-2R	1000	16	5/8	10	3/8	0.2	6	0.34	Aircraft, aged and selected ±10% cp
1784-1784D	T-1 3/4	Wire Term.	C-2R	1000	13	1/2	—	—	0.2	6	0.6	Indicator
1847	T-3 1/4	Min. Bay.	C-2R	8333	31	1 7/32	20	25/32	0.15	6.3	0.38	Radio, TV and indicator
1866	T-3 1/4	Min. Bay.	C-2R	5000	31	1 7/32	20	25/32	0.25	6.3	0.65	Radio
159	T-3 1/4	Wedge	C-2R	5000	27	1 1/16	13	1/2	0.15	6.3	0.34	Radio, TV and indicator
259	T-3 1/4	Wedge	C-2R	5000	27	1 1/16	17	11/16	0.25	6.3	0.65	Radio, TV and indicator

755	T-3$\frac{1}{4}$	Min. Bay.	C-2R	20,000	31	1$\frac{7}{32}$	20	$\frac{25}{32}$	0.15	6.3	0.33	Indicator
40	T-3$\frac{1}{4}$	Min. Screw	C-2R	3000	31	1$\frac{7}{32}$	25	$\frac{31}{32}$	0.15	6.3	0.51	Radio and indicator
47	T-3$\frac{1}{4}$	Min. Bay.	C-2R	3000	31	1$\frac{7}{32}$	20	$\frac{25}{32}$	0.15	6.3	0.51	Radio, TV and indicator
44	T-3$\frac{1}{4}$	Min. Bay.	C-2R	3000	31	1$\frac{7}{32}$	20	$\frac{25}{32}$	0.25	6.3	0.9	Radio, TV and indicator
46	T-3$\frac{1}{4}$	Min. Screw	C-2R	3000	31	1$\frac{7}{32}$	25	$\frac{31}{32}$	0.25	6.3	0.9	Radio, TV and indicator
380	T-1$\frac{3}{4}$	S.C. Mid. FL.	C-2V	20,000	16	$\frac{5}{8}$	10	$\frac{3}{8}$	0.04	6.3	0.03	Indicator
2180-2180D	T-1$\frac{3}{4}$	Wire Term.	C-2V	20,000	13	$\frac{1}{2}$	—	—	0.04	6.3	0.02	Indicator
381	T-1$\frac{3}{4}$	S.C. Mid. FL.	C-2F	20,000	16	$\frac{5}{8}$	10	$\frac{3}{8}$	0.2	6.3	0.4	Indicator
2181-2181D	T-1$\frac{3}{4}$	Wire Term.	C-2F	20,000	13	$\frac{1}{2}$	—	—	0.2	6.3	0.4	Indicator
455‡	G-4$\frac{1}{2}$	Min. Bay.	C-2R	500	27	1$\frac{1}{16}$	14	$\frac{9}{16}$	0.5	6.5	1.9	Indicator (flasher)
50	G-3$\frac{1}{2}$	Min. Screw	C-2R	1000	24	$\frac{15}{16}$	18	$\frac{23}{32}$	0.22	7.5	1	Toy train
344	T-1$\frac{3}{4}$	S.C. Mid. FL.	C-2F	50,000	16	$\frac{5}{8}$	10	$\frac{3}{8}$	0.014	10	0.006	Indicator
1869-1869D	T-1$\frac{3}{4}$	Wire Term.	C-2F	50,000	13	$\frac{1}{2}$	—	—	0.014	10	0.003	Indicator, 5/8″ leads A. = ±10%, blue bead
428	G-4$\frac{1}{2}$	Min. Screw	C-2V	250	27	1$\frac{1}{16}$	18	$\frac{23}{32}$	0.25	12.5	2.4	Toy train
382	T-1$\frac{3}{4}$	S.C. Mid. FL.	C-2F	27,500	16	$\frac{5}{8}$	10	$\frac{3}{8}$	0.08	14	0.3	Indicator
2182-2182D	T-1$\frac{3}{4}$	Wire Term.	C-2F	40,000	13	$\frac{1}{2}$	—	—	0.08	14	0.3	Indicator
430	G-4$\frac{1}{2}$	Min. Screw	C-2V	250	27	1$\frac{1}{16}$	18	$\frac{23}{32}$	0.25	14	2.7	Toy train
1891	T-3$\frac{1}{4}$	Min. Bay.	C-2F	500	30	1$\frac{3}{16}$	16	$\frac{5}{8}$	0.24	14	2.033	Auto, radio and indicator
1893	T-3$\frac{1}{4}$	Min. Bay.	C-2F	7500	30	1$\frac{3}{16}$	16	$\frac{5}{8}$	0.33	14	2	Auto, heavy duty
257‡	G-4$\frac{1}{2}$	Min. Bay.	C-2R	500	27	1$\frac{1}{16}$	14	$\frac{9}{16}$	0.27	14	2.35	Auto, toy train; flasher
256‡	T-3$\frac{1}{4}$	Min. Bay.	C-2R	500	30	1$\frac{3}{16}$	16	$\frac{5}{8}$	0.27	14	0.8	Auto flasher
1892	T-3$\frac{1}{4}$	Min. Bay.	C-2F	1000	31	1$\frac{7}{32}$	16	$\frac{5}{8}$	0.12	14.4	0.75	Auto, Radio
1156	S-8	S.C. Bay.	C-6	1200	51	2	32	1$\frac{1}{4}$	2.1	12.8	32	Auto frnt. turn indic.
1458	G-5	Min. Bay.	C-2V	250	30	1$\frac{3}{16}$	16	$\frac{5}{8}$	0.25	20	4.2	Coin Machine
327	T-1$\frac{3}{4}$	S.C. Mid. FL.	C-2F	4000	16	$\frac{5}{8}$	10	$\frac{3}{8}$	0.04	28	0.34	Aircraft
1762-1762D-1762U	T-1$\frac{3}{4}$	Wire Term.	C-2F	4000	13	$\frac{1}{2}$	—	—	0.04	28	0.34	Indicator
387	T-1$\frac{3}{4}$	S.C. Mid. FL.	C-2F	7000	16	$\frac{5}{8}$	10	$\frac{3}{8}$	0.04	28	0.3	Indicator
1829	T-3$\frac{1}{4}$	Min. Bay.	C-2F	1000	31	1$\frac{7}{32}$	16	$\frac{5}{8}$	0.07	28	1	Indicator
757	T-3$\frac{1}{4}$	Min. Bay.	C-2F	11,250	30	1$\frac{3}{16}$	16	$\frac{5}{8}$	0.08	28	0.62	Indicator
Halogen indicator lamps												
H3-55	T-3$\frac{1}{2}$	PK22S	C-6	100	42	1$\frac{21}{32}$	18	$\frac{23}{32}$	66W	12	115	Auto aux.
H3-100	T-3$\frac{1}{2}$	PK22S	C-6	50	42	1$\frac{21}{32}$	18	$\frac{23}{32}$	100W	12	187	Off-road aux.
767	T-2$\frac{1}{4}$	Min. Bay.	C-6	50	29	1$\frac{1}{8}$	14	$\frac{9}{16}$	1.12	6	19	Instrument halogen
777	T-2$\frac{1}{4}$	G-4 2 pin	C-6	275	25	1	20	$\frac{25}{32}$	0.924	4	5.5	Flashlight halogen
778	T-2$\frac{3}{4}$	G-4 2 pin	C-6	100	27	1$\frac{1}{16}$	20	$\frac{25}{32}$	2.57026	6	32	Instrument

Fig. 6-103. *Continued*

Lamp number	Bulb	Base	Filament	Rated life (h)	Maximum over-all length (mm)	(in.)	Light center length (mm)	(in.)	Design amperes of watts	Design volts	Luminous intensity (cd) MSCP	Primary application
784	T-2$\frac{1}{4}$	G-4 2 pin	C-6	50	25	1	20	$\frac{25}{32}$	0.77	6	9	Emergency light halogen
1945	T-4	2-pin	CC-6	200	57	2$\frac{1}{4}$	33	1$\frac{5}{16}$	200W	32	360	Marine quartz
1946	T-3	Wire Term.	CC-6	50	37	1$\frac{15}{32}$	22	$\frac{7}{8}$	250W	28	660	Aircraft
1962TY	T-3	Wire Term.	C-6	50	21	1$\frac{27}{32}$	7	$\frac{9}{32}$	62W	8.5	110	Medical-quartz
1962BG	T-3	Wire Term.	C-6	50	21	1$\frac{27}{32}$	7	$\frac{9}{32}$	62W	8.5	110	Aircraft
1968	T-3	Double Slide	C-2V	500	30	1$\frac{3}{16}$	10	$\frac{3}{8}$	25W	28	15	Aircraft gunsight
1970	T-3	Special	CC-8	1000	57	2$\frac{1}{4}$	29	1$\frac{1}{8}$	100W	28	150	Aircraft
1978X	T-3	Special	C-8	2000	55	2$\frac{5}{32}$	29	1$\frac{1}{8}$	100W	10	130	Aircraft navigation
2082	T-2$\frac{1}{4}$	G5.3	CC-6	100	38	1$\frac{1}{2}$	25	$\frac{31}{32}$	12W	12	20	Halogen
HR9000	PAR-18	G-6 2 pin	C-6	50	56	2$\frac{7}{32}$	—	—	7W	6	—	Emergency light

Light Emitting Diodes (LEDs)§

Lamp number (Part No.)	Description Emitted color	Description Package (bulb diameter)	Description Lens	Bulb diameter (mm)	Peak forward current (mA)	Maximum overall length (mm)	(in.)	Luminous intensity (cd @20 mA) Min.	Luminous intensity (cd @20 mA) Max.	IF (mA)	Max. Forward Voltage	Viewing Angle 2θ$\frac{1}{2}$ (degrees)	Peak Wavelength (nm)	Features
HLMP-8100§	Red	T-1$\frac{3}{4}$	Clear	5.6	300	9	$\frac{11}{32}$	—	2	0.02	2.4	24	650	Wide angle
HLMP-8104§	Red	T-1$\frac{3}{4}$	Clear	5.6	300	9	$\frac{11}{32}$	3	8.4	0.02	2.4	7	650	
HLMP-8150§	Red	T-4	Clear	12.7	300	19	$\frac{23}{32}$	8	36	0.04	2.4	4	650	
HLMP-3850§	Yellow	T-1$\frac{3}{4}$	Clear	5.6	60	6	$\frac{7}{32}$	—	0.14	—	3	24	583	
HLMP-3950§	Green	T-1$\frac{3}{4}$	Clear	5.6	90	9	$\frac{11}{32}$	—	0.12	—	3	24	565	
HLMP-D400§	Orange	T-1$\frac{3}{4}$	Clear	5.6	90	9	$\frac{11}{32}$	—	—	—	3	60	600	Diffuse
C470-5C14 ‖	Blue	T-1$\frac{3}{4}$	Clear	5.6	50	—	—	—	0.13	20	3	16	470	
C470-5D16 ‖	Blue	T-1$\frac{3}{4}$	White Diff.	5.6	50	—	—	—	0.05	45	3.4	34	470	Diffuse

*General Electric.
†Sylvania.
‡Flasher lamp.
§LED information from Hewlett Packard.
‖ LED information from Cree Research Inc.

Fig. 6-104. Specifications of Flasher-Filament Lamps

Lamp No.	Bulb	Base	Filament	Approximate flashes per minute	Useful life (h)	Maximum Overall length (mm)	Maximum Overall length (in.)	Bulb diameter (mm)	Bulb diameter (in.)	Design volts	Design amperes or watts	Mean spherical candlepower	Primary application
256	T-3$\frac{1}{4}$	Min. Bay.	C-2R	—	500	30	1$\frac{3}{16}$	10	$\frac{13}{32}$	14	0.27	—	Auto flasher
257	G-4$\frac{1}{2}$	Min. Bay.	C-2R	—	500	27	1$\frac{1}{16}$	14	$\frac{9}{16}$	14	0.27	1.8	Auto, toy train
258	G-4$\frac{1}{2}$	Min. Screw	C-2R	—	500	27	1$\frac{1}{16}$	14	$\frac{9}{16}$	14	0.27	1.6	Toy train
267	T-3$\frac{1}{4}$	Min. Bay.	C-2R	—	5000	30	1$\frac{3}{16}$	10	$\frac{13}{32}$	6.3	0.15	0.33	Flasher
405	G-4$\frac{1}{2}$	Min. Screw	C-2R	45	500	27	1$\frac{1}{16}$	14	$\frac{9}{16}$	6	0.5	—	Signal
406	G-4$\frac{1}{2}$	Min. Screw	C-2R	40–160	50	27	1$\frac{1}{16}$	14	$\frac{9}{16}$	2.6	0.3	—	Toy, flasher
407	G-4$\frac{1}{2}$	Min. Screw	C-2R	40–160	50	27	1$\frac{1}{16}$	14	$\frac{9}{16}$	4.9	0.3	1.3	Flasher-4F cells
425	G-4$\frac{1}{2}$	Min. Screw	C-2R	—	15	27	1$\frac{1}{16}$	14	$\frac{9}{16}$	5	0.5	2.3	Hand lantern-4F cells
455	G-4$\frac{1}{2}$	Min. Bay.	C-2R	40–160	500	27	1$\frac{1}{16}$	14	$\frac{9}{16}$	6.5	0.5	1.9	Indicator
D26	C-7$\frac{1}{2}$	Cand. Screw	—	—	750	54	2$\frac{1}{8}$	24	$\frac{15}{16}$	120	7W	—	Twinkle lamp (in and out)
D27	C-9$\frac{1}{2}$	Inter. Screw	—	—	750	79	3$\frac{1}{8}$	30	1$\frac{3}{16}$	120	7W	—	Twinkle lamp (outdoor)

Fig. 6-105. Lamps for Flashlight, Handlantern, Bicycle and Other Services

Lamp No.	Bulb	Base	Filament	Rated life (h)	Maximum overall length (mm)	(in.)	Light center length (mm)	(in.)	Design volts	Design amperes or watts	Luminous intensity (cd)	Use with cell type	Primary application
PR2	B-3½	S.C. Min. FL.	C-2R	15	32	1¼	6	¼	2.38	0.50	0.73	2-D	Flashlight
PR3	B-3½	S.C. Min. FL.	C-2R	15	32	1¼	6	¼	3.57	0.50	1.50	3-D	Flashlight
PR4	B-3½	S.C. Min. FL.	C-2R	10	32	1¼	6	¼	2.33	0.27	0.40	2-C	Flashlight
PR6	B-3½	S.C. Min. FL.	C-2R	30	32	1¼	6	¼	2.47	0.30	0.45	2-D	Flashlight (industrial)
PR7	B-3½	S.C. Min. FL.	C-2R	30	32	1¼	6	¼	3.70	0.30	0.90	3-D	Flashlight (industrial)
PR12	B-3½	S.C. Min. FL.	C-2R	15	32	1¼	6	¼	5.95	0.50	3.10	5-D	Flashlight
PR13	B-3½	S.C. Min. FL.	C-2R	15	32	1¼	6	¼	4.75	0.50	2.20	4-F	Flashlight
13	G-3½	Min. Screw	C-2R, 2B	15	24	15/16	18	23/32	3.70	0.30	0.98	3-D	Flashlight
14	G-3½	Min. Screw	C-2R	15	24	15/16	18	23/32	2.47	0.30	0.50	2-D	Flashlight
PR15	B-3½	S.C. Min. FL.	C-2R	20	32	1¼	6	¼	4.82	0.50	1.90	8-F‡	Hand lantern
PR18	B-3½	S.C. Min. FL.	C-2R	3	32	1¼	6	¼	7.20	0.53	5.50	6-D	Flashlight
PR20	B-3½	S.C. Min. FL.	C-2R	15	32	1¼	6	¼	4.32	0.25	2.50	7-D	Hand lantern
27	G-4½	Min. Screw	C-2R	30	27	1 1/16	18	23/32	4.90	0.30	1.40	4-F	Flashlight
112	TL-3	Min. Screw§	S-2	5	24	15/16	22	7/8	1.20	0.22	0.09	1 AA, C, D	Flashlight
131	G-3½	Min. Screw	S-2	50	24	15/16	18	23/32	1.30	0.10	0.03	1-D	Bicycle
KPR140	B-3½	S.C. Min. FL.	C-2R	15	32	1¼	6	¼	4.00	0.90	4.00	Recharg.	Flashlight, krypton
222	TL-3	Min. Screw§	C-2R, 6	5	24	15/16	—	—	2.25	0.25	—	2-AA	Flashlight
223	FE-3¾	Min. Screw	C-6	5	21	13/16	17	21/32	2.25	0.25	0.4	2-AA	Flashlight
233	G-3½	Min. Screw	C-2R	10	24	15/16	18	23/32	2.33	0.27	0.42	2-C	Flashlight
401∥	G-4½	Min. Screw	S-2	15	27	1 1/16	—	—	1.25	0.22	0.09	1-D	Toy flasher
406∥	G-4½	Min. Screw	C-2R	50	27	1 1/16	—	—	2.60	0.30	0.43	2-D	Toy flasher
407∥	G-4½	Min. Screw	C-2R	50	27	1 1/16	21	13/16	4.90	0.30	—	4-F	Flasher
502	G-4½	Min. Screw	C-2R	100	27	1 1/16	18	23/32	5.10	0.15	0.60	4-F	Hand lantern
605	G-4½	Min. Screw	C-2R	15	27	1 1/16	18	23/32	6.15	0.50	3.20	5-D	Flashlight
HPR-40#	T-3	S.C. Min. FL.	C-6	50	32	1¼	6	¼	6.00	6.70	6.00	—	Flashlight halogen
HPR-41#	T-3	S.C. Min. FL.	C-6	100	32	1¼	6	¼	3.75	0.75	3.10	—	Flashlight halogen

* Laboratory test.
‡ Two 4 cell groups in parallel.
§ Lens and lamp.
∥ Flasher lamp.
Philips.

Fig. 6-106. Lamps for 6-, 12-, and 24-Volt Automotive and Heavy Duty Truck Service

Lamp No.	Bulb	Base	Filament	Design amperes	Design volts	Luminous intensity (cd)	Related life (h)	Maximum overall length (mm)	(in.)	Light center length (mm)	(in.)	Atmosphere B-Vac C-Gas	Service*
1445	G-3½	Min. Bay.	C-2V	0.13	14.40	0.70	2000	24	15/16	13	½	B	A, C, H
53	G-3½	Min. Bay.	C-2V	0.12	14.40	1	1000	24	15/16	13	½	B	A, C
182	G-3½	Min. Bay.	C-2F	0.18	14.40	1	2000	24	15/16	13	½	B	A, C, H
53X	G-3½	Min. Bay.	C-2F	0.12	14.40	0.92	1000	24	15/16	13	½	B	A, C
161	T-3¼	Wedge	C-2F	0.19	14.00	1	4000	27	1 1/16	14	9/16	B	A, C, H
184	T-3¼	Wedge	C-2F	0.16	9.60	1.05	4000	27	1 1/16	14	9/16	B	A, C, H
257	G-4½	Min. Bay.	C-2R	0.27	14.00	2.35	500	27	1 1/16	14	9/16	B, C	C (flasher)
57	G-4½	Min. Bay.	C-2V	0.24	14.00	2	500	27	1 1/16	14	9/16	B	A, C
57X	G-4½	Min. Bay.	C-2F	0.24	14.00	2	500	27	1 1/16	14	9/16	B	A, C, H
158	T-3¼	Wedge	C-2V	0.24	14.00	2	500	27	1 1/16	14	9/16	B	A, C
194	T-3¼	Wedge	C-2F	0.27	14.00	2	4000	27	1 1/16	14	9/16	B	A, C, H
193	T-3¼	Wedge	C-2F	0.33	14.00	2	9167	27	1 1/16	14	9/16	B	A, C, H
1895	G-4½	Min. Bay.	C-2F	0.27	14.00	2	2500	27	1 1/16	14	9/16	B	A, C, H
293	G-4½	Min. Bay.	C-2F	0.33	14.00	2	6667	27	1 1/16	14	9/16	B	A, C, H
168	T-3¼	Wedge	C-2F	0.35	14.00	3	1500	27	1 1/16	14	9/16	B	A, C, H, M
97	G-6	S.C. Bay.	C-2V	0.69	13.50	4	5000	37	1 7/16	21	13/16	C	A, C, H, L, M, T, P
67	G-6	S.C. Bay.	C-2R	0.59	13.50	4	5000	37	1 7/16	21	13/16	C	A, L M, P, T
68	G-6	D.C. Bay.	C-2R	0.59	13.50	4	5000	37	1 7/16	21	13/16	C	A, C, E, M
96	G-6	D.C. Bay.	C-2V	0.69	13.50	4	5000	37	1 7/16	21	13/16	C	A, C, E, H, M
1155	G-6	S.C. Bay.	2C-2R	0.59	9.00	4	5000	37	1 7/16	21	13/16	C	A, H, L, M, T
89	G-6	S.C. Bay.	C-2R	0.58	13.00	6	750	37	1 7/16	19	¾	C	E, M
631	G-6	S.C. Bay.	2C-2R	0.63	14.00	6	1000	37	1 7/16	19	¾	C	A, E, M, T, H
98	G-6	S.C. Bay.	C-2V	0.62	13.00	6	967	37	1 7/16	19	¾	C	E, H, M
90	G-6	D.C. Bay.	C-2R	0.58	13.00	6	750	37	1 7/16	19	¾	C	A, E, M
99	G-6	D.C. Bay.	C-2V	0.62	13.00	6	700	37	1 7/16	19	¾	C	A, E, H, M
105	B-6	S.C. Bay.	C-6	1.00	12.80	12	733	44	1 ¾	27	1 1/16	C	E, F, H
104	B-6	D.C. Bay.	C-6	0.67	8.53	8	850	44	1 ¾	27	1 1/16	C	E, F, H
93	S-8	S.C. Bay.	C-2R	1.04	12.80	15	700	51	2	29	1 ⅛	C	D, E
1093	S-8	S.C. Bay.	C-2R	0.79	8.53	10	1000	51	2	32	1 ¼	C	D, E, H
94	S-8	D.C. Bay.	C-2R	1.04	12.80	15	700	51	2	29	1 ⅛	C	E
1003	B-6	S.C. Bay.	C-6	0.94	12.80	15	167	44	1 ¾	27	1 1/16	C	E
1004	B-6	D.C. Bay.	C-6	0.94	12.80	15	167	44	1 ¾	27	1 1/16	C	E
1034	S-8	D.C. Index	C-6/C-6	1.8/0.59	12.8/14	32/3	200/5000	51	2	32	1 ¼	C	D, L, S, T, P
1073	S-8	S.C. Bay.	C 6	1.80	12.80	32	200	51	2	32	1 ¼	C	D, D, S
1141	S-8	S.C. Bay.	C-6	1.44	12.80	21	1000	51	2	32	1 ¼	C	B, D, S
1159	S-8	S.C. Bay.	C-6	1.07	8.53	14	500	51	2	32	1 ¼	C	D, H, S
1142	S-8	D.C. Bay.	C-6	1.44	12.80	21	1000	51	2	32	1 ¼	C	B, D, S
1176	S-8	D.C. Bay.	C-6/C-6	1.34/0.59	12.8/14	21/6	275/1250	51	2	32	1 ¼	C	E
1376	S-8	D.C. Bay.	C-6/C-6	1.60/0.64	12.8/14	21/6	1500/2000	51	2	32	1 ¼	—	E, H
1156	S-8	S.C. Bay.	C-6	2.10	12.80	32	1200	51	2	32	1 ¼	C	B, D, H, S
199	S-8	S.C. Bay.	C-6	2.25	12.80	32	1300	51	2	32	1 ¼	C	B, D, H, S
1157	S-8	D.C. Index	C-6/C-6	2.10/0.59	12.8/14	32/3	1200/5000	51	2	32	1 ¼	C	D, H, L, P, S, T
198	S-8	D.C. Index	C-6/C-6	2.25/0.59	12.8/14	32/3	1200/5000	51	2	32	1 ¼	C	D, H, L, P, S, T
1293	RP-11	S.C. Bay.	C-2R	1.00	4.17	16.67	300	57	2 ¼	32	1 ¼	—	B, G
1195	RP-11	S.C. Bay.	C-2V	3.00	12.50	50	300	57	2 ½	32	1 ¼	C	G
1295	S-8	S.C. Bay.	C-2R	2.00	8.33	33.33	250	51	2	32	1 ¼	C	B, G

*Letter designations are defined as follows:
A-Instrument.
B-Back-up.
C-Indicator or pilot.
D-Turn signal.
E-Interior.
G-Auxiliary service.
H-Heavy duty.
L-License.
M-Marker, clearance and identification.
P-Parking.
S-Stop.
T-Tail.

Fig. 6-107. Sealed Beam and Bonded Beam Lamps for Land Vehicles

Lamp No.	Bulb	Base				Rated life (h)*	Maximum overall length		Design watts	Design volts	Approx. Total Spread to 10% Max. C.P. (degrees)		Luminous intensity (cd) BCP	Type of service
		S.A.E. Type	Terminals	Contacts	Filament		(mm)	(in.)			Horizontal	Vertical		
6006	PAR-56	H-3	Lugs	3	C-6	300 500	134	$5\frac{1}{4}$	50 40	6.1 6.2	— —	— —	— —	Auto headlamp upper beam lower beam
4012†	PAR-46	G-2	Screw	2	C-6	190	95	$3\frac{3}{4}$	35	6.2	—	—	—	
4535	PAR-46	G-2	Screw	2	C-6	84	95	$3\frac{3}{4}$	30	6.4	5.25	2	95,000	Spotlamp
4515	PAR-36	G-2	Screw	2	C-6	59	70	$2\frac{3}{4}$	30	6.4	5	5	40,000	Spotlamp
4013	PAR-46	G-2	Screw	2	C-6	250	95	$3\frac{3}{4}$	25	6.4	25	25	860	Tractor flood
4019	PAR-46	G-2	Screw	2	C-6	245	95	$3\frac{3}{4}$	30	6.2	—	—	2767	Tractor
4015†	PAR-36	G-2	Screw	2	C-6	190	70	$2\frac{3}{4}$	35	6.2	—	—	8600	Auto fog
4419	PAR-46	G-2	Screw	2	C-6	300	95	$3\frac{3}{4}$	35	12.8	—	—	1600	Tractor
4413	PAR-46	G-2	Screw	2	C-6	300	95	$3\frac{3}{4}$	50	12.8	80	20	1167	Tractor flood
4001‡	PAR-46	H-2	Lugs	2	C-6	300	102	4	37.5	12.8	—	—	—	
4000‡	PAR-46	H-3	Lugs	3	C-6 C-6	320 200	102	4	60 37.5	12.8 12.8	—	—	—	Auto headlamp upper beam lower beam Type 2C1
4040‡	PAR-46	H-3	Lugs	3	C-6 C-6	300 500	102	4	37.5 60	12.8 12.8	—	—	—	Truck headlamp
6014†	PAR-56	H-3	Lugs	3	C-6 C-6	200 320	134	$5\frac{1}{4}$	60 50	12.8 12.8	—	—	—	Auto headlamp upper beam lower beam

	Shape		Base		Filament								Life	Application
6015	PAR-56	H-3	Lugs	3	C-6 C-6	283 467	134	$5\frac{1}{4}$	56.7 50	12.8 12.8	— —	— —	— —	Truck headlamp upper beam lower beam
6016	PAR-56	—	Lugs	3	C-6 C-6	300 500	134	$5\frac{1}{4}$	60 50	12.8 12.8	— —	— —	— —	Auto fleet service High / low beam headlamp
4405	PAR-36	G-2	Screw	2	C-6	100	70	$2\frac{3}{4}$	30	12.8	6	5	50,000	Spotlight
4420	PAR-46	H-3	Lugs	3	C-6 C-6	300 300	102	4	30	12.8 12.8	—	—	—	Cycle headlamp
4412†	PAR-46	G-2	Screw	2	C-6	250	102	4	35	12.8	40	6.5	10,667	Foglight
4415†	PAR-36	G-2	Screw	2	C-6	250	70	$2\frac{3}{4}$	35	12.8	40	5	9000	Foglight
4651	Rectangular	—	Lugs	2	C-6	200	121	$4\frac{3}{4}$	50	12.8	—	—	—	Auto headlamp upper beam
4652	Rectangular	—	Lugs	3	C-6 C-6	230 290	121	$4\frac{3}{4}$	50 50	12.8 12.8	—	—	—	Auto headlamp upper beam lower beam
6052	Rectangular	—	Lugs	3	C-6 C-6	150 260	143	$5\frac{5}{8}$	65 55	12.8 12.8	—	—	—	Auto headlamp upper beam lower beam
H4651	Rectangular	—	Lugs	2	C-6	200	121	$4\frac{3}{4}$	50	12.8	—	—	—	Auto headlamp upper beam Type 1A Halogen
H4656	Rectangular	—	Lugs	3	C-6 C-6	200 320	121	$4\frac{3}{4}$	35 35	12.8 12.8	—	—	—	Auto headlamp upper beam lower beam
H4701	Rectangular	—	Lugs	2	C-8	150	88	$3\frac{7}{16}$	65	13.2	—	—	—	Auto headlamp high halogen
H4703	Rectangular	—	Lugs	2	C-8	500	88	$3\frac{7}{16}$	55	13.2	—	—	—	Auto headlamp low halogen

*Lab rating; at 7.0 volts for 6.0 – 6.4 volt lamps; 14.0 volts for 12.8 volt lamps.

†Available with clear or amber lens.

‡Dual headlamp system (one unit of each type as a pair on each side on the front of vehicle.)

Fig. 6-108. Commonly Used Projection Lamps

Watts	Bulb	ANSI Code	Volts	Base	Filament	Rated life (h)	Maximum overall length (mm)	(in.)	Light center length (mm)	(in.)	Approximate color temperature (K)	Initial lumens	Initial lumens per watt	Description[†]
30	S-11	BLC	115–125	D.C. Bay.	CC-2V	50	60	$2\frac{3}{8}$	35	$1\frac{3}{8}$	2775	400	13.3	h, c
50	S-11	BLX	115–125	D.C. Bay.	CC-2V	50	60	$2\frac{3}{8}$	35	$1\frac{3}{8}$	2850	780	15.6	h, d
50	T-8	CAX	115–125	D.C. Bay.	CC-13	50	79	$3\frac{1}{8}$	35	$1\frac{3}{8}$	2900	775	15.5	e, h
80	T-12	DFE	30	4-pin	CC-8	15	81	$3\frac{3}{16}$	40	$1\frac{9}{16}$	3400	—	—	k, d
80	T-12	DGB/DMD	30	4-pin	CC-6	15	90	$3\frac{9}{16}$	40	$1\frac{9}{16}$	3400	—	—	k, e
80	T-14	DLD/DFZ	30	4-pin	CC-6	15	89	$3\frac{1}{2}$	40	$1\frac{9}{16}$	3400	—	—	l, d
150	T-10	CAR	120	4-pin	2CC-8	15	79	$3\frac{1}{8}$	33	$1\frac{5}{16}$	3100	3500	23.3	b, e, i
150	T-12	DCH/DJA/DFP	120	4-pin	CC-6	15	90	$3\frac{9}{16}$	40	$1\frac{9}{16}$	3150	—	—	k, e
150	T-12	DFN/DFC	125	4-pin	CC-8	15	81	$3\frac{3}{16}$	40	$1\frac{9}{16}$	3167	—	—	k, d
150	T-14	DJL	120	4-pin	CC-8	15	89	$3\frac{1}{2}$	40	$1\frac{9}{16}$	3150	—	—	j, d
150	MR-16	DNE	120	2-pin vent	CC-8	12	51	2	16	$1\frac{5}{8}$	3350	—	—	a, f, p, s
150	MR-16	ELD/EJN	21	2-pin	CC-6	40	47	$1\frac{7}{8}$	45	$1\frac{3}{4}$	3350	—	—	a, d, m, s
150	MR-16	EJN	21	Rim mnt.	CC-6	40	44	$1\frac{3}{4}$	—	—	3400	—	—	a, d, m, s
150	MR-16	ELD	21	Rim mnt.	C-8	40	44	$1\frac{3}{4}$	—	—	3350	—	—	a, d, m, s
150	T-4	FCS	24	Glass 2-pin	C-6 oval	50	51	2	30	$1\frac{3}{16}$	3350	5100	34	a, d, g, s
200	MR-16	EJL	24	2-pin	CC-6	50	47	$1\frac{7}{8}$	—	—	3400	—	—	a, d, n, s
250	MR-14	EMM/EKS	24	2-pin vent	CC-6	50	48	$1\frac{7}{8}$	16	$\frac{5}{8}$	3400	—	—	a, d, s, t
250	MR-16	ENH	120	Oval 2-pin	CC-8	175	45	$1\frac{3}{4}$	—	—	3250	—	—	a, d, q, s
300	T-10	CAL	120	4-pin	C-13	25	102	4	40	$1\frac{9}{16}$	2900	—	—	b, e, i
300	$T-8\frac{1}{2}$	CLS/CLG	120–125	S.C. Bay.	C-13	25	105	$4\frac{1}{8}$	35	$1\frac{3}{8}$	3200	7650	22.5	b, e, h
300	MR-16	ELH	120	Oval 2-pin	CC-8	35	47	$1\frac{7}{8}$	—	—	3350	—	—	a, d, q, s

				R.S.C.*									
420	T-4	FAL	120	CC-8	75	67	$2\frac{5}{8}$	—	—	3200	11,000	26.2	a, c, g, s
500	T-6	CBA	120	4-pin	50	92	$3\frac{5}{8}$	45	$1\frac{3}{4}$	3200	10,000	20	b, d, g, i
500	T-10	CZA/CZB	120, 125	4-pin	25	102	4	40	$1\frac{9}{16}$	3300	—	—	b, e, i
500	T-10	CZX/DAB	115–120, 125	Med. Pref.	25	146	$5\frac{3}{4}$	60	$2\frac{3}{8}$	3200	12,562.5	25.1	b, e, g
500	T-10	DAY/DAK	120	4-pin	30	105	$4\frac{1}{8}$	40	$1\frac{9}{16}$	3200	12,733	25.5	b, e, g
500	T-12	DEK/DFW	120	4-pin	25	92	$3\frac{5}{8}$	45	$1\frac{3}{4}$	3200	—	—	b, f, i
500	T-6	EHA	120	2-pin	50	76	3	37	$1\frac{7}{16}$	3300	11,000	—	a, d, g, i, s
600	G-7	DYS/DYV/GHC	120	Pref. 2-pin	75	64	$2\frac{1}{2}$	37	$1\frac{7}{16}$	3200	17,125	28.5	a, f, g, s
750	T-12	CWA	115–125	Pref. 4-pin	25	118	$4\frac{5}{8}$	40	$1\frac{9}{16}$	3250	—	—	b, e, g, i
750	T-12	DDB	115–120, 125	Med. Pref.	25	146	$5\frac{3}{4}$	60	$2\frac{3}{8}$	3250	19,700	26.3	b, e, g
1000	T-12	CTT/DAX	115–125	4-pin	25	118	$4\frac{5}{8}$	40	$1\frac{9}{16}$	3300	—	—	b, e, g, i

*Recessed single contact.
†Terms described as follows:
a Tungsten-halogen lamp.
b Opaque top.
c Burning position-any.
d Burning position-base down to horizontal.
e Burning position-base down.
f Burning position-horizontal.
g Heat-resistant bulb.
h Base pins of lamp are approximately parallel to plane of lead wires.
i Proximity reflector.
j Internal reflector-focal distance, 44.5 mm ($1\frac{3}{4}$ in.).
k Internal dichroic reflector-focal distance 44.5 mm ($1\frac{3}{4}$ in.).
l Internal dichroic reflector-focal distance 44.5 mm ($1\frac{3}{4}$ in.).
m Mounted in dichroic reflector, 50 mm (2 in.) diameter.
n Mounted in dichroic reflector, 50 mm (2 in.) diameter Mounting distance 32 mm ($1\frac{1}{4}$ in.).
o Mounted in dichroic reflector, 50 mm (2 in.) diameter Mounting distance 65.9 mm ($2\frac{19}{32}$ in.).
p Mounted in dichroic reflector, 50 mm (2 in.) diameter Mounting distance 68 mm ($2\frac{23}{32}$ in.).
q Mounted in dichroic reflector, 50 mm (2 in.) diameter Mounting distance 142 mm ($5\frac{19}{32}$ in.).
r On these "non-jacketed" tungsten-halogen lamps, screening techniques should be used where appropriate to protect people and surroundings in case of shattering.
s Lamps should be protected from scratches and abrasions and should not be used at over 110% of rated voltage.
t Mounted in dichroic reflector, 44 mm ($1\frac{3}{4}$ in.) in diameter. Mounting distance 65.9 mm.

Fig. 6-109. Examples of Variations in Range and Specifications of Miniature Lamps

Lamp no.	Watts	Bulb	Base	Filament or electrode	Approximate life (h)	Design volts	Design amperes (A)	Maximum overall length (mm)	Maximum overall length (in.)	Light center length (mm)	Light center length (in.)	Luminous intensity (cd) (MSCP)	Battery	Maximum safe temperature (°C)	Maximum safe temperature (°F)	Primary use
A9A (NE-2E)	0.08	T-2	Wire Term.	—	25,000	105–125	0.0007	19	$\frac{3}{4}$	—	—	—	—	150	300	Neon glow
B7A (NE-45)	0.25	T-4$\frac{1}{2}$	Cand. Screw	—	5000	105–125	0.002	39	1$\frac{17}{32}$	—	—	—	—	150	300	Neon glow
14	—	G-3$\frac{1}{2}$	Min. Screw	C-2R	15	2.47	0.3	24	$\frac{15}{16}$	18	$\frac{23}{32}$	0.90	2-D cells	175	350	Flashlight
44	—	T-3$\frac{1}{4}$	Min. Bay.	C-2R	3000	6.3	0.25	24	$\frac{15}{16}$	20	$\frac{25}{32}$	0.90	—	175	350	Indicator
51	—	G-3$\frac{1}{2}$	Min. Bay.	C-2R	1000	7.5	0.22	15	$\frac{19}{36}$	13	$\frac{1}{2}$	1	—	175	350	Indicator
194	—	T-3$\frac{1}{4}$	Wedge	C-2F	2500	14	0.27	21	$\frac{13}{16}$	14	$\frac{9}{16}$	2	—	315	600	Auto Instrument
222	—	TL-3	Min. Screw	C-6	5	2.25	0.25	24	$\frac{15}{16}$	—	—	—	2-AA cells	175	350	Flashlight
259	—	T-3$\frac{1}{4}$	Wedge	C-2R	5000	6.3	0.25	21	$\frac{13}{16}$	17	$\frac{21}{32}$	0.65	—	315	600	Radio
327	—	T-1$\frac{3}{4}$	S.C. Mgt. Flg.	C-2F	4000	28	0.34	16	$\frac{5}{8}$	10	$\frac{3}{8}$	0.34	—	150	300	Aircraft
1157	—	S-8	D.C. Indexing	C-6	1200	12.8	2.1	32	1$\frac{1}{4}$	45	1$\frac{3}{4}$	32	—	175	350	Auto park two filament
1157				C-6	5000	14	0.59	—	—	—	—	3	—	—	—	Tail signal
4535[a,b,c,d,e]	30	PAR-46	Screw Term.	C-6	100	6.4	—	—	—	95	3$\frac{3}{4}$	95,000	—	175	350	Spotlamp
	—	T-$\frac{3}{4}$	Wire Term.	C-2R	60,000	5	0.06	5	$\frac{3}{16}$	—	—	0.03	—	—	—	Indicator
8270	—	T-$\frac{3}{4}$	Mic. Mgt. Flg.	C-2R	3000	5	0.08	8	$\frac{5}{16}$	4	$\frac{5}{32}$	0.15	—	—	—	Indicator
PR2	—	B-3$\frac{1}{2}$	S.C. Mgt. Flg.	C-2R	15	2.38	0.5	32	1$\frac{1}{4}$	6	$\frac{1}{4}$	0.80	2-D cells	—	—	Flashlight

[a]Maximum luminous intensity in beam.
[b]PAR type lamp with reflector.
[c]Bulb has built-in lens.
[d]Hemispherical shield in front of filament.
[e]Approximate beam size to 10% max. CP $= 5\frac{1}{2}^{\circ}$ horiz. $\times 4^{\circ}$ vert.

Fig. 6-110. Infrared Energy Sources

A. Tungsten filament lamps (500 – 4000 nm)*

Watts	Bulb and other description	Voltage range	Base	Filament	Bulb finish	Maximum overall length (mm)	(in.)	Light center length (mm)	(in.)	Radient energy 500 to 4000 nm	Type of service
125	G-30 clear	115 – 125	Med. Skt.	C-7A, C-11	Clear	186	$7\frac{5}{16}$	127	5	—	Industrial
125	R-40 reflector frosted	115 – 125	Med. Skt.	C-9, C-11	I.F.	184	$7\frac{1}{4}$	—	—	—	Industrial
250	G-30 clear	120	Med. Skt.	C-7A	Clear	187	$7\frac{3}{8}$	127	5	—	Industrial
250	R-40 reflector frosted	115 – 125	Med. Skt.	C-9, C-11	I.F.	187	$7\frac{3}{8}$	—	—	—	Industrial
250	R-40 reflector frosted	115 – 125	Med.	C-6, C-8	I.F.	167	$6\frac{9}{16}$	—	—	—	Home and farm
250	R-40 reflector red glass	115 – 125	Med.	CC-6, C-9	Red bowl	171	$6\frac{3}{4}$	—	—	—	Home and farm
375	G-30 clear	115 – 125	Med.	C-7A, C-11	Clear	186	$7\frac{5}{16}$	127	5	—	Industrial
375	R-40 reflector frosted	115 – 125	Med. Skt.	C-9, C-11	I.F.	187	$7\frac{3}{8}$	—	—	—	Industrial
375	R-40 reflector red glass	115	Med. Skt.	C-9	Red bowl	191	$7\frac{1}{2}$	—	—	—	Industrial
500	G-30 clear	115 – 125	Med. Skt.	C-7A, C-11	Clear	202	$7\frac{15}{16}$	127	5	—	Industrial
1000	T-40 clear	115 – 125	Mog. Bip.	Triangular	Clear	184	$7\frac{1}{4}$	78	$3\frac{1}{16}$	—	Industrial

B. Tubular quartz heat lamps (operating position — horizontal except as noted). Color temperature 2500K except as noted.*

Watts	Bulb and other description	Voltage range	Base	Filament	Type of seal	Maximum overall Length (mm)	(in.)	Approximate Heated Length (mm)	(in.)	Radient energy (watts per inch of filament)	Type of service
300	T-3†	115 – 125§	Sleeve§	C-8	Regular	224	$8\frac{13}{16}$	127	5	100	General service
375	T-3†	115 – 125§	Sleeve§	C-8	Regular	224	$8\frac{13}{16}$	127	5	75	General service
375	T-3†	115 – 125 ‖	RSC ‖	C-8	Regular	219	$8\frac{5}{8}$	127	5	75	General service
500	T-3†	115 – 125	Sleeve§	C-8	Regular	224	$8\frac{13}{16}$	127	5	100	General service
500	T-3 clear†	115 – 125	Sleeve§	C-8	Regular	224	$8\frac{13}{16}$	127	5	100	General service
500	T-31	115 – 125	RSC ‖	C-8	Regular	219	$8\frac{5}{8}$	127	5	100	General service
500	T-3 clear†‡	115 – 125	Sleeve§	C-8	—	224	$8\frac{13}{16}$	127	5	—	General service
500	T-3 clear†‡	120	Sleeve§	C-8	—	71	$2\frac{13}{16}$	—	—	—	Special equipment
600	T-3 clear	104	Sleeve§	C-8	—	303	$11\frac{15}{16}$	152	6	—	—
800	T-3 frosted	115 – 125	Sleeve§	C-8	—	303	$11\frac{15}{16}$	203	8	—	—
900	T-3 clear	215	Sleeve§	C-8	—	405	$15\frac{15}{16}$	229	9	—	—
1000	T-31‡	100 – 120	Sleeve§	C-8	Regular	351	$13\frac{13}{16}$	254	10	100	Infrared
1000	T-3 clear	230 – 250	Sleeve§	C-8	High temp.	405	$15\frac{15}{16}$	254	10	100	H.T., application
1000	T-3 clear‡	230 – 250	Sleeve§	C-8	High temp.	351	$13\frac{13}{16}$	254	10	100	H.T., application
1200	T-3 clear‡	144	Sleeve§	C-8	High temp.	225	$8\frac{7}{8}$	156	6	200	H.T., application
1600	T-3 frosted	230 – 250	Sleeve§	C-8	Regular	503	$19\frac{13}{16}$	406	16	200	Special equipment
1600	T-3 frosted	277	Sleeve§	C-8	Regular	503	$19\frac{13}{16}$	406	16	100	General service
1600	T 3 frosted	208, 230 250	RSC ‖	C-8	Regular	498	$19\frac{5}{8}$	406	16	100	General service
1600	T-3 clear	230 – 250	Sleeve§	C-8	—	498	$19\frac{5}{8}$	406	16	—	—
1600	T-3 clear‡	230 – 250	Sleeve§	C-8	—	456	$17\frac{15}{16}$	406	16	—	—
2000	T-3 clear	230 – 250	Sleeve§	C-8	—	303	$11\frac{15}{16}$	248	10	—	—
2000	T-3 clear‡	230 – 250	Sleeve§	C-8	High temp.	303	$11\frac{15}{16}$	248	10	200	H.T., application
2000	T-3 clear‡	230 – 250	Sleeve§	C-8	High temp.	325	$12\frac{13}{16}$	254	10	200	H.T., application
2500	T-3	460 – 500	Sleeve§	C-8	Regular	732	$28\frac{13}{16}$	632	25	100	Infrared
2500	T-3 frost	460 – 500	RSC ‖	C-8	Regular	727	$28\frac{5}{8}$	635	25	100	Infrared
2500	T-3 clear vert. oper.	460 – 500	Sleeve§	C-8	—	727	$28\frac{5}{8}$	635	25	—	—
2500	T-3 clear	460 – 500	Sleeve§	C-8	—	732	$28\frac{13}{16}$	635	25	—	—
2500	T-3 clear‡	460 – 500	Sleeve§	C-8	Regular	732	$28\frac{13}{16}$	635	25	100	Special equipment
3650	T-3 clear	480	Special	C-8	Regular	1057	$41\frac{5}{8}$	965	38	100	Infrared
3800	T-3 frost	550 – 600	Sleeve§	C-8	—	1062	$41\frac{13}{16}$	965	38	—	—
3800	T-3 clear	550 – 600	Sleeve§	C-8	Regular	1062	$41\frac{13}{16}$	965	38	100	Industrial
3800	T-3 frost. vert. oper.	550 – 600	Sleeve§	C-8	Regular	1062	$41\frac{13}{16}$	965	38	100	Industrial
5000	T-3 clear‡	575 – 625	Sleeve§	C-8	Regular	732	$28\frac{13}{16}$	635	25	200	Special equipment
5000	T-3 clear	920 – 1000	Sleeve§	C-8	Regular	1367	$53\frac{13}{16}$	1270	50	100	Industrial
6000	T-3 clear‡	480	Sleeve§	C-8	High temp.	303	$11\frac{15}{16}$	248	10	600	Industrial

＊Rated life in excess of 5000 hours.
†Operating position: any.
‡High temperature construction.
§With flexible connectors.
‖ Recessed single contact.

Fig. 6.111. Typical Photoflash Lamps

Class	Description	Approximate time to peak (ms)	Duration at 1/2 peak (ms)	Approximate lumen seconds or beam candela seconds	Voltage range for operation	Approximate peak beam candlepower*	Bulb or shape	Maximum overall length (mm)	(in.)	Base
— Clear lacquer-coated for black and white film (approximate color temperature — 3800 K)										
M	M3	17	—	16,000	—	—	T-6$\frac{1}{2}$	46	1 $\frac{13}{16}$	Min. Bay. Pinless
M	Press 25	20	—	21,000	—	—	B-12	67	2 $\frac{5}{8}$	S.C. Bay.
M	2 (PF-200)†	20	—	70,000	3 – 125	—	A-19	121	4 $\frac{3}{4}$	Med. screw
S	3 (PF-300)†	30	—	110,000	3 – 125	—	A-23	151	5 $\frac{15}{16}$	Med. screw
FF	FF-33 (PF-330)†	50	1750	140,000	4.5 – 45	—	A-23	151	5 $\frac{15}{16}$	Med. screw
FP	FP26	—	—	18,000	—	—	B-12	67	2 $\frac{5}{8}$	S.C. Bay.
— Blue lacquer-coated for daylight color film (approximate color temperature — 6600 — 6000 K)										
MF	AG-1B‡	12	15	5300	4 – 45	250,000	T-3$\frac{3}{4}$	33	1 $\frac{5}{16}$	Glass groove
M	M3B	17	—	10,000	—	—	T-6$\frac{1}{2}$	44	1 $\frac{3}{4}$	Min. Bay. Pinless
M	5B, 25B	20	—	10,000	—	—	B-11, B-12	67	2 $\frac{5}{8}$	S.C. Bay.
M	2B	20	—	33,500	—	—	A-19	121	4 $\frac{3}{4}$	Med.
S	3B	30	—	53,000	—	—	A-23	151	5 $\frac{15}{16}$	Med.
FP	FB26B	—	—	98,000	—	—	B-12	67	2 $\frac{5}{8}$	S.C. Bay.
— Multiple flash (5500 K)										
MF	Flashcube‡	13	15	—	4 – 45	130,000	Cube	34	1 $\frac{11}{32}$	Plastic; indexing post
MF	Hi-Power.	13	—	48,000	No voltage	—	Cube	36	1 $\frac{13}{32}$	Plastic
MF*	Magicube‡§	7	10	2000	No voltage	(44,000) 150,000	Cube	42	1 $\frac{21}{32}$	Plastic; indexing post
MF	Flashbar	16	—	36,000	—	—	Array	108	4 $\frac{1}{4}$	Contact tab
MF*	Flipflash‡§	13	10	1800	2200	(32,000) 140,000	Ver. array	140	5 $\frac{1}{2}$	Contact tab
S*	Flash 600 (flashbar)‡§	25	20	1400	3 – 45	(15,000) 70,000	Array	51	2	Contact tab
M*	Flashbar‡§	17	14	3600	3 – 45	(50,000) 200,000	Array	48	1 $\frac{7}{8}$	Contact tab

*Intensity for GE product is average for 40° × 40° zone.
†EG & G.
‡GTE Sylvania.
§General Electric.

Fig. 6-112. Sign Lamps

Watts	Bulb and other description*	Base	Filament	Rated life (h)	Maximum overall length (mm)	Maximum overall length (in.)	Light center length (mm)	Light center length (in.)	Total lumens†	Initial lumens per watt
7.5	S-11 Clear	Medium	C-9	1400	57	$2\frac{1}{4}$	40	$1\frac{9}{16}$	49	6.5
10	S-11 Clear	Intmed. BE	C-7A	1500	59	$2\frac{5}{16}$	41	$1\frac{5}{8}$	80	8.0
10	S-11 Blue*‡	Intmed. BE	C-7A	1500	59	$2\frac{5}{16}$	41	$1\frac{5}{8}$	—	—
10	S-14 Clear	Medium	C-6	1500	89	$3\frac{1}{2}$	64	$2\frac{1}{2}$	100	10.0
11	S-14 Clear*	Medium	C-9	3000	89	$3\frac{1}{2}$	64	$2\frac{1}{2}$	80	7.3
11	S-14 Blue*‡	Medium, BB	C-9	3000	89	$3\frac{1}{2}$	64	$2\frac{1}{2}$	—	—
15	A-15 Clear 130 V	Medium, BB	C-9	3000	89	$3\frac{1}{2}$	64	$2\frac{1}{2}$	—	—
15	A-15 Inside frost	Medium	C-9	3000	89	$3\frac{1}{2}$	60	$2\frac{3}{8}$	125	8.3
15	S-14 Clear 130 V	Medium	C-9	3000	89	$3\frac{1}{2}$	64	$2\frac{1}{2}$	120	8.0
25	A-15 I.F. Reflector	Medium	C-9	2500	89	$3\frac{1}{2}$	—	—	—	—
25	A-19 Clear	Medium	C-9	3000	100	$3\frac{15}{16}$	64	$2\frac{1}{2}$	205	8.2
30	R-20 I.F.‡	Medium, BB	C-9	2000	100	$3\frac{15}{16}$	—	—	210	7.0
32	A-19 Clear	Medium	C-9	3000	108	$4\frac{1}{4}$	73	$2\frac{7}{8}$	255	8.0
33	A-19 Clear 130 V	Medium, BB	C-9	2000	98	$3\frac{7}{8}$	—	—	—	—
33	R-17 Reflector (frosted)	Medium	C-9	2500	70	$2\frac{3}{4}$	—	—	225	6.8
40	A-21 Clear 130 V	Medium	C-9	3000	114	$4\frac{1}{2}$	73	$2\frac{7}{8}$	352	8.8
40	A-21	Medium	C-9	3000	73	$2\frac{7}{8}$	114	$4\frac{1}{2}$	352	8.8
60	R-20 Reflector (blue)	Medium	C-9	6000	100	$3\frac{15}{16}$	—	—	—	—
65	R-30 Reflector (frost)	Medium	C-17A	5000	132	$5\frac{3}{16}$	—	—	—	—

*Also Ceramic colors; blue, green, orange, red and yellow.
†Ratings are for clear lamps.
‡General Electric.

Fig. 6-113. Typical Enlarger Lamps

Manufacturer designation	Rated watts	Bulb and other description	Base	Nominal voltage	Rated life (h)*	Maximum overall length (mm)	Maximum overall length (in.)	Bulb diameter (mm)	Bulb diameter (in.)	Approximate color temperature (K)	Rated lumens*	Burning position§
PH / 111A	75	S-11 white	S.C. Bay.	120	25	60	$2\frac{3}{8}$	35	$1\frac{3}{8}$	2900	1120	BDTH
PH / 113†	50	S-11 white	S.C. Bay.	115–125	25	60	$2\frac{3}{8}$	35	$1\frac{3}{8}$	—	700	BDTH
PH / 140	75	S-14 white	Medium	120	50	89	$3\frac{1}{2}$	41	$1\frac{5}{8}$	2900	1200	Any
PH / 211	75	A-21 (F-10) white	Medium	115–125	100	125	$4\frac{15}{16}$	67	$2\frac{5}{8}$	2975	1200	Any
PH / 212	150	A-21 (E-11) white	Medium	115–125	100	125	$4\frac{15}{16}$	67	$2\frac{5}{8}$	3000	2825	Any
PH / 213†	250	A-21 white	Medium	115–125	3	125	$4\frac{15}{16}$	67	$2\frac{5}{8}$	3400	7000	Any
PH / 300‡	150	PS-30 (E-14) white	Medium	115–125	100	205	$8\frac{1}{16}$	95	$3\frac{3}{4}$	3100	2700	—
300C‡	300	A-21 (E-13) white	Medium	115	20	135	$5\frac{5}{16}$	67	$2\frac{5}{8}$	3200	7650	—
PH / 302	500	PS-30	Medium	115-125	100	—	—	95	$3\frac{3}{4}$	—	11,000	—
PH / 1400†	75	S-14 white	Medium	230	25	86	$3\frac{3}{8}$	44	$1\frac{3}{4}$	2900	1100	Any
BEV†	150	G-16$\frac{1}{2}$ printer	S.C. Pref.	20	25	76	3	52	$2\frac{1}{16}$	3300	4000	BU
DLS / DLG / DHX†	150	T-14 int. dic. reflector	4 pin	22	7.5	37	$1\frac{7}{16}$	44	$1\frac{3}{4}$	3250	—	BDTH
EJL†	200	MR-16 Multi-Mirror™	2 pin	24	25	44	$1\frac{3}{4}$	51	2	3400	—	BDTH
EJV†	150	MR-16 reflector	2 pin	21	20	44	$1\frac{3}{4}$	51	2	3350	—	BDTH
ELC†	250	MR-16 Multi-Mirror™	2 pin	24	25	44	$1\frac{3}{4}$	51	2	3400	—	BDTH
ESD†	150	MR-16 Multi-Mirror™	Oval 2 pin	120	6	44	$1\frac{3}{4}$	51	2	3350	—	BDTH

*At 118 volts.
†General Electric.
‡Sylvania.
§BDTH — base down to horizontal.
BU — base up.

Fig. 6-114. Compact Fluorescent Lamps*

Generic designation NEMA	Lamp watts	Bulb type	Base	Rated life† (h)	Maximum overall length (mm)	Maximum overall length (in.)	Lamp current (A)	Lamp voltage (V)	Approx. initial lumens‡	Lumens per watt	Color§ temperature and/or CRI
Twin tube 2700K, 3500K, 4100K, 5000K§ CRI 80 +											
CFT5W/G23	5	T-4	G23	7500	105	$4\frac{1}{4}$	0.180	38	250	50	82
CFT7W/G23	7	T-4	G23	10,000	135	$5\frac{7}{16}$	0.180	45	400	57	82
CFT9W/G23	9	T-4	G23	10,000	167	$6\frac{9}{16}$	0.180	59	600	67	82
CFT13W/GX23	13	T-4	GX23	10,000	191	$7\frac{1}{2}$	0.285	60	888	68	82
CFT5W/2G7	5	T-4	2G7	10,000	85	$3\frac{11}{32}$	0.180	35	250	50	82
CFT7W/2G7	7	T-4	2G7	10,000	115	$4\frac{17}{32}$	0.180	45	400	57	82
CFT7W/2G7[1, ||]	9	T-4	2G7	10,000	145	$5\frac{23}{32}$	0.180	59	600	67	82
CFT13W/2GX7	13	T-4	2GX7	10,000	175	$6\frac{29}{32}$	0.285	59	900	69	82
FT18W/2G11[2]	18	T-5	2G11	12,000	229	9	0.375	60	1250	69	82
FT18W/2G11RS	18	T-5	2G11	20,000	267	$10\frac{1}{2}$	0.250	76	1250	69	82
FT24W/2G11	24 – 27	T-5	2G11	12,000	328	$12\frac{29}{32}$	0.340	91	1800	69	82
FT36W/2G11	36 – 39	T-5	2G11	12,000	422	$16\frac{5}{8}$	0.430	111	2900	76	82
FT40W/2G11	40	T-5	2G11	20,000	574	$22\frac{19}{32}$	0.270	169	3150	79	82
FT50W/2G11	50	T-5	2G11	14,000	574	$22\frac{19}{32}$	0.43	147	4000	80	—
Quad 2700K, 3500K, 4100K, 5000K; CRI 80 +											
CFQ9W/G23	9	T-4	G23-2	10,000	111	$4\frac{3}{8}$	0.180	15	575	21	82
CFQ13W/GX23	13	T-4	GX23-2	10,000	125	$4\frac{29}{32}$	0.285	15	860	59	82
CFQ10W/G24d	10	T-4	G24d-1	10,000	118	$4\frac{5}{8}$	0.140	64	600	60	82
CFQ13W/G24d	13	T-4	G24d-1	10,000	152	6	0.170	91	900	69	82
CFQ18W/G24d	18	T-4	G24d-2	10,000	175	$6\frac{29}{32}$	0.220	100	1250	69	82
CFQ28W/G24d	26	T-4	G24d-3	10,000	196	$7\frac{23}{32}$	0.315	105	1800	69	82
CFQ15W/GX32d	15	T-5	GX32d-1	10,000	140	$5\frac{1}{2}$	—	60	900	60	—
CFQ22W/GX32d	20	T-5	GX32d-2	10,000	151	$5\frac{15}{16}$	—	53	1200	60	—
CFQ26W/GX32d	27	T-5	GX32d-3	10,000	173	$6\frac{13}{16}$	—	54	1600	59	—
CFQ10W/G24q	10	T-4	G24q-1	10,000	117	$4\frac{5}{8}$	0.190	64	600	60	82
CFQ13W/G24q	13	T-4	G24q-1	10,000	152	6	0.170	77	900	69	82
CFQ18W/G24q	18	T-4	G24q-2	10,000	173	$6\frac{13}{16}$	0.110	80	1250	69	82
CFQ26W/G24q	26	T-4	G24q-3	10,000	194	$7\frac{5}{8}$	0.158	80	1800	69	82

Typical incandescent lamp substitutes (Compact fluorescent lamps, internal ballast)#

Generic designation	Ballast type	Incandescent equivalent (W)	Lamp watts	Bulb type	Base	Related life† (h)	Maximum overall length** (mm)	(in.)	Lamp current (A)	Lamp voltage (V)	Approx. initial lumens‡ (Candlepower)	lumens per watt	Color* temperature and / or CRI
7 W[3]	Electronic	25	7	T-4	Med. Screw	10,000	140	$5\frac{1}{2}$	0.140	120	400	57	—
11 W[3]	Electronic	40	11	T-4	Med. Screw	10,000	140	$5\frac{1}{2}$	0.170	120	600	55	—
11 W reflector[3]	Electronic	50W. R30	11	R-35	Med. Screw	10,000	148	$5\frac{13}{16}$	0.170	120	(315)	—	
11 W globe[3]	Electronic	30	11	G-32	Med. Screw	10,000	168	$6\frac{9}{16}$	0.170	120	450	41	—
15 W[1,2,3]	Electronic	60	15	T-4	Med. Screw	10,000	172	$6\frac{25}{32}$	0.240	120	900	60	81
15 W reflector[3]	Electronic	75W. R40	15	RSB	Med. Screw	10,000	183	$7\frac{7}{32}$	0.240	120	(1335)	—	—
15 W globe[3]	Electronic	50	15	G-38	Med. Screw	10,000	188	$7\frac{13}{32}$	0.240	120	700	47	—
15 W globe[2]	Magnetic	40 – 60	18	G-30	Med. Screw	9000	160	$6\frac{5}{16}$	—	120	700	47	82
17 W decorative diffuser[1]	Electronic	60	17	T-24	Med. Screw	10,000	149	$5\frac{7}{8}$	0.265	120	950	57	—
18 W decorative diffuse[2]	Electronic	75	18	T-24	Med. Screw	10,000	183	$7\frac{7}{32}$	0.240	120	1100	61	—
18 W reflector	Electronic	75W. R40	18	R-40	Med. Screw	10,000	142	$5\frac{19}{32}$	0.240	120	800	44	—
18 W[4]	Electronic	75	18	T-4	Med. Screw	10,000	175	$6\frac{7}{8}$	—	120	1100	61	—
20 W[1,2,3]	Electronic	75	20	T-4	Med. Screw	10,000	203	8	0.265‡‡	120	1200	60	—
22 W circular lamp[2]	Magnetic	75	22	T-9	Med. Screw	10,000	130	$5\frac{1}{8}$	—	120	1200	54	52
23 W[1,3]	Electronic	90	23	T-4	Med. Screw	10,000	176	$6\frac{5}{16}$	0.325	120	1550	67	—
26 W[2]	Electronic	90	26	T-5	Med. Screw	10,000	203	8	0.430	120	1500	58	—
Square 2700 K and 3500 K[2]													
F102D/827/4P			10	2D	GR10Q 4Pl	8000	94	$3\frac{23}{32}$	0.18	72	650	65	82
F162D/827/4P			16	2D	GR10Q 4Pl	8000	140	$5\frac{1}{2}$	0.195	103	1050	66	82
F212D/827/4P			21	2D	GR10Q 4Pl	8000	140	$5\frac{1}{2}$	0.26	101	1350	64	82
F282D/827/4P			28	2D	GR10Q 4Pl	10,000	203	8	0.32	107	2050	73	82
F382D/827/4P§§,‖‖			38	2D	GR10Q 4Pl	10,000	203	8	0.43	110	2850	79	82

Note. Many Compact Fluorescent Lamps come equipped with normal (formally called low) power-factor ballasts, either intergral or as auxiliaries. To minimize line losses and to maximize energy savings and lamp efficiency specifiers should require high power factor ballasts and should insist that luminaires, utilizing these lamps, be so equipped.
* These values are the averages of several manufactures data.
†At 3 hours per start.
‡Values for reflector lamps are in beam candlepower.
§Not all color temperatures available from each manufacturer.
‖ Also available in red, blue, green.
#Screw base adaptors with integral ballasts are available for retrofitting twin and quard tube lamps into incandescent fixtures.
** Some lamps are available with shorter MOL's.
††LLD's not yet available for these lamps.
‡‡Lamps are available with higher power factors and lower line currents.
§§Add 2 watts for cathodes when operating on rapid-start circuits.
‖‖ Rapid start life is estimated as 12000 hours @ 3 or more hours per start.
[1]Philips
[2]General Electric
[3]Osram
[4]Sylvania

Fig. 6-115. Energy-Saving Fluorescent Lamps*

Lamp description	Lamp watts	Lamp watts replaced	Lamp current (A)	Lamp volts (V)	Lamp life† (h)	Nominal length (mm)	Nominal length (in.)	Base (end caps)	Nominal lumens‡§						
									3000K RE70	3500K RE70	4100K RE70	3000K RE80	3500K RE80	4100K RE80	5000K RE80
Rapid start															
F17T8	17	—	0.265	70	20,000	610	24	Med. Bipin	1325	1325	1325	1375	1375	1375	—
F25T8	25	—	0.265	100	20,000	914	36	Med. Bipin	2125	2125	2125	2200	2200	2200	—
F32T8	32	—	0.265	137	20,000	1219	48	Med. Bipin	2850	2850	2850	2975	2975	2975	2700[b]
F40T8	40	—	0.265	172	20,000	1524	60	Med. Bipin	3600	3600	3600	3725	3725	3725	—
F40T12/U/3	36	40	—	—	12,000	610	24	Med. Bipin	2800[b]	2800[b]	—	—	—	—	—
F40T12/U/6	34	40	0.45	84	16,000	610	24	Med. Bipin	2090	2090	2025[a]	—	—	—	—
F30T12	25	30	0.453	64	18,000	914	36	Med. Bipin	2800	2800	2800	2880	2880	2880	—
F40T12	34–36‖	40	0.46	73	20,000	1219	48	Med. Bipin	2800	2800	2800	2880	2880	2880	—
F48T12/HO	55	60	—	—	12,000	1219	48	Reces. DC	3850[a]	4075	3850[a]	4400[b]	—	—	—
F96T12/HO	95	110	0.83	126	12,000	2438	96	Reces. DC	8430	8430	8430	8620	8500[a]	8600[c]	—
F96T12/1500	195	215	1.58	137	12,000	2438	96	Reces. DC	—	—	—	—	—	—	—
F48PG17	95	110	1.53	64	12,000	1219	48	Reces. DC	—	—	—	—	—	—	—
F96PG17	185	215	1.57	144	12,000	2438	96	Reces. DC	—	—	—	—	—	—	—
Preheat start															
F40T12	34	40	0.45	84	15,000	1219	48	Med. Bipin	—	—	—	—	—	—	—
F90T17	86	90	—	—	9000	1524	60	Mog. Bipin	—	—	—	—	—	—	—
Instant start (Slimline)															
F48T12	30–32	38–40	—	—	9000	1219	48	Single pin	2610	2610	2610	2700[b]	—	—	—
F96T8	40–41	50–51	—	—	7500	2438	96	Single pin	—	—	—	—	—	—	—
F96T8[b]	56	—	0.26	267	15,000	2438	96	Single pin	—	—	5675	5800	5800	5800	—
F96T12	60	75	0.44	153	12,000	2438	96	Single pin	5675	5675	5675	5850	5850	5850	—

Nominal Lumens†§

Lamp description	Lamp watts‡	Lamp watts replaced	4150K CRI 60 + Cool white	3000K CRI 50 + Warm white	3470K CRI 60 + White	6380K CRI 70 + Daylight	5000K CRI 90 + C50	4160K CRI 80 + Deluxe cool white	2990K CRI 70 + Delux warm white (soft white)	4200K CRI 40 + Lite-white	3200K CRI 80 + Optima 32™d	3570K CRI 80 + Natural	7500K CRI 90 + C75	5500K CRI 90 + Vita-lite d
Rapid start														
F17T8	17	—	—	—	—	—	—	—	—	—	—	—	—	—
F25T8	25	—	—	—	—	—	—	—	—	—	—	—	—	—
F32T8	32	—	—	—	—	—	—	—	—	—	—	—	—	—
F40T8	40	—	—	—	—	—	—	—	—	—	—	—	—	—
F40T12/U/3	36	40	2350[a]	2425[a]	—	—	—	—	—	2500[a]	—	—	—	—
F40T12/U/6	34	40	2480	2530	2550	—	—	—	—	2620	—	—	—	—
F30T12	25	30	1975	2025	—	—	—	—	—	—	—	—	—	—
F40T12	34–36[b]	40	2670	2730	2700	2310	2010	1930	1925	2800	2010	—	—	—
F48T12HO	55	60	—	—	—	—	—	—	—	3900[a]	—	—	—	—
F96T12HO	95	110	8020	8130	8000	6750[c]	—	5750	—	8400	—	—	—	6000[d]
F96T12/1500	188	215	13430	—	—	—	—	—	—	13,880	—	—	—	—
F48PG17	95	110	5700[a]	—	—	—	—	—	—	—	—	—	—	—
F96PG17	185	215	13,500[a]	—	—	—	—	—	—	14,100[a]	—	—	—	—
Preheat start														
F40T12	34	40	2700	—	—	—	—	—	—	—	—	—	—	—
F90T17	86	90	5765	—	—	—	—	—	—	—	—	—	—	—
Instant start (Slimline)														
F40T12	30.7	40	2475	2575[a]	—	—	—	—	—	2525	—	—	—	—
F96T8	40	50	3450[a]	—	—	4730	4050	3950	3900	—	4200	—	—	4015
F96T12	60	75	5430	5570	5370	—	—	—	—	5670	—	—	—	—

*The life and light output ratings of fluorescent lamps are based on their use with ballasts that provide proper operating characteristics. Ballasts that do not provide proper electrical values may substantially reduce lamp life, light output or both.

†Rated life under specified test conditions at 3 hours per start. At longer burning intervals per start, longer life can be expected.

‡"RE" indicates "RARE EARTH" type phosphors. This nomenclature has been developed by NEMA to define a system of color rendering information. RE 70 designates a CRI range of 70 – 79, RE 80 a range of 80 – 89, and RE 90 ≥ 90.

§At 100 hours.

‖ Also in 32 watt cathode-cutout but with reduced life.

[a] General Electric.
[b] Sylvania.
[c] Phillips.
[d] Duro-Test.

Fig. 6-116. Typical Hot-Cathode Fluorescent Lamps (Rapid Start)*

Lightly loaded lamps (under 500 mA)

Lamp description	Lamp watts†	Lamp lumen depreciation‡	Lamp life (h)§	Nominal length (mm)	(in.)	Base (end caps)	3000K RE70	3500K RE70	4100K RE70	3000K RE80	3500K RE80	4100K RE80	5000K RE80
									Nominal lumens ‖ #				
Circline; diameters 6″, 8″, 12″, 16″													
FC6T9 /15a**††	20		12,000	165	6.5	4-Pin	1150[b]				1100[c]		
FC8T9	22	72	12,000	210	8.25	4-Pin	2100[b]				1885[c]		
FC12T9	32	82	12,000	305	12	4-Pin							
FC16T9	40	77	12,000	406	16	4-Pin							
U lamp; leg spacing 1 5/8″, 3 5/8″, 6″													
F16T8/U/1 5/8	16	90	20,000	267	10.5	Med. Bipin				1250[b]	1250[b]	1250[b]	
F24T8/U/1 5/8	24	90	20,000	419	16.5	Med. Bipin				2050[b]	2050[b]	2050[b]	
F31T8/U/1 5/8	31	90	20,000	572	22.5	Med. Blpin				2800[b]	2800[b]	2800[b]	
F40T12/U/3	40	84	12,000	610	24	med. Bipin			2925	3000	3000		
F40T12/U/6	40	84	16,000	610	24	Med. Pipin			3085	3150	3100	3100[c]	

Continued below

Lamp Description	Lamp watts†	Lamp lumen depreciation‡	Lamp life (h)§	Nominal length (mm)	(in.)	Base (end caps)	4150K CRI 60+ Cool white	3000K CRI 50+ Warm white	3470K CRI 60+ White	6380K CRI 70+ Daylight	2750K CRI 80+ Incandescent fluorescent	4160K CRI 80+ Deluxe cool white	2990K CRI 70+ Deluxe warm white (soft white)	4200K CRI 40+ Lite-white	3200K CRI 80+ Optima 32[d],™	3570K CRI 80+ Natural	7500K CRI 90+ C 75
											Nominal lumens§ #						
Circline; diameters 6″, 8″, 12″, 16″																	
FC6T9	20		12,000	165	6.5	4-Pin	775	820		895		875	785				
FC8T9	22	72	12,000	210	8.25	4-Pin	1035	1035		1590		1488	1400				
FC12T9	32	82	12,000	305	12	4-Pin	1850	1875		2200		2000	1858				
FC16T9	40	77	12,000	406	16	4-Pin	2650	2700									
U lamp; leg spacing 1 5/8″, 3 5/8″, 6″																	
F16T8/U/1 5/8	16	90	20,000	267	10.5	Med. Bipin											
F24T8/U/1 5/8	24	90	20,000	419	16.5	Med. Bipin											
F31T8/U/1 5/8	31	90	20,000	572	22.5	Med. Bipin											
F40T12/U/3	40	84	12,000	610	24	Med. Bipin	2680	2770	2725	2400[c]		2025[a]	2000[a]				
F40T12/U/6	40	84	16,000	610	24	Med. Bipin	2817	2883	2880			2085	2010				

Lamp description	Lamp watts†	Lamp lumen depreciation‡	Lamp life (h)§	Nominal length (mm)	(in.)	Base (end caps)	3000K RE70	3500K RE70	4100K RE70	3000K RE80	3500K RE80	4100K RE80	5000K RE80	5000K CRI 90+ C 50
										Nominal lumens ‖ #				
Lightly loaded lamps (under 500 mA) Subminiature														
F6T7MM	6		10,000	203	8	Special					310			
F8T7MM	8		10,000	305	12	Special					500			
F10T7MM	10		10,000	406	16	Special					680			
F13T7MM	13		10,000	508	20	Special					860			
Lightly loaded lamps (under 500 mA) regular														
F30T12	30	81	18,000	914	36	Med. Bip.	2350	2350	2350	2390	2390	2400[c]	2380[c]	
F40T12	40	84	20,000	1219	48	Med. Bip.	3200	3200		3280	3280	3280	3280	2200
F40T10	40		24,000	1219	48	Med. Bip.				3700[c]	3700[c]	3700[c]	3700[c]	1650[c]

Nominal lumens ∥ #

Lightly loaded lamps (under 500mA) Subminiature

Lamp Description	Lamp watts†
F6T7MM	6
F8T7MM	8
F10T7MM	10
F13T7MM	13

Lightly loaded lamps (under 500mA) regular

Color columns under "Nominal lumens ∥ #"

Lamp description	Lamp watts†	Lamp lumen depreciation‡	4150K CRI 60+ Cool white	3000CK CRI 50+ Warm white	3470K CRI 60+ White	6380K CRI 70+ Daylight	2750K CRI 80+ Incandescent fluorescent	4160K CRI 80+ Delue cool white	2990K CRI 70+ Deluxe warm white (soft white)	4200K CRI 40+ Lite-white	3200K CRI 80+ Optima 32	3570K CRI 80+ Natural	7500K CRI 90+ C 75	5500K CRI 90+ Vita-Lite™
F30T23	30	81	2225	2260	2230	1910	1550[b]	1580	1570		1700			1600
F40T12	40	84	3050	3115	3075	2600		2215	2165		2260	2100	1975	2180
F40T10	40		3100[c]	3150[c]	3100[c]	2700[c]				3300[n]				

Medium Loaded Lamps (500 to 1000 mA)

Color columns under "Nominal lumens ∥ #"

Lamp description	Lamp watt	Lamp lumens depreciation‡	Lamp life (h)§	Nominal length (mm)	Nominal length (in.)	Base (end caps)	3000K RE70	3500K RE70	4100K RE70	3000K RE80	3500K RE80	4100K RE80	5000K RE80	5000K CRI 90+ C 50
F24T12/HO	35	77	9000	610	24	Reces. D.C.								1200[b]
F30T12/HO	41	—	9000	762	30	Reces. D.C.								2100[b]
F36T12/HO	47	77	9000	914	36	Reces. D.C.								2550[b]
F42T12/HO	55	77	9000	1067	42	Reces. D.C.								2925
F48T12/HO	60	82	12000	1219	48	Reces. D.C.		4250	4267	4250	4350[a]	4400[c]		3850[b]
F60T12/HO	73	82	12000	1524	60	Reces. D.C.								4200[b]
F64T12/HO	78	82	12000	1626	64	Reces. D.C.								4200[b]
F72T12/HO	85	82	12000	1829	72	Reces. D.C.	6680	6680	6680	6817	6817	6800		4700[b]
F84T12/HO	100	82	12000	2134	84	Reces. D.C.								5600[b]
F96T12/HO	110	82	12000	2438	96	Reces. D.C.	9250	9250	9250	9417	9417	9400[c]	9350[c]	6300

Medium loaded lamps (500 to 1000 mA)

Color columns under "Nominal lumens ∥ #"

Lamp Description	Lamp watt†	Lamp lumen depreciation‡	4150K CRI 60+ Cool white	3000K CRI 50+ Warm white	3470K CRI 60+ White	6380K CRI 70+ Daylight	2750K CRI 80+ Incandescent fluorescent	4160K CRI 80+ Delue cool white	2990K CRI 70+ Deluxe warm white (soft white)	4200K CRI 40+ Lite-white	3200K CRI 80+ Optima 32	3570K CRI 80+ Natural	7500K CRI 90+ C 75	5500K CRI 90+ Vita-Lite™
F24T12/HO	35	77	1650	1650[b]		1400								
F30T12/HO	41	—	2270			1920[c]								
F36T12/HO	47	77	2815			2400								
F42T12/HO	55	77	3430			2980								
F48T12/HO	60	82	4067	4133		3467		2867				2750		
F60T12/HO	73	82	5200	5250[b]		4550				4200[b]				
F64T12/HO	78.7	82	5650			4850								
F72T12/HO	85	82	6367	6483		5517		4517				4300		
F84T12/HO	100	82	7700			6700								
F96T12/HO	110	82	8830	8850	8875	7675		6433	6437			6167		

Fig.6-116. *Continued*

Highly loaded Lamps (over 1000 ma)

Lamp description	Lamp watts†	Lamp lumens depreciation‡	Lamp life (h)§	Nominal length (mm)	Nominal length (in.)	Base (end caps)	Nominal lumens ‖ # 3000K RE70	3500K RE70	4100K RE70	3000K RE80	3500K RE80	4100K RE80	5000K RE80
F48T10/1.5A**††	110‡‡	66	9000	1219	48	Reces. D.C.	8500[a]						
F60T10/1.5I**††	135‡‡	—	9000	1524	60	Reces. D.C.							
F72T10/1.4A**††	160‡‡	66	9000	1829	72	Reces. D.C.							
F96T10/VHO**††	295‡‡	66	9000	2438	96	Reces. D.C.							
F48T12/1.5A**††	110	69	10667	1219	48	Reces. D.C.							
F60T12/1.5A**††	135	69	11000	1524	60	Reces. D.C.							
F72T12/1.5A**††	165	72	10667	1829	72	Reces. D.C.							
F96T12/1.5A**††	217	72	10667	2438	96	Reces. D.C.							
F48PG17/1.5A	110	72	12000	1219	48	Reces. D.C.							
F72PG17/1.5A	165	69	12000	1829	72	Reces. D.C.							
F96PG17/1.5A	215	69	12000	2438	96	Reces. D.C.							

Highly loaded lamps (over 100 mA)

Lamp Description	Lamp watts†	Lamp lumen depreciation‡	Nominal lumens ‖ # 4150K CRI 60 + Cool white	3000K CRI 50 + Warm white	3470K CRI 60 + White	6380K CRI 70 + Daylight	2750K CRI 80 + Incandescent fluorescent	2990K CRI 70 + Deluxe warm white (soft white)	4160K CRI 80 + Deluxe cool white	4200K CRI 40 + Optima 32[d]	3200K CRI 80 + Optima 32[d]	3570K CRI 80 + Natural	7500K CRI 90 + C 75	5500K CRI 90 + Vita-Lite
F48T10/1.5A**††	110‡‡	66	6200[a]						4500[a]					
F60T10/1.5I**††	135‡‡	66	8200[a]						7500[a]					
F72T10/1.5A**††	160‡‡	66	9700[a]											
F96T10/VHO**††	295‡‡	66	13500[a]											
F48T12/1.5A**††	110	69	6617	6683		5600[b]								
F6012/1.5A**††	135	72	11000	8850		9250								
F72T12/1.5A**††	165	72	10617	10650		12167			10500					
F96T12/1.5A**††	217	69	14400	14567										
F48PG17/1.5A	110	69	6800[a]			5700[a]								
F72PG17/1.5A	165	69	11000[a]			9000[a]								
F96PG17/1.5A	215	69	15300[a]	15700[a]		12700[a]			11000[a]					

Note: all electrical and lumen values apply only under standard photometric conditions. Ballasts that do not provide proper electrical values may substantially reduce lamp life, light output or both.
[a]General Electric.
[b]Sylvania.
[c]Philips.
[d]Duro-Test.
*The life and light output ratings of fluorescent lamps are based on their use with ballasts that provide proper operating characteristics.
†Includes watts for cathode heat.
‡Per cent of initial light output at 70% rated life at three hours per start. Average for cool white lamps.
§Rated life under specified test conditions at three hours per start. At longer operating intervals per start, longer life can be expected.
⊥ "RE" indicates "RARE EARTH" type phosphers.
#RE 70 designates a CRI range of 70–79, RE 80 is a range of 80–89, and RE 90 range ≥ 90. This nomenclature has been developed by NEMA to define a system of color rendering information.
** Jacketed lamp designs are available for use in applications where bare lamps are directly exposed to temperatures below 50° F and with winds above 5 mph.
††These lamps are available in several variations (i.e., outdoor and low temperature) with the same or slightly different ratings.
‡‡Peak value. At 25° C (77° F) lumen and wattage values are lower.

Fig. 6-117. Typical Hot Cathode Fluorescent Lamps (Preheat Starting)*

Lamp description	Lamp watts	Lamp lumen depreciation†	Lamp life (h)‡	Nominal length (mm)	Nominal length (in.)	Base (end caps)	Nominal lumens§							
							3000K RE70	3500K RE70	4100K RE70	2700K RE80	3000K RE80	3500K RE80	4100K RE80	5000K RE80
F4T5	4	67	6000	152	6	Min. Bipin								
F6T5	6	67	7500	229	9	Min. Bipin								
F8T5	8	75	7500	305	12	Min. Bipin								
F13T5	13	72	7500	533	21	Min. Bipin				450[c]	450[c]			
F14T12	14	82	9000	381	15	Med. Bipin	735[b]		940[a]	1000[c]	1000[c]	1000[a]	1000	1000[c]
F15T8	15	79	7500	457	18	Med. Bipin	920	940			973			
F15T12	15	81	9000	457	18	Med. Bipin	830[b]	820[c]						
F20T12	20	85	9000	610	24	Med. Bipin	1283	1283	1275[a]		1333	1325	1350[c]	1340[c]
F25T12	25	79	9000	838	33	Med. Bipin					2330			
F30T8	30	79	7500	914	36	Med. Bipin								
F40T12	40	82	15,000	1219	48	Med. Bipin								
F90T17	90	85	9000	1524	60	Mog. Bipin								

Lamp description	Lamp watts	Nominal lumens§												
		5000K CRI 90+ C50	4150K CRI 60+ Cool White	3000K CRI 50+ Warm white	3470K CRI 50+ White	6380K CRI 70+ Daylight	2750K CRI 80+ Incandescent Fluorescent	4160K CRI 80+ Deluxe cool white	2990K CRI 70+ Deluxe warm white (soft white)	4200K CRI 40+ Lite-white	3200K CRI 80+ Optima 32™[d]	3570K CRI 80+ Natural	7500K CRI 90+ C75	5500K CRI 90+ Vita-Lite™
F4T5	4		135		140[b]	115	—							
F6T5	6		290	275[b]	275[b]	240	—							
F8T5	8	280[b]	400	400	400[b]	340	—							
F13T5	13		840	875			—	205[a]	272					
F14T12	14		680	700	690[b]	590	—	480[b]						465
F15T8	15		850	800	855	730	—	600	605		675	595		610
F15T12	15		780	790	790[b]	630	—	550[b]	545					535
F20T12	20		1200	1250	1255	1058	—	885	867		960	850		855
F25T12	25		1875	1925		1550	—							
F30T8	30		2185	2240	2215[b]	1750	—	1560	1500[a]		1650	1500		1585
F40T12	40		3050	3115	3075	2600	—	2150	2150					2180
F90T17	90		6025			5275								

*The life and light output ratings of fluorescent lamps are based on the ballasts that provides its operating characteristics. Ballasts that do not provide proper electrical values may substantially reduce lamp life, light output or both.
†Percent of initial light output at 70% of rated life at 3 hours per start. Average for cool white lamps. Approximate values.
‡Rated life under specified test conditions at 3 hours per start. At longer burning intervals per start, longer life can be expected.
§At 100 hours. When lamp is made by more than one manufacturer, light output is the average of all manufacturers submitting data.
[a]General Electric.
[b]Sylvania.
[c]Philips.
[d]Duro-Test.

Fig. 6-118. Typical Hot Cathode Fluorescent Lamps (Instant Starting)*

Lamp description	Lamp watts	Lamp lumen depreciation†	Lamp life (h)‡	Nominal length (mm)	Nominal length (in.)	Base (end caps)	Nominal lumens§ 3000K RE70	3500K RE70	4100K RE70	3000K RE80	3500K RE80	4100K RE80	5000K RE80
F42T6 ||	24	76	7500	1067	42	Single Pin							
F64T6 ||	38	77	7500	1626	64	Single Pin							
F72T8 ||	37	83	7500	1854	73	Single Pin							
F96T8 ||	50	89	7500	2438	96	Single Pin							
F48T12	40	83	8250	1219	48	Med. Bipin							
F60T17	40	89	7500	1524	60	Mog. Bipin							
F24T12	20	81	7500	610	24	Single Pin							
F36T12	30	82	7500	914	36	Single Pin							
F42T12	35	80	7500	1067	42	Single Pin							
F48T12	39	82	9000	1219	48	Single Pin	3000[a]	3017		3075	3050[a]	3150[c]	
F60T12	50	78	12,000	1524	60	Single Pin							
F64T12	51	78	12,000	1626	64	Single Pin							
F72T12	55	89	12,000	1829	72	Single Pin	4700	4700	4700[a]	4817	4817	4825	4800[c]
F84T12	67	91	12,000	2134	84	Single Pin							
F96T12	75	89	12,000	2438	96	Single Pin	6450	6450	6450	6617	6617	6575	6500[c]

Lamp description	Lamp watts	Base (end caps)	Nominal lumens§ 4150K CRI 60 + Cool white	3000K CRI 50 + Warm white	3470K CRI 60 + white	6380K CRI 70 + Daylight	5000K CRI 90 + C50	4160K CRI 80 + Deluxe cool white	2990K CRI 70 + Deluxe warm white (soft white)	3200K CRI 80 + Optima 32™ᵈ	3570K CRI 80 + Natural	5500K CRI 90 + Vita-Lite™ᵈ
F42T6	24	Single Pin	1840	1880	1920	1620[b]		1300				
F64T6	38	Single Pin	2925	3000		2700[b]		2140				
F72T8	37	Single Pin	3025	3100								
F96T8	50	Single Pin	4025	4050[b]		3550[b]						
F48T12	40	Med. Pipin	3000									
F60T17	40	Mog. Bipin	2850									
F24T12	20	Single Pin	1150	2050[a]		940[c]						
F36T12	30	Single Pin	1940			1655						
F42T12	35	Single Pin	2350			1990						
F48T12	39	Single Pin	2890	2940	2890	2480		2070			1975	2120
F60T12	50	Single Pin	3580			3120						2700
F64T12	51	Single Pin	3830			3270						
F72T12	55	Single Pin	4480	4600	4600[b]	3830	4550	3180		3250	3030	3335
F84T12	67	Single Pin	5280	5280		4480					4250	
F96T12	75	Single Pin	6620	6270	6175	5280		4470		4750		4475

* The life and light output ratings of fluorescent lamps are based on their use with ballasts that provide proper operating characteristics. Ballasts that do not provide proper electrical values may substantially reduce lamp life, light output or both.
† Percent of initial light output at 70% of rated life at 3 hours per start. Average for cool white lamps. Approximate values.
‡ Rated life under specified test conditions at 3 hours per start.
§ At 100 hours. When lamp is made by more than one manufacturer, light output is the average of all manufacturers submitting data.
|| These lamps can also be operated 120 and 300 mA.
[a] General Electric.
[b] Sylvania.
[c] Philips.
[d] Duro-Test.

Fig. 6-119. Typical Cold-Cathode Instant-Starting Fluorescent Lamps

Lamp description	Bulb	Lamp power (watts)		Lamp base (end caps)	Open circuit starting voltage (rms)		Lamp current* (mA)	Lamp voltage		Rated life† (thousands of hours)		Overall length‡		Initial Lumens§			
		Type LP	Type HP		Type LP	Type HP		Type LP	Type HP	Type LP	Type HP	(mm)	(in.)	Warm white	3500K white	4500K white	Daylight
48T8	25 mm T-8	26	28	Ferrule	450	600	120	250	270	15	25	1140	45	4040	3940	3770	3730
72T8	25 mm T-8	34	37	Ferrule	600	750	120	320	350	15	25	1753	69	4350	4250	4145	4080
96T8	25 mm T-8	42	46	Ferrule	750	835	120	420	450	18	30	2362	93	4490	4385	4280	4210
U6-96T8	25 mm T-8	42	46	Ferrule	750	835	120	420	450	18	30	1140	45‖	4490	4385	4280	4210

*Lamps can be operated up to 200 mA.
†Life not affected by number of starts.
‡Length of lamp without lamp holders.
§Initial rating after 100 hours for types LP and HP. Other color lamps are available.
‖Extended lamp length 2325 millimeters (93 inches) formed to U shape with 180 degrees, 150 millimeter (6 inch) arc.

Fig. 6-120. Fluorescent Lamp Electrical Characteristics

Lamp description	Bulb diameter (in.)[b]	Bulb watts	Base (end caps)	Nominal length (mm)	Nominal length (in.)	Min. required rms voltage across lamp for reliable starting*	Operating current (mA)	Operating voltage	Cathode heaters (low resistance) volts	Cathode heaters (low resistance) Maximum watts	One lamp circuit Ballast	One lamp circuit Total	Two lamp circuit (lead-lag and series) Ballast	Two lamp circuit (lead-lag and series) Total
Rapid start‡														
Lightly loaded (under 500 mA)														
FC6T9 Circular§	1 1/8	19	4-Pin	165	6.5	150	380	49	3.6	2	11	30	—	—
FC8T9 Circular§	1 1/8	22.5	4-Pin	210	8.2	180	370	61	3.6	2	7.5	30	—	—
F25T8	1	25	Med. Bipost	900	36	170	265	170	3.6	1.5	5	30	8	58
F28T12||	1 1/2	28	Med. Bipost	1200	48	231	390	135	3.6	—	9	37	4	60
F32T8	1	32	Med. Bipost	1200	48	200	265	137	3.6	1.7	5	37	7	71
FC12T9 Circular§	1 1/8	32	4-Pin	305	12	200	425	84	3.6	2	16	10	42	—
FC16T9 Circular§	1 1/8	40	4-Pin	406	16	205	430	109	3.6	2	—	56	—	—
F30T12	1 1/2	30	Med. Bipost	900	36	150	430	77	3.6	2	11.5	44	13	78
F40T12 ||	1 1/2	32	Med. Bipost	1200	48	—	—	—	—	2	—	—	—	76
F40T12	1 1/2	34	Med. Bipost	1200	48	200	430	236	3.6	1.5	—	—	—	—
F40T8	1	40	Med. Bipost	1500	60	250	265	172	3.6	2	6	46	11	91
F40T10	1 1/4	41	Med. Bipost	1200	48	200	420	104	3.6	2	13	54	13	95
F40T1	1 1/2	41	Med. Bipost	1200	48	200	430	101	3.6	2	13	54	13	95
F40T12/U/3#	1 1/2	41	Med. Bipost	584	23	200	420	103	3.6	2	13	54	13	95
F40T12/U/6#	1 1/2	40.5	Med. Bipost	600	24	200	430	100	3.6	2	13	53.5	13	94
F6T7MM	7mm	6	Special	203	8	130	100	—	7	0.7	—	—	—	—
F8T7MM	7mm	8	Special	305	12	190	100	—	7	0.7	—	—	—	—
F10T7MM	7mm	19	Special	406	16	250	100	—	7	0.7	—	—	—	—
F3T7MM	7mm	13	Special	508	20	310	100	—	7	0.7	—	—	—	—
FT8W/2G11RS	5/8	18	2G11	267	11	210	250	76	—	—	9	27	10	46
FT4W/2G11RS	5/8	24–27	2G11	311	12	220	340	89	—	—	7	34	6	60
FT36W/2G11RS	5/8	36–39	2G11	419	17	230	430	110	—	—	11	48	11	85
FT40W/2G11RS	5/8	40	2G11	572	23	275	270	170	—	—	5	44	4	82
FT50W/2G11RS	5/8	50	2G11	572	23	275	430	147	—	—	4	54	—	—

Lamp description	Bulb diameter (in.)	Bulb watts	Base (end caps)	Nominal length (mm)	Nominal length (in.)	Min. required rms voltage across lamp for reliable starting*	Operating current (mA)	Operating voltage	Cathode heaters (high resistance) volts	Cathode heaters Maximum watts	One lamp circuit Ballast	One lamp circuit Total	Two lamp circuit (lead-lag and series) Ballast	Two lamp circuit Total
Medium loaded (500 – 1000 mA)												*Approximate watts†*		
F24T12/HO	1½	35	Rec. DC	610	24	85	800	41	3.6	7	33	70	41	115
F30T12/HO	1½	41	Rec. DC	762	30	—	—	—	—	—	—	—	—	—
F36T12/HO	1½	47	Rec. DC	914	36	115	800	59	3.6	7	—	—	—	—
F42T12/HO	1½	55	Rec. DC	1067	42	—	—	—	—	—	—	—	—	—
F48T12/HO	1½	60	Rec. DC	1219	48	155	800	78	3.6	7	22	85	20	146
F60T12/HO	1½	73	Rec. DC	1524	60	210	800	98	3.6	7	—	—	—	—
F64T12/HO	1½	78	Rec. DC	1626	64	—	—	—	—	—	—	—	—	—
F72T12/HO	1½	85	Rec. DC	1829	72	260	800	117	3.6	7	48	135	36	210
F84T12/HO	1½	100	Rec. DC	2134	84	280	800	135	3.6	7	19	119	13	213
F96T12/HO	1½	110	Rec. DC	2438	96	295	790	153	3.6	7	27	140	20	246
Highly loaded (over 1000 mA)														
F48T10/1.5A	1½	110	Rec. DC	1219	48	160	1500	84	3.6	7	—	—	—	—
F60T10/1.5A	1½	135	Rec. DC	1524	60	—	—	—	—	—	—	—	—	—
F72T10/1.5A	1½	160	Rec. DC	1829	72	—	—	—	—	—	—	—	—	—
F96T10/1.5A	1½	205	Rec. DC	2438	96	—	—	—	—	—	—	—	—	—
F48T12/1.5A	1½	110	Rec. DC	1219	48	160	1500	84	3.6	7	28	139	27	247
F60T12/1.5A	1½	135	Rec. DC	1524	60	—	—	—	—	—	—	—	—	—
F72T10/1.5A	1½	165	Rec. DC	1829	72	225	1500	125	3.6	7	40	200	40	360
F96T12/1.5A	1½	215	Rec. DC	2438	96	300	1500	163	3.6	7	20	235	20	450
F48PG17	2⅛	116	Rec. DC	1219	48	160	1500	84	3.6	7	30	146	20	252
F72PG17	2⅛	168	Rec. DC	1800	72	225	1500	125	3.6	7	48	213	—	328
F96PG17	2⅛	215	Rec. DC	2400	96	300	1500	163	3.6	7	—	260	—	450
Preheat start														
F4T5	5/8	4	Min. Bipin	152	6	108[b]	170	29	8	0.25	2	6.5	—	—
F6T5	5/8	6	Min. Bipin	229	9	108[b]	160	42	8	0.25	2	8	—	—
F8T5	5/8	8	Min. Bipin	305	12	108[b]	145	57	8	0.25	2	9.2	—	—
F13T5	5/8	13	Min. Bipin	533	21	180	165	94	8	0.27	5	18	—	—
F14T12	1½	14	Med. Bipin	381	15	108[b]	380	40	8	0.65	5	19	5	33

Lamp description	Bulb diameter (in.)	Bulb watts	Base (end caps)	Nominal length (mm)	Nominal length (in.)	Min. required rms voltage across lamp for reliable starting*	Operating current (mA)	Operating voltage	Cathode heaters (high resistance) volts	Cathode heaters Maximum watts	One lamp circuit Ballast	One lamp circuit Total	Two lamp circuit (lead-lag and series) Ballast	Two lamp circuit Total
Preheat start														
F15T8	1	15	Med. Bipin	457	18	108[b]	305	55	8	0.65	4.5	19.5	9	39
F15T12	1½	15	Med. Bipin	457	18	108[b]	325	47	8	0.65	4.5	19	9	38
F20T12	1½	20	Med. Bipin	610	24	108[b]	380	57	8	0.75	5	25.5	10	41
F25T12	1½	25	Med. Bipin	838	33	108[b]	460	61	—	0.95	6	31.5	—	—
F30T8	1	30	Med. Bipin	914	36	108	355	99	—	0.65	10.5	41	17	78
F40T12	1½	40	Med. Bipin	1219	48	176	430	101	3.6	0.75	10	50	16	96
F90T17	2⅛	90	Mog. Bipin.	1524	60	132	1500	65	—	2.2	20	110	33	213
Instant start with bipin base														
F40T12	1½	40	Med. Bipin*	1200	48	385	425	104	—	—	20	60	25	105
F40T17	2⅛	40	Mog. Bipin*	1500	60	385	425	107	—	—	20	60	25	105
Instant start with single pin base (Slimline lamps)														
F42T6**	⅝	25	Single pin	1050	42	405	200	145	—	—	16	41	16	66
F64T6**	⅝	38	Single pin	1600	64	540	200	225	—	—	17	55	30	106
F72T8**	1	38	Single pin	1800	72	540	200	218	—	—	17	55	30	106
F96T8**	1	51	Single pin	2400	96	675	200	290	—	—	19	70	30	132
F96T8	1	40	Single pin	2400	96	—	—	—	—	—	—	—	—	—
F48T12 (lead-lag)	1½	39	Single pin	1200	48	385	425	100	—	—	20	59	30	108
(series)				1200	48	385	425	—	—	—	—	—	20	98
F48T12 (energy saving)	1½	30 — 32	Single pin	1200	48	—	—	—	—	—	—	—	—	—
F72T12 (lead-lag)	1½	55	Single pin	1800	72	475	425	149	—	—	26	81	33	143
(series)				1800	72	475	425	—	—	—	—	—	27	137
F96T12 (lead-lag)	1½	75	Single pin	2400	96	565	425	197	—	—	26	101	33	183
(series)				2400	96	565	425	—	—	—	—	—	27	177
F96T12 (energy saving)	1½	60	Single pin	2400	96	565	440	160	—	—	—	—	8	128
F96T8 (electronic)††	1	56	Single pin	2400	96	—	265	—	—	—	—	—	—	105

Typical cold cathode

Lamp description	Bulb diameter (in.)	Bulb watts	Base (end caps)	Nominal length (including lampholders) (mm)	(in.)	Minimum required rms voltage across lamp for reliable starting*	Operating current (mA)	Operating voltage	Cathode heaters volts	Cathode heaters Maximum watts	One lamp circuit Ballast	One lamp circuit Total	Two lamp circuit (lead-lag and series) Ballast	Two lamp circuit Total
96T8LP	25 mm	42 49 59	Ferrule	2400	96	750	120 150 200	420	NA	NA	9 19	51 78	17 30	101 148
96T8HP	25 mm	46 54 65	Ferrule	2400	96	835	120 150 200	450	NA	NA	12	58	24 28 30	115 136 160

Using energy-saving ballasts‡‡

Lamp description	Bulb diameter (in.)	Bulb watts	Base (end caps)	Nominal length (mm)	(in.)	Minimum required rms voltage across lamp for reliable starting*	Operating current (mA)	One lamp circuit Ballast	One lamp circuit Total	Two lamp circuit Ballast	Two lamp circuit Total
Rapid start‡‡											
40T12		40		1200	48	200	430	7	47	6	86
40T12§§		34 – 35		1200	48	200	460		41		74
Slimline											
96T12		75		2400	96	565	425				160
96T12§§		60		2400	96	565	440				178
Rapid start (800 mA)‡											
96T12		113		2400	96	296	800				237
96T12§§		95		2400	96	296	840				207

*Between 10° C (50°) and 43° C (110° F). The voltage shown is that required across one lamp. A ballast designed to operate two rapid-start lamps in series will require an open circuit voltage roughly 40% higher than that shown here. Consult lamp manufacturer for information.

†Lamp watts and light output will vary with lamp temperature.

‡Requires starting aid.

a Circular lamp: dimension given is nominal outside diameter.

‖ Cathode-cutout type.

U-shaped lamp.

** T-6 and T-8 slimline lamps also operate at 120 and 300 mA.

†† Suitable for operation on 120 volt ac lines with series reactor as ballast.

‡‡ Energy-saving CBM rated ballasts are designed to operate standard fluorescent lamps at CBM rated light output with lower ballast losses than ballasts which do not bear the "Energy Saving" label. The data shown here are typical for this type of ballast when used with the three most common energy-saving fluorescent lamp approved by the manufacturer for use with such a ballast.

§§ Energy-saving fluorescent lamp.

b Inches except where noted.

Fig. 6-121. Representative Fluorescent Lamp Ballast Factors

Lamp	Ballast		
	Standard	Low loss	High performance
		4 ft rapid-start system (F40T12)	
Standard	0.95	0.95	0.97
Reduced wattage	0.89	0.87	0.95
		8 ft slimline systems (F96T12)	
Standard	0.94	0.93	0.97
Reduced wattage	0.87	0.85	0.96
		8 ft high-output systems	
Standard	0.98	—	1.03
Reduced wattage	0.93	—	0.98

Fig. 6-122. Typical High-Intensity Discharge Lamps

I. HIGH PRESSURE SODIUM*

A. Compact double-ended high pressure sodium lamps

Lamp watts	ANSI no. and other description	Bulb type	Base	Rated life (h)†	Max overall length (mm)	Max overall length (in.)	Light center length (mm)	Light center length (in.)	Nominal lamp efficacy (LPW)	Nominal lumens Clear 1900-2000K CRI 20+	Nominal lumens Coated 1900-2000K CRI 20+
70[d]	S88-70[2]	T-7	RSC	10,000	114	4.5	57	2.25	100	7000	
150[d]	NA-150[2]	T-7	RSC	10,000	132	5.1875	67	2.625	107	16,000	
250[b]	S50-250	T-7	RSC	24,000	256	10.0625	—	—	102	25,500	
400[b]	S51-400	T-7	RSC	24,000	256	10.0625	—	—	115	46,000	

B. Compact single-ended high pressure sodium lamps

Lamp watts	ANSI no. and other description	Bulb type	Base	Rated life (h)†	Max overall length (mm)	Max overall length (in.)	Light center length (mm)	Light center length (in.)	Nominal lamp efficacy (LPW)	Nominal lumens Clear 1900-2000K CRI 20+	Nominal lumens Coated 1900-2000K CRI 20+
35	S76HA(HB)-35	ED(B)-17	Medium	24,000	140	5.5	89	3.5	63	2250	2150
35	S76-35	T-10	Medium	24,000	130	5.125	80	3.1562	60	2100	
50	S68-50	ED(B)-17	Medium	24,000	140	5.5	89	3.5	78	4000	3800
50	S68-50	T-10	Medium	24,000	130	5.125	80	3.1562	74	3700	
70	S62LG(LH)-70	ED(E)-17	Medium	24,000	140	5.5	89	3.5	88	6400	5950
70	S62-70	T-10	Medium	24,000	130	5.125	80	3.1562	87	6100	
100	S54SG(SH)-100	ED(E)-17	Medium	24,000	140	5.5	89	3.5	92	9500	8800
150	S55RN(RP)-150	ED(E)-17	Medium	24,000	146	5.75	89	3.5	103	16,000	15,000
750[b]	S111NH-750	BT-37	Mogul	24,000	292	11.5	175	6.875	147	110,000	
1000[c]	S52-1000	ED-37	Mogul	24,000	292	11.5	178	7	125	125,000	

C. Standard high pressure sodium lamps

Lamp watts	ANSI no. and other description	Bulb type	Base	Rated life (h)†	Max overall length (mm)	Max overall length (in.)	Light center length (mm)	Light center length (in.)	Nominal lamp efficacy (LPW)	Nominal lumens Clear 1900-2000K CRI 20+	Nominal lumens Coated 1900-2000K CRI 20+
50	S68MS(MT)-50	E(ED,ET)-23$\frac{1}{2}$	Mogul	24,000	197	7.75	127	5	78	4000	3800
70	S62ME(MF)-70	E(ED,ET)-23$\frac{1}{2}$	Mogul	24,000	197	7.75	127	5	88	6400	5950
100	S54SB(MC)-100	E(ED,ET)-23$\frac{1}{2}$	Mogul	24,000	197	7.75	127	5	92	9500	8800
150	S55SC(MD)-150 55 volt	E(ED,ET)-23$\frac{1}{2}$	Mogul	24,000	197	7.75	127	5	103	16,000	15,000
150	S56SD-150 100 volt	E(ED,BT)-28	Mogul	24,000	211	8.3125	127	5	100	15,000	
200	S66MN-200	E(ED,ET)-18	Mogul	24,000	248	9.75	146	5.75	110	22,000	
250	S50VA-250	E(ED,ET)-18	Mogul	24,000	248	9.75	146	5.75	110	27,500	26,000
250	S50VC-250	E(ED,BT)-28	Mogul	24,000	229	9	127	5	104	27,500	
310	S67MR-310	E(ED,ET)-18	Mogul	24,000	248	9.75	146	5.75	119	37,000	
400	S51WA-400	E(ED,ET)-18	Mogul	24,000	248	9.75	146	5.75	125	50,000	47,500
400	S51WB-400	E(ED,BT)-37	Mogul	24,000	287	11.3125	178	7	119	50,000	
600[d]	S106-600	T-16	Mogul	18,000	284	11.1875	168	6.625	150	90,000	
1000[d]	S52-1000	T-21	Mogul	24,000	378	14.875	222	8.75	140	140,000	
1000	S52XB-1000	E-25	Mogul	24,000	383	15.0625	222	8.75	140	140,000	

Fig. 6-122. *Continued*

I. HIGH PRESSURE SODIUM*

D. Reflector high pressure sodium lamps
E. Dual arc tube high pressure sodium lamps
F. High color rendering high pressure sodium lamps

Lamp watts	ANSI no. and other description	Bulb type	Base	Rated life (h)†	Max overall length (mm)	Max overall length (in.)	Light center length (mm)	Light center length (in.)	Nominal lamp efficacy (LPW)	Clear 1900-2000K CRI 20+	Clear 2200-2300K CRI 60+	Clear 2600-2700K CRI 80+	Clear 4200K CRI 80+	Clear 3600-4000K CRI 60+	Clear 4100-4400K CRI 60+	Clear 5400K CRI 93	Coated 1900-2000K CRI 20+	Coated 2200-2300K CRI 60+	Coated 2600-2700K CRI 80+
35	S76-35§ (reflec. 150° beam)	R-38	Medium	16,000	156	6.125	—	—	40	420									
70	S62-70§ (reflec. 150° beam)	R-38	Medium	16,000	156	6.125	—	—	49	1300									
70	S62-70§ (reflec. 150° beam)	R-38	Medium	10,000	156	6.125	—	—	37		1000								
70	S62-70	E(ET)-23½	Mogul	24,000	191	7.5	127	5	80	5600									
100	S54-100	E(ET)-23½	Mogul	24,000	191	7.5	127	5	91	9100									
150	S55-150	E(ET)-23½	Mogul	24,000	191	7.5	127	5	104	15600									
200^b	S66-200	ET-18	Mogul	40,000	248	9.75	146	5.75	110	22000									
250	S50-250	E(ET)-18	Mogul	24,000	248	9.75	146	5.75	110	27500									
400	S51-400	E(ET)-18	Mogul	24,000	248	9.75	146	5.75	125	50000									
1000^b	S52-1000	E-25	Mogul	24,000	383	15.0625	222	8.75	140	140000									S52-10
35^c	S99AF-35	T-10	PG-12	10,000	149	5.875	90	3.5625	36			1250							
50^c	S104AF-50	T-10	PG-12	10,000	149	5.875	90	3.5625	46			2300							
50^c	S104-50	ED-17	Medium	10,000	138	5.4375	87	3.4375	44		3800								
70	S62LG-70	B(ED)-17	Medium	15,000	140	5.5	64	2.5	53										2190
100^c	S105NZ-100	T-10	PG-12	10,000	149	5.875	90	3.5625	47			4700							
100^c	S105-100	ED-17	Medium	10,000	138	5.4375	87	3.4375	25										2470
150	S55RN(RP)-150./C 55 v	B(ED)-17	Medium	15,000	146	5.75	89	3.5	68		10,500							9900	
150	S55SC(MD)-150 55 v	E(ED)-23½	Mogul	15,000	197	7.75	127	5	68		10,500							9900	
250	S50VA-250 100 v	E(ED)-18	Mogul	15,000	248	9.75	146	5.75	90		22,500							20,000	
250^a	S50-250	E-28	Mogul	15,000	229	9	127	5	80		37,500								
400^c	S51WA-400 100 v	ED-18	Mogul	15,000	248	9.75	146	5.75	94									35,500	
400^a	S51-400	E-28	Mogul	10,000	229	9	133	5.25	91		37,400								

a General Electric.
b Sylvania.
c Philips.
d OSRAM.
* Actual lamp watts may vary depending on the ballast characteristic curve. Use only on ballasts that provide proper electrical values.
† Horizontal ± 45°.
‡ Instant restart with special ignitor.
§ Luminous output is shown in candlepower; other wattage ratings are available.

II. METAL HALIDE

A. Compact metal halide lamps double ended

Lamp watts	ANSI no. and other description	Bulb type	Base	Rated Life[3] (h)[+]	MOL (mm)	MOL (in.)	LCL (mm)	LCL (in.)	Nominal lamp efficacy (LPW)	Clear 3000-3200K CRI 60	Clear 3000-3200K CRI 70	Clear 3000K CRI 80+	Clear 4200K CRI 80+	Clear 3800-4000K CRI 60+	Clear 4100-4400K CRI 60+	Clear 5400K CRI 93	Clear 3000-3200K CRI 60+	Clear 3700-4100K CRI 60+	Coated 3000K CRI 70+	Coated 3200-3600K CRI 70+	Coated 3700/4200K CRI 70+
70**	M85PX-70	T-6(6½)	RSC (R7s)	7000	121	4.75	60	2.375	75	5000	5200	5000	5500								
100b**	M91TN-100	T-6	RSC (R7s)	7500	121	4.75	60	2.375	85	11,250	8500	11,000	11,250								
150**	M85PS-150	T-7(7½)	RSC (R7s)	8375	138	5.437E	67	2.625	78	11,250	13,000	11,000	11,250			19,000					
250d**	M80	T-9½	Fc2	10,000	164	6.437E	81	3.1875	78				20,000			19,000					
400d**	M86	T-10	Fc2	10,000	206	8.125	103	4.0625	63							25,000					
1000b*	Not available	T-7	Rect. RSC	7500	256	10.062E	124	4.875	100					100,000							
1500b*	Not available	T-7	Rect. RSC	3000	256	10.062E	178	7	100					150,000							
2000b*	Not available	T-8	Rect. RSC	3000	273	10.75	184	7.25	100					200,000							

B. Compact metal halide lamps single ended

Lamp watts	ANSI no. and other description	Bulb type	Base	Rated Life[3] (h)[+]	MOL (mm)	MOL (in.)	LCL (mm)	LCL (in.)	Nominal lamp efficacy (LPW)	Clear 3000-3200K CRI 60	Clear 3000-3200K CRI 70	Clear 3000K CRI 80+	Clear 4200K CRI 80+	Clear 3800-4000K CRI 60+	Clear 4100-4400K CRI 60+	Clear 5400K CRI 93	Clear 3000-3200K CRI 60+	Clear 3700-4100K CRI 60+	Coated 3000K CRI 70+	Coated 3200-3600K CRI 70+	Coated 3700/4200K CRI 70+
32[a]	M100GZ-32/VBU	E-17	Med. Screw	10,000	138	5.437E	87	3.4375	78		3300			3400			2500				3400
50	M110-50/U	ED-17	Med. screw	5000	138	5.437E	87	3.4375	67	6000	3300	5200	5000	3400	5000			5000		5000	3400
70	M98SJ(SK)-70	ED-17	Med. screw	6250	138	5.437E	87	3.4375	55	6000	5200	5200	5000	5600	5000			5000		5000	5000
70[d]	M85	T-8	G12	6000	84	3.312E	56	2.1875	74	9000	8500	8500	7800	7800	7800			7800		8500	7800
100	M90SJ(SK)-100/U	ED-17	Med. screw	7500	138	5.437E	87	3.4375	81	9000	8500	8500	7800	7800	7800			7800		8500	7800
100	M90-100/BU/BD	B-17	Med. screw	10,000	138	5.437E	87	3.4375	88	8500	13000			10,125			8500			9000	9720
150	M102TW(TX)-150	ED-17	Med. screw	10,000	138	5.437E	87	3.4375	74		13000	12000	12000	10,125			8500			9000	9720
150[d]	M81	T-8	G12	6000	84	3.312E	56	2.1875	80			12000	12000	15,000	14000			14000		14,000	15,000
175	M57-175/U	ED-17	Med. screw	10,000	138	5.44	87	3.44	86					15,000			15750				15,000
175[e]	M57-175/BU	ED-17	Med. screw	10,000	138	5.44	87	3.44	86	16,600				16,000			15750			14,000	
175	M57PE(PF)-175/XBU/BD	E-23½	Mogul	10,000	197	7.75	127	5	92	16,600						19,000					
250[d]	M80	T14½	Mogul	9000	219	8.625	149	5.875	76					20,500		19,000					
250[e]	M58-250/U	ED-18	Mogul	10,000	248	9.75	146	5.75	82	20,500				20,500							
250[e]	M58-250/HOR	ED-18	Mogul	10,000	248	9.75	146	5.75	87	20,500				23,000							
250	M58-250/U	T-15	Mogul	10,000	248	9.75	146	5.75	84					21,000		25,000					
400[d]	M86	T14½	Mogul	9000	286	11.25	175	6.875	62.5					40,000		25,000				36,000	40,000
400[e]	M59-400/HOR	ED-28	Mogul[q]	20,000	211	8.31	127	5	97					40,000						36,000	40,000
400	M59PJ-400/U	ED-28	Mogul	16,000	211	8.3125	127	5	90					36,000							36,000
400	M59PL-400	T-15	Mogul	10,000	248	9.75	146	5.75	90					36,000							
1000[e]	M47-1000/HOR	BT-37	Mogul[q]	12,000	292	11.5	178	7	117	117,000				110,000							
1000	M47-1000/U	BT-37	Mogul	11,000	292	11.5	178	7	110	117,000				110,000		90,000					
1000[d]	M83	T-24	Mogul	12,000	340	13.375	221	8.6875	90	155,000						90,000					
1500[e]	M48-1500/U	BT-37	Mogul	3000	292	11.5	178	7	103	155,000											

Fig. 6-122. *Continued*

II. METAL HALIDE

C. Standard metal halide lamps

Lamp watts	ANSI no. and other description	Bulb type	Base	Rated life (h)†	Max. overall length (mm)	(in.)	Light center length (mm)	(in.)	Nominal lamp efficacy (LPW)	Clear 1900-2000K CRI 20+	Clear 2200-2300K CRI 60+	Clear 2600-2700K CRI 80+	Clear 4200K CRI 80+	Clear 3600-4000K CRI 60+	Clear 4100-4400K CRI 60+	Clear 5400K CRI 93	Coated 1900-2000K CRI 20+	Coated 2200-2300K CRI 60+	Coated 2600-2700K CRI 80+
70	M98-70/U (clear or coat.)	ED-17	Med. screw	5000	138	5.4375	87	3.4375	71					5000					5000
100	M90-100/U (clear or coat.)	ED-17	Med. screw	10,000	138	5.4375	87	3.4375	78					7800					7800
150[c]	M107-150/U	ED-28	Mogul	10,000	211	8.31	127	5	90					13,500					
175[d]	M57-175/U (clear or coat.)	ED-17	Med. screw	10,000	138	5.4375	87	3.4375	80					14,000					14,000
175	M57PE(PF)-175/U	E-28	Mogul	10,000	211	8.3125	127	5	76					13,500	14,000				14,000
175	M57PE(PF)-175	BT-28	Mogul	10,000	211	8.3125	127	5	81					13,500					14,000
250	M58PG(PH)-250/U	E(BT)-28	Mogul	10,000	211	8.3125	127	5	63					20,500	20,500			12,000	20,500
250[d]	M58-250/U (clear or coat.)	BT-28	Mogul	10,000	210	8.25	127	5	100					13,500	14,000			12,000	20,500
400[2]	M59PJ(PK)-400/U	BT-37	Mogul	20,000	292	11.5	178	7	92					36,000	20,500			33,000	36,000
1000[b]	M47-1000/U	BT-37	Mogul	12,000	292	11.5	178	7	105					20,500				20,500	20,500
1000[b]-2	M47PA(PB)-1000/U	BT-56	Mogul	13,600	391	15.375	241	9.5	109					110,000		125,000			110,000
1500[e]	M48PC-1500/HBU	BT-56	Mogul	2812.5	391	15.375	241	9.5	98		155,000			36,000				33,000	36,000

D. Metal halide high output

Lamp watts	ANSI no. and other description	Bulb type	Base	Rated Life[3] (h)†	Max. overall length (mm)	(in.)	Light center length (mm)	(in.)	Nominal lamp efficacy (LPW)	Clear 3000-3200K CRI 60	Clear 3000-3200K CRI 70	Clear 3000K CRI 80+	Clear 4200K CRI 80+	Clear 3800-4000K CRI 60+	Clear 4100-4400K CRI 60+	Clear 5400K CRI 93	Coated 3000-3200K CRI 60	Coated 3000K CRI 70+	Coated 3200-3600K CRI 70+	Coated 3700-4200K CRI 70+
175[a]	M57PE(PF)-175/XBU-BD	E-23½	Mogul	10000	197	7.75	127	5	92	16600							15750			
175	M57PE(PF)-175/HOR	BT-28	Mogul[q]	8333.3	211	8.3125	127	5	75					15,000	15,000			14,000		15,000
250**	M58PG(PH)-250/HOR	BT-28	Mogul[q]	10000	211	8.3125	127	5	90					23,000	23,000				23,000	22,000
400**	M59P(JPK)-400/HOR	BT-37	Mogul[q]	20000	292	11.5	178	7	97					40,000	40,000				36,000	40,000
400***	M59PJ(PK)-400/BU(BD)	ED-37	Mogul	20000	292	11.5	178	7	86		36000			40,000	40,000				36,000	40,000
1000***	M47PA(PB)-1000/BU(BD)	BT-56	Mogul	11333	391	15.375	241	9.5	125	155000				125,000						125000

E. Metal halide reflector lamps

Lamp watts	ANSI no. and other description	Bulb type	Base	Rated Life[3] (h)†	Max. (inches) length (mm)	(in.)	Light (inches) length (mm)	(in.)	Nominal lamp efficacy (LPW)	Clear 3000-3200K CRI 60	Clear 3000-3200K CRI 70	Clear 3000K CRI 80+	Clear 4200K CRI 80+	Clear 3800-4000K CRI 60+	Clear 4100-4400K CRI 60+	Clear 5400K CRI 93	Coated 3000-3200K CRI 60+	Coated 3000K CRI 70+	Coated 3200-3600K CRI 70+	Coated 3700-4200K CRI 70+
70[e]	M98 (15° reflector)§	R-40	Med. screw	10000	165	6.5	—	—	—					60,000						
70[e]	M98 (70° reflector)§	R-40	Med. screw	10000	165	6.5	—	—	—					2300						
100[e]	M90 (15° reflector)§	R-40	Med. screw	10000	165	6.5	—	—	—					80,000						
100[e]	M90 (70° reflector)§	R-40	Med. screw	10000	165	6.5	—	—	—					3300						
100[e]	M90 (15° reflector)§	R-40	Med. screw	10000	165	6.5	—	—	—					95,000						

Watts	Designation	Bulb	Base	Lumens	MOL	LCL		CP	CP	Life
175[e]	M90 (70° reflector)§	R-40	Med. screw	10000	165	6.5	—	6500		
250[c]	M58 Reflector (19° beam)§	RD-40	Mogul	7500	191	7.5	—	65,000		
400[c]	M59 Reflector (16° beam)§	R-60	Mogul	15000	276	10.875	—	120,000		
70[c]	M98 (15° reflector)§	PAR-38	Med. screw	7500	135	5.31	—		40,000	18000
70[b]	M98 (20° reflector)§	PAR-38	Med. Skirted	7500	135	5.3125	—		12,000	10000
70	M98 (35° reflector)§	PAR-38	Med. Skirted	7500	135	5.3125	—			3000
70[b]	M98 (65° reflector)§	PAR-38	Med. Skirted	7500	135	5.3125	—		105,000	
70[c]	M98 (20° reflector)§	PAR-56	Mog. E. Prg.	5000	127	5	—			
100	M90 (20° reflector)§	PAR-38	Med. Skirted	6250	135	5.3125	—		106,000	26000
100[b]	M90 (35° reflector)§	PAR-38	Med. Skirted	7500	135	5.3125	—		12,000	12000
100[b]	M90 (65° reflector)§	PAR-38	Med. Skirted	7500	135	5.3125	—	10000		4500
175[c]	M57 Reflect. (50° beam)§	PAR-38	Med. screw	7500	148	5.8125	—	60000		
175[c]	M57 Reflect. (16° beam)§	Med. screw7500	148	148	5.8125	—			108,000	
175[c]	M57 (20° Reflector)§	PAR-56	Mog. E. Prg.	5000	127	5	—		210,000	
250[c]	M58 (15° reflector)§	PAR-64	Mog. E. Prg.	5000	152	6	—			
400[c]	M59 (30° reflector)§	PAR-64	Mog. E. Prg.	5000	152	6	—		12,000	

F. Metal halide instant restart

Watts	Designation	Bulb	Base	Lumens	MOL	LCL				CP
175[e]	M57-175/U	BT-28	Mogul	10000	211	8.31	127	5	80	14,000
250[e]	M58-250/U	ED-28	Mogul	10000	211	8.31	127	5	82	20,500
400[e]	M59-400/U	BT-37	Mogul	20000	292	11.5	178	7	88	35,000
1000[e]	M47-1000/U	BT-56	Mogul	12000	391	15.375	241	9.5	110	110,000
1500[e]	M48-1500/BU	BT-56	Mogul	3000	391	15.375	241	9.5	103	155,000
1500[e]	M48-1500/HOR	BT-56	Mogul[q]	3000	391	15.375	241	9.5	108	162,000
1650[e]	M112-1650/HOR	BT-56	Mogul[q]	3000	391	15.375	241	9.5	107	177,000

[a] General Electric.
[b] Sylvania.
[c] Philips.
[d] OSRAM.
[e] Venture.
[1] Lamp efficacy, lumen output and beam candlewpoer are the average values for all products submitted.
[2] May be used in open fixtures if operated vertical ± 15.
[3] Lamp life shown is for vertical operation unless otherwise noted.
[q] These ma ¶ Base up (Base down) to Horz.
¶ Base up § Luminous output shown in candlepower.
§ Luminouq These manufacturers use a position oriented mogul.
* Horizontal ± 4°
** Horz. ± 45°
*** Base up ± 15°
* Horizontal ± 4°
** Horz. ± 45°
*** Base up ± 15°

Fig. 6.122. *Continued*

III. MERCURY VAPOR

A. Standard mercury

Lamp watts	ANSI no. and other description	Bulb type	Base	Rated Life‡ (h)†	Maximum overall length (mm)	Maximum overall length (in.)	Light center length (mm)	Light center length (in.)	Nominal lamp efficacy (LPW)	Nominal lumens§ Clear 5700 (Clear)[a] CRI 15	Nominal lumens§ Clear 5900K (Clear)[b] CRI 22	Nominal lumens§ Clear 6300-7000K (Clear)[c] CRI 25	Nominal lumens§ Coated 4000K (DX)[b] CRI 40+	Nominal lumens§ Coated 3000-3300K N(WDX) CRI 50+	Nominal lumens§ Coated 3600-3900K DX[a,c] CRI 50+
40,50	H45AY-40/50/DX	ED(B)-17	Medium	24,000	130	5.125	79	3.125	32				1650		1578
75	H43AV-75DX	ED(B)-17	Medium	24,000	138	5.4375	95	3.75	40				3150		2800
75[b]	H38AV-75/N	ED-17	Medium	24,000	138	5.4375	95	3.75	44					4400	
100	H38AV-100/DX	ED(B)-17	Medium	24,000	138	5.4375	95	3.75	42				4400		4000
100	H38MP-100/DX	A-23 (A-23$\frac{1}{2}$)	Medium	18,000	130	5.125	89	3.5	43				4500	4400	4250
100	H38HT-100	E(ED)(ET)-23$\frac{1}{2}$	Mogul	24,000	191	7.5	127	5	40	3850	4100	4100			
100	H38JA-100/DX	E(ED)(ET)-23$\frac{1}{2}$	Mogul	24,000	191	7.5	127	5	44				4500		4300
100[a]	H38JA-100/WDX	E(ED)(ET)-23$\frac{1}{2}$	Mogul	24,000	191	7.5	127	5	34					3400	
100[b]	H38JA-R100/WDX(N)	ET-23$\frac{1}{2}$	Mogul	24,000	191	7.5	127	5	46					4600	
100[b]	H44GS-100	PAR-38	Medium	16,000	138	5.4375	—	—	25		2500				
100	H44GS-100MDSK	PAR-38	Med. skt.	16,000	138	5.4375	—	—	27		2500	2800			
100	H44GS-100 30° Spot	PAR-38	Admed.	16,000	138	5.4375	—	—	26	2450	2500	2800			
100	H44JM-100 90° Med. Fl.	PAR-38	Admed.	16,000	138	5.4375	—	—	25	2450	2500				
100[a]	H38BM-100	R-40	Medium	24,000	178	7	—	—	29	2850					
100	H38BP-100/DX	R-40	Medium	24,000	191	7.5	—	—	29				2900		
100[c]	H38BP-100/N	R-40	Medium	24,000	191	7.5	—	—	25					2450	
175	H39KB-175	BT(ED)-28	Mogul	24,000	211	8.3125	127	5	45	7950	7850	7900			
175	H39KC-175/DX	BT(ED)-28	Mogul	24,000	211	8.3125	127	5	49				8500		8550
175	H39KC-R175/WDX/(N)	BT(ED)-28	Mogul	24,000	211	8.3125	127	5	40					7000	
175	H39BP-175DX 160° V WFL	R-40	Medium	24,000	191	7.5	—	—	33				5800		5725

Watts	Designation	Bulb	Base	Rated life (hr)					lm/W						
175	H39BM-175	R-40	Medium	24,000	191	7.5	—	—	34	5700		6100			
250	H37KB-250	E(BT)(ED)-28	Mogul	24,000	211	8.3125	77	5	47	11,200	12,000	12100			
250	H37KC-250/DX	E(BT)(ED)-28	Mogul	24,000	211	8.3125	77	5	51				13,000		12,550
250	H37KC-R250/WDX(N)	E(BT)(ED)-28	Mogul	24,000	211	8.3125	77	5	45					11333	
400	H33CD-400	E(BT)(ED)-37	Mogul	24,000	292	11.5	108	7	52	21,000	20,500	21000			
400	H33GL-400/DX	E(BT)(ED)-37	Mogul	24,000	292	11.5	108	7	57				23,000		22,750
400	H33GL-R400/DX(N)	E(BT)(ED)-37	Mogul	24,000	292	11.5	108	7	53					21,250	
400	H33AR-400	T-16	Mogul	12,000	279	11	108	7	49		19,500				
400[a]	H33DN-400/DX Reflector	R-52	Mogul	24,000	298	11.75	—	—	55						22,000
400[a]	H33FS-400/DX Reflector WFL	R-60	Mogul	24,000	257	10.125	—	—	39						15,500
400[c]	H33GL-400/DX/BT	BT-37	Mogul	24,000	292	11.5	178	7	58						23,000
400[c]	H33DN-400/DX	R-57	Mogul	24,000	324	12.75	—	—	58						23,000
700	H35ND-700/DX	BT-46	Mogul	24,000	364	14.3125	241	9.5	60						42,000
1000	H34GW-1000/DX	BT-56	Mogul	24,000	383	15.0625	241	9.5	62						62,000
1000	H36GV-1000	BT-56	Mogul	24,000	383	15.0625	241	9.5	57	57,000					
1000	H36GW-1000DX	BT-56	Mogul	24,000	383	15.0625	241	9.5	63						63,000
1000[a]	H36 — 1000DX Reflector I.F.	R-80	Mogul	24,000	352	13.875	—	—	43						43,000
B. Mercury (self-extinguishing)															
100	H38JA-T100/DX	ED(ET)-23½	Mogul	24,000	191	7.5	127	5	38				3700		3950
175	H39KC-T175/DX	E(BT)(ED)-28	Mogul	24,000	211	8.31225	127	5	44				7700		7700
250	H37KC-T250/DX	E(BT)(ED)-28	Mogul	24,000	211	8.31225	127	5	46				11,200		11,200
400	H33GL-T400/DX	E(BT)(ED)-37	Mogul	24,000	292	11.5	178	7	50				20,000		20,000
1000	H36GW-T1000/DX	BT-56	Mogul	24,000	391	15.375	241	9.5	55				55,450		55,450

*The life and light output ratings of mercury vapor lamps are based on their use with ballasts that provide proper operating characteristics. Ballasts that do not provide proper electrical values may substantially reduce either lamp life, light output or both. Unless otherwise noted, ratings apply to operation on ac circuits.

†All bulbs are made from heat-resistant glass.

‡Lamp life shown is for vertical operation unless otherwise noted.

§Lamp efficacy; lumen output and beam candlepower are the average values of all products submitted.

[a]General Electric.

[b]Sylvania.

[c]Philips.

Fig. 6-123. Self-Ballasted Mercury Lamps Used for General Lighting*

Watts	ANSI No. and other description	Bulb	Bulb finish	Base	Rated lumens† Initial (100 h)	Rated lumens† Mean	Rated life (h)‡	Max. overall length (mm)	Max. overall length (in.)	Light center length (mm)	Light center length (in.)	Nominal lumens† 4000K (DX)b CRI 40 +	Nominal lumens† Coated 3200-3300K N(WDX)b,c CRI 50 +	Nominal lumens† Coated 3700-3900K DXa,c CRI 50 +
160c,d	B87YL-160	E-23(E-23½)	—	Medium	2800	2250	12,000	178	7	116	$4\frac{9}{16}$		2800	
160a,d	B87YM-160 120V	E-24	Phosphor	Med. NPBB	2300	1600	12,000	178	7	116	$4\frac{9}{16}$			2300
160c	B87YR-160	PAR-38	—	Med. Skt.	—	—	12,000	168	$6\frac{5}{8}$	—	—			
160c	B87YS-160 Reflector flood	R-40	Inside frosted	Medium	1970	—	12,000	178	7	—	—		1970	
160d	B87YT-160	R-40	—	Medium	—	—	12,000	184	$7\frac{1}{4}$	132	$5\frac{3}{16}$			
250a	B94HM-250 120 V	E-28	Phosphor	Med. NPBB	5000	3750	12,000	216	$8\frac{1}{2}$	146	$5\frac{3}{4}$			5000
250c	—	E-28	—	Medium	5990	—	12,000	216	$8\frac{1}{2}$	132	$5\frac{3}{16}$		5990	
250a,d	B94HP-250 120V	E-28	Phosphor	Mog. NPBB	5000	3750	12,000	216	$8\frac{1}{2}$	146	$5\frac{3}{4}$			5000
250c	—	E-28	—	Mogul	5990	—	12,000	211	$8\frac{5}{16}$	—	—		5990	
250c	B94HZ-250 Reflector flood	R-40	—	Mogul	3450	—	12,000	187	$7\frac{3}{8}$	—	—		3540	
250d	B94HD-250	PS-30	—	Medium	4800	—	12,000	205	$8\frac{1}{16}$	—	—			
250d	B94HE-250	PS-35	—	Medium	4800	—	14,000	227	$8\frac{15}{16}$	—	—			
250d	B94HG-250	PS-35	—	Mogul	4800	—	14,000	238	$9\frac{3}{8}$	—	—			
250d	B94HN-250 Reflector	R-40	—	Medium	3540	—	14,000	184	$7\frac{1}{4}$	—	—			
450a,c,d	B75JB-450 220-230 V	BT-37	—	Mogul	11,800	—	16,000	292	$11\frac{1}{2}$	—	—			
450d	B75JD-450 220-230 V	BT-37	—	Mogul	12,000	—	16,000	292	$11\frac{1}{2}$	—	—			
450d	B75JF-450 220-230 V	PS-40	—	Mogul	12,200	—	16,000	248	$9\frac{3}{4}$	—	—			
450d	B75JK-450 220-230 V	R-60	—	Mogul	—	—	16,000	260	$10\frac{1}{4}$	—	—			
750a,d	B78YF-750 120 V	R-57	Phosphor	Mog. NPBB	14,000	11,200	16,000	324	$12\frac{3}{4}$	213	$8\frac{3}{8}$			14,000
750a,d	Reflector FL. 240 V	R-57	Phosphor	Mog. NPBB	17,300	15,400	16,000	324	$12\frac{3}{4}$	213	$8\frac{3}{8}$			17,300
1250d	BT-56 DX 200-280 V	BT-56	—	Mogul	40,500	—	16,000	388	$15\frac{9}{32}$	—	—			

*All values are the average of manufactures submitted data.

†Values apply at lower voltage when two different voltage lamps are listed.

‡Life expectancy dependent on line voltage.

a General Electric

b Sylvania.

c Philips.

d Duro-Test.

Fig. 6-124. Characteristics of Typical Low-Pressure Mercury Sources of Ultraviolet Energy

A. Near Ultraviolet Output (320 – 420 nm)

Nominal lamp watts	Lamp and other description	Bulb type	Base	Rated life (h)*	Relative black light energy (100 h)†	Nominal overall length‡ (mm)	Nominal overall length‡ (in.)	Useful arc length (mm)	Useful arc length (in.)	Diameter (mm)	Diameter (in.)	Minimum rms starting voltage§	Lamp volts (V)	Lamp arc current (A)
Preheat start lamps														
4	F4T5/BL	T-5	Min. Bipost	6000	4	152	6	64	2.5	16	$\frac{5}{8}$	120	29	0.17
4	F4T5/BLB (blue glass)	T-5	Min. Bipost	6000	3	152	6	64	2.5	16	$\frac{5}{8}$	120	29	0.17
6	F6T5BL	T-5	Min. Bipost	7500	7	229	9	140	5.5	16	$\frac{5}{8}$	120	42	0.16
6	F6T5/BLB (blue glass)	T-5	Min. Bipost	7500	6	229	9	140	5.5	16	$\frac{5}{8}$	120	42	0.16
8	F8T5/BL	T-5	Min. Bipost	7500	13	305	12	216	8.5	16	$\frac{5}{8}$	120	57	0.145
8	F8T5/BLB (blue glass)	T-8	Min. Bipost	7500	8	305	12	216	8.5	16	$\frac{5}{8}$	120	57	0.145
9	PL9W/10 (compact)	PL-9	G23	10,000	—	154	$6\frac{1}{2}$	—	—	—	—	—	59	0.18
12	F12T8/350BL/PH	T-8	Med. Bipost	7500	—	305	12	—	—	25	1	—	—	—
15	F15T8/BL	T-8	Med. Bipost	7500	25	457	18	330	13	25	1	120	55	0.305
15	F15T8/BLB (blue glass)	T-8	Med. Bipost	7500	20	457	18	330	13	25	1	120	55	0.305
20	F20T12/BL	T-12	Med. Bipost	9000	42	610	24	483	19	38	$1\frac{1}{2}$	120	56	0.38
20	F20T12/BLB (blue glass)	T-12	Med. Bipost	9000	31	610	24	483	19	38	$1\frac{1}{2}$	120	56	0.38
22	F15 & 12″/350BL/500/PH	T-12	Med. Bipost	—	—	381	15	—	—	38	$1\frac{1}{2}$	—	—	—
25	F25T8/350BL/18″	T-8	Med. Bipost	—	—	457	18	—	—	25	1	—	—	—
30	F30T8/BL	T-8	Med. Bipost	7500	65	914	36	787	31	25	1	176	98	0.355
30	F30T8/BLB (blue glass)	T-8	Med. Bipost	7500	54	914	36	787	31	25	1	176	98	0.355
32	F18T12/350BL/700PH	T-12	Med. Bipost	—	—	457	18	—	—	38	$1\frac{1}{2}$	—	—	—
U-shaped lamps (preheat start)														
20/25	F20T12/BL/U/3	T-12	Med. Bipost	9000	—	305	12	—	—	—	—	—	—	—
35/40	F35T12/BL/U/3	T-12	Med. Bipost	7500	—	305	12	—	—	38	$1\frac{1}{2}$	—	—	—
40	F40BL/U/3	T-12	Med. Bipost	12,000	—	610	24	—	—	38	$1\frac{1}{2}$	—	—	—
Rapid start lamps														
22	Blacklight circline	T-8	4 pin	12,000	—	203	8	—	—	29	$1\frac{1}{8}$	—	—	—
40	F40BL	T-12	Med. Bipost	12,000	—	1219	48	—	—	38	$1\frac{1}{2}$	—	—	—
40	F40BLB (blue glass)	T-12	Med. Bipost	20,000	—	1219	48	—	—	38	$1\frac{1}{2}$	—	—	—
85	F72T12/BL/HO	T-12	RDC	12,000	—	1829	72	—	—	38	$1\frac{1}{2}$	—	—	—

*At 3 hours per start. Useful life may be less, depending on the requirements of the application.
†Relative value of 100 equals 100 flcrens.
‡One lamp plus two standard lampholders.
§Minimum required rms voltage between lamp electrodes for reliable starting from 10°C (50°F) to 45°C (110°F).

B. Germicidal Ultraviolet Output (253.7 nm)

Nominal Lamp watts	Lamp, bulb and cathode type, and other description	Glass transmission below 200 nm*	Base	Rated life (h)†	Approx. 254 nm UV output (100 hrs.) (mW/cm² at one meter)	Nominal overall length‡ (mm)	(in.)	Useful arc length (mm)	(in.)	Diameter (mm)	(in.)	Approx. lamp voltage (V)	Approx. 254 nm UV output (W)	Lamp arc current (A)
Preheat start lamps														
4	G4T4/1 U shape (hot)	—	4 pin	4000	8	146	$5\frac{3}{4}$	152	6	13	$\frac{1}{2}$	52	0.6	0.11
4.5	G4T5 T-5 (hot)	Very low	Min. Bipost	—	5.4	140	$5\frac{1}{2}$	64	2.5	16	$\frac{5}{8}$	120	0.5	—
6	G6T5 T-5 (hot)	Very low	Min. Bipost	—	11	210	$8\frac{9}{32}$	140	5.5	16	$\frac{5}{8}$	120	1.2	—
7.2	G8T5 T-5 (hot)	Very low	Min. Bipost	6000	16	305	12	216	8.5	16	$\frac{5}{8}$	57	1.4	0.17
9	TUV PLS 9 W (compact)	Very low	2 pin G23	—	—	210	$8\frac{9}{32}$	—	—	10	$\frac{13}{32}$	60	2.5	—
15	G15T8 T-8	Very low	Med. Bipost	7500	35	457	18	356	14	26	1	56	3.3	0.3
25	G25T8 T-8	—	Med. Bipost	7500	—	457	18	—	—	26	1	—	—	—
30	G30T8 T-8	Very low	Med. Bipost	7500	80	914	36	813	32	26	1	100	8.4	0.36
36	TUV 36 W T-8	Very low	Med. Bipost	—	—	1200	$44\frac{1}{4}$	—	—	26	1	103	14	—
55	TUV 55 W HO T-8	Very low	Med. Bipost	—	—	900	$35\frac{7}{16}$	—	—	26	1	83	17	—
75	TUC 75 W HO T-8	Very low	Med. Bipost	—	—	1200	$47\frac{1}{4}$	—	—	26	1	108	25	—
115	TUV 115 W VHOT-12	Very low	Med. Bipost	—	—	1200	$47\frac{1}{4}$	—	—	38	$1\frac{1}{2}$	92	32	—
Instant start lamps														
3.8	G4S11 S-11 Bulb (ozone)	Very high	Inter. screw	6000	1.5	57	$2\frac{1}{4}$	10	0.375	35	$1\frac{3}{8}$	24	0.1	0.35
65	G64T6 T-6 hot	Very low	Sgl. Pin	7500	200	1626	64	1470	58	19	$\frac{3}{4}$	180	25	0.425

*Low pressure mercury discharges generate some energy at 184.9 nm. In most lamps this is filtered out by the glass bulb. Germicidal lamps are made with several different glass types to allow transmission of more or less of this short wave UV energy. UV at wavelengths below 200 nm can convert oxygen (O_2) to ozone (O_3). Ozone is a toxic gas even in relatively low concentrations and care should be taken in using germicidal lamps that transmit large amounts of this radiation.

†At 8 hours per start except for the G4T4/1 lamp which is at 3 hours per start.

‡With double-ended lamps, MOL includes two standard lampholders.

Luminaires

7

A luminaire is a complete lighting unit consisting of one or more lamps (light sources) together with the parts designed to distribute the light, to position and protect the lamps and to connect the lamps to the power supply. This chapter primarily deals with the parts other than lamps. For the latter see chapter 6, Light Sources. Also, for luminaire photometric data for calculation purposes, such as coefficients of utilization, see chapter 9, Lighting Calculations.

CONSIDERATIONS IN DESIGNING AND SELECTING LUMINAIRES[1]

Some of the factors to be considered in luminaire design and selection include: (1) codes and standards relative to their construction and installation (see chapter 14, Codes and Regulations), (2) their physical and environmental characteristics, (3) electrical and mechanical considerations, (4) thermal properties, (5) safety and (6) economic factors.

Luminaire Characteristics

The luminaire and light source to be employed for a given application depend upon many factors. In addition to the illumination aspects (such as luminance, glare, uniformity, illuminance), consideration should be given to appearance, color of light, heating effect, noise level, efficiency, life and economics.

Reflector Design Considerations

Most lamps do not act as point sources in the size of reflectors into which they are placed. Physically large arcs or coated bulbs require larger reflectors to control light to the same degree as obtained from small arcs or sources. Generally, the larger the source, the larger the reflector required for equivalent control.

Secondary effects of reflector or housing design can often be detrimental to the performance of a luminaire. As an example, if reflected energy is concentrated on the lamp, lamp parts may fail or reduced lamp life may be experienced; if the beam is concentrated on a lens front, the glass may fail from thermal stress.

When fluorescent lamps are used in confining luminaires, two effects take place. The buildup of heat in the lamp compartment raises the bulb wall temperature, which may reduce the light output. See chapter 6, Light Sources. As lamps are moved closer together, a mutual heating occurs and, beyond this, light which might have been redirected out of the luminaire is trapped between lamps, or between lamps and reflector. Both conditions lower luminaire efficiency.

Lamp Position and Replacement

The lamp operating position is important. Many lamps are designed only for base up, base down or some other specified operating position. Ignoring such limitations will normally result in unsatisfactory lamp performance, reduced lamp life or both.

A basic consideration is that of easy lamp insertion and removal. Recognition should be made of possible lamp changing devices that might be used, and space should be allowed for this purpose.

Effects of Radiant Energy

Consideration must be given to the effects of lamp energy in the nonvisible regions of the electromagnetic spectrum on luminaire materials and performance. Some plastics and rubber materials, for example, can be altered by ultraviolet (UV) energy. Some reflector materials are excellent for visible light but absorb infrared (IR), thus creating thermal problems.

If the intended lamp can present a hazard to people or objects under some conditions of operation (for example, some high-intensity discharge lamps operated with broken envelopes), protective devices which switch the lamp off should be designed into the luminaire or lamp.

Lamp Wattages

Lamp dimension is rarely the sole criterion in determining luminaire size. Careful consideration must be given to heat dissipation to ensure normal lamp life and luminaire performance.

Luminaire Efficiency

This is normally a function of physical configuration and the selection of materials used. It should be recognized that many materials will change to some extent with use.

Appearance

The luminaire designer must coordinate technical, safety and economic considerations with the final appearance. Where the lighting is primarily functional, performance has maximum importance. Design efforts will probably be concentrated on reflectors, refractors and shielding elements.

Decorative luminaires are often selected because of their appearance. In this case, not unlike a piece of jewelry, they may serve to complement or accent a decorative scheme. It may be desirable to sacrifice optimum performance in order to attain pleasing proportions and shapes. Sometimes both can be coordinated into a single luminaire.

Color, texture and form all play an important role in the attempt to achieve either of the above goals.

Glare

Light sources and luminaires are potential sources of discomfort and disability glare. The degree of brightness control to be designed into a luminaire depends upon its intended use and the luminous environment within which it will be used. Frequently, design compromises are required between visual comfort, utilization and esthetics.

Computational and measurement systems exist to evaluate the potential glare from luminaires. See chapter 3, Vision and Perception, and chapter 9, Lighting Calculations. They establish criteria commonly used to guide the luminaire designer in determining acceptable limits of maximum and average luminances. A thorough understanding of the principles involved is essential.

The problem of glare and its control should be recognized for both interior and exterior luminaires.

Thermal Distribution

The integration of luminaires into the air handling and architectural aspects of a building greatly influences their basic construction. Some materials used in luminaires can be good reflectors of light and good absorbers of IR radiation. For reflectance data see figure 7-1.

Ventilation and Circulation

Air movement through the lamp compartment of a luminaire may result in the lowering of light output due to accumulation of dust and dirt, or it may main-

Fig. 7-1. Properties of Materials used in Luminaires (*T* = Percent Transmittance and *R* = Percent Reflectance at the Selected Wavelength)

Material	Visible Wavelengths						Near Infrared Wavelengths						Far Infrared Wavelengths							
	400 nm		500 nm		600 nm		1000 nm		2000 nm		4000 nm		7000 nm		10,000 nm		12,000 nm		15,000 nm	
	R	T	R	T	R	T	R	T	R	T	R	T	R	T	R	T	R	T	R	T
Specular aluminum	87	0	82	0	86	0	97	0	94	0	88	0	84	0	27	0	16	0	14	0
Diffuse aluminum	79	0	75	0	84	0	86	0	95	0	88	0	81	0	68	0	49	0	44	0
White synthetic enamel	48	0	85	0	84	0	90	0	45	0	8	0	4	0	4	0	2	0	9	0
White porcelain enamel	56	0	84	0	83	0	76	0	38	0	4	0	2	0	22	0	8	0	9	0
Clear glass-3.2 millimeters (.125 inch)	8	91	8	92	7	92	5	92	23	90	2	0	0	0	24	0	6	0	5	0
Opal glass-3.9 millimeters (.155 inch)	28	36	26	39	24	42	12	59	16	71	2	0	0	0	24	0	6	0	5	0
Clear acrylic-3.1 millimeters (.120 inch)	7	92	7	92	7	92	4	90	8	53	3	0	2	0	2	0	3	0	3	0
Clear polystyrene-3.1 millimeters (.120 inch)	9	87	9	89	8	90	6	90	11	61	4	0	4	0	4	0	4	0	5	0
White acrylic-3.2 millimeters (.125 inch)	18	15	34	32	30	34	13	59	6	40	2	0	3	0	3	0	3	0	3	0
White polystyrene-3.1 millimeters (.120 inch)	26	18	32	29	30	30	22	48	9	35	3	0	3	0	3	0	3	0	4	0
White vinyl-0.76 millimeters (.030 inch)	8	72	8	78	8	76	6	85	17	75	3	0	2	0	3	0	3	0	3	0

Measurements in the visible range were made with a General Electric recording spectrophotometer. The reflectance was measured with a black velvet backing behind the samples. Measurements at 1000 and 2000 nm were made with a Beckman DK2-R spectrophotometer. Measurements at wavelengths greater than 2000 nm were made with a Perkin-Elmer spectrophotometer. Reflectances in the infrared region are relative to evaporative aluminum on glass.

tain the lumen output by the cleaning action of air moving past the lamps.

In fluorescent heat transfer luminaires a reverse airflow is sometimes used to trap dirt and dust before it enters the lamp compartment. Consideration must also be given to the effect air currents have on bulb wall temperature, since this affects light output. See chapter 6, Light Sources. Ambient temperature affects the striking voltage of all discharge lamps.[2]

Acoustics

Undesirable sound generation is sometimes a problem with fluorescent or other discharge lamps ballasted with electromagnetic or solid-state devices. Luminaires can transmit this sound to the rest of the space and, in some cases, add luminaire vibration to it. Large, flat surfaces and loose parts amplify the sound. Steps taken to minimize transmission of sound from the ballast to the luminaire may affect heat transfer characteristics.

Where luminaires are used as air supply or air return devices, the air-controlling surfaces should be designed with full consideration for air noise. In this case, there are well-accepted criteria for permissible sound levels.[3, 4]

Some ballast hum is inevitable in view of the electromagnetic principle involved, and each ballast type has a different sound rating. Where low noise levels are necessary, consideration should be given to mounting the ballasting equipment remotely or using light sources having inherently quieter operation. Remote locations of ballasts may involve complications of wiring, voltage, thermal considerations and code restrictions. See the National Electrical Code (NEC)[5] for details.

Vibration

Incandescent lamps are normally made smaller for vibration service (up to 150 W) and for rough service (up to 500 W). Where more severe vibration is present or larger wattages are required, vibration-resisting sockets or shock-absorbing mountings may be used. For high bay mounting on a building's steel structure, a spring steel loop of proper size and tension for the luminaire's weight usually solves even the most difficult vibration problems.

High-intensity discharge lamps are less fragile than most incandescent lamps and will consequently stand more vibration. If vibration is severe, then shocks absorbers should be used.

For fluorescent luminaires that may be installed in vibration areas, spring-loaded lampholders should be used, rather than those of the twist type. There are conditions of very high frequencies, such as turbine deck areas, where special lampholders may be required.

Radiation Interference

Electromagnetic radiation from gaseous discharge lamps, especially of the fluorescent type, and auxiliary components such as starters and phase control devices may be sufficient to cause interference with nearby radios, television receivers, sound amplifying equipment, electrocardiograph devices, sensitive electronic equipment and certain military radar and tracking equipment. This interference is transmitted in two ways: (1) by direct radiation through the face of the luminaire and (2) by conduction through ballast and supply line.

To eliminate direct electromagnetic radiation the luminaire should be entirely metal enclosed, except for the light-transmitting opening. Normal tolerances on the fit of parts are acceptable, but there should be no large open holes in any of the metal parts, and the electrical service should be brought in through grounded conduit or shielded cable. Conducted interference can be isolated by proper line filters located at the luminaire.

Life and Maintenance

The life of any luminaire is dependent primarily upon its ability to withstand the environmental conditions in which it is installed. To ensure reasonable life, appropriate treatment of all materials should be considered. Where conditions are such that electrolytic action may occur, the use of dissimilar metals and high-copper-content alloys of aluminum should be avoided where possible.

Maintenance may be a problem unless proper consideration is given to minimizing luminaire light loss factors at the time the luminaire is designed. Ventilation, gasketing and filtering, in addition to the selection of materials to diminish the effect of dust and dirt, should be utilized. Ease of relamping and of access to auxiliary components are important considerations as well.

Environmental Conditions

Ambient Temperature. The most obvious influence of ambient temperature is its effect on the starting and the operating characteristics of fluorescent lamps. The effect of high and low temperatures on other luminaire components should also be considered. Excess heat generated by internal heat sources such as lamps, and in some cases ballasts, must be transferred to the environment.

Surface-mounted luminaires and recessed equipment, especially when operating in nonventilated plenums, are often exposed to high ambient temperatures. Some industrial areas may be 65° C (150° F), or even higher. Refrigerated storage areas, and in some climates unheated storage areas, attain temperatures of $-29°$ C ($-20°$ F) or lower. Proper design and component selection will result in luminaires that operate efficiently through these extremes.

Incandescent Filament Lamps. An incandescent filament operates at a very high temperature, near $2620°$ C ($4750°$ F) for a 200-W lamp. Normal changes in ambient temperature will not appreciably affect its light output or life.

Fluorescent Lamps. The performance of fluorescent lamps is affected by ambient temperature and convection. See chapter 6, Light Sources. In totally enclosed interior luminaires, fluorescent lamps usually operate at temperatures above those for optimum light output. Ventilation and other means of heat dissipation are helpful and should be considered.

High-Intensity Discharge Lamps. Ambient temperature is not normally a significant factor in the light output of conventional high-intensity discharge lamps. Starting requirements are sometimes affected at low temperatures, and ballasts meeting such requirements must be used. Special auxiliary equipment also may be required at elevated temperatures. The relationships between temperature and service life (wiring and components) must be considered. There are Underwriters Laboratories (UL), NEC and Canadian Electrical Code (CEC)[8] requirements which apply in some cases.

Radiation. Certain areas of buildings, especially laboratories with specialized equipment, may emit radiation which will have a detrimental effect on the luminaire. These are special cases, and the possible effects of fading or color change of paints, and degradation of plastics should be studied. In these cases, special consideration should be given to selection of luminaire materials.

Air Movement. Outdoor luminaires should be designed to withstand wind loading. In indoor locations, such as subway stations or small offices, the air pressure on a fluorescent troffer lens or a luminous ceiling component can dislodge a diffuser when doors are suddenly opened.

Miscellaneous Environmental Effects. A complete listing of the possible effects of the environment on luminaire design is impossible. The designer, however, should be alert to the possibilities of many others not specifically covered, such as the effect of UV energy on outdoor components, thermal shock, extremes in humidity and foreign substances in the atmosphere.

Electrical Considerations

Sockets and lampholders, wire, ballasts and other controls are parts of electrical circuits of luminaires. All gas discharge lamps require some form of ballast or control equipment to provide adequate starting voltage and to limit the current after the lamp has started.

Lamp Circuits. Each type of lamp requires a specific ballast circuit. See chapter 6, Light Sources.

Ballast Quality. Rated lamp life and light output for fluorescent and HID lamps are directly dependent on the ballast's ability to meet specified limits set by the American National Standards Institute (ANSI) standards. Ballasts not meeting ANSI standards may reduce lamp life as much as 50% and light output by more than 30%.

The life of ballasts made with $105°$ C (Class A) insulation is approximately 45,000 h (continuous operation not exceeding $105°$ C). Ballast coil temperatures will not exceed the $105°$ C rating in properly designed ballasts when luminaires maintain a maximum ballast case temperature of $90°$ C. Other factors affecting ballast life are input voltage, luminaire heat dissipation characteristics, luminaire mounting and the environment. Field data indicate a 12-yr median ballast life for a duty cycle of 16 h per day, 6 days per week, or 5000 h per year. This life rating assumes that because of ballast warmup time, the ballast only operates at peak temperatures for 12 h out of the 16-h duty cycle, or 3750 h per year.

Ballast safety standards are set by UL. Case temperatures of fluorescent lamp ballasts are limited to $90°$ C with the ballast mounted in a luminaire and the luminaire operated in an ambient temperature of $25°$ C. Ballasts for HID lamps have limits that apply to the coil and core temperatures, depending upon the insulation system used; that is, whether it is rated for 105, 130 or $180°$ C.

Excessive ballast operating temperatures cause ballast insulation deterioration, resulting in short life and possible activation of the ballast protective device. A convenient rule of thumb is that every $10°$ C increment above $90°$ C results in a 50% reduction in life. Luminaire design should limit heating within the luminaire.

Thermally Protected Ballasts. The NEC requires that thermally protected ballasts be used in some fluorescent and HID luminaires. For fluorescent lamp ballasts, UL requires that the protector open so that maximum ballast case temperature does not exceed $90°$ C when the luminaire is in service. Protected ballasts for fluorescent lamps are called *Class P* ballasts and are listed by UL as such. All new fluorescent luminaires must use UL-listed Class P ballasts in order to carry the UL label. The intent is to limit the maximum temperature a ballast case can reach in a luminaire under any condition. All recessed HID ballasts, both integral and remote, must be thermally protected.

High-Frequency Operation. Most fluorescent lamps can be operated on higher frequencies, resulting in increased luminous efficacy (see chapter 6). As a rule, high-frequency ballasts are smaller, lighter and more efficient.

Low-Temperature Operation. Fluorescent and HID lamps require higher open-circuit voltages for low-temperature starting. Low-temperature ballasts should be used where ambient temperatures are below 10° C.

Sockets and Lampholders. The ratings of voltage, current and wattage should not be exceeded for any socket or lampholder. Limitations also usually exist for operations. Specific consideration should be given to the following:

1. The UL or Canadian Standards Association (CSA) listing and ratings should be followed for the specific application of any socket or lampholder.
2. The materials used for contacts and screw shells, such as aluminum, copper, brass, nickel, stainless steel, silver or plated metals and their alloys, will limit the operating temperature, wattage and current during use.
3. The metallic, porcelain, plastic, or other nonmetallic housings have temperature limits that affect usage.
4. Where high voltage or starting pulses are required in lamp operation, the lampholder or socket, as well as associated wire, should be rated for these voltages or pulses.
5. High temperatures occur with some lamps, such as tungsten halogen, and the wire, contacts and housing should be rated for the temperatures that occur during lamp operation.
6. Spring tension at lamp contacts may deteriorate under excessive temperatures or abuse, causing contact loss and deterioration, and resulting in socket failure. Improper seating of lamps into a socket, as well as vibrations, can also cause arcing and contact deterioration. Arcing of lamp base pins, screw shells and other lamp or socket contacts can be detected through the burning or pitting of the material. Any lamps or sockets found with such deterioration should be replaced.
7. Wet, damp or hazardous environment applications, as well as usage in outdoor, mining, stage, or photographic locations, may require special consideration for sockets and lampholders.

Wire. The ratings of voltage and current should not be exceeded in the use of any wire. The material used for the conductor(s) and insulation may limit wire application, both indoors and outdoors. Specific considerations should be given to the following:

1. The local, state and national electric codes designate types of wire and their usage in various applications. Further limits are designated in UL and CSA standards for wire in specific luminaires.
2. Some common limitations include:
   a. Wire smaller than no. 18 American Wire Gauge (AWG) may not be used for line circuits of 120 V or higher.
   b. Luminaire wires have designations of 300, 600 or 1000 V, and for some special applications, higher-voltage wire may be required.
   c. Wire temperature designations range from 60 to 200° C.
   d. Some applications require stranded wire, especially where it must flex.
   e. Nickel-plated conductors are common in high-temperature applications.
   f. Grounded cord sets are common.
   g. When luminaires are not wired through metallic conduit, a metallic luminaire should be grounded using acceptable ground wire.
   h. Users and specifiers should be familiar with electric codes, requirements for which include the use of at least no. 14 AWG wire for the supply leads of a recessed luminaire, despite a low-current requirement.

Starters and Ignitors. Fluorescent, HID and specialty arc lamps may be operated on circuits that include starters and ignitors. They provide voltage pulses to start lamps, or a time delay to heat cathodes prior to lamp starting. They can also disconnect lamps from the circuit when the lamp fails. Accessibility is necessary for any that are replaceable or contain an element such as a spark gap that may fail and require replacement. Temperature limits must be observed for starters and ignitors, and they must be used only with the lamps and ballasts designated for them. The various circuits and lamp starter and ignitor requirements are found in chapter 6, Light Sources.

Mechanical Considerations

Tolerances. It is necessary to establish suitable dimensional tolerances for both the component parts and the final assembly. This includes allowances for the different rates of thermal expansion of the various parts. An industry standard[9] defines tolerances of recessed fluorescent luminaires. Surface- and pendant-mounted luminaires may have less critical tolerances. When using recessed luminaires, availability of plenum space should be considered.

Strength. All luminaires should have housings of sufficient rigidity to withstand normal handling and installation. Luminaires intended for outdoor use should incorporate mounting and design features suitable to withstand high winds and rain and snow accumulation.

Luminaires recessed in poured concrete should have an enclosure of suitable strength, tightness and rigidity for the application.

Surface-mounted luminaires should be strong enough so that they will not excessively distort when mounted on uneven ceilings.

Suspended luminaires should have adequate strength to limit vertical sag between supports as well as lateral distortion and twist. Provision must be made for attachment of supports at suitable locations.

Local conditions, such as in earthquake areas, sometimes require conformity with special local codes.

Component Support. Lampholders and sockets should be fixed in place to prevent movement and to maintain good lamp contact in luminaires with double-ended fluorescent, tungsten-halogen or HID lamps. To hold large, high-wattage incandescent and HID lamps, gripping sockets are often helpful. Large horizontally operated HID mogul base lamps benefit from the use of an end support. Ballasts should be securely fastened to the luminaire housing for good thermal contact. Door glasses, lenses and refractors should be securely fastened to withstand the effects of wind, rain and shock.

Mounting. Mounting components should satisfy the requirements of UL, CSA, local codes and end-use environmental conditions. Tamper-proof fastenings may be required in public areas as well as in correctional institutions and mental hospitals. Wire guards may be required around exposed lamps in accessible locations. Local codes should be considered with regard to power supply, continuous row wiring and grounding of the luminaire. Instructions and warnings should be marked in a readily discernible and permanent manner. The text and physical dimensions may be governed by code requirements.

Maintenance. Ease of maintenance is an important consideration. Instructions for maintenance and correct lamping should be provided to prevent luminaire damage and ensure performance. Electrical components should be replaceable without removing the luminaire from its mounting. Where ceiling plenums are not otherwise accessible, provision must be made for access through the luminaire to splice boxes that connect to the branch circuit.

Size. The size of a luminaire is usually controlled by components such as lamps, ballasts and reflectors.

Mounting limitations and building modules can also limit the size.

Thermal Considerations

The temperature of a luminaire will be affected by the lamp efficacy, wattage and type. Ballasts and transformers will also affect the temperature, as will the luminaire's environment. Finally, the heat-dissipating properties of the luminaire itself will affect its temperature.

Very high or low ambient temperatures may cause electrical components to fail. For example, contact of hot glass with cold air or water may result in breakage, and excess heat may cause thermoplastics to distort. Satisfactory performance at the luminaire interior temperature is a major consideration in selecting components and finishes.

Higher than nominal line voltages usually cause higher temperatures within electrical components. Lower voltages do not necessarily produce lower temperatures.

Metal components and their finishes may be affected by temperature within a luminaire. Thought must also be given to metals as conductors of heat either to or from component parts.

Glass and plastic components should be very carefully chosen to prevent cracking, shattering, deformation or other deterioration. This may be either or both long and short term.

Expansion or contraction of components due to thermal changes should be considered. Different coefficients of expansion between materials in close contact can lead to serious problems.

Safety Considerations

The need for attention to safety considerations, particularly in the design stage, cannot be overemphasized. Usually, if the design meets applicable code requirements, it will conform to the following criteria.

Electrical. The safe conversion of electrical energy to light is of utmost importance. In this context important wiring considerations are:

1. Current-carrying capacity of the conductors
2. Insulation rating of the conductors
3. Grounding. In most cases portable lighting equipment is required to have a polarized plug cap such that the screwshell of the socket is neutral or electrically dead. All permanently installed lighting equipment must be provided with grounding to eliminate shock hazard.
4. Temperature rating of the conductors

5. Connections to the junction boxes. Where supplied, connections must be in conformance with local codes.
6. Wire termination color coding in conformance with code requirements for safe field installation
7. Mechanical strength and flexing requirements
8. Safety interlocks. These are advisable in equipment where high open-circuit voltages are present for protection during servicing and are often advisable in damp areas and basements.
9. Fuses and thermal protectors. Where required, these must be included in the design of the equipment.
10. Applicable UL, CSA and ANSI requirements for splices, clearances and sockets
11. Low-voltage units. These should be considered for outdoor applications, and may be required around pools and hot tubs.

Thermal. Luminaires should be designed to meet the requirements of the thermal environment and use. If the unit is to be firmly mounted and will not be handled during operation, it can operate at a higher temperature than a unit which must be held or moved by hand.

The NEC,[5] the Canadian Electrical Code (CEC)[8] and their respective testing laboratories set specific temperature limits for electrical components and critical areas immediately surrounding a luminaire. Much of their testing is performed at an ambient temperature of 25° C (77° F). Code requirements usually do not relate to performance characteristics, and thermal considerations are regarded solely from a safety standpoint.

Ballasts and other auxiliary equipment, sockets and wires have definite safe operating temperature limits defined by UL, CSA, ANSI and the manufacturer. Special electrical components may have to be specified for extreme temperatures.

Ultraviolet. An enclosure and cover glass that absorbs UV radiation may be required for some types of luminaires. Safety interlock switches are required to disconnect the lamps upon opening the luminaire, or upon breakage of the glass cover. Labels should be provided with such luminaires to warn users of this hazard.

Many lamps produce some UV, but of insufficient quantities to require total enclosure and interlock switches. In applications such as museums, the long-term exposure to such UV radiation is considered a hazard (see chapter 17). Most glass or plastic lenses do not transmit significant quantities of UV; hence there is little hazard except for long-term display exposure.

MATERIALS USED IN LUMINAIRES[10]

The materials most commonly used in luminaires are glass, plastics, metals and applied finishes and coatings. Each of these materials is briefly described here. For more specific applications the material manufacturer's data should always be consulted.

Glass

Glass is an inorganic product of fusion which has been cooled to a rigid condition without crystallizing. Chemically, glasses are mixtures of oxides such as silicon, boron, aluminum, lead, sodium, magnesium, calcium and potassium. The chemical and physical properties of glasses, such as color, refractive index, thermal expansion, hardness, corrosion resistance, dielectric strength and elasticity, are obtained by varying the composition, heat treatment and surface finish.

Types. Glasses used in luminaires can be classified into several groups with characteristic properties.

Soda-Lime. Soda-lime glasses (or lime glasses), used for windows, incandescent lamp bulbs, lens covers and cover glasses (tempered), are easily formed when heated, and are usually specified for service where high heat resistance and chemical stability are not required.

Lead-Alkali. Lead-alkali glasses (or lead glasses) are used for fluorescent and HID lamp bulbs, neon sign tubing and certain optical components. They are useful because they are easy to form and have high electrical resistivity and high refractive indices. When formed, however, they will not withstand high temperatures or sudden temperature changes. UV radiation is absorbed by this type of glass.

Borosilicate. Borosilicate glasses are used for refractors, reflectors and sealed beam lamp parts because of their high chemical stability, high heat shock resistance and excellent electrical resistivity. They may be used at higher temperatures (about 230° C) than soda-lime or lead-alkali glasses, but they are not as convenient to fabricate. Near UV radiation is transmitted by this glass.

Aluminosilicate. Aluminosilicate glasses are used where high thermal shock resistance is required. They have good chemical stability, high electrical resistivity, and a high softening temperature enabling use at moderately high temperatures (about 400° C).

Ninety-Six Percent Silica. Ninety-six percent silica glasses are used where high operating temperatures are required. They may be regularly used at 800° C. They are also useful because of their extremely high chemical stability, good transmittance to UV and IR radiation, and resistance to severe thermal shock. They are considerably more expensive than soda-lime and borosilicates, and are more difficult to fabricate. Due to their low coefficient of thermal expansion, these glasses cannot be tempered to increase mechanical strength.

Vitreous Silica. Vitreous silica is a glass composed essentially of SiO_2. It is used for lamp bulbs and arc tubes where high-temperature operation and excellent chemical stability are required. It has high resistance to severe thermal shock, high transmission to UV, visible and IR radiation, and excellent electrical properties. However, due to its low coefficient of thermal expansion, it cannot be tempered to increase mechanical strength. Depending on the method of manufacture, this glass may be known as fused silica, synthetic fused silica or fused quartz.

Manufacturing Techniques. Glass may be formed by several techniques: pressing, blowing, rolling, drawing, centrifugal casting and sagging. These operations may be performed by hand methods or by automatic machines, depending on volume.

After being formed, many glass products must be annealed to relieve excessive stress. Additional finishing operations may be required, such as cutting, grinding, polishing and drilling. Further treatment, such as tempering or chemical strengthening, may be required to obtain the desired physical properties.

The finishes for glass surfaces are varied in nature, depending on the forming technique. The surfaces may be subsequently altered by chemical etching, sandblasting or shot blasting, polish-staining and coating. These operations are used to obtain reflection, control radiation or make a surface electrically conductive.

Functions. The functions of glass in lighting may be divided into the following general categories:

1. Control of light and other radiant energy
2. Protection of the light source
3. Safety
4. Decoration

These functions may be combined for a particular application. Typical properties of glasses are shown in figure 7-2.

Plastics

Plastics generally are high-molecular-weight organic compounds that can be, or have been, changed by application of heat and pressure, or by pressure alone, and once formed retain their shape under normal conditions.

They can be broadly classified as thermoplastic or thermosetting. *Thermoplastic resins* may be repeatedly softened and hardened by heating and cooling. No chemical change takes place during such actions. *Thermosetting resins* cannot be softened and reshaped once they have been heated and set, since their chemical structure has changed. Some of the commercially important thermoplastics are acrylonitrile butadiene styrenes (ABS), acrylics, cellulosics, acetals, fluorocarbons, nylons, polyethylenes, polycarbonates, polypropylenes, polystyrenes and vinyls. In the thermosetting group, resins of importance are epoxies, melamines, phenolics, polyesters, ureas and silicones.

Most resins, whether thermoplastic or thermosetting, can be processed into structural or low-ratio expanded foams. Among the important properties of many foams are stress-free parts, improved insulation characteristics and lighter weight, and sometimes greater strength and toughness than the unfoamed form of the material.

Fillers and reinforcing agents are frequently added to plastics to obtain improved heat resistance, strength, toughness, electrical properties and chemical resistance, and to alter formability characteristics. Some of the fillers and reinforcements in general use are aluminum powder, asbestos, calcium carbonate, clay, cotton fibers, fibrous glass, graphite, nylon, powdered metals and wood flour.

The basic compounds from which today's plastics are produced are obtained from such sources as air, water, natural gas, petroleum, coal and salt. The required chemicals are reacted in large closed vessels under controlled heat and pressure with the aid of catalysts. The resultant solid product is then subjected to such further operations as reduction of particle size, addition of fillers, softeners and modifiers, and conversion of form to granules, pellets and film.

If the plastic surfaces need protection from UV radiation, a UV-resistant film is sometimes laminated onto the surface facing the energy source. UV-resistant clear coatings may also be applied on the interior and exterior surfaces of transparent plastic materials to retard discoloration.

The forming and converting of plastics into end products is a highly specialized field. Some of the more important processes are as follows:

Injection Molding. Fluid plastic is forced under pressure into a controlled-temperature mold.

Compression Molding. Resin is placed in the mold, and the cavity filled by application of heat and pressure.

Blow Molding. A thin cylinder of plastic is placed in a mold and inflated by air pressure to conformity with the mold cavity.

Extrusion. Fluid plastic is forced through a die.

Thermoforming. A sheet, heated to a state of limpness, is draped over a mold and forced into close conformity with it by pressure or vacuum.

Fig. 7-2. Properties of Glasses Used in Luminaires

Type of Glass	Color[a]	Coefficient of Thermal Expansion per °C[b] (× 10^{-7})	Upper Working Temperatures °C(°F) (Mechanical Considerations Only)				Thermal Shock[a,f] Resistance Plates 15 cm × 15 cm × 0.64 cm (6 in × 6 in × 1/4 in) thick	Impact Abrasion Resistance[g]	Density (grams per cc)	Young's Modulus		Poisson's Ratio[h]	Refractive Index (589.3 nm)
			Annealed		Tempered					(10^6 kg/cm²)	(10^6 lb/in²)		
			Normal Service[c,e]	Extreme Limit[d,e]	Normal Service[c,e]	Extreme Limit[d,e]							
Soda-Lime	Clear	85–97	110 (230)	430–460 (806–860)	200–240 (392–464)	250 (482)	50	1.0–1.2	2.47–2.49	0.7–0.71	10–10.2	.24	1.512–1.514
Lead-alkali	Clear	85–91	110 (230)	370–400 (698–752)	220 (428)	240 (464)	45	.56	2.85–3.05	0.61–0.62	8.7–8.9	.22	1.534–1.56
Borosilicate	Clear	32–46	230 (446)	460–490 (860–914)	250–260 (482–500)	250–290 (482–554)	100–150	3.1–3.2	2.13–2.43	0.65–0.66	9.3–9.5	.20	1.474–1.488
Aluminosilicate	Clear	34–52	200 (392)	650 (1202)	400 (752)	450 (842)	100–150	2.0	2.43–2.64	0.87–0.89	12.5–12.7	.25	1.524–1.547
96% Silica	Clear	8	800–900 (1472–1652)	1090–1200 (1994–2192)			1000	3.5–3.53	2.18	0.67	9.6	.18	1.458
Vitreous Silica	Clear	5.5	1000 (1832)	1200 (2192)			1000	3.6	2.2	0.73	10.4	.16	1.458

[a] All glasses can be colored by the addition of metallic oxides that become suspended or dissolved in the parent glass usually without substantially changing its chemical composition or physical properties.
[b] From 0° to 300°C, in/in/°C, or cm/cm/°C.
[c] Normal Service: no breakage from excessive thermal shock is assumed. Glass will be very vulnerable to thermal shock; tests should be made before adopting final designs.
[d] Extreme Limits: depends on the atmosphere in which the material operates.
[e] These data approximate only.
[f] Based on plunging sample into cold water after oven heating. Resistance of 100°C means no breakage if heated to 110°C and plunged into water at 10°C. Tempered samples have over twice the resistance of annealed glass.
[g] Data show relative resistance to sandblasting.
[h] Value applies to only one glass of group.

Spray Coating. A solution or emulsion is sprayed on a prepared surface.

Machining. Solid plastic is shaped by usual wood- or metal-working operations.

Rotational Molding. Resin is charged into a mold rotated in an oven, centrifugal forces distribute the resin, and the heat melts and fuses the charge to the shape of the cavity.

Cold Stamping. Stamping and forming of cold plastic sheet.

Ultrasonic Welding. Bonding of plastics by conversion of sonic vibrations to heat.

Coextrusion. This is performed with a twin-head extruding machine, whereby two compatible plastics are extruded simultaneously to produce a finished profile.

Two-Color Molding. This method uses a twin-head injection molding machine, or two machines and dies, to mold one part and then inject a second material or color into designated areas of the part.

Transfer Molding. A decorating film or ink is placed on a tape, which is spooled through the mold. The tape indexes to the desired position, and the material is then injected into the mold, against the underside of the tape. When the mold opens for ejection of the part, the tape is stripped away, leaving a completed, decorated part.

Secondary operations for molded plastics include vacuum metallizing for reflectors, painting, silk-screening, hot stamping, decorative or protective pad printing, plating for chemical resistance, sonic welding for bonding, laser cutting for hole piercing or machining, and the use of high-pressure water jets for custom fabrication. Dichroic coating can be applied to some plastic materials to produce cold-mirror reflectors.

Important resins and properties of plastics used in lighting are shown in figures 7-3 and 7-4, respectively.

Steel

In the fabrication of lighting equipment, steel serves primarily in a structural capacity. Sheet steel, while having the great strength and low cost needed for a large-volume material, must be processed additionally with platings or applied coatings before it can serve as a light-controlling medium. Many grades and types of sheet steel are available, in a variety of forms.

Sheet steel used in lighting equipment is of three basic types: hot-rolled steel, cold-rolled steel and porcelain enameling sheets.

Hot-rolled steel, because of the rolling process at elevated temperatures, carries an oxide coating (mill scale). It is not normally used where a smooth appearance is desired. The scale can be removed in an acid bath (pickling), but the surface is still somewhat rough.

Fig. 7-3. Uses of Resins in Lighting Applications

Resin	Uses
Thermoplastics	
Acrylics	louvers, formed light diffusers, prismatic lenses, diffusers, film
Cellulosics	sign faces, vacuum formed diffusers, globes, light shades, light supports
Flexible vinyls	gaskets, wire coating
Nylons	electro-mechanical parts, wire insulation, coil forms
Polycarbonates	insulators, globes, diffusers, anti-vandalism street lighting globes
Polyethylenes	(high density)—wire coatings, housings
Polyethylenes	(low density)—formed light diffusers, blow molded globes
Polystyrenes	same as acrylic
Rigid vinyls	formed lighting diffusers, corrugated sheet for luminous ceilings
Thermosetting	
Melamines	switches, insulators
Phenolics	wire connectors, switches, sockets, shades
Polyesters	(glass reinforcing)—shades, reflector housings, diffusers
Ureas	louvers, lamp holders, shades
Filled reinforced plastics	insulators, reflectors, housings, globes, light shades, switch bases

Cold-rolled steel is used primarily because of its smooth surface appearance. It is also available in thinner gauges than hot-rolled steel. It is usually obtained by pickling hot-rolled steel coil and further reducing the thickness without heating.

Porcelain enameling sheets have very low carbon content, in order to prevent mill scale beneath the porcelain coating.

All of these steels are available in several grades and finishes. The types of finishes include galvanized sheet, prepainted sheet, aluminum-clad sheet and plastic-coated sheet. Preplated sheets are also available, the platings including chrome, brass and copper.

Steel sheet used in lighting is often referred to by its thickness, or *gauge*. The metal gauge most commonly used is the Manufacturer's Standard Gauge for Steel Sheets.

Aluminum

Aluminum is a nonferrous, corrosion-resistant, lightweight, nonmagnetic metal having good thermal and electrical conductivity. It is high in the electro-chemical series, but resists attack by either air or water because of the formation of an invisible protective covering of aluminum oxide.

Uses in Lighting. Aluminum is used in lighting for structural parts such as tubes or poles, housings, channels, mechanical parts and trim; and light-controlling surfaces such as reflectors, louvers and decorative surfaces. Aluminum is also used as a reflecting surface

Fig. 7-4. Properties of Plastics Used in Luminaires

Materials	Castings	Compression Moldings	Extrusions	Fiber	Film	Foam	Injection Moldings	Sheet	Reinforced Plastic Moldings	Industrial Laminates	Chemical Resistance	Colorability	Flammability Rating*	Flexibility	High Dielectrics	Low Moisture Absorption	Clarity	Strength and Rigidity	Toughness	Effect of Ultraviolet†	Resistance to Heat °C Continuous
Thermoplastics																					
ABS‡			X				X	X			X	X	HB-VO		X			X	X	NP	60–110
Acetals‡			X				X				X	X	HB		X			X	X	C	80
Acrylics	X		X	X			X	X			X	X	HB				X	X		N	60–90
Acrylic-styrene copolymers			X				X	X			X	X	HB		X	X	X	X		NP-SL	80–95
Cellulose acetates			X	X	X		X	X				X	HB-VO		X		X	X	X	SL	65–105
Cellulose acetate butyrates			X		X		X	X				X	HB		X		X	X	X	NL	60–105
Cellulose propionates			X		X		X	X				X	HB		X		X	X	X	SL	70–105
TFE-fluorocarbons			X		X			X			X		VO		X	X				N	260
Nylons‡			X	X	X		X	X			X		HB-VO		X			X	X	CO	80–150
Polycarbonates‡			X				X				X	X	HB-VO			X		X	X	SL	120
Polyethylenes			X	X	X	X	X	X			X	X	HB-VO	X	X	X		X	X	NP	80–120
Polypropylenes‡			X	X	X		X	X			X	X	HB-VO		X	X		X	X	NP	120–160
Polystyrenes‡	X		X	X	X		X	X			X	X	HB-VO		X		X	X	X§	NP	75–95
Styrene acrylonitrile copolymers‡			X	X			X	X			X	X	HB-VO		X		X	X		NP	80–95
Vinyls	X		X	X	X	X	X	X			X	X	HB-VO	X	X	X		X	X	SL	65–95
Polysulfones			X			X	X				X	X	V1-VO		X			X	X		150–175
Thermosetting Plastics																					
Epoxies	X					X			X	X	X	X	HB-VO		X	X		X		SL	120–290
Melamines		X				X			X	X	X	X	VO		X	X		X	X	SL	100
Phenolics	X	X				X			X	X	X	X	HB-VO		X			X	X	D	120
Polyesters (other than molding compounds)	X			X	X				X	X	X	X	HB-VO		X		X		X	SL	150–210
Polyesters		X					X				X	X	HB-VO		X	X				SL	150–175
Silicones	X	X				X					X	X	HB-VO		X	X				SL-N	315
Ureas		X									X	X	V1-VO							G	75

** For general guidance only—Evaluate suitability of specific compounds upon detailed data from manufacturer.

*Per UL 94. Because of the complexity of flammability ratings, exact information on specific compounds should be obtained from the supplier of the plastic resins.

† NP-needs protection, C-chalks, N-none, SL-slight, NL-nil, CO-colors, D-darkens, G-grays.

‡ Available in glass filled forms which, in general, yield parts with improved toughness, higher rigidity, significantly higher heat resistance and slower burning rates.

§ Rubber modified form.

when vaporized on glass and plastic, and as a paint when in fine powder form and suspended in a suitable liquid vehicle.

An aluminum reflector can have a high-permanence, high-reflectance, diffuse or semidiffuse surface of graduated reflectance.

Types of Aluminum. Aluminum is used in its near-pure state or may be alloyed by the addition of other elements to improve its mechanical, physical and chemical properties. Silicon, iron, copper, manganese, magnesium, chromium, nickel and zinc are the most common elements used. Aluminum alloys may be cast, extruded and rolled as shapes or sheets. In sheet form, aluminum is available in a variety of alloys and finishes.

Finishes. The final finish on aluminum parts will depend on service requirements. Aluminum may be etched, polished, brushed, plated, anodized, vacuum coated with a dielectric, color anodized, brightened, plastic coated with or without vaporization, coated with clear or dye lacquers, finished with baked or porcelain enamel or given some combination of these finishes. Reflector finishes may range from diffuse, such as baked enamel or etched surfaces, to highly specular, such as polished, anodized or coated surfaces. Aluminum paint, made of aluminum as a fine powder suspended in a suitable liquid vehicle, has found wide use as an attractive and practical finish for many surfaces.

Processing. Anodizing, an electrochemical process, is used to form a protective surface of aluminum oxide of a thickness greater than 100 times that formed naturally in air. The aluminum oxide surface is smooth, continuous and inseparable, and has a particle hardness with a Mohs value of 9. Anodizing combined with chemical or electrochemical brightening provides surface finishes of uniformly high reflectance and permanence.

High-purity aluminum must be used if a clear, colorless transparent, high-reflectance oxide surface is required. Impurities and alloying materials will result in lower reflectance, cloudiness, dullness or streaking of the oxide surface. Prefinished anodized sheet is available for forming simple reflector elements.

In the anodizing process, colored surfaces may be obtained by depositing dyes or pigments within the open pores of the aluminum oxide just before the final sealing of the surface. A wide range of colors and tints are available.

Physical Characteristics. Properties of several alloys of aluminum that may be of interest to the designer are shown in figure 7-5. The types and values shown are intended as typical illustrations. New alloys are being developed continually, and any contemporary listing rapidly becomes out of date.

Other Metals

Stainless Steel. Stainless steel includes those iron-base alloys which contain sufficient chromium to render them corrosion resistant. The classification "stainless" is usually reserved for those steels having 12–30% chromium; those with more than 30% are classed as heat-resisting alloys and not as stainless. The family of stainless steels may be divided into three main groups:

Straight chrome group. The steels in this group are all magnetic. They may rust on exposure to corrosive atmospheres; however, the rusting is only a superficial film and acts as a barrier to further corrosive action. These are identified by the American Iron and Steel Institute (AISI) as AISI Type 400 Series.
Chrome-nickel group. These steels are nonmagnetic. They do not rust, but some alloys may not be satisfactory in certain corrosive atmospheres. These steels are designated as AISI Type 300 Series.
Chrome-nickel-manganese group. These steels are nonmagnetic. In this group, manganese substitutes for part of the nickel. These steels do not rust, but some alloys may not be satisfactory in certain corrosive atmospheres. These steels are designated as AISI Type 200 Series.

Stainless steels are widely used in luminaires intended for outdoor installation or in other corrosive atmospheres. Some applications of stainless steel are for housings, springs, latches, mounting straps, hinges, fittings, fasteners and lampholder screw shells.

Copper. Copper is used extensively for the conductors, bus bars and associated switchgear necessary for the distribution and control of electrical energy used for lighting. Copper is ductile, malleable, flexible and fairly strong, and may be formed by a variety of standard machines and processes.

Nonferrous Alloys. Bronze, an alloy of copper and tin, and brass, an alloy of copper and zinc, are often used in special luminaires where the attractive color is a prime consideration. A more utilitarian use of bronze and brass is in luminaires for marine use, where

Fig. 7-5. Typical Physical Properties of Aluminum

Type	Alloy	Federal Specification Number	Average Coefficient of Thermal Expansion*	Specific Gravity**	Thermal Conductivity at 25°C (CGS units)	Reflectance (per cent)
Specular, processed sheet	#12 Reflector sheet		23.6	2.71	0.53	80–95
Diffuse, processed sheet	#31 Reflector sheet		23.6	2.71	0.53	75–80
Mill finish sheet	#1100-H14	QQ-A-561c	23.6	2.71	0.53	70
Extruded	#6061-T4	QQ-A-270a	23.4	2.7	0.37	
Extruded	#6063-T4	QQ-A-274	23.4	2.7	0.46	
Extruded	#6463-T4		23.4	2.7	0.52	
Cast, sand, or permanent	#43-F	QQ-A-371c	22.1	2.69	0.34	
Cast, sand, or permanent	#214-F	QQ-A-371c	22.3	2.89	0.29	
Cast, sand (heat treat)	#220-T4	QQ-A-371c	24.7	2.57	0.29	
Cast, die	#360	QQ-A-591a-2	20.9	2.64	0.27	
Cast, die	#380	QQ-A-591a-2	20.9	2.72	0.23	

* μcm/cm·°C, 20 to 100°C.
** Also weight in g/cm³.

strength and resistance to saltwater corrosion are highly important.

Chromium copper and beryllium copper are often used for conducting springs, contacts and similar highly stressed members that have to be formed in manufacture. The parts are shaped soft and then stiffened by heat treatment.

Manufacturing Techniques for Metals

Spinning. In this process a metal blank in the form of a thin disk is mounted against a wood or steel chuck between the headstock and the tailstock of a lathe. While the blank and chuck are rotating, the metal is forced against the chuck by means of a tool held by the operator. The blank assumes the shape of the chuck. Automatic equipment exists which forms the metal against the chuck by means of rollers. This is called autospinning. This process is characterized by low tool investment. Manual spinning is usually performed only for low quantities and for special or prototype pieces.

Stamping. Also know as drawing or deep drawing, this metal-forming process places a metal blank on top of a negative cavity die, usually a cast block of steel. While the perimeter of the blank is held firmly by a ring, a positive die forces the blank into the negative cavity. The blank assumes the shape of the matching positive and negative dies. This process is characterized by high tool and setup costs, but low piece costs in high-volume production.

Hydroforming. In this process a metal blank is placed on a die plate and forced against a diaphragm of synthetic material, behind which is a large container filled with oil. The oil container is called the pressure dome. A positive die is forced against the metal blank. The oil is nearly incompressible and helps form the metal blank to the shape of the die. Water, rather than oil, was originally used in this process; thus its name. This process is characterized by low tool costs and low piece costs in high-volume production.

Die Casting. In this process molten metal is pumped at high pressure into a two-piece die. The die halves open when the part is sufficiently cooled, and ejector pins push the part out of one of the die halves. This process is characterized by very high tool costs but low piece costs in very high volume production.

FINISHES USED IN LUMINAIRES[10]

A *finish* is the final treatment given to the surface of a material in the course of manufacturing to render it ready for use. Three major purposes for finishes on lighting equipment are the control of light, the protection of material and the enhancement of appearance.

In addition, there are several special applications, such as flame-retardant and color-stabilizing treatments.

Finishes are classified both by the method of application and by the kind of material applied. The three basic types are coatings, laminates and chemical conversion finishes. Coatings can be divided into four general classes as organic, ceramic, metallic and other.

Typical characteristics of finishes are indicated in figure 7-6. Because of the great number of possible variations in composition and application of all types of finishes, numerical values are not shown and relative gradings only are used. For more details on finishes, technical assistance should be obtained from suppliers and available literature.

Coatings

Organic Coatings. *Lacquers* may be clear, transparent or opaque and will cure rapidly at room temperature. They may be used for decoration or protection. *Enamels* are pigmented coatings and are applied for protection, decoration or reflectance. They cure by oxidation (air or forced drying) or polymerization (baking or catalytic action) and result in tougher finishes than lacquers. *Baked clear coatings*, sometimes called baking lacquers, are used for decoration and protection. They cure by polymerization (baking or catalytic action).

Organisols and *plastisols* are usually applied by dipping and spraying. These plastic dispersion coatings offer good exterior corrosion as well as scratch and abrasion resistance and are also able to conceal many surface defects.

Ceramic Coatings. Ceramic coatings, including porcelain enamels, are fired on glass and metals at temperatures above 540° C. Primary features include high resistance to corrosion, good reflectance and easy maintenance on metals; and reduction of brightness and increase of diffusion on glass.

Metallic Coatings. Electrochemical deposition, commonly called electroplating, causes a second metal to be deposited over the first by means of an electrolytic action. Zinc, cadmium or nickel is used to provide protection. Brass and silver finishes are primarily decorative.

Vacuum metallizing consists of vaporizing a metal, usually aluminum, in a vacuum chamber and depositing it on surfaces of plastic, glass or metal. Finishes of high specular reflectance are obtained and can be used for either light control or decorative purposes. Dip and spray coatings, as in galvanizing, are deposits of a second metal to protect the base metal against corrosion.

Other Coatings. Semiconductors, such as silicon and germanium, and inorganic dielectrics, such as magne-

Fig. 7-6. Properties of Finishes Used in Luminaires

Type of Finish	Method of Application[a]	Principal Uses[b]	Colors Possible	Character of Reflected Light	Per Cent Reflectance[d]	Resistance[c]				Stability[c]	Flammability
						Heat	Corrosion	Abrasion	Impact		
Organic coatings											
Lacquers	D, B, S	A, P	Colorless or any color	Mixed to diffuse	10–90	F	F	P	F	F	Slow burn
Emulsions	D, B, S	A, P	All colors	Mixed to diffuse	10–90	G	G	G	G	G	Slow burn
Enamels	D, B, S	A, P, R	All colors	Mixed to diffuse	10–90	G	G	G	G	G	Slow burn
Baked clear coatings	D, B, S	A, P	Colorless, clear color	Diffuse to specular	0	G	G	G	G	G	Slow burn
Organisols	D, S	A, P	All colors	Mixed to diffuse	10–90	F	E	G	G	F	None
Ceramic coatings											
Vitreous enamels	D, S	A, P, R	All colors	Diffuse to specular	10–90	E	E	E	P	E	None
Ceramic enamels	D, S, B	A, R	All colors	Mixed to specular	10–90	E	E	E	P	E	None
Metallic coatings											
Chrome plate	Electrochemical	A, P	Fixed; depending on color of plated metal	Specular to diffuse	60–88	E	E	E	E	E	None
Nickel plate	Electrochemical	A, P		Specular to diffuse	55	E	G	E	E	E	None
Cadmium plate	Electrochemical	P		Specular to diffuse	85	G	G	F	P	E	None
Brass plate	Electrochemical	A		Specular to diffuse	55–80	P	P	F	P	F	None
Silver plate	Electrochemical	A, R		Specular	85–95	P	P	F	P	E	None
Laminates	Laminate	A, P, R	All colors of metallic effects	Mixed	10–90	Depends on nature of laminate					Slow burn
Conversion coatings											
Anodized aluminum	Electrochemical	A, P, R	Natural aluminum (or a wide variety of colors)	Diffuse to specular	60–90	E	E	E	E	E	None
Vacuum metalizing	Vacuum chamber	A, R	Natural aluminum (or a wide variety of colors)	Specular	10–70	Depends on nature of protective coating					None
Vacuum deposition	Vacuum chamber	A, R, T	Colorless to interference effects	Diffuse to specular	0–99	E	E	E	E	E	None

[a] D—dip, S—spray, B—brush.
[b] A—appearance, P—protection, R—reflectance, T—transmittance.
[c] P—poor, F—fair, G—good, E—excellent.
[d] Depends upon color.

sium fluoride and titanium dioxide, are vacuum deposited on such materials as glass, aluminum and plastics. The coatings of interest for lighting uses are multilayered and less than 1 μm thick.

Laminates

This type of finish is created by bonding a thin layer to a base material, such as a plastic film to sheet metal. The laminate can be a decorative material or it can be a light-controlling material.

Chemical Conversion Finishes

Anodizing converts an aluminum surface by an anodic process to aluminum oxide, which has outstanding protective qualities against corrosion and abrasion. The resultant finish may be clear or can be dyed in a variety of colors.

REFLECTOR DESIGN[11]

The design of reflector contours is an extensive subject because the possible shapes for a particular application are almost limitless. The end use, however, usually limits the choice.

For design purposes, reflector contours can be divided into two classes, basic and general contours. Basic contours may be defined as those which are highly predictable as to light distribution and can be designed mathematically. General contours are those required to satisfy many intensity distribution curves, but which do not conform to any of the basic contours.

Basic Reflector Contours

Basic contours that are used very frequently are the conic sections and the spherical reflector.

A conic section is, by definition, the locus of points having distances from a fixed point that are in a constant ratio to the distances from a fixed straight line. The fixed point is called the focus of the conic section; the fixed line is its directrix. The constant ratio is the *eccentricity e* of the conic section.

If $e = 1.0$ then the section is called a *parabola*.
If $e < 1.0$ then the section is an *ellipse*.
If $e > 1.0$ then the section is a *hyperbola*.

Parabolic Reflectors. An inherent property of the parabola is its ability to redirect a ray of light originating at its focal point along a direction parallel to the axis of the parabola. The proof of the property is shown in figure 7-7, where $A'A''$ is tangent to the curve at A, BA is perpendicular to DD', and $BA = FA$. If the parabola is rotated about its axis (the line indicated by the X), a *paraboloid* is swept out. Assume a per-

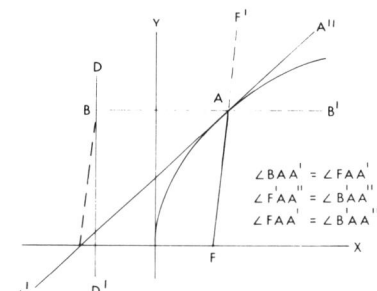

Fig. 7-7. Parabolic conic section. DD' is the directrix; F is the focus.

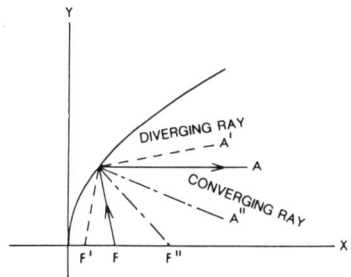

Fig. 7-8. Diverging or converging rays from a point source on the axis of a parabolic reflector, but behind or ahead of the focal point F.

fectly specular mirror is made to this shape, and that a point source is at the focus (F). All light from the source striking the mirror is redirected as a beam of light parallel to the parabolic axis. The ideal conditions of perfect specularity and a point source cannot be reached in practice, nor, in most cases, would this be desirable. The further conditions deviate from these, the greater will be the deviation of the light from a parallel beam. Formulas have been derived expressing the light divergence fromshallow mirrors when sources of various shapes are used. Figure 7-8 illustrates the action of point sources lying on the axis of the parabola (line X) but ahead of (F'') or behind (F') the focal point F.

Ellipsoidal Reflectors. If an ellipse is rotated about its major axis, a surface is swept out which is an *ellipsoid*. This surface, having two foci, will take light from one focus and reflect it through the other focus. Ellipsoidal reflectors are an efficient means for producing beams of controlled divergence and for collecting light to be controlled by a lens or lens system.

The ellipse shown in figure 7-9 can be described as the set of points (x, y) on the X, Y plane such that the following equation is satisfied:

$$\frac{x^2}{a^2} + \frac{y^2}{b^2} = 1 \qquad (7\text{-}1)$$

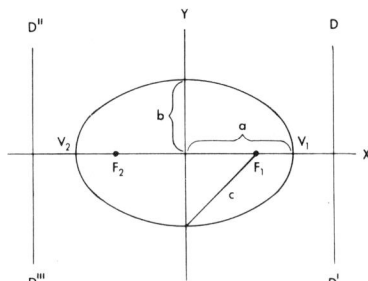

Fig. 7-9. The foci (F_1 and F_2), directrices (DD' and D"D'''), and axes of an ellipse.

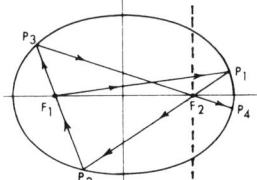

Fig. 7-10. The action of a perfect ellipsoidal mirror.

Useful working equations are

$$y = \pm \frac{b}{a}\sqrt{a^2 - x^2} \qquad (7\text{-}2)$$

$$x = \pm \frac{a}{b}\sqrt{b^2 - y^2} \qquad (7\text{-}3)$$

$$b^2 = a^2 - \left(\frac{\overline{F_1 F_2}}{2}\right)^2 \qquad (7\text{-}4)$$

Figure 7-10 illustrates the action of a perfect complete ellipsoidal mirror with a light source at F_1 and a ray of light striking the mirror at P_1, passing through F_2 (the conjugate focus) to P_2, and being reflected again through F_1 to P_3 and on to P_4. If the mirror is "chopped off" at F_2 (the dashed line) or at a point closer to F_1, all of the light from the theoretical source at F_1 will leave the mirror either directly or after one reflection. By moving the opening back along the major axis, the beam limits of the reflected light are narrowed. When the plane of the opening reaches the center of the ellipse, the maximum angle of the reflected light coincides with the angle of direct emission from the source.

Hyperbolic Reflectors. The diverging beam typical of the ellipsoidal reflector can also be produced by a reflector having a hyperbolic contour. The main difference, as shown in figure 7-11, is that the hyperbolic reflector produces a virtual image, F_2, behind the focus, whereas the ellipsoidal reflector produces a real image in front of the focus.

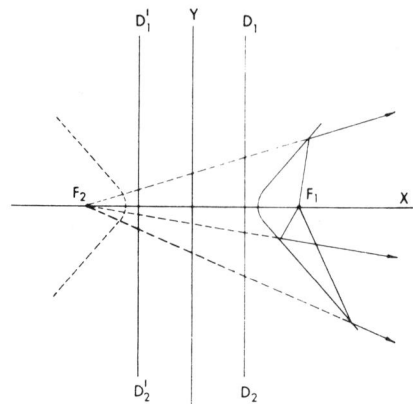

Fig. 7-11. Hyperbolic reflector action.

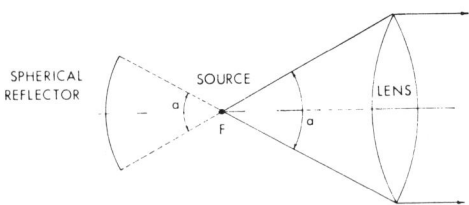

Fig. 7-12. Projecting device with a spherical reflector.

Spherical Reflectors. A spherical reflector can be considered as a special form of the ellipsoidal reflector where the two foci are coincident. Any light leaving the source located at the focus will return and pass through the same point. This has obvious disadvantages when dealing with practical sources, since the concentration of energy can often damage the source or the bulb wall surrounding it. The principle is, however, often used in projecting devices to increase the amount of light collected by a lens as shown in figure 7-12.

General Reflector Contours

For many applications, reflectors can be designed which are mathematically predictable as to contour and action. A more general problem is that of determining the contour of a reflector which does not meet these conditions. Usually there are two specified factors: an approximate luminous intensity distribution for the finished reflector, and the material from which it is to be manufactured.

Diffuse Reflecting Surfaces. In the rare case of surfaces with perfectly diffuse reflection, the contour of the reflector has very little effect on the distribution of light. The luminous intensity distribution of such a reflector (after that portion due to the bare lamp has been deducted) is very nearly spherical, with the maximum value normal to the plane of the opening. The distribution is not perfectly spherical, because portions of the reflector are not uniformly illuminated. A strip of unit area near the lower edge of the reflector, being farther from the source, receives less light than a similar strip higher in the reflector. Since these lower portions are the parts directing light out at the upper angles, the intensity decreases faster than the cosine of the angle. In this case, there is little that can be done by the designer in the way of light control except by aiming the entire reflector.

Reflectors with Specular and Semispecular Surfaces. General contours for specular reflectors are usually obtained through graphical or computational methods. The problem consists in determining what reflector shape is necessary to redirect luminous flux from the lamp into the proper directions to achieve a predetermined luminous intensity distribution.

The basic steps in one method of determining a reflector contour are shown below.[12] In this method, the lamp is approximated by a point source with an axially symmetric luminous intensity distribution. Additionally, the required luminous intensity distribution is assumed to be axially symmetric. This simple procedure lends itself to computer implementation, resulting in an effective way to automate the reflector shape synthesis process:

1. Select the width, in degrees, of the annular zones to be considered. From the required candela distribution, calculate the luminous flux required in each zone. (Flux in each zone = candelas × zonal constant.) See chapter 9, Lighting Calculations. Tabulate these values.
2. Calculate the luminous flux emitted by the bare lamp in each zone, using the luminous intensity distribution of the bare lamp and the zonal constants, and tabulate.
3. Find the reflected lumens needed in each zone by subtracting the bare-lamp lumens (data from step 2) from the required luminous flux (data from step 1) in those zones where no reflection will take place; in other words, from nadir up to cutoff. Tabulate these values.

4. Decide upon the general action of the reflector. There are, in general, four basic actions of the reflectors as shown in figure 7-13. For a given cutoff, the forms shown in figure 7-13c and d usually require a very large reflector. The form in figure 7-13b has the disadvantage that much of the light is passed through the lamp bulb. For most cases, the form in figure 7-13a results in the smallest reflector and redirects the least light back through the lamp.
5. Plot a curve of the reflected flux obtained in step 3. Starting at 0°, show cumulative sums of lumens required to be reflected into each zone from nadir up to cutoff; see figure 7-14. Similarly, plot a curve of available lamp flux (from the step 2 data). Starting at cutoff, show how many lumens are incident on the reflector progressively from cutoff to 180° (figure 7-14b). Since all flux considered here must be reflected from the reflector surface, the available lamp lumens must be multiplied by the reflectance of the surface and by other loss factors. It is convenient to work with rectangular coordinates, plotting the lumens along the horizontal axis and degrees along the vertical axis. Plot the reflected-flux curve (figure 7-14a) to the same scale and directly below the curve of available lamp flux (bare-lamp flux corrected for losses). If the reflector action illustrated in figure 7-13b or d was selected, the horizontal (lumen) scales of the two curves will be in the same direction. If figure 7-13a or c was selected, the scales will be reversed as shown in figure 7-14. Take intercepts at intervals (one for each zone) along the reflected-flux curve (figure 7-14a), and project upward to the available-lamp-flux curve as shown in figure 7-14. At the point where each intercept cuts the available-lamp-flux curve (figure 7-14b), project horizontally to degrees on the vertical axis. The spacings between intercepts on the vertical axis indicate how large an angular zonal segment of the reflector is required to

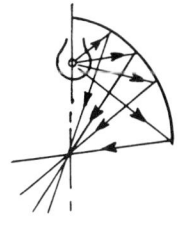 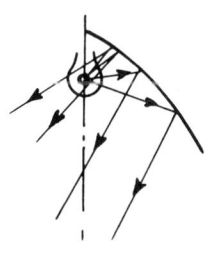 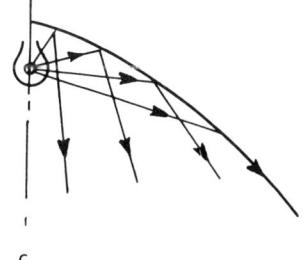 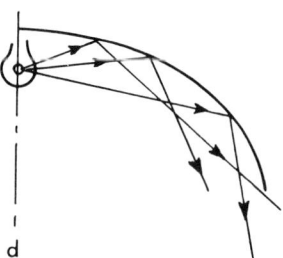

a   b   c   d

Fig. 7-13. Four basic reflector actions.

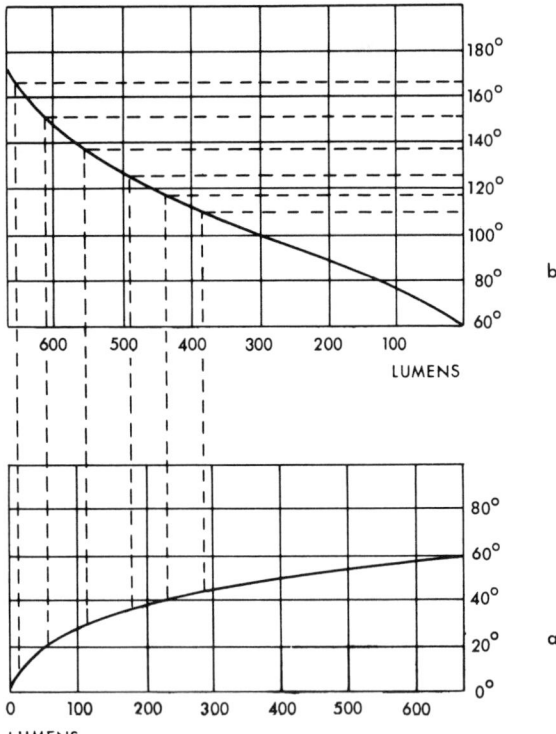

Fig. 7-14. Reflection plan of available lamp luminous flux (shown for a 60° cutoff). (a) Reflected flux curve. (b) Incident or available flux curve (corrected for losses).

direct enough light at a particular angle to satisfy the requirements of the reflected-flux curve.

6. Lay out the reflector contour by starting at the point nearest the lamp and progressively drawing small, straight segments (one segment for each zone). Each segment must be of the required length, and placed in the correct position for the flux striking it to be reflected in the amount and direction determined in step 5. Obtain the final contour by drawing a smooth curve tangent to the segments.

The procedure outlined above assumes a point source and true specular reflection. The effect of a real filament will be to smooth out the final distribution, rounding off sharp points. This effect will be more noticeable as the reflector gets smaller in comparison with the source.

Departures from true specularity will have a similar effect, which will increase as the proportion of diffuse to total reflection increases. With semispecular surfaces, the effect of specularity of the surface increases as the angle of incident light increases. Hence, for accurate control of the light, it is good to keep the angle of incidence as large as possible for semispecular surfaces or to use highly specular high-reflectance surfaces when multiple reflection exists.

REFRACTOR DESIGN[11]

Optic Surface to Redirect Light Rays

A common problem, illustrated in figure 7-15, is the determination of an optic surface to cause the eventual refraction of a light ray from a source to a required direction. Initially, five elements of this problem are known:

1. The exit surface S, which is the side of the lens away from the source. This surface can be flat, spherical, cylindrical or irregularly shaped, the fundamentals being the same.
2. The optic surface T to which an optical configuration must be designed in order to create the required distribution of light rays. The surface T is normally parallel to the exit surface S.
3. The location of the light source
4. The incident ray from the source to the lens
5. The required emergent ray. The angle θ of the optic surface T' which will change the incident ray to the direction of the emergent ray is the unknown quantity in this problem.

The first step is to draw all the known components of the problem: the exit surface S, optic surface T, incident ray, emergent ray required and source. Note that the surface T is represented by a dashed line, indicating that at the end of the complete design this

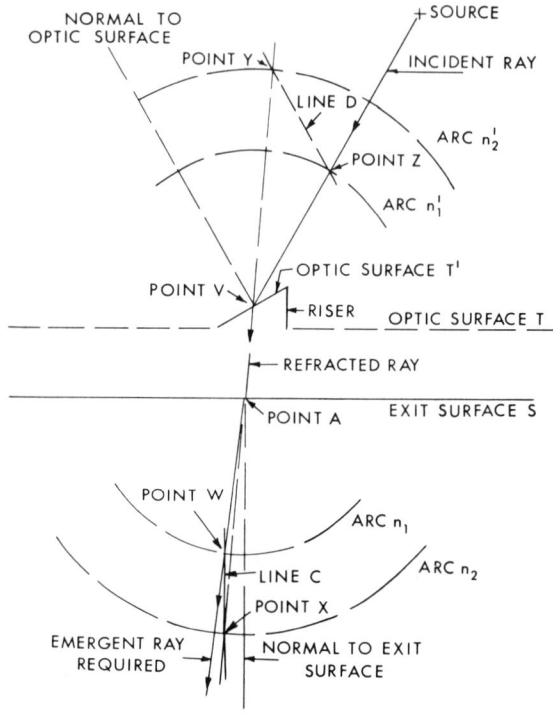

Fig. 7-15. Design of an optical element to redirect a light ray.

surface will no longer be continuous, but will contain optic elements.

To point *A*, the intersection of the emergent ray and exit surface *S*, draw the normal to *S*; with point *A* as center, strike arc n_1 with radius proportional to n_1, the refractive index of the outside medium (probably air with $n_1 = 1$). Again with point *A* as center, strike arc n_2 with radius proportional to the refractive index of the optical medium. Through point *W*, the intersection of arc n_1 and the emergent ray required, draw line *C* parallel to the normal to the exit surface *S*. Through the intersection of arc n_2 and line *C*, which is indicated as point *X*, draw the construction line to point *A* on the exit surface *S*. Extended, this becomes a refracted ray through the optic surface *T*. Further extended, it intersects arc n_2' at point *Y*. The radius of arc n_2' is proportional to the refractive index of the optical medium. Note that the center of the arc, point *V*, lies on the optic surface, which has not yet been established. Thus a few trials are necessary for this solution.

The initial steps are repeated until point *V* coincides with the intersection of the incident ray and the optic surface *T'*. With point *V* as center, strike an arc n_1', whose radius is proportional to the refractive index of the outside medium. Draw line *D* between point *Y* and point *Z*, the intersection of arc n_1' and the incident ray. The normal to the optic surface *T'* is then drawn parallel to line *D* and intersecting point *V*. The optic surface *T'* is then perpendicular to this normal.

All rays at an internal angle to the normal greater than the critical angle θ ($\sin \theta = n_1/n_2$) are internally reflected from the inside of the surface.

This procedure can be implemented on computer-aided drafting systems to help automate the refractor design process.

Refraction-Reflection System

Total internal reflection is used extensively in lens design when rays must be bent at an angle larger than is possible to accomplish with refraction alone. Total internal reflection problems can be solved graphically by methods similar to those used in solving refraction problems.

Figure 7-16 illustrates the solution of a typical problem involving both refraction and total internal reflection. A ray of light from the source passes through the system in the following manner:

1. Ray 1 is refracted at surface *S*.
2. The refracted ray becomes incident to surface *T* at an angle greater than the critical angle of the medium.
3. Total internal reflection occurs at surface *T*, so that $r' = r$.

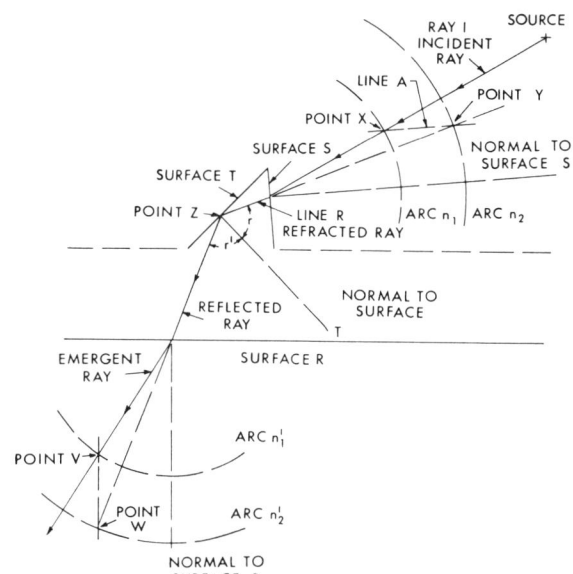

Fig. 7-16. The path of a light ray through a refraction-reflection system.

4. The reflected ray becomes incident on surface *R*.
5. The ray is refracted at surface *R* and emerges from the system.

The graphical method of determining the refracted rays has been described in the previous section. It is accomplished by constructing the angle from the reflected ray to normal equal to the angle from the incident ray to normal.

LUMINOUS AND LOUVERED CEILING DESIGN

Luminous ceiling systems employ translucent media with lamps installed in the cavity above. Luminous ceiling systems employing diffusing media produce results similar to that of well-designed indirect lighting from conventional suspended luminaires (or coves), but with generally greater uniformity of ceiling luminance than is possible with the latter method. Luminous ceilings that employ prismatic materials give generally higher utilization than those that employ diffusing materials; they also have better direct-glare control.

Either glass or plastic of proper optical characteristics may be used as the translucent medium. This material is usually supported in a structural framework and is formed in panels or rolls of a size which is convenient for handling. The diffusing material should have the highest possible transmittance consistent with adequate concealment of the lamps. Experience indicates that the material should have a transmittance of about 50% and as low an absorptance as possible. Prismatic materials should have as high a transmittance as is compatible with the degree of light control desired. In general, such materials will have an effective transmittance of 70–75%.

Ideally, the cavity above the diffuser should be of depth just sufficient to obtain the proper relation between spacing of lamps and vertical distance from the diffuser to produce acceptably uniform luminance. The luminous efficiency of the system decreases as the depth of the cavity is increased with respect to its length and width. The cavity should be unobstructed, and all surfaces painted in a white paint of at least 80% reflectance. All dust leaks in cavity walls and ceilings should be sealed. Where deep, heavily obstructed cavities occur, it is wise to consider the possibility of furring down the cavity ceiling to a reasonable level. The cost of such construction may be less than the additional cost of equipment, power and maintenance required to force an otherwise inefficient system to deliver a given illuminance level.

Successful luminous ceilings have been designed using practically all types of lamps; however, fluorescent is generally used. A typical arrangement of lamps within the cavity is shown in figure 7-17. For uniform brightness appearance over a diffusing ceiling, the spacing of the lamp(s) should not exceed 1.5–2 times their height above the diffuser (L); that is, $S/L \leqslant 2.0$. Where the plenum is shallow, the plenum ceiling painted white and the lamps mounted against the plenum ceiling, S/L can be greater than when the plenum above the lamps is deep, or dark, or obstructed. Also, when it is necessary to use luminaires with reflectors such as those in figure 7-18, the ratio S/L should not exceed 1.5. With ceilings of prismatic materials, S/L should rarely exceed 1.0 if acceptable luminance uniformity is to be achieved.

For greater uniformity of luminance over the entire ceiling, it is recommended that the lamp rows be spaced closer together at the sides of the cavity. The ends of the rows should be carried all the way to the ends of the cavity. In some instances it is desirable to install extra lamps between the rows at the end of the cavity, or across the ends of the rows, to increase the luminance at those points.

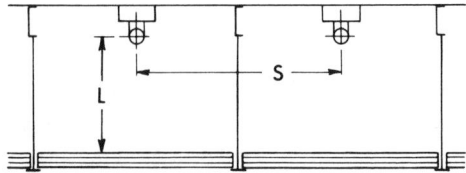

Fig. 7-17. Section of a portion of a luminous ceiling. The distance S should not exceed 1.5L to 2L.

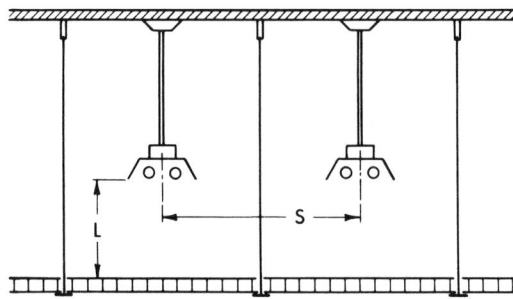

Fig. 7-18. Section of a portion of a louvered ceiling. For both translucent and opaque louvers, the ratio of S to L should not exceed 1.5:1.

Luminous ceiling systems are often used for the dual purpose of providing light and concealing the visual clutter of beams and building services. Aside from the reduction in system efficiency caused by these obstructions, there is the possibility that they will cast shadows on the translucent medium. It is good to place the prime sources of light below, or at right angles to, such obstructions wherever possible.

Obtaining proper acoustical treatment of a room with a luminous ceiling can be difficult. In many cases, it is better to obtain the required results by treating other room surfaces. Generally this means wall surfaces in small rooms, and floors in large ones.

Louvered ceiling systems consist of an open network of translucent or opaque vanes through which light passes from the lighting recess above to the area below. The louver cells can be made in a number of shapes and sizes, depending upon mechanical design relationships and desired architectural effects, with various degrees of shielding. Fluorescent lamps are generally used with this type of ceiling. Here, the lighted appearance of the louvers is dependent on the conditions within the cavity, the spacing of the lamps, the height of the lamps above the louvers, the size of the louver cells and the characteristics of the louver blades themselves. The transmittance (if any) of the blades, and both the type of reflectance (specular, spread or diffuse) and its amount (percent), are important. Louvers of the parabolic wedge type have yet different requirements.

As a guide, in unobstructed, shallow plenums with white-painted surfaces and ceiling-mounted strip luminaires, S/L should not exceed 1.5 for translucent louvers, and 1 for opaque louvers. See figure 7-18. For other conditions, closer spacings are the rule.

Pipes, ducts and beams should be considered in their relationship to the louvered ceiling system in order to avoid the forming of unsightly shadows.

The lighting equipment should be mounted high enough above the louvers to permit ease of access and relamping. Means for removing the louvers in sections small enough for ease of handling facilitates the rather infrequent cleaning necessary.

The acoustical effect of louvers depends on the cell size and the louver material. In most cases, however, it is best to ignore the louvers and apply acoustical material to the ceiling of the plenum, or to other room surfaces.

The efficiency and effective reflectance of luminous and louvered ceilings vary with the cavity proportions and reflectances, the type of lighting equipment used, the reflectance and transmittance of the ceiling material, the shielding angle of louvers, and the amount and kind of obstruction within the cavity. Chapter 9, Lighting Calculations, gives coefficients of utilization for typical ceilings of these types. Performance data for other ceilings can be determined by photometric tests or by zonal-cavity calculations for coupled enclosures. The ceiling cavity reflectance for a room with a luminous or louvered ceiling can be found by

$$\rho_{eff} = \rho_d + T^2\left(\frac{\rho_{cc}}{1 - \rho_d\rho_{cc}}\right) \qquad (7\text{-}5)$$

where

T = ceiling material transmittance,
ρ_d = ceiling material reflectance,
ρ_{cc} = effective reflectance of ceiling cavity,
ρ_{eff} = effective reflectance of luminous ceiling seen from below.

The effective transmittance and reflectance for opaque

louvers can be estimated using the curves of figure 7-19.

COVES

Coves may be used for illumination or for the creation of a decorative effect. In most instances, an efficient lighting system and a more pleasing brightness pattern are obtained if the brightness of the ceiling and the brightness of the wall above the cove are similar. Usually these objectives are more easily attained if the cove is not located too close to the ceiling. The brightness of the wall above the cove and that of the ceiling near the cove are produced largely by direct illumination from the light source and from reflections between the cove, wall and ceiling. The brightness of the ceiling at the far end of the room is largely dependent upon the general room surface reflectances. To attain more uniform wall and ceiling brightness, it is recommended that the lamps be mounted away from the wall and that the wall adjacent to the source be shielded in part from the direct radiation from the lamp. The channel serves this purpose very well. In general, the further the cove is located from the ceiling, the further the lamp and channel should be located from the wall. See figure 7-20.

If the cove is 300 mm (12 in.) from the ceiling (H), the lamp center should be 60 mm (2.5 in.) or more from the wall (S); if the cove is 380–500 mm (15–20 in.) from the ceiling, the lamp center should be 90 mm (3.5 in.) or more from the wall; and if the cove is 530–760 mm (21–30 in.) from the ceiling, the lamp center should be 110 mm (4.5 in.) or more from the wall.

Reflectors can be used in fluorescent coves to obtain very pleasing results when the reflector is aimed about 20° above the horizontal.

LUMINAIRE CLASSIFICATION

Lighting systems are often classified in accordance with their layout or location with respect to the visual task

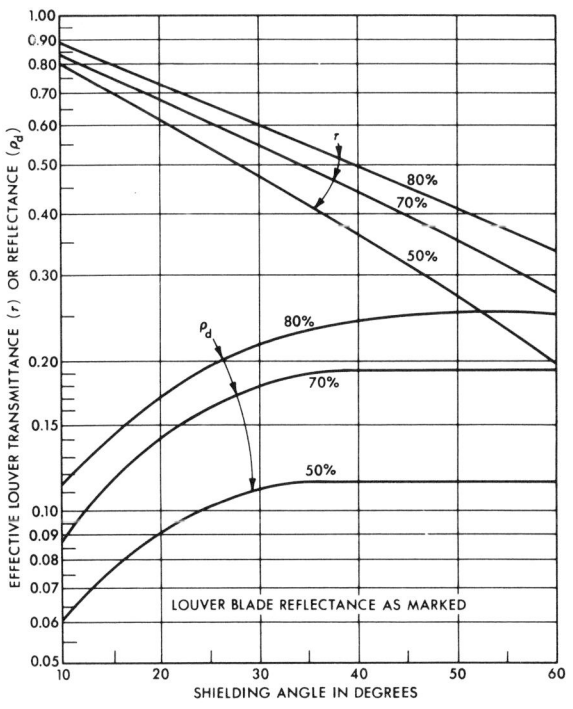

Fig. 7-19. Graph for obtaining effective transmittance and reflectance for square-cell opaque louvers.

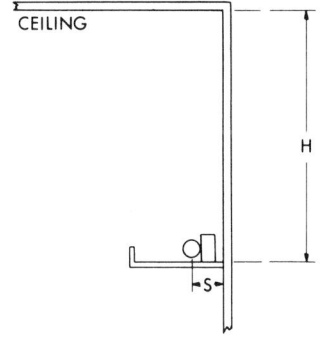

Fig. 7-20. Section through a fluorescent cove.

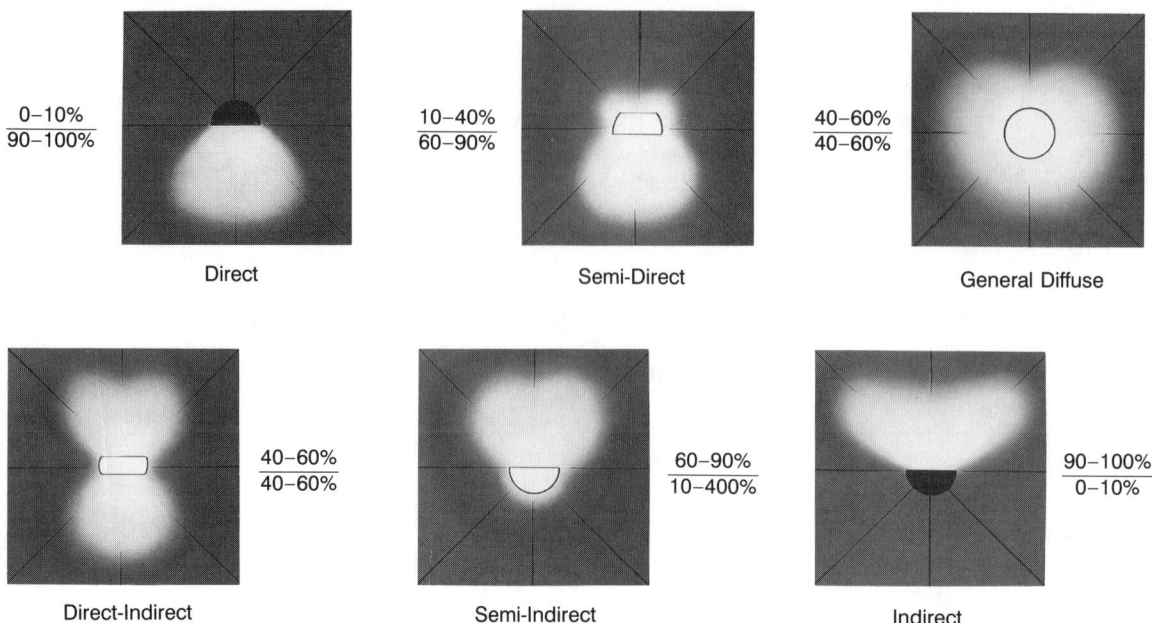

Fig. 7-21. Luminaires for general lighting are classified by the CIE in accordance with the percentages of total luminaire output emitted above and below horizontal. The light distribution curves may take many forms within the limits of upward and downward distribution, depending upon the type of light source and the design of the luminaire.

or object lighted: general lighting, localized general lighting, local (supplementary) lighting and task-ambient lighting. They are also classified in accordance with the Commission Internationale de l'Éclairage (CIE) type of luminaire used: direct, semidirect, general diffuse (direct-indirect), semi-indirect and indirect. See figure 7-21.

Classification by Layout and Location

General Lighting. Lighting systems which provide an approximately uniform illuminance on the workplane over the entire area are called general lighting systems. The luminaires are usually arranged in a symmetrical plan fitted to the physical characteristics of the area. Such installations are simple to install and are not coordinated with furniture or machinery. Perhaps the greatest advantage of general lighting systems is that they permit complete flexibility in task location.

If partitions are planned for the space, the actual illuminance will be lower than in the open space. To accurately predict the illuminance, the location of partitions must be included in the lighting calculations for the space.

Localized General Lighting. A localized general lighting system consists of a luminaire arrangement coordinated with the location of visual tasks or work areas as well as illumination for the entire area. Such a system uses light more effectively for visual tasks and provides the designer with the opportunity to locate the luminaires to prevent annoying shadows, direct glare, veiling reflections and partition interference.

Local Lighting. A local lighting system provides lighting only over a relatively small area occupied by the task and its immediate surroundings. The illumination may be from luminaires mounted near the task or from more remote locations. It is an economical means of providing higher illuminances over a small area, and it usually permits some adjustment of the lighting to suit the requirements of the individual. Improper adjustments may, however, cause annoying glare for nearby workers.

Local lighting by itself is seldom desirable. To limit luminance ratios, it should be used in conjunction with general lighting that is at least 20–30% of the local lighting level; it then becomes *supplementary lighting*.

Task-Ambient Lighting. Task-ambient lighting is often built into the furniture in an open-plan office layout. Luminaires are located close to work areas (as in local lighting, above) and are supplemented by direct or indirect ambient illumination. Electrical service to furniture-mounted lighting equipment is often through the floor.

Classification by CIE Luminaire Type

Direct Lighting. When luminaires direct 90–100% of their output downward, they form a *direct* lighting system. The distribution may vary from widespread to highly concentrated, depending on the reflector material, finish and contour and on the shielding or optical control media employed.

Direct-lighting luminaires can have the highest efficiency, but this efficiency may be reduced by brightness control media needed to minimize direct glare. Direct glare may also be reduced by using fewer lamps.

Veiling reflections and reflected glare and shadows may also be problems with direct lighting unless the luminaire has been designed to reduce these effects.

High-reflectance, matte room surfaces are particularly important with direct lighting to improve light distribution and thus brightness relationships. Higher illuminances will also result for the same number of luminaires. With very concentrating distributions, techniques should be found to provide adequate illuminances on vertical surfaces.

Luminous ceilings, louvered ceilings and large-area modular lighting elements are forms of direct lighting having luminous characteristics similar to those of indirect lighting discussed below. Care should be taken with these forms of lighting to limit the luminance of the shielding medium to 850 cd/m^2 or less, to prevent direct glare. Reflected glare, particularly for VDTs, may be a problem with systems employing cellular louvers as the shielding medium, since the images of the light sources above the louvers may be seen at some angles.

Semidirect Lighting. The distribution from semidirect units is predominantly downward (60–90%) but with a small upward component to illuminate the ceiling and upper walls. The characteristics are essentially the same as for direct lighting except that the upward component will tend to soften shadows and improve room brightness relationships. Care should be exercised with close-to-ceiling mounting of some types to prevent overly bright spots directly above the luminaires. Efficiencies can approach, and sometimes exceed, that of well-shielded direct units.

General Diffuse Lighting. When the downward and upward components of light from luminaires are about equal (each 40–60% of total luminaire output), the system is classified as general diffuse. *Direct-indirect* is a special (non-CIE) category within this classification; in it, the luminaires emit very little light at angles near the horizontal. Since this characteristic results in lower luminances in the direct-glare zone, direct-indirect luminaires are usually more suitable than general diffuse luminaires which distribute the light about equally in all directions.

General diffuse luminaires combine the characteristics of direct lighting described above and indirect lighting described below. Their efficiencies are somewhat lower than for direct or semidirect luminaires, but are still quite good in rooms with high-reflectance matte surfaces. Brightness relationships throughout the room are generally good, and shadows from the direct component are softened by the upward light reflected from the ceiling. Excellent direct-glare control can be provided by well-shielded luminaires, but short suspen-

sions can result in ceiling luminances that exceed luminaire luminances. Reflected glare from the downward component can be a problem, but it is mitigated by the reflected upward light; close spacings or layouts that locate luminaires so that they are not reflected in the task may be used to limit this problem.

Luminaires designed to provide a general-diffuse or direct-indirect distribution when pendant mounted are frequently installed on or very close to the ceiling. It should be recognized that such mountings change the distribution to direct or semidirect, since the ceiling acts as a top reflector redirecting the upward light back through the luminaire. Photometric data obtained with the luminaire equipped with top reflectors or installed on a simulated ceiling board should be employed to determine the luminaire characteristics for such applications.

Semi-Indirect Lighting. Lighting systems which emit 60–90% of their output upward are classified as semi-indirect. The characteristics of semi-indirect lighting are similar to those of indirect systems discussed below, except that the downward component usually produces a luminaire luminance that closely matches that of the ceiling. However, if the downward component becomes too great and is not properly controlled, direct or reflected glare may result. An increased downward component improves the utilization of light over that for indirect lighting. This factor makes higher illuminances possible with fewer semi-indirect luminaires and without excessive ceiling luminance.

Indirect Lighting. Lighting systems classified as indirect are those which direct 90–100% of the light upward to the ceiling and upper side walls. In a well-designed installation the entire ceiling becomes the primary source of illumination, and shadows in the space will be virtually eliminated. Also, since the luminaires direct very little light downward, both direct and reflected glare will be minimized if the installation is well planned. It is also important to suspend the luminaires a sufficient distance below the ceiling to obtain reasonable uniformity of ceiling luminance without excessive luminance immediately above the luminaires.

Since with indirect lighting the ceiling and upper walls must reflect light to the workplane, it is essential that these surfaces have high reflectances. Even then, the efficiency is low compared to that of other systems. Care should also be exercised to prevent overall ceiling luminance from becoming too high and thus glaring.

APPLICATIONS: INDOOR LUMINAIRES

Recessed Luminaires

Wide-distribution recessed luminaires using incandescent A lamps and compact fluorescent lamps are suit-

Fig. 7-22 Recessed Lighting Equipment

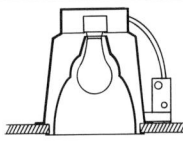

INCANDESCENT DOWNLIGHT

A frosted A lamp is used in the luminaire. Corridors, auditoriums, lobbies and public spaces are common applications. A scalloped effect may also be achieved by close placement to walls.

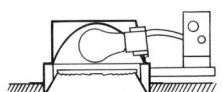

LENSED INCANDESCENT DOWNLIGHT

A general service A lamp is used in the luminaire. The refractor provides a wide distribution. Corridors, lobbies and exterior soffits are common applications.

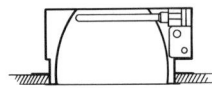

COMPACT FLUORESCENT, WIDE DISTRIBUTION

Two 9-W or 13-W compact fluorescent lamps are commonly used in the luminaire. Corridors, lobbies, stores and public spaces are typical applications.

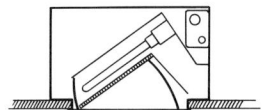

COMPACT FLUORESCENT, WALL WASHER

Two 13-W compact fluorescent lamps are commonly used in the luminaire. Both a reflector and a refractor are used to provide a uniform distribution of light onto vertical surfaces in offices, lobbies and stores.

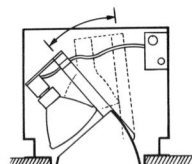

INCANDESCENT, ADJUSTABLE ACCENT

A PAR 38 spot or flood lamp is used in the luminaire. The former is used for a narrow distribution to highlight objects in stores, museums, restaurants or residences. The latter is used to highlight vertical or horizontal surfaces where a narrow beam is not required.

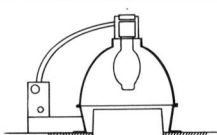

RECESSED HID DOWNLIGHT

A metal halide lamp is commonly used in the luminaire. Applications with high ceilings, such as industrial spaces, some retail stores and atriums are appropriate. High pressure sodium versions are also available.

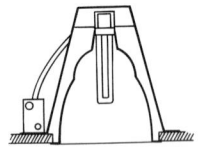

COMPACT FLUORESCENT, NARROW DISTRIBUTION

A 26-W compact fluorescent lamp is commonly used in the luminaire. Applications include downlighting in corridors, auditoriums, lobbies and public spaces. A scalloped effect may also be achieved by close placement to walls.

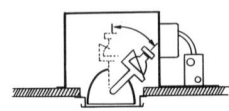

ADJUSTABLE, LOW VOLTAGE

A low voltage MR16 lamp is used in the luminaire. A very narrow distribution of light is often used to highlight objects in stores, museums, restaurants, or residences. This luminaire is sometimes used to illuminate horizontal or vertical surfaces where a very specific beam is desired.

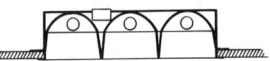

PARABOLIC THREE LAMP, 2′ × 4′ FLUORESCENT TROFFER

Three T-8, T-10 or T-12 fluorescent lamps, four feet in length, are used in the luminaire. General illumination for offices, especially where computer terminals are present, is the most common application.

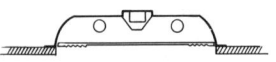

TWO LAMP, LENSED 2′ × 4′ FLUORESCENT TROFFER

Two T-8, T-20 or T-12 fluorescent lamps, four feet in length, are used in the luminaire. General illumination for offices and corridors is the most common application.

able for general illumination in circulation or activity areas. Narrow-distribution luminaires with reflectors or reflector lamps are used for accent lighting (see figure 7-22).

Accent luminaires are used to highlight sculpture, enhance texture and form or provide functional light for small tasks. Special asymmetric recessed luminaires can have adjustable lamp, shutter and lens assemblies to shape the beam of emitted light (see figure 7-22).

When a uniform wash of light on a vertical surface is desired, an asymmetric distribution of wallwashers is recommended. Spacing between luminaires and distance from walls are both critical when trying to achieve uniformity.

Recessed luminaires using T-12, T-10 and T-8 fluorescent lamps commonly supply general illumination to commercial spaces. These luminaires may utilize one, two, three or four 4-ft long lamps; the overall dimensions of these luminaires are typically 1×4 ft or 2×4 ft. The 4×4 ft luminaire is becoming much less common in new construction and renovation due to growing trends toward lower illuminances and lower energy costs.

The 2×2 ft luminaire is growing in popularity with specifiers. These luminaires may utilize two T-12 U-shaped fluorescent lamps, or two or three T-8 U-shaped or T-5 compact fluorescent lamps. The three lamp compact fluorescent luminaire is typically used where the space requires a relatively high illuminance.

Many forms of optical control are found with recessed luminaires. Prismatic refractors have been widely utilized in the past because they provide high luminaire efficiency and uniform illuminance distribu-

tion in the work space. More recently, due to concern with reflected glare in VDT screens, sharp-cutoff louvers are being specified with recessed luminaires. Well-designed luminaires of this type minimize or eliminate the brightness of the reflected image of the luminaire in the VDT screen (see chapter 15, Office Lighting).

Ceiling-Mounted Luminaires

General diffuse ceiling-mounted luminaires (see figure 7-23b, c and e) direct their light in a wide pattern and are normally used for general illumination. In general, the light source should not be visible through the luminaire, and their luminances should be carefully balanced within the room. This may be less important, however, in an industrial space with high ceilings because the luminires are well above the usual lines of sight. See figure 7-24. The close-to-ceiling position of luminaires of this type does allow them to have a higher luminance than similar ones hung lower into the

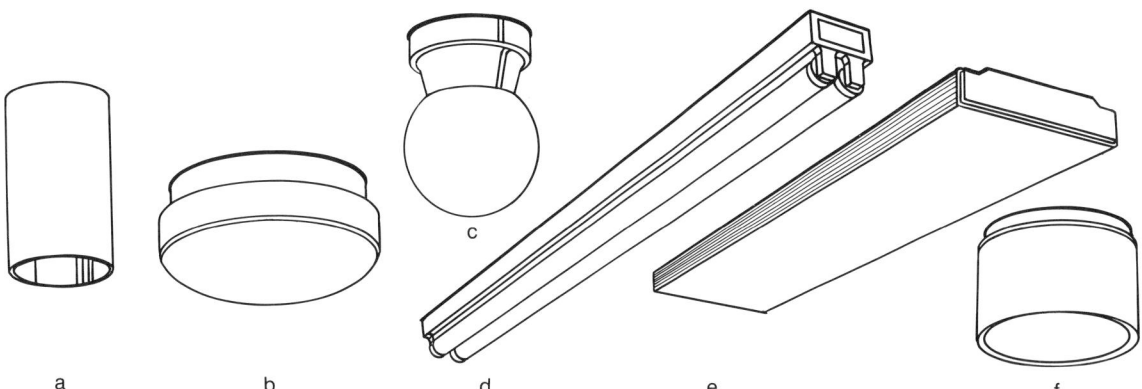

Fig. 7-23. Ceiling-mounted luminaires. Diffuse types: b, c and e. Downlighing types: a, d and f.

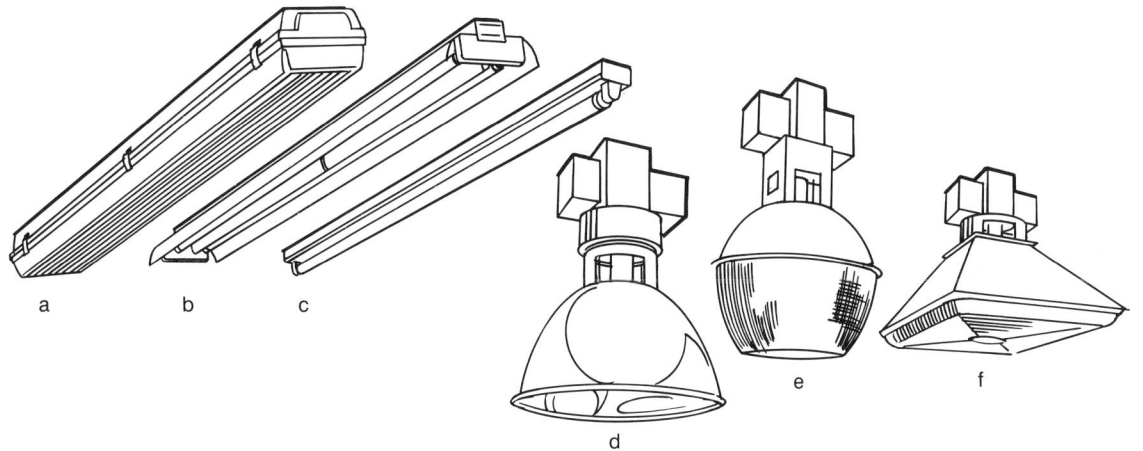

Fig. 7-24. Types of industrial luminaires. (a) Damp and wet location, (b) two-lamp slimline, (c) one-lamp slimline, (d) high bay, (e) warehouse and (f) low bay.

line of sight. Ideally, though, every ceiling-mounted luminaire should provide some illuminance on the ceiling to balance brightnesses within the field of view.

Ceiling-mounted downlights or directional luminaires (see figure 7-23a, d and f) are designed to be used for accent lighting or supplementary illumination for critical visual tasks, such as preparing food at counter tops.

Track-Mounted Luminaires

Track-mounted luminaires use track which is generally made of linear extruded aluminum, containing copper wires to form a continuous electrical raceway. Available in nominal lengths of 0.6, 1.2 and 2.4 m (2, 4 and 8 ft), it can be joined or cut, or set into a variety of patterns with connectors in the shape of L's, T's, or X's, or with flexible connectors for irregular patterns. Track is available in a one-, two-, three- or four-circuit mode for greater capacity and added flexibility in control and switching. Single-circuit tracks usually have a rating of 20 A at 120 V, with a theoretical maximum load of 1920 W on a 20-A circuit. Low-voltage track with remote transformers is also available.

Track can be mounted at or near the ceiling surface, recessed into the ceiling plane with special housing or clips, or mounted on stems in high-ceiling areas. It can also be used horizontally or vertically on walls. It can be hardwired at one end or anywhere along its length. Flexibility can be added if a cord-and-plug assembly rather than hardwiring is used to supply power.

A variety of adjustable track-mounted luminaires are available (see figure 7-25) for attachment at any point along the track. These luminaires come in many shapes and styles, housing a large assortment of lamps, including line and low voltage. Low-voltage track systems can be equipped with integral transformers at each luminaire or with remote power to provide low-voltage power along the entire length of track. In addition, a number of luminaires are designed to create special effects for decorative applications.

Wall-Mounted Luminaires

Wall-mounted luminaires (see figure 7-26) can be diffuse or directional. In light distribution, they are similar to luminaires mounted on the ceiling. Since they are often mounted low, they are often in the field of view, and therefore the designer should be aware of the potential for glare.

Wall-mounted luminaires often have exposed clear lamps for decorative purposes. Additional room lighting is important to provide general illumination in order to maintain a low luminance and to prevent glare from the exposed lamps. Translucent shields, which vary in size or shape, are often used for lighting hallways, stairways, doorways and mirrors.

Wall-mounted luminaires with opaque shielding completely conceal the source from normal viewing angles, and are strongly directional in light distribution. Downlight luminaires are often mounted on the wall

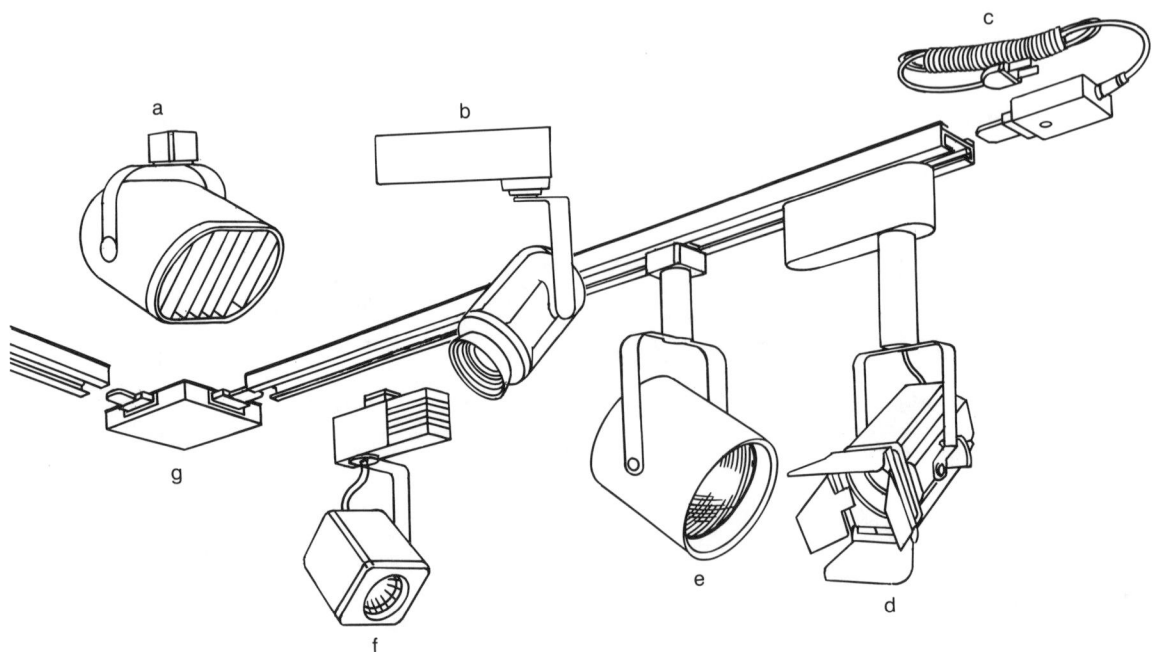

Fig. 7-25. Track-mounted luminaires and feeds. Examples shown are (a) compact fluorescent, (b) MR 16, (c) plug-in feed, (d) MR 16 projector, (e) PAR, (f) MR 16 and (g) corner connector feed.

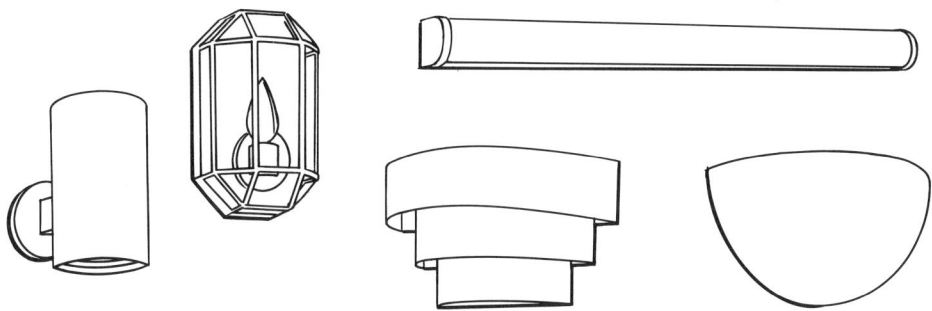

Fig. 7-26. Wall-mounted luminaires.

for accent and display lighting, whereas uplight luminaires can be used for general, indirect illumination.

Suspended Luminaires

Suspended luminaires are hung by chain, aircraft wire, cord, or stems from the ceiling. They can have single or multiple arms or a single lamp holder and diffuser. See figure 7-27

Suspended luminaires that diffuse the light are used for both functional and decorative purposes. For functional purposes, the luminance should be optically controlled to prevent glare and ensure proper luminance ratios, particularly if hung low enough to be in the line of sight.

Indirect and direct-indirect luminaires are being more commonly used in commercial environments where VDT screens are extensively used by the occupants. Properly specified and installed, these suspended luminaires provide a relatively high, uniform illuminance without bright reflections on the VDT screen.

Direct-indirect suspended luminaires with opaque or slightly luminous shades or shields may be placed in the direct line of sight. Glass or plastic diffusers should not be visible below the shade or shield. Shielding the top of the luminaire is important if it is viewed from

above. Likewise, a louver at the bottom is important if it is viewed from below.

The main function of suspended downlights is to provide accent illumination, and they are generally suspended at or below eye level. When mounted above eye level, as in stairways, halls and entryways, they require some bottom shielding (louver or diffuser). Almost without exception, luminaires of this type need additional general room illumination for visual comfort.

The main function of exposed-lamp suspended luminaires is to provide decorative highlights, sparkle and accent. They are not suitable for general room illumination or for lighting specific tasks. The lamps should have low luminance and should be mounted above the normal line of sight. When such luminaires must be mounted at or below the line of sight, the lamps should be dim and should be viewed against walls which have a high reflectance.

Portable Luminaires

Portable luminaires (table or floor lamps) are frequently used as decorative elements in a furnishing scheme. In many interior spaces, portable luminaires make a major contribution to the general illumination, as well as provide illumination for visual activities.

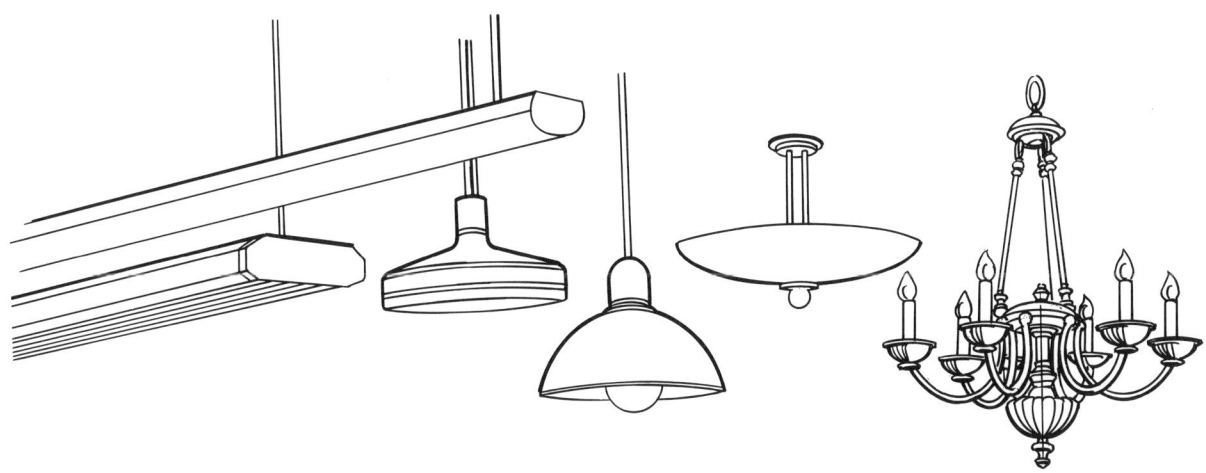

Fig. 7-27. Suspended luminaires.

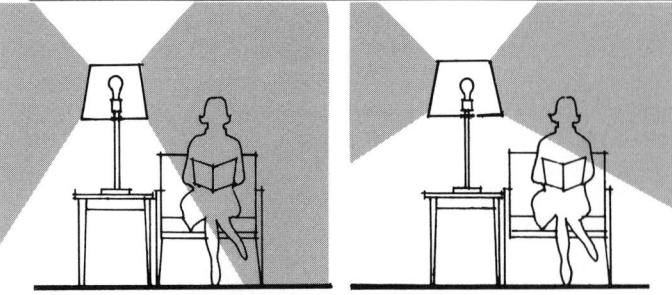

Fig. 7-28. Influence of shade dimensions on light distribution of portable luminaires. Shade on the left is 360 mm (14 in.) wide. Shade on the right is 410 mm (16 in.) wide.

If the room is evenly illuminated and the room reflectances are high, the optical performance of the portable luminaire is less important. In a room lighted exclusively by table or floor lamps, the type of shade and location of the light sources becomes more critical. Deep, narrow shades do not provide useful task illumination; they restrict the spread of both downward and upward light. Figure 7-28 illustrates the difference in performance between a 360-mm (14-in.) and a 410-mm (16-in.) shade.

Opaque shades create pools of light above and below, and unless there are other light sources in the room, the effect can be visually uncomfortable. On the other hand, shades of too high transmittance and too little diffusion show "hot spots" that are unattractive and distracting. The inner surface of the shade should have a high reflectance; otherwise light is lost by ab-

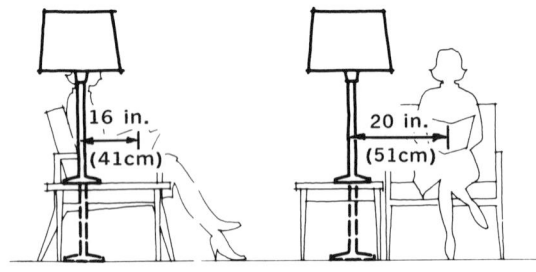

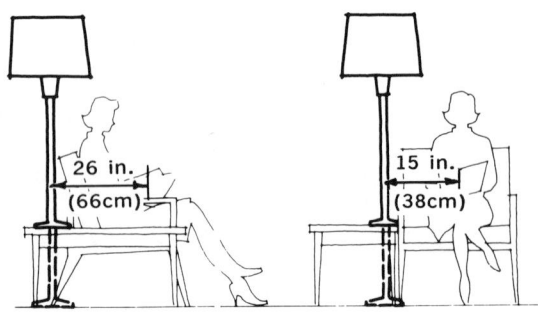

Fig. 7-29. Recommended placement of common types of portable luminaires for the task of reading in a chair.

sorption. The shade material should have good diffusing quality and suitable transmittance.

The light source, if there is only one, should be centered within the shade so that the luminance of the shade is nearly uniform from top to bottom. A better solution is to mount one source high in the shade to provide upward light, and another source near the lower edge of the shade for illumination of the task plane.

Placement of portable luminaires may be a difficult issue, especially since these luminaires might be moved often. Figure 7-29 shows the recommended placement of different types of portable luminaires for the common task of reading in a chair.

APPLICATIONS: OUTDOOR LUMINAIRES

Classification

Outdoor luminaires are classified by the manner in which they are mounted, by the type of intensity distribution they exhibit and by the degree to which they provide cutoff.[13] Following are the IESNA outdoor luminaire classifications by intensity distribution (see figure 24-6 in chapter 24, Roadway Lighting):

Type I or	Narrow, symmetric distribution, highest intensity usually at nadir
Type II	Wider distribution than Type I, highest intensity between 10° and 20° from nadir
Type III	Wide distribution, highest intensity between 25° and 35° from nadir
Type IV	Widest distribution
Type V	Symmetrical; produces circular illuminance pattern
Type VS or VQ	Produces an almost symmetrically square illuminance pattern

More detailed information on these luminaire types is found in chapter 24, Roadway Lighting. Cutoff classifications are as follows:

Cutoff	Intensity at 80° from nadir does not exceed 100 cd per 1000 lamp lumens, nor at 90° from nadir does intensity exceed 25 cd per 1000 lamp lumens
Semicutoff	Intensity at 80° from nadir does not exceed 200 cd per 1000 lamp lumens, nor at 90° from nadir does intensity exceed 50 cd per 1000 lamp lumens
Noncutoff	No intensity limitations

Most outdoor luminaires use one of three kinds of high-intensity discharge lamps: high-pressure sodium, metal halide and mercury vapor. Low-pressure sodium lamps are sometimes used for parking lot lighting, though the poor color properties of these lamps limit their application.

Pole-Mounted Luminaires

Pole-mounted luminaires are commonly used for roadway and parking lot lighting (see chapter 24, Roadway Lighting). These luminaires have wide distributions to permit large pole spacings. In most cases, minimum horizontal illuminance and uniformity of horizontal illuminance are the most important design criteria. For this reason, the intensity distributions used have maximum values at angles above 75° from the nadir.

Luminaires with *dropped-dish*, or *ovate*, refractors are commonly used in roadway applications. They are mounted on long arms off the pole. Because of their appearance they are referred to as "cobra head" luminaires. Poles for roadway applications are usually mounted well back from the roadside to avoid damage to both the luminaire and oncoming traffic.

This kind of refractor optical system can cause glare. Roadway glare can be reduced by using cutoff luminaires. Luminaires with the same "cobra head" form but without refractors are available for this purpose.

Parking lot lighting often uses cutoff luminaires with flat-bottomed lenses (see figure 7-30). These luminaires are mounted on short arms and can be arranged in single, twin or quad configurations. Symmetric and asymmetric intensity distributions and mounting configurations are used to provide the necessary flexibility in pole placement for parking lots.

Small pole-mounted luminaires are also used with short poles to provide walkway and grounds lighting. Sometimes referred to as *post top* luminaires, they can satisfy functional as well as esthetic purposes.

Surface-Mounted Luminaires

Wall-mounted luminaires are often used for small parking lots immediately adjacent to a building or in parking structures. Often referred to as "wall packs," wall-mounted luminaires have an asymmetric distribu-

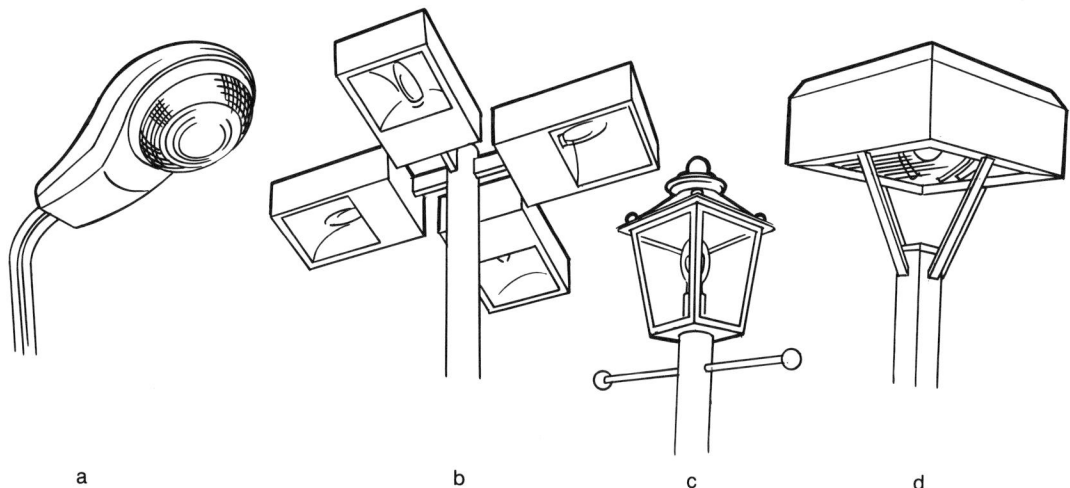

Fig. 7-30. Outdoor pole-mounted luminaires. Examples shown are (a) "cobra head" type for roadways, (b) cutoff luminaires in a quad configuration for parking lots and (c and d) post top types for walkways and grounds.

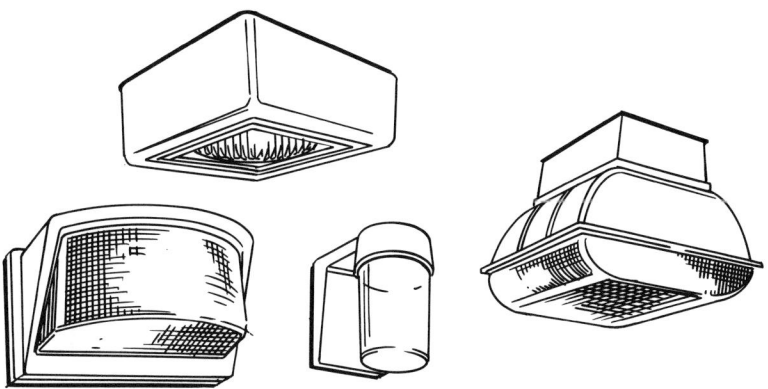

Fig. 7-31. Ceiling- and wall-mounted luminaires for parking lots.

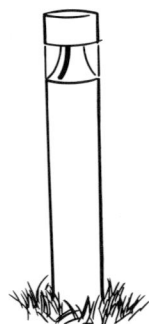

Fig. 7-32. Bollard luminaire for walkway or grounds lighting.

tion necessary for lighting adjacent parking lots. See figure 7-31.

Surface-mounted luminaires in parking structures are mounted on walls or ceilings and are designed to produce a considerable amount of interreflected light in the structure.

Bollard Luminaires

Walkway and grounds lighting is often accomplished with bollards. These luminaires have the form of a short thick post similar to that found on a ship or wharf; hence the name. The optical components are usually at the top, producing an illuminated area in the immediate vicinity. Bollards are used for localized lighting. Their size is appropriate for the architectural scale of walkways and other pedestrian areas. See figure 7-32.

Floodlight Luminaires

These luminaires are often used for building facade lighting, sports lighting and other special applications. See chapters 22 and 23 and figure 7-33. These applications can have intensity distributions that range from

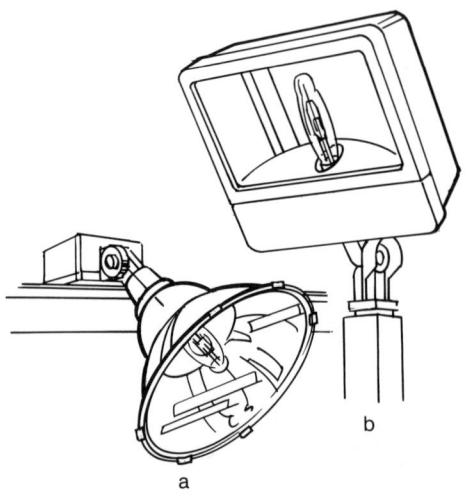

Fig. 7-33. Floodlight luminaires for (a) sports lighting and (b) building facade lighting.

very narrow to very wide, depending upon the angular size of the object being illuminated and the effect to be achieved. The intensity distributions are usually not symmetric.

Sports lighting usually uses luminaires with very narrow intensity distributions, mounted to the side of the playing area, and luminaires with medium distributions and sharp cutoff mounted over the playing area. Use of the narrow-intensity-distribution luminaires almost always requires careful computations at the design stage to ensure proper overlapping of beams as well as proper horizontal and vertical illuminances. See chapter 9, Lighting Calculations, and chapter 23, Sports and Recreation Areas.

Building facade lighting uses luminaires with narrow and wide distributions, depending upon the portion of the building being illuminated and the distance to the luminaire mounting location. Column lighting, accent lighting and distant mounting locations require narrow distributions. Lighting large areas with near mounting locations requires very wide distributions. This type of luminaire often has an intensity distribution that produces a square or rectangular illuminance pattern. See chapter 22, Exterior Lighting.

The mounting for floodlight luminaires usually contains a mechanical arrangement that permits aiming. In banks flood light luminaires are often grouped, since their application usually involves limited mounting and access availability, however, each luminaire is aimed independently. Both sports and building facade luminaires require careful aiming after installation.

APPLICATIONS: WIRING

Every luminaire, as part of a lighting system, should also be considered part of a well-designed, trouble-free electrical wiring system.

Branch-circuit panel boards and the feeders that serve them must be designed to carry the lighting load to be connected. The characteristics of the electrical system (such as voltage, phases and capacity), should be known prior to designing the circuit or choosing any of the controls such as switches, dimmers or occupancy sensors. These control devices must match the electrical system characteristics to achieve a coordinated electrical system.

Designers should know the fundamentals of electrical systems design to ensure that they can optimize flexibility and cost. All electrical systems in the United States must be designed and installed in accordance with the provisions and requirements of the NEC[5] as well as state and local codes. To assure that these requirements are met, the electrical system should always be designed by a licensed professional engineer.

The first step in the design of a coordinated lighting and electrical system is to determine the utilization voltage of the system. For new buildings, this information may be obtained from the utility company or from the engineer. In existing buildings, the information may be obtained from the maintenance engineer by measurement, or by reading the name plate data on existing panel boards.

The electrical characteristics most often encountered in the United States are:

- 120/240 V, single phase, three wire for residential buildings
- 120/208 V, three phase, four wire for older or small commercial buildings
- 277/480 V, three phase, four wire for many newer and large commercial buildings

In Canada, the voltages are:

- 120/240 V, single phase, three wire for residential buildings
- 347/600 V, three phase, four wire for commercial buildings

In Mexico, the electrical characteristics are:

- 127/220 V, three phase, four wire for residential and commercial buildings
- 220/440 V, three phase, four wire for industrial buildings

It should be noted, however, that branch-circuit wiring for lighting in residential and commercial applications in Mexico utilizes 127 V, single phase.

When the designer is faced with a 277/480-V source of power, step-down transformers, to obtain 120/208 V, will be required for use with incandescent sources. The designer must exercise caution, as these step-down transformers may also be used for power to appliance and receptacle circuits, leaving little or no power for incandescent lighting. If involved in a project early enough, the designer may wish to request that a portion of the transformer kilovoltamperes be held in reserve for "special lighting."

The location(s) of the panel boards and transformers will probably be dictated by the architecture of the building, as usable and rentable space is not easily given up. To exemplify, a high-rise office building will probably have one electrical room per floor, with vertical electrical distribution of 277/480 V and a step-down transformer for 120/208 V on each floor.

Very often, the lighting designer will be requested to state the power density prior to the completion of the design process. There are several sources of information available to assist in obtaining an answer; they

include, in addition to past experience, the NEC,[5] ASHRAE/ANSI/IES 90.1,[14] and state and local codes.

Due to the increased awareness of the need for effective energy utilization, the control of lighting has become a more integral part of the design. Various techniques for control are at the disposal of designers. These lighting control tools include two- or three-level switching of three- or four-lamp fluorescent lighting luminaires, and photoelectric control for daylight and occupancy/motion sensors. See chapter 31, Lighting Controls, for a discussion of control strategies.

There are economies in the circuiting of lighting of which designers should be aware. A 277- or 120-V single-phase circuit to a panel board (homerun) will require one phase conductor and one neutral conductor. It is, however, possible to "trunk" three single-phase circuits to make one three-phase homerun if the electrical distribution system is three phase. This three-phase homerun will consist of one neutral conductor and three phase conductors, thereby saving two neutral conductors.

Other economic issues that should be considered include the use of high-power-factor ballasts for compact fluorescent luminaires and the use of 208 or 480 V for HID sources both indoors and outdoors. There are some code restrictions on the use of 480-V lighting equipment.

The importance of using high-power-factor ballasts can be demonstrated by comparing them with normal-power-factor ballasts with the help of an example. Using two 26-W quad compact fluorescent lamps operating at 120 V, the electrical characteristics and hence the electrical circuit data will be as indicated in the following table:

	Normal Power Factor	High Power Factor
Ballast loss	22 W	22 W
Total fixture draw	74 W	74 W
Starting current	1.20 A	0.6 A
Operating current	1.20 A	0.6 A
Voltamperes	144 VA	72 VA

Although the total fixture draw remains constant, the operating current increases and therefore the voltamperes increase. The net result in this example is that using normal-power-factor ballasts will allow a maximum of 13 luminaires on a 20-A, 120-V circuit. Using a high-power-factor ballast will allow a maximum of 20 luminaires on the same circuit.

Caution is required in the use of square wave inverters for emergency power with high-power-factor, compact fluorescent ballasts. The power-factor-correcting capacitor used in the ballast may look like a short circuit to the square wave output of the inverter and create circuit breaker problems.

With the increase in the use of electronic ballasts, the designer and the engineer should work as a team to ensure that the inherent harmonic distortions of these ballasts do not damage the neutral conductor(s) of the electrical system. In some cases, it may become necessary to oversize the neutral conductor. See chapter 6, Light Sources, for further information on electronic ballasts.

Minimum wiring capacity requirements are given in the NEC.[5] The purpose of the NEC is the practical safeguarding of persons and buildings and their contents from hazards arising from the use of electricity for light, heat, power, radio, signaling and other purposes, and compliance with its requirements does not ensure adequacy either for present use or future growth.

APPLICATIONS: THERMAL INTERACTION OF LUMINAIRES AND BUILDINGS

The Building Environment

Building spaces are designed to provide pleasing and productive conditions for the occupants. A building consists of a variety of components and systems, including structural, architectural, electrical, mechanical and control systems, and interior furnishings and equipment. The interactions between building systems, and the response of the building to exterior conditions and occupant activities, influence the performance of each of the building components. In this regard, lighting system performance is also dependent on the building's thermal environment.

The major thermal considerations related to the performance of a lighting system are the dependence of its light output and efficiency on lamp temperature, and the cooling load due to energy dissipated by it. The effects of the thermal environment on light output and efficiency fall primarily within the realm of the lighting designer; the cooling load due to lighting is of more interest to the mechanical systems designer. Unless proper consideration is given to the interactions between the lighting, heating and cooling systems and their effect on light output and efficiency, accurate predictions of system performance cannot be achieved.

Essentially all of the electrical power provided to the lighting system is dissipated into the building space as heat, the exception being any visible light radiated directly out of the building through transparent surfaces. The heat gain from the lighting system contributes to the cooling load, or helps satisfy the heating requirements, depending on the building conditions. Most large commercial buildings have large interior

heat sources, such as computers and other electrical equipment, and need to be cooled throughout the year. Exterior zones in large buildings, and smaller buildings with high ratios of surface area to volume, may require heating in winter. In buildings without air conditioning, the heat from lighting systems can overheat occupant spaces.

Lighting can account for 25–50% of building electrical energy usage. Electrical energy to meet the cooling loads imposed by lighting can add another 10–20%. Another important factor is that the time of day when the lighting load is greatest corresponds to the time of peak building cooling load demand and electric utility demand and of greatest electrical energy unit cost. Thus, any improvement in lighting system efficiency can save lighting energy, cooling energy and energy costs, and also reduce cooling equipment capacity requirements.

Thermal Effects on Lighting System Performance

The performance of many lamp types is dependent on the lamp wall temperature. This is particularly true for fluorescent lamps, for which both light output and electrical power input, and thus luminous efficacy, vary with the temperature of the coldest spot on the lamp wall. The lamp temperature in turn is a function of the heat balance between the lamp and its surroundings. Electrical energy provided to the lamp is partly converted into visible light, the balance being dissipated through the mechanisms of thermal (infrared) radiation, convection and conduction.

Even the most efficient lamps convert only a moderate percentage of their electrical power input into visible light, as shown in figures 7-34, 7-35 and 7-36. The efficacy varies from a low of 10% for incandescent lamps, to approximately 19% for fluorescent lamps, to a high of 28% for low-pressure sodium lamps. With the exception of low-pressure sodium lamps, the greatest

Fig. 7-34. Energy Output for Some Fluorescent Lamps of Cool White Color

Type of Energy	40WT12	96 Inch T12 (800 mA)	PG17† (1500 mA)	T12 (1500 mA)	T8 F32 rare earth
Light	19.0%	19.4%	17.5%	17.5%	23.4%
Infrared (est.)*	30.7	30.2	41.9	29.5	29.0
Ultraviolet	0.4	0.5	0.5	0.5	0.4
Conduction-convetion (est.)	36.1	36.1	27.9	40.3	34.2
Ballast	13.8	13.8	12.2	12.2	13.0
Approximate average bulb wall temperature	41°C (106°F)	45°C (113°F)	60°C (140°F)		37°C 99°F

*Principally far infrared (wavelengths beyond 5000 nanometers).
†Grooves sideways.
Note: Lamps are operated on high-power-factor, 120-V, 2-lamp ballasts under ambient temperatures of 25°C (77°F) in still air.

Fig. 7-35. Energy Output for Some Incandescent Lamps

Type of Energy	100-Watt* (750-hour life)	300-Watt (1000-hour life)	500-Watt (1000-hour life)	400-Watt ‡ (2000-hour life)
Light	10.0%	11.1%	12.0%	13.7%
Infrared†	72.0	68.7	70.3	67.2
Conduction-convention	18.0	20.2	17.7	19.1

* Coiled-coil filament.
† Principally near infrared (wavelengths from 700 to 5000 nanometers).
‡ Tungsten-halogen lamp.

Fig. 7-36. Energy Output for Some High Intensity Discharge Lamps

Type of Energy	400-Watt Mercury	400-Watt Metal Halide	400-Watt High Pressure Sodium	180-Watt Low Pressure Sodium
Light	14.6%	20.6%	25.5%	29.0%
Infrared	46.4	31.9	37.2	3.7
Ultraviolet	1.9	2.7	0.2	0
Conduction-convention	27.0	31.1	22.2	49.1
Ballast	10.1	13.7	14.9	18.2

percentage of energy converted by most lamps is dissipated as infrared radiation. The relative energy dissipation by convection and conduction depends on airflow conditions and the temperature around the lamp, and on the details of the lamp mounting and fixture design.

Since lamps emit energy in infrared as well as visible wavelengths, it is useful to examine the radiant properties of materials used in luminaires. The transmittance and reflectance of most materials are wavelength dependent. Thus, for example, a lens material can be selected which has high visible transmittance but low

infrared transmittance, thereby reducing the amount of heat radiated from the luminaire. However, the heat which is trapped in the luminaire will cause the fixture and lamp temperature to be greater than it would be otherwise. This may be desirable if higher lamp temperatures are needed to boost efficiency, but consideration should be given to the possibility of increased thermal stresses within the luminaire. Figure 7-37 lists the radiant properties of several materials which are commonly used in lighting systems, including the percentage reflectance and transmittance at selected wavelengths.

Lighting Energy Distribution Fractions

In general, the electrical energy input to a luminaire will be dissipated via the following mechanisms:

- Downward visible light
- Upward visible light
- Downward infrared radiation
- Upward infrared radiation
- Downward convection
- Upward convection
- Convection to return air
- Conduction

The magnitude of each of these components depends on the type of lamp and luminaire, the HVAC design and the design of the building space, particularly the presence or absence of a ceiling plenum. Some of the fractions may be zero for some configurations. Figure 7-38 lists typical values of the lighting energy distribution fractions for various luminaire, HVAC and room types.[15] In this table, all visible light output, both up and down, is lumped together, since the split can vary

Fig. 7-37. Lighting Energy Distribution Percentages

Plenum	none	none	static	vented	vented	static
Air return	ceiling grill or sidewall	ceiling grill or sidewall	ducted or sidewall	ceiling grill	lamp compartment extract	ducted lamp compartment extract
visual/room	18	18	18	18	18	18
IR/room	32	72	30	25	15	5
IR/plenum	0	0	4	9	5	5
convection/room	40	10	42	39	0	0
convection/plenum	0	0	3	6	59	5
convection/return	0	0	0	0	0	54
conduction	10	0	3	3	3	3

Fig. 7-38. Lamp Temperature Elevations

Number of lamps	Lamp type	Luminaire type	Air return	Temperature elevation (°C)
4	40 W	acrylic	ceiling grill	26-28
4	40 W	acrylic	lamp compartment	22-25
4	40 W	parabolic	ceiling grill	20-22
4	40 W	parabolic	lamp compartment	14-17
2	40 W	acrylic	ceiling grill	21-24
2	40 W	acrylic	lamp compartment	15-19
2	40 W	parabolic	ceiling grill	10-16
2	40 W	parabolic	lamp compartment	10-12
2	20 W	acrylic	ceiling grill	15-18
2	20 W	acrylic	lamp compartment	10-14

Note: A side slot return is similar to ceiling grill.

greatly depending on the luminaire photometric distribution.

Several test methods have been employed to assess the total energy distribution from a particular luminaire. One involves an adaptation of photometric techniques. Two others involve calorimetry, including the use of continuous-water-flow[16] and continuous-airflow[17,18] calorimeters. In one study, though procedures and equipment varied widely, the test results were of the same order of magnitude.[19]

Testing guides for determining the thermal performance of luminaires have been published by IESNA, the Air Diffusion Council (ADC) and the National Electrical Manufacturers Association (NEMA). The IESNA approved a new test method in 1978 which considers the effect of plenum temperature and air return on the light output. The test also provides data on the manner in which heat distribution and power input depend upon the return airflow through the luminaire.[20]

Lamp Temperature as a Function of Design

Fluorescent lamps are widely used in commercial and industrial spaces, and their performance is strongly dependent on lamp wall temperature. The type of fixture and its location relative to supply and return air ducts influence the lamp temperature and therefore performance. A convenient way of characterizing lamp thermal performance is in terms of the elevation of lamp temperature above ambient air temperature for each luminaire and HVAC configuration. This allows the determination of the lamp temperature for any ambient air temperature by adding the lamp temperature elevation to the air temperature.

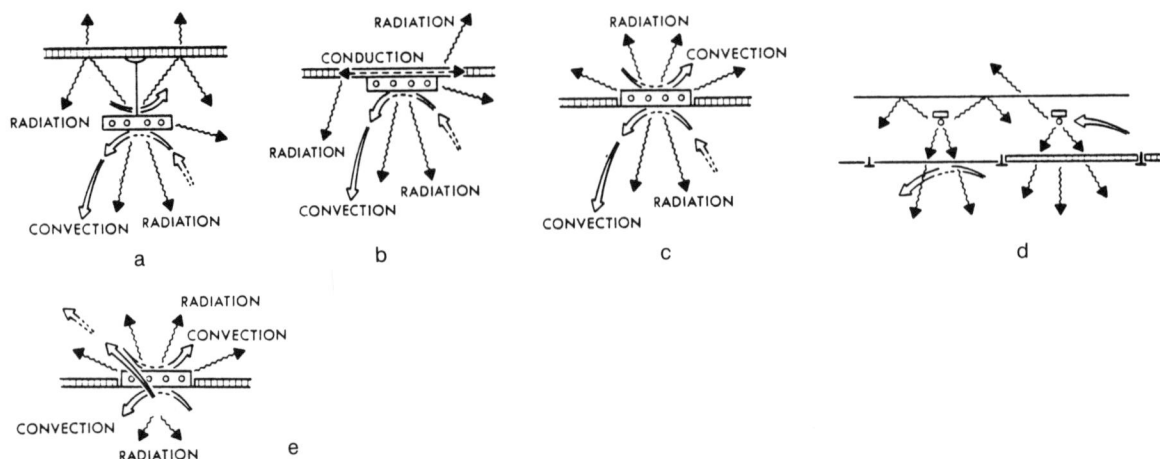

Fig. 7-39. Effect of the ceiling-to-luminaire relationship upon the lighting system heat transfer. The fluorescent luminaire has a direct-indirect total energy distribution classification. (a) Suspension-mounting, (b) surface-mounting, (c) recessed, (d) luminous and louvered ceiling, and (e) heat transfer luminaire.

For example, an unvented four-lamp fixture with an acrylic lens will usually have hotter lamps than the same fixture if vented, or than a similar fixture with two lamps, or than a fixture with an open-cell diffuser. For each fixture type and airflow configuration, the possible lamp temperatures span a fairly narrow range, approximately 3–6° C. Some variation in lamp temperature can be obtained by changing the airflow rate, but this has a limited effect unless lamp compartment extract is used.

Most fluorescent lamps are designed to operate most efficiently with a minimum lamp wall temperature of about 40° C. A fixture with an acrylic lens will operate about 6–8° C warmer than a similar open-cell parabolic fixture. Lamp compartment air return reduces the lamp temperature by about 4–6° C. A two-lamp fixture will operate about 4–7° C cooler than a similar four-lamp fixture. Lamp temperatures are very similar with ceiling grill and side slot returns.

Figure 7-39 lists ranges of minimum lamp wall temperature elevations above ambient air temperature for various luminaire and HVAC design configurations. These values were determined from full-scale testing, and actual values for specific equipment may vary.[21]

Cooling Load Due to Lighting

The ASHRAE Fundamentals Handbook covers the calculation of the space load due to lighting for various luminaires and ventilation arrangements.[22] Generally, the instantaneous heat load from the lighting system is expressed using the relationship

$$P_i = P_l \times BLF \times CLF \times UF$$

where

P_i = instantaneous heat load from the lighting system, in W (multiply by 3.41 to get Btu/h),

P_l = total lamp power, in W,

BLF = ballast load factor (1.00 for incandescent, 1.08–1.30 for rapid start fluorescent, 1.04–1.37 for HID),

CLF = cooling load factor, which allows for luminaire type, room envelope and hours of operation (see reference 22),

UF = utilization factor, the fraction of installed power in use (for many commercial applications such as stores, UF = 1.0).

The luminaire mounting has an important role in the distribution of thermal energy. Figure 7-39 illustrates typical heat flows for various types of ceiling-to-luminaire relationships. The total energy distribution involves all three mechanisms of heat transfer: radiation, conduction and convection. The illustration shows a fluorescent luminaire, but HID luminaires exhibit similar patterns. The input of the suspended luminaire in figure 7-39a would be convected and radiated in all directions, to be reflected or absorbed and reradiated. Essentially all of the input energy would remain within the occupied space.

Heat transfers from the surface-mounted semidirect luminaire in figure 7-39b involve radiation, conduction and convection. Assuming good contact with the ceiling, upper surfaces of the luminaire will transfer energy to or from the ceiling by conduction. Since many acoustical ceiling materials are also good thermal insulators, it may be assumed that temperatures within the luminaire will be elevated. Thus, lower luminaire surfaces will tend to radiate and convect to the space below at a somewhat higher rate. Unless the ceiling material is a good heat conductor and can reradiate above, essentially all of the input energy will remain in the space.

A different situation exists when components of the system are separated from the space. The recessed luminaire in figure 7-39c distributes some portion of its input wattage above the suspended ceiling. The actual ratio is a function of the luminaire design and plenum and ambient conditions. For most recessed static luminaires, the ratio is very nearly 50% above the ceiling and 50% below.

Lighting systems of luminous and louvered ceiling types are illustrated in figure 7-39d. A similarity with the heat transfers of figure 7-39a is noted. Although the luminaires are separated from the occupied space, the plastics and glass used in luminous ceilings are good absorbers of infrared. White synthetic enameled louvers are also good absorbers, whereas aluminum louvers reflect a high percentage of infrared. Unless some means of controlling the energy is employed, all of the electrical input energy again remains in the occupied space.

Heat transfer recessed luminaires are illustrated in figure 7-39e. Here, the convected and the radiated component to the space has been reduced considerably, while the upward energy has increased correspondingly. Under certain conditions it is possible for the space load to consist almost entirely of light energy. The majority of the power input to the luminaire is directed upward, where it can be captured by the system and be subject to some form of control. Laboratory tests conducted in accordance with IESNA procedures[20] will provide energy distribution data for evaluative purposes. However, the total system must be evaluated, because heat removal to the plenum may raise plenum temperatures, causing conductive heat transfer back through the ceiling and floor to the space below and above, and thereby adding thermal load back to the space.

Task-ambient lighting systems have a different lighting energy distribution. Care must be exercised in the selection of the cooling load factor (CLF). Depending on the installation, it may be necessary to calculate task and ambient heat loads separately.

It is possible to have both systems completely within the space. This will be the case if suspended or surface-mounted luminaires are used for ambient lighting, with task lighting being incorporated into the furniture or with suspended or surface-mounted luminaires being used for both. In this case, the entire input power is an instantaneous space load.

With recessed luminaires utilized for ambient lighting and either suspended or furniture-mounted ones for task lighting, the heat loads must be figured separately, as only the task lighting load is entirely instantaneous space load. The recessed luminaire heat contribution may be considerably less, depending upon the CLF.

Systems can also utilize recessed luminaires for both task and ambient lighting. Here, both will impose a heat load which will be reduced by the CLF.

Benefits of Integrated Design

The benefits of integrating building heat into lighting design are:

- Improved performance of the air-conditioning system
- More efficient handling of lighting heat
- More efficient lamp performance

The control and removal of lighting heat can lower heat in the occupied space, reduce air changes and fan horsepower, lower temperature differentials required in the space, enable a more economical cooling coil selection because of the higher temperature differential across the coil, and reduce luminaire and ceiling temperature, thereby minimizing radiant effects.

The degree to which any of these benefits may be realized depends on many variables, such as the quantity of energy involved, the type of heat transfer mechanism, the temperature difference between source and sink, and the velocity and quantity of fluids or air available for heat transfer. However, in most applications, luminaire temperature will be higher than room temperature, so fluids at room temperature can be effective in heat transfer. Any unwanted heat that can be removed at room temperature or above can be removed much more economically than at lower temperatures.

The full benefits of integrated design can be achieved only through the combined efforts of a design team, which should include architects, space planners, interior designers, electrical engineers, mechanical engineers, lighting designers and cost analysts.

REFERENCES

1. IES. Committee on Light Control and Equipment Design. 1970. IES guide to design of light control. Part IV: Practical concepts of equipment design. *Illum. Eng.* 65(8):479–494.
2. Underwriters Laboratories. 1972. *Standard for safety: Electric lighting fixtures, UL-57.* Northbrook, IL: Underwriters Laboratories.
3. American Society of Heating, Refrigerating and Air-Conditioning Engineers. 1972. *Methods of testing for sound rating heating, refrigerating and air-conditioning equipment, ASHRAE 36-72.* New York: American Society of Heating, Refrigerating and Air-Conditioning Engineers.
4. American Society of Heating, Refrigerating and Air-Conditioning Engineers. 1976. Systems. In *ASHRAE Handbook and Product Directory 1976*, chapter 35. American Society of Heating, Refrigerating and Air-Conditioning Engineers.
5. National Fire Protection Association. 1978. *National electrical code, NFPA 70.* Quincy, MA: National Fire Protection Association.
6. Underwriters Laboratories. 1974. *Standard for safety: Marine-type electric lighting fixtures, UL-595.* Northbrook, IL: Underwriters Laboratories.
7. Underwriters Laboratories. 1976. *Standard for safety: Electric lighting fixtures for use in hazardous locations, UL-844.* Northbrook, IL: Underwriters Laboratories.
8. Canadian Standards Association. 1975. *Canadian electrical code: Safety standard for electrical installations, CSA standard C22.1-1975.* Rexdale, Ont.: Canadian Standards Association.
9. National Electrical Manufacturers Association. 1974. *Fluorescent luminaires.* NEMA LE1-1974. Washington: National Electrical Manufacturers Association.
10. IES. Committee on Light Control and Equipment Design. 1967. IES guide to design of light control. Part III: Materials used in light control. *Illum. Eng.* 62(8):483–510.
11. IES. Committee on Light Control and Equipment Design. 1959. IES guide to design of light control. Part I: Physical principles. *Illum. Eng.* 54(2):722–727. Part II: Design of reflector and optical elements. *Illum. Eng.* 54(12):778–786.
12. Jolley, L. B. W., J. M. Waldram, and G. H. Wilson. 1930. *The theory and design of illuminating engineering equipment.* London: Chapman and Hall.

Daylighting

8

Daylight[1] is distinguished as a light source by its unique, changing spectra and distributions. It can increase occupant satisfaction and conserve energy if considerations such as view design, glare control, human factors and integration of building systems are properly addressed. It is essential that daylight effects be considered in any space where daylight is admitted, even if it is not exploited as a light source, in order to avoid problems with glare and damage to materials.

To use daylight effectively, the following factors should be taken into account:

- Human factors, including physiology, perception, preferences and behavior
- Effects of daylight on all materials, including furniture, artwork and plants
- Controlled admission of direct sunlight
- Controlled admission of diffuse daylight
- Effects of local terrain, landscaping and nearby buildings on the available light
- Integration of building systems, including the electric lighting, fenestration, interior geometry and finishes, manual and automatic control systems, and active climate control systems

DAYLIGHT SOURCES AND AVAILABILITY

The daily and seasonal movements of the sun with respect to a particular geographic location produce a predictable pattern of amount and direction of potentially available daylight. A random pattern coexists with this predictable pattern and is caused by changes in the weather, temperature and air pollution.

Of the solar energy received at the earth's surface, 40% is visible radiation. The rest is invisible shorter (ultraviolet) and longer (infrared) wavelengths. When absorbed, virtually all the radiant energy from the sun is converted to heat. The amount of usable visible energy in the solar spectrum varies with the depth and condition of the atmosphere which the light traverses. Because the spectral distribution of daylight changes continuously with sun position and sky conditions, the Commission Internationale de l'Éclairage (CIE) has adopted three standard spectral radiant power distributions for daylight; see figure 8-1.

The Sun as a Light Source

The rotation of the earth about its axis, as well as its revolution about the sun, produces an apparent motion of the sun with respect to any point on the earth's surface. The position of the sun with respect to such a point is expressed in terms of two angles: the *solar altitude*, which is the vertical angle of the sun above the horizon, and the *solar azimuth*, which is the horizontal angle of the sun from due south in the northern hemisphere (figure 8-2).

The Sky as a Light Source

As sunlight passes through the atmosphere, a portion is scattered by dust, water vapor and other suspended particles. This scattering, acting in concert with clouds, produces sky luminance. Skies are divided into three categories: (1) clear, (2) partly cloudy and (3) cloudy.

When the sky is not completely overcast, the sky luminance distribution may change rapidly and by large amounts as the sun is alternately obscured, partly obscured or fully revealed.

The Ground as a Light Source

Light reflected from the ground may be important in daylighting design. Such light is, in turn, reflected from the ceiling or walls onto other interior surfaces. On sunlighted elevations, the light reflected from the ground typically represents 10–15% of the total daylight reaching a window. It frequently exceeds this with light-colored ground surfaces such as sand and snow. On shaded exposures, it may account for even more of the total light reaching a window, depending on the sky condition and building design.

Daylight Availability

Calculation of the light received from the "source" is considerably more complex for daylight than for electric sources. Determination of the illuminance incident on windows and skylights must take account of the

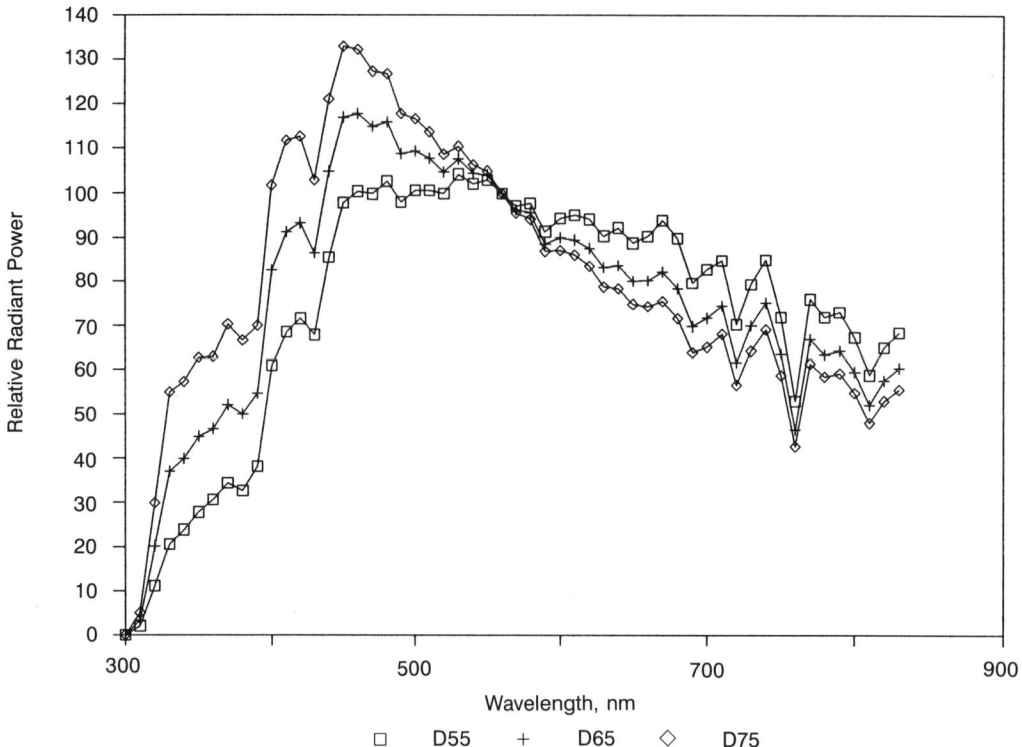

Fig. 8-1. Three spectral radiant power distributions of daylight.

time-varying characteristics of the sky and sun, including the changing spatial relationship between the sun and daylighting apertures.

The phrase *daylight availability* refers to the amount of light from the sun and the sky for a specific location, time, date and sky condition. Measurements of daylight illuminance by various researchers in numerous worldwide locations over the past 60 years have resulted in very similar mean values.[2] Equations giving available daylight illuminance are determined from these values.

Daylight availability data, and the equations derived from them, do not express instantaneous values of illuminance and luminance; they give mean values. That is, the equations provide best fits to data averaged over time and measurement sessions. For this reason, measured instantaneous luminances and illuminances may differ widely from those determined by calculation methods based on daylight availability. It is not unusual for the instantaneous values to be more than twice or less than half the mean design values.

Calculation of daylight availability at a site begins with a determination of the solar position, which is a function of:

- Latitude and longitude of the site
- Day of the year (Julian date)
- Local time

The local time is converted to solar time. Angles are computed that give the position of the sun in the sky. Finally, for a particular sky condition, the daylight availability equations are used to compute the daylight illuminance. All angles are expressed in radians.

Site Location

The site location is specified by a latitude l and a longitude L. Latitudes and longitudes may be found in any standard atlas or almanac. Figure 8-3 shows the latitudes and longitudes of some North American cities.[3]

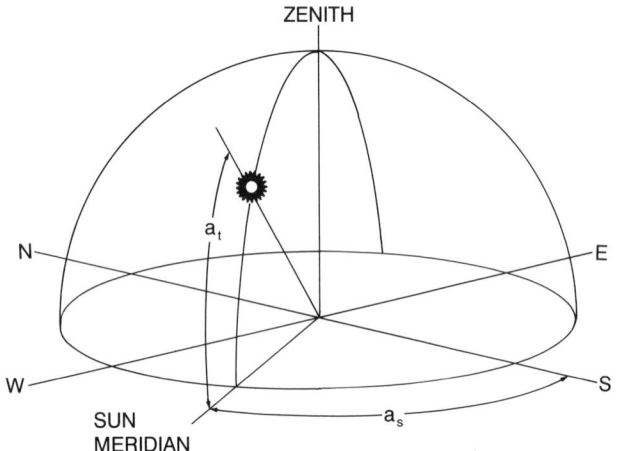

Fig. 8-2. Solar altitude (a_t) and azimuth (a_s).

Fig. 8-3. Latitude and Longitude of Some North American Cities

Country/City	Latitude Degrees	Latitude Radians	Longitude Degrees	Longitude Radians
Canada				
Ottawa, ON	45	0.79	76	1.33
Montreal, PQ	46	0.80	74	1.29
Toronto, ON	44	0.77	79	1.38
Vancouver, BC	49	0.85	123	2.15
Winnipeg, MB	50	0.87	97	1.69
Mexico				
Mexico City	19	0.33	99	1.73
United States				
Anchorage, AK	61	1.06	150	2.62
Big Rapids, MI	44	0.77	85	1.48
Boulder, CO	40	0.70	105	1.83
Chicago, IL	42	0.73	88	1.54
Cleveland, OH	41	0.72	82	1.43
Dallas, TX	33	0.58	97	1.69
Honolulu, HI	21	0.37	158	2.76
Los Angeles, CA	34	0.59	118	2.06
Miami, FL	26	0.45	80	1.40
New York, NY	41	0.72	74	1.29
Philadelphia, PA	40	0.70	75	1.31
Seattle, WA	48	0.84	122	2.13
Troy, NY	43	0.75	74	1.29
Washington, DC	39	0.68	77	1.34

Conventions used in expressing latitudes are:
Positive = northern hemisphere
Negative = southern hemisphere

Conventions used in expressing longitudes are:
Positive = west of prime meridian (Greenwich, U.K.)
Negative = east of prime meridian

Time

A 24-h clock is used to express time. Solar time can be determined from standard time (or daylight time) by correcting (1) for site longitude within a time zone and (2) for the equation of time. The equation of time gives the difference between solar time and clock time due to:

• Elliptical orbit of the earth
• Solar declination of the axis

The value for the equation of time may be determined from:

$$ET = 0.170 \sin\left(\frac{4\pi(J-80)}{373}\right)$$
$$- 0.129 \sin\left(\frac{2\pi(J-8)}{355}\right) \quad (8\text{-}1)$$

where

ET = time expressed in decimal hours (for example, 1:30 p.m. = 13.5),
J = Julian date, a number between 1 and 365.

Fig. 8-4. Time Zone Standard Meridians

Time Zone	Standard Meridian Degrees	Standard Meridian Radians
Atlantic	60	1.05
Eastern	75	1.31
Central	90	1.57
Mountain	105	1.83
Pacific	120	2.09
Yukon	135	2.36
Alaskan-Hawaiian	150	2.62
Bering	165	2.88

This equation is a least-squares best fit to a very precise equation of time given by Lamm.[4] It is sufficiently accurate for daylighting calculations.

Each time zone has a reference longitude that is used in calculating solar time. These standard meridians are given in figure 8-4.

The relationship between standard time and daylight time is given by

$$t_s = t_d - 1 \quad (8\text{-}2)$$

where

t_s = standard time in decimal hours,
t_d = daylight time in decimal hours.

Solar time is calculated from standard time by the equation

$$t = t_s + ET + \frac{12(SM - L)}{\pi} \quad (8\text{-}3)$$

where

t = solar time in decimal hours,
t_s = standard time in decimal hours,
ET = time from eq. 8-1 in decimal hours,
SM = standard meridian for the time zone in rad,
L = site longitude in rad.

Solar Position

The position of the sun is specified by the solar altitude and solar azimuth, and is a function of site latitude, solar time and solar declination. The solar declination can be closely approximated by

$$\delta = 0.4093 \sin\left(\frac{2\pi(J-81)}{368}\right) \quad (8\text{-}4)$$

where

δ = solar declination in rad,
J = Julian date.

The solar altitude is given by

$$a_t = \arcsin\left(\sin l \sin \delta - \cos l \cos \delta \cos \frac{\pi t}{12}\right) \quad (8\text{-}5)$$

where

a_t = solar altitude in rad,
l = site latitude in rad,
δ = solar declination in rad,
t = solar time in decimal hours.

The solar altitude has a range of 0 to $\pi/2$. If the sun is below the horizon, eq. 8-5 gives a negative value.

The solar azimuth is given by

$$a_s = \arctan\left(\frac{-[\cos\delta\sin(\pi t/12)]}{-[\cos l\sin\delta + \sin l\cos\delta\cos(\pi t/12)]}\right)$$

(8-6)

where

a_s = solar azimuth in rad,
l = site latitude in rad,
δ = solar declination in rad,
t = solar time in decimal hours.

Positive solar azimuthal angles indicate a direction west of south, while negative angles indicate a direction east of south. The arctangent must be placed in the proper quadrant by assessing the signs of the numerator and denominator of its argument.

In many daylighting calculations, it is necessary to calculate the daylight on a vertical surface, such as a wall or a window. The elevation azimuth angle is needed for this calculation. It is the angle, measured in the horizontal plane, between the normal to the vertical surface and south (in the northern hemisphere). See figure 8-5. It is measured clockwise from south.

The solar-elevation azimuth gives the azimuthal angle between the sun and the normal to a vertical

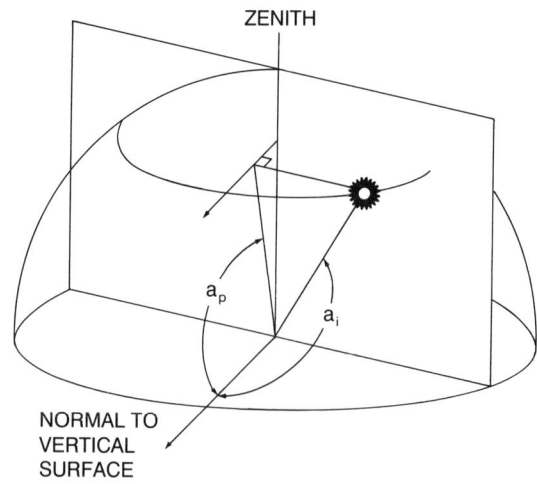

Fig. 8-6. Incident and profile angles.

surface of interest (figure 8-5). It is given by

$$a_z = a_s - a_e$$

(8-7)

where

a_z = solar-elevation azimuth in rad,
a_s = solar azimuth in rad,
a_e = elevation azimuth in rad.

The incident angle is the angle between the normal to a vertical surface of interest and the direction to the sun (figure 8-6) and can be computed from

$$a_i = \arccos(\cos a_t \cos a_z)$$

(8-8)

where

a_i = incident angle in rad,
a_t = solar altitude in rad,
a_z = solar-elevation azimuth in rad.

The profile angle is the apparent altitude of the sun relative to a vertical surface of interest (figure 8-6) and is calculated by eq. 8-9a or 8-9b below. It is used primarily to determine shadows and to plot direct beam penetration on building sections:

$$a_p = \arctan\left(\frac{\sin a_t}{\cos a_i}\right)$$

(8-9a)

$$a_p = \arctan\left(\frac{\tan a_t}{\cos a_z}\right)$$

(8-9b)

where

a_p = profile angle in rad,
a_t = solar altitude in rad,
a_i = incident angle in rad,
a_z = solar-elevation azimuth in rad.

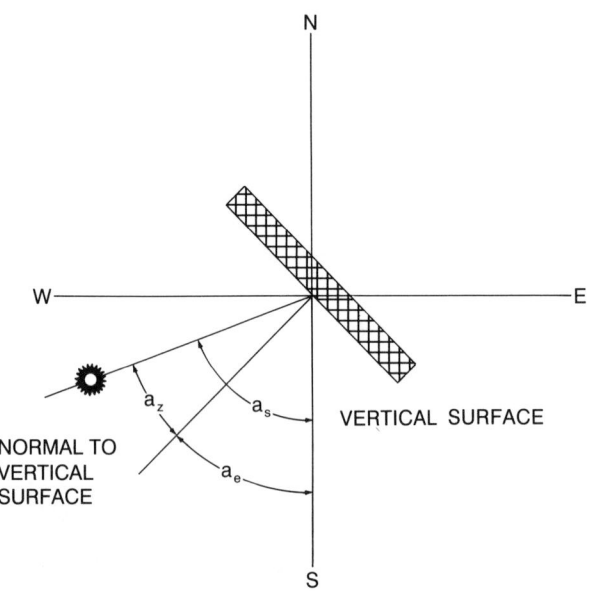

Fig. 8-5. Azimuth angles (plan view).

Sunlight

For the purpose of most basic daylighting calculations, the sun is considered to be a point source that provides a constant illuminance at a point on a plane that is normal to the direction of the sun and near the earth's orbit. The solar illumination constant is the total solar illuminance at normal incidence on a surface in free space at the earth's mean distance from the sun. It is obtained from

$$E_{sc} = K_m \int_{380}^{770} G_\lambda V_\lambda \, d\lambda \qquad (8\text{-}10)$$

where

E_{sc} = solar illumination constant in klx,
K_m = spectral luminous efficacy of radiant solar flux in lm/W,
G_λ = solar spectral irradiance at wavelength λ in W,
V_λ = photopic vision spectral luminous efficiency at wavelength λ,
λ = wavelength in nm (for photopic vision at 380–770 nm).

The following are important solar parameters based on current standards:[5,6]

Solar illumination constant:	128 klx
Solar irradiation constant:	1350 W/m² (126 W/ft²)
Solar luminous efficacy:	94.2 lm/W

To calculate the sunlight reaching the ground, the following must be considered:

- Varying distance of the earth to the sun caused by the earth's elliptical orbit
- Effect of the earth's atmosphere

The extraterrestrial solar illuminance, corrected for the earth's elliptical orbit, is

$$E_{xt} = E_{sc}\left(1 + 0.034 \cos \frac{2\pi(J-2)}{365}\right) \quad (8\text{-}11)$$

where

E_{xt} = extraterrestrial solar illuminance in klx,
E_{sc} = solar illumination constant in klx,
J = Julian date.

The direct normal illuminance at sea level, E_{dn}, corrected for the attenuating effects of the atmosphere, is given by[7]

$$E_{dn} = E_{xt} e^{-cm} \qquad (8\text{-}12)$$

Fig. 8-7. Daylight Availability Constants

Sky Condition	c	A (klx)	B (klx)	C
Clear	0.21	0.8	15.5	0.5
Partly Cloudy	0.80	0.3	45.0	1.0
Cloudy	*	0.3	21.0	1.0

*No direct sun; $E_{dn} = 0$.

where

E_{dn} = direct normal solar illuminance in klx,
E_{xt} = extraterrestrial solar illuminance in klx,
c = atmospheric extinction coefficient (see figure 8-7),
m = optical air mass (dimensionless).

Values for the atmospheric extinction coefficient, discussed below, vary with the sky condition. The equation that is the simplest, and the most often used,[8] representation for the optical air mass is

$$m = \frac{1}{\sin a_t} \qquad (8\text{-}13)$$

where

m = optical air mass (dimensionless),
a_t = solar altitude in rad.

The direct sunlight on a horizontal plane is expressed by

$$E_{dh} = E_{dn} \sin a_t \qquad (8\text{-}14)$$

where

E_{dh} = direct horizontal solar illuminance in klx,
E_{dn} = direct normal solar illuminance in klx,
a_t = solar altitude in rad.

The direct sunlight on a vertical elevation is expressed by

$$E_{dv} = E_{dn} \cos a_i \qquad (8\text{-}15)$$

where

E_{dv} = direct vertical solar illuminance in klx,
E_{dn} = direct normal solar illuminance in klx,
a_i = incident angle in rad.

Skylight

Either the sky ratio method or the sky cover method is used to classify a sky. The sky ratio is determined by dividing the horizontal sky irradiance by the global horizontal irradiance. Since the sky ratio approaches 1.0 when the solar altitude approaches zero (regardless of the sky condition), this method is not accurate for low solar altitudes. The sky conditions are defined as follows:

Clear:	Sky ratio $\leqslant 0.3$
Partly cloudy:	$0.3 <$ sky ratio < 0.8
Cloudy:	Sky ratio $\geqslant 0.8$

The sky cover method uses estimates of the amount of cloud cover. Cloud cover is estimated in tenths and is expressed on a scale from 0.0 for no clouds to 1.0 for complete sky cover. The sky conditions are as follows:

Clear:	0.0–0.3
Partly cloudy:	0.4–0.7
Cloudy:	0.8–1.0

The horizontal illuminance produced by the sky can be expressed as a function of solar altitude:[2]

$$E_{kh} = A + B \sin^C a_t \qquad (8\text{-}16)$$

where

E_{kh} = horizontal illuminance due to
      unobstructed skylight in klx,
A = sunrise/sunset illuminance in klx,
B = solar altitude illuminance coefficient in klx,
C = solar altitude illuminance exponent,
a_t = solar altitude in rad.

The form of the equation is the same for all three sky conditions, with different constants for different sky conditions (figure 8-7).

A different equation is used to represent the mean luminance distribution of each of the three sky conditions. The luminance of the sky is a function of:

• Luminance distribution with respect to zenith luminance
• Absolute value of the zenith luminance

In the method used here, a zenith luminance factor is used to calculate the zenith luminance from the horizontal sky illuminance:

$$L_z = E_{kh}\,\text{ZL} \qquad (8\text{-}17)$$

where

L_z = zenith luminance in kcd/m^2,
E_{kh} = horizontal illuminance due to unobstructed
      skylight from eq. 8-16, in klx,
ZL = zenith luminance factor at the same solar
      altitude as E_{kh}, in kcd/(m$^2 \cdot$ klx).

Values for the zenith luminance factor can be found in figure 8-8. More detailed equations for the zenith luminance have been developed, which include effects such as differences in atmospheric turbidity.[9]

Fig. 8-8. Sky Zenith Luminance (ZL) Constants for Overcast Sky, ZL = 0.409 for any Solar Altitude

Solar Altitude (degrees)	Clear Sky ZL	Partly Cloudy Sky ZL
90	1.034	.637
85	.825	.567
80	.664	.501
75	.541	.457
70	.445	.413
65	.371	.375
60	.314	.343
55	.269	.315
50	.234	.292
45	.206	.272
40	.185	.255
35	.169	.241
30	.156	.230
25	.148	.221
20	.142	.214
15	.139	.209
10	.139	.205
5	.140	.202
0	.144	.201

The angles used in sky luminance determinations are shown in figure 8-9. The position of the sun in figure 8-9 is given by the solar azimuth a_s and zenithal sun angle Z_0. Note that Z_0 is related to the solar altitude a_t by the simple formula

$$Z_0 = \frac{\pi}{2} - a_t \qquad (8\text{-}18)$$

The position of a point P in the sky (at which the sky luminance is calculated) is given by angles ζ, the zenithal point angle in radians, and α, the azimuth angle from the sun in radians.

A standard clear-sky luminance distribution function was developed by Kittler[10] and adopted by the CIE:[11]

$$L_{\zeta,\alpha} = L_z \frac{(0.91 + 10e^{-3\gamma} + 0.45\cos^2\gamma)(1 - e^{-0.32/\cos\zeta})}{(0.91 + 10e^{-3Z_0} + 0.45\cos^2 Z_0)(1 - e^{-0.32})}$$

$$(8\text{-}19)$$

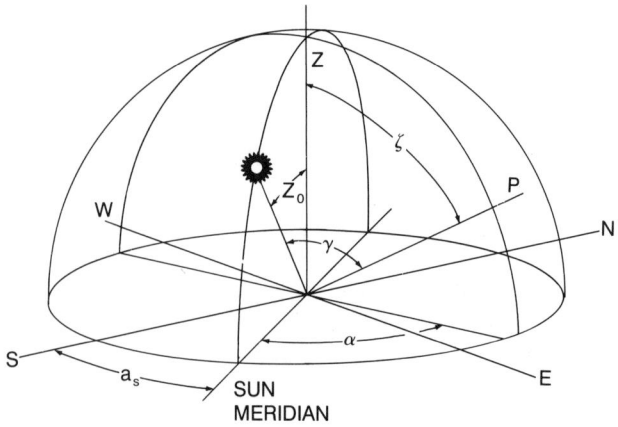

Fig. 8-9. Sky angles.

where

$L_{\zeta,\alpha}$ = sky luminance at point p with spherical coordinates ζ and α, in kcd/m²,

L_z = sky zenith luminance in kcd/m²,

γ = angle between the sun and sky point p in rad (eq. 8-20),

ζ = zenithal point angle in rad,

α = azimuth angle from the sun in rad,

Z_0 = zenithal sun angle in rad.

The angle γ between the sun and sky point p is given by

$$\gamma = \arccos(\cos Z_0 \cos \zeta + \sin Z_0 \sin \zeta \cos \alpha) \quad (8\text{-}20)$$

where Z_0, ζ, α are defined as in eq. 8-19. This equation does not take account of changes in the luminance distribution due to changes in atmospheric turbidity, which can substantially alter the luminance distribution of the sky.

The equation for a partly cloudy sky[12] is similar in form to the clear-sky distribution, but has different values of the constants based on mean data for partly cloudy skies:

$$L_{\zeta,\alpha} = L_z \frac{(0.526 + 5e^{-1.5\gamma})(1 - e^{-0.80/\cos \gamma})}{(0.526 + 5e^{-1.5Z_0})(1 - e^{-0.80})} \quad (8\text{-}21)$$

where the symbols have the same meaning as above. The overcast-sky equation is

$$L_{\zeta,\alpha} = L_z \left(0.864 \frac{e^{-0.52/\cos \zeta}}{e^{-0.52}} + 0.136 \frac{1 - e^{-0.52/\cos \zeta}}{1 - e^{-0.52}} \right)$$

$$(8\text{-}22)$$

where the symbols have the same meaning as above in eq. 8-19.

The form of the overcast-sky equation can be derived from first principles.[12] The first term provides the luminance contribution of the cloud layer, and the second term provides the luminance contribution of the atmosphere between the bottom of the cloud layer and the ground. Constants have been chosen to give a best fit to the original data used by Moon and Spencer[13] in their treatment of the overcast sky.

The empirical Moon-Spencer[13] equation for the luminance distribution of an overcast sky is

$$L_{\zeta,\alpha} = \frac{L_z}{3}(1 + 2\cos \zeta) \quad (8\text{-}23)$$

where

$L_{\zeta,\alpha}$ = sky luminance in kcd/m²,

L_z = sky zenith luminance in kcd/m²,

ζ = zenithal point angle in rad.

This equation has been almost universally used to represent overcast skies for the past 40 years and was adopted by the CIE in 1955.[14] It is historically significant in that a large number of daylight calculation methods are based on it. There is very little numerical difference between eq. 8-22 and eq. 8-23 for the appropriate constants.

The illuminance on a horizontal surface produced by a differential element of the sky is given by

$$dE_{kh} = L_{\zeta,\alpha} \cos \zeta \, d\omega = L_{\zeta,\alpha} \cos \zeta \sin \zeta \, d\zeta \, d\alpha \quad (8\text{-}24a)$$

where

E_{kh} = illuminance on the horizontal surface in klx,

$L_{\zeta,\alpha}$ = sky luminance at point p with spherical coordinates ζ and α, in kcd/m²,

$d\omega$ = differential element of solid angle in the direction to point p,

ζ = zenithal point angle in rad,

α = azimuth angle from the sun in rad.

This equation assumes spherical coordinates. It can be integrated to give the horizontal illuminance produced by an area of sky:

$$E_{kh} = \frac{1}{\pi} \iint L_{\zeta,\alpha} \sin \zeta \cos \zeta \, d\zeta d\alpha \quad (8\text{-}24b)$$

where

E_{kh} = illuminance on the horizontal surface in klx,

$L_{\zeta,\alpha}$ = sky luminance at point p with spherical coordinates ζ and α, in kcd/m²,

ζ = zenithal point angle in rad,

α = azimuth angle from the sun in rad.

The limits of integration depend upon the position and extent of the sky patch. In the limit of the entire sky, the integration is over a hemisphere. This gives

$$E_{kh} = \frac{1}{\pi} \int_0^{2\pi} \int_0^{\pi/2} L_{\zeta,\alpha} \sin \zeta \cos \zeta \, d\zeta \, d\alpha \quad (8\text{-}25)$$

Similarly, the illuminance on a vertical surface due to the sky only is given by

$$E_{kv} = \frac{1}{\pi} \int_{a_z-\pi/2}^{a_z+\pi/2} \int_0^{\pi/2} L_{\zeta,\alpha} \sin^2 \zeta \sin \alpha \, d\zeta \, d\alpha \quad (8\text{-}26)$$

In numerical methods, Equations 8-25 and 8-26 are usually approximated by finite sums of products of differentials and discrete values.

For those cases where the illuminance is desired at a point on a horizontal or vertical plane that has unobstructed access to the sky and the sun, illumi-

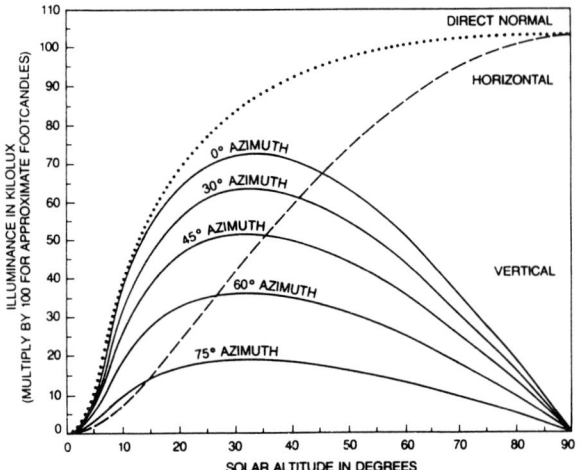

Fig. 8-10. Illuminance from the sun under clear sky conditions as a function of solar altitude and azimuth.

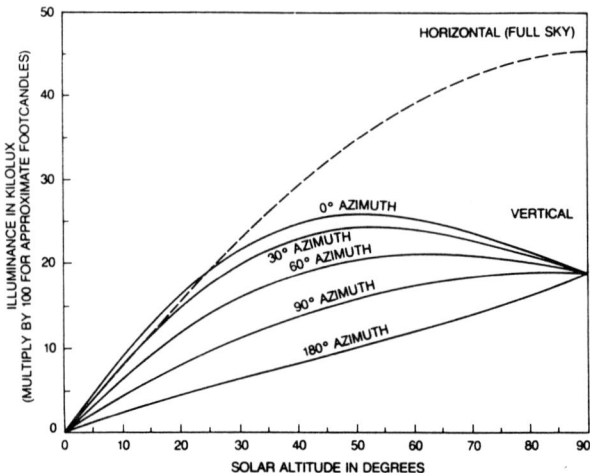

Fig. 8-13. Illuminance on vertical surfaces from partly cloudy sky conditions as a function of solar altitude and azimuth.

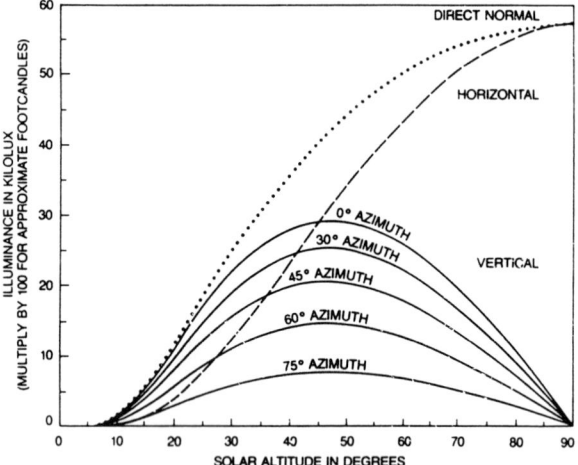

Fig. 8-11. Illuminance from the sun under partly cloudy sky conditions as a function of solar altitude and azimuth.

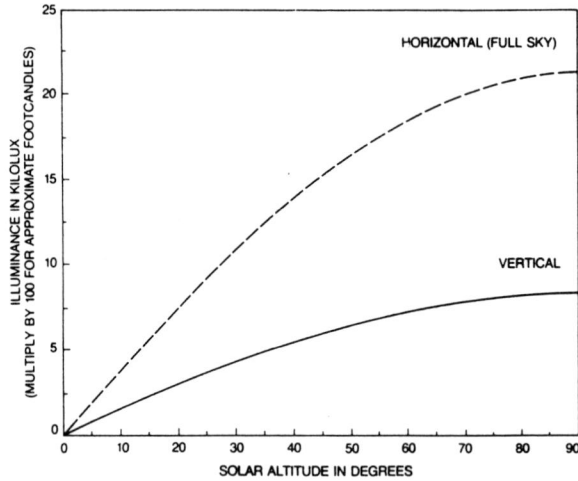

Fig. 8-14. Illuminance on vertical surfaces from overcast sky conditions as a function of solar altitude.

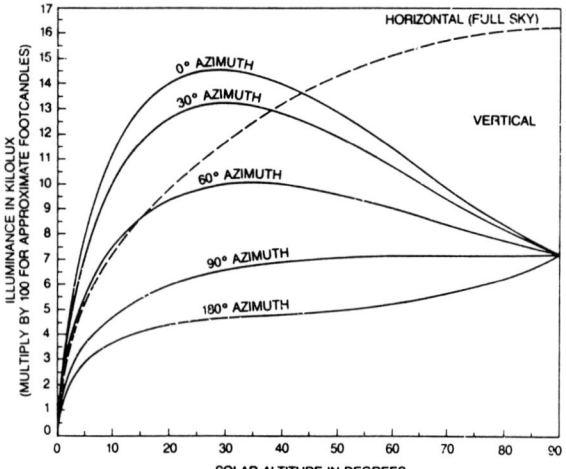

Fig. 8-12. Illuminance on vertical surfaces from clear sky conditions as a function of solar altitude and azimuth.

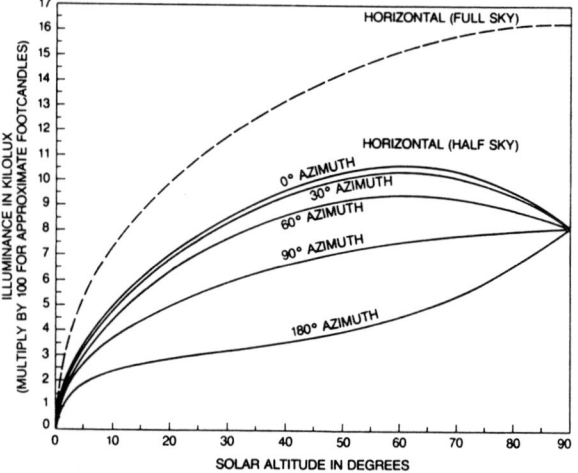

Fig. 8-15. Illuminance on horizontal surfaces from clear sky conditions as a function of solar altitude and azimuth.

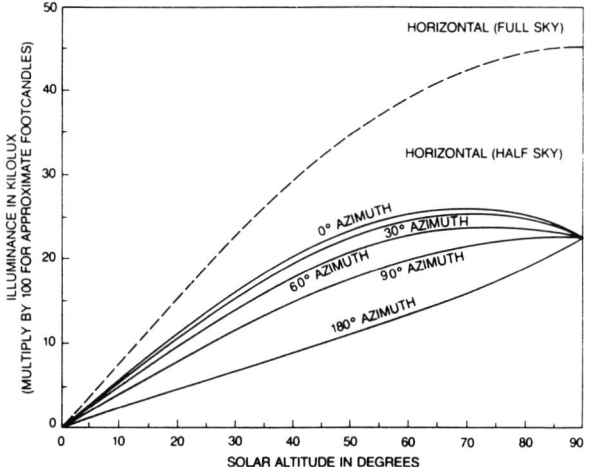

Fig. 8-16. Illuminance on horizontal surfaces from partly cloudy sky conditions as a function of solar altitude and azimuth.

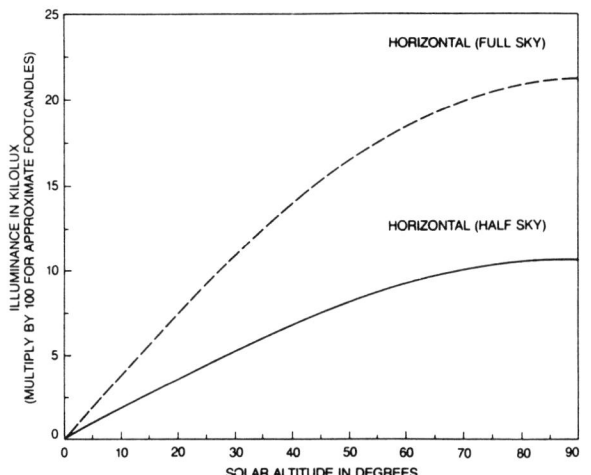

Fig. 8-17. Illuminance on horizontal surfaces from overcast sky conditions as a function of solar altitude.

nances for given sky conditions and sun positions can be obtained from graphs (figures 8-10 through 8-17). These are based on eqs. 8-25 and 8-26.

DAYLIGHTING AND HUMAN FACTORS

View Design and Human Reaction to Windows

It is important that the provision of view and the delivery of daylight be clearly differentiated. Although the terms "view" and "daylighting" are sometimes used interchangeably, the view function of windows is very different from the daylight delivery function. The provision of daylight alone (for example, through skylights) will not satisfy user desires for views including sky, horizon, and ground.[15]

It has been suggested that, to satisfy most workers, windows must cover at least 20% of the window wall

area.[16-18] Heavily tinted glass, used to reduce glare and solar heat gain from such windows, gives outdoor areas an overcast and gloomy appearance, even on sunny days.[19]

Glare from Daylight

Daylighting systems can produce discomfort glare. Very high luminance ratios are produced unless care is taken to balance and reduce luminances. Increased interior electric lighting may be required to balance luminances and reduce glare produced by daylight, thus *increasing* energy use when daylighting is used. Glare is critically dependent on the luminance of the window. Methods for predicting the presence of glare from large area sources have been developed.[20]

Because of its intensity, direct sunlight must also be considered in glare control. While it may be used as an amenity, it should be excluded from critical task areas. The duration of sunshine, rather than its intensity or the size of the patch of sunlight, correlates best with the appreciation of interior sunlight.[21-23]

Human Behavior with Respect to Blinds and Shades

Venetian blinds and curtains are commonly used devices for adjusting the amount of natural light entering spaces and reducing window luminance to control glare. These devices can drastically reduce the amount of daylight admitted to a space, so occupant use of blinds is an important consideration in estimating energy savings from daylighting. Occupants adjust venetian blinds infrequently, having preferred blind positions that are dependent on the orientation of the facade and the season of the year.[24, 25]

DAYLIGHT EFFECTS ON BUILDING CONTENTS

Daylight Effects on Materials and Artwork

Daylight is of particular concern with respect to light damage to materials and artwork because of its high intensity relative to light from electric sources. Light at all frequencies, not just in the ultraviolet (UV) range, contributes to fading, bleaching and other damage.[26] However, UV is known to be especially active in the fading and bleaching process. Unfiltered daylight has about ten times as much UV radiation per lumen as electric light. The length of time that materials are exposed to daylight is a factor in fading; the longer the exposure time, the greater the damage. Exposure of items such as sensitive display merchandise to daylight should therefore be minimized. Fading and bleaching are discussed in chapter 5, Nonvisual Effects of Radiant Energy and in chapter 17, Institution and Public Building Lighting (Museum Lighting).

Daylight Effects on Plants

Daylight provides the full spectrum that plants need for all photoresponses in order to maintain health. Lighting for plant health is discussed in chapter 5.

DAYLIGHTING DESIGN

The provision of apertures for daylighting must be considered in conjunction with decisions regarding building economics, architectural composition, thermal control, ventilation, acoustics and other design factors. Even if windows and skylights are provided for amenity lighting only, daylighting effects must be considered in order to avoid glare and thermal problems. A wide range of approaches has been taken to daylighting as a primary means of illuminating spaces.[27-31]

Effective daylighting design requires consideration of the interaction of building systems. For instance, the installation of energy-conserving dimmable lighting systems may provide only minimal savings if heavily tinted glazing, used to control glare, excessively reduces the admission of daylight.

It is essential that the continuous time variation of daylight be considered in design. No single static condition can provide a reasonable basis for assessing a daylighting design.

Daylight Penetration and Glare Control

Glare control is a major consideration in daylighting, because of the intensity of the source (especially in the case of direct sunlight) and because, in many situations (for example, sidelighting of deep plan buildings) achieving spatially balanced illumination is difficult with a source that is unevenly distributed through the space. A rule of thumb is that the distance of useful daylight penetration with sidelighting is usually not more than twice the window head height. Room furnishings in particular may drastically reduce daylight penetration in sidelit spaces.[32, 33]

Control of Glare from Direct Sunlight. Because of the intensity of direct sunlight, direct and indirect glare can be serious problems. Designs should be developed such that direct sunlight is, or can be, excluded from critical task areas. Sources of reflection should also be identified and eliminated or their reflectance reduced insofar as is possible. Glare produced by reflected sunlight, even for only a few minutes per day, may lead users to take measures that reduce the admission of light for a long time.[34]

Control of Glare from Diffuse Daylight. Glare increases substantially with larger views of the upper portion of the sky. This can be avoided by limiting the height of the view window head in critical task areas, by screening upper window areas from view, or by placing daylighting apertures high enough to be out of the normal field of vision. The task may also be arranged so that the user does not face the window, although this may conflict with user view preferences. Glare can also be reduced by using light colors on interior surfaces. This is critical for areas adjacent to windows, which are typically the surfaces of highest luminance.[20]

Evaluation of Designs

A logical sequence in evaluating a proposed design is the following:

1. Determine whether sunlight will fall on any areas where it should be excluded, and address any resulting problems by changing the daylighting apertures or providing fixed or movable controls.
2. Determine whether sky glare will be a problem, and make adjustments to the design to control glare, or provide fixed or movable controls.
3. Evaluate the performance of the daylighting system acting in concert with any electric lighting, using illuminances and energy use as measures of performance. This includes investigating the pattern of sunlight in spaces where it is being provided as an amenity.

A guide to daylighting design tools is available.[35]

Evaluation of Designs at the Conceptual Stage

Serious glare problems must be identified and addressed early in the design process, because fenestration must often be modified to correct problems created by sunlight penetration.

For a minimum investigation at the conceptual stage, daylighting should be evaluated with solar altitudes corresponding to the solstices, around December 21 and June 21, and the equinoxes, around March 21 and September 22. A range of sky conditions should be tested, including, at least, the extremes for a particular orientation (such as solar noon and the earliest and darkest hours when daylighting occurs for a south-facing facade).

It is important that designs be checked for critical conditions, when sunlight may enter spaces. For instance, at northern latitudes, direct sunlight may strike the north-facing facades of buildings on summer evenings. In the winter, the sun will be low in the sky, resulting in deep penetration of shading systems and sidelit spaces. At southern latitudes, the high summer sun can more readily enter spaces through skylights.

Manual Methods. Sun penetration may be assessed by plotting profile angles on building sections.

Computer Methods. A number of general-purpose three-dimensional modeling programs for architectural design are now available that allow the user to model complex spaces and determine patterns of sunlight penetration through apertures in the envelope. Most of these do not calculate illuminances, but that is not required at this stage of design.

Scale Models. Scale models may be used in conjunction with direct sunlight or lamps to simulate conditions of interest. This does not provide accurate estimates of illuminance, but does allow the assessment of patterns of sunlight penetration.

Evaluation of Designs During Design Development

In addition to estimating illuminances, it is often desirable to perform visual assessments of daylighting systems. Scale models and full-scale mockups were, until recently, the sole means of conducting such assessments. Computer-based visualization systems are now offering an alternative means of conducting visual assessments in addition to computing illuminance patterns.[36]

The aids that may be used in more detailed analysis of daylighting systems are:

- Manual calculation methods (see Calculation of Interior Illuminances below)[37]
- Computer simulation programs (see Calculation of Interior Illuminances below)[36,38,39]
- Graphical methods[28]
- Scale models evaluated under real or artificial skies, which may be used to determine sun penetration and illuminance. Models are also useful in performing visual assessments of lighting systems (see Measurement of Interior Illumination below).[28-30,40]

Assessment of Daylighting Effects on Energy Utilization

Daylighting is sometimes used as an energy conservation measure, because electric lighting is typically the major energy end use in commercial buildings. The Illuminating Engineering Society of North America (IESNA) and the American Society of Heating, Refrigerating and Air-Conditioning Engineers (ASHRAE) have produced a guide for energy-efficient design.[41] This provides procedures for estimating the contribution of daylighting to energy conservation. A method has also been devised for using postconstruction en-ergy-use data to estimate the contribution of daylighting to energy savings.[42]

Photoelectric Control of Electric Lighting Systems

Daylighting will provide energy savings primarily through reductions in the operation of electric lighting. For this purpose, photoelectric control is an alternative to manual switching of lights. The subdivision of the building into sufficiently small control zones is an important consideration. Large zones may not adequately respond to different lighting conditions within them. For instance, some offices may receive too little light when part of a zone is shaded by an adjacent building.

It is important that building operators and occupants be educated as to the purpose and function of daylighting controls if they are to be used. Automatic controls may be deactivated by persons who fail to understand their purpose and function.

Maintenance

If the planned results of the daylighting system are to be achieved, maintenance is required. This will involve periodic cleaning. Light loss factors due to dirt depreciation are given in figure 8-18 below.

DAYLIGHTING SYSTEMS

Several fenestration designs are used to provide a view and deep penetration of daylight while controlling glare.[27,28,43-48]

Fenestration and Building Sections

Some common approaches include:

Unilateral Sidelighting. This design (see figure 8-19a) lends itself to continuous fenestration and curtain wall construction. To avoid large ranges in daylight illuminances (greater than 25:1), the distance from the window wall to the inner wall should normally be limited to twice the window head height with clear glazing. Deeper spaces may be created if additional lighting opposite the window wall is used to balance illuminances. For this reason, window heads are often placed close to the ceiling, although the resulting increase in the view of the sky also increases glare.

Fig. 8-18. Typical Light Loss Factors for Daylighting Design

Locations	Light Loss Factor Glazing Position		
	Vertical	Sloped	Horizontal
Clean Areas	0.9	0.8	0.7
Industrial Areas	0.8	0.7	0.6
Very Dirty Areas	0.7	0.6	0.5

Window with Overhang. Overhangs (see figures 8-19a and b) may be used to reduce sunlight penetration in latitudes where the sun is high in the sky during the times spaces are occupied. This reduces the view of the upper portion of the sky and provides a less drastic range of illuminances across a space. However, overhangs also reduce daylight penetration, although this may be offset to some degree by the redirection of ground-reflected light into the space.

Simple Window with Blinds. Venetian blinds can be effective in controlling the entry of sunlight, reducing sky glare and redirecting light to the ceiling. They can provide a shading effect equivalent to a very substantial overhang. However, users tend to adjust blinds infrequently. Blinds may substantially reduce the amount of daylight admitted and significantly reduce the effectiveness of energy-saving dimming electric lighting controls.

Split Window with Upper and Lower Blinds. This allows for different adjustments for the upper and lower portions of the glazing. For instance, daylight can still be admitted deep into the space when the lower blinds are closed to exclude sunlight from a task area.

Split Window with Upper Pane Tinted. This reduces glare from the upper portion of the sky while providing a minimally distorted view of the ground plane.

Window with Vertical Shading Elements. Devices such as fins are effective sun controls on east and west walls. Combinations of vertical and horizontal elements (for example, "egg crate" shades) as sun controls are most common in southern latitudes.

Window with Light Shelf. Light shelves are fixed exterior and interior shading systems used in combination with glazing placed above the view glazing in sidelighting systems. By screening the upper portion of the sky, they allow the exploitation of higher window heads, providing deeper and more uniform daylighting while eliminating the glare that would normally accompany the use of tall windows.

Bilateral. Bilateral daylighting (see figure 8-19b) balances the admission of light. This system permits doubling of the room width possible with unilateral daylighting. The second set of windows often occupies only the upper part of the wall. A reflecting roof below the secondary windows acts as a ground plane, contributing materially to the light entering the room. At least one set of windows is exposed to the sun, necessitating glare control. Sloping ceilings, sometimes employed with this design, have little effect on the quantity or quality of illumination except where they can allow a higher window head.

Roof Monitor. This daylighting system is most frequently used in industrial buildings where a central high bay is set between two lower flanking areas (see figure 8-19c). Providing high-reflectance roof surfaces below the monitors increases interior illuminances.

Clerestory. Additional windows on the roof facing the same direction as the main window aid in overcoming the daylight penetration limitations of the unilateral section (see figure 8-19d).

Staggered Building Sections. Staggered building sections can allow for deep penetration of daylight along with greater flexibility in the layout of spaces. They are a variation on combinations of clerestory lighting and other sidelighting systems.

Sawtooth. This fenestration (see figure 8-19e) is used principally in large-area industrial buildings. Slanting the windows to face the sky increases the potential daylighting contribution, but this may be offset by increased dirt collection on the glazing; heat gain may also be increased.

Skylights. Skylights assume many forms, including domes, panels with integral sun and brightness control, panels of fiber-glass-reinforced plastic, and louvers for heat and glare control. Skylight detailing requires spe-

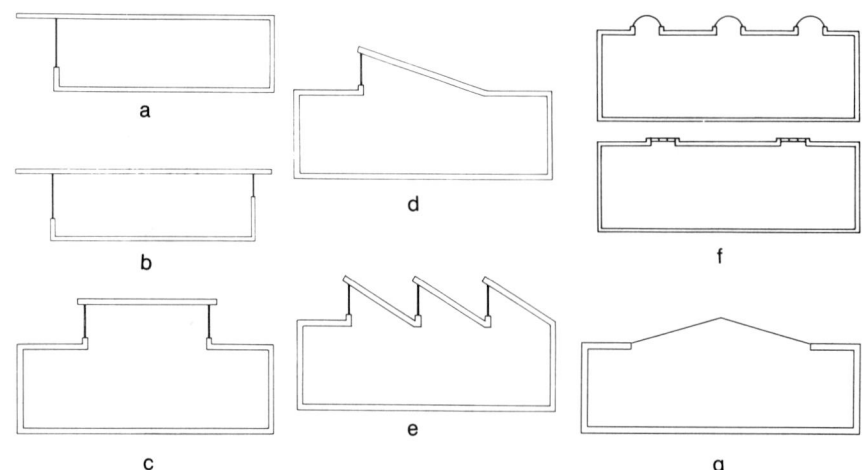

Fig. 8-19. a. Unilateral lighting section. b. Bilateral lighting section. c. Roof monitor lighting section. d. Clerestory lighting section. e. Sawtooth lighting section. f. Skylight sections. g. Atrium section.

cial attention to prevent moisture penetration and dripping due to condensation. Openable skylights may also provide ventilation and cooling (see figure 8-19f).[49]

Atria.[50] Large area daylighting sources that have several forms such as ridge type (see figure 8-19g), sheds, pyramids and domes. Because of the large area, lower range (10-25%) light transmissions are used. Translucent sandwich panels with high diffusing glass-fiber reinforced polymer faces are especially suitable for diffuse shadow-free daylighting with light and heat control.

Materials and Control Elements

The materials and shading systems used in daylighting are characterized by the following properties: transmission, absorption, reflection, diffusion, refraction, cost, thermal properties and appearance.

Transmittance data for several materials are provided in figure 8-20. It should be noted that the transmittance of materials is a function of the incident angle of the light (see the subsection on the Lumen Method, below, for an example of the application of this fact in computing illuminances).[51]

Transparent (High-Transmittance) Materials. These transmit light without appreciably changing its direction or color; they are image preserving. Common types are sheet, polished plate, and float and molded glass as well as some rigid plastic materials and formed panels. Windows may include multiple glazings and spaces to reduce heat transfer.

Transparent (Low-Transmittance) Materials. Low-transmittance glasses and plastics offer a measure of brightness reduction that increases as their transmit-

Fig. 8-20. Transmittance Data of Glass and Plastic Materials

Material	Approximate Transmittance (percent)
Polished Plate/Float Glass	80–90
Sheet Glass	85–91
Heat Absorbing Plate Glass	70–80
Heat Absorbing Sheet Glass	70–85
Tinted Polished Plate	40–50
Figure Glass	70–90
Corrugated Glass	80–85
Glass Block	60–80
Clear Plastic Sheet	80–92
Tinted Plastic Sheet	42–90
Colorless Patterned Plastic	80–90
White Translucent Plastic	10–80
Glass Fiber Reinforced Plastic	5–80
Translucent Sandwich Panels	2–67
Double Glazed–2 Lights Clear Glass	77
Tinted Plus Clear	37–45
Reflective Glass*	5–60

*Includes single glass, double glazed units and laminated assemblies. Consult manufacturer's material for specific values.

tance decreases. During daylight hours, the ability to view into a room is reduced. At night, the view into a room is apparent while the view from a room to the outdoors is reduced. Lower transmittances, below 0.5, can give a gloomy appearance to outdoor views.

Electrically Controlled Glazings. Electrically controlled glazings have transmittance properties that are a function of an applied voltage. Currently available products require the application of a low voltage to render them opaque and become clear when the voltage is switched off.[52]

Diffusing Materials. The amount of diffusion in materials varies over a wide range, depending on the material and its surface treatment. Generally, transmittance and luminance decrease as diffusion increases. The luminance of highly diffusing materials is nearly constant from all viewing angles. Diffusing materials include translucent and surface-coated or patterned glass, plastics, translucent sandwich panels[53] with fiberglass reinforced polymer faces and diffusing glass block.

High-Reflectance, Low-Transmittance Materials. Reflective glasses and plastics provide luminance control by having high exterior reflectances. These materials act as one-way mirrors, depending on the ratio of indoor to outdoor illumination. Their low transmittance gives outdoor areas an overcast appearance, even on sunny days.[19] Some selectively admit visible light while reflecting infrared wavelengths that would otherwise add to the cooling load.

Directional Transmitting Materials. These include glasses and plastics with prismatic surfaces that are used to obtain the desired directional control of light and luminance. They are used in either horizontal or vertical panels.

Specularly Selective Transmitting Materials. These include the various heat-absorbing and reflecting materials that are designed to pass most visible radiation, but absorb or reflect a portion of the infrared radiation, which would otherwise contribute to cooling loads. Absorbed heat is reradiated indoors and outdoors in approximately equal proportions. Stained glass comes under this classification, as it is selective in the visible portion of the spectrum, though primarily for reasons of appearance rather than as a means of illumination control.

Shades and Draperies. These include opaque and diffusing shades and draperies for excluding or moderating daylight and sunlight. To darken a room, as for projection, the system must be opaque and completely cover the window.

Louvers. Louvers may be fixed or adjustable, horizontal or vertical. They are capable of excluding direct sunlight and reducing radiant heat while reflecting a large portion of sun, sky and ground light into the interior. In the case of fixed louvers, the spacing and height of the slats should be designed to exclude direct sunlight at normal viewing angles. Overhangs for sun control are often made with louver elements so that light from the rest of the sky can reach the windows. Louvers are also employed in top-lighting arrangements, sometimes with two sets of slats set at right angles to form an egg crate. Matte textures and high reflectances should be used where possible.

Landscaping. Trees can be effective shading devices for buildings of low elevation if placed in an appropriate position with respect to windows. Deciduous trees provide protection against glare due to direct sun during the warm months, but transmit sunlight during the winter. Deciduous vines on louvered overhangs or arbors provide similar seasonal shade.

Exterior Reflecting Elements. Reflective pavements and similar surfaces increase the amount of ground light entering the building. Reflecting materials or finished roofs below windows have the same effect.

Interior Reflecting Elements. In general, most interior elements should have a high reflectance. This reduces contrast and glare, and is especially important for elements near windows, such as mullions. In particular, ceiling reflectance has a large influence on the amount of daylight (sunlight, skylight and ground-reflected light) delivered to parts of rooms far from windows and light shelves.

Superglazings. High-performance glazings use multiple cavities separated by films and filled with special gases, as well as low-emissivity coatings, to reduce heat transfer.

CALCULATION OF INTERIOR ILLUMINANCES

Calculation methods can be useful in comparing alternative daylight delivery systems or considering the limits of daylight utilization for various systems under average lighting conditions. Illuminance computation involves determination of the sky, sun and interreflected components of daylight. The sky and sun components are due to flux that reaches a point directly. The interreflected component results from sunlight and skylight that have initially reached other surfaces and then been reflected to the point of interest. Computation of the sky, sun and interreflected components may be used to calculate illuminances at points or average illuminances over surfaces.

Computer Calculations

Because of the speed with which alternative scenarios can be explored and the complexity of the situations that can be evaluated, computer methods are becoming more widely used. Capabilities for visualization of inte-

riors with combined electric sources and daylighting are also increasing.[36]

Calculation of illuminances at points is usually done with computer software because of the complexity of the required calculations.

In most computer programs used for daylighting, the sky and sun components at the points of interest are determined using a finite-sum approximation for eqs. 8-25 and 8-26. The summation is performed using only those (small) sections of the sky that illuminate the points directly.

The interreflected component of illuminance at the points of interest is determined using the finite-element radiative transfer method. This process is described in detail in chapter 9 on Lighting Calculations. In its application to daylight calculations, the initial exitances of room surfaces are determined from the flux input from windows and skylights. It is usual to assume room surface reflectances are diffuse.

Calculation of the direct and interreflected components can be very complicated for elaborate fenestration and skylight systems, if space contents are to be modeled (for example, partitions), or if the space geometry is complicated.

Factors affecting the accuracy of computer simulations are discussed in references 54 and 55.

Lumen Method

The lumen method for calculation of interior illuminances is similar to the zonal cavity method for electric lighting, and is simple enough to permit manual computation. It provides a simple way to predict interior daylight illumination through skylights and windows. It assumes an empty rectangular room with simple fenestration and shading devices. Room cavity obstructions substantially reduce illuminances, especially in sidelit spaces,[32, 33] but must be considered using other methods.

The method consists of four basic steps:

1. The exterior illuminances at the window or skylight are determined. These can be calculated as shown in the subsection on Daylight Availability above.
2. The net transmittance of the fenestration reduces the amount of light that reaches the interior of the room. It includes the transmittance of the glazing, the light loss factor and other factors that may be required, depending on the sophistication of the fenestration controls used.
3. Coefficients of utilization are multiplying factors that relate the daylight entering the room to the average daylight illuminance on the workplane (lumen method for toplighting) or

to the daylight illuminance at five predetermined points in the room (lumen method for sidelighting).

4. The interior illuminance is calculated by taking the product of the factors determined in the first three steps.

The basic equation for the illuminance at a prescribed point using the lumen method is the simple formula

$$E_i = E_x(NT)(CU) \qquad (8\text{-}27)$$

where

E_i = interior illuminance in lx,
E_x = exterior illuminance in lx,
NT = net transmittance,
CU = coefficient of utilization.

The procedures for determining the net transmittance and the coefficient of utilization differ for toplighting and sidelighting. If both types of systems are being employed, the illuminance can be computed for each and the illuminances added to give the combined effect.

In calculating illuminances for toplighting and sidelighting, the basic lumen method equation generally shows up in a more complicated form, but it is still derived from these few primary elements.

Lumen Method for Toplighting

For daylighting systems employing horizontal apertures such as skylights at or slightly above roof level, the lumen method for toplighting is used. It is assumed that the skylights are positioned uniformly across the ceiling. The average horizontal illuminance on the workplane is

$$E_i = E_{xh}\tau \, CU \, \frac{A_s}{A_w} \qquad (8\text{-}28)$$

where

E_i = average incident illuminance on the workplane from skylights in lx,
E_{xh} = horizontal exterior illuminance on the skylights in lx,
A_s = gross projected horizontal area of all the skylights in m^2,
A_w = area of the workplane in m^2,
τ = net transmittance of the skylights and light well, including losses because of solar control devices and maintenance factors,
CU = coefficient of utilization.

Equation 8-28 can be used to determine the average workplane illuminance if the total skylight area and the

horizontal exterior illuminance are known. Conversely, the required skylight area can be determined if the required average workplane illuminance and the horizontal exterior illuminance are known.

The exterior horizontal illuminance is the sum of the illuminances from the sun and sky. These are determined using the procedures given in the subsection on Daylight Availability above.

The net transmittance is determined from a direct transmittance T_D and a diffuse transmittance T_d.[56] The direct transmittance is used for the sun component and is a function of the angle of incidence. The diffuse transmittance is single-valued and is used for the sky component, which is treated as diffuse. Generally, manufacturers provide transmittance data for flat sheets of their glass or plastic in the form of a single value of T_d and a curve showing the variation of T_D with incidence angle.

The net transmittance is also affected by the shape of a skylight, multiple layering, the presence of a skylight well, the presence of louvers or other shades, and light loss factors.

Most skylights are domed. This decreases the sheet thickness at the center of the dome, modifying the dome transmittance to

$$T_{DM} = 1.25 T_{FS}(1.18 - 0.416 T_{FS}) \qquad (8\text{-}29)$$

where

T_{DM} = dome transmittance,
T_{FS} = flat-sheet transmittance.

This does not change the transmittance of the transparent sheet (T_{FS} = 0.92), but increases the transmittance of a translucent sheet (T_{FS} = 0.44) by about 25%, in conformity with what actually happens in practice.

Doming also causes the angle of incidence of the direct sunlight to vary over the dome's surface. As well, the dome has greater light-gathering surface area than a flat sheet. Both these factors may be considered together by noting that the effect of doming is to cause T_D to become constant within 10% for all angles of incidence less than 70° (sun angles greater than 20°).[56] Thus, for most dome applications, a single number for T_D equal to its value at 0° angle of incidence can be used.

To reduce heat gains and heat losses, most contemporary skylights are double domed, most often a transparent dome over a translucent dome. The overall transmittance of such a unit may be obtained from the following equation:[57]

$$T = \frac{T_1 T_2}{1 - \rho_1 \rho_2} \qquad (8\text{-}30)$$

where

T_1, T_2 = diffuse transmittances of the individual domes,

ρ_1 = reflectance from the bottom side of the upper dome,

ρ_2 = reflectance from the top side of the lower dome.

Equation 8-30 takes into account the interreflections between the two domes.

Reflective loses and interreflections in any light well between the dome and the ceiling plane of the room reduce the net transmittance. This reduction is expressed as a well efficiency N_w, which can be obtained from figure 8-21 if well wall reflectance and the well cavity ratio (WCR) are known. The well cavity ratio is given by

$$\text{WCR} = \frac{5h(w + l)}{wl} \qquad (8\text{-}31)$$

where

h = well height,
w = well width,
l = well length.

In eq. 8-31, h, w, and l must be expressed in the same units.

The net transmittance should also take into account the ratio of net to gross skylight area (R_a). If any diffusers, lenses, louvers or other controls are present,

their transmittances (T_c) must be included. Finally, the light loss factor (LLF) must be included to take account of dirt depreciation of the skylight and well surfaces. Typical values are given in figure 8-18. The net transmittances of the skylight-well system are found from

$$\tau_d = T_d N_w R_a T_c \text{ LLF} \qquad (8\text{-}32a)$$

$$\tau_D = T_D N_w R_a T_c \text{ LLF} \qquad (8\text{-}32b)$$

where T_d is equal to the diffuse transmittance and T_D is equal to the direct transmittance of the dome.

Coefficients of utilization (CU) are given in figure 8-22. These are based on a spacing-to-mounting-height ratio of 1.5 : 1, a lambertian distribution from the skylight, and a floor reflectance of 0.2. The wall and ceiling reflectances, as well as room cavity ratios (RCR),

Fig. 8-22. Room Coefficients of Utilization for Skylighting (based on a 20% floor reflectance)

Ceiling Reflectance (Percent)	RCR	Wall Reflectance (Percent)		
		50	30	10
80	0	1.19	1.19	1.19
	1	1.05	1.00	0.97
	2	0.93	0.86	0.81
	3	0.83	0.76	0.70
	4	0.75	0.67	0.60
	5	0.67	0.59	0.53
	6	0.62	0.53	0.47
	7	0.57	0.49	0.43
	8	0.54	0.47	0.41
	9	0.53	0.46	0.41
	10	0.52	0.45	0.40
50	0	1.11	1.11	1.11
	1	0.98	0.95	0.92
	2	0.87	0.83	0.78
	3	0.79	0.73	0.68
	4	0.71	0.64	0.59
	5	0.64	0.57	0.52
	6	0.59	0.52	0.47
	7	0.55	0.48	0.43
	8	0.52	0.46	0.41
	9	0.51	0.45	0.40
	10	0.50	0.44	0.40
20	0	1.04	1.04	1.04
	1	0.92	0.90	0.88
	2	0.83	0.79	0.76
	3	0.75	0.70	0.66
	4	0.68	0.62	0.58
	5	0.61	0.56	0.51
	6	0.57	0.51	0.46
	7	0.53	0.47	0.43
	8	0.51	0.45	0.41
	9	0.50	0.44	0.40
	10	0.49	0.44	0.40

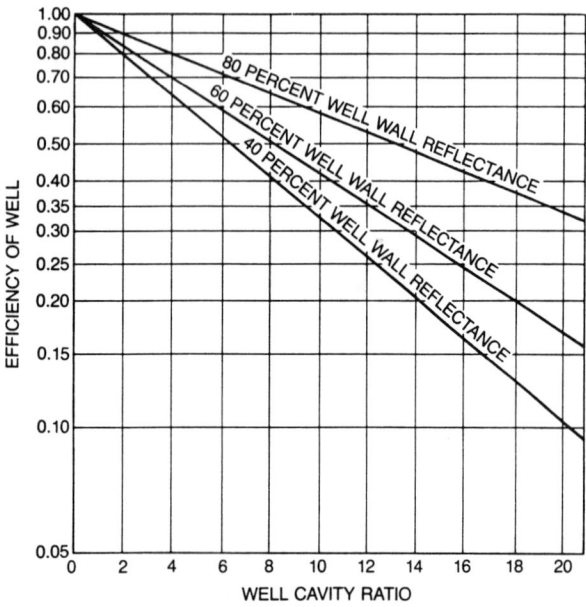

Fig. 8-21. Efficiency factors for various depths of light wells, based on well-intereflectance values, where:

$$\text{WCR} = \frac{5 \times \text{Well Height} \times (\text{Well Width} + \text{Well Length})}{\text{Well Width} \times \text{Well Height}}$$

are required. Room cavity ratios may be obtained from

$$\mathrm{RCR} = \frac{5h_\mathrm{c}(l + w)}{lw} \qquad (8\text{-}33)$$

where

h_c = height from the workplane to the bottom of the skylight well,
l = length of the room,
w = width of the room.

All three parameters must have the same units.

The general lumen method for toplighting (eq. 8-28) can now be applied. For overcast skies, this is

$$E_\mathrm{i} = E_\mathrm{xh\,sky}\tau_\mathrm{d}\,\mathrm{CU}\,N\frac{A}{A_\mathrm{w}} \qquad (8\text{-}34)$$

For a clear or partly cloudy sky, the equation is

$$E_\mathrm{i} = (E_\mathrm{xh\,sky}\tau_\mathrm{d} + E_\mathrm{xh\,sun}\tau_\mathrm{D})\,\mathrm{CU}\,N\frac{A}{A_\mathrm{w}} \qquad (8\text{-}35)$$

where

$E_\mathrm{xh\,sky}$ = exterior horizontal illuminance due to the sky only, in lx,
$E_\mathrm{xh\,sun}$ = exterior horizontal illuminance due to the sun only, in lx,
τ_d = net diffuse transmittance,
τ_D = net direct transmittance,
CU = coefficient of utilization,
N = number of skylights,
A = area of each skylight in m^2,
A_w = area of the workplane in m^2.

Note that because the net transmittance depends in part on the well efficiency and the ratio of net to gross skylight area, these factors must be recalculated if the skylight size changes.

Lumen Method for Sidelighting

The prediction of interior daylight illumination from sidelighting has been simplified by using the standard conditions shown in figure 8-23. The floor cavity extends from the window sill to the floor and has a reflectance of 30%. The ceiling cavity extends from the top of the windows to the ceiling and has a reflectance of 70%. The room cavity extends in height (H) from the top of the floor cavity to the bottom of the ceiling cavity, in width (W) along the window wall and in depth (D) from the window wall to the rear wall; it has a wall reflectance of 50%. The interior daylight illumination is calculated at five reference points located on a line perpendicular to the window wall across the center of the room at the same height as the window sill. The five points are located along a line at 0.1D, 0.3D, 0.5D, 0.7D and 0.9D.

The procedure described here provides for shades, drapes, solar film or other simple daylight controls on or at the fenestration. It does not provide for horizontal or vertical window blinds, nor for exterior elements such as sidewalks, streets, other buildings and overhangs. A more elaborate procedure is available to take account of such elements.

The basic formula used to calculate the horizontal interior daylight illuminance at one of the five refer-

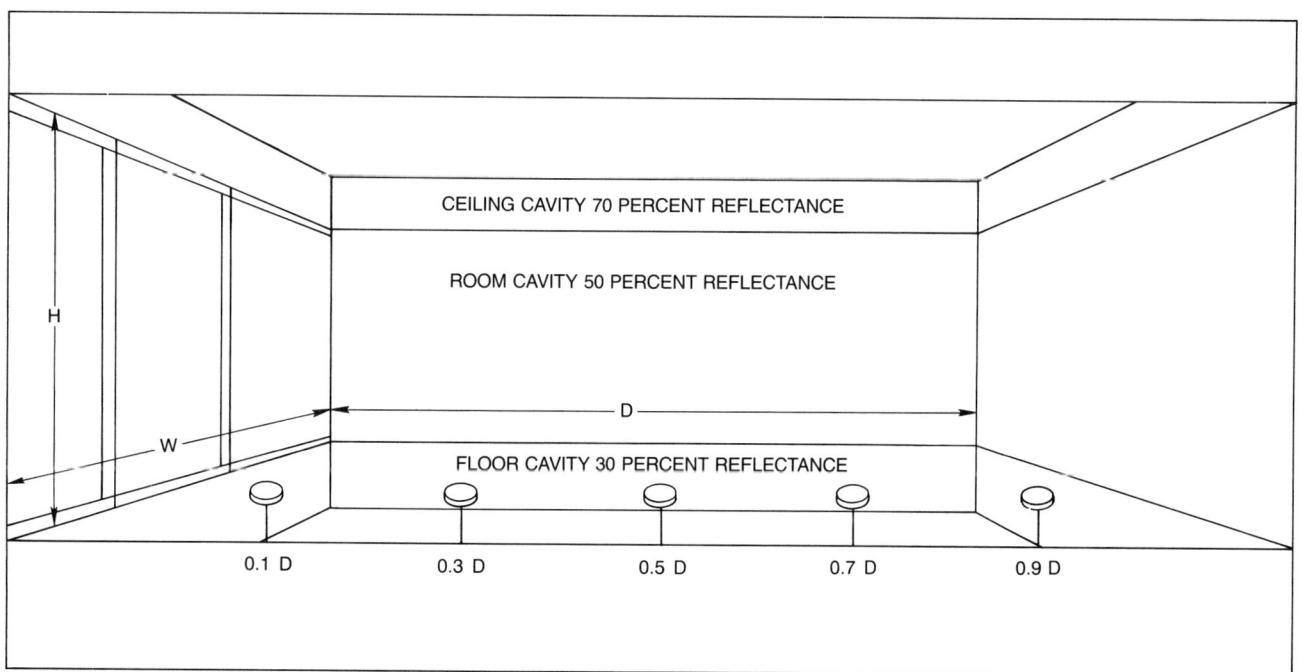

Fig. 8-23. Standard conditions in a room for calculating sidelighting.

ence points is

$$E_i = E_{xv}\tau\, CU \qquad (8\text{-}36)$$

where

E_i = interior horizontal illuminance on a reference point from sidelighting, in lx,

E_{xv} = exterior vertical illuminance on the window wall in lx,

τ = net transmittance of the window wall,

CU = coefficient of utilization.

Superposition is used to obtain the final interior illuminance at a reference point due to multiple sets of daylighting apertures. For instance, the illuminations from the sky and ground are calculated separately and added together to determine the combined effect. The lumen method does not provide for direct sunlight entering into the room cavity.

The exterior vertical illuminance E_{xv} is the illuminance on the vertical aperture, excluding direct sunlight. For simple exterior situations, that is, with no obstructions, this illuminance is from the sky and ground. That portion due to the sky can be determined using the procedures in the subsection on Daylight Availability above. The illuminance on the vertical aperture due to the ground can be determined using the method of configuration factors (see Chapter 9,

Lighting Calculations), in which exitances and configuration factors are used to calculate the illuminance produced at a point by a large diffuse source. The ground is assumed to be such a source and to exhibit a diffuse exitance, which is given by

$$M_g = \rho_g\big(E_{xh\,sky} + E_{xh\,sun}\big) \qquad (8\text{-}37)$$

where

M_g = exitance from the ground in lm/m^2,

ρ_g = reflectance of the ground in lm/m^2,

$E_{xh\,sky}$ = horizontal illuminance from the sky in lx,

$E_{xh\,sun}$ = horizontal illuminance from the sun in lx.

The net transmittance is the product of the transmittance (T) of the glazing, a light loss factor (LLF) representing dirt accumulation, the net-to-gross window area ratio (R_a), representing such elements as mullions and glazing bars, and a factor T_c representing other elements such as shades and drapes which reduce the transmittance of the window. The net transmittance of the window wall is found from

$$\tau = TR_aT_c\, LLF \qquad (8\text{-}38)$$

The coefficients of utilization (CU) for each of the five reference points in the room are given in figure 8-24.[58] If the fenestration is transparent (view preserv-

Fig. 8-24a. Coefficient of Utilization from Window Without Blinds. Sky Component $E_{xv\,sky}/E_{xh\,sky} = 0.75$

Room Depth/ Window Height	Percent D	.5	1	2	3	4	6	8	Infinite
1	10	.824	.864	.870	.873	.875	.879	.880	.883
	30	.547	.711	.777	.789	.793	.798	.799	.801
	50	.355	.526	.635	.659	.666	.669	.670	.672
	70	.243	.386	.505	.538	.548	.544	.545	.547
	90	.185	.304	.418	.451	.464	.444	.446	.447
2	10	.667	.781	.809	.812	.813	.815	.816	.824
	30	.269	.416	.519	.544	.551	.556	.557	.563
	50	.122	.204	.287	.319	.331	.339	.341	.345
	70	.068	.116	.173	.201	.214	.223	.226	.229
	90	.050	.084	.127	.151	.164	.167	.171	.172
3	10	.522	.681	.739	.746	.747	.749	.747	.766
	30	.139	.232	.320	.350	.360	.366	.364	.373
	50	.053	.092	.139	.163	.174	.183	.182	.187
	70	.031	.053	.081	.097	.106	.116	.116	.119
	90	.025	.041	.061	.074	.082	.089	.090	.092
4	10	.405	.576	.658	.670	.673	.675	.674	.707
	30	.075	.134	.197	.224	.235	.243	.243	.255
	50	.028	.050	.078	.094	.104	.112	.114	.119
	70	.018	.031	.048	.059	.065	.073	.074	.078
	90	.016	.026	.040	.048	.053	.059	.061	.064
6	10	.242	.392	.494	.516	.521	.524	.523	.588
	30	.027	.054	.086	.102	.111	.119	.120	.135
	50	.011	.023	.036	.044	.049	.055	.056	.063
	70	.009	.018	.027	.032	.035	.040	.041	.046
	90	.008	.016	.023	.028	.031	.034	.035	.040
8	10	.147	.257	.352	.380	.387	.391	.392	.482
	30	.012	.026	.043	.054	.060	.067	.070	.086
	50	.006	.013	.021	.026	.029	.333	.035	.043
	70	.005	.011	.017	.021	.023	.026	.027	.034
	90	.004	.010	.015	.019	.021	.023	.025	.030
10	10	.092	.168	.248	.275	.284	.290	.291	.395
	30	.006	.014	.026	.032	.036	.041	.044	.059
	50	.003	.008	.014	.017	.019	.022	.024	.032
	70	.003	.007	.012	.014	.016	.018	.019	.026
	90	.003	.006	.011	.013	.015	.016	.017	.024

Fig. 8-24b. Coefficient of Utilization from Window Without Blinds. Sky Component $E_{xv\,sky}/E_{xh\,sky} = 1.00$

Room Depth/ Window Height	Percent D	.5	1	2	3	4	6	8	Infinite
1	10	.671	.704	.711	.715	.717	.726	.726	.728
	30	.458	.595	.654	.668	.672	.682	.683	.685
	50	.313	.462	.563	.589	.598	.607	.608	.610
	70	.227	.362	.478	.515	.527	.530	.532	.534
	90	.186	.306	.424	.465	.481	.468	.471	.472
2	10	.545	.636	.658	.660	.661	.665	.666	.672
	30	.239	.367	.459	.484	.491	.499	.501	.506
	50	.121	.203	.286	.320	.335	.348	.351	.355
	70	.074	.128	.192	.226	.243	.259	.264	.267
	90	.058	.101	.156	.188	.207	.215	.221	.223
3	10	.431	.561	.607	.613	.614	.616	.615	.631
	30	.133	.223	.306	.337	.348	.357	.357	.366
	50	.058	.103	.155	.183	.197	.211	.213	.218
	70	.037	.064	.098	.119	.132	.147	.150	.154
	90	.030	.051	.079	.098	.110	.122	.126	.129
4	10	.339	.482	.549	.560	.563	.566	.565	.593
	30	.078	.139	.204	.234	.247	.258	.260	.272
	50	.033	.060	.094	.114	.126	.139	.143	.150
	70	.022	.039	.061	.074	.083	.095	.099	.104
	90	.019	.032	.050	.061	.070	.080	.084	.089
6	10	.211	.343	.433	.453	.458	.461	.461	.518
	30	.033	.065	.103	.123	.135	.145	.148	.167
	50	.015	.029	.047	.057	.064	.073	.077	.086
	70	.011	.021	.033	.040	.045	.051	.054	.060
	90	.010	.019	.028	.034	.038	.044	.046	.052
8	10	.135	.238	.326	.353	.362	.366	.367	.452
	30	.016	.034	.058	.072	.080	.090	.094	.116
	50	.008	.017	.027	.034	.039	.045	.048	.059
	70	.006	.013	.021	.026	.028	.032	.035	.043
	90	.005	.012	.019	.023	.025	.029	.031	.038
10	10	.090	.165	.244	.272	.283	.290	.291	.395
	30	.009	.020	.036	.045	.052	.060	.064	.087
	50	.005	.010	.019	.023	.026	.030	.033	.044
	70	.004	.009	.015	.018	.020	.023	.025	.033
	90	.003	.008	.014	.016	.018	.020	.022	.030

Fig. 8-24c. Coefficient of Utilization from Window Without Blinds. Sky Component $E_{xv\,sky} / E_{xh\,sky} = 1.25$

Room Depth/ Window Height	Percent D	Window Width / Window Height							
		.5	1	2	3	4	6	8	Infinite
1	10	.578	.607	.614	.619	.621	.633	.634	.635
	30	.405	.525	.580	.594	.599	.612	.614	.615
	50	.287	.423	.519	.547	.556	.569	.571	.573
	70	.218	.347	.461	.501	.515	.522	.525	.526
	90	.186	.307	.428	.473	.491	.483	.486	.487
2	10	.472	.549	.566	.569	.570	.574	.575	.581
	30	.221	.337	.422	.447	.456	.465	.467	.472
	50	.120	.202	.285	.321	.337	.353	.357	.361
	70	.078	.136	.204	.242	.261	.281	.287	.290
	90	.064	.112	.174	.211	.233	.244	.251	.253
3	10	.377	.488	.527	.533	.534	.536	.536	.549
	30	.130	.217	.298	.329	.341	.352	.353	.362
	50	.062	.110	.165	.195	.211	.228	.231	.237
	70	.040	.070	.109	.132	.147	.166	.171	.175
	90	.033	.057	.090	.112	.127	.142	.148	.152
4	10	.300	.424	.484	.494	.497	.499	.499	.524
	30	.080	.143	.209	.240	.255	.267	.269	.283
	50	.036	.066	.104	.126	.140	.156	.160	.168
	70	.024	.043	.068	.083	.094	.109	.115	.120
	90	.021	.036	.056	.070	.080	.092	.099	.103
6	10	.193	.314	.395	.415	.420	.423	.423	.476
	30	.036	.071	.113	.136	.149	.161	.165	.186
	50	.017	.033	.053	.065	.074	.084	.089	.100
	70	.012	.024	.037	.045	.050	.058	.061	.069
	90	.011	.021	.031	.038	.043	.049	.053	.060
8	10	.128	.226	.310	.337	.346	.351	.352	.433
	30	.019	.039	.066	.082	.092	.104	.109	.134
	50	.009	.019	.031	.040	.045	.052	.056	.069
	70	.007	.015	.023	.029	.032	.037	.040	.049
	90	.006	.013	.021	.025	.028	.032	.035	.043
10	10	.088	.164	.241	.270	.282	.290	.291	.396
	30	.011	.024	.043	.054	.062	.071	.076	.103
	50	.005	.012	.022	.026	.030	.035	.038	.052
	70	.004	.010	.017	.020	.023	.026	.028	.038
	90	.004	.009	.016	.018	.020	.023	.025	.034

Fig. 8-24d. Coefficient of Utilization from Window Without Blinds. Sky Component $E_{xv\,sky} / E_{xh\,sky} = 1.50$

Room Depth/ Window Height	Percent D	Window Width / Window Height							
		.5	1	2	3	4	6	8	Infinite
1	10	.503	.528	.536	.541	.544	.557	.558	.559
	30	.359	.464	.514	.528	.534	.549	.550	.552
	50	.261	.384	.471	.499	.508	.524	.526	.527
	70	.204	.325	.432	.470	.485	.497	.499	.500
	90	.179	.295	.412	.456	.475	.474	.477	.478
2	10	.412	.477	.490	.492	.493	.498	.499	.505
	30	.201	.304	.379	.402	.410	.422	.424	.429
	50	.115	.192	.269	.304	.320	.339	.343	.347
	70	.078	.136	.204	.241	.261	.286	.292	.295
	90	.066	.117	.183	.221	.246	.262	.271	.273
3	10	.331	.426	.458	.461	.462	.465	.465	.477
	30	.121	.202	.275	.304	.316	.327	.329	.337
	50	.062	.109	.164	.193	.209	.228	.232	.238
	70	.041	.073	.114	.138	.154	.176	.183	.188
	90	.035	.062	.099	.123	.141	.159	.169	.173
4	10	.265	.372	.422	.430	.433	.435	.435	.456
	30	.077	.137	.199	.229	.243	.256	.259	.272
	50	.037	.069	.107	.130	.144	.161	.167	.175
	70	.026	.046	.073	.089	.101	.119	.126	.132
	90	.022	.039	.063	.078	.090	.106	.114	.120
6	10	.173	.281	.351	.368	.373	.375	.375	.422
	30	.037	.073	.115	.137	.151	.164	.168	.189
	50	.018	.035	.058	.071	.080	.092	.098	.110
	70	.013	.026	.040	.049	.056	.064	.069	.078
	90	.012	.023	.035	.043	.048	.057	.062	.070
8	10	.117	.207	.282	.305	.314	.319	.320	.393
	30	.020	.042	.071	.087	.098	.111	.116	.143
	50	.010	.021	.035	.044	.050	.058	.063	.078
	70	.007	.016	.026	.032	.036	.041	.045	.055
	90	.076	.014	.023	.028	.031	.036	.040	.049
10	10	.082	.153	.224	.250	.262	.269	.271	.368
	30	.012	.026	.047	.059	.068	.078	.084	.114
	50	.006	.014	.024	.030	.034	.040	.044	.060
	70	.005	.011	.019	.022	.025	.029	.032	.043
	90	.004	.010	.017	.020	.023	.026	.028	.038

Fig. 8-24e. Coefficient of Utilization from Window Without Blinds. Sky Component $E_{xv\,sky} / E_{xv\,sky} = 1.75$

Room Depth/ Window Height	Percent D	Window Width / Window Height							
		.5	1	2	3	4	6	8	Infinite
1	10	.435	.457	.465	.471	.474	.486	.488	.489
	30	.317	.407	.452	.466	.471	.486	.488	.489
	50	.234	.343	.422	.447	.456	.472	.475	.476
	70	.187	.297	.395	.430	.445	.458	.461	.462
	90	.168	.276	.384	.426	.444	.447	.450	.451
2	10	.357	.412	.422	.424	.424	.430	.431	.436
	30	.180	.271	.335	.356	.363	.375	.378	.381
	50	.106	.177	.246	.278	.293	.313	.318	.321
	70	.074	.130	.194	.229	.249	.274	.282	.284
	90	.065	.116	.181	.219	.244	.264	.273	.276
3	10	.288	.369	.394	.397	.397	.400	.401	.411
	30	.110	.183	.247	.272	.282	.294	.296	.304
	50	.058	.104	.154	.181	.196	.215	.221	.226
	70	.040	.072	.112	.136	.152	.176	.184	.188
	90	.035	.063	.101	.126	.144	.165	.177	.182
4	10	.232	.324	.365	.371	.373	.375	.375	.394
	30	.071	.127	.183	.209	.222	.235	.238	.250
	50	.036	.067	.104	.125	.139	.157	.163	.171
	70	.025	.046	.072	.089	.101	.119	.127	.134
	90	.022	.041	.065	.082	.095	.114	.124	.130
6	10	.153	.247	.307	.320	.324	.326	.327	.367
	30	.035	.070	.109	.130	.143	.155	.160	.180
	50	.018	.036	.058	.071	.080	.091	.098	.110
	70	.013	.026	.041	.051	.058	.067	.073	.082
	90	.012	.023	.037	.046	.052	.062	.069	.078
8	10	.104	.184	.249	.269	.276	.281	.282	.346
	30	.020	.042	.070	.086	.096	.109	.115	.141
	50	.010	.022	.036	.046	.052	.060	.066	.081
	70	.008	.017	.027	.033	.038	.044	.048	.059
	90	.007	.015	.024	.030	.034	.040	.044	.054
10	10	.074	.138	.201	.223	.233	.240	.242	.328
	30	.012	.027	.048	.059	.067	.078	.084	.114
	50	.006	.014	.026	.032	.036	.043	.047	.064
	70	.005	.011	.020	.024	.027	.031	.034	.046
	90	.004	.010	.018	.022	.024	.028	.031	.042

Fig. 8-24f. Coefficient of Utilization from Window Without Blinds (Ground Component)

Room Depth/ Window Height	Percent D	Window Width / Window Height							
		.5	1	2	3	4	6	8	Infinite
1	10	.105	.137	.177	.197	.207	.208	.210	211
	30	.116	.157	.203	.225	.235	.241	.243	.244
	50	.110	.165	.217	.241	.252	.267	.269	.270
	70	.101	.162	.217	.243	.253	.283	.285	.286
	90	.091	.146	.199	.230	.239	.290	.292	.293
2	10	.095	.124	.160	.178	.186	.186	.189	.191
	30	.082	.132	.179	.201	.212	.219	.222	.225
	50	.062	.113	.165	.189	.202	.214	.218	.220
	70	.051	.093	.141	.165	.179	.194	.198	.200
	90	.045	.079	.118	.140	.153	.179	.183	.185
3	10	.088	.120	.157	.175	.183	.185	.163	.167
	30	.059	.107	.154	.176	.187	.198	.193	.198
	50	.039	.074	.113	.134	.146	.157	.166	.170
	70	.031	.055	.085	.101	.111	.122	.127	.130
	90	.028	.047	.070	.083	.092	.107	.113	.115
4	10	.073	.113	.154	.174	.183	.187	.176	.184
	30	.040	.082	.127	.148	.159	.170	.177	.185
	50	.025	.049	.078	.094	.103	.113	.117	.123
	70	.020	.036	.054	.065	.071	.079	.083	.087
	90	.019	.032	.046	.054	.060	.069	.073	.076
6	10	.056	.106	.143	.164	.175	.184	.173	.194
	30	.021	.050	.081	.098	.107	.117	.123	.138
	50	.013	.027	.041	.049	.054	.060	.064	.072
	70	.011	.021	.029	.033	.035	.039	.041	.046
	90	.011	.020	.026	.030	.032	.035	.037	.042
8	10	.036	.082	.122	.143	.156	.166	.170	.208
	30	.011	.029	.050	.062	.070	.078	.082	.101
	50	.007	.016	.024	.028	.031	.035	.038	.046
	70	.006	.013	.018	.020	.021	.023	.025	.030
	90	.006	.013	.017	.019	.020	.022	.023	.028
10	10	.024	.061	.109	.120	.131	.144	.147	.200
	30	.006	.017	.034	.040	.046	.053	.056	.076
	50	.004	.010	.016	.018	.020	.024	.024	.033
	70	.004	.009	.013	.014	.015	.016	.016	.022
	90	.004	.009	.013	.013	.014	.015	.016	.021

ing), then the horizontal and vertical exterior illuminances from the half-sky are calculated for the center of the window. Based on a ratio of vertical to horizontal illuminance at the window of 0.75, 1.00, 1.25, 1.50 or 1.75, the coefficients of utilization from figures 8-24a through 8-24e are used. The ground component coefficient of utilization is given in figure 8-24f.

If the fenestration is not image preserving, as would be expected from frosted glass, shades or drapes, then the vertical illuminances from the sky and ground are added. Half of this value is used for each of the sky illuminance and the ground illuminance. Use figure 8-24b, based on a uniform sky distribution, for the coefficient of utilization of the sky component, and figure 8-24f for the coefficient of utilization of the ground component.

Equations 8-39 and 8-40 are used to calculate the illuminance at each of the five reference points in the room. If the window is image preserving, then the illuminances are given by

$$E_i = \tau \left(E_{xv\,sky} \, CU_{sky} + E_{xvg} \, CU_g \right) \qquad (8\text{-}39)$$

and for a diffuse window by

$$E_i = 0.5\tau \left(E_{xv\,sky} + E_{xvg} \right) \left(CU_{sky} + CU_g \right) \quad (8\text{-}40)$$

where

E_i = interior illuminance at a reference point in lx,
τ = net transmittance of the window wall,
$E_{xv\,sky}$ = exterior vertical illuminance from the sky on the window in lx,
CU_{sky} = coefficient of utilization from the sky,
E_{xvg} = exterior vertical illuminance from the ground on the window in lx,
CU_g = coefficient of utilization from the ground.

MEASUREMENT OF INTERIOR ILLUMINATION

Scale model and full-scale photometry allow the investigation of spaces and fenestration systems that are more complex than can be evaluated using lumen methods or currently available computer programs. However, photometry requires the use of special-purpose equipment, and illuminances can only be determined for the sky conditions under which measurements are made. They may not be representative of average conditions, because instantaneous sky conditions can vary considerably from long-term averages. The measured sky conditions can be compared with daylight availability measurements, as is discussed below. In making this comparison, it is desirable to obtain

measurements for a range of sky conditions (that is, overcast and clear), and, in the case of clear skies, for a range of sun positions (for example, at 4-min intervals from 0800 to 2000, 4 min being the interval in which the sun changes position by 1°). Measurements under overcast skies are discussed in reference 59.

Considerations in Using Photometric Instruments

Because of the short-term variability of daylight, it is usually necessary to use sensors connected to a data logger with recording capability. An alternative is the use of artificial skies and suns, although only a few such facilities exist, mostly at universities or research institutions. Artificial skies and suns also have limitations.[59]

Some factors contributing to error in scale model photometry[54, 60] are substantially under the control of the user, including relative calibration of sensors, surface reflectances and the fidelity with which the model replicates the space and fenestration of interest (although this can become quite difficult with complex fenestration systems). Other factors to consider are listed below.

Photocell Leveling. At the rear of deep sidelit spaces, where much of the light striking a photocell does so at an oblique angle, small errors in leveling a photocell may produce large errors in illuminance measurements; for an incidence angle of 85°, a sensor misalignment of 2° will result in an error of 40% for the sky component.[61]

Photocell Size. A given sensor has a different view of the sky in a model than in a full-scale space. Where illuminances are changing rapidly and by large amounts (for example, close to a window without shading controls), significant error may result.

Sensor Placement. While it is not difficult to place photocell faces with sufficient accuracy for most conditions, small placement errors in models may result in relatively large errors where flux gradients are steep.

Effects of Space Contents. Space contents, such as sensor holders in scale models, may increase internal reflections and lead to significant overestimates. Such holders should be painted matte black unless their luminous characteristics correspond to features that would exist in the proposed design.

Luminance-based measurements using calibrated video cameras can record thousands of luminance measurements in a physical model, allowing evaluation of lighting attributes such as luminance distribution, color and visual performance. These video-based systems can also assist the designer in recording subjective evaluations of the model.

Measurement of Sky Conditions

It is generally necessary to make measurements of the total illuminance on an unobstructed horizontal surface (the global illuminance) simultaneously with interior measurements as a record of daylight availability. Other important measures are the diffuse illuminance on an unobstructed horizontal surface and the zenith luminance. The most basic means of determining the diffuse illuminance is screening a sensor with a shadow band and using a correction factor to compensate for the diffuse daylight obstructed by the shadow band.[62] It may also be useful to record daylight on vertical planes of interest, usually facing one or more of the cardinal directions, which necessitates the use of screening devices to cut off ground-reflected light.[33]

THE DAYLIGHT FACTOR

The *daylight factor method*, which has been adopted by the CIE,[14] treats the illuminance that occurs at a point inside a room as a fraction of the simultaneous illuminance on an unobstructed horizontal plane outdoors. This ratio is called the daylight factor. Direct sunlight is excluded for both interior and exterior values of illumination.

The advantage of the daylight factor as an indicator of daylighting performance is that it expresses the efficiency of a room and its fenestration as a natural lighting system.[28] The use and limitations of the daylight factor are related to its variability over time when determined from measured values (even under overcast skies), its variability under clear and partly cloudy skies due to the constantly changing sky luminance distribution, its failure to correlate with human assessment of the general brightness of spaces, and practical differences in its determination by the field measurement of illuminances.[63]

REFERENCES

1. IES. Daylighting Committee. 1979. Recommended practice of daylighting. *Light. Des. Appl.* 9(2):25–60.
2. Gillette, G., W. Pierpoint, and S. Treado. 1984. A general illuminance model for daylight availability. *J. Illum. Eng. Soc.* 13(4):330–340.
3. Lane, H. U., ed. 1981. Latitude, longitude, and altitude of North American cities. In *The world almanac and book of facts 1982*, 768–769. New York: Newspaper Enterprise Association.
4. Lamm, L. O. 1981. A new analytic expression for the equation of time. *Sol. Energy* 26(5):465.
5. American Society for Testing and Materials. 1974. *Standard solar constant and air mass zero solar spectral irradiance tables.* ASTM E490-73a. Philadelphia: American Society for Testing and Materials.
6. Illuminating Engineering Society of North America. 1981. *Nomenclature and Definitions for Illuminating Engineering, ANSI / IES RP-16-1980.* New York: Illuminating Engineering Society of North America.
7. Stephenson, D. G. 1965. Equations for solar heat gain through windows. *Sol. Energy* 9(2):81–86.
8. American Society of Heating, Refrigerating and Air-Conditioning Engineers. 1981. Fenestration. Chapter 27 in *ASHRAE Handbook: 1981 Fundamentals.* Atlanta: American Society of Heating, Refrigerating and Air-Conditioning Engineers.
9. Karayel, M., M. Navvab, E. Ne'eman, and S. Selkowitz. 1984. Zenith luminance and sky luminance distributions for daylighting calculations. *Energy Build.* 6(3):283–291.
10. Kittler, R. 1967. Standardisation of outdoor conditions for the calculation of daylight factor with clear skies. In *Sunlight in buildings: Proceedings of the CIE Intercessional Conference, Newcastle-Upon-Tyne, April 5–9, 1965.* Amsterdam: Bouwcentrum.
11. Commission Internationale de l'Éclairage. 1973. *Standardization of luminance distribution of clear skies.* CIE Publication No. 22. Paris: Bureau Central de la CIE.
12. Pierpoint, W. 1983. A simple sky model for daylighting calculations. *General proceedings: 1983 International Daylighting Conference*, Phoenix, AZ, February 16–18, 1983. T. Vonier, ed. Washington: American Institute of Architects.
13. Moon, P., and D. E. Spencer. 1942. Illumination from a nonuniform sky. *Illum. Eng.* 37(12):707–726.
14. Commission Internationale de l'Éclairage. 1970. *International recommendations for the calculation of natural daylight.* CIE Publication No. 16. Paris: Bureau Central de la CIE.
15. McFadden, P., and M. Fontoynont. 1987. Occupant response to daylighting: Results from a valence school. In *Solar 87: Proceedings of the 12th Passive Solar Conference, Portland, OR, July 11–16, 1987.* Boulder, CO: The American Solar Energy Society.
16. Ne'eman, E., and R. G. Hopkinson. 1970. Critical minimum acceptable window size: A study of window design and provision of a view. *Light. Res. Tech.* 2(1):17–27.
17. Keighley, E. C. 1973. Visual requirements and reduced fenestration in offices: A study of multiple apertures and window area. *Build. Sci.* 8(4):321–331.
18. Ludlow, A. M. 1976. The functions of windows in buildings. *Light. Res. Tech.* 8(2):57–68.
19. Flynn, J. E., A. W. Segil, and G. R. Steffy. 1988. *Architectural interior systems: Lighting, acoustics, air conditioning.* 2nd ed. New York: Van Nostrand Reinhold.
20. Chauvel, P., J. B. Collins, R. Dogniaux, and J. Longmore. 1982. Glare from windows: Current views of the problem. *Light. Res. Tech.* 14(1):3146.
21. Ne'eman, E., J. Craddock, and R. G. Hopkinson. 1976. Sunlight requirements in buildings I: Social survey. *Build. Environ.* 11(4):217–238.
22. Ne'eman, E. 1977. Sunlight requirements in buildings II: Visits of an assessment team and experiments in a controlled room. *Build. Environ.* 12(3):147–157.

23. Ne'eman, E., W. Light, and R. G. Hopkinson. 1976. Recommendations for the admission and control of sunlight in buildings. *Build. Environ.* 11(2):91–101.

24. U.S. National Bureau of Standards. 1978. Window blinds as a potential energy saver: A case study. Prepared by A. I. Rubin, B. L. Collins and R. L. Tibbott. Washington: National Bureau of Standards.

25. Rea, M. S. 1984. Window blind occlusion: A pilot study. *Build. Environ.* 19(2):113–137.

26. Taylor, A. H., and W. G. Pracejus. 1950. Fading of colored materials by light and radiant energy. *Illum. Eng.* 45(3):149–151.

27. Lam, W. M. C. 1986. *Sunlighting as formgiver for architecture.* New York: Van Nostrand Reinhold.

28. Hopkinson, R. G., P. Petherbridge, and J. Longmore. 1966. *Daylighting.* London: William Heineman.

29. Robbins, C. L. 1986. *Daylighting: Design and analysis.* New York: Van Nostrand Reinhold.

30. Evans, B. H. 1981. *Daylight in architecture.* New York: Architectural Record Books.

31. Selkowitz, S. E., and J. W. Griffith. 1986. Effective daylighting in buildings: Revisited. *Light. Des. Appl.* 16(3):34–47.

32. Siminovitch, M., M. Navvab, and F. Rubenstein. 1987. The effects of interior room cavity obstructions on the illuminance distribution characteristics in task-station applications. *Conference Record of the 1987 IEEE Industry Applications Society Meeting, Part II,* Atlanta, GA, October 18–23, 1987. Piscataway, NJ: Institute of Electrical and Electronics Engineers.

33. Love, J. A. 1990. The vertical-to-horizontal illuminance ratio: Development of a new indicator of daylighting performance. Dissertation, University of Michigan.

34. Thomas, G. P., S. P. Manwell, and L. F. Kinney. 1986. Development of a monitoring system and evaluation method for a daylighting retrofit. In *1986 International Daylighting Conference: Proceedings I, Long Beach, CA, November 4–7, 1986.* M. S. Zdepsik, and R. McCluney, eds. McLean, VA: International Daylighting Organizing Committee.

35. Lawrence Berkeley Laboratory. 1992. *Daylighting design tool survey,* DA170 Summary. Berkeley, CA: Lawrence Berkeley Laboratory.

36. Ward, G. J. 1990. Visualization. *Light. Des. Appl.* 20(6):4–5, 14–20.

37. IES. Committee on Calculation Procedures. 1989. *IES recommended practice for the lumen method of daylight calculations.* IES RP-23-1989. New York: Illuminating Engineering Society of North America.

38. Lawrence Berkeley Laboratory. 1985. *Superlite 1.0 program description summary.* DA 205. Berkeley: Lawrence Berkeley Laboratory.

39. DiLaura, D. L. 1982. On the simplification of radiative transfer calculations. *J. Illum. Eng. Soc.* 12(1):12–16.

40. Leslie, R. P., and C. J. Sher DeCusatis. 1992. The daylight modeling probe. In *Proceedings of the 17th National Passive Solar Conference, Cocoa Beach, FL, June 15–18, 1992.* S. M. Burley and M. E. Arden, eds. Boulder, CO: American Solar Energy Society.

41. American Society of Heating, Refrigerating and Air-Conditioning Engineers and Illuminating Engineering Society of North America. 1989. *Energy efficient design of new buildings except new low-rise residential buildings, ASHRAE / IES 90.1-1989.* Atlanta, GA: American Society of Heating, Refrigerating and Air-Conditioning Engineers.

42. Lawrence Berkeley Laboratory. 1987. *Daylighting performance evaluation method: Summary report,* LBL-24002. Prepared by B. Andersson, R. Hitchcock, D. B. Erwine, R. Kammerud, A. Seager, and A. Hildon. Berkeley, CA: Lawrence Berkeley Laboratory.

43. Heap, L. J., J. Palmer, and A. Hildon. 1988. Redistributed daylight: A performance assessment. In *National Lighting Conference and Daylighting Colloquium, Cambridge, U.K., March 27–30, 1988.* London: Chartered Institute of Building Services Engineers.

44. Magnusson, M. 1983. Window configuration: Designing for daylighting and productivity. *General proceedings: 1983 International Daylighting Conference,* Phoenix, AZ, February 16–18, 1983. T. Vonier, ed. Washington: American Institute of Architects.

45. Windheim, L. S., R. J. Riegel, K. V. Davy, M. D. Shanus, and L. A. Daly. 1986. Case study: Lockheed Building 157 deep daylighting/innovative lighting concepts for a large office building. *General proceedings: 1983 International Daylighting Conference,* Phoenix, AZ, February 16–18, 1983. T. Vonier, ed. Washington: American Institute of Architects.

46. Love, J. A., D. Edmunds, and M. Navvab. 1988. A preliminary assessment of daylighting at Calgary's Olympic Oval. *Energy solutions for today: Proceedings of the 14th annual Conference of the Solar Energy Society of Canada,* Ottawa, Ont., 1988. Ottawa: Solar Energy Society of Canada.

47. Brown, J. P. 1983. Problems in the design and analysis of the Pacific Beach Post Office San Diego. *General proceedings: 1983 International Daylighting Conference,* Phoenix, AZ, February 16–18, 1983. T. Vonier, ed. Washington: American Institute of Architects.

48. Ellinwood, S. 1983. Daylight in the design process. *General Proceedings: 1983 International Daylighting Conference,* Phoenix, AZ, February 16–18, 1983. T. Vonier, ed. Washington: American Institute of Architects.

49. Navvab, M. 1988. Daylighting techniques: Skylights as a light source. *Archit. Light.* 2(8):46–47, 50.

50. Navvab, M. 1990. Outdoors indoors: Daylighting within atrium spaces. *Light. Des. Appl.* 20(5):6–7, 24–31.

51. Navvab, M. 1988. Daylighting techniques: Light transmission and reflection. *Archit. Light.* 2(2):36–37.

52. Navvab, M. 1988. Daylighting techniques: Translucent and transparent daylighting systems. *Archit. Light.* 2(5):48–55.

53. Murdoch, J. B., T. W. Oliver and G. P. Reed. 1991. Luminance and illuminance characteristics of translucent daylighting sandwich panels. *J. Illum. Eng. Soc.* 20(2):69–79.

54. Love, J. A., and M. Navvab. 1991. Daylighting estimation under real skies: A comparison of full-scale photometry, model photometry, and computer simulation. *J. Illum. Eng. Soc.* 20(1):140–156.

55. Saraiji, R. M. N., and R. G. Mistrick. 1993. The evaluation of determinant sky parameters for daylighting CUs. *J. Illum. Eng. Soc.* 22(1):131–138.

56. Linforth, E. 1958. Efficiency of domed acrylic skylights. *Illum. Eng.* 53(10):544–546.

57. Kreider, J. F., and F. Kreith. 1982. *Solar heating and cooling: Active and passive design*, 2nd ed. New York: McGraw-Hill.

58. U.S. Naval Civil Engineering Laboratory. 1983. *Daylighting coefficient of utilization tables.* NCEL CR 83.038. Prepared by W. E. Brackett. Port Hueneme CA: Naval Civil Engineering Laboratory.

59. Love, J. A. 1993. Determination of the daylight factor under real and overcast skies. *J. Illum. Eng. Soc.* 22(2).

60. Love, J. A. 1993. Daylighting estimation under real skies: Further comparative studies of full-scale and model photometry. *J. Illum. Eng. Soc.* 22(2).

61. Walsh, J. W. T. 1961. *The science of daylight.* London: Macdonald.

62. LeBaron, B. A., J. J. Michalsky, and R. Perez. 1990. A simple procedure for correcting shadowband data for all sky conditions. *Sol. Energy* 44(5):249–256.

63. Love, J. A. 1992. The evolution of performance indicators for the evaluation of daylighting systems. In *Conference Record of the IEEE Industry Applications Society Annual Meeting, Houston, TX, October 4–9, 1992.* Piscataway, NJ: Institute of Electrical and Electronics Engineers.

Lighting Calculations

9

INTRODUCTION

Lighting calculations are performed during the design process to obtain information about lighting system performance. A designer can use the results of calculations to choose between design alternatives or to refine a particular design. Lighting calculations are mathematical models of the complex physical processes that occur within a lighted space. Since these models can never be correct in every detail, the computations are approximations of real situations.

This chapter contains many of the fundamental calculation methods that are used in lighting system analysis, including both simple and complex methods. For methods that apply to specific applications, such as luminaire design, daylighting, floodlighting, roadway lighting, sports lighting or merchandise lighting, see the special chapters for procedures particular to those areas.

The simplest lighting calculation methods can be performed by hand, while the more advanced methods can only be performed using a computer. More advanced models generally provide more accurate information. Accuracy, for the purpose of this discussion, is defined as the degree to which the calculations agree with reality. In actuality, it is very difficult to achieve perfect agreement, as will be discussed later in this chapter.

Lighting calculation methods are application driven. The type of information that is desired about a lighting system and the complexity of the lighting condition being analyzed determine which calculation method is best applied to the problem. The aspects that must be evaluated in determining the lighting analysis model to use are the following:

- Information desired
- Equipment choice
- Equipment number and placement
- Space characteristics

It is the responsibility of the designer to determine which calculation model is the most appropriate one to use in such situations and to apply it. The material presented in this chapter will provide the general light-

ing practitioner with information that can be used in making these decisions.

This chapter will provide general calculation procedures that are used in the analysis of direct and reflected light. In general, these are fundamental procedures that can be applied to all lighting analysis situations. Also included are specialized calculations for metrics that are commonly used in the evaluation of lighting systems.

BASIC PRINCIPLES

Predicting the radiative transport of luminous flux (or more briefly, flux transfer) from a source to a receiving surface is fundamental to all lighting calculations. This transport is through air, which is assumed to be nonabsorbing and nonscattering.

Flux transfer is categorized into six types by geometry and emitter type:

1. Point source to a point or differential receiving area
2. Point source to a receiving area
3. Diffuse area source to a point or differential receiving area
4. Diffuse area source to a receiving area
5. Nondiffuse area source to a point or differential receiving area
6. Nondiffuse area source to a receiving area

Transfer type 1 is conceptually the simplest and is the easiest to formulate. Transfer types 2, 3 and 4 are obtained from the formulation of type 1 by integrating over the source, the receiving area, or both. Transfer types 5 and 6 are the most complicated, but are also the most commonly encountered in practice.

Light reaching a point or an area is described by *illuminance*—a measure of flux density, the incident flux per unit area. Illuminance is determined using methods for predicting flux transfer of types 1 through 4.

It is often necessary to know how light reflects from a point or an area. *Exitance* is the simplest case, and is measured as flux density leaving the surface. More complicated is *luminance*, which describes the flux leaving a surface in a particular direction. For exitance and luminance calculations the reflecting properties of the surface must be known. In these cases, methods for predicting illuminance are combined with reflectance information to predict exitances and luminances.

Photometric measurement of a luminaire provides a luminous intensity distribution from which the spatial distribution of flux from the luminaire is obtained. For calculations, the simplest cases are those when the luminaire is small and can be considered a point. Flux transfer types 1 and 2 can be used. In many cases, the luminaires are large and flux transfer types 3 and 4 are required to provide adequate accuracy. Methods for assessing luminaire size are given below.

Interreflection is the multiple reflection of light among surfaces. It is an important aspect of most interior lighting systems, since it is by interreflection that many interior architectural surfaces acquire a luminance. It is by these luminances that architecture is also revealed and given perceptual form. For some, less common interior lighting systems, interreflection is the only process by which the illuminance on the visual task is produced. Such is the case for indirect electric lighting and many daylighting systems.

Direct Flux Transfer

Flux Transfer Type 1, Point Source to a Point. The illuminance E produced on an area A centered at a point P is related to the luminous intensity of a light source, $I(\theta, \psi)$, as follows. Given the intensity distribution of the light source in spherical coordinates (θ, ψ), the geometric arrangement is shown in figure 9-1.

The illuminance E is defined in terms of the flux Φ incident on an area A:

$$E = \frac{\Phi}{A} \qquad (9\text{-}1)$$

That flux can also be analyzed directionally in terms of

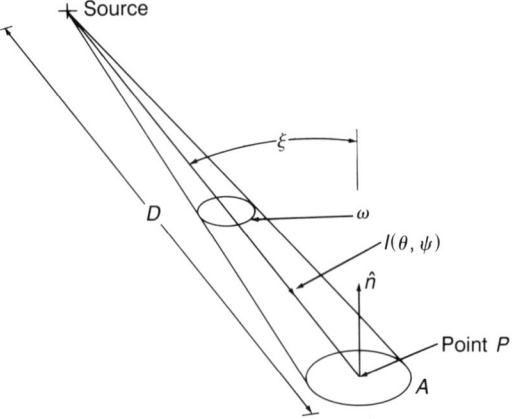

Fig. 9-1. Geometric arrangement for the inverse square cosine law.

the solid angle ω. If the origin of a spherical coordinate system is located at the source, and the area A is small with respect to the distance D, then

$$\omega = \frac{A}{D^2} \cos \xi \qquad (9\text{-}2)$$

where

D = distance between the source and point P,
ξ = angle between the normal ($\hat{n}$) to the surface A and direction of the distance D.

The definition of the luminous intensity from the source is used to related equations 9-2 and 9-1:

$$I(\theta, \psi) = \frac{\Phi}{\omega}$$

or

$$\Phi = I(\theta, \psi)\omega \qquad (9\text{-}3)$$

Substituting this into equation 9-1 gives

$$E = \frac{I(\theta, \psi)\omega}{A}$$

Substituting equation 9-2 into this gives

$$E = \frac{I(\theta, \psi) \cos \xi}{D^2} \qquad (9\text{-}4)$$

Equation 9-4 is the fundamental equation of flux transfer, the so-called inverse square cosine law.[1] Its validity assumes that of equation 9-2 and that the luminous intensity is (nearly) constant in the neighborhood of the direction (θ, ω).

As the area A (the neighborhood around point P) is made smaller, the solid angle ω becomes smaller and equation 9-2 becomes more accurate. In the limit of a differential area, dA, the solid angle becomes differential, $d\omega$, and equation 9-2 is exactly correct. The computational consequence of this consideration is that equation 9-4 describes the illuminance at a differentially small neighborhood around point P, or more briefly, gives the illuminance at P.

Equation 9-2 expresses the solid angle subtended by the area A at a point; the light source is assumed to be coincident with this point. The computational consequence is that equation 9-4 describes the illuminance from a point source.

The intensity value used in equation 9-4 is most often obtained by interpolation from values in a table. Intensity distributions are almost always expressed using the two angles of spherical coordinates; thus the required interpolation is over these two angles. Bilinear splines, bicubic splines and double Fourier series are among the methods used.

Flux Transfer Type 2, Point Source to a Receiving Area. The flux transferred from a point source to a differential area can be expressed using equation 9-4. This is integrated over the receiving area to give the flux received by the entire area:

$$d\Phi = E \, dA$$

$$\Phi = \int E \, dA$$

$$\Phi = \int \frac{I(\theta,\psi)\cos\xi}{D^2} \, dA \qquad (9\text{-}5)$$

The integration is over the receiving area A.

Analytic integration of equation 9-5 is possible only if the intensity distribution is a simple function and the geometric arrangement is simple.[2] Otherwise it is necessary to approximate the area integral of equation 9-5 with a finite sum. In this case the receiving surface is broken up into small areas, or *discretized*, and equation 9-4 is applied to each. The smaller and more numerous the discrete areas, the more accurate the result:

$$\Phi = \sum_i I(\theta_i,\psi_i)\cos\xi_i \frac{a_i}{D_i^2} \qquad (9\text{-}6)$$

where

$I(\theta_i,\psi_i)$ = intensity of the point source in the direction of the ith piece of area A,

ξ_i = incident angle at the ith piece of area A,

a_i = area of the ith piece of area A,

D_i = distance between the source and the ith piece of area A.

The average illuminance, $\overline{E}$, can be obtained from either equation 9-5 or 9-6:

$$\overline{E} = \frac{\Phi}{A}$$

Flux Transfer Type 3, Diffuse Area Source to a Point. In many applications the light source is too large, or the point at which the illuminance is to be calculated is too close, for the conditions of validity for direct use of equation 9-4 to be met. However, if the source is a diffuse emitter, equation 9-4 can be used indirectly.

The intensity distribution of a diffuse emitter, in spherical coordinates, is given by

$$I(\theta,\psi) = I_n \cos\theta$$

The distribution is axially symmetric about the direction (0,0), which is also the surface normal (perpendicular). I_n is the luminous intensity in the direction of the surface normal.

Because each differential element dA of the source is a diffuse emitter, the intensity distribution of such an element is

$$dI(\theta,\psi) = \frac{M_{dA}\cos\theta}{\pi} \, dA$$

where M_{dA} is the exitance of the source at the differential element dA. The illuminance produced at the point P is

$$dE = \frac{M_{dA}\cos\theta\cos\xi}{\pi D^2} \, dA$$

and the illuminance produced by the entire source is

$$E = \frac{1}{\pi}\int \frac{M_{dA}\cos\theta\cos\xi}{D^2} \, dA \qquad (9\text{-}7)$$

If the source exhibits a constant exitance M over its extent, then

$$E = \frac{M}{\pi}\int \frac{\cos\theta\cos\xi}{D^2} \, dA \qquad (9\text{-}8)$$

The integration is over the extent of the source.

The quantity which multiplies the exitance M is purely geometric and is called the *configuration factor*[3] C. More simply,

$$E = MC \qquad (9\text{-}9)$$

where

$$C = \frac{1}{\pi}\int \frac{\cos\theta\cos\xi}{D^2} \, dA \qquad (9\text{-}10)$$

The configuration factor relates the exitance of a diffuse area emitter to the illuminance it produces at a point. It has the limiting values

$$0 \leqslant C \leqslant 1$$

Alternative definitions of the configuration factor are possible. It can be defined as that fraction of the total flux emitted by a differential diffuse emitter which is received directly by an area. The analytic result of this definition is equation 9-10. This configuration factor has been evaluated for a large number of geometric conditions.[4] A selection of these equations is given in figures 9-30 and 9-31 at the end of this chapter.

Equation 9-9 can be used to calculate the illuminance at a point produced by any diffuse emitter having a shape for which the configuration factor is known or can be calculated. Note that the emitter is assumed to have a uniform diffuse exitance.

Flux Transfer Type 4, Diffuse Area Source to a Receiving Area. If the emitting surface is specified as A_1 and the receiving surface as A_2, then the flux sent from A_1 to A_2, Φ_2, is

$$\Phi_2 = \int E_{dA_2} dA_2$$

where E_{dA_2} is the illuminance at element dA_2 from all of source A_1. Substituting for E_{dA_2} using equation 9-7 gives

$$\Phi_2 = \int \frac{1}{\pi} \int \frac{M_{1\,dA_1} \cos\theta \cos\xi}{D^2} dA_1\, dA_2$$

If the source exhibits a constant exitance M_1 over its extent, then

$$\Phi_2 = \frac{M_1}{\pi} \iint \frac{\cos\theta \cos\xi}{D^2} dA_1\, dA_2 \qquad (9\text{-}11)$$

The integration is over the extent of the source and the extent of the illuminated area. The quantity which multiplies the exitance M_1 is purely geometric. It is customary to divide it by the area A_1 so that it is the fraction of flux leaving surface A_1 which reaches A_2. This is called the *form factor* $F_{1 \to 2}$.[3] Subscripts for form factors are necessary to indicate the direction in which flux is transferred. We have

$$F_{1 \to 2} = \frac{1}{\pi A_1} \iint \frac{\cos\theta \cos\xi}{D^2} dA_1\, dA_2 \qquad (9\text{-}12)$$

With this definition, equation 9-11 becomes

$$\Phi_2 = M_1 A_1 F_{1 \to 2}$$

The average illuminance, $\bar{E}_2$, produced on surface A_2 is then

$$\bar{E}_2 = \frac{\text{flux emitted by } A_1 \text{ reaching } A_2}{A_2}$$

$$\bar{E}_2 = \frac{M_1 A_1 F_{1 \to 2}}{A_2}$$

Form factors and areas relate the exitance of a diffuse area emitter to the average illuminance produced on a receiving surface. The form factors have the limiting values

$$0 \leqslant F \leqslant 1$$

and exhibit *reciprocity*:

$$A_1 F_{1 \to 2} = A_2 F_{2 \to 1}$$

Application of reciprocity gives

$$\bar{E}_2 = M_1 F_{2 \to 1} \qquad (9\text{-}13)$$

The equation for the form factor has been evaluated for a large number of geometric conditions. A selection of these equations is given in figures 9-32 and 9-33 at the end of this chapter.

Equations 9-9 and 9-13 have wide application for the calculation of illuminance and average illuminance produced by any form of diffuse emitter. Most large architectural surfaces exhibit a diffuse reflectance and therefore are diffuse emitters by reflection. The illuminance produced by such surfaces can be calculated using equations 9-9 and 9-13. This includes surfaces made luminous by interreflection of light and indirectly lighted surfaces.

Diffuse skylights or windows are diffuse emitters by reason of the type of transmittance they exhibit. Equations 9-9 and 9-13 can be used in these cases also.

If an area diffuse emitter does not have a uniform exitance, it can be discretized into smaller elements, each of which has a nearly uniform exitance. The illuminance produced by each element is then calculated by repeated application of equation 9-9 or 9-13. The total effect is obtained by adding the individual illuminances.

Flux Transfer Type 5, Nondiffuse Area Source to a Point. Nondiffuse area emitters are significantly more difficult to treat than diffuse emitters. If a far-field intensity distribution is available for the luminaire, equation 9-4 can be used in certain cases. If the distance from the luminaire to the calculation point is greater than 5 times the largest dimension of the luminaire, then treating the luminaire as a point source using equation 9-4 will give a computational accuracy of approximately 5% or better.

For points closer to the luminaire, an assumption can be made about homogeneity (surface uniformity) which permits a useful approximation to be made.[2] Under this assumption, the intensity distribution, $dI(\theta, \psi)$, of any differential element of the emitter is proportional to the intensity distribution, $I(\theta, \psi)$, of the entire luminaire. The constant of proportionality is the ratio of the area dA of the differential element to the area A of the entire luminaire. That is,

$$dI(\theta, \psi) = I(\theta, \psi) \frac{dA}{A}$$

The differential element is then treated as a point

source, and equation 9-4 is used to express the differential illuminance it produces:

$$dE = \frac{dI(\theta, \psi) \cos \xi}{D^2}$$

$$= \frac{1}{A} \frac{I(\theta, \psi) \cos \xi}{D^2} dA$$

Integration over the surface of the luminaire gives

$$E = \frac{1}{A} \int \frac{I(\theta, \psi) \cos \xi}{D^2} dA \qquad (9\text{-}14)$$

Analytic integration of equation 9-14 is possible only if the intensity distribution is a simple function and the geometric arrangement is simple. Otherwise it is necessary to approximate the area integral of equation 9-14 with a finite sum. In this case, the luminaire is discretized into small areas. The smaller and more numerous the discrete areas, the more accurate the result will be:

$$E = \frac{1}{A} \sum_i I(\theta_i, \psi_i) \cos \xi_i \frac{a_i}{D_i^2} \qquad (9\text{-}15)$$

where the summation is over all the discrete pieces of the luminaire, and

$I(\theta_i, \psi_i) =$ intensity of the ith piece of the luminaire surface to point P,
$\xi_i =$ incident angle for flux from the ith piece of the luminaire surface,
$a_i =$ area of the ith piece of the luminaire surface,
$D_i =$ distance between the ith piece of the luminaire surface and point P,
$A =$ area of the luminaire surface.

Equation 9-15 has wide application for the calculation of illuminance produced by luminaires with nondiffuse distributions.

Flux Transfer Type 6, Nondiffuse Area Source to a Receiving Area. If the nondiffuse emitting surface is specified as A_1 and the receiving surface as A_2, then the flux Φ_2 sent from A_1 to A_2 is

$$\Phi_2 = \int E_{dA_2} dA_2$$

where E_{dA_2} is the illuminance at element dA_2 from all of source A_1.

Under the same assumption of luminaire homogeneity described above, equation 9-14 can be used to express E_2:

$$E_2 = \int \frac{1}{A_2} \int \frac{I(\theta, \psi) \cos \xi}{D^2} dA_1 dA_2 \qquad (9\text{-}16)$$

The double area integrals usually cannot be evaluated analytically, and a double area summation is used as an approximation. In this case the luminaire and the receiving surface are discretized into small areas. The smaller and more numerous the discrete areas, the more accurate the result:

$$E_2 = \frac{1}{A_2} \sum_i \sum_j I(\theta_{ij}, \psi_{ij}) \cos \xi_{ij} \frac{a_{1i} a_{2j}}{D_{ij}^2} \qquad (9\text{-}17)$$

where the summation is over all the discrete pieces of luminaire and the discrete pieces of the receiving surface, and

$I(\theta_{ij}, \psi_{ij}) =$ intensity of the ith piece of the luminaire in the direction of the jth piece of the receiving surface,
$\xi_{ij} =$ incident angle of flux from the ith piece of the luminaire,
$a_{1i} =$ area of the ith piece of luminaire,
$a_{2j} =$ area of the jth piece of the receiving surface,
$D_{ij} =$ distance between the ith piece of the luminaire and the jth piece of the receiving surface,
$A_1 =$ area of the luminaire surface,
$A_2 =$ area of the receiving surface.

All of the previous types of analyses are summarized in figure 9-2. The equation to be used for illuminance calculations is determined by the size of the source, the size of the receiving element and the nature of the intensity distribution of the source. If the distance between the source and the analysis point is less than five times the largest dimension of the source, the

Fig. 9-2. Flux Transfer Equations

An asterisk (*) signifies that these equations are available for specific geometries. See figures 9-30 through 9-33.

Size of Source	Size of Receiving Element	Distribution	Appropriate Equation
Point	Point	Diffuse	(9-4)
	Point	Nondiffuse	(9-4)
	Area	Diffuse	(9-9)*
Area	Point	Diffuse	(9-9)*
	Point	Nondiffuse	(9-15)
	Area	Diffuse	(9-13)*
	Area	Nondiffuse	(9-17)

source is considered an area source for the purposes of calculation. This "five times" rule is discussed in the next section.

Photometry from a Calculation Standpoint

Intensity distributions are used to specify the spatial distribution characteristics of a source of light. This description treats the source as a point and gives the luminous intensity in a set of directions. The set is sufficiently large to provide a complete description of the spatial distribution of flux.

Photometry determines intensity by calculation, using an illuminance measurement and a test distance. For most photometry, the test distance is constant for all measurement points. Thus, illuminance measurements are made at positions on an imaginary sphere with a radius equal to the test distance. The sphere center coincides with a fiducial point inside the luminaire. This so-called photometric center is often the origin of the coordinate system used for calculations.[5]

If the source is assumed to be a point, then the intensity and the illuminance are related by equation 9-4. If the illuminance measurements are made with the surface normal of the illuminance probe oriented to the photometric center, then the cosine of the viewing angle equals 1 and equation 9-4 becomes

$$E_t = \frac{I}{D_t^2}$$

or

$$I = E_t D_t^2 \qquad (9\text{-}18)$$

where

$$I = \text{luminous intensity,}$$
$$E_t = \text{illuminance measurement,}$$
$$D_t = \text{measurement (test) distance.}$$

The luminous intensity is distance invariant, since the product $E_t D_t^2$ is distance invariant. Thus, the illuminance at any distance is given by equation 9-4.

Far-Field Photometry

Assuming the luminaire to be a point permits the illuminance produced under any geometric circumstance to be calculated. The computational value of intensity distributions rests on the assumption that illuminance varies proportionally to the reciprocal of the distance squared and to the cosine of the incident angle.

Only a point light source produces illuminances that always vary as the inverse squared distance. However, regardless of the luminaire size, it is always possible to

choose a distance, D_t, sufficiently large so that illuminances produced at distances greater than D_t do vary (nearly) as the inverse squared distance. Yamauti[6] and Fock[7] first showed this for diffuse emitters. For these emitters D_t is five times the maximum dimension of the emitter. This "five times" rule permits a computational accuracy of at worst 2% for diffuse emitters. In far-field photometry, a distance of at least D_t is used to make the illuminance measurements from which the luminous intensities are calculated. These intensities can then be used to calculate illuminances at distances greater than D_t, treating the luminaire as a point source. Most commercial photometry is far-field photometry.

Illuminance calculations at distances less than D_t, and which assume the luminaire to be a point source, are likely to be inaccurate. As a guide to the inaccuracies that can be expected, figure 9-3 shows an illuminance error curve for a square diffuse emitter. The error, in percent of the correct value, is given as a function of the ratio of the calculation distance D to the luminaire dimension. The "five times" rule requires this ratio to be 5 or larger. Comparison between measurements and predictions using real luminaires gives similar results.[8]

It should be noted that intensity distributions other than that of a diffuse emitter have different values of D_t.[9] However, it is customary to apply the "five times" rule to all luminaire photometry.

Near-Field Photometry

Near-field photometry describes the spatial flux distribution of a luminaire in a manner permitting accurate illuminance calculations at distances less than D_t. Near-field photometry is particularly important for analyzing indirect lighting systems. Two types of near-field photometry have been developed expressly for improving computational accuracy.

Application-distance photometry uses test distances that are equal to the distances at which illuminance calculations will be made.[10-12] No assumptions about distance invariance are made. In this case the luminaire must be treated as a point source for calculations. Since illuminance calculations are likely to be made at many distances, application-distance photometry provides intensity distributions for several test distances.

Luminance field photometry[9,13,14] measures and reports the luminance distribution of the luminaire, as viewed from a set of points completely surrounding the luminaire. All points are the same distance from the luminaire photometric center. Precisely stated, the data describe a four-dimensional scalar field of luminance. From these luminance data, illuminance can be calculated for any geometric condition.

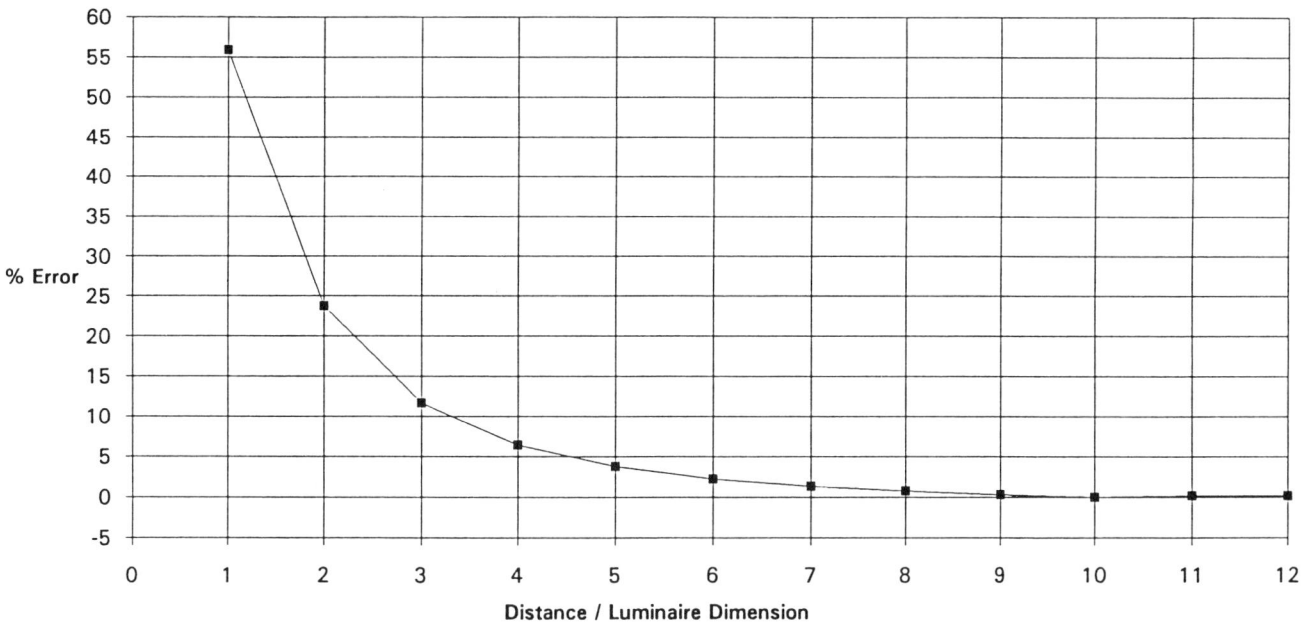

Fig. 9-3. Demonstration of the five-times rule for photometric measurements.

Reflection Properties of Surfaces

Useful special cases of reflectance are perfectly diffuse and perfectly specular reflectances. These cases of the spatial distribution permit great simplification of calculations involving the reflection of light from surfaces.

Perfectly diffuse reflection is that in which the amount of flux reflected in a given direction is proportional to the cosine of the declination angle from the perpendicular to the surface. The flux reflected from a diffuse surface is not a function of the incident direction or the azimuthal angle. Thus, the reflecting surface exhibits a luminance independent of viewing angle.

Perfectly specular reflection is that in which flux is reflected at the mirror angle to the incident direction. That is, the angle of the reflected flux is equal to that of the incident direction with respect to the direction perpendicular to the surface, and the azimuthal separation of the exitant and incident flux is exactly 180°.

Many surfaces and finishes used in architecture exhibit a reflectance that is sufficiently diffuse to be considered perfectly diffuse. This is important for computational purposes, since they can be considered diffuse emitters regardless of the incident direction of the light.

In some cases, assumptions about diffuseness will lead to very inaccurate results. An example of this is the calculation of the luminance of visual tasks, such as pencil marks on paper, etched marks on a rule and roadway surfaces. The *bidirectional reflectance distribution function* (BRDF) of a surface must be used in these cases.[15]

In addition to simplifying the spatial distribution characteristics of reflectance, it is often permissible (and necessary) to simplify its spectral characteristics. All surfaces exhibit a reflectance that varies with the wavelength of the incident light. The reflectance reported for a particular surface is usually obtained by integrating the proportion of light reflected from the surface at all visible wavelengths. Although the reflectance so defined changes if the spectrum of the illuminant changes, it is a useful approximation to assume that the reflectance is spectrally flat. The surface is assigned a "gray reflectance" equal to the integrated value. Thus, it is assumed that the surface will exhibit the same reflectance regardless of the spectral power distribution of incident light used in calculations. This is referred to as the "gray assumption."

Although this simplifies calculations and usually introduces only small errors, difficulties can arise. The reflectance of a surface with a deeply saturated color usually has a significant spectral reflectance only in a narrow band of wavelengths. Use of a light source spectrally different from that used in making a reflectance standard can then lead to large errors.

Interreflection of Light

Some of the light incident on an architectural surface will be absorbed and some reflected. The reflected portion will radiate to other surfaces, where it will be absorbed and reflected again. This can be thought of as happening an infinite number of times. The phenomena of repeated exchange of light by multiple reflection is called *interreflection*.[16-19] Architectural surfaces are made luminous by interreflection, as well as by light which reaches them directly from sources such as luminaires and windows. The exitances that these surfaces exhibit under these circumstances are said to be those at *luminous equilibrium*. That is, they are the exitances present when the rate at which light is being provided by luminaires and daylighting is balanced by the rate at which it is being absorbed by surfaces. These exitances are called *final exitances*, in contrast with *initial exitances*, which are those produced directly by light from luminaires or daylighting, before the process of interreflection.

Surfaces made luminous by interreflections become additional sources of light that should be considered when determining illuminance. The illuminance produced by reflected light is termed the interreflected component. In most architectural settings it is usually assumed that the surfaces involved exhibit a diffuse reflectance and therefore are diffuse emitters. They can then be treated as diffuse area sources, and the illuminance is calculated using the equations for a diffuse area source, involving configuration factors and surface exitance. The total interreflected component at an analysis point is

$$E_{\text{inter}} = \sum_{i=1}^{N} C_{i \to p} M_i \qquad (9\text{-}19)$$

where

$C_{i \to p}$ = configuration factor from surface i to point p,
M_i = diffuse exitance of surface i.

Thus, calculating the interreflected component of illuminance requires the determination of the final exitance of surfaces that are luminous by interreflection.

The most useful calculation procedure for determining the final exitances is the finite-element method.[20-22] The surfaces in the space are discretized, and each element is assumed to have a different, but uniform, exitance. In most cases it also can be assumed that the reflectances are perfectly diffuse. The accuracy of the calculated luminance pattern depends on the size of the zones and on the degree to which the reflectances are diffuse.

Modeling room surfaces as discrete elements not only allows an approximation to the actual exitance pattern in the room, but can represent the effect of doors, windows, bulletin boards and chalkboards.[20] Since these surfaces generally differ from the walls in reflectance, their exitance is also different, and likewise their effect on the illuminance within the space.

The degree to which the pattern of exitance in the enclosure is represented by the assemblage of discrete zone exitances depends upon the zone size. A highly variable directional component, such as can be produced by an indirect lighting or wallwash system, may require a small discretization of surfaces. This permits an accurate model of the large luminance gradient.

In advanced models, interior obstructions such as partitions and shelves can also be considered.[23,24] The execution times of computer programs based on these complex models can be very long because of the need to test for shadowing between elements. Other methods have been developed to further reduce the amount of work required to solve such systems.[25-27] Approximations for calculations in spaces with interior obstructions have also been developed.[28]

To obtain the equations for calculating interreflection, a flux balance equation is written for each element. It equates the total flux leaving an element to the total incident flux multiplied by the element's reflectance. The total incident flux has a direct component due to electric and daylight sources, and an interreflected component due to the flux from all the other elements. The equality expressing the flux balance exists when all interreflections are taken into account. For the ith element of a radiative transfer system the equation is

$$M_i = M_{0i} + \rho_i (F_{i \to 1} M_1 + F_{i \to 2} M_2 + \cdots$$

$$+ F_{i \to m} M_{m-1} + F_{i \to m} M_m) \quad (9\text{-}20)$$

This can be written for each surface element in the system, and a set of linear, independent, simultaneous equations results. Expressed in matrix form, this gives

$$\begin{bmatrix} M_1 \\ M_2 \\ \vdots \\ M_m \end{bmatrix} = \begin{bmatrix} M_{01} \\ M_{02} \\ \vdots \\ M_{0m} \end{bmatrix}$$

$$+ \begin{bmatrix} \rho_1 F_{1 \to 1} & \rho_1 F_{1 \to 2} & \cdots & \rho_1 F_{1 \to m-1} & \rho_1 F_{1 \to m} \\ \rho_2 F_{2 \to 1} & \rho_2 F_{2 \to 2} & \cdots & \rho_2 F_{2 \to m-1} & \rho_2 F_{2 \to m} \\ \vdots & \vdots & & \vdots & \vdots \\ \rho_m F_{m \to 1} & \rho_m F_{m \to 2} & \cdots & \rho_m F_{m \to m-1} & \rho_m F_{m \to m} \end{bmatrix}$$

$$\times \begin{bmatrix} M_1 \\ M_2 \\ \vdots \\ M_m \end{bmatrix} \qquad (9\text{-}21)$$

where

m = number of zones in the system,

M_i = exitance of the ith zone, due to direct and interreflected flux (the equation is solved for these values),

ρ_i = diffuse reflectance of the ith zone,

M_{0i} = exitance due to the direct component on the ith zone (due to luminaires and daylight sources),

$F_{i \to j}$ = form factor from zone i to zone j (note that for planar zones, $F_{i \to i} = 0$).

The form factors can be computed using the equations found for parallel and orthogonal rectangles in figures 9-32 and 9-33.

The above matrix equation can also be rewritten in terms of the illuminance on each surface. This form is particularly valuable when one or more of the reflectances is assigned a value of zero, since then the illuminance striking each element is independent of the element's reflectance:

$$\begin{bmatrix} E_1 \\ E_2 \\ \vdots \\ E_m \end{bmatrix} = \begin{bmatrix} E_{01} \\ E_{02} \\ \vdots \\ E_{0m} \end{bmatrix}$$

$$+ \begin{bmatrix} \rho_1 F_{1 \to 1} & \rho_2 F_{1 \to 2} & \cdots & \rho_{m-1} F_{1 \to m-1} & \rho_m F_{1 \to m} \\ \rho_1 F_{2 \to 1} & \rho_2 F_{2 \to 2} & \cdots & \rho_{m-1} F_{2 \to m-1} & \rho_m F_{2 \to m} \\ \vdots & \vdots & & \vdots & \vdots \\ \rho_1 F_{m \to 1} & \rho_2 F_{m \to 2} & \cdots & \rho_{m-1} F_{m \to m-1} & \rho_m F_{m \to m} \end{bmatrix}$$

$$\times \begin{bmatrix} E_1 \\ E_2 \\ \vdots \\ E_m \end{bmatrix} \qquad (9\text{-}22)$$

The simplest way to solve these large matrix finite-element systems is to use the method of iteration. The iteration begins by setting the vector M equal to the exitance vector M_0 in equation 9-21, using this as an initial estimate of the solution. This initial estimate is then used on the right-hand side of the equation to generate another estimate of the solution vector on the left. Convergence is achieved rapidly, with five iterations being sufficient for most lighting applications. Convergence is guaranteed by the nature of the transfer matrix; its size, in terms of matrix multiplication, is less than 1, since the sum of elements in any of its rows is always less than 1.

It should be noted that maintained values of the exitance may differ from initial values. Should computation of maintained values be required, the surface reflectances used in the computation of the reflected component should be the reflectances expected under maintained conditions in the environment. Additionally, a light loss factor should be used in the calculation of the initial exitances.

Implementation of the Flux Balance Model

The simplest example of a radiative transfer problem solved by this method is a system with two surfaces. In this case, two equations in two unknowns result. The solution is

$$M_1 = \frac{M_{01} + M_{02}\rho_1 F_{1 \to 2}}{1 - \rho_1\rho_2 F_{1 \to 2} F_{2 \to 1}} \qquad (9\text{-}23a)$$

$$M_2 = \frac{M_{02} + M_{01}\rho_2 F_{2 \to 1}}{1 - \rho_1\rho_2 F_{1 \to 2} F_{2 \to 1}} \qquad (9\text{-}23b)$$

where

M_1 = final exitance of surface 1, taking account of interreflection,

M_2 = final exitance of surface 2, taking account of interreflection,

M_{01} = initial exitance of surface 1,

M_{02} = initial exitance of surface 2,

ρ_1 = diffuse reflectance of surface 1,

ρ_2 = diffuse reflectance of surface 2,

$F_{2 \to 1}$ = form factor from surface 2 to surface 1,

$F_{1 \to 2}$ = form factor from surface 1 to surface 2.

These equations provide a way to estimate the effects of interreflection in situations involving only two surfaces, or where only two elements of a large system will participate in interreflection.

Another example of how a simple flux balance model can be applied to the analysis of a lighting system is the three-surface model used in the lumen method.[29-31] The geometric arrangement is an empty rectangular room with recessed lighting equipment. The lighting system provides a general uniform illuminance on the workplane. Perfectly diffuse reflectances on all surfaces are assumed, and the same reflectance is assumed for the four wall surfaces. This allows the four walls to be treated as one surface. The average illuminance on the floor is to be calculated. See figure 9-4.

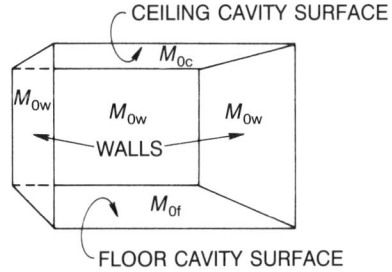

Fig. 9-4. Radiative transfer theory diagram.

For the purposes of the finite-element procedure, then, there are three elements or zones in this room: ceiling, walls and floor. The surfaces have initial exitances M_{0c}, M_{0w} and M_{0f} respectively. These initial exitances are due to the flux falling on the surfaces from the luminaires within the room.

Since there will be interreflections, the final exitances M_c, M_w and M_f can be expressed as follows:

$$M_c = M_{0c} + \rho_c(M_w F_{c \to w} + M_f F_{c \to f}) \quad (9\text{-}24)$$

$$M_w = M_{0w} + \rho_w(M_c F_{w \to c} + M_w F_{w \to w} + M_f F_{w \to f}) \quad (9\text{-}25)$$

$$M_f = M_{0f} + \rho_f(M_c F_{f \to c} + M_w F_{f \to w}) \quad (9\text{-}26)$$

where

M_c = final ceiling exitance,
M_w = final wall exitance,
M_f = final floor exitance,
M_{0c} = initial ceiling exitance,
M_{0w} = final wall exitance,
M_{0f} = final floor exitance,
ρ_f = floor reflectance,
ρ_w = wall reflectance,
ρ_c = ceiling reflectance,
$F_{f \to c}$ = form factor from floor to ceiling,
$F_{f \to w}$ = form factor from floor to walls,
$F_{w \to c}$ = form factor from walls to ceiling,
$F_{w \to w}$ = form factor from walls to walls,
$F_{w \to f}$ = form factor from walls to floor,
$F_{c \to w}$ = form factor from ceiling to walls,
$F_{c \to f}$ = form factor from ceiling to floor.

With these three equations and the form factors, any interior illuminance or exitance can be determined. The above set of simultaneous equations is the basis for generating the tables of the coefficients of utilization, the wall exitance coefficients and the ceiling cavity exitance coefficients.

The simple geometry permits six of the seven form factors to be calculated from the single form factor $F_{c \to f}$:

$$F_{f \to c} = F_{c \to f} \quad (9\text{-}27)$$

$$F_{c \to w} = F_{f \to w} = 1 - F_{c \to f} \quad (9\text{-}28)$$

$$F_{w \to c} = F_{w \to f} = \frac{A_c}{A_w}(1 - F_{c \to f}) \quad (9\text{-}29)$$

$$F_{w \to w} = 1 - 2F_{w \to c} \quad (9\text{-}30)$$

This three-surface model is the simplest of all flux transfer models for interior lighting calculations. It assumes that flux strikes each surface in a uniform manner and does not include variations in illuminance

Fig. 9-5. Form Factors for Zonal-Cavity System. The Length:Width Ratio is 1.6:1

RCR	$F_{w \to w}$	$F_{w \to c}$ $F_{w \to f}$	$F_{c \to w}$ $F_{f \to w}$	$F_{c \to f}$ $F_{f \to c}$
0	0.000	0.500	0.000	1.000
1	.133	.434	.173	.827
2	.224	.388	.311	.689
3	.298	.351	.421	.579
4	.361	.320	.511	.489
5	.415	.292	.585	.415
6	.463	.269	.645	.355
7	.504	.248	.694	.306
8	.540	.230	.735	.265
9	.573	.214	.769	.231
10	.601	.199	.798	.202

across any surface. In accordance with the Commission Internationale de l'Éclairage (CIE) practice and for the lumen method described below, the standard lighting coefficient tables are based upon a length-to-width ratio of 1.6 and given as a function of the room cavity ratio (RCR) only. Figure 9-5 gives numerical values for the various form factors.

The lumen method extends the utility of this three-surface model by letting the ceiling and floor surfaces be virtual surfaces that are actually openings into rectangular cavities. These virtual surfaces are assigned effective reflectances. The top virtual surface is a plane containing the luminaires, and the cavity that this virtual surface represents extends from the luminaires up to the ceiling. The bottom virtual surface is the workplane, and the cavity that this virtual surface represents extends from the workplane down to the floor. Note that the average illuminance onto the workplane will be its final exitance divided by its effective reflectance.

Although more complicated, exactly the same procedure can be used for models of radiative transfer in a room that uses more than three surfaces (the finite-element method). Complex models can have thousands of discrete elements as each surface in the room is divided into a collection of smaller zones.[25-27] The result is a more detailed knowledge of the room surface exitance distributions.

APPLICATION ISSUES

This section contains information on the application of lighting calculations.

Characterizing Light for Calculation Purposes

Lighting calculations are generally divided into two components for the purpose of determining the amount of light reaching a point in space. The *direct component* is that light reaching the point directly from the luminaires or windows. The *interreflected component* is that light reaching the same point from surfaces due to interreflections.

Direct Component. The direct component must be determined for points of interest on the workplane and for any reflecting surfaces that are being considered in the analysis. The contribution to the reflecting surfaces is used to provide the starting condition for interreflections. On the workplane, the direct component may have special importance because it is the principal component responsible for veiling reflections. Under a typical direct lighting system, the direct component will provide the majority of the total illuminance on the workplane. In outdoor lighting situations, the direct component may be the only light that a point receives. The direct component can be determined using the inverse square law or one of the area source methods if the luminaires are large compared to the distances involved. Methods have been developed which take advantage of either spectral geometries or intensity distributions.[32-36]

Interreflected Component. In most lighting calculations, the interreflected component requires the most time-consuming calculation. The amount of work involved in solving the large matrix problem is proportional to the square of the number of elements involved. To determine the interreflected component, the initial illuminance or direct component must first be determined at each of the discrete elements. In most cases, the value at the center of each element is used as an approximation of the average illuminance across an element. If the elements are sufficiently small, the error involved in this assumption is minimal. Large elements require more careful determinations of the average initial exitance, such as integration methods or calculation of several points to get an average.

Determination of the interreflected component is critical in situations where it is likely to be large relative to the direct component. Situations where this may be true include coves, valences and indirect lighting applications. It is important that the discretization scheme and calculation model being used for the direct component be capable of providing a light distribution which accurately models that provided by the lighting system.[23] Near-field photometry may be required for such calculations.

In some cases, a much less rigorous interreflection model may be applied. If the direct component is certain to dominate at the analysis points of interest, it may be possible to use a rather simple interreflected component calculation method involving larger and fewer room surface elements. When using large elements, it is important to remember that the value at the center of a large surface does not necessarily

approximate the average across it. The total luminous flux striking the surface should be determined and then divided by the area to determine the average illuminance on the surface.

In the simplest approximation, the room is approximated with three surfaces, as used in the lumen method described below, and the interreflected component is calculated using the three surface exitances that result from the lumen method approximation.

Light Loss Factors[37-39]

Light loss factors adjust lighting calculations from controlled laboratory to actual field conditions. They represent differences in lamp lumen output, luminaire output and surface reflectances between the two conditions. Calculations based on laboratory data alone are likely to provide unrealistically high values if not modified by light loss factors.

Light loss factors are divided into two groups: recoverable and nonrecoverable (see figure 9-6). Recoverable factors are those that can be changed by regular maintenance, such as cleaning and relamping luminaires and cleaning or painting room surfaces. Nonrecoverable factors are those attributed to equipment and site conditions and cannot be changed with normal maintenance.

Light loss factors are assumed to represent independent effects and are therefore multiplicative. The *total light loss factor* (LLF) is the product of all the applicable factors listed in figure 9-6. No factor should be ignored (set equal to 1) until investigations justify doing so. Lighting calculations should not be attempted until all light loss factors are considered.

Nonrecoverable Factors. The nonrecoverable factors usually are not controlled by lighting maintenance procedures. Some will exist initially and continue through the life of the installation, either being of such little effect as to make correction needless, or being too costly to correct. However, all should be studied, be-

Fig. 9-6. Light Loss Factors

Nonrecoverable

    Luminaire ambient temperature factor
    Heat extraction thermal factor
    Voltage-to-luminaire factor
    Ballast factor
    Ballast-lamp photometric factor
    Equipment operating factor
    Lamp position (tilt) factor
    Luminaire surface depreciation factor

Recoverable

    Lamp lumen depreciation factor
    Luminaire dirt depreciation factor
    Room surface dirt depreciation factor
    Lamp burnout factor

cause they can diminish the planned luminous output of the lighting system.

Luminaire Ambient Temperature Factor. The effect of ambient temperature on the output of some luminaires is considerable. Variations in temperature, within the range of those normally encountered in interiors, have little effect on the light output of incandescent and high-intensity discharge lamp luminaires, but appreciably affect the light output of fluorescent luminaires. The *luminaire ambient temperature factor* is the fractional lumen loss of a fluorescent luminaire due to internal luminaire temperatures differing from the temperatures at which photometry was performed. This factor should take into consideration any variation in the temperature around the luminaire, the means and conditions of mounting the luminaire, and the use of any insulation in conjunction with the application of the luminaire.

Generally, firm data on this factor are not available, but can be estimated on the following basis. Luminaire photometry is performed in 25° C (77°F) ambient still air. For each degree of rise in ambient temperature above this value, the cold-spot temperature on the lamp rises by about 0.6° C (1°F). The effect of lamp temperature rise can be estimated from the manufacturer's literature, recognizing that lamps in luminaires generally operate at temperatures greater than the optimum. Judgment must be applied to factors such as the effect of open versus enclosed luminaires, possible air movement and the fact that the plenum temperature will have a greater effect than the room temperature on recessed luminaires.

Heat Extraction Thermal Factor. Air-handling fluorescent luminaires are integrated with the HVAC system as a means of introducing or removing air. This will have an effect on lamp temperature and consequently on lamp lumens. The *heat extraction thermal factor* is the fractional lumen loss or gain due to the air flow. Generally, manufacturers provide specific luminaire test data for this factor at various air flows. Typically, the factor approaches a constant value for air flows in excess of 10–20 ft^3/min through the lamp compartment of a luminaire.

Voltage-to-Luminaire Factor. In-service voltage is difficult to predict, but high or low voltage at the luminaire will affect the luminous output of most luminaires. For incandescent units, small deviations from rated lamp voltage cause approximately a 3% change in lumen output for each 1% of voltage deviation. For mercury lamp luminaires with high-reactance ballasts there is a change in lumen output of approximately 3% for each 1% change in primary voltage deviation from rated ballast voltage. When regulated-output ballasts are used, the lamp lumen output is relatively independent of primary voltage within the design range. The luminous output of fluorescent luminaires using con-

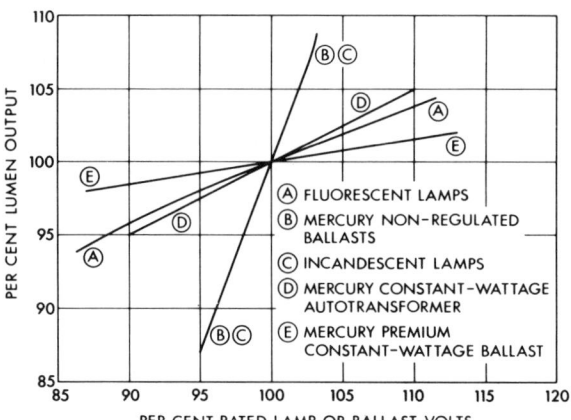

Fig. 9-7. Light output change due to voltage change.

ventional magnetic ballasts changes approximately 1% for each 2.5% change in primary voltage. Figure 9-7 shows these variations in graphic form. Different characteristics apply to electronic or energy-conserving magnetic ballasts and depend on specific design parameters. See Chapter 6, Light Sources.

Ballast Factor. The lumen output of fluorescent lamps depends on the ballast used to drive the lamps. The lumen output from lamps on commercial ballasts generally differs from that of lamps on the standard reference ballast used for determining rated lumens. For this reason, a multiplicative *ballast factor* is required to correct nominal rated lamp lumens to actual luminaire performance. The ballast factor is the fractional flux of a fluorescent lamp or lamps operated on the actual ballast divided by the flux when operated on the standard (reference) ballasting specified for rating lamp lumens. Ballast factors are determined in accordance with the American National Standard Methods of Measurement of Fluorescent Lamp Ballasts.[40] Manufacturers should be consulted for necessary factors. Data on ballast factors for electronic ballasts are available.[41] Some representative values are shown in chapter 6, Light Sources. Note that when uncertified ballasts are used, there may be no reliable data available.

The ballast factor depends on the lamp as well as on the ballast, so that a ballast factor developed for a standard lamp does not apply when, say, an energy-conserving lamp is used, even though the ballast is the same. Magnetic ballasts bearing the label of Certified Ballast Manufacturers (CBM) have a ballast factor which is not less than 0.925 for standard 30- and 40-W rapid start lamps; the ballast factor for such ballasts is frequently estimated at between 0.94 and 0.95. The ballast factor for highly loaded rapid start lamps is 0.95, and for various low-wattage lamps is 0.90.

However, the American National Standards Institute (ANSI) test method for the ballast factor specifies that the test be performed on a cold ballast (for convenience in testing). Significant temperature rise occurs for operating ballasts in luminaires. This causes additional lumen loss, usually on the order of 1.5%, but values as high as 2.5 to 3.5% have been reported.

Consequently, a conservative estimate of the operational ballast for a CBM certified ballast would be 0.93. It should be noted that only conventional magnetic ballasts can have CBM certification at this time. Collectively, the various energy-conserving ballasts and electronic ballasts have no expected minimum ballast factor, and the values may be as low as 0.7.

Ballast-Lamp Photometric Factor. Fluorescent luminaire photometry is performed at a standard ambient temperature of 25° C (77° F). The lamp temperature will differ from its value when rated lamp lumens are determined. The consequent lamp lumen change from rated lumens is incorporated in the photometric data. The lamp temperature within the luminaire depends on the particular combination of ballasting (standard magnetic, "energy-efficient" magnetic or electronic) and lamps (standard loading, reduced-power and "energy-efficient"). For this reason the photometric data apply only to the specific lamp and ballast types used in the tests. This also applies to the derived data such as coefficients of utilization and exitance coefficients.

Lamp lumen variations cause a change in the magnitude but not in the spatial distribution of fluorescent luminaire intensity. Consequently, all photometric data can be corrected by a multiplicative factor for ballast and lamp types that differ from those used in the photometric tests. This factor is the *ballast-lamp photometric factor*, and it is measured for a specific ballast-lamp combination in relation to those used in the luminaire photometry. Values for it are available as part of the luminaire photometric report or from the manufacturer. Note that this factor includes adjustment for lamp and ballast changes at the photometric test temperature of 25° C (77° F). The *luminaire ambient temperature factor* is a separate correction for differences between the laboratory and the expected luminaire installation temperature.

Equipment Operating Factor. The lumen output of high-intensity discharge (HID) lamps depends on the ballast, the lamp operating position and the effect of power reflected from the luminaire back onto the lamp. These effects are collectively incorporated in the *equipment operating factor* (EOF), which is defined as the ratio of the flux of an HID lamp-ballast-luminaire combination, in a given operating position, to the flux of the lamp-luminaire combination operating in the position for rating the lamp lumens and using the standard (reference) ballasting specified for rating lamp lumens. Equipment operating factors are determined in accordance with the IES Approved Method for Determining Luminaire-Lamp-Ballast Combination Operating Factors for High Intensity Discharge Luminaires.[42]

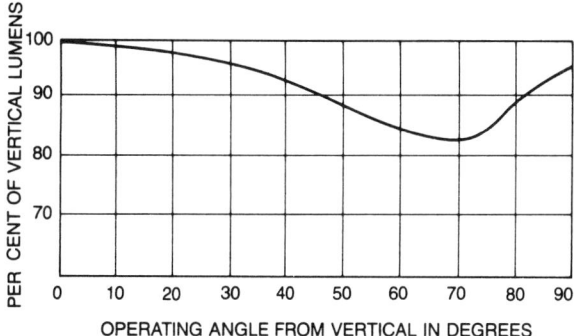

Fig. 9-8. Lumen output for HID lamps as a function of operating position.

Lamp Position or Tilt Factor (Part of EOF). For HID lamps, the *lamp position factor* (sometimes known as the *tilt factor*) is the ratio of the flux of an HID lamp in a given operating position to the flux when the lamp is operated in the position at which the lamp lumens are rated. This factor is determined at constant lamp wattage and constitutes part of the equipment operating factor. The lamp position factor is reasonably consistent for mercury lamp types. However, for metal halide lamps it is variable from lamp to lamp and depends on the operating history; thus, it is not actually a constant even for a given lamp.[43, 44] Figure 9-8 presents typical average data for the lamp position factor; manufacturers should be consulted regarding specific lamp types.

Luminaire Surface Depreciation Factor. Luminaire surface depreciation results from adverse changes in metal, paint and plastic components which result in reduced light output. Surfaces of glass, porcelain or processed aluminum have negligible depreciation and can be restored to original reflectance. Baked enamel and other painted surfaces have a permanent depreciation because all paints are porous to some degree. Among plastics, acrylic is least susceptible to change, but its transmittance may be reduced by use over a period of 15–20 yr in certain atmospheres. For the same usage, polystyrene will have lower transmittance than acrylic and will depreciate faster.

Because of the complex relationship between the light-controlling elements of luminaires using more than one type of material (such as a lensed troffer), it is difficult to predict losses due to deterioration of materials. Also, for luminaires with one type of surface the losses will be affected by the type of atmosphere in the installation. No factors for this effect are available at present.

Recoverable Factors. The recoverable factors that follow always need to be considered in determining the total light loss factor. The magnitude of each will depend on the maintenance procedures to be used in addition to the physical environment and the lamps and luminaires to be installed.

Lamp Lumen Depreciation Factor. The lumen outputs of lamps change gradually and continuously over their operating lives, even with constant operating conditions. In almost all cases, the lumens will decrease. The lamp lumen depreciation (LLD) factor is the fraction of the initial lumens produced at a specific time during the life of the lamp. Information about LLD as a function of the hours of lamp operation is available from manufacturers' tables and graphs for lumen depreciation and mortality of the chosen lamp. The rated average life should be determined for the expected number of hours per start; it should be known when burnouts will begin in the lamp life cycle. From these facts, a practical group relamping cycle can be established, and then, based on the hours elapsed to lamp removal, the LLD factor can be determined. Consult the tables in chapter 6 (Light Sources) or manufacturers' data for LLD factors. 70% of average rated life is the recommended criterion for lamp replacement for both group and spot relamping programs. It should be noted that some electronic ballasting systems compensate to varying degrees for change in lamp lumen output through life, either by an average correction or by feedback control.

Luminaire Dirt Depreciation Factor. The accumulation of dirt on luminaires results in a loss in light output, and therefore a loss on the workplane. This loss is known as the luminaire dirt depreciation (LDD) factor and is determined as follows:

1. The luminaire maintenance category is selected from manufacturers' data or by using figure 9-9.
2. The atmosphere (one of five degrees of dirt conditions) in which the luminaire will operate is found as follows. Dirt in the atmosphere will have come from two sources: that passed from adjacent air, and that generated by work done in the vicinity. Dirt may be classified as adhesive, attracted or inert, and it may come from intermittent or constant sources. *Adhesive* dirt clings to luminaire surfaces by its stickiness, while *attracted* dirt is held by electrostatic force. *Inert* dirt will vary in accumulation, from practically nothing on vertical surfaces, to as much as a horizontal surface will hold before the dirt is dislodged by gravity or air circulation. Examples of adhesive dirt are grease from cooking, particles from machine operation borne by oil vapor, particles borne by water vapor as in a laundry, and times from metal-pouring operations or plating tanks. Examples of attracted dirt are hair, lint, fibers, and dry particles which are electrostatically charged from machine operations. Examples of inert dirt are nonsticky, uncharged particles

Fig. 9-9. Procedure for Determining Luminaire Maintenance Categories

To assist in determining Luminaire Dirt Depreciation (LDD) factors, luminaires are separated into six categories (I through VI). To arrive at categories, luminaires are arbitrarily divided into sections, a Top Enclosure and a Bottom Enclosure, by drawing a horizontal line through the light center of the lamp or lamps. The characteristics listed for the enclosures are then selected as best describing the luminaire. Only one characteristic for the top enclosure and one for the bottom enclosure should be used in determining the category of a luminaire. Percentage of uplight is based on 100‰ for the luminaire. The maintenance category is determined when there are characteristics in both enclosure columns. If a luminaire falls into more than one category, the lower numbered category is used.

Maintenance Category	Top Enclosure	Bottom Enclosure
I	1. None.	1. None
II	1. None 2. Transparent with 15 per cent or more uplight through apertures. 3. Translucent with 15 per cent or more uplight through apertures. 4. Opaque with 15 per cent or more uplight through apertures.	1. None 2. Louvers or baffles
III	1. Transparent with less than 15 per cent upward light through apertures. 2. Translucent with less than 15 per cent upward light through apertures. 3. Opaque with less than 15 per cent uplight through apertures.	1. None 2. Louvers or baffles
IV	1. Transparent unapertured. 2. Translucent unapertured. 3. Opaque unapertured.	1. None 2. Louvers
V	1. Transparent unapertured. 2. Translucent unapertured. 3. Opaque unapertured.	1. Transparent unapertured 2. Translucent unapertured
VI	1. None 2. Transparent unapertured. 3. Translucent unapertured. 4. Opaque unapertured.	1. Transparent unapertured 2. Translucent unapertured 3. Opaque unapertured

such as dry flour, sawdust and fine cinders. Figures 9-10 and 9-11 may be useful for evaluating the atmosphere. Figure 9-10, Evaluation of Operating Atmosphere, is intended to evaluate the atmosphere-dirt category. Factors 1–5 should be assessed and inserted into the spaces in the table as they are required to describe the conditions of the space. The "Area Adjacent to Task Area" column represents the area separated from but adjacent to the area

Fig. 9-10. Evaluation of Operating Atmosphere

Type of Dirt*	Area Adjacent to Task Area					Filter Factor (per cent of dirt passed)			Area Surrounding Task						Sub Total
	Intermittent Dirt		Constant Dirt		Total				From Adjacent		Intermittent Dirt		Constant Dirt		
Adhesive Dirt		+		=		×		=		+		+		=	
Attracted Dirt		+		=		×		=		+		+		=	
Inert Dirt		+		=		×		=		+		+		=	
											Total of Dirt Factors				
0–12 = Very Clean		13–24 = Clean			25–36 = Medium		37–48 = Dirty			49–60 = Very Dirty					

* See step 2 under Luminaire Dirt Depreciation

Factors for use in the table below are 1: Cleanest conditions imaginable; 2: Clean, but not the cleanest; 3: Average; 4: Dirty, but not the dirtiest; 5: Dirtiest conditions imaginable.

in which the luminaire operates (which is the "Area Surrounding Task"). The "Filter Factor" column contains the percentages of dirt allowed to pass from the adjacent atmosphere to the surrounding atmosphere. The "From Adjacent" column indicates the net amount of such dirt which can pass through. This category might include, for example, an open window with a filter factor of 1.0 (no filtering at all), or an air-conditioning system with a filter factor of 0.1 (90% of dirt is filtered out). The total of all the numbers in the "Subtotal" column will be a number up to 60 and can be translated into the applicable atmosphere-dirt category listed at the bottom of the table.

3. From the appropriate luminaire maintenance category curve of figure 9-12, the applicable dirt condition curve and the proper elapsed time in months of the planned cleaning cycle, the LDD factor is found. For example, if the category is I, the atmosphere dirty and cleaning every 20 months, the LDD is approximately 0.80. An alternative procedure to figure 9-12 is to use the fitted equation

$$LDD = e^{-At^B} \qquad (9\text{-}31)$$

where the constants A and B are found from figure 9-13, based on the luminaire maintenance category and the atmosphere condition involved, and t is time in decimal years; that is, 1 yr 6 mo is entered as 1.5 yr.

Room Surface Dirt Depreciation Factor. The accumulation of dirt on room surfaces reduces the amount of luminous flux reflected and interreflected to the workplane. To take this into account, figure 9-14 has been developed to provide room surface dirt depreciation (RSDD) factors for use in calculating maintained average illuminance levels. These factors are determined as follows:

1. From one of the five curves in figure 9-14, find the expected dirt depreciation using figure 9-10 or 9-11 as a guide to atmospheric dirt conditions, together with an estimate of the time

Fig. 9-11. Five Degrees of Dirt Conditions

	Very Clean	Clean	Medium	Dirty	Very Dirty
Generated Dirt	None	Very little	Noticeable but not heavy	Accumulates rapidly	Constant accumulation
Ambient Dirt	None (or none enters area)	Some (almost none enters)	Some enters area	Large amount enters area	Almost none excluded
Removal or Filtration	Excellent	Better than average	Poorer than average	Only fans or blowers if any	None
Adhesion	None	Slight	Enough to be visible after some months	High—probably due to oil, humidity or static	High
Examples	High grade offices, not near production; laboratories; clean rooms	Offices in older buildings or near production; light assembly; inspection	Mill offices; paper processing; light machining	Heat treating; high speed printing; rubber processing	Similar to Dirty but luminaires within immediate area of contamination

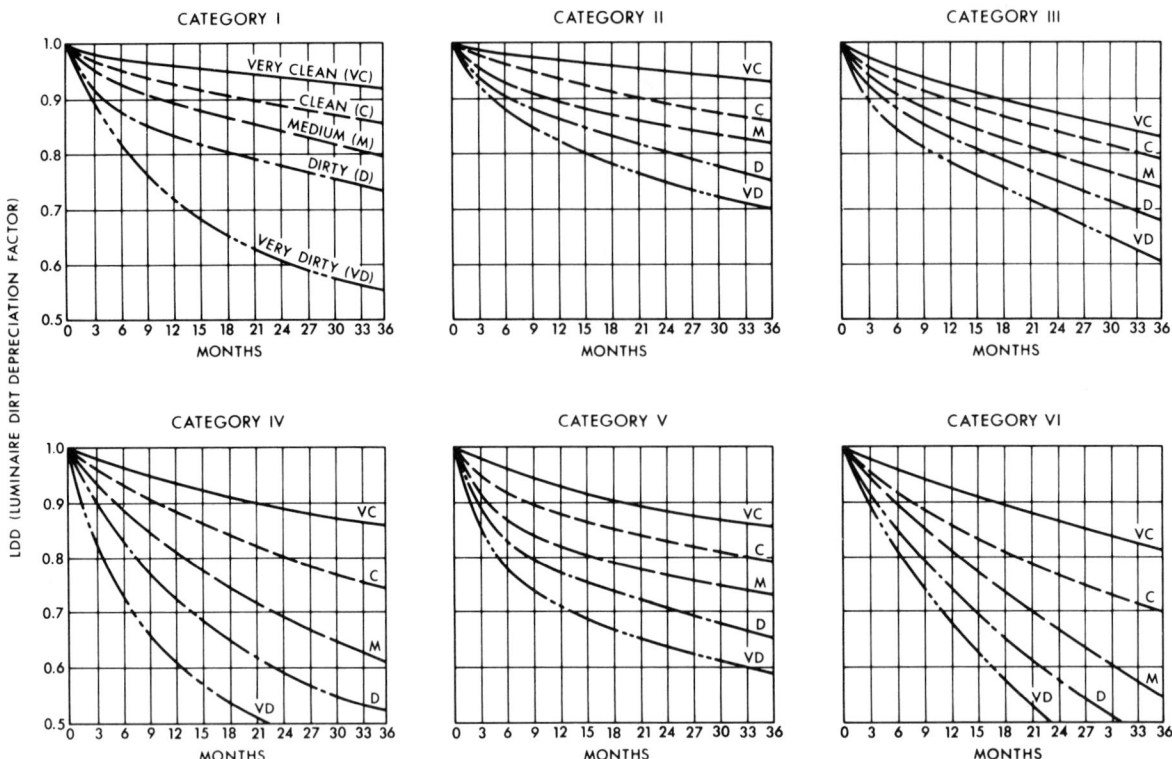

Fig. 9-12. Luminaire Dirt Depreciation (LDD) factors for six luminaire categories (I through VI) and for five degrees of dirtiness as determined from figures 9-10 or 9-11.

between cleanings. For example, if the atmosphere is dirty and room surfaces are cleaned every 24 months, the expected dirt depreciation is approximately 30%.

2. Knowing the expected dirt depreciation (step 1), the type of luminaire distribution (see chapter 7, Luminaires) and the room cavity ratio, determine the RSDD factor from figure 9-14. For example, for a dirt depreciation of 30%, a direct luminaire and a room cavity ratio (RCR) of 4, the RSDD would be 0.92.

Fig. 9-13. Luminaire Dirt Depreciation Constants Used for Calculating the LDD for Six Luminaire Categories and Five Fegrees of Dirtiness

Luminaire Maintenance Category	B	A				
		Very Clean	Clean	Medium	Dirty	Very Dirty
I	.69	.038	.071	.111	.162	.301
II	.62	.033	.068	.102	.147	.188
III	.70	.079	.106	.143	.184	.236
IV	.72	.070	.131	.216	.314	.452
V	.53	.078	.128	.190	.249	.321
VI	.88	.076	.145	.218	.284	.396

Lamp Burnout Factor. Lamp burnouts contribute to light loss. If lamps are not replaced promptly after burnout, the average illuminance will be decreased proportionally. In some instances, more than just the faulty lamp may be lost. For example, when series sequence fluorescent ballasts are used and one lamp fails, both lamps go out. The *lamp burnout* (LBO) *factor* is the ratio of the number of lamps remaining lighted to the total, for the maximum number of burnouts permitted.

Manufacturers' mortality statistics should be consulted for the performance of each lamp type to determine the number expected to burn out before the time of planned replacement is reached. In practice, the number of lamp burnouts will be a reflection of the quality of the lighting services program.

Total Light Loss Factor. The *total light loss factor* (LLF) is simply the product of all the contributing factors described above. Where factors are not known, or not applicable, they are assumed to be unity. At this point, if it is found that the total light loss factor is excessive, it may be desirable to reselect the luminaire.

STATISTICAL QUANTITIES

When lighting calculations and system modeling are required, it is important that an appropriate method be

Fig. 9-14. Room Surface Dirt Depreciation (RSDD) Factors

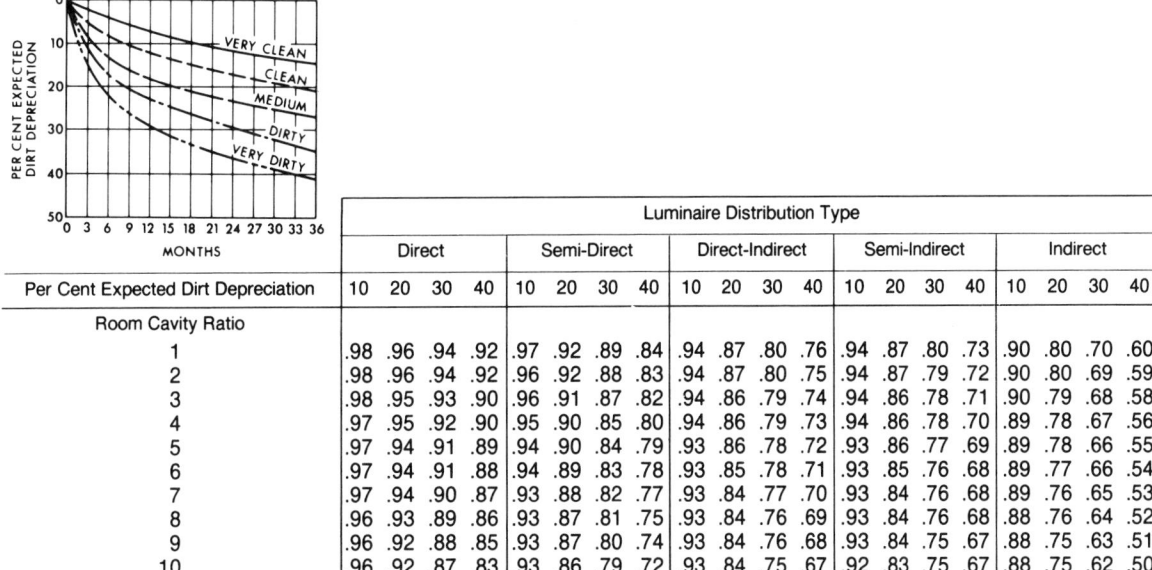

Per Cent Expected Dirt Depreciation	Direct				Semi-Direct				Direct-Indirect				Semi-Indirect				Indirect			
Room Cavity Ratio	10	20	30	40	10	20	30	40	10	20	30	40	10	20	30	40	10	20	30	40
1	.98	.96	.94	.92	.97	.92	.89	.84	.94	.87	.80	.76	.94	.87	.80	.73	.90	.80	.70	.60
2	.98	.96	.94	.92	.96	.92	.88	.83	.94	.87	.80	.75	.94	.87	.79	.72	.90	.80	.69	.59
3	.98	.95	.93	.90	.96	.91	.87	.82	.94	.86	.79	.74	.94	.86	.78	.71	.90	.79	.68	.58
4	.97	.95	.92	.90	.95	.90	.85	.80	.94	.86	.79	.73	.94	.86	.78	.70	.89	.78	.67	.56
5	.97	.94	.91	.89	.94	.90	.84	.79	.93	.86	.78	.72	.93	.86	.77	.69	.89	.78	.66	.55
6	.97	.94	.91	.88	.94	.89	.83	.78	.93	.85	.78	.71	.93	.85	.76	.68	.89	.77	.66	.54
7	.97	.94	.90	.87	.93	.88	.82	.77	.93	.84	.77	.70	.93	.84	.76	.68	.89	.76	.65	.53
8	.96	.93	.89	.86	.93	.87	.81	.75	.93	.84	.76	.69	.93	.84	.76	.68	.88	.76	.64	.52
9	.96	.92	.88	.85	.93	.87	.80	.74	.93	.84	.76	.68	.93	.84	.75	.67	.88	.75	.63	.51
10	.96	.92	.87	.83	.93	.86	.79	.72	.93	.84	.75	.67	.92	.83	.75	.67	.88	.75	.62	.50

applied to predict system performance. If an inappropriate model is used, the results can be inaccurate. A designer should therefore have knowledge of the capabilities and limitations of the different modeling options and their applications.

Averages

An average value is the simplest way of specifying the performance of a lighting system. "Average" usually refers to the mean of several calculated or measured values. The average illuminance (or an average of any other quantity) should be used only when the distribution is expected to be unimodal and normally distributed (that is, the common bell-shaped distribution). When a localized lighting system is desired, such as for a reception desk in a lobby, bimodal or multimodal distributions will result, and an average-illuminance calculation method should not be used. An average value can be used to design the system for the general circulation space, but for the task area, individual point source calculations should be used to characterize the task lighting.

In general, an average value alone is not sufficient to fully describe or evaluate lighting system performance. Information on the uniformity of the lighting is also important. The following two subsections consider methods for describing the uniformity of lighting across an area.

Minima and Maxima

If a large number of analysis points are used for calculation, then the variability of the lighting can be evaluated and the minimum and maximum values can be determined and located. The minima and maxima can be important indicators of the quality of the design, particularly if they deviate significantly from the desired average. In some design situations, maximum and minimum design values may be specified. In evaluating whether or not a particular design is acceptable, it is important to focus on the critical task areas within a space. Minima often occur around the perimeter of a room or lighted area, where tasks may not be located. Levels below the target level may be acceptable if they are not at actual task locations. In other design situations, the maximum value may be critical. For example, it may not be desirable to have room surface luminances that exceed a particular value. This is the case in the lighting recommendations for spaces with visual display terminals (VDTs).

Uniformity is often expressed in terms of a ratio of two quantities. Examples are maximum to minimum, maximum to average, and average to minimum. Different design situations warrant different use of these metrics.

Criterion Ratings

The maximum and minimum values provide little information about the overall distribution of a particular photometric or derived quantity across a space. The criterion rating is a convenient way to obtain greater detail regarding the distribution of a quantity across a space. The *criterion rating* is the probability that a specific criterion will be met or exceeded anywhere within a defined area. It can be used in addition to (or instead of) concepts such as averages or minimum and maximum levels. Lighting criteria to which this technique may be applied include luminance, illuminance, visual comfort probability (VCP), contrast, visibility metrics and visual performance metrics.

The criterion rating assumes the name of the criterion being rated. For example, the criterion rating for illuminance is called the illuminance rating; for VCP, the VCP rating. Assume, for example, that an illuminance of 500 lx has been established as the design criterion for a space. The illuminance rating defines the likelihood that at any point on the workplane the illuminance will be equal to or greater than 500 lx. This criterion rating is determined by evaluating the appropriate quantity (by calculation or measurement) at a grid of points covering the area in question. The distance between evaluation points must not exceed one-fifth the distance from any luminaire to the evaluation plane. The percentage of points that comply with the criterion is the criterion rating:

$$\text{criterion rating} = \frac{(\text{number of points satisfying criterion}) \times 100\%}{\text{number of points computed or measured}} \qquad (9\text{-}32)$$

Criterion ratings may be expressed using a notation which lists the rating, in percent, followed by the criterion, separated by the symbol @, which stands for "at." For example, a lighting system producing a luminance of 20 cd/m^2 over 60% of the specified area may have its luminance rating expressed as 60%@20 cd/m^2. For dimensionless criteria, such as contrast and VCP, the shorthand form for the criterion rating must include the name and value of the criteria; for example, 92%@70 VCP means 92% of the area has a VCP of 70 or better. The desired coverage area for a particular criterion value is determined by the designer.

As an example of the use of the criterion rating technique (using the foot as the unit of length), consider a square room 30 ft on a side, as shown in figure 9-15, with an 8-ft ceiling height, a 3-ft-high workplane and recessed luminaires. The tabulated values in figure 9-15 are calculated illuminances in the 8 × 12-ft shaded area. The required illuminance is 50 fc in the shaded area. The distance from the workplane to the luminaires is 5 ft (8 ft − 3 ft). Thus, the distance between rows and columns of analysis points must be no greater than 1 ft (5 ft/5). To determine the criterion rating, the calculated illuminance values are examined for criterion compliance. It is found that 47 of the 96 locations receive an illuminance of 50 fc or more. The illuminance rating of this lighting system for the shaded area is then 48.9% [(47/96) × 100%]. This can be expressed as 48.9%@50 fc.

Fig. 9-15. Example of Criterion Rating Technique.

The numbers in the grid represent the calculated illuminances, in fc, in the center of each ft^2 of the shaded portion of the work plane.

24	28	35	45	52	56	61	60
24	29	38	50	53	55	60	63
23	28	38	50	53	55	60	63
23	28	36	48	51	52	54	55
24	29	37	51	53	55	58	59
22	27	34	44	48	51	54	55
23	28	35	48	51	54	57	58
24	28	38	52	53	56	59	60
24	29	40	55	55	58	62	64
23	25	37	50	52	54	56	57
20	23	32	44	49	47	50	54
18	22	30	37	42	45	48	49

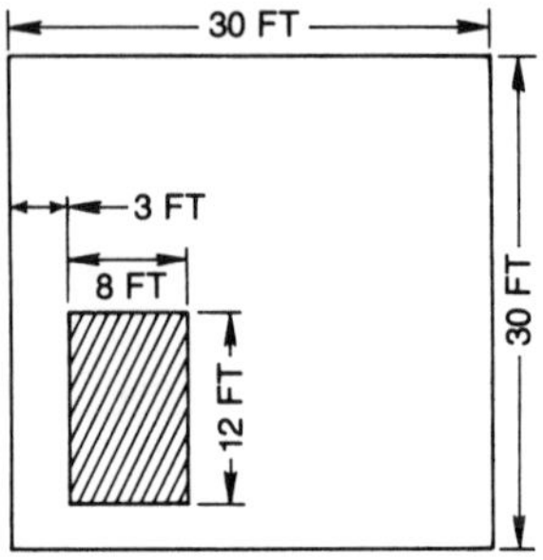

CALCULATION OF BASIC QUANTITIES

The basic quantities that are discussed in this section are illuminance, luminance and exitance.

Illuminance

Illuminance is one of the fundamental quantities used in designing and evaluating lighting systems. To determine the direct illuminance at a point on an area, one must determine that either a point or an area source method is applicable to the situation. To obtain the total illuminance at any point or on any surface, the interreflected component must be appropriately determined and added to the direct component.

Luminance

As a primary visual stimulus, luminance is the most important and useful calculated quantity. One of the most common situations in which luminance must be calculated is for the evaluation of visual tasks, such as for print on paper. Methods for evaluating the visual performance or visibility of a task require a value for the task contrast, size and adaptation luminance. The luminances of both the task (L_t) and the background (L_b) are needed to determine the task contrast. The quantities L_t and L_b are specific to a particular task location, lighting condition and viewer orientation.

Luminance calculations are performed whenever it is necessary to calculate the luminance of a surface that exhibits a directionally sensitive reflectance. A calculation model that computes luminance should be able to predict the luminance at any point. While it is not required that any given method be able to take all possible ranges of the following nine parameters into account, any restrictions which the method imposes should be adequately noted:

- Room size and shape.
- Room surface reflectances.
- Luminaire characteristics.
- Number and location of luminaires.
- Nature of the given surface.
- Observer location, line of sight and viewing angle.
- Nature and luminance of all other surfaces in the environment.
- Body shadow effects.
- Polarization effects.

Because of the complexity involved in calculating luminance, this calculation is generally performed on a computer.

The luminance in a particular luminous environment at a particular location is given by

$$L = \int dE(\theta, \psi) \, f_r(\theta, \psi) \qquad (9\text{-}33)$$

where

$L =$ luminance at a point on a surface in a particular viewing direction,

$\theta, \psi =$ spherical coordinates, declination and azimuth, respectively,

$dE(\theta, \psi) =$ differential amount of illuminance at the point in the plane of the surface from a direction indicated by (θ, ψ),

$f_r(\theta, \psi) =$ bidirectional reflectance distribution function (BRDF) of the surface material for a particular viewing direction.

Figure 9-16 indicates the necessary coordinates. This expression represents the total effect of all components of illuminance multiplied by the appropriate BRDF, to give the luminance of the surface. The BRDF is dependent upon the surface reflectance characteristics, the

Fig. 9-16. Task and illumination coordinates

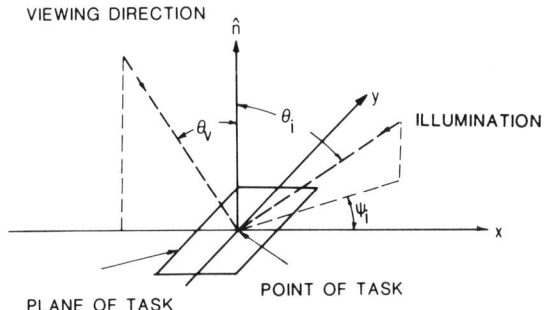

VIEWING DIRECTION

viewing angle and the size of the light source used to measure it.

It should be noted that unlike perfectly diffuse reflectances, the BRDF is sensitive to both incident light and viewing directions. This can be expressed as

$$f_r(\theta_v, \psi_v, \theta_i, \psi_i)$$

where the subscript i represents the incident direction and v the viewing direction. In many cases only the difference in azimuthal angle between the incident and exitant directions is required. Then the specification of the BRDF becomes

$$f_r(\theta_v; \theta_i, \psi_i)$$

where ψ_i is the difference in azimuthal angle between the incident and exitant directions. This simplification is not possible for non-axially-isotropic materials such as brushed metal surfaces. In such cases, the azimuthal incident and viewing angles cannot be made relative, but must have a fixed orientation with respect to the surface. For many surfaces, however, the simplification can be made and the equation for luminance becomes

$$L(\theta_v) = \int dE(\theta_i, \psi_i) \, f_r(\theta_v; \theta_i, \psi_i) \qquad (9\text{-}34)$$

The viewing angle θ_v is normally held constant.

Some surfaces exhibit sensitivity to polarization. It is then possible to separate the BRDF into two orthogonal components associated with orthogonal planes of polarization (p_1 and p_2). The BRDFs are

$$f_{rp_1}(\theta_v; \theta_i, \psi_i)$$

$$f_{rp_2}(\theta_v; \theta_i, \psi_i)$$

In a complementary fashion, two orthogonal components of the illuminance can be considered separately, and will be indicated by dE_{p_1} and dE_{p_2}. This gives

$$L(\theta_v) = \int \left[dE_{p_1}(\theta_i, \psi_i) \, f_{rp_1}(\theta_v; \theta_i, \psi_i) \right.$$

$$\left. + dE_{p_2}(\theta_i, \psi_i) \, f_{rp_2}(\theta_v; \theta_i, \psi_i) \right] \qquad (9\text{-}35)$$

The expression for L is general and applicable to all situations. Since the illuminance values and luminance factors must be expressed as analytic functions in order to attempt integration of these expressions, there can be, in general, no closed-form analytic expression for L. Approximation by the method of finite elements allows an evaluation of the equation. The BRDFs now take the form of a set of discrete values that sample the continuous BRDF. The resulting approximation is

$$L(\theta_v) \approx \sum \left[\Delta E_{p_1}(\theta_i, \psi_i) f_{rp_1}(\theta_v; \theta_i, \psi_i) \right.$$

$$\left. + \Delta E_{p_2}(\theta_i, \psi_i) f_{rp_2}(\theta_v; \theta_i, \psi_i) \right] \quad (9\text{-}36)$$

The sum is taken over all the discrete values of illuminance. The number of discrete steps determines the accuracy of the approximation. The step size in these approximations is determined by the need to model high gradients of either the illuminance or the BRDFs.

In the case of calculations of luminance for visual tasks, a modification can be applied to the BRDF to take account of a body shadow.

Exitance

If room surfaces are considered to be lambertian, then the exitances of discrete elements can be found using a flux transfer model described above. Exitance distributions across a room surface can be determined at an array of points that cover it, using lighting analysis software. For rooms with a uniform lighting system, average room surface exitances can be determined using the lumen method.

CALCULATION OF DERIVED QUANTITIES

From the photometric quantities—illuminance, luminance and exitance—it is possible to calculate other quantities that characterize how the human visual system interprets or is affected by a visual scene. This section discusses a number of different quantities of this type and provides equations or references for use in their computation.

Contrast

Contrast represents the difference in luminance between the task detail and its background relative to the luminance of the background or the luminances in the visual scene. There are three different formulas for computing contrast, each of which will provide a slightly different answer. See chapter 3, Vision and Perception, for definitions.

Visual Performance and Visibility Metrics

Relative visual performance (RVP) and equivalent sphere illumination (ESI) are metrics for the evaluation of visual performance and visibility, respectively. The calculation of these quantities requires the determination of the task and background luminances (to obtain the task contrast). The task size and adaptation luminance are also needed. The equations needed to

compute these quantities are provided in the references of chapter 3, Vision and Perception, where they are discussed in more detail.

Visual Comfort Probability (VCP)

Discomfort glare is the sensation of discomfort caused by luminances which are high relative to the average luminance in the field of view. The *visual comfort probability* (VCP) is the probability that a normal observer will not experience discomfort when viewing a lighting system under defined conditions.

Equations for the calculation of the VCP were derived from correlating photometric and geometric characteristics of simple lighting patterns with discomfort glare assessments of observers.[45-52] Experiments in simulated rooms have been used to confirm the extension from the laboratory to actual lighting installations.[53,54] This system was tested and validated using lensed direct fluorescent systems only. VCP should not be applied to very small sources such as incandescent, to very large sources such as the ceiling in indirect systems, or to nonuniform sources such as parabolic reflectors.

To calculate the VCP[55-61] several intermediate calculations must first be performed. The position index of a source, P, is an inverse measure of the relative sensitivity to a glare source at different positions throughout the field of view. Selected values or families of curves were published in early references. P is given by the formula[62]

$$P = \exp\left[(35.2 - 0.31889\alpha - 1.22e^{-2\alpha/9}) \, 10^{-3}\beta \right.$$

$$\left. + (21 + 0.26667\alpha - 0.002963\alpha^2) \, 10^{-5}\beta^2 \right] \quad (9\text{-}40)$$

where

α = angle from vertical of the plane containing the source and the line of sight (see figure 9-17), in degrees,

β = angle between the line of sight and the line from the observer to the source.

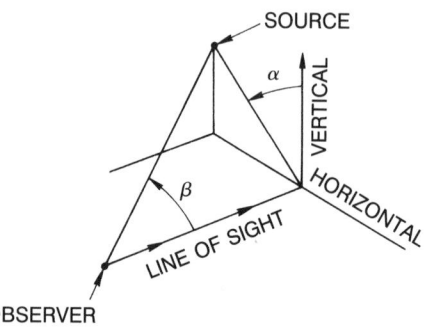

Fig. 9-17. Geometry defining position index as used in VCP calculations.

The average luminance for the entire field of view, F_v, is approximated by the following equation:

$$F_v = \frac{L_w \omega_w + L_f \omega_f + L_c \omega_c + \Sigma L_s \omega_s}{5} \quad (9\text{-}41)$$

where

L_w = average luminance of the walls in cd/m^2,
L_f = average luminance of the floor in cd/m^2,
L_c = average luminance of the ceiling in cd/m^2,
L_s = average luminance of the source in cd/m^2,
ω_w = solid angle subtended at the observer by the walls in sr,
ω_f = solid angle subtended at the observer by the floor in sr,
ω_c = solid angle subtended at the observer by the ceiling in sr,
ω_s = solid angle subtended at the observer by the source in sr.

The 5 in the denominator arises from the assumption that the total field of view is 5 sr.[63]

A function Q has been developed which is used in the calculation of the VCP. This function is given by

$$Q = 20.4\omega_s + 1.52\omega_s^{0.2} - 0.075 \quad (9\text{-}42)$$

where ω_s is the solid angle subtended at the observer by the source, in steradians. The values of P, F_v and Q are used to determine the index of sensation, M:

$$M = \frac{0.50 L_s Q}{P F_v^{0.44}} \quad (9\text{-}43)$$

The luminance in the above equation is expressed in cd/m^2. The factor 0.50 in the numerator allows for the use of these units.

From the index of sensation of each source, a discomfort glare rating (DGR) can be calculated for the full field of view. The DGR is a metric of discomfort which increases as discomfort increases; it is also used in calculating the VCP. It is given by

$$\text{DGR} = \left(\sum_{i=1}^{n} M_i \right)^{n^{-0.0914}} \quad (9\text{-}44)$$

where

n = number of sources in the field of view,
M_i = index of sensation for the ith source.

The relation between DGR and VCP may be found from a graph such as figure 9-18 or may be calculated by[64]

$$\text{VCP} = \frac{100}{\sqrt{2\pi}} \int_{-\infty}^{6.374 - 1.3227 \ln \text{DGR}} e^{-t^2/2} \, dt \quad (9\text{-}45)$$

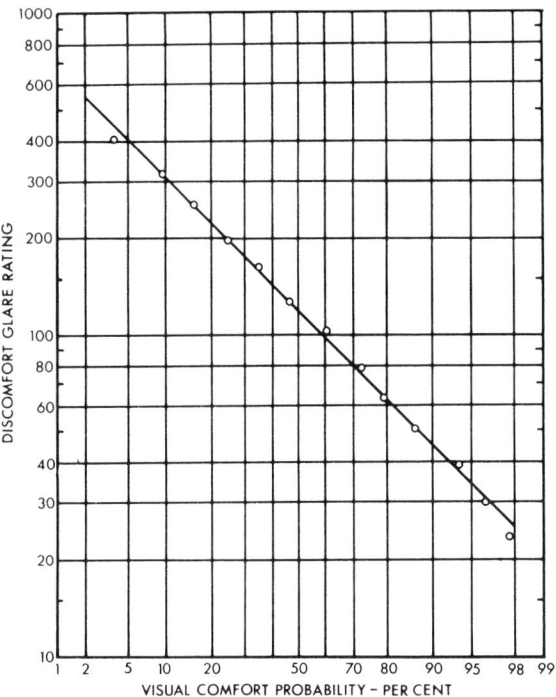

Fig. 9-18. A chart for converting discomfort glare ratings (DGR) to VCP (the percentage of observers expected to judge a given lighting condition to be either comfortable or at the borderline between comfort and discomfort).

These basic relations may be applied through a variety of techniques. Generally, the room cavity concept is used, in which the actual ceiling and floor luminances and solid angles are replaced by their equivalent cavity values. The computation can be performed by summing throughout the enclosure.[65]

VCP values are frequently associated with luminaires under standardized conditions of use. In this method, the luminaires are fractionally apportioned over the ceiling according to a standard scheme. VCP values are determined for:

1. An initial average horizontal illuminance of 1000 lx (100 fc)
2. Room reflectances of $\rho_{CC} = 0.80$, $\rho_W = 0.50$ and $\rho_{FC} = 0.20$
3. Luminaire mounting heights above the floor of 2.6, 3, 4 and 4.9 m (8.5, 10, 13 and 16 ft)
4. A (given) range of room dimensions including square, long narrow and short wide rooms
5. An observation point 1.2 m (4 ft) in front of the center of the rear wall and 1.2 m (4 ft) above the floor
6. A horizontal line of sight, directly forward
7. An upward limit to the field of view corresponding to an angle of 53° above and directly forward from the observer

This standardized procedure is extensively treated in references 53, 54, 55, 58 and 59.

Fig. 9-19. Example of a Tabulation of VCP Values

This example is for use when the units of length and illuminance are the foot (ft) and footcandle (fc). VCP values will be identical if units of length and illuminance are the meter (m) and the lux (lx).

Wall Reflectance-50%, Effective Ceiling Cavity Reflectance-80%, Effective Floor Cavity Reflectance-20%. Luminaire No. 000 Work-Plane Illuminance-100 fc

Room		Luminaires Lengthwise				Luminaires Crosswise			
W	L	8.5	10.0	13.0	16.0	8.5	10.0	13.0	16.0
20	20	78	82	90	94	77	81	89	93
20	30	73	76	82	88	72	75	81	86
20	40	71	73	78	82	70	72	76	80
20	60	69	71	74	78	68	70	73	76
30	20	78	82	88	92	77	81	87	92
30	30	73	75	80	85	72	74	79	84
30	40	70	72	75	78	69	71	74	77
30	60	68	69	71	74	67	69	70	73
30	80	67	69	69	72	67	68	68	71
40	20	79	82	87	92	79	82	87	91
40	30	74	76	79	84	73	75	78	83
40	40	71	72	74	77	70	71	73	76
40	60	68	69	70	72	68	69	69	71
40	80	67	68	68	70	67	68	67	69
40	100	67	68	67	69	67	67	66	68
60	30	75	76	79	83	74	76	78	82
60	40	71	72	74	76	71	72	73	76
60	60	69	69	69	71	68	69	68	70
60	80	68	68	67	69	67	68	66	68
60	100	67	67	66	67	67	67	65	66
100	40	74	75	75	78	74	74	75	77
100	60	71	71	71	72	71	71	70	72
100	80	70	70	68	69	70	69	67	69
100	100	69	68	66	67	69	68	66	67

There are two objectives in applying the standardized procedure. First, it simplifies calculations by permitting organization of various procedural steps. Second, it allows comparisons between those luminaires for which the standardized values have been tabulated even before a specific lighting layout has been made. Figure 9-19 illustrates a typical tabulation of visual comfort probabilities as developed by the standardized procedure.

Unified Glare Rating (UGR)

The CIE has recently developed a unified glare rating (UGR) system. This system is intended for discomfort glare prediction and is likely to be adopted by many nations. The IESNA is currently considering its attitude to this development for future recommendations.

Average Illuminance Calculation: The Lumen Method

The lumen method is used in calculating the average illuminance $\overline{E}$ on the workplane in an interior. This is

defined as

$$\overline{E} = \frac{\text{total flux onto workplane}}{\text{workplane area}} \qquad (9\text{-}46)$$

A coefficient of utilization gives the fraction of lamp lumens that reach the workplane, directly from sources and from interreflections. Thus the number of lumens produced by the lamps, multiplied by this coefficient of utilization (CU), determines the number that reaches the workplane:

$$\overline{E}_{\text{initial}} = \frac{(\text{total lamp lumens}) \times \text{CU}}{\text{workplane area}} \qquad (9\text{-}47)$$

Since the design objective is usually maintained illuminance, a light loss factor must be applied to allow for the estimated depreciation in lamp lumens over time, the estimated losses from dirt collection on the luminaire surfaces (including lamps) and other factors which affect luminaire lumen output over time. The formula thus becomes

$$\overline{E}_{\text{maintained}} = \frac{(\text{total lamp lumens}) \times \text{CU} \times \text{LLF}}{\text{workplane area}}$$

$$(9\text{-}48)$$

where

$$\text{CU} = \text{coefficient of utilization},$$
$$\text{LLF} = \text{light loss factor}.$$

The lamp lumens in the formula are most conveniently taken as the total rated lamp lumens in the luminaires:

$$\overline{E}_{\text{maintained}} = \frac{1}{\text{workplane area}}$$

$$\times [(\text{number of luminaires})$$

$$\times (\text{lamps per luminaire})$$

$$\times (\text{lamp lumens}) \times \text{CU} \times \text{LLF}]$$

$$(9\text{-}49)$$

If the desired maintained illuminance is known, this equation can be solved for the total number of luminaires needed:

number of luminaires

$$= \frac{\overline{E}_{\text{maintained}} \times (\text{workplane area})}{(\text{lamps per luminaire}) \times (\text{lamp lumens}) \times \text{CU} \times \text{LLF}}$$

$$(9\text{-}50)$$

For a typical form for calculating illuminance, see figure 9-20.

GENERAL INFORMATION

Project identification: _____

(Give name of area and/or building and room number)

Average maintained illuminance for design:___ lux or
                                        :___ footcandles

Lamp data:

   Type and color:_____

Luminaire data:

   Number per luminaire:_____

  Manufacturer: _____

   Total lumens per luminaire: _____

  Catalog number: _____

SELECTION OF COEFFICIENT OF UTILIZATION

Step 1: Fill in sketch at right

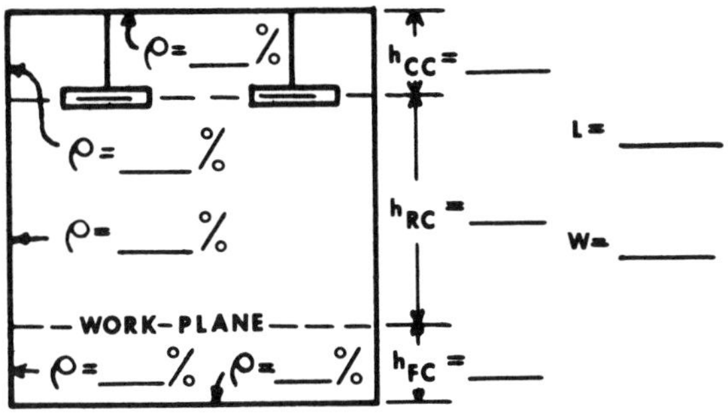

Step 2: Determine Cavity Ratios

     Room Cavity Ratio, RCR = _____

     Ceiling Cavity Ratio, CCR = _____

     Floor Cavity Ratio, FCR = _____

Step 3: Obtain Effective Ceiling Cavity Reflectance (ρ_{CC}) ρ_{CC} = ____

Step 4: Obtain Effective Floor Cavity Reflectance (ρ_{FC}) ρ_{FC} = ____

Step 5: Obtain Coefficient of Utilization (CU) from Manufacturer's Data   CU = ____

SELECTION OF LIGHT LOSS FACTORS

Nonrecoverable

Luminaire ambient temperature   _____

Voltage to luminaire   _____

Ballast factor   _____

Luminaire surface depreciation   _____

Recoverable

Room surface dirt depreciation RSDD   _____

Lamp lumen depreciation LLD   _____

Lamp burnouts factor LBO   _____

Luminaire dirt depreciation LDD   _____

Total light loss factor, LLF (product of individual factors above) = _____

CALCULATIONS

(Average Maintained Illuminance)

$$\text{Number of Luminaires} = \frac{(\text{Illuminance}) \times (\text{Area})}{(\text{Lumens per Luminaire}) \times (\text{CU}) \times (\text{LLF})}$$

$$= \underline{\hspace{5cm}} =$$

$$\text{Illuminance} = \frac{(\text{Number of Luminaires}) \times (\text{Lumens per Luminaire}) \times (\text{CU}) \times (\text{LLF})}{(\text{Area})}$$

$$= \underline{\hspace{5cm}} =$$

Calculated by: _____   Date: _____

Fig. 9-20. Average illuminance calculation sheet.

Limitations. The illuminance computed by the lumen method is an average value that will be representative only if the luminaires are spaced to obtain reasonably uniform illuminance. The calculation of the coefficients of utilization is based on empty interiors having surfaces that exhibit perfectly diffuse reflectance. The average illuminance determined by the lumen method is defined to be the total lumens reaching the workplane, divided by the area of the workplane. The average value determined this way may vary considerably from that obtained by averaging discrete values of illuminance at several points.

Calculation Procedure. Figure 9-20 provides a procedure for calculating average maintained illuminance using the zonal-cavity method.[30–32]

Cavity Ratios. The radiative exchange between the top and the base of a rectangular space is a function of the proportions of its length, width and height. Cavity ratio values approximate this effect by combining these proportions into a single quantity.

In the zonal-cavity method, the effects of room proportions, luminaire suspension length and workplane height upon the coefficient of utilization are respectively represented by the room cavity ratio, ceiling cavity ratio and floor cavity ratio. These ratios are determined by dividing the room into three cavities, as shown by figure 9-21, and substituting dimensions (in feet or meters) into the following formula:

$$\text{cavity ratio} = \frac{5h(\text{cavity length} + \text{cavity width})}{\text{cavity length} \times \text{cavity width}}$$

$$(9-51)$$

where

$$h = \begin{cases} h_{RC} & \text{for the room cavity ratio (RCR)} \\ h_{CC} & \text{for the ceiling cavity ratio (CCR)} \\ h_{FC} & \text{for the floor cavity ratio (FCR)} \end{cases}$$

The illuminance in rooms of irregular shape can be determined by calculating the room cavity ratio using the following formula and solving the problem in the usual manner:

cavity ratio

$$= \frac{2.5 \times (\text{cavity height}) \times (\text{cavity perimeter})}{\text{area of cavity base}}$$

$$(9-52)$$

Effective Cavity Reflectances. Figure 9-22 provides a means of converting the combination of wall and ceiling or wall and floor reflectances into a single effective ceiling cavity reflectance, ρ_{CC}, and a single effective floor cavity reflectance, ρ_{FC}. In lumen method calculations, the ceiling, wall and floor reflectances should be initial values. The RSDD factor compensates for the decrease of reflectance with time. Note that for surface-mounted and recessed luminaires, the CCR equals 0 and the actual ceiling reflectance may be used for ρ_{CC}.

A rectangular cavity consists of four walls, each having a reflectance of ρ_W, and a base of reflectance ρ_B (ceiling or floor reflectance). The effective reflectance, ρ_{eff}, of this cavity is the ratio of the flux reflected out to the flux entering the cavity through its opening. If the reflectances are assumed to be perfectly diffuse and the flux is assumed to enter the cavity in a perfectly diffuse way, it is possible to calculate the effective cavity reflectance using flux transfer theory. The result is

$$\rho_{eff} = \frac{\rho_B\rho_W F\left(\frac{2A_B}{A_W}(1 - F) - F\right) + \rho_B F^2 + \rho_W \frac{A_B}{A_W}(1 - F)^2}{1 - \rho_B\rho_W \frac{A_B}{A_W}(1 - F)^2 - \rho_W\left(1 - 2\frac{A_B}{A_W}(1 - F)\right)}$$

$$(9-53)$$

where

A_B, A_W = areas of the cavity base and walls, respectively,

ρ_B, ρ_W = reflectances of the cavity base and walls, respectively,

F = form factor between the cavity opening and the cavity base.

The form factor F in the above equation is given by

$$F = \frac{2}{\pi xy} \ln\left(\frac{(1 + x^2)(1 + y^2)}{1 + x^2 + y^2}\right)^{1/2}$$
$$+ \frac{2}{\pi x}(1 + x^2)^{1/2} \arctan\left(\frac{y}{(1 + x^2)^{1/2}}\right)$$
$$+ \frac{2}{\pi y}(1 + y^2)^{1/2} \arctan\left(\frac{x}{(1 + y^2)^{1/2}}\right)$$
$$- \frac{2}{\pi x} \arctan y - \frac{2}{\pi y} \arctan x \qquad (9-54)$$

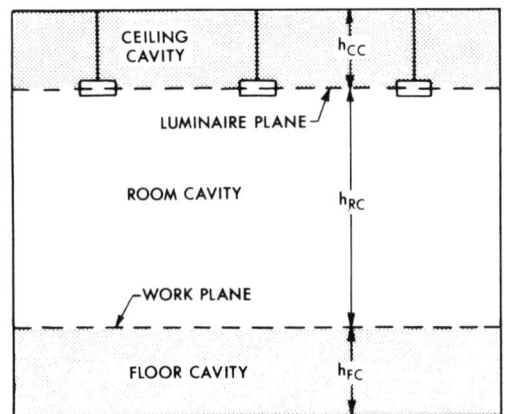

Fig. 9-21. The three cavities used in the zonal-cavity method.

Fig. 9-22. Percent Effective Ceiling or Floor Cavity Reflectances for Various Reflectance Combinations*

Per Cent Base† Reflectance	90										80										70										60										50									
Per Cent Wall Reflectance / Cavity Ratio	90	80	70	60	50	40	30	20	10	0	90	80	70	60	50	40	30	20	10	0	90	80	70	60	50	40	30	20	10	0	90	80	70	60	50	40	30	20	10	0	90	80	70	60	50	40	30	20	10	0
0.2	89	88	88	87	86	85	85	84	84	82	79	78	78	77	77	76	76	75	75	72	70	69	69	69	68	67	67	66	65	64	60	59	59	59	58	57	56	56	55	53	50	50	49	49	48	48	47	46	46	44
0.4	88	87	86	85	84	83	81	80	79	76	79	77	76	75	74	73	72	71	69	68	69	68	68	67	65	64	63	62	61	58	60	59	58	57	57	55	54	53	52	50	50	49	48	48	47	46	45	45	44	42
0.6	88	86	85	84	82	81	79	78	77	73	78	76	75	73	71	70	68	67	65	63	69	67	66	64	63	61	59	58	57	54	60	58	57	56	55	53	51	51	50	46	50	48	48	47	45	44	43	42	41	38
0.8	87	85	83	82	80	79	77	76	75	69	78	75	73	71	69	67	65	63	61	57	68	66	64	62	60	58	56	55	53	50	60	58	56	55	54	51	48	47	46	43	50	48	47	46	44	43	40	39	38	36
1.0	86	85	82	80	78	77	75	73	72	67	77	74	72	69	67	65	62	60	57	55	68	65	62	60	58	55	53	52	50	47	59	57	55	53	51	48	45	44	43	41	50	48	47	46	44	43	41	38	37	34
1.2	85	82	78	75	72	69	66	63	60	57	76	73	70	67	64	61	58	55	53	51	67	64	61	59	57	54	51	50	48	44	59	56	54	51	49	46	44	42	40	38	50	47	45	43	41	39	36	35	34	29
1.4	85	80	77	73	69	65	62	59	57	52	76	72	68	65	62	59	55	53	50	48	67	63	60	58	55	51	49	47	45	41	59	56	53	49	47	44	41	39	38	36	50	47	45	42	40	38	35	34	32	27
1.6	84	79	75	71	67	63	59	56	53	50	75	71	67	63	60	57	53	50	47	44	67	62	59	56	53	47	45	43	41	38	59	55	52	48	45	42	39	37	35	33	50	47	44	41	39	36	33	32	30	26
1.8	83	78	73	69	64	60	56	53	50	48	75	70	66	62	58	54	50	47	44	41	66	61	58	54	51	46	43	40	38	35	58	54	51	47	44	40	37	35	33	31	50	46	43	40	38	35	31	30	28	25
2.0	83	77	72	67	62	58	53	50	47	43	74	69	64	60	56	52	48	45	41	38	66	60	56	52	49	45	40	38	36	33	58	54	50	46	43	39	35	33	31	29	50	46	43	40	37	34	30	28	26	24
2.2	82	76	70	65	59	54	50	47	44	40	74	68	63	58	54	49	45	42	38	35	66	60	55	51	48	43	38	36	34	32	58	53	49	45	42	38	34	31	29	28	50	46	42	38	36	33	29	27	24	22
2.4	82	75	69	64	58	53	48	45	41	37	73	67	61	56	52	47	43	39	36	33	65	60	54	50	46	41	37	35	32	30	58	53	48	44	41	37	32	30	27	26	50	46	42	37	35	31	27	25	23	21
2.6	81	74	67	62	56	51	46	42	38	35	73	66	60	55	50	45	41	37	34	31	65	59	54	49	45	40	35	33	30	28	58	53	48	43	39	35	31	28	26	24	50	46	41	37	34	30	26	23	21	20
2.8	81	73	66	60	54	49	44	40	36	34	73	65	59	53	48	43	38	35	32	29	65	59	53	48	43	38	33	30	28	26	58	52	47	42	38	34	29	27	24	22	50	46	41	36	33	29	24	22	19	19
3.0	80	72	64	58	52	47	42	38	34	30	72	65	58	52	47	42	37	34	30	27	64	58	52	47	42	37	32	29	27	24	57	52	46	41	37	32	28	25	23	20	50	45	40	36	32	28	24	21	17	17
3.2	79	71	63	56	50	45	40	36	32	28	72	65	57	51	45	40	35	33	28	25	64	58	51	46	40	36	31	28	25	23	57	51	45	40	36	31	27	23	22	18	50	44	38	34	31	27	23	20	18	16
3.4	79	70	62	54	48	43	38	34	30	27	71	64	56	49	44	39	34	32	27	24	64	57	50	45	39	35	29	27	24	22	57	51	45	39	35	30	26	23	20	17	50	44	39	34	30	26	22	19	17	15
3.6	78	69	61	53	47	42	36	32	28	25	71	63	54	48	43	38	32	29	25	23	63	56	49	44	38	33	28	25	22	20	57	50	44	39	34	30	25	22	19	16	50	44	39	33	29	25	21	18	16	14
3.8	78	69	60	51	45	40	35	31	27	23	70	62	53	47	41	36	31	28	24	22	63	56	49	43	37	32	27	24	21	19	57	50	43	38	33	29	24	21	18	15	50	44	38	33	28	25	21	17	15	13
4.0	77	69	58	50	44	39	33	29	25	22	70	61	53	46	40	35	30	26	23	20	63	55	48	42	36	31	26	23	20	17	57	49	42	37	32	28	23	20	18	14	50	44	38	32	28	24	20	17	15	12
4.2	77	62	57	50	43	37	32	28	24	21	69	60	52	45	39	34	29	25	21	18	62	55	47	41	35	30	25	22	19	16	56	49	42	36	32	27	22	19	17	14	50	43	37	32	28	24	20	17	14	12
4.4	76	61	56	49	42	36	31	27	23	20	69	60	51	44	38	33	28	24	20	17	62	54	46	40	34	29	24	21	18	15	56	49	42	36	31	27	22	19	16	13	50	43	37	32	27	23	19	16	13	11
4.6	76	60	55	47	40	35	30	26	22	19	69	59	50	43	37	32	27	23	19	17	62	53	45	39	33	28	24	20	16	13	56	49	41	35	30	26	21	18	15	13	50	43	36	31	26	22	18	15	13	10
4.8	75	59	54	46	39	34	28	25	21	18	68	58	49	42	36	31	26	22	18	14	62	53	45	38	32	27	23	19	16	13	56	48	41	34	29	25	21	18	15	12	50	43	36	31	26	22	18	15	12	09
5.0	75	59	53	44	38	33	28	24	20	16	68	58	48	41	35	30	25	21	18	14	61	52	44	36	31	26	22	19	16	12	56	48	40	34	28	24	20	17	14	11	50	42	35	30	25	21	17	14	12	09
6.0	73	65	50	41	34	29	24	20	16	11	66	55	44	38	31	27	22	19	15	11	60	51	41	35	28	24	19	16	13	09	55	45	37	31	25	21	17	14	11	07	50	42	34	29	23	19	15	13	10	06
7.0	70	64	48	38	30	27	21	18	14	08	64	53	41	35	28	24	18	16	12	08	58	48	38	32	26	22	17	14	11	06	54	43	35	30	24	20	15	12	09	05	49	41	32	27	21	18	14	11	08	05
8.0	68	62	42	35	27	23	18	15	11	06	62	50	38	32	25	21	17	14	11	06	57	46	35	29	23	19	14	13	10	05	53	42	33	28	22	18	14	11	08	04	49	40	30	25	19	16	12	10	07	03
9.0	66	60	40	31	25	21	16	14	11	05	61	49	36	30	23	19	15	12	10	05	56	45	33	27	21	18	14	12	09	04	52	40	31	26	20	16	12	10	07	03	48	39	29	24	18	15	12	09	07	03
10.0	65	58	36	29	22	19	15	11	09	04	59	46	33	27	21	18	14	11	08	04	55	43	31	25	19	16	12	10	08	03	51	39	29	24	18	15	11	09	07	02	47	37	27	22	17	14	10	08	06	02

* Values in this table are based on a length to width ratio of 1.6.
† Ceiling, floor or floor of cavity.

Fig. 9-22. *Continued**

Cavity Ratio	Base 40: 90	80	70	60	50	40	30	20	10	0	Base 30: 90	80	70	60	50	40	30	20	10	0	Base 20: 90	80	70	60	50	40	30	20	10	0	Base 10: 90	80	70	60	50	40	30	20	10	0	Base 0: 90	80	70	60	50	40	30	20	10	0
0.2	40	40	39	39	39	38	38	37	36	36	31	31	30	30	29	29	28	28	28	27	21	20	20	20	20	20	19	19	19	17	11	11	11	10	10	10	09	09	09	09	02	02	02	01	01	01	01	00	00	0
0.4	41	40	39	38	38	38	37	35	34	34	31	31	30	30	29	28	28	27	26	25	22	21	20	20	20	19	19	18	18	16	12	11	11	11	11	11	10	09	09	08	04	03	03	02	02	01	01	01	00	0
0.6	41	40	38	38	37	36	34	33	32	31	32	31	30	29	28	27	26	25	24	23	23	21	21	20	19	19	18	18	17	15	13	13	12	11	11	11	10	09	08	08	05	05	04	03	03	02	02	01	01	0
0.8	41	40	39	37	36	35	33	32	31	29	32	31	30	29	28	26	25	24	23	22	24	22	21	20	19	19	18	17	16	14	14	13	13	12	12	11	10	09	08	07	07	06	05	04	04	03	02	02	01	0
1.0	42	40	38	37	35	33	32	31	29	27	33	32	30	29	27	25	24	23	21	20	25	23	22	20	19	18	17	16	15	12	16	14	13	13	12	11	11	09	08	07	08	07	06	05	04	03	03	02	02	0
1.2	42	40	38	36	34	32	30	29	27	25	33	32	30	28	26	24	23	22	20	19	25	23	22	20	19	17	17	16	14	12	17	15	14	13	12	11	10	09	08	06	10	08	07	06	05	04	03	02	02	0
1.4	42	39	37	35	33	31	29	27	25	23	34	32	30	28	26	24	22	21	19	18	26	24	22	20	18	17	16	15	13	12	18	16	14	14	12	11	10	09	07	06	11	09	08	07	06	04	03	03	02	0
1.6	42	39	37	35	32	30	27	25	23	21	34	33	29	28	25	23	22	20	18	17	26	24	22	20	18	17	16	15	13	11	19	17	15	14	13	11	10	08	07	06	12	10	09	07	06	05	04	03	02	0
1.8	42	39	36	35	32	29	26	24	22	20	35	33	29	27	25	23	21	19	17	16	27	25	23	20	18	16	15	14	12	11	19	17	15	15	13	12	10	08	07	05	13	11	09	08	07	05	04	03	03	0
2.0	42	39	36	34	31	28	25	23	21	19	35	33	29	27	24	22	20	18	16	14	28	25	23	20	18	16	15	13	11	09	20	18	16	16	13	12	10	08	06	05	14	12	10	09	07	05	04	03	03	0
2.2	43	39	36	33	30	27	24	22	19	18	36	32	29	26	24	22	19	17	15	13	28	25	23	20	18	16	14	12	11	09	21	19	16	14	13	11	09	08	06	05	15	13	11	09	08	06	04	03	03	0
2.4	43	39	35	33	29	27	24	21	18	17	36	32	29	26	24	21	19	16	14	12	29	26	23	20	18	16	14	12	10	08	22	19	17	15	13	11	09	08	06	05	16	13	11	09	08	06	04	03	03	0
2.6	44	39	35	32	29	26	23	20	17	15	36	32	25	25	23	21	18	16	13	11	29	26	23	20	18	16	14	12	10	08	23	20	17	15	13	11	09	07	05	04	17	14	12	10	08	06	05	04	03	0
2.8	43	39	35	32	28	25	22	19	16	14	37	37	29	25	23	20	17	15	13	11	30	27	24	20	18	15	13	11	09	07	23	20	18	16	13	11	09	07	05	03	17	15	12	10	08	07	05	04	03	0
3.0	43	39	35	31	27	24	21	18	16	13	37	33	29	25	22	20	17	15	12	10	30	27	23	20	17	15	13	11	09	07	24	21	18	16	13	11	09	07	05	03	18	16	13	11	09	07	05	04	03	0
3.2	43	39	35	31	27	23	20	17	15	13	37	33	29	25	22	19	16	14	12	10	31	27	23	20	17	15	12	11	09	06	25	21	18	16	13	11	09	07	05	03	19	16	13	11	09	07	05	04	03	0
3.4	43	39	34	30	26	23	20	16	14	12	37	33	29	25	22	19	16	14	11	09	31	27	23	20	17	15	12	10	08	06	26	22	18	16	13	11	09	07	05	03	20	17	13	11	09	07	05	04	03	0
3.6	44	39	34	30	26	22	19	16	14	11	38	33	29	24	21	18	15	13	10	09	32	28	24	20	17	15	12	10	08	05	26	22	19	15	13	11	09	06	04	02	20	17	14	12	10	08	05	04	04	0
3.8	44	38	33	29	25	21	18	16	13	10	38	33	28	24	21	18	15	13	10	08	32	28	24	20	17	14	12	10	08	05	27	23	19	17	14	11	09	06	04	02	21	18	15	12	10	08	06	04	04	0
4.0	44	38	33	29	25	21	18	15	13	10	38	33	28	24	21	18	15	12	10	07	33	28	23	20	16	14	11	09	07	05	27	23	20	17	14	11	09	06	04	02	22	18	15	13	10	08	06	04	04	0
4.2	44	38	33	29	24	21	17	15	12	10	38	33	28	24	20	17	14	12	09	07	33	28	23	20	17	14	11	09	07	04	28	24	20	17	14	11	09	06	04	02	22	19	16	13	10	08	06	04	04	0
4.4	44	38	33	28	24	20	17	14	11	09	39	33	28	24	20	17	14	11	08	06	34	28	24	20	15	14	11	09	07	04	28	24	20	17	14	11	08	06	04	02	23	19	16	13	11	08	06	04	04	0
4.6	44	38	32	28	23	20	16	14	11	08	39	33	28	24	20	17	13	11	08	06	34	29	24	20	15	14	11	09	07	04	29	25	20	17	13	11	08	06	03	02	23	20	16	13	11	08	06	05	04	0
4.8	44	38	32	27	22	19	16	13	10	08	39	33	24	24	20	16	13	10	08	05	35	29	24	20	14	13	10	08	06	04	29	25	20	17	13	10	08	06	03	02	24	20	17	14	11	08	06	05	04	0
5.0	45	38	31	27	22	19	15	13	10	07	39	33	28	24	19	16	12	10	08	05	35	29	24	20	13	13	10	08	06	04	30	25	20	17	13	10	08	06	03	02	25	21	17	14	11	08	06	05	04	0
6.0	44	37	30	25	20	17	13	11	08	05	39	33	27	23	18	15	11	09	07	04	36	30	24	20	16	13	09	07	05	02	31	26	21	18	14	11	08	05	03	01	27	23	18	15	12	09	06	05	04	0
7.0	44	36	29	24	19	16	12	10	07	04	40	36	26	22	17	14	10	08	07	04	36	30	23	19	15	12	08	06	04	02	32	27	21	17	13	11	08	05	03	01	28	24	19	15	12	09	06	05	04	0
8.0	44	35	28	23	18	15	11	09	06	03	40	35	25	21	16	13	09	07	04	02	37	30	23	19	14	12	08	06	03	01	33	27	20	17	13	10	07	05	02	01	30	25	20	15	12	09	06	05	04	0
9.0	44	35	26	21	16	13	10	08	05	02	40	33	20	20	15	12	09	07	04	02	37	29	23	18	13	11	07	06	03	01	34	28	20	17	13	10	07	04	02	01	31	25	20	15	12	09	06	05	04	0
10.0	43	34	25	20	15	12	08	07	05	02	40	32	24	19	14	11	08	06	03	01	37	29	22	18	13	10	07	05	03	01	34	28	21	17	12	10	07	05	02	01	31	25	20	15	12	09	06	05	04	0

* Values in this table are based on a length to width ratio of 1.6.
† Ceiling, floor or floor of cavity.

where x and y have the following values:

$$x = \frac{\text{cavity length}}{\text{cavity depth}} \quad (9\text{-}55\text{a})$$

$$y = \frac{\text{cavity width}}{\text{cavity depth}} \quad (9\text{-}55\text{b})$$

The arctangents are expressed in radians. If it is assumed that the cavity is square, then

$$x = y = \frac{10}{\text{cavity ratio}} \quad (9\text{-}56)$$

The effective ceiling cavity reflectance of nonhorizontal ceilings can be determined by the following formula. The illuminance problem is then solved in the usual manner:

$$\rho_{CC} = \frac{\rho}{\frac{A_s}{A_o} - \rho\left(\frac{A_s}{A_o} - 1\right)} \quad (9\text{-}57)$$

where

A_o = area of the ceiling opening,
A_s = area of the ceiling surface,
ρ = reflectance of the ceiling surface.

The formula for ρ_{CC} applies to concave ceilings such as a hemispherical dome where all parts of the ceiling are exposed to all other parts. If the ceiling surface reflectance is not the same for all parts of the ceiling, an area-weighted average should be used. Thus, if the ceiling has n sections, then

$$\rho = \frac{\sum_{i=1}^{n} \rho_i A_i}{\sum_{i=1}^{n} A_i} \quad (9\text{-}58)$$

where

ρ_i = reflectance of the ith section of the ceiling,
A_i = area of the ith section of the ceiling.

Luminaire Coefficients of Utilization. Absorption of light in a luminaire is allowed for in the computation of coefficient of utilization (CU) for that luminaire. Figure 9-34 is a tabulation of coefficients of utilization calculated by the zonal-cavity method for representative luminaire types. These coefficients are for an effective floor cavity reflectance of 20%, but any CU obtained from the table may be corrected for a different value of ρ_{FC} by applying the appropriate multiplier from figure 9-23.

Figure 9-34 is based on generic luminaires that can be readily identified. As an example, there are many variations of the flat-bottom fluorescent troffer using prismatic lenses, and since there are no well-established subgroups, a single set of entries for wide and narrow cutoffs (luminaires 42 and 43) is given, using data averaged over the entire class. The luminaires in figure 9-34 are not to be considered as recommended luminaires. The entries for some present useful data even though the luminaires concerned are no longer commonly used. For example, luminaires 2 and 33 are largely out of use; however, the coefficients apply to any indirect luminaire of similar efficiency and direct component, since they do not depend on the shape of the upward intensity distribution. An important feature of these coefficients is that the performance of luminaires of similar distributions but different efficiencies may also be analyzed with their use by making a simple multiplicative correction (see note 3 of figure 9-34).

Since the light loss factor includes the effect of dirt deposited on wall surfaces, the selection of the proper column of wall reflectances, ρ_W, should be based upon the initial values expected. The wall reflectance should also represent the weighted average of the reflectances of the painted areas, fenestration or daylight controls, chalkboards, shelves and so forth in the area to be lighted. The weighting should be based on the relative areas of each type of surface within the cavity being considered. In using figure 9-23, it will often be necessary to interpolate between room cavity ratios and effective ceiling cavity reflectances. This is most easily accomplished by interpolating first between RCRs to obtain CUs for effective ceiling cavity reflectances that straddle the actual ρ_{CC}, and then interpolating between these CUs.

Average Exitance Calculations: The Lumen Method

Exitance calculations are greatly simplified through the use of exitance coefficients (ECs). These coefficients, like coefficients of utilization, may be computed for any luminaire, although they are somewhat rare in manufacturers' literature. The wall and ceiling cavity exitance coefficients for a group of generic luminaires are found in figure 9-34.

Exitance coefficients are similar to coefficients of utilization, except that they apply to the surfaces of the room cavity. They may be substituted into a variation of the lumen method formula in place of the coefficient of utilization. The result obtained is either the average wall exitance or the average ceiling cavity exitance, rather than illuminance on the workplane. Thus

average initial wall exitance

= total bare-lamp lumens

$$\times \frac{\text{ceiling exitance coefficient}}{\text{floor area}} \quad (9\text{-}59)$$

Fig. 9-23. Multiplying Factors for Effective Floor Cavity Reflectances Other than 20% (0.2)

% Effective Ceiling Cavity Reflectance, ρcc	80				70				50			30			10		
% Wall Reflectance, ρw	70	50	30	10	70	50	30	10	50	30	10	50	30	10	50	30	10
For 30 Per Cent Effective Floor Cavity Reflectance (20 Per Cent = 1.00)																	
Room Cavity Ratio																	
1	1.092	1.082	1.075	1.068	1.077	1.070	1.064	1.059	1.049	1.044	1.040	1.028	1.026	1.023	1.012	1.010	1.008
2	1.079	1.066	1.055	1.047	1.068	1.057	1.048	1.039	1.041	1.033	1.027	1.026	1.021	1.017	1.013	1.010	1.006
3	1.070	1.054	1.042	1.033	1.061	1.048	1.037	1.028	1.034	1.027	1.020	1.024	1.017	1.012	1.014	1.009	1.005
4	1.062	1.045	1.033	1.024	1.055	1.040	1.029	1.021	1.030	1.022	1.015	1.022	1.015	1.010	1.014	1.009	1.004
5	1.056	1.038	1.026	1.018	1.050	1.034	1.024	1.015	1.027	1.018	1.012	1.020	1.013	1.008	1.014	1.009	1.004
6	1.052	1.033	1.021	1.014	1.047	1.030	1.020	1.012	1.024	1.015	1.009	1.019	1.012	1.006	1.014	1.008	1.003
7	1.047	1.029	1.018	1.011	1.043	1.026	1.017	1.009	1.022	1.013	1.007	1.018	1.010	1.005	1.014	1.008	1.003
8	1.044	1.026	1.015	1.009	1.040	1.024	1.015	1.007	1.020	1.012	1.006	1.017	1.009	1.004	1.013	1.007	1.003
9	1.040	1.024	1.014	1.007	1.037	1.022	1.014	1.006	1.019	1.011	1.005	1.016	1.009	1.004	1.013	1.007	1.002
10	1.037	1.022	1.012	1.006	1.034	1.020	1.012	1.005	1.017	1.010	1.004	1.015	1.009	1.003	1.013	1.007	1.002
For 10 Per Cent Effective Floor Cavity Reflectance (20 Per Cent = 1.00)																	
Room Cavity Ratio																	
1	.923	.929	.935	.940	.933	.939	.943	.948	.956	.960	.963	.973	.976	.979	.989	.991	.993
2	.931	.942	.950	.958	.940	.949	.957	.963	.962	.968	.974	.976	.980	.985	.988	.991	.995
3	.939	.951	.961	.969	.945	.957	.966	.973	.967	.975	.981	.978	.983	.988	.988	.992	.996
4	.944	.958	.969	.978	.950	.963	.973	.980	.972	.980	.986	.980	.986	.991	.987	.992	.996
5	.949	.964	.976	.983	.954	.968	.978	.985	.975	.983	.989	.981	.988	.993	.987	.992	.997
6	.953	.969	.980	.986	.958	.972	.982	.989	.977	.985	.992	.982	.989	.995	.987	.993	.997
7	.957	.973	.983	.991	.961	.975	.985	.991	.979	.987	.994	.983	.990	.996	.987	.993	.998
8	.960	.976	.986	.993	.963	.977	.987	.993	.981	.988	.995	.984	.991	.997	.987	.994	.998
9	.963	.978	.987	.994	.965	.979	.989	.994	.983	.990	.996	.985	.992	.998	.988	.994	.999
10	.965	.980	.989	.995	.967	.981	.990	.995	.984	.991	.997	.986	.993	.998	.988	.994	.999
For 0 Per Cent Effective Floor Cavity Reflectance (20 Per Cent = 1.00)																	
Room Cavity Ratio																	
1	.859	.870	.879	.886	.873	.884	.893	.901	.916	.923	.929	.948	.954	.960	.979	.983	.987
2	.871	.887	.903	.919	.886	.902	.916	.928	.926	.938	.949	.954	.963	.971	.978	.983	.991
3	.882	.904	.915	.942	.898	.918	.934	.947	.936	.950	.964	.958	.969	.979	.976	.984	.993
4	.893	.919	.941	.958	.908	.930	.948	.961	.945	.961	.974	.961	.974	.984	.975	.985	.994
5	.903	.931	.953	.969	.914	.939	.958	.970	.951	.967	.980	.964	.977	.988	.975	.985	.995
6	.911	.940	.961	.976	.920	.945	.965	.977	.955	.972	.985	.966	.979	.991	.975	.986	.996
7	.917	.947	.967	.981	.924	.950	.970	.982	.959	.975	.988	.968	.981	.993	.975	.987	.997
8	.922	.953	.971	.985	.929	.955	.975	.986	.963	.978	.991	.970	.983	.995	.976	.988	.998
9	.928	.958	.975	.988	.933	.959	.980	.989	.966	.980	.993	.971	.985	.996	.976	.988	.998
10	.933	.962	.979	.991	.937	.963	.983	.992	.969	.982	.995	.973	.987	.997	.977	.989	.999

and

average initial ceiling cavity exitance

= total bare-lamp lumens

$$\times \frac{\text{ceiling cavity exitance coefficient}}{\text{floor area}} \quad (9\text{-}60)$$

If the maintained average wall exitance or the maintained average ceiling cavity exitance is required, a light loss factor is introduced into these equations in the same manner as for maintained average illuminance. For suspended luminaires, the average ceiling cavity exitance obtained is the average exitance of the imaginary plane at the level of the luminaires. This exitance does not include the weighted average exitance of the luminaires as seen from below. It is rather the average exitance of the background against which the luminaires are seen. In the case of recessed or ceiling-mounted luminaires, the average ceiling cavity exitance obtained is the average exitance of the ceiling between luminaires.

Limitations. The limitations for exitance calculations are similar to those for average illuminance. In addition, the wall reflectance used to enter the tables is a weighted average of the reflectances for the various parts of the walls; the wall exitance found from the wall exitance coefficient is the value that would occur if the walls were of a uniform and perfectly diffuse reflectance equal to the average reflectance used. Thus, many parts of the wall may have exitance values that differ from the calculated average value. A correction can be applied to determine the approximate exitance of any part of the wall. For any area on the wall,

exitance

$$= \frac{(\text{average wall exitance}) \times (\text{reflectance of area})}{\text{average wall reflectance}}$$

$$(9\text{-}61)$$

The Lumen Method Applied to Partitioned Spaces

The lumen method can also be applied to partitioned spaces by separating the room cavity into an upper cavity that extends from the top of the partitions to the luminaire plane, and a second cavity that is the cavity within the partitioned area. The upper cavity has an area that is equal to the area of the room, while the lower cavity covers only the area included within a single partitioned zone. Two lumen method calculations need to be made in order to perform a complete analysis.

First, the calculation is performed for the upper cavity to determine the illuminance falling on the top of the partitions. The floor cavity for this analysis is the area below the top of the partitions, and the effective floor cavity reflectance is that of a single partitioned space as viewed from above. All of the room's luminaires are used in this analysis, since presumably they all contribute to the illuminance on the plane at the top of the partitions. The coefficient of utilization is determined for the appropriate cavity ratio, and the average illuminance on the top of the partitions is then determined.

Next, the coefficient of utilization for the lower cavity, the area within a single partition, is considered. The coefficient of utilization is determined for a "virtual" luminaire that has a lambertian distribution, using figure 9-24. The appropriate wall and effective floor cavity reflectances are used to obtain this value. The effective ceiling cavity reflectance assumed in this table is zero, since interreflections between the upper and lower room cavities were already considered in the determination of the illuminance on the top of the partitions. In many partitioned spaces, each cubicle only has three sides formed by the partitions, with the fourth side being open. For the wall reflectance, an area-weighted average of the cubicle walls should be used, where the opening is assigned a reflectance of zero. The illuminance obtained at the top of the partitions is then multiplied by the coefficient of utilization obtained for the cubicle area to obtain the average illuminance on the workplane. The equation is summarized below:

$$E = \frac{\left(\begin{array}{c}\text{total bare}\\\text{lamp lumens}\end{array}\right) \times CU_{\text{upper cavity}} \times CU_{\text{cubicle}} \times LLF}{\text{area of work plane}}$$

$$(9\text{-}62)$$

CALCULATION OF EQUIPMENT-RELATED QUANTITIES

So far in this chapter, quantities that evaluate the lighting within a room have been discussed. Another set of quantities comprises those that are computed for the luminaire. These include coefficients of utilization, optical efficiency and the spacing criterion.

Lumen Method Coefficients of Utilization[22, 30, 66–68]

Tables of coefficients of utilization (CUs), wall exitance coefficients and ceiling cavity exitance coefficients can be prepared by systematic procedures. It is desirable to standardize the process for producing published tables of these values to prevent misunderstandings and to facilitate direct comparisons of the data for different luminaires. These coefficients are derived from the equations described under radiative transfer theory in the section on Basic Principles above. The basic assumptions used to develop the zonal-cavity coefficients are:

- Room surfaces are lambertian reflectors.
- The incident flux on each surface is uniformly distributed over that surface.
- The luminaires are uniformly distributed throughout the room (uniformly dense but not necessarily in a uniform pattern).
- The room is empty.
- The room surfaces are spectrally neutral.

Figure 9-34 shows the recommended form for unabridged tables. It is recognized that space limitations often necessitate abridgements. In that case, only the columns for $\rho_{CC} = 80$, 50, and 10% are recommended for luminaires having 0–35% of their output in the 90–180° zone; and 80, 70, and 50% for luminaires having over 35% of their output in that zone. Also, the $\rho_{CC} = 10\%$ columns are not required for

Fig. 9-24. Coefficients of Utilization for a Perfectly Diffuse Emitter

Floor Cavity Reflectance (ρcc = 20 Per Cent)					
Wall Reflectance ρw (Per Cent)	70	50	30	10	0
RCR					
0	1.00	1.00	1.00	1.00	1.00
1	.90	.88	.86	.84	.84
2	.81	.77	.74	.71	.70
3	.74	.69	.64	.61	.59
4	.67	.61	.56	.52	.50
5	.61	.54	.49	.44	.42
6	.56	.44	.43	.38	.36
7	.52	.44	.38	.33	.31
8	.48	.39	.33	.29	.27
9	.44	.35	.29	.25	.23
10	.41	.32	.26	.22	.20

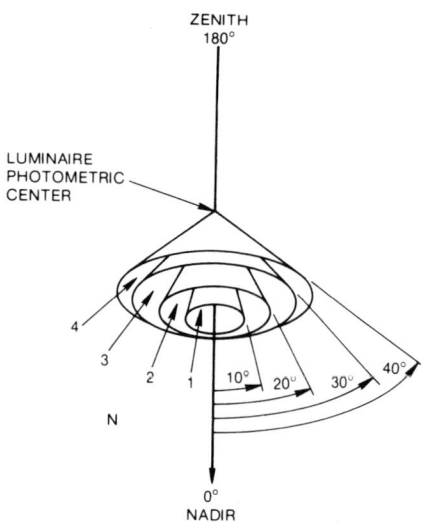

Fig. 9-25. Conic solid angle zones of 10° width for use in calculating zonal flux.

abridged tables. It is recommended that CUs be published to two decimal places, wall exitance coefficients to three decimal places and ceiling cavity exitance coefficients to three decimal places. A wall direct radiation coefficient (WDRC) should be published to three decimal places for every room cavity ratio, adjacent to the wall exitance coefficient table. The three significant figures are not justified in terms of coefficient accuracy, but are required because certain computational methods require the small differences between these coefficients.

Computation

1. Define 18 conic solid angle zones of 10° width from the nadir to the zenith about the luminaire as shown in figure 9-25, where the index of each zone, N, is an integer between 1 and 18 inclusive.
2. Determine the flux Φ_N (lumens) in the various zones:
   a. The flux in a conic solid angle (see figure 9-26) is given by

$$\Phi_N = 2\pi I_{\theta_N}(\cos \theta_N - \cos \theta_{N+1}) \quad (9\text{-}63)$$

   where

I_{θ_N} = midzone intensity, in cd, for the Nth zone,

θ_N, θ_{N+1} = bounding cone angles.

   b. If the intensity is not rotationally symmetric about the vertical axis, average the intensity about the vertical axis at each vertical angle θ. Note that

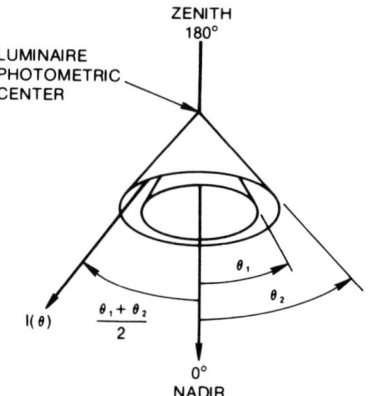

Fig. 9-26. Angles used in calculating zonal flux.

the intensity must be sampled at equal angular intervals about the vertical axis. For example, if the intensity is known for three vertical planes $[I_{\theta, 90°}$ (perpendicular), $I_{\theta, 45°}$ and $I_{\theta, 0°}$ (parallel)], then

$$I_\theta = \tfrac{1}{4}(I_{\theta, 0°} + 2I_{\theta, 45°} + I_{\theta, 90°}) \quad (9\text{-}64)$$

While three planes are sufficient for luminaires of nominal rotational symmetry, photometric data at 15° or 22.5° increments about the vertical axis are preferred for luminaires without this symmetry.

   c. If the intensity is taken at 10° vertical intervals ($\theta = 5°, 15°, 25°, \ldots$), then the flux Φ_N is determined by the application of the equation in part a above to the full zone. It is preferred to have intensity values at 5° vertical angles ($\theta = 2.5°, 7.5°, 12.5°, \ldots$). Then zone N is divided into two parts, the equation is applied to each part, and the resulting flux is summed.

3. Determine the additional flux functions:

$$\Phi_{\text{total}} = \sum_{N=1}^{18} \Phi_N \quad (9\text{-}65)$$

$$\Phi_{\text{down}} = \frac{1}{\Phi_{\text{total}}} \sum_{N=1}^{9} \Phi_N \quad (9\text{-}66)$$

$$\Phi_{\text{up}} = \frac{1}{\Phi_{\text{total}}} \sum_{N=10}^{18} \Phi_N \quad (9\text{-}67)$$

where

Φ_{total} = total flux of the lamps in the luminaire,

Φ_{down} = proportion of lamp flux leaving the luminaire in a downward direction,

Φ_{up} = proportion of lamp flux leaving the luminaire in an upward direction.

Fig. 9-27. Constants for the Zonal Multiplier Equation

Zone (N)	A	B
1	0.	0.
2	0.041	0.98
3	0.070	1.05
4	0.100	1.12
5	0.136	1.16
6	0.190	1.25
7	0.315	1.25
8	0.640	1.25
9	2.10	0.80

4. Determine the direct ratio, D_G, related to the fraction of luminaire flux below the horizontal which is directly incident on the workplane:

$$D_G = \frac{1}{\Phi_{\text{down}}\Phi_{\text{total}}} \sum_{N=1}^{9} K_{GN}\Phi_N \quad (9\text{-}68)$$

where

G = room cavity ratio (RCR), between 1 and 10 inclusive,

K_{GN} = zonal multipliers.

The zonal multiplier is the fraction of downward-directed flux directly incident on the workplane (lower surface of room cavity) for each zone N. The zonal multipliers are functions of the RCR:

$$K_{GN} = e^{-AG^B} \quad (9\text{-}69)$$

where A and B are constants and are given in figure 9-27.

5. Determine the parameters C_1, C_2, C_3, and C_0 as an intermediate step. In the formulas below, ρ_W is the wall reflectance, ρ_{CC} is the ceiling cavity reflectance, and ρ_{FC} is the floor cavity reflectance, which is taken as 0.2 for standard coefficient tables. $F_{CC \rightarrow FC}$ is the form factor from the ceiling cavity to the floor cavity, described above in the discussion of flux transfer theory in the section on Basic Principles:

$$C_1 = \frac{(1 - \rho_W)(1 - F_{CC \rightarrow FC}^2)G}{2.5\rho_W(1 - F_{CC \rightarrow FC}^2) + GF_{CC \rightarrow FC}(1 - \rho_W)}$$
$$(9\text{-}70)$$

$$C_2 = \frac{(1 - \rho_{CC})(1 + F_{CC \rightarrow FC})}{1 + \rho_{CC}F_{CC \rightarrow FC}} \quad (9\text{-}71)$$

$$C_3 = \frac{(1 - \rho_{FC})(1 + F_{CC \rightarrow FC})}{1 + \rho_{FC}F_{CC \rightarrow FC}} \quad (9\text{-}72)$$

$$C_0 = C_1 + C_2 + C_3 \quad (9\text{-}73)$$

6. Determine the coefficient of utilization (CU), the wall exitance coefficient (WEC) and the ceiling cavity exitance coefficient (CCEC) for each applicable combination of reflectances and RCR:

$$CU = \frac{2.5\rho_W C_1 C_3 (1 - D_G)\Phi_{\text{down}}}{G(1 - \rho_W)(1 - \rho_{FC})C_0}$$

$$+ \frac{\rho_{CC}C_2 C_3 \Phi_{\text{up}}}{(1 - \rho_{CC})(1 - \rho_{FC})C_0}$$

$$+ \left(1 - \frac{\rho_{FC}C_3(C_1 + C_2)}{(1 - \rho_{FC})C_0}\right)\frac{D_G \Phi_{\text{down}}}{1 - \rho_{FC}} \quad (9\text{-}74)$$

$$WEC = \frac{2.5\rho_W(1 - D_G)\Phi_{\text{down}}}{G(1 - \rho_W)}$$

$$\times \left(1 - \frac{2.5\rho_W C_1(C_2 + C_3)}{G(1 - \rho_W)C_0}\right)$$

$$+ \frac{2.5\rho_W \rho_{CC}C_1 C_2 \Phi_{\text{up}}}{G(1 - \rho_W)(1 - \rho_{CC})C_0}$$

$$+ \frac{2.5\rho_W \rho_{FC}C_1 C_3 D_G \Phi_{\text{down}}}{G(1 - \rho_W)(1 - \rho_{FC})C_0} \quad (9\text{-}75)$$

$$CCEC = \frac{2.5\rho_W \rho_{CC}C_1 C_2(1 - D_G)\Phi_{\text{down}}}{G(1 - \rho_W)(1 - \rho_{CC})C_0}$$

$$+ \frac{\rho_{CC}\Phi_{\text{up}}}{1 - \rho_{CC}}\left(1 - \frac{\rho_{CC}C_2(C_1 + C_3)}{(1 - \rho_{CC})C_0}\right)$$

$$+ \frac{\rho_{CC}\rho_{FC}C_2 C_3 D_G \Phi_{\text{down}}}{(1 - \rho_{CC})(1 - \rho_{FC})C_0} \quad (9\text{-}76)$$

7. Determine the wall direct radiation coefficient (WDRC) for each RCR:

$$WRDC = \frac{2.5\Phi_{\text{down}}(1 - D_G)}{G} \quad (9\text{-}77)$$

8. The above equations can be used to calculate the CU, WEC and CCEC when the RCR equals zero, but the forms of the equations must be arranged to avoid division by zero. It is simplest to use the

following relationships:

$$\text{CU}_{G=0} = \frac{\Phi_{\text{down}} + \rho_{\text{CC}}\Phi_{\text{up}}}{1 - \rho_{\text{CC}}\rho_{\text{FC}}} \quad (9\text{-}78)$$

$$\text{CCEC}_{G=0} = \frac{\rho_{\text{CC}}(\Phi_{\text{up}} + \rho_{\text{FC}}\Phi_{\text{down}})}{1 - \rho_{\text{CC}}\rho_{\text{FC}}} \quad (9\text{-}79)$$

Luminaire Optical Efficiency

The luminaire optical efficiency is simply the ratio of the lumens leaving the luminaire to the total lumens produced by the lamps. From the expressions above, this quantity is

$$\text{luminaire optical efficiency} = \frac{\Phi_{\text{total}}}{\text{total lamp lumens}}$$

$$(9\text{-}80)$$

Average Luminaire Luminance

The average luminaire luminance is a means of evaluating the effect that a luminaire will have on visual comfort, as well as veiling reflections on task surfaces such as VDTs. A value can be easily determined in any direction, given the photometric characteristics of the luminaire. Since luminance is expressed in candelas per unit area, the average luminance in a direction (θ, ψ) (specified in spherical coordinates) is

$$L(\theta, \psi)_{\text{avg}} = \frac{I(\theta, \psi)}{A_{\text{luminaire}} \cos \theta} \quad (9\text{-}81)$$

where

$I(\theta, \psi)$ = intensity of the luminaire in the direction (θ, ψ),
$A_{\text{luminaire}}$ = surface area of the luminous element(s) of the luminaire.

Luminaire Spacing Criterion

The *luminaire spacing criterion*[69] (SC) is a classification technique for interior luminaires relating to the spread or distribution of the direct illuminance on a horizontal plane. It tests the uniformity of horizontal illuminance at two pairs of selected points to estimate the probable extreme limit of acceptable luminaire spacing. It is not a specification of the spacing-to-mounting-height ratio to be used in a lighting installation, and in fact, installation of luminaires at this nominal value may produce a poor lighting system.

The purpose of this classification technique is to aid designers in rapidly assessing one aspect of the potential of a luminaire with respect to its applications. It gives some idea about the distribution of flux from a luminaire and its subsequent effect on lighting system parameters, using only a single number. The basis of the luminaire spacing criterion is the horizontal illuminance on the workplane due to direct illuminance from nearby luminaires. As a first approximation, it is assumed that this represents a limiting case, since the reflected component of illuminance and the illuminance due to more distant luminaires generally will increase the uniformity of horizontal illuminance from point to point.

When two similar conventional luminaires are near their maximum spacing, the illuminance directly under a luminaire (P) is principally due to the overhead luminaire (A) (see figure 9-28a). Further, a very probable point of low illuminance will be at the midpoint between two luminaires (Q). The maximum spacing at a given mounting height above the workplane is chosen such that the illuminance halfway between the two luminaires (Q) due to both luminaires (A and B) equals the illuminance under one (P) due to that one luminaire (A) only. Another likely point (R) for low

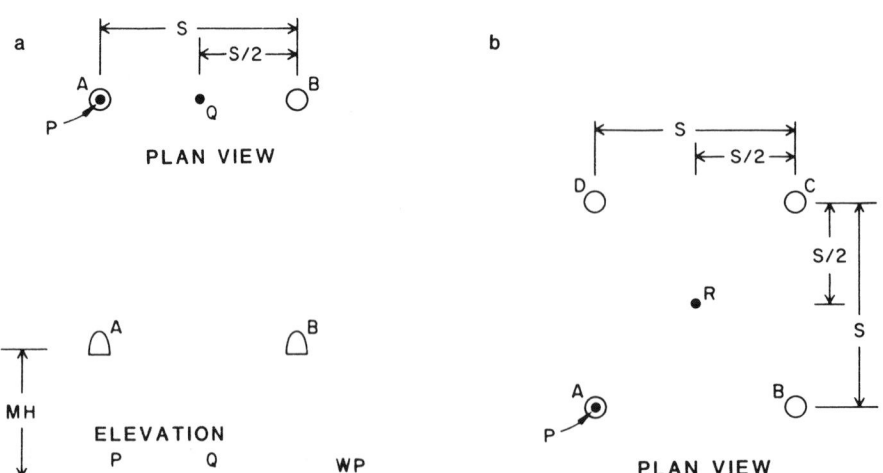

Fig. 9-28. Points Q and R represents points of most probable low illuminance for: (a) a configuration of 2 luminaires, and (b) a square array of 4 luminaires.

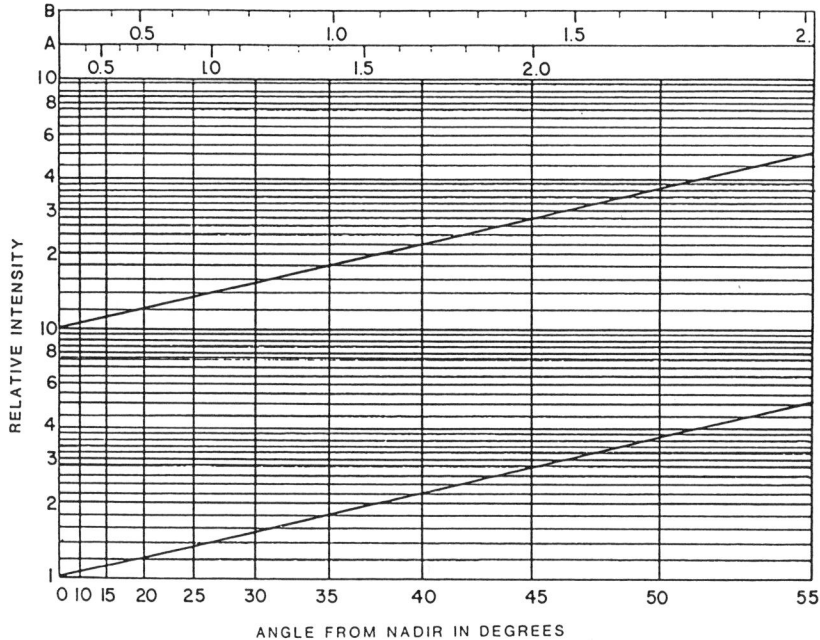

Fig. 9-29. Chart for determining the luminaire spacing criterion.

illuminance is at the center of a square array of adjacent luminaires (see figure 9-28b). The maximum spacing at a given mounting height above the workplane is chosen such that the illuminance at the center of the luminaires (R) due to all four luminaires (A, B, C and D) equals the illuminance under one (P) due to that one luminaire (A) only. The maximum spacing (expressed as a spacing-to-mounting-height ratio) that fulfills each of the above conditions is easily determined on a special graph (figure 9-29) using the intensity distribution of the luminaire. For the purpose of establishing this criterion, it is assumed that the inverse square law is valid. This is the only assumption for the computations.

Procedure. The procedure for calculating the Luminaire Spacing Criterion is as follows:

A. For luminaires whose intensity distribution is nominally symmetric about the nadir:
  1. Plot the relative intensity of the luminaire on the chart of figure 9-29.
  2. Locate the point of one-half the intensity at 0° on the ordinate, and draw a line through that point and parallel to the diagonal lines. If the intensity varies significantly in the vicinity of 0°, use an average of the intensity over the 0–5° polar angle.
  3. Read scale A above the intersection of this line with the intensity curve.
  4. Repeat step 2 using the point of one-quarter the intensity at 0°.

5. Read scale B above the intersection of this line with the intensity curve.
6. The lower of the values found in steps 3 and 5 is the luminaire spacing criterion. Round off the value to the nearest 0.1.

B. For luminaires with significantly asymmetric intensity distributions about the nadir:
  1. Independently evaluate the longitudinal and transverse (parallel and perpendicular, 0° and 90°) intensity distributions.
  2. Apply steps 1, 2 and 3 from part A above for each of the intensity curves. Round off to the nearest 0.1.

Interpretation. The value from scale A corresponds to the luminaire spacing criterion at point Q (figure 9-28a), and the value from scale B corresponds to this criterion at point R (figure 9-28b). Thus for symmetrical intensity distributions, the luminaire spacing criterion requires the direct horizontal illuminance at both test points not to be less than the illuminance directly below a single luminaire. For nonsymmetrical intensity distributions, it is generally found that independent testing at point Q for each orientation will be adequate. A point directly under a luminaire will have relatively high illuminance and receive its principal contribution from the luminaire overhead when the spacing is large. If the illuminance at a probable low point due to the closest luminaires is no lower than that at a probable high point, due to the main component, then it is likely that reasonable uniformity will be achieved over the entire workplane. The luminaire spacing criterion only suggests a maximum spacing at which the horizontal illuminance will be reasonably uniform. When other criteria are considered, such as overlap between luminaires, vertical illuminance, shadowing and illuminance distribution above the workplane, it generally is found that luminaires must be installed at some spacing-to-mounting-height ratio less than the value of the luminaire spacing criterion.

In cases where uniformity is particularly important, the lighting designer must calculate the illuminance at several points throughout the room. It is suggested that a maximum value of 1.5 be assigned as the luminaire spacing criterion for any luminaire, since the use of larger values frequently does not produce acceptable lighting installations when all performance criteria are examined. Also, certain luminaires are designed to be installed only with specific spacing relations, and neither larger nor smaller spacings are desirable. In such cases, a luminaire spacing criterion is not applicable. Specific limits or ranges for the spacing-to-mounting-height ratios should be recommended by the manufacturer, and the basis for the recommendation should be stated, such as a certain degree of horizontal illuminance uniformity (determined by point calculations). In addition to the luminaire spacing criterion, it is possible to determine illuminance uniformity for specific installation conditions and report spacing-to-mounting-height limits for such conditions. If that is done, the luminaire layout, the room conditions, the uniformity criteria and any application restrictions should be explicitly described.

INTERPRETATION AND LIMITS OF CALCULATED QUANTITIES

Calculated quantities can be used to provide the designer of a lighting system with information that could not otherwise be obtained except with an actual mock-up of a lighting installation. Information on illuminance, luminance, exitance, contrast, visual comfort probability, visibility and visual performance metrics can be used to compare alternative designs and to verify that design criteria are met. These calculated quantities can also be used to protect or challenge a specification. Calculations are often required to meet strict design requirements imposed by labor unions, owners, local codes, or the like. If used correctly, computer models can be a valuable asset in designing a lighting system to meet particular design criteria.

With recent advances in the field of computer graphics, it is now possible to view the effects of a lighting system on a room through a computer-generated rendering of a space. At the heart of these renderings is a complex lighting analysis. The transformation from luminance data to a realistic-looking synthetic image requires special attention, since a computer screen has a limited range of available luminances. These tools are now being used by lighting professionals to evaluate and market their designs. Further improvements in this process will certainly make computer-generated visual methods more popular in the future.

In reviewing any lighting calculations, the results should first be screened for possible errors. Improper orientation or placement of a luminaire may produce incorrect results. Improper photometry, lamp lumen output or light loss factors may also cause errors. If the results appear unreasonable, an error may be producing an inaccurate result. Assuming that the results are for the proper arrangement of lighting equipment and room surfaces, some advice is provided below to help evaluate computer output.

Illuminance

Often a designer has selected a target illuminance, and a detailed analysis is performed to determine if the target value is provided. For maintained illuminance, a design is generally acceptable if the illuminance is within 10% of the target value. For energy conservation purposes, values below the target value are preferred over values above.

It is difficult, however, to achieve a uniform value everywhere within a space, or even across a desk or workplane. A 15% variation in illuminance is generally considered to be tolerable. In all cases it is the responsibility of the designer to determine if a particular variation is acceptable.

In evaluating illuminance, it is important to focus on the actual task locations. Most general lighting systems will provide a higher illuminance in the middle of the room than near the walls. If the principal task locations are against the walls, a more detailed analysis may be needed to properly evaluate the illuminance at those areas.

Obstructions in a space, such as partitions, should be considered in a lighting calculation model if possible. If a simple empty room approach is used, the illuminance near a vertical partition is likely to be much lower than predicted.

Luminances

Luminances can be used to evaluate the appearance of a space. Scallops, sharp luminaire cutoffs, and the general pattern of brightnesses can be studied through numerical and graphical models. Computer renderings or simple luminance contours for room surfaces can provide the needed information for a designer to evaluate the performance of lighting equipment.

Luminances can also be evaluated with respect to a luminance ratio criterion. In the lighting of spaces containing VDTs, the uniformity of the luminance on the ceiling and the maximum ceiling luminance are critical aspects to study (see chapter 15, Office Lighting).

Contrast

The calculation of task contrast, particularly for specular tasks, will provide an indication of where veiling reflections occur within a space. Contrast can also be used to compare the performance of two different lighting systems. Visibility and visual performance metrics that utilize task contrast can provide some insight into the significance of the contrast and the task luminance provided by a lighting system.

Visual Comfort Probability

Visual comfort probability (VCP) is a metric with limited application. It was developed for lensed fluorescent lighting equipment. It is not valid for use with incandescent or high-intensity discharge equipment. It also cannot be used with luminaires that have an upward component. The procedure has never been proven to accurately model the discomfort caused by parabolic fluorescent luminaires, although many lighting professionals continue to apply it in such situations. Parabolic luminaires are much less uniform in luminance than lensed luminaires, and the difference can have a noticeable effect on the comfort of occupants.

Small differences in VCP are not significant. VCP differences of less than 5 points do not indicate a meaningful difference in discomfort glare potential.

Comparison of Calculated and Measured Quantities

Although it seems reasonable to expect calculated values of quantities to be reproduced in the field, in practice it is very difficult to reconcile measured quantities with those provided by calculation. Assumptions inherent in any calculational model often represent conditions very different from those in an actual lighting installation.[70] Some of these conditions are:

- Lambertian surfaces are assumed in most computer programs. Real-world surfaces may contain some degree of specularity.

- The room surface reflectance input to analysis software may not accurately represent what is present in the field.
- Reduced electrical voltage in the power system may produce reduced light output.
- The assumed ballast factor may be much different from that present in the field.
- Thermal effects in an installed luminaire may alter light output.
- Minor differences incurred in the manufacturing process or in the positioning of the lamp within a luminaire may alter the luminaire's photometric distribution.
- Furniture and other absorbing and reflecting surfaces may not have been considered in the computer model.
- No analysis model is an exact representation of any real room. Simplifying assumptions in the calculation method may limit the accuracy of the results.
- Far-field photometric methods applied in a near-field situation may not accurately model the luminaire performance.

Another reason for disagreement can be errors in the measurement process. It is important to follow strict guidelines when measuring the photometric performance of lighting systems. For example, it is important that the lighting system be measured at a temperature that is representative of its thermal equilibrium condition. New lamps should operate for at least 100 h before measurements are taken. The operator of a photometer must ensure that his or her own presence does not influence the reading. Orientation and positioning of the photometer are also critical; a tripod with a leveling device is particularly useful when conducting horizontal illuminance measurements. Finally, all daylight should be eliminated from the measurements on interior lighting systems, perhaps by conducting measurements at night. Any attempt to subtract out daylight levels will be difficult and likely introduce errors because of the temporal variations in daylight illuminance.

The magnitude of the differences between detailed analysis methods and field measurements will vary. In general, differences of less than 20% can be expected, but in extreme cases, where a calculation method simply cannot handle the complexity of the lighting system, they may be greater. For a more complete discussion of the uncertainties, see reference 70.

Fig. 9-30. Configuration Factors (C) for Diffuse Line and Area Sources

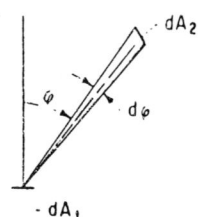

Area dA_1 of differential width and any length, to infinitely long strip dA_2 of differential width and with parallel generating line to dA_1.

$$C = \frac{\cos\varphi}{2}\,d\varphi$$

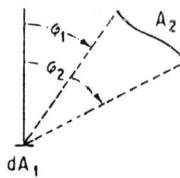

Area dA_1 of differential width and any length to any cylindrical surface A_2 generated by a line of infinite length moving parallel to itself and parallel to the plane of dA_1.

$$C = \frac{1}{2}(\sin\varphi_2 - \sin\varphi_1)$$

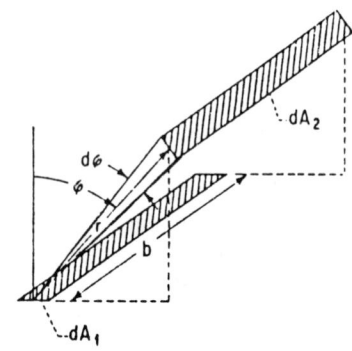

Strip A_1 of length b and differential width, to differential strip dA_2 of same length on parallel generating line.

$$C = \frac{\cos\varphi}{\pi}\,d\varphi\,\arctan\frac{b}{r}$$

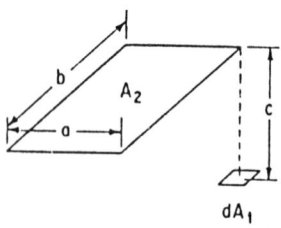

Plane element dA_1 to plane parallel rectangle A_2; normal to element passes through corner of rectangle. $X = a/c$; $Y = b/c$.

$$C = \frac{1}{2\pi}\left(\frac{X}{\sqrt{1+X^2}}\arctan\frac{Y}{\sqrt{1+X^2}} + \frac{Y}{\sqrt{1+Y^2}}\arctan\frac{X}{\sqrt{1+Y^2}}\right)$$

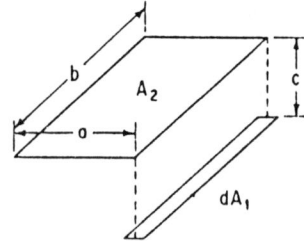

Strip element dA_1 to rectangle A_2 in plane parallel to strip; strip is opposite one edge of rectangle. $X = a/c$; $Y = b/c$.

$$C = \frac{1}{\pi Y}\left[\sqrt{1+Y^2}\arctan\frac{X}{\sqrt{1+Y^2}} - \arctan X + \frac{XY}{\sqrt{1+X^2}}\arctan\frac{Y}{\sqrt{1+X^2}}\right]$$

Fig. 9-30. *Continued*

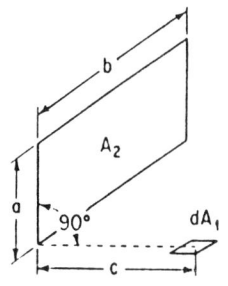

Plane element dA_1 to rectangle A_2 in plane 90° to plane of element. $X = a/b$; $Y = c/b$.

$$C = \frac{1}{2\pi}\left[\arctan\frac{1}{Y} - \frac{Y}{\sqrt{X^2 + Y^2}}\arctan\frac{1}{\sqrt{X^2 + Y^2}}\right]$$

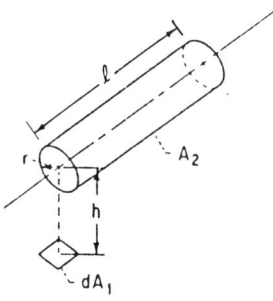

Plane element dA_1 to right circular cylinder A_2 of finite length ℓ and radius r; normal to element passes through one end of cylinder and is perpendicular to cylinder axis. $L = \ell/r$; $H = h/r$; $X = (1 + H^2) + L^2$; $Y = (1 - H^2) + L^2$.

$$C = \frac{1}{\pi H}\arctan\frac{L}{\sqrt{H^2 - 1}} +$$
$$\frac{L}{\pi}\left[\frac{(X - 2H)}{H\sqrt{XY}}\arctan\sqrt{\frac{X(H - 1)}{Y(H - 1)}} - \frac{1}{H}\arctan\sqrt{\frac{H - 1}{H + 1}}\right]$$

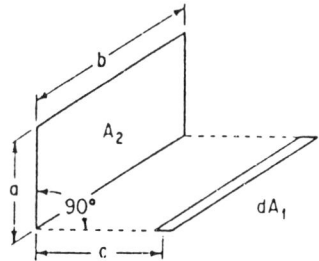

Strip element dA_1 to rectangle A_2 in plane 90° to plane of strip. $X = a/b$; $Y = c/b$.

$$C = \frac{1}{\pi}\left\{\arctan\frac{1}{Y} + \frac{Y}{2}\ln\left[\frac{Y^2(X^2 + Y^2 + 1)}{(Y^2 + 1)(X^2 + Y^2)}\right] - \frac{Y}{\sqrt{X^2 + Y^2}}\arctan\frac{1}{\sqrt{X^2 + Y^2}}\right\}$$

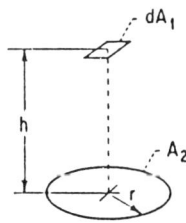

Plane element dA_1 to circular disk A_2 in plane parallel to element; normal to element passes through center of disk.

$$C = \frac{r^2}{h^2 + r^2}$$

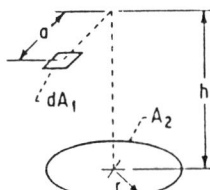

Plane element dA_1 to circular disk A_2 in plane parallel to element. $H = h/a$; $R = r/a$; $Z = 1 + H^2 + R^2$.

$$C = \frac{1}{2}\left(1 - \frac{1 + H^2 - R^2}{\sqrt{Z^2 - 4R^2}}\right)$$

Fig. 9-30. *Continued*

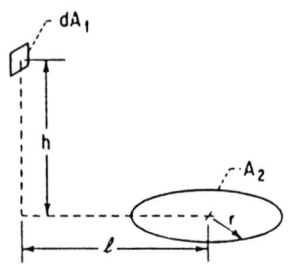

Plane element dA_1 to circular disk A_2; planes containing element and disk intersect at 90°. $H = h/\ell$; $R = r/\ell$; $Z = 1 + H^2 + R^2$.

$$C = \frac{H}{2}\left(\frac{Z}{\sqrt{Z^2 - 4R^2}} - 1\right)$$

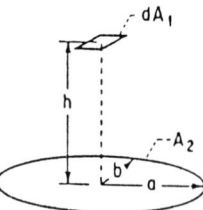

Plane element dA_1 to elliptical plate A_2 in plane parallel to element; normal to element passes through center of plate.

$$C = \frac{ab}{\sqrt{(h^2 + a^2)(h^2 + b^2)}}$$

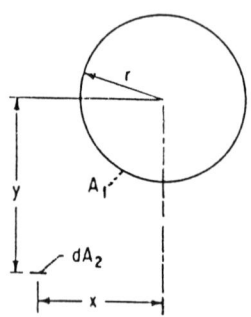

Strip element dA_2 of any length to infinitely long cylinder A_1. $X = x/r$; $Y = y/r$.

$$C = \frac{Y}{X^2 + Y^2}$$

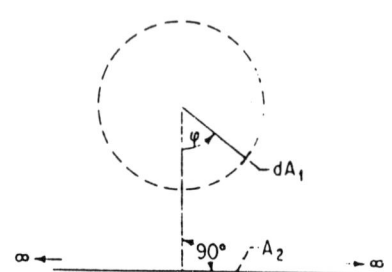

Element dA_1 of any length on cylinder to plane A_2 of infinite length and width.

$$C = \frac{1}{2}(1 + \cos\varphi)$$

Fig. 9-31. General Configuration Factors (C) for Parallel and Perpendicular Rectangles

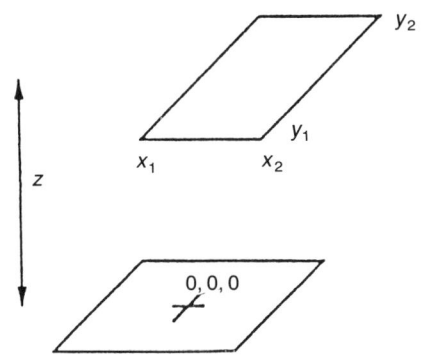

$$C = \frac{1}{2\pi}\sum_{i=1}^{2}\sum_{j=1}^{2} F(x_i, y_j)\,(-1)^{i+j}$$

$$F(x_i, y_j) = \frac{x_i}{\sqrt{x_i^2 + z^2}}\arctan\frac{y_j}{\sqrt{x_i^2 + z^2}} + \frac{y_j}{\sqrt{y_j^2 + z^2}}\arctan\frac{x_i}{\sqrt{y_j^2 + z^2}}$$

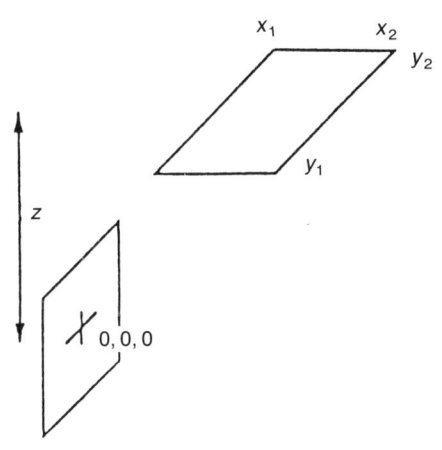

$$C = \frac{z}{2\pi}\sum_{i=1}^{2}\sum_{j=1}^{2} F(x_i, y_j)\,(-1)^{i+j}$$

$$F(x_i, y_j) = \frac{-1}{\sqrt{x_i^2 + z^2}}\arctan\frac{y_j}{\sqrt{x_i^2 + z^2}}$$

Fig. 9-32. Radiative Transfer Theory Form Factors (*F*) for Diffuse Area Sources

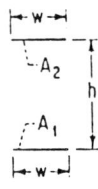

Two infinitely long, directly opposed plates A_1 and A_2 of the same finite width. $H = h/w$.

$$F_{1-2} = F_{2-1} = \sqrt{1 + H^2} - H$$

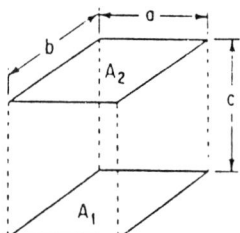

Identical, parallel, directly opposed rectangles A_1 and A_2.
$X = a/c$; $Y = b/c$.

$$F_{1-2} = \frac{2}{\pi XY}\left\{ \ln\left[\frac{(1 + X^2)(1 + Y^2)}{1 + X^2 + Y^2} \right]^{1/2} + X\sqrt{1 + Y^2}\arctan\frac{X}{\sqrt{1 + Y^2}} \right.$$
$$\left. Y\sqrt{1 + X^2}\arctan\frac{Y}{\sqrt{1 + X^2}} - X\arctan X - Y\arctan Y\right\}$$

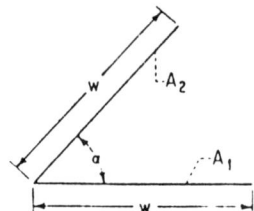

Two infinitely long plates A_1 and A_2 of equal finite width w, having one common edge, and at an included angle a to each other.

$$F_{1-2} = F_{2-1} = 1 - \sin\frac{\alpha}{2}$$

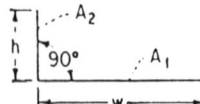

Two infinitely long plates A_1 and A_2 of unequal widths h and w, having one common edge, and at an angle of 90° to each other. $H = h/w$.

$$F_{1-2} = \frac{1}{2}\left[1 + H - \sqrt{1 + H^2} \right]$$

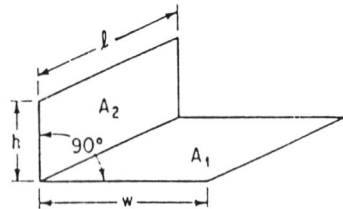

Two finite rectangles A_1 and A_2 of same length, having one common edge, and at an angle of 90° to each other.
$H = h/\ell$; $W = w/\ell$.

$$F_{1-2} = \frac{1}{\pi W}\left(W\arctan\frac{1}{W} + H\arctan\frac{1}{H} - \sqrt{H^2 + W^2}\arctan\frac{1}{\sqrt{H^2 + W^2}} + \right.$$
$$\left. \frac{1}{4}\ln\left\{ \frac{(1 + W^2)(1 + H^2)}{(1 + W^2 + H^2)}\left[\frac{W^2(1 + W^2 + H^2)}{(1 + W^2)(W^2 + H^2)} \right]^{W^2}\left[\frac{H^2(1 + H^2 + W^2)}{(1 + H^2)(H^2 + W^2)} \right]^{H^2}\right\}\right)$$

Fig. 9-32. *Continued*

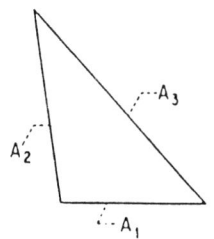

Infinitely long enclosure formed by three plane areas A_1, A_2 and A_3.

$$F_{1\text{-}2} = \frac{A_1 + A_2 - A_3}{2A_1}$$

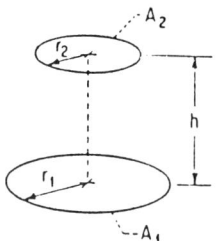

Parallel circular disks A_1 and A_2 with centers along the same normal. $R_1 = r_1/h$; $R_2 = r_2/h$; $X = 1 + (1 + R_2{}^2)/R_1{}^2$.

$$F_{1\text{-}2} = \frac{1}{2}\left[X - \sqrt{X^2 - 4\left(\frac{R_2}{R_1}\right)^2}\right]$$

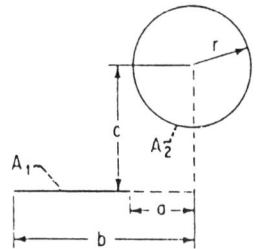

Infinitely long plane A_1 of finite width to parallel infinitely long cylinder A_2.

$$F_{1\text{-}2} = \frac{r}{b - a}\left[\arctan\frac{b}{c} - \arctan\frac{a}{c}\right]$$

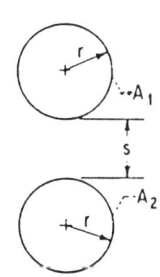

Infinitely long parallel cylinders A_1 and A_2 of the same diameter. $X = 1 + s/2r$.

$$F_{1\text{-}2} = F_{2\text{-}1} = \frac{1}{\pi}\left[\sqrt{X^2 - 1} + \arcsin\left(\frac{1}{X}\right) - X\right]$$

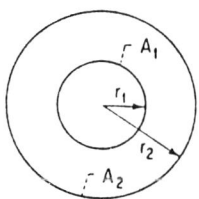

Concentric cylinders A_1 and A_2 of infinite length.

$$F_{1\text{-}2} = 1$$
$$F_{2\text{-}1} = \frac{r_1}{r_2}$$
$$F_{2\text{-}2} = 1 - \frac{r_1}{r_2}$$

Fig. 9-33 General Expressions for Form Factors (F) Between Parallel and Perpendicular Rectangles

Parallel rectangles A_1 and A_2.

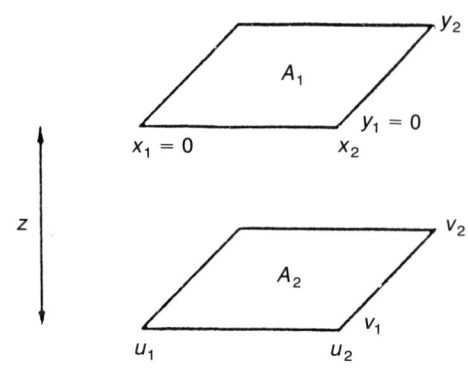

$$F_{1\text{-}2} = \frac{z^2}{\pi A_1^2} \sum_{i=1}^{2}\sum_{j=1}^{2}\sum_{k=1}^{2}\sum_{m=1}^{2} H(u_i, v_j, x_k, y_m)(-1)^{i+j+k+m}$$

$$H(u_i, v_j, x_k, y_m) = b\sqrt{1+a^2}\arctan\frac{b}{\sqrt{1+a^2}} + a\sqrt{1+b^2}\arctan\frac{a}{\sqrt{1+b^2}} - \frac{1}{2}\ln(1+a^2+b^2)$$

$$a = (x_k - u_i)/z \qquad b = (y_m - v_j)/z$$

Perpendicular rectangles A_1 and A_2.

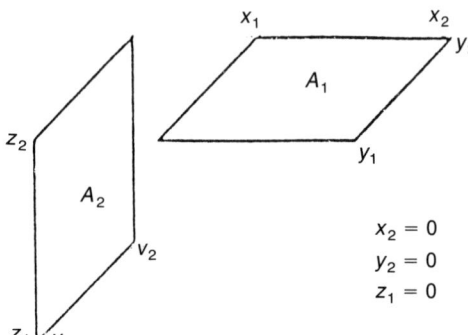

$$F_{1\text{-}2} = \frac{1}{2\pi A_1}\sum_{i=1}^{2}\sum_{j=1}^{2}\sum_{k=1}^{2}\sum_{m=1}^{2} G(v_i, z_j, x_k, y_m)(-1)^{i+j+k+m}$$

$x_2 = 0$
$y_2 = 0$
$z_1 = 0$

$$G(v_i, z_j, x_k, y_m) = a\sqrt{c^2+b^2} + \frac{1}{4}(a^2 - b^2 - c^2)\ln(a^2+b^2+c^2)$$

$a = y_m - v_i \qquad b = \bar{z} - z_j \qquad c = x_k - \bar{x}$
$\bar{z} = z\text{-coordinate of surface } A_1$
$\bar{x} = x\text{-coordinate of surface } A_2$

Instructions and Notes: Tables of Coefficients of Utilization (Figure 9-34)

1. The luminaires in this table are organized by source type and luminaire form rather than by application, for convenience in locating luminaires. In some cases, the data are based on an actual typical luminaire; in other cases, they represent a composite of generic luminaire types. Therefore, whenever possible, specific luminaire data should be used in preference to this table.

2. The polar intensity sketch (candlepower distribution curve) and the corresponding luminaire spacing criterion are representative of many luminaires of each type shown. A specific luminaire may differ in perpendicular-plane (crosswise) and parallel-plane (lengthwise) intensity distributions and in spacing criterion from the values shown. However, the various coefficients depend only on the average intensity at each polar angle from nadir. The average intensity values used to generate the coefficients are given at the end of the table, normalized to 1000 lamp lumens for reference.

3. The various coefficients depend only on the average intensity distribution curve and are linearly related to the total luminaire efficiency. Consequently, the tabulated coefficients can be applied to luminaires with similarly shaped average intensity distributions along with a correcting multiplier equal to the new luminaire total efficiency divided by the tabulated luminaire total efficiency. The use of polarizing lenses on fluorescent luminaires has no effect on the coefficients given in this table except as they affect the total luminaire efficiency.

4. Satisfactory installations depend on many factors, including the environment, space utilization and luminous criteria, as well as the luminaire itself. Consequently, a definitive spacing recommendation cannot be assigned to the luminaire as such. The spacing criterion (SC) values given are only general guides. SC values are not assigned to semi-indirect and indirect luminaires, since the basis of this technique does not apply to such situations. Also, SC values are not given for those bat-wing luminaires which must be located by criteria other than that of horizontal illuminance.

5. Key:

$$\rho_{CC} = \text{cciling cavity reflectance (percent),}$$
$$\rho_{W} = \text{wall reflectance (percent),}$$
$$\rho_{FC} = \text{floor cavity reflectance (percent),}$$
$$\text{RCR} = \text{room cavity ratio,}$$
$$\text{WDRC} = \text{wall direct radiation coefficient,}$$
$$\text{SC} = \text{luminaire spacing criterion,}$$
$$\text{NA} = \text{not applicable.}$$

6. Many of the luminaires in this figure appeared in earlier editions of the *IES Lighting Handbook*. The identifying number may be different due to a re-ordering of the luminaires. In some cases, the data have been modified in view of more recent or more extensive information. The user should specifically refer to this Handbook when referencing luminaires. Fluorescent luminaire efficiencies, and consequently the coefficients, are a function of the number of lamps in relation to the size of the luminaire. This is due to temperature changes and to changes in the blocking of light. In this figure, fluorescent luminaires have been chosen with typical luminaire sizes and numbers of lamps; these are identified under the typical luminaire drawings. Variations of the coefficients with size and number of lamps depend on the many details of luminaire construction. The following correction factors are average values to apply to a four-lamp luminaire 610 mm (2 ft) wide:

No. of lamps	Width		Multiply by
	mm	ft	
8	1220	4	1.05
3	610	2	1.05
2	610	2	1.1
2	300	1	0.9

Multiply the entries for two-lamp wraparound luminaires by 0.95 for four lamps.

7. Photometric data for fluorescent luminaires in this table are based upon tests using standard-wattage fluorescent lamps. Reduced-wattage fluorescent lamps cause lower lamp operating temperatures with some luminaires. Consequently, the efficiency and coefficients may be slightly increased. It is desirable to obtain specific correction factors from the manufacturers. Typical factors for reduced-wattage fluorescent lamps (approximately 10% below standard lamp wattages) are as follows:

Luminaire	Multiply by
2-lamp strip, surface mounted	1.03
4-lamp troffer, enclosed, non-air-handling	1.07
4-lamp wraparound, surface mounted	1.07
2-lamp industrial, vented	1.00

Electronic ballasts can be designed for any arbitrary operating condition. The manufacturer must be consulted for specific data.

Fig. 9-34. Coefficients of Utilization, Wall Luminance Coefficients, Ceiling Cavity Luminance Coefficients, Luminaire Spacing Criteria and Maintenance Categories Typical Luminaires

Typical Luminaire	Typical Intensity Distribution and Per Cent Lamp Lumens		ρ_{CC} →	80			70			50			30			10			0	WDRC	ρ_{CC} →
			ρ_W →	50	30	10	50	30	10	50	30	10	50	30	10	50	30	10	0		ρ_W →
	Maint. Cat.	SC	RCR ↓	Coefficients of Utilization for 20 Per Cent Effective Floor Cavity Reflectance (ρ_{FC} = 20)																	RCR ↓
1	V	1.5	0	.87	.87	.87	.81	.81	.81	.70	.70	.70	.59	.59	.59	.49	.49	.49	.45		
	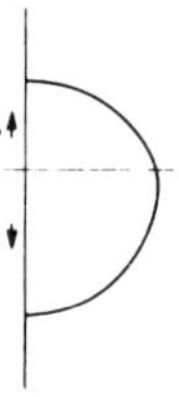		1	.71	.66	.62	.65	.61	.58	.55	.52	.49	.46	.44	.42	.38	.36	.34	.30	.368	1
			2	.60	.53	.48	.55	.50	.45	.47	.42	.38	.39	.35	.32	.31	.29	.26	.23	.279	2
	35½% ↑		3	.52	.44	.38	.48	.41	.36	.40	.35	.31	.33	.29	.26	.27	.24	.21	.18	.227	3
			4	.45	.37	.32	.42	.35	.29	.35	.30	.25	.29	.25	.21	.23	.20	.17	.14	.192	4
			5	.40	.32	.27	.37	.30	.25	.31	.25	.21	.26	.21	.18	.21	.17	.14	.12	.166	5
	45% ↓		6	.35	.28	.23	.33	.26	.21	.28	.22	.18	.23	.19	.15	.19	.15	.12	.10	.146	6
			7	.32	.25	.19	.29	.23	.18	.25	.20	.16	.21	.16	.13	.17	.13	.11	.09	.130	7
			8	.29	.22	.17	.27	.20	.16	.23	.17	.14	.19	.15	.12	.15	.12	.09	.07	.117	8
Pendant diffusing sphere with incandescent lamp			9	.26	.19	.15	.24	.18	.14	.21	.16	.12	.17	.13	.10	.14	.11	.08	.07	.107	9
			10	.24	.17	.13	.22	.16	.12	.19	.14	.11	.16	.12	.09	.13	.10	.08	.06	.098	10
2	II	N.A.	0	.83	.83	.83	.72	.72	.72	.50	.50	.50	.30	.30	.30	.12	.12	.12	.03		
			1	.72	.69	.66	.62	.60	.57	.43	.42	.40	.26	.25	.25	.10	.10	.10	.03	.018	1
			2	.63	.58	.54	.54	.50	.47	.38	.35	.33	.23	.22	.20	.09	.09	.08	.02	.015	2
			3	.55	.49	.45	.47	.43	.39	.33	.30	.28	.20	.19	.17	.08	.07	.07	.02	.013	3
			4	.48	.42	.37	.42	.37	.33	.29	.26	.23	.18	.16	.15	.07	.06	.06	.02	.012	4
	83% ↑		5	.43	.36	.32	.37	.32	.28	.26	.23	.20	.16	.14	.12	.06	.06	.05	.01	.011	5
			6	.38	.32	.27	.33	.28	.24	.23	.20	.17	.14	.12	.11	.06	.05	.04	.01	.010	6
	3½% ↓		7	.34	.28	.23	.30	.24	.21	.21	.17	.15	.13	.11	.09	.05	.04	.04	.01	.009	7
			8	.31	.25	.20	.27	.21	.18	.19	.15	.13	.12	.10	.08	.05	.04	.03	.01	.008	8
Concentric ring unit with incandescent silvered-bowl lamp			9	.28	.22	.18	.24	.19	.16	.17	.14	.11	.10	.09	.07	.04	.03	.03	.01	.008	9
			10	.25	.20	.16	.22	.17	.14	.16	.12	.10	.10	.08	.06	.04	.03	.03	.01	.007	10
3	IV	1.3	0	.99	.99	.99	.97	.97	.97	.93	.93	.93	.89	.89	.89	.85	.85	.85	.83		
	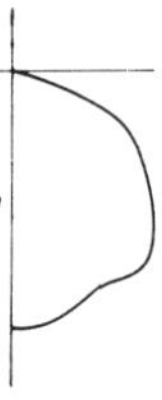		1	.87	.84	.81	.85	.82	.79	.82	.79	.77	.79	.76	.74	.76	.74	.72	.71	.323	1
	0% ↑		2	.76	.70	.65	.74	.69	.65	.71	.67	.63	.69	.65	.62	.66	.63	.60	.59	.311	2
			3	.66	.59	.54	.65	.59	.53	.62	.57	.53	.60	.56	.52	.58	.54	.51	.49	.288	3
			4	.58	.51	.45	.57	.50	.45	.55	.49	.44	.53	.48	.44	.51	.47	.43	.41	.264	4
			5	.52	.44	.39	.51	.44	.38	.49	.43	.38	.47	.42	.37	.46	.41	.37	.35	.241	5
	83½% ↓		6	.46	.39	.33	.46	.38	.33	.44	.38	.33	.43	.37	.33	.41	.36	.32	.31	.221	6
			7	.42	.34	.29	.41	.34	.29	.40	.33	.29	.39	.33	.29	.38	.32	.28	.27	.203	7
			8	.38	.31	.26	.37	.31	.26	.36	.30	.26	.35	.30	.25	.34	.29	.25	.24	.187	8
Porcelain-enameled ventilated standard dome with incandescent lamp			9	.35	.28	.23	.34	.28	.23	.33	.27	.23	.32	.27	.23	.32	.26	.23	.21	.173	9
			10	.32	.25	.21	.32	.25	.21	.31	.25	.21	.30	.24	.21	.29	.24	.20	.19	.161	10
4	V	1.3	0	.89	.89	.89	.85	.85	.85	.77	.77	.77	.70	.70	.70	.63	.63	.63	.60		
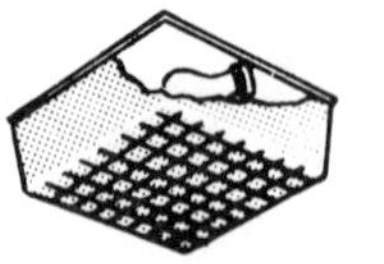			1	.77	.74	.71	.74	.71	.68	.67	.65	.63	.61	.59	.57	.55	.54	.53	.50	.264	1
	18½% ↑		2	.68	.63	.59	.65	.61	.57	.59	.56	.53	.54	.51	.49	.49	.47	.45	.42	.224	2
			3	.61	.55	.50	.58	.53	.48	.53	.49	.45	.49	.45	.42	.44	.42	.39	.37	.197	3
			4	.54	.48	.43	.52	.46	.42	.48	.43	.39	.44	.40	.37	.40	.37	.34	.32	.176	4
			5	.49	.42	.38	.47	.41	.37	.43	.38	.35	.40	.36	.33	.37	.33	.31	.29	.159	5
	60½% ↓		6	.44	.38	.33	.43	.37	.32	.39	.34	.31	.36	.32	.29	.34	.30	.27	.26	.145	6
			7	.40	.34	.30	.39	.33	.29	.36	.31	.27	.33	.29	.26	.31	.27	.25	.23	.133	7
			8	.37	.31	.27	.36	.30	.26	.33	.28	.25	.31	.27	.24	.29	.25	.22	.21	.124	8
			9	.34	.28	.24	.33	.27	.24	.31	.26	.22	.29	.24	.21	.27	.23	.20	.19	.115	9
Prismatic square surface drum			10	.32	.26	.22	.30	.25	.21	.28	.24	.21	.27	.23	.20	.25	.21	.19	.17	.108	10
5	IV	0.8	0	1.19	1.19	1.19	1.16	1.16	1.16	1.11	1.11	1.11	1.06	1.06	1.06	1.02	1.02	1.02	1.00		
	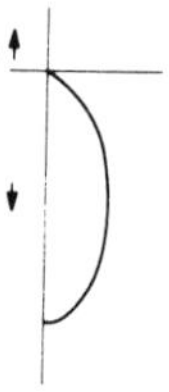		1	1.08	1.05	1.03	1.06	1.03	1.01	1.02	1.00	.98	.98	.97	.95	.95	.93	.92	.90	.241	1
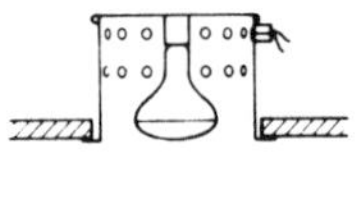	0% ↑		2	.99	.94	.89	.97	.92	.88	.93	.90	.86	.90	.87	.84	.88	.85	.83	.81	.238	2
			3	.90	.84	.79	.88	.83	.78	.86	.81	.77	.83	.79	.76	.81	.77	.74	.73	.227	3
			4	.82	.75	.70	.81	.75	.70	.79	.73	.69	.77	.72	.68	.75	.71	.67	.66	.215	4
	100% ↓		5	.76	.68	.63	.75	.68	.63	.73	.67	.62	.71	.66	.62	.69	.65	.61	.59	.202	5
			6	.70	.62	.57	.69	.62	.57	.67	.61	.57	.66	.60	.56	.64	.60	.56	.54	.191	6
			7	.65	.57	.52	.64	.57	.52	.62	.56	.52	.61	.56	.52	.60	.55	.51	.50	.180	7
			8	.60	.53	.48	.59	.53	.48	.58	.52	.48	.57	.52	.47	.56	.51	.47	.46	.169	8
			9	.56	.49	.44	.55	.49	.44	.54	.48	.44	.53	.48	.44	.52	.47	.44	.42	.160	9
R-40 flood without shielding			10	.52	.46	.41	.52	.45	.41	.51	.45	.41	.50	.45	.41	.49	.44	.41	.39	.152	10
6	IV	0.7	0	1.01	1.01	1.01	.99	.99	.99	.94	.94	.94	.90	.90	.90	.87	.87	.87	.85		
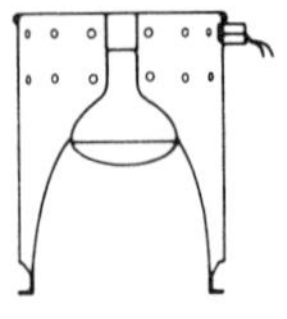			1	.95	.93	.91	.93	.91	.89	.89	.88	.87	.86	.85	.84	.83	.82	.82	.80	.115	1
	0% ↑		2	.89	.86	.83	.87	.84	.82	.85	.82	.80	.82	.80	.79	.80	.78	.77	.76	.115	2
			3	.83	.80	.77	.82	.79	.76	.80	.77	.75	.78	.76	.74	.76	.74	.72	.71	.113	3
			4	.79	.74	.71	.78	.74	.71	.76	.73	.70	.74	.71	.69	.73	.70	.68	.67	.110	4
	85% ↓		5	.74	.70	.67	.74	.69	.66	.72	.68	.66	.71	.68	.65	.69	.67	.65	.63	.107	5
			6	.70	.66	.62	.70	.65	.62	.68	.65	.62	.67	.64	.61	.66	.63	.61	.60	.104	6
			7	.67	.62	.59	.66	.62	.59	.65	.61	.58	.64	.61	.58	.63	.60	.58	.57	.100	7
			8	.63	.59	.56	.63	.58	.55	.62	.58	.55	.61	.58	.55	.60	.57	.55	.54	.097	8
R-40 flood with specular anodized reflector skirt; 45° cutoff			9	.60	.56	.53	.60	.56	.53	.59	.55	.52	.58	.55	.52	.58	.54	.52	.51	.094	9
			10	.57	.53	.50	.57	.53	.50	.56	.52	.50	.56	.52	.50	.55	.52	.49	.48	.091	10

Fig. 9-34. *Continued*

80			70			50			30			10			80			70			50			30			10		
50	30	10	50	30	10	50	30	10	50	30	10	50	30	10	50	30	10	50	30	10	50	30	10	50	30	10	50	30	10
Wall Exitance Coefficients for 20 Per Cent Effective Floor Cavity Reflectance (ρ_{FC} = 20)															Ceiling Cavity Exitance Coefficients for 20 Per Cent Floor Cavity Reflectance (ρ_{FC} = 20)														
															.423	.423	.423	.361	.361	.361	.246	.246	.246	.142	.142	.142	.045	.045	.045
.328	.187	.059	.311	.178	.056	.280	.161	.051	.252	.145	.047	.226	.131	.042	.422	.396	.373	.361	.340	.321	.247	.234	.222	.142	.135	.129	.046	.044	.042
.275	.150	.046	.259	.143	.044	.231	.129	.040	.205	.115	.036	.181	.102	.032	.417	.379	.347	.357	.327	.300	.245	.226	.209	.141	.131	.123	.045	.043	.040
.240	.128	.038	.226	.121	.036	.200	.108	.033	.176	.097	.030	.154	.085	.026	.412	.367	.332	.353	.317	.287	.242	.220	.202	.140	.128	.119	.045	.042	.039
.214	.111	.033	.201	.105	.031	.177	.094	.028	.155	.083	.025	.135	.073	.022	.406	.358	.321	.348	.309	.279	.239	.215	.196	.138	.126	.116	.045	.041	.038
.193	.098	.028	.181	.093	.027	.160	.083	.024	.139	.073	.022	.120	.064	.019	.400	.350	.314	.343	.303	.273	.236	.212	.193	.137	.124	.114	.044	.041	.038
.176	.088	.025	.165	.084	.024	.145	.074	.022	.126	.066	.019	.109	.057	.017	.394	.344	.309	.338	.298	.269	.234	.209	.190	.135	.123	.113	.044	.040	.037
.162	.080	.023	.152	.076	.022	.133	.067	.019	.116	.059	.017	.100	.052	.015	.388	.339	.305	.334	.294	.266	.231	.206	.188	.134	.122	.112	.043	.040	.037
.150	.073	.021	.140	.069	.020	.123	.062	.018	.107	.054	.016	.092	.047	.014	.383	.335	.302	.330	.291	.264	.228	.204	.187	.133	.120	.111	.043	.039	.037
.139	.067	.019	.131	.064	.018	.115	.057	.016	.099	.050	.014	.085	.043	.013	.378	.332	.300	.326	.288	.262	.226	.202	.186	.131	.119	.111	.043	.039	.037
.130	.062	.017	.122	.059	.016	.107	.052	.015	.093	.046	.013	.080	.040	.011	.374	.328	.298	.322	.285	.260	.223	.201	.185	.130	.119	.110	.042	.039	.037
															.796	.796	.796	.680	.680	.680	.464	.464	.464	.267	.267	.267	.085	.085	.085
.226	.128	.041	.195	.111	.035	.137	.078	.025	.083	.048	.015	.034	.020	.006	.790	.772	.756	.676	.663	.651	.462	.456	.450	.266	.264	.262	.085	.085	.085
.207	.114	.035	.179	.099	.030	.126	.070	.022	.077	.043	.013	.031	.018	.006	.784	.755	.731	.671	.650	.632	.460	.450	.441	.265	.262	.258	.085	.085	.084
.191	.102	.030	.165	.088	.027	.116	.063	.019	.071	.039	.012	.029	.016	.005	.778	.743	.715	.667	.641	.620	.458	.445	.435	.265	.260	.256	.085	.084	.084
.177	.092	.027	.153	.080	.024	.108	.057	.017	.066	.035	.011	.027	.014	.004	.773	.734	.703	.664	.634	.611	.456	.442	.430	.264	.259	.255	.085	.084	.084
.164	.084	.024	.142	.073	.021	.100	.052	.015	.061	.032	.010	.025	.013	.004	.768	.726	.696	.660	.629	.605	.455	.439	.427	.263	.258	.253	.085	.084	.084
.153	.077	.022	.133	.067	.019	.094	.048	.014	.057	.030	.009	.023	.012	.004	.764	.721	.690	.656	.624	.601	.453	.437	.425	.263	.257	.253	.085	.084	.083
.143	.071	.020	.124	.062	.018	.088	.044	.013	.054	.027	.008	.022	.011	.003	.759	.716	.686	.653	.621	.598	.451	.435	.423	.262	.256	.252	.085	.084	.083
.134	.066	.018	.116	.057	.016	.082	.041	.012	.050	.026	.007	.020	.010	.003	.755	.712	.683	.650	.618	.595	.450	.434	.422	.262	.256	.252	.085	.084	.083
.126	.061	.017	.109	.053	.015	.077	.038	.011	.047	.024	.007	.019	.010	.003	.751	.709	.680	.647	.615	.593	.448	.432	.421	.261	.255	.251	.085	.084	.083
.119	.057	.016	.103	.050	.014	.073	.036	.010	.045	.022	.006	.018	.009	.003	.747	.706	.678	.644	.613	.592	.447	.431	.421	.261	.255	.251	.084	.084	.083
															.159	.159	.159	.136	.136	.136	.093	.093	.093	.053	.053	.053	.017	.017	.017
.248	.141	.045	.242	.138	.044	.231	.133	.042	.221	.128	.041	.212	.123	.040	.150	.130	.113	.128	.112	.097	.088	.077	.067	.050	.045	.039	.016	.014	.013
.240	.131	.040	.235	.129	.040	.225	.125	.039	.216	.121	.038	.208	.117	.037	.143	.110	.082	.123	.095	.071	.084	.066	.050	.048	.038	.029	.016	.012	.009
.225	.120	.036	.220	.118	.036	.212	.115	.035	.204	.112	.034	.196	.109	.034	.137	.095	.062	.118	.082	.054	.081	.057	.038	.047	.033	.022	.015	.011	.007
.209	.109	.032	.205	.107	.032	.197	.105	.031	.190	.102	.031	.184	.100	.030	.131	.084	.048	.113	.073	.042	.077	.051	.030	.045	.030	.018	.014	.010	.006
.194	.099	.029	.191	.098	.029	.184	.096	.028	.177	.094	.028	.171	.092	.028	.125	.076	.039	.108	.065	.034	.074	.046	.024	.043	.027	.014	.014	.009	.005
.181	.091	.026	.177	.090	.026	.171	.088	.026	.166	.086	.025	.160	.084	.025	.119	.069	.032	.103	.060	.028	.071	.042	.020	.041	.025	.012	.013	.008	.004
.168	.083	.024	.165	.082	.023	.160	.081	.023	.155	.079	.023	.150	.078	.023	.114	.063	.027	.098	.055	.024	.068	.038	.017	.039	.023	.010	.013	.007	.003
.157	.077	.022	.155	.076	.022	.150	.075	.021	.145	.074	.021	.141	.072	.021	.109	.058	.024	.093	.050	.021	.065	.035	.015	.038	.021	.009	.012	.007	.003
.147	.071	.020	.145	.071	.020	.141	.070	.020	.136	.068	.020	.133	.067	.019	.103	.054	.021	.089	.047	.018	.062	.033	.013	.036	.019	.008	.012	.006	.003
.138	.066	.018	.136	.066	.018	.132	.065	.018	.129	.064	.018	.125	.063	.018	.099	.051	.018	.085	.044	.016	.059	.031	.011	.034	.018	.007	.011	.006	.002
															.290	.290	.290	.248	.248	.248	.169	.169	.169	.097	.097	.097	.031	.031	.031
.243	.138	.044	.232	.132	.042	.211	.121	.039	.192	.111	.036	.175	.101	.033	.283	.264	.247	.242	.227	.213	.166	.156	.147	.095	.090	.085	.031	.029	.028
.216	.118	.036	.206	.114	.035	.187	.104	.032	.170	.095	.030	.154	.087	.027	.276	.246	.221	.236	.212	.191	.162	.147	.133	.093	.085	.078	.030	.028	.025
.196	.104	.031	.187	.100	.030	.170	.092	.028	.154	.085	.026	.140	.077	.024	.269	.233	.204	.231	.201	.177	.158	.139	.124	.092	.081	.073	.029	.026	.024
.180	.093	.027	.171	.090	.027	.156	.083	.025	.142	.076	.023	.128	.070	.021	.263	.223	.192	.226	.192	.167	.155	.134	.117	090	.079	.069	.029	.026	.023
.166	.084	.024	.158	.081	.024	.144	.075	.022	.131	.069	.021	.119	.064	.019	.257	.215	.183	.221	.186	.160	.152	.130	.113	.088	.076	.067	.028	.025	.022
.154	.077	.022	.147	.074	.021	.134	.069	.020	.122	.064	.019	.111	.058	.017	.252	.208	.177	.216	.180	.154	.149	.126	.109	.087	.074	.065	.028	.024	.021
.143	.071	.020	.137	.068	.019	.125	.063	.018	.114	.059	.017	.104	.054	.016	.246	.203	.173	.212	.176	.151	.146	.123	.107	.085	.073	.063	.027	.024	.021
.134	.066	.018	.129	.063	.018	.118	.059	.017	.108	.055	.016	.098	.050	.015	.242	.199	.169	.208	.172	.148	.144	.121	.105	.084	.071	.062	.027	.023	.021
.126	.061	.017	.121	.059	.017	.111	.055	.016	.102	.051	.015	.093	.047	.014	.237	.195	.166	.204	.169	.145	.142	.119	.103	.083	.070	.061	.027	.023	.020
.119	.057	.016	.114	.055	.015	.105	.051	.014	.096	.048	.014	.088	.044	.013	.233	.192	.164	.201	.167	.143	.139	.117	.102	.081	.069	.061	.026	.023	.020
															.190	.190	.190	.163	.163	.163	.111	.111	.111	.064	.064	.064	.020	.020	.020
.220	.125	.040	.213	.122	.039	.200	.115	.037	.189	.109	.035	.178	.103	.033	.174	.157	.141	.149	.135	.122	.102	.093	.084	.059	.054	.049	.019	.017	.016
.212	.116	.036	.206	.114	.035	.195	.109	.034	.185	.104	.033	.176	.099	.031	.161	.132	.107	.138	.114	.093	.095	.079	.065	.055	.046	.038	.018	.015	.012
.202	.107	.032	.197	.105	.032	.187	.101	.031	.178	.098	.030	.170	.094	.029	.151	.114	.084	.130	.098	.073	.089	.068	.051	.051	.040	.030	.017	.013	.010
.191	.099	.029	.186	.098	.029	.178	.094	.028	.170	.091	.028	.163	.089	.027	.142	.100	.067	.122	.086	.058	.084	.060	.041	.049	.035	.024	.016	.011	.008
.180	.092	.027	.176	.091	.026	.169	.088	.026	.162	.086	.025	.156	.083	.025	.135	.088	.055	.116	.077	.047	.080	.053	.033	.046	.031	.020	.015	.010	.007
.171	.086	.024	.167	.084	.024	.161	.082	.024	.155	.080	.024	.149	.078	.023	.128	.080	.045	.110	.069	.039	.076	.048	.028	.044	.028	.017	.014	.009	.005
.162	.080	.023	.158	.079	.022	.153	.077	.022	.147	.075	.022	.142	.074	.022	.121	.072	.038	.104	.063	.033	.072	.044	.024	.042	.026	.014	.014	.008	.005
.153	.075	.021	.150	.074	.021	.145	.073	.021	.140	.071	.021	.136	.070	.020	.115	.066	.033	.099	.058	.029	.069	.040	.020	.040	.024	.012	.013	.008	.004
.145	.070	.020	.143	.070	.020	.138	.068	.019	.134	.067	.019	.130	.066	.019	.110	.061	.029	.095	.053	.025	.066	.037	.018	.038	.022	.011	.012	.007	.003
.138	.066	.018	.136	.066	.018	.132	.065	.018	.128	.064	.018	.124	.062	.018	.105	.057	.025	.091	.050	.022	.063	.035	.016	.037	.021	.009	.012	.007	.003
															.162	.162	.162	.138	.138	.138	.094	.094	.094	.054	.054	.054	.017	.017	.017
.139	.079	.025	.133	.076	.024	.123	.070	.022	.113	.065	.021	.104	.060	.019	.144	.133	.124	.123	.115	.106	.084	.079	.074	.049	.046	.043	.016	.015	.014
.132	.072	.022	.127	.070	.022	.119	.066	.020	.110	.062	.019	.103	.058	.018	.131	.112	.097	.112	.097	.084	.077	.067	.059	.044	.039	.034	.014	.013	.011
.126	.067	.020	.122	.065	.020	.114	.062	.019	.107	.059	.018	.101	.056	.017	.120	.096	.078	.102	.083	.067	.070	.058	.047	.041	.034	.028	.013	.011	.009
.119	.062	.018	.116	.061	.018	.110	.058	.017	.104	.056	.017	.098	.053	.016	.110	.084	.063	.095	.072	.055	.065	.050	.039	.038	.029	.023	.012	.010	.008
.114	.058	.017	.111	.057	.017	.105	.055	.016	.100	.053	.016	.095	.051	.015	.103	.074	.052	.088	.064	.045	.061	.044	.032	.035	.026	.019	.011	.009	.006
.109	.055	.016	.106	.054	.015	.101	.052	.015	.097	.050	.015	.093	.049	.014	.096	.066	.044	.083	.057	.038	.057	.040	.027	.033	.023	.016	.011	.008	.005
.104	.052	.015	.102	.051	.014	.098	.049	.014	.094	.048	.014	.090	.047	.014	.091	.059	.037	.078	.051	.032	.054	.036	.023	.031	.021	.014	.010	.007	.004
.100	.049	.014	.098	.048	.014	.094	.047	.013	.090	.046	.013	.087	.045	.013	.086	.054	.032	.074	.047	.028	.051	.033	.020	.030	.019	.012	.010	.006	.004
.096	.046	.013	.094	.046	.013	.091	.045	.013	.087	.044	.013	.084	.043	.012	.081	.049	.027	.070	.043	.024	.049	.030	.017	.028	.018	.010	.009	.006	.003
.092	.044	.012	.091	.044	.012	.088	.043	.012	.085	.042	.012	.082	.041	.012	.077	.045	.024	.067	.039	.021	.046	.028	.015	.027	.016	.009	.009	.005	.003

Fig. 9-34. *Continued*

Typical Luminaire	Typical Intensity Distribution and Per Cent Lamp Lumens		RCR ↓	ρCC → 80			70			50			30			10			0	WDRC	RCR ↓
	Maint. Cat.	SC		ρW → 50	30	10	50	30	10	50	30	10	50	30	10	50	30	10	0		

7 — EAR-38 lamp above 51 mm (2″) diameter aperture (increase efficiency to 54½% for 76 mm (3″) diameter aperture)* — Maint. Cat. IV, SC 0.7, 0%↑, 43½%↓

RCR	80 (50)	80 (30)	80 (10)	70 (50)	70 (30)	70 (10)	50 (50)	50 (30)	50 (10)	30 (50)	30 (30)	30 (10)	10 (50)	10 (30)	10 (10)	0	WDRC	RCR
0	.52	.52	.52	.51	.51	.51	.48	.48	.48	.46	.46	.46	.45	.45	.45	.44		0
1	.49	.48	.47	.48	.47	.46	.46	.45	.45	.44	.44	.43	.43	.43	.42	.41	.055	1
2	.46	.44	.43	.45	.44	.43	.44	.43	.42	.43	.42	.41	.41	.41	.40	.39	.054	2
3	.43	.41	.40	.43	.41	.40	.42	.40	.39	.41	.39	.38	.40	.39	.38	.37	.053	3
4	.41	.39	.37	.41	.39	.37	.40	.38	.37	.39	.37	.36	.38	.37	.36	.35	.052	4
5	.39	.37	.35	.39	.37	.35	.38	.36	.35	.37	.36	.34	.36	.35	.34	.34	.051	5
6	.37	.35	.33	.37	.35	.33	.36	.34	.33	.35	.34	.33	.35	.34	.32	.32	.049	6
7	.35	.33	.31	.35	.33	.31	.34	.33	.31	.34	.32	.31	.33	.32	.31	.30	.048	7
8	.34	.31	.30	.33	.31	.30	.33	.31	.30	.32	.31	.29	.32	.31	.29	.29	.046	8
9	.32	.30	.28	.32	.30	.28	.31	.30	.28	.31	.29	.28	.31	.29	.28	.28	.045	9
10	.31	.28	.27	.31	.28	.27	.30	.28	.27	.30	.28	.27	.30	.28	.27	.26	.043	10

8 — Medium distribution unit with lens plate and inside frost lamp — Maint. Cat. V, SC 1.0, 0%↑, 54½%↓

RCR	80 (50)	80 (30)	80 (10)	70 (50)	70 (30)	70 (10)	50 (50)	50 (30)	50 (10)	30 (50)	30 (30)	30 (10)	10 (50)	10 (30)	10 (10)	0	WDRC	RCR
0	.65	.65	.65	.63	.63	.63	.60	.60	.60	.58	.58	.58	.55	.55	.55	.54		0
1	.59	.57	.56	.58	.56	.55	.56	.54	.53	.53	.52	.52	.52	.51	.50	.49	.133	1
2	.54	.51	.49	.53	.50	.48	.51	.49	.47	.49	.47	.46	.48	.46	.45	.44	.130	2
3	.49	.46	.43	.48	.45	.43	.47	.44	.42	.45	.43	.41	.44	.42	.41	.40	.123	3
4	.45	.41	.38	.44	.41	.38	.43	.40	.38	.42	.39	.37	.41	.39	.37	.36	.116	4
5	.41	.37	.35	.41	.37	.34	.40	.36	.34	.39	.36	.34	.38	.35	.33	.32	.109	5
6	.38	.34	.31	.38	.34	.31	.37	.33	.31	.36	.33	.31	.35	.33	.31	.30	.103	6
7	.35	.31	.29	.35	.31	.29	.34	.31	.28	.33	.30	.28	.33	.30	.28	.27	.097	7
8	.33	.29	.26	.32	.29	.26	.32	.28	.26	.31	.28	.26	.31	.28	.26	.25	.092	8
9	.31	.27	.24	.30	.27	.24	.30	.26	.24	.29	.26	.24	.29	.26	.24	.23	.087	9
10	.29	.25	.22	.28	.25	.22	.28	.25	.22	.27	.24	.22	.27	.24	.22	.21	.082	10

9 — Recessed baffled downlight, 140 mm (5½″) diameter aperture—150-PAR/FL lamp — Maint. Cat. IV, SC 0.5, 0%↑, 68½%↓

RCR	80 (50)	80 (30)	80 (10)	70 (50)	70 (30)	70 (10)	50 (50)	50 (30)	50 (10)	30 (50)	30 (30)	30 (10)	10 (50)	10 (30)	10 (10)	0	WDRC	RCR
0	.82	.82	.82	.80	.80	.80	.76	.76	.76	.73	.73	.73	.70	.70	.70	.69		0
1	.78	.77	.75	.76	.75	.74	.74	.73	.72	.71	.70	.70	.69	.68	.68	.67	.051	1
2	.74	.72	.71	.73	.71	.70	.71	.70	.68	.69	.68	.67	.67	.66	.66	.65	.050	2
3	.71	.69	.67	.71	.68	.67	.69	.67	.66	.67	.66	.65	.66	.65	.64	.63	.049	3
4	.69	.66	.64	.68	.66	.64	.67	.65	.63	.66	.64	.63	.64	.63	.62	.61	.048	4
5	.67	.64	.62	.66	.63	.62	.65	.63	.61	.64	.62	.61	.63	.61	.60	.59	.047	5
6	.64	.62	.60	.64	.61	.60	.63	.61	.59	.62	.60	.59	.61	.60	.59	.58	.045	6
7	.63	.60	.58	.62	.60	.58	.61	.59	.57	.61	.59	.57	.60	.58	.57	.56	.044	7
8	.61	.58	.56	.60	.58	.56	.60	.58	.56	.59	.57	.56	.59	.57	.56	.55	.043	8
9	.59	.56	.55	.59	.56	.55	.58	.56	.54	.58	.56	.54	.57	.55	.54	.54	.042	9
10	.58	.55	.53	.57	.55	.53	.57	.55	.53	.56	.54	.53	.56	.54	.53	.52	.041	10

10 — Recessed baffled downlight, 140 mm (5½″) diameter aperture—75ER30 lamp — Maint. Cat. IV, SC 0.5, 0%↑, 85%↓

RCR	80 (50)	80 (30)	80 (10)	70 (50)	70 (30)	70 (10)	50 (50)	50 (30)	50 (10)	30 (50)	30 (30)	30 (10)	10 (50)	10 (30)	10 (10)	0	WDRC	RCR
0	1.01	1.01	1.01	.99	.99	.99	.95	.95	.95	.91	.91	.91	.87	.87	.87	.85		0
1	.96	.94	.93	.94	.93	.91	.91	.89	.88	.88	.87	.86	.85	.84	.83	.82	.085	1
2	.91	.88	.86	.90	.87	.85	.87	.85	.83	.84	.83	.81	.82	.81	.80	.79	.084	2
3	.87	.83	.81	.86	.83	.80	.83	.81	.79	.81	.79	.78	.80	.78	.77	.75	.082	3
4	.83	.79	.76	.82	.79	.76	.80	.77	.75	.79	.76	.74	.77	.75	.73	.72	.080	4
5	.79	.76	.73	.79	.75	.72	.77	.74	.72	.76	.73	.71	.75	.72	.71	.70	.078	5
6	.76	.72	.70	.76	.72	.69	.74	.71	.69	.73	.71	.68	.72	.70	.68	.67	.076	6
7	.73	.69	.67	.73	.69	.67	.72	.69	.66	.71	.68	.66	.70	.68	.66	.65	.073	7
8	.71	.67	.64	.70	.67	.64	.69	.66	.64	.69	.66	.64	.68	.65	.63	.62	.071	8
9	.68	.64	.62	.68	.64	.62	.67	.64	.62	.66	.63	.61	.66	.63	.61	.60	.069	9
10	.66	.62	.60	.66	.62	.60	.65	.62	.59	.64	.61	.59	.64	.61	.59	.58	.067	10

11 — Wide distribution unit with lens plate and inside frost lamp — Maint. Cat. V, SC 1.4, 0%↑, 53½%↓

RCR	80 (50)	80 (30)	80 (10)	70 (50)	70 (30)	70 (10)	50 (50)	50 (30)	50 (10)	30 (50)	30 (30)	30 (10)	10 (50)	10 (30)	10 (10)	0	WDRC	RCR
0	.63	.63	.63	.62	.62	.62	.59	.59	.59	.57	.57	.57	.54	.54	.54	.53		0
1	.57	.55	.54	.56	.54	.53	.54	.52	.51	.52	.51	.50	.50	.49	.48	.47	.153	1
2	.51	.48	.46	.50	.48	.45	.48	.46	.44	.47	.45	.43	.45	.44	.42	.41	.150	2
3	.46	.42	.40	.45	.42	.39	.44	.41	.39	.42	.40	.38	.41	.39	.37	.36	.142	3
4	.42	.38	.35	.41	.37	.34	.40	.36	.34	.39	.36	.33	.37	.35	.33	.32	.133	4
5	.38	.34	.30	.37	.33	.30	.36	.33	.30	.35	.32	.30	.34	.32	.29	.28	.124	5
6	.34	.30	.27	.34	.30	.27	.33	.29	.27	.32	.29	.27	.31	.28	.26	.25	.117	6
7	.31	.27	.24	.31	.27	.24	.30	.27	.24	.29	.26	.24	.29	.26	.24	.23	.109	7
8	.29	.25	.22	.28	.24	.22	.28	.24	.22	.27	.24	.22	.27	.24	.21	.20	.103	8
9	.26	.22	.20	.26	.22	.20	.26	.22	.20	.25	.22	.20	.25	.22	.19	.19	.097	9
10	.24	.21	.18	.24	.20	.18	.24	.20	.18	.23	.20	.18	.23	.20	.18	.17	.091	10

12 — Recessed unit with dropped diffusing glass — Maint. Cat. V, SC 1.3, 1½%↑, 50½%↓

RCR	80 (50)	80 (30)	80 (10)	70 (50)	70 (30)	70 (10)	50 (50)	50 (30)	50 (10)	30 (50)	30 (30)	30 (10)	10 (50)	10 (30)	10 (10)	0	WDRC	RCR
0	.62	.62	.62	.60	.60	.60	.57	.57	.57	.54	.54	.54	.52	.52	.52	.51		0
1	.52	.50	.48	.51	.49	.47	.49	.47	.45	.46	.45	.43	.44	.43	.42	.40	.256	1
2	.45	.41	.38	.44	.40	.37	.42	.39	.36	.40	.37	.35	.38	.36	.34	.33	.222	2
3	.39	.35	.31	.38	.34	.31	.37	.33	.30	.35	.32	.29	.33	.31	.28	.27	.195	3
4	.35	.30	.26	.34	.29	.26	.32	.28	.25	.31	.27	.25	.29	.27	.24	.23	.173	4
5	.31	.26	.22	.30	.25	.22	.29	.25	.22	.28	.24	.21	.26	.23	.21	.20	.154	5
6	.28	.23	.19	.27	.22	.19	.26	.22	.19	.25	.21	.19	.24	.21	.18	.17	.139	6
7	.25	.20	.17	.24	.20	.17	.24	.20	.17	.23	.19	.16	.22	.19	.16	.15	.127	7
8	.23	.18	.15	.22	.18	.15	.22	.18	.15	.21	.17	.15	.20	.17	.14	.13	.116	8
9	.21	.16	.14	.21	.16	.13	.20	.16	.13	.19	.16	.13	.18	.15	.13	.12	.107	9
10	.19	.15	.12	.19	.15	.12	.18	.15	.12	.18	.14	.12	.17	.14	.12	.11	.099	10

Coefficients of Utilization for 20 Per Cent Effective Floor Cavity Reflectance (ρFC = 20)

* Also, reflector downlight with baffles and inside frosted lamp.

Fig. 9-34. *Continued*

80			70			50			30			10			80			70			50			30			10		
50	30	10	50	30	10	50	30	10	50	30	10	50	30	10	50	30	10	50	30	10	50	30	10	50	30	10	50	30	10
Wall Exitance Coefficients for 20 Per Cent Effective Floor Cavity Reflectance (ρ_{FC} = 20)															Ceiling Cavity Exitance Coefficients for 20 Per Cent Floor Cavity Reflectance (ρ_{FC} = 20)														
															.083	.083	.083	.071	.071	.071	.048	.048	.048	.028	.028	.028	.009	.009	.009
.069	.039	.012	.066	.038	.012	.061	.035	.011	.056	.032	.010	.051	.030	.010	.074	.069	.064	.063	.059	.055	.043	.041	.038	.025	.023	.022	.008	.008	.007
.065	.036	.011	.063	.035	.011	.058	.032	.010	.054	.030	.010	.050	.028	.009	.067	.058	.050	.057	.050	.043	.039	.034	.030	.023	.020	.018	.007	.006	.006
.062	.033	.010	.060	.032	.010	.056	.030	.009	.052	.029	.009	.049	.027	.008	.061	.050	.040	.052	.043	.035	.036	.030	.025	.021	.017	.014	.007	.006	.005
.059	.031	.009	.057	.030	.009	.054	.028	.009	.051	.027	.008	.048	.026	.008	.056	.043	.033	.048	.037	.029	.033	.026	.020	.019	.015	.012	.006	.005	.004
.056	.029	.008	.054	.028	.008	.052	.027	.008	.049	.026	.008	.046	.025	.007	.052	.038	.027	.045	.033	.024	.031	.023	.017	.018	.013	.010	.006	.004	.003
.053	.027	.008	.052	.026	.008	.050	.025	.007	.047	.025	.007	.045	.024	.007	.049	.034	.023	.042	.029	.020	.029	.020	.014	.017	.012	.008	.005	.004	.003
.051	.025	.007	.050	.025	.007	.048	.024	.007	.046	.023	.007	.044	.023	.007	.046	.030	.019	.039	.026	.017	.027	.018	.012	.016	.011	.007	.005	.004	.002
.049	.024	.007	.048	.024	.007	.046	.023	.007	.044	.022	.006	.043	.022	.006	.043	.027	.017	.037	.024	.014	.026	.017	.010	.015	.010	.006	.005	.003	.002
.047	.023	.006	.046	.023	.006	.044	.022	.006	.043	.021	.006	.041	.021	.006	.041	.025	.014	.035	.022	.013	.024	.015	.009	.014	.009	.005	.005	.003	.002
.045	.022	.006	.045	.022	.006	.043	.021	.006	.041	.021	.006	.040	.020	.006	.039	.023	.013	.034	.020	.011	.023	.014	.008	.014	.008	.005	.004	.003	.002
															.104	.104	.104	.088	.088	.088	.060	.060	.060	.035	.035	.035	.011	.011	.011
.121	.069	.022	.117	.067	.021	.110	.063	.020	.104	.060	.019	.098	.057	.018	.095	.085	.077	.081	.073	.066	.055	.050	.046	.032	.029	.027	.010	.009	.009
.116	.063	.019	.113	.062	.019	.107	.059	.018	.101	.057	.018	.096	.054	.017	.088	.072	.058	.075	.062	.051	.052	.043	.035	.030	.025	.021	.010	.008	.007
.110	.058	.017	.107	.057	.017	.102	.055	.017	.097	.053	.016	.092	.051	.016	.082	.062	.046	.070	.053	.040	.048	.037	.028	.028	.022	.016	.009	.007	.005
.103	.054	.016	.101	.053	.016	.097	.051	.015	.092	.050	.015	.088	.048	.015	.077	.054	.036	.066	.047	.032	.046	.033	.022	.026	.019	.013	.008	.006	.004
.098	.050	.014	.096	.049	.014	.092	.048	.014	.088	.046	.014	.084	.045	.014	.073	.048	.030	.063	.042	.026	.043	.029	.018	.025	.017	.011	.008	.006	.004
.092	.046	.013	.091	.046	.013	.087	.045	.013	.084	.043	.013	.081	.042	.013	.069	.043	.025	.060	.038	.021	.041	.026	.015	.024	.015	.009	.008	.005	.003
.088	.043	.012	.086	.043	.012	.083	.042	.012	.080	.041	.012	.077	.040	.012	.066	.039	.021	.057	.034	.018	.039	.024	.013	.023	.014	.008	.007	.005	.003
.083	.041	.011	.082	.040	.011	.079	.039	.011	.076	.039	.011	.074	.038	.011	.063	.036	.018	.054	.031	.016	.037	.022	.011	.022	.013	.007	.007	.004	.002
.079	.038	.011	.078	.038	.011	.075	.037	.011	.073	.036	.010	.070	.036	.010	.060	.033	.016	.052	.029	.014	.036	.020	.010	.021	.012	.006	.007	.004	.002
.075	.036	.010	.074	.036	.010	.072	.035	.010	.069	.035	.010	.067	.034	.010	.057	.031	.014	.049	.027	.012	.034	.019	.008	.020	.011	.005	.006	.004	.002
															.131	.131	.131	.112	.112	.112	.076	.076	.076	.044	.044	.044	.014	.014	.014
.090	.051	.016	.086	.049	.016	.077	.044	.014	.069	.040	.013	.062	.036	.012	.115	.108	.102	.099	.093	.088	.068	.064	.061	.039	.037	.035	.012	.012	.011
.083	.046	.014	.079	.044	.013	.072	.040	.013	.066	.037	.012	.060	.034	.011	.103	.091	.082	.088	.078	.070	.060	.054	.049	.035	.032	.029	.011	.010	.009
.077	.041	.012	.074	.040	.012	.068	.037	.011	.063	.034	.011	.058	.032	.010	.092	.078	.066	.079	.067	.058	.054	.047	.040	.031	.027	.024	.010	.009	.008
.072	.038	.011	.070	.036	.011	.065	.034	.010	.060	.032	.010	.056	.030	.009	.083	.067	.055	.072	.058	.048	.049	.040	.034	.028	.024	.020	.009	.008	.007
.068	.035	.010	.066	.034	.010	.062	.032	.009	.058	.030	.009	.054	.029	.009	.076	.059	.046	.065	.051	.040	.045	.035	.028	.026	.021	.017	.008	.007	.006
.064	.032	.009	.062	.031	.009	.059	.030	.009	.055	.029	.008	.052	.028	.008	.070	.052	.039	.060	.045	.034	.041	.031	.024	.024	.018	.014	.008	.006	.005
.061	.030	.009	.059	.030	.008	.056	.028	.008	.053	.027	.008	.051	.026	.008	.064	.046	.033	.055	.040	.029	.038	.028	.020	.022	.016	.012	.007	.005	.004
.058	.028	.008	.057	.028	.008	.054	.027	.008	.052	.026	.008	.049	.025	.007	.060	.041	.029	.052	.036	.025	.036	.025	.018	.021	.015	.011	.007	.005	.003
.056	.027	.008	.054	.026	.007	.052	.026	.007	.050	.025	.007	.048	.024	.007	.056	.037	.025	.048	.032	.022	.033	.023	.015	.019	.013	.009	.006	.004	.003
.053	.026	.007	.052	.025	.007	.050	.025	.007	.048	.024	.007	.046	.023	.007	.053	.034	.022	.045	.030	.019	.032	.021	.014	.018	.012	.008	.006	.004	.003
															.162	.162	.162	.139	.139	.139	.095	.095	.095	.054	.054	.054	.017	.017	.017
.123	.070	.022	.117	.067	.021	.107	.061	.020	.097	.056	.018	.088	.051	.016	.144	.134	.126	.123	.115	.108	.084	.079	.075	.048	.046	.043	.016	.015	.014
.115	.063	.019	.110	.061	.019	.102	.057	.018	.094	.053	.016	.086	.049	.015	.129	.113	.100	.110	.097	.086	.076	.067	.060	.044	.039	.035	.014	.013	.011
.108	.058	.017	.104	.056	.017	.097	.052	.016	.090	.049	.015	.084	.046	.014	.117	.097	.081	.100	.083	.070	.069	.058	.049	.040	.034	.029	.013	.011	.009
.102	.053	.016	.099	.052	.015	.092	.049	.015	.087	.046	.014	.081	.044	.013	.106	.084	.066	.091	.072	.057	.063	.050	.040	.036	.029	.024	.012	.010	.008
.096	.049	.014	.094	.048	.014	.088	.046	.014	.083	.044	.013	.079	.042	.013	.098	.073	.055	.084	.063	.048	.058	.044	.034	.034	.026	.020	.011	.008	.007
.092	.046	.013	.089	.045	.013	.085	.043	.013	.080	.042	.012	.076	.040	.012	.091	.065	.046	.078	.056	.040	.054	.039	.029	.031	.023	.017	.010	.008	.006
.087	.043	.012	.085	.042	.012	.081	.041	.012	.077	.040	.012	.074	.038	.011	.084	.058	.039	.073	.050	.034	.050	.035	.024	.029	.021	.015	.009	.007	.005
.084	.041	.011	.082	.040	.011	.078	.039	.011	.075	.038	.011	.072	.037	.011	.079	.052	.034	.068	.045	.030	.047	.032	.021	.027	.019	.013	.009	.006	.004
.080	.039	.011	.078	.038	.011	.075	.037	.011	.072	.036	.010	.069	.035	.010	.074	.048	.030	.064	.041	.026	.044	.029	.018	.026	.017	.011	.008	.006	.004
.077	.037	.010	.075	.036	.010	.072	.036	.010	.070	.035	.010	.067	.034	.010	.070	.044	.026	.061	.038	.023	.042	.027	.016	.025	.016	.010	.008	.005	.003
															.101	.101	.101	.087	.087	.087	.059	.059	.059	.034	.034	.034	.011	.011	.011
.131	.074	.024	.127	.072	.023	.120	.069	.022	.114	.066	.021	.108	.062	.020	.094	.084	.074	.080	.072	.064	.055	.049	.044	.032	.029	.026	.010	.009	.008
.126	.069	.021	.123	.068	.021	.117	.065	.020	.111	.062	.020	.106	.060	.019	.088	.070	.050	.075	.061	.048	.062	.042	.034	.030	.024	.020	.010	.008	.006
.119	.064	.019	.117	.062	.019	.111	.060	.018	.107	.058	.018	.102	.057	.017	.083	.061	.043	.071	.052	.037	.049	.036	.026	.028	.021	.015	.009	.007	.005
.113	.059	.017	.110	.058	.017	.106	.056	.017	.101	.054	.016	.097	.053	.016	.079	.053	.034	.067	.046	.030	.046	.032	.021	.027	.019	.012	.009	.006	.004
.106	.054	.016	.104	.053	.016	.100	.052	.015	.096	.051	.015	.093	.050	.015	.075	.048	.028	.064	.041	.024	.044	.029	.017	.026	.017	.010	.008	.006	.003
.100	.050	.014	.098	.050	.014	.095	.049	.014	.091	.047	.014	.088	.046	.014	.071	.043	.023	.061	.037	.020	.042	.026	.014	.024	.015	.008	.008	.005	.003
.095	.047	.013	.093	.046	.013	.090	.045	.013	.087	.044	.013	.084	.044	.013	.068	.039	.019	.058	.034	.017	.040	.024	.012	.023	.014	.007	.008	.005	.002
.090	.044	.012	.088	.043	.012	.085	.043	.012	.082	.042	.012	.080	.041	.012	.065	.036	.016	.056	.031	.014	.039	.022	.010	.022	.013	.006	.007	.004	.002
.085	.041	.011	.083	.041	.011	.081	.040	.011	.078	.039	.011	.076	.039	.011	.062	.034	.014	.053	.029	.013	.037	.020	.009	.022	.012	.005	.007	.004	.002
.081	.039	.011	.079	.038	.011	.077	.038	.011	.075	.037	.011	.073	.037	.010	.059	.031	.013	.051	.027	.011	.035	.019	.008	.021	.011	.005	.007	.004	.002
															.112	.112	.112	.095	.095	.095	.065	.065	.065	.037	.037	.037	.012	.012	.012
.187	.106	.034	.182	.104	.033	.174	.100	.032	.167	.096	.031	.160	.093	.030	.108	.094	.080	.092	.080	.069	.063	.055	.048	.036	.032	.028	.012	.010	.009
.168	.092	.028	.164	.090	.028	.157	.087	.027	.150	.084	.026	.144	.082	.026	.104	.081	.062	.089	.070	.053	.061	.048	.037	.035	.028	.022	.011	.009	.007
.151	.081	.024	.148	.079	.024	.142	.077	.023	.136	.074	.023	.130	.072	.022	.100	.072	.050	.086	.062	.043	.059	.043	.030	.034	.025	.018	.011	.008	.006
.138	.072	.021	.135	.070	.021	.129	.068	.020	.124	.066	.020	.119	.065	.020	.096	.065	.042	.083	.057	.036	.057	.039	.026	.033	.023	.015	.011	.008	.005
.126	.064	.019	.123	.063	.018	.118	.062	.018	.113	.060	.018	.109	.058	.018	.092	.060	.036	.079	.052	.032	.055	.036	.022	.032	.021	.013	.010	.007	.004
.116	.058	.017	.113	.057	.016	.109	.056	.016	.105	.054	.016	.101	.053	.016	.088	.056	.032	.076	.048	.028	.052	.034	.020	.030	.020	.012	.010	.007	.004
.107	.053	.015	.105	.052	.015	.101	.051	.015	.097	.050	.014	.094	.049	.014	.085	.052	.030	.073	.045	.026	.050	.032	.018	.029	.019	.011	.009	.006	.004
.100	.049	.014	.098	.048	.014	.094	.047	.013	.091	.046	.013	.087	.045	.013	.081	.049	.027	.070	.043	.024	.048	.030	.017	.028	.018	.010	.009	.006	.003
.093	.045	.013	.091	.044	.012	.088	.043	.012	.085	.043	.012	.082	.042	.012	.078	.047	.026	.067	.040	.022	.046	.028	.016	.027	.017	.009	.009	.006	.003
.087	.042	.012	.086	.041	.012	.083	.040	.011	.080	.040	.011	.077	.039	.011	.075	.044	.024	.064	.039	.021	.045	.027	.015	.026	.016	.009	.008	.005	.003

Fig. 9-34. *Continued*

Typical Luminaire	Maint. Cat.	SC	RCR ↓	80 / 50	80 / 30	80 / 10	70 / 50	70 / 30	70 / 10	50 / 50	50 / 30	50 / 10	30 / 50	30 / 30	30 / 10	10 / 50	10 / 30	10 / 10	0	WDRC
13 Bilateral batwing distribution—clear HID with dropped prismatic lens (2½% ↑, 71% ↓)	V	N.A.	0	.87	.87	87	.85	.85	.85	.80	.80	.80	.76	.76	.76	.73	.73	.73	.71	
			1	.75	.72	.69	.73	.70	.68	.70	.67	.65	.66	.64	.63	.63	.62	.60	.59	.312
			2	.66	.60	.56	.64	.59	.55	.61	.57	.54	.58	.55	.52	.56	.53	.51	.49	.279
			3	.58	.51	.47	.56	.51	.46	.54	.49	.45	.51	.47	.44	.49	.46	.43	.41	.251
			4	.51	.44	.39	.50	.44	.39	.48	.42	.38	.46	.41	.37	.44	.40	.37	.35	.226
			5	.45	.39	.34	.44	.38	.33	.42	.37	.33	.41	.36	.32	.39	.35	.32	.30	.206
			6	.41	.34	.29	.40	.33	.29	.38	.33	.28	.37	.32	.28	.35	.31	.28	.26	.188
			7	.37	.30	.26	.36	.30	.25	.35	.29	.25	.33	.28	.25	.32	.28	.24	.23	.173
			8	.33	.27	.23	.33	.27	.23	.31	.26	.22	.30	.25	.22	.29	.25	.22	.20	.159
			9	.30	.24	.20	.30	.24	.20	.29	.23	.20	.28	.23	.19	.27	.22	.19	.18	.148
			10	.28	.22	.18	.27	.22	.18	.26	.21	.18	.26	.21	.17	.25	.20	.17	.16	.138
14 Clear HID lamp and glass refractor above plastic lens panel (0% ↑, 66% ↓)	V	1.3	0	.78	.78	.78	.77	.77	.77	.73	.73	.73	.70	.70	.70	.67	.67	.67	.66	
			1	.71	.69	.67	.69	.67	.65	.67	.65	.63	.64	.63	.61	.62	.61	.60	.58	.188
			2	.64	.60	.57	.62	.59	.56	.60	.57	.55	.58	.56	.54	.56	.54	.53	.51	.183
			3	.57	.53	.49	.56	.52	.49	.54	.51	.48	.53	.50	.47	.51	.49	.46	.45	.173
			4	.52	.47	.43	.51	.46	.43	.49	.46	.42	.48	.45	.42	.47	.44	.41	.40	.161
			5	.47	.42	.38	.46	.42	.38	.45	.41	.38	.44	.40	.37	.43	.40	.37	.36	.151
			6	.43	.38	.34	.42	.38	.34	.41	.37	.34	.40	.36	.34	.39	.36	.33	.32	.141
			7	.39	.34	.31	.39	.34	.31	.38	.34	.30	.37	.33	.30	.36	.33	.30	.29	.132
			8	.36	.31	.28	.36	.31	.28	.35	.31	.28	.34	.30	.27	.34	.30	.27	.26	.124
			9	.34	.29	.25	.33	.28	.25	.32	.28	.25	.32	.28	.25	.31	.28	.25	.24	.117
			10	.31	.26	.23	.31	.26	.23	.30	.26	.23	.30	.26	.23	.29	.25	.23	.22	.110
15 Enclosed reflector with an incandescent lamp (0% ↑, 71½% ↓)	V	1.4	0	.85	.85	.85	.83	.83	.83	.80	.80	.80	.76	.76	.76	.73	.73	.73	.72	
			1	.77	.75	.73	.76	.74	.72	.73	.71	.69	.70	.69	.67	.67	.66	.65	.64	.189
			2	.70	.66	.63	.68	.65	.62	.66	.63	.60	.64	.61	.59	.61	.60	.58	.56	.190
			3	.63	.58	.54	.62	.57	.54	.60	.56	.53	.58	.54	.52	.56	.53	.51	.50	.183
			4	.56	.51	.47	.56	.51	.47	.54	.50	.46	.52	.49	.46	.51	.48	.45	.44	.174
			5	.51	.46	.42	.50	.45	.41	.49	.44	.41	.48	.44	.40	.46	.43	.40	.39	.164
			6	.46	.41	.37	.46	.41	.37	.45	.40	.36	.43	.39	.36	.42	.39	.36	.34	.155
			7	.42	.37	.33	.42	.37	.33	.41	.36	.33	.40	.36	.32	.39	.35	.32	.31	.146
			8	.39	.33	.30	.38	.33	.29	.37	.33	.29	.37	.32	.29	.36	.32	.29	.28	.137
			9	.36	.30	.27	.35	.30	.27	.35	.30	.27	.34	.30	.26	.33	.29	.26	.25	.129
			10	.33	.28	.24	.33	.28	.24	.32	.27	.24	.31	.27	.24	.31	.27	.24	.23	.122
16 "High bay" narrow distribution ventilated reflector with clear HID lamp (1½% ↑, 77% ↓)	III	0.7	0	.93	.93	.93	.90	.90	.90	.86	.86	.86	.82	.82	.82	.78	.78	.78	.77	
			1	.86	.84	.82	.84	.82	.80	.80	.79	.78	.77	.76	.75	.74	.74	.73	.71	.138
			2	.79	.76	.73	.78	.75	.72	.75	.73	.71	.73	.71	.69	.70	.69	.67	.66	.136
			3	.74	.70	.66	.73	.69	.66	.70	.67	.65	.68	.66	.63	.66	.64	.62	.61	.132
			4	.69	.64	.61	.68	.64	.60	.66	.62	.60	.64	.61	.59	.63	.60	.58	.57	.126
			5	.64	.60	.56	.63	.59	.56	.62	.58	.55	.60	.57	.55	.59	.56	.54	.53	.120
			6	.60	.55	.52	.60	.55	.52	.58	.54	.51	.57	.54	.51	.56	.53	.50	.49	.115
			7	.57	.52	.49	.56	.52	.48	.55	.51	.48	.54	.50	.48	.53	.50	.47	.46	.109
			8	.53	.49	.45	.53	.48	.45	.52	.48	.45	.51	.47	.45	.50	.47	.44	.43	.104
			9	.51	.46	.43	.50	.46	.43	.49	.45	.42	.48	.45	.42	.48	.44	.42	.41	.100
			10	.48	.43	.40	.48	.43	.40	.47	.43	.40	.46	.42	.40	.45	.42	.40	.39	.095
17 "High bay" intermediate distribution ventilated reflector with clear HID lamp (1% ↑, 76% ↓)	III	1.0	0	.91	.91	.91	.89	.89	.89	.85	.85	.85	.81	.81	.81	.78	.78	.78	.76	
			1	.83	.81	.79	.81	.79	.77	.78	.76	.75	.75	.74	.72	.72	.71	.70	.68	.187
			2	.75	.71	.68	.74	.70	.67	.71	.68	.65	.68	.66	.64	.66	.64	.62	.61	.189
			3	.68	.63	.59	.67	.62	.59	.65	.61	.58	.62	.59	.57	.61	.58	.56	.54	.183
			4	.62	.56	.52	.61	.56	.52	.59	.54	.51	.57	.53	.50	.55	.52	.50	.48	.174
			5	.56	.50	.46	.55	.50	.46	.54	.49	.45	.52	.48	.45	.51	.47	.44	.43	.165
			6	.51	.46	.41	.51	.45	.41	.49	.44	.41	.48	.44	.40	.47	.43	.40	.39	.155
			7	.47	.41	.37	.47	.41	.37	.45	.40	.37	.44	.40	.37	.43	.39	.36	.35	.147
			8	.43	.38	.34	.43	.37	.34	.42	.37	.33	.41	.36	.33	.40	.36	.33	.32	.138
			9	.40	.35	.31	.40	.34	.31	.39	.34	.31	.38	.34	.30	.37	.33	.30	.29	.131
			10	.37	.32	.28	.37	.32	.28	.36	.31	.28	.35	.31	.28	.35	.31	.28	.27	.124
18 "High bay" wide distribution ventilated reflector with clear HID lamp (½% ↑, 77½% ↓)	III	1.5	0	.93	.93	.93	.91	.91	.91	.87	.87	.87	.83	.83	.83	.79	.79	.79	.78	
			1	.84	.81	.79	.82	.80	.78	.79	.77	.75	.76	.74	.73	.73	.72	.70	.69	.217
			2	.75	.71	.67	.74	.70	.66	.71	.68	.65	.68	.66	.63	.66	.64	.62	.60	.219
			3	.67	.62	.57	.66	.61	.57	.64	.59	.56	.61	.58	.55	.59	.56	.54	.52	.211
			4	.60	.54	.50	.59	.54	.49	.57	.52	.48	.55	.51	.48	.54	.50	.47	.46	.200
			5	.54	.48	.43	.53	.47	.43	.52	.46	.42	.50	.45	.42	.49	.45	.41	.40	.189
			6	.49	.42	.38	.48	.42	.38	.47	.41	.37	.45	.41	.37	.44	.40	.37	.35	.177
			7	.44	.38	.34	.44	.38	.33	.42	.37	.33	.41	.36	.33	.40	.36	.33	.31	.166
			8	.40	.34	.30	.40	.34	.30	.39	.33	.30	.38	.33	.29	.37	.32	.29	.28	.156
			9	.37	.31	.27	.37	.31	.27	.36	.30	.27	.35	.30	.26	.34	.29	.26	.25	.146
			10	.34	.28	.24	.34	.28	.24	.33	.28	.24	.32	.27	.24	.31	.27	.24	.22	.138

Notes on column headers: ρCC → 80, 70, 50, 30, 10, 0; ρW → 50 30 10 (for each ρCC except ρCC = 0 which has a single "0" column). Coefficients of Utilization for 20 Per Cent Effective Floor Cavity Reflectance (ρFC = 20).

Fig. 9-34. *Continued*

80			70			50			30			10			80			70			50			30			10		
50	30	10	50	30	10	50	30	10	50	30	10	50	30	10	50	30	10	50	30	10	50	30	10	50	30	10	50	30	10
Wall Exitance Coefficients for 20 Per Cent Effective Floor Cavity Reflectance (ρ_{FC} = 20)															Ceiling Cavity Exitance Coefficients for 20 Per Cent Floor Cavity Reflectance (ρ_{FC} = 20)														
															.159	.159	.159	.136	.136	.136	.093	.093	.093	.053	.053	.053	.017	.017	.017
.238	.135	.043	.232	.132	.042	.220	.126	.040	.210	.121	.039	.201	.116	.038	.152	.134	.117	.130	.115	.101	.089	.079	.070	.051	.046	.041	.016	.015	.013
.218	.119	.037	.212	.117	.036	.202	.113	.035	.193	.108	.034	.185	.105	.033	.146	.116	.091	.125	.100	.079	.086	.069	.055	.050	.040	.032	.016	.013	.010
.200	.106	.032	.195	.105	.031	.186	.101	.031	.178	.098	.030	.171	.095	.029	.141	.103	.074	.121	.089	.064	.083	.062	.045	.048	.036	.026	.015	.012	.009
.184	.096	.028	.180	.094	.028	.172	.091	.027	.165	.089	.027	.158	.086	.026	.135	.094	.062	.116	.081	.054	.080	.056	.038	.046	.033	.022	.015	.011	.007
.170	.087	.025	.167	.086	.025	.160	.083	.024	.153	.081	.024	.147	.079	.024	.130	.086	.054	.111	.075	.047	.077	.052	.033	.044	.031	.020	.014	.010	.006
.158	.079	.023	.155	.078	.023	.149	.076	.022	.143	.074	.022	.137	.072	.021	.125	.080	.048	.107	.069	.042	.074	.049	.030	.043	.029	.018	.014	.009	.006
.147	.073	.021	.144	.072	.021	.139	.070	.020	.133	.068	.020	.128	.067	.020	.120	.075	.044	.103	.065	.038	.071	.046	.027	.041	.027	.016	.013	.009	.005
.138	.067	.019	.135	.067	.019	.130	.065	.019	.125	.063	.018	.121	.062	.018	.115	.071	.041	.099	.061	.035	.068	.043	.025	.040	.025	.015	.013	.008	.005
.129	.063	.017	.127	.062	.017	.122	.060	.017	.118	.059	.017	.114	.058	.017	.111	.067	.038	.095	.058	.033	.066	.041	.024	.038	.024	.014	.012	.008	.005
.122	.058	.016	.119	.058	.016	.115	.056	.016	.111	.055	.016	.107	.054	.015	.106	.064	.036	.092	.056	.031	.064	.039	.022	.037	.023	.013	.012	.008	.004
															.126	.126	.126	.107	.107	.107	.073	.073	.073	.042	.042	.042	.013	.013	.013
.161	.091	.029	.156	.089	.028	.148	.085	.027	.140	.081	.026	.133	.077	.025	.116	.103	.092	.099	.089	.079	.068	.061	.055	.039	.035	.032	.013	.011	.010
.154	.085	.026	.151	.083	.026	.143	.080	.025	.136	.077	.024	.130	.074	.023	.109	.087	.069	.093	.075	.060	.064	.052	.042	.037	.030	.024	.012	.010	.008
.146	.078	.023	.143	.076	.023	.136	.074	.022	.130	.071	.022	.125	.069	.021	.102	.075	.054	.088	.065	.046	.060	.045	.033	.035	.026	.019	.011	.009	.006
.138	.072	.021	.135	.070	.021	.129	.068	.020	.124	.066	.020	.119	.065	.020	.097	.066	.042	.083	.057	.037	.057	.040	.026	.033	.023	.015	.011	.008	.005
.130	.066	.019	.127	.065	.019	.122	.063	.019	.117	.062	.018	.113	.060	.018	.092	.059	.034	.079	.051	.030	.054	.036	.021	.032	.021	.013	.010	.007	.004
.122	.061	.018	.120	.061	.017	.115	.059	.017	.111	.058	.017	.107	.056	.017	.087	.053	.028	.075	.046	.025	.052	.032	.018	.030	.019	.010	.010	.006	.003
.115	.057	.016	.113	.056	.016	.109	.055	.016	.106	.054	.016	.102	.053	.016	.083	.048	.024	.072	.042	.021	.050	.029	.015	.029	.017	.009	.009	.006	.003
.109	.053	.015	.107	.053	.015	.104	.052	.015	.100	.051	.015	.097	.050	.015	.080	.045	.021	.068	.039	.018	.047	.027	.013	.028	.016	.008	.009	.005	.003
.103	.050	.014	.102	.050	.014	.098	.049	.014	.095	.048	.014	.093	.047	.014	.076	.041	.018	.065	.036	.016	.045	.025	.011	.026	.015	.007	.009	.005	.002
.098	.047	.013	.097	.047	.013	.094	.046	.013	.091	.045	.013	.088	.044	.013	.073	.039	.016	.063	.033	.014	.043	.024	.010	.025	.014	.006	.008	.005	.002
															.137	.137	.137	.117	.117	.117	.080	.080	.080	.046	.046	.046	.015	.015	.015
.167	.095	.030	.162	.092	.029	.152	.087	.028	.144	.083	.027	.136	.079	.025	.126	.113	.102	.108	.097	.087	.074	.067	.060	.043	.039	.035	.014	.012	.011
.163	.089	.027	.159	.088	.027	.151	.084	.026	.143	.080	.025	.137	.077	.024	.118	.096	.077	.101	.082	.066	.069	.057	.046	.040	.033	.027	.013	.011	.009
.157	.083	.025	.153	.082	.025	.146	.079	.024	.139	.076	.023	.133	.074	.023	.112	.083	.059	.096	.071	.051	.066	.049	.036	.038	.029	.021	.012	.009	.007
.149	.077	.023	.146	.076	.023	.139	.074	.022	.134	.072	.022	.128	.070	.021	.106	.073	.047	.091	.063	.041	.063	.044	.029	.036	.026	.017	.012	.008	.006
.141	.072	.021	.138	.071	.021	.133	.069	.020	.128	.067	.020	.123	.066	.020	.101	.065	.038	.087	.056	.033	.060	.039	.023	.035	.023	.014	.011	.008	.005
.134	.067	.019	.131	.066	.019	.126	.065	.019	.122	.063	.019	.117	.062	.018	.096	.059	.032	.083	.051	.028	.057	.036	.020	.033	.021	.012	.011	.007	.004
.127	.063	.018	.124	.062	.018	.120	.061	.017	.116	.059	.017	.112	.058	.017	.092	.054	.027	.079	.047	.023	.055	.033	.017	.032	.019	.010	.010	.006	.003
.120	.059	.016	.118	.058	.016	.114	.057	.016	.110	.056	.016	.107	.055	.016	.088	.049	.023	.076	.043	.020	.052	.030	.014	.030	.018	.009	.010	.006	.003
.114	.055	.015	.112	.055	.015	.108	.054	.015	.105	.053	.015	.102	.052	.015	.084	.046	.020	.072	.040	.018	.050	.028	.013	.029	.017	.007	.009	.005	.002
.108	.052	.014	.106	.051	.014	.103	.051	.014	.100	.050	.014	.097	.049	.014	.081	.043	.018	.069	.037	.016	.048	.026	.011	.028	.016	.007	.009	.005	.002
															.158	.158	.158	.135	.135	.135	.092	.092	.092	.053	.053	.053	.017	.017	.017
.147	.084	.026	.141	.081	.026	.131	.075	.024	.121	.070	.022	.112	.065	.021	.144	.133	.122	.123	.114	.105	.084	.078	.073	.049	.045	.042	.016	.015	.014
.140	.077	.024	.136	.075	.023	.127	.070	.022	.118	.066	.021	.111	.063	.020	.133	.113	.097	.114	.097	.084	.078	.067	.058	.045	.039	.034	.014	.013	.011
.133	.071	.021	.129	.069	.021	.121	.066	.020	.114	.063	.019	.107	.059	.018	.123	.099	.079	.106	.085	.068	.073	.059	.048	.042	.035	.028	.013	.011	.009
.126	.066	.019	.123	.064	.019	.116	.061	.018	.110	.059	.018	.104	.056	.017	.116	.087	.066	.099	.075	.057	.068	.053	.040	.039	.031	.024	.013	.010	.008
.120	.061	.018	.117	.060	.017	.111	.058	.017	.105	.055	.016	.100	.053	.016	.109	.078	.056	.094	.068	.049	.064	.047	.034	.037	.028	.020	.012	.009	.007
.114	.057	.016	.111	.056	.016	.106	.054	.016	.101	.052	.015	.096	.051	.015	.103	.071	.048	.089	.062	.042	.061	.043	.030	.035	.025	.018	.011	.008	.006
.108	.053	.015	.106	.053	.015	.101	.051	.015	.097	.050	.014	.092	.048	.014	.098	.065	.042	.084	.057	.037	.058	.040	.026	.034	.023	.016	.011	.008	.005
.103	.050	.014	.101	.050	.014	.097	.048	.014	.093	.047	.014	.089	.046	.013	.093	.060	.038	.080	.052	.033	.056	.037	.023	.032	.022	.014	.010	.007	.005
.098	.048	.013	.096	.047	.013	.093	.046	.013	.089	.045	.013	.086	.043	.013	.089	.056	.034	.077	.049	.030	.053	.034	.021	.031	.020	.013	.010	.007	.004
.094	.045	.013	.092	.045	.012	.089	.043	.012	.086	.042	.012	.082	.041	.012	.086	.053	.031	.074	.046	.027	.051	.032	.019	.030	.019	.012	.010	.006	.004
															.153	.153	.153	.131	.131	.131	.089	.089	.089	.051	.051	.051	.016	.016	.016
.171	.098	.031	.166	.095	.030	.156	.089	.029	.146	.084	.027	.137	.080	.026	.140	.127	.115	.120	.109	.099	.082	.075	.068	.047	.043	.040	.015	.014	.013
.168	.092	.028	.163	.090	.028	.154	.086	.027	.146	.082	.026	.138	.078	.025	.131	.108	.089	.113	.093	.077	.077	.064	.053	.044	.037	.031	.014	.012	.010
.161	.086	.026	.157	.084	.025	.149	.081	.025	.142	.078	.024	.135	.075	.023	.124	.094	.070	.106	.081	.061	.073	.056	.043	.042	.033	.025	.014	.011	.008
.153	.080	.023	.149	.078	.023	.143	.076	.023	.136	.073	.022	.130	.071	.022	.118	.083	.057	.101	.072	.050	.069	.050	.035	.040	.029	.021	.013	.010	.007
.145	.074	.021	.142	.073	.021	.136	.071	.021	.130	.069	.020	.125	.067	.020	.112	.075	.048	.096	.065	.041	.066	.045	.029	.038	.027	.017	.012	.009	.006
.138	.069	.020	.135	.068	.020	.129	.066	.019	.124	.065	.019	.120	.063	.019	.107	.068	.041	.092	.059	.035	.063	.041	.025	.037	.024	.015	.012	.008	.005
.131	.065	.018	.128	.064	.018	.123	.062	.018	.119	.061	.018	.114	.059	.017	.102	.063	.035	.088	.055	.031	.061	.038	.022	.035	.023	.013	.011	.007	.004
.124	.061	.017	.122	.060	.017	.117	.059	.017	.113	.057	.017	.109	.056	.016	.098	.058	.031	.084	.051	.027	.058	.036	.019	.034	.021	.012	.011	.007	.004
.118	.057	.016	.116	.056	.016	.112	.055	.016	.108	.054	.015	.104	.053	.015	.094	.055	.028	.081	.047	.024	.056	.033	.017	.033	.020	.010	.011	.006	.003
.112	.054	.015	.110	.053	.015	.106	.052	.015	.103	.051	.015	.100	.050	.014	.090	.051	.026	.078	.045	.022	.054	.031	.016	.031	.019	.009	.010	.006	.003
															.154	.154	.154	.132	.132	.132	.090	.090	.090	.052	.052	.052	.017	.017	.017
.188	.107	.034	.183	.104	.033	.172	.099	.032	.162	.094	.030	.154	.089	.029	.143	.128	.115	.122	.110	.099	.084	.076	.068	.048	.044	.040	.015	.014	.013
.186	.102	.031	.181	.100	.031	.172	.095	.030	.163	.092	.029	.155	.088	.028	.135	.109	.087	.115	.094	.076	.079	.065	.053	.046	.038	.031	.015	.012	.010
.178	.095	.028	.174	.093	.028	.166	.090	.027	.158	.087	.027	.152	.084	.026	.128	.095	.068	.110	.082	.059	.075	.057	.042	.043	.033	.024	.014	.011	.008
.170	.088	.026	.166	.087	.026	.159	.084	.025	.152	.082	.025	.146	.079	.024	.122	.084	.055	.105	.073	.048	.072	.051	.034	.042	.030	.020	.013	.010	.007
.161	.082	.024	.157	.081	.024	.151	.079	.023	.145	.076	.023	.139	.074	.022	.117	.076	.045	.100	.065	.039	.069	.046	.028	.040	.027	.017	.013	.009	.005
.152	.076	.022	.149	.075	.022	.143	.073	.021	.138	.072	.021	.133	.070	.021	.112	.069	.038	.096	.060	.033	.066	.042	.024	.038	.025	.014	.012	.008	.005
.143	.071	.020	.141	.070	.020	.136	.069	.020	.131	.067	.020	.126	.066	.019	.107	.064	.033	.092	.055	.029	.064	.039	.020	.037	.023	.012	.012	.007	.004
.136	.066	.019	.133	.066	.019	.129	.064	.018	.124	.063	.018	.120	.062	.018	.102	.059	.029	.088	.051	.026	.061	.036	.018	.036	.021	.011	.011	.007	.004
.128	.062	.017	.126	.062	.017	.122	.060	.017	.118	.059	.017	.1'4	.058	.017	.098	.055	.026	.085	.048	.023	.059	.034	.016	.034	.020	.010	.011	.007	.003
.122	.058	.016	.120	.058	.016	.116	.057	.016	.112	.056	.016	.109	.055	.016	.094	.052	.024	.081	.045	.021	.056	.032	.015	.033	.019	.009	.011	.006	.003

Fig. 9-34. *Continued*

Typical Luminaire			ρcc →	80			70			50			30			10			0	WDRC	ρcc →
	Maint. Cat.	SC	ρw →	50	30	10	50	30	10	50	30	10	50	30	10	50	30	10	0		ρw →
			RCR ↓	Coefficients of Utilization for 20 Per Cent Effective Floor Cavity Reflectance (ρFC = 20)																	RCR ↓
19 "High bay" intermediate distribution ventilated reflector with phosphor coated HID lamp	III 6½%↑ 75½%↓	1.0	0	.96	.96	.96	.93	.93	.93	.88	.88	.88	.83	.83	.83	.78	.78	.78	.76		0
			1	.88	.86	.83	.86	.83	.81	.81	.79	.78	.77	.75	.74	.73	.72	.71	.69	.167	1
			2	.80	.76	.73	.78	.74	.71	.74	.71	.69	.71	.68	.66	.68	.66	.64	.62	.168	2
			3	.73	.68	.64	.71	.67	.63	.68	.64	.61	.65	.62	.60	.63	.60	.58	.56	.162	3
			4	.67	.61	.57	.65	.60	.57	.63	.59	.55	.60	.57	.54	.58	.55	.52	.51	.155	4
			5	.61	.56	.52	.60	.55	.51	.58	.53	.50	.56	.52	.49	.54	.50	.48	.46	.147	5
			6	.57	.51	.47	.56	.50	.46	.54	.49	.45	.52	.48	.45	.50	.46	.44	.42	.139	6
			7	.52	.47	.43	.51	.46	.42	.50	.45	.42	.48	.44	.41	.47	.43	.40	.39	.132	7
			8	.49	.43	.39	.48	.42	.39	.46	.42	.38	.45	.41	.38	.44	.40	.37	.36	.125	8
			9	.45	.40	.36	.45	.39	.36	.43	.39	.35	.42	.38	.35	.41	.37	.34	.33	.118	9
			10	.42	.37	.33	.42	.37	.33	.41	.36	.33	.39	.35	.32	.38	.35	.32	.31	.112	10
20 "High bay" wide distribution ventilated reflector with phosphor coated HID lamp	III 12%↑ 69%↓	1.5	0	.93	.93	.93	.90	.90	.90	.83	.83	.83	.77	.77	.77	.72	.72	.72	.69		0
			1	.85	.82	.80	.82	.79	.77	.76	.74	.73	.71	.70	.69	.66	.65	.65	.62	.168	1
			2	.76	.72	.69	.74	.70	.67	.69	.66	.64	.65	.63	.61	.61	.59	.58	.56	.168	2
			3	.69	.64	.60	.67	.62	.59	.63	.59	.56	.59	.56	.54	.56	.54	.51	.49	.163	3
			4	.62	.57	.52	.61	.55	.51	.57	.53	.50	.54	.51	.48	.51	.48	.46	.44	.156	4
			5	.57	.51	.46	.55	.50	.46	.52	.48	.44	.49	.46	.43	.47	.44	.41	.39	.148	5
			6	.52	.45	.41	.50	.45	.40	.48	.43	.39	.45	.41	.38	.43	.40	.37	.35	.141	6
			7	.47	.41	.37	.46	.40	.36	.44	.39	.35	.42	.37	.34	.40	.36	.33	.32	.133	7
			8	.43	.37	.33	.42	.36	.33	.40	.35	.32	.38	.34	.31	.37	.33	.30	.29	.126	8
			9	.40	.34	.30	.39	.33	.29	.37	.32	.29	.35	.31	.28	.34	.30	.27	.26	.120	9
			10	.37	.31	.27	.36	.30	.27	.34	.29	.26	.33	.28	.25	.31	.28	.25	.23	.114	10
21 "Low bay" rectangular pattern, lensed bottom reflector unit with clear HID lamp	V 0°▲ 68½°▼ 45° 11,⊥	1.8	0	.82	.82	.82	.80	.80	.80	.76	.76	.76	.73	.73	.73	.70	.70	.70	.68		0
			1	.73	.70	.68	.71	.69	.67	.68	.66	.64	.65	.64	.62	.63	.62	.61	.59	.231	1
			2	.64	.60	.56	.63	.59	.55	.60	.57	.54	.58	.55	.53	.56	.54	.52	.50	.227	2
			3	.56	.51	.47	.55	.51	.47	.53	.49	.46	.52	.48	.45	.50	.47	.44	.43	.213	3
			4	.50	.44	.40	.49	.44	.40	.48	.43	.39	.46	.42	.39	.44	.41	.38	.37	.199	4
			5	.45	.39	.34	.44	.38	.34	.42	.38	.34	.41	.37	.33	.40	.36	.33	.32	.184	5
			6	.40	.34	.30	.39	.34	.30	.38	.33	.29	.37	.33	.29	.36	.32	.29	.28	.171	6
			7	.36	.30	.26	.36	.30	.26	.35	.29	.26	.34	.29	.26	.33	.29	.25	.24	.159	7
			8	.33	.27	.23	.32	.27	.23	.31	.26	.23	.31	.26	.23	.30	.26	.23	.21	.148	8
			9	.30	.24	.20	.29	.24	.20	.29	.24	.20	.28	.23	.20	.27	.23	.20	.19	.138	9
			10	.27	.22	.18	.27	.22	.18	.26	.22	.18	.26	.21	.18	.25	.21	.18	.17	.129	10
22 "Low bay" lensed bottom reflector unit with clear HID lamp	V 3▲ 68▼	1.9	0	.83	.83	.83	.81	.81	.81	.77	.77	.77	.73	.73	.73	.70	.70	.70	.68		0
			1	.72	.69	.66	.70	.67	.65	.67	.64	.62	.63	.62	.60	.60	.59	.57	.56	.302	1
			2	.62	.57	.53	.61	.56	.52	.58	.54	.50	.55	.52	.49	.52	.50	.47	.46	.279	2
			3	.54	.48	.43	.53	.47	.43	.50	.45	.41	.48	.44	.40	.46	.42	.39	.38	.253	3
			4	.47	.41	.36	.46	.40	.35	.44	.39	.35	.42	.37	.34	.40	.36	.33	.31	.229	4
			5	.42	.35	.30	.41	.34	.30	.39	.33	.29	.37	.32	.29	.36	.31	.28	.26	.208	5
			6	.37	.30	.26	.36	.30	.25	.35	.29	.25	.33	.28	.25	.32	.27	.24	.23	.189	6
			7	.33	.27	.22	.33	.26	.22	.31	.26	.22	.30	.25	.21	.29	.24	.21	.19	.173	7
			8	.30	.24	.19	.29	.23	.19	.28	.23	.19	.27	.22	.19	.26	.22	.18	.17	.159	8
			9	.27	.21	.17	.26	.21	.17	.26	.20	.17	.25	.20	.17	.24	.19	.16	.15	.147	9
			10	.25	.19	.15	.24	.19	.15	.24	.18	.15	.23	.18	.15	.22	.18	.15	.13	.137	10
23 Wide spread, recessed, small open bottom reflector with low wattage diffuse HID lamp	IV 0°▲ 56°▼	1.7	0	.67	.67	.67	.65	.65	.65	.62	.62	.62	.60	.60	.60	.57	.57	.57	.56		0
			1	.60	.58	.56	.58	.57	.55	.56	.55	.53	.54	.53	.52	.52	.51	.50	.49	.177	1
			2	.53	.49	.46	.52	.48	.46	.50	.47	.45	.48	.46	.44	.46	.44	.43	.42	.179	2
			3	.46	.42	.39	.46	.42	.38	.44	.41	.38	.42	.40	.37	.41	.39	.37	.35	.172	3
			4	.41	.36	.33	.40	.36	.33	.39	.35	.32	.38	.34	.32	.37	.34	.31	.30	.161	4
			5	.37	.32	.28	.36	.31	.28	.35	.31	.28	.34	.30	.27	.33	.30	.27	.26	.150	5
			6	.33	.28	.24	.32	.28	.24	.31	.27	.24	.30	.27	.24	.30	.26	.24	.23	.139	6
			7	.30	.25	.21	.29	.25	.21	.28	.24	.21	.28	.24	.21	.27	.23	.21	.20	.129	7
			8	.27	.22	.19	.26	.22	.19	.26	.22	.19	.25	.21	.19	.24	.21	.19	.17	.120	8
			9	.25	.20	.17	.24	.20	.17	.24	.20	.17	.23	.19	.17	.22	.19	.17	.16	.112	9
			10	.22	.18	.15	.22	.18	.15	.22	.18	.15	.21	.18	.15	.21	.17	.15	.14	.105	10
24 Open top, indirect, reflector type unit with HID lamp (mult. by 0.9 for lens top)	VI 78°▲ 0°▼	N.A.	0	.74	.74	.74	.63	.63	.63	.43	.43	.43	.25	.25	.25	.08	.08	.08	.00		0
			1	.64	.62	.59	.55	.53	.51	.38	.36	.35	.22	.21	.20	.07	.07	.07	.00	.000	1
			2	.56	.52	.48	.48	.45	.42	.33	.31	.29	.19	.18	.17	.06	.06	.06	.00	.000	2
			3	.49	.44	.40	.42	.38	.35	.29	.26	.24	.17	.15	.14	.05	.05	.05	.00	.000	3
			4	.43	.38	.34	.37	.33	.29	.26	.23	.20	.15	.13	.12	.05	.04	.04	.00	.000	4
			5	.38	.33	.28	.33	.28	.25	.23	.20	.17	.13	.12	.10	.04	.04	.03	.00	.000	5
			6	.34	.28	.24	.29	.25	.21	.20	.17	.15	.12	.10	.09	.04	.03	.03	.00	.000	6
			7	.31	.25	.21	.26	.22	.18	.18	.15	.13	.11	.09	.08	.03	.03	.03	.00	.000	7
			8	.28	.22	.18	.24	.19	.16	.16	.13	.11	.10	.08	.07	.03	.03	.02	.00	.000	8
			9	.25	.20	.16	.21	.17	.14	.15	.12	.10	.09	.07	.06	.03	.02	.02	.00	.000	9
			10	.23	.17	.14	.20	.15	.12	.14	.11	.09	.08	.06	.05	.03	.02	.02	.00	.000	10

Fig. 9-34. *Continued*

80			70			50			30			10			80			70			50			30			10		
50	30	10	50	30	10	50	30	10	50	30	10	50	30	10	50	30	10	50	30	10	50	30	10	50	30	10	50	30	10
Wall Exitance Coefficients for 20 Per Cent Effective Floor Cavity Reflectance (ρ_{FC} = 20)															Ceiling Cavity Exitance Coefficients for 20 Per Cent Floor Cavity Reflectance (ρ_{FC} = 20)														
															.207	.207	.207	.177	.177	.177	.121	.121	.121	.069	.069	.069	.022	.022	.022
.176	.100	.032	.168	.096	.030	.154	.088	.028	.141	.081	.026	.128	.074	.024	.194	.180	.168	.166	.155	.144	.113	.106	.100	.065	.062	.058	.021	.020	.019
.170	.093	.029	.163	.090	.028	.150	.084	.026	.139	.078	.024	.128	.073	.023	.184	.160	.140	.157	.138	.121	.108	.095	.085	.062	.055	.050	.020	.018	.016
.162	.086	.026	.156	.083	.025	.145	.078	.024	.135	.074	.023	.125	.069	.021	.175	.145	.121	.150	.125	.105	.103	.087	.074	.060	.051	.043	.019	.017	.014
.153	.080	.023	.148	.078	.023	.138	.073	.022	.129	.069	.021	.121	.066	.020	.168	.134	.107	.144	.116	.093	.099	.081	.066	.057	.047	.039	.018	.015	.013
.145	.074	.021	.141	.072	.021	.132	.069	.020	.124	.065	.019	.116	.062	.019	.162	.125	.097	.139	.108	.085	.096	.075	.060	.055	.044	.035	.018	.014	.012
.138	.069	.020	.133	.067	.019	.126	.064	.019	.118	.061	.018	.111	.058	.017	.156	.118	.090	.134	.102	.078	.093	.071	.055	.054	.042	.033	.017	.014	.011
.131	.065	.018	.127	.063	.018	.120	.060	.017	.113	.058	.017	.106	.055	.016	.151	.112	.084	.130	.097	.073	.090	.068	.052	.052	.040	.031	.017	.013	.010
.124	.061	.017	.120	.059	.017	.114	.057	.016	.108	.055	.016	.102	.052	.015	.147	.107	.080	.126	.093	.069	.087	.065	.049	.051	.038	.029	.016	.013	.010
.118	.057	.016	.115	.056	.016	.109	.054	.015	.103	.052	.015	.098	.050	.014	.142	.103	.076	.123	.089	.066	.085	.063	.047	.049	.037	.028	.016	.012	.009
.112	.054	.015	.109	.053	.015	.104	.051	.014	.099	.049	.014	.094	.047	.014	.138	.099	.073	.119	.086	.064	.083	.061	.046	.048	.036	.027	.016	.012	.009
															.244	.244	.244	.209	.209	.209	.143	.143	.143	.082	.082	.082	.026	.026	.026
.183	.104	.033	.174	.099	.032	.157	.090	.029	.141	.081	.026	.127	.073	.024	.232	.218	.205	.199	.187	.177	.136	.129	.122	.078	.075	.071	.025	.024	.023
.177	.097	.030	.168	.093	.029	.153	.085	.026	.139	.078	.024	.126	.071	.023	.223	.199	.178	.191	.171	.154	.131	.118	.107	.076	.069	.063	.024	.022	.021
.168	.090	.027	.161	.086	.026	.148	.080	.024	.135	.074	.023	.123	.068	.021	.216	.184	.159	.185	.159	.138	.127	.111	.097	.073	.065	.057	.024	.021	.019
.160	.083	.024	.154	.080	.024	.141	.075	.022	.130	.070	.021	.119	.065	.020	.209	.173	.146	.180	.150	.127	.124	.104	.089	.071	.061	.053	.023	.020	.017
.152	.077	.022	.146	.075	.022	.135	.070	.021	.125	.066	.020	.115	.061	.018	.204	.165	.136	.175	.143	.119	.121	.100	.084	.070	.059	.050	.023	.019	.016
.144	.072	.021	.139	.070	.020	.129	.066	.019	.119	.062	.018	.110	.058	.017	.199	.158	.129	.171	.137	.112	.118	.096	.080	.068	.056	.047	.022	.018	.016
.137	.068	.019	.132	.066	.019	.123	.062	.018	.114	.058	.017	.106	.055	.016	.194	.153	.124	.167	.132	.108	.115	.093	.076	.067	.055	.045	.022	.018	.015
.130	.063	.018	.125	.062	.017	.117	.058	.017	.109	.055	.016	.101	.052	.015	.190	.148	.120	.163	.128	.104	.113	.090	.074	.066	.053	.044	.021	.017	.015
.124	.060	.017	.119	.058	.016	.112	.055	.016	.104	.052	.015	.097	.049	.014	.186	.144	.116	.160	.125	.101	.111	.088	.072	.065	.052	.043	.021	.017	.014
.118	.056	.016	.114	.055	.015	.106	.052	.015	.100	.049	.014	.093	.047	.013	.182	.141	.114	.157	.122	.099	.109	.086	.071	.063	.051	.042	.021	.017	.014
															.130	.130	.130	.112	.112	.112	.076	.076	.076	.044	.044	.044	.014	.014	.014
.186	.106	.033	.181	.103	.033	.172	.099	.032	.164	.094	.030	.156	.091	.029	.122	.107	.094	.104	.092	.081	.071	.063	.056	.041	.037	.033	.013	.012	.011
.181	.099	.030	.177	.097	.030	.169	.094	.029	.162	.091	.028	.155	.088	.028	.115	.090	.069	.099	.078	.060	.068	.054	.042	.039	.031	.025	.013	.010	.008
.171	.091	.027	.168	.090	.027	.161	.087	.026	.154	.085	.026	.148	.082	.025	.110	.078	.053	.094	.067	.046	.065	.047	.032	.037	.027	.019	.012	.009	.006
.161	.084	.025	.158	.083	.024	.152	.081	.024	.146	.078	.024	.141	.076	.023	.105	.069	.041	.090	.060	.036	.062	.042	.025	.036	.024	.015	.012	.008	.005
.151	.077	.022	.148	.076	.022	.143	.074	.022	.138	.073	.022	.133	.071	.021	.100	.062	.033	.086	.053	.029	.059	.037	.020	.034	.022	.012	.011	.007	.004
.142	.071	.020	.139	.070	.020	.134	.069	.020	.130	.067	.020	.126	.066	.020	.096	.056	.027	.082	.049	.024	.057	.034	.017	.033	.020	.010	.011	.007	.003
.133	.066	.019	.131	.065	.019	.127	.064	.018	.122	.063	.018	.119	.062	.018	.092	.051	.023	.079	.045	.020	.054	.031	.014	.032	.018	.009	.010	.006	.003
.125	.061	.017	.123	.061	.017	.119	.060	.017	.116	.059	.017	.112	.058	.017	.088	.047	.020	.075	.041	.017	.052	.029	.012	.030	.017	.007	.010	.006	.002
.118	.057	.016	.116	.057	.016	.113	.056	.016	.109	.055	.016	.106	.054	.016	.084	.044	.017	.072	.038	.015	.050	.027	.011	.029	.016	.006	.009	.005	.002
.112	.053	.015	.110	.053	.015	.107	.052	.015	.104	.051	.015	.101	.051	.015	.080	.041	.015	.069	.036	.013	.048	.025	.010	.028	.015	.006	.009	.005	.002
															.156	.156	.156	.133	.133	.133	.091	.091	.091	.052	.052	.052	.017	.017	.017
.230	.131	.041	.224	.128	.041	.213	.122	.039	.203	.117	.038	.194	.112	.036	.149	.131	.115	.128	.113	.099	.087	.078	.069	.050	.045	.040	.016	.014	.013
.216	.118	.036	.210	.116	.036	.201	.112	.035	.192	.108	.034	.183	.104	.033	.144	.114	.089	.124	.099	.077	.085	.068	.054	.049	.040	.032	.016	.013	.010
.200	.106	.032	.195	.104	.031	.186	.101	.031	.178	.098	.030	.171	.094	.029	.139	.102	.073	.119	.088	.063	.082	.061	.044	.047	.036	.026	.015	.012	.009
.184	.096	.028	.180	.094	.028	.172	.091	.027	.165	.089	.027	.158	.086	.026	.134	.093	.061	.115	.080	.053	.079	.056	.038	.046	.033	.022	.015	.011	.007
.170	.087	.025	.166	.085	.025	.159	.083	.024	.153	.081	.024	.147	.078	.024	.129	.086	.054	.111	.074	.047	.077	.052	.033	.044	.030	.020	.014	.010	.006
.158	.079	.023	.154	.078	.022	.148	.076	.022	.142	.074	.022	.137	.072	.021	.124	.080	.048	.107	.069	.042	.074	.049	.030	.043	.029	.018	.014	.009	.006
.147	.072	.021	.144	.072	.020	.138	.070	.020	.132	.068	.020	.127	.066	.019	.120	.075	.044	.103	.065	.039	.071	.046	.027	.041	.027	.016	.013	.009	.005
.137	.067	.019	.134	.066	.019	.129	.064	.018	.124	.063	.018	.119	.061	.018	.115	.071	.041	.099	.062	.036	.069	.043	.026	.040	.026	.015	.013	.008	.005
.128	.062	.017	.125	.061	.017	.121	.060	.017	.116	.058	.017	.112	.057	.016	.111	.068	.039	.095	.059	.034	.066	.041	.024	.039	.024	.014	.012	.008	.005
.120	.058	.016	.118	.057	.016	.113	.056	.016	.109	.054	.015	.106	.053	.015	.107	.065	.037	.092	.056	.032	.064	.040	.023	.037	.023	.014	.012	.008	.005
															.107	.107	.107	.091	.091	.091	.062	.062	.062	.036	.036	.036	.011	.011	.011
.146	.083	.026	.142	.081	.026	.135	.077	.025	.128	.074	.024	.122	.071	.023	.099	.088	.077	.085	.075	.067	.058	.052	.046	.033	.030	.027	.011	.010	.009
.145	.079	.024	.141	.078	.024	.135	.075	.023	.129	.072	.023	.123	.070	.022	.094	.074	.057	.080	.064	.049	.055	.044	.034	.032	.026	.020	.010	.008	.007
.138	.074	.022	.136	.073	.022	.130	.070	.021	.125	.068	.021	.120	.066	.021	.090	.064	.043	.077	.055	.038	.053	.038	.026	.030	.022	.016	.010	.007	.005
.131	.068	.020	.128	.067	.020	.123	.065	.020	.119	.064	.019	.114	.062	.019	.086	.056	.034	.074	.049	.029	.051	.034	.021	.029	.020	.012	.009	.006	.004
.123	.063	.018	.121	.062	.018	.116	.061	.018	.112	.059	.018	.108	.058	.017	.082	.050	.027	.070	.044	.024	.048	.031	.017	.028	.018	.010	.009	.006	.003
.116	.058	.017	.114	.057	.017	.110	.056	.016	.106	.055	.016	.102	.054	.016	.078	.046	.022	.067	.040	.020	.046	.028	.014	.027	016	.008	.009	.005	.003
.109	.054	.015	.107	.053	.015	.103	.052	.015	.100	.051	.015	.097	.050	.015	.075	.042	.019	.064	.036	.017	.044	.026	.012	.026	.015	.007	.008	.005	.002
.102	.050	.014	.101	.050	.014	.097	.049	.014	.094	.048	.014	.091	.047	.014	.071	.039	.016	.062	.034	.014	.043	.024	.010	.025	.014	.006	.008	.005	.002
.096	.047	.013	.095	.046	.013	.092	.045	.013	.089	.045	.013	.087	.044	.013	.068	.036	.014	.059	.031	.012	.041	.022	.009	.024	.013	.005	.008	.004	.002
.091	.044	.012	.090	.043	.012	.087	.043	.012	.084	.042	.012	.082	.041	.012	.065	.034	.013	.056	.029	.011	.039	.021	.008	.023	.012	.005	.007	.004	.002
															.743	.743	.743	.635	.635	.635	.433	.433	.433	.249	.249	.249	.080	.080	.080
.201	.114	.036	.172	.098	.031	.117	.067	.022	.068	.039	.013	.022	.013	.004	.737	.721	.707	.631	.619	.609	.431	.426	.421	.248	.247	.245	.080	.079	.079
.184	.101	.031	.158	.087	.027	.108	.060	.019	.062	.035	.011	.020	.011	.004	.732	.706	.685	.627	.608	.592	.430	.421	.413	.248	.245	.242	.079	.079	.079
.170	.091	.027	.146	.078	.024	.100	.054	.017	.058	.032	.010	.019	.010	.003	.727	.695	.670	.623	.600	.581	.428	.417	.408	.247	.243	.240	.079	.079	.079
.158	.082	.024	.135	.071	.021	.093	.049	.015	.054	.029	.009	.017	.009	.003	.723	.687	.660	.620	.594	.573	.426	.414	.404	.247	.242	.239	.079	.079	.079
.147	.075	.022	.126	.065	.019	.087	.045	.013	.050	.027	.008	.016	.009	.003	.718	.681	.653	.617	.589	.568	.425	.411	.401	.246	.242	.238	.079	.079	.078
.137	.069	.020	.117	.059	.017	.081	.042	.012	.047	.024	.007	.015	.008	.002	.714	.676	.648	.614	.585	.564	.423	.410	.399	.246	.241	.237	.079	.079	.078
.128	.063	.018	.110	.055	.016	.076	.038	.011	.044	.023	.007	.014	.007	.002	.710	.671	.644	.611	.582	.562	.422	.408	.398	.245	.240	.237	.079	.079	.078
.120	.059	.016	.103	.051	.014	.071	.036	.010	.042	.021	.006	.013	.007	.002	.706	.668	.642	.608	.579	.559	.421	.407	.397	.245	.240	.236	.079	.079	.078
.113	.054	.015	.097	.047	.013	.067	.033	.009	.039	.020	.006	.013	.006	.002	.703	.665	.639	.605	.577	.558	.419	.406	.396	.244	.240	.236	.079	.079	.078
.106	.051	.014	.091	.044	.012	.063	.031	.009	.037	.018	.005	.012	.006	.002	.699	.662	.638	.603	.575	.556	.418	.405	.395	.244	.239	.236	.079	.079	.078

Fig. 9-34. *Continued*

ρcc →		80			70			50			30			10			0	ρcc →
ρw →		50	30	10	50	30	10	50	30	10	50	30	10	50	30	10	0	**ρw →**

Coefficients of Utilization for 20 Per Cent Effective Floor Cavity Reflectance (ρFC = 20)

25 — Porcelain-enameled reflector with 35°CW shielding · Maint. Cat. II · SC 1.3 · 22½%↑ · 65%↓

RCR	80-50	80-30	80-10	70-50	70-30	70-10	50-50	50-30	50-10	30-50	30-30	30-10	10-50	10-30	10-10	0	WDRC
0	.99	.99	.99	.94	.94	.94	.85	.85	.85	.77	.77	.77	.69	.69	.69	.65	
1	.87	.84	.81	.83	.80	.77	.75	.73	.71	.68	.66	.65	.62	.60	.59	.56	.236
2	.77	.71	.67	.73	.68	.64	.67	.63	.60	.60	.58	.55	.55	.53	.51	.48	.220
3	.68	.62	.56	.65	.59	.54	.59	.55	.51	.54	.50	.47	.49	.46	.44	.41	.203
4	.61	.54	.48	.58	.52	.47	.53	.48	.44	.48	.44	.41	.44	.41	.38	.35	.186
5	.54	.47	.42	.52	.46	.41	.48	.42	.38	.44	.39	.36	.40	.36	.33	.31	.170
6	.49	.42	.37	.47	.40	.36	.43	.38	.34	.40	.35	.32	.36	.33	.30	.27	.157
7	.45	.37	.32	.43	.36	.32	.39	.34	.30	.36	.32	.28	.33	.29	.26	.24	.145
8	.41	.34	.29	.39	.33	.28	.36	.31	.27	.33	.29	.25	.31	.27	.24	.22	.135
9	.37	.31	.26	.36	.30	.25	.33	.28	.24	.31	.26	.23	.28	.24	.22	.20	.126
10	.34	.28	.24	.33	.27	.23	.31	.25	.22	.28	.24	.21	.26	.22	.20	.18	.118

26 — Diffuse aluminum reflector with 35°CW shielding · Maint. Cat. II · SC 1.5/1.3 · 17%↑ · 66%↓

RCR	80-50	80-30	80-10	70-50	70-30	70-10	50-50	50-30	50-10	30-50	30-30	30-10	10-50	10-30	10-10	0	WDRC
0	.95	.95	.95	.91	.91	.91	.83	.83	.83	.76	.76	.76	.69	.69	.69	.66	
1	.85	.82	.79	.81	.79	.76	.75	.73	.71	.69	.67	.66	.63	.62	.61	.58	.197
2	.75	.71	.67	.72	.68	.65	.67	.63	.61	.62	.59	.57	.57	.55	.53	.51	.194
3	.67	.61	.57	.65	.59	.55	.60	.56	.52	.55	.52	.49	.51	.49	.46	.44	.184
4	.60	.54	.49	.58	.52	.48	.54	.49	.45	.50	.46	.43	.46	.43	.41	.39	.173
5	.54	.47	.43	.52	.46	.42	.49	.43	.40	.45	.41	.38	.42	.39	.36	.34	.162
6	.49	.42	.37	.47	.41	.37	.44	.39	.35	.41	.37	.33	.38	.35	.32	.30	.151
7	.44	.38	.33	.43	.37	.32	.40	.35	.31	.38	.33	.30	.35	.31	.28	.27	.141
8	.40	.34	.29	.39	.33	.29	.37	.31	.28	.34	.30	.27	.32	.28	.26	.24	.132
9	.37	.31	.26	.36	.30	.26	.34	.29	.25	.32	.27	.24	.30	.26	.23	.21	.124
10	.34	.28	.24	.33	.27	.23	.31	.26	.23	.29	.25	.22	.28	.24	.21	.19	.117

27 — Porcelain-enameled reflector with 30°CW × 30°LW shielding · Maint. Cat. II · SC 1.0 · 23½%↑ · 57%↓

RCR	80-50	80-30	80-10	70-50	70-30	70-10	50-50	50-30	50-10	30-50	30-30	30-10	10-50	10-30	10-10	0	WDRC
0	.91	.91	.91	.86	.86	.86	.77	.77	.77	.68	.68	.68	.61	.61	.61	.57	
1	.80	.77	.75	.76	.74	.71	.69	.67	.65	.62	.60	.59	.55	.54	.53	.50	.182
2	.71	.67	.63	.68	.64	.60	.61	.58	.55	.55	.53	.51	.50	.48	.46	.43	.174
3	.63	.58	.53	.60	.55	.51	.55	.51	.47	.50	.46	.44	.45	.42	.40	.38	.163
4	.57	.51	.46	.54	.49	.44	.49	.45	.41	.45	.41	.38	.41	.38	.35	.33	.151
5	.51	.45	.40	.49	.43	.39	.45	.40	.36	.41	.37	.34	.37	.34	.31	.29	.140
6	.46	.40	.35	.44	.38	.34	.41	.36	.32	.37	.33	.30	.34	.30	.28	.26	.130
7	.42	.36	.31	.40	.35	.30	.37	.32	.29	.34	.30	.27	.31	.28	.25	.23	.121
8	.38	.32	.28	.37	.31	.27	.34	.29	.26	.31	.27	.24	.29	.25	.23	.21	.113
9	.35	.29	.25	.34	.28	.25	.31	.27	.23	.29	.25	.22	.27	.23	.21	.19	.106
10	.33	.27	.23	.31	.26	.22	.29	.24	.21	.27	.23	.20	.25	.21	.19	.17	.099

28 — Diffuse aluminum reflector with 35°CW × 35°LW shielding · Maint. Cat. II · SC 1.5/1.1 · 17%↑ · 56½%↓

RCR	80-50	80-30	80-10	70-50	70-30	70-10	50-50	50-30	50-10	30-50	30-30	30-10	10-50	10-30	10-10	0	WDRC
0	.83	.83	.83	.79	.79	.79	.72	.72	.72	.65	.65	.65	.59	.59	.59	.56	
1	.74	.72	.70	.71	.69	.67	.65	.63	.62	.59	.58	.57	.54	.53	.52	.50	.160
2	.66	.62	.59	.64	.60	.57	.58	.56	.53	.54	.51	.49	.49	.47	.46	.44	.158
3	.59	.54	.50	.57	.53	.49	.53	.49	.46	.48	.46	.43	.45	.42	.40	.38	.150
4	.53	.48	.44	.51	.46	.42	.47	.43	.40	.44	.41	.38	.40	.38	.36	.34	.141
5	.48	.42	.38	.46	.41	.37	.43	.39	.35	.40	.36	.33	.37	.34	.32	.30	.132
6	.44	.38	.34	.42	.37	.33	.39	.35	.31	.36	.33	.30	.34	.31	.28	.27	.124
7	.40	.34	.30	.38	.33	.29	.36	.31	.28	.33	.30	.27	.31	.28	.25	.24	.116
8	.36	.31	.27	.35	.30	.26	.33	.28	.25	.31	.27	.24	.29	.25	.23	.21	.109
9	.33	.28	.24	.32	.27	.24	.30	.26	.23	.28	.24	.22	.26	.23	.21	.19	.102
10	.31	.25	.22	.30	.25	.22	.28	.24	.21	.26	.22	.20	.25	.21	.19	.18	.096

29 — Metal or dense diffusing sides with 45°CW × 45°LW shielding · Maint. Cat. II · SC 1.1 · 39%↑ · 32%↓

RCR	80-50	80-30	80-10	70-50	70-30	70-10	50-50	50-30	50-10	30-50	30-30	30-10	10-50	10-30	10-10	0	WDRC
0	.75	.75	.75	.69	.69	.69	.57	.57	.57	.46	.46	.46	.37	.37	.37	.32	
1	.66	.64	.62	.61	.59	.57	.51	.50	.48	.42	.41	.40	.33	.33	.32	.28	.094
2	.59	.55	.52	.54	.51	.48	.46	.43	.41	.38	.36	.34	.30	.29	.28	.25	.091
3	.52	.48	.44	.48	.44	.41	.41	.38	.35	.34	.32	.30	.27	.26	.25	.22	.085
4	.47	.42	.38	.43	.39	.35	.37	.33	.31	.31	.28	.26	.25	.23	.22	.19	.079
5	.42	.37	.33	.39	.34	.31	.33	.30	.27	.28	.25	.23	.23	.21	.20	.17	.073
6	.38	.33	.29	.35	.31	.27	.30	.27	.24	.25	.23	.21	.21	.19	.18	.16	.068
7	.35	.29	.26	.32	.28	.24	.28	.24	.21	.23	.21	.19	.19	.17	.16	.14	.063
8	.32	.26	.23	.29	.25	.22	.25	.22	.19	.21	.19	.17	.18	.16	.15	.13	.059
9	.29	.24	.21	.27	.23	.20	.23	.20	.17	.20	.17	.15	.17	.15	.13	.12	.056
10	.27	.22	.19	.25	.21	.18	.22	.18	.16	.19	.16	.14	.16	.14	.12	.11	.052

30 — Same as unit #29 except with top reflectors · Maint. Cat. IV · SC 1.0 · 6%↑ · 46%↓

RCR	80-50	80-30	80-10	70-50	70-30	70-10	50-50	50-30	50-10	30-50	30-30	30-10	10-50	10-30	10-10	0	WDRC
0	.61	.61	.61	.58	.58	.58	.55	.55	.55	.51	.51	.51	.48	.48	.48	.46	
1	.54	.52	.50	.52	.50	.49	.49	.47	.46	.46	.45	.43	.43	.42	.41	.40	.159
2	.48	.45	.42	.46	.44	.41	.44	.41	.39	.41	.39	.38	.39	.37	.36	.34	.145
3	.43	.39	.36	.42	.38	.35	.39	.36	.34	.37	.35	.33	.35	.33	.31	.30	.132
4	.39	.35	.32	.38	.34	.31	.36	.32	.30	.34	.31	.29	.32	.30	.28	.27	.121
5	.35	.31	.28	.34	.30	.27	.32	.29	.27	.31	.28	.26	.29	.27	.25	.24	.111
6	.32	.28	.25	.31	.27	.25	.30	.26	.24	.28	.25	.23	.27	.25	.23	.22	.102
7	.29	.25	.22	.29	.25	.22	.27	.24	.22	.26	.23	.21	.25	.23	.21	.20	.095
8	.27	.23	.20	.27	.23	.20	.25	.22	.20	.24	.21	.19	.23	.21	.19	.18	.088
9	.25	.21	.19	.25	.21	.18	.24	.20	.18	.23	.20	.18	.22	.19	.17	.16	.083
10	.23	.20	.17	.23	.19	.17	.22	.19	.17	.21	.18	.16	.20	.18	.16	.15	.077

Fig. 9-34. *Continued*

80			70			50			30			10			80			70			50			30			10		
50	30	10	50	30	10	50	30	10	50	30	10	50	30	10	50	30	10	50	30	10	50	30	10	50	30	10	50	30	10
Wall Exitance Coefficients for 20 Per Cent Effective Floor Cavity Reflectance ($\rho_{FC} = 20$)															Ceiling Cavity Exitance Coefficients for 20 Per Cent Floor Cavity Reflectance ($\rho_{FC} = 20$)														
															.339	.339	.339	.290	.290	.290	.198	.198	.198	.114	.114	.114	.036	.036	.036
.243	.138	.044	.230	.131	.042	.206	.118	.038	.184	.106	.034	.163	.095	.031	.329	.311	.293	.282	.267	.253	.193	.183	.175	.111	.106	.102	.036	.034	.033
.228	.125	.038	.216	.119	.037	.195	.108	.034	.174	.098	.031	.156	.088	.028	.322	.290	.264	.276	.250	.228	.189	.173	.159	.109	.101	.093	.035	.033	.030
.212	.113	.034	.202	.108	.032	.182	.098	.030	.163	.090	.027	.146	.081	.025	.315	.275	.244	.270	.238	.212	.185	.165	.148	.107	.096	.087	.034	.031	.029
.197	.102	.030	.187	.098	.029	.169	.090	.027	.153	.082	.025	.137	.074	.023	.308	.264	.231	.265	.228	.200	.182	.159	.141	.105	.093	.083	.034	.030	.027
.183	.093	.027	.175	.090	.026	.158	.082	.024	.143	.075	.022	.129	.069	.021	.302	.255	.221	.260	.221	.192	.179	.154	.136	.104	.091	.081	.033	.030	.027
.171	.086	.025	.163	.082	.024	.148	.076	.022	.134	.070	.020	.121	.064	.019	.297	.248	.214	.255	.215	.186	.176	.151	.132	.102	.089	.078	.033	.029	.026
.160	.079	.022	.153	.076	.022	.139	.070	.020	.126	.065	.019	.114	.059	.017	.291	.243	.209	.250	.210	.182	.173	.148	.129	.101	.087	.077	.032	.028	.025
.150	.073	.021	.144	.071	.020	.131	.065	.019	.119	.060	.017	.107	.055	.016	.286	.238	.205	.246	.206	.179	.170	.145	.127	.099	.085	.076	.032	.028	.025
.141	.068	.019	.135	.066	.018	.123	.061	.017	.112	.056	.016	.101	.052	.015	.281	.234	.202	.242	.203	.176	.168	.143	.125	.098	.084	.075	.032	.028	.025
.133	.064	.018	.128	.062	.017	.117	.057	.016	.106	.053	.015	.096	.048	.014	.277	.230	.199	.239	.200	.174	.165	.141	.124	.097	.083	.074	.031	.027	.024
															.286	.286	.286	.244	.244	.244	.167	.167	.167	.096	.096	.096	.031	.031	.031
.209	.119	.038	.198	.113	.036	.178	.102	.033	.159	.092	.029	.142	.082	.027	.275	.259	.244	.235	.222	.210	.161	.153	.145	.093	.088	.084	.030	.028	.027
.200	.110	.034	.191	.105	.032	.173	.096	.030	.156	.087	.027	.140	.079	.025	.267	.239	.216	.229	.206	.187	.157	.143	.130	.090	.083	.076	.029	.027	.025
.190	.101	.030	.181	.097	.029	.164	.089	.027	.149	.082	.025	.135	.075	.023	.260	.225	.197	.223	.194	.171	.153	.135	.120	.088	.079	.071	.028	.026	.023
.178	.093	.027	.170	.089	.026	.156	.083	.025	.142	.076	.023	.129	.070	.021	.254	.214	.184	.218	.185	.159	.150	.129	.112	.087	.076	.066	.028	.025	.022
.168	.085	.025	.161	.082	.024	.147	.077	.023	.134	.071	.021	.123	.065	.020	.248	.206	.174	.213	.178	.151	.147	.124	.107	.085	.073	.063	.027	.024	.021
.158	.079	.023	.151	.076	.022	.139	.071	.021	.127	.066	.019	.116	.061	.018	.243	.199	.167	.209	.172	.145	.144	.121	.103	.084	.071	.061	.027	.023	.020
.148	.073	.021	.142	.071	.020	.131	.066	.019	.120	.062	.018	.110	.057	.017	.238	.193	.162	.205	.168	.141	.142	.118	.100	.082	.069	.060	.027	.023	.020
.140	.068	.019	.135	.066	.019	.124	.062	.018	.114	.058	.017	.105	.054	.016	.234	.189	.158	.201	.164	.138	.139	.115	.098	.081	.068	.058	.026	.022	.019
.132	.064	.018	.127	.062	.017	.118	.058	.016	.108	.054	.016	.100	.051	.015	.229	.185	.155	.197	.160	.135	.137	.113	.096	.080	.067	.057	.026	.022	.019
.125	.060	.017	.121	.058	.016	.112	.055	.015	.103	.051	.015	.095	.048	.014	.225	.182	.153	.194	.158	.133	.135	.111	.095	.079	.066	.056	.025	.022	.019
															.334	.334	.334	.286	.286	.286	.195	.195	.195	.112	.112	.112	.036	.036	.036
.210	.119	.038	.197	.113	.036	.173	.099	.032	.151	.087	.028	.131	.076	.025	.325	.308	.294	.278	.265	.253	.190	.182	.175	.109	.105	.102	.035	.034	.033
.199	.109	.033	.187	.103	.032	.166	.092	.029	.146	.082	.026	.127	.072	.023	.317	.290	.267	.272	.249	.231	.186	.173	.161	.107	.100	.094	.034	.032	.031
.186	.099	.030	.176	.094	.028	.156	.085	.026	.138	.076	.023	.121	.067	.021	.311	.276	.249	.266	.238	.215	.183	.165	.151	.106	.097	.089	.034	.031	.029
.174	.090	.027	.164	.086	.025	.146	.078	.023	.130	.070	.021	.115	.062	.019	.305	.266	.236	.261	.230	.205	.180	.160	.144	.104	.094	.085	.033	.031	.028
.162	.083	.024	.154	.079	.023	.137	.072	.021	.122	.065	.019	.108	.058	.017	.299	.258	.227	.257	.223	.198	.177	.156	.139	.103	.091	.083	.033	.030	.027
.152	.076	.022	.144	.073	.021	.129	.066	.019	.115	.060	.018	.102	.054	.016	.294	.251	.221	.253	.218	.192	.174	.152	.136	.101	.090	.081	.033	.029	.027
.143	.071	.020	.135	.067	.019	.122	.062	.018	.109	.056	.016	.097	.050	.015	.289	.246	.216	.249	.213	.188	.172	.149	.133	.100	.088	.079	.032	.029	.026
.134	.066	.018	.128	.063	.018	.115	.057	.016	.103	.052	.015	.091	.047	.014	.284	.241	.212	.245	.209	.185	.169	.147	.131	.099	.087	.078	.032	.028	.026
.127	.061	.017	.120	.059	.016	.109	.054	.015	.097	.049	.014	.087	.044	.013	.280	.238	.209	.241	.206	.182	.167	.145	.129	.097	.086	.077	.032	.028	.026
.120	.057	.016	.114	.055	.015	.103	.050	.014	.092	.046	.013	.082	.041	.012	.276	.234	.207	.238	.204	.180	.165	.143	.128	.096	.085	.077	.031	.028	.025
															.268	.268	.268	.229	.229	.229	.156	.156	.156	.090	.090	.090	.029	.029	.029
.180	.103	.032	.170	.097	.031	.151	.087	.028	.134	.077	.025	.118	.068	.022	.259	.245	.232	.221	.210	.200	.151	.144	.138	.087	.084	.080	.028	.027	.026
.173	.095	.029	.164	.090	.028	.146	.081	.025	.131	.073	.023	.116	.066	.021	.251	.227	.207	.215	.196	.179	.148	.135	.125	.085	.079	.073	.027	.025	.024
.163	.087	.026	.155	.083	.025	.139	.076	.023	.125	.069	.021	.112	.062	.019	.245	.215	.191	.210	.185	.165	.144	.129	.116	.083	.075	.068	.027	.024	.022
.153	.080	.023	.146	.076	.023	.132	.070	.021	.119	.064	.019	.107	.058	.018	.240	.205	.179	.206	.177	.156	.141	.124	.110	.082	.072	.065	.026	.024	.021
.144	.074	.021	.138	.071	.021	.125	.065	.019	.113	.060	.018	.102	.054	.016	.235	.198	.171	.202	.171	.148	.139	.120	.105	.080	.070	.062	.026	.023	.020
.136	.068	.019	.130	.065	.019	.118	.060	.018	.107	.056	.016	.097	.051	.015	.230	.192	.165	.198	.166	.143	.136	.116	.101	.079	.068	.060	.026	.022	.020
.128	.063	.018	.122	.061	.017	.111	.056	.016	.101	.052	.015	.092	.048	.014	.226	.187	.160	.194	.162	.139	.134	.114	.099	.078	.067	.059	.025	.022	.019
.121	.059	.017	.116	.057	.016	.106	.053	.015	.096	.049	.014	.087	.045	.013	.222	.183	.156	.191	.159	.136	.132	.111	.097	.077	.066	.058	.025	.022	.019
.114	.055	.015	.109	.053	.015	.100	.050	.014	.091	.046	.013	.083	.042	.012	.218	.180	.154	.188	.156	.134	.130	.110	.095	.076	.065	.057	.025	.021	.019
.108	.052	.014	.104	.050	.014	.095	.047	.013	.087	.043	.012	.079	.040	.011	.214	.177	.152	.185	.153	.132	.128	.108	.094	.075	.064	.056	.024	.021	.019
															.433	.433	.433	.370	.370	.370	.253	.253	.253	.145	.145	.145	.046	.046	.046
.180	.102	.032	.163	.093	.030	.132	.076	.024	.103	.060	.019	.077	.044	.014	.426	.411	.399	.364	.353	.343	.249	.243	.237	.143	.141	.138	.046	.045	.045
.168	.092	.028	.153	.084	.026	.125	.069	.022	.098	.055	.017	.074	.042	.013	.419	.396	.377	.359	.341	.326	.246	.236	.227	.142	.137	.133	.046	.044	.043
.157	.083	.025	.143	.077	.023	.117	.063	.019	.093	.051	.016	.070	.039	.012	.414	.385	.362	.355	.332	.314	.244	.231	.220	.141	.135	.130	.045	.044	.042
.146	.076	.022	.133	.070	.021	.109	.058	.017	.087	.047	.014	.066	.036	.011	.409	.376	.351	.351	.325	.305	.241	.227	.215	.140	.133	.127	.045	.043	.042
.136	.069	.020	.125	.064	.019	.102	.053	.016	.082	.043	.013	.063	.034	.010	.404	.370	.344	.347	.320	.299	.239	.223	.211	.139	.131	.125	.045	.043	.041
.127	.064	.018	.117	.059	.017	.096	.049	.014	.077	.040	.012	.059	.031	.009	.400	.364	.339	.344	.315	.295	.237	.221	.209	.138	.130	.124	.044	.042	.041
.119	.059	.017	.109	.055	.016	.091	.046	.013	.073	.037	.011	.056	.029	.009	.396	.360	.335	.341	.312	.292	.235	.219	.207	.137	.129	.123	.044	.042	.041
.112	.055	.015	.103	.051	.014	.085	.043	.012	.069	.035	.010	.053	.027	.008	.392	.356	.331	.338	.309	.289	.234	.217	.205	.136	.128	.122	.044	.042	.040
.106	.051	.014	.097	.047	.013	.081	.040	.011	.065	.033	.009	.051	.026	.007	.388	.353	.329	.335	.306	.287	.232	.215	.204	.135	.127	.122	.044	.042	.040
.100	.048	.013	.092	.044	.012	.077	.037	.011	.062	.031	.009	.048	.024	.007	.385	.350	.327	.332	.304	.286	.230	.214	.203	.134	.127	.121	.044	.042	.040
															.145	.145	.145	.124	.124	.124	.085	.085	.085	.049	.049	.049	.016	.016	.016
.142	.081	.026	.137	.078	.025	.127	.073	.023	.117	.068	.022	.108	.063	.020	.139	.128	.118	.119	.110	.102	.081	.076	.070	.047	.044	.041	.015	.014	.013
.132	.072	.022	.127	.070	.022	.118	.066	.020	.109	.061	.019	.102	.058	.018	.134	.116	.100	.115	.099	.087	.079	.069	.060	.045	.040	.035	.015	.013	.012
.122	.065	.019	.118	.063	.019	.109	.059	.018	.102	.056	.017	.095	.053	.016	.129	.106	.088	.111	.092	.077	.076	.064	.054	.044	.037	.032	.014	.012	.010
.113	.059	.017	.109	.057	.017	.102	.054	.016	.095	.051	.015	.089	.048	.015	.125	.099	.000	.107	.000	.070	.074	.000	.040	.040	.005	.020	.014	.011	.010
.105	.054	.016	.102	.052	.015	.095	.050	.015	.089	.047	.014	.083	.044	.013	.121	.094	.074	.104	.081	.065	.071	.057	.046	.041	.033	.027	.013	.011	.009
.098	.049	.014	.095	.048	.014	.089	.046	.013	.083	.043	.013	.078	.041	.012	.117	.090	.070	.101	.078	.061	.069	.054	.043	.040	.032	.026	.013	.010	.008
.092	.045	.013	.089	.044	.013	.084	.042	.012	.079	.040	.012	.074	.038	.011	.114	.086	.067	.098	.075	.058	.068	.052	.041	.039	.031	.024	.013	.010	.008
.086	.042	.012	.084	.041	.012	.079	.039	.011	.074	.038	.011	.070	.036	.010	.111	.083	.064	.095	.072	.056	.066	.051	.040	.038	.030	.024	.012	.010	.008
.081	.039	.011	.079	.039	.011	.074	.037	.010	.070	.035	.010	.066	.034	.010	.108	.080	.062	.093	.070	.054	.064	.049	.038	.037	.029	.023	.012	.010	.008
.077	.037	.010	.075	.036	.010	.071	.035	.010	.067	.033	.009	.063	.032	.009	.105	.078	.060	.091	.068	.053	.063	.048	.037	.037	.028	.022	.012	.009	.007

LIGHTING CALCULATIONS

Fig. 9-34. *Continued*

	ρCC → 80	70	50	30	10	0	
Typical Luminaire / Maint.Cat. / SC / RCR	ρW → 50 30 10	50 30 10	50 30 10	50 30 10	50 30 10	0	WDRC

31 — 150 mm × 150 mm (6 × 6″) cell parabolic wedge louver—multiply by 1.1 for 250 × 250 mm (10 × 10″) cells. Maint. Cat. IV, SC 1.5/1.2, 0% up, 58% down.

RCR	80: 50 30 10	70: 50 30 10	50: 50 30 10	30: 50 30 10	10: 50 30 10	0	WDRC
0	.69 .69 .69	.67 .67 .67	.64 .64 .64	.62 .62 .62	.59 .59 .59	.58	
1	.62 .61 .59	.61 .59 .58	.59 .57 .56	.57 .55 .54	.55 .54 .53	.52	.159
2	.56 .53 .50	.55 .52 .50	.53 .50 .48	.51 .49 .47	.49 .48 .46	.45	.160
3	.50 .46 .43	.49 .46 .43	.48 .44 .42	.46 .43 .41	.45 .42 .41	.39	.155
4	.45 .41 .37	.44 .40 .37	.43 .39 .36	.42 .38 .36	.40 .38 .36	.34	.147
5	.40 .36 .32	.40 .36 .32	.39 .35 .32	.38 .34 .32	.37 .34 .31	.30	.139
6	.37 .32 .29	.36 .32 .28	.35 .31 .28	.34 .31 .28	.33 .30 .28	.27	.131
7	.33 .29 .25	.33 .28 .25	.32 .28 .25	.31 .28 .25	.30 .27 .25	.24	.123
8	.30 .26 .23	.30 .26 .22	.29 .25 .22	.28 .25 .22	.28 .25 .22	.21	.115
9	.28 .23 .20	.27 .23 .20	.27 .23 .20	.26 .23 .20	.26 .22 .20	.19	.109
10	.26 .21 .18	.25 .21 .18	.25 .21 .18	.24 .21 .18	.24 .20 .18	.17	.102

32 — 2-lamp, surface mounted, bare lamp unit—photometry with 460 mm (18″) wide panel above luminaire—lamps on 150 mm (6″) centers. Maint. Cat. I, SC 1.3, 9½% up, 78% down.

RCR	80: 50 30 10	70: 50 30 10	50: 50 30 10	30: 50 30 10	10: 50 30 10	0	WDRC
0	1.02 1.02 1.02	.99 .99 .99	.92 .92 .92	.86 .86 .86	.81 .81 .81	.78	
1	.85 .80 .76	.82 .78 .74	.76 .73 .70	.71 .68 .66	.67 .64 .62	.60	.467
2	.72 .65 .59	.70 .63 .58	.65 .60 .55	.61 .56 .52	.57 .53 .50	.47	.387
3	.63 .55 .48	.60 .53 .47	.56 .50 .45	.53 .47 .43	.49 .45 .41	.38	.331
4	.55 .46 .40	.53 .45 .39	.50 .43 .37	.46 .41 .36	.43 .38 .34	.32	.289
5	.49 .40 .34	.47 .39 .33	.44 .37 .32	.41 .35 .31	.39 .34 .29	.27	.255
6	.43 .35 .29	.42 .34 .29	.40 .33 .28	.37 .31 .27	.35 .30 .26	.23	.228
7	.39 .31 .25	.38 .30 .25	.36 .29 .24	.34 .28 .23	.32 .26 .22	.20	.206
8	.36 .28 .22	.35 .27 .22	.33 .26 .21	.31 .25 .21	.29 .24 .20	.18	.188
9	.33 .25 .20	.32 .25 .20	.30 .24 .19	.28 .23 .18	.27 .22 .18	.16	.173
10	.30 .23 .18	.29 .22 .18	.28 .21 .17	.26 .21 .17	.25 .20 .16	.14	.159

33 — Luminous bottom suspended unit with extra-high output lamp. Maint. Cat. VI, SC N.A., 66% up, 12% down.

RCR	80: 50 30 10	70: 50 30 10	50: 50 30 10	30: 50 30 10	10: 50 30 10	0	WDRC
0	.77 .77 .77	.68 .68 .68	.50 .50 .50	.34 .34 .34	.19 .19 .19	.12	
1	.67 .64 .61	.59 .56 .54	.43 .42 .41	.29 .29 .28	.17 .16 .16	.10	.048
2	.58 .54 .50	.51 .48 .44	.38 .36 .34	.26 .24 .23	.14 .14 .13	.08	.045
3	.51 .46 .42	.45 .41 .37	.33 .30 .28	.23 .21 .19	.13 .12 .11	.07	.041
4	.45 .39 .35	.40 .35 .31	.30 .26 .24	.20 .18 .17	.11 .10 .10	.06	.037
5	.40 .34 .30	.35 .30 .26	.26 .23 .20	.18 .16 .14	.10 .09 .08	.05	.034
6	.36 .30 .25	.31 .26 .23	.24 .20 .17	.16 .14 .12	.09 .08 .07	.04	.031
7	.32 .26 .22	.28 .23 .20	.21 .18 .15	.15 .12 .11	.08 .07 .06	.04	.028
8	.29 .23 .19	.26 .21 .17	.19 .16 .13	.13 .11 .09	.08 .06 .06	.04	.026
9	.26 .21 .17	.23 .18 .15	.17 .14 .12	.12 .10 .08	.07 .06 .05	.03	.024
10	.24 .19 .15	.21 .17 .13	.16 .13 .10	.11 .09 .07	.06 .05 .04	.03	.022

34 — Prismatic bottom and sides, open top, 4-lamp suspended unit—see note 7. Maint. Cat. VI, SC 1.4/1.2, 33% up, 50% down.

RCR	80: 50 30 10	70: 50 30 10	50: 50 30 10	30: 50 30 10	10: 50 30 10	0	WDRC
0	.91 .91 .91	.85 .85 .85	.74 .74 .74	.64 .64 .64	.54 .54 .54	.50	
1	.80 .77 .74	.75 .72 .70	.65 .63 .61	.57 .55 .54	.49 .47 .47	.43	.179
2	.70 .65 .61	.66 .62 .58	.58 .54 .52	.50 .48 .46	.43 .42 .40	.37	.166
3	.62 .56 .51	.58 .53 .49	.51 .47 .44	.45 .42 .39	.39 .37 .35	.32	.153
4	.55 .49 .44	.52 .46 .42	.46 .41 .38	.40 .37 .34	.35 .32 .30	.27	.140
5	.50 .43 .38	.47 .41 .36	.41 .37 .33	.36 .33 .30	.32 .29 .26	.24	.129
6	.45 .38 .33	.42 .36 .32	.37 .33 .29	.33 .29 .26	.29 .26 .23	.21	.119
7	.40 .34 .29	.38 .32 .28	.34 .29 .26	.30 .26 .23	.26 .23 .21	.19	.111
8	.37 .30 .26	.35 .29 .25	.31 .26 .23	.28 .24 .21	.24 .21 .19	.17	.103
9	.34 .27 .23	.32 .26 .22	.29 .24 .21	.25 .22 .19	.22 .19 .17	.15	.096
10	.31 .25 .21	.29 .24 .20	.26 .22 .19	.23 .20 .17	.21 .18 .15	.14	.090

35 — 2-lamp prismatic wraparound—see note 7. Maint. Cat. V, SC 1.5/1.2, 11½% up, 58½% down.

RCR	80: 50 30 10	70: 50 30 10	50: 50 30 10	30: 50 30 10	10: 50 30 10	0	WDRC
0	.81 .81 .81	.78 .78 .78	.72 .72 .72	.66 .66 .66	.61 .61 .61	.59	
1	.71 .68 .66	.68 .66 .63	.63 .61 .59	.58 .57 .56	.54 .53 .52	.50	.223
2	.63 .58 .55	.60 .56 .53	.56 .53 .50	.52 .50 .47	.48 .46 .45	.43	.201
3	.56 .50 .46	.54 .49 .45	.50 .46 .43	.47 .43 .41	.43 .41 .39	.37	.183
4	.50 .44 .40	.48 .43 .39	.45 .40 .37	.42 .38 .35	.39 .36 .34	.32	.167
5	.45 .39 .34	.43 .38 .34	.40 .36 .32	.38 .34 .31	.35 .32 .30	.28	.153
6	.40 .34 .30	.39 .34 .30	.37 .32 .28	.34 .30 .27	.32 .29 .26	.25	.142
7	.37 .31 .27	.35 .30 .26	.33 .29 .25	.31 .27 .24	.30 .26 .23	.22	.131
8	.33 .28 .24	.32 .27 .23	.30 .26 .23	.28 .24 .22	.27 .24 .21	.20	.122
9	.31 .25 .21	.30 .25 .21	.28 .24 .20	.26 .23 .20	.25 .22 .19	.18	.114
10	.28 .23 .19	.27 .22 .19	.26 .21 .18	.24 .21 .18	.23 .20 .17	.16	.107

36 — 2-lamp prismatic wraparound—see note 7. Maint. Cat. V, SC 1.2, 24% up, 50% down.

RCR	80: 50 30 10	70: 50 30 10	50: 50 30 10	30: 50 30 10	10: 50 30 10	0	WDRC
0	.82 .82 .82	.77 .77 .77	.69 .69 .69	.61 .61 .61	.53 .53 .53	.50	
1	.71 .67 .65	.67 .64 .61	.59 .57 .55	.52 .51 .49	.46 .45 .44	.40	.234
2	.62 .57 .53	.59 .54 .51	.52 .49 .46	.46 .44 .41	.41 .39 .37	.34	.194
3	.55 .49 .45	.52 .47 .43	.46 .42 .39	.41 .38 .36	.37 .34 .32	.30	.168
4	.49 .43 .39	.47 .41 .37	.42 .37 .34	.37 .34 .31	.33 .30 .28	.26	.150
5	.44 .38 .34	.42 .36 .32	.38 .33 .30	.34 .30 .27	.30 .27 .25	.23	.135
6	.40 .34 .29	.38 .32 .28	.34 .30 .26	.31 .27 .24	.28 .25 .22	.20	.123
7	.36 .30 .26	.35 .29 .25	.31 .27 .23	.28 .24 .22	.26 .23 .20	.18	.112
8	.33 .27 .23	.32 .26 .23	.29 .24 .21	.26 .22 .20	.23 .20 .18	.16	.104
9	.30 .25 .21	.29 .24 .20	.26 .22 .19	.24 .20 .18	.22 .19 .16	.15	.097
10	.28 .23 .19	.27 .22 .18	.25 .20 .17	.22 .19 .16	.20 .17 .15	.14	.090

Coefficients of Utilization for 20 Per Cent Effective Floor Cavity Reflectance ($\rho_{FC} = 20$)

436

Fig. 9-34. *Continued*

80			70			50			30			10			80			70			50			30			10		
50	30	10	50	30	10	50	30	10	50	30	10	50	30	10	50	30	10	50	30	10	50	30	10	50	30	10	50	30	10
Wall Exitance Coefficients for 20 Per Cent Effective Floor Cavity Reflectance (ρ_{FC} = 20)															Ceiling Cavity Exitance Coefficients for 20 Per Cent Floor Cavity Reflectance (ρ_{FC} = 20)														
															.111	.111	.111	.094	.094	.094	.064	.064	.064	.037	.037	.037	.012	.012	.012
.138	.078	.025	.134	.076	.024	.126	.072	.023	.119	.069	.022	.113	.065	.021	.102	.091	.081	.087	.078	.070	.060	.054	.048	.034	.031	.028	.011	.010	.009
.136	.074	.023	.132	.073	.022	.126	.070	.022	.120	.067	.021	.114	.065	.020	.095	.077	.061	.082	.066	.053	.056	.046	.037	.032	.027	.022	.010	.009	.007
.130	.069	.021	.127	.068	.021	.122	.066	.020	.117	.064	.020	.112	.062	.019	.090	.066	.047	.077	.057	.041	.053	.040	.028	.031	.023	.017	.010	.008	.005
.124	.065	.019	.122	.064	.019	.117	.062	.018	.112	.060	.018	.108	.058	.018	.086	.058	.037	.074	.050	.032	.051	.035	.023	.029	.021	.013	.009	.007	.004
.118	.060	.017	.115	.059	.017	.111	.058	.017	.107	.056	.017	.103	.055	.017	.082	.052	.030	.070	.045	.026	.049	.031	.018	.028	.018	.011	.009	.006	.004
.112	.056	.016	.109	.055	.016	.105	.054	.016	.102	.053	.016	.098	.052	.015	.078	.047	.024	.067	.041	.021	.046	.028	.015	.027	.017	.009	.009	.005	.003
.106	.052	.015	.104	.052	.015	.100	.051	.015	.097	.050	.014	.094	.049	.014	.075	.043	.021	.064	.037	.018	.044	.026	.013	.026	.015	.008	.008	.005	.003
.100	.049	.014	.098	.048	.014	.095	.047	.014	.092	.047	.013	.089	.046	.013	.072	.040	.018	.062	.034	.015	.043	.024	.011	.025	.014	.007	.008	.005	.002
.095	.046	.013	.093	.045	.013	.090	.045	.013	.087	.044	.013	.085	.043	.012	.068	.037	.015	.059	.032	.013	.041	.022	.010	.024	.013	.006	.008	.004	.002
.090	.043	.012	.088	.043	.012	.086	.042	.012	.083	.041	.012	.081	.041	.012	.066	.034	.014	.057	.030	.012	.039	.021	.008	.023	.012	.005	.007	.004	.002
															.239	.239	.239	.205	.205	.205	.140	.140	.140	.080	.080	.080	.026	.026	.026
.345	.196	.062	.335	.191	.061	.318	.182	.058	.302	.174	.056	.287	.166	.054	.236	.209	.185	.202	.180	.159	.138	.123	.110	.080	.071	.064	.025	.023	.021
.300	.164	.050	.292	.161	.049	.276	.153	.048	.262	.147	.046	.248	.140	.044	.230	.189	.154	.197	.163	.133	.135	.112	.093	.078	.065	.054	.025	.021	.018
.267	.142	.043	.259	.139	.042	.245	.133	.040	.232	.127	.039	.220	.122	.038	.224	.174	.135	.192	.150	.117	.132	.104	.082	.076	.061	.048	.024	.020	.016
.240	.125	.037	.233	.122	.036	.220	.117	.035	.209	.112	.034	.198	.107	.033	.217	.163	.122	.186	.141	.106	.128	.098	.075	.074	.058	.044	.024	.019	.015
.218	.111	.032	.212	.109	.032	.200	.104	.031	.190	.100	.030	.180	.096	.029	.210	.154	.113	.180	.134	.099	.124	.093	.070	.072	.055	.041	.023	.018	.014
.199	.100	.029	.194	.098	.028	.183	.094	.027	.174	.090	.027	.165	.087	.026	.203	.147	.107	.175	.128	.093	.121	.089	.066	.070	.053	.039	.023	.017	.013
.184	.091	.026	.179	.089	.025	.169	.086	.025	.160	.082	.024	.152	.079	.023	.197	.141	.103	.169	.123	.089	.117	.086	.063	.068	.051	.038	.022	.017	.012
.170	.083	.023	.166	.082	.023	.157	.078	.022	.149	.075	.022	.141	.073	.021	.191	.137	.099	.164	.118	.086	.114	.083	.061	.066	.049	.037	.021	.016	.012
.158	.077	.021	.154	.075	.021	.146	.072	.021	.139	.070	.020	.132	.067	.019	.185	.132	.096	.160	.115	.084	.111	.081	.060	.064	.048	.036	.021	.016	.012
.148	.071	.020	.144	.070	.019	.137	.067	.019	.130	.065	.018	.124	.062	.018	.180	.129	.094	.155	.112	.082	.108	.079	.058	.063	.046	.035	.020	.015	.012
															.653	.653	.653	.558	.558	.558	.381	.381	.381	.219	.219	.219	.070	.070	.070
.206	.117	.037	.181	.103	.033	.133	.077	.024	.090	.052	.017	.049	.029	.009	.647	.631	.616	.553	.541	.530	.378	.372	.367	.218	.215	.213	.070	.069	.069
.191	.104	.032	.167	.092	.028	.124	.069	.021	.084	.047	.015	.047	.026	.008	.641	.615	.593	.549	.529	.512	.376	.366	.357	.217	.213	.209	.070	.069	.068
.176	.094	.028	.155	.083	.025	.115	.062	.019	.078	.043	.013	.043	.024	.007	.636	.603	.577	.545	.521	.501	.374	.362	.351	.216	.211	.207	.069	.069	.068
.163	.085	.025	.144	.075	.022	.107	.057	.017	.072	.039	.012	.040	.022	.007	.631	.595	.567	.542	.514	.493	.373	.358	.347	.216	.210	.205	.069	.068	.067
.152	.077	.022	.133	.069	.020	.099	.052	.015	.067	.036	.011	.038	.020	.006	.627	.588	.560	.538	.509	.487	.371	.356	.344	.215	.209	.204	.069	.068	.067
.141	.071	.020	.124	.063	.018	.093	.047	.014	.063	.033	.010	.035	.019	.006	.623	.583	.554	.535	.505	.483	.369	.353	.342	.214	.208	.203	.069	.068	.067
.132	.065	.018	.116	.058	.017	.087	.044	.013	.059	.030	.009	.033	.017	.005	.618	.578	.551	.532	.501	.480	.367	.352	.340	.214	.207	.202	.069	.068	.067
.124	.060	.017	.109	.054	.015	.081	.041	.012	.055	.028	.008	.031	.016	.005	.614	.575	.548	.529	.499	.478	.366	.350	.339	.213	.206	.202	.069	.068	.067
.116	.056	.016	.103	.050	.014	.077	.038	.011	.052	.026	.007	.029	.015	.004	.611	.572	.545	.526	.496	.476	.364	.349	.338	.212	.206	.201	.069	.068	.067
.109	.052	.015	.097	.047	.013	.072	.035	.010	.049	.025	.007	.028	.014	.004	.607	.569	.544	.523	.494	.474	.363	.348	.337	.212	.206	.201	.069	.068	.067
															.409	.409	.409	.350	.350	.350	.239	.239	.239	.137	.137	.137	.044	.044	.044
.226	.129	.041	.210	.120	.038	.181	.104	.033	.154	.089	.028	.129	.075	.024	.401	.383	.367	.343	.329	.316	.235	.226	.219	.135	.131	.127	.043	.042	.041
.210	.115	.035	.196	.108	.033	.169	.094	.029	.145	.081	.025	.122	.069	.022	.394	.365	.340	.337	.314	.294	.231	.217	.205	.133	.126	.120	.043	.041	.039
.195	.104	.031	.182	.098	.029	.158	.086	.026	.135	.074	.023	.115	.063	.020	.388	.351	.322	.332	.303	.279	.228	.211	.196	.132	.123	.116	.042	.040	.038
.182	.094	.028	.170	.089	.026	.147	.078	.023	.127	.068	.021	.107	.058	.018	.382	.341	.310	.328	.295	.269	.225	.205	.190	.130	.120	.112	.042	.039	.037
.169	.086	.025	.158	.081	.024	.138	.072	.021	.119	.063	.019	.101	.054	.016	.376	.333	.301	.323	.288	.262	.223	.201	.185	.129	.118	.110	.042	.039	.036
.158	.079	.023	.148	.075	.022	.129	.066	.019	.111	.058	.017	.095	.050	.015	.371	.327	.295	.319	.283	.257	.220	.198	.182	.128	.116	.108	.041	.038	.036
.148	.073	.021	.139	.069	.020	.121	.061	.018	.105	.054	.016	.089	.046	.014	.366	.321	.290	.315	.279	.253	.218	.195	.179	.126	.115	.107	.041	.038	.035
.139	.068	.019	.130	.064	.018	.114	.057	.016	.099	.050	.014	.084	.043	.013	.361	.317	.286	.311	.275	.250	.215	.193	.177	.125	.114	.106	.041	.037	.035
.131	.063	.018	.123	.060	.017	.108	.053	.015	.093	.047	.013	.080	.041	.012	.357	.313	.284	.308	.272	.247	.213	.191	.176	.124	.113	.105	.040	.037	.035
.123	.059	.016	.116	.056	.016	.102	.050	.014	.089	.044	.012	.076	.038	.011	.353	.310	.281	.304	.269	.246	.211	.189	.174	.123	.112	.104	.040	.037	.035
															.221	.221	.221	.189	.189	.189	.129	.129	.129	.074	.074	.074	.024	.024	.024
.202	.115	.036	.193	.110	.035	.178	.102	.033	.163	.094	.030	.150	.087	.028	.213	.198	.183	.183	.170	.158	.125	.117	.109	.072	.068	.064	.023	.022	.021
.186	.102	.031	.178	.098	.030	.164	.091	.028	.151	.085	.027	.139	.079	.025	.207	.181	.160	.177	.156	.138	.121	.108	.096	.070	.063	.056	.022	.020	.018
.172	.091	.027	.165	.088	.027	.153	.083	.025	.141	.077	.024	.130	.072	.022	.201	.169	.144	.172	.146	.125	.118	.101	.087	.068	.059	.051	.022	.019	.017
.159	.083	.024	.153	.080	.024	.142	.075	.022	.131	.071	.021	.121	.066	.020	.196	.160	.133	.168	.138	.115	.115	.096	.081	.067	.056	.048	.021	.018	.016
.148	.076	.022	.143	.073	.021	.133	.069	.020	.123	.065	.019	.114	.061	.018	.191	.153	.125	.164	.132	.109	.113	.092	.077	.065	.054	.045	.021	.018	.015
.139	.069	.020	.134	.068	.019	.124	.064	.019	.115	.060	.018	.107	.056	.017	.186	.147	.119	.160	.127	.104	.110	.089	.073	.064	.052	.044	.021	.017	.014
.130	.064	.018	.125	.062	.018	.117	.059	.017	.108	.056	.016	.101	.052	.015	.182	.142	.115	.156	.123	.100	.108	.087	.071	.063	.051	.042	.020	.017	.014
.122	.060	.017	.118	.058	.016	.110	.055	.016	.102	.052	.015	.095	.049	.014	.178	.138	.112	.153	.120	.097	.106	.084	.069	.062	.050	.041	.020	.016	.014
.115	.056	.016	.111	.054	.015	.104	.051	.015	.097	.048	.014	.090	.046	.013	.174	.135	.109	.150	.117	.095	.104	.082	.068	.060	.049	.040	.020	.016	.013
.108	.052	.014	.105	.051	.014	.098	.048	.014	.092	.046	.013	.086	.043	.012	.170	.132	.107	.147	.115	.094	.102	.081	.066	.059	.048	.040	.019	.016	.013
															.324	.324	.324	.277	.277	.277	.189	.189	.189	.108	.108	.108	.035	.035	.035
.232	.132	.042	.219	.125	.040	.196	.112	.036	.175	.101	.032	.155	.090	.029	.318	.300	.284	.272	.257	.244	.186	.177	.169	.107	.102	.098	.034	.033	.032
.204	.112	.034	.193	.106	.033	.172	.096	.030	.152	.086	.027	.134	.076	.024	.312	.283	.260	.267	.244	.224	.183	.169	.157	.105	.098	.092	.034	.032	.030
.185	.098	.029	.174	.093	.028	.155	.084	.026	.137	.075	.023	.121	.067	.021	.305	.271	.244	.262	.234	.211	.180	.163	.148	.104	.095	.087	.033	.031	.029
.169	.088	.026	.160	.083	.025	.142	.075	.022	.126	.067	.020	.111	.060	.018	.300	.262	.233	.257	.226	.202	.177	.158	.143	.102	.092	.084	.033	.030	.028
.156	.079	.023	.147	.076	.022	.131	.068	.020	.116	.061	.018	.102	.055	.016	.294	.255	.225	.253	.220	.196	.174	.154	.138	.101	.090	.082	.033	.029	.027
.144	.072	.021	.136	.069	.020	.122	.062	.018	.108	.056	.016	.095	.050	.015	.289	.249	.220	.249	.216	.191	.172	.151	.135	.100	.089	.080	.032	.029	.027
.134	.066	.019	.127	.063	.018	.114	.057	.017	.101	.052	.015	.089	.046	.014	.285	.244	.216	.245	.212	.188	.169	.148	.133	.098	.087	.079	.032	.029	.026
.126	.061	.017	.119	.059	.017	.107	.053	.015	.095	.048	.014	.084	.043	.012	.280	.240	.212	.241	.208	.185	.167	.146	.131	.097	.086	.078	.031	.028	.026
.118	.057	.016	.112	.055	.015	.100	.050	.014	.089	.045	.013	.079	.040	.012	.276	.237	.210	.238	.205	.183	.165	.144	.130	.096	.085	.078	.031	.028	.026
.111	.053	.015	.106	.051	.014	.095	.046	.013	.084	.042	.012	.075	.038	.011	.272	.234	.208	.235	.203	.181	.163	.143	.129	.095	.084	.077	.031	.028	.026

Fig. 9-34. *Continued*

Typical Luminaire	Typical Intensity Distribution and Per Cent Lamp Lumens		ρcc →	80			70			50			30			10			0	WDRC	ρcc →
	Maint. Cat.	SC	ρw →	50	30	10	50	30	10	50	30	10	50	30	10	50	30	10	0		ρw →
			RCR ↓	Coefficients of Utilization for 20 Per Cent Effective Floor Cavity Reflectance (ρFC = 20)																	RCR ↓
37 2-lamp diffuse wraparound—see note 7 (8%↑ 37½%↓ II ⊥)	V	1.3	0	.52	.52	.52	.50	.50	.50	.46	.46	.46	.43	.43	.43	.39	.39	.39	.38		0
			1	.44	.42	.40	.42	.40	.39	.39	.37	.36	.36	.35	.33	.33	.32	.31	.30	.201	1
			2	.38	.35	.32	.37	.33	.31	.34	.31	.29	.31	.29	.27	.28	.27	.25	.24	.171	2
			3	.33	.29	.26	.32	.28	.25	.29	.26	.24	.27	.25	.22	.25	.23	.21	.20	.149	3
			4	.29	.25	.22	.28	.24	.21	.26	.23	.20	.24	.21	.19	.22	.20	.18	.17	.132	4
			5	.26	.22	.19	.25	.21	.18	.23	.20	.17	.21	.18	.16	.20	.17	.15	.14	.117	5
			6	.23	.19	.16	.22	.18	.16	.21	.17	.15	.19	.16	.14	.18	.15	.13	.12	.106	6
			7	.21	.17	.14	.20	.16	.14	.19	.15	.13	.17	.15	.12	.16	.14	.12	.11	.096	7
			8	.19	.15	.12	.18	.15	.12	.17	.14	.12	.16	.13	.11	.15	.12	.11	.10	.088	8
			9	.17	.14	.11	.17	.13	.11	.16	.13	.10	.15	.12	.10	.14	.11	.09	.09	.081	9
			10	.16	.12	.10	.15	.12	.10	.14	.11	.09	.14	.11	.09	.13	.10	.09	.08	.075	10
38 4-lamp, 610 mm (2') wide troffer with 45° plastic louver—see note 7 (0%↑ 50%↓)	IV	1.0	0	.60	.60	.60	.58	.58	.58	.56	.56	.56	.53	.53	.53	.51	.51	.51	.50		0
			1	.53	.51	.49	.52	.50	.49	.50	.48	.47	.48	.47	.46	.46	.45	.44	.43	.168	1
			2	.47	.44	.42	.46	.43	.41	.44	.42	.40	.43	.41	.39	.41	.40	.38	.37	.159	2
			3	.42	.38	.36	.41	.38	.35	.40	.37	.36	.39	.36	.34	.37	.35	.34	.32	.146	3
			4	.38	.34	.31	.37	.34	.31	.36	.33	.30	.35	.32	.30	.34	.32	.30	.29	.135	4
			5	.34	.30	.27	.34	.30	.27	.33	.29	.27	.32	.29	.27	.31	.28	.26	.25	.124	5
			6	.31	.27	.24	.31	.27	.24	.30	.27	.24	.29	.26	.24	.28	.26	.24	.23	.114	6
			7	.29	.25	.22	.28	.24	.22	.28	.24	.22	.27	.24	.21	.26	.23	.21	.20	.106	7
			8	.26	.22	.20	.26	.22	.20	.25	.22	.20	.25	.22	.20	.24	.21	.19	.19	.099	8
			9	.24	.21	.18	.24	.21	.18	.24	.20	.18	.23	.20	.18	.23	.20	.18	.17	.092	9
			10	.23	.19	.17	.22	.19	.17	.22	.19	.16	.22	.19	.16	.21	.18	.16	.16	.086	10
39 4-lamp, 610 mm (2') wide troffer with 45° white metal louver—see note 7 (0%↑ 46%↓)	IV	0.9	0	.55	.55	.55	.54	.54	.54	.51	.51	.51	.49	.49	.49	.47	.47	.47	.46		0
			1	.49	.48	.46	.48	.47	.46	.46	.45	.44	.45	.44	.43	.43	.42	.42	.41	.137	1
			2	.44	.42	.40	.43	.41	.39	.42	.40	.38	.40	.39	.37	.39	.38	.37	.36	.131	2
			3	.40	.37	.34	.39	.36	.34	.38	.36	.33	.37	.35	.33	.36	.34	.32	.32	.122	3
			4	.36	.33	.30	.36	.33	.30	.35	.32	.30	.34	.31	.29	.33	.31	.29	.28	.113	4
			5	.33	.30	.27	.33	.29	.27	.32	.29	.27	.31	.28	.26	.30	.28	.26	.25	.104	5
			6	.30	.27	.24	.30	.27	.24	.29	.26	.24	.29	.26	.24	.28	.25	.24	.23	.097	6
			7	.28	.25	.22	.28	.24	.22	.27	.24	.22	.26	.24	.22	.26	.23	.22	.21	.090	7
			8	.26	.23	.20	.26	.22	.20	.25	.22	.20	.25	.22	.20	.24	.22	.20	.19	.085	8
			9	.24	.21	.19	.24	.21	.19	.23	.20	.18	.23	.20	.18	.23	.20	.18	.18	.079	9
			10	.23	.19	.17	.22	.19	.17	.22	.19	.17	.22	.19	.17	.21	.19	.17	.16	.075	10
40 Fluorescent unit dropped diffuser, 4-lamp 610 mm (2') wide—see note 7 (1%↑ 60½%↓)	V	1.2	0	.73	.73	.73	.71	.71	.71	.68	.68	.68	.65	.65	.65	.62	.62	.62	.60		0
			1	.63	.60	.58	.62	.59	.57	.59	.57	.55	.56	.55	.53	.54	.53	.51	.50	.259	1
			2	.55	.51	.47	.54	.50	.46	.51	.48	.45	.49	.46	.44	.47	.45	.43	.42	.236	2
			3	.48	.43	.39	.47	.42	.39	.45	.41	.38	.43	.40	.37	.42	.39	.36	.35	.212	3
			4	.43	.37	.33	.42	.37	.33	.40	.36	.32	.39	.35	.32	.37	.34	.31	.30	.191	4
			5	.38	.33	.29	.37	.32	.28	.36	.31	.28	.35	.31	.28	.33	.30	.27	.26	.173	5
			6	.34	.29	.25	.34	.29	.25	.33	.28	.24	.31	.27	.24	.30	.27	.24	.23	.158	6
			7	.31	.26	.22	.31	.26	.22	.30	.25	.22	.29	.25	.21	.28	.24	.21	.20	.144	7
			8	.28	.23	.20	.28	.23	.20	.27	.23	.19	.26	.22	.19	.25	.22	.19	.18	.133	8
			9	.26	.21	.18	.26	.21	.18	.25	.21	.17	.24	.20	.17	.24	.20	.17	.16	.123	9
			10	.24	.19	.16	.24	.19	.16	.23	.19	.16	.22	.19	.16	.22	.18	.16	.15	.115	10
41 Fluorescent unit with flat bottom diffuser, 4-lamp 610 mm (2') wide—see note 7 (0%↑ 57½%↓)	V	1.2	0	.69	.69	.69	.67	.67	.67	.64	.64	.64	.61	.61	.61	.59	.59	.59	.58		0
			1	.60	.58	.55	.59	.57	.55	.56	.55	.53	.54	.53	.51	.52	.51	.50	.49	.227	1
			2	.52	.49	.45	.51	.48	.45	.49	.46	.44	.47	.45	.43	.46	.44	.42	.40	.214	2
			3	.46	.41	.38	.45	.41	.37	.43	.40	.37	.42	.39	.36	.40	.38	.35	.34	.196	3
			4	.41	.36	.32	.40	.35	.32	.39	.34	.31	.37	.34	.31	.36	.33	.30	.29	.178	4
			5	.36	.31	.28	.36	.31	.27	.35	.30	.27	.33	.30	.27	.32	.29	.26	.25	.162	5
			6	.33	.28	.24	.32	.27	.24	.31	.27	.24	.30	.26	.23	.29	.26	.23	.22	.148	6
			7	.30	.25	.21	.29	.25	.21	.28	.24	.21	.28	.24	.21	.27	.23	.21	.20	.136	7
			8	.27	.22	.19	.27	.22	.19	.26	.22	.19	.25	.21	.19	.25	.21	.19	.17	.126	8
			9	.25	.20	.17	.25	.20	.17	.24	.20	.17	.23	.20	.17	.23	.19	.17	.16	.116	9
			10	.23	.18	.15	.23	.18	.15	.22	.18	.15	.22	.18	.15	.21	.18	.15	.14	.108	10
42 Fluorescent unit with flat prismatic lens, 4-lamp 610 mm (2') wide—see note 7 (0%↑ 63%↓ II ⊥ 60°)	V	1.4/1.2	0	.75	.75	.75	.73	.73	.73	.70	.70	.70	.67	.67	.67	.64	.64	.64	.63		0
			1	.67	.64	.62	.65	.63	.61	.63	.61	.59	.60	.59	.58	.58	.57	.56	.55	.208	1
			2	.59	.56	.52	.58	.55	.52	.56	.53	.51	.54	.52	.49	.52	.50	.48	.47	.199	2
			3	.53	.48	.45	.52	.48	.44	.50	.46	.43	.48	.45	.42	.47	.44	.42	.41	.186	3
			4	.47	.42	.38	.46	.42	.38	.45	.41	.38	.44	.40	.37	.42	.39	.37	.35	.172	4
			5	.43	.37	.34	.42	.37	.33	.41	.36	.33	.39	.36	.33	.38	.35	.32	.31	.160	5
			6	.39	.33	.30	.38	.33	.29	.37	.32	.29	.36	.32	.29	.35	.31	.29	.27	.148	6
			7	.35	.30	.26	.35	.30	.26	.34	.29	.26	.33	.29	.26	.32	.28	.26	.24	.138	7
			8	.32	.27	.24	.32	.27	.23	.31	.26	.23	.30	.26	.23	.29	.26	.23	.22	.128	8
			9	.30	.25	.21	.29	.24	.21	.28	.24	.21	.28	.24	.21	.27	.24	.21	.20	.120	9
			10	.27	.22	.19	.27	.22	.19	.26	.22	.19	.26	.22	.19	.25	.22	.19	.18	.113	10

Fig. 9-34. *Continued*

80			70			50			30			10			80			70			50			30			10		
50	30	10	50	30	10	50	30	10	50	30	10	50	30	10	50	30	10	50	30	10	50	30	10	50	30	10	50	30	10
Wall Exitance Coefficients for 20 Per Cent Effective Floor Cavity Reflectance (ρ_{FC} = 20)															Ceiling Cavity Exitance Coefficients for 20 Per Cent Floor Cavity Reflectance (ρ_{FC} = 20)														
															.147	.147	.147	.125	.125	.125	.085	.085	.085	.049	.049	.049	.016	.016	.016
.162	.092	.029	.156	.089	.028	.145	.083	.027	.136	.078	.025	.127	.073	.024	.144	.131	.120	.123	.113	.103	.084	.077	.071	.048	.045	.041	.016	.014	.013
.144	.079	.024	.139	.076	.024	.129	.072	.022	.120	.068	.021	.112	.064	.020	.141	.121	.104	.120	.104	.090	.083	.072	.063	.048	.042	.037	.015	.014	.012
.130	.069	.021	.125	.067	.020	.116	.063	.019	.108	.059	.018	.101	.056	.017	.137	.113	.094	.118	.098	.081	.081	.068	.057	.047	.040	.034	.015	.013	.011
.118	.061	.018	.114	.059	.018	.106	.056	.017	.098	.053	.016	.092	.050	.015	.134	.107	.087	.115	.093	.076	.079	.065	.053	.046	.038	.032	.015	.012	.010
.108	.055	.016	.104	.053	.016	.097	.050	.015	.090	.048	.014	.084	.045	.013	.130	.103	.083	.112	.089	.072	.077	.062	.051	.045	.037	.030	.014	.012	.010
.099	.050	.014	.096	.048	.014	.089	.046	.013	.083	.043	.013	.077	.041	.012	.127	.099	.079	.109	.086	.069	.075	.060	.049	.044	.035	.029	.014	.012	.010
.092	.045	.013	.088	.044	.013	.083	.042	.012	.077	.039	.011	.072	.037	.011	.124	.096	.077	.107	.083	.067	.074	.059	.047	.043	.034	.028	.014	.011	.009
.085	.042	.012	.082	.041	.011	.077	.038	.011	.072	.036	.010	.067	.034	.010	.121	.094	.075	.104	.081	.065	.072	.057	.046	.042	.034	.028	.014	.011	.009
.080	.038	.011	.077	.037	.011	.072	.036	.010	.067	.034	.010	.063	.032	.009	.118	.092	.074	.102	.079	.064	.071	.056	.046	.041	.033	.027	.013	.011	.009
.075	.036	.010	.072	.035	.010	.067	.033	.009	.063	.031	.009	.059	.030	.009	.116	.090	.072	.100	.078	.063	.069	.055	.045	.040	.032	.027	.013	.011	.009
															.095	.095	.095	.082	.082	.082	.056	.056	.056	.032	.032	.032	.010	.010	.010
.135	.077	.024	.132	.075	.024	.125	.072	.023	.119	.069	.022	.114	.066	.021	.089	.078	.069	.076	.067	.059	.052	.046	.041	.030	.027	.024	.010	.009	.008
.128	.070	.022	.125	.069	.021	.120	.066	.021	.114	.064	.020	.109	.062	.020	.084	.066	.051	.072	.057	.044	.049	.039	.031	.028	.023	.018	.009	.007	.006
.120	.064	.019	.117	.063	.019	.112	.061	.018	.108	.059	.018	.103	.057	.018	.079	.057	.039	.068	.049	.034	.047	.034	.024	.027	.020	.014	.009	.006	.005
.112	.058	.017	.109	.057	.017	.105	.056	.017	.101	.054	.016	.097	.053	.016	.075	.050	.031	.065	.043	.027	.044	.030	.019	.026	.018	.011	.008	.006	.004
.104	.053	.015	.102	.052	.015	.098	.051	.015	.094	.050	.015	.091	.049	.015	.071	.045	.025	.061	.039	.022	.042	.027	.016	.024	.016	.009	.008	.005	.003
.097	.049	.014	.095	.048	.014	.092	.047	.014	.089	.046	.014	.086	.045	.013	.068	.041	.021	.058	.035	.018	.040	.025	.013	.023	.014	.008	.008	.005	.003
.091	.045	.013	.089	.045	.013	.086	.044	.013	.083	.043	.012	.081	.042	.012	.065	.037	.018	.056	.032	.015	.038	.023	.011	.022	.013	.007	.007	.004	.002
.086	.042	.012	.084	.041	.012	.081	.041	.012	.079	.040	.012	.076	.039	.011	.062	.034	.015	.053	.030	.013	.037	.021	.009	.021	.012	.006	.007	.004	.002
.081	.039	.011	.079	.039	.011	.077	.038	.011	.075	.037	.011	.072	.037	.011	.059	.032	.013	.051	.027	.012	.035	.019	.008	.020	.011	.005	.007	.004	.002
.076	.037	.010	.075	.036	.010	.073	.036	.010	.071	.035	.010	.069	.035	.010	.056	.029	.012	.048	.026	.010	.033	.018	.007	.020	.011	.004	.006	.003	.001
															.088	.088	.088	.075	.075	.075	.051	.051	.051	.029	.029	.029	.009	.009	.009
.115	.065	.021	.112	.064	.020	.106	.061	.019	.100	.058	.019	.095	.055	.018	.081	.072	.064	.069	.062	.055	.048	.043	.038	.027	.025	.022	.009	.008	.007
.109	.060	.018	.107	.059	.018	.102	.056	.018	.097	.054	.017	.092	.052	.016	.076	.061	.048	.065	.052	.042	.045	.036	.029	.026	.021	.017	.008	.007	.006
.103	.055	.016	.100	.054	.016	.096	.052	.016	.092	.050	.015	.088	.049	.015	.072	.053	.037	.061	.045	.032	.042	.031	.023	.024	.018	.013	.008	.006	.004
.096	.050	.015	.094	.049	.015	.090	.048	.014	.086	.046	.014	.083	.045	.014	.068	.046	.030	.058	.040	.026	.040	.028	.018	.023	.016	.011	.007	.005	.004
.090	.046	.013	.088	.045	.013	.085	.044	.013	.081	.043	.013	.078	.042	.013	.064	.041	.024	.055	.036	.021	.038	.025	.015	.022	.015	.009	.007	.005	.003
.084	.042	.012	.083	.042	.012	.080	.041	.012	.077	.040	.012	.074	.039	.012	.061	.037	.020	.052	.032	.017	.036	.022	.012	.021	.013	.007	.007	.004	.002
.079	.039	.011	.078	.039	.011	.075	.038	.011	.073	.037	.011	.070	.036	.011	.058	.034	.017	.050	.029	.015	.034	.021	.010	.020	.012	.006	.006	.004	.002
.075	.037	.010	.074	.036	.010	.071	.035	.010	.069	.035	.010	.067	.034	.010	.055	.031	.015	.047	.027	.013	.033	.019	.009	.019	.011	.005	.006	.004	.002
.071	.034	.010	.070	.034	.010	.067	.033	.009	.065	.033	.009	.063	.032	.009	.052	.029	.013	.045	.025	.011	.031	.018	.008	.018	.010	.005	.006	.003	.002
.067	.032	.009	.066	.032	.009	.064	.031	.009	.062	.031	.009	.060	.030	.009	.050	.027	.011	.043	.023	.010	.030	.016	.007	.017	.010	.004	.006	.003	.001
															.123	.123	.123	.105	.105	.105	.072	.072	.072	.041	.041	.041	.013	.013	.013
.196	.111	.035	.191	.109	.035	.182	.105	.033	.174	.101	.032	.167	.097	.031	.118	.102	.089	.101	.088	.076	.069	.060	.053	.040	.035	.031	.013	.011	.010
.181	.099	.030	.177	.098	.030	.170	.094	.029	.163	.091	.029	.156	.088	.028	.113	.087	.066	.096	.075	.057	.066	.052	.040	.038	.030	.023	.012	.010	.008
.167	.089	.027	.163	.087	.026	.156	.085	.026	.150	.082	.025	.144	.080	.025	.108	.077	.052	.092	.066	.045	.063	.046	.032	.037	.027	.019	.012	.009	.006
.153	.080	.023	.150	.079	.023	.144	.076	.023	.139	.074	.022	.133	.072	.022	.103	.069	.042	.088	.059	.037	.061	.041	.026	.035	.024	.015	.011	.008	.005
.141	.072	.021	.139	.071	.021	.133	.069	.020	.128	.068	.020	.124	.066	.020	.098	.062	.036	.085	.054	.031	.058	.038	.022	.034	.022	.013	.011	.007	.004
.131	.066	.019	.128	.065	.019	.124	.063	.018	.119	.062	.018	.115	.061	.018	.094	.057	.031	.081	.050	.027	.056	.035	.019	.032	.020	.011	.010	.007	.004
.122	.060	.017	.119	.060	.017	.115	.058	.017	.111	.057	.017	.107	.056	.016	.090	.053	.027	.077	.046	.024	.053	.032	.017	.031	.019	.010	.010	.006	.003
.114	.056	.016	.112	.055	.016	.108	.054	.015	.104	.053	.015	.101	.052	.015	.086	.049	.024	.074	.043	.021	.051	.030	.015	.030	.018	.009	.010	.006	.003
.106	.051	.014	.105	.051	.014	.101	.050	.014	.098	.049	.014	.095	.048	.014	.082	.046	.022	.071	.040	.019	.049	.028	.014	.029	.017	.008	.009	.005	.003
.100	.048	.013	.098	.048	.013	.095	.047	.013	.092	.046	.013	.089	.045	.013	.079	.044	.021	.068	.038	.018	.047	.027	.013	.027	.016	.008	.009	.005	.003
															.110	.110	.110	.094	.094	.094	.064	.064	.064	.037	.037	.037	.012	.012	.012
.174	.099	.031	.170	.097	.031	.162	.093	.030	.155	.089	.029	.149	.086	.028	.104	.090	.078	.089	.077	.067	.061	.053	.046	.035	.031	.027	.011	.010	.009
.165	.090	.028	.161	.089	.027	.155	.086	.027	.149	.083	.026	.143	.081	.025	.099	.076	.057	.085	.065	.049	.058	.045	.034	.033	.026	.020	.011	.009	.007
.153	.082	.024	.150	.080	.024	.144	.078	.024	.139	.076	.023	.134	.074	.023	.094	.066	.043	.081	.057	.037	.056	.039	.026	.032	.023	.015	.010	.007	.005
.142	.074	.022	.139	.073	.022	.134	.071	.021	.129	.069	.021	.124	.068	.021	.090	.058	.034	.077	.050	.029	.053	.035	.021	.031	.021	.012	.010	.007	.004
.131	.067	.019	.129	.066	.019	.124	.065	.019	.120	.063	.019	.116	.062	.019	.086	.052	.027	.074	.045	.024	.051	.032	.017	.029	.018	.010	.009	.006	.003
.122	.061	.018	.120	.061	.017	.116	.059	.017	.112	.058	.017	.108	.057	.017	.082	.047	.023	.070	.041	.020	.048	.029	.014	.028	.017	.008	.009	.006	.003
.114	.056	.016	.112	.056	.016	.108	.055	.016	.104	.054	.016	.101	.053	.015	.078	.043	.019	.067	.038	.017	.046	.026	.012	.027	.016	.007	.009	.005	.002
.106	.052	.015	.104	.051	.015	.101	.051	.014	.098	.050	.014	.095	.049	.014	.074	.040	.017	.064	.035	.014	.044	.024	.010	.026	.014	.006	.008	.005	.002
.100	.048	.013	.098	.048	.013	.095	.047	.013	.092	.046	.013	.090	.046	.013	.070	.037	.015	.061	.032	.013	.042	.023	.009	.025	.013	.005	.008	.004	.002
.094	.045	.012	.092	.045	.012	.090	.044	.012	.087	.043	.012	.085	.043	.012	.067	.035	.013	.058	.030	.011	.040	.021	.008	.023	.013	.005	.008	.004	.002
															.120	.120	.120	.103	.103	.103	.070	.070	.070	.040	.040	.040	.013	.013	.013
.168	.096	.030	.164	.093	.030	.156	.089	.029	.148	.085	.027	.141	.082	.026	.112	.099	.087	.096	.085	.075	.065	.058	.052	.038	.034	.030	.012	.011	.010
.161	.088	.027	.157	.087	.027	.150	.083	.026	.143	.080	.025	.137	.078	.024	.105	.083	.064	.090	.072	.056	.062	.050	.039	.036	.029	.023	.011	.009	.007
.152	.081	.024	.148	.079	.024	.142	.077	.023	.136	.075	.023	.131	.072	.022	.100	.072	.049	.086	.062	.043	.059	.043	.030	.034	.025	.018	.011	.008	.006
.142	.074	.022	.139	.073	.022	.134	.071	.021	.128	.069	.021	.124	.067	.020	.095	.063	.039	.082	.055	.034	.056	.038	.024	.032	.022	.014	.010	.007	.005
.133	.068	.020	.131	.067	.020	.126	.065	.019	.121	.064	.019	.117	.062	.019	.091	.057	.031	.078	.049	.027	.054	.034	.019	.031	.020	.011	.010	.007	.004
.125	.063	.018	.123	.062	.018	.118	.061	.018	.114	.059	.017	.110	.058	.017	.086	.051	.026	.074	.044	.023	.051	.031	.016	.030	.018	.010	.010	.006	.003
.117	.058	.016	.115	.057	.016	.111	.056	.016	.108	.055	.016	.104	.054	.016	.082	.047	.022	.071	.041	.019	.049	.028	.014	.028	.017	.008	.009	.005	.003
.110	.054	.015	.109	.053	.015	.105	.052	.015	.102	.052	.015	.099	.051	.015	.079	.043	.019	.068	.037	.016	.047	.026	.012	.027	.016	.007	.009	.005	.002
.104	.050	.014	.102	.050	.014	.099	.049	.014	.096	.048	.014	.093	.047	.014	.075	.040	.017	.065	.035	.014	.045	.024	.010	.026	.014	.006	.008	.005	.002
.098	.047	.013	.097	.047	.013	.094	.046	.013	.091	.045	.013	.089	.045	.013	.072	.037	.015	.062	.032	.013	.043	.023	.009	.025	.014	.005	.008	.004	.002

Fig. 9-34. *Continued*

Typical Luminaire	Maint. Cat.	SC	RCR ↓	ρCC→ 80 ρW→50	30	10	70 50	30	10	50 50	30	10	30 50	30	10	10 50	30	10	0	WDRC	RCR ↓
43 — 4-lamp, 610 mm (2′) wide unit with sharp cutoff (high angle—low luminance) flat prismatic lens—see note 7	V	1.4/1.3	0	.78	.78	.78	.76	.76	.76	.73	.73	.73	.70	.70	.70	.67	.67	.67	.66		
			1	.71	.68	.66	.69	.67	.65	.66	.65	.63	.64	.63	.61	.62	.61	.60	.58	.181	1
			2	.63	.60	.57	.62	.59	.56	.60	.57	.55	.58	.56	.54	.56	.54	.52	.51	.180	2
			3	.57	.52	.49	.56	.52	.48	.54	.51	.48	.52	.49	.47	.51	.48	.46	.45	.173	3
			4	.51	.46	.43	.50	.46	.42	.49	.45	.42	.47	.44	.41	.46	.43	.41	.39	.164	4
			5	.46	.41	.37	.46	.41	.37	.44	.40	.37	.43	.39	.36	.42	.39	.36	.35	.154	5
			6	.42	.37	.33	.41	.37	.33	.40	.36	.33	.39	.35	.32	.38	.35	.32	.31	.145	6
			7	.38	.33	.29	.38	.33	.29	.37	.32	.29	.36	.32	.29	.35	.32	.29	.28	.136	7
			8	.35	.30	.26	.35	.30	.26	.34	.29	.26	.33	.29	.26	.33	.29	.26	.25	.127	8
			9	.32	.27	.24	.32	.27	.24	.31	.27	.24	.31	.27	.24	.30	.26	.24	.22	.120	9
			10	.30	.25	.22	.30	.25	.22	.29	.25	.22	.28	.24	.22	.28	.24	.21	.20	.113	10
44 — Bilateral batwing distribution—louvered fluorescent unit	IV	N.A.	0	.71	.71	.71	.70	.70	.70	.66	.66	.66	.64	.64	.64	.61	.61	.61	.60		
			1	.64	.62	.60	.63	.61	.60	.60	.59	.58	.58	.57	.56	.56	.55	.54	.53	.167	1
			2	.57	.54	.51	.56	.53	.51	.54	.52	.50	.52	.50	.48	.51	.49	.47	.46	.170	2
			3	.51	.47	.44	.50	.46	.43	.49	.45	.43	.47	.44	.42	.46	.43	.41	.40	.165	3
			4	.46	.41	.38	.45	.41	.37	.44	.40	.37	.42	.39	.36	.41	.38	.36	.35	.157	4
			5	.41	.36	.33	.40	.36	.32	.39	.35	.32	.38	.35	.32	.37	.34	.31	.30	.148	5
			6	.37	.32	.28	.36	.32	.28	.35	.31	.28	.34	.31	.28	.34	.30	.28	.27	.139	6
			7	.33	.29	.25	.33	.28	.25	.32	.28	.25	.31	.27	.25	.30	.27	.24	.23	.130	7
			8	.30	.26	.22	.30	.25	.22	.29	.25	.22	.28	.25	.22	.28	.24	.22	.21	.122	8
			9	.28	.23	.20	.27	.23	.20	.27	.23	.20	.26	.22	.20	.25	.22	.19	.18	.115	9
			10	.25	.21	.18	.25	.21	.18	.25	.20	.18	.24	.20	.18	.23	.20	.18	.17	.108	10
45 — Bilateral batwing distribution—4-lamp, 610 mm (2′) wide fluorescent unit with flat prismatic lens and overlay—see note 7	V	N.A.	0	.57	.57	.57	.56	.56	.56	.53	.53	.53	.51	.51	.51	.49	.49	.49	.48		
			1	.50	.48	.46	.49	.47	.45	.47	.45	.44	.45	.43	.42	.43	.42	.41	.40	.204	1
			2	.43	.40	.37	.42	.39	.36	.39	.37	.35	.39	.37	.35	.37	.36	.34	.33	.192	2
			3	.37	.33	.30	.37	.33	.30	.35	.32	.29	.34	.31	.29	.33	.30	.28	.27	.175	3
			4	.33	.28	.25	.32	.28	.25	.31	.27	.24	.30	.27	.24	.29	.26	.24	.23	.159	4
			5	.29	.24	.21	.28	.24	.21	.27	.24	.21	.26	.23	.20	.25	.23	.20	.19	.145	5
			6	.26	.21	.18	.25	.21	.18	.24	.21	.18	.24	.20	.18	.23	.20	.17	.16	.132	6
			7	.23	.19	.16	.23	.18	.15	.22	.18	.15	.21	.18	.15	.21	.17	.15	.14	.122	7
			8	.21	.17	.14	.21	.16	.14	.20	.16	.13	.19	.16	.13	.19	.16	.13	.12	.112	8
			9	.19	.15	.12	.19	.15	.12	.18	.14	.12	.18	.14	.12	.17	.14	.12	.11	.104	9
			10	.17	.13	.11	.17	.13	.11	.17	.13	.11	.16	.13	.11	.16	.13	.10	.10	.096	10
46 — Bilateral batwing distribution—one-lamp, surface mounted fluorescent with prismatic wraparound lens	V	N.A.	0	.87	.87	.87	.84	.84	.84	.77	.77	.77	.72	.72	.72	.66	.66	.66	.64		
			1	.75	.72	.69	.72	.69	.66	.67	.64	.62	.62	.60	.58	.57	.56	.54	.52	.296	1
			2	.65	.60	.56	.63	.58	.54	.58	.54	.51	.54	.51	.48	.50	.47	.45	.43	.261	2
			3	.57	.51	.46	.55	.49	.45	.51	.46	.42	.47	.43	.40	.44	.41	.38	.36	.232	3
			4	.50	.44	.39	.48	.42	.38	.45	.40	.36	.42	.38	.34	.39	.35	.32	.30	.209	4
			5	.45	.38	.33	.43	.37	.32	.40	.35	.31	.37	.33	.29	.35	.31	.28	.26	.189	5
			6	.40	.33	.28	.39	.32	.28	.36	.31	.26	.34	.29	.25	.31	.27	.24	.22	.172	6
			7	.36	.29	.25	.35	.29	.24	.32	.27	.23	.30	.26	.22	.28	.24	.21	.19	.158	7
			8	.33	.26	.22	.31	.25	.21	.29	.24	.20	.28	.23	.20	.26	.22	.19	.17	.146	8
			9	.30	.23	.19	.29	.23	.19	.27	.22	.18	.25	.21	.17	.24	.20	.17	.15	.135	9
			10	.27	.21	.17	.26	.21	.17	.25	.20	.16	.23	.19	.16	.22	.18	.15	.13	.126	10
47 — Radial batwing distribution—4-lamp, 610 mm (2′) wide fluorescent unit with flat prismatic lens—see note 7	V	1.7	0	.71	.71	.71	.69	.69	.69	.66	.66	.66	.63	.63	.63	.61	.61	.61	.60		
			1	.62	.59	.57	.60	.58	.56	.58	.56	.54	.55	.54	.52	.53	.52	.51	.50	.251	1
			2	.53	.49	.46	.52	.48	.45	.50	.47	.44	.48	.45	.43	.46	.44	.42	.41	.237	2
			3	.46	.41	.37	.45	.41	.37	.44	.40	.36	.42	.39	.36	.40	.38	.35	.34	.216	3
			4	.41	.35	.31	.40	.35	.31	.38	.34	.30	.37	.33	.30	.36	.32	.30	.28	.196	4
			5	.36	.30	.26	.35	.30	.26	.34	.29	.26	.33	.29	.26	.32	.28	.25	.24	.178	5
			6	.32	.27	.23	.32	.26	.23	.31	.26	.22	.29	.25	.22	.29	.25	.22	.21	.162	6
			7	.29	.24	.20	.28	.23	.20	.28	.23	.19	.27	.22	.19	.26	.22	.19	.18	.149	7
			8	.26	.21	.18	.26	.21	.17	.25	.20	.17	.24	.20	.17	.24	.20	.17	.16	.137	8
			9	.24	.19	.15	.24	.19	.15	.23	.18	.15	.22	.18	.15	.22	.18	.15	.14	.127	9
			10	.22	.17	.14	.22	.17	.14	.21	.17	.14	.20	.16	.14	.20	.16	.14	.12	.118	10
48 — 2-lamp fluorescent strip unit	I	1.6/1.2	0	1.01	1.01	1.01	.96	.96	.96	.87	.87	.87	.79	.79	.79	.72	.72	.72	.68		
			1	.84	.79	.75	.80	.76	.72	.72	.69	.66	.65	.63	.60	.59	.57	.55	.52	.414	1
			2	.72	.65	.59	.68	.62	.57	.62	.57	.52	.56	.52	.48	.50	.47	.44	.41	.343	2
			3	.62	.54	.48	.59	.52	.46	.53	.47	.42	.48	.43	.39	.43	.39	.36	.33	.293	3
			4	.54	.46	.39	.52	.44	.38	.47	.40	.35	.42	.37	.33	.38	.34	.30	.27	.255	4
			5	.48	.40	.33	.46	.38	.32	.41	.35	.30	.38	.32	.28	.34	.29	.26	.23	.225	5
			6	.43	.35	.29	.41	.33	.28	.37	.31	.26	.34	.28	.24	.30	.26	.22	.20	.202	6
			7	.38	.30	.25	.37	.29	.24	.34	.27	.22	.31	.25	.21	.28	.23	.19	.17	.182	7
			8	.35	.27	.22	.33	.26	.21	.31	.24	.20	.28	.22	.18	.25	.21	.17	.15	.166	8
			9	.32	.24	.19	.30	.24	.19	.28	.22	.18	.26	.20	.16	.23	.19	.15	.13	.152	9
			10	.29	.22	.17	.28	.21	.17	.26	.20	.16	.24	.18	.15	.22	.17	.14	.12	.140	10

Coefficients of Utilization for 20 Per Cent Effective Floor Cavity Reflectance (ρFC = 20)

Fig. 9-34. *Continued*

80			70			50			30			10			80			70			50			30			10		
50	30	10	50	30	10	50	30	10	50	30	10	50	30	10	50	30	10	50	30	10	50	30	10	50	30	10	50	30	10
Wall Exitance Coefficients for 20 Per Cent Effective Floor Cavity Reflectance (ρ_{FC} = 20)															Ceiling Cavity Exitance Coefficients for 20 Per Cent Floor Cavity Reflectance (ρ_{FC} = 20)														
															.125	.125	.125	.107	.107	.107	.073	.073	.073	.042	.042	.042	.013	.013	.013
.156	.089	.028	.152	.087	.028	.143	.082	.026	.136	.078	.025	.128	.074	.024	.115	.103	.092	.098	.088	.079	.067	.061	.055	.039	.035	.032	.012	.011	.010
.153	.084	.026	.149	.082	.025	.142	.079	.024	.135	.076	.024	.129	.073	.023	.108	.087	.069	.092	.075	.060	.063	.052	.042	.037	.030	.024	.012	.010	.008
.146	.078	.023	.143	.076	.023	.136	.074	.022	.130	.071	.022	.125	.069	.021	.102	.075	.053	.087	.065	.046	.060	.045	.032	.035	.026	.019	.011	.008	.006
.139	.072	.021	.136	.071	.021	.130	.069	.021	.125	.067	.020	.120	.065	.020	.097	.066	.042	.083	.057	.036	.057	.040	.026	.033	.023	.015	.011	.008	.005
.131	.067	.019	.129	.066	.019	.124	.064	.019	.119	.063	.019	.115	.061	.018	.092	.059	.034	.079	.051	.029	.055	.035	.021	.032	.021	.012	.010	.007	.004
.124	.062	.018	.122	.061	.018	.117	.060	.017	.113	.059	.017	.109	.057	.017	.088	.053	.028	.076	.046	.024	.052	.032	.017	.030	.019	.010	.010	.006	.003
.117	.058	.016	.115	.057	.016	.111	.056	.016	.107	.055	.016	.104	.054	.016	.084	.048	.024	.072	.042	.021	.050	.029	.015	.029	.017	.009	.009	.006	.003
.111	.054	.015	.109	.054	.015	.105	.053	.015	.102	.052	.015	.099	.051	.015	.080	.045	.020	.069	.039	.018	.048	.027	.013	.028	.016	.007	.009	.005	.002
.105	.051	.014	.103	.050	.014	.100	.050	.014	.097	.049	.014	.094	.048	.014	.077	.041	.018	.066	.036	.015	.046	.025	.011	.027	.015	.006	.009	.005	.002
.100	.048	.013	.098	.047	.013	.095	.047	.013	.092	.046	.013	.090	.045	.013	.073	.039	.016	.063	.034	.014	.044	.024	.010	.026	.014	.006	.008	.005	.002
															.114	.114	.114	.097	.097	.097	.066	.066	.066	.038	.038	.038	.012	.012	.012
.144	.082	.026	.140	.080	.025	.132	.076	.024	.125	.072	.023	.118	.069	.022	.105	.094	.084	.090	.080	.072	.061	.055	.050	.035	.032	.029	.011	.010	.009
.142	.078	.024	.139	.076	.024	.132	.073	.023	.126	.071	.022	.120	.068	.021	.099	.079	.063	.085	.068	.054	.058	.047	.038	.033	.027	.022	.011	.009	.007
.137	.073	.022	.134	.072	.022	.128	.069	.021	.123	.067	.021	.118	.065	.020	.094	.068	.048	.080	.059	.042	.055	.041	.029	.032	.024	.017	.010	.008	.006
.131	.068	.020	.128	.067	.020	.123	.065	.019	.118	.063	.019	.113	.062	.019	.089	.060	.038	.077	.052	.033	.053	.036	.023	.030	.021	.014	.010	.007	.004
.124	.063	.018	.122	.062	.018	.117	.061	.018	.113	.059	.018	.109	.058	.017	.085	.054	.030	.073	.046	.026	.050	.032	.019	.029	.019	.011	.009	.006	.004
.117	.059	.017	.115	.058	.017	.111	.057	.017	.107	.056	.016	.104	.055	.016	.082	.049	.025	.070	.042	.022	.048	.029	.015	.028	.017	.009	.009	.006	.003
.111	.055	.016	.109	.054	.015	.105	.053	.015	.102	.052	.015	.099	.051	.015	.078	.044	.021	.067	.039	.018	.046	.027	.013	.027	.016	.008	.009	.005	.003
.105	.051	.014	.103	.051	.014	.100	.050	.014	.097	.049	.014	.094	.048	.014	.075	.041	.018	.064	.036	.016	.044	.025	.011	.026	.015	.007	.008	.005	.002
.100	.048	.013	.098	.048	.013	.095	.047	.013	.092	.046	.013	.089	.045	.013	.071	.038	.016	.062	.033	.014	.043	.023	.010	.025	.014	.006	.008	.005	.002
.094	.045	.013	.093	.045	.013	.090	.044	.012	.088	.044	.012	.085	.043	.012	.068	.036	.014	.059	.031	.012	.041	.022	.009	.024	.013	.005	.008	.004	.002
															.092	.092	.092	.078	.078	.078	.053	.053	.053	.031	.031	.031	.010	.010	.010
.153	.087	.027	.149	.085	.027	.143	.082	.026	.137	.079	.025	.131	.076	.025	.087	.075	.064	.074	.064	.055	.051	.044	.038	.029	.026	.022	.009	.008	.007
.145	.079	.024	.142	.078	.024	.136	.076	.024	.131	.074	.023	.126	.071	.023	.084	.063	.047	.072	.055	.040	.049	.038	.028	.028	.022	.016	.009	.007	.005
.135	.072	.022	.132	.071	.021	.127	.069	.021	.123	.067	.021	.118	.065	.020	.080	.055	.035	.069	.048	.030	.047	.033	.021	.027	.019	.013	.009	.006	.004
.125	.065	.019	.123	.064	.019	.118	.063	.019	.114	.061	.018	.110	.060	.018	.077	.049	.027	.066	.042	.024	.045	.029	.017	.026	.017	.010	.008	.006	.003
.116	.059	.017	.114	.058	.017	.110	.057	.017	.106	.056	.017	.102	.055	.016	.073	.044	.022	.063	.038	.019	.043	.026	.014	.025	.016	.008	.008	.005	.003
.107	.054	.015	.106	.053	.015	.102	.052	.015	.099	.051	.015	.096	.050	.015	.070	.040	.018	.060	.035	.016	.042	.024	.011	.024	.014	.007	.008	.005	.002
.100	.049	.014	.098	.049	.014	.095	.048	.014	.092	.047	.014	.089	.046	.014	.067	.037	.015	.057	.032	.013	.040	.022	.010	.023	.013	.006	.007	.004	.002
.093	.046	.013	.092	.045	.013	.089	.044	.013	.086	.044	.013	.084	.043	.013	.064	.034	.013	.055	.029	.012	.038	.021	.008	.022	.012	.005	.007	.004	.002
.087	.042	.012	.086	.042	.012	.083	.041	.012	.081	.041	.012	.079	.040	.012	.061	.031	.012	.052	.027	.010	.036	.019	.007	.021	.011	.004	.007	.004	.001
.082	.039	.011	.081	.039	.011	.079	.038	.011	.076	.038	.011	.074	.037	.011	.058	.029	.010	.050	.026	.009	.035	.018	.006	.020	.011	.004	.007	.003	.001
															.236	.236	.236	.201	.201	.201	.138	.138	.138	.079	.079	.079	.025	.025	.025
.247	.140	.044	.238	.136	.043	.221	.127	.040	.205	.118	.038	.191	.111	.036	.230	.210	.193	.196	.181	.166	.134	.124	.115	.077	.072	.067	.025	.023	.022
.224	.123	.038	.216	.119	.037	.201	.112	.035	.187	.105	.033	.174	.098	.031	.224	.193	.167	.192	.166	.144	.131	.115	.101	.076	.067	.059	.024	.022	.019
.205	.109	.033	.198	.106	.032	.184	.100	.030	.171	.094	.029	.160	.088	.027	.218	.180	.150	.187	.155	.130	.128	.108	.091	.074	.063	.054	.024	.020	.018
.188	.098	.029	.182	.095	.028	.169	.090	.027	.158	.085	.026	.147	.080	.024	.213	.170	.138	.182	.147	.120	.125	.103	.084	.073	.060	.050	.023	.020	.016
.174	.089	.026	.168	.086	.025	.157	.082	.024	.146	.077	.023	.136	.073	.022	.207	.163	.130	.178	.141	.113	.123	.098	.080	.071	.058	.047	.023	.019	.016
.161	.081	.023	.156	.079	.023	.146	.075	.022	.136	.071	.021	.127	.067	.020	.202	.157	.124	.174	.136	.108	.120	.095	.076	.069	.056	.045	.022	.018	.015
.150	.074	.021	.145	.072	.021	.136	.069	.020	.127	.065	.019	.119	.062	.018	.197	.152	.120	.169	.131	.104	.117	.092	.074	.068	.054	.044	.022	.018	.015
.140	.069	.019	.136	.067	.019	.127	.063	.018	.119	.060	.017	.111	.057	.017	.192	.147	.117	.166	.128	.102	.115	.090	.072	.067	.053	.043	.022	.017	.014
.132	.064	.018	.127	.062	.017	.119	.059	.017	.112	.056	.016	.105	.053	.015	.188	.144	.114	.162	.125	.100	.112	.088	.071	.065	.052	.042	.021	.017	.014
.124	.059	.016	.120	.058	.016	.112	.055	.016	.106	.052	.015	.099	.050	.014	.184	.141	.112	.158	.122	.098	.110	.086	.070	.064	.051	.041	.021	.017	.014
															.114	.114	.114	.097	.097	.097	.066	.066	.066	.038	.038	.038	.012	.012	.012
.188	.107	.034	.184	.105	.033	.176	.101	.032	.169	.097	.031	.162	.094	.030	.108	.093	.080	.092	.080	.069	.063	.055	.047	.036	.032	.028	.012	.010	.009
.179	.098	.030	.176	.097	.030	.169	.094	.029	.162	.091	.028	.156	.088	.028	.103	.079	.058	.080	.068	.060	.061	.047	.035	.035	.027	.020	.011	.009	.007
.167	.089	.027	.163	.087	.026	.157	.085	.026	.151	.083	.025	.146	.081	.025	.099	.068	.043	.085	.059	.038	.058	.041	.026	.034	.024	.016	.011	.008	.005
.154	.080	.024	.151	.079	.023	.145	.077	.023	.140	.075	.023	.136	.074	.022	.095	.060	.034	.081	.052	.029	.056	.036	.021	.032	.021	.012	.010	.007	.004
.142	.073	.021	.140	.072	.021	.135	.070	.021	.130	.069	.020	.126	.067	.020	.091	.054	.027	.078	.047	.024	.054	.033	.017	.031	.019	.010	.010	.006	.003
.132	.066	.019	.130	.065	.019	.125	.064	.019	.121	.063	.018	.117	.062	.018	.086	.049	.023	.074	.043	.020	.051	.030	.014	.030	.018	.008	.010	.006	.003
.123	.061	.017	.121	.060	.017	.117	.059	.017	.113	.058	.017	.110	.057	.017	.082	.045	.019	.071	.039	.017	.049	.027	.012	.028	.016	.007	.009	.005	.002
.115	.056	.016	.113	.055	.016	.109	.055	.016	.106	.054	.015	.103	.053	.015	.078	.042	.017	.068	.036	.014	.047	.025	.010	.027	.015	.006	.009	.005	.002
.107	.052	.014	.106	.051	.014	.102	.051	.014	.099	.050	.014	.097	.049	.014	.075	.039	.015	.064	.034	.013	.045	.024	.009	.026	.014	.005	.008	.005	.002
.101	.048	.013	.099	.048	.013	.096	.047	.013	.094	.046	.013	.091	.046	.013	.071	.036	.013	.061	.032	.011	.043	.022	.008	.025	.013	.005	.008	.004	.002
															.325	.325	.325	.278	.278	.278	.189	.189	.189	.109	.109	.109	.035	.035	.035
.335	.191	.060	.323	.184	.058	.299	.172	.055	.277	.160	.051	.257	.149	.048	.321	.295	.272	.275	.253	.234	.188	.174	.162	.108	.101	.094	.035	.032	.030
.293	.161	.049	.282	.155	.048	.260	.145	.045	.241	.135	.042	.222	.126	.040	.316	.275	.241	.270	.237	.208	.185	.164	.145	.107	.095	.085	.034	.031	.028
.262	.139	.042	.251	.135	.040	.232	.126	.038	.214	.117	.036	.197	.109	.034	.309	.261	.222	.265	.225	.192	.182	.156	.135	.105	.091	.080	.034	.030	.026
.236	.123	.036	.226	.119	.035	.209	.111	.033	.192	.103	.031	.177	.096	.029	.303	.250	.209	.260	.216	.182	.179	.150	.128	.103	.088	.076	.033	.029	.025
.215	.109	.032	.206	.106	.031	.190	.099	.029	.175	.092	.027	.161	.086	.026	.296	.241	.201	.254	.209	.175	.175	.146	.123	.101	.086	.073	.033	.028	.024
.197	.099	.028	.189	.095	.027	.174	.089	.026	.160	.083	.024	.147	.078	.023	.289	.234	.195	.249	.203	.169	.172	.142	.120	.100	.084	.071	.032	.027	.024
.181	.090	.025	.174	.087	.025	.161	.081	.023	.148	.076	.022	.136	.071	.021	.283	.228	.190	.244	.198	.166	.168	.139	.117	.098	.082	.070	.032	.027	.023
.168	.082	.023	.162	.080	.022	.149	.075	.021	.137	.070	.020	.126	.065	.019	.277	.224	.187	.239	.194	.163	.165	.136	.115	.096	.080	.069	.031	.026	.023
.157	.076	.021	.151	.073	.021	.139	.069	.020	.128	.064	.018	.118	.060	.017	.272	.219	.184	.234	.190	.160	.162	.134	.114	.095	.079	.068	.031	.026	.023
.147	.070	.020	.141	.068	.019	.130	.064	.018	.120	.060	.017	.111	.056	.016	.267	.216	.182	.230	.187	.159	.160	.132	.113	.093	.078	.067	.030	.026	.022

Fig. 9-34. *Continued*

Typical Luminaire	Typical Intensity Distribution and Per Cent Lamp Lumens		ρcc →	80			70			50			30			10			0	WDRC	ρcc →
			ρw →	50	30	10	50	30	10	50	30	10	50	30	10	50	30	10	0		ρw →
	Maint. Cat.	SC	RCR ↓	Coefficients of Utilization for 20 Per Cent Effective Floor Cavity Reflectance (ρFC = 20)																	RCR ↓
49	I	1.4/1.2	0	1.13	1.13	1.13	1.09	1.09	1.09	1.01	1.01	1.01	.94	.94	.94	.88	.88	.88	.85		0
			1	.95	.90	.86	.92	.87	.83	.85	.82	.78	.79	.76	.74	.74	.72	.69	.66	.464	1
	12½° ▲		2	.82	.74	.68	.79	.72	.66	.73	.68	.63	.68	.64	.60	.63	.60	.56	.53	.394	2
			3	.71	.62	.55	.69	.61	.54	.64	.57	.52	.59	.54	.49	.55	.51	.47	.44	.342	3
			4	.62	.53	.46	.60	.52	.45	.56	.49	.43	.52	.46	.41	.49	.44	.40	.37	.300	4
	85° ▼		5	.55	.46	.39	.54	.45	.39	.50	.43	.37	.47	.40	.36	.44	.38	.34	.32	.267	5
			6	.50	.41	.34	.48	.40	.33	.45	.38	.32	.42	.36	.31	.39	.34	.30	.27	.240	6
			7	.45	.36	.30	.43	.35	.29	.41	.34	.28	.38	.32	.27	.36	.30	.26	.24	.218	7
			8	.41	.32	.26	.40	.32	.26	.37	.30	.25	.35	.29	.24	.33	.27	.23	.21	.199	8
2-lamp fluorescent strip unit with 235° reflector fluorescent lamps			9	.37	.29	.24	.36	.28	.23	.34	.27	.22	.32	.26	.22	.30	.25	.21	.19	.183	9
			10	.34	.26	.21	.33	.26	.21	.32	.25	.20	.30	.24	.20	.28	.23	.19	.17	.170	10

Typical Luminaires	ρcc →	80			70			50			30			10			0
	ρw →	50	30	10	50	30	10	50	30	10	50	30	10	50	30	10	0
	RCR ↓	Coefficients of utilization for 20 Per Cent Effective Floor Cavity Reflectance, ρFC															
50	1	.42	.40	.39	.36	.35	.33	.25	.24	.23	Coves are not recommended for lighting areas having low reflectances.						
	2	.37	.34	.32	.32	.29	.27	.22	.20	.19							
	3	.32	.29	.26	.28	.25	.23	.19	.17	.16							
	4	.29	.25	.22	.25	.22	.19	.17	.15	.13							
	5	.25	.21	.18	.22	.19	.16	.15	.13	.11							
	6	.23	.19	.16	.20	.16	.14	.14	.12	.10							
	7	.20	.17	.14	.17	.14	.12	.12	.10	.09							
	8	.18	.15	.12	.16	.13	.10	.11	.09	.08							
Single row fluorescent lamp cove without reflector, mult. by 0.93 for 2 rows and by 0.85 for 3 rows.	9	.17	.13	.10	.15	.11	.09	.10	.08	.07							
	10	.15	.12	.09	.13	.10	.08	.09	.07	.06							
51 ρcc from below ~65%	1				.60	.58	.56	.58	.56	.54							
	2				.53	.49	.45	.51	.47	.43							
	3				.47	.42	.37	.45	.41	.36							
	4				.41	.36	.32	.39	.35	.31							
	5				.37	.31	.27	.35	.30	.26							
	6				.33	.27	.23	.31	.26	.23							
Diffusing plastic or glass	7				.29	.24	.20	.28	.23	.20							
1) Ceiling efficiency ~60%; diffuser transmittance ~50%; diffuser reflectance ~40%. Cavity with minimum obstructions and painted with 80% reflectance paint—use ρc = 70.	8				.26	.21	.18	.25	.20	.17							
	9				.23	.19	.15	.23	.18	.15							
2) For lower reflectance paint or obstructions—use ρc = 50.	10				.21	.17	.13	.21	.16	.13							
52 ρcc from below ~60%	1				.71	.68	.66	.67	.66	.65	.65	.64	.62				
	2				.63	.60	.57	.61	.58	.55	.59	.56	.54				
	3				.57	.53	.49	.55	.52	.48	.54	.50	.47				
	4				.52	.47	.43	.50	.45	.42	.48	.44	.42				
	5				.46	.41	.37	.44	.40	.37	.43	.40	.36				
	6				.42	.37	.33	.41	.36	.32	.40	.35	.32				
Prismatic plastic or glass.	7				.38	.32	.29	.37	.31	.28	.36	.31	.28				
1) Ceiling efficiency ~67%; prismatic transmittance ~72%; prismatic reflectance ~18%. Cavity with minimum obstructions and painted with 80% reflectance paint—use ρc = 70.	8				.34	.28	.25	.33	.28	.25	.32	.28	.25				
	9				.30	.25	.22	.30	.25	.21	.29	.25	.21				
2) For lower reflectance paint or obstructions—use ρc = 50.	10				.27	.23	.19	.27	.22	.19	.26	.22	.19				
53 ρcc from below ~45%	1							.51	.49	.48				.47	.46	.45	
	2							.46	.44	.42				.43	.42	.40	
	3							.42	.39	.37				.39	.38	.36	
	4							.38	.35	.33				.36	.34	.32	
	5							.35	.32	.29				.33	.31	.29	
Louvered ceiling.	6							.32	.29	.26				.30	.28	.26	
1) Ceiling efficiency ~50%; 45° shielding opaque louvers of 80% reflectance. Cavity with minimum obstructions and painted with 80% reflectance paint—use ρc = 50.	7							.29	.26	.23				.28	.25	.23	
	8							.27	.23	.21				.26	.23	.21	
	9							.24	.21	.19				.24	.21	.19	
2) For other conditions refer to Fig. 6–18.	10							.22	.19	.17				.22	.19	.17	

Fig. 9-34. *Continued*

80			70			50			30			10			80			70			50			30			10		
50	30	10	50	30	10	50	30	10	50	30	10	50	30	10	50	30	10	50	30	10	50	30	10	50	30	10	50	30	10
Wall Exitance Coefficients for 20 Per Cent Effective Floor Cavity Reflectance (ρ_{FC} = 20)															Ceiling Cavity Exitance Coefficients for 20 Per Cent Floor Cavity Reflectance (ρ_{FC} = 20)														
															.280	.280	.280	.239	.239	.239	.163	.163	.163	.094	.094	.094	.030	.030	.030
.357	.203	.064	.346	.197	.063	.326	.187	.060	.307	.177	.057	.290	.168	.054	.275	.247	.222	.235	.212	.191	.161	.146	.132	.093	.084	.077	.030	.027	.025
.316	.173	.053	.306	.169	.052	.288	.160	.050	.271	.152	.048	.256	.145	.046	.268	.224	.188	.230	.193	.162	.157	.134	.113	.091	.078	.066	.029	.025	.022
.284	.151	.045	.275	.147	.044	.259	.140	.043	.243	.133	.041	.229	.127	.039	.261	.208	.166	.224	.180	.144	.154	.125	.101	.089	.073	.060	.028	.024	.019
.257	.134	.039	.249	.130	.039	.234	.124	.037	.221	.118	.036	.208	.113	.034	.253	.196	.152	.217	.169	.132	.150	.118	.093	.086	.069	.055	.028	.022	.018
.235	.120	.035	.227	.117	.034	.214	.111	.033	.202	.106	.032	.190	.101	.030	.246	.186	.142	.211	.161	.123	.145	.112	.087	.084	.066	.052	.027	.022	.017
.215	.108	.031	.209	.106	.030	.197	.101	.029	.185	.096	.028	.175	.092	.027	.239	.178	.135	.205	.154	.117	.142	.108	.083	.082	.064	.049	.027	.021	.016
.199	.098	.028	.193	.096	.027	.182	.092	.027	.172	.088	.026	.162	.084	.025	.232	.172	.130	.199	.149	.113	.138	.104	.080	.080	.061	.048	.026	.020	.016
.185	.090	.025	.180	.088	.025	.169	.085	.024	.160	.081	.023	.151	.077	.023	.225	.166	.126	.194	.144	.109	.134	.101	.078	.078	.060	.046	.025	.020	.016
.172	.083	.023	.168	.082	.023	.158	.078	.022	.150	.075	.021	.141	.072	.021	.219	.161	.122	.189	.140	.107	.131	.099	.076	.076	.058	.045	.025	.019	.015
.162	.077	.022	.157	.076	.021	.149	.073	.020	.140	.070	.020	.133	.067	.019	.214	.157	.120	.184	.137	.105	.128	.096	.074	.074	.057	.044	.024	0.19	.015

54

910 mm x 910 mm (3′ x 3′) fluorescent troffer with 1220 mm (48″) lamps mounted along diagonals—use units 40, 41 or 42 as appropriate

55

610 mm x 610 mm (2′ x 2′) fluorescent troffer with two "U" lamps—use units 40, 41 or 42 as appropriate

Tabulation of Luminous Intensities Used to Compute Above Coefficients
Normalized Average Intensity (Candelas per 1000 lumens)

Angle ↓	Luminaire No.													
	1	2	3	4	5	6	7	8	9	10	11	12	13	14
5	72.5	6.5	256.0	238.0	808.0	1320.0	695.0	374.0	2680.0	2610.0	208.0	152.0	190.0	316.0
15	72.5	8.0	246.0	264.0	671.0	1010.0	630.0	357.0	1150.0	1200.0	220.0	148.0	196.0	311.0
25	72.5	9.5	238.0	248.0	494.0	584.0	286.0	305.0	209.0	411.0	254.0	141.0	199.0	301.0
35	72.5	10.0	238.0	191.0	340.0	236.0	88.0	212.0	13.5	97.0	220.0	125.0	212.0	271.0
45	72.5	8.0	203.0	122.0	203.0	22.0	5.0	81.0	0	15.0	130.0	106.0	206.0	156.0
55	72.0	6.5	168.0	62.5	91.0	0	0	40.5	0	0	59.0	87.5	125.0	63.0
65	71.5	4.5	130.0	45.5	33.0	0	0	20.5	0	0	26.0	69.5	68.5	31.5
75	70.5	2.5	34.0	38.0	12.5	0	0	9.5	0	0	11.0	47.0	41.5	17.5
85	70.0	2.0	7.0	32.0	4.0	0	0	2.5	0	0	3.5	23.5	26.0	4.0
95	67.0	15.0	0	28.0	0	0	0	0	0	0	0	9.5	12.5	0
105	62.5	147.0	0	28.0	0	0	0	0	0	0	0	4.5	6.0	0
115	58.0	170.0	0	41.0	0	0	0	0	0	0	0	1.0	3.5	0
125	54.5	168.0	0	42.5	0	0	0	0	0	0	0	0	1.5	0
135	51.0	183.0	0	33.0	0	0	0	0	0	0	0	0	0	0
145	48.0	159.0	0	22.5	0	0	0	0	0	0	0	0	0	0
155	46.5	139.0	0	9.0	0	0	0	0	0	0	0	0	0	0
165	45.0	94.5	0	3.0	0	0	0	0	0	0	0	0	0	0
175	44.0	50.5	0	1.0	0	0	0	0	0	0	0	0	0	0

Angle ↓	Luminaire No.													
	15	16	17	18	19	20	21	22	23	24	25	26	27	28
5	288.0	999.0	470.0	294.0	576.0	274.0	203.0	136.0	155.0	0	263.0	246.0	284.0	244.0
15	321.0	775.0	384.0	282.0	519.0	302.0	192.0	151.0	169.0	0	258.0	260.0	262.0	248.0
25	331.0	475.0	344.0	294.0	426.0	344.0	194.0	171.0	185.0	0	236.0	264.0	226.0	242.0
35	260.0	188.0	290.0	294.0	274.0	321.0	252.0	175.0	188.0	0	210.0	248.0	187.0	218.0
45	202.0	90.5	210.0	246.0	127.0	209.0	230.0	182.0	162.0	0	163.0	192.0	145.0	152.0
55	114.0	32.0	86.5	137.0	69.5	45.5	119.0	158.0	119.0	0	98.0	98.0	83.0	70.0
65	13.5	8.5	18.0	26.0	20.0	8.0	52.5	90.0	57.0	0	55.5	32.5	36.5	26.0

Fig. 9-34. *Continued*

Angle ↓	Luminaire No.													
	15	16	17	18	19	20	21	22	23	24	25	26	27	28
75	6.0	6.0	5.0	6.5	2.5	3.0	21.0	41.0	4.5	0	29.5	12.5	18.5	10.0
85	2.0	1.0	1.0	1.0	1.5	2.5	3.5	17.0	0	0	11.0	4.0	5.5	3.0
95	1.0	0.5	0.5	0.5	0.5	3.5	0	8.0	0	19.0	8.0	3.5	3.5	2.5
105	0	0.5	0.5	0.5	0.5	8.0	0	7.0	0	64.0	14.5	6.5	11.0	6.0
115	0	0.5	0.5	0.5	4.5	15.5	0	7.0	0	212.0	21.5	12.0	21.0	13.0
125	0	1.0	0.5	0.5	10.5	22.5	0	5.0	0	205.0	31.0	21.5	34.5	24.0
135	0	1.5	1.0	0.5	16.5	29.0	0	0	0	160.0	47.0	33.5	51.5	36.0
145	0	8.0	3.0	1.5	20.5	33.5	0	0	0	128.0	59.5	50.0	71.5	49.5
155	0	8.5	8.0	7.5	32.0	42.0	0	0	0	115.0	82.5	70.5	92.0	70.0
165	0	0.5	0.5	0.5	33.0	27.5	0	0	0	106.0	105.0	92.0	109.0	88.5
175	0	0.5	0.5	0.5	16.5	2.5	0	0	0	102.0	111.0	102.0	115.0	95.5

Angle ↓	Luminaire No.																				
	29	30	31	32	33	34	35	36	37	38	39	40	41	42	43	44	45	46	47	48	49
5	189.0	270.0	218.0	199.0	41.5	194.0	210.0	206.0	107.0	272.0	312.0	218.0	206.0	253.0	288.0	197.0	90.0	132.0	135.0	157.0	238.0
15	176.0	249.0	220.0	194.0	38.5	192.0	211.0	199.0	104.0	244.0	268.0	207.0	202.0	249.0	284.0	196.0	104.0	144.0	142.0	156.0	232.0
25	147.0	200.0	224.0	184.0	35.5	187.0	212.0	185.0	98.5	202.0	213.0	187.0	183.0	236.0	271.0	199.0	125.0	181.0	167.0	153.0	218.0
35	110.0	144.0	222.0	170.0	32.5	169.0	204.0	158.0	90.0	156.0	148.0	164.0	162.0	214.0	246.0	235.0	140.0	202.0	171.0	147.0	200.0
45	64.0	86.5	187.0	154.0	29.0	123.0	164.0	108.0	79.5	106.0	87.0	135.0	133.0	172.0	190.0	223.0	131.0	173.0	151.0	137.0	176.0
55	34.5	53.5	99.0	137.0	22.0	77.5	78.5	51.5	66.5	68.0	51.0	106.0	104.0	95.5	97.0	99.5	104.0	113.0	120.0	122.0	149.0
65	20.5	34.0	15.5	117.0	14.5	37.5	36.5	35.5	52.0	42.0	30.0	74.0	70.5	45.0	25.0	18.5	65.5	63.0	82.0	104.0	119.0
75	10.0	20.5	3.5	88.5	7.0	18.5	26.0	34.5	36.0	21.5	15.5	42.5	36.5	19.0	6.0	3.0	27.5	42.5	41.5	79.0	86.5
85	2.5	10.0	1.0	59.0	2.0	10.5	17.5	32.0	21.5	6.0	4.0	15.5	7.0	7.0	2.5	0.5	8.0	27.5	7.5	52.5	50.5
95	4.0	7.0	0	49.5	11.0	14.5	15.5	32.5	14.5	0	0	5.5	0	0	0	0	0	23.0	0	45.0	32.5
105	19.0	8.5	0	32.5	49.5	40.0	22.0	49.0	14.5	0	0	2.5	0	0	0	0	0	31.0	0	43.5	27.5
115	40.5	9.5	0	6.5	96.0	57.0	27.0	49.0	14.0	0	0	0	0	0	0	0	0	30.0	0	38.5	22.0
125	67.0	10.0	0	0	130.0	68.5	23.0	44.5	13.0	0	0	0	0	0	0	0	0	19.5	0	33.0	17.5
135	93.0	11.0	0	0	155.0	71.5	18.5	36.0	12.0	0	0	0	0	0	0	0	0	10.0	0	27.0	13.5
145	117.0	11.0	0	0	172.0	67.5	12.0	28.5	10.0	0	0	0	0	0	0	0	0	7.5	0	20.0	10.5
155	136.0	11.5	0	0	183.0	65.0	7.5	24.0	8.5	0	0	0	0	0	0	0	0	4.5	0	13.0	7.5
165	151.0	12.0	0	0	189.0	67.5	4.5	21.0	6.5	0	0	0	0	0	0	0	0	1.5	0	7.0	5.0
175	155.0	13.0	0	0	201.0	73.5	4.0	18.0	5.5	0	0	0	0	0	0	0	0	0	0	2.5	2.5

REFERENCES

1. Lambert, J. H. 1892. *Lamberts Photometrie (Photometria, sive De mensura et gradibus luminis, colorum et umbrae).* E. Anding, trans. Leipzig: W. Engelmann.

2. DiLaura, D. L. 1975. On the computation of equivalent sphere illumination. *J. Illum. Eng. Soc.* 4(2):129–149.

3. Hamilton, D. C., and W. R. Morgan. 1952. *Radiant-Interchange Configuration Factors.* Technical Note 2836. Washington: National Advisory Committee for Aeronautics.

4. Siegel, R., and J. R. Howel. 1980. *Thermal radiation heat transfer.* 2nd ed. New York: McGraw-Hill.

5. IES. Design Practice Committee. 1970. General procedure for calculating maintained illumination. *Illum. Eng.* 65(10):602–617.

6. Yamauti, Z. 1924. *Geometrical calculation of illumination due to light from luminous sources of simple forms.* Researches of the Electrotechnical Laboratory, 148. Tokyo: Electrotechnical Laboratory.

7. Fock, V. 1924. Zur Berechnung der Beleuchtungsstärke. *Z. Phys.* 28:102–113.

8. Mistrick, R. G., and C. R. English. 1990. A study of near-field indirect lighting calculations. *J. Illum. Eng. Soc.* 19(2):103–112.

9. Levin, R. E. 1971. Photometric characteristics of light controlling apparatus. *Illum. Eng.* 66(4):205–215.

10. Lautzenheiser, T., G. Weller, and S. Stannard. 1984. Photometry for near field applications. *J. Illum. Eng. Soc.* 13(2):262–269.

11. Stannard, S., and J. Brass. 1990. Application distance photometry. *J. Illum. Eng. Soc.* 1918(1):39–46.

12. Ngai, P. Y., J. X. Zhang, and F. G. Zhang. 1992. Near-field photometry: Measurement and application for fluorescent luminaires. *J. Illum. Eng. Soc.* 21(2):68–83.

13. Yamauti, Z. 1932. *Theory of field of illumination.* Researches of the Electrotechnical Laboratory, 339. Tokyo: Electrotechnical Laboratory.

14. Gershun, A. 1939. The light field. P. Moon and G. J. Timoshenko, trans. *J. Math. Phys.* 18(2):51–151.

15. Murray-Coleman, J. F., and A. M. Smith. 1990. The automated measurement of BRDFs and their application to luminaire modeling. *J. Illum. Eng. Soc.* 19(1):87–99.

16. Moon, P. 1940. On interreflections. *J. Opt. Soc. Am.* 30(5):195–205.

17. Moon, P. 1941. Interreflections in rooms. *J. Opt. Soc. Am.* 31(5):374–382.

18. IES. Committee on Standards of Quality and Quantity for Interior Illumination. 1946. The interreflection method of predetermining brightness and brightness ratios. *Illum. Eng.* 41(5):361–385.

19. Moon, P., and D. E. Spencer. 1950. Interreflections in coupled enclosures. *J. Franklin Inst.* 250(2):151–166.

20. O'Brien, P. F. 1955. Interreflections in rooms by a network method. *J. Opt. Soc. Am.* 45(6):419–424.

21. O'Brien, P. F., and J. A. Howard. 1959. Predetermination of luminances by finite difference equations. *Illum. Eng.* 54(4):209–281.

22. O'Brien, P. F. 1960. Lighting calculations for thirty-five thousand rooms. *Illum. Eng.* 55(4):215–226.

23. DiLaura, D. L. 1982. On the simplification of radiative transfer calculations. *J. Illum. Eng. Soc.* 12(1):12–16.

24. DiLaura, D. L. 1992. On the development of a recursive method for the solution of radiative transfer problems [abstract]. *J. Illum. Eng. Soc.* 21(2):115.

25. Mistrick, R. G., and D. L. DiLaura. 1987. A new finite orthogonal transform applied to radiative transfer calculations. *J. Illum. Eng. Soc.* 16(2):115–128.

26. Mistrick, R. G. 1989. A priority based dual density finite element inerreflected component calculation. *J. Illum. Eng. Soc.* 18(2):16–22.

27. Zhang, J. X., and P. Y. Ngai. 1991. Lighting calculations in a multi-partitioned space. *J. Illum. Eng. Soc.* 20(1):32–43.

28. Ballman, T. L., and R. E. Levin. 1987. Illumination in partitioned spaces. *J. Illum. Eng. Soc.* 16(2):31–49.

29. O'Brien, P. F., and E. Balogh. 1967. Configuration factors for computing illumination within interiors. *Illum. Eng.* 62(4):169–179.

30. IES. Lighting Design Practice Committee. 1964. Zonal-cavity method of calculating and using coefficients of utilization. *Illum. Eng.* 59(5):309–328.

31. Jones, J. R., and B. F. Jones. 1964. Using the zonal-cavity system in lighting calculations: Part I. *Illum. Eng.* 59(5):413–415; Part II. *Illum. Eng.* 59(6):448–450; Part III. *Illum. Eng.* 59(7):501–503; Part IV. *Illum. Eng.* 59(8):556–561.

32. IES. Committee on Lighting Design Practice. 1974. The determination of illumination at a point in interior spaces. *J. Illum. Eng. Soc.* 3(2):170–201.

33. Jones, J. R., R. C. LeVere, N. Ivanicki, and P. Chesebrough. 1969. Angular coordinate system and computing illumination at a point. *Illum. Eng.* 64(4):296–308.

34. Illuminating Engineering Society (London). 1968. *The calculation of direct illumination from linear sources.* IES Technical Report 11. London: Illuminating Engineering Society.

35. Burnham, R. D. 1950. The illumination at a point from an industrial fluorescent luminaire. *Illum. Eng.* 45(12):753–757.

36. Murdoch, J. B. 1984. Extension of the configuration factor method to strip sources. *J. Illum. Eng. Soc.* 13(3):290–295.

37. IES. Design Practice Committee. 1970. General procedure for calculating maintained illumination. *Illum. Eng.* 65(10):602–617.

38. Clark, F. 1963. Accurate maintenance factors. *Illum. Eng.* 58(3):124–131.

39. Clark, F. 1968. Light loss factor in the design process. *Illum. Eng.* 63(11):575–581.

40. American National Standards Institute. 1977. *American national standard methods of measurement of fluorescent lamp ballasts, ANSI C82.2-1977.* New York: American National Standards Institute.

41. National Lighting Product Information Program. 1991. *Specifier reports: Electronic ballasts.* Guest Contributor R. Verderber. Troy, NY: Rensselaer Polytechnic Institute.

42. IES. Committee on Testing Procedures. Subcommittee on Photometry of Outdoor Luminaires. 1970. IES approved method for determining luminaire-lamp-ballast combination operating factors for high intensity discharge luminaires. *Illum. Eng.* 65(12):718–721.

43. McNamara, A. C., C. R. Snyder, and J. T. Oliver. 1974. High wattage HID lamp fixture coordination: Vertical versus horizontal versus somewhere in between. *IEEE Trans. Ind. Appl.* IA-10(5):618–623.

44. Levin, R. E., and T. M. Lemons. 1971. High-intensity discharge lamps and their environment. *IEEE Trans. Ind. Gen. Appl.* 7(2):218–224.

45. Luckiesh, M., and S. K. Guth. 1949. Brightness in visual field at borderline between comfort and discomfort (BCD). *Illum. Eng.* 44(11):650–670.

46. Hopkinson, R. G. 1957. Evaluation of glare. *Illum. Eng.* 52(6):305–316.

47. Guth, S. K., and J. F. McNelis. 1959. A discomfort glare evaluator. *Illum. Eng.* 54(6):398–406.

48. Guth, S. K., and J. F. McNelis. 1961. Further data on discomfort glare from multiple sources. *Illum. Eng.* 56(1):46–57.

49. Bradley, R. D., and H. L. Logan. 1964. A uniform method for computing the probability of comfort response in a visual field. *Illum. Eng.* 59(3):189–206.

50. Guth, S. K. 1963. A method for the evaluation of discomfort glare. *Illum. Eng.* 57(5):351–364.

51. Allphin, W. 1966. Influence of sight line on BCD judgments of direct discomfort glare. *Illum. Eng.* 61(10):629–633.

52. Allphin, W. 1968. Further studies of sight line and direct discomfort glare. *Illum. Eng.* 63(1):26–31.

53. Allphin, W. 1961. BCD appraisals of luminaire brightness in a simulated office. *Illum. Eng.* 56(1):31–44.

54. Allphin, W. 1961. Further appraisals of luminaire brightness. *Illum. Eng.* 56(12):701–707.

55. IES. Committee on Recommendations of Quality and Quantity of Illumination. Subcommittee on Direct Glare. 1966. Outline of a standard procedure for computing visual comfort ratios for interior lighting: Report No. 2. *Illum. Eng.* 61(10):643–666.

56. Guth, S. K. 1966. Computing visual comfort ratings for a specific interior lighting installation. *Illum. Eng.* 61(10):634–642.

57. McGowan, T. K., and S. K. Guth. 1969. Extending and applying the IES visual comfort rating procedure. *Illum. Eng.* 64(4):253–270.

58. IES. Committee on Recommendations of Quality and Quantity of Illumination. 1969. A statement concerning visual comfort probability (VCP): Naive vs experienced observers. *Illum. Eng.* 64(9):604.

59. IES. Testing Procedures Committee. Subcommittee on Photometry of Indoor Luminaires. 1972. Determination of average luminance of luminaires. *J. Illum. Eng. Soc.* 1(2):181–184.

60. IES. Committee on Recommendations of Quality and Quantity of Illumination. Subcommittee on Direct Glare. 1973. RQQ Report No. 2 (1972): Outline of a standard

procedure for computing visual comfort ratings for interior lighting. *J. Illum. Eng. Soc.* 2(3):328–344.

61. IES. Committee on Recommendation of Quantity and Quality of Illumination. 1973. Appendix to RQQ Report No. 2 (1972): Determination of effective candlepower of modular and linear regressed systems. *J. Illum. Eng. Soc.* 2(4):504–505.

62. Fry, G. A. 1976. A simplified formula for discomfort glare. *J. Illum. Eng. Soc.* 8(1):10–20.

63. Levin, R. E. 1975. Position index in VCP calculations. *J. Illum. Eng. Soc.* 4(2):99–105.

64. Levin, R. E. 1973. An evaluation of VCP calculations. *J. Illum. Eng. Soc.* 2(4):355–361.

65. DiLaura, D. L. 1976. On the computation of visual comfort probability. *J. Illum. Eng. Soc.* 5(4):207–217.

66. O'Brien, P. F. 1965. Numerical analysis for lighting design. *Illum. Eng.* 60(4):169–173.

67. IES. Lighting Design Practice Committee. 1968. Calculation of luminance coefficients based upon the zonal-cavity method. *Illum. Eng.* 63(8):423–432.

68. IES. Calculation Procedures Committee. 1982. Recommended procedure for calculating coefficients of utilization, wall exitance coefficients, and ceiling cavity exitance coefficients. *J. Illum. Eng. Soc.* 12(1): 3–11.

69. IES. Design Practice Committee. 1977. Recommended practice for classification of interior luminaires by distribution: Luminaire spacing criterion. *Light. Des. Appl.* 7(8):20–21.

70. Levin, R. E. 1982. The photometric connection. Part 1: *Light. Des. Appl.* 12(9):28–35; Part 2: *Light. Des. Appl.* 12(10):60–63; Part 3: *Light. Des. Appl.* 12(11):42–47; Part 4: *Light. Des. Appl.* 12(12):16–18.

Elements
of Design

III

Lighting Design Process 10

INTRODUCTION

Lighting design is a process of informed decision making, involving a sequence of creative and practical choices that support the goals of the project. This chapter introduces the design steps and some considerations essential for successful results.

OVERVIEW

Lighting design is the creative process for developing lighting solutions for safe, productive and enjoyable use of the built environment. In the past there has been an overwhelming emphasis on assuring that an appropriate *quantity* of light is delivered to the task or work surface. *Quality* of light has been considered mainly in the limited sense of controlling direct glare from luminaires or reflected glare from surfaces and objects. However, lighting design extends far beyond these factors. Light is one of the tools used to shape our environment, visually and emotionally. Lighting design is a synthesis of light and shadow, color, form, space, rhythm, texture and proportion, achieved through an understanding of the technology necessary to produce these effects. Working with all of these elements is what distinguishes the work of the lighting designer from that of the artist, from whom the lighting designer draws inspiration; and from that of the engineer, from whom the designer learns practical problem-solving techniques.

Part of the appeal of designing with light is its elusive nature: its effect can be almost palpable and may be visually arresting, yet the rays of light themselves are usually invisible. When designers or users talk of "light," they often mean the effect of light on a surface or object: highlight and shadow, soft gradations of light, or the sharp definition that comes with focused point sources. Light reveals form: wall planes, three-dimensional space, architectural details, furnishings, sculpture, the branching structure of trees. Light can enhance or diminish elements of the built environment as well as the natural environment.

Light profoundly affects our feelings of well-being, of awe and wonder, of mood, of comfort, of motivation.

It influences how we perceive all the other elements. Light patterns evoke psychological responses such as "bright," "dim," "magical," "dull," "mysterious," "pleasant" and "forbidding."

The associations we have with light are inevitably made early on, more so than with many other aspects of architecture. Light can symbolize dignity and mystery to those who first became aware of its special qualities in the soft, mysterious light of a church. It can symbolize excitement to those whose early memories of light are the dazzling, never touchable lights of Broadway or Times Square, to those to whom the glow of neon marked the first place in which they realized that light was much more than what happened when you flipped a wall switch. On the other hand, light can symbolize comfort and security to those whose recollections are of lamps left on at night to guide them home or just to make a house feel warm. And comfort mixed with a hint of the exotic, for those whose early memories are of candlelight and the glow of a fire.

What is most important about all of these things is that they deal with emotional associations. They are not pure fact, the recollection of the knowledge that one plus one equals two, but something that strikes much deeper than empirical knowledge... light inevitably has these kinds of associations for people. However much we can quantify light and talk of things like task lighting, and footcandles, and wattage, light remains an emotional thing. It transcends the scientific, even as ... designers require more and more scientific knowledge every day. The heart of the issue with lighting is still the emotional associations it engenders, the way lighting "feels." For what changes in a room when the lighting changes are not the hard facts, not the length or the width or the height or where the door and windows are. It is the way the room "feels."

Paul Goldberger
Address to Lighting World III
April 1985

THE PROCESS

There are many factors that must be considered together in order to form a lighting design that provides the proper quantity and quality of light, and is appropriate in terms of cost, energy, maintenance, style, availability and a dozen other considerations. Because there are so many aspects to weigh together, there is no one perfect solution to a single lighting problem. There are a multitude of solutions, and they will be more or less successful depending on how well the designer has synthesized the solution, and depending on whose criteria are used in the judging.

The lighting design process is not a predictable, linear process. It begins with the formation of a design concept from a myriad of design considerations. Then, as it proceeds, it is filled with cross-checking and doubling back. However, most lighting design projects follow the phases that occur in architectural design:

- Programming
- Schematic design
- Design development
- Contract documents
- Bidding and negotiation
- Construction
- Postoccupancy evaluation

See figure 10-1 for a schematic presentation of the lighting design process.

The players involved in the design process will vary according to the size and complexity of the project. Sometimes the lighting designer is hired by and works directly with a building owner or the owner's representative (called "client" in this chapter). Other times, the lighting designer is hired by the architect or interior designer and works with the owner and other team members, such as the electrical engineer or landscape architect. Design team meetings may include the client and all team designers and engineers, or may be as small as just the architect and the lighting designer. Good communication among all parties is one key to successful design.

Programming

This is the important initial phase of a project when the lighting designer gathers information about user and client needs, preferences and constraints. The lighting designer looks to the client and the design team for design objectives, such as image, maintenance, flexibility and budget. This information is exchanged through meetings, written inquiries or telephone conversations. Site visits to observe similar installations can be helpful for communication, since the client can point to what is and is not liked in both function and appearance. The site visit also gives the lighting designer a chance to see and experience the visual tasks involved. Interviews with users of similar spaces can help identify potential lighting problems.

Here is a list of issues to address during the programming stage for either new or existing spaces:

A. Owner and design team preferences and impressions
   1. Space function, use
   2. Building materials, room finishes, architectural style
   3. Space plan, furniture style
   4. Important features such as art locations and signage
   5. Comfort level and satisfaction of occupants, workers and users
   6. Need for flexibility of space function and users
   7. Exterior features such as image, security and landscape
B. Visual and perception needs
   1. Age of occupants
   2. Tasks to be performed: their importance and duration
   3. Times of occupancy during the day and year
   4. Psychological needs for light
   5. The shape of the task, particularly in industrial areas
C. Security issues
   1. Personal safety, including dangerous conditions, rotating parts, assault and theft potential
   2. Vandalism
D. Architectural opportunities and constraints
   1. Architectural features, interior and exterior
   2. Historical constraints
   3. Ceiling heights, type of ceiling
   4. Plenum depth
   5. Location and size of structural members and mechanical ducts
   6. Window and skylight locations and orientations
      a. Types of glazing, wall configurations
      b. Shades, blinds, drapes, other sun control media
   7. Construction and safety codes
   8. Electrical system
      a. Voltage
      b. Circuit capacity
      c. Lighting controls, including likely locations and appropriate types
      d. Energy management system or other automatic controls for building
   9. Construction schedule
   10. Landscape features
E. Photometric considerations (illuminance, luminance, task size and contrast) of existing installation and at similar sites during both day and night

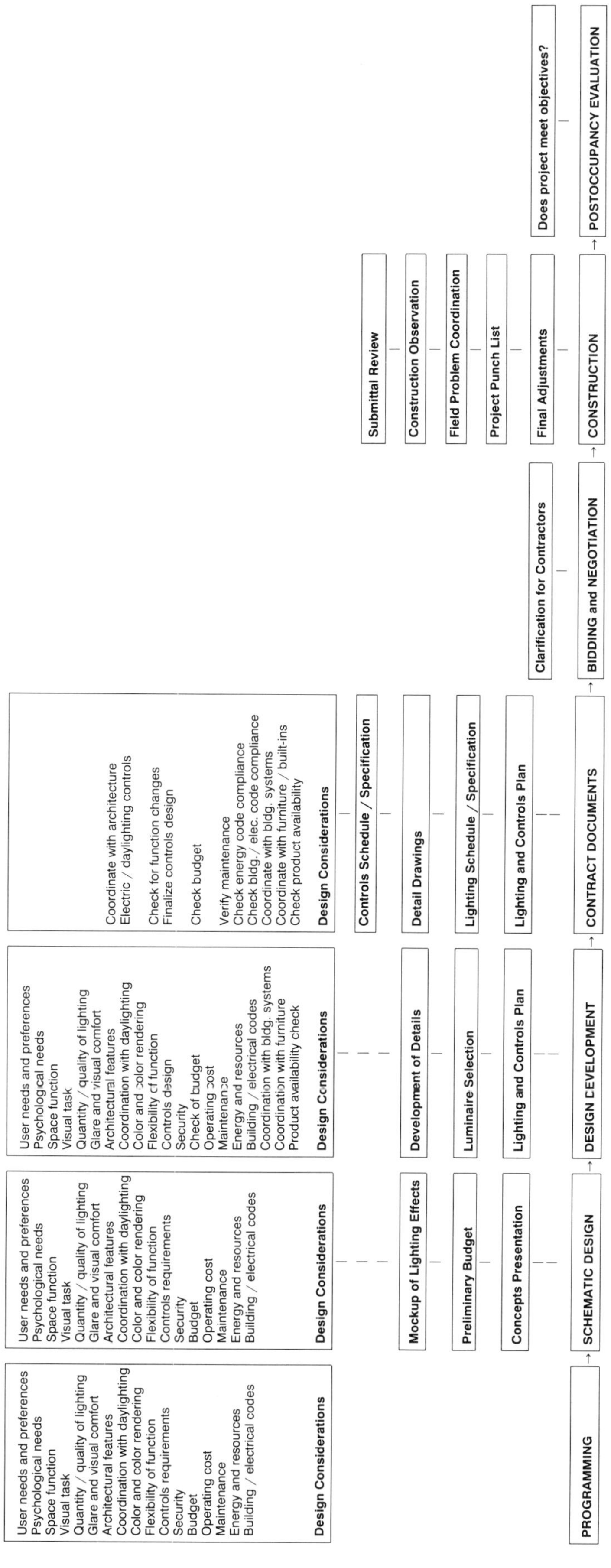
PROGRAMMING
Design Considerations
User needs and preferences
Psychological needs
Space function
Visual task
Quantity / quality of lighting
Glare and visual comfort
Architectural features
Coordination with daylighting
Color and color rendering
Flexibility of function
Controls requirements
Security
Budget
Operating cost
Maintenance
Energy and resources
Building / electrical codes
SCHEMATIC DESIGN
Concepts Presentation
Preliminary Budget
Mockup of Lighting Effects
Design Considerations
User needs and preferences
Psychological needs
Space function
Visual task
Quantity / quality of lighting
Glare and visual comfort
Architectural features
Coordination with daylighting
Color and color rendering
Flexibility of function
Controls requirements
Security
Budget
Operating cost
Maintenance
Energy and resources
Building / electrical codes
DESIGN DEVELOPMENT
Lighting and Controls Plan
Luminaire Selection
Development of Details
Design Considerations
User needs and preferences
Psychological needs
Space function
Visual task
Quantity / quality of lighting
Glare and visual comfort
Architectural features
Coordination with daylighting
Color and color rendering
Flexibility of function
Controls design
Security
Check of budget
Operating cost
Maintenance
Energy and resources
Building / electrical codes
Coordination with bldg. systems
Coordination with furniture
Product availability check
CONTRACT DOCUMENTS
Lighting and Controls Plan
Lighting Schedule / Specification
Detail Drawings
Controls Schedule / Specification
Design Considerations
Coordinate with architecture
Electric / daylighting controls
Check for function changes
Finalize controls design
Check budget
Verify maintenance
Check energy code compliance
Check bldg. / elec. code compliance
Coordinate with bldg. systems
Coordinate with furniture / built-ins
Check product availability
BIDDING and NEGOTIATION
Clarification for Contractors
CONSTRUCTION
Final Adjustments
Project Punch List
Field Problem Coordination
Construction Observation
Submittal Review
POSTOCCUPANCY EVALUATION
Does project meet objectives?

Fig. 10-1. The Lighting Design Process

 1. Critical vision: task areas and immediate surrounds
 2. General field of view: highlights, ambient levels
 3. Distant surrounds: circulation areas, transition areas
F. Budget
 1. Initial cost (installed)
 2. Maintenance and energy cost
 3. Life-cycle cost
G. Energy limitations
 1. Energy code requirements (federal, state or province, local)
 2. Utility incentive programs
H. Maintenance considerations

The programming phase results in a list of project needs, preferences, constraints and design goals.

Schematic Design (Developing the Lighting Concept)

Probably no phase of the science and art of illumination, briefly called "illuminating engineering," has been so much discussed as its relation to the science and art of building, briefly called "architecture." The fact that a building can fulfill no purpose, either utilitarian or artistic, without the use of light sufficiently indicates the importance of the correlation of the two sciences. A complete discussion of an architectural work therefore necessitates an examination of the methods of supplying both natural and artificial light, and, conversely, the study of lighting of a building demands a general analysis of its architectural motives and details.

Louis Sullivan
"Lighting the People's Savings Bank"
in *The Public Papers*
ed. Robert Twombly, 205
University of Chicago Press, 1988

Once the programming phase data are gathered, the lighting designer starts thinking about the needs and requirements of the space and how they work together, including architectural needs and the psychological and visual needs of the people using the space. During the development of the lighting concept, the designer establishes a framework to judge how a lighted space will feel to the user of that space. This concept provides a reference against which the final design can be judged.

The nature, feeling, quality and other intangible aspects of light in the space are often given only perfunctory attention, and most time is consumed analyzing the quantifiable aspects of the lighting system envisioned. However, methods of lighting design based on calculating various quantities to avoid fundamental mistakes, such as an inadequate amount of light, are not sufficient. The question asked and answered is "will it work?" The question that is not asked is "is it appropriate?" (or, as Louis Kahn used to say, "what does the space want to be?").

To answer the question of appropriateness will require a fundamental change in the way the designer thinks about lighting a space. Instead of starting with a particular task and its characteristics, one will start with the needs and requirements of the space as a whole. These needs will be architectural needs, that is to say, based on the internal logic of the space as a volume in which people engage in various activities, rather than simply the technical requirements having to do with human performance of a visual task. Once this concept of the nature and feeling of the space (whether interior or exterior) is established, a much stronger schematic design can result. The designer will also have a basis upon which lighting design schemes may be evaluated. The following questions are relevant to all lighting design projects:

Who uses the space? What are their ages and visual needs? The lighting designer needs to understand human vision (see chapter 3, Vision and Perception). What are their activities? What do they like or not like in lighting?

How is the space used? What activities will take place? At what times of day? What are the visual tasks? Lighting techniques have evolved for different applications, based on a synthesis of theory, engineering and proven experience. (See the application chapters.) Once the visual tasks have been identified, then ask:

How critical is the task being performed? A pharmacist could easily fill a prescription incorrectly if she misreads the doctor's handwriting. A bank clerk could make an expensive mistake if he has difficulty reading a check. If accuracy in performing the visual task is important, extra attention should be paid to providing an appropriate quality and quantity of light which will aid performance and minimize the fatigue that can result from visual effort. Speed and accuracy can make the difference in being competitive or noncompetitive in our global economy.

However, in many spaces visual tasks are less important. In a romantic restaurant, reading the menu is secondary to creating an ambiance where patrons will feel relaxed and unhurried, enjoy a sense of privacy, and be visually entertained.

Where is the visual task located? It is important to remember that light need not be evenly spread across rooms. Energy-efficient lighting design often means putting high light levels only where the critical visual tasks will be located, and lower ambient levels elsewhere. Also, it is important to remember that not all tasks occur in the horizontal plane (that is, on the desktop). Storage racks and bookstack lighting are two examples of vertical-plane visual tasks. The lighting designer must select luminaires and locate them carefully so that the light is put where the user needs it. (See the application chapters.)

What is the proper quality and quantity of light for the task? The lighting designer must understand the characteristics of visual tasks and know what direction and quality of lighting will make the task easy to see. This includes determining the luminance of each task, the areas surrounding the task, and the luminances in the user's peripheral view, since luminance values affect visual comfort as well as task performance. The geometric relationship between the lighting system, the user's eye and the visual task is a critical factor in visibility. See chapter 3, Vision and Perception, and the application chapters for information on how to avoid reflections that reduce task contrast and for recommendations on balancing luminances for user comfort.

Will the space be a pleasant place for users to enter and spend time in? Often, the appropriate question to ask during the design process is not "can the user perform the visual task in this luminous environment?" but "would the user want to?" The designer must understand how people perceive and interpret light patterns, and then know how to create luminous environments that evoke the desired response. It is most often the vertical surfaces in an environment (walls, columns, beams, windows and sculptures in an interior space; trees, signage and building walls in an exterior space) that determine whether the space seems bright or dim, intriguing or mysterious, pleasant or forbidding.

Will the lighting installation be compatible with the architecture? The lighting design does not exist independently. It must coordinate with the design of the building and work to reveal that design. It must be detailed as an integral part of the building, rather than appearing to be an afterthought.

This question, along with several others in this list, is a primary reason for the development of a strong conceptual design. The answers to these types of subjective questions are best tested by evaluating them against the overall lighting concept created at the onset of the project. Although they may have no absolute numeric basis, they still may be tested for appropriateness, if the original concept is clear to all parties involved.

Will the lighting system work with available daylight? Will it work at night? Electric lighting systems can be controlled to lower the output when there is a useful daylight contribution from windows or skylights. This can reduce energy loads during peak demand hours for the electric utility. See chapter 8, Daylighting, and chapter 31, Lighting Controls. Also, the lighting designer needs to be concerned about the effect of both interior and exterior luminaires and light patterns on the nighttime appearance of the building. See chapter 22, Exterior Lighting.

What color of light is appropriate? Consider the objects, surfaces and people that will be lighted in the space. Should the color of the light be warm or cool or something in between? How important is the color rendering ability of the light source? Will the light source color coordinate well with available daylight? Sources with good color rendering make merchandise look more appealing, and can help people feel better about themselves because their skin tones look healthier. Plant foliage can appear dead under sources deficient in the short-wavelength (blue) region of the spectrum, so light sources used for landscape lighting must be carefully selected for spectral composition. See chapter 5, Nonvisual Effects of Radiant Energy. Warmer color temperatures of light can help people feel relaxed because it reminds them of the warm light sources used in their homes. Where color is critical, there is no substitute for viewing objects, skin tones, fabrics and finishes under the intended light source in a color booth or full-scale mockup. See chapter 4, Color.

Will glare be a problem? The lighting designer must evaluate the lighting system under design so that uncomfortable or distracting glare is minimized for the user. This involves knowing the location of the user, the angles of view and the distribution of light on the room surfaces, as well as familiarity with the specified lighting products. Maximum luminaire brightness cannot always be derived from photometric reports, so the designer may have to view luminaire samples or rely on past experience to determine whether glare from a particular luminaire will be a problem. See chapter 7, Luminaires. Windows and skylights may produce a glare problem that requires an architectural solution. See chapter 3, Vision and Perception, for issues connected with glare.

Is the proposed lighting system within budget? Are its operating costs appropriate? Life-cycle costing is often the best way to examine the expense of lighting. These numbers should then be discussed with the owner or client. There is no easy way to predict the exact value of a commercial or industrial lighting system in terms of production, safety, quality control, employee morale or employee health; however, employee costs far outweigh both initial and operating costs of lighting. Small improvements in employee morale due to a comfortable and effective lighting system could quickly pay for the incremental lighting cost. See chapter 13, Lighting Economics.

Is the lighting system using energy and resources responsibly? Electrical energy use affects environmental pollution and costs the building owner energy dollars. Disposal of lamps and ballasts may also contribute to hazardous waste disposal problems. The deleterious environmental effects must be balanced with the human benefits of the lighting system. See chapter 34, Environmental Issues.

Is the lighting system flexible? If the client's needs are likely to change often, the lighting system should be designed to accommodate changes easily. Workstations may be shifted in an office. Merchandise displays may be moved in a retail store. Plants may grow and necessitate lighting system modifications in an outdoor installation. Stack locations may change in a library. The likelihood of change must be weighed against the increased lighting system cost and energy cost that may result from the more flexible lighting design. See chapter 31, Lighting Controls.

How will the lighting system be controlled? Lighting may be switched or dimmed, and this affects both the control devices and the ballasts. The lighting designer will often be involved in determining where the controls are located, and this necessitates questioning the client about how the space will be used. In most cases the controls should be located so that they are as convenient as possible for the clients to use. In some cases, however, it is better for the controls to be hidden or locked to prevent the lights from being turned off in areas where security is a problem, or to prevent users from adjusting the lights. (Imagine a restaurant where patrons turn the lights up and down, distracting other patrons.) The designer frequently decides which lights will be controlled together, and specifies wall-box controls, architectural dimming systems and preset dimming controls. The designer may —independently or together with the electrical engineer—gauge whether automatic controls, such as occupancy sensors, programmable time clocks or energy management systems, will save a sufficient amount of energy to justify their initial cost. See chapter 31, Lighting Controls.

What are the applicable building, handicap, electrical and energy codes? With the assistance of the architect and engineer, the designer must become familiar with all of the applicable codes pertaining to lighting for the locality of the project. These will include egress requirements, circuiting requirements, and, in some areas, energy restrictions. Among the newest government regulations are the Americans with Disabilities Act (ADA) handicap requirements, and the component requirements for lamps and ballasts. The ADA

requirements pertain to the allowable projection of wall-mounted fixtures. The component regulations cover lamp and ballast efficacy. See chapter 14, Codes and Regulations.

The idea that lighting codes and illuminance measurements alone can achieve effective and comfortable results is the "illuminance illusion." Design must address the entirety of the visual environment and all its nuances—factors which can be gleaned from sources other than energy tables. Lighting can only play an essential role in the creation of a positive experience when it is seen as part of a total environment.
Peter Boyce
"Reflections on the 1988/89 Lecture Series"
Lighting Research Center

What are the lighting considerations particular to an industrial area? Lighting for industrial areas has many of the needs discussed above. In addition, it may be necessary to consider conditions which are unique to the industrial workplace. The following are indicative of the special conditions which occur in the industrial workplace.

The tasks found in many locations are two-dimensional, whereas those in industry are often three-dimensional. This requires special consideration when designing lighting to assure that the proper illuminances are provided to allow the worker to see all aspects of the task. In addition, care must be taken in industrial lighting designs to assure that a stroboscopic effect does not create a dangerous condition where rotating parts or machine components are involved. For a complete discussion, see chapter 20, Industrial Lighting.

Design Development

The lighting designer is now ready to formulate design concepts. There are many ways to develop such ideas. Visiting sites with similar features and visual tasks helps the designer learn about lighting systems that worked or did not work in those spaces. Photographs are a quick way to document the lighting solutions in these existing spaces. The designer can also search for photographs and descriptions of similar installations in magazines and books. These can provide inspiration, although it may be impossible to judge from a photograph whether the lighting system satisfied the task requirements or created uncomfortable glare for the users.

The lighting designer's own sketches are invaluable tools in the schematic design process because they illustrate the designer's mental images of the lighted environment. The space may be imagined as the inside of a box with its surfaces painted with light. The light can be applied to the walls, the desk top, the ceiling or the floor. It can be applied in a regular or irregular pattern. It must provide an appropriate quality of light for the visual tasks performed, respond to the psychological needs of the users and enhance architectural design features. The lighting designer may visualize an evenly lighted scene or one with notable contrasts in light and shadow. (Some of the design effects that can be achieved with light, such as "enlarging space with light" or "grazing," are discussed in figure 10-2 and illustrated with sketches.) The lighting sketches often show which surfaces are illuminated and the relative brightness of each. The designer should be aware of the psychological and spatial effects created by the lighting patterns. Will users find this space "open," "bright," "intimate," "public," "restful," "gloomy," "stimulating," "comfortable," "dramatic" or "business-like"? See chapter 3, Vision and Perception, and also John Flynn's work:

> *Light can have a strengthening or reinforcing effect similar to that of background music in creating an appropriate emotional environment and a complementary psychological setting. The impression of pleasantness and well-being that an individual receives in a space may influence his attitude, and in the final analysis, attitude is the major factor in maintaining effective interest in an activity or task. In this sense, visual impressions induced by the lighting system are fundamental in planning and design, and they become a functional part of the activity.*
> John E. Flynn
> in Flynn and Mills:
> *Architectural Lighting Graphics*
> Reinhold Publishing Company, 1962

Any step which helps the designer develop a design concept can also be a communication tool. Photographs of analogous installations, design sketches and magazine photographs can all be used to illustrate the ideas to other design team members, the client and the end users. This material should be saved for presentations.

Once the desired light patterns are established and the special needs of the area have been considered, the designer determines the appropriate distribution of light, direction of light, and light source. Light may emanate from a luminaire in a concentrated beam or as diffuse blob or wash; from a point source, linear source or area source. The luminaire may be visible or concealed. It may be recessed, wall-mounted or suspended from the ceiling. It may be portable or mounted to the furniture. These requirements lead the lighting designer toward specific lighting products; but actual product selection takes place during the design development phase.

Lighting design concepts developed through this process must be tested and retested against the project's objectives and constraints. Concepts which continue to satisfy the programming requirements are presented to the design team and the client, and once approved, move on to the design development stage.

In the design development phase, the lighting design concept is refined, and documentation is initiated. Mounting details are developed as well as detailing of any custom luminaires. More precise lighting calculations and energy use calculations may be performed. Lighting layouts (with exact luminaire lengths, lamp counts, spacings, and so forth) are firmed up.

Luminaire selection requires an understanding of photometric reports and the characteristics of light sources, and in many cases it requires an evaluation of a sample luminaire, either on the table top or in a mockup. The style of the luminaires should relate to the architecture, and must be appropriate in terms of cost and energy use. See chapter 7, Luminaires.

The lighting designer often finds that the desired luminaire does not exist as a standard, cataloged product. The designer may want a special look or finish or optical distribution, and this necessitates working with a manufacturer to create a custom or modified lighting product. Many manufacturers are willing to engineer and fabricate a custom product if the number of units is large, or if it involves a minor modification to a product in their standard line. A smaller group of manufacturers are set up to produce small numbers of custom luminaires. Designers should be aware that custom luminaires have potential problems that standard products may avoid: long lead times for delivery, additional cost, UL listing complications, and poor product engineering (such as clumsy relamping). However, custom luminaires frequently contribute a unique look to the exterior or interior of a building. The premium in cost is often minor or may be well justified. The designer, in conjunction with the project team, usually makes the decision on the utilization of custom luminaires.

During the design development phase there may be extensive communication and coordination with other design team members (architect, interior designer, engineers and landscape architect) to ensure that the lighting is integrated into the whole of the building or site. Here are some additional issues to investigate in this phase:

Is the lighting system coordinated with other building systems? The lighting system must integrate with the structural, mechanical, acoustical, electrical, fire protection and life safety systems in the building. Lighting hardware can be combined with air supply and extraction systems, for example, which may result in a more economical building and an architecturally coordinated ceiling appearance. By code, the luminaire housing must be rated for the area where it is mounted in the

Fig. 10-2. Creating Effects with Light

Effect	Created by	Light Sources	Visual Effects	Effects on People, Objects, and Tasks	Suggestions	Sketched Illustration
Enlarging space	Indirect or ambient light. Brightly and evenly lighted ceiling, wall or floor surfaces. Surfaces should have high reflectance.	Diffuse, point or linear sources. Incandescent, fluorescent or HID.	Room dimensions appear larger. Lighting more uniform. Less drama, less contrast in room. Colors less vibrant.	Contrast and shadows are diminished. Objects become less prominent than surfaces. Sparkle from jewelry, crystal, hair sheen, shiny finishes is reduced. Architectural form of space is more visible. Space appears less "crisp." Quality of light for reading tasks can be excellent, but is dependent on illuminance level and luminaire placement.	Direct shielded light helps focus attention on objects or work surfaces. Use accent light 2 to 20 times as bright on special objects.	 Enlarging Space with Light
Making space look smaller or more intimate	Direct, shielded luminaires, recessed in ceiling, or surface-mounted on wall or ceiling.	Point sources, concentrated beam spreads. Usually incandescent.	Room dimensions appear smaller. High contrast. Vibrant color and glitter.	Creates dramatic, stimulating atmosphere. Creates mood of intimacy. Sparkle and glitter enhanced. Attracts attention to bright objects. Prominent shadows can enhance texture, but render faces harshly. High contrast may not be conducive to long-term performance of visual tasks. Position of luminaire and angle of light affect task visibility.	Add ambient light to soften contrasts and improve appearance of faces. High-contrast setting may be one of several options on a programmable dimmer.	 Making Spaces Smaller
Grazing	Well-shielded directional luminaires, recessed or surface-mounted downlight, wall-mounted uplight. Sharp angle of incidence of light against surface.	Point source, high or low intensity. Sometimes achievable with linear source. Incandescent, HID, or fluorescent.	Expands space. Emphasizes texture and color of surface. Reduces reflections on specular grazed surfaces such as picture glass or shiny marble walls.	Adds visual interest. Draws attention to special surfaces. Adds ambient light to space. Can balance light from other lighting systems. Will accentuate flaws and unevenness in gypboard walls.	Use with other lighting systems for balance. Highly textured wall coverings, brick patterns or stone patterns will produce pleasing shadow patterns.	 Grazing
Washing	Well-shielded directional luminaires, recessed, surface-mounted, wall-mounted, or floor-mounted.	Point or linear source, high or low intensity. Incandescent, fluorescent or HID.	Provides even lighting across wall or ceiling surfaces. Softens shadows. Extends space.	Calls attention to lighted surfaces. Soft, reflected light on faces. Bright surfaces make space feel cheerful. Adds ambient light.	Recommended for matte surfaces only, or else glary reflections may occur. Use with other lighting systems for balance.	 Wall Washing

	Equipment	Light source	Light characteristics	Effect	Usage notes
Framing	Recessed or surface-mounted framing projector with adjustable shutters.	Point source, high intensity. Low-voltage or line-voltage incandescent.	Lights painting or object only. Background goes dark, creating very high contrast. Shutters allow confining light to the artwork. No spill light.	Very dramatic effect on artwork. Artwork seems to glow. Sharp shadows on frame. Focuses attention an art. Can be used for wall-hung art, sculpture, rectangular dining tables and other horizontal surfaces. This technique may give an artificial look to artwork if the contrast between art and background is too high.	Use with other lighting systems for balance.
Accent	Narrow-beam recessed downlights or surface-mounted luminaires. Adjustable aiming.	Point source, high intensity. Low-voltage or line-voltage incandescent, or compact metal halide.	Focuses light on object with little spill light on background. Creates high contrast.	Dramatic effect that draws attention to the lighted object or surface. Enhances color. Creates sharp shadows which often enhance the form in sculpture. Adds visual interest to the space.	Use with other lighting systems for balance. Direct glare or reflected glare may be a problems if light is not carefully aimed away from normal viewing angles.
Ambient	General lighting, nondirectional.	Diffuse, point or linear sources. Incandescent, fluorescent or HID.	Light is nondirectional, unconcentrated. Look may be soft or, if too uniform, bland.	Objects and background equally visible. Soft shadows. No highlights. Helpful in washing out harsh shadows and veiling reflections that could reduce visibility of some tasks.	Use with other lighting systems for balance.
Visible fixtures	Wall-mounted or hanging luminaires. Permanently installed, or portable table lamps or floor lamps.	Diffuse, point or linear sources. Incandescent, HID or fluorescent. Shielded or unshielded.	Contributes to decorative style of space. May add sparkle or glare. May add ambient light.	Decorative luminaires add visual interest. If lamps are visible and wattage is too high, luminaire may be glary and distracting. Well-shielded lamps and chandeliers can provide needed ambient light.	Reduce lamp wattage to a minimum if lamps are exposed. Use other lighting system to provide task lighting.

Framing

Accent

Ambient

Visible Fixtures

building—for wet, damp or dry locations, hazardous locations, or insulated or noninsulated ceilings, for example. See chapter 14, Codes and Regulations.

Is the lighting system coordinated with the furniture? In open office areas, workstation partitions may interfere with the distribution of light from ceiling-mounted luminaires. This may call for specialized ambient lighting systems and task lighting built into the workstation. Veiling reflections, brightness ranges and energy use must be evaluated both for task lighting and for ambient lighting. Lighting is often built into retail display cases. The built-in lighting product must be detailed so that it does not obscure the view of the merchandise, but enhances the displayed goods with color, sparkle and highlight. See chapter 18, Lighting for Merchandise Areas.

Localized and task lighting should be included in the design of industrial lighting systems, where required, to properly illuminate a task which may be located out of the normal distribution pattern for the general lighting system.

Is the lighting system easy to maintain? The lighting designer should imagine the job of the lighting maintenance person. How often does the lamp have to be changed? How difficult is it to get into the luminaire to change the lamp? Does it require special tools? Does it require special lifts, scaffolding or intrepid workers? Are the lamps hard to order or find? Is the number of different lamps on the job so large that it is impractical or confusing to stock them all? If any lighting products have special maintenance problems, the designer should change the specifications or else work with the client to set up a system for maintenance. See chapter 32, Lighting Maintenance.

Will the specified products be available in time? If there is a short lead time on a construction project, it may be necessary to specify quick-ship products. There may also be a backlog in production of new, popular or customized lamps, ballasts, controls or luminaires. Verifying availability early on will help forestall urgent calls from electrical contractors during the construction phase.

Significant redesign may occur during the design development phase, as a result of coordination activities or more precise cost estimates. At the completion of this phase, the lighting design should be well established and the design documentation well underway.

Contract Documents

In this phase of the lighting design process, effort is concentrated on producing a set of documents which are sufficiently clear and complete for the electrical contractor to bid the project, order the lighting and controls products, and install the lighting with a mini-

mum of conflicts with other systems in the building or on the site.

Lighting design documents will vary from project to project, but normally will include:

- Electrical lighting plan (usually a modified reflected-ceiling plan) to indicate the locations and luminaire types for all lighting within the scope of work. Control locations and circuits are also shown on the lighting plan.
- Drawings that show mounting details, building sections and elevations, custom luminaire details and other supplemental information
- Luminaire schedule to specify luminaire attributes, catalog numbers and lamping
- Lighting specifications to outline general requirements for the lighting system, such as ballasting, electrical requirements, applicable codes and standards, approved manufacturers, mounting restrictions and custom fixture requirements
- Dimming and controls schedule to specify control attributes and catalog numbers
- Dimming and controls specifications to outline general requirements of the controls system
- Catalog "cuts" package to illustrate specified luminaires and controls

The lighting designer may be retained to review contract documents prepared by other design team members for coordination. At the conclusion of the contract documents phase, the package of lighting documents is turned over to the owner or owner's representative for bidding.

Bidding and Negotiation

During this phase, the lighting designer may be called upon to clarify points that the bidding contractors do not understand. He or she may also be asked to preapprove lighting products other than those specified. The contractor may offer these substitutions in order to reduce the contractor's cost, improve availability or facilitate ordering of the product. The designer must review substitutions carefully to ensure that the design intent and photometric performance characteristics are met. The construction and reliability of the product must also be checked.

Construction

At this point, the bid has been awarded to an electrical contractor. The lighting designer is usually retained to review *submittal drawings* to ensure that the products the contractor is ordering comply with the intent of the contract documents. Product substitutions may be offered at this time, and it is the designer's responsibility to review carefully the substituted product's construction, appearance and photometric performance so that the client receives a product that will perform just as well as the one specified. By approving the substitution, the designer accepts responsibility for the performance of that product.

The designer may be called upon to help resolve field problems that arise when construction conflicts occur, or when unanticipated product and design problems manifest themselves. This coordination and resolution may occur through written communication, telephone exchanges or site visits. During the final site visit, the designer may prepare a *punch list* which enumerates any errors, flaws or omissions that the designer can spot in the installation of the lighting system.

If there are aimable interior or exterior lighting products on the project, or if there are controls that require the programming of presets, the designer may return to the job site for these adjustments after construction is complete. Often the aiming takes place after the client has moved in furnishings and artwork, so that lights can be aimed to produce the intended visual effect. Proper aiming of exterior facade or landscape lighting is extremely important in order to obtain successful results.

Postoccupancy Evaluation (POE)

After the lighting is installed and in use, it is important for the lighting designer to evaluate how well the lighting installation is performing. Put simply, the POE goal is to determine whether the general design objectives of the lighted space have been met. The designer may ask, in the case of an office building: Does the lighting design work well for the various activities performed? Is it attractive and flattering to the architecture? Does the lighted environment satisfy human needs? Is it comfortable? Is it stimulating? Will people enjoy spending time there? If the answers are yes and the design has stayed within budget, complied with energy constraints and satisfied the objectives established during the programming and design phases, the lighting design has been successful.

[We] see a vast number of projects per year and constantly learn by critical observation and client feedback. It is this experience—not handbook, not research, not other data—that is the principal reference in our prac-

tice. In addition, it is not intuition and definitely not computers.

Howard Brandston
"Lighting Design—The Creative Process"
November 1990

INTERNATIONAL ILLUMINATION DESIGN AWARDS

The purpose of the International Illumination Design Awards program of the IESNA is to advance the appreciation and recognition of lighting design in all its facets and applications. This program provides a unique opportunity for public recognition of professionalism, ingenuity and originality in lighting design, based upon the individual merit of each project submitted and judged against specific criteria.

Judges are selected from a broad professional spectrum that represents knowledge of lighting and design excellence. The judging system, which occurs at local, regional and international levels, is based entirely on how well the lighting design meets the program criteria. These criteria include such considerations as the complexity of the program, lighting concepts and originality of the design approach, architectural integration of lighting equipment, energy effectiveness of the solution and performance criteria achieved.

Contained within the program are parallel awards, judged at the final international level. These were created to recognize outstanding lighting design in their respective categories.

Commercial / Industrial:
   Edwin F. Guth Memorial Awards
Outdoor Lighting:
   Paul Waterbury Awards
Residential Design:
   Aileen Page Cutler Awards
Energy Efficiency in Commercial Buildings:
   Electric Power Research Institute Awards

A special Howard Brandston Student Lighting Design Education Grant has been established to encourage and recognize students who have evidenced high professional promise. Full-time students in an approved academic degree program have the opportunity to submit a presentation of an original and ingenious solution to a supplied lighting design problem.

Illuminance Selection

11

SELECTION PROCEDURE

In 1979 the Illuminating Engineering Society of North America established a procedure[1] for selecting illuminances, based upon factors important to visual performance. This illuminance selection procedure is flexible in that it provides the designer with an opportunity to tailor the illuminance to a specific set of conditions. Such flexibility requires the designer to assess the following factors:

1. *Type of activity within a space.* Activities are considered in the illuminance selection procedure as having varying degrees of emphasis on visual performance.
2. *Characteristics of the visual task.* Target contrast and size as well as the time allowed to perform the visual task are important.
3. *Age of the occupant.* As one ages, it is more difficult to see.
4. *Importance of visual performance in terms of speed and accuracy.* How quickly and accurately one can see are the main visual performance criteria in the procedure.
5. *Reflectance.* People see brightness, which is affected by room and task surface reflectances as well as the illuminance. Therefore, the reflectance of the task surface is important.

Consideration of these factors has been systematized into the following four steps, which can be executed by using figures 11-1 and 11-2.

Step 1: Define the Visual Task

Determine the type of activity for which the illuminance is being selected (for example, reading typed originals). At the same time, establish the plane in which the visual task will be performed (workplane). Document the visual task and the workplane as part of the illuminance selection procedure.

Step 2: Select the Illuminance Category

Nine illuminance categories have been established by the IESNA, which are patterned after those in CIE

Report No. 29.[2] They are designated A through I and cover illuminances from 20 to 20,000 lx (2 to 2000 fc). Each of these nine categories is associated with a range of three target illuminances; the categories and the target illuminances are shown in part I of figure 11-1. The application committees of the IESNA have either adopted these categories by listing different types of areas and activities as intended in parts II and III of figure 11-1, or have provided a different set of illuminance recommendations, which may be found in the appropriate chapters of this Handbook.

Following step 1, where the visual task has been defined, refer to parts II and III of figure 11-1 for the closest corresponding description of the "area/activity." If no satisfactory description can be found in parts II or III, refer to the first column labeled "Type of Activity" in part I of figure 11-1 for a generic description of the visual task.

Step 3: Determine the Illuminance Range

Every illuminance category has a corresponding range of three target illuminances, listed in lux and in footcandles.

Due to the nature of the activities listed in categories A through C, general lighting is required over the entire area of the interior space considered. For instance, in a lobby area one visual task is walking through the lobby. The visual task is to circulate through a space containing large, high-contrast objects; therefore, a low level of general illumination should be selected for the entire lobby.

Categories D through F, however, are for tasks which remain fixed at one location, and where visual performance is a more critical consideration. From location to location, tasks may also vary considerably. For example, an accounting office may have a secretarial pool where reading notes handwritten in felt-tipped pen and proofreading typed originals are prominent tasks, while at the same time accountants in another location may be reading low-contrast computer printouts. Each task calls for a particular illuminance for satisfactory visual performance, and so each task should be lighted accordingly. Therefore, categories D through F should be applied only to the appropriate task area.

Fig. 11-1. Currently Recommended Illuminance Categories and Illuminance Values for Lighting Design —
Targeted Maintained Levels

The following table is a consolidated listing of the IESNA's current illuminance recommendations. This listing is intended to guide the designer in selecting an appropriate illuminance.

Guidance is provided in two forms: (1), in Parts I, II and III as an *Illuminance Category*, representing a range of illuminances; and (2), in Parts IV, V and VI as an *Illuminance Value*. Illuminance categories are represented by letter designations A through I. Illuminance Values are given in *lux* with equivalents in *footcandles* and as such are intended as *target* values with deviations expected. These target values also represent *maintained* values.

This table has been divided into six parts for ease of use. Part I lists both Illuminance Categories and Illuminance Values for generic types of interior activities and normally is to be used when Illuminance Categories for a specific Area/Activity cannot be found in Parts II and III. Parts IV, V and VI provide target maintained Illuminance Values for outdoor facilities, sports and recreational areas, and transportation vehicles where special considerations apply as discussed.

In all cases the recommendations in this table are based on the assumption that the lighting will be properly designed to take into account the visual characteristics of the task.

I. Illuminance Categories and Illuminance Values for Generic Types of Activities in Interiors

Type of Activity	Illuminance Category	Ranges of Illuminances		Reference Work-Plane
		Lux	Footcandles	
Public spaces with dark surroundings	A	20-30-50	2-3-5	General lighting throughout spaces
Simple orientation for short temporary visits	B	50-75-100	5-7.5-10	
Working spaces where visual tasks are only occasionally performed	C	100-150-200	10-15-20	
Performance of visual tasks of high contrast or large size	D	200-300-500	20-30-50	
Performance of visual tasks of medium contrast or small size	E	500-750-1000	50-75-100	Illuminance on task
Performance of visual tasks of low contrast or very small size	F	1000-1500-2000	100-150-200	
Performance of visual tasks of low contrast and very small size over a prolonged period	G	2000-3000-5000	200-300-500	
Performance of very prolonged and exacting visual task	H	5000-7500-10000	500-750-1000	Illuminance on task, obtained by a combination of general and local (supplementary lighting)
Performance of very special visual tasks of extremely low contrast and small size	I	10000-15000-20000	1000-1500-2000	

II. Commercial, Institutional, Residential and Public Assembly Interiors

Area/Activity	Illuminance Category	Area/Activity	Illuminance Category
Accounting (see **Reading**)		**Churches and synagogues** . . (see chapter 17)[4]	
Air terminals (see **Transportation terminals**)		**Club and lodge rooms**	
Armories	C[1]	Lounge and reading	D
Art galleries (see **Museums**)		**Conference rooms**	
Auditoriums		Conferring.	D
Assembly	C[1]	Critical seeing (refer to individual task)	
Social activity	B	**Court rooms**	
Banks (also see **Reading**)		Seating area.	C
Lobby		Court activity area	E[3]
General	C	**Dance halls and discotheques**	B
Writing area	D		
Tellers'stations	E[3]	**Depots, terminals and stations** (see **Transportation terminals**)	
Barber shops and beauty parlors	E		

For footnotes, see end of table.

Fig. 11-1. *Continued*

II. *Continued*

Area/Activity	Illuminance Category	Area/Activity	Illuminance Category
Drafting		**Health care facilities**	
Mylar		Ambulance (local)	E
High contrast media; India ink, plastic		Anesthetizing	E
leads, soft graphite leads	E[3]	Autopsy and morgue[17, 18]	
Low contrast media; hard graphite leads	F[3]	Autopsy, general	E
Vellum		Autopsy table	G
High contrast	E[3]	Morgue, general	D
Low contrast	F[3]	Museum	E
Tracing paper		Cardiac function lab	E
High contrast	E[3]	Central sterile supply	
Low contrast	F[3]	Inspection, general	E
Overlays[5]		Inspection	F
Light table	C	At sinks	E
Prints		Work areas, general	D
Blue line	E	Processed storage	D
Blueprints	E	Corridors[17]	
Sepia prints	F	Nursing areas—day	C
		Nursing areas—night	B
Educational facilities		Operating areas, delivery, recovery, and	
Classrooms		laboratory suites and service	E
General (see **Reading**)		Critical care areas[17]	
Drafting (see **Drafting**)		General	C
Home economics (see **Residences**)		Examination	E
Science laboratories	E	Surgical task lighting	H
Lecture rooms		Handwashing	F
Audience (see **Reading**)		Cystoscopy room[17, 18]	E
Demonstration	F	Dental suite[17]	
Music rooms (see **Reading**)		General	D
Shops (see Part III, Industrial Group)		Instrument tray	E
Sight saving rooms	F	Oral cavity	H
Study halls (see **Reading**)		Prosthetic laboratory, general	D
Typing (see **Reading**)		Prosthetic laboratory, work bench	E
Sports facilities (see Part V, Sports		Prosthetic laboratory, local	F
and Recreational Areas)		Recovery room, general	C
Cafeterias (see **Food service facilities**)		Recovery room, emergency examination	E
Dormitories (see **Residences**)		Dialysis unit, medical[17]	F
		Elevators	C
Elevators, freight and passenger	C	EKG and specimen room[17]	
		General	B
Exhibition halls	C[1]	On equipment	C
		Emergency outpatient[17]	
Filing (refer to individual task)		General	E
		Local	F
Financial facilities (see **Banks**)		Endoscopy rooms[17, 18]	
		General	E
Fire halls (see **Municipal buildings**)		Peritoneoscopy	D
		Culdoscopy	D
Food service facilities		Examination and treatment rooms[17]	
Dining areas		General	D
Cashier	D	Local	E
Cleaning	C	Eye surgery[17, 18]	F
Dining	B[6]	Fracture room[17]	
Food displays (see **Merchandising spaces**)		General	E
Kitchen	E	Local	F
		Inhalation therapy	D
Garages—parking	(see chapter 14)	Laboratories[17]	
		Specimen collecting	E
Gasoline stations (see **Service stations**)		Tissue laboratories	F
		Microscopic reading room	D
Graphic design and material		Gross specimen review	F
Color selection	F[11]		
Charting and mapping	F		
Graphs	E		
Keylining	F		
Layout and artwork	F		
Photographs, moderate detail	E[13]		

For footnotes, see end of table.

Fig. 11-1. *Continued*

II *Continued*

Area/Activity	Illuminance Category	Area/Activity	Illuminance Category
Chemistry rooms	E	Radiological suite[17]	
Bacteriology rooms		Diagnostic section	
General	E	General[18]	A
Reading culture plates	F	Waiting area	A
Hematology	E	Radiographic/fluoroscopic room	A
Linens		Film sorting	F
Sorting soiled linen	D	Barium kitchen	E
Central (clean) linen room	D	Radation therapy section	
Sewing room, general	D	General[18]	B
Sewing room, work area	E	Waiting area	B
Linen closet	B	Isotope kitchen, general	E
Lobby	C	Isotope kitchen, benches	E
Locker rooms	C	Computerized radiotomography section	
Medical illustration studio[17, 18]	F	Scanning room	B
Medical records	E	Equipment maintenance room	E
Nurseries[17]		Solarium	
General[18]	C	General	C
Observation and treatment	E	Local for reading	D
Nursing stations[17]		Stairways	C
General	D	Surgical suite[17]	
Desk	E	Operating room, general[18]	F
Corridors, day	C	Operating table	(see chapter 17)
Corridors, night	A	Scrub room[18]	F
Medication station	E	Instruments and sterile supply room	D
Obstetric delivery suite[17]		Clean up room, instruments	E
Labor rooms		Anesthesia storage	C
General	C	Substerilizing room	C
Local	E	Surgical induction room[17, 18]	E
Birthing room	F[7]	Surgical holding area[17, 18]	E
Delivery area		Toilets	C
Scrub, general	F	Utility room	D
General	G	Waiting areas[17]	
Delivery table	(see chapter 17)	General	C
Resuscitation	G	Local for reading	D
Postdelivery recovery area	E		
Substerilizing room	B	**Homes (see Residences)**	
Occupational therapy[17]		**Hospitality facilities (see Hotels, Food service facilities)**	
Work area, general	D		
Work tables or benches	E	**Hospitals (see Health care facilities)**	
Patients' rooms[17]		**Hotels**	
General[18]	B	Bathrooms, for grooming	D
Observation	A	Bedrooms, for reading	D
Critical examination	E	Corridors, elevators and stairs	C
Reading	D	Front desk	E[3]
Toilets	D	Linen room	
Pharmacy[17]		Sewing	F
General	E	General	C
Alcohol vault	D	Lobby	
Laminar flow bench	F	General lighting	C
Night light	A	Reading and working areas	D
Parenteral solution room	D	Canopy (see Part IV, Outdoor Facilities)	
Physical therapy departments		**Houses of worship** (see chapter 17)	
Gymnasiums	D	**Kitchens (see Food service facilities or Residences)**	
Tank rooms	D		
Treatment cubicles	D	**Libraries**	
Postanesthetic recovery room[17]		Reading areas (see **Reading**)	
General[18]	E	Book stacks (vertical 760 millimeters (30 inches) above floor)	
Local	H	Active stacks	D
Pulmonary function laboratories[17]	E	Inactive stacks	B

For footnotes, see end of table.

Fig. 11-1. *Continued*

II. *Continued*			
Area/Activity	Illuminance Category	Area/Activity	Illuminance Category
Book repair and binding	D	Thermal copy, poor copy	F[3]
Cataloging	D[3]	Xerograph	D
Card files	E	Xerography, 3rd generation and greater	E
Carrels, individual study areas (see **Reading**)		Electronic data processing tasks	
Circulation desks	D	CRT screens	B[12, 13]
Map, picture and print rooms (see **Graphic design and material**)		Impact printer	
Audiovisual areas	D	good ribbon	D
Audio listening areas	D	poor ribbon	E
Microform areas (see **Reading**)		2nd carbon and greater	E
		Ink jet printer	D
Locker rooms	C	Keyboard reading	D
		Machine rooms	
Merchandising spaces		Active operations	D
Alteration room	F	Tape storage	D
Fitting room		Machine area	C
Dressing areas	D	Equipment service	E[10]
Fitting areas	F	Thermal print	E
Locker rooms	C	Handwritten tasks	
Stock rooms, wrapping and packaging	D	#2 pencil and softer leads	D[3]
Sales transaction area (see **Reading**)		#3 pencil	E[3]
Circulation . . . . (see chapter 18)[8]		#4 pencil and harder leads	F[3]
Merchandise . . . . (see chapter 18)[8]		Ball-point pen	D[3]
Feature display . . . . (see chapter 18)[8]		Felt-tip pen	D
Show windows . . . . (see chapter 18)[8]		Handwritten carbon copies	E
		Non photographically reproducible colors . . .	F
Motels (see **Hotels**)		Chalkboards	E[3]
		Printed tasks	
Municipal buildings—fire and police		6 point type	E[3]
Police		8 and 10 point type	D[3]
Identification records	F	Glossy magazines	D[13]
Jail cells and interrogation rooms	D	Maps	E
Fire hall	D	Newsprint	D
		Typed originals	D
Museums		Typed 2nd carbon and later	E
Displays of non-sensitive materials	D	Telephone books	E
Displays of sensitive materials . . . (see chapter 17)[2]			
Lobbies, general gallery areas, corridors	C	**Residences**	
Restoration or conservation shops and			
laboratories	E	General lighting	
		Conversation, relaxation and entertainment . .	B
Nursing homes (see **Health care facilities**)		Passage areas	B
		Specific visual tasks [20]	
Offices		Dining	C
Accounting (see **Reading**)		Grooming	
Audio-visual areas	D	Makeup and shaving	D
Conference areas (see **Conference rooms**)		Full-length mirror	D
Drafting (see **Drafting**)		Handcrafts and hobbies	
General and private offices (see **Reading**)		Workbench hobbies	
Libraries (see **Libraries**)		Ordinary tasks	D
Lobbies, lounges and reception areas	C	Difficult tasks	E
Mail sorting	E	Critical tasks	F
Off-set printing and duplicating area	D	Easel hobbies	E
Spaces with VDTs . . . . (see chapter 15)[13]		Ironing	D
		Kitchen duties	
Parking facilities . . . . (see chapter 24)		Kitchen counter	
		Critical seeing	E
Post offices (see **Offices**)		Noncritical	D
		Kitchen range	
Reading		Difficult seeing	E
Copied tasks		Noncritical	D
Ditto copy	E[3]		
Micro-fiche reader	B[12, 13]		
Mimeograph	D		
Photograph, moderate detail	E[13]		

For footnotes, see end of table.

Fig. 11-1. *Continued*

II. *Continued*

Area/Activity	Illuminance Category	Area/Activity	Illuminance Category
Kitchen sink		Safety . . . . (see chapter 33)	
Difficult seeing	E	Schools (see **Educational facilities**)	
Noncritical	D	Service spaces (see also **Storage rooms**)	
Laundry		Stairways, corridors	C
Preparation and tubs	D	Elevators, freight and passenger	C
Washer and dryer	D	Toilets and washrooms	C
Music study (piano or organ)		**Service stations**	
Simple scores	D	Service bays (see Part III, Industrial Group)	
Advanced scores	E	Sales room (see **Merchandising spaces**)	
Substand size scores	F	**Show windows** . . . . (see chapter 18)	
Reading		**Stairways** (see **Service spaces**)	
In a chair			
Books, magazines and newspapers	D	**Storage rooms** (see Part III, Industrial Group)	
Handwriting, reproductions and poor		**Stores** (see **Merchandising spaces** and **Show windows**)	
copies	E		
In bed		**Television** . . . . (see chapter 21)	
Normal	D	**Theatre and motion picture**	
Prolonged serious or critical	E	** houses** . . . . (see chapter 21)	
Desk			
Primary task plane, casual	D	**Toilets and washrooms**	C
Primary task plane, study	E	**Transportation terminals**	
Sewing		Waiting room and lounge	C
Hand sewing		Ticket counters	E
Dark fabrics, low contrast	F	Baggage checking	D
Light to medium fabrics	E	Rest rooms	C
Occasional, high contrast	D	Concourse	B
Machine sewing		Boarding area	C
Dark fabrics, low contrast	F		
Light to medium fabrics	E		
Occasional, high contrast	D		
Table games	D		
Restaurants (see **Food service facilities**)			

III. Industrial Group

Area/Activity	Illuminance Category	Area/Activity	Illuminance Category
Aircraft maintenance . . . . (see chapter 20)[21]		Mechanical	D
		Hand	E
Aircraft manufacturing . . . . (see chapter 20)[21]		Scales and thermometers	D
		Wrapping	D
Assembly			
Simple	D	**Book binding**	
Moderately difficult	E	Folding, assembling, pasting	D
Difficult	F	Cutting, punching, stitching	E
Very difficult	G	Embossing and inspection	F
Exacting	H		
		Breweries	
Automobile manufacturing . . . . . . (see chapter 20)[21]		Brew house	D
		Boiling and keg washing	D
Bakeries		Filling (bottles, cans, kegs)	D
Mixing room	D		
Face of shelves	D	**Building construction** (see Part IV, Outdoor Facilities)	
Inside of mixing bowl	D		
Fermentation room	D	**Building exteriors** (see Part IV, Outdoor Facilities)	
Make-up room			
Bread	D	**Candy making**	
Sweet yeast-raised products	D	Box department	D
Proofing room	D	Chocolate department	
Oven room	D	Husking, winnowing, fat extraction, crushing	
Fillings and other ingredients	D	and refining, feeding	D
Decorating and icing			

For footnotes, see end of table.

Fig. 11-1. *Continued*

III. *Continued*

Area/Activity	Illuminance Category	Area/Activity	Illuminance Category
Bean cleaning, sorting, dipping, packing, wrapping	D	Examining (perching)	I
Milling	E	Sponging, decating, winding, measuring	D
Cream making		Piling up and marking	E
Mixing, cooking, molding	D	Cutting	G
Gum drops and jellied forms	D	Pattern making, preparation of trimming, piping, canvas and shoulder pads	E
Hand decorating	D	Fitting, bundling, shading, stitching	D
Hard candy		Shops	F
Mixing, cooking, molding	D	Inspection	G
Die cutting and sorting	E	Pressing	F
Kiss making and wrapping	E	Sewing	G
Canning and preserving		**Control rooms** (see **Electric generating stations—interior**)	
Initial grading raw material samples	D		
Tomatoes	E	**Corridors** (see **Service spaces**)	
Color grading and cutting rooms	F	**Cotton gin industry**	
Preparation		Overhead equipment—separators, driers, grid cleaners, stick machines, conveyers, feeders and catwalks	D
Preliminary sorting		Gin stand	D
Apricots and peaches	D	Control console	D
Tomatoes	E	Lint cleaner	D
Olives	F	Bale press	D
Cutting and pitting	E		
Final sorting	E	**Dairy farms** (see **Farms**)	
Canning		**Dairy products**	
Continuous-belt canning	E	Fluid milk industry	
Sink canning	E	Boiler room	D
Hand packing	D	Bottle storage	D
Olives	E	Bottle sorting	E[22]
Examination of canned samples	F	Bottle washers	
Container handling		Can washers	D
Inspection	F	Cooling equipment	D
Can unscramblers	E	Filling: inspection	E
Labeling and cartoning	D	Gauges (on face)	E
		Laboratories	E
Casting (see **Foundries**)		Meter panels (on face)	E
		Pasteurizers	D
Central stations (see **Electric generating stations**)		Separators	D
		Storage refrigerator	D
Chemical plants (see **Petroleum and chemical plants**)		Tanks, vats	
		Light interiors	C
Clay and concrete products		Dark interiors	E
Grinding, filter presses, kiln rooms	C	Thermometer (on face)	E
Molding, pressing, cleaning, trimming	D	Weighing room	D
Enameling	E	Scales	E
Color and glazing—rough work	E		
Color and glazing—fine work	F	**Dispatch boards** (see **Electric generating stations—interior**)	
Cleaning and pressing industry		**Dredging** (see Part IV, Outdoor Facilities)	
Checking and sorting	E		
Dry and wet cleaning and steaming	E	**Electrical equipment manufacturing**	
Inspection and spotting	G	Impregnating	D
Pressing	F	Insulating: coil winding	E
Repair and alteration	F		
		Electric generating stations—interior (see also **Nuclear power plants**)	
Cloth products		Air-conditioning equipment, air preheater and fan floor, ash sluicing	B
Cloth inspection	I		
Cutting	G	Auxiliaries, pumps, tanks, compressors, gauge area	C
Sewing	G		
Pressing	F		
Clothing manufacture (men's) (see also **Sewn Products**)			
Receiving, opening, storing, shipping	D		

For footnotes, see end of table.

Fig. 11-1. *Continued*

III. *Continued*			
Area/Activity	Illuminance Category	Area/Activity	Illuminance Category
Battery rooms	D	Silo	A
Boiler platforms	B	Silo room	C
Burner platforms	C	Feed storage area—rain and concentrate	
Cable room	B	Grain bin	A
Coal handling systems	B	Concentrate storage area	B
Coal pulverizer	C	Feed processing area	B
Condensers, deaerator floor, evaporator floor, heater floors	B	Livestock housing area (community, maternity, individual calf pens, and loose housing holding and resting areas)	B
Control rooms		Machine storage area (garage and machine shed)	B
Main control boards	D[23]	Farm shop area	
Auxiliary control panels	D[23]	Active storage area	B
Operator's station	E[23]	General shop area (machinery repair, rough sawing)	D
Maintenance and wiring areas	D	Rough bench and machine work (painting, fine storage, ordinary sheet metal work, welding, medium benchwork)	D
Emergency operating lighting	C		
Gauge reading	D		
Hydrogen and carbon dioxide manifold area	C	Medium bench and machine work (fine woodworking, drill press, metal lathe, grinder)	E
Laboratory	E		
Precipitators	B	Miscellaneous areas	
Screen house	C	Farm office (see **Reading**)	
Soot or slag blower platform	C	Restrooms (see **Service spaces**)	
Steam headers and throttles	B	Pumphouse	C
Switchgear and motor control centers	D		
Telephone and communication equipment rooms	D	**Farms—poultry** (see **Poultry industry**)	
Tunnels or galleries, piping and electrical	B	**Flour mills**	
Turbine building		Rolling, sifting, purifying	E
Operating floor	D	Packing	D
Below operating floor	C	Product control	F
Visitor's gallery	C	Cleaning, screens, man lifts, aisleways and walkways, bin checking	D
Water treating area	D		
		Forge shops	E
Electric generating stations—exterior (see Part IV, Outdoor Facilities)		**Foundries**	
		Annealing (furnaces)	D
Elevators (see **Service spaces**)		Cleaning	D
		Core making	
Explosives manufacturing		Fine	F
Hand furnaces, boiling tanks, stationary driers, stationary and gravity crystallizers	D	Medium	E
		Grinding and chipping	F
Mechanical furnace, generators and stills, mechanical driers, evaporators, filtration, mechanical crystallizers	D	Inspection	
		Fine	G
		Medium	F
Tanks for cooking, extractors, percolators, nitrators	D	Molding	
		Medium	F
		Large	E
Farms—dairy		Pouring	E
Milking operation area (milking parlor and stall barn)		Sorting	E
General	C	Cupola	C
Cow's udder	D	Shakeout	D
Milk handling equipment and storage area (milk house or milk room)		**Garages—service**	
General	C	Repairs	E
Washing area	E	Active traffic areas	C
Bulk tank interior	E	Write-up	D
Loading platform	C		
Feeding area (stall barn feed alley, pens, loose housing feed area)	C	**Glass works**	
Feed storage area—forage		Mix and furnace rooms, pressing and lehr, glass-blowing machines	C
Haymow	A		
Hay inspection area	C		
Ladders and stairs	C		

For footnotes, see end of table.

Fig. 11-1. *Continued*

III. *Continued*

Area/Activity	Illuminance Category	Area/Activity	Illuminance Category
Grinding, cutting, silvering	D	**Meat packing**	
Fine grinding, beveling, polishing	E	Slaughtering	D
Inspection, etching and decorating	F	Cleaning, cutting, cooking, grinding, canning, packing	D
Glove manufacturing		**Nuclear power plants** (see also **Electric generating stations**)	
Pressing	G	Auxiliary building, uncontrolled access areas	C
Knitting	F	Controlled access areas	
Sorting	F	Count room	E[23]
Cutting	G	Laboratory	E
Sewing and inspection	G	Health physics office	F
Hangars (see **Aircraft manufacturing**)		Medical aid room	F
Hat manufacturing		Hot laundry	D
Dyeing, stiffening, braiding, cleaning, refining	E	Storage room	C
Forming, sizing, pouncing, flanging, finishing, ironing	F	Engineered safety features equipment	D
Sewing	G	Diesel generator building	D
Inspection		Fuel handling building	
Simple	D	Operating floor	D
Moderately difficult	E	Below operating floor	C
Difficult	F	Off gas building	C
Very difficult	G	Radwaste building	D
Exacting	H	Reactor building	
Iron and steel manufacturing . . . (see chapter 20)[21]		Operating floor	D
Jewelry and watch manufacturing	G	Below operating floor	C
Laundries		**Packing and boxing** (see **Materials handling**)	
Washing	D	**Paint manufacturing**	
Flat work ironing, weighing, listing, marking	D	Processing	D
Machine and press finishing, sorting	E	Mix comparison	F
Fine hand ironing	E	**Paint shops**	
Leather manufacturing		Dipping, simple spraying, firing	D
Cleaning, tanning and stretching, vats	D	Rubbing, ordinary hand painting and finishing art, stencil and special spraying	D
Cutting, fleshing and stuffing	D	Fine hand painting and finishing	E
Finishing and scarfing	E	Extra-fine hand painting and finishing	G
Leather working		**Paper-box manufacturing**	E
Pressing, winding, glazing	F	**Paper manufacturing**	
Grading, matching, cutting, scarfing, sewing	G	Beaters, grinding, calendering	D
Loading and unloading platforms (see Part IV, Outdoor Facilities)		Finishing, cutting, trimming, papermaking machines	E
Locker rooms	C	Hand counting, wet end of paper machine	E
Logging (see Part IV, Outdoor Facilities)		Paper machine reel, paper inspection, and laboratories	F
Lumber yards (see Part IV, Outdoor Facilities)		Rewinder	F
Machine shops		**Parking facilities** . . . (see chapter 24)	
Rough bench or machine work	D	**Petroleum and chemical plants** . . (see chapter 20)[21]	
Medium bench or machine work, ordinary automatic machines, rough grinding, medium buffing and polishing	E	**Plating**	D
Fine bench or machine work, fine automatic machines medium grinding, fine buffing and polishing	G	**Polishing and burnishing** (see **Machine shops**)	
Extra-fine bench or machine work, grinding, fine work	H	**Power plants** (see **Electric generating stations**)	
Materials handling		**Poultry industry** (see also **Farm—dairy**)	
Wrapping, packing, labeling	D	Brooding, production, and laying houses	
Picking stock, classifying	D	Feeding, inspection, cleaning	C
Loading, inside truck bodies and freight cars	C	Charts and records	D
		Thermometers, thermostats, time clocks	D
		Hatcheries	
		General area and loading platform	C

For footnotes, see end of table.

Fig. 11-1. *Continued*

III. *Continued*

Area/Activity	Illuminance Category	Area/Activity	Illuminance Category
Inside incubators	D	Rough lumber grading	D
Dubbing station	F	Finished lumber grading	F
Sexing	H	Dry lumber warehouse (planer)	C
Egg handling, packing, and shipping		Dry kiln colling shed	B
General cleanliness	E	Chipper infeed	B
Egg quality inspection	E	Basement areas	
Loading platform, egg storage area, etc.	C	Active	A
Egg processing		Inactive	A
General lighting	E	Filing room (work areas)	E
Fowl processing plant			
General (excluding killing and unloading area)	E	**Service spaces** (see also **Storage rooms**)	
		Stairways, corridors	B
Government inspection station and grading stations	E	Elevators, freight and passenger	B
		Toilets and wash rooms	C
Unloading and killing area	C		
Feed storage		**Sewn products**	
Grain, feed rations	C	Receiving, packing, shipping	E
Processing	C	Opening, raw goods storage	E
Charts and records	D	Designing, pattern-drafting, pattern grading and marker-making	F
Machine storage area (garage and machine shed)	B	Computerized designing, pattern-making and grading digitizing, marker-making, and plotting	B
Printing industries		Cloth inspection and perching	I
Type foundries		Spreading and cutting (includes computerized cutting)	F[26]
Matrix making, dressing type	E	Fitting, sorting and bundling, shading, stitch marking	G
Font assembly—sorting	D	Sewing	G
Casting	E	Pressing	F
Printing plants		In-process and final inspection	G
Color inspection and appraisal	F	Finished goods storage and picking orders	F[27]
Machine composition	E	Trim preparation, piping, canvas and shoulder pads	F
Composing room	E	Machine repair shops	G
Presses	E	Knitting	F
Imposing stones	F	Sponging, decating, rewinding, measuring	E
Proofreading	F	Hat manufacture (see **Hat manufacture**)	
Electrotyping	F	Leather working (see **Leather working**)	
Molding, routing, finishing, leveling molds, trimming	E	Shoe manufacturing (see **Shoe manufacturing**)	
Blocking, tinning	D	**Sheet metal works**	
Electroplating, washing, backing	D	Miscellaneous machines, ordinary bench work	E
Photoengraving		Presses, shears, stamps, spinning, medium bench work	E
Etching, staging, blocking	D	Punches	E
Routing, finishing, proofing	E	Tin plate inspection, galvanized	F
Tint laying, masking	E	Scribing	F
Quality control (see **Inspection**)		**Shoe manufacturing—leather**	
		Cutting and stitching	
Receiving and shipping (see **Materials handling**)		Cutting tables	G
		Marking, buttonholing, skiving, sorting, vamping, counting	G
Railroad yards (see Part IV, Outdoor Facilities)		Stitching, dark materials	G
Rubber goods—mechanical (see chapter 20)[21]		Making and finishing, nailers, sole layers, welt beaters and scarfers, trimmers, welters, lasters, edge setters, sluggers, randers, wheelers, treers, cleaning, spraying, buffing, polishing, embossing	F
Rubber tire manufacturing (see chapter 20)[21]			
Safety (see chapter 33)			
Sawmills			
Secondary log deck	B	**Shoe manufacturing—rubber**	
Head saw (cutting area viewed by sawyer)	E	Washing, coating, mill run compounding	D
Head saw outfeed	B		
Machine in-feeds (bull edger, resaws, edgers, trim, hula saws, planers)	B		
Main mill floor (base lighting)	A		
Sorting tables	D		

For footnotes, see end of table.

Fig. 11-1. *Continued*

III. *Continued*		
Area/Activity		Illuminance Category

Area/Activity	Illuminance Category	Area/Activity	Illuminance Category
Varnishing, vulcanizing, calendering, upper and sole cutting	D	Drawing (gilling, pin drafting)	D
Sole rolling, lining, making and finishing processes	E	Combing	D[24]
		Roving (slubbing, fly frame)	E
Soap manufacturing		Spinning (cap spinning, twisting, texturing) . .	E
Kettle houses, cutting, soap chip and powder . .	D	Yarn preparation	
Stamping, wrapping and packing, filling and packing soap powder	D	Winding, quilling, twisting	E
		Warping (beaming, sizing)	F[16]
Stairways (see **Service spaces**)		Warp tie-in or drawing-in (automatic)	E
		Fabric production	
Steel (see **Iron and steel**)		Weaving, knitting, tufting	F
		Inspection	G[16]
Storage battery manufacturing	D	Finishing	
		Fabric preparation (desizing, scouring, bleaching, singeing, and mercerization) . . .	D
Storage rooms or warehouses		
Inactive	B	Fabric dyeing (printing)	D
Active		Fabric finishing (calendaring, sanforizing, sueding, chemical treatment)	E[16]
Rough, bulky items	C	
Small items	D	Inspection	G[11, 16]
Storage yards (see Part IV, Outdoor Facilities)		**Tobacco products**	
		Drying, stripping	D
Structural steel fabrication	E	Grading and sorting	F
Sugar refining		**Toilets and wash rooms** (see **Service spaces**)	
Grading	E	
Color inspection	F	**Upholstering**	F
Testing		**Warehouse** (see **Storage rooms**)	
General	D	
Exacting tests, extra-fine instruments, scales, etc.	F	**Welding**	
		Orientation	D
		Precision manual arc-welding	H
Textile mills			
Staple fiber preparation		**Woodworking**	
Stock dyeing, tinting	D	Rough sawing and bench work	D
Sorting and grading (wood and cotton)	E[16]	Sizing, planing, rough sanding, medium quality machine and bench work, gluing, veneering, cooperage	D
Yarn manufacturing		
Opening and picking (chute feed)	D	Fine bench and machine work, fine sanding and finishing	E
Carding (nonwoven web formation)	D[24]	

IV. Outdoor Facilities					
Area/Activity	Lux	Footcandles	Area/Activity	Lux	Footcandles
Advertising Signs (see **Bulletin and poster boards**			Medium light surfaces . .	200	20
			Medium dark surfaces . .	300	30
Bikeways (see chapter 24)			Dark surfaces	500	50
			Dark surroundings		
Building (construction)			Light surfaces	50	5
General construction	100	10	Medium light surfaces . .	100	10
Excavation work	20	2	Medium dark surfaces . .	150	15
			Dark surfaces	200	20
Building exteriors					
Entrances			**Bulletin and poster boards**		
Active (pedestrian and/or conveyance)	50	5	Bright surroundings		
			Light surfaces	500	50
Inactive (normally locked, infrequently used)	10	1	Dark surfaces	1000	100
Vital locations or structures	50	5	Dark surroundings		
Building surrounds	10	1	Light surfaces	200	20
			Dark surfaces	500	50
Buildings and monuments, floodlighted					
Bright surroundings			**Central station** (see **Electric generating stations—exterior**)		
Light surfaces	150	15			

For footnotes, see end of table.

Fig. 11-1. *Continued*

IV. *Continued*

Area/Activity	Lux	Footcandles	Area/Activity	Lux	Footcandles
Coal yards (protective)......	2	0.2	Focal points, large	100	10
Dredging	20	2	Focal points, small........	200	20
Electric generating stations— exterior			**Gasoline station (see Service stations** in Part II)		
Boiler areas			**Highways** (see chapter 24)		
Catwalks, general areas .	20	2	**Loading and unloading**		
Stairs and platforms	50	5	Platforms	200	20
Ground level areas in- cluding precipitators, FD and ID fans, bottom ash hoppers	50	5	Freight car interiors	100	10
Cooling towers			**Logging** (see also **Sawmills**)		
Fan deck, platforms, stairs, valve areas .	50	5	Yarding	30	3
Pump areas...........	20	2	Log loading and unloading .	50	5
Fuel handling			Log stowing (water)	5	0.5
Barge unloading, car dump- er, unloading hoppers, truck unloading, pumps, gas metering	50	5	Active log storage area (land)	5	0.5
Conveyors	20	2	Log booming area (water)— foot traffic	10	1
Storage tanks	10	1	Active log handling area (water)	20	2
Coal storage piles, ash dumps...........	2	0.2	Log grading—water or land	50	5
Hydroelectric			Log bins (land)...........	20	2
Powerhouse roof, stairs, platform and intake decks	50	5	**Lumber yards**	10	1
Inlet and discharge water area...........	2	0.2	**Parking areas** (see chapter 24)		
Intake structures			**Piers**		
Deck and laydown area .	50	5	Freight	200	20
Value pits.............	20	2	Passenger	200	20
Inlet water area	2	0.2	Active shipping area surrounds	50	5
Parking areas			**Prison yards**	50	5
Main plant parking	20	2	**Quarries**	50	5
Secondary parking	10	1	**Railroad yards**		
Substation			Retarder classification yards		
Horizontal general area .	20	2	Receiving yard		
Vertical tasks	50	5	Switch points	20	2
Transformer yards			Body of yard	10	1
Horizontal general area .	20	2	Hump area (vertical)	200	20
Vertical tasks	50	5	Control tower and retarder area (vertical)	100	10
Turbine areas			Head end.............	50	5
Building surrounds	20	2	Body	10	1
Turbine and heater decks, unloading bays....	50	5	Pull-out end...........	20	2
Entrances, stairs and platforms[9]	50	5	Dispatch or forwarding yard	10	1
Flags, floodlighted (see Bulle- tin and poster boards)			Hump and car rider classifi- cation yard		
Gardens[19]			Receiving yard		
General lighting	5	0.5	Switch points	20	2
Path, steps, away from house	10	1	Body of yard	10	1
Backgrounds—fences, walls, trees, shrubbery ...	20	2	Hump area	50	5
Flower beds, rock gardens .	50	5	Flat switching yards		
Trees, shrubbery, when emphasized	50	5	Side of cars (vertical) ...	50	5
			Switch points	20	2
			Trailer-on-flatcars		
			Horizontal surface of flatcar	50	5
			Hold-down points (vertical)	50	5
			Container-on-flatcars	30	3
			Roadways (see chapter 24)		

For footnotes, see end of table.

Fig. 11-1. *Continued*

IV. *Continued*

Area/Activity	Lux	Footcandles	Area/Activity	Lux	Footcandles
Sawmills (see also **Logging**)			Service areas	70	7
Cut-off saw	100	10	Landscape highlights . . .	50	5
Log haul	20	2	**Ship yards**		
Log hoist (side lift)	20	2	General	50	5
Primary log deck	100	10	Ways	100	10
Barker in-feed	300	30	Fabrication areas	300	30
Green chain[26]	200 to 300	20 to 30	**Signs**		
Lumber strapping[26]	150 to 200	15 to 20	Advertising (see **Bulletin and**		
Lumber handling areas	20	2	**poster boards**)		
Lumber loading areas	50	5	Externally lighted roadway		
Wood chip storage piles . . .	5	0.5	(see chapter 24)		
Service station (at grade)			**Smokestacks with advertising**		
Dark surrounding			**messages** (see		
Approach	15	1.5	**Bulletin and**		
Driveway	15	1.5	**poster boards**)		
Pump island area	200	20	**Storage yards**		
Building faces (exclusive			Active	200	20
of glass)[14]	100	10	Inactive	10	1
Service areas	30	3	**Streets** (see chapter 24)		
Landscape highlights . . .	20	2			
Light surrounding			**Walkways** (see chapter 24)		
Approach	30	3	**Water tanks with advertising**		
Driveway	50	5	**messages** (see **Bulle-**		
Pump island area	300	30	**tin and poster boards**)		
Building faces (exclusive					
of glass)[14]	300	30			

V. Sports and Recreational Areas

Area/Activity	Lux	Footcandles	Area/Activity	Lux	Footcandles
Archery (indoor)			Junior league (Class I and		
Target, tournament[14]	500	50	Class II)		
Target, recreational[14]	300	30	Infield	300	30
Shooting line, tournament . . .	200	20	Outfield	200	20
Shooting line, recrational	100	10	On seat during game	20	2
Archery (outdoor)			On seats before & after game	50	5
Target, tournament[14]	100	10	**Basketball**		
Target, recreational[14]	50	5	College and professional	500	50
Shooting line, tournament . . .	100	10	College intramural and high		
Shooting line, recreational . . .	50	5	school	300	30
Badminton			Recreational (outdoor)	100	10
Tournament	300	30	**Bathing beaches**		
Club	200	20	On land	10	1
Recreational	100	10	150 feet from shore[14]	30	3
Baseball			**Billiards** (on table)		
Major league			Tournament	500	50
Infield	1500	150	Recreational	300	30
Outfield	1000	100	**Bowling**		
AA and AAA league			Tournament		
Infield	700	70	Approaches	100	10
Outfield	500	50	Lanes	200	20
A and B league			Pins[14]	500	50
Infield	500	50	Recreational		
Outfield	300	30	Approaches	100	10
C and D league			Lanes	100	10
Infield	300	30	Pins[14]	300	30
Outfield	200	20	**Bowling on the green**		
Semi-pro and municipal league			Tournament	100	10
Infield	200	20	Recreational	50	5
Outfield	150	15	**Boxing or wrestling (ring)**		
Recreational			Championship	5000	500
Infield	150	15			
Outfield	100	10			

For footnotes, see end of table.

Fig. 11-1. *Continued*

V. *Continued*					
Area/Activity	Lux	Footcandles	Area/Activity	Lux	Footcandles
Professional	2000	200	**Golf**		
Amateur	1000	100	Tee ..... [14]	50	5
Seats during bout.........	20	2	Fairway[14]	10–30	1–3
Seats before and after bout ..	50	5	Green	50	5
Casting—bait, dry-fly, wet-fly			Driving range		
Pier or dock	100	10	At 180 meters [200 yards][14]	50	5
Target (at 24 meters [80 feet]			Over tee area	100	10
for bait casting and 15			Miniature	100	10
meters [50 feet] for wet or			Practice putting green	100	10
dry-fly casting)[14]	50	5	**Gymnasiums** (refer to individual		
Combination (outdoor)			sports listed)		
Baseball/football			General exercising and		
Infield	200	20	recreation	300	30
Outfield and football	150	15	**Handball**		
Industrial softball/football			Tournament...............	500	50
Infield	200	20	Club		
Outfield and football	150	15	Indoor—four-wall or squash	300	30
Industrial softball/6-man foot-			Outdoor—two-court	200	20
ball			Recreational		
Infield	200	20	Indoor—four-wall or squash	200	20
Outfield and football	150	15	Outdoor—two-court	100	10
Croquet or Roque			**Hockey, field**	200	20
Tournament...............	100	10	**Hockey, ice (indoor)**		
Recreational	50	5	College or professional	1000	100
Curling			Amateur	500	50
Tournament			Recreational	200	20
Tees	500	50	**Hockey, ice (outdoor)**		
Rink	300	30	College or professional	500	50
Recreational			Amateur	200	20
Tees	200	20	Recreational	100	10
Rink	100	10	**Horse shoes**		
Fencing			Tournament	100	10
Exhibitions	500	50	Recreational	50	5
Recreational	300	30	**Horse shows**	200	20
Football			**Jai-alai**		
Distance from nearest side-			Professional	1000	100
line to the farthest row			Amateur	700	70
of spectators			**Lacrosse**	200	20
Class I Over 30 meters [100			**Playgrounds**	50	5
feet]	1000	100	**Quoits**	50	5
Class II 15 to 30 meters [50			**Racing (outdoor)**		
to 100 feet]	500	50	Auto.....................	200	20
Class III 9 to 15 meters [30			Bicycle		
to 50 feet	300	30	Tournament	300	30
Class IV Under 9 meters			Competitive	200	20
[30 feet]	200	20	Recreational	100	10
Class V No fixed seating			Dog	300	30
facilities	100	10	Dragstrip		
It is generally conceded that the distance between the			Staging area	100	10
spectators and the play is the first consideration in deter-			Acceleration, 400 meters		
mining the class and lighting requirements. However,			[1320 feet]............	200	20
the potential seating capacity of the stands should also			Deceleration, first 200		
be considered and the following ratio is suggested:			meters [660 feet]	150	15
Class I for over 30,000 spectators;Class II for 10,000 to			Deceleration, second 200		
30,000; Class III for 5000 to 10,000; andClass IV for			meters [660 feet]	100	10
under 5000 spectators.			Shutdown, 250 meters		
Football, Canadian—rugby			[820 feet]	50	5
(see **Football**)			Horse	200	20
Football, six-man			Motor (midget of motorcycle) .	200	20
High school or college......	200	20			
Jr. high and recreational	100	10			

For footnotes, see end of table.

Fig. 11-1. *Continued*

V. *Continued*

Area/Activity	Lux	Footcandles	Area/Activity	Lux	Footcandles
Racquetball (see **Handball**)			Infield	300	30
Rifle 45 meters [50 yards]—outdoor)			Outfield	2000	20
On targets[14]	500	50	Industrial league		
Firing point	100	10	Infield	200	20
Range	50	5	Outfield	150	15
Rifle and pistol range (indoor)			Recreational (6-pole)		
On targets[14]	1000	100	Infield	100	10
Firing point	200	20	Outfield	70	7
Range	100	10	Slow pitch, tournament—see		
Rodeo			industrial league		
Arena			Slow pitch, recreational		
Professional	500	50	(6-pole)—see recreational		
Amateur	300	30	(6-pole)		
Recreational	100	10	**Squash** (see **Handball**)		
Pens and chutes	50	5	**Swimming (indoor)**		
Roque (see **Croquet**)			Exhibitions	500	50
Shuffleboard (indoor)			Recreational	300	30
Tournament	300	30	Underwater—1000 [100] lamp		
Recreational	200	20	lumens per square meter		
Shuffleboard (outdoor)			[foot] of surface area		
Tournament	100	10	**Swimming (outdoor)**		
Recreational	50	5	Exhibitions	200	20
Skating			Recreational	100	10
Roller rink	100	10	Underwater—600 [60] lamp		
Ice rink, indoor	100	10	lumens per square meter		
Ice rink, outdoor	50	5	[foot] of surface area		
Lagoon, pond, or flooded area	10	1	**Tennis (indoor)**		
Skeet			Tournament	1000	100
Targets at 18 meters [60 feet][14]	300	30	Club	750	75
Firing points	50	5	Recreational	500	50
Skeet and trap (combination)			**Tennis (outdoor)**		
Targets at 30 meters [100 feet]			Tournament	300	30
for trap, 18 meters [60 feet]			Club	200	20
for skeet[14]	300	30	Recreational	100	10
Firing points	50	5	**Tennis, platform**	500	50
Ski slope	10	1	**Tennis, table**		
Soccer (see **Football**)			Tournament	500	50
Softball			Club	300	30
Professional and championship			Recreational	200	20
Infield	500	50	**Trap**		
Outfield	300	30	Targets at 30 meters [100 feet][14]	300	30
Semi-professional			Firing points	50	5
			Volley ball		
			Tournaments	200	20
			Recreational	100	10

VI. Transportation Vehicles

Area/Activity	Lux	Footcandles	Area/Activity	Lux	Footcandles
Aircraft			Fare box (rapid transit train)	150	15
Passenger compartment			Vestibule (commuter and in-		
General	50	5	tercity trains)	100	10
Reading (at seat)	200	20	Aisles	100	10
Airports			Advertising cards (rapid tran-		
Hangar apron	10	1	sit and commuter trains)	300	30
Terminal building apron			Back-lighted advertising		
Parking area	5	0.5	cards (rapid transit and		
Loading area[14]	20	2	commuter trains)—860		
Rail conveyances			cd/m^2 (80 cd/ft^2) average		
Boarding or exiting	100	10	maximum.		
			Reading[3]	300	30

For footnotes, see end of table.

Fig. 11-1. *Continued*

VI. *Continued*					
Area/Activity	Lux	Footcandles	Area/Activity	Lux	Footcandles
Rest room (inter-city train) . . .	200	20	Toilets	200	20
Dining area (inter-city train) . .	500	50	Libraries and lounges		
Food preparation (inter-city			General lighting	200	20
train)	700	70	Reading[3,16]	300	30
Lounge (inter-city train)			Prolonged seeing[3,16] . .	700	70
General lighting	200	20	Purser's office[16]	200	20
Table games	300	30	Shopping areas	200	20
Sleeping car			Smoking rooms	150	15
General lighting	100	10	Stairs and foyers	200	20
Normal reading[3]	300	30	Recreation areas		
Prolonged seeing[3]	700	70	Ball rooms[15]	150	15
Road conveyances			Cocktail lounges[15]	150	15
Step well and adjacent			Swimming pools		
ground area	100	10	General[15]	150	15
Fare box	150	15	Underwater		
General lighting (for seat			Outdoors—600 [60] lamps lumens/square meter [foot]		
selection and movement)			of surface area		
City and inter-city buses at			Indoors—1000 [100] lamp lumens/square meter		
city stop	100	10	[foot] of surface area		
Inter-city bus at country			Theatre		
stop	20	2	Auditorium		
School bus while moving .	150	15	General[15]	100	10
School bus at stops	300	30	During picture	1	0.1
Advertising cards	300	30	Navigating Areas		
Back-lighted advertising cards			Chart room		
(see **Rail conveyances**)			General	100	10
Reading[3]	300	30	On chart table[3,16]	500	50
Emergency exit (school bus) .	50	5	Gyro room	200	20
Ships			Radar room	200	20
Living Areas			Radio room[16]	100	10
Staterooms and Cabins			Radio room, passenger		
General lighting	100	10	Foyer	100	10
Reading and writing[3,15] . .	300	30	Ship's offices		
Prolonged seeing[3,16] . .	700	70	General[16]	200	20
Baths (general lighting) .	100	10	On desks and work		
Mirrors (personal groom-			tables[3,16]	500	50
ing)	500	50	Wheelhouse	100	10
Barber shop and beauty			Service Areas		
parlor	500	50	Food preparation[16]		
On subject	1000	100	General	200	20
Day rooms			Butcher shop	200	20
General lighting[15]	200	20	Galley	300	30
Desks[3,16]	500	50	Pantry	200	20
Dining rooms and mess-			Thaw room	200	20
rooms	200	20	Sculleries[16]	200	20
Enclosed promenades			Food storage nonrefriger-		
General lighting	100	10	ated)	100	10
Entrances and			Refrigerated spaces (ship's		
passageways			stores)	50	5
General	100	10	Laundries		
Daytime embarkation . . .	300	30	General[16]	200	20
Gymnasiums			Machine and press		
General lighting	300	30	finishing, Sorting	500	50
Hospital			Lockers	50	5
Dispensary (general			Offices		
lighting)[16]	300	30	General	200	20
Operating room			Reading[3,16]	500	50
General lighting[16] . .	500	50	Passenger counter[3,16] .	500	50
Doctor's office[16]	300	30	Storerooms	50	5
Operating table	20000	2000	Telephone exchange	200	20
Wards			Operating Areas		
General lighting	100	10	Access and casing	100	10
Reading	300	30	Battery room	100	10
			Boiler rooms[16]	200	20

For footnotes, see end of table.

Fig. 11-1. *Continued*

VI. *Continued*

Area/Activity	Lux	Footcandles	Area/Activity	Lux	Footcandles
Cargo handling (weather deck)[16]	50	5	Motor generator rooms (cargo handling)	100	10
Control stations (except navigating areas)			Pump room	100	10
General			Shaft alley	100	10
Control consoles	200	20	Shaft alley escape	30	3
Gauge and control	300	30	Steering gear room	200	20
boards	300	30	Windlass rooms	100	10
Switchboards	300	30	Workshops[16]		
Engine rooms[16]	200	20	General	300	30
Generator and switchboard rooms[16]	200	20	On top of work bench . .	500	50
Fan rooms (ventilation & air conditioning)	100	10	Tailor shop[16]	500	50
			Cargo holds		
			Permanent luminaires[16]	30	3
Motor rooms	200	20	Passageways and trunks	100	10

[1]Include provisions for higher illuminances for exhibitions.

[2]Specific limits are provided to minimize deterioration effects.

[3]Task subject to veiling reflections.

[4]Illuminances are based on experience and consensus. Values relate to needs during various religious ceremonies.

[5]Degradation factors: Overlays--add 1 weighting factor for each overlay; Used material--estimate additional factors.

[6]Provide higher illuminance over food service or selection areas.

[7]Supplementary lighting as in delivery rooms must be available.

[8]Illuminances developed for various degrees of store activity.

[9]Or not less than 1/5 the level in adjacent areas.

[10]Only when actual equipment service is in progress. May be achieved by a general lighting system or by localized or portable equipment.

[11]For color matching, the spectral quality of the light source is important.

[12]Because veiling reflections may be produced on glass surfaces, it may be necessary to treat positive weighting factors as negative in order to obtain proper illuminance.

[13]It may be advisable to shield or reorient the task.

[14]Vertical illuminance.

[15]Illuminances may vary widely, depending on the desired effect, the decorative scheme, and the specific activities within the room.

[16]Supplementary lighting should be provided in this space to produce the higher levels required for specific seeing tasks involved.

[17]Good to high color rendering capability should be considered in these areas.

[18]Variable (switching or dimming).

[19]Values based on a 25 percent reflectance, which is average for vegetation and typical outdoor surfaces. These figures must be adjusted to specific reflectances of materials lighted for equivalent brightness. Levels give satisfactory brightness patterns when viewed from dimly lighted terraces or interiors. When viewed from dark areas they may be reduced by at least 1/2; or they may be doubled when a high key is desired.

[20]General lighting should not be less than 1/3 of visual task illuminance nor less than 200 lx (20 fc).

[21]Industry representatives have established a table of single illuminance values which, in their opinion, can be used in preference to employing reference 1. Illuminances for specific operations can also be determined using categories of similar tasks and activities found in this table and the application of the appropriate weighting factors.

[22]Special lighting such that (1) the luminous area is large enough to cover the surface which is being inspected and (2) the luminance is within the limits necessary to obtain comfortable contrast conditions. This involves the use of sources of large area and relatively low luminance in which the source luminance is the principal factor rather than the illuminance produced at a given point.

[23]Maximum levels--controlled system.

[24]Additional lighting needs to be provided for maintenance only.

[25]Select upper level for high speed conveyor systems. For grading redwood lumber, 3000 lx (300 fc) is required.

[26]Higher levels from local lighting may be required for manually operated cutting machines.

[27]Use illuminance category G if color matching is critical.

Categories G through I are for extremely difficult visual tasks, and may be difficult to illuminate. For practical and economic reasons, lighting systems for these tasks will visually require a combination of general overall illumination and higher task illuminance. Because of the unusual conditions associated with tasks in these categories, very careful analysis is recommended.

Step 4: Establish Target Illuminance

Target illuminances are established somewhat differently for categories A through C than for categories D through I, based upon the series of weighting factors shown in figure 11-2.

Categories A Through C. To establish an appropriate target illuminance the designer should be familiar with the interior design and with the characteristics of the intended occupants to the extent that room surface reflectances, from 0 to 1, and occupant ages, in years, can be correctly specified. From this information, the designer can determine the appropriate weighting factors for the application from figure 11-2a and the following three steps:

Step 4.A.1. From the occupants' ages and the room surface reflectances, determine both of the weighting factors (−1, 0, +1).

Step 4.A.2. Add the two weighting factors together.

Step 4.A.3. If the sum of the two weighting factors is −2, use the lowest of the three illuminances in the range; if +2, use the highest; if −1, 0 or +1, use the middle illuminance.

Categories D Through I. To establish an appropriate target illuminance, the designer should be familiar with some further characteristics of the task than those considered in step 1. The background reflectance of the task, from 0 to 100%, is important in illuminance selection. In addition, the designer should be able to specify the workers' ages and, with the client, the importance of speed and accuracy for the performance of the task. From this information the designer can determine the appropriate weighting factors for the application from figure 11-2b.

Step 4.B.1. Given that the appropriate illuminance category has been selected, determine each of the three weighting factors (−1, 0, +1), one each for the workers' ages, the importance of speed and accuracy, and the reflectance of the task background.

Step 4.B.2. Add the three weighting factors together.

Step 4.B.3. If the sum of the three weighting factors is −2 or −3, use the lowest of the three illuminances in the range; if +2 or +3, use the highest; if −1, 0 or +1, use the middle illuminance.

A simpler version of steps 3 and 4 is given in figure

Fig. 11-2. Weighting Factors to be Considered in Selecting Specific Illuminance Within Ranges of Values for Each Category

a. For illuminance categories A through C			
Room and occupant characteristics	**Weighting factor**		
	-1	0	+1
Occupant ages	Under 40	40-55	Over 55
Room surface reflectances*	Greater than 70 percent	30 to 70 percent	Less than 30 percent
b. For illuminance categories D through I			
Task and worker characteristics	**Weighting factor**		
	-1	0	+1
Worker's ages	Under 40	40-55	Over 55
Speed and/or accuracy[1]	Not important	Important	Critical
Reflectance of task background[2]	Greater than 70 percent	30 to 70 percent	Less than 30 percent

*Average weighted surface reflectances, including wall, floor and ceiling reflectances, if they encompass a large portion of the task area or visual surround. For instance, in an elevator lobby, where the ceiling height is 7.6 meters [25 feet], neither the task nor the visual surround encompass the ceiling, so only the floor and wall reflectances would be considered

[1]In determining whether speed and / or accuracy is not important, important or critical, the following questions need to be answered: What are the time limitations? How important is it to perform the task rapidly? Will errors produce an unsafe condition or product? Will errors reduce productivity and be costly? For example, in reading for leisure there are no time limitations and it is not important to read rapidly. Errors will not be costly and will not be related to safety. Thus, speed and / or accuracy is not important. If however, a worker is involved in exacting work, accuracy is critical because of the close tolerances, and time is important because of production demands.

[2]The task background is that portion of the task upon which the meaningful visual display is exhibited. For example, on this page the meaningful visual display includes each letter which combines with other letters to form words and phrases. The display medium, or task background, is the paper, which has a reflectance of approximately 85 percent.

11-2. This figure should be used only if the bases for steps 3 and 4 are clearly understood.

EXAMPLE

A classroom in a high school is to be relighted. The designer, in consultation with the teacher and school administrators, has determined the following:

1. The task is reading photocopied material with a reflectance of about 80% on a horizontal desk surface.
2. The students are teenagers.
3. The students practice typing to improve speed and accuracy; thus speed and accuracy are considered to be important, but not critical.

Using the above step-by-step procedure:

Step 1. The visual task and the workplane are defined above.

Step 2. Referring to figure 11-1, the illuminance category D is found under "Reading, Photocopies" in the table.

Step 3. Referring to part I of figure 11-1, the illuminance range is found to be 200–300–500 lx (20–30–50 fc).

Step 4. Referring to figure 11-2b and the above information, the weighting factors selected are −1 for age; 0 for speed and accuracy; −1 for reflectance of task background. The sum of the weighting factors is −2. therefore, the illuminance to be selected is the lowest value, 200 lx (20 fc).

If the task were reading no. 3 pencil handwriting on 80% reflectance paper and the students were older (as in an adult education course), the illuminance category would change to E, and the illuminance range would become 500–750–1000 lx (50–75–100 fc). The weighting factor for age would be 0; the importance of speed and accuracy and the background reflectance would remain as before. The new sum of the weighting factors would be −1. Therefore, the illuminance to be selected would be the middle value in the new range, that is, 750 lx (75 fc).

APPLICATION OF THE PROCEDURE

Before the selected illuminance is applied, the following issues should be understood by the designer:

1. The IESNA is recommending a *procedure* for selecting illuminance rather than an illuminance per se. It is incumbent upon the designer to use the procedure properly and to determine the factors in each of the four steps accurately. The ranges of illuminance provided in figure 11-1 should enable the designer to have the flexibility to work with the client for the best results.

2. This procedure is intended for use in interior environments where visual performance,[1] based upon speed and accuracy of visual response, is an important consideration. It is a consensus procedure which includes illuminances deemed appropriate for given task activities and areas.

3. The selected illuminance is to be maintained in service, either as the average maintained illuminance for categories A through C or as the local maintained illuminance for categories D through I. It is not the initial illuminance; appropriate light loss factors should be used in calculating the maintained value.

4. The selected illuminances, for categories D through I, are specific to a given task. Where multiple tasks are performed, either at the same location or at other locations in the same space, different illuminances may be required. The designer must work with the client to establish priorities in selecting a final illuminance. Where deemed appropriate, multiple illuminances, that is, task tuning, may be employed in a space.

5. a. Implicit in the illuminance selection procedure is that the quality of the lighting system has been considered. In this context, quality refers to an absence of direct glare and veiling reflections which will impair visual performance. For example, the same horizontal illuminance may be incident on a matte and on a glossy surface, with very different visual effects. In the latter case the correct illuminance may have been selected using this procedure, but veiling reflections may completely obscure the visual task. In this case, illuminance is not a reliable indicator of visual performance.

   b. More sophisticated procedures are available which will enable the designer to evaluate the impact of lighting geometry, polarization and distribution on visual performance. Equivalent sphere illuminance (ESI)[3,4,5] and relative visual performance (RVP)[6,7] take into account the same visual factors important in the illuminance selection procedure. To use these procedures successfully, contrast, size, background reflectance and the age of the worker must be specified precisely. Measurement tools and computer programs are available to the designer to determine values of the ESI and

RVP. Currently, however, experience with the use of ESI and RVP is insufficient to justify their inclusion in the IESNA's recommendations.

6. Illuminance selection, based upon visual performance, is only one lighting design criterion to be considered. There are many applications where other design criteria, such as glare or color rendering, are more important to a successful lighting design.

   a. In merchandising, for example, the luminance ratios in the space are more important than absolute illuminance values; higher relative brightness is more attractive to customers. Similarly, architectural details should be highlighted only if the relative brightness of these features is greater than their surround.

   b. Often light can create artistic effects, as with holiday decorations. For these applications the illuminance selection procedure is not relevant.

   c. Minimum illuminances are recommended for safe egress from buildings. These are not based upon the speed and accuracy of visual response per se, but rather upon the need to see obstructions and exit ways in the space.

   d. In some spaces, such as theatre lobbies, occupants must move from bright areas to dark areas and vice versa. For these spaces speed and accuracy are less important than the transition in brightness between the two extremes for occupant safety and comfort.

   e. Sometimes photosensors other than the human eye are important. Animals, plants and even television cameras have different spectral sensitivities than those of the human eye. In such cases illuminance, based upon human spectral sensitivity, is an inappropriate design criterion.

   f. Some materials degrade with exposure to light. In museums, for example, strict exposure criteria are established to preserve archival specimens. Here, too, the illuminance selection procedure is an inappropriate design criterion.

The illuminance selection procedure, which is based upon the speed and accuracy of visual response, may often be less important than the other criteria for a successful lighting design. For a complete discussion of design criteria, see chapter 10, Design Process.

REFERENCES

1. IES. Committee on Recommendations for Quality and Quantity of Illumination. 1980. Selection of illuminance values for interior lighting design (RQQ Report No. 6). *J. Illum. Eng. Soc.* 9(3):188–189.
2. Commission Internationale de l'Éclairage. 1975. *Guide on interior lighting.* CIE Publication No. 29. Prepared by CIE Committee TC-4.1. Paris: Bureau Central de la CIE.
3. Commission Internationale de l'Éclairage. 1981. *An analytic model for describing the influence of lighting parameters upon visual performance. Volume 1: Technical foundations.* CIE Publication No. 19/2.1. Paris: Bureau Central de la CIE.
4. IES. Design Practice Committee. 1977. Recommended practice for the specification of an ESI rating in interior spaces when specific task locations are unknown. *J. Illum. Eng. Soc.* 6(2):111–123.
5. DiLaura, D. L. 1975. On the computation of equivalent sphere illumination. *J. Illum. Eng. Soc.* 4(2):129–149.
6. Rea, M. S., and M. J. Ouellette. 1988. Visual performance using reaction times. *Light. Res. Tech.* 20(4):139–153.
7. Rea, M. S., and M. J. Ouellette. 1991. Relative visual performance: A basis for application. *Light. Res. Tech.* 23(3):135–144.

Basic Lighting Calculations 12

OVERVIEW

The purpose of this chapter is to show how to apply some of the basic equations in lighting. The following outline helps organize these different equations, and in fact represents the order in which the calculations are often performed.

- First-order calculations: illuminance
  1. Direct calculations
     A. Diffuse, Lambert emission
     B. Real emission distributions
  2. Interreflection calculations
- Second-order calculations: luminance
  1. Diffuse, Lambert reflection
  2. Real, bidirectional reflectance distributions

The first-order calculations are used to characterize the light reaching a surface, that is, the illuminance. The illuminance on a surface is a result of the light reaching that surface directly and by interreflections from surrounding surfaces. Luminance describes how light makes objects and surfaces appear and includes determination of contrast and luminance ratios. The determination of luminance is a second-order calculation because it almost always follows an illuminance calculation.

The first-order (illuminance) calculations are of two types. The first type is used to determine how much light reaches a surface or a point directly from a luminous source. The second type is used to determine how much light reaches the same surface or point from a secondary source of light which is, in fact, luminous by reflection.

Illuminance, either averaged over a surface or at a point on a surface, is treated as if produced by light emitted directly from a point source (as in the case of an incandescent downlight), a line source (a fluorescent luminaire) or an area source (a window). These direct illuminance calculations assume one of two types of emitters, diffuse or real.

Diffuse emitters are actually idealized approximations of reality intended to make the calculations simpler to perform. Such emitters follow Lambert's cosine law of emission. This approximation is useful and appropriate for some reflective materials, such as cloth-covered partitions and flat-latex-painted walls, and for some transmissive materials, such as the face of a white plastic sign. Some self-luminous sources, such as the surface of a fluorescent lamp, can also be considered diffuse emitters.

Luminaires are almost always treated as real emitters. These emitters have specific luminous intensity distributions determined by photometric measurement.

Diffuse exitance values from diffuse emitters or luminous intensity values from real emitters are used to calculate what is termed the *direct component* in the illuminance calculation.

Interreflection is the repeated reflection of light among surfaces. For interreflection calculations, surfaces are always assumed to be diffuse reflectors. These surfaces are of finite area, their number and sizes dictated by the accuracy needed for the calculation. More surfaces of smaller size are specified for more accurate interreflection calculations. Interreflection calculations lead to surface exitance values, which are then used as sources of illumination. These values produce a quantity called the *interreflected component* in the illuminance calculation.

For some illuminance calculations, such as those for an indirect electric lighting system, only the interreflections are relevant. For some direct lighting systems, interreflections are negligible contributors to the total illuminance; in these cases, an experienced designer will not bother to calculate them.

Once light reaches a surface, the reflection characteristics of the surface determine its luminance. There are two types of luminance calculations: those for surfaces which can be approximated by diffuse reflection (that is, those which follow Lambert's cosine law of reflection), and those requiring specificity as to the bidirectional reflectance characteristics of the surface. Bidirectionality means that the reflectance of the surface depends on both the incident and the exitant directions of light. All real surfaces are characterized by a bidirectional reflectance distribution function (BRDF). Luminance calculations for real surfaces are the only ones for which the direction of incident light is important.

A GENERAL ALGORITHM FOR LIGHTING CALCULATIONS

The following discussion presents a general algorithm for lighting calculations. It consists of six steps:

1. Determine the quantity to be calculated.
2. Identify luminaires and the information describing them.
3. Determine the accuracy, complexity and detail of the calculation.
4. Identify required geometric, reflectance and other ancillary data.
5. Determine the appropriate equations or computational procedure.
6. Solve the equations or complete the procedure.

1. Determine the Quantity to Be Calculated

An evaluation of the proposed lighting system is the first step in the lighting calculation process. This evaluation includes a determination of what needs to be calculated and the required accuracy of the calculation. Listed in order of increasing complexity are the quantities considered in this section of example calculations:

- Average illuminance on a surface
- Illuminance at a point
- Average exitance and average diffuse luminance of a surface
- Exitance and diffuse luminance at a point
- Nondiffuse luminance

These basic quantities are used in a wide range of lighting applications. Computational procedures to determine them are independent of the specific lighting application in which they are used. Some applications, such as sports and roadway lighting (see chapters 23 and 24), use coordinate systems and light loss factors in ways characteristic to those applications.

The value in performing these calculations is that they help demonstrate what is and is not important for a lighting design. For example, surface reflectances can significantly affect the lighting power density required to bring the illuminance levels to those required in an indoor space.

2. Identify Luminaire Geometry and Luminous Intensity Distribution

For computational purposes, sources can be categorized by the size and the dimensions they exhibit relative to the distances involved in the computation. It is usual to use the *five-times rule* to make this determination. This rule states that if the distance between the luminaire and the computation point is more than five times a luminaire's largest dimension, the luminaire can be treated as a point source. Thus, it is the ratio of luminaire size to computation distance which governs the "computational size" or geometry category of the luminaire. See chapter 9, Lighting Calculations. Assuming a luminaire to be a luminous rectangle, the following criteria hold:

- If both of its dimensions are smaller than one-fifth the computation distance, the luminaire is considered a *point* source.
- If only one dimension is larger than one-fifth the computation distance, the luminaire is considered a *line* source.
- If both dimensions are larger than one-fifth the computation distance, the luminaire is considered an *area* source.

Some examples of point, line and area sources are:

Geometry	Examples
Point	75-W incandescent A lamp in an 8-in.-diameter downlight, used in an office with 8-ft ceilings.
	1000-W metal halide industrial luminaire with a 24-in. reflector mounted 25 ft above the floor.
Line	4-ft unshielded T-12 fluorescent lamp in a small machine shop.
	6-in. × 4-ft wallwasher luminaire with two T-8 fluorescent lamps.
Area	2 × 4-ft troffer with three T-12 fluorescent lamps and a prismatic lens in a classroom with 9-ft ceilings.
	2 × 2-ft parabolic troffer with two 39-W compact fluorescent lamps, recessed in a 10-ft ceiling and 4 ft from a wall on which luminances are to be calculated.
	4-in. × 2-ft luminaire with a 20-W T-5 fluorescent lamp and a prismatic lens mounted under a bookshelf over a desk.

For computational purposes, luminous intensity distributions are considered either diffuse or nondiffuse. For computational purposes a diffuse luminous intensity distribution (see figure 12-1) is defined as

$$I(\theta, \psi) = I_n \cos \theta$$

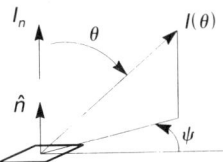

Fig. 12-1. Illustration of angles for a diffuse intensity distribution.

where

I_n = luminous intensity normal ($\hat{n}$) to the luminous surface,

θ = declination angle measured from the normal,

ψ = azimuthal angle.

35100127

A diffuse luminous intensity distribution does not depend on the azimuthal angle ψ and is axially symmetric about the normal to the luminous surface. It exhibits an intensity that varies only with the cosine of the declination angle θ.

If a luminaire has a luminous intensity distribution given by $I(\theta,\psi)$ and the ratio

$$\frac{I(\theta,\psi)}{I(0°,0°)\cos\theta}$$

differs from 1.0 by more than 10% for any of the intensities, the distribution is considered to be nondiffuse. Large errors may result if such a distribution is treated as diffuse. Most luminous intensity distributions exhibited by electric lighting equipment are nondiffuse.

3. Determine the Accuracy and the Complexity

Accuracy. Accuracy requirements are different for different stages in the lighting design process. A preliminary determination of the type of source and required luminaire efficiency can be made, knowing the average illuminance that will be required. An accuracy of $\pm100\%$ is generally sufficient for this determination. Then a preliminary choice of the general type and number of luminaires can be made, knowing the average illuminance that will be required. An accuracy of $\pm25\%$ is generally sufficient for this stage. Illuminance calculations at a point require that both the specific luminous intensity distribution and location of the luminaire(s) be known.

Figure 12-2 provides guidance about the required accuracy at different stages of the design process.

The accuracy required of a calculation is determined by the importance of the result and the consequences of uncertainty. The accuracy, in turn, determines the complexity and cost of the calculation. For purposes of assessing illuminance as it relates to vision-

Fig. 12-2. Expected Accuracy of Lighting Calculations

Available Information	Assumptions Needed to Perform the Calculations	Types of Calculations Possible	Approximate Accuracy
Lamp wattage and efficacy	Luminaire efficiency	Average illuminance	$\pm100\%$
Lumen output of luminaire	Luminous flux between 0° and 45°	Average illuminance	$\pm25\%$
Lamp lumens, coefficients of utilization	None	Average illuminance, exitance or diffuse exitance	$\pm10\%$
Luminous intensity distribution	None	Illuminance, exitance or luminance at a point	$\pm5\%$

and visibility-related lighting system characteristics, an accuracy of $\pm25\%$ is probably sufficient. Luminances used for determining the contrast of reading materials should be calculated with an accuracy of $\pm10\%$. For specification, legal or comparison purposes, calculations of $\pm5\%$ accuracy are often desired. A reasonable upper limit to what can be expected from computational accuracy is established by the uncertainty in measurement. Even with high-quality light measurement equipment, $\pm5\%$ accuracy is the best that can usually be expected. Computational accuracy greater than this cannot be verified by measurement.

Complexity. Calculation complexity is determined by the geometry of the problem. For example, an L-shaped room is computationally more complex than a rectangular room. Similarly, partition shadows and reflections add considerable complexity to the calculations; however, the complex calculations are more accurate.

The need for accuracy is often different for the direct and interreflected components. Although it may be necessary to calculate both the direct and interreflected components, the dominant component should always be calculated with much more accuracy. This, in turn, will affect the complexity of the calculation.

4. Identify Required Geometric, Reflectance and Ancillary Data

Geometric Data. Room dimensions, partition sizes and locations, and surface orientation information such as the slope of a ceiling are necessary geometric information for calculations. Similarly, the luminaire sizes and locations must be determined.

Reflectance Data. Surface reflectances are often unknown at lighting design and calculation time. Unknown reflectances produce an uncertainty that can be determined by calculation. In such cases, those quantities affected by reflectance are calculated twice, using the lowest and highest reasonable values of reflectance that are likely to be present. If these two values lie outside the accuracy requirements listed in figure 12-2 and below in step 5, then a specification for surface reflectance will be required. If the range is small, on the other hand, the reflectances can remain unknown, their values having been found not to significantly affect the lighting system's performance.

Ancillary Data. These data are often specific to a particular application. Examples of such data are BRDFs for visual tasks, *r* tables for roadway luminance calculations, application adjustment factors (AAFs) for sports lighting, and climate and site data for daylighting calculations. See the application chapters of this handbook for complete information on the ancillary data which might be required for a particular situation.

5. Determine Appropriate Equations

The appropriate equations for *average workplane illuminance* calculations are determined by the required accuracy. Note that the following equations should also include light loss factors in order to be accurate.

For direct lighting systems with an accuracy of $\pm 100\%$,

$$E_{ave} = \frac{\substack{\text{lamp watts} \times \text{efficacy} \\ \times \text{luminaire efficiency} \\ \times \text{number of lamps}}}{\text{lighted area}}$$

For indirect lighting systems with an accuracy of $\pm 100\%$,

$$E_{ave} = \frac{\substack{\text{lamp watts} \times \text{efficacy} \\ \times \text{luminaire efficiency} \\ \times \text{number of lamps} \times 0.80 \\ \times \text{ceiling reflectance}}}{\text{lighted area}}$$

The factor 0.80 above is a reasonable average value in most rooms for what is termed the *form factor* between the ceiling and floor. That is, for typical rooms, the fraction of luminous flux emitted by the ceiling which reaches the floor is 0.80.

For direct lighting systems and an accuracy of $\pm 25\%$,

$$E_{ave} = \frac{\substack{\text{lamp lumens} \times \text{luminaire efficiency} \\ \times \text{number of lamps} \\ \times \text{fraction of luminaire lumens} \\ \text{between } 0° \text{ and } 45°}}{\text{lighted area}}$$

The amount between 0° and 45° is a reasonable value for the luminaire lumens which reach the floor directly, in rooms of typical proportions.

Fig. 12-3. Equations for Direct Component Calculations

Source Geometry	Equation	
	Diffuse distribution	Nondiffuse distribution
Point	Inverse square cosine law (see chapter 9, Lighting Calculations)	Inverse square cosine law (see chapter 9, Lighting Calculations)
Line	Configuration factor for a line to a point (see chapter 9, Lighting Calculations)	Inverse square cosine law, where the line is discretized into pieces which are treated as point sources
Area	Configuration factor for an area to a point (see chapter 9, Lighting Calculations)	Inverse square cosine law, where the area is discretized into pieces which are treated as point sources

There is no equation for indirect lighting systems and an accuracy of $\pm 25\%$.

For both direct and indirect lighting systems and an accuracy of $\pm 10\%$,

$$E_{ave} = \frac{\substack{\text{lamp lumens} \\ \times \text{coefficient of utilization} \\ \times \text{number of lamps}}}{\text{lighted area}}$$

For an accuracy of $\pm 5\%$ the luminous intensity distribution must be known. The appropriate equations for direct component calculations follow from the geometry of the source, as shown in figure 12-3.

The appropriate equations for interreflected component calculations are obtained from radiative transfer theory (see chapter 9, Lighting Calculations). The room surfaces are divided into discrete elements and an exitance is calculated for each. More and smaller elements are required for more accurate interreflection calculations.

6. Solve the Equations

Hand calculation is appropriate for small problems with straightforward equations. Spreadsheet programs can often be used. They are the useful option to specialized software, are easy to learn and use, and can be very powerful. More sophisticated computer programs are essential for complex, repetitive or extended calculations.

COORDINATE SYSTEMS FOR LUMINAIRE PHOTOMETRY

Many calculations for lighting involve using luminous intensity distribution data provided by manufacturers in photometric reports.

Directions relative to a lamp or luminaire are specified in a spherical coordinate system by angles θ (altitude) and ψ (azimuth). The convention often is used that an azimuth direction along the lamp axis is $\psi = 0°$ or $\psi = 180°$, but when referring to data in a photometric report it is necessary to give careful attention to how the origin of ψ is defined. The following terms and symbols are used to describe a direction along the lamp axis:

along, parallel, ∥

and across the lamp axis:

across, perpendicular, ⊥

A *polar curve* specifies the variation with θ of $I(\theta, \psi)$ in a vertical plane for a stated angle ψ. The polar curve is scaled in candelas (cd) measured radially from the photometric center. If the luminous intensity distribution is constant about the vertical axis (as with a round downlight having a vertical lamp orientation), only one polar curve is given and the angle ψ is not specified. If the luminous intensity distribution is symmetric about both the parallel and perpendicular horizontal axes (as with a horizontally mounted fluorescent lamp), polar curves may be given only for angles from 0 to 90°. Such a distribution is called *quadrilaterally symmetric*. In this case, equivalent values of ψ for angles which are between 90° and 360° are calculated as follows:

Range of ψ	Equivalent Angle
90°–180°	$180° - \psi$
180°–270°	$\psi - 180°$
270°–360°	$360° - \psi$

This equivalent angle is the lookup angle used in the table of luminous intensity values.

With lesser symmetry and increasing complexity of optical control, polar curves are required in more vertical planes to adequately define the performance of the luminaire. Sometimes the luminous intensity of a luminaire is required at an angle which is not listed in the photometric report. In such cases linear interpolation will be necessary to obtain accurate results. Figure 12-4 contains a partial luminous intensity table for an imagi-

nary luminaire. Altitude angles are given at 10° intervals, and three azimuth angles are given (0°, 45° and 90°). To determine the luminous intensity for an azimuth angle of 45° and an altitude angle of, say, 42.7°, the following procedure can be used.

The fraction equal to the difference between 40° and 42.7° over the difference between 40° and 50° should be calculated:

$$\frac{42.7° - 40°}{50° - 40°} = \frac{2.7°}{10°} = 0.27$$

From the table, the intensity at 40° is 3012 cd and the intensity at 50° is 3133 cd. The difference between these two values is $3133 - 3012 = 121$ cd. 27% of this difference is 32.7 cd. This value is then added to the intensity at 40°. Thus the intensity at an altitude of 42.7° and an azimuth of 45° is estimated to be $3012 + 32.7 = 3044.7$, or 3045 cd.

A way to check that the interpolated value is correct is that it must lie between the bounding points in the table (3045 cd lies between 3012 and 3133 cd).

EXAMPLES OF BASIC LIGHTING CALCULATIONS

The examples which follow are taken from actual applications. They are intended to illustrate the general algorithm for lighting calculations discussed above. Only rarely would these examples represent a complete lighting calculation analysis. It is hoped, however, that the preceding discussion and the following examples will lead to or augment an understanding of the invisible process of computer calculations.

All of the following examples use English units of measurement (such as feet, inches, footcandles). This is

Fig. 12-5. Example Calculations and Their Applications

Quantity Calculated	Possible Applications	Example*
Average illuminance	Large room with several luminaires and uncertain task locations	1
Illuminance at a point	Localized, known task locations, accent lighting, or evaluation of lighting system uniformity	2 (point) 3 (line) 4 (area)
Average exitance	When interreflections are critical to the illuminance calculations above (exitance is the fundamental quantity for calculating diffuse luminance)	5
Exitance at a point	Calculation of luminance, contrast or luminance ratios at a point for diffuse surfaces	6
Nondiffuse luminance	Reading materials (signs, print) and glossy surfaces	7

*1: Lumen method for average illuminance in a room with partitions. 2: Parking lot lighting. 3: Lighting a chalkboard in a classroom. 4: Diffuse skylight illuminating a desk. 5: Interreflections from daylight. 6: Luminances produced by a point source for task lighting at a desk. 7: Evaluating contrast produced on printed material.

Fig. 12-4. Partial Example of a Luminous Intensity Distribution

Altitude	Intensity (cd) at Azimuth, ψ		
θ	0°	45°	90°
0°	1866	1866	1866
10°	2019	2653	2304
20°	2431	2721	2512
30°	2512	2964	2581
40°	2639	3012	2744
50°	2818	3133	3008

done to help facilitate an understanding of the basic calculations for the audience familiar with this system of units.

Figure 12-5 summarizes the example calculations and their applications. The most useful and most widely applied calculations are those for illuminance, both at a point and averaged over a surface. All illustrations for these examples have been made using a computer drafting system similar to that which might be used in many architectural and lighting design firms.

Example 1: Lumen Method for Average Illuminance

Setting: A small open plan office with six workstations formed by partitions. VDTs will be used extensively in this space.

The office measures 36 × 30 ft with a 9.5-ft floor-to-ceiling height. The partitions are 5 ft high, and each workstation is 12 × 12 ft. The layout of the partitions and desks is shown in figure 12-6a. The section showing the room cavities to be used is in figure 12-6b.

1. Determine the Quantity to be Calculated. It is decided that an indirect lighting system will be used in the space, with the goal of providing a maintained illuminance of 40 fc on the horizontal desk surfaces, which are 2.5 ft above the floor. High-angle light control is needed to suit VDT use in the space.

The number of luminaires required to produce this illuminance on the desktops inside the partitioned workstations is the quantity to be calculated.

2. Identify Luminaires and the Information Describing Them. An indirect luminaire will be used. The luminaire uses single in-line T-8 fluorescent lamps (lamp lumens = 2900 lm) and is available in continuous lengths that are multiples of 4 ft, up to a maximum length of 24 ft. A 1.5-ft pendant length is recommended by the manufacturer. Photometric data in-

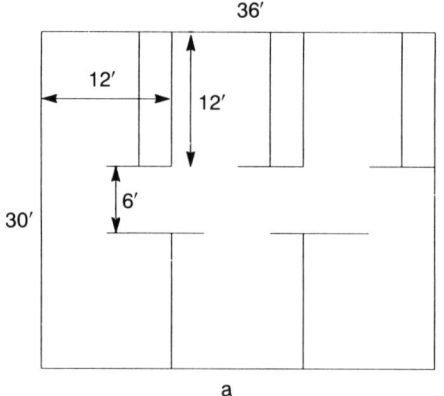

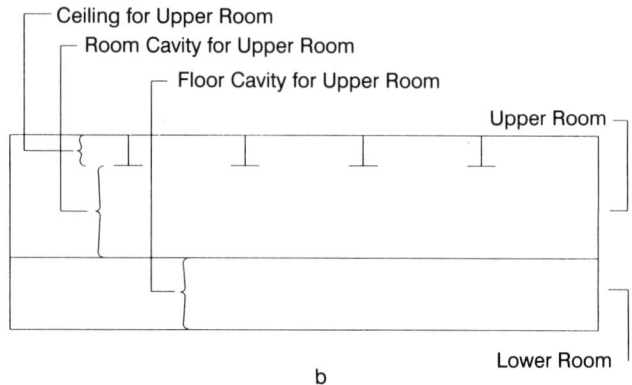

Fig. 12-6. Open plan office for example 1: (a) layout, (b) section.

clude the coefficients of utilization which are shown in figure 12-7.

3. Determine the Accuracy, Complexity and Detail of the Calculation. The lumen method (described in chapter 9, Lighting Calculations) will be used to determine the number of luminaires required, and the following light loss factors will be defined:

• Luminaire dirt depreciation factor
• Lamp lumen depreciation factor
• Ballast factor

Fig. 12-7. Coefficients of Utilization for Indirect Luminaire Used in Example 1

				$\rho_{floor} = 20$				
	$\rho_{ceiling} = 80$			70			50	
RCR	$\rho_{wall} = 70$	50	30	70	50	30	50	30
0	75	75	75	73	73	73	70	70
1	71	69	68	70	68	66	65	64
2	67	64	61	66	63	61	61	59
3	64	59	56	62	58	55	57	54
4	60	55	51	59	54	51	53	50
5	56	50	46	55	50	46	49	45
6	53	47	43	52	46	42	45	42
7	50	43	39	49	43	39	42	38
8	46	39	35	45	39	35	38	35
9	43	36	32	42	36	32	35	31
10	40	33	29	39	33	29	32	28

Other light loss factors are assumed to have a value of 1.0 for this example.

The following calculation strategy is used to take account of the light losses and shadowing produced by the partitions:

1. An individual partitioned workstation is treated as a small room.
2. An imaginary horizontal plane at the level of the top of the partitions represents the ceiling of an individual workstation. The partitions form the walls of this workstation, and the actual working plane is considered as the floor in the calculations. The ceiling reflectance is the effective cavity reflectance of the upper portion of the room, and the floor reflectance is the surface-area-weighted average of the desktop reflectance and effective cavity reflectance of the surfaces below the workplane. In both cases, the effective cavity reflectance is considered from a viewpoint between the workstation ceiling plane and the workplane.
3. The required illuminance on the desk surface will be produced if, taking account of inter-reflections within the workstation, sufficient light crosses the workstation ceiling plane. This light will be directed onto the ceiling plane from the portion of the room above the partitions.
4. Light crossing the workstation ceiling plane can be characterized both as an exitance from a viewpoint inside the workstation and as an illuminance from a viewpoint above the workstation ceiling plane. It is assumed that the distribution of the light crossing the workstation ceiling plane is diffuse.
5. For the purpose of lumen calculations within the workstation, the workstation ceiling plane can be considered a perfectly diffuse luminaire. Thus, the coefficients of utilization of a perfectly diffuse emitter can be used.
6. Working back from the illuminance required on the desk, the luminous output of the diffuse luminaire (that is, the diffuse exitance of the workstation ceiling plane) is calculated.
7. This exitance is numerically equal to the illuminance which must be produced by the upper part of the room onto the workstation ceiling plane. That is, the workstation ceiling plane can be considered the floor of the upper part of the room with a required illuminance. It will have a reflectance that is the effective cavity reflectance of the partitioned workstation.
8. The lumen method is applied to the space above the partitions to determine the number of indirect luminaires required to produce this illuminance. Coefficients of utilization for the indirect luminaire are used for this calculation.

4. Identify Required Geometric, Reflectance and Other Ancillary Data. The diffuse reflectances of the room surfaces are listed as follows:

Floor	0.25
Walls	0.60
Ceiling	0.80
Partitions	0.65
Desktops	0.35

It is assumed that the fluorescent lighting system will operate continuously through the working day, corresponding to 10 h of operation per start. A maintenance schedule whereby lamps and luminaires will be cleaned every 12 mo is also assumed.

The luminaire dirt depreciation light loss factor is determined following the procedure given in figure 9-9 in chapter 9, Lighting Calculations. Since the luminaire has an opaque bottom surface and no top enclosure, it is in maintenance category VI. Using the method given in figure 9-10, the operating atmosphere must be classified, and for this situation is determined to be "clean." The luminaire dirt depreciation light loss factor is then determined from figure 9-12 and the depreciation curve for luminaires operating in a "clean" atmosphere. For a 12-mo maintenance cycle, the luminaire dirt depreciation factor is determined to be 0.85.

Approximate values of the lamp lumen depreciation factor are given in the tables at the end of chapter 6, Light Sources. A more accurate determination can be made by referring to manufacturer's data for the specific lamp type to be used. Allowance can be made for the assumption that the lamps will be operated for 10 h per start. The data in chapter 6 are based on 3 h per start; thus it is assumed that the lamp lumen depreciation factor should be slightly adjusted to 0.88.

The ballast factor for the magnetic ballasts used in this luminaire is 0.95.

The total light loss factor (LLF) is thus

$$\text{LLF} = 0.85 \times 0.88 \times 0.95 = 0.711$$

5. Determine Appropriate Equations. From chapter 9, Lighting Calculations, the lumen method equation for determining the required number of luminaires is

number of luminaires

$$= \frac{\overline{E}_{\text{maintained}} \times \text{workplane area}}{\text{lamps per luminaire} \times \text{lamp lumens} \times \text{CU} \times \text{LLF}}$$

6. Solve the Equations. The lumen method is applied first to a workstation. The coefficient of utilization

(CU) is determined from the room cavity ratio (RCR) and the surface reflectances (determined as shown in chapter 9, Lighting Calculations):

$$RCR = \frac{5h(l + w)}{lw}$$

where

$$h = \text{cavity height,}$$
$$l = \text{cavity length,}$$
$$w = \text{cavity width.}$$

Because the ceiling of a workstation is at the level of the top of the partitions and the floor is at workplane level, the cavity height is $5 - 2.5 = 2.5$ ft. This value and the workstation dimensions give

$$RCR = \frac{5 \times 2.5 \times (12 + 12)}{12 \times 12} = 2.08$$

Below the workplane level is a floor cavity, for which the effective cavity reflectance must be determined. It has a base reflectance of 0.25 (the actual floor) and a wall reflectance of 0.60, and the floor cavity ratio is given by

$$FCR = \frac{5 \times 2.5 \times (12 + 12)}{12 \times 12} = 2.08$$

Figure 9-22 in chapter 9, Lighting Calculations, is read to determine the effective floor cavity reflectance (ρ_{FC}), using the floor cavity ratio 2.08 and the reflectances 0.25 and 0.60. By linear interpolation, the result is

$$\rho_{FC} = 0.23$$

In an area as small as the workstation, the size of the desk is significant. A surface-area-weighted average reflectance (ρ_{FCave}) can be determined for the floor or base of the cavity as shown in chapter 9, Lighting Calculations. In this way,

$$\rho_{FCave} = \frac{A_{FC}\rho_{FC} + A_{DT}\rho_{DT}}{A_{FC} + A_{DT}}$$

where the subscript DT indicates the desktop. If the area of the desktop is 18 ft^2, the effective floor cavity reflectance is

$$\rho_{FCave} = \frac{(12 \times 12 - 18) \times 0.23 + 18 \times 0.35}{(12 \times 12 - 18) + 18} = 0.245$$

The reflectance assigned to the workstation ceiling plane is the effective cavity reflectance of the upper portion of the room from a viewpoint inside the workstation. As the room height is 9.5 ft and the partitions are 5 ft tall, the cavity height is 4.5 ft. The room cavity ratio is given by

$$RCR = \frac{5 \times 4.5 \times (36 + 30)}{36 \times 30} = 1.37$$

The base reflectance of this cavity is the ceiling reflectance of the room, 0.80, and the wall reflectance is the wall reflectance of the room, 0.60. Referring to chapter 9, Lighting Calculations, the effective ceiling cavity reflectance for the work space is 0.65.

Thus, the parameters for determining the coefficient of utilization in the workstation are

$$RCR = 2.08$$

$$\rho_{ceiling} = 0.65$$

$$\rho_{walls} = 0.60$$

$$\rho_{floor} = 0.245$$

A table of coefficients of utilization for a perfectly diffuse emitter is given in figure 9-24 in chapter 9, Lighting Calculations. Linear interpolation gives the value

$$CU = 0.80$$

As stated in the table of coefficients of utilization, all values assume a floor cavity reflectance of 0.20. Thus in this situation the CU value must be modified to take account of the high floor cavity reflectance. The multiplier for this purpose is interpolated from the table of multipliers in figure 9-23 in chapter 9. For $\rho_{FC} = 0.245$, the result is

$$\text{multiplier} = 1.06$$

and so the correct coefficient of utilization is

$$CU = 0.80 \times 1.06 = 0.85$$

From the lumen method equation, the number of lumens required to pass through the workstation ceiling plane is

lumens required

$$= \frac{E_{maintained} \times \text{workplane area}}{CU}$$

$$= \frac{40 \times 12 \times 12}{0.85} = 6776 \text{ lm}$$

The illuminance that must be produced on this plane is thus

$$E_{required} = \frac{\text{required lumens}}{\text{area of workstation}}$$

$$= \frac{6776}{12 \times 12} = 47 \text{ fc}$$

The lumen method is now applied to the upper portion of the room. The room cavity height is the distance between the partition tops and suspended luminaires, 3 ft. The room cavity ratio is

$$RCR = \frac{5 \times 3 \times (36 + 30)}{36 \times 30} = 0.916$$

Since the luminaires are suspended, an effective ceiling cavity reflectance must be determined. The ceiling cavity ratio is

$$CCR = \frac{5 \times 1.5 \times (36 + 30)}{36 \times 30} = 0.458$$

The base reflectance of this cavity is the room ceiling reflectance, 0.80, and the wall reflectance is the room wall reflectance, 0.60. Referring to chapter 9, Lighting Calculations, the effective ceiling cavity reflectance is

$$\rho_{CC} = 0.74$$

The effective floor reflectance of the room is determined from the data on the workstations. The effective reflectance of the workplane has been calculated to be 0.245, and this plane forms the cavity base. The partitions, having a reflectance of 0.65, form the cavity walls. The cavity height is the height between the workplane and the workstation ceiling plane, 2.5 ft. The cavity ratio is

$$CR = \frac{5 \times 2.5 \times (12 + 12)}{12 \times 12} = 2.08$$

Referring again to chapter 9, the effective floor cavity reflectance is

$$\rho_{FC} = 0.24$$

Thus, the parameters for determining the coefficient of utilization are

$$RCR = 0.916$$

$$\rho_{CC} = 0.74$$

$$\rho_{walls} = 0.60$$

$$\rho_{FC} = 0.24 \qquad \text{\small 35100056}$$

Interpolation in the table of coefficients of utilization for the indirect luminaire (figure 12-7) gives

$$CU = 0.67$$

As previously, a multiplier must be determined to correct for the difference between the assumed floor reflectance of 0.20 and the value 0.24. From figure

9-23, the result is

$$\text{multiplier} = 1.08$$

The corrected coefficient of utilization is

$$CU = 0.67 \times 1.08 = 0.72$$

The other parameters for the lumen method equation are

$$\text{lamps per luminaire} = 1$$

$$\text{lamp lumens} = 2900 \text{ lm}$$

Finally, the number of luminaires is

number of luminaires

$$= \frac{\overline{E}_{\text{maintained}} \times \text{workplane area}}{\text{lamps per luminaire} \times \text{lamp lumens} \times CU \times LLF}$$

$$= \frac{47 \times 36 \times 30 \times}{1 \times 2900 \times 0.72 \times 0.771} = 31.5$$

An architecturally practical layout of these luminaires would involve 32 luminaires. One such arrangement is four rows, each 32 ft long, consisting of eight luminaires per row.

Example 2: Lighting a Small Parking Area

Setting: A small parking lot near an office building.

The parking lot measures 100×100 ft and is adjacent to a three-story office building. It is desired to keep the height of equipment consistent with the architectural scale of the building. An analysis is to be performed to see if a single luminaire on a pole can sufficiently illuminate the entire parking lot. The pole will be placed at the center of the area.

1. Determine the Quantity to be Calculated. A diagram of the parking area and the proposed lighting system appears in figure 12-8.

To evaluate the effectiveness of a single pole location, the illuminances are calculated at the points of a 5×5-ft rectangular grid on the pavement surface. This analysis will be performed with three typical pole heights: 15, 20 and 25 ft. The evaluation criterion is the illuminance recommendation (see chapter 24, Roadway Lighting) for a low-activity-level, open parking facility: a minimum illuminance of 0.2 fc with a uniformity criterion that the ratio of average to minimum illuminance is to be no greater than $4:1$.

2. Identify Luminaires and the Information Describing Them. The luminaire to be used in the analysis is type VS with a square distribution, using a clear metal halide lamp, and having a lumen rating of 23,000 lm. Photometric data are available and are shown in figure 12-9 as they might appear in a photometric report.

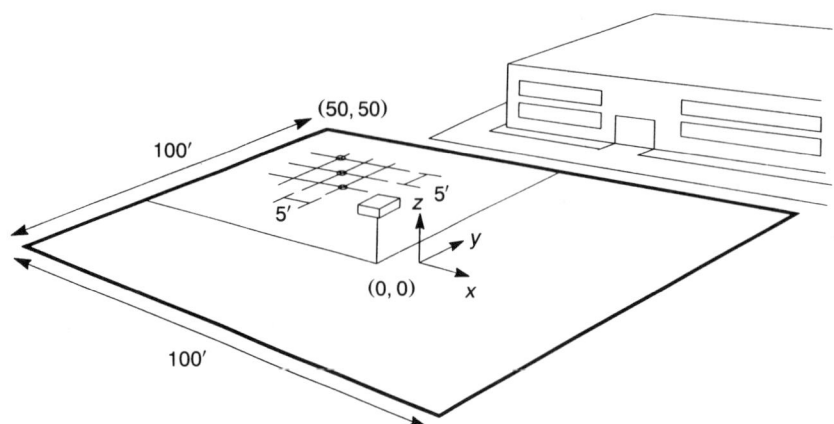

Fig. 12-8. Diagram of parking area for example 2.

Fig. 12-9. Parking Lot Luminaire Luminous Intensity Distribution for Type A Photometry*

Vertical Angle	Intensity (cd) at Lateral Angle										
	0°	5°	15°	25°	35°	45°	55°	65°	75°	85°	90°
0.0°	2886	2886	2886	2886	2886	2886	2886	2886	2886	2886	2886
2.5°	2879	2887	2887	2904	2921	2929	2946	2954	2954	2954	2963
5.0°	2846	2854	2879	2904	2921	2938	2946	2963	2963	2963	2963
7.5°	2829	2829	2862	2879	2896	2896	2904	2912	2921	2929	2929
10.0°	2779	2795	2812	2820	2829	2837	2854	2854	2879	2871	2879
12.5°	2745	2745	2762	2779	2779	2795	2812	2837	2846	2854	2846
15.0°	2678	2678	2695	2728	2753	2762	2787	2812	2820	2812	2812
17.5°	2628	2628	2645	2678	2712	2737	2770	2795	2812	2795	2787
20.0°	2578	2578	2603	2636	2670	2712	2779	2837	2854	2829	2804
22.5°	2561	2553	2553	2611	2653	2728	2812	2904	2921	2837	2804
25.0°	2544	2553	2544	2628	2703	2753	2804	2879	2879	2804	2762
27.5°	2461	2477	2511	2620	2720	2770	2829	2896	2887	2804	2770
30.0°	2427	2435	2461	2611	2720	2812	2904	3021	2963	2829	2812
32.5°	2578	2569	2494	2728	2779	2904	3046	3155	3021	2871	2837
35.0°	2712	2678	2561	2929	2896	3080	3297	3356	3138	3046	2996
37.5°	3046	2921	2653	3122	3063	3406	3599	3691	3373	3306	3339
40.0°	3565	3331	2912	3456	3389	4051	3967	4268	3590	3490	3565
42.5°	3733	3456	3122	3892	3825	4695	4293	4670	3749	3574	3724
45.0°	4118	3599	3189	4067	4101	5030	4729	4812	3984	3833	4109
47.5°	4185	3841	3297	4469	4377	5097	4896	5214	4101	3833	4327
50.0°	3749	3565	3482	4570	4494	5038	4871	5381	4101	3691	4293
52.5°	3314	3097	3465	4327	4243	4829	4645	5281	4385	3716	4770
55.0°	3046	3097	3758	3992	4093	5088	4888	5842	5139	4067	5164
57.5°	2142	2544	3130	4084	5088	6955	5716	5591	4553	3825	4151
60.0°	1741	2134	2410	3281	4461	5323	4385	4143	3808	3197	3448
62.5°	1490	1942	2260	2820	4076	4235	3716	3348	3908	3021	3557
65.0°	1205	1657	2402	2293	3724	3515	3540	3389	3858	3180	4235
67.5°	1038	1398	2193	2151	3574	4009	4452	3816	4921	3222	4143
70.0°	836	1105	1774	1967	3565	4645	5189	4093	4720	3339	3532
72.5°	619	795	1205	1758	2753	3657	4185	3607	3549	2059	2360
75.0°	418	460	518	1138	2025	3021	3063	1891	2092	1013	1364
77.5°	234	192	200	309	535	1029	1071	594	493	326	251
80.0°	117	100	108	142	175	184	209	167	108	92	100
82.5°	50	58	50	50	58	66	50	50	41	33	41
85.0°	33	16	41	16	25	16	16	16	16	16	16
87.5°	0	0	0	0	0	0	0	0	0	0	0
90.0°	0	0	0	0	0	0	0	0	0	0	0

*Total lumen output is 23,000 lm.

3. Determine the Accuracy, Complexity and Detail of the Calculation. Initial calculations will be performed at the points along the diagonal of this grid. It is anticipated that the illuminance is likely to be lowest at the corners of the parking area because the distance from the luminaire is greatest at the corners.

4. Identify Required Geometric, Reflectance and Other Ancillary Data. The necessary dimensions are shown in the figure. On their photometric reports, manufacturers often recommend a total light loss factor to be used with their luminaires. In this case, the manufacturer recommended a total light loss factor of 0.83.

Reflectances are unimportant, since this is an outdoor application.

5. Determine Appropriate Equations. The smallest mounting height to be used is 15 ft, which is more than 5 times the largest dimension of the luminaire. Thus, the five-times rule will be satisfied for any point on the calculation grid, and the luminaire can be treated as a point source. The inverse square cosine law can be used for illuminance computations:

$$E = \frac{I(\theta, \phi) \cos \xi}{D^2}$$

The geometry of this problem allows each of the trigonometric and distance quantities in this equation to be expressed in rectangular coordinates (see figure 12-8):

$$\theta = \arctan\left(\frac{\sqrt{x^2 + y^2}}{z}\right)$$

$$\psi = \arctan\left(\frac{x}{y}\right)$$

$$\cos \xi = \frac{z}{\sqrt{x^2 + y^2 + z^2}}$$

$$D^2 = x^2 + y^2 + z^2$$

These combine to give the following expression for the illuminance:

$$E = I(\theta, \phi) \frac{z}{(x^2 + y^2 + z^2)\sqrt{x^2 + y^2 + z^2}}$$

6. Solve the Equations. An analysis will be performed at the grid points along a diagonal. Referring to the figure, the rectangular coordinates can be determined with respect to the luminaire. Three values of z are used for each pair of x and y coordinates, each value of z representing one of the three pole heights to be evaluated. The point $(x = 0, y = 0)$ is directly under-

Fig. 12-10. Intermediate Calculations for Example 2

x (ft)	y (ft)	z (ft)	θ	ψ	I (cd)	D (ft)	E (fc)
0.0	0.0	15.0	0.0°	0.0°	2886	15.0	12.83
0.0	0.0	20.0	0.0°	0.0°	2886	20.0	7.22
0.0	0.0	25.0	0.0°	0.0°	2886	25.0	4.62
5.0	5.0	15.0	25.2°	45.0°	2754	16.6	9.03
5.0	5.0	20.0	19.5°	45.0°	2717	21.2	5.70
5.0	5.0	25.0	15.8°	45.0°	2754	26.0	3.92
10.0	10.0	15.0	43.3°	45.0°	4802	20.6	8.23
10.0	10.0	20.0	35.3°	45.0°	3119	24.5	4.24
10.0	10.0	25.0	29.5°	45.0°	2804	28.7	2.96
15.0	15.0	15.0	54.7°	45.0°	5057	26.0	4.32
15.0	15.0	20.0	46.7°	45.0°	5076	29.2	4.08
15.0	15.0	25.0	40.3°	45.0°	4128	32.8	2.92
20.0	20.0	15.0	62.1°	45.0°	4409	32.0	2.02
20.0	20.0	20.0	54.7°	45.0°	5057	34.6	2.44
20.0	20.0	25.0	48.5°	45.0°	5073	37.7	2.37
25.0	25.0	15.0	67.0°	45.0°	3910	38.4	1.04
25.0	25.0	20.0	60.5°	45.0°	5105	40.6	1.53
25.0	25.0	25.0	54.7°	45.0°	5057	43.3	1.56
30.0	30.0	15.0	70.5°	45.0°	4147	45.0	0.68
30.0	30.0	20.0	64.8°	45.0°	3573	46.9	0.69
30.0	30.0	25.0	59.5°	45.0°	5649	49.2	1.19
35.0	35.0	15.0	73.1°	45.0°	3504	51.7	0.38
35.0	35.0	20.0	68.0°	45.0°	4136	53.4	0.54
35.0	35.0	25.0	63.2°	45.0°	4437	55.5	0.65
40.0	40.0	15.0	75.1°	45.0°	2941	58.5	0.22
40.0	40.0	20.0	70.5°	45.0°	4147	60.0	0.38
40.0	40.0	25.0	66.2°	45.0°	3752	61.8	0.40
45.0	45.0	15.0	76.7°	45.0°	1666	65.4	0.09
45.0	45.0	20.0	72.6°	45.0°	3632	66.7	0.24
45.0	45.0	25.0	68.6°	45.0°	4289	68.4	0.34
50.0	50.0	15.0	78.0°	45.0°	860	72.3	0.03
50.0	50.0	20.0	74.2°	45.0°	3225	73.5	0.16
50.0	50.0	25.0	70.5°	45.0°	4147	75.0	0.25

neath the luminaire. The point $(x = 50, y = 50)$ is at the corner of the parking lot. The luminous intensity values are obtained by linear interpolation from figure 12-9.

The intensity at $(\theta = 43.3°, \psi = 45.0°)$ is estimated as 4802 cd. The results of all intermediate calculations are summarized in figure 12-10. The illuminance at each position is calculated for each of the three pole heights.

At a distance of 50 ft, the illuminance near the corner of the lot is below 0.2 fc for a pole height of 15 or 20 ft. Only for a pole height of 25 ft is the minimum illuminance requirement of 0.2 fc met over the entire parking lot. This pole height also minimizes the average-to-minimum illuminance ratio over the parking area, but does not meet the required ratio of 4:1 from chapter 24, Roadway Lighting, as will be demonstrated below.

Two methods may be used to estimate the average illuminance on the parking lot. The first method assumes that all of the lumens from the luminaire reach the parking lot surface. The lumen output is 23,000 lm, and the area of the parking lot is 10,000 ft² (100 × 100 ft). The average illuminance can be estimated as follows:

$$\text{average illuminance} = \frac{\text{incident flux} \times \text{LLF}}{\text{surface area}}$$

$$= \frac{23{,}000 \times 0.83}{10{,}000} = 1.91 \text{ fc}$$

The second method simply takes the mean of the 11 point illuminances calculated above. This method gives an average illuminance of

$$\tfrac{1}{11}(4.62 + 3.92 + 2.96 + 2.92 + 2.37$$

$$+ 1.56 + 1.19 + 0.65 + 0.40 + 0.34 + 0.25) = 1.93 \text{ fc}$$

The average-to-minimum ratio for the pole height of 25 ft is calculated as follows:

$$\frac{\text{average illuminance}}{\text{minimum illuminance}} = \frac{1.91 \text{ fc}}{0.25 \text{ fc}} = \frac{7.6}{1}$$

or

$$= \frac{1.93 \text{ fc}}{0.25 \text{ fc}} = \frac{7.7}{1}$$

Thus the ratio is 7.6:1 or 7.7:1, neither of which meets IESNA recommendations for uniformity.

Example 3: Calculation of Illuminance at a Point: Direct and Interreflected Components

Setting: Lighting a chalkboard.

1. Determine the Quantity to Be Calculated. The quantity of interest is the illuminance at a point on a chalkboard. This will be used to determine if a design illuminance criterion of 20 fc on the chalkboard is met. It is assumed that the point at the center of the chalkboard is representative; this point will be used for calculations. The layout is shown in figures 12-11 and 12-12.

2. Identify Luminaires and the Information Describing Them. A pair of 1 × 4-ft recessed troffers, each with

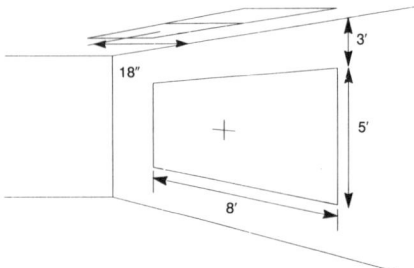

Fig. 12-11. Pertinent room dimensions for example 3, lighting a chalkboard.

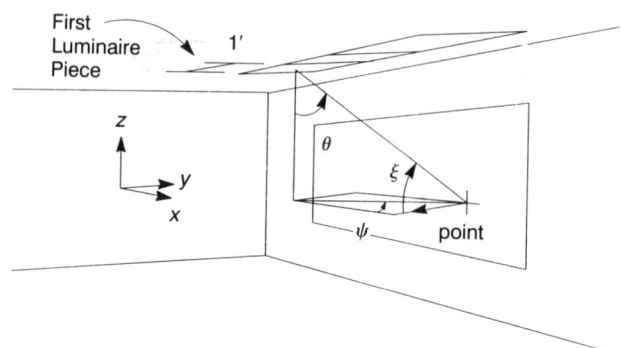

Fig. 12-12. Illustration of angles and dimensions for example 3.

Fig. 12-13. Luminous Intensity Distribution for Schoolroom Luminaire

Angle θ	Intensity (cd)		
	Along ($\psi = 0°$)	$\psi = 45°$	Across ($\psi = 90°$)
0°	1531	1531	1531
5°	1440	1554	1547
15°	1357	1495	1523
25°	1238	1401	1519
35°	1072	1331	1652
45°	852	1242	1259
55°	586	771	612
65°	155	205	216
75°	26	31	26
85°	4	13	9
90°	0	0	0

two T-12 fluorescent lamps, will be used. The total produced by a single luminaire is 3791 lm. The luminous intensity distribution for this luminaire is shown in figure 12-13 as it might appear in a photometric report.

3. Determine the Accuracy, Complexity and Detail of the Calculation. The direct component of illuminance will be calculated from the two luminaires. The luminaires will not be able to be treated as point sources, because of their size and proximity to the chalkboard. Because of their shape, they are determined to be line sources. Therefore the five-times rule will be used to determine the number of discrete pieces of luminaire that must be considered.

The distance D from the center of one of the luminaires to the center of the chalkboard, as can be seen in figures 12-11 and 12-12, is

$$D = \sqrt{x^2 + y^2 + z^2}$$

$$D = \sqrt{2^2 + 1.5^2 + 5.5^2} = 6.04 \text{ ft}$$

The five-times rule requires the dimensions of the discrete pieces of the luminaire to be no greater than $6.04/5 = 1.2$ ft. Since the luminaires measure approximately 1 × 4 ft, each can be discretized into four sections of 1 ft² along its length. Each discrete piece of the luminaire is assumed to emit $\frac{1}{4}$ of the luminaire lumens. Therefore, each has a luminous intensity distribution equal to $\frac{1}{4}$ that of the entire luminaire.

The interreflected component will be determined using the average interreflected illuminance over the chalkboard, since the average interreflected illuminance variation is likely to be small. It is assumed that the principal interreflection will be between the chalkboard and a section of the ceiling nearby. The floor is very likely to have a low reflectance, and will be ignored for purposes of interreflected component calculations. Other walls are assumed to be sufficiently far from the chalkboard to give a negligible contribution to the interreflected component. Note that luminaires in the room other than those used to directly light the chalkboard may also produce direct and interreflected illuminance on the chalkboard. Other sources of illumination are not considered in this example.

4. Identify Required Geometric, Reflectance and Other Ancillary Data.
The chalkboard reflectance ρ_1 is 0.25. The ceiling reflectance ρ_2 is 0.80. The pertinent room dimensions are as shown in figure 12-11.

5. Determine Appropriate Equations
Direct Component. The discrete luminaire pieces are small enough for the inverse square cosine law to be applied for each of the eight pieces, and the illuminances (calculated using eq. 9-4 in chapter 9, Lighting Calculations) added together to give the total illuminance:

$$E = \sum_{i=1}^{8} \frac{I_i \cos \xi_i}{D_i^2}$$

where

I_i = intensity of the ith piece in the direction to the center of the chalkboard,

ξ_i = angle between the normal to the chalkboard surface and a line from the ith piece to the center of the chalkboard,

D_i = distance between the center of the chalkboard and the ith piece.

Interreflected Component. A general equation for interreflected illuminance between two diffuse surfaces is used, based on eq. 9-23a in chapter 9, Lighting Calculations:

$$\bar{E}_{1\,\text{inter}} = \frac{\bar{E}_{1\,\text{dir}} + \bar{E}_{2\,\text{dir}} F_{1\to 2}}{1 - \rho_1 \rho_2 F_{1\to 2} F_{2\to 1}} - \bar{E}_{1\,\text{dir}}$$

where

$\bar{E}_{1\,\text{dir}}$ = direct illuminance onto surface 1,
$\bar{E}_{2\,\text{dir}}$ = direct illuminance onto surface 2,
$F_{1\to 2}$ = radiative exchange form factor from surface 1 to surface 2,

$F_{2\to 1}$ = radiative exchange form factor from surface 2 to surface 1,
ρ_1, ρ_2 = diffuse reflectances of surfaces 1 and 2.

In the present application, surface 1 is the chalkboard and surface 2 is the ceiling near the chalkboard. In this case only the chalkboard has an initial illuminance, and the general equation becomes

$$\bar{E}_{\text{inter}} = \frac{\bar{E}_{\text{dir}}}{1 - \rho_{\text{cb}} \rho_{\text{c}} F_{\text{cb}\to \text{c}} F_{\text{c}\to \text{cb}}} - \bar{E}_{\text{dir}}$$

where

$\bar{E}_{\text{dir}}$ = direct illuminance on the chalkboard,
$F_{\text{cb}\to \text{c}}$ = radiative exchange form factor between the chalkboard (cb) and the ceiling (c) (see chapter 9, Lighting Calculations, for discussion of form factors),
$F_{\text{c}\to \text{cb}}$ = radiative exchange form factor between the ceiling and the chalkboard,
$\rho_{\text{cb}}, \rho_{\text{c}}$ = diffuse reflectances of the chalkboard and ceiling.

6. Solve the Equations
Direct Component. The intermediate quantities required to calculate the direct component of illuminance are shown below and in figure 12-14:

$$D_i = \sqrt{x_i^2 + y_i^2 + z_i^2}$$

$$\cos \xi_i = \frac{y_i}{D_i}$$

$$\theta_i = \arccos\left(\frac{z_i}{D_i}\right)$$

$$\psi_i = \arctan\left(\frac{y_i}{x_i}\right)$$

The angle ψ is measured from the lamp axis of the luminaire. The plane of data corresponding to a value of zero for this angle is identified as "along" in figure 12-13.

Intensities for angles not between 0 and 90° are obtained as discussed above. Negative angles can be converted to positive angles by adding 360°.

The luminous intensities are linearly interpolated from the luminous intensity distribution data in figure 12-13 and divided by 4 on account of the discretization of the luminaire into four pieces.

All of the calculated values for each of the eight luminaire pieces are shown in figure 12-14. The total direct illuminance is then the sum of the partial illuminances in the column at the far right of the table, or 18.5 fc.

Fig. 12-14. Intermediate Calculations for Example 3

Luminaire Piece (i)	x_i	y_i	z_i	D_i	$\cos \xi_i$	θ_i	ψ_i	I_i	E_i
1	−3.5	1.5	5.5	6.69	0.224	34.7°	−23.2°	302	1.51
2	−2.5	1.5	5.5	6.22	0.241	27.8°	−31.0°	331	2.06
3	−1.5	1.5	5.5	5.89	0.255	21.0°	−45.0°	360	2.65
4	−0.5	1.5	5.5	5.72	0.262	15.9°	−71.6°	377	3.02
5	0.5	1.5	5.5	5.72	0.262	15.9°	71.6°	377	3.02
6	1.5	1.5	5.5	5.89	0.255	21.0°	45.0°	360	2.65
7	2.5	1.5	5.5	6.22	0.241	27.8°	31.0°	331	2.06
8	3.5	1.5	5.5	6.69	0.224	34.7°	23.2°	302	1.51

Interreflected Component. As shown above, this calculation requires the initial average illuminance on the chalkboard. For the purpose of calculating the interreflected component, it is assumed to be the same as the average illuminance on the entire wall. This average illuminance can be calculated from (luminaire lumens incident onto the chalkboard)/(area of the chalkboard wall). The luminaires have intensity distributions which are symmetric both along and across the lamp axis, and are mounted close to the chalkboard wall. Thus it can be assumed that approximately 50% of the luminaire lumens reach this surface directly. For each luminaire, 50% of 3791, or 1895.5 lm, will reach the chalkboard wall directly. Because there are two luminaires, the total flux incident on the chalkboard wall is assumed to be 3791 lm. The area of the chalkboard wall is 64 ft^2 (8 × 8 ft). Therefore,

$$\overline{E}_{\text{dir}} = \frac{\text{incident flux}}{\text{area}} = \frac{3791 \text{ lm}}{64 \text{ ft}^2} = 59 \text{ fc}$$

Solving for the interreflected illuminance component gives

$$\overline{E}_{\text{inter}} = \frac{\overline{E}_{\text{dir}}}{1 - \rho_{\text{cb}}\rho_{\text{c}}F_{\text{cb}\rightarrow\text{c}}F_{\text{c}\rightarrow\text{cb}}} - \overline{E}_{\text{dir}}$$

where $\overline{E}_{\text{dir}}$, ρ_{cb} and ρ_{c} have been previously defined, and $F_{\text{cb}\rightarrow\text{c}}$ and $F_{\text{c}\rightarrow\text{cb}}$ are both assumed to equal 0.2. Hence

$$\overline{E}_{\text{inter}} = 0.5 \text{ fc}$$

The total illuminance at the point is then

$$E = \overline{E}_{\text{dir}} + \overline{E}_{\text{inter}}$$

$$= 18.5 \text{ fc} + 0.5 \text{ fc} = 19 \text{ fc}$$

Given the accuracy of the equations used (which is no better than 5%, as discussed in the description of the algorithm above), the calculated illuminance of 19 fc may or may not meet the established design criterion of 20 fc. Further analysis on the part of the designer is probably necessary in this borderline case.

Note that the interreflected component is significantly smaller than the direct component. Because of

this, a more elaborate calculation of the interreflected component produced by these luminaires is not required.

Example 4: Calculation of Illuminance at a Point from an Area Source: Direct Component Only

Setting: Skylights in a small classroom in Denver, Colorado.

1. Determine the Quantity to Be Calculated. The quantity of interest is the direct component of illuminance at a point on a desk in a small classroom. This calculation will be used to determine if the IESNA recommended illuminance for classrooms is obtained.

The calculation point will be at the center of the room on a desk 2.5 ft high. The room is 28 × 28 ft with

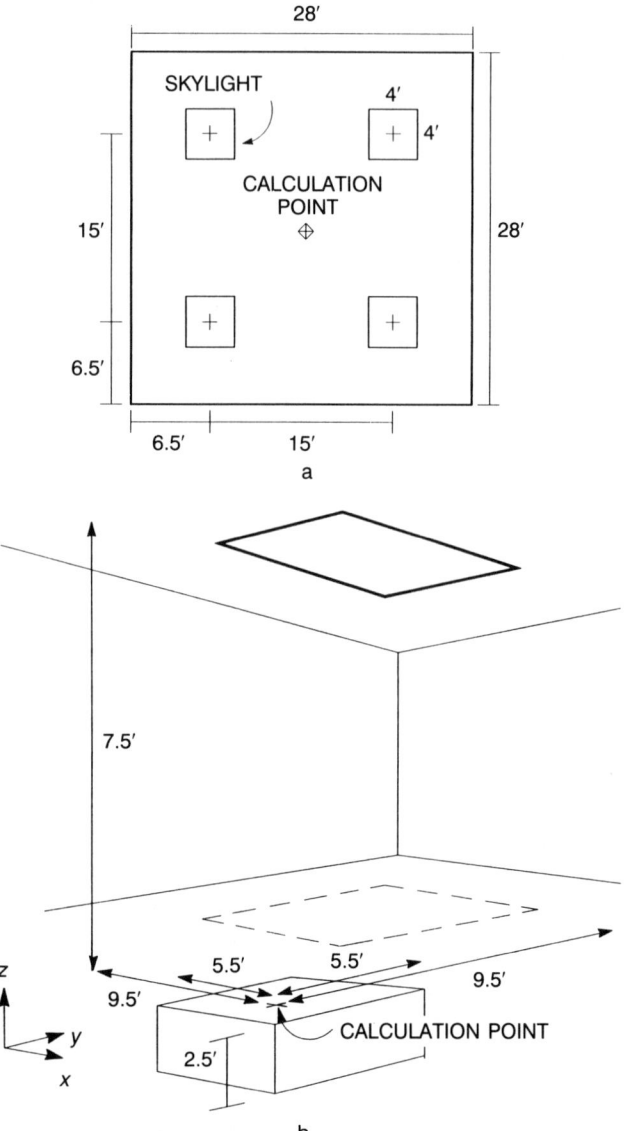

Fig. 12-15. Classroom and skylights for examples 4 and 5: (a) plan, (b) perspective.

a floor-to-ceiling height of 10 ft. It has a ceiling reflectance of 0.80, a wall reflectance of 0.46 and a floor reflectance of 0.20.

2. Identify Sources and the Information Describing Them. The room is lighted by an array of four domed skylights, as shown in figure 12-15. Each skylight is made of plastic which exhibits a diffuse transmittance of 0.15 for light incident perpendicular to the surface. For light incident at other angles, the transmittance is diffuse but the value is reduced. This diffuse directional transmittance $T(\theta)$ is given by

$$T(\theta) = 0.15 \cos^2 \theta$$

where θ is the angle of incidence.
This equation will be used for the direct solar contribution. The total diffuse transmittance T for light incident equally from all directions is 0.10.

3. Determine the Accuracy and Complexity. The direct component will be calculated from the skylights, assuming that they are diffuse area sources. The equation for the illuminance produced by a diffuse area source is used (see chapter 9, Lighting Calculations). This equation requires the source exitance, which in this case is the skylight exitance. This exitance is produced by sunlight and sky light transmitted through the dome of the skylight, and is affected by the skylight's transmittance.
Since the skylight is domed, the transmittance is almost independent of the direction from which the light arrives onto the skylight. This would not be true if the skylight were flat. Domed skylights exhibit a transmittance change due to the thinning of material at the top of the dome. The effect of domed skylights will be determined by evaluating the change in transmittance.
The illuminance produced by the skylights is a function of their exitance, which in turn is a function of the daylight illuminance on them and their transmittance. Both of these quantities are affected by the sun's position. Thus the calculation must be made for a specific date, time and sky condition as described in chapter 8, Daylighting.
The calculation for the interreflected component is shown in example 5.

4. Identify Required Geometric, Reflectance and Other Ancillary Data. The date and time of the example calculation is April 10, 12 noon for Denver, Colorado. The sky condition is assumed to be clear. The available horizontal illuminance, as calculated according to the method described in chapter 8, Daylighting, is

$$E_{\text{sun}} = 9150 \text{ fc}$$

$$E_{\text{sky}} = 1400 \text{ fc}$$

The solar altitude for these conditions is 57.5°, so the sun is 32.5° from the zenith.

5. Determine Appropriate Equations. The equation for the illuminance produced by a diffuse area source, E, is

$$E = MC$$

where

M = diffuse exitance of the source,
C = configuration factor for the area to the point.

In this case the configuration factor is for a rectangle to a point in a plane parallel to the plane of the rectangle. The general equation is in chapter 9, Lighting Calculations:

$$C = \frac{1}{2\pi} \sum_{i=1}^{2} \sum_{j=1}^{2} F(x_i, y_j) \cdot (-1)^{i+j}$$

where

$$F(x_i, y_j) = \frac{x_i}{\sqrt{x_i^2 + z^2}} \arctan \frac{y_j}{\sqrt{x_i^2 + z^2}} + \frac{y_j}{\sqrt{y_j^2 + z^2}} \arctan \frac{x_i}{\sqrt{y_j^2 + z^2}},$$

x_1 = distance from the calculation point to the first edge of the rectangular source in the x direction,
x_2 = distance from the calculation point to the second edge of the rectangular source in the x direction,
y_1 = distance from the calculation point to the first edge of the rectangular source in the y direction,
y_2 = distance from the calculation point to the second edge of the rectangular source in the y direction,
z = distance between the plane containing the calculation point and the plane of the source.

Since there is more than one diffuse area source, the total direct component of illuminance is

$$E = \sum_{i=1}^{4} M_i C_i$$

All four skylights have the same transmittance characteristics, and their proximity means that they will have the same sky and sun illuminance. Thus they will exhibit the same exitance. This gives

$$E = M \sum_{i=1}^{4} C_i$$

In the present example, the calculation point is at the center of the room and is thus symmetrically placed with respect to the skylights. Thus, for this calculation point, the four configuration factors are the same. The illuminance is then

$$E = 4MC$$

The exitance M of the skylight within the room is

$$M = E_{sun}T_{net} + E_{sky}T$$

where

E_{sun} = horizontal illuminance produced by the sun,
E_{sky} = horizontal illuminance produced by the sky,
T_{net} = net directional transmittance of the skylight,
T = total diffuse transmittance of the skylight.

The equation for the net directional transmittance T_{net} of a domed skylight for directional light (that is, from the sun) is (see chapter 8, Daylighting)

$$T_{net} = 1.25\,T(0)\,[1.18 - 0.416T(0)]$$

where $T(0)$ is the diffuse transmittance for light incident perpendicularly to the surface of the plastic.

6. Solve the Equations. The skylight net transmittance is

$$T_{net} = 1.25(0.15)[1.18 - 0.416(0.15)] = 0.210$$

The skylight exitance M is

$$M = (9150)(0.210) + (1400)(0.10) = 2057\ \text{lm/ft}^2$$

The configuration factor from one of the skylights to the point is calculated from the equation shown above in step 5. The distances involved are

$$x_1 = 5.5\ \text{ft}, \qquad x_2 = 9.5\ \text{ft}$$
$$y_1 = 5.5\ \text{ft}, \qquad y_2 = 9.5\ \text{ft}$$
$$z = 7.5\ \text{ft}$$

The resulting configuration factor C is 0.0104. The illuminance at the calculation point from the four skylights is

$$E = 4MC = 4(2057)(0.0104) = 85.5\ \text{fc}$$

Thus, for a clear sky condition at 12 noon on April 10 in Denver, the four skylights will produce a direct illuminance of 86 fc on the desk in the middle of the room.

Example 5: Calculation of Illuminance at a Point from an Area Source: Interreflected Component

Setting: Skylights in a small classroom in Denver, Colorado.

1. Determine the Quantity to Be Calculated. The quantity of interest is the interreflected component of illuminance at a point on a desk in a small classroom. This will be used to determined if a design criterion of 100 fc is met. The direct illuminance component has been calculated in example 4 and is 86 fc.

The calculation point is the same as for example 4: at the center of the room, on a desk 2.5 ft above the floor. The room is 28 × 28 ft with a floor-to-ceiling height of 10 ft. It has a ceiling reflectance of 0.80, a wall reflectance of 0.46 and a floor reflectance of 0.20.

2. Identify Sources and the Information Describing Them. The room is lighted by an array of four domed skylights, as shown in figure 12-15. The skylights are described in example 4.

3. Determine the Accuracy and Complexity. The interreflected component due to the skylights will be calculated assuming that they are diffuse area sources. The interreflections in the room are likely to produce uniform room surface exitances, so a simple three-surface radiative transfer model will be used. That is, the ceiling and floor will each be treated as a separate surface, and the four walls will be grouped together and treated as the third surface. Calculating the interreflection of light will result in a single final exitance for the floor, walls and ceiling.

The ceiling and walls are then treated as diffuse area sources, and the illuminance they produce at the calculation point is the interreflected component. The equation for the illuminance produced by a diffuse area source is used.

4. Identify Required Geometric, Reflectance and Other Ancillary Data. The date and time of the example calculation is April 10, 12 noon for Denver, Colorado. The sky condition is assumed to be clear. The available horizontal illuminance, calculated as described in chapter 8, Daylighting, is

$$E_{sun} = 9150\ \text{fc}$$
$$E_{sky} = 1400\ \text{fc}$$

The reflectance data are described above in step 1.

5. Determine Appropriate Equations. From chapter 9, Lighting Calculations, the equations governing the in-

terreflection of light in a three-surface model are

$$M_c = M_{0c} + \rho_c(M_w F_{c \to w} + M_f F_{c \to f})$$

$$M_w = M_{0w} + \rho_w(M_c F_{w \to c} + M_w F_{w \to w} + M_f F_{w \to f})$$

$$M_f = M_{0f} + \rho_f(M_c F_{f \to c} + M_w F_{f \to w})$$

where

M_c = final ceiling exitance,
M_w = final wall exitance,
M_f = final floor exitance
M_{0c} = initial ceiling exitance,
M_{0w} = initial wall exitance,
M_{0f} = initial floor exitance,
ρ_c = ceiling reflectance,
ρ_w = wall reflectance,
ρ_f = floor reflectance,
$F_{f \to c}$ = form factor from the floor to the ceiling,
$F_{f \to w}$ = form factor from the floor to the walls,
$F_{w \to c}$ = form factor from the walls to the ceiling,
$F_{w \to w}$ = form factor from the walls to the walls,
$F_{w \to f}$ = form factor from the walls to the floor,
$F_{c \to w}$ = form factor from the ceiling to the walls,
$F_{c \to f}$ = form factor from the ceiling to the floor.

As discussed in chapter 9, Lighting Calculations, reciprocity between radiative exchange form factors and the simple geometry of the three-surface model permits six of the seven form factors to be calculated from the single form factor $F_{f \to c}$, the radiative exchange form factor between floor and ceiling. This is the fraction of flux leaving the ceiling which reaches the floor directly. $F_{f \to c}$ is calculated using the equation for identical, parallel, directly opposed rectangles.

The initial exitances M_{0c}, M_{0w} and M_{0f} are determined from

$$M = \frac{\phi_{\text{onto}} \rho}{\text{arca}}$$

where ϕ_{onto} is, in this case, the flux directly from the skylights onto the surface.

The three simultaneous equations can then be solved for the final exitances M_c, M_w and M_f. Finally, the illuminance produced at the desk by the ceiling and walls is calculated from

$$E = M_c C_{c \to p} + M_w C_{p \to w}$$

where

$C_{c \to p}$ = configuration factor from the ceiling to the point,
$C_{p \to w}$ = configuration factor from the walls to the point.

In this case the configuration factor is for a rectangle

to a point in a plane parallel to the plane of the rectangle. This equation is found in chapter 9, Lighting Calculations.

Since the sum of the configuration factors from all the surfaces enclosing a point is 1.0,

$$C_{p \to w} = 1.0 - C_{c \to p}$$

6. Solve the Equations. The radiative exchange form factor between floor and ceiling, $F_{f \to c}$, is calculated using figure 9-32 in chapter 9, Lighting Calculations. Substituting the dimensions determined in step 1 into the appropriate equation, it is determined that $F_{f \to c} = 0.52571$.

We now use the relationships among the other form factors (from equations 9-27 through 9-30):

$$F_{c \to f} = F_{f \to c} = 0.52571$$

$$F_{c \to w} = F_{f \to w} = 1 - F_{c \to f} = 0.47429$$

$$F_{w \to c} = F_{w \to f} = \frac{A_c}{A_w}(1 - F_{c \to f}) = 0.33200$$

$$F_{w \to w} = 1 - 2F_{w \to c} = 0.33599$$

where A_c is the area of the ceiling and A_w is the area of the walls. The equations for M_c, M_w and M_f become

$$M_c = M_{0c} + 0.80(M_w\,0.47429 + M_f\,0.52571)$$

$$M_w = M_{0w} + 0.46(M_c\,0.33200 + M_w\,0.33599 + M_f\,0.33200)$$

$$M_f = M_{0f} + 0.20(M_c\,0.52571 + M_w\,0.47429)$$

The initial exitance of the ceiling, M_{0c}, is zero, since the skylights cannot directly illuminate the ceiling:

$$M_{0c} = 0.0$$

The initial exitance of the floor, M_{0f}, is given by

$$M_{0f} = \frac{\Phi_{\text{skylights} \to \text{floor}}\,\rho_f}{A_f}$$

where

$\Phi_{\text{skylights} \to \text{floor}}$ = flux emitted by the skylights that reaches the floor directly,
A_f = area of the floor.

The flux from the skylights to the floor is calculated from the total flux leaving the skylights and the radiative exchange form factors from the skylights to the floor:

$$\Phi_{\text{skylights} \to \text{floor}} = \sum_{i=1}^{4} \Phi_{\text{skylight}} F_{\text{skylight} \to \text{floor}}$$

The summation is over the four skylights in the room. Since the skylights are identical, and placed symmetrically with respect to the calculation point and the center of the room, each will emit the same number of lumens, and the form factors from each skylight to the floor will be identical. Thus

$$\Phi_{\text{skylights} \to \text{floor}} = 4\Phi_{\text{skylight}} F_{\text{skylight} \to \text{floor}}$$

Φ_{skylight} is calculated from

$$\Phi_{\text{skylight}} = M_{\text{skylight}} A_{\text{skylight}}$$

Thus

$$M_{0f} = \frac{4M_{\text{skylight}} A_{\text{skylight}} F_{\text{skylight} \to \text{floor}} \rho_f}{A_f}$$

The skylight exitance M_{skylight}, as calculated in example 4, is 2057 lm/ft^2. The radiative exchange form factor from a skylight to the floor is calculated from the appropriate equation in figure 9-33 in chapter 9, Lighting Calculations. The resulting value of $F_{\text{skylight} \to \text{floor}}$ is 0.556.

Solving for M_{0f}, then, we have

$$M_{0f} = \frac{4(2057)(16)(0.556)(0.20)}{(28)(28)} = 18.7 \text{ lm/ft}^2$$

The initial wall exitance is treated similarly:

$$M_{0w} = \frac{4M_{\text{skylight}} A_{\text{skylight}} F_{\text{skylight} \to \text{walls}} \rho_w}{A_w}$$

The radiative exchange form factor from the skylight to the walls is found by closure; that is, all of the flux emitted by a skylight which does not reach the floor must reach the walls:

$$F_{\text{skylight} \to \text{walls}} = 1 - F_{\text{skylight} \to \text{floor}} = 1 - 0.556 = 0.444$$

Thus

$$M_{0w} = \frac{4(2057)(16)(0.444)(0.50)}{(4)(28)(10)} = 26.1 \text{ lm/ft}^2$$

With these three values of initial exitance the three simultaneous equations become

$$M_c = \quad 0.0 \qquad\qquad\quad + M_w 0.37943 + M_f 0.42057$$

$$M_w = 26.1 + M_c 0.15372 + M_w 0.15556 + M_f 0.15372$$

$$M_f = 18.7 + M_c 0.10514 + M_w 0.09486$$

The solution of these three equations yields:

$$M_c = 25.87 \text{ lm/ft}^2$$

$$M_w = 40.21 \text{ lm/ft}^2$$

$$M_f = 25.23 \text{ lm/ft}^2$$

The configuration factor from the calculation point to the ceiling, $C_{c \to p}$, is calculated as described in figure 9-30 in chapter 9, Lighting Calculations. Its value is 0.811. By closure, the configuration factor from the calculation point to the walls, $C_{p \to w}$, equals

$$1.0 - C_{c \to p} = 0.189$$

Finally, solving for the interreflected illuminance E, we have

$$E = M_c C_{c \to p} + M_w C_{p \to w}$$

$$= 25.87(0.811) + 40.21(0.189) = 28.76 \text{ fc}$$

The sum of the direct (from example 4) and interreflected illuminance components is

$$E_{\text{total}} = 86 + 28.76 = 115 \text{ fc}$$

The calculated value 115 fc for the prescribed time, location and sky condition exceeds the design illuminance criterion of 100 fc.

Example 6: Calculation of Luminances Produced by a Point Source

Setting: Task lighting analysis of a desk. A small desk luminaire is to be used for lighting desks in workstations.

1. Determine the Quantity to be Calculated. The analysis of the performance of a task light on a desk consists, in part, of a determination of the luminance of a white piece of paper.

2. Identify Luminaires and the Information Describing Them. The luminaire that will be used is a single 13-W compact fluorescent lamp with a reflector which produces a very directional luminous intensity distribution. The luminaire is 6 in. long, 3 in. wide and 1.5 in. high. It is mounted on a movable arm designed to permit it to be placed off to the side of the desk. The photometric data are shown in figure 12-17.

3. Determine the Accuracy, Complexity and Detail of the Calculation. The luminance of the paper is assumed to be diffuse, so the luminance calculation requires only a determination of the illuminance and a measurement of the paper's diffuse reflectance.

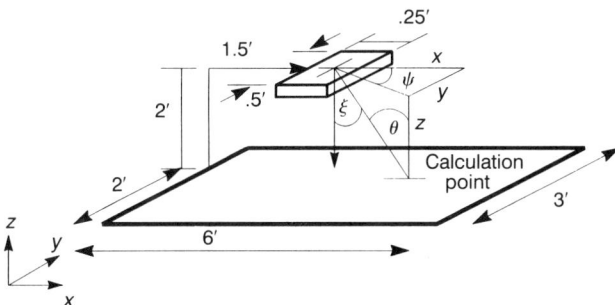

Fig. 12-16. Desk layout for example 6.

Fig. 12-17. Luminous Intensity Distribution of Desk Luminaire

Elevation Angle θ	Intensity (cd) at Azimuthal Angle ψ				
	0.0°	22.5°	45.0°	67.5°	90.0°
0.0°	450	450	450	450	450
5.0°	453	457	453	445	442
15.0°	437	446	450	454	451
25.0°	406	422	447	470	478
35.0°	362	391	443	497	523
45.0°	302	350	448	551	592
55.0°	233	310	474	624	678
65.0°	158	284	505	651	691
75.0°	81	263	432	529	559
85.0°	20	134	178	192	193
90.0°	1	4	5	8	10

As shown in figure 12-16, the luminaire arm is mounted at the side of a desk whose dimensions are 6×3 ft. The luminaire is located at a height of 2 ft above the desk surface, 1.5 ft to the left of the center of the desk, and 2 ft from the front of the desk. The distance from the center of the luminaire to the center of the desk is given by

$$D = \sqrt{x^2 + y^2 + z^2} = \sqrt{1.5^2 + 0.5^2 + 2^2} = 2.55 \text{ ft}$$

This distance is larger than 5 times the maximum luminous dimension of the luminaire (6 in.), so the inverse square cosine law for the illuminance from a point source can be used.

4. Identify Required Geometric, Reflectance and Other Ancillary Data. The geometric dimensions are shown in figure 12-16. The white paper is a diffusely reflecting object with a reflectance $\rho = 0.83$.

5. Determine Appropriate Equations. The luminance L of a diffusely reflecting surface is given by the following formula:

$$L = \frac{M}{\pi} = \frac{\rho_{\text{paper}} E}{\pi}$$

The illuminance at the center of the desk is given by

$$E = \frac{I(\theta, \psi) \cos \xi}{D^2}$$

The luminous intensity distribution data are shown in figure 12-17. The angles required to determine the luminous intensity are calculated as follows from geometric principles (see figure 12-16):

$$\theta = \arctan\left(\frac{\sqrt{x^2 + y^2}}{z}\right)$$

$$\psi = \arctan\left(\frac{y}{x}\right)$$

The incident angle ξ is given by the following expression:

$$\xi = \arctan\left(\frac{\sqrt{x^2 + y^2}}{z}\right)$$

6. Solve the Equations. First, the illuminance produced by the luminaire is calculated. Using the dimensions in figure 12-16,

$$\theta = \arctan\left(\frac{\sqrt{1.5^2 + 0.5^2}}{2}\right) = 38.3°$$

$$\psi = \arctan\left(\frac{0.5}{1.5}\right) = 18.4°$$

Linearly interpolating in the table of luminous intensities (figure 12-17), the intensity at ($\theta = 38.3°$, $\psi = 18.4°$) has a value of 356 cd.

The incident angle is given by

$$\xi = \arctan\left(\frac{\sqrt{1.5^2 + 0.5^2}}{2}\right) = 38.3°$$

The illuminance E is calculated as follows:

$$E = \frac{I(\theta, \psi) \cos \xi}{d^2} = \frac{356 \cos 38.3°}{1.5^2 + 0.5^2 + 2^2} = 42.9 \text{ fc}$$

The luminance of the paper is

$$L_{\text{paper}} = \frac{\rho_{\text{paper}} E}{\pi} = \frac{(0.83)(42.9)}{\pi} = 11.4 \text{ cd/ft}^2$$

Example 7: Calculation of Contrast Produced on Printed Material

Setting: Task lighting analysis of a desk. A small desk luminaire is to be used for task lighting desks in workstations.

1. Determine the Quantity to be Calculated. The analysis of the performance of a task light on a desk consists, in part, of a determination of the visual task contrast that is produced on the horizontal desk surface. The contrast determined here is that for black print on white glossy paper, such as is commonly found in journals and magazines.

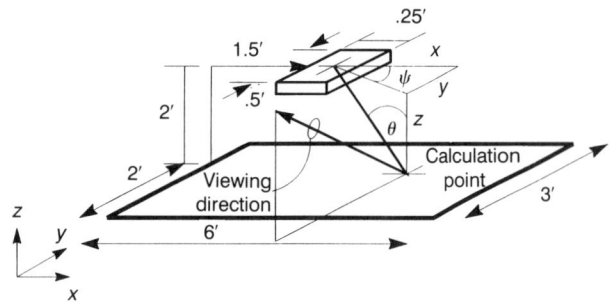

Fig. 12-18. Desk lamp drawing for example 7.

2. Identify Luminaires and the Information Describing Them. The same luminaire will be used for this example as for example 6. The luminous intensity distribution is shown in figure 12-17.

3. Determine the Accuracy, Complexity and Detail of the Calculation. Calculating the contrast requires determining the luminance of both the task and its background. Neither the paper nor the print ink is assumed to have a diffuse reflectance for this example. Therefore, the calculation of these luminances requires both the illuminance and the bidirectional reflectance distribution function (BRDF) of each.

The layout of the task is shown in figure 12-18. As calculated in example 6, the distance from the task (at the center of the desk) to the center of the luminaire is 2.55 ft, which is larger than 5 times the maximum luminous dimension of the luminaire. Thus the inverse square cosine law is valid in this case.

4. Identify Required Geometric, Reflectance and Other Ancillary Data. The necessary dimensions are shown in the figure. The BRDFs for the paper and for the printed ink are shown in figures 12-19 and 12-20, for a typical viewing angle of 10° from vertical. The irregular spacing of the azimuth and declination angles in the BRDF tables reflects the degree of specularity for the material. Where angles are spaced closer together, the BRDF is more sensitive to small changes in these angles.

5. Determine Appropriate Equations. The luminance contrast C of a task is given by

$$C = \frac{|L_b - L_t|}{L_b}$$

where

L_b = luminance of the background,
L_t = luminance of the target.

In this example, the luminances are of nondiffusely reflecting surfaces. The luminance of a nondiffusely reflecting surface illuminated by an unpolarized source is discussed in chapter 9, Lighting Calculations, and is

$$L(\theta_v) = \sum_i E(\theta_i, \psi_i) f_r(\theta_v; \theta_i, \psi_i)$$

where

θ_v = viewing declination angle, in this case equal to 10°,
θ_i = incident declination angle,
ψ_i = incident azimuthal angle, measured from the plane containing the direction of view and given by

$$\psi_i = 90° + \arctan\left(\frac{y}{x}\right)$$

The sum is taken over all the discrete values of illuminance. The number of discrete steps determines the accuracy of the approximation. The step size in these approximations is determined by the need to model high gradients of either the illuminance or the BRDFs. In the present case, the largest declination angle subtended by the luminaire to the calculation point is 6.9°, and the largest azimuthal angle subtended by the luminaire is 19.9°. The azimuthal and declination incident angles from the center of the luminaire are used to determine the region of the BRDFs being used. Examination of this region reveals whether discretization is necessary for an illuminating field which measures 6.9° × 19.9°.

Fig. 12-19. Partial Bidirectional Reflectance Distribution Function (BDRF) Data for White Paper*

Azimuth	BDRF (sr⁻¹) at Declination					
	24°	28°	34°	44°	52°	60°
0°	0.226	0.221	0.215	0.216	0.205	0.194
130°	0.240	0.226	0.220	0.217	0.208	0.197
150°	0.249	0.231	0.224	0.214	0.208	0.196
160°	0.252	0.231	0.221	0.214	0.200	0.196
170°	0.253	0.233	0.222	0.216	0.212	0.196
176°	0.250	0.234	0.223	0.216	0.206	0.197
177°	0.261	0.235	0.224	0.217	0.205	0.198
178°	0.262	0.236	0.223	0.218	0.211	0.198
179°	0.263	0.235	0.223	0.219	0.213	0.200
180°	0.263	0.234	0.222	0.219	0.210	0.193

*Viewing declination agle = 10°, viewing azimuth angle = 0°.

Fig. 12-20. Partial BRDF Data for Black Printed Ink*

Azimuth	BRDF (sr⁻¹) at Declination					
	22°	28°	36°	44°	52°	60°
0°	0.004	0.003	0.002	0.001	0.000	0.000
130°	0.013	0.002	0.000	0.000	0.000	0.000
150°	0.034	0.006	0.000	0.000	0.000	0.000
160°	0.056	0.010	0.000	0.000	0.000	0.000
170°	0.089	0.015	0.001	0.000	0.000	0.000
176°	0.109	0.018	0.001	0.000	0.000	0.000
177°	0.111	0.019	0.001	0.000	0.000	0.000
178°	0.113	0.019	0.002	0.000	0.000	0.000
179°	0.116	0.020	0.002	0.000	0.000	0.000
180°	0.118	0.020	0.002	0.000	0.000	0.000

*Viewing declination angle = 10°, viewing azimuth angle = 0°.

6. Solve the Equations. The illuminance at the center of the desk is 42.9 fc, as shown in example 6. The luminances of task and background require determining the BRDFs of the paper and of the printed ink at the specified angles. The incident azimuthal angle ψ_i must be determined:

$$\psi_i = 90° + \arctan\left(\frac{1.5}{0.5}\right) = 161.5°$$

The incident declination angle has been determined to be 38.3° in example 6. Given the viewing angle of 10°, the BRDF tables in figures 12-19 and 12-20 for the paper and ink are interpolated to obtain the values

$$f_{ink}(10°; 38.3°, 161.5°) = 0.0001$$

$$f_{paper}(10°; 38.3°, 161.5°) = 0.2182$$

The units of BRDFs are inverse steradians (sr⁻¹). The luminance of the ink at the calculation point is then

$$L_{ink} = E(\theta_i, \psi_i)f_r(\theta_v; \theta_i, \psi_i)$$
$$= (42.9 \text{ fc})(0.0001 \text{ sr}^{-1}) = 0.0043 \text{ cd/ft}^2$$

The luminance of the paper at the calculation point is

$$L_{paper} = E(\theta_i, \psi_i)f_r(\theta_v; \theta_i, \psi_i)$$
$$= (42.9 \text{ fc})(0.2182 \text{ sr}^{-1}) = 9.36 \text{ cd/ft}^2$$

The luminance contrast of the task and background is then

$$C = \frac{|9.36 - 0.0034|}{9.36} = 0.999$$

Calculations of contrast for the extreme azimuth and declination angles subtended by the luminaire result in the following contrasts at the calculation point:

$$C(38.3° + 3.45°, 161.5° + 9.95°)$$
$$= C(41.75°, 171.45°) = 0.999$$
$$C(38.3° + 3.45°, 161.5° - 9.95°)$$
$$= C(41.75°, 151.55°) = 1.000$$
$$C(38.3° - 3.45°, 161.5° + 9.95°)$$
$$= C(34.85°, 171.45°) = 0.986$$
$$C(38.3° - 3.45°, 161.5° - 9.95°)$$
$$= C(34.85°, 151.55°) = 0.970$$

Each of these lies within 10% of the contrast calculated using a single point at the center of the luminaire, so discretization of the luminaire into several elements is not required.

Lighting Economics

13

THE ROLE OF ECONOMIC ANALYSIS IN LIGHTING[1-5]

Lighting must be responsive to all of the needs of the user, including economic ones. In fact, it is economic needs which often drive the decision-making process when lighting systems are designed and purchased. Unfortunately, economic concerns are often thought of as the antagonist of esthetic and visual concerns. The lighting professional tends to draw up a list of those criteria and needs thought to be essential, then begins the tedious process of identifying priorities and determining which can be accommodated by the budget.

Rather than considering economic analysis as the antithesis of engineering analysis or esthetic design, it should be thought of as a framework within which all of the needs of the various clientele can be taken properly into account. For example, when a worker's vision is impaired by disability glare, reduced productivity is an economic consequence. A decision to improve the lighting could be based on the economic needs of the owner. When the lighting of an office building atrium fails to complement the architecture of the space, the rental value will fail to achieve its potential. Again, a decision to improve the lighting is an economic decision. Thus, taking care of economic needs, when done correctly, can assure that the other lighting needs are properly considered.

Specifically, several rationales can be given for a comprehensive lighting economic analysis. These include (for new or existing systems):

- Comparing alternative systems as part of a decision-making process.
- Evaluating maintenance techniques and procedures.
- Evaluating energy conservation and demand-side management technologies and strategies.
- Determining the effect of lighting on other building systems.
- Budgeting and cash flow planning.
- Simplifying and reducing complex lighting system characteristics to a generally understandable common measure: cost.
- Helping to determine the benefit of lighting (cost-benefit analysis).

LIGHTING COST COMPARISONS

Many metrics and techniques have been proposed over the years for comparing the cost of one lighting system with that of another. These methods can be classified into two categories: first-level and second-level analysis methods (see figure 13-1). The distinction between the two groups is that the first-level methods do not consider the time value of money. The term "time value of money" refers to the fact that one dollar today is not equivalent to the promise of one dollar at a specified time in the future.

The Cost of Light

The simplest economic analysis consists of one rule: the initial costs are compared and the least expensive is chosen. Thus, if lamp A costs $1.20 and lamp B costs $1.00, lamp B will be selected. If the lamps are identical in performance, then this may be a sufficient analysis. However, if lamp A produces 1000 lm and lamp B produces only 800 lm, then one might choose A based on a comparison of the cost per lumen (A, 0.12 ¢/lm; B, 0.125 ¢/lm). On the other hand, lamp A might have a rated life of 1000 h as compared with 1100 h for lamp B, so a further refinement of the calculation would be necessary.

Both costs and benefits must enter the analysis in order to obtain a meaningful result. The process of providing the desired lighting involves the expenditure of money for a number of products such as lamps, luminaires and wire, and services such as labor and electricity, to obtain certain benefits, namely light. This was recognized early in the history of electrical light-

Fig. 13-1. Lighting Cost Comparison Methods

First-Level Analysis Methods*
Cost of light
Simple payback
Simple rate of return

Second-Level Analysis Methods
Life-cycle cost-benefit analysis
Savings-investment ratio
Internal rate of return

*Generally not recommended for large or complex projects.

ing, and basic measures of lighting value have been developed, based upon the idea of cost per unit of lighting delivered. This is the traditional "cost of light" and would logically be expressed in dollars per lumen hour. Because the cost per lumen hour of typical general lighting systems is very small, the unit of dollars per million lumen hours is usually used instead.

The cost of light may be expressed by the following equation:

$$U = \frac{10}{Q}\left(\frac{P + h}{L} + WR\right) \qquad (13\text{-}1)$$

where

U = unit cost of light for a lamp, in $\$/10^6$ lm · h,
Q = mean lamp flux, in lm,
P = lamp price, in ¢,
h = labor cost to replace one lamp, in ¢,
L = average rated lamp life, in kh,
W = mean input power per lamp (lamp and losses), in W,
R = energy cost, in ¢/kW · h.

The cost of light is calculated by multiplying the average light output in lumens by the life of the lamps and dividing the result into the total owning and operating costs for the same time period. Equation 13-1 shows the simplest formulation. A good use for the cost-of-light method is the comparison of two competing lamps for use in the same lighting system, or in evaluating a retrofit lamp such as a compact fluorescent as an alternative to an existing incandescent lamp.

Note that this equation contains no information about the luminaire in which the lamp is housed. Therefore care must be exercised in extending its use to choices between systems containing different luminaires. Suppose, for example, a manufacturer introduces a new lamp as an efficient replacement for metal halide lamps. By performing the calculation of equation 13-1 twice, once for a metal halide lamp and once for the new lamp, one could see approximately how much it costs each of the two lamps to produce one million lumen hours. However, if the lamps differed appreciably in physical characteristics such as size, shape and operating temperature, the luminaires that house them might also differ appreciably in efficiency, cleaning requirements, intensity distribution or maintenance characteristics. Each of these differences could affect the cost of owning and using the system.

Another weakness of the cost-of-light method is that it does not consider the time value of money. However, when the life of the project is short (say, two years or less), as occurs in seasonal or other temporary lighting, interest rates have little effect on the analysis and a method which ignores them can still be useful. Also, if interest rates are very low or are considered separately

(as in a project involving an expense rather than a capital expenditure), then ignoring the time value of money may be appropriate.

Simple Payback

Simple payback is a first-level method commonly used in the lighting industry today for comparing and evaluating a lighting project or proposal. Payback offers information about the amount of time it will take for an investment or initial outlay to be paid off. It is defined as the initial cost of a system divided by the annual cash flow or saving which the system engenders.

Simple payback is calculated by the following formula:

$$P = \frac{I}{A} \qquad (13\text{-}2)$$

where

P = payback period, in years,
I = incremental investment, in dollars,
A = incremental annual cash flow.

The term "incremental" in the above definition indicates a comparison of one system with another. Two types of comparisons are possible: comparing a proposed replacement system with an existing system, or comparing design alternatives for a new space in which there is no existing system. The former is the more common use of the simple payback concept in lighting.

Frequently, questions arise concerning the desirability of replacing existing lighting with a new technology. Whether a system will "pay for itself" and how long it will take to do so are the most commonly asked such questions. For example, an owner of an office building may estimate that a certain lighting modification will save about $2000 in energy costs annually. The expense associated with purchasing and installing the modification is estimated at $11,000. Then the simple payback period would be

$$P = \$11{,}000/\$2000 = 5.5 \text{ yr}$$

Those who like the simple payback method argue that it is easy to use and a simple way to determine the profitability of a proposed action. In fact, however, it is actually a risk assessment tool posing as a profitability metric. This is seen by examining the question the method answers. It does not answer the question "is a certain investment profitable?"; rather, it responds to the concerns of the person who is unsure about the future and hopes to recoup the investment as soon as possible. If getting money back is the primary concern, why invest at all? If no investment is made, then that money is available immediately and the payback is zero years, the ideal result of a simple payback calculation.

Another problem with this method is that it fails to consider what happens after the investment is paid back. For example, if the savings from system A (which has a shorter payback than system B) decline sharply each year after the payback period, but the savings of system B remain steady, the payback method has led to the choice of an inferior alternative. A similar situation will be encountered if the systems have different lengths of economic life. Therefore the payback method cannot be used when the alternatives have nonuniform cash flows, nor is it appropriate for assessing options having different lives.

As with all first-level methods, simple payback does not consider the time value of money. Therefore, like the cost-of-light method, simple payback is best suited for short-lived projects for which interest rates have little importance. Simple payback can also be helpful as an initial screening method for projects of longer duration: if a system pays back within some specified short period (typically one or two years), then it is extremely likely to be profitable and can be accepted with no further analysis. However, a project which does not pass such a test should not be rejected, since it may still be profitable. Instead, such a project should be subjected to more rigorous analysis based on a second-level method.

Simple Rate of Return

The simple rate of return is simply the reciprocal of the payback:

$$\text{ROR} = \frac{A}{I} \qquad (13\text{-}3)$$

where

$\quad$ ROR = rate of return,
$\qquad A$ = incremental annual cash flow,
$\qquad I$ = incremental investment.

Thus if a system saves \$20,000/yr and requires an initial investment of \$100,000, its simple rate of return is \$20,000/\$100,000, or 20%, equivalent to a 5-yr payback. The advantages and disadvantages of this method are identical to those of the payback method. It is simple to apply and understand, but it cannot deal with nonuniform savings streams or unequal lives.

Life-Cycle Cost-Benefit Analysis (LCCBA)

The first-level methods are attractive due to their simplicity. However, they may lead to serious errors, and thus they are generally not recommended for large or complex projects. Of the second-level methods, life-cycle cost-benefit analysis (LCCBA) has emerged as the most robust method, and one that is approved by experts in managerial economics from all industries.[6-8]

Therefore, LCCBA is presented here as the economic analysis method recommended by IESNA. For a more thorough treatment of LCCBA and a discussion of some of the other methods listed in figure 13-1, see references 6, 7 and 8.

LCCBA is a comprehensive example of the second-level methods. This method uses a differential cost to give a direct comparison of systems under consideration. As with all second-level methods, the time value of money is considered. An outline of this method for comparing new interior lighting systems is illustrated by the worksheet in figure 13-2. Within the format of that figure, two lighting system alternatives (systems 1 and 2) are compared. In order to do so it must be assumed that the systems provide equal functional benefits, or that they both fulfill all functional requirements and any additional benefits which one or the other system may provide have no economic value to the owner. The method is easily expanded using the same format if comparison of additional options is desired.

The first step in the LCCBA process is to complete the worksheet in figure 13-2 for each system under consideration. The notes give estimates and default values to be used only as a last resort for values that are not available by any other means. Since initial costs and annual power and maintenance costs occur at different times, they cannot be directly compared. The second step, then, is to put all terms into their time equivalents to allow comparison. The following equations are used to take into consideration the time value of money.

The *single present-worth factor* is calculated by

$$P = F \times \frac{1}{(1+i)^y} \qquad (13\text{-}4)$$

where

$\quad P$ = present worth, or the equivalent value at present, in dollars,
$\quad F$ = future worth, or the amount in the future, in dollars,
$\quad y$ = number of years,
$\quad i$ = opportunity or interest rate as a decimal fraction (5% equals 0.05).

The single present-worth factor finds a value today, P, which is equivalent to a value in the future, F. That is to say, one would be equally willing to be paid P dollars today, or F dollars at a time y years in the future.

The *uniform present-worth factor* is determined by the following equation:

$$P = A \times \frac{(1+i)^y - 1}{i(1+i)^y} \qquad (13\text{-}5)$$

Fig. 13-2. Worksheet for LCCBA. In section C, *P* represents the present worth factor, and *A* represents the annual cost factor described in the text

	System 1	System 2
A. Initial Costs		
1. Lighting system: initial installed costs, all parts and labor:	_____	_____
2. Total power used by lighting system (kW):	_____	_____
3. Air conditioning tons required to dissipate heat from lighting (kW / 3.516):	_____	_____
4. First cost of air conditioning tons in line A3 @ $_____ / ton:	_____	_____
5. Reduction in first cost of heating equipment:	_____	_____
6. Utility rebates:	_____	_____
7. Other first costs engendered by the presence of the lighting systems:	_____	_____
8. Subtotal mechanical and electrical installed cost:	_____	_____
9. Initial taxes:	_____	_____
10. Total costs:	_____	_____
11. Installed cost per square meter (memo):	_____	_____
12. Watts of lighting per square meter (memo):	_____	_____
13. Residual (salvage) value at end of economic life:	_____	_____
B. Annual Power and Maintenance Costs		
1. Luminaire energy (operating hours × kW × $ / kWh):	_____	_____
2. Air conditioning energy (operating hours × tons × kW / ton × $ / kWh):	_____	_____
3. Air conditioning maintenance (tons × $ / ton):	_____	_____
4. Reduction in heating cost:	_____	_____
5. Reduced heating maintenance (MBtu × $ / MBtu):	_____	_____
6. Other annual costs engendered by the lighting system:	_____	_____
7. Cost of lamps annually (see notes):	_____	_____
8. Cost of ballast replacement (see notes):	_____	_____
9. Luminaire washing cost (number of luminaires × cost per luminaire):	_____	_____
10. Annual insurance cost:	_____	_____
11. Annual property tax cost:	_____	_____
12. Subtotal, annual power and maintenance (with income tax):	_____	_____
13. Income tax effect of depreciation:	_____	_____
C. Comparisons		
1. Present worth: *A*10 + *P*(*A*13) + *P*(*B*12 + *B*13)	_____	_____
2. Annual cost: *A*(*A*10) + *A*(*A*13) + *B*12 + *B*13	_____	_____

where

> P = present worth, or the amount at present, in dollars,
> A = amount of an annual payment, in dollars,
> y = number of years,
> i = opportunity or interest rate as a decimal fraction.

This equation converts a stream of equal annual amounts into a single present value. One would be indifferent if offered the choice of equal annual payments of A dollars for the next y years, or P dollars today.

The *uniform capital recovery factor* is

$$A = P \times \frac{i(1 + i)^y}{(1 + i)^y - 1} \qquad (13\text{-}6)$$

where

> A = amount of an annual payment, in dollars,
> P = present worth, or amount at present, in dollars,
> y = number of years,
> i = opportunity or interest rate as a decimal fraction.

The reciprocal of the uniform present-worth factor, the *uniform capital recovery factor*, is the annual amount which, in a uniform stream, is equivalent to P dollars today.

The *uniform sinking fund factor* is determined by

$$A = F \times \frac{i}{(1 + i)^y - 1} \qquad (13\text{-}7)$$

where

> F = future worth, or amount in the future, in dollars,
> A = amount of an annual payment, in dollars,
> y = number of years,
> i = opportunity or interest rate as a decimal fraction.

This equation finds an equal stream of annual amounts which is equivalent to some specified amount at a specific time in the future. Again, one is indifferent between the offer of F dollars y years from now and the offer of A dollars each year for y years.

The present worth of an escalating annual cost can be determined by one of several formulas. The general form is

$$P = \sum_{k=1}^{y} A \frac{(1 + r)^k}{(1 + i)^k} \qquad (13\text{-}8a)$$

where

P = present worth, or amount at present, in dollars,
A = *initial* annual payment, in dollars,
y = number of years,
i = opportunity or interest rate,
r = *rate of escalation*, or percentage by which the annual payment increases each year, as a decimal fraction (5% equals 0.05).

If i (the interest rate) and r (the rate of escalation) are the same, the above equation becomes

$$P = Ay \qquad (13\text{-}8b)$$

If i and r are different, it becomes

$$P = A \times \frac{(1 + r)\left[(1 + i)^y - (1 + r)^y\right]}{(1 - r)(1 + i)^y} \qquad (13\text{-}8c)$$

The systems from the worksheet can now be compared in either of two ways. Either the residual value (line A13 from figure 13-2) and annual costs (lines B12 and B13) can be converted to their present values using equations 13-4 and 13-5 respectively, or the total initial cost (line A10 from figure 13-2) and the residual value (line A13) can be converted to annualized amounts using equations 13-6 and 13-7, respectively. Once all costs for a system have been converted to either annual equivalents or present-worth equivalents, they can be summed to obtain a single value for each system. Systems can now be compared on the basis of a single number. These approaches are summarized in section C of figure 13-2.

An additional subtlety can be injected if an estimate is available for the expected rate of cost increase over time for any of the costs (for example, if it is predicted that the cost of energy will increase 5% each year over the planning horizon). Using equation 13-8a, b or c, escalation rates of this type can be applied to the annual costs of lines B1 through B11 of figure 13-2.

Notes on the Use of Equations 13-4 through 13-8: Equations 13-4 through 13-8 serve to make explicit the notion that one dollar today is not equal in value to one dollar a year from now. This is easily seen from the example of $100 deposited in an account which bears 5% annual interest. At the end of one year, the amount has grown to $100 plus 5%, or $105. Thus it can be said that $100 today is in some sense *equivalent* to $105 one year from today. In terms of equation 13-4,

$$P = F \times \frac{1}{(1 + i)^y} \qquad (13\text{-}4)$$

$$\$100 = \$105 \times \frac{1}{(1 + 0.05)^1}$$

If it is desired to know how much would need to be deposited in this account today in order to yield $100,000 20 years from now, equation 13-4 can again be applied:

$$P = \$100,000 \times \frac{1}{(1 + 0.05)^{20}}$$

$$P = \$37,689$$

Again, $37,689 today and $100,000 20 years from now are considered equivalent at an interest rate of 5%. This equivalence holds for any 20-year investment at 5% interest, including lighting systems.

Similarly, time equivalents can be computed for streams of equal annual payments or receipts. For example, if the depositor in the previous example does not have $37,689 today to deposit in an account, it might be desirable to know how much money must be set aside each year over the next 20 years in order to have $100,000 on hand at the end of that period. Equation 13-7 is used:

$$A = F \times \frac{i}{(1 + i)^y - 1} \qquad (13\text{-}7)$$

$$A = \$100,000 \times \frac{0.05}{(1 + 0.05)^{20} - 1}$$

$$A = \$3024$$

Twenty annual payments of $3024 are equivalent to $100,000, 20 years from now, if the interest rate is 5%. One might be willing to pay $3024 annually in maintenance costs to avoid the need to replace a lighting system at a cost of $100,000 after 20 years.

To illustrate the use of equation 13-5, consider a lighting retrofit that will save $10,000 per year in energy costs each year over the next 10 years. How much should one be willing to pay for this retrofit today if the interest rate is 6%?

$$P = A \times \frac{(1 + i)^y - 1}{i(1 + i)^y} \qquad (13\text{-}5)$$

$$P = \$10,000 \times \frac{(1 + 0.06)^{10} - 1}{0.06(1 + 0.06)^{10}}$$

$$P = \$73,601$$

So $73,601 today is equivalent to a stream of equal payments (or receipts) of $10,000 annually for 10 years at 6% interest.

NOTES ON THE LCCBA WORKSHEET

General Note: This section contains some explanatory information for using the LCCBA worksheet in figure 13-2. Since the analysis of lighting system economics is predominantly the analysis of costs, the convention is used that costs are positive and revenues, savings and benefits are negative. Estimates and default values listed should only be used as a last resort if actual figures are not available.

Section A

1. An estimate is prepared for material and labor of the installation. This amount is in dollars.
2. Enter the connected load of the lighting system, including ballasts and transformers, if any. This line should be in kilowatts.
3. Each lighting system introduces heat into the building which must be dissipated by the air-conditioning system. One ton of air conditioning can dissipate the heat generated by 3.516 kW of lighting (equivalent to 12,000 Btu/h). Enter the number of tons the lighting system will require.
4. Enter the first cost of the air-conditioning equipment in line A3. It will be from $1000 to $2000 per ton. Use the same value for each system. If the cooling requirements of the systems only differ by a few tons, the same nominal-size cooling plant may be used for both. For example, if one system requires 62 tons of cooling and another requires 64, then both designs might call for a 65-ton unit, and no first-cost differential would be realized. A similar caveat applies to item A5. The value on this line should be in dollars.
5. The heat generated by each lighting system will reduce the heating load on the building. This means that the heating plant can be smaller and thus the first cost of the heating plant is reduced. Enter on line A5 the amount of that reduction for each lighting system, as a negative number. Heating equipment costs range from approximately $15 to $25 per kBtu it consumes. Each kilowatt of lighting will reduce the heating needed by about 3.4 kBtu/h. This line should be in dollars. Note: If daylighting is used, it is possible that the

air-conditioning first costs may also be reduced due to exterior shading.[9]

6. In order to reduce peak demand, many electric utility companies in the United States offer lighting rebate programs which provide incentives for end users who retrofit or install energy-efficient lighting equipment in their buildings. Two types of programs are currently available: technology-based and performance-based. The technology-based programs offer cash rebates for each energy-efficient component installed. These include energy-saving lamps, electronic ballasts, reflectors and controls. The performance-based programs offer a rebate for reductions in the total lighting energy load. In some areas, rebates are available for new construction as well as retrofit. In either case, they depend on the utility company. Therefore, the designer should consult the utility which serves the site under analysis. Enter any rebates as a negative number in dollars.
7. Any other differential costs to be included, such as insulation, solar power, or tax credits, in dollars.
8. The subtotal will be the sum of lines A1, A4, A5, A6 and A7, taking proper note of signs.
9. Usually 6–8% of the first cost (line A8). Enter as a dollar amount.
10. The sum of lines A8 and A9.
11. The installed cost per square meter can be included as a memo; it does not enter into the LCCBA calculation.
12. The power density can be included as a memo; it does not enter into the LCCBA calculation.
13. The amount the system will be worth at the end of its economic life (as scrap, for example). Use the same life for each system under comparison. Note that this value is negative if money is received for the salvage; it is positive if a cost is incurred to dispose of the system at the end of its life. This amount is in dollars.

Section B

1. The number of operating hours and cost per kilowatthour will depend upon occupancy schedules and local power rates. Ten hours a day, five days a week, 52 weeks per year represents 2600 h. In the United States, the average energy cost for commercial, institutional and industrial customers is on the order of 8–9 ¢/kWh. This line will be in dollars.

2. The number of tons of air conditioning should come from line A3. The number of kilowatts per ton for a central plant will be approximately 1.25. The value in this line is in dollars.
3. This value can be approximated by $150/ton times the air conditioning tons from line A3, in dollars.
4. This is the reduction in the annual cost of fuel for heating equipment due to increased heat obtained from the lighting system. The number of heating hours can be obtained by the formula

$$\text{heating hours} = (\text{lighting hours}) \times 0.85$$
$$- (\text{cooling hours})$$

The heat from the lighting system in MBtu is given by

$$(\text{kW of lighting}) \times (3.413 \text{ MBtu/kWh})$$
$$\times (\text{heating hours})$$

To convert costs of typical fuels to dollars per MBtu, multiply the cost of fuel (such as $0.80/gal for fuel oil) by the corresponding value in column 4 of figure 13-3 (such as 10 gal/MBtu). For example, if the price of electricity is $0.10/kWh, the cost per MBtu is ($0.10/kWh) × (293 kWh/MBtu) = $29.30/MBtu. If the price of fuel oil is $0.80/gal, the cost per MBtu is ($0.80/gal) × (10 gal/MBtu) = $8.00/MBtu. The annual reduction in heating energy costs then becomes

$$(\text{MBtu of heat from lighting})$$
$$\times (\text{fuel cost per MBtu})$$

This value should be in dollars. Note: If daylighting is used, the effects of shading devices on air conditioning costs should also be considered.[9]
5. Heating maintenance costs can be approximated by $2/MBtu. Multiply by the number of MBtu of heat from lighting to get a dollar amount.

Fig. 13-3. Conversion Factors for Various Fuels

Fuel	Fuel Efficiency	Unit Energy	Fuel to obtain 1 MBtu
Electric heat	1.0	0.0034 MBtu / kWh	293 kWh
Coal	0.65	30 MBtu / ton	0.05 ton
No. 2 fuel oil	0.70	0.14 MBtu / gal	10 gal
Natural gas	0.70	1.0 MBtu / mCF	1.4 mCF / MBtu

6. Other costs may include costs, in dollars, for inspection of the lighting system.
7. The cost of lamps per year will depend on the relamping strategy. If spot relamping is used, then the lamp cost per year is figured from

$$\frac{(\text{cost for spot replacement of one lamp}) \times (\text{number of lamps in the system})}{(\text{lamp life})/(\text{annual burning hours})}$$

For group relamping, use

$$(\text{number of lamps replaced per year})$$
$$\times (\text{cost per lamp of group relamping})$$

Either way, the number on this line should be a dollar amount.
8. To annualize ballast costs, use

$$\frac{(\text{cost to replace one ballast}) \times (\text{number of ballasts in the system})}{(\text{ballast life})/(\text{annual burning hours})}$$

This amount is in dollars.
9. Multiply the number of luminaires by the cost to clean a single luminaire to obtain the annual cost in dollars.
10. Approximately 1–1.5% of first cost.
11. Approximately 4–6% of first cost.
12. The annual expenses of lines B1 through B11 serve to reduce the owner's income tax liability based on the income tax rate (ITR). The net cost of these items is entered as

$$(B1 + B2 + B3 + B4 + B5 + B6$$
$$+ B7 + B8 + B9 + B10 + B11) \times (1 - \text{ITR})$$

13. Depreciation reduces the owner's income tax liability. Assuming the asset is depreciated by the same amount each year (straight-line depreciation), the annual depreciation amount is given by

$$D = \frac{\text{initial cost from line A10}}{\text{economic life of system}}$$

If the owner's income tax rate (ITR) is expressed as a decimal fraction, then the tax effect is $T = D \times \text{ITR}$. This should be entered as a negative dollar amount, since it is a benefit or saving.

Section C

1. A present-worth comparison is done by finding "time zero" equivalents of all future costs and adding those to the initial costs of line A10.

Equation 13-5 is used to convert the annual values in B12 and B13 to their equivalents at time zero. Use equation 13-1 to convert the residual value (A13).

2. An annual-cost comparison requires that all one-time costs (initial costs and residual values) be converted to annual equivalents. These are then added to the annual energy and maintenance costs. Use equation 13-6 to convert the initial cost of line A10 to its annual equivalent. The residual value (line A13) is converted to an annual value using equation 13-7.

REFERENCES

1. Mangold, S. A. 1974. Lighting economics based on proper maintenance. *Light. Des. Appl.* 4(8):6–11.

2. Merril, G. S. 1937. The economics of light production with incandescent lamps, with particular reference to operating voltage. *Trans. Illum. Eng. Soc.* 32(10):1077–1090.

3. Helms, R. N., and M. C. Belcher. 1991. Lighting economics. In *Lighting for energy-efficient luminous environments,* chapter 14. Englewood Cliffs, NJ: Prentice-Hall.

4. Belcher, M. C. 1989. Lighting cost analysis: Is there a better way? *Light. Des. Appl.* 19(6):14–21.

5. Belcher, M. C. 1989. MCSEALS: A Monte Carlo simulation for economic analysis of lighting systems. *J. Illum. Eng. Soc.* 18(2):40–51.

6. IES. Design Practice Committee. 1980. Life cycle cost analysis of electric lighting systems. *Light. Des. Appl.* 10(5):43–48.

7. Horngren, C. T. 1982. *Cost accounting: A managerial emphasis.* 5th ed. Englewood Cliffs, NJ: Prentice-Hall.

8. DeLaney, W. B. 1973. How much does a lighting system really cost? *Light. Des. Appl.* 3(1):22–28.

9. IES. Daylighting Committee. 1979. *Recommended practice of daylighting, IES RP 5-1979.* New York: Illuminating Engineering Society of North America.

Codes and Standards

14

A myriad of codes, regulations and standards affect lighting design and the choice of lighting equipment. These include local, state, national and international codes and professional and manufacturers' standards. Standards do not bear the force of law, but are generally followed by the lighting industry. Anything written into law is, of course, mandatory. Because the laws differ geographically and with the end use of equipment, it is imperative to be familiar with those that are applicable.

Codes and regulations fall essentially within two categories:

- Energy-saving codes
- Safety and construction codes

The first category covers any type of code or regulation dealing with ways to save energy through the efficient use of electric lighting. The codes establish limitations which set maximum power density values for lighting systems used in buildings, and codes that set minimum efficiency or efficacy (lumens per watt) values for lighting equipment.

The second category of codes relates to specific safety and construction requirements which must be met in the construction, installation and maintenance of a luminaire.

Another important code in the United States is the Americans With Disabilities Act (ADA) of 1990,[1] which deals with many issues, including accessibility for all persons in public areas and commercial facilities. The guidelines of the ADA are to be applied during the design, construction and renovation of public buildings and facilities. The technical specifications of these guidelines are generally the same as those of the American National Standards Institute (ANSI) A117.1-1986[2] with a few exceptions. Issues that pertain to lighting include regulations for the positioning and visibility of signals for elevators as well as prescribed illumination levels for elevator interiors and thresholds; specifications for visual alarm signals; recommendations for visibility of signage; and requirements for mounting heights and projections of wall-mounted luminaires.

ENERGY-SAVING CODES

In October 1992, the U.S. federal government passed the Energy Policy Act of 1992 (PL102-486)[3] as an amendment to the Energy Policy and Conservation Act originally passed in 1975. The legislation includes provisions that encourage electric utilities to invest in conservation and energy efficiency, as well as funding for establishing energy-efficient lighting and building centers. There are also regulations mandating energy-efficient lighting, including:

1. Prescriptive (application) codes requiring states to establish energy standards for lighting in buildings
2. Component codes requiring efficacy standards and labeling for lamps manufactured or imported for sale in the United States and calling for development of a voluntary national testing and information program for luminaires

State laws are directly affected by the Energy Policy Act.

Lighting Application Codes for Buildings

Currently, many states in the United States have no lighting application codes designed to save energy, or base their codes on outdated standards. In most states, the lighting code appears within an energy code that is part of a building construction code. Usually lighting application codes apply only to new buildings or substantial renovations. The most common approach is to limit the amount of power allowed for a lighting system.

PL102-486 requires each state to review the energy efficiency provisions of its building code by October 1994. State codes must then meet or exceed these standards:

- For residential buildings: Council of American Building Officials (CABO) Model Energy Code[4] (latest revision)

- For commercial buildings: American Society of Heating, Refrigerating, and Air-Conditioning Engineers/Illuminating Engineering Society of North America (ASHRAE/IES) Standard 90.1-1989[5] (or subsequent revisions)

In addition, new federal buildings, homes financed with federal mortgages, and improvements in federal facilities must comply with the appropriate standard(s).

Chapter 30, Energy Management, gives a detailed description of the methodology of ASHRAE/IES Standard 90.1-1989, which is an application code. The CABO code is a revised method of lighting evaluation based on previous ASHRAE/IES standards. An ASHRAE committee was appointed in 1993 to develop a code language for ASHRAE/IES 90.1-1989. The CABO Model Energy Code is a model code that can be adopted by a state directly, in whole or in part, as an application code.

California Code. An example of a state performance code is the California State Building Code Title 24,[6] which gives mandatory efficiency requirements for non-residential lighting. It applies whenever a permit is required for work within a building. Lighting power levels can be checked for compliance in any one of three ways: complete building, area category or tailored (room by room). Credits are given for lighting controls.

The whole-building method requires comparison of the adjusted actual power (power minus control credits) with the power allowed for the building. However, in many cases, buildings are built without all the lighting designed and installed, so this method is difficult to use. In such cases, the area category method is the simplest: the square footages of all spaces in each category are totaled and multiplied by the lighting power density allowed for each area. Details on room cavity ratios and specific tasks and locations are not required.

The tailored approach is the most complicated, but is useful when there are special lighting requirements for a space.

California's Title 24 requires automatic shutoff controls for lighting on each floor of a building, except for buildings or separately metered spaces under 5000 sq. ft. Such lighting controls must be certified as meeting the specified minimum requirements.

Equipment Codes: National

A component approach to energy saving requires the use of efficient lighting equipment. For example, the National Appliance Energy Conservation Amendments of 1988 mandate the use of efficient ballasts for fluorescent lighting systems.

Fig. 14-1. Effective Dates for Lamp Requirements According to the Energy Policy Act of 1992

Lamp Efficacy (LPW) Standards	
Incandescent reflector and selected fluorescent lamps:	
Minimum standards issued:	October 1992
Lamps in compliance:	
244-cm (96-in.) slimline; 244-cm (96-in.) high-output fluorescent	April 1994
122-cm (48-in.) medium bipin; 61-cm (24-in.) U-shaped fluorescent	October 1995
Incandescent reflector lamps	October 1995
Selected HID lamps:*	
Testing requirements prescribed:	April 1995
Minimum standards issued:	October 1996
Lamps in compliance:	October 1999
Lamp Labeling Requirements	
General-service incandescent and general-service and medium-base compact fluorescent lamps:	
Requirements prescribed:	April 1994
Lamps in compliance:	April 1995
Selected HID lamps:*	
Requirements prescribed:	April 1997
Lamps in compliance:	October 1997

*This standard will apply only if the U.S. Department of Energy decides to prescribe efficacy standards and labeling requirements for HID lamps.

The National Energy Policy Act of 1992 requires conformance with performance standards, as described above, and also mandates component standards in the United States. The new component requirements include labeling and minimum efficacy (lm/W) values for specific lamp types, along with plans for energy efficiency testing procedures and labeling for luminaires. Testing, efficacy and labeling requirements will be phased in over a period of time, as shown in figure 14-1.

Lamp Standards. The labeling portion of the Act covers these lamps (other than exempted types):

- Nonreflector general-service incandescent lamps (30 W and up, medium base, 115–130 V)
- PAR, R, and similar reflector incandescent lamps (40 W and up, medium base, 115–130 V)
- General-service fluorescent lamps (122-cm [48-in.] medium bipin, 61-cm [24-in.] U-shaped, 244-cm [96-in.] slimline, 244-cm [96-in.] high-output)
- Medium-base compact fluorescent lamps

Within 12 months of publication of labeling requirements, these lamps must bear conspicuous labels giving such information as is deemed necessary to enable consumers to select the most energy-efficient lamps which meet their requirements. The required label information for incandescent lamps will be based on 120-V operation regardless of rated voltage. Excluded are specialty incandescent lamps, such as those in-

Fig. 14-2. Standards for Fluorescent Lamps According to the Energy Policy Act of 1992

Lamp Type	Nominal Lamp Wattage	Minimum CRI	Minimum Efficacy	Effective Date
122-cm (4-ft)	over 35	69	75	October 1995
medium bipin	35 or less	45	75	October 1995
61-cm (2-ft)	over 35	69	68	October 1995
U-shaped	35 or less	45	64	October 1995
244-cm (8-ft)	over 65	69	80	April 1994
slimline	65 or less	45	80	April 1994
244-cm (8-ft)	over 100	69	80	April 1994
high output	100 or less	45	80	April 1994

Fig. 14-3. Standards for Incandescent Reflector Lamps According to the Energy Policy Act of 1992*

Nominal Lamp Wattage	Minimum Lamp Efficacy (LPW)	Effective Date
40 – 50	10.5	October 1995
51 – 66	11.0	October 1995
67 – 85	12.5	October 1995
86 – 115	14.0	October 1995
116 – 155	14.5	October 1995
156 – 205	15.0	October 1995

*These standards apply to lamps with a medium base, voltage between 115 and 130 V and diameter greater than 7 cm (2.75 in.).

tended for traffic signals, aviation service, photography, dental service, microscopes or swimming pools. Fluorescent lamps for specialized applications are also not covered (for example, lamps for plant growth and for low-temperature applications, impact-resistant lamps and high-color-rendering lamps with a color rendering index of at least 82).

Minimum lamp efficacy (LPW) values for general-service fluorescent lamps and incandescent reflector lamps were established in the Act (see figures 14-2 and 14-3). "Minimum lamp efficacy" is the minimum average lumen-per-watt readings taken over a statistically significant period of manufacture.

The only incandescent reflector lamps that must conform to the standards are those between 40 and 205 W, medium screw base, 115 to 130 V, with diameters greater than 7 cm (2.75 in.). Some types of reflector lamps are exempted. Incandescent lamps other than reflector lamps are not covered.

Lamps must meet these standards by specified dates (see figure 14-1). In addition, the fluorescent lamps mentioned in the Act must have a minimum color rendering index (CRI), as shown in figure 14-2.

The United States Department of Energy (DOE) will prescribe efficacy standards and testing requirements for HID lamps if such standards would be "technologically feasible and economically justified and would result in significant energy savings."[3] If such standards are deemed appropriate, testing procedures must be developed by April 1995. The government will have then issued energy conservation standards by October 1996, with compliance required within three

years. The DOE will mandate labeling requirements for HID lamps within six months after publication of the standards, if such standards are developed.

Luminaire Standards. The Energy Policy Act of 1992 calls for a voluntary national testing and information program for luminaires. The DOE and the lighting industry will work together to determine which luminaires are covered and to specify test procedures and appropriate written information for labels and publications. The goal is to facilitate consumer assessment of energy consumption and potential cost savings with alternative products. Luminaires to be evaluated are those that are "widely used and for which there is a potential for significant energy savings as a result of such a program."[3]

DOE will monitor the voluntary program until October 1995. At that time, if DOE decides the program is working, it will continue as a voluntary effort. If not, DOE will take over and mandate test procedures and labeling requirements for luminaires.

As with the lamp standards, this is a component approach to energy saving.

Equipment Codes: State[7]

Most states have codes mandating an application approach to energy conservation. An exception is New York State, which has a comprehensive code based on both an application and an equipment approach. The New York State Energy Conservation Construction Code of 1991 establishes minimum efficacies for fluorescent lamps and minimum total efficiency values for luminaires used for general lighting and for fluorescent lamp ballasts. The standards for fluorescent lamps and ballasts are the same as the federal standards.

Lamp regulations set minimum values for efficacy and for color rendering indices (CRI). In New York, as well as in the federal standard, CRI values are included to preclude the use of full-wattage halophosphor fluorescent lamps, which have lower CRIs and lower lamp efficacies than triphosphor fluorescent lamps.

Luminaire standards set minimum total luminaire efficiencies based on the lumen distribution, categorized as narrow, moderate or wide. The New York code also establishes minimum ballast efficiencies for some types of fluorescent lamp ballasts. Automatic controls are required for some applications.

SAFETY AND CONSTRUCTION CODES

The second category of codes and regulations does not involve power considerations. These codes set minimum standards for safety or construction. Some codes and standards deal with electrical, mechanical and thermal safety. Others mandate the use of certain materials or finishes in construction.

Local, State and National Standards

The National Electrical Code (NEC),[8] the Canadian Electrical Code (CEC),[9] and similar codes in most major countries throughout the world state specific electrical requirements which must be met by all electrical equipment, including luminaires. They have been developed by safety protection and inspection agencies in conjunction with fire protection associations.

The NEC is a minimum standard for safety in the design, installation, use and maintenance of electrical systems. It is specific, covering each requirement in detail. For example, see chapter 7, Luminaires, for a discussion of thermal considerations and codes.

Local agencies may or may not accept the NEC in whole or in part. Information regarding local codes may be obtained from electrical inspection departments.

Most state, county and city code jurisdictions also operate under one of the following codes:

- Building Officials and Code Administrators International (BOCA), Basic Building Code
- Southern Building Code Congress International (SBCC), Standard Building Code
- International Conference of Building Officials (ICBO), Uniform Building Code

All these codes contain sections controlling the use of materials in luminaires and luminous ceilings.

Conformance to the appropriate set of specifications is often determined by certified laboratory tests. These tests can be performed following standards set by Underwriters Laboratories, Inc. (UL), the Canadian Standards Association (CSA) or similar laboratories or associations in other countries. These organizations publish minimum safety standards for electrical and associated products; the standards are in conformance with the electrical code of the country of origin.

These associations have laboratories to which luminaires and their component parts must be submitted for listing. Certification is often denoted by an identifying label showing that a product has passed the tests needed for that particular listing. Most manufacturers design luminaires to meet UL, CSA or similar standards.

Industry Standards

Industry standards are published by professional societies, associations and institutes, in most cases utilizing national technical committees. Represented on these committees are inspection and safety protection agencies, manufacturers, professionals and consumers. Conformance to such standards may be desirable or specified, but is otherwise not binding.

Such organizations include:

- ASTM (American Society for Testing and Materials)
- CBM (Certified Ballast Manufacturers)
- IEEE (Institute of Electrical and Electronic Engineers)
- IESNA (Illuminating Engineering Society of North America)
- NEMA (National Electrical Manufacturers Association)
- ANSI (American National Standards Institute)
- ASHRAE (American Society of Heating, Refrigerating, and Air-Conditioning Engineers)

United States Government Standards

Standards written by the following and similar federal agencies are usually for their own requirements:

- BuShips (Bureau of Ships)
- CAB (Civil Aeronautics Board)
- FAA (Federal Aviation Administration)
- GSA (General Services Administration)
- USCG (US Coast Guard)
- CE (Corps of Engineers)

Sometimes these and similar agencies write regulations concerning nonfederal commercial applications. For instance, chapter 25, Aviation Lighting, gives information about regulations for safety lighting on aircraft and other safety requirements specified by federal or international law. Regulations concerning automotive and ship lighting are discussed in chapter 26, Transportation Lighting.

Codes Regulating Luminaire Choice or Construction

It is important to choose the correct luminaire for a particular application. The NEC includes definitions of different types of ordinary and hazardous or other specialized locations and specifies which UL listings lighting equipment must have to be used safely in each type of situation.

Damp Locations. The NEC defines a damp location as one that is partially protected, such as an open porch with a roof, or an area covered by a canopy or marquee. Some interior spaces subject to moderate degrees of moisture are also damp locations. Examples include barns, basements and cold-storage warehouses. Luminaires used for these and similar situations should be UL listed and labeled "Suitable for Damp Locations." A luminaire listed for use in wet locations is also suitable is also suitable for damp locations. Section 410-4 of the NEC gives guidelines for installation in these environments.

Wet Locations. As defined by the NEC, a wet location is one with installations underground, in concrete slabs or masonry in direct contact with the earth, in locations subject to saturation with water or other liquids, and in unprotected locations exposed to weather.

The NEC requires that luminaires for wet locations be so labeled by the manufacturer under authority from the UL. UL Standards 1570, 1571 and 1572 cover the minimum design requirements of such luminaires in detail. Article 680 of the NEC and UL Standard 676 specifically cover swimming pools. See also NEC, Articles 410-4.

Corrosive Locations. In some areas, lighting equipment is subject to unusually corrosive atmospheres. The presence of airborne corrosive or abrasive agents or salt water can lead to rapid depreciation of exposed or unprotected surfaces. Smoke- and grease-laden atmospheres can also be damaging.

The NEC gives guidelines for the characteristics of all materials used where corrosive or severe local atmospheric conditions are anticipated. Luminaires must be UL listed for use in such environments. For marine use, consult UL-595.[10]

Hazardous (Classified) Locations. The NEC defines hazardous (classified) locations as those in which there is danger of fire or explosion because of the presence or possible presence of flammable gases or vapors (Class I), combustible dusts (Class II) or easily ignitable fibers or flyings (Class III).[11] These three classes are further divided into divisions and then into groups (see figure 14-4). Division 1 areas are those where the flammable materials are continuously present. A Division 2 classification means that the flammable materials are not normally present, but may be.

Groups are letter designations denoting the physical properties of the hazardous materials. There are no groups given for Class III locations. It is up to the authority having jurisdiction (AHJ) to classify an area, but the NEC gives detailed guidelines.

There are also Canadian equivalents to these classifications, requiring labeling by the CSA.

Lighting equipment for hazardous locations must bear a label showing that it is approved by the UL for the environment in which it is to be used or installed. To obtain approval for such labeling, the construction

Fig. 14-4. Classifications for Hazardous Locations Based on the National Electrical Code (NEC)

NEC Class	Division		Group*
I Flammable gases or vapors	1	Normally hazardous	A, B, C, D
	2	Not normally hazardous	A, B, C, D
II Combustible dusts	1	Normally hazardous	E, F, G
	2	Not normally hazardous	G
III Easily ignitable fibers or flyings	1, 2		None

*Group designations are based on the particular properties of the specific hazardous agent(s) present.

must comply with UL Standard 844, "Electric Lighting Fixtures for Use in Hazardous Locations." General requirements for hazardous locations are covered in articles 500 through 517 of the NEC.

Some industries have additional requirements. For example, flour mills and elevators are covered by the Electrical Code of the Mill Mutual Fire Prevention Bureau, 2 North Riverside Plaza, Chicago, IL 60606.

There are also more restrictive local codes, such as in New York City, Chicago and Los Angeles.

The design of lighting equipment for hazardous locations is a highly specialized topic. It is imperative that the designer be completely familiar with the latest versions of the applicable codes and regulations.

Emergency Lighting. Requirements for emergency lighting are covered in chapter 33, Safety, Security and Emergency Lighting. For instance, the chapter includes detailed information on exit-sign characteristics mandated by codes and standards.

The lighting designer should be aware of the following North American codes applicable to emergency lighting:

- NFPA 101—National Fire Protection Association Life Safety Code
- BOCA—Building Officials and Code Administrators International, Inc., Basic Building Code
- UBC—Uniform Building Code—International Conference of Building Officials
- Standard Building Code—Southern Building Code Congress International
- NFPA 70—National Electrical Code
- NFPA 99—Standard for Health Care Facilities
- NFPA 497M—Standard for Electrical Installation for Hazardous (Classified) Location—Gases, Vapors, Dust

- NFPA 110—Standard for Emergency and Standby Power Systems
- NFPA 171—Standard for Fire Safety Symbols
- Canadian Occupational Safety and Health (COSH)—Standard issued by Labour Canada in 1989, applicable for federal work places.
- National Building Code of Canada, Associate Committee of the National Building Code, National Research Council Canada, Institute for Research in Construction, Ottawa, 1990. Recommended practice for building construction, used as a model for most jurisdictions.
- National Fire Code of Canada—Associate Committee of the National Fire Code, National Research Council Canada, Institute for Research in Construction, Ottawa, 1990. Recommended practice for fire prevention, including maintenance of emergency lighting equipment and backup power supplies.
- Canadian National Master Construction Specification C-NMS16519. Specification for products purchased by the Canadian Government.
- Canadian Standards Association C22.1-1986—Canadian Electrical Code, Part 1, 1986.
- Mexico—Authorities state they use emergency products and leave the standard to the consulting engineers.
- Commission Internationale de l'Éclairage (CIE), *Guide on the Emergency Lighting of Building Interiors*. CIE No. 49 (TC4-1). Paris, 1981.
- Underwriters Laboratories (UL) Inc., *Emergency Lighting and Power Equipment, UL 924, Exit Fixture and Exit Light Visibility*. March 2, 1989. Copyright 1973, 1989.

This list represents suggested codes to consult, but is by no means all-inclusive. These codes are often modified by the authorities having jurisdiction (local, county, city or state). Other sources to consult are Department of Health and Human Services Guidelines and local or state board of education requirements, as applicable to the occupancy.

Wiring Codes and Standards

Although the National Electrical Code does not purport to be a design manual, the lighting designer and engineer should be familiar with recommended minimum lighting circuit capacities. The circuit capacities required are frequently far in excess of that required by modern efficient lighting systems.

Wiring design information based on current good practice for specific applications may be found in the latest editions of the following publications:

- *IEEE Recommended Practice for Electric Power Systems in Commercial Buildings*, IEEE No. 241, Institute of Electrical and Electronic Engineers, New York
- *IEEE Recommended Practice for Electric Power Distribution for Industrial Plants*, IEEE No. 141, Institute of Electrical and Electronic Engineers, New York
- *Standard Handbook for Electrical Engineers*, McGraw-Hill, New York
- *Electrical Engineers' Handbook*, Wiley, New York
- *American Electricians' Handbook*, McGraw-Hill, New York

Codes Regulating Disposal of Ballasts and Lamps

Another safety consideration is the disposal of materials considered to be hazardous waste. According to U.S. law, leaking ballasts containing PCBs (polychlorinated biphenyl compounds) are classified as hazardous waste and must be disposed of in the manner prescribed by the law. Some states and municipalities have stringent laws covering the disposal of any ballasts containing PCBs. Chapter 34, Environmental Issues, gives information on proper disposal methods.

That chapter also covers the disposal of lamps containing mercury, which is currently regulated by law in California and Minnesota. Other states are considering such legislation.

REFERENCES

1. U.S. Congress. *Americans with disabilities act of 1990, PL101-336.* Washington: U.S. Government Printing Office.
2. American National Standards Institute. 1986. *American national standard for buildings and facilities: Providing accessibility and usability for physically handicapped people, ANSI A117.1–1986.* New York: American National Standards Institute.
3. U.S. Congress. 1992. *Energy policy act of 1992, PL 102–486.* Washington, DC: U.S. Government Printing Office.
4. Council of American Building Officials. 1989. *Model energy code.* Falls Church, VA: Council of American Building Officials.
5. American Society of Heating, Refrigerating and Air-Conditioning Engineers and Illuminating Engineering Society of North America. 1989. *Energy efficient design of new buildings except new low-rise residential buildings, ASHRAE / IES 90.1-1989.* Atlanta, GA: American Society of Heating, Refrigerating and Air-Conditioning Engineers.
6. Berryman, F. W. 1992. California's new Title 24 lighting energy standards: A golden opportunity for lighting management companies. *Lighting Management & Maintenance (LM & M)* 20(11):14–15, 18–19.

7. Davis, R. G., and S. A. Meyers. 1992. *Lighting regulation in the United States.* Troy, NY: Rensselaer Polytechnic Institute.

8. National Fire Protection Association. 1990. *National electrical code, NFPA 70.* Quincy, MA: National Fire Protection Association.

9. Canadian Standards Association. 1975. *Canadian electrical code: Safety standard for electrical installations, CSA standard C22.1-1975.* Rexdale, Ont.: Canadian Standards Association.

10. Underwriters Laboratories. 1974. *Standard for safety: Marine-type electric lighting fixtures, UL-595.* Northbrook, IL: Underwriters Laboratories.

11. Underwriters Laboratories. 1976. *Standard for safety: Electric lighting fixtures for use in hazardous locations, UL-844.* Northbrook, IL: Underwriters Laboratories.

Lighting Applications

Office Lighting

15

This chapter deals with the lighting of working and associated circulation spaces found in office buildings.

THE IMPORTANCE OF LIGHTING IN THE OFFICE ENVIRONMENT

Offices are designed to house working people engaged in thought and in a number of forms of communication (written, visual, telephone, computer and face to face). Office lighting should enable workers (who typically spend one-third of their waking hours there) to perform these tasks effectively.

Since feelings of well-being, interest and enthusiasm, which tend to enhance productivity, are affected by the environment, consideration should be given to the design of office interiors in an effort to achieve a stimulating work place. The visual effect of lighting is of major importance as part of the total office environment.

Office lighting affects the appearance of the space and its occupants, mood or affect, and productivity level. An equally important consideration, however, is to provide for visibility of the visual tasks to be performed. Both visibility values (quantity and quality of light) and aesthetic values (occupant perceptions and mood) must be considered in lighting the environment.

It is convenient to consider the luminous environment and the lighting of visual tasks separately. However, these aspects must work together to provide both a stimulating and comfortable environment and good visibility. Indeed, the same lighting system may contribute to both (as in general lighting), or separate luminaires may provide or augment the lighting for the visual task.

Efficient energy use in achieving these goals is critical to office lighting design. Reduced operating costs and reductions in environmental pollution are worthy benefits of a conscientious energy philosophy.

THE LUMINOUS ENVIRONMENT

Composition of the Luminous Environment

The visual effect of an office space depends on variations in perceived luminance and color. These may be achieved by varying surface reflectance, color or illuminance. Shadow, as a design element, is just as important as light. One commonly employed example of varying luminance, called *wall washing*, provides a greater luminance of the wall than of the ceiling or floor. Another example is local task lighting that provides pools of higher luminance within a large space. This kind of luminance variation at the workstation helps give office workers a sense of place within an open office. Careful design will provide interesting variations without producing distracting or uncomfortable luminance differences.

Color

Both surface color and light source color play important roles in the office lighting environment. Color adds visual interest to a space, making it a more inviting and pleasant place in which to work. The spectral composition of the light source is critical if detailed color work is being performed. The spectral composition of the light source can determine the general overall appearance of people, furnishings and room surfaces and should therefore be selected carefully.

Surface Colors. In the office, where workers are exposed to the same environment for long periods of time, the color in that environment can affect performance positively or negatively, even if workers are not aware of this effect. Small offices can be made to appear larger and less crowded if woodwork and furniture placed against walls have the same hue or a similar reflectance. Touches of accent color will give vitality and dramatic interest to any office area. Contrasting colors, or light and dark values of the same color, may be used at some point or points in the room. These may be in wall coverings, furniture upholstery, or pictures or tapestries. Colors selected for large surface areas should have reflectances as recommended in figure 15-1. At low illuminance levels, interior spaces may be made to appear sharper or brighter by creating more color contrast through the use of more colorful surfaces.

Light Source Color. There are two distinct application considerations with respect to color and light sources,

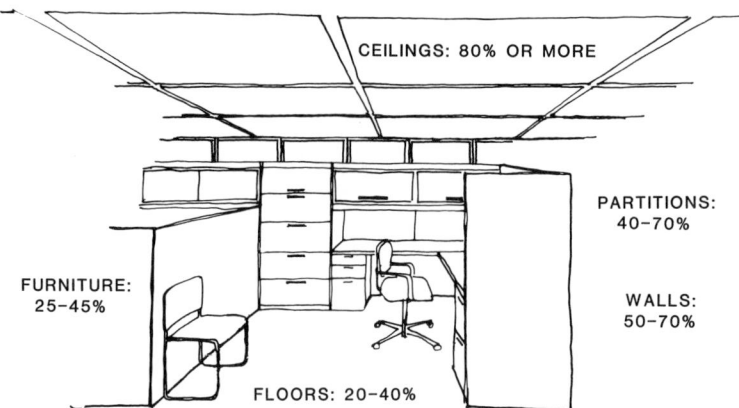

Fig. 15-1. Reflectances recommended for room and furniture surfaces in offices.

namely, the chromaticity (correlated color tempera-ture) and the color rendering properties of the light source.

Chromaticity refers to the color appearance of the lighted source and is designated by its correlated color temperature in kelvins. See chapter 4, Color. In inte-rior spaces such as offices, a source will create a "warm" environment if its correlated color tem-perature is about 3000 K or lower, and a "cool" en-vironment if 4000 K or higher. A correlated color temperature between these two is considered neutral. Individuals will vary in their preference for warm, neutral or cool environments. See chapter 6, Light Sources.

The perceived color of an object will be affected by the color rendering properties of the lamp. The color rendering index (CRI) is a measure of the color shift induced by a given lamp relative to a standard lamp of the same correlated color temperature. The maximum CRI value is 100. Where color discrimination is an important part of the work (for example, color match-ing in an advertising agency), a source with a color rendering index of 90 or higher should be employed.

Two lamps with the same chromaticity may have different color rendering characteristics. Fluorescent lamps are now available that offer the designer several chromaticities with good to excellent color rendering and high luminous efficacy. The color rendering prop-erties of various lamps can be demonstrated by in-stalling them in display boxes or rooms, each having an identical presentation of colored objects.

Light source selection depends on the importance given to color rendering, the initial cost, the lamping and maintenance costs, and the energy costs. Because different sources render colors differently, it is impor-tant that the sources scheduled by the designer be used in the actual lighting system implementation to achieve the desired effects. If daylight will be present in the office, the colors should be viewed under the electric light source with and without the expected daylight

contribution (taking into account possible tinting of the fenestration).

Luminance Differences

Luminance differences are usually necessary for vision. Print may be seen and interpreted because of the difference in luminance between the white page and black print. Similarly, an interior space will be seen and interpreted because of the luminance differences of the surfaces. Luminance variations are a function of both the reflectances of the surfaces and the distribu-tion of light on those surfaces.

Large luminance variations can be problematic. Of-fice interiors should be lighted to provide for good visibility with no distracting glare. Direct and reflected glare should be avoided; however, it is important to provide enough variation in luminance (or color) to contribute to a stimulating, attractive environment. Where there are no prolonged visual tasks, as in lob-bies, corridors, and reception, conference, lounge and dining areas, greater variations in luminance are en-couraged, using attractive colors and appropriate focal points of high contrast to catch the eye.

Luminance-Ratio Limits. For a working office environ-ment, luminances near each task and in other parts of the office interior within the field of view should be balanced with the task luminance. Two separate phe-nomena are influenced by the luminance ratios within the field of view: transient adaptation and disability glare. To limit the effects of these phenomena, the luminance ratios generally should not exceed the fol-lowing:

Between paper task and adjacent VDT screen:	3:1	or 1:3
Between task and adjacent dark surroundings:	3:1	or 1:3
Between task and remote (nonadjacent) surfaces:	10:1	or 1:10

It is not, however, practical or esthetically desirable to maintain these ratios throughout the entire environment. For visual interest and distant eye focus (for periodic eye muscle relaxation throughout the day), small visual areas which exceed the luminance-ratio recommendations are desirable. This would include artwork, accent finishes on walls, ceilings or floors, small window areas, accent finishes on chairs and accessories, and accent focal lighting.

Transient Adaptation. The visual system adjusts its operating characteristics as a result of changes in the brightnesses within the field of view. Photochemical, neurological and pupillary changes occur in this adaptation process. Neural changes occur most quickly, though while the visual system readjusts, visual capabilities are temporarily impaired. This is known as transient adaptation, and takes a very short time (less than 200 ms) for completion. Photochemical changes occur much more slowly and are most noticeable when there is a dramatic change in ambient light level, such as moving from full daylight into a dark theater. Pupillary changes are relatively insignificant in the adaptation process. See chapter 3, Vision and Perception.

Disability Glare. Glare sources within the field of view may cause stray light within the ocular media of the eye. This light is in turn superimposed upon the retinal image. This reduces the contrast of the image and may thus reduce visibility and performance.

Reflectances and Finishes. The brightnesses of objects depend upon illuminance as well as surface reflectance. For example, reading 80%-reflectance white paper on an evenly illuminated desk top will require that the desk top have a reflectance of at least 27% (one-third of 80%) in order to comply with the 3:1 guideline for the ratio between the luminance of the task and its immediate surrounding. Thus, reflectance as well as illuminance levels are important in office lighting design.

Surface specularity, or gloss, must also be considered. Glossy surfaces are more mirrorlike and produce images of the luminaires that can result in reflected glare, a *patch* of very high luminance. Glossy horizontal work surfaces are particularly troublesome. They may reflect bright images of ceiling-mounted downlighting luminaires to the worker. For this reason, shiny work surfaces should be avoided. See figure 15-2.

If shiny horizontal surfaces cannot be avoided for some reason, a relatively low-luminance indirect lighting system may be used to provide ambient illuminance. It is important that the luminaires have a broad light distribution pattern to provide essentially even luminance of the ceiling. Even though there will be a brightness contrast between the illuminated ceiling and the underside of the indirect luminaire, the ceiling

Fig. 15-2. The streaks of light are reflected images of two continuous rows of luminaires. A very severe glare condition is produced by a desk top which is both dark and specular. The reflected glare disappears when a piece of light matte material is placed over the dark, specular top.

reflections from the glossy work surface will be limited to a low, even luminance, and reflected glare will be avoided. Local task lighting located on one or both sides of the task may be used to supplement the ambient illuminance. By placing this lighting to the sides of the work area, reflected glare from the shiny desk top will be minimized for the worker's viewing position.

In private offices, direct ceiling-mounted luminaires may be located beside or behind shiny work surfaces so that, again, specular reflections of the luminaires in the desk top are directed away from the viewing position.

Visual Comfort

Discomfort glare is a sensation of annoyance produced by light in the visual field that is significantly higher than the luminance to which the visual system is adapted. The magnitude of the sensation depends upon the size, position, relative luminance and number of sources in the field of view.

Luminaires. A comparison of glare control from various luminaires can be made from photometric reports by comparing the average luminance values produced at 0° (vertical), 45°, 55°, 65°, 75° and 85° in the lengthwise, crosswise and (sometimes) diagonal planes.

A more comprehensive comparison can be made by using the *visual comfort probability* (VCP) calculation. See chapter 9, Lighting Calculations. It is recommended that office lighting systems should have a VCP of 70 or greater. Since the operation of a visual display terminal (VDT) requires a heads-up, near-horizontal viewing position, several luminaires may be in view behind the VDT. To minimize discomfort glare for VDT tasks, a VCP of 80 or greater is recommended. VCP tables are available from most luminaire manufacturers.

Discomfort glare becomes less important as the light source is removed farther from the line of sight. However, sources of intense brightness, even well above the line of sight, can be distracting or unpleasant.

Fenestration. Windows and skylights have variable luminance. Frequently their luminance is high enough to cause glare, particularly for windows which are more directly in the field of view than skylights or ceiling-mounted luminaires. They can also cause a problem as reflected glare in VDTs. It is therefore advisable to have exterior shading or some interior device to variably control the luminance of each window.

Electric Lighting and Daylight. Office lighting with some daylight contribution must also be adequate for work after dusk. During the day, with proper controls, daylight can replace some electric lighting. One way of integrating daylight with electric light is to circuit perimeter luminaires on a separate switch which may be manually or photoelectrically switched or dimmed. Horizontal blinds or refractors can control brightness or, to some extent, redirect light in useful directions.

VISUAL TASK CONSIDERATIONS

The Importance of Visual Tasks in Offices

Office work entails a variety of difficult visual tasks. Thus, besides creating a pleasant and stimulating environment, lighting for offices should provide adequate luminous conditions for the various visual tasks performed. The visibility of task details is determined by their size and their contrast with the background, the absolute luminance of the background and the viewing duration. Although visual performance follows a law of diminishing returns, one can say in general that the

greater the contrast and size of the task details, the higher the background luminance, and the longer the viewing duration, the higher the level of visual performance.[1-3]

Within limits, a given level of visual performance can be maintained by trading off reductions in the magnitude of one factor with improvements in another. So, for example, leaning forward to make task details look larger can offset reduced background luminance caused by a low illuminance level.[4]

Visibility also depends upon the age of the worker. As a person ages, the pupil becomes progressively smaller (for a fixed level of ambient illumination) and the crystalline lens becomes thicker and less transparent. For example, a typical 50-year-old will need twice the illuminance falling on a task that a typical 20-year-old will need for the same task to provide the same amount of light falling on the retina.[5,6] The illuminance selection procedure (see chapter 11) provides a means to take age into account.

Illuminance Selection Procedure

Illuminance should be determined based on visual performance research[1,2,6,7] as well as on design experience. The procedure is task specific, and knowledge of the task is important. If a specific task is unknown, then the designer must design for typical office tasks. If possible, a survey of future occupants should be conducted to gather information about the activities that will occur in the space and the ages of the people who will perform them.

For a given office task, three illuminance design values are provided. Following the illuminance selection procedure, the designer can tailor the illuminance to the specific situation. The designer is provided with this flexibility in order to specify a level that is suited to the visual task, keeping in mind the age of the worker or occupant, the importance of speed and accuracy, the task background reflectance and the room surface conditions.

Illuminance is measured on the plane of the task. This means that horizontal tasks require horizontal illuminance. For vertical surfaces, such as bookshelves, vertical illuminance is required. For drafting tables, the illuminance is measured on the tilted surface of the drafting board.

If there is more than one task in the space, and each requires a different illuminance, the designer must choose among them. There are several alternative methods for combining many criteria.

The illumination requirements of different tasks may be satisfied by the use of a flexible lighting system. For example, if one designs for the highest level and provides dimming capabilities, the user may adjust the lighting level in various areas to suit particular tasks. Multilevel lighting systems may also be appropriate. If

Fig. 15-3. In a VDT screen, veiling reflections from bright objects, which reduce contrast, are prominent on a white-on-black display (right side of screen). These reflections are less noticeable on a black-on-white display (left side of screen).

flexibility is not possible, the designer may be forced to choose one criterion over another for the entire system. There are various ways in which this may be done.

The designer may set the illuminance equal to that required for the most difficult visual task. This may not be the best decision if, for example, the difficult task is performed for only twenty minutes per week. It may be wasteful of client costs and energy usage. An aggregate value may be developed based upon some average of the individual task illuminances. This method, however, may not take into account the relative importance or frequency of performing specific tasks. A weighted

average of time and importance may be appropriate here.

Often, office buildings are built on speculation, so that the visual tasks and the occupants are unknown. A logical recourse in such buildings is to design for the modern electronic office in which a combination of paper and VDT tasks will be performed. A building in which the lighting has been thoughtfully designed will be more attractive for prospective tenants.

Illuminance levels should be chosen with attention to the effects of light loss over time. Light loss factors such as luminaire dirt depreciation and lamp lumen depreciation must be considered, so that desired lighting levels are maintained.

Quality of Lighting

It should be remembered that, in addition to the quantity of illuminance reaching a task, the task visibility will be affected by the location of the luminaires relative to the task, the distribution of the luminaires, and the specific properties of the task and of the work surface. These factors can cause veiling reflections, reflected glare and shadows, resulting in reduced contrast and visibility.

Veiling Reflections, Reflected Glare and Shadows. As discussed earlier, the contrast of the visual task affects visibility. The contrast will depend in part upon the glossiness of the task surface and upon the geometric relationships between the light sources, the task and the eyes. If the visual task produces a mirror angle

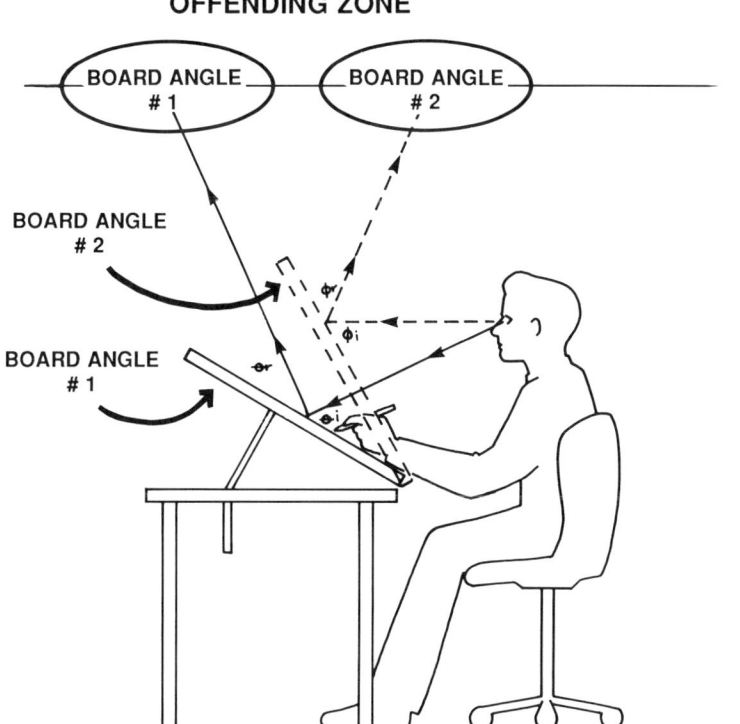

Fig. 15-4. The offending zone moves with board angle changes and with eye movements relative to the task surface.

between the eye and the luminaire or another bright object, contrast can be reduced. This effect is called *veiling reflections*, because the luminances of the task details and their backgrounds become more alike due to reflections of the object in the task area. See figure 15-3. Usually one luminaire among many is largely responsible for causing veiling reflections. The area of the ceiling where the problem luminaire is located is termed the *offending zone*. See figure 15-4.

Like ceiling luminaires, task lighting, either as desk luminaires or as part of open-plan furniture systems, should not ordinarily be placed in the offending zone. However, the light distribution characteristics of some luminaires minimize veiling reflections through optical design elements. Such luminaires may be placed in the offending zone.

The designer should always consider multiple working areas within the space. In open office areas, for example, one luminaire placed outside the offending zone for one worker may be in the offending zone for another. Luminaire light output should be limited at angles greater than 55° from vertical, in order to prevent veiling reflections[8,9] and to reduce discomfort glare.

Reflected Glare. Reflected glare is usually caused by a mirror image of the light source in the offending zone reflected from highly polished wood or glass-covered desk tops to the worker's eyes. It can be reduced by the use of matte surfaces and by carrying out the procedures for reducing veiling reflections on the task. Large-area low-luminance luminaires or indirect luminaires may be used when specular surfaces cannot be avoided.

Shadows on the visual task reduce the luminance of the task, and may impair effective seeing. In addition, when shadows are sharply defined at or near the task, they may be annoying and cause high luminance ratios. Shadows will be softened if the light comes from many directions. High-reflectance matte finishes on room surfaces become effective secondary light sources and materially reduce shadows by reflecting a significant amount of diffuse light into the space. Large-area luminaires and indirect lighting luminaires can provide shadowless environments.

THE PSYCHOLOGICAL EFFECT OF LIGHTING IN OFFICES

Subjective Responses

Although office spaces are primarily task oriented, more subtle effects of lighting on users' satisfaction and well-being must also be considered during the lighting design process. A body of literature exists which discusses the subjective responses to lighting.[10-14]

Although this literature is not extensive, some trends are present which suggest guidelines to the lighting system designer. In general, the underlying principle is that light not only provides the physical stimulus necessary for visual task performance, but also communicates certain cues which influence people's subjective impressions of the environment surrounding them.

Four characteristics of lighting systems have been shown to be important in influencing subjective impressions.[13] These characteristics are defined in general terms as overhead/peripheral, bright/dim, uniform/nonuniform and visually warm/visually cool. By varying the emphasis of the lighting system in each of these lighting modes, the designer can influence the types of impressions he or she believes are desirable for the particular project being developed.

Of course, people's impressions of architectural interior environments are influenced by many factors in addition to lighting, such as room size and proportions, type of space, furnishings and finishes used, and furniture layout. In many cases, these other factors will provide a stronger influence on some subjective responses than the lighting will. In spite of this, variations in the intensity, distribution and color tone of the lighting will exert some influence on subjective impressions such as spaciousness, relaxation, visual clarity and pleasantness. These influences must be carefully considered as an integral part of the office lighting design process. A detailed discussion of these influences can be found in chapter 10, Lighting Design Process.

Admittedly, these guidelines are qualitative in nature, and the actual psychological effects of a particular lighting design solution are difficult to predict with much confidence. However, ongoing research is taking place to develop methods for predicting these effects during the design process. Efforts to define quantitative aspects of the lighted environment or to develop computer graphic models of lighted spaces show potential in providing design tools which assist the designer in predicting the subjective effects of lighting.[15,16] These tools may well stimulate greater consideration of these types of effects of lighting.

ECONOMICS AND ENERGY CONSIDERATIONS

General

No lighting design is complete unless it has been subjected to a careful evaluation of its utilization of energy. The energy management checklist suggested in chapter 30, Energy Management, can be used by the designer and owner in assessing key energy issues for the project. In order to select proper energy-saving options, the designer should determine the payback criteria the building owner desires to be used for economic evaluations. A life-cycle cost evaluation should be performed. See chapter 13, Lighting Economics.

When making a cost comparison, it is important to be aware of local utility rate structures. For example, utilities' time-of-day pricing policies and their projections of future energy costs need to be used to make an accurate cost-benefit analysis. Other important factors to consider, in addition to direct lighting energy savings, include energy savings for air conditioning and maintenance costs for lamp and ballast replacements.

If energy economics are ignored, a designer may produce a wasteful lighting system that will cause the owner to pay an ever-increasing financial penalty. Energy waste will occur when any of the following conditions exist:

1. A light is energized when not needed (poor lighting controls).
2. The lighting system is inefficient or of poor quality.
3. The amount of lighting exceeds that needed.

These three items encompass energy management problems that must be resolved in designing a quality lighting system. The losses that result from poor control, system inefficiency and excessive lighting are direct costs for wasted electrical energy. Each of these can be evaluated on a quantitative basis. Actual energy and related costs can be established when comparing the effectiveness of various design approaches.

Prior to the heightened societal concern for energy, it was reasonable and practical to provide high illuminances as insurance against any potential productivity problem. Further, if tasks were not known or if changes in use were unpredictable, the design could be tailored to the most severe visual needs that might be encountered. As the politics and economics of energy continue to change, designs must be more closely tailored to the actual and demonstrable needs of the client.

Energy management topics addressed in this section can be applied to new construction, renovation or retrofit design.

Controls

The ability to manage the operation of an installed lighting system properly is a very important factor in determining the energy consumed by that system. With the departure from uniform lighting designs to localized lighting and from continuously operated lighting systems to those designed to match lighting operation with occupancy, lighting controls have become more prevalent and more complex. It is important that an

adequate amount of engineering time be devoted to careful analysis of the control system.

Most office lighting is manually controlled to provide users and occupants with flexibility and simplicity of light operation. The design of the manual control (number, location, ergonomic factors) affects the energy consumption of the building. Automatic controls can reduce lighting energy consumption caused by occupants' failure to use lighting controls properly. These automatic controls can range from timed switches to central building control systems. See chapter 31, Lighting Controls, for detailed information.

The following general provisions should be considered for both manual and automatic controls:

1. Each separate office or area should have its own control switch(es).
2. In large open spaces, work areas should be grouped and switched independently.
3. When single- or two-lamp fluorescent luminaires are used, adjacent luminaires should be placed on alternate circuits.
4. When three-lamp fluorescent luminaires are used, the inside lamp should be connected to a separate circuit from the outside lamps.
5. When four-lamp fluorescent luminaires are used, the inside pair of lamps should be connected to a circuit separate from the outside lamp pair.
6. When electronic ballasts are used, considerations should be given to high-low switching and dimming.
7. Task areas requiring higher illuminances should be on separate circuits.
8. Luminaires along window walls should be switched separately.

When energy was not a significant factor in lighting design, first-cost considerations would favor manual switching of large blocks of luminaires and maximum loading of circuit switches. Today, the energy savings achievable through local switching and automatic control systems should be an initial consideration in developing the plan for lighting systems. The expanding resource of innovative lighting control systems can be expected to play an increasingly important role in the management of lighting energy. It is important to maintain up-to-date data on this technology and associated cost evaluations. Further information on control devices can be found in chapter 31, Lighting Controls.

The usefulness of a lighting system can be enhanced by installing dimmers in rooms where there will be widely variable lighting requirements. Dimming systems are available that can provide uniform dimming without problems of flicker or radio interference. Manufacturers can supply data on energy consumed at reduced levels. Dimming is available with both manual and automatic control systems.

Lighting System Efficiency

The efficiency of a lighting system is the result of the combination of component efficiencies incorporated in the luminaire as well as the organization of the office environment.

Most office lighting design continues to utilize fluorescent lamps as the primary light source. However, HID lamps are also being incorporated in interior lighting designs. The efficacy (lumens per watt) will differ for various lamp groups (incandescent, fluorescent, mercury, metal halide, high-pressure sodium). It will also vary within a lamp group, depending upon wattage. For HID lamps, higher wattages are generally more efficient. For fluorescent lamps, variations in efficacy are numerous. In addition to efficacy differences between wattages, the efficacy of fluorescent lamps can vary significantly with bulb diameter (T-5, T-8 and T-10 designs being generally more efficient than T-12 designs) and phosphor coatings (triphosphor lamps provide greater efficacy than halophosphate lamps). The designer should select the most efficacious source that will satisfy the lighting requirements for the space involved. However, lamp selection will also depend upon color requirements, switching frequency and desired distribution (see chapter 6, Light Sources).

It should be noted, though, that when calculating illuminances for a space using newer, more efficacious lamps, it is necessary to base the calculations upon specific lamp output data, rather than general lumen values established for fluorescent lamps of a given wattage.

Ballasts. Presently, a high percentage of office lighting utilizes 40-W rapid-start fluorescent lamps and low-efficacy magnetic ballasts. Improvements in ballast design have produced more efficient magnetic, hybrid and electronic products.

In particular, advances in solid-state technology have produced electronic ballast systems for both fluorescent and HID lamps. Ballast efficiency can be significantly improved with this technology. These systems can also provide many design options, including multi-level switching, continuous photocell-controlled dimming and addressable preset output levels. Electronic ballasts operate at high frequencies, typically 18–30 kHz, and virtually eliminate audible noise and lamp flicker. The ballast weight is considerably less than for core-and-coil magnetic models, which results in lighter-weight luminaires. Many of these systems will operate with a reduced amount of harmonic distortion, thus improving the power factor and avoiding current overload on the neutral wire of a three-phase electrical system, as well as possible interference with a building's

time clocks, communication systems and computing systems. As the technology evolves over the next several years, control alternatives will expand and further innovation in energy management capabilities can be anticipated.

Luminaires. The luminaire optical system is an important element to consider in developing specifications for energy-efficient lighting. Lamp light output is directed to the task by the different elements of the optical system. These are the reflector and, if used, the lens, refractor or louver.

The design of the optical system will also affect the luminaire's coefficient of utilization (CU), which is the number of lumens delivered from the luminaire to the workplane divided by the lumen output from the lamps alone. The CU is often used as a measure of luminaire efficiency, but it is not the only measure of effectiveness of an optical system. In general, a luminaire with a high CU will also contribute more to discomfort glare, so care should be taken in the selection and placement of such luminaires.

Task Location and Quality. Task locations should be planned to relate to the most efficient lighting layout. It may be possible to group tasks having similar visual difficulty to realize efficiency improvements.

Another opportunity may exist by bringing together functions that can be expected to operate before or after normal business hours. It may be beneficial, for example, to locate difficult seeing tasks along window walls to benefit from higher illuminances produced by daylighting.

Reflectances and Dirt Depreciation. The owner should be encouraged to approve the use of high-reflectance colors for all surfaces in the work space. To achieve savings, illuminance calculations should be made with actual reflectance values rather than "rule of thumb" values.

In regard to the luminaire dirt depreciation factor, improved filtering in the building air supply system and prohibition of smoking should be recommended. This will result in less luminaire dirt accumulation.

Daylighting. Daylighting can be an important energy-saving feature for the office environment. Coordination of window location, orientation, size and transmission characteristics, along with daylight-responsive sensors or window shading devices, can result in significant cost savings in the work space. Daylighting can not only reduce energy usage, but can also lower peak power demands, resulting in further cost savings for the owner.

Air Conditioning. An added benefit can be realized from an energy-efficient lighting design in the form of a reduction in the size of air-conditioning equipment, if the lighting design is completed prior to the final sizing of cooling equipment.

Every watt of power supplied for lighting introduces approximately 3.41 Btu/h of heat into the building envelope. Heat produced by the lighting components can be handled in a variety of ways by the building's mechanical system. Frequently, the heat is removed from the occupied space through an air-return ceiling plenum or ducted heat-extracting luminaires. In some systems, the heat generated by lighting can be used elsewhere in the building or even on the same floor to fulfill heating requirements. Most luminaire manufacturers publish information on the equipment's thermal characteristics and air-handling capabilities.

Mechanical engineers have sized air conditioning according to "rule of thumb" power density values for the lighting load. By using actual design values as well as information on expected use (switching), significant oversizing of cooling equipment can be prevented. This will save on the initial equipment investment and can be expected to improve the operating efficiency of the air conditioning.

Government Energy Regulations.

It is incumbent upon the lighting designer to investigate all energy-related codes which may apply to a project. A wide range of federal, state and local codes exist that regulate various aspects of energy used in building lighting. See chapter 30, Energy Management.

Codes are no substitute, however, for a proper, comprehensive analysis of the lighting system's energy and economic relationships. It should be recognized that a design which fulfills the requirements of applicable energy codes does not assure a successful solution.

Lighting Methods

General Lighting Versus Localized Lighting.

There are basically two methods for lighting office tasks. One is to design the general lighting so that required illuminances are provided at the various tasks. This is most appropriate for private offices or special situations where task lighting is inappropriate. The other is to supply most of the task illuminance with localized lighting from task lighting luminaires, and provide a lower level of general illumination. In open-plan arrangements not only can this be more desirable, but it is often necessary. If vertical partitions or storage cabinets over work surfaces cause shadows, localized lighting becomes essential to provide adequate task illumination and reduce the shadows.

When localized lighting is used, the general illumination does not have to provide the required illuminance on the task. It should be designed with a lower illuminance appropriate for circulation, for casual viewing of tasks, and to provide the recommended luminance ratios between the task and other areas within the field of view. Additionally, the design of the general illumination can now become more coordinated with the interior design and architecture, requiring less attention to illuminance considerations.

Indirect, Direct and Direct / Indirect Lighting.

Broad alternatives for general lighting are direct (downward) lighting, indirect (upward) lighting, or a combination of the two in which the luminaire or luminaires direct light in both directions. See figure 15-5.

Indirect Lighting.

Indirect lighting illuminates the ceiling, which in turn reflects light downwards. Thus, the ceiling becomes the brightest surface in the visual field. See figure 15-6. To avoid excessive luminance, the illumination on the ceiling should be evenly distributed. Two criteria that should be established in evaluating an indirect lighting approach are maximum ceiling brightness, typically directly above the luminaire, and uniformity ratios. The maximum allowable ceiling luminance should be determined by the task.

If the primary task in a large office space is reading a dark-background VDT screen, the maximum allowable ceiling luminance should not exceed 850 cd/m². The *uniformity ratio* is the ratio of the brightest area of

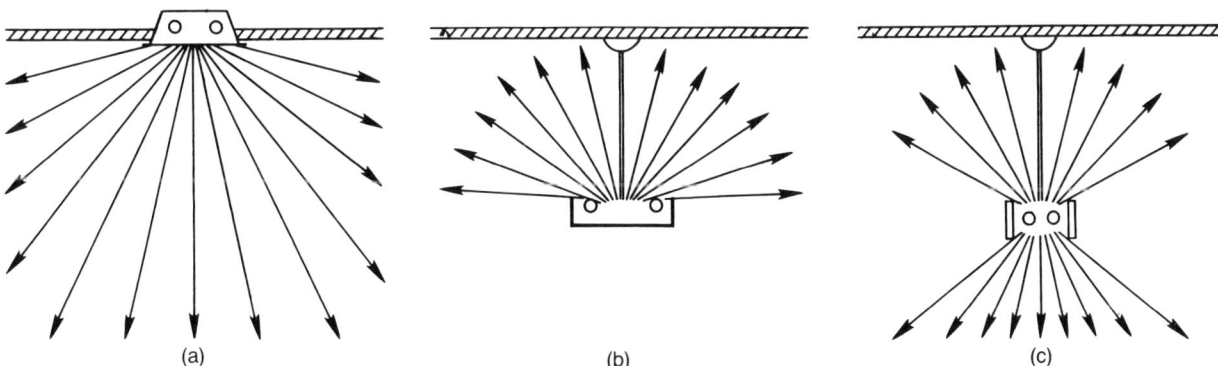

(a)   (b)   (c)

Fig. 15-5. Luminaires for general lighting are classified in accordance with the percentage of total light output emitted above and below the horizontal. Three of the classifications are (a) direct lighting, (b) indirect lighting and (c) direct-indirect lighting.

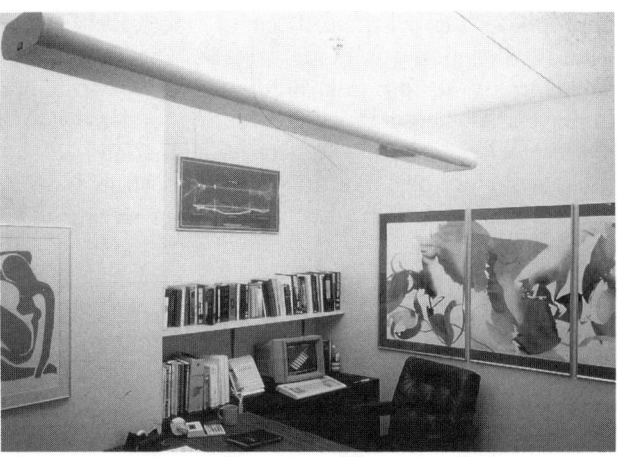

Fig. 15-6. Pendant luminaires are the most common method for providing indirect illumination.

the ceiling, typically above the fixture, to the darkest area of the ceiling, that between fixtures—in other words, the ratio of the maximum to the minimum. In a VDT-intensive environment, better uniformity will result in less noticeable indirect glare on the screen. Ratios up to 8 : 1 are acceptable; however, 4 : 1 is achievable and more desirable. The designer should attempt to provide as smooth a gradient as possible between the high and the low luminance.

If VDTs are not present, higher ceiling luminance may be allowed. The ratio (R) of the maximum average ceiling luminance to the luminance of the task should not exceed 10 : 1. For example, a 75% reflectance task ($\rho = 0.75$) illuminated to 500 lx (E) would limit the ceiling luminance to approximately 1200 cd/m^2, according to the following equation:

$$L_{c\,max} = \frac{\rho ER}{\pi}$$

$$L_{c\,max} = \frac{(0.75)(500)(10)}{\pi} = 1194 \text{ cd/m}^2$$

Ceiling uniformity also should be assessed in terms of esthetic considerations and of acceptable luminance ratios between the task and more remote surfaces. If the extremes in ceiling luminance are present, lower visual comfort may result.

Many indirect luminaires emit light below the horizontal plane. This can provide both an increased sense of perceived brightness and a recognizable source of light.[17] If a luminaire does emit light below the horizontal plane, the average luminance in the lengthwise, crosswise and 45° horizontal planes, at angles between 55 and 90° from vertical, should be controlled to avoid direct glare.

Indirect lighting can provide a calm, diffuse light, void of highlights and shadows, similar to the light of an overcast day. Indirect lighting can provide good visual task illumination, since it tends not to cause bright images in VDT screens, nor appreciable veiling reflections on paper-based tasks. It may be especially good for drafting tasks because it will not create shadows from the tools used to perform the task. It may, however, reduce the sense of visual clarity, depth perception or orientation. The lack of highlight and shadow eliminates visual cues. This problem can be addressed by using more color, adding accent lighting, or wall washing, all of which will establish visual cues and make it easier to interpret the visual environment, as well as contribute to the pleasantness of the space.

A major consideration in designing an indirect lighting scheme is the selection of lamps. The most common choices are metal halide and fluorescent. These sources differ greatly as to luminaire size and color. Luminaire size varies because of the inherent difference in the lamp sizes. It may determine fixture location and appropriateness of the design. Color is the most noticeable difference between the two lamp types, and therefore the most important consideration when lighting a flat, white plane, such as the ceiling. The potential color shift in metal halide lamps through their life may thus be more noticeable when illuminating a ceiling plane than with a downlight illuminating the floor.

Direct Lighting. Direct (downward) lighting deemphasizes the ceiling surface and (with low-brightness luminaires) the luminaires themselves, and emphasizes horizontal planes, such as work surfaces and the floor. See figure 15-7. Floor colors are reflected and may actually tint the ceiling. With wider-spread luminaires, or perimeter placement, luminaires may also emphasize vertical surfaces.

There is a wide range of direct-type luminaires with a variety of distribution characteristics. These characteristics are dependent on lamp type, size, and reflector and shielding material. Light distributions range from very broad, using translucent diffusing shielding, to tightly concentrated, using specular reflectors and louvers.

Luminaire light distributions may be compared by reference to the candela distribution curve and related numbers on a photometric report. Luminaire luminances can also be compared by referring to the luminance summary section of a photometric report. This information is typically given in two or three horizontal planes (lengthwise, crosswise, 45°) at angles of 0 (vertical), 45, 55, 65, 75 and 85°.

Several types of optical controls are available for direct lighting systems; most are also available for direct/indirect systems.

Diffusers. A diffuser scatters the light emitted by the lamps before it leaves the luminaire. Since the area of the diffuser is much larger than the area of the

Fig. 15-7. Low-brightness, direct luminaires deemphasize the ceiling surface.

lamps, the total flux is more evenly distributed, and thus the average luminance will be less than that of bare lamps. Nevertheless, the average luminance of a diffuser is still rather high and nearly constant for all viewing angles. In a large office, diffusers may have low *visual comfort probability* (VCP) ratios as well as producing unacceptable reflections in VDT screens. Diffusers are not recommended for open office environments, except when a special effect is desired, such as with a luminaire that mimics a skylight. In small private offices, they may be appropriate if they are not visible at viewing angles required for visual tasks. Their broad distribution does not create excessive brightness on the walls.

Lenses. A lens incorporates a series of small prisms which reduce the apparent brightness of the luminaire at the near-horizontal viewing angles of 45 to 90° from vertical. Depending on the specific optical characteristics of a lens, acceptable glare ratings may be obtained. However, most lenses do not reduce glare sufficiently to prevent luminaire reflections in VDT screens. The efficiency will depend on the specific lens.

Polarizers. Polarized light can reduce veiling reflections and reflected glare under special conditions. Some commercially available luminaire lenses are designed

to polarize the emitted illumination by transmitting light through multiple refractive layers (see chapter 1, Light and Optics). The degree of polarization in the illumination is dependent upon the number of layers through which the light is transmitted, as well as the angle of transmission. There is no polarization produced at the angle perpendicular to the transmission plane, that is, directly below the luminaire. As the angle of transmission increases, for a given number of layers, the degree of polarization increases up to Brewster's angle, approximately 60° for these lenses. At this angle, and depending upon the number of transmission layers, the light can be polarized by between 30 and 50%.

The benefits of polarized light in reducing veiling reflections and reflected glare are dependent upon the degree of polarization in the illumination, the luminaire-task-eye geometry, and the specular characteristics of the task surface.[18-21] Because the effectiveness of polarized light depends upon all of these factors, it is difficult to provide a general statement on polarized light that is correct for every application. Guidance on the significance of polarized light for a specific application can be obtained from the literature.[22-27]

The luminances of luminaires using polarizing materials should also comply with VCP recommendations for typical offices, and luminance guideline for spaces with VDTs.

Parabolic Louvers. Luminaires with a grid of parabolic louvers having a specular finish can control brightness precisely. The louver is an array of open cells, the walls of which form parabolic reflectors. The cells range in size from 1.25 × 1.25 cm to almost 30 × 30 cm. The smaller cell types are usually injection-molded plastic, which is then vacuum metallized with aluminum. The larger cell types are usually fabricated from aluminum sheets, usually anodized prior to forming. When either type is made with a specular finish, the light output can be precisely controlled so that practically no light is emitted at angles above the cutoff angle. When this is the case, the louver can look darker than the ceiling. This precise light cutoff angle also darkens walls near the ceiling and places greater importance on illuminating vertical surfaces.

Parabolic louvers do not always have a sharp cutoff or a low luminance. Their optical performance depends upon the degree of specularity of the louver surface and the optical cutoff of the louver. A semispecular finish diffuses the light reflected from the louver surfaces, and at angles of view above the nominal cutoff angle provides some luminance rather than the dark surface achieved with very specular surfaces. A semispecular finish also tends to hide imperfections in the reflector surface, dust and fingerprints. However, the semispecular luminance may show up as a reflection on VDT screens.

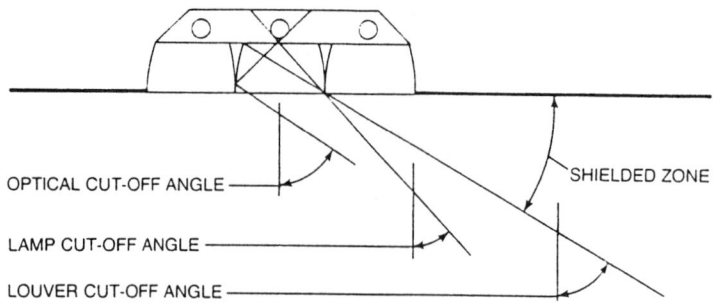

Fig. 15-8. The blades of a parabolic louver provide a physical cutoff in the same way as an ''egg-crate'' louver; however, a parabolic louver with a specular finish reflects light from its curved blades at an angle equal to or less than the louver cutoff angle.

Parabolic louvers actually have two cutoff angles. The first is the physical cutoff angle, which is the angle from vertical that just occludes a view of the lamp. The second is the optical cutoff, which is the angle from vertical at which light reflected from the parabolic surfaces is just occluded. This angle depends on the precise shape of the reflector surfaces and is not always the same as the physical cutoff angle. For a precise cutoff, the two cutoff angles should be the same. See figure 15-8.

The degree of specularity and the louver cutoff angles are not usually included in luminaire specifications. The shielding angle sometimes given in photometric reports refers to the angle from the horizontal at which a direct view of the bare lamp first becomes visible. However, the performance of a luminaire resulting from the degree of louver specularity and from the louver cutoff characteristics can be determined from the luminaire photometric report. The luminance summary table in the report can be used to compare and select direct-lighting luminaires, especially for offices with VDTs. The luminance summary table shows the luminaire luminance at various angles measured from the vertical. The table typically shows these values in the lengthwise and crosswise horizontal planes. It is an advantage when the table also gives values for the 45° plane, as this may reveal a higher luminance at a given angle than for lengthwise and crosswise planes. See figure 15-9.

Conclusion. In establishing luminaire brightness criteria, both the task and the room size characteristics must be considered. If a large space contains many VDT tasks, then restrictive criteria need to be established. The often glossy, vertical VDT has a high potential for reflecting ceiling luminance, and this "heads-up" task needs more demanding VCP standards. If the VDT task is performed in a small private office, luminaire luminance is less important.

Direct / Indirect Lighting. A combination of direct and indirect approaches can produce excellent results. See

figures 15-10 and 15-11. This combination can be provided by using two different luminaire types within the same area, one providing uplight, the other providing downlight. Obviously, the downlight luminaire should be positioned so as not to interfere with the indirect luminaire, and vice versa. The other approach is to provide both upward and downward light from the same luminaire. If this is done, the criteria for both individual approaches should apply. The indirect portion should have distribution characteristics so as to not create hot spots or excessive luminance on the ceiling. The direct portion should provide adequate shielding to provide good visual comfort and avoid glare.

Although direct/indirect lighting may be more difficult to achieve, the results can be quite satisfactory. Typically this design solution obscures the inadequacies of each individual approach and maximizes the advantages of each, creating both a pleasant and a functional environment.

Light Source. The selection of an appropriate light source may be the single most important aspect of implementing a design concept, and may, in fact, be an integral part of the design concept. The choices available for light sources are increasing at a rapid rate, and there are sometimes only subtle differences between lamps.

This increase in source choices may make the job of developing the lighting design more difficult, since the evaluation process becomes lengthier. The end result should be successful, however, with appropriate lighting designs that more closely match the needs of the client.

In selecting light sources several variables must be evaluated. These include lamp intensity, lamp lumens and efficacy, all of which dramatically affect the lighting design. Lamp efficacy will not only influence operating costs, but may determine whether or not a design is suitable to meet energy consumption guidelines that are either self-determined or legislated by code. Other

XYZ PHOTOMETRIC LABORATORIES
CERTIFIED TEST PROGRAM
COMPUTED BY XYZ PROGRAM

REPORT NO: ABC COMPANY: 00001
PREPARED FOR ABC COMPANY
CATALOG NO: ABC00000
LUMINAIRE: FABRICATED METAL HOUSING, WHITE PAINTED REFLECTOR, SPECULAR
PARABOLIC LOUVER
LAMPS: THREE F40T12/CW, EACH RATED 3150 LUMENS
BALLASTS: ONE X000, ONE CDE X003Z
MOUNTING: RECESSED
LUMEN TO CANDELA RATION USED = 9.17
TOTAL INPUT WATTS = 131.1 AT 120.0 VOLTS
THE 0-DEGREE PLANE IS PARALLEL WITH THE LAMPS

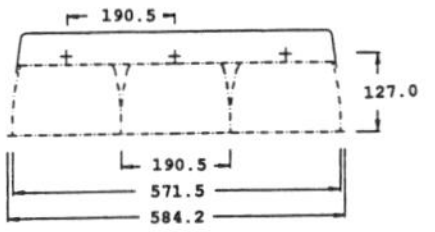

CANDELA DISTRIBUTION   FLUX
        0.0   22.5   45.0   67.5   90.0
  0   2876   2876   2876   2876   2876
  5   2875   2887   2899   2919   2915   278
 15   2739   2831   2982   3102   3122   844
 25   2485   2700   3197   3703   3767   1462
 35   2150   2532   3074   2939   2835   1706
 45   1545   1987   1688   1302   1290   1208
 55   24   108   295   159   120   214
 65   0   0   0   0   0   0
 75   0   0   0   0   0   0
 85   0   0   0   0   0   0
 90   0   0   0   0   0

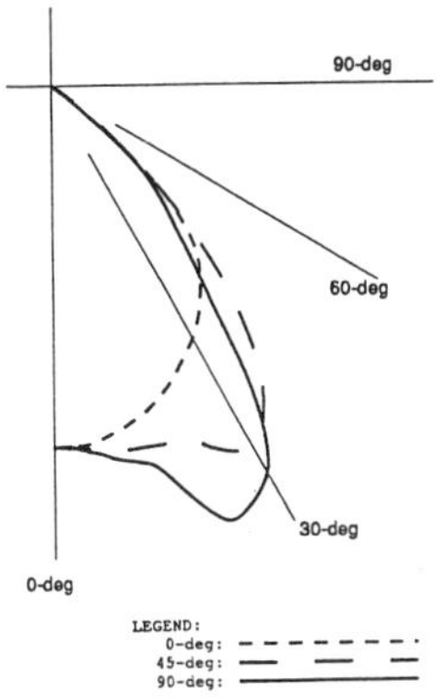

ZONAL LUMEN SUMMARY
ZONE   LUMENS   %LAMP   %FIXT
  0- 30   2584   27.3   45.2
  0- 40   4290   45.4   75.1
  0- 60   5711   60.4   100.0
  0- 90   5711   60.4   100.0
 90-180   0   0.0   0.0
  0-180   5711   60.4   100.0

TOTAL LUMINAIRE EFFICIENCY =   60.4 %
TOTAL REFLECTANCE OF PAINT =   91.3 %
CIE TYPE - DIRECT
PLANE   : 0-DEG   90-DEG
SPACING CRITERIA :   1.2   1.4
LUMINANCE DATA IN CANDELAS PER SQUARE METER
ANGLE AVERAGE   AVERAGE   AVERAGE

LUMINANCE DATA IN CANDELAS PER SQUARE METER			
ANGLE	AVERAGE	AVERAGE	AVERAGE
IN DEG	0-DEG	45-DEG	90-DEG
45	3240	3535	2700
55	60	760	310
65	0	0	0
75	0	0	0
85	0	0	0

Fig. 15-9. A typical photometric report showing the luminance summary table.

Fig. 15-10. Direct / indirect lighting can be produced from two independent sources as shown. The direct portion is produced from a continuous linear trough with a parabolic baffle, and the indirect component is produced by bouncing light off the ceiling and structural elements from independent indirect coves.

factors that should be considered are lamp size (which will influence luminaire types), lamp life, lamp color, initial costs, replacement costs and maintenance characteristics.

Photometric Data. A candela distribution curve, which is a part of the luminaire photometric report, will show how light exits the luminaire. This will help determine luminaire placement, layout and uniformity, and will help determine whether or not the luminaire can achieve the desired results for illuminance and luminance objectives.

Along with candela distribution, a photometric report can also provide information on luminaire brightness or luminance. The luminance summary data provide information on the average luminance of the luminaire at a variety of angles in several planes. This information will help determine how noticeable a direct luminaire, or how noticeable or appropriate the side brightness of some indirect luminaires, may be. A

Fig. 15-11. Direct / indirect lighting can be produced from a single luminaire which emits light from the same source in both an upward and a downward direction.

survey of three horizontal planes—lengthwise, cross-wise and 45°—should be examined. Along with the luminance summary, visual comfort probability (VCP) data will give further information on luminaire brightness for direct luminaires within the context of a given set of spatial dimensions. It should be noted that most VCP data are reported for 1000-lx (100-fc) conditions. For lower-illuminance applications, additional VCP data should be requested. Within open-plan offices where large ceiling areas are within typical fields of view, and especially in VDT-task environments, where the tasks are typically performed in a "heads up" position, the VCP should be at or above 80. In smaller private offices, VCP data are less significant unless full-height walls are grazed and ceiling luminaires are visible from a distance.

Luminaire Efficiency. The *luminaire efficiency* is the percentage of lamp lumens that exit the luminaire. Although efficiency is very important in determining the appropriateness of the luminaire and its ability to meet energy consumption objectives, it should not be interpreted by itself, but must be evaluated in the context of the candela distribution and luminance summary. Often, higher efficiencies are obtained through greater output at angles which cause glare and are not beneficial for the lighting design.

Layout, Integration and Design Appropriateness. It is possible for a luminaire to meet illuminance and energy design objectives, yet not integrate functionally or esthetically within the environment. The luminaire must also integrate mechanically, electrically and acoustically with the architectural design.

System Operation and Maintenance. An important consideration in a lighting design is the expected maintenance of the luminaire, including the lamp and ballast. Once it has been determined that a design meets the objectives established in these areas, a maintenance plan should be developed with the owner and occupants of the space. If the lighting system is to perform as designed, the user must assume some responsibility for maintenance. At the very least, the maintenance plan should specify the lamps and include cleaning and relamping schedules. If layout changes will be required in the future, an explanation of how luminaires will be relocated should be included if flexibility is part of the original design.

Final Selection Process. Although much of a luminaire's performance can be evaluated through data analysis, the final selection process should include more than just reviewing printed information or photographs. Whenever possible, actual luminaire samples should be obtained and examined. Physical inspection of the luminaire can reveal aspects of both performance and quality.

A further step to assure the quality of both the design and the luminaire selection can be a mock-up. A mock-up should duplicate the characteristics of the final space as closely as possible. Variations in finishes or ceiling heights, for example, may greatly influence perceptions. Also, a mock-up should contain a suitable number of luminaires so that appropriate judgments can be made concerning illuminance values under realistic conditions. If a mock-up is not feasible, visits to installations with the same luminaires will give both designer and client the opportunity to see the luminaires function, even if the spatial conditions are different.

DESIGN ISSUES FOR SPECIFIC AREAS

Open-Plan Office Lighting

General Considerations. Open, or *open-plan*, offices are areas that accommodate workers in a common space with few, if any, floor-to-ceiling partitions or walls. There can be many different kinds of seeing tasks and activities, and the furniture configurations may be specific to the activity. Individual work areas can consist of:

- Bullpen-like desk arrangements
- Desk-and-credenza combinations
- Floor-standing panels partially enclosing a space, often supporting work surfaces and storage components
- Freestanding screens or panels between desks

The office configurations will have a significant effect on the lighting requirements. As much information as possible should be obtained about the plan anticipated.

Panels and storage shelves above work surfaces may create undesirable shadows on the visual task and on adjacent surfaces. Panel heights and workstation density and size will change the distribution of the general illumination and affect luminance and illuminance uniformity at the work surface. As the number of vertical partitions increases, their reflectance becomes more significant; dark finishes absorb more light and lower the general impression of brightness as well as the actual illuminance on the task.

Calculating Illuminance. Accurately calculating illuminances in open-plan office areas can become most complex. The empty-room assumption is not a valid approximation of the environmental condition; in fact, predictions based on that assumption can be very misleading. Vertical obstructions such as partitions and filing cabinets play an important role in determining the lighting within and surrounding a workstation. For example, an average density of partitions 150 cm (60 in.) high may decrease illuminances by 10–50% (depending on reflectances and illuminance distribution characteristics). Since classical room zonal cavity computations cannot include these obstructions, their use, even as an approximation tool, is limited. A better approximation can be made through the coupled-cavities extension of the standard method.[28–30] See chapter 9, Lighting Calculations.

Since a partitioned work space takes on many of the visual aspects of a small room, the importance of surface reflectances, color and height should be stressed. Point-by-point computer calculations may be required if an accurate prediction of illuminances is desired. An alternative might be a controlled mock-up in which illuminance readings can be taken.

It may be desirable to plan general illumination separately from task illumination, given the limits of calculation procedures and the expense of a mock-up. In this way, localized illuminance calculations can be performed from the photometric characteristics of the task luminaire and the reflectance characteristics of the workstation.

Luminance Considerations. The background luminance at the visual task may be considered from two perspectives. Luminance within the immediate task surround should maintain a maximum bright-to-dark ratio of 3:1 with respect to the task. Away from the immediate task surround (within the field of view), greater contrast may be desirable to enhance visual clarity, depth perception and a sense of spatial orientation. In these areas a maximum ratio of 10:1 with respect to the task is recommended.

Consideration of task versus background luminance will be different for visual display terminals (VDT screens) than for paper tasks and different for partitioned workstations than for visually open spaces. In the open office the immediate surround will be the work surface for horizontal paper tasks. For tasks with an elevated line of sight, such as VDT screens or vertical copy stands, the immediate surround will be part of more remote room and furniture surfaces or the panel surface of a partitioned workstation.

Flexibility. In the design of the lighting for an open-plan office, the permanence of workstation location must be considered. A planned design or layout may be quite different from the actual furniture layout six months after initial occupancy. A lighting design tailored to a specific furniture orientation, such as rectilinear or diagonal, may create glare or low illuminances if furniture is moved.

Psychological and Design Issues. One of the most overlooked design aspects of open-plan office lighting is the consideration of the psychological effect of all the elements in the space. The spatial arrangement and the lighting distribution become integrated by the user, whether the interior and lighting designs were integrated or not, causing a psychological effect.

Large open spaces create an entirely different feeling from that of partitioned workstations. The lighting, the furniture layout and the room and furniture finishes must work together to communicate to the occupant the sense of the design concept.

In open-plan offices, another major objective is the identification of circulation patterns and activity areas. Users need to have a sense of orientation with respect to their environment. This may involve the ability to locate exits, reception areas, specific departments, individual offices, and locations of adjacent areas like the copy machine room and the conference room quickly. The lighting system, in conjunction with the interior design, can provide the appropriate visual cues to communicate orientation and circulation. As open-plan offices become larger, the need for users to understand the limits of space and their relationship to the space becomes increasingly important.

Acoustical Aspects. The acoustical criteria for open-plan offices are often quite stringent. Of special concern is the acoustical privacy between workstations. In closed office spaces this is provided by permanent walls, but in their absence, the ceiling takes on increased importance along with the space dividers. Luminaires, either recessed or surface mounted, can have an adverse effect on acoustical absorption. Lensed luminaires can reflect sound to adjacent workstations, while louvered units will "break up" the reflected sound. To ensure a completely satisfactory open-plan installation, the designer should work with an acoustical consultant.

Alternative Design Methods. There are several generic approaches to lighting an open-plan office. There is no specific approach that always provides the best design, and there is no formula that will always give the best answer. Proper analysis and a design process that includes the above-mentioned concerns is the best formula for success. Design approaches generally fall into one of several categories. These include uniform, nonuniform and task/ambient lighting.

Uniform Lighting. Uniform lighting means that the general or ambient lighting delivers consistent illuminance throughout the space. It may provide sufficient task illumination or a level which requires supplemental lighting at task locations. Uniform lighting at high illuminances can be quite costly in terms of lighting equipment and energy use. If it is to provide task illuminance, it should be considered only if the task requires low illuminance, the task is performed throughout or in a large area of the space, or task lighting is not feasible.

Nonuniform Lighting. Nonuniform lighting means that pools of high illuminance are intermixed with areas of lower illuminance. An example of this type of design approach is a three-level illumination plan. The lowest illuminance is found in circulation areas or corridors between pools of nonuniform general illumination at workstation locations. The highest illuminance levels are then at specific work surfaces lighted

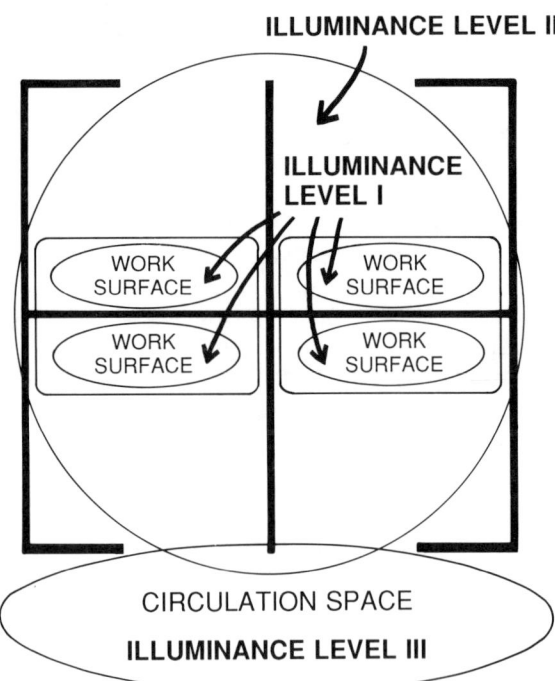

Fig. 15-12. Illuminance level I is the highest level, which is provided by a task-oriented luminaire. Illuminance level II is within the workstation and has a lower illuminance. Illuminance level III is the lowest and is located between workstations, typically in circulation areas.

by task-oriented luminaires within these workstations. See figure 15-12. Illuminances and surface reflectances must be chosen carefully to stay within the recommended luminance ratios.

Whenever any type of nonuniform approach is considered, maintenance must be a concern. If variations in illuminance are provided, there must be a direct relationship between the lighting and the furniture (and task locations). With even the most flexible lighting systems, a commitment must be made to make the required lighting changes when necessary. This may mean additional planning time and expense, longer "change times," and additional costs to make the changes. In spaces that are often reconfigured, these costs may be prohibitive. In more stable spaces, nonuniformity may offer lower initial equipment costs and greater long-term energy savings.

Task/Ambient Lighting. Task/ambient lighting is an approach by which a uniform or a nonuniform general illuminance level is lower than that required for the task and higher illuminance levels are provided in task areas. It includes many different types of systems and can be extremely effective for illuminating an open-plan environment. The general or ambient lighting may be direct, indirect, or direct/indirect and should provide an illuminance level which is lower than the task illuminance level (maintaining a 3:1 luminance ratio between task and surround). *Task lighting*, or task-oriented lighting, may be mounted on or in the furniture or ceiling. Recommendations for task illumination should be applied. The advantage of this approach is that the highest illuminance is provided at the task. Since the general or ambient illumination does not provide the major portion of the task illuminance, it can be more responsive to requirements such as visual comfort and enhancement of interior architecture and design objectives.

Private Offices

A private office is generally a fairly small space (8–12 m²) with floor-to-ceiling partitions and one occupant. Ceiling-mounted direct luminaires are typical of the lighting. Usually luminaires outside the private office cannot be seen by the occupant, so the luminaire brightness may be less important than it is for larger spaces. If, however, the partition walls are grazed, or contain clerestory windows, overhead lighting within the private office may affect those outside and vice versa. In this case, the overhead lighting should be treated as in open-plan areas.

As in open-plan offices, task lighting, combined with low-level general illumination, can be used for private offices. Because the wall area of a private office is large relative to the room size, there is opportunity for wall lighting to provide all or part of the general lighting, whether or not additional task lighting is provided. The result will often be more pleasing in appearance than lighting from ceiling sources alone. Wall washing with individual luminaires or continuous linear sources produces a more open, brighter appearance; highlighting features such as art work or creating patterns of brightness on the walls also lend variety and interest.

Alternatives that should be considered include indirect lighting from wall-mounted or ceiling-suspended luminaires, wall coves to provide both wall luminance and task illumination, and direct/indirect illumination from suspended or wall-mounted luminaires.

Downlighting from either incandescent, compact fluorescent or low-wattage HID luminaires should not be used to provide task illumination. The point source nature of these types of luminaires is likely to cause harsh hand shadows on the task. Additionally, if these luminaires are placed in the offending zone, a very high degree of veiling reflection will occur. They may, however, be appropriate for wall washing or accent lighting.

Conference Rooms

Visual tasks in conference rooms range from casual to difficult. Two or more lighting systems should be

planned to provide flexibility for this range:

1. A general lighting system, in which control is provided by switching, or dimmers to vary the illuminance
2. A supplementary lighting system, consisting of downlighting with dimmer control for slide projection and other low-level illumination requirements. Due to improved technology and the reduced cost of electronic dimming systems for fluorescent lamps, it is sometimes effective to incorporate dimming into the general fluorescent system. Then the need for a second system is eliminated.
3. A perimeter or wall wash lighting system for better visual appeal and where presentation materials may be mounted on the walls, controlled with dimmers

Drafting and Graphic Production Rooms

Visual requirements for drafting demand high-quality illumination, since discrimination of fine detail is frequently required for extended periods of time. Significant graduation of shadows along T squares and triangles reduces visibility. Harsh directional shadows from drawing instruments and hands may reduce productivity. Lighting systems that avoid reflected glare, veiling reflections and task shadows are very important in providing maximum visibility. The requirements for computer-aided drafting (CAD) are very different, and are similar to but often more demanding than those for VDT tasks, due to the use of large color monitors and very fine detailing and line weight.

Quality of Lighting. The use of large-luminous-area systems or of indirect, semidirect or other forms of overall ceiling lighting will minimize shadows. When ceiling heights or energy constraints do not permit the use of these systems, direct lighting systems can be applied where the drafting board is illuminated from both sides. In such a system, the absence of any luminaire in the offending zone also minimizes veiling reflections and reflected glare. Referring to figure 15-4, note that the offending zone varies with board angle.

Supplementary Lighting. Supplementary lighting equipment with user-adjustable support stems may be attached to the drafting table, allowing the worker to position the light for critical task requirements or to overcome shadows or reflections. Some lighting systems are attached to drafting machines so that the light moves with the task.

Reception Areas

Reception areas are designed for people who are waiting for their appointments. While they are waiting, they can read or converse with others. The lighting should be restful yet provide enough illumination for reading.

One way to provide a restful atmosphere without direct glare is by illuminating one or more of the walls. Another way is to light the ceiling and part of the walls. Accent lighting for pictures or for a piece of sculpture enlivens the appearance of the room. If there is a receptionist located in the area, the ambient light may need to be augmented, depending on the visual tasks involved. Care should also be taken to light the receptionist's face, so as to make this person look approachable, and also to eliminate harsh shadows caused by the downlights directly overhead.

Files

Files are primarily vertical work surfaces. In active filing areas, the work is likely to be long and visually difficult. Illumination should be directed onto the opened file drawers to minimize shadowing within the drawer. Where files are located in a general office environment and vertical illumination may also cause glare, consideration should be given to local illumination at the files, with individual manual or automatic switching located nearby.

Rest Rooms

Uniform illumination is not required in rest rooms. Luminaires should provide light in the vicinity of the mirrors to illuminate the face adequately. Other luminaires should illuminate bathroom fixtures and stalls; partitions should not cast heavy shadows on the fixtures or stalls. Concentration of light in these areas also has a tendency to encourage cleanliness.

Public Areas

Public areas in a building include entrance and elevator or escalator lobbies, corridors and stairways. Since many people move through these areas, lighting considerations should include safety requirements and luminance balance with respect to adjacent areas, in addition to the appearance of the space. Public areas must remain illuminated for long periods, if not continuously. Therefore, serious consideration should be given to energy-efficient systems. Since many public areas are egress areas, an auxiliary lighting system is required to cope with power outages and system fail-

ures. These auxiliary systems can also serve as security lighting.

Entrance Lobbies. First impressions of office buildings are often perceived in entrance lobbies. The lighting should complement the architecture and provide for safe transition from the exterior to the interior. Consideration must be given to readaptation by the visual system from bright daylight conditions to darker interior lighting conditions, or vice versa. The degree of readaptation depends upon the fenestration and the changing exterior lighting conditions.

Perhaps the most important element in a lobby is the walls. Some may be of glass and some of opaque materials. Walls, if they are of high reflectance, may be wall washed, and the wall luminance can provide all of the light for the lobby and provide orientation for those moving through it. If specular materials are used, possible unwanted reflections from luminaires must be considered. Grazing light from luminaires close to such surfaces will minimize visible specular reflections.

If the lobby is enclosed with glass, the interior walls need to be at a higher luminance during the day in order to be seen from outside against the high luminance of daylight. At night, a much lower luminance is required. The variable luminance also makes it easier for eyes to adapt to the luminance difference when entering or leaving a building. For these reasons, the lobby lighting should incorporate dimming or switching controls. Since surfaces have a profound effect upon the interaction of light and the space, the designer should work with the architect to choose building materials and lighting systems that will work together to achieve the desired appearance from different perspectives and at different times.

Corridors. Corridor illumination should provide at least one-fifth the illuminance of adjacent areas. (Illuminances are typically calculated with respect to the floor.) This illuminance will be both safe and energy-efficient and will not cause a high degree of eye readaptation upon entering and leaving the corridor.

Wall finish reflectance values should equal or exceed those of adjacent areas. Linear luminaires oriented crosswise to the corridor generally make it appear wider. Continuous linear luminaires located adjacent to the sidewalls provide high wall luminance, generally giving a feeling of spaciousness. Corridors, which are paths of egress, must be provided with emergency lighting.

Elevator Lobbies. These are classified as casual seeing areas, so high luminance differences are acceptable. Relatively high illuminance should be provided at the elevator threshold to call attention to possible differences in elevation between the elevator cab and the floor.

Elevators. Luminances equal to those provided in the building corridors should be provided in elevators. Elevators are small confined spaces often shared by strangers, so the lighting should help people feel comfortable. Bright ceilings and walls will give a feeling of increased size and will also indirectly light people's faces. One method of accomplishing this is through the use of a luminous ceiling. The lighting in an elevator should always be connected to the building's emergency power supply to help alleviate distress in the event of an elevator power failure or malfunction.

Stairways. The stair treads should be well illuminated, and the luminaires should be located so as to avoid glare and shadows cast by occupants onto the stairs. Luminaires should be easy to maintain; ladders are difficult to use in stairways. Emergency lighting should be provided in all public stairways. Although the lighting requirements are the same for all stairways, the lighting design solutions may be different.

OFFICES WITH VIDEO DISPLAY TERMINALS

General Considerations

The VDT is a major element in today's office and presents the design team with unique problems which must be addressed to create an acceptable work environment. In creating lighting design objectives to take into account the unique physical characteristics of VDT screens, many previously discussed recommendations also apply, but several may need to be altered. In specific terms, the lighting design must control direct and reflected glare, and must limit luminance both in the immediate task surround and within the field of view.

The lighting design process for offices containing VDT screens should begin with an analysis. It is important to understand how the VDT screen is used, what type of visual image it displays, and the angular relationship between the user, the VDT screen, and the hardcopy task. The VDT screen tilt is important; angles range from vertical to a tilt of 45° from vertical away from the operator. Many terminals offer vertical adjustment, so that the angles may not be fixed. Ergonomics typically suggests a tilt angle of 5–15° from vertical, and this value seems to be quite common. The tilt angle, along with eye height and screen height, will determine the geometry and location of the area from which brightness can cause reflected glare. Screen backgrounds and characters can display either positive contrast (light letters on a dark background) or negative contrast (dark letters on a light background). Screen surfaces can be specular or diffuse, flat or

convex. As a result, the VDT screen interacts with room surfaces, fenestration and luminaire luminance in a different manner than conventional paper tasks.

The location of the VDT screen is important, and the design of the entire work area will affect the success of the lighting design. In open-plan offices, it should be assumed that the VDT can be located anywhere within the space and that the lighting conditions outside the defined workstation will affect VDT screen visibility. Panel or partition heights behind the VDT screen can mitigate screen reflections. Partitions in front of the screen can limit direct glare from luminaires and windows. Windows are the most difficult problem to address. Short of using curtains or blinds, an orientation of the screen perpendicular to the window may limit both reflected brightness and excessive luminance contrast. In private offices the ceiling luminaires are almost directly overhead, and therefore they will not cause direct glare at normal viewing angles. Nor will they cause reflected glare in a VDT screen.

Illuminance and Luminance

The most common complaint about office lighting is reflected glare and veiling reflections on VDT screens. Luminaires, bright ceilings, the operator's clothing, walls or windows may be seen by a VDT viewer as bright patches of light reflected in the screen. Reflected glare results from brightness in the offending zone (see figures 15-4 and 15-15). The reflecting characteristics of the screen and the actual luminances determine the type of glare and the severity of problems that may result.

Negative-contrast VDT screens (dark characters on light background) can reduce the effect of reflections because they are much less visible on a light background. It should be noted that when the entire screen background is bright, flicker is more likely to be seen due to the 60-Hz refresh rate. This is especially true if the VDT screens are seen in the periphery of the field of vision, where the visual system is most sensitive to flicker.

In an office containing VDT screens, particularly in open-plan environments, it is appropriate for the general lighting to be kept at relatively low levels, and supplemental task lighting to be applied where required for paper tasks. Average maintained illuminance levels should not exceed 500 lx (50 fc) on the horizontal workplane. Typically, a low light level will have less effect on the screen contrast than higher illuminances, because the luminances of the reflected images will be lower. Although the illuminance should never exceed this value where VDT tasks predominate, it may be appropriate to provide a still-lower level if reflected luminances remain high. Windows can be a particular problem with regard to bright reflections.

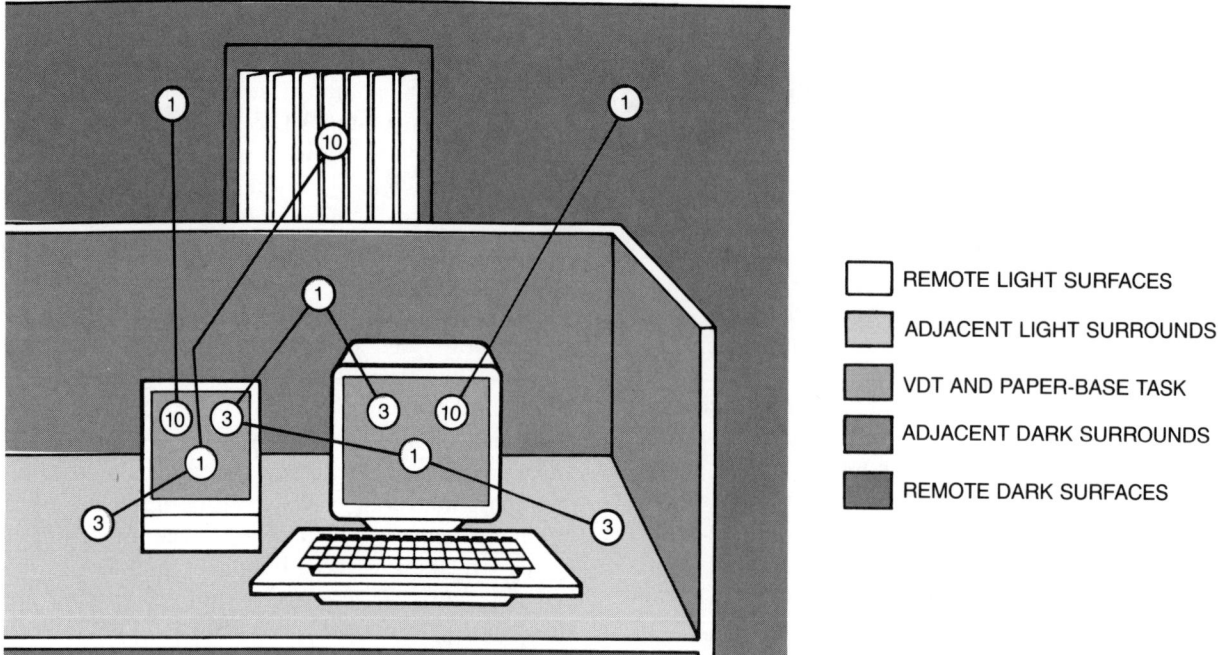

Fig. 15-13. Maximum luminance ratios recommended for a VDT workstation. The values joined by lines illustrate the maximum recommended luminance ratios between various surfaces.

Although not often recognized, direct sunlight reflecting off even a low-reflectance carpet can be a problem. If paper tasks are being performed that require higher illuminances, particular attention should be paid to the quality of the localized task lighting. Other luminances in the field of view should not exceed the recommendations for luminance ratios established for any office environment. See figure 15-13.

VDT visual tasks differ from conventional paper tasks in another significant manner. Whereas paper tasks are typically performed looking down on the horizontal task, a typical VDT visual task is performed in a "heads-up" position. Because of this, in large open offices, a significant portion of the ceiling may be in the field of view. For this reason, it is important to limit luminance on the ceiling plane in order to prevent discomfort glare or adaptation problems. See figure 15-14. Windows, again, can be a particular problem when they are located behind the VDT screen.

Visual comfort probability (VCP) data can help provide useful information for direct luminaires, but actual luminaire average luminance values at specific angles are more useful. The ceiling brightness of indirect lighting may also cause problems. As the ceiling can typically be considered a remote luminous surface, the maximum ceiling luminance should not exceed 10

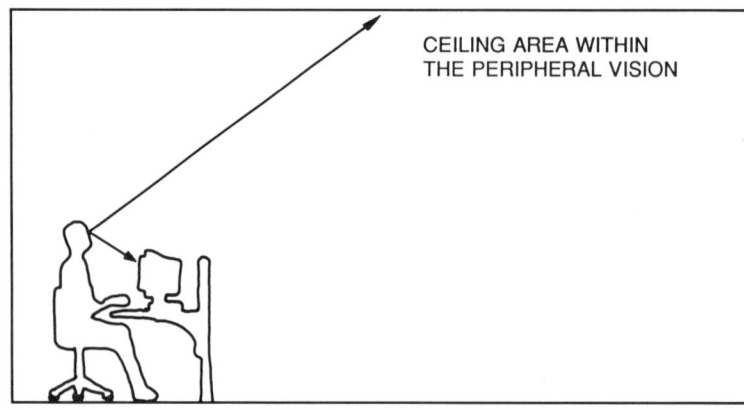

Fig. 15-14. Viewing a VDT usually requires a nearly horizontal line of sight; thus, a large area of the ceiling will be within the peripheral vision.

Fig. 15-15. Depending on the eye-screen geometry, the offending zone may be located on the ceiling plane, a wall or a partition. Screen curvature may enlarge or change the location of the offending zone.

times that of the VDT screen if the luminance ratio standards are to be maintained.

Paper Tasks. Paper tasks adjacent to VDT screens can cause a direct conflict between illuminance and luminance ratio recommendations. An 80%-reflectance, white background paper illuminated to 750 lx will result in a luminance level of roughly 200 cd/m². If the VDT screen's average luminance is, say, 50 cd/m², the paper task is four times brighter. This exceeds the recommended 3:1 luminance ratio between the paper task and adjacent VDT screens. To avoid this problem, task illuminance requirements should be more rigorously examined, and if luminance values require illuminance to be other than optimum, the quality of the task lighting should be as good as possible (no veiling reflections). Another solution to this problem is to use a VDT with a negative-contrast screen that provides greater luminance.

Direct Lighting

Specific luminance-value limitations are important for designs using direct luminaires. The geometry shown in figure 15-15 illustrates the offending zone for VDT lighting. Since screens provide a wide-angle reflection of the space, many luminaires may be in the offending zone in an open-plan environment. When a luminaire is viewed lengthwise, crosswise, or from 45°, the average luminances should be constrained by the values shown in figure 15-16.

The average luminance of a luminaire is shown on its associated photometric report in the luminance summary table (figure 15-9). Some reports may show values in footlamberts (1 fL = 3.43 cd/m²), whereas the recommendations above are made in the preferred units of candelas per square meter (cd/m²). Although

Fig. 15-16. Recommended Preferred and Maximum Average Luminance for Luminaires Used in the Direct Lighting of a VDT Environment

Angle from Vertical (deg)	Average Luminance,* cd / m²	
	Preferred	Maximum
55	850	—
65	350	850
75	175	350
≥ 85	175	175

*Luminance is measured along the lengthwise, crosswise and 45° horizontal planes.

average luminaire luminance values are a critical part of lighting guidelines, it may actually be the maximum luminaire luminance that is most meaningful in determining the potential for reflected glare. However, since there is currently no acceptable method for measuring maximum luminance, further research is required.

Utilizing low-brightness luminaires may solve the technical problems associated with VDT glare, but the resulting environmental impact may be severe. Eliminating glare does not in itself result in a pleasant environment. Additional design efforts are needed to create an appropriate perceived brightness and a sense of well-being.

Indirect Lighting

With indirect lighting, luminaire distribution characteristics, luminaire spacing and the distance between the luminaires and ceiling become critical (figure 15-17). This is especially true if, while viewing a VDT screen, the offending zone is the ceiling plane, and indirect luminaires light this plane. The maximum ceiling luminance should not exceed 850 cd/m². Also to be considered is the relationship between the ceiling luminance and the task luminance. Since the VDT task is typically a "heads-up" task, the ceiling may be visible in the peripheral view while looking at the screen. To avoid adaptation problems, the ceiling luminance should not exceed 10 times the average screen luminance.

Additionally, since it is an *area* of the ceiling and not a single point that will be reflected in the screen, that area should have uniform brightness so as not to create distracting reflection in the VDT screen. An 8:1 uniformity ratio between the brightest area, typically directly above the luminaire, and the least bright area, typically between luminaires, should be the maximum allowed. A 4:1 ratio is a more desirable goal, and 2:1 should be achievable with the appropriate equipment and layout. (As stated above, control of overhead brightness in a private office is far less important than it is in large spaces. Therefore, these guidelines are primarily for large spaces.)

In addition to ceiling luminance, the luminaire itself must also be considered. The luminaire will create contrast when seen against an illuminated ceiling. When reflected in the VDT screen, the image of the

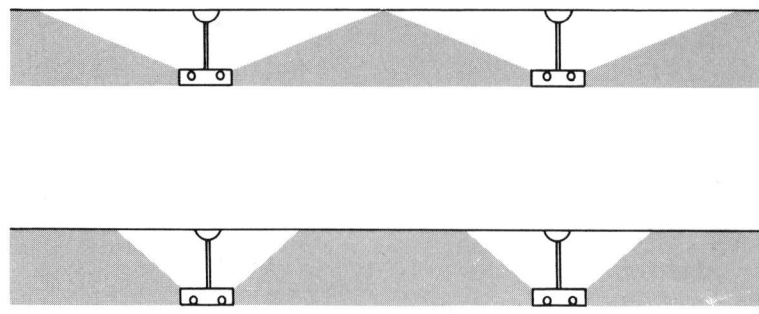

Fig. 15-17. Indirect luminaires should have a widespread light distribution as shown in the upper sketch. A narrow light distribution as shown in the lower sketch may cause patches of brightness.

luminaire can be distracting and can alter the task contrast when compared to other areas of the screen. To avoid this problem, the luminaire itself should have a high reflectivity, and the reflectivity of the surfaces below the luminaire should be considered as well. Some luminaire luminance may be useful, however, in enhancing the perceived brightness of the space. This luminance should be evaluated to assure that it is not excessive and will not be reflected as glare on the VDT screen. Because this brightness is viewed against the background of a luminous ceiling, it does not have to meet the full guidelines for direct luminaires.

Direct/Indirect Lighting

An approach that can combine the positive attributes of both direct and indirect lighting, and often eliminate the shortcomings of each, is a direct/indirect system. With this approach, either one luminaire produces both direct and indirect illumination or different luminaires are used to create different distributions. This approach may be difficult to implement, because the recommendations for both direct and indirect lighting need to be considered.

EMERGENCY LIGHTING

Emergency lighting helps ensure the safety of building occupants when the normal lighting system fails. The illumination provided by the emergency lighting system should permit an orderly accident-free exit from the office during the emergency condition. If exiting is not required, the system will operate to provide security to the remaining occupants until the general lighting can be restored. See the section on Emergency Lighting in chapter 33, as well as the National Electrical Code and individual state and local codes.

Fig. 15-18. Levels of Illumination for Safety*

Normal activity level†	Hazard requiring visual detection			
	Slight		High	
	Low	High	Low	High
Areas	Conference rooms Reception areas Exterior floodlighting Closets	Lobbies Corridors Concourse Restrooms Telephone switchboards Exterior entrances Exterior floodlighting	Freight elevators File rooms Mail rooms Offices Stairways Stockrooms Exterior entrance with stairs	Elevators Escalators Computer rooms Drafting rooms Stairways Transformer vaults Engine rooms Electrical, mechanical, plumbing rooms
Illuminance, lx (fc)	5.4 (0.5)	11 (1.0)	22 (2.0)	54 (5.0)

*Minimum illuminance for safety of personnel: absolute minimum at any time and at any location on any plane where safety is related to seeing conditions. For recommended illuminances for efficient visual performance of tasks rather than for safety alone, consult the illuminance selection procedure.
†Special conditions may require different levels of illumination. In some cases higher levels may be required, as in areas where security is a factor. In some other cases, greatly reduced illuminance levels, including complete darkness, may be necessary, specifically in situations involving manufacturing, handling, use or processing of light-sensitive materials (notably in connection with photographic film). In these situations, other methods of ensuring safe operations must be employed.

SAFETY

Importance of Safety

Safe working conditions are essential in any office arca, and the effect of light on safety must be considered. Light aids seeing and thus increases the probability that an occupant will detect the cause of a potential accident and act to avert it.

When accidents are attributed to lighting, the cause is usually very low illuminance. However, other factors associated with poor illumination can contribute to office accidents. Direct glare, reflected glare and harsh shadows hamper seeing. Accidents can also be caused by the delayed eye adaptation that a person experiences when moving from bright surroundings into dark ones and vice versa. Some accidents that are attributed to an individual's carelessness can actually be traced to difficulty in seeing, due to one or more of the above causes.

Illuminance

The illuminance recommendations provided in this Handbook serve as a guide for efficient visual performance rather than for safety; therefore, they should not be interpreted as requirements for regulatory minimum illuminances.

Figure 15-18 lists illuminances required for safety alone. To assure these values at all times, higher initial levels need to be provided as required by the maintenance conditions. See the section on Emergency Lighting in chapter 33.

Glare and Luminance Ratios

In addition to adequate illuminance, a visually safe area must not have excessive glare, nor should there be large differences in luminance within the area. Due to changes in eye adaptation when looking between areas of widely different luminance, the luminance ratio between luminaires, windows or skylights and adjacent surfaces should not exceed 40 : 1 anywhere in the field of view.

Lighting Evaluation

Although an office area may be designed for the proper quantity and quality of illumination for safety, it is necessary to know whether the requirements actually have been met in the field. To provide a standard method of evaluation, a publication entitled "How to Make a Lighting Survey" has been developed in cooperation with the U.S. Public Health Service.[31] This procedure is to be used in surveys of lighting for safety.

END-USER RESPONSIBILITY: MAINTENANCE

General Considerations

If the lighting system is to perform as designed, maintenance information must be transferred to the user for implementation. This is extremely important in that the lighting system is designed with light loss factors (LLF) that require periodic maintenance for the life of the installation. Maintenance statistics should be recorded so that the designed illuminances, capital investment and energy can be evaluated.

The designer has to be responsible for communicating the lighting service program and its importance to the user. If a tenant is new to an existing building, or an existing tenant changes the task requirements, then the lighting maintenance program needs to be reviewed and updated to suit the new office arrangements and tasks. LLFs are an important aspect of the service program, since these are part of the basic design in new or retrofit installations. The LLFs involve lamp lumen depreciation (LLD), luminaire dirt depreciation (LDD), burnouts, voltage, temperature, room dirt depreciation and other factors. An appropriate maintenance procedure and schedule for each area should be prepared. The frequency and duration of use as well as the nature of the task influence the schedule for cleaning and relamping. The practice of overdesigning lighting systems to compensate for dirt, lumen depreciation and reduced maintenance is no longer acceptable because of restrictions on energy usage and costs. To make the most of the lighting, the maintenance schedule needs to be refined and followed much more closely. See chapter 32, Lighting Maintenance.

REFERENCES

1. Weston, H. C. 1935. *The relation between illumination and visual efficiency: The effect of size of work.* Prepared for Industrial Health Research Board (Great Britain) and Medical Research Council (London). London, England: Her Majesty's Stationery Office.
2. Weston, H. C. 1945. *The relation between illumination and visual efficiency: The effect of brightness contrast*, Report No. 87. Prepared for Industrial Health Research Board (Great Britain) and Medical Research Council (London). London, England: Her Majesty's Stationery Office.
3. Rea, M. S., and M. J. Ouellette. 1991. Relative visual performance: A basis for application. *Light. Res. Tech.* 23(3):135–144.
4. Rea, M. S., M. J. Ouellette, and M. E. Kennedy. 1985. Lighting and task parameters affecting posture, performance, and subjective ratings. *J. Illum. Eng. Soc.* 15(1):231–238.
5. Weale, R. A. 1961. Retinal illumination and age. *Trans. Illum. Eng. Soc. (London)* 26(2):95–100.
6. Blackwell, O. M., and H. R. Blackwell. 1980. Individual

responses to lighting parameters for a population of 235 observers of varying ages. *J. Illum. Eng. Soc.* 9(4):205–232.

7. Blackwell, O. M., and H. R. Blackwell. 1971. Visual performance data for 156 normal observers of various ages. *J. Illum. Eng. Soc.* 1(1):3–13.

8. Allphin, W. 1963. Sight lines to desk tasks in schools and offices. *Illum. Eng.* 58(4):244–249.

9. Crouch, C. L., and J. E. Kaufman. 1963. Practical application of polarization and light control for reduction of reflected glare. *Illum. Eng.* 58(4):277–291.

10. Davis, R. G. 1987. Closing the gap: Research, design, and the psychological aspects of lighting. *Light. Des. Appl.* 17(5):14–15, 52.

11. Flynn, J. E., A. W. Segil, and G. R. Steffy. 1988. *Architectural interior systems: Lighting, acoustics, air conditioning.* 2nd ed. New York: Van Nostrand Reinhold.

12. Flynn, J. E., C. Hendrick, T. Spencer, and O. Martyniuk. 1979. A guide to methodology procedures for measuring subjective impressions in lighting. *J. Illum. Eng. Soc.* 8(2):95–110.

13. Flynn, J. E. 1977. A study of subjective responses to low energy and nonuniform lighting systems. *Light. Des. Appl.* 7(2):6–15.

14. Rowlands, E., D. L. Loe, R. M. McIntosh, and K. P. Mansfield. 1985. Lighting adequacy and quality in office interiors by consideration of subjective assessment and physical measurement. *CIE J.* 4(1):23–37.

15. Bernecker, C. A. 1980. The potential for design applications of luminance data. *J. Illum. Eng. Soc.* 10(1):8–16.

16. Davis, R. G. 1986. Computer graphics as a design tool. *Light. Des. Appl.* 16(6):38–40.

17. Bernecker, C. A., and J. M. Mier. 1985. The effect of source luminance on the perception of environment brightness. *J. Illum. Eng. Soc.* 15(1):253–271.

18. Blackwell, H. R., and I. Goodbar. 1964. Letters to the Editor. *Illum. Eng.* 59(4):13A, 59(5):10A–11A, 59(8):28A–29A, 59(11):32A–33A, and 59(12):18A–19A.

19. Rea, M. S. 1981. Visual performance with realistic methods of changing contrast. *J. Illum. Eng. Soc.* 10(3):164–177.

20. Rea, M. 1982. Photometry and visual assessment of polarized light under realistic conditions. *J. Illum. Eng. Soc.* 11(3):135–139.

21. Lawrence Berkeley Laboratory. 1979. *Can polarized lighting panels reduce energy consumption and improve visibility in building interiors?* LBL-8671. Prepared by S. Berman and R. Clear. Berkeley, CA: Lawrence Berkeley Laboratory.

22. Blackwell, H. R., and R. N. Helms. 1973. Application procedures for evaluation of veiling reflections in terms of ESI: I. General principles. *J. Illum. Eng. Soc.* 2(3):230–327.

23. Blackwell, H. R., and D. L. DiLaura. 1973. Application procedures for evaluation of veiling reflections in terms of ESI: II. Gonio data for the standard pencil task. *J. Illum. Eng. Soc.* 2(3):254–283.

24. Blackwell, H. R., R. N. Helms, and D. L. DiLaura. 1973. Application procedures for evaluation of veiling reflections in terms of ESI: III. Validation of a predetermination method for luminaire installations. *J. Illum. Eng. Soc.* 2(3):284–298.

25. Blackwell, H. R., R. N. Helms, and D. L. DiLaura. 1973. Application procedures for evaluation of veiling reflections in terms of ESI: IV. Final validation of measurement and predetermination methods for luminaire installation. *J. Illum. Eng. Soc.* 2(3):299–327.

26. Blackwell, H. R. 1963. A general quantitative method for evaluating the visual significance of reflected glare, using visual performance data. *Illum. Eng.* 58(4):161–243.

27. DiLaura, D. L. 1975. On the computation of equivalent sphere illumination. *J. Illum. Eng. Soc.* 4(2):129–149.

28. Ballman, T. L., and R. E. Levin. 1987. Illumination in partitioned spaces. *J. Illum. Eng. Soc.* 16(2):31–49.

29. Brackett, W. E., W. L. Fink, and W. Pierpoint. 1983. Interior point-by-point calculations in obstructed spaces. *J. Illum. Eng. Soc.* 13(1):14–25.

30. Briggs, J. F. 1984. An illuminance survey and analysis of partitioned spaces. *J. Illum. Eng. Soc.* 14(1):63–119.

31. Joint Lighting Survey Committee. IES. Lighting Survey Committee and U.S. Department of Health, Education and Welfare. Public Health Service. 1963. How to make a lighting survey. *Illum. Eng.* 58(2):87–100.

Educational Facility Lighting

16

There are continuing challenges and opportunities for the designer in the field of educational facility lighting. New educational buildings will result from new needs, while others will be replacements for obsolete structures. There are many existing educational buildings that are in need of retrofitting to improve the visual environment and to reduce energy usage; however, it is not sufficient simply to replace old lighting equipment. Innovative lighting designs are also required to meet new needs and to reduce energy consumption.

THE GOAL OF EDUCATIONAL FACILITY LIGHTING

The goal of educational facility lighting is to provide in each school situation a visual environment for both student and instructor that is supportive of the learning processes. This can only be achieved if the occupants can see their visual tasks accurately, quickly and comfortably. Uniform horizontal illuminance throughout an educational facility does not assure high levels of visual performance, because of the great variety of visual tasks found in a school. The visual tasks become more varied as the pupil moves from the elementary school through high school to college.

Lighting must also be visually comfortable and be responsive to the psychological and emotional needs of learners. Lighting can make a school more pleasant and attractive, reinforce feelings of spaciousness, delineate areas of different functions, stimulate learning and improve behavior.

ENERGY MANAGEMENT

Energy can be better utilized in providing an optimum visual environment by careful selection, use and control of efficient light sources and luminaires, along with the use of daylight, to provide the proper quantity of high-quality, comfortable lighting (see chapter 30, Energy Management). Daylight must, however, be carefully controlled if it is to be effectively used (see chapter 8, Daylighting).

With the emergence of energy codes on local and state levels, the issues of effective energy use cannot be overemphasized. The designer must also provide written information for each building to enable administrators, instructors, students and custodians to operate and maintain the lighting systems in the most visually effective, energy-efficient and cost-effective manner.

The designer should prepare written instructions for the maintenance of the lighting system, covering such major items as: (1) listing of specific lighting equipment used, (2) the cleaning schedule for lamps and luminaires, (3) the relamping schedule and (4) the room surface maintenance schedule, including repainting.[1] If such information is not made available, neglect will result in decreased illumination while using the same amount of energy (see chapter 30, Energy Management).

Consideration should be given to lighting control methods such as multiple-level switching, daylight and motion sensors, and whole building controls.

VISUAL TASKS

Visual tasks in educational facilities vary in size, contrast, viewing direction and distance.[2] Major critical tasks are reading and writing, commonly requiring prolonged and close attention. There are both near and far visual tasks, of small and large size, on matte and glossy surfaces. Students are often required to adapt from reading at a desk to reading from a chalkboard; from looking almost straight down to looking along or above the horizontal.

Educators have a basic responsibility to help students see well. This may be accomplished by providing tasks having high contrast and low specularity and by properly designed illumination. With regard to the major school tasks of reading and writing, the steps that educators can take to improve visibility include:

1. Felt-tipped pens and No. 2 pencils are not shiny and provide high contrast with the paper. Other writing materials should be selected similarly.
2. Ten-point type is the minimum size recommended for textbooks. Younger pupils will require a larger type size. Adequate spacing between the lines of type and low-gloss ink will aid readability.

3. Opaque matte paper should be used in text-books and workbooks, for tablets and note-books, and for tests and other reproduced materials.
4. A proper combination of high-grade chalk, chalkboard and illumination should be provided. White chalk is more visible than other light-colored chalks on most colors of chalk-board. Chalkboards should be kept clean and periodically restored or resurfaced. Teachers should be encouraged to use large letters and figures when writing on chalkboards. Supplementary lighting is advised for chalkboards to provide adequate vertical illumination.

QUALITY AND QUANTITY OF ILLUMINATION

Quality and quantity of illumination are interdependent. Illuminance levels may be appropriate for the task, but reflected glare, veiling reflections and excessive luminance in the field of view all compromise visibility and therefore reduce lighting quality.

Illuminance

Illuminance recommendations for a few of the tasks found in educational facilities are listed in chapter 11, Illuminance Selection. In order to select suitable illuminance values for the many other tasks and areas it is necessary to consult the illuminance selection procedure found in chapter 11. From this procedure, a suitable illuminance can be determined.

Because it is uncommon for learning spaces to contain a single visual task, the determination of appropriate illuminance must begin by evaluating each visual task in terms of such variables as size, contrast and time. Then the illuminance can be selected in relation to the most demanding visual task that occupies a significant part of the time spent in the space.

The usual approach is to select the most difficult commonly occurring task and to provide an adequate level for that task. Reading pencil writing is most often the task selected. Where reading printed materials of high contrast is the commonly occurring, most difficult task, lower levels would be considered adequate. As other, more difficult tasks are attempted, assuming a constant illuminance level, a smaller percentage of the most difficult students will be provided with adequate light to reach a given performance level.

In some cases, selection of the most difficult commonly occurring task in a classroom or other teaching station can result in uneconomically high illuminances. In such cases it is preferable to provide a level that is adequate for the less demanding tasks and to provide increased illuminance at each specific task location where a higher level is needed. Thus the ambient

lighting in the space can provide adequate general illumination, with task lighting only at specific points. Drafting tables and chalkboards, for example, need higher levels, but the remainder of the space need not be lighted to the same level. School shops, sewing rooms, art classrooms, areas for the partially sighted, and many other educational spaces can and should be adequately lighted by means of a proper combination of task and ambient lighting.

Reflectances

Walls, including tackboards and large cabinets or cupboards mounted on the wall, should have nonspecular surfaces with 40–60% reflectance (see figure 16-1). Blinds or drapes, like walls, should be light colored, with similar reflectances. Walls adjacent to windows should also have very high, nonspecular reflectances, to avoid excessive luminance ratios between the windows and the wall surface. That portion of the wall above the level of the luminaires should have a reflectance of 80%. The ceiling should be highly reflective (white) and nonspecular, because this surface is most important in reflecting light downward toward tasks on desk tops when using direct/indirect or indirect luminaires. It is also necessary to avoid obvious brightness differences between the ceiling and the luminaires, whether located within or below the ceiling. Ideally, the ceiling should have a luminance greater than, or at least equal to, that of the side walls. It is desirable to have the luminance of the side walls at least one-half that of the immediate surround.

Floors provide the secondary background for desk-top tasks; thus, floors should have a nonspecular, high reflectance but should be of lower luminance than the walls. Floor coverings, whether carpet, resilient tile or some other material, should be light in color. While there are floor coverings with soil-resistant finishes, there are no soil-resistant colors, and dark colors become soiled as readily as do light, higher-reflectance colors.

Luminance Ratios

The brightnesses of the various surfaces in the normal field of view in a space must be kept within accepted limits. When the eye fixates on a task, an adaptation level is established. As the eye shifts from one luminance, such as a book, to another luminance, such as the chalkboard, it must readapt to the new luminance level. If there is much difference between the two levels, a period of time is required for the eye to adjust itself to the new situation. Further, if the difference is too great, some discomfort will be experienced.

In order to avoid this, and for good visual performance, the luminance of any surface normally viewed directly should not be greater than five times the luminance of the task (see figure 16-2). No large area,

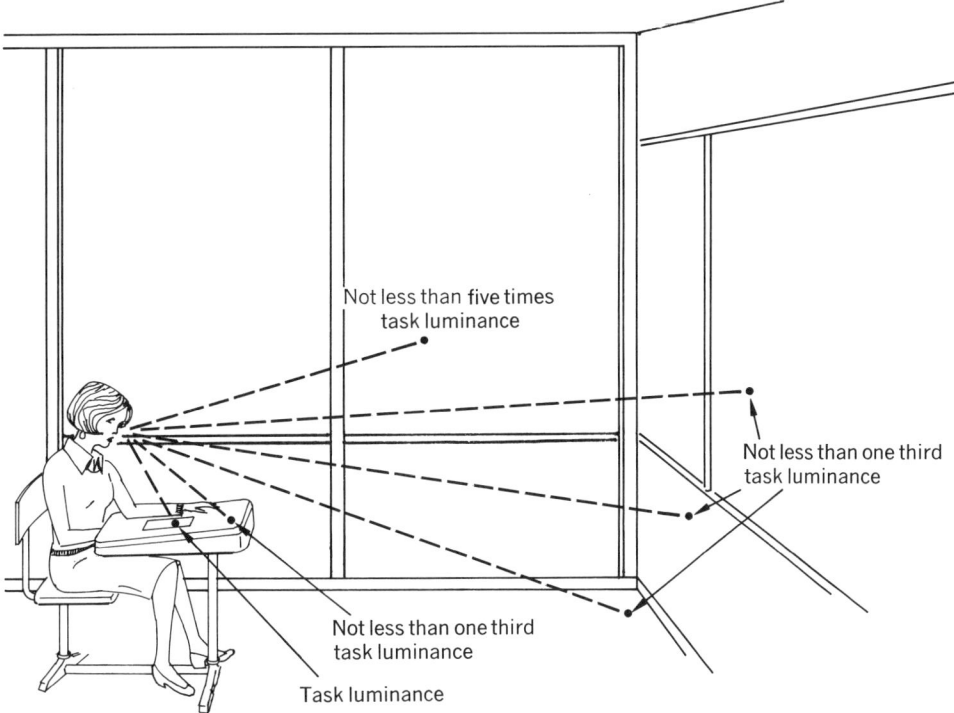

Not less than five times
task luminance

Not less than one third
task luminance

Not less than one third
task luminance

Task luminance

Fig. 16-1. In a classroom the luminance of significant surfaces should not differ greatly from that of the visual task. The luminance of the surface immediately surrounding the task should be less than the task luminance but not less than one-third the task luminance. The lowest luminance of any significant surface should not be less than one-third the task luminance. The highest luminance should not be greater than five times the task luminance.

regardless of its position in the room, should have less than one-third the luminance of the task. The luminance of surfaces immediately adjacent to the visual task is more critical in terms of visual comfort and performance than that of more remote surfaces in the visual surround. Surfaces, such as desk tops, immediately adjacent to the visual task should not exceed the luminance of the task, but should have at least one-third the luminance of the task. The difference in luminance between adjacent surfaces in the visual surround should be kept as low as possible.

The general approach in providing low luminance ratios over the entire visual field is to limit the luminance of luminaires and of fenestration and to increase the luminance of all interior surfaces. There are two methods to increase surface luminance: increase the reflectance of the surface, and select luminaires which distribute more light onto the surface.

Glare

An educational space should limit glare. When light sources, electric or daylight, are too bright, they can produce discomfort or impair vision. The *visual comfort probability* (VCP), which predicts the relative freedom from discomfort glare of a lighting system, is used in evaluating lighting systems in many educational facility spaces. The system takes into account the size and shape of the space, surface reflectances, illuminances,

luminaire type (including size and light distribution), luminance of the entire field of view, observer location and line of sight. The VCP system yields the percentage of people who, if seated in the most undesirable location, will be expected to find it acceptable. See chapter 3, Vision and Perception.

In order to prevent glare, windows must be either located outside the normal field of view or provided with means of optical control. Shades, blinds, louvers, baffle systems or roof overhangs can be used (see chapter 8, Daylighting). Luminaires with a high luminance will also produce discomfort glare. Optical control devices, such as louvers, must be incorporated into the luminaires.

Reflections of light sources from specular surfaces in the field of view are referred to as *reflected glare*. Reflected glare can be reduced by using matte finishes on furniture, equipment and room surfaces and by using low-luminance sources.

This does not mean that *sparkle* must be eliminated. A small patch of sunlight, a brilliant view, or bright holiday decorations may be relevant at a particular time and should not be considered as unacceptable glare. Some sparkle may be a permanent feature, but much will be transitory, providing a welcome variation in the visual environment.

Losses in task contrast can result when light is reflected from the task. These reflections act as a luminous veil superimposed on the task. The veiling

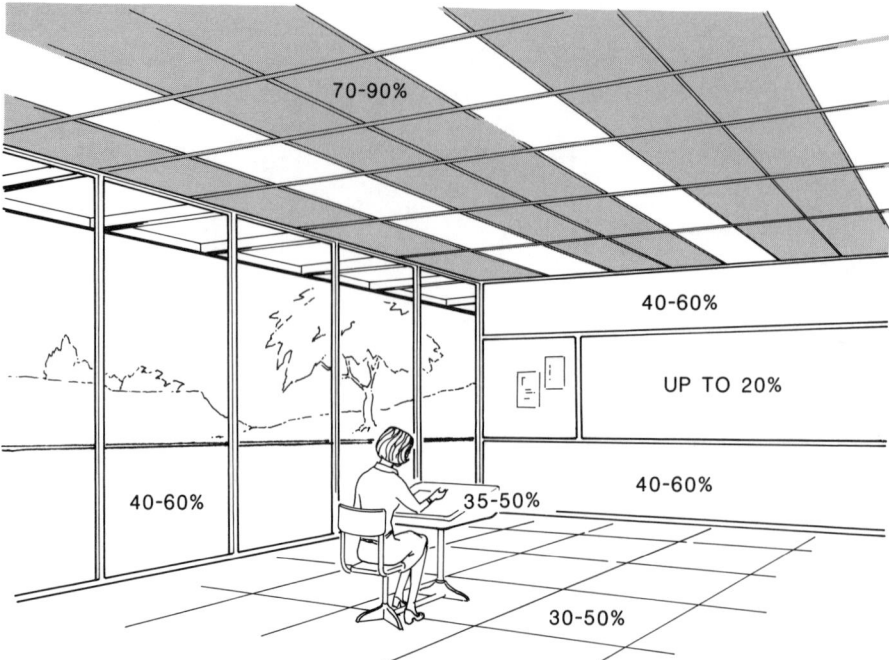

Fig. 16-2. Recommended reflectances for surfaces and furnishings in the classroom. (Note the control media used at windows to reduce exterior luminances so that they are in balance with interior luminances.)

reflection may be quite apparent, as it is when a page in a magazine printed on glossy paper becomes obscured by a reflected source of light. It may be quite subtle, as when written material on matte paper is just slightly obscured or veiled. People are quick to move the task or their posture to overcome deleterious veiling reflections. Such changes may not be easy to achieve or may cause discomfort, so care must be taken to prevent veiling reflections whenever possible.

Shadows cast on visual tasks may impair effective seeing. Sharply defined shadows or ones too close to the task may be particularly annoying. This does not mean that shadows must be completely eliminated, but that shading and shadows must not be excessively dense or confusing. Effective use of shadows is important in rooms where modeling of three-dimensional surfaces is desirable.

Sharply defined shadows are usually produced by direct luminaires; indirect or diffuse luminaires tend to eliminate shadowing.

Color in classrooms and other educational spaces is an important consideration for the designer. Light colors should predominate to provide adequate levels of illuminance and brightness. Wall, floor and furniture colors that conform to the reflectances and to the luminance ratios recommended will necessarily be the lighter colors. Light colors carried to an extreme, however, may lead to bland and uninteresting results. Touches of accent color or limited areas of relatively bright color, not conforming to the general recommendations given above, can give vitality and dramatic

interest to a space, if used with discretion.

Where good color rendering is very important, as in art education rooms, it is advisable that light sources be selected that will make materials appear as they do under daylight. Where good color rendering is less important, as in workshops, light sources having a more limited spectrum may be considered. These sources must be utilized with caution, with proper consideration given to the activities to be carried on in the space. This is particularly true of spaces from which daylight is largely excluded, or which are used as much at night as during the day.

LIGHTING SYSTEMS FOR EDUCATIONAL FACILITIES

Daylighting

There are numerous aspects of daylight that make its use in educational facilities desirable as a light source and valuable from a psychological, esthetic and economic viewpoint. Well-designed fenestration systems can serve a number of purposes in educational facilities:

- Admission, control and distribution of daylight for the performance of visual tasks
- A distant focus for the eye, relaxing the eye muscles
- The psychological benefit of an exterior view

Since daylight is a variable source, it must be controlled and supplemented by an electric lighting system.

Means of controlling potential glare from daylight include exterior architectural appendages, such as screens, overhangs or awnings, and interior devices such as shades, blinds, drapes and solar-reflecting or -reducing glazing materials. Blinds or drapes can be managed by the occupants so as to compensate for changes in daily orientation and for seasonal differences in daylight. Both manual and automatic control systems for the electric lights can be used to compensate for inadequate daylight and reduce energy costs when daylight provides sufficient illumination.

Finally, daylight systems should be coordinated within the total building design, including heating, cooling, ventilating and electric lighting. Its value must be evaluated using life-cycle cost-benefit analyses (see chapter 13, Lighting Economics) to assure proper trade-offs between the various elements of the total design.

Electric Lighting

Light Source Selection. At the heart of any electric lighting system is the light source itself. Of the three main categories, fluorescent, high-intensity discharge and incandescent, the most frequently used in classrooms is the fluorescent lamp. Fluorescent lamps have many advantages, including high efficacy, low brightness, and long life (see chapter 6, Light Sources). The 1200-mm (4-ft) and 2400-mm (9-ft) lamps are the most popular.

The standard cool white halophosphate lamp has historically seen significant use due to its low cost. However, in recent years, superior efficacy, higher-color-rendering rare-earth phosphor lamps have emerged as the preferred light source. These lamps can be employed where good color rendering is required. Indeed, with new legislation, halophosphate lamps will no longer be available.

Deluxe and other specialized high-color-rendering lamps are also used where good to excellent color rendering is specified. These lamps are available in both "cool" (above 4000 K) and "warm" (3000 K) correlated color temperatures and are suitable for art, fashion, science and other classroom areas where color is important.

High-intensity discharge (HID) lamps have long been used in school gymnasiums and outdoor applications. Their high efficacy, compact size and long life make them the most economical and practical lamps for use in high-ceiling interior spaces and for almost all exterior applications. Care should be taken in the selection of HID sources with regard to color rendering, color temperature and flicker. It should be pointed out that

while HID lamps are highly efficacious, they also require startup times which can range from 2 to 12 min.

For quiet areas, such as libraries and study halls, HID lamp ballasts should be remotely located in order to minimize hum or buzzing.

Tungsten halogen lamps are excellent supplemental light sources for the classroom, but should not be used for general lighting. The optical compactness of tungsten halogen lamps allows for a high degree of light control, making them excellent choices for highlighting, for display lighting and for featuring instructional aids in the classroom. They are switched on and off instantly and are inexpensively dimmed.

For more information on the characteristics of each type of light source see chapter 6, Light Sources.

Luminaire Selection. In selecting appropriate luminaires for any educational space, the designer should be aware of the purpose of the lighting, whether to maximize visibility, to attract attention, to establish a mood, to create interest, or to unify or separate spaces. Factors to be considered in selecting luminaires can be found in reference 1 and in chapter 7, Luminaires.

SPECIFIC APPLICATIONS

The modern educational facility, whether an elementary school, a comprehensive high school or a university building, contains a variety of lighting needs. A few specific applications are reviewed here to emphasize the unique requirements of educational facility lighting. See reference 2 for further information.

Lighting the Classroom

Lighting the conventional, or academic, classroom is the most common lighting design problem in educational facilities. Classrooms can, however, be any space within the building. These classrooms are those in the elementary school in which pupils spend a major portion of their school day, those in the middle and senior high schools in which pupils study the academic subjects, and similar classrooms found throughout the college and university campus.

Regular classroom floor areas range from 61 to 83 m² (660 to 900 ft²) or more. Windows range from a "vision strip" the length of one wall, but only a meter (a few feet) high, to a full floor-to-ceiling window wall. Some classrooms are windowless or have a small window in one corner. More typically, classroom windows reach almost to the ceiling above a solid spandrel usually 760–910 mm (30–36 in.) high. Classrooms of the future may have somewhat different window areas to minimize heat loss and gain and electric lighting loads and thus conserve energy.

Open-plan arrangements found in many schools utilize movable partitions and portable chalkboards, desks, demonstration tables and book shelving. These can be relocated and regrouped as needed. The lighting system should be equally flexible and responsive. Luminaires should be arranged so that desk locations will not be dictated by the lighting, because regular rows of desks are rarely found today, at least in the lower grades.

The required classroom illuminance is dependent upon the tasks to be performed. The task in most regular classrooms, which occupies at least one-third of each pupil's time, involves writing, such as completing a spelling test or taking notes during a college lecture. If the most difficult common task to be encountered is reading good-quality printed material, then the illuminance should be designed for that task. See chapter 11, Illuminance Selection.

Type and Placement of Luminaires. Once the desired illuminance has been determined, other factors, such as glare, shadows and color should be considered in the luminaire and lamp selection.

The type of luminaire selected also depends on the ceiling height and type. In high-ceiling spaces, suspended direct/indirect luminaires provide for reflected light from the ceiling and downlighting (see figure 16-3). Well-designed indirect lighting systems provide good shadow-free illumination. A great many school class rooms, however, have low ceilings that necessitate ceiling-mounted or recessed luminaires. Recessed luminaires are less obtrusive than surface-mounted luminaires of the same size.

Classroom luminaires can be arranged in a variety of patterns; however, special consideration should be given to the orientation of the luminaires with regard

to the following factors:

- Predictable or unpredictable position and orientation of desks
- Location of chalkboard
- Location and proximity of windows
- Ceiling height
- Photometric characteristic of luminaires
- Flexibility of the space for other functions

Lighting for Audiovisual Presentations. Television, motion pictures, slides and film strips are used extensively in classrooms.[3] For effective viewing it is necessary to reduce or to turn off the general overhead lighting. The room should not be completely darkened; blackout drapes are not recommended for use in the classroom. Careful adjustment of drapes or blinds can usually provide adequate daylight control. Any needed light can be provided by the regular luminaires if those over the screen can be turned off, while others are operated at the lowest level available. If students are expected to take notes during the audiovisual presentation, an alternative solution may be to switch or dim certain selected luminaires or lamps.

Task/Ambient Lighting

Numerous areas in schools have lighting design criteria different from those of regular classrooms. These criteria may put a greater emphasis on the discrimination of color, three-dimensional modeling or variations in brightness. While it may be necessary to provide fairly high, uniformly distributed levels in regular classrooms, it is sometimes practical, and in the interest of wise energy use, to reduce illuminance to areas suitable for general activities and then provide supplementary lighting only where it is needed. Thus, the ambient lighting should be suitable for reading high-contrast printed material, and the supplementary lighting, often in the form of *task lighting*, should provide a higher illuminance where it is needed. This task lighting can be supplied by small sources concentrated on these areas. At times this supplementary lighting includes a directional component to provide modeling or to serve some other need.

Sewing Rooms. One of the most difficult visual tasks is that of sewing. The process of seeing fine stitching on cloth where the thread matches the cloth is inherently difficult and fatiguing. The stitching is seen in part by the reflected glint from the thread. Task lighting is needed which can provide the high illuminances required.

Shops. The lighting of each school shop should follow the industrial lighting practice for the types of activities provided in the shop, with special emphasis on assisting the effectiveness of manual operations and on

Fig. 16-3. Direct-indirect lighting for an elementary school classroom.

making all elements of danger visually obvious (see chapter 20, Industrial Lighting and chapter 33, Emergency, Safety and Security Lighting). Special paint colors should be adopted for machine controls and for machine parts which represent a hazard for the student.[4] Important work points on each machine should be painted to make them stand out. Flicker from lamps (for example, HID lamps) should be minimized.

Art Rooms. Because the appearance of colors in an art room is paramount, the light sources used should render colors well. Lamps with high color rendering capability will be required. See chapter 4, Color. This is true of both the ambient and the task lighting. Supplementary lighting from concentrating directional sources is useful with displays and models, for it provides improved visibility and creates desired highlights and shadows needed for modeling purposes. Adjustable luminaires can be used to provide this type of lighting.

Classrooms for the Handicapped

Certain classrooms may be specifically designed for handicapped pupils.[5] In most cases partially sighted individuals benefit from high illuminance levels. There are some exceptions, however, and special provisions should be made for those who need lower levels. Information on such special cases should be provided by the school authorities, and the designer may find it necessary to arrange specialized lighting.

Pupils having impaired hearing often depend upon speech reading (lip reading) for much of their understanding. It is necessary that the speaker's face be well lighted. The illumination should provide sufficient modeling for the movements of the lips and other facial features to be readily perceived.

Spaces with Visual Display Terminals

Many schools have classrooms for computer training. Visual display terminals (VDTs) used in these rooms have special lighting needs. For a discussion of lighting of spaces with VDTs, see chapter 15, Office Lighting.

Learning Resources Centers and Libraries

Libraries in schools range from very simple rooms in the elementary school with a reading area surrounded by book stacks to the very complex learning resources centers in high schools and the general, special and technical libraries in colleges and universities. Many libraries include a reading area requiring uniform illumination, adequate for reading printed materials, plus stack areas with special lighting to make possible the reading of information on the spines of shelved books (see figure 16-4). Libraries may include such spaces as a circulation desk and card catalogs, conference and seminar rooms, display and exhibition areas, mi-

Fig. 16-4. Luminaires housing T-8 fluorescent lamps are mounted to the top of the shelves to illuminate book stacks.

crofiche viewing areas, audiovisual rooms, technical processing areas and offices. Some may have word-processing equipment rooms for the students' use. Each of these areas presents different and, often, unique lighting problems.

Reading, by far the most common visual task in the reading and reference area, requires that the lighting be suited to the wide range of materials to be read (see figure 16-5). Type smaller than that on a newspaper page may be encountered. Considerable handwriting is performed, so lighting adequate for reading pencil writing should be provided. Room surface reflectances recommended for school classrooms will usually provide satisfactory luminance ratios. Some special areas of task lighting will be required, for example, adjacent

Fig. 16-5. A library reading area lighted with a direct-indirect fluorescent luminaire and natural light from a nearby window.

to the machines in the microform viewing area, so that the machines themselves can be located in an area of reduced lighting. If proper precautions are not taken in the reading areas, veiling reflections may greatly reduce visibility. Additional information on the special problems of large libraries will be found in chapter 17, Institutions and Public Buildings.

Physical Education and Multipurpose Spaces

Physical education spaces in schools are usually the largest spaces in the building. For this reason they may be planned and used as multipurpose spaces to accommodate large groups for many activities not related to physical education and athletics.

The elementary multipurpose room is often planned to provide for physical education classes, after-school recreation, dining and auditorium activities, including musical and dramatic rehearsals and presentations. Community activities can also be accommodated. The lighting should be appropriate for the uses planned and should be adaptable to levels suited to assemblies and other activities. If there is a stage, either built-in or portable, suitable stage lighting of an appropriate type should be provided.[6] See chapter 21, Theatre, Television and Photographic Lighting, for more information on stage lighting.

The high school gymnasium or college field house is a multipurpose space. Besides physical education and athletics, it is used for graduations, assemblies, dances, concerts and community meetings. The resulting diversity of visual tasks and lighting needs dictates a choice of illuminances. A good design technique is the provision of the highest illuminance needed together with flexible circuitry to reduce it where appropriate. Supplementary low-level lighting may also be appropriate. Portable or temporary lighting equipment should be included so that special effects can be obtained for the nonathletic events.

HID or fluorescent light sources are normally suitable for gymnasium lighting (see figure 16-6). These should be supplemented by sources which restart more rapidly and are suited to the other uses of the gymnasium. Gymnasium luminaires should be covered with protective grids. See chapter 23 for further information on sports and recreational area lighting.

College and University Applications

The recommendations given above for lighting classrooms and other school spaces are applicable to community college, college and university classrooms. Though more typical of the college or university, the following may be found in some high schools.

Lecture Rooms. Lecture room capacities range from 50 occupants or less to several hundred. Floors may be

Fig. 16-6. A gymnasium lighted with recessed HID luminaires.

flat, slightly sloping or steeply ramped. The problems of lighting lecture rooms become more complex with an increase in floor area and the demand for good observation of demonstrations. A lecture room should have a general lighting system which is flexible enough to provide at least two illuminances, the higher level for note-taking and a subdued one for demonstrations. An intermediate level is also desirable. When downlighting is used, it should be very carefully designed to avoid loss of visibility due to veiling reflections.

If a demonstration table is to be used, directional downlights should be located at a 40–60° angle above the horizontal in relation to the location of the lecturer. This minimizes glare and provides good lighting for the speaker's face. Such lighting can be arranged to allow use of an audiovisual screen at the same time that the lecturer is speaking.

Dormitory Rooms. Dormitory rooms are commonly provided with two systems of illumination, a low-level one for general illumination and a higher level of task lighting for study purposes. Direct/indirect table or floor luminaires are suited to reading and study. If study carrels are used, the luminaires should be mounted at the sides.[7] Illuminances on desk tops should be adequate for pencil tasks. When the room is shared by two or more students, it should be possible for one to retire, after turning off the ambient lighting, and for the other to continue to study by the task illumination alone. This situation may partially violate the desirable luminance relationships between the task and the visual surround, but it is a necessary condition of dormitory life.

Corridors and Stairs

No single illuminance is applicable to all corridors or all stairways. Each must be considered in relation to the occupants of the building and their needs.

Corridors. During daylight hours, corridors are the transition areas from the higher luminances of the out-of-doors to the lower luminances of the interior spaces of a school. Corridors adjacent to entrances can be lighted to a slightly higher level with daylight and electric lighting to aid in alleviating transient adaptation phenomena. This will also serve to indicate the location of exits at night. Corridors should be adequately lighted to promote safety and discipline. Corridors lined with lockers require higher levels than those used simply for passage. Supplementary lighting may be required at the positions where monitors or security personnel are stationed. When corridors are used also as work or study areas, as is true in some elementary schools, they become extensions of the classrooms and so should be appropriately lighted.

Corridor lighting also provides an opportunity to add visual interest to school environments and emphasis to displays, bulletin boards and posters. Special attention to the lighting of architectural elements will add to the pleasantness and visual vitality of corridors.

Stairs. The lighting of stairwells must be very carefully planned so that the edge of each step is properly illuminated, there are no high luminances in the line of vision, landings are adequately lighted, and occupants do not cast shadows on the stairs. Corridor lighting seldom illuminates stairs and stairwells adequately, so it is important that corridor and stair lighting be coordinated to eliminate dark areas, especially where there are fire doors.

Emergency Lighting. The illumination provided by the emergency lighting system should be adequate to permit an orderly, accident-free exit from anywhere in the building. Sufficient illumination must be provided on the exit route to make it readily identifiable. Emergency general lighting should be provided for windowless classrooms and offices and for auditoriums, cafeterias, multipurpose rooms and other large-group spaces.

Care in specifying emergency lighting luminaires suited to the location is very important. Emergency lighting luminaires should be protected in school situations where mischief-prone youngsters may find the unit or its test switch an attraction. The units selected should be capable of resisting such actions and remain in working condition. See chapter 33, Emergency, Safety and Security Lighting for further information.

Outdoor Lighting and Security Lighting

Many educational buildings are used after dark, and it is therefore important to give careful consideration to the various aspects of outdoor lighting. Building facades, approaches and outdoor activity areas should be illuminated both for the activity itself and for general safety, as well as for protection against vandalism and theft. Lighting of outdoor areas such as parking lots, roadways and athletic fields is discussed in chapters 22 and 24. Outdoor lighting and security lighting are so closely related that they must be considered together. Often the same installation will serve both purposes.

Outdoor Lighting. Outdoor lighting for schools should facilitate legitimate nighttime approach and entry, whether on foot or by vehicle, provide security for the building and its contents, and enhance the architectural features of the building. In many cases the last purpose will be largely achieved by proper provision for the other two. Walks, driveways, internal streets and parking lots should be illuminated at night. They may be lighted using conventional walkway, roadway and parking lot luminaires. Entrance and exit areas of the building should be more brightly illuminated with efficient light sources.

Security Lighting. The need for and definition of security lighting must first be clearly established. One effective security lighting strategy for a school building is facade lighting. Such lighting, supplied by luminaires located away from the building, facilitates security in the following ways:

- By providing direct viewing of persons and of the structure
- By allowing indirect viewing of the enlarged shadows cast by intruders as they approach the lighted surface of the building
- By permitting observation of intruders in silhouette against the lighted background before they are in range of the illumination from the luminaires
- By reducing or eliminating the glare distraction which often accompanies floodlighting mounted anywhere on the building itself

Facade lighting for security purposes can be placed on poles, trees, adjacent walls or special pedestals. Often low-level luminaires on pedestals can be hidden behind plantings so that the sources are not readily apparent. Available high-efficacy sources, such as high-intensity discharge, are well suited to the type of dusk-to-dawn security lighting required. Combined with properly located and vandal-proof luminaires, the result can be an attractive, efficient and functional nighttime security lighting system. Lamps need not provide high color rendition to be effective. See chapter 33 for additional information on security lighting.

REFERENCES

1. IES. Design Practice Committee. 1974. Factors to be considered in lighting design. *Light. Des. Appl.* 4(4):38–39.
2. IES. School and College Lighting Committee. 1978. American national standard guide for school lighting, ANSI/IES RP-3-1977. *Light. Des. Appl.* 8(2):12–42.

3. IES. School and College Committee. Subcommittee on Lighting for Audiovisual Aids. 1966. Guide for lighting audiovisual areas in schools. *Illum. Eng.* 61(7):477–491.

4. American National Standards Institute. 1980. *American national standard safety color code for marking physical hazards, ANSI Z53.1-1979.* New York: American National Standards Institute.

5. Herron, P. L., and F. F. LaGiusa. 1975. Brightness variations affect deaf learners' attention. *Light. Des. Appl.* 5(2):30–34.

6. IES. Theater, Television and Film Lighting Committee. CP-34 Task Group. 1983. Addendum to "Lighting for theatrical presentations on educational and community proscenium-type stages," IES CP-34A. *Light. Des. Appl.* 13(9):27.

7. LaGiusa, F. F., and J. F. McNelis. 1971. Guides for evaluating the effectiveness of supplementary lighting for study carrels. *Light. Des. Appl.* 1(5):6–11.

Institution and Public Building Lighting

17

Financial facilities, houses of worship, health care facilities, hospitality facilities (such as hotels, motels and food service facilities), libraries, and museums and art galleries are usually considered to be institutions or public buildings. The lighting of the spaces peculiar to these buildings is included in this section.

Appropriate design illuminances for areas and tasks in institutions and public buildings are given in chapter 11, Illuminance Selection. Within this chapter specific illuminance values are given based on criteria other than visual task performance.

For the lighting of office areas, merchandising areas and exteriors of institutions and public buildings, see chapters 15, 18 and 22, respectively. For general information on interior lighting design and energy management, see chapters 10 and 30.

FINANCIAL FACILITIES

The various functions, tasks and spatial arrangements that are found in financial facilities are mainly the same as those that occur in offices—conference areas, accounting, general and private offices, including bookkeeping and VDT use (see chapter 15, Office Lighting). There are, however, several areas that are special to banking functions where the lighting needs may be different.

Specific Areas

Illuminance recommendations for areas and associated seeing tasks are given in chapter 11, Illuminance Selection. Special areas are treated below.

Lobbies. In the past, many bank lobbies had very high ceilings. (See figure 17-1.) Today, because of increased building and operating costs, they are usually no more than 3.5–4.5 m (12–15 ft) high. Where very high ceilings exist, the use of high-intensity discharge lamps should be considered to help control construction, energy and maintenance costs.

Special attention should be given to adequate illumination in writing areas. This can be accomplished with additional ceiling-mounted luminaires or local counter-mounted task lights. When promotional incentives, such as merchandise, are located in the lobby, there should be provisions for highlighting to create a focal point (see chapter 18, Lighting for Merchandise Areas).

Network Control. The bank's *network control* area is usually a continuously occupied space in a major banking facility. Because of the large numbers of VDT data screens and electronic displays present in these areas, it is advisable to treat these spaces in the same way as a VDT office (see chapter 15, Office Lighting).

Tellers' Stations. The most active areas in a bank are the tellers' stations. Here the lighting should provide for fast, accurate transactions. Because of highly polished material often used for the deal plate, reflections from ceiling-mounted lights may be problematic. One way to reduce reflections is to utilize large-area, low-brightness luminaires at the tellers' stations. Luminaires mounted to either side of the deal plate directing light on the plate can also be effective. See figure 17-2. Recessed downlight luminaires directly over the deal plates should be avoided, as they tend to cause shadows and reflected glare. Stations are also equipped with VDT screens to access account information. This also requires special attention in luminaire selection and location to assure good screen visibility (see chapter 15, Office Lighting).

The interior lighting at a drive-up window should be similar to other tellers' stations; however, because of the sloping window glass in many of these areas, luminaires behind the drive-up teller should be of low brightness to minimize reflections from the glass itself.

Possibly the most neglected area of bank lighting is the outdoor drive-up area. The illuminance outside this area should be about the same as that in the interior to avoid a mirror effect on the glass looking into or out from the drive-up teller's position. The luminaires should be located to light the person in the car, not the top of the car. In addition to the "visual" drive-up teller facilities, where the teller sees the client or customer directly, there are special luminaires to provide lighting for cameras.

Automatic Teller (Transaction) Machines (ATM). Since this equipment is in operation 24 hours a day and may

Fig. 17-1. The lighting design for this monumental-style high-ceiling bank accentuates the renaissance-style architecture: downlights and pendant luminaires with metal halide lamps provide general lighting in the lobby area, and incandescent uplights emphasize the vaulted windows.

be located either inside or outside the building, special considerations should be given to the lighting. First, one must provide adequate lighting at the keypad and on the writing shelf, so that the client will be able to read and prepare transactions. Second, the area at and in the vicinity surrounding the ATM should be illuminated to give users a feeling of security. See figure 17-3.

Security Lighting. Security lighting should be incorporated in accordance with the latest edition of the 1968 Bank Protection Act, whereby adequate night lighting, exit lighting and lighting on the vault are required to be on at all times. Also, there must be adequate interior lighting for an alarm camera system. Lighting requirements for cameras should be obtained from the

Fig. 17-2. The tellers' stations in this modern-style bank are lighted with recessed fluorescent luminaires with prismatic lenses to provide large-area, low-brightness illumination for transactions. Recessed incandescent downlights on either side of the deal plate also provide effective lighting.

Fig. 17-3. ATM illuminated with a side-mounted HID light source that provides proper lighting to the user of the machine with no veiling glare. In addition, the light source is properly directed to highlight such potential obstructions as the desk and the planter.

manufacturer. Lighting should also be provided for night deposit areas. Dark corners and shadows should be eliminated in the surrounding area.

HOUSES OF WORSHIP[1]

One of the most important aspects of the successful design of a worship facility is the method employed to provide illumination. Skillfully used lighting makes services at houses of worship (such as churches, synagogues and mosques) more meaningful and enhances the architectural design. An important consideration is the strategic and feasible use of daylight. In conceiving a design program for the lighting of houses of worship, the designer should begin with daylighting and consider the use of electric lighting to augment the daylight.

There is no aspect of the space for which daylighting cannot be considered. Daylight can be used for task lighting, accent lighting, and architectural and celebration lighting. Consideration of daylighting must be related to the time of day. Daylighting can be used for task or general lighting in the nave area, as well as accent lighting in the leadership areas (sanctuary, chancel or bema). Sources of daylighting are the roof (skylights or dormer windows) and the walls (windows or full walls). Such lighting may be direct or indirect. It should be used with care so that glare does not reduce its usefulness by creating visual competition during the religious service.

For every lighting system controls are required, the simplest being blinds for daylighting and on-off switches for electric light sources. Consideration of more sophisticated control methods is strongly suggested. The ultimate success of the lighting system is enhanced by a more sophisticated control system.

The owner, architect and lighting designer should work closely to achieve a good solution. Since there is a wide range of equipment and lamps available, mock-ups at the site are recommended for existing facilities.

There are state and local energy codes governing lighting installations. Refer to chapter 14, Codes and Regulations. As lamp efficacy, luminaire efficiency and dimming control systems continue to improve, they provide opportunities for energy savings, especially for television and video lighting and in peripheral spaces having higher use (longer burning hours).

Interior Lighting

Main Worship Areas. The interior lighting system is generally considered to consist of four components (see figures 17-4 and 17-5):

1. *Light for reading.* Congregational and leadership function lighting
2. *Accent lighting.* Lighting for focus on the speaker, leader and religious objects (vertical surfaces)
3. *Architectural lighting.* General ambient illumination that will light the ceiling (indirect) and wash the walls to reveal the religious interior, and to highlight the architectural features such as arches and trusses
4. *Celebration lighting.* The festive and joyous light from candles, reflections in polished metal and, sometimes, chandeliers and

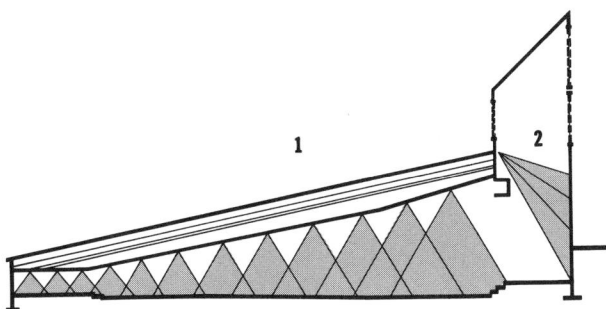

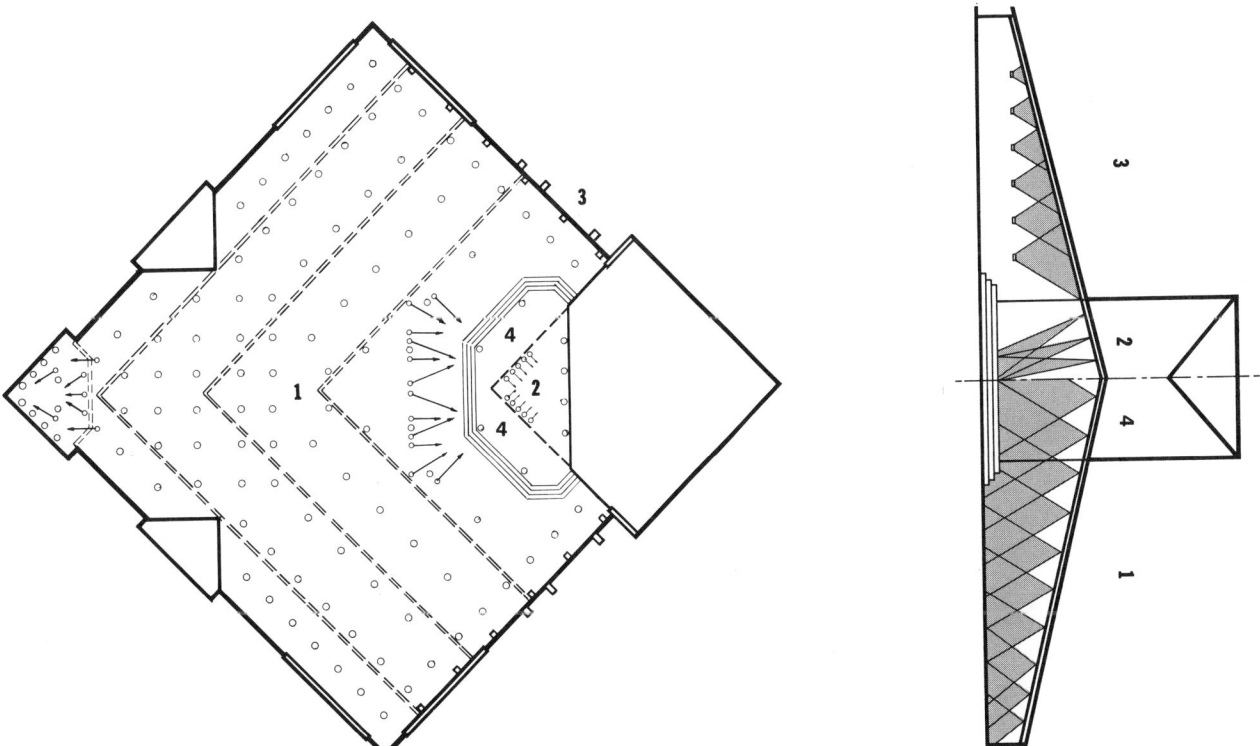

Fig. 17-4. A possible system of lighting for a modern fan-shaped church: (1) Task reading light from recessed downlights. (2) Accent light from recessed adjustable spotlights. (3) Architectural light from wall-mounted urns. (4) Celebration light utilizing candles with polished brass to add sparkle.

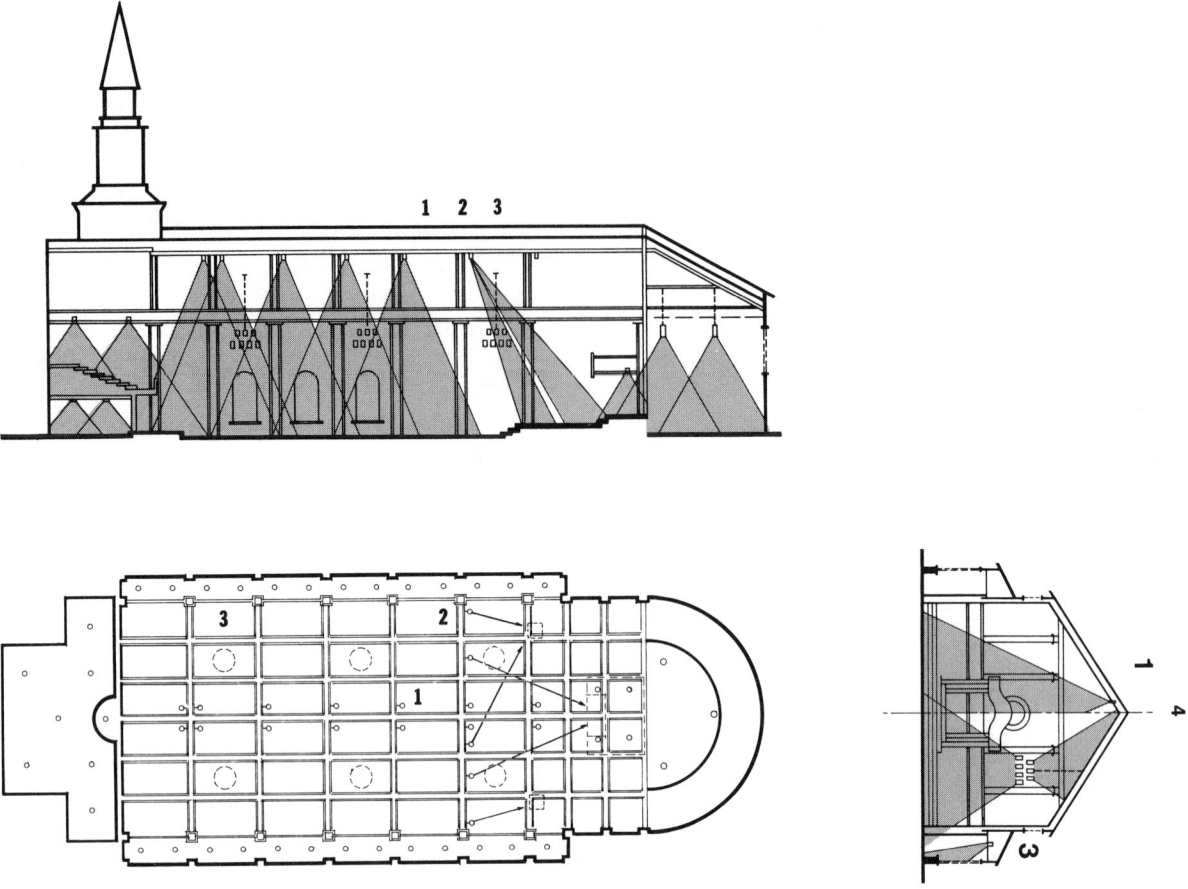

Fig. 17-5. A possible lighting system for a modified traditional church: (1) Task reading light from bracketed downlights. (2) Accent lighting with bracketed spotlights. (3) Architectural light with uplighting in a chandelier and side-aisle wallwashers. (4) Celebration light with controlled adjustable chandeliers.

lanterns at a very low luminance in relation to the surround

Seventy-five to one hundred years ago, all four components came from one source, consisting of bulbs installed in gas luminaires and, later on, in pendant church lanterns. Today, with modern technology, it is appropriate for the lighting designer to design for as sophisticated a level of lighting flexibility as the budget will allow.

Relative values of lighting in main worship areas are more important than absolute levels. Many architecturally rich interiors (particularly older structures with darker marbles and mosaics) have been found to have low illuminances. More modern facilities and those associated with less liturgical groups often use higher illuminances.

The base level of lighting for reading (task lighting) is the illuminance in the seating area. This is the illuminance to which all other design levels are related. See chapter 11, Illuminance Selection. Suggested relationships are:

1. *Accent lighting.* Approximately 3 times the illuminance for reading in the seating area, on the vertical plane

2. *Architectural lighting.* Approximately 25% or less of the illuminance for reading in the seating area

Television Lighting. Supplementary accent lighting used for video cameras and television broadcasting can be part of the original design if required; thus, it can be architecturally integrated so that it will not create glare or other unpleasantness for those in attendance. Luminaire positions and illuminances must be reviewed to provide adequate vertical surface illuminance for the equipment utilized. This component of the lighting system should be separately controlled, as it may be used only occasionally.

Lighting Controls. Good practice calls for the consideration of lighting control systems which can entirely change the appearance of the worship space. There are various types of equipment that can be part of a lighting control system to produce different lighting effects, for example: (1) simple switches to turn lights on and off; (2) time clocks to control interior and exterior lights automatically; (3) sensors that respond to occupant motion; (4) wallbox dimmers, motorized louvers and shades for daylighting; or (5) a modern dimming control system that combines all of the above controls. See also chapter 31, Lighting Controls.

A modern dimming control system allows all the lighting to be grouped into control channels, and *scenes* created so that one preset button allows for easy shifting of all the relative light levels. At the installation stage, the designer will set the relative levels for each control channel (groups of lights) so the lighting system will best support the different functions. Suggested preset functions (or moods) are:

1. *Visiting hours.* When the church is open to the public, a low level of architectural lighting with accent lighting on the devotional shrines
2. *Before and after service.* Lighting at low level for movement of the congregation
3. *Service.* Accent lighting in the leadership area; reading lighting increased; lighting on devotional areas diminished
4. *Sermon.* Accent lighting on the speaker, with all other lighting at a low level
5. *Service at focal point.* Downlights and accents combined on processional and focal areas
6. *Weddings and funerals.* Celebration and architectural lighting with selected accent lights for the specific ceremony
7. *Major feasts and concerts.* Downlighting and accent lighting for the performance area only
8. *Manual.* The ability to override presets for direct control of the lighting

These are only a few of the possible choices for preset functions.

However, not all interiors need the full capabilities of a dimming control system. A small church may only use a set of master controls that provide direct control over groups of lights. Larger churches may need a preset system with remote activator buttons at door entry, pulpit, organ and other locations.

In all cases, when dimming controls are used energy is saved, since modern dimmers reduce wattage throughout the dimming range. Further, dimming prolongs lamp life and reduces maintenance.

Exterior Lighting

Factors Governing Exterior Lighting. When designing lighting for the exterior of a house of worship, some questions to consider are:

1. From what directions will the building be viewed?
2. What effect will seasonal change have upon the lighting system?
3. What other visual competition exists?

Fig. 17-6. Steeple uplighted with narrow-beam floodlights.

4. What energy codes are applicable to exterior lighting?
5. What precautions are required to avoid unwanted spill light?

In addition to the above, specific design objectives should be established for the following:

• Facade illumination
• Entrance and walkways
• Spire and steeple illumination
• Art glass window illumination
• Sign illumination
• Driveway and parking illumination
• Security lighting
• Maintenance concerns
• Lighting for special functions
• Esthetic considerations

Building Lighting. Facade lighting is generally direct lighting aimed at a target area, an object or building. Another technique, silhouette lighting, can be very effective. Individual project analysis is necessary to determine the methods to be used.

Spire and steeple lighting is nearly always directional (narrow-beam floodlights), although installation of an internal illuminator has been successful where the surface materials are translucent. (See figure 17-6 and chapter 22, Exterior Lighting.)

Art Glass Window Lighting

Lighting specialists should work closely with the art window designer to determine the desired appearance of the lighted window. In all stained art glass windows the density, diffusion and refractive qualities of the glass will determine the light source luminance and size to be used. The selection of the type of source also should be based on the predominant colors of the glass. Incandescent and high-pressure sodium sources are more suitable for red and yellow glasses; metal halide and fluorescent sources, for blue and green. A combination of sources may give the best results.

It is not necessary or desirable to achieve perfectly flat or uniform lighting effects. It is recommended that a mock-up of the lighting system be built to determine how the glass will respond. Attention should be given to the color temperature of the light source. Generally, the lighting of art windows serves for: (1) general viewing from inside during nighttime services, and (2) viewing from outside for passing traffic at night.

Viewing from Inside. The window can be lighted with outside floodlighting units if the glass has sufficient diffusion and refracting qualities (from irregularities on the surface of the glass and within the glass). If the glass is not extremely diffuse, the units should be located so that they are not seen through the glass and do not produce visual "hot spots." Clear stained glass needs a luminous background, such as a closed light box around the outside of the window, or a diffuse protective layer, such as frosted or opalescent protective glass; however, these solutions eliminate the view of the window from the exterior.

Viewing from Outside. The floodlighting approach discussed above also can be used, with equipment carefully located inside the building. The luminaires' positions are often limited. The most convenient location often is on the ceiling, but the viewer is usually below the window, making bright spots a potential problem. A larger number of lower-intensity floodlights can make the spots less apparent. For transparent stained glass, a scrim, movable screen or drape can be placed inside and lighted to form a luminous background. This element can be moved away when the window is to be viewed from the inside.

Security Lighting

Interior. In some areas it may be desirable to provide motion sensors to energize selected interior luminaires that will alarm an intruder and give notice to passersby that someone is inside the space. A path of light also can be provided automatically to authorized occupants entering the facility. This can obviate night lighting.

Exterior. Consideration should be given to exterior security lighting. This can be achieved through the use of (1) a site lighting system, (2) building-mounted luminaires, or (3) interior lighting that illuminates the exterior through the windows.

Special Exterior Use or Functions

An exterior devotional grotto, facility or shrine should be lighted in a manner that will not subject the visitor or worshiper to glare and will provide the proper reverent atmosphere. Low-profile landscape and walkway lighting can be incorporated into most designs for general area lighting, with the grotto or shrine lighted from within.

Additional circuits can be supplied to parking area lighting or driveway poles to connect temporary lighting for church festivals and seasonal outdoor events. (See chapter 24, Roadway Lighting, for parking and walkway lighting.)

Design Checklist for Church Lighting

The best approach to lighting design for worship spaces is a complete, comprehensive, long-range plan that may be implemented one phase at a time. This encourages the best lighting results and allows the cost to be worked into several annual budgets or gifts and memorials. A church may renovate or redecorate only once every generation (20–30 yr). Therefore, care should be taken so that the latest proven technologies are used and that sufficient electrical service capacity is provided for interim requirements. The following should be given consideration:

1. An earliest possible consultation among clergy, laity, architect, engineer, lighting designer and electrical contractor is recommended.
2. The use of daylighting should be planned.
3. The various techniques of downlighting, uplighting and accent lighting should be evaluated to provide reading light, architectural enhancement and emphasis for clergy, shrines and celebrations.
4. The requirements of energy efficiency codes must be considered and efficient equipment selected that is easy to maintain, architecturally compatible and readily available.
5. Dimming control capability and flexibility is strongly recommended.
6. All spaces related to worship, social and educational activities, and their needs as related to television, security, emergency and safety should be studied in the initial design. Windows, facades, walkways, driveways, parking, grottos and festivals should not be overlooked.

HEALTH CARE FACILITIES[2]

The lighting of health care facilities presents many problems involving a wide range of seeing conditions. Optimum visual conditions should be provided for doctors, nurses, technicians, maintenance workers and patients. For a better appreciation of the principles involved, a review should be made of chapter 3, Vision and Perception; chapter 4, Color; and chapter 10, Design Process.

Many activities in health care facilities are not related directly to patient care but are necessary as supportive institutional functions, such as business offices and laundries. Lighting for these activities is not discussed in this chapter. Some of them, such as libraries and kitchens, are identical or similar to those in other institutions. There will be some locations in which there is overlap in recommendations. For example, a patient room may be similar in its lighting requirements to a hotel room when it is used for minimal-care patients, yet the lighting must be different in a patient room for the sick, aged or infirm.

Illuminance recommendations for health care facilities are given in chapter 11, Illuminance Selection. Where higher illuminances from localized lighting are required, as in surgery, obstetrics, dentistry, emergency treatment, trauma rooms and autopsies, it is desirable to ensure comfortable lighting conditions by limiting luminance ratios between the task and other areas in the normal field of view. In other words, the luminance ratio between the task and adjacent surrounding should be no greater than $1:\frac{1}{3}$; between the task and remote darker surfaces, no greater than $1:\frac{1}{5}$; and between the task and remote lighter surfaces, no greater than $1:5$. To help achieve these ratios, room surface reflectances should be within the following percentage ranges: ceilings, 80–90%; walls, 40–60%; furniture and equipment, 25–45%; and floors, 20–40%.

Types of Facilities

Health care facilities include acute general hospitals, chronic general and chronic special institutions for the care of the physically and mentally ill, and the extension of these services into other facilities which offer more than the patient's own residence in professional care.

In considering the lighting of such institutions, the designer should take into account not only the immediate objectives, but also the services which might be required in the future. For example, a facility designed as an extended care unit in conjunction with an acute care hospital may find its beds recertified as acute care beds.

The Acute Care Hospital. While an acute care hospital may be faced with all of the diverse lighting design considerations of a complete multidisciplinary hospital, there are some that will not. Obstetric and pediatric departments are being allocated to certain hospitals and abandoned in others. This trend toward specialization will result in greater demand upon the support facilities, but will reduce the need for flexibility in services.

Outpatient services, particularly those considered to be in-hospital functions, are expanding. Many procedures being performed on an outpatient basis today require the same quality and quantity of illumination as that found in the general operating room. Some operations are now being carried out in special ambulatory operating rooms located in free-standing clinics or office buildings designed for physicians and dentists. All of these facilities require special illumination.

There are also continual changes in the instrumentation of medical, surgical and dental practice. The computer and its application to patient imaging may entirely alter that specialty's lighting requirements.

Where once there were large multibed open wards, now there are either single- or double-occupancy rooms. Where, in intensive care areas, there were multibed spaces individualized by curtains, there are now either semienclosures with glass observation windows or cubicles acting as bed bays opening onto a central hall or workspace. By federal guideline these spaces must be located close to windows to afford the patient access to daylighted surroundings for orientation. Night and task illumination, however, presents some problems for the designer.

The Chronic Care Hospital. The chronic long-term care facility is largely disappearing. The psychiatric institution is being replaced by mental health units, often situated in general acute hospitals. This means that psychiatric and contagion units must be provided in the acute care hospital.

The Extended Care Facility. Extended care facilities, specifically nursing homes, are proliferating. Most of these are inhabited by the elderly whose vision difficulties, including cataracts, presbyopia, aphakia, yellowed lenses, glaucoma, retinitis pigmentosa and macular degeneration, pose special problems for the designer.

General recommendations for lighting these facilities include:

1. Use indirect lighting whenever possible.
2. Provide consistent floor illumination.
3. Use higher illuminance appropriate to the task, or highlight important information.
4. Specify high-color-rendering sources or incandescent lighting.
5. Arrange luminaires to provide luminance patterns that aid in environmental orientation and minimize confusion.
6. Place control of lighting with the aging patient.
7. Provide adjustable task-oriented luminaires whenever appropriate.

In general, for patients with preretinal disease, contrast should be maximized while the total flux entering the eye should be minimized. Special attention to control disability glare is critical. For patients with central retinal disease, provisions should be made for significantly higher illuminances than are provided for the normally sighted. For further information on the aging eye, see chapter 3, Vision and Perception.

Other Facilities. Free-standing ambulatory surgical centers, emergency centers, medical office buildings and clinics warrant special attention, as they form an appreciable and growing part of the health care network. Illumination requirements range from simple examination to major surgical lighting. Every doctor's office should contain lighting equipment that will enable the physician to perform all tasks with ease.

Lighting Objectives

In recent years there have been many changes in lighting concepts and in solutions to lighting problems. Basic research has increased our knowledge of visual requirements, industry has provided new equipment for producing light and modifying its quality, and energy conservation and management are of great concern (see chapter 30, Energy Management).

Recent medical practices have created special challenges for the lighting designer to provide the best lighting for new visual tasks. For example, constant monitoring of patients in intensive care units is required under meticulous visual and auditory surveillance conditions. The illumination must be unobtrusive yet fully adequate to avoid observer visual fatigue.

The color rendering of the light source should be sufficient for accurate diagnosis. For the morale of patient and visitor, the color rendering should make patients look as good as possible to themselves and to their visitors. These requirements do not conflict—lamps with better color rendering also ease diagnosis.

The designer should also consider the sensibilities of the patient. Although the lighting should serve the demands of the medical and nursing attendants, it also should contribute to the patient's comfort and help him or her feel at ease. The illumination in multibed rooms should be designed to be unobtrusive to each roommate while remaining adequate for all.

Lighting Design Considerations

In designing the lighting system for a new or renovated space, consideration should be given to the needs of the occupant of that space, the visual tasks to be performed, the desired appearance of that space, and energy and economic constraints.

The wide use of computers requires the assumption that visual display terminals (VDTs) may be used in every administrative and functional support space. For lighting areas where VDTs may be used, see chapter 15, Office Lighting.

Personnel working in diagnostic and therapeutic facilities encompass a wide variety of ages, as do patients. Consequently, lighting should be planned to be adequate for all. In particular, the need for good color rendering is clear in most task-related areas of the hospital.[4]

Task Lighting. In spaces where visual tasks from surgical procedures to patient reading are performed, the task areas are the focal points. Less light may be required in the surround. Lighting for task performance depends upon (1) the importance and delicacy of the particular task with regard to both time allowed and accuracy required, (2) the person performing the task, and (3) the task itself.

Seeing is a dynamic activity. The eyes do not remain fixed upon a single point, but move to all parts of the task area. For this reason, consideration should be given to three zones of lighting, particularly for the operating room. The highest level should be in the operative field; a second lower level should surround the table; and a third level should light the peripheral area.

Hospitals contain areas designated for specific activities, and for these, some specifications of lighting requirements, both quantitative and qualitative, are suggested below.[5, 6]

Adult Patient Rooms. For patient rooms, the designer must reconcile the need for lighting at different times for various people and, usually, provide such lighting as simply and economically as possible. The nurse, doctor and housekeeping personnel require different illuminances in a given room to perform their various services. These illuminances should be rendered acceptable to all patients occupying the room, and satisfy the lighting needs and desires of the patients, whose only field of view may be the ceiling.

Nursing Services. Since the primary purpose of the hospital is to restore the patient to health, lighting for nursing services and critical examinations is common to all hospitals. The variation is in the provision for patient comfort during convalescence. This may vary greatly, depending upon the health and mobility of the patient, the quality of services supplied by the hospital, whether the hospital is public or private, and perhaps most importantly, on whether a room is for single or multiple occupancy.

Routine Nursing. General lighting should be comfortable for the patient. Variable-control dimmers or multiple switching, located at the door of the room, provide flexibility. The nurse should never have to search for light to read charts and thermometers. Should more lighting be needed, the patient's reading light may be used. The luminance of luminaires and nearby surroundings should be less than 310 cd/m^2 (30 cd/ft^2) as seen from the patient's bed or any normal reading position.

Luminaires to meet these conditions should have low luminance. One or more such luminaires in a single- or multiple-occupancy room may be needed to provide general lighting 760 mm (30 in.) above the floor for normal use. To prevent excessive spottiness of general lighting, the installation should provide a lighting level ratio of not more than 1:5 on a horizontal plane 760 mm (30 in.) above the floor within a radial distance of 2.4 m (8 ft) from the point of maximum illuminance on that plane.

Observation of Patients. Provision should be made for local low-level illumination of a color quality that will allow for proper diagnosis of the patient's appearance. There should be lighting at each bed and its floor area so that the nurse can frequently observe the patient and equipment, such as drainage tubes and containers, during the night, with minimum disturbance to patients. This light should be switched at the door, and may also be controlled by a dimmer. When the observation lighting must be left on all night, or when higher levels are needed, temporary screening from other patients may be necessary.

NIGHT LIGHTING. Wall-bracket combination lighting units for patients' use frequently incorporate a night light with switch at the bed. Such a light is desirable for occasional use by patient or nurse; however, when left on continuously, its luminance in the surrounding field of darkness is sometimes a source of annoyance to patients wishing to sleep.

For continuous use, the night light recommended incorporates a low-brightness luminaire with louvered or refractive cover, flush wall type, installed so that its center is approximately 360 mm (14 in.) above the floor, to direct a low illuminance along the floor where it is needed for moving about the room.

For night lighting it is most important to limit the source luminance. This luminance should not exceed 70 cd/m^2 (6.5 cd/ft^2) for continuous use, or 200 cd/m^2 (19 cd/ft^2) for a short time.

EXAMINATION LIGHTING. The lighting for *examining* patients in their rooms should be of a color quality that will not distort skin or tissue color, of a directionality to permit careful inspection of surfaces and cavities, and shadowless. When curtains are used to isolate a patient, others in the room are protected from the examining lamp; however, whether fixed or portable, the examination lighting should be confined to the bed area and provide adequate lighting over a circular area 0.6 m (2 ft) in diameter.

Examination lights are defined as those luminaires used for minor medical procedures outside the operating room. Examples of these procedures are tissue examination and suture removal. Examination/treatment units range from a simple gooseneck lamp to a luminaire similar to an operating room unit, depending on the complexity and nature of the visual task. The following criteria should be considered when selecting luminaires for examination:

1. *Distance.* Adequate illumination should be available at a distance of 1070 mm (42 in.). In treatment rooms, the focal length of the luminaire should be compatible with the task to be observed, typically 600–910 mm (24–36 in.).
2. *Radiation.* For patient safety and comfort, the luminaire should be designed with a heat filtration system. At maximum intensity, the lighting unit at a distance of 1060 mm (42 in.) from the field should produce no more than 25,000 μW/cm^2 in the field.
3. *Color Correction.* The luminaire should provide good color rendering of tissue. The color temperature should be between 3500 and 6700 K.
4. *Mobility.* The unit should move freely and be easily positioned with one hand. Once the luminaire is positioned, the mounting system should permit it to remain stationary without drifting. Articulation of the unit should require 23 kg (5 lb) or less of force by the user.
5. *Safety.* Safety of the user and patient should be addressed by considering (a) the surface temperatures of the luminaire, (b) the tipping hazard, (c) electrical safety and (d) the durability of external surfaces. The placement of fixed, flexible arm units should be reviewed carefully, especially with older patients who may reach out to use the arm for support, which it will not provide.

Patient Use. Patient use implies control by the patient for reading, visiting, self-care or viewing television. This control must be limited to prevent annoyance to other patients.

The reading light should provide light at the normal reading position, assumed to be 1140 mm (45 in.) above the floor. To allow the patient freedom to turn in bed without moving out of the reading light zone, the area of the reading plane (lighted by an adjustable unit) should be approximately 0.3 m^2 (3 ft^2), and for a nonadjustable unit the area should be approximately 0.7 m^2 (6 ft^2). To provide a reasonable degree of uniformity of light over these recommended areas, the lighting level at the outer edge of each area should not be less than two-thirds of the lighting level at the center. To provide comfortable lighting conditions for reading, the luminance in candelas per square meter on the ceiling, provided by some means of general

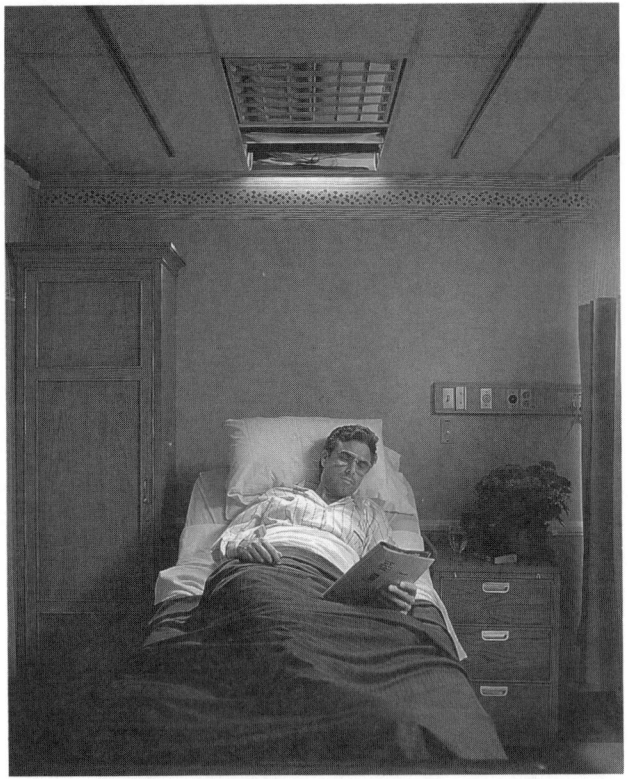
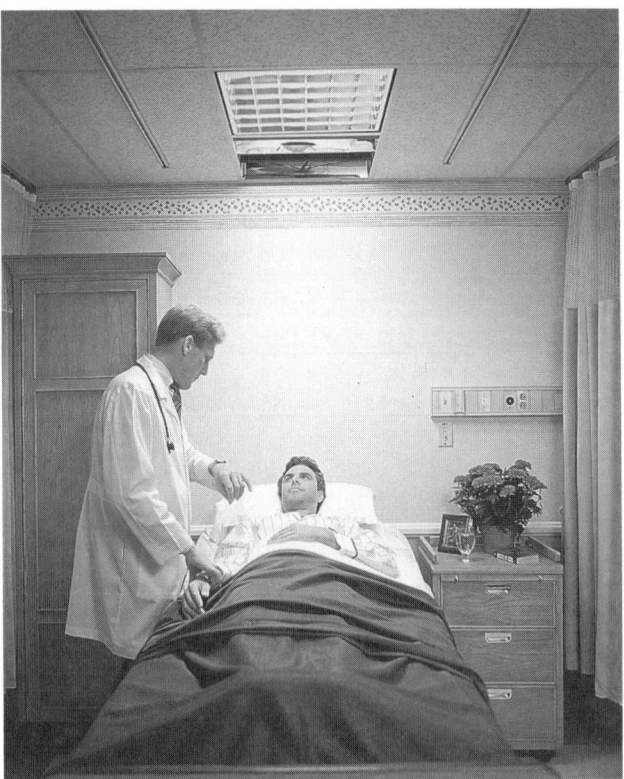

Fig. 17-7. Patient room lighting. Left: Reading light, which positions light directly onto the patient's reading material with no reflected glare. Right: Examination light, which can be controlled with a wall switch by hospital staff, utilizes compact fluorescent lamps for excellent color rendition.

lighting, should be at least equal to the illuminance in 1/p lux on the reading matter.

The luminance of the reading lamp and of any surface illuminated by it, as seen from the patient's bed or any normal reading position, should be less than 310 cd/m^2 (30 cd/ft^2). This condition is admittedly difficult to satisfy and entails a careful choice of luminaire and built-in limitations to its movement. See figure 17-7.

Housekeeping. A very important consideration is the lighting for housekeeping functions. Housekeepers need to see dust or dirt to remove it, including that beneath the furniture. Oblique lighting should be provided over horizontal surfaces to observe dust.

Nursing Stations. In most hospitals a nursing unit is coordinated around a nursing station (see figure 17-8). Here charts are stored, read and written. A desk or shelf is invariably provided, usually against some type of counter or below a hung cabinet. Lighting mounted beneath this counter should provide for the task. It should be so arranged that it supplements the overall illumination of the station.

Some of this lighting will be in continuous use, night and day, and this should be considered in the lighting plan for the station. Usually, although by no means universally, when the nursing station is not visible from any of the patient accommodations, general ceiling

Fig. 17-8. Lighting at a nurses' station is multilevel, to allow for a higher illumination during the day and a lower level at night. The lighting is designed to allow for the critical task of reading patient information from the computer screen. Undercounter task lights also function as night lights.

sources remain lighted during the night hours. Also the luminaires beneath counters, placed so that a person sitting at the desk is shielded from glare, should not be within the patient's direct view.

As the nurse must make frequent trips from the station to patient's rooms as well as to service locations, the corridors between should have transition lighting: a higher level during the day, switched or dimmed to a lower level at night. For safety, the illumination at the nursing stations is usually on an emergency auxiliary lighting system.

Critical Care Areas. The term critical care is replacing many former names such as intensive care. Critical care areas are specially designed for the very ill, and may be highly specialized or be quite flexible in their acceptance of such patients. These accommodations have been designed for postsurgical patients and patients with coronary disease, respiratory disease, burns or acute childhood and neonatal problems. All of these require physical and instrument monitoring, and the capability to provide for resuscitation, control of hemorrhage, or other emergency measures.

The illumination should enable the observer to note (1) changes in contour and color, (2) the prominence of veins on the neck, and (3) the presence of yellow tints in the patients' eyes, if possible. Good color rendering is important so that the patients' complexion will have a true appearance. Thus, only improved-color fluorescent lamps should be used. See figure 17-9.

While the demands for visual tasks in these units may be great, the well-being of the patient must also be carefully considered in planning. Health Resources Administration (HRA) standards (79-1450) require windows in patient rooms to enable each patient to be cognizant of the outdoor environment, though the provision of illumination by this means is not important. The general lighting should be dimmable. It should be located so that neither a supine patient nor one sitting

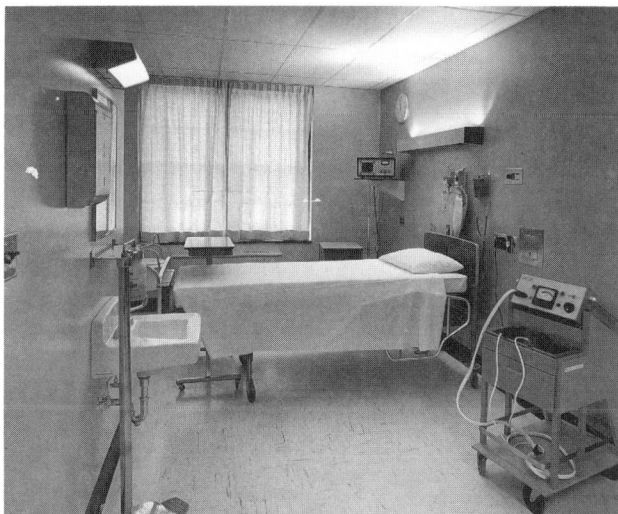

Fig. 17-9. Critical care room. Wall brackets contain two fluorescent lamps for indirect general lighting, one fluorescent lamp as a downlight for reading, and an incandescent night light for surveillance from the nursing station. Two 325-W tungsten-halogen lamps in ellipsoidal reflectors are also provided for examination light.

with an elevated backrest will be subjected to glare. In addition to general lighting, there should be lighting for examinations by the physician. Also, some type of surgical task light should be readily available to provide higher illuminances for emergency procedures. Most of these facilities contain a handwashing area.

The nursing station is usually fully visible to the patient, so that luminaires below the counter or shelf should be shielded.

Monitoring devices should be studied so that there will be adequate illumination for reading them. This also includes a review of their placement and whether or not they are internally illuminated.

Children's Section (Pediatric). A child admitted to the hospital for the first time may feel overwhelmed by its huge size and depressed from seeing so many sick people. Strange equipment may be frightening and may alarm ill patients or intensify anxiety. For this reason the pediatric section or department should be provided with ample space for diversions and educational projects and materials. The lighting should be planned with this in mind, but should be similar to that in adult areas.

The use of daylight is essential. There should be a bright and sunny atmosphere. Corridors should be pleasant, with warm colors on surfaces and objects, and diffused lighting should be used. Spots of lighting and patterns with interesting views seem to shorten the apparent times of waiting and distances of travel down hospital corridors. Arrangements for varying the lighting by multiple switching or dimming are often worthwhile.

Children play and sit on the floor, and often use it as a table. For this reason the lighting should be planned for reading, looking at pictures, drawing and other visual activity on the floor level.

Nurseries. Nursery lighting should be designed so that infants in cribs and in incubators can be observed easily (see figure 17-10). Lighting is often needed for careful observation, but should not be kept at high levels too long because infants do not have the ability to employ adult protective mechanisms to avoid retinal exposure. This must be taken into account when planning the illumination. Luminaires for general lighting should be of such a type or so installed that the luminance of any luminaires, ceiling or wall surface, seen from a working or normal bassinet position, will be less than 310 cd/m² (30 cd/ft²).

In order to recognize minor changes in the color of the skin or sclera, light sources should have good color rendering capabilities.

For information on the treatment of infantile jaundice with fluorescent light, particularly the precautions that are recommended for such therapy,[7,8] and on the use of ultraviolet bactericidal barriers in pediatric sec-

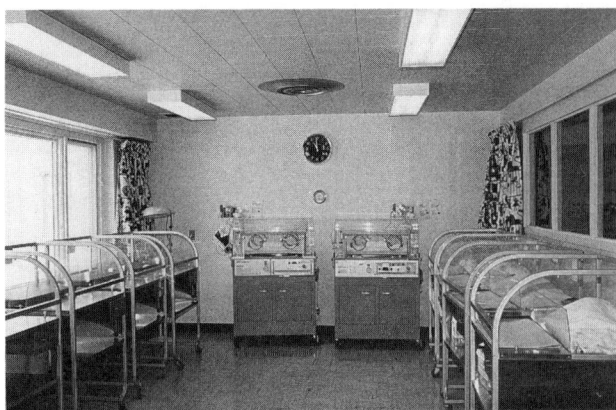

Fig. 17-10. Infant nursery. Windows at right permit relatives to view the babies.

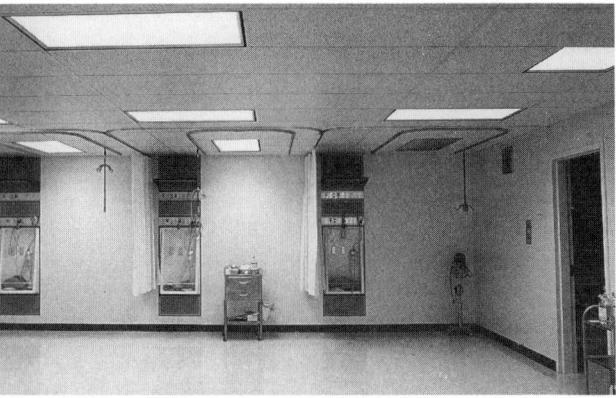

Fig. 17-11. Surgical holding area where patients are kept before being taken into the operating room. Note that each unit here is separately dimmable. Surgical recovery areas are similar.

tions,[9] consult the recommended publications as well as chapter 5, Nonvisual Effects of Radiant Energy.

Mental Health Facilities. Facilities for mentally or emotionally disturbed patients are either "open," in which the patients are unrestricted, or "closed," where access is controlled. Either type may house patients who are considered to be under maximum security. The lighting should be designed to be inaccessible to such patients, in order to protect them from injuring themselves or others, and yet designed to avoid a prisonlike effect. Lighting should be provided by nonadjustable luminaires recessed in the ceiling, not only out of reach of the patient, but protected from impact by objects thrown. These luminaires should be controlled by key switches, preferably mounted in hallways outside of the detention areas.

Most mental health facilities today handle patients who are not severely disturbed. Regardless of the type of patient, proper lighting depends on knowledgeable selection of patterns and areas of illumination to calm rather than disturb them. A general, basic guideline is that the lighting of these facilities should provide interest, warmth, definition of spaces, and illumination for tasks and safety. It is particularly important that the color rendering of the illumination be good, both to ensure that objects are seen in their normal coloration and to provide a pleasant, colorful surround. Flickering fluorescent lamps should be replaced immediately.

Surgical Holding Areas. These areas (see figure 17-11) are designed primarily for the retention of patients, nearly always supine on wheeled stretchers (gurneys) after sedative premedication. They are kept in these areas out of the traffic stream for periods ranging from a few minutes to as long as 30 min.

The patient's eyes should not be exposed to a luminance of more than 100 cd/m^2 (10 cd/ft^2). Most of the time a subdued illumination for slumber is advisable; it should be designed to be out of the recumbent

patient's line of sight. A higher illuminance is needed for supervision and observation.

The holding area is not usually designed for surgical induction; however, some hospitals will use it for that purpose, and the planner must give such an arrangement additional consideration. Some type of lighting is useful for starting intravenous lines and for other preanesthetic activities such as shaving. This purpose might well be served by a flexible wall-hung bracket luminaire, which will allow a patient to be prepped without disturbing another. Bright, cheerful, colorful surroundings, with illumination of adequate color rendering, is important.

Surgical Induction Room. The patient is transferred here from a stretcher to an operating table, the anesthesia started, needles placed in the patient's veins, and the patient maneuvered into a variety of positions by manipulations of the operating table. Connections to monitoring devices are attached to the patient. The positioning of the patient may take a considerable time, but for this the patient is usually already partially anesthetized.

Ideally the patient is brought into this room under subdued light. The anesthesia can be induced after placement of a needle in the vein. For this, a task light of some type must be available. Once the patient is unconscious, the illumination can be increased to serve the staff tasks. It should be possible, however, to reduce the light in the room again while the anesthesiologist inserts a tube into the trachea (windpipe), utilizing a lighted laryngoscope. This device provides only about 50–100 lx (5–10 fc), and thus a low ambient level is preferred.

Surgical Suite

Operating Room. For the designer lighting the operating room presents a difficult challenge, not because of the number of people to be satisfied but because of the importance of the work performed there. Emergency lighting should be a major concern in case of power outage, and should be a consideration in the original design.

There should be no dense shadows to prevent the surgeon from seeing past his own hands and instruments or to prevent him or her from adequately seeing the patient's tissue, organs and blood with correct coloration. Sometimes the surgeon must see into deep body cavities, natural or artificial. To enhance physical comfort for the surgical team, heat reaching the back of the surgeon's head and neck from the overhead surgical light must be minimized. The surgeon must be able to work for hours, if necessary, without any discomfort and must be able to glance to and from the work without having to take time for the eyes to adjust to large differences in luminance. Luminance ratios between areas of appreciable size within view of the surgeon and his team should be no greater than 1:3 between the wound and the surgical field and 5:1 between the surgical field and the instrument table. The luminance ratio between the surgical field and the room's lighter surfaces also should be no greater than 1:5. Visual comfort is probably greatest when there are no excessively bright reflections in the field.

Even more important than the comfort of the surgeon and the surgical team is the safety of the patient. Body tissues exposed during an operation must not be excessively heated, dried or irradiated with ultraviolet energy.

Colors and reflectances of operating and delivery room interior surfaces, draping and gown fabrics should be somewhat as follows: ceilings, a near-white color with 90% or more reflectance; walls, nonglossy surfaces of any light color with 60% reflectance; floor reflectance preferably in the range of 20–30%, but may be as low as 8%, depending on the selection of flooring materials available; and fabrics for gowns and surgical drapes, colored, usually in a dull shade of blue-green, turquoise or pearl gray, with 30% or less reflectance. Surgical instruments should be of a nonreflecting matte finish to minimize reflected glare in the area of the operative cavity. Any plastic materials used in draping should also be of matte finish.

Equipment such as that for X rays, anesthesia and ventilation competes with the lighting system for the limited ceiling space available. Therefore, to achieve the desired illuminance, the location and arrangement of the lighting system should be carefully planned. Because of the variety of surgical procedures, the general illumination in the operating room should provide a uniformly distributed illuminance with provisions for changing the level. Luminaires should be equipped with elements to diffuse the light and to prevent glare.

When fluorescent luminaires are utilized in the surgical suite, they should be designed to reduce electro-magnetic interference to a level that will not interfere with the operation of delicate electronic equipment in a life support system. This may require welded construction to minimize radio-frequency leakage through openings, lenses with an electrically grounded conductive coating, and radio-frequency filters to reduce the radio energy getting into the electric wiring. The appearance of the patient should not differ significantly when viewed under the surgical light or under the general room illumination. This is best achieved by matching the color temperature and color rendering of the two types of lights. For example, if the main surgical light has a color temperature of 4000 K, general room illumination should be provided by fluorescent lamps with similar color temperature—in this case, deluxe cool white fluorescent lamps. In all cases fluorescent lamps should have excellent color rendering capabilities.

The surgical task lighting system (see figure 17-12) should be capable of providing a minimum of 27 klx (2500 fc) directed to the center of a 500-cm^2 (78-in.^{2}) or larger pattern on a surgical table with the top 990 mm (39 in.) from the floor. This pattern is defined as an area within which the illuminance tapers from center to edge so that at the edge it is no less than 20% of that at the center. For ceiling-suspended surgical lighting systems, the illuminance and patterns are measured 1070 mm (42 in.) from the face of the lamp cover glass,

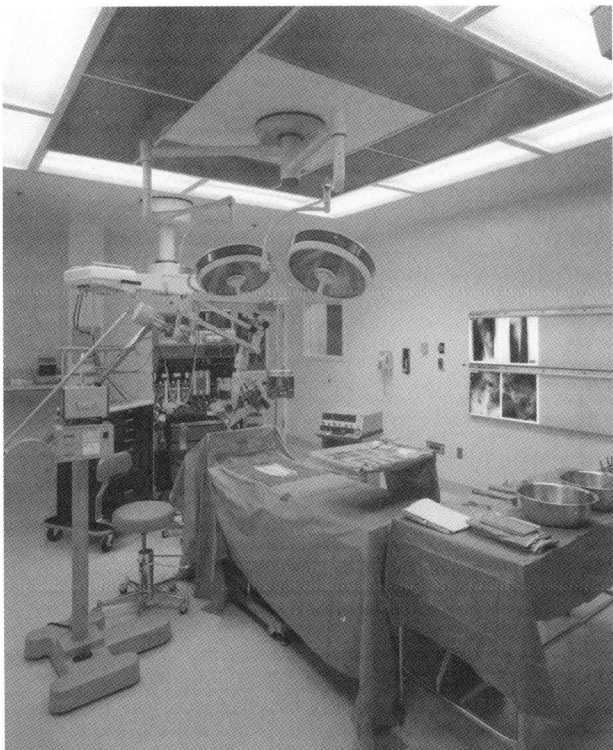

Fig. 17-12. An operating room, showing state-of-the-art surgical lights.

if a cover glass is used, or from the lower edge of the outer reflectors in a multiple-reflector unit with an individual cover over each lighting source.

The above is intended as minimum for general surgical procedures. In many specialized instances higher illuminances and various pattern sizes and shapes are desirable, as well as control of the illuminance level. Variable pattern sizes are provided by moving the light closer to or farther from the patient. Some lights provide, in addition, a focusing control which varies the pattern size. Users should determine the depth of field required for their work and evaluate the luminaires available that will give a usable pattern over the depth of field required. All illuminance measurements should be made with a color- and cosine-corrected light-sensing element that will indicate the average level over a 38-mm (1.5-in.) diameter area.

To prevent obscuring shadows from the surgeon's hands, head, and instruments, the light should reach the operating area from wide angles. Shadow reduction depends on the optical design, positioning, reflector size and number of lamp heads. A recommended test for the relative shadow reduction ability of various lights and configurations of light is discussed in the following paragraph.

For test purposes, the lighting system should provide a minimum level of 10% of the unshadowed level inside and at the bottom of a tube 50 mm (2 in.) in diameter and 76 mm (3 in.) long, finished flat black inside, from a distance of 1070 mm (42 in.) when the beam is obstructed by a disk 254 mm (10 in.) in diameter, 580 mm (23 in.) above the operating table, and normal to the axis of the tube. When multiple lamp heads constitute the system to be tested, the 1070-mm (42-in.) distance should be measured from the center face of each lamp head to the photocell (see figure 17-13). The designer should also compare the ability of various lamps to allow the surgeon to discriminate the color and texture of tissue adequately: neither illuminance nor color temperature is necessarily indicative of this most important characteristic of the surgical illumination.

Precautions should be taken to avoid a total lamp failure, for example, by having multiple lamps in a single lighthead unit, or a multiple lighthead unit.

The radiant energy produced by surgical lights must be minimized for protection of surgically exposed tissues and the comfort and efficiency of the surgeon and assistants. For most operations the radiant energy in the spectral region of 800–1000 nm should be kept at a minimum. This is the band of infrared absorption by flesh and water; hence it will heat the surgeon noticeably and, more importantly, may cause drying of exposed tissues. Current research suggests that in certain neurosurgical or intestinal procedures on delicate, thin, dry or abnormal tissue, the user of surgical lights should take care not to exceed approximately 25,000

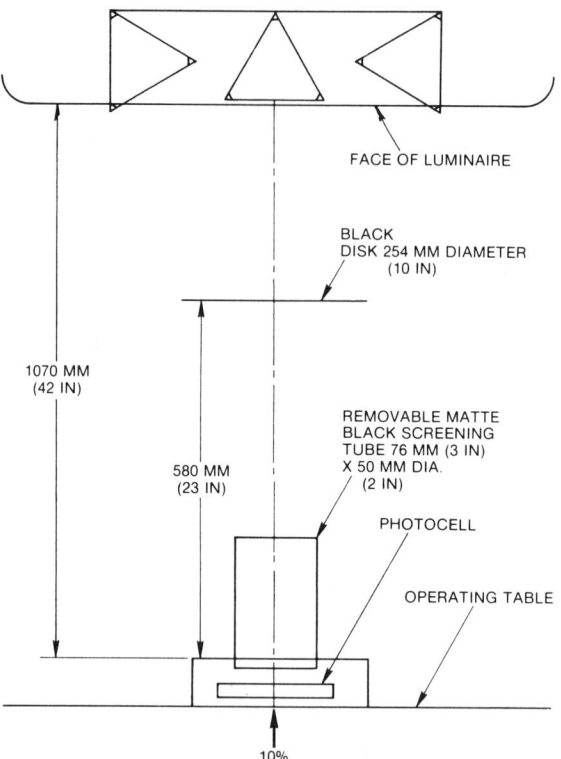

Fig. 17-13. The test for shadow reduction. Distance and sizes of objects are as shown above. Ten percent of the incident light should be seen at the bottom of the tube.

μW/cm^2 at maximum intensity in the light pattern. Manufacturers of surgical lighting should provide information on conditions under which their equipment can exceed these energy levels. An irradiance factor in μW/cm^2 per lux or per footcandle would be helpful in determining the total irradiance of the lighting system.

For general surgery, the light from the luminaire should have a color within an area described by a five-sided polygon on the 1931 CIE x, y chromaticity diagram (see chapter 4, Color). The range of CIE coefficients is appropriately defined by the following x and y values:

x	y
.310	.310
.400	.375
.400	.415
.375	.415
.310	.365

When plotted, the above points will result in correlated color temperatures between 3500 and 6700 K. The spectral power distribution should be designed to provide color rendition satisfactory to the surgeon.[10]

Second only to its unusual optical quality is the flexibility designed into the surgical lighting unit. This may be accomplished mechanically on units suspended from the ceiling, or by electrical switching arrangements in stationary units in the ceiling. Directionality is sometimes achieved by permitting the scrubbed surgeon to adjust a sterile handle, but the asepsis of this technique has been questioned. If handles are used, they should be demountable for sterilization, be smooth to avoid glove puncture, and have a guard to prevent contact with a nonsterile area.

The requirements for directional flexibility in the main task lighting system will vary with the surgeons and the type of surgical procedures to be performed, and limited by the "five-foot rules"[11] imposed on the use of flammable anesthetic agents. The directionality requirements for orthopedic operations differ greatly from those for cardiovascular and neurosurgical operations, which in turn differ from those for gynecological procedures. Thus, the selection of the lighting system cannot be simply prescribed, and the prospective purchaser must be aware of the limitations of all of the equipment.

Two-team surgery is now frequently practiced for many procedures. For example, one team may remove a vein from the thigh while another implants it into the heart. For this purpose additional lightheads or satellite units may extend from the primary luminaire mounting. On the other hand, the use of two or more luminaires on one surgical field requires special care; see the discussion above relating to the heating of tissues.

Supplemental surgical task luminaires are of two main types: those with a beam encompassing the entire field and those that operate by directing light through a glass or plastic fiber-optic bundle. Both types, when used where flammable anesthetic gases are employed, must be explosion proof or limited in movement to 1.5 m (5 ft) above the floor. The electrical system must be in accordance with the Standard for Health Care Facilities (NFPA 99).[11]

Free-standing lights must conform with safety standards to avoid tipping, as prescribed in NFPA 99, part 3-3.5.1.6, and must have a reasonable ability to retain their position. No part of a portable wide-beam lamp housing should project below 1.5 m (5 ft) from the floor. The entire unit must be grounded through a third wire in the flexible cable (NFPA 99, Part 3-2.5.1.3).

A fiber-optic unit, for use in a sterile field must be capable of sterilization or be encased in a waterproof and sterile static-free barrier. At the exit face of the fiber-optic device the irradiance should be no more than 25,000 μW/cm^2 if actually intended for insertion in the wound.

Low-voltage lighting equipment (less than 8 V) may be used in accordance with NFPA 99, if supplied by an individual isolating transformer "connected by an anesthetizing location cord and plug" or from dry cell batteries or transformer above the 1.5-m level. Isolat-

ing transformers should have a grounded case and core.

The anesthesiologist usually sits behind a tent of surgical drapes that prevent an accurate assessment of the patient's face color. Most of the monitoring instruments and dials that must constantly be observed are hard to see. Their cover glasses usually are very reflective and may well produce veiling reflections or reflected glare. Furthermore, the anesthesiologist should be shielded from the operating task light. Shielding of the general illumination system and other special lighting considerations also may be needed.

Scrub Area. Scrub areas and corridors adjacent to the operating room are areas where personnel can accommodate their eyes to the illuminances of the operating room. Both illuminance levels and color rendering of the illumination are important. While scrubbing before an operation, the surgical team should be exposed to light of the same level that they will encounter in the operating room. This will not only ensure a good job of scrubbing, but will allow them to enter the operating room fully light adapted. These illuminance levels will also promote a cleaner scrub area and consequently more aseptic conditions. This same reasoning holds for corridors leading to the operating room. These are the areas where the surgical team adapts to the operating room environment.

It should be possible to reduce the illumination in the scrub area when surgical light levels are reduced.

Special Lighting

Photography and Television. Operating room television and film camera systems can be grouped into three categories:

1. That which is built into the lighthead, that always coordinates the angle of viewing for light and camera field. Upright image orientation is important for a television system.
2. That which is attached to a separate arm mechanism, that is part of the surgical light system. This type allows more control of the viewing angle, but requires more operator skill.
3. That which is separate from the lighting system on booms, dollies or platforms. This type allows higher-quality imaging, but requires more space and good camera-operator skills.

For a given installation, the photographic needs can range from basic before-and-after documentation to sophisticated teaching films (the latter requiring the most versatile equipment). See figure 17-12.

Headlights. Headlights are often used by surgeons to supplement the illumination from overhead surgical lights, or provide light from angles that overhead lights cannot achieve, such as upward from a low position. Typical headlight-to-task distances range from 300 to

600 mm (12 to 24 in.). Headlights are especially useful for seeing in small, narrow or deep cavities where the beam of light must be parallel to the surgeon's line of sight (coaxial). A typical surgical headlight system consists of a headlight mounted on a headband, a cable and a power or light source. There are two common styles of headlight: (1) a coaxial type that projects a beam forward or down from a location directly between the surgeon's eyes, and (2) a direct type that projects a beam generally downward from a location on the forehead.

Headlights are usually illuminated through a flexible fiber-optic cable that plugs into an illuminator or light source box. A few headlights use low-voltage lamps and wires from a battery or small transformer. Factors to consider in evaluating headlights include:

- Spot size at anticipated working distance
- Spot size adjustability
- Illuminance at anticipated working distance
- Ability to pivot and aim the light beam in various directions
- Weight of both headlight and cable
- Comfort and adjustments of the headband
- Cable size, durability and ease of maintenance (Some cables have clips to transfer the cable's weight to the surgical gown.)
- Ease of aiming by a scrubbed surgeon using sterile handling

Factors to consider in evaluating fiber-optic illuminators to power headlights include:

- Size, weight and mobility
- Ease of lamp replacement
- Light intensity and color
- Intensity adjustment
- Number of fiber-optic cables the light source can power at the same time

Specialized Operating Rooms

Eye Surgery. Rooms for eye surgery contain some type of fixed pedestal or columns connected with an operating microscope. This equipment may contain its own luminaires and frequently contains beam-splitting devices to permit viewing by more than one person. There may be film or television camera equipment attached. Various lasers may be present, as well as an electromagnet for removing ferrous foreign material from the eye.

The general room illumination is planned to give the same level as in the general operating room. The surgeon, however, will sometimes require less general illumination and may prefer almost complete darkness to reduce reflections from the curved surface of the

eye; therefore, a method for reducing the illumination becomes mandatory in the eye room. Separate lighting may be necessary for the anesthesiologist so that equipment may be observed. Pendant ceiling-mounted surgical lights are also used in eye surgery for work on muscles, tissue and lachrymal glands surrounding the eye itself. These should be selected by applying the criteria for surgical suite lighting to the requirements of the ophthalmologist.

The levels of heat production from microscope lighting need to be considered.

Ear, Nose and Throat Surgery. The requirements for this specialty are identical to those for eye surgery. Microscopic surgery is used for operations on the inner ear.

Neurosurgery. In general a neurosurgery operating room is no different in its visual requirements from a general surgery operating room. Some neurosurgeons prefer to use headlamps, frequently fiber-optic ones. Recently, surgical microscopes have been employed in a darkened room. These operating microscopes contain their own illumination and may be ceiling or wall mounted. Neurosurgeons often require a horizontal rather than a vertical beam of light. Thus, luminaires that can be brought as low as the codes allow, or are flexible, are needed.

Orthopedic Surgery. In general, orthopedic operating room visual needs are no different from those of general surgery, but better facilities for X-ray equipment may be necessary. The type of X-ray equipment and the mounting needed should be coordinated with the lighting systems. Particular attention should be paid to flexibility of the luminaires, for orthopedic surgery frequently requires special positioning on the side of the operating (fracture) table for low lighting of the patient's hip. Fluoroscopy with image intensification and television screening will permit the use of a room that is not darkened. The orthopedic surgeon also uses the surgical microscope.

For implantable-joint replacement, the orthopedist sometimes employs laminar airflow chambers, and surgical luminaires pose a problem both from their disturbance of the laminarity of the airflow and from the convection currents they cause. These situations are difficult to avoid, as the necessity for illumination of the surgical task is paramount.

Postanesthetic Recovery Room. This is an area of meticulous monitoring and equipment observation; it must also include the capability of carrying out certain emergency procedures. Color recognition for changes in the patient's skin must be facilitated; therefore, adequate light with good color rendering is important. Lighting should be variable, so that presentations on the face of oscilloscopes (electroencephelographic and electrocardiographic) can be interpreted.

Cystoscopy Room. Cystoscopy is normally carried out in a dark room. The cystoscope is introduced, however, in a lighted room. For female patients a gynecologic examining light should be provided. Flammable anesthetics are not usually used in the area; in such cases the light should be available at a level just above the sitting urologist's shoulder.

Darkening of the room should be possible by switching or dimming. The illuminance, though low, should be adequate in magnitude and color rendering for the anesthesiologist to see the equipment and to evaluate the patient's color. Surgical lighting capability should be available, as some operative procedures are performed here. It should be centered to illuminate the lower end of the cystoscopic table.

Obstetric Delivery Suite

Labor Rooms. Monitoring apparatus is often applied to the patient to observe uterine contractions and the heart tones and responses of the unborn child. These data are usually recorded on paper and observed by attendants. Examinations performed in this room are usually manual and do not require visual control. However, observation of the patient includes blood pressure measurement and the patient's general status; therefore, lighting with good color rendering is preferred so that any cyanosis (blueness) will be obvious. Patient morale tends to be heightened to the extent that a colorful, noninstitutional environment is provided.

Some facilities use a single labor and delivery room, called a birthing room. See figure 17-14. This may be situated in a hospital or in an ambulatory facility, called a childbearing center, with lighting similar to a hotel room, except that a portable surgical lamp should

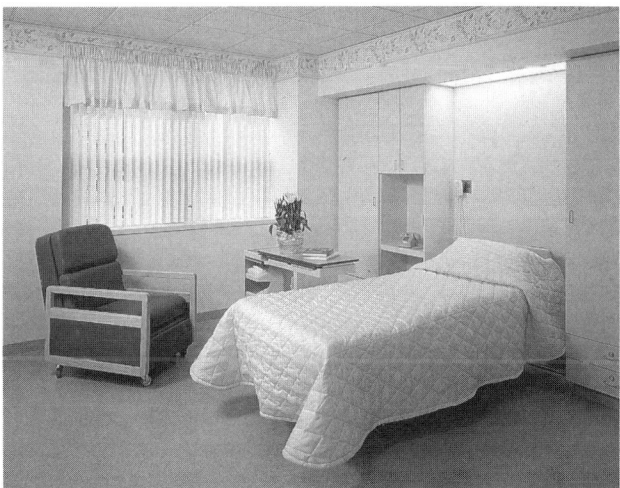

Fig. 17-14. A birthing room, with its soothing colors, inviting textures and soft lighting, is reminiscent of a residential bedroom. The patient can control the glare-free reading lamp positioned over the head of the bed.

be available.[3] The patient's consciousness is complete, so that high luminance should not be in the visual field of the recumbent patient. Cleanliness is imperative; a luminaire that can be easily cleaned should be selected. In addition to the general lighting, reading lights can be provided. Task lighting should be able to flood the lower abdomen and perineum with illumination. This can be provided by a portable task lamp.

Delivery Area. The area for delivery scrub should be identical in its illumination to the surgical scrub area. The general illumination of the delivery room should be achieved by recessed luminaires providing light throughout, the same as in the operating room.

The task luminaire should be capable of focusing and producing an illuminance of 25 klx (2500 fc) at its center. Ideally, the lamp should have the capability of being centered over the shoulder of a sitting obstetrician. Explosion-proof portable units are also available. In some institutions the anesthesiologist will ban the use of flammable anesthetic agents in the delivery suite because of the explosion hazard.

A special lighting plan should exist for the area in which the newborn infant is resuscitated. The lighting should have good color rendering capability, both for pleasing appearance of mother and baby, and for the detection of cyanosis and jaundice.

General Radiographic / Fluoroscopic Room. The modern radiographic suite includes a great variety of viewing tasks and a multitude of equipment that requires good lighting for effective use. Much of the equipment is mounted on movable arms to give both vertical and horizontal flexibility in locational adjustment. This makes it difficult to avoid glare to the patient unless the overhead fixtures are effectively shielded.

Another consideration is the use of incandescent or color-improved fluorescent lighting to provide the most flattering quality of lighting for the patients. Patients awaiting radiology are often apprehensive and the lighting should be used to enhance their appearance, both to themselves and to others, as much as possible.

Laboratories

Specimen Collecting (Venipuncture) and Donor Areas for the Blood Bank. Lighting should be provided for the site of the venipuncture, at the height of the arm of an armchair. Veins are best seen in light that is not flat; therefore, ceiling luminaires or task lights should be placed to provide oblique illumination. Bright and cheerful surroundings are important. Good color rendering enhances the appearance of patient and staff and allows for easy detection of the vein pattern. The walls in this area should be pastel shades of low reflectance for donor comfort and reassurance.

Tissue Laboratory. Lighting in a tissue laboratory should provide excellent color rendering. There are usually two counter heights, 760 mm (30 in.) and 910 mm (36 in.), the former to be used sitting, the latter standing. The same lighting arrangements are valuable in the room devoted to the preparation of cytology specimens. Backgrounds for microscope viewing should be dark in color and of very low reflectance to avoid glare.

Microscopic Reading Room. A pathologist spends a considerable amount of time reading microscopic material. For this purpose the table tops upon which the microscopes are placed are usually 810 mm (32 in.) from the floor and are of low reflectance, often in a mahogany or walnut finish. Room lighting should be adjustable for long periods of viewing. In facilities where microscope slides are viewed on a video monitor, special lighting is not required.

Central Sterile Supply. The inspection area of the central processing department should have general lighting; in special areas where delicate instruments and other equipment are inspected, the illumination should be increased and its quality be such as to give good clarity.

Dental Suites. In the dental operatory the luminance ratios between the patient's mouth and face, the patient's bib, the instrument tray and the surrounding areas should be no greater than 3:1.

Lighting should be provided at the level of the patient's face and the instrument tray. Lighting inside the oral cavity should be supplied from a luminaire easily adjustable to keep high luminance from the patient's eyes and at the same time provide such lighting as is needed by the dentist to see fine details over long periods of time. The dentist must be able to judge accurately the depth of drilling and the preparation for retention of fillings. The light should have good color rendering characteristics so the dentist can judge the matching of colors of teeth and fillings, and occlusions of dentures in any place within the mouth.

A luminaire for producing such a penetrating light, reasonably free of shadows at the oral cavity, must produce a convergent beam, and at a distance of about 1 m (3–4 ft) should be capable of lighting a semicircular area with a cutoff to exclude the bright light from the patient's eyes.

Prosthetic work in the laboratory requires speed, accuracy, close inspection and a very close color match between the prosthesis and the patient's own coloring. Therefore, general lighting with excellent color rendering should be provided at the workbench, at one or more points depending on the number of people using the laboratory at a time.

Color matching is a particular problem in dental prosthetics. Metamerism of artificial versus natural teeth poses a great challenge. Matching should take place in a light environment like that in which the patient normally will be seen.

If a dental suite is large enough to have a separate recovery room with a lower level of lighting, provision can be made for higher illuminances for emergency examination or special treatment.

Examination and Treatment Rooms. For examination and nonsurgical treatment there should be general lighting with supplementary lighting on the table.

Emergency Suites and Trauma Units. Emergency suites are generally self-sufficient. Fixed ceiling-mounted directional luminaires or portable lights that provide lighting at the center of the operating area, in combination with a lower level of general illumination, are usually adequate for examination and emergency surgery. Illumination should offer excellent color rendering, since rapid and accurate diagnoses are required.

Autopsy Room and Morgue. Good lighting is imperative in the autopsy room. A surgical type of dissection must be performed there. However, it is performed in the open rather than in a restricted cavity as in surgical exposure; therefore, the highest levels of surgical illumination are not needed. While some of the dissection should be meticulous in order to expose the tissue planes, the placement of sutures and of instruments to control bleeding from fine blood vessels is not necessary. Some of the contouring so advantageous when performing surgery on the living can be sacrificed.

The task light of the autopsy room can therefore be a nonadjustable large unit, with good-color-rendering lamps augmented by spotlights providing illumination at a level on the autopsy table 760 mm (30 in.) above the floor. Surgical lights are not necessary in this room. A single spot with filters to greatly reduce infrared radiation is valuable for the skull portion of the autopsy. Additional lighting for a scale placed over a counter is also valuable.

Scanning Rooms. Various types of scanning machines are used for diagnostic purposes. The patient is usually prone on a table that either moves under or into the scanning device, or the device may move over the patient. Light in these rooms is usually indirect so that the light source is not in the patient's direct line of sight. Many scanning rooms have valance or perimeter lighting with both upward and downward components. Some general lighting may be installed for cleanup.

Computerized tomography (CT) units and magnetic resonance imaging (MRI) systems are usually housed in three basic rooms: control, computer and scanning. Equipment consoles with cathode-ray tube (CRT) monitors are typically located in the control room, with a viewing window connecting to the scanning room for

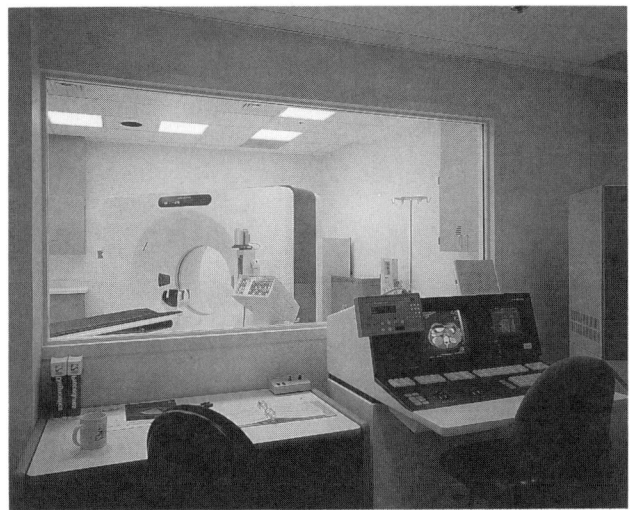

Fig. 17-15. The control room of a diagnostic scanning unit, with lights switched off to reveal the image on the CRT monitor. A viewing window allows for patient observation during the procedure.

direct observation of the patient. See figure 17-15. General lighting on a dimming system or a combination of switched and dimmed lighting zones in the control and scanning rooms will provide lower illuminances during treatments and higher illuminances for equipment maintenance and setup.

System equipment and power supplies are typically located in the computer room, where only general lighting is required for equipment maintenance. MRI utilizes powerful magnetic fields in the diagnostic process. Therefore, nonferrous, direct-current-powered incandescent luminaires should be used in the scanning room as much as possible, to eliminate the effects of the magnetic fields on the lighting system and also to reduce the interference of magnetic objects in the diagnostic image produced during the scanning process.

The psychological effect of lighting can be very important for scanning rooms where the patient is required to spend long periods lying inside the equipment, as in CT and MRI scanning. Windows to allow daylight, combined with lower light levels, can do much to alleviate some of the patient's apprehension, by softening the hard look of the somewhat intimidating equipment.

Pharmacy. The pharmacy should be well illuminated so that the pharmacist can easily read labels and fine print of precautionary literature supplied with the medications. Illumination should be provided at the workbench level 910 mm (36 in.) from the floor to allow prescriptions to be filled rapidly and accurately.

Emergency Lighting. Emergency lighting is needed to perform two categories of essential tasks: evacuating

the building under adverse conditions and providing life support services to the patients who cannot be evacuated. These two categories may be thought of as requiring two lighting systems. The first is a relatively low-level emergency light for ambulatory mobility of patients and staff; the second is a light of higher illuminance level that, in most applications, will be equal to that provided by the regular lighting system. Safety markings must be rendered in their true colors to give their intended indications.

With the increased use of electrical power in operating rooms and critical care areas, there is a need to increase the reliability of the electrical service to these areas. The regular room lighting becomes the emergency lighting whenever the power supply to the critical care areas switches from the normal source to the emergency source.[9]

The remaining areas of the hospital should have low-level emergency lighting as recommended in figure 17-16.

Fig. 17-16. Current Recommended Illuminances, in Lux and Footcandles, on Tasks for Emergency or Continuity Service (for Use when Normal Service is Interrupted)

	Lux	Footcandles
Exit Ways		
Corridors leading to exits, at floor	30	3
Stairways leading to exits, at floor	30	3
Exit direction signs, on face of luminaire	50	5
Exit doorway, at floor	30	3
Operating Room, surgical table	27000	2500
Operating Room, emergency table	22000	2000
Delivery Room, obstetrical table	27000	2500
Recovery Rooms for operating rooms and obstetrical suites	100	10
Nurseries, infant, 760 millimeters (30 inches) above floor	100	10
Nurseries, premature, 760 millimeters (30 inches) above floor	100	10
Nurseries, pediatric, 760 millimeters (30 inches) above floor	20	2
Medication Preparation Area, local	300	30
Nurses' Station	50	5
Pharmacy	50	5
Blood Bank Area	50	5
Central Suction Pump Area	50	5
Telephone Switchboard, face of board	50	5
Central Sterile Supply, issuing area	50	5
Psychiatric Patient Bed Area	20	2
Main Electrical Control Center	50	5
Hospital Elevator—Exit Lighting	50	5
Stairwells	50	5
Life Safety Areas (Life Support Areas)	50	5
Cardiac Catheter Laboratories	100	10
Coronary Care Units	300	30
Dialysis Units	200	20
Emergency Room Treatment Areas	500	50
Intensive Care Units	300	30

* These are minimum lighting levels. It is particularly desirable that they be increased to as near the levels normally provided in these areas as the available capacity of the emergency electrical supply will permit.

HOSPITALITY FACILITIES[12]

In designing lighting for hospitality facilities, which include hotels, motels and food service facilities, the first task is to identify those items that the staff and users want or need to see. Both groups must be able to see and comprehend their environment in order to move about and work within it. In addition, they should enjay doing so. In facilities such as hotels and restaurants, the psychological effects of lighting are particularly important. By creating an attractive, comfortable and functional environment, the lighting design becomes a marketing tool. Moreover, the lighting design must be integrated with the overall architectural design.

Lighting that is inappropriate in quality or quantity can ruin an otherwise successful installation. Using an appropriate combination of daylight and electric lighting, the designer can develop and reinforce almost any visual mood and satisfy the visual needs in any space by day and by night. The lighting system must be compatible with acoustic, thermal, spatial and esthetic requirements and objectives for each area. A successful total environment requires a cooperative effort by the owner, facility manager, architect, engineer, interior designer and consultants who work to integrate all concepts into a harmonious final solution. In hospitality facilities, where architectural treatment is critical, the lighting designer must strike an appropriate balance between efficiency and esthetics while considering energy management. See chapter 30, Energy Management.

The following general objectives should be addressed:

- Achieving harmony with the architectural and decorative character of the facility
- Providing high-quality illumination for visual tasks
- Controlling glare and luminance ratios
- Providing an adequate quantity of illumination
- Optimizing costs to maximize net revenues, including first costs, operating costs and maintenance costs
- Using energy efficiently

Consideration must be given to the desired appearance of each space and to the seeing tasks to be performed. The factors that affect task visibility and performance are discussed in chapter 3, Vision and Perception. All potential hazards such as changes in floor level should be well lighted for safety of guests and staff. If thought out in advance, such highlighting of potential hazards can be made part of any decorative scheme.

Hospitality spaces often have different visual tasks at different times. Function rooms, for example, are used for banquets, meetings, lectures, conferences, classroom applications, exhibitions and entertainment. To accommodate all these different uses with their various illuminances and distribution patterns, several lighting systems may be required with multiple switching and dimming.

Design Considerations for Specific Locations

Specific visual tasks and design considerations for different areas are discussed below. Illuminance recommendations are given in chapter 11, Illuminance Selection. The levels for specific spaces and activites selected from figure 11-1 should be based on an evaluation of the needs of the occupant and on management experience.

Exterior and Site. The total exterior lighting system should identify the facility at night and create a favorable visual impression for welcoming patrons (see figure 17-17). Building facade lighting and marquee,

Fig. 17-17. Halos of clear decorative lamps operated at reduced voltage define the room towers of this hotel and, combined with the uplighted alley of trees framing the entrance drive and the line of glittering sources over the entry, create a distinctive image for the facility.

walkway and parking lighting should be coordinated with signage to produce an effective and coherent overall impression. Grounds of buildings should be lighted:

- To merchandise the property (when warranted)
- To provide for the safety of guests and property, especially in parking areas and along pedestrian paths, steps, walkways and entries
- To eliminate areas that would otherwise be inviting to vandalism or pose a security problem
- To make all areas of barrier-free design accessible to the handicapped

All entryways should be well lighted to make them "landmarks" that may be used safely by guests. Lighting should be used to provide orientation and to reinforce intended traffic patterns. Marquees, taxi stands, drive-ups, registration areas and unloading areas should be lighted in such a way as to distinguish them clearly from surrounding areas.

Lighting of parking areas should provide for traffic and pedestrian safety, visual security and protection from assault, theft and vandalism. Luminaire place-ment and elevation should be coordinated with buildings and plantings in such a way as to minimize shadows. Light sources should provide adequate color rendering for easy vehicle identification.

Public Spaces. The lobby typically establishes the main design themes for the facility and houses a number of areas that can be differentiated and enhanced with appropriate lighting techniques. These include the elevator lobby, reception desk, lounge areas and bell captain's desk. See figure 17-18. The entrance foyer is a transition space between the outdoors and the interior space, so foyer lighting should promote a sense of security and welcome while allowing adaptation between high and low illuminances. In the lounge area both casual and prolonged reading tasks must be anticipated, though these can usually be accommodated with fairly low illuminances. A residential treatment may be appropriate to create an inviting ambiance.

Where information television monitors are located in public spaces, care should be taken to avoid distraction or excessive veiling reflections on the monitor's tube-face from luminaires, lamps or high-brightness surfaces.

Fig. 17-18. By day shafts of sunlight make this clear-glazed atrium dramatic. The high-level daylight illumination is beneficial to the large trees. At night, the elevators become moving illuminated sculptures against the neutral sculptural background created by the gentle glow from fluorescent coves concealed in the handrails of the balconies and bridges. Uplighted trees and low mushroom lights reinforce the exterior imagery created by careful selection and detailing of materials. Pendant high-intensity discharge downlights, required for tree maintenance, are only turned on late at night after the public has left the space.

Fig. 17-19. At the registration desk, concealed fluorescent sources are used to provide task light on the desk. The back wall is lighted indirectly to create a glowing band that draws the visitor to the desk. This is reinforced by the concealed fluorescent cove at the lower edge of the desk, which washes the carpet. Low-brightness downlights put an even wash of low illumination on a richly colored carpet.

Many visual tasks are performed at the registration desk. To make this area easy to locate and to use (see figure 17-19), the designer may designate a high general lighting level to accommodate all tasks; however, a lower overall level with a system of local task lighting should be considered, especially where VDTs are to be used. Care should be taken so that the lighting will be compatible with surrounding areas.

Areas for storage of luggage should be lighted so that labels and other means of identification can be quickly and easily seen. In enclosed storage areas the color rendering qualities of the light should be adequate to permit correct identification of stored items. If not separated from the main lobby, storage areas should have somewhat higher illuminance than the ambient level.

The lighting for elevator lobby areas should be designed to orient people to the elevators and should enable them to read directional signage and instructions and select the proper controls to signal the elevator. Internally illuminated signage and controls should be considered.

Corridor lighting should illuminate room numbers, room name identification signs and the locks in doors. Lighting should be designed to make the passage through hallways, on stairs and to elevators a pleasant and safe experience. It should make guests feel secure. It should call attention to circulation modes such as elevators and vending areas. The tunnel effect associated with long corridors should be minimized by creating areas of varying luminance.

Suitable lighting for shops, newsstands and other specialized services (including cleaning and maintenance) may require sophisticated equipment and controls. Such merchandise lighting should be considered as part of the overall interior lighting scheme (see figure 17-20), and should be balanced with adjacent public areas. It may be possible to use display lighting that remains on 24 hours a day to light adjacent corridors, eliminating corridor luminaires.

In most cases, the lighting of ballrooms,[13] function and meeting rooms, and conference areas should be related to the overall design themes for the hotel. (See figure 17-21.) These rooms are used for meetings,

Fig. 17-20. In this commercial corridor, all corridor lighting is provided with spill light from displays.

Fig. 17-21. Left: Sections of tubing were flocked and hung from the structure over this ballroom to create a richly colored decorative ceiling in scale with the size of the room. Downlights, accent lights and air registers are concealed in and between the tubes. The large contemporary chandelier is made of planes of woven wire mesh, highlighted from lines of R-type lamps above. All circuits are dimmer controlled. Right: Concealed in the decorative ceiling of this function room are several independently controlled lighting systems. Effects include wallwashing, accent lighting for art and speakers, and neutral downlighting for projection and note-taking. The ceiling is fabricated of bronze acrylic cubes, the walls of which multiply the sparkle of incandescent sources.

exhibits, dancing, dining and other functions, which makes it important to provide a variety of lighting levels and effects. If decorative luminaires such as chandeliers are used, at least one or two supplementary lighting systems will usually be required. Dimming and multiple switching should be provided, organized and clearly labeled for easy operation by banquet and function personnel. Lighting must be adequate for critical tasks such as reading and note-taking. Adjustable accent lighting should be provided at speaker's areas, head-table locations and likely locations for displays. Outlets for local lighting should be provided in exhibit areas. Highest illuminances will be required for setup and cleaning purposes.

In public lavatories, visual tasks include grooming, which requires shadowless illumination on both sides of the face. Color rendition is important. Lounge areas in restrooms require only low levels of light.

Guest Rooms. The guest room is one of the major commodities of a hospitality facility. Since it is frequently used for small business conferences, flexibility is needed in the lighting plan. General illumination from ceiling- or wall-mounted luminaires provides a background for task lighting, aids housekeeping and gives a feeling of cheer, as well as providing the needed flexibility for nonresidential uses. To establish an inviting, homelike atmosphere a variety of lighting equipment, some decorative in appearance, is usually needed. Visual tasks in the guest room include: reading in a chair or in bed, desk work, television viewing, and grooming at the mirror both in the bathroom and at the dresser. See chapter 19, Residential Lighting.

The small entry foyer, which is typically part of the guest room, should have its own source of general illumination that reflects light from the ceiling or walls. Recessed incandescent luminaires are not usually suitable because the distribution of light is too narrow. Often the foyer lighting can be designed to illuminate closets, luggage storage and grooming areas as well (see figure 17-22). Self-luminous switches with lighted handles are a convenience for guests in unfamiliar surroundings. Low-wattage switch-controlled night lights should be installed in each guest room, usually in the bathroom, so that guests do not leave other lights on all night long.

Mirror lighting generally provides adequate illumination in bathrooms. If, however, there are separate compartments for toilet, tub or dressing, each space should have a separately switched source of general illumination adequate for safety when the door or curtain is closed.

Entertainment and Food Service Spaces. Entertainment and food service spaces within the hospitality facility are complex and energy-intensive areas in which lighting plays a key role in establishing the mood or atmosphere. The success of lighting effects depends on the appropriateness of the illuminance, color of light, luminaire candlepower distribution, type of luminaire and its locations in relation to the architecture, and source size. In addition to creating an intimate feeling, well-shielded downlights, for example, can produce a pleasing sparkle in reflective objects such as table settings. (See figure 17-23.) On the other hand, indirect lighting or large-area diffuse sources, such as fluores-

Fig. 17-23. In this bar, an indirect cove provides a gentle glow from the fabric ceiling. Clear decorative sources provide sparkle and light the walls. A central chandelier over the bar, consisting of downlighted plastic balls, makes the theme design statement for the room.

Fig. 17-22. A fluorescent luminaire concealed in the header of the closet door in this guest room foyer provides light for both closet and foyer (there is no wall above the luminaire). In the room beyond, a ceramic shade covers an inexpensive porcelain socket, creating a decorative pattern of projected light and providing indirect ambient room illumination as well as reading light for the chair below.

cent luminaires, typically define a brighter-looking space and call more attention to the whole room.

The decorative features in the dining area may require special lighting, which can range from highlighting a picture or sculpture to lighting a full luminous wall. The effects can range from dramatic and sophisticated to cozy and cheerful.

The luminaires themselves may, if used decoratively, become distinctive features in their own right. Many suspended decorative luminaires, regardless of shape, size or style, have a general diffuse distribution that can produce dull, uniformly lighted spaces when used as the sole source of illumination. Unless low-wattage lamps are used, permitting these luminaires to act only as luminous decorative elements, and supplementary lighting is provided, the luminance of such suspended luminaires can be uncomfortably high.

In a general food service facility, switching, supplemental systems and the use of dimmers may be required to make the same space comfortable for breakfast, lunch and dinner. Variation in the quantity and quality of light may be needed, both to change the environment at different times of the day and to permit a higher illuminance for cleanup than would be desir-

able for dining. Automatic preset, programmable dimming control is preferable to switching, since a smooth transition between levels is desirable.

The success of display lighting is best measured by how well it helps to sell merchandise. Food displays should be so lighted that attention is placed on them and the details are clearly seen. Color rendering is even more important over fresh foods than it is over packaged foods. A good rule of thumb is that the illuminance level used in food displays should be at least twice that of surrounding areas. However, heat from luminaires should be a major consideration over fresh, cooled or frozen foods.

The mood established by lighting can vary from subdued and relaxing to bright and lively, depending on the type of facility and the intended clientele. Dining spaces are usually grouped into three categories: intimate, leisure and quick service.

Intimate types of dining spaces, which include cocktail lounges, nightclubs and some restaurants (see figure 17-23), are those places where people congregate as much to visit, be entertained and be seen as to eat and drink. These spaces characteristically have a subdued atmosphere with low luminances throughout, accented with subtly lighted feature elements. The lighting must be well controlled in level and distribution.

Leisure types include most restaurants and many dining rooms, places where eating is the most important activity and time is often a factor. A restful atmosphere, but interesting decor is called for. Lighting should generally be unobtrusive except where decorative luminaires or highlighted features are used as part of the theme decor. Moderate illuminance levels are typical. Good control of glare is required.

Quick service types include lunchrooms, cafeterias, snack bars, coffee shops and franchise menu restaurants, where the diner and management are both intent on fast service and quick customer turnover. Higher illuminances and uniform distribution can be used to suggest a feeling of economy and efficiency.

Kitchen and Food Preparation Areas. Well-designed lighting helps to create a bright, hygienic atmosphere in a kitchen and, by revealing dirt and the presence of debris, can stimulate good housekeeping. Food preparation involves peeling, slicing, dicing and cutting operations, both by machine and by hand. These are obviously hazardous, and lighting for safety must be a strong consideration.

Good lighting can reduce accidents, reveal spills that make floors slippery, and emphasize hazardous areas. In kitchen and associated support areas there is a need to eliminate shadows and to provide illumination on both vertical and horizontal surfaces. While kitchens contain difficult and demanding tasks that may require relatively high illuminances, luminaires should be placed and shielded so as not to create glare or "blasts of light" into adjacent intimate dining areas when kitchen doors are opened. This is particularly important when the adjacent dining area has lower light levels. Color rendering is important in food preparation and inspection areas.

Visibility can be reduced by great variations in luminance in the visual field. Direct and reflected glare can be significant obstacles to employee comfort, productivity and safety; therefore, exposed lamps in direct luminaires should not be used. In most food preparation areas, gasketed, damp-labeled luminaires are preferred. This allows for easy cleaning and prevents dirt and grease from entering the luminaires. Although glare can be controlled in direct luminaires by effective shielding of the lamps, indirect or semi-indirect lighting is preferable because it turns the entire ceiling into a large, low-brightness area source (see figure 17-24).

Light-colored walls will further diffuse the general lighting, reducing shadows. Because vertical surfaces of equipment and furnishings typically occupy a significant portion of the visual field, especially in kitchens, light finishes are recommended for these surfaces.

Horizontal surfaces, such as table tops in restaurants and equipment tops in kitchens, are important because they serve as backgrounds for critical tasks. Whenever possible, matte finishes are preferable because they minimize reflected glare which can produce discomfort and fatigue. Stainless steel kitchen equipment is a common offender in this respect. Matte or brushed finishes combined with careful placement of luminaires and good glare control can minimize these

Fig. 17-24. Indirect fluorescent valances are arranged around the venting hoods to define the work islands in this commercial kitchen. High-reflectance surfaces are used throughout. Sources are shielded from adjacent dining spaces.

problems. The same principles apply elsewhere. Lighting near specular surfaces, such as mirrored ceilings or glazed walls, must be very carefully planned if one is to avoid unintended reflections of sources.

In areas such as bakeries and dishwashing areas that have inherent dust or moisture conditions, the use of enclosed dustproof or vapor-tight luminaires is recommended. Where open-type fluorescent luminaires are located directly over food storage, preparation, service or display areas, plastic sleeve protectors should be used to prevent glass and phosphor from falling into the food in case of breakage.

In receiving and storage areas, lights should be installed in the aisles rather than near the walls, so that stacked shelves do not block the illumination.

Support Areas. Support areas include such spaces as key shops, plan rooms and paint shops. The visual tasks in such areas are often demanding and sometimes dangerous. Where flammable materials are stored or used, explosion-proof luminaires should be used. Task lighting using localized luminaires should be considered as an alternative to general higher-level lighting.

Refuse Areas. The maintenance of safe and sanitary conditions in refuse areas is extremely important. Illumination should permit all hazardous or unsanitary conditions such as slippery spots, foul waste and evidence of insects, rodents or mold to be seen. Corners and other out-of-the-way places should be well lighted.

Merchandising Areas, Offices, Laundry and Valet Areas, and Indoor and Outdoor Recreation Areas. For lighting recommendations for these spaces see chapters 18, 15, 19 and 23, respectively.

General Design Considerations

Selection of Architectural Finishes. The factors that influence how well people perceive a task or space include the luminance distribution, the task contrast and the size, color, form, texture, familiarity and length of time for viewing. Some specific recommendations can be made here with regard to hotel, motel and food service facilities.

Because these facilities typically include adjacent areas with very different illuminances, readaptation in moving from one space to another can be a problem for both staff and patrons. The designer must, therefore, provide appropriately lighted transition spaces. For example, a patron who has been registering at the front desk adapts to a relatively high luminance. Turning back into the lobby, the person may be momentarily unable to distinguish the location of steps or to recognize faces if the difference in luminance varies greatly between the two areas. As the potential hazard or task difficulty increases, it is important to keep luminance ratios within recommended limits.

Room surfaces exert an important influence on luminance ratios between luminaires and their surroundings, and between tasks and their backgrounds. On large surfaces the use of matte finishes with recommended reflectance helps to prevent excessive luminance ratios and undesirable specular reflections. Light-colored matte surfaces serve as effective secondary light sources that can materially reduce shadows. Soft shadows generally accentuate the form and depth of objects, supporting rather than hindering the process of perception.

Selection of Light Sources. Both daylight and electric lighting systems are used in hospitality facilities. Each has its own characteristics. The lighting systems should integrate the two.

Most hospitality facility spaces have windows. The opportunity to look through windows can be psychologically satisfying. It permits relaxation when the eyes can shift focus occasionally from nearby to distant objects. However, windows can bring large areas of high luminance into the field of view, causing discomfort. Good glare control is important. The designer should not locate very brightly lighted areas next to dimly lighted interior spaces without allowing adequate transition spaces between them. Proper daylight control is preferable to increasing the level of electric lighting.

Enhancement of public spaces and provision of proper task lighting are the two principal considerations in the design of lighting systems for hospitality facilities. Three families of electric light sources are used: incandescent, fluorescent and high-intensity dis-

charge (HID). Choice of source depends on the particular requirements of each space, the economics, energy considerations and the personal preference of the system designer and the facility operator. Generally, for public spaces, incandescent or rare-earth fluorescent lamps are recommended.

In these facilities, the chief advantages of incandescent lighting are low initial cost, good color rendering properties, and excellent optical control inherent in such a small source. Because they are so easily dimmed, it is recommended that all incandescent luminaires in public areas be dimmer controlled. Drawbacks of incandescent lamps are their short life, low efficacy and high energy use.

In support areas, where optical control and good color rendering may be less critical, the designer should consider the more efficient, longer-life fluorescent and HID sources. When using these sources, the designer should always be aware of ballast hum, temperature effects, restrike times and color rendering. Ballasts can generally be mounted remotely from critical areas if ballast noise will be objectionable. When using fluorescent sources outdoors and in unheated spaces such as garages, only lamps and ballasts rated for low ambient temperature should be used. HID lamps may take 15 min to come back to full output following a power interruption. The designer should verify the appropriateness of the color temperature and color rendering of each source selected.

Color of Surfaces and Light. In any hospitality facility space, the color of the finishes will affect both patrons and workers. While no hard and fast rules exist, it is generally accepted that strong colors are more stimulating, while less intense colors are more restful and tend to expand the perceived size of a space.

Whatever the colors selected, it is imperative that they be evaluated under the light source or mix of sources that will be used in the finished space, since light sources vary significantly in their color rendering qualities.

The use of colored light is often overlooked as a design tool. Strong colors of light can create interesting effects when surfaces are illuminated for decorative purposes, but should not be used to light food or people because of the color distortion that will result.

Emergency Lighting. In public areas in hospitality facilities, the designer must provide lighting for public safety during emergency conditions, without either disorienting the users or causing them to panic. Emergency systems for public facilities should be designed to provide lighting for short durations during evacuation and safety of guests and staff. For security purposes and to assure continuity of critical operations, emergency lighting of longer duration may be required at hazardous locations. A common error is the installation of "permanently on" emergency luminaires in restaurants. Since these luminaires cannot be switched off or dimmed at night, they are sure to disrupt an intimate dining atmosphere.

While it may be possible in a small facility to meet emergency lighting needs with independent battery-powered units, a central emergency generator or battery installation may be required in a hospitality facility. Options, of which the designer should be aware, include double-circuiting of luminaires and the use of transfer relays to provide power to emergency-only sources during power failures.

LIBRARIES[14]

Libraries have a variety of seeing tasks. Among them are: (1) reading matter, (2) browsing or searching through book stacks or storage areas, (3) studying at a carrell or other work surface, (4) viewing microform or computer retrieval systems, (5) working on computers, (6) meeting or conferring, (7) general office and clerical work, and (8) repair and inspection work. These tasks, along with general illumination for circulation spaces or audio booths, special lighting for audiovisual areas, and accent lights for exhibits and displays, provide a variety of lighting problems.

Seeing Tasks in Libraries

Reading is the visual task performed most often in a library. Reading tasks vary from children's books printed in 10- to 14-point type on matte paper, to newspapers printed in 7-point type on low-contrast off-white pulp paper, to law books with long paragraphs in condensed type, to rare books with unusual type faces printed on old paper. There are also handwriting tasks involving pencils and pens, and computer tasks. Details about the general principles which must be considered to provide the quantity and quality of illumination needed for these tasks may be found in chapter 11, Illuminance Selection and chapter 15, Office Lighting.

A task that is fairly specific to the library is that of browsing and/or searching in a stack or other form of storage space. In public spaces some material may be on low shelves, on tables, on racks or in bins that are very accessible. However, the vast majority of books, magazines and reference materials are stored in shelving that is tightly spaced and up to 2.5 m (8 feet) high, or in compact shelving with limited aisles. The task involves reading a title or author's name, assisted perhaps by an index number applied to the material. The books or other material are often worn or old, causing the title or other means of identification to be of very poor contrast.

When a library is associated with an educational institution, it contains areas used for studying, which involves reading, writing and computer tasks. Such areas may contain several work stations or constitute an individual work station such as a study carrel. Task lighting is often provided at these locations, and veiling reflections should be minimized. Computer stations have very specific requirements. These are discussed in chapter 15, Office Lighting.

Lighting Systems

A variety of lighting systems are used in libraries. Many libraries make use of daylight through windows or skylights. In all cases the luminance comfort recommendations should be the same as for offices and educational facilities. See chapters 15 and 16.

In areas where architectural features are dominant, design concepts may require sacrifice of efficiency for esthetics when translating the architect's concepts into practical lighting designs. In areas that do not have dominant architectural features, the lighting systems should be selected to provide comfortable seeing conditions, and more emphasis should be placed on economics and luminaire design features. See figure 17-25.

For library lighting applications, there are three basic types of light sources in use today: incandescent, fluorescent and high-intensity discharge. (See chapter 6 for light source data.) No one lighting system can be recommended exclusively. Each system has qualities that match the requirements for a given situation. The first consideration in choosing a lighting system should be to allow the library user to see efficiently and without distraction. The second should be the appearance of the installation within the architectural and

Fig. 17-25. Direct lighting in a library using fluorescent luminaires for general illumination and recessed downlights for highlighting the circulation desk.

decorative design concepts of the library. The third consideration is for the energy efficiency of the system.

The designer should aim to provide sufficient illumination for the most common seeing task performed in an area. If a more difficult visual task is to be done in a small portion of that area, additional illumination should be specified in the form of extra overhead luminaires or supplementary lighting equipment located close to the task. Higher illuminance should also be provided in areas that will be used by persons with impaired vision. When relighting existing traditional-type library reading rooms, supplementary lighting equipment consistent with the decorative treatment of the room is sometimes required. It is especially important to avoid direct and reflected glare and to avoid veiling reflections when using supplementary lighting.

Specific Areas

Reading Areas. Reading areas in a library, including main reading rooms and reference rooms, are found throughout the entire library. Reading is usually done on either side of long tables, in lounge chairs, in study carrels or at the circulation desk. Care should be taken to locate the luminaires to avoid veiling reflections on the seeing tasks and to use luminaires that reduce the luminance in the direct glare zones.

Individual Study Areas. Individual study areas, or carrels, may be found in almost any public area of the library building, such as main reading rooms, enclosed individual rooms and stack areas. See figure 17-26. One of the most serious lighting problems for carrels is the shadows produced by dividing walls. To avoid shadows it is desirable to provide lighting from as many directions as practicable. Special care should be taken to avoid veiling reflections, especially from local luminaires. Individual task lighting should be considered.

Shelving and Stack Areas. Such areas contain shelving and storage units for all types of materials in addition to books. The visual tasks in book stacks can be very difficult, for example, to identify a book by number and author on the lowest shelf. As a result of studies made of typical books at actual viewing angles, it is recommended that, when practical, nonglossy plastic book jackets should be used rather than glossy, and that large and legible nonglossy lettering should be used for authors' names, book titles and index numbers. Dark book, shelf and floor surfaces reflect very little light; therefore, the use of light-colored surfaces should be encouraged.

Open-Access Stacks. Open-access stacks are open to the public for finding their own books or for browsing. Book stacks can be arranged in rows with continuous rows of fluorescent luminaires located along the center of each aisle. An alternative is to locate luminaires at right angles to the stacks (see figure 17-27). Obtaining maximum illumination on the lower shelves is the greatest concern.

Fig. 17-26. Study carrels outfitted with individual task lights. An indirect lighting system provides general illumination.

Fig. 17-27. Low-ceiling library, where open-access stacks are lighted with rows of fluorescent luminaires at right angles to the stacks.

Limited-Access or Closed Stacks. These stacks are used primarily by library personnel. The aisles are usually narrower, which increases the problem of obtaining illumination on the lower shelves. Compact shelves may also be used for limited-access or closed stacks. Luminaires controlled by occupancy sensors for energy conservation may be considered for these stack areas.

Card Catalogs. Files of card indexes are usually located in the main reading rooms. Location of overhead general lighting luminaires at right angles to the file cards rather than parallel to them will provide slightly better illumination on the vertical surfaces of the cards. An alternative solution is to use indirect lighting.

Computer catalog systems, which are becoming common, require the same considerations in lighting as VDT workstations. See chapter 15, Office Lighting.

Circulation Desks. Circulation desks are usually located near the entrance to the main reading room. Often the general overhead lighting system will be sufficient to illuminate the desk. When it is not adequate, the designer should provide supplementary lighting, such as task lighting, or an architectural element that will easily identify the circulation desk.

Conference and Seminar Rooms. Conferences and seminars are frequently scheduled in libraries. In addition to general overhead lighting, provision should be made, at potential locations, to illuminate the speakers and their materials. Sources and controls should be selected to modulate levels and provide for multiple uses.

Display and Exhibition Areas. Many libraries have display and exhibition areas. These may be in glass-covered horizontal cases or mounted on vertical walls or dividers. See the section on Museums and Art Galleries below for techniques for lighting such displays.

Audiovisual Rooms. For effective viewing of visual presentations it is necessary to reduce or turn off general overhead lighting. Needed light can be provided by the regular luminaires if those located near the screen can be turned off, while others are operated at a low level. See also chapter 31, Lighting Controls.

Lighting for VDT and Microform Viewing Areas. Computers and microform materials permit much larger holdings of newspaper files, rare books, special collections and technical publications. Microform materials include rolls and cartridges of microfilms on strips, aperture cards containing single frames, or microfilm and microfiche cards or sheets containing a series of highly reduced microimages. One of the most difficult seeing tasks is reading a screen filled with a printed page located in an area lighted to high levels required for other tasks in the area. Reflections, diffuse and specular, tend to wash out the already poor image on the screen. See the section on Offices with Video Display Terminals in chapter 15, Office Lighting. When notes must be taken over long periods of time, task illumination should be provided on the note pad, controlled to reduce reflections on the screen. The task luminaire should be movable so that it may be individually located to accommodate both right- and left-handed operators.

Higher illuminances are needed for files of microforms than are needed for viewing individual microforms. Where viewers must be placed in reading areas or work areas with higher-level general illumination and no controlled lighting or dimming is available, machines should be selected that are hooded and have screens that are treated to reduce reflections.

Offices. Office areas in libraries should be illuminated in accordance with the recommendations in chapter 15.

Rare-Book Rooms. Higher illuminances are recommended for rare-book rooms because of the poor quality of printing often found in rare books; however, lighting techniques such as those used in museums and art galleries should be used for books displayed in glass cases. These include means of reducing the amount of deleterious radiation.

Archives. Archives are for the storage and examination of public documents of all kinds. They include legal documents, minutes of meetings, legislative actions and other historical papers. Pencil writing, small letters and condensed type are used in many of these documents.

Map Rooms. Map rooms have both storage and reading areas. The wide aisles should be sufficiently illuminated to permit easy selection of a map when drawers are open for access. Vertical surface lighting should be provided on map hanging areas.

Fine Arts, Picture and Print Rooms. See the section on Museums and Art Galleries for the proper lighting of displays, paintings and art objects.

Group Study Rooms. Sometimes students are assigned group projects. Isolated rooms that will accommodate four to six people may be provided for this purpose. Techniques used for classroom lighting are recommended for these rooms. See chapter 16, Educational Facilities Lighting.

Overnight Study Halls. Sometimes students prefer to work all night when preparing for examinations or using word-processing equipment. Libraries may provide a portion of the building that can be isolated for this purpose. Lighting for these areas is similar to that required for reading areas, individual study areas or

VDT spaces (see the section on Offices with Video Display Terminals in chapter 15).

Entrance Vestibules and Lobbies. Lighting in entrance vestibules and lobbies should create an atmosphere suitable for the particular type of library. The lighting may emphasize the architectural features and provide a transition to the functional areas.

MUSEUMS AND ART GALLERIES

Museums and art galleries collect, preserve, analyze and display the past, present and future of the human race, its achievements and the worlds around it. These institutions need lighting designs which complement the collections, extend the preservation and enhance the display of artifacts.

Exhibit lighting must be achieved within the constraints necessary for the conservation of artifacts. The designer should determine the appropriate visual effect, and apply principles of display lighting while understanding the susceptibilities of the artifacts to light exposure. In addition, the designer should evaluate the efficiency and maintainability of the specified system.

Principles of Museum and Art Gallery Lighting

Lighting in the museum should provide visibility of the exhibit in an unobtrusive manner and without causing undue damage to the collections. It is believed that high contrasts of light and dark produce tension and drama; overall soft lighting and pastel colors create relaxation. Either treatment carried to extremes can produce fatigue or boredom, while variety can increase interest. The designer should employ the artistic standards of form, color and content to arrive at a finished design.

Artifacts are classified according to their susceptibilities to degradation and are illuminated accordingly. All susceptible artifacts will experience some degradation when exposed to light, even in small amounts. The decision to display an artifact recognizes that some damage to it can be tolerated.[15] The displayed artifact must have sufficient illumination to be not only visible but also appreciated. Otherwise, the artifact's display does not justify the inevitable damage. See figure 17-28.

Adjacent spaces with different artifacts and various artifacts within the same space may require disparate illuminances. Transitional lighting that provides a gradual change between the two levels is the preferred method of handling special requirements. Good practice indicates that luminance ratios of successively viewed fields should not exceed 10:1. For example, a transitional display of replica costume pieces illuminated strongly could provide the visual transition between a daylighted court devoted to frontier artifacts, such as plows and locomotives, and an adjacent enclosed space with low illuminance devoted to native objects such as furs, robes and feathers.

Museum Lighting Applications

Exhibit displays can be categorized into the following four groups:

- Three-dimensional objects
- Flat displays on vertical surfaces
- Realistic environments
- Display cases

Three-Dimensional Objects. Irrespective of size, a three-dimensional object must have some variation of illumination from different directions in order to provide the essential highlights and shadows which reveal the object's shape or texture. This can be accomplished by using different lamps, color filters or beam patterns

Fig. 17-28. Recommended Total Exposure Limits in Illuminance Hours per Year to Limit Light Damage to Susceptible Museum and Art Gallery Objects*

Material	Lux-hours per year	Footcandle-hours per year
Highly susceptible displayed materials: textiles, cotton, natural fibers, furs, silk, writing inks, paper documents, lace, fugitive dyes, watercolors, wool	54,000†	5,000†
Moderately susceptible displayed materials: textiles with stable dyes, oil paintings, wood finishes, leather, some plastics	500,000‡	48,000‡
Least susceptible displayed materials: metal, stone, ceramic, most minerals	Dependent on exhibition situation	Dependent on exhibition situation

*All ultraviolet radiation (below 400 nm) should be eliminated.
†Approximately 54 lx (5 fc) × 8 h / day × 125 days / yr. Different levels (higher or lower) and different periods of display (e.g., 4 h / day for 250 days) may be appropriate, depending upon the material. If in doubt, consult a conservator.
‡Approximately 220 lx (20 fc) × 8 h / day × 300 days / yr. Lower levels may be appropriate, depending upon the material. If in doubt, consult a conservator.

from different angles. For example, a patined bronze sculpture may appear light blue, green or gray, depending upon the light source. Directional lighting will model sculptures, expressing depth and highlighting some areas while allowing others to fall into shadow.

Shadows are indicators of surface form and texture, as long as they are not so dark as to conceal important details. Highlights are also good visual clues to surface characteristics, but should not dazzle or cause uncomfortable glare. When gems are to be displayed, they are usually illuminated by spotlights to emphasize glitter, but when gems are to be examined or graded, the lighting must be diffuse so that the interior of the stone may be seen.

If an object is lighted from all sides, there will be few problems for the viewer when the object is at eye level or lower, but there may be a considerable problem with glare when the object is tall. When the object is low and small, the luminaires may be angled steeply from above, and because the viewer is not looking upward, glare is not a problem. When the object is high, some of the light may go past the display and cause glare for the viewer located on the other side of

the display looking upward. Some solutions to this problem are listed below. See figure 17-29a–f.

- Angle the luminaires sharply downward, and relieve shadows with a high-reflectance pedestal.
- Keep the light beams entirely within the mass of the display.
- Illuminate the objects from below if that will not distort their appearance.
- Combine ambient, diffuse lighting (fill light) in the space with narrow beam lighting (key light) on important parts of the objects.

Outdoor monuments and sculptures require the same principles as above. See chapter 22, Exterior Lighting.

Flat Displays on Vertical Surfaces. Illuminating a large vertical display uniformly is often desired, but is one of the more difficult lighting problems. Paintings, prints, documents and explanatory labels are objects in this important category. Preferences for various lighting distributions have been studied by Loe, Rowlands and

a

b

c

d

Fig. 17-29. Sculpture lighting: Alan Houser's Apache Warrior. Los Angeles County Museum of Natural History, 1982. (a) Key, fill and back light. (b) Key light only. (c) Fill light only. (d) Back light only.

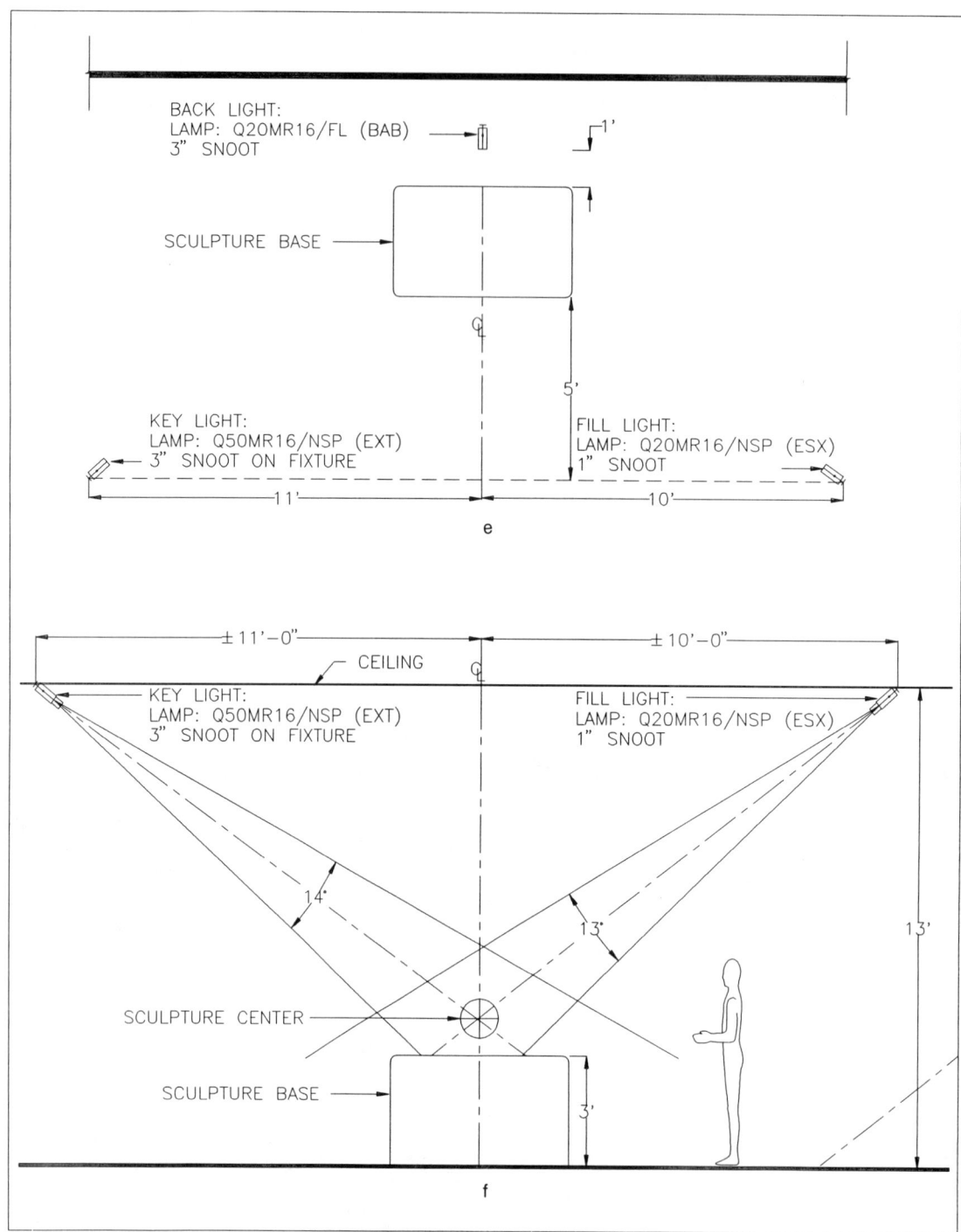

Fig. 17-29. *Continued.* (e) Plan view. (f) Front elevation.

Watson.[16] Generally, the lighting should provide uniform illumination over the entire surface. Occasionally one feature of the object may need to be highlighted. This can be done with spotlights.

A good method of providing vertical illumination is to employ wallwasher luminaires. Such luminaires mounted far from the surface will mute the texture; mounted close to it, they will accentuate the texture (see figure 17-30). Wallwashers are usually the lumi-

naires of choice for murals, particularly tall murals where spotlights or floodlights would cause unwanted highlights. Many types of lamps can be used with wallwasher luminaires. Choose the luminaire that provides the color, the intensity distribution and the lamp life required.

For small and medium-size pictures or label panels mounted on a wall, spotlights or floodlights are usually selected. The mounting position can be determined by

Fig. 17-30. Left: Raking of weave of renaissance tapestry by high-angle directional light. Right: Same tapestry with concentrated light at 60° incident angle. (Courtesy of the Metropolitan Museum of Art. Bequest of George Blumenthal, 1941.)

following the diagram in figure 17-31. It is also possible to use optical projectors which can delineate the object in a "frame." Framing can cause the object to appear self-luminous or translucent. Such effects are rarely desired, and it will be necessary to provide additional diffuse lighting. With less beam control, light will spill over into adjacent areas. This spill light reduces the self-luminous effect. If a separate label is used to describe the object, it should be located in the spill-light area.

Either diffuse light, or a directed beam that illuminates the display from the direction perpendicular to the display, will reduce shadows and texture and provide flat lighting. Flat lighting enhances the color and detail of patterns in tapestries and similar displays where the texture is uniform. In contrast, directional lighting that is nearly parallel to the display will enhance texture, and will mute the color and detail of the pattern.

Realistic Environments. Museums sometimes re-create realistic environments, where the space itself becomes the message, such as period rooms, outdoor scenes, or historic houses. Lighting in character with the original purpose of the space would seem desirable, within reason. For example, the Museum of Science and Industry in Chicago has a simulated coal mine. A true coal mine's underground lighting would be too dark for

visitor safety, much less convey the exhibit's intended message. Miners wear lighted helmets and require very little light because they are familiar with the environment. Clearly, realistic environments in museums require compromises.

The designer can employ at least two techniques to achieve realistic lighting: concealed lighting positions and dual lighting systems. Concealed lighting locations require known viewing positions, the highlighting of prominent display features, and sufficient light for visitor safety. Good examples are many of the rides at theme parks. A dual lighting system utilizes control equipment to alternate, either automatically or manually, between realistic lighting and display lighting. The display lighting should complement the realistic lighting in color and style. Reproducing realistic lighting requires extensive research and observation by the designer, as has been described by Robinson.[17]

Exhibit Cases. Museum display cases often contain small, delicate and valuable artifacts. The case allows a visitor to approach the objects closely while maintaining a barrier against touching or taking. The display case can range from a 5-cm acrylic cover holding a jewel to a 3-m cube holding rare clothing. The case can either have mullions at the corners, or be made of clear acrylic or glass panels glued at the edges. Vitrines

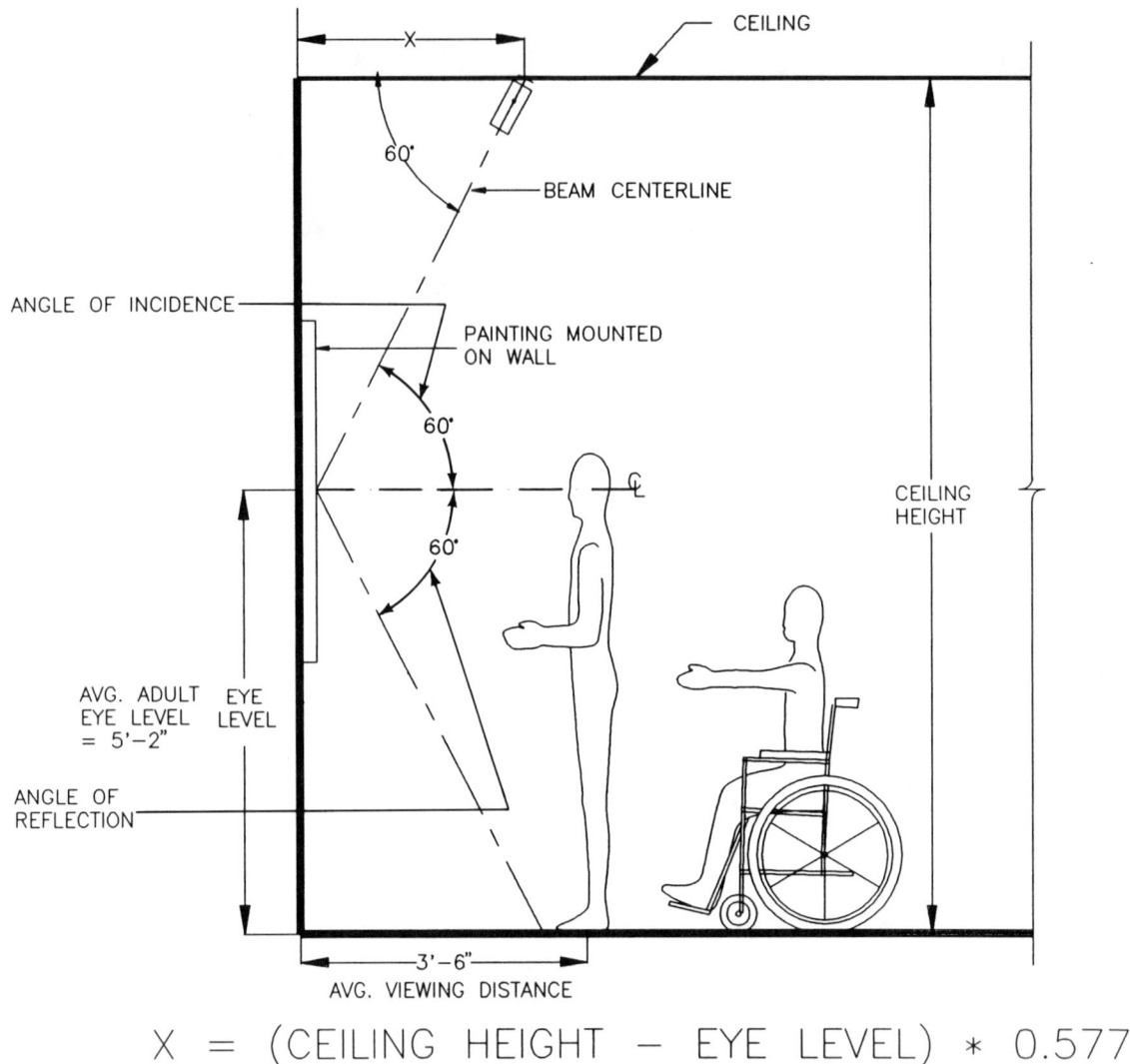

$$X = (CEILING\ HEIGHT - EYE\ LEVEL) * 0.577$$

NOTE: USE ABOVE FORMULA AS A GUIDE.   INCREASE OR DECREASE "X" AS REQUIRED TO AVOID
SHADOWS FROM OVERSIZE FRAMES ON PAINTINGS.   COMPUTE ANGLE OF INCIDENCE/REFLECTION
TO AVOID GLARE TO VIEWER.

Fig. 17-31. Guidelines for luminaire mounting position.

can be shaped to fit the pieces on display. An object can also be placed in a niche, which constitutes a display case set flush into the wall.

Exhibit cases may have internal or external lighting. The types of lamps used vary, including low-voltage incandescent, fluorescent and high-intensity discharge. The principal problems with display case lighting are heat transfer, reflections in the front glazing, and shadows either from the visitor or from one of the displayed objects on another. Reflections are most troubling with cases that have dark interiors. It may be necessary to have such cases face a black wall, and to minimize outward light spill so that the visitor's image is not reflected. Other possible lighting solutions are:

- Use glass which is angled inward at the bottom of the case so that the principal reflections are of the gallery floor, which is kept dark.

- Use specially curved viewing glass which reflects a dark surface.
- Eliminate the glass in favor of some other kind of barrier such as railings or taut wires.
- Keep the case interior strongly lighted, and keep the public space as dark as practical.

It is likely that some reflections will occur in most instances, but if the actual displayed material is brighter than the reflections, they are tolerated. In fact, total elimination of all reflections may lead the viewer to touch the glass for assurance that the display is indeed protected. Be aware that laminated glass will have multiple reflections, one from each surface.

Externally Lighted Cases. When cases are lighted with an external light source, the lights should be above the front of the case and directed straight down. Other luminaire positions will produce shadows within the case from the case edges or corners, even if there are no opaque supporting structures. Diffusing material placed across the top of the case reduces distinct shadows and produces the effect of a self-lighted case. The diffusion material also reduces the reflection of the top of the case onto the ceiling.

External light sources will still produce heat within the case. The use of dichroic reflector (cool beam) lamps or heat filters will reduce this problem. It is important to realize, however, that radiation even in the visible wavelength region is converted to heat when it strikes dark surfaces within the case.

Externally lighted cases usually employ reflector lamps of various beam patterns. Use caution when mounting heavy lamps such as PAR-38 lamps directly above a glass case. If the lamp is dropped during servicing, it can damage the case. Guard against this hazard by incorporating a clear safety barrier between the lamp and the case.

Internally Lighted Cases. Freestanding or built-in cases frequently have light attics or light boxes overhead. These luminaire positions offer the advantage of concealment of various light sources. Cases that can be viewed only from one direction may have a light attic just above the viewing window. This light attic may contain fluorescent lamps for diffuse illumination, fixed or adjustable incandescent lights for directional illumination, or a lighting track which can accommodate both. Luminaires used in a light attic should be simple and easily maintained. Since the luminaires are not seen by the viewer, their appearance is not important. Choice of the surface reflectance (black or white) can affect the amount of stray light from the attic.

Cases intended to be seen from all sides will require a light box the same size as the top of the case. Fluorescent lighting can provide diffuse, even illumination. Where spotlights are required, a deep light attic should be used, and the spots of light should be directed either through small apertures in an opaque material or through a louver. This will eliminate glare to the viewer. Also, locate the spotlights carefully to avoid projecting the pattern of the apertures or louver.

Supplementary lighting from the side, back or bottom of the case can enhance the modeling of three-dimensional objects. Such lighting can also highlight ceramic, glass or polished metallic objects (see figure 17-32). Again, the light source should be shielded to limit direct glare from the viewer.

Luminaires built into the case should be accessible for maintenance through their own door. Lamp changing should not jeopardize the contents of the display case, so the lamp chamber should be separated from the case contents by a secured glazing material.

Lamp chambers require ventilation to dissipate heat. They should always have vents to allow air exchange and convection cooling. In extreme situations, chambers may require conditioned air or electric fans to

Fig. 17-32. Sculpture lighting inside case: Alan Houser's Warm Springs Apache, Los Angeles County Museum of Natural History, 1991. One luminaire on the right provides key light and bounce light inside the case as well as exterior fill light.

improve air flow. All chamber openings should be filtered to prevent dirt deposits from forming on the luminaires and on the glazing.

Ultraviolet (UV) radiation should not enter the case. The case should be constructed from material that filters UV radiation, or UV-reducing lenses should be installed on the luminaires.

For a case that has a front that opens, the evenness of lighting should not be assessed when the front is open. Closing the front glass will reflect light into the lower area of the case, and the top-to-bottom gradient may be greatly improved. If the lower portion of the case seems dark, the case finishes may be too dark, the case may be too tall, or the case may be too shallow for top lighting alone. In these instances one should provide side lighting, repaint the interior of the case, or add internal or external spotlights.

Fiber Optics. Fiber optics represents a new tool for museum lighting. A fiber-optic system consists of a clear glass or polycarbonate extrusion, either solid core or multicore, an end fitting, and an illuminator or light source. The fibers can either provide a point source at its end, or a linear light source along a prescribed length. Extrusions are manufactured in diameters from 0.75 mm ($\frac{1}{32}$ in.) to 12 mm ($\frac{1}{2}$ in.).

Fiber optics provides distinct advantages for lighting cases. Low-level light can be piped directly into a case and focused onto a specific object while maintaining a sealed case. The illuminator itself can be positioned outside the case, dramatically limiting heat within. Virtually no ultraviolet light is transmitted through the strand. The light delivered through the strand can be varied continuously in color by inserting a color wheel in the illuminator. Several fiber-optic strands can emanate from one illuminator. Fiber optics tends to be inefficient over large distances, but new technology has increased its efficiency.

Color

The color rendering properties of the lamp and its correlated color temperature (CCT) will affect the color appearance of objects. Daylight, or lamps with color rendering index (CRI) values of 85 or greater, should be used. The CCT of the light source will determine whether the display takes on a "cool" or a "warm" appearance. Noontime daylight is cool and has a CCT of about 5000 K; a deluxe cool white fluorescent lamp has a CCT of about 4100 K; and an incandescent lamp is warm and has a CCT of about 2800 K. Triphosphor fluorescent lamps are manufactured in many correlated color temperatures.

Mixing lamps of different CCTs in a single display will accentuate their color differences. For example, a cool white fluorescent source in a space dominated by warm incandescent sources will appear cool, whereas the same lamp seen in daylight will appear warm.

Galleries for Changing Exhibits

Galleries for special exhibitions will usually have flexible lighting systems. Flexible lighting systems may include:

- Lighting track throughout the space
- Ample electrical power supply in both ceiling and floor
- Installation of lighting equipment only where needed
- Modular ceiling panels, which facilitate substitution of different luminaires
- Exhibit furniture that provides both display and ambient lighting or only display lighting
- General lighting for the space

Track lighting is the most common form of flexible directional lighting. The luminaire positioning is determined by the surface to be illuminated, the object being illuminated and the lamp intensity distribution. For illuminating vertical surfaces, the angle of incidence at eye level should be between 50 and 60°. Reducing the angle of incidence to 30° will minimize the apparent texture of vertical surfaces but may cause reflected glare. Increasing the angle of incidence to 70° will accentuate texture (see figure 17-31).

Spacing refers to the distance from one luminaire to another or from the luminaire to the wall. Luminaires in a track should be positioned parallel to the display surfaces. Concentric tracks located in the center of the room can be used to illuminate displays which are not located on permanent walls. Track mounted 45–60 cm (1.5–2 ft) above can provide top lighting for cases. Track may also be suspended from a ceiling, but will then require special reinforcement.

Light Damage to Artifacts

Photochemical and Thermal Damage. The principal conservation risks associated with lighting a museum or an art gallery are the photochemical and thermal effects of radiant energy. Since wavelengths shorter than 315 nm are normally absent from daylight that has passed through glass and from electric light sources with glass bulbs (quartz bulbs being a notable exception), the primary concern is with the near-ultraviolet radiation spectrum, 315–400 nm, and the visible radiation spectrum, 400–760 nm. Thermal effects are associated with infrared (IR) radiation. Damage from both photochemical and thermal radiation is irreversible and cumulative.

Current knowledge on the effects of light exposure on the fading of dyes[18-20] has been reviewed by Henderson, LaGiusa and McGowan.[21] Refer to chapter 5, Nonvisual Effects of Radiant Energy, for an additional discussion regarding fading and bleaching.

Materials Subject to Light Damage

Materials subject to light damage include nearly all organic substances and composite materials containing organic substances, such as plastics and synthetic fabrics. Materials highly susceptible to damage include textiles and fibers such as cotton, wool and furs, and some writing inks. Examples include silk costumes, watercolor paintings, hand-written documents and paper. Moderately susceptible materials subject to light damage include oil paintings, tempera, finished wood, ivory, leather and reeds. The least susceptible materials to light damage include inorganic materials, such as metal, stone, glass, ceramic and most minerals.

Minimizing Damage

Ultraviolet Spectrum (315–400 nm). Energy in the ultraviolet (UV) part of the spectrum is invisible and contributes nothing to the vision process. Its photons, having high energy, are destructive and should be eliminated. Clear glass absorbs much, but not all, UV radiation. There are many dichroic and absorbing filters which can block all UV energy while reducing energy in the visible spectrum by less than 10%.

Incandescent light has approximately 75 microwatts (μW) of long-wavelength UV per lumen (75 μW/lm). Most fluorescent lamps fall in a higher range of UV content, and unfiltered daylight can be even higher. It is therefore important to have a UV meter which reads in microwatts per lumen to ascertain the radiation striking an artifact. This meter will be in addition to an illuminance meter, which is sensitive only to the visible spectrum.

Visible Spectrum (400–770 nm). Recommended exposure limits for the visible spectrum are given in figure 17-25. To apply these limits, the designer must calculate the annual hours of exposure, and divide the limit by this value to obtain the maximum recommended illuminance.

Consider a highly susceptible material to be displayed in a museum that is open for 8 hours per day, 300 days per year. If the amount of light incident on the artifact at other times will be negligible, then the annual duration of exposure is 2400 hours. From figure 17-25, the recommended limit is 54,000 lx · hr/yr (5000 fc · hr/yr), and the maximum recommended illuminance for permanent display is 54 lx (5 fc). The annual time of operation of the museum multiplied by the illuminance of 54 lx yields an annual exposure of nearly 130,000 lx · hr/yr (12,000 fc · hr/yr), well over twice the recommended limit. An illuminance substantially less than 54 lx is unlikely to provide for a satisfying display, so to limit damage to a highly susceptible artifact, the hours during which the artifact is displayed must be reduced.

For example, the Star-Spangled Banner from Fort McHenry, Maryland, is on permanent display in the Museum of American History in Washington, but only for five minutes each hour on the half hour. At all other times, the flag is covered by an opaque canvas with an artist's rendition of the flag. At thirty minutes past each hour, the canvas is lowered to reveal the flag and expose it to an illuminance of 540 lx (50 fc). Over a span of 10 h, the flag is exposed to 50 min of light at an average of 25 fc or less. This results in an annual exposure of approximately 80,700 lx · hr/yr (1,500 fc · hr/yr). This scheme permits the flag to be viewed by millions of visitors each year while severely limiting its exposure to light.

Illuminance can be controlled by luminaires with integral dimmers, area master dimmers, mechanical light-blocking screens on luminaires, reduced-wattage lamps, electromechanical shutter devices, glass or plastic filters, or any combination of these. The display time can be reduced by rotation of artifacts, shorter viewing hours, and controlling the on time of the light with sensors or mechanical devices. Some of these reductions carry the possibility of adverse side effects such as alternate contraction and expansion of the artifact and shifting of the lamp's chromaticity.

Infrared Spectrum (770–5000 nm). The absorption of visible energy is an unavoidable consequence of display, but the heating effects by infrared (IR) radiation should be minimized, since they can cause considerable damage. Infrared-absorbing filters ("heat filters") or dichroic infrared reflector glass can be used, but usually it is preferable to select a source which has been designed to minimize IR radiation, such as cool beam PAR and MR lamps.

The absorption of any radiant energy (UV, visible spectrum or IR) on the surface of an artifact will raise its temperature, even in an environment where the air temperature is precisely controlled. Heat can dry or damage the artifact. The daily switching on and off of illumination equipment may be particularly problematic because the alternate heating and cooling may result in cracking or flaking, particularly in leather or wood artifacts.

Light Sources

Electric light sources, or lamps, for museum applications fall into three main categories: incandescent, fluorescent and high-intensity discharge. Incandescent and fluorescent lamps are generally best suited for interior display applications. See chapter 6, Light Sources.

When designing natural lighting systems, the challenge is to retain the positive aspects associated with daylight—such as its ever-changing directional, spectral and temporal qualities—while controlling illuminances within acceptable ranges. This challenge must start with a clear definition of the permitted cumulative annual exposure.

Maintenance

Maintenance of lighting in a museum requires a trained technical staff member who not only understands the physics of electricity and illumination, but also appreciates the sensitivity of the artifacts displayed. The designer should be sensitive to ease of lamp and socket replacement, potential wear points, breakable parts and parts which require cleaning. The designer and the technician should work together from the inception of the project to assure ease of maintenance. Below is a simple checklist to assist them:

1. Allow sufficient access space for lamp replacement and luminaire repairs.
2. Ensure available ladders, rolling towers, catwalks or self-propelled machinery which are sufficient for luminaire maintenance.
3. Minimize the number of lamp types used in the exhibition.
4. Design a safety and security barrier between the artifact and the lighting chamber.
5. Evaluate each luminaire with respect to the maintenance time and skill required to keep it functioning.
6. Provide adequate storage space for replacement lamps, luminaires and cleaning supplies.
7. Provide adequate work space and proper equipment for repair and preparation of luminaires.
8. Provide a lamp and luminaire maintenance schedule.

Simplicity of design promotes easy and continuous maintenance. Specialty and precision luminaires can enhance a display, but maintenance for these types of units requires trained museum staff. Simple, uncomplicated pieces of equipment help ensure that the lighting design presented on the first day of the exhibition will remain operational until its close. For additional information, see chapter 32, Lighting Maintenance.

REFERENCES

1. IES. Committee on Lighting for Houses of Worship. 1991. *Lighting for houses of worship.* IES RP-25-91. New York: Illuminating Engineering Society of North America.
2. IES. Health Care Facilities Committee. 1985. *Lighting for health care facilities.* IES CP-29-1985. New York: Illuminating Engineering Society of North America.
3. Beck, W. C. 1984. The lighting of the birthing room. *Light. Des. Appl.* 14(7):40–41.
4. Beck, W. C., and W. H. VanSlyke. 1976. Light, color, and lamps in the hospital. *Guthrie Bul.* 45(3):129–136.
5. Beck, W. C., and R. H. Meyer, eds. 1982. *Health care environment: The user's viewpoint.* Boca Raton FL: CRC Press.
6. Burton, C. 1986. Lighting for health care facilities. *Construction Specifier* 39(4):44–51.
7. Sisson, T. R. C. 1976. Visible light therapy of national hyperbilirubinemia. In *Photochemical and photobiological reviews,* vol. 1, chapter 6. K. C. Smith, ed. New York: Plenum.
8. Kethley, T. W., and K. Branch. 1972. Ultraviolet lamps for room air disinfection. *Arch. Environ. Health* 25(3):205–214.
9. U.S. National Institute for Occupational Safety and Health. 1972. *Occupational exposure to ultraviolet radiation: Criteria for a recommended standard.* DHEW publication HSM 73-11009. [Rockville, MD]: National Institute for Occupational Safety and Health.
10. Beck, W. C., J. Schreckendgust, and J. Geffert. 1979. The color of the surgeon's task light. *Light. Des. Appl.* 9(7):54–57.
11. National Fire Protection Association. [Latest edition]. *Standard for health care facilities, NFPA 99.* Quincy, MA: National Fire Protection Association.
12. IES. Committee on Hospitality Facilities. [To be published]. *Lighting for hospitality facilities.* New York: Illuminating Engineering Society of North America.
13. Kling, C. 1986. Before the ball begins: Lighting for ballrooms and meeting rooms. *Light. Des. Appl.* 16(5):27–30.
14. IES. Committee on Institutions. Subcommittee on Library Lighting. 1974. Recommended practice of library lighting. *J. Illum. Eng. Soc.* 3(3):253–281.
15. Michalski, S. 1989. *Draft: Light and conservation guidelines.* Ottawa: Canadian Conservation Institute.
16. Loe, D. L., E. Rowlands, and N. F. Watson. 1982. Preferred lighting conditions for the display of oil and watercolour paintings. *Light. Res. Tech.* 14(4):173–192.
17. Robinson, E. K. 1986. Spotlight on "After the Revolution." *Light. Des. Appl.* 16(5):23–25.
18. Feller, R. L. 1964. Control of deteriorating effects of light upon museum objects. *Museum* 17(2):57–98.
19. Thomson, G. 1986. *The museum environment.* 2nd ed. London, Boston: Butterworths.
20. Cuttle, C. 1988. Lighting works of art for exhibition and conservation. *Light. Res. Tech.* 20(2):43–53.
21. Henderson, A. J., F. F. LaGiusa, and T. K. McGowan. 1991. Dye fading. *Light. Des. Appl.* 21(5):16–25.

Plate 1. This large church in Orlando, FL, which seats 6200 people, is illuminated by tungsten-halogen downlighting for reading light in the pews as well as indirect lighting for ambient light and wall-washing for drama. A sophisticated accent lighting system allows for live television broadcasting. Behind the back-lighted stained glass window in the baptistery is a projection screen.

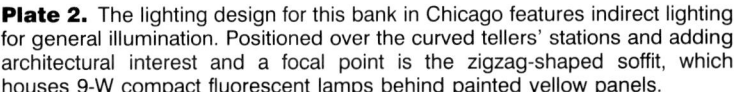

Plate 2. The lighting design for this bank in Chicago features indirect lighting for general illumination. Positioned over the curved tellers' stations and adding architectural interest and a focal point is the zigzag-shaped soffit, which houses 9-W compact fluorescent lamps behind painted yellow panels.

Plate 3. This airline hospitality suite in Cincinnati, with its soft colors and inviting textures, features daylighting, fluorescent cove lighting, and accent lighting. The sculptured ceiling is softened by louvers and frosted acrylic overlays. A chandelier and reading lamps were added for warmth and comfort.

Plate 4. The 244 by 21 m (800 by 68 ft) pedestrian tunnel at O'Hare Airport features a colorful undulating glass block wall, which is lighted with fluorescent lamps and assymetric reflectors. Above the 76-m (250-ft) long people movers is a neon sculpture, which adds excitement to the space and has an energizing effect on weary travelers.

Plate 5. The new lighting design for this Byzantine revival style temple in San Francisco included the creation of an oculus at the peak of the dome in which supplementary 1000-W PAR64 flood lamps were installed to increase the downlighting for the reading of prayer books. An uplight component was added to the four major chandeliers. Accent lighting was added to highlight the central altar and other architectural and liturgical features.

Plate 6. This atrium inside a Kentucky hotel is visually exciting with "holiday" lights, tubes of neon outlining the balconies, and scallops of downlight creating interest.

Plate 7. A multisource lighting design was used in this hotel ballroom in Hawaii. The decorative crystal luminaires, outfitted with scores of individual A lamps, give the room sparkle. Supplementary lighting is provided by downlights and accent lights for special occasions. The lighting is controlled by a four scene preset system with divisible ballroom assigner panels.

Plate 8. Dining becomes high drama in this California restaurant which is illuminated with an indirect system for general lighting. Also included are accent lights on the decorative elements, pendant luminaires at the tables, and neon tube lighting for whimsy.

Lighting for Merchandise Areas

18

New lighting techniques and equipment as well as more efficient light sources provide the designer with tools to meet the challenge of the ever changing requirements of the merchandising world and the increasing cost of energy.[1]

Careful consideration must be given to visual cues which will aid in establishing the image a store wishes to project. The lighting system should be designed to create a pleasant and secure environment in which to do business.

Sophisticated consumers and the tendency toward fewer trained sales personnel make it essential to present merchandise under lighting that will help increase sales. Thus, attention should be given to the quality, quantity and effectiveness of lighting and its ability to render the color of the task area or displayed merchandise.

GOALS OF MERCHANDISE LIGHTING

The primary goals common in the lighting of merchandising areas are to attract the customer, to initiate purchases and to facilitate the completion of the sale.

Lighting to Attract and Guide the Customer. The first step in the merchandising process is to attract the customer to the retail space and merchandise. Light attracts. The quantity and quality of illumination, the impression of the merchandise that it creates and the effect it has on the appearance of the area (show window or store interior) are factors in the effective sale of merchandise.

Lighting to Evaluate the Merchandise. Buying decisions start when the customer is visually attracted. However, the actual purchase is not accomplished until the customer can visually evaluate the merchandise for characteristics such as texture, color and quality and read labels under adequate illumination.

Lighting to Complete the Sale. Proper lighting at the point of sale is necessary to complete a transaction. Proper lighting should enable the customer to make a final decision, and sales personnel to perform quickly and accurately services such as recording sales on the register, preparing paperwork, reading prices, using credit card transaction tools, and packaging. Good lighting design will also help minimize returned merchandise, since the customer is able to evaluate the merchandise as to color, texture and quality at the point of sale and is less likely to be disappointed with his or her purchases when viewing them at home.

Lighting design for retail interiors, exteriors, show windows and other merchandising spaces should take into account the appearance of the space, impact on the merchandise and graphics, operational and maintenance methods, and physical, environmental and economic aspects of the space and merchandise. See Chapter 10, Design Process, for a general discussion of lighting design.

LIGHTING DESIGN CRITERIA

Characteristics of the Visual Systen

The appearance of merchandise and merchandising spaces, the sale of merchandise and the performance of tasks are affected by basic factors important to any visual task.

As the size of the visual target increases, it becomes easier to see, at least up to a certain point. When an object is small or contains fine detailing, visibility can be improved by increasing illuminance. To see each critical detail of a piece of merchandise, such as gray thread on black cloth, the object must differ in luminance or color from its background. Visibility is improved when the luminance contrast of details with their background increases. Where poor contrast conditions exist, visibility can be improved, if deemed necessary, by increasing the illuminance or by using a more effective lighting technique such as directional lighting to highlight fabric texture.

As the brightness of merchandise and task areas is increased, seeing is made easier. For example, under the same lighting conditions, the pattern on a light-colored suit is easier to see than that on a dark-colored suit, because the reflectance of the light-colored suit is higher, causing it to be of higher luminance and thus appear brighter. Luminance is increased by increasing the illuminance.

Broadly speaking, one's ability to see an object is best when the luminances within the space are nearly

Fig. 18-1. Linen household items (left) are of higher luminance than the surroundings to attract attention; (right) silhouette lighting is another effective method for attracting attention, as shown for a chair display.

the same. If fine inspection or careful reading is required, the ratio of the luminances within the merchandising space should be less than 3 : 1. On the other hand, for the customer to be attracted to the merchandise, the display should have at least 5 times the luminance of the surround. On special or key displays, luminance of the merchandise should be closer to 10 times the surround luminance. Small areas of higher or lower luminance within the merchandising space may not appreciably affect the visual process but will create interest (see figure 18-1).

As one ages, less light reaches the eye, and that which does reach it is of lower quality. Thus, the older person sees less brightness and contrast in objects than does a young person looking at the same objects. There is some evidence, too, that older people are troubled more by high illuminance ratios, including glare, than younger people. Care should be taken to provide the proper quantity and quality of illuminance and to reduce glare in spaces frequented by the elderly.

Characteristics of Merchandise Lighting

Light Sources for Retail Spaces. When lighting retail spaces, there are three families of light sources from which to choose: incandescent, fluorescent and high-intensity discharge. Selecting the most appropriate light source will be based on many factors: cost, energy, color, illuminance, startup time, flicker, store image, environmental concerns, users' needs and wants—along with the lighting consultant's personal preferences. For a complete discussion on light sources, see chapter 6.

Distribution and Direction of Electric Light.[2] Luminaires are characterized according to the percentage of

light emitted above and below the horizontal plane (see chapter 7, Luminaires). Luminaires such as spotlights, floodlights and wallwashers for specific merchandise highlighting are not classified in the same manner, but are described according to performance characteristics, beam spread, focusing ability and sharpness of cutoff. Performance characteristics are dependent on the light source type and housing and on auxiliary devices such as louvers, lenses, reflectors and diffusers.

Lighting systems provide either diffuse or directional light. The form of objects and texture of surfaces can be revealed by directional lighting like that from small, highly focused light sources. Diffuse light from wide-distribution downlights or large-area light sources, such as fluorescent luminaires or indirect lighting systems, tends to reduce the variations in form and texture. Three-dimensional merchandise, for example, should generally be displayed with some mix of directional lighting to accent form, and with significant diffuse lighting to relieve the harshness produced by dark shadows (see the section on museums and art galleries in chapter 17, Institution and Public Building Lighting). The appearance of customers and sales personnel (facial forms and expressions) is best treated with a similar combination of directional and diffuse lighting. Directional lighting may cause harsh shadows on areas where visual tasks are performed, reducing the luminance of the task area. High-reflectance matte finishes on room surfaces act as effective secondary sources, reducing the shadows.

Daylighting. In open-front stores, or where there are windows or skylights, it is necessary to avoid large differences in luminance between daylit areas and interior areas illuminated to recommended levels. This may be accomplished by controlling the daylight, increasing the level of electric illumination or both.

The amount and distribution of daylight received in store interiors depends on the orientation and total area of windows, their light transmission properties and the relationship of the window height to the room width. Comfortable seeing conditions in merchandising areas result from careful consideration of the types of glass used in windows, the method and degree of daylight control, such as overhangs, awnings or internal window treatments, and the reflectance values of surrounding surfaces.

Draperies, shades, baffles or louvers should be used for windows in areas where sky luminance or sunlight becomes uncomfortable or glaring to persons within. Horizontal or vertical overhangs outside the windows can eliminate glare from direct sunlight. Sales personnel should be oriented so that bright windows are not within the normal field of view, and shadows are not cast on reading material.

Glare. When overly bright light sources, windows or lighted surfaces are within the visual field of the shopper or clerk and can be seen directly or by reflection, they may produce glare that will divert attention from the merchandise displayed. When they are near the line of sight of the merchandise or sales tasks, they can reduce one's ability to see. Luminaires or luminous elements near the line of sight should not be so bright as to distract from or compete with the merchandise or impede circulation flow. When retrofitting existing luminaires, make sure that the luminaires are outfitted for glare control. To reduce offending reflections of luminaires in the glass lenses of surveillance equipment and in computer screens at the registers, attach glare shields or louvers to the luminaires. See the discussion of lighting for VDT screens in chapter 15, Office Lighting.

Light source reflections from specular or semispecular materials can also be a problem. Large-area, low-luminance luminaires are used when shiny surfaces cannot be avoided. High-reflectance matte surfaces can also be used to reduce reflected glare.

Color. Knowledge of the principles of light and color is very important in merchandise lighting design. See chapter 4, Color. Although personal tastes in color vary with climate, nationality, age, gender and personality, there is almost universal agreement to call yellows, yellow-reds, reds and red-purples "warm colors" and to call greens, blue-greens, blues and purple-blues "cool colors." All gray colors approach neutral in character, whether from the warm or the cool side.

Color, as one of the most powerful of all merchandising tools, can attract attention, create an ambiance, stimulate sales or guide customers. See plate 1 in this chapter. A positive psychological affect can be introduced in special merchandising areas by creating warm or cool color ambiance. In areas that have mirrors, however, it is important that the customer have a natural appearance. The light source selected for general illumination should render acceptable skin tones as well as enhance the merchandise.

Color of Area Surfaces. In merchandising areas where customers are exposed to an environment for long periods, the colors of surfaces can have an effect on their buying attitudes—positively or negatively, consciously or subconsciously. The colors of merchandise should be considered in the selection of colors of large area surfaces. The use of large areas of strong colors can clash with the color of the merchandise displayed and can adversely affect the color of reflected light reaching the merchandise. In general, where the merchandise is colorful and varied, the background should be of light reflectance and neutral color. Should stronger surface color be desired for display lighting, it can be provided by the light source. Small areas of accent color will give vitality and dramatic interest.

Color of Light Sources. The color of area surfaces and merchandise is a function of the spectral composition of the light source and the pigment, and the surface properties of the viewed object. For example, a surface is seen as red when the light source contains some energy in the long-wavelength region of the spectrum and the object predominantly reflects energy in that same region. A "white" light source, such as daylight or sunlight, usually contains energy throughout the visible spectrum, ranging from 380 to 770 nm.

Fluorescent, incandescent and high-intensity discharge lamps, as well as daylight, are all considered as broad-band sources of light; however, these "white" light sources vary significantly in the relative amount of energy in each portion of the spectrum. The spectral composition determines not only the color appearance of the lamp (warm or cool), but also its color rendering properties. Recent developments have improved the color rendering capability of many of these lamps. In addition, a wide range of fluorescent, HID and incandescent lamps are available to produce different color effects. Colored filters are also available for fluorescent and incandescent sources.

Besides attracting attention, it may be desirable for a lighting system to show merchandise under conditions similar to those under which it will be viewed (illuminance and light source). This will help minimize customer dissatisfaction and returns.

Characteristics of the Surfaces

Surface textures vary from mirrored (specular) to diffuse (matte). The brightness of matte surfaces, such as carpeting, appears nearly uniform from every viewing direction and independent of the direction of illumina-

Fig. 18-2. Veiling reflections on specular transparent display cases can obscure the merchandise. Here a horizontal counter displays images of the ceiling luminaires, which compete with the merchandise.

tion. For specular surfaces such as flatware, the brightness varies with the viewing direction, the location, size and intensity of the light source, and the degree of specularity of the surface being viewed. Where reflectances of the surfaces within the merchandising areas can be selected, they should be chosen to provide luminance ratios within the recommended limits. When reflectances cannot be selected, the luminance ratios can be controlled to some extent by varying the illuminances on the surfaces.

Reflections of light sources from specular, transparent surfaces, such as counter tops, show windows, wall cases and packaging materials, can be particularly problematic (see figure 18-2). These reflections can cause glare and reduce the visibility of objects beneath or behind the surface.

The designer may deliberately locate a luminaire to produce reflections from a surface; for example, a light source reflected in a silver tureen emphasizes the form of the object as well as its patina. Points of brightness from light source images reflected in shiny surfaces appear as highlights or streaks of brightness and are often used as elements of sparkle to enhance the appearance of merchandise.

Whether reflections are desired or not, the designer must be careful to locate the luminaires with respect to the specular surface and the expected location of the customer.

Illuminance and Energy[3,4]

When formulating a lighting plan for a merchandise area, the designer should consider all of the following: merchandising techniques and goals, the types of activities within the store, illuminance recommendations and energy efficiency.

Illuminance for actual merchandising (selling) areas and for the specific visual tasks performed by sales and support personnel should be evaluated when developing a lighting design. The designer should refer to the recommendations for task-oriented lighting on the merchandise and for the surrounding circulation spaces listed in figure 18-3.

Merchandising and Associated Areas. Figure 18-3 lists current recommended illuminances for merchandising areas. These values are intended as a guide. Current practice indicates a strong trend to variations in illumination for different kinds of stores and for various departments within a store. These considerations, plus those of competition, need for distinctive effects and store design, may make it desirable to vary the levels at specific locations from the values shown.

When merchandise is displayed in one location and evaluated in another (an example being removal of an item from a showcase to show a customer), it is desirable not to exceed a 3 : 1 ratio in illuminance between the two locations.

To assure that the appropriate lighting levels are provided every time, the probable procedures for lighting maintenance should be reflected in the lighting calculations.

Sales and Support Areas. The quantity of light in the support areas in stores is just as important as in the merchandise areas. See chapter 11, Illuminance Selection, for recommended illuminance categories for many commonly occurring tasks such as writing, reading or wrapping; however, many of the tasks will be performed in merchandising locations. If more than one task is performed within a space, and these tasks require different illuminances, the designer must choose between them.

Regulation. Energy regulations for lighting vary from state to state. Lighting is also subject to federal legislation. Some regulations are based on power density (watts per square meter); others are based on requirements for lamp efficacy or, in some cases, overall system efficiency of lamp and luminaire or of lamp, ballast and luminaire. The designer must determine what local, state and federal codes apply to each specific design. The following energy management considerations apply specifically to the merchandising spaces.

Since displays are frequently changed, lighting for the activity areas within the store should be periodically evaluated (see figure 18-3). In some cases rearrangement of store space may result in different usage (for example, from medium to low activity), and the illuminance should then be changed accordingly.

Ratios between illuminance on merchandise on display and in the customer evaluation location should be determined. If ratios exceed the recommended 3 : 1, the display levels should be reduced to fall within the recommendation.

Fig. 18-3. Currently Recommended Illuminances for Lighting Design in Merchandising, Sales and Support Services Areas — Target Maintained Levels

Areas or Tasks	Description	Type of Activity Area*	Illuminance†	
			Lux	Foot-candles
Circulation	Area not used for display or appraisal of merchandise or for sales transactions	High activity Medium activity Low activity	300 200 100	30 20 10
Merchandise† (including showcases & wall displays)	That plane area, horizontal to vertical, where merchandise is displayed and readily accessible for customer examination	High activity Medium activity Low activity	1000 750 300	100 75 30
Feature displays‡	Single item or items requiring special highlighting to visually attract and set apart from the surround	High activity Medium activity Low activity	5000 3000 1500	500 300 150

Show windows
  Daytime lighting
    General
    Feature
  Nighttime lighting
    Main business districts (highly competitive)
      General
      Feature
    Secondary business districts or small towns
      General
      Feature
			
			2000
			10000
			
			2000
			10000
			
			1000
			5000
				
				200
				1000
				
				200
				1000
				
				100
				500

Sales Transactions	Areas used for employee price verification and for recording transactions	Reading of copied, written, printed or electronic data processing information	See Fig 2-1	
Support Services	Store spaces where merchandising is not the prime consideration	Alteration rooms, fitting rooms, stock rooms, locker areas, wrapping and packaging	See Fig. 2-1	

*One store may encompass all three types within the buildings.

High activity: Merchandise is usually displayed in bulk and is readily recognizable as to its use. Evaluation and viewing time is short. Minimal sales assistance and few customer amenities are available. Included in this category are mass merchandisers, warehouse sales, grocery and discount stores, auto parts departments, and hardware departments.

Medium Activity: Merchandise is familiar, but the customer may require time or help in evaluation of quality or usage or in the decision to buy. Some sales assistance and customer amenities are available. Included in this category are department and specialty stores.

Low activity: Merchandise is generally exclusive, of the finest quality and highest price. Personal services and premium customer amenities are expected. Shopping is generally unhurried. Included in this category are fashion boutiques, designer signature shops, jewelry stores, fur salons, and fine art galleries.

†Maintained on the task or in the area at any time.
‡Lighting levels to be measured in the plane of the merchandise.

Lamps and Ballasts. A periodic review of new light sources is advised to determine if more effective types can be substituted for older ones. In evaluating lamps and ballasts, the luminous intensity as well as overall power density for the space should be considered. This is particularly important in applications where small displays require special emphasis lighting from distant luminaire locations. An efficient, but diffuse light source would be totally unacceptable here. Color rendering of merchandise is also of importance in selecting a light source and may be the deciding factor in changing from one light source family to another, or within one family. Additional information on light sources can be found in chapter 6.

Luminaire Layout and Control. Each time displays are changed, the lighting system should be checked for its suitability, so that the merchandise is always appropriately lighted. Specific highlighting units not required for the changed display should be removed if mounted on a track or other flexible installation, or shut off if part of a permanent installation.

Lighting Controls. Consideration should also be given to controlling the lighting system. Lighting controls within merchandising areas can be used to decrease operating costs and increase flexibility of the lighting system. Controls allow for selective switching and dimming of the luminaires during different operational periods. For example, accent lighting can be switched off during periods of security and surveillance, cleanup and maintenance, as well as stocking and tagging. Entrances and windows may, however, require a higher illuminance from electric lighting in daytime to compensate for high daylight illuminance.

Typical methods include light control with low-voltage switching, programmable microprocessor light control, time clocks, photocells, motion and occupancy sensors, and dimmers. See chapter 31 for additional information on controls.

Area Surfaces. Lighter finishes are preferred for greater utilization of reflected light, but excessive luminance ratios should be avoided, keeping in mind the suitability of background surfaces for the merchandise.

Maintenance Program. Coordination between maintenance and display personnel is important. Lighting system maintenance, which includes relamping, cleaning, aiming and focusing, is required in order to maintain the effect of the original design and maximize system efficiency. Lighting design and retrofit projects should include a maintenance procedures manual to assure implementation of an ongoing maintenance program. Refer to chapter 32 on lighting system maintenance for further information.

System Utilization. Consideration should be given to the use of the space so that the most energy-effective lighting solutions for the application may be achieved. For example, spill light from feature displays may be sufficient for delineating circulation areas without the necessity of providing separate aisle lighting systems.

Acoustical and Thermal Factors

Today's store frequently requires integration of the lighting, acoustical and HVAC systems. Acoustical treatment of ceiling surfaces is important, because the reflectance of the acoustical material affects the performance of the lighting system. Luminaire material, in turn, can affect the acoustics of the space.

Heat generated from light sources can have an effect on the air conditioning systems. Air-handling luminaires are also available which handle supply, return and heat removal as part of the comfort control system. These systems may also improve the efficiency of the lighting system by operating fluorescent lamps at the optimal temperature. See Part III, Elements of Design.

Economics

The total cost of a lighting system is the sum of owning and operating charges. While initial investment may in some cases be a dominant factor in selecting specific luminaires or lamp types, there are capital expenses (amortization, interest, taxes and insurance) that also should be considered.[5]

Maintenance

All lighting systems depreciate in light output with the passage of time; see chapter 30, Energy Management. Lighting equipment and room surfaces should be well maintained if design efficiency and appearance are to be obtained. Of course, consideration should be given to the accessibility of luminaires for cleaning and relamping, especially in high mounting areas.

Fading, Bleaching and Spoilage

When an item of merchandise is put on display, its color stability should be considered. Fading of merchandise will be caused by exposure to high illuminances for extended periods of time. Other factors that contribute to fading are the spectral distribution of radiation (particularly in the ultraviolet region), moisture, and temperature variation. Depending on the chemical composition of merchandise, the saturation of dyes in the merchandise, and the composition of the weave of fabrics, these effects may be more or less important. See chapter 5, Nonvisual Effects of Radiant Energy.

INTERIOR SPACES

Lighting Methods for Merchandising Spaces

Once the type of store, class of merchandise to be handled and clientele desired are determined, the lighting should be designed in keeping with their character. The lighting design should consider all surfaces in the customers' fields of view. Merchandise should dominate the scene.

There are three basic approaches to the lighting of merchandise areas in stores: the general pattern system, the specific system and the flexible system. Each system should have supplemental lighting to attract attention to featured displays, to influence traffic circulation and to create added interest.

General Pattern System. The general pattern system employs a pattern of luminaires to provide general lighting throughout the sales area, with or without display lighting, and without regard for the location of the merchandise (see figure 18-4). The system should include switching or dimming controls for flexibility of space use and for efficient energy utilization. If neither display lighting nor switching or dimming controls are used, the store will lack areas of emphasis or focal points.

Fig. 18-4. Downlights in a general pattern provide general illumination in this book store. Light sources concealed above the wall book shelves provide a uniform wash of light on the books to attract attention to the merchandise and facilitate customer selection.

Fig. 18-6. In this jewelry store a specific lighting system is used, determined by the location of the showcase. Downlights accent the jewelry, and chandeliers provide for general illumination, as well as add sparkle and elegance.

Specific System. The specific system employs a layout of luminaires determined by the location of the merchandise displays (store fixtures, showcases or gondolas). It is tailored to emphasize the merchandise and delineate sales areas (see figures 18-5 and 18-6).

Flexible System. The flexible system employs a pattern of electric outlets of the continuous or individual type for nonpermanent installation of luminaires. These may be wired for multiple-circuit application and control. This system may be used for a general pattern lighting or for specific lighting and offers the added advantage of interchangeability of luminaire types to create lighting tailored to the merchandise display. See figure 18-7.

In choosing a system or combination of systems to be used, consideration must be given to the architectural interior design requirements as well as to the

flexibility and adjustment required for the merchandising task. The following three types of lighting are frequently used in flexible systems: recessed adjustable luminaires, recessed adjustable pulldown luminaires and track lighting. Recessed adjustable luminaires have the appearance of recessed downlights, but provide aiming adjustability of 30–45° from the vertical and usually 355° of rotation about the vertical. The recessed adjustable pulldown luminaire adds the flexibility of being able to position the light source below the ceiling line and hence allows much greater vertical adjustment (0–90°). The most flexible system is a track lighting installation where the luminaire can be positioned at any point on a linear electrified track of arbitrary length, and the luminaire is adjustable both horizontally (355°) and vertically (0–90°). The recessed adjustable luminaire provides a clean ceiling line. Re-

Fig. 18-5. A wine cellar has been created as a focal center in this liquor store, and the lighting system has been designed specifically to illuminate the vertical surfaces of the wine racks.

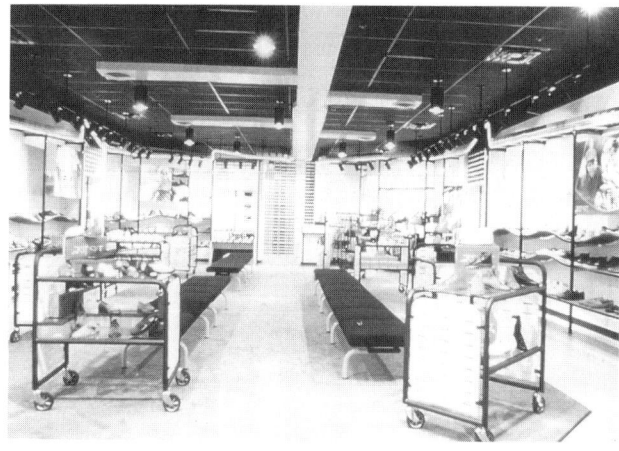

Fig. 18-7. Track lighting provides the flexibility desired by many stores to accommodate frequently changing displays.

cessed adjustable pulldown luminaires provide more adjustability and, when properly positioned, appear as semirecessed on the ceiling. The track lighting system provides the most flexibility but may appeared cluttered on the ceiling. Although pulldown and track luminaires are the most flexible, care must be taken when using these types of luminaires to assure that aiming angles do not create objectionable glare. (For information on modular wiring, see chapter 7, Luminaires.)

Feature and Supplementary Lighting

The proper balance of a general pattern or specific lighting system depends on the type of store and merchandise and the methods of presentation. Special consideration should be given to the store's most prominent feature, and supplementary lighting should be added to attain the results desired. Each specific area must receive individual consideration in lighting design, selection of lighting equipment and illuminances. Specific consideration should be given to placing and aiming the light sources at angles to prevent direct and reflected glare from reaching the eyes of customers and sales personnel. The following is a discussion of merchandising areas that will generally require supplementary lighting.

Show Windows. The show window should be a powerful attraction, providing the link between the potential customer passing by and the merchandise within the store. Each of the following factors should be considered in the design of show-window lighting: merchandise strategy; merchandise type and characteristics; location of the show window (outdoor or enclosed mall area, urban or suburban setting, free-standing store or shopping-center unit); night and day use and associated ambient illuminances (see figure 18-5), including the nature of the competition; open back or enclosed configuration; size and shape; contour and slant of the glazing, and brightness from daytime and nighttime reflections; interior surface reflectances and colors; flexibility requirements; and size and location of display graphics. See chapter 9 for calculation techniques.

Counter Lighting. Counter lighting is a form of accent lighting in which merchandise displayed on counter tops, or at the point of sale near the counter tops, receives three to five times the circulation-area illuminance. This is usually accomplished with focused downlight equipment.

Mirror Lighting. Lighting at a mirror is important because here shoppers make their final appraisal of hats, clothing, shoes and cosmetics in terms of color, fit and appearance. When a shopper evaluates wearing apparel, the face is generally observed first. The following

factors should be considered when lighting mirrors:

1. The face should be softly lighted with light sources that flatter skin tones, and from a direction that minimizes harsh lines or shadows. Special consideration should be given to areas requiring selection or appraisal of colors —for example, cosmetics.
2. The sales item should lighted so that all important areas of the product can be seen.
3. The lighting should be of a quality consistent with the illumination under which the merchandise will be worn.

In fitting rooms or special selling alcoves, side lighting can be used and confined directly to the garment. This technique is especially effective in departments featuring coats and furs. In the case of triple mirrors, side lighting can be reflected from the wing mirrors. Downlighting can be used effectively in confined selling spaces such as fitting rooms. The reflectance, color and illumination of the background are important. See Fitting Rooms, below, and chapter 19, Residential Lighting, for mirror lighting.

Showcase Lighting. Another commonly used technique in retail spaces is to light merchandise displayed in showcases. Generally, showcase lighting requires three times the illuminance of the circulation-area lighting. Fluorescent lamps may be employed for a continuous line of light, and to minimize the heat created in enclosed spaces. The major objective of showcase lighting is to attain maximum light on merchandise without obstruction from lighting equipment; thus, small-diameter lamps are usually preferred. Despite the general use of fluorescent lamps, incandescent and miniature halogen lamps are sometimes used for more acceptable color rendition and sparkle, especially for items such as jewelry and glassware. For a curved or irregular case, miniature halogen, compact fluorescent and cold-cathode tubing can be used to conform to the shape of the case. See figure 18-8, the section in chapter 17 on Museum Lighting, and chapter 29, Lighting for Advertising.

Modeling Lighting. The form and texture of merchandise may be more apparent through the use of directional lighting to supplement the general diffuse lighting needed for the overall effect. However, light should not be directed too obliquely, since unilateral or otherwise objectionable shadows may be cast.

Wall-Case Lighting. Wall-case lighting is similar in concept to showcase lighting. It falls into three categories: (1) the free-standing vertical display mounted against a wall; (2) the encased, open-front, wall-mounted display; and (3) the glass-door, wall-mounted

Fig. 18-8. Fluorescent sources beneath diffusing material produce a transilluminated display for a cosmetic counter showcase. Perfume bottles appear to glow and float.

Fig. 18-9. Lighting on the vertical plane emphasizes the color and polish of the china and increases the feeling of depth.

display case. Wall-case lighting is usually used in merchandise displays in upscale stores. Though it stands alone as a feature, it is often used within standard perimeter lighting.

Accent lighting of the free-standing vertical display offers the greatest freedom in expression to the lighting designer. This type of lighting may be accomplished by flush, surface-mounted or suspended adjustable luminaires, strategically located to produce highlights and shadows so as to create a three-dimensional display. Colored lamps instead of clear lamps may further dramatize or accent the displayed merchandise.

The open-front, wall-case display follows the lighting methods of the free-standing vertical displays. See figure 18-9. The system should be planned to project light within the encased area. In this type of display, added flexibility can be obtained by using adjustable luminaires installed at locations and aimed at angles that avoid veiling reflections.

Display cases with glass doors present a different problem, namely, the merchandise displayed behind the glass panel is obscured by surface reflections from the glass. This is virtually a show-window problem, and the best way to overcome annoying reflections is to increase the illuminance within the case. Spotlighting can accomplish this; however, extended use of spotlighting can cause fading of merchandise.

As with showcase lighting, a multitude of light sources and equipment is available to light wall cases. In general, compact fluorescent lamps with good color rendering should be used for fill lighting or base lighting. Accent and feature lighting are best achieved with miniature halogen lamps and small-scale luminaires such as PAR 20 and PAR 16 line-voltage lamps or MR 16 and MR 11 low-voltage lamps. There are several miniature low-voltage lamp and holder systems (with remote transformers) that are particularly well suited to lighting wall cases. For definitions of fill, base,

accent and feature, consult the Glossary of Lighting Terminology at the end of this book.

Rack Lighting (Clothing). Rack lighting should be designed to attract customers and for easy evaluation of the merchandise. Racks located in large, cased wall areas may be lighted from above by concealed, baffled light sources. Where linear light sources are used, the color should render merchandise in the same way as the ambient lighting in the fitting rooms. The lighting system chosen should be one that fully illuminates the articles of clothing and accurately reveals color and texture. An illuminance should be provided that will permit quick and discerning selection by the customer.

In the open rack areas, flush or surface-mounted adjustable ceiling downlights should be directed obliquely onto the displayed merchandise. The illuminance on the clothing should be greater than that of the general or ambient lighting of the aisles between racks. In aiming the downlights, caution must be exercised to avoid directing the light beam into the eyes of customers viewing clothing on the opposite side of the rack or at adjacent racks. The use of louvers, baffles or lenses helps to alleviate this situation.

Perimeter Lighting. Perimeter lighting is an asset to a store environment, contributing to a sense of pleasantness and adding to the visibility and visual impact of displays at the walls (see figure 18-10). In addition, effective perimeter lighting will draw attention to the merchandise and reinforce the design esthetics. Vertical surface brightness plays a significant part in the

Fig. 18-10. A store, seen from the outside, utilizing perimeter lighting to produce vertical surface luminances for attraction and to overcome potential veiling reflections in the windows.

shopper's impression of the store. Vertical surfaces should be lighted for visual comfort, pleasantness, spaciousness, and visual and directional cues.

Perimeter wall lighting can be achieved by various techniques using either linear or point sources to create continuous or individual patterns of light. Some of the equipment and techniques to achieve a continuous, even wash of light are:

1. Architectural cornices, soffits or valances with concealed fluorescent, cold cathode or linear incandescent strip luminaires
2. Fluorescent, incandescent or HID wallwash luminaires spaced to provide a continuous luminous pattern

Patterns of light, and concentrated accent light, which require precise beam control, can be accomplished by:

1. Incandescent or HID track or monopoint luminaires
2. Recessed adjustable incandescent or HID luminaires
3. Compact fluorescent directional luminaires. (Note: Precise beam control is not usually associated with this design.)

Fitting Rooms. The fitting-room area in a clothing store is one of the most critical sales areas. This is where the final decision to buy is often made. Lighting this space requires the utmost sensitivity from the designer to ensure appropriate illuminance, good color rendering and the elimination of harsh shadows. Lighting solutions should provide a combination of diffuse and directional light to accentuate facial features and fabric texture without deep shadows.

Careful choice and placement of overhead luminaires will add to color vibrancy, texture enhancement, sheen or glitter of hair and materials and will create modeling effects. Lighting at the mirror should be used to compliment and soften facial shadows without reflected glare. Vertical illumination should extend far enough down to enable the customer to easily evaluate full-length garments.

Background finishes should be light colored, matte, and simple in design to avoid color distortion or distraction from the merchandise.

Other Store Spaces

In addition to the lighting consideration for merchandising areas, attention should be given to other spaces used by customers and store personnel. The following is a list of those spaces:

Entrances, Escalators, Elevators and Stairways. First impressions of a merchandising area or store are often made in entrance lobbies. The luminous environment should be esthetically pleasing, complement the architecture and the merchandise and fulfill primary visual requirements. The lighting should provide safe and attractive transition from the entrance into the merchandise area.

To aid circulation and draw attention to functional areas, nonuniform lighting is often desirable in entrance lobbies. Consideration should be given to supplementary adjustable lighting equipment for displays or graphics. Escalators, elevators and stairways must have adequate illuminance to accommodate all means of egress. Under normal operating conditions, the illuminance should be no less than one-third of that in adjacent spaces. For a discussion of energy-saving conditions, see chapter 30, Energy Management.

Alteration Rooms. General lighting should provide the required illuminance for most sewing and pressing tasks. Supplementary or localized general lighting should be used to provide additional illuminance for tasks such as hand or machine sewing, which are often done with low-contrast dark thread on dark material. For handwork diffuse light is preferred. Supplementary illumination is recommended for the needle of the sewing machine.

Food Service Facilities. See chapter 17, Institution and Public Building Lighting.

Offices. See chapter 15, Office Lighting.

Rest Rooms and Locker Rooms. Mirror and sink areas, lounge facilities, sanitary maintenance and accessibility to lockers are concerns for lighting rest rooms and locker rooms. Uniform illumination is not required in rest rooms. Luminaires should be located to provide enough light in the vicinity of the mirror for adequate illumination of the face. See chapter 19, Residential Lighting, for mirror lighting. In public lavatories, visual tasks include grooming, which requires shadowless illumination on both sides of the face. Color rendering is important. Lounge areas in rest rooms require only low levels of light; other luminaires should be located so that their maximum light output will be concentrated in areas of the urinals and toilet stalls. Concentration of light in these areas has a tendency to encourage cleanliness. In locker rooms, the lighting of lockers and dressing areas is principally a matter of arranging the lighting equipment so that the interiors of the lockers are illuminated and general lighting is supplied for safe movement about the dressing areas.

Stock Rooms. Storage shelves, bins, racks, etc., should be lighted so that labels and other means of identification can be readily seen. In enclosed storage areas, the color rendering qualities of the light should be adequate to permit correct identification of stored items. Storage areas should have somewhat higher illuminances than that provided by the general ambient lighting.

LIGHTING FOR INTERIOR MALLS

In mall design the lighting helps to define architectural forms, draw people to certain areas and reinforce the identity of the specific facility. Light affects the way people see, the way they feel and the way they move through a space. By manipulation of form, texture and color through lighting techniques, the designer can evoke different desired responses. The purpose of the enclosed mall is to draw patrons into the center and entice them into the stores, so that they will make purchases. Lighting can help to reinforce this purpose.

Lighting Design Techniques

The basic steps in mall lighting design consist of the following:

- Determine the desired mood or atmosphere by evaluating the type of clientele and tenant. The atmosphere should be tailored to fit the retailer's level; if the stores are high-end boutiques, it is more appropriate to use an elegant approach than a carnival theme.
- Respond to the architecture and focus on the space as a whole composition, not just parts and pieces. Highlighting forms that define space, such as feature columns, changing ceiling planes or elevation changes, will add interest to the mall.
- Decide on the paths and directions of movement through the mall. Light will attract, darkness will deter. People will linger in areas of higher light levels and move quickly through those that are dark by comparison.

Building Entrances

Other than site signage, building entrances are the first lighted areas to welcome patrons to the mall. It is important that they act as beacons inviting the public inside during both daylight and nighttime hours. (See plate 5 in this chapter.) Mall entries should be clearly visible from any location in the parking lot, and during the day the architecture and signage play a large part in the task. At night the use of warm-color-temperature sources in canopies, decorative elements and vertical surfaces will provide a very inviting entry. Vestibules are transition spaces through which people move quickly and therefore can be lighted to lower levels with less vertical surface illumination.

Entry Mall Corridors

Entry mall corridors should be brightly lighted to provide good visibility to the retail stores located here. Higher illuminances, brightly colored ceilings or walls, color, or any form of sparkle will entice patrons down side concourses.

Main Mall Circulation

Main circulation routes through the mall are intermediate spaces between the courts. Their brightness should be low enough so as not to compete with the storefronts and signage. Spill light from the stores can provide the path illumination in the adjacent circulation zone. This heightens the contrast with the surrounding mall and shifts the focus to the retailer.

Courts

Courts are usually the main focus of the lighting design. They can be divided into three general categories: department store courts, center courts and food courts. Each court in the mall should have its own identity, yet all courts should have a common theme. Giving courts individuality helps identify retailers in the area and orient shoppers within the mall. Lighting can alter the perception of the court and change the focus in the space. See plate 7 in this chapter.

Lighting department store courts is complicated by the influence of the major tenants. Their areas are forecourts to the retailers around them. Since the department store is often the end of a view, this storefront should be highlighted. The lighted terminus attracts people to the ends of the mall, benefiting retailers along the way.

Center courts house various functions and activities. People use the center court to rest and congregate. Lighting must address a variety of purposes: to provide general ambient lighting, to add highlight and to be flexible enough to accommodate special functions. Through the use of circuiting and controls, in conjunction with a flexible lighting system such as track lighting, the lighting in the center court can be reconfigured to accommodate special displays or seasonal attractions. Center courts are often landscaped, and lighting for both highlight and plant growth should be provided. See plate 6 in this chapter. Vendor carts and kiosks should be considered in the design with lighting that can be adjusted and altered to fit their changing needs.

Food courts are similar to center courts in their function as a meeting and resting place. However, food courts have one primary function and do not require as much flexibility as center courts. The perimeter of the court consists of open counters which are the tenant "storefronts" and the focus of the court. Lighting should be designed to draw attention away from tables and toward the food vendors. Highlighting can be used to direct patrons to centrally located amenities, such as condiment stands and trash receptacles, or to distinguish between various seating areas. Highlighting should be subdued and should not compete with tenants or their signage.

Daylighting

Some common architectural features of malls are skylights and clerestory windows. The balance of all the components of the mall must be maintained by modulating the contrast between daylighted and nonday-lighted areas. Circuits and control systems can be used to balance the illuminances provided by daylight and by electric lighting. Illuminances can be raised in the darker spaces during the day to compensate for the daylight in adjacent areas. Simultaneously, lighting in areas with daylight can be reduced by dimming, switching or photocell controls during the day (see chapter 31, Lighting Controls).

At night, skylights and windows become dark holes, or they act as mirrors reflecting lighted objects below. Various techniques should be evaluated to mitigate this effect. For example, banners hung in skylights will help filter sunlight during the day while adding color and interest at night. Care should be taken in positioning luminaires to prevent source reflections in the glass at night.

Ambient Lighting

Ambient lighting is typically accomplished by direct downlighting or indirect uplighting. Equipment can be recessed or surface mounted, depending on structural conditions and architectural details. Both techniques can be implemented using a variety of sources, including incandescent, fluorescent and HID lamps. For efficiency in high-ceiling areas (3 m or more), recessed HID downlights are the most common solution. Compact fluorescent sources are increasing in popularity for downlighting because of their high efficiency, good color rendering and long life. These work best in ceiling heights of 3 m or less.

All of these sources can be used in indirect lighting. Linear indirect lighting, as in architectural coves, is best handled with fluorescent sources to provide uniformity.

Highlighting

For highlighting, the featured object should be at least 3 and at most 10 times brighter than its surroundings. For example, if the average luminance in the space is 25 cd/m^2, highlighted objects should be lighted so that they have a luminance between 75 and 250 cd/m^2.

Accent lighting is typically done with incandescent sources, because of the variety of beam patterns available. However, as HID sources become more compact, fixture manufacturers are developing the highly controlled optical systems necessary to provide higher levels of illumination and broader spectral distributions. Some HID sources are particularly good for plant growth and maintenance.

Both recessed and surface-mounted equipment can be used for highlighting, the most common being track lighting for flexibility. Clamp-mounted track heads and theatrical spotlights can be attached to space frames or joist structures.

Plate 1. An example of a strong focal center. The silverware display, through spotlighting and color, is the eye-catching feature.

Plate 2. Quiet elegance is the feeling inside this high-end glass shop. PAR 36 lamps on the ceiling and perimeter highlight the glass items displayed on tables and stands. Low-voltage lamps are built into the shelves, which wash the merchandise with light.

Plate 3. A Ralph Lauren retail store was created from a former private home. The residential ambiance was maintained by the use of chandeliers, sconces, and picture lights for ambient light. MR-16 lamps, which are used throughout the store, were selected for their excellent color rendition, flexibility and variety of beam spreads.

Plate 4. Drama is created in a supermarket deli department by a dark ceiling, false skylight and neon-lit signs. The recessed fixtures, 3000K metal halides, brightly light the merchandise.

Plate 5. Sixth Street Marketplace, Richmond, VA illuminated to create an exciting shopping experience and restore life to the downtown area.

Plate 6. Grand Court at the Sixth Street Marketplace, lighted with 100-W mercury vapor uplights with deep blue filters. Palm trees are accented with 5000K metal halide luminaires to create the feeling of a sunny day.

Plate 7. An indirect lighting system employing metal halide lamps was used in this mall center court. Flexible downlights and neon tubes at the column capitals were used for accent.

Plate 8. The customer screening area of this video store was illuminated by theatrical-style accent lights, which highlight the video display screens as well as the glass-block wall. For accent lighting neon waves were integrated throughout the perforated sheet-metal wall and ceiling-truss system.

Low-voltage tungsten-halogen sources are excellent for water features. Water can be very effectively lighted from above or below. For more information on lighting water features, refer to the Exterior Lighting section in chapter 19, Residential Lighting.

Decorative Elements

Decorative luminaires, such as sconces, pendants and torchieres, can be used to add scale, color and sparkle. Placement of these elements must be evaluated to prevent interference with sight lines of storefronts and signage. Exposed sources, such as neon and incandescent striplight or holiday-type "twinkle" lights, can also add color and sparkle.

Maintenance

One of the most important considerations in mall lighting design is maintenance. Equipment selection and placement must ensure accessibility using available lifts or ladders. Floor structures must also be strong enough to handle the load of this equipment. Adjustable luminaires should be locked in place to ensure that aiming angles will remain fixed during regular maintenance.

Long-life sources, such as rapid-start fluorescent or HID lamps, typically rated at 10,000–24,000 h, should be used to provide ambient illumination. Lamp types should be kept at a minimum so that a large inventory is not needed and to facilitate ease of maintenance. Group schedules should be established and followed to maintain proper illuminance and source color consistency. On an annual basis, group relamping is more economical.

EXTERIOR SPACES

Store and Wall Exteriors

The roles of outdoor lighting at stores and shopping centers are numerous and varied. The lighting should attract customers to the center and then to specific stores; identify key areas such as entrances, exits, parking and the various stores; facilitate safe passage of motorists and pedestrians on the grounds; contribute to effective security and surveillance of people and property; and visually unify the shopping area, providing a positive contribution to the surrounding areas without causing light trespass problems. See chapter 24, Roadway Lighting, for parking facilities. When the potential customer arrives in the vicinity of the shopping center (or free-standing store), there is a pattern of progression to arrive at the point of purchase. Lighting plays a major role in leading the shopper from one zone to another and eases the identification process through each step from locating the shopping center site, the entrance to the center, the parking area and the store (all vehicular circulation) to locating the store entrance, departments and finally the merchandise (all pedestrian circulation).

Exterior Retail Selling Areas

Exterior retail lighting includes the illumination of auto dealerships, gas station convenience stores, fast food facilities, and pool and garden centers. The goals of outdoor retail lighting are similar to those of retail interiors, but in addition the designer should consider such issues as light pollution, light trespass and glare.

Luminaire selection and position are critical factors. Light pollution and trespass can be minimized by using cut-off luminaires, optically controlled luminaires, and louvers and shields on floodlights. The floodlight or area-light angle of maximum candela (candlepower) should be aimed within the property line to minimize glare in surrounding areas, especially roadways. Luminaire selection should also take into consideration the specific environmental requirements of the site, in particular, temperature, wind and corrosive factors.

To select the appropriate illuminance for outdoor merchandise and display areas (see recommended illuminance levels for outdoor merchandising areas, chapter 22), the designer should consider the luminance ratios between the merchandise and the surrounding area (the surrounding area refers to a specific location). For instance, a rural road will have a very low luminance. The illuminance in these areas should not be greater than 10 times the surrounding area. Measurements should be referenced from the roadway.

REFERENCES

1. IES. Merchandising Lighting Committee. 1985. *Lighting merchandising areas: A store lighting guide.* IES RP-2-86. New York: Illuminating Engineering Society of North America.
2. LaGuisa, F. F. 1983. A new generation of low voltage lighting. *Vis. Merch. Store Des.* 114(3):40–44.
3. American Society of Heating, Refrigeration and Air-Conditioning Engineers and Illuminating Engineering Society of North America. 1985. *Energy conservation in existing buildings: Commercial, ANSI / ASHRAE / IES 100.3.* Atlanta, GA: American Society of Heating, Refrigerating and Air-Conditioning Engineers.
4. American Society of Heating, Refrigerating and Air-Conditioning Engineers and Illuminating Engineering Society of North America. 1989. *Energy efficient design of new buildings except new low-rise residential buildings, ASHRAE / IES 90.1-1989.* Atlanta, GA: American Society of Heating, Refrigerating and Air-Conditioning Engineers.
5. Feltman, S. 1986. A designer's checklist for merchandise lighting. *Light. Des. Appl.* 16(5):18–21.

Residential Lighting

19

This chapter serves as a guide for lighting interior residential spaces—and other spaces, such as waiting rooms, reception areas, eating spaces, executive suites and lounges, where a residential atmosphere may be desired—as well as exterior residential spaces.[1] The chapter is intended to help create lighted spaces that have richness and variety, adequate task lighting where needed, general illumination, sparkle and shadow where suitable, and good color rendition for pleasing and flattering living environments. It covers design objectives, criteria for the quantity and quality of illumination, lighting methods, typical equipment and electrical energy considerations. Methods for lighting specific visual tasks, such as reading, sewing or shaving, are presented task by task. Each presentation includes a description of the task details, the task plane, the range of recommended illuminances, lighting design considerations and typical equipment locations.

FACTORS AFFECTING THE INTERIOR LIGHTING PLAN

Human Factors

Light is an element of design. Like other design elements (texture, line, shadow and form), light influences the emotional responses of the people who occupy the space. The definition and character of a space is greatly dependent on the distribution and pattern of light and shadow. Luminaires have design qualities that may be used to strengthen or minimize architectural line, form, pattern and texture. Lighting solutions should not only provide the needed illumination, but also enhance the basic architectural and decorative design of the space. Lighting design does not start with the selection of luminaires, but with an evaluation of the occupants' needs, their visual and physical capabilities and their lifestyles. Because needs, lifestyles and occupants can change, consideration should be given to the use of portable, modular and easily controlled luminaires.

Design Factors

The designer must gather information to identify the client's needs and develop solutions. Those elements that contribute to the design solution are the design factors (see chapter 10, Lighting Design Process). Following the evaluation of the design factors, the designer should then select the light sources and luminaires and finally determine quantity, location and appropriate controls.

Several important criteria must be considered in residential lighting design. They include the need to move quickly and safely from one space to another, the importance of lighting people as well as objects, the requirements for flexibility in multipurpose spaces such as kitchens and activity rooms, the desire for lighting installations which exhibit a sense of quality and esthetics, and the concern for energy efficiency.[2-4]

Finally, the designer should consider how alternative sources, equipment, placement or controls would improve the end results and affect costs. The designer should provide a maintenance schedule and lamp replacement list for the client to help keep the lighting system equipped to perform as planned. See chapter 32, Lighting Maintenance.

LIGHTING CRITERIA FOR INTERIOR SPACES

Quality of Light

Lighting may be broadly described as *diffuse* or *directional.* Diffuse light minimizes shadows and provides a more relaxing and less visually compelling atmosphere. When diffuse light is used alone, none of the objects in the visual scene is given prominence. The artful use of directional light can provide highlights and shadows that emphasize texture and form. Brilliance or sparkle can be obtained from small unshielded sources, such as a bare lamp or a candle flame. These light sources are seldom used as primary sources of illumination; they are generally decorative, and must be supplemented by other means. The glitter of crystal and polished brass, the luster of table settings, and the sheen of some types of surface materials can be heightened by directional lighting to create a sense of warmth and festivity in a space.

In many residential spaces, it is desirable to create more than one mood or to be able to vary the atmo-

Fig. 19-1. Seeing zones and luminance ratios for visual tasks

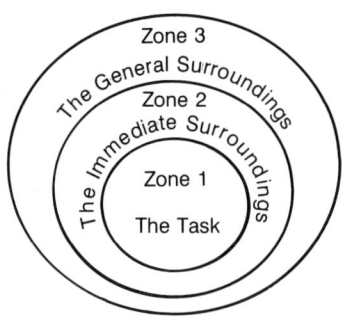

Zone	Luminance Ratios
2 — Area adjacent to the visual task	
a) Desirable ratio	$\frac{1}{3}$ to equal to task†
b) Minimum acceptable ratio	$\frac{1}{5}$ to equal to task†
3 — General surrounding	
a) Desirable ratio	$\frac{1}{5}$ to 5 times task†
b) Minimum acceptable ratio	$\frac{1}{10}$ to 10 times task†

†Typical task luminance range is 40 to 120 candelas per square meter [4 to 12 candelas per square foot] (seldom exceeds 200 candelas per square meter [20 candelas per square foot]).

sphere. Lighting control systems can provide this flexibility and should be an integral part of the design. See chapter 31, Lighting Controls.

Brightness Relationships

Brightness is an impression of the appearance of a light source or an illuminated surface, described in terms of its perceived relative luminosity. This subjective impression can be correlated with light-measuring instruments (see chapter 2, Measurement of Light and Other Radiant Energy) that determine the luminance of the surface or of the source. Luminance is expressed in candelas per square meter (cd/m^2). Luminance ratios play an important role in the comfort, eye fatigue and difficulty of visual tasks.

Seeing Zones

A person's visual field consists of three major zones (see figure 19-1):

• Zone 1: The task area itself
• Zone 2: The area immediately surrounding the task
• Zone 3: The general surroundings

For visual comfort the luminance of the immediate surround (zone 2) should range between $\frac{1}{3}$ of the task luminance and 3 times the task luminance. The luminances of areas in the general surround (zone 3) should range between $\frac{1}{10}$ of the task luminance and 10 times the task luminance. These relationships should not be

Fig. 19-2. Recommended Reflectances for Interior Surfaces of Residences

Surface	Reflectance (%)	Approximate Munsell Value
Ceiling	60 – 90	8 and above
Curtain and drapery treatment on large wall areas	35 – 60	6.5 – 8
Walls	35 – 60*	6.5 – 8
Floors	15 – 35*	4.0 – 6.5

*In areas where lighting for specific visual tasks takes precedence over lighting for the environment, the minimum reflectance should be 40% for walls, 25% for floors.

exceeded for visual comfort in visually demanding tasks such as studying, sewing or reading.

Reflectance

Reflectance is the ratio of the amount of light leaving a surface to the amount of light incident on it. Reflectance can be expressed as a percentage or more roughly as a Munsell value. Pale, high-reflectance colors for room surfaces and furnishings are important and often essential in achieving desirable luminance ratios. To assist the designer in obtaining the recommended luminance ratios, recommended surface reflectances with approximate Munsell values are listed in figure 19-2.

Veiling Reflections

Light reflected from the task which partially or totally obscures the details by reducing the contrast is called veiling reflection. When tasks involve specular glossy surfaces, such as high-gloss photographs and slick magazines, veiling reflections can be a problem (see chapter 3, Vision and Perception).

Reflected Glare

When the reflections of light sources are imaged in glossy glass-top tables or mirror-like surfaces in or near the visual task, the condition is known as reflected glare. If these reflections are excessively bright, they will cause visual discomfort (see chapter 3, Vision and Perception).

Light and Color[5]

Color recognition depends on the spectral characteristics of the light source and the spectral reflection characteristics of the object. These two factors provide object color to the observer.

Surface or object colors may match under one light source but not under another. For example, two colors may match under incandescent lighting but not under daylighting (see chapter 4, Color). Note should be made of this fact when selecting materials, pigments or dye lots for interior surfaces.

Surface Finish. Colors of objects often appear to change with surface finish. Specular or mirror reflections from glossy surfaces may, in extreme cases, increase the chroma and saturation at one angle and obscure color at other angles. A matte finish reflects light diffusely and will appear more or less the same for any viewing angle. Deeply textured finishes, such as velvet or deep-pile carpeting, cause shadows within the fibers that make the materials appear darker than smooth-surfaced materials such as satin, silk or plastic laminates of the same color.

Fading. Light will fade fabrics and furnishings. Ultraviolet (UV) energy is one cause of fading (see chapter 5, Nonvisual Effects of Radiant Energy). Since UV radiation cannot be completely eliminated, the amount, frequency and length of exposure should be considered when materials or objects are of great value or irreplaceable. Visible light will also cause fading, and exposure to it should also be considered; for a further discussion, see the section on Museum Lighting in chapter 17, Institution and Public Building Lighting.

Quantity of Light

Visual activities in living spaces range from simple to extremely difficult tasks. Sewing is an activity with small visual details and low contrast which requires higher illuminance than simple orientation as in an entry foyer. See chapter 3, Vision and Perception, for a discussion of the factors involved in seeing and recommended quantities of illumination.

LIGHTING METHODS

General Lighting

Areas with Visual Activities. Residential lighting is planned on the basis of activities, not on the basis of rooms. Many visual tasks can be, and are, performed in almost any part of the home. The designer must determine what activities are to be performed in each room, and provide light for them first. See figure 19-3. The individual task areas are then tied together by means of a general lighting system. This is essential in order to prevent a spotty effect, to maintain recommended luminance ratios in the field of view, and to provide light throughout the interior for safety and housekeeping activities. The general lighting system should also help to avoid excessive differences in illuminance between adjacent rooms.

In some spaces, particularly utility areas, a general lighting system can be designed to supply all, or nearly all, of the illumination needed for visual activities. However, a high level and uniform distribution of general lighting would be unacceptable in most living areas. The equipment most commonly used to light

Fig. 19-3. A kitchen with downlights that illuminate the work spaces of the kitchen and graze the cabinets, and recessed adjustable accent lights that highlight the pictures on the wall.

room surfaces and create a satisfactory background for visual work includes general-diffuse ceiling luminaires, wall luminaires, indirect portable luminaires and coves. In small rooms, general illumination may even be supplied by the luminaires used for specific task lighting, such as lighting for the use of a mirror or lighting from an open-shade portable luminaire used for reading or studying. In any case, for these kinds of demanding visual tasks, portable task lighting may be needed in addition to a system which provides general illumination.[6]

Areas for Relaxation. For periods of relaxation, when prolonged and exacting visual task performance is at a minimum, or for various rooms designed solely for relaxation, a low level of general illumination creates a pleasant atmosphere for conversation, watching television or listening to music. See figure 19-4. Uniformity of illumination need not be an objective here. On the contrary, moderate variations create a more attractive pattern of light. The primary considerations for these spaces are comfort and esthetic satisfaction. See chapter 10, Lighting Design Process, for further information on different lighting effects.

Halls and Stairways. Changes in visual adaptation are important in setting the proper illuminance levels for halls and stairways. If they adjoin an interior area with a higher illuminance, the level in the hall or stair should be no less than one-fifth that of the adjacent area. Wall luminances are crucial in creating a sensation of lightness and reducing shadows on the stairs. Therefore, luminaires should direct light to the walls, and wall and floor finishes should have high reflectance values. See figure 19-5. Lighting in the entry hall should be flexible so that adjustments can be made

Fig. 19-4. This sitting room offers a quiet retreat from the bustle of the city with its subdued lighting scheme, a combination of indirect lighting and portable luminaires. Fluorescent lighting is used at the desk top.

for visual adaptation during both the daytime and the nighttime. On stairs, it is critical that tread edges be emphasized, and that the top and bottom steps be well lighted for safety. Under no circumstances should a built-in wall-mounted luminaire or portable luminaire be located where a person descending the stairway can look directly at the light source.

Garages. The major areas where light is needed in a garage are on both sides of the automobile and between automobiles, especially over the front and rear. Luminaires are usually located slightly to the rear of the trunk area and approximately in line with the front wheels. A portable trouble light can be provided for repair work.

Closets. Light sources in closets should be located out of the normal view, generally to the front of the closet

Fig. 19-5. A large entry hall illuminated with recessed wall washers that graze the wall and highlight the paintings.

and above the door. In walk-in closets, a ceiling luminaire should be mounted at the center of the traffic area so that shelves do not block the lighting of the garments. The positioning of unprotected lamps relative to shelving must meet national and local electrical code requirements.[7]

Lighting for Common Visual Tasks

In providing the recommended illuminance on the task, which corresponds to zone 1 in figure 19-1, the essentials of good lighting quality, as previously discussed, must not be overlooked. Rarely can the desired illuminance be provided by general lighting alone. At the same time, local lighting by itself is seldom totally satisfactory or comfortable; therefore, a combination of local and general lighting is needed. Daylighting also adds to the quality of the lighting in a residence.

The common residential visual tasks are discussed in figures 19-6 through 19-23. Included in this discussion is a description of the task and task plane, special design considerations and typical equipment locations. For illuminance values see chapter 11, Illuminance Selection.

OTHER INTERIOR LIGHTING DESIGN CONSIDERATIONS

Sparkle, Highlight and Spatial Effects

In addition to lighting tasks and providing general illumination, lighting can play an important role in reinforcing spatial perception, activity and mood. These effects depend upon a person's previous experience, perception, attitude and expectations. Specific impressions include perceptual clarity, spaciousness, relaxation, privacy and pleasantness (see chapter 3, Vision and Perception). Lighting can set a mood for the use of the space, render people flatteringly and enhance colors and textures in a space. See figure 19-24. To create these effects, many factors have to be considered. One is luminance contrast among the spaces of interest and their adjacent spaces. The contrast of a brightly lighted area adjacent to a dim area can create a dramatic effect. A minimum ratio of 10:1 is required for dramatic effects and to focus attention.

Sparkle is a small brilliance of light and is often considered for creating festive or romantic moods. Sparkle adds visual interest to objects in a space and attracts attention. Glare will result if the source is too bright or adjacent reflective surfaces are mirrorlike. The angle, intensity and shielding of the source must be evaluated to assure visual comfort.

Playing light against darkness within a space can create a striking visual effect. See figure 19-25. The

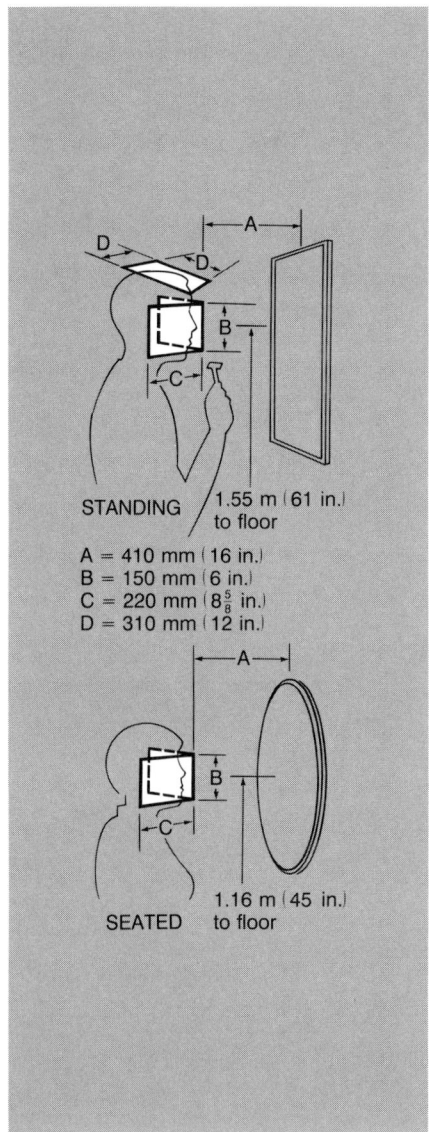

STANDING / 1.55 m (61 in.) to floor

A = 410 mm (16 in.)
B = 150 mm (6 in.)
C = 220 mm ($8\frac{5}{8}$ in.)
D = 310 mm (12 in.)

SEATED   1.16 m (45 in.) to floor

Fig. 19-6. Grooming

1. *The task:* The chief tasks are shaving and makeup. Because the apparent distance of the face or figure as viewed in the mirror is twice its actual distance from the mirror, and because the details to be seen in shaving or makeup are usually small and of low contrast with their background, the visual task may be critical. Skin and hair reflectance can be quite low, below 30%, and the speed and accuracy can be critical for a fastidious person rushed for time.

2. *Description of the tasks planes:*
   (a) Standing position: The task area consists of two 150 × 220-mm (6 × $8\frac{5}{8}$-in.) planes at right angles with each other, converging at a point 410 mm (16 in.) out from the mirror, and centered vertically 1550 mm (61 in.) above the floor. They represent the front and sides of the face. A third plane 310 mm (12 in.) square, its front edge also 410 mm (16 in.) out from the mirror, is tilted up 25° above the horizontal and represents the top of the head.
   (b) Seated position: The two facial planes are identical in size and position to those mentioned above, except that the center of the planes is 1160 mm (45 in.) above the floor. The size of the third, top-of-the-head plane is the same as above.

3. *Special design considerations:* Lighting equipment at a mirror should direct light toward the person and not onto the mirror. The luminance of surfaces reflected in the mirror and seen adjacent to the face reflection should not be in distracting contrast with it.
   (a) Adjacent walls should have a 50% or higher reflectance.
   (b) Luminaires should be mounted outside the 60° visual cone, the centerline of which coincides with the line of sight.
   (c) No luminaire should exceed 2100 cd/m² (190 cd/ft²) in luminance, that is, an illuminance meter held against it should not read more than 6500 lx (600 fc).

4. *Typical equipment locations:*
   (a) Wall-mounted linear or nonlinear luminaires over the mirror
   (b) Wall-mounted linear or nonlinear luminaires over and at the sides of the mirror
   (c) Combination of wall- and ceiling-mounted luminaires flanking the mirror and over the head of the user
   (d) Structural devices (such as soffits) extending the length of the mirror
   (e) Portable luminaires with luminous shades flanking the mirror
   (f) Pendant luminaires with luminous sides flanking the mirror

Note: If grooming is performed in a seated position, the relationship of the luminaires to the face should remain as specified above for standing.

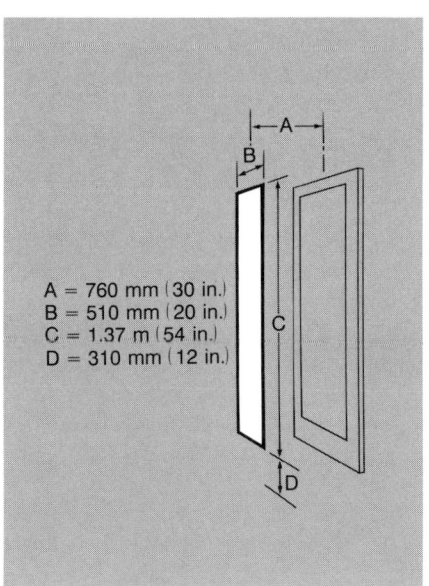

A = 760 mm (30 in.)
B = 510 mm (20 in.)
C = 1.37 m (54 in.)
D = 310 mm (12 in.)

Fig. 19-7. Full-length mirror

1. *The task:* The task is the alignment of clothing, commonly with reflectance between 30 and 70%, and casual overall appraisal. Speed and accuracy may or may not be important.

2. *Description of the task plane:* The task area is a plane 510 mm (20 in.) wide by 1370 mm (54 in.) high with the lower edge 310 mm (12 in.) above the floor; it is centered on and parallel with the mirror, 760 mm (30 in.) from the mirror surface.

3. *Special design considerations:* Lighting equipment at the mirror should direct light toward the person and not onto the mirror. The luminance of surfaces reflected in the mirror and seen adjacent to the face reflection should not be distracting.
   (a) Luminaires should be mounted outside the 60° visual cone, the centerline of which coincides with the line of sight.
   (b) No luminaire should exceed 2100 cd/m² (190 cd/ft²) in luminance, that is, an illuminance meter in contact with the surface should not read more than 6500 lx (600 fc).

4. *Typical equipment locations:* Vertical linear luminaires wall mounted beside the mirror. The same, supplemented by wall-mounted or ceiling-mounted over-mirror luminaires.

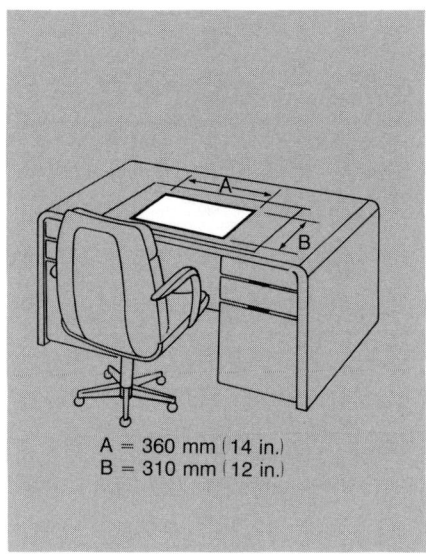

A = 360 mm (14 in.)
B = 310 mm (12 in.)

Fig. 19-8. Desk

1. *The task:* The tasks range from casual to prolonged and difficult reading of printed material, handwriting, typing and drawings. When studying, the task may involve fine print and close detail. Task reflectances are usually between 30 and 70%. Speed and accuracy may not be important for casual tasks, but may be important or critical for study.

2. *Description of the task planes:* The primary task plane is 360 × 310 mm (14 × 12 in.) parallel with the desk top. The bottom edge of the task plane is 76 mm (3 in.) from the front edge of the desk. A secondary task plane for reference books, large drawings, etc., measures 610 mm (24 in.) deep by 910 mm (36 in.) wide with the front edge at the front of the desk top.

3. *Special design considerations:* Equipment should be located so that shadows are not cast on the task area by the user's hand. The surface of the desk top should be nonglossy and light in color (30–50% reflectance). The luminance of any luminaire visible from a normal seated position should be no more than 510 cd/m² (50 cd/ft²) and no less than 170 cd/m² (16 cd/ft²).

4. *Typical equipment locations:* Desk-mounted (one or more luminaires). Wall-mounted (one or more luminaires). Ceiling-mounted (one or more luminaires). Floor-mounted.

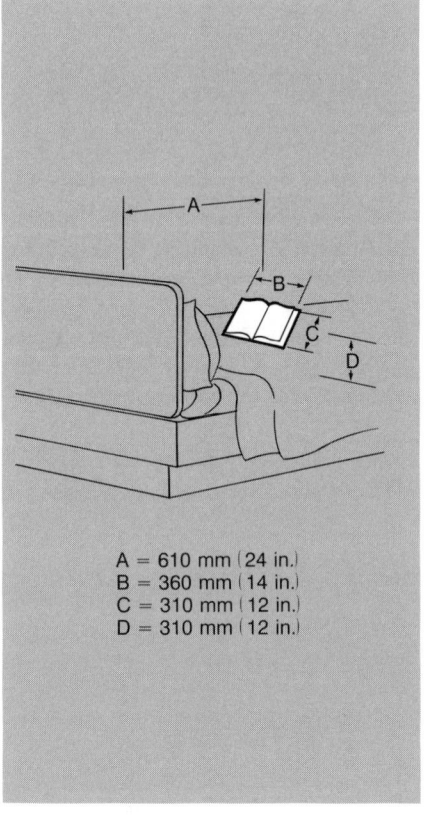

A = 610 mm (24 in.)
B = 360 mm (14 in.)
C = 310 mm (12 in.)
D = 310 mm (12 in.)

Fig. 19-9. Reading in bed

1. *The task:* The majority of people who read in bed are only casual readers, perhaps reading for a few minutes before going to sleep. They are often interested in closely confining the light distribution so as not to disturb another occupant of the room. Such lighting arrangements are not satisfactory for comfortable reading over a long period. The following recommendations are for the person who reads for a more extended period, or for the person who performs critical seeing tasks while confined to bed. The normal materials vary from books and magazines to pocket editions and to newspaper print, with reflectances of 30–70%. Speed and accuracy will vary from not important (for leisure reading) to important to critical (for critical tasks).

2. *Description of the task plane:* The task plane is 310 × 360 mm (12 × 14 in.), tilted at an angle of 45° from the vertical. The center of the task plane is 610 mm (24 in.) out from the headboard or wall and 310 mm (12 in.) above the mattress top. There are no customary reading positions or habits. These recommendations assume that the reader is in an upright or semireclined position.

3. *Special design considerations:* Equipment should be located so that no shadows are cast on the reading plane by the head or body, and so that the luminaire does not interfere with a comfortable position.

4. *Typical equipment locations:*
   (a) Wall-mounted directly in back of or to one side of the user (both linear and nonlinear designs)
   (b) Luminaire on bedside table or storage headboard
   (c) Ceiling-mounted: (1) Suspended: adjustable or stationary; (2) Surface-mounted: directional or nondirectional; (3) Recessed: directional or nondirectional
   (d) Luminaire incorporated into furniture design

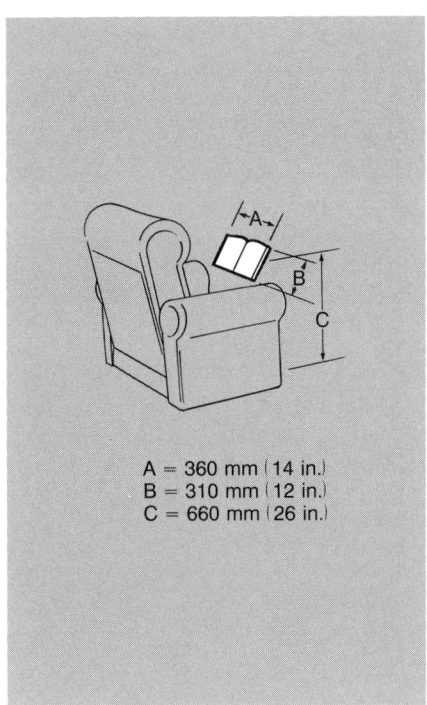

A = 360 mm (14 in.)
B = 310 mm (12 in.)
C = 660 mm (26 in.)

Fig. 19-10. Reading in a chair

1. *The task:* Typical reading tasks in a home encompass a wide range of seeing difficulty, from short-time casual reading of material with good visibility (large print on white paper) to prolonged reading of poor material (small type on low-contrast paper). The majority of tasks have reflectances between 30 and 70% or higher. Speed and accuracy may not be important for casual reading, and may or may not be important for prolonged reading.

2. *Description of the task plane:* The task plane measures 360 mm (14 in.) wide by 310 mm (12 in.) high with the center of the plane approximately 660 mm (26 in.) above the floor. The plane is tilted at 45° from the vertical. The reader's eyes are approximately 1 m (40 in.) above the floor.

3. *Special design considerations:* The normal seated eye level is 0.97–1.07 m (38–42 in.) above the floor and is a critical consideration when the light source is to be positioned beside the user. The lower edge of the shielding device should not be materially above or below eye height. This will prevent discomfort from bright sources in the periphery of the visual field and yet permit adequate distribution of light over the task area. Variations in chair and table heights necessitate selection and placement of equipment to achieve this relationship for each individual case.

4. *Typical equipment locations:*
   (a) Table-mounted, floor-mounted and wall-mounted beside or behind the user
   (b) Ceiling-mounted: suspended beside or behind the user
   (c) Directional small-area luminaires may be used (wall-, ceiling-, pole-mounted)

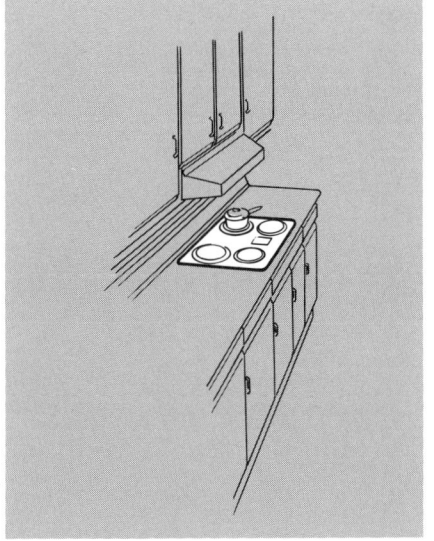

Fig. 19-11. Kitchen range or cooktop

1. *The task:* Typical seeing tasks at the kitchen range or cooking top are the determination of the condition of foods in all stages of the cooking process (color and texture evaluation) and reading controls, instructions and recipes. Food often has a reflectance of less than 30%. Speed and accuracy can be critical for some difficult preparation tasks.

2. *Description of the task plane:* The task area is a range top. Generally this is located 910 mm (36 in.) above the floor.

3. *Special design considerations:* Reflected glare is inherent in the shiny finish of utensils and range tops. Some reduction in the luminance of reflected images may be obtained by the use of diffuse luminaires or sources. Color rendering qualities of light sources are especially important in the kitchen. Controls, such as multiple-position switching and dimming equipment, can be utilized to lower the illuminance when there are no difficult seeing tasks.

4. *Typical equipment locations:*
   (a) Range hood
   (b) Ceiling—recessed, surface-mounted or suspended
   (c) Structural—lighted soffits, wall brackets, canopies
   (d) Underside of wall cabinets

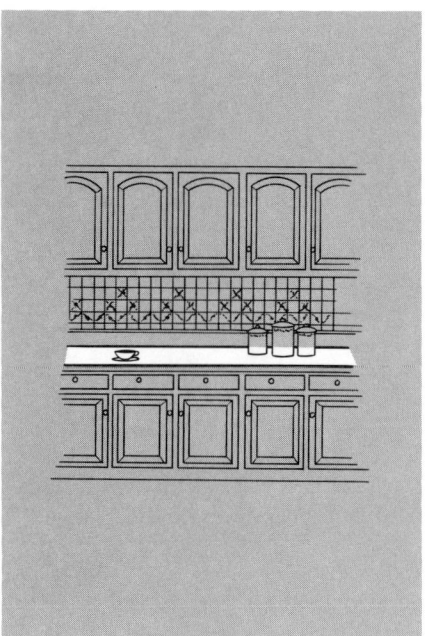

Fig. 19-12. Kitchen counter

1. *The task:* Typical seeing tasks at the kitchen counter include reading fine print on packages and cookbooks, handwritten recipes in pencil and ink, and numbers for speeds and temperatures on small appliances. Other tasks include measuring and mixing, color and texture evaluation of foods, safe operation of small appliances, and cleanup. Task reflectances are usually less than 70% and often below 30%. Speed and accuracy may not be important for noncritical tasks, but critical for the difficult preparation and cleaning tasks.

2. *Description of the task plane:* The task area is a plane 510 mm (20 in.) deep (starting at the front edge of the counter) and as long as the counter.

3. *Special design considerations:* Although there are a great many ways in which counter surfaces may be lighted, luminaires are commonly mounted under the wall cabinets, above the counter. These may be well shielded because of the cabinet structure itself, but if not, there is need for added shielding. Also, care should be exercised to see that the luminance of the luminaires is comfortable to other users of the room, particularly in seated positions. Controls, such as multiple-position switching and dimming equipment, can be utilized to lower the illuminance when there are no difficult seeing tasks.

4. *Typical equipment locations:*
   (a) Underside of wall cabinets
   (b) Ceiling—recessed, surface-mounted or pendant
   (c) Structural—lighted soffits, wall brackets

Fig. 19-13. Kitchen sink

1. *The task:* Typical seeing tasks at the kitchen sink involve cleaning and inspection of dishes and utensils, evaluation of color and texture of foods in preparation, reading and measuring. Task reflectances and speed and accuracy needs are similar to those at the counters.

2. *Description of the task plane:* The task area is determined by sink dimensions. It is usually at a height of 910 mm (36 in.) above the floor.

3. *Special design considerations:* Color rendering qualities of the light source are particularly important in kitchen illumination. The limited space available for luminaire mounting at the sink location increases the possibility of shadows being cast on the workplane by the head or body of the user. Controls, such as multiple-position switching and dimming equipment, can be utilized to lower the illuminance when there are no difficult seeing tasks.

4. *Typical equipment locations:*
   (a) Ceiling—recessed, surface-mounted or pendant
   (b) Structural—lighted soffits, wall brackets
   (c) Underside of wall cabinets

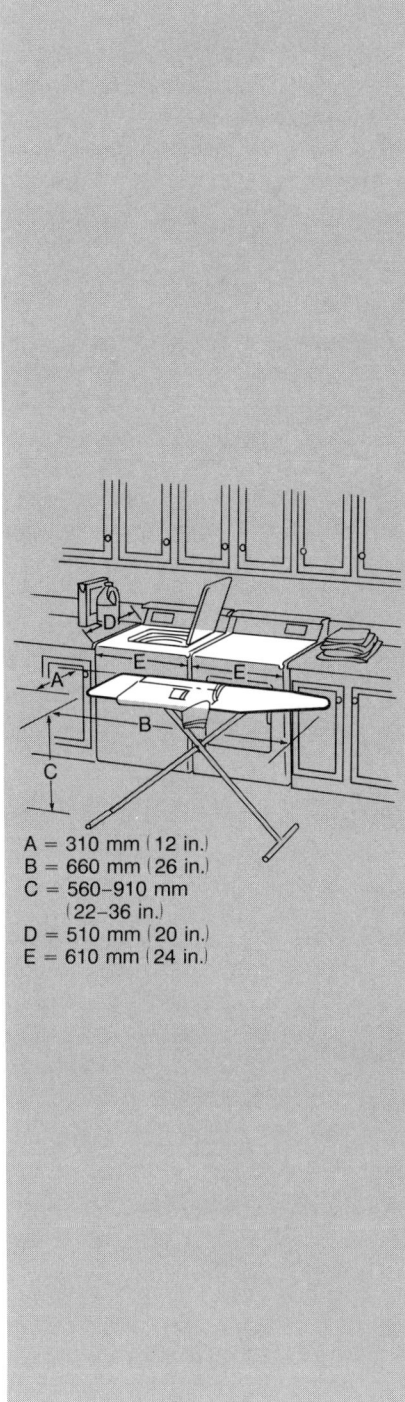

A = 310 mm (12 in.)
B = 660 mm (26 in.)
C = 560–910 mm
    (22–36 in.)
D = 510 mm (20 in.)
E = 610 mm (24 in.)

Fig. 19-14a. Ironing

1. *The task:* The basic visual task in ironing is the detection and removal of wrinkles from garments and the detection of possible scorches. The majority of fabrics have a reflectance between 30 and 70%, but dark clothes have less than 30%. Speed and accuracy may be important.

2. *Description of the task plane:* The task plane is 310 × 660 mm (12 × 26 in.) and varies in its height, depending upon the ironing board. In general, such boards are adjustable from 560 to 910 mm (22 to 36 in.) in height, for use either standing or sitting. The seat of the average stool is located 610 mm (24 in.) above the floor, which places the average seated person's eye level at 1350 mm (53 in.). In a standing position the eye level is 1550 mm (61 in.).

3. *Special design considerations:* A light source with directional quality may frequently reveal shadows cast by small wrinkles, or creases, to the advantage of the user. Ironing and television viewing are often done at the same time. Under these circumstances it is important to ensure a good balance among the luminances of task, television screen and other room surfaces in the line of sight.

4. *Typical equipment locations:*
   Ceiling-mounted:
   (a) Suspended, adjustable
   (b) Fixed, directional
   (c) Fixed, nondirectional
   (d) Combination of luminaires (general diffusing plus directional component)

Fig. 19-14b. Laundry

1. *The task:* In the preparation area, the tasks are sorting of fabrics by color and type, determination of location and type of soil, prewash treatment, tinting, bleaching and starching. In the tub area, the tasks are soaking, hand washing, tinting, rinsing, bleaching and starching. In the washer and dryer area, the tasks are loading, setting of dials and controls, and removal of clothes. Speed and accuracy may be important in the preparation and tub areas, but not important at the washer and dryer. Reflectances of fabrics and packaging vary widely but most are within 30–70%.

2. *Description of the task planes:* In the preparation area, the general task area is 510 × 610 mm (20 × 24 in.) with a critical seeing area 310 × 310 mm (12 × 2 in.). In the tub area, the task area is 510 × 610 mm (20 × 24 in.) on a single laundry tub, with a critical seeing area 310 × 310 mm (12 × 12 in.) in the middle. The washing machine and dryer area has no definable boundaries and can be illuminated by the general room lighting.

3. *Special design considerations:* Totally direct and not highly diffused light sources can contribute to the visibility of certain laundry tasks. In most laundry locations, task lighting equipment also must provide the general room illumination. Luminaires should in this case be selected and positioned to illuminate the ceiling and side walls for comfortable luminance relationships.

4. *Typical equipment locations:*
   (a) Ceiling-mounted (suspended, surface or recessed) linear or nonlinear luminaires centered over the front edge of the laundry equipment. As above, supplemented by wall-mounted or cabinet-mounted linear luminaires.
   (b) Large-area luminous panels

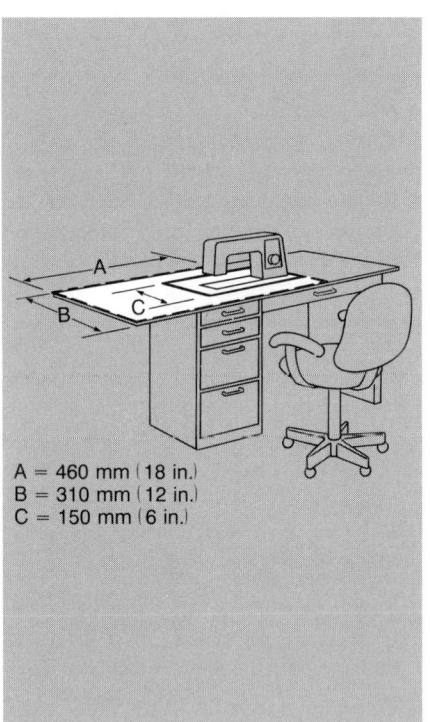

A = 460 mm (18 in.)
B = 310 mm (12 in.)
C = 150 mm (6 in.)

Fig. 19-15. Machine sewing

1. *The task:* The small detail and low contrast between thread and material usually involved in machine sewing make it a visually difficult task. The degree of difficulty varies with thread and stitch size, reflectance of materials and contrast between thread and fabric. Speed and accuracy may be critical.

2. *Description of the task plane:* The primary task area is a plane 150 mm (6 in.) square located so that the needle point is 50 mm (2 in.) forward from the center of the back edge. The secondary task area of less critical seeing measures 310 × 460 mm (12 × 18 in.) with the needle point centered on the shorter dimension and 150 mm (6 in.) in from the right-hand edge.

3. *Maximum illuminance on the primary task plane* should not exceed the minimum by more than 3 : 1. The minimum illuminance level on the secondary task plane should not be less than $\frac{1}{3}$ of the minimum on the primary task plane, and not less than 200 lx (20 fc). Special design considerations: Equipment should be located so that shadows are not cast on the task area by the user's hand. The use of light with a moderate directional component increases the visibility of threads by casting slight shadow to increase contrast.

4. *Typical equipment locations* (other than the light built into the machine):
   (a) Wall-mounted directly in front of the user (both linear and nonlinear sources).
   (b) Ceiling-mounted (location of luminaire and machine should avoid the possibility of the user's head blocking out light or casting a shadow on the task): (1) Suspended, adjustable; (2) fixed, directional (surface or recessed) or track-mounted; (3) fixed, nondirectional; (4) luminous area.
   (c) Floor-mounted or pole-mounted.

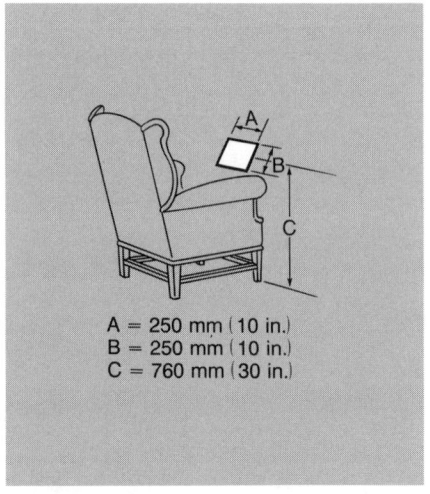

A = 250 mm (10 in.)
B = 250 mm (10 in.)
C = 760 mm (30 in.)

Fig. 19-16. Hand sewing

1. *The task:* The seeing task encompasses a wide range of difficulty from coarse threads to fine, from light materials to very dark and from high contrast to virtually no contrast at all. Speed and accuracy may be important.

2. *Description of the task plane:* The task area is a plane 250 mm (10 in.) square tilted at 45° toward the eye. The plane is centered at 760 mm (30 in.) from the floor. The eye position is approximately 1000 mm (42 in.) from the floor.

3. *Maximum illuminance on the task plane* should not exceed the minimum by more than 3 : 1. Special design considerations: Equipment should be located opposite the hand being used, so that shadows are not cast on the task area.

4. *Typical equipment locations:*
   (a) Floor-mounted or pole-mounted
   (b) Ceiling-mounted: (1) suspended, adjustable; (2) fixed, directional (surface or recessed); (3) fixed, luminous area; (4) combination luminaire (general diffusing plus directional component).
   (c) Wall-mounted (both linear and nonlinear) sources located beside or behind the user.

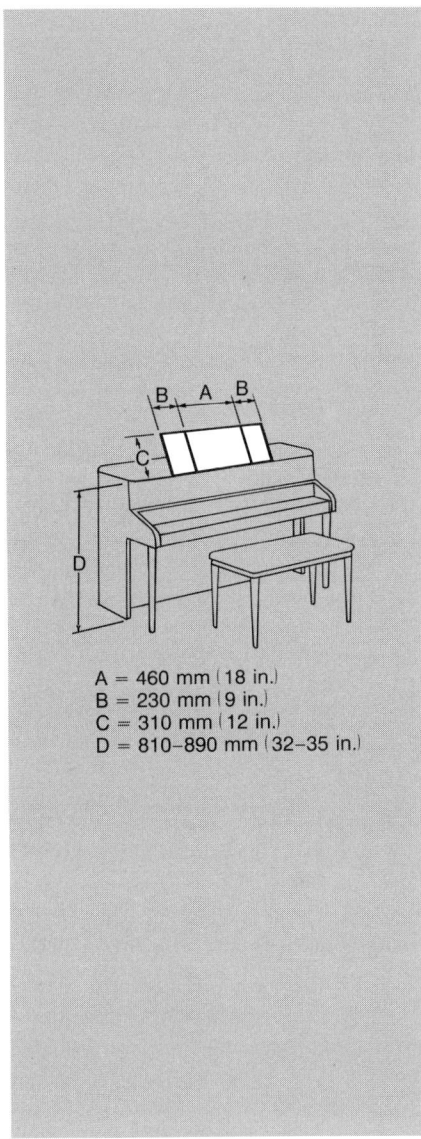

A = 460 mm (18 in.)
B = 230 mm (9 in.)
C = 310 mm (12 in.)
D = 810–890 mm (32–35 in.)

Fig. 19-17. Music study at piano or organ

1. *The task:* The task is the reading of musical scores, usually 30–70% reflectance or higher, ranging from very simple ones with large notes and staff lines to very difficult substandard-size scores with notations printed on the lines. Speed and accuracy may not be important for very simple scores, but are important for advanced and critical for professional.

2. *Description of the task plane:* The primary task plane is on the music rack in an area 310 × 460 mm (12 × 18 in.); it is tilted back from the viewer about 17°. The lower edge is 810–890 mm (32–35 in.) from the floor. The secondary plane includes an additional 230 × 310 mm (9 × 12 in.) on each side of the primary plane. The piano keyboard, typically 1220 mm (48 in.) long and 710 mm (28 in.) above the floor, is also a secondary plane. Note: These dimensions will vary greatly with electric organs and miniature pianos.

3. *Special design considerations:* The maximum task illuminance should not exceed the minimum by more than 3:1. The minimum on the secondary task plane should not be less than one-third the minimum on the primary task plane. The musical instrument is in the best position for control of luminance values if the player faces a wall.

4. *Typical equipment locations:*
   (a) Ceiling-mounted or recessed above ceiling:
      (1) Directional source:
         (i) Should be adjustable to strike the plane of the task at about 90°
         (ii) Should be located above the user's head to avoid a shadow of his or her body
         (iii) Should be located and shielded to prevent glare to other persons occupying or passing through the area
         (iv) Downlights are not desirable; their distribution is not good, and reflected glare and veiling reflections may be a problem.
      (2) Large-area nondirectional source: The luminance should be within the comfort range and esthetic considerations of the room.
   (b) Mounted on the instrument:
      (1) Uniformity of distribution over the task plane may be difficult to achieve.
      (2) There should be no luminous part within the user's field of view having a luminance of more than 170 cd/m^2 (16 cd/ft^2).
   (c) Pole-type luminaires: Because of the directional quality of this type of light source, it is possible to get acceptable illuminance on the task as well as general surround light. Care should be exercised to avoid glare to other occupants in the room as well as veiling reflections on the task area.

Fig. 19-18. Dining area

1. *The task:* The task is essentially one of creating the desired mood or atmosphere for dining; therefore, the illuminance, the luminance in the room, and the choice of luminaire are largely matters of personal taste.

2. *Description of the task plane:* The entire table top should be considered as the task plane. If carving and serving are done at a separate location, this becomes another task area and can generally be equated with the task plane for a kitchen counter.

3. *Controls:* Controls, such as multiposition switching and dimming equipment, can often add to the enjoyment of dining-area lighting by adapting the level of illuminance to the particular occasion. Room surface reflectances will influence the selection of the level.

4. *Special design considerations:* Lighting with a strong downward component will accent the table setting, creating attractive focal highlights; however, this type of distribution, if used alone, will render faces poorly, causing harsh shadows. Strong downward lights should be kept away from people's faces (that is, confined within the perimeter of the table itself), or should be well balanced by indirect light from table top, walls or ceiling. The nature of the table top may also influence the choice of lighting distribution: downlighting may cause annoying specular reflections from glossy table tops such as glass or marble, and if all the light is directed on the table, a colored tablecloth may appreciably tint the light by reflection. Exposed sources such as unshielded low-wattage bulbs can often be tolerated, especially if some general lighting is provided and the background is not too dark. The darker the walls, the more general lighting is required to keep luminance relationships in the room within a comfortable range. In situations where the dining table is moved from time to time, a flexible means of mounting a pendant luminaire is desirable.

5. *Typical equipment locations:*
   (a) Task area—over-center-of-table luminaires:
       (1) Recessed (a group of recessed units is generally required)
       (2) Surface-mounted
       (3) Suspended, generally mounted so that the bottom of the luminaire is 690–910 mm (27–36 in.) above the table top
   (b) Area surrounding the task:
       (1) Luminous ceiling or large luminous area
       (2) Luminous wall
       (3) Cornice
       (4) Valance
       (5) Cove
       (6) Brackets, for example, linear fluorescent or decorative incandescent
       (7) Recessed luminaires, for example, incandescent downlights or wall-washers
       (8) Ceiling-mounted luminaires, for example, shallow large-area types
       (9) Suspended luminaires, for example, small pendants
       (10) Table lamp
       (11) Floor lamp or torchiere

Fig. 19-19. Multipurpose table

1. *The task:* The task includes both the creation of the desired mood or atmosphere for dining (see figure 19-18) and provision for other general visual tasks such as sewing, reading, hobbies and table games. Task reflectances are generally 30–70%, and speed and accuracy can be important, particularly when sewing.

2. *Description of the task plane:* The entire table top must be considered as the task plane.

3. *Special design considerations:*
   (a) A broad distribution pattern of light is required to illuminate the entire table top rather uniformly. To minimize veiling reflections, the light sources should have a high degree of diffusion or have substantial direct components.
   (b) It is difficult for a single static light source to provide drama and atmosphere for dining and widespread, diffused lighting (at a higher level) for other table activities; therefore, a multipurpose table usually requires more than one lighting system or a means of switching from one effect to another.

4. *Typical equipment locations:*
   (a) Task area—over-center-of-table luminaires:
       (1) Recessed (a group of recessed units is generally required)
       (2) Surface-mounted
       (3) Suspended–generally mounted so the bottom of the luminaire is 690–910 mm (27–36 in.) above the table top.
       (4) Track-mounted luminaires
   (b) Area surrounding the task:
       (1) Large luminous area
       (2) Luminous wall
       (3) Cornice
       (4) Valance
       (5) Cove
       (6) Brackets, for example, fluorescent or decorative incandescent
       (7) Recessed luminaires, for example, incandescent downlights or wall-washers
       (8) Ceiling luminaires, for example, shallow large-area types
       (9) Track-mounted luminaires
       (10) Pendant luminaires, for example, small pendants
       (11) Table lamp and floor lamp or torchiere
       (12) Chandelier with or without downlight

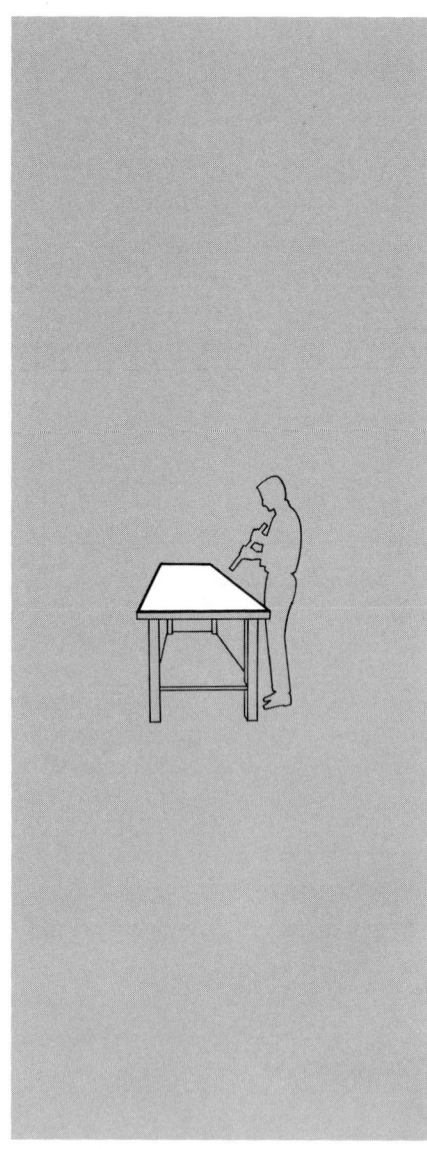

Fig. 19-20. Workbench hobbies

1. *The task:* Activities carried on at the workbench include woodworking (sawing, hammering, vise operation, planing, assembling parts and drilling) and craft hobbies. The majority of task reflectances may be below 30%, and speed and accuracy can be critical for power-tool operation. Hobbies vary greatly in visual difficulty, and often require additional illumination and consideration of directional quality. Leather work, ceramic enameling, pottery, mosaics, wood carving, block cutting (linoleum-wood), model assembly, electrical and electronic assembly, and fly tying are considered to be difficult tasks. Metal engraving, embossing, lapidary work (gem polishing) and jewelry making are considered to be critical tasks. Among these, block cutting and jewelry making require large-area low-luminance reflections in order to see fine detail, which shows up as an interruption in a surface sheen.

2. *Description of the task plane:* The task plane area is 510 mm (20 in.) wide and 1220 mm (48 in.) long, 910 mm (36 in.) above the floor. (Home workbenches vary in length. The task plane extends the full length of the bench.)

3. *Special design considerations:* Luminance balance within the visual field:

   (a) The wall immediately behind the workbench should have a reflectance above 40%. The light reflected is necessary to provide illumination on the task plane as well as eye comfort from the standpoint of luminance differences.

   (b) Additional room illumination should be provided to contribute to the luminance balance in the visual surroundings when the worker faces into the room.

   (c) If the user is facing a window while working, then (1) daylight glare should be controlled by blinds or shades, and (2) light-colored window coverings should be used at night. The light source should be so positioned that its image reflected in glossy materials is not visible to the user in normal position, unless desired for some special application.

5. *Typical equipment locations:*

   (a) Ceiling-mounted track or suspended linear luminaire running parallel with the task plane

   (b) Ceiling-mounted or suspended nonlinear luminaires in a symmetrical arrangement over the work area to provide uniform distribution of light

   (c) Wall- or shelf-mounted luminaire or luminaires with adequate shielding directly in front of the user

   (d) Luminous ceiling area

   (e) Portable equipment to provide added directional lighting for special conditions as indicated in the table above

Fig. 19-21. Table tennis

1. *The task:* The basic game of table tennis, although it always has the same rules and table size, varies greatly in its visual difficulty according to the skill of the players. Lighting recommendations here are for recreational play, where the speed of play is not high and the players' skill is minimal.

2. *Description of the task plane:* In recreational play the task plane area is to be considered as the 1.5 × 2.7-m (5 × 9-ft) table only.

3. *Special design considerations:* Although the general guides for luminance balance within the visual field still hold true in table tennis, the background surfaces seen by the player should not be too light, or they will not provide sufficient contrast with the white ball for good visibility. Wall and ceiling surfaces must not have strong, distracting patterns. Spottiness or uneven distribution of light can cause seeing difficulty. In table tennis, since the ceiling plane is the major part of the visual field, the luminance ratios at the ceiling become more important than usual.

4. *Typical equipment locations:*
   (a) Ceiling-mounted linear sources with the centerlines of the luminaires crosswise over the table, located approximately 0.3 m (1 ft) in from each end, plus one or more in each runback area
   (b) Ceiling-mounted linear sources positioned lengthwise above the table, centered over its outer edges and extending into the runback areas
   (c) Ceiling-mounted nonlinear sources arranged in a symmetrical pattern over the entire task area
   (d) Large-area luminaires of low luminance symmetrically located to cover the task area, and equipped with louvers or other material providing a minimum of 45° shielding

Fig. 19-22. Easel hobbies

1. *The task:* Easel hobbies include painting, sketching and collage. Unlike most tasks, which can be described in relatively exact terms, easel hobbies include widely diverse activities. In many cases the task reflectance can be less than 30%, and speed and accuracy can be important. A definition of a "standard painting" would be absurd. If it is assumed the artist wishes to see small applications of nearly identical colors, a standard task may be described as the application of a spot of color 6.4 mm (0.25 in.) in diameter on a background of the next nearest color in a scale comprising 1800 different colors (Munsell).

2. *Description of the task plane:* The task area is a surface up to 0.9 m (3 ft) square. The plane of the task is inclined from the vertical to suit the user and the task. The average eye height is 1220 mm (48 in.) sitting, 1580 mm (62 in.) standing. There is also a palette and often an object being copied. The locations of these are not fixed.

3. *Special design considerations:* Luminance balance within the visual field:
   (a) The reflectance of wall surfaces should be above 35%.
   (b) Additional room illumination should be provided to contribute to the luminance balance in the visual surroundings when the painter looks away from his or her work.
   (c) If the artist faces a window while working, the (1) glare should be controlled by blinds or shades, and (2) light-colored window coverings should be used.
   (d) The light source should be so positioned that its image reflected in glossy materials is not visible to the artist in normal working position, unless specifically desired. For instance, a large low-luminance reflection may be required in order to see fine detail in a glossy paint surface; the detail shows up as an interruption on a surface sheen. A general recommendation is to paint under the light source by which the painting will ultimately be seen.

4. *Typical equipment locations:*
   (a) Ceiling-mounted track, or suspended linear luminaires running parallel with the task plane
   (b) Ceiling-mounted or suspended nonlinear luminaires in a line to provide uniform distribution of light
   (c) Portable equipment to provide added lighting for fine detail

Fig. 19-23. Home Electronic Office

1. *The task:* The tasks are reading information on a computer terminal screen, keys and templates on the keyboard, and written or printed information on paper. In addition, printer and fax machine status settings must be read. Speed and accuracy may not be important for casual operation, but may be important when doing work at home. Reflectances of equipment surfaces (other than the screen) are between 30 and 70%.

2. *Description of the task plane:* The terminal screen usually is in a vertical to near-vertical plane, while the keyboard is on a near-horizontal plane. The paper-based tasks may be on any plane from horizontal to vertical. Printer and fax status settings are usually in a near-horizontal plane.

3. *Special design considerations:* Luminance ratios between the terminal screen, the paper-based tasks and the equipment and surface in the surround should be limited (see chapter 15, Office Lighting). Luminaire, ceiling and window brightness should be controlled to avoid reflections on the screen and specular surfaces of equipment.

4. *Typical equipment locations:*
   (a) Desk-mounted or floor-mounted task lights for paper and keyboard tasks
   (b) Wall-mounted direct/indirect luminaires at the front or side of the desk for ambient and task lighting
   (c) Ceiling-mounted low-brightness luminaires

Fig. 19-24. Downlight illuminates the piano keyboard and accent lighting highlights the artwork in this California living room.

Fig. 19-25. Drama is created with adjustable accent lighting in the alcoves that house the life-size sculptures. Recessed wall washers highlight the paintings, and downlights illuminate the seating areas.

brightness ratios between luminaires and their background are very important. For example, the brightness of a translucent, portable luminaire against a dark wall may result in a dramatic effect, but it can cause discomfort if the shade is excessively bright.

Lighting can reinforce spatial perceptions. It can make a space appear larger or smaller (see chapter 3, Vision and Perception). Uniform lighting can make a space seem larger, but at the same time it can make the space seem flat or dull if there are no shadows. In contrast, nonuniform lighting can make a space seem smaller, particularly if walls and corners are dark, and can also create a sense of intimacy.

Refer to chapter 10, Lighting Design Process, for a discussion of the many factors important in altering the perceived size of a space. Pretesting spatial effects is always recommended.

Art Created by Light

Light as an art medium is a way to enhance interior spaces. The art medium can be flat works created by projections onto surfaces or transmission through surfaces, or three-dimensional sculptures in glass, acrylic or neon. The selection of these pieces can be personal, as with any work of art, or can be designed as part of the overall luminous environment. The effect that a luminous piece of art will have on the space must be evaluated by the same criteria as other lighting effects. Luminous contrast, glare, and day and nighttime impact are a few of the considerations.

Design Effects

The visual effects that can be created with lighting are almost limitless. Some of these possibilities are charted for easy reference in chapter 10, Lighting Design Process.

LIGHT SOURCES FOR INTERIOR SPACES

The most common electric light sources used in residential interiors are incandescent, tungsten-halogen, fluorescent and compact fluorescent lamps. Tungsten-halogen sources provide whiter light, longer life and higher efficacy than standard incandescent lamps. Incandescent and tungsten-halogen lamps are available for line voltage as well as low voltage, and are used extensively in portable luminaires, recessed downlights, track lights, wall sconces and chandeliers.

Standard T-12 linear fluorescent lamps and the more energy-efficient, smaller-diameter T-8 lamps are available in versions with very good color rendering properties. Linear fluorescent sources are appropriate in kitchens, bathrooms, utility rooms and any setting where valances, coves or soffits are used.

Compact fluorescent lamps can be effectively used in residences, offering good color rendering and an energy-efficient alternative to standard incandescent lamps. For best results, luminaires designed specifically for compact fluorescent lamps should be used.

See chapter 6, Light Sources, for further information on incandescent, tungsten-halogen, fluorescent and compact fluorescent sources.

Retrofitting

Compact, screw-base, self-ballasted fluorescent lamps are commonly used to replace standard incandescent A-type lamps. These lamps can reduce energy consumption. They are often physically longer than standard incandescents and may not fit properly in existing luminaires. Typical applications are downlighting, wall sconces and portable luminaires (for example, table lamps). Compact fluorescents often require a special harp or extender for portable luminaires. In downlighting luminaires and wall sconces, the dimension of the luminaire must also be checked to assure proper fit. The operating temperature may cause the lumen output to be lower than expected. The color appearance of compact fluorescents differs slightly from incandescent sources. Fluorescent retrofit kits for downlights, available from luminaire manufacturers, include ballast, cone, lamp and trim.

Many "energy saver" incandescent lamps reduce the wattage while producing nearly the same light output as their equivalent standard lamp. Further, by using tungsten-halogen lamps wattage can be reduced. For example, halogen PAR lamps are more efficient than standard R lamps and have more precise beam control, allowing the use of reduced wattages to achieve the same light on a surface.

LUMINAIRES FOR INTERIOR SPACES

Luminaires for interior living spaces range from portable luminaires to custom-made architectural lighting. Luminaires are categorized by their different light distributions by CIE designation as to the type of luminaire used (direct, semidirect or general diffuse). The choice depends upon structural conditions, esthetics and economics. To select lighting equipment wisely, the designer must be able to interpret manufacturers' literature, including photometric data and charts for estimating illuminance.

Several types of luminaires are used in residences. A discussion of their applications may be found in chapter 7, Luminaires.

In typical residential applications, the average luminance of the luminaire which provides general illuminance to the space should not exceed 1700 cd/m^2, except in utility areas. For equipment used in utility spaces, luminances as high as 2700 cd/m^2 are acceptable. Within the diffusing element, the luminance of the brightest 645 mm^2 (1 in^2) should not exceed twice the average luminance of the overall element. Luminance ratios between the luminaire and the ceiling should not exceed 20:1. Even with the best diffusing glass or plastic, spottiness will occur if the lamps are widely spaced or too close to the diffuser.

EXTERIOR LIGHTING

Definition

Exterior residential lighting includes the functional and esthetic lighting of buildings and structures, landscape areas, planting, and focal points such as sculptures, water features and specimen trees. Although the bulk of exterior residential lighting is concentrated in back yard areas, the potential benefits of lighting front yards and structures should not be ignored. See chapter 22, Exterior Lighting.

Purpose

Residential landscape lighting serves several purposes. It provides safety, security and esthetics for both the family and guests. Each of these three issues addresses specific needs, and all can be integrated into a cohesive, pleasing lighting composition. Safety lighting addresses the visibility of potential obstacles in the landscape such as the edges of pools, changes in elevation such as stairs, and other objects, whether permanent features of the landscape or children's toys left outside. Security lighting allows people to feel free from threat by eliminating hiding places and identifying boundaries. The main purposes of night lighting are esthetic, to accentuate the features of the landscape and to expand the hours of enjoyment of residential property. A lighting composition integrating safety, security and esthetics allows the option of having several lighting schemes within the overall composition through the inclusion of multiple control options.

Exterior lighting addresses specific needs and uses, including welcoming people to a residence with walkway and entry lighting, providing views from the interior to the exterior (and vice versa), and allowing nighttime activities. The overall effect may be subdued, stimulating or dramatic, depending on the design and application of light.

Guiding Principles

Lighting ideas develop from an evaluation of the daytime landscape composition and the elements within the landscape. Nonuniform lighting provides the most interesting visual composition. The designer needs to assess the visual importance of all the elements and assign a nighttime role to each element in the composition. This process will establish a hierarchy of luminance values to create order and cohesion in the nighttime scene.

Concept development must consider the following:

1. The users' preferences and feelings about light
2. The atmosphere they would like to create in the landscape
3. The uses they intend for the space
4. The frequency of their use of it
5. The condition of their eyes

While visual task needs such as food preparation, dining and sports need to be considered, the view through windows, in many cases, has greater significance.

In many locations, landscape areas cannot be used during much of the year due to weather restrictions (snow, low temperatures, wind and rain). However, a view of the landscape can be retained at night by balancing luminances on both sides of the windows to eliminate reflections that make them appear as black mirrors. Landscape lighting can serve as an extension of the interior lighting, expanding the apparent visual size of the interior space. To achieve this, luminances need to be balanced according to the direction of view. In most cases, the primary view is from interior to exterior, requiring the landscape lighting levels to match or exceed those of the interior. When the primary view is from the landscape into the interior, the interior lighting levels need to be the higher ones. When the two directions of view are equally important, the lighting levels on the two sides of the window need to be nearly equal.

To create the desired composition, the designer must know the layout of pavement, plant materials and features in the landscape. Knowing the reflectances of all elements in the landscape to be lighted is important. The lighting effects evolve from the reflection of light off the elements in the landscape. The importance of an object in the landscape depends on the contrast of brightness between it and the other elements in the composition. Contrast is the most important element in landscape lighting, as it directs where and how people see the features of the landscape.

Elements that serve as primary focal points can be as much as 10 times brighter than the general grounds, and 3–5 times brighter than secondary focal points. To achieve these ratios, higher illuminance may be required on background elements that have lower reflectances than focal points. Providing fill lighting between focal points is critical to creating cohesion. The actual level of light required depends on the ambient level of the surrounding community. Residential areas in downtown areas of cities tend to have higher street lighting levels than suburban and rural areas. In these areas, the exterior lighting levels can be higher without creating visual disturbance in the neighborhood.

Locating and aiming the lighting equipment should be done in such a way as to avoid creating glare in the landscape area or in surrounding properties.

Techniques

Consider the texture, form, line, reflectance and relationship to the background of all objects to be lit in the landscape. Head-on floodlighting tends to make objects appear flat; modeling is obtained by lighting from one or more sides with either equal or unequal illuminance levels. Light striking a surface at a near-grazing angle emphasizes texture. Lighting a surface behind the object accentuates form. The last technique works best when objects have strong shapes and the detail and color are not important.

Walkways. Providing a clear view of walkways constitutes an important aspect of all landscape lighting. Walkway lighting works best when the lighting is as even as possible. For example, luminaires should be

Fig. 19-26. Vertical downlight is used to illuminate the front entrance of this Florida residence. Accent lighting highlights some of the plants and shrubs.

placed on one side of the walk, rather than alternating sides along its length.

Decorative path luminaires need not provide good path lighting. However, locating adjustable accent luminaires either in trees or on a structure such as a roof overhang, a side of a wall or a trellis to downlight a path can accentuate the landscape and light the path at the same time. This provides visual interest and increases psychological comfort by identifying the boundaries of the walk.

Entrances. Light is needed at doorways to help people identify the entrance, for safety of passage and for identifying callers. See figure 19-26. Vertical surface lighting of the doorway accomplishes each of these goals by visually directing the callers through the landscape to the door and providing light on the caller's face.

Steps and Staircases. To provide for safe movement in a landscape, all changes in elevation must be clearly identified. The light on stairs must differentiate between risers and treads. As with pathway lighting, even illumination along the length of the staircase provides the most comfortable effect. Lighting the entire width of the staircase is typically less important; however, it becomes more important as traffic frequency and the occurrence of two-way traffic on the staircase increase.

Buildings and Structures. Incorporating the residence as a part of the landscape lighting composition is important. If the home is not lighted, its identification and location will be lost. Structural lighting includes not only brackets, cornices, coves, panels and soffits, but also lighted bookshelves, display cabinets, lighted niches, coffers, artificial skylights, extended soffits, lighted mantels, handrails and luminous ceilings.

The importance of the house and all its structures needs to be considered along with the other elements in the composition. Often just a shadow pattern from an uplighted tree may be enough. In other cases, the architectural shape requires or deserves enhancement. The lighting on buildings should be planned to enhance their appearance. This does not require even floodlighting, but visually disjointed lighting can distort the nighttime appearance of the building rather than enhancing it.

Plant Materials. The lighting of plant materials requires more attention than other elements in the landscape. The designer should strive to understand the characteristics of all plants to be used in the landscape, even those that will not be lit. The characteristics important to consider include: overall shape and size; growth rate; mature height and width; trunk and branching structure; leaf characteristics, including shape, size, density, translucence and color; flowering characteristics; and dormancy. These issues affect which plants to light, where to locate luminaires, what type of light source to use, and how to light specific plants.

One of the most important issues to understand in landscape lighting is that plants are alive and continually change over time. The changes that occur in plants over time require careful planning in the initial design stages and, often, flexibility to change the luminaire aiming angle or location, the lamp beam spread or wattage, or the number of luminaires lighting the plant.

The physical characteristics of plants affect the types of lighting. For example, dense trees or those that produce branches close to the ground, such as junipers, must be lit with fixtures located away from the tree and aimed towards it. Birches, maples and other trees with an open trunk form or translucent leaves will glow when lit from inside the tree canopy. The trunk should have some light on it to tie the tree visually to the ground.

When the tree serves as a focal point, the designer must consider the overall appearance of the lighting on it. To make it appear natural, luminaires must be placed around the canopy to show the overall shape and provide depth. When the tree is seen from limited viewing angles, lighting only one side may be acceptable.

Sculptures. When lighting a sculpture, the designer should consider its size, its physical characteristics and any special features that might be accentuated. When the sculpture represents a life form, such as a human or animal, the sculpture should not be uplighted or downlighted from a grazing angle. This will create unnatural shadows that detract from the appearance. Luminaires should be positioned far enough away from the sculpture to avoid creating exaggerated shadows.

Life forms should be lighted from one or more sides, as with theatrical lighting. One-side lighting can enhance movement. Lighting from two sides provides the most natural appearance. See the remarks on sculpture lighting in the section on Museums in chapter 17, Institution and Public Building Lighting, and in chapter 22, Exterior Lighting.

Water Features. Lighting of water features such as fountains, pools, waterfalls and ponds differs from other landscape lighting in that the luminaires used must be rated for submersible use. Lighting water features also requires a greater maintenance commitment than other kinds of landscape lighting. A burned-out lamp can ruin the entire effect. As with any element, the importance of the water feature must be evaluated. Often, water features represent the primary focal point and need to have the highest luminance.

Some physical characteristics of light must be understood in order to provide effective lighting of water features. As light moves from water into air, the angle at which it is traveling will change. This affects the placement of luminaires for lighting objects outside the water such as sculptures or plant materials. Light also loses intensity by approximately 10% for every 5 cm (2 in.) of water it travels through.

To make a fall of water visible the characteristics of the water must be understood. Water falling over a rough surface will have air bubbles in it. The bubbles catch light and make the water glow. Therefore, the luminaire needs to be located directly beneath where the falling water will hit the surface of the lower water body. When water falls over a smooth edge, there are no air bubbles in it. This application requires luminaire

placement in front of the falling water and aimed at it so that light will be reflected back.

Water features do not always have to be lighted from beneath the water surface. Downlighting from a tree or nearby structure can be very effective, especially if air bubbles are present. Typically downlighting will not create as dramatic an effect, but it will be less costly and maintenance will be easier. Another approach is to use a remote-mounted light source with a collecting lens and fiber-optic cabling to deliver light into the water feature. The benefit of this system is simplified maintenance.

Lighting Equipment

Light Sources. The appropriate lamps to be used in landscape lighting depend on the size of the project and the desired effects. A white-light source will vary depending on the color of the elements that will be used. See figure 19-27 for an overview of which light sources will accentuate various elements. Typically, lower-wattage lamps work best in small landscapes to integrate with the surrounding community light levels. On large properties, higher-wattage lamps may be beneficial, as this will decrease the number of fixtures required to provide ambient lighting.

Luminaires. The selection of luminaires constitutes perhaps the most important decision in landscape lighting. The daytime appearance of luminaires needs to complement the landscape or disappear from view. All the equipment must be able to stand up to the weather conditions. Rain, snow, fog, temperature variation and other outdoor conditions encourage corrosion. Lamps should be protected from weather, since even lamps

Fig. 19-27. Objects or Materials Typically Found in Outdoor Landscaped Areas, Along with Light Sources Used to Illuminate Them*

Color	Objects / Materials	Light Sources	CRI
Warm	Red brick	High-pressure sodium (HPS)	22
	Red or yellow blossoms	Color-corrected HPS	70
	Autumn foliage		
		Line-voltage incandescent	95
	Redwood bark	Line-voltage halogen	100
		Low-voltage halogen	99
	Cypress bark	D827 compact fluorescent	81
	Pine bark		
	Concrete	3200-K coated metal halide	75
Neutral			
	Birch tree bark	3500-K compact fluorescent	74
	Variegated foliage		
	Most green plant material		
		Standard metal halide	65
		Color-corrected DX mercury	45
		4100-K compact fluorescent	70
		4100-K HQI metal halide	88
	Bermuda grass		
	Bluegrass	Clear mercury	15
Cool	Blue blossoms	Daylight metal halide	80

*The most appropriate sources are those within six rows (up or down) of the object or material and with the highest color rendering index (CRI).

rated as weatherproof may fail sooner if exposed to water.

The construction of luminaires needs to be evaluated. The outdoor environment can damage the appearance and structure of luminaires and cause them to stop functioning. Since the landscape will be continually changing due to plant growth, luminaire maintenance needs to be simple. Lamp access should be easy, requiring no tools and little disturbance of other components.

CONTROLS

Controls should be installed to make a lighting system easy to operate and flexible. A control should be conveniently located at the entry point of every space (both indoors and outdoors) and, ideally, luminaires should be controlled separately or collectively to achieve a desired lighting effect. Well designed and conveniently located controls save energy by allowing the user to operate only those luminaries necessary to produce the desired effect.

ENERGY CONSIDERATIONS

Lighting decisions should include energy considerations. The criteria and information in Chapter 30, Energy Management, can be used to develop the most energy-efficient solutions. In new construction, early planning will enable the use of energy-efficient techniques. In existing structures, luminaires and light sources previously installed will influence how energy efficiency can be achieved. The choices are: retrofitting with more efficient sources, modifying the existing lighting systems, or replacing luminaires and controls. In addition, in interior spaces, daylight can be used to reduce dependence upon electric light whenever it is suitable to the task and to the space.

CODES AND STANDARDS

Several types of codes and approvals affect residential lighting design both indoors and out. They can be federal, state or locally based. See Chapter 14, Codes and Standards, and check with local code enforcement agencies to determine which regulations apply to the area.

Most electrical codes merely set minimum requirements for electrical wiring methods. But others may dictate specific requirements for lighting systems. Examples are types of lighting systems used in kitchens and storage closets. Additional requirements relate to energy consumption, minimum amount of light and lamp or luminaire efficiencies.

REFERENCES

1. IES. Residence Lighting Committee. 1980. Design criteria for lighting interior living spaces. *Light. Des. Appl.* 10(2):31–61; 10(3):35–63.

2. Caminada, J. F., and W. J. M. van Bommel. 1984. New lighting criteria for residential areas. *J. Illum. Eng. Soc.* 13(4):350–358.

3. Christensen, N. 1986. Homelighting: Focus on aesthetics energy and quality. *Light. Des. Appl.* 16(5):33–39.

4. IES. Residence Lighting Committee. 1974. Energy-saving tips for home energy lighting. *Light. Des. Appl.* 4(4):40–42.

5. IES. Color Committee. 1993. *Color and illumination.* New York: Illuminating Engineering Socitey of North America.

6. Crouch, C. L., and J. E. Kaufman. 1965. Illumination performance for residential study tasks. *Illum. Eng.* 60(10):591–596.

7. American Society of Heating, Refrigerating and Air-Conditioning Engineers and Illuminating Engineering Society of North America. 1989. *Energy efficient design of new buildings except new low-rise residential buildings, ASHRAE / IES 90.1-1989.* Atlanta, GA: American Society of Heating, Refrigerating and Air-Conditioning Engineers.

8. Illuminating Engineering Society of North America. 1965. IES lighting performance requirements for table study lamps. *Illum. Eng.* 60(7):463–464.

Industrial Lighting

20

INTRODUCTION

In this revision of the Handbook, several changes have been made which are intended to improve its value for all users. As a result, some material which has appeared in previous volumes of the *IESNA Lighting Handbook* has been omitted from this revision. Among the industries which are not represented in this revision are candy manufacturing, cotton ginning, cleaning and pressing, dairy and poultry, flour mills, fruit and vegetables, men's clothing and shoe manufacturing. Material for some of these industries appears in other publications,[1] and material previously contained in the *IESNA Lighting Handbook* can be found in its previous volumes.

PURPOSE

Industry encompasses a wide range of visual tasks, operating conditions and economic considerations.[2-7] Visual tasks may be small or large; dark or light; opaque, transparent or translucent; on specular or diffuse surfaces; and involving flat or contoured shapes. In addition, the task may involve movement of the object or the viewer or both. With each of the various task conditions, the lighting must provide adequate visibility in transforming raw materials into finished products. Physical hazards exist in manufacturing processes, and therefore lighting is of the utmost importance as a safety factor in preventing accidents. The speed of operations may be such as to allow only minimum time for visual perception, and therefore lighting must be a compensating factor to increase the speed of vision (see chapter 3, Vision and Perception).

Various topics related to industrial lighting, such as economics, emergency and safety lighting, security lighting and energy management, may be found in separate chapters of this Handbook.

FACTORS OF GOOD INDUSTRIAL LIGHTING

Quality of Illumination

Quality of illumination pertains to the distribution of luminances in the visual environment. The term im-plies that all luminances contribute favorably to visual performance, visual comfort, ease of seeing, safety and aesthetics for the specific visual task involved. Glare, diffusion, direction, uniformity, color, luminance and luminance ratios all have a significant effect on visibility and the ability to see accurately and quickly. See chapter 3, Vision and Perception. Certain seeing tasks, such as discernment of fine details, require much more careful analysis and higher-quality illumination than others. Areas where the seeing tasks are severe and performed over long periods of time require much higher quality than where seeing tasks are casual or of relatively short duration.

Industrial installations of very poor quality are easily recognized as uncomfortable and are possibly hazardous. Unfortunately, moderate deficiencies are not readily detected, although even minimal glare can result in material loss of seeing efficiency and undue fatigue.

Direct Glare. When glare is caused by the source of lighting within the field of view, whether daylight or electric, it is described as direct glare.

To reduce direct glare in industrial areas, the following steps may be taken: (1) decrease the luminance of light sources or lighting equipment, or both; (2) reduce the area of high luminance causing the glare condition; (3) increase the angle between the glare source and the line of vision; (4) increase the luminance of the area surrounding the glare source and against which it is seen; (5) place louvers between the glare source and the line of sight.

Unshaded factory windows are frequent causes of direct glare. They may permit direct view of the sun, bright portions of the sky or bright adjacent buildings. These often constitute large areas of very high luminance in the normal field of view.

Luminaires that are too bright for their environment may produce *discomfort* glare or *disability* glare, or both. The former produces visual discomfort without necessarily interfering with visual performance or visibility. Disability glare reduces both visibility and visual performance and is often accompanied by visual discomfort. To reduce direct glare, luminaires should be mounted as far as possible above the normal line of sight. They should be designed to limit both the luminance and the quantity of light emitted in the 45–85° zone, because such light, likely to be well within the field of view, may interfere with vision. Luminaires with louvers can also be used to control glare. These precautions may require the use of supplementary task lighting equipment.

There is such a wide divergence of industrial tasks and environmental conditions that it may not be economically feasible to recommend a degree of quality satisfactory for all needs. The required luminance control depends on the task, the length of time to perform it and those factors which contribute to direct glare. In production areas, luminaires within the normal field of view should be shielded to at least 25° from the horizontal—preferably to 45°.

Luminance and Luminance Ratios. The ability to see detail depends upon the contrast between the detail and its background. The greater the contrast or difference in luminance, the more readily the seeing task is performed. However, the eyes function more comfortably and efficiently when the luminances within the remainder of the environment are fairly uniform. Therefore, all luminances in the field of view should be carefully controlled. In manufacturing there are many areas where it is not practical to achieve the same luminance relationships as are easily achieved in areas such as offices. But between the extremes of heavy manufacturing and office spaces lie the bulk of industrial areas. Therefore, figure 20-1 has been developed as a practical guide to recommended maximum luminance ratios for industrial areas.

To achieve the recommended luminance relationships, it is necessary to select the reflectances of all the finishes of the room surfaces and equipment as well as control the luminance distribution of the lighting equipment. Figure 20-2 lists the recommended reflectance values for industrial interiors and equipment. High reflectance surfaces are generally desirable to provide the recommended luminance relationships and utilization of light. They also improve the appearance of the work space.

In many industries machines are painted so that they present a completely harmonious environment from the standpoint of color. It is desirable that the background be slightly darker than the seeing task. It appears desirable to paint stationary and moving parts of machines with contrasting colors to reduce accident hazard by aiding identification.

Veiling Reflections. Where seeing-task details are specular, veiling reflections which will decrease task visibility should be minimized. See chapter 3, Vision and Perception.

Reflected Glare. Reflected glare is caused by the reflection of high-luminance light sources from shiny

Fig. 20-1. Recommended Maximum Luminance Ratios

	Environmental Classification*		
	A	B	C
1. Between tasks and adjacent darker surroundings	3 to 1	3 to 1	5 to 1
2. Between tasks and adjacent lighter surroundings	1 to 3	1 to 3	1 to 5
3. Between tasks and more remote darker surfaces	10 to 1	20 to 1	†
4. Between tasks and more remote lighter surfaces	1 to 10	1 to 20	†
5. Between luminaires (or windows, skylights, etc.) and surfaces adjacent to them	20 to 1	†	†
6. Anywhere within normal field of view	40 to 1	†	†

* Classifications are:
  A—Interior areas where reflectances of entire space can be controlled in line with recommendations for optimum seeing conditions.
  B—Areas where reflectances of immediate work area can be controlled, but control of remote surround is limited.
  C—Areas (indoor and outdoor) where it is completely impractical to control reflectances and difficult to alter environmental conditions.
  † Luminance ratio control not practical.

Fig. 20-2. Recommended Reflectance Values (Applying to Environmental Classifications A and B in Figure 20-1)

Surfaces	Reflectance* (percent)
Ceiling	80 to 90
Walls	40 to 60
Desk and bench tops, machines and equipment	25 to 45
Floors	not less than 20

*Reflectance should be maintained as near as practical to recommended values.

surfaces. In manufacturing processes this may be a particularly serious problem where critical seeing is involved with highly polished surfaces such as polished or machined metal, vernier scales and digital displays.

Reflected glare can be minimized or eliminated by using light sources of low luminance or by orienting the work so reflections are not directed in the normal line of vision. Often it is desirable to use reflections from a large-area, low-luminance luminaire located over the work. The section that follows on supplementary lighting covers in detail the solutions to such problems.

In special cases it is practical to reduce the specular reflection (and the resultant reflected glare) by changing the specularity of the offending surface.

Distribution, Diffusion and Shadows. Uniform horizontal illuminance (where the maximum level is not more than one-sixth above the average level, and the minimum, not more than one-sixth below) is frequently appropriate for specific industrial interiors where tasks are closely spaced and where there are similar tasks requiring the same amount of light. In such instances, uniformity permits flexibility of functions and equipment and assures more uniform luminances. Neighboring areas with extreme luminance differences are undesirable because it tires the eyes to adjust to them.

Maintaining uniformity between contiguous areas which have significantly different visibility (and illumination) requirements may be wasteful of energy—for example, a storage area adjacent to a machine shop. In such instances, it is prudent to design and apply nonuniform lighting between those areas. This may be accomplished by using luminaires of different wattage or by adjusting the number of luminaires per unit area. Local lighting restricted to a small work area is unsatisfactory unless there is sufficient general illumination.

Harsh shadows should be avoided, but some shadow effect may be desirable to accentuate the depth and form of objects. There are a few specific visual tasks where clearly defined shadows improve visibility, and such effects should be provided by supplementary lighting equipment arranged for the particular task.

Color Quality of Light. For general seeing tasks in industrial areas there appears to be no effect upon visual acuity due to variations in color of light. However, where color discrimination or color matching is a part of the work, the color of the light should be selected very carefully. This is also the case when color differentiation or color matching is a part of the work. One example is in the printing industry, covered in a section below.

Color, of course, has an effect upon the appearance of the work space, the complexions of personnel and the appearance of safety colors, especially under high pressure sodium lights. Therefore, the selection of the lighting system and the decorative scheme should be carefully coordinated. See chapter 4, Color.

Quantity of Illumination

The desirable quantity of light (illuminance) for an installation depends primarily upon the seeing task, the worker and the importance of speed and accuracy in performing the task (see chapter 11, Illuminance Selection).

Illuminance recommendations for industrial tasks and areas are given in chapter 11. In addition, in several instances industry representatives have established tables of single illuminance values which, in their opinion, can be used in preference to employing the illuminance selection procedure. However, illuminance values for specific operations can also be determined using illuminance categories of similar tasks and

activities, and the application of the appropriate weighting factors in chapter 11. In either case, the values given are considered as target maintained illuminances. If it is desired to determine the illuminance produced by an existing installation, the measurement procedure outlined in chapter 11 should be followed.

Recommendations for illuminance uniformity can be found in CIE publication 29.2. In locations where dirt will collect very rapidly on luminaire surfaces and where adequate maintenance is not provided, the initial illuminance should be even higher than the maintained value. For typical light loss data and a further discussion see chapter 6, Light Sources, chapter 7, Luminaires and chapter 9, Lighting Calculations.

Where workers wear eye-protective devices with occupationally required tinted lenses that materially reduce the light reaching the eye, the illuminance for the tasks should be increased accordingly.

General Considerations of Design for Lighting Industrial Areas

The designer of an industrial lighting system should consider the following factors as the first and all-important requirements of good planning.

1. Determine the quantity and quality of illumination desirable for the manufacturing processes involved and needed to produce a suitable and safe environment.
2. Select lighting equipment that will provide the quantity and quality requirements by considering photometric characteristics as well as the mechanical performance that will meet installation, operating and actual maintenance conditions.
3. Select and arrange equipment so that it will be safe, easy and practical to maintain. Certain lamps may be prone to explosion in adverse conditions and should be shielded from workers. See chapter 6, Light Sources.
4. Weigh all of the energy management considerations discussed in chapter 30 and economic factors against the quantity and quality requirements for optimum visual performance. The choice of the electric distribution system may affect overall economics.

Although not specifically mentioned in the discussions of the lighting for each industry that follow, the use of daylighting should be considered for area lighting in all industries.

Types of Lighting Equipment. The manner in which the light from the lamps is controlled by the lighting

Fig. 20-3. The importance of a white ceiling in an industrial facility is shown in this plant under construction. Note the improved visual environment in the right bay (where the painters have finished the ceiling) compared to that in the left (as yet, unpainted). The illuminance in the right is substantially higher, too.

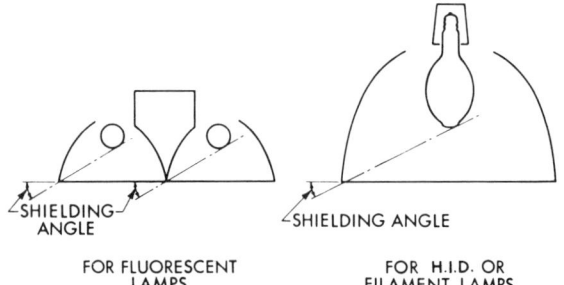

FOR FLUORESCENT LAMPS

FOR H.I.D. OR FILAMENT LAMPS

Fig. 20-4. Luminaires require adequate shielding for visual comfort. This is particularly important for higher luminance sources. An upward component also contributes to visual comfort by balance of luminances between luminaires and their backgrounds. Top openings help minimize dirt accumulation.

equipment governs to a large extent the important effects of glare, shadows, distribution and diffusion. Luminaires are classified in accordance with the way in which they control the light. Chapter 7, Luminaires gives the standard CIE classifications for interior lighting equipment.

Most industrial applications call for either the direct or the semidirect type. Luminaires with upward components of light are preferred for most areas, because an illuminated ceiling or upper structure reduces luminance ratios between luminaires and the background. The upward light reduces the "dungeon" effect of totally direct lighting and creates a more comfortable and more cheerful environment as shown in figure 20-3. Industrial luminaires for fluorescent, high-intensity discharge and incandescent filament lamps are available with upward components. See figure 20-4. Good environmental luminance relationships can also often be achieved with totally direct lighting if the illuminances and room surface reflectances are high.

In selecting industrial lighting equipment, it will be noted that other factors leading to more comfortable installations include:

1. Light-colored finishes on the outside of luminaires to reduce luminance ratios between the outside of the luminaire and the inner reflecting surface and light source.
2. Higher mounting heights to raise luminaires out of the normal field of view.
3. Better shielding of the light source by deeper reflectors, cross baffles or louvers. This is particularly important with high-wattage incandescent filament or high-intensity discharge sources and the higher-output fluorescent lamps.
4. Selecting light control material, such as specular or nonspecular aluminum or prismatic configurated glass or plastic, that can limit the luminaire luminance in the shielded zone.

Top openings in luminaires generally minimize dirt collection on the reflector and lamp by allowing an air draft path to move dirt particles upward and through the luminaire to the outer air. Therefore, ventilated types of luminaires have proven their ability to minimize maintenance of fluorescent, high-intensity discharge and incandescent filament types of luminaires. Gasketed dust-tight and dirt- and moisture-resistant luminaires are also effective in minimizing dirt collection on reflector surfaces.

Direct Lighting Equipment. Distributions of direct industrial lighting equipment vary from wide to narrow (see chapter 7, Luminaires). The wide distribution types include porcelain enameled reflectors and various other types of diffuse and diffuse-specular white reflecting surfaces. Aluminum, mirrored glass, prismatic glass and other similar materials may also be used to provide a wide distribution when the reflector is designed with the proper contour. This type of light distribution is advantageous in industrial applications where a large proportion of the seeing tasks are vertical or nearly vertical.

Narrow distributions are obtained with prismatic-glass, mirrored-glass and aluminum reflectors. This type of light distribution is useful where the mounting height is approximately equal to or greater than the width of the room or where high machinery and processing equipment necessitate directional control for efficient illumination between the equipment.

In making a choice between wide- and narrow-distribution equipment on the basis of horizontal illuminances, a comparison of coefficients of utilization for the actual room conditions involved will serve as a guide in selecting the most effective distribution. The coefficients of utilization should be based on values as close as practical to those for actual ceiling, wall and floor reflectances as well as actual room proportions.

If, however, it is desired to determine illuminances at specific points, then a point calculation method should be used to obtain accurate results (see chapter 9, Lighting Calculations). This is particularly true for high mounting heights.

Other Types of Direct Lighting Equipment. Where low reflected luminance is a necessity, large-area types of low-luminance luminaires should be used. Such a luminaire may consist of a diffusing panel on a standard type of fluorescent reflector, an indirect light hood or a completely luminous ceiling.

Semidirect Lighting Equipment. This classification of distribution is useful in industrial areas because the upward component (10–40%) is particularly effective in creating more comfortable seeing conditions. A vari-

Fig. 20-6. Semidirect HID warehouse lighting.

ety of fluorescent and high-intensity discharge luminaires of this distribution are available and designed specifically for industrial application. See figures 20-5 and 20-6.

While the semidirect type of distribution has a sufficient upward component to illuminate the ceiling, the downward component of 90–60% of the output contributes to good illumination efficiency, particularly where ceiling obstructions may lessen the effectiveness of the indirect component.

Industrial Applications of Other Distribution Classifications

The general diffuse, semiindirect and indirect systems are suitable for industrial applications where a superior quality of diffused, low-luminance illumination is required and where environmental conditions make such systems practical. An example of such applications includes the precision industries where a completely controlled environment is important, including lighting, air conditioning and carefully planned decoration.

Building Construction Features That Influence Luminaire Selection and Luminaire Placement

The skeletal framework used in the construction of industrial buildings forms interior subspaces called bays. The selection and placement of luminaires in a bay is strongly influenced by the height of the bay. For this reason the interior spaces in industrial buildings are classified as low-bay, medium-bay and high-bay areas. Low-bay areas are generally considered to be those where the bottom of the luminaire is approximately 5.5 m (18 ft) or less above the floor (see figure 20-5). When the bottom of the luminaire is 5.5–7.5 m (18–25 ft) above the floor, the space is defined to be a medium-bay area. In a high-bay area (figure 20-6) the

Fig. 20-5. Semidirect fluorescent lighting provides vertical illuminance on stacked boxes in a warehouse.

bottom of a luminaire is more than 7.5 m (25 ft) above the floor.

Luminaires are usually mounted from the ceiling, or from bar joists, beams or other overhead structural elements, in a uniform array called the ceiling plane. The lighting provided by this type of luminaire placement is called *general lighting*. General lighting is intended to provide substantially uniform illumination throughout an area, exclusive of any provision for special local requirements (see the subsection on Distribution, Diffusion and Shadows, above). *Localized general lighting* may be used for areas containing visual tasks that require illuminance values that are higher than the levels provided by general lighting. This additional illuminance may be achieved by increasing the numbers (or rows) of luminaires, the light output per luminaire, or both. For more difficult visual tasks, *supplementary task lighting* may be required (see the section on Supplementary Task Lighting in Industry, below).

Factors of Special Consideration

Lighting and Space Conditioning. With the use of higher illuminances, it may be practical to combine the lighting, heating, cooling and atmospheric control requirements in an integrated system. The lighting system can often provide most of the energy during the heating period. When cooling is required, much of the lighting heat can be removed by the air exhaust system. See chapter 7, Luminaires, for further details on thermal considerations.

High Humidity or Corrosive Atmosphere and Hazardous Location Lighting. Enclosed gasketed luminaires are used in nonhazardous areas where atmospheres contain nonflammable dusts and vapors, or excessive dust. Enclosures protect the interior of the luminaire from conditions prevailing in the area. Steam processing, plating areas, wash and shower rooms and other areas of unusually high humidity are typical areas that require enclosed and gasketed luminaires. Severe corrosive conditions necessitate knowledge of the atmospheric content to permit selection of proper material for the luminaire.

Hazardous locations are areas where atmospheres contain flammable dusts, vapors or gases in explosive concentrations. They are grouped by the National Electrical Code on the basis of their hazardous characteristics, and all electrical equipment must be approved for use in specific classes and groups. Luminaires are available that are specifically designed to operate in these areas, which are noted in Article 500 of the National Electrical Code as Class I, Class II and Class III locations (divisions).

For definitions of luminaires used in these areas, such as *explosion-proof*, *dust-tight*, *dust-proof* and *enclosed and gasketed*, see the Glossary in this Handbook.

Abnormal Temperature Conditions. Low ambient temperatures exist in such areas as unheated heavy industrial plants, frozen food plants and cold storage warehouses. Equipment has to be selected to operate under such conditions, and particular attention should be given to lamp starting and light output characteristics if fluorescent equipment is considered. With high-intensity discharge equipment, temperature variations have practically no effect on light output, but the proper starting conditions must be provided. With incandescent filament lamp equipment, neither the starting nor the operation is a problem at low temperature.

Abnormally high temperatures are common at truss height in foundries, steel mills and forge shops. Caution should be observed in selecting lighting equipment for mounting in such locations. It is particularly important to consider the temperature limitations of fluorescent and high-intensity discharge ballasts under such conditions. Often ballasts should be remotely located at a lower and cooler level or special high-temperature equipment should be used. The reduction in fluorescent lamp output at high operating temperatures should be recognized. See the section on Luminaire Design in chapter 7.

Maintenance. Regular cleaning and prompt replacement of lamp outages is essential in any well-operated industrial lighting system. It is important for the lighting designer to analyze luminaire construction and reflector finish and also to make provisions for maintenance access so the system can be properly serviced. Another point that should be considered is that it may often be necessary to do the servicing during the plant operating hours. Further details on maintenance, access methods and servicing suggestions are found in chapter 32.

SUPPLEMENTARY TASK LIGHTING IN INDUSTRY[8]

Difficult visual tasks often require a specific amount or quality of lighting which cannot readily be obtained by general lighting methods. To solve such problems supplementary luminaires often are used to provide higher illuminances for small or restricted areas. Also, they are used to furnish a certain luminance or color, or to permit special aiming or positioning of light sources to produce or avoid highlights or shadows so as to best portray the details of the visual task.

Before supplementary task lighting can be specified it is necessary to recognize the exact nature of the visual task and to understand its light-reflecting or -transmitting characteristics. An improvement in the visibility of the task will depend upon one or more of the four fundamental visibility factors—luminance, contrast, size and time. Thus, in analyzing the problem,

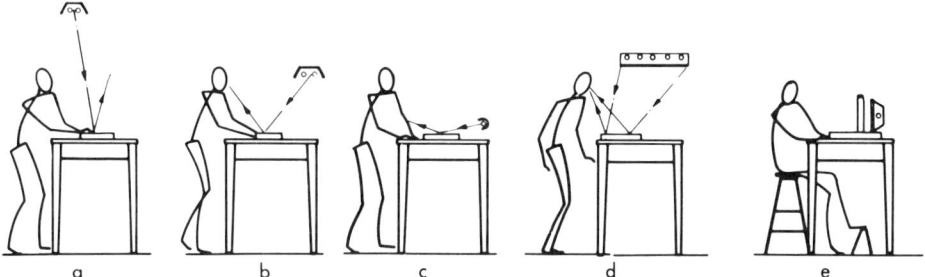

Fig. 20-7. Examples of placement of supplementary luminaires: a. Luminaire located to prevent veiling reflections and reflected glare; reflected light does not coincide with angle of view. b. Reflected light coincides with angle of view. c. Low-angle lighting to emphasize surface irregularities. d. Large-area surface source and pattern are reflected toward the eye. e. Transillumination from diffuse source.

the lighting designer may find that difficulty in seeing is caused by insufficient luminance, poor contrast (veiling reflections), small size or task motion too fast for existing seeing conditions.

The planning of supplementary task lighting also entails consideration of the visual comfort of both those workers who benefit directly and those who are in the immediate area. Supplementary equipment must be carefully shielded to prevent glare for the user and his or her neighbors. Luminance ratios should be carefully controlled. Ratios between task and immediate surroundings should be limited as recommended in figure 20-1. To attain these limits it is necessary to coordinate the design of supplementary task lighting and general lighting.

Luminaires for Supplementary Task Lighting

Supplementary task lighting units can be divided into five major types according to candlepower distribution and luminance. These are:

Type S-I – Directional. Includes all concentrating units. Examples are reflector or projection spot lamps or units that employ concentrating reflectors or lenses. Also included in the group are concentrating longitudinal units such as a well-shielded fluorescent lamp in a concentrating reflector.

Type S-II – Spread, High-Luminance. Includes small-area sources, such as incandescent or high-intensity discharge. An open-bottom, deep-bowl diffusing reflector with a high-intensity discharge lamp is an example of this type.

Type S-III – Spread, Moderate-Luminance. Includes all fluorescent units having a variation in luminance greater than 2:1.

Type S-IV – Uniform-Luminance. Includes all units having less than 2:1 variation of luminance. Usually this luminance is less than 6800 cd/m². An example of

Fig. 20-8. Small portable luminaires provide localized lighting on the task.

this type is an arrangement of lamps behind a diffusing panel.

Type S-V – Uniform-Luminance with Pattern. A luminaire similar to Type S-IV except that a pattern of stripes or lines is superimposed.

See figure 20-7 for a graphic representation of the different types of supplementary lighting.

Portable Luminaires

Wherever possible, supplementary luminaires should be permanently mounted in the location to produce the best lighting effect. Adjustable arms and swivels will often adapt the luminaires to provide flexibility. Portable equipment (see figure 20-8), however, can be used to good advantage where it must be moved in and around movable machines or objects, as in airplane assembly, in garages or where internal surfaces must be viewed. The luminaires must be mechanically and electrically rugged to withstand possible rough handling. Lamps should be guarded and of the rough-service type. Guards or other means should protect the user from excessive heat. Precautions, such as ground fault

Fig. 20-9. Classification of Visual Tasks and Lighting Techniques

Part 1—Flat surfaces

Classification of visual task	Example	Lighting technique	
General characteristics — Description	Description — Lighting requirements	Luminaire type	Locate luminaire
A. Opaque materials			
1. Diffuse detail & background			
a. Unbroken surface — Newspaper proofreading	High visibility with comfort	S-III or S-II	To prevent direct glare & shadows (Fig. 20-7a)
b. Broken surface — Scratch on inglazed tile	To emphasize surface break	S-I	To direct light obliquely to surface (Fig. 20-7c)
2. Specular detail & background			
a. Unbroken surface — Dent, wraps, uneven surface	Emphasize unevenness	S-V	So that image of source & pattern is reflected to eye (Fig. 20-7d)
b. Broken surface — Scratch, scribe, engraving, punch marks	Create contrast of cut against specular surface	S-III or	So detail appears bright against a dark background
		S-IV or S-V when not practical to orient task	So that image of source is reflected to eye & break appears dark (Fig. 20-7d)
c. Specular coating over specular background — Inspection of finish plating over underplating	To show up uncovered spots	S-IV with color of source selected to create maximum color contrast between two coatings	For reflection of source image toward the eye (Fig. 20-7d)
3. Combined specular & diffuse surfaces			
a. Specular detail on diffuse light background — Shiny ink or pencil marks on dull paper	To produce maximum contrast without veiling reflections	S-III or S-IV	So direction of reflected light does not coincide with angle of view (Fig. 20-7a)
b. Specular detail on diffuse dark background — Punch or scribe marks on dull metal	To create bright reflection from detail	S-II or S-III	So direction of reflected light from detail coincides with view (Fig. 20-7b)
c. Diffuse detail on specular, light background — Graduation on a steel scale	To create a uniform, low-brightness reflection from specular background	S-IV or S-III	So reflected image of source coincides with angle of view (Fig. 20-7b or d)
d. Diffuse detail on specular, dark background — Wax marks on auto body	To produce high brightness of detail against dark background	S-III or S-II	So direction of reflected light does not coincide with angle of view (Fig. 20-7a)
B. Translucent materials			
1. With diffuse surface — Frosted or etched glass or plastic, lightweight fabrics hosiery	Maximum visibility or surfaces detail	Treat as opaque, diffuse surface—See A-1	
	Maximum visibility of detail within material	Transilluminate behind material with S-II, S-III, or S-IV (Fig. 20-7e)	
2. With specular surface — Scratch on opal glass or plastic	Maximum visibility of surface detail	Treat as opaque specular surface—See A-2	
	Maximum visibility of detail within material	Transilluminate behind material with S-II, S-III or S-IV (Fig. 20-7e)	
C. Transparent materials			
Clear material with specular surface — Plate glass	To produce visibility or details within material such as bubbles & details on surface such as scratches	S-V and S-I	Transparent material should move in front of Type S-V., then in front of black background with Type S-I directed to prevent reflected glare
D. Transparent over opaque materials			
1. Transparent material over diffuse background — Instrument panel	Maximum visibility of scale & pointer without veiling reflections	S-1	So reflection of source does not coincide with angle of view (Fig. 20-7a)
Varnished desk top	Maximum visibility of detail on or in transparent coating or on diffuse background	S-V	So that image of source & pattern is reflected to the eye (Fig. 20-7d)
	Emphasis of uneven surface		

Fig. 20-9. *Continued*

| Classification of visual task | Example | Lighting requirements | Lighting technique | |
General characteristics	Description		Luminaire type	Locate luminaire
D. Continued				
2. Transparent material over a specular background	Glass mirror	Maximum visibility of detail on or in transparent material	S-I	So reflection of source does not coincide with angle of view. Mirror should reflect a black background (Fig. 20-7d)
		Maximum visibility of detail on specular background	S-V	So that image of source & pattern is reflected to the eye (Fig. 20-7d)
Part II—Three-dimensional objects				
A. Opaque materials				
1. Diffuse detail & background	Dirt on a casting or blow holes in a casting	To emphasize detail with a poor contrast	S-III or S-II or	To prevent direct glare & shadows (Fig. 20-7a)
			S-I or	In relation to task to emphasize detail by means of highlight & shadow (Fig. 20-7b or c)
			S-III or S-II as a "black light" source when object has a fluorescent coating	To direct ultraviolet radiation to all points to be checked
2. Specular detail & background				
a. Detail on the surface	Dent on silverware	To emphasize surface unevenness	S-V	To reflect image of source to eye (Fig. 20-7d)
	Inspection of finish plating over underplating	To show up areas not properly plated	S-IV plus proper color	To reflect image of source to eye (Fig. 20-7d)
b. Detail in the surface	Scratch on a watch case	To emphasize surface break	S-IV	To reflect image of source to eye (Fig. 20-7d)
3. Combination specular & diffuse				
a. Specular detail on diffuse background	Scribe mark on casting,	To make line glitter against dull background	S-III or S-III	In relation to task for best visibility. Adjustable equipment often helpful
				Overhead to reflect image of source to eye (Fig. 20-7b or d)
b. Diffuse detail on specular background	Micrometer scale	To create luminaous background against which scale markings can be seen in high contrast	S-IV or S-III	With axis normal to axis of micrometer
	Coal picking	To make coal glitter in contrast to dull impurities	S-I, S-II	To prevent direct glare (Fig. 20-7b)
B. Translucent materials				
1. Diffuse surface	Lamp shade	To show imperfections in material	S-II	Behind or within for transillumination (Fig. 20-7e)
2. Specular surface	Glass enclosing globe	To emphasize surface irregularities	S-V	Overhead to reflect image of source to eye (Fig. 20-7e)
		To check homogeneity	S-II	Behind or within for transillumination
C. Transparent materials				
Clear material with specular surface	Bottles, glassware—empty or filled with clear liquid	To emphasize surface irregularities	S-I	To be directed obliquely to objects
		To emphasize cracks, chips, and foreign particles	S-IV or S-V	Behind for transillumination. Motion of objects is helpful (Fig. 20-7e)

circuit protection, should be taken to prevent electrical shock.

Classification of Visual Tasks and Lighting Techniques

Visual tasks are unlimited in number, but can be classified according to certain common characteristics. The detail to be seen in each group can be emphasized by an application of certain lighting fundamentals. Figure 20-9 classifies tasks according to their physical and light controlling characteristics and suggests lighting techniques for good visual perception. It should be noted when using figure 20-9 that the classification of visual tasks is based on their fundamental characteristics and not on their general applications. For example, on a drill press the visual task will often be the discernment of a punch mark on metal. This could be specular detail with a diffuse, dark background, classification A-3(b) in figure 20-9. Luminaire type S-II or S-III is recommended. S-II on an adjustable arm bracket is a practical recommendation in view of space limitations. Several or all of the luminaire types are applicable for many visual task classifications, and the best luminaire for a particular job will depend upon physical limitations, possible placements of luminaires and the size of the task to be illuminated.

Special Effects and Techniques

Color as a part of the seeing task can be very effectively used to improve contrast. While black and white are the most desirable combinations for continual tasks such as reading a book, it has been found that certain color combinations have a greater attention value. Black on yellow is most legible, and the next combinations in order of preference are green on white, red on white, blue on white, white on blue and finally black on white.

The color of light can be used to increase contrast by either intensifying or subduing certain colors inherent in the seeing task. To intensify a color, the light source should be strong in that color; to subdue a color the source should have relatively low output in it. For example, it has been found that imperfections in chromium plating over nickel plating can be emphasized by using a bluish light such as a daylight fluorescent lamp.

Three-dimensional objects are seen in their apparent shapes because of the shadows and highlights resulting from certain directional components of light. This directional effect is particularly useful in emphasizing texture and defects on uneven surfaces. See figure 20-10.

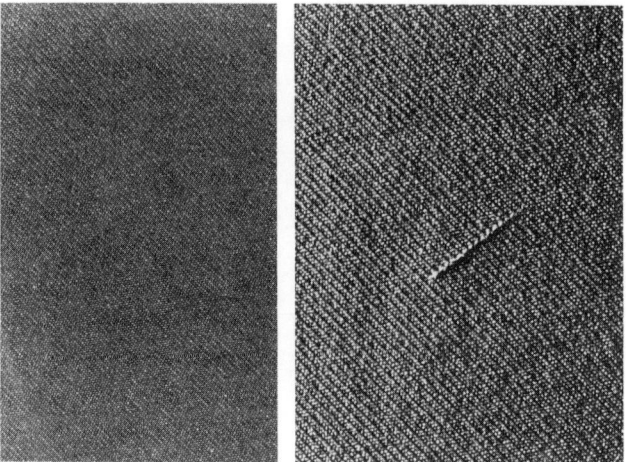

Fig. 20-10. Directional lighting (right) reveals a pulled thread unseen by diffuse lighting (left).

Silhouette is an effective means of checking contour with a standard template. Illumination behind the template will show brightness where there is a difference between the contour of the standard and the object to be checked. Fluorescence under ultraviolet radiation is often useful in creating contrast. Surface flaws in metal and nonporous plastic and ceramic parts can be detected by the use of fluorescent materials.

The detection of internal strains in glass, mounted lenses, lamp bulbs and transparent plastics may be facilitated by transmitted polarized light. The nonuniform spectral transmittance of strained areas causes the formation of color fringes that are visible to an inspector. With transparent models of structures and machine parts, it is possible to analyze strains under operating conditions.

Inspection of very small objects may be greatly simplified by viewing them through lenses. For production work the magnified image may be projected on a screen. Because the projected silhouette is many times the actual size of the object, any irregular shapes or improper spacings can be detected readily. Similar devices are employed for the inspection of machine parts where accurate dimensions and contours are essential. One typical device now in common use projects an enlarged silhouette of gear teeth on a profile chart. The meshing of these production gears with a perfectly cut standard is examined on the chart.

It is sometimes necessary to inspect and study moving parts while they are operating. This can be done with stroboscopic illumination, which can be adjusted to "stop" or "slow" the motion of constant-speed rotating and reciprocating machinery. Stroboscopic lamps give flashes of light at controllable intervals (frequencies). The flashing can be so timed that when the flash occurs an object with rotating or reciprocating motion is always in exactly the same position and appears to remain stationary. There is a potentially dangerous stroboscopic effect produced by HID lamps and other sources which flicker on rotating equipment such as drilling, milling and lathe machines.

SPECIFIC INDUSTRY LIGHTING INFORMATION

Specific lighting recommendations have been developed through a consensus process for several particular industries. These recommendations are included here to give the lighting practitioner guidance in the unique requirements of these industries. While these recommendations have been supplied by those with special knowledge in their fields, they may well have application in other industries using similar processes. For this reason, even if the industry of interest is not listed here, there may still be valuable information under another heading that appears related.

AIRCRAFT / AIRLINE INDUSTRIES[9]

The aircraft and airline operations covered below consist of aircraft manufacturing and aircraft maintenance. The illuminance recommendations listed in figure 20-11 represent those established by aircraft/airline industry representatives and, in their opinion, may be used in preference to employing the illuminance selection procedure in chapter 11; however, values can still be determined using chapter 11 for similar tasks and activities.

Aircraft Manufacturing

Aircraft manufacturing consists basically of the following functions: fabrication, subassembly, assembly, final assembly, painting and flight test. The lighting problems encountered in the areas where fabrication is carried out are, in many cases, similar to those found in other manufacturing plants. Fabrication of parts and processing of materials is accomplished in open-bay, medium-height buildings, similar to structures used by other related industries. Assembly, painting and flight test functions are not necessarily similar to other manufacturing processes; therefore, special lighting applications are required in many instances.

Fabrication. Lighting techniques for many of the general fabrication and processing operations are covered under other headings in this chapter, such as machining metal parts and fabricating sheet metal parts. In aircraft manufacturing, these same machines and operations are used, but often for more precise work than in other industries. The problem of weight reduction in aircraft design has created many special operations in the manufacturing and processing of many parts, from minute ones to large metal skins.

An overall general lighting level is required for work areas, together with supplementary lighting for the most critical seeing tasks (see figure 20-12).

Subassembly and Final Assembly. This phase of aircraft manufacturing has special requirements not usually found in other types of manufacturing. The age of the airbus has necessitated the construction of hangar-type buildings with clear bay areas exceeding 26,000 m^2 (300,000 ft^2) and truss heights of more than 24 m (80 ft) from floor level. (See figure 20-13.) The lighting problems in buildings of this size are not confined to the engineering and design concepts but include the task of maintenance and lamp replacement. The use of either a system of catwalks or traveling-bridge cranes should be relied upon to allow access to the lighting units. In some cases, mobile telescoping cranes can be used to reach luminaires from the floor, but the heights involved and obstructions on the floor make this method of maintenance generally impractical.

One special problem in lighting certain tasks in assembly areas is that the lighting is designed to specific task levels as if the areas were to be completely open whereas in reality that is seldom so. The lighting from overhead systems is often reduced by large assembly equipment. Typical examples of such assembly tasks are riveting, bolting and hydraulic and electric work. They are all done in confined areas, and special or supplementary lighting usually is needed.

Exterior lighting for joining together large aircraft sections requires both horizontal and vertical illumination as well as lighting installed in such a manner that it will light the underside of the body and wings. Use of floodlights can give both components of light on the exterior body and also provide light to the undersides of the body and wings. Specially mounted luminaires or portable lighting is required to light areas such as landing-gear pockets.

Materials used in the wing-body join section are hazardous. The lighting for these areas must recognize this hazard and make the necessary provisions to prevent explosions. Portable explosion-proof work lights are awkward to use, require the use of explosion-proof cord and plug sets and are generally not very satisfactory.

Interior illumination of the body sections for the tasks required to install electrical systems, tubing controls, ventilation, insulation, floors and interior paneling and trim is difficult to achieve. General and task illumination is required to light the overhead, sides and floor. Temporary light sources must be rugged, be easy to move, have no sharp edges and be free of glare.

Fig. 20-11. Illuminance Values Currently Recommended by Industry Representatives for Aircraft Maintenance and Manufacturing (Maintained on Tasks)

Area and Task	Illuminance on Task		Area and Task	Illuminance on Task	
	Lux	Footcandles		Lux	Footcandles
Aircraft Maintenance					
Close up			Check, operate, pre-inspect, record	750	75
Install plates, panels, fairings, cowls, etc.	750	75	Install safety devices (lockpins-sleeves, etc.)	750	75
Seal plates	750	75	Drain tanks, relieve struts	500	50
Paint (exterior or interior of aircraft) where plates, panels, fairings, cowls, etc., must be in place before accomplishing	750	75	Remove any plates, doors, cowls, fairings, etc. required for precleaning	750	75
			Install protective covers and masking	750	75
Stencils, decals, seals, etc., where final paint coat needed before applying	750	75	Strip paint	750	75
			Clean	750	75
Final "fly-away" outfitting (trays, loose gear, certs, includes final cleaning)	750	75	Install personnel protective devices (sharp edge covers, people barriers, etc.)	300	30
Docking			**Preparation for dedock**		
Position doors and control surfaces for docking	300	30	Remove shoring	750	75
Move aircraft into position in dock	500	50	Remove workstands, ladders, etc.	750	75
Attach grounding wires and other safety equipment	300	30	Close aircraft doors and position control surfaces	300	30
Jack and level aircraft	750	75	Let aircraft down off jacks	750	75
Shore aircraft	750	75	Dedock	750	75
Position ramps, walk-overs and other work facilities and equipment	750	75	**Preparation for maintenance and modification**		
Systems deactivation and safety locks installed	750	75	Check, operations, recordings—required in dock prior to power shutdown	750	75
Removals—prior to power shutdown	750	75	Draining	750	75
Reposition doors, flaps, etc. after docking	750	75	Shutdown aircraft power systems	750	75
Maintenance, modification and repairs to airframe structures			Remove plates, panels, cowls, fairings, linings, etc., for accessibility	750	75
Jacking and shoring not accomplished during docking phase	750	75	Vent, purge, flush, etc., any tanks, lines, systems, etc., drain systems, drain and cap off not previously accomplished	750	75
Remove any carrier or energy transmission portions or systems	750	75	Precleaning prior to removals	750	75
Remove any linings, insulation, blankets, etc., to expose structure	750	75	Disconnect lines, cables, ducts, linkages, etc., required for accessibility	750	75
Remove any minor structures (brackets, clips, angles, boxes, shelves, etc.) that attach to, obstruct or cover up major structure to be replaced, modified or repaired	750	75	Remove components	750	75
			Install protective covers, masking, or devices	750	75
Remove any sealant necessary to expose structures	750	75	Dock cleaning and/or stripping required for inspection, later modification, maintenance and/or painting	750	75
Remove any major structural members (spars, stringers, longerons, circumferentials, etc.) that will be replaced with new ones	750	75	Sand painted areas	750	75
			Area inspection		
Install new structural members	750	75	Ordinary	500	50
Sealant installation after structural member adjustment, modification or repair	1000	100	Difficult	1000	100
			Highly difficult	2000	200
Install any linings, insulation, blankets, etc.	750	75	**Specialty shops**		
			Instruments, radio	1500	150
Prime paint exterior	750	75	Electrical	1500	150
Top coat paint exterior	1000	100	Hydraulic and pneumatic	1000	100
Modifications or repairs to systems			Components	1000	100
Install those carrier or energy transmission portions of systems previously removed which do not require modifications. (Elec. wires, hyd. lines, ducts, fuel lines, cables, etc.)	750	75	Upholstery, chairs, rugs	1000	100
			Sheet metal fabrication, repairs, welding	1000	100
			Paint	1000	100
			Parts inspection	1000	100
Modify any energy transmission or carrier portion of a system or add new ones previously nonexistent (Electrical, mechanical, liquid, pneumatic)	750	75	Plastics	1500	150
			System operations and functional checks requiring aircraft power systems activation to perform		
Repair any carrier or energy transmitting portions of any systems	750	75	Activate any aircraft power system	300	30
Post overhaul—ramp	50	5	Block areas for operationals	750	75
Predocking			Functional check of any system that prohibits other operations or actions within that system	750	75
Convert hanger to fit incoming plane	300	30	Operational or functional check of any system not a part of or requiring sequential accomplishment	750	75
			Test sequentially required operation of systems	750	75

Fig. 20-11. *Continued*

Area and Task	Illuminance on Task		Area and Task	Illuminance on Task	
	Lux	Footcandles		Lux	Footcandles
Aircraft Maintenance					
Release areas after operationals	300	30	Re-install components of systems that do not require a system check or ring-out before component installation	750	75
Nonpressure lube after operations	300	30			
Cleaning after operations	750	75	Install components requiring preliminary checks and ring-outs	750	75
System repairs after operations and close up preparation			Hook up systems (wires, lines, pipes, ducts, cables, etc.) other than rigging	750	75
Repairs after system operationals	750	75			
Corrosion treatment	750	75	Physically block areas for dangerous operations	750	75
Apply masking	750	75			
Painting and/or chromating	750	75	Rig cable systems that do not require sequential rigging	750	75
Removing masking	500	50			
Final inspections prior to close			Rig cable systems in step sequences	750	75
Ordinary	500	50	Operate any system for checking that can be operated from power source other than aircraft power	750	75
Difficult	1000	100			
Highly difficult	2000	200			
System restoration or new system component installation			Clear blocked area	300	30
			Reconnect lines to aircraft systems	750	75
Hook up any lines, cables, ducts, panels and insulation to be covered by later component installation	750	75	Install cavity or tank covers or plates necessary to filling	750	75
			Precheck before filling	500	50
Install any components previously removed that must be in place for others to attach to, or subsequent components which when installed would obstruct or cover	750	75	Fill tanks. Service or lube tanks, struts, accumulators, etc.	500	50
			Static leak checks	500	50
Paint	750	75	Pressure check systems from pressure sources external to the aircraft	750	75
Paint preparation and clean up	500	50			
Aircraft Manufacturing					
Fabrication (preparation for assembly)			General		
Rough bench work and sheet metal operations such as shears, presses, punches, countersinking, spinning	500	50	Rough easy seeing	300	30
			Rough difficult seeing	500	50
			Medium	1000	100
Drilling, riveting, screw fastening	750	75	Fine	5000[a]	500[a]
Medium bench work and machining such as ordinary automatic machines, rough grinding, medium buffing and polishing	1000	100	Extra fine	10000[a]	1000[a]
			First manufacturing operations (first cut)		
			Marking, shearing, sawing	500	50
Fine bench work and machining such as ordinary automatic machines, rough grinding, medium buffing and polishing	5000[a]	500[a]	**Flight test and delivery area**		
			On the horizontal plane	50	5
			On the vertical plane	20	2
Extra fine bench and machine work	10000[a]	1000[a]	**General warehousing**		
Layout and template work, shaping and smoothing of small parts for fuselage, wing sections, cowling etc.	1000[a]	100[a]	High activity		
			Rough bulky	100	10
			Medium	200	20
Scribing	2000[a]	200[a]	Fine	500	50
Plating	300	30	Low activity	50	5
Final assembly such as placing of motors, propellers, wing sections, landing gear	1000	100	**Outdoor receiving and storage areas**		
			Unloading	200	20
			Storage		
			High activity	200	20
			Low activity	10	1

[a] Obtained with a combination of general lighting plus specialized supplementary lighting. Care should be taken to keep within the recommended luminance ratios (see figure 20-1). These seeing tasks generally involve the discrimination of fine detail for long periods of time and under conditions of poor contrast. The design and installation of the combination system must not only provide a sufficient amount of light, but also the proper direction of light, diffusion, color and eye protection. As far as possible it should eliminate direct and reflected glare as well as objectionable shadows.

Luminaires are designed for hanging from the airframe or for floor mounting. Uniformity is difficult to obtain because of the limited space and the need to mount the luminaires close to the task location. This may require the use of several luminaires of lower wattage to provide the desired uniformity.

Aircraft Painting. Commercial aircraft painting is done in a hangar designed specifically for that purpose. The entire hangar, therefore, becomes a large paint spray booth. In view of this, the entire area in and around the aircraft is classified as hazardous, and all electrical systems must conform to the requirements of the National Electrical Code (NFPA 70) for areas of this hazard classification.

It is necessary that all surfaces of the airplane be adequately lighted for proper painting. This means the lighting system must provide both horizontal and vertical illuminance. The lighting must also be designed to reduce shadowing which may be caused by the painter and the necessary scaffolding used during the preparation, painting and inspection.

Fig. 20-12. Typical area for component fabrication.

Fig. 20-13. Metal halide lamps and skylights used in lighting for aircraft assembly and maintenance.

More time is spent in the preparation of the airplane for painting than in actually painting. Preparation includes cleaning, abrading and masking. Application of one coat of paint to a Boeing 747 aircraft takes less than two hours, whereas preparation takes about three days.

Color is critical, particularly in the painting of a commercial aircraft, where the color forms an integral part of the image of the airline. In order to achieve the finished color the customer expects, it is necessary for the lighting in the areas being used for color matching and color evaluation to render colors in a uniform manner. (For more information see chapter 4, Color).

HID luminaires, preferably utilizing a metal halide source, are recommended for the general lighting system in a painting hangar. The luminaire should have a wide distribution to reduce shadowing and provide adequate amounts of both horizontal and vertical illuminance. Louvered luminaires have been found to be effective in reducing glare and improving the environment for the painter. Mixing of metal halide and

high-pressure sodium sources is not recommended. Reflections of the source in the painted surface can be undesirable.

To aid in the lighting of the underside of the aircraft, it is recommended that light colors be used on all of the surfaces of the hangar, including the floor. Light reflected off the floor can be effective in lighting areas which are difficult to reach on the underside of the airplane.

It is common to raise the temperature and humidity in the hangar to aid in the curing of the paint. The ambient temperature at the luminaire mounting location can reach 140° F. The luminaire and ballast must be suitable for the temperatures to be encountered.

Flight Test and Delivery. Flight testing is the final phase of aircraft manufacturing and is conducted outdoors on concrete ramps and taxi strips. The mounting height is critical not only from the standpoint of adequate dispersion of light, but to provide clearance for maneuvering the aircraft and to meet National Electrical Code requirements for classified areas. It should be noted that in most cases aircraft have been fueled when reaching this phase of production.

The height of floodlight poles may be limited by the proximity of adjoining airfields, traffic patterns and maintenance facilities. Federal Aviation Administration Advisory Circulars should be checked prior to determining the location and height of poles.

Explosion-proof portable equipment may be required to provide supplementary lighting under wings and fuselage areas to illuminate access hatches and landing gear fittings.

Illumination of the interior of the aircraft is usually accomplished by energizing the craft's electrical system with external 400 Hz ground power and utilizing the cockpit and cabin lighting systems.

Aircraft Engine Maintenance. The maintenance of an aircraft jet engine consists of several tasks.

Disassembly. Turbojet and turbofan engines are designed to break into sections and subsections that may be separated or joined by three different basic techniques or variations thereof. These techniques are known as vertical assembly, horizontal assembly and combined assembly.

The design of the engine lends itself to dismantling into subassemblies, simultaneous operations and a proper sequence of operations to quickly reach those engine sections that will be needed first at assembly. Normally these will be the compressor sections.

Overhaul of Accessory Components. The overhaul and testing of accessories and components is a large enough operation to warrant a completely separate shop. The testing of the components involves several expensive test stands. In addition, the fire and explosion hazards present special problems in the planning of an accessory component overhaul and test shop.

Inspection. For engine maintenance, inspection falls into two broad categories: line inspection and parts inspection. Line inspection covers the quality of assembly and test. Parts inspection covers the serviceability of parts. Parts inspection is subdivided into two categories, generally called crack detection and table inspection. Crack detection employs the aid of magnetic flux and penetrant dyes or fluorescent particles to detect cracks and defects not easily visible to the naked eye. In general, table inspection covers the visual and dimensional checks required to determine the serviceability of parts.

Cleaning. The function of cleaning of engine parts for maintenance is to permit proper inspection to determine serviceability. At the present time chemical cleaning is the most widely accepted method. A pitfall in the selection of a good cleaning process is the tendency to assume that the process that makes the parts look the cleanest, brightest or smoothest to the eye is the best one. However, some processes, in achieving this look, may make the visual task more difficult by smearing cracks or leaving a crack or surface in such a condition that a fluorescent penetrant inspection is not possible.

Repair. The majority of the parts rejected by the parts inspectors may be returned to service after a suitable repair. The range of repairs and reconditioning of parts is such that a fully equipped overhaul shop will have a plate shop, a machine shop and a weld shop. Owing to the size of jet engine parts, large tanks, ovens and machine tools are required. However, except in the larger maintenance facilities, only a minimum of such equipment is needed.

Spare Parts. Beyond simply storing parts, spare parts supply has many related tasks such as procuring, recording, shipping, receiving and preserving them.

Marshaling. Marshaling is the term applied to the making up of the engine parts and subassemblies into complete sets prior to assembly. Usually the first marshaling area is located adjacent to the parts-inspection and minor-rework area where stock chasers and expediters hunt down missing parts, expedite repair work and procure new parts as necessary to make up an engine into assembly groups ready for subassembly.

Assembly. Assembly is like disassembly, but requires higher-quality workmanship and miscellaneous inspections and checks. In general, it can be expected to take about three times as many worker-hours as disassembly to accomplish. Probably the most critical assembly operation is the assembly and balance of the compressor and turbine rotors. In order to attain the desired freedom from vibration, it is necessary to weight blades to obtain an even distribution of forces in the disks;

statically balance disk and blade assemblies; and, finally, dynamically balance the rotor assemblies.

Airframe Maintenance Operations. Aircraft are designed so that maintenance work can be performed at different levels of complexity. The work is either inside or outside the hangar, and the aircraft is either jacked up or on its tires and may or may not require auxiliary electrical power. The overhaul consists of cleaning, disassembly for inspection, disassembly for replacement of parts, repair, replacement of parts, inspection, assembly and test of aircraft. Also, while the aircraft is in the dock for inspection, other work is done that falls within this time restraint. Such work includes component replacements, modifications and repairs of defects.

Disassembly. Certain work performed to gain access to functional parts of the aircraft is done so frequently as to be routine:

1. *Cabin.* Remove and overhaul (at "component shop") chairs, rugs, class dividers, curtains, galleys and toilets. On those items where a match fit is required, the items are tagged to facilitate reinstallation in the exact location.
2. *Fuel tanks.* Remove access plates from all tanks, and install purging equipment to purge fuel vapor from tanks.
3. *Structural inspection.* Remove plates and components as required to perform the necessary inspections.
4. *Engines.* The maintenance work required on engines is so repetitive that removal of plates and components for access is nearly a fixed routine.
5. *Paint stripping.* Although paint stripping is done primarily in conjunction with decorative painting of the airplane, some paint is protective only. In these cases, a paint-stripping operation may be performed to bare the metal for an inspection.

Maintenance, Modification and Repairs to Airframe Structures. Normally, the term "maintenance of structures" refers to protection from corrosion, removal of corrosion or replacement of decorative parts such as cabin wall panels. "Modifications and repairs" are a much more elaborate process. They frequently involve specialized shoring to support the structural members being worked on. Invariably, components and outer skin must be removed to get at primary structures. The modification and repair process usually involves either the installation of doublers to strengthen members or replacement of these members.

Modifications or Repairs to Systems; System Restoration; Installation of New System Components. The inspection of *systems* is somewhat different than that of *structures*. "System" refers to an aggregate of structures such as the landing gear system or the flap system, or to a larger entity such as the entire hydraulic system. "Structures" refer to the parts or components that make up these systems. Some system inspection tasks are performed before the system is disassembled, but usually the inspection is performed after all replacements have been made to the system and it is intact once again.

System Operational and Functional Checks Requiring Aircraft Power Systems Activation. After each system has been repaired and restored, it must be tested to see that it performs according to specifications. Such checks are called operational checks and almost always come at the end of the overhaul. While the operational check is conducted by a mechanic with an inspector controlling the test from the cockpit, several mechanics, stationed at strategic locations throughout the aircraft, observe conditions during the test. As the test proceeds, the observers report to the cockpit what is happening. During the test, adjustments may be made and lock fasteners installed to secure the system in proper operation condition.

System Repairs After Operationals and Close-Up Preparation. The successful accomplishment of system operational checks signals the end of the overhaul. At this point everything of major consequence has been done. Only cleaning up and the closing of access doors and plates remain. One significant operation performed at this time is the application of protective paint. This requires cleaning, masking, painting and removing masking, primarily performed on high-strength steel parts of the landing gear. Before closing of doors or plates, an inspection determines that no debris has been left in an area and that all wires are hooked up.

AUTOMOTIVE INDUSTRY

The automotive industry consists of many facilities devoted to parts manufacturing or assembly. Each facility is dynamic: processes and systems are frequently modified, added, removed or renovated because of technological changes and marketplace demands. The visual tasks at these facilities are dynamic, too: the product is frequently in motion. Thus, the visual tasks include the product, the manufacturing process, the process equipment and the transitions between work stations.

Several support activities involve visual tasks. These activities include, but are not limited to, maintenance, machine repair, tool and die work, equipment calibration, utility generation and distribution and construction work.

General, localized general and supplementary lighting techniques are used at automotive facilities. The selection, design and operation of the lighting systems are complicated, in part because of the many light sources and variety of lighting systems (particularly luminaires) that can be applied. Each system is unique in its design, application and operation. No single system is ideal for the full range of this industry's lighting needs.

High-intensity discharge (HID) lamps of 400- or 1000-W ratings can be used effectively to illuminate areas with high mounting heights. Fluorescent lamps are used by this industry primarily for task lighting. Care must be exercised in selecting the appropriate emergency lighting system for areas illuminated with HID lamps in order to respond properly to the delayed restrike time experienced with these lamps. For more information, see chapter 33, Emergency, Safety and Security Lighting.

Illuminance Levels. Recommended maintained illuminances for automotive parts manufacturing and assembly facilities are shown in figure 20-14. The values listed represent a consensus of industry representatives on the IESNA Automotive Subcommittee. Should designers or owners elect, they may use the procedures for selecting illuminances given in chapter 11.

Automotive Parts Manufacturing

The major operations-related seeing tasks and typical lighting systems are as follows:

Incoming Raw Materials. Raw materials are delivered to manufacturing facilities by truck or rail shipment. Both open-top and closed-top vehicles are used.

- *Seeing Task:* To identify the materials and correlate the material and shipping documents
- *Lighting:* General lighting with supplementary lighting for trailer or rail car interiors

Active Storage Areas. Raw materials are unloaded in the receiving areas by lift trucks or overhead cranes. They are transported to the active storage areas or directly to the production process by the same means.

- *Seeing Tasks:* To identify the materials (labels or markings) from the cab of an overhead crane or lift truck and to move the materials and deposit them at a designated location
- *Lighting:* General illumination

Parts Manufacturing Processes. Parts facilities manufacture several different products using many unique

Fig. 20-14. Illuminance Values Currently Recommended by Industry Representatives for Automotive Industry Facilities (Maintained on Tasks)

Area and task	Illuminance on task	
	Lux	Footcandles
Coal yards, oil storage	5	0.5
Exterior inactive storage, railroad switching points, outdoor substations, parking areas	15	1.5
Inactive interior storage areas, exterior pedestrian entrances, truck maneuvering areas	50	5
Elevators, steel furnace areas, locker rooms, exterior active storage areas	200	20
Waste treatment facilities (interior), clay mold and kiln rooms, casting furnace area, glass furnace rooms, HVAC and substation rooms, sheet steel rolling, loading docks, general paint manufacturing, plating, toilets and washrooms ...	300	30
Frame assembly, powerhouse, forgings, quick service dining, casting pouring and sorting, service garages, active storage areas, press rooms, battery manufacturing, welding area.	500	50
Control and dispatch rooms, kitchens, large casting core and molding areas (engines), machining operations (engine and parts)	750	75
Chassis, body and component assembly, clay enamel and glazing, medium casting core and molding areas (crankshaft), grinding and chipping, glass cutting and inspection, hospital examination and treatment rooms, ordinary inspection, maintenance and machine repair areas, polishing and burnishing, upholstering	1000	100
Parts inspection stations	1500	150
Final assembly, body finishing and assembly, difficult inspection, paint color comparison	2000	200
Fine difficult inspection (casting cracks)	5000	500

processes. The designer should refer to other sections of this chapter for major activities that occur in an automotive manufacturing plant: machining, sheet metal shops, castings.

- *Seeing Tasks:* A number of different tasks may be performed.
- *Lighting:* General lighting with supplementary lighting in areas or on equipment requiring increased illuminance levels

Parts Assembly. In many manufacturing plants, individual components are assembled into subassemblies (wiring harness, engine, transmission, leaf spring or carburetor). The assembly processes combine manual, semiautomatic and automatic activities.

- *Seeing Tasks:* To select, orient, install and fasten a component to the subassembly
- *Lighting:* General lighting with supplementary lighting added to specific work stations

Testing. Highly diversified and complicated procedures and test equipment determine compliance with design specifications for the many mechanical, electrical and electromechanical subassemblies. Testing activities are manual, semiautomatic and automatic.

- *Seeing Tasks:* To secure the subassembly to the test fixture; to make electrical or mechanical connections; to run tests and read gauges and meters; to perform mechanical or electrical adjustments as required; to complete test reports; to disconnect and remove the subassembly from the test fixture
- *Lighting:* General and supplementary lighting

Final Inspection. This determines if the manufactured part or subassembly is in total compliance with the design specification.

- *Seeing Tasks:* To visually inspect the part or subassembly for specification compliance and to ensure that all intermediate inspections and tests are satisfactory
- *Lighting:* General lighting with supplementary lighting as required to inspect the part or subassembly

Packing. Parts are manually or semiautomatically placed in boxes, metal shipping containers or shipping racks for shipment.

- *Seeing Tasks:* To identify the part and place it in a destination-designated shipping container or rack
- *Lighting:* General area lighting

Shipping. Parts are usually shipped to assembly plants or warehouses in enclosed rail cars and trucks. Lift trucks are generally used to load these vehicles.

- *Seeing Tasks:* To identify a shipping container or rack by part and destination and load it into the designated rail car or truck
- *Lighting:* General lighting with adjustable or portable supplementary lighting provided for the rail car or truck trailer interior

Automobile Assembly

The automotive assembly process is continuous and requires both general and supplementary lighting to illuminate the many difficult seeing tasks along the major portion of the assembly line. The maze of ducts, piping, supporting steel and conveyors around the assembly line reduces the effectiveness of the general lighting system. There are currently two methods of automotive assembly: (1) frame and body drop and (2) unibody.

Mobile assembly platforms and elevating assembly luminaires are beginning to be used in manufacturing facilities to increase productivity and to provide more comfortable working conditions for the employees. Lighting for these tasks must recognize these new assembly features. The major operations, related seeing tasks and typical lighting systems are as follows:

Frame and Body Drop Assembly

Body Framing Area. Metal parts are placed in large jigs or fixtures and automatically or manually welded.

- *Seeing Tasks:* Alignment of mating parts in jigs; welding and inspection of welding tips
- *Lighting:* Localized general lighting with luminaires positioned slightly behind the operator

Body Soldering Area. Joints (between welded parts), dents and scratches are filled with solder to give a smooth appearance to welded body parts.

- *Seeing Tasks:* To see all welds, joints, dents and scratches and to cover them with solder
- *Lighting:* Luminaires are positioned on both sides of the line and oriented above and behind the worker. Usually, luminaires are built into the exhaust canopy over this area.

Metal Finishing Area. Raw metal and solder are ground and polished to the desired surface contour.

- *Seeing Tasks:* To inspect all welds and soldered areas and to grind and polish to desired contour and smoothness
- *Lighting:* Luminaires are mounted parallel or perpendicular along both sides of the assembly line.

Body Inspection Area. The body is inspected to locate all metal defects. Defects are marked for correction so that when paint is applied, the surface will be uniform.

- *Seeing Tasks:* To locate and mark all metal body defects (dents, scratches and high spots) so that they can be repaired before painting

- *Lighting:* Illumination is provided along both sides of the assembly line. Luminaires are mounted at an angle with the horizontal to provide illumination for the hood, roof and upper vertical surfaces. Luminaires are also positioned to illuminate the lower vertical surfaces and quarter panels.

Body Repair Area. Defects that have been marked by inspection personnel are repaired.

- *Seeing Tasks:* To see and distinguish the various marks that identify the location and nature of the defect; also, to see that the surface of the body is smooth and uniform after grinding or polishing
- *Lighting:* Same quantity and quality of illumination as for the body inspection area

Painting Area. Paint is applied automatically and manually to all body surfaces.

- *Seeing Tasks:* To see identification marks so that paint of the proper color is applied; to see that paint is applied completely and evenly over the entire surface; to eliminate running and insufficient coverage
- *Lighting:* Luminaires are installed in spray booth walls and ceiling so that illumination is provided over all horizontal and vertical body surfaces.

After-Paint Inspection Area. The work is inspected for proper paint coverage and for defects not identified and corrected prior to painting.

- *Seeing Tasks:* To detect any irregularities in body surface or color and any insufficient coverage
- *Lighting:* Luminaires usually mounted at an angle, along both sides of the body and perpendicular to the assembly line. Luminaires should be positioned to enable inspectors to see defects by observing distortion of the reflected light-source image in the specular body surface.

Frame and Chassis Area. The frame of the automobile is started down the assembly line. The fuel tank, exhaust system and suspension are all assembled on the frame during this phase of the assembly operation.

- *Seeing Tasks:* There are no critical seeing tasks in this area. Parts are generally large, and alignment is usually all that is required.
- *Lighting:* General or local lighting

Engine Drop Area. The engine is placed on the frame, fuel lines connected and miscellaneous other parts bolted into position.

- *Seeing Tasks:* Large parts are bolted in place with hand tools.
- *Lighting:* Luminaires on both sides of the line, angled to provide horizontal and vertical illumination

Body Drop Area. The body is lowered onto the chassis and fastened into position.

- *Seeing Tasks:* The alignment of the body is a very important seeing task.
- *Lighting:* General and vertical illumination are required. The illumination must be sufficient to ensure proper positioning of the body and to bolt it in place with hand tools.

Pit Area. The body is bolted to the frame. Other operations on the undercarriage are accomplished by workers with hand tools.

- *Seeing Tasks:* To see that bolts are properly installed and tightened
- *Lighting:* Luminaires are usually recessed in the walls on both sides of the pit to provide light over the worker's shoulder.

Inside Trim Areas. Seats, head liner, instrument panel and other interior accessories are installed.

- *Seeing Tasks:* To identify proper positions and fasten seats, instrument panel, accessories and interior head liner
- *Lighting:* Luminaires are located along both sides of the assembly line. General illumination in this area will satisfy seeing requirements inside the automobile.

Final Inspection Area. The automobile is inspected for all defects (body and trim), so that repairs can be effected.

- *Seeing Tasks:* The most critical task is identification of body defects and surface damage which may have occurred during the assembly process.
- *Lighting:* Luminaires are installed above and to the side of the automobile so that all surfaces can be inspected. Inspection personnel spot body defects by viewing distorted reflected lamp images in specular surfaces.

Unibody Assembly

Underbody Area. Metal parts are automatically or manually welded to form the underbody.

- *Seeing Tasks:* Alignment of mating parts in jigs; welding and inspection of weld tips
- *Lighting:* Localized general lighting with luminaires positioned above and behind workers

Body Weld Area. Floor, side and roof panels are welded automatically or manually to form the vehicle body.

- *Seeing Tasks:* Same as for the underbody area
- *Lighting:* Same quality and quantity of illuminance as for the underbody area

Panel Line. Doors, lids and hoods are mounted on the vehicle body. Voids between welded parts are brazed. Minor metal defects are ground and polished to desired body finish.

- *Seeing Tasks:* Workers manually fasten panels to the body using hand tools. Voids are identified and manually filled using wire (mig) welders. Brazing and metal imperfections are finished to desired contour and smoothness.
- *Lighting:* Luminaires are mounted along both sides of the line and oriented above and behind the worker. Luminaires are normally built into the booth ceiling in the brazing area.

Body Inspection and Repair Area. The body is inspected to locate metal defects. Defects are marked for correction, and repairs are made before the body is sent for painting.

- *Seeing Tasks:* To locate and mark all body defects, distinguish the various marks that identify the location and nature of defects, and repair defects
- *Lighting:* Luminaires are mounted along both sides of the line and oriented at an angle to the horizontal to provide illumination for hood, roof and both upper and lower vertical surfaces.

Undercoat/Prime Area. The metal body is cleaned and washed, and the undercoat and prime coat of paint are applied.

- *Seeing Tasks:* To make certain that the undercoat and prime coat are properly applied
- *Lighting:* General and local supplemental lighting

Sealer Line. Soundproofing and waterproofing materials are automatically and manually applied.

- *Seeing Tasks:* There are no critical seeing tasks in this area.
- *Lighting:* General or local supplemental lighting

Masking and Prep Area. The body is inspected for defects in the prime coat, surfaces are cleaned to ensure smooth application of paint, and areas are masked manually.

- *Seeing Tasks:* To locate and repair imperfections in the prime coat, wipe body clean, and mask surfaces for proper paint application
- *Lighting:* Luminaires are mounted on enclosure walls and across open top of enclosures to provide illumination over all horizontal and vertical body surfaces.

Paint/Oven Area. Paint is automatically applied to all body surfaces with robots or bell applicators.

- *Seeing Tasks:* To make certain that the paint is properly applied
- *Lighting:* Luminaires are installed in spray booth ceilings and walls. (Luminaires are sometimes installed outside the paint booth itself, to reduce the hazard and permit the use of non-hazardous-rated luminaires.)

Paint Inspection Area. The work is inspected for proper paint coverage and for defects not corrected prior to painting.

- *Seeing Tasks:* To detect any irregularities in the body surface, color and coverage
- *Lighting:* Luminaires are located along both sides of the body and perpendicular to the assembly line. They are positioned so that the entire body surface is illuminated and inspectors can detect defects by observing distortion of the reflected light source image in the specular body surface. Special high-color-rendering lamps (5000 K) are used for color matching.

There is a growing tendency to prepaint parts in the automotive industry, and if this trend continues, it will have an effect on how painted parts are treated and inspected in the future.

Chassis Line. The gas tank, brake lines and suspension are assembled on the body. The engine is mounted

in place, and the hydraulic and fuel lines are connected.

- *Seeing Tasks:* Large parts are bolted in place with hand tools.
- *Lighting:* Luminaires are installed on both sides of the line and are angled to provide both horizontal and vertical illumination.

Trim Line. Seats, headliners, instrument panels, mirrors, tires and other interior and exterior accessories are installed.

- *Seeing Tasks:* To identify the proper positions, and fasten interior and exterior accessories into position
- *Lighting:* Luminaires are located along both sides of the assembly line and angled so they will accommodate the seeing requirements outside and inside the vehicle.

Final Inspection Area. Fuel, engine and transmission fluids are dispensed; the automobile is started and inspected for all defects (body and trim) so that any repairs necessary may be effected.

- *Seeing Tasks:* The most critical seeing task in this area is identification of body defects and surface damage which may have occurred during the assembly process.
- *Lighting:* Luminaires are installed above and to the side of the automobile so that all surfaces can be inspected.

BAKERIES[10]

Visual tasks in bakeries are not critical. Most hand operations are almost automatic with little attention to detail. General lighting systems provide adequate illumination for most functions; a few will need supplementary lighting. For selection of illuminance levels, see chapter 11.

Lighting is also an aid to sanitation, safety and morale.[10] Cleanliness, of great importance in all food-producing establishments, is much easier to maintain in well-lighted interiors. In bakeries a large part of production areas is occupied by trucks, racks, mixing bowls and other equipment. Adequate illumination can help prevent injuries due to congestion in these areas and enhance the safety of employees operating moving machinery, working adjacent to hot surfaces and handling hot pans.

Mixing Room. Flour, normally stored in bins directly above the mixers, can be weighed and sifted directly into the mixing bowl. Sometimes it is conveyed to scale hoppers located above the mixers. Standard dial or beam scales are used to weigh the flour, with meters to measure the liquid ingredients. Some mixing rooms have a side bench where additional ingredients are mixed and weighed. General illumination with vertical illumination on the face of the shelves is required. For vertical mixers, supplementary lighting should be provided to light the inside of the mixing bowl.

Fermentation Room. From the mixing room, bread dough or sponges are taken in large troughs (holding 550–680 kg [1200–1500 lb]) to the fermentation room, which is maintained at about 27°C (80°F) and 80% humidity. Since little attention is paid to the dough during fermentation, only sufficient light is required to ensure safe handling of the equipment. High humidity requires the use of enclosed and gasketed luminaires. Experiments have shown that ultraviolet radiation can control wild molds in the fermentation room.

Makeup Room. The dough is divided, shaped and panned preparatory to baking. Modern bakeries use production-line procedures. Operations are largely mechanical and require very little handling.

Proofing Room. During proofing the panned dough rises to its final shape. Local general illumination is required directly in front of the tray racks to permit a quick inspection of the panned dough. Because of the low ceilings in most proofing rooms, symmetrical, angular-directional luminaires or luminaires with asymmetric distribution can be used; because of the high humidity, enclosed and gasketed luminaires are recommended.

Oven Room. Ovens present a special lighting problem because (1) many of them are finished in black and white and (2) they are lighted on the interior by lamps with high-temperature bases in glass enclosures. The front of the oven should be illuminated to balance the luminances of the lighted oven opening so as to keep luminance ratios below 10:1. Luminaires must be mounted so that tray trucks placed near the oven mouth do not cause shadows when the oven is being filled or emptied.

Fillings and Other Ingredients. Preparation of fillings involves accurate weighing and mixing of various ingredients. Many ingredients are perishable and must be carefully inspected. Luminaires should be placed to provide illumination for cleaning the inside of the mixing bowl. For cooking fruit fillings, an exhaust fan and canopy are usually provided above the kettles. Auxiliary luminaires can be mounted inside the canopy to provide good shielding and to properly direct the light. Enclosed and gasketed luminaires protect the lamps.

Tables for fruit washing, cutting and mixing are normally placed near the windows. Venetian blinds or shades control outside glare for any workers who must face such windows.

Decorating and Icing. In many large bakeries, icing is mechanically applied to the products. The lighting problem is similar to that in the makeup room.

Hand decorating and icing, however, require greater skill and care. Because of the detail involved in hand decorating and the necessity for working rapidly, quick and accurate seeing is required. Lighting on the decorating benches can be best provided by industrial luminaires. Properly shielded fluorescent luminaires will minimize reflected brightness from the glossy icings.

If the operators are stationed on only one side of the decorating benches, luminaires may be placed above the heads of the operators and parallel to the benches. With this location, illumination of the vertical surfaces of the product will be improved and the slight shadows produced will bring out the detail of the decoration. Also, reflections from the highly reflective surfaces of the icing will be directed away from the operator. The luminaires may be tilted slightly toward the decorating benches if the benches are so located that a single lighting unit is not expected to illuminate more than one bench. If operators are located on both sides of the benches, the luminaires should be placed across the benches and between the operators.

The color of the light sources in the decorating and icing department should match that under which the product will be purchased or consumed.

Consideration should be given to heat radiation produced by the lighting equipment. It is important to avoid concentrated beams of light, and to avoid reflectors with dichroic filters when concentrated supplementary task lighting is required.

Illumination of Scales and Thermometers. Illuminated instruments permit quick, accurate reading of the graduations; however, one should be careful to avoid direct or reflected glare from luminaires or windows. See figure 20-15. Where local luminaires are impractical, suitable shielded spotlights are recommended.

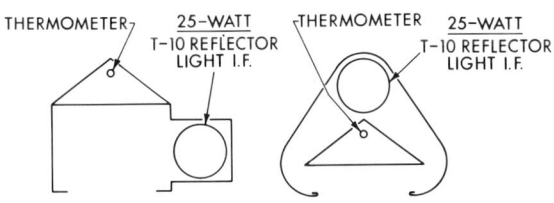

Fig. 20-15. Two suggested methods for illuminating thermometers. Care should be taken to dissipate heat away from the thermometers.

Wrapping Room. Wrapping is done by automatic machines. Interruptions may be caused by torn wrappers which clog the mechanism. General lighting expedites locating and removing obstructions and cleaning, oiling and adjusting the machines.

Germicidal (bactericidal) lamps can be used to control mold in packaged bakery goods.

Storage. A correct illuminance level promotes good housekeeping and tends to decrease storage losses. Because storage rooms frequently have low ceilings, attention should be paid to proper shielding of lamps. Correct placing of the units with regard to the bins and platforms is essential to prevent blocking light from the working areas.

Shipping Room. The finished product is delivered to the shipping room by tray trucks or conveyors. Shipping room tasks include keeping records, loading trucks and, in some places, maintaining and cleaning the trucks.

Truck Platform. Truck bodies are enclosed and are loaded from the rear door. It is necessary to use appropriately located angle or projector equipment permanently attached to walls, columns or other facilities to provide adequate seeing within the truck body. Sufficient illumination is necessary in the garage for cleaning the trucks.

CARGO HANDLING AND PORT SHIPPING

The pertinent areas and seeing tasks peculiar to port shipping facilities are described below along with suggested specific general lighting recommendations. The recommendations are based upon a study of existing installations and practices and represent a consensus of the members of the IESNA Cargo Handling and Port Shipping Subcommittee. Areas considered common to the shipping industry and other manufacturing operations are not included.

Port Cargo Handling Facilities

Port cargo handling facilities can be classified by type and divided into general areas which have different seeing tasks. By separately considering each type of facility, and by further breaking down each type into areas involving specialized seeing tasks, specific illuminances that cover most variations can be recommended.

Many port areas are used for one type of cargo handling only—such as containers, bulk or automobiles—while other port areas may be used for a combination of operations.

Types of Facilities

Bulk Cargo. These commodities are received by truck or rail for loading aboard ship or are discharged from the ship, using cargo handling devices that include dump pits, rail car shakers and rotating dumpers, suction devices, conveyor systems, gantry cranes fed by conveyors through pouring spouts, or clamshell or magnet cranes.

Container / Automobile. This cargo is received by truck or rail for loading aboard ship or is discharged from the ship, using bridge-type ramps.

General Cargo. This class includes all types of cargo such as break bulk (small packages, boxes, bagged), packaged lumber and steel products, palletized loads, refrigerated cargoes not in containers, machinery, and similar cargoes not specifically defined.

Oil Transfer Terminals. In the United States, illumination requirements for these facilities are provided by the U.S. Department of Transportation (Coast Guard–enforced regulations) under 33 CFR 126.

Areas of Operation

Facility Entrance. A controlled or designated entrance or exit, such as locations where pedestrians or vehicle traffic have access to the facility.

Open Dock / Storage Yard. An area where cargo is placed prior to loading or after discharge from the ship. Includes traffic lanes and means of access to the dock area adjacent to the ship.

Front (Dock Adjacent to Ship, High Line). The location where cargo is landed from the ship or placed for hoisting/driving aboard the ship.

Transit Shed / Stuffing Station. An indoor cargo storage facility used prior to loading or after discharge for the receiving and delivering of cargo.

Employee Parking. A designated area that may be located within the facility or immediately outside the facility entrance.

Low Line. An area, usually on landside of a transit shed, with a truck loading dock.

Dumping Pit. Where bulk commodities are received from rail hopper cars or trucks, either by bottom drop, rotary dumping, scoop, clamshell or magnet.

Conveyor Transfer System. A system that moves and piles bulk commodities using endless belts, pockets or scoops.

Safety

Figure 20-16 lists the minimum illuminances required for safety in cargo handling and port shipping areas. To assure these values are maintained, higher initial illuminances must be provided as required by the maintenance conditions. In those areas which do not have fixed lighting, local illumination needs to be pro-

Fig. 20-16. Categorization of Port Cargo Handling and Shipping Facilities with Recommended Illuminances for Safety*

Area*	Activity	IESNA class	Illuminance	
			lux	footcandles
General cargo				
Employee parking	Pedestrian traffic, security	Slight hazard / low activity	5	0.5
Facility entrance	Pedestrian access, traffic control, security	Slight hazard / low activity	5	0.5
Open dock area	Equipment operator moving cargo with machine. Dockman piling cargo, setting blocks, etc.	Slight hazard / low activity	5	0.5
Transit shed	Placing cargo, piling cargo, building loads, hand handling	Slight hazard / high activity	10	1.0
Front	Landing / hoisting loads, equipment operators, frontman	Slight hazard / high activity	10	1.0
Transit shed	Inactive, security only	Slight hazard / low activity	5	0.5
Low line	Receiving / delivering of cargo from trucks, rail cars	Slight hazard / low activity	5	0.5
Container / automobile				
Employee parking	Pedestrian access, security	Slight hazard / low activity	5	0.5
Facility entrance	Truck traffic, pedestrian walkways, weighing scales, security	Slight hazard / high activity	10	1.0
Storage yard, open dock	Equipment operator moving cargo	Slight hazard / low avtivity	5	0.5
Transit shed / stuffing station	Loading / discharging containers, piling cargo, equipment operations	Slight hazard / high activity	10	1.0
Front / container—wharf	Landing / hoisting cargo, securing / releasing chassis devices, pedestrian vehicle traffic	High hazard / high activity	50	5.0
Front / automobile	(Same as front / container)	High hazard / low activity	20	2.0
Walkways through traffic lanes	Pedestrian traffic, vehicle operations	Slight hazard / low activity	5	0.5
Perimeter walkways	Pedestrian foot traffic, security	Slight hazard / low activity	5	0.5
Transit shed / stuffing station	Inactive, security only	Slight hazard / low activity	5	0.5
Bulk cargo				
Employee parking	Pedestrian traffic, security	Slight hazard / low activity	5	0.5
Facility entrance	Pedestrian access, traffic control security	Slight hazard / low activity	5	0.5
Open dock area	Moving rail cars, truck dump traffic	Slight hazard / low activity	5	0.5
Dumping pit	Opening hoppers, rotary and shaking operations	Slight hazard / high activity	10	1.0
Conveyor system point of operation / transfer	Observing flow of cargo, control belt system	Slight hazard / low activity	5	0.5

* In areas not defined, or where IESNA hazard class does not agree with an operation or activity, refer to chapter 33, Emergency, Safety and Security Lighting.

vided during occupancy, either by portable luminaires or by luminaires mounted on material-handling or other vehicles. A visually safe installation must also be free of excessive glare and of uncontrolled large differences in luminances within the area.

Tasks

The following is a description of the tasks performed by workers in general cargo and container operation facilities. These descriptions may be helpful in determining illuminance values for design purposes when using the illuminance selection procedure in chapter 11.

General Cargo

Frontman. The frontman's function includes securing and removing stevedore gear to vessels' hoisting equipment or cranes, using shackles and hooks; landing cargo or slinging cargo; placing hooks, bridles, clamps and slings to hoist cargo or removing them from loads. Work is performed in the vicinity of fork lifts, tow tractors, pipe trucks and other vehicles which serve the front.

Dockman. The dockman's duties include placing blocks, cones and stickers for landing loads from fork lifts and shed or open dock storage areas; manually handles cargo in palletizing or sorting; working directly with fork lift operators; and loading and unloading rail cars. The size of the objects varies.

Combination Lift Driver. This employee is an equipment operator for fork lifts, Ross carriers, tow tractors and other miscellaneous haulage equipment, ranging from small to very large. The driver picks up and transports cargo in terminals and shed areas, driving in forward and reverse; often carries wide and bulky objects which impair visibility; and must maneuver in close quarters and coordinate vehicle handling with other equipment operators and personnel working on foot. The equipment is operated at low speed. It is not usually provided with driving lights.

Clerk. This employee performs seeing tasks related to the paperwork necessary to cargo documentation. It involves the reading of lot numbers, seals and other identifying marks on cargo and cargo packaging, and directing equipment operators to the proper locations for the pickup and delivery of such cargo. The task requires being able to properly read all types of documentation, including computer printout and carbon copies. This employee works in the vicinity of equipment operators and is required to make written notations and pencil and chalk marks.

Foreman. This employee is responsible for the supervision of other employees, handles paperwork pertaining to payrolls and hatch logs, is responsible for utilization of testing equipment such as carbon monoxers, and must be able to observe all operations.

Security Officer. The security officer is responsible for security and traffic control in longshore operations. Duties may include vehicle, bicycle and foot patrols; handling cargo or other objects in addition to a clipboard and keys; and working in the vicinity of other employees and equipment operators.

Container Operations

Dockman. The duties of this employee are to place and remove lashing materials on vans being hoisted to and from the vessel and to release and secure locking devices on the chassis in a truck-tractor operation. The work is usually located in the congested area on the front.

Semitractor Operator. This truck-tractor operator handles long chassis with loaded and empty containers by driving a yard hustler tractor. The required skills include the maneuvering of these large rigs in close quarters and within the traffic pattern established in container yards.

Straddle Truck Operator. The operator drives a piece of equipment located 3–9 m (10–30 ft) above the ground; handles large objects, such as long containers, with this machine; must locate and identify, by reading numbers, places within the yard and vans to be handled; and must operate in the vicinity of other employees and equipment.

Crane Operator. Crane operators handle a variety of container cranes; however, they usually are similar to a bridge-type gantry crane, either rubber-tire or rail-track mounted. They must operate from a height up to 27 m (90 ft) above ground, and are responsible for the safe movement of long containers around other employees and equipment and for the loading and unloading of chassis.

Clerk. The clerk generally operates a small vehicle and is responsible for the paperwork connected with receiving, delivering and loading of containers aboard ship. This involves the use of various documents and notations. The clerk is also required to maneuver throughout the yard, directing other operators to the location of their cargoes.

Security Officer. The security officer may be located at the gate entrance or be on roving patrol throughout the yard. Duties include security and traffic control within the yard, and involve both operating equipment and working on foot around other equipment operators.

Foreman. The foreman is responsible for the foregoing duties being properly performed as well as for doing paperwork and for maintaining testing procedures when necessary. The foreman is often provided with a small vehicle. The foreman works in the congested area around the crane, as well as throughout the yard.

ELECTRIC GENERATING STATIONS

Electric power generating stations may be classified by their types of primary energy: fossil fuel, hydroelectric and nuclear. This classification is convenient because while such spaces as turbine buildings, transformer yards and switchyards have similar lighting problems, the lighting in the various types of power production areas may be quite different. For illuminance recommendations see chapter 11.

Switchyards, Substations and Transformer Yards[11]

These areas are occupied by station transformers; oil, gas, vacuum or air circuit breakers; disconnect switches; high-voltage buses; and their auxiliary equipment. In addition, there often is a small building housing transmission lines and substation relays, batteries and communication equipment. Lighting outdoor substations presents a peculiar problem because the seeing tasks are frequently a considerable distance above eye level and the contrast varies greatly.

Two kinds of lighting are required: general illumination for the movement of occupants, and directed illumination for seeing fans, bushings, oil gauges, panels, disconnect switch jaws, high-voltage bus and other live parts.

Specially designed stanchion or bracket-mounted substation luminaires are available to provide the required upward lighting component, although floodlights and spotlights are often used. Because of their long life, high-intensity discharge lamps help to reduce the maintenance problem caused by the difficult access to lighting equipment.

Control Rooms and Load Dispatch Rooms[12]

The *control room* is the nerve center of the power plant and must be continuously monitored. Its lighting must be designed with special attention to the comfort of the operator: direct and reflected glare and veiling reflections must be minimized, and luminance ratios must be low.

Along with ordinary office-type seeing tasks, it is necessary to read meters, often 3–4.5 m (10–15 ft) away. Reflected glare and veiling reflections must be eliminated from meters, including those with curved glass faces.

While the practice is not standardized, most control-room lighting involves one of two general categories: diffuse lighting or directional lighting. Diffuse lighting may be from low-luminance, luminous indirect lighting equipment, solid luminous plastic ceilings or louvered ceilings (see figure 20-17). Directional lighting may be from recessed troffers which follow the general contour of the control board. (These luminaires must be accurately located to keep reflected light away from the glare zone.) Illumination for the rest of the room may utilize any type of low-luminance general lighting equipment.

Giving operators full control of illuminance levels through the use of multiple switching or dimming systems increases lighting flexibility.

Load dispatch rooms resemble control rooms and may be illuminated similarly.

Fig. 20-17. Control room of a nuclear generating station with a louvered ceiling.

Turbine Buildings[11, 13]

Turbine buildings usually have medium-to-high ceilings. Seeing tasks include general inspection, meter and gauge reading and pedestrian movement. Where there is detailed maintenance or inspection, higher-level portable lighting equipment is recommended.

In low- and medium-bay areas, high-intensity discharge or fluorescent industrial luminaires installed below major obstructions are appropriate for general illumination (see figure 20-18). If there are structural limitations, it may be necessary to use floodlights mounted on walls or platforms. Supplementary lighting is recommended for vertical illumination on such equipment as control panels, switchgear and motor control centers. Luminaires with an upward component contribute to improved visual comfort.

For high-bay areas (generally 7.6 m [25 ft] or higher) it may be appropriate to use either high-intensity discharge or fluorescent luminaires. Lighting continuity must be maintained during any power interruptions. See chapter 33, Emergency, Safety and Security Lighting.

Fossil Fuel Areas[11]

Fossil fuel plants (those which use gas, coal, oil or lignite) require facilities to receive, store and transport the fuel. Coal handling usually involves extensive outdoor storage areas. High-intensity discharge floodlights will provide the required illumination for stacker, reclaimer and bulldozer operations. Post-top luminaires often provide the light required for both pedestrian traffic and conveyor inspections. Crusher houses, transfer towers, thaw sheds, unloading hoppers and other enclosures usually require indoor industrial luminaires. Once these areas are classified, they should be lighted

Fig. 20-18. View of condenser well lighted from general lighting system in turbine room ceiling. Lighting layout keyed to special acoustical treatment of ceiling and light tile walls. Note visitors' gallery.

with equipment that meets the applicable provisions of the National Electrical Code.

Oil-fired stations have large oil storage tanks and many pumps which must be illuminated for inspection, and may have barge or tanker unloading facilities, whereas gas-fired stations usually have gas metering areas. Illumination for these areas should be provided by floodlights. It is mandatory to comply with the requirements of the National Electrical Code.

Boilers in fossil-fuel stations have a series of indoor and outdoor platforms. These platforms (and their associated stairs and landings) should be illuminated for safe pedestrian passage and for inspection of burners, pumps, valves, gauges, soot blowers, etc. Where no overhead structure is available for the support of general-purpose industrial luminaires, stanchion-supported luminaires may be used. The extreme heat associated with certain indoor boiler areas necessitates the use of luminaires that are designed to operate in high ambient temperatures.

Hydroelectric Stations[11]

The turbine building of a hydroelectric station, commonly called the "powerhouse," has lighting requirements generally the same as those previously outlined in the subsection on Turbine Buildings. Lighting of the intake and discharge areas, where applicable, is best accomplished with floodlighting.

Nuclear Stations[14]

The selection of lighting equipment for nuclear stations is often limited by factors other than economy or efficiency. There are extensive station areas, especially the containment building around the reactor and fuel storage facilities, where there may be a restriction on the kinds of lamps and metals used in the luminaires;

thus, luminaire and lamp selection should be coordinated with the appropriate authorities.

Emergency Lighting[11]

In certain areas, if the normal system fails, standby lighting is needed for the continued performance of critical functions and for safe building egress. Emergency lighting (see chapter 33) should be considered for control rooms, first aid rooms, turbine rooms, exit stairs and passages, battery rooms and emergency generator rooms.

In nuclear stations it is recommended that emergency lighting be provided in all areas subject to contamination, especially the decontamination room and laboratory area.

FOUNDRIES[15, 16]

The design, construction and operation of modern foundries have provided for improvements in materials handling and in dust control. It is common to find semiautomatic production conducted in a nearly clear atmosphere.

Although materials handling and atmospheric conditions have been improved, it is necessary to carefully select the following when lighting foundries:

- Proper light sources
- Luminaires with acceptable performance characteristics
- Luminaire locations that assure ease of installation and maintenance

Metal castings are made in a variety of sizes and shapes, from a few ounces to many tons. Some are made to very close tolerances, others require less accuracy. The lighting requirements for foundry operations vary with the required accuracy and the severity of the seeing task.

Melting, molding and coremaking usually involve equipment with nonspecular surfaces. Where such work is done in high-bay areas, high-intensity discharge luminaires may be installed without introducing reflected glare.

Maintenance may be minimized by the use of ventilated luminaires, or enclosed and gasketed luminaires. Some luminaires have filters which permit "breathing" but minimize the ingress of dust. It is prudent to install the least practicable number of luminaires which will provide the recommended illuminances.

Coremaking

Three general methods are used to form sand cores: hand ramming, machine ramming and blowing.

Rammed cores are formed by packing sand in the core boxes by hand or by machine. Core-blowing machines use compressed air to inject the sand into the core box and pack it tightly.

The most critical seeing tasks in coremaking are:

- Inspecting empty core boxes for foreign material or sand
- Inspecting the cores for such defects as missing sand or heavy parting lines

The severity of the seeing task varies with the size of the cores and with the degree of tolerance. Coremaking is a rapid and continuous operation which requires almost instantaneous inspection at frequent intervals.

Contrast is fairly good between light sand and metal boxes; it is extremely poor between brown sand and orange shellacked boxes or between black sand and black boxes. Contrast and seeing conditions may be improved by finishing the inner surfaces of wooden boxes with white paint.

Bench tops having a light, natural wood finish are both practical and desirable. They can be kept clean and will provide a comfortable visual environment with low luminance ratios. Benches lighted with ventilated, uplight industrial fluorescent luminaires provide good visibility. Centering the luminaires on a line above and parallel to the worker's edge of the bench will minimize reflected glare and shadows.

Molding

The visual tasks in forming molds from treated sand are:

- Inspecting the pattern for foreign material
- Setting the pattern in the flask and packing sand around it
- Removing the pattern and inspecting the mold for loose sand and for accuracy of mold contour
- Inserting core supports and cores (the operator must be able to see the core supports)
- Smoothing mold surfaces, checking core position and checking clearance between parts

The critical seeing tasks are:

- Inspecting the mold
- Placing the cores (and chaplet supports, if employed)

The size and detail of the seeing tasks may vary. The smallest task has a visual angle of about 10 minutes of arc, corresponding to the size of separate grains of sand. A defect involving the misplacement of only five or six grains of sand will cause imperfections in small

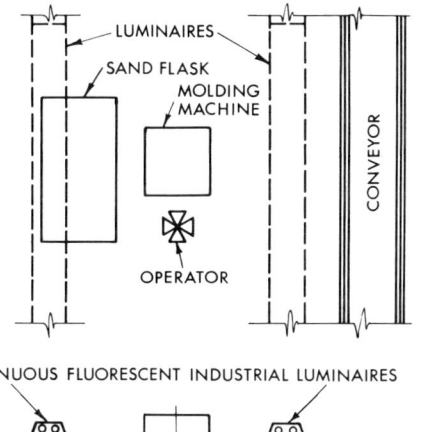

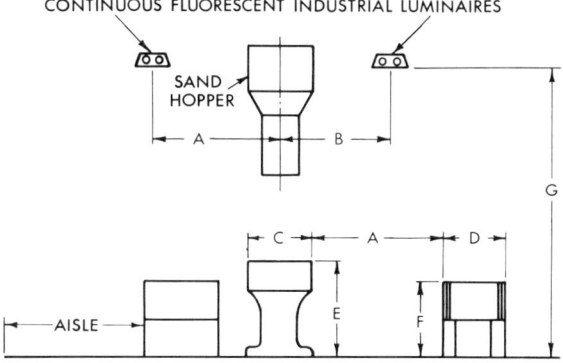

Fig. 20-19. Lighting layout for molding machines used for small castings. A = 1070(42), B = 910(36), C = 560(22), D = 510(20), E = 760(30), F = 610(24) and G = 2440 millimeters (96 inches).

castings. The more exacting seeing tasks are repetitive and of interrupted short-time duration.

Lighting should be designed for the intermittent, critical seeing of materials which have low reflectances and unfavorable contrasts. The varying depths of mold cavities demand adequate vertical illumination which does not produce harsh shadows. Figure 20-19 illustrates an example of good lighting practice for molding machine areas where small castings of 460 mm (18 in.) maximum dimension are made.

Deep pit molds require additional consideration in planning proper lighting. The walls of the pit may block some of the light from the general lighting system and result in shadows and lower luminance, especially on the vertical surfaces of the molds. The pit areas will benefit by the installation of additional general-lighting luminaires, located to avoid conflict with materials-handling equipment.

Supplementary lighting is sometimes recommended for locations where sand is supplied from overhead ducts and conveyors (figure 20-20); however, it is usually preferable to install a general lighting system which satisfies these requirements.

Charging Floor

The weighing and handling of metal for charging furnaces is a simple, nonexacting task; thus, lighting should be primarily guided by safety considerations.

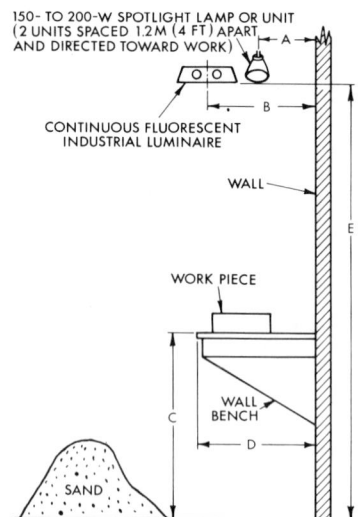

Fig. 20-20. A lighting layout for core or bench molding (wall area). A = 300(12), B = ⟨FT56⟩560(22), C = ⟨FT56⟩910(36), D = ⟨FT56⟩610(24) and E = ⟨FT56⟩2130 millimeters (84 inches).

Pouring

The most crucial seeing task in pouring is that of directing the molten metal into the pouring basin. If the flow is not directed accurately, splashing may occur and cause injury to the workers. It can also displace sand in the mold and spoil the casting.

Proper general illumination contributes to safety. The eyes of the workers often become adapted to the bright, molten metal contrasted with dark surroundings. This adaptation may cause difficulty in seeing any obstructions on a poorly illuminated, dark-colored floor. Adequate lighting reveals such obstructions.

To improve visibility within the mold, contrast is sometimes increased by placing white *parting sand* around the opening. When weights are used, the opening in the weight indicates the general location of the pouring basin.

Shake-Out

Castings are removed from the molds and freed of sand in the shake-out area. The most critical seeing task occurs during removal of the gates and risers. Where a ventilation hood is used over the shake-out grate, the latter should be illuminated with a supplementary lighting system.

Heat Treating

In malleable-iron foundries, small castings are prepared in annealing ovens. The primary lighting requirement is for safety and for the packing of castings (to prevent warping during annealing).

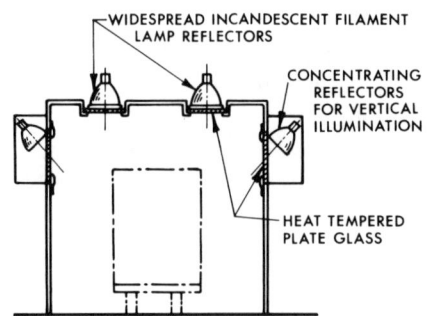

Fig. 20-21. Supplementary lighting for a sandblast house.

Sandblasting or Cleaning

Three methods are used for cleaning castings:

- Sandblasting in a blast room
- Sandblasting in a cabinet or on a rotary table
- Eroding by friction in a tumbling barrel

The principal tasks are:

- Handling castings
- Directing (manually) the sandblast stream
- Inspecting the castings to see that they are clean

Where workers wear goggles or helmets, additional lighting should be provided to compensate for the reduction in visibility.

The use of blast cleaning requires that the room general lighting be supplemented by luminaires which are mounted outside the cabinet but which project their light inside through tempered glass windows (see figure 20-21).

Grinding and Chipping

Excess metal is usually removed from castings by:

- Breaking off the greater part of fins, sprues, risers and gates with a hammer
- Chipping remaining projections with a hand or power chisel
- Grinding to a finish

Cleaning by a tumbling operation may remove all or most of the excess metal from small castings.

Grinding operators remove excess metal and fins from castings by grinding to a contour, to a mark or to a gauge. Protective glasses worn by the operators often become fogged, so that the seeing task becomes fairly severe. For stationary grinders, both general and supplementary lighting systems should be used. It is good practice to locate the centerline of the supplementary luminaires approximately 150 mm (6 in.) from the edge of the wheel on the side toward the operator. See figure 20-22.

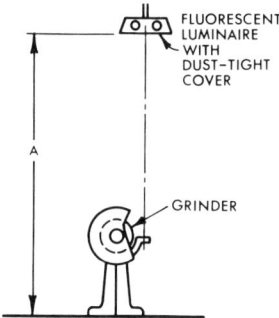

Fig. 20-22. Lighting for a stand grinder. Luminaire mounting height A is 2.1 to 2.4 meters (7 to 8 feet).

Inspection

Quality control depends largely on visibility. A casting meets the specified tolerances when:

- Patterns are carefully checked against the drawings
- Flasks are inspected for fit
- Cores and molds are inspected for size, accuracy and alignment
- Core clearances are gauged prior to mold closing
- Castings are checked against templates and gauges
- Surfaces are inspected and defective castings are culled

Inspections are generally conducted at intermediate stages during the manufacture of the product. The inspections at some stages are either combined with the functional operation or performed in the same area. The type of inspection will dictate the proper quality and quantity of illumination.

A typical inspection is that of cores by the core-maker prior to baking. Later, the castings may be inspected and scrapped by the shake-out handlers or by the grinder operators, avoiding subsequent waste of labor on defective parts. Small castings are frequently inspected and sorted simultaneously.

In sorting areas, a simple, general lighting system of ventilated fluorescent industrial luminaires may be mounted 1.2 m (4 ft) or more above the sorting table or conveyor. Atmospheric and maintenance conditions will determine the type of luminaires (open, enclosed or filtered) to be used.

For medium inspections, fluorescent luminaires may reduce reflected glare and improve diffusion of light. Medium-fine and fine inspection sometimes require special lighting equipment.

GRAPHIC ARTS AND PRINTING[17]

The graphic arts industry is one of the oldest. Its history includes that period when daylighting was a major source of interior illumination. Experience in the industry has shown, however, that a modern, well-designed lighting installation, excluding daylighting, has a beneficial effect upon quantity and consistent quality of work.

Receiving Area

The most difficult tasks in this area are those of reading markings on shipments, labels and bills of lading. General illumination will provide sufficient light for these tasks and for the operation of manual or powered forklift trucks, as well as for general traffic in the area.

Supplementary illumination may be necessary for the interior of transport carriers bringing material to the plant. Angle or projector-type luminaires may be utilized, but care must be taken to avoid glare from these sources. If the conveyances are deep, reel-type or other portable equipment may be necessary. Yard or loading-dock lighting should be installed for night operation.

Stockroom Area

Identification marks on the sides of bulky materials, rolls of paper, and crates or boxes require vertical illumination. Additional illumination should be provided over the aisles where high piles of stock interfere with general lighting.

Local building code requirements should be checked as to permissible luminaires for lighting areas where volatile materials are stored.

Copy Preparation Area

Functions preliminary to printing take place here (paste-up, layout, art and designing), as do decisions about point size and style of type, size and placements of cuts (pictures, drawings and charts) and size of page. Colors are specified (color work requires special lighting techniques; see the section on the Color Appraisal Area below). Well-diffused, glare-free illumination is essential.

Composing Room Area

In printing plants where type composition is by machines such as Ludlow, Monotype and Linotype, the operator uses a keyboard similar to that of a typewriter. General illumination from well-shielded luminaires with a good upward component is recommended.

Compositors performing manual tasks incur special lighting problems. In inspecting type, the visibility varies with the number of times the type is run (impressions made), its reflectance, and the contrast between its face and shoulder and between its spacing and size.

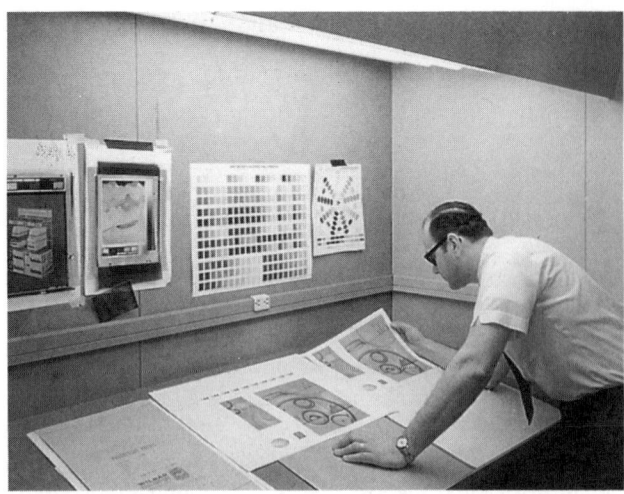

Fig. 20-23. Color appraisal area using a high color rendering fluorescent source.

Lighting should be provided by large-area, high-luminance sources. The high luminance, reflected from the shoulder, gives the necessary contrast between the mirrorlike shoulder and the type face. Research has indicated that the downward luminance of the large-area source should be at least 10,000 cd/m². Care must be taken to select and locate the luminaires to provide a well-diffused glare-free system throughout the composing room.

Proofreading is also done in this area. Well-shielded diffuse illumination is recommended.

Color Appraisal Area

In 1959 a joint report was prepared by the Illuminating Engineering Society and the Research and Engineering Council of the Graphic Arts Industry[17] to define a standard light source for the color appraisal of reflection-type material. In 1872 a more comprehensive report, incorporating the CIE color rendering system, was issued.[18] It suggests a light source (luminaire) with a correlated color temperature of 5000 K for appraisal of color quality and 7500 K for appraisal of color uniformity. Both sources should have a color rendering index of 90 or higher. See figure 20-23.

Plate Preparation Area

The visual task in this area is severe and prolonged. However, the galley (camera) area needs only enough general illumination for traffic. Light source glare must be kept away from the camera lens. Packaged lighting units for photography are usually furnished by the camera supplier.

Stripping and opaquing are done on a luminous-top table. The table design should provide good, low-luminance diffusion to assure visual comfort. Any part of the luminous area not covered by the negative should

be masked. General overhead, low-level lighting for traffic in this area should be so located as to eliminate table-top reflections.

Platemaking requires low levels of illumination. Higher levels are injurious to plates requiring extended processing. Colored lamps are frequently utilized.

Pressroom Area

The pressroom is usually a large, high-ceiling area (necessitated by the dimensions of the equipment), which reduces the utilization of light. The tasks can be divided into three groups:

1. Tasks with type for make-ready, register and correction of errors in both the proof press and the production press. Included are the movement of semifinished products from one press to another, the movement of finished sheets from presses to other departments, and the movement of raw materials to the presses.
2. Mechanical functions such as adjusting the presses, installing frames and cylinders on the presses, adjusting ink fountains for the inking rollers, and feeding the paper.
3. The inspection of semifinished and finished products. (If this involves color appraisal, see the section on the Color Appraisal Area above.)

General illumination is recommended, using a luminaire with good shielding and with a minimum 10% upward component.

Ink and drying compounds in the atmosphere make frequent maintenance necessary; therefore, ease of maintenance is an important factor in luminaire selection. Supplementary lighting is often required, and the need for it can be determined only by careful examination of the equipment. Low-mounted luminaires, tilted at an angle to penetrate recesses in the presses, may be necessary. Workers in this area need a large-area high-luminance light source (as recommended above for inspecting type).

Bindery Area

After printing is completed, if binding or any other bindery function is required, the finished product of the printing plant becomes the raw product of the bindery.

Practically all bindery production involves hand labor: collating, folding, stapling, stitching, gluing, backing and trimming pages. In many operations, critical seeing is not important, but speed is. Diffuse general lighting should be provided by well-shielded luminaires with an upward component.

In bookbinding, there are frequent additional operations which are more tedious and exacting, such as corner rounding, indexing, cover imprinting and applying gold leaf or gold ink. Additional luminaires (or closer spacing) are necessary to provide a higher level of lighting for these activities.

Shipping Area

The tasks in this area are similar to those in the receiving area, but include wrapping, packaging, labeling, typing and weighing. It is a more critical area than receiving because it is especially important to avoid damage to the finished product being sent to the customer.

LOGGING AND SAWMILL INDUSTRIES[19, 20]

The conversion of living trees into lumber involves two basic industries, the manufacturing of logs (logging) and the manufacture of lumber (sawmilling).

Logging, traditionally done during daylight hours, presents the worker with basically simple seeing tasks —the handling of trees and logs—with adequate time to see necessary detail. Some functions of the logging industry are accomplished under electric lighting.

Sawmilling has become a high-speed production process almost entirely under electric lighting. There is a wide range of visual tasks, from assessing the lumber content of logs on the mill log deck to discriminating fine detail under poor contrast as the log is broken down into finished lumber.

Since the seeing tasks in both logging and sawmilling involve viewing logs and lumber from the side as well as from above, a relatively high vertical illuminance component is required. In general, a 2 : 1 ratio of horizontal to vertical illuminance is recommended.

Logging

Yarding. This is the moving of logs from the logging area to the logging road. Logs yarded under electric lighting will have been felled, limbed and bucked during daylight hours. The general illumination must be adequate to enable the logger to move about safely over rough terrain covered with a confusion of logs and limbs. This general illumination will normally be provided by floodlights mounted either on poles or masts attached to movable platforms or trunks, or on the boom of the yarding machine.

Mounting heights in excess of 15 m (50 ft) are difficult to obtain in the usual logging operations; thus, the effective area of yarding is limited to about 180 m (600 ft) from the yarding machine or spar.

The general illumination must be supplemented by light from portable spotlights attached to the loggers' hard hats and by headlights and spotlights mounted on trucks, tractors and specialized yarding and loading equipment.

Loading. Loading requires adequate general illumination to enable the operator of the loading machine to hoist the logs deposited by the yarding operation from the landing to the waiting trucks or railroad flat cars. The illumination should also be adequate for the safe movement of men throughout the area and to enable the head loader to direct the operation efficiently. General lighting in the loading area is usually provided by floodlights mounted on the boom of the loading machine and on special poles or masts mounted on movable platforms or trucks.

Supplementary illumination, provided by portable spotlights attached to the loggers' hard hats, is required for strapping or chaining the logs securely to the trucks and stamping or painting logs and for general utility operations in the loading area.

Unloading. Lighting requirements for unloading are similar to those for loading. As in loading, the floodlight mounting height governs the lighting effectiveness. Both sides of the loaded truck or flatcar should be illuminated to facilitate the release of cable or chain clamps. Supplementary lighting mounted on the workers' hard hats will not normally be required.

Dry-Land Sorting. The sorting of logs as to species, size and grade on land rather than in water is increasing in popularity in the industry. The logs are usually sorted on a conveyor system which allows the operators to cut the logs to suitable lengths and to route them to stockpiles or *bins*, from where they are taken (usually by loaders) either to a log dump on the water or to a stockpile on land.

Floodlighting must provide adequate visibility for safe movement of workers using heavy loading equipment, and for releasing tiedown cable clamps. Seeing is most critical at the log-handling conveyor system, where the sorting is carried out at high speed. The sorting machine operator must be able to quickly recognize the species of a log and any major defects.

Water Sorting and Booming. The water sorting and booming operation starts at the log dump area where logs are unloaded, or dumped, from trunks or flat cars. Often a large crane is used to offload logs, sometimes as a large "bundle." Adequate illumination assists the crane operator and enables workers to safely release tiedown cables. Once the logs are in the water, they are moved according to species and size by boom operators or boom workers to specified storage areas and assembled into booms or rafts.

Lighting in the log dump, sorting and booming areas is usually provided by floodlights mounted on poles or towers at the shoreline or on dolphins in the water.

Following transport to the sawmill boom storage area, booms are dismantled and the logs moved to a sorting and grading area prior to moving up the log haul or jackladder. The seeing tasks in this operation are generally more critical than during boom assembly. Boom workers and boom boat operators must be able to quickly and safely recognize log species and spot cables and chains. Floodlights mounted on poles or dolphins should be located to minimize direct glare and shadows, and should provide relatively high illuminances in key areas where logs are graded and scaled or where cables are released from log bundles.

Log Haul, Side Lift, Log Deck. Seeing tasks in these areas involve recognition of large objects such as cables, pieces of steel or rocks (which could damage saws or equipment) as the logs move to the barkers and the head saw. The movement of the logs is accelerated on the log deck, requiring a higher illuminance for safety and productivity.

Debarkers. Bark is removed by rotating knives in mechanical debarkers and by high-pressure water jets in hydraulic debarkers. The debarker operator must clearly see all surfaces of the logs to determine when the bark is being removed effectively. Lighting will normally be provided by luminaires mounted on the mill frame, or on poles if the debarkers are exposed to the weather.

Sawmilling

Head Saw. Converting logs into lumber commences at this point. The head sawyer must see the complete log clearly and quickly while making decisions on the cuts to make in order to obtain the best use of the log. Illumination in both the horizontal and vertical planes must be adequate for quick recognition of major defects in the log. The seeing requirements for using either band or circular saw head rigs have been found to be more critical than for mills processing smaller logs using a gang saw head rig.

General Sawmill Lumber Processing Areas. Once the log has passed through the head saw, the large slabs or cants are progressively passed through the edger, resaws, trim saws, rough grading station and green chain. The seeing tasks are similar and involve the machine operators' high-speed recognition of lumber characteristics and defects. High luminance in both horizontal and vertical planes is required, particularly on the intake side of the machines.

Wastewood Collecting and Conveyors (Basement). Seeing tasks in these areas are generally less demanding and involve clearing blockages in conveyors and routine maintenance. Conveyor intakes to chippers require a higher illuminance to ensure safe working conditions and to enable the operators to feed material into the chipper.

Planer Mill. The planing or sizing and surfacing operation is usually located in a separate building, particularly if the rough-sawn lumber is dried before planing. The planing machine is often enclosed in a soundproof room because of the high-frequency noise produced by the planer heads. The lighting system should enable the operator to move safely around the planer, to spot imperfections in the planed lumber caused by nicked planer blades, and to do routine maintenance work during shutdown. A portable trouble light is often required for setting up the planer heads or repairing the machine.

Lumber Grading. Lumber is graded or sorted in the sawmill and the planer mill to meet quality standards established by the industry and grading agencies or to meet customer specifications. Usually, lumber moves past the grading station on a conveyor system at a rate of up to 30 pieces per minute. Graders must recognize a great number of defects in the lumber which, in turn, enable them to determine the correct class or grade of lumber for each board. The grader must be able to spot defects at distances of up to 7.3 m (24 ft) and must examine all four surfaces of each board.

Grading of rough-sawn lumber requires high illuminance, primarily on the horizontal plane. This will generally be provided by supplementary lighting and should illuminate a section of the conveyor system of 3-m (10-ft) minimum width for the full depth of the conveyor. Improved-color mercury, fluorescent or metal halide lamps in well-shielded industrial luminaires should be used for this system.

The grading of planed lumber requires high illuminance with a strong unidirectional component aimed at an angle of 20–45° below horizontal to enable the grader to quickly recognize surface defects in the lumber. See figure 20-24.

Filing Room. The primary functions in the filing room are the grinding or filing of the teeth of both circular and band saws, the grinding of planer or sticker knives, the swaging of sawteeth, and the leveling or truing of saws. The seeing task in sharpening saws or planer knives is to determine that the sawtooth or the planer knife has been ground to a sharp and accurately shaped cutting edge. The filer recognizes proper grinding by observing the reflection of the light source on the ground surrounding the saw teeth. Low-brightness luminaires (such as industrial units) are recommended to minimize reflected glare.

Fig. 20-24. Grading planed lumber under a combination fluorescent and incandescent filament lighting system. The incandescent lamps are mounted in a shielded trough, directing light on the lumber at an angle of about 20 degrees to accentuate surface defects.

THE PULP AND PAPER INDUSTRY

Papermaking is a technical process that utilizes highly sophisticated equipment in the manufacture of thousands of varieties of paper and paperboard. The process begins in scientifically managed timberlands where trees suitable for pulpwood are harvested, cut into short lengths and transported to the paper mill. The bark is removed from the pulpwood, which is then chipped into small pieces about the size of a quarter (2 cm). The chips are mixed with chemicals and then fed into pressure cookers called *digesters*, to soften the adhesive that binds the fibers together. After this cooking process, the cellulose fibers are separated and processed through several stages of washing, screening and, if necessary, bleaching to the required brightness. After further refining, the fibers are combined with pigments, dyes, sizing and resins, depending on the type of paper or paperboard required. This mixture, which is more than 99% water and less than 1% fiber and other solids, is now ready to be formed on the paper machine.

The mixture flows onto a moving wire screen on which the fibers mat, forming a continuous sheet of paper, and much of the water is drawn through the wire into collection tanks for recycling. Water-laden, the web of pulp passes through heavy rollers that press most of the moisture from the sheet. This sheet then proceeds over steam-heated cylinders to complete the drying process by evaporation. The paper or board is rewound into small rolls or cut into sheets, ready for shipment.

Illuminance recommendations for the various mill locations are listed in figure 20-25. These recommendations represent consensus values established by the pulp and paper industry.

Lighting Application by Major Mill Areas

Groundwood Area. Once the bark is removed from the logs, they are sent to the grinders to separate the wood fibers mechanically. The personnel working in the grinder area need an illuminance of 700 lx (70 fc) on the work platforms to enable safe movement for observation of hoppers and efficient shifting or handling of logs. The luminaires used in the high-bay, medium-bay, or low-bay areas should be industrial-type direct units or enclosed and gasketed luminaires designed for low-ceiling areas.

Brown Stock Washers. General lighting illuminance values of 500 lx (50 fc) should be provided in this high-bay area, using industrial-type direct luminaires. The process taking place in this area is generally carried on under hoods. It may be necessary to provide supplementary task lighting on the stock located under these hoods. This is usually accomplished by attaching incandescent reflector lamps to the outside of the hood enclosure and projecting the lamp beam inward onto the stock.

Soft and Hardwood Kraft Bleaching. Bleaching areas are highly corrosive. Luminaires in these areas should be enclosed and gasketed, and the luminaire finish and hardware should be corrosion resistant. The basement region of the bleaching area should be designed for an illuminance of 300 lx (30 fc), and the operating floor area should have 500 lx (50 fc).

Digester Areas. The operating floor is the most visually critical region in a digester area. An illuminance of 300 lx (30 fc) is recommended for this space. The ground or chip conveyor floor should have 200 lx (20 fc), and 100 lx (10 fc) should be provided on the inactive floors. Enclosed and gasketed luminaires with corrosion-resistant finish and hardware should be used, and upper-level luminaires should be rated for elevated ambient temperatures.

The Lime Kiln. A lime kiln is joined on one end with a mud filter and on the opposite end with a firing area. In all areas the recommended illuminance value is 300 lx (30 fc), and the luminaires should be enclosed and gasketed. The finish and hardware on each luminaire should be corrosion-resistant, and if the kiln area is covered, each luminaire should be rated for elevated ambient temperatures.

Paper Machine: Wet End. The wet end of the paper machine is high in humidity and temperature. Avoid placing luminaires over the fourdrinier wires and

Fig. 20-25. Illuminance Values Currently Recommended by the Pulp and Paper Industry

Area /Activity	Lux	Footcandles	Area/Activity	Lux	Footcandles
Indoors			**Power plant—interior (power boiler, recovery boiler, etc.)**		
Paper mill—preparation			Air-conditioning equipment, air preheater and fan floor, ash sluicing	100	10
Groundwood mill grinder room	700	70	Auxiliaries, pumps, tanks, compressors, gauge area	200	20
Beater room	300	30			
Brown stock washers	500	50	Battery rooms	300	30
SW & HW Kraft bleaching operating floor	500	50	Boiler platforms	200	20
SW & HW Kraft bleaching basement	300	30	Burner platforms	300	30
Lime kiln	300	30	Cable room	100	10
Color plant	1000	100	Coal handling systems	100	10
Digester operating floors	300	30	Coal pulverizer	200	20
Digester inactive floors	200	20	Condensers, deaerator floor, evaporator floor, heater floors ...	100	10
Paper mill—machine room			Control rooms:		
Paper machine room basement	300	30	Main control boards**	500	50
Headbox, slice, wire and press	700	70	Auxiliary control panels**	500	50
Working aisle	700	70	Operator's station**	1000	100
Roll dryer	500	50	Maintenance and wiring areas ...	300	30
Calender, reel, winder	1000	100	Emergency operating lighting	30	3
Rewinder	1000	100	Gauge reading	300	30
Mezzanines	300	30	Hydrogen and carbon dioxide manifold area	200	20
Paper mill—finishing, inspection, shipping			Laboratory	700	70
Coater and supercalender	700	70	Precipitators	100	10
Finished rool storage	300	30	Screen house	200	20
Cutting and sorting	700	70	Soot or slay blower platform	150	15
Trimming	700	70	Steam headers and throttles	100	10
Inspection	1000	100	Switchgear and motor control centers	300	30
Storage room or warehouse:			Telephone and communication equipment rooms	200	20
Inactive	10	1	Tunnels or galleries, piping and electrical	100	10
Active	50	5	Turbine building:		
Shipping railroad shed	50	5	Operating floor	500	50
Shipping truck shed	50	5	Below operating floor	200	20
Maintenance shops and stores			Visitor's gallery	200	20
Medium benchboard and machine work	500	50	Water treatment area	300	30
Fine benchboard and machine work	1000	100	**Outdoors**		
Instrument repair	750	75	**Roadways**	4	0.4
Electrical rooms	300	30	Parking lots	8	0.8
Heating & ventilating rooms	300	30	Log unloading	50	5
Laboratories			Log pile—active	30	3
Close work	1000	100	Log pile—storage	5	0.5
General	500	50	Conveyors	20	2
Services spaces					
Stairways, corridors***	100	10			
Elevators, freight and passenger***	100	10			
Toilets and wash rooms	200	20			
Locker rooms	200	20			

** Maximum levels — controlled system
*** Or not less than $\frac{1}{5}$ the level in the adjacent area.

presses. Most mills have a drop cover ceiling over the fourdrinier to help collect condensation that might form and drop into the wire area.

For lighting the high-bay paper machine operating floor, an illuminance value of 700 lx (70 fc) is recommended, using industrial-type direct luminaires rated for elevated ambient temperatures. Supplementary task lighting under the wire must be tailored to the job, depending on the equipment and mounting points available. Low-voltage luminaires are best suited for this task.

Dry End. The dryer section is the start of the dry end of a paper machine. Hoods are utilized to contain the heat, and only aisle lighting, from the ceiling area, is necessary. The use of industrial-type direct luminaires rated at elevated ambient temperatures with an illuminance value of 500 lx (50 fc) is recommended. Supplementary task lighting is needed inside the dryer hood. The luminaires used for this task must be carefully chosen to suit the high-temperature environment formed under the dryer hood.

The calender, reel and winder area at the dryer end is an active area and very dangerous. The use of industrial-type direct luminaires with an illuminance of 1000 lx (100 fc) is recommended. Avoid placing luminaires over the sheet of paper.

Rewinders and inspection stations should also be designed with an illuminance of 1000 lx (100 fc). Areas for coaters, supercalenders, cutting and trimming should have an illuminance of 700 lx (70 fc), provided by industrial-type direct luminaires.

Mezzanines. Auxiliary equipment (such as heating and ventilating equipment and pumps) are located on the mezzanines. An illuminance of 300 lx (30 fc) is recommended, and the luminaires providing this illuminance should be enclosed and gasketed.

Basement. Basements are usually very wet areas, and basement aisles are covered with pipes, trays, conduits, and heating and ventilating ducts. Luminaires should be located as high as possible: usually 2.5–3 m (8–10 ft) above the floor. These luminaires must be sufficiently high to be clear of fork lift truck traffic. Use enclosed and gasketed luminaires in wet areas and open luminaires in dry areas; an illuminance of 300 lx (30 fc) is recommended.

Power Plant. Power complexes need light primarily for maintenance. The tasks of inspection and operation are performed at only a few points, and these can be supplied with recommended illuminance values, varying from 500 lx (50 fc) in the turbine area to 300 lx (30 fc) for inspection work. General area lighting can be accomplished at 100–200 lx (10–20 fc).

Industrial-type direct luminaires are appropriate in high-bay areas, and enclosed and gasketed luminaires are recommended in low-bay areas. Ballasts must be rated for high ambient temperatures; this is especially true on the top levels.

Storage Rooms and Warehouses. Properly illuminated storage rooms and warehouses will help reduce product damage caused by fork lift truck drivers. Care must be taken to locate luminaires in the aisles well away from the paper storage areas.

Active storage areas and warehouses should have illuminances of 50 lx (5 fc), and 10 lx (1 fc) is recommended in inactive storage spaces. Storage spaces are usually high-bay areas using industrial-type widespread direct unit luminaires.

Additional information on lighting storage areas and warehouses can be found in the Warehouse and Storage Area Lighting section of this chapter.

Control Rooms. The most common luminaires used in control room lighting are sharp cutoff fluorescent fixtures. The placement of these luminaires must be coordinated with the control panels to provide vertical illuminance on the panel faces.

If video display terminals (VDTs) are used in control rooms, care must be taken to avoid reflected glare on terminal screens, that is, reflection of light from the sources by the surface of the control display into the operator's eyes. Indirect lighting systems provide excellent control of discomfort reflections and the veiling of display information from VDTs. In order to enhance the clarity of the visual tasks displayed on VDT screens, an illuminance of 200–400 lx (20–40 fc) is required. The fluorescent luminaires used to provide this illuminance should be dimmer controlled, or multiple-level switching should be used to allow the operator to adjust the illuminance.

Information that may be relevant to lighting control rooms containing VDT screens can be found in the *IESNA Recommended Practice for Lighting Offices Containing Computer Visual Display Terminals*.[21]

Woodyard. Most woodyards operate 24 hours a day. Closed-circuit television is used to monitor the barking drums, chip piles, and various other systems found in woodyards. Tower or high-mast lighting, usually 100 ft high, is the most popular and least expensive way to light a woodyard.

Minimum interior illuminances around the woodyard should be 50 lx (5 fc), and in areas where active equipment is utilized 200 lx (20 fc) is recommended. Careful placement of the luminaires to avoid glare in the operator's eyes is important. Supplementary lighting for areas that require higher illuminance can be mounted on buildings, structures, pipe bridges and conveyor supports.

Offices. For office lighting refer to chapter 15 and to the *IESNA Recommended Practice for Lighting Offices Containing Computer Visual Display Terminals*.[21]

MACHINING METAL PARTS[22]

Machining of metal parts consists of the preparation and operation of machines such as lathes, grinders (internal, external and surface), millers (universal and vertical), shapers and drill presses; bench work; and inspection of metal surfaces. The precision of such machine operation usually depends upon the accuracy of the setup and the careful use of the graduated feed-indicating dials rather than the observation of the cutting tool or its path. The work is usually checked by portable measuring instruments, and only in rare cases is a precision cut made to a scribed line. The fundamental seeing problem is the discrimination of detail on plane or curved metallic surfaces.

Visibility for Specific Seeing Tasks

Convex Surfaces. The discrimination of detail on a convex surface, as in reading a convex scale on a micrometer caliper, is a typical seeing task. The reflected image of a large-area low-luminance source on the scale provides excellent contrast between the dark figures and divisions and the bright background without producing reflected glare. The use of a near-point source for such applications results in a narrow, brilliant (glaring) band that obscures the remainder of the scale because of the harsh specular reflection and loss of contrast between the figures or divisions and the background. See figure 20-26.

Flat Surfaces. In viewing a flat surface, such as a flat scale, the seeing task is similar to that in reading a convex scale. With a flat scale, however, it is possible,

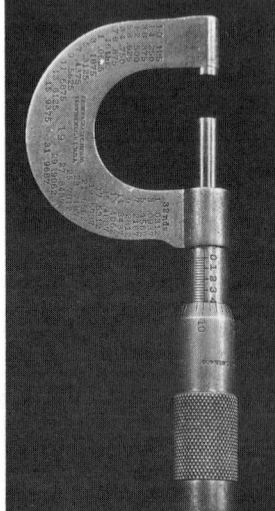 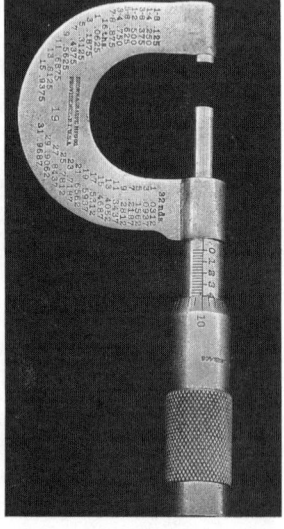

Fig. 20-26. (Left) Micrometer illuminated with a system of small, bright sources is seen with bright streak reflections against a dark background. (Right) When illuminated with a large area, low-luminance source, the micrometer graduations are seen in excellent contrast against a luminous background.

depending on the size, location and shape of the source, to reflect the image of the source either on the entire scale, or only on a small part of it. If the reflected image of the source is restricted to too small a part of the scale, the reflection is likely to be glaring.

Scribed Marks. The visibility of scribed marks depends upon the characteristics of the surface, the orientation of the scribed mark and the nature of the light source. Directional light produces good visibility of scribed marks on untreated cold-rolled steel if the marks are oriented for maximum visibility, so that the brightness of the source is reflected from the side of the scribed mark to the observer's eye. Unfortunately, this technique reduces the visibility of other scribed marks. Better average results are obtained with a large-area low-luminance source. If the surface to be scribed is treated with a low-reflectance dye, the process of scribing will remove the dye and expose the surface of the metal. Such scribing appears bright against a dark background. The same technique is appropriate for lighting specular or diffuse aluminum. In this case, the scribed marks will appear dark against a bright background.

Center-Punch Marks. A visual task quite similar to scribing is that of seeing center-punch marks. Maximum visibility is obtained when the side of the punch opposite the observer reflects the brightness of a light source. A directional source located between the observer and the task provides excellent results when the light is at an angle of about 45° with the horizontal.

Concave Specular Surfaces. The inspection of concave specular surfaces is difficult because of reflections from surrounding light sources. Large-area, low-luminance sources provide the best visibility.

Lighting for Specific Visual Tasks

In the machining of small metal parts, a low-luminance source of approximately 1700 cd/m^2 is desirable. The size of the source required depends on the shape of the machined surface and the area from which it is desired to reflect the brightness. The techniques applicable to specular reflections can also be applied to semispecular surfaces.

Flat Specular Surfaces. The geometry for determining luminous source size is illustrated in figure 20-27. First, draw lines from the extremities of the surface that is to reflect the source, to the location of the observer's eye, forming angle α. At the intersections of these lines with the plane of the surface, erect normals to that plane, forming angles β_1 and β_2. Project these lines to the established luminaire location to define the luminaire width; extend them in the opposite direction until they intersect, forming angle θ equal to angle α.

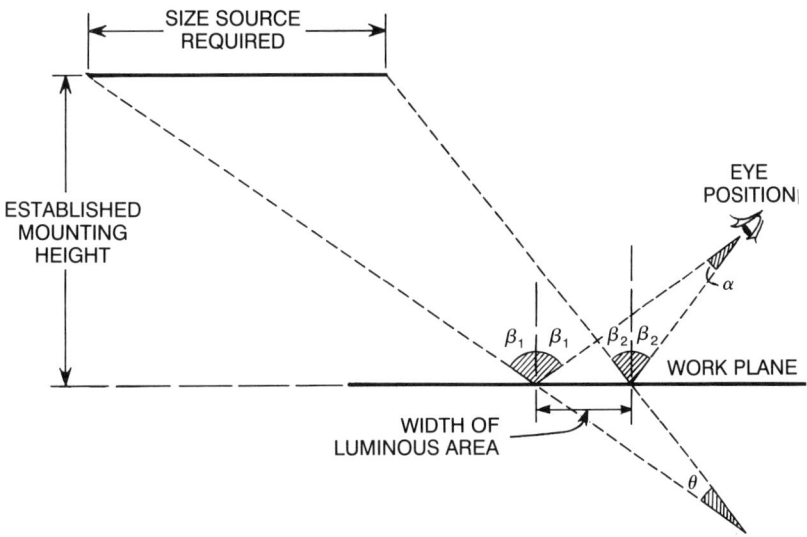

Fig. 20-27. Procedure used for establishing the luminaire size necessary to obtain source reflections on a flat specular surface. In the diagram, $\alpha = \theta$.

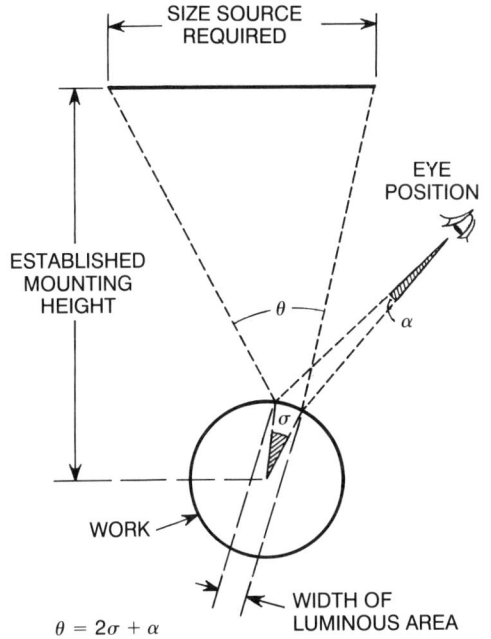

Fig. 20-28. Procedure used for establishing the luminaire size necessary to obtain source reflections on a convex specular surface. In the diagram, $\theta = 2\sigma + \alpha$.

Convex Specular Surfaces. The appropriate width of the luminous area of the convex surface is shown in figure 20-28. Draw lines from the location of the observer's eye to the edges of the surface's luminous area, forming angle α. Erect normals at intersections of lines with the surface.

At these intersections and on the other side of the normals, construct lines to form angles equal to those to the eye (the same procedure as that for flat surfaces described above). Project lines (as for flat surfaces) to

define the luminaire width. The same general procedure can be applied to concave surfaces.

General Lighting

There is a distinct advantage in the use of large-area low-luminance sources for most of the visual tasks in the machining of metal parts. The ideal general lighting system is one having a large indirect component. While both fluorescent and high-intensity discharge sources are used for general lighting, fluorescent luminaires, particularly in a grid pattern, are preferred by many specifiers for low mounting heights.

High-reflectance room surfaces improve utilization of illumination and visual performance.

MINING INDUSTRY[23]

The mining industry offers many diverse environmental conditions for lighting. Underground mining, surface mining and processing facilities are unique areas that present their own special lighting problems.

Underground mines contain miles of infrequently used haulage and travel areas as well as high-activity restricted work areas. The area in which material is being extracted from its natural deposit is a highly mobile one; it usually advances as the material is extracted and transported to the surface. Extraction is accomplished by drilling and blasting or by ripping the material with rotating steel drums laced with carbide bits. Extracted material is then loaded onto the haulage equipment, which is either rail, conveyor belt, water slurry, pneumatic or elevator, or by a combination, depending upon the mining conditions. The haulage equipment that bridges the distance between those permanent conveying installations and the advancing extraction work areas usually consists of diesel- or electric-powered vehicles or mobile conveyor systems.

Surface facilities include storage areas, loading points, maintenance shops, railroad yards, offices, bath houses and both elevated and surface walkways. The mined material is stored in silos, storage barns or yard areas. Transportation is usually via conveyor belts. Large buildings contain facilities to wash, size, refine, separate and process the mined material.

Surface mining is conducted in quarries, in open pits and by other types of stripping operations. Some of the equipment, larger than a house, consumes more energy than a small town. The operation may cover many square kilometers (square miles) of active workings, or it may be confined to the small area of a mountain ledge. Haulage is usually by large trucks with limited visibility or by overland conveyors.

Underground Mining

Illumination of underground mines involves many diverse areas that are covered in other portions of this Handbook. Some of the work areas in underground mining are the maintenance shop, electrical substations, track switch points, track loading points, pumping stations, storage rooms, loading platforms and battery-charging stations.

Providing illumination for underground work areas requires giving particular thought to worker mobility. In maintenance shops or medical facilities (where personnel are present for extended periods of time), standard lighting practices are appropriate. Areas such as track loading points (where personnel visit only a few times during a working shift) can be illuminated to a very low luminance level. Personnel are usually adapted to the luminance produced from their cap lamps when they approach a lighted work area (for safety it is critical that they experience minimum adaptation); hence, these areas should be illuminated to approximately the same level as provided by the individual cap lamps. In addition to maintaining an overall low illuminance level, care must be used in the selection of the luminaire. The mounting height may be restricted in many areas underground; therefore, a diffused, low-level light source is desirable.

Coal Mine Face Illumination (Coal Extraction Areas). Coal mine face illumination is applied to the most difficult lighting environment in the world. There are five distinct contributing conditions:

1. The low surface reflectance, usually less than 5%, almost eliminates secondary reflections and indirect lighting.

2. Mounting-height restrictions and job tasks place the luminaires in the workers' direct line of sight.
3. Suspended dust and water vapor cause backscattering which obscures task surfaces.
4. Mounting positions restrict the size, location and light distribution of the luminaires.
5. Luminaires must meet the safety requirements of the US Department of Labor's Mine Safety and Health Administration for use in hazardous locations (methane and air-and-coal-dust atmospheres).

These problems require unique lighting systems for each size of entry and for each type of machine being used in that entry. With the luminaires mounted at or below eye level, discomfort and disability glare present real problems and are dominant design considerations in any lighting system.

Typical entry dimensions are 1.5 m (5 ft) high, 6 m (20 ft) long and 6 m (20 ft) wide. Luminaire mounting positions are usually available only in the middle 2.4 m (8 ft) of the length (on board the mining equipment). Work tasks and safety hazards can be located anywhere and on any surface within the entry. The most difficult problems involve the low mounting heights and the varied positions of mining personnel in the entry.

One advantage in underground lighting is that most tasks (usually involving large tools or equipment) do not require the high illuminances that are needed to see fine detail. Also, many hazards in the face area involve equipment motion that can easily be detected at low illuminance.

Even though a lighting system has been designed and installed and has gained worker acceptance, the job may not yet be completed. The face can move 30 m (100 ft) a day and change in height from 600 mm (24 in) to 3.7 m (12 ft). Roof conditions can force a decrease in the mining width of an entry from 9 m (30 ft) to 4.3 m (14 ft). Lighting design must be flexible enough to adapt to the changing conditions and still provide minimum illuminances for safety.

Other Extraction Areas. The natural deposit of materials usually dictates the most economic method of mining. Salt, for example, is often found in large nodes or domes, which may result in mining areas hundreds of meters (feet) high and hundreds of meters (feet) wide. High-intensity discharge sources can be mounted in elevated positions to provide good general illumination. The high reflectance of salt helps to provide uniform lighting.

Other materials lie in horizontal, vertical or sloping veins. Each requires its own approach to mining and illumination. In many instances, only hydraulic or pneumatic power is available to generate electricity to operate the lighting system in the extraction areas. These power sources limit the design choices. The problems of maintaining very low illuminances, of restricted mounting heights and locations, and of utilizing luminaires with low brightness are thereby made more difficult, but remain no less important in lighting design for underground mining.

Surface Mining

Stripping Operations. Surface stripping involves equipment that operates 24 hours a day, six days a week. Illuminances must be sufficient so that tasks can be performed safely around the equipment and in the stripping area. If the work area is limited, high-wattage, mast-mounted luminaires can provide good general illumination. Examples of tasks in such an area are scraping topsoil prior to stripping or spreading topsoil during reclamation. The area being worked for either of these instances is limited, and general illumination will help in equipment control and contribute to general safety, especially with large equipment such as scrapers or trucks, or with machines operated in close proximity to each other.

Equipment. Large excavating equipment requires a variety of luminaires for safe lighting. Interior work areas should have heavy-duty, shock-mounted luminaires for general walkway lighting. Tasks should be accented according to the safety conditions surrounding the accomplishment of those tasks. In exterior work areas the lighting designer can use high-intensity discharge sources mounted on the equipment superstructure. These luminaires should also include heavy shock mounting. Pieces of large excavating equipment, including draglines, shovels and wheel excavators, are subject to high vibration during normal operation. Shock mounting will increase the life of the luminaire and decrease maintenance costs. This is particularly important on the booms of draglines and shovels, where high-impact loading on luminaires shortens lamp life.

Other equipment used in surface mining includes diesel fueled apparatus, such as front-end loaders, bulldozers, scrapers, haulage trucks and drill rigs. To supply high-intensity discharge lighting for these types of equipment, special inverter ballasts or rotary converters develop the required voltages. This equipment also requires shock-mounted luminaires for adequate lamp and luminaire life.

In lighting interior tasks in control rooms, general lighting may not be appropriate for gauges, meters and controls. In many instances, the operator has two tasks. One is to monitor the gauges and meters and to operate the controls; the other is to monitor the equipment operation outside the control room. An example is a dragline operator, who sits in the control room while controlling the operation of the bucket, which may be as much as 45 m (150 ft) away from the mainframe of the machine. Controls and indicators are usually self-luminous, and all interior control room lighting is subdued.

Surface Facilities

Interior. Surface facilities wash, crush, size, separate, mill and perform other processes on the mined material. These facilities are usually large, damp, dusty, noisy and subject to vibrations. Within the buildings are many support structures and large pieces of equipment that restrict light distribution. Luminaires should be adequate in number and in distribution to eliminate shadows that could cause safety problems. For ease of cleaning, moisture-proof and dust-proof luminaires will allow the use of water sprays during maintenance shifts.

Exterior. Exterior areas around surface facilities are used for equipment storage, mined-material storage, train and truck loading and unloading, travelways and conveyor haulage systems. Many of these areas require lighting for safety. Unloading areas, for example, contain open dumping pits, surge bins, crushers, belt feeders, conveyor belts and walkways. General lighting or specific task lighting can be used for illuminating these tasks and their safety hazards.

PETROLEUM, CHEMICAL AND PETROCHEMICAL PLANTS[24]

A petroleum, chemical or petrochemical plant converts raw material (gas, liquid or solid) into a usable product. At each plant there is some form of receiving and shipping, storage, removal of impurities and processing. It is common to find several different process units in a single plant. Frequently, several processes are combined in an integrated unit.

The modern plant is a highly automated, continuous process operation. Each unit is controlled from a local control house by one or two operators. A central control house may be used instead of unit control houses to operate several process units. It is apparent that there are very few people in a modern chemical plant.

The seeing tasks in the process units are reduced to very basic operations such as turning a valve, starting a pump, taking a sample, or just walking through a unit to sense some disorder. More critical seeing tasks require supplementary local illumination.

Most modern continuous process plants have preventive maintenance programs scheduled during daytime shifts. When unusual maintenance is required at night, portable illumination may be necessary.

Petroleum, chemical and petrochemical plants are restricted to the employees. Many areas are further restricted to personnel specially trained and assigned to the area. Most visual tasks are greatly simplified by sophisticated automatic control systems. Many areas require illumination only for the safe movement of personnel; many have only daytime occupancy and do not require lighting. Like electric generating stations, those facilities with continuous operation may benefit from information on the effects of light on circadian rhythms.

Most processes in chemical plants involve elevated temperatures and pressures and are designed for the continuous flow of vapor, liquid or solid from one vessel to another. Many of these materials are highly toxic and highly flammable. For these reasons, most process streams are contained entirely within closed piping systems and vessels. Outdoor luminaires are appropriate to such equipment and construction.

Illuminance recommendations are listed in figure 20-29. They represent those established by petroleum, chemical and petrochemical industry representatives and in their opinion can be used in preference to the general illuminance selection procedure.

Corrosive Areas. A variety of corrosive chemicals is generally present in each plant. Further, outdoor plants are exposed to the elements of rain, snow, fog, high humidity and salt-laden sea air. The usual methods to protect against these are to use metals that resist attack, special surface preparation, epoxy finishes, polyvinyl chloride coatings or nonmetallic parts. In addition to these protections, it is common to hose down an area. Luminaires should be selected that are protected against the prevalent corrosion.

Classified Areas. Some areas may be exposed to the release of flammable gases, vapors or dusts. The National Electrical Code[25] requires that these areas be classified and sets forth rules for the type of luminaire that may be installed. These luminaires must be approved for the class, group and division in which they are to be used. Improper application of a lighting unit can result in fire or explosion.

Classification of these areas within a plant must be made prior to selection of equipment. A general classification is shown in figure 20-30.

Designers should investigate the feasibility of floodlighting outdoor classified locations by locating nonexplosion-proof floodlights beyond the boundaries.

General Practice. Once the environmental conditions of classified locations, corrosive vapors, and other ambient atmospheric conditions such as moisture and temperature have been considered, task lighting follows accepted industrial practice.

The outdoor process unit, storage areas, loading and unloading areas and other areas can be effectively illuminated by combinations of high-wattage floodlights and low-wattage local luminaires (the latter for shadowed areas). The use of exterior floodlighting entails preventing light pollution or spill light that will cause annoyance outside the facility.

The industry currently uses high-intensity discharge lamps for process and other industrial areas. Fluorescent lamps are utilized in control rooms, switch rooms, shops and administration areas.

Luminaires within reach of personnel, or where exposed to breakage, should always be equipped with strong metal guards.

Outdoor Tower Platforms, Stairways, and Ladders. Luminaires should provide uniform illumination and be shielded from direct view of persons using these facilities. Enclosed and gasketed or weatherproof luminaires equipped with refractors or clear, gasketed covers may be used for reading gauges. Luminaires above top platforms or ladder tops should be equipped with refractors or reflectors. Reflectors may be omitted on intermediate platforms around towers so that the sides of the towers will receive some illumination and the reflected light therefrom will mitigate sharp shadows. If luminaires are attached to equipment, care should be taken to avoid damaging vibration.

Special Equipment. Special lighting equipment may be needed for such functions as illuminating the insides of filters or other equipment whose operation must be inspected through observation ports. If the equipment does not include built-in luminaires, concentrating-type reflector luminaires should be mounted at ports in the equipment housing.

Portable luminaires are utilized where access holes are provided for inside cleaning and maintenance of tanks and towers. Explosion-proof types (where hazardous conditions may exist) with 15 m (50 ft) portable cables are connected at industrial receptacles (either explosion-proof or standard) located near tower access holes or at other locations.

RAILROAD YARDS[26]

The lighting of railroad yards, storage areas and platforms is essential to personnel safety, to expedite operations, and to reduce theft and damage to equipment. Illuminance recommendations for these functions are listed in the illuminance selection procedure in chapter 11.

Because light is absorbed by moisture, smoke and dust particles, the amount of absorption must be considered even in an apparently clean atmosphere, especially when luminaires are located at a distance from

Fig. 20-29. Illuminances Currently Recommended by the Petroleum, Chemical and Petrochemical Industry Representatives

Area or Activity	Illuminance Lux (Foot-candles)	Elevation Millimeter (Inches)
I. Process areas		
A. General process units		
Pump rows, valves, manifolds	50 (5)	Ground
Heat exchangers	30 (3)	Ground
Maintenance platforms	10 (1)	Floor
Operating platforms	50 (5)	Floor
Cooling towers (equipment areas)	50 (5)	Ground
Furnaces	30 (3)	Ground
Ladders and stairs (inactive)	10 (1)	Floor
Ladders and stairs (active)	50 (5)	Floor
Gage glasses	50 (5)[b]	Eye level
Instruments (on process units)	50 (5)[b]	Eye level
Compressor houses	200 (20)	Floor
Separators	50 (5)	Top of bay
General area	10 (1)	Ground
B. Control rooms and houses		
Ordinary control house	300 (30)	Floor
Instrument panel	300 (30)[b]	1700 (66)
Console	300 (30)[b]	760 (30)
Back of panel	100 (10)[b]	760 (30)
Central control house	500 (50)	Floor
Instrument panel	500 (50)[b]	1700 (66)
Console	500 (50)[b]	760 (30)
Back of panel	100 (10)[b]	900 (36)
C. Specialty process units		
Electrolytic cell room	50 (5)	Floor
Electric furnace	50 (5)	Floor
Conveyors	20 (2)	Surface
Conveyor transfer points	50 (5)	Surface
Kilns (operating area)	50 (5)	Floor
Extruders and mixers	200 (20)	Floor
II. Nonprocess areas		
A. Loading, unloading, and cooling water pump houses		
Pump area	50 (5)	Ground
General control area	150 (15)	Floor
Control panel	200 (20)[b]	1100 (45)
B. Boiler and air compressor plants		
Indoor equipment	200 (20)	Floor
Outdoor equipment	50 (5)	Ground
C. Tank fields (where lighting is required)		
Ladders and stairs	5 (0.5)	Floor
Gaging area	10 (1)	Ground
Manifold area	5 (0.5)	Floor
D. Loading racks		
General area	50 (5)	Floor
Tank car	100 (10)	Point
Tank trucks, loading point	100 (10)	Point
E. Tanker dock facilities[c]		
F. Electrical substations and switch yards[d]		
Outdoor switch yards	20 (2)	Ground
General substation (outdoor)	20 (2)	Ground

Area or Activity	Illuminance Lux (Foot-candles)	Elevation Millimeter (Inches)
Substation operating aisles	150 (15)	Floor
General substation (indoor)	50 (5)	Floor
Switch racks	50 (5)[b]	1200 (48)
G. Plant road lighting (where lighting is required[d]		
Frequent use (trucking)	4 (0.4)	Ground
Infrequent use	2 (0.2)	Ground
H. Plant parking lots[d]	1 (0.1)	Ground
I. Aircraft obstruction lighting[e]		
III. Buildings[d]		
A. Offices (see chapter 15)		
B. Laboratories		
Qualitative, quantitative and physical test	500 (50)	900 (36)
Research, experimental	500 (50)	900 (36)
Pilot plant, process and specialty	300 (30)	Floor
ASTM equipment knock test	300 (30)	Floor
Glassware, washrooms	300 (30)	900 (36)
Fume hoods	300 (30)	900 (36)
Stock rooms	150 (15)	Floor
C. Warehouses and stock rooms[d]		
Indoor bulk storage	50 (5)	Floor
Outdoor bulk storage	5 (0.5)	Ground
Large bin storage	50 (5)	760 (30)
Small bin storage	100 (10)[a]	760 (30)
Small parts storage	200 (20)[a]	760 (30)
Counter tops	300 (30)	1200 (48)
D. Repair shop[d]		
Large fabrication	200 (20)	Floor
Bench and machine work	500 (50)	760 (30)
Craneway, aisles	150 (15)	Floor
Small machine	300 (30)	760 (30)
Sheet metal	200 (20)	760 (30)
Electrical	200 (20)	760 (30)
Instrument	300 (30)	760 (30)
E. Change house[d]		
Locker room, shower	100 (10)	Floor
Lavatory	100 (10)	Floor
F. Clock house and entrance gatehouse[d]		
Card rack and clock area	100 (10)	Floor
Entrance gate, inspection	150 (15)	Floor
General	50 (5)	Floor
G. Cafeteria		
Eating	300 (30)	760 (30)
Serving area	300 (30)	900 (36)
Food preparation	300 (30)	900 (36)
General, halls, etc.	100 (10)	Floor
H. Garage and firehouse		
Storage and minor repairs	100 (10)	Floor
I. First aid room[d]	700 (70)	760 (30)

[a] These illumination values are not intended to be mandatory by enactment into law. They are a recommended practice to be considered in the design of new facilities. For minimum levels for safety, see chapter 33, Emergency, Safety and Security Lighting.

[b] Indicates vertical illumination.

[c] Refer to local Coast Guard, Port Authority, or governing body for required navigational lights.

[d] The use of many areas in petroleum and chemical plants is often different from what the designation may infer. Generally, the areas are small, occupancy low (restricted to plant personnel), occupancy infrequent and only by personnel trained to conduct themselves safely under unusual conditions. For these reasons, illuminances may be different from those recommended for other industries, commercial areas, educational areas or public areas.

[e] Refer to local FAA regulations for required navigational and obstruction lighting and marking.

Fig. 20-30. Area Classifications (Based on the 1990 National Electrical Code)

Flammable	Flammable Mixture	Classification	Basic Type of Fixed Luminaire†
Gas	Normally hazardous	Class I, Division 1 *	Explosion-proof
	Occasionally hazardous	Class I, Division 2	Enclosed and gasketed
Dust	Normal	Class II, Division 1	Dust-ignition proof
	Occasionally hazardous	Class II, Group G Division 2 only	Enclosed and gasketed
Fibers or flyings		Class III	Enclosed and gasketed

* Group and temperature markings shown on the luminaire establish its classification.

† The terms *explosion proof*, *dust-ignition proof* and *enclosed and gasketed* are types of construction only. The Class, Group, Division and operating temperature must be known to select the appropriate luminaire.

For portable lighting units, there is only Class I or II; Division 1 listed construction is permitted.

the task or the task is viewed from a distance. For example, if the atmospheric transmittance were 80% per 3 m (10 ft) distance and the task were viewed from 30 m (100 ft), the illuminance on the task would have to be increased by a factor of 10 to obtain the same visibility as at 100% atmospheric transmittance.

Seeing Tasks

Railroad yards can be divided into general areas that have different seeing tasks.

Retarder Classification Yard. The large and often highly automated retarder classification yard, with its supporting yards and servicing facilities, presents a variety of seeing tasks.

Receiving Yard. Seeing tasks throughout the area include walking between cars, bleeding air systems, opening journal-box covers, and observing air hoses, safety appliances, etc.

Hump Area. Seeing tasks in this area are diverse. The scale operator and hump conductor are usually required to check each car number. Illumination on the underneath surfaces of the cars and on the running gear is necessary for inspectors' ready and precise inspection of a car that is in motion. There also should be enough light at the tops of cars to permit judgment of height. Personnel uncoupling cars should be able to see the coupling mechanism. The hump conductor, the car inspector and the car uncoupler should have specifically directed lighting of a higher level than that provided by the general lighting in other parts of the hump area.

Control Tower and Retarder Area. Modern retarder classification yards are computer controlled and equipped with various methods for determining car speed, "rollability," track occupancy, etc. These de-

vices automatically set retarders to permit a car to roll from the hump to its proper position in the yard without action by the control-tower operator. In other, less automated yards, it may be necessary that the operator check the extent of track occupancy, gauge the speed of the car coming from the hump and manually set the amount of retardation to be applied to the car. Even in an automated yard, the operator may also be required to do this manually in the event one or more of the automatic features fail. In many yards, the control-tower operator is expected to check the car number against a switching list and to see that the car goes to the correct track. Accordingly, it is essential that the operator be able to quickly and accurately identify the moving car. Under clear atmospheric conditions, it is therefore important that there be no direct light projected toward the operator (this may cover a considerable angle). However, under adverse atmospheric conditions (dense fog, for example) it is general practice to utilize auxiliary lighting equipment on the side of the tracks opposite the control tower to reveal the outlines of cars in silhouette. In this situation, the tower operator cannot check car numbers, but can observe and regulate the movement of the cars.

Head End of Classification Yard. The operator should be able to see that cars entering the classification yard actually clear switch points and clearance points so that following cars will not be impeded or perhaps wrecked.

Body of Classification Yard. Frequently, the operator must be able to see the body of the yard sufficiently to determine the extent of track occupancy. On some railroads, personnel are required to move along cars in the body of the classification yard to couple air hoses and to close journal-box covers.

Pullout End of Classification Yard. In this area, switchpersons are required to walk along tracks to determine switch positions and, if necessary, to operate them. Illumination should provide safe walking conditions along the switch tracks.

Departure or Forwarding Yard. Some railroads make up departing trains by having cars pulled from the classification yard into a departure yard. Here, minor repairs made to the cars avoid the delay of switching cars to a repair track. Air hoses may be coupled, journals lubricated and journal boxes closed, and any necessary tests or inspections effected. Lighting should be sufficient to permit work to progress with a minimum amount of auxiliary or portable lighting.

Hump-and-Car-Rider Classification Yard. The seeing tasks here and around the hump are considerably different from those in a retarder yard. Around the hump area, a yard clerk should be able to read car numbers. Cars must be uncoupled, and car riders must be able to see grab irons and ladders sufficiently well to climb safely onto the cars. Switchpersons along the lead track must have visibility adequate for walking safely along it and for operating switches. Car riders on any cars rolling into the yard should be able to see any cars on the track ahead so that they can brake adequately to reduce impact and prevent damage to lading. The rider must then be able to see to get off the car and walk along yard tracks to the hump.

Flat Switching Yards. The only seeing requirements in most of these yards are for safe walking by switchpersons around the switches at the head end and pullout end, and for pulling pins or throwing switches. A yard supervisor may also be required to read car numbers at the head end of the yard in order to assign cars to their proper tracks. A locomotive pushes cars into the body of the yard. In most instances, the locomotive headlight furnishes sufficient light for the locomotive engineer. Illumination is needed at clearance points to prevent interference with cars going to adjoining tracks. General lighting is recommended in the area of the switches at both the head end and the pullout end of the yard. If a supervisor must read car numbers, local lighting should be added.

Intermodal Facilities. There has been rapid growth in the hauling of highway trailers and standard containers loaded on special railroad flatcars. There are several types of rail equipment and several methods of loading and unloading the trailers and containers. Also, many railroads operate large automobile transloading facilities. Security lighting is very important at all intermodal facilities.

Trailer-on-Flatcar Yards. These areas include a ramp leading from the ground level up to the body level of the flatcars. To load the cars, each trailer is backed up the ramp by a standard highway tractor, then backed or pushed from one flatcar to the next until it is on its prescribed car, working from the back car forward; to unload, the process is reversed, beginning with the front car. Mechanized loading methods are used in most large facilities to lift and pivot the trailer onto or off the sides of the flatcars. When the trailers are loaded, most railroads use special tiedown equipment and methods to secure them for shipment. At most trailer-on-flatcar loading and unloading facilities, there is a parking area for trailers that either are waiting to be loaded or have been unloaded.

The tractor operator must be able to see to back up or drive along the tops of the flatcars, uncouple the tractor when loading, couple the tractor when unloading, and pull off. The trailers must be tied down to the flatcars when loading or unfastened when unloading. To do this, one must be able to see beneath the trailers at the tiedown points. Tractor operators must be able to see to back up and to couple a trailer parked in the parking area when preparing to load a trailer on a flatcar; likewise, they must be able to see to park and uncouple the trailer in the parking area when unloading. Clerks checking the yard walk between the trailers and must read the numbers on them.

Container-on-Flatcar Yards. In these yards, cranes load or unload demountable containers and trailers from flatcars. Usually, trailers are lined up parallel to a row of flatcars. A crane straddling both the trailer and the flatcar lifts the demountable containers or trailers and places them on the flatcar. There is usually a parking area for trailers at such intermodal facilities.

The crane operators must see to pick up containers (1) from any part of the trailer parking yard and place them in precise locations on the flatcars, or (2) from the flatcars and place them in precise locations on the trailers. In addition to general area lighting, local lighting from luminaires located near the top of the four corners of the crane should provide light on all sides of the vehicles.

Vehicle Loading and Unloading Facilities. Transporting automobiles on railroads is accomplished by using special multilevel railroad cars or vertically packed cars for small automobiles. On multilevel cars, automobiles are secured by a special tiedown. They are loaded or unloaded from ramps that move from track to track and that can be adjusted to different levels.

A vertically packed car has bottom-hinged sides that open outward to become a platform. The automobiles are driven or pushed onto the platform and secured by brackets on the automobile frame that engage hooks built into the platform.

Both types of loading and unloading facilities usually have areas for parking the automobiles. Security lighting is particularly important in these parking areas.

Lighting should be provided at the tiedown spots at each level. The drivers should be able to drive the automobiles on or off the multilevel cars, up and down the ramps, and to or from the parking areas. To reduce over-the-road vandalism, many automobile rack railcars are now equipped with sides. Special lighting may be needed for visual inspection to determine if there has been any kind of damage during shipment.

Lighting Systems

Two different systems of lighting are commonly used to illuminate railroad yards: *projected* (long-throw) lighting and *distributed* lighting. Each has its advantages under specific yard situations.

In general, the principles in lighting railroad yards are the same as those for other outdoor locations; however, it is necessary to observe railroad regulations with respect to the location of any lighting equipment above or adjacent to the tracks.

Projected Lighting System. The function of this system is to provide illumination from a minimum of locations throughout the various work areas of the yard. See figure 20-31. Advantages are:

1. Use of high poles on towers reduces the number of mounting sites.
2. The light distribution is flexible. Both general and local lighting are readily achieved. (Aiming of projectors, however, may be more critical.)
3. The projectors are effective over long ranges.
4. Maintenance problems are restricted to a few concentrated areas.
5. Physical and visual obstructions are minimized.
6. The electrical distribution system serves a small number of concentrated loads.

Distributed Lighting System. Distributed lighting differs from projected lighting in that luminaires are at many locations. Advantages are:

1. Good illuminance uniformity on the horizontal
2. Good utilization of light
3. Reduction of undesirable shadows
4. Less critical aiming
5. Lower mounting heights (floodlight maintenance is facilitated)
6. Reduced losses to atmospheric absorption and scattering
7. The electrical distribution system serves a large number of small, distributed loads

Security Lighting. Security lighting is an auxiliary to task lighting and is important in railroad facilities for reducing theft and vandalism. Two basic systems (or a

Fig. 20-31. A projected high mast lighting system using 1000 watt, metal halide luminaires to illuminate retarder area and head end of classification yard.

combination of both) may be used to provide practical and effective protective lighting: lighting the boundaries and approaches, or lighting the area and structures within the general boundaries.

Boundary lighting involves directing light toward approaching trespassers so that they can be seen by security personnel. This light also serves as a glare source that reduces the trespassers' ability to see; guards are not affected in the same way because the light comes from behind them.

RUBBER TIRE MANUFACTURING[27]

Illuminance recommendations for the manufacture of rubber tires are listed in figure 20-32 along with those for mechanical rubber goods. These recommendations

Fig. 20-32. Illuminance Values Currently Recommended by Industry Representatives for the Manufacture of Rubber Tires and Mechanical Rubber Goods (Maintained on Tasks)

Area and Task	Illuminance on Task	
	Lux	Footcandles
Rubber tire manufacturing		
Banbury	300	30
Tread stock		
General	500	50
Booking and inspection, extruder, check weighing, width measuring	1000*	100*
Calendering		
General	300	30
Letoff and windup	500	50
Stock cutting		
General	300	30
Cutters and splicers	1000*	100*
Bead Building	500	50
Tire Building		
General	500	50
At machines	1500†	150†
In-process stock	300	30
Curing		
General	300	30
At molds	750†	75†
Inspection		
General	1000	100
At tires	3000‡	300‡
Storage	200	20
Rubber goods—mechanical		
Stock preparation		
Plasticating, milling, Banbury	300	30
Calendering	500	50
Fabric preparation, stock cutting, hose looms	500	50
Extruded products	500	50
Molded products and curing	500	50
Inspection	2000†	200†

* Refer to local FAA regulations for required navigational and obstruction lighting and making.
† Obtained with a combination of general lighting plus specialized supplementary lighting. Care should be taken to keep within the recommended luminance ratios.
‡ Localized general lighting.

represent those established by rubber tire industry representatives and in their opinion can be used in preference to employing the illuminance selection procedure in chapter 11; however, values can still be determined using the illuminance selection procedure for similar tasks and activities.

Some manufacturers have developed their own lighting standards for their facilities. At least one manufacturer has selected an illuminance of 500 lx (50 fc) of uniform lighting for all production areas, with 1000 lx (100 fc) of task lighting being provided in selected areas where improved visibility is required, such as the tire machine operator's position or the finish inspection area.

Much of the area within a tire manufacturing plant is not color sensitive, and therefore energy efficiency is the main consideration in the design of the lighting system. This has led to the use of high-pressure sodium luminaires in many sections of the plant. There are at least two areas where fluorescent lighting is used extensively. One is in the finish area. Because of the high density of conveyors in this area, fluorescent fixtures allow good distribution of the light without providing excessive illuminance. In the press area, where there is a high concentration of smoke and fumes, fluorescent lighting is sometimes used to improve the visibility and appearance of the space.

Processes and Flowchart

The following descriptions pertain to the processes that convert raw materials to finished tires. Figure 20-33 is a flowchart showing the major areas. It should be noted that not all tire manufacturers are currently using the same manufacturing processes. Therefore, variations may be found in some plants. As an example, there are some tire manufacturing processes which do not currently use pelletizers. In some cases, extruders with roller heads are used in place of mills.

Banbury Area (1). Bales of synthetic and natural rubber are removed from storage and split into small pieces. Various grades of rubber are blended to meet specific compound requirements, then charged into a *Banbury mixer* together with carbon black, oil and dry pigments. The resulting blend of rubber and precise amounts of carbon black and pigments are emptied from a conveyor into a *Banbury machine*. After mixing, this *master batch* drops from the Banbury machine into a *pelletizer*, where it is cut into small marble-like pellets of uniform size and shape to facilitate cooling, handling and processing. Sulfur and accelerators are added to the pellets in a final mixing process, and, after a trip through the Banbury mixer, the *final batch* drops onto an automatic mill, where it is rolled into a thick continuous sheet and conveyed to a *wig-wag loader*, which places it on a skid, ready for further processing.

When needed for the preparation of treads, sidewalls, plies or beads, a batch of compounded rubber stock is conveyed to a warming mill, where it is kneaded and heated to make it more workable. It is then removed in continuous strips on conveyor belts to the machines which turn out the components.

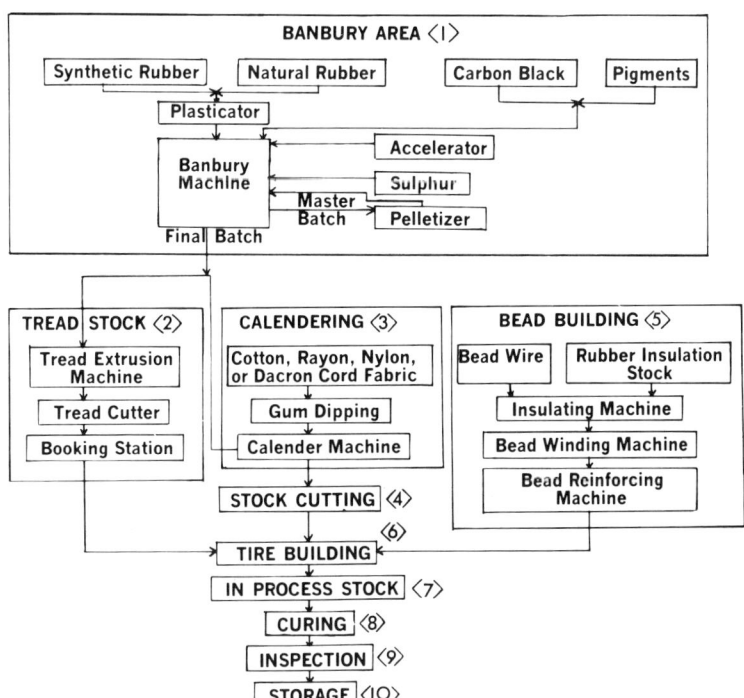

Fig. 20-33. Flow chart for the manufacturing of rubber tires. Numbers in parentheses refer to sections of the text.

Tread Stock (2). Rubber stocks are pulled from storage skids into cold feed extruders, either multiple or single, and then extruded through a common die in a continous strip onto a series of conveyors. During this process, an identifying code is printed on the extruded material, a gum cushion is applied, the underside is coated with liquid cement, and the strip is subjected to water cooling and automically cut into precise lengths, which are placed on storage skids. These skids are trucked to storage for aging before going to the tire assembly operation.

Calendering (3). Huge rolls containing rayon, nylon, dacron or other cord fabric are taken to a gum-dipping operation, where the cord fabric is dipped in a special compound, heat treated and dried under tension. Steel cord is processed from a multiple-roll creel directly into the calender without treating.

The fabric passes on to calendering machines, where rubber stock from warmup mills, fed automatically into the calender rolls, is pressed onto both sides and between the cords of the fabric as it passes between the rolls. The fabric goes over cooling drums and is rolled into cloth liners to prevent sticking.

Square-yard weights and widths are recorded at the control board. Many quality checks, including use of the beta gauge and statistical quality control charts, aid the calender operations. Accuracy of these measurements is very important to ensure a quality product.

Stock Cutting (4). From calendering, the rolls of fabric are trucked to the stock cutting operation, where the fabric is cut on the bias (diagonally across the cords). Cut to specific widths and bias angles, these pieces, known as plies, pass from the cutting table, are turned end to end and are precision spliced into continuous strips ready for tire assembly.

Bead Building (5). Copper-plated high-tensile-strength steel wire is brought in on large reels. A specified number of strands are brought together from the reels and guided through a die in the head of a small tube machine. Here, a special rubber insulation stock is squeezed around and between the separate strands of wire.

The rubber-covered wire strip is then run into a bead-winding machine, where it is wound on a chuck or collapsible ring. The machine automatically winds the proper number of turns, cuts the wire and ejects the wound bead on to a storage arm. In the next operation, bead reinforcing, the wound bead wire is covered with a strip of calendered fabric called a *reinforce*. The reinforce not only ties the bead into the tire but also plays a vital part in giving the tire added strength and stability.

Tire Building (6). All the parts of a tire are brought together in the tire assembly operation and are com-

Fig. 20-34. Forming and curing presses where "green" tires are fed in to be formed and vulcanized.

bined on a semiautomatic precision machine with a collapsible drum.

In-Process Stock (7). Green tires are accumulated along with other parts still in process, such as fabrics and calendered stock.

Curing (8). Green tires are sprayed automatically with lubricants, inside and out, to aid in molding. They are then conveyed to long batteries of automatic forming and curing presses, where they are transformed into tires. See figure 20-34.

Inspection (9). Tires are subjected to a series of quality checks. Passenger tires arriving from the curing room pass along a conveyor to automatic trimmers and on to spray painting machines for identification symbols. The tires are then conveyed to inspectors who check each tire inside and out.

The entire tread is examined to see that its angles are sharply molded so that they will grip the road. Sidewalls are inspected for gouges, pinvents and whitewall adhesion. The bead is examined for wrinkles or any defects that might prevent the tire from seating tightly and securely when mounted on a wheel or in any other way affect the service of the tire. Tire inner liners are inspected for any separations.

Finished Tire Storage (10). Tires are stored for later shipment.

Lighting Design for Specific Tasks

Banbury Area (1). Banbury materials are weighed and charged automatically, but certain tasks are performed manually by the operator. The operator should be able to read temperature recorders, time clocks and scale dials during each machine cycle.

General lighting should be provided with particular attention to locations where the operators perform their task. Also, it should be noted that there will be high dirt accumulation on luminaires and room surfaces because there are large quantities of carbon black in the air.

Tread Stock (2). General lighting is required in this area, with a higher level at the extruder, over the check-weighing and width-measuring station, and over the booking and inspection station where the tread is inspected for physical defects, weight, length and width.

Calendering (3). General lighting should be provided in the calendering area, with a higher level at the letoff and windup, where the crew handle the fabric; and at the instrumentation panel and over the measurement and inspection area, where the operator looks for such imperfections as bare cords.

Stock Cutting (4). This area should have both general and local lighting, with a higher level from the local units over the splicing table. The operator should be able to inspect fabric for bare cords, to make manual splices, or to set up an automatic splicer machine.

Bead Building (5). General lighting is needed in the bead room to permit proper machine setup, the inspection of coatings on the wire and the work of reinforcing.

Tire Building (6). General lighting should be provided throughout the entire area, with supplementary lighting at the tire-building machines to enable the operator to properly feed the materials onto the drum and to inspect laps.

In-Process Stock (7). General lighting is needed for reading tags or color codes on items in this active storage area.

Curing (8). In addition to general lighting, supplementary lighting is required at the molds. Supplementary luminaires should be so positioned that molds may be readily inspected during cleaning and coating. An alternative to permanently mounted inspection lights is the use of hand-held lights which can be better positioned by the operator to illuminate the area of concern, wherever it may be in the process.

Inspection (9). This area should be provided with general and supplementary illumination or localized general illumination at each inspection stand. Luminaires should be positioned on both sides of the tires to illuminate both the inside and the outside of the casings. Luminaires should be shielded and installed so as to eliminate as much glare as possible.

Finished Tire Storage (10). See the subsection on In-Process Stock above.

SHEET METAL SHOPS

Visual tasks in the sheet metal shop are often difficult because sheet metal (after pickling and oiling) has a reflectance similar to the working surface of the machine, resulting in poor contrasts between the machine and work; low reflectance of the metal results in a low task luminance; high-speed operation of small presses reduces the available time for seeing; bulky machinery obstructs the distribution of light from general-lighting luminaires; and noise contributes to fatigue.

Punch Press

The seeing task is essentially the same for a large press as it is for a small press, except that with a small press less time is available for seeing. The shadow problem, however, is much greater with a large press. With either, the operator must have adequate illumination to move the stock into the press, inspect the die for scrap after the operating cycle is completed and inspect the product. Where an automatic feed is employed, the speed of operation is so great that the operator has time only to inspect the die for scrap clearance.

The general lighting system in press areas should provide the illuminance selected from chapter 11, Illuminance Selection. This is necessary for the safe and rapid handling of stock in the form of unprocessed metal, scrap or finished products. In large press areas, such as that shown in figure 20-35, illumination should be furnished by high-bay lighting equipment or by a combination of high-bay and supplementary task lighting as shown in figure 20-36. For medium-bay areas (figure 20-37), the illumination should be supplied by luminaires having a widespread distribution to provide uniform illuminance for the bay and the die surface area. Where the mounting height exceeds 6 m (20 ft),

Fig. 20-35. High-bay large press shop lighted with 1000-watt improved color mercury lamp units.

Fig. 20-36. Large press with built-in supplementary lighting to facilitate setup and operation.

Fig. 20-37. Low-bay press shop with fluorescent lighting. Note: upward component and center shield for better comfort.

careful consideration should be given to maintenance costs.

The operator's ability to inspect the die is more directly related to the reflected brightness of the die surface than to the amount of light incident upon it. For example, a concentrated light placed on the operator's side of the press and directed toward the die may produce results much less satisfactory than a large-area source of low luminance placed at the back or side of the press. See figure 20-38. The luminance required for optimum visibility of the die has not been established; consensus suggests that 1700 cd/m^2 is satisfactory.

Paint applied to both the exterior and the throat surfaces of a press contributes to the operator's ability to see. The reflectance of the paint selected for the exterior of the press should be not less than 40%. This treatment of vertical surfaces on the exterior provides for maximum utilization of light from the general lighting system. Similarly, the paint selected for throat surfaces should have a reflectance of 60% or higher.

Shear

The operator must be able to see a measuring scale in order to set the stops for gauging the size of cut. When a sheet has to be trimmed, either to square the sides or to cut off scrap from the edges, the operator must be able to see the location of the cut in order to minimize scrap.

The general lighting system should provide the illuminance selected from chapter 11 in the area around the shear for safely feeding the sheets at the front, collecting the scrap at the back and stacking the finished pieces in preparation for removal.

Local lighting, as shown in figure 20-39, produces a line of light to indicate where the cut will be made and the amount of scrap that will be trimmed. It also provides light to enable the operator who is responsible for pressing the foot-release bar to see quickly that all hands are clear of the guard.

STEEL MILLS[28]

The manufacture of steel is an integrated process involving three major steps: the blast furnaces refine the iron ore into pig iron; the pig iron is transferred to an open-hearth furnace, basic oxygen furnace or electric furnace, where it is converted into steel; and the steel ingots are sent to various rolling mills, where they are formed into sheets, bars, rails and structural forms. See

Fig. 20-38. Highlights and shadows on the die of a small press are produced by supplementary or general lighting at the rear of the press. The operator can quickly inspect the open die for loose pieces of scrap.

Fig. 20-39. Shear. Six 150-watt floodlamps provide a narrow line of light on the metal sheet to indicate where the cut will be made. Sockets are mounted in channel supported by springs. A 2-lamp fluorescent ventilated industrial luminaire will also provide good illumination and is less subject to short lamp life due to vibration.

Fig. 20-40. Steel mill area producing cold rolled sheet in coils. Deep reflectors shield the lamps in normal field of view. Left outer row of reflectors are located close to the wall to maintain better illumination along the edge of the space.

Fig. 20-41. Illuminance Values Currently Recommended by Representatives from the Iron and Steel Industry (Maintained on Tasks)

Area/Activity	Illuminance	
	Lux	Foot-candles
Open hearth		
Stock yard	100	10
Charging floor	200	20
Pouring slide		
Slag pits	200	20
Control platforms	300	30
Mold yard	50	5
Hot top	300	30
Hot top storage	100	10
Checker cellar	100	10
Buggy and door repair	300	30
Stripping yard	200	20
Scrap stockyard	100	10
Mixer building	300	30
Calcining building	100	10
Skull cracker	100	10
Rolling mills		
Blooming, slabbing, hot strip, hot sheet	300	30
Cold strip, plate	300	30
Pipe, rod, tube, wire drawing	500	50
Merchant and sheared plate	300	30
Tin plate mills		
Tinning and galvanizing	500	50
Cold strip rolling	500	50
Motor room, machine room	300	30
Inspection		
Black plate, bloom and billet chipping	1000	100
Tin plate and other bright surfaces	2000*	200b

*The specular surface of the material may necessitate special consideration in selection and placement of lighting equipment, or orientation of work.

figure 20-40. Each one of these processes can be considered as a separate operation. They may be located anywhere from a few hundred meters (yards) to many kilometers (miles) apart.

Regardless of any other consideration, enough lighting equipment should be provided to satisfy minimum safety requirements. Also, there are certain areas of critical seeing where higher levels and proper quality are important. See figure 20-41 for recommended illuminances representing those established by iron and steel industry representatives, which in their opinion can be used in preference to the standard illuminance selection procedure; however, values can still be determined using the illuminance selection procedure in chapter 11 for similar tasks and activities. Beyond these values, there are some examples of far-reaching management policies which also recognize good lighting as a useful tool to aid the production of increased outputs of higher-quality material. Since considerable capital expenditures are authorized for lighting systems, the selection of the most practical and trouble-free lighting system pays off when preliminary planning is complete in every detail.

First costs of lighting systems are not a true measure of the systems' effectiveness, especially when steel mills operate at full capacity. Prime study should be given to the annual operating costs of these systems. In virtually all cases, lighting equipment which performs efficiently with dependable and trouble-free operation will prove economically sound for steel mill application.

The following characteristics are common to steel mill building construction and to the operation of the industry, and each has its influence on the design of practical lighting systems:

1. All production areas have overhead cranes which must be used to move raw materials and finished products.
2. The raw materials and finished products are of such composition and size as to require considerable headroom, with the result that lighting units must be installed 9 m (30 ft) or higher above the floor.
3. Arrangement of equipment on floor plans influences the sizes and spans of overhead cranes, and the flow of products from raw material to finished form dictates the locations of lighting outlets to a degree seldom, if ever, found in any other industry.
4. The range of ambient temperatures where lighting equipment must operate runs from $-18°C$ ($0°F$) in unheated rolling and beam mills during winter months, to soaking pit and hot top areas where readings of $60°C$ ($140°F$) are common above crane cabs during the summer.
5. Atmospheric conditions are poor even in the most modern mills, where well-planned ventilating systems are installed. The basic production methods, which employ a succession of heating and cooling cycles, make for conditions which induce fast-rising air currents which carry metal dust, products of combustion, and oil vapors upward to locations where lighting equipment must be installed.
6. Instead of finished ceilings with high reflectances of 60–80%, there are open truss frameworks below metal roof decks; instead of smooth, light-colored walls with 30–50% reflectances, there are corrugated metal sidings

and a succession of columns marking the boundaries between bays; and finally, instead of floors with smooth finishes rated at 10–30% reflectance, there are pieces or stacks of dark-colored material and equipment in most locations, or black dirt and unswept concrete where parts of the floor are visible.

In many areas, the high mounting heights favor the use of 400- and 1000-W high-intensity discharge lamps. High-pressure sodium sources should be used where conditions permit. Special consideration should be given to maintaining lighting continuity in case of momentary or long-term power outages. See the section on Emergency Lighting in chapter 33.

The choice of light source will depend upon the power supply available. High-intensity discharge lamps installed on cranes served by direct current should use appropriate ballasts. Extreme vibration and voltage variation may make resistor-ballasted mercury vapor lamps the most reliable choice. Care should also be taken to use shock and vibration damping mounts for crane-mounted luminaires.

Open Hearth[28]

Stock Yard. Scrap metal, ore and limestone are loaded by overhead cranes. Generally, overhead lighting should be provided. In outdoor areas in which no overhead framing is available, directional lighting units having wide distribution can be installed on the underside of crane girders.

Charging Floor. Charging boxes are emptied into the furnaces by machine and alloy materials added by shovel or machine. In addition to general lighting, localized lighting should be provided on the instrument panel which controls the furnace operation. Additional lighting should be provided over the small material storage bins. This usually can be best accomplished by mounting directional lighting equipment on the steel columns or on the underside of the crane girders.

Pouring Side. The molten metal is an area of very concentrated high luminance. When the furnaces are tapped and the ladles emptied into molds, there are clouds of fumes and vapor. General overhead lighting is recommended. Auxiliary lighting may be provided for the slag pits in either of two ways: directional lighting equipment can be mounted permanently on the steel columns above the platform level which is part of the charging-floor area, or, if this is not feasible, portable units mounted on a standard having either a tripod or a flat platform with castors can be set on the platform above the slag pit area. At the ingot pouring platform supplementary lighting is necessary and can be obtained by mounting directional lighting equipment on the columns back of the platform. Portable lighting is not satisfactory on account of its low mounting height and the glare from the pour and rear directional light sources.

Mold Yard. The ingot molds are cleaned, coated, sprayed and stored. This is a very dirty area with a high concentration of fumes from the spraying operation. General overhead lighting with supplementary lighting on the underside of the crane is recommended. Consideration should be given to suitable maintenance features such as dirt-resistant design and dust-tight covers.

Hot Top Relining and Repairing. General overhead lighting should be provided. Supplemental lighting at the point of hot top repairs and mold relining is also necessary. Directional lighting equipment can be mounted on the overhead beams; for close inspection of the lining it is necessary to use extension cords.

Hot Top Storage. The operator must be able to see in order to place a thin steel gasket accurately between the hot top and mold. General overhead lighting plus lighting units under the crane are required.

Checker Cellar. Brick repair work is sometimes done in this low-ceiling area. Overhead lights should be placed wherever possible, and portable work lights provided.

Buggy and Door Repair Shop. This is a repair shop for charging boxes, buggies and furnace doors. Operations include rough machine and bench work, cutting and welding. General lighting is required.

Stripping Yard. The molds are removed from the ingots by a stripping machine. For indoor locations high-bay general lighting is required. Outdoors, directional lighting equipment should be mounted under crane girders; overhead units mounted on messenger cable are also satisfactory.

Scrap Stock Yard. In this outdoor area with overhead cranes, scrap is cut by torch and shears and then stored. Standard industrial lighting equipment can be mounted on messenger cable strung between the crane-supporting steel structure, with floodlights on towers or poles erected beside the crane runway.

Mixer Building. Molten metal from blast furnaces is poured into a tilting vessel which acts as a reservoir. The vessel, called a *mixer*, has a capacity of 300–1500 tons. Owing to the very large mixers and the bins containing raw material mounted above them, it is almost impossible to provide general illumination over the entire area. Lighting equipment should be located where possible and convenient. Supplementary lighting should be provided for important areas such as the top of mixers, the pouring level, walkways and stairwells.

Calcining Building. This is a very dirty high-bay area in which limestone is stored and crushed. General overhead lighting is not advisable, due to the height of the crushing machinery and the bins for feeding it. Industrial lighting units should be provided at convenient locations on all working platforms or levels.

Skull Cracker. In this outdoor area old ingot molds, as well as solid material which freezes on the bottom or sides of ladles, are broken up. Directional lighting equipment should be mounted on the underside of crane girders. Lighting is also necessary under the cranes.

Cinder Dump. Furnace cinders are stored outside. General lighting from overhead or directional lighting equipment and additional units under the cranes are necessary.

Basic Oxygen Furnace Plant

The lighting techniques are much the same as with the open hearth. Mounting heights are very high, and servicing is accomplished from cranes or disconnecting and lowering hangers. The high concentration of graphite particles and dust dictates use of ventilated luminaires, gasketed enclosed luminaires or reflector lamps for this facility.

Continuous Casting

The continuous casting process takes molten steel and produces the required cross sections of slabs or blooms; it therefore bypasses the soaking pits and blooming or slabbing mills. The tundish area can be lighted similarly to other hot-metal-handling facilities. Vertical machines will usually require directional lighting from the sides. The needed luminaires can be mounted on building columns or structural supporting members of the casting units.

Casting Floor Areas. General overhead lighting with supplemental lighting is required. Supplemental lighting below the tundish and at the mold can be obtained from directional lighting on portable stands or mounted to structural members.

Spray Chambers. The spray chamber is the area where steel below the mold is water cooled to achieve proper solidification. During operation, this area is exposed to high temperatures, steam and water mist. Lighting in this area for viewing the cooling spray pattern and for machine maintenance can be obtained from permanently mounted protected directional luminaires mounted as far from the bloom or slab as practical, or from portable luminaires.

Instrument Areas. Modern continuous casting machines utilize many sensors, transmitters and valves for controlling the water systems. Lighting for these typically congested areas can be provided by high-output fluorescent luminaires to minimize shadows and allow switching the lighting on and off when required.

Electric Arc Furnaces

The lighting techniques for this process are much the same as for the basic oxygen and the open-hearth processes. The scrap metal charge is loaded into the top of the arc furnace with the roof swung to the side. This practice results in flame and considerable dirt directly over the furnace. The lighting must be designed to avoid placing luminaires in that unfriendly location.

TEXTILE INDUSTRY

The textile industry is composed of firms which convert staple fibers and continuous filament fibers into yarns and fabrics and furnish these products to apparel, industrial, and other customers, who in turn convert the product for an end use. Originally, the term "textile" referred only to fabrics made by interlacing (weaving) yarns. Today, knitted fabrics formed by interlooping yarns and nonwoven fabrics formed by a random deposition of fiber to create a web, as well as various combinations of all the above types, are included in the textile industry. The intended end use and the type of fiber used determine the exact nature of the intermediate processing steps.

Staple fiber yarn production involves alignment, attenuation, evening and twisting of short, fine natural and synthetic fibers. *Filament* yarn production involves converting synthetic fiber raw stock to a yarn with added bulk, stretch and texture; these operations occur mainly in a segment of the industry known as *throwing*, and the converters are called *throwsters*—a term dating back to those who twisted and folded continuous-filament silk.

The description of processes given below identifies major process areas, and relates yarn production terminology to the most common yarn-processing systems, for example, the short-staple cotton system. The terminology used in North American woolen and worsted (long-staple) yarn production is included. Textile terminology may be obtained from standard sources such as the *Man-Made Fiber and Textile Dictionary*, published by the Hoechst Celanese Corporation, Charlotte, NC (1990); and *Textile Terms and Definitions*, published by the Textile Institute, Manchester, England. The descriptive organization follows the flow of input fiber to the finished fabric.

A natural fiber such as cotton is very light in weight and of very small diameter. Even the finest (smallest-diameter) yarns can contain over a thousand fibers in a cross section. The yarn diameter depends on the end use. Small diameters are used for shirting and blouse fabrics; coarser yarns are used for denim, heavy industrial canvases and the like. Even for fine yarns, the processing machinery is large and robust; for economic reasons, it operates at high speed. Lighting requirements are dictated by the need to have operators interact with the flow of fiber into yarn, yarn into fabric, and so on through to final shipping. With the drive to automate and use robots whenever possible, there are dreams of operations with "lights out." In the meantime, illumination may well shift to overall HID with task lighting to assist operators in identifying and repairing broken ends, initiating thread-up and recognizing off-quality production and defects.

Staple Fiber Preparation

Stock Dyeing, Tinting. For industries where large quantities of the same color are needed (for example, contract carpet) and where extreme fastness to light is required (for example, automotive), coloration, in the form of pigments, may be added to the synthetic fiber melt prior to extrusion to form fiber. Special "heather" effects can also be obtained by blending pigment yarn with undyed yarn.

When several fibers in a manufacturing operation are likely to become confused by operators, fugitive tints may be added to the fiber surface to identify and separate the various process streams through the plant. These tints are polymeric in nature, do not penetrate into the fiber, and are thus easily removed in subsequent washing operations. General lighting is adequate in a localized special area for color matching (separate booths are used, with standard illuminants in a gray surround).

Most wool preprocessing—for example, degreasing and scouring—requires similar lighting, except that wool sorting (like cotton grading) requires a higher level, including specialized lighting. When wool is stock dyed (in fiber form) and later blended to achieve the desired shade, lighting again is critical for color evaluation of the resulting blend.

Yarn Manufacturing — Short Staple

Opening and Picking (Chute Feed). Staple natural and synthetic fiber is shipped to a mill in bales weighing approximately 230 kg (500 lb) and of density 320–480 kg/m^3 (20–30 lb/ft^3). The opening process separates the condensed fibers by producing small tufts, blends various lots of fiber and removes large particles of leaf and stem trash—the last being extremely important for cotton.

Some mills convert continuous-filament (for example, acrylic) bundles of fiber (tow) to a staple or short-length form (top). Top has a longer staple length than cotton.

Increasingly, opened fiber stock is sent directly to the next process by pneumatic chute to reduce air contamination; or it may be further processed through a picker to produce a card lap. The picker removes more trash, blends the fiber stock and evens out variations in its linear density (mass per unit length). The high degree of automation involved in the opening process lessens the amount of lighting needed. However, good lighting is required during maintenance and repairs.

Carding (Nonwoven-Web Formation). The purpose of cards, whether roller top (long staple), granular (synthetics) or flat top (cotton), is to clean and attenuate the stock to produce a yarn intermediate termed *sliver*. Sliver is a loose collection of fibers of long length and of diameter 25–76 mm (1–3 in.), cotton being fine and wool coarse, which is formed as the web exits the card. This normally enclosed process requires a moderate illuminance as well as additional supplementary task lighting during machine maintenance. Maintenance includes setting the critical space between the central drum and planetary card components to less than 0.03 mm (0.001 in.) tolerance.

Drafting. Normally, eight card slivers are drafted into one sliver to achieve better blending. At this point, slivers of different fibers, such as polyester and cotton, are blended to get the commercial blends required. The process further aligns fibers, blends the different fibers and attenuates them to achieve the approximate sliver linear density achieved by a card. The lighting needs are similar to those of carding. Increased automation in recent times has meant that lighting is needed only for maintenance.

Combing. This process is used only for fine, long-staple cotton (for example, high-quality shirting) and for worsted suiting material. The card slivers are formed by a *sliver lapper* into a lap (blanket) for input to the comber. Combing achieves a high level of parallelization of the fibers while cleaning and removing short fiber from the stock. The result gives a higher luster to the combed yarn. The comber output is a sliver which is fed to the drafting frame. While moderate lighting is adequate during regular operation, additional switched or supplementary task lighting is required for maintenance.

Roving. In this process, the roving frame attenuates sliver input by a factor of eight to ten and produces an output also called *roving*. Because roving is unable to support its own weight as a parallel fiber bundle, a small amount of twist is added to enable material handling into the spinning operation. Both the roving *bobbin* and the large device termed a *flyer* rotate at high speed. Lighting must be increased for operators to fix broken ends: supplementary task lighting may be the best answer.

Ring Spinning. Yarn is produced from roving on a spinning frame, where final attenuation up to a factor of 100 occurs along with a twist to provide final yarn strength. If the twist direction runs from upper left to lower right along the yarn, it is *S twist*; if from upper right to lower left, it is *Z twist*. See figure 20-42.

Open-End Spinning. Open-end spinning, whether with a spindle, with an air jet spinning or by friction, converts sliver directly to yarn without the intermediate roving process. In general the result is a coarser yarn than those produced by ring spinning. Lighting should be concentrated along the aisles between machines and also on the thread lines.

Fig. 20-42. Spinning room with continuous rows of luminaires running perpendicular to machines to prevent machine shadows.

Yarn Preparation

Winding. The product of ring spinning is a low-mass bobbin which usually is made into a larger package for later use in weaving, knitting or beaming. Most winding is done automatically, including the tying of knots. Task illumination is not critical.

Beaming. In weaving or warp knitting, several thousand parallel yarns are required to weave or knit today's wide fabrics. Yarn from winding is placed in a *creel* containing hundreds of yarn packages, which are unwound simultaneously to make a section beam. Section beams are also used in warp knitting. Task illumination is critical; good lighting in the take-up and reed areas is highly recommended.

Slashing (Sizing). Prior to weaving, a number of section beams (four to six) are brought together and the parallel yarns unwound and pulled through a sizing solution of starch (for cotton), polyvinyl alcohol (for blends of polyester and cotton) or polyacrylic acid (for polyesters). The solution is dried, leaving behind a flexible coating which protects the yarn during weaving. The loom beam is taken to a drawing-in operation which prepares the warp for weaving by bringing each yarn through a *heddle eye* in a harness and a dent in the reed. This arrangement allows the loom to interlace the filling yarns with the warp yarns to form the woven fabric.

Slashing requires good task lighting in the take-up and reed areas.

Fabric Production

Weaving. Weaving is the interlacing of the parallel yarns from the warp beam and the usual perpendicular yarns, called *filling*, in a machine called a loom. A special type, *triaxial* weaving, allows three sets of yarns to interact. Other special looms are used for terry toweling and three-dimensional constructs.

Originally, small bobbins from spinning were used directly to make quills of yarn for use in the shuttles which carried the filling yarns across the warp. Shuttleless looms have emerged which operate much faster, with less noise, and consume less energy because energy is not lost in accelerating and decelerating the heavy shuttle. Small projectiles, jets of air, jets of water, or rapiers are used to transport the yarn across the machine hundreds of times per minute. The operation is still slow, producing fabric at rates of centimeters per minute per loom. Good illumination is highly recommended, especially in producing fancy, dobby, and Jacquard fabrics (see figure 20-43).

Knitting. Knitting is the interlooping of yarns. Warp knitting is performed on flat bed machines using section beams of parallel yarns, resulting in a flat, open-

Fig. 20-43. Weave room of a textile mill. Note rows of luminaires are perpendicular to looms to prevent harsh line shadows from upper parts of loom.

width fabric often used industrially for automotive head liner and for ladies' lingerie. In weft knitting, yarns are fed from individual yarn packages into a circular or flat bed of knitting needles. The resulting fabric is tubular or flat and is often used for T shirts, jogging outfits and hosiery. Production is measured in meters per minute. Lighting is critical for on-line inspection of knitting. A lamp is usually placed in the circular knitting machine to help identify defects before the fabric is removed.

Tufting. Most carpets are made by a nonweaving technique called tufting. A woven jute or polypropylene web or a randomly made nonwoven polypropylene web serves as the medium; yarn is punched from one side of this backing to the face. By controlling the amount of yarn punched through, the height of the pile, or tuft, can be controlled to give either an even pile height or a patterned height. A rubber backing is eventually applied to lock the tufts in place. Production is measured in meters per minute.

Task lighting on the tufting machine is critical for on-line inspection and quality control.

Finishing

Fabrics produced by the previously described processes, called *greige* or *gray* goods, are typically *finished* by passing through a number of chemical and mechanical processes.

Preparation. The first series of operations for a cotton or polyester-cotton woven fabric is called *preparation* and is typically a continuous process operating at speeds of 100 m/min or higher. Fabric is held open to the desired width and (if it contains polyester) heat set to stabilize it; it is then singed to remove surface fuzz, desized to remove the protective size from the warp yarn, scoured to remove oils and waxes, bleached to remove colored impurities, and often mercerized using caustic solution to swell the cotton fiber, thereby making it easier to dye.

Many of these processes are done inside enclosed machines to conserve thermal energy and contain chemicals. The fabric is kept thoroughly wet from singeing onward. Lighting is not critical.

Knits and small batches of woven fabric can be prepared in batches in a machine capable of performing those several operations in series. Treatment baths of different chemicals are added and drained in sequence to treat the fabric.

Lighting is not critical except at the end of continuous ranges, where on-line inspection is performed.

Fabric Dying and Printing. If coloration is required following preparation, the dyes can be applied continuously (dye range or in batch form, beck, jet beck or jig). To conserve thermal energy and in some cases to allow the dye to penetrate the fiber, these machines are enclosed, and the fabric is mostly out of sight. When wet, it is currently impossible to determine the final, dry color by an extrapolation technique. In order to assess the color, the fabric must be dried and observed under controlled lighting conditions. The color temperature of the light source is of great importance for color matching.

Printing is a form of localized coloration. Once the pigment (the most common type of printing) is mixed into a paste, there is little that can be done to alter the shade. Lighting on the print machine is critical to ensure good pattern registration as each color is printed.

Fabric Finishing. Fabrics from preparation or from dyeing and printing now are given the final processing to improve esthetics or utility. These steps may include mechanical finishing: calendering, Sanforizing™, napping, shearing, or sueding. Chemical treatment is needed for flameproofing, durable press, soil release, water repellency and softening. Most such processing is done inside enclosed machines and at high speeds (100 m/min). Normal lighting is sufficient.

In final inspection, color and type of illuminant are critical. Final decisions on color may often be made in the laboratory, where color temperature and color rendering properties of the light source and the color of the surround are rigidly controlled.

WAREHOUSE AND STORAGE AREA LIGHTING

Placing items in storage, accounting for them and later retrieving them are some of the most widespread activities requiring electric lighting in North America today. Storage activities are found in business operations of every type, ranging from small local operations to multinational corporations.

Since rapid changes are taking place, the traditional concept of the warehouse must be expanded to encompass new techniques, including automation, high-rise storage, barcoding, cold storage, shrink-wrap packaging, etc.

A variety of specific tasks may occur in warehouse usage:

Open Storage. Areas of material stored without the use of rack systems. This includes storage on the floor and on pallets which may be stacked on each other.

High Rise. Areas generally automated, where storage bins may be rotated so that unused bins are kept high up, and with storage levels rising to over 100 ft.

Offices. Paperwork areas located within warehouses.

Cold Storage. Areas that warehouse normally perishable food items and require low (sometimes below freezing) temperatures.

Hazardous Materials Storage. Areas where there is storage of hazardous gases, vapors, or dust requiring specific methods of storage.

Exit and Emergency. Areas within warehouses that must provide safe exit from the building or that must conform to the Life Safety Code in case of emergency.

Shipping and Receiving. Areas where materials are received into the warehouse for sorting and placement in storage areas. Such areas also serves as staging areas for coordination of products to be sorted and placed on trucks or trains for shipping.

Loading Docks and Staging Areas. Areas, generally just outside the shipping area, that may be outdoors but are often covered and that are used to place items on and off trucks and railroad cars and to assemble goods.

Maintenance Shops, Fork Lift Recharging Areas and Refrigeration Equipment Rooms. Locations where general plant housekeeping activities occur. Separate areas or rooms are generally set aside for this purpose.

Mobile Racking. A facility widely used outside North America and being introduced here. Entire blocks of racking move on floor-mounted rails to open and close aisles as needed. In order to obtain maximum use from any lighting provided, the definition of the actual seeing task should be considered.

From the tasks encountered in the warehouse, it can be concluded that the majority of critical seeing tasks occur on a vertical plane. The major consideration for appropriate illumination in the warehouse is that of lighting the vertical surfaces of stored goods. However, adequate horizontal illumination for aisle activities must also be provided.

Care must be taken that adequate illumination is distributed uniformly over the entire vertical seeing surface from top to bottom and along the entire length of storage aisles. This requires special care when discrete HID luminaires are used, because there may be unacceptable dropoff of illuminance between luminaires.

Another possibility that needs to be considered during design is that some racks and storage locations may be partly or wholly empty at times, and the darkness of the empty shelves may reduce the illuminance. This effect should be anticipated and included in the design parameters.

Horizontal-plane illuminance must be adequate for safety and navigation, as well as the reading of documents, and is therefore also important, though not as critical as the light required on vertical task surfaces.

For recommended illuminances for various warehouse situations, see chapter 11, Illuminance Selection.

The reflectances of exposed surfaces can significantly affect lighting results. While these reflecting characteristics of stored goods cannot be controlled at the warehouse operating level, they should be taken into consideration when cartoning and container decisions are being made. Light-colored packing material can contribute to efficient utilization and increase visibility through greater contrast.

Since storage in fixed-location racking results generally in long narrow aisles, lighting layout and calculation procedures should be based on the dimensions of the aisle space rather then the overall building size parameters. Lighting fixtures should be located over the aisles (generally in the middle), regardless of the overall building configuration. Because of the special geometry of aisle space and because the determination of vertical footcandles is a key task, the standard zonal cavity method of illuminance determination is not useful in such warehouse calculations. Fortunately, computer programs for the point-by-point calculation of delivered illuminance are now generally available throughout the industry.

To assure a productive work environment, glare from light sources should be minimized. This becomes particularly important with concentrated HID sources, especially for operators located beneath luminaires while looking at the tops of stacks, since they may encounter total disabling glare under such conditions. Proper shielding of the source needs to be considered here, as well as viewing along the aisles.

Indirect lighting systems for warehouses, while not as efficient in overall illuminance production, can be useful in providing excellent seeing results and have proven particularly useful in areas with computer terminals and where storage and selling both take place.

Aisles or narrow "rooms" can be served by HID sources with classical high-bay-type luminaires spaced reasonably closely together. The spacing can be increased with luminaires that have a substantial uplight component when the ceilings have high reflectance, or with special aisle luminaires, having an asymmetric light distribution, that are available from a variety of commercial sources. Special care must be taken at higher mounting heights that sufficient illumination levels are still reached when the wider spacings are used.

To shield warehouse operating personnel who will be looking directly into open HID luminaires when working directly under them and viewing stack tops, special protective lenses should be considered.

While HID sources in appropriate luminaires can be used at various mounting heights, they are generally most effective at mounting heights of 15 ft or more.

Fluorescent lighting is also frequently used for warehouse aisles. While it can be applied at various mounting heights, it is generally most effective in low-mounting-height installations. Fluorescent designs are implemented either with continuous rows along an aisle (in reflector, lensed, or open strip types) or with individually mounted units.

Since storage spaces may be used intermittently, it is possible to save energy by controlling light sources to be switched off or to operate at reduced output at inactive times and to operate at full output only when the space is in use. Multilevel HID ballasts have been developed for this purpose. These ballasts are utilized at reduced levels when there is no activity, and a sensor activates the circuit when someone is present in the space; significant energy savings are thereby realized.

REFERENCES

1. IES. Committee on Industrial Lighting. 1991. *American national standard practice for industrial lighting, ANSI / IES RP-7-1991.* New York: Illuminating Engineering Society of North America.
2. Illuminating Engineering Society of North America. 1991. *Lighting economics: An intermediate approach to economics as applied to the lighting practice.* IES ED-150.9. New York: Illuminating Engineering Society of North America.
3. IES. Energy Management Committee. 1982. *IES recommended procedure for lighting power limit determination.* IES LEM-1-1982. New York: Illuminating Engineering Society of North America.
4. IES. Energy Management Committee. 1984. *IES recommended procedure for lighting energy limit determination for buildings.* IES LEM-2-1984. New York: Illuminating Engineering Society of North America.
5. IES. Energy Management Committee. 1987. *IES design considerations for effective building lighting energy utiliza-*

tion. IES LEM-3-1987. New York: Illuminating Engineering Society of North America.

6. IES. Energy Management Committee. 1984. *IES recommended procedure for energy analysis of building design and installations.* IES LEM-4-1982. New York: Illuminating Engineering Society of North America.

7. IES. Energy Management Committee. *IES recommendations for building lighting operation and maintenance for effective energy utilization.* IES LEM-5. New York: Illuminating Engineering Society of North America.

8. IES. Committee on Lighting Study Projects in Industry. Subcommittee on Supplementary Lighting. 1952. Recommended practice for supplementary lighting. *Illum. Eng.* 47(11):623–635.

9. IES. Industrial Lighting Committee. Aircraft Industry Subcommittee. 1975. Lighting for the aircraft/airline industries: Manufacturing and maintenance. *J. Illum. Eng. Soc.* 4(3):207–219. IES. Industrial Lighting Committee. Aircraft Industry Subcommittee. 1978. Lighting for the aircraft/airline industries: Airframe maintenance. *Light. Des. Appl.* 8(6):41–47.

10. IES. Committee on Lighting Study Projects in Industry. Subcommittee on Lighting in Bakeries. 1950. Lighting in bakeries. *Illum. Eng.* 45(6):387–397.

11. IES. Industrial Lighting Committee. Electric Generating Stations Subcommittee. 1975. Lighting outdoor locations of electric generating stations. *J. Illum. Eng. Soc.* 4(3):220–228.

12. IES. Committee on Lighting of Central Station Properties. 1951. *Lighting of central station properties. Part I: Lighting of control rooms. Part II: Lighting of load dispatch rooms.* New York: Illuminating Engineering Society of North America. IES. Committee on Lighting of Central Station Properties. Subcommittee on Lighting of Indoor Locations. 1957. Lighting indoor locations of central station properties. *Illum. Eng.* 52(8):423–438.

13. IES. Committee on Lighting of Central Station Properties. Subcommittee on High Bay Lighting. 1955. Lighting of central station high bay areas. *Illum. Eng.* 50(8):395–403.

14. IES. Industrial Lighting Committee. Electric Generating Station Subcommittee. 1986. Nuclear power plant lighting. *J. Illum. Eng. Soc.* 5(2):107–116.

15. IES. Committee on Lighting Study Projects in Industry. Subcommittee on Lighting for Foundries. 1953. Lighting for foundries. *Illum. Eng.* 48(5):279–290.

16. Ruth, W., L. Carlsson, R. Wibom, and B. Knave. 1979. Work place lighting in foundries. *Light. Des. Appl.* 9(11):22–29.

17. IES. Industrial Committee. Graphic Arts Subcommittee. Color Appraisal Task Committee. 1957. Lighting for the color appraisal of reflection-type materials in graphic arts. *Illum. Eng.* 52(9):493–500.

18. American National Standards Institute. 1972. *American national standard viewing conditions for the appraisal of color quality and color uniformity in the graphic arts.* ANSI PH2.32-1972. New York: American National Standards Institute.

19. IES. Industrial Lighting Committee. Subcommittee on Logging and the Sawmill Industries. 1986. *Lighting in the logging and sawmill industries.* IES CP-42-1986. New York: Illuminating Engineering Society of North America.

20. IES. Industrial Lighting Committee. Subcommittee on Sawmill Lighting. 1957. Lighting for sawmills: Redwood green chain. *Illum. Eng.* 52(7):381–392.

21. IES. Committee on Office Lighting. Subcommittee on Visual Display Terminals. 1989. *IES recommended practice for lighting offices containing computer visual display terminals.* IES RP-24-1989. New York: Illuminating Engineering Society of North America.

22. IES. Committee on Lighting for the Machining of Small Metal Parts. 1949. Lighting for the machining of small metal parts. *Illum. Eng.* 44(10):615–626.

23. Mayton, A. G. 1991. Investigation of task illumination for surface coal mining equipment operators. *J. Illum. Eng. Soc.* 20(1):2–18.

24. IES. Industrial Lighting Committee. Petroleum, Chemical and Petrochemical Subcommittee. 1977. Lighting for petroleum and chemical plants. *J. Illum. Eng. Soc.* 6(3):184–192.

25. National Fire Protection Association. 1990. *National electrical code, ANSI / NFPA 70.* Quincy, MA: NFPA.

26. IES. Industrial Lighting Committee. Subcommittee on Outdoor Productive Areas. 1962. Railroad yard lighting. *Illum. Eng.* 57(3):239–251.

27. IES. Industrial Committee. Subcommittee on Lighting for the Rubber Industry. 1969. Lighting for manufacturing rubber tires. *Illum. Eng.* 64(2):112–125.

28. IES. Committee on Lighting Study Projects in Industry. Subcommittee on Lighting in Steel Mills. 1952. Lighting for steel mills. Part 1: Open hearth. *Illum. Eng.* 47(3):165–171.

Theatre, Television and Photographic Lighting

21

Editor's Note: Material on motion picture lighting and projection lighting, which was previously contained in this chapter, has been omitted from this revision to allow inclusion of additional lighting information of interest to a broader range of readers. The information on these subjects is available in the 1987 Volume of the *IESNA Lighting Handbook Application Volume.* For the latest information on these subjects, it is suggested you contact the Society of Motion Picture and Television Engineers (SMPTE).

Even though lighting problems for theatre, television and film have many similarities, they also have many differences. In theatre, one lights a three-dimensional subject for the eye. In television and film, one lights for a camera to transform a two dimensional medium (height and width) into a three-dimensional look, adding depth.

For theatre, television and film, the lighting system design and luminaire choice is based on production plans. The size and complexity of the system are based on production needs, from elementary training facilities to professional facilities. In all facilities, however, the budget usually determines the degree of complexity.

The theatre design requires information concerning types of programs (opera, orchestra, choral, dance, drama, variety) which will be produced by resident groups or touring companies. Television design requires information concerning types of productions (variety shows, dramas, news, soap operas, panel shows) that will be produced for network or local broadcasting or for closed-circuit or syndication release. The actual illuminance levels for television vary from under 1000 lx (100 fc) to several thousand lux (several hundred footcandles), depending upon the type of video camera in use.

In lighting for film, both still and motion picture, the function of the lighting is not only to give the third dimension, but to produce the photochemical changes on the film required to produce the image. Thus, the illuminance required is determined largely by the type of film, that is, its sensitivity.

LUMINAIRES, LAMPS AND CONTROL SYSTEMS

Luminaires for Theatre, Television and Photographic Lighting

In theatre, television and photographic (film) lighting, different types of luminaires are used to produce a quality of light output that falls generally within three basic categories:

1. *Key light*—illumination with defined margins. Its output produces defined, but soft-edged shadows and highlights. (Typical luminaire: Fresnel spotlight.)
2. *Soft-edged light*—diffuse illumination with indefinite margins. Its output produces poorly defined shadows, and softens and fills the shadows produced by key light. Sometimes referred to as "fill light." (Typical luminaire: scoop, soft light.)
3. *Hard-edged light*—illumination which produces sharply defined, geometrically precise shadows. (Typical luminaire: ellipsoidal spotlight.)

The basic types of luminaires used in theatre, television and film production have a variety of optical characteristics (see figure 21-1). Most luminaires contain provisions for the use of color filters or diffusion materials. Some special luminaires, or accessory devices, have the ability to remotely control the aiming, focus or color. The characteristics of these luminaires are described in the following paragraphs.[1]

Nonlens Luminaires. The *nonlens* luminaire (primarily used in film location applications) embodies a lamp, a reflector and frequently a focus mechanism to change the light output by varying the field and beam angles. Those points on the candela distribution curve at which the intensity is at least 10% of its maximum define the *field angle* of a light source. The points at which the

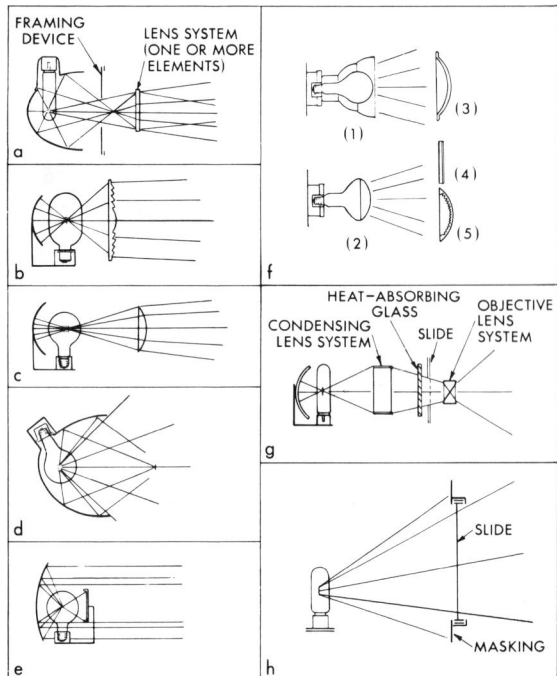

Fig. 21-1. Optical characteristics of stage lighting equipment. (a) Ellipsoidal reflector spotlight. (b) Fresnel-lens spotlight. (c) Plano-convex lens spotlight. (d) Scoop-type floodlight. (e) Parabolic-reflector floodlight. (f) Striplight: (1) reflector with general service lamp; (2) reflector lamp; (3) glass roundel; (4) sheet color medium, (5) spread lens roundel, plain or colored. (g) Lens-type scenic slide projector. (h) Nonlens-type scenic slide projector (Linnebach type).

intensity is at least 50% of maximum define the *beam angle*. The quality of the illumination produced by a nonlens luminaire can vary from soft to hard, depending on lamp type and reflector finish. External beam control is possible with *barn doors* (swinging flaps attached to the front of a luminaire to control the shape and spread of the light beam); however, the degree of control is somewhat limited. In addition, the luminaires can be equipped with scrims, heat filters, daylight correction filters or color frames.

There are many different types of nonlens luminaires that can be considered as spotlights or floodlights. They utilize tungsten-halogen lamps from 100 to 2000 W, and discharge sources from 200 to 4000 W. Nonlens luminaires include scoops, parabolic-reflector spots, soft lights, broads and cyc lights.

Scoop. The *scoop* is a floodlight consisting of a lampholder, lamp and reflector with a matte or brushed finish. The lamp and reflector may have a fixed or variable relationship. Scoops are equipped with front clips to hold a color frame containing either color media or diffusion material. The scoop produces illumination having a field angle of 90–180°. The quality of the illumination is considered soft, and the shadow sharpness depends primarily on the texture of the reflector. Scoops are available from 250 to 450 mm (10

to 18 in) in diameter and are usually equipped with tungsten-halogen lamps from 500 to 2000 W. The lamps are usually frosted for further softening of illumination. In general, the larger the diameter of the scoop, the softer the light output. There are variable-focus scoops which can also vary the beam characteristics.

Parabolic (Reflector) Spotlight. The parabolic spotlight consists of a lamp and a parabolic specular reflector. Some luminaires have a reflector in front of the lamp to redirect light into the main reflector. Other luminaires are equipped with spill rings to minimize spill light and glare. In most types of parabolic spotlights, the lamp and reflector are adjustable to produce a wide or a narrow beam of light; the closer the lamp is to the reflector, the wider the beam. This luminaire produces a hard-edged beam of illumination that cannot be easily controlled, except, in part, by spill rings. A parabolic spotlight is also known as a sun spot or beam projector. Parabolic spotlights have not enjoyed great interest in North America, but they are becoming more popular.

Soft Light. A soft-light luminaire is a well-diffused, almost shadow-free, light source used in special applications. All of the light in these units is reflected off a matte-finish reflector before reaching the subject, and due to this design, they are not efficient sources of illumination.

The soft light is the most common fill light chosen for television studio applications. Soft lights are available from 500 to 8000 W and are used where either shadows or reflections must be minimized.

Broad. Generally, a broad is a small, rectangular floodlight and is used primarily in television for a very wide, soft lighting effect and as a fill light. Broads are available in ratings up to 1500 W and are generally designed to use double-ended tungsten-halogen lamps. They commonly have different distributions in the horizontal and vertical directions. Horizontal spreads of over 100° and vertical distributions of near 90° are common.

Cyclorama Light. Cyclorama, or cyc, lights provide an overall wash of illumination over the cyclorama curtain for background. There are two types of cyc lights: strip cyc lights, which are compartmentalized luminaires with lamps on 200–300 mm (8–12 in.) centers, and cluster lights, mounted on 1.8–2.4 m (6–8 ft) centers.

Strip cyc lights, when mounted either from above or on the floor, can generally light a cyclorama which is 3.6–6.0 m (12–20 ft) high. If lights are used on both top and bottom, or if they have an asymmetrical reflector to improve the beam distribution, even higher surfaces can be suitably lighted. Normally a single group, either suspended from above or floor mounted, will have an illuminance falloff greater than 50% from the top of the space to the bottom. Lamps for these luminaires are available in wattages from 300 to 2000. The striplights have the advantage of much closer mounting to the cyclorama than the cluster lights. This can be critical in those theatres where stage space is limited.

Cluster lights will light a cyclorama up to 9 m (30 ft) high by lighting from the top only, and the illuminance falloff is less than 5%. Since these lights are mounted on 1.8–2.4 m (6–8 ft) centers, rather than the 300 mm (12-in.) centers for striplights, the power saving is substantial. This type of cyc light will usually require greater stage depth than striplights.

Striplights for two-color luminaires use 3300 W/m (1000 W/ft), whereas cluster lights use 820 W/m (250 W/ft) for the same two-color coverage.

Lens Luminaires. The lens luminaire used in theatre, film and television embodies a lamp, a reflector, a system of one or more lenses and, frequently, a focus mechanism to change the light output by varying the field and beam angles. The quality of the illumination produced by a lens luminaire can vary from soft to hard, depending on lamp type and reflector finish. External beam control is possible with barn doors, gobos (devices which allow patterns to be projected onto the stage or curtain, usually cut into a flat metal sheet), irises, shutters, color frames and, in some cases, adjustable-focal-length arrangements to permit zoom control.

There are many different types of lens luminaires that can be considered as spotlights or floodlights. They utilize tungsten-halogen lamps in the range of 100–6000 W. Among those luminaires considered "lens" are Fresnel and ellipsoidal spotlights, PAR luminaires, striplights and follow spots. *Plano-convex* spotlights also fall into this category; however, while they are popular in other parts of the world, they get little use in North America, and for that reason they are not included here.

Fresnel Spotlight. The Fresnel spotlight is a luminaire that embodies a lamp, a Fresnel lens and, generally, a spherical reflector behind the lamp. The field and beam angles can be varied by changing the distance between the lamp and the lens. This action is called *focusing*. The distance between the lamp and the reflector is fixed by the optical design and cannot be changed.

The quality of illumination produced by a Fresnel spotlight tends to be intermediate or hard, and the beam angle is soft-edged. The illumination varies considerably depending on the optics of the luminaire. Typical luminaires of this type have a beam angle of 10–50°, depending on the relative position of the lamp and lens.

Fresnel spotlights are generally equipped with tungsten-halogen lamps with C-13 or C-13D planar fila-

ments. Many Fresnel spotlights are now available using a compact-source metal halide lamp as well. In order to shape the light beam, barn doors are used, as well as *snoots* (metal tubes mounted on the front of spotlights to control stray light—also called funnels, top hats, or high hats). The light beam may also be colored or diffused by means of materials placed in its color frame.

Fresnel spotlights are manufactured in lens diameters from 75 to 610 mm (3 to 24 in.) and in wattages from 75 to 12,000 W. Remote operation (pan, tilt, focusing, on/off) is available on some luminaires. Remote operation of these units can be achieved manually by using a pole, or electrically by use of servomotor-equipped units.

These units are generally designed to be operated within approximately 45° of horizontal, particularly in the higher wattages in the range of 1–2 kW. Operating Fresnel luminaires in this wattage range for long periods of time in a vertical position can cause damage to the luminaire and reduce lamp life (which is fairly short anyway), because the fixture cannot dissipate heat well in that position.

Ellipsoidal Spotlight. The ellipsoidal spotlight, or pattern light, consists of a lamp and ellipsoidal reflector mounted in a fixed relationship. The light is focused through the gate of the unit, where the beam can be shaped with the use of shutters, a gobo or an iris. The shaped beam is then focused by the lens system.

The output of the ellipsoidal spotlight is a hard-edged light with precise beam control. By defocusing the lens system, the hard edge can be softened somewhat. Variable-beam angle units are also available. The lens diameter and focal length will determine the throw and coverage of the unit.

For example, a 6 × 9-in. ellipsoidal has an objective lens with a 6-in. diameter and a focal length of 9 in. These units are sometimes identified by their field angle. This, the 6 × 9-in. ellipsoidal may also be identified as a 30° ellipsoidal.

Ellipsoidal spotlights are available in sizes from 90 mm (3.5 in.), 400 W, to 300 mm (12 in.), 2000 W. Units are also available employing metal halide lamps as the source. The effective throw of the larger units is about 30 m (100 ft).

PAR Luminaire. PAR luminaires embody a PAR lamp, lampholder and housing. The performance of the luminaire depends upon the type of lamp selected. As the beam pattern of most PAR lamps tends to be oval, the luminaire is designed so that the lamp may be rotated to cover the desired area. The beam of a PAR lamp can be controlled somewhat, and glare reduced, by barn doors, and the intensity may be modestly increased by applying a top hat.

PAR luminaires using 650-, 1000- or 1200-W lamps are designed to accommodate either single lamps or groups of lamps in clusters of 3, 6, 9, 12 or more. For special effects, the use of low-voltage, narrow-beam aircraft landing lights is common.

The PAR-64 luminaire is used in many theatres because it can do many jobs and is fairly inexpensive. It is popular with traveling road shows because it can withstand physical abuse.

Striplight or Borderlight. A striplight is a compartmentalized luminaire. Each compartment contains a reflector lamp, or a lamp and reflector, and a color frame. The compartments are arranged in line and wired on two, three or four alternate circuits, each circuit producing a different color.

Striplights provide an overall wash of illumination on a stage. They may also be located at the front of a stage (*footlights*) to provide an overall low illuminance level.

While striplights have been replaced in many applications by more versatile individual units such as Fresnel and ellipsoidal spotlights, they do still find use in those applications where cost is a consideration. Striplights and borderlights are less expensive than Fresnel and ellipsoidal lights. They are also used in some applications where labor costs are high and the use of the more flexible units would increase the labor required to set up a show.

Luminaires using PAR-38, PAR-46 and PAR-56 lamps may be arranged in linear strips functioning as borderlights or striplights.

There are striplights available which use 12-V MR-16 lamps wired in series. While these units are useful in applications where space is at a premium, they are generally not considered a suitable substitute for full-size striplights. In addition, cost and required maintenance are relatively high for these units.

Follow Spot. A follow spot is a special type of spotlight, stand mounted, with a shutter (commonly a douser), an iris, and a color frame, or "boomerang," to hold color media. Most follow spots utilize a tungsten-halogen lamp, a metal halide lamp or an arc source and a lens system. For high-intensity follow spots, the carbon arc has been almost totally replaced by compact metal halide or xenon lamps.[2] All of these arc units produce more output, watt for watt, than the tungsten-halogen units. Follow spots are selected to provide the throws required for the application.

Arc Light Luminaire. There are still some arc units in use today, although they are not popular in new installation. An arc light luminaire uses a carbon electrode arc as the source of illumination. These produce carbon monoxide as a by-product. This is, in some concentrations, a deadly gas. In addition, the operators required for these luminaires can be expensive, particularly for the small theatre or school auditorium.

Such luminaires are manufactured in two basic forms: (1) equipped with a Fresnel lens for general illumination, and (2) equipped with a reflector and optical system for follow spot operation. Carbons available for these luminaires are of various types, producing different intensities and color temperatures. Carbons and ballasts are available for either dc or ac operation.

Lamps for Theatre, Television and Photographic Lighting

The most prevalent light sources for theatre stages are tungsten-halogen lamps that have been designed especially for these types of service. For television and film lighting, tungsten-halogen and hydrargyrum medium-arc-length iodide (HMI) discharge lamps are the two most common sources. In still photography, tungsten-halogen and variable-output xenon strobe are the most common lamps. Conventional incandescent spotlight lamps have been supplanted by tungsten-halogen lamps designed to retrofit into existing luminaires. Discharge sources such as DMI and CID lamps, both in the same group as HMI, are also popular. Ballasts for these discharge sources have been developed which produce no noticeable flicker, for use in television and film lighting.

Carbon arcs are still used occasionally, principally for motion picture production, but have been supplanted to a great extent by multiple lamp arrays of 650- or 1000-W tungsten-halogen or PAR lamps, often with integral daylight filters, and (more commonly) by compact-source metal halide lamps.

Virtually all types of light sources find occasional use in theatre, television and film production. For example, metal halide HID lamps are used to light such areas as stadiums and arenas, providing illuminances and color quality suitable for televising performances. They also have the capability of providing "daylight fill" for movie and television productions. Fluorescent lamps with a variety of spectral power distributions, often on special dimming systems, may light cycloramas in television studios or theatre stages, or backings of motion picture sets. Fluorescent lamps are also used as television and motion picture base lights.

Both fluorescent and HID lamps for use in television and film work require high-frequency ballasts to overcome the flicker effect inherent in these lamps when operated on 60-Hz power.

Xenon flash tubes, similar to those for photo studios, may be used in a repetitive-flash mode for theatrical effects. Lasers and light-emitting diodes may also be used for spectacular effects. Standard PAR and R lamps, as well as sign, decorative and indicator lamps, have a variety of common theatrical applications.

Fiber optics are employed in many stage settings for special effects such as star curtains or irregular linear shapes.

Extensive data on all types of light sources are found in chapter 6, Light Sources, including lamp operating principles, physical and performance characteristics, and tables of commonly available types.

Tungsten-Halogen and Incandescent Lamps.[3-6] Data

for lamps most frequently used in lighting for theatre stages, television and motion picture production, and professional still photography are found in chapter 6. In many cases lamps may appear to be mechanically interchangeable with each other, that is, they have the same base and light source location. However, caution should be exercised. For example, in luminaires designed specifically for tungsten-halogen lamps, the bulbs of some incandescent lamps may be too large to fit within the luminaire. Furthermore, there may be differences in filament configuration that could affect the luminaire's optical performance.

Also, some luminaires may not provide adequate heat dissipation for higher-wattage lamps. Lighting equipment manufacturers should be consulted for the maximum allowable wattage.

High-Intensity Discharge Lamps. A wide variety of

HID lamps, employing metal halides as the light-generating medium, are used for general interior and exterior lighting systems. These compact arc lamps are also used to provide supplementary light of approximate daylight color for television and film production, and have been adapted into such specialized equipment as scenic projectors and follow spots. Xenon short arcs of the types commonly used for motion picture projection are also used in some follow spots and scenic projectors.

Special types of metal halide lamps have been developed with characteristics that are often better suited to the requirements of lighting for film and television production outside of the studios, and for scenic projectors and follow spots. The two principal groups[7] of lamps are commonly known as HMI[8] and CSI. Two additional types are DMI and CID[9], both in the same group as HMI.

HMI, DMI and CID lamps are available in a range of sizes, from 200 to 18,000 W. HMI and DMI lamps are of double-ended construction, CID are of single-ended construction, and both have short arc gaps, such that their arc luminance is several times that of typical incandescent spotlight lamps. This feature makes them useful in follow spots and effects projectors. There are also single-ended HMI lamps available from 575 to 4000 W. CID and HMI lamps are also available in PAR configurations. HMI and DMI have a broad spectrum (see figure 21-2) with a very high color rendering index, making them well suited as sources for "daylight fill" in movie and television shooting. Effective service lives range from 300 to 2000 h. After ignition, they require a minute or so to warm up. Most ballast and igniter equipment can restrike the lamp

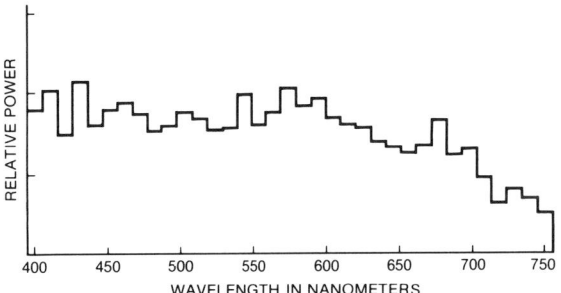

Fig. 21-2. Relative spectral power distribution for a typical HMI lamp.

immediately after it has been turned off. The flicker produced by these ac-operated lamps is not generally a problem for television, but for motion pictures requires careful coordination of frame rates and shutter angles to render it inconspicuous. Ballasts are available which provide waveform and frequency modifications that will minimize or eliminate flicker in motion pictures.

CSI lamps are available in 400 and 1000 W. The latter wattage is also furnished in a PAR-64, over which interchangeable spread lenses may be used. Life ratings range from 500 to 1500 h. CSI lamps also have relatively high source luminances that permit effective image projection and follow spot applications. Their spectral composition (see figure 21-3) departs substantially from a blackbody radiator and has a correlated color temperature somewhere between daylight and incandescent. Filters are often used to blend with daylight (blue) or incandescent (yellow). As with other metal halide lamps, a warmup of a few minutes is required; however, CSI lamps with mogul bipost bases will restrike when hot if suitable igniters are included with the ballast. Electronic, dimmable ballasts for CID and HMI lamps are available which can reduce flicker.

HMI lamps are far more common in the various performance industries than CID, CSI or DMI. Refer to the lamp information tables in chapter 6 for infor-

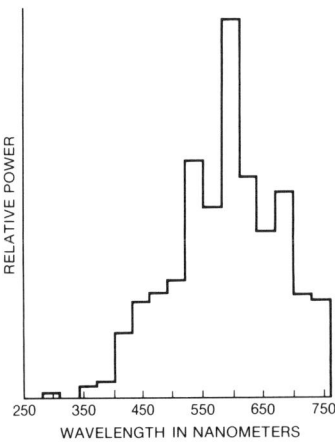

Fig. 21-3. Relative spectral power distribution for a typical CSI lamp.

mation on lamp color temperature, color rendering and life.

ANSI Codes. The American National Standards Institute (ANSI) assigns three-letter designations to incandescent lamps, including tungsten-halogen lamps, used in photographic, theatre and television lighting applications. The letters are arbitrarily chosen and do not, in themselves, describe the lamps. Neither do they imply tolerances or minimum levels of performance with respect to such nonmechanical characteristics as life and light output. When an ANSI code number is assigned to a lamp type at the request of a lamp manufacturer, it may be used by all manufacturers as a commercial ordering code. The assignment of an ANSI code number means that the basic parameters of the coded lamps, such as nominal wattage, type of base, size of bulb, light center length and approximate color temperature, are specified so that physical interchangeability of lamps is assured. However, the ANSI code does not guarantee equal performance of lamps from different manufacturers. Furthermore, lamp manufacturers sometimes make improvements in lamp performance characteristics, including life and lumens, beyond the values that are stated on the original ANSI code application.

Manufacturer's Ordering Codes. The lamp manufacturer's ordering code is another type of lamp designation. Often two or more manufacturers will agree on the code designation for a lamp type. Manufacturer's codes are usually descriptive of some of the lamp characteristics, and often include lamp wattage and bulb size and shape. Some manufacturers of lighting equipment supply lamps marked with their own private codes to identify the proper lamps for their equipment.

Low-Noise Construction. Most tungsten-halogen lamps for theatre, television and film, and many of the incandescent lamps for such applications, have special low-noise construction to minimize audible noise generation when operated on ac circuits. The lamp manufacturer should be consulted for information on which lamps have low-noise construction. Lamps, sockets and wiring all tend to generate more audible noise when used with dimmers that distort the normal ac sine wave (solid-state dimmers) than with ordinary autotransformer or resistance dimmers. Generally noise is not generated on dc circuits. Recent developments in dimmer choke design and firing techniques greatly reduce the noise generated by lamps operating on dimmers which distort the waveform.

Caution Notices. Caution notices are generally provided with most lamps for stage and studio service. Virtually all tungsten-halogen lamps operate with internal pressure above atmospheric; therefore, protection from lamp abrasion and avoidance of overvoltage operation is advised. The use of screening is advised where appropriate to protect people and surroundings in case a lamp shatters.

Control Systems for Theatre and Television Lighting

The design of a lighting control system is based on the artistic and technical needs of projected productions.[10-14] It is related to the building architecture, luminaire rigging system and density of electrical outlet distribution. Design parameters are expressed in terms of power capability, number of lighting outlets, dimmer bank capacity, interconnection system and lighting control facilities.

The performance requirements for a lighting control system must provide the designers with total flexibility of control over all of the luminaires lighting the set. There must, therefore, be adequate dimmers, circuits and control equipment to establish the number of lighting channels required, to assemble those channels into cues, and to switch and fade from one cue to another, thus achieving the desired lighting changes.

Lighting control systems for the theatre and for television differ slightly. Theatre lighting control systems make extensive use of memory, require accurately timed faders and must be capable of complex simultaneous operations, while television lighting control systems generally require less memory and fewer operational features, and benefit from automated dimmer channels.

Lighting control systems divide into two basic categories, described as *dimmer-per-circuit* (sometimes also called "dimmer-per-outlet") and *power programming* (sometimes called "line-voltage-patch"). Dimmer-per-circuit systems provide a dimmer of adequate capacity for every lighting outlet and use a "soft" (or electronically generated) patch at the control console to assign dimmers to control channels. It is usual for the dimmer number and the outlet, or circuit, number to be the same. If budgets are low, cost is sometimes reduced by connecting more than one outlet or fixture to the same circuit. Power programming systems employ a cord-and-jack or slider-and-bus system to switch individual outlets to larger-capacity dimmers.

Dimmers. Almost all of the lighting control devices used in theatre and television lighting use *silicon-controlled-rectifier* (SCR) dimmers, which are manufactured in a range of 1–12 kW. Triac dimmers, manufactured in a nominal capacity of 2 kW, are used occasionally in inexpensive portable dimming equipment. Dimmers are rated by Underwriters Laboratory (UL) for continuous operation at 100% of their rating.

For good lighting operation, it is essential that electronic dimmers have stable output, cause no interference to audio and video circuits or to other dimmers, be insensitive to load and have high efficiency. The *dimmer curve*,[15,16] that is, the relation of the dimmer line voltage output on the control input voltage, is usually fixed. Some systems allow alternative dimming curves to be selected via software in the dimmer rack or at the control console.

Dimmers are assembled in portable packs of 6 to 24 or into racks which may contain several hundred dimmers custom built to suit the installation.

All electronic dimmers require ventilation to maintain components within specified operating temperature ranges. The amount of ventilation required is dependent on the dimmer's efficiency and the individual manufacturer's recommendations. A 97% efficient dimmer will produce approximately 100–120 Btu/h for each kilowatt of connected load.

Distributed dimming systems, those in which individual dimming modules are at the lighting instrument location rather than in a centralized dimmer enclosure, are becoming more common. They are particularly cost effective in older houses where existing wiring is to be reused and is limited in capacity. The controls can follow a common protocol which can be easily "daisy-chained" to reduce the cost of installation and maintenance.

Electrical Installation. A major expenditure in any lighting system, whether theatrical or architectural, is the cost of the electrical distribution. To minimize this cost, care should be taken to locate the dimmer racks so as to achieve the most economical balance between the cost of the electrical feeders to the dimmer racks and the cost of the distribution wiring from there to the individual lighting positions or outlet boxes. For solid-state dimming systems it is required to install a "hot" wire and a neutral from each dimmer module to its outlet. Therefore, the distribution wiring required for an electronically dimmed lighting system requires more wires than for a typical room lighting system. The cost of installing these additional wires must be included in the studies when determining the best location for major system components.

In determining the size of power distribution feeders for electronic dimming systems—that is, the wiring from the building electrical system to the dimming rack —the United States Institute of Theatre Technology (USITT) recommends that the neutral conductor be sized for 130% of the rated capacity of circuit conductors. This is to allow for the effect of the harmonic frequencies generated by the electronic dimmers during operation. In portable installations, many municipalities have mandated two parallel neutral conductors, each sized the same as the individual feeder conductors, to provide adequate capacity for this neutral current.

Dimmer-Per-Circuit. Technology now allows a properly sized dimmer to be directly connected to the various lighting outlets. While this method leads to a large number of small dimmers, the improvement in wiring efficiency and the elimination of enclosures and power interconnect panels, when considered in conjunction with the added flexibility of these systems, usually amount to a cost saving and significant operating advantages. The control console, whether computerized or manual, generally contains an electronic soft patch that connects the control channels to the dimmers, performing much the same function as the power interconnect panels formerly did.

Power Programming System. This technique uses a smaller number of large dimmers, normally with one dimmer per control channel, and permits designated outlets to be connected to selected dimmers with a power switching system. This system is not often used, since the price of dimming equipment relative to the total theatrical lighting system cost has come down.

Manual Preset Lighting Control System. The basic form of lighting control is the manual preset system, which employs groups of manual controllers for each dimmer or control channel. These controllers are arranged in horizontal rows termed *presets*. Presets are connected to submaster faders that are, in turn, switched to paired master faders for proportional, dipless (smooth dimming curve) cross fades between presets. Lighting levels are set as required on individual controllers in each preset, and lighting cues are achieved through submaster and master controllers.

Memory Lighting Control Systems. Memory lighting control systems are, in general, programmed software based systems. In such a system, the operational program is permanently stored in a read-only-memory (ROM) section, which may be updated by the manufacturer to provide additional operational facilities as they are developed. These systems may incorporate video monitors for displaying cue information and have a floppy disk or cassette for storage of program information. Peripheral equipment used with memory lighting control consoles may include hand-held remote controllers used with remote receptacles at lighting positions to assist in focusing lights, designer's remote consoles (used in conjunction with the console in the operator's booth), printers and remote monitors.

Communications between control positions and the dimmers can be accomplished by discrete analog signals or by multiplexed control signals. Industry standards exist for digital and analog multiplexed protocols as well as for discrete analog methods. These standard protocols provide for interchangeable hardware, and may reduce the complexity and cost of wiring.

LIGHTING FOR THEATRES

Theatres are of two basic types, for live productions and for film (motion picture). The former can be further classified as legitimate, community and school theatres. The term *live productions* refers to the presence of live actors on stage. In the case of motion picture theatres, there is only one classification to consider, and that is the indoor auditorium. Drive-in theatres, which were popular several years ago, have all but disappeared.

Lighting requirements for the marquee, lobby and foyer are similar for live and for film auditorium theatres. An important goal common to both types of theatre is to reduce the illuminance as a patron proceeds from the brightly lighted marquee and street area to the lobby, the foyer and eventually the auditorium. The lighting requirements for the various types of spaces within the theatres are quite different, however.

Marquee. Attracting attention is one of the motives in the design of theatre exteriors. Much of the selling for current and coming attractions can be done here. Flashing signs, running borders, color-changing effects, floodlighting and architectural elements are but a few of the many techniques employed. See chapter 29, Lighting for Advertising. As styles, and tastes, change, it is necessary to design the exterior elements of a theatre to convey the feeling of the neighborhood. Many marquee "current attraction" panels are lighted with incandescent filament lamps, fluorescent sign tubing or fluorescent lamps behind diffusing glass or plastic. Opaque or colored letters on a lighted field are generally more effective than luminous letters on a dark field. The principal requirement is uniformity of luminance, because luminance differences across the face of the sign which exceed a ratio of 3:1 from the brightest to the darkest area will be noticeable and will detract from the message being presented. See figure 21-4.

Infrared units for heating and snow melting may be considered in areas where warranted by climatic conditions. (See chapter 5, Nonvisual Effects of Radiant Energy, for further discussion.)

Lobby. An illuminance of 200 lx (20 fc) is desirable in theatre lobbies. The ceiling treatment is often inte-

grated with the marquee soffit. Many lighting treatments are applicable here; some considerations are easy maintenance, designs that retain appearance and architectural suitability, and a pattern of luminances that attracts as well as influences the flow of traffic. Built-in lighting with fluorescent lamps, spotlighting or transillumination has been successful for poster panels. Luminances range from 70 to 350 cd/m², depending on surroundings and brightness competition. An important consideration is to allow sufficient depth behind the illuminated panel so fairly uniform illuminance may be obtained. (See chapter 29 for further information on sign construction.)

Foyer. Usually a restful, subdued atmosphere is desirable in the foyer. Illumination from large, low-luminance elements, such as coves, is one successful method. Wall lighting and accents on statuary, paintings, posters and plants are important in developing atmosphere. Light must not spill into the auditorium. General illuminance levels from 50 lx (5 fc) for motion picture theatres to 150 lx (15 fc) for live production theatres are recommended.

Both lobbies and foyers may be used as public gathering places and as places of assembly for civic and business events. All of the ultimate uses to which the space will be put must be considered in the design of the interior, including the lighting.

Live Production Theatres

Although there are many varieties of indoor and outdoor live production theatres, such as amphitheatre, music tent, arena and open stage, the most common are the traditional proscenium and the open stage or thrust type. (See figure 21-5.)

The proscenium-type theatre is composed, typically, of a seating area and a stage area. It may serve not only as a theatre, but also as an assembly and lecture hall, a study room, and a concert or audiovisual aids area as well as for numerous other activities. Considerable attention is being given to the development of speech and theatre arts programs not only in schools but also as a community activity among adult groups. The many uses of the theatre require well-planned facilities which are properly lighted.

It is important to provide the proper quantity and locations of power outlets, and the proper luminaires and control equipment, so that the stage lighting designer has the tools to create dramatic lighting for all stage performances. The necessary structural provisions must be made to allow placement of the lighting equipment and access for installation, operation and maintenance.

Seating Area. The seating area should be provided with diffuse, comfortable illumination. Because of the many purposes the seating area often serves, different

Fig. 21-4. Recommended Illuminances and Theatre Advertising Sign Luminances in Various Locations

Type of Area in Which Theatre Is Located	Range of Ambient Horizontal Illuminances, lx (fc)		Recommended Sign Luminance, cd/m²
City center	50 – 100	(5 – 10)	500 – 1200
Shopping mall	20 – 70	(2 – 7)	400 – 700
Residential	10 – 50	(2 – 5)	300 – 500
Under marquee	200 – 500	(20 – 50)	2000 – 5000

Fig. 21-5. Two common types of live producton theatre stages. The upper photograph shows the traditional proscenium stage in New York State Theatre in Lincoln Center; the lower photograph shows the open or thrust-type stage.

illuminances are necessary. An illuminance of 100–200 lx (10–20 fc) should always be provided in the seating area. This basic lighting should be under dimmer control, preferably from several stations, such as the stage lighting control board, the projection booth and a staff entrance. There should be transfer capabilities, however, so that the lighting will not be accidentally turned on during performances. Lighting equipment for the seating area may include general downlight luminaires, coves, sidewall urns, and curtain and mural lights. Higher illuminances may be required for visual tasks to

be performed in the space, such as reading or the taking of examinations. If such tasks are expected to take place, the illuminance should be designed for at least 300 lx (30 fc). Selected lighting system circuits may also be used as work lights for cleaning and rehearsals. Separate control of certain circuits should be provided for emergency conditions. "Panic" switches should be provided which will allow the operator to bring on selected lights in the house in case of emergency. This control must be independent of dimmer or switch settings. In accordance with local and national codes, an alternate electrical supply for emergency lighting must be provided. This system may include emergency house lights, exit lights, shielded aisle and step lights, and other required lighting.

Stage Area.[17-19] Proper lighting for dramatic presentations extends beyond visibility to the achievement of artistic composition, the production of mood effects, the revelation of forms as three-dimensional, and movement. These functions of stage lighting result from the manipulation of various qualities, quantities, colors and directions of light. They vary from one performance to the next as well as throughout a single performance. The lighting layout may be affected by the use planned for the theatre and by the frequency of use.

Stage areas to be lighted include the stage apron, or forestage; acting areas upstage from the proscenium arch, including areas above and below the stage floor; extension stage areas; auxiliary acting areas in the auditorium; foreground scenery and properties; and background scenery and properties.

Basic Lighting Functions

An appreciation of the dramatic potential of lighting begins with an understanding of its four basic functions:

Visibility. This is the most basic function of lighting in the theatre. For the audience to hear and understand in the theatre, they must be able to see.

Motivation. Motivation or naturalism is the term given to the expression of time and place.

Composition. Composition is revealed artistically through the proper use of light and shadow. Warm and cool light give plasticity and composition to the visual effect. The concept of the production as indicated by the playwright and implemented by the director determines the approach of the designer.

Mood. Mood, or atmosphere, as created by the total visual effect, brings the stage into focus with the meaning of the play. The final visual effect is provided by equipment that has been chosen by the designer because it supplies the desired output of light in terms of intensity, form, color and movement.

Properties of Stage Lighting

The controllable properties of light, as it applies to the theatre, include intensity, color, distribution and movement. The control exercised by the designer over these properties has a direct bearing on the success of the performers in achieving the intended response from the audience.

Intensity. Intensity control is achieved by the use of various types of luminaires, lamps, mounting positions and color media, and, of course, by altering the illuminance through the use of dimmers. Precise, consistent dimmer control is essential for establishing and maintaining various intensity levels.

Form. Form, meaning the density, spread and direction of the light, calls for a wide variety of luminaire types and mounting positions. The angle of the light relative to the object and the viewer creates dimensionality, which in turn is a function of the fixture type, location, focus and dimmer balance.

Color. Color in lighting design is used to accent, enhance, distort and motivate the scene. Color is controlled by means of lamp selection, dimmers and separate filters which may be placed in front of each source. Incandescent lamps, in particular, will become much warmer as they are dimmed. A tonal quality can be obtained by the additive mixture of two or more sources.

Movement. Movement consists of a change in one or all of the qualities of light. Aside from a manually operated follow spot or special units with which the aiming or color filters can be remotely controlled and changed, this is accomplished by means of dimming individual luminaires rather than by luminaire movement.

The Need for Stage Lighting

To determine what stage lighting positions are required, it is first necessary to determine the use to which the space will be put. Regardless of size or budget, stages may be used for a variety of performances or purposes. These include drama, comedy, dance, civic functions and music, both choral and instrumental. In addition, the stage may be in a variety of locations, from elementary schools to major legitimate theatres. The principles of stage lighting will not change for any of the various functions or venues, but the budget and complexity of the program may determine the extent to which the various techniques will be employed.

For theatre, dance, opera and similar programs, the lighting must come from the front, to light for the audience, and from the back, sides and top, to produce the effects needed to model and create mood and dimensionality.

For musical programs, both choral and instrumental, it is necessary to light from the front for the audience, but light must also be provided from above and behind so the performers can read their music.

Lighting Locations.[20] Basic locations for lighting equipment (see figure 21-6) may be divided into two groups as follows: (1) locations in front of the proscenium opening (which include the auditorium ceiling, side walls of auditorium or proscenium or both, balcony front, follow-spot booth, and edge of the stage apron); and (2) locations behind the proscenium opening, such as tormentor pipes for side lights, overhead cyclorama pipes for top lights, and cyclorama pit for base lights, as well as special locations employed as needed, such as overhead light pipes (stage electrics), free space at the sides and rear of the stage main acting area for floor-mounted or hanging equipment, and below-stage areas. Though the positions may be fixed, virtually every luminaire is portable and gets shifted around for each production. The focus, direction, intensity and color are generally different for each production.

To determine the lighting positions required, the stage may be divided into lighting areas. While each project has its own unique requirements, the following is indicative of an approach which could be used.

A typical multipurpose stage can be divided into lighting areas of 3–4-m (10–12-ft) diameter. Therefore, a stage 12 m (40 ft) wide by 9 m (30 ft) deep would have three rows of four lighting areas each, for a total of 12 lighting areas. From the center of each position, luminaires may be placed in the following locations relative to each of the 12 lighting areas (see figure 21-6):

1. Two luminaires 35–45° above horizontal, one located 45° to each side of the lighting area. Ellipsoidal and, possibly, Fresnel spotlights can be used at these locations. They should be located on a "front-of-house" ceiling bridge, box boom, stage electric or tormentor position.
2. One luminaire 35–45° above horizontal and directly in front of each lighting area. These could be the same as the luminaires in item 1 above, with the possible addition of PAR-type luminaires for the upstage positions. Mounting locations would be similar to those in item 1 above.
3. One luminaire directly above the lighting area. It can be an ellipsoidal spotlight, a PAR, a striplight or borderlight, or, possibly, a scoop. The mounting should be from the stage electrics.

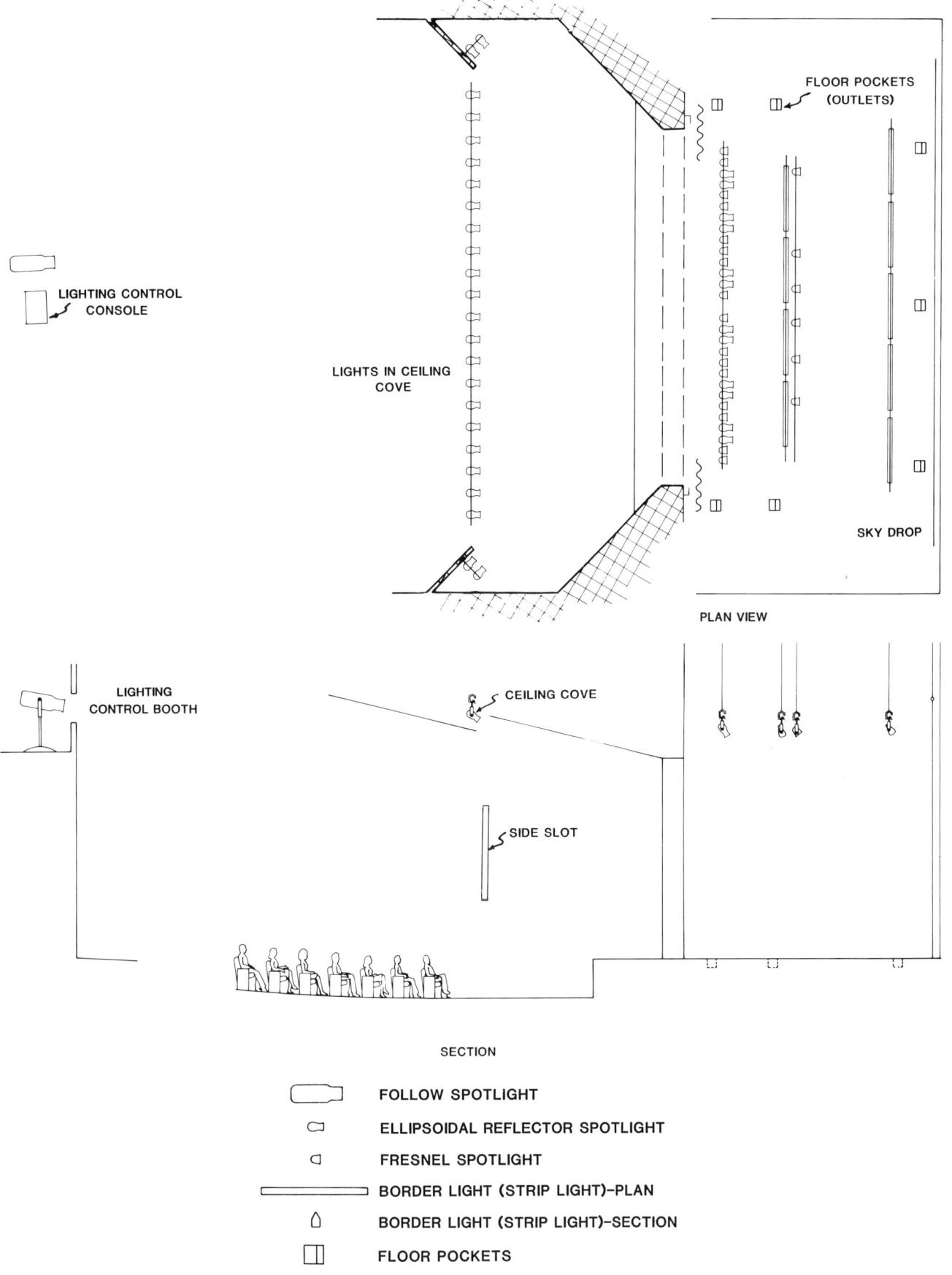

PLAN VIEW

SECTION

FOLLOW SPOTLIGHT

ELLIPSOIDAL REFLECTOR SPOTLIGHT

FRESNEL SPOTLIGHT

BORDER LIGHT (STRIP LIGHT)–PLAN

BORDER LIGHT (STRIP LIGHT)–SECTION

FLOOR POCKETS

Fig. 21-6. Typical plan and section of an average size theatre.

4. One luminaire 45–75° above the horizontal and located directly behind the lighting area as a back light. An ellipsoidal spotlight or a PAR can be used for this purpose. If on hand, or if lowest cost is a consideration, striplights (borderlights) can be used in this position. The mounting should be from the stage electrics.

In addition to the positions listed above, a row of cyc lights located at the top of the cyclorama and, ideally, about 2.5 m (8 ft) in front of it can be used to provide light on the background. Many times this space will not be available, and compromises will have to be made or equipment selected which will be more effective in the space available. In the case of high cycloramas, or where necessary for an effect, another row of cyc lights can be placed at the bottom of the cyclorama.

This is not intended to be a comprehensive list of all stage lighting positions. There are many other positions, such as 25–35° above the horizontal at (for instance) the front of a balcony, which can be effective in reducing shadows, particularly for television work. The side-wall slots and tormentor positions are effective for modeling and for dance productions. The goal of the stage lighting system design is to provide the capacity and flexibility to permit the stage lighting designer to be as creative as necessary to provide the lighting required for the full range of activities envisioned for the stage.

Locations of Luminaires in Front of the Proscenium Opening

Luminaires in the Auditorium Ceiling. Stage-lighting luminaires in the auditorium ceiling are generally used for the basic purpose of lighting downstage and apron acting areas. Each luminaire should produce a clearly defined light beam that can provide an average illuminance of 500–1000 lx (50–100 fc) of white light on a vertical plane, with adjustable means for a controlled cutoff, so that the beam can be varied in shape to cover a desired area with little or no spill onto adjacent areas. (See figure 21-1.) These spotlights are best located behind slots, or coves, in the ceiling and are ideally mounted in a continuous slot stretching across the ceiling from side wall to side wall.

Luminaires in Auditorium and Proscenium Side Walls. Luminaires located on or in the side walls, although not absolutely required, are recommended. They are used mainly as a supplement to the ceiling spotlights, and are of a similar type. Preferably, these luminaires should be recessed into wall slots. They provide lower angles of throw than the ceiling units and offer an excellent opportunity for side lighting with a wide range of different angles of throw.

Luminaires on the Balcony Front. Angle lighting from spotlights in the side walls or ceiling will provide effective front lighting for most purposes, but there are occasions when the balcony position affords desirable low angles of throw or a soft wash of directional front lighting. Attention must be paid to where the shadows fall. There is a danger that shadows from low-angle front spots may fall on the scenery and move as the actor moves. This will cause an unacceptable distraction. (Effect projectors, however, are not often put in this location.) Proper access must be provided to these spaces so that lights can be readily put in place, focused and lamped.

Follow Spot Booth. Follow spots are used to highlight selected performers. A follow spot should be capable of providing a level of at least 2000 lx (200 fc) in an area of 2.5 m (8 ft) diameter, and should embody means to enable the size and shape of the light beam to be varied so that it may be reduced to cover the head of a person only, or be widened to flood a considerable portion of the stage. In addition to the usual accessories, such as an iris, spread lens or horizontal paired shutters, follow spot equipment often includes either a color wheel or a multislide color boomerang (a device for inserting individual filters of several different colors into the follow spot) that can be operated from either the side or the rear of the spotlight in order to change the color of the light. Light sources for follow spots are usually incandescent, xenon or compact-source metal halide. Follow spot positions should be near the center of the house at the rear. It should be possible for the beam of light to reach all areas of the stage and, ideally, the orchestra pit in front of the stage. Care must be taken to allow for any portable stage which may be designed to fit over the orchestra pit to assure the follow spot can reach the front of the portable stage.

Footlights. Footlights are a set of striplights, sometimes multicolored, at the front edge of the stage platform, used to soften face shadows cast by overhead luminaires and to add general tone-lighting from below. Footlights may be used to light large flat scenery, for special effects, for mood or to duplicate period scenes.

Locations Behind the Proscenium Opening

Overhead Locations. The greatest number of luminaires in any one location upstage of the proscenium will be mounted on the first pipe or bridge immediately upstage. The luminaires for this position may include spotlights, borderlights and scenic projectors. The majority of the spotlight units are required to produce a soft-edged beam that is widely variable in focus. A number of ellipsoidal reflector spotlights or PARs are usually mounted in this row. There should be provisions for mounting additional rows of lights on pipes parallel with the proscenium opening every 2–2.5 m (6–8 ft) of stage depth.

Connector Strips and Drop Boxes for Stage-Light Pipes (Stage Electric). The basic purpose of a connector strip or drop box is to provide a simple and quick method of electrically connecting a number of lighting units, wherever mounted on an associated pipe, by means of a series of outlets. The length of a connector strip mounted on a pipe or bridge (sometimes called a *stage electric*) should approximate the width of the stage proscenium opening. Outlets should not be spaced closer than 300 mm (12 in) apart, and each outlet or group of outlets should be on an individual circuit with a separate neutral. So that any available pipe may be used for luminaires, a more flexible alternative, or supplement, to connector strips fixed to specified light pipes is a number of multiconductor cables, permanently attached to the gridiron, with a box of minimum proportions housing an appropriate number of outlets at the other end. Every cable is long enough so the outlet box can be lowered and attached to either end of a stage pipe. Floor and wall boxes are positioned throughout the stage to provide for a range of portable lights.

Border Lighting and Scoops for Stage Light Pipes. While Fresnel and ellipsoidal luminaires are commonly used on stage light pipes, there are additional luminaires which find use in these locations, also. A borderlight or series of scoops provides general downlighting across an area of the stage and provides overhead illumination of hanging curtains and scenery. They contribute tonal quality to the overall lighting effect. Separated control of different sections of the borderlight or scoops enables parts of the stage width to be variously accented in brightness and color. Borderlights, other than those for cyclorama illumination, should be wired on three or four separate color circuits and should be capable of providing illumination of the whole width of a curtain or flat scenic drop. They should be mounted 1.2 m (4 ft), or more, upstage of the borderlight equipment. The illuminance provided by borderlights or scoops in the center of the vertical surface should be not less than 250 lx (25 fc) of white light when measured at a point 1.8 m (6 ft) from the stage floor.

Cyclorama Top Lighting. Cyclorama borderlights must be long enough to illuminate the whole of the visible width of the background, independent of illumination from cyclorama bottom lighting. Cyclorama lighting requires at least twice the illuminance provided by other borderlights. When the cyclorama is an important feature and deep color filters are used, then the wattage of the associated borderlight equipment may be from 2 to 4 times that of a regular borderlight, depending on the density of the filter. The required illuminance may necessitate two parallel rows of borderlights, using, for example, 250-W PAR-38 lamps on 150-mm (6-in.) centers or 500-W PAR-56 lamps on 200-mm (8-in.) centers in each strip. An alternative is the use of compact lamp striplights using series-wired MR-16 lamps.

Backlighting from an Upstage Pipe. It is desirable to provide a row of high-intensity, narrow-beam luminaires, such as Fresnel spotlights, parabolic spotlights, or PAR luminaires, suspended on an upstage pipe, and directed downstage to provide backlighting of artists in the main acting area. For example, there may be one 500–750-W luminaire for every 1.2–1.8 m (4–6 ft) of effective stage width.

Mounting for Stage Side Lights. Although other mounting methods may be used where conditions permit, there are two general methods of providing side stage lighting: either on suspended three- or four-rung ladders, or from vertical, floor-mounted boomerangs or tormentor pipes. These positions are essential to provide side and modeling light.

Special Theatrical Effects. Fluorescent paints, fabrics or other materials responding to UV radiation are often used for special theatrical effects. Sources for exciting the fluorescent materials include mercury lamps with filters for absorbing visible radiation, fluorescent "black light" lamps, which also require a filter, and integral-filtered fluorescent "black light" lamps. Carbon arc follow spots are sometimes filtered for "black light" effects. Strobe lights and lasers are used in today's theatre. Great care must be exercised where using UV and lasers to comply with all government and municipal regulations and to avoid operations which could cause permanent eye damage to the audience, the performers or the operators.

Automated Luminaires and Accessories. Many theatrical and television productions use luminaires that can be moved or steered, or whose color, pattern and beam edge, and focus can be changed to achieve the effect of moving light. These luminaires will generally be mounted in the same way as fixed luminaires, but require additional power and control wiring.

Lens accessories for traditional fixed-type luminaires are available to allow alternative colors of gels to be fitted to the luminaire and allow remote selection of the colors. These often require additional power and control wiring.

Scenic Projectors. An increased understanding of the techniques of slide projection by theatre personnel has led to an improvement of the basic optical design for projection in the live theatre. Some of the principal improvements include: increased projector lamp wattages up to 10 kW; the introduction of new compact metal halide lamps to provide additional scene illumination and coverage; improved methods for slidemaking; remote, programmed slide changing; wide-angle projection to screen widths of 1.5 times the projection distance; standardization of units to permit easy interchangeability; and the availability of relatively simple and inexpensive remote-control 35-mm projectors.

The general availability of the 35-mm, 2×2-in. slide projector, as well as the increased availability of larger units, has led to much experimentation in this field. Multisources, wide ranges in composition and buildup of the total picture, multiscreens and mosaic designs, fractured pictures, time and dimming variants, and adjustment of the controllable properties of auxiliary light sources all combine to make projection an exciting light tool in theatrical presentations.[21].

Motion Picture Theatres

Auditorium-Type Theatres. The objectives of auditorium lighting in the motion picture theatre may be outlined as follows:

- To create a pleasing, distinctive environment
- To retain brightness and color contrasts inherent in the motion picture
- To create adequate visibility for safe and convenient circulation at all times
- To provide comfortable viewing conditions

For general lighting during intermission, 50 lx (5 fc) is considered the minimum. During the picture, illumination is necessary for safe and convenient circulation of patrons. Illuminances between 1 and 2 lx (0.1 and 0.2 fc) represent good practice. The screen luminance with the picture running is between 3 and 20 cd/m^2. The need to eliminate stray light on the screen dictates controlled lighting for at least the front section of the auditorium. Downlighting is one of the most effective methods for this purpose. In general, diffusing elements, such as coves, allow too much light to fall on the screen if they provide adequate illumination in the seating area. Diffusing wall brackets, semidirect luminaires and luminous elements are generally too bright to be used for supplying illumination during the picture presentation.

The luminous contrast between the screen and its black border is sometimes more than 1000:1, creating uncomfortable viewing conditions. The luminances of areas around the screen can be raised; however, they should not have decorations which may be distracting. Light for this purpose may be reflected from the screen under special conditions, or it may be supplied by supplementary projectors or by elements behind the screen.

Curtains may be lighted in color with a projector border during intermissions. Adequate spotlighting on the stage is desirable for announcements and special occasions.

Aisle lights should be low in luminance and spaced close enough to give fairly uniform illuminance in the aisle. House lights should be dimmer controlled, rather than controlled merely by on-off switches.

Meetings, Conventions and Industrial Show Facilities[22-24]

Lighting for meetings and conventions requires comfortable illumination and accent lighting for nontheatrical participants. Where open discussion takes place between speakers and audience, the lighting should be free of glare so that prompt recognition of each speaker occurs. Lighting for industrial shows, new-product presentations and similar groups may require theatre lighting.

Stage locations may vary considerably from meeting to meeting. A show that uses rear projection may move the stage area 4.5–6 m (15–20 ft) forward. Another meeting may require a simple platform with maximum space for an audience seated in schoolroom or conference style. Many meetings use a center area, or theatre-in-the-round arrangement. Other producers find a projected stage along a wall more satisfactory for their presentation.

Many meetings are conducted in multipurpose spaces that are used for food service, fashion shows, motion pictures, social events and meetings. The ease and speed with which these areas can be changed from one arrangement to another is an important economic operating factor.

Lighting must be coordinated with many other elements. These include wall surface brightness, projection screen location, communications and sound systems, to mention a few. Projection from audiovisual equipment and follow spots requires unobstructed views of screens, stages and acting areas. Chandeliers must not be placed in locations that will interfere with the projection or "stage" lighting. A sufficient number of dimmers, as well as flexible distribution of wiring and luminaire mounting locations, should be provided. For the required flexibility, not fewer than 24 dimmers should be available for spaces intended to be used for complex presentations.

Theatre-Restaurants, Lounges and Discos

Stage lighting design criteria for theatres and auditoriums are generally applicable to theatre restaurants, night clubs and lounges. Theatrical lighting in small areas such as lounges will, however, utilize more compact luminaires. For low ceilings, a basic luminaire is an "inky" with a 76-mm (3-in.) Fresnel lens or an adapter accessory having individually adjustable framing shutters, and with lamps up to 375 W. In larger spaces with longer throws, a Fresnel spotlight or a floodlight for 250–400-W lamps and a beamshaper accessory may be used. An alternative is a small ellipsoidal framing spot of 650 W or less, available with wide-, medium- and narrow-beam lens systems.

Discos use many stage lighting techniques and equipment. Additionally, a tremendous amount of movement in lights is introduced. Mirror shower balls, spinners, rotators, police emergency lights and more are used. Control systems include presets, chasers and programmers.

Luminaire Locations. Lights can normally be used at sharp angles, the limit being closer to 30° than to the 45° prevailing in theatrical work. Downlights are used to produce pools of light on dancers and set pieces. Uplights, recessed in the stage floor, can also be used. Side-mounted luminaires, located from 45° in front of to 45° behind the performer, are essential for three-dimensional effects, particularly in dance and production numbers. Floor-mounted linear strips can be used for horizon effects on cycloramas. These may be of the disappearing type or recessed with expanded metal covers to permit performers to walk over them.

Follow Spots. Locations for several follow spots should be provided to light the performers from all viewing directions. One or more follow spots should be able to cover audience areas. Some performers enter from the audience, and runways are frequently used to bring the chorus closer to the viewers. Side stages on each side of the main stage are frequently used for bands and stage action and provision should be made for adequate lighting of these areas.

Transparencies. Scrims are frequently used to hide the band when playing for a show. On the other hand, the band and performers are frequently revealed by bringing up lighting behind the scrim and keeping light off the front of the scrim. These changes may occur on the side or the principal (center) stage.

Special Effects. Mounting devices and nondimmed control circuits and receptacles are required for "black lights," projectors, electronic flash, motor-driven color wheels, and for dissolves, fog and smoke machines, mirrorballs and similar equipment. Color organs are used to pulsate lights with music. Plastic-covered floors for dancing and entertainment should provide selectable color and pattern effects. In small spaces, fluorescent lamps and dimming ballasts are used. If ventilation can be provided, incandescent lamps can be used for special effects.

Controls. Single lights are frequently used. Receptacles should be on individual dimmer circuits. Permanent grouping should be avoided. Nondimmed controls should be integrated with the dimmer controls, that is, they should be switched with voltage-sensitive relays controlled by potentiometers of the same type as those used for the dimmer controls.

LIGHTING FOR TELEVISION

Television broadcasting requires extensive preplanning of the lighting arrangements, switching, dimming, color and more, due to the necessity of continuous dramatic action. An exceptionally high degree of mechanical and electrical flexibility is necessary. Multiple scenes are arranged for continuous camera switching. Consequently, the lighting for each scene is preset without interference with adjoining sets. The quantity and quality of the lighting needed for television production depends upon the type of camera tube used and the spectral properties of the object. A limiting factor for any camera is the contrast range that the camera will accommodate. The choice of lenses is governed by the same optical principles applied to all photographic devices.

There are two aspects of lighting which must be considered for television production. First, the light must be controlled in terms of quantity, color and distribution to produce a technically satisfactory picture. Second, the lighting design must produce the desired dramatic and artistic visual effect.

Studio Lighting for Color Television

The spectral response characteristics of cameras are critical to color reproduction, and experience has shown that the light sources used for television should have very broad spectral power distributions. While the gains of the red, blue and green channels of a camera can be adjusted to operate with almost any continuous-spectrum light source, a wide variation in the spectral characteristics of the light sources used to illuminate a scene will cause unpredictable changes in color reproduction. Where filament lamps are used, current practice also indicates the correlated color temperature of all lamps used in a scene should be within a 300-K range for accurate color rendering.

Incandescent filament lamps have been favored for color studio lighting due to their continuous spectrum, their low cost, and the fact that they are available in a wide range of sizes with approximately the same correlated color temperature. Incandescent filament lamps having correlated color temperatures between 2900 and 3200 K are currently used. These lamps are favored because their housing equipment is generally less bulky and of lighter weight, and the smaller filament allows for better optical control of the light beam. Furthermore, color filters are easily used with these luminaires.

Mixed light sources, such as incandescent, high-intensity discharge and fluorescent, ordinarily should not be used to light a scene, because the camera will not transmit a good color picture where the spectral power distribution of the light source varies greatly. However, new developments in fluorescent and high-intensity discharge light sources are now providing greater flexibility for mixing sources. In particular, discharge lamps are now being manufactured with much better, and in some cases continuous, spectral power distributions. Some sports arenas have successfully mixed 75% high-intensity discharge and 25% incandescent sources.

For televising color pictures, luminances between 350 and 3500 lx (35 and 350 fc) are satisfactory. Many studios, especially those producing color spectaculars, have found it desirable to provide up to 5000 lx (500 fc). This is done to compensate for older-model color cameras or to provide greater depth of field. In scenes employing a very low light level, the problems of focus may be complicated by the very narrow depth of field afforded by wide-open lenses.

Video Recordings

The same requirements as given above apply to video recording. In addition, it is recommended the contrast range should not exceed 20:1.

Television Film Production

The significant element in lighting for television film production is the control of the contrast range. Most television film reproduction systems require a picture luminance range not exceeding 25:1. This contrasts with the current theatre projection range of about 100:1. It is important, therefore, to limit the luminance range of filmed subjects. Such control can be obtained by the introduction of fill light to raise the luminances of areas in shadow. This does not mean that flat lighting is desirable, but rather that the lighting ratios used for modeling should be lower than is normally used when making films for theatrical projection.

In shooting color film for television, the same general rules apply. Additionally, it is necessary to bear in mind that color contrast is not enough to ensure an acceptable signal. Brightness contrasts essentially constitute the signal seen on a monochrome receiver tuned to a color broadcast. Consequently, it may be necessary to light in such a way that areas differing only in hue are placed at different lighting illuminances. A poor monochrome picture is particularly conspicuous when

scenery is painted in several pastel shades, all having similar reflectances.

Projected Backgrounds

A scene may be projected onto a translucent screen from behind. This technique is used to simulate background scenery, which may take the form of stationary objects as produced by a slide, moving effects such as clouds and water, or continuous motion simulating moving trains or motion from an automobile as produced by a motion picture film.

For realism, projected highlight levels should be within a 2:1 ratio of live highlight levels. As a rule, it is desirable to have a projected highlight luminance of 250 cd/m² when the acting area is illuminated to 1000 lx (100 fc).

Chroma Key

The production technique known as chroma key is a special effect that enables any background material to be matted into a scene. In the studio, a color camera views the subject against a backdrop of a primary color that has sufficient saturation to produce a full output level in the corresponding channel of the camera. This signal output is used to key a special effects generator so that all information except the wanted subject is matted out of the original studio scene. Information from any other source, such as a film chain or video tape recorder, can then be inserted in the matted portions of the signal.

The primary color used in the backdrop is chosen on the basis that it is not present in the color of the wanted subject. When human subjects are used, blue is usually the best background color because it is absent in flesh tones. Additional precaution must be taken to avoid the use of the background color in costumes or stage props.

The illuminance on the backdrop must be high enough to produce a full output signal from the camera without excessive noise. Light should not be reflected from the background onto the subject, because it will create spurious keying signals.

Types of Illumination

A graphic representation of the following types of lighting is shown in figure 21-7.

Base Light or Fill Light. Base light or fill light is usually supplied by floodlights that supply broad, soft illumination. It is desirable to aim base lights at a 12–15° angle below horizontal.

Key or Modeling Light. Key or modeling light is usually supplied by Fresnel lens spotlights ranging in lamp size from 500 to 10,000 W. Fresnel luminaires are equipped to hold supplementing masking devices, such

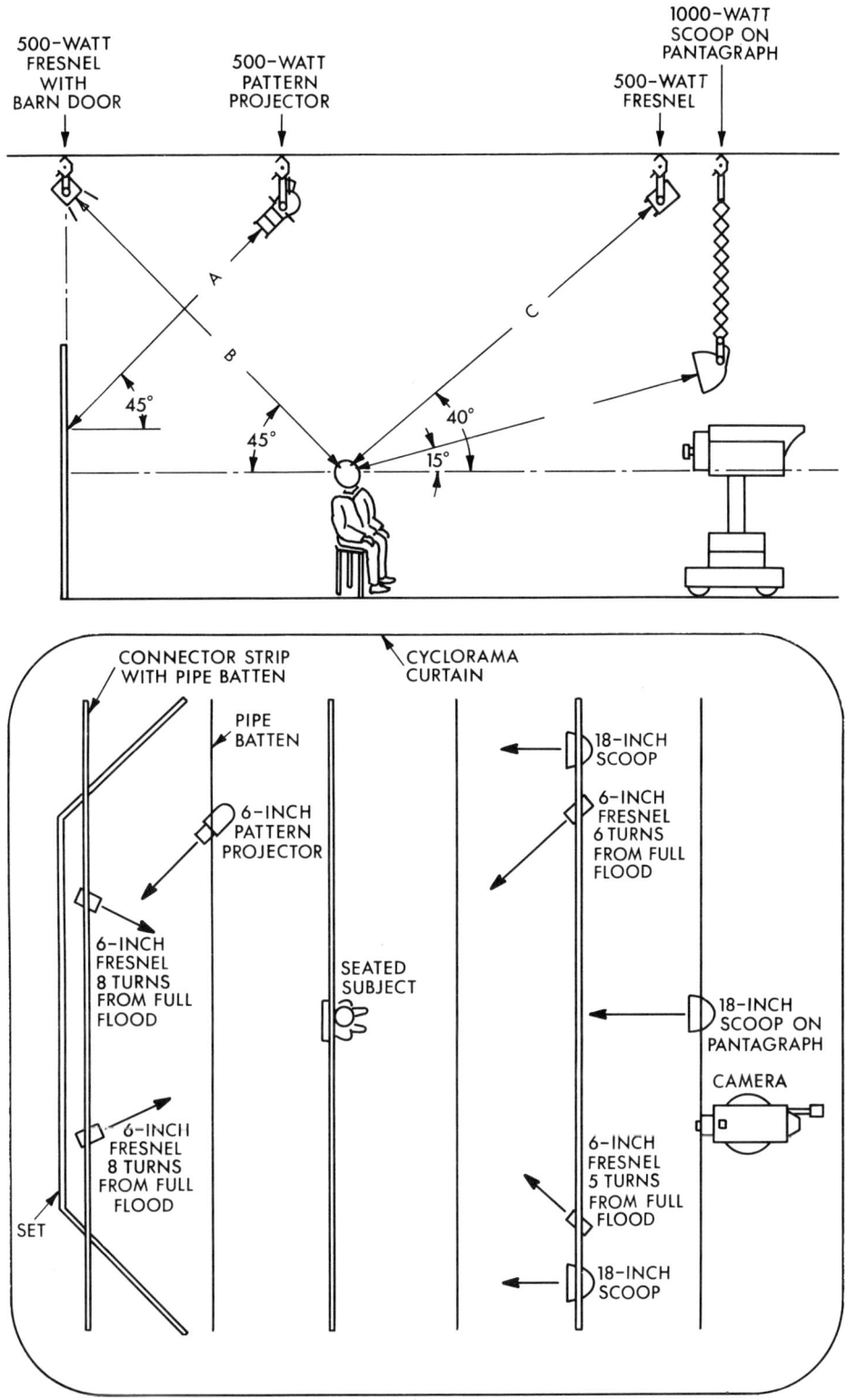

Fig. 21-7. Diagrams showing good practice in luminaire location and aiming angles. In the top diagram $A = 3$ m (10 ft), $B = 3.7$ m (12 ft) and $C = 4$ m (13 ft).

as barn doors, snoots and color frames. The barn door fits in front of the lens and is used to limit the bottom, top or sides of the light beam. These units can either be hung or used on floor stands and are generally aimed at a 20–40° angle below horizontal. Back light is used for separation. Back lights are hung behind a subject and are aimed at approximately a 45° angle to light the back of the head and shoulders, and to separate the subject from the background. Back light luminances should be from one-half to the same as that of the front light, depending upon the reflectance of the hair and the costume.

Set Light. Set light is used to decorate or help give dimension to scenery. The amount of light necessary is totally dependent on the reflectance of the scenery. It must be kept in mind that a typical skin tone, such as a person's face, reflects 40–45% of the light falling upon it. Therefore, the major part of the background must be kept below the luminance of the face. A gray-scale value of 75% of the skin reflectance is an adequate average value for the background.

There are many other luminaires that can be used to help dramatize a show, such as sun spots, ellipsoidal spots, follow spots, pattern projectors and striplights. These luminaires are described above under Lighting for Theatres.

Balancing for Correct Contrast. It is important to have the proper balance among the different types of light-

ing discussed above. If, for instance, the set is painted in a color value that reflects more light than the flesh of the actor, skin tones may appear darker than desired in the picture. This means that the set light should be reduced. A quick way to do this is to cover the set lighting luminaires with a spun-glass diffuser material. This is available in 1 × 4-m (3 × 12-ft) rolls and can be cut to fit the luminaire. One 0.38-mm (0.015-in.) thickness cuts about 20% of the light. Additional thicknesses can be used until the correct contrast is obtained. The problem in using spun glass is that the character of the light has been altered from somewhat firm image-forming to soft, diffuse, flood and less directional ambient light. However, if the front, or fill, light is brighter than the key light, the use of spun glass will help, too, in solving that problem.

Another medium that is sometimes used to balance the lighting is one or more layers of ordinary house window screening. Black window screening material has the virtue of minimizing changes to the optical characteristics of the light.

If the installation includes dimmers and a cross-connecting system, the different luminaires can be grouped and then dimmed until the desired contrast is obtained. There is no apparent color effect due to dimming in black-and-white television. In the case of color television, the color temperature decreases 10 K per volt for lamps operated at 120 V. As stated before, differences of 300 K contained in one scene will be

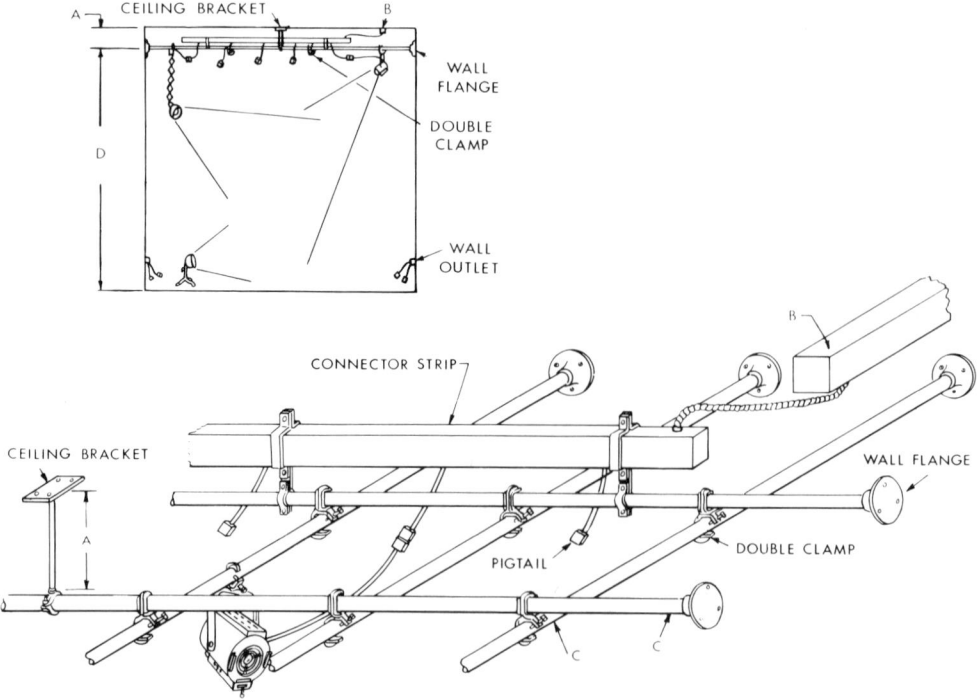

Fig. 21-8. Diagram showing a typical overhead grid system for mounting lighting equipment in a small low-ceiling studio. Typical systems for larger studios with higher ceilings can be raised and lowered. In the drawings $A = 300$ mm (12 in.), $B = 100 \times 100$ mm (4 × 4 in.) duct, $C = 32$ mm (1.5 in.) ID pipe, and $D = 3$ to 3.7 m (10 to 12 ft).

perceptible. A very low color temperature contains little short-wave energy and may introduce unwanted noise into the picture.

Lighting Equipment Installation

The method of supporting the luminaires depends to a great extent on the ceiling height and the intended use of the studio. Where the height is low, in the range of 3.5–5 m (12–16 ft), a permanent pipe or track grid is usually installed, from which the luminaires are hung directly or through pantographs which permit individual vertical setting. See figure 21-8. The luminaires are capable of complete rotation and tilting. In high-ceiling studios and in television theatres, the luminaires are supported either from fixed pipe or track grids or on counterweighted pipe or track battens (see figure 21-8).

Television Control-Room Lighting

The lighting system for use during control-room operating periods should meet the following requirements:

1. *General illumination.* A diffuse, evenly distributed illuminance of 50 lx (5 fc) should be provided by low-intensity sources located so as to avoid any specular reflections in picture monitors, clock faces, windows, control panels, console desks or similar surfaces, as seen from normal positions occupied by operation personnel.
2. *Work illumination.* Localized higher illuminances of approximately 250 lx (25 fc) should be provided on the production consoles, control consoles, switching consoles and announcer's desk.
3. *Correlated color temperature.* The correlated color temperature of control-room operating lights should be nearly constant.
4. *Emergency lighting.* Emergency power from a separate source should be provided.

The lighting system used during maintenance of the area should have an illuminance of approximately 250 lx (25 fc). This system would be independent of the production lighting outlined above and is for use when installing equipment, repairing equipment, moving equipment or cleaning.

Educational Television

In addition to commercial television channels, there are certain channels that have been allocated for educational broadcasting exclusively. Most of these are owned and operated by universities or other educa-

Illuminance Readings in Lux (Footcandles) at Test Positions						
	1	2	3	4	5	6
A	—	1000 (100)	1000 (100)	1000 (100)	—	—
B	—	—	—	—	1000 (100)	—
C	1250 (125)	1250 (125)	1250 (125)	1250 (125)	—	1000 (100)
D	1250 (125)	1500 (150)	1500 (150)	1250 (125)	—	1000 (100)
E	—	1500 (150)	1500 (150)	1250 (125)	—	1000 (100)
F	1250 (125)	—	1250 (125)	1250 (125)	—	—

Distance	Meters	Feet
V	9.1	30
W	27.4	90
X	30.5	100
Y	45.7	150
Z	9.1	30

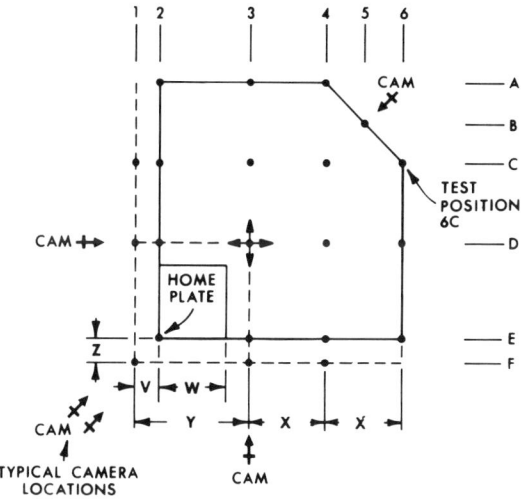

Fig. 21-9. Recommended minimum illuminance levels and survey test position for television pickup of baseball.

tional bodies. Their operations closely parallel the commercial stations in that cameras and lighting of the same type are used.

Field Pickups of Sporting Events

The lighting recommendations for sports (see chapter 23, Sports and Recreation Lighting) are based upon player and spectator visibility needs. A more complete discussion of sports lighting for TV may be found in chapter 23. When telecasting, especially in color, or filming is involved, additional factors must be considered. These include (1) providing a directional balance to the vertical illumination, (2) providing the quantity of illumination required by zoom lens systems, (3) providing uniformity of illuminance within a 2:1 maximum-to-minimum ratio and (4) providing good color quality.

Television systems and motion picture film are sensitive enough to obtain quality pictures at levels of 750–1500 lx (75–150 fc). This corresponds to the normal illuminances required in large sports facilities such as college or major league football stadiums and major league ballparks. The main source of variations in the normal lighting requirements that are needed for television and film is the need to consider vertical illumination and the more restrictive uniformity limit.

It is also important to provide illumination in the spectator area adjacent to the playing field for crowd shots and for wide-angle shots of the playing field. This is best accomplished from behind the spectators, to limit glare for both the spectators and camera positions in the spectator seating area. Glare is an important consideration for players too, and it can be minimized if the light comes from the sides of the normal direction of play. This is easily identified in a football

stadium; in a baseball park the light direction is best taken at right angles to a line from home plate to center field.

Modeling. Layouts for a baseball and football field, indicating the normal camera locations, are shown in figures 21-9 and 21-10. Since both vertical and horizontal illumination are important, a typical test location and vertical illuminance test direction are illustrated. The vertical illuminances should be recorded along with their directions as illustrated; however, only two of the four directions need to meet the illuminance requirement. Measurements of horizontal and vertical illuminances in four directions should be made at a height of 900 mm (36 in.) above the playing surface. The visibility for players and spectators is dependent upon the values of horizontal- and vertical-plane illuminance, since modeling of an object is related to the

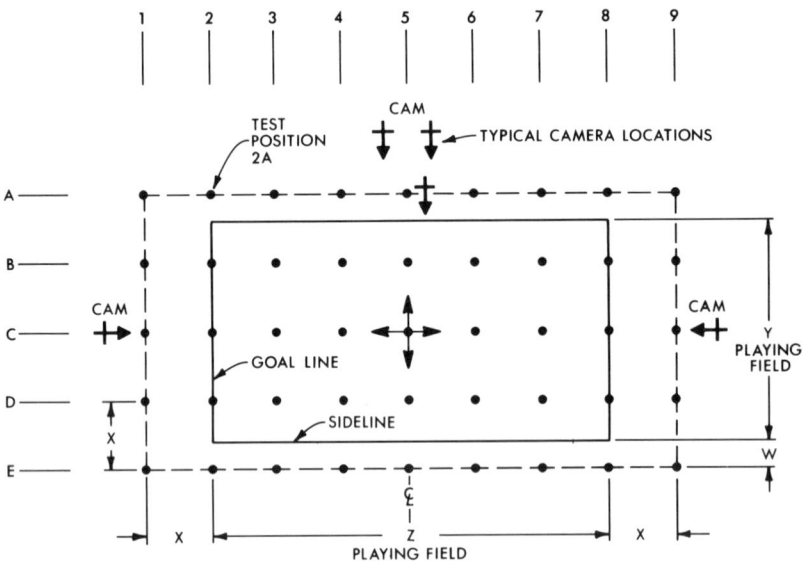

Illuminance Readings in Lux (Footcandles) at Test Positions									
	1	2	3	4	5	6	7	8	9
A	1000 (100)	1000 (100)	1000 (100)	1000 (100)	1000 (100)	1000 (100)	1000 (100)	1000 (100)	1000 (100)
B	1100 (110)	1250 (125)	1350 (135)	1350 (135)	1350 (135)	1350 (135)	1350 (135)	1250 (125)	1100 (110)
C	1250 (125)	(1500 (150)	1500 (150)	1500 (150)	1500 (150)	1500 (150)	1500 (150)	1500 (150)	1250 (125)
D	1100 (110)	1250 (125)	1350 (135)	1350 (135)	1350 (135)	1350 (135)	1350 (135)	1250 (125)	1100 (110)
E	1000 (100)	1000 (100)	1000 (100)	1000 (100)	1000 (100)	1000 (100)	1000 (100)	1000 (100)	1000 (100)

Distance	Meters	Feet
W	6.1	20
X	15.2	50
Y	48.8	160
Z	91.4	300

Fig. 21-10. Recommended minimum illuminance levels and survey test position for television pickup of football.

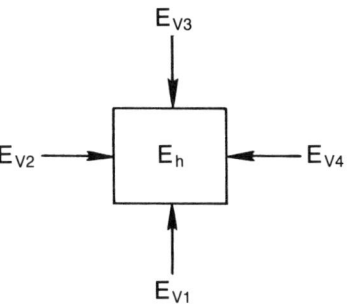

Fig. 21-11. Five illuminance measurements used to determine acceptable modeling for sports lighting.

proportion of horizontal to vertical illuminance reaching an object from different directions. As the number of vertical planes at any one point is infinite, it is convenient to consider only faces of two vertical planes at right angles (see figure 21-11).

If E_h, E_{v1}, E_{v2}, E_{v3}, and E_{v4} (where E_h is the horizontal illuminance at the point under study and E_{v1} through E_{v4} are the four vertical-plane illuminances at that point separated by 90°) are approximately the same, the modeling (or revealing power of the lighting) will be poor, that is, it will be difficult to see objects in three dimensions. On the other hand, excessive difference in these five values will give harsh modeling that can distort the appearance of the object. For the purpose of sports lighting, since viewing is from all directions, it is usual to take the average of the values at a number of points over the area. Acceptable modeling will generally be achieved if E_{hav} (the average horizontal illuminance over the area) is no greater than twice the average value in any one of the four vertical planes.

Glare Control. Glare makes visual observation more difficult and reduces visual comfort. It must therefore be controlled for both players and spectators by controlling the apparent brightness of light sources in the main direction of view.

This is relatively easy to achieve for sports facilities that have a main direction of view below the horizontal. Glare control is achieved in a number of ways:

1. Select luminaires with an intensity distribution suited to the required illuminance, uniformity, size of area and mounting height.
2. Mount luminaires out of the main field of view of players and spectators, and if necessary use additional screening devices on the luminaire to control the brightness in certain directions.
3. For indoor areas, ensure adequate illumination of spectator areas, upper walls and roof; select suitable surface reflectances to ensure that the lighting equipment is not seen against a dark background.

The reflectances recommended for major surfaces are 60% for ceilings and 30–60% for walls.

The reflectance of the ceiling should be high, so that the difference between the luminance of luminaires and that of the ceiling is as small as possible. Where it is difficult to achieve an effective ceiling reflectance as high as 60%, the luminance contrast can be improved by directing light on the roof area.

Reflected glare can be caused by reflection of the luminaires off surfaces such as ice or polished wood courts. This should be avoided by suitable positioning of the luminaires and appropriate screening.

PHOTOGRAPHIC LIGHTING

Photographic lighting is used by amateur photographers, portrait and commercial photographers, industrial photographers and cinematographers. The needs

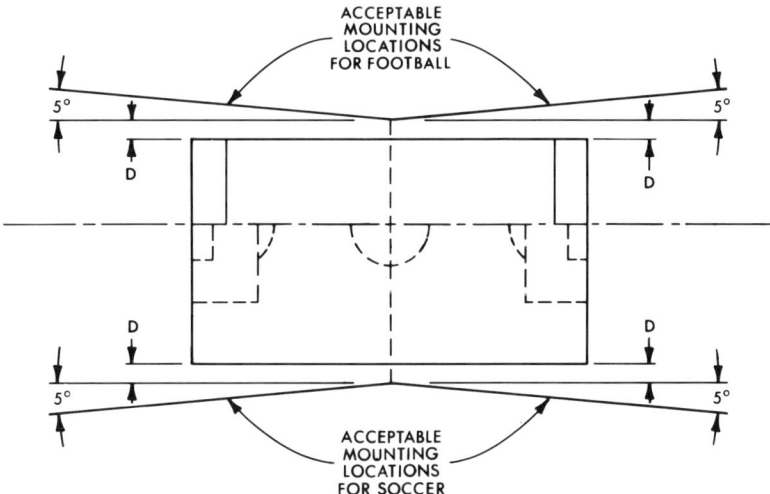

Fig. 21-12. Recommended pole locations for television pickup of football and soccer. Mounting locations are defined in Figure 21-10; minimum mounting height is addressed in Chapter 23, Sports and Recreation Area Lighting. $D = 4.6$ m (15 ft).

of these photographers vary considerably, as do the film materials and lighting systems. A portrait photographer may use flashlights to minimize the discomfort for the subject. Strobes and flashbulbs will stop the motion of moving objects. Color photography requires compatibility between the film spectral sensitivity and the light source spectral output. In motion picture photography, the stroboscopic effect of fluorescent and high-intensity discharge light sources must be minimized with special ballasts or synchronized with the film speed and shutter angle. The lighting requirements are therefore many and varied.

Photosensitive Materials[25]

Commonly used photosensitive films and plates include the following:

- Panchromatic (sensitive to all colors, produces a black-and-white image).
- Orthochromatic (sensitive to all colors except orange and red, produces a black-and-white image).
- Color (sensitive to all colors, produces a color image).
- Infrared (sensitive to red and infrared, produces a black-and-white image).

Spectral sensitivity curves are given in figure 21-13.

For photography, light sources must emit energy in the spectral region in which the photographic material is sensitive. Even in black-and-white photography, color delineation in the form of faithful gray values is required. In black-and-white photography, photographers endeavor to secure a scale of grays in their negatives corresponding to the various brightnesses of the subject; thus, it is necessary that the film and the light source complement each other. Where this is not

possible, it is general practice to employ a filter at the camera lens.

For color photography, the spectral quality of the illumination is even more critical. Color emulsions are "balanced" for use with a particular quality of light. Because most color photography materials are based on three emulsion layers, each sensitive to a narrow spectral band, adjustment by filtering to a light source other than the one for which the material was originally intended calls for precise filter selection.

Photographic Lighting Equipment

Still camera lenses ordinarily cover an angle of about 45°; therefore, for lighting equipment placed at or near the camera, reflector beam patterns for complete light utilization should fill an angle of about 45°. However, difficulties caused by inaccurate aiming of the reflector and other variables are minimized by filling a 60° cone with reasonably uniform illuminance. A luminaire with a 60° beam angle usually provides lower illuminances toward the edges of the scene, but this is seldom objectionable, since the point of interest in a picture is generally in the middle.

The shadows and contrasts that help to light a person as normally seen are usually "soft," such as those produced by a light source of appreciable angular size. Large reflectors 400–600 mm (16–24 in.) in diameter produce more natural modeling and are used in portrait studios or other applications where their size is not a handicap. Flashlamp equipment used with smaller-format cameras necessarily have smaller reflectors, which produce somewhat sharper, and less natural, shadows.

Photographic Lighting Techniques

The lighting required will depend on the final effect desired from a photograph. If good rendering of shadow

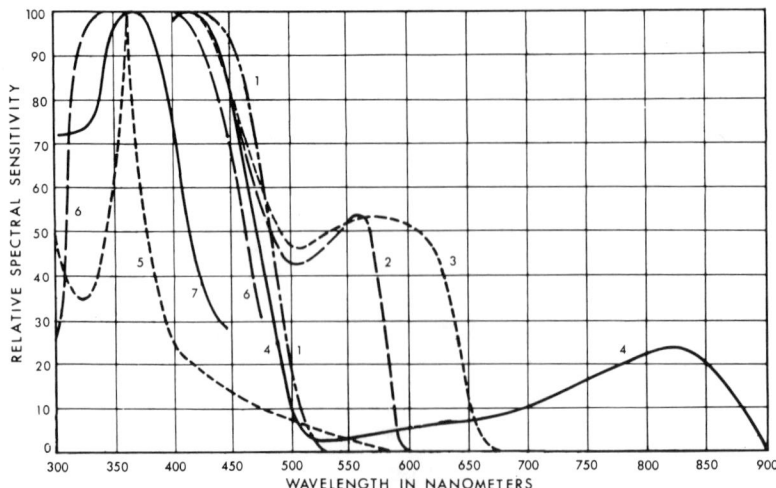

Fig. 21-13. Spectral sensitivity curves for common types of photographic and photoprocess materials. (1) blue sensitives; (2) orthochromatic; (3) panchromatic; (4) infrared sensitive, (5) bichromate coating; (6) diazotype paper; (7) blueprint paper.

detail is desired, a rather narrow range of illuminances is required so that both the brightest parts (highlights) and the darkest parts (shadows) of the scene will be fully rendered in the final print or transparency. The brightness range reproduced on film is much narrower than that which can be perceived by the human eye, particularly in the case of color photography. With typical subject reflectance ranges, the recommended maximum illuminance range within the scene is 10:1 for black-and-white and 4:1 for color film.

In color photography, the correlated color temperature of all of the light sources used must be the same. The eye readily accepts illumination of mixed color temperature, but photographic film does not.

The monocular vision of the camera tends to render subjects flat. That is, they tend not to have a three-dimensional look. To compensate for the lack of stereo depth, the best lighting on photographic subjects emphasizes their roundness, form and spatial relationship. This is largely a matter of lighting direction, such as lighting from the side or the back.

In photography, both general and modeling illumination are needed to produce a natural-appearing likeness of a subject. General illumination, if used alone, produces a negative that is flat and without modeling. Such illumination does not produce prominent shadows. Density differences in the negative are created by differences in the reflectance of various portions of the subject. This general illumination goes by several names, among which are front light, broad light, flat light, camera light and basic light. Modeling light, if used alone, produces a negative in which the highlights can be well exposed but the shadows show no detail at all. Modeling lights are usually highly directional and are used for the express purpose of creating shadows and highlights.

For ordinary subjects, the background should not be very dark, very light or too close behind the subject. Neither should it be of exactly the same luminance as important parts of the subject, because such a condition would have the effect of merging the subject with the background. Better photographs result where less detail and fewer distracting spots are in the background.

Photography of Lighting Installations

The photography of installations by "existing light" does not require special photographic materials or equipment. Attention to focus, proper exposure and composition is necessary, and the use of a tripod is recommended.

The finished picture should represent the actual installation as closely as possible.[26, 27] Because most installations have a luminance range that exceeds the acceptance of the film, various techniques in photographing and photographic finishing are used to

compensate and so produce a more natural-appearing photograph.

In taking the picture, exposures may be split (meaning a separate exposure will be used on the same film frame for each different source of light), fill light may be introduced, lampshades may be lined, and bulbs may be substituted to reduce brightness. When fill light is used, great care must be taken to avoid unnatural shadows. This may mean bouncing light off of walls or the ceiling. In black-and-white photography, a 10:1 ratio of scene illuminance is desirable. In color photography, the ratio should not exceed 4:1.

The rule of exposing for shadows and developing for highlights is still valid for black-and-white photography. Through experience and testing, the photographer finds the best combination of lighting technique, film and processing that yields an easily printed negative. The printer can also use various methods of compensation, such as dodging, flashing and burning in, to overcome the deficiencies of a poorly executed negative.

When using color film, exposure should be for the highlight areas where detail is desired. It is also imperative that all the light sources be similar in color. Fluorescent lamps generally should not be combined with incandescent fill light, since this will usually produce a noticeable color mismatch in the final photograph.

Installations of discharge lamps photographed with color-positive material present color balancing problems. Because all films are designed to respond to a continuous spectrum and high-intensity discharge lamps generally do not have continuous spectra, filtration in some form is required to produce an acceptable color balance.

Lamps and film manufacturers can generally furnish recommendations for suitable filters to balance the various color-positive films to specific discharge lamps, both fluorescent and HID.

Another, and usually much simpler, method of color photography is to photograph the installation on unfiltered color-negative material and work with a professional color laboratory to produce prints or slides with the correct color, the necessary filtration being done in the photofinishing laboratory.

Darkroom Lighting

In general, any type of darkroom safelight filter must transmit light which will have the least effect on the photographic material and yet will provide the most illumination for the eye. Any photographic material will fog if left long enough under even the best safelight illumination.

The placement, as well as the size and type, of safelight lamp will depend on the purpose which the light is to serve. The two types of darkroom illumination are general, to supply subdued illumination over

Fig. 21-17. Types of Safelight Filters

Color	Material Used with
Clear yellow	Contact printing papers
Bright orange	Bromide and other fast papers and lantern slide plates
Greenish yellow	(Better than orange for judging print quality)
Orange-red	Ordinary films and plates
Deep red	Orthochromatic films and plates
Green	Panchromatic films and plates
Yellowish green	X-ray film
Special green	Infrared films and plates

the whole room without concentration at any one point, and local, to supply higher illumination on some particular point or object. These are combined, dependent upon the size of the room and the type of work.

Because of the varying sensitivities of the different classes of photographic materials, several safelight filters are available, differing in both color and intensity. These have been produced by the manufacturers of the luminaires, and it is never safe to use substitutes. Other materials may appear to the eye to have the same color as a tested safelight filter, but they will frequently have a much greater effect on the exposed, unprocessed film. The use of makeshift safelight substitutes is not recommended.

Figure 21-17 indicates available types of safelight filters. Film manufacturers should be consulted for more complete information.

REFERENCES

1. IES. Theatre, Television and Film Lighting Committee. 1983. A glossary of commonly used terms in theatre, television and film lighting. *Light. Des. Appl.* 13(11): 43–48.
2. Hatch, A. J. 1974. Updating the follow spot. *Light. Des. Appl.* 4(3):54–56.
3. Clark, C. N., and T. F. Neubecker. 1967. Evolution in tungsten lamps for television and film lighting. *J. Soc. Mot. Pict. Tel. Eng.* 76(4):347–360.
4. Levin, R. E. 1968. New developments in tungsten-halogen lamps. *Ind. Photogr.* 17(11):38.
5. Lemons, T. M., and R. E. Levin. 1968. Tungsten-halogen replacement lamps for standard incandescent types. *J. Soc. Mot. Pict. Tel. Eng.* 77(11):1194–1198.
6. Lemons, T. M., and R. E. Levin. 1969. The rating problem: Lamps in luminaires. *J. Soc. Mot. Pict. Tel. Eng.* 78(12):1064–1069.
7. Schelling, W. F. 1979. HID lamps for television remotes. *Light. Des. Appl.* 9(4):2–5.
8. Lemons, T. M. 1978. HMI lamps. *Light. Des. Appl.* 8(8):32–37.
9. Hall, R. and B. Preston. 1981. High-power single-ended discharge lamps for film lighting. *J. Soc. Mot. Pict. Tel. Eng.* 90(8):678–685.
10. Rubin, J. E., and W. E. Crocken. 1972. Q-file random access memory control for theatre and television. *J. Illum. Eng. Soc.* 1(4):329–333.
11. Pincu, T. L. 1974. Memory-assisted dimming. *Light. Des. Appl.* 4(3):50–53.
12. Pearlman, G. 1979. Functional criteria for memory lighting control systems. *Light. Des. Appl.* 9(3):27–28.
13. Garrard, M., Ghent Emmanuel, and J. Seawright. 1974. A high-speed digital control system. *Light. Des. Appl.* 4(3):14–21.
14. Miller, K. H., and L. J. Wittman. 1979. A dimmer-per-circuit approach to stage lighting. *Light. Des. Appl.* 9(3):29–31.
15. Shearer, C. W. 1972. Which dimmer curve: Why? *J. Illum. Eng. Soc.* 1(4):325–328.
16. Otto, F. B. 1974. A curve for theatrical dimmers. *Light. Des. Appl.* 4(3):44–46.
17. IES. Committee on Theatre, Television and Film Lighting. Educational and Community Theatre Stages Subcommittee. 1968. Lighting for theatrical presentations on educational and community proscenium-type stages. *Illum. Eng.* 63(6):327–336. IES. Theater, Television and Film Lighting Committee. CP-34 Task Group. 1983. Addendum to "Lighting for theatrical presentations on educational and community proscenium-type stages" IES CP-34A. *Light. Des. Appl.* 13(9):27.
18. Bentham, F. 1969. *The art of stage lighting.* New York: Taplinger.
19. IES. Theatre, Television and Film Lighting Committee. Theatre Lighting Subcommittee. 1983. Stage lighting: A guide to the planning of theatres and public building auditoriums [IES CP-45-1983]. *Light. Des. Appl.* 13(9):17–26.
20. Davis, B. 1975. Frontlight positions: An informal plea for diversity. *Light. Des. Appl.* 5(6):62–68.
21. Tawil, J. N. 1978. Staging with light patterns and scenic projections. *Light. Des. Appl.* 8(1):26–33.
22. Gill, G., and C. E. Sorensen. 1966. Making available light available. *J. Soc. Mot. Pict. Tel. Eng.* 75(3):310, 312.
23. Moody, J. L. 1979. "Hanging" a one-night stand. *Light. Des. Appl.* 9(3):22–25.
24. Fiorentino, I. 1974. Lighting for mixed media. *Light. Des. Appl.* 4(3):22–25.
25. Jones, L. A. 1937. Measurements of radiant energy with photographic materials. In *Measurement of radiant energy,* chapter 8. W. E. Forsythe, ed. New York: McGraw-Hill.
26. Jones, B. F. 1963. Good color slides without gadgetry. *Illum. Eng.* 58(3):116–117.
27. Ulrich, J. D. 1974. The lighting of lighting. *Light. Des. Appl.* 4(3):33–39.

Exterior Lighting

22

INTRODUCTION

Lighting for exterior environments involves a multitude of issues. This section will help guide the lighting designer through the critical issues and then address specific areas of exterior lighting design: structures, softscapes, hardscapes and specialty lighting.

Community-Responsive Design

Community-responsive design addresses how well an exterior lighting design will be accepted by neighbors and the community. Project locations challenging to the designer may include an open parking structure located in a residential neighborhood, building lighting in a historic district, and a car dealership in a rural community. These and many more difficult project locations can be successfully designed by following some basic design steps.

The first step in designing exterior lighting is to examine the *community theme*. Community themes in architecture and lighting help establish local identities. Examples of community themes are "casino and entertainment excitement" and "gaslight quietness and intimacy." All exterior lighting designs should blend into the community theme where the project is located.

The second step is to discover any community *lighting ordinances* which may affect the lighting design. Lighting ordinances have many scopes and purposes. Examples are lighting ordinances addressing light pollution, light trespass or minimum illuminance levels and uniformities for parking lots. Some ordinances even address community theme.

The third step is to identify the immediate *surrounding brightness*. Surrounds can be classified as dark, medium and bright. Examples of a dark surround are a rural town, a national park and a residential neighborhood. An example of a medium surround is an urban setting in a medium-size community, or in a community where lighting ordinances dictate energy-responsive designs. Examples of bright surrounds are the downtown of a large metropolitan area and the middle of a large industrial park area.

Identification of *neighboring areas* is also a crucial step. Identify the luminance of adjacent roadways,

walkways and properties. Once these have been identified, the luminance ratios of the design should take into consideration the effects listed in Fig. 22-1.

Attention must be given to the safety of motorists. If a 1:10 ratio is exceeded, the motorist may be distracted and have a difficult time identifying objects on the roadway. In the same way, a home that is floodlighted to 10 times the level of adjacent homes may be a distraction and a source of complaint.

The fourth step is to check whether the project location is in close proximity to an airport. Flight patterns may dictate pole height restrictions. Care should be taken to minimize uplight light pollution which could cause glare to the pilots.

Light Pollution and Light Trespass

As a result of efforts to increase the use of facilities during the night, light pollution and light trespass have become extremely important issues that should be considered when preparing an outdoor lighting design.

Light pollution, sometimes called atmospheric or astronomical light pollution, is caused by stray or reflected light that is emitted into the atmosphere. Dust, water vapor and other atmospheric pollutants reflect and scatter this light, causing the sky glow found over all urban areas. Although this sky glow is not injurious to the populace, it does deprive urban residents of the opportunity to stargaze.

Light pollution is of special concern in areas where astronomical observatories are located. The use of a monochromatic light source such as low-pressure sodium (LPS) is preferred by astronomers because it can be easily filtered, but the use of spectral composition does not completely eliminate atmosphere light pollution.

Several methods to help control light pollution are:

1. Street and area lighting systems, including lighting for sports and commercial areas such as parking lots and vehicle sales lots, should be designed to minimize or eliminate direct upward light emission. This will not eliminate all light emission above the horizontal plane, since

Fig. 22-1. Recommended Luminance Ratios for Exterior Lighting Effects

Lighting Effect	Maximum Luminance Ratio
Blending in with surrounds	1 : 2
Softly accented	1 : 3
Accented	1 : 5
Strongly accented	1 : 10

reflected light from the ground or pavement is an important portion of the upward emission.

2. Lighting systems that project light upward, such as architectural and sign lighting, should be designed to minimize light that does not illuminate the target area.

3. All outdoor lighting, including advertising sign lighting and interior high rise office building lighting, should be turned off after use or by 11:00 p.m. unless needed for safety and security. Usually safety and security illuminance, with the exception of street lighting, can be at a much lower level than that needed when the area is in use.

Light trespass is a somewhat subjective topic, since it relates in many cases to an unmeasurable or even undefinable quantity, which sometimes cannot be controlled. A typical example is the "light shining in my window" complaint. To eliminate the complaint might require the elimination of a luminaire deemed essential for the safety and security of a street or off-street area. The elimination of the offending unit might satisfy the original complainant but result in a new complaint from an adjacent property resident about the darkness without the unit in place.

Light trespass usually can be classified into one of three categories:

• The classic "light shining in a window"
• Unwanted light on an adjacent property
• Excessive brightness in the normal field of vision (nuisance glare)

Efforts have been made in numerous jurisdictions to write ordinances or laws controlling light trespass, with little success, since enforcement is difficult. An ordinance defining trespass in terms of horizontal illuminance misses the point entirely, since vertical luminance often creates the problem. A bright object against a dark background may be an annoyance, even though there is no horizontal illuminance at the viewing location.

The following recommendations will help control light trespass problems:

1. Inspecting areas adjacent to the design location to identify and consider any sensitive loca-

tions in the lighting system design, such as residences, roadways and airports.

2. Selecting luminaires which have tightly controlled candela distributions, using sharp-cutoff reflectors or refractors.

3. Containing the light within the design area by careful selection, location and mounting of the luminaires.

4. Selecting equipment which can be shielded, if a potential problem exists, after installation.

5. Keeping floodlight aiming angles as low as possible during both design and installation.

Energy-Responsive Design

Energy-responsive design involves several issues, which turn out to be related to mitigating light trespass and pollution and to community-responsive design.

The first issue is lamp and ballast selection. Attention should be given to selecting high-efficacy lamps and efficient ballasts. Beam spreads should be carefully selected for the application to ensure that light is directed only where it is needed.

The second issue is luminaire selection. As with the lamp, the luminaire should be correctly specified for the design application. The combination of lamp and luminaire should have the correct distribution for the application in order to further reduce energy consumption by placing the light only where it is needed.

The third issue is the relative brightness used in the design. If careful consideration is given to figure 22-1, exterior lighting designs will not be too bright for their surroundings.

The fourth issue is lighting control. Illuminance levels should be reduced when the property is not occupied or when few people are present. All nonessential exterior lighting should be turned off during the late night hours in order to conserve energy and to accommodate local observatories.

Maintenance

Exterior lighting maintenance issues include accessibility, lamp and ballast life, exposure to adverse weather conditions, dirt, animal deposits, bird nests, vandalism and water collection. Refer to chapter 32, Lighting Maintenance.

Specific Exterior Lighting Applications

Other chapters in this Handbook, such as chapters 20 on Industrial Lighting, 24 on Roadway Lighting, 18 on Lighting for Merchandise Areas, and 25 on Aviation Lighting, are devoted to specific lighting applications. Care should be taken in applying the principles of community-responsive design to the lighting design for these applications.

STRUCTURE LIGHTING

This section will discuss the illumination of architectural structures. Building lighting is primarily discussed here, but the theory and approaches can be implemented for other structures as well. See figure 22-2 for a demonstration of floodlighting principles and figures 22-3 through 22-12 for examples of structure lighting.

Basic Design Principles

One of the most important decisions to be made when considering the lighting of a building facade is the effect on the surrounding area. Certain areas may not lend themselves to this type of lighting. Floodlighted buildings may not fit into the community. The designer has an obligation, not only to the building owner, but to everyone in the community, to provide a design that is in keeping with the civic atmosphere.

Several elements enter into the synthesis of a building lighting design. Equipment-mounting locations, lamps and desired light effects must all be considered when designing the system.

Equipment Location

Luminaires may be mounted either on the structure or remotely. Mounting on the structure is most easily accomplished with new construction, where luminaires can be integrated into the architecture. Luminaires may be hidden in cornices, on or behind parapets or on roof setbacks. Luminaires can also be attached to the facade, but this is usually not appropriate unless the luminaire has a decorative quality. Luminaires mounted remotely from the structure can be grade mounted, pole mounted or mounted to an adjacent structure. If luminaires are to be mounted on adjacent structures, coordination with the owner of the other structures will be required. In all cases, luminaires should be installed in such a way that glare is minimized from expected viewing directions and from adjacent properties and roadways.

Lighting Effects

The distance of the luminaire from the structure will influence the final lighting effect. The photometric distribution of the luminaire will determine the necessary setbacks required to achieve the desired effect.

Luminaires mounted close to the structure tend to emphasize the texture of the material being illuminated. The grazing of light off a surface also emphasizes the distribution of the luminaire, causing scalloping on the surface. This may or may not be the desired effect. Scalloping can be helpful in creating a rhythmic organization to break up large uninteresting surfaces. If the luminaires are pointed upward, the undersides of building projections will be emphasized by creating a

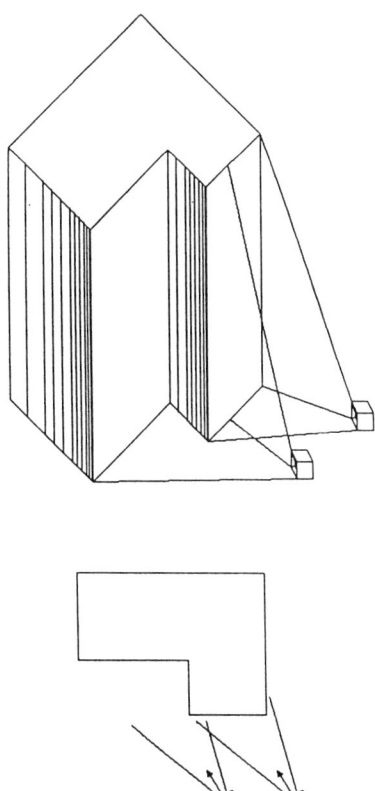

Fig. 22-2. Floodlighting from an angle helps define building structure and reduce a flattened appearance.

high illuminance level on the bottom of horizontal surfaces which contrast to shadows thrown on the vertical surface above the projection. Luminaires mounted close to the structure offer the easiest control of glare from inside the structure, as there will be little light passing through the fenestration.

Luminaires mounted remotely from the structure create a more even distribution of illuminance, tending to deemphasize the articulation of the structure. One way to decrease the flattening of the elevation being lighted is to aim the luminaires at an angle to the vertical surface (see figure 22-2). Remote mounting also makes light trespass into the interior of the structure more difficult to control. The further the luminaires are mounted away from the structure, the greater the penetration of light through the fenestration.

Luminance, or more correctly exitance, levels play a large role in structure lighting design. The exitance levels of surrounding structures should be determined before the design for a new structure is undertaken. The exitance of these surrounding structures should be used as a guideline for determining the levels for the new design and should be considered in the context of other architectural spaces. See figure 22-1.

Other visibility issues must be analyzed as well when determining appropriate exitance levels for the structure. For example, when lighting bridges, the structure luminance levels must be maintained within the stringent constraints of roadway lighting so as not to produce glare for the driver.

Lamp selection is an important component of a structure lighting system. The spectral compositions of lamps vary greatly, even between manufacturers of the same lamp type. See chapter 6, Light Sources. It is important to visually test the lamps being considered for an architectural interior to assure that these materials being illuminated will be an appropriate color.

SOFTSCAPE LIGHTING

Softscape lighting includes a variety of outdoor areas: private yards, parks, garden areas, and earth features such as water. In each case the lighting designer must take into account the surroundings so that the lighting design blends with the rest of the composition.

Controlling glare is a major issue in designing softscape lighting. Concealing the light source with trees, shrubs, plants, buildings or rocks helps to control glare. When concealing a luminaire, avoid bright "hot spots" on these objects. If the luminaire is placed too close to the object, reflected glare can be as much of a problem as viewing the source directly. Spill light also creates an undesirable effect and can be controlled with louvers and shields. The designer's main task is to create a safe, attractive nighttime environment using an energy-efficient system. See figure 22-13.

Evaluating Plant Materials

The designer should have knowledge of the characteristics of the plant materials being lighted, as they will dictate the selection and location of equipment. Information concerning plant characteristics can be obtained from the architect, landscape designer or ANSI (American National Standards Institute). The designer should be aware that the following characteristics vary by region:

- Growth rate (how quickly and how much)
- Overall shape, height and width
- Texture
- Leaf type
- Branch characteristics and branching pattern
- Foliage color (reflectance)
- Trunk characteristics (striped, thorny, peeling, cracked, multicolored or flaking bark)
- Flowering characteristics (when, how long, size and shape)
- Light requirements (plants require a regular cycle of light and darkness for strength, bloom and growth)

- Dormancy characteristics (will the design work year round?)

Additionally, coordination should take place with the designer of the landscape in planning a maintenance and pruning schedule[1] (see chapter 32, Lighting Maintenance).

General Design Guidelines

Use the following guidelines to aid in the design process.

1. Determine the areas of importance. Realize that significant areas in the day may not be the same as the ones at night. Determine:

   - Focal point(s) (major/minor)
   - Transition elements
   - Background elements

2. Determine the amount of light required to illuminate each area of importance; take into consideration the foliage color and reflectance.
3. For each area of importance, determine if the plant will have a natural or a dramatic appearance.
4. Determine the location of the equipment by choosing a desired effect:

   - Frontlighting shows or creates shapes, highlights details and colors, and reduces or emphasizes texture, depending on the distance of the luminaire from the plant.
   - Backlighting shows only detail, adds depth by separating the plant from background, and creates drama by eliminating colors and details.
   - Sidelighting emphasizes textures on plants and creates shadows that can be used to tie areas together.

5. Decide if uplighting or downlighting is to be used. This will be determined by the availability of mounting locations and the desired appearance of the composition. The following describes the effects created by each:

   - Uplighting provides a glow within the branches and casts shadows on vertical surfaces.
   - Downlighting is the most natural approach to lighting, since it imitates the sun and moon. Downlighting accents details, colors and textures.

6. The luminance ratio between the focal points should be between 5:1 and 10:1.

Fig. 22-3. (left) Cincinnati's City Hall is illuminated with high pressure sodium and metal halide sources, which highlight the building's splendid architectural features and unique stone carving.

Fig. 22-4. (above) The lighting system for the Aerial Lift Bridge, Duluth, MN, was designed to withstand ice buildup and high winds. It is floodlighted with 32 400-W high pressure sodium lamps. The roadway across the bridge is lighted with 100 and 150-W high pressure sodium lamps.

Fig. 22-5. The newly relighted Swann Memorial Fountain, Philadelphia, PA, is now illuminated with long-life, energy-efficient metal halide sources. The fountain serves as a festive backdrop for numerous city-wide celebrations.

Fig. 22-6. CenTrust Savings Bank, Miami, employs metal halide lamps and a special color gel system for displaying messages or graphics, which can be changed to publicize events or send holiday messages.

Fig. 22-7. The new lighting for the Statue of Liberty utilizes two types of metal halide lamps, each with a different color temperature, carefully aimed to emphasize the folds of the gown with shadows and highlights.

Fig. 22-8. Festive holiday lighting emphasizes the architectural details of this historic building. C-9 lamps were fastened to soft copper tubing, which was then fastened to the structure.

Fig. 22-9. Terminal tower, Cleveland, floodlighted with high pressure sodium lamps.

Fig. 22-10. The Custom House Clock and Tower, Boston, was lighted with incandescent sources selected for their color rendering qualities and beam control. Luminaires were custom made and painted to match the granite facade of the building. The flat gold hands of the clock are now visible at night, lit from above and below with narrow beam lamps.

Fig. 22-11. Several different light sources were used to light the exterior of the Mall of the Americas, Miami. The stunning facade is illuminated by 400-W metal halide ultraflood lights. Alternate floods have glass lens filters on separate color circuits so that red, blue or purple light can be used. A blue 15-mm neon (argon) band delineates the facade. Translucent awnings are backlit with C-150 Par 38 floodlights.

Fig. 22-12. Lamps for the Canadian War Memorial, Ottawa, were positioned in four corners of the landscape and focused to reveal the forms and balance the contrast between the white stone and dark bronze figures. Sixteen 6-V, 120-W very narrow spot PAR 64 lamps in metal box housings were positioned just above hedge height, so that beams of light can be angled above people's heads.

Fig. 22-13. Creative lighting was used to illuminate the exotic landscaping of this Florida residence. Compact 50-W MR-16s were selected for their good color rendition and 5000 h ratings to light individual trees and shrubs.

Design Guidelines for Various Types of Trees

Tree Trunks. Always include the trunk when accenting the tree, or the canopy will appear detached from the ground. Sidelighting the trunk will display crisp edges, whereas frontlighting will reveal details and color. See figure 22-14 for an example of tree lighting.

Tree Shape. The location of the luminaires will depend on the overall shape of the tree and the leaf and branch patterns (open or dense). The following list describes how to approach each category of trees:

Vase, fountain or umbrella trees such as palm, cherry or crabapple. If open, light from within the canopy near the trunk. If dense, highlight from outside the canopy.

Pyramidal, columnar or upright trees such as beech, elm or cedar. Locate luminaires outside the branch structure. Luminaires placed close to the tree will emphasize texture, while luminaires located farther away highlight the shape.

Rounded trees such as oak, maple or poplar. For dense growth use a wash from outside the canopy to accentuate the shape and diminish texture. For open growth locate the luminaires inside the canopy of trees to give depth.

Trees weeping or branching to the ground, such as willow, birch or ash. For weeping trees, place luminaires toward the edge of the canopy, and uplight to give depth and highlight the texture. For trees branching to the ground the luminaires should be placed outside the canopy.

Earth Features

Earth features include waterfalls, ponds, streams and ocean fronts. Evaluate the surroundings and determine whether the earth feature is to be a focal point, transition or background element in the scene. If placing

Fig. 22-14. Dramatic frontlighting of trees at the entrance to a country club in Dallas emphasizes their color, size and shape.

equipment under water, consider the effect of light and heat on the organisms living there. All such equipment must be listed for submersible use, and all electrical codes for underwater lighting followed precisely. Underwater luminaires used in lighting waterfalls need strong locking mechanisms to maintain the aiming angle.

Waterfalls. To light a waterfall, determine the weir or type of edge over which the water falls. If the weir is rough, the water will be agitated and aerated. Luminaires placed directly below the point where the water hits the surface allow the light to travel up the falls, reacting with the bubbles to give the water a glow. The water will take on the color of the light shining into it. If the weir is a smooth surface, the water will fall in sheets. This type of waterfall should be lighted from the front with the luminaires placed far enough away to cover the entire height of the falls.

Streams and Ponds. Streams and ponds rarely represent the most important element in the landscape composition. However, if they are to be lighted it is best to do so externally. Internal lighting tends to draw too much attention away from other areas.

Oceanfront. The only part of the ocean that can be lit is the foam on the surf. A great deal of light must be thrown at the ocean, since most of it will be absorbed. High-wattage metal halide lamps are the best source for this application.

Lighting for other natural features, those found in national parks, geysers and rock faces, should be designed on a case-by-case basis and should take into account the basic design principles previously discussed.

Lamps

When choosing a lamp, consider its spectral characteristics and the desired color of the highlighted object. See chapter 6, Light Sources, for more detailed information on lamps. To add a sense of fun and fantasy, color filters can be added to completely change the atmosphere of the landscape. In equipment selection, consider the heat output from the source. Heat can burn or kill plants. See chapter 5, Nonvisual Effects of Radiant Energy, for further information.

HARDSCAPE LIGHTING

Hardscape lighting is a special category of landscape lighting which is associated with architectural features. This discussion will focus on fountains, outdoor sculpture and traveled ways.

Fountains

Fountains are constructed in a variety of forms, but the following design issues should be considered for all types. Determine which parts of the fountain need to be lighted—the water or the structure. Ascertain the viewing geometry and the type of lighting effects that will surround the fountain. If color is desired, care must be taken to keep other lighting from overpowering or washing out the colored effects. Constructed waterfalls can be treated as fountains, or they may be illuminated in a similar fashion to natural waterfalls.

Light interacts with water in three different ways (see figures 22-15 and 22-16). Light is *refracted* (changes direction) on passing from air into water or vice versa. This is why there can be a shift of apparent location of a submerged object. Refraction causes rainbows or sparkle in water droplets or in turbulent water.

Reflection also occurs when light strikes the surface of water: it is redirected back into the air or water in which it had been traveling. As with a mirror, the angle of incidence equals the angle of reflection. This is an important consideration for determining equipment location, since it is possible to see luminaires as reflected images in a pool. Reflection can also play a role in displaying the lighted structure. When lighting objects from underwater sources in calm water, one must consider that total internal reflection will occur at the water surface if the angle of incidence is greater than the critical angle of about 48° (see figure 22-17).

Depending on the particulate matter content and the air bubble content in a body of water, a certain amount of light *diffusion* will take place. This occurs because the light traveling through the water strikes the particles or bubbles, and is then reflected in a different direction. This may be a help or a hindrance.

For example, a laser light show requires smoke or fog in the air for the light to be seen. On the other hand, if the desired effect is lighting ornate tile at the bottom of a fountain, the water may end up looking murky, thus obscuring the tile. For more information on the optical effects of water on light, see chapter 1, Light and Optics.

For location of equipment, several factors should be considered, including critical angles, viewing angles and whether the equipment is above or under water. When positioning equipment, make sure the luminaires are aimed so that the source cannot be seen—either directly, or indirectly as a result of the reflection and refraction angles.

Lighting equipment installed under water must be accompanied by a maintenance commitment, as it is very complicated to service. All the equipment must be watertight and approved for submerged locations. An exception to these two constraints is in the use of fiber optics. This technology separates the electric lighting equipment from the water, so that it need not be water resistant. Note that all submersible equipment is about three to five times more expensive than normal wet-location outdoor equipment.

If equipment is not installed under water, it can be installed in trees, on nearby structures, in the ground surrounding the fountain, or on the fountain structure. Again, maintenance and access issues should be kept in mind when locating equipment. This approach may yield a less dramatic solution than submerged equipment, but it may be more practical and less expensive.

For general notes on equipment and source selection, refer to the section on Lighting Equipment and Maintenance in this chapter. As with natural-water features, all safety codes should be met as set forth by the National Electrical Code and any local authorities. See chapter 14, Codes and Regulations, for more information.

Sculpture

Exterior sculpture can be illuminated in much the same way as interior sculpture. The level of drama in the design should be adequate at night, but should also be appropriate to the theme of the immediate surroundings. Publications on museum lighting are also helpful for conveying ideas on sculpture lighting (see the discussion of Museum Lighting in chapter 17, Institution and Public Building Lighting). The three basic methods employed are key, fill and back (silhouette) light.

Key light is usually the most intense concentration of light, and it is usually direct and from a location in front of or to the side of, and slightly above, the sculpture. It focuses attention on what the designer

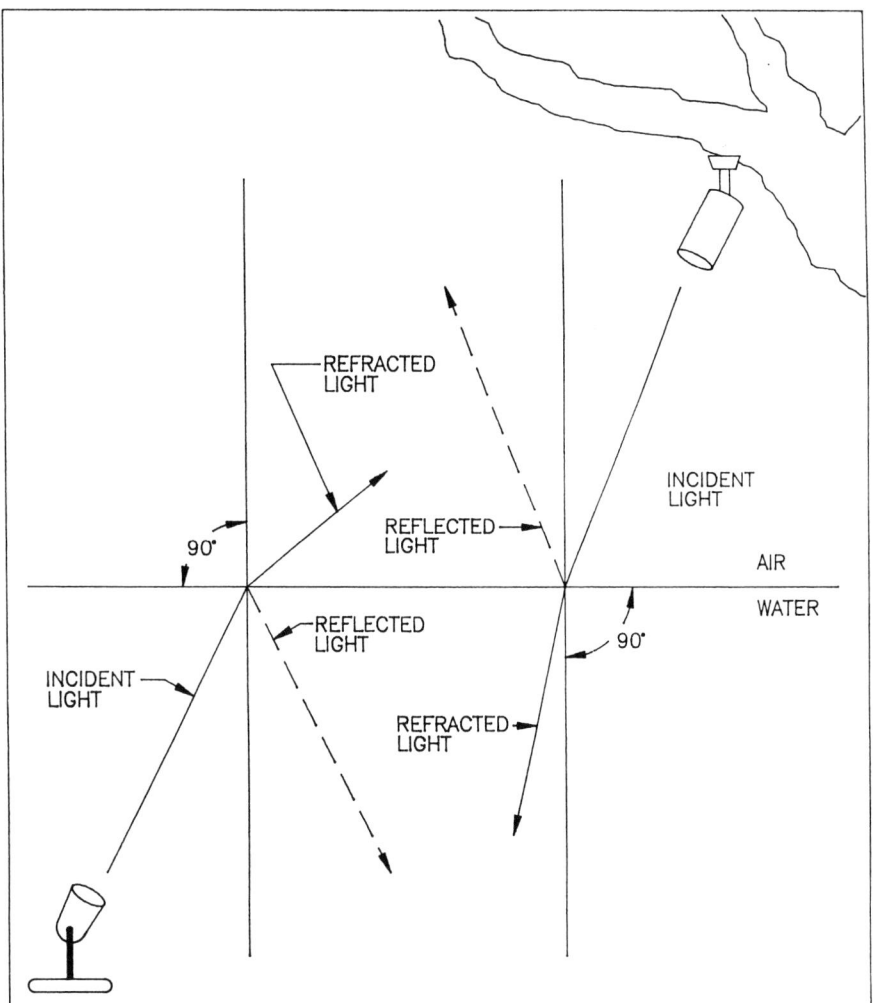

Fig. 22-15. Light travelling between air and water is refracted or "bent," causing an apparent shift in an object's location.

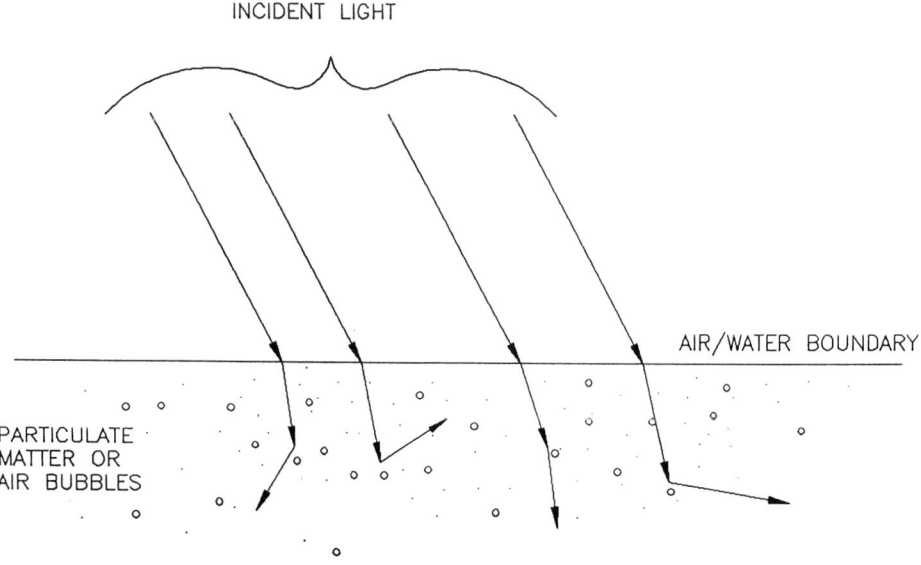

DIFFUSED LIGHT

Fig. 22-16. Diffused light is created when small particulate matter or air bubbles reflect light in all directions.

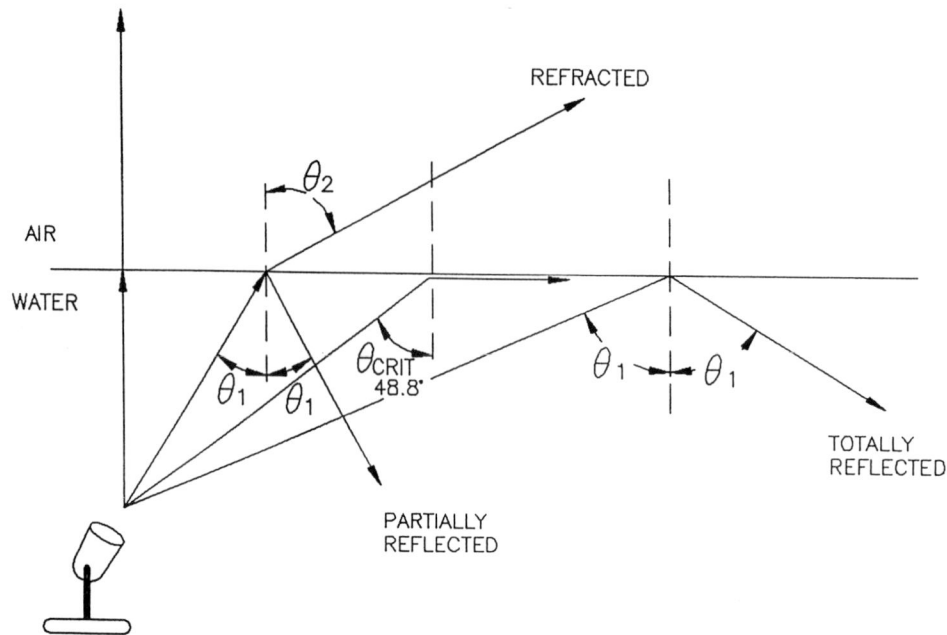

Fig. 22-17. Underwater light rays can be refracted or reflected depending on the incident angle with which they strike the surface of the water.

believes is the most important aspect of the piece. Fill light is less bright and helps to fill the direct shadows left by the key light. It can be direct, but can also be in the form of ambient landscape light or moonlight. Back light creates a halo or silhouette effect and helps define outline, but does not reveal detail. Note that if the key light from the front of a sculpture is too intense, it may tend to reduce shadows so much that the object will appear flat.

In addition to the angle of lighting, its beam spread, color and motion can also be controlled. Beam spreads can range from very narrow to very wide. Colored filters are available in a variety of shades. Motion can be created by using lighting controls or, simply, a color wheel with a multiple-fiber-optic system.

Walkways and Bikeways

Walkways and bikeways should be illuminated as an integral part of the surrounding landscape, but there are a few specific issues which need to be addressed. These will focus on traveled ways which are distant from roadways. For those near roadways, refer to chapter 24, Roadway Lighting, for details.

Minimum average maintained illuminance levels of 5 lx (0.5 fc) are important for identifying obstacles on the pavement. Visual identification of other pedestrians and bicyclists is dependent to a great degree on vertical surface illuminance. It is also dependent on the uniformity of this vertical illuminance. Uniformity is important for eliminating dark areas and potential security problems. Special security areas should have an average-to-minimum illuminance uniformity ratio,

both horizontal and vertical, which does not exceed 5:1 for any walkway or bikeway. Also important to security and a general sense of well-being is a luminous environment which extends out from the pavement and for a reasonable distance into the surrounding area. This border should extend at least 2 m (6 ft) on either side of the pavement, and have at least one-third the lighting level of the path.

In addition to security, scale is important in designing a lighting system for walkways and bikeways. Roadway lighting techniques are not appropriate for this application. Low-level lighting equipment such as bollards, step lights and decorative landscape lights, in conjunction with low pole-mounted luminaires, is appropriate. The pole-mounted system can provide the uniform ambient lighting, while the low-level equipment can add variety and contribute to identifying obstacles.

Stairways, intersections and sharp curves require special attention, as they are the areas with the highest potential for mishap. Stumbling down stairways and colliding with fellow pedestrians or bicyclists can often be avoided if the area is well lighted. Stairways should be illuminated so that each level change has definition, and so that the shadows which define these changes do not overlap too much and cause confusion. Usually the run of stairs can be illuminated to a lower average than the landing, which represents a change in the rhythm of travel. Average illuminances for stairways should be two to three times higher than the ambient level of the walkway. Stairways can be illuminated with any of the systems discussed for walkway and bikeway equipment. Similarly, intersections can be illuminated with the same equipment, and should also have levels two to three times higher than the walkway and bikeway.

Marina Lighting

Architectural environmental lighting in and around a marina must be designed in such a way as not to conflict with the navigation equipment lights and markings.

All equipment must be chosen and installed to help guide the boats and simplify docking. Docks and walkways adjacent to bodies of water should be lighted to create enough contrast to enhance the visibility of small objects, ropes and cleats on docks which could cause tripping and accidental falls.

The final installation should avoid the use of beacons, or red and green lights, which could be mistaken for navigational lights. The lights used for lighting the marina or dock must be visible from distances of one nautical mile or more. The lighting design should also ensure that the background created does not produce glare and light pollution, which would limit the visibility of the navigation equipment, or cause veiling luminance across the water, preventing a safe approach to the marina and dock for an incoming boat.

Agencies such as the U.S. Coast Guard and the U.S. Army Corps of Engineers can provide additional information on navigational lights. See also chapter 26, Transportation Lighting.

When lighting a marina, the following recommendations must be taken into consideration:

- Refer to the U.S. Coast Guard's standard for marinas, 33 CFR62.
- Refer to the appropriate chapters of this Handbook and to IES Recommended Practices for lights for adjacent structures, parking lots and access roads.
- Keep the environment free of glare to maintain good visibility of navigation equipment.
- Do not use colored lights that mimic colors used in standard navigational equipment.
- Make sure that all structures, docks and walkways next to bodies of water are illuminated to assure visibility of small objects that may cause tripping.
- When positioning the luminaire, take great care to minimize reflections from the water, which could create glare and render operations unsafe.

SPECIALTY LIGHTING

Many exterior lighting designs involve specialty areas. Examples of these are gazebos, follies, ice structures and displays. Sometimes the lighting design is tempo-

rary, as for holiday lighting, concerts or light displays. The lighting may be a static design or a dynamic design with color and movement. Specialty lighting can add life and even be the main feature of the outdoor setting.

Temporary Lighting

Holiday displays can be modern, traditional, whimsical or religious. The effects can be subtle or strong, taking many forms from the simplest outlining techniques to three-dimensional luminous structures.

Holiday Trees. The most popular holiday display is the traditional Christmas tree. Most trees are randomly lighted, and the total required number of lights is approximately equal to the height of the tree times the width times three. Large trees, above 15 m (50 ft), may need larger-scale medium-base lamps. Small trees, shorter than 3 m (10 ft), may be more attractively lighted with midget lamps, but will require two or three times as many lamps as stated in the formula above.

Color impact may be enhanced by using one or only a few colors on each tree. Multicolored sets with equal numbers of differently colored lamps may lose their individuality and appear yellowish-white when viewed at a distance.

Holiday Displays. Outlining structures with bare lamps is simple and effective. Festooning lights is the easiest approach. A touch of visual liveliness can be achieved in the following ways:

- Install a blinking "twinkle lamp" in every fifth or sixth socket of a string of decorative lamps, or entire strings of such lamps throughout trees and structures.
- Use fiber-optic materials or light pipes with a changing color wheel to outline or enhance features or structures.
- Utilize sequential switching for strings of lighting, light pipes or fiber-optic materials.

Temporary Structures. A temporary structure may be an ice structure or a theatrical building. Refer to the section on Structure Lighting for techniques. Consideration must be given to the location of the equipment in order to minimize electrical hazards from the temporary lighting. The heat of the lamps is very critical when lighting ice structures.

Flags

Flags should be illuminated from different directions. It is usually not possible to predict in which direction the wind will carry the flag. Therefore, an array of luminaires to cover all directions is most effective. A luminaire located at the base of the flagpole will graze the flag and create deeper shadows as the flag waves in the wind. Spotlights located on either side of the flag will enhance the visibility of the flag from many directions. Lamp intensities and beam spreads should be selected to minimize spill light.

Other Areas

There are a multitude of specialty areas which should be considered on a case-by-case basis, such as outdoor concert theaters, display areas and theme parks.

LIGHTING EQUIPMENT AND MAINTENANCE

The selection of lighting equipment must include consideration of durability and maintenance for the environment in which it has been placed. Ultimately, exterior lighting equipment is judged on its ability to continue to perform in a harsh environment and with less than rigorous maintenance.

Performance

Many exterior luminaires require precise aiming to effectively perform their intended function. Landscape luminaires may have to be periodically re-aimed in response to growing foliage. High winds or driving rain will necessitate strong locking devices for aimed luminaires to maintain their objective.

Lighting equipment should also integrate with the architecture of its surround. A luminaire's scale, proportion, finish and style should complement the architecture.

Lamps

Lamp selection is an important consideration for a lighting system. The spectral composition of lamps varies greatly, even between manufacturers of the same type of lamp. It is important to test the lamps being considered to assure that the material being illuminated will be rendered properly. The efficacy of the source is also of great importance. High-intensity discharge sources are available which will render many surfaces with pleasing results. The higher efficacy of the HID system will usually result in lower energy consumption of the system.

Lighting Equipment and Climate

Exterior lighting equipment must withstand an abusive and corrosive environment while achieving its intended goal. Location, moisture, dirt, equipment construction and finish all affect luminaire performance. See chapter 7, Luminaires, and chapter 9, Lighting Calculations.

The design and construction of lighting equipment must be suited for the particular environment. Luminaires located below grade may require more resistance against moisture than those mounted above grade or under cover. Some luminaires are carefully sealed against moisture, while others provide drainage for inevitable water accumulation. Yet, luminaires with drainage may also invite insects to enter and die within the lamp housing, thereby increasing luminaire dirt depreciation. Luminaires designed for water runoff may aid in keeping the luminaire clean by allowing dirt and debris to be washed away. Equipment seals and finishes should adequately withstand the heat and ultraviolet radiation of the lamps with which they are recommended. Sharp luminaire edges should be avoided where a finish might easily deteriorate. All materials and finishes must be sufficient to bear the structural abuse and corrosion occasioned by the environment.

Maintenance

Luminaire location and construction must be reviewed from the maintenance perspective to ensure continued performance consistent with the design parameters. See chapter 32, Lighting Maintenance.

When possible, luminaire locations should be easily accessible to allow for cleaning and group relamping. Inaccessible luminaires should not be placed where debris, dirt and snow will easily accumulate, rendering the luminaire useless until maintenance is performed. Fallen foliage and animal matter can quickly compromise the performance of an ill-placed luminaire. Furthermore, lighting equipment and luminaire locations should not impede the regular maintenance of the surrounding structures, landscapes or traveled ways.

Construction assembly should facilitate lamp replacement. Complex disassembly will reduce the chance that a luminaire is correctly reassembled after relamping. Luminaire components should be as few as possible, since parts may be easily lost outdoors. Luminaire construction should also be sturdy enough to withstand vandalism.

REFERENCES

1. Moyer, J. L. 1992. *The landscape lighting book.* New York: Wiley.

Sports and Recreational Area Lighting

23

Note: As in other chapters of this Handbook, illuminance recommendations are presented in a lux (footcandle) format, wherein we take 1 fc ≈ 10 lx (rather than the more exact relationship 1 fc = 10.76 lx). Because many sports facilities are laid out in terms of Imperial units (yards, feet, inches), the designer may prefer to use the footcandle version.

OVERVIEW[1-4]

Advancements in illuminating engineering design and technology have allowed sporting events to be increasingly played and watched at night. During the last decade, light source efficacies have more than doubled; thus, the electrical power and energy required for a sports facility have been drastically reduced in spite of increased illuminances required to serve the elevated skill level of athletes.

Associated with improved illuminances are increased problems of glare and color rendering for better visual performance and quality television broadcasting. Sports lighting design can no longer be accomplished by methods of approximation but requires sophisticated computations. Therefore, designers need a thorough understanding of illuminating engineering principles and associated computer programs.

For more information on computer algorithms, illuminance calculation methods, equipment installation, field measurements and illuminance criteria for various sports, the reader is referred to the IES Recommended Practice for Sports and Recreational Area Lighting (RP-6).[1]

CLASS OF PLAY AND FACILITIES

The traditional way of classifying sports as *amateur* and *professional* is no longer meaningful. Modern practices allow both amateurs and professionals to compete in the same event, as in golf and tennis. Furthermore, some amateur sports, such as basketball and football, are played at practically the same skill level and in the same facilities as professional sports.

In general, as the skill level of play is elevated, players and spectators require a better-lighted environment. A correlation exists between the size of a facility and the skill level of play, that is, the number of spectators is directly related to the skill level of play. Accordingly, facilities should be designed to satisfy the highest skill level to be played as well as the greatest spectator capacity. To determine illumination criteria, facilities are grouped into four classes:

- *Class I*—for competition play in large-capacity arenas and stadiums with up to 200,000 spectators. (In this chapter, the recommendations of illumination criteria for individual sports are limited to audiences of 10,000 or less. Stadiums with spectator capacity greater than 10,000 generally require considerably higher horizontal and vertical illuminances due to the needs of spectators seated farthest from the playing field and of the camera for television broadcasting. The required illuminances under these circumstances are frequently more than double those recommended in this section.)
- *Class II*—for competition play with less than 5,000 spectators.
- *Class III*—for competition play primarily for players, though with due consideration for spectators.
- *Class IV*—for social and recreational play only, with secondary consideration for spectators.

There is, of course, some overlap between illumination criteria for various skill levels of play and facility sizes (see figure 23-1).

TYPES OF SPORTS

Based on illumination requirements, sports may be divided into two groups—aerial sports and ground level sports—and within these two groups, they can be further divided into multidirectional sports and unidirectional sports.

Aerial Sports

Aerial sports involve the playing of an object (usually a ball) in the air as well as on the ground.

Fig. 23-1. Classes of Play and Facilities

Facility	Class			
	I	II	III	IV
International	X			
National	X			
Professional	X			
College	X	X		
Semi-professional	X	X		
Sports clubs	X	X		
Amateur leagues		X	X	
High schools		X	X	
Training facilities			X	X
Elementary schools			X	X
Recreational Events				X
Social events				X

Class I—Facilities with spectator capacity of 5000 to 200,000.
Class II—Facilities for spectators of 5000 or less.
Class III—No special provision for spectators.
Class IV—Social and recreational, i.e., noncompetitive.

- *Multidirectional aerial sports:* The players and spectators view the playing object from multiple positions and viewing angles. For aerial sports, vertical illumination over the playing field is more critical than horizontal illumination at ground level. It is important to control direct glare from luminaires by locating the luminaires away from the most frequent viewing directions of players and spectators. Typical multidirectional aerial sports include badminton, baseball, basketball, football, handball, jai alai, soccer, squash, tennis and volleyball.

- *Unidirectional aerial sports:* The playing object is viewed in the air from a fixed position on the ground. General horizontal illumination is required at the starting end and vertical illumination at the finishing end. This is normally done by aiming some luminaires downward at the starting end and at high angles toward the finishing end. Luminaires must be shielded from the player's view. Typical unidirectional sports include golf, skeet and trap shooting and ski jumping.

Ground Level Sports

These sports are played on the ground or a few feet above the ground. Players and spectators in the normal course of play do not look upward.

- *Multidirectional ground level sports:* The players and spectators view the playing object from multiple positions, normally looking downward or horizontally, but occasionally upward. These sports require well-distributed horizontal illu-

mination, although vertical illumination should be considered. Typical multidirectional ground level sports include boxing, curling, field hockey, ice hockey, skating, swimming (excluding high board diving) and wrestling.

- *Unidirectional ground level sports:* The object is aimed at a fixed position, usually in a vertical plane close to ground level. For these sports, vertical illumination is critical at this vertical plane. This is normally accomplished by aiming luminaires toward the plane, shielded from view of the players and spectators at the starting end. Typical unidirectional ground level sports include archery, bowling and pistol shooting. Skiing is also a unidirectional ground level sport, but for it the sloped ground surface is the illuminated plane and the luminaire beam is directed down the slope.

POWER AND ENERGY

Since most sports involve the critical viewing of a fast-moving object, such as a baseball or an ice hockey puck, sports facilities normally require high illuminance, ranging from 300 to 1500 lx (30 to 150 fc). The lighting load requires high power densities (watts per unit area) and high power demand (kilowatts), and in some facilities, high energy consumption (kilowatt-hours). It is noteworthy that power is consumed only when the system is being operated. For major sports facilities, the lighting load may require high power demand for short periods of time, and thus have fairly low energy consumption.

For example, a major league stadium for professional baseball and football might be lighted with 700 luminaires equipped with 1.5-kW metal halide lamps. The power demand would be approximately 1130 kW. If the operating schedule of the stadium is 40 night games annually for an average of 5 h per game, the annual energy consumption for arena lighting will be in the range of $1130 \times 40 \times 5 = 226,000$ kWh.

In comparison, a municipal park might consist of four softball fields and be lighted with only 240 luminaires equipped with 1-kW metal halide lamps. The power demand would be only 260 kW for the lighting. However, the operating schedule of a typical complex might be 200 nights per year for an average of 5 h per night. This would result in an annual energy consumption for the field lighting of $260 \times 200 \times 5 = 260,000$ kWh.

For every professional sports stadium, there are hundreds of public parks and municipal recreational facilities. The lighting energy consumption due to these recreational facilities is considerably greater than that of a few stadiums. Thoughtful design, circuiting and control of lighting installations are the keys to energy conservation.

QUALITY AND QUANTITY OF ILLUMINATION

The goal of sports lighting is to provide an appropriate luminous environment by controlling the brightness of an object and its background so the object will appear clear and sharp to the players, spectators and television viewers. To achieve this goal, both qualitative and quantitative factors of illumination must be considered.

Illuminance

The illuminance must satisfy the requirements of the players and the spectators, as well as the television cameras if any. These requirements should be known at the beginning of the design process, since lighting needs for spectators and television cameras frequently exceed the suggested level for the sport itself. Factors affecting illuminance levels for all sports are determined by:

- *Speed of sport*. Visual tasks of various sizes must be seen when playing sports at a wide range of speeds against various background brightnesses and colors.
- *Skill level of players*. As the skill level of players increases, the speed of objects and the importance of accuracy also increase, which in turn calls for higher illuminances. Professional or competitive playing requires higher illuminance than unskilled or recreational playing.
- *Age of players*. It has been recognized that older players require a higher illuminance and are less tolerant of glare than younger players.
- *Spectator capacity*. The visual size of tasks diminishes as the inverse square of the distance. This demands increased illuminance to compensate. For sport stadiums, the illuminance is determined by the lighting required for the spectators seated farthest from the playing area.
- *Television broadcasting*. The illuminance required for television cameras and photographic film depends on the sensitivity of the photosensitive media, aperture of the camera, and depth of field to be rendered. Television cameras using an extended telephoto lens may require twice the illuminance required for a regular telephoto lens.

Horizontal Illuminance. The horizontal illuminance specified for sports as target illuminance is normally taken on the ground or 3 ft above the ground. It should be noted that for most aerial sports, the task is played and viewed in the air rather than on the ground. Therefore, vertical illuminances should be of primary concern. However, horizontal illuminance is normally used in design calculations for two reasons:

- Horizontal illuminance values are much less complicated and time consuming to compute and to measure in the field.
- The vertical illuminance values are acceptable when the horizontal illuminance meets the recommended criteria and the design complies with recommended design factors, such as mounting height, aiming and beam spread.

Vertical Illuminance. Factors to be considered when determining vertical target luminance values specified for sports are:

- *Viewing direction*. There are an infinite number of vertical planes from the perspective of players, spectators or television cameras. Generally, the planes normal to the four principal directions of the playing field are considered adequate for calculation. Vertical illuminances at given points in space from different directions are not additive. Vertical illuminance must occur on the different viewing planes to be effective.
- *Elevation*. Elevations vary with the sport and skill level of play, and the background luminance varies with facility design and whether it is indoors or outdoors. For example, major league baseball requires high vertical illuminance, up to 150 ft above the ground; whereas the height needed for basketball is only around 20 ft.
- *Illuminance relations*. For multidirectional sports, the ratio of illuminances at ground level is also important and should be less than 3:1 between horizontal and vertical planes as well as between vertical illuminances in the four primary viewing directions.

Initial Illuminance. The initial illuminance is that calculated or measured for new installations using rated lamp lumens provided at 100 h of operation (corrected for any lamp position or tilt factor, ballast factor and voltage variation losses).

Maintained Illuminance. The maintained illuminance is the average illuminance at a point, or throughout an area, after a specific period of time or after relamping and cleaning. Based upon a designated maintenance schedule and using known light loss and field factors, a close approximation of the actual maintained value can be calculated. The values used to approximate the light loss and field factors should always be identified when calculating maintained illuminance values.

Target Illuminance. The target illuminance is the value used for calculations during system design to determine if the system meets a desired performance standard. This value may be the initial illuminance, but more often an initial value is reduced by a designated percentage to approximate maintained values. Initial field measurements of the resultant system are then corrected by this reduction to evaluate whether the design criteria have been achieved. Target illuminances for various sports recommended in this section are based on 70% of rated life. If the designer chooses to use the "mean lumens" of a lamp as a basis for design calculations, the illuminances should be modified accordingly.

For example, suppose the lamp to be used for the design is rated for 10,000 h and initially delivers 90,000 lm. However, the lamp manufacturer's lumen maintenance data also indicate the lumen output at 70% of rated life (7000 h) is only 75,000 lm. Then the designed target illuminance should be based on 75,000 rather than 90,000 lm. Note that field measurement for verification usually takes place shortly after installation. The initial illuminance measured will naturally be higher than the target illuminance by a factor of 90,000/75,000 as well as other light loss factors (LLFs). Refer to chapter 6, Light Sources, and chapter 9, Lighting Calculations, for further discussion of LLFs.

Uniformity (Horizontal). Uniformity is a measure of relationships of the illuminances over an area. It is particularly important for high-speed sports on a large playing field, such as baseball, football, ice hockey and tennis. Poor uniformity may distort the visual perception of tasks both in speed and in position, thus affecting player performance.

There are many methods to express uniformity. These include:

- Coefficient of variation (CV)
- Ratio of maximum to minimum illuminance (M/M)
- Uniformity gradients (UG)
- Ratio of maximum to average illuminance
- Ratio of minimum to average illuminance
- Ratio of minimum to target illuminance

The first three methods are most useful for expressing the quality of uniformity. One or more of these methods may be used to evaluate an installation, but not all are required for every sport.

Coefficient of Variation (CV). This method is a measure of the weighted average of all relevant illuminance values and is commonly used in statistics, where the variance of a set of values is calculated as the ratio of

standard deviation σ of all values to the mean $\bar{x}$. We have

$$\sigma = \sqrt{\frac{\sum_{i=1}^{n}(x_i - \bar{x})^2}{n}} \qquad (23\text{-}1)$$

where

x_i = illuminance at point i,
n = number of points measured (see the section on Field Measurements and Performance Evaluation, below, for guidance on the number and distribution of points to be measured),
$\bar{x}$ = mean illuminance.

Then

$$CV = \frac{\sigma}{\bar{x}} \qquad (23\text{-}2)$$

As a rule, the value of the CV for Classes I, II, III and IV should not exceed 0.15, 0.25, 0.30 and 0.35 respectively.

Maximum to Minimum (M/M). The uniformity U can also be defined in terms of the extremes, that is, the highest and lowest values of the calculated or measured illuminances:

$$U = \frac{E_{max}}{E_{min}} \qquad (23\text{-}3)$$

The uniformity ratio for Classes I, II, III and IV should not exceed 2.0, 2.5, 3.5 and 5.0 respectively.[1] This limit needs to be tightened for some high-speed sports if play is televised.

Uniformity Gradient. The uniformity gradient (UG) is the rate of change of illuminance on the playing field. It is extremely important for high-speed sports, because a fast-moving object passing from a light to a dark space may appear to change speeds due to different visual processing times for different adaptation levels; the visual system responds more slowly at lower adaptation levels. The UG is expressed as a ratio between the illuminances of adjacent measuring points on a uniform grid. The recommended upper limit of

Fig. 23-2. Upper Limit of Uniformity Gradient, for Comparing Two Adjacent Areas. The Corresponding Upper Limit for the Uniformity Gradient in Diagonal Positions can be 1.4 Times the Given Values if the Grid is Square

Speed of Sport	Player	Spectator	Television
Fast (e.g., baseball or tennis)	1.5	1.5	1.5
Moderate (e.g., football)	2.1	1.5	1.5
Slow (e.g., gymnastics)	2.0	2.0	2.0

Fig. 23-3. Recommended Field-Measuring Grids of Typical Class I and II Facilities

Sport	Court Boundary (CBA)		Lighted Area (PPA)		Grids	
	Typical Dimensions (Feet)	Court Boundary Area (Sq. Ft.)	Typical Dimensions (Feet)	Primary Playing Area (Sq. Ft.)	Quantity	Grid Size (Feet)
Badminton	20 × 44	880	30 × 50	1,500	15	10 × 10
Baseball						
Infield	90 × 90	8,100	150 × 150	22,500	25	30 × 30
Outfield	*	*	*	*	*	30 × 30
Basketball	50 × 90	4,500	75 × 105	7,875	35	15 × 15
Bowling						
Lane	6 × 70	420	Same	Same	8	6 × 10
Pins (Vertical)	6 × 3	18	Same	Same	6	3 × 2
Boxing / Wrestling	24 × 24	576	36 × 36	1,296	36	6 × 6
Field Hockey	180 × 300	54,000	210 × 330	69,300	77	30 × 30
Football	160 × 360	57,600	180 × 360	64,800	72	30 × 30
Ice Hockey	85 × 200	17,000	90 × 210	18,900	84	15 × 15
Lacrosse	180 × 330	59,400	210 × 330	69,300	77	30 × 30
Soccer	200 × 330	66,000	210 × 330	69,300	77	30 × 30
Softball						
Infield	60 × 60	3,600	120 × 120	14,400	16	30 × 30
Outfield	*	*	*	*	*	30 × 30
Tennis	36 × 78	2,808	60 × 100	6,000	15	20 × 20 ~
Volleyball	30 × 60	1,800	45 × 90	4,050	18	15 × 15

*Baseball and softball fields are pie-shaped. Outfield areas are derived from the overall area less the lighted infield area.

~ The intersection points of the baselines, double lines, centerline and service lines can be utilized as reading locations. This is a convenient walk-on-grid in lieu of the 20 by 20 foot grid.

UG values varies with the speed of the sport and is shown in figure 23-2.[1]

For most sports, the recommended field measurement grid is in a pattern of squares, say 20 ft × 20 ft each (see figure 23-3). The illuminance values at the adjacent grid points can be compared along the X and Y directions to determine the UG values. When comparing illuminance values along the diagonal directions, the UG criteria should be increased proportionately.

Some sports fields have more than one design illuminance. In that case, the transitions between design illuminances should be gradual. For example, if the infield of a major baseball stadium is designed for 1500 lx (150 fc) and the outfield for 1000 lx (100 fc), the illuminance at the grid points in the outfield adjacent to the infield should be higher than 1000 lx (100 fc), say 1250 lx (125 fc), in order to achieve an acceptable UG.

Glare

Glare is particularly important in sports lighting in that it can impair visibility (and thus the level and quality of play) and can cause discomfort to both players and spectators. These two types of glare are classically known as disability glare and discomfort glare, respec-

a   b

Fig. 23-4. Luminaires directly over the basket (a), or windows behind the basketball board (b) produce direct glare to players.

tively (see chapter 3, Vision and Perception). Glare of both types can result either from directly viewing the luminaire (direct glare) or from viewing its reflection in a glossy or semiglossy surface (reflected glare).

Direct Glare. The present methods of assessing disability and discomfort glare for sports lighting are inadequate because of the very large number of viewing positions required to perform and to view the various sports. The Commission Internationale de l'Éclairage (CIE) is, however, currently working on a system to assess direct glare for sports lighting.

Whenever possible, it is imperative to diminish the effects of glare by locating the luminaires or daylight sources away from the normal lines of sight. For example, luminaires should not be located directly above the basket on a basketball court, because players can then be blinded when looking up at the basket. (See figure 23-4a.) In those instances where glare cannot be avoided in positioning the luminaires, consideration should be given to the type of lamp and the use of glare control devices on the luminaires to reduce the luminance.

Windows in an indoor sports facility are not considered desirable, particularly behind the basket of a basketball court and at either end of an indoor tennis court. (See figure 23-4b.) Skylights should be screened and be placed away from the normal line of sight.

Reflected Glare. To reduce reflected glare, surfaces within the field of view should have low reflectance values, preferably in matte finishes. See figure 23-5a (reflection of luminaires and players on a basketball court) and figure 23-5b (reflection on the water surface from windows at an indoor swimming pool).

Contrast

Contrast is the relationship between the luminances of an object and its immediate background. It is essential to have contrast to see. For example, it would be difficult to detect a fast-moving white baseball against a white background (see figure 23-6a), or even against a predominantly white background, such as the seating area of a baseball stadium during hot summer days when many spectators wear white clothing (see figure 23-6b). However, too much contrast, such as using a black background on a baseball field, may be esthetically unpleasant. The use of harmonious color combi-

a

b

Fig. 23-5. (a) Specular surfaces can cause reflected glare as illustrated on the floor of a gymnasium. (b) Windows can produce unwanted glare from the water surface of a swimming pool and will reduce the ability of the lifeguard to see beneath the surface or even some objects on the water surface.

a

b

Fig. 23-6. The visibility of a white baseball can be seriously reduced against a predominantly white background (a) where many spectators are wearing white clothing during warm weather (b).

nations, such as a dark green court surface with a yellow tennis ball, can significantly improve the seeing tasks.

Modeling

Modeling is the ability of the lighting system to reveal the three-dimensional form of an object, such as a ball, target or player. With regard to modeling, illumination may be described as flat or directional.[1] Effective illumination for sports depends in large part on modeling. This is especially important for high-quality television broadcasting. Lighting from two or more directions is required to eliminate deep shadows and separate the visual target, such as a ball, from its background. Variations in intensity also accentuate changes in shape.

Flicker

The lumen output of a lamp varies with its power input on a 50- or 60-Hz ac circuit; the light varies 100 or 120 times per second, respectively. The cyclic variation of light, termed *flicker*, can cause a stroboscopic effect (see chapter 6, Light Sources, for further information). Incandescent lamps produce the least flicker, since the filament retains the incandescent heat during the cyclic variation in current. High-pressure sodium lamps have the greatest flicker. Illuminating a plane with lamps controlled by ballasts which shift the lamp current (and thus the light output), either leading or lagging the voltage, will minimize flicker. Luminaires connected on different phases of a three-phase power system can also minimize flicker. Metal halide lamps have the least flicker among the HID sources and can be used on single-phase systems.

Spill Light

Spill light, sometimes referred to as "light trespass," is light shining beyond the sports facility that may annoy occupants of the adjacent property. Because spill light frequently creates political issues, many municipalities have enacted ordinances to limit it.

Spill light may be controlled by a number of design considerations:

1. Select luminaires with an intensity distribution that does not illuminate areas outside the sports facility.
2. Use cutoff luminaires or, where direct glare from luminaires is not a problem, high mounting poles with luminaires having a low aiming angle.

A combination of design factors must be evaluated in order to achieve optimum solutions.

Television Broadcasting

The illumination criteria for television broadcasting of a sport are much more complicated than the criteria for playing it. Detailed information on illumination criteria and recommendations are contained in IESNA Publication RP-6[1] and in chapter 21, Theater, Television and Photographic Lighting.

LIGHT SOURCES

Three basic types of light sources are commonly used for sports lighting applications: incandescent, fluorescent and high-intensity discharge. Each type has advantages and disadvantages. The proper selection depends upon particular requirements of the installation being considered, economics and the designer's preference.

Detailed information on light sources is given in chapter 6, Light Sources. As a general comparison, the relative ratings of light sources are summarized in figure 23-7.

LUMINAIRES

General

A luminaire is a complete lighting unit consisting of one or more lamps (light sources) together with the parts designed to control the light distribution and other mechanical and electrical components. The opti-

Fig. 23-7 Light Source Ratings

Light Source	Lumen Output per Lamp	Efficacy (Lumens per Watt)	Life	Color Acceptability	Degree of Light Control	Maintenance of Lumen Output
Incandescent*	Fair	Low	Low	High	High	Fair
Mercury (Coated)	Good	Fair	High	Fair to Good	Fair	Fair
Metal Halide	High	Good	Good	Good	Good	Good
High Pressure Sodium	High	High	High	Fair	Good	High
*Includes tungsten-halogen.						

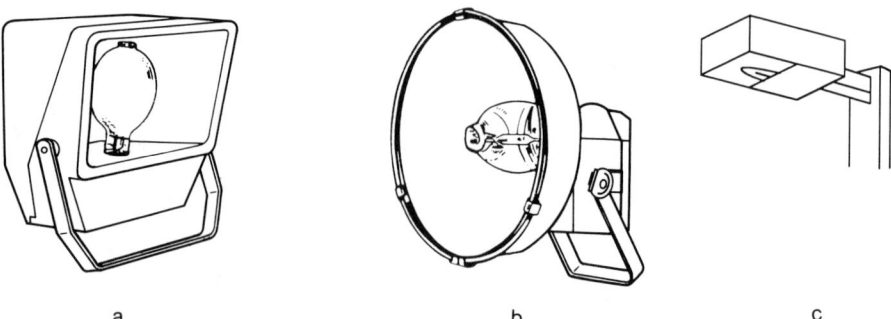

Fig. 23-8. Types of floodlights used for sports lighting. (a) Enclosed rectangular type. (b) Enclosed round type. (c) Shielded type.

cal characteristics of a luminaire affect the direct and reflected glare, shadows, distribution and pattern, which all should be considered when selecting the correct luminaire for a particular application. See chapter 7, Luminaires, for more information.

Floodlights

Floodlights are the most common type of luminaire used for sports lighting. Some types of floodlights are:

1. *Enclosed rectangular type.* This class of luminaire includes a substantially constructed housing in which a separate reflector is placed. The assembly is enclosed by a weatherproof hinged door with a cover glass to provide an unobstructed light opening at least equal to the effective dimensions of the reflector (figure 23-8a).
2. *Enclosed round type.* This class is weatherproof and may be constructed so the housing forms the reflecting surface. The assembly is enclosed by a cover glass (figure 23-8b).
3. *Shielded type.* This class is designed to shield the light source and reflector above a certain vertical angle. This shielding angle is chosen so as to minimize the direct glare to the observer at a normal viewing angle but still provide broad coverage on the sports field (figure 23-8c).
4. *Reflectorized lamps.* This class consists of a lamp holder and a lamp with an integral reflector.

Beam and Field Angles

The light distribution of a luminaire may be classified by its beam and field angles. The beam and field angles are determined from the intensity distribution pattern, there being one of each value for circular beams, and separate horizontal and vertical values for oval beams. The beam angle is the included angle between points

of 50% intensity, and field angle is the included angle between points of 10% intensity. See figure 23-9.

The NEMA field angle classification, as shown in figure 23-10, is widely used by the lighting industry to classify the overall candlepower distribution pattern of a floodlight. It is also useful to the designer for preliminary design selections. However, the coefficient of utilization (CU) of each design application should be based on the total luminous flux (in lumens) of the luminaire rather than the NEMA field angle.

Asymmetrical beam floodlights may be designated according to the horizontal and vertical beam spreads in that order; that is, a floodlight with a horizontal beam spread of 75° (Type 5) and a vertical beam spread of 35° (Type 3) may be designated as a Type 5 × 3 floodlight.

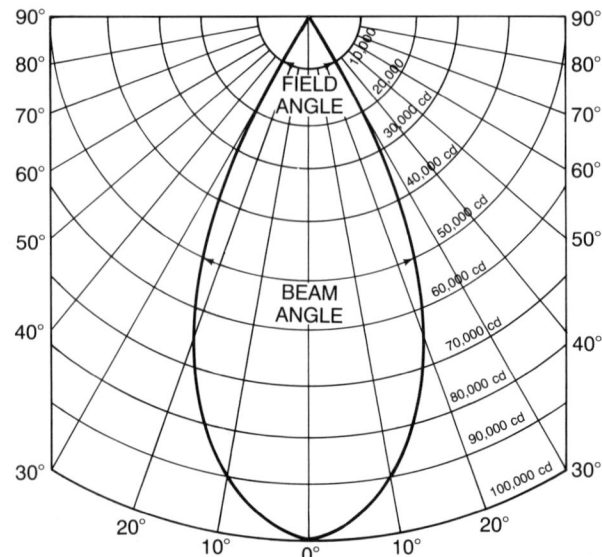

Fig. 23-9. As illustrated from this intensity distribution curve on polar coordinates, the maximum intensity is 100,000 cd. The field angle is 60°, the angle included between the intersecting points of the curve at 10,000 cd (10% of 100,000 cd). The beam angle is 48°, the angle included between the intersecting points of the curve at 50,000 cd (50% of 100,000 cd). According to NEMA classification, the illustrated floodlight is classified as Type 4 having a field angle between 46° and 70°.

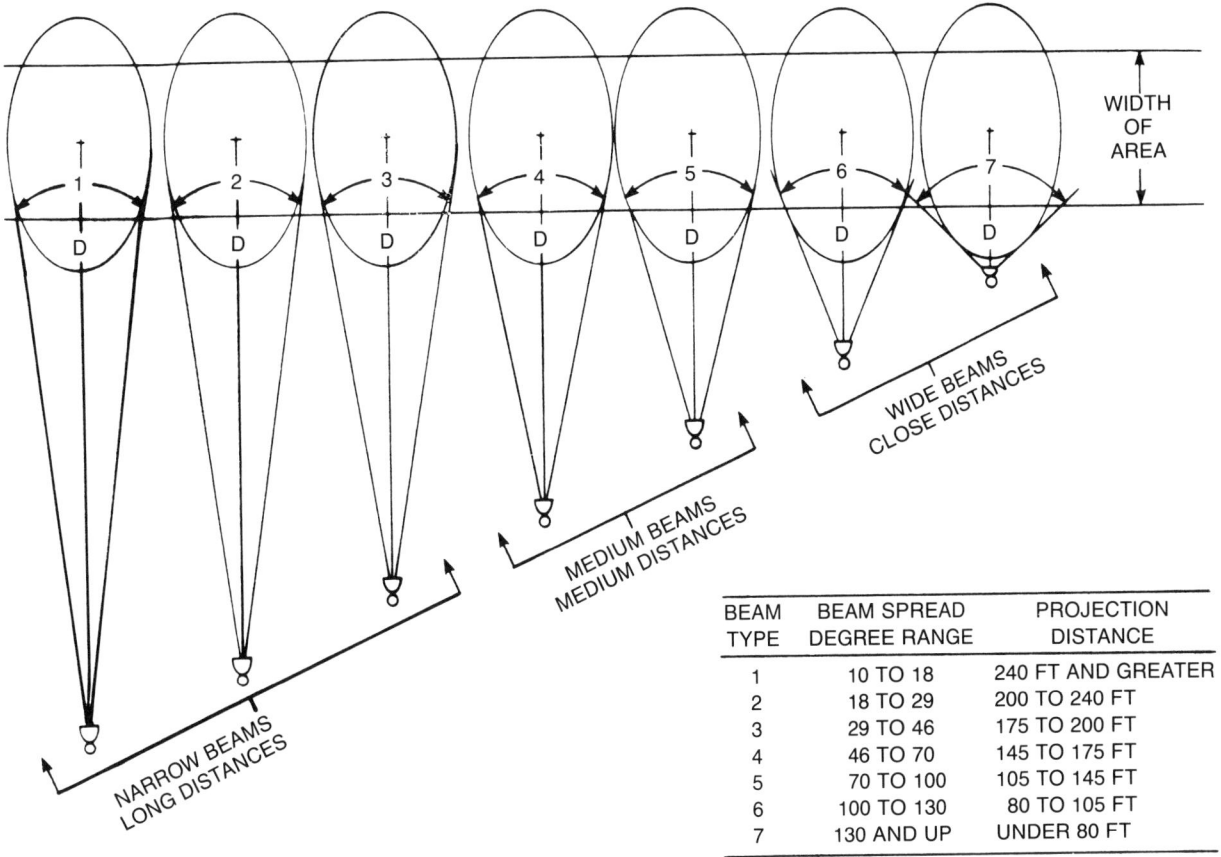

Fig. 23-10. NEMA field angle (formerly beam spread) classifications and their effective projection distances.

BEAM TYPE	BEAM SPREAD DEGREE RANGE	PROJECTION DISTANCE
1	10 TO 18	240 FT AND GREATER
2	18 TO 29	200 TO 240 FT
3	29 TO 46	175 TO 200 FT
4	46 TO 70	145 TO 175 FT
5	70 TO 100	105 TO 145 FT
6	100 TO 130	80 TO 105 FT
7	130 AND UP	UNDER 80 FT

Luminance Control

Glare and spill light control devices include visors, internal and external louvers, lamps and special lamp shields. They should be considered during design, because some of them cannot be retrofitted after initial installation. The use of such control devices will reduce the efficiency of luminaires. Proper lighting design should minimize their use by selecting luminaires that provide the desired beam control.

DESIGN CONSIDERATIONS FOR SPORTS FACILITIES

Sports lighting design follows the same principles and practices as the design for other spaces or facilities given in chapter 10, Design Process. Chapter 31, Lighting Controls, and chapter 30, Energy Management, provide additional information on the techniques and economics of controls and operations. Included below are considerations that are particularly applicable to sports lighting design.

General-Purpose Facilities

Most sports facilities, especially indoor facilities, are intended to be used for various sports, social, educa-tional or entertainment functions. The lighting, therefore, must be adaptable to all intended functions. General-purpose facilities, ordered by size and spectator capacity, may be classified as exercise rooms, gymnasiums, field houses, arenas and stadiums.

1. *Exercise rooms.* These rooms are usually small, for general exercise such as physical fitness, aerobic dancing, weight lifting and machine exercise. General uniform and diffuse lighting of 300 lx (30 fc) is recommended.

2. *Gymnasiums.* Gymnasiums are generally a part of a school facility designed to serve school programs during the day and community functions at night. A wide choice of illuminances may be desirable because of the diverse seeing tasks and activities that can be encountered. Variations in general illumination can be achieved through dimming, split switching, or other means of lighting control between 50 and 500 lx (5 and 50 fc).

3. *Field Houses.* Field houses and gymnasiums have common uses; however, field houses are generally larger and serve a wider range of sports, such as indoor track and field events. Illuminance levels are normally 500–1000 lx (50–100 fc).

4. *Arenas.* Arenas are large multipurpose facilities. Playing areas of arena floors are generally 50 m (150 ft) or more in each direction, with seating spaces designed to serve a few thousand to 20,000 spectators. Vertical and horizontal target illuminances for arenas are normally in excess of 1000 lx (100 fc) and are suitable for a variety of sports.
5. *Stadiums.* Stadiums are large, completely open facilities for major league baseball and football and can accommodate up to 100,000 spectators. Their lighting design should be similar to that of arenas. Multiple light sources, distributions and controls must be used to provide illuminances suitable for players, spectators and television cameras.

System Selection Considerations

Outdoor Facilities. A direct lighting system is the only kind that can be used for outdoor facilities. When the facility contains roofed areas covering spectator seating, the roof structure is normally utilized to serve as structural support for the lighting system. Lighting underneath the covered roof can also serve to soften the glare of the luminaires.

Since outdoor lighting is generally visible at distances far beyond the boundary of the facility and is subject to environmental conditions, careful consideration should be given to:

• Spill light on neighboring property
• Light added to the sky glow
• Durability of equipment and wiring under the continuous exposure to the environment

Indoor Facilities. There are more system choices in indoor applications. The system may be a totally indirect distribution system for a small multipurpose facility, a direct-indirect system for an indoor tennis center, or a direct system for arenas and stadiums which demand a high level of illuminance not economically achievable by other systems. The design of lighting systems must be closely interfaced with the architectural and structural design of the facility to form an integrated design. The design should also include the coordination of interior finishes (colors, reflectances and textures), daylighting (if desired), and acoustics. For most facilities, the use of light finished surfaces enhances the appearance of the space and minimizes direct glare. The addition of supplementary uplights (indirect lighting) reduces direct glare by softening the contrast between the bright luminaires and their background.

Luminaire Selection Considerations

Photometric Data. These data are the important technical information about a luminaire, specifying and

illustrating its optical performance characteristics, such as its intensity distribution (figure 23-9), isocandela curve and lumen distribution (figure 23-11). These data should be obtained from manufacturers.

Beam and Field Angles and Lamp Wattage. The selection of the floodlight beam and field angles is determined by the design illuminance on the playing field and the distance from the floodlight to its aiming point on the ground. The maximum beam intensity should not produce an illuminance on the field greater than the average design level. Thus, the distributions from adjacent luminaires must overlap to some extent. The lamp wattage and lumen output are chosen so that the playing field can be uniformly lighted with the minimum number of floodlights. Manufacturer's recommendations and photometric data should be consulted.

Ballast. All HID and fluorescent light sources require ballasting. Ballasts are designed to work with available, nominal voltages. Voltage fluctuation and voltage drop directly affect light output; thus, branch circuit and feeder wiring should be designed to minimize the voltage drop, normally less than 5% of the system voltage.

Structural. The location of the ballast should be considered as to whether it is to be integral in the luminaire or remotely mounted. The size and shape of the luminaire determine the effective projected area (EPA), which should be considered when determining the structural strength needed to support the luminaires under wind loading in outdoor applications.

Lamp Tilt Factor. The lumen output of a lamp may be sensitive to its operating position. The lowest output for a metal halide lamp is usually at a tilt of 60–75° off vertical, that is, when the lamp is closer to horizontal than to vertical. Normally, the tilt factor, which is to be included in determining the overall light loss factor (LLF), ranges from 0.8 to 1.0. Tilt factor information should be obtained from the supplier.

Light Source Selection Considerations

The selection of light sources (lamps) goes hand in hand with the selection of luminaires. Metal halide lamps are used for most sports. Incandescent or tungsten-halogen lamps are used for sports requiring lower initial illuminance and for facilities with limited annual usage. Fluorescent lamps are normally used indoors or where the lamp is less than 20 ft from the lighted area. Standard high-pressure sodium lamps are used for applications where color rendition is less critical and where three-phase power is available, and at least two beams are aimed in the same direction from luminaires operated on different phases. Consideration should be given to:

1. The methods to minimize flicker of HID light sources

2. The effect of ballast noise, especially in indoor facilities
3. The effect of ambient temperature on the performance of the lamps, on the lumen output, and on starting characteristics
4. The estimated annual operating hours, which may influence the economics of the lamp selection
5. The starting and restarting characteristics of lamps (For applications where starting and restarting is frequent, HID lamps should be avoided.)
6. The effect of color shift (Some HID lamps have a significant color shift during their life; the color of a lamp may also be affected by the input voltage. Color shift may be minimized by better voltage regulation of the power system and by group relamping.)

ILLUMINANCE CALCULATIONS

The general methods of illuminance calculation are given in chapter 9, Lighting Calculations, and chapter 11, Illuminance Selection. However, for sports lighting calculations, more specific methods and algorithms are necessary. A more complete description of these algorithms is given in RP-6.[1] The following factors should be understood when making sports lighting design calculations.

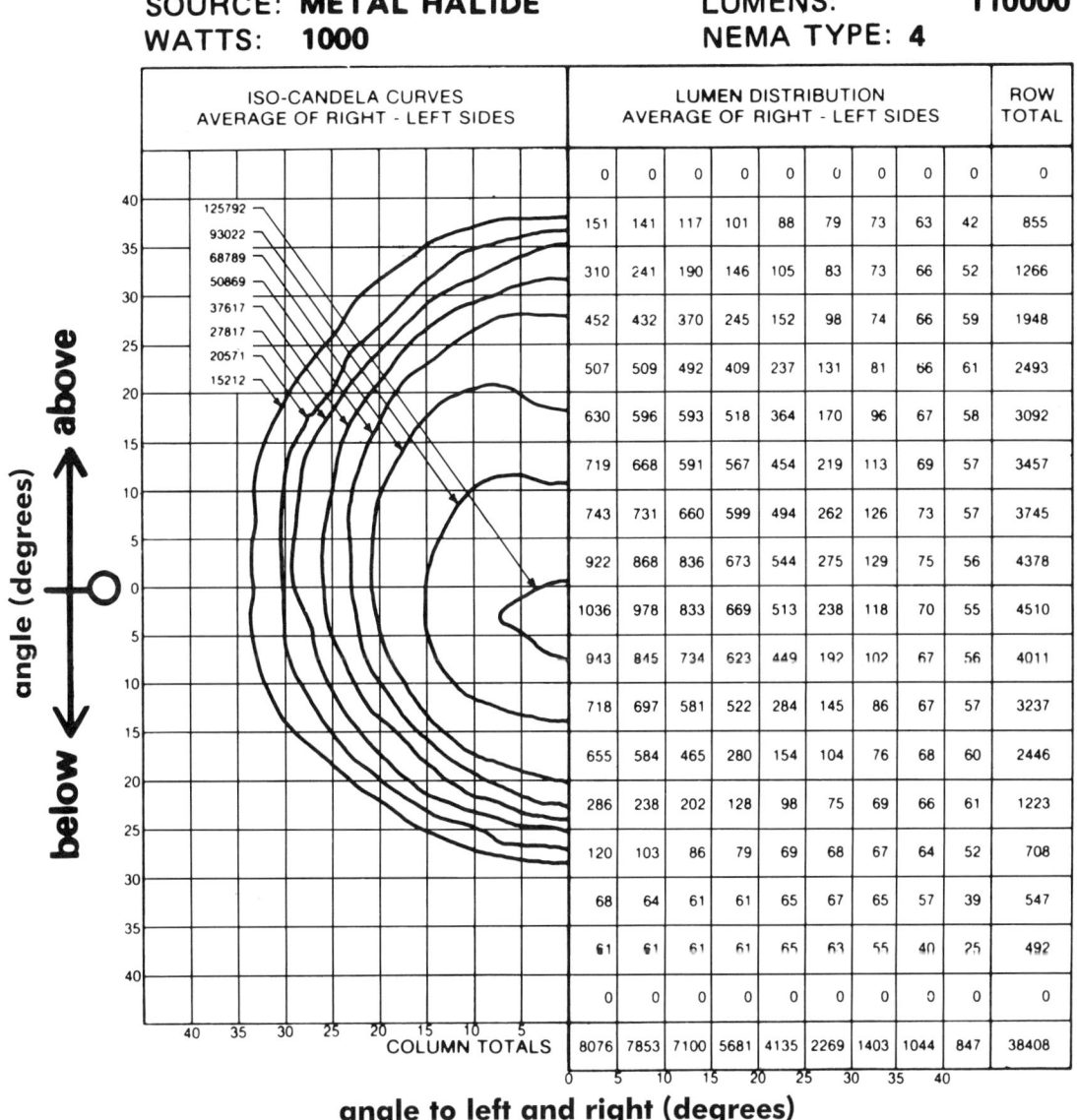

Fig. 23-11. Photometric data of a typical sports luminaire indicating the isocandela curves on the left side and Lumen Depreciation values on the right side. The last column at the extreme right indicates the accumulated lumens within each horizontal row. These values should be doubed to obtain the total accumulated lumens for both sides of the luminaire.

Fig. 23-12. Primary Playing Areas for Class I or Class II Facilities Beyond Court Boundaries that Require Equal Illuminances

Sport	Distance (Feet)	Sport	Distance (Feet)
Baseball Infield Outfield	30 10 to 30	Racquetball	
Basketball	10 to 15	Soccer	10 to 15
Badminton	5 to 10	Softball Infield Outfield	20 10 to 20
Boxing	5	Swimming	Full deck
Football	10 to 15	Volleyball	10 to 20
Ice Hockey		Track and Field	5 to 10
Jai Alai		Tennis	6 to 10

Playing Area

Although every sport has a defined dimension and court boundary, some sports require an additional area outside the court boundaries for the sport to be played. Perhaps baseball requires more outside playing area than any other sport. Others, such as badminton, football, tennis, and volleyball, also require some additional area to allow unobstructed play. For illumination design purposes, the playing field can be divided into three areas.

1. *Court boundary area (CBA).* The area within the prescribed boundaries at the playing field.
2. *Primary playing area (PPA).* The total area extending beyond the playing boundary in which a nearly equal illuminance level must be maintained. For example, in baseball the foul zone must be counted as PPA. This zone extends a minimum of 30 ft behind home base, up to the end of the infield, and gradually diminishes to about 10 ft in depth at the far end of the outfield. The recommended minimum dimensions of the PPA beyond the court boundary for some major sports are given in figure 23-12.
3. *Secondary playing area (SPA).* The playing area between the PPA and a physical barrier, such as a fence or a spectator stand. For example, the court boundary of a tennis court is 78 × 36 ft, having an area of 2808 ft². The PPA of a tennis court, as defined by United States Tennis Association (USTA), is the area bounded by lines 6 ft beyond the sidelines and 10 ft behind the baselines, having an area of 4704 ft². (Use 4700 ft² as an approximate value.) However, the overall playing area of a tennis court is considerably larger, ranging

from 7200 to 10,000 ft², depending on the class of the facility. Thus, the SPA will vary from 2500 to 5300 ft². The illumination for the SPA should not be less than 50% of that for the PPA, with a gradual transition complying with the guidelines for the uniformity gradient (UG) discussed earlier in this chapter.

Calculation Procedure

The following procedure applies to sports lighting design using the point method calculations with direct distribution luminaires.

1. Based on the type of sport, skill level of play, size of the facility, television broadcasting and architectural or structural requirements, determine the illumination criteria, such as illuminances, uniformity and coefficients of variation.
2. Make a preliminary selection of light sources and luminaires based on their photometric data, such as lumen output, beam angle, candela and lumen distributions, color rendition and lamp life.
3. Use the modified lumen method to determine the approximate number of luminaires with one or more luminaire selections. This and the next four steps may be bypassed if the designer is experienced; go to step 8.
4. Assign locations and mounting heights of these luminaires based on the guidelines given.
5. Determine the grid pattern or number of uniform areas for which the illuminance value should be calculated (see figure 23-3).
6. Confirm the selection of beam spread and rough aiming by manual calculations at a few selected grid points.
7. Determine the applicable light loss and field factors to be used.
8. Use a computer program to calculate the illuminance values, uniformity ratios, coefficients of variation and so forth at the recommended grid points.
9. Repeat the process by varying the number of luminaires, locations, mounting heights and aiming directions, until the target illuminance levels at each grid point meet the design criteria for illuminances, uniformity and other quality factors.

MODIFIED LUMEN METHOD

Although the lumen (zonal cavity) method described in chapter 9, Lighting Calculations, is applicable in principle to determine the average illuminance for sports lighting design, it is difficult to determine the coeffi-

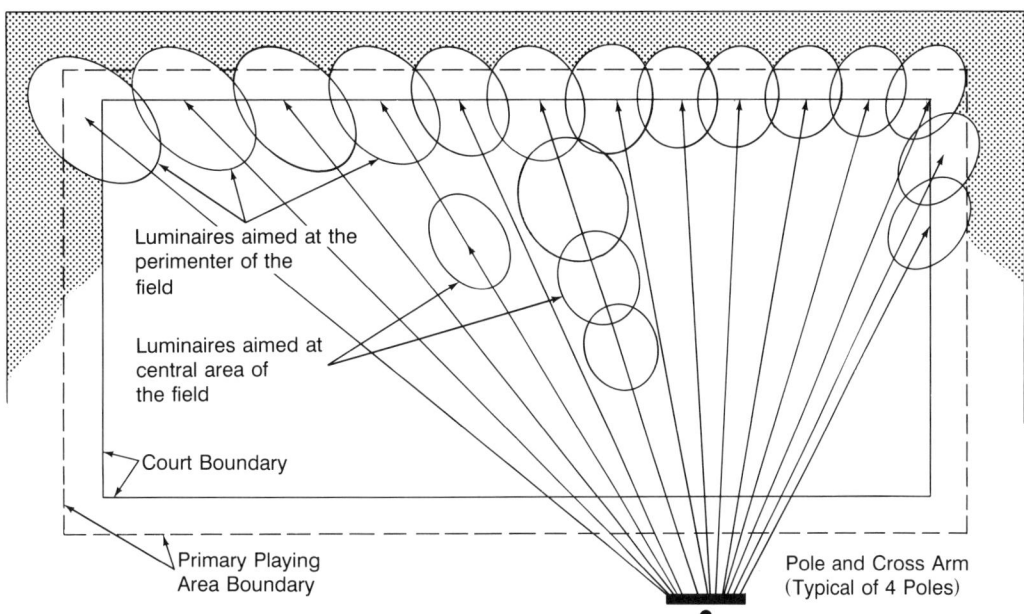

Fig. 23-13. The effects of floodlight aiming on the CU of a sports lighting design. Floodlights aimed toward the center of the field will have high CUs since nearly all of the beam lumens are utilized, and those aimed toward the perimeter will have lower CUs which may vary between 0.4 and 0.9 depending on location and beam angle of the luminaires selected.

cient of utilization (CU) when many of the floodlights must be aimed beyond the court boundary line for vertical illuminance and uniformity. Figure 23-13 illustrates this condition in sports lighting design.

Introduced here is a modified lumen method which should be simple to use for evaluating preliminary luminaire and mounting location selections prior to the use of the more accurate point method in detailed calculations. The modified lumen method is applicable to all rectangular playing fields with floodlights installed along the long dimensions of the field. The formula for calculating the average horizontal illuminance on the playing field is

$$E = \frac{N \times \Phi \times \text{PCU} \times \text{AAF} \times \text{LLF}}{A} \quad (23\text{-}4)$$

where

E = illuminance in lx or fc
N = number of luminaires
Φ = lamp lumens per luminaire
PCU = preliminary coefficient of utilization
AAF = application adjustment factor
LLF = light loss factor
A = area in m² or ft²

The *preliminary coefficient of utilization* (PCU) is defined as the ratio of the beam lumens that fall within the area to be illuminated to the total lamp lumens of each floodlight. It assumes that all spill light will be lost beyond the near and far sides of the field, and there is no spill light along the long dimension (length) of the field. The vertical angle covered by each floodlight is ∠ *MFN* in figure 23-14, with the beam center at

point *P*, which bisects ∠ *MFN*. The light flux (lumens) included within ∠ *MFN* is determined from the photometric data on the selected luminaire (figure 23-11). Based on the cumulative lumens in figure 23-15, a PCU curve is then plotted as shown in figure 23-16. The PCU is determined by the intersection points of $\frac{1}{2}$∠MFN with the PCU curves above and below the beam center.

The *application adjustment factor* (AAF) is applied to correct the initial assumption that there is no spill light along the long dimension of the field. The AAF is affected by the following:

- *Intensity distribution.* The AAF depends on the degree of beam spread of the luminaire, with higher AAF for narrower beam spread.
- *Field Factor (FF).* This factor is related to the angle subtended at the luminaire by the near corners (*A* and *B*) of the playing field; it is equal to the ratio of the length of the field (*L*) to the square root of the sum of the squares of the luminaire mounting height *h* and the pole setback *s*:

$$\text{FF} = \frac{L}{\sqrt{h^2 + s^2}} \quad (23\text{-}5)$$

Larger field factors will yield higher AAF values. Figure 23-17 provides recommended AAF values empirically determined.

As an example, refer to the football field in figure 23-14. Based on the luminaire data in figure 23-11, the

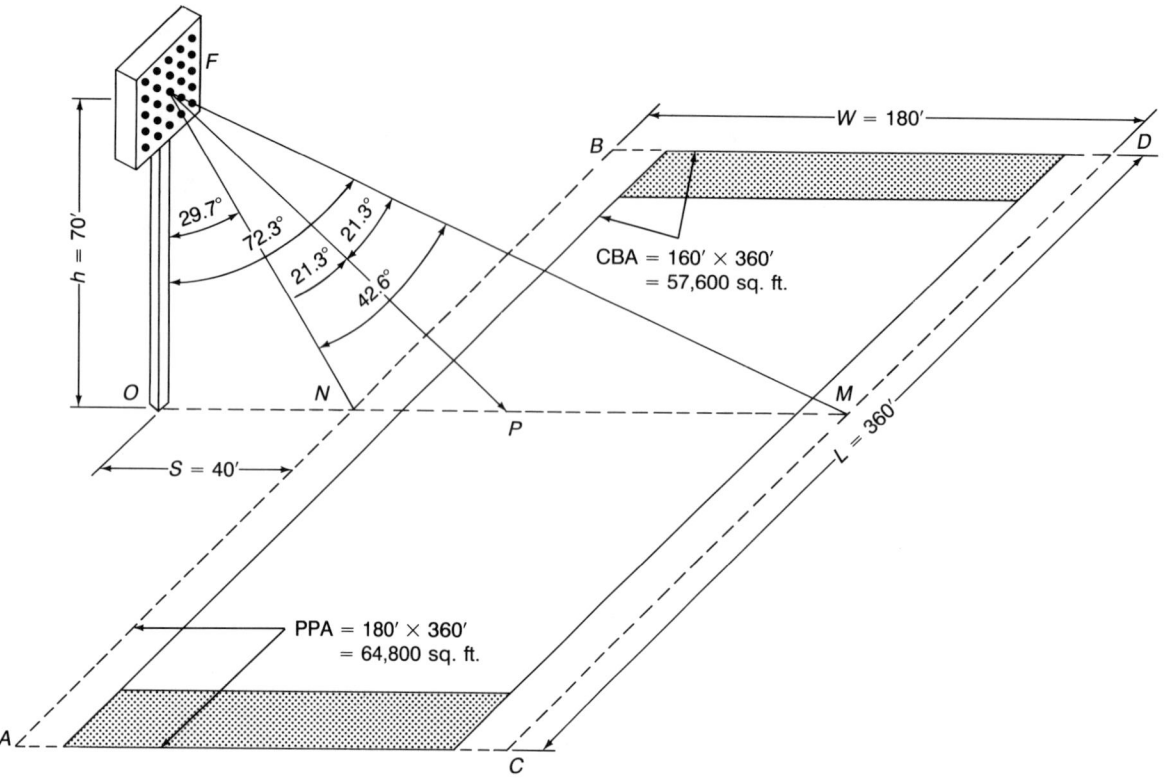

Fig. 23-14. Typical floodlighted football field.

distribution of lumens above and below beam center is summarized in figure 23-15. The number of lumens between 0° and 5° above beam center for one side only is 4378. Doubling this value to obtain both the left and the right half of the floodlight pattern yields 8756 lm between 0° and 5°. This represents 8.0% of the total 110,000 lamp lumens.

From figure 23-15, a curve of the preliminary coefficient of utilization is generated as presented in figure 23-16. The curve shows the portion of lamp lumens that falls upon an infinitely long field with a width subtending a constant angle ($\angle MFN$) across the field.

In figure 23-14, $\angle OFN$ is $\arctan(40/70) = 29.7°$, and $\angle OFE$ is $\arctan(220/70) = 72.3°$. The vertical an-

Fig. 23-15. Determination of Coefficients of Utilization from Photometric Data in Fig. 23-11. Total Lumens Equals 100,000 lm

	Degrees Interval	Lumens One Side	Lumens Both Sides	Cumu-lative Lumens	% Lamp Lumens
above	35-40	855	1710	42468	38.6
	30-35	1266	2532	40758	37.1
	25-30	1948	3896	38226	34.8
	20-25	2493	4986	34330	31.2
	15-20	3092	6184	29344	26.7
	10-15	3457	6914	23160	21.1
	5-10	3745	7490	16246	14.8
	0-5	4378	8756	8756	8.0
	Beam Center				
below	0-5	4510	9020	9020	8.2
	5-10	4011	8022	17042	15.5
	10-15	3237	6474	23516	21.4
	15-20	2446	4892	28408	25.8
	20-25	1223	2446	30854	28.0
	25-30	708	1416	32270	29.3
	30-35	547	1094	33364	30.3
	35-40	492	984	34348	31.2

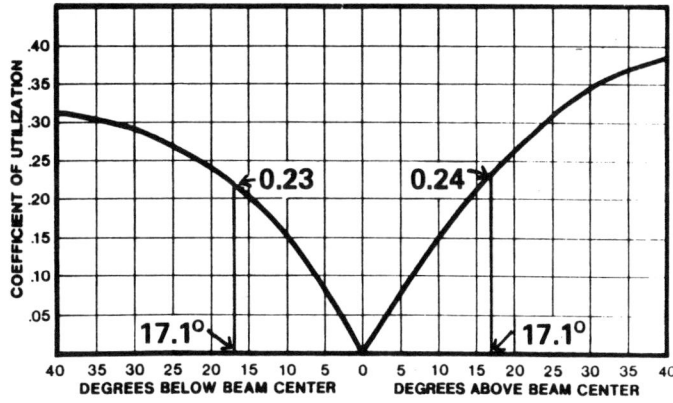

Fig. 23-16. Preliminary coefficient of utilization (PCU) curve as generated from figure 23-15.

Fig. 23-17. Recommended values for Application Adjustment Factors (AAFs)

Field Factor (FF)	NEMA Field Angle Classification		
	(1 and 2)	(3 and 4)	(5,6 and 7)
4.5 and up	.95	.85	.80
3.0 to 4.4	.90	.80	.75
2.0 to 2.9	.85	.75	.70
1.9 or below	.75	.65	.55

gle, $\angle MFN$, subtended by the field at the floodlight then must be $72.3° - 29.7° = 42.6°$. For approximation, each floodlight would be aimed so that the angle subtended would be bisected by the aiming point P. Based on figure 23-16, the preliminary coefficients of utilization at 21.3° above and below beam center are 0.27 and 0.24, for a total PCU of 0.51.

As shown in figure 23-14, we have field length $L = 360$ ft, mounting height $h = 70$ ft, setback distance $S = 40$ ft; therefore, the field factor is equal to 4.5. The horizontal beam spread of the luminaires used in the example is NEMA Type 4. Hence, the AAF is equal to 0.85. (See equation 23-5 and figure 23-17.)

If the football field is designed for an average maintained 50 fc and a 70% LLF, then

$$N = \frac{E \times A}{\Phi \times PCU \times AAF \times LLF}$$

$$= \frac{50 \times (360 \times 180)}{110,000 \times 0.51 \times 0.85 \times 0.7}$$

$$= 97.1 \qquad (23\text{-}6)$$

The number of floodlights may be rounded up or down to achieve symmetry. If four poles are used, then one might choose either 24 luminaires per pole for a total of 96, or 25 luminaires per pole for a total of 100.

POINT METHODS

Point methods are the most accurate methods for sports lighting applications. The trigonometric and vector expressions for the tilt, rotation and point of aiming of a floodlight are illustrated in IES Publication RP-6.[1] Included here is a treatment of the trigonometric method based on Type B photometry.

For Type B photometry, the quantitative relationship of dimensions is illustrated in figure 23-18. As shown there, luminaire F is rotated horizontally by an angle α from the x axis, and tilted vertically by an angle γ from the z axis. In Type B photometry, the zero angle of elevation faces horizontally, that is, the elevation angle is measured from a horizontal line; therefore, the luminaire tilt angle is normally the complement of γ. The line $P'P$ is normal to plane FAC. The horizontal angle β and vertical angle φ are calculated by using equations 23-7 and 23-9 below.

Illuminance Determination

To determine the illuminance at point P from the luminaire, the following steps are required:

1. From the horizontal angle β and elevation angle φ, determine the intensity value (in candelas) from photometric data on the luminaire provided by the manufacturer. Linear interpolation may be used.
2. Determine the angle θ between the incident light ray and the normal to the target surface (plane).
3. Calculate the illuminance E according to the inverse square law (see equation 23-10).
4. Repeat the same steps to determine the accumulated illuminance at point P due to all other luminaires.

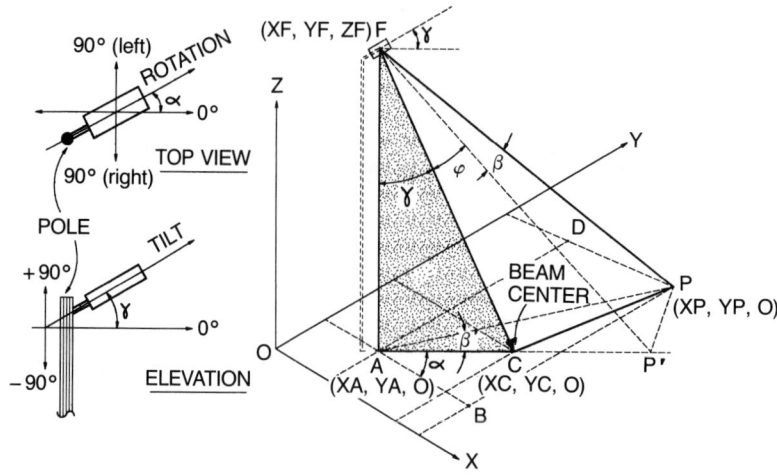

Fig. 23-18. Trigonometric method based on Type B photometry.

We have

$$\beta = \arcsin\left(\frac{\overline{AP}\,\sin\beta'}{\overline{FP}}\right) \qquad (23\text{-}7)$$

where

$$\beta' = \arctan\left(\frac{\overline{AD}}{\overline{AB}}\right) - \alpha \qquad (23\text{-}8)$$

Furthermore, from the geometric properties of triangles,

$$XA = XF, \qquad YA = YF$$

$$\overline{AB} = XP - XA$$

$$\overline{AD} = YP - YA$$

$$\overline{AP} = \sqrt{\overline{AB}^2 + \overline{AD}^2}$$

$$\overline{FP} = \sqrt{(ZF)^2 + \overline{AB}^2 + \overline{AD}^2}$$

and

$$\varphi = \arctan\left(\frac{\overline{AP'}}{ZF}\right) - \gamma \qquad (23\text{-}9)$$

where

$$\overline{AP'} = \overline{AP}\cos\beta'$$

Finally,

$$E = \frac{I\cos\theta}{D^2} \qquad (23\text{-}10)$$

DESIGN AND LAYOUT RECOMMENDATIONS

With the availability of choices of light sources, luminaires and mounting techniques, there are a large number of design options to achieve excellent results for both illuminance distribution and glare control. Representative layouts for several major sports are given in reference publication IES-RP-6.[1] Two of the representative layouts are included here (figures 23-19 and 23-20).

ILLUMINANCE RECOMMENDATIONS

It is important that illuminances be sufficient for comfortable and accurate seeing by the players, the spectators and the television viewers. In those sports where large numbers of spectators are expected, as in large football and baseball stadiums, the illuminance required is the amount for the spectators seated farthest from the playing area to follow the course of play. This condition may require several times the amount of light found satisfactory to the players. The illuminances suggested here for sports are those that are currently considered good practice, taking into consideration both players and up to 10,000 spectators.

Professional sports in facilities designed for more than 10,000 spectators require higher illuminances than those recommended in the tables. For example, current practice for National Football League (NFL) facilities is 2000 lx (200 fc) vertical and 3000 lx (300 fc) horizontal, and for the National Basketball Association (NBA) is 1250 lx (125 fc) vertical and 2500 lx (250 fc) horizontal.

The recommended illuminances given in the tables below are, in most cases, stated as horizontal illuminances in service. It is recognized that the vertical

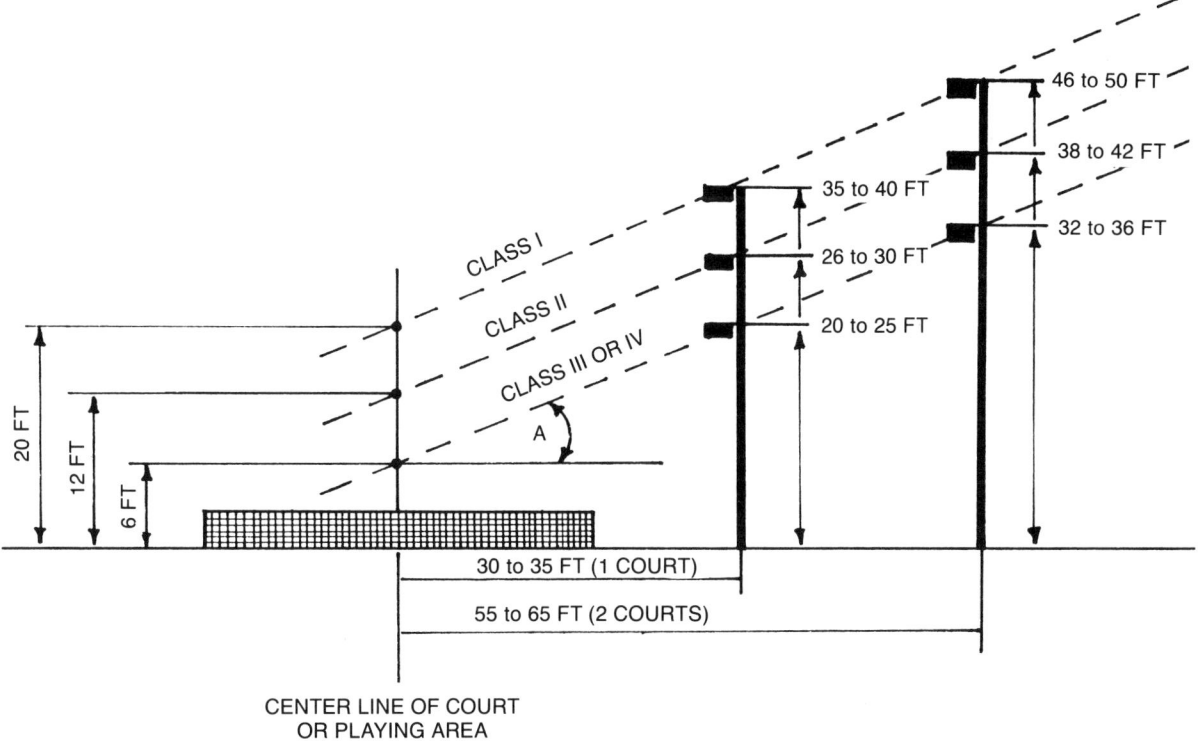

Fig. 23-19. Outdoor tennis. Recommended mounting heights of luminaires on pole for various setbacks, classes of play and facilities. Angle *A* should be a minimum of 25° for sharp cutoff-type luminaires and a minimum of 30° for floodlights.

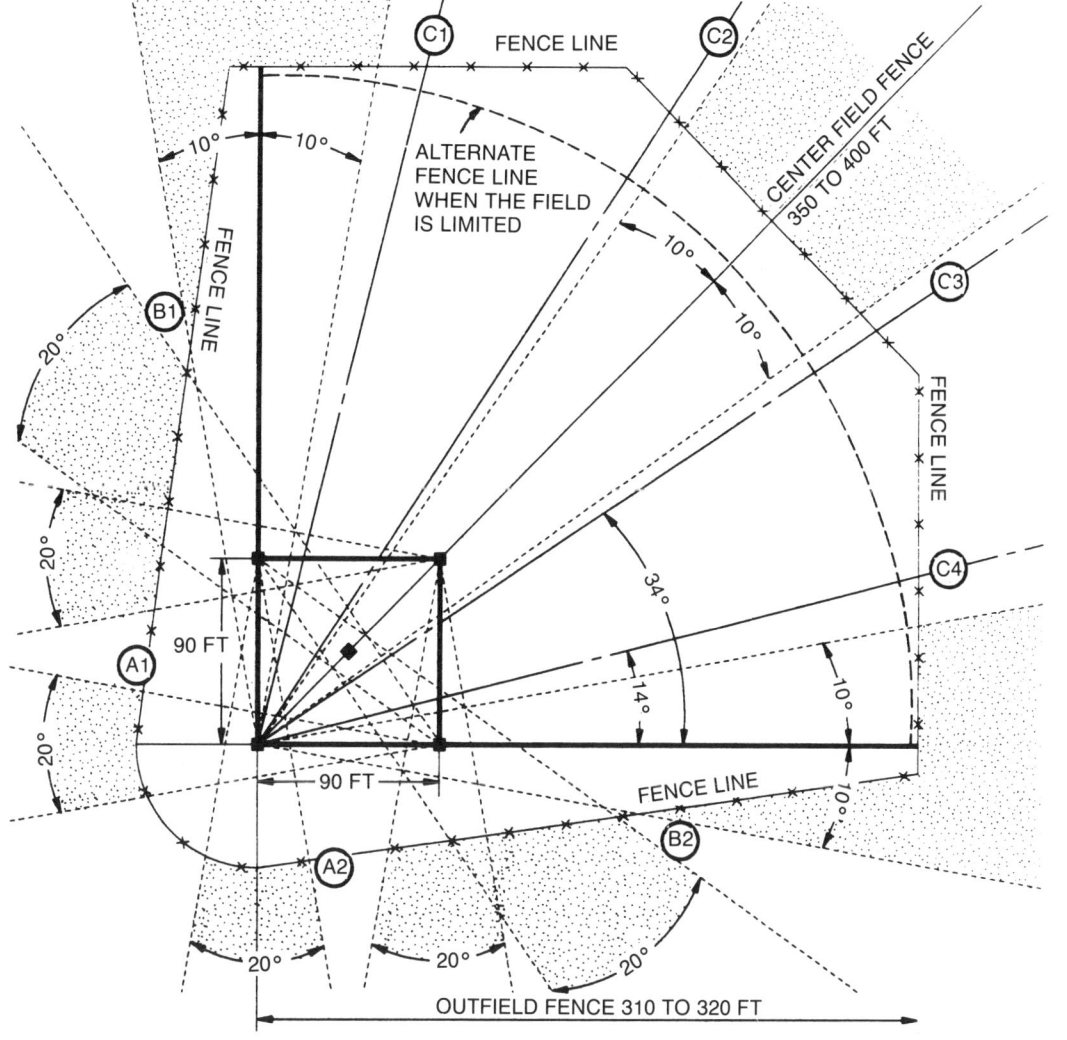

Fig. 23-20. Recommended location of poles for a regulation-size baseball field. Shaded area indicates critical glare zone where poles should not be located.

Fig. 23-21. Illuminance Criteria for Indoor Archery*

Class of Play	Horizontal Footcandles		Vertical Footcandles on target at	
	Target	Range	98 Feet	300 Feet
I	20	5	50	200
II	20	5	50	100
IV	10	3	30	50

*For outdoor archery, use illuminances approximately one-half those listed above.

component of the illumination on the playing area is important in most sports. This is particularly true in the aerial games, where both players and spectators rely, to a considerable degree, on the vertical illumination on or near the playing area, and in some cases well above the playing area. The vertical components of illuminance have usually been found adequate where the horizontal illuminances meet the values in the table, except where noted otherwise, and the lighting equipment is positioned at mounting heights and locations conforming to accepted good practice.

Recommended Illuminances for Indoor Sports

The recommended illuminance for popular indoor sports are given in figures 23-21 through 23-35. All entries are target values. It should be noted that the recommended value for underwater illumination is in lumens per square meter (or square foot) of swimming surface area. The reader should refer to IES Publication RP-6[1] for additional recommendations.

Recommended Illuminances for Outdoor Sports

The recommended illuminances for popular outdoor sports are given in figures 23-36 through 23-53. All illuminances are target values. The reader should refer to IES Publication RP-6[1] for additional recommendations.

FLOODLIGHT AIMING

Aiming floodlights is the final step in completing a floodlighting installation. Only with proper aiming can

the original design objectives for illuminances and uniformity be met.

Aiming Methods

There are two methods used for floodlight aiming: target aiming and degree aiming.

- *Target aiming* (floodlights in place): For target aiming, the primary playing area (PPA) to be lighted is divided into a uniform grid. Targets large enough to be seen from the floodlight location are placed on the grid line intersections or at the center of each grid area. The grids are identified with the actual field dimensions from a given reference point.
- *Degree aiming* (floodlights preset on poles, usually prior to poles being installed): Degree (or preset) aiming orients the floodlight by setting a horizontal and vertical protractor supplied with the floodlight. The angles must be set in reference to one of the field dimensions. Normally, the horizontal degree setting is defined with 0° along the line drawn perpendicular to the sideline of the field. For baseball outfield poles, 0° is along the line drawn from the pole to home plate. The vertical setting is based on 0° being directly below the floodlight. Degree aiming is less accurate than target aiming and is normally not used for larger fields.

Aiming Considerations

The following guidelines should be considered when establishing floodlight aiming:

- Be familiar with the intensity distributions of the floodlights, as these will be critical in determining the illuminance and amount of spill light.
- The initial aiming may often be accomplished by aiming consecutive floodlights so that the

Fig. 23-22. Illuminance Criteria for Basketball

Class of Play	Applications	Horizontal Footcandles	Vertical Footcandles	Uniformity (Maximum to Minimum)
I	Television and Professional	125	125	1.5
	College	100	100	1.5
II	High School	75		2.1
III	Elementary School and Club	50		3.0
IV	Recreational	30		3.0

Fig. 23-23. Illuminance Criteria for Bowling

Class of Play	Horizontal Footcandles		Vertical Footcandles	Uniformity (Maximum to Minimum)
	Approach	Lane		
I	75	100	200	1.5
II	50	75	150	1.5
III	30	50	100	2.0
IV	30	50	100	3.0

Fig. 23-24. Illuminance Criteria for Boxing and Wrestling

Class of Play	Horizontal Footcandles	Vertical Footcandles	Uniformity (Maximum to Minimum)
I	500	200	1.5
II	200		2.0
III	100		3.0

Fig. 23-25. Illuminance Criteria for Curling

Class of Play	Application	Footcandles	
		Hack to Hog	Hog to Hog
I	Professional	125	100
II	Tournament	50	30
III	Amateur	50	30
IV	Recreational	20	10

Fig. 23-26. Illuminance Criteria for Gymnastics

Class of Play	Application	Footcandles	Uniformity (Maximum to Minimum)
I	Television	100	1.5
II	Competition	50	2.0
III	Competition	30	2.5

angular positions of the half-maximum candle-power points coincide.

- In general it has been found that the actual final aiming points needed to achieve the expected illuminances over the playing field tend to be further from the poles than the calculations predict.
- The presence of television cameras or spectators may influence the aiming selection. Television cameras and spectators require a greater degree of vertical illuminance than may be necessary just to meet the horizontal illuminance criterion.

Fig. 23-27. Illuminance Criteria for Ice Hockey

Class of Play	Application	Horizontal Footcandles	Vertical Footcandles	Uniformity (Maximum to Minimum)
I	Professional	125	100	2.0
II	College	100	75	3.0
III	Amateur	75	50	4.0
IV	Recreational	50	25	4.0

Fig. 23-28. Illuminance Criteria for Ice (Speed) Skating

Class of Play	Applications	Horizontal Footcandles	Vertical Footcandles	Uniformity (Maximum to Minimum)
I	Competition	100	70	2.0
II	Competition	30	20	2.5
III	Training	10		3.0

Fig. 23-29. Illuminance Criteria for Racquetball and Squash

Class of Play	Application	Horizontal Footcandles	Vertical Footcandles	Uniformity (Maximum to Minimum)
I	Professional	100	75	1.5
II	Tournament	75	50	2.0
III	Club	50	30	2.5

Fig. 23-30. Illuminance Criteria for Roller Skating

Class of Play	Application	Footcandles
I	Professional	125
II	Racing	50
III	Commercial	30
IV	Recreational	20

Fig. 23-31. Illuminance Criteria for Tennis Courts

Class	Horizontal-Footcandles within Primary Playing Area		Uniformity (Maximum to Minimum)	
	Average	Minimum	Within Lines	Within Primary Playing Area
I	125	100	1.2	1.5
II	75	60	1.5	1.7
III	50	35	1.7	2.0
IV	40	30	2.0	2.5

Fig. 23-32. Recommended Surface Reflectance (in percent) for Tennis Courts

Area	Outdoor		Indoor	
	One Color	Two-Tone	One Color	Two-Tone
Court Boundary Area	10 to 15	10 to 15	15 to 20	10 to 15
Outside Court Boudary Area	10 to 15	20 to 30	15 to 20	30 to 40
Rear Screening				
Below 15 feet	5 to 15	5 to 15	5 to 15	5 to 15
At 15 feet and above	5 to 15	5 to 15	50 to 80	50 to 80
Side Screening or Wall				
Below 8 feet	5 to 30	5 to 30	30 to 50	30 to 50
At 8 feet and above	5 to 30	5 to 30	50 to 80	50 to 80
Ceiling			70 to 80	70 to 80

Fig. 23-33. Recommended Lamp Lumens for Underwater Lighting

Class	Application	Per Square Foot of Pool Surface Area		Uniformity (Maximum to Minimum)
		Indoor	Outdoor	
I	International, professional and tournament	100	60	2.0
II	College and Diving	75	50	2.5
III	High school without diving	50	30	3.0
IV	Recreational	30	15	4.0

Fig. 23-34. Recommended Illuminance Criteria for Above-Pool Lighting

Class	Surface in Horizontal Footcandles			Vertical Footcandles	Uniformity (Maximum to Minimum)
	Indoor	Outdoor	Deck	Platform	
I	70		50	70*	2.0
II	50	30	20	30	2.5
III	30	20	10		3.0
IV	30	10	10		4.0

*The platform in the principal viewing direction should have 70 to 100 footcandles without direct glare to the divers.

Fig. 23-35. Illuminance Criteria for Volleyball

Class of Play	Horizontal Footcandles	Vertical Footcandles	Uniformity (Maximum to Minimum)
I	100	50	1.5
II	50	30	2.0
III	30	20	3.5
IV	20	15	4.0

Fig. 23-36. Illuminance Criteria for Automobile Racing

Class	Application	Horizontal Footcandles		Uniformity Ratio (Maximum to Minimum)	
		Track	Finish	Track	Finish
I	Professional/International	30	75	2.0	1.5
II	Competition	20	50	2.5	2.0
IV	Recreational	10	25	3.0	2.0

Fig. 23-37. Illuminance Criteria for Baseball Fields

Class of play	Horizontal Footcandles		Vertical Footcandles		Horizontal Uniformity (Maximum to Minimum)		Vertical Uniformity (Maximum to Minimum)	
	Infield	Outfield	Infield	Outfield	Infield	Outfield	Infield	Outfield*
I	150	100	100	70	1.5	1.5	1.5	2.0
II	100	70	70	50	1.5	1.7	1.7	2.5
III	50	30	40	25	2.0	2.5		
IV	30	20	25	15	3.0	3.5		

* Acceptable vertical uniformity is 4.0 from outfield camera locations.

Fig. 23-38. Illuminance Criteria for Bicycle Racing

Class	Applications	Horizontal Footcandles		Uniformity Ratio (Maximum to Minimum)	
		Track	Finish	Track	Finish
I	Professional/International	30	50	2.0	1.5
II	Competition	20	30	2.5	2.0
IV	Recreational	10	10	3.0	2.0

Fig. 23-39. Recommended Illuminance Values for Field Hockey

Class	Application	Horizontal Footcandles	Uniformity (Maximum to Minimum)
II	College	30	2.0
III	High School	20	3.0

Fig. 23-40. Illuminance Criteria for Football (American)

Class of Play	Horizontal Footcandles	Vertical Footcandles	Uniformity (Maximum to Minimum)
I	100	80	1.5
II	50	40	2.0
III	30		2.5
IV	20		3.0

Fig. 23-41. Illuminance Criteria for Handball

Class of Play	Application	Horizontal Footcandles	Vertical Footcandles	Uniformity (Minimum to Maximum)
II	Tournament	30	20	2.0
IV	Recreational	15	10	3.0

Fig. 23-42. Illuminance Criteria for Ice Hockey

Class	Application	Horizontal Footcandles	Vertical Footcandles	Uniformity (Minimum to Maximum)
II	College/Professional	50	40	2.0
III	High School	30	20	2.0
IV	Recreational	20	15	3.0

Fig. 23-43. Illuminance Criteria for Ice Skating

Class	Application	Horizontal Footcandles	Uniformity (Minimum to Maximum)
II	Competition	30	2.0
III	Training	20	3.0
IV	Recreational	10	

Fig. 23-44. Illuminance Criteria for Platform Tennis

Class of Play	Application	Horizontal Footcandles	Vertical Footcandles
II	Tournament	50	30
III	Club	30	20
IV	Recreational	20	15

Fig. 23-45. Illuminance Criteria for Rifle and Pistol Ranges

Class of Play	Horizontal Footcandles	Vertical Footcandles
I		
At firing line	10	
At target		50
II		
At firing line	10	
At target		50
III		
At firing line	10	
At target		30

Fig. 23-46. Illuminance Criteria for Rodeo and Animal Shows

Class	Application	Horizontal Footcandles	Uniformity (Maximum to Minimum)
I	Professional (Television)	100	2.0
II	Professional	50	3.0
III	Semi-Professional/Amateur	30	4.0

Fig. 23-47. Illuminance Criteria for Skeet and Trap Shooting

Class	Application	Horizontal Illuminance*		Uniformity (Maximum to Minimum) at Target
		Skeet at 60 Feet	Trap at 100 Feet	
III	Competition/tournaments	30	30	2.0
IV	Recreational	20	15	3.0

*There should be five footcandles of horizontal illuminance at the firing point.

Fig. 23-48. Illuminance Criteria for Soccer

Class	Application	Horizontal Footcandles	Vertical Footcandles*	Uniformity (Minimum to Maximum)
I	Professional	100	80	1.5
II	College/Municipal	50	35	1.5
III	Schools/Amateur/Leagues	30	25	2.0
IV	Recreational	20	15	3.0

*At 3 feet above the field.

Fig. 23-49. Illuminance Criteria for Outdoor Tennis

Class	Horizontal Footcandles*		Uniformity (Maximum to Minimum)	
	Average	Minimum	Within Lines	Within PPA
I	125	100	1.2	1.5
II	60	40	1.5	1.7
III	40	30	1.7	2.0
IV	30	20	2.0	2.5
*Within principal playing area (PPA).				

Fig. 23-50. Illuminance Criteria for Track and Field

Class	Application	Horizontal Footcandles	Uniformity (Maximum to Minimum)
II	College\Profesional	50	2.0
III	School/Competition	30	2.5
IV	Recreation/Training	10	3.0

- All systems should be fine tuned after the aiming is complete. The fewer the floodlights, the greater the need to fine tune.

Aiming Examples

Figures 23-54 and 23-55 illustrate the aiming diagrams for typical football and baseball fields.

Fig. 23-51. Illuminance Criteria for Volleyball

Class	Application	Horizontal Footcandles	Uniformity (Maximum to Minimum)
III	Competition/Tournament	20	2.0
IV	Recreational	10	3.0

LIGHTING ECONOMICS

Lighting design should be evaluated in terms of its economic feasibility. Analysis of costs associated with the design, purchase, ownership and operation of a lighting system assists in comparing alternatives. Analysis should also include evaluating maintenance techniques and procedures, determining the effect of lighting on other building systems, and budgeting and cash flow planning and cost-benefit evaluation. See chapter 13, Lighting Economics, and IES RP-6[1] for more details on economic analysis in sports lighting applications.

FIELD MEASUREMENTS AND PERFORMANCE EVALUATIONS

To evaluate the actual performance of a lighting installation in comparison with the design intent, illumi-

Fig. 23-52. Illuminance Criteria for Various Recreational Areas and Activities

Activity	Horizontal Footcandles		Uniformity (Maximum to Minimum)
	Minimum	Average	
Bicycle paths*	0.2	1.0	4.0
Game areas			
Children's Play	0.5	2.0	6.0
Croquet	1.0	5.0	6.0
Horseshoes	1.0	5.0	6.0
Jungle Gyms†	0.5	2.0	4.0
Swings and Seesaws	0.5	2.0	6.0
Washer Pitching	1.0	5.0	4.0
Jogging Trails			
General	0.2	1.0	4.0
Bridges and Tunnels†	1.0	2.0	4.0
Traffic Areas	1.0	2.0	4.0
Lawn Area	0.2	0.5	6.0
Nature Trails	0.2	0.5	6.0
Pavilions, covered	0.5	2.0	4.0
Picnic, uncovered	0.2	1.0	4.0
Rest Rooms			
Exterior†	0.5	2.0	4.0
Interior	1.0	5.0	6.0
*See also Reference 22.			
†Indicates areas where the avoidance of glare is important for the seeing task or for security.			
‡See also Reference 23.			
§See also Reference 24.			

Fig. 23-53. Illuminance Criteria for Recreational and Specialty Sports

Sport and Tasks	Horizontal Footcandles		Uniformity (Maximum to Minimum)
	Class II	Class III	
Badminton (general area)	30	10	2.0
Beaches (at beach and at surf)		2	4.0
Bowling green (general area)	10	5	3.0
Casting (at dock)	10	10	
Golf			
Miniature		10	
Par-3		1	3.0
Putting green		5	
Horseshoes (at pit)	10	5	
Jogging track (along track)		1	10.0
Park lighting (general area)		5	5.0
Quoits (general area)	10	5	
Shuffleboard (general area)	10	5	
Skating pond (general area)	1	1	3.0

nances and uniformity measurements should be made with the field divided into a uniform grid. Each grid cell should be square in shape whenever practical.

This section provides guidelines for the location of calculation points and measurement point stations for various sports. By following these guidelines, it is possible to compare the performance of alternative lighting systems on a common basis at the design stage of a project and relate it directly to the illuminance measurements made on the field of the completed lighting installation.

Measurement and Report Procedure

Careful documentation should be made and consistent measurement techniques used in all measurements for sports lighting installations, noting carefully:

- Selection of measuring equipment
- Measuring procedures
- Reporting format and data
- Recommended measuring stations for specialty sports

Area to be Measured

Although most sports have well-defined court boundaries and thus court boundary areas (CBAs), the play-

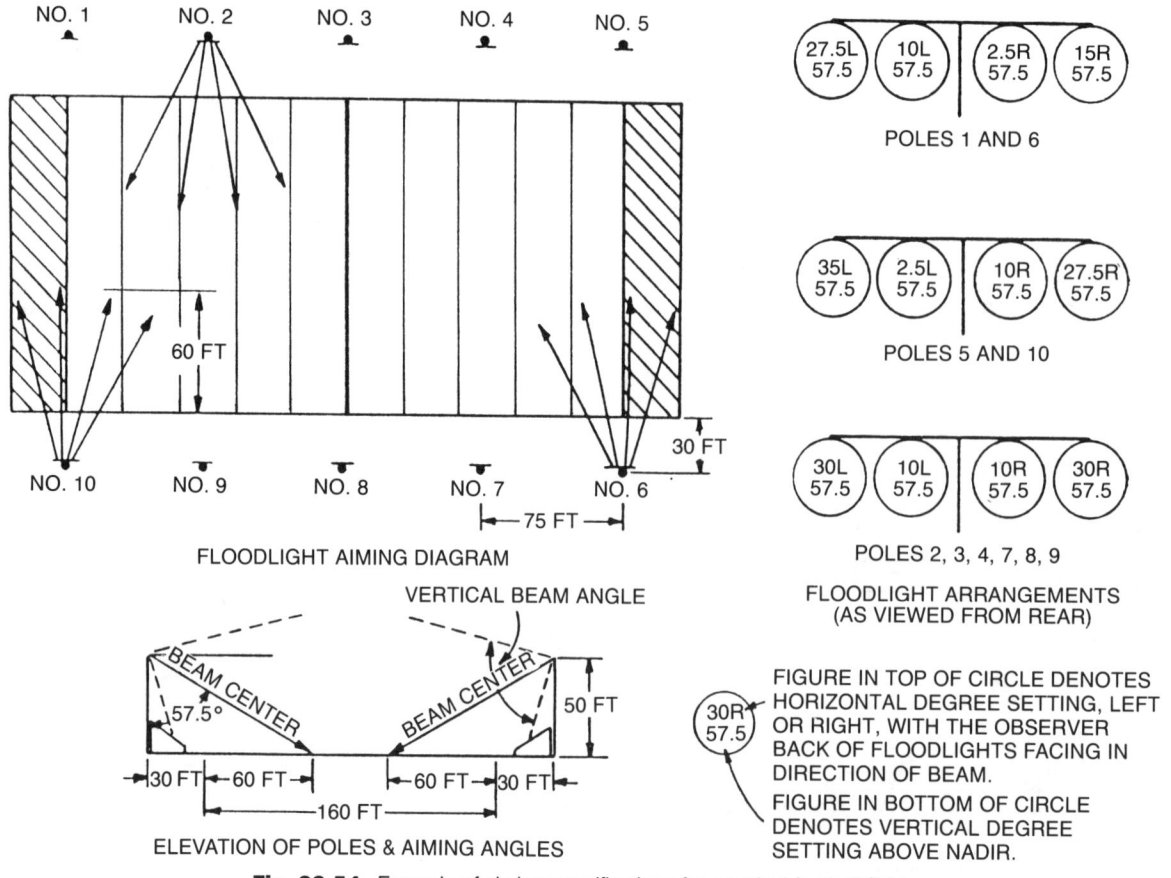

FLOODLIGHT AIMING DIAGRAM

VERTICAL BEAM ANGLE

ELEVATION OF POLES & AIMING ANGLES

| 27.5L 57.5 | 10L 57.5 | 2.5R 57.5 | 15R 57.5 |

POLES 1 AND 6

| 35L 57.5 | 2.5L 57.5 | 10R 57.5 | 27.5R 57.5 |

POLES 5 AND 10

| 30L 57.5 | 10L 57.5 | 10R 57.5 | 30R 57.5 |

POLES 2, 3, 4, 7, 8, 9

FLOODLIGHT ARRANGEMENTS (AS VIEWED FROM REAR)

FIGURE IN TOP OF CIRCLE DENOTES HORIZONTAL DEGREE SETTING, LEFT OR RIGHT, WITH THE OBSERVER BACK OF FLOODLIGHTS FACING IN DIRECTION OF BEAM.

FIGURE IN BOTTOM OF CIRCLE DENOTES VERTICAL DEGREE SETTING ABOVE NADIR.

Fig. 23-54. Example of aiming specifications for a typical football field.

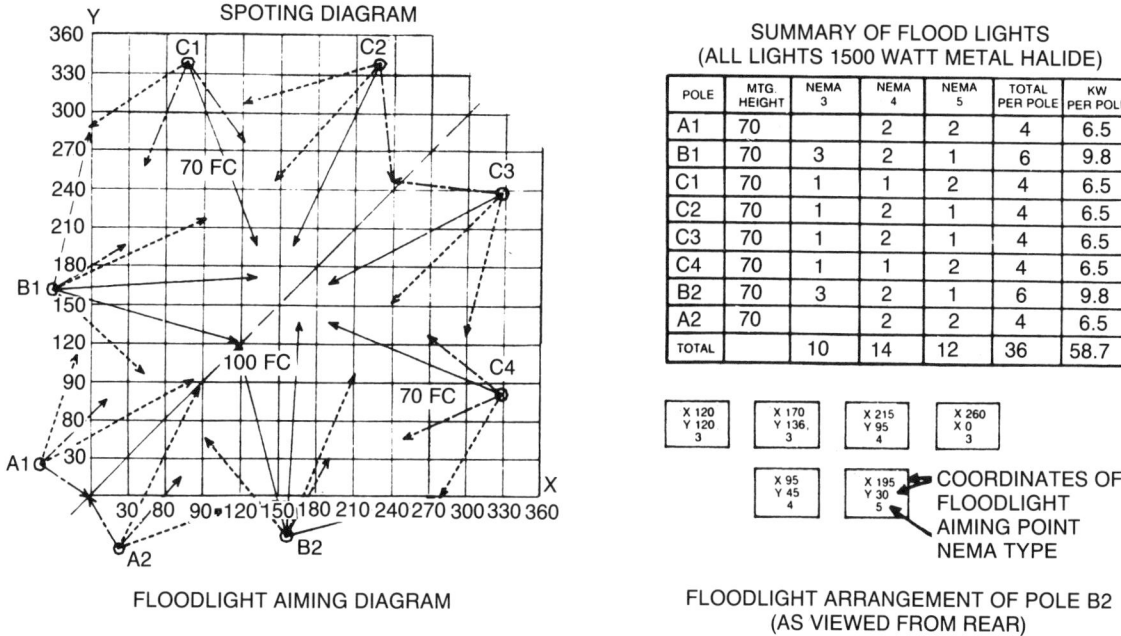

SUMMARY OF FLOOD LIGHTS
(ALL LIGHTS 1500 WATT METAL HALIDE)

POLE	MTG. HEIGHT	NEMA 3	NEMA 4	NEMA 5	TOTAL PER POLE	KW PER POLE
A1	70		2	2	4	6.5
B1	70	3	2	1	6	9.8
C1	70	1	1	2	4	6.5
C2	70	1	2	1	4	6.5
C3	70	1	2	1	4	6.5
C4	70	1	1	2	4	6.5
B2	70	3	2	1	6	9.8
A2	70		2	2	4	6.5
TOTAL		10	14	12	36	58.7

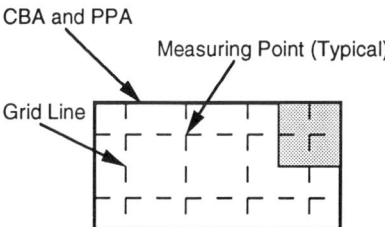

FLOODLIGHT AIMING DIAGRAM

FLOODLIGHT ARRANGEMENT OF POLE B2
(AS VIEWED FROM REAR)

Fig. 23-55. Example of aiming specifications for a typical baseball field.

ing action of many sports is extended far beyond the CBA. Depending on the sport, the extended area may be further divided into primary playing area (PPA) and secondary playing area (SPA). Baseball and tennis are typical sports with considerable PPAs and SPAs that must be lighted. However, there are sports with play action totally confined within the court boundary, such as racquetball, squash, ice hockey and bowling. For such sports, the CBA is equal to the PPA. Lighting measurements should cover the whole PPA, with spot checking in the SPA.

Location of Test Station

The illuminance obtained at a test station is the representative or average value of illuminance for the area bounded by the grid lines. The question arises whether the grid lines should coincide with, or be offset from, the boundary lines. The answer depends on the sport.

- *Where the PPA is equal to the CBA.* For sports such as ice hockey where all action is within the court boundary, the grid lines should be established so that the edge of the grid area coincides with the edge of the court boundary. The court boundary area should then be divided into as many square, or nearly square, grid cells as practical. See figure 23-56.
- *Where the PPA is greater than the CBA.* For these sports the grid lines should be located to adequately cover the overall primary playing area. For most sports, the measuring stations will likely be offset from the court boundary

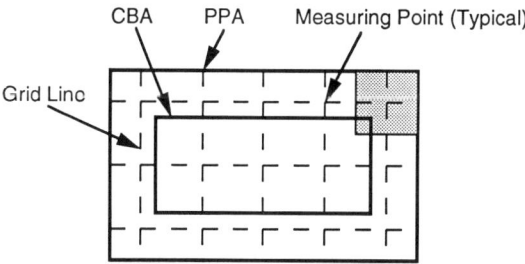

Fig. 23-56. Typical grid lines and measuring points where the court boundary area (CBA) is equal to the primary playing area (PPA). The shaded area indicates the area represented by the measuring point within it.

Fig. 23-57. Typical grid lines and measuring points where the PPA extends beyond the CBA. The shaded area indicates the area represented by the measuring point within it.

lines. See figure 23-57. If the primary playing area is included in the lighting measurement, it is conceivable that the measuring points will be located on the court boundary lines.

Most of the major sports have defined standardized reading points as shown in IES RP-6.[1] These test locations should be used in both the design and the

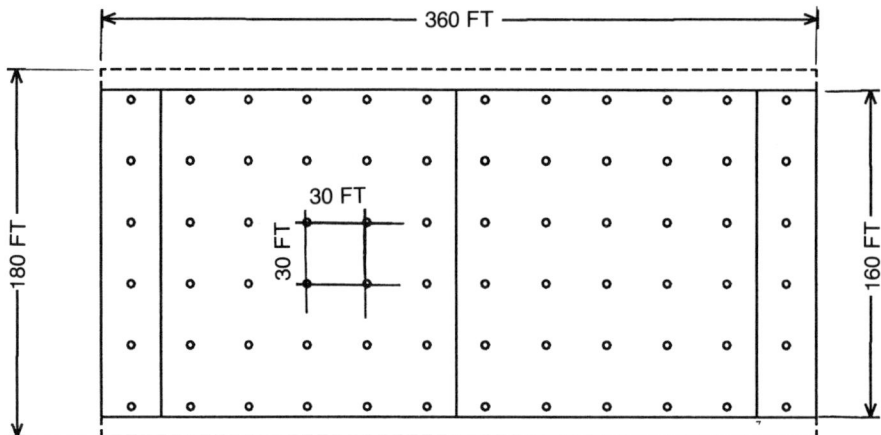

Fig. 23-58. Illuminance measuring points for American football (lighted area equals 64,800 ft^2).

testing of the illumination on a sports field. For those sports for which a standardized layout is not available, the test locations should be selected and reviewed with the owner or other responsible person in charge of the illumination system. The selected points should be reasonably uniform and include all of the area on which play can be expected to occur. The distance between points should normally not exceed the mounting height of the luminaires and ideally would be about half of the mounting height. Again the selected test points should be used in both the design and the testing of the illumination system.

Layouts of Measuring Grids

Probably the most important factor in determining the spacing of measurement points is the luminaire mounting height. The lower the mounting height, the closer together the measuring stations should be to ensure a representative average and that important peaks and

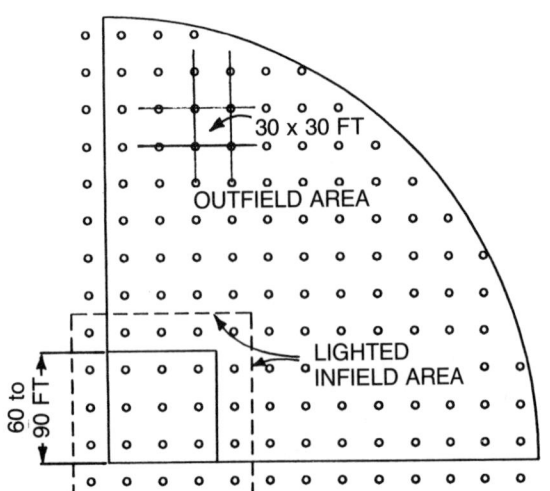

Fig. 23-59. Illuminance measuring points for baseball and softball.

valleys are not missed because the measurement grid is too coarse. Figure 23-3 provides recommended grids for popular sports. Figures 23-58 and 23-59 show layouts of several typical sports frequently played at night.

Field Verification

Every sports lighting installation must be verified by a site survey to achieve the following objectives:

1. Confirm performance of the luminaires, the electrical system and the accuracy of the aiming.
2. Provide the owner with a benchmark for future evaluation of maintenance programs and their effectiveness.
3. Provide the lighting design practitioner feedback on the accuracy and effectiveness of the designs for evaluation.

The values measured in the site survey are less accurate than laboratory photometry and computer calculations. This is due to the many uncontrollable factors, such as product tolerance, electrical power variations and small errors in aiming the floodlights. Every effort should be made to keep these inaccuracies to a minimum and to record all conditions so that a proper evaluation can be made. The following is a checklist for field verification or survey. Refer to chapter 6, Light Sources, regarding product tolerance guidelines.

1. All luminaires should be operating and properly aimed.
2. HID lamps should have been operating for 50–100 h prior to testing. If the lamps and luminaires have been operated for substantially more than 100 h, the approximate operating hours should be recorded.

3. For HID lamps, the system should be turned on at least 30 min prior to testing.
4. Tests should be taken when the air is clear and extraneous light is at a minimum.
5. Care should be taken that the operator and other test personnel do not cast shadows or reflected light from clothing on the measurement instruments.
6. The photometer should be of good quality and accuracy, recently calibrated or its accuracy otherwise verified. The meter should also be cosine corrected for incident light up to an incident angle of 80°.

The measurement record should include the following information:

- Name of the installation
- Date and time of the measurements
- Description of the illumination system, including luminaire and lamp type, mounting heights, quantities and other pertinent details
- Age of the system and number of operating hours since the last lamp change
- Type, make and serial number of the photometer, and date and source of the calibration

Evaluation of the Measured Results

Plans or other design documents should show the computer-predicated performance of the installation, including the calculated mean, the calculated coefficient of variation (CV) and the initial and maintained illuminances. The values of the light loss factor (LLF) and field factors (FF) used in calculating the maintained illuminance should be identified. A discrepancy between predicated performance and the actual site survey results is to be expected. However, the actual results should be within ±10% of the expected illumination.

REFERENCES

1. IES. Committee on Sports and Recreational Areas Lighting. 1989. *Current recommended practice for sports lighting.* IES RP-6-88. New York: Illuminating Engineering Society of North America.
2. Commission Internationale de l'Éclairage. 1978. *Lighting for tennis.* CIE Publication 42. Paris: Bureau Central de la CIE. Commission Internationale de l'Éclairage. 1979. *Lighting for ice sports.* CIE Publication 45. Paris: Bureau Central de la CIE. Commission Internationale de l'Éclairage. 1983. *Lighting for football.* CIE Publication 57. Paris: Bureau Central de la CIE. Commission Internationale de l'Éclairage. 1983. *Lighting for sports halls.* CIE Publication 58. Paris: Bureau Central de la CIE. Commission Internationale de l'Éclairage. 1984. *Lighting for swimming pools.* CIE Publication 62. Paris: Bureau Central de la CIE. Commission Internationale de l'Éclairage. 1986. *Guide for the photometric specification and measurement of sports lighting installations.* CIE Publication 67. Paris: Bureau Central de la CIE. Commission Internationale de l'Éclairage. 1989. *Guide for the lighting of sports events for colour television and film systems.* CIE Publication 83. Paris: Bureau Central de la CIE.
3. Armstrong, J. D. 1990. A new measure of uniformity for lighting installations. *J. Illum. Eng. Soc.* 19(2):84–89.
4. Frier, J. P. 1990. Common sense techniques for sports lighting. *Architectural Lighting* 4(6):54–59.

Roadway Lighting

24

Fixed lighting of public ways for both vehicles and pedestrians can create a nighttime environment in which people can see comfortably and can quickly and accurately identify objects on the roadway being travelled. Roadway lighting can improve traffic safety, achieve efficient traffic movement and promote the general use of the facility during darkness and under a wide variety of weather conditions.

As a supplement to vehicular headlight illumination, fixed lighting can enable the motorist to see details more distinctly, locate them with greater certainty and react safely to roadway and traffic conditions present on or near the roadway facility. Pedestrians must be able to see with sufficient detail to readily negotiate the pedestrian facility and recognize the presence of other pedestrians, vehicles and objects in their vicinity. When fixed-lighting principles and techniques are properly applied, the visibility provided on these public ways can provide economic and social benefits to the public, including:

- Reduction in nighttime accidents
- Aid to police protection
- Facilitation of traffic flow
- Promotion of business and industry during nighttime hours
- Inspiration for community spirit and growth

This chapter considers only fixed lighting for the different kinds of public roads, pedestrian walkways and bikeways of a quality considered appropriate to modern requirements for night use. See chapter 26, Transportation Lighting, for information on vehicle headlighting.

Background for Design Criteria

The criteria for roadway lighting in previous editions of this Handbook were based on horizontal illuminance. However, it is known that pavement luminance and veiling luminance (glare) criteria provide a better correlation with the visual impression of roadway lighting quality. It is possible to satisfy illuminance criteria and fall far short of the luminance criteria. It is also recognized that luminance criteria do not constitute a direct measure of the visibility of features of traffic routes, such as the traffic and fixed hazards on these routes. Unfortunately, not enough research and evaluation data are available to permit the use of visibility criteria at this time. For this reason, and because luminance criteria correlate with the visual impression of roadway lighting quality, pavement luminance and veiling luminance recommendations are currently considered to be the preferred method of specifying roadway lighting.

The visual process permits detection of lower contrasts as the background luminance for those contrasts becomes higher (see chapter 3, Vision and Perception). Since the pavement often serves as the background for the detection of objects, it is important to consider the average level of pavement luminance and its uniformity in roadway lighting design. Pavement luminance is affected by the location of the observer, the direction of the light reaching the pavement, its incidence relative to the observer, and the reflection characteristics of the pavement.

Visual performance is also affected by glare from the fixed lighting system. Disability glare has been quantified to give the designer information to identify the veiling effect of the glare as a percentage of the average overall luminance. This gives a better means of evaluating the glare from a lighting system than classifying a single luminaire distribution as to the amount of luminous flux above certain vertical angles. For further information on glare, see chapter 3, Vision and Perception.

Horizontal illuminance is a function of the amount of light striking various parts of the surface and on the vertical angle at which the light travels to the pavement. Illuminance criteria can provide acceptable visual performance if good design judgment is used in their application. As a result, even though visual performance cannot be as well controlled, the use of illuminance criteria can be an effective alternative to luminance criteria.

Energy Management Implications

The use of the design criteria in this chapter should result in good lighting and achieve effective energy management if the designer and user will utilize:

1. Efficient luminaires, lamps, photoelectric controls or other suitable control devices for the area to be lighted
2. A good maintenance program to ensure system integrity and to maintain the design level
3. Appropriate mounting heights and luminaire positioning

CLASSIFICATION DEFINITIONS[1]

Roadway: Pedestrian Walkway and Bikeway Classifications

Freeway. A divided major roadway with full control of access and with no crossings at grade. This definition applies to toll as well as nontoll roads as follows:

Freeway A. Roadways with visual complexity and high traffic volumes. Usually this type of freeway is found in major metropolitan areas in or near the central core and operates through much of the early evening hours of darkness at or near design capacity.

Freeway B. All other divided roadways with full control of access where lighting is needed.

Expressway. A divided major roadway for through traffic with partial control of access and generally with interchanges at major crossroads. Expressways for noncommercial traffic within park areas are generally known as parkways.

Major. The part of the roadway system that serves as the principal network for through traffic flow. The routes connect areas of principal traffic generation and important rural highways entering the city.

Collector. The roadways serving traffic between major and local roadways. These are roadways used mainly for traffic movements within residential, commercial and industrial areas.

Local. Roadways used primarily for direct access to residential, commercial, industrial or other abutting property. They do not include roadways carrying through traffic. Long local roadways will generally be divided into short sections by a system of collector roadway systems.

Alley. Narrow public ways within a block, generally used for vehicular access to the rear of abutting properties.

Sidewalk. Paved or otherwise improved areas for pedestrian use, located within public street rights-of-way which also contain roadways for vehicular traffic.

Pedestrian Walkway. A public walk for pedestrian traffic, not necessarily within the right-of-way for a

vehicular traffic roadway. Included are skywalks (pedestrian overpasses), subwalks (pedestrian tunnels), walkways giving access to parks or block interiors, and midblock street crossings.

Isolated Interchange. A grade-separated roadway crossing which is not part of a continuously lighted system, with one or more ramp connections with the crossroad.

Isolated Intersection. The general area where two or more noncontinuously lighted roadways join or cross at the same level. The intersection includes the roadway and roadside facilities for traffic movement in that area. A special type is the *channelized* intersection, in which traffic is directed into definite paths by islands with raised curbing.

Bikeway. Any road, street, path or way that is specifically designated as being open to bicycle travel, regardless of whether such facilities are designed for the exclusive use of bicycles or are to be shared with other transportation modes.

Type A: Designated Bicycle Lane. A portion of roadway or shoulder which has been designated for use by bicyclists. It is distinguished from the portion of the roadway for motor vehicle traffic by a paint stripe, curb or other similar device.

Type B: Bicycle Trail. A separate trail or path from which motor vehicles are prohibited and which is for the exclusive use of bicyclists or the shared use of bicyclists and pedestrians. Where such a trail or path forms a part of a highway, it is separated from the roadways for motor vehicle traffic by an open space or barrier.

Area Classifications (Abutting Land Uses)

Certain land uses, such as office and industrial parks, may fit into any of the classifications below. The classification selected should be consistent with the expected night pedestrian activity.

Commercial. A business area of a municipality where ordinarily there are many pedestrians during night hours. This definition applies to densely developed business areas outside, as well as within, the central part of a municipality. The area contains land use which frequently attracts a heavy volume of nighttime vehicular and pedestrian traffic.

Intermediate. Those areas of a municipality characterized by frequent moderately heavy nighttime pedestrian activity, as in blocks having libraries, community recreation centers, large apartment buildings, industrial buildings or neighborhood retail stores.

Residential. A residential development, or a mixture of residential and small commercial establishments, characterized by few pedestrians at night. This definition includes areas with single-family homes, town houses and small apartment buildings.

Pavement Classifications

The calculation of pavement luminance requires information about the surface reflectance characteristics of the pavement. Studies have shown that most common pavements can be grouped into a limited number of standard road surfaces having specified reflectance data given by reduced luminance coefficient tables (r tables). In this section, pavement reflectance characteristics follow the established CIE document.[2] A description of road surface classifications is given in figure 24-1. The r tables quantifying the pavement class are shown in figure 24-2.

Luminaire Light Distribution Classifications

Proper distribution of the light flux from luminaires is one of the essential factors in efficient roadway lighting. The light emanating from the luminaires is directionally controlled and proportioned in accordance with the roadway width, the spacing between luminaires, and the mounting locations where the luminaires are expected to be used. Therefore, there is a need for a luminaire light distribution classification system to aid the user or designer to narrow down the selection of luminaires that might meet the requirements specified for a given roadway system.

Several methods have been devised for showing the light distribution pattern from a luminaire. (See figures 24-3 through 24-7.) For practical operating reasons, the range in luminaire mounting heights may be limited. Therefore, it becomes necessary to have several different light distributions in order to light different roadway widths effectively, while using various luminaire spacing distances at a fixed luminaire mounting height. All luminaires can be classified according to their lateral and vertical distribution patterns. Different lateral distributions are available for different street-width-to-mounting-height ratios. Different vertical distributions are available for different spacing-to-mounting-height ratios.

Distributions with higher vertical angles of maximum candlepower emission are necessary to obtain the required uniformity of illuminance where longer luminaire spacings are used (as on residential and light-traffic roadways). These higher vertical emission angles produce a more favorable pavement luminance, which may be desired for silhouette seeing where the traffic volume is low. Distributions with lower vertical angles of maximum candlepower emission are used in order to reduce system glare. This becomes more important when using high-lumen-output lamps. The lower the emission angle, the closer the luminaire spacing must be to obtain required illuminance uniformity.

Luminaire light distribution may be classified in respect to three criteria:

1. Vertical light distribution
2. Lateral light distribution
3. Control of light distribution above maximum candlepower

Classification of the light distribution should be made on the basis of an isocandela diagram which, on its rectangular coordinate grid, has superimposed a series of longitudinal roadway lines (LRL) in multiples of the mounting height (MH) and a series of transverse roadway lines (TRL), also in multiples of the MH. The relationship of LRL and TRL to an actual street and the representation of such a web are shown in figures 24-3 through 24-7. The minimum information which should appear on such an isocandela diagram for classification is as follows:

1. LRL lines at 1.0, 1.75 and 2.75 MH
2. TRL lines at 1.0, 2.25, 3.75, 6.0 and 8.0 MH
3. Maximum-candlepower location and half-maximum-candlepower trace
4. Candlepower lines at the numerical values of 2.5, 5, 10 and 20% of the rated bare lamp lumens

Fig. 24-1. Road Surface Classifications

Class	Q_o	Description	Mode of Reflectance
R1	0.10	Portland cement, concrete road surface. Asphalt road surface with a minimum of 15 percent of the aggregates composed of artificial brightener and aggregates	Mostly diffuse
R2	0.07	Asphalt road surface with an aggregate composed of a minimum 60 percent gravel (size greater than 10 milimeters). Asphalt road surface with 10 to 15 percent artificial brightener in aggregate mix. (Not normally used in North America.)	Mixed (diffuse and specular)
R3	0.07	Asphalt road surface (regular and carpet seal) with dark aggregates (e.g., trap rock, blast furnace slag); rough texture after some months of use (typical highways).	Slightly specular
R4	0.08	Asphalt road surface with very smooth texture.	Mostly specular

Note: Q_o = representative mean luminance coefficient.

Fig. 24-2. The *r*-Tables for Standard Surfaces: (a) R1, (b) R2, (c) R3, (d) R4. All values must be Multiplied by 10,000. Angles are shown in (e). (Adapted from reference 2.)

tan γ \ β	0	2	5	10	15	20	25	30	35	40	45	60	75	90	105	120	135	150	165	180
0	655	655	655	655	655	655	655	655	655	655	655	655	655	655	655	655	655	655	655	655
0.25	619	619	619	619	610	610	610	610	610	610	610	610	610	601	601	601	601	601	601	601
0.5	539	539	539	539	539	539	521	521	521	521	521	503	503	503	503	503	503	503	503	503
0.75	431	431	431	431	431	431	431	431	431	431	395	386	371	371	371	371	371	386	395	395
1	341	341	341	341	323	323	305	296	287	287	278	269	269	269	269	269	269	278	278	278
1.25	269	269	269	260	251	242	224	207	198	189	189	180	180	180	180	180	189	198	207	224
1.5	224	224	224	215	198	180	171	162	153	148	144	144	139	139	139	144	148	153	162	180
1.75	189	189	189	171	153	139	130	121	117	112	108	103	99	99	103	108	112	121	130	139
2	162	162	157	135	117	108	99	94	90	85	85	83	84	84	86	90	94	99	103	111
2.5	121	121	117	95	79	66	60	57	54	52	51	50	51	52	54	58	61	65	69	75
3	94	94	86	66	49	41	38	36	34	33	32	31	31	33	35	38	40	43	47	51
3.5	81	80	66	46	33	28	25	23	22	22	21	21	22	22	24	27	29	31	34	38
4	71	69	55	32	23	20	18	16	15	14	14	14	15	17	19	20	22	23	25	27
4.5	63	59	43	24	17	14	13	12	12	11	11	11	12	13	14	14	16	17	19	21
5	57	52	36	19	14	12	10	9.0	9.0	8.8	8.7	8.7	9.0	10	11	13	14	15	16	16
5.5	51	47	31	15	11	9.0	8.1	7.8	7.7	7.7										
6	47	42	25	12	8.5	7.2	6.5	6.3	6.2											
6.5	43	38	22	10	6.7	5.8	5.2	5.0												
7	40	34	18	8.1	5.6	4.8	4.4	4.2												
7.5	37	31	15	6.9	4.7	4.0	3.8													
8	35	28	14	5.7	4.0	3.6	3.2													
8.5	33	25	12	4.8	3.6	3.1	2.9													
9	31	23	10	4.1	3.2	2.8														
9.5	30	22	9.0	3.7	2.8	2.5														
10	29	20	8.2	3.2	2.4	2.2														
10.5	28	18	7.3	3.0	2.2	1.9														
11	27	16	6.6	2.7	1.9	1.7														
11.5	26	15	6.1	2.4	1.7															
12	25	14	5.6	2.2	1.6															

Q0 = 0.10; S1 = 0.25; S2 = 1.53

(a)

tan γ \ β	0	2	5	10	15	20	25	30	35	40	45	60	75	90	105	120	135	150	165	180
0	294	294	294	294	294	294	294	294	294	294	294	294	294	294	294	294	294	294	294	294
0.25	326	326	321	321	317	312	308	308	303	298	294	280	271	262	258	253	249	244	240	240
0.5	344	344	339	339	326	317	308	298	289	276	262	235	217	204	199	199	199	199	194	194
0.75	357	353	353	339	321	303	285	267	244	222	204	176	158	149	149	149	145	136	136	140
1	362	362	352	326	276	249	226	204	181	158	140	118	104	100	100	100	100	100	100	100
1.25	357	357	348	298	244	208	176	154	136	118	104	83	73	70	71	74	77	77	77	78
1.5	353	348	326	267	217	176	145	117	100	86	78	72	60	57	58	60	60	60	61	62
1.75	339	335	303	231	172	127	104	89	79	70	62	51	45	44	45	46	45	45	46	47
2	326	321	280	190	136	100	82	71	62	54	48	39	34	34	34	35	36	36	37	38
2.5	289	280	222	127	86	65	54	44	38	34	25	23	22	23	24	24	24	24	24	25
3	253	235	163	85	53	38	31	25	23	20	18	15	15	14	15	15	16	16	17	17
3.5	217	194	122	60	35	25	22	19	16	15	13	9.9	9.0	9.0	9.9	11	11	12	12	13
4	190	163	90	43	26	20	16	14	12	9.9	9.0	7.4	7.0	7.1	7.5	8.3	8.7	9.0	9.0	9.9
4.5	163	136	73	31	20	15	12	9.9	9.0	8.3	7.7	5.4	4.8	4.9	5.4	6.1	7.0	7.7	8.3	8.5
5	145	109	60	24	16	12	9.0	8.2	7.7	6.8	6.1	4.3	3.2	3.3	3.7	4.3	5.2	6.5	6.9	7.1
5.5	127	94	47	18	14	9.9	7.7	6.9	6.1	5.7										
6	113	77	36	15	11	9.0	8.0	6.5	5.1											
6.5	104	68	30	11	8.3	6.4	5.1	4.3												
7	95	60	24	8.5	6.4	5.1	4.3	3.4												
7.5	87	53	21	7.1	5.3	4.4	3.6													
8	83	47	17	6.1	4.4	3.6	3.1													
8.5	78	42	15	5.2	3.7	3.1	2.6													
9	73	38	12	4.3	3.2	2.4														
9.5	69	34	9.9	3.8	3.5	2.2														
10	65	32	9.0	3.3	2.4	2.0														
10.5	62	29	8.0	3.0	2.1	1.9														
11	59	26	7.1	2.6	1.9	1.8														
11.5	56	24	6.3	2.4	1.8															
12	53	22	5.6	2.1	1.8															

Q0 = 0.07; S1 = 1.11; S2 = 2.38

(b)

tan γ \ β	0	2	5	10	15	20	25	30	35	40	45	60	75	90	105	120	135	150	165	180
0	390	390	390	390	390	390	390	390	390	390	390	390	390	390	390	390	390	390	390	390
0.25	411	411	411	411	411	411	411	411	411	411	379	368	357	357	346	346	346	335	335	335
0.5	411	411	411	411	403	403	384	379	370	346	325	303	281	281	271	271	271	260	260	260
0.75	379	379	379	368	357	346	325	303	281	260	238	216	206	206	206	206	206	206	206	206
1	335	335	335	325	292	291	260	238	216	195	173	152	152	152	152	152	141	141	141	141
1.25	303	303	292	271	238	206	184	152	130	119	108	100	103	106	108	108	114	114	119	119
1.5	271	271	260	227	179	152	141	119	108	93	80	76	76	80	84	87	89	91	93	95
1.75	249	238	227	195	152	124	106	91	78	67	61	52	54	58	63	67	69	71	73	74
2	227	216	195	152	117	95	80	67	61	52	45	40	41	45	49	52	54	56	57	58
2.5	195	190	146	110	74	58	48	40	35	30	27	24	26	28	30	33	35	38	40	41
3	160	155	115	67	43	33	26	21	18	17	16	16	17	17	18	21	22	24	26	27
3.5	146	131	87	41	25	18	15	13	12	11	11	11	11	11	12	14	15	17	18	21
4	132	113	67	27	15	12	10	9.4	8.7	8.2	7.9	7.6	7.9	8.7	9.6	11	12	13	15	17
4.5	118	95	50	20	12	8.9	7.4	6.6	6.3	6.1	5.7	5.6	5.8	6.3	7.1	8.4	10	12	13	14
5	106	81	38	14	8.2	6.3	5.4	5.0	4.8	4.7	4.5	4.4	4.8	5.2	6.2	7.4	8.5	9.5	10	11
5.5	96	69	29	11	6.3	5.1	4.4	4.1	3.9	3.8										
6	87	58	22	8.0	5.0	3.9	3.5	3.4	3.2											
6.5	78	50	17	6.1	3.8	3.1	2.8	2.7												
7	71	43	14	4.9	3.1	2.5	2.3	2.2												
7.5	67	38	12	4.1	2.6	2.1	1.9													
8	63	33	10	3.4	2.2	1.8	1.7													
8.5	58	28	8.7	2.9	1.9	1.6	1.5													
9	55	25	7.4	2.5	1.7	1.4														
9.5	52	23	6.5	2.2	1.5	1.3														
10	49	21	5.6	1.9	1.4	1.2														
10.5	47	18	5.0	1.7	1.3	1.2														
11	44	16	4.4	1.6	1.2	1.1														
11.5	42	14	4.0	1.5	1.1															
12	41	13	3.6	1.4	1.1															

Q0 = 0.07; S1 = 0.58; S2 = 1.80

(c)

tan γ \ β	0	2	5	10	15	20	25	30	35	40	45	60	75	90	105	120	135	150	165	180
0	264	264	264	264	264	264	264	264	264	264	264	264	264	264	264	264	264	264	264	264
0.25	297	317	317	317	317	310	304	290	284	277	271	244	231	224	224	218	218	211	211	211
0.5	330	343	343	343	330	310	297	284	277	264	251	218	198	185	178	172	172	165	165	165
0.75	376	383	370	350	330	304	277	251	231	211	198	165	139	132	132	125	125	125	119	119
1	396	396	396	330	290	251	218	198	185	165	145	112	86	86	86	86	86	87	87	87
1.25	403	409	370	310	251	211	178	152	132	115	103	77	66	65	65	63	65	66	67	68
1.5	409	396	356	284	218	172	139	115	100	88	79	61	50	50	50	50	52	55	55	55
1.75	409	396	343	251	178	139	108	88	75	66	59	44	37	37	37	38	40	41	42	45
2	409	383	317	224	145	106	86	71	59	53	45	33	29	29	29	30	32	33	34	37
2.5	396	356	264	152	100	73	55	45	37	32	28	21	20	20	20	21	22	24	25	26
3	370	304	211	95	63	44	30	25	21	17	16	13	12	12	13	13	15	16	17	19
3.5	343	271	165	63	40	26	19	15	13	12	11	9.8	9.1	8.8	8.8	9.4	11	12	13	15
4	317	238	132	45	24	16	13	11	9.6	9.0	8.4	7.5	7.4	7.4	7.5	7.9	8.6	9.4	11	12
4.5	297	211	106	33	17	11	9.2	7.9	7.3	6.6	6.3	6.1	6.1	6.2	6.5	6.7	7.1	7.7	8.7	9.6
5	277	185	79	24	13	8.3	7.0	6.3	5.7	5.1	5.0	5.0	5.1	5.4	5.5	5.8	6.1	6.3	6.9	7.7
5.5	257	161	59	19	9.9	7.1	5.7	5.0	4.6	4.2										
6	244	140	46	13	7.7	5.7	4.8	4.1	3.8											
6.5	231	122	37	11	5.9	4.6	3.7	3.2												
7	218	106	32	9.0	5.0	3.8	3.2	2.6												
7.5	205	94	26	7.5	4.4	3.3	2.8													
8	193	82	22	6.3	3.7	2.9	2.4													
8.5	184	74	19	5.3	3.2	2.5	2.1													
9	174	66	16	4.6	2.8	2.1														
9.5	169	59	13	4.1	2.5	2.0														
10	164	53	12	3.7	2.2	1.7														
10.5	158	49	11	3.3	2.1	1.7														
11	153	45	9.5	3.0	2.0	1.7														
11.5	149	41	8.4	2.6	1.7															
12	145	37	7.7	2.5	1.7															

Q0 = 0.08; S1 = 1.55; S2 = 3.03

(d)

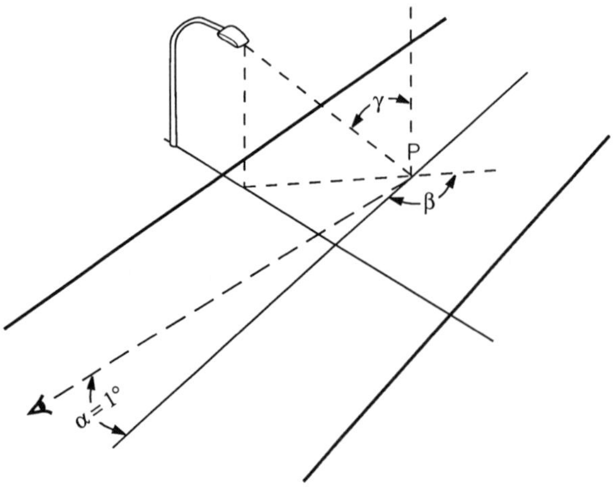

(e)

Vertical Light Distributions. Vertical light distributions are divided into three groups: short (S), medium (M) and long (L). See figures 24-3 and 24-6.

- Short distribution: A luminaire is classified as having a short light distribution when its maximum-candlepower point lies in the S zone of the grid, which is from the 1.0-MH TRL up to the 2.25-MH TRL. The maximum luminaire spacing is generally less than 4.5 times the mounting height. See figures 24-3 and 24-4.
- Medium distribution: A luminaire is classified as having a medium light distribution when its maximum-candlepower point lies in the M zone

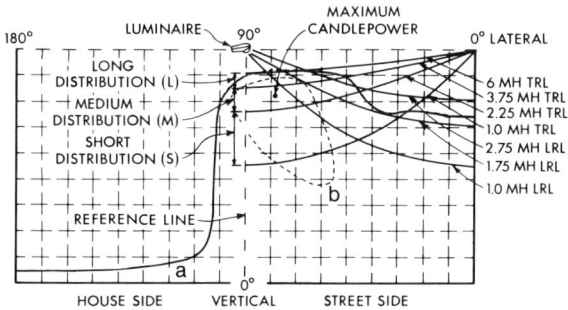

Fig. 24-3. Recommended vertical light distribution boundaries on a rectangular coordinate grid (representation of a sphere). Lines a and b are isocandela traces.

of the grid, which is from the 2.25-MH TRL up to the 3.75-MH TRL. The maximum luminaire spacing is less than 7.5 times the mounting height. See figures 24-3 and 24-4.

• Long distribution: A luminaire is classified as having a long light distribution when its maxi-

mum-candlepower point lies in the L zone of the grid, which is from the 3.75-MH TRL up to the 6.0-MH TRL. The maximum luminaire spacing is less than 12 times the mounting height. See figures 24-3 and 24-4.

Lateral Light Distributions. Lateral light distributions (see figures 24-5 and 24-6) are divided into two groups based on the location of the luminaire in relation to the area to be lighted. Each group may be subdivided into divisions with regard to the width of the area to be lighted in terms of the MH ratio. Only the segments of the half-maximum-candlepower isocandela trace which fall within the longitudinal distribution range, as determined by the point of maximum candlepower (S, M or L), are used for establishing the luminaire distribution width classification.

Luminaires At or Near Center of Area. The group of lateral width classifications that deals with luminaires intended to be mounted at or near the center of the

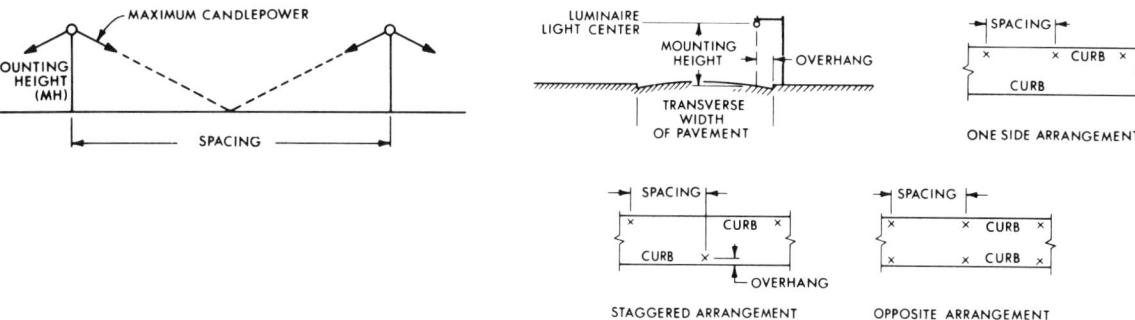

Fig. 24-4. Typical lighting layouts showing spacing-to-mounting height relationships and terminology with respect to luminaire arrangement and spacing. Short Distribution — for luminaires which are designed to be located less than 4.5 × MH between luminaires. Medium Distribution — for luminaires which are designed to be located in the range of 4.5 × MH to 7.5 × MH between luminaires. Long Distribution — for luminaires which are designed to be located in the range of 7.5 × MH to 12 × MH between luminaires.

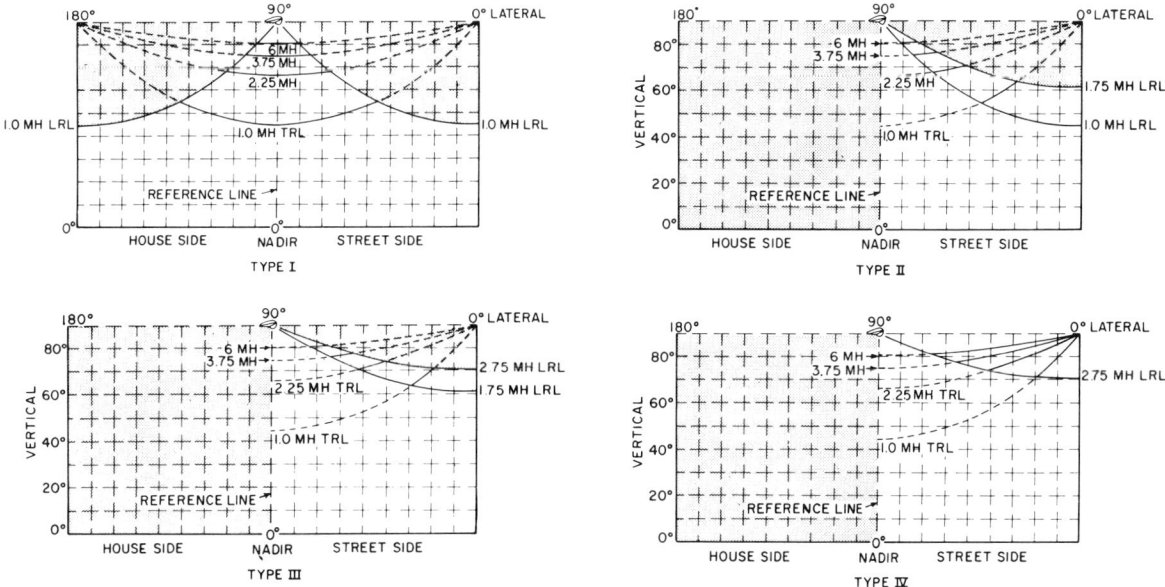

Fig. 24-5. Recommended lateral light distribution boundaries on a rectangular coordinate grid (representation of a sphere). Some information omitted for clarity. See Fig. 24-3 for complete diagram.

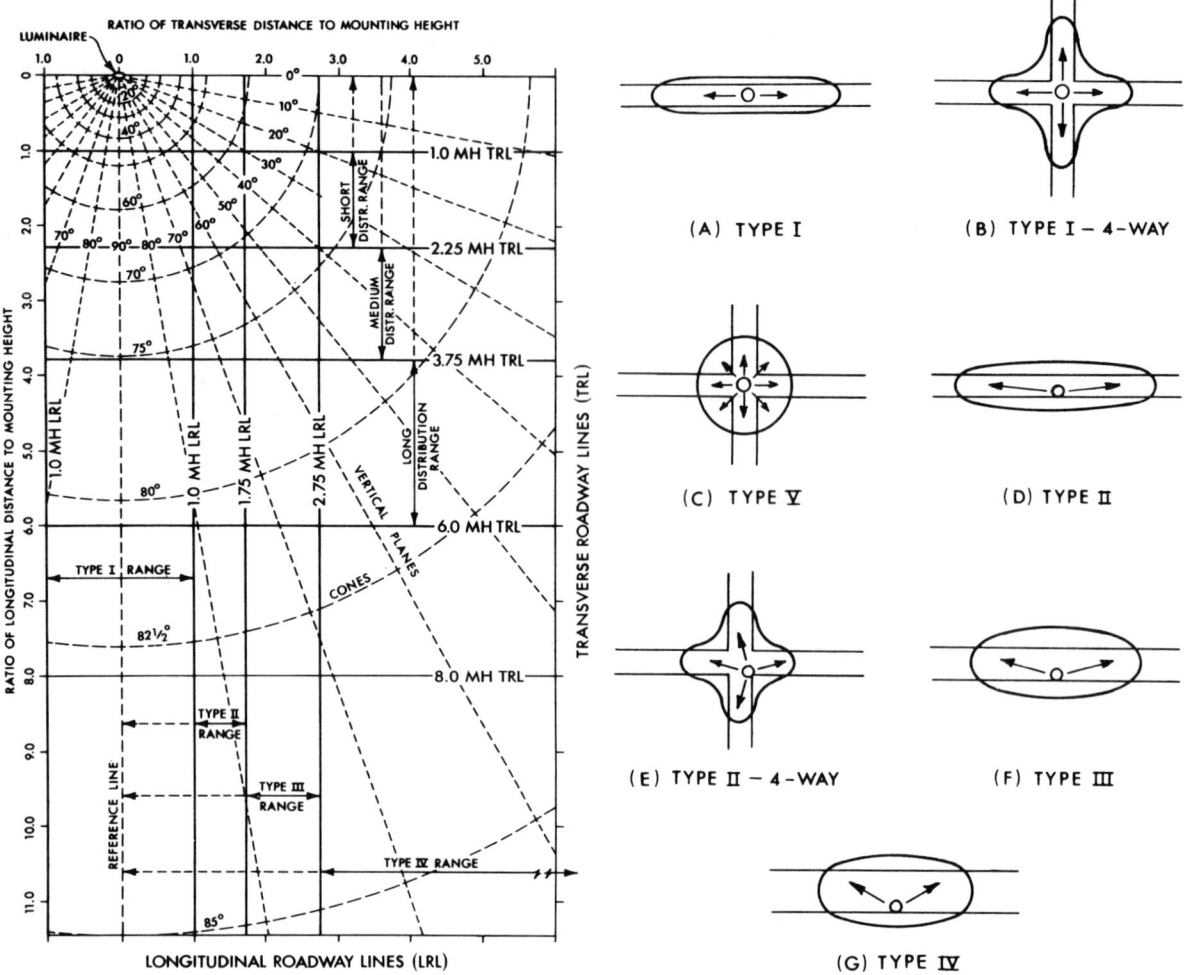

Fig. 24-6. Plan view of roadway coverage for different types of luminaires.

area to be lighted has similar light distributions on both the house side and the street side of the reference line.

- Type I: A distribution is classified as Type I when its half-maximum-candlepower isocandela trace lies within the Type I width range on both sides of the reference line which is bounded by 1.0-MH house side LRL and 1.0-MH street side LRL within the longitudinal distribution range (S, M or L) where the point of maximum candlepower falls. (See figure 24-6a.)
- Type I four-way: A distribution is classified as a Type I four-way when it has four beams of the width as defined for Type I above. (See figure 24-6b.)
- Type V: A distribution is classified as Type V when it has circular symmetry, being essentially the same at all lateral angles around the luminaire. (See figure 24-6c.)

Luminaires Near Side of Area. The lateral width classifications that deal with luminaires intended to be

mounted near the side of the area to be lighted vary as to the width of distribution range on the street side of the reference line. The house side segment of the half-maximum-candlepower isocandela trace within the longitudinal range in which the point of maximum candlepower falls (S, M or L) may or may not cross the reference line. In general it is preferable that the half-maximum-candlepower isocandela trace remain near the reference line. The variable width on the street side is as defined by the following.

- Type II: A distribution is classified as Type II when the street side segment of the half-maximum-candlepower isocandela trace within the longitudinal range in which the point of maximum candlepower falls (S, M or L) does not cross the 1.75-MH street side LRL. (See figure 24-6d.)
- Type II four-way: A distribution is classified as a Type II four-way when it has four beams, each of the width on the street side as defined for Type II above. (See figure 24-6e.)

- Type III: A distribution is classified as Type III when the street side segment of the half-maximum-candlepower isocandela trace within the longitudinal range in which the point of maximum candlepower falls (S, M or L) lies partly or entirely beyond the 1.75-MH street side LRL, but does not cross the 2.75-MH street side LRL. (See figure 24-6f.)
- Type IV: A distribution is classified as Type IV when the street side segment of the half-maximum-candlepower isocandela trace within the

longitudinal range in which the point of maximum candlepower falls (S, M or L) lies partly or entirely beyond the 2.75-MH street side LRL. (See figure 24-6g.)

Control of Distribution Above Maximum Candlepower. Although the pavement luminance generally increases on increasing the vertical angle of light flux emission, it should be emphasized that the disability and discomfort glare also increase. However, since the rates of increase and decrease of these factors are not

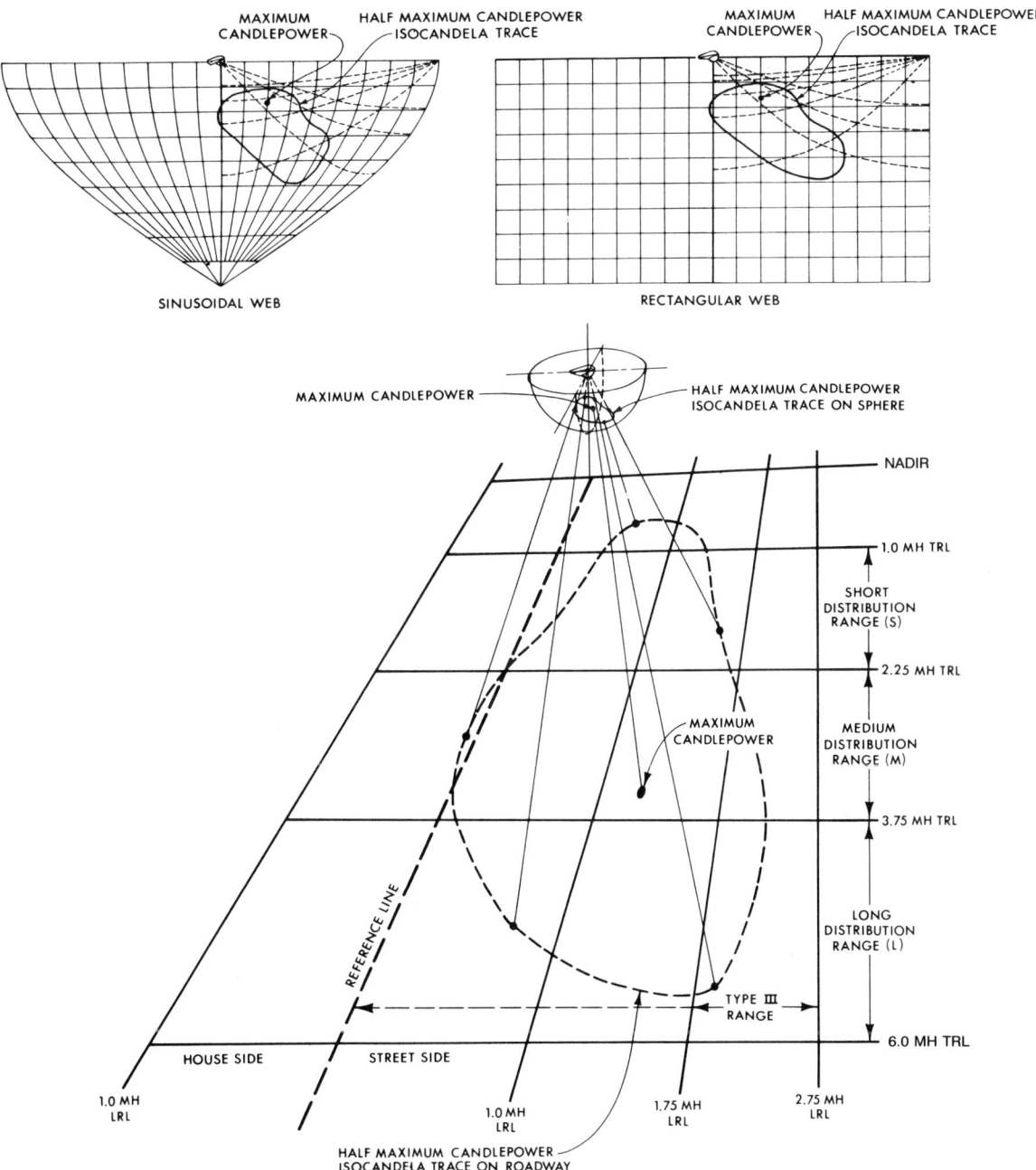

Fig. 24-7. Diagram showing projection of maximum candlepower and half-maximum candlepower isocandela trace from a luminaire having a Type III — Medium distribution, on the imaginary sphere and the roadway. Sinusoidal web and rectangular web representation of sphere are also shown with maximum candlepower and half-maximum candlepower isocandela trace.

the same, design compromises become necessary in order to achieve balanced performance. Therefore, varying degrees of control of candlepower in the upper portion of the beam above maximum candlepower are required. This control of the candlepower distribution is divided into three categories.

Cutoff. A luminaire light distribution is designated as cutoff when the candlepower per 1000 lamp lumens does not numerically exceed 25 (2.5%) at an angle of 90° above nadir (horizontal), and 100 (10%) at a vertical angle of 80° above nadir. This applies to any lateral angle around the luminaire. (In some cases the cutoff distribution may meet the requirements of the semicutoff distribution.)

Semicutoff. A luminaire light distribution is designated as semicutoff when the candlepower per 1000 lamp lumens does not numerically exceed 50 (5%) at an angle of 90° above nadir (horizontal), and 200 (20%) at a vertical angle of 80° above nadir. This applies to any lateral angle around the luminaire. (In some cases the semicutoff distribution may meet the requirements of the noncutoff distribution.)

Noncutoff. This is the category in which there is no candlepower limitation in the zone above maximum candlepower.

Variations. With the variations in roadway width, type of surface, luminaire mounting height and spacing found in actual practice, there are a large number of "ideal" lateral distributions. For practical applications, however, a few types of lateral distribution patterns may be preferable to many complex arrangements. This simplification of distribution types will be more easily understood, and consequently there will be greater assurance of proper installation and more reliable maintenance.

When luminaires are tilted upward, it raises the angle of the street side light distribution. Features such as cutoff or width classification may be changed appreciably. When the tilt is planned, the output of the luminaire should be measured and the light distribution classified in the position in which it will be installed.

Type I, II, III and IV lateral light distributions should vary across transverse roadway lines other than that including the maximum candlepower in such a way as to provide adequate coverage of the rectangular roadway area involved. The width of the lateral angle of distribution required to cover adequately a typical width of roadway varies with the vertical angle or length of distribution as shown by the TRL (transverse roadway line). For a TRL at 4.5 MH, the lateral angle of distribution for roadway coverage is obviously narrower than that required for a TRL at 3.0 MH or 2.0 MH.

Other variations from the distributions specified here may be useful for special applications.

Luminaire Selection

Luminaire light distribution classification will help to determine the optical and economical suitability of a luminaire for lighting a particular roadway from the proposed mounting height and location. A wide selection of light distribution systems is available.

Simply because a luminaire is assigned a particular classification, there is no assurance that it will produce the recommended quantity and quality of lighting for all roadway configurations and mountings shown in figure 24-4. The relative amount and control of light in areas other than the cone of maximum candlepower are equally important in producing good visibility in the final system, but are not considered in the classification system.

LIGHTING DESIGN

The lighting system of a specific road section should accommodate the visual needs of night traffic (vehicular and pedestrian) and be expressed in terms clearly understandable by lighting designers, traffic engineers and highway administrators.

The visual environmental needs along the roadway may be described in terms of pavement luminance, luminance uniformity and disability veiling glare produced by the system light sources. Figure 24-8a provides recommended luminance design requirements and uniformity. It also specifies the relationship between the average luminance L_{avg}, which is the average of all of the luminances values calculated for the section of roadway under consideration, and the veiling luminance L_v, which is defined later in this chapter.

The visual needs along the roadway may also be satisfied by the use of illuminance criteria. Figure 24-8b provides the recommended illuminance design requirements, considering the differences in roadway reflectance characteristics. The designer should not expect the lighting systems designed under the two sets of criteria to correlate perfectly.

The design of a roadway lighting system involves consideration of visibility, economics, esthetics, safety and environmental conditions, as well as appropriate material and equipment. The design process follows these major steps:

1. Determination of roadway classification and adjacent area classification along the specific road section to be lighted. There are three types of area classification: commercial, intermediate and residential. If the pavement classification is unknown, use the R3 values of figure 24-8.
2. (a) Selection of the level and uniformity of pavement luminance and assessment of the relationship between the veiling luminance

Fig. 24-8. Recommended Maintained Luminance and Illuminance Values for Roadways

(a) Maintained Luminance Values (L_{avg}) in Candelas per Square Meter*

Road and Area Classification		Average Luminance L_{avg}	Luminance Uniformity L_{avg} to L_{min}	L_{max} to L_{min}	Veiling Luminance Ratio (maximum) L_v to L_{avg}
Freeway Class A		0.6	3.5 to 1	6 to 1	0.3 to 1
Freeway Class B		0.4	3.5 to 1	6 to 1	0.3 to 1
Expressway	Commercial	1.0	3 to 1	5 to 1	
	Intermediate	0.8	3 to 1	5 to 1	0.3 to 1
	Residential	0.6	3.5 to 1	6 to 1	
Major	Commercial	1.2	3 to 1	5 to 1	
	Intermediate	0.9	3 to 1	5 to 1	0.3 to 1
	Residential	0.6	3.5 to 1	6 to 1	
Collector	Commercial	0.8	3 to 1	5 to 1	
	Intermediate	0.6	3.5 to 1	6 to 1	0.4 to 1
	Residential	0.4	4 to 1	8 to 1	
Local	Commercial	0.6	6 to 1	10 to 1	
	Intermediate	0.5	6 to 1	10 to 1	0.4 to 1
	Residential	0.3	6 to 1	10 to 1	

(b) Average Maintained Illuminance Values (E_{avg}) in Lux†

Road and Area Classification		Pavement Classification R1	R2 and R3	R4	Illuminance Uniformity Ratio E_{avg} to E_{min}
Freeway Class A		6	9	8	3 to 1
Freeway Class B		4	6	5	
Expressway	Commercial	10	14	13	
	Intermediate	8	12	10	3 to 1
	Residential	6	9	8	
Major	Commercial	12	17	15	
	Intermediate	9	13	11	3 to 1
	Residential	6	9	8	
Collector	Commercial	8	12	10	
	Intermediate	6	9	8	4 to 1
	Residential	4	6	5	
Local	Commercial	6	9	8	
	Intermediate	5	7	6	6 to 1
	Residential	3	4	4	

Notes

L_v = veiling luminance

1. These tables do not apply to high mast interchange lighting systems, *e.g.*, mounting heights over 20 meters. See Fig. 24-9.

2. The relationship between individual and respective luminance and illuminance values is derived from general conditions for dry paving and straight road sections. This relationship does not apply to averages.

3. For divided highways, where the lighting on one roadway may differ from that on the other, calculations should be made on each roadway independently.

4. For freeways, the recommended values apply to both mainline and ramp roadways.

   * For approximate values in candelas per square foot, multiply by 0.1.

   † For approximate values in footcandles, multiply by 0.1.

and the average pavement luminance, as recommended in figure 24-8a for each different area classification along the section, or

(b) Determination of the roadway pavement classification, desired average horizontal illuminance and uniformity for design as recommended in figure 24-8b.

3. Preliminary selection of several luminaires and light sources.

4. Preliminary selection of one or more lighting system geometries, including mounting heights and lateral luminaire positions, that may provide an acceptable design based on recommended level, uniformity and veiling luminance control.

5. Calculation of pole spacing for the various luminaire and lamp combinations under study, if for a new system, or of lamp output requirements, if existing poles are to be reused, based

on illuminance values. Mounting height and lateral luminaire positions may also be considered to verify meeting the requirements of figure 24-8a or b.

6. When luminaires have been selected, borderline situations quickly become evident during the application stage. In most cases, skilled judgment must be exercised when considering luminaires for a specific system. It may not be appropriate to specify only one light distribution when it is obvious that several different luminaire light distributions will provide improved performance for a specific application.

7. Selection of final decision or reentry of the design process at any step above to achieve an optimal design.

8. Selection of luminaire supports (pole and bracket) that result in an acceptable esthetic appearance, adherence to traffic safety practice, low initial construction cost, and minimal operation and maintenance expenses.

The formation of a preliminary design involves many variables not explicitly described here. The choice of light source, the extent to which available electrical distribution facilities are used, and the types of poles, brackets and luminaires selected are some of the factors that will influence the economics of lighting. Any consideration of appearance must be resolved by professional judgment and can only be justified if the basic requirements of good visibility have first been attained. It is important that roadway lighting be planned on the basis of traffic and past accident information, which includes the factors necessary to provide for traffic safety and nighttime pedestrian security.

Roadway conditions—such as width of pavement and location of curbs adjacent and within the roadway (island and medians); pavement reflectance; severe grades and curves; location and width of sidewalks and shoulders; type and location of very high volume driveways, intersections and interchanges; underpasses and overpasses; and trees—may also affect the final design.

Lighting System Depreciation

The recommended values of figures 24-8, 24-9 and 24-10 represent the lowest in-service luminance or illuminance values for the type of maintenance to be given to the system. Prior to beginning the design of a lighting system it is necessary to determine the expected light losses. Since luminance or illuminance values can depreciate by 50% or more between relamping and luminaire washing cycles, it is imperative to use lamp lumen depreciation (LLD) and luminaire dirt depreciation (LDD) factors which are valid and based on realistic information or judgment. See chapter 9,

Fig. 24-9. Recommended Maintained Illuminance Design Levels for High Mast Lighting* in Lux†

Road Classification	Horizontal Illuminance (E_{avg}) in Lux		
	Commercial Area	Intermediate Area	Residential Area
Freeways	6	6	6
Expressways	10	8	6
Major	12	9	6
Collector	8	6	6

* Recommended uniformity of illumination is 3 to 1 or better; average-to-minimum for all road classifications at the illuminance levels recommended above. These design values apply only to the travelled portions of the roadway. Interchange roadways are treated individually for purposes of uniformity and illuminance level analysis.
† For approximate values in footcandles, multiply by 0.1.

Fig. 24-10. Recommended Average Maintained Illuminance Level for Pedestrian Ways* in Lux†

Walkway and Bikeway Classification	Minimum Average Horizontal Levels (E_{avg})	Average Vertical Levels For Special Pedestrian Security (E_{avg})‡
Sidewalks (roadside) and Type A bikeways:		
Commercial areas	10	22
Intermediate areas	6	11
Residential areas	2	5
Walkways distant from roadways and Type B bikeways:		
Walkways, bikeways, and stairways	5	5
Pedestrian tunnels	43	54

* Crosswalks traversing roadways in the middle of long blocks and at street intersections should be provided with additional illumination.
† For approximate values in footcandles, multiply by 0.1.
‡ For pedestrian identification at a distance. Values at 1.8 meters (6 feet) above walkway

Lighting Calculations, for the use of light loss factors in calculations.

Changes in Pavement Reflectance

Pavement luminance values also may be changed by wear on the road surface, resulting in modifications of the reflectance coefficient. For example, asphalt tends to lighten because of exposure of aggregate, and Portland cement darkens because of carbon and oil deposits.

Quality

Quality lighting relates to the ability of the lighting system to provide target and obstacle contrast so that people can make decisions based on fast and accurate obstacle detection and recognition. If the quality of one lighting installation is higher than that of a second installation for the same average luminance (or illuminance) level, then visual detection of typical tasks will be faster and easier under the first installation.

Uniformity

Uniformity is usually expressed in one of three ways: the average-to-minimum, minimum-to-maximum or maximum-to-average ratio. In roadway lighting, the average-to-minimum and maximum-to-minimum ratios are the usual criteria of interest. The average-to-minimum point method uses the average luminance of the roadway design area between two adjacent luminaires, divided by the lowest value at any point in the area. The maximum-to-minimum point method uses the maximum and minimum values between the same adjacent luminaires.

The luminance values provided in figure 24-8a are considered to be satisfactory only if the average-to-minimum and maximum-to-minimum uniformity ratios do not exceed the limits specified in this figure. The illuminance values given in figure 24-8b are satisfactory if the average-to-minimum uniformity ratios are not exceeded.

The luminance uniformity (average-to-minimum and maximum-to-minimum) considers the traveled portion of the roadway, except for divided highways, which may have different design requirements on each side of the roadway.

It is important in the actual design of the roadway lighting system that actual photometric data be used for the calculations rather than generic data, so as to assure that the lighting results achieved will match, within the normal limits of the calculations, with the predicted values.

Luminaire Mounting Height

Mounting heights of luminaires have, in general, increased substantially during the past several decades. The advent of more efficient, higher-lumen lamps has been the primary reason. Designers have increased mounting heights in order to obtain economic and esthetic gains in addition to increased uniformity of luminance and illuminance values when utilizing modern, high-wattage lamps. Mounting heights of 12 m (40 ft) and higher are used along roadways, and the cluster mounting of luminaires is used at interchanges. The advent of suitable servicing equipment and lowering devices has made this practical.

During this same period, there has been another trend to lower mounting heights in some cases. In general, this has been due to esthetic considerations. An example is the use of pole-top-mounted luminaires in residential areas.

When designing a system, mounting height should be considered in conjunction with spacing and lateral

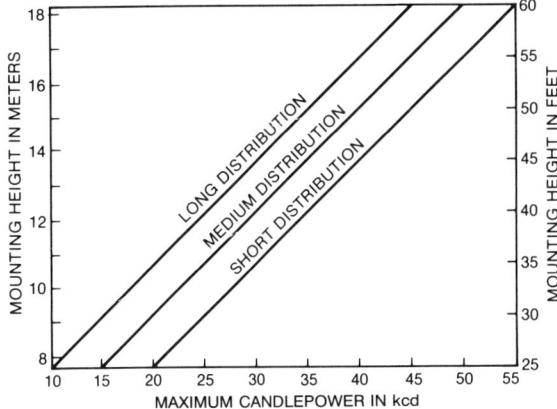

Fig. 24-11. Minimum luminaire mounting heights based on current practice and veiling luminance calculations.

positioning of the luminaires as well as the luminaire type and distribution. (See figure 24-11.) Uniformity and levels of luminance and illuminance should be maintained as recommended regardless of the mounting height selected.

Increased mounting height may, but will not necessarily, reduce discomfort glare and veiling luminance. It increases the angle between the luminaires and the line of sight to the roadway; however, luminaire light distributions and candlepower also are significant factors. Glare is dependent on the flux reaching the observer's eyes from all luminaires in the visual scene.

High-Mast Interchange Lighting

High-mast interchange lighting is defined as the use of a group of luminaires mounted more than 20 m [60 ft] in height, and is intended to light multiple sections of the paved roadway of an interchange.

The design levels of figure 24-8 have not been proven to apply to high-mast interchange lighting systems. This is due to a lack of applicable experience in the design of such lighting on a luminance basis. Experience indicates that a system designed to the illuminance criteria in figure 24-9 will give satisfactory results.

Luminaire Spacing

The spacing of luminaires is often influenced by the location of utility poles, block lengths, property lines and roadway geometry. It is generally more economical to use lamps with high lumen output at longer intervals and higher mounting heights than to use lamps with lower lumen output at more frequent intervals with lower mounting heights. Higher mounting is usually in the interest of good lighting, provided the spacing-to-mounting-height ratio is within the range of lighting distribution for which the luminaire is designed. Termi-

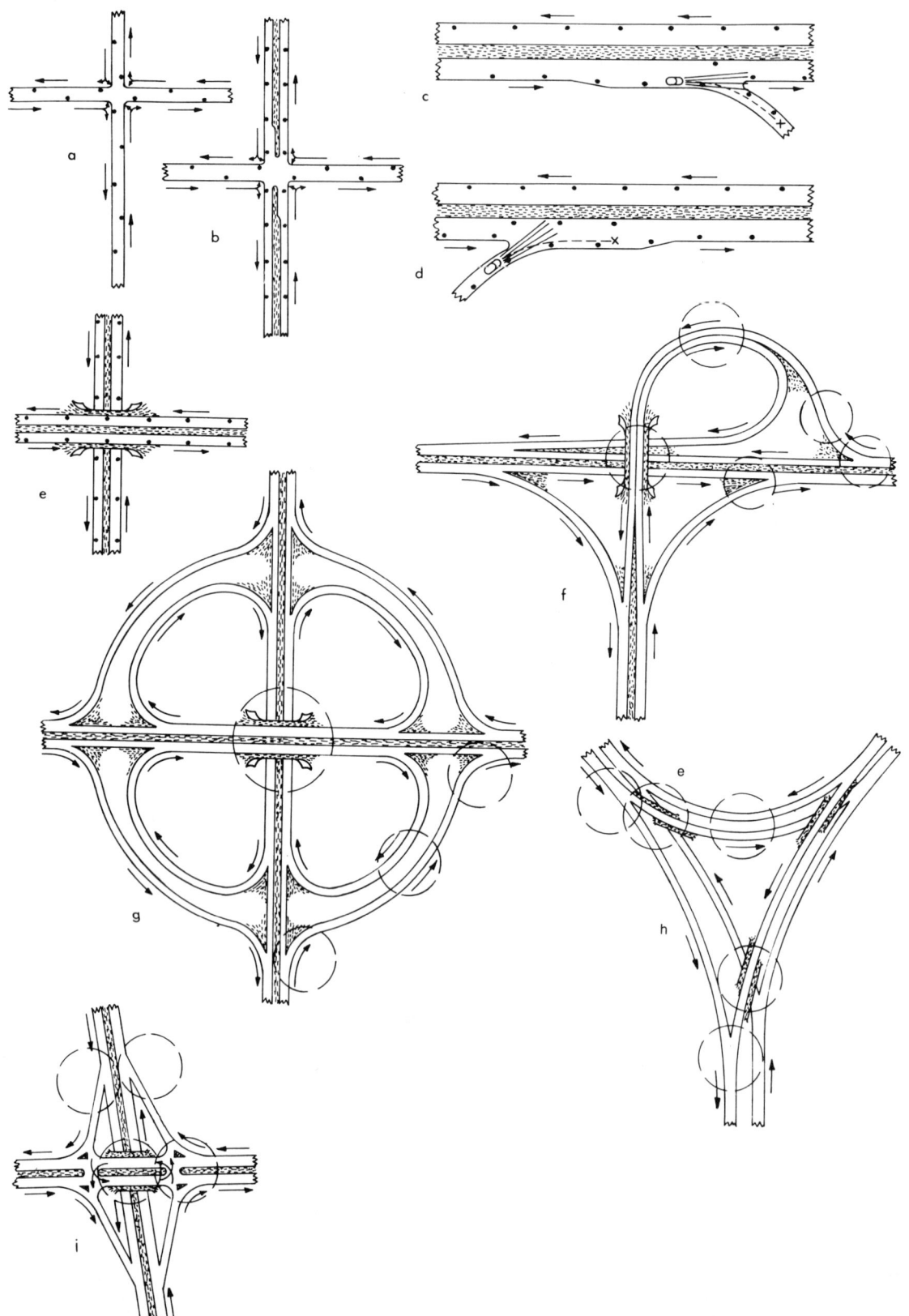

Fig. 24-12. Roadway complexities. (a) Grade intersection, balanced heavy traffic. (b) Larger, more complex grade intersection. (c) Diverging traffic lanes. (d) Converging traffic lanes. (e) Underpass — overpass. (f) to (i) Traffic interchanges. Note: Arrows indicate traffic flow directions. Pole location will depend on local practice and physical conditions of the area.

nology with respect to luminaire arrangement and spacing is shown in figure 24-4.

Other factors to be considered are:

- Access to luminaires for servicing
- Vehicle-pole collision probabilities
- System glare aspects
- Visibility (both day and night) of traffic signs and signals
- Esthetic appearance
- Trees
- Locations of poles at intersections to allow joint use for traffic signals

Situations Requiring Special Consideration

Roadways have many areas where the problems of vision and maneuvering of motor vehicles are complex, such as grade intersections, abrupt curves, underpasses, converging traffic lanes, diverging traffic lanes and various types of complicated traffic interchanges. The values in figure 24-8 are for roadway sections that are continuous and nearly level. Intersecting, merging or diverging roadway areas require special consideration. The luminance or illuminance levels for these areas should be at least equal to the sum of the recommended values associated with each roadway that forms the intersection. Very high volume driveway connections to public streets and midblock pedestrian crosswalks should be lighted to at least 50% higher level than the average route value.

The lighting of such areas, at first glance, appears to be a very complicated problem. It becomes apparent upon analysis, however, that all such areas consist of one of several basic types of situations or a combination of these.

Grade Intersections, Balanced Heavy Traffic. See figure 24 12a. These intersections may have unrestricted traffic flow on both roadways, restriction by means of stop signs on one or both of the roadways, or control of the traffic by signal lights, by police officers or by other means. Some intersections are complicated by pedestrian traffic as well as vehicular traffic. The lighting problems on all of these, however, are fundamentally the same. The luminance level in these areas should be higher than that on either intersecting road. See also the subsections on converging and diverging traffic lanes below.

Luminaires should be located so that illumination will be provided on vehicles and pedestrians in the intersection area, on the pedestrian walkways and on the adjacent roadway areas. Of particular importance here is the amount of light falling on the vertical surfaces of such objects that differentiates them from the pavement background against which they are seen.

Figure 24-12b shows a larger, more complex grade intersection. The lighting problems and techniques here are similar to those at the smaller intersections. The size, however, may make the use of more and larger luminaires mandatory.

Curves and Hills. See figure 24-13. The visual problems in motor vehicle operation increase on curves and hills. In general, gradual large-radius curves, roadways with appropriate super elevation (the vertical distance between the inner and outer edges of the roadway), and gently sloping grades are lighted satisfactorily if treated like straight, level roadway surfaces. Sharper curves and steeper grades, especially at the crests of hills, warrant closer spacing of luminaires in order to provide higher pavement luminance and improved uniformities. See figure 24-13e and f.

The geometry of abrupt curves, such as those found on traffic interchanges and many roadway areas, requires careful analysis. Headlighting is not effective in these situations, and silhouette seeing (a condition where the target, or obstacle, has a lower luminance than the background) cannot be provided in some instances. Luminaires should be located to provide ample illumination on vehicles, road curbing and berms, guard rails, etc. Poles should be located to provide adequate, safe clearance behind guardrails or any natural barriers that may exist. There is some evidence that poles are more likely to be involved in accidents if placed on the outside of curves. Many vehicle operators may be unfamiliar with these areas, and illumination on the surround greatly helps their discernment of the roadway path. See figure 24-13c and d.

Proper horizontal orientation of luminaire supports and poles on curves is important to assure balanced distribution of the light flux on the pavement. See figure 24-13a.

When luminaires are located on grade inclines, it is desirable to orient the luminaire so that the light beams strike the pavement equidistant from the luminaire. This assures maximum uniformity of light distribution and keeps glare to a minimum. See figure 24-13b.

Underpass-Overpass. See figure 24-12e. Short underpasses such as those encountered where a roadway goes beneath a two- or four-lane roadway can generally be lighted satisfactorily with standard luminaires if they are properly positioned. Luminaires on the lower roadway should be positioned so that there are not large discontinuities in the pavement lighting from that on either side of the overpass and so that the recommended levels are provided. Care should be taken so that the uniformity does not fall below the minimum values recommended in figure 24-8. These luminaires should also provide adequate vertical illumination on the supporting structures.

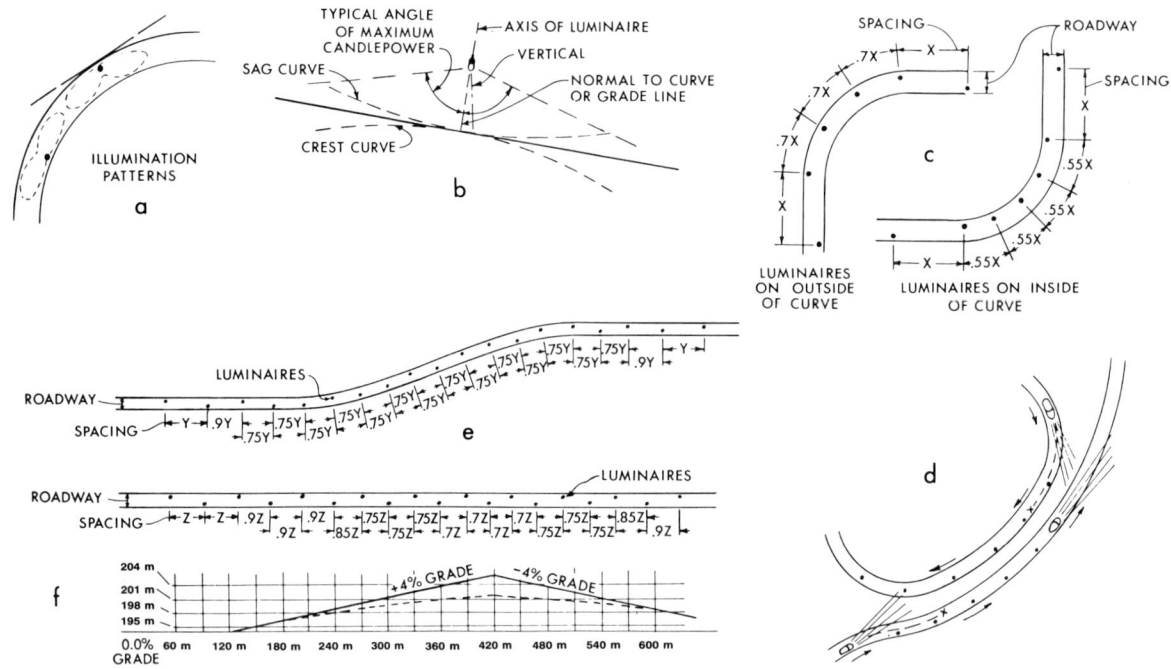

Fig. 24-13. Typical lighting layouts for horizontal curves and vertical curves. (a) Luminaires oriented to place reference plane perpendicular to radius of curvature. (b) Luminaire mounting on hill (vertical curves and grade). (c) Short radius curves (horizontal). (d) Vehicle illumination will fall outside the roadway when approaching a curve. Roadway luminaires must be located to compensate for the illumination lost when this occurs. (e) Horizontal curve, radius 305 meters (1000 feet), super elevation six percent per foot. (f) 380-meter (1250-foot) vertical curve with four percent grade and 230-meter (750 foot) sight distance. (In this illustration, 30 m = 100 ft.)

Longer underpasses, where such overlapping of the illumination from the street luminaires cannot be accomplished, require special treatment. Such underpasses also greatly reduce the entrance of daylight, warranting illumination during the daytime. Very high luminance levels can be justified in order to reduce the required adaptation, particularly during daylight hours. In many cases, the techniques used for tunnel lighting can be used effectively for lighting these longer underpasses.

Diverging Traffic Lanes. See figure 24-12c. Diverging traffic lanes warrant extremely careful consideration because these are areas where motorists are most frequently confused. Luminaires should be placed to provide illumination on curbs, abutments, guardrails and vehicles in the area of traffic divergence. Poles should be located to provide adequate safety clearance for vehicles that may cross the gore area. Lighting also should be provided in the deceleration zone. Diverging roadways frequently have all the problems of abrupt curves and should be treated accordingly.

Converging Traffic Lanes. See figure 24-12d. Converging traffic lanes frequently have all the problems of abrupt curves. Here, automobile headlighting is inef-

fective, and silhouette seeing cannot be provided for many of the situations. It is also essential to provide good direct side illumination on the vehicles entering the main traffic lanes.

Interchanges: High-Speed, High-Traffic-Density Roadways. See figure 24-12f, g, h and i. Interchanges at first glance appear to be complex lighting problems. Analysis, however, shows that they are composed of one or more of the basic problems that are dealt with in previous paragraphs and may be treated accordingly.

When designing lighting for interchanges, the regular roadway lighting system will usually provide sufficient surround illumination in the field of view to reveal features of the entire scene and allow drivers to know at all times where they are and where they are going. An inadequately lighted interchange with too few luminaires may lead to confusion for the driver, by giving misleading clues due to the random placement of the luminaires. (This does not apply to high-mast lighting.)

When continuous illumination for the entire interchange area cannot be provided, it may be desirable to illuminate intersections, points of access and egress, curves, hills and similar areas of geometrical and traffic complexity. In these cases, illumination should be extended beyond the critical areas. Two fundamental reasons for this are:

1. The eyes of the driver, adapted to the level of the lighted area, need about 1 s to adjust to changes in the illumination upon leaving the lighted area and must maintain vision during this period of dark adaptation. There is no evidence that a gradual reduction at the levels used in roadway lighting has any practical advantage over a sudden ending of the lighted area. This end, however, should be beyond the end of the maneuver area.

2. Traffic merging into a major roadway from an access road is often slow in accelerating to the speed on the major roadway. The lighting along this area for a distance beyond the access point extends visibility and facilitates the acceleration and merging process.

The placement of luminaires should be carefully considered so as to minimize glare for the drivers and, especially, so as not to detract from sign legibility or block the view of signs.

Railroad Grade Crossings. Railroad grade crossings should be adequately lighted to allow identification of the crossing, any irregularities in the pavement surface,

and the presence or absence of the train in or approaching the crossing, and to allow recognition of unlighted objects or vehicles at or near the railroad crossing.

Grade crossings are normally identified by means of signs with the message on a vertical face, as well as markings on the pavement surface. The lighting direction and level should permit visual recognition of such signs and markings. Minor variation of the basic lighting layouts shown in figure 24-14 may be desirable, depending on the exact locations of the signs or markings.

General principles to be followed in selecting and locating equipment are as follows:

1. The illuminance level on a track area starting 30 m (100 ft) before the crossing and ending 30 m (100 ft) beyond it should be in accordance with figure 24-8, but never less than a luminance of 0.8 cd/m^2 or an illuminance of 8 lx (0.8 fc) (see figure 24-14a).
2. Pole location should provide uniformity (figure 24-14b through f) as outlined above under Uniformity.
3. Vertical illumination of a train in a crossing is important for adequate visibility. However, care must be used in locating the luminaire so

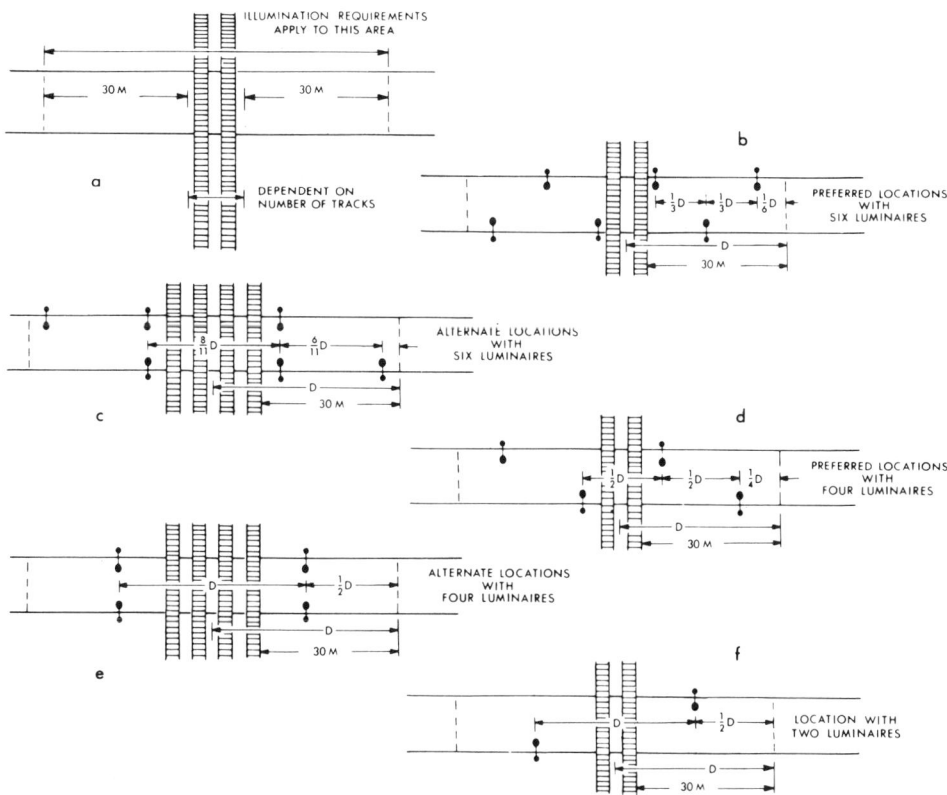

Fig. 24-14. Railroad grade crossings.

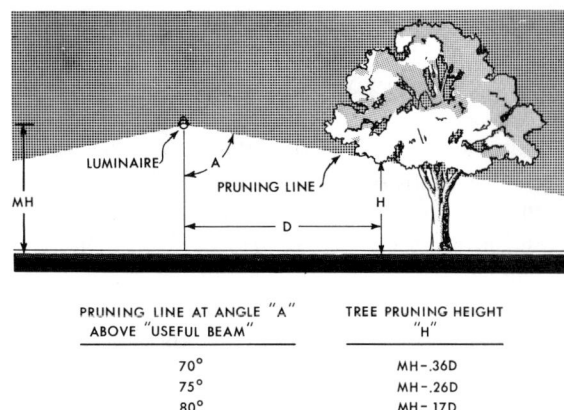

PRUNING LINE AT ANGLE "A" ABOVE "USEFUL BEAM"	TREE PRUNING HEIGHT "H"
70°	MH−.36D
75°	MH−.26D
80°	MH−.17D

Fig. 24-15. Recommended tree pruning to minimize conflict with roadway lighting. "Above useful beam" may be considered that light above the 50% max CP distribution for the luminaire being used.

that glare is not a problem to the drivers approaching the crossing from the opposite direction.

Trees. Trees are important community assets. Careful placement of luminaires and regular tree pruning (see figure 24-15) will not only enhance traffic safety and pedestrian security but will also preserve the character and appearance of a neighborhood. Figures 24-16 and 24-17 can help a designer determine suitable overhang distances of luminaires for different mounting heights with different types of trees.

Deviations from ideal luminaire spacing may be necessary to accommodate trees. Generally, a 10% deviation in longitudinal spacing of luminaires will not seriously affect lighting uniformity. For certain luminaires, deviations up to 20% can be tolerated, provided no two consecutive luminaires are involved. Only as a last resort should deviation be permitted in the transverse overhang of the luminaires. This positioning is important for effectiveness of the lighting and appearance of the system. Although foliage mostly affects light on the roadway pavement, it can also affect light

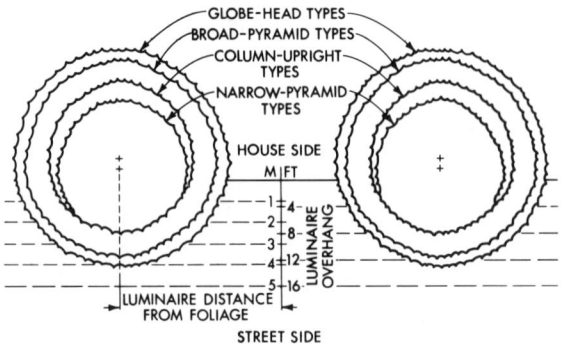

Fig. 24-16. Overhang distances for luminaires to assure maturing trees will not interfere with the luminaire distribution.

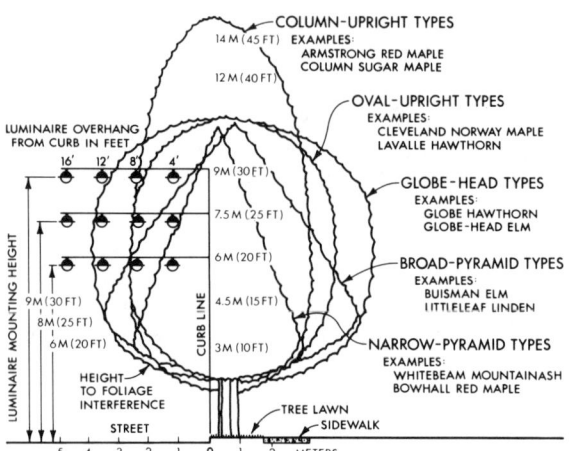

Fig. 24-17. Height of foliage interference for different types of trees. Luminaire overhang must be selected to assure luminaire distribution will not be obstructed by the foliage as the tree matures. (tree examples by E. H. Scanlon.)

on adjoining sidewalks. This latter point can be very important in regard to local residential streets.

Roadside Border Areas

Visibility for drivers can be improved if areas beyond the roadway proper are illuminated. It is desirable to widen the narrow visual field into the peripheral zone in order to reveal adjacent objects. Such conditions also improve depth perception and perspective, thereby facilitating the judgment of speed and distance. The luminance of border areas should diminish gradually and uniformly away from the road. Of course, these points must be considered in the context of local property owners; the design must eliminate objectionable light trespass.

Transition Lighting

Transition lighting is a technique intended to provide the driver with a gradual reduction in illuminance when traveling from one roadway area into another. Factors that may influence the decision to provide a transition lighting area are:

- Significant reduction in roadway cross section
- Severe horizontal or vertical curvature of the roadway
- Change from a very high lighting level to a lower level

The use of transition lighting is the option of the designer after a study of the conditions at a specific location.

Gradual decreases in pavement luminance are usually accomplished by extending the lighting system beyond the normal limits and partially interrupting the required geometric arrangement of luminaires. For example, a two-side opposite or staggered spacing arrangement could be continued to the normal lighting limits, where luminaires would be omitted from the exiting side of the roadway but continued for one to six cycles beyond the normal limits on the approach side, depending on road speed and luminaire coverage. Designer judgment should be used and various geometric arrangements considered.

Alleys

A well-lighted alley increases the perception of safety and reduces criminals' opportunities to operate and hide under the cover of darkness. Alleys should be lighted to facilitate police patrolling from sidewalks and cross streets, especially in commercial areas. Generally, such lighting also meets the vehicular traffic needs in these low-traffic areas.

Pedestrian Walkways and Bikeways

Proper lighting of walkway and bikeway areas is essential to the safe and comfortable use of such areas by pedestrians (herein assumed to include bicyclists) at night. Many walkways and bikeways are located adjacent to lighted roadways and no specific or separate lighting is required. All too often, however, the roadway spill light is inadequate for the comfort and safety of pedestrians on the walkway or bikeway.

It is recommended that all lighting designs conform to the illuminance requirements shown in figure 24-10. If the roadway illumination does not provide the recommended walkway or bikeway levels, revisions or additions to the roadway lighting will be necessary.

The photometric data provided by the supplier of the roadway luminaires can be used for evaluating Type A or Type B sidewalk or roadway bikeway illuminance recommendations.

The recommended levels of walkway and bikeway illuminance listed in figure 24-10 represent average

maintained illuminance levels and should be considered as minimum, particularly when security and pedestrian identification at a distance is important. Visual identification of other pedestrians and objects along walkways is dependent to a great degree on vertical surface illuminance; therefore, different values are shown in the table.

To provide well-lighted surroundings for such pedestrian ways as walkways and bikeways through parks (Type B), it is further recommended that the area bordering these pedestrian ways for a width of 2–5 m (6.5–16 ft) on each side be lighted to levels of at least one-third the level suggested for the walkway or bikeway. This is also applicable to similar marginal areas such as below-grade entrances to building basements, gaps between building fronts, dense shrubbery and other locations where criminals might hide.

The average-to-minimum uniformity ratio in illuminating pedestrian ways where special pedestrian security is not essential should not exceed 4:1, except for residential sidewalks and Type A bikeways in residential areas, where a ratio of 10:1 is acceptable. Where increased pedestrian security is desired, the uniformity ratio should not exceed 5:1 for any walkway or bikeway.

Tunnels[3]

Tunnel lighting should provide good visibility for drivers, both day and night. The many factors that contribute to or detract from visibility need to be identified and their specific importance determined for each tunnel.

Physical Characteristics. For lighting purposes a tunnel is an enclosure over a roadway that restricts the normal illumination of the roadway by daylight, thus requiring an evaluation of the need for supplemental lighting. This enclosure may be created either by boring through natural materials such as earth and rock, or by construction using materials such as steel and

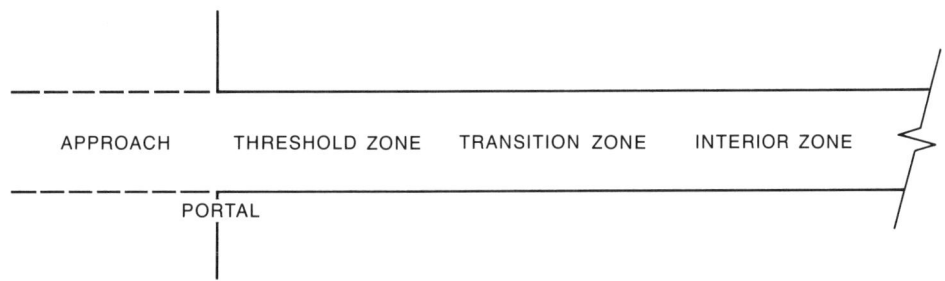

Fig. 24-18. Descriptive terms associated with tunnel lighting:
Approach: The external roadway area leading to the tunnel;
Portal: The plane of entrance into the tunnel;
Threshold Zone: The first part of the tunnel where, during daytime, the highest level of the lighting is provided;
Transition Zone: The area where a transition is made from the high lighting level of the threshold to the lower lighting level of the interior.
Interior Zone: The innermost part of the tunnel where the lowest level of lighting is provided.
Note: Lengths of zones will vary with the design parameters.

Fig. 24-19. Safe Stopping Sight Distance.*

Traffic Speed		Minimum Safe Stopping Sight Distance (SSSD)†	
Kilometers per Hour	Miles Per Hour	Meters	Feet
48	30	60	200
64	40	90	300
80	50	140	450
88	55	165	540
96	60	200	650
104	65	220	720

* Based on American Association of State Highway and Transportation Officials (AASHTO) recommendations. See *A Policy on Geometric Design of Highways and Streets*, 1984, AASHTO, 444 No. Capitol Street N.W., Suite 225, Washington, DC 20001.

† Assumes average prevailing speeds in a straight and level tunnel approach roadway are at, or near, the posted speed limit of the facility. For other geometric conditions, refer to the AASHTO standard as referenced.

concrete. The terminology associated with tunnels for the purpose of lighting design is described in figure 24-18.

Depending upon the length and the safe-stopping sight distance (SSSD; see figure 24-19), tunnels may be classified in two categories:

1. *Short tunnel.* A tunnel having an overall length, from portal to portal along the center-line, equal to or less than the SSSD.
2. *Long tunnel.* a tunnel with an overall length greater than the SSSD.

The critical task facing the driver approaching the tunnel entrance portal during the daytime is to overcome the "black hole" effect created by the high ratio of external to internal luminance. The use of dark finish material on the approach road surface to the tunnel portal, and light finish material on the road surface inside the portal, for a distance at least equal to the SSSD, will reduce the difference between external and internal luminances. The darkening of these external surfaces reduces the luminance level to which the eye is adapted prior to entering the tunnel, thus shortening the time to adapt to the lower luminance levels within the tunnel. For tunnels with a prominent sky background immediately above their entrance portals, plants, screens or panels can increase the size of the darkened area above the portals.

To effectively use daylight and supplemental electric lighting, it is recommended that interior wall surfaces be of an easily maintained, high-reflectance, nonspecular finish having a reflectance of at least 50% initially. In tunnels having curved roadways or having curved approach roadways, development of high wall luminance is of great value in meeting visibility needs. Relatively narrow tunnels, where the width-to-height ratios are approximately 3 or less, will normally develop good tunnel visibility as a result of reflected light from high-reflectance walls. Tunnels having greater width-to-height ratios will normally require supplemental lighting of the roadway surface.

The amount and extent of daylight penetration into the tunnel entrance is largely dependent upon the orientation of the tunnel with respect to the sun's path in the sky. Since the orientation of a tunnel is generally directed by criteria other than illumination considerations, the tunnel lighting system must be able to accommodate the entrance orientation conditions. In entrance portal areas, sunlight penetration can be improved by use of wall, ceiling and roadway surface texture control.

Lighting Design Considerations. Tunnel lighting design should take into account the following considerations:

- Volume and speed of traffic
- External luminance
- Tunnel classification
- Tunnel luminances during both daytime and nighttime conditions
- Lighting and electrical equipment

Volume and Speed of Traffic. Tunnels with high traffic volume and with high-speed traffic require higher luminance levels than those with lower volume and slower traffic to aid the motorist in performing more difficult driving tasks. High-volume traffic increases the probability of having to stop quickly or take evasive action. Higher speeds reduce the time available for eye adaptation and reaction to driving difficulties.

External Luminance. Since approaching drivers are looking at the tunnel entrance prior to entering the tunnel, they are adapted to the luminance of the portal area and the surrounding visual scene.

Tunnel Classification. Short tunnels, with a length of less than the SSSD and having straight, level approach alignment and a straight and level tunnel roadway, may have adequate visibility without supplemental daytime lighting. In these cases, visibility can be provided by negative contrast (silhouette), with high luminance values provided by the exit portal. In tunnels with curved roadways, where the exit portal is not visible, supplemental lighting may be required. These short tunnels should have a single lighting zone equal in luminance to the threshold zone as shown in figure 24-20. Long tunnels require several zones of lighting.

Tunnel Luminance. Tunnels have several different areas with different lighting requirements. In addition, the time of day plays an important role in the lighting of tunnels. Topics discussed below include the threshold zone, the interior zone, the transition zone, nighttime tunnel lighting, uniformity rules and maintenance considerations.

- Threshold zone: Daytime tunnel luminance in the threshold zone must be relatively high to

Fig. 24-20. Recommended Maintained Threshold Zone Average Payment Luminance Values
for Tunnel Roadways during Daylight

| Characteristics of Tunnel | Traffic Speed | | Traffic Volume AADT* | | | |
| | Kilometers per Hour | Miles per Hour | <25,000 | 25-89,999 | 90-150,000 | >150,000 |
			Candelas per Square Meter†			
Mountain tunnels, gradual slopes where snow can accumulate or river tunnels with few surrounding buildings. East/west tunnel orientation.	≥81	50	210	250	290	330
	61-80	38-49	180	220	260	300
	≤60	37	140	185	230	270
Mountain tunnels with steep, dark slopes or climate conditions where snow cannot accumulate. Portal surroundings have medium brightness year round.	≥81	50	145	175	205	235
	61-80	38-49	130	160	190	220
	≤60	37	105	140	170	200
Concealed portals, dark surfaces or buildings surrounding entrance. Artificial measures taken to reduce exterior brightnesses. North/south orientation.	≥81	50	80	100	115	130
	61-80	38-49	70	90	105	120
	≤60	37	60	80	95	110

* Average Annual Daily Traffic in both directions.
† For approximate values in candelas per square foot, multiply by 0.1.

provide visibility during eye adaptation as the motorist enters the tunnel. Figure 24-20 gives appropriate daytime threshold zone luminances. During nighttime, the motorist's eyes are adapted to the low ambient exterior luminance; therefore, a nighttime minimum luminance of 2.5 cd/m^2 is recommended for the entire length of the tunnel, including the threshold. Since the illuminance required at the tunnel threshold during nighttime hours will be significantly lower than that required during daytime hours, it may be appropriate to provide for dimming or switching the tunnel lighting system to permit adjusting the threshold illuminance to provide appropriate daytime and nighttime levels. As indicated, the required luminance level is dependent upon both the characteristics of the tunnel and the traffic speed and volume in the tunnel. The length of the threshold zone lighting should be 15 m (50 ft) less than the SSSD. At approximately 15 m (50 ft) before the portal, the tunnel dominates the visual scene.

• Interior zone: Daytime lighting in the interior of a long tunnel can be reduced, since the motorist's eyes will have adapted to the lower luminance of the threshold zone. Luminance of the tunnel interior zone should be a minimum of 5 cd/m^2 with a uniformity not exceeding 3:1 average-to-minimum.

• Transition zone: Daytime luminance in the transition zone should taper from the threshold zone luminance to the interior zone luminance over a length equal to the SSSD. Transition zone lighting can be accomplished in various ways: greater spacing between luminaires, fewer

lamps per luminaire (in the case of fluorescent lamps), lower-wattage lamps or combinations of the above. The number of sections within the transition zone using different lighting arrangements should be such that an even transition will occur. The transition zone should first be divided into segments of equal length. The first segment after the threshold zone should have a pavement luminance of no less than 25% that of the threshold zone. Each subsequent section should have a pavement luminance no less than 33% that of the previous segment. The last segment before the interior zone should have a pavement luminance no greater than twice that of the interior zone.

Nighttime. During nighttime, the motorist's eyes are adapted to the low ambient exterior luminance; therefore, a nighttime minimum luminance of 2.5 cd/m^2 is recommended for the entire length of the tunnel.

Uniformity Ratios. Uniformity ratios within the tunnel zones should be the same as those used for general roadway lighting as shown in figure 24-8.

Maintenance Considerations. The recommended luminance values given for tunnels in figure 24-20 represent the lowest in-service values that should be allowed throughout the operating life of the system. Therefore, the initial luminance in the tunnel may have to be higher to compensate for lamp lumen depreciation, luminaire dirt depreciation and tunnel surface dirt depreciation.

Lighting and Electrical Equipment. Fluorescent, HID and low-pressure sodium lamps are the light sources used most commonly for tunnel lighting installations. Incandescent lamps are seldom used in new installations, due to their lower efficacy and shorter life.

Tunnel lighting luminaires must be ruggedly constructed to withstand the harsh environment found in most tunnels. Vibration, air turbulence caused by vehicles, vehicle exhaust fumes, road dirt, salt and the periodic washing of tunnels with industrial detergents and high-pressure jet spray equipment are some of the conditions to which luminaires are exposed.

The power supply for tunnel lighting must be very reliable. Even a momentary loss of power cannot be tolerated, since it can lead to serious accidents if people enter complete darkness. Safety can be greatly improved by providing power from two separate sources to the entire tunnel lighting system with transfer devices which automatically switch from one power source to the other in the event of power failure. Consideration should be given to the installation of an emergency power supply to luminaires providing at least one-fifth of the design nighttime lighting level.

Tunnel lighting requirements may vary during daily operation as a result of external luminances varying with weather or the position of the sun. Installations may be provided with luminaires which can be switched or dimmed automatically with changes in the outdoor luminance or with changes in the effective light output of the luminaires. Tunnel systems may also have a manned control room with closed-circuit television surveillance that allows monitoring of tunnel conditions and provides for manual override of the automatic operations.

Flicker Effect. In the interior of a lighted tunnel, where luminaires or their reflected images are in full or partial view of the vehicle occupants, the flicker effect of passing closely spaced light sources may produce undesirable behavioral sensations. The significance of this effect depends upon the brightness of the source to the observer, the location of the source in the motorist's viewing field, and the frequency or rate at which successive light sources appear to be moving. The designer should avoid luminaire spacings that produce drive-by frequencies of 5–10 Hz.[4]

Rest Areas[5]

Rest areas on limited access highways are an important feature to the motorist, and there is general agreement that for the public to obtain maximum benefits from the construction of a rest area, it must be available 24 hours a day, and be considered safe to enter and stay in at least for short periods of time. To obtain this condition, these areas must be adequately lighted for nighttime use. Figure 24-21 shows a typical layout for a roadway rest area.

In designing a lighting system for a rest area, geographical location, topographical location, motorists' comfort and safety, landscaping and architectural treatment, and appearance to pedestrians must be considered. An important benefit to be derived from proper lighting is ease of policing these areas during nighttime hours.

One of the prime design considerations is the motorist's view while traveling along an unlighted main highway or in the rest area. The motorist should not be disturbed by glare or spill light from luminaires placed adjacent to the roadway within the rest areas. While traversing the entire length of the adjacent rest area, the motorist should be able to discern any vehicle leaving the rest area, as well as the traffic moving along the main roadway.

The overall design of the lighting is divided into general areas as follows:

- Entrance and exit
- Interior roadways
- Parking areas
- Activity areas

These have been defined for separate consideration because each is to be used for a different purpose.

The illuminances recommended in figure 24-22 are minimum maintained values.

Entrance and Exit. Entrance and exit areas are defined as the deceleration and acceleration lanes adjacent to the main roadway, leading to and from the gore area. These lanes should be lighted so that the driver entering or leaving the rest area can safely make the transition from the main roadway to the rest area and vice versa. At the same time, drivers electing to continue along the main roadway should be able to do so without impairment of their vision by luminaire brightness or spill light. Drivers should likewise be able to discern vehicles leaving or entering the roadway. The assumption is often made that access lanes to rest areas should be lighted in the same manner as ramps at interchanges; however, interchange ramps are usually designed for higher speeds and traffic densities. Rest area entrances and exits, with relatively low traffic density, are deceleration and acceleration lanes leading to and from low-speed roadways within the area, and thus must be designed with this purpose in mind.

It is recommended that the illuminance along the deceleration lane be allowed to vary (see figure 24-22), but the maximum illuminance should occur at the gore point between the deceleration lane and the beginning of the interior roadways. Similarly, a high illuminance level should occur at the exit gore. Illumination may decrease from this point to a point where the motorist can be considered to have merged with the through traffic. The motorist on the through lanes must be able to see an exiting vehicle, make a proper decision and adjust to the traffic flow. The decreased illuminance is desirable for the merging motorist because it facilitates

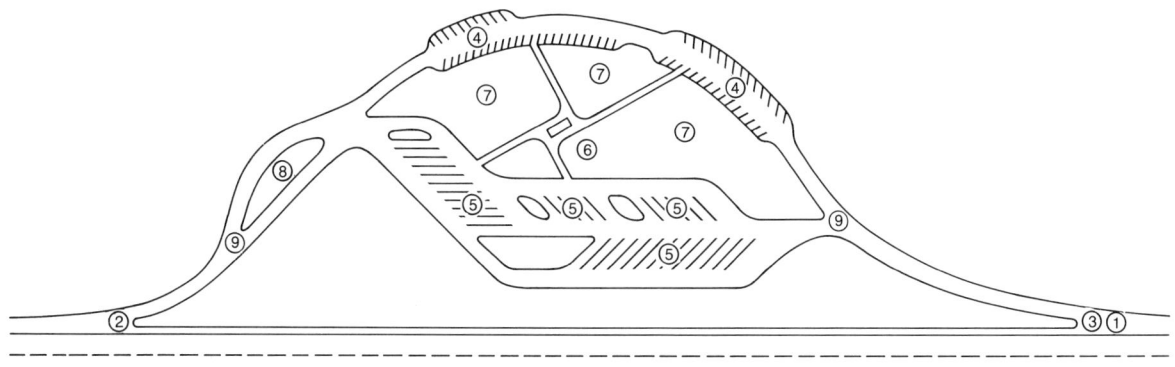

Fig. 24-21. Typical layout of roadway rest area, (1) deceleration lanes; (2) acceleration lanes; (3) gore area; (4) automobile parking; (5) truck parking; (6) comfort station; (7) picnic area; (8) waste station; and (9) interior roadway.

adaptation from the illuminated rest area to the unlighted roadway.

It is recommended that luminaires be used that confine the main light to the deceleration and acceleration lanes and restrict high-angle brightness. In the event that the main roadway is continuously lighted beyond the confines of the rest area, deceleration and acceleration lanes should be lighted to a level equal to that of the main roadway.

Interior Roadways. Interior roadways are those between the entrance or exit points and the parking areas.

As these roadways are off the main highway, the designer may select another type of luminaire than that used on the highway. The designer should keep in mind, however, that there may be an added maintenance problem when several different types of luminaires and lamps are required within one area.

Parking Areas. Illumination of both automobile and truck parking areas should be designed so that, from the vehicle, the motorist can distinguish features of the area including pedestrians. The area should be lighted

so that a motorist can read signage and be directed by it to various parts of the area.

Careful attention should be paid to areas, such as handicap ramps and sanitary disposal stations, which may require special detailing.

Activity Areas. Activity areas are those designed for pedestrian use. Major activity areas are those which include such structures as comfort stations and information centers, as well as the walkways between those locations and the parking area. Minor activity areas are those which include picnic tables and dog walks, and their associated walkways and facilities. Generally, the illuminance in the major activity areas will be higher than those in the minor areas.

Area floodlighting may be provided for architectural or other purposes. Care should be taken to ensure that stray light is not directed toward, or reflected from, the main roadway toward the passing motorist.

Maintenance. Rest areas are frequently in remote, isolated regions and require more rigid maintenance and supervision than facilities which can be visited more regularly by maintenance and security personnel.

Parking Facility Lighting[6]

Objectives. Parking facility lighting is vital for traffic safety, for protection against assault, theft and vandalism, for convenience and comfort to the user, and, in many instances, for business attraction.

Types of Facilities. For lighting purposes, parking facilities can be classified as either *open* or *covered*. Most parking facilities will be either one type or the other, but in a multilevel parking structure, the roof level will be considered open while the lower levels will be considered covered.

Open Parking Facilities. The illumination requirements of an open parking facility depend on the amount of usage it receives. Three levels of activity have been established and are designated as *high*, *medium* and

Fig. 24-22. Recommended Illuminance Levels for Roadway Rest Areas*

Rest Area	Illuminances**		Uniformity† Ratio
	Lux	Footcandles	
Entrance and Exit			
Access Lanes	3 to 6	.3 to .6	6:1 to 3:1
Gores	6	.6	3:1
Interior Roadways	6	.6	3:1
Parking Areas‡	11	1.0	
Activity Areas			
Major	11	1.0	3:1
Minor	5	.5	6:1

* The illuminance values recommended represent the condition just prior to cleaning and/or group relamping as calculated and planned in the design procedure.
** Average.
† Average to minimum.
‡ 6 lux [0.6 footcandles] minimum.

low. These levels reflect both traffic and pedestrian activity and are illustrated by, but not limited to, the following examples:

High activity:

- Major league athletic events
- Major cultural or civic events
- Regional shopping centers
- Fast food facilities

Medium activity:

- Community shopping centers
- Office parks
- Hospital parking areas
- Transportation parking (airports, commuter lots, etc.)
- Cultural, civic or recreational events
- Residential complex parking

Low activity:

- Neighborhood shopping
- Industrial employee parking
- Educational facility parking
- Church parking

If the level of nighttime activity involves a large number of vehicles, then the examples above for low and medium activity properly belong in the next higher level.

Covered Parking Facilities. Four critical areas can be identified within covered parking facilities: general parking and pedestrian areas; ramps and corners; entrance areas; and stairways. These critical areas can require lighting both day and night. The first of these areas is considered to be the same as for an open parking facility. The second area is self-explanatory. The third area (entrance) is defined as the entryway into the covered portion of the parking structure from the portal to a point 15 m (50 ft) beyond the edge of covering on the structure. The fourth area again is self-explanatory.

Illuminance Recommendations. Recommendations have been established for both open parking facilities (outdoor) and covered parking facilities (structures), as shown in figure 24-23. These recommendations are given to provide for the safe movement of traffic, for satisfactory vision for pedestrians and for the guidance of both vehicles and pedestrians. They are the lowest acceptable levels consistent with the seeing task involved and the need to deter vandalism while at the same time meeting energy constraints. Customer convenience, closed circuit television surveillance and customer attraction may require a higher level of lighting in some circumstances.

In open parking facilities, a *general parking and pedestrian area* is defined as one where pedestrian conflicts with vehicles are likely to occur. A *vehicular use area (only)* is defined as one where conflicts with pedestrians are not likely to occur. These are areas such as service areas or access roads.

It should be noted that, whereas figure 24-23 specifies *average* levels for the vehicular area in open park-

Fig. 24-23. Recommended Maintained Horizontal Illuminances for Parking Facilities

(a) Open Parking Facilities

	General Parking and Pedestrian Area			Vehicle Use Area (only)		
Level of Activity	Lux (Minimum on Pavement)	Footcandles (Minimum on Pavement)	Uniformity Ratio (Average:Minimum)	Lux (Average on Pavement)	Footcandles (Average on Pavement)	Uniformity Ratio (Average:Minimum)
High	10	0.9	4:1	22	2	3:1
Medium	6	0.6	4:1	11	1	3:1
Low*	2	0.2	4:1	5	0.5	4:1

(b) Covered Parking Facilities

	Day		Night		
Areas	Lux (Average on Pavement)†	Footcandles (Average on Pavement)†	Lux (Average on Pavement)	Footcandles (Average (Average:Minimum)	Uniformity Ratio
General parking and Pedestrian areas	54	5	54	5	4:1
Ramps and corners	110	10	54	5	4:1
Entrance areas Stairways	540	50	54	5	4:1

* This recommendation is based on the requirement to maintain security at any time in areas where there is a low level of nighttime activity.
† Sum of electric lighting and daylight.
   See chapter 11, Illuminance Selection.

ing facilities and for covered parking facilities, it specifies *minimum* levels for the pedestrian areas of open parking facilities. The reason for this is that an absolute minimum of lighting is considered necessary for the identification of features or pedestrian safety, which should be achieved at all points.

Special Considerations. Lighting of access roads to all types of parking facilities should match the local highway lighting, as much as possible. The average maintained illuminance should be compatible with local conditions. The average-to-minimum uniformity ratio should not exceed 3 : 1.

In all parking facilities, consideration should be given to color rendition, uniformity of lighting and minimizing glare. Users sometimes have trouble identifying their cars under light sources with poor color rendering characteristics. Uniformities less than recommended can detract from safety and security. Glare can affect the ability to perceive objects or obstructions clearly.

In many parking facilities, closed-circuit television is deemed necessary. When the camera tube is specified, the lighting level, the type of light source, the distribution pattern of luminaires and the aiming of the camera must be considered in order to ensure effective results.

From the standpoint of energy management, it may be desirable to reduce the lighting levels in certain parking facilities during periods of reduced activity. For example, during peak use, the high-activity lighting levels may be required. During inactive periods only security lighting will be necessary.

Special Considerations for Open Facilities. In open parking facilities, exits, entrances, loading zones, pedestrian crossings and collector lanes should be given special consideration to permit ready identification and to enhance safety.

Lighting for outdoor pedestrian stairways may require a luminaire on every landing with additional units in between if required for safety. It may be necessary to call attention to changes in elevation where steps are present.

Parking facilities for rest or scenic areas adjacent to roadways generally employ lower illuminances. See the subsection on Rest Areas.

Support poles should be located so as not to be damaged by automobiles being parked. The overhang of a typical automobile is approximately 0.5–1.0 m (1.5–3.3 ft) in front, and 1.5 m (5 ft) in the rear.

Vandalism is an important consideration with open parking facilities. Damage can generally be reduced by mounting luminaires at least 3 m (10 ft) above grade. However, greater mounting heights are recommended.

Special Consideration for Covered Facilities. In covered parking facilities, vertical illuminances of objects

such as columns and walls should be equal to the horizontal values given in figure 24-23. These vertical values should be for a location 1.8 m (6 ft) above the pavement.

In covered parking facilities the design should be arranged so that some lighting can be left on for security reasons. The low level from figure 24-23 for open parking facilities can be used for this purpose.

Emergency luminaires in covered parking facilities should be located so as to provide a minimum lighting level in case of an interruption to the normal power supply. In general, these units should provide approximately 10% of the levels in figure 24-23, or applicable local code requirements.

Illuminated Roadway Signs[7]

Motorists may stop or reduce speed at roadway signs that are difficult to read, and thus create a hazardous condition. Proper sign lighting can aid rapid and accurate recognition of the sign shape, color and message.

Lighting for roadway signs becomes more significant as: (1) volume of traffic increases, (2) complexity of highway design increases, (3) likelihood of adverse weather increases and (4) ambient luminance increases.

Ambient Luminance. The background luminance against which a sign will be viewed by a motorist is called its *ambient luminance*. Three categories of ambient luminance (high, medium and low) can be identified:

- High: Areas with high street lighting levels and brightly lighted advertising signs
- Medium: Areas with small commercial developments and lighted roadways and interchanges
- Low: Rural areas without lighting or areas with very low levels of lighting

High levels of ambient luminance can make sign lighting mandatory in order to ensure sign legibility for decisive driver action.

Light Source Selection. Energy consumption is a major consideration that must be balanced by other factors, such as color rendering, ambient temperature and maintenance. Selection should be based on efficacy and lamp life in addition to careful evaluation of color rendering abilities. Lighting must maintain the color rendering as close as practical to that seen under daylight conditions.

Illumination Recommendations. There are three types of lighted signs: *externally lighted signs, internally lighted signs,* and *luminous source message signs* (where the message is formed by lamps).

Fig. 24-24. Recommended Maintained Levels for Externally Lighted Roadway Signs

Ambient Light Level	Sign Illuminance		Sign Luminance*
	lux	footcandles	Candelas per square meter
Low	100-200	10-20	22-44
Medium	200-400	20-40	44-89
High	400-800	40-80	89-178

* Based on maintained reflectance of 70 percent for white sign letters.

Fig. 24-25. Recommended Maintained Luminance for Internally Lighted Roadway Signs

	Ambient light level		
	Low	Medium	High
Candelas per square meter	240	520	1000
Candelas per square foot	24	52	100

Externally Lighted Signs. Recommended illuminances for externally lighted signs are shown in figure 24-24. A maximum-to-minimum illuminance uniformity ratio of 6:1 should not be exceeded for acceptable appearance of the sign face. Lower ratios will produce a more legible sign.

Internally Lighted Signs. Recommended luminances for internally lighted signs are shown in figure 24-25. These luminance values are for a white translucent material forming the legend and the border. For colors other than white, higher luminance values may be required to obtain the same contrast with the background.

The maximum-to-minimum luminance ratio of the sign background should not exceed 6:1, and no adjacent areas 0.3×0.3 m (1×1 ft) should have a luminance difference greater than 20%. The maximum-to-minimum luminance ratio for the entire sign legend should not exceed 6:1. Lastly, the average luminance contrast between legend and background should be greater than 10:1.

Luminous Source Message Signs. Recommended levels have been established only for a variable message sign composed of a matrix of luminous sources that can be selectively lighted. These levels are the same as those given in figure 24-25.

COMPUTATIONAL METHODS

The basic computations that follow apply to conventional roadway lighting systems mounted alongside the street or highway at heights of 5–20 m (15–60 ft) above the pavement. The data and techniques can also be applied to adjacent walkways, median strips and other areas. Illuminance, light loss factors and luminance are

important in roadway lighting, but because of their general nature, illuminance calculations and light loss factors are discussed in chapter 9. Roadway luminance calculations, because of their unique r tables and roadway coordinate system, are included in this chapter. Special computations relating to area lighting with high-mast equipment over 20 m (60 ft) above the pavement, to walkways and bikeways and to veiling luminance are also covered in this chapter.

The recommended design values, as well as uniformity ratios, are given in figures 24-8, 24-9 and 24-10. These represent the lowest maintained values that are currently considered appropriate for the kinds of roadways or walkways in various areas. Numerous installations have been made at higher levels. Furthermore, the recommendations assume the use of applicable types of luminaire light distribution, lamp size, mounting heights, spacing and transverse locations. These figures do not represent initial readings, but should be the lowest in-service values of systems designed with the proper light loss factors. The tables indicate whether the values are averages or minima for each area.

Light Loss Factors

Once design values for illuminance or luminance are established and a preliminary choice of a luminaire is made, light loss factors (LLF) can be evaluated. Several of these factors are affected by time-dependent depreciation effects. Others will exist initially and continue through the life of the installation. However, all factors should be studied and attempts should be made to improve LLFs wherever possible. Consult chapter 9 for details on LLFs that are not included in this chapter.

The following LLFs are applicable to roadway lighting:

Lamp Lumen Depreciation. Consult the manufacturer.

Luminaire Dirt Depreciation. The accumulation of dirt on luminaires results in a loss in light output. This loss is known as the luminaire dirt depreciation (LDD) factor and is estimated by dirt category (very clean, clean, moderate, dirty, or very dirty) from definitions given in figure 24-26. The LDD is found from the appropriate dirt category curve in figure 24-26 and the proper elapsed time in years of the planned cleaning cycle.

Luminaire Ambient Temperature. Consult the manufacturer.

Voltage to Luminaire. Consult the utility.

Ballast and Lamp Factor.[8,9] Consult the manufacturer.

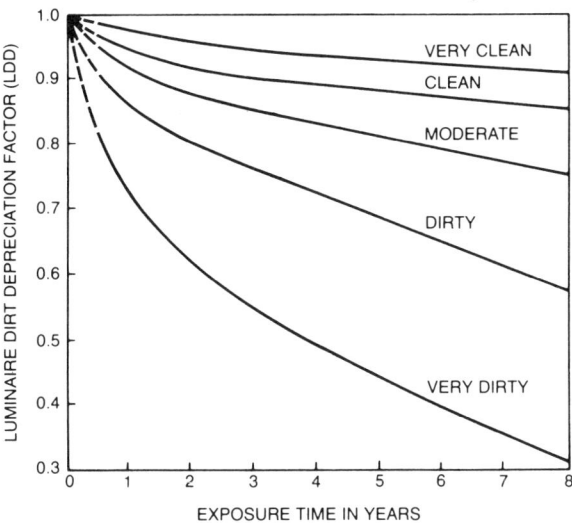

SELECT THE APPROPRIATE CURVE IN ACCORDANCE WITH THE TYPE OF AMBIENT AS DESCRIBED BY THE FOLLOWING EXAMPLES:

VERY CLEAN—No nearby smoke or dust generating activities and a low ambient containment level. Light traffic. Generally limited to residential or rural areas. The ambient particulate levels is no more than 150 micrograms per cubic meter.

CLEAN—No nearby smoke or dust generating activities. Moderate to heavy traffic. The ambient particulate level is no more than 300 micrograms per cubic meter.

MODERATE—Moderate smoke or dust generating activities nearby. The ambient particulate level is no more than 600 micrograms per cubic meter.

DIRTY—Smoke or dust plumes generating by nearby activities may occasionally envelope the luminaires.

VERY DIRTY—As above but the luminaires are commonly enveloped by smoke or dust plumes.

Fig. 24-26. Chart for estimating roadway luminaire dirt depreciation factor for enclosed and gasketed luminaires.

Luminaire Surface Depreciation. Experience is the best predictor; no factors are available at present.

Burnouts. Routine maintenance is required.

Total Light Loss Factor. The total light loss factor is simply the product of all the contributing factors described above. Where factors are not applicable, they are omitted. If, at this point, it is found that the total light loss factor is excessive, it may be desirable to reselect the luminaire or lamp, or modify the cleaning and maintenance schedule.

Another factor which must be considered in the calculation is the change in the performance of individual components as a result of operation with a range of different associated luminaire components. For example, a lamp will not always have the same lumen output when used with ballasts of different manufacturers or when installed in luminaires of different design or manufacturer. This should be taken into account in the calculations for luminance or illuminance. The factor used for calculations can be in the range of 5–15%.

Determination of Average and Point Illuminance

The average illuminance over a large pavement area may be calculated by means of an average-footcandle calculation, a "utilization curve" (which is almost never used today) or an isolux (isofootcandle) curve, or by computing the illuminance at a large number of points and averaging the values found.

Average-Lux (Average-Footcandle) Computation. The formulas for determination of average horizontal illuminance in roadway lighting are the same ones used

for average illuminance in chapter 9. See chapter 9, and the associated sample calculations in that chapter, for roadway applications.

Utilization Curves. Utilization curves, available for various types of luminaires, afford a practical method for the determination of average illuminance over the roadway surface where lamp size, mounting height, width of roadway, overhang and spacing between luminaires are known or assumed. Conversely, the desired spacing or any other unknown factor may readily be determined if the other factors are given.

A *coefficient of utilization* is derived from the utilization curve and is the percentage of rated lamp lumens which will fall on either of two striplike areas of infinite length, one extending in front of the luminaire (street side), and the other behind the luminaire (house side), when the luminaire is level and oriented over the roadway in a manner equivalent to that in which it was tested. Since the roadway width is expressed in terms of a ratio of luminaire mounting height to roadway width, the term has no dimensions.

Isolux (Isofootcandle) Diagram. An isolux diagram is a graphical representation of points of equal illuminance connected by a continuous line. Such diagrams are convenient for making point illuminance determinations, and are provided by the manufacturer of the luminaire under consideration. They have become less common since the introduction of powerful computer programs which can quickly and easily make point-by-point roadway lighting calculations.

Point-by-Point Calculation Method. For a complete description of the classical point-by-point calculation method and an example of its application to roadway lighting, see chapter 9.

Determination of Luminance

Luminance values at a point may be calculated from photometric data obtained and provided by most manufacturers for luminaires associated with roadways. Parameters of position are important determinations that should be consistently applied for both luminance calculations and measurements.

The luminance of a point P (see figure 24-2e) can be written as a sum of contributions from all n luminaires:

$$L_P = \sum_{i=1}^{n} \frac{r(\beta_i, \gamma_i) I(\phi_i, \gamma_i)}{10,000 H^2} \qquad (24\text{-}1)$$

where all symbols, except luminous intensity (I), are defined in figure 24-2. The factor 10,000 appears in the denominator because the values in figure 24-2 should have been multiplied by 10,000. (If the values are taken directly from Fig. 24-2 without multiplying by 10,000, the factor 10,000 in the denominator of Equation 24-1 should be omitted.) The value of I must be depreciated by the light loss factor times any equipment factors.

Calculation and Measurement Parameters. (See figures 24-2 and 24-27.)

- Observer eye height: 1.45 m (4.75 ft) above grade
- Line of sight of observer: downward 1° below horizontal over a distance of 83 m (272 ft); parallel to edge of roadway along lines $\frac{1}{4}$ roadway line width from edges of each lane (two lines per lane)
- Lighting system to be measured: smooth and level, at least 10 mounting heights long

- Number of points per line: at least 10, not more than 5 m (16.5 ft) apart
- Area covered by measurement and calculations: all points between two luminaires on one side of roadway (see figure 24-27)
- Calculation-point location with respect to contributing luminaires: at least one luminaire behind, and at least three ahead of the calculation point P
- Luminaire light distribution data: based on initial installed values using actual lamp-luminaire performance
- Luminance values: to be calculated using the r tables in figure 24-2
- Horizontal illuminance E_h: to be printed and recorded at the same points as the luminance values, as a reference
- Luminance L: to be printed and recorded at the same points as the horizontal illuminance values
- Average luminance L_{avg}: to be determined by averaging all values of the evaluated roadway section
- Longitudinal luminance uniformity: lane uniformity L_L to be determined as the ratio of the maximum to the minimum luminance in any one quarter-lane line, taking the worst (highest) ratio as the rating for the roadway
- Average luminance uniformity: to be determined by rating the average luminance L_{avg} to the minimum found in any of the lines within the roadway
- Maximum luminance uniformity: to be determined by rating the maximum luminance found in any of the lines to the minimum found in any of the lines within the roadway

For a simplified graphical method of luminance calculations see reference 3.

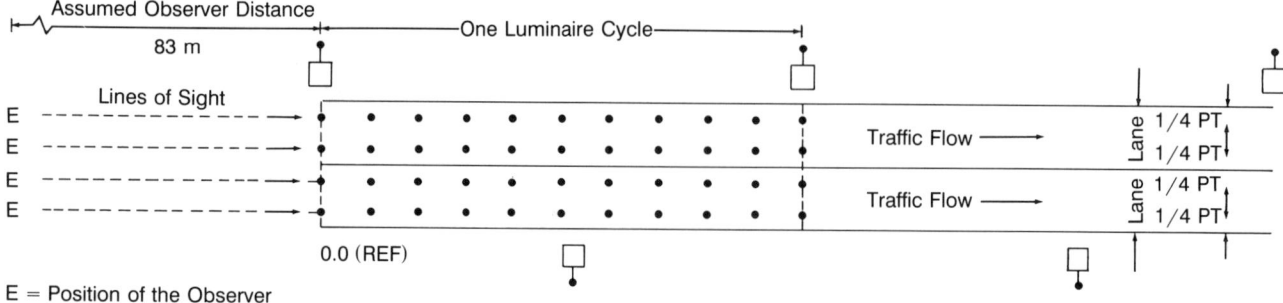

Fig. 24-27. Luminance calculation points.

Veiling Luminance

The L_v (expressed in cd/m^2) of a roadway lighting system can be determined from the observer's position by using the following empirically derived formula[11] to calculate the L_v contributed by each luminaire separately, and then summing the individual L values:

$$L_v = \frac{10E_v}{\theta^2 + 1.5\theta} \qquad (24\text{-}2)$$

where

E_v = vertical illuminance in the plane of the pupil of the observer's eye,

θ = angle between the line of sight and the luminaire in degrees.

Note that the line of sight is a line parallel to the curb line of the roadway and located away from the edge of the roadway in one of the quarter-lane planes, at an eye height of 1.45 m (4.75 ft) above the road. (See figure 24-28.)

The number of luminaire cycles is to be the same as that for determining the pavement luminance. The L_v for an entire system of n luminaires is therefore

$$L_v = \sum_{i=1}^{n} \frac{10E_{vi}}{\theta^2 + 1.5\theta} \qquad (24\text{-}3)$$

Walkway and Bikeway Lighting

The procedure to determine the horizontal illuminance values on pedestrian ways for safe and comfortable use is similar to that followed for roadways.

Because the design of roadway lighting places greater emphasis on achieving proper illuminance on the roadway, it is customary for the lighting system to be initially selected to suit the needs of the roadway. Then, the system is checked to determine if the sidewalk illuminance levels and uniformity are adequate. If not, the designer may modify the luminaire type or spacing, may provide supplemental lighting primarily for the sidewalk area, or may do both in order to achieve proper illuminance on both roadway and sidewalk.

In some areas where personal security is a problem and identification of another pedestrian at a distance is important, the recommended levels on the right side of figure 24-10 apply. These recommendations are stated in terms of the average vertical illuminance reaching a plane surface 1.8 m (6 ft) above the walkway and perpendicular to the centerline of the walkway.

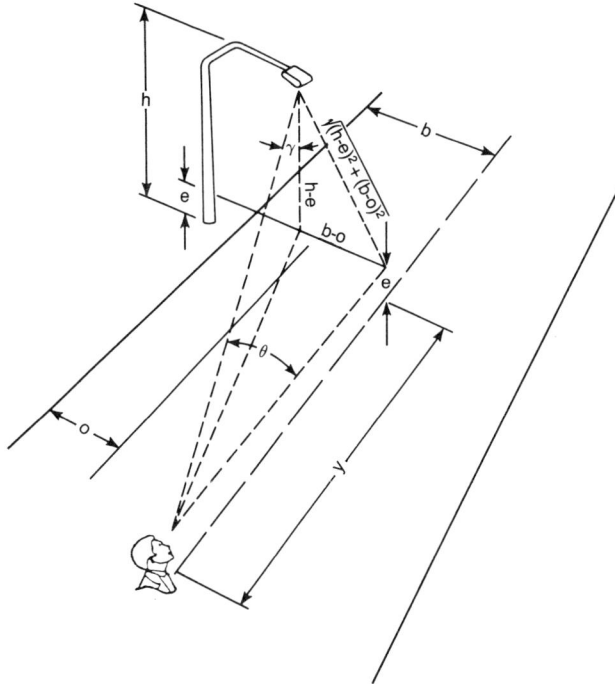

Fig. 24-28. Angular relationships for calculating L_v (Veiling Luminance) from a single luminaire.
Note:

$$\gamma\,\arctan \frac{\sqrt{y^2 + (b-o)^2}}{h-e}$$

$$\times\,\theta\,\arctan \frac{\sqrt{(h-e)^2 + (b-o)^2}}{y}$$

where

h = mounting height of luminaire above the road surface in meters.

e = eye height above the road surface in meters.

The calculation procedure for vertical illuminance may be found in chapter 9.

LIGHT POLLUTION AND LIGHT TRESPASS[11]

As people increasingly use facilities of many types during hours of darkness, the issues of light pollution and light trespass become extremely important. These issues should be considered any time an outdoor lighting design, including roadway lighting, is prepared.

Light pollution can be either astronomical or atmospheric, or both. It is caused by stray or reflected light. Dust, water vapor and other atmospheric pollutants reflect this light, causing the sky glow found over many urban areas. Although this sky glow is not injurious to people, it can interfere with astronomical observations and animal behavior patterns.

Astronomical light pollution is of concern in areas where astronomical observatories are located. In addition to major observatories, there are many small optical observatories at or near universities used for instruction and research. The use of a monochromatic light source such as low-pressure sodium (LPS), which can be excluded by special filters, is preferred by astronomers. However, this expedient will not reduce *atmospheric* light pollution. Recommendations to help control light pollution include:

1. Street and area lighting systems, including lighting for sports and commercial areas such as parking lots and vehicle sales lots, should be designed to minimize or eliminate light emission above the horizontal plane. It must be realized that this will not completely eliminate upward light, since reflected light from the ground or pavement is an important contributor to upward emission.
2. Lighting systems that project light upward, such as architectural and sign lighting, should be designed to minimize the amount of light that does not illuminate the target area. Where possible, sign lighting should be from luminaires positioned above the sign rather than below.
3. All outdoor lighting, including advertising sign lighting and interior high-rise office building lighting, should be switched off after use, unless needed for safety and security. Usually safety and security lighting, with the exception of street lighting, can be at a lower level than that needed when the area is in general use.

Light trespass is a subjective notion, since it relates to an unmeasurable or undefinable quantity in many cases, and often cannot be controlled. A typical example is the "light shining in my eye" complaint. Responding to this complaint might require the elimination of a luminaire deemed essential for the safety and security of a street or off-street area, but it could result in an additional complaint from a neighboring resident about the lack of illumination without the luminaire in place.

Light trespass complaints can usually be classified into one of two categories:

- Unwanted light illuminating an area or property
- Excessive brightness in the normal field of vision (nuisance glare)

Efforts have been made in numerous jurisdictions to write ordinances or laws controlling light trespass. It is essential that ordinances be written by those who understand the problems and can write an ordinance which is comprehensive and enforceable. An ordinance which defines trespass only in terms of horizontal illu-

minance may miss the point entirely, because it is often vertical illuminance that creates the problem. A bright object against a dark background may be an annoyance, even though there is no horizontal illuminance at the location of the complainant.

Recommendations for the control of light trespass are:

1. Follow the recommendations provided above to control light pollution.
2. Inspect the areas adjacent to the design location to identify potential problems, and consider them in the lighting design.
3. Select equipment which does not have a high-angle, high-candela distribution.
4. Try to contain light within the design area by careful selection of luminaire location, mounting height and light distribution. Choose equipment which can be shielded if an anticipated problem occurs.
5. Keep floodlighting aiming angles as low as possible during both design and installation.

REFERENCES

1. Illuminating Engineering Society of North America. 1983. *American national standard practice for roadway lighting, ANSI / IES RP-8-1983.* New York: Illuminating Engineering Society of North America.
2. Commission Internationale de l'Éclairage. 1982. *Calculation and measurement of luminance and illuminance in road lighting.* CIE Publication 30.2. Paris: Bureau Central de la CIE.
3. IES. Roadway Lighting Committee. 1984. *Graphical methods for designing with the 1983 standard practice for tunnel lighting.* New York: Illuminating Engineering Society.
4. IES. Roadway Lighting Committee. [To be published.] *American national standard practice for tunnel lighting (proposed).* New York: Illuminating Engineering Society of North America.
5. Lott, L. 1976. King's Cross tunnel lighting. *IES Light. Rev. (Australia)* 30(3):61.
6. IES. Roadway Lighting Committee. Subcommittee on Off Roadway Facilities. 1985. *Lighting roadway safety rest areas.* IES CP-38-1985. New York: Illuminating Engineering Society of North America.
7. IES. Roadway Lighting Committee. Highway Signs Subcommittee. 1983. Recommended practice for roadway sign lighting [IES RP-19-1983]. *J. Illum. Eng. Soc.* 12(3):141–145.
8. IES. Roadway Lighting Committee. Subcommittee on Off-Roadway Facilities. 1985. Lighting for parking facilities [IES RP-20-1984]. *J. Illum. Eng. Soc.* 14(2):616–623.
9. IES. Committee on Testing Procedures. Subcommittee on Photometry of Outdoor Luminaires. 1970. IES approved method for determining luminaire-lamp-ballast combination operating factors for high intensity dis-

charge luminaires. *Illum. Eng.* 65(12):718–721. IES. Testing Procedures Committee. Subcommittee on Photometry of Outdoor Luminaires. 1986. *IES approved guide for identifying operating factors for installed high intensity discharge (HID) luminaires.* IES LM-61-1986. New York: Illuminating Engineering Society of North America.

10. Fry, G. A. 1954. A re-evaluation of the scattering theory of glare. *Illum. Eng.* 49(2):98–102.

11. IES. Roadway Lighting Committee. Subcommittee on Light Trespass. 1985. A statement on astronomical light pollution and light trespass [IES CP-46-1985]. *J. Illum. Eng. Soc.* 14(2):658–662.

Aviation Lighting

25

Aviation lighting falls into two principal categories: aircraft lighting, on or inside the aircraft, and aviation ground lighting, on the landing facility or in the airport.

Aircraft lighting, categorized by location as exterior lighting, crew station lighting and passenger interior lighting, covers a broad spectrum of lighting equipment, ranging from that used for visual collision avoidance to instrument lighting to decorative lighting in the passenger cabins.

Aviation ground lighting provides for the illumination of aprons, hardstands, parking areas, taxiways and runways and for signal lighting. Signal lighting conveys information to pilots by means of color, location, flash characteristics and pattern rather than by illumination of areas or objects. To provide additional visual guidance to pilots, other visual aids such as reflectors and markings are also used.

Standardization

In both ground lighting and aircraft lighting, standardization is absolutely essential. The interstate and international scope of operations make the establishment of color and pattern standards imperative for all of the visual aid systems necessary to operate aircraft safely. These regulations and standards are originated by government agencies and by military and international organizations such as the International Civil Aviation Organization (ICAO) and the North Atlantic Treaty Organization (NATO). In this section, the relevant regulations or regulating body is usually mentioned; before planning or modifying any aviation lighting or visual aid, the appropriate agency or standards must be consulted.

AIRCRAFT LIGHTING

Aircraft lighting equipment, particularly that used on the exterior surfaces of the airplane, must perform satisfactorily over a wide range of environmental conditions, including temperatures, pressures and vibration, not normally found in most lighting applications.

For the most part, luminaires are designed to perform a specific function when installed in specific loca-

tions in specific types of airplanes. For example, all airplanes are equipped with position lights and, for airplanes carrying passengers, small luminaires for reading. Usually position lights are designed to fit within the wing tip area, which is different for each type of airplane. The needs of the passenger dictate interior design such as luminaires for reading. Designs may vary among the different airline companies operating the same type of aircraft; therefore, there is little opportunity to achieve significant standardization in luminaires for interior aircraft lighting. It is more likely that lighting functions will be performed by luminaires that can be adapted to different space configuration and environmental requirements.

Aircraft Categories

The broad categories of aircraft are general aviation, commercial and military.

General Aviation Categories. General aviation includes small private, single-engine airplanes and sophisticated multiengine, turbine-powered airplanes used for business. Also included are those aircraft used for air taxi and charter operations.

The minimum lighting requirements for these aircraft are found in Part 23 of the United States Federal Aviation Regulations (FAR) for fixed-wing airplanes, and in Part 27 for helicopters. Part 91 (Operating Requirements) requires the use of position or navigation lights and anticollision lights for night operations. Position lights (red and green wing tip lights and white tail light) are so named because they are intended to indicate to an observer the position of the aircraft. Landing lights are required on aircraft for some commercial operations.

Commercial Category. Commercial, or airline, aircraft must include luminaires meeting FAR Part 25 for fixed-wing aircraft and Part 29 for transport-type helicopters. Operating requirements for airline operations are found in Part 121 of the FAR. These include minimum lighting requirements for and use of position, anticollision, landing, instrument and indicator lights, wing ice floodlights and signage (emergency egress, no-smoking and fasten-seat-belt signs). One large wide-bodied transport aircraft has more than 560 individual luminaires of 55 different types.

Military Category. Military aircraft also consist of a wide variety of types, ranging from relatively simple, small trainers to high-performance fighters, bombers, large transport aircraft and helicopters. While military aircraft have many of the same lighting requirements as general aviation or commercial ones, they will frequently require special luminaires for military functions such as formation flying, in-flight refueling and approach to aircraft carrier decks. In the United States, there are differences in requirements for intensity distribution for both position and anticollision lights among the FAR, Navy, Air Force and Army specifications. Navy exterior lighting requirements are generally covered in Specification MIL-L-006730; navy interior lighting requirements, in Specification MIL-L-18276. Requirements for lighting of Air Force and Army airplanes are described in Specification MIL-L-6503H. Other specifications, usually referenced in these documents, have been issued for various detail lighting requirements.

Some international standardization is attempted by use of documents published by the ICAO for civil aviation and NATO for military aviation.

Aircraft Electrical Systems

Most new aircraft are now equipped with either 28-V dc or 120/208-V, 400-Hz, three-phase electrical systems. Until recently all small single-engine airplanes were equipped with 14-V dc systems. In some cases, the same luminaires can be used with appropriate lamps to produce the same lighting performance on either 14 or 28 V. In many cases lamps for aircraft using 400-Hz systems may be lower voltage (6–10 V) and operated from individual transformers. Low-voltage incandescent filaments can have increased strength for resistance to shock and vibration as well as more compact size for improved optical efficiencies.

Exterior Lighting of Aircraft

Position Lights. For many years, aircraft have been equipped with a system of navigation lights, or *position lights*, consisting of red lights on the left wing tip, green lights on the right wing tip and white lights on the tail of the aircraft—or, more recently, on the trailing edge of each wing tip. These lights are basic to all systems and are required for night operation. Intensities of red and green position lights in the forward direction on different aircraft range from 40 cd (minimum required by FAR) to more than 300 cd in some cases. Commercial aircraft are commonly equipped with dual position lights for redundancy. Having the white tail lights on the trailing edge of the wing tips or on the outboard

trailing edges of the horizontal stabilizer permits easier maintenance and also provides a better assessment of attitude when the aircraft is viewed from the rear.

Anticollision Lights. Anticollision lights may be either red or white. Current Federal Aviation Regulations require that these lights produce a minimum of 400 cd of effective intensity near the horizontal plane and 20 cd at vertical angles of 75° up or down. Condenser discharge flashtubes (strobes) are commonly used for both red and white anticollision lights. Many aircraft are equipped with anticollision light systems which include red flashing lights located top and bottom of the fuselage and supplemented with white flashing lights on the wing tips. Strobe lights are operated at energy levels of 15–100 J per flash and flash rates of 50–80 flashes per minute. Effective intensities range from 100 to more than 4000 cd. Locating the white high-intensity flashing lights on the wing tips produces significantly fewer problems caused by reflections or backscatter which may interfere with the crew's vision from the cockpit.

High-intensity white lights must not be used during taxiing operations at the airport, because they may be only a few meters (a few feet) from the pilot of another aircraft. It has become common practice at airports to operate the red anticollision lights to indicate that turbine engines are operating while an airplane is stationary.

Landing Lights. Landing lights are commonly equipped with 400–1000-W PAR-46 sealed-beam lamps. Large aircraft will commonly be equipped with four of these lamps in a landing light system with one in each outboard wing section in retractable luminaires and one in a fixed unit in each inboard wing root. On some aircraft, fixed lighting is located on the landing gear struts. Landing lights are commonly used to improve the aircraft's visibility, particularly when aircraft are within 16 km (10 mi) of a tower-controlled airport or lower than 3000 m (10,000 ft). To avoid having to extend landing gear prematurely, some airplanes are now being equipped with fixed recognition lights in the wing tips or wing leading edges for identification purposes. These lights will usually produce a relatively narrow beam with an intensity of approximately 70,000 cd.

Helicopters are equipped with search and landing lights which are controlled in both elevation and azimuth by operating a four-way switch, commonly located on the collective pitch control.

Taxi Lights. Taxi lights normally have a wide horizontal and a narrow vertical beam and are commonly mounted on landing gear struts. In some cases, they are mounted on the movable section of a nose wheel strut as shown in figure 25-1. Dual-filament sealed-

Fig. 25-1. Taxi light mounted on nose wheel strut.

beam lamps are commonly used, where operation of one or both filaments will provide a specified taxi or landing light pattern. In other cases, there are fixed taxi lights located in wing root cavities to illuminate areas outboard and ahead of the aircraft so as to identify taxiway turnoff areas.

Auxiliary Lights. All large aircraft are equipped with fixed floodlights arranged so that the crew may visually inspect wing leading-edge surfaces and nacelles at night to assess ice buildup. These lights are usually located in the side of the fuselage or in the outboard sides of the engine nacelles. Another type of exterior floodlight that has become popular consists of lights arranged to illuminate the sides of the vertical fin. These are commonly called *logo lights* and may be located on the surface of the horizontal stabilizer or, in some cases, in units on the trailing edge of the wing tips, aimed at the vertical fin.

Electroluminescent lamp strips have become very common for use as formation lights. Strips up to 100 mm (4 in.) wide and up to 1.5 m (5 ft) long are placed on the sides of the fuselage and the vertical fin and on the top and bottom surfaces of the wing tips. Modern fighter aircraft may use as much as 0.45 m^2 (700 in^2) of green electroluminescent lamps for this purpose. The luminance of these lights may be continuously varied from 0 to about 70 cd/m^2.

For in-flight refueling, tanker airplanes are equipped with a variety of incandescent floodlights and signal lights supplemented with electroluminescent striplights. The lights are designed to make it possible for the pilot of the refueling airplane to maintain the proper location with respect to the tanker and to receive pertinent information on the progress of the refueling. Modern tanker airplanes are equipped with a special anticollision or rendezvous light that consists of dual red and white flashtubes coded by a flashing color sequence. This provides a signal that unmistakably identifies the aircraft as a tanker airplane. These light assemblies have also been designed and qualified to meet stringent lightning-strike requirements.

Carrier-based aircraft are normally equipped with red, green and amber lights that can be seen in the daytime during landing operations by the landing signal officer aboard the carrier. These lights will indicate to the landing signal officer the approach attitude of the aircraft.

Crew Station Lighting[1, 2]

In sophisticated aircraft, crew station lighting has become rather complex. Self-luminous devices such as cathode-ray tubes contribute to the lighting problems of the cockpit areas. In most multiengine aircraft, the lighting is an integral part of the instrument. Switch panels are normally plastic panels about 5 mm (0.19 in.) thick that are lighted with small embedded subminiature or electroluminescent lamps. See figure 25-2.

Red instrument and panel lighting is used where the mission of the aircraft may require the pilot to maintain dark adaptation. Many U.S. Air Force airplanes are equipped with blue-white instrument lighting. The blue filters were originally added to permit operation at very low levels without the extreme yellow color associated with operation of dimmed incandescent lamps. Commercial airplanes usually use white unfiltered light from long-life 5-V subminiature incandescent lamps. See figure 25-3.

Night vision goggles (NVG) greatly amplify near-infrared energy and are commonly used by cockpit crews in various military-type airplanes. If NVG are used with ordinary instrument lights, the infrared energy from the light sources, even when dimmed virtually to extinction, will overwhelm the NVG and cause them to shut down; therefore, all instrument lighting, when used in conjunction with NVG, must be carefully limited spectrally to the shorter wavelengths with very

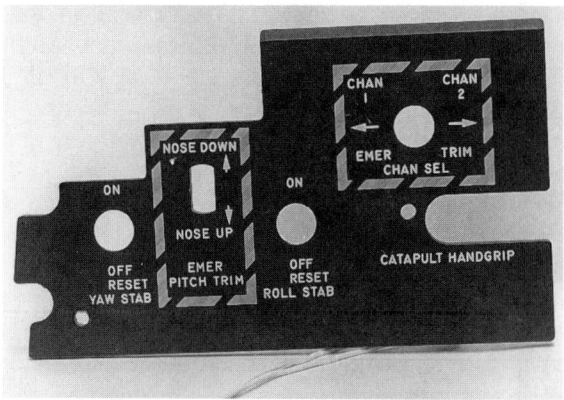

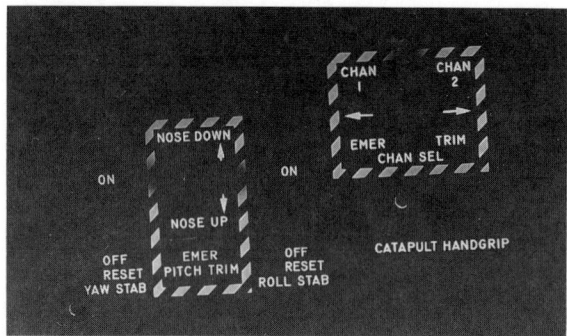

Fig. 25-2. Electroluminescent control panel. Top: unlighted daylight view. Bottom: lighted night view.

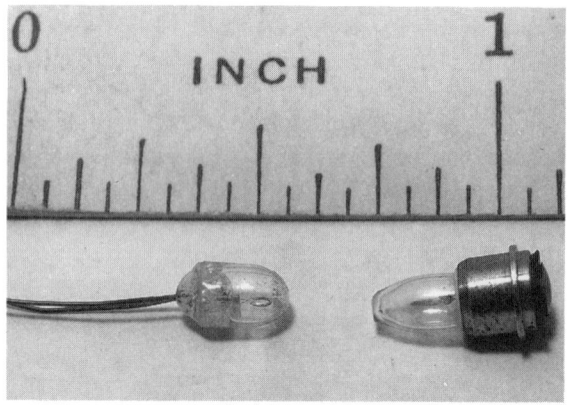

Fig. 25-3. Subminiature lamps (T-1, 5.0 V) for instrument and control-panel lighting.

little energy emitted above 600 nm. The objective is to provide illumination that is compatible with the NVG by providing approximately the same apparent visibility through the NVG as with the unaided eye. This must be accomplished without affecting the operating capabilities of the NVG.

Most aircraft are also equipped with instrument floodlighting systems in addition to integral instrument and panel lighting. This system provides low-level background lighting in order to avoid any autokinetic effect that may be produced when lighted markings are

viewed against a perfectly black background. Also, aircraft are commonly equipped with "thunderstorm" floodlights capable of providing about 1000 lx (100 fc). These lights ensure the continued visibility of instruments in case dark adaptation is suddenly destroyed by bright light such as a lightning flash.

Another important part of crew station lighting is the indicator or annunciator lights. Annunciator lights should be readable in bright sunlight producing incident illumination of 100 klx (10,000 fc).

Most airplanes are also equipped with map lights that are easily controlled by the pilot to provide a desired level of illumination on navigational charts.

Passenger Interior Lighting

Passenger interior lighting varies from one aircraft to another, since considerable use is made of lighting in conjunction with the decorative designs in the cabin. Figure 25-4 illustrates some of the cabin lighting in a wide-body jet aircraft.

Individually controlled passenger reading lights are an important part of the cabin lighting system. These lights provide a level of 250–300 lx (25–30 fc) on the reading plane. They must provide carefully controlled beam patterns to avoid interference with adjacent passengers. The distance between the luminaire and the reading plane may be less than 760 mm (30 in.) or as much as 2 m (80 in.).

A variety of lighted signs are used in the passenger interiors of airplanes. These include "no smoking," "fasten seat belts" and "return to seat" signs. In some cases, large signs are located on the forward bulkheads of compartments; in others, smaller signs are located in passenger service units for each row of seats. Frequently, the design of the sign is part of the decorative scheme in the airplane interior. Sign symbols have also become quite common.

Passenger cabins are usually equipped with general fluorescent or incandescent lighting. Valance lights over window reveals on either side of the cabin are very common. Also, many airplanes are equipped with striplights that illuminate the ceilings of the cabins from locations above the bag racks. Both incandescent and fluorescent lamps are used for this application.

Other than signs and luminaires for reading, cabin lights are dimmable by the cabin crew either continuously or in steps. Both hot- and cold-cathode fluorescent lamps are used.

Emergency Egress Lighting. Emergency egress lighting has become an important part of safety equipment in modern airline aircraft. Luminaires are installed in the ceiling to provide illuminances of more than 0.5 lx (0.05 fc) at seat arm-rest level. Other luminaires are installed to illuminate the exit areas. The Federal Aviation Administration (FAA) specifies minimum

Fig. 25-4. A portion of a modern commercial airplane, showing some of the passenger cabin lighting. (1) Individual passenger reading lights. (2) Incandescent downlights. (3) Pendant sign: No Smoking/Fasten Seat Belt. (4) Fluorescent indirect luminaire operated from inverter ballasts, fully dimmable. (5) Information sign. (6) Emergency exit signs operated from separate battery power supplies. (7) Fluorescent window reveal lights, fully dimmable.

lighting requirements for area lighting as well as the size, luminance and contrast of signs marking exits and directing passengers to these exits.

Recently adopted FAA regulations require floor-proximity emergency escape path marking. These markings must provide emergency evacuation guidance for passengers when all sources of illumination more than 1.2 m (4 ft) above the cabin aisle floor are totally obscured. All commercial airlines are now installing systems to meet this requirement. One system consists of small lamps, low on the sides of aisle seats; another consists of extruded plastic strips, including wiring and small lamps, on about 500-mm (20-in.) centers in the carpet along one side of the aisle. Small exit signs are located adjacent to all floor-level exits and over wing exits. Electroluminescent strips are used in some cases on the linoleum floor across the galley from the aisle to the exit.

All safety luminaires and signs are powered by batteries which can be activated manually or automatically on failure of the aircraft electrical power system. Areas outside the airplane such as escape slides and over-wing exit paths are also illuminated.

AVIATION GROUND LIGHTING[3-6]

Airport / Runway Classification

The ground lighting and other visual aids required at an airport are usually based upon the visibility conditions under which operations are conducted and the types of electronic navigational aids available at the airport to support such operations.

Fig. 25-5. Airport/Runway Visibility Condition Categories

Category	Runway Visual Range		Decision Height	
	Meters	Feet	Meters	Feet
I	720	2400	60	200
II	360	1200	30	100
IIIA	210	700	—	—
IIIB	45	150	—	—
IIIC	0	0	—	—

Visibility conditions are categorized according to the distance from which a pilot can detect a 10,000-cd light source (*runway visual range*, RVR) and the decision height above the runway at which a missed approach is initiated if the required visual reference has not been established (*decision height*). See figure 25-5.

Depending on the types of navigational aids available, runways are classified as visual or instrument. A *visual runway* is one intended solely for the operation of aircraft using visual approach procedures. An *instrument runway* is one suitable for an instrument approach procedure utilizing electronic navigational facilities. If these facilities provide only horizontal guidance or area navigational information, the runway is called a *nonprecision runway*. If the runway has instrument landing systems (ILS), microwave landing systems (MLS) or a precision approach radar (PAR), the runway is called a *precision instrument runway*.

Taxiway Guidance Systems

Visual taxi guidance between the runways and the destination on the airport is provided by centerline

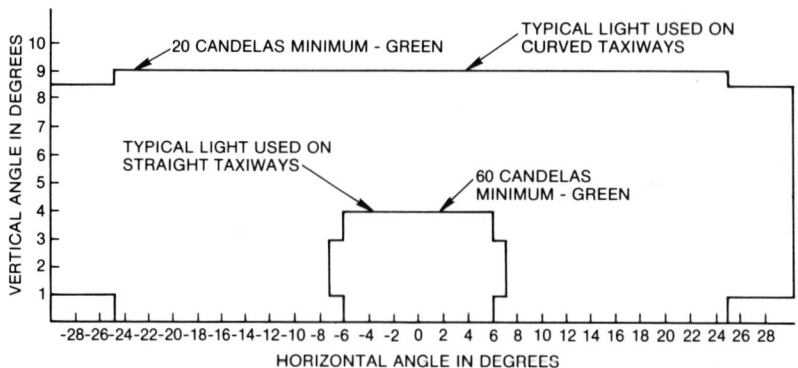

Fig. 25-6. Typical photometric characteristics for taxiway centerline lights.

luminaires, edge luminaires, reflectors, signs and markings.

Taxiway Centerline Lighting. A taxiway centerline lighting system is designed to facilitate aircraft ground traffic movements.

Centerline luminaires are provided on taxiways intended for use in conditions where the visual range will be less than 360 m (1200 ft) and are recommended for all airports with runways having precision approach procedures, particularly at high-traffic-density airports.

Taxiway centerline luminaires are green and operate continuously. The luminous intensity is varied according to the ambient conditions. Figure 25-6 shows typical photometric characteristics for a centerline luminaire.

Centerline luminaires on a straight section of a taxiway are spaced at longitudinal intervals of not more than 30 m (100 ft), except:

1. On short, straight sections, additional luminaires are provided at intervals less than 30 m (100 ft).
2. On a taxiway intended for use in runway visual range conditions of less than 360 m (1200 ft), the longitudinal spacing is not to exceed 15 m (50 ft).
3. On a curved section of taxiway intended for use in runway visual range conditions of less than 360 m (1200 ft), the lights are not to exceed a spacing of 15 m (50 ft), and on a curve of radius less than 360 m (1200 ft), the lights are spaced at intervals not greater than 7.5 m (25 ft). This spacing extends for 60 m (200 ft) on both ends of the curve.
4. Unidirectional centerline luminaires on a high-speed exit taxiway commence at a point at least 60 m (200 ft) before the beginning of the taxiway centerline curve and continue beyond the end of the curve to a point on the centerline of a taxiway where the aircraft can be expected to reach normal taxi speed. The luminaires on that portion of the runway parallel to the centerline should be either on the runway centerline or, if runway centerline lights are provided, offset from the runway centerline up to 900 mm (36 in.).
5. At other exit taxiways, unidirectional taxiway luminaires should commence at the point where the taxiway centerline marking begins to curve from the runway centerline and follow the curved taxiway centerline marking at least to the point where the marking leaves the runway. The first luminaire should be at least 0.6 m (2 ft) from any row of runway centerline luminaires. The exit taxiway luminaires should be spaced at longitudinal intervals of not more than 8 m (25 ft). The colors should alternate sequentially between green and yellow, and the first light should be green.
6. At taxiway intersections, centerline luminaires may be installed around the curves at the spacing indicated above or by using the straight-through method (see figure 25-7).

Taxiway Edge Luminaires. A taxiway edge lighting system is a configuration of luminaires which define the lateral limits of the usable taxiing area.

Taxiway edge luminaires are provided along taxiways intended for use at night and along taxiways not provided with centerline lights. Taxiway edge luminaires are required for airline night operations. However, edge luminaires need not be provided where only general aviation operations occur and, considering the nature of the operations, adequate guidance can be achieved by other means, such as reflectors.

Taxiway edge lights are continuously burning blue lights but may be varied in intensity. The lights show up to at least 30° above the horizontal and at all angles of azimuth necessary to provide guidance to a pilot taxiing in either direction. Luminaires should be shielded at angles of azimuth that may cause confusion with other lights.

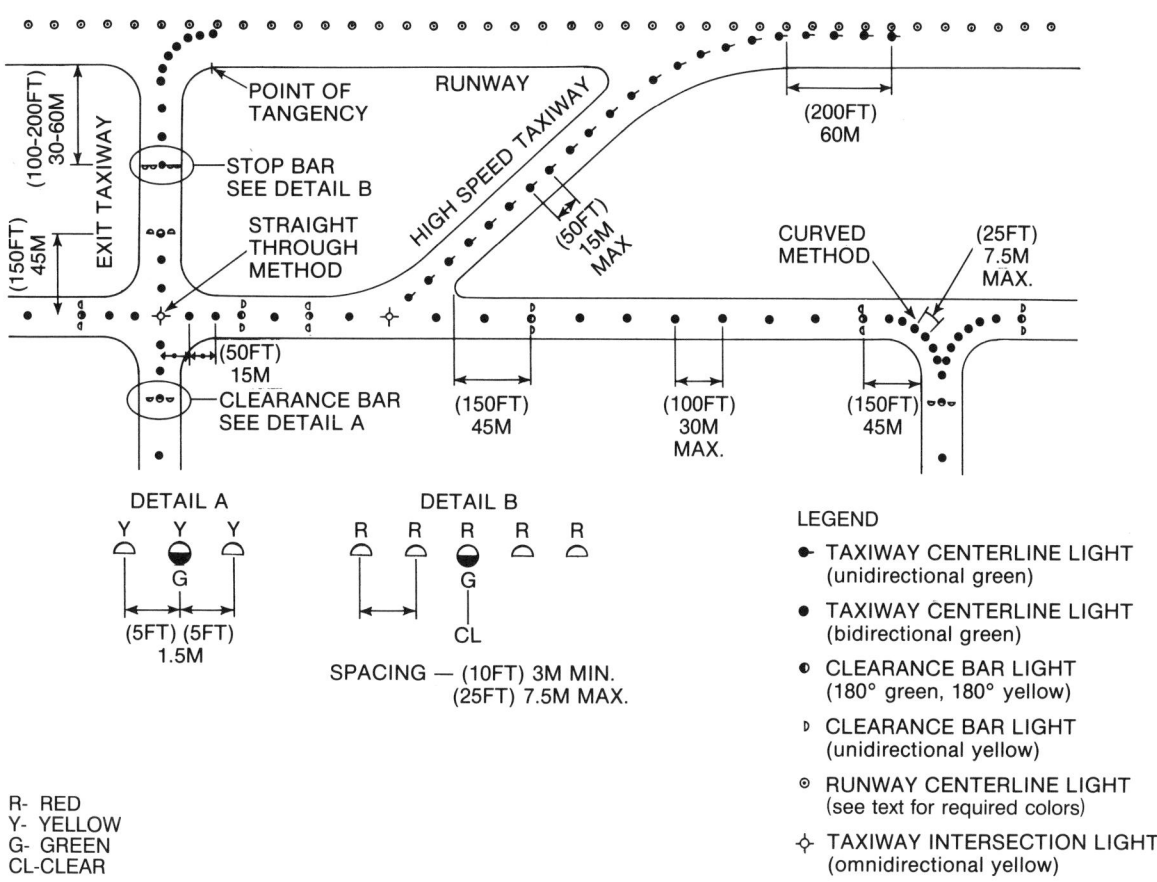

Fig. 25-7. Typical centerline lighting configurations.

Taxiway edge luminaires on a straight section of a taxiway are spaced at uniform longitudinal intervals of not more than 60 m (200 ft). The luminaires on a curve are spaced at intervals less than 60 m (200 ft), so that a clear indication of the line of the curve is provided. The luminaires are to be located 3 m (10 ft) from the edge of the taxiway.

Stop Bars and Taxi-Holding Position Luminaires. Under low-visibility conditions, that is, for Categories II and III on figure 25-5, the conspicuity of the taxi-holding position marking should be improved by installing stop bars and taxi-holding position luminaires. This is particularly important to prevent inadvertent passing of a taxi-holding position by an aircraft.

Stop bar luminaires consist of unidirectional lights, showing red in the direction of approach to the intersection or taxi-holding position, spaced at intervals of 3 m (10 ft) across the entire width of the taxiway. The intensity and beam spreads of stop bar lights should not be less than that of the taxiway lights. A taxi-holding position should consist of a pair of unidirectional yellow luminaires aligned so as to be visible to the pilot of an aircraft taxiing to the taxi-holding position.

Stop bars are located across the taxiway at the point where it is desired that traffic stop (see figure 25-7). A taxi-holding position luminaire should be located at each side of a stop bar and as close as possible to the taxiway edge.

Clearance Bars. A clearance bar is a series of luminaires provided at a taxiway intersection where it is desired to define a specific aircraft holding position. See figure 25-7. Clearance bars consist of at least three fixed unidirectional lights showing yellow in the direction of approach to the intersection, with a light distribution similar to that of taxiway lights. The lights are installed symmetrically about the taxiway centerline with individual lights spaced 1.5 m (5 ft) apart.

Clearance bars are normally located at a point between 30 m (100 ft) and 60 m (200 ft) from the near edge of the intersecting taxiway or runway.

Taxiway Centerline Reflectors. Centerline reflectors are installed to improve the conspicuity of the taxiway centerline during the hours of darkness.

Centerline reflectors may be provided on taxiways not equipped with centerline lights. In snow areas, special reflectors that are compatible with snow removal equipment are preferred. Centerline reflectors normally supplement other taxiway visual aids.

Taxiway centerline reflectors are bidirectional green reflectors capable of withstanding normal operations of aircraft and maintenance vehicles. The reflectors are small units with a maximum height of 15.9 mm (0.625 in.), and designed for cementing on the taxiway surface. The reflectors should have a wide divergence angle of light return to meet most operational requirements.

Centerline reflectors on straight sections and large areas of taxiway and on high-speed exits are spaced at longitudinal intervals of not more than 15 m (50 ft). On tight taxiway curves having a radius of 120 m (400 ft) or less, reflectors are spaced at 7.5-m (25-ft) intervals. The layout of centerline reflectors is similar to the layout described for centerline luminaires.

Taxiway Edge Reflectors. Elevated edge reflectors are installed to improve the conspicuity of taxiway edges during the hours of darkness.

Edge reflectors may be provided along unlighted taxiways to supplement centerline lighting systems, and to supplement taxiway edge lighting systems at low-density general aviation airports.

Elevated taxiway edge reflectors are generally cylindrical in shape and blue in color, with 360° reflective bands. They may be flexible or rigid (with frangible mounts), and are constructed to withstand aircraft blast.

The spacing of elevated edge reflectors is not greater than that specified for taxiway edge luminaires.

Taxi Guidance Signs. The purpose of the taxi sign system is to give guidance within the aircraft operating area. Signs also substantially aid the traffic controller by simplifying instructions for taxiing clearances and for routing and holding aircraft. The classes and types of signs constituting a sign system will vary according to the operational needs of an airport.

Taxiway guidance sign planning should be in accordance with requirements of the governing agency (FAA Advisory Circular 150/5340-18). A taxi guidance sign system consists of five basic classes of signs:

1. *Holding position signs* indicate the location for a taxiing aircraft to hold prior to entering (1) a runway, (2) the boundary of an ILS critical area or (3) a runway approach area where specific clearances are required. These signs are mandatory and must not be ignored. A holding position sign and taxiway location sign should be installed at the holding position on any taxiway that provides access to a runway and on any runway that intersects another runway.
2. *Destination signs* aid pilots in their inbound and outbound taxiing routes. These signs al-

ways include arrows to aid pilots in taxiing. The airport owner should consult with the local aviation authority for specific requirements.
3. *Location signs* identify the taxiway or runway upon which an aircraft is located. Location signs are also used to identify the boundary of the runway safety area for a pilot exiting a runway. Taxiway location signs are black with yellow letters or numerals. Runway location signs are red with white numerals and letters. These signs do not contain arrows.
4. *Direction signs* indicate to the pilot other taxiways leading out of an intersection. Direction signs have black inscriptions on a yellow background and always contain arrows. Runway exit signs indicate the direction of normally used runway exit taxiways.
5. *Roadway signs* are used for ground vehicles that cross runways and taxiways. These signs should be located at the edge of the applicable runway or taxiway safety area.

Signs are lightweight and frangibly mounted. Retaining cables are used to prevent signs which have broken from their mountings from blowing away. Two types of signs installed on airports are:

1. *Mandatory signs*, which, if ignored by a pilot in an aircraft on the ground, could cause a hazard involving an aircraft landing or taking off. Mandatory signs have white letters on a red background and are illuminated. Runway intersection and special-purpose signs are mandatory signs.
2. *Information signs*, which provide specialized information such as taxiing routes and noise abatement. They have yellow background with black legend. In general, they are illuminated; those that are not illuminated are retroreflective. Destination, location, direction and roadway signs are information signs.

All signs are located as near as possible to the edge of the pavement, but at sufficient distance to be clear of jet engine pods and engine blast effects. Sign locations are dependent on sign size, with larger signs being located farther from pavement edges:

1. *Destination signs* are installed on the far side of the intersection and in the most visible location, usually the left side of the taxiway.
2. *Intersection signs* are installed on the near side of the intersection on the side toward which traffic normally turns. If traffic turns both left and right, the sign is installed on the left.

3. A *runway exit sign* is usually located at the near side of the exit and marked with taxiway identification and an arrow depicting the exact angle of egress.

4. *Special-purpose signs* are located to best identify special-condition areas such as Category II (figure 25-5) and ILS clearance areas.

Taxiway Markings. Taxiway markings are provided to meet operational needs and are applied in an aviation-yellow surface color meeting the chromaticity and luminance factors given in *Appendix 1, Annex 14, Aerodromes*, a publication of the International Civil Aviation Organization (ICAO). General guidance follows:

1. *Taxiway centerline markings* are applied to paved taxiways.
2. *Taxiway edge markings* are applied to the edge of the full-strength pavement of a taxiway where it may not otherwise be readily apparent to the pilot.
3. *Taxiway holding-line markings* are applied to a taxiway pavement where it is desirable to hold aircraft clear of an active runway.
4. *Critical-area holding-line markings* are applied to pavement where it is necessary to keep aircraft clear of electronically sensitive and obstacle free areas.
5. *Taxiway identification markings* are applied to taxiway pavement to aid the pilot in locating taxiway identification signs.

Runway Guidance Systems

Runway visual aids are installed to provide guidance during landings and takeoffs. These visual aids consist of reflectors, signs and painted markings as well as edge, centerline, touchdown zone, approach slope and approach lights.

Approach Lighting Systems. An approach lighting system is a configuration of lights, usually disposed symmetrically about the extended runway centerline. The system starts at the beginning of the usable landing runway surface (threshold) and extends horizontally out toward the aircraft approaching for a landing. Approach lights provide visual information on runway alignment, roll guidance and horizon reference during the final stages of approach to a landing.

The selection of an approach lighting system is based on the worst-case meteorological visibility conditions permissible for operations conducted on the particular runway.

An approach lighting system comprises white or colored nonflashing lights, white sequentially flashing lights or a combination of both. The nonflashing lights

Fig. 25-8. Runway Approach-Light Applications

Runway Usage		Approach Light System
Instrument Systems	Categories II & III	High Intensity Approach Light System with Sequenced Flashers (ALSF-2)
	Category I*	Calvert System (High Intensity)
		Alpha System (High Intensity)
		Medium Intensity Approach Light System with Runway Alignment Indicator Lights (MALSR)
	Other Instrument not Categories I, II, or III*	Omnidirectional Approach Light System (ODALS)
		Medium Intensity Approach Light System (MALS)
		Medium Intensity Approach Light System with Sequenced Flashers (MALSF)
Visual Flight Only*		Non-Instrument Approach System (Low Intensity)

* The use of an individual approach light system for this runway usage is subject to approval by the local authority having jurisdiction.

may be unidirectional or omnidirectional, and are usually of variable intensity, depending on the system used. The sequentially flashing lights may be unidirectional or omnidirectional. They have a definite flash duration, intensity and spatial orientation. They may be of variable intensity and will flash sequentially, starting with the luminaire furthest from the landing threshold or end of the pavement used for landing operations, and flashing inward toward the threshold at the rate of either one or two flashes per luminaire per second, depending on the system. The azimuth and elevation orientations of directional lights use the extended runway centerline and the horizontal plane as their respective references. Most systems incorporate the use of frangible or low-mass structures to hold the individual luminaires in proper orientation; these structures are designed to minimize damage to landing aircraft if the structures are inadvertently struck.

Approach lighting systems are listed in figure 25-8 and are described below.

1. The approach-light system for *Category II and III operations* (see figure 25-5) uses white, green and

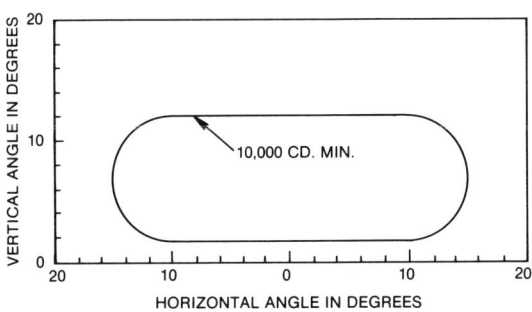

Fig. 25-9. Photometric characteristics of a typical white approach light (steady burning).

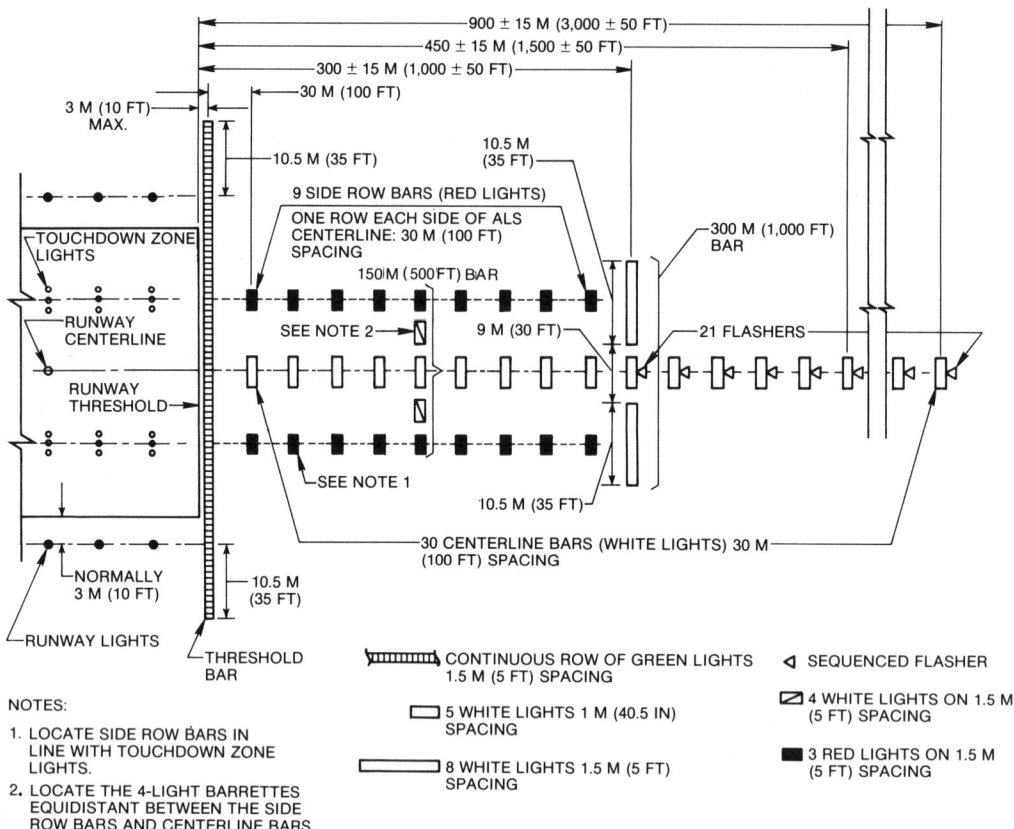

Fig. 25-10. Approach-light system with sequenced flashers: ALSF-2.

red unidirectional, nonflashing lights and white unidirectional sequenced flashers, all of variable intensity. The photometric properties of a typical nonflashing white light are shown in figure 25-9. The photometric properties for the flashing white light have the same shape as shown in figure 25-9, but the intensity is 20,000 maximum and 8000 minimum effective cd within the area shown. The flash rate for each luminaire is two flashes per second. The system layout is shown on figure 25-10.

2. Approach-light systems for *Category I operations* (see figure 25-5) have three configurations for instrument approach. All three are termed centerline crossbar systems. Two of these systems are classed as high-intensity systems, and the third as a medium-intensity system.

   a. The *Calvert system* uses white and green nonflashing lights of variable intensity. The white nonflashing lights have the following minimum intensity characteristics: $\pm7.5°$ divergence in the horizontal plane at 20,000 cd, $\pm12.5°$ divergence in the horizontal plane at 5000 cd; beam spread in the vertical plane may be up to 30% less than that of the horizontal plane. See figure 25-11.

   b. The *alpha system*, also known as ALSF-1 (high-intensity approach-light system with sequenced flashers), differs from the ALSF-2 shown in figure 25-10 in that ALSF-1 does not have the "row bars." The luminaires have the same photometric characteristics as in the ALSF-2 system.

   c. The *medium-intensity approach-light system* with runway alignment indicator lights (MALSR) uses nonflashing unidirectional white and green lights and white sequenced flashers which are usually unidirectional, and all lights are of variable intensity. The white nonflashing luminaires are five lights grouped together in a horizontal bar. Figure 25-12 shows the MALSR layout.

3. There are three types of approach lights for other instrument runways. Two systems may be thought of as simplified versions of the MALSR system. The other system is unique in that it uses only omnidirectional sequenced flashers.

   a. The *omnidirectional approach-light system* (ODALS) consists of seven white omnidirectional sequenced flashing lights of variable intensity and having a flash rate of one flash per second per luminaire. The two lights on the

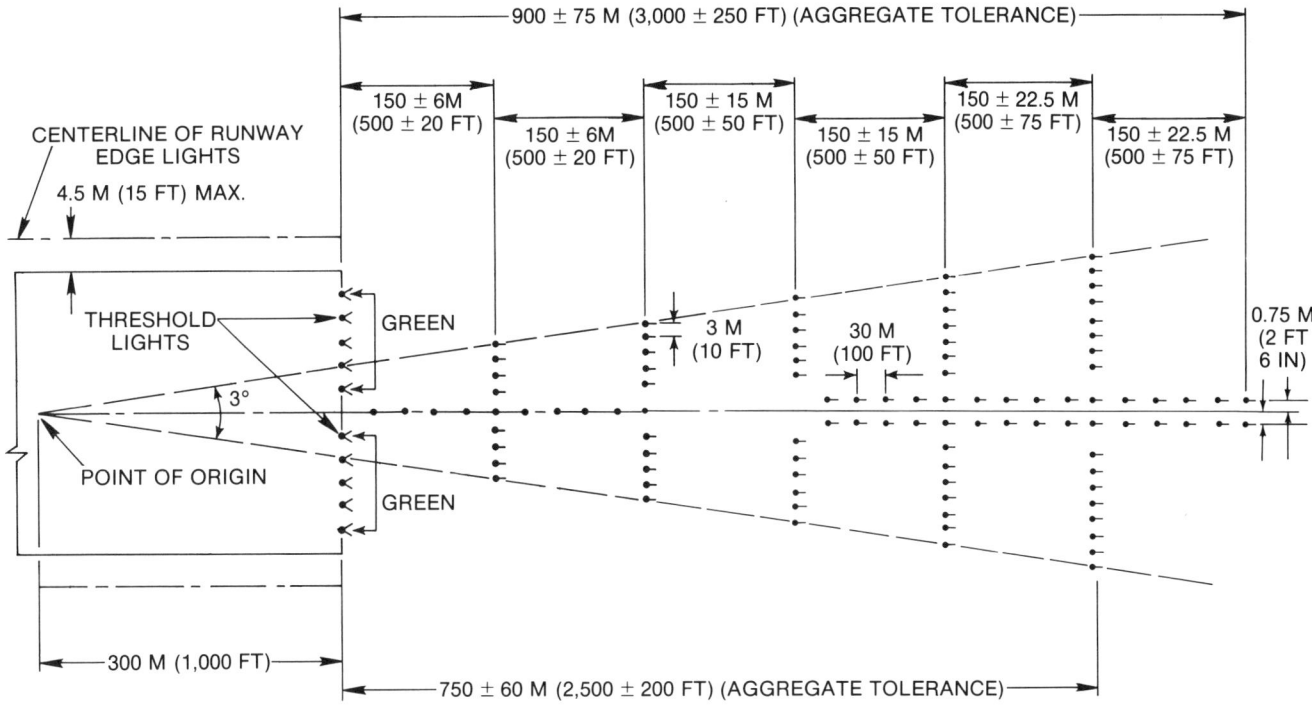

Fig. 25-11. Calvert system.

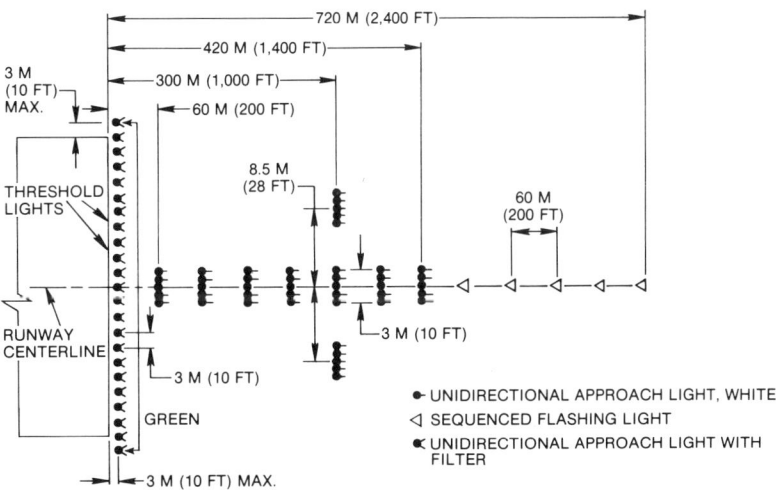

Fig. 25-12. Medium-intensity approach-light system with runway alignment indicator lights (MALSR).

threshold flash in unison. The layout is shown in figure 25-13.

b. The *medium-intensity approach-light system* (MALS) is identical to the first 420 m (1400 ft) of the MALSR shown in figure 25-12 and may be considered a building block of a MALSR for phased development of a runway lighting system.

c. The *medium-intensity approach-light system with sequenced flashers* (MALSF) consists of a MALS with three sequenced flashers at the three outer light-bar locations. These flashers are added to the MALS at locations where, because of high ambient background lighting or for other reasons, these lights are required to assist pilots in making an earlier identifica-

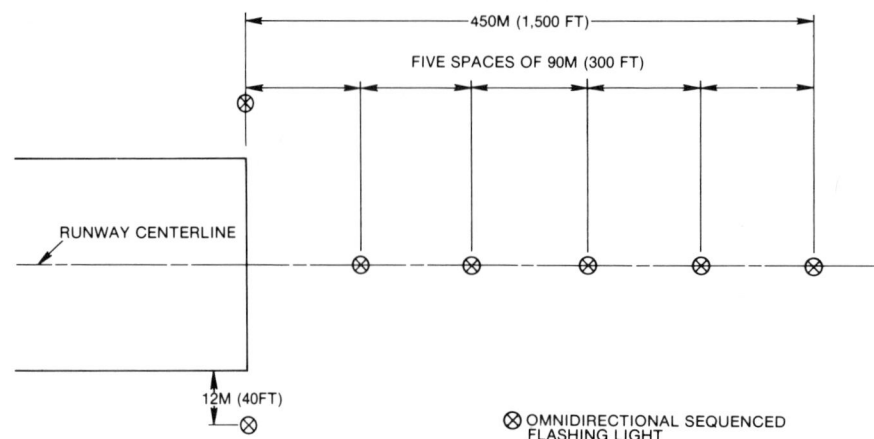

Fig. 25-13. Omnidirectional approach-light system (ODALS).

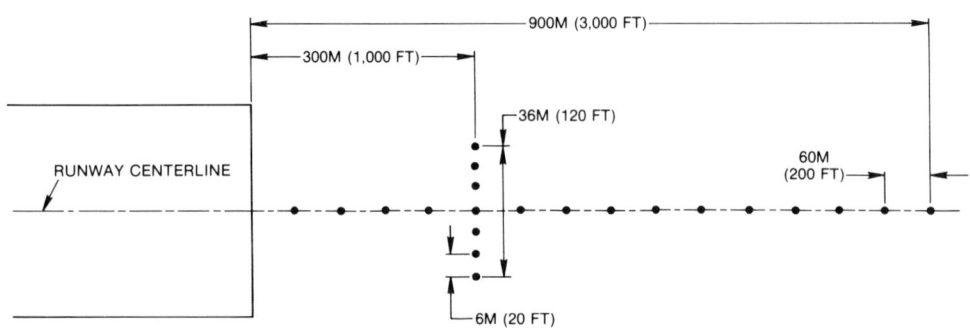

Fig. 25-14. Noninstrument approach system.

tion of the system. These lights flash in sequence toward the threshold at a rate of twice per second per luminaire, and are the same as the flashers used in the MALSR.

4. The *noninstrument* approach-light system is also a centerline cross-bar system. It consists of a single or double omnidirectional, nonflashing aviation yellow or aviation red light. The system layout is shown in figure 25-14.

Visual Approach Descent Indicators (VADI). The VADI is a configuration of lights that furnish the pilot with approach slope information during the landing descent. The VADI is intended for day and night use during visual flight rule (VFR) weather conditions. The most common systems are the red-white *visual approach slope indicator* (VASI) and the *precision approach path indicator* (PAPI). The PAPI has supplanted the VASI as the predominant system for new VADI installations and is the ICAO and FAA standard.

The use and configurations of the various systems of red-white VADI are shown in figure 25-15.

In the basic PAPI four-box system (PAPI-4) each luminaire projects a split beam of light consisting of

Fig. 25-15. Configurations and Usage for the Various Types of Red-White (VADI) Visual Approach Descent Indicator Systems. The Horizontal Bars Represent Approach Lights for "Runway R."

Type	Configuration	Usage
VASI-16		Wide Bodied Jet Operations at Major International Airports
VASI-12		Conventional Jet Operations at Major International Airports
VASI-6		Wide Bodied Jet Operations at Domestic Airports
VASI-4		Conventional Jet Operations at Domestic Airports
VASI-2		Smaller Airports Having no Turbojet Operations
PAPI-4		Runways for International or Air Carrier Use
PAPI-2		Other Types of Runways

white above the aiming line and red below. When the aircraft is on the proper glide path, the pilot will observe the two units nearest the two runway edges as red, and the two units farthest from the runway edge as white. When above the approach path, the unit nearest to the runway will be seen as red and the three units farthest from the runway will be seen as white. When farther above the approach path, all boxes will be seen as white. Conversely, when below the approach path, the three units nearest the runway will be seen as red and the unit farthest from the runway will be seen as white. When farther below the approach path, all boxes will be seen as red.

The basic two-box system (PAPI-2) is similar to the PAPI-4 with only two boxes instead of four on each side of the runway.

The *visual approach slope indicator* (VASI) projects a split red-and-white beam of light similar to that in the PAPI system. There are several different configurations of the VASI system, which are shown in figure 25-15. The *two-bar system* has the boxes running in two parallel bars across the runway, one ahead of the other. The *three-bar system* is similar but with three parallel bars across the runway. These systems are used to provide the following signal information to the pilot during landing approach:

1. For the VASI-2, -4 and -12 (two-bar system). (1) When the aircraft is on the proper glide path, the pilot will observe the downwind light bar (nearest the runway threshold) to be white and the upwind bar (farthest from the threshold) to be red. (2) If the approach is too high, both bars will appear white. (3) If the approach is too low, both bars will appear red.
2. For the VASI-6 and -16 (three-bar systems). An additional bar is added upwind of the standard two-bar configuration. This is intended to serve as a second on-course indication for the higher threshold clearance needed by large jets with greater wheel-to-cockpit heights.

Generic Visual Approach Descent Indicator (GVADI). The smaller configurations of PAPI and VASI, such as PAPI-2 and VASI-2, are typically considered suitable for this category. This category also includes the *pulse-light approach-slope indicator* (PLASI). The PLASI is a single-point projector such that when an aircraft is on the established approach path, the light will be steady-burning white. When above the approach path, the light will pulse white, the pulse rate increasing with height above the proper glide path. When below the approach path, the light will be steady-burning red; and when farther below the approach path, the light

will pulse red, the pulse rate increasing with distance below the proper glide path.

Siting considerations vary with the type of aircraft and in particular the cockpit-to-wheel height when operating on the runway. FAA Advisory Circulars AC 150/5345-28 and AC 150/5340-14 detail the system design considerations. When PAPI or VASI is used on a runway equipped with an ILS or MLS, the PAPI/VASI touchdown point is to be within 17 m (50 ft) of the ILS/MLS touchdown point.

Runway End Identifier Lights (REIL). Runway end identifier lights are a pair of white flashing lights located near the runway threshold. They provide rapid and positive identification of the threshold. They are most effective in identifying runways surrounded by a preponderance of other lighting, or runways lacking contrast with surrounding terrain.

REILs are two simultaneously flashing white lights, and may be either unidirectional or omnidirectional. Intensity may be variable. The flash rate is one flash per second for the omnidirectional and two flashes per second for the unidirectional REIL. The omnidirectional REILs provide excellent circling guidance, while the unidirectional REILs provide limited circling guidance.

A typical REIL layout is two lights located 12–22.5 m (40–75 ft) on both sides of the runway, a maximum of 3 m (10 ft) ahead of the runway threshold and turned 15° away from the runway centerline.

Runway Edge Lights. A runway edge light system is a configuration of luminaires used to outline the lateral and longitudinal limits of usable landing or takeoff area during periods of darkness and during restricted visibility conditions both day and night.

The selection of a lighting system is based on the type of operations conducted on the particular runway. *Low-intensity runway lights* (LIRL) are installed on runways at visual flight rule (VFR) airports. *Medium-intensity runway lights* (MIRL) may be installed on runways having a nonprecision instrument flight rule (IFR) procedure for either circling or straight-in approaches, as well as VFR runways. *High-intensity runway lights* (HIRL) are installed on runways having precision IFR procedures and on runways utilizing runway visual range (RVR) instrumentation.

Runway edge lights are nonflashing white lights of variable intensity, with the following exceptions:

- In the case of a displaced landing threshold, red lights are placed between the beginning of the runway and the displaced threshold in the aircraft landing approach direction.
- For a runway with an instrument approach, yellow lights are used for the last 600 m (2000 ft) or the last half of the runway length,

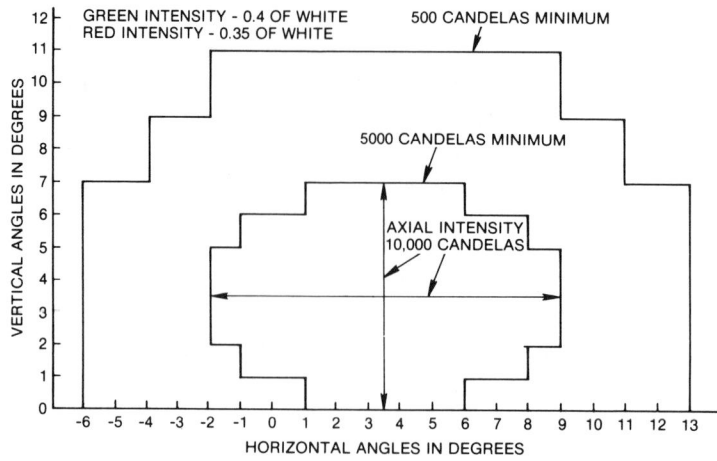

Fig. 25-16. Photometric characteristics of typical high-intensity runway edge, threshold and end lights.

whichever is less, at the opposite end of the runway from which the instrument approach is made.

Runway threshold lights are fixed green unidirectional lights oriented toward the approach to the runway. The intensity and beam spread of the lights are designed for the visibility and ambient illumination conditions under which the runway is intended to be used.

Runway end lights are fixed red unidirectional lights oriented toward the takeoff direction of the runway. The intensity and beam spread of the lights are designed for the visibility and ambient illumination conditions under which the runway is intended to be used.

The runway threshold and end lights, except where a displaced threshold might exist, are usually combined in one luminaire. Typical photometric characteristics of high-intensity edge, threshold and end lights are shown in figure 25-16.

The runway edge lights are located on a line not more than 3 m (10 ft) from the edge of the full-strength pavement which is designated for runway use. The longitudinal spacing of the luminaires should not exceed 60 m (200 ft), and they should be located on both sides of the runway on a line perpendicular to the centerline.

The threshold and runway end lights are located on a line perpendicular to the extended runway centerline not less than 0.6 m (2 ft) or more than 3 m (10 ft) beyond the designated threshold of the runway. The designated threshold is the end of the pavement surface used for aircraft operations. The lights are installed in two groups located symmetrically about the extended runway centerline. For instrument runways each group of lights contains not fewer than four lights; for other runways, no fewer than three lights. In either case, the outermost light in each group is located in line with the runway edge lights. The other lights in each group are located on 3-m (10-ft) centers.

For a displaced threshold, the threshold lights flank the runway and are separate and distinct from the runway end lights. The innermost light of each group is located in line with the runway edge lights, and the remaining lights are located further out from the runway on 3-m (10-ft) centers on a line perpendicular to the runway centerline. As the displaced runway area is usable for certain operations (takeoff, rollout, taxiing), runway edge lights are installed to delineate this area.

Runway Centerline Lights. Runway centerline lights are intended to provide after-touchdown rollout and takeoff guidance. They are provided on Category II and III instrument runways and on runways used for takeoff in visibility less than 480-m (1600-ft) runway visual range (RVR). Lights are recommended on Category I instrument approach runways. Refer to figure 25-5 for the classification of runway visibility conditions.

Runway centerline lights are white, nonflashing, variable-intensity luminaires except for the last 900 m (3000 ft) of the runway. They alternate red and white between 300 and 900 m (1000 and 3000 ft) from the runway end and are all red for the last 300 m (1000 ft) of the runway. Runway centerline lights should not be visible on approach in the area that may be displaced from landing on the full-strength runway due to navigational hazards. The photometric properties of typical runway centerline lights are shown in figure 25-17.

Runway centerline lights are located along the centerline of the runway at a uniform longitudinal spacing of 15 m (50 ft).

Runway Touchdown Zone Lights. The runway touchdown zone lights are landing aids located in the area of the runway where aircraft would normally land. They are provided on instrument runways.

Touchdown zone lights are nonflashing white lights of variable intensity. Photometric properties of typical touchdown zone lights are shown in figure 25-18. These

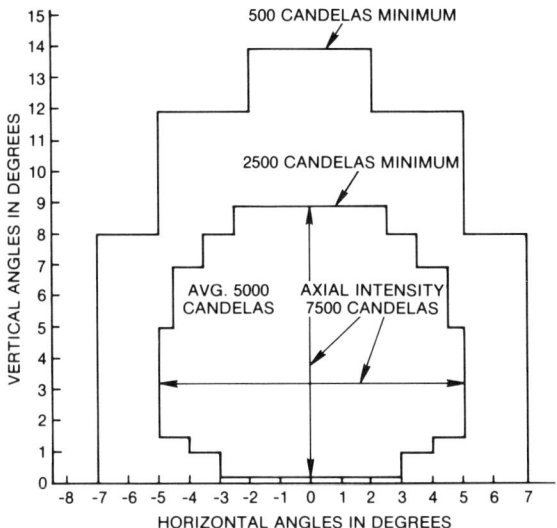

Fig. 25-17. Photometric characteristics of typical high-intensity runway centerline lights.

lights extend for 900 m (3000 ft) from the landing threshold.

Runway Centerline Reflectors. Centerline reflectors are installed to improve the conspicuity of the runway centerline during hours of darkness.

Centerline reflectors may be provided on runways not equipped with centerline lights. In snow areas, special reflectors that are compatible with snow removal equipment are used. Centerline reflectors normally do not replace centerline lights or painted markings, but rather supplement these visual aids.

Runway centerline reflectors are bidirectional white reflectors or red-and-white reflectors. They must be capable of withstanding operations of aircraft and maintenance vehicles. The reflectors are small units

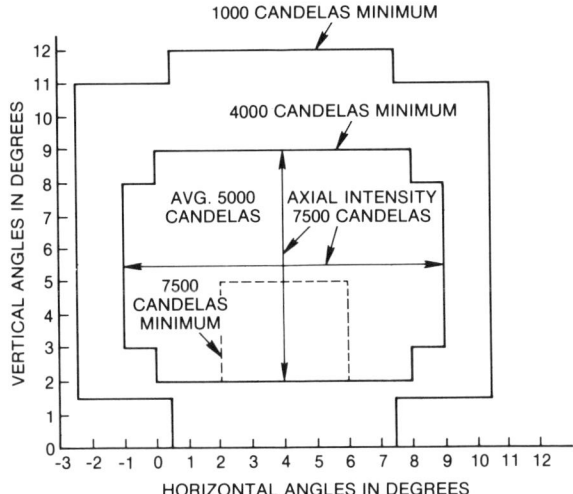

Fig. 25-18. Photometric characteristics of typical high-intensity runway touchdown zone lights.

with a maximum height of 15.9 mm (0.625 in.) and cement onto the runway surface. To meet operational requirements, the reflectors should have a wide angle of divergence for the reflected light.

The color coding of the reflectors is identical to the color coding used for runway centerline lighting. For displaced thresholds, markers are blanked out in the direction of aircraft approach on pavements denied for landings.

Runway centerline reflectors are spaced at longitudinal intervals of not more than 15 m (50 ft).

Runway Markings. Runway markings are provided to enhance the safety and efficiency of aircraft operations and are normally white in color.

Runway Distance Markers. *Runway distance markers* provide the pilot with an indication of the remaining operational length of the runway during takeoff or landing.

Pairs of signs (one on each side of the runway) are located every 300 m (1000 ft) to show the remaining distance to the end of the runway. All are located the same distance, at least 15 m (50 ft), from the runway edge. A marker is omitted where its position would fall on an intersecting runway or taxiway.

Markers are painted with a flat black background and white numbers. Markers can be one of two sizes. The smaller size is used on airports that do not have large jet operations. These small signs can be located as close as 7 m (20 ft) to the runway edge, whereas the large signs must be located at least 15 m (50 ft) from the edge. Markers are illuminated and frangibly mounted.

Barrier Engagement Markers. Hookcable, or *barrier engagement*, markers are of a similar configuration to distance markers, but with a large illuminated orange circle instead of numbers. They are used to mark the position of arresting gear.

Gate, Service-Area and Parking Guidance[7]

The gate, service-area and aircraft parking system is designed to give pilots visual guidance to the gate and to parking positions and should provide final alignment and stop indicators.

A visual docking, or parking, guidance system is installed when it is necessary to position an aircraft by visual aids on a hardstand. This hardstand provides space for loading and unloading of passengers and cargo, for refueling and for rapid maintenance. These visual aids are in addition to the guidance provided by the apron and ramp floodlighting and consist of symbols, lighted targets and markings mounted at varying heights on concourse or terminal walls. They are usable for daytime or nighttime operations.

The system provides alignment and stopping guidance. The azimuth guidance unit provides left and right guidance so that the pilot is informed of the position of the aircraft in relation to the longitudinal guidance line. The stopping position indicator shows the stopping position for the aircraft for which the hardstand is intended and also provides closing rate information near the stopping position.

The azimuth, or alignment, guidance unit is so located that its signals are visible from the cockpit of an aircraft and aligned for use by the pilot occupying the left seat. The stopping position indicator is so located that its signals are visible from the cockpit of an aircraft and should preferably be usable by the pilot and the copilot. It is located in conjunction with the azimuth guidance unit.

Apron and Ramp Floodlighting and Ground Lighting and Marking[8]

Apron and ramp lighting is provided at night or during low-visibility conditions. This lighting may include both apron and ramp taxi route guidance and general area floodlighting.

When operations are conducted in conditions where visibility is 360 m (1200 ft) RVR or less, the most effective route guidance within apron and ramp areas is provided with taxiway centerline lights. With visibilities greater than 360 m (1200 ft) RVR, taxiway centerline lighting is also recommended, especially if complex routes must be delineated. The edges or boundaries of apron and ramp areas are usually delineated by elevated blue edge lights. Boundary and edge guidance lights or reflectors should not be spaced more than 30 m (100 ft) apart. Route guidance within apron and ramp areas may also be provided by centerline reflectors, elevated edge reflectors and painted markings, as used on taxiways.

Apron floodlighting is located so as to provide adequate illuminances on all apron service areas, with a minimum of glare to pilots of aircraft in flight and on the ground, airport controllers and personnel on the apron. High-mounted luminaires with a good optical cutoff will guard against glare for pilots. Floodlights are aimed toward the aircraft hardstand so that it receives light from two or more directions, thus minimizing shadows. Low-mounted lights are required for work under the aircraft and for baggage handling, refueling and ground maintenance.

The color rendering of the apron and ramp floodlights is very important and should be such that the colors used for markings connected with routing and servicing and for surface and obstacle marking can be correctly identified.

Recommended horizontal and vertical illuminances are provided to perform tasks such as aircraft taxiing, fueling both on top and under wing, baggage loading

and unloading, mechanical checks, passenger loading and unloading, ramp service vehicles and baggage carts, and night cargo operations.

The average illuminance provided by the floodlighting system for tasks should be:

- Aircraft hardstand: Horizontal illuminance of 20–50 lx (2–5 fc) with a uniformity ratio (average to minimum) of 4 : 1. Vertical illuminance on the task surface of 20 lx (2 fc) at a height of 2 m (6 ft) above the apron.
- Other apron areas: Horizontal illuminance 50% of the illuminance on the aircraft hardstands.
- Adequate floodlighting is essential for aircraft equipment and personnel safety. The minimum recommended illuminance from the nose to the tail of an aircraft should be 50 lx (5 fc) or more for both horizontal and vertical tasks.

Airport Beacons

An airport beacon is installed on or adjacent to the airport to aid the pilot in visually locating the airport after dark. Sometimes a beacon is not required, however, if other aids are available for locating the airport.

Airport beacons show alternating white and green flashes. The frequency of the flashes is from 12 to 30 per minute and preferably not less than 20 per minute. The light from the beacon shows at all angles of azimuth. The minimum effective intensity of the white flash at various elevations should be as shown in figure 25-19. The intensity of the green flash should be at least 20% of the value in figure 25-19. See reference 9 and chapter 3, Vision and Perception for the method of obtaining the effective intensity of a light flashed at a known rate from measurements of the average intensity. The configuration of the beacon flashes gives information about the airport and must be suitable for the particular installation.

The beacon should be located as follows:

1. Minimum distance:

   a. For airports with runways 960 m (3200 ft) or less in length, the beacon should be located at least 105 m (350 ft) from the nearest runway centerline.

Fig. 25-19. Minimum Effective Intensity of White Flashes for an Airport Beacon at Various Elevations

Elevation Angle (degrees)	Minimum Effective Intensity of White Flash (candelas)
1 to 2	25,000
2 to 8	50,000
8 to 10	25,000
10 to 15	5,000
15 to 20	1,000

b. For airports with runways over 960 m (3200 ft) in length, the beacon should be located at least 225 m (750 ft) from the runway centerline.

c. The beacon must be located at a distance from runway centerlines to provide the clearance required of FAR Part 77 surfaces. This determination is beyond the scope of this Handbook, and the reader is referred to the FAR documents for a complete explanation.

2. Maximum distance: For all airports, the beacon should not be located more than 1500 m (5000 ft) from the nearest point of the usable landing areas, except in cases where surrounding terrain will unduly restrict the visibility of the beacon. In these cases, the distance may be increased to a maximum of 3.2 km (2 mi) from the usable landing area provided that the airport itself is readily identifiable from the beacon location.

Wind Direction Indicators

Airports are equipped with one or more wind direction indicators. If only one wind indicator is provided, it is located near the center of the runway complex. It should be visible to aircraft in flight or in movement areas on the ground. It should be installed in such a manner as to be free from the effects of air disturbances caused by nearby objects. If more than one wind indicator is provided, they should be located at both ends of the runway, in an area 45–90 m (150–300 ft) from the runway edge and 150–450 m (500–1500 ft) down the runway from the landing threshold. The wind indicator must be located to clear FAR Part 77 surfaces and should not be located in any ILS glide area.

The wind direction indicator is in the form of a truncated cone made of fabric. The cone is at least 2.5 m (8 ft) in length but not more than 4 m (12 ft). The diameter at the larger end may range from 450 to 900 mm (18 to 36 in.). A framework is provided for a portion of the length of the cone to permit viewing in calm wind conditions. The color is international orange, or orange and white bands with five alternating bands, the first and last being orange. The wind indicator is capable of indicating the correct wind direction at a speed of 3.5 km/h (2.2 mph) and fully streaming at a speed of 10.5 km/h (6.5 mph). The wind indicator is lighted for night use and mounted on a lightweight frangible tower when installed near a runway.

Electrical Circuits for Lighting[10]

Except for small airports with few lighting devices, which usually use multiple (parallel) circuits, the power to approach, runway, taxiway and other field lighting

equipment is distributed underground by series lighting circuits. Electric power is usually made available for the following facilities:

- Lighting to enable air traffic service personnel to carry out their duties
- All obstruction lights that are essential to ensure safe operation
- Meteorological equipment
- Security lighting
- Field lighting (all lighting aids discussed in this section)

Power Source Requirements and Characteristics

For air traffic safety, power supplies should be of the highest reliability. Normal power is often furnished by a minimum of two feeders, preferably from independent power sources. An emergency power supply is normally used to maintain service in the event of loss of the main utility feeders. Emergency power supplies are usually provided by standby engine generator sets that may be supplemented with battery-backed uninterruptable power supply (UPS) systems. Transfer of power between different sources should be automatic, with maximum transfer times no longer than indicated in figure 25-20.

Typical transfer devices are automatic transfer switches and automatic circuit breakers suitably interlocked. The type, size and rating of the emergency power source required is dependent upon the minimum power necessary to operate the essential visual aids to permit safe operations under expected visibility conditions.

The field lighting power system should be installed in vaults located to minimize the length of cable runs to the lighting loads and control wiring to the control

Fig. 25-20. Emergency Power Switchover Time for Airport Lighting

Runway	Aids Requiring Power	Maximum Switch-Over Time (seconds)
Non-Instrument	VASIS*	No Requirement
	Runway edge	
	Obstruction*	
Instrument Approach	Approach lighting system	15
	VASIS*	15
	Obstruction*	15
Precision Approach Category I	Approach lighting system	15
	Runway edge	15
	Essential taxiway	15
	Obstruction*	15
Precision Approach Category II and III	Approach lighting system	1
	Runway edge	1
	Runway centerline	1
	Runway touchdown zone	1
	Essential taxiway	15
	Obstruction*	15

*VADI and obstruction lights should be supplied with secondary power when the appropriate authority considers their operation essential to the safety of flight operations.

tower. Some systems are installed with vaults at each end of the runway wired to keep alternate lights energized from different vaults for added reliability.

Series Lighting Equipment[11]

Most airport lighting circuits are powered by constant-current (series circuit) regulators. This results in uniform brightness of all lights in the circuit. Regulators are designed to produce constant current output under variations in field circuit loads and in the voltage of the power source. Regulators can be set to operate one, three or five different current outputs, corresponding to one, three or five steps of brightness.

A field lighting control panel is normally located remotely to operate the regulators from the control tower. This allows the air traffic controller to select and control power and brightness to the approach, runway and taxiway lighting systems as well as other essential systems, including wind-cone direction indicators, beacons and obstruction lights. Mimic control boards provide a lighted display of the field lighting system, and can be designed to actually monitor the condition of each system and provide a warning when any regulator fails to operate properly. Local control at each vault should be provided to prevent a complete system shutdown in the event of a malfunction in the control equipment.

The primary function of an isolation transformer is to provide continuity in a series lighting circuit so that the failure of a lamp does not interrupt the primary circuit. Another important function of the isolation transformer is to provide electrical isolation of the lamp in the luminaire from the high voltage in the primary wiring, and thereby provide safety to the maintenance personnel. It is suggested that one side of the secondary wiring and the core be grounded for safety.

Primary wires are usually installed in ducts with splices in accessible handholds or boxes so as to facilitate quick repairs. A counterpoise (ground) wire installed with primary wiring provides added protection for safety and lightning strikes and for better electrical fault detection. Secondary wiring can be installed in conduits or pavement saw cuts. All lighting devices should be effectively grounded. Splicing is made with premolded plug-type splice kits that allow for quick replacement, reconnection and troubleshooting.

All electrical systems for airport lighting should be properly maintained and periodically tested in order to maintain their integrity. Wiring must be checked for grounds; generators must be started and operated under actual load conditions, usually at least weekly; and transfer equipment must be checked for proper operation. The design of the electrical systems should be carefully evaluated so that failure of any component, including wiring, will not black out an entire lighting system.

AIRPORT PARKING AREAS[12, 13]

The lighting of automobile parking areas and roadways in and around an airport must provide sufficient illumination on the roadways and parking areas to promote safe, secure and efficient movement of motor vehicles and pedestrians without interfering with nighttime visibility of the control tower operators and of the pilots.

At night, control tower operators work in semidarkness. Their eyes must be dark adapted to enable them to see aircraft maneuvering in the air and on the ground. Any appreciable amount of brightness in their fields of view will greatly reduce their ability to see. The same is true for incoming pilots. The roadway and parking area luminaires in the vicinity of the airport should not be visible above the horizontal, to avoid confusion between the pattern that the luminaires form and the pattern of runway marker lights.

For the automobile parking area, the major considerations in providing illumination are to eliminate accidents, to make it easier to locate parking spaces and locate cars on return, and to enhance security and discourage petty larceny and criminal assault.

Illuminance Recommendations. It is good practice to provide a minimum of 10 lx (1 fc) and a maximum of 20 lx (2 fc) average maintained in service, with a uniformity ratio not greater than 3:1 between the average and minimum point anywhere on the roadway, and 4:1 in the parking area.

Focal points in parking areas, such as entrances, toll plazas and exits, should have an average illuminance at least twice that of the general parking area. Also, points of heavy pedestrian crossing should have twice the parking area illuminance.

Special Requirements. It is desirable to limit the ambient light on the control tower windows to no more than 1 lx (0.1 fc). The vertical illumination on the control tower windows is ambient light accumulated from all sources, including reflected light from paved surfaces and direct high-angle light from luminaires. In areas that are subject to snowfall, the reflected light may become a significant factor.

Although it is difficult to control reflected light and glare, some factors that contribute to reflected light can be controlled at least partially. These include the location of lighting equipment with relation to the control tower, the candlepower and the angle at which the light is directed in relation to the control tower. Angles which will reflect light toward the control tower should be avoided.

Direct light or stray light directed at the tower may be controlled in several ways. Luminaire position is important, as is optical control that limits direct or stray light emitted above the horizontal plane. The view of the runways and runway approaches, taxiways, and aircraft or apron ramp areas should also be considered when locating luminaires. The poles must also be designed so that specified obstruction clearance and height requirements are met.

HELIPORTS[14]

Heliport lighting and markings provide visual operational guidance to heliport operators for landing and takeoff from a helipad. Heliports consist of one or more helipads and may or may not be associated with an airport. Heliports intended only for daytime use are usually provided with helipad markings and wind indicator. If the heliport is to be used at night, it should have, as a minimum, markings, a lighted wind indicator, perimeter lights and a heliport beacon.

Markings for helipads should clearly identify the area as a facility for the landing and departure of helicopters. The basic marking is a large, white letter H located at the center of the helipad or landing and takeoff area. The marking for a hospital helipad is a large red H at the center of a white cross. The boundaries of the landing area are outlined with a white stripe that may be continuous or segmented.

Perimeter lights around the landing area form a square, rectangle or circle made up of evenly spaced lights. For squares or rectangles, an odd number of lights per side are used, with a minimum of five lights on each side. A circular area will have a minimum of eight lights spaced around the circumference. A typical layout is shown in figure 25-21. Perimeter lights are omnidirectional, are yellow in color, may be semiflush or elevated, and may be provided with intensity con-

trol. The beam peak is between 7 and 9° of elevation, with a minimum of 40 cd between 3 and 15° of elevation, 15 cd between 15 and 25° of elevation, and 5 cd between 25 and 90° of elevation.

A heliport beacon is used to identify the location of the heliport. It is located within 0.8 km (0.5 mi) of the helipad, and flashes a color code green-yellow-white at a rate of between 30 and 60 flashes per minute. A heliport beacon is not required for heliports located on a lighted airport.

Wind indicators for helipads are usually 2.5-m (8-ft) wind cones that are lighted if the helipad is lighted.

Helipad floodlighting is used to illuminate the helipad landing area to augment the guidance of perimeter lights. It also aids in depth perception. Helipad floodlights are white in color with a wide beam spread and aimed to provide no distribution above the horizontal plane.

Helipad landing direction lights are provided to indicate the preferred final direction of approach to the landing pad. Landing direction lights are yellow in color, normally elevated and five to seven in number. A typical installation is shown in figure 25-21. While there may be more than one set of landing direction lights, only one set is illuminated at any given time. The landing direction lights have the same photometric characteristics as the perimeter lights.

Helipad approach lights provide identification of the preferred approach to the helipad in the initial stages. They may be omnidirectional or unidirectional elevated units, white in color. For unidirectional lights, the peak beam should be adjustable between 3° and 12° elevation, and have an intensity not less than twice that of the perimeter lights. Intensity control should be provided for the perimeter, landing direction and approach lights.

OBSTRUCTION IDENTIFICATION

Any object that penetrates an established set of imaginary planes or exceeds a height of 60 m (200 ft) at the airport site may be required to be marked or lighted so that the obstruction will be conspicuous both day and night. However, whether an obstruction is to be marked or lighted, and the extent thereof, is determined as part of an aeronautical study conducted by the proper authority.

Marking

The purpose of marking a structure is to warn of its presence during daylight hours. Two types of markings are used:

1. *Painting.* Objects with essentially unbroken surfaces are painted to show alternately aviation surface orange and aviation white.

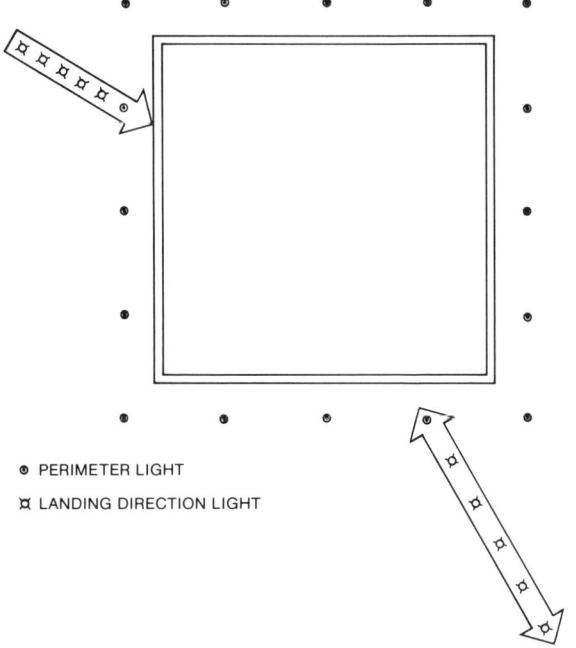

● PERIMETER LIGHT

¤ LANDING DIRECTION LIGHT

Fig. 25-21. A typical layout for helipad lighting.

Fig. 25-22. Standards for Lighting an Obstruction More Than 60 m (200 ft) and Less Than 275 m (900 ft). The Height of the Obstruction is *h*.

Height of Obstruction (h)	Obstruction Classification				
	60 – 92 m (200 – 300 ft)	92 – 137 m (300 – 450 ft)	137 – 183 m (450 – 600 ft)	183 – 229 m (600 – 750 ft)	229 – 275 m (750 – 900 ft)
Beacon Light	h	h	h	h	h
Placement (distance from ground)			1/2 h	2/5 h	2/3 h
					1/3 h
Obstruction Light	1/2 h	2/3 h	3/4 h	4/5 h	5/6 h
Placement (distance from ground)		1/3 h	1/4 h	3/5 h	1/2 h
				1/5 h	1/6 h

2. *Markers.* Markers should be used to mark obstructions when it has been determined that it is impracticable to mark them by painting. Two types of markers are used: spherical markers not less than 500 mm (20 in.) in diameter and colored aviation surface orange, and colored flags. The flags may be of checkerboard pattern, solid aviation orange or two triangular sections.

Spherical markers are normally displayed on overhead wires at equal intervals.

Lighting

The purpose of lighting a structure is to warn of its presence during both day and night conditions. Three commonly used obstruction lighting systems are:

1. Aviation red obstruction lights, consisting of flashing beacons and steady burning lights, are used for night operations and during periods of limited daytime visibility.
2. High-intensity white obstruction lights consisting of variable-intensity, flashing white light are used for both day and night operations.
3. Dual lighting is used, consisting of aviation red obstruction lights for night operations and high-intensity white lights for day operations.

Figure 25-22 contains typical standards for lighting an obstruction with height more than 60 m (200 ft) and less than 275 m (900 ft) with aviation red obstruction lights. For example, a 150 m tower (h = 150 m) would require *beacon* lights at heights of 150 m (h) and 75 m ($\frac{1}{2}$ h), and *obstruction* lights at 38 m ($\frac{1}{4}$ h) and 112 m ($\frac{3}{4}$ h).

REFERENCES

1. Lauritzen, P. O., J. A. Jorgensen, S. D. Meyer, and J. G. Osborn. 1983. A dimmable (1000:1 range) fluorescent ballast for instrument panel lighting. *J. Illum. Eng. Soc.* 12(2):86–90.
2. U.S. National Aeronautics and Space Administration. 1981. *Optical fiber illumination system for visual flight simulation.* NASA CR-3409. Prepared by R. H. Hollow. Washington: National Aeronautics and Space Administration.
3. Witteveen, N. D. 1985. US airport runway and taxiway lighting systems. *Light. Des. Appl.* 15(5):36–38.
4. Feldman, J. M., and A. A. Skavenski. 1982. A study of the environmental impact of an intense flashing airport lighting system. *J. Illum. Eng. Soc.* 12(1):17–28.
5. Marsh, B. E. 1980. Hong Kong Airport taxiway and approach lighting control system. In *International Conference on Power System Monitoring and Control, London, June 24–26, 1980.* London: Institution of Electrical Engineers.
6. Matsunaga, N., Y. Hosokawa, and O. Takemoto. 1980. Automatic monitoring system for the CCR and aerodrome lighting system on airport systems. In *Applications of mini and microcomputers: 1980 IECI proceedings, Philadelphia, PA, March 17–20, 1980.* Piscataway, NJ: Institute of Electrical and Electronics Engineers.
7. IES. Aviation Lighting Committee. Recommended Practice Subcommittee. 1987. *IES recommended practice for airport service area lighting.* IES RP-14-1987. New York: Illuminating Engineering Society of North America.
8. Controlling apron lighting at Terminal C. 1982. *Light. Des. Appl.* 12(10):14–16.
9. IES. Aviation Committee. 1964. IES guide for calculating the effective intensity of flashing signal lights. *Illum. Eng.* 59(11):747–753.
10. Glaser, H. 1980. New constant-current regulator for airport lighting. *Siemens Power Eng.* 2(12):355.
11. Vellaye, K. H. 1981. Monitoring insulation resistance in the series circuits of airport lighting systems. *Siemens Power Eng.* 3(5):149.
12. IES. Aviation Lighting Committee. Recommended Practices Subcommittee. 1987. *IES recommended practice for airport road automobile parking area lighting.* IES RP-17-1987. New York: Illuminating Engineering Society of North America.
13. High-mast luminaires light up Miami Airport parking. 1979. *Light. Des. Appl.* 9(7):34–36.
14. Downing, J. R. 1978. Systems approach to heliport lighting. *Vertiflite* 24(5):8.

Transportation Lighting

26

The general principles established for good interior and exterior lighting apply also in the transportation field. However, the limited supply of electric power and the special characteristics of this power in automobiles, buses and railway cars often make it more difficult and expensive to provide interior illumination of recommended quantity and quality. Also, the tremendous length of roadways and railways, the fact that they are used intermittently, and their exposure to a wide variety of weather conditions are important factors that complicate the lighting problem.

The following requirements are of special importance in the road and rail transportation fields. They apply to the lighting of practically all types of vehicles, but are more essential in some than in others:

1. Adequate illuminance on the task. Where the task tends to vibrate, a higher level is needed than for a fixed seeing task
2. Adequate illuminance at special locations to permit safe entrance, exit and movement of passengers
3. Lighting for fare and ticket collection
4. Adequate vision of the operator, particularly freedom from reflections or glare in the field of view
5. Minimum glare and luminance ratios for passengers' seeing comfort
6. Cheerful and attractive appearance of the vehicle, both inside and as seen from outside

Most vehicles are long and narrow with low ceilings and large windows. The desires of the passengers and the loading of the conveyance vary. The positions of the occupants and the operator are generally known and fixed, so that good lighting is obtainable through a careful study of all phases of the problem.

In the transportation field, direct-current power supplies predominate and a wide variety of voltages are involved. For these reasons, one of the principal problems is to adapt lamps and lighting equipment to the power available and in particular to provide suitable power for fluorescent lighting.

AUTOMOBILE LIGHTING

Most automobiles depend on a 12-V wet storage battery kept charged by a generator or alternator driven by the engine. In addition to the lighting, the electrical system must supply power for starting, ignition, heater blowers, radios, air conditioners, power seats, power windows, defrosters and other special equipment. A single-wire grounded wiring system is commonly used. With the use of structural plastics, which are nonconducting, two-wire systems are sometimes used.

Exterior Lighting

Two categories of exterior lighting equipment are used on motor vehicles: luminaires to see by and ones to be seen. The first group includes headlights, backup lights, cornering lights, fog lights and spotlights. The second group includes a variety of signal and position or presence lights whose function is to convey information between drivers of vehicles.

Headlighting.[1-8] The most difficult and important illuminating problem on the automobile is the headlighting system. It is not easy to provide good road lighting without creating glare for an approaching driver.

The simplest headlighting system currently in use comprises two identical two-filament sealed-beam units, each of which provides an upper and a lower beam. Four-lamp, or dual, headlighting systems are also used. There are several different four-lamp systems in use. They consist of rectangular sealed-beam units of two types, with one of each type mounted on either side on the front of the vehicle. Further details are summarized in figure 26-1. A toe-board-mounted foot-operated switch or a steering-column-mounted hand-operated switch permits the use of either the lower beams or the upper beams.

The sealed-beam unit construction consists of a lens and reflector hermetically sealed together with one or two filaments enclosed within. They have a standardized two- or three-blade connector and are usually filled with an inert gas under some pressure. Those

Fig. 26-1. Lamps Used in the Four-Lamp Headlighting System

Lamp Type	No. of Filaments	Filament Position	Provides
Mounted inner or lower position			
1C1 (round)	1	At focus	Primary part of
1A1 (rectangular)	1	At focus	upper beam
UF (rectangular)	1	At focus	Total upper beam
Mounted outer or upper position:			
2C1 (round)	2	At focus &	Lower beam & part
2A1 (rectangular)	2	below focus	of upper beam
LF (rectangular)	1	At focus	Lower beam

units utilizing tungsten-halogen light sources contain a small tubular envelope that encloses the tungsten filament and is filled with one of the halogens under pressure. Each sealed-beam unit has three raised bosses on the lens face. These are used in conjunction with a mechanical aiming device to provide correct aim without the necessity of a darkroom or aiming screen.

Another type of headlamp now in use consists of a lens and reflector joined together, but with a replaceable halogen bulb. Three halogen headlamp bulbs have been approved by the National Highway Traffic Safety Administration (NHTSA) for use in the United States. In this type of construction the headlamp can be any size or shape and the bulb is the common standardized part.

The total maximum luminous intensity of all the high-beam lamps on a vehicle must not exceed 150,000 cd. This maximum was increased from 75,000 cd in 1978, and by now almost all vehicles manufactured utilize tungsten-halogen light sources.

A new lighting system is about to make its way to the automobile markets of the world: fiber optics. This system will employ a metal halide lamp with near-instant start and restart, in wattages which will initially be in the range of 60–150 watts. The light from the lamp will be piped by optical-grade fiber from the light source to all of the internal and external lighting systems normally found on a passenger car. The size or number of fibers will determine the intensity of light produced at each position on the vehicle. The fibers have the ability to emit light which is reasonably well focused through the use of either a lens attached to the end of the fiber or a lens placed in front of the fiber. Most of the fibers used for automotive lighting will be end emitting rather than side emitting. Therefore, the light will be concentrated at the end of the fiber rather than being distributed along its length.

These systems will permit switching individual automobile lights on and off for applications such as turn signals and will also have the ability to concentrate light in a very narrow band when used for headlighting.

In that application, the light produced by the fiber-optic system will provide twice as much light on the road as the traditional sealed-beam or tungsten-halogen lamps which have been in use up to the early 1990s. This will be done with better efficiency and less glare to the oncoming motorists than has been possible in the past. The small size of the new fiber headlights will also open new possibilities in design for the front end of the automobile.

There will also be the possibility of producing units with spare lamps which may be energized in the event of failure of the primary lamp. The almost instant starting capability of the lamps will make this practical.

The increase in seeing distance is not nearly in proportion to the increase in intensity. Higher intensity also means more glare and the necessity to change to lower beam at greater distances.

Signal Lighting. Signal lamps include tail lights, stop lights, turn signals, front position lights, parking lights, side marker lights and reflex reflectors. The U.S. Department of Transportation has mandated that all new vehicles be equipped with a third stop light mounted near the center of the rear window.

Signal indications must be unmistakable. The number of indications or messages conveyed must be kept to a minimum to avoid confusion. The following indications cover most situations:

1. Indications of the presence of a vehicle proceeding in a normal manner and its direction of travel
2. Indication that the brakes are being applied and the vehicle is stopping or is stopped
3. Indication that the vehicle is disabled or obstructing a traffic lane
4. Indication that the driver intends to change the direction of travel

Effective signal indications may be accomplished by the means described in the following paragraphs.

Color of Signal Indication. For automotive use the colors available are uncolored (white), yellow, red and blue. The usually accepted meaning of these colors is: (1) uncolored—indication of the presence of the vehicle, commonly considered as approaching; (2) yellow—indication that caution is needed in approaching the vehicle; (3) red—indication that the vehicle displaying the red light is a traffic hazard and that the approaching vehicle may have to stop.

Fire and police vehicles use many combinations of these colors; blue in combination with red and white is common for police vehicles. Very high intensity gaseous discharge or rotating colored spotlights add much attention-getting quality to these lights.

Alternately flashing yellow or red lights are used on school buses to alert motorists to the presence of children and indicate in many states that the motorist must stop until the lights are turned off.

Lamps in specific configurations and locations are used on trucks, trailers and other vehicles over 2 meters (6.6 feet) wide to indicate wide and possibly slow-moving vehicles.

Intensity of Signal Light. The intensity of a signal light has a definite bearing on its conspicuity. The signal indication on automobiles must be recognized easily when first seen. Consider the situation where a car is coming over the brow of a hill or around a sharp curve and suddenly the driver sees a vehicle ahead. The driver must know at once whether this vehicle is proceeding normally or is stopping or has stopped. Drivers not in sight of the car ahead when the intensity change occurred have no sure way of knowing whether they are looking at a bright tail light or a dim stop light unless the intensity differences are large.

To be a reliable means of conveying different indications from the same luminaire, a ratio of intensities not less than 5:1 should be used. Larger ratios are desirable.

Pattern of Display. Patterns of display, such as a single unit for one indication, two units, one above the other, for another indication, or three units in a triangular pattern for still another indication, are not good signals, since they are not distinguishable at great distances.

Method of Display. The signal light may be displayed as a steady-burning light or as a flashing light. Two luminaires may be displayed by alternate or simultaneous flashing.

Canadian, Mexican and European Regulations

Canadian Regulations. Canadian automotive lighting regulations are almost identical to those in the United States, except that Canada permits the use of either European headlamp beam patterns or those of the U.S. sealed-beam units. All new Canadian automobiles must now be furnished with low-intensity headlamps which operate any time the engine is running, day or night.

Canadian federal regulations as established by Transport Canada control the equipment on new vehicles built in or imported into Canada. The individual provinces, however, regulate the use of lighting equipment. As a result, many variations of lighting devices are permitted to be sold for aftermarket installation.

Mexican Regulations. Mexico has no federal regulations regarding automotive lighting equipment. It is expected that all new vehicles will have basic lighting equipment such as headlamps and parking, tail, stop, license and turn signal lights. However, not all vehicles have hazard warning, backup and side marker lights. The Mexican government is developing a proposal to require these in the future.

The Department of Transportation and police departments do have subjective performance regulations for lighting equipment on vehicles purchased for their use. Vehicles complying with either U.S. or European regulations will meet these requirements.

European Regulations. Most European countries follow the recommendations of the United Nations Committee WP29 or the regulations of the Common Market. These are either identical or very similar, but they differ from U.S. regulations as follows:

1. European headlamp lower beams have a sharp top-of-beam cutoff with less glare light above the horizontal than the U.S. beam. The seeing ability is roughly comparable to that for the U.S. beam, each having advantages in certain areas.
2. The European upper-beam system maximum is 225,000 cd, while the U.S. maximum is 150,000 cd. The upper-beam patterns of the two systems are quite similar.
3. Sealed-beam headlamp units are not required in Europe, and lenses and reflectors are of many shapes and sizes. In addition to clear lenses, selective yellow (a very pale yellow) is permitted or, in some countries, required. Several different standardized lamps are used. Tungsten-halogen lamps are the most common.
4. In a few north European countries lower beams or a pair of special front running lamps must be used in the daytime during winter months as an aid to being seen.
5. European regulations for rear position tail lamps, front position parking lamps, stop lamps and turn signal lamps generally have lower candela requirements than those in the United States. Rear turn signals must be yellow and front turn signals must be white, whereas in the United States rear turn signals may be either red or yellow and front turn signals must be yellow. Side marker lamps and hazard warning lamps are not required. Rear fog lamps are required in a few countries. These are manually switched, steady-burning, red lamps about the intensity of a stop lamp. Trucks must have triangular reflex reflectors, but do not use clearance or identification lamps as in the United States. Special large reflective

panels are required in some countries on long vehicles.

Interior Illumination

Reading and writing are not generally requirements in a passenger automobile either while driving or while the vehicle is parked. Standards of luminance and illuminance have not been established for the interiors of passenger cars. Installations should be planned, however, to provide illumination for casual inspection of road maps and other printed matter, and for safety in getting out. The installation should be in harmony with the style of the interior. Lamps employed range from 1.5 to 21 cd and should be shielded to prevent direct glare. In addition, all lamps should be located or shielded to prevent reflections in the windshield from obscuring the driver's view of the road if the lamps are turned on while the car is in motion.

Panel-board or instrument lighting for automobiles should be designed for utility, with decorative considerations given second place. The typical driver uses the various instruments for reference rather than continuous viewing; nevertheless they should be easily and quickly readable. It is essential that luminaires and instrument faces be placed so they are not reflected from the windshield or shiny trim surfaces into the driver's eyes. Provision for dimming panel lights is desirable to avoid excessive brightness and interference with the driver's view of the road at night. Illumination is provided by: (1) small lamps recessed behind glass, plastic or other light-transmitting materials; (2) similar lamps used for edge lighting of recessed or raised numerals; (3) lamps located at the top, at the bottom or in front of the panel faces; or (4) ultraviolet excitation of fluorescent numerals and pointers. Electroluminescent lamps have also been used. Fiber optics will find increased application in this type of lighting.

SPECIFICATIONS FOR EXTERIOR LIGHTING OF MOTOR VEHICLES[9-13]

The mass production methods characteristic of the automotive industry encourage extensive standardization, and through the cooperation of the Society of Automotive Engineers (SAE), the Illuminating Engineering Society of North America (IESNA), safety engineers and state motor vehicle administrators, standards have been developed over the years covering the characteristics and procedures for testing automotive lighting equipment. The U.S. Department of Transportation has issued standards for automotive lighting equipment, in general following the SAE standards with some variations and additions. The SAE standards are published annually in the SAE Handbook

and are reviewed at least once every five years and continued or revised. The standards outline specifications and tests for the various lighting devices, covering such details as photometry, color, vibration, moisture, dust and corrosion.

Original and replacement lamps for vehicular lighting are regulated in the United States by the Federal Motor Vehicle Safety Standard No. 108. These regulations, established by the National Highway Traffic Safety Association (NHSTA), cover headlighting, signaling and marking lamps, reflective devices and assorted equipment necessary for the safe operation of vehicles after darkness and under other conditions of reduced visibility.

Since NHTSA regulations change from time to time, that agency should be contacted for the latest information before proceeding with new designs. The NHTSA frequently specifies an older SAE standard (as indicated by an earlier suffix letter) than that published in the latest SAE Handbook.

Devices such as fog lamps and auxiliary driving lamps are regulated by the individual states. The American Association of Motor Vehicle Administration coordinates most regulations of the states and maintains a listing of recognized lighting devices not covered by Federal Motor Vehicle Safety Standard No. 108.

REFLEX DEVICES IN TRANSPORTATION LIGHTING

Retroreflecting devices, or reflex reflectors, are important in transportation lighting and signaling and for directional guides. Other applications include reflector flares for highway emergency markers; railway switch signals; clearance markers for commercial vehicles; luminous warnings and direction signs; delineators of highway contours; marine buoys; contact markers for airplane landing strips; bicycle front, rear and side markers; belts and markers for traffic officers; luminous paving strips; and luminous advertising display signs.

Principles of Operation

A reflex reflector is a device that turns light back toward its source. There are several specific types of these devices; however, the principle of operation—the production of brightness in the direction of the source, as shown in figure 26-2—is the same for all types. The greater the accuracy of the design of the reflex reflector, the narrower will be the cone of reflected visual brightness. The narrower the cone, the brighter will be the signal. Two optical systems in use are the triple reflector (corner of a cube) and the lens-mirror device.

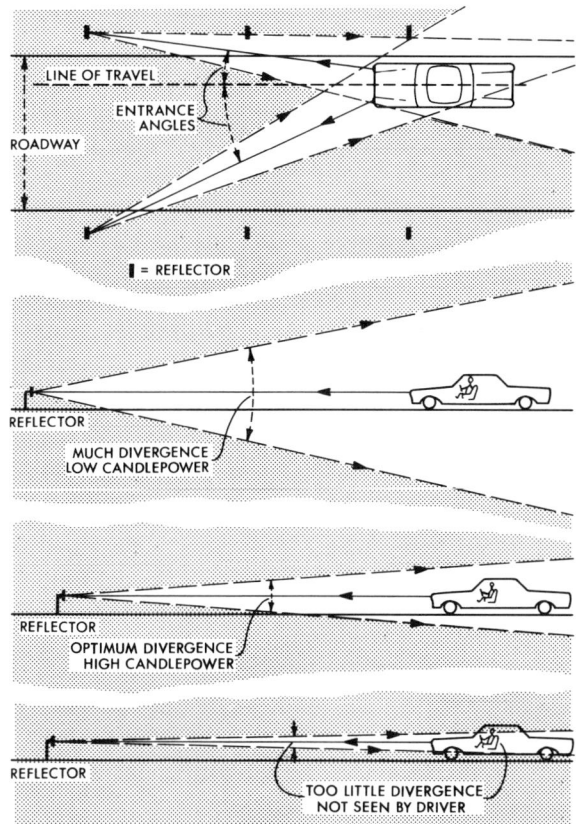

Fig. 26-2. Effect of the divergence of reflex devices on their angular coverage and intensity.

The triple reflector is most commonly used in automotive devices.

Triple Reflectors

The triple reflector makes use of the principle of reflection from plane surfaces where the angle of incidence is such that total reflection takes place. Three optically flat surfaces arranged mutually at right angles, as the inside corner of a cube, form a system such that any ray of light that has been successively internally reflected from the three surfaces will be reflected back upon the source.

A plaque of transparent glass or plastic with a continuous pattern of small adjacent cube corners molded into the back, as shown in figure 26-3, is a commonly used form of reflex reflector. Acrylic or polycarbonate plastics are the most commonly used plastics and are more adaptable than glass to accurate shaping of the prisms, resulting in greater intensity of the return beam. Economy of manufacture, lightness, and shatter resistance are other advantages of plastic. A 76-mm (3-in.) plastic reflex reflector can be seen from up to 300 m (1000 ft) from an automobile using high-beam headlights.

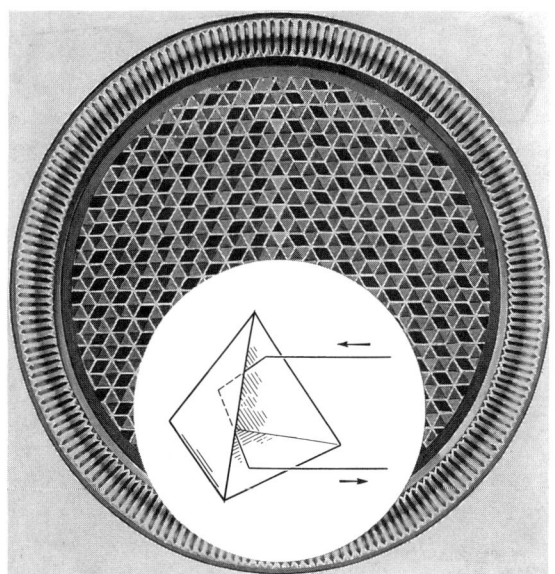

Fig. 26-3. Triple mirror reflectors comprise aggregates of concave cube corners.

Lens-Mirror Reflex

The lens-mirror button consists of a short-focal-length lens-and-mirror combination designed, to some extent with regard to chromatic and spherical aberration, so that the lens focuses the light source upon the mirror, the mirror and lens returning the reflection in the direction of the source. See figure 26-4. An aggregate of small lenses pressed into a plaque with a mirrored backing formed into concave surfaces, properly designed, will produce a very satisfactory reflex reflector.

Another device that produces a wide spread of light, but lower luminance, is a spherical transparent glass bead embedded in a diffuse reflecting material such as white or aluminum paint. This type of reflex reflector is used largely in signboards and in center stripes on highway pavements.

Maintenance and Construction

For good maintenance, all the reflecting and transmitting surfaces should be kept clean and, where possible,

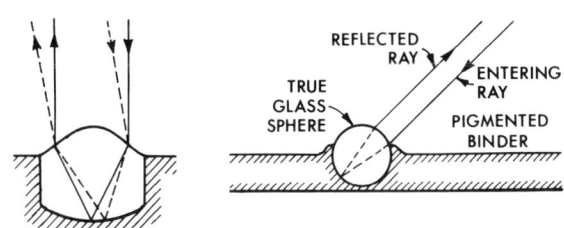

Fig. 26-4. Light paths in button and spherical ball lens-mirror reflexes.

free from moisture. The construction should be such that the rear surfaces are either sealed and water-proofed integrally, or open to a sealed compartment, as when the reflector forms part of a lamp lens. Moisture on a totally reflecting surface will lessen the reflection. If moisture should accumulate on a dusty surface, optical contact takes place and light passes through the surface rather than being reflected. Any roughening or etching of the transmitting surface also tends to reduce the efficiency.

PUBLIC CONVEYANCE LIGHTING FOR ROAD AND RAIL[14]

The general principles established for lighting of fixed interiors covered in other chapters may be applied to the lighting of public conveyance interiors. This has been made possible through the development of solid-state devices and the availability of new light sources and luminaires.

Illuminances. In modern road and rail conveyances, passenger seeing tasks vary widely, from ordinary tasks such as boarding and exiting, depositing fares or having them collected, finding one's seat, reading and writing, and viewing advertising cards, to residential-type tasks on intercity trains such as are found in dining cars, lounges and washrooms. Illuminances for the special tasks found in road and rail conveyances listed in chapter 11, Illuminance Selection represent values that have been found to be satisfactory in practice. In general, they are consistent with similar tasks in other land applications and have been tempered only to recognize the factors of adaptation and comfort where the exterior surround is in darkness and when passengers must move from lighted to unlighted areas.

The illuminance values in chapter 11, Illuminance Selection are maintained values that are to be provided on the visual tasks regardless of their location or plane. To ensure these values, the original lighting design should make allowance for the decrease in light output caused by luminaire dirt accumulations and depreciation of other interior surfaces such as walls, ceilings, floors and upholstery and by depreciation in light source output.

Quality of Illumination. High luminances of luminaires and windows and high luminance ratios will produce uncomfortable seeing conditions (see figure 26-5), and prolonged exposure will generally result in eye fatigue. To avoid discomfort from high luminances that reach the eyes directly or indirectly through reflections from shiny surfaces or from improperly shielded light sources, lighting equipment should be located as far from the line of sight as possible. Glossy reflecting surfaces should be covered or modified to reduce glare,

Fig. 26-5. Recommended Luminance Ratios for Public Conveyances

To achieve a comfortable balance of luminances, it is desirable to limit luminance ratios between areas of appreciable size from normal viewing points as follows:

Areas involved	Acceptable Limit
Between task and adjacent surroundings	1 to 1/5
Between task and more remote darker surfaces	1 to 1/10
Between task and more remote lighter surfaces	1 to 10
Between luminaire or windows and surfaces adjacent to them	20 to 1
Anywhere within the normal visual field	40 to 1

and luminaires and windows should have proper brightness control.

In passenger spaces, the average luminaire luminance should not exceed 1700 cd/m^2. The luminance of the brightest 645-mm^2 (1-in^2) area of the luminaire diffuser should not exceed twice the average value. In strictly utility spaces, luminances as high as 2700 cd/m^2 are acceptable. In either case, the luminance ratio between the luminaire and the ceiling should not be more than 20:1, as shown in figure 26-5. Luminances within the remainder of the environment also should be balanced in accordance with figure 26-5. The use of matte finishes of reflectances recommended in figure 26-6 will help to achieve this balance.

Colors of objects appear to change with the surface finish of the object. It should be noted that matte finishes will reflect diffuse light and give an object a more consistent color appearance, while glossy surfaces may lose their color when viewed in a direction near the specular angle. Finishes such as velvet and deep-pile carpeting appear darker than smooth-surface materials such as vinyl or plastic laminate of the same color.

Choice of Light Source. Incandescent and fluorescent lamps are normally used in the lighting of public conveyance interiors. Incandescent lamps are usually considered where (1) operating hours are short, (2) a high degree of light control is necessary, (3) interior surfaces are warm in color and (4) general illuminance values are low. Fluorescent lamps are considered where (1) operating hours are long, (2) general illuminance values are higher, (3) the linear shape is desired and (4) surface colors are cool.

Fig. 26-6. Suggested Reflectance Values for Surfaces in Public Conveyance Interiors

Surface	Reflectance
Ceilings	60-90%
Walls	
Upper	35-90%
Lower	35-60%
Floors	15-35%
Upholstery	15-35%
Furniture	25-45%

Road Conveyances: City, Intercity and School

General lighting is provided for passenger movement along aisles and for seat selection. City buses leave general lighting on at all times because of the frequent movement of passengers when boarding and exiting the bus. Intercity buses usually turn general lighting off when on the road to allow the driver's eyes to adjust to the outside luminances. For school bus lighting, the general principles and requirements are the same as those for city buses and intercity buses; however, higher levels of general lighting are provided for surveillance of active children, whether the bus is moving or stopped, being boarded or exited. Lighting should be directed or shielded in such a way that the driver's vision is not impaired by reflections or glare spots in the field of view.

Boarding and Exiting. The seeing tasks are on the steps and the ground or platform area. The steps and an area extending 1.2 m (4 ft) outside the door should be illuminated to allow passengers to see the base of the steps and the curb or platform area. The plane of the task is horizontal and on steps, curbs or platforms, with the viewing distance varied according to the height of the individual.

Illumination (see chapter 11, Illuminance Selection, for values) should be provided at the center of each step and 450 mm (18 in.) from the bottom step on the ground, centered on the doorway.

Fare Collection. The seeing task is one of identifying money or tickets and depositing fares, and therefore the fare box and the immediate area around the box should be illuminated. The plane of the task is horizontal and at the top of the fare box. Illumination should be provided at the top of the fare box on a horizontal plane.

Aisle Lighting. The task is one of observing the floor area for obstacles and the seat area for accommodation, generally while the vehicle is moving. The plane of the task for walking is at floor level, and for seat selection at the back of seats.

Illumination should be provided on a horizontal plane at the centerline of the aisle floor and, for seat selection, on a horizontal plane at the top center of each seat back.

Advertising Cards. The seeing task is viewing opaque or backlighted translucent advertising cards placed at the top of side walls. The plane of the task is vertical to 45°.

Illumination on opaque cards should be provided on the face of the card. Luminance values of backlighted advertising cards should be measured at the face of the

Fig. 26-7. Articulated city bus. Fluorescent luminaires mounted end to end over the passenger seats provide diffuse semidirect illumination. Dome lights are incandescent.

luminaire without the card over the diffuser. Within the diffuser area, the maximum luminance should not exceed twice the average.

Reading. The seeing task is generally one of reading newspapers, magazines and books and is generally the most difficult seeing task encountered in conveyances. The task plane, which is at 45°, should be as free from reflection as possible.

For a seated passenger, the illumination should be provided on a plane 430 mm (17 in.) above the front edge of the seat on a 45° angle. For the standing passenger, the measurement should be taken 1420 mm (56 in.) above the floor on a 45° plane at the edge of the aisle seat as if a passenger were reading facing the seat.

Typical Lighting Methods

City Buses. For boarding and exiting, luminaires should be designed, located and arranged so as to minimize shadows, prevent glare for both passenger and driver, maintain a uniform illuminance and remain permanently in adjustment. Typical luminaire locations are the ceiling, over the steps and at the side of the step well.

For fare collection, luminaires can be ceiling mounted, or a local light can be used. Figure 26-7 illustrates one approach to general lighting for aisle seat selection and reading.

Transportation of handicapped persons has been made less complicated with the use of small paratransit vehicles which can more easily travel city streets, especially those in residential areas, than full-size buses. This type of bus can hold up to twelve people and accomodate several wheelchairs. It is equipped with a lift and seat belts. Lighting is provided by ceiling-mounted fluorescent luminaires. See figure 26-8.

Fig. 26-8. Interior of twelve-passenger paratransit vehicle, equipped with a lift to accomodate wheelchairs. Ceiling-mounted fluorescent luminaires provide diffuse semidirect illumination.

Intercity Buses. For boarding and exiting, the lighting of step wells and the outside ground area is the same as for city buses. Figure 26-9 is an example of luminaires located for reading. Illumination for fare collection, aisle lights and seat selection is provided by an indirect system. A low-level night light system is often desirable so that the driver may clearly see throughout the entire bus. At intermediate stops, a special aisle lighting system of moderate level is turned on to facilitate passenger movement without disturbing those who are sleeping. Special luminaires are often provided for the baggage compartment above the seats.

Rail Conveyances: Rapid Transit

Rapid transit means intracity rail service such as subway or surface railways. It is generally characterized by fast trips ranging from a few minutes to an hour. Standing passengers are a normal condition of this service. The seeing tasks and their lighting are the same as those described for Road Conveyances, except

that the illumination for boarding and exiting should be provided on the tread of the entrance and platform areas.

Typical Lighting Methods. For boarding and exiting, provisions should be made for illumination of the threshold and the steps of the car. In addition, car illumination should supplement platform illumination for at least 1.2 m (4 ft) from the car body at the location of the doors. In general, fare collection is made before entering the boarding platform; however, where rapid transit cars have fare collection facilities, it is necessary to provide illumination by an internal light in the fare box or a ceiling light.

The use of incandescent sources for aisle, seat selection, advertising cards and reading generally has been superseded by fluorescent luminaires. This is due, primarily, to the efficiency, long life and general diffused type of illumination which is available from fluorescent luminaires. The common installations use a row of luminaires down the center of a car, or a row of luminaires on each side of the car center, or a cornice on each side of the car. In some cars a third row of fluorescent luminaires is added between the outside rows, often with an air distributor combined for an integrated ceiling.

Where transverse seats are installed in the car, the lighting can be accomplished by use of transverse luminaires. They can be mounted above each seat provided there are no difficulties in connection with the car structural elements and air distribution system.

Some luminaires for backlighted advertising cards are designed to provide adequate lighting for both standees and seated passengers (figure 26-10). Supplementary center strip luminaires are also needed.

In cars using opaque cards, illumination can be supplied from two rows of continuous fluorescent luminaires over the passenger seats as in figure 26-9.

Fig. 26-9. Intercity bus. Individually controlled beam-type incandescent lights are mounted over the seats to provide each passenger with a reading light.

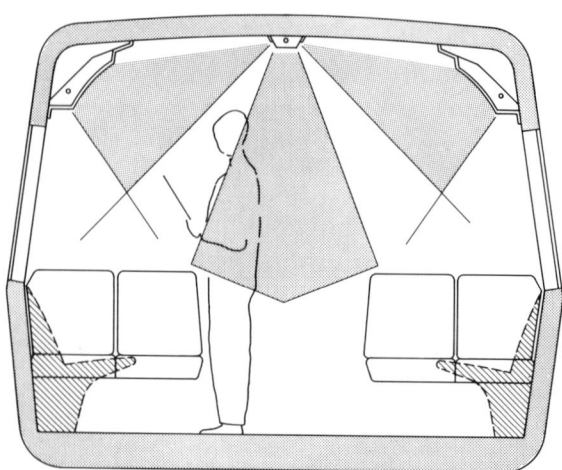

Fig. 26-10. Backlighted car-card luminaires with supplementary center strip lighting.

Rail Conveyances — Intercity and Commuter

Seeing tasks on intercity and commuter trains are much the same as on other public conveyances. The only differences are those additional tasks in the facilities provided for passenger comfort during long-distance travel, such as food preparation areas, diners and washrooms. Some tasks described here do not apply to commuter trains.

Boarding and Exiting. The seeing tasks are on the platform, steps and vestibule floor, and all are horizontal at floor level. The viewing angle is practically vertical for the person to observe the condition of the tread surface and platform alignment with the car floor.

Illumination should be provided at the center of the vestibule floor and at the longitudinal centerline of the steps.

Fare or Ticket Collection. There are no special lighting requirements for fare or ticket collection, since this normally takes place while passengers are seated.

Aisle Lighting and Seat Selection. The seeing task is one of observing the floor area for obstacles and the seat area for accommodations. The plane of the task is at floor level for walking and at the top center of each seat back for seat selection.

Illumination should be provided on a horizontal plane at the centerline of the floor. For seat selection, illuminance should be measured on a horizontal plane at the top center of each seat back.

Advertising Cards. The seeing task is the same as for road conveyances except that some cards may be placed on bulkheads at the end of passenger compartments.

Reading. The task is one of reading magazines, newspapers, books or business correspondence for an extended period of time. The plane of the task and measurement of illuminances are the same as those for road conveyances.

Food Preparation. The work performed is preparing foods and beverages and cleaning the area. The task plane is horizontal on work counters 910 mm (36 in.) from the floor. Illumination should be provided on the work counters from the front to the back edge.

Dining. Passengers need light for eating and drinking and for reading menus and checks. The task plane is horizontal to 45° from the horizontal, 200 mm (8 in.) in from the front edge of the table at each seat position.

Illumination should be provided on a plane 45° up facing the seated diner, 200 mm (8 in.) from the front edge of the table or counter.

Lounge. In addition to relaxing and conversing, there are seeing tasks such as reading and card playing. For reading, the task plane is the same as for road conveyances. For card playing the task is horizontal at the playing surface.

General illumination should be provided on a horizontal plane 760 mm (30 in.) from the floor.

Washrooms. The most demanding tasks usually are shaving and applying makeup. Because the apparent distance of the face or figure as viewed in the mirror is twice its actual distance from the mirror, and because the details to be seen in shaving and critical inspection are usually small and of low contrast with the background, the visual task may be a difficult one. The task area in a standing position consists of two 150 × 220-mm (6 × 8.7-in.) planes at right angles to each other, converging at a point 410 mm (16 in.) out from the mirror, and centered vertically 1550 mm (61 in.) above the floor (see chapter 19, Residential Lighting). They represent the front and sides of the face. A third plane 300 mm (12 in.) square, its front edge also 410 mm (16 in.) out from the mirror, is tilted up 25° above the horizontal and represents the top of the head.

Recommended illuminances should be provided 1550 mm (61 in.) above the floor and 410 mm (16 in.) from the mirror, with the plane facing in the direction of the light source.

Typical Lighting Methods. The interior lighting systems of intercity and commuter coaches are designed in much the same way. However, intercity trains have additional facilities such as washrooms and lounges that provide passenger comfort during long-distance travel.

All of the general requirements of good lighting, such as elimination of direct and reflected glare or deep shadows and excessive luminance ratios that will interfere with good vision, apply to railway cars. A railway passenger car, however, has certain fundamental limitations that affect the design of lighting systems. The length, height and width of the car are fixed by the track gauge and clearances. The inherent physical characteristics of the car, crowded with air ducts, wire ways and structural members, and the limitations of power supply also may complicate the lighting design.

Boarding and Exiting. Vestibule and platform lighting should be designed so that passengers board and detrain safely. Both track and vestibule levels are generally provided with a luminaire over each trapdoor, illuminating vestibule and step areas. Supplementary lighting may be provided by step lights located in the step well to increase illumination over steps, and a leading light located adjacent to steps, directed to give increased illumination in front of the steps.

Fare or Ticket Collection. See the subsection on Intercity Buses above.

Fig. 26-11. Intercity railway passenger coach. Fluorescent luminaires are mounted on the baggage racks to provide general lighting. Individual reading lights are located under the baggage rack.

Aisle and Seat Selection. General lighting can be provided indirectly by luminaires mounted in the extreme corner of the baggage rack and the outer wall of the car, by ceiling-mounted luminaires that direct the light to the desired areas as in figure 26-11, and by luminous ceilings. Individual reading lights are desirable as shown in the figure, since the baggage rack casts shadows on the window seats.

Reading. Illumination for reading and writing can be accomplished by individually controlled reading lights mounted either in the aisle edge of the baggage rack, or at the line of the baggage rack and the outer wall of the car. In the case of the closed type of baggage rack, these lights are mounted directly above the seats.

Food Preparation. Higher illuminances are given in these areas for the utmost efficiency of operating personnel and to ensure good appearance of food and its proper inspection. Quality of lighting is important, especially in regard to color. In addition to general lighting, usually supplied by ceiling-mounted luminaires, supplementary lighting should be provided over all work areas. The service window between the kitchen and pantry should be well lighted to facilitate food inspection. Refrigeration cabinets should have at least one lamp per compartment, operated by automatic door switches.

Dining Area Lighting. The functions of the lighting system in dining areas are to enhance the appeal of the interior decorations, table settings and food, and to assist in providing a comfortable, pleasant atmosphere for the diners. Quality and color of light under these circumstances are of more importance than quantity, which should, however, be adequate for safety and

convenience. The design of the lighting system should be governed by the overall decor of the car and the effects desired. Direct incandescent downlighting on a table provides sparkle to the silverware and glassware that cannot be obtained from diffuse illumination, and is an important aid to eye appeal.

Lounge. General illumination should be such as to meet the requirements for relaxing or card playing and to provide sufficient illumination to the upper walls and ceiling for the elimination of high luminance ratios. Supplementary luminaires may be required to furnish a higher level for prolonged reading and typing or processing business forms.

Sleeping Car (Pullman). The bedroom compartment for all intents and purposes can be considered the passenger's traveling apartment. Lighting should add to the comfort, convenience and beauty of the accommodations. As in any good lighting installation, the ability to perform the visual task is the primary consideration. The visual tasks in sleeping accommodations are similar to those in the home.

The arrangement of berths and provisions for upper storage in the daytime severely limits the ceiling area available for luminaires. Structural members, air ducts and conduit runs also limit the usable ceiling area. In general, the location and maximum size of a luminaire in the ceiling are fixed by the space available. Figure 26-12 shows a typical sleeping car with supplementary downlights for reading.

Berth lighting units should be designed to provide suitable illumination for reading in bed. Here again, as in the case of the ceiling luminaires, freedom of design and optimum use of materials are limited by the physical characteristics of the application. Berth lighting

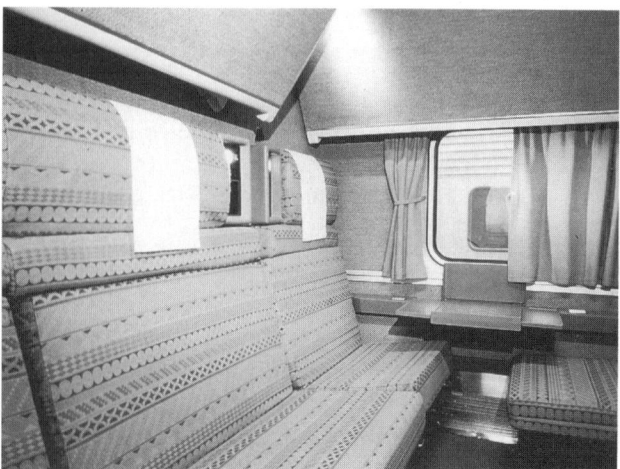

Fig. 26-12. Sleeping car illuminated with a ceiling-mounted luminaire for general lighting and and individually controlled beam-type lights for reading.

units should be so designed as to provide a concentrated beam of light for the reading task and a component for general illumination to relieve excessive luminance ratios.

Washrooms and Toilet Sections. The lighting design should provide general illumination and mirror lighting from luminaires on the ceiling, side walls or both. A luminaire, generally located in the ceiling, should be provided in the toilet section.

LAMPS AND ELECTRIC POWER SYSTEMS FOR TRANSPORTATION LIGHTING

Lamps

Both incandescent and fluorescent lamps are used for public conveyance lighting, but there is a trend toward more fluorescent lighting. The high efficacy, linear shape and low luminance of the fluorescent lamp make it well suited to vehicular lighting. However, few public conveyances have the normal 60-Hz, 120-V alternating current for which most fluorescent lamps and accessories are designed. Consequently, special electrical systems have been devised to facilitate the use of fluorescent lamps in this field.

Multiple incandescent filament lamps suitable for transportation are described in the chapter on light sources.

Electric Systems for Operating Fluorescent Lamps in Public Conveyances

Fluorescent lamps were primarily developed for ac operation and are generally more efficient and satisfactory when operated on ac, but a dc power supply for lighting has been the accepted standard in the transportation field until recent years. Certain sizes of fluorescent lamps may be operated directly on the dc power available on the vehicle, or ac may be generated from the dc supply by means of various types of conversion units.[15]

With dc operation of fluorescent lamps, a resistance-type ballast is used to control the current. Ballast loss should be included when determining the total power required for the lighting. Also, in lamps over 600 mm (24 in.) in length, the direction of the current flow through the lamps should be periodically reversed to prevent the reduction in light output at the positive end of the lamp caused by the gradual drift of the mercury to the negative end. The useful lamp life on dc burning is reduced to approximately 80% of that on ac burning. Also, special provisions are needed to assure dependable lamp starting at low line voltage and at lower ambient temperatures.

The use of power conversion equipment to convert from dc to ac is common practice. See figure 26-13.

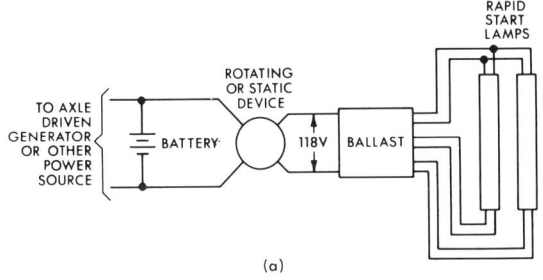

(a)

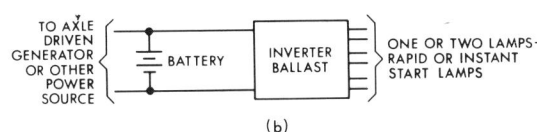

(b)

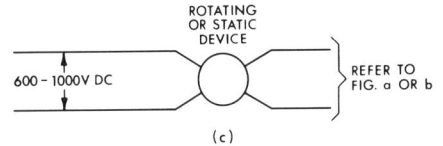

(c)

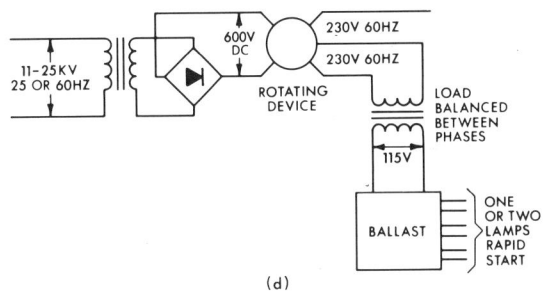

(d)

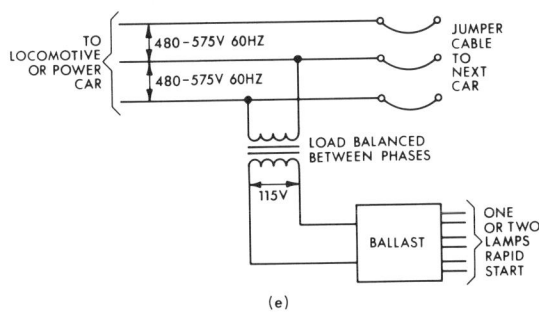

(e)

Fig. 26-13. Typical circuits for operating fluorescent lamps in the transportation field: (a) circuit for converting available dc to 60-Hz ac; (b) circuit using available dc; (c) circuit for converting high-voltage dc; (d) circuit for converting high-voltage ac; and (e) circuit used with power from locomotive.

The conversion may be to 60 Hz; however, the trend is toward higher frequencies in order to gain overall efficiency and reduced weight in the auxiliary equipment.

Two common methods of conversion in use to produce ac from the dc power source are available. They are described in the following paragraphs.

Rotary Machines. Devices such as rotary converters,[16] motor alternators and booster inverters are being used on dc voltages to generate various ac output voltages. Gasoline-electric or diesel-electric equipment is available for mounting beneath a car and for a "head-end" ac power system.

Inverter Systems. These systems produce ac power, usually of a high frequency ranging from 400 Hz to 25 kHz. The lower frequencies are sometimes used in applications where the noise of the vehicle overcomes the resulting hum. Optimum frequencies, however, are above the hearing range. These frequencies also provide minimum size of equipment and maximum overall system efficiency.

Any standard fluorescent lamp can be used to advantage on high-frequency power; however, the ballast and all component equipment should be designed for good lamp performance, taking into consideration ample open circuit voltage and correct operating watts for the fluorescent lamp involved.

MARINE LIGHTING

Objectives

Marine lighting encompasses the illumination provided aboard ships and illuminated aids to marine navigation. The objectives of shipboard lighting are to provide illumination for the safety and well-being of passengers and crew, for the accomplishment of visual tasks aboard the vessel, for the safe navigation of the vessel and for a pleasant and comfortable visual environment. Lighted aids to marine navigation are installed to aid in the piloting and navigation of the vessel and to indicate areas of danger and restricted passage.

Regulatory-Body Requirements, Other Standards and Guidance

Technical guidance for the design and installation of marine lighting is contained in the *Marine Lighting Standard Practice*[17] published by the Illuminating Engineering Society.

The lighting requirements for life safety for ships of U.S. registry are established by the U.S. Coast Guard. Regulations regarding ships' electrical plants and lighting are contained in the *U.S. Coast Guard Electrical Engineering Regulations*.[18] The lighting regulations reflect the lighting requirements published by the International Conference on the Safety of Life at Sea.

Lighting requirements for navigation lights are contained in the *Rules of the Road*,[19] which is published by the U.S. Coast Guard.

Complete details for the design and application of lighting equipment for aids to marine navigation are contained in the latest edition of the U.S. Coast Guard Ocean Engineering Report Number 37 (CG-250-37), *Visual Signalling: Theory and Application to Aids to Navigation*.[20]

Detailed guidance for the construction of luminaires for marine applications is contained in the *Standard for Marine-type Electric Lighting Fixtures*[21] and the *Standards for Electrical Lighting Fixtures for Use in Hazardous Locations*.[22] Both documents are published by Underwriters Laboratories.

The American Bureau of Shipping has established requirements for the construction of vessels in order that they may be certified as being eligible for insurance issued by members of the Marine Insurance Underwriters.[23]

The Committee on Marine Transportation of the Institute of Electrical and Electronics Engineers (IEEE) has published the *Recommended Practice for Electric Installations on Shipboard*.[24] It serves as a guide for the installation of electrical equipment on merchant vessels having an electric plant system.

For U.S. naval vessels, the lighting specification for a ship is derived from either the *General Specifications for Ships of the U.S. Navy* (NAVSEA S9AAO-AA-SPN-010/GEN-SPEC)[25] or other documents published by the Naval Sea Systems Command of the U.S. Navy.

Marine Lighting Equipment

Commercially available luminaires for marine lighting are tested in accordance with procedures established by the Underwriters Laboratories (UL) in the United States and the Canadian Standards Association (CSA) in Canada. While the two agencies use similar tests and criteria, the specifier should ensure that the correct certifications are provided by manufacturers.

Luminaires which have been examined and found to comply with the Underwriters Laboratories standards are identified in two different ways:

1. *Underwriters Laboratories service label.* The label is provided for most luminaires, with the exception of utilitarian desk and bulkhead luminaires. Labeled luminaires are identified by the Underwriters Laboratories service mark together with the designation "Marine-type Electric Fixture" or "Marine-type Recessed

Electric Fixture." The labels also include other applicable luminaire information such as "Inside-type," "Inside Dripproof-type," "Outside-type (Salt Water)" or "Outside-type (Fresh Water)."

2. *Underwriters Laboratories reexamination service.* This category designates unwired general utilitarian luminaires, deck or bulkhead mounted, which may be exposed to the weather or mounted in other wet or damp locations. Such luminaires are not labeled; rather, they are listed by catalog number in the *Electrical Construction Materials List*[26] published by Underwriters Laboratories. Listed luminaires are characterized by features including junction boxes, protective glassware and, often, protective guards.

Special luminaires which do not fall within the scope of the UL standards or for which inspection and certification by UL would be uneconomical may be given special consideration by the U.S. Coast Guard.

Lighting equipment installed aboard U.S. Navy ships is manufactured to end-item specifications which are identified in the U.S. Navy publications described above, as well as to suitable Commercial Item Descriptions approved by the Naval Sea Systems Command.

Seeing Tasks in Marine Lighting

General Considerations

Tasks. Shipboard lighting tasks are similar to those encountered on land. Additional considerations are imposed by night vision requirements and the limited locations available to install luminaires due to reduced ceiling heights, machinery placement and the constraints and inaccessibility of topside locations including the mast and superstructure.

Environmental Considerations. Both fresh and salt water may be encountered. The effects of waves as well as exposure to the elements affect fixture design. The illumination must be adequate when surfaces are either wet or dry. Lamps and luminaires must withstand the vibration and shock loading imposed by ship motion, sea conditions, mooring or anchoring and the vessel's anticipated operations. Many locations and spaces also require the installation of hazardous-location luminaires.

Interior Lighting

Space Considerations. The lighting techniques utilized in the interior spaces of a vessel are very similar to those encountered ashore. Low ceilings, obstructions and the requirements for watertight luminaires are added considerations for the designer. As electric energy supplies are limited, luminaires should utilize

the most efficient sources and optical assemblies consistent with the application.

Design Guidance. The techniques and principles delineated in this Handbook for lighting ashore are applicable to marine lighting applications. The illuminance required for tasks aboard ship are the same as shown in figure 11-1 for tasks ashore. The values shown represent maintained values, measured without consideration of daylight or supplementary sources (unless they are installed for the task being measured). Recommended values are based on safety and functional requirements. Design consideration must be given to esthetic and decorative requirements as appropriate.

Living, Office and Public Spaces. Stateroom, dining, recreation, office and medical spaces for passengers, officers and crew should have general as well as local or task lighting. Direct or indirect luminaires may be used to provide illumination without glare and to allow safe movement throughout such areas. They also will provide adequate illumination for cleaning and maintenance purposes. Areas in which supplementary illumination is indicated include reading, serving, dressing and makeup. Controls for general lighting should be placed at principal entrances. Controls for supplementary lighting should be located conveniently to the task.

Passageways, stair foyers and stairs should be uniformly illuminated by luminaires installed overhead, in the corner between the bulkhead and overhead, or in other suitable locations which will not pose a hazard. Care should be taken to light the entire width of passageways and stairs as well as compartment numbers and other signage. Minimum illuminances for safety should be provided by luminaires connected to the emergency power system or battery backup. For fire safety on passenger vessels, emergency egress lighting may be provided by luminaires located near the deck and powered from the emergency power system with battery backup.

Passenger entrances are the first to be seen by the passenger. Accordingly, careful attention must be paid to the quality of their illumination. Emergency lighting should also be provided to permit emergency egress.

Passengers' dining rooms, the wardroom, the crew's mess, lounges, libraries and recreational spaces are all public spaces for lighting design purposes. The same principles and techniques as are utilized ashore apply to provide quality illumination. Special consideration should be given to the emergency lighting requirements, as shipboard spaces are more restricted or obstructed than similar spaces ashore.

Navigation Spaces. During nighttime operations, the pilot house, bridge and navigation areas must be in complete darkness with the exception of instrument lights and the chart table. Such lights must provide "red" illumination at the minimum levels necessary to perform the seeing tasks. Dimming controls are recommended. White lights as required for cleaning and maintenance should also be provided.

Lighting in passageways and spaces adjacent to the pilot house and bridge should be equipped with controls which extinguish the lights when doors to those areas are opened at night. As an alternative, light traps may be provided.

To prevent interference with dark adaptation, red illumination should provide light at wavelengths greater than 590 nm with a luminance not greater than 0.3 cd/m².

General lighting in the chart room should be provided by ceiling luminaires. For night operation, red filters or separate task sources should be provided. The task luminaire for the chart table should be fed from the emergency power system or a battery backup. A task light may be installed to illuminate the chronometer and controlled with a momentary contact switch.

Operating and Service Spaces. Careful attention should be paid to the quality of illumination in galleys, shops and service spaces. Glare and high luminance are to be avoided. Low overhead heights and obstructions can create difficulties in luminaire placement. General lighting should be provided from overhead-mounted luminaires with supplementary task illumination provided at workstations.

Machinery spaces, including steering-gear, auxiliary spaces and engine rooms, should be provided with overhead-mounted general illumination with supplementary and task lighting installed to illuminate obscured areas, control and gauge panels and other surfaces having special visual tasks. Illumination should be designed to prevent veiling reflections on instrument and control surfaces. Figure 26-14 illustrates typical engine-room lighting. Emergency lighting should be provided for instruments and controls as well as for emergency egress. Vapor- and waterproof luminaires are typically required in hazardous locations. Haz-

ardous-rated luminaires may also be required in spaces where hazardous cargo and fuel are handled. Protective guards or impact-resistant lenses are recommended.

Exterior Lighting

Special Considerations. Lighting is required while the ship is in port and when it is underway. In-port exterior lighting is used for cargo handling, passenger boarding, security and maintenance. Decorative lighting may also be provided for entertainment or advertising. Luminaires should be waterproof and located for ease of maintenance. During underway periods, many similar activities may be undertaken; in addition, however, stray light must not interfere with the recognition of navigation lights of other vessels by officers and crew on the bridge. Light sources should be selected for long life and stability under expected electrical system and operating performance characteristics.

Design Guidance. The lighting design should be based on the comparable tasks ashore. These are typically found in industrial and recreational applications. Care should be taken to illuminate railings and other hazards for safety.

General Topside Lighting. The outside lighting of decks should utilize watertight deck and bulkhead luminaires. Protective guards or lenses should be provided. Illuminances should be held to the minimum required for safe passage.

Cargo Handling. Ships are usually fitted with permanent lighting in cargo holds. Receptacles are placed adjacent to hatches for the installation of temporary or portable lighting equipment. Floodlighting is recommended in the vicinity of cargo hatches. Fixed lighting for this purpose can be mounted on the superstructure, masts or booms. Tankers should have lighting for valves, piping and gauges.

Aircraft and Night Operations Underway. Many vessels are engaged in special operations at night. They include fishing boats, military vessels, dredges and research ships. Both military and commercial vessels operate aircraft at night. Fixed-wing operations are limited to aircraft carriers, on which airport lighting has been adapted to the marine environment. However, helicopter operations are common on fishing boats, passenger vessels and Coast Guard cutters. Lighting for helicopter operations should conform to good aviation lighting practice. Care should be taken to avoid blinding or misleading the pilot with stray light. For fishing vessels, illumination should cover the entire fantail and nets in the vicinity of the hull. Such operations are inherently dangerous. Illumination should provide clear visual cues.

Recreation Areas. The nighttime illumination of recreation areas should follow comparable practices ashore, with care being paid to the cautions stated previously.

Fig. 26-14. Ship's engine room. General lighting is provided by water-tight fluorescent luminaires, installed so that piping and other equipment do not obstruct light.

Lifeboat and Life Raft Launching. Incandescent floodlights should be provided at each lifeboat or life raft launching station. The luminaires should be adjustable so as to illuminate the boat during all steps of launching and recovery. Power should be provided from the emergency system with battery backup.

Stack Lighting. Where stack lighting is desired, floodlights equipped with shielding and focusing capability are recommended. The luminaires should uniformly illuminate the stack area and minimize spill light.

Searchlights. Where a navigational searchlight is desired, it should be located above the pilothouse and be remotely operable from within the pilothouse. Portable searchlights for signaling should be provided for operation from bridge wings. They should be energized from either the ship's emergency system or be battery operated. Signaling may be effected by keying the power to the light with a momentary contact switch or through the use of shutters fitted to the luminaire. The latter is the preferred method to maximize lamp life.

Navigation Lights. Requirements for running, anchor and signal lights are delineated in the *Rules of the Road*[19] and should be installed to conform to the specific rules governing the waters in which it is expected the vessel will navigate. A running-light indicator panel, equipped with both visible and audible indications of lamp failure, should be provided for the masthead, range, side, stern and special occupation lights. All navigation and other special purpose lights used for navigation purposes should be powered from the emergency system. Dual-filament lamps, switched at the navigating light panel, allow a second filament to be switched on should a lamp fail.

Naval, Coast Guard and Other Military Vessels

All the considerations previously discussed apply to vessels constructed for military service or to support military operations. There are, however, additional considerations that must be taken into account when designing and specifying lighting for such vessels. The first consideration is the illumination required for special operations. They include aircraft operations, underway replenishment, search and rescue, and surveillance. The second consideration is survivability. It encompasses criteria dictated by combat conditions such as shock, vibration, fragmentation hazards and "darken ship" operations.

In addition to conventional illumination, red, yellow and blue light sources are used for general lighting in areas having special tasks. The need for topside operations at night dictates that large portions of the vessels be capable of being darkened to permit access and passage of personnel without loss of night adaptation.

Marine Electrical Systems

Marine electrical systems may be either grounded or ungrounded (floating neutral). Additionally, both alternating and direct current are encountered. Both standard and low-voltage systems are encountered.

For the designer, care must be taken to ensure that the equipment is acceptable for the electrical system and that the correct switching and protection devices have been specified.

Selected lighting applications are fed from the emergency power distribution system. They also may be provided with a local battery backup. The lighting design is driven by considerations of safety of the personnel and the vessel.

Aids to Marine Navigation

The operation and maintenance of marine aids to navigation in U.S. waters is the responsibility of the U.S. Coast Guard. There are over 16,000 lighthouses, buoys and beacons in U.S. navigable waters. Other visual aids to navigation are maintained by state and local agencies on lakes and rivers used for recreational boating.

Most lighted aids to marine navigation utilize incandescent filament lamps. New and modernized aids to navigation are being equipped with gaseous discharge light sources. In all cases, emphasis is placed on reliability, long service life and maintainability.

There is a continuing trend to replace manned facilities with automatic equipment due to continuing shortages of qualified personnel and the need for cost savings. Accordingly, navigation aids must operate for very long periods between scheduled maintenance.

Energy considerations weigh heavily in design decisions. Many navigation aids are located in areas inaccessible to electric distribution facilities. Batteries and photovoltaic generation are used for such facilities. Light sources must have both high efficiency and long life with a low premature-failure rate.

Optical control is a key factor in the efficiency of a visual aid to navigation. Complex Fresnel lenses concentrate the light into a tight pattern with very little light directed above or below the horizontal plane. The lenses may also concentrate the light into horizontal arcs to provide a characteristic pattern. Modern aids are placed at or near the water level. Older luminaires placed high above the water provide visibility at a distance, but are ineffective at close range. As a rule, visual aids to navigation are no longer intended for piloting beyond the horizon distance (about 25 km).

Color specifications for navigation aids are very demanding to ensure both visibility and discrimination. Guidance for the specification of lenses is found in U.S. Coast Guard publications.[20]

The light beams projected by lighthouse beacons may be produced by one of the following types of apparatus: (1) flashing incandescent filament lamps, flash tubes or flashing xenon short-arc lamps mounted in fixed cylindrical Fresnel lens assemblies; and (2) steady-burning incandescent filament lamps, mercury lamps or mercury-xenon short-arc lamps mounted in assemblies of rotating Fresnel flash panels and/or reflectors. Both types of apparatus produce a distinctive flashing characteristic which permits ready sighting and quick identification of the light by reference to the appropriate navigational charts.

Some lighthouses and other lighted aids to marine navigation are characterized by steady-burning or flashing lights projecting distinctive colors over various sectors of azimuth. The effect is produced by one of the two types of apparatus described above in conjunction with suitable opaque screens and color filters.

RAILWAY GUIDANCE SYSTEMS

Railway train operating personnel receive guidance through three main categories of luminaires:

1. Exterior lights on the train, including headlights and marker lights
2. Interior cab signals
3. Wayside signals

Voice communications by wire and radio serve various crew coordinating functions and yard movements; however, actual train movement into any main line segment of the rail system is normally directed by a signal light indication.

Exterior Lights on Trains

Locomotive headlights are classified either as road service, giving 240-m (800-ft) object visibility, or as switching service, giving 90-m (300-ft) object visibility, as governed by the regulations of the Federal Railroad Administration, Department of Transportation. Headlight equipment consists of two all-glass sealed-beam lamps mounted in a single housing, each lamp projecting a 300,000-cd beam about 5° wide. The pair of lamps exceeds the performance and reliability of the old single-reflector headlight. Shielding is provided to minimize veiling glare from stray light illuminating atmospheric particles in the line of sight. In addition to lighting possible obstructions on the right of way, the headlight also activates colored reflectorized markers at switch locations.

Locomotive Cab Signals

With suitable track circuits and electric receiving equipment, automatic signal lights inside the cab can be made to show signal aspects corresponding to those

Fig. 26-15. In this type of rapid transit cab signal, lighted segments on the speedometer show the highest speed permitted. The six windows below the speedometer light to show yellow, green and red aspects and speed limits.

of the wayside signals. This is useful in times of poor visibility due to atmospheric conditions or other obstructions. Changes of wayside signals ahead of the train may be displayed promptly in the cab, thus expediting response to the change. When cab signals are supplemented with speed control, the engineer is required to limit the train speed to that prescribed by the cab signal to prevent automatic brake application.

Rapid Transit Cab Signals

In rapid transit systems, speed commands are continuously transmitted, through the rails, precisely and exclusively to the train intended. Onboard, the cab signal displays the commands, and the overspeed control system compares the actual train speed with the maximum speed allowed by the cab signal. See figure 26-15. If the actual speed exceeds the limit displayed, the system warns the motor operator, audibly, that a brake application is required. If the operator fails to take action immediately, the control system automatically stops the train.

Wayside Signals

The movement and speed of trains into each segment of trackage is permitted only by the adjacent signal indication, with some advance information provided by the range of the signal beam and the preceding signal.

Wayside Signal Range. The beam intensity and range considerations for a lighted signal are based upon the estimated safe visual range by day in clear weather. For red and green signals it is common to use the formula

$$D = \sqrt{186I} \qquad (26\text{-}1)$$

where

$$D = \text{range in m,}$$
$$I = \text{intensity in cd;}$$

or

$$D = \sqrt{2000I} \qquad (26\text{-}2)$$

where

D = range in ft,
I = intensity in cd of the same type of signal when equipped with colorless optical parts.

Yellow and lunar white lenses provide a somewhat longer range, but blue ones provide only about one-third the distance D.

By the use of these formulas and the candlepower distribution curve of a signal beam, it is possible to lay out a chart or plan that shows the ground area over which a particular signal will be within visible range in clear weather. This signal range plan can be superimposed on a track plan to see whether the signal will have visibility over a particular track approach. See figure 26-16. Signal manufacturing companies have prepared range charts for their various signal units embodying the large variety of horizontal beam-spreading and beam-deflecting auxiliary lenses available.

A horizontal deflecting or spreading prismatic element may be chosen to provide visibility along a curved track approach. A vertical deflecting prismatic element is necessary to enable an engineer to see a signal at very close range high overhead or to see a signal close to the ground.

External Light Interference. By making the front surface of lenses and roundels convex rather than flat, it is possible to redirect most of the reflected ambient light away from the direction of the beam, thus improving signal visibility. Together with hoods or visors, which are always used, this assures that daylight will produce negligible interference with the signal under most conditions. Occasionally, flat auxiliary roundels are inclined at selected angles.

The incorporation of reflectors in the optics of a signal involves particularly careful analysis to prevent reflected external light. A typical deep parabolic reflector, as used in ordinary spotlights, could flash false indications from external light if used in signals.

Color.[27-29] Train operating personnel are selected to have normal color vision. The colors used by railways in North America are, with very few exceptions, governed by the Signal Manual Part of the Association of American Railroads. See figure 26-17. These color specifications contain basic definitions for the colors to be displayed in service and the tolerances for color-limit filters to be used to inspect signal glassware. The primary standard filters controlling these inspection filters are maintained by the National Institute of Standards and Technology (NIST) in Washington, D.C.

The Association of American Railroads currently specifies five colors: red, yellow, green, blue and lunar white; however, only red, yellow and green are used for long-range color signals. Both the red and the yellow are somewhat more saturated than those used in street traffic signals. Blue signals are not used frequently because of the very low short-wavelength emission of incandescent signal lamps and the low transmission of light, about 2%, by blue glass. Lunar white is the term applied to white light as filtered by a bluish glass which raises the apparent color temperature, or "whiteness." The lunar white aspect from an incandescent signal lamp will appear about 4000–5000 K, and from a kerosene lamp about 3000–4000 K. Purple is no longer recommended as a signal color, because the filter has low transmission and because the color makes different impressions upon different observers.

As is commonly understood, red is associated with the most restrictive signal indications, green with the least restrictive, and yellow intermediate. For the specific meaning of the signal aspects, many of which involve two or more lights shown together, see *American Railway Signalling Principles and Practices*, Chapter II, published by the Association of American Railroads.

Wayside Signal Types. Modern signal units and their arrangement on a mast all have some feature suggestive of the early semaphore unit, which had a blade for day viewing and associated color disks that swung in

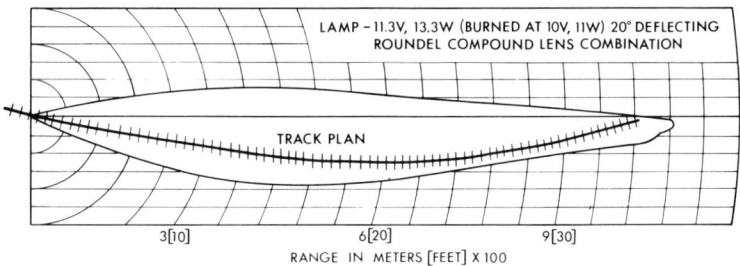

Fig. 26-16. Range chart for searchlight-type signal unit with part of a track plan superimposed to show range of useful coverage.

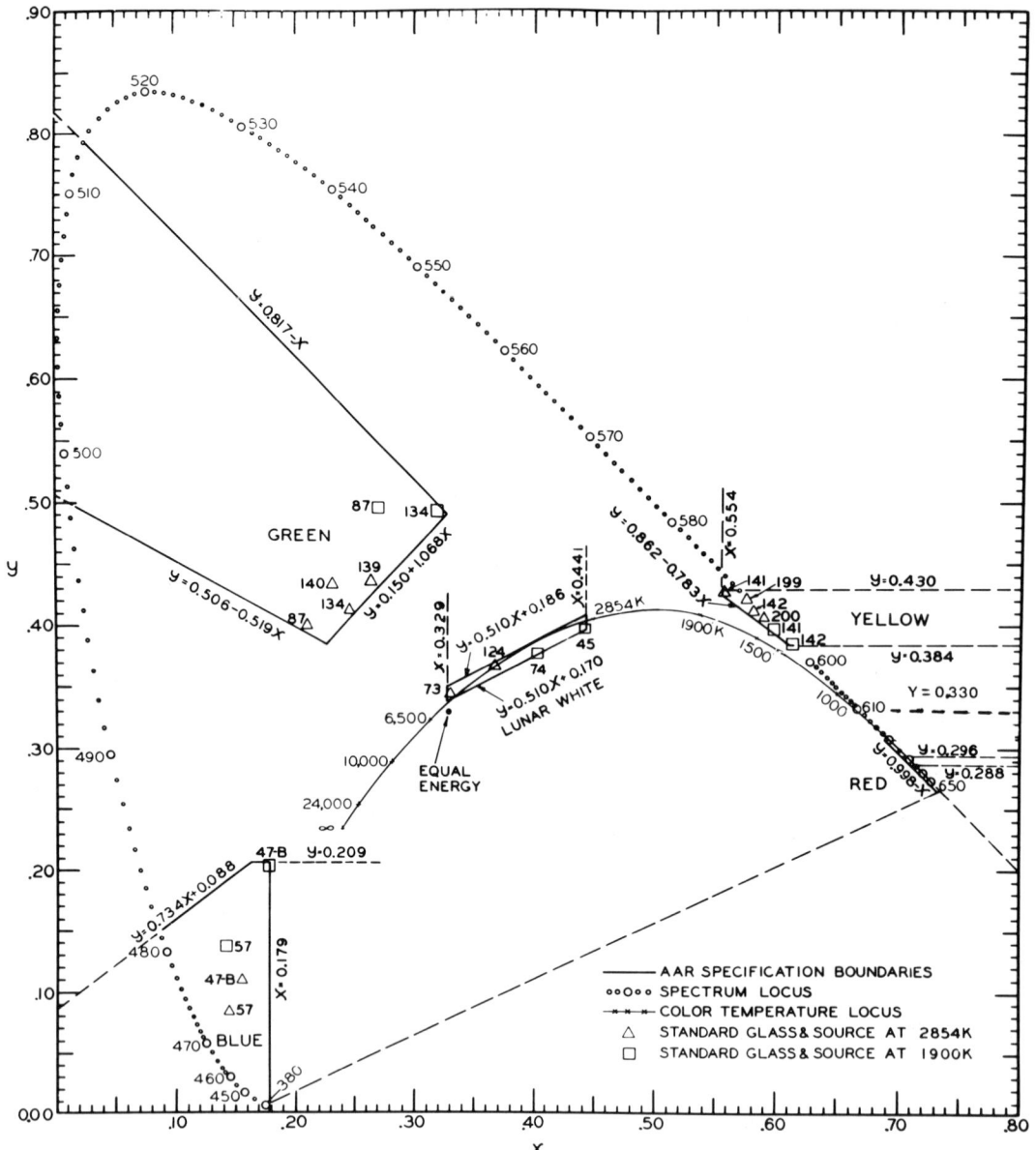

Fig. 26-17. Railway signal color specifications plotted on a CIE chromaticity diagram.

front of a lamp for night viewing. The three types of signals that depend entirely upon light are described below as position-light signal, color-light signal and color-position-light signal. See figure 26-18. All utilize large targets or black backgrounds to permit low-wattage lamps to show up without blending into the sky. Lamps are usually of 18–25 W with very small filaments that must be precisely located at the focal point by a prefocus base.

Every signal unit is accurately aimed using a sighting device during installation or is adjusted according to radio instructions from a viewer down the track.

Color-Light Signal. A color-light signal may involve separate lights with colored lenses for each color, or the signal lighting units may have internal mechanisms

and movable filters to change the color within each unit. This latter movable filter unit is called a search-light signal and permits three units on a mast to display the widest variety of color combinations, for instance, "red over yellow over yellow," "green over yellow over red," etc.

Position-Light Signal. The position-light signal is a type of wayside signal that does not depend upon color discrimination by the engineer. In this type, a number of lamps (maximum nine) are mounted on a circular target—eight lights arranged in a circle, one at the center. By operating three lamps at a time, the aspect of the signal may be a vertical, a horizontal or a diagonal row. Each of the target lights is aligned by its own projector system in the direction of the approach-

Fig. 26-18. (a) Position-light signal. (b) Color-light signal. (c) Color-position-light signal. (d) Searchlight-type color-light signals.

ing train. Yellow lenses are normally used to achieve distinctiveness from other, nonsignal lights.

Color-Position-Light Signal. The color-position-light signal utilizes a combination of the principles of the color-light and the position-light systems. Here also there are several lights on a target. These may be lighted in pairs: vertical pair (green), horizontal pair (red), and right and left diagonal pairs (yellow and lunar white, respectively).

Power Sources for Signals. The lighted aspect displayed is controlled by relays at the signal, actuated by coded impulses in the track circuit; however, for complete dependability, power for the lamp comes from storage batteries at the location. The batteries may be used alone or as standby for ac service. To provide long lamp life and reduce the probability of a dark signal, lamps are usually burned at 90% of rated voltage.

Control Panels for Signal Systems

The movement of trains and the sections of track thus occupied are represented on control panels at *interlocking* or at *centralized traffic control* centers. On such a panel the operator is presented with push buttons that operate relays for switches and signals along a portion of the rail line that may be a local yard or several hundred kilometers (several hundred miles) of track. Lights indicate the response of the switches and signals.

A track diagram for the territory is studded with indicator lights which show when a train occupies certain sections of track along the line or what route has been established.

Railway-Highway Grade Crossing Lights

Warnings for highway traffic at grade crossings are provided by train-actuated flashing red lights. Generally four pairs of horizontally spaced alternately flashing red lights of 18–25 W are used. Track circuits which sense the presence of an approaching train control the lights. The light beam width is usually 30° and provides usable visibility of 300 m (1000 ft). The lights normally operate from ac with dc standby.

REFERENCES

1. Roper, V. J. and E. A. Howard. 1938. Seeing with motor car headlamps. *Trans. Illum. Eng. Soc. (London)* 33(4):417–438.

2. Roper, V. and K. D. Scott. 1939. Silhouette seeing with motor car headlamps. *Trans. Illum. Eng. Soc.* 34(9):1073–1084.

3. Roper, V. and G. E. Meese. 1952. Seeing against headlamp glare. *Illum. Eng.* 47(3):129–134.

4. Land, E. H., J. H. Hunt, and V. J. Roper. 1948. *The polarized headlight system.* Highway Research Board Bulletin, No. 11. Washington: National Research Council.

5. Davis, D. D., F. A. Ryder, and L. M. K. Boelter. 1939. Measurements of highway illumination by automobile headlamps under actual operating conditions. *Trans. Illum. Eng. Soc.* 34(7):761–782.

6. de Boer, J. B. and D. Vermeulen. 1951. On measuring the visibility with motorcar headlighting. In *Proceedings. Commission Internationale de l'Éclariage 12th Session, Stockholm.* Paris: Bureau Central de la CIE.

7. de Boer, J. B. and D. Vermeulen. 1951. Motorcar headlights. *Philips Tech. Rev.* 12(11):305–317.

8. Bone, E. P. 1951. *Automobile glare and highway visibility measurements.* Highway Research Board Bulletin, No. 34. Washington: National Research Council.

9. Boelter, L. M. K. and F. A. Ryder. 1940. Notes on the behavior of a beam of light in fog. *Illum. Eng.* 35(3):223–235.

10. Finch, D. M. 1950. Lighting design for night driving. *Illum. Eng.* 45(6):371–386.

11. IES. Committee on Motor Vehicle (Exterior) Lighting. 1964. Lighting study project report on motor vehicle (exterior) lighting. *Illum. Eng.* 59(10):660–662.

12. Society of Automotive Engineers. 1971. *Service performance requirements for motor vehicle lighting devices and components, SAE J256a.* SAE Handbook. Warrendale, PA: Society of Automotive Engineers.

13. Spencer, D. E. and R. E. Levin. 1966. Guidance in fog on turnpikes. *Illum. Eng.* 61(4):251–265.

14. IES. Committee on Interior Lighting for Public Conveyances. 1974. Interior lighting of public conveyances: Road and rail. *J. Illum. Eng. Soc.* 3(4):381–396.

15. Brady, C. I., Jr., R. G. Slauer, and R. R. Wylie. 1948. Fluorescent lamps for high voltage direct current operation. *Illum. Eng.* 43(1):50–64.

16. Hill, E. P. 1927. Rotary converters, their principles, construction and operation. London: Chapman and Hall, Ltd.

17. IES. Committee on Interior Lighting of Public Conveyances. Subcommittee on Marine Transportation. 1974. Recommended practice for marine lighting. *J. Illum. Eng. Soc.* 3(4):397–410.

18. U.S. Coast Guard. [Latest issue.] *Electrical engineering, 46 CFR 110 to 113.* Washington: U. S. Government Printing Office.

19. U. S. Coast Guard. [Latest issue.] *Navigation rules: International-inland, COMDTINST M16672.2 B.* Washington: Coast Guard.

20. U. S. Coast Guard. 1964. *Visual signalling: Theory and application to aids to navigation.* USCG 250-37. Washington: Coast Guard.

21. Underwriters Laboratories. [Latest issue.] *Standard for safety: Marine-type electric lighting fixtures, UL-595.* Northbrook, IL: Underwriters Laboratories, Inc.

22. Underwriters Laboratories. [Latest issue.] *Standard for safety: Electric lighting fixtures for use in hazardous locations, UL-844.* Northbrook, IL: Underwriters Laboratories, Inc.

23. American Bureau of Shipping. [Latest edition.] *Rules for building and classing steel vessels.* Paramus, NJ: American Bureau of Shipping.

24. Institute of Electrical and Electronics Engineers. [Latest issue.] *IEEE recommended practice for electrical installation on shipboard, ANSI / IEEE 45.* New York: Institute of Electrical and Electronics Engineers.

25. U. S. Navy. *General specifications for ships of the U.S. Navy, NAVSEA S9AAO-AA-SPN-010 / GEN-SPEC.* Washington: Navy.

26. Underwriters Laboratories. [Latest issue.] *Electrical construction materials list.* Northbrook IL: Underwriters Laboratories, Inc.

27. Association of American Railroads. 1992. *Signal manual of recommended practices.* Washington: Association of American Railroads.

28. Gage, H. P. 1928. Practical considerations in the selection of standards for signal glass in the United States. In *Proceedings of the International Congress on Illumination, Saranac Inn, NY, September 1928.* New York: International Congress on Illumination.

29. Gibson, K. S., G. W. Haupt, and H. J. Keegan. 1946. Specification of railroad signal colors and glasses [RP 1688]. *J. Res. Natl. Bur. Stand.* 36:1–30.

Searchlights

27

Prior to the 1940s, searchlights were in general use in military operations primarily for coastal defense, anti-aircraft operations and miscellaneous signaling purposes. The use of searchlights for such purposes has been, or is being, phased out because of the rapid development of such replacements as image intensifiers, heat detectors, radar and other electronic aids. At the same time, civil uses of ground-based, airborne and marine searchlights have greatly increased.

Projectors are similar to searchlights. They are used to cast an image onto a remote surface or to light irregularly shaped objects without spill light.

The type A/N TVS-3 searchlight, originally intended for battlefield illumination, is now being used as a mobile general-purpose unit. See figure 27-1. This unit has a 20-kW liquid-cooled xenon short-arc lamp and has a maximum beam intensity of 800 Mcd. An illuminance of approximately 1350 lx (125 fc) has been achieved with multiple units to provide camera and television coverage. These units may operate continuously for periods up to 90 h unattended.

Searchlights utilized in helicopter operations range from a 450-W, 100-kcd unit using a PAR-46 incandescent lamp (see figure 27-2) up to a 30-kW, xenon-lamped unit with an elliptical reflector producing a 35° beam with a peak intensity of 1 Mcd (see figure 27-3). These searchlights are utilized in such night operations

Fig. 27-2. Aircraft search-landing light, retractable and designed for rotational capacity in the extended position. This light uses a 450 W PAR-46 lamp.

as search-and-rescue, police surveillance and disaster-area lighting.

Shipboard searchlights are used extensively by vessels traveling inland waterways of North America to illuminate navigation aids indicating the navigable channels, in addition to search-and-rescue operations and general-purpose illumination. Typical maritime searchlights range from 30 to 60 cm (12 to 24 in.) in diameter and use incandescent, carbon arc and xenon lamps as sources. See figures 27-4 and 27-5.

SEARCHLIGHT CHARACTERISTICS

Because of the high luminance of the carbon arc, it has been used extensively where maximum beam intensity

Fig. 27-1. Army A / N TVS-3 20 kW searchlight with liquid cooled xenon short-arc lamps, with spread lens in the open position (U.S. Army photograph *H-06618*).

Fig. 27-3. Airborne application of a gimbal-mounted 30 kW xenon searchlight. It provides 1 Mcd and a 35° beam spread.

Fig. 27-5. A searchlight with remote electric control using a 1000 W xenon arc lamp. Spread of the beam can be changed from the operator's position.

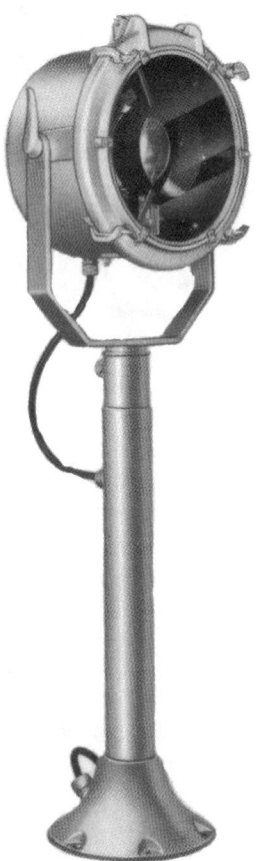

Fig. 27-4. A pedestal-mounted, hand operated 30 cm (12 in.) searchlight with a 500 W incandescent lamp.

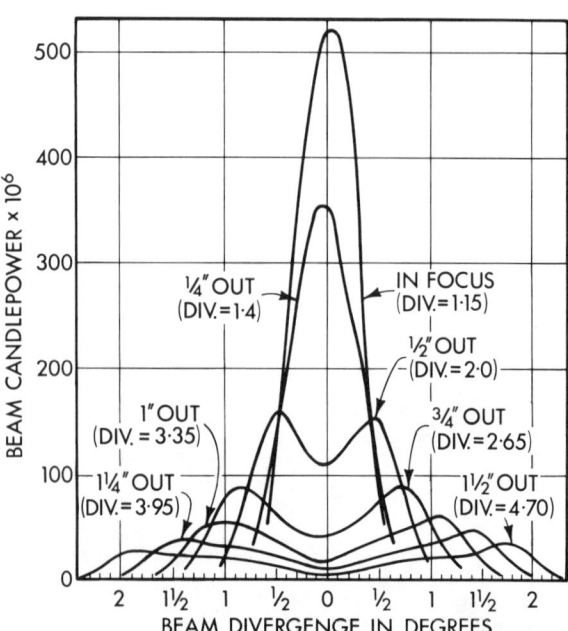

Fig. 27-6. Luminous intensity distributions of a 152 cm (60 in.) searchlight with the lamp in focus and out of focus by varying amounts. The lamp is a carbon arc with a 16 mm positive operated at a current of 150 A. The focal length of the reflector is 660 mm (26 in.).

Fig. 27-7. Characteristics of typical searchlights

Type	Optics	Light Source	Electrical Characteristics	Peak Intensity (approx. mega-candelas)	Beam Divergence (degrees)	
					Horizontal	Vertical
Marine	30-cm (12-in) parabolic reflector	Incandescent filament lamp	500W, 120V	0.8	5	5
	46-cm (18-in) parabolic reflector	Incandescent filament lamp	1000W, 120V	3	4½	4¾
	60-cm (24-in) parabolic reflector	Incandescent filament lamp	1000W, 30V	5	3½	3
	36-cm (14-in) short-focus parabolic reflector	Xenon short-arc	1kW, 45A	43	1½	1½
Airborne	15-cm (5.8-in) PAR-46	Incandescent filament	450W, 28V	0.4	13	14
	25-cm (10-in) parabolic reflector	Xenon short-arc	1.6kW, 63A	4	14	4
	76-cm (30-in) elliptical reflector	Xenon plasma-arc	30kW, 620A	1	35	35
General purpose and military	58- x 36-cm (23- x 14-in) parabolic reflector	Xenon short-arc	2.2kW, 95A	100	¾ *	¾ *
	60-cm (24-in) parabolic reflector	Xenon short-arc	5kW, 140A	250	1⅓ *	1⅓ *
	76-cm (30-in) parabolic reflector	Xenon short-arc	20kW, 450A	800	1¾	1¾
	152-cm (60-in) parabolic reflector	Carbon-arc	12kW, 150A	500	1¼	1½
Hand-held	14-cm (5.5-in) parabolic reflector**	Incandescent filament lamp	12.5V, 3A	0.2	2	2
	38-cm (15-in) parabolic reflector	Xenon short-arc	150W	1	3	3

* Minimum, adjustable   ** Light-signal gun in airport control towers.

is required (mainly in high-intensity searchlights and motion picture equipment). The carbon arc lamp mechanism is complex and difficult to maintain, and the carbon electrodes are consumed rapidly. Automatic magazine-fed lamp mechanisms have been developed to provide operation over longer periods of time; however, the unattended operating time is still fairly short. Carbon arc searchlights are rarely used today and are no longer manufactured in North America.

Other high-intensity sources such as mercury, mercury-xenon, and xenon short-arc lamps are being used increasingly in a wide variety of searchlight applications. These sources have become available in ratings up to 30 kW. Lamps of this type can operate unattended for long periods of time and do not require the complex feed mechanisms common with carbon arcs; however, they have disadvantages, such as high-voltage ignition circuitry for starting (up to 50 kV) and average luminances less than those of the carbon arc.

Searchlights may be defocused to increase the beam spread (divergence), but at considerable sacrifice of intensity. Figure 27-6 shows the effect of defocusing in a typical searchlight. Figure 27-7 gives important characteristics of several representative searchlights.

SEARCHLIGHT CALCULATIONS

Visual Range of Searchlights

Searchlight applications fall into two general categories: signal lights that are to be seen, and sources of illumination by which distant targets are to be seen. Signal lights are discussed in chapter 3, Vision and Perception.

A discussion of sources of illumination involves numerous variables that are not independent in their effect:

- The peak intensity of the searchlight
- The relative intensity distribution of the searchlight
- The atmospheric transmittance
- The polar scattering function of the atmosphere
- The size and shape of the target
- The reflectance of the target
- The location of the target within the beam of the searchlight; that is, whether it is near the beam axis, the near edge of the beam or the far edge

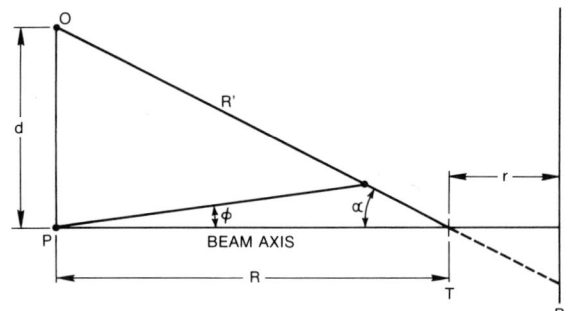

Fig. 27-8. Geometry of target within a searchlight beam. Points P, O, T and B represent the searchlight, observer, target and background locations.

- The distance between the target and its background
- The reflectance of the background
- The lateral offset distance of the observer from the searchlight
- The luminance of the target and its background with the searchlight off
- The visual capabilities of the observer
- The effect of binoculars, if used

The visual range of a target in a searchlight beam has been studied by several researchers; each was restricted to a few selected conditions.[1-6] A summary of the analyses of references 2, 3, 4 and 5 has been prepared by Middleton.[7] It is possible, however, to develop equations based upon the referenced studies which, when used in conjunction with data on contrast thresholds and on threshold illuminances (see chapter 3, Vision and Perception), facilitate the computation of the visual range of targets illuminated by searchlight beams.

Let the arrangement of searchlight, target, background and observer be that shown in figure 27-8, where P is the position of a searchlight having an axial intensity I_0 (in candelas) and an intensity distribution which can be approximated by[3,6]

$$I(\varphi) = I_0 e^{-K\varphi^2} \qquad (27\text{-}1)$$

where K is a constant for a particular beam chosen so that

$$K = \frac{\ln 0.1}{\varphi_0^2} \qquad (27\text{-}2)$$

where φ_0 is the half angle (in radians) of the beam at which the intensity of the light is 10% of the axial intensity I_0. In figure 27-8,

- O is the position of the observer at a distance d from the searchlight,
- T is the target located on the axis of the searchlight beam, a distance R from the

searchlight and having a reflectance ρ_T in the direction of point O, and
- B is the background of the target, located a distance r behind the target and having a reflectance ρ_B in the direction of point O.

If the apparent contrast C' between the target T and its background B is equal to ϵ, the contrast threshold, then the distance R' is the visual range of the target from the position O. The apparent contrast is given by

$$C' = \frac{L'_T - L'_B}{L'_B} \qquad (27\text{-}3)$$

where L'_T and L'_B are the apparent luminances of the target and its background at the position O.

If σ is the atmospheric attenuation coefficient (per unit length) and is constant throughout the region of interest, then

$$L'_T = L_T e^{-\sigma R'} + L_R \qquad (27\text{-}4)$$

where L_T is the inherent luminance of the target and L_R is the luminance added by light scattered from the searchlight beam in the direction of O from points along the line of sight between O and the target. The inherent luminance of the target in candelas per unit area is given by

$$L_T = \frac{\rho_T}{\pi} \left(\frac{I_0 e^{-\sigma R}}{R^2} + E_a \right) \qquad (27\text{-}5)$$

where E_a is the ambient illuminance on the target, and R and ρ_T are defined as above.

If the atmospheric attenuation is caused solely by scattering, and R is large in comparison with d, the luminance added by the light scattered from the searchlight beam is

$$L_R = \frac{I_0 \sigma}{\alpha \pi d} \int_0^{\pi/2} S_\varphi \, d\varphi \qquad (27\text{-}6)$$

where

$$S_\varphi = e^{-K\varphi^2 - 2\sigma R d/(R\varphi + d)} \qquad (27\text{-}7)$$

Similarly, the apparent luminance of the background, L'_B, is

$$L'_B = L_B e^{-\sigma(R'+r')} + L_R + L_r \qquad (27\text{-}8)$$

where L_B is the inherent luminance of the background, L_R and E_a are as previously defined, and L_r is the luminance added by light from the searchlight beam scattered in the direction of O from points along the line of sight between the target and its background. Also,

$$L_B = \frac{\rho_B}{\pi}\left(\frac{I_0 e^{-\sigma(R+r)}}{(R+r)^2} + E_a\right) \quad (27\text{-}9)$$

and

$$L_r = \frac{I_0 \sigma}{8\pi d}\int_\alpha^0 S_\varphi \, d\varphi \quad (27\text{-}10)$$

where, from figure 27-8, α is given by

$$\alpha = arctan(d/R) \quad (27\text{-}11)$$

Usually the value of E_a is so small in comparison with the values of the other pertinent terms in eqs. 27-5 and 27-8 that it may be neglected. Doing so, combining terms, and simplifying yields

$$C' = \frac{\left(\dfrac{\rho_T}{R^2} - \dfrac{\rho_B}{(R+r)^2}e^{-2\sigma r}\right)e^{-2\sigma R} - \dfrac{\sigma}{8d}\displaystyle\int_\alpha^0 S_\varphi \, d\varphi}{\dfrac{\rho_B}{(R+r)^2}e^{-2\sigma}(R+r) + \dfrac{\sigma}{8d}\displaystyle\int_\alpha^{\pi/2} S_\varphi \, d\varphi}$$

$$(27\text{-}12)$$

If the target is viewed against a sky or a very distant background, r becomes infinite and eq. 27-12 simplifies to

$$C' = \frac{\dfrac{\rho_T}{R^2}e^{-2R} - \dfrac{\sigma}{8d}\displaystyle\int_{\alpha'}^0 S_\varphi \, d\varphi}{\dfrac{\sigma}{8d}\displaystyle\int_{\alpha'}^{\pi/2} S_\varphi \, d\varphi} \quad (27\text{-}13)$$

where

$$\alpha' \approx d/R \quad (27\text{-}14)$$

Note that the apparent contrast is independent of the axial intensity of the searchlight, but is a function of its intensity distribution.

The contrast threshold ϵ applicable to the viewing situation is a function of the apparent background luminance L'_B and the angular size of the target. As stated, if C' is equal to ϵ, the distance R' is the visual range of the target.

When the target is viewed against a terrestrial background,

$$L'_B = \frac{I_0}{\pi}\left(\frac{\rho_B}{(R+r)^2}e^{-2\sigma(R+r)} + \frac{\sigma}{8d}\int_{\alpha'}^{\pi/2} S_\varphi \, d\varphi\right)$$

$$(27\text{-}15a)$$

and when the target is viewed against a sky back-

ground,

$$L'_B = \frac{I_0 \sigma}{8\pi d}\int_{\alpha'}^{\pi/2} S_\varphi \, d\varphi \quad (27\text{-}15b)$$

The visual range of a target is affected by its position within the searchlight beam. The magnitude of the effect is a function of most of the parameters listed above. Although quantitative generalizations are not possible, the following qualitative generalizations may be made. Illuminating the target with the "far" side of the beam (the part away from the position of the observer) may lead to losses in range as great as 40%. Small offsets of the target into the "near" side of the beam produce marked increases in range when the observer is close to the searchlight. These increases diminish and finally become decreases as the offset of the target from the beam axis and the displacement of the observer from the searchlight increase.[4-6]

The visual range of the target is highly dependent upon the displacement of the observer from the searchlight. For example, with a small target on the axis of the beam of a typical searchlight viewed against the sky in a clear atmosphere, the range increases about 25% as the observer moves from a position 9 m (30 ft) from the searchlight to a distance of 30 m (100 ft) from the searchlight, and about 50 and 75% when the displacement is 60 and 150 m (200 and 500 ft) respectively. The increase is even greater in hazy atmospheres.[4,5]

For small targets in a clear atmosphere, the range increases roughly as the fourth root of the area and of the reflectance of the target, and with the eighth root of the peak intensity of the searchlight; in haze the increase in range is even less rapid.[3,4]

The effects of intensity and atmospheric clarity on range are illustrated in figure 27-9, based upon the work of Rocard.[2] The figure should be considered only as an illustrative example because of the marked effect on range of the parameters discussed above.

The range is also affected by the beam spread of the searchlight, especially in hazy weather with targets of low reflectance.[5,6] For example, a decrease from a beam spread of 9.6° to 0.6° can increase the range by a factor of 3.[5]

The use of binoculars will increase the range of small targets by decreasing the illuminance threshold. For properly designed binoculars the threshold illuminance is inversely proportional to the square of the magnification.[8]

Peak Intensity of Projectors

Projectors differ from searchlights in that they produce a beam suitable for displaying images at great distances. A useful rough approximation of the peak intensity of a projector may be obtained from the formula

$$I = L\rho AF \quad (27\text{-}16)$$

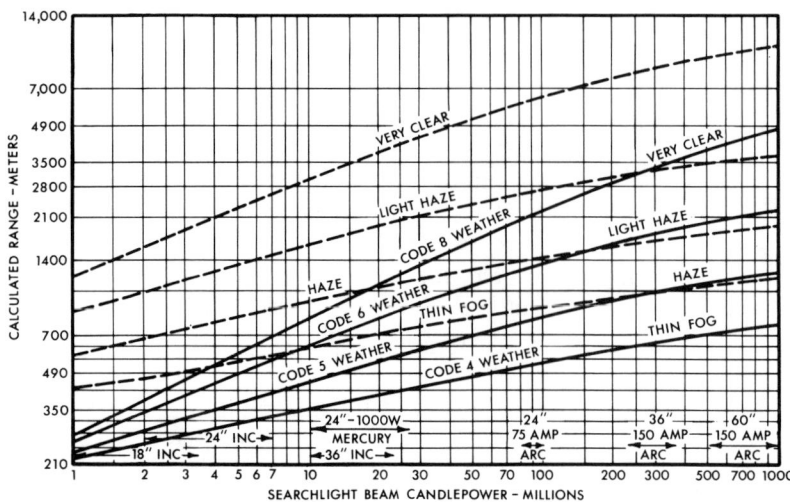

Code Number	Weather	Maximum Daylight Visibility
0	dense fog	50 meters
1	thick fog	200 meters
2	mod. fog	500 meters
3	light fog	1000 meters
4	thin fog	2 km
5	haze	4 km
6	light haze	10 km
7	clear	20 km
8	very clear	50 km
9	except. clear	over 50 km

Fig. 27-9. The effect of atmospheric clarity on the useful range of targets in searchlight beams. The solid lines represent small or low contrast targets, such as a person or a dark-colored automobile against a similarly dark background. The dashed lines represent large or high contrast targets, such as a ship or a building tower viewed against the sky.

where

I = peak intensity,
L = peak luminance of the source within the collecting angle of the optic,
ρ = reflectance of the reflector or transmittance of the refractor,
A = area of the projector aperture,
F = ratio of the flashed area to the total area of the aperture (the *flashed area* is the area of the reflector, seen from the front of the projector, in which the reflection of the source can be seen).

The factor F is dependent not only upon the proportion of the aperture obscured by the lamp and its supports, but also upon the size of the source and the accuracy of the optics. This factor typically varies from about 0.9 for projectors with precision optics and large sources to about 0.3 for projectors with nonprecision optics and small sources. If the beam is spread by use of spreader lenses or by moving the source away from the focus, F is given roughly by the relation

$$F = F_0 \theta_0 \phi_0 / \theta \phi \qquad (27\text{-}17)$$

where F_0 is the factor that would be applicable if the beam were made collimated by removing the spread lens or by placing the source at the focus, θ_0 and ϕ_0 are the horizontal and vertical beam spreads that would be obtained if the beam were collimated, and θ and ϕ are the horizontal and vertical spreads of the actual beam.

Benford[9] has made a very comprehensive study of light and its distribution in a searchlight beam.

Beam Spread (Divergence) of Projectors

To a first approximation, the beam spread of a projector producing a collimated beam can be obtained from the relation

$$\theta = \arctan \frac{l}{f} \qquad (27\text{-}18)$$

where

θ = horizontal or vertical beam spread,
l = width or height of the source, as applicable,
f = focal length of the optic.

Aberrations, imperfections and incorrect adjustments tend to increase the beam spread. If a collimated beam is made more divergent by the addition of a spreader lens, then a rough approximation of the beam spread may be obtained from the relation

$$\theta' = \theta + \arctan \frac{w}{f'} \qquad (27\text{-}19)$$

where

θ' = spread of the divergent beam,
w = width of a single flute (rounded narrow groove) of the spread lens,
f' = focal length of the flute in the plane perpendicular to its axis.

If the additional spread is obtained by moving the source away from the focus, the following relation is applicable:

$$\theta' = \arctan \frac{l}{u} \qquad (27\text{-}20)$$

where

l = width or height of the source, as applicable,
u = distance between the optic and the source.

See also references 9 through 11.

REFERENCES

1. Blondel, A. 1915. A method for determining the visual range of searchlights. *Illuminating Engineer (London)* 8:85; 8:153.
2. Rocard, Y. 1932. Visibilité des buts éclairés par un projecteur. *Revue d'Optique* 11(May):193; 11(June–July):257; 11(October):439; 13(April):160; 13(May):204.
3. Hampton, W. M. 1933. The visibility of objects in a searchlight beam. *Proc. Phys. Soc. (London)* 45(5): 663–672. Discussion. 1948. In *Symposium on Searchlights, London, April 15, 1947.* London: Illuminating Engineering Society (London).
4. Hulburt, E. O. 1946. Optics of searchlight illumination. *J. Opt. Soc. Am.* 36(8):483–491.
5. Chesterman, W. D., and W. S. Stiles. 1948. The visibility of targets in a naval searchlight beam. In *Symposium on Searchlights, London, April 15, 1947.* London: Illuminating Engineering Society (London). Beggs, S. S., and J. M. Waldram. 1948. Some visibility problems associated with anti-aircraft searchlight beams. In *Symposium on Searchlights, London, April 15, 1947.* London: Illuminating Engineering Society (London).
6. Blackwell, H. R., S. Q. Duntley, and W. M. Kincaid. 1953. *Characteristics of tank-mounted searchlights for detection of ground targets.* Washington: Armed Forces. National Research Council. Vision Committee.
7. Middleton, W. E. K. 1952. The visual range of light sources. In *Vision through the atmosphere*, Section 7.2. Toronto: Univ. of Toronto Press.
8. Tousey, R., and E. O. Hulburt. 1948. The visibility of stars in the daylight sky. *J. Opt. Soc. Am.* 38(10):886–896. Tousey, R., and M. J. Koomen. 1953. The visibility of stars and planets during twilight. *J. Opt. Soc. Am.* 43(3):177–183.
9. Benford, F. 1945. The projection of light. *J. Opt. Soc. Am.* 35(2):149–156. Benford, F. 1923–1924. Studies in the projection of light. *Gen. Elec. Rev.*, Part 1, 26(2):75–82; Part 2, 26(3):160–167; Part 3, 26(4):230–234; Part 4, 26(5):280–290; Part 5, 26(8):575–582; Part 6, 26(9):624–631; Part 7, 26(11):780–787; Part 8, 26(12):818–827; Part 9, 27(3):199–207; Part 10, 27(4):252–260.
10. Benford, F., and J. E. Bock. 1948. The normal probability curve as an approximation to the distribution curve of the high intensity searchlight. *J. Opt. Soc. Am.* 38(6):527–531.
11. IES. Testing Procedures Committee. Subcommittee on Photometry of Outdoor Luminaires. 1983. *IES guide for photometric testing of searchlights.* IES LM-11. New York: Illuminating Engineering Society of North America.

Underwater Lighting

28

Divers, manned submersible vehicles, unmanned instrument platforms and permanent bottom installations use underwater lighting[1-5] for a variety of tasks. Underwater television as well as motion picture and still photography are dependent on light for successful pictures.

Seeing ranges in water vary from a few centimeters (or inches) in contaminated waters to a few hundred meters (or feet) in unusually clear parts of the oceans. The underwater world differs in color appearance from that above water, looking yellow, yellow-green or green in bays or coastal areas and blue-green in deep, clear ocean water. The external pressure of water at great depths and the corrosive effects of seawater also provide unusual challenges to the designer of lighting equipment or lighting systems for underwater applications.

TERMS AND DEFINITIONS

The terms and definitions given here are peculiar to underwater lighting. The definitions generally follow the recommendations of the Committee on Ocean Optics of the International Association for the Physical Sciences of the Ocean (IAPSO). Neither the notation nor the units are universal, but they are widely used. Additional terms and definitions useful in underwater lighting are found in the Glossary.

It should be noted that in the past some authors have used terms such as "absorption" or "extinction" to mean "beam attenuation" as it is defined here, and that sometimes decade values for the beam attenuation, absorption or scattering coefficients have been given, with values smaller by the factor $1/\log_e 10$. To further confuse matters, both "extinction coefficient" and "vertical extinction coefficient" have sometimes been used for the term "diffuse attenuation coefficient."

The definitions used here are as follows:

Absorption Coefficient. The ratio of the radiant flux lost through absorption (dF_a), in an infinitesimally thin layer of medium normal to the beam, to the incident flux F, divided by the thickness of the layer (dx):

$$a = -\frac{1}{F}\frac{dF_a}{dx} \qquad (28\text{-}1)$$

The unit for a is m^{-1}. The symbol F for radiant flux is an IAPSO standard. The corresponding IES symbol for radiant flux is Φ.

Volume Scattering Function. The radiant intensity $dI(\theta)$ from a volume element dV in a given direction θ, per unit of irradiance E of a beam incident on the volume, per unit volume (θ is ordinarily measured from the forward direction):

$$\beta(\theta) = \frac{1}{E}\frac{dI(\theta)}{dV} \qquad (28\text{-}2)$$

The unit for $\beta(\theta)$ is m^{-1}.

(Total) Scattering Coefficient. The ratio of radiant flux lost through scattering in an infinitesimally thin layer of the medium normal to the beam (dF_s) to the incident flux F, divided by the thickness of the layer (dx); equivalent to the integral of the volume scattering function over all directions:

$$b = -\frac{1}{F}\frac{dF_s}{dx} = \int_0^{4\pi}\beta(\theta)\,d\omega$$
$$= 2\pi\int_0^{\pi}\beta(\theta)\sin\theta\,d\theta \qquad (28\text{-}3)$$

The unit for b is m^{-1}.

Beam Attenuation Coefficient. The sum of the absorption coefficient a and the scattering coefficient b:

$$c = a + b \qquad (28\text{-}4)$$

The unit for c is m^{-1}. Note: Sometimes the symbol α is used instead of c. Hence, a transmissometer is often called an "alphameter."

Diffuse Attenuation Coefficient for Irradiance. The ratio of irradiance lost through absorption and scattering in an infinitesimally thin horizontal layer of the medium (dE) to the incident irradiance E, divided by the thickness of the layer (dz).

$$K = -\frac{1}{E}\frac{dE}{dz} \qquad (28\text{-}5)$$

FILTERING PROPERTIES OF WATER[6]

Different wavelengths of light are absorbed by different amounts in water. Seawater that is both deep and clear has an absorption spectrum that closely resembles distilled water, with a peak transmission at 480 nm.

The absorption curves for other bodies of water differ greatly from those of distilled water due to the presence of silt, plant and animal material, pollution and living organisms. A widespread effect on the absorption characteristics of water comes from plankton. Plankton absorbs short wavelengths much more than long wavelengths. Therefore, the peak of the transmission curve in a body of water that includes plankton moves from 480 to between 510 and 570 nm. The degree to which the peak transmission shifts depends upon the density of the plankton.

Some typical spectral transmittance curves for different types of water are shown in figure 28-1.[7] The shapes of the spectral transmittance curves result primarily from absorption, but the curves include losses from both absorption and scattering processes. Since scattering in distilled water is nearly independent of wavelength, it affects the level of the curves and not their shapes.

The curve for Morrison Springs, Florida is essentially the same as for distilled water and has a maximum transmittance of over 90% at 480 nm. The main difference between the samples from Morrison Springs and the Gulf of Mexico is a lower transmittance in the short wavelengths for the latter, presumably due largely to plankton. The Long Island Sound water shows lower transmittance throughout the spectrum, with the greatest loss in the short wavelengths.

Waters in heavily polluted areas such as the Thames River in Connecticut[7] transmit very little light, and the curves will be completely different from those for distilled water.

Since light transmittance in water is related to distance by an exponential function, the spectral absorption becomes extreme as the distance the light travels increases. Therefore, the relative visibility of different colors can be expected to vary considerably in different types of water and at different distances.

SEEING DISTANCE IN WATER

Assuming a sufficient quantity of light, the seeing distance in water is limited by scattering. The loss of contrast and limited seeing distance in water are like those encountered in fog.

At short distances one can see reasonably well in water with almost any lighting arrangement. At longer distances, the quality of underwater images received by a sensor (eye or camera) located in the same volume of water and near the light source is seriously degraded by scattered light. Long-range underwater viewing can only be achieved when light scattering is minimal.

Two simple techniques are recommended to suppress underwater light scattering from electric light sources:

1. A light shield (septum) can be used to shield most of the line of sight from the direct field of the lamp or the optical control (reflector or refractor).

2. The light source can be offset to one side of the sensor. Then no part of the line of sight is close to the lamps; therefore, the inverse-square law and attenuation by absorption and scattering operate to avoid intense lighting of the water close to the sensor. Offset of the lamp may also be to the rear or to the front of the sensor. Offset to the rear offers good illuminance uniformity for large fields of view, but requires increased light source intensity to compensate for the longer distance between the light source and the viewed object. Offset to the front (source between sensor and object) is effective and efficient, but requires more complex light control to achieve illuminance uniformity.

3. A technique using crossed polarizers can be used. The lamp and the sensor must have orthogonally oriented polarizers, and the object must depolarize the light upon reflection in order for it to be visible. Each polarizer absorbs about half the light, so the light source

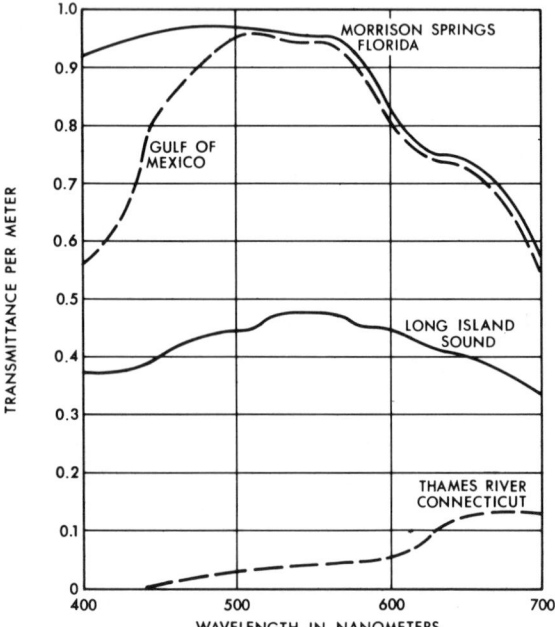

Fig. 28-1. Spectral transmittance of 1 m of various bodies of water.

Fig. 28-2. Values of One Attenuation Length
for Several Bodies of Water

Location	Attenuation Length (m)
Caribbean Sea	8
Pacific N. Equatorial Current	12
Pacific Countercurrent	12
Pacific Equatorial Divergence	10
Pacific S. Equatorial Current	9
Gulf of Panama	6
Galapagos Islands	4

intensity must be increased or the camera must have longer integration times, faster lens speed or greater film sensitivity.

To simplify quantitative discussion of seeing distance in water, the concept of attenuation length is often used. The attenuation length is defined as the reciprocal of the beam attenuation coefficient and is the distance in which the radiant flux is reduced to $1/e$, or about 37%, of its initial value. The attenuation length is analogous to the mean free path in physics and the time constant in electronics. Typical values of the attenuation length are shown in figure 28-2.[8]

Most underwater photography and viewing is done at distances of less than the attenuation length, because image contrast through such distances is acceptable even when the light source is very close to the camera. With daylight and horizontal viewing, a swimmer can detect a dark object at a maximum of about 4 attenuation lengths and a light object at about 4 to 5 attenuation lengths.[8] At 3 to 4 attenuation lengths, good images can be obtained with the aid of the polarizer and septum techniques. Good images can be obtained at 6 attenuation lengths with the light moved near the object in combination with the septum and polarizers. With an ideally arranged combination of these aids and high-contrast film developing, usable photographs have been obtained at a distance of 12 attenuation lengths corresponding to 120 m (394 ft) in average clear ocean water.

There is a limit to the underwater viewing range which becomes apparent at slightly greater distances. Even with unlimited sensor integration time, self-luminous objects, and silhouetted objects in otherwise unlighted water, objects disappear in their own forward-scattered light beyond approximately 15 attenuation lengths. Contrast enhancement techniques extend this limit only slightly.

The laboratory experiments from which the above numbers were derived were performed with stationary objects, moderate-sensitivity film (ASA 160), an $f/2$ lens, and a DVY lamp. At distances of 1 or 2 attenuation lengths the exposure times were small fractions of a second, but at 5 or 6 attenuation lengths several minutes were required. A time exposure of several

hours was needed in order to obtain a picture at 12 attenuation lengths. Such sensor integration times are not usually feasible, but they give an idea of the amount of light or sensor sensitivity required for viewing under water.

Another technique to suppress scattering can be used where its complexity and cost are justifiable. A scanned narrow-beam light source synchronized with the sensor system can reduce scattering to a minimum.[9]

SENSOR CHARACTERISTICS

A wide variety of sensors is available for underwater usc. The choice of sensor type will depend on the overall system requirements and will have a bearing on the characteristics required of the associated underwater lighting equipment.

These sensors may be divided into two general categories: imaging, as in the case of television or film; and nonimaging, for use in instrumentation applications such as photometry and attenuation or scattering measurement.

Photographic Films

Black-and-white films used in underwater photography have ASA ratings between 12 and 400, and with special development, ASA ratings up to 3200 can be obtained. Negative and positive color films are available with ASA ratings from 25 to 400, and again, special processing can push these film speeds even higher. It is best to discuss the application with the film manufacturer to determine the best film for use in a given application. The spectral responses of typical films are shown in figure 28-3.

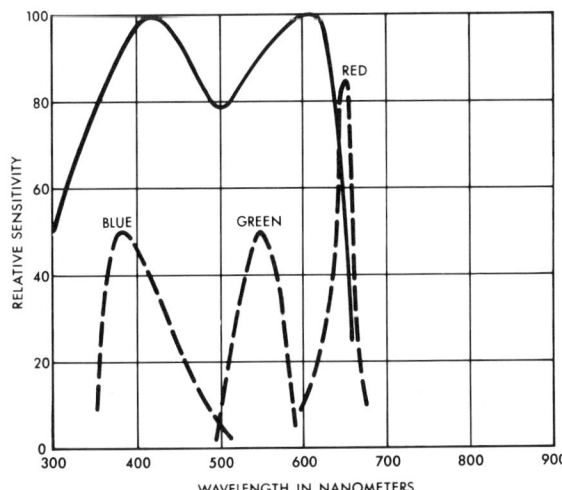

Fig. 28-3. Spectral responses of black and white panchromatic negative film (solid line) and of a typical color reversal film (dashed line).

Television Sensors

Over the past several years the devices used to obtain television pictures have changed dramatically. The devices of the past, such as vidicons, image orthicons and isocons, are used very little today and have been displaced by newer technology. They suffer from high lag time (the time required between images, resulting from the persistence of the previous image), low sensitivity and high power requirements.

The *secondary-electron conduction* (SEC) camera tube is of moderate size and sensitivity. It has a low lag time (10% or less) and is not affected much by relative scene motion.

The *electron-bombarded silicon target* and *silicon intensified target* (SIT) tubes are still used in security and military applications. They have extremely high sensitivity and operate in ambient light environments such as moonlight or starlight. They are highly burn-resistant diode array targets. These tubes are intermediate in size and provide a higher signal-to-noise ratio than some of the obsolete tubes.

Charge-coupled devices (CCD) have become the most common imaging devices. They are sensitive and operate at reduced power levels. They also have the advantage of being able to acquire a "snapshot" image in a variable time frame and have the equivalent of shutter speeds in the range of $\frac{1}{1000}$ s. The image cannot be downloaded to the video electronic package in that short a time, but it can be stored in digital buffer memory for later transmission as a video signal timed to produce a picture in the standard $\frac{1}{60}$-s interlacing video system common to the industry. The ability to acquire information at such a high speed allows the CCD imaging device to stop action and produce very clear, high-speed pictures.

Nonimaging Sensors

Photodiodes and photomultipliers available for use in underwater instrumentation generally employ semitransparent photocathodes with a spectral response similar to those shown in figure 28-4. Characteristics of other types of photosensitive devices are described in chapter 2, Measurement of Light and Other Radiant Energy. Because of the extreme variations possible in the spectral transmittance of water, it is often necessary to match the sensor spectral response to the system application or to make a number of narrow-band measurements.

LIGHT SOURCES FOR UNDERWATER USE

Many kinds of light sources are used in underwater lighting systems in a wide range of wattages for television and photography as well as for visual inspection.

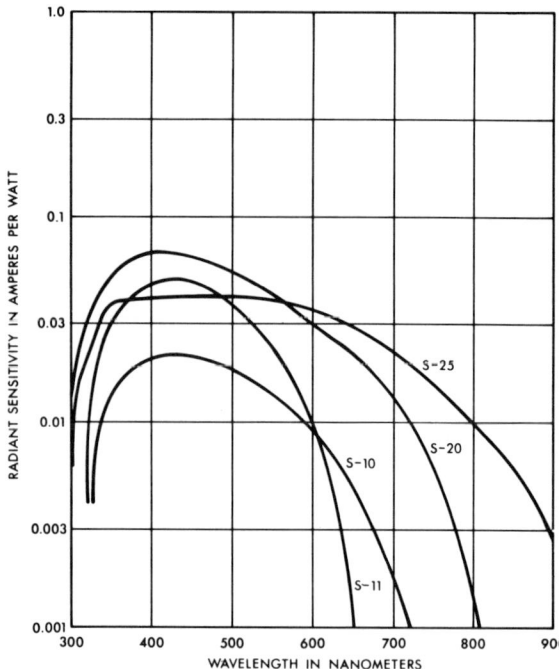

Fig. 28-4. Absolute spectral response of some semitransparent photocathodes.

Incandescent sources are used where instantaneous starting, simplicity and small size are requirements. Arc discharge sources are used where their higher efficacy is required. Typical underwater lighting units are shown in figure 28-5.

In choosing light sources for underwater applications, one should consider the filtering properties of the water. Theoretically it should be possible to maximize the color rendering of any underwater scene by proper choice of a light source. In clear ocean water, for example, a tungsten lamp with high output in the long wavelengths might be used to replace the wavelengths absorbed by the water. In turbid water, on the other hand, a mercury source with its preponderance of blue and green light could bring a better color balance. In all practicality, however, the balance may have to be achieved on a trial-and-error basis, since waters vary so much among themselves and since the exponential absorption of light with both lighting and viewing distances makes the actual underwater ranges very important.

Although not commonly available in underwater lighting equipment, other light sources applicable to underwater systems, and now found in one-of-a-kind custom-built systems, include the scandium sodium metal halide, mercury short arc and xenon short arc. These have been found to be effective for visual, photographic and television uses.

Electrical characteristics and power supplies for the various light sources are discussed in chapter 6, Light Sources. Also, there are auxiliary circuits available

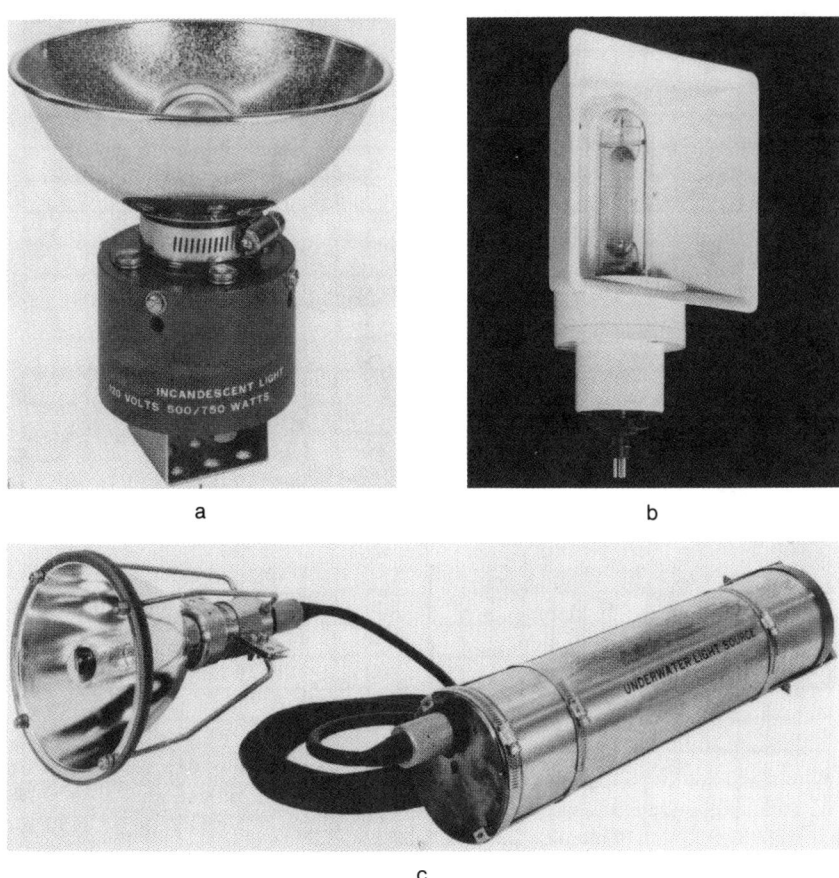

Fig. 28-5. Typical underwater lighting units. (a) Incandescent. (b) Arc discharge. (c) Pulsed xenon.

from underwater lighting equipment manufacturers which are especially designed for the unusual requirements of various underwater lighting applications. Information pertaining to the design of pressure housings for underwater lights is available.[10]

Lasers are also coming into increasing use in underwater systems.[11]

UNDERWATER LIGHTING CALCULATIONS

The amount of light needed for an underwater task is difficult to predict with any accuracy. Wide variations exist in the color filtering and contrast-reducing properties of water from place to place, and from day to night and season to season in the same place. For these reasons, the calculations described here are approximations, but they are often sufficient for these purposes.

Daylighting Calculations

The illuminance due to daylighting on a surface parallel to the water surface can be calculated by

$$E = E_0 e^{-Kd} \qquad (28\text{-}6)$$

where E_0 is the illuminance at the surface of the water, K is the diffuse attenuation coefficient for irradiance, and d is the depth from the water surface to the illuminated surface. An observer looking at this surface would see an apparent luminance

$$L = E\rho e^{-cr_2} \qquad (28\text{-}7)$$

where ρ is the reflectance of the illuminated surface, c is the beam attenuation coefficient, and r_2 is the distance from the illuminated surface to the underwater observer. Extensive studies of daylight in water have been made.[8]

Electric Lighting Calculations

The luminance observed by an underwater viewer or camera is

$$L = \frac{I\rho\tau}{r_1^2} \qquad (28\text{-}8)$$

where I is the source luminous intensity, ρ is the object reflectance, τ is the water transmittance (two-way path), and r_1 is the source-to-object distance. The water transmittance can be approximated by

$$\tau = e^{-c(r_1 + r_2)} \qquad (28\text{-}9)$$

where c is the beam attenuation coefficient of the water, and r_2 is the object-to-sensor distance. If $r_1 + r_2$ equals one meter, this equation also defines the relation between c and τ for figure 28-1. Two factors must be considered in evaluating the validity of using these equations in this simple form: spectral effects (that is, c, I, ρ, and the sensor response are functions of wavelength) and scattering.

A semiempirical formula has been developed[8] to allow approximate calculation of the amount of scattered light that illuminates the object. This forward-scattered component is not included in the simple expression given above for τ, but it can become quite large. The proportion of scattered light in the object illumination increases with range. At 1 attenuation length, the unscattered object illuminance (calculated by the simple expression given above) is nearly equal to the illuminance due to scattering. At 4 attenuation lengths, the scattered illumination is about 10 times the unscattered illumination. The increase in calculated object luminance due to scattering is partially offset by losses due to spectral filtering (see figure 28-1).

The value of the beam attenuation coefficient, c, used in approximate calculations (eqs. 28-7 and 28-9) is usually the minimum value with respect to wavelength (maximum value in the transmittance curves of figure 28-1). For photometric calculations, figure 28-1 shows that this choice is a reasonable approximation, because the curves are nearly flat in the region of photopic spectral sensitivity. When the sensor has a spectral response much different from that of the eye or when more accurate predictions are needed, the radiance observed by the underwater sensor at each wavelength can be calculated as

$$L_\lambda = \frac{\rho_\lambda \tau_\lambda I_\lambda}{r_1^2} \qquad (28\text{-}10)$$

where I_λ is the spectral radiant intensity of the source. The expression for τ_λ is the same as for τ except that the attenuation coefficient c is now c_λ, a function of wavelength. The symbol ρ_λ refers to the spectral reflectance. The response of the underwater sensor is

$$S = \int_{\lambda_1}^{\lambda_2} S_\lambda E_\lambda \, d\lambda \qquad (28\text{-}11)$$

where S_λ is the spectral response of the sensor (see figures 28-3 and 28-4) and E_λ is the irradiance of the sensor due to L_λ. E_λ and L_λ are related by the usual imaging equation:

$$E_\lambda = \frac{\pi t_\lambda L_\lambda}{4(f\text{-number})^2} \qquad (28\text{-}12)$$

where t_λ is the lens spectral transmittance. Further discussion of spectral calculations can be found in the references.[12–14]

Additional discussion of underwater lighting calculations can be found in the references.[8, 9, 15–17]

MEASUREMENT TECHNIQUES AND INSTRUMENTATION

The performance of underwater light sources has been tested according to standard measuring techniques for light sources used in air. These data are usually supplied on the product information sheets, but can be misleading because, as pointed out above, light absorption is relative to the wavelength. The photometric units often given do not apply when these light sources are used in water.

There are no established methods of instrumentation to evaluate a light source in the water environment. A number of research programs by light source manufacturers are underway, but standardization is distant.

REFERENCES

1. Spinrad, R. W., ed. 1991. *Underwater Imaging, Photography and Visiblity. Proceedings 23 July 1991.* San Diego: Society of Photo-optical Engineers.
2. Hersey, J. B. 1967. *Deep-sea Photography.* Baltimore: Johns Hopkins Press.
3. Duntley, S. Q. 1977. An overview of the basic parameters controlling underwater visibility. In *Oceans '77 Conference Record, Los Angeles, October 17–19, 1977.* Piscataway, NJ, and Washington: Institute of Electrical and Electronics Engineers and Marine Technology Society.
4. Jerlov, N. G. 1976. *Marine optics.* 2nd ed. Elsevier Oceanography Series, No. 14. Amsterdam: Elsevier.
5. Lankes, L. R. 1970. Optics and the physical parameters of the sea. *Opt. Spect.* 4(5):42–49.
6. Smith, R. C., and K. S. Baker. 1981. Optical properties of the clearest natural waters (200–800 nm). *Appl. Opt.* 20(2):177–184.
7. Kinney, J. A. S., S. M. Luria, and D. O. Weitzman. 1967. Visibility of colors underwater. *J. Opt. Soc. Am.* 57(6):802–809.
8. Duntley, S. Q. 1963. Light in the sea. *J. Opt. Soc. Am.* 53(2):214–233.
9. Mertens, L. E. 1970. *In-water photography: Theory and practice.* New York: Wiley-Interscience.
10. Stachiw, J. D. and K. O. Gray. 1967. *Light housings for deep submergence applications.* Part I, Report TR-532; Part II, Report TR-559. Naval Civil Engineering Laboratory.

11. Eastman Kodak Company. Professional, Commercial, and Industrial Markets Division. 1972. *Bibliography on underwater photography and photogrammetry.* Kodak Pamphlet P-124. Rochester, NY: Eastman Kodak.

12. ITT. 1966. *Source-detector spectral matching factors.* Technical Note 100. Fort Wayne, IN: ITT Industrial Laboratories.

13. Biberman, L. M. 1967. Apples, oranges and unlumens. In *Long abstracts: 1967 spring meeting program, Columbus OH, April 12-14, 1967.* [Washington]: Optical Society of America.

14. Moon, P. 1936. *The scientific basis of illuminating engineering.* 1st ed. New York: McGraw-Hill.

15. Austin, R. W. 1970. Assessing underwater visibility. *Opt. Spect.* 4(5):34–39.

16. Jerlov, N. G., and E. Steemann Nielsen, eds. 1974. *Symposium on Optical Aspects of Oceanography, June 19–23, 1972, Copenhagen.* New York: Academic Press.

17. Kinney, J. A. S. 1985. *Human underwater vision: Physiology and physics.* Bethesda, MD: Undersea Medical Society.

Lighting for Advertising

29

Through the knowledge and use of materials, light sources and techniques, a wide variety of signs can be produced for today's needs. Illuminated advertising signs, whether exposed lamp, luminous tube or luminous element, while differing in several respects from other forms of advertising, definitely tie in with any overall promotional activity. Signs can quickly gain the observers' attention through the combined use of size, color and motion.

SIGN CHARACTERISTICS

Electric signs may be classified by illumination method:

- *Luminous-letter signs* have illuminated letters and a nonilluminated background, such as those with exposed lamps, exposed luminous tubes, raised glass or plastic letters.
- *Luminous-element signs* have panels of translucent plastic or glass, which are illuminated by interior light sources such as HID, fluorescent or incandescent lamps or luminous tubing.
- *Floodlighted signs* are those such as painted bulletins and poster panels.

Signs may also be classified by their application—for example, as single-faced with luminous elements or as double-faced projecting.

Physical location, desired legibility range and brightness determine the minimum letter height required for legibility. To attain advertising effectiveness, letter heights of twice the minimum height for legibility are generally employed. Vertical columns of letters, though usually an aid in increasing the apparent size of a sign, are more difficult to read than horizontal arrangements.

Brightness. Letter or background brightness and contrast between letter and background are factors influencing the legibility of a letter and the speed with which it is recognized. The contrast between the average brightness of a sign and that of its surround determines, in large measure, the manner in which the sign stands out. Brightness and contrast attract attention.

Location and Position. The advertising value of a sign depends on the greatest possible number of persons seeing it. This is a function of its location.

Distinctiveness. One of the elements of a good electric sign is that it is distinctive and individual. It should create a pleasing, favorable impression, should have public appeal and should be remembered easily.

Motion. Motion increases the attracting power and memory value of a sign. It capitalizes on the instinctive trait of people to be aware of and to give heed to moving things.

Color. Color is an important factor in legibility. Often color is incorporated in a sign because it provides contrast. It may aid in attracting attention and may make a sign more distinctive.

EXPOSED-LAMP SIGNS

Signs with Exposed Incandescent Filament Lamps

These signs are constructed so that the lamps are exposed to direct view. This type is well suited to applications where long viewing distances are involved, as well as for small, high-brightness signs. Motion and color can be incorporated in such signs as shown in figure 29-1.

Legibility. The legibility of a sign is primarily a function of letter size and design, letter spacing, contrast between letter and background, and sign brightness.

Block letters possess greater legibility than ornamental styles, script or special forms, although the latter types may be used to increase distinctiveness. Wide, extended letters are more legible than tall, thin letters.

Reflectors. When wide-angle viewing is relatively unimportant, reflector lamps or reflectors may be used to enhance the lamp's directional candlepower. Reflectors can greatly increase brightness at the intended viewing angle as well as the sign's effectiveness during daylight hours. They can also lower lamp wattage for the same advertising effectiveness.

Fig. 29-1. Spectacular signs located in a highly competitive advertising area where close to half a million people pass daily. Computer programmed red, blue, green and white incandescent filament 30- and 50-watt R-20 lamps provide a colorful, animated display for day and night viewing.

Letter Size. The letter height employed on an exposed-lamp sign usually is greater than the minimum height necessary to gain recognition. For quick reading of advertising, it is common practice to provide exposed-lamp signs with letter heights that are $1\frac{1}{2}$ to 2 times greater than those necessary for legibility.

For simple block letters where the width is equal to 60% of the height, and having a single row of lamps, in typical locations the minimum height for legibility is given by the formula

$$H_r = \frac{D}{500} \qquad (29\text{-}1)$$

where

H_r = minimum vertical height of the letter, for recognition, from top lamp to bottom lamp, m (ft),

D = maximum distance at which the letter is legible to a majority of people, m (ft).

For letters with strokes consisting of multiple rows of lamps, the height should be increased by three times W, the distance between outside rows of lamps in a stroke:

$$H_r = \frac{D}{500} + 3W \qquad (29\text{-}2)$$

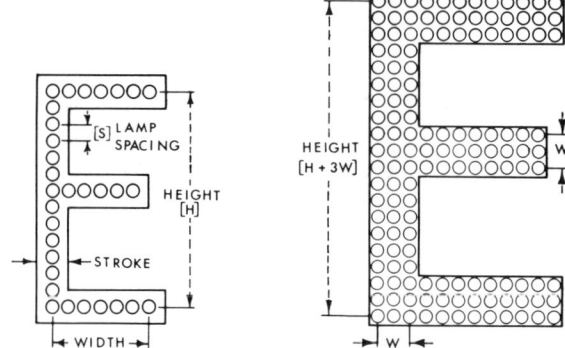

Fig. 29-2. Important dimensions in the design of exposed lamp letters.

Letter width, height, stroke width and lamp spacing are illustrated in figure 29-2.

Lamp Spacing. The proper spacing between lamps to obtain an apparently continuous line of light is determined by the minimum viewing distance. Lamp spacing may be estimated by the following formula:

$$S = D\frac{D_{\min}}{1500} \qquad (29\text{-}3)$$

where

S = spacing between centerlines of lamps, m (ft),

$D_{\min}$ = minimum viewing distance, m (ft).

In very bright locations the above spacing should be decreased by 25–35%.

To produce a *smooth* line of light, the above spacing should be decreased by 50%. At viewing distances of less than 150 m (500 ft), a smooth line of light will generally not be possible, because low-wattage, medium-based lamps (6-, 11- or 15-W S-14) require spacings of 50–60 mm [2–2.5 in] to permit easy maintenance.

Lamp Wattage Rating. The incandescent lamp wattage employed depends upon the general brightness of the surroundings and background against which the sign is viewed. Thus, a roof sign, even if located in a brightly lighted district in the business center of a city, might always be viewed against a dark sky at night. Such a sign would require the same lamps called for in low-brightness areas.

Figure 29-3 indicates the typical lamp wattages found in signs in various areas, classified according to district brightness.

Fig. 29-3. Lamp Wattages for Various District Brightnesses

District Brightness	Typical Sign Lamp Wattages
Low [E_v < 10 lx (1 fc)]	6, 10, 11
Medium [E_v = 10 – 50 lx (1 – 5 fc)]	10, 11, 15, 25
Bright [E_v > 50 lx (5 fc)]	25, 40

Fig. 29-4. Relative Wattage of Clear and Transparent Colored Incandescent Filament Lamps Required for Approximately Equal Advertising Value

Color	clear	yellow	orange	red	green	blue
Wattage	10-11	10-11	15	25	25	40

If incandescent lamps with colored bulbs or clear bulbs with colored accessories are employed, lower letter brightness will result than when equal-wattage lamps with clear bulbs are used alone. However, less colored light is necessary to create equal advertising effectiveness. It is therefore not necessary to increase wattage in direct proportion to the output of the colored lamps. This is taken into account in figure 29-4.

Both transparent and ceramic coatings are used to color bulbs. In general, the transparent coatings have higher transmittances than the ceramic; thus the transparent coated lamps appear brighter. In addition, the filament is visible for added "glitter" at near viewing distances.

Note that signs lighted in cool colors, blue and green for example, will generally be less legible than those with clear or warm-colored lamps, because cool colors appear to "swell" or "irradiate" more than warm.

Lamp Types. For exposed-lamp signs located where rain or snow can fall on the hot glass, vacuum-type incandescent lamps are recommended. They are available in 6-, 10-, 11-, 15-, 25- and 40-W ratings in both clear and colored bulbs.

For high-speed motion effects, a 20-W gas-filled clear lamp is available. The filament heats and cools very rapidly, producing a clean, sharp on-off action. It is used for scintillation effects, running borders and traveling message signs, and wherever afterglow is undesirable.

Channels. Incandescent lamps are often set into channels. This improves the legibility of the sign when viewed at an angle, and increases contrast by reducing background spill light. It does not prevent the strokes of the letters from merging together when viewed at a distance, since this phenomenon occurs in the eye.

It is desirable to employ electrically grounded metal channels to separate incandescent filament lamps and luminous tubing when combined in a sign. Without the channel, the electric field generated by the tubing causes the filament to vibrate, thereby reducing the life of the lamp.

Effective Daytime Exposed-Lamp Signs

Exposed, high-candlepower light sources can be used to create electric signs that have as much, or more,

Fig. 29-5. Animation panel with constantly changing graphics and messages.

advertising value during the day as do conventional exposed-lamp signs at night. Since traffic is generally greater during daylight hours, greatly increased readership usually results, so that the cost per advertising impression remains comparable to that of night-viewed lamp signs. The technique is adaptable to signs ranging in size from small store signs to community bulletin boards (see figure 29-5) to major spectaculars (see figure 29-1).[1]

The letter height and lamp spacing in a daytime lamp sign depend primarily on the lamp candlepower and on the maximum and minimum viewing distances.[2]

For the great majority of daytime sign applications, 75-W PAR-38 floodlamps on 150-mm (6-in.) centers will adequately meet advertising and identification needs. Higher-candlepower sources should be used with care, since there is a possibility of making the sign too bright for comfort. A guide for choosing lamp size is given in figure 29-6.

The minimum letter height for legibility is the same as for nighttime exposed-lamp signs.

It should be recognized that a daytime sign utilizing PAR-type lamps is a highly directional display. The sign's luminance is a function of the candlepower distribution of the lamp. With a PAR flood, for example, the luminance is reduced to 10% of maximum when viewed 30° off axis. This characteristic also provides automatic dimming of the sign as a motorist drives toward it and under the beam of the lamp.

Nighttime Viewing. A sign of sufficient brightness to compete successfully with daylight will, in most cases, require dimming at night in order to prevent loss of legibility due to irradiation and the possibility of excessive glare. The need for dimming appears to occur for the 75-W PAR-38 flood at about 250-lx (25-fc) daylight illumination, vertically, on the back of the sign. Except for the highest-candlepower lamps, dimming by reduc-

Fig. 29-6. Daytime Attraction Power of Several Lamp Types (Viewed Perpendicular to Plane of Sign)

Lamp	Spacing		Distance (meters [feet])		
	millime-ters	inches	330 [1100]	750 [2500]	1300 [4300]
25-watt PAR-38 Flood	150	6	F	P	NR
	305	12	P	NR	NR
	460	18	—	—	NR
75-watt PAR-38 Flood	150	6	E	E	G
	305	12	G	G	F
	460	18	—	—	NR
150-watt PAR-38 Flood	150	6	*	E	E
75-watt PAR-38 Spot	305	12	*	E	G
	460	18	—	—	F
150-watt PAR-38 Spot	150	6	*	E	E
	305	12	*	E	E
	460	18	—	—	E

——Spacing inadequate.
*—Brighter than normally necessary.
E—Excellent.
G—Good.
F—Fair.
P—Poor.
NR—Not recommended

ing the line voltage 50% has generally proved satisfactory. An inexpensive and effective dimming method is to place the primary windings of 120–240-V supply transformers in series. Greater dimming, especially for very high candlepower sources, through multiple-tap or variable transformers may be required. Continuously variable brightness depending on the sky brightness may be accomplished by regulating a dimming system with a photocell.

LUMINOUS-TUBE SIGNS[3]

Luminous-tube signs (see figure 29-7) are constructed of gas-filled glass tubing which, when subjected to high voltage, becomes luminescent in a color characteristic of the particular gas used, of the gas and the color of the tubing combined, or of the fluorescent phosphors coating the inner wall.

Color. Fluorescent tubing may be made to emit almost any desired color by mixing different phosphors. Most coated tubings have a higher lumen output per watt than the gaseous tubing without a fluorescent coating. Color produced by any one of the gases may be modified by using colored glass tubing, which will transmit only certain colors.

Effective Range. The range of effectiveness for advertising purposes of tube signs is approximately that of exposed-incandescent-lamp signs of the same size, color and luminance, from 75 m (250 ft) to over 3 km (2 mi).

Legibility. For block letters of width equal to three-fifths of their height, the minimum letter height that will be legible to most people is approximately the same as that for exposed-lamp signs.

Fig. 29-7. Luminous letter sign provides a distinctive and recognizable identification for pedestrians and motorists.

Tubing Sizes. Standard sizes of tubing for signs range from 9 to 15 mm (outside diameter), but larger tubing is available.

Transformers. Several forms of high-leakage-reactance transformers are manufactured to supply the high voltage necessary to start and operate sign tubing. This voltage is of the order of 3000–15,000 V. After a tube sign is lighted, 60% of the starting voltage is necessary to keep it operating. The usual range of operating currents for tube signs is between 10 and 60 mA.

Additional information on luminous-tube lighting for advertising may be obtained from the National Electric Sign Association.

LUMINOUS-ELEMENT SIGNS

A luminous-element sign can be created by transilluminating or backlighting a plastic or glass panel that may be either integrally pigmented, externally painted or opaqued. The pigmentation or paint film diffuses the light, providing uniform brightness over the desired portion of the sign face. See figure 29-8. A wide variety of colors is possible with both the integrally pigmented media and the available translucent lacquers and films.

Design Data for Luminous Elements

Proper lighting is important to assure the best attraction and readability for these signs. Other points, however, must be considered along with the lighting.

Contrast. High contrast, either in color or brightness, between message and background panels should be provided. Opaque letters on a light background are generally preferred for commercial signs because of their attractiveness. Where communication is of prime

Fig. 29-8. Luminous sign for attraction both day (left) and night (right).

importance, as with rental car return signs, very light letters on dark backgrounds are generally specified.

Light Sources. Selection of the light source is based on the brightness required, size and shape of the sign, desired color effects, flashing or dimming requirements, environmental temperature conditions, and service access requirements. Linear sources, such as fluorescent lamps, luminous tubing or custom sign tubing, may be used as the lighting element. Special diffusing materials should be used with spot sources, such as incandescent or high-intensity discharge lamps, to prevent "hot spots" of brightness on sign faces. Specially designed HID luminaires are available for internally illuminated signs which do not require diffusing screens because of a refractor designed specifically for this application. These luminaires effectively distribute the light from a single HID lamp across the entire face of such signs. Their use leads to cost- and energy-efficient signs.

Sign Brightness. Adequate sign brightness should be provided, but it is important that it should not be overdone. The best brightness depends primarily upon the desired sign visibility, its use and the environment in which it is to be seen. See figure 29-9.

Calculating the Number of Linear Lamps Needed. When white, yellow or ivory backgrounds are used, a formula for estimating the spacing of linear lighting elements (usually fluorescent lamps) in millimeters (inches) is as follows:

$$d = \frac{K\tau \times \Phi/l}{L} \qquad (29\text{-}4)$$

where

K = 250 when l is in meters, 9.4 when l is in feet (a constant for the combined interreflectance characteristics of the sign enclosure),

l = length of the lamp in meters (feet)

L = luminance required (from figure 29-9),

τ = transmittance of the medium (from manufacturer's literature or measurement),

Φ/l = number of lumens per meter (foot) of lamp to be used. This is obtained by dividing the manufacturer's initial lumen output for the lamp by the length in meters (feet). (This formula may be modified for maintained lumens by including an appropriate factor for lamp lumen depreciation [LLD] in the numerator.)

This spacing is based on providing a clearance between the lighting elements and the sign face material equal to the center-to-center spacing value. However, with both internally pigmented media and with lacquer coatings, it is possible to obtain satisfactory diffusion in many cases with a smaller clearance. There is, of course, a minimum clearance distance, whereby an

Fig. 29-9. Recommended Luminous Background Sign Luminances

Range of Sign Luminance		Potential Areas of Application
Candelas/ square meter	Candelas/ square foot	
70 to 350	7 to 35	Lighted facades and fascia signs
250 to 500	25 to 50	Bright fascia signs as in shopping centers
450 to 700	45 to 70	"Low" brightness areas where signs are relatively isolated or have dark surrounds
700 to1000	70 to 100	Average commercial sign such as for gas station identification
1000 to 1400	100 to 140	High rise signs and signs in areas of high sign competition
1400 to 1700	140 to 170	For emergency traffic control conditions where communication is critical

image of the light elements will be seen through the sign face. Clearances between the lamps and the sign face can be determined in a test mockup when experience and published data are lacking.

Adaptation of Formulas for Point Sources. The formulas above may be adapted for point sources by using the following form:

$$\text{spacing between lamps (mm)} = 1000\sqrt{\frac{K\tau\Phi}{L}} \quad (29\text{-}4a)$$

$$\text{spacing between lamps (in.)} = 12\sqrt{\frac{K\tau\Phi}{L}} \quad (29\text{-}4b)$$

This gives the same spacing in the vertical and horizontal directions. The clearance between the surface of the lamps and the sign face media should be not less than that derived from the following formulas:

$$\text{minimum clearance (mm)} = 12.5\sqrt{\text{lamp wattage}}$$
$$(29\text{-}5)$$

$$\text{minimum clearance (in.)} = 0.5\sqrt{\text{lamp wattage}}$$
$$(29\text{-}6)$$

This prevents overheating of the sign face media by direct radiation from the lamp. Having determined the necessary spacing, the number of lamps can be readily calculated.

Obscuring Lamp Sockets. Where fluorescent lamps are to be used, the dimensions of the sign should be such that the lamp sockets are located just beyond the translucent face area. This will prevent shadows at the edges directly over the lamp sockets. Series arrangement of tubes in large signs using more than one tube per row requires overlapping of the tubes by at least 76 mm (3 in.) to prevent shadows similar to those at the sockets. All internal sign components such as structural framing, sheet metal backgrounds and ballasts should be coated with at least two coats of high-reflectance (85% or higher) white paint to derive maximum lighting efficiency and prevent shadows.

Venting. Provision for venting and air circulation may be necessary, depending upon the environmental temperature conditions of the sign. This is primarily to maintain the efficiency and to prolong the life of the lighting elements and supporting equipment such as ballasts. In signs with lamps close together, forced ventilation may be necessary to prevent overheating of the sign face media.

Legibility. The legibility of a luminous panel sign depends primarily on four factors:

1. The size and proportions of the letters and the letter design configuration
2. The letter spacing
3. The color and brightness contrast between letter and background
4. The brightness of the sign face

Size and Proportions of Letters. With dark letters and light background colors, the following formula may be used to determine the minimum letter height:

$$H = \frac{D}{600} \quad (29\text{-}7)$$

where
H = letter height, m (ft),
D = maximum distance of legibility, m (ft).

For maximum readability, the width of a letter should be 60% of the height, and a stroke should equal 15% of the height in a sans serif (block Gothic) style.

Spacing of Letters. The above width and stroke proportions are effective in preventing blending of letter lines where legibility at a distance is required. Considerable license is possible with the spacing of painted letters; however, for maximum legibility distance, the spacing between letters should be 15% of the letter height, with allowance for visual equalization of white masses, such as between a letter W and a letter A.

Letters and illustrations, or insignia, of bold silhouette rather than fine detail are preferable for long-distance legibility. Fine detail and stylized script letters find their greatest use where they will normally be observed from a relatively close distance, as in downtown shopping areas and in shopping malls. Three-dimensional formed and fabricated letters should be spaced on the basis of their depth of forming and the minimum observation angle acuteness, that is, the minimum angle parallel to the sign which will allow the sign to be read. See figure 29-10.

The ratios given in figure 29-10 are also useful in the design of letters to be formed or fabricated so that their legibility is a function of the observation angle. For example, based on a minimum observation angle of 10° and a proposed depth of forming of 50 mm (2 in.),

Fig. 29-10. Maximum Spacing of Three-Dimensional Letters

Observation Angle (degrees from plane of sign)	Minimum Spacing*
5	12 D
10	6 D
15	4 D
20	3 D

* D = depth of formed or fabricated letter.

the minimum opening in a letter such as O should be 6 times 5, or 300 mm (6 × 2 = 12 in.). Hence, for minimum observation angles letters will be extended, and the average letter width will be as large as the letter height, or more, to meet the requirements of acute observation angles.

Luminance and Readability of Sign Face. The brightness of the sign face has a significant influence on the readability of the sign. A sign which is too bright can suffer loss of readability from a halo effect around the letters. Insufficient lighting will reduce the legibility distance. The recommendations for sign luminance in given districts, shown in figure 29-9, are suitable guides. In some cases, where high background brightness is required, elimination of the halo effect is achieved by applying a stripe of opaque black paint, 13 mm (0.5 in) wide, around the outline of the letter. This applies particularly to those signs employing flat cut-out, formed or fabricated letters attached to light-colored backgrounds. In signs using dark backgrounds with light letters, *debossing*, or forming depressed areas rather than the conventional raised letter areas, eliminates halation.

Luminous Building Fronts or Facades

The same basic data for design of luminous elements applies, in general, to luminous portions of building fronts. However, the surface luminances need not be designed for more than 350 cd/m². In an area of low-level environmental lighting, 85 cd/m² of surface luminance will be adequate.

Building Fascia (Belt) Signs

Lamps may be placed at either the top, the bottom or the top and bottom of long fascia, or *belt*, signs installed on the face of a building. It is necessary to locate the lamps in such a way that they can be serviced. By selecting the dimensions of the sign carefully, it is possible to produce acceptable luminous uniformity over the entire face of the sign with lamps located in any of the above configurations. These configurations will produce a low, but acceptable, sign luminance. This system produces a front surface luminance in the range of 70–350 cd/m². A double row raises the surface luminance to between 250 and 500 cd/m².

Major design considerations in systems for obtaining uniform light distribution or even lighting of the fascia surface are:

- The depth of the sign cabinet (from the face of the sign to the back of the cabinet)
- Specially shaped sign enclosures with sloping, parabolic or elliptical contoured backs do not

improve the light distribution over the straight-back sign cabinet.
- Luminous uniformity can be improved with special reflectors at the light source (in a shallow sign cabinet, a parabolic-reflector fluorescent-lamp luminaire can, for example, provide more uniform illumination on the fascia than bare lamps alone).
- The luminance uniformity ratio, maximum to minimum, of the sign face medium can be determined from the following formula:

$$\frac{\text{highest sign face luminance}}{\text{lowest sign face luminance}} = \text{uniformity ratio}$$

$$(29\text{-}8)$$

A ratio of 1 is best. A ratio of 2 may be tolerated in some installations, but should be considered the maximum allowable. Ratios of 1.3–1.5 will be satisfactory for most installations.
- Very high output fluorescent lamps are as efficient in obtaining uniform light distribution as aperture lamps.

Examples of fascia signs may be found on automobile dealerships, food chain stores and discount stores.

Luminous Fascia Colors Other Than White. The information shown above is for signs using integrally pigmented sign face media, 3.2 mm (0.125 in.) thick, having a 40% transmittance. Other whites and other colors with lower transmittance values will produce surface luminance values below those shown. When using colors other than white, it is necessary to apply a spray coating of white paint to the inside surface of the sign cabinet in order to obtain comparable light distribution qualities.

FLOODLIGHTED SIGNS[4,5]

Lighting Poster Panels, Painted Bulletins and Vertical Surface Signs

There are no hard rules in creating an outdoor advertisement. Since outdoor messages will be viewed at distances ranging from 30 to 120 m (100 to 400 ft) by people in motion, logic dictates the need for brevity, simplicity and clarity. In general, fewer words, larger illustrations, bolder colors, simpler backgrounds and clearer product identification produce better outdoor advertisements.

The most important factors contributing to the conspicuity of an illuminated sign are area and brightness.

Fig. 29-11. Recommended Illuminances for Poster Panels, Painted Bulletins and Other Advertising Signs

Average Reflectance of Advertising Copy	Recommended Illuminance in Lux [Footcandles]	
	Bright Surrounds	Dark Surrounds
Low	1000[100]	500[50]
High	500[50]	200[20]

However, several relatively complex factors affect legibility of signs, many of which are psychological as well as physical. See the section on Sign Characteristics at the beginning of this chapter.

General Guides for Lighting Signs. The following is a list of recommendations to be considered in designing floodlighting of signs.

1. The brightness of the sign panel should be sufficient for it to stand out from its surroundings. Figure 29-11 lists recommended illuminances.
2. The luminance should be sufficiently uniform to provide equal legibility over the message area. A maximum-to-minimum luminance ratio of 4:1 is desirable. Sharp shadows should be avoided on the sign face. Uneven brightnesses detract from the communication impact of the sign.
3. The lighting should cause neither direct nor reflected glare at the normal viewing positions.
4. The lighting equipment should not obstruct the reading of the sign from normal viewing positions, nor produce daytime shadows on the sign.
5. The lighting equipment should require minimal maintenance and have low annual operating cost.
6. The system should be maintained to achieve the designed illuminances.

Location of Lighting Equipment. Some of the factors to be considered when determining whether luminaires should be mounted across the top or bottom of a sign are:

1. For top-mounted units:

Advantages

- The luminaire cover may collect less dirt, snow and debris.
- Luminaires will not hide the message.
- The sign will usually shield a direct view of lamps from opposing traffic.

Disadvantages

- Reflected glare is more apparent.
- Luminaires may produce daytime shadows.

- Luminaires may be more difficult to service.
- The sign is more difficult to post (poster panels).
- The panels are more difficult to change (painted bulletins).

2. For bottom-mounted units:

Advantages

- Reflected glare is minimized.
- No daytime shadows are produced.
- Luminaires may be easier to service.
- Posting and message changing are more simply accomplished.

Disadvantages

- The luminaire cover may collect more dirt, snow or debris.
- Luminaires may hide the message from some viewing angles.
- Shielding may be necessary to hide direct view of the lamp or luminaire optical system from opposing traffic.

Light Sources for Floodlighted Signs

There is no single type of source that can be described as best for sign floodlighting. Most lamps, regardless of type, can be used with different reflector and lens combinations to realize various beam patterns which may be required. Therefore, choices of light source for a given sign are generally made for reasons of initial cost, operating cost (including maintenance), end result desired, color or novelty. Chapter 6, Light Sources, contains a detailed discussion of available sources.

The following lamp types are used in sign floodlighting:

Metal Halide. Advantages are good lamp life, efficacy and color rendering capability as well as low operating cost. A disadvantage is the high initial cost.

High-Pressure Sodium. Advantages are good lamp life and efficacy, but color rendering is poor.

Incandescent. Advantages include good color rendering, small size, accurate beam control and very good cold-weather operation. Disadvantages are low efficacy, short lamp life and high operating costs.

Mercury. Advantages include long lamp life, high efficacy and low operating cost. Disadvantages are high initial cost, fair beam control and only fair color rendering capability below that of incandescent or tungsten-halogen lamps.

Tungsten-Halogen. Advantages include good color rendering, high lumen maintenance and very good cold-weather operation. Disadvantages are low efficacy, medium lamp life and high operating costs.

Fluorescent. Advantages are long life, high efficacy and low operating cost. Disadvantages are high initial cost, lack of beam control and variable output due to changing temperatures.

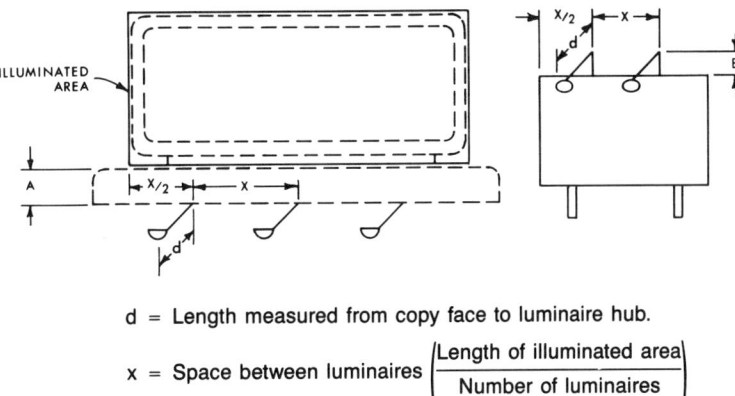

d = Length measured from copy face to luminaire hub.

x = Space between luminaires $\left(\dfrac{\text{Length of illuminated area}}{\text{Number of luminaires}}\right)$

x (max.) = 2.5d

Fig. 29-12. Typical floodlighted sign installation and illuminance results. Dimension A = 0.76 to 1.0 m (2.5 to 3.5 ft) and B = 0.76 m (2.5 ft).

Lighting Systems for Floodlighted Signs

Concurrent with consideration of a particular light source, there should be an evaluation of other elements such as lamp housing, mounting arrangements and auxiliary equipment. Due to improved lamp performance, metal halide lamp systems are becoming more prevalent. Many existing signs, however, are still lighted by fluorescent equipment. Incandescent and tungsten-halogen lamps with their associated housings are, in general, less expensive to install initially, since they do not require auxiliaries such as ballasts, but their use has dwindled considerably in favor of the longer-life and more energy-efficient sources.

Application Data. Regardless of which system is used, the most economical floodlighting system is one which utilizes the fewest floodlights containing the highest-wattage lamps. Such a system is easiest to install, control and maintain. It also uses less power for the same illuminance than a system using more but smaller units. However, illuminance uniformity and appearance may require the selection of a system using a larger number of smaller units. It may be necessary to draw a careful balance between the two extremes. Particularly with shorter-lived lamps, such as incandescent and tungsten-halogen, the beam patterns should be overlapped so that any given area receives light from at least two units. This requirement is usually satisfied if an acceptable uniformity ratio is achieved.

Metal Halide Systems. The metal halide lamp, with increasingly longer life, is supplanting the mercury lamp in many installations. The 400-W metal halide lamp is most frequently used for sign lighting, although the 250-W is also popular. Figure 29-12 includes information on positioning a typical luminaire for both top and bottom mounting and shows the maintained illuminance obtained with specific luminaire location data. Figure 29-13 is a view of a typical sign.

Mercury Systems. Deluxe mercury lamps in 175, 250, and 400 W have many applications in sign lighting where long life is essential, maintenance is infrequent, or the signs are inaccessible. The luminaire location is usually determined in the same manner as for metal halide systems. Maintained illuminance values for typical signs are shown in figure 29-12.

Fig. 29-13. View of lighted sign using four luminaires with clear metal halide lamps.

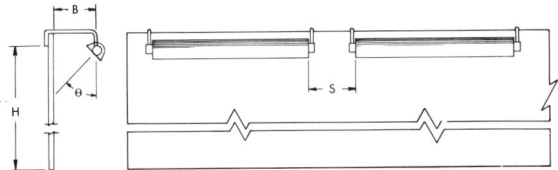

Fig. 29-14. General rules for applying fluorescent floodlights.*

1. S should not exceed B.
2. Overhang B should not be less than approximately 0.4H.
3. If H exceeds 4.5 meters (15 feet), floodlights are recommended across both bottom and top of area in order to assure an acceptable uniformity ratio.

*These "rules of thumb" are based upon the use of a white enameled reflector that produces a symmetrical distribution in a plane perpendicular to the lamp. B and θ may vary with specific reflector types.

Fig. 29-15. Illuminance Obtained on Vertical Surfaces from Enclosed Fluorescent Floodlights[a]

Display	Number of Lamps[b]	Average Illuminance Maintained in Service in Lux (Footcandles)[c] (Approximate mA—Rating[d])	
		800	1500
Poster Panel	2-units	140(13)	250(23)
	3-units	220(20)	360(33)
Painted Bulletin	3-units	120(11)	190(18)
	4-units	140(13)	250(23)
	5-units	180(17)	310(29)

[a] Calculations of illuminance based upon B = 1.5 meters (5 feet).
[b] See Fig. 17-17 for general overhangs B and aiming angles θ.
[c] Assuming a light loss factor of 0.65. Uniformity ratio max/min should be less than 4/1.
[d] Assumed are F96T12 fluorescent lamps at 10°C(50°F).

Tungsten-Halogen Systems. Both 500- and 1500-W tungsten-halogen lamps are used for sign lighting. See figure 29-12 for typical location details for bottom- or top-mounted units and the maintained illuminance for typical signs.

Fluorescent Systems. General rules for applying fluorescent floodlights are shown in figure 29-14. The aiming angle is usually near 45°. One important consideration is that fluorescent lamps are sensitive to temperature and to air currents. Most photometric data are obtained at an ambient temperature of 25°C (77°F). Illuminance values obtained on typical signs are shown in figure 29-15. For higher illuminance values, twin units are used or units are added to the bottom of the sign and aimed upward.

REFERENCES

1. Baird, N. F., and R. B. Schmitz. 1978. Effective use of colored lamps on a computerized, animated sign. *Light. Des. Appl.* 8(10):38–47.

2. Hart, A. L. 1956. Some factors that influence the design of daytime effective exposed lamp signs. *Illum. Eng.* 51(10):677–682.

3. Peek, S. C., and J. P. Keenan. 1959. Outdoor applications of new reflector contour designs for higher output fluorescent lamps. *Illum. Eng.* 54(2):77–80.

4. Agnew, H. E. 1985. *Outdoor advertising.* New York: Garland. [Reprint. Originally published: New York: McGraw-Hill, 1938.]

5. Boddewyn, J. J. 1979. *Outdoor-billboard advertising regulations.* New York: International Advertising Association.

Special Topics V

Energy Management

30

INTRODUCTION

Energy management has gained in importance since the early 1970s, stimulated by the escalation of energy costs, the depletion of certain energy sources and the concern for the protection of our environment. As a result, the way buildings are constructed, lighted, heated and cooled has been closely examined. Criteria for new building design and for existing buildings have been developed to ensure that energy resources are used effectively and efficiently. This chapter discusses lighting energy management, and describes important influences on lighting energy use.

Electric lighting consumes a significant amount of energy. About 20–25% of all energy used in buildings and about 5% of total energy consumption in the United States is used for lighting. Lighting also produces additional heat in buildings, increasing the load on air conditioning systems, but is sometimes effective in cool climates. The heat from lighting accounts for 15–20% of a building's cooling load.

Two forces are exerting increasing influence on lighting energy management: codes and standards, and demand-side management (DSM) programs. Energy codes and standards are developed to minimize lighting energy waste and assure the use of efficient lighting systems. An overview of codes and standards is provided in chapter 14, Codes and Regulations, as well as a detailed discussion of the development of the ASHRAE/IES Standard 90.1.[1] Capital may not always be available for replacement of old lighting equipment, and some relighting proposals may not meet a company's criteria for cost-effectiveness. DSM programs from utilities and government agencies provide incentives to encourage energy-efficient solutions. These programs are also discussed in this chapter.

For new buildings, standards are designed to limit the amount of power available for lighting, while still enabling the designer to provide a lighting system suitable for the task requirements of the occupants. A saving in energy (kilowatt-hours) can be achieved by reducing either the amount of connected power for the lighting system, or the time the lighting system is operating. The energy consumed by a lighting system can be minimized without compromising the quality of the lighting design. Considerations for energy management when designing a new building will be reviewed in this chapter. These include: (1) components: luminaires, sources and controls; (2) space parameters: room surfaces, furniture, partition and space plan, tasks, and space utilization; and (3) operation and maintenance.

In existing buildings, it is desirable that the lighting comply with the same energy standards as in new buildings. Improved energy utilization options include modifying or replacing the lighting system with a more efficient one, using replacement components which use less power in spaces which are overlighted, and modifying the operating characteristics of the building to reduce hours of use. Energy management strategies for existing buildings are covered in this chapter, as well as techniques and tools for surveying and evaluating existing lighting systems.

ENERGY CODES AND STANDARDS

Energy use for lighting systems is often regulated through building codes enacted by the federal government, by the state or provincial government, or by a local regulatory authority. Codes and incentives establish minimum requirements which support the use of efficient lighting systems and design principles. Lighting system evaluation using a life cycle cost basis is a method of weighing equipment efficiency and cost. Less expensive equipment is not always the most cost-effective (see chapter 13, Lighting Economics).

Two approaches are common for regulating lighting energy use: the use of application standards which limit the total power allowed for the lighting system, and component regulations which mandate minimum efficiencies for system components. In the United States, legislation governing lighting energy consumption varies from state to state.[2] Federal legislation has recently been enacted which establishes minimum lighting code requirements to be met by October 1994.

Most states have adopted codes based on one of three standards: ASHRAE 90-75, ANSI/

ASHRAE/IES 90A-1980 or ASHRAE/IES 90.1-1989. The Model Energy Code (MEC 1983, 1986, 1989, 1992), which has been developed by the Council of American Building Officials (CABO) with participation from other building code organizations, codifies the ASHRAE standards. The MEC is widely used by states in developing their codes. Some states have chosen to deviate somewhat from the ASHRAE/IES standards and have adopted codes with modifications of the determination procedures for lighting power budgets or of the lighting power budget allowances themselves. A small number of states have imposed codes which include lighting equipment component regulations. These codes have imposed minimum allowable efficiencies for lamps, ballasts or luminaires. Approximately three-fourths of the states have adopted lighting energy legislation or criteria. This percentage will continue to increase as energy conservation and environmental issues become a higher priority.

In Canada, energy management is mainly a provincial issue, and a number of provinces have enacted energy efficiency legislation. These regulations specify requirements for energy-efficient products. An example of this is the recent filing by most provinces of a Canadian Standards Association (CSA) standard on energy-efficient ballasts as a regulation under the relevant act.

The Canadian national building code is also used as a mechanism for assuring energy efficiency in buildings. This code is adopted, with minor changes, by the provinces as a regulation. It is expected that standards such as ASHRAE/IES 90.1 will be incorporated in the national code. Canadian municipal governments also have by-laws containing local energy efficiency requirements. Building owners and operators must check with local municipal authorities, as well as provincial ones, to assure that all legal conditions are met.

In Mexico, there is currently no code-writing body and no formal energy legislation.

Application Standards

The most common application standards are the ASHRAE/IES series. ASHRAE/IES 90.1-1989, "Energy Efficient Design of New Buildings Except Low-Rise Residential," is intended to encourage efficient lighting design for both interior and exterior spaces. This is achieved both through mandatory requirements for controls and ballasts and through lighting power density allowances. The designer is given a power allowance based on the space or building use. Compliance with the ASHRAE/IES standard is achieved by installing a lighting system that requires lower lighting power density than the allowance and that meets the other mandatory requirements. This approach provides

design flexibility while limiting the total power load. ASHRAE/IES 90.1-1989 applies only to new buildings and the tenant improvements of core and shell buildings.

Meeting the requirements of this standard assures only a base level of energy efficiency. Greater efficiency is often possible and will be cost-effective in many buildings. Designers are encouraged to go beyond the minimum levels of efficiency required by the standard whenever possible.

While ASHRAE/IES 90.1-1989 applies to new buildings, ASHRAE/IES Standard 100 applies to existing buildings. It provides requirements for retrofit lighting modifications. In general, the required changes can be done easily by maintenance personnel. When major renovations are made to existing buildings, for example when the entire lighting system is replaced, it is recommended that the designer meet the requirements for new construction even though compliance may not be required.

Compliance with Standard 90.1 or Standard 100 does not ensure lighting quality or quantity of illuminance. The purpose of these standards is to set limits on the amount of power that may be used for lighting. While it is the consensus of experts that lighting quality can be achieved within the limits set by Standard 90.1-1989, it is the responsibility of the designer to provide lighting quality and adequate illuminance for all visual work.

Much of the material in the 90.1 Standard is incorporated in the DOE Standard for Federal Buildings (10 CFR Part 435 Subpart A). There are a few differences, however:

- The unit power density (UPD) tables for the system performance method contain different values for some activities and building types.
- Lighting power allowances which are more stringent took effect in 1993.

Equipment Regulations

The U.S. Federal Government has been playing an increasing role in mandating the conservation of lighting energy. Two recent acts mandate the use of more efficient lighting components: The U.S. National Appliance Energy Conservation Act Amendment of 1988, and the national Energy Policy Act of 1992.

The U.S. National Appliance Energy Conservation Act Amendment mandates the manufacture and sale of efficient electromagnetic and electronic ballasts. Ballasts used in commercial fluorescent lighting installations must meet or exceed the minimum *ballast efficiency factors* (BEF) established by this legislation. The law exempts ballasts used for dimming and for use at ambient temperatures of $-18°C$ ($0°F$) or less, and ballasts with low power factor (less than 0.90) for residential use.

The National Energy Policy Act mandates energy efficiency standards that affect the manufacture and sale of lamps and lighting systems. The National Energy Policy Act also requires that the Federal Trade Commission (FTC) establish labeling rules for lamps.

The luminaire efficiency rating and labeling program is a voluntary effort by the lighting industry initiated by the Department of Energy (DOE). This program will become effective by the end of 1995. The labeling will allow for easy comparisons between the efficiencies of different luminaires. Labeling rules for incandescent, incandescent reflector, and general-service (A) and compact fluorescent lamps are effective at the end of 1994. These rules will help consumers to make more informed decisions on what type of lamp to purchase.

Efficiency standards have been developed for specific lamp types within the categories of incandescent, fluorescent and high intensity discharge (HID). The standards for incandescent and fluorescent lamps will be phased in between 1993 through 1996. HID lamp standards are scheduled to become effective in 1998.

The Act includes incandescent lamps of the reflector types, R (reflector) and PAR (parabolic reflector). Lamps that are acceptable must meet specific lumen-per-watt (LPW) ratings. Most ER (ellipsoidal reflector) and tungsten halogen PAR lamps meet the requirements. General-service, ER and some specialty incandescent lamps are excluded from the efficiency standards.

Fluorescent lamps included in the Act are full-wattage F40T12 (4 ft), F96T12 (8 ft), and F96T12/HO (8 ft). Types that meet the standard are those that surpass specific LPW ratings and have a high color rendering index (CRI). Standards for HID lamps will be established by 1996. Lamp manufacturers can provide specific lists of lamp types that meet the standards.

In addition, the Act provides for the establishment of Energy Efficient Lighting Demonstration Centers. Ten of these centers are being established by various nonprofit utility, state and local organizations. The centers will provide information, education, demonstrations and training to promote lighting efficiency.

Finally, the Act includes provisions to encourage utilities to provide more incentive and rebate programs. This is accomplished by mandates for utility least-cost planning and by requiring the state Public Utility Commissions to allow the utilities to earn a return on conservation and demand-side management programs.

In Canada, national harmonization of equipment standards is achieved through adoption of CSA standards. Individual provinces are then required to include these in the standards in their provincial energy efficiency acts.

DEMAND-SIDE MANAGEMENT LIGHTING

Utility Programs

Utilities plan for future load growth in order to ensure that there is enough electricity generating and distribution capacity to meet demand and allow for repairs or equipment failure. Since electricity is so important to society, much utility planning addresses how to provide enough reliable electricity at the lowest reasonable cost. Utility planners look at modifying customers' energy use as a quicker, easier and sometimes less costly method of adjusting the balance of supply and demand. Thus, demand-side management (DSM) attempts to influence utility customers to achieve the most cost-effective overall supply of electricity.

DSM programs include a wide variety of options which alter customers' demand, resulting in more efficient use of energy. They also include strategies for shifting the time pattern of electricity use. Energy efficiency is one of the most important criteria in DSM lighting programs. Energy-efficient lighting can reduce the total energy requirements of the electrical system, conserving precious natural resources and the environment.

The concept of avoided cost is used as a tool by utilities and utility regulators for evaluating the economic merits of lighting conservation. The following equation defines the two main components of utility savings due to avoided costs:

$$\text{avoided cost} = \text{avoided energy cost}$$
$$+ \text{avoided capacity cost}$$

These components reflect the reduction in energy costs required to produce electricity and the potential to postpone new generation facilities.

Two major economic tests have been developed to evaluate the viability of DSM programs: the *total resource test* and the *ratepayer impact measure* (RIM). The total resource test is used to compare the costs saved by DSM and conservation with the costs of providing these measures. The RIM is more complex and includes not only the resource cost savings associated with DSM, but also the lost revenues to utilities associated with the conservation of energy. As a consequence, the RIM is a tougher conservation standard than the Total Resource Cost test. This is because the lost revenues to utilities, associated with the reduction in demand, need to be offset by the benefits of conservation in delaying new construction or mitigating pollution.

Traditional ratemaking principles have been an impediment to the development of DSM programs. It has been difficult to overcome the simple notion that the utility makes its profits on the sale of electricity, and that for each kilowatt hour of electricity that is conserved, utility profitability will be reduced. In order to counter this disincentive among utilities, public utility commissions have been developing new ratemaking principles. By these principles, the utility's profitability is not based simply on sales levels. For example, many regulatory commissions have created incentive programs that encourage utilities to conserve power. As a consequence, many utilities in the United States have a growing interest in pursuing DSM and conservation programs. Lighting plays a major role in most of these programs.

One way in which the appropriate levels of DSM are now being evaluated is through integrated resource planning. Within integrated resource planning, electric supply and DSM options are looked at consistently as resources to the utility. The least expensive option is selected from among the array of DSM and supply-side options—the latter meaning the building of new generation facilities. This makes it possible to provide service to utility ratepayers at the lowest cost. It is likely that efficient lighting will be an increasingly important option in meeting customers' demand for service in the future.

The concept of avoided cost is an integral part of evaluating utility incentive programs. In its simplest form, the utility may pay up to the avoided cost of generation, for example, paying the value of each kilowatt of lighting load reduced by the customer. In practice, DSM programs are often implemented at a lower kilowatt payout. This payout is based on the amount acceptable to the customer to reduce the first cost of the installation, and on the payback period as well. Incentives may be provided for lighting products, systems or designs, and often take the form of direct cash rebates to the customer.

Nonregulatory Government Programs

Government agencies also encourage DSM through programs designed to promote energy efficiency and energy conservation. One notable example is the Green Lights Program, administered by the U.S. Environmental Protection Agency (EPA). This program is a voluntary, nonregulatory initiative designed to reduce lighting energy use on a national scale. The objective of Green Lights is to minimize pollution associated with the generation of energy required to operate both new and existing lighting systems.

Corporations that sign the Green Lights voluntary agreement commit themselves to surveying the lighting systems in their facilities, and converting to efficient lighting systems within five years when economically viable. The EPA also provides a variety of services to Green Lights Partners to assist them in their lighting system upgrades.

Energy Management Guidelines for New Construction and Existing Spaces

This section describes the key elements of lighting energy management for both new construction and major renovation. Additional considerations specific to existing buildings are addressed later in this chapter. The checklist at the end of this chapter (figure 30-4) may also be referred to for suggestions about energy management for most applications and additional suggestions for existing spaces.

KEY ELEMENTS OF LIGHTING ENERGY MANAGEMENT[3]

The key elements of lighting energy managment are outlined in figure 30-1.

Lighting Needs

First and foremost, the lighting needs of a space must be defined to ensure the optimum allocation and management of energy. Lighting needs may range from simple orientation to specific visual tasks. Important considerations for prolonged visual tasks associated with work environments include adequate illuminance on the task surface, a proper balance of luminance between the task surface and surrounding horizontal and vertical surfaces, adequate control of direct and reflected glare from all sources of light, and adequate color rendering of task elements and surrounds. Other

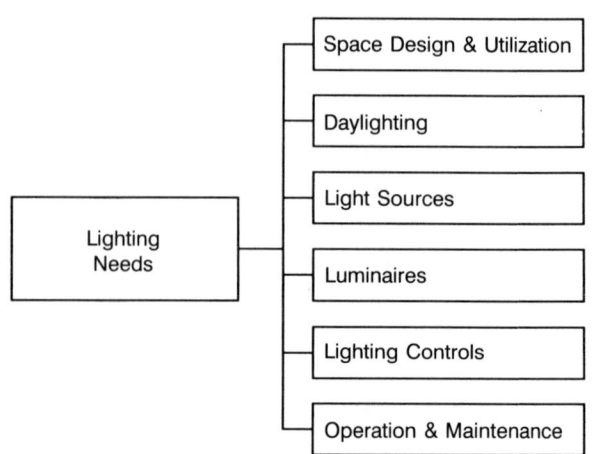

Fig. 30-1. Key elements of lighting energy management.

considerations also apply, depending on details of the specific visual task performed.

When the nature and location of visual tasks can be identified, it is usually possible to reduce ambient illuminances and corresponding energy consumption by providing light more selectively where and when it is needed. When specific tasks and their locations cannot be identified, a more uniform pattern of ambient illumination is generally provided, along with provisions for task lighting and local control. In applications where there are no prolonged visual tasks, lighting for emphasis, esthetics and safety are prime considerations.

Other sections of this Handbook may be consulted for assistance in determining lighting needs for specific applications. In addition, there are numerous IESNA publications that provide guidance in identifying and addressing lighting needs. The ASHRAE/IES 90.1 Standard and its compliance manual may be consulted for guidelines in determining lighting energy allocations for specific applications.

Space Design and Utilization. Space design and utilization are characteristics of a space that are often determined before the lighting system is considered. However, it is necessary to coordinate the design of lighting and control systems with these characteristics in order to maximize the energy efficiency potential. For interior spaces, particularly those of large size, reflectances of room surfaces should be high (above 0.7). This will increase the brightness within the space and will reduce the amount of electric lighting needed to produce a given illuminance.

The design and utilization of a space may also facilitate effective use of daylight. High-reflectance interior finishes can enhance the effectiveness of daylighting for offsetting electric lighting. Applications which involve similar visual tasks should be grouped in order to optimize the energy used for lighting. This is known as task tuning. Using low ambient illumination and open-plan modular furniture with task lighting can also reduce the use of energy for lighting. Modular branch circuit wiring for ambient lighting provides an additional degree of flexibility by allowing luminaires to be easily relocated when the design or function of a space changes.

Occupancy schedules of a space may be planned to optimize the effectiveness of lighting controls. Traffic patterns may be predetermined so that logical applications for occupancy sensors may be identified.

Daylighting. Daylight can be an excellent source of ambient illumination. The potential for daylight utilization should be evaluated early in the design development of a space. Architectural features such as overhangs, light shelves, and window treatments may be incorporated into the design to enhance daylight utilization and control. For effective use of daylight in energy management, the levels and hours of daylight availability must be determined. Also, the manner in which daylight is distributed in the space is important. Glare from fenestration should be controlled to the same degree as glare from luminaires.

The heat gain or loss through fenestration must be coordinated with the building envelope and HVAC systems. The use of exterior sun control devices and "high-performance" heat-reflecting and insulating glass in windows should also be considered to minimize solar heat gain in the summer and heat loss in the winter without obstructing views of the exterior. Daylighting reduces energy consumption primarily if electric lighting can be reduced. The electric lighting design should be coordinated with available daylight so that illuminance and distribution are integrated. Automatic dimming controls should be considered in order to continuously adjust electric lighting levels for maximum energy savings and occupant acceptance.

Chapter 8, Daylighting, can provide useful information on the availability of daylight, daylight control systems, and design and evaluation methods. Recent published data from manufacturers of fenestration materials and controls may also be consulted.

Light Sources. Electric light sources should be selected to maintain the highest efficacy, while providing appropriate color qualities, physical and optical size, life expectancy and warm-up time for the specific application. These attributes are closely related to decisions on luminaires, lighting controls, and operation and maintenance.

Figure 30-2 shows the relative efficacy ranges of commonly used light sources, including ballast losses. Within a range, the higher-wattage sources are generally more efficient than the lower-wattage sources. High-pressure sodium, metal halide and fluorescent are the most efficient light sources; mercury vapor and incandescent are the least efficient. Except for incandescent and halogen light sources, each light source requires a specific ballast. Ballast efficiencies also vary and can have a large effect on the total lighting system efficacy.

Chapter 6, Light Sources, provides detailed information pertaining to the operation and performance of various lamp types. Lamp manufacturers' published data provide specific information relative to lumen output, efficacy, life expectancy, lumen maintenance and costs.

Luminaires. A luminaire is an assembly of individual components including lamps, ballasts, sockets, wiring, and optical media such as reflectors, louvers and lenses. The efficiency of the luminaire is affected by the performance of these individual components. Typically, luminaire configurations are constructed to perform specific functions for specific applications. Application

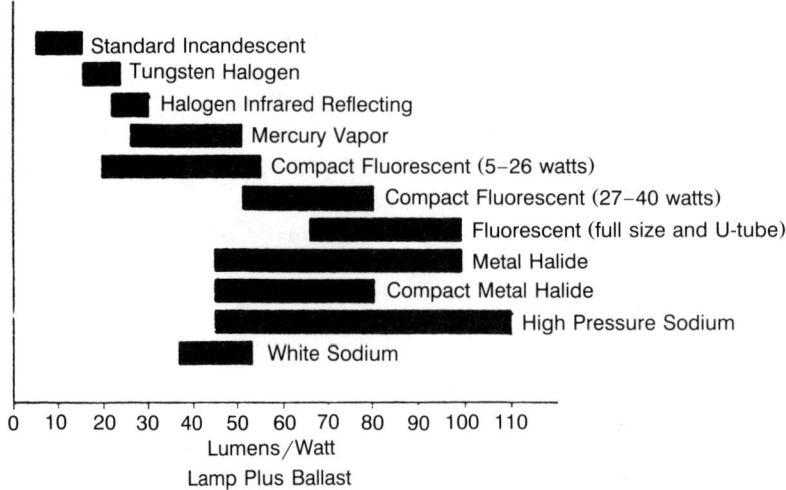

Fig. 30-2. Light source efficacies.

constraints, such as ambient temperature, color requirements, accessibility and glare control needs, may require the use of certain components or preclude the use of others. The efficiency of a luminaire must be evaluated relative to specific application criteria.

In spaces that contain visual tasks, a primary objective of the lighting system is to illuminate the task effectively. In addition, the system must illuminate the ambient space effectively to balance task lighting and create a comfortable work environment. The system which provides task illuminance may be independent of that which provides ambient illuminance, or the same system may provide both. In either case, it is important that the luminaires perform their functions efficiently and that the designer understand their optical performance and its impact on the overall environment.

Luminaires that can be cleaned easily and those with low dirt accumulation will maintain greater efficiency and reduce maintenance costs over the system life. When possible, luminaires with heat transfer capabilities should be considered for interior applications, so that heat generated by the lighting system can be effectively utilized or removed from a space and coordinated with the overall building HVAC design.

Data from luminaire manufacturers are useful for determining how efficiently luminaires meet lighting needs. It is very important to understand that efficiency alone should not be the determining factor in luminaire selection.

Chapter 7, Luminaires, should be consulted for further information about luminaire energy management issues. There are also numerous IESNA publications that recommend performance guidelines for luminaires relative to specific lighting needs.

Lighting Controls. The most efficient luminaires and light sources can be utilized even more effectively by integrating them with lighting controls that make the lighting more responsive to changing requirements. Lighting control strategies may be implemented either centrally over an entire building or locally in individual areas. Some combination of these two levels of control is also common.

Central lighting control systems allow for lighting load scheduling to reduce peak demand as well as providing the ability to monitor and control total energy use. Central lighting control systems may be interfaced with overall building management systems.

A building may also be divided into areas that have different lighting needs and require different control strategies. For example, perimeter areas consisting mainly of private offices and core areas consisting of open-plan space are good candidates for local lighting control, because they have predictable occupancy schedules, they are low-traffic areas requiring task-level illumination only when occupied, and they utilize a significant daylight contribution. Lighting control strategies are closely related to space utilization. It is very important to coordinate the two in order to optimize the effectiveness of the former (refer to the discussion on Space Design and Utilization above).

For a more detailed discussion of lighting controls for energy management, refer to chapter 31, Lighting Controls. Information from manufacturers may also be consulted for performance data and application assistance on various control technologies.

Operation and Maintenance. All lighting systems require maintenance. A planned maintenance program will augment the ability of a lighting system to meet design objectives effectively and efficiently. Scheduled maintenance should include lamps, ballasts, luminaires, controls, fenestration and room surfaces. Group relamping and cleaning cycles are recommended for maximum maintained efficiency.

A planned, systematic maintenance schedule will save significant energy and operating costs over time. If the commitment to implement scheduled maintenance is made in the initial stage of design, a significant capital cost saving is also possible because less equipment is required initially. Refer to chapter 32, Lighting Maintenance, for a more detailed discussion relative to efficient operation and maintenance of lighting systems.

Energy Management Procedures for Existing Buildings

Evaluating lighting system changes for existing spaces can be more accurate than for new construction because the actual space can be surveyed, eliminating the need for assumptions. An existing building is evaluated from the standpoint of power and energy by the following methods:

- Building survey
- Power budget and limit determination
- Energy limit determination
- Energy limit analysis

Building Survey. An examination of the building to determine the connected power, time scheduling and controls for lighting involves a survey of all spaces. The wattage of each connected luminaire, including lamp watts, ballast watts and losses introduced by dimming devices, is verified and totaled. The power for portable and supplementary lighting devices also should be included in the total. Factors related to occupancy, daylighting and controls should be included as outlined in the discussion on Energy Limit Analysis below. Specific information on surface finishes and reflectances should also be recorded. Sampling procedures have been used to avoid measuring every feature of the space.[4]

Power Budget and Limit Determination. By using the power density (unit power density procedure) in the local energy code or ASHRAE/IES 90.1-1989, the budgets for individual spaces and the limit for the building are calculated.

Energy Limit Determination. Beginning with the power budgets for each space, determined by the UPD procedure,[5] energy budgets are determined by adjusting for occupancy schedules and the use of daylight and lighting controls. Reference 6 contains the full procedure which results in a total energy limit for the building or facility.

Energy Limit Analysis. The actual current energy use for the facility is determined and compared with the energy limit. The difference is the energy saving from the retrofits. The resulting revised energy use estimate

can be compared with the recommended energy limit.[6] If it exceeds the limit, the lighting systems should be reevaluated. Spaces or strategies which are inefficient should be identified and modified to reduce the estimated energy below the calculated limit. Reference 7 contains the full procedure and energy management forms to estimate and evaluate lighting energy use for buildings.

METHODOLOGY OF THE ASHRAE / IES 90.1 STANDARD

As a combined effort of the Illuminating Engineering Society of North America (IESNA) and the American Society of Heating, Refrigeration and Air Conditioning Engineers (ASHRAE), the first energy conservation standard was published in 1975. This standard, "Energy Conservation in New Building Design," was developed as a national voluntary consensus standard. The 1980 version of this standard was approved as an ANSI standard; later versions have not been approved. During the 1980s many states enacted regulations based directly or indirectly on this standard. The standard has been updated twice; the current version is ASHRAE/IES 90.1-1989.

The purposes of the standard are to:

- Set minimum requirements for the energy-efficient design of new buildings so that they may be constructed, operated and maintained in a manner that minimizes the use of energy without constraining the building function or the comfort or productivity of the occupants
- Provide criteria for energy-efficient design and methods for determining compliance with these criteria
- Provide sound guidance for energy-efficient design

The organization of ASHRAE/IES 90.1 is shown in figure 30-3. All buildings must meet the *basic requirements*. The basic requirements with respect to lighting, pursuant to the above purposes, include:

- Minimum criteria for lighting controls
- Power allowance for external building lighting
- Minimum ballast efficiency and tandem wiring

Beyond the basic requirements, Standard 90.1 allows several methods of compliance. First, the designer, working in conjunction with other team members, must decide whether to use the *building energy cost budget* approach or one of the two paths shown under the *system-component method* in figure 30-3.

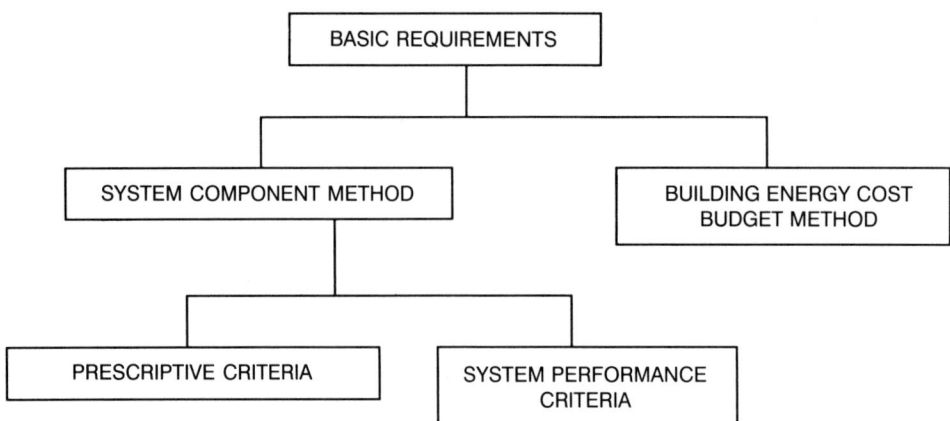

Fig. 30-3. The structure of ASHRAE / IES Standard 90.1-1989.

The cost budget approach is the most encompassing and complex method of compliance. It allows the designer to trade off lighting energy use against other energy factors—HVAC and building envelope. To accomplish this analysis, a whole-building energy model must be used to predict energy use. Although the method is flexible, it requires sophisticated analysis tools and is time consuming.

Two paths were developed in response to the demand of code officials for more simplified methods of showing compliance. The *prescriptive criteria method* specifically addresses the need for a very quick and simple process for calculating the allowable connected lighting load for building interiors. This method does not address unique project requirements, and is intended primarily for core and shell buildings or during the preliminary design phase. Eight of the most common building types currently under construction were chosen, and budgets for the maximum allowable power density were developed for each building type and for a range of six different building sizes. This prescriptive unit power allowance, selected from a table in the standard, is multiplied by the total lighted area of the building to give the interior lighting power allowance in watts. This allowance is then the metric against which the actual design is measured. To comply, a project must meet the basic requirements and not exceed the interior lighting power allowance.

A more accurate and detailed calculation procedure is contained in the *system performance criteria method*. The lighting power budget is calculated room by room and is more task specific. The process is more involved, since the unit power density is calculated for each space or activity area and also takes the room geometry into account through an area factor which is provided in graphic form in the standard. Individual areas are summed to obtain the allowable interior lighting power.

The 1989 version of the standard helped to both simplify the process and decrease the time involved by including a computer program. This program can be used for both the prescriptive and the system performance method. In addition, it contains the data to quickly obtain the basic requirements for controls and exterior lighting.

Lighting Energy Management Documents

The Energy Management Committee of the IESNA has developed several publications related to building energy utilization. The first in the series of these publications is the Lighting Power Limit Determination (LEM-1).[5] This publication describes the method for determining the lighting power limit as approved and published in the joint ANSI/ASHRAE/IES Standard 90A-1980, which is being used in many states. Tables and an example are included in LEM-1[5] to assist in understanding the methodology and in performing the calculations.

A pair of publications is available to deal with energy limitations. The first[6] contains the method for determining an energy limit for a new or existing building, based on the power limit determined in LEM-1. A companion booklet describes how to check a lighting design against established budgets. If the budget is exceeded, the publication provides a method to institute changes which will decrease energy use and maintain cost-effectiveness. Both publications include worksheets and sample forms.

To obtain further information on all of the design factors that influence connected lighting load and lighting energy, a publication on Design Considerations for Effective Building Lighting Energy Utilization is also available (LEM-3).[3]

CHECKLIST OF ENERGY-SAVING GUIDELINES

Figure 30-4 contains recommendations for the development of an energy management program for new con-

Fig. 30-4. Checklist of Energy-Saving Guidelines for New Construction and Existing Spaces

Lighting Needs

☐	Visual tasks: specification	Identify specific visual tasks and locations to determine recommended illuminances for tasks and for surrounding areas.
☐	Safety and esthetics	Review lighting requirements for given applications to satisfy safety and esthetic criteria.
☐	Overlighted application	In existing spaces, identify applications where maintained illumination is greater than recommended. Reduce energy by adjusting illuminance to meet recommended levels.
☐	Groupings: similar visual tasks	Group visual tasks having the same illuminance requirements, and avoid widely separated workstations.
☐	Task lighting	Illuminate work surfaces with luminaires properly located in or on furniture; provide lower ambient levels.
☐	Luminance ratios	Use wallwashing and lighting of decorative objects to balance brightnesses.

Space Design and Utilization

☐	Space plan	When possible, arrange for occupants working after hours to work in close proximity to one another.
☐	Room surfaces	Use light colors for walls, floors, ceilings and furniture to increase utilization of light, and reduce connected lighting power to achieve required illuminances. Avoid glossy finishes on room and work surfaces to limit reflected glare.
☐	Space utilization branch circuit wiring	Use modular branch circuit wiring to allow for flexibility in moving, relocating or adding luminaires to suit changing space configurations.
☐	Space utilization: occupancy	Light building for occupied periods only, and when required for security or cleaning purposes (see chapter 31, Lighting Controls).

Daylighting

☐	Daylight compensation	If daylighting can be used to replace some electric lighting near fenestration during substantial periods of the day, lighting in those areas should be circuited so that it may be controlled manually or automatically by switching or dimming.
☐	Daylight sensing	Daylight sensors and dimming systems can reduce electric lighting energy.
☐	Daylight control	Maximize the effectiveness of existing fenestration-shading controls (interior and exterior) or replace with proper devices or shielding media.
☐	Space utilization	Use daylighting in transition zones, in lounge and recreational areas, and for functions where the variation in color, intensity and direction may be desirable. Consider applications where daylight can be utilized as ambient lighting, supplemented by local task lights.

Lighting Sources: Lamps and Ballasts

☐	Source efficacy	Install lamps with the highest efficacies to provide the desired light source color and distribution requirements.
☐	Fluorescent lamps	Use T8 fluorescent and high-wattage compact fluorescent systems for improved source efficacy and color quality.
☐	Ballasts	Use electronic or energy efficient ballasts with fluorescent lamps.
☐	HID	Use high-efficacy metal halide and high-pressure sodium light sources for exterior floodlighting.
☐	Incandescent	Where incandescent sources are necessary, use reflector halogen lamps for increased efficacy.
☐	Compact fluorescent	Use compact fluorescent lamps, where possible, to replace incandescent sources.
☐	Lamp wattage reduced-wattage lamps	In existing spaces, use reduced-wattage lamps where illuminance is too high but luminaire locations must be maintained for uniformity. *Caution:* These lamps are not recommended where the ambient space temperature may fall below 16°C (60°F).

Fig. 30.4. *Continued*

Lighting Sources: Lamps and Ballasts

☐	Control compatibility	If a control system is used, check compatibility of lamps and ballasts with the control device.
☐	System change	Substitute metal halide and high-pressure sodium systems for existing mercury vapor lighting systems.

Luminaires

☐	Maintained efficiency.	Select luminaires which do not collect dirt rapidly and which can be easily cleaned.
☐	Improved maintenance	Improved maintenance procedures may enable a lighting system with reduced wattage to provide adequate illumination throughout system or component life.
☐	Luminaire efficiency replacement or relocation	Check luminaire effectiveness for task lighting and for overall efficiency; if ineffective or inefficient, consider replacement or relocation.
☐	Heat removal	When luminaire temperatures exceed optimal system operating temperatures, consider using heat removal luminaires to improve lamp performance and reduce heat gain to the space. The decrease in lamp temperature may, however, actually increase power consumption.
☐	Maintained efficiency	Select a lamp replacement schedule for all light sources, to more accurately predict light loss factors and possibly decrease the number of luminaires required.

Lighting Controls

☐	Switching: local control	Install switches for local and convenient control of lighting by occupants. This should be in combination with a building-wide system to turn lights off when the building is unoccupied.
☐	Selective switching	Install selective switching of luminaires according to groupings of working tasks and different working hours.
☐	Low-voltage switching systems	Use low-voltage switching systems to obtain maximum switching capability.
☐	Master control system	Use a programmable low-voltage master switching system for the entire building to turn lights on and off automatically as needed, with overrides at individual areas.
☐	Multipurpose spaces	Install multicircuit switching or preset dimming controls to provide flexibility when spaces are used for multiple purposes and require different ranges of illuminance for various activities. Clearly label the control cover plates.
☐	"Tuning" illuminance	Use switching and dimming systems as a means of adjusting illuminance for variable lighting requirements.
☐	Scheduling	Operate lighting according to a predetermined schedule.
☐	Occupant / motion sensors	Use occupant / motion sensors for unpredictable patterns of occupancy.
☐	Lumen maintenance	Fluorescent dimming systems may be utilized to maintain illuminance throughout lamp life, thereby saving energy by compensating for lamp-lumen depreciation and other light loss factors.
☐	Ballast switching	Use multilevel ballasts and local inboard-outboard lamp switching where a reduction in illuminances is sometimes desired.

Operation and Maintenance

☐	Education	Analyze lighting used during working and building cleaning periods, and institute an education program to have personnel turn off incandescent lamps promptly when the space is not in use, fluorescent lamps if the space will not be used for 5 min or longer, and HID lamps (mercury, metal halide, high-pressure sodium) if the space will not be used for 30 min or longer.

Fig. 30.4. *Continued*

Operation and Maintenance

☐	Parking	Restrict parking after hours to specific lots so lighting can be reduced to minimum security requirements in unused parking areas.
☐	Custodial service	Schedule routine building cleaning during occupied hours.
☐	Reduced illuminance	Reduce illuminance during building cleaning periods.
☐	Cleaning schedules	Adjust cleaning schedules to minimize time of operation, by concentrating cleaning activities in fewer spaces at the same time and by turning off lights in unoccupied areas.
☐	Program evaluation	Evaluate the present lighting maintenance program, and revise it as necessary to provide the most efficient use of the lighting system.
☐	Cleaning and maintenance	Clean luminaires and replace lamps on a regular maintenance schedule to ensure proper illuminance levels are maintained.
☐	Regular system checks	Check to see if all components are in good working condition. Transmitting or diffusing media should be examined, and badly discolored or deteriorated media replaced to improve efficiency.
☐	Renovation of luminaires	Replace outdated or damaged luminaires with modern ones which have good cleaning capabilities and which use lamps with higher efficacy and good lumen maintenance characteristics.
☐	Area maintenance	Trim trees and bushes that may be obstructing outdoor luminaire distribution and creating unwanted shadows.

struction or existing spaces. The list can be scanned quickly to determine which ideas may be applicable for a particular installation. The designer should review these guidelines in consultation with the client and consider those which meet the needs of the client and occupants.

REFERENCES

1. American Society of Heating, Refrigerating and Air-Conditioning Engineers and Illuminating Engineering Society of North America. 1989. *Energy efficient design of new buildings except new low-rise residential buildings, ASHRAE / IES 90.1-1989.* Atlanta, GA: American Society of Heating, Refrigerating and Air-Conditioning Engineers.

2. Davis, R. G., and S. A. Meyers. 1992. *Lighting regulation in the United States.* Troy, NY: Rensselaer Polytechnic Institute.

3. IES. Energy Management Committee. [To be published.] *IES design considerations for effective building lighting energy utilization.* IES LEM-3. New York: Illuminating Engineering Society of North America.

4. Rea, M. S., I. Pasini, and L. Jutras. 1990. Lighting performance measured in a commercial building: Strengths and weaknesses pinpointed. *Light. Des. Appl.* 20(1):22–32.

5. IES. Energy Management Committee. 1982. *IES recommended procedure for lighting power limit determination.* IES LEM-1-1982. New York: Illuminating Engineering Society of North America.

6. IES. Energy Management Committee. 1984. *IES recommended procedure for lighting energy limit determination for buildings.* IES LEM-2-1984. New York: Illuminating Engineering Society of North America.

7. IES. Energy Management Committee. 1984. *IES recommended procedure for energy analysis of building design and installations.* IES LEM-4-1982. New York: Illuminating Engineering Society of North America.

Lighting Controls

31

The lighting controls covered in this section are controls for electric lighting. They provide desired illuminance at appropriate times while reducing energy use and operating costs of lighting systems.

In the past, controls were used primarily to turn lights on or off, or for special purposes such as stage, theater or conference room lighting. Lately the use of controls has become an essential element of good lighting design and an integral part of energy management programs for lighting of commercial, residential, industrial and exterior areas. Lighting controls for specific applications are described in chapters 15, Office Lighting; 16, Educational Facilities Lighting; 21, Theatre, Television and Photographic Lighting; and 30, Energy Management.

A variety of strategies and techniques have been developed to control a building's power demand, energy consumption, lighting equipment, and working environment. Some equipment is best suited for new construction and renovation, while other equipment is better suited for retrofit. This section describes different types of lighting control strategies, techniques and equipment and their effects on building systems and occupants.

Studies of buildings that have implemented control strategies have shown that it is possible to reduce overall lighting energy consumption by as much as 70% in some areas.[1,2] Cumulative savings are dependent on the building configuration, the control hardware specified, the combination of control strategies selected and the extent to which each of the control strategies is available for use within a building.

LIGHTING CONTROL STRATEGIES

There are two major benefits from the application of lighting controls: energy management and esthetics. Energy-management controls for lighting systems provide energy and cost savings through reduced illuminance or reduced time of use. Esthetic controls provide the ability to change space functions and can create emotional appeal. These benefits are not necessarily in conflict. Energy management control strategies may significantly improve the esthetic quality of a space, and controls installed for esthetic purposes may pro-

duce significant energy savings. Here, however, the two benefits are discussed separately.

Energy Management Strategies[3,4]

Predictable Scheduling. Where activities in a building occur routinely during the day, luminaires throughout the space can be operated on a fixed schedule (with overrides). For example, staff arrival and departure times, lunch periods and cleaning hours are predictable for weekdays, weekends and holidays in many manufacturing plants, offices, schools, libraries and retail stores. Predictable-scheduling strategies are particularly effective when work schedules are well defined for the entire area. Such strategies can reduce energy by as much as 40% by eliminating energy waste on lights operating in unoccupied spaces. Automatic scheduling also relieves staff of the burden of operating lighting controls and can be used to signal times of particular activities, such as the opening and closing of retail stores. It is unacceptable, however, to plunge occupants into darkness when scheduling the operation of the lighting system.

Unpredictable Scheduling. Many events are unpredictable and unscheduled, such as workstation vacancies due to sickness, vacations, staff meetings, and business trips. Unassigned areas such as copy centers, filing areas, conference rooms, and dressing rooms in retail stores are used sporadically and are not readily scheduled. Though these areas may not be amenable to tightly scheduled lighting operation, local automatic techniques may be more cost-effective than the usual reliance on manual operation of lights. Unpredictable scheduling strategies using occupancy/motion sensors have yielded energy savings over 60% in areas well suited for their use. To assess the benefits of automatic controls, it is important first to determine the proportion of time the space will be vacant. It is also important to consider that switching lights on and off may disturb occupants of adjacent spaces, as in an open-plan office. For reasons of esthetics, safety and user acceptance, lights in these spaces may be dimmed rather than switched off completely.

Daylighting.[5-7] In the perimeter areas of buildings, part of the desired illumination can often be supplied

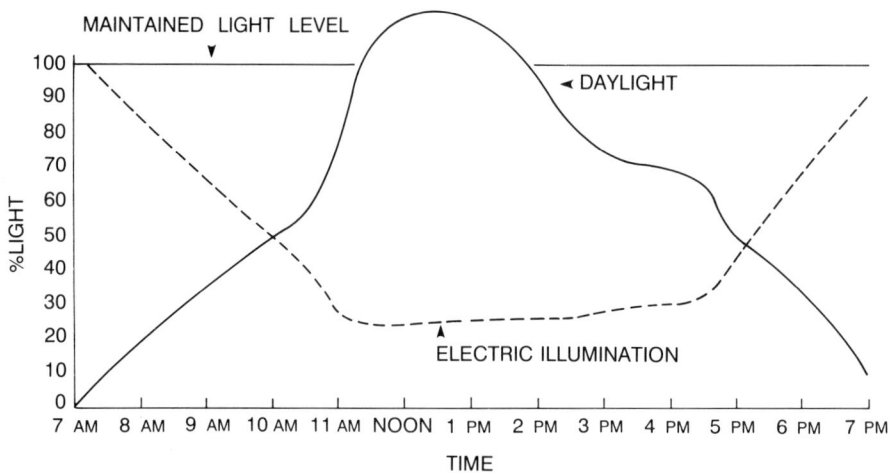

Fig. 31-1. Photocell-activated dimmers maintain a constant light level by adjusting the output of electric illumination according to changing ambient illuminance.

by daylight. See figure 31-1. In these areas, reducing the electric lighting in proportion to the amount of available daylight will reduce energy consumption.

The energy savings realized from daylighting depend on many factors, such as the climatic conditions, the building form, orientation and design, the sensor and control design, and the activities within the building. Under suitable conditions, daylight can reduce electric energy costs significantly when photoelectric sensor controls are used. This is particularly important during peak power demand hours when the cost of electric energy may be much higher than during off-peak hours. It is essential that control of the electric lighting be properly integrated with the daylight illumination pattern to maintain adequate quantity and quality of lighting.

With respect to photosensor controls, the size and shape of control zones are usually constrained by the rapid falloff of horizontal illuminance from the window wall. Although lighting zones can be laid out to cover a single task area, a room or an entire building, in practice the lighting zones should be close to the daylight-admitting elements. For typical spaces illuminated by daylight from a side window, the lighting zones should be adjacent to the window wall and no more than 4 m (13 ft) deep. The row of luminaires nearest the window should be controlled on a separate circuit from those in the interior area. If manually operated shading devices are used, smaller control zones may be required for daylighting to be effective.

Brightness Balance. Lighting design often dictates limits to the brightness within or among spaces. One design goal is to balance different brightness levels so that glare and shadows are reduced. For example, lighting controls can be used to mitigate the very high brightness produced by windows in interior spaces. One control technique is to limit light entering the space with blinds or louvers. Another, possibly counter-intuitive approach for interior spaces is to increase the illuminance produced by the electric lights. Often controls can be used to provide a luminous transition between two spaces having very different brightness levels. Perhaps the most common example is tunnel lighting. The illuminance produced by the electric lights in the entry zone of the tunnel will depend upon the level of daylight illuminance; higher illuminances are produced by the electric lights in this zone on sunny days than on cloudy days.

Lumen Maintenance

Lighting systems are usually designed for a minimum maintained illuminance level. This requires the level of a new lighting system to exceed the design minimum by 20–35% to allow for lumen depreciation (lamp lumen depreciation, luminaire dirt depreciation, and room surface dirt depreciation: see also chapter 9, Lighting Calculations and chapter 30, Energy Management). Lumen depreciation control strategy calls for reducing the initial illumination of a new system to the designed minimum level. As lumen depreciation occurs, more power is applied to the lamps in order to maintain constant output. Thus, full power is applied only near the end of the lumen maintenance period, significantly reducing energy use over the life of the lamp.[2] See figure 31-2.

Lumen maintenance can be accomplished through the use of a dimming system with a photosensor input. The control system for lumen maintenance is most cost-effective when large blocks of luminaires are controlled together. Group relamping to maintain all of the lamps at virtually the same lumen output is required for the system to be effective in reducing both energy and maintenance costs.

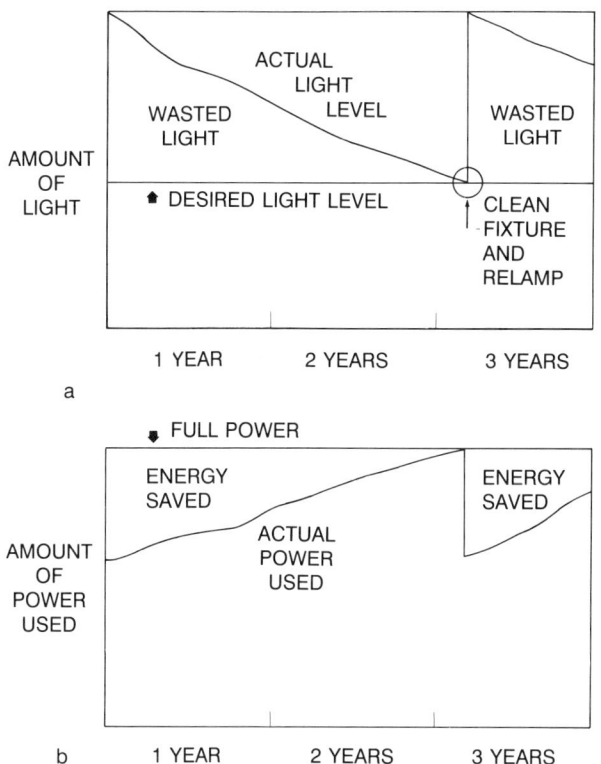

Fig. 31-2. Lumen Maintenance Control Strategy. a) Light levels drop over time with conventional lighting systems, but power remains constant; b) with a lumen maintenance system, light levels stay constant and energy is saved.

Task Tuning

Uniform illuminances are often provided throughout a space. With a task-tuning control strategy, however, the lighting system can be adjusted, or tuned, to provide local illumination as needed. Levels can be lowered in areas such as aisles and reception rooms, and raised in areas where more difficult visual tasks occur. Considerable savings are possible through task tuning.[2] This strategy results in the efficient use of energy for lighting without sacrificing occupant visual performance.

Tuning is accomplished by varying the light output of individual or small groups of luminaires. Since it is necessary to tune the lighting only occasionally, upon a change in the space utilization or in the task being performed, the adjustment often can be done manually. A number of light controllers are capable of tuning a zone of luminaires. Some electronic ballasts incorporate a built-in potentiometer to permit tuning.

Load Shedding and Demand Reduction

A building's lighting electrical bill can be effectively reduced by controlling lighting power demand for short periods of time. Selective reduction of illuminance in less critical areas may be particularly effective in re-

gions where the peak electric power demand occurs in summer, because a reduction in lighting load will also reduce the cooling load. Peak power demand charges are employed by many utilities to help avoid brownouts and blackouts, so the savings at peak periods are substantial.

Esthetic Control Strategies

Many spaces in commercial, institutional and residential applications are used for more than one purpose. Different tasks require a variety of lighting conditions. Esthetic controls provide the means to adjust the lighting to suit the purpose, to maintain human visual performance and to change the mood of the space.

Esthetic controls include switching and dimming. Dimming controls can provide dynamic effects or create strong focal points. Changes can occur rapidly to create excitement, or subtly to create a smooth transition between different room functions.

For many esthetic applications it is necessary to control illuminance over a wide range. In a conference room, for example, a high illuminance may be required for reading tasks, whereas for a slide presentation the illuminance should be one-tenth or less of the reading level. The differences in needed illuminance are due to the differences in the task visibility and the adaptation of the eye to changes in illuminance. The *square law* curve for adaptation used by most controls manufacturers is shown in figure 31-3. The curve shows, for example, that a measured illuminance of 25% of the original illuminance is perceived as a brightness of 50% of the original level. Audiovisual applications for controls generally require a measured illuminance of less than 10%.

It is important to use a source that can be appropriately dimmed. Incandescent and low-voltage incandescent sources can dim to zero output. Fluorescent sources can be dimmed to 1% output when used with proper dimming ballasts. Neon and cold cathode lamps can be dimmed to approximately 10% ot maximum light output. HID sources can be dimmed to approximately 20% of maximum light output, but they have a slow response time and strong color shifts that make them poorly suited for esthetic applications.

The strategies used for esthetic control include:

- Manual controls
- Preset control systems
- Central control systems

Manual controls (switches and dimmers) are commonly used in commercial, institutional, industrial and residential buildings. If they are to be effective, manual controls should be simple and convenient to use. The number of control channels should be minimized to

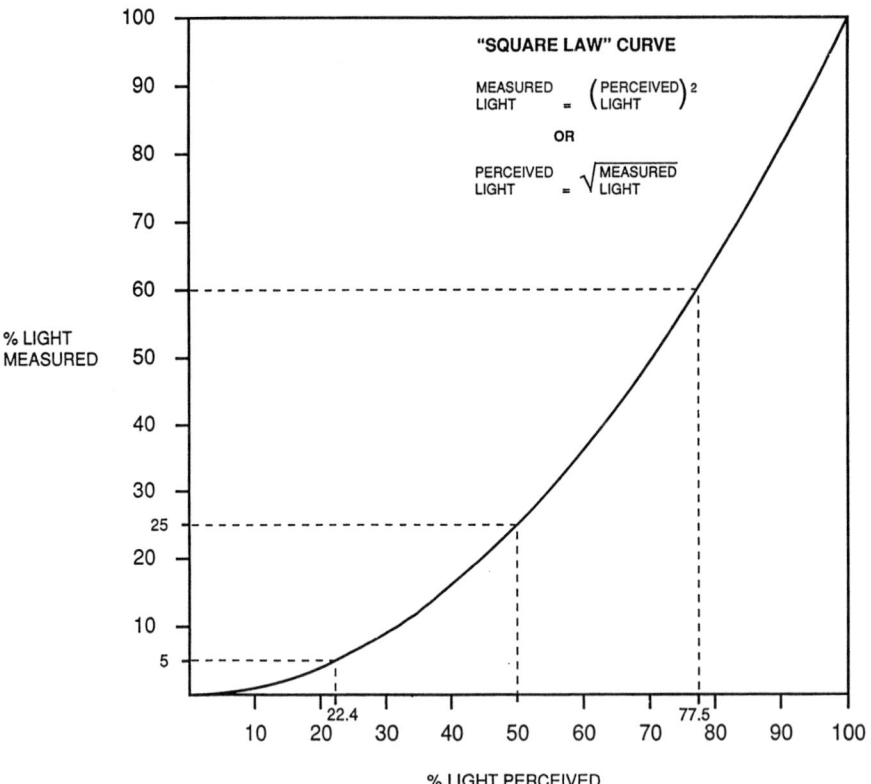

Fig. 31-3. Square Law Curve — A presumed relationship between perceived illuminance and measured illuminance.

Fig. 31-4. Switches and dimmers, clearly labeled for easy use.

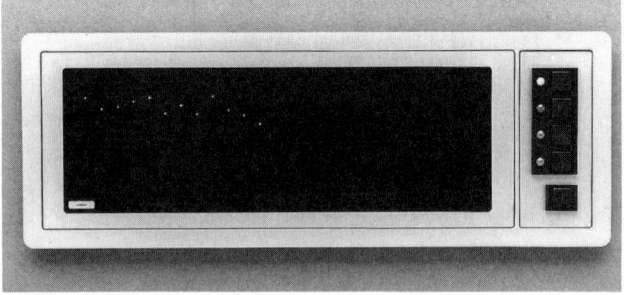

Fig. 31-5. Example of multi-channel preset station that provides four scenes of control for 12 channels of lighting.

avoid confusing choices. Control panels should be clearly and permanently labeled. See figure 31-4.

The appearance of the controls is also important. Switches and dimmers should match each other and fit into the overall architectural style of the space.

Preset control systems allow for several lighting channels to be controlled simultaneously. All channels are programmed to provide two or three moods or scenes. Each of these scenes can be recalled with the touch of one button. See figure 31-5. Preset systems are valuable in multifunction commercial spaces such

as conference rooms and ballrooms. They are also used in residential applications for areas such as living rooms, dining rooms and media rooms.

Central dimming systems are the most powerful of the group of dimming options. Like theatrical dimming systems, they have at least one central dimming panel. The dimmers themselves are the power-handling devices. The control-function logic is typically in the control stations, which can include processors and several forms of manual or preset controls.

Local, single-room systems typically consist of one control station with manual sliders or nondimming switches that can control large amounts of power. The dimmable wattage is limited only by the number of modules a dimmer panel can hold. These systems are easily expanded to multiple rooms and customized to offer many combinations of manual, preset, assigned and time-clock control. They can incorporate energy reduction controls such as occupancy/motion sensors and photosensors, and can handle emergency power functions. Some systems allow wireless remote control and can interface to audiovisual and other systems in both commercial and residential applications.

In divisible rooms, assignment control stations allow several independent lighting systems to be joined together through flexible master control. Hotel function rooms and convention center meeting rooms are the most common applications.

Whole-house systems are being used more frequently. Using local or small modular dimmers, a central computer and master control stations, these systems can control every lighting feature. Many of these systems can also operate other electrical systems such as motorized curtains or Jacuzzi pumps, and they interface easily with burglar alarms, smart home systems and other electrical control systems.

LIGHTING CONTROL TECHNIQUES[2,3]

Selection of the major control techniques is particularly important in the specification process. The following three categories establish the major choices: *switching or dimming control*, *local or central control*, and *degree of control automation*. After the strategy or strategies are decided, it is necessary to select the specific lighting control equipment to be employed.

Switching or Dimming

With switching control, lighting loads are switched on and off. This switching can be done manually with simple wall-box switches or via relays by the control system. It has been found that the use of local switching controls can save energy. Two-level switching in private offices is an inexpensive way to give the occupant the ability to modulate the environment in response to daylight or specific task needs.

Central switching systems are less expensive to install per unit area than equivalent dimming systems and are most appropriate for strategies such as scheduling, where the switching action can be confined to unoccupied times. Switching techniques should be treated cautiously for other purposes, especially if the switching action can occur when the space is occupied, because sudden changes in the electric lighting may annoy building occupants, thus affecting productivity.[3]

In multiballasted lighting systems, switching can be used most effectively if the luminaires are split wired. By split-wiring three- and four-lamp luminaires (figures 31-6 and 31-7), multiple intensities can be provided in

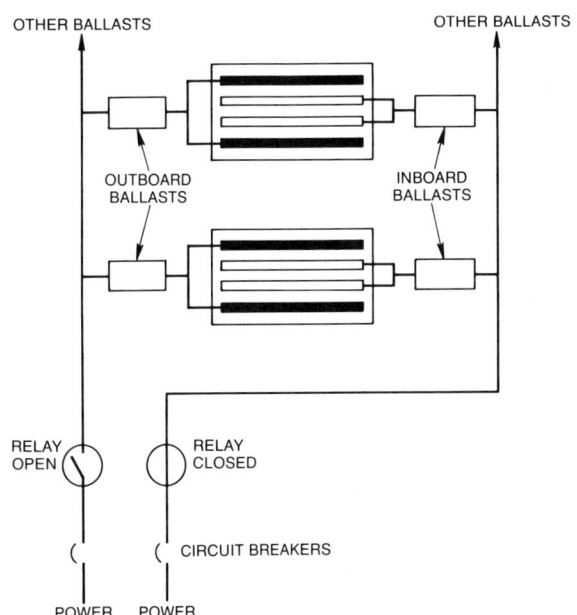

Fig. 31-6. Split-level wiring scheme that permits three lighting levels (0, 50 and 100 percent) with four-lamp luminaires. Above luminaires are shown at 50 percent lighting levels.

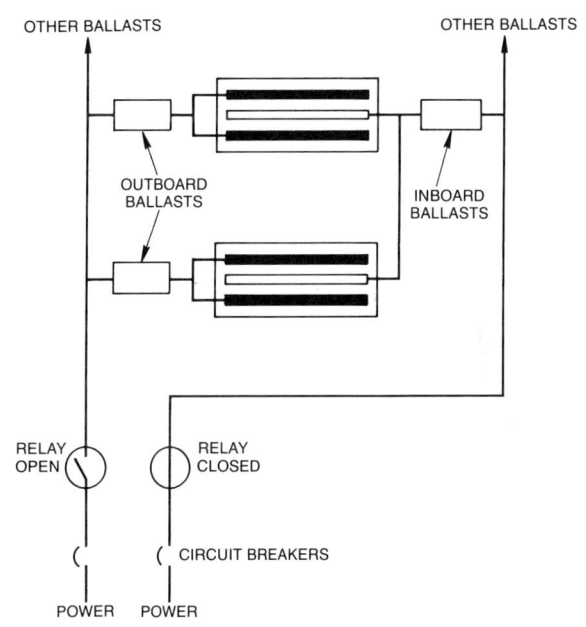

Fig. 31-7. Split-level wiring scheme that permits four lighting levels (0, $33\frac{1}{3}$, $66\frac{2}{3}$ and 100%) with three-lamp luminaires. The above luminaires are shown at $33\frac{1}{3}$% light levels.

a single zone. With the help of a relay-based control system, full lighting can be provided for certain portions of the day while allowing a reduced lighting level (at reduced power) for times when less demanding tasks are performed. In retrofit applications, split wiring can be expensive. Depending on the wiring system in place, relays may be installed near the circuit breaker panels to permit automatic control of blocks of lighting (figure 31-8).

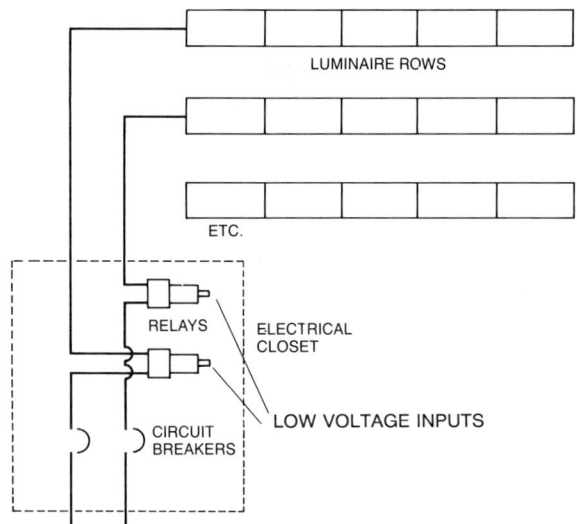

Fig. 31-8. Installation of low voltage relays in an electric closet controlling different banks of luminaires.

With dimming control, the illuminance in each zone may be varied smoothly and continuously to dynamically match visual requirements. Dimming is consequently well suited to daylighting applications, since daylight varies continuously. Similarly, dimming is effective in saving energy by compensating for the gradual light losses that occur over time with all electric lighting systems (lumen maintenance strategy).

Local or Central

Lighting controls can be implemented in buildings using either a local approach, a central system, or some combination of the two. The two approaches are distinguished both by the size of the controlled areas and by how the control inputs are integrated into the system.

A local lighting system is divided into small, independently controllable zones, their size and shape typically dictated by the geometry of the building spaces (such as the locations of ceiling-high partitions, windows or skylights) or according to functional need. Sensor inputs are wired directly to the localized control

rather than to a central location. Thus each module is essentially independent of other modules.

Central systems generally combine many local zones. Some central microprocessor systems are intended to handle either or both lighting and mechanical (HVAC) systems. Total building energy-management control and monitoring functions are easier with central systems.[4]

System Integration. One major advantage of a lighting control system is that the illuminance can be automatically adjusted to suit the activity or tasks at hand. With proper programming and sensors, some processors can control the lighting systems as well as the mechanical systems of the building. A common system permits the optimum control of energy use and also minimizes programming and training requirements. Through the use of a distributive processing configuration the differences between mechanical and lighting inputs and control strategies are easily overcome. The local processor can be designed for the specific inputs and control outputs as well as the required interface with the central processor.

All lighting control systems contain three major components: (1) a power controller, (2) a logic circuit and (3) a sensing device. The communication and wiring system must link these components. The controller, such as a dimmer, relay, or switch, is the "business end" of a control system that electrically changes the output of the light source. The logic circuit is the intelligence that decides when, and how much, electric lighting to supply. The logic circuit receives its information from a sensing device, such as a photosensor, an occupancy/motion sensor, or a timing device. Two or more of these elements may be combined in a single system. See figure 31-9.

Control strategies may have different but overlapping sets of hardware requirements. For some combination of strategies, such as daylighting and lumen maintenance, the hardware required for either is essentially identical to that required for both. Thus, the economic benefit of employing several strategies with

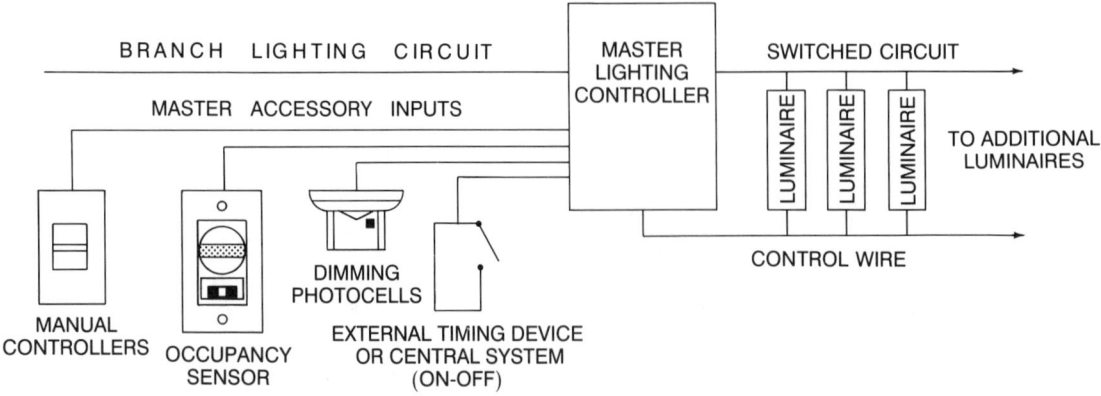

Fig. 31-9. Diagram of a lighting control system.

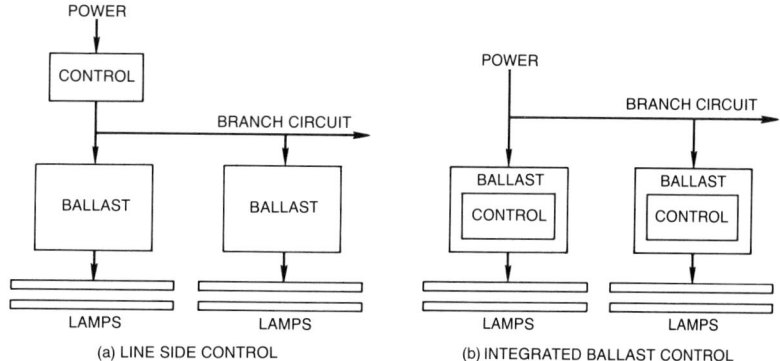

Fig. 31-10. Lighting control operating lamps from (a) the line side of the luminaire; (b) integrated internally with the ballast circuitry.

the same hardware can increase the cost-effectiveness of the control system investment.

Hardwiring. There are many methods available for linking the lighting control system components. The control device itself (dimmer, relay or switch) is usually hardwired to a lighting system before the supply and the ballast (line-side controls) as shown in figure 31-10a. Some electronic ballasts incorporate circuitry to vary the output of the lamps over a wide range, effectively combining the control device and ballast in one integrated package (figure 31-10b).

Power Line Carrier. The power line carrier is a communication method that is finding increased application in retrofit control installations. By allowing communication between the processor and the control device directly over the existing power lines, extensive rewiring is avoided. However, some wiring systems in older buildings may significantly reduce the effective range of communications between the sensor, the processor and the controller. Care must be taken to ensure that all of the control devices on the power line are compatible as a system.

Radio Links. Radio-controlled systems eliminate the need for wiring between the sensor, the processor and the controller. These systems are relatively expensive, but have found application in outdoor systems and high-bay warehouses where the controlled luminaires are difficult to access.

Control System Selection

There are many variables to consider when designing the appropriate system for a specific building. When selecting the type of local or central system the designer should answer the following questions:

1. *What functions will the processor perform?* Determine the control needs for each space,

such as daylight control, occupancy sensors, dimming, scheduling or space flexibility.

2. *What output functions are required?* If a dimming strategy is used, the system should support dimming functions. If a daylighting strategy is used, consider the need to control banks of luminaires separately.

3. *What is the size and complexity of the space being controlled?* The building geometry plays a large role in determining control zones; select control systems suitable for these zones.

4. *How much change is anticipated for the space and lighting system?* If the facilities or building functions are expected to change, select a system flexible enough to respond to these changes.

5. *What other systems are proposed for the facility?* Choose a system that will interact with other functions and building systems without interference.

6. *What is the expertise level of the system operators and maintainers?* Consider available personnel and abilities, and either select a system which conforms to the skills and schedules of the facility managers or establish a training program for them.

7. *Is a dedicated processor required; or is processing shared with a central mainframe unit; or is processing done by a standard, off-the-shelf microcomputer or minicomputer?* Consider the computing resources in the building, the cost of new computers, and the effects of reliability of the central building system on lighting control.

8. *Does the system meet all code and safety requirements?* Review all applicable code and safety standards and requirements.

9. *What are the economics for the system?* An economic analysis will determine whether the system will meet the owner's financial criteria. See chapter 13, Lighting Economics.

10. *What is the reliability of the system?* Select manufacturers with the ability to assure long-term reliability and availability of components.
11. *What are the warranty and service commitments from the vendor?* These issues are critical to ensure the owner will be served over the life of the system.

When answering the questions it is important to consider the needs of the occupants. This will help qualify the functional requirements as well as making sure the system can be effectively implemented and used in the particular application. A system selected with these considerations will help ensure that the system is efficient, reliable and cost-effective.

Degree of Control Automation and Zoning

Controls vary greatly in degree of automation, ranging from manual (wall switches) to highly automated. In terms of energy conservation, automatic controls are most effective in reducing energy consumption, since they do not rely on human initiative. In terms of cost and occupant response, automatic controls are not always the most effective. Allowing occupants to override the automatic operation when required is very important, especially when programmable controls are used for scheduling purposes. A strict lighting schedule can be employed if automatic control can be locally overridden when necessary.[2]

Zoning. In designing a lighting control system, the size and distribution of the control zones in the building space have an important effect on both the success and the cost-effectiveness of the final system. There is a tradeoff between the size of the control zone and the system cost. Smaller zones are more expensive (both in equipment and in installation costs) but offer greater flexibility and potential for reducing lighting operating costs. Some control strategies, particularly daylighting and task tuning, are best implemented with small control zones, 10–40 m^2 (100–400 ft^2), while scheduling and lumen maintenance can be used effectively even if the control zones correspond to the area illuminated by an entire branch circuit, approximately 100–400 m^2 (1000–4000 ft^2).

LIGHTING CONTROL EQUIPMENT

Manual Switching

The energy savings achievable through switching should be the initial consideration in developing the plan for lighting circuits. The most common practice is to allow manual control of lighting. The design and the location of the manual control affects the energy consumption of the building. Since the energy savings depend upon the willingness of individuals to use the switching system, the convenience and flexibility of switching greatly affects the extent of any lighting energy savings. Occupants of private offices are the most likely to use the switches to modulate the illuminance in their space and to do their part in saving energy.

Each lighting plan will present a unique set of switching circumstances. The following general provisions should be considered:

1. Each separate office or area should have its own control switch, and those with daylighting should have at least two-level switching.
2. In large open spaces, similar work areas should be grouped together on one circuit.
3. When single- or two-lamp luminaires are used, adjacent luminaires should be placed on alternate circuits to provide for half and full light level.
4. When three-lamp fluorescent luminaires are used, the middle lamps should be connected to a separate circuit from the outside lamps. This will produce three-level lighting systems with one-third, two-thirds and full light level.
5. When four-lamp fluorescent luminaires are used, the inside pair of lamps should be connected to a circuit separate from the outside pair to provide half and full light level.
6. Task areas with high levels of lighting should be on separate switches.
7. Luminaires along window walls should be wired on separate circuits and be controlled independently.

Timing and Sensing Devices

Timing Devices. The function of the timer is to control lighting in response to known or scheduled sequences of events, that is, to turn off the lighting which is not needed. Timers range in complexity from simple integral timers (spring-wound) to microprocessors that can program a sequence of events for years at a time. Coupled with microprocessors, timers can control multiple events and lighting effects. As a general rule, some form of override must be provided to accommodate deviations from the preset schedule. The override should automatically reset to the programmed functions after a suitable period.

With a simple *integral timer*, the load is switched on and held energized for a preset period of time. Timer limits range from a few minutes to twelve hours. Some models have a hold position for continuous service. For lighting loads these units will handle a current of up to 20 A.

An *electromechanical time clock* is driven by an electric motor, with contactors actuated by mechanical stops or arms affixed to the clock face. Time clocks have periods from 24 hours to 7 days and may include astronomical correction to compensate for seasonal changes. They can initiate numerous on-off operations. Some units are available with up to 16 h of backup power on the timing mechanism in case of power failure. Some can actuate a momentary contact switch to provide on and off pulses for actuating low-voltage relays or contactors. Wall-mounted (outlet box) units are also available to control local loads such as security lighting.

Electronic time clocks provide programmable selection of many switching operations, and typically may be controlled to the nearest minute over a 7-day period. These devices offer the same switching options as the electromechanical time clock. Battery backup is available to protect the system from power outages.

Photosensors. Photosensors utilize electronic components that transform visible radiation (light) into an electrical signal. Most sensors generate a current proportional to the irradiance. The output signal can activate two modes of operation. In the first, the photosensor output activates a simple on-off switch or relay. In the second, a variable output signal is established and sent to a controller that will continuously adjust the output of electric lighting.

When photosensors for interior applications are used in conjunction with relays for on-off control, they should utilize a *dead band*, that is, the illuminance above which the lamps are switched off should be higher than the illuminance below which they are switched on. This will prevent unnecessary on-off cycling near the threshold illuminance levels. It is also important to consider that switching lights on and off may disturb occupants. A photosensor may be an integral part of a luminaire, it may be remote from the luminaire that it controls, or it may control a circuit relay that operates several luminaires. A photosensor can also be used in conjunction with a time clock which can switch lights off or reduce their output.

Photosensors used in outdoor applications are usually oriented to the north (in the northern hemisphere). This assures more constant illumination on the sensor, as there is no sunlight contribution. The sensors are adjustable with respect to light levels for activation. Photosensors designed for outdoor lighting should not be used to control interior lighting, due to their limited sensitivity and adjustability.

Systems that continuously vary their output in response to the varying photosensor response are most effective when employed for lumen maintenance or daylighting strategies. The photosensor will detect a change in illuminance and send a signal to the controller to increase or decrease the illuminance. In response to the signal, the lighting system may be adjusted by stepped or continuous dimming.

The use of photosensors to control interior lighting is not trivial; proper design, placement and calibration of them are critical.[8] Several techniques are currently employed. Placement of the sensor on the task surface has the advantage of direct measurement of task illuminance, but there may be difficulty in wiring the sensor to the controller and in ensuring that the sensor does not damage and is not damaged by the task materials. The second and most common method places the sensor on the ceiling, oriented toward the task. A third method measures the daylight entering through the fenestration. The best results for this method are achieved when direct sunlight cannot fall on the sensor. A fourth method measures the external illuminance directly. All methods require the sensor output to be adjusted to match the illuminance on the task as closely as possible. An accurate and easy means to calibrate the response of the sensor is essential. Lumen maintenance strategies typically use the second method, while daylighting strategies may use any of the last three methods.

A further consideration with interior lighting is the amount of area controlled by one photosensor. The most important guideline is that the areas controlled by a single sensor should all have the same general task activity, illuminance requirements and surround. The space controlled should have the same daylight illumination conditions (amount and direction). The entire area should be contiguous, having no high walls or partitions to divide it.

Occupancy / Motion Sensors.[9] The primary function of occupancy sensors is to automatically switch luminaires off when spaces are unoccupied, so as to reduce energy use. Electrical consumption is reduced by cutting the number of hours that luminaires remain on, and electrical demand is reduced by taking advantage of incomplete occupancy loads during periods of peak electrical use.

Occupancy/motion sensors provide local on-off control of luminaires in response to the presence or absence of occupants in a space. Occupancy is sensed by audio, ultrasonic, passive infrared or optical means. These devices are designed to switch lights on as an occupant enters and keep them on while he or she remains in the space; lights are switched off after a preset time following the departure of the occupant. The normal movements of a person should sustain lighting in the occupied space. Quiet activities such as word processing, reading, or using the telephone, however, are often not detected, and lights being switched

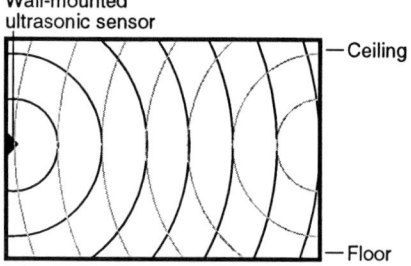

Wall-mounted ultrasonic sensor

—Ceiling

—Floor

This figure shows a simplified wave pattern in an empty room.Ultrasonic waves (black) are emitted by the sensor and reflect off the back wall. The reflected waves (gray) then return to the sensor.

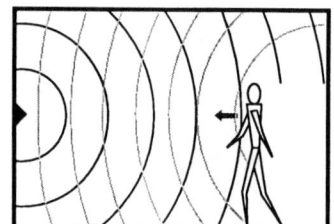

A person, or any object in the room, reflects waves emitted by the sensor. As a person moves in the space, the frequency of the waves reflected off the person changes. The sensor detects this change in frequency and the luminaires are turned on.

Fig. 31-11. Example of Motion Detection with Ultrasonic Sensors.

off can frustrate occupants in these situations.

There are a variety of mounting configurations for occupancy/motion sensors; they can be recessed or surface mounted on the ceiling or wall, can replace wall switches, or can plug into receptacles. The floor area covered by individual sensors can range from 15 m² (150 ft²) in individual offices or work stations to 200 m² (2000 ft²) in large classroom or assembly spaces. Larger areas can be controlled by adding more sensors. Occupancy/motion sensors can be used in combination with timers, daylighting sensors, dimmers and central lighting controls.

Ultrasonic sensors transmit ultrasound and receive a reflected signal to sense the presence of occupants in a space. The frequency of ultrasonic sensors is usually between 25,000 and 40,000 Hz. (See figure 31-11.) Passive infrared sensors detect the changes in infrared patterns across their segmented detection regions.[10] (See figure 31-12.)

When selecting a sensor and planning for its location, the designer should ensure that all important movements within the controlled area will be detected, subject to the avoidance of false positive responses, that is, responses to movement by inanimate objects inside the room or by people outside the entrance. It should also be recognized that the operating life of fluorescent lamps is reduced by increased switching. The amount of the reduction will depend upon the type of lamp and the frequency of switching. The actual service life of the lamps, however, may be increased by the elimination of unnecessary burning hours.

Central Processors

Function. For central systems, the processor is the device which assimilates the data inputs, determines the required change, and initiates action to effect the change. The more sophisticated processors can re-

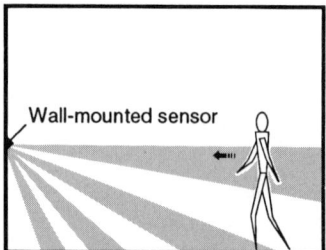

Wall-Mounted Sensor: Section View Vertical Fan Patterns

Wall-mounted sensor

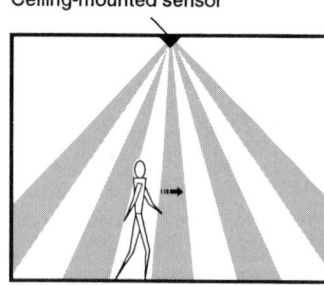

Ceiling-mounted sensor

Ceiling-Mounted Sensor: Section View Vertical Fan Patterns

Fig. 31-12. Example of Motion Detection with Infrared Sensors. The motion of a person through the pattern of receiver areas is detected as a change, and the luminaires are turned on.

spond to a number of complex lighting conditions in the space, collect power and energy-use data, and supply summary reports for building management and tenant billing. Processors range in complexity from a microchip in a controller to a mainframe computer. Simplicity of operation and control, coupled with automatic operation in response to the actual environment, is essential.

Operation. In general, all processors operate in the same way. Input is received from a sensor, such as a photosensor or clock, data are analyzed in accordance with a predetermined set of rules, and a system change is initiated. Systems can respond to manual switches as well as to automatic functions such as the time of day and to illuminance conditions. Outputs can include switching, dimming, and adjusting daylighting shading or reflection devices.

Processor Type. There are three types of processors: local, central and distributed. In the local type, the processor is located in, or adjacent to, the device it controls. Sensor inputs go to a signal conditioner, either analog or digital, and are then fed to the processor. The central processor receives all inputs, analyzes the data, and then sends instructions to controllers located throughout a facility. This method allows coordinated control of all system elements. In distributed processing, the ongoing decision making is left to local processors, but a central processor orchestrates the entire system. It provides a time signal, operating parameters, and direction to specific points on an *exception* basis, that is, one which overrides the normal routine. Most inputs are directed to the local processor. Analysis is done locally, with only exception data being sent to the central processor. The advantage of this system is that it will not collapse from the loss of any one processor, and only the local processor has to be reprogrammed to accommodate changes.

DIMMING CONTROLS

Controllers for Incandescent Lamps

Equipment to control the light output of incandescent lamps is readily available. Early lamp dimming controls were simply variable resistances connected in series with the lamps. The method wasted energy, as some of the power saved in the lamp was dissipated in the resistor. An alternative to resistive dimmers was the autotransformer, which reduced voltage to the lamps more efficiently, that is, the transformer losses are relatively small. The autotransformer offers smooth, quiet, reliable dimming without introducing line interference, but it is bulky and heavy. Today, the majority of dimming equipment relies on solid-state switching components that offer small size, design flexibility, and lower cost. This technology employs thyristors or transistors as the switching element to efficiently control the power to the lamps. However, the fast switching of these electronic devices can generate electromagnetic and audible noise as well as harmonic distortion which must be filtered.

Dimming incandescent lamps affects the light output, life and color temperature of the lamp. For example, a 12% power reduction decreases light output by 25%, and the lamp life triples. Figure 31-13 illustrates the effects of reduced voltage on light output, correlated color temperature, lamp life and efficacy. Note

Fig. 31-13. Change in Characteristics of Typical Incandescent Lamps Operated Below Rated Voltage

Input to Lamp (volts)	Light Output (percent)	Watts (percent)	Color Change (kelvin)	Life* (percent)	Relative Efficacy
120	100	100	0	100	1.00
110	75	88	-100	300	0.85
100	55	76	-200	1000	0.72
90	38	64	-300	4000	0.59

* Based on filament temperature only. Other factors, shock and vibration will also affect lamp life.

that as the voltage is decreased, the light appears warmer.

Controllers for Fluorescent Lamps

The fluorescent lamp is the primary light source for commercial and retail applications. Equipment is available to dim these lamps when operated with standard magnetic ballasts, magnetic dimming ballasts, or electronic dimming ballasts. Unlike the incandescent lamp, which is a pure resistive load, the fluorescent lamp is a complex negative-resistance load requiring a ballast to maintain the proper electrical input for both starting and operation. Simply reducing the input voltage, as is done to dim incandescent lamps, will extinguish the arc at some point, as well as reduce the life of the lamp.

Another factor affecting lamp life that must be considered is the lamp current-crest factor (CCF). This, together with the line power factor and line harmonics (power quality), affects the whole distribution system and needs to be taken into account in control and ballast design. The methods to control fluorescent lamps operated with standard, dimming magnetic and electronic ballasts are described below.

Standard Magnetic Ballasts. Rapid-start fluorescent lamps operated with standard magnetic core-coil ballasts are dimmed by changing the power supplied to the ballasts. This is done either by reducing the input voltage within a limited range or by electronically modifying the voltage waveform. Both of these methods involve switching of electrical power at high voltages or high current. In order to be cost-effective, the equipment is usually designed to switch large groups of lamps. Typically, equipment is designed to handle a current of 20 A. Such control systems are usually located centrally in the electrical closet, require a minimum of rewiring, and have low installation cost, since no hard-wiring is required at the luminaire. This makes them particularly attractive for retrofit.

While it is technically possible to dim fluorescent lamps over a wide range of illuminances, there is a practical limitation because lamp life will be reduced if illuminances go too low. When the input power is significantly reduced by voltage reduction or waveform modification, the filament voltage will also be reduced.

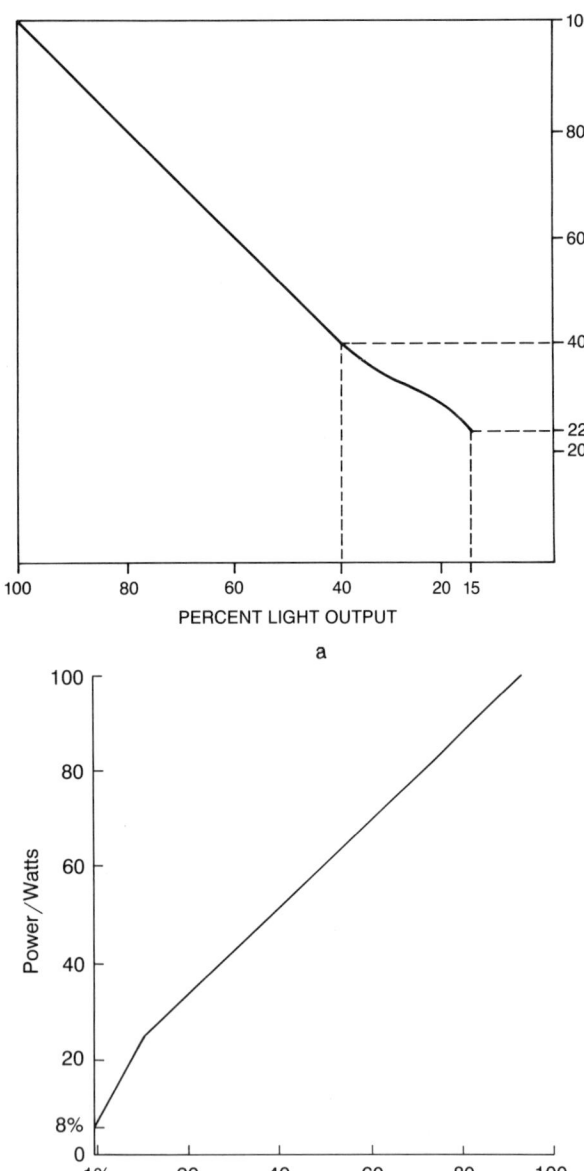

Fig. 31-14. Relative light output as a function of power for (a) a two-lamp, 34-W, rapid-start fluorescent system with standard core-coil ballast. Minimum level of lighting adjustment is shown as 15% light output at 22% power; (b) three-lamp, 32-W, T-8 rapid-start fluorescent system with electronic ballast. Minimum level of lighting adjustment is shown as 1% light output at 8% power.

If the filament temperature is reduced more than about half, lamp life will be significantly curtailed. Thus, the practical dimming range of lamps operated with magnetic ballasts is limited to approximately 40% of full light output.

Figure 31-14a shows the performance of a particular waveform-modifying system. This system behaves in such a way that relative decreases in light output and power are approximately linear down to 40% of full light output (the system efficacy is constant). This type of performance does not accurately characterize all dimming systems, and the efficacy of each system has to be evaluated separately.

Dimming equipment that reduces the input voltage generally cannot dim fluorescent lamps as well as waveform modification systems can. Such equipment has to maintain the peak voltage to the lamp that is necessary to maintain the arc. In addition, standard magnetic ballasts have voltage regulation such that a 10% change in supply voltage changes the light output by about 5%. These two factors generally limit the voltage reduction techniques to dimming rapid-start fluorescent lamps to about 70% of full light output. Slimline instant-start lamps also have a limited dimming range, between 100 and 50%.

Also, when lamps are off and set in the dimmed mode, the controller must restore full power when starting the lamps. Otherwise, lamps may not start, and lamp life will be reduced.

Special Magnetic Dimming Ballasts. The control systems designed to dim lamps with standard magnetic ballasts have a limited dimming range. Special magnetic dimming ballasts are available, however, that permit fluorescent lamps to be safely dimmed to 10% of full light output. These systems have two power feeds to the ballast. One feed powers the filaments; the other controls the current to the lamp. These dimming ballasts are available for 30- and 40-W rapid-start lamps. Such systems are less efficient and more expensive than standard ballasts, since they require installation of ballasts with a third wire as well as the installation of the controller. Because of the added installation costs, they lend themselves to renovation or new installations rather than retrofit, and are used primarily in applications where dimming to very low illuminances is required.

Electronic Dimming Ballasts. The electronic ballast serves the same function as the standard magnetic ballast for fluorescent lamps. The electronic ballast circuit employs active semiconductor devices such as transistors and thyristors to transform the 60-Hz input power to a high frequency (20–30 kHz). Operating fluorescent lamps at high frequency increases their efficacy by 20–25% over standard 60-Hz systems.

Most electronic ballasts are dedicated systems and cannot be dimmed. There are special dimming electronic ballasts for fluorescent lamps in which a low-level signal to the inverter controls the lamp arc current and hence the lamp's light output (see figure 31-15).[11] Fluorescent lamps operated with electronic dimming ballasts can be dimmed to less than 1% of full light output without producing flicker. Some electronic ballasts are also designed to reduce the electrode filament voltage at full light output, and restore it when the lamps are

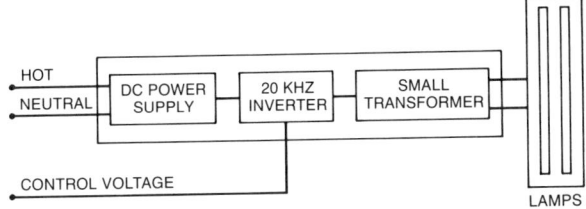

Fig. 31-15. Schematic illustration of an electronic dimming ballast showing the essential circuit elements and the method used to control the light output of the lamps through the inverter circuit.

operated in the dimmed mode at low arc current. This extends the lamp life and reduces the power consumption at full light output (see figure 31-14b).

Some electronic dimming ballasts have potentiometers to dim the lamps manually. This provides manual "tuning" of the ballast. Controlling the light output via low-level signals allows electronic dimming ballast systems to be more flexible than magnetic ballast systems based on conditioning the ballast input power. Large banks of electronic ballasts can be controlled as readily as a few. Thus, lighting control strategies such as task tuning, daylighting and load shedding generally require modular control. Scheduling and lumen maintenance can be readily accomplished with electronic dimming ballast systems, since the ballast is controlled independently of the distribution system.

Electronic dimming ballasts are more costly than standard magnetic dimming ballasts. However, the control equipment needed to dim electronic dimming ballasts is less expensive, since there is no need for the high-power switching devices required to dim magnetic ballasts. The added initial cost of these systems can be justified by the increased lamp-ballast efficacy, energy savings for the various strategies, and greater dimming range.

Multilevel Ballasts. Both magnetic and electronic multilevel ballasts are available. These provide the ability to be switched between two or more illuminances. They provide a low-cost, but limited control approach for dimming and can be used in some cases to satisfy energy codes.

Controllers for HID Lamps

High-intensity discharge (HID) lamps can be controlled using equipment similar to that used for dimming fluorescent lamps. The long warmup and restrike times associated with HID lamps, however, may limit their applications. On-off control of HID lamps is most commonly used where there are long on and off periods, as for outdoor and roadway applications, where switching generally occurs twice a day. These typically use a photocell.

Multilevel ballasts are available for HID lamps, allowing the illuminance to be reduced. This technique is practical in warehouses, parking garages, tunnels and daylighting applications. Equipment is available to dim HID lamps continuously to less than 20% of full light output. Color shift limits the range that can be used in some applications. Metal halide lamps shift color toward blue-green, and high-pressure sodium lamps shift color to yellow. The change in color becomes noticeable below 60% of rated lamp power for metal halide and 40% for high-pressure sodium lamps. See chapter 6, Light Sources, for information on the relative change in power and light output for the three types of HID lamps: (a) mercury, (b) metal halide and (c) high-pressure sodium.

COST ANALYSIS

The general approach used to evaluate the economics of lighting systems may be extended to include systems with controls.[12, 13] Fundamentally, the procedure involves adding the cost of the control system to the rest of the lighting system equipment costs and determining how the use of the controls affects operating costs. Since lighting controls may not only affect the operation of the lighting system, but also other building energy systems, care must be taken to consider all of the interrelationships. In office buildings, for example, lighting controls that vary the output of the general lighting, perhaps in response to daylight, also change the amount and location of heat generated in the building. As the building's heating and cooling systems take this into account, the HVAC costs will also be affected. Some lighting control systems may also affect the electrical system, for example by changing the power factor, or may alter the performance of the lighting system itself in terms of efficacy, lamp life and ballast life.

The actual energy savings are entirely dependent on the size of the space, the availability of daylight, the work schedule, the kinds of activities performed, and the attitude and training of the occupants. For example, if the users are very conscious of energy concerns and are motivated to switch lights off each time they exit the area, then the installation of occupancy/motion sensors will not result in significant energy savings.

To estimate the energy that could be saved by using automatic controls, the areas to be controlled should be broken down into smaller areas of similar function and occupancy, such as private offices with windows and open-plan sales offices. Users should establish a plausible use scenario for each small area, including:

- Hours of use
- Fixed or flexible work schedules

- Weekly, monthly or yearly changes in the schedule
- Periods when areas are unoccupied, such as breaks, lunch, end of day, before cleaning
- Cleaning crew schedules
- Use of daylight to permit reducing electric light levels during daylight hours

The sum of the projected savings from small areas provides the total potential savings.

Cost Considerations

Some costs normally associated with the installation and operation of lighting control systems include:

- Control hardware, including sensors, control and monitoring station equipment, cabling and overcurrent protection
- Interface equipment, such as multiplexers in cases where control signals are carried by the power wiring, or data links and interconnection devices between controls and the telephone or on-site computer system
- Installation and setup labor, since several different skills (and therefore costs) may be involved in handling both signal and power-level wiring, calibration and checkout
- Maintenance labor and spare parts
- Energy costs and utility rate structures

Economic Analysis Techniques. Lighting controls are frequently cost justified on the basis of expected energy cost savings over a period of time. Methods of comparing the cost with the savings are explained in chapter 13, Lighting Economics.[12, 13]

The *life-cycle cost-benefit analysis* method is the cost model typically used when a thorough analysis, including the cost of money, is required. It lends itself particularly well to the financial decision-making process because it easily incorporates both one-time and recurring costs and puts them into perspective over the life of the investment. In contrast to analyzing initial or annual costs, the focus is on long-term rather than short-term costs. Details of how the present-worth method can be applied to lighting system analysis are presented in chapter 13.

Sources of Cost and Performance Data. While cost information for lighting control hardware is easily obtained, performance information that affects operating and other system costs is not as available and may be very site specific. The most important information to determine is the system input power and operating hours, since these are usually the main operating-cost factors. Fairly accurate estimates for on-off control

systems can be made if the operating period of the system is known, but systems with variable power inputs must be measured or carefully simulated. It may be helpful to construct a profile of system input power versus time or use computer modeling, especially if daylighting, time-of-day utility rates or other special considerations apply.

IMPACT OF LIGHTING CONTROLS

Effects on the Whole Building

HVAC Effects. Lighting can be responsible for a major portion of a building's HVAC load. Thus, lighting loads have a major influence on both the air conditioning loads and fan operation. Lighting loads affect the initial cost of the HVAC system as well as its annual energy consumption. If lighting controls are utilized to reduce the lighting energy consumption, it is important that the HVAC system and controls be designed to respond to changes in the operation of the lighting system. Furthermore, with the trend toward the use of daylighting to augment the electric lighting system, it is also necessary to consider the effects of the glazing system on the heating and air conditioning system and its controls. The use of daylighting can increase the initial cost and the annual energy consumption if the daylighting system is not carefully designed. For example, a daylighting system may increase the necessary summertime cooling load of a building by letting more heat into the building.

By properly integrating the HVAC system and its controls with the lighting system and its controls, both the initial cost of the HVAC system and the energy consumption can often be reduced. In order to achieve these benefits, it is necessary that the HVAC system be properly designed with zoning and effective controls. The type of HVAC system is extremely important if full savings are to be achieved from lighting controls, especially in existing buildings where the air distribution system is either a multizone, a double-duct or a terminal reheat system; these systems supply a constant amount of air and vary the supply air temperature in order to maintain the space temperature.

In recent building designs, the use of multizone and terminal reheat systems has been eliminated by building energy codes. Most commercial systems utilize numerous small single-zone units or variable-air-volume (VAV) systems where the space temperature is maintained by utilizing a constant supply air temperature and varying the volume of air.

Since the HVAC system is affected by the lighting system, the most effective lighting control systems will interact with HVAC conditions in the space. The point where the lighting controls can be integrated with the

HVAC system is the building energy management and control system (EMCS). The primary application is the time scheduling of the start and stop of the various loads. The EMCS computer can also be used to consider the time of imposition of the various loads required for optimal start and stop and the thermal storage effects of the building mass.

Another consideration which affects the energy consumption of the HVAC system is the part-load efficiency of the heating and air conditioning, including the energy dissipated by fans and motors. Unless the HVAC system components and controls are designed with consideration for the part-load efficiency, it is possible that much of the potential HVAC energy savings from the lighting controls will not be realized.

Electrical Equipment Effects

Switching. Electrical control equipment that switches lamps on and off excessively can reduce fluorescent and HID lamp life.[14] There is no discernable decrease in ballast life or reliability due to increased cycling. The actual service life of lamps may be extended by the elimination of unnecessary burning hours.

Interference. Radio frequency interference (RFI) or electromagnetic interference (EMI) is inherent in all control systems that rapidly switch a portion of input power. There are specific standards and limits to the radio noise permitted in the United States. The Federal Communications Commission (FCC) publishes these standards (FCC, Part 15 or 18) and regulates manufacturers of devices that may emit radio noise. The Food and Drug Administration (FDA) publishes separate standards for radio noise for devices used in hospital environments. The FCC is concerned with all types of radiating devices, including various types of occupant/motion sensors.

There are two areas of concern with regard to radio noise: conducted emission and radiated emission. Conducted emission is the noise fed directly into the power line by the device drawing power from that line. Radiated emission is the electrical noise radiated by the lamps in the luminaire, with the power line possibly acting as an antenna. Conducted emission follows the power line itself as a path of propagation. Generally, at high frequencies this noise is limited to the downstream portion of the circuit, from the branch transformer to the devices in question.

In most commercial and industrial buildings the lighting power circuits are contained within metal conduits. These conduits attenuate radiated electromagnetic energy and limit the radio noise to the circuits contained within the same conduit. Conducted emissions are of concern to the extent that they interfere with the lighting control system and any other devices

on the same branch circuit feeds, such as computers or security systems. Control systems use passive and active filters to keep the conducted emissions within the allowable limits.

With shielded power lines, radiated noise is limited to the radio noise emitted directly from the controller and luminaire. It is of concern to the extent that other devices within the immediate area of the controller and luminaire may be affected. The primary antenna within the luminaire is the lamp itself. While all ballasts, lamps and control systems emit radio noise that may interfere with some equipment, there are precautions that ballast and control manufacturers can take to reduce such noise. For conventional ballasts, noise filters are available. For solid-state high-frequency ballasts, which emit more radio noise than conventional ones, the noise is of a type and magnitude that can be more easily suppressed or designed out of the ballast. There are also luminaires with conductive lenses specifically designed to attenuate the EMI radiated by the lamps.

Power Quality

The power quality of electrical switching systems has become a concern to utilities with regard to power factor, safety, and interference. Most incandescent dimming techniques utilize *phase control*, in which the rms voltage to the lamp is reduced by high-speed switching. This will distort the sinusoidal line current, producing other frequencies and leading to a decrease in the power factor.

The designer should be aware of potential harmonics, as they can overload the neutral conductor in three-phase electrical distribution systems, which can damage its insulation, overheat transformers, and distort the voltage at points of coupling. In addition, if only a single leg of a three-phase system is dimmed, the system will become unbalanced, further increasing the neutral current. In practice no problems have actually been attributed to the generation of harmonics by lighting control systems to date, but designers and engineers should become familiar with the issues when using these advanced lighting technologies.

Human Performance Effects

Lighting control systems can have a positive effect on the working environment, provided that they alter lighting unobtrusively while adding to the comfort and the esthetics of a space. These factors have further economic implications for controls, reflected in increased productivity of the occupants. This is particularly true in spaces where visual display terminals (VDTs) are used but tasks requiring high illuminance also occur. The ceiling and task lighting can be controlled in zones over a wide range of illuminance to tune the space to these specific needs.

Care should be taken when attempting to reduce peak power demand or energy usage to ensure that illuminance is not reduced below that required for visual tasks in the space. In addition, there are three other effects of dimmer controls that can degrade human performance. They are audible noise, flicker, and source color changes.

Illuminance. The illuminance determines the visual adaptation level, which has been demonstrated to affect performance in a number of visual tasks, such as reading, inspecting and assembling. Control systems must be designed so that the lighting system can provide proper illuminance for these tasks.

Audible Noise. Lighting control systems may produce audible noise in the environment, which can be a source of annoyance. The manufacturer should be consulted to minimize the noise produced by the control system.

Flicker. Controls that modify the waveform can cause excessive flicker. Flicker will be noticeable if the variation in light amplitude is sufficiently high (see chapter 6 on Light Sources). Even imperceptible flicker may cause eyestrain and fatigue.[14] Proposed control systems should therefore be examined for their effect on flicker.

Flicker is typically greater with HID lamps than with fluorescent lamps. This is because the phosphors in a fluorescent lamp continue to generate light throughout the ac cycle. HPS lamps have high flicker because of the rapid recombination rates of sodium ions. Solid-state ballasts should be selected which drive the lamps without flicker.

Color Changes. During lamp dimming, there is a small, unnoticeable shift in lamp color with fluorescent lamps. This color shift is not usually considered significant. Other light sources, including incandescent lamps, exhibit a more significant color shift. Care must be exercised when employing such lamps. They should not be dimmed to levels that alter the esthetics of the space, cause discomfort to the occupants, or affect tasks in which color rendition or discrimination are essential. One acceptable approach is to limit the range of dimming so that no color shift is apparent.

The shift in incandescent lighting to a lower color temperature by dimming may actually be desirable in certain applications, such as restaurants, where a warmer atmosphere may be wanted.

REFERENCES

1. Illuminating Engineering Society of North America. 1991. *Lighting economics: An intermediate approach to economics as applied to the lighting practice.* IES ED-150.9. New York: Illuminating Engineering Society of North America.

2. Rubinstein, F., M. Karayel, and R. Verderber. 1984. Field study on occupancy scheduling as a lighting management strategy. *Light. Des. Appl.* 14(5):34–38, 40–45.

3. Rea, M. S., ed. 1984. *Lighting Control: Proceedings of the CEA / DBR Symposium, Ottawa, June 28, 1984.* Ottawa: National Research Council Canada.

4. IES. Energy Management Committee. 1987. *IES design considerations for effective building lighting energy utilization.* IES LEM-3-1987. New York: Illuminating Engineering Society of North America.

5. Lawrence Berkeley Laboratory. 1985. *Controlite 1.0: Lighting control systems and daylighting analysis program.* LBL-17444. Berkeley, CA: Lawrence Berkeley Laboratory.

6. IES. Daylighting Committee. 1979. *Recommended practice of daylighting.* IES RP-5. New York: Illuminating Engineering Society of North America.

7. U.S. Department of Commerce. National Bureau of Standards. 1977. *Window design strategies to conserve energy.* Prepared by S. R. Hastings and R. W. Crenshaw. Building Science Series, 104. Washington: U. S. Government Printing Office.

8. Rubinstein, F. 1984. Photoelectric control of equi-illumination lighting systems. *Energy Build.* 6(2):141–150.

9. New York State Energy Research and Development Authority. 1982. *Occupancy controlled lighting: Energy savings demonstration and analysis.* ERDA 82-83. Prepared by O. Turner. Albany, NY: New York State Energy Research and Development Authority.

10. National Lighting Product Information Program. 1992. *Specifier reports: Occupancy sensors.* Prepared by D. Maniccia. Troy, NY: Rensselaer Polytechnic Institute.

11. Alling, W. R. 1983. The integration of microcomputers and controllable output ballasts: "A new dimension in lighting control." In *Conference record: Industry Applications Society, IEEE, IAS-1983 annual meeting, [Mexico], October 3–7, 1983.* New York: Institute of Electrical and Electronics Engineers.

12. McGowan, T. K. 1983. *The economic analysis of lighting systems with controls. Proceedings: 20th session. Commission Internationale de l'Éclairage, Amsterdam, August 31–September 8, 1983.* Paris: Bureau Central de la CIE.

13. Verderber, R. R., and O. Morse. 1981. Cost-effectiveness: Long-life incandescent, circular fluorescents and energy buttons. *Elec. Constr. Maint.* 80(11):55–58, 81.

14. Wilkins, A. J., I. Nimmo-Smith, A. I. Slater, and L. Bedocs. 1989. Fluorescent lighting, headaches and eyestrain. *Light. Res. Tech.* 21(1):11–18.

Lighting Maintenance   *32*

Lighting systems must be maintained to assure the lighting quantity and quality intended, whether for task performance, safety or esthetic reasons.[1] System components have a finite life and at some point in time must be replaced. Lamp performance changes over time before failure. Dirt accumulates on luminaire and room surfaces. All of these factors tend to reduce illuminance or change the lighting quality.

Lack of maintenance can have a negative effect on human performance, perception of an area, safety and security. It can also waste energy. The combined effect of equipment age and dirt depreciation can reduce illuminance by 25–50% or more, depending on the application and equipment used. At the same time, the owner of the lighting system will continue to pay the same amount for electricity as if the lamps were new and the lamp, luminaire and room surfaces were clean.[2]

To take the above causes of light loss into account, lighting systems are generally designed with a light loss factor to provide from the onset a higher illuminance than that recommended for the task in the space.[3]

The most effective method of consistently maintaining illuminance and lighting quantity at the lowest operating and maintenance cost is through a planned program. Planned lighting maintenance entails group relamping, cleaning lamps and luminaires, and replacing defective or broken components on a scheduled basis. Painting and maintaining room surfaces are also important.[4]

CAUSES OF LIGHT LOSS

Lighting maintenance means action to recover light loss due to the following:[5]

- Lamp lumen depreciation
- Dirt accumulation on lamps and luminaires
- Lamp burnouts
- Luminaire surface deterioration
- Room surface dirt accumulation

Lamp Lumen Depreciation. As a lamp is operated, its lumen output gradually decreases until failure occurs. This is called lamp lumen depreciation and is characteristic of all lamps, although the rate of decrease and the overall lamp life differ for each lamp type. See chapter 6 on Light Sources.

Dirt Accumulation on Lamps and Luminaires.[6] As dirt accumulates on a lamp, it reduces the amount of light being emitted. As dirt accumulates on luminaire surfaces, it acts to reduce the amount of light reflected or transmitted by those surfaces. Dirt buildup on the luminaire's surfaces can also affect light distribution; for example, dirt on a specular aluminum reflector in a high-bay luminaire can widen the lighting distribution of that luminaire. Such a change will result in lower illuminance on the workplane. The total amount of light loss due to dirt depreciation depends on the type and amount of dirt accumulated, the lamp's type and shape, and the luminaire's design and finish.

Two types of luminaires built to resist dirt accumulation are ventilated luminaires and filtered or dust-tight luminaires. Ventilated luminaires tend to collect less dirt than those with closed tops. The temperature difference between the lamp and the surrounding air causes convection currents which help carry dirt through the luminaire openings rather than allowing it to accumulate on the reflector. Filtered or dust-tight luminaires or reflector lamps minimize dirt accumulation because the lamp and reflecting surfaces are protected from dusty air.

The light loss due to dirt depends on the rate of accumulation and the characteristics of the dirt. For example, dirt buildup occurs much faster in a foundry than in a well-ventilated office. The dirt found in a suburban office is different in amount and type from dirt in an office located in an industrial area. Black steel-mill dirt is very different from the light-colored dust found in a woodworking shop. Thus, dirt accumulation will affect luminaire performance differently in each of these situations.

Lamp Burnout. A lamp burnout (a failed lamp) decreases the local illuminance and thus affects lighting uniformity. It can also pose a hazard to other luminaire components. For example, in some fluorescent circuits, when one lamp fails, others on the same ballast will glow dimly and may also fail. This can also cause rectification and high ballast current, causing the ballast either to fail immediately or to experience reduced life.

Luminaire Surface Deterioration. Luminaire construction materials differ in their ability to reflect light and resist deterioration. Porcelain enamel, for example, retains its high reflectance and is relatively easy to clean. Processed aluminum finishes tend to depreciate at a lower rate than painted finishes. Plastics (acrylics,

cellulosics, polycarbonates and vinyls), as light-controlling materials, change over time. Exposure to ultraviolet and infrared radiation causes the color and transmittance of plastics to change. The rate of this change depends on the type of lamp used, its distance from the plastic, and the temperature to which the plastic is subjected during operating periods. Additionally, improper cleaning materials and techniques can cause added changes in transmittance due to chemical action or surface scratching.

Room Surface Dirt Accumulation. Light reaching the workplane comes directly from the luminaires in the

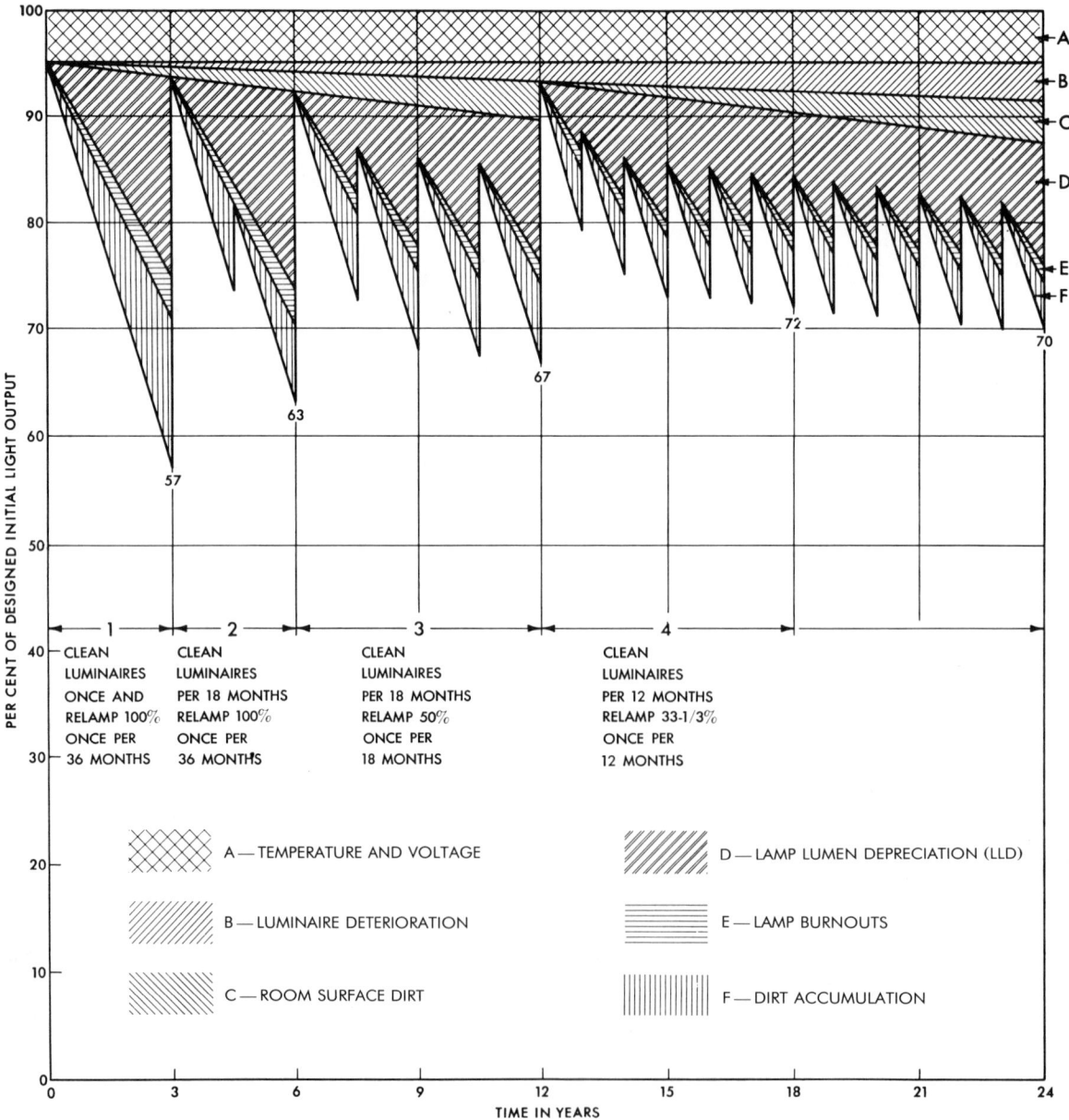

Fig. 32-1. Effect of light loss on illuminance level. Example above used 40-watt T-12 cool white rapid start lamps in enclosed surface mounted luminaires, operated 10 hours per day, 5 days per week, 2600 hours per year. All four maintenance systems are shown on the same graph for convenience. For a relative comparison of the four systems, each should begin at the same time and cover the same period of time.

room and from the reflected light from room surfaces. Thus, dirt accumulation on room surfaces will reduce the amount of light on the workplane. Cleaning and regular repainting of walls and other surfaces will reduce the effect of dirt accumulation on these surfaces.

These light loss factors are shown in figure 32-1. These and others are discussed in chapter 9 on Lighting Calculations.

PLANNED MAINTENANCE TECHNIQUES

During the design of a new or retrofit lighting system, an effective maintenance plan, properly executed, can minimize the required number of luminaires needed for a space, thus minimizing costs and energy usage.[4,7] The primary maintenance techniques are group relamping and cleaning. During and between relamping and cleaning, the system can be inspected for defective or broken components and other problems.

Group Relamping

Group relamping entails replacing all of the lamps in a system together after a fixed interval, called the *economic group relamping interval*. Group relamping can reduce the cost of operating a lighting system while improving illuminance. As discussed above, if a lighting system is analyzed during the design phase and group relamping is judged economical, then less overdesign can be built into the system (that is, a higher light loss factor can be used in calculating the maintained illuminance) while still maintaining the design illuminance level. This can save initial, operating and maintenance costs.

The savings resulting from group relamping come from labor costs. It typically costs less per lamp to replace all of the lamps in a system at one time than it does to replace them one by one as they fail. If the labor savings are worth more than the value of the used lamps, then from an economic standpoint it makes sense to discard used and depreciated lamps, even though they may still have some burning hours remaining. A useful rule of thumb is that group relamping should be examined if the labor cost of spot-replacing one lamp, less the cost of group-relamping one lamp, exceeds the cost of one new lamp.

Analysis techniques are available which determine the economic group relamping interval. These are based on the mortality rates of the lamp (the probability of failure as a function of time), the labor rates involved, the cost of the lamp and its depreciation rate. Typically, the most economical time to group relamp is between 70 and 80% of rated life. This is just before the majority of lamps are expected to fail, when the greatest labor costs can be saved, and when lamp

lumen depreciation makes the lamps uneconomical to continue operating from a cost-per-lumen standpoint. The calculations should take into account the cost of replacing spot failures between group relampings so lighting quality and appearance are also maintained.

Group relamping also presents a scheduled period where relamping can be economically combined with installation of new luminaire components such as specular reflectors, energy-efficient lamps, energy-efficient ballasts and other components which optimize the performance of the system.[2]

Periodic Planned Cleaning

Cleaning the lighting system usually entails washing or otherwise removing dirt from the luminaires, occasionally cleaning and repainting room surfaces and occasionally cleaning air supply vents to prevent unnecessary dirt distribution.

Periodically cleaning the lamp and the luminaire will reduce the depreciation in light output from accumulated dirt. Periodically cleaning the luminaire also maintains its intended distribution and increases reflectance. Regularly cleaning or repainting room surfaces increases reflectance and thereby increases overall illuminance in the space. Cleaning is particularly important in environments susceptible to dirt buildup such as industrial facilities. In indirect lighting systems, the luminaires are often open and the illuminance depends heavily on reflections from the room surfaces and on keeping the luminaire clean.

Cleaning is another service which can economically be combined with group relamping, although in environments with high concentrations of dirt or dust in the air, it should be performed more often. As in the case of group relamping, periodically cleaning luminaires delivers more light per lighting dollar and ensures more consistent illuminance through the life of the lamps.

OPERATIONS: PROGRAMS AND METHODS

Planning

Lighting systems are becoming more complex. As a result, the requirements for resources, expertise and competence are increasing. Often it is desirable for an organization to use a lighting maintenance company if it does not have the proper equipment and trained staff to maintain the system properly itself.

Planning Factors

The most economical group relamping and cleaning interval must be established. Many factors are involved and the facilities manager must:

- Establish the maintenance cycle so that there is neither excessive light loss nor wasted equipment.
- Determine the rate at which dirt accumulates in the environment.
- Evaluate the impact of dirt on luminaires and room surfaces for the specific lighting system.

Several options with factors applicable to the facility should be considered, and results compared to determine the best maintenance interval.

In addition, the application will also dictate other maintenance requirements. Luminaire accessibility and rate of dirt accumulation vary in almost every circumstance. Planning must take account of these conditions. For example, in many industrial areas, not only is the rate of dirt accumulation high and the dirt dark and adhesive, but the luminaires are usually mounted high up, so that mechanized lifts are needed to reach them.

Plan Execution

The building's environmental characteristics will greatly affect how maintenance is performed. Generally, cleaning and relamping operations require several basic steps:

1. *Making luminaires shock free.* Lamp sockets present an electric shock threat to the maintenance technician. The electrical circuit must be turned off when working on luminaires.
2. *Removing shielding material and lamps.* Louvers and plastic or glass lenses or diffusers are removed from the luminaire and passed to the technician on the floor. Lamps are then removed and also passed down to the technician, who cleans or discards them.
3. *Cleaning basic unit.* If present, heavy deposits of dirt should be wiped or brushed from the top of the channel, reflector or other surfaces. The entire unit is then ready to be washed with a suitable solution. The cleaner may apply the solution with a brush, sponge or cloth. After washing, the entire unit should then be rinsed to remove any residue of dirt or solution. Indirect luminaires should have the dust and dirt blown out with an antistatic nozzle.
4. *Cleaning shielding material and lamps.* While the reflective surface is being cleaned, the technician on the floor cleans shielding materials. During relamping, the old lamps should be placed in a disposal area, then new lamps brought in for installation. Plastic lenses or louvers should be dried with a damp cloth.

Dry wiping can cause electrostatic charging, which attracts dust. Drip drying can leave streaks on prismatic lenses. Shielding material can be cleaned with devices such as ultrasonic machines. Antistatic fluid should be applied to the shielding material, except for glass, to retard dust accumulation.

5. *Replacing lamps and shielding material.* The clean shielding and new or cleaned lamps are passed up to the technician at the luminaire for installation.
6. *Troubleshooting.* During the above steps, the technician at the luminaire should check for damaged or defective components and be prepared to replace them with new ones. The lighting system should then be tested and checked for defective lamps, ballasts, sockets and wiring.

Safety Considerations

During cleaning and relamping, the cleaner and the floor technicians should observe all safety precautions. For specific professional safety requirements, the U.S. Occupational Safety Health Administration (OSHA) in Washington should be consulted.

Equipment Disposal.[8] Replaced lamps and ballasts should be disposed of per state and federal guidelines. Precautions should be taken when disposing of older PCB-containing ballasts. While the manufacture and distribution of PCB-containing ballasts was banned in the United States in 1978, they can still be found in luminaires. A non-PCB ballast is appropriately labeled, "No PCBs." If PCB ballasts are encountered, a lighting management and maintenance professional, a hazardous-waste treatment professional or any state or federal organization which offers resources in these situations should be contacted. PCB ballasts must be disposed of in accordance with state and federal guidelines. The U.S. Environmental Protection Agency in Washington should be contacted for more information.

CLEANING COMPOUNDS

Different cleaning applications require different cleaning compounds. Improperly selected or used compounds can scratch or otherwise deteriorate the luminaire surface. For each application, the manufacturer's recommendations should be followed for best results. Listed below are several general tips:

Aluminum. Very mild soaps and cleaners followed by a thorough rinse with clean water prove effective with aluminum. Strong alkaline cleaners should never be used.

Silver Film. Silver film is commonly coated with plastic or acrylic material. To clean this material without scratching the surface, it is extremely important that manufacturer's recommendations be followed. Generally, applying a 0.5% nonabrasive solution of mild liquid detergent and water with a soft, damp rag is satisfactory.

Porcelain Enamel. Nonabrasive cleaners can be used on porcelain. Detergents and most automobile and glass cleaners are effective.

Synthetic Enamel. Some strong cleaners may injure this finish, particularly in cases where the enamel is left to soak in the solution. Alcohol or abrasive cleaners should not be used. Detergents produce no harmful effects.

Glass. As with porcelain enamel, most nonabrasive cleaners will prove effective. Most detergents will work well; after cleaning, however, the lens must be rinsed. Glass reflectors may simply be wiped dry.

Plastics. A static charge may develop on plastic, attracting dust. Most common detergents do not provide a high degree of permanence in their antistatic protection. Other antistatic compounds are available which have greater permanence. Plastic should not be dry wiped after application of a rinse solution, as this will cause the formation of electrostatic charges. They should also not be drip dried, as this will result in streaks. The most effective method of drying plastics is vacuuming.

CLEANING EQUIPMENT

Cleaning, group relamping and new equipment installation can be performed more efficiently if proper equipment is chosen. The choice of equipment depends on several factors, such as safety, luminaire mounting height, size of area, accessibility of the lighting system, and obstacles in the area.

Ladders and Stilts. Ladders are often chosen for their low weight, low cost and simplicity (see figure 32-2). Safety, mobility and height restrictions limit their use, however. Aluminum or other conductive ladders must not be used. Wood or fiber-glass ladders should only be used if they are OSHA approved.

Stilts are also used for maintenance in spaces with relatively low ceilings (see figure 32-3).

Scaffolding. Portable scaffolding is generally safer and more mobile than ladders. The scaffold provides more room for equipment and firm footing for technicians. Scaffolds generally should be light, sturdy, adjustable, mobile and easy to assemble and dismantle. The right type of scaffolding often depends on special requirements, such as mounting on uneven surfaces or clearance of obstacles such as tables or machines. In all

Fig. 32-2. A ladder is used to change a ballast.

Fig. 32-3. Stilts used for maintenance in spaces with low ceiling heights.

Fig. 32-4. Telescoping scaffold.

Fig. 32-5. Mobile platform lift.

aspects, the scaffold must conform to OSHA standards.

Telescoping Scaffolding. The telescoping scaffold (see figure 32-4) provides a quick and versatile method for reaching a variety of mounting heights. This equipment, which comes in various sizes, has platforms which can be raised and lowered either manually or electrically.

Personnel Lift. The personnel lift has proven itself as one of the quickest and most efficient maintenance devices (see figure 32-5). The platform is raised and lowered automatically. Some types of personnel lifts can be driven from the platform.

Bucket Truck. The bucket truck (see figure 32-6) is used in many outdoor applications, such as sign lighting, street lighting and parking lot lighting.

Disconnecting Hangers. Disconnecting hangers allow the technician to lower the luminaire to a convenient work level (see figure 32-7). The luminaire's electrical circuit connection is automatically disconnected for safety. When the luminaire is raised after the work is complete, the hanger positions the luminaire and reconnects the electrical circuit automatically.

Lamp Changers. Lamp changers simplify lamp replacement. They grip lamps either mechanically or with air suction. Lamp changers usually are on a pole and are used from the ground (see figure 32-8).

Catwalks, Cranes and Cages. These types of equipment can be incorporated as an integral part of the lighting system for servicing (see figure 32-9). They enable luminaires to be maintained speedily and safely. Power to a crane must be turned off before lighting maintenance work is begun.

Vacuum Cleaners and Blowers. A vacuum cleaner or blower is sometimes used to remove dust from luminaires. While some of the dirt can be removed this way, the luminaires should also be washed. The periodic use of a vacuum cleaner or blower, however, can prolong the period of time between washings and, with the addition of an antistatic nozzle, is very effective for indirect luminaires.

Ultrasonic Cleaning. This method removes dirt and dust from metals, plastics, glass and other materials by high-frequency sound waves. A generator, a transducer and a suitable tank constitute the ultrasonic cleaning system. The generator produces high-frequency electri-

Fig. 32-6. Bucket truck.

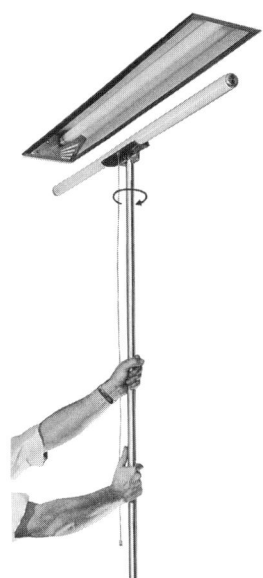

Fig. 32-8. Pole lamp changer.

Fig. 32-9. Maintenance cage.

Fig. 32-7. Disconnecting and lowering hangers.

cal energy, which the tank-mounted transducer converts to high-frequency sound waves. These sound waves travel through the cleaning solution and cause *cavitation*, the formation of countless microscopic bubbles which grow in size, then violently collapse. This phenomenon creates a scrubbing action which rapidly and forcefully removes dirt from the material immersed in the solution. Ultrasonic cleaning proves extremely effective with aluminum parabolic louvers. Nonmetallic louvers, however, may be damaged by this method over time. Ultrasonically cleaned parts should be rinsed in clean water.

TROUBLESHOOTING AND MAINTENANCE TIPS

Planned lighting maintenance entails more than simply changing lamps and cleaning. It is also an opportunity to efficiently locate and repair defective or broken components causing system problems. See chapter 6 on Light Sources for diagrams and explanations of the circuits described in this section.

Preheat Fluorescent Lamp Circuits

Troubleshooting

1. Replace existing lamps with lamps known to be operative.
2. Use only lamp types that are listed on the ballast label. Check to make certain lamps can be used on preheat circuits.
3. Replace existing starters with starters known to be operative and of proper rating. Refer to chapter 6 on Light Sources for description of various types and the features of each.
4. Check luminaire wiring for incorrect connections, loose connections or broken lampholders or wires. Refer to the wiring diagram printed on the ballast.
5. Check the ballast to see if the label agrees with the application with regard to temperature limitations and lamps. Replace the ballast if faulty or inappropriate.

Maintenance Hints

1. Deactivated lamps should be replaced as quickly as possible. Cycling lamps cause abnormal currents to flow in the ballast which will cause ballast heating and thereby reduce ballast life.
2. Lamp cycling will also reduce starter life.

Rapid-Start Fluorescent Lamp Circuits

Constant heater current is essential for proper starting of all rapid-start lamps. It is also essential for proper lamp operation.

Troubleshooting

1. If a lamp requires 5–6 s to start, one electrode may not be receiving the cathode heating current. This usually results in excessive darkening of that end of the lamp, which is visible after a short period of operation. With lamps removed from the sockets, check heater voltages. This can be done with available testers which have a flashlight lamp mounted on a

fluorescent lamp base. If a voltmeter is used, a 10-Ω, 10-W resistor should be inserted in parallel with the meter. The meter should measure at least 3 V. If proper voltage is found, check for poor contact between lamp holder and base pins or contacts on the lamp. Also check for proper spacing of lamp holders. If no voltage is measured, check for open circuit caused by poor or improper connections, broken or grounded wires, or open heater circuit on the ballast. Verify that the wiring conforms exactly to the ballast label diagram.

2. If one lamp is out and the other lamp is operating at low brightness or if both lamps are out, only one lamp may have failed. Refer to the circuit diagram in chapter 6, and note that two-lamp magnetic and some electronic circuits are of a series design.
3. Replace the ballast if the output voltage is not within its rated voltage, or if no voltage is present after determining that the input voltage to the ballast is correct.

Maintenance Hints

1. Failed lamps should be replaced as quickly as possible. Rapid-start lamps require both heater current and starting voltage for proper operation. If either is missing, poor starting or short lamp life will result. In a two-lamp series circuit, one lamp can fail and the second lamp will operate at reduced current. This condition will reduce the life of the second lamp.
2. Lamps should be kept reasonably clean. All rapid-start lamps are coated with a silicone to provide reliable starting in conditions of high humidity. However, dirt can collect on the lamp surface and then absorb moisture when the humidity is high, thus nullifying the silicone coating and making the starting unreliable.

Instant-Start Fluorescent Lamp Circuits

Two-lamp circuits can be of either lead-lag or series-sequence design. Lead-lag ballasts operate lamps in a parallel circuit, meaning that if one lamp fails, the other should continue to operate properly. Series-sequence ballasts operate lamps in series, meaning that if one lamp fails, the other will fail or glow dimly.

Troubleshooting

1. Replace existing lamps with lamps known to be operative.
2. Check lampholders for broken or burned contacts or discolored plastic in the holders, indi-

cating high temperature. Check circuit for improper or broken wires. Refer to the wiring diagram on the ballast.

3. If the ballast is suspected of being defective, replace it with one known to be operative. Measurement of output ballast voltages in the luminaire is difficult because the primary circuit of the ballast is automatically disconnected when a lamp is removed. Refer to the circuit diagram in chapter 6.

Maintenance Hints

1. Deactivated lamps should be replaced as soon as possible. In a two-lamp series magnetic circuit, one lamp can fail and the second lamp will operate at low brightness. This condition will reduce the life of the second lamp and also will cause an abnormal current to flow in the ballast, giving rise to ballast heating and a reduction in ballast life.

2. Flickering instant-start or "slimline" lamps, which show heavy end blackening, should be replaced, even if the lamps are lighted. This condition is known as *lamp rectification* and will cause reduced ballast life if it is allowed to persist.

Incandescent Lamps

Troubles with incandescent lamps are usually the result of misapplication, improper operating conditions or poor maintenance. Apply the hints below to avoid most problems.

Maintenance Hints

1. *Overvoltage operation.* Overvoltage operation drastically shortens lamp life. For example, a 120-V lamp operated on a 125-V circuit suffers a 40% loss in life. Refer to chapter 6.

2. *Shock and vibration conditions.* Under such conditions, the use of vibration-service or rough-service lamps is recommended. The use of general-service lamps under these conditions results in short life.

3. *Sockets.* Lamps of higher wattage should not be operated in sockets designed for a specified wattage, or excessive lamp and socket temperatures may result. Excessive temperatures may affect lamp performance or may shorten the life of insulated wire and sockets.

4. *Luminaires.* Only the proper lamps for which the luminaire was designed should be used. Contact of any metal part of a luminaire with a hot lamp may result in violent failure of the lamp.

5. *Cleaning lamps.* A wet cloth should not be used to clean a hot lamp. A violent failure may result.

6. *Proper burning position.* Lamps should be operated in their proper burning position as specified by the lamp manufacturer. Operation of the lamps in the wrong position may cause a lamp to fail prematurely or immediately.

7. *Replacing lamps.* Whenever possible, lamps should be replaced with power switched off. Replacing lamps with power switched on, particularly high-voltage types, can result in the drawing of an arc between the lamp base and the socket.

8. *Tungsten-halogen lamps.* These lamps should always be installed with the power switched off. It is also recommended that the bulb be held with a clean cloth or tissue or gloves to avoid fingerprints, which will result in bulb discoloration, subsequent reduction in light output, short life and possible violent failure. Follow lamp manufacturers' instructions on the carton.

9. *Dichroic reflector lamps.* Certain lamps utilize a dichroic reflector designed to radiate heat back through the reflector portion of the bulb. Luminaires using these lamps should be ventilated or otherwise designed to provide adequate cooling of the socket and wiring adjacent to the bulb.

Mercury Lamps

Troubleshooting

1. Replace the lamp with one known to be operative. Be sure the operative lamp is cool, as hot lamps will not restart immediately.

2. Check that the lamp is properly seated and that its base eyelet and shell make proper contact in the lampholder.

3. Check the ballast nameplate. Make sure that ballast and lamp designations match. Refer to the system of lamp and ballast designations developed by the lamp industry and American National Standards Institute (ANSI).

4. Check the ballast wiring. If a multiple-tapped primary-winding ballast is used, be sure the connected tap matches the supply voltage.

5. Check the supply circuit wiring for open circuit or incorrect connections.

6. Replace the ballast if no output voltage can be obtained and make sure that line voltage is properly connected to the ballast input terminals.

7. If a lamp fails prematurely, especially if it does so repeatedly in the same way in the same luminaire, check for the following:

    a. Cracks or breaks in the bulb will allow air to enter the lamp and cause arc tube seal failure. They can be caused by rough handling, by contact with metal surfaces of a bulb changer or metal parts of the luminaire, or by water droplets falling on an operating lamp.

    b. Overly blackened or swollen arc tubes may indicate excessive lamp current and over-wattage operation. See items 3, 4 and 5 above. Also, the ballast may have failed due to a component failure, such as a shorted capacitor or core winding.

If the power is lost in an HID ballast-lamp combination for even a few cycles, the lamp will extinguish itself and then have to cool down somewhat, reignite, and warm up again before reaching maximum light output.

Caution: To prevent electric shock hazard, always turn off the power before removing or installing lamps. This is especially important when removing lamps that may have cracked or broken outer envelopes. Unless the power is turned off, the exposed metal parts of the internal lamp structure will be connected to power and touching them will cause an electric shock. Always follow OSHA guidelines.

Maintenance Hints

1. If multiple-tapped ballasts are used, check to be sure that the tap matches the supply voltage to which the ballast tap is connected. Connecting a given line voltage to a tap marked for a higher voltage will give low light output due to underwattage operation. Connecting it to a tap marked for a lower voltage will cause poor lamp lumen maintenance and short lamp and ballast life due to overwattage operation.

2. The line voltage should be reasonably free of voltage fluctuations. A variety of ballast types are available that provide an appropriate percentage of lamp wattage regulation with respect to the percentage of line voltage variation.

3. Lamp-and-ballast combinations must be chosen so that their electrical characteristics match. This can be assured by following the system of lamp and ballast designations developed by the lamp industry and ANSI. Incorrect matching of lamp and ballast may result in short life and equipment damage.

4. Lamps should be handled carefully. Rough handling can cause scratches or cracks in outer

glass envelopes, resulting in short lamp life and possible injury.

Caution: If the outer envelope of a lamp is broken or punctured, the arc tube will continue to burn for many hours. Turn off the power and replace the lamp immediately. Certain types of lamps are available that will automatically extinguish if the outer envelope is broken or punctured.

Metal Halide Lamps

Follow the recommendations and all cautionary measures given for mercury lamps, as these also apply to metal halide lamps. The following additional information is also pertinent.

Troubleshooting

1. Many metal halide lamps are to be used only in specified operating positions. Short life and improper light and color output will result if this is not done.

2. The time to restart automatically after a short power interruption may be much longer than for mercury lamps. This is not a lamp defect or a cause for lamp replacement.

3. It is normal for metal halide lamps to have a short delay between the time the circuit is energized and the time the lamp starts.

4. Slight color shifts from lamp to lamp are characteristic of metal halide lamps. Also, one to two days of burning in an installation may be required to stabilize the color of a lamp and the uniformity among a group of lamps.

Caution: Follow lamp manufacturers' recommendations with respect to allowed use of metal halide lamps in open or enclosed luminaires.

Maintenance Hints

1. If a metal halide lamp is to be moved from one luminaire to another, keep it in the orientation in which it was installed while transferring it. If the lamp is rotated, its color will take time to restabilize.

2. Operate metal halide lamps only in their allowed operating positions.

High-Pressure Sodium Lamps

Troubleshooting

1. Follow steps 1 through 6 listed for mercury lamps.

2. If lamps fail prematurely, especially if they do so repeatedly in the same way or in the same

luminaire, check the following:
   a. Same as item 7a under Mercury Lamps.
   b. Excessive discoloration of the arc tube or a metallic deposit on the inside walls of the outer envelope may indicate overwattage operation. See items 3, 4 and 5 under Mercury Lamps. Also, ballast components may have failed; for example, a capacitor or a core winding may be shorted.
3. A high-pressure sodium lamp must be started with an igniter. If both the old and a known good lamp fail to start, steps must be taken to determine if the igniter or the ballast or perhaps both are defective. First make certain that the proper line voltage is correctly connected to the ballast input. Obtain a ballast tester (a flashlight lamp mounted on a fluorescent lamp base) or voltmeter and follow the manufacturer's instructions to determine the defect. Do not connect a voltmeter or multimeter to an open or inoperative high-pressure sodium socket. The high-voltage pulse from the igniter will damage the meter.

Maintenance Hints

1. Follow steps 1 through 4 for mercury lamps.
2. High-pressure sodium lamps have a vacuum in the space between the ceramic arc tube and the outer envelope. Handle these lamps carefully, since vacuum lamps are known to make an inordinately loud noise if the glass should break when dropped.
3. In case the outer envelope breaks during lamp operation, ultraviolet emission is not a problem.
   Caution: To prevent electric shock, always turn off the power before removing or installing lamps. This is especially important when removing lamps that may have cracked or broken outer envelopes. Unless the power is turned off, the exposed metal parts of the internal lamp structure will be live, and touching them will cause an electric shock.

Self-Ballasted Mercury Lamps

Although the use of self-ballasted mercury lamps has declined as new technologies become more popular, troubleshooting procedures for them are important, as many installations continue to use these lamps.

Troubleshooting

1. Items 1, 2 and 5 and the Caution given under Mercury Lamps apply.

2. Self-ballasted lamps are rated by voltage. They should be used in installations in which available socket voltages correspond to the allowed voltage range recommended by the manufacturer of the lamp.
3. In general, self-ballasted mercury lamps take longer than mercury lamps, but not as long as metal halide lamps, to restart automatically after a short power interruption.
4. Lamps rated for 120-V line voltage operation are constructed with an internal thermostatic switch to preheat the arc tube starting electrode(s). The action of the switch may result in blinking during lamp starting and restarting. The blinking will occur about 7–30 s after the lamp is energized and in less than that time during automatic restarting.
5. Starting temperature limits published by the manufacturers should be carefully followed. Since these lamps operate directly from the available line voltage, no step-up voltage can be introduced as is done for mercury, metal halide and high-pressure sodium lamps, where ballasts must be used and step-up transformers can be incorporated in them.

Maintenance Hints

1. Lamps should be handled carefully. Rough handling can cause scratches or cracks, resulting in short life and possible injury.
2. As self-ballasted mercury lamps are likely to be replaced into existing incandescent sockets, they will be installed in old luminaires. The rating of the socket should not be exceeded, and moisture falling on the bulb must be prevented. Follow manufacturers' recommendations for indoor and outdoor burning positions in open and closed luminaires.

Low-pressure Sodium Lamps

Troubleshooting

1. Replace the lamp with a lamp known to be operative.
2. Check the lampholder for proper seating of the lamp and for proper contact.
3. Check the ballast nameplate reading for compatibility.
4. Check the ballast wiring. If a multiple-tapped ballast is used, be sure the ballast tap matches the supply voltage at the ballast.
5. Check the circuit wiring for open circuit or incorrect connections.

6. Check the grounding of the luminaires.
7. Replace the ballast.
8. If lamps fail prematurely, check for the following:
  a. Lamp breakage. Check lamps for cracks or scratches in the outer bulb. These can be caused by rough handling, by contact with metal surfaces in the bulb changer or luminaire, or by moisture falling on an overheated bulb.
  b. Bulb touching the luminaire, the lampholder or any other hard surface.
9. If the arc tube is cracked, blackened or swollen early in life, or if the connecting leads inside the outer bulb are damaged, check for the following:
  a. Overwattage operation. Check the ballast rating, the voltage at the ballast and whether the proper tap on the ballast is being used.
  b. Excessive current. Check if the ballast is shorted. Check for possible voltage surges or transients on the supply line.
Caution: Do not replace the bulb until the circuit is checked and the cause of the trouble has been corrected.

Maintenance Hints

1. If multiple-tapped ballasts are used, check to be sure the tap matches the supply voltage at the ballast. Low voltage will cause low light output, poor lumen maintenance and reduced lamp life. High voltage will cause short lamp life.
2. The circuit should be reasonably free from voltage fluctuations. Replacement ballasts should match the particular voltage, frequency and lamp type.
3. The proper lamp type should be used for the ballast in installation. Incorrect matching of lamp and ballast may result in short lamp life or lamps going on and off repeatedly.
4. Lamps should be handled carefully to avoid breakage.

REFERENCES

1. Finn, J. F. 1973. Servicing: a design priority. *Light. Des. Appl.* 3(9):28–30.
2. Barnhart, J. E., C. DiLouie, and T. Madonia. 1993. *Lighten up: A training textbook for apprentice lighting technicians.* Princeton, NJ: interNational Association of Lighting Management Companies.
3. Clark, F. 1968. Light loss factor in the design process. *Illum. Eng.* 63(11):575–581.
4. Barnhart, J. E., C. DiLouie, and T. Madonia. 1993. *Illuminations: A training textbook for senior lighting technicians.* Princeton, NJ: interNational Association of Lighting Management Companies.
5. Clark, F. 1963. Accurate maintenance factors. *Illum. Eng.* 58(3):124–131.
6. Clark, F. 1966. Accurate maintenance factors. Part two (luminaire dirt depreciation). *Illum. Eng.* 61(1):37–46.
7. ASHRAE and Illuminating Engineering Society of North America. 1989. *Energy efficient design of new buildings except new low-rise residential buildings.* ASHRAE/IES 90.1-1989. Atlanta, GA: American Society of Heating, Refrigerating and Air-Conditioning Engineers.
8. Lighting Research Center. 1992. *Guide to responsible disposal of fluorescent lighting ballasts.* Schenectady, NY: Niagara Mohawk Power Corporation.

Emergency, Safety and Security Lighting

33

EMERGENCY LIGHTING

The designer faces no greater challenge and, possibly, no more important responsibility than making provisions for reliable lighting and marking of means of egress. In many situations occupants of a building need to evacuate the premises because of fires or power failures. Such occasions can become times of great danger if emergency lighting is not available. Therefore, it is the designer's responsibility to provide carefully designed egress route lighting and well-conceived informational signage.

Not every lighting failure is accompanied by a need for rapid evacuation, and not every evacuation need be accomplished without utility power present. Yet other factors, such as the presence of smoke, the operation of sprinkler systems, hazards presented by manufacturing equipment or architectural features, and handicaps or special needs of building occupants, can reduce the effectiveness of simplistic lighting solutions. The designer must anticipate the full range and diversity of possible conditions present in a facility and design an appropriate egress lighting system.

Collaboration between the lighting designer, building owner, occupants, architects, fire officials and utilities is highly recommended as a means of understanding and planning for the variables that might interfere with the the operation and effectiveness of the egress lighting system. Careful consideration should be given to these variables early in the building design stage so that the egress lighting system can be most effectively integrated into the design of other building systems.

The purpose of this chapter is to provide assistance in identifying these important design considerations and to make recommendations, where practical, on appropriate specifications.

Though an airplane is not a building, many of the recommendations in this chapter also apply to emergency lighting on aircraft. For more information, see chapter 25, Aviation Lighting.

Several terms are unique to emergency lighting. Definitions for most such terms may be found in the Glossary.

CODES AND STANDARDS

Chapter 14, Codes and Standards, contains an extensive list of codes and regulations with which the designer should be familiar when designing emergency lighting. These codes have been developed by a number of governmental and private organizations, including the National Fire Protection Association (NFPA), Canadian Occupational Safety and Health Board, Building Officials and Code Administrators (BOCA) International, Commission Internationale de l'Éclairage (CIE) and Underwriters Laboratories (UL). Other sources to consult are Department of Health and Human Services guidelines, local or state board of education requirements and local fire departments as applicable to the occupancy.

Some codes have been incorporated into legislation which is enforced by national or local officials. Others represent guidelines which contain no specific mandates to the designer. Careful consideration of the specific applications and the requirements of the applicable laws must be made before developing emergency lighting for any building.

DESIGN CONSIDERATIONS FOR EMERGENCY EGRESS LIGHTING

Illuminance

By itself, illuminance is not an adequate measure of visibility, since it refers only to the quantity of light falling on a surface and not the amount reflected back to the eye. Luminance is more closely correlated with visibility; however, it is more difficult to predict and specify for emergency lighting applications. Nevertheless, illuminance does influence the speed of egress from furnished and cluttered spaces,[1-5] as illustrated in figure 33-1.[4] Furthermore, an average illuminance of 0.5 lx can provide sufficient visibility to permit people to exit without colliding with furniture and other obstacles.[1,3-6]

Based on this information and adding a safety factor to take account of less than perfect field conditions, it

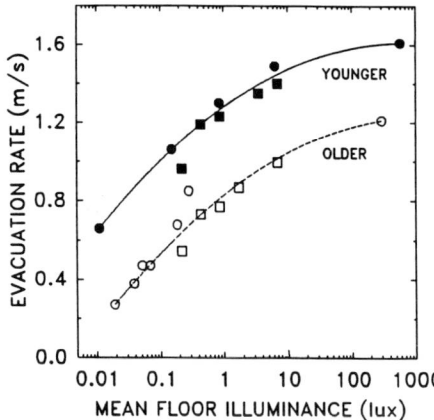

Fig. 33-1. Rates of evacuation of both older and younger people in cluttered spaces.[4]

is recommended that minimum horizontal illuminance measured at the floor be at least 1 lx (0.1 fc) at all points along the means of egress, and that the minimum maintained illuminance at the beginning of emergency operation should be at least 10 lx (1 fc). Illuminance values should be determined in a manner consistent with recommended IESNA field measurement practices. See chapter 2, Measurement of Light and Other Radiant Energy.

Health care facilities require more illuminance in emergency situations because of the need to evacuate under adverse conditions and to provide life support services to patients who cannot be evacuated. Chapter 17, Institution and Public Building Lighting, gives current recommended illuminances for use when normal service is interrupted.

In making calculations the designer should remember that isolux distribution curves for sealed beam incandescent lamps typically show illuminance on a plane perpendicular to the lamp axis. Since such equipment is usually aimed at angles off the vertical, the cosine factor must be taken into account (see chapter 2, Measurement of Light and Other Radiant Energy). It is also important to note that zonal cavity methods or point-by-point illuminance calculations are generally not applicable when making calculations for fluorescent emergency luminaires. Layouts of fluorescent emergency luminaires are often too widely spaced, and therefore nonuniform, for these methods to be valid.

Duration

The time required for occupants to evacuate a space will depend upon its size and complexity. Codes specify minimum operating periods from 30 min to 8 h, with 90 min being the most common. (Minimum code requirements are 90 min in the United States and 30 min in Canada.) Relevant codes such as BOCA, NFPA and

local codes should also be consulted (see chapter 14, Codes and Standards).

The designer should also give consideration to extending the operating time if unusual field factors, such as limited mobility and complex facilities, dictate. Such circumstances might include a high occupancy rate by older persons, occupancy by the handicapped and facilities requiring a long shutdown process.

In hospitality facilities, there is a special need for long-lasting emergency lighting in such areas as restaurants; see chapter 17, Institution and Public Building Lighting.

The light output of some emergency lighting systems will decline during the course of operation. Care should be taken to design systems so that illuminance levels do not fall below 60% of the initial levels for the full duration of emergency operation. In the United States, the National Electrical Code (NEC) requires a minimum of 60% of the initial illuminance to be maintained.[7]

Illuminance Uniformity

Providing a minimum degree of uniformity will keep adaptation to changing illuminances from becoming a factor in the speed or safety of movement along the path of egress, and help eliminate shadows in the means of egress.

An illuminance uniformity ratio (E_{avg}/E_{min}) not exceeding 10:1 will provide excellent uniformity for safe movement. Even ratios in excess of 40:1 may be acceptable, but an attempt to minimize this ratio should be made.

Illuminance uniformity is more easily achieved by using a greater number of luminaires with lower light output than by employing fewer but more widely spaced luminaires with higher light output.

Visibility of Hazards

Specification of floor-level illuminance is not itself adequate to provide assurance that all hazards are properly lighted. Visibility is largely dependent on the contrast between the hazard and its background. Attention should be given to the identification and lighting of hazards to ensure adequate visibility. Hazard areas include any area in which a change in direction or level occurs along the path of egress.

Some examples of such hazard areas are:

• Intersections of corridors
• Abrupt changes of direction of the egress path
• Staircases
• Changes of floor level
• Exits and areas adjacent to exits
• Obstructions along the means of egress

Every potential obstruction in a means of egress should contrast with its surroundings. Such obstructions include the nosings of stair treads, as well as short barriers and walls at right angles to the direction of movement.

In addition to providing enhanced illuminance and high contrast for the kinds of hazards described above, consideration should be given to vertical surface illumination. All vertical surfaces along the means of egress should be well lighted to assist in defining the escape route. Such vertical surface illumination will also provide the occupant with greater confidence that obstructions and hazards are visible and therefore they can exit with greater speed.

For additional security, preliminary evidence[8-13] indicates that photoluminescent paints and adhesive products can supplement electric lighting evacuation systems. They can be applied to hazards, baseboards, door frames, stairs and walls in a manner that will clearly delineate the means of egress in the event of complete power failure and allow the evacuee to develop a more coherent image of the space. Sufficient illumination should be provided throughout non-emergency periods to keep the photoluminescent pigments completely "charged." Such systems may require at least 200 lx, 24 hours per day, for proper operation. The manufacturer of the material should be consulted to verify requirements.

Illumination of Fire-Alarm Call Points and Fire-Fighting Equipment

Fire-alarm call points and fire-fighting equipment provided along the means of egress should be illuminated by either emergency lighting, normal electric lighting or daylight at all times while the premises are occupied.

Location and Application of Egress Luminaires

The purpose of this subsection is to identify those factors unique to the design of emergency egress lighting.

Path Delineation. The first and perhaps best cues provided to evacuees regarding the path to safety can come from the egress lighting system itself (independent of signage). Care should be taken to design the lighting system in such a way that the brightness and location of delivered light gives a clear, unambiguous and conspicuous indication of the location of the path of egress. Illuminances on the egress path higher than those on immediately surrounding areas can help guide occupants to the exits, in a *path-making* approach. Similarly, relatively high illuminances near the exit

door can make this area more conspicuous and quickly identifiable.

Coverage. It is important to provide adequate lighting in all areas that constitute the means of egress. Exit access and discharge areas are frequently difficult to define with certainty, but agreement can and should be reached between the designer and the authority having jurisdiction. It is also important to remember that the exit discharge extends outside the building and that luminaires appropriate for outdoor application are required. Many jurisdictions also require emergency lighting and exit marking at all changes of direction of travel, in windowless or underground buildings and at elevation changes in stairwells or corridors. Locally applicable codes should always be consulted to verify that equipment is provided in all required locations.

Glare Control. Inadequate control of glare can substantially degrade the quality of an emergency egress lighting system. Disability glare will reduce the visibility of hazards. Directional, sealed beam lighting commonly used for emergency lighting will create disability glare unless carefully positioned and aimed.

To reduce glare, the designer should select luminaire types with appropriate photometric distributions, and specify aiming angles which minimize direct glare in the direction of oncoming foot traffic. Mounting locations and aiming angles should be chosen which position luminaires well off the line of sight to exit signage. This helps to reduce the effects of scattered ambient light that would decrease the visibility of signs in the presence of smoke.[4, 14-18] Eliminating competing sources of brightness along the same line of sight aids in keeping exit signage adequately conspicuous and easy to locate.

Shadowing. When using highly directional light sources or when obstructions such as partitions or merchandise racks are present in a space (see figure 33-2), consideration should be given to the shadowing which may result. An example of effects to be avoided is the body shadow created by an evacuee on stairs lighted by a single directional light source. Each flight of stairs should be illuminated by more than one luminaire to minimize shadows on nosings and treads. In addition, improperly located luminaires may become ineffective if the partitions in open-plan offices create shadows along the means of egress. This problem is compounded by partitions which are moved to accommodate new office layouts. Easy-to-move luminaires or broad general coverage from overhead diffuse luminaires should be provided to minimize this problem.

Smoke. The possible presence of smoke along the path of egress poses a difficult problem for the designer. The dynamics of smoke vary with the burning

Fig. 33-2. Emergency lighting for merchandising areas must be carefully aimed and positioned to avoid shadowing and obstruction from partitions and displays, as are these column-mounted luminaires to the left.

materials and conditions in the building. Smoke varies in temperature, color, rate of development, degree of stratification, particulate content and optical density.[19, 20] All of these properties can hinder the effectiveness of the egress lighting system.

Given the inherent variability and instability of smoke, recommendations for emergency lighting during smoke-filled conditions are currently somewhat limited. One promising design avenue in this regard is a supplemental lighting delivery system mounted near the floor. Such systems can light the path while avoiding light absorption and scattering in smoke stratified at higher levels. In addition, such equipment delineates the path for the evacuee crawling beneath the smoke layer.

Areas Outside the Means of Egress. Codes may require lighting outside the means of egress itself. A well-designed egress lighting system should include

emergency lighting in areas which might enhance the safety and functionality of the building during loss of power. Examples of such applications include:

- Public restrooms
- Generator rooms
- Elevator equipment rooms
- Cold storage rooms
- Computer and communications equipment rooms
- Tool storage and maintenance facilities
- Classrooms
- Electrical equipment rooms
- Health care facilities
- Hazardous manufacturing equipment
- Underground corridors and other windowless spaces

Architectural Factors

Exteriors. Most codes enforced by the local *authorities having jurisdiction* (AHJ) require an emergency "white light" at the exit discharge from a building. This source provides the transition from the interior egress path to the exterior. The exterior source should provide a minimum of 10 lx at the exit. Currently, there is no distance requirement for emergency lighting beyond the exit discharge.

Exterior sources should be located either above the door or to one side, to reduce glare. Different sources are available to accomplish exit discharge lighting, and the designer should be aware of the pros and cons of each.

Incandescent lamps are short lived but may be a good choice when used only as an interim source during HID lamp restrike times or in a low-voltage dc battery-powered source during power failures. Since egress lighting may be required to be on during all times of occupancy, not just during power failures, a battery-powered source must be used in conjunction with a "normally on" source. This "normally on" source should have long life, such as HID or compact fluorescent. With any power failure, the HID arc will extinguish, so the restrike time must be covered with a backup "instant on" lamp, or else "instant restrike" lamps should be employed.

With compact fluorescent lamps, low ambient temperatures may affect lamp lumen performance. The proper ballast and lamp must be specified for the expected temperature range.

Environmental conditions such as damp, wet and hazardous locations require the additional consideration of the suitability of the equipment for use in such locations. The AHJs usually refer to the listing or labeling practices of a product testing and certification organization, acceptable to them, in determining the acceptability of the installation. The listed or labeled equipment should be marked for use in locations of the kind.

Partially protected exterior locations under canopies, marquees, roofed open porches and the like, as well as interior locations subject to moderate degrees of moisture (such as some basements, some barns and some cold storage warehouses), constitute *damp* locations. Exterior locations exposed to weather and unprotected, and interior locations subject to saturation with water or other nonflammable liquids, such as vehicle washing areas, are classified as *wet* locations. Locations where fire or explosion hazards may exist due to flammable gases or vapors, flammable liquids, combustible dust or ignitible fibers in the air constitute *hazardous* locations. For information on the codes applicable to these situations, see chapter 14, Codes and Standards.

"Normally on" exterior luminaires may be controlled by photocells and time clocks to conserve energy during nonoccupied periods.

Many interior and exterior locations require equipment which is safe from tampering and vandalism. Schools and many outdoor locations are examples of applications often requiring vandal-resistant equipment (see chapter 16, Educational Facilities Lighting, and chapter 22, Exterior Lighting).

Interiors. Typically, emergency lighting and exit marking are required at all changes of direction or level, in windowless or underground buildings, in stairwells and corridors, and in rooms leading to the exit path when separated from the exit path by two rooms or by passing through two doors. Remodeling, such as relocating movable office partitions, may invalidate existing emergency and exit lighting.

In the United States, the Americans with Disabilities Act (ADA) prohibits wall objects such as luminaires from projecting more than 10 cm (4 in.) into walks, corridors, hallways, or aisles when these objects are mounted between 67 and 200 cm (27 and 80 in.) above the finished floor. Under the ADA, the designer should also be aware of special areas which may require additional emergency lighting, such as toilet rooms.

Night-light circuits—those in use to provide minimal light during unoccupied time—are commonly used when the designer selects unitary battery equipment or other "normally off" (units only turned on during power failure) systems for emergency lighting. The "normally off" system does not provide egress or walkaround illumination when interior luminaires are turned off and the building is occupied by night watchmen or maintenance personnel. These night-light circuits need not be part of the emergency lighting system, but as a minimum should meet recommendations for egress lighting.

When using sealed beam lamps, the angle of incidence should be corrected to the horizontal. The narrow beam from sealed beam lamps may create extremely narrow patterns of light on the path of egress, requiring multiple units or special types of beam patterns to achieve egress lighting objectives.

When using fluorescent battery-inverter units to power a fluorescent lamp during normal power failure, the lamp lumens will be substantially reduced, unless full lumen output fluorescent battery inverter units are used.

Emergency lamps and luminaires should be marked as being part of the emergency lighting system. These markings should appear on the exterior of the luminaires to be readily apparent. Unit equipment and central dc systems are not always compatible with the interior design of a space. For some spaces this is not important. For others, where the appearance of battery-operated equipment is objectionable, a generator or inverter system can power selected luminaires that are already part of the lighting system.

Failure of one luminaire should never leave a space in total darkness. In stairwells, alternating a normal source with an emergency source at each landing should provide a reliable system. Also, emergency egress lighting circuits usually are not permitted to be switched, except where the controls are accessible only to an "authorized" person as defined by the AHJ.

In places of assembly, such as theatres and auditoriums, some jurisdictions permit egress illuminance to be reduced to 2 lx during performances or projections but require 10 lx at all other times. Manufacturers of dimming or other control systems may provide an emergency transfer module or contactors to transfer selected luminaires to "full on" upon failure of the normal power source to the dimming control cabinet. In this way the emergency luminaires can become an integral part of the lighting system and function with the other, "normal" luminaires.

Floor proximity lighting systems are commonly used in theatres, auditoriums and even places of worship to provide egress lighting. These systems may consist of step-lighting luminaires to define each stair riser, aisle seating-mounted luminaires, or an assembly of low-voltage miniature lamps housed in a flexible clear plastic tube. Other typical systems consist of electroluminescent lamps or LEDs in a tube or extruded housing. The path of egress can be defined in this way, with additional lighting provided from ceiling- or wall-mounted luminaires (being sure to consider ADA restrictions).

Architectural Obstructions. Ceiling soffits and bulkheads can completely block unitary sealed beam lamps and other luminaires, interfering with the ability of the emergency lighting system to produce sufficient illumination. The designer should coordinate the location of these luminaires with ceiling plans. Minimum ceiling clearances in egress corridors are prescribed by NFPA, BOCA and ADA (see chapter 14, Codes and Standards, for further information). The designer should locate egress luminaires, especially the sealed beam type, so that they are not obscured by soffits, bulkheads or suspended luminaires and do not protrude below the code-set minimum headroom. Supplementary egress luminaires may be necessary if examination of lines of sight along a corridor shows that bulkheads or suspended luminaires obstruct the function of emergency egress luminaires.

Emergency Lighting Equipment. Power supply sources and lighting equipment for an emergency lighting system can be divided into six general categories:

- Unit equipment
- Unit inverters
- Central dc systems
- Central inverter systems
- Standby generators
- Floor proximity path marking

Unit Equipment. Unit equipment consists of a self-contained rechargeable battery, a battery charger, a battery status indicator, a transfer device, a test switch and pilot lamp, and provisions for either integral or remote lamps or both. This equipment charges a battery when normal ac power is available and transfers battery power to the emergency light source during a power outage. These luminaires operate only during normal power failures. Both halogen and incandescent sealed beam types, and a variety of low-voltage lamps and reflector combinations, are used in these luminaires.

Unit Inverter. The unit inverter system consists of a battery, a battery dc-to-ac inverter charger, a transfer device, a pilot lamp and a test switch. During a power interruption, it operates one or more fluorescent lamps from an internal battery by converting dc power to ac power at a frequency of 60 Hz or higher. When the power is returned, battery charging occurs. During a power outage, the emergency luminaire will operate with the circuit switched on or off.

Unit inverter systems operate the fluorescent luminaires used for general lighting in a building. Most units fit into the luminaire ballast channel. High temperatures in this space may shorten the life of the battery. An externally mounted system should be used if high temperatures are expected.

With unit inverters, the required test switch and ready light must be easily visible.

The combination of unit inverter and lamp should also be compatible. Inverters that accommodate different lamp types provide different lumen outputs that can be a low percentage of the initial lamp lumens.

Central DC Systems. A "normally off" central dc system contains a battery, a battery charger, a test switch, a transfer device and a pilot lamp. The system powers remote incandescent (including halogen) lamps during a power interruption. Normal emergency supply voltages are 12, 24 and 120 V dc. Older systems using 32, 36, and 48 V still exist.

Lamps for dc systems can be any filament lamp of equal voltage rating. However, it is important to note that most commonly available 24-, 32-, 36- and 48-V lamps are for applications other then emergency lighting and should be reviewed for life, lumen output and future availability.

Central Inverter Systems. A central inverter system contains a battery, a battery charger, a dc-to-ac inverter and a transfer means, plus appropriate test and monitoring equipment. The system incorporates electronic devices to convert battery dc voltage to 60-Hz line voltage. Standard transfer systems (those with transfer time over 8 ms) can operate incandescent and fluorescent lamps without significant off time. Fast-transfer and uninterruptable systems can operate HID sources that need a transfer or "off" time of 4–8 ms or less. These systems can also power fire-alarm systems and other crucial 60-Hz equipment.

Standby Generator. The standby generator includes a starter battery, a battery charger and a transfer means, plus test and monitoring equipment. An engine generator produces 60-Hz line voltage. This kind of system powers incandescent and fluorescent lamps and other 60-Hz life safety loads. It is not suitable for HID unless supplementary incandescent or fluorescent sources are used. A standby generator system provides ac power backup as an emergency source in large buildings. Check the Life Safety Code for the maximum allowable startup time.

Floor Proximity Path Marking. Several marking systems designed for use in smoke have recently become available. These systems are covered in the Life Safety Code[21] and may be mounted in the floor or on the wall nearby. Some states, such as California, are considering requirements for such systems, and the designer should remain alert for codes adopting this emerging technology, keeping in mind that it is a supplementary rather than an alternative emergency lighting system. In the meantime considerations should be given to applying such systems where enhanced safety can result.

Light Sources. Incandescent lamps used in "normally off" emergency lighting applications differ in design from those used for general illumination. These usually have a lamp life of roughly 50 h and provide significantly more lumens per watt than their longer-lived general-illumination counterparts. These high-output lamps are particularly useful when operated from unit equipment and central low-voltage dc systems. Low-wattage lamps reduce current requirements and make large conductors unnecessary, both for internal and for remote lamp wiring.

Emergency lamps used in "normally on" applications should have high reliability and long life expectancy. Because of their short lives, general-illumination incandescent and halogen lamps are not good choices if an inverter or a generator is the emergency supply. Reliable lamps are less susceptible to filament damage from vibration, have long life, can operate over a wide range of temperatures, have good socket contact, and have short (less than 10 s) restrike time.

If general-illumination lamps are required for emergency lighting, the physical and electrical characteristics of candidate lamps should be checked to ensure that a reliable lamp is selected.

Compact fluorescent lamps are becoming much more common in emergency applications. These lamps offer long lamp life, high color rendering characteristics and high efficacy to reduce the power requirement. It is often easier to achieve good illuminance uniformity and low glare with such lamps, since luminaires utilizing them provide broader photometric distributions than more concentrated incandescent lamps. The designer should be aware that low-temperature or high-humidity exterior applications may not be suitable for these lamps, and the manufacturer should be consulted for assistance with such applications.

Caution is required in the use of square wave inverters for emergency power with high-power-factor, compact fluorescent ballasts. The power-factor-correcting capacitor in the ballast may look like a short circuit to the square wave output of the inverter and create problems by tripping the circuit breaker.

HID lamps may be suitable for use as emergency light sources if the designer recognizes and adapts to the special operating characteristics of these lamps. HID lamps are generally incompatible with conventional emergency power sources such as dc systems, generators or ac inverters. None of these systems will maintain lamp operation during transfer from normal to emergency power, so the long cooldown and restrike times will prevent emergency lighting from being available within the 10 s required by the Life Safety Code. Fast-transfer and UPS (uninterruptible power supply) ac inverters are available to prevent this problem and are the only emergency power sources compatible with HID lamps. "Instant restrike" HID lamps are available, as are systems which incorporate incandescent lamps during HID off periods.

If HID sources are selected, the designer should be sure that the spectral characteristics of the source do not degrade the visibility of exit markings and should select a system appropriate for the expected ambient temperature.

Full-size fluorescent lamps are also used in emergency lighting systems, particularly for marking the pathways of egress.

Batteries. The emergency power systems described above use batteries as a source of backup power, except for the standby generator, which uses a battery for engine cranking. The information that follows is a summary of the extensive literature on the subject.

A battery consists of one or more connected cells. Batteries used for backup power are either rechargeable or, by definition, secondary batteries. Two categories of rechargeable cells found in emergency lighting systems contain lead-based plates with an acid electrolyte and nickel-cadmium with an alkaline electrolyte. The major groups of commercially available cells are pure lead (lead-acid), lead-calcium, lead-antimony, and nickel-cadmium cells. All can be manufactured as wet type (with liquid electrolyte), and most have a means for adding water; that is, they require maintenance. Also in production is a sealed type (starved electrolyte or gelled electrolyte) which are said to be "maintenance-free." The advantages of sealed cells are that they are easy to ship and virtually eliminate the chance of injury from electrolyte splash. However, sealed cells have shorter life than well-maintained wet cells. Wet lead-based cells offer greater plate thickness and a mid-range specific gravity, both indicators of longer life.

Batteries are classified as short-, medium- and long-discharge types. A 90-min operating time corresponds to a medium discharge rate. Equal initial ampere-hour ratings do not mean equal battery capacities. Available amperes at a specific time are the only way to compare battery output. Manufacturer information should be reviewed before a battery is chosen. Data from the battery manufacturer represent ideal temperatures and the most favorable charging and discharging conditions. A reasonable safety factor should be added to compensate for conditions other than ideal.

The battery must be compatible with its charger, and it must operate efficiently in the application temperature range at the expected maintenance intervals. In addition, the battery must meet all load requirements. Underwriters Laboratories Standard 924 allows the battery to reach 87.5% of normal voltage for minimum current capacity. In no case can the discharge time be less than 90 min, per UL and NFPA 70.

Lead-based cells and, to a lesser extent, nickel-cadmium cells emit hydrogen gas during charging and discharging. Sealed cells also provide blowout vents in case severe overcharging occurs. The worst-case hydrogen emission information on large battery installation should be checked to determine if exhaust fans are needed.

Because batteries are perishable, and because the time between manufacture and installation can be substantial, shelf life and no-load recharge intervals are important. For long intervals without charging after system installation, it is best to disconnect the battery to prevent deep discharge and then give boost charges at the recommended intervals.

Chargers. Battery chargers for emergency lighting systems must conform to the UL 924 standard. This ensures that the combination of battery and charger has met the time requirements for the initial charge and recharge and that the charger has passed normal UL safety tests.

Three common emergency lighting chargers are:

- Pulse
- Constant current
- Constant voltage

Most use a two-rate charge: a high rate for initial charging and quick recharge after a discharge, and a float or trickle rate to maintain the battery at maximum capacity. The time needed to recharge depends on the charger's current-producing capacity and the battery's ability to accept that current. A fast recharge requirement can shorten battery life. If the current supplied is too great, the heat created causes a subsequent loss of electrolyte. Battery charging tolerances are critical. A 2.5% increase in float voltage significantly reduces the battery life through overcharging; a 2.5% decrease does so through self-discharge. If both battery and charger are acquired from one manufacturer, the float charge and the high-charge characteristics should be fixed before shipment. Standalone chargers may require field adjustments for best operation. Nickel-cadmium designs, which produce 1.2 V per cell, use different charging techniques than lead-based ones at 2.0 V per cell, even when the total battery voltage is the same. For example, a 12-V nickel-cadmium battery has different charge set point than a lead-cadmium battery.

DESIGN CONSIDERATIONS FOR EXIT MARKING

Legibility and Visibility of Exit Signs

The legibility, visibility and conspicuity of exit signs are determined by three primary factors; namely, sign characteristics, observer variables, and location and application conditions. Sign characteristics include sign luminance, contrast, color, uniformity, graphics and location; observer variables include adaptation state, visual capacity, expectations and familiarity with the space; environmental considerations include viewing distance, sign position, ambient illuminance, veiling luminance, veiling reflections, glare, competing graphics, colors, and contrast of the surroundings. These factors do not affect visibility equally.

Sign Characteristics

Graphics. Both NFPA 101[21] and UL 924[22] specify the following criteria for exit sign graphics. The word EXIT is specified in the United States, while both EXIT and SORTIE are specified in Canada.

- Stroke width should be 19 mm (0.75 in.).
- Letter height should be 152 mm (6 in.).
- Letter width should be 50 mm (2 in.), except for the letter "I" in EXIT and SORTIE, which should be 19 mm (0.75 in.) wide.
- Interchanacter spacing should be 10 mm (0.37 in.).
- Optional directional indicator should be a chevron (arrow or other symbol) located to the left or right of the word EXIT, consistent with the direction of travel.

Several codes, such as CIE,[23] ISO[24] and NFPA,[25] have provisions for an optional pictograph for exit markings. Its graphic content contains a human figure exiting through a door.[26]

Viewing Distance. The ability to locate and read an exit sign decreases as the distance of the viewer from the sign increases. The current maximum spacing between signs, or between a sign and the exit, is 30 m (100 ft). This translates into a visual angle of about 17.2 min of arc for a 150-mm (6-in.) letter height, and 5.6 min of arc for a 50-mm (2-in.) letter width. Visual angles of this size should be resolvable by those with 20/100 or better vision,[27] about 95% of the population,[28] although questions remain about which features of the word EXIT constitute the critical detail necessary for recognition.

Luminance. Sign luminance is not directly specified by the Life Safety Code[21] or the National Building Code of Canada.[29] The Life Safety Code does state that exit signs which are externally lighted shall have a minimum contrast of 0.50 and be lighted to a level of 50 lx (5 fc). Internally lighted signs are required to exhibit visibility which is equivalent to such externally lighted signs. It can be concluded that the luminance levels required to meet this requirement are on the order of 15–17 cd/m^2. The Life Safety Code presently allows an exception to this requirement for self-luminous signs which have a minimum letter brightness of 0.2 cd/m^2.

Recent research, however, has shown such signs to be significantly less visible and conspicuous than signs meeting the 50-lx standard.[30, 31]

In other codes, specifications are given for sign luminance. UL-924, for example, specifies two methods for making comparisons. Thus, the CIE specifies a minimum luminance of 15 cd/m^2 and a maximum of 300 cd/m^2 for pictographs,[23] while a United States Aeronautics and Space code specifies 89 cd/m^2 as a minimum.[32] The preponderance of research has demonstrated that increasing sign luminance can increase visibility and conspicuity in both clear and smoke conditions,[15, 16, 30, 31, 33–36] although the existence of an upper limit remains uncertain.

Contrast. The contrast between an exit sign's graphic and its background is very important in determining its visibility. The contrast can be calculated with the formula $|L_t - L_b|/L_b$, where L_t is the luminance of the character and L_b is the background luminance. NFPA specifies that an exit sign must have a minimum contrast of at least 0.5. Available research, however, indicates that increasing contrast beyond the minimum should increase sign visibility.[31, 37]

Color. Neither NFPA nor UL provides specifications for exit sign color, although many local jurisdictions do. Color combinations are typically some combination of red or green letters on a contrasting background (often white), although the letter and background color can be reversed. In other countries, codes specify green and white for exit signs.[23, 24, 38] Research on the visibility of exit signs of different colors has been somewhat inconclusive,[30, 31] possibly because contrast has often varied along with color.

Configuration and Uniformity. Other sign factors that determine visibility include the configuration and uniformity of the sign. Recent research has hinted that stencil-faced signs, in which the letters are illuminated and the background is opaque, may be somewhat more visible in both smoke and clear conditions.[15, 30, 33] Sign uniformity has not been studied systematically enough to provide reliable luminance ratios, although some have suggested variations of no more than 3, 4 or 5 : 1 above the average level over the brightest area of the sign. An Australian standard specifies ratios of no more than 4 or 5 : 1 for internally lighted signs,[38] while the CIE suggests no more than 10 : 1.[23] Excessive nonuniformity may lead to obscuration of letters or critical details on the sign.

Observer Characteristics

Handicaps in the population must be considered. For example, between 0.5 and 1% of the population can be considered legally blind,[28] even with corrective lenses. About 8–10% of the male Caucasian population suf-

fers from color vision defects which can result in inability to identify colors accurately, or confusions between colors such as red and green.[39] Other observers may suffer mobility impairments which lead to longer egress times. All observers will suffer from problems due to changes in their adaptation during the first several seconds after building lighting is extinguished. For example, normal building illuminance levels can range from 100 to 1000 lx or more for offices. The time to adjust to emergency lighting varies with the level of the emergency lighting; the lower the level, the longer the time. As a result, signs of very low luminance, such as self-luminous signs at 0.2 cd/m^2, may be invisible during the early stages of a power failure or similar building emergency.[2] Beneficial effects have been reported from using photoluminescent markings and signs under such conditions.[11, 12]

Location and Application of Exit Marking Equipment

Exit signs are required in all buildings, and rooms or spaces must have more than one access. Exit signs should be located along the required means of egress and at all exit doors or access areas. Directional exit signs should be located at changes of direction in the egress path. Entrances to egress stairs should also be indicated with exit signs.

Exit signs are usually mounted above exit doors to allow passage beneath, and no lower than 2 m (80 in.) above the finished floor to the bottom of the sign. Signs must be visible over the heads of others located in the path of egress. Exit signs should not be more than 30 m (100 ft) apart along the egress path at each exit door,[21] at each change of direction, at entrances to stairwells and at changes of elevation. Check local codes for other required locations. During a fire emergency, smoke may obscure signs mounted above doors. One solution has been the use of supplemental floor proximity signs, located about 200 mm (8 in.) above the floor (see figure 33-3). These signs are intended to be visible to a person crawling along the floor, just below the smoke.[40] Recent research suggests such signs should have high luminance, because low-luminance signs are obscured very rapidly in smoke.[30, 31] Some incandescent and many electroluminescent and self-powered (tritium) exit signs have low sign luminances. Certification or listing by a recognized agency does not ensure proper application of an exit sign.

The same types of problems are encountered when locating exit signs as with egress luminaires. Ceiling soffits and bulkheads may block the line of sight for exit signs. Other types of luminaires, such as surface and suspended linear, may block the view of the sign. Hindrances to proper location and mounting of exit signs are very large doors, glass above doors, insuffi-

Fig. 33-3. Supplemental exit signs mounted near the floor can be seen by occupants crawling along the floor in smoky conditions.

cient recessing or surface mounting depth to mount exit signs above doors, business signs, and emergency egress luminaires. Exit signs with battery packs may be four or more inches deeper than nonbattery types, making the exit sign extend lower into the corridor headroom or door opening space. The location of LED exit signs should be checked for viewing angles, as these signs are less visible when viewed from oblique angles. It should be noted, too, that emergency egress luminaires may produce sufficient glare to obscure the exit sign. Other competing light sources and building finishes may also interfere with sign visibility. Ambient illumination may change sign contrast, reflectance, brightness and conspicuity as well. In exterior applications, certain light sources may not be suitable; electroluminescent signs, for example, are affected by high humidity. Also, incandescent sources may be affected by high vibration, which may damage both the source and the socket.

Choice of Exit Marking Equipment

Although exit marking equipment is controlled by many standards, many different products meet the legal criteria. Therefore, specifiers have a large selection of equipment from which to choose. Internally lighted, edge-lighted, and externally lighted signs, both self-contained and remote powered, abound. Light sources for exit signs include incandescent (high or low voltage), fluorescent and halogen lamps, light-emitting diodes, electroluminescent panels, and phosphors energized by tritium gas.

Options for exit signs include flashing, possibly combined with audible signaling. These options alert the visually impaired via sound and the hearing impaired via flashing. The UL-924 standard specifies the on-off duty cycle times for these accessories.[22] Some local codes require exit signs with these options to interface with a fire-alarm system as a way to provide additional information to the occupants. Again, local codes are the best source of review for facilities that require these options.

Self-Contained Signs. Self-contained illuminated exit signs maintain sign luminance during normal power loss without the need for an external power source. Battery, battery charger and transfer systems stay ready to sense a power outage and switch to battery backup. Higher-frequency operation during power outages is common.

Remote-Powered Signs. Unit equipment, dc systems, inverters and generators are all sources of emergency power for remote-powered exit signs. With unit equipment or dc systems a separate circuit feeds directly to the exit to power emergency lamps. In these systems, the emergency lamp voltage must match the supply. Inverters or generators used as emergency power sources will continue to operate the "normally on" lamp without need for additional circuits.

Because remote-powered signs do not contain a dedicated battery and charger, they are less expensive than self-contained signs. The total system cost depends upon the remote power source, the distance from that source, and the voltage needed to power the sign. For example, an inverter- or generator-powered system using the same distribution as the utility adds no cost, but dc power needs additional wiring from the emergency source.

Exit Sign Lamps

Long-life lamps are essential for both safety and economical maintenance. A building emergency can occur without immediate power interruption. Therefore, the "normally on" exit source should be designed for high reliability and reasonably long life.

Many incandescent exit signs have extended-life "normally on" lamps and low-voltage emergency lamps that operate at the battery voltage. Refer to the characteristics of incandescent sources for emergency lighting above. The burn cycle for the battery-operated incandescent lamp or lamps is short, and therefore a short-life, high-lumen-output source may be used. Incandescent lamps will provide extended life and lower light output when operated below their rated voltage. Long-life incandescent lamps designed for exit applications have a rated life ten or more times that of standard lamps and still provide needed exit luminance. One advantage of filament lamps is that they can be easily circuited to flash within the specified duty cycle. High-voltage long-life lamps have thin filaments, so shock and vibration can be a problem with these lamps. Vibration may also cause screw base lamps to back out of the lampholders. Lamps with a dc bayonet base or fluorescent lamps should be considered for such applications.

Fluorescent sources are popular choices for exit signs. Low-wattage tubular and compact types are reliable, can provide good luminance uniformity, have a reasonably long life, and are more efficacious than incandescent sources. Total efficacy calculations for fluorescent sources should include ballast loss, which can be as much as 50% of the listed lamp wattage. The power factor is usually low for compact fluorescent lamps and must be considered in circuit sizing. The luminous output of fluorescent lamps depends upon temperature, so care should be taken to avoid excessively high or low temperatures.

Electroluminescent lamps operate between 80 and 200 V ac, require less than 1 W of power per exit face, and yield a completely uniform luminance pattern. Light is produced by phosphors serving as a dielectric between a conductive foil or metal-sputtered back electrode and a clear front electrode. Lamp life can be 5 years or more when operating at a low frequency and low power density. Exit signs with these sources operate the lamp at line frequency during normal times. If self-contained, they switch to a higher frequency and higher light output during emergencies.

Electroluminescent lamps exhibit a brightness decay characteristic such that their luminance gradually declines over their life. The lamp should certainly be replaced before the luminance falls below the 0.21 cd/m^2 specified by the Life Safety Code.[21] Different types of lamps decay at different rates, and the manufacturer should be consulted for information pertaining to expected lamp life and brightness decay.

Light-emitting diodes (LED) use 2–8 W per exit face. LEDs are highly resistant to vibration, temperature and humidity because of their solid-state structure. Proper voltage and current transient protection is necessary to achieve long lamp life and good lumen maintenance. These small point sources are used in an array to spell EXIT in English-language signs. These lamps also have flashing capabilities and can be circuited to vary in intensity. Viewing angles should be checked when using LED signs, or diffusion material should be added, because the luminous intensity of the LED varies with the viewing angle.

Self-luminous signs depend on the decay of tritium gas and the resultant electrons striking a phosphor-coated glass tube to produce visible radiation. The published life expectancy of these sources is 5–15 yr.

This light source may be useful in explosion-prone areas. Areas which require expensive electrical distribution systems also benefit from this nonelectrical exit sign. These signs must be registered with the U.S. Nuclear Regulatory Commission or the Atomic Energy Control Board of Canada for use and proper disposal at end of life. The designer should make sure that the chance of breakage and exposure to the general public is minimal.

As stated in previous sections, the luminance of such signs is very low and decays exponentially. Higher-brightness signs should be used when the application allows.

MAINTENANCE REQUIREMENTS

A permanent record of all maintenance and inspections should be kept in a log book or computer file for review by the local inspection agency, in compliance with the National Electric Code (NEC), NFPA 70;[7] National Life Safety Code, NFPA 101;[21] National Fire Code Canada; and NFPA 110, Emergency & Standby Power Systems.

All self-contained emergency lighting and exit signs, including units with "maintenance-free" batteries, should be inspected and tested every 30 days or oftener. This inspection should include, but not be limited to, depressing the test switch a minimum of 90 s, and checking for lamp operation (including remotely mounted lamps) and pilot light operation. Luminaires containing wet batteries should be inspected for electrolyte level in each cell and for electrolyte leakage.

Central systems powered by ac or dc supplies or by "maintenance-free" batteries should also be inspected and tested at least every 30 days. The system's output voltage, frequency and current should also be checked against the data on the nameplate, and should be within the tolerance specified when connected to the full emergency lighting load.

Every 12 months the emergency lighting and exit marking equipment should be disconnected from the normal ac supply and allowed to operate for a period of 90 min, during which time all emergency light sources should be in continuous operation. When selecting a time for the 90-min test for battery-operated units, consideration should be given to the occupancy pattern in the space in which the test is performed. To ensure that the space will always have emergency lighting, the test should be conducted at a time when the batteries can be recharged before the building is occupied.

As part of the 12-month inspection and testing, the battery terminals should also be checked for corrosion and cleaned if necessary. Also, wet-cell battery vent caps should be visually inspected for blockage and cleaned if necessary.

For large installations where reliable skilled maintenance personnel are not available, a service contract with a responsible service organization should be provided.

Where the designer anticipates little or no maintenance and inspection, self-diagnostic or self-testing emergency lighting equipment should be considered. A multitude of "smart" equipment is currently available. It automatically monitors various vital functions of the equipment and indicates failures via visual and audible indicators. It typically runs an automatic test and diagnostic program at least once each month.

When replacing lamps, batteries or any other parts, the maintenance personnel must select replacement parts with identical ratings in order to maintain the proper visibility, illuminance and duration of operation in accordance with code requirements. Field-installed diodes used in series with an incandescent lamp to extend lamp life and reduce power consumption should be avoided in exit signs. The diodes reduce the lumen output of the lamp, possibly affecting the visibility of the exit sign as tested by the independent testing laboratories.

Emergency lighting should be treated as life safety equipment, for without its proper function, an area can be left in total darkness, causing confusion, collisions with obstacles, panic, and even loss of life.

LIGHTING FOR SAFETY

Lighting for safety is different from emergency lighting in that it involves ensuring proper illumination to provide safe working conditions, safe passage and the identification of any hazards or obstructions, indoors or outdoors.

Importance

Safe conditions are essential in any areas where there are people, and the effects of lighting on safety must be considered. The environment should be designed to help compensate for the limitations of human capability. Any factor that aids visual effectiveness increases the probability that a person will avoid an accident or detect the potential cause of an accident and act to correct it.

In many instances where illumination is associated with accidents, they are attributed to inadequate illuminance or poor quality of illumination. However, there are many less tangible factors associated with poor illumination which can contribute to many accidents. Some of these are direct glare, reflected glare and harsh shadows, all of which hamper seeing and can cause visual confusion. Excessive visual fatigue itself may be an element leading toward accidents. Accidents may also be prompted by the delayed eye adaptation a person experiences when moving from bright to dark surroundings and vice versa. Some accidents which have been attributed to an individual's carelessness could have been partially due to difficulty in seeing from one or more of the above-mentioned factors. The accidents might have been avoided through the use of good lighting principles.

Lighting for safety is a concern that must be addressed in both outdoor and indoor locations. Persons must be made aware of such hazards as curbs, steps, sloped walkways and obstacles in one's path (see figure 33-4). Where the illumination is very low or designed to create a special effect, such as in hotels, restaurants, theatres, museums, art galleries and aquariums, care must be taken to identify changes in elevation and direction without detracting from the visual effectiveness of the lighting.

The industrial environment presents many special concerns with respect to lighting for safety. Physical hazards are marked according to American National Standards Institute (ANSI) documents.[41] The color rendering properties of the light source should be considered with regard to the physical hazards present in the particular installation.[42]

Illuminance Levels

The lighting recommendations in chapter 11 provide a guide for efficient visual performance rather than for safety alone; therefore, they are not to be interpreted as requirements for regulatory minimum illuminance levels.

Fig. 33-4. Adequate safety lighting must be used in spaces with obstructions or changes in direction or level, such as stairwells.

Fig. 33-5. Illuminance Levels for Safety

Hazards Requiring Visual Detection	Slight		High	
Normal Activity Level Illuminance Levels	Low	High	Low	High
Lux	5.4	11	22	54
Footcandles	0.5	1	2	5

These values represent absolute minimum illuminances at any time and location where safety is related to visibility. However, in some cases higher levels may be required (such as where security is a factor). In other conditions, especially involving work with light-sensitive materials such as photographic film, much lower illuminances must be used. In these cases, alternate methods of ensuring safety must be employed.

Figure 33-5 lists illuminance levels regarded as absolute minima for safety alone. To assure these values are maintained, higher initial levels must be provided as required by the maintenance conditions. In those areas which do not have fixed lighting, local illumination should be provided during occupancy by means of luminaires that are portable or mounted on material-handling equipment and vehicles.

Other Factors

A visually safe installation must be free of excessive glare and of uncontrolled, large differences in luminances. Appropriate guides to limiting glare and adaptation effects are given earlier in this section in discussions of luminance ratios and visual comfort. Maximum luminance ratios are important to avoid temporary reductions in visibility because of changes in eye adaptation when alternately looking at areas of widely different luminance.

Illumination Evaluation

Although the quality and quantity of illumination may be designed for safety in an area, it is necessary to know whether the design meets requirements. A standard procedure, titled "How to Make a Lighting Survey,"[43] has been developed in cooperation with the U.S. Public Health Service. This standard procedure is recommended for use in surveys of lighting for safety.

SECURITY LIGHTING

Definition

Security lighting is exterior lighting installed solely to enhance the security of people and property. Other forms of exterior lighting, such as outdoor display lighting, decorative floodlighting and park lighting, can serve the same purpose, but they are designed with additional criteria in mind. Nonetheless, the principles

discussed here are relevant to the security aspect of these other applications (see chapter 18, Lighting for Merchandise Areas, and chapter 22, Exterior Lighting).

Objectives

Security lighting is installed to enhance the security of people and property. To achieve this objective, it is designed to:

- Deter any would-be criminal by making detection seem more likely.
- Allow guards to search a large area, either by direct visual surveillance or, indirectly, by closed-circuit television (CCTV) surveillance.

Principles

The basic principles of security lighting are:

- To provide enough light over the secure area so that anyone moving in or around it can be seen easily.
- Wherever possible, to limit the view of any would-be intruders into the secure area so that they are uncertain if anyone is watching.

These two principles require the designer to pay attention to the illuminance provided, the uniformity of the illuminance distribution, the effect of obstructions, the surface reflectances, the degree of glare, the light source color, the interaction with electronic surveillance systems and the effect on the surrounding area.

Security Systems

It should be emphasized that lighting is only a part of a security system. The complete system usually includes a physical element, such as fences, gates and locks; a detection element, involving guards patrolling or remote surveillance; and a response element, which determines what is to be done after detection occurs. Unless security lighting is integrated into the complete system, it is unlikely to be successful. For example, good lighting in a storage area which nobody is watching, and hence in which there is no possibility of a response, will simply help intruders do what they want to do, more quickly.

Site Considerations

The characteristics of the lighting to be used as part of the security system will be determined by several different aspects of the site. The factors which need to be considered are as follows:

Ambient Brightness of the Surrounding Area. If the surrounding area is brightly lighted, the security lighting needs to at least match or preferably exceed that brightness. If the surrounding area is dimly lighted, such as by moonlight, then almost any form of security lighting will make the site look well lighted.

Crime Status of the Area. If the site is in a high-crime area, it is likely that the physical defenses will be extensive. The security lighting should be used to support those defenses by ensuring that anyone tampering with them is easily detectable.

Shape of Site. If the site is large and open, then area lighting is required. However, if the site is largely filled with a building, floodlighting of the building is a better approach. In either case, unless it is economically impossible, the whole site should be lighted. There is little point in lighting part of a secure site.

Degree of Obstruction. In sites which have a high degree of obstruction, such as container terminals, the method of lighting should be designed to avoid strong shadows.

Applications

Given the wide range of site characteristics which may be encountered, it is not realistic to specify one general-purpose security lighting system for all sites. It is better to set out approaches to lighting the different elements which form a security system. This approach is used below.

Large Open Areas: Storage Yards, Container Terminals. The lighting of these areas is basically area lighting. Typically such areas are lighted by floodlighting or road luminaires on poles 10 m (30 ft) high or higher. The recommended average illuminance on the surface of large open areas is given in figure 33-6. Figure 33-7 shows a typical layout. As a rule of thumb, a ratio of average to minimum illuminance of 8:1 should be achieved. For typical road-lighting and floodlighting luminaires, mounted singly on poles, this can be done by the spacing the luminaires at 6 times their mounting height.

The designer of area lighting is faced with a choice of the number of poles, the number of luminaires attached to each pole, the wattage and type of lamp to be used and the mounting height of the luminaires. If the area is unobstructed, the choice will be largely determined by economic considerations. Relevant rules of thumb are that it is more economic to use the most efficient type of lamp, it is usually more economic to use a small number of large-wattage lamps than a large number of small-wattage lamps, and it is often more economic to mount a number of luminaires on one pole than to mount each lamp individually. However, if these rules of thumb were followed to their logical conclusion, the result would be one pole with all the

Fig. 33-6. Recommended Average Illuminances for Security Lighting

Application	Illuminance, lx (fc)	Notes
Large open areas	5 – 20 (0.5 – 2)	The greater the brightness of the surrounding area, the higher the illuminance required to balance the brightnesses in the space.
Buildings	5 – 20 (0.5 – 2)	Vertical illuminance on the building facade. The greater the brightness of the surrounding area, the higher the illuminance required to balance the brightnesses in the space.
Perimeter fence	5 (0.5)	Illuminance on the ground on either side of the fence.
Entrances	100 (10)	Illuminance on the ground in the inspection area.
Gatehouses	300 (30)	Illuminance on the workplane in the gatehouse. This lighting must be dimmable to low levels at night so the guard can see outside the gatehouse.

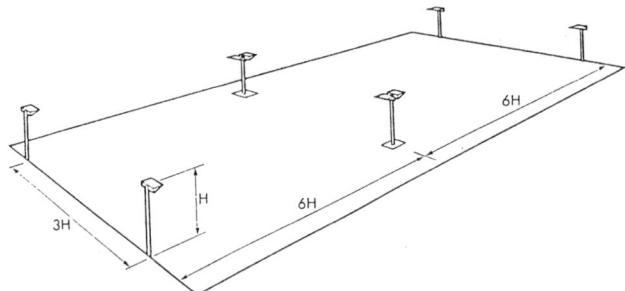

Fig. 33-7. Typical layout for floodlighting open areas. *H* is the pole height for the luminaires.

luminaires mounted on it. This is unlikely to be effective, because unless the pole height were great compared with the size of the secure area, it would create a very nonuniform illuminance distribution which would be detrimental to security. Therefore these rules of thumb need to be applied with care for illuminance uniformity.

This is particularly true if the area contains obstructions, as in container areas, because then having all the light sources in one location will lead to extensive shadowed areas. Two rules apply to the lighting of obstructed areas. The first is that increasing the mounting height will reduce the size of shadows cast by the obstructions. The second is that every point in the area should receive light from at least two directions. One should also remember the value of increasing the reflectance of the surface. For example, a concrete surface will reflect much more light than a blacktop surface. This reflected light will also diminish the strength of shadows.

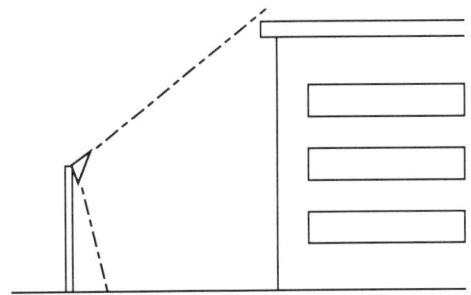

Fig. 33-8. Use of pole-mounted luminaires to provide uniform illumination on and around a building.

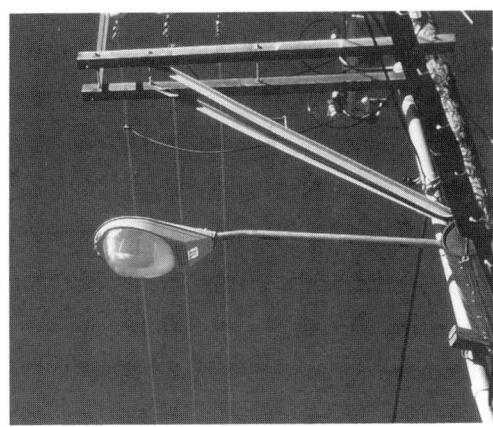

Fig. 33-9. Use of a pole-mounted luminaire to light fenced perimeter areas.

An alternative system which is sometimes suggested for large open areas is the glare system. In this system, a line of low-intensity floodlights is mounted at eye level and aimed out of the secure area. The idea is to create disability glare for any would-be intruder and also to make the position of any guard difficult to discern. Such a system has several disadvantages. It can be ineffective if the secure area is lighted as well, the disability glare being much reduced by the other lighting. The disability glare can also be diminished if the would-be intruder shields the view of the glare sources. Overall, the glare system is of limited usefulness unless the secure area is remote from other lighted areas such as working areas, roads and buildings.

Buildings. Some sites consist of a sealed building with a narrow open area around it. In this situation, a useful approach is to light the building and rely on reflectance from it to light the surrounding area. The building can be lighted either by luminaires mounted on the building or by luminaires mounted on poles and aimed at the building (see figure 33-8). The important point for both approaches is to ensure that all points of entry to the building are lighted. As points of entry consist of not only the doors and windows but also the roof, this usually means uniformly lighting the whole building. The illuminance to be provided on the face of the building is given in figure 33-6. The ratio between the average and the minimum illuminance on the building facade should not be greater than 8:1. Again, It is useful to have a high surface reflectance either adjacent to the building (such as stone chippings) or on the building facade itself.

Perimeter Fences. The purpose of lighting perimeter fences is to enable guards to detect anybody loitering outside the fence or attempting to get over or through it. Fences come in several different forms, which vary in their obstruction to vision. Masonry walls are opaque. Chain link fences allow some vision through them, but this will vary with the angle of view. The form of lighting used will depend on the possibility of seeing through the fence and whether one or both sides of the fence line are to be patrolled.

If the fence is solid, there is no possibility of seeing through it. Nonetheless, lighting can be provided on both sides by positioning a luminaire over the top of the fence. This is particularly useful if CCTV surveillance on both sides is to be used.

If a view through the fence is possible and if the fence is patrolled from either inside or outside the secure area, it is useful to be able to see both sides of the fence. For this, lighting needs to be provided on both sides. This can be done from pole-mounted fixtures set back from the fence (see figure 33-9). However, it will be most effective if the luminance of the fence is lower than the luminance of the area on the side being viewed through the fence. This objective can be achieved by using a low-reflectance fence material such as black or green coated chain link rather than galvanized chain link. If galvanized chain link is used, care should be taken with the aiming of the luminaires to reduce the illuminance directly onto the fence.

The glare system described in this chapter can also be used for perimeter fences enclosing large areas in remote locations. In this situation any patrol road should be set behind the glare lights.

Entrances. The entrance to a secure site (see figure 33-10) can be the most vulnerable area. It is the area where crime by deception will be attempted. This means that the lighting provided has to be matched to the type of inspection that occurs in the entrance. That can range from the examination of documents to the inspection of the underside of vehicles. The illuminance recommendation for secure entrances is given in figure 33-6, but illuminance alone is not enough. The lighting should have good color rendering properties so that the color of people, documents, goods and vehicles can be easily discriminated. Further, the distribution of light is important, particularly if vehicles or their contents are to be inspected. Again, having a concrete road surface to increase the reflected light

Fig. 33-10. Secure entrances must be sufficiently illuminated to enable inspection of visitors or automobiles.

will help in the inspection of the underside of vehicles; luminaires set into the road surface will be even better.

Gatehouses. A gatehouse is usually an element in an entrance and a base for guards. A common mistake in the lighting of gatehouses is to light the inside brightly. This reduces the dark adaptation of the guard and allows anyone outside to see how many guards are in the gatehouse and what they are doing. A better approach is to light the inside of the gatehouse much more dimly than the area outside. This can be achieved by fitting the gatehouse with specular-reflecting, low-transmission glass at a tilted angle, painting the inside of the gatehouse in dark colors and ensuring that its lighting is dimmable. Figure 33-11 shows a typical installation.

CCTV Surveillance. The surveillance of a large area can be most economically done with a number of CCTV cameras feeding pictures to a central control room, provided always that there is some method of response established for those occasions when an intruder is detected. CCTV cameras do not have the same spectral sensitivity as the human eye and therefore respond differently to light sources. Most CCTV camera manufacturers specify a minimum illuminance

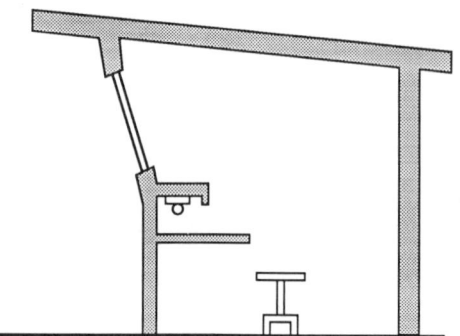

Fig. 33-11. Gatehouses should be painted in dark colors and use well-shielded luminaires and tilted windows to minimize reflections and disability glare.

Fig. 33-12. CCTV surveillance stations such as this airport installation should use luminaires and room surfaces which produce low luminances to prevent glare in monitor screens.

needed for their cameras to produce a clear picture. These illuminances are usually given for an incandescent lamp. Higher illuminance will be required for other light sources. Further, if moving objects are to be easily seen, illuminances above the minimum will be required, whatever the light source. The camera manufacturer should be consulted before selecting the light source to be used if there is any doubt about the sensitivity of the camera. As a last resort, the performance of most CCTV cameras used in surveillance systems can be improved by the addition of some tungsten-halogen floodlighting.

The other aspect of CCTV cameras which needs care is their rather limited dynamic range. Care should be taken to mount surveillance cameras below the lighting fixtures so that they do not receive any light directly from the fixtures. This is necessary if "white-out" of part of the image is to be avoided. As for the lighting, care should be taken to evenly light all the surfaces which are to be seen by the camera.

The security station containing the monitors for CCTV surveillance should also be carefully lighted to avoid reflections from interior luminaires in the monitor screens. See figure 33-12.

Interaction with Adjacent Areas. The influence of the ambient lighting on the choice of security lighting has already been mentioned. However, the reverse should also be considered, namely, the influence of the security lighting system on the surrounding area. Such effects as local light pollution can give rise to complaints from neighbors. Other possibilities concern safety effects on neighboring roads and railroads due to glare. Further, where signal lights are used to control traffic on roads, railroads or rivers or at sea, care should be taken to avoid confusion caused by either disability glare directly from the security lighting, veiling reflections on the signals from the security lighting, or the identification of the security lighting as a signal. This involves making sure that the security lighting is limited to the secure area. If there is any doubt about this question, the appropriate authorities should be consulted, such as the U.S. Coast Guard for navigable channels and waterways.

Equipment

Light Sources. The factors which should be considered in selecting a light source are its luminous efficacy, its color properties, its restrike and runup times and its performance at temperatures likely to occur on the site. Luminous efficacy obviously has a major influence on the cost of operating the security lighting installation. The color properties are important for the accurate description of people and objects, though not necessarily for the detection of their presence. Restrike and runup times are important because they relate to how rapidly the security lighting will respond following an interruption of electric supply. The sensitivity to temperature is important because not all lamps operate well at very low or very high temperatures. Light sources suitable for security lighting are all reviewed in chapter 6, Light Sources.

Luminaires. All the luminaires suitable for security lighting are reviewed generically in chapter 7, Luminaires. Luminaires should be evaluated in terms of their efficiency and light distribution. Inefficient equipment is wasteful, and luminaires with inappropriate light distribution can give very nonuniform lighting and may produce light pollution of the surrounding area.

REFERENCES

1. Boyce, P. R. 1985. Movement under emergency lighting: The effect of illuminance. *Light. Res. Tech.* 17(2):51–71.
2. Boyce, P. R. 1986. Movement under emergency lighting: The effects of changeover from normal lighting. *Light. Res. Tech.* 18(1):1–18.
3. Jaschinski, W. 1982. Conditions of emergency lighting. *Ergonomics* 25(5):363–372.
4. Ouellette, M. J., and M. S. Rea. 1989. Illuminance requirements for emergency lighting. *J. Illum. Eng. Soc.* 18(1):37–42.
5. Simmons, R. C. 1975. Illuminance, diversity and disability glare in emergency lighting. *Light. Res. Tech.* 7(2):125–132.
6. Nikitin, V. D. 1973. Minimum required level of illumination intensity for emergency illumination in evacuation of persons. *Svetotechnica* 6:9–10.
7. National Fire Protection Association. *National electrical code, ANSI / NFPA 70.* Quincy, MA: National Fire Protection Association.
8. Webber, G. M. B. 1985. Emergency lighting recommendations. In *Proceedings of the International Conference on Building Use and Safety Technology, Los Angeles CA, March 12–14, 1985.* National Institute of Building Sciences.
9. Webber, G. M. B., P. J. Hallman, and A. C. Salvidge. 1988. Movement under emergency lighting: Comparison between standard provisions and photoluminescent markings. *Light. Res. Tech.* 20(4):167–175.
10. Webber, G. M. B. 1987. Way out lighting. *Build. Serv.* 9(8):39–40.
11. Webber, G. M. B., and P. J. Hallman. 1987. Emergency lighting and movement through corridors and stairways. In *Contemporary Ergonomics: Proceedings of the Ergonomic Society's 1987 Annual Conference, Swansea, Wales, April 6–10, 1987.* E. D. Megaw, ed. London: Taylor & Francis.
12. Webber, G. M. B., and P. J. Hallman. 1988. Movement under various escape route lighting conditions. In *Safety in the built environment.* J. D. Sime, ed. London: E. & F. N. Spon.
13. Green, L. 1986. Emergency lighting. *Specif. Eng.* 55(4):117–119.
14. Clark, F. R. S., M. S. Rea, and M. J. Ouellette. 1985. Visibility of exit signs through smoke. In *Pre-conference proceedings: International Conference on Building Use and Safety Technology, Los Angeles CA, March 12–14, 1985.*
15. Ouellette, M. J. 1988. Exit signs in smoke: Design parameters for greater visibility. *Light. Res. Tech.* 20(4):155–160.
16. U.S. Department of Transportation. Federal Aviation Administration. 1979. *Readability of self-illuminated signs in a smoke-obscured environment.* FAA-AM-79-22, FAA-ARD-79-108. Prepared by P. G. Rasmussen, J. D. Garner, J. G. Blethrow, and D. L. Lowrey. Washington: Federal Aviation Administration.
17. Rea, M. S. 1985. How good are emergency lighting systems? *Light. Des. Appl.* 15(9):26–27.
18. Jin, T., S. Takahashi, S. Kawai, Y. Takeuchi and R. Tanabe. 1983. Experimental study on visibility and conspicuousness of an exit sign. *Proceedings: 21st session. Commission Internationale de l'Eclairage,* Venice, June 1987. Vienna: Bureau Central de la CIE.
19. U.S. National Bureau of Standards. 1978. *Smoke measurements in large and small scale fire testing.* NBSIR 78-1502. Prepared by R. W. Bukowski. Gaithersburg, MD: National Bureau of Standards.
20. Cooper, L. Y. 1988. Compartment fire-generated environment and smoke filling. In *SFPE handbook of fire protection engineering.* 1st ed., chapter 7. Quincy, MA: National Fire Protection Association.
21. National Fire Protection Association. 1991. Illumination of means of egress, emergency lighting, and markings of means of egress. In *Life safety code, NFPA 101,* sections 5-8–5-10. Quincy, MA: National Fire Protection Association.
22. Underwriters Laboratories. 1989. *Exit fixture and exit light visibility. Standard for safety: Emergency lighting and power equipment, UL-924.* Northbrook, IL: Underwriters Laboratories, Inc.

23. Commission Internationale de l'Éclairage. 1981. *Guide on the Emergency Lighting of Building Interiors.* CIE Publication 49. Paris: Bureau Central de la CIE.

24. International Standardization Organization. 1984. *Safety colours and safety signs, ISO 3864.* Geneva, Switzerland: International Standardization Organization.

25. National Fire Protection Association. 1991. *Standard Public Fire Safety Symbols, NFPA 170.*

26. U.S. National Bureau of Standards. 1983. *Evaluation of exit symbol visibility.* NBSIR 83-2675. Prepared by B. L. Collins and N. D. Lerner. Washington: National Bureau of Standards.

27. U.S. National Bureau of Standards. 1983. *Size of letters required for visibility as a function of viewing distance and observer visual acuity.* NBS TN 1180. Prepared by G. L. Howett. Washington: National Bureau of Standards.

28. U.S. National Eye Institute. 1983. *Vision research: A national plan 1983–1987: Vol. 1.* NIH/PUB 83-2469; NEI 80-306-1. Washington: National Institutes of Health.

29. Associate Committee on the National Building Code of Canada. 1990. Lighting and emergency power systems, Subsection 3.2.7; Exit signs, Subsection 3.4.5. *National Building Code of Canada 1990.* Ottawa: National Research Council, Institute for Research in Construction.

30. U.S. National Institute of Standards and Technology. 1990. *Evaluation of exit signs in clear and smoke conditions.* NISTIR 4399. Prepared by B. L. Collins, M. S. Dahir, and D. Madrzykowski. Gaithersburg, MD: National Institute of Standards and Technology.

31. Rea, M. S., F. R. S. Clark and M. J. Ouellette. 1985. *Photometric and psychophysical measurements of exit signs through smoke.* NRCC 24627. [Ottawa]: National Research Council Canada.

32. U.S. Department of Transportation. Federal Aviation Administration. 1989. *Emergency exit marking, emergency lighting, and emergency exit access.* 14 CFR 25.811–25.813. Washington: U.S. Government Printing Office.

33. Wilson, I. 1990. The effectiveness of exit signs in smoke. *Light. Aust.* (February):14–19.

34. Jin, T., and T. Yamada. 1985. Irritating Effects of Fire Smoke on Visibility. *Fire Sci. Tech.* 5(1):79–90.

35. U.S. Department of Transportation. Federal Aviation Administration. 1982. *Examination of aircraft interior emergency lighting in a postcrash fire environment.* DOT/FAA/CT-82/55. Prepared by J. Demaree. Washington: Federal Aviation Administration.

36. Beyreis, J. R., and T. G. Castino. 1974. Safety in sight. *Labdata* 5(1):14–19.

37. Collins, B. L. 1991. Visibility of exit signs and directional indicators. *J. Illum. Eng. Soc.* 20(1):117–133.

38. Standards Association of Australia. 1983. *Emergency evacuation lighting in buildings. Part 1: Installation requirements, AS2293, Part 1-1983.* North Sydney, N.S.W.: Standards Association of Australia.

39. Hurvich, L. M. 1981. *Color vision.* Sunderland, MA: Sinauer Associates.

40. California. Office of State Fire Marshall. [1985]. *A feasibility study on the placement of egress signage at lower positions than is currently common: A report to the California State Legislature by the Office of the State Fire Marshal in response to SCR 32.* [Sacramento]: Office of State Fire Marshall.

41. American National Standards Institute. 1979. *American national standard safety color code for marking physical hazards, ANSI Z53.1-1979.* New York: American National Standards Institute.

42. IES. Color Committee. 1980. Potential misidentification of industrial safety colors with certain lighting. *Light. Des. Appl.* 10(11):20.

43. Joint Lighting Survey Committee. IES. Lighting Survey Committee, and U.S. Department of Health, Education and Welfare. Public Health Service. 1963. How to make a lighting survey. *Illum. Eng.* 58(2):87–100.

Environmental Issues

34

LIGHTING AND AiR POLLUTION

Electricity generation produces pollution, so reducing energy consumption can significantly reduce pollution over the long term. This is the basic concept behind the U.S. Environmental Protection Agency (EPA) Green Lights Program,[1,2] which encourages every American organization to switch to more energy-efficient lighting.

Many power plants burn coal, oil or natural gas to generate electricity, and in so doing add carbon dioxide (CO_2), sulfur dioxide (SO_2) and nitrogen oxides (NO_x) to the atmosphere. Carbon dioxide contributes to global warming; sulfur dioxide, to acid rain; and nitrogen oxides, to both acid rain and smog.

On a national average basis, taking into account all power plants (including nuclear and hydroelectric), each kilowatthour of electricity *not sold* eliminates the emission of 680 g (1.5 lb) of CO_2, 5.8 g of SO_2 and 2.5 g of NO_x compounds. The U.S. government estimates that if all of the profitable energy-efficient lighting upgrades were implemented by the year 2000, power plant CO_2 emissions would be reduced by 202 million metric tons (equivalent to those produced by 44 million automobiles); SO_2 emissions by 1.3 million metric tons; and NO_x compounds by 0.6 million metric tons. For more information on reducing energy consumption in lighting systems, refer to chapter 30, Energy Management, and chapter 31, Lighting Controls.

BALLAST DISPOSAL

The main factor to consider in the disposal of ballasts for fluorescent lighting systems is whether or not the ballasts contain polychlorinated biphenyl (PCB) compounds, which have been linked to cancer in animals and are also suspected of causing cancer in humans. The capacitors found in most ballasts manufactured through 1979 are filled with about 30–90 g (1–3 oz) of virtually pure PCB fluid. Through the Toxic Substances Control Act (TSCA) of 1976, the United States Government declared PCBs to be hazardous waste and banned their manufacture and sale.

Later ballasts made without PCBs are labeled "No PCBs." Any ballast not so labeled should be assumed to contain PCBs and should be disposed of according to the regulations in effect in the state where the ballasts will be discarded.

Many states in the United States have enacted legislation to ban PCB ballasts from municipal sanitary landfills, and several more are considering such legislation. Many municipal landfills in other states refuse to accept any PCB waste, including ballasts, because of fear of potential liability in the event that PCB leakage will contaminate the entire landfill. A 0.45-kg (1-lb) spill of PCBs, the amount contained in as few as 12–16 ballasts, is sufficient under the Comprehensive Environmental Response, Compensation, and Liability Act for the U.S. federal government to declare a Superfund hazardous waste cleanup site. The parties responsible for the spill would share liability for the cleanup costs and environmental damage. Thus, only very small quantities of ballasts may legally be disposed of at a municipal landfill, and only in some states. In the United States, for additional information on Superfund issues, contact personnel at the EPA Resource Conservation and Recovery Act (RCRA)/Superfund hotline at (800) 424-9346.

In Canada, disposal in sanitary landfills of any component containing PCBs is prohibited. In Mexico, the disposal of ballasts containing PCBs is unregulated.

Ballasts Without PCBs

If ballasts are PCB free, disposal at any municipal landfill or incinerator is probably the least expensive option. As a more environmentally responsible choice, non-PCB ballasts may be recycled to recover the asphalt, copper, steel and aluminum they contain. This costs approximately $1–2 per ballast.

Leaking Ballasts with PCBs

Under U.S. law, leaking PCB ballasts are classified as hazardous waste and must be incinerated at an EPA-approved high-temperature incinerator. The condition of ballasts should be determined before they are removed from luminaires, because any materials that come in contact with leaking ballasts are also considered hazardous waste and must be disposed of according to federal regulations.

Handling of leaking PCB ballasts should be performed only by trained, authorized personnel. For packing, storage, transportation and disposal information, contact the EPA Toxic Substances Control assistance hotline at (202) 554-1404.

Nonleaking Ballasts with PCBs

If the ballasts contain PCBs and are not leaking, the disposer has several options:

- *Leave disconnected ballasts in luminaires.* Although this option is temptingly simple, the National Fire Protection Agency (NFPA) recommends against it. In the event of a fire, PCBs may burn incompletely, posing a serious health threat to building occupants and fire fighters. Utilities that offer rebates for energy-efficient ballasts are also wary of this option, because of the possibility that an old ballast will be reconnected when a new ballast fails. When upgrading a lighting system, the lighting engineer should ensure that all disconnected ballasts containing PCBs are removed and properly disposed of.
- *Sanitary landfill.* The relatively low short-term costs of this option are offset by the potential liability in the event that the landfill is declared a hazardous waste cleanup site. Even if a spill is never reported, the probability is high that the ballasts will eventually rupture and release PCBs into the environment. Increasingly few municipal landfills are willing to accept PCB ballasts in any quantity.
- *Municipal incinerator.* Because the incomplete burning of PCBs breaks them down into substances which are even more toxic, this is one of the worst ways to dispose of PCB ballasts.
- *Hazardous-waste landfill.* PCB ballasts can be packed into 55-gal drums and shipped to designated hazardous-waste landfills by hazardous-waste disposal companies. Although such landfills are sealed to prevent chemical leaks, they are not designed to handle the 70–100%-pure PCB fluid contained in ballasts. A ruptured drum could result in a severe PCB spill requiring Superfund cleanup, for which the disposer would be partly liable.
- *High-temperature incineration.* PCBs can be destroyed when burned under the proper high-temperature conditions. Incineration is the only method of disposal that removes the hazardous

materials from the environment and also eliminates the threat of future liability if PCBs should be released. Incinerating the entire ballast is the most expensive disposal option, costing $6–10 per ballast, largely because of the scarcity of operational incinerators.
- *High-temperature incineration and recycling.* The most environmentally responsible method of disposal is to incinerate only the PCB-laden capacitor while recycling the nonhazardous materials (such as copper and aluminum) from the remainder of the ballast. Several firms offer this service, typically at a cost of $2–4 per ballast.

Documentation

When disposing of ballasts which contain PCBs, be sure to document fully all aspects of the disposal process, including:

- Year, make and quantity of ballasts
- Documentation from hazardous-waste haulers
- Certificates of destruction from the contractor, validating the disposal of the ballasts by high-temperature incineration or their placement in a hazardous-waste landfill

Nonleaking Small-Capacitor Fluorescent Lamp Ballasts

Nonleaking small-capacitor fluorescent ballasts that contain PCBs are not covered under U.S. federal law. Ballasts are classified as "small-capacitor" ballasts if the weight of the dielectric fluid in the capacitor is less than 1.36 kg (3 lb). Generally, a capacitor with a total volume of less than 1639 cm^3 (100 in^3) contains less than the specified amount, and one over 3278 cm^3 (200 in^3) contains more. Ballasts with a total volume between these two values are considered to contain less than 1.36 kg of dielectric fluid if the total weight of the capacitor is less than 4.08 kg (9 lb).

The Environmental Protection Agency (EPA) encourages disposal of these small-capacitor PCB ballasts in the same responsible manner as larger ballasts that contain PCBs. Large quantities (more than 25 ballasts) should be sent to hazardous-waste landfills or high-temperature incinerators.

LAMPS CONTAINING MERCURY

Fluorescent and high-intensity discharge (HID) lamps contain small quantities of mercury, cadmium and antimony. Disposal of mercury-containing lamps is covered in the United States by federal regulations only if the quantity of mercury exceeds that allowed under the

Resource Conservation and Recovery Act. Determining how much mercury is in a batch of lamps is difficult because the amount per lamp can vary, even in the same installation. When a material fails one of the hazard characterization tests (toxicity, flammability, corrosivity and ignitability), it must be handled as a hazardous waste material. The EPA completed tests indicating that its sample of fluorescent lamps failed the test for toxicity and therefore constituted hazardous waste materials. Additional information on the management of hazardous wastes may be obtained from the EPA RCRA/Superfund hotline described above in the section on Ballast Disposal.

Several states have policies concerning the disposal of fluorescent lamps. In those states, used mercury-containing lamps are classified as hazardous waste and their disposal is regulated. Other states are considering enacting similar regulations. Consult with regional EPA offices and state agencies before disposing of fluorescent or HID lamps.

Glass from fluorescent lamps can be remanufactured for nonfood containers or reused as fillers in cement and asphalt. End caps can be sent to an aluminum recycler for remanufacturing. Mercury can be recovered by a mercury distiller and then reused for thermometers and other products. The cost of recycling or properly disposing of a fluorescent lamp is between \$0.50 and \$1.00. This cost is quite low in comparison with the total cost of lamp purchase, installation and operation.

Some companies also recycle HID lamps. The EPA publishes lists of recycling facilities, although the organization does not screen them and such listing is not an endorsement of their recycling methods.

When planning a lighting upgrade, all disposal options should be thoroughly investigated. Include recycling of fluorescent lamps in specifications, and ask for certification, licenses and references from all contractors or subcontractors providing waste disposal services. Be specific in your requests, and insist on documentation to show that all hazardous wastes have been disposed of properly.

REFERENCES

1. U.S. Environmental Protection Agency. Global Change Division. 1991. Green Lights Program. In *Green Lights Program lighting upgrade manual.* 1st ed., chapter 1. Washington: Environmental Protection Agency.

2. U.S. Environmental Protection Agency. Global Change Division. 1991. Waste disposal. In *Green Lights Program lighting upgrade manual.* 1st ed., chapter 8. Washington: Environmental Protection Agency.

Glossary of Lighting Terminology

As the title implies, this last chapter contains terminology directly related to light and lighting practice. All terms are presented in alphabetical order and are followed by their standard symbols or abbreviations and their defining equations where applicable, by their definitions and by other related terms of interest. No attempt has been made to provide information on pronunciations or etymologies. Definitions of electrical terms common to lighting and to other fields are available in the *American National Standard Dictionary of Electrical and Electronics Terms* (ANSI/IEEE 100-1984).

Any of the radiometric and photometric quantities that follow may be restricted to a narrow wavelength interval $\Delta\lambda$ by the addition of the word "spectral" and the specification of the wavelength λ. The corresponding symbols are changed by adding a subscript λ, as in Q_λ for a spectral concentration, or a λ in parentheses, as in $K(\lambda)$ for a function of wavelength. The appendix is a tabulated summary of standard units, symbols and defining equations for the fundamental photometric and radiometric quantities. Other symbols, abbreviations and conversion factors are also given in the appendix.

Most of the definitions in this glossary have been adapted from ANSI/IES RP-16-1986, *Nomenclature and Definitions for Illuminating Engineering*. Those marked with a dagger (†) do not appear in the ANSI standard.

A

absolute luminance threshold the luminance threshold for a bright object like a disk on a totally dark background.

absorptance, $\alpha = \Phi_a/\Phi_i$ the ratio of the flux absorbed by a medium to the incident flux. See *absorption*.
  Note The sum of the hemispherical reflectance, the hemispherical transmittance and the absorptance is one.

absorption a general term for the process by which incident flux is converted to another form of energy, usually and ultimately to heat.
  Note All of the incident flux is accounted for by the processes of reflection, transmission and absorption.

accent lighting directional lighting to emphasize a particular object or to draw attention to a part of the field of view. See *directional lighting*.

accommodation the process by which the eye changes focus from one distance to another.

actinic photochemically active.

action spectrum the quantitative actinic response of a chemical or biological substance or living organism as a function of an appropriate spectral parameter such as wavelength or photon energy.

adaptation the process by which the retina becomes accustomed to more or less light than it was exposed to during an immediately preceding period. It results in a change in the sensitivity to light. See *scotopic vision, photopic vision, chromatic adaptation*.
  Note "Adaptation" is also used to refer to the final state of the process, as in "reaching a condition of adaptation to a specific luminance level."

adaptive color shift the change in the perceived object color caused solely by change of the state of chromatic adaptation.

adverse weather lamp See *fog lamp*.

aerodrome beacon an aeronautical beacon used to indicate the location of an aerodrome.
  Note An *aerodrome* is any defined area on land or water, including any buildings, installations and equipment, intended to be used either wholly or in part for the arrival, departure and movement of aircraft.

aeronautical beacon an aeronautical ground light visible at all azimuths, either continuously or intermittently, to designate a particular location on the surface of the earth. See *aerodrome beacon, airway beacon, hazard or obstruction beacon* and *landmark beacon*.

aeronautical ground light any light specially provided as an aid to air navigation, other than a light displayed on an aircraft. See *aeronautical beacon, angle-of-approach lights, approach lights, approach-light beacon, bar (of lights), boundary lights, circling guidance lights, course light, channel lights, obstruction lights, runway alignment indicator, runway end identification light, perimeter lights, runway lights, taxi-channel lights* and *taxiway lights*.

aeronautical light any luminous sign or signal specially provided as an aid to air navigation.

after image a visual response that occurs after the stimulus causing it has ceased.

aircraft aeronautical light any aeronautical light specially provided on an aircraft. See *navigation light system, anti-collision light, ice detection light, fuselage lights, landing light, position lights* and *taxi light*.

airway beacon an aeronautical beacon used to indicate a point on the airway.

alphanumeric display (digital display)   an electrically operated display of characters. Tungsten filaments, gas discharges, light-emitting diodes, liquid crystals, projected or illuminated characters and other principles of operation may be used.

altitude (in daylighting)   the angular distance of a heavenly body measured on the great circle that passes perpendicular to the plane of the horizon through the body and through the zenith. It is measured positively from the horizon to the zenith, from $0°$ to $90°$.

ambient lighting   lighting throughout an area that produces general illumination.

anchor light (aircraft)   an aircraft light designed for use on a seaplane or amphibian to indicate its position when at anchor or moored.

angle-of-approach lights   aeronautical ground lights arranged so as to indicate a desired angle of descent during an approach to an aerodrome runway. (Also called optical glide path lights.)

angle of collimation   the angle subtended by a light source at a point on an irradiated surface.

angstrom, Å   a unit of wavelength equal to 10^{-10} m (one ten-billionth of a meter).

anticollision light   a flashing aircraft aeronautical light or system of lights designed to provide a red signal throughout $360°$ of azimuth for the purpose of giving long-range indication of an aircraft's location to pilots of other aircraft.

aperture color[†]   the perceived color of the sky or of a patch seen through an aperture and not identifiable as belonging to a specific object.

apostilb (asb)   a lambertian unit of luminance equal to $1/\pi$ (0.3183) cd/m^2. This term is obsolete and its use is deprecated.

approach-light beacon   an aeronautical ground light placed on the extended centerline of the runway at a fixed distance from the runway threshold to provide an early indication of position during an approach to a runway.
Note   The runway threshold is the beginning of the runway usable for landing.

approach lights   a configuration of aeronautical ground lights located in extension of a runway or channel before the threshold to provide visual approach and landing guidance to pilots. See angle-of-approach lights, approach-light beacon and VASIS.

arc discharge   an electric discharge characterized by high cathode current densities and a low voltage drop at the cathode.
Note   The cathode voltage drop is small compared with that in a glow discharge, and secondary emission plays only a small part in electron emission from the cathode.

arc lamp   a discharge lamp in which the light is emitted by an arc discharge or by its electrodes.
Note   The electrodes may be either of carbon (operating in air) or of metal.

artificial pupil   a device or arrangement for confining the light passing through the pupil of the eye to an area smaller than the natural pupil.

atmospheric transmissivity   the ratio of the directly transmitted flux incident on a surface after passing through unit thickness of the atmosphere to the flux that would be incident on the same surface if the flux had passed through a vacuum.

average luminance   the luminous intensity at a given angle divided by the projected area of the luminaire at that angle. Luminance is a property of a geometric ray. Luminance as measured by conventional meters is averaged with respect to two independent variables, area and solid angle; both must be defined for a complete description of a luminance measurement.

azimuth   the angular distance between the vertical plane containing a given line or celestial body and the plane of the meridian.

B

back light   illumination from behind (and usually above) a subject to produce a highlight along its edge and consequent separation between the subject and its background. See side back light.

backing lighting   the illumination provided for scenery in off-stage areas visible to the audience.

backup lamp   a lighting device mounted on the rear of a vehicle for illuminating the region near the rear of the vehicle while moving or about to move in reverse. It normally can be used only while backing up.

bactericidal (germicidal) effectiveness   the capacity of various portions of the ultraviolet (UV) spectrum to destroy bacteria, fungi and viruses.

bactericidal (germicidal) efficiency of radiant flux (for a particular wavelength)   the ratio of the bactericidal effectiveness at a particular wavelength to that at wavelength 265.0 nm, which is rated as 1.0.
Note   Tentative values of the bactericidal efficiency of various wavelengths of radiant flux are given in chapter 5, Nonvisual Effects of Radiant Energy.

bactericidal (germicidal) exposure   the product of bactericidal flux density on a surface and time. It usually is expressed in bactericidal $\mu W \cdot min/cm^2$ or bactericidal $W \cdot min/ft^2$.

bactericidal (germicidal) flux   radiant flux evaluated according to its capacity to produce bactericidal effects. It usually is measured in microwatts of UV radiation weighted in accordance with its bactericidal efficiency, cited as "bactericidal microwatts."
Note   Radiated UV power at wavelength 253.7 nm usually is referred to as "ultraviolet microwatts" or "UV watts." These terms should not be confused with "bactericidal microwatts," because they refer to radiation that has not been weighted in accordance with the values given in chapter 5, Nonvisual Effects of Radiant Energy.

bactericidal (germicidal) flux density   the bactericidal flux per unit area of the surface being irradiated. It is equal to the incident bactericidal flux divided by the area of the surface when the flux is uniformly distributed. It usually is measured in $\mu W/cm^2$ or W/ft^2 of bactericidally weighted UV radiation (bactericidal $\mu W/cm^2$ or bactericidal W/ft^2).

bactericidal lamp   a UV lamp that radiates a significant portion of its radiative power in the UV-C band (100–280 nm).

baffle a single opaque or translucent element to shield a source from direct view at certain angles, to absorb or block unwanted light, or to reflect and redirect light.

balcony lights luminaires mounted on the front edge of an auditorium balcony.

ballast a device used with an electric-discharge lamp to obtain the necessary circuit conditions (voltage, current and waveform) for starting and operating. See *reference ballast*.

ballast factor the flux of a fluorescent lamp(s) operated on a ballast as a fraction of the flux when operated on the standard (reference) ballasting specified for rating lamp lumens.

Note The lamp(s) are at specified ambient temperature conditions for photometric testing.

ballast-lamp photometric factor the ratio of fluorescent luminaire lumen output with a given ballast and lamp type under photometric conditions to that with the lamp type used to generate a photometric test.

Note This factor is applicable when "energy-conserving" lamps and ballasts are used in a luminaire photometered with standard lamps and conventional ballasts, and vice versa.

bar (of lights) a group of three or more aeronautical ground lights placed in a line transverse to the axis, or extended axis, of the runway. See *barrette*.

bare (exposed) lamp a light source with no shielding.

barn doors a set of adjustable flaps, usually two or four (two-way or four-way), that may be attached to the front of a luminaire (usually a Fresnel spotlight) in order to alter the shape and spread of the light beam.

barrette (in aviation) a short bar in which the lights are closely spaced so that from a distance they appear to be a linear light.

Note Barrettes are usually no longer than 4.6 m (15 ft).

base light uniform, diffuse, near-shadowless illumination sufficiently intense for a television or film picture of acceptable quality at a desired lens opening. The acceptable base level of unaccented base illumination.

beacon a light (or mark) used to indicate a geographic location. See *aerodrome beacon, aeronautical beacon, airway beacon, approach-light beacon, hazard or obstruction beacon, identification beacon* and *landmark beacon*.

beam angle the angle between the two directions for which the intensity is 50% of the maximum intensity as measured in a plane through the nominal beam centerline. For beams that do not possess rotational symmetry, the beam angle is generally given for two planes at 90°, typically the maximum and minimum angles.

Note In certain fields of application, the beam angle was formerly measured to 10% of maximum intensity.

beam axis of a projector a line midway between two lines that intersect the intensity distribution curve at points equal to a stated percentage of its maximum (usually 50%).

beam lumens the total flux in that region of space where the intensity exceeds 50% of the maximum intensity.

beam projector a luminaire with the light source at or near the focus of a paraboloidal reflector, producing near-parallel rays of light in a beam of small divergence. Some are equipped with spill rings to reduce spill and glare. In most types, the lamp may be moved toward or away from the reflector to vary the beam spread.

beam spread (in any plane) the angle between the two directions in the plane in which the intensity is equal to a stated percentage of the maximum beam intensity.

biconical reflectance, $\rho(\omega_i; \omega_r)$ the ratio of the reflected flux collected through a conical solid angle to the incident flux limited to a conical solid angle.

Note The directions and extent of each cone must be specified; the solid angle need not be a right circular cone.

biconical transmittance, $\tau(\omega_i; \omega_t)$ the ratio of the transmitted flux collected through a conical solid angle to the incident flux limited to a conical solid angle.

Note The directions and extent of each cone must be specified; the solid angle need not be a right circular cone.

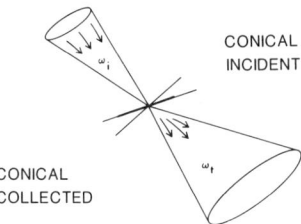

bidirectional reflectance, $\rho(\theta_i, \phi_i; \theta_r, \phi_r)$ the ratio of the reflected flux collected over an element of solid angle surrounding the given direction to the essentially collimated incident flux.

Note The directions of incidence and collection and the size of the solid angle element of collection must be specified. In each case of conical incidence or collection, the solid angle need not be a right circular cone, but may be of any cross section, including a rectangle, a ring, or a combination of two or more solid angles.

bidirectional reflectance distribution function (BRDF), f_r *the ratio of the differential luminance* $dL_r(\theta_r, \phi_r)$ *of a ray reflected in a given direction* (θ_r, ϕ_r) *to the differential luminous flux density* $dE_i(\theta_i, \phi_i)$ *incident from a given direction of incidence,* (θ_i, ϕ_i), *which produces it:*

$$f_r(\theta_i, \phi_i; \theta_r, \phi_r) \equiv \frac{dL_r(\theta_r, \phi_r)}{dE_i(\theta_i, \phi_i)} \qquad (\text{sr}^{-1})$$

$$= \frac{dL_r(\theta_r, \phi_r)}{L_i(\theta_i, \phi_i)\, d\Omega_i}$$

where $d\Omega \equiv d\omega \cos \theta$.

Note This distribution function is the basic parameter for describing (geometrically) the reflecting properties of an opaque surface element (negligible internal scattering). It may have any positive value and will approach infinity in the specular direction for ideally specular reflectors. The spectral and polarization aspects must be defined for complete specification, since the BRDF as given above only defines the geometric aspects.

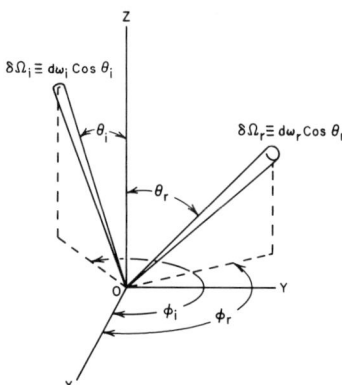

bidirectional transmittance, $\tau(\theta_i, \phi_i; \theta_t, \phi_t)$ The ratio of the incident flux collected over an element of solid angle surrounding the given direction to the essentially collimated incident flux.
Note The direction of incidence, direction of collection and size of the solid angle element must be specified.

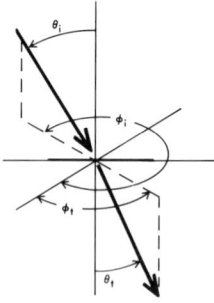

bidirectional transmittance distribution function (BTDF), f_t the ratio of the differential luminance $dL_t(\theta_t, \phi_t)$ of a ray transmitted in a given direction (θ_t, ϕ_t) to the differential luminous flux density $dE_i(\theta_i, \phi_i)$ incident from a given direction of incidence (θ_i, ϕ_i) that produces it:

$$f_t(\theta_i, \phi_i; \theta_t, \phi_t) \equiv \frac{dL_t(\theta_t, \phi_t)}{dE_i(\theta_i, \phi_i)} \quad (sr^{-1})$$

$$= \frac{dL_t(\theta_t, \phi_t)}{L_i(\theta_i, \phi_i)\, d\Omega_i}$$

where $d\Omega \equiv d\omega \cos \theta$.
Note This distribution is the basic parameter for describing (geometrically) the transmitting properties of a thin scattering film (with negligible internal scattering) so that the transmitted radiation emerges from a point that is not significantly separated from the point of incidence of the incident ray(s). The governing considerations are similar to those for application of the *bidirectional reflectance distribution function* (BRDF), rather than the bidirectional scattering-surface reflectance distribution function (BS-

SRDF). This function may have any positive value and will approach infinity in the direction for regular transmission (possibly with refraction but without scattering). The spectral and polarization aspects must be defined for complete specification, since the BTDF as given above only defines the geometrical aspects.

bihemispherical reflectance, $\rho(2\pi; 2\pi)$ The ratio of the reflected flux collected over an entire hemisphere to the incident flux from the entire hemisphere.

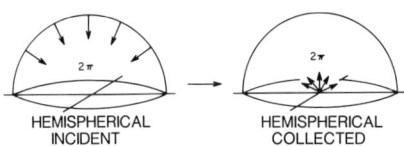

bihemispherical transmittance, $\tau(2\pi; 2\pi)$ The ratio of the transmitted flux collected over an entire hemisphere to the incident flux from the entire hemisphere.

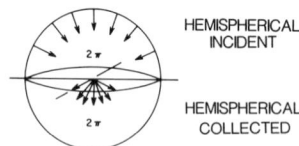

binocular portion of the visual field that portion of space where the fields of the two eyes overlap.
biological rhythm a characteristic periodic change in a living organism or life-related process. Some biological rhythms are induced or synchronized by light.
blackbody a temperature radiator of uniform temperature whose radiant exitance in all parts of the spectrum is the maximum obtainable from any temperature radiator at the same temperature. Such a radiator is called a blackbody because it will absorb all the radiant energy that falls upon it. All other temperature radiators are called nonblackbodies. They radiate less in some or all wavelength intervals than a blackbody of the same size and the same temperature.
Note The blackbody is practically realized over limited solid angles in the form of a cavity with opaque walls at a uniform temperature and with a small opening for observation. It also is called a full radiator, standard radiator, complete radiator or ideal radiator.
blackbody (planckian) locus the locus of points on a chromaticity diagram representing the chromaticities of blackbodies having various (color) temperatures.
"black light" the popular term for UV energy near the visible region.
Note For engineering purposes the wavelength range 320–400 nm has been found useful for rating lamps and their effectiveness upon fluorescent materials (excluding phosphors used in fluorescent lamps). By confining "black light" applications to this region, germicidal and erythemal effects are, for practical purposes, eliminated.
"black light" flux radiant flux within the wavelength range 320–400 nm. It is usually measured in milliwatts. See *fluoren*.
Note Because of the variability of the spectral sensitivity of materials irradiated by "black light" in practice, no attempt is made to evaluate "black light" flux according to its capacity to produce effects.

"black light" flux density the "black light" flux per unit area of the surface being irradiated. It is equal to the incident "black light" flux divided by the area of the surface when the flux is uniformly distributed. It usually is measured in milliwatts per unit area of flux.

"black light" lamp An ultraviolet lamp that emits a significant portion of its radiative power in the UV-A band (315–400 nm).

blending lighting general illumination used to provide smooth transitions between the lighting areas on a stage.

blinding glare glare which is so intense that for an appreciable length of time after it has been removed, no object can be seen.

Blondel-Rey law an expression for the ratio of the thresholds of a squareform flashing light (E_a) and of a steady light (E_o), in point vision conditions at night, as a function of the duration in seconds of the flash (t):

$$\frac{E_o}{E_a} = \frac{t}{0.21 + t}$$

borderlight a long continuous striplight hung horizontally above a stage and aimed down to provide general diffuse illumination or to light the cyclorama or a drop; usually wired in three or four color circuits.

borderline between comfort and discomfort (BCD) the average luminance of a source in a field of view which produces a sensation between comfort and discomfort.

boundary lights aeronautical ground lights delimiting the boundary of a land aerodrome without runways. See *range lights.*

bowl an open-top diffusing glass or plastic enclosure used to shield a light source from direct view and to redirect or scatter the light.

bracket (mast arm) an attachment to a lamp post or pole from which a luminaire is suspended.

brightness (of a perceived aperture color) the attribute by which an area of color of finite size is perceived to emit, transmit or reflect a greater or lesser amount of light. No account is taken of whether the light comes from a reflecting, transmitting or self-luminous object. See also *subjective brightness, luminance, veiling luminance* and *brightness of a perceived light source color.*

brightness contrast threshold the just-detectable contrast between two patches of color separated by a brightness contrast border, as in the case of a bipartite photometric field or of a disk-shaped object surrounded by its background.

brightness of a perceived light source color[†] the attribute in accordance with which the source seems to emit more or less luminous flux per unit area.

bulb[†] See *lamp.*

C

candela, cd the SI unit of luminous intensity, equal to one lumen per steradian (lm/sr). Formerly "candle." See chapter 2, Measurement of Light and Other Radiant Energy.

Note The candela is the luminous intensity, in a given direction, of a source that emits monochromatic radiation of frequency 540×10^{12} Hz (wavelength approximately 555 nm) that has a radiant intensity in that direction of $\frac{1}{683}$ (0.001464) W/sr. The candela so defined is the base unit applicable to photopic, scotopic and mesopic quantities. From 1909 until January 1, 1948, the unit of luminous intensity in the United States, as well as in France and Great Britain, was the *international candle,* which was maintained by a group of carbon-filament vacuum lamps. From 1948 to 1979 the unit of luminous intensity was defined in terms of a complete (blackbody) radiator. 1 cd was defined as the luminous intensity of $1/600,000$ m^2 of projected area of a blackbody radiator operating at the temperature of solidification of platinum, at a pressure of 101,325 Pa. The difference between the candela and the old international candle is so small that only measurements of high accuracy are affected.

candlepower, $I = d\Phi/d\omega$; cp. luminous intensity expressed in candelas.

candlepower distribution curve See *intensity distribution curve.*

carbon-arc lamp an electric-discharge lamp employing an arc discharge between carbon electrodes. One or more of these electrodes may have cores of special chemicals that contribute importantly to the radiation.

cavity ratio (CR)[†] a number indicating cavity proportions calculated from length, width and height. See *ceiling cavity ratio, floor cavity ratio* and *room cavity ratio.*

ceiling area lighting a general lighting system in which the entire ceiling is, in effect, one large luminaire.
    Note Ceiling area lighting includes luminous ceilings and louvered ceilings.

ceiling cavity[†] the cavity formed by the ceiling, the plane of the luminaires and the wall surfaces between these two planes.

ceiling cavity ratio (CCR) a number indicating ceiling cavity proportions calculated from length, width and height. See chapter 9, Lighting Calculations.

ceiling projector a device designed to produce a well-defined illuminated spot on the lower portion of a cloud for the purpose of providing a reference mark for the determination of the height of that part of the cloud.

ceiling ratio the ratio of the luminous flux reaching the ceiling directly to the upward component from the luminaire.

central (foveal) vision the seeing of objects in the central or foveal part of the visual field, approximately 2° in diameter. It permits seeing much finer detail than does peripheral vision.

central visual field that region of the visual field corresponding to the foveal portion of the retina.

channel an enclosure containing the ballast, starter, lamp holders and wiring for a fluorescent lamp, or a similar enclosure on which filament lamps (usually tubular) are mounted.

channel lights aeronautical ground lights arranged along the sides of a channel of a water aerodrome. See *taxi-channel lights.*

characteristic curve a curve which expresses the relationship between two variable properties of a light source, such as candlepower and voltage, flux and voltage, etc.

chromatic adaptation the process by which the chromatic properties of the visual system are modified by the observation of stimuli of various chromaticities and luminances. See *state of chromatic adaptation.*

chromatic color   perceived color possessing a hue. In everyday speech, the term color is often used in this sense in contradistinction to white, gray or black.

chromatic contrast threshold (color contrast threshold)[†]   a threshold of chromaticity difference between two patches of color juxtaposed and separated only by a color contrast border, below which they cannot be perceived as different in chromaticness or separated by a contrast border. A contrast border can involve differences both in luminance and in chromaticity between the two sides.

chromaticity coordinates (of a color), x, y, z the ratios of the three tristimulus values of the color to their sum.

chromaticity diagram   a plane diagram formed by plotting one of the three chromaticity coordinates against another.

chromaticity difference threshold   the smallest difference in chromaticity between two colors of the same luminance that makes them perceptibly different. The difference may be a difference in hue or saturation, or a combination of the two.

chromaticity of a color   the dominant or complementary wavelength and purity aspects of the color taken together, or the aspects specified by the chromaticity coordinates of the color taken together.

chromaticness   the attribute of a visual sensation according to which the (perceived) color of an area appears to be more or less chromatic.

CIE ($L*, a*, b*$) uniform color space (CIELAB)   a transformation of CIE tristimulus values X, Y, Z into three coordinates that define a space in which equal distances are more nearly representative of equal magnitudes of perceived color difference. This space is specially useful in cases of colorant mixtures.

CIE ($L*, u*, v*$) uniform color space (CIELUV)   a transformation of CIE tristimulus values X, Y, Z into three coordinates that define a space in which equal distances are more nearly representative of equal magnitudes of perceived color difference. This space is specially useful in cases where colored lights are mixed additively, such as color television.

CIE standard chromaticity diagram   a diagram in which the x and y chromaticity coordinates are plotted in rectangular coordinates.

circling guidance lights   aeronautical ground lights provided to supply additional guidance during a circling approach when the circling guidance furnished by the approach and runway lights is inadequate.

clear sky   a sky that has less than 30% cloud cover.

clearance lamp   a lighting device mounted on a vehicle for the purpose of indicating the overall width and height of the vehicle.

clerestory   that part of a building rising clear of the roofs or other parts and whose walls contain windows for lighting the interior.

cloudy sky   a sky having more than 70% cloud cover.

coefficient of attenuation, f   the decrement in flux per unit distance in a given direction within a medium, defined by the relation $\Phi_x = \Phi_0 e^{-\mu x}$, where Φ_x is the flux at any distance x from a reference point having flux Φ_0. More generally,

$$\Phi_x = \Phi_0 e^{-\int_0^x \mu(x)\,dx}$$

where the coefficient varies from point to point; $\mu = \mu(x)$ along the path.

coefficient of beam utilization (CB)   the ratio of the luminous flux (lumens) reaching a specified area directly from a floodlight or projector to the total beam luminous flux (lumens).

coefficient of utilization (CU)   the ratio of the luminous flux (lumens) from a luminaire calculated as received on the workplane to the luminous flux emitted by the luminaire's lamps alone. See chapter 9, Lighting Calculations.

coffer   a recessed panel or dome in a ceiling.

cold-cathode lamp   an electric-discharge lamp whose mode of operation is that of a glow discharge, and having electrodes so spaced that most of the light comes from the positive column between them.

color[†]   the characteristic of light by which a human observer may distinguish between two structure-free patches of light of the same size and shape. See *light source color* and *object color*.

color difference threshold   the difference in chromaticity or luminance between two colors that makes them just perceptibly different. The difference may be in hue, saturation, brightness (lightness for surface colors) or a combination of the three.

color comparison, or color grading (CIE, object color inspection)   the judgment of equality, or of the amount and character of difference, of the color of two objects viewed under identical illumination.

color contrast thresholds   See *chromaticity difference threshold*.

color correction (of a photograph or printed picture)   the adjustment of a color reproduction process to improve the perceived-color conformity of the reproduction to the original.

color discrimination   the perception of differences between two or more colors.

color matching   the action of making a color appear the same as a given color.

color-matching functions (spectral tristimulus values), $\bar{x}(\lambda) = X_\lambda / \Phi_{r\lambda}$, $\bar{y}(\lambda) = Y_\lambda / \Phi_{r\lambda}$, $\bar{z}(\lambda) = Z_\lambda / \Phi_{e\lambda}$ the tristimulus values per unit wavelength interval and unit spectral radiant flux.

Note   Color-matching functions have been adopted by the Commission Internationale de l'Éclairage (CIE). They are tabulated as functions of wavelength throughout the spectrum and are the basis for the evaluation of radiant energy as light and color. The standard values adopted by the CIE in 1931 are given in chapter 4, Color. The $\bar{y}$ values are identical with the spectral luminous efficiency for photopic vision. The $\bar{x}$, $\bar{y}$ and $\bar{z}$ values for the 1931 Standard Observer are based on a 2° bipartite field, and are recommended for predicting matches for stimuli subtending between 1 and 4°. Supplementary data based on a 10° field were adopted in 1964 for use for angular subtenses greater than 4°. Tristimulus computational data for CIE standard color sources A and C are given in chapter 5.

color preference index (CPI)   See *flattery index*.

color rendering[†]   a general expression for the effect of a light source on the color appearance of objects in conscious or subconscious comparison with their color appearance under a reference light source.

color rendering improvement (of a light source)[†] the adjustment of spectral composition to improve color rendering.

color rendering index (of a light source) (CRI) a measure of the degree of color shift objects undergo when illuminated by the light source as compared with those same objects when illuminated by a reference source of comparable color temperature.

color temperature of a light source the absolute temperature of a blackbody radiator having a chromaticity equal to that of the light source. See also *correlated color temperature* and *distribution temperature*.

colorfulness See *chromaticness*.

colorfulness of a perceived color the attribute according to which it appears to exhibit more or less chromatic color. For a stimulus of a given chromaticity, colorfulness normally increases as the absolute luminance is increased.

colorimetric purity (of a light), ρ_c the ratio L_1/L_2, where L_1 is the luminance of the single-frequency component that must be mixed with a reference standard to match the color of the light, and L_2 is the luminance of the light. See *excitation purity*.

colorimetric shift the change of chromaticity and luminance factor of an object color due to change of the light source. See *adaptive color shift* and *resultant color shift*.

colorimetry the measurement of color.

compact-arc lamp See *short-arc lamp*.

compact source iodide (CSI) an arc source utilizing a mercury vapor arc with metal halide additives to produce illumination in the 5000–6000-K range. Requires a ballast and ignition system for operation.

comparison lamp a light source having a constant, but not necessarily known, luminous intensity with which standard and test lamps are compared successively.

complementary wavelength (of a light), r_c the wavelength of radiant energy of a single frequency that, when combined in suitable proportion with the light, matches the color of a reference standard. See *dominant wavelength*.

complete diffusion diffusion in which the diffusing medium completely redirects the incident flux by scattering so that no incident flux can remain in an image-forming state.

cones retinal receptors that dominate the retinal response when the luminance level is high and provide the basis for the perception of color.

configuration factor, $C_{1\to2}$ the ratio of the illuminance on a surface at point 1 (due to flux directly received from lambertian surface 2) to the exitance of surface 2:

$$C_{1\to2} = E_1/M_2$$

It is used in flux transfer theory. Also, the ratio of the differential flux directly received by surface 2 (and due to element 1) to the total differential flux emitted by differential lambertian surface element 1:

$$C_{1\to2} = \frac{d\Phi_{1\to2}}{d\Phi_1}$$

Note In the literature this ratio is also called the *angle factor*, *illumination factor*, *point configuration factor*, and *sky factor*.

conical-directional reflectance, $\rho(\omega_i; \theta_r, \phi_r)$ the ratio of the reflected flux collected over an element of solid angle surrounding the given direction to the incident flux limited to a conical solid angle.

Note The direction and extent of the cone must be specified, and the direction of collection and size of the solid angle element must be specified.

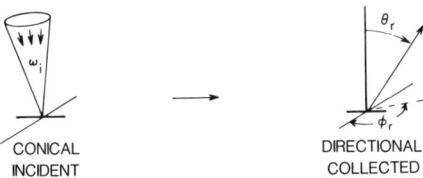

conical-directional transmittance, $\tau(\omega_i; \theta_t, \phi_t)$ the ratio of the transmitted flux collected over an element of solid angle surrounding the direction to the incident flux limited to a conical solid angle.

Note The direction and extent of the cone must be specified, and the direction of collection and size of the solid angle element must be specified.

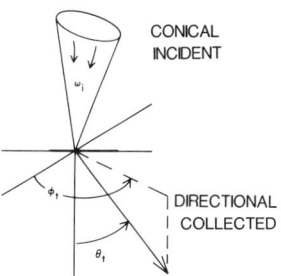

conical-hemispherical reflectance, $\rho(\omega_i; 2\pi)$ the ratio of the reflected flux collected over the entire hemisphere to the incident flux limited to a conical solid angle.

Note The direction and extent of the cone must be specified.

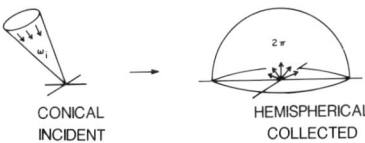

conical-hemispherical transmittance, $\tau(\omega_t; 2\pi)$ the ratio of the transmitted flux collected over the entire hemisphere to the incident flux limited to a conical solid angle.

Note The direction and extent of the cone must be specified.

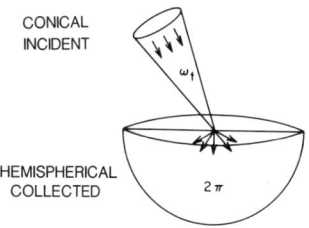

conspicuity the capacity of a signal to stand out in relation to its background so as to be readily discovered by the eye.

contrast See *luminance contrast*.

contrast rendition factor (CRF) the ratio of the visual task contrast with a given lighting environment to the contrast with sphere illumination. Also known as the *contrast rendering factor*.

contrast sensitivity the ability to detect the presence of luminance differences. Quantitatively, it is equal to the reciprocal of the brightness contrast threshold.

cornice lighting lighting comprising sources shielded by a panel parallel to the wall and attached to the ceiling, and distributing light over the wall.

correlated color temperature (of a light source) the absolute temperature of a blackbody whose chromaticity most nearly resembles that of the light source.

cosine law the law that the illuminance on any surface varies as the cosine of the angle of incidence. The angle of incidence θ is the angle between the normal to the surface and the direction of the incident light. The inverse square law and the cosine law can be combined as $E = (I\cos\theta)/d^2$. See *cosine-cubed law* and *inverse square law*.

cosine-cubed law an extension of the cosine law in which the distance d between the source and surface is replaced by $h/\cos\theta$, where h is the perpendicular distance of the source from the plane in which the point is located. It is expressed by $E = (I\cos^3\theta)/h^2$.

counter-key light illumination on a subject from a direction that is opposite to that of the key light.

country beam See *upper (driving) beams*.

course light[†] an aeronautical ground light, supplementing an airway beacon, for indicating the direction of the airway and to identify by a coded signal the location of the airway beacon with which it is associated.

cove lighting lighting comprising sources shielded by a ledge or horizontal recess, and distributing light over the ceiling and upper wall.

criteria rating a technique that determined the probability that a specific criterion will be met anywhere in a defined area. The name of the criteria rating includes the name of the criterion being rated. It is expressed in shorthand notation by listing the rating in percent followed by the criterion itself and separated by an "@." For example, a lighting system producing a luminance of 100 cd/m² over 60% of the specified area could have its luminance rating expressed as 60%@100 cd/m².

critical flicker frequency (cff) See *flicker fusion frequency*.

critical fusion frequency (cff) See *flicker fusion frequency*.

cross lighting illumination from two sources on opposite sides of the subject. Often different color media are used in the luminaires for the same area to give the illusion of shadow while providing sufficient illumination for good visibility.

cucoloris an opaque cutout panel mounted between a light source (sun or arc) and a target surface in order to project a shadow pattern (clouds or leaves are typical) upon scenery, cyclorama or acting area.

cutoff angle (of a luminaire) the angle, measured up from nadir, between the vertical axis and the first line of sight at which the bare source is not visible.

D

dark adaptation the process by which the retina becomes adapted to a luminance less than about 0.034 cd/m².

daylight availability the luminous flux from the sun and the sky at a specific location, time, date and sky condition.

daylight factor a measure of daylight illuminance at a point on a given plane, expressed as the ratio of the illuminance on that plane at that point to the simultaneous exterior illuminance on a horizontal plane from the whole of an unobstructed sky of assumed or known luminance distribution. Direct sunlight is excluded from both interior and exterior values of illuminance.

daylight lamp a lamp producing a spectral distribution approximating that of a specified daylight.

densitometer a photometer for measuring the optical density (common logarithm of the reciprocal of the transmittance or reflectance) of materials.

diffuse reflectance the ratio of the flux leaving a surface or medium by diffuse reflection to the incident flux.
Note Provision for the exclusion of regularly reflected flux, which is nearly always present, must be clearly described.

diffuse reflection the process by which incident flux is redirected over a range of angles.

diffuse transmission the process by which the incident flux passing through a surface or medium is scattered.

diffuse transmittance the ratio of the diffusely transmitted flux leaving a surface or medium to the incident flux.
Note Provision for the exclusion of regularly transmitted flux must be clearly described.

diffused lighting lighting, provided on the workplane or on an object, that is not predominantly incident from any particular direction.

diffuser a device to redirect or scatter the light from a source, primarily by the process of diffuse transmission.

diffusing panel a translucent material covering the lamps in a luminaire to reduce the luminance by distributing the flux over an extended area.

diffusing surfaces and media those that redistribute at least some of the incident flux by scattering in all directions. See *complete diffusion, incomplete diffusion, perfect diffusion, narrow-angle diffusion* and *wide-angle diffusion*.

digital display See *alphanumeric display*.

dimmer a device used to control the intensity of light emitted by a luminaire by controlling the voltage or current available to it.

direct component that portion of the light from a luminaire which arrives at the workplane without being reflected by any room surfaces. See *indirect component*.

direct glare glare resulting from high luminances or sufficiently shielded light sources in the field of view. It is usually associated with bright areas, such as luminaires, ceilings and windows, which are outside the visual task or region being viewed. A direct glare source may also affect performance by distracting attention.

direct-indirect lighting a variant of general diffuse lighting in which the luminaires emit little or no light at angles near the horizontal.

direct lighting lighting by luminaires distributing 90–100% of the emitted light in the general direction of the surface to be illuminated. The term usually refers to light emitted in a downward direction.

direct ratio the ratio of the luminous flux reaching the workplane directly to the downward component from the luminaire.

directional-conical reflectance, $\rho(\theta_i, \phi_i; \omega_r)$ the ratio of reflected flux collected through a conical solid angle to essentially collimated incident flux.
Note   The direction of incidence must be specified, as must the direction and extent of the cone.

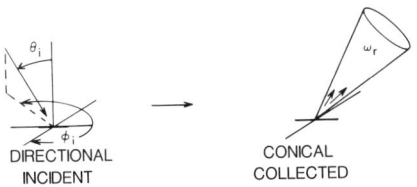

directional-conical transmittance, $\tau(\theta_i, \phi_i; \omega_r)$ the ratio of transmitted flux collected through a conical solid angle to essentially collimated incident flux.
Note   The direction of incidence must be specified, as must the direction and extent of the cone.

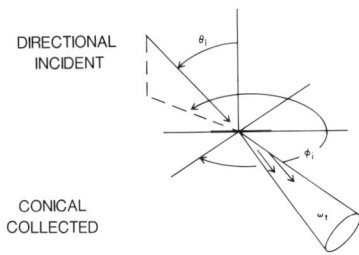

directional-hemispherical reflectance, $\rho(\theta_i, \phi_i; 2\pi)$ the ratio of reflected flux collected over the entire hemisphere to essentially collimated incident flux.
Note   The direction of incidence must be specified.

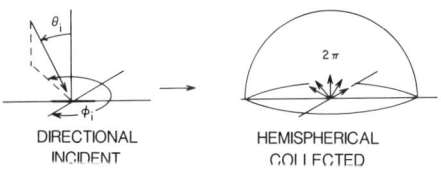

directional-hemispherical transmittance, $\tau(\theta_i, \phi_i; 2\pi)$ the ratio of transmitted flux collected over the entire hemisphere to essentially collimated incident flux.
Note   The direction of incidence must be specified.

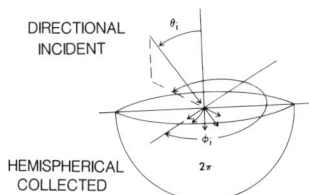

directional lighting   lighting provided on the workplane or on an object predominantly from a preferred direction. See *accent lighting*, *key light* and *cross light*.

disability glare   the effect of stray light in the eye whereby visibility and visual performance are reduced. A direct glare source that produces discomfort may also produce disability glare by introducing a measurable amount of stray light in the eye.

disability glare factor (DGF)   a measure of the visibility of a task in a given lighting installation in comparison with its visibility under reference lighting conditions, expressed in terms of the ratio of luminance contrasts having an equivalent effect upon task visibility. The definition of the DGF takes account of the equivalent veiling luminance produced in the eye by the pattern of luminances in the task surround.

discomfort glare   glare producing discomfort. It does not necessarily interfere with visual performance or visibility.

discomfort glare factor   the numerical assessment of the capacity of a single source of brightness, such as a luminaire, in a given visual environment for producing discomfort (this term is obsolete and is retained only for reference and literature searches). See *glare* and *discomfort glare*.

discomfort glare rating (DGR)   a numerical assessment of the capacity of a number of sources of luminance, such as luminaires, in a given visual environment for producing discomfort. It is the net effect of the individual values of the index of sensation for all luminous areas in the field of view. See *discomfort glare factor*. See also chapter 9, Lighting Calculations.

distal stimuli   any of the points, lines and surfaces and three-dimensional arrays of scattering particles which one can identify in the physical space in front of the eye and which form optical images on the retina. Each element of a surface or volume to which an eye is exposed subtends a solid angle at the entrance pupil. Such elements of solid angle make up the field of view, and each has a specifiable luminance and chromaticity. Points and lines are specific cases which have to be dealt with in terms of total intensity and intensity per unit length.

distribution temperature (of a light source)   the absolute temperature of a blackbody whose relative spectral distribution is most nearly the same in the visible region of the spectrum as that of the light source.

dominant wavelength (of a light), λ_d the wavelength of radiant energy of a single frequency that, when combined in suitable proportion with the radiant energy of a reference standard, matches the color of the light. See *complementary wavelength*.

downlight   a small direct lighting unit which directs the light downward and can be recessed, surface mounted or suspended.

downward component   that portion of the luminous flux from a luminaire emitted at angles below the horizontal. See *upward component*.

driving beam   See *upper (driving) beams*.

dual headlighting system   headlighting by means of two double units, one mounted on each side of the front end of a vehicle. Each unit consists of two sealed beam lamps mounted in a single housing. The upper or outer lamps may have two filaments supplying the lower beam and part of the upper beam, respectively. The lower or inner lamps have one filament providing the primary source of light for the upper beam.

dustproof luminaire   a luminaire so constructed or protected that dust will not interfere with its successful operation.

dust-tight luminaire   a luminaire so constructed that dust will not enter the enclosing case.

E

effective ceiling cavity reflectance, ρ_{CC} a number giving the combined reflectance effect of the wall and ceiling reflectance of the ceiling cavity. See *ceiling cavity ratio*.

effective floor cavity reflectance, ρ_{FC} a number giving the combined reflectance effect of the floor cavity. See *floor cavity ratio*.

effective intensity, I_e a quantity conventionally defined for a flashing light by

$$I_e = \frac{I_0 t}{t + 0.2\,\text{s}}$$

where the source has constant magnitude I_0 over a time duration t. For a time-varying source $I(t)$,

$$I_e = \frac{\int_{t_1}^{t_2}}{t_2 - t_1 + 0.2\,\text{s}}$$

The unit of I_e is the candela. The times t_1 and t_2 are chosen to maximize the calculated effective intensity. It is then found that the actual intensity I_t at time t_1 or t_2 is equal to the calculated equivalent intensity I_e.

efficacy   See *luminous efficacy of a source of light* and *spectral luminous efficacy of radiant flux*.

efficiency   See *luminaire efficiency, luminous efficacy of a source of light* and *spectral luminous efficiency of radiant flux*.

egress   See *means of egress*.

egress lighting   emergency lighting for egress.

electric discharge   See *arc discharge, gaseous discharge* and *glow discharge*.

electric-discharge lamp   a lamp in which light (or radiant energy near the visible spectrum) is produced by the passage of an electric current through a vapor or gas. See *fluorescent lamp, cold-cathode lamp, hot-cathode lamp, carbon-arc lamp, glow lamp, fluorescent lamp* and *high-intensity discharge (HID) lamp*.

   Note   Electric-discharge lamps may be named after the fill gas or vapor that is responsible for the major portion of the radiation, as with mercury lamps, sodium lamps, neon lamps and argon lamps.

electroluminescence   the emission of light from a phosphor excited by an electromagnetic field.

electromagnetic spectrum[†]   a continuum of electric and magnetic radiation encompassing all wavelengths. See *regions of the electromagnetic spectrum*.

elevation   the angle between the axis of a searchlight drum and the horizontal. For angles above the horizontal, elevation is positive; for angles below, negative.

ellipsoidal reflector spotlight   a spotlight in which a lamp and an ellipsoidal reflector are mounted in a fixed relationship directing a beam of light into an aperture, where it may be shaped by a pattern, iris, shutter system or other insertion. The beam then passes through a single or com-

pound lens system that focuses it as required, producing a sharply defined beam with variable edge definition.

emergency   any condition, external or internal to the premises, that would compromise the effectiveness of the lighting in an occupied area for safe movement within and out of that area and safe operation of equipment within the space. An emergency may include any or all of the following:
   1. utility power failure.
   2. utility power voltage reduction (brownout) below the minimum required to support the arc in fluorescent or HID lamps.
   3. power interruption within the premises including total power loss or individual phase or branch circuit failure.
   4. fire or smoke.

emergency exit   a way out of the premises that is intended to be used only during an emergency.

emergency lighting   lighting designed to supply illumination essential to safety of life and property in the event of failure of the normal supply. Emergency lighting may include any or all of the following:
   1. Illumination of the means of egress of the premises during an emergency.
   2. Illumination of the signs which mark the means of egress.
   3. Safety lighting necessary to enhance the safety of occupants remaining on the premises during an emergency.
   4. Standby lighting to provide the illumination necessary to enable normal activities to continue during an emergency.

emissivity, ϵ [†]   the ratio of the radiance (for directional emissivity) or radiant exitance (for hemispherical emissivity) of an element of surface of a temperature radiator to that of a blackbody at the same temperature.

emittance, ϵ (1) The ratio of the radiance in a given direction (for directional emittance) or radiant exitance (for hemispherical emittance) of a sample of a thermal radiator to that of a blackbody radiator at the same temperature. (2) See *exitance*. Use of the term with this meaning is deprecated.

enclosed and gasketed   See *vapor-tight*.

equal interval (isophase) light   a rhythmic light in which the light and dark periods are equal.

equipment operating factor   the flux of a high-intensity discharge (HID) lamp-ballast-luminaire combination in a given operating position as a fraction of the flux of the lamp-luminaire combination (1) operated in the position for rating lamp lumens and (2) using the reference ballasting specified for rating lamp lumens.

   Note   If the given lamp operating position is not the same as the lamp rating position, the ratio of the flux for the operating ballast to that for the standard rating ballast is determined in the given operating position. This ratio is multiplied by the lamp position factor to obtain the equipment operating factor.

equivalent contrast, $\tilde{C}$ a numerical description of the relative visibility of a task. It is the contrast of the standard visibility reference task giving the same visibility as that of a task whose contrast has been reduced to threshold when the background luminances are the same. See *visual task evaluator*.

equivalent contrast, actual, $\tilde{C}_e$ the equivalent contrast in a real luminous environment with nondiffuse illumination. This quantity may be less than the equivalent contrast defined above, on account of veiling reflection. We have $\tilde{C}_e = \tilde{C} \times$ CRF. See *contrast rendition factor*.

equivalent luminous intensity (of an extended source at a specified distance) the intensity of a point source which would produce the same illuminance at that distance. Formerly, the apparent luminous intensity of an extended source.

equivalent sphere illumination (ESI) the level of sphere illumination which would produce task visibility equivalent to that produced by a specific lighting environment.

equivalent veiling luminance the luminance of the reflected image of a bright surface that is superimposed on a test object to measure the veiling effect equivalent to that produced by stray light in the eye produced by a disability glare source. The disability glare source is turned off when the reflected image is turned on.

erythema a temporary reddening of the skin such as produced by exposure to actinic UV radiation. UV-induced erythema is due to actinic action and is a delayed effect occurring several hours after exposure. This differs from IR-induced erythema, a thermal effect occurring only for the duration of time that the skin temperature is elevated.
Note The degree of erythema is used as a guide to dosages applied in UV therapy.

erythemal effectiveness the capacity of various portions of the ultraviolet spectrum to produce erythema.

erythemal efficiency of radiant flux (for a particular wavelength) the ratio of the erythemal effectiveness of a particular wavelength to that of wavelength 296.7 nm, which is rated as 1.0.
Note This quantity formerly was called the "relative erythemal factor." The erythemal efficiency of radiant flux of various wavelengths for producing a minimum perceptible erythema (MPE) is given in chapter 5, Nonvisual Effects of Radiant Energy.

erythemal exposure the product of erythemal flux density on a surface and time. It usually is measured in erythemal μW · min/cm^2.
Note For average untanned skin a minimum perceptible erythema requires about 300 μW · min/cm^2 of radiation at 296.7 nm.

erythemal flux radiant flux evaluated according to its capacity to produce erythema of the untanned human skin. It usually is measured in microwatts of UV radiation weighted in accordance with its erythemal efficiency. Such quantities of erythemal flux are said to be in erythemal microwatts. See *erythemal efficiency of radiant flux* and *erythemal unit*.

erythemal flux density the erythemal flux per unit area of the surface being irradiated. It is equal to the incident erythemal flux divided by the area of the surface when the flux is uniformly distributed. It usually is measured in μW/cm^2 of erythemally weighted UV radiation (erythemal μW/cm^2). See *finsen*.

erythemal threshold See *minimal perceptible erythema*.

erythemal unit (EU) a unit of erythemal flux that is equal to the amount of radiant flux that will produce the same erythemal effect as 10 μW of radiant flux at wavelength 296.7 nm. Also called *E-viton*.

E-viton (erytheme) See *erythemal unit*.

exit the portion of a means of egress that segregates all other spaces in the building or structure by fire resistant construction in order to provide a protected way of travel to the exit discharge. Exits include exterior exit doors, exit passageways, horizontal exits, and separated exit stairs or ramps.

exit access the portion of a means of egress that leads to an exit.

exit discharge the portion of a means of egress between the conclusion of an exit and a public way.

exit sign a graphic device including words or symbols that indicates or identifies an escape route or the location of, or direction to, an exit or emergency exit.

exitance See *luminous exitance* and *radiant exitance*.

exitance coefficient the ratio of the average initial (time zero) wall or ceiling cavity exitance to the lamp flux per unit floor area.
Note Exitance is measured in lumens per unit area, where the units of area agree with those of the floor area. Average wall or ceiling cavity luminances can be determined by noting the underlying assumption of lambertian room surfaces where $L = M/\pi$; here L is in candelas per unit area, where the units of area agree with those of M. The exitance coefficients are numerically identical to what were formerly called luminance coefficients.

excitation purity (of a light), p_e the ratio of the distance on the CIE x, y chromaticity diagram between the reference point and the light point to the distance in the same direction between the reference point and the spectrum locus or the purple boundary. See *colorimetric purity*.

explosion-proof luminaire a luminaire which is completely enclosed and capable of withstanding an explosion of a gas or vapor that may occur within it, and preventing the ignition of a gas or vapor surrounding the enclosure by sparks, flashes or explosion of the gas or vapor within. It must operate at such an external temperature that a surrounding flammable atmosphere will not be ignited thereby.

externally illuminated exit sign an exit sign with an externally mounted light source. The exit legend and background are typically opaque and rely on reflected light for visibility.

eye light illumination on a person to provide a specular reflection from the eyes, teeth, or jewelry without significantly increasing the total illumination of the subject.

F

far (long-wavelength) infrared the region of the electromagnetic spectrum extending from 5000 to 1,000,000 nm.

far ultraviolet the region of the electromagnetic spectrum extending from 100 to 200 nm.

fay light a luminaire that uses incandescent parabolic reflector lamps with a dichroic coating to provide "daylight" illumination.

fenestra method a procedure for predicting the interior illuminance received from daylight through windows.

fenestration any opening or arrangement of openings (normally filled with media for control) for the admission of daylight.

field angle the angle between the two directions for which the intensity is 10% of the maximum intensity measured in a plane through the nominal beam centerline. For beams that do not possess rotational symmetry, the beam angle is generally given for two planes at 90°, typically the maximum and minimum angles. Note that in certain fields of applications the angle of the 10%-of-maximum directions was formerly called the beam angle.

fill light supplementary illumination to reduce shadow or contrast range.

film (or aperture) color[†] the perceived color of the sky or a patch of color seen through an aperture.

filter a device for changing, by transmission or reflection, the magnitude or spectral composition of the flux incident upon it. Filters are called *selective* (or *colored*) or *neutral*, according to whether or not they alter the spectral distribution of the incident flux.

filter factor, f_f the transmittance of "black light" by a filter. Note The relationship between glow factor and filter factor is illustrated by the following formula for determining the luminance of fluorescent materials exposed to "black light":

$$L = \frac{E}{\pi} f_g f_f \quad (\text{cd/m}^2)$$

where E is in fluorens per square meter, f_g is the glow factor, and f_f is the filter factor. When integral-filter "black light" lamps are used, the filter factor is dropped from the formula because it already has been applied in assigning fluoren ratings to these lamps.

finsen a suggested practical unit of erythemal flux density equal to one E-viton per square centimeter.

fixed light a light having a constant luminous intensity when observed from a fixed point.

fixture See *luminaire*.

flashing light a rhythmic light in which the periods of light are of equal duration and are clearly shorter than the periods of darkness. See *group flashing light*, *interrupted quick-flashing light* and *quick-flashing light*.

flashtube a tube of glass or fused quartz with electrodes at the ends and filled with a gas, usually xenon. It is designed to produce high-intensity flashes of light of extremely short duration.

flattery index (of a light source), R_f[†] a measure appraising a light source for appreciative viewing of colored objects, or for promoting an optimistic viewpoint by flattery (making the view more pleasant), or for enhancing the perception of objects in terms of color. Also sometimes called *color preference index* (CPI).

flicker fusion frequency (fff) the frequency of intermittent stimulation of the eye at which flicker disappears. It also is called the *critical fusion frequency* (cff) or *critical flicker frequency* (cff).

flicker index a measure of the cyclic variation in output of a light source, taking into account the waveform of the light output. It is the ratio of the area under the light output curve that is above the average light output level to the total area under the light output curve for a single cycle. See chapter 6, Light Sources.

flicker photometer See *visual photometer*.

floodlight a projector designed for lighting a scene or object to a luminance considerably greater than its surroundings. It usually is capable of being pointed in any direction and is of weatherproof construction. The beam spread of flood-

lights may range from narrow field angles (10°) to wide ones (more than 100°). See *heavy-duty floodlight*, *general-purpose (GP) floodlight*, *ground-area open floodlight* and *ground-area open floodlight with reflector insert*. In theatre lighting, a floodlight (or flood) is a luminaire consisting of a lamp and spread reflector with resultant field angle greater than 100°. Fixed and variable beam types are available.

floodlighting a system designed for lighting a scene or object to a luminance greater than its surroundings. It may be for utility, advertising or decorative purposes.

floor cavity[†] the cavity formed by the workplane, the floor, and the wall surfaces between those two planes.

floor cavity ratio (FCR)[†] a number indicating floor cavity proportions calculated from length, width and height. See chapter 9, Lighting Calculations.

floor lamp a portable luminaire on a high stand suitable for standing on the floor. See *torchère*.

fluoren a unit of "black light" flux equal to one milliwatt of radiant flux in the wavelength range 320–400 nm.

fluorescence the emission of light (luminescence) as the result of, and only during, the absorption of radiation of shorter wavelengths (time scale less than approximately 10^{-8} s).

fluorescent lamp a low-pressure mercury electric-discharge lamp in which a fluorescing coating (phosphor) transforms some of the UV energy generated by the discharge into light. See *instant start fluorescent lamp*, *preheat (switch start) fluorescent lamp* and *rapid start fluorescent lamp*.

flush-mounted or recessed luminaire a luminaire which is mounted above the ceiling (or behind a wall or other surface) with the opening of the luminaire level with the surface.

flux transfer theory a method of calculating the illuminance in a room by taking into account the interreflection of the light flux from the room surfaces based on the average flux transfer between surfaces.

fog (adverse-weather) lamps units which may be used in lieu of headlamps or in connection with the lower beam headlights to provide road illumination under conditions of rain, snow, dust or fog.

follow spot any instrument operated so as to follow the movement of an actor. Follow spots are usually high-intensity controlled-beam luminaires.

footcandle, fc a unit of illuminance, equal to 1 lm/ft² or 10.76 lx.

footcandle meter See *illuminance (lux or footcandle) meter*.

footlambert, fL a lambertian unit of luminance equal to $1/\pi$ (0.3183) cd/ft². This term is obsolete, and its use is deprecated.

footlights a set of striplights at the front edge of the stage platform used to soften face shadows cast by overhead luminaires and to add general toning lighting from below.

form factor, $F_{1 \to 2}$ the ratio of the flux directly received by surface 2 (and due to lambertian surface 1) to the total flux emitted by surface 1:

$$F_{1 \to 2} = \Phi_{1 \to 2}/\Phi_1$$

It is used in *flux transfer theory*. Also, the ratio of the average illuminance on surface 1 to the causative exitance of lambertian surface 2:

$$F_{1 \to 2} = E_1/M_2$$

Note In the literature, this quantity is also called the *angle factor*, *configuration factor*, *geometrical factor*, *I-factor*, *illumination factor*, and *shape modulus*.

formation light a navigation light especially provided to facilitate formation flying.

fovea a small region at the center of the retina, subtending about 2°, containing cones but no rods and forming the site of most distinct vision.

foveal vision See *central (foveal) vision*.

Fresnel spotlight a luminaire containing a lamp and a Fresnel lens (stepped "flat" lens with a textured back) which has variable field and beam angles obtained by changing the spacing between lamp and lens (flooding and spotting). The Fresnel spotlight produces a beam of light with a smooth, soft edge.

fuselage lights aircraft aeronautical lights, mounted on the top and bottom of the fuselage, used to supplement the navigation light.

G

gas-filled lamp an incandescent lamp in which the filament operates in a bulb filled with one or more inert gases.

gaseous discharge the emission of light from gas atoms excited by an electric current.

general color rendering index, R_a a measure of the average shift of eight standardized colors chosen to be of intermediate saturation and spread throughout the range of hues. If a color rendering index is not qualified as to the color samples used, R_a is assumed.

general diffuse lighting lighting involving luminaires which distribute 40–60% of the emitted light downward and the balance upward, sometimes with a strong component at 90° (horizontal). See *direct-indirect lighting*.

general lighting lighting designed to provide a substantially uniform level of illumination throughout an area, exclusive of any provision for special local requirements. See *direct lighting, semidirect lighting, general diffuse lighting, direct-indirect lighting, semi-indirect lighting, indirect lighting, ceiling area lighting* and *localized general lighting*.

general-purpose (GP) floodlight a weatherproof unit so constructed that the housing forms the reflecting surface. The assembly is enclosed by a cover glass.

germicidal effectiveness See *bactericidal (germicidal) effectiveness*.

germicidal efficiency of radiant flux See *bactericidal (germicidal) efficiency of radiant flux*.

germicidal exposure See *bactericidal (germicidal) exposure*.

germicidal flux and flux density See *bactericidal (germicidal) flux* and *bactericidal (germicidal) flux density*.

germicidal lamp a low-pressure mercury lamp in which the envelope has high transmittance for 254-nm radiation. See *bactericidal lamp*.

glare the sensation produced by luminance within the visual field that is sufficiently greater than the luminance to which the eyes are adapted to cause annoyance, discomfort or loss in visual performance and visibility. See *blinding glare, direct glare, disability glare* and *discomfort glare*.

Note The magnitude of the sensation of glare depends upon such factors as the size, position and luminance of a source, the number of sources and the luminance to which the eyes are adapted.

globe a transparent or diffusing enclosure intended to protect a lamp, to diffuse and redirect its light or to change the color of the light.

glossmeter an instrument for measuring gloss in terms of the directionally selective reflecting properties of a material at angles near to and including the direction giving specular reflection.

glow discharge an electric discharge characterized by a low, approximately constant current density at the cathode (on the order of 10 μA/mm^2) at low cathode temperature, and a high voltage drop (typically 50 V or more). The secondary emission from the cathode is much greater than the thermionic emission.

Note A distinction is made between the normal cathode drop (potential difference due to space charge near the cathode) that occurs when the glow does not cover the cathode completely (with constant current density) and that is independent of the discharge current, and the abnormal cathode drop that occurs when the glow covers the cathode completely (with increased current density) and that depends on the discharge current.

glow factor a measure of the visible light response of a fluorescent material to "black light." It is equal to π times the luminance in cd/m^2 produced on the material divided by the incident "black light" flux density in mW/m^2. It may be measured in lm/mW.

glow lamp an electric-discharge lamp whose mode of operation is that of a glow discharge, and in which light is generated in the space close to the electrodes.

goniophotometer a photometer for measuring the directional light distribution characteristics of sources, luminaires, media and surfaces.

graybody a temperature radiator whose spectral emissivity is less than unity and the same at all wavelengths.

ground-area open floodlight (O) a unit providing a weatherproof enclosure for the lamp socket and housing. No cover glass is required.

ground-area open floodlight with reflector insert (OI) a weatherproof unit so constructed that the housing forms only part of the reflecting surface. An auxiliary reflector is used to modify the distribution of light. No cover glass is required.

ground light visible radiation from the sun and sky reflected by surfaces below the plane of the horizon.

group flashing light a flashing light in which the flashes are combined in groups, each including the same number of flashes, and in which the groups are repeated at regular intervals. The duration of each flash is clearly less than the duration of the dark periods between flashes, and the duration of the dark periods between flashes is clearly less than the duration of the dark periods between groups.

H

hard light light that causes an object to cast a sharply defined shadow.

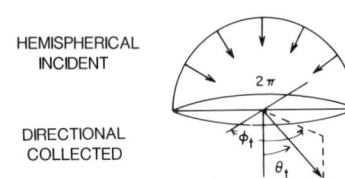

hazard or obstruction beacon an aeronautical beacon used to designate a danger to air navigation.

hazardous location an area where ignitable vapors or dust may cause a fire or explosion created by energy emitted from lighting or other electrical equipment or by electrostatic generation.

headlamp a major lighting device mounted on a vehicle and used to provide illumination ahead of it. Also called headlight. See *multiple-beam headlamp* and *sealed beam headlamp*.

headlight an alternative term for headlamp.

heat extraction thermal factor the fractional lumen loss or gain due to passage of room air being returned to the plenum through the lamp compartment of a luminaire.

heavy-duty floodlight (HD) a weatherproof unit having a substantially constructed metal housing in which is placed a separate and removable reflector. A weatherproof hinged door with cover glass encloses the assembly but provides an unobstructed light opening at least equal to the effective diameter of the reflector.

hemispherical-conical reflectance, $\rho(2\pi; \omega_r)$ the ratio of reflected flux collected over a conical solid angle to the incident flux from the entire hemisphere.

Note The direction and extent of the cone must be specified.

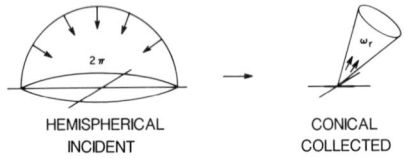

hemispherical-conical transmittance, $\tau(2\pi; \omega_t)$ the ratio of transmitted flux collected over a conical solid angle to the incident flux from the entire hemisphere.

Note The direction and extent of the cone must be specified.

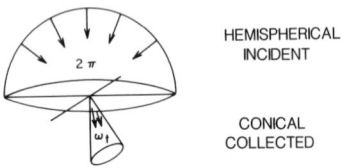

hemispherical-directional reflectance, $\rho(2\pi; \theta_r, \phi_r)$ The ratio of reflected flux collected over an element of solid angle surrounding the given direction to the incident flux from the entire hemisphere.

Note The direction of collection and the size of the solid angle element must be specified.

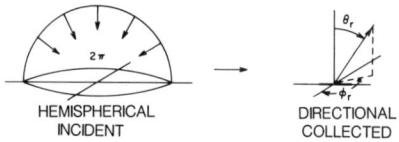

hemispherical-directional transmittance, $\tau(2\pi; \theta_t, \phi_t)$ The ratio of transmitted flux collected over an element of solid angle surrounding the given direction to the incident flux from the entire hemisphere.

Note The direction of collection and size of the solid angle element must be specified.

hemispherical reflectance the ratio of all of the flux leaving a surface or medium by reflection to the incident flux. The use of this term is deprecated. See *hemispherical transmittance*.

Note If "reflectance" is not preceded by an adjective descriptive of the angles of view, hemispherical reflectance is implied.

hemispherical transmittance the ratio of the transmitted flux leaving a surface or medium to the incident flux. The use of this term is deprecated.

Note If "transmittance" is not preceded by an adjective descriptive of the angles of view, hemispherical reflectance is implied.

high-bay lighting interior lighting where the roof truss or ceiling height is greater that approximately 7.6 m (25 ft) above the floor.

high-intensity discharge (HID) lamp an electric-discharge lamp in which the light-producing arc is stabilized by wall temperature, and the arc tube has a bulb wall loading in excess of 3 W/cm². HID lamps include groups of lamps known as mercury, metal halide and high-pressure sodium.

high-key lighting a type of lighting that, applied to a scene, results in a picture having gradations from middle gray to white with limited areas of dark gray and black. Also, intense, overall illumination. In motion pictures, high-level accent lighting with strong contrast (dark deep shadows with little or no middle gray). See *low-key lighting*.

high-mast lighting† illumination of a large area by means of a group of luminaires which are designed to be mounted in fixed orientation at the top of a high mast, generally 20 m (65 ft) or higher.

high-pressure sodium (HPS) lamp a high-intensity discharge (HID) lamp in which light is produced by radiation from sodium vapor operating at a partial pressure of about 1.33×10^4 Pa (100 Torr). Includes clear and diffuse-coated lamps.

horizontal exit an escape route from one building to an area of refuge in another building on approximately the same level. It also is an escape route through or around a fire barrier to an area of refuge on approximately the same level in the same building.

horizontal plane of a searchlight the plane which is perpendicular to the vertical plane through the axis of the searchlight drum and in which the train lies.

hot-cathode lamp an electric-discharge lamp whose mode of operation is that of an arc discharge. The cathodes may be heated by the discharge or by external means.

house lights the general lighting system installed in the audience area (house) of a theatre, film or television studio or arena.

hue of a perceived color the attribute that determines whether the color is red, yellow, green, blue or the like.

hue of a perceived light-source color† the attribute that determines whether the color is red, yellow, green, blue or the like. See *hue of a perceived color*.

hydrargyrum, medium-arc-length iodide (HMI) lamp an arc light source utilizing mercury vapor and metal halide additives for an approximation of daylight (5000–6000-K) illumination. Requires a ballast and ignition system for operation.

I

ice detection light an inspection light designed to illuminate the leading edge of an aircraft wing to check for ice formation.

ideal radiator See *blackbody*.

identification beacon an aeronautical beacon emitting a coded signal by means of which a particular point of reference can be identified.

ignitor a device, either by itself or in association with other components, that generates voltage pulses to start discharge lamps without preheating of electrodes.

illuminance, $E = d\Phi / dA$ the areal density of the luminous flux incident at a point on a surface.

illuminance (lux or footcandle) meter an instrument for measuring illuminance on a plane. Instruments which accurately respond to more than one spectral distribution are color corrected, that is, the spectral response is balanced to $V(\lambda)$ or $V'(\lambda)$. Instruments which accurately respond to more than one spatial distribution of incident flux are cosine corrected, that is, the response to a source of unit luminous intensity, illuminating the detector from a fixed distance and from different directions, decreases as the cosine of the angle between the incident direction and the normal to the detector surface. The instrument comprises some form of photodetector, with or without a filter, driving a digital or analog readout through appropriate circuitry.

illumination an alternative, but deprecated, term for illuminance. It is frequently used because "illuminance" is subject to confusion with "luminance" and "illuminants," especially when not clearly pronounced.

Note The term "illumination" also is commonly used in a qualitative or general sense to designate the act of illuminating or the state of being illuminated. Usually, the context will indicate which meaning is intended, but occasionally it is desirable to use the expression *level of illumination* to indicate that the quantitative meaning is intended.

incandescence the self-emission of radiant energy in the visible spectrum due to the thermal excitation of atoms or molecules.

incandescent filament lamp a lamp in which light is produced by a filament heated to incandescence by an electric current.

Note Normally, the filament is of coiled or coiled-coil (doubly coiled) tungsten wire. However, it may be uncoiled wire, a flat strip or of material other than tungsten.

incomplete diffusion (partial diffusion) that in which the diffusing medium partially redirects the incident flux by scattering while the remaining fraction of incident flux is redirected without scattering, that is, a fraction of the incident flux can remain in an image-forming state.

index of sensation, *M* **(of a source)** a number which expresses the effects of source luminance, solid angle factor, position index and field luminance on discomfort glare rating. See chapter 9, Lighting Calculations.

indirect component the portion of the luminous flux from a luminaire arriving at the workplane after being reflected by room surfaces. See *direct component*.

indirect lighting lighting by luminaires distributing 90–100% of the emitted light upward.

infrared lamp a lamp that radiates predominately in the infrared region of the spectrum; the visible radiation is not of principal interest.

infrared (IR) radiation for practical purposes any radiant energy within the wavelength range of 770–10^6 nm. This radiation is arbitrarily divided as follows:

Near (short-wavelength) IR	770–1400 nm
Intermediate IR	1400–5000 nm
Far (long-wavelength) IR	5000–1,000,000 nm

Note In general, unlike UV energy, IR energy is not evaluated on a wavelength basis but rather in terms of all of such energy incident upon a surface. Examples of these applications are industrial heating, drying, baking and photoreproduction. However, some applications, such as IR viewing devices, involve detectors sensitive to a restricted range of wavelengths; in such cases the spectral characteristics of the source and receiver are of importance.

inhibition (visual) reduction in magnitude of the sensation aroused by the stimulus (or a reduction in visual sensitivity) caused by some other situation that is adjacent spatially or temporally.

initial luminous exitance the density of luminous flux leaving a surface within an enclosure before interreflections occur.

Note For light sources this is the luminous exitance defined as the luminous flux density at a surface. For non-self-luminous surfaces it is the reflected luminous exitance of the flux received directly from sources within the enclosure or from daylight.

instant-start fluorescent lamp a fluorescent lamp designed for starting by a high voltage without preheating of the electrodes.

Note Also known as a cold-start lamp in some countries.

integrating photometer a photometer that enables total luminous flux to be determined by a single measurement. The usual type is the Ulbricht sphere with associated photometric equipment for measuring the indirect luminance of the inner surface of the sphere. (The measuring device is shielded from the source under measurement.)

intensity† a shortening of the terms *luminous intensity* and *radiant intensity*. Often misused for level of illumination or illuminance.

intensity distribution curve a curve, often polar, that represents the variation of luminous intensity of a lamp or luminaire in a plane through the light center.

Note A vertical intensity distribution curve of a luminaire is obtained by taking measurements at various angles of elevation in a vertical plane through the light center; unless the plane is specified, the curve is assumed to represent an average such as would be obtained by rotating the lamp or luminaire about its vertical axis. A horizontal intensity distribution curve represents measurements made at various angles of azimuth in a horizontal plane through the light center.

internally illuminated exit sign a transilluminated exit sign containing its own light source.

interreflected component the portion of the luminous flux from a luminaire arriving at the workplane after being reflected one or more times from room surfaces, as determined by the *flux transfer theory*.

interreflection   the multiple reflection of light by the various room surfaces before it reaches the workplane or other specified surface of a room.

interrupted quick-flashing light   a quick-flashing light in which the rapid alternations are interrupted by periods of darkness at regular intervals.

inverse square law   the law stating that the illuminance E at a point on a surface varies directly with the intensity I of a point source, and inversely as the square of the distance d between the source and the point. If the surface at the point is normal to the direction of the incident light, the law is expressed by $E = I/d^2$.
Note   For sources of finite size having uniform luminance, this gives results that are accurate within 1% when d is at least 5 times the maximum dimension of the source as viewed from the point on the surface. Even though practical interior luminaires do not have uniform luminance, this distance d is frequently used as the minimum for photometry of such luminaires, when the magnitude of the measurement error is not critical.

iris   an assembly of flat metal leaves arranged to provide an easily adjustable near-circular opening, placed near the focal point of the beam (as in an ellipsoidal reflector spotlight) or in front of the lens to act as a mechanical dimmer (as in older types of carbon arc follow spotlights).

irradiance, E the density of radiant flux (power) incident on a surface.

isocandela line   a curve plotted on any appropriate set of coordinates to show the distances in various directions in space, about a source of light, at which the intensity is the same. A series of such curves, often for equal increments of intensity, is called an isocandela diagram.

isolux (isofootcandle) line   a line plotted on any appropriate set of coordinates to show all the points on a surface where the illuminance is the same. A series of such lines for various illuminance values is called an isolux (isofootcandle) diagram.

K

key light   the apparent principal source of directional illumination falling upon a subject or area.

kicker   a luminaire used to provide an additional highlight or accent on a subject.

klieg light   a high-intensity carbon arc spotlight, typically used in motion picture lighting.

L

laboratory reference standard   the highest-ranking order of standards at each laboratory.

lambert, L a lambertian unit of luminance equal to $1/\pi$ (0.3183) cd/cm^2. This term is obsolete and its use is deprecated.

lambertian surface   a surface that emits or reflects light in accordance with Lambert's cosine law. A lambertian surface has the same luminance regardless of viewing angle.

Lambert's cosine law, $I_\theta = I_0 \cos\theta$ the law stating that the luminous intensity in any direction from an element of a perfectly diffusing surface varies as the cosine of the angle between that direction and the perpendicular to the surface element.

lamp   a generic term for an artificial source of light. By extension, the term is also used to denote sources that radiate in regions of the spectrum adjacent to the visible.
Note   A lighting unit consisting of a lamp with shade, reflector, enclosing globe, housing or other accessories is also sometimes called a "lamp." In such cases, in order to distinguish between the assembled unit and the light source within it, the latter is often called a "bulb" or "tube," if it is electrically powered. See also *luminaire*.

lamp burnout factor   the fractional loss of task illuminance due to burned-out lamps left in place for long periods.

lamp lumen depreciation factor (LLD)   the fractional loss of lamp lumens at rated operating conditions that progressively occurs during lamp operation.

lamp position factor   The ratio of the flux of a high-intensity discharge (HID) lamp at a given operating position to the flux when the lamp is operated in the position at which the lamp lumens are rated.

lamp post   a standard support provided with the necessary internal attachments for wiring and the external attachments for the bracket and luminaire.

lamp shielding angle   the angle between the plane of the baffles or louver grid and the plane most nearly horizontal that is tangent to both the lamps and the louver blades. See figure 1.
Note   The lamp shielding angle is formed by a straight line tangent to the lowest part of the brightness area to be shielded. If H is the vertical distance from the brightness source to the bottom of the shielding element, and D is the horizontal distance from the brightness source to the shielding element, then the lamp shielding angle $\Phi = \arctan(H/D)$. The lamp shielding angle frequently is larger than the louver shielding angle, but never smaller. See *louver shielding angle*.

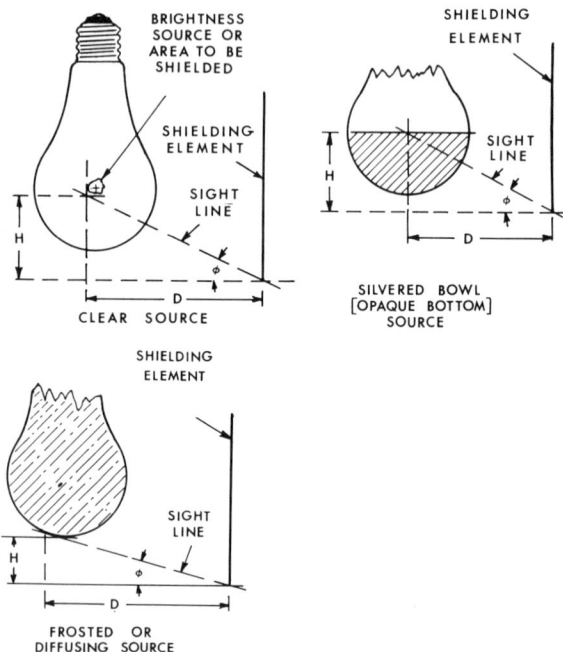

Fig. 1. The lamp shielding angle is formed by a sight line tangent to the lowest part of the brightness area to be shielded. H is the vertical distance from the brightness source to the bottom of the shielding element. D is the horizontal distance from the brightness source to the shielding element. Lample shielding element ϕ = arctan H / D.

landing direction indicator a device to indicate visually the direction currently designated for landing and takeoff.

landing light an aircraft aeronautical light designed to illuminate a ground area from the aircraft.

landmark beacon an aeronautical beacon used to indicate the location of a landmark used by pilots as an aid to en route navigation.

laser an acronym for "light amplification by stimulated emission of radiation." The laser produces a highly monochromatic and coherent (spatially and temporally) beam of radiation. A steady oscillation of nearly a single electromagnetic mode is maintained in a volume of an active material bounded by highly reflecting surfaces, called a resonator. The frequency of oscillation varies according to the material used and the methods of initially exciting or pumping the material.

lateral width of a light distribution in roadway lighting, the lateral angle between the reference line and the width line, measured in the cone of maximum candlepower. This angular width includes the line of maximum candlepower. See *reference line* and *width line*.

lens† a glass or plastic element used in luminaires to change the direction and control the distribution of light rays; also, that part of the eye which allows objects at different distances to be focused onto the retina.

level of illumination See *illuminance*.

life performance curve a curve which represents the variation of a particular characteristic of a light source (such as luminous flux or intensity) throughout the life of the source.
Note Life performance curves sometimes are called maintenance curves, as, for example, lumen maintenance curves.

life test of lamps a test in which lamps are operated under specified conditions for a specified length of time, for the purpose of obtaining information on lamp life. Measurements of photometric and electrical characteristics may be made at specified intervals of time during this test.

light radiant energy that is capable of exciting the retina and producing a visual sensation. The visible portion of the electromagnetic spectrum extends from about 380 to 770 nm.
Note The subjective impression produced by stimulating the retina is also sometimes called light. Visual sensations are sometimes arbitrarily defined as sensations of light, and in line with this concept it is sometimes said that light cannot exist until an eye has been stimulated. Electrical stimulation of the retina or the visual cortex is described as producing flashes of light. In illuminating engineering, however, light is a physical entity—radiant energy weighted by the luminous efficiency function. It is a physical stimulus which can be applied to the retina. (See *spectral luminous efficacy of radiant flux* and *values of spectral luminous efficiency for photopic vision*.)

light adaptation the process by which the retina becomes adapted to a luminance greater than about 3.4 cd/m². See also *dark adaptation*.

light center (of a lamp) the center of the smallest sphere that would completely contain the light-emitting element of the lamp.

light center length (of a lamp) the distance from the light center to a specified reference point on the lamp.

light-emitting diode (LED) a p-n junction solid-state diode that emits light depending on its physical construction, material used and exciting current. The output may be in the IR or in the visible region of the spectrum.

light loss factor (LLF) Formerly called "maintenance factor." The ratio of illuminance (or exitance or luminance) for a given area to the value that would occur if lamps operated at their (initial) rated lumen output and if no system variation or depreciation had occurred. Components of this factor may be either initial or maintained.
Note The light loss factor is used in lighting calculations as an allowance for lamp(s) or luminaire(s) operating at other than rated conditions (initial) and for the depreciation of lamps, light control elements and room surfaces to values below the initial or design conditions, so that a minimum desired level of illuminance may be maintained in service. However, this phrase was formerly often defined as the ratio of average illuminance in service to initial illuminance.

light meter See *illuminance (lux or footcandle) meter*.

light source color the color of the light emitted by a source.
Note The color of a point source may be defined by its luminous intensity and chromaticity coordinates; the color of an extended source may be defined by its luminance and chromaticity coordinates. See *perceived light source color*, *color temperature* and *correlated color temperature*.

lighting effectiveness factor (LEF_V) the ratio of equivalent sphere illumination to ordinary measured or calculated illumination.

lightness (of a perceived patch of surface color) the brightness of an area judged relative to the brightness of a similarly illuminated area that appears to be white or highly transmitting.

linear light a luminous signal having a perceptible physical length.

linear polarization the process by which the transverse vibrations of light waves are oriented in or parallel to a specific plane. Polarization may be obtained by using either transmitting or reflecting media.

Linnebach projector a lensless scenic projector, using a concentrated source in a black box and a slide or cutout between the source and the projection surface.

liquid crystal display (LCD) a display made of material whose reflectance or transmittance changes when an electric field is applied.

local lighting lighting providing illuminance over a small area or confined space without providing any significant general surrounding lighting.

localized general lighting lighting utilizing luminaires above the visual task and contributing also to the illumination of the surround.

long-arc lamp an arc lamp in which the distance between the electrodes is large.
Note This type of lamp (such as xenon) is generally of high pressure. The arc fills the discharge tube and is therefore wall stabilized.

longitudinal roadway line (LRL) any line along a roadway that is parallel to the curb line.

louver a series of baffles used to shield a source from view at certain angles, to absorb or block unwanted light or to reflect or direct light. The baffles usually are arranged in a geometric pattern.

louver shielding angle, θ the angle between the horizontal plane of the baffles or louver grid and the plane at which the louver conceals all objects above. See figure 2 and *lamp shielding angle*.
Note The planes usually are so chosen that their intersection is parallel with the louvered blade.

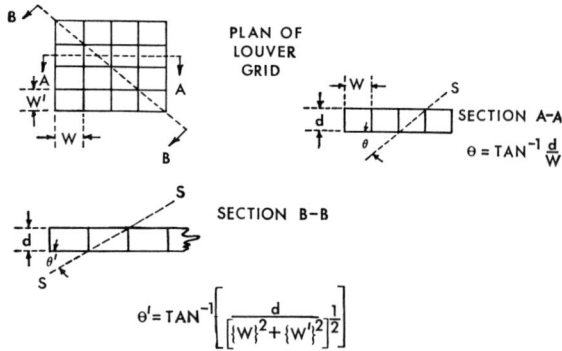

Fig. 2. Louver shielding angles θ and θ'.

louvered ceiling   a ceiling area lighting system comprising a wall-to-wall installation of multicell louvers shielding the light sources mounted above it. See *luminous ceiling.*

low-bay lighting   interior lighting where the roof truss or ceiling height is approximately 7.6 m (25 ft) or less above the floor.

low-key lighting   a type of lighting that, applied to a scene, results in a picture having gradations from middle gray to black, with comparatively small areas of light grays and whites. See *high-key lighting.*

low-pressure mercury lamp   a discharge lamp (with or without a phosphor coating) in which the partial pressure of the mercury vapor does not exceed 100 Pa during operation.

low-pressure sodium lamp   a discharge lamp in which light is produced by radiation from sodium vapor operating at a partial pressure of 0.1–1.5 Pa (approximately 10^{-3}–10^{-2} Torr).

lower (passing) beams   one or more beams directed low enough on the left to avoid glare in the eyes of oncoming drivers, and intended for use in congested areas and on highways when meeting other vehicles within a distance of 300 m (1000 ft). Formerly "traffic beam."

lumen, lm   the SI unit of luminous flux. Radiometrically, it is determined from the radiant power. Photometrically, it is the luminous flux emitted within a unit solid angle (1 sr) by a point source having a uniform luminous intensity of 1 cd.

lumen (or flux) method   a lighting design procedure used for predetermining the relation between the number and types of lamps or luminaires, the room characteristics and the average illuminance on the workplane. It takes into account both direct and reflected flux.

lumen-second, lm · s   a unit of quantity of light, the SI unit of luminous energy (also called a talbot). It is the quantity of light delivered in one second by a luminous flux of one lumen.

luminaire (light fixture)   a complete lighting unit consisting of a lamp or lamps and ballasting (when applicable) together with the parts designed to distribute the light, to position and protect the lamps and to connect the lamps to the power supply.

luminaire ambient temperature factor   the fractional lumen change of a fluorescent luminaire due to internal luminaire temperatures differing from the temperatures at which photometry was performed. This factor takes into consid-

eration a variation in ambient temperature surrounding the luminaire, the means and the conditions of mounting the luminaire, and the use of any insulation in conjunction with the application of the luminaire.

luminaire dirt depreciation factor (LDD)   the fractional loss of task illuminance due to luminaire dirt accumulation.

luminaire efficiency   the ratio of luminous flux (lumens) emitted by a luminaire to that emitted by the lamp or lamps used therein.

luminaire spacing criterion (SC)   a classification parameter for indoor luminaires relating to the distribution of the direct illuminance component produced on the workplane. The SC of a luminaire is an estimated maximum ratio of spacing to mounting height above the workplane for a regular array of that luminaire such that the workplane illuminance will be acceptably uniform.

Note   The SC is not a recommendation for the spacing-to-mounting-height ratio for an installation. It is a characteristic that assists in identifying appropriate luminaires when illuminance uniformity is a design goal. The SC evolved but is distinctly different from an obsolete luminaire parameter called the spacing-to-mounting-height ratio. See chapter 9, Lighting Calculations, for the SC algorithm.

luminaire surface depreciation factor   the fractional loss of task illuminance due to permanent deterioration of luminaire surfaces.

luminance, $L = d^2\Phi \, / \, (d\omega \, dA \cos\theta)$ (in a direction and at a point of a real or imaginary surface)   the quotient of the luminous flux at an element of the surface surrounding the

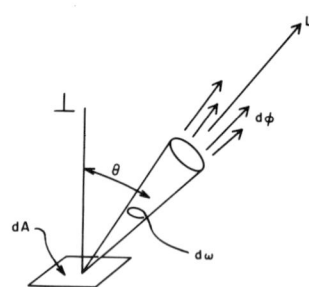

point, and propagated in directions defined by an elementary cone containing the given direction, by the product of the solid angle of the cone and the area of the orthogonal projection of the element of the surface on a plane perpendicular to the given direction. The luminous flux may be leaving, passing through or arriving at the surface. Formerly, "photometric brightness." By introducing the con-

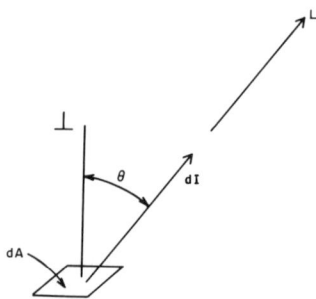

cept of luminous intensity, luminance may be expressed as $L = dI/(dA \cos\theta)$. Here, the luminance at a point of a surface in a direction is interpreted as the quotient of luminous intensity in the given direction produced by an element of the surface surrounding the point by the area of the orthogonal projection of the element of surface on a plane perpendicular to the given direction. [Luminance may be measured at a receiving surface by using $L = dE/(dA \cos \theta)$. This value may be less than the luminance of the emitting surface, due to the attenuation of the transmitting media.]

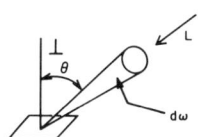

Note   In common usage the term "brightness" usually refers to the magnitude of sensation which results from viewing surfaces or spaces from which light comes to the eye. This sensation is determined in part by the definitely measurable luminance defined above and in part by conditions of observation such as the state of adaptation of the eye. In much of the literature "brightness," used alone, refers to both luminance and sensation. The context usually indicates which meaning is intended. Previous usage not withstanding, neither the term "brightness" nor the term "photometric brightness" should be used to denote the concept of luminance.

luminance coefficient   a coefficient similar to the coefficient of utilization used to determine wall and ceiling luminances. An obsolete term; see *exitance coefficient*.

luminance contrast   the relationship between the luminances of an object and its immediate background. It is equal to $|L_1 - L_2|/L_1 = \Delta L/L_1$, where L_1 and L_2 are the luminances of the background and object, respectively. It must be specified which of L_1 and L_2 is greater. The ratio $\Delta L/L_1$ is known as Weber's fraction.
Note   See note under *luminance*. Because of the relationship among luminance, illuminance and reflectance, contrast often is expressed in terms of reflectance when only reflecting surfaces are involved. Thus, the contrast is equal to $|\rho_1 - \rho_2|/\rho_1$, where ρ_1 and ρ_2 are the reflectances of the background and object, respectively. This method of computing contrast holds only for perfectly diffusing (matte) surfaces; for other surfaces it is only an approximation unless the angles of incidence and view are taken into consideration. (See *reflectance*.)

luminance difference[†]   the difference in luminance between two areas. It usually is applied to contiguous areas, such as the detail of a visual task and its immediate background, in which case it is quantitatively equal to the numerator in the formula for luminance contrast.
Note   See note under *luminance*.

luminance factor, β the ratio of the luminance of a surface or medium under specified conditions of incidence, observation and light source to the luminance of a completely reflecting or transmitting, perfectly diffusing surface or medium under the same conditions.
Note   The reflectance or transmittance cannot exceed 1, but the luminance factor may have any value greater than 0.

luminance ratio   the ratio between the luminances of any two areas in the visual field.

luminance threshold[†]   the minimum perceptible difference in luminance for a given state of adaptation of the eye.

luminescence   any emission of light not ascribable directly to incandescence. See *electroluminescence*, *fluorescence* and *phosphorescence*.

luminous ceiling   a ceiling area lighting system comprising a continuous surface of transmitting material of a diffusing or light-controlling character with light sources mounted above it. See *louvered ceiling*.

luminous density, $\omega = dQ/dV$ quantity of light (luminous energy) per unit volume.

luminous efficacy of radiant flux   the quotient of the total luminous flux by the total radiant flux. It is expressed in lumens per watt.

luminous efficacy of a source of light   the total luminous flux emitted by a lamp divided by the total lamp power input. It is expressed in lumens per watt.
Note   The term "luminous efficiency" has in the past been extensively used for this concept.

luminous efficiency   See *spectral luminous efficiency of radiant flux*.

luminous energy   See *quantity of light*.

luminous exitance, $M = d\Phi/dA$ the areal density of luminous flux leaving a surface at a point. Formerly "luminous emittance" (deprecated).
Note   This is the total luminous flux emitted, reflected and transmitted from the surface and is independent of direction.

luminous flux, Φ radiant flux (radiant power); the time rate of flow of radiant energy, evaluated in terms of a standardized visual response:

$$\Phi_v = K_m \int \Phi_{e,\lambda} V(\lambda) \, d\lambda$$

where Φ_v is in lumens, $\Phi_{e,\lambda}$ is in watts per nanometer, λ is in nanometers, $V(\lambda)$ is the spectral luminous efficiency, and K_m is the maximum spectral luminous efficacy in lumens per watt. Unless otherwise indicated, the luminous flux is defined for photopic vision. For scotopic vision, the corresponding spectral luminous efficiency $V'(\lambda)$ and the corresponding maximum spectral luminous efficacy K'_m are substituted into the above equation. K_m and K'_m are derived from the basic SI definition of luminous intensity and have the values 683 and 1754 lm/W, respectively.

luminous flux density at a surface, $d\Phi/dA$ the luminous flux per unit area at a point on a surface.
Note   This need not be a physical surface; it may also be a mathematical plane. See also *illuminance* and *luminous exitance*.

luminous intensity, $I = d\Phi/d\omega$ (of a point source of light in a given direction)   the luminous flux per unit solid angle in the direction in question. Hence, it is the luminous flux on a small surface centered on and normal to that direction divided by the solid angle (in steradians) which the surface subtends at the source. Luminous intensity may be expressed in candelas or in lumens per steradian (lm/sr).
Note   Mathematically a solid angle must have a point as its apex; the definition of luminous intensity, therefore, applies strictly only to a point source. In practice, however, light emanating from a source whose dimensions are negligible in comparison with the distance from which it is observed may be considered as coming from a point. Specifically, this implies that with change of distance, (1) the variation in solid angle subtended by the source at the receiving point approaches 1/distance², and (2) the average luminance of the projected source area as seen from the receiving point does not vary appreciably. The bare word "intensity" is

sometimes used to designate luminous intensity. However, it is also widely used in other ways, either formally or informally, in other disciplines. "Stimulus intensity" may mean either the retinal illuminance of a proximal stimulus or the luminance of a distal stimulus. "Intensity" is used in the same sense with respect to other modulates such as audition (sound). The same word has been used to designate the level of illuminance on a surface or the flux density in the cross section of a beam of light. In physical optics, "intensity" usually refers to the square of the wave amplitude.

luminous intensity distribution curve   See *intensity distribution curve*.

luminous reflectance   any of the geometric aspects of reflectance in which both the incident and the reflected flux are weighted by the spectral luminous efficiency of radiant flux, $V(\lambda)$.
   Note   Unless otherwise qualified, the term "reflectance" means luminous reflectance.

luminous transmittance   any of the geometric aspects of transmittance in which the incident and transmitted flux are weighted by the spectral luminous efficiency of radiant flux, $V(\lambda)$.
   Note   Unless otherwise qualified, the term "transmittance" means luminous transmittance.

lux, lx   the SI unit of illuminance. One lux is one lumen per square meter (lm/m^2). (See the Appendix for conversion values.)

lux meter   See *illuminance (lux or footcandle) meter*.

M

maintenance factor (MF)   a factor formerly used to denote the ratio of the illuminance on a given area after a period of time to the initial illuminance on the same area. This term is obsolete and is no longer valid. See *light loss factor*.

matte surface   a surface from which the reflection is predominantly diffuse, with or without a negligible specular component. See *diffuse reflection*.

mean horizontal intensity (candlepower)   the average intensity (in candelas) of a lamp in a plane perpendicular to the axis of the lamp and which passes through the luminous center of the lamp.

mean spherical luminous intensity   the average value of the luminous intensity in all directions for a source. Also, the total emitted luminous flux of the source divided by 4π.

mean zonal candlepower   the average intensity (candelas) of a symmetrical luminaire or lamp at an angle to the luminaire or lamp axis which is in the middle of the zone under consideration.

means of egress   An unobstructed and continuous way of exit from any point in a building or structure to a public way. It consists of three distinct parts:
   • the exit access
   • the exit
   • the exit discharge
A means of egress consists of the vertical and horizontal travel ways including intervening room spaces, doorways, hallways, corridors, passageways, ramps, stairs, lobbies, horizontal exits, escalators, enclosures, courts, balconies and yards.

mercury lamp   a high-intensity discharge (HID) lamp in which the major portion of the light is produced by radia-

tion from mercury operating at a partial pressure in excess of 10^5 Pa (approximately 1 atm). Includes clear, phosphor-coated (mercury-fluorescent) and self-ballasted lamps.

mercury fluorescent lamp (phosphor mercury lamp)   an electric-discharge lamp having a high-pressure mercury arc in an arc tube, and an outer envelope coated with a fluorescing substance (phosphor) which transforms some of the ultraviolet energy generated by the arc into light.

mesopic vision   vision with fully adapted eyes at luminance conditions between those of photopic and scotopic vision, that is, between about 3.4 and 0.034 cd/m^2.

metal halide lamp   a high-intensity discharge (HID) lamp in which the major portion of the light is produced by radiation of metal halides and their products of dissociation—possibly in combination with metallic vapors such as mercury. Includes clear and phosphor-coated lamps.

metamers   lights of the same color but of different spectral power distribution.
   Note   The term is also used to denote objects which, when illuminated by a given source and viewed by a given observer, produce metameric lights.

middle ultraviolet   a portion of the electromagnetic spectrum in the range of 200–300 nm.

minimal perceptible erythema (MPE)   the erythemal threshold.

mired   See *reciprocal color temperature*.

modeling light   that illumination which reveals the depth, shape and texture of a subject. Key light, cross light, counter-key light, side light, back light and eye light are types of modeling light.

modulation threshold   threshold value of the quantity

$$\text{modulation} = \frac{L_{max} - L_{min}}{L_{max} + L_{min}}$$

in terms of which manipulation of luminance differences can be specified in the case of a sine wave grating. Periodic patterns that are not sinusoidal can be similarly specified in terms of the modulation of the fundamental sine wave component. The number of periods or cycles per degree of visual angle represents the spatial frequency.

monocular visual field   the visual field of a single eye. See *binocular portion of the visual field*.

mounting height (roadway)[†]   the vertical distance between the roadway surface and the center of the apparent light source of a luminaire.

mounting height above the floor (MH_f)[†]   the distance from the floor to the light center of the luminaire, or to the plane of the ceiling for recessed equipment.

mounting height above the workplane (MH_{wp})[†]   the distance from the workplane to the light center of the luminaire, or to the plane of the ceiling for recessed equipment.

multiple-beam headlamp   a headlamp designed to permit the driver of a vehicle to use any one of two or more distributions of light on the road.

Munsell chroma, C   an index of perceived chroma of the object color, defined in terms of the luminance factor Y and chromaticity coordinates x, y for CIE Standard Illuminant C and the CIE 1931 Standard Observer.

Munsell color system a system of surface-color specification based on perceptually uniform color scales for the three variables: Munsell hue, Munsell value and Munsell chroma. For an observer of normal color vision, adapted to daylight and viewing a specimen when illuminated by daylight and surrounded with a middle-gray to white background, the Munsell hue, value and chroma of the color correlate well with the hue, lightness and perceived chroma.

Munsell hue, *H* an index of the hue of the perceived object color defined in terms of the luminance factor *Y* and chromaticity coordinates *x, y* for CIE Standard Illuminant C and the CIE 1931 Standard Observer.

Munsell value, *V* an index of the lightness of the perceived object color defined in terms of the luminance factor *Y* for CIE Standard Illuminant C and the CIE 1931 Standard Observer.

> Note   The exact definition gives *Y* as a fifth-power function of *V*, so that tabular or iterative methods are needed to find *V* as a function of *Y*. However, *V* can be estimated within ± 0.1 by $V = 11.6(Y/100)^{1/3} - 1.6$ or within ± 0.6 by $V = Y^{1/2}$, where *Y* is the luminance factor expressed in percent.

N

nanometer, nm a unit of wavelength equal to 10^{-9} m. See the Appendix for conversion values.

narrow-angle diffusion that in which flux is scattered at angles near the direction that the flux would take by regular reflection or transmission. See *wide-angle diffusion.*

narrow-angle luminaire a luminaire that concentrates the light within a cone of small solid angle. See *wide-angle luminaire.*

national standard of light† a primary standard of light which has been adopted as a national standard. See *primary standard of light.*

navigation lights an alternative term for *position lights.*

navigation light system a set of aircraft aeronautical lights provided to indicate the position and direction of motion of an aircraft to pilots of other aircraft or to ground observers.

near infrared the region of the electromagnetic spectrum from 770 to 1400 nm.

near ultraviolet the region of the electromagnetic spectrum from 300 to 380 nm.

night the hours between the end of evening civil twilight and the beginning of morning civil twilight.

> Note   Civil twilight ends in the evening when the center of the sun's disk is 6° below the horizon, and begins in the morning when the center of the sun's disk is 6° below the horizon.

nit, nt a unit of luminance equal to 1 cd/m^2.

> Note   The candela per square meter (cd/m^2) is the International Standard (SI) unit of luminance.

nonrecoverable light loss factors (initial or maintained) factors that give the fractional light loss that cannot be recovered by cleaning or lamp replacement, consisting of those components that are due to the lamps operating at other than their rated luminous value. These factors are applied to lighting calculations irrespective of the age of the lighting system.

normal ac power power supplied to a facility during non-emergency situations. It is usually supplied by a local electric utility.

normal lighting permanently installed task and corridor electric lighting normally for use when the premises are occupied.

numerical display (digital display) an electrically operated display of digits. Tungsten filaments, gas discharges, light-emitting diodes, liquid crystals, projected numerals, illuminated numbers and other principles of operation may be used.

O

object color the color of the light reflected or transmitted by an object when illuminated by a standard light source, such as CIE source A, B, C or D_{65}. See *standard source* and *perceived object color.*

obstruction beacon See *hazard beacon.*

obstruction lights aeronautical ground lights provided to indicate obstructions.

occulting light a rhythmic light in which the periods of light are clearly longer than the periods of darkness.

orientation the relation of a building with respect to compass directions.

Ostwald color system a system of describing colors in terms of color content, white content and black content. It is usually exemplified by color charts in triangular form with full color, white and black at the apices providing a gray scale of white and black mixtures, and parallel scales of constant white content as these grays are mixed with varying proportions of the full color. Each chart represents a constant dominant wavelength (called *hue*), and the colors lying on a line parallel to the gray scale represent constant purity (called *shadow series*).

overcast sky one that has 100% cloud cover; that is, no sun is visible.

overhang† the distance between a vertical line passing through a luminaire and the curb or edge of a roadway.

ozone-producing radiation UV energy of wavelength shorter than about 220 nm that decomposes oxygen (O_2), thereby producing ozone (O_3). Some UV sources generate energy at 184.9 nm that is particularly effective in producing ozone.

P

panel (open) face exit sign† a transilluminated sign where both the exit legend and background are translucent.

PAR lamp See *pressed reflector lamp.*

parking lamp a lighting device placed on a vehicle to indicate its presence when parked.

partial diffusion See *incomplete diffusion.*

partly cloudy sky one that has 30–70% cloud cover.

passing beams See *lower (passing) beams.*

pendant luminaire See *suspended (pendant) luminaire.*

perceived light source color the color perceived to belong to a light source.

perceived object color† the color perceived to belong to an object, resulting from characteristics of the object, of the incident light and of the surround, the viewing direction and observer adaptation. See *object color.*

percent flicker   a relative measure of the cyclic variation in output of a light source (percent modulation). It is given by the expression

$$100\frac{A - B}{A + B}$$

where A is the maximum and B is the minimum output during a single cycle. See chapter 6, Light Sources.

perfect diffusion   that in which flux is uniformly scattered in accord with Lambert's cosine law (such that the luminance or radiance is the same in all directions).

perimeter lights   aeronautical ground lights provided to indicate the perimeter of a landing pad for helicopters.

period life   the time interval until lamps are replaced or luminaires are cleaned.

peripheral vision   the seeing of objects displaced from the primary line of sight and outside the central visual field.

peripheral visual field   that portion of the visual field that falls outside the region corresponding to the foveal portion of the retina.

phosphor mercury lamp   See *mercury fluorescent lamp.*

phosphorescence   the emission of light as the result of the absorption of radiation, and continuing for a noticeable length of time after excitation (longer than approximately 10^{-8} s).

phot, ph   the unit of illuminance when the centimeter is taken as the unit of length; it is equal to one lumen per square centimeter.

photobiology   a branch of biology that deals with the effects of optical radiation on living systems.

photochemical radiation   energy in the ultraviolet, visible and infrared regions capable of producing chemical changes in materials.

   Note   Examples of photochemical processes are accelerated fading tests, photography, photoreproduction and chemical manufacturing. In many such applications a specific spectral region is of importance.

photoelectric receiver[†]   a device that reacts electrically in a measurable manner in response to incident radiant energy.

photoflash lamp   a lamp in which combustible metal or other solid material is burned in an oxidizing atmosphere to produce light of high intensity and short duration for photographic purposes.

photoflood lamp   an incandescent filament lamp of high color temperature for lighting objects for photography or videography.

photometer   an instrument for measuring photometric quantities such as luminance, luminous intensity, luminous flux or illuminance. See *densitometer, goniophotometer, illuminance (lux or footcandle) meter, integrating photometer, reflectometer, spectrophotometer* and *transmissometer.*

photometry   the measurement of quantities associated with light.

   Note   Photometry may be visual, in which the eye is used to make a comparison, or physical, in which measurements are made by means of physical receptors.

photometric brightness[†]   a term formerly used for *luminance.*

photoperiod   the environmental (natural or artificial) light-dark cycle to which living organisms may be exposed, as for example the natural cycle at the earth's equator of light (L) for 12 h and darkness (D) for 12 h, expressed as LD 12 : 12.

photopic vision   vision mediated essentially or exclusively by the cones. It is generally associated with adaptation to a luminance of at least 3.4 cd/m². See *scotopic vision.*

photosynthetic irradiance   irradiance within the wavelength band 400–700 nm, measured in W/m².

photosynthetic photon flux density (PPFD)   the number of photons per unit time and per unit area in the wavelength band 400–700 nm. It is measured in units of micromoles (formerly microeinsteins) per second per square meter [μmol/(s · m²)]. One mole contains 6.022×10^{23} photons.

photosynthetically active radiation (PAR)   photon flux in the wavelength band 400–700 nm.

phototherapy   the treatment of disease involving the use of optical radiation.

physical photometer   an instrument containing a physical receptor (such as a photoemissive cell, barrier-layer cell or thermopile) and associated filters that is calibrated so as to read photometric quantities directly. See *visual photometer.*

pilot house control   a mechanical means for controlling the elevation and train of a searchlight from a position on the other side of the bulkhead or deck on which it is mounted.

Planck radiation law   an expression representing the spectral radiance of a blackbody as a function of the wavelength and temperature. This law commonly is expressed by the formula

$$L_\lambda = \frac{dI_\lambda}{dA'} = c_{1L}\lambda^{-5}\left(e^{c_2/\lambda T} - 1\right)^{-1}$$

in which L_λ is the spectral radiance, dI_λ is the spectral radiant intensity, dA' is the projected area ($dA \cos \theta$) of the aperture of the blackbody, e is the base of natural logarithms (2.71828), T is the absolute temperature in kelvins, and c_{1L} and c_2 are constants called the first and second radiation constants.

Note   The symbol c_{1L} is used to indicate that the equation in the form given here refers to the radiance L, or to the intensity I per unit projected area A', of the source. Numerical values are commonly given not for c_{1L} but for c_1, which applies to the total flux radiated from a blackbody aperture, that is, in a hemisphere (2π sr), so that, with the Lambert cosine law taken into account, $c_1 = \pi c_{1L}$. The currently recommended value of c_1 is 3.741832×10^{-16} W · m², or 3.741832×10^{-12} W · cm². Then c_{1L} is $1.1910621 \times 10^{-16}$ W · m² · sr⁻¹, or $1.1910621 \times 10^{-12}$ W · cm² · sr⁻¹. If, as is more convenient, wavelengths are expressed in micrometers and area in square centimeters, then $c_{1L} = 1.1910621 \times 10^4$ W · μm⁴ · cm⁻² · sr⁻¹, L_λ being given in W · cm⁻² · sr⁻¹ · μm⁻¹. The currently recommended value of c_2 is 1.438786×10-2 m · K.

The Planck law in the following form gives the energy radiated from the blackbody in a given wavelength interval (λ_1, λ_2):

$$Q = \int_{\lambda_1}^{\lambda_2} Q_\lambda \, d\lambda = Atc_1 \int_{\lambda_1}^{\lambda_2} \lambda^{-5}\left(e^{c_2/\lambda T} - 1\right)^{-1} d\lambda$$

If A is the area of the radiation aperture or surface in square centimeters, t is the time in seconds, λ is the wavelength in micrometers, and $c_1 = 3.7418 \times 10^4$ W $\cdot$ $\mu m^4 \cdot cm^{-2}$, then Q is the total energy in watt-seconds, or joules (J), emitted from this area (that is, in the solid angle 2π), in time t, within the wavelength interval (λ_1, λ_2).

planckian locus See *blackbody (planckian) locus.*

planoconvex spotlight a spotlight embodying a planoconvex lens and a lamp movable within the housing in relation to the lens in order to vary beam and field angles.

point of fixation a point or object in the visual field at which the eyes look and upon which they are focused.

point of observation a point at which luminance distributions are calculated. For most purposes it may be assumed that the distribution of luminance in the field of view can be described as if there were a single point of observation located at the midpoint of the baseline connecting the centers of the entrance pupils of the two eyes. For many problems it is necessary, however, to regard the centers of the entrance pupils as separate points of observation for the two eyes.

point-by-point method a method of lighting calculation, now called the *point method.*

point method a lighting design procedure for predetermining the illuminance at various locations in lighting installations, by use of luminaire photometric data.
  Note The direct component of illuminance due to the luminaires and the interreflected component of illuminance due to the room surfaces are calculated separately. The sum is the total illuminance at the point.

point source a source of radiation the dimensions of which are small enough, compared with the distance between the source and the irradiated surface, for them to be neglected in calculations and measurements.

point vision the mode of vision of a small source of light such that the sensation is determined by its intensity rather than by its size. Point vision occurs with sources so small that their form or shape is not perceived and that they appear as points of light; this generally means less than 1′ angular subtense.

polarization the process by which unpolarized radiation is polarized. It can be accomplished by either a reflection or a transmission process.

polarized radiation radiation whose electromagnetic field, which is transverse, is oriented in defined directions. The polarization can be rectilinear, elliptic, or circular.

pole (roadway lighting) a standard support generally used where overhead lighting distribution circuits are employed.

portable lighting lighting involving equipment designed for manual portability.

portable luminaire a lighting unit that is not permanently fixed in place. See *table lamp* and *floor lamp.*

portable traffic control light a signaling light designed for manual portability that produces a controllable distinctive signal for purposes of directing aircraft operations in the vicinity of an aerodrome.

position index, P a factor which represents the relative average luminance for a sensation at the borderline between comfort and discomfort (BCD), for a source located anywhere within the visual field.

position lights aircraft aeronautical lights forming the basic, internationally recognized navigation light system.
  Note The system is composed of a red light showing from dead ahead to 110° to the left, a green light showing from dead ahead to 110° to the right, and a white light showing to the rear through 140°. Position lights are also called *navigation lights.*

prefocus lamp a lamp in which, during manufacture, the luminous element is accurately adjusted to a specified position with respect to the physical locating element (usually the base).

preheat (switch start) fluorescent lamp a fluorescent lamp designed for operation in a circuit requiring a manual or automatic starting switch to preheat the electrodes in order to start the arc.

pressed reflector lamp an incandescent filament or electric-discharge lamp of which the outer bulb is formed of two pressed parts that are fused or sealed together; namely, a reflectorized bowl and a cover, which may be clear or patterned for optical control.
  Note Often called a projector or PAR lamp.

primary (light) any one of three lights in terms of which a color is specified by giving the amount of each required to match it by additive combination.

primary line of sight the line connecting the point of observation and the point of fixation. For a single eye, it is the line containing the point of fixation and the center of the entrance pupil.

primary standard of light a light source by which the unit of light is established and from which the values of other standards are derived. See *national standard of light.*
  Note A satisfactory primary (national) standard must be reproducible from specifications (see *candela*). Primary (national) standards usually are found in national physical laboratories such as the National Institute of Standards and Technology in the United States.

projection lamp a lamp with physical and luminous characteristics suited for projection systems such as motion picture projectors, slide projectors and microfilm viewers.

projector a lighting unit that, by means of mirrors and lenses, concentrates the light to a limited solid angle so as to obtain a high value of luminous intensity. See *floodlight, searchlight* and *signaling light.*

protective lighting a system intended to facilitate the nighttime policing of industrial and other properties.

proximal stimulus the distribution of illuminance on the retina

public way any road, alley, or other similar parcel of land essentially open to the outside air, permanently appropriated for public use and having a clear height and width of not less than 3 m (10 ft).

pupil (pupillary aperture) the opening in the iris that admits light into the eye. See *artificial pupil.*

Purkinje phenomenon the reduction in subjective brightness of a red light relative to that of a blue light when the luminances are reduced in the same proportion without changing the respective spectral distributions. In passing from photopic to scotopic vision, the curve of spectral luminous efficiency changes, the wavelength of maximum efficiency being displaced toward the shorter wavelengths.

purple boundary the straight line drawn between the ends of the spectrum locus on a chromaticity diagram.

Q

quality of lighting favorable distribution of luminance in a visual environment, with regard to visual performance, visual comfort, ease of seeing, safety and esthetics or the specific visual tasks involved.

quantity of light (luminous energy), $Q = \int \Phi \, dt$ the product of the luminous flux by the time it is maintained. It is the time integral of luminous flux (compare *light* and *luminous flux*).

quartz-iodine lamp an obsolete term for the tungsten halogen lamp.

quick-flashing light a single flashing light at a frequency equal to or greater than 1 Hz. There is no agreed verbal differentiation between lights that flash at 1 Hz and those that flash more rapidly (a quick-flashing light may be a sequence of single flashes or a sequence of multiflick flashes, at 1-s intervals; there is no restriction on the ratio of the durations of the light to the dark periods).

R

radiance, $L = d^2\Phi/(d\omega \, dA \cos\theta) = dI/(dA \cos\theta)$ (in a direction, at a point of the surface of a source, of a receiver or of any other real or virtual surface) the quotient of the radiant flux leaving, passing through or arriving at an element of the surface surrounding the point, and propagated in directions defined by an elementary cone containing the given direction, by the product of the solid angle of the cone and the area of the orthogonal projection of the element of the surface on a plane perpendicular to the given direction.

   Note In the defining equation θ is the angle between the normal to the element of the source and the given direction.

radiant energy density, $\omega = dQ/dV$ radiant energy per unit volume; typical units, joules per cubic meter (J/m^3).

radiant energy, Q energy traveling in the form of electromagnetic waves. It is measured in units of energy such as joules, ergs or kilowatthours. See *spectral radiant energy*.

radiant exitance, M the density of radiant flux leaving a surface. It is expressed in watts per unit area of the surface.

radiant flux (radiant power), $\Phi = dQ/dt$ the time rate of flow of radiant energy. It is expressed preferably in watts (W), that is, joules per second. See *spectral radiant flux*.

radiant flux density at a surface the quotient of radiant flux of an element of surface to the area of that element, in units such as W/m^2. When referring to radiant flux emitted from a surface, this has been called "radiant emittance" (deprecated); the preferred term is *radiant exitance*. The radiant exitance per unit wavelength interval is called *spectral radiant exitance*. The radiant flux density incident on a surface is called *irradiance* (E).

radiant intensity, $I = d\Phi/d\omega$ the radiant flux proceeding from a source per unit solid angle in the direction considered, often measured in W/sr. See *spectral radiant intensity*.

   Note Mathematically, a solid angle must have a point at its apex; the definition of radiant intensity, therefore, applies strictly only to a point source. In practice, however, radiant energy emanating from a source whose dimensions are negligible in comparison with the distance from which it is observed may be considered as coming from a point. Specifically, this implies that with change of distance (1) the variation in solid angle subtended by the source at the receiving point approaches $1/\text{distance}^2$, and that (2) the average radiance of the projected source area as seen from the receiving point does not vary appreciably.

radiator an emitter of radiant energy.

radiometry the measurement of quantities associated with radiant energy and power.

range lights groups of color-coded boundary lights provided to indicate the direction and limits of a preferred landing path, normally on an aerodrome without runways, but exceptionally on an aerodrome with runways.

rapid-start fluorescent lamp a fluorescent lamp designed for operation with a ballast that provides a low-voltage winding for preheating the electrodes and initiating the arc without a starting switch or the application of high voltage.

rated lamp life the life value assigned to a particular type lamp. This is commonly a statistically determined estimate of average or of median operational life. For certain lamp types other criteria than failure to light may be used; for example, the life may be based on the average time until the lamp type produces no more than a given fraction of the initial luminous flux.

reaction time the interval between the beginning of a stimulus and the beginning of the response of an observer.

recessed luminaire See *flush-mounted or recessed luminaire*.

reciprocal color temperature color temperature T_k expressed on a reciprocal scale ($1/T_k$). An important use stems from the fact that a given small increment in reciprocal color temperature is approximately equally perceptible regardless of the color temperature itself. Also, color temperature conversion filters for sources approximating graybody sources change the reciprocal color temperature by nearly the same amount anywhere on the color temperature scale.

   Note The unit is the reciprocal megakelvin (MK^{-1}). The reciprocal color temperature expressed in MK^{-1} has the numerical value of $10^6/T_k$ when T_k is expressed in kelvins. The acronym "mirek" (for micro-reciprocal-kelvin) occasionally has been used in the literature. The acronym "mired" (for micro-reciprocal-degree) is now considered obsolete as the name for this unit.

recoverable light loss factors factors which give the fractional light loss that can be recovered by cleaning or lamp replacement.

redirecting surfaces and media those surfaces and media that change the direction of the flux without scattering the redirected flux.

reference ballast a ballast specially constructed to have certain prescribed characteristics for use in testing electric-discharge lamps and other ballasts.

reference line (roadway lighting) either of two radial lines where the surface of the cone of maximum candlepower is intersected by a vertical plane parallel to the curb line and passing through the light center of the luminaire.

reference standard[†] an alternative term for secondary standard.

reflectance of a surface or medium, $\rho = \Phi_r/\Phi_i$ the ratio of the reflected flux to the incident flux. Reflectance is a

function of:
1. Geometry:
   a. of the incident flux;
   b. of collection for the reflected flux.
2. Spectral distribution:
   a. characteristic of the incident flux;
   b. weighting function for the collected flux.
3. Polarization:
   a. of the incident flux;
   b. component defined for the collected flux.

Note Unless the state of polarization for the incident flux and the polarized component of the reflected flux are stated, it should be considered that the incident flux is unpolarized and that the total reflected flux (including all polarization) is evaluated. Spectral reflectance depends only on the beam geometry and the character of the reflecting surface (and on polarization). Luminous reflectance also is a function of the spectral distribution of the incident flux. If no qualifying geometric adjective is used, the reflectance for hemispherical collection is meant. Certain of the reflectance terms are theoretically imperfect and are recognized only as practical concepts to be used when applicable. Physical measurements of the incident and reflected flux are always biconical in nature. Directional reflectances cannot exist, since one component would be finite while the other was infinitesimal; here the reflectance distribution function is required. However, the concepts of directional and hemispherical reflectance have practical application in instrumentation, measurements and calculations when including the effect of the nearly zero or nearly 2π conical angle would increase complexity without appreciably affecting the immediate results. In each case of conical incidence or collection, the solid angle need not be a right cone, but may be of any cross section, including a rectangle, a ring or a combination of two or more solid angles. For many geometrically specified reflectance properties it is assumed that the radiance (luminance) is isotropic over the specified solid angle of incidence. Otherwise, the property is a function of the directional distribution of incident radiance (luminance) as well as the beam geometry and the character of the reflecting surface.

reflectance factor, R the ratio of the flux actually reflected by a sample surface to that which would be reflected into the same reflected-beam geometry by an ideal (glossless), perfectly diffuse (lambertian) standard surface irradiated in exactly the same way as the sample. Note the analogies to reflectance in the fact that nine canonical forms are possible, that "spectral" may be applied as a modifier, and that one may have a luminous or radiant reflectance factor, for example. Note also that reflectance cannot exceed 1, but the reflectance factor may have any nonnegative value.

reflected glare glare resulting from reflections of high luminances in polished or glossy surfaces in the field of view. It usually is associated with reflections from within a visual task or areas in close proximity to the region being viewed. See *veiling reflection*.

reflection a general term for the process by which the incident flux leaves a surface or medium from the incident side, without change in frequency.
Note Reflection is usually a combination of regular and diffuse reflection. See *regular (specular) reflection*, *diffuse reflection* and *veiling reflection*.

reflectivity[†] reflectance of a layer of a material of such a thickness that there is no change of reflectance with increase in thickness.

reflectometer a photometer for measuring reflectance.
Note Reflectometers may be visual or physical instruments.

reflector a device used to redirect the flux from a source by the process of reflection. See *retro-reflector*.

reflector lamp an incandescent filament or electric-discharge lamp in which the outer blown glass bulb is coated with a reflecting material so as to direct the light (such as R- or ER-type lamps). The light-transmitting region may be clear, frosted, patterned or phosphor coated.

reflex reflector See *retro-reflector*.

refraction[†] the process by which the direction of a ray of light changes as it passes obliquely from one medium to another in which its speed is different.

refractor a device used to redirect the luminous flux from a source, primarily by the process of refraction

regions of the electromagnetic spectrum for convenience of reference the electromagnetic spectrum is arbitrarily divided as follows:

Vacuum ultraviolet:	
Extreme ultraviolet	10–100 nm
Far ultraviolet	100–200 nm
Middle ultraviolet	200–300 nm
Near ultraviolet	300–380 nm
Visible	380–770 nm
Near (short-wavelength) infrared	770–1400 nm
Intermediate infrared	1400–5000 nm
Far (long-wavelength) infrared	5000–1,000,000 nm

Note The spectral limits indicated above have been chosen as a matter of practical convenience. There is a gradual transition from region to region without sharp delineation. Also, the division of the spectrum is not unique. In various fields of science the classifications may differ according to the phenomena of interest. Another division of the UV spectrum often used by photobiologists is given by the CIE:

UV-A	315–400 nm
UV-B	280–315 nm
UV-C	100–280 nm

regressed luminaire a luminaire mounted above the ceiling with its opening above the ceiling line. See *flush-mounted*, *surface-mounted*, *suspended* and *troffer*.

regular (specular) reflectance the ratio of the flux leaving a surface or medium by regular (specular) reflection to the incident flux. See *regular (specular) reflection*.

regular (specular) reflection that process by which incident flux is redirected at the specular angle. See *specular angle*.

regular transmission that process by which incident flux passes through a surface or medium without scattering. See *regular transmittance*.

regular transmittance the ratio of the regularly transmitted flux leaving a surface or medium to the incident flux.

relative contrast sensitivity (RCS) the relation between the reciprocal of the luminous contrast of a task at visibility threshold and the background luminance expressed as a percentage of the value obtained under a very high level of diffuse task illumination.

relative erythemal factor See *erythemal efficiency of radiant flux*.

relative luminosity an obsolete term for the spectral luminous efficiency of radiant flux.

relative luminosity factor an obsolete term for the spectral luminous efficiency of radiant flux.

resolving power the ability of the eye to perceive the individual elements of a grating or any other periodic pattern with parallel elements. It is measured by the number of cycles per degree that can be resolved. The *resolution threshold* is the period of the pattern that can be just resolved. The *visual acuity*, in such a case, is the reciprocal of one-half the period expressed in minutes. The resolution threshold for a pair of points or lines is the distance, in minutes of arc, between their centers when they can just be distinguished as two objects.

resultant color shift the difference between the perceived color of an object illuminated by a test source and that of the same object illuminated by the reference source, taking account of the state of chromatic adaptation in each case; that is, the resultant of colorimetric shift and adaptive color shift.

retina a membrane lining the posterior part of the inside of the eye. It comprises photoreceptors (cones and rods) that are sensitive to light, and nerve cells that transmit to the optic nerve the responses of the receptor elements.

retro-reflector (reflex reflector) a device designed to reflect light in a direction close to that at which it is incident, whatever the angle of incidence.

rhythmic light a light that, when observed from a fixed point, has a luminous intensity that changes periodically. See *equal interval (isophase) light*, *flashing light*, *group flashing light*, *interrupted quick-flashing light*, *quick-flashing light* and *occulting light*.

ribbon filament lamp an incandescent lamp in which the luminous element is a tungsten ribbon.
   Note   This type of lamp is often used as a standard in pyrometry and radiometry.

rods retinal receptors which respond at low levels of luminance, even below the threshold for cones. At these levels there is no basis for perceiving differences in hue and saturation. No rods are found near the center of the fovea.

room cavity[†] the cavity formed by the plane of the luminaires, the workplane, and the wall surfaces between these two planes.

room cavity ratio (RCR) a number indicating room cavity proportions, calculated from the length, width and height. See *zonal-cavity interreflectance method*.

room utilization factor (utilance) the ratio of the luminous flux (lumens) received on the workplane to that emitted by the luminaire.
   Note   This ratio sometimes is called "interflectance." It is based on the flux emitted by a complete luminaire, whereas the coefficient of utilization is based on the flux generated by the bare lamps in a luminaire.

room surface dirt depreciation (RSDD) the fractional loss of task illuminance due to dirt on the room surface.

runway alignment indicator a group of aeronautical ground lights arranged and located to provide early direction and roll guidance on the approach to a runway.

runway centerline lights lights installed in the surface of the runway along the centerline, indicating the location and direction of the centerline; of particular value in conditions of very poor visibility.

runway edge lights lights installed along the edges of a runway marking its lateral limits and indicating its direction.

runway end identification light a pair of flashing aeronautical ground lights symmetrically disposed on each side of the runway at the threshold to provide additional threshold conspicuity.

runway exit lights lights placed on the surface of a runway to indicate a path to the taxiway centerline.

runway lights aeronautical ground lights arranged along or on a runway. See *runway centerline lights*, *runway edge lights*, *runway end identification light* and *runway exit lights*.

runway threshold[†] the beginning of the part of the runway usable for landing.

runway visibility the meteorological visibility along an identified runway. Where a transmissometer is used for measurement, the instrument is calibrated with respect to a human observer: for example, the sighting of dark objects against the horizon sky during daylight and the sighting of moderately intense unfocused lights of the order of 25 candelas at night. See *visibility (meteorological)*.

runway visual range (RVR) in the United States, an instrumentally derived value, based on standard calibrations, representing the horizontal distance a pilot will see down the runway from the approach end; it is based either on the sighting of high-intensity runway lights or on the visual contrast of other targets, whichever yields the greater visual range.

S

saturation of a perceived color the attribute according to which it appears to exhibit more or less chromatic color, judged in proportion to its brightness. In a given set of viewing conditions, and at luminance levels that result in photopic vision, a stimulus of a given chromaticity exhibits approximately constant saturation for all luminances.

scoop a floodlight consisting of a lamp in an ellipsoidal or paraboloidal matte reflector, usually in a fixed relationship, though some types permit adjustment of the beam shape.

scotopic vision vision mediated essentially or exclusively by the rods. It is generally associated with adaptation to a luminance below about 0.034 cd/m^2. See *photopic vision*.

sealed beam lamp A pressed-glass reflector lamp (PAR) that provides a closely controlled beam of light.
   Note   This term is generally applied in transportation lighting (such as automotive headlamps or aircraft landing lights) to distinguish such lamps from similar devices in which the light source is replaceable within the reflector-lens unit.

sealed beam headlamp an integral optical assembly designed for headlighting purposes, identified by the name "Sealed Beam" branded on the lens.

searchlight a projector designed to produce an approximately parallel beam of light, and having an optical system with an aperture of 20 cm (8 in.) or more.

secondary standard source a constant and reproducible light source calibrated directly or indirectly by comparison with a primary standard. This order of standard is also called a *reference standard*.

Note National secondary (reference) standards are maintained at national physical laboratories; laboratory secondary (reference) standards are maintained at other photometric laboratories. A self-calibrated detector may be used as a secondary standard.

self-ballasted lamp any arc discharge lamp of which the current-limiting device is an integral part.

Note Known as a "blended lamp" in some countries.

self-luminous exit sign† an exit sign consisting of phosphor-coated glass tubes filled with a radioactive tritium gas. When the radioactive gas bombards the phosphor, the tube emits light (luminescence) and illuminates the exit legend, typically between 0.2 and 0.7 cd/m².

semidirect lighting lighting by luminaires distributing 60–90% of their emitted light downward and the balance upward.

semi-indirect lighting lighting by luminaires distributing 60–90% of their emitted light upward and the balance downward.

service period the number of hours per day for which daylighting provides a specified illuminance. It often is stated as a monthly average.

set light in theatrical lighting, the separate illumination of the background or scenic elements.

shade a screen made of opaque or diffusing material designed to prevent a light source from being directly visible at normal angles of view.

shielding angle (of a luminaire) the angle between a horizontal line through the light center and the line of sight at which the bare source first becomes visible. See *cutoff angle (of a luminaire)*.

short-arc lamp an arc lamp in which the distance between the electrodes is small (on the order of 1–10 mm).

Note This type of lamp (often xenon or mercury) generally has an arc tube containing gas at very high pressure.

side back light illumination from behind the subject in a direction not parallel to a vertical plane through the optical axis of the camera. See *back light*.

side light lighting from the side to enhance subject modeling and place the subject in depth (apparently separated from the background).

side marker lamps lamps indicating the presence of a vehicle when seen from the front and sometimes serving to indicate its width. When seen from the side they may also indicate its length.

signal shutter a device that modulates a beam of light by mechanical means for the purpose of transmitting intelligence.

signaling light a projector used for directing light signals toward a designated target zone.

size threshold the minimum perceptible size of an object. It also is defined as the size that can be detected some specific percentage of the times it is presented to an observer, usually 50%. It usually is measured in minutes of arc. See *visual acuity*.

sky factor the ratio of the illuminance on a horizontal plane at a given point inside a building due to the light received directly from the sky, to the illuminance due to an unobstructed hemisphere of sky of uniform luminance equal to that of the visible sky.

sky light visible radiation from the sun redirected by the atmosphere.

sky luminance distribution function for a specified sky condition, the luminance of each direction of the sky relative to the zenith luminance.

soft light diffuse illumination that produces soft-edged, poorly defined shadows on the background when an object is placed in its path. Also, a luminaire designed to produce such illumination.

solar efficacy the ratio of the solar illuminance constant to the solar irradiance constant. The current accepted value is 94.2 lm/W.

solar illuminance constant the solar illuminance at normal incidence on a surface in free space at the earth's mean distance from the sun. The currently accepted value is 127.5 klx (11,850 fc).

solar (irradiance) constant the irradiance, averaging 1353 W/m² (125.7 W/ft²), from the sun at its mean distance from the earth, 1.5×10^{11} m (92.9×10^6 mi), before modification by the earth's atmosphere.

solar radiation simulator a device designed to produce a beam of collimated radiation having a spectrum, flux density and geometric characteristics similar to those of the sun outside the earth's atmosphere.

solid angle, ω† a measure of that portion of space about a point bounded by a conic surface whose vertex is at the point. It is defined as the ratio of intercepted surface area of a sphere centered on that point to the square of the sphere's radius. It is expressed in steradians.

Note Solid angle is a convenient way of expressing the area of light sources and luminaires for computations of discomfort glare factors. It combines into a single number the projected area A_p of the luminaire and the distance D between the luminaire and the eye. It usually is computed by means of the approximate formula

$$\omega = \frac{A_p}{D^2}$$

in which A_p and D_2 are expressed in the same units. This formula is satisfactory when the distance D is greater than about three times the maximum linear dimension of the projected area of the source. Larger projected areas should be subdivided into several elements.

solid angle factor, Q a function of the solid angle ω subtended by a source at a viewing location, given by $Q = 20.4\omega + 1.52\omega^{0.2} - 0.075$. See *index of sensation*.

spacing† for roadway lighting, the distance between successive lighting units, measured along the centerline of the street. For interior applications see chapter 9, Lighting Calculations.

spacing-to-mounting-height ratio, S/MH_{wp} the ratio of the actual distance between luminaire centers to the mounting height above the workplane. Also, an obsolete term that described a characteristic of interior luminaires. See *luminaire spacing criterion*.

special color rendering index, R_i a measure of the color shift of various standardized special colors, including saturated colors, typical foliage and Caucasian skin. It also can be defined for other color samples when the spectral reflectance distributions are known.

spectral directional emissivity, $\epsilon(\theta, \phi, \lambda, T)$ (of an element of surface of a temperature radiator at any wavelength and in a given direction) the ratio of its spectral radiance at that wavelength and in the given direction to that of a blackbody at the same temperature and wavelength.

spectral hemispherical emissivity, $\epsilon(\lambda, T)$ (of an element of surface of a temperature radiator) the ratio of its spectral radiant exitance to that of a blackbody at the same temperature.

Note Hemispherical emissivity is frequently called "total" emissivity. However, the word "total" is ambiguous and should be avoided, since it may also refer to the *spectral total* (all wavelengths) or to the *directional total* (all directions).

spectral (spectroscopic) lamp a discharge lamp that radiates a significant portion of its radiative power in a line spectrum and that, in combination with filters, may be used to obtain monochromatic radiation.

spectral luminous efficacy of radiant flux, $K(\lambda) = \Phi_{v\lambda}/\Phi_{e\lambda}$ the quotient of the luminous flux at a given wavelength by the radiant flux at that wavelength. It is expressed in lm/W.

Note This quantity formerly was called the "luminosity factor." The reciprocal of the maximum luminous efficacy of radiant flux, that is, the ratio between radiant and luminous flux at the wavelength of maximum luminous efficacy, is sometimes called the "mechanical equivalent of light." The most probable value is 0.00146 W/lm, corresponding to 683 lm/W as the maximum possible luminous efficacy. For scotopic vision values the maximum luminous efficacy is 1754 lm/W.

spectral luminous efficiency for photopic vision, $V(l)$ See *values of spectral luminous efficiency for photopic vision.*

spectral luminous efficiency for scotopic vision, $V'(\lambda)$ See *values of spectral luminous efficiency for scotopic vision.*

spectral luminous efficiency of radiant flux the ratio of the luminous efficacy for a given wavelength to the value for the wavelength of maximum luminous efficacy. It is dimensionless.

Note This term replaces the previously used terms "relative luminosity" and "relative luminosity factor."

spectral radiant energy, $Q_\lambda = dQ/d\lambda$ radiant energy per unit wavelength interval at wavelength λ; typical units are J/nm.

spectral radiant exitance See *radiant flux density.*

spectral radiant flux, $\Phi_\lambda = d\Phi/d\lambda$ radiant flux per unit wavelength interval at wavelength λ; typical units are W/nm.

spectral radiant intensity, $I_\lambda = dI/d\lambda$ radiant intensity per unit wavelength interval; typical units are W/(sr · nm).

spectral reflectance of a surface or medium, $\omega(\lambda) = \Phi_{r\lambda}/\Phi_{i\lambda}$ the ratio of the reflected flux to the incident flux at a particular wavelength, λ, or within a small band of wavelengths, $\Delta\lambda$, about λ.

Note The various geometrical aspects of reflectance may each be considered restricted to a specific region of the spectrum and may be so designated by the use of the adjective "spectral."

spectral-total directional emissivity, $\epsilon(\theta, \phi, T)$ (of an element of surface of a temperature radiator in a given direction) the ratio of the radiance of the thermal radiator at temperature T, at a point (x, y) and in the given direction (θ, ϕ), to that of a blackbody at the same temperature T:

$$\epsilon(x, y, \theta, \phi, T) = \frac{L(x, y, \theta, \phi, T)}{L_{\text{blackbody}}(T)}$$

where θ and ϕ are directional angles and T is temperature.

spectral-total hemispherical emissivity, ϵ (of an element of surface of a temperature radiator) the ratio of its radiant exitance to that of a blackbody at the same temperature:

$$\epsilon(x, y, 2\pi, T) = \frac{1}{\pi}\int_{2\pi} \epsilon(x, y, \theta, \phi, T)\cos\theta\, d\omega$$

$$= \frac{1}{\pi}\int_0^\infty \int_{2\pi} \epsilon(\lambda x, y, \theta, \phi, T)\cos\theta\, d\omega\, d\lambda$$

$$= \frac{M(x, y, T)}{M_{\text{blackbody}}(T)}$$

spectral transmittance of a medium, $\tau(\lambda) = \Phi_{t\lambda}/\Phi_{i\lambda}$ the ratio of the transmitted flux to the incident flux at a particular wavelength λ or within a small band of wavelengths, $\Delta\lambda$, about λ.

Note The various geometrical aspects of transmittance may each be considered restricted to a specific region of the spectrum and may be so designated by the use of the adjective "spectral."

spectral tristimulus values See *color-matching functions.*

spectrophotometer an instrument for measuring the transmittance and reflectance of surfaces and media as a function of wavelength.

spectroradiometer an instrument for measuring radiant flux as a function of wavelength.

spectrum locus the locus of points representing the colors of the visible spectrum in a chromaticity diagram.

specular angle the angle between the perpendicular to a surface and the reflected ray; it is numerically equal to the angle of incidence, and it lies in the same plane as the incident ray and the perpendicular but on the opposite side of the perpendicular to the surface.

specular reflectance See *regular (specular) reflectance.*

specular reflection See *regular (specular) reflection.*

specular surface one from which the reflection is predominantly regular. See *regular (specular) reflection.*

speed of light[†] the speed of all radiant energy, including light, is 2.9979258×10^8 m/s in vacuum (approximately 186,000 mi/s). In all material media the speed is less and varies with the material's index of refraction, which itself varies with wavelength.

speed of vision the reciprocal of the duration of the exposure required for something to be seen.

sphere illumination illumination on a task from a source providing equal luminance in all directions about that task, such as an illuminated sphere with the task located at the center.

spherical reduction factor an obsolete term: the ratio of the mean spherical luminous intensity to the mean horizontal intensity.

spotlight any of several different types of luminaires with narrow beam angle designed to illuminate a well-defined area. In motion pictures, generic for Fresnel lens luminaires. Also, a form of floodlight, usually equipped with lenses and reflectors to give a fixed or adjustable narrow beam.

standard illuminant A a blackbody at a temperature of 2856 K. It is defined by its relative spectral power distribution over the range from 300 to 830 nm.

standard illuminant B a representation of noon sunlight with a correlated color temperature of approximately 4900 K. It is defined by its relative spectral power distribution over the range from 320 to 770 nm.

standard illuminant C a representation of daylight having a correlated color temperature of approximately 6800 K. It is defined by its relative spectral power distribution over the range from 320 to 770 nm.

standard illuminant D_{65} a representation of daylight at a correlated color temperature of approximately 6500 K. It is defined by its relative spectral power distribution over the range from 300 to 830 nm.

Note At present, no artificial source for matching this illuminant has been recommended.

standard source in colorimetry, an artificial source that has a specified spectral distribution and is used as a standard.

standard source A a tungsten filament lamp operated at a color temperature of 2856 K, and approximating a blackbody operating at that temperature.

standard source B an approximation of noon sunlight having a correlated color temperature of approximately 4874 K. It is obtained by a combination of source A and a special filter.

standard source C an approximation of daylight provided by a combination of direct sunlight and clear sky, having a correlated color temperature of approximately 6774 K. It is obtained by a combination of source A plus a special filter.

starter a device used in conjunction with a ballast for the purpose of starting an electric-discharge lamp.

state of chromatic adaptation the condition of the chromatic properties of the visual system at a specified moment as a result of exposure to the totality of colors of the visual field currently and in the past.

Stefan-Boltzmann law the statement that the radiant exitance of a blackbody is proportional to the fourth power of its absolute temperature; that is,

$$M = \sigma T^4$$

Note The currently recommended value of the Stefan-Boltzmann constant σ is 5.67032×10^{-8} W $\cdot$ m^{-2} $\cdot$ K^{-4}, or 5.67032×10^{-12} W $\cdot$ cm^{-2} $\cdot$ K^{-4}.

stencil face exit sign a transilluminated sign where either the exit legend or the background are opaque. Usually the exit legend is translucent and the background is die cut from an opaque medium such as plastic or metal.

steradian, sr (unit of solid angle)† the solid angle subtended at the center of a sphere by an area on the surface of the sphere equal to the square of the sphere radius.

stilb a cgs (cm-gram-second) unit of luminance. One stilb equals 1 cd/cm^2. The use of this term is deprecated.

Stiles-Crawford effect the reduced luminous efficiency of rays entering the peripheral portion of the pupil of the eye. This effect applies only to cones and not to rods. Hence, there is no Stiles-Crawford effect in scotopic vision.

stop lamp a device giving a steady warning light to the rear of a vehicle or train of vehicles, to indicate the intention of the operator to diminish speed or to stop.

stray light (in the eye) light from a source that is scattered onto parts of the retina lying outside the retinal image of the source.

street lighting luminaire a complete lighting device consisting of a light source and ballast, where appropriate, together with its direct appurtenances such as globe, reflector, retractor housing and such support as is integral with the housing. The pole, post or bracket is not considered part of the luminaire.

Note Modern street lighting luminaires contain the ballasts for high-intensity discharge lamps where they are used; a light-activated switch may be mounted on the luminaire.

street lighting unit the assembly of a pole or lamp post with a bracket and a luminaire.

striplight (theatrical) once an open trough reflector containing a series of lamps; now usually a compartmentalized luminaire with each compartment containing a lamp, reflector and color frame holder, wired in rotation in three or four circuits and used as borderlights, footlights or cyclorama lighting from above or below.

stroboscopic lamp (strobe light) a flash tube designed for repetitive flashing.

subjective brightness the subjective attribute of any light sensation giving rise to the perception of luminous magnitude, including the whole scale of qualities of being bright, light, brilliant, dim or dark. See *saturation of a perceived color*.

Note The term "brightness" often is used when referring to the measurable luminance. While the context usually makes it clear as to which meaning is intended, the term "luminance" should be used for the photometric quantity, thus reserving "brightness" for the subjective sensation.

sun bearing the angle measured in the plane of the horizon between a vertical plane at a right angle to the window wall and the position of this plane after it has been rotated to contain the sun.

sunburn inflammation with reddening (erythema) of the skin, of variable degree, caused by exposure to direct or diffuse solar radiation or artificial optical radiation.

sunlamp an ultraviolet lamp that radiates a significant portion of its radiative power in the UV-B band (280–315 nm).

sunlight direct visible radiation from the sun.

suntan a darkening of the skin due to an increase of melanin pigmentation above constitutive level and induced by UV radiation.

supplementary lighting lighting used to provide an additional quantity and quality of illumination that cannot readily he obtained by a general lighting system and that supplements the general lighting level, usually for specific work requirements.

supplementary standard illuminant D_{55} a representation of a phase of daylight at a correlated color temperature of approximately 5500 K.

supplementary standard illuminant D_{75} a representation of a phase of daylight at a correlated color temperature of approximately 7500 K.

surface-mounted luminaire a luminaire mounted directly on a ceiling.

suspended (pendant) luminaire a luminaire hung from a ceiling by supports.

switch start fluorescent lamp See *preheat (switch start) fluorescent lamp*.

T

table lamp   a portable luminaire with a short stand, suitable for standing on furniture.

tail lamp   a lighting device used to identify the rear of a vehicle by a warning light.

talbot, T   a unit of light, equal to one lumen-second.

tanning lamp   an ultraviolet lamp that radiates a significant portion of its radiative power in the UV-A or UV-B band.

task lighting   lighting directed to a specific surface or area that provides illumination for visual tasks.

task-ambient lighting   a combination of task lighting and ambient lighting within an area such that the general level of ambient lighting is lower than and complementary to the task lighting.

taxi-channel lights   aeronautical ground lights arranged along a taxi channel of a water aerodrome to indicate the route to be followed by taxiing aircraft.

taxi light   an aircraft aeronautical light designed to provide necessary illumination for taxiing.

taxiway lights   aeronautical ground lights provided to indicate the route to be followed by taxiing aircraft. See *taxiway centerline lights, taxiway edge lights* and *taxiway holding-post light*.

taxiway centerline lights   taxiway lights placed along the centerline of a taxiway except on curves or corners having fillets, where they are placed a distance equal to half the normal width of the taxiway from the outside edge of the curve or corner.

taxiway edge lights   taxiway lights placed along or near the edges of a taxiway.

taxiway holding-post light   a light or group of lights installed at the edge of a taxiway near an entrance to a runway, or to another taxiway, to indicate the position at which the aircraft should stop and obtain clearance to proceed.

temperature radiator   an ideal radiator whose radiant flux density (radiant exitance) is determined by its temperature and the material and character of its surface, and is independent of its previous history. See *blackbody* and *graybody*.

thermopile   a thermal radiation detector consisting of a number of thermocouples interconnected in order to increase the sensitivity to incident radiant flux.

threshold   the value of a variable associated with a physical stimulus (such as size, luminance, contrast or time) that permits the stimulus to be seen a specific percentage of the time or at a specific accuracy level. In many psychophysical experiments, thresholds are presented in terms of 50% accuracy, that is, accuracy 50% of the time. However, the threshold can also be defined as the value of the physical variable that permits the object to be just barely seen. The threshold may be determined by merely detecting the presence of an object, or it may be determined by discriminating certain details of the object. See *absolute luminance threshold, brightness contrast threshold, luminance threshold* and *modulation threshold*.

threshold lights   runway lights placed to indicate the longitudinal limits of that portion of a runway, channel or landing path usable for landing.

top light   illumination of a subject directly from above, employed to outline the upper margin or edge of the subject.

torchère   an indirect floor lamp sending all or nearly all of its light upward.

tormentor light   a luminaire mounted directly behind the sides of the stage arch.

total emissivity   See *spectral-total directional emissivity* and *spectral-total hemispherical emissivity*.

touchdown zone lights   barrettes of runway lights installed in the surface of the runway between the runway edge lights and the runway centerline lights to provide additional guidance during the touchdown phase of a landing in conditions of very poor visibility.

traffic beam   See *lower (passing) beams*.

train   the angle between the vertical plane through the axis of a searchlight drum and the corresponding plane when the searchlight is in a position designated as having zero train.

transient adaptation factor (TAF)   a factor which reduces the equivalent contrast due to readaptation from one luminous background to another.

transition lighting   in roadway lighting, lighting gauged to compensate for visual adaptation between regions of high and low light level, as when entering tunnels.

transmission   a general term for the process by which incident flux leaves a surface or medium on a side other than the incident side, without change in frequency.
Note   Transmission through a medium is often a combination of regular and diffuse transmission. See *regular transmission, diffuse transmission* and *transmittance*.

transmissometer   a photometer for measuring transmittance.
Note   Transmissometers may be visual or physical instruments.

transmittance, $\tau = \Phi_t/\Phi_i$ the ratio of the transmitted flux to the incident flux. It should be noted that transmittance refers to the ratio of flux emerging to flux incident; therefore, reflections at the surface as well as absorption within the material operate to reduce the transmittance. Transmittance is a function of:

1. Geometry:
    a. of the incident flux;
    b. of collection for the transmitted flux.
2. Spectral distribution:
    a. characteristic of the incident flux;
    b. weighting function for the collected flux.
3. Polarization:
    a. of the incident flux;
    b. component defined for the collected flux.

Note   Unless the state of polarization for the incident flux and the polarized component of the transmitted flux are stated, it should be considered that the incident flux is unpolarized and that the total transmitted flux (including all polarization) is evaluated. Spectral transmittance depends on the beam geometry and the character of the transmitting surfaces and media (and on polarization). In addition, luminous transmittance is a function of the spectral distribution of the incident flux. If no qualifying geometric adjective is used, transmittance for hemispherical collection is meant. In each case of conical incidence or collection, the solid angle need not be a right cone, but may be of any cross section, including a rectangle, a ring, or a combination of two or more solid angles. These concepts must be applied with care if the area of the transmitting element is not large compared to its thickness, in view of internal transmission across the boundary of the area. For many geometrically specified transmittance properties it is assumed that the radiance (luminance) is isotropic over the specified solid angle of incidence. Otherwise, the property is a function of the directional distribution of incident radiance (luminance) as well as the beam geometry and the character of the transmitting surfaces or media. Most transmittance quantities are applicable only to the transmittance of thin films with negligible internal scattering, so that the transmitted radiation emerges from a point that is not significantly separated from the point of incidence of the incident ray that produces the transmitted ray or rays. The governing considerations are similar to those for application of the bidirectional reflectance distribution function (BRDF), rather than the bidirectional scattering-surface reflectance distribution function (BSSRDF).

transverse roadway line (TRL) any line across a roadway that is perpendicular to the curb line.

tristimulus values of a light, X, Y, Z the amounts of each of three specific primaries required to match the color of the light.

troffer a recessed lighting unit, usually long and installed with the opening flush with the ceiling. The term is derived from "trough" and "coffer."

troland a unit of retinal illuminance which is based upon the fact that retinal illuminance is proportional to the product of the luminance of the distal stimulus and the area of entrance pupil. One troland is the retinal illuminance produced when the luminance of the distal stimulus is 1 cd/m^2 and the area of the pupil is 1 mm^2.
   Note The troland makes no allowance for interocular attenuation or for the Stiles-Crawford effect.

tube See *lamp*.

tungsten-halogen lamp a gas-filled tungsten incandescent lamp containing a certain proportion of halogens in an inert gas whose pressure exceeds 3 atm.
   Note The tungsten-iodine lamp (U.K.) and quartz iodine lamp (U.S.) belong to this category.

turn signal operating unit that part of a signal system by which the operator of a vehicle indicates the direction a turn will be made, usually by a flashing light.

U

ultraviolet lamp a lamp which radiates a significant portion of its radiative power in the ultraviolet (UV) part of the spectrum; the visible radiation is not of principal interest.

ultraviolet radiation for practical purposes any radiant energy within the wavelength range 10–380 nm. See *regions of the electromagnetic spectrum*.
   Note On the basis of practical applications and the effect obtained, the ultraviolet region often is divided into the following bands:

Ozone-producing	180–220 nm
Bactericidal (germicidal)	220–300 nm
Erythemal	280–320 nm
"Black light"	320–400 nm

There are no sharp demarcations between these bands, the indicated effects usually being produced to a lesser extent by longer and shorter wavelengths. For engineering purposes, the "black light" region extends slightly into the visible portion of the spectrum. Another division of the ultraviolet spectrum often used by photobiologists is given by the CIE:

UV-A	315–400 nm
UV-B	280–315 nm
UV-C	100–280 nm

units of luminance† the luminance of a surface in a specified direction may be expressed as luminous intensity per unit of projected area of surface or as luminous flux per unit of solid angle and per unit of projected surface area. Note Typical units are the cd/m^2 [lm/(sr · m^2)] and the cd/ft^2 [lm/(sr · ft^2)]. The luminance of a surface in a specified direction is also expressed (incorrectly) in lambertian units as the number of lumens per unit area that would leave the surface *if the luminance in all directions within the hemisphere on the side of the surface being considered were the same as the luminance in the specified direction*. A typical unit in this system is the footlambert (fL), equal to 1 lm/ft^2. This method of specifying luminance is equivalent to stating the number of lumens that would leave the surface *if the surface were replaced by a perfectly diffusing surface with a luminance in all directions within the hemisphere equal to the luminance of the actual surface in the direction specified*. In practice no surface follows exactly the cosine formula of emission or reflection; hence the luminance is not uniform, but varies with the angle from which it is viewed. For this reason, this practice is denigrated.

unrecoverable light loss factors See *nonrecoverable light loss factors*.

upper (driving) beams one or more beams intended for distant illumination and for use on the open highway when not meeting other vehicles. Formerly "country beams." See *lower (passing) beams*.

upward component that portion of the luminous flux from a luminaire emitted at angles above the horizontal. See *downward component*.

utilance See *room utilization factor*.

V

vacuum lamp an incandescent lamp in which the filament operates in an evacuated bulb.

valance a longitudinal shielding member mounted across the top of a window or along a wall and usually parallel to the wall, to conceal light sources giving both upward and downward distributions.

valance lighting lighting comprising light sources shielded by a panel parallel to the wall at the top of a window.

values of spectral luminous efficiency for photopic vision, V(l) values for spectral luminous efficiency at 10-nm intervals (see chapter 1, Light and Optics) were provisionally adopted by the CIE in 1924 and were adopted in 1933 by the International Committee on Weights and Measures as a basis for the establishment of photometric standards of types of sources differing from the primary standard in spectral distribution of radiant flux.

Note The standard values of spectral luminous efficiency were determined by observations with a 2° photometric field having a moderately high luminance, and photometric evaluations based upon them consequently do not apply exactly to other conditions of observation. Power in watts weighted in accord with these standard values is often referred to as being measured in "light watts."

values of spectral luminous efficiency for scotopic vision $V'(\lambda)$ values of spectral luminous efficiency at 10-nm intervals (see chapter 1, Light and Optics) were provisionally adopted by the CIE in 1951.

Note These values of spectral luminous efficiency were determined by observation by young dark-adapted observers using extrafoveal vision at near-threshold luminance.

vapor-tight luminaire a luminaire designed and approved for installation in damp or wet locations. It also is described as "enclosed and gasketed."

VASIS (Visual Approach Slope Indicator System) the system of angle-of-approach lights accepted as a standard by the International Civil Aviation Organization, comprising two bars of lights located at each side of the runway near the threshold and showing red or white or a combination of both (pink) to the approaching pilot, depending upon his or her position with respect to the glide path.

veiling luminance a luminance superimposed on the retinal image which reduces its contrast. It is this veiling effect produced by bright sources or areas in the visual field that results in decreased visual performance and visibility.

veiling reflection regular reflections that are superimposed upon diffuse reflections from an object and that partially or totally obscure the details to be seen by reducing the contrast. This sometimes is called *reflected glare*. Another kind of veiling reflections occurs when one looks through a plate of glass. A reflected image of a bright element or surface may be seen superimposed on what is viewed through the glass plate.

vertical plane of a searchlight the plane through the axis of the searchlight drum which contains the elevation angle. See *horizontal plane of a searchlight*.

visibility the quality or state of being perceivable by the eye. In many outdoor applications, visibility is defined in terms of the distance at which an object can be just perceived by the eye. In indoor applications it usually is defined in terms of the contrast or size of a standard test object, observed under standardized view conditions, having the same threshold as the given object. See *visibility (meteorological)*.

visibility (meteorological) the greatest distance, expressed in kilometers or miles, that selected objects (visibility markers) or lights of moderate intensity (25 cd) can be seen and identified under specified conditions of observation.

visibility level (VL) a contrast multiplier to be applied to the visibility reference function to provide the luminance contrast required at different levels of task background luminance to achieve visibility for specified conditions relating to the task and observer.

visibility performance criteria function, VL8 a function representing the luminance contrast required to achieve 99% visual certainty for the same task used for the visibility reference function, including the effects of dynamic presentation and uncertainty in task location.

visibility reference function, VL1 a function representing the luminance contrast required at different levels of task background luminance to achieve visibility threshold for the visibility reference task consisting of a 4' disk exposed for 0.2 s.

vision See *central (foveal) vision, mesopic vision, peripheral vision, photopic vision* and *scotopic vision*.

visual acuity a measure of the ability to distinguish fine details, measured with a set of optotypes (test types for determining visual acuity) of different sizes. Quantitatively, it is the reciprocal of the minimum angular size in minutes of the critical detail of an object that can just be seen.

visual angle the angle subtended by an object or detail at the point of observation. It usually is measured in minutes of arc.

visual approach slope indicator system See *VASIS*.

visual comfort probability (VCP) the rating of a lighting system expressed as a percentage of people who, when viewing from a specified location and in a specified direction, will be expected to find it acceptable in terms of discomfort glare. It is related to the discomfort glare rating (DGR).

visual field the locus of objects or points in space that can be perceived when the head and eyes are kept fixed. The field may be monocular or binocular. See *monocular visual field, binocular portion of the visual field, central visual field* and *peripheral visual field*.

visual perception the interpretation of impressions transmitted from the retina to the brain in terms of information about a physical world displayed before the eye.

Note Visual perception involves any one or more of the following: recognizing the presence of something (object, aperture or medium); identifying it; locating it in space; noting its relation to other things; identifying its movement, color, brightness or form.

visual performance the quantitative assessment of the performance of a visual task, taking into consideration speed and accuracy.

visual photometer a photometer in which the equality of brightness of two surfaces is established visually. See *physical photometer*.

Note The two surfaces usually are viewed simultaneously side by side. This method is used in portable visual luminance meters. It is satisfactory when the color difference between the test source and comparison source is small. However, when there is a substantial color difference, a flicker photometer provides more precise measurements. In this type of photometer the two surfaces are viewed alternately at such a rate that the color sensations either nearly or completely blend, and the flicker due to brightness difference is balanced by adjusting the comparison source.

visual range of a light or object the maximum distance at which it can be seen and identified.

visual surround all portions of the visual field except the visual display used in performing a task.

visual task conventionally, those details and objects that must be seen for the performance of a given activity, including their immediate background.

Note This term is a misnomer in that it refers to the visual display itself and not the task of extracting information from it. That task in turn has to be differentiated from the overall task performed by the observer.

visual task evaluator (VTE) a form of visibility meter that measures the level of contrast of a given visual display above the threshold of visibility. The ratio of the contrast of a display to its threshold contrast represents its visibility level (VL).

voltage-to-luminaire factor   the fractional loss of illuminance due to improper voltage at the luminaire.

W

wavelength   the distance between two successive points of a periodic wave, in the direction of propagation, at which the oscillation has the same phase. The three commonly used units are listed in the following table:

Name	Symbol	Size
micrometer (micron)	μm	10^{-6} m
nanometer	nm	10^{-9} m
angstrom	Å	10^{-10} m

The use of the terms *micron* and *angstrom* is deprecated.

Weber's fraction   See *luminance contrast*.

wide-angle diffusion   diffusion in which flux is scattered at angles far from the direction that it would take by regular reflection or transmission. See *narrow-angle diffusion*.

wide-angle luminaire   a luminaire that concentrates the light within a cone of large solid angle. See also *narrow-angle luminaire*.

width line (roadway lighting)   the radial line (the one that makes the larger angle with the reference line) that passes through the point of half-maximum candlepower on the lateral candlepower distribution curve plotted on the surface of the cone of maximum candlepower.

Wien displacement law   an expression representing, in a functional form, the spectral radiance of a blackbody as a function of the wavelength and the temperature:

$$L_\lambda = \frac{dI_\lambda}{dA'} = c_{1L}\lambda^{-5}f(\lambda T)$$

The two principal corollaries of this law are

$$\lambda_m T = b$$

$$\frac{L_m}{T^5} = b'$$

which show how the maximum spectral radiance L_m and the wavelength λ_m at which it occurs are related to the absolute temperature T. See *Wien radiation law*.

Note   The currently recommended value of b is 2.8978×10^{-3} m $\cdot$ K or 2.8978×10^{-1} cm $\cdot$ K. From the Planck radiation law, and with the use of the values of b, c_1 and c_2 as given above, b' is found to be 4.0956×10^{-14} W $\cdot$ cm^{-2} $\cdot$ sr^{-1} $\cdot$ μm^{-1} $\cdot$ K^{-5}.

Wien radiation law   an expression representing approximately the spectral radiance of a blackbody as a function of its wavelength and temperature. It commonly is expressed by the formula

$$l_\lambda = \frac{dI_\lambda}{dA'} = c_{1L}\lambda^{-5}e^{-c_2/\lambda T}$$

This formula is accurate to 1% or better for values of λT less than 3000 μm $\cdot$ K.

wing clearance lights   aircraft lights provided at the wing tips to indicate the extent of the wing span when the navigation lights are located an appreciable distance inboard of the wing tips.

workplane   the plane at which work usually is done, and on which the illuminance is specified and measured. Unless otherwise indicated, this is assumed to be a horizontal plane 0.76 m (30 in.) above the floor.

working standard   a standardized light source for regular use in photometry.

Z

zonal-cavity interreflectance method   a procedure for calculating coefficients of utilization, wall exitance coefficients and ceiling cavity exitance coefficients, taking into consideration the luminaire intensity distribution, room size and shape (cavity ratio concepts) and room reflectances. It is based on flux transfer theory.

zonal constant   a factor by which the mean intensity emitted by a source of light in a given angular zone is multiplied to obtain the lumens in the zone. See chapter 2, Measurement of Light and Other Radiant Energy.

zonal-factor interreflection method   a formerly used procedure for calculating coefficients of utilization, based on integral equations.

zonal-factor method   a procedure for predetermining, from typical luminaire photometric data in discrete angular zones, the proportion of luminaire output which would be incident initially (without interreflections) on the workplane, ceiling, walls and floor of a room.

zonal multipliers   multipliers for the flux in each 10° conical zone from 0° (nadir) to 90° (horizontal) from a luminaire, expressing the fraction of that zonal flux that is directly incident on the floor of a room cavity. These multipliers are a function of the room cavity ratio and are used to determine the direct ratio.

Appendix

Appendix Fig. 1. Partial List of Abbreviations, Symbols and Acronyms Used in This Handbook

A

A	ampere
Å	angstrom unit
ac	alternating current
AIA	American Institute of Architects
ANSI	American National Standards Institute
ASID	American Society of Interior Designers
ASTM	American Society for Testing and Materials
ASHRAE	American Society of Heating, Refrigerating and Air-Conditioning Engineers
atm	atmosphere

B

BCD	borderline between comfort and discomfort
BCP	beam candlepower
BL	"black light"
BRDF	bidirectional reflectance distribution function
Btu	British thermal unit

C

°C	degree Celsius
cal	calorie
CBM	Certified Ballast Manufacturers
CBU	coefficient of beam utilization
CCR	ceiling cavity ratio
cgs	centimeter-gram-second (system)
CIE	Commission Internationale de l'Éclairage (International Commission on Illumination)
cm	centimeter
cos	cosine
cp	candlepower
CPI	color preference index
CRF	contrast rendition factor
CRI	color rendering index
CRT	cathode-ray tube
CSA	Canadian Standards Association
CSI	compact source iodide
CU	coefficient of utilization
CW	cool white
CWX	cool white deluxe

D

dB	decibel
dc	direct current
DGF	disability glare factor
DIC	direct illumination component

E

emf	electromotive force
ESI	equivalent sphere illumination
EU	erythemal unit

F

°F	degree Fahrenheit
fc	footcandle
FCR	floor cavity ratio
fff	flicker fusion frequency
ft	foot
ft^2	square foot

H

h	hour
HID	high-intensity discharge
HMI	hydragyrum medium-arc-length iodide
hp	horsepower
HPS	high-pressure sodium
Hz	hertz

I

IALD	International Association of Lighting Designers
IDSA	Industrial Designers Society of America
IEEE	Institute of Electrical and Electronics Engineers
IERI	Illuminating Engineering Research Institute
in.	inch
in.^{2}	square inch
IR	infrared
ISO	International Organization for Standarization

J

J	joule

K

K	kelvin
kcal	kilocalorie
kg	kilogram
kHz	kilohertz
km	kilometer
km^2	square kilometer
km / s	kilometer per second
kV	kilovolt
kVA	kilovoltampere
kVAr	reactive kilovoltampere
kW	kilowatt
kWh	kilowatthour

L

LBO	lamp burnout
LCD	liquid crystal display
LDD	luminaire dirt depreciation
LED	light-emitting diode
LEF$_v$	lighting effectiveness factor
LLD	lamp lumen depreciation
LLF	light loss factor
lm	lumen
ln	logarithm (natural)
LPS	low-pressure sodium
lx	lux

Appendix Fig. 1. *Continued*

M

m	meter
m^2	square meter
mA	milliampere
max	maximum
MF	maintenance factor
MH	mounting height
MHz	megahertz
min	minimum
min	minute (time)
mm	millimeter
mm^2	square millimeter
mol wt	molecular weight
MPE	minimal perceptable erythema
mph	miles per hour

N

NBS	National Bureau of Standards
NEC	National Electrical Code
NEMA	National Electrical Manufacturers Association
nm	nanometer

O

OSA	Optical Society of America

P

PAR	pressed-reflector lamp
pf	power factor

R

R	reflectance lamp
rad	radian
RCR	room cavity ratio
RCS	relative contrast sensitivity
rms	root mean square
RSDD	room surface dirt depreciation
RTP	relative task performance
RVP	relative visual performance
RVR	runway visual range

S

s	second
sin	sine
SPD	spectral power distribution
sq	square
sr	steradian

T

TAF	transient adaptation factor
tan	tangent
temp	temperature

U

UV	ultraviolet
UL	Underwriters Laboratories

V

V	volt
VA	voltampere
VAr	reactive voltampere
VASIS	visual approach slope indicator system
VCP	visual comfort probability
VDU	visual display unit
VHO	very high output (lamp)
VI	visibility index
VL	visibility level
VTE	visual task evaluator
VTP	visual task photometer

W

W	watt
WW	warm white
WWX	warm white deluxe
mA	microampere
μV	microvolt
μW	microwatt
ρ_{CC}	effective ceiling cavity reflectance
ρ_{FC}	effective floor cavity reflectance
'	minute (angular measure)
''	second (angular measure)
°	degree

Appendix Fig. 2. Units, Symbols and Defining Equations for Fundamental Photometric and Radiometric Quantities*

Quantity†	Symbol†	Defining Equation	Unit	Symbol
Radiant energy	Q, (Q_e)		erg joule‡ calorie kilowatt-hour	erg J cal kWh
Radiant energy density	w, (w_e)	$w = dQ/dV$	joule per cubic meter‡ erg per cubic centimeter	J/m^3 erg/cm^3
Radiant flux	Φ, (Φ_e)	$\Phi = dQ/dt$	erg per second watt‡	erg/s W
Radiant flux density at a surface 　Radiant exitance (Radiant emittance§) 　Irradiance	M, (M_e) E, (E_e)	$M = d\Phi/dA$ $E = d\Phi/dA$	watt per square centimeter, watt per square meter,‡ etc.	W/cm^2 W/m^2
Radiant intensity	I, (I_e)	$I = d\Phi/d\omega$ (ω = solid angle through which flux from point source is radiated)	watt per steradian‡	W/sr
Radiance	L, (L_e)	$L = d^2\Phi/(d\omega dA \cos\theta)$ $= dI/(dA \cos\theta)$ (θ = angle between line of sight and normal to surface considered)	watt per steradian and square centimeter watt per steradian and square meter‡	W/sr·cm^2 W/sr·m^2

Appendix Fig. 2. *Continued*

Emissivity, spectral-total hemispherical	ϵ	$\epsilon = M/M_{blackbody}$ (M and $M_{blackbody}$ are respectively the radiant exitance of the measured specimen and that of a blackbody at the same temperature as the specimen)	one (numeric)	
Emissivity, spectral-total directional	$\epsilon(\theta, \phi, T)$	$\epsilon(\theta, \phi, T) = L(T)/L_{blackbody}(T)[L(T)$ and $L_{blackbody}(T)$ are, respectively, the radiance of the measured specimen and that of a blackbody at the same temperature (that of the specimen)].	one (numeric)	
Emissivity, spectral directional	$\epsilon(\theta, \phi, \lambda, T)$	$\epsilon(\lambda, \theta, \phi, T) = L_\lambda(\lambda, \theta, \phi, T)/L_{\lambda,blackbody}(\lambda, T)$ (L_λ and $L_{\lambda blackbody}$ are respectively the spectral radiance of the measured specimen and that of a blackbody at the same temperature of the specimen)	one (numeric)	
Emissivity, spectral hemispherical	$\epsilon(\lambda, T)$	$\epsilon(\lambda, T) = M_\lambda(\lambda, T)/M_{\lambda,blackbody}(\lambda, T)$ are respectively the spectral radiant exitance of the measured specimen and that of a blackbody at the same temperature of the specimen	one (numeric)	
Absorptance	α	$\alpha = \Phi_a/\Phi_i\|$	one (numeric)	
Reflectance	ρ	$\rho = \Phi_r/\Phi_i\|$	one (numeric)	
Transmittance	τ	$\tau = \Phi_t/\Phi_i\|$	one (numeric)	
Luminous efficacy	K	$K = \Phi_v/\Phi_e$	lumen per watt‡	lm/W
Luminous efficiency	V	$V = K/K_{maximum}$ ($K_{maximum}$ = maximum value of $K(\lambda)$ function)	one (numeric)	
Luminous energy (quantity of light)	$Q, (Q_v)$	$Q_v = \int_{380}^{770} K(\lambda)Q_{e\lambda}d\lambda$	lumen-hour lumen-second‡ (talbot)	lm·h lm·s
Luminous energy density	$w, (w_v)$	$w = dQ/dV$	lumen-hour per cubic centimeter	lm·h/cm³
Luminous flux	$\Phi, (\Phi_v)$	$\Phi = dQ/dt$	lumen‡	lm

Luminous flux density at a surface
  Luminous exitance (Luminous emittance§)
  Illuminance (Illumination§)
	
	$M, (M_v)$
	
	$E, (E_v)$
		
		$M = d\Phi/dA$
		
		$E = d\Phi/dA$
			
			lumen per square foot
			
			{ footcandle (lumen per square foot)
			lux (lm/m²)‡
			phot(lm/cm²)
				
				lm/ft²
				
				fc
				lx
				ph

Luminous intensity (candlepower)	$I, (I_v)$	$I = d\Phi/d\omega$ (ω = solid angle through which flux from point source is radiated)	candela‡ (lumen per steradian)	cd
Luminance	$L, (L_v)$	$L = d^2\Phi/(d\omega dA \cos\theta)$ $= dI/(dA \cos\theta)$ (θ = angle between line of sight and normal to surface considered)	candela per unit area stilb (cd/cm²) nit (cd/m²‡) footlambert (cd/πft²)§ lambert (cd/πcm²)§ apostilb (cd/πm²)§	cd/in², etc. sb nt, cd/m² fL§ L§ asb§

* The symbols for photometric quantities are the same as those for the corresponding radiometric quantities. When it is necessary to differentiate them the subscripts v and e respectively should be used, *e.g.*, Q_v and Q_e.

† Quantities may be restricted to a narrow wavelength band by adding the word spectral and indicating the wavelength. The corresponding symbols are changed by adding a subscript λ, *e.g.*, Q_λ, for a spectral concentration or a λ in parentheses, *e.g.*, $K(\lambda)$, for a function of wavelength.

‡ International System (SI) unit

§ Use is deprecated

‖ Φ_i = incident flux, Φ_a = absorbed flux, Φ_r = reflected flux, Φ_t = transmitted flux

Appendix Fig. 3. Conversion Factors for Units of Length

Multiply Number of → / To Obtain Number of ↓ (By)	Angstroms	Nanometers	Micrometers (Microns)	Millimeters	Centimeters	Meters	Kilometers	Mils	Inches	Feet	Miles
Angstroms	1	10	10^4	10^7	10^8	10^{10}	10^{13}	2.540×10^5	2.540×10^8	3.048×10^9	1.609×10^{13}
Nanometers	10^{-1}	1	10^3	10^6	10^7	10^9	10^{12}	2.540×10^4	2.540×10^7	3.048×10^8	1.609×10^{12}
Micrometers (Microns)	10^{-4}	10^{-3}	1	10^3	10^4	10^6	10^9	2.540×10	2.540×10^4	3.048×10^5	1.609×10^9
Millimeters	10^{-7}	10^{-6}	10^{-3}	1	10	10^3	10^6	2.540×10^{-2}	2.540×10	3.048×10^2	1.609×10^6
Centimeters	10^{-8}	10^{-7}	10^{-4}	10^{-1}	1	10^2	10^5	2.540×10^{-3}	2.540	3.048×10	1.609×10^5
Meters	10^{-10}	10^{-9}	10^{-6}	10^{-3}	10^{-2}	1	10^3	2.540×10^{-5}	2.540×10^{-2}	3.048×10^{-1}	1.609×10^3
Kilometers	10^{-13}	10^{-12}	10^{-9}	10^{-6}	10^{-5}	10^{-3}	1	2.540×10^{-8}	3.048×10^{-5}	3.048×10^{-4}	1.609
Mils	3.937×10^{-6}	3.937×10^{-5}	3.937×10^{-2}	3.937×10	3.937×10^2	3.937×10^4	3.937×10^7	1	10^3	1.2×10^4	6.336×10^7
Inches	3.937×10^{-9}	3.937×10^{-8}	3.937×10^{-5}	3.937×10^{-2}	3.937×10^{-1}	3.937×10	3.937×10^4	10^{-3}	1	12	6.336×10^4
Feet	3.281×10^{-10}	3.281×10^{-9}	3.281×10^{-6}	3.281×10^{-3}	3.281×10^{-2}	3.281	3.281×10^3	8.333×10^{-5}	8.333×10^{-2}	1	5.280×10^3
Miles	6.214×10^{-14}	6.214×10^{-13}	6.214×10^{-10}	6.214×10^{-7}	6.214×10^{-6}	6.214×10^{-4}	6.214×10^{-1}	1.578×10^{-8}	1.578×10^{-5}	1.894×10^{-4}	1

Appendix Fig. 4. Conversion from Values in SI Units

Left labels point to output columns as follows: m → ft, cm → in, kcd/m² → cd/in², cd/m² → fL, lx* → fc (for both panels).

lx*	fc	fL	cd/in²	in	ft	lx*	fc	fL	cd/in²	in	ft
1	.09	.29	.65	.39	3.3	500	46.5	146.0	322.5	196.9	1641
2	.19	.58	1.29	.79	6.6	510	47.4	148.9	329.0	200.8	1673
3	.28	.88	1.94	1.18	9.8	520	48.3	151.8	335.4	204.7	1706
4	.37	1.17	2.58	1.57	13.1	530	49.2	154.7	341.9	208.7	1739
5	.47	1.46	3.23	1.97	16.4	540	50.2	157.6	348.3	212.6	1772
6	.56	1.75	3.87	2.36	19.7	550	51.1	160.5	354.8	216.5	1805
7	.65	2.04	4.52	2.76	23.0	560	52.0	163.5	361.2	220.5	1837
8	.74	2.34	5.16	3.15	26.2	570	53.0	166.4	367.7	224.4	1870
9	.84	2.63	5.81	3.54	29.5	580	53.9	169.3	374.1	228.3	1903
						590	54.8	172.2	380.6	232.3	1936
100	9.3	29.2	64.5	39.4	328	600	55.7	175.1	387.0	236.2	1969
110	10.2	32.1	71.0	43.3	361	610	56.7	178.1	393.5	240.2	2001
120	11.1	35.0	77.4	47.2	394	620	57.6	181.0	399.9	244.1	2034
130	12.1	37.9	83.9	51.2	427	630	58.5	183.9	406.4	248.0	2067
140	13.0	40.9	90.3	55.1	459	640	59.5	186.8	412.8	252.0	2100
150	13.9	43.8	96.8	59.1	492	650	60.4	189.7	419.3	255.9	2133
160	14.9	46.7	103.2	63.0	525	660	61.3	192.7	425.7	259.8	2165
170	15.8	49.6	109.7	66.9	558	670	62.2	195.6	432.2	263.8	2198
180	16.7	52.5	116.1	70.9	591	680	63.2	198.5	438.6	267.7	2231
190	17.7	55.5	122.6	74.8	623	690	64.1	201.4	445.1	271.7	2264
200	18.6	58.4	129.0	78.7	656	700	65.0	204.3	451.5	275.6	2297
210	19.5	61.3	135.5	82.7	689	710	66.0	207.2	458.0	279.5	2330
220	20.4	64.2	141.9	86.6	722	720	66.9	210.2	464.4	283.5	2362
230	21.4	67.1	148.4	90.6	755	730	67.8	213.1	470.9	287.4	2395
240	22.3	70.1	154.8	94.5	787	740	68.7	216.0	477.3	291.3	2428
250	23.2	73.0	161.3	98.4	820	750	69.7	218.9	483.8	295.3	2461
260	24.2	75.9	167.7	102.4	853	760	70.6	221.8	490.2	299.2	2494
270	25.1	78.8	174.2	106.3	886	770	71.5	224.8	496.7	303.1	2526
280	26.0	81.7	180.6	110.2	919	780	72.5	227.7	503.1	307.1	2559
290	26.9	84.7	187.1	114.2	951	790	73.4	230.6	509.6	311.0	2592
300	27.9	87.6	193.5	118.1	984	800	74.3	233.5	516.0	315.0	2625
310	28.8	90.5	200.0	122.0	1017	810	75.2	236.4	522.5	318.9	2658
320	29.7	93.4	206.4	126.0	1050	820	76.2	239.4	528.9	322.8	2690
330	30.7	96.3	212.9	130.0	1083	830	77.1	242.3	535.4	326.8	2723
340	31.6	99.2	219.3	133.9	1116	840	78.0	245.2	541.8	330.7	2756
350	32.5	102.2	225.8	137.8	1148	850	79.0	248.1	548.3	334.6	2789
360	33.4	105.8	232.2	141.7	1181	860	79.9	251.0	554.7	338.6	2822
370	34.4	108.0	238.7	145.7	1214	870	80.8	254.0	561.2	342.5	2854
380	35.3	110.9	245.1	149.6	1247	880	81.8	256.9	567.6	346.5	2887
390	36.2	113.8	251.6	153.5	1280	890	82.7	259.8	574.1	350.4	2920
400	37.2	116.8	258.0	157.5	1312	900	83.6	262.7	580.5	354.3	2953
410	38.1	119.7	264.5	161.4	1345	910	84.5	265.6	587.0	358.3	2986
420	39.0	122.6	270.9	165.4	1378	920	85.5	268.5	593.4	362.2	3019
430	39.9	125.5	277.4	169.3	1411	930	86.4	271.5	600.0	366.1	3051
440	40.9	128.4	283.8	173.2	1444	940	87.3	274.4	606.3	370.1	3084
450	41.8	131.4	290.3	177.2	1476	950	88.3	277.3	612.8	374.0	3117
460	42.7	134.3	296.7	181.1	1509	960	89.2	280.2	619.2	378.0	3150
470	43.7	137.2	303.2	185.0	1542	970	90.1	283.1	625.7	381.9	3183
480	44.6	140.1	309.6	189.0	1575	980	91.0	286.1	632.1	385.8	3215
490	45.5	143.0	316.1	192.9	1608	990	92.0	289.0	638.6	389.8	3248

* Also useful for converting from ft² to m².

Appendix Fig. 5. Conversion to Values in SI Units

Left columns headers (arrows): ft, in, cd/in², fL, fc*
Right columns headers (arrows): ft, in, cd/in², fL, fc*

	lx	cd/m²	kcd/m²	cm	m		lx	cd/m²	kcd/m²	cm	m
1	10.76	3.4	1.55	2.54	.30	500	5380	1713	775.0	1270	152.4
2	21.5	6.9	3.00	5.08	.61	510	5488	1747	790.5	1295	155.4
3	32.3	10.3	4.65	7.62	.91	520	5595	1782	806.0	1321	158.5
4	43.0	13.7	6.20	10.16	1.22	530	5703	1816	821.6	1346	161.5
5	53.8	17.1	7.75	12.70	1.52	540	5810	1850	837.0	1372	164.6
6	64.6	20.6	9.30	15.24	1.83	550	5918	1884	852.5	1397	167.6
7	75.3	24.0	10.85	17.78	2.13	560	6026	1919	868.0	1422	170.7
8	86.1	27.4	12.40	20.32	2.44	570	6133	1953	883.5	1448	173.7
9	96.8	30.8	13.95	22.86	2.74	580	6241	1987	899.0	1473	176.8
						590	6348	2021	914.5	1499	179.8
100	1076	343	155.0	254	30.5	600	6456	2056	930.0	1524	182.9
110	1184	377	170.5	279	33.5	610	6564	2090	945.5	1549	185.9
120	1291	411	186.0	305	36.6	620	6671	2124	961.0	1575	189.0
130	1399	445	201.5	330	39.6	630	6779	2158	976.5	1600	192.0
140	1506	480	217.0	356	42.7	640	6886	2193	992.0	1626	195.1
150	1614	514	232.5	381	45.7	650	6994	2227	1007.5	1651	198.1
160	1722	548	248.0	406	48.8	660	7102	2261	1023.0	1676	201.2
170	1829	582	263.5	432	51.8	670	7209	2295	1038.5	1702	204.2
180	1937	617	279.0	457	54.9	680	7317	2330	1054.0	1727	207.3
190	2044	651	294.5	483	57.9	690	7424	2364	1069.5	1753	210.3
200	2152	685	310.0	508	61.0	700	7532	2398	1085.0	1778	213.4
210	2260	719	325.5	533	64.0	710	7640	2432	1100.5	1803	216.4
220	2367	754	341.0	559	67.1	720	7747	2467	1116.0	1829	219.5
230	2475	788	356.5	584	70.1	730	7855	2501	1131.5	1854	222.5
240	2582	822	372.0	610	73.2	740	7962	2535	1147.0	1880	225.6
250	2690	857	387.5	635	76.2	750	8070	2570	1162.5	1905	228.6
260	2798	891	403.0	660	79.2	760	8178	2604	1178.0	1930	231.6
270	2905	925	418.5	686	82.3	770	8285	2638	1193.5	1956	234.7
280	3013	959	434.0	711	85.3	780	8393	2672	1209.0	1981	237.7
290	3120	994	449.5	737	88.4	790	8500	2702	1224.5	2007	240.8
300	3228	1028	465.0	762	91.4	800	8608	2741	1240.0	2032	243.8
310	3336	1062	480.5	787	94.5	810	8716	2775	1255.5	2057	246.9
320	3443	1096	496.0	813	97.5	820	8823	2809	1271.0	2083	249.9
330	3551	1131	511.5	838	100.6	830	8931	2844	1286.5	2108	253.0
340	3658	1165	527.0	864	103.6	840	9038	2878	1302.0	2134	256.0
350	3766	1199	542.5	889	106.7	850	9146	2912	1317.5	2159	259.1
360	3874	1233	558.0	914	109.7	860	9254	2946	1333.0	2184	262.1
370	3981	1268	573.5	940	112.8	870	9361	2981	1348.5	2210	265.2
380	4089	1302	589.0	965	115.8	880	9469	3015	1364.0	2235	268.2
390	4196	1336	604.5	991	118.9	890	9576	3049	1379.5	2261	271.3
400	4304	1370	620.0	1016	121.9	900	9684	3083	1395.0	2286	274.3
410	4412	1405	635.5	1041	125.0	910	9792	3118	1410.5	2311	277.4
420	4519	1439	651.0	1067	128.0	920	9899	3152	1426.0	2337	280.4
430	4627	1473	666.5	1092	131.1	930	10010	3186	1441.5	2362	283.5
440	4734	1507	682.0	1118	134.1	940	10110	3220	1457.0	2388	286.6
450	4842	1542	697.5	1143	137.2	950	10220	3255	1472.5	2413	289.6
460	4950	1576	713.0	1168	140.2	960	10330	3289	1488.0	2438	292.6
470	5057	1610	728.5	1194	143.3	970	10440	3323	1503.5	2464	295.7
480	5165	1644	744.0	1219	146.3	980	10540	3357	1519.0	2489	298.7
490	5272	1679	759.5	1245	149.4	990	10650	3392	1534.5	2515	301.8

* Also useful for converting from m² to ft²

Appendix Fig. 6. Luminance Conversion Factors

1 nit = 1 candela/square meter
1 stilb = 1 candela/square centimeter
1 apostilb (international) = 0.1 millilambert = 1 blondel
1 apostilb (German Hefner) = 0.09 millilambert
1 lambert = 1000 millilamberts

Multiply Number of → To Obtain Number of ↓	Footlambert*	Candela/ square meter	Millilambert*	Candela/ square inch	Candela/ square foot	Stilb
Footlambert*	1	0.2919	0.929	452	3.142	2,919
Candela/square meter	3.426	1	3.183	1,550	10.76	10,000
Millilambert*	1.076	0.3142	1	487	3.382	3,142
Candela/square inch	0.00221	0.000645	0.00205	1	0.00694	6.45
Candela/square foot	0.3183	0.0929	0.2957	144	1	929
Stilb	0.00034	0.0001	0.00032	0.155	0.00108	1

* Deprecated unit of luminance.

Appendix Fig. 7. Illuminance Conversion Factors

1 lumen = 1/683 light-watt
1 lumen-hour = 60 lumen-minutes
1 footcandle = 1 lumen/square foot
1 watt-second = 10^7 ergs
1 phot = 1 lumen/square centimeter
1 lux = 1 lumen/square meter = 1 metercandle

Multiply Number of → To Obtain Number of ↓	Foot- candles	Lux	Phot	Milliphot
Footcandles	1	0.0929	929	0.929
Lux	10.76	1	10,000	10
Phot	0.00108	0.0001	1	0.001
Milliphot	1.076	0.1	1,000	1

Appendix Fig. 8. Angular Measure, Temperature, Power and Pressure Conversion Equations

Angle
1 radian = 57.29578 degrees
Temperature
(F to C) $C = 5/9 (F - 32)$
(C to F) $F = 9/5\ C + 32$
(C to K) $K = C + 273$
Power
1 kilowatt = 1.341 horsepower
= 56.89 Btu per minute
Pressure
1 atmosphere = 760 millimeters of mercury at 0°C
= 29.92 inches of mercury at 0°C
= 14.7 pounds per square inch
= 101.3 kilopascals

Appendix Fig. 9. Greek Alphabet (Capital and Lowercase)

Capital	Lower Case	Greek Name
A	α	Alpha
B	β	Beta
Γ	γ	Gamma
Δ	δ	Delta
E	ϵ	Epsilon
Z	ζ	Zeta
H	η	Eta
Θ	θ	Theta
I	ι	Iota
K	κ	Kappa
Λ	λ	Lambda
M	μ	Mu
N	ν	Nu
Ξ	ξ	Xi
O	o	Omicron
Π	π	Pi
P	ρ	Rho
Σ	σ, s	Sigma
T	τ	Tau
Υ	υ	Upsilon
Φ	φ, ϕ	Phi
X	χ	Chi
Ψ	ψ	Psi
Ω	ω	Omega

Appendix Fig. 10. Unit Prefixes

Prefix	Symbol	Factor by Which the Unit is Multiplied
exa	E	$1,000,000,000,000,000,000 = 10^{18}$
peta	P	$1,000,000,000,000,000 = 10^{15}$
tera	T	$1,000,000,000,000 = 10^{12}$
giga	G	$1,000,000,000 = 10^{9}$
mega	M	$1,000,000 = 10^{6}$
kilo	k	$1,000 = 10^{3}$
hecto	h	$100 = 10^{2}$
deka	da	$10 = 10^{1}$
deci	d	$0.1 = 10^{-1}$
centi	c	$0.01 = 10^{-2}$
milli	m	$0.001 = 10^{-3}$
micro	μ	$0.000,001 = 10^{-6}$
nano	n	$0.000,000,001 = 10^{-9}$
pico	p	$0.000,000,000,001 = 10^{-12}$
femto	f	$0.000,000,000,000,001 = 10^{-15}$
atto	a	$0.000,000,000,000,000,001 = 10^{-18}$

Appendix Fig. 11. Base Luminaire Symbols

LUMINAIRE; POINT SOURCE SURFACE MOUNTED, (DRAWN TO SCALE OR LARGE ENOUGH FOR CLARITY)

LUMINAIRE; EXTENDED SOURCE, SURFACE MOUNTED (DRAWN TO SCALE)

LUMINAIRE; STRIP TYPE (LENGTH DRAWN TO SCALE)

LUMINAIRE; FLOOD TYPE

LINEAR SOURCE; i.e. LOW VOLTAGE STRIP, NEON, FIBER OPTIC, ETC. (LENGTH DRAWN TO SCALE)

EXIT SIGN; MOUNTING, # OF FACES AND ARROWS AS SHOWN

Appendix Fig. 12. Base Luminaire Symbol Modifiers

OR RECESSED

OR WALL MOUNTED

OR PENDANT, CHAIN OR STEM MOUNTED

OR POLE MOUNTED WITH ARM

OR POLE MOUNTED ON TOP

OR ACCENT/DIRECTIONAL ARROW (DRAWN FROM PHOTOMETRIC CENTER IN DIRECTION OF OPTICS OR PHOTOMETRIC ORIENTATION)

DIRECTIONAL AIMING LINE (DRAWN FROM PHOTOMETRIC CENTER TO ACTUAL AIMING POINT)

TRACK MOUNTED; LENGTH, LUMINAIRE TYPES AND QUANTITIES AS SHOWN (TRACK LENGTH DRAWN TO SCALE)

OR LUMINAIRE PROVIDING EMERGENCY ILLUMINATION (FILLED IN)

NOTE: MODIFIERS ARE SHOWN WITH SPECIFIC BASE SYMBOLS FOR CLARITY. EACH MODIFIER CAN BE USED WITH ANY OF THE BASE SYMBOLS.

Appendix Fig. 13. Optional Luminaire Symbol Modifiers

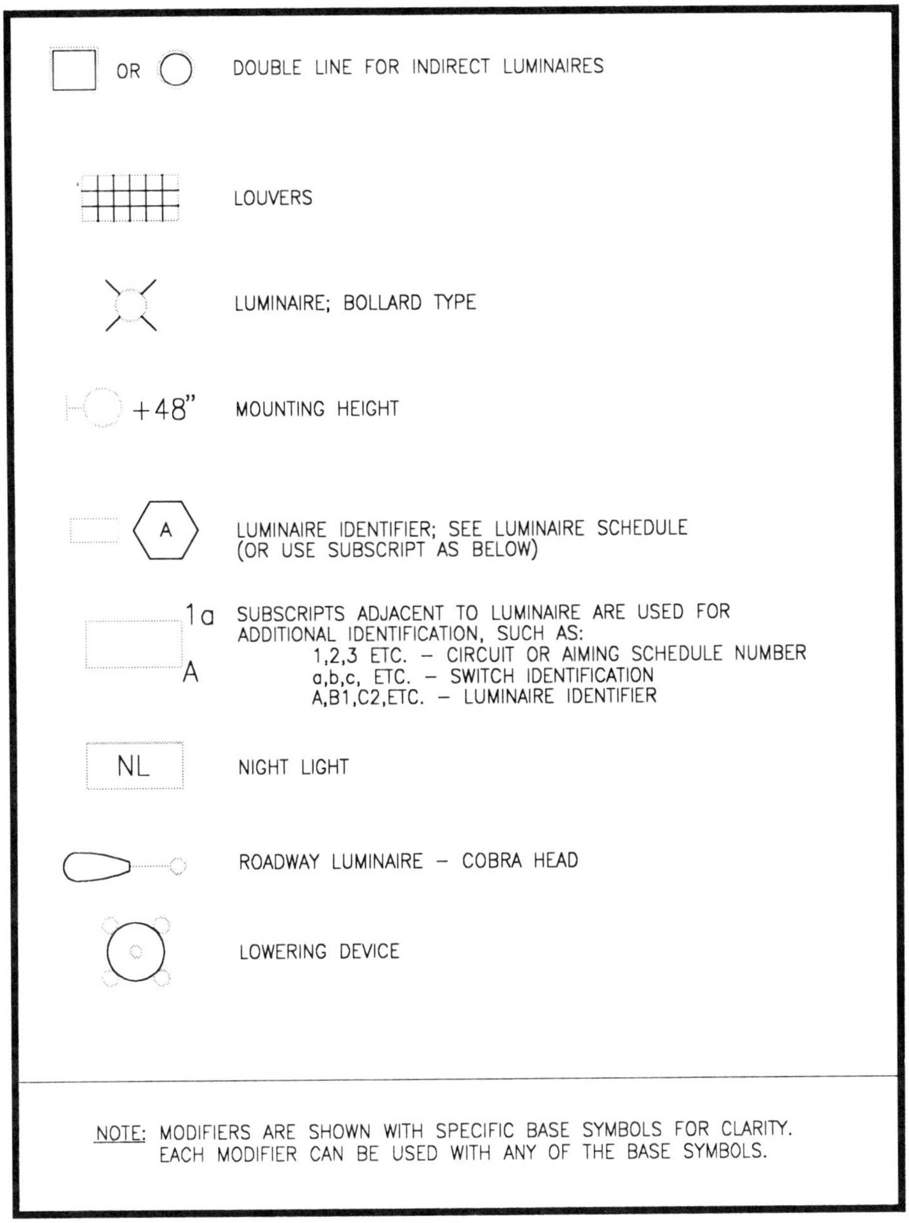

DOUBLE LINE FOR INDIRECT LUMINAIRES

LOUVERS

LUMINAIRE; BOLLARD TYPE

+48" MOUNTING HEIGHT

LUMINAIRE IDENTIFIER; SEE LUMINAIRE SCHEDULE
(OR USE SUBSCRIPT AS BELOW)

1a   SUBSCRIPTS ADJACENT TO LUMINAIRE ARE USED FOR
ADDITIONAL IDENTIFICATION, SUCH AS:
     1,2,3 ETC. — CIRCUIT OR AIMING SCHEDULE NUMBER
A   a,b,c, ETC. — SWITCH IDENTIFICATION
     A,B1,C2,ETC. — LUMINAIRE IDENTIFIER

NL   NIGHT LIGHT

ROADWAY LUMINAIRE — COBRA HEAD

LOWERING DEVICE

NOTE: MODIFIERS ARE SHOWN WITH SPECIFIC BASE SYMBOLS FOR CLARITY.
EACH MODIFIER CAN BE USED WITH ANY OF THE BASE SYMBOLS.

Appendix Fig. 14. Sample Luminaire Symbols

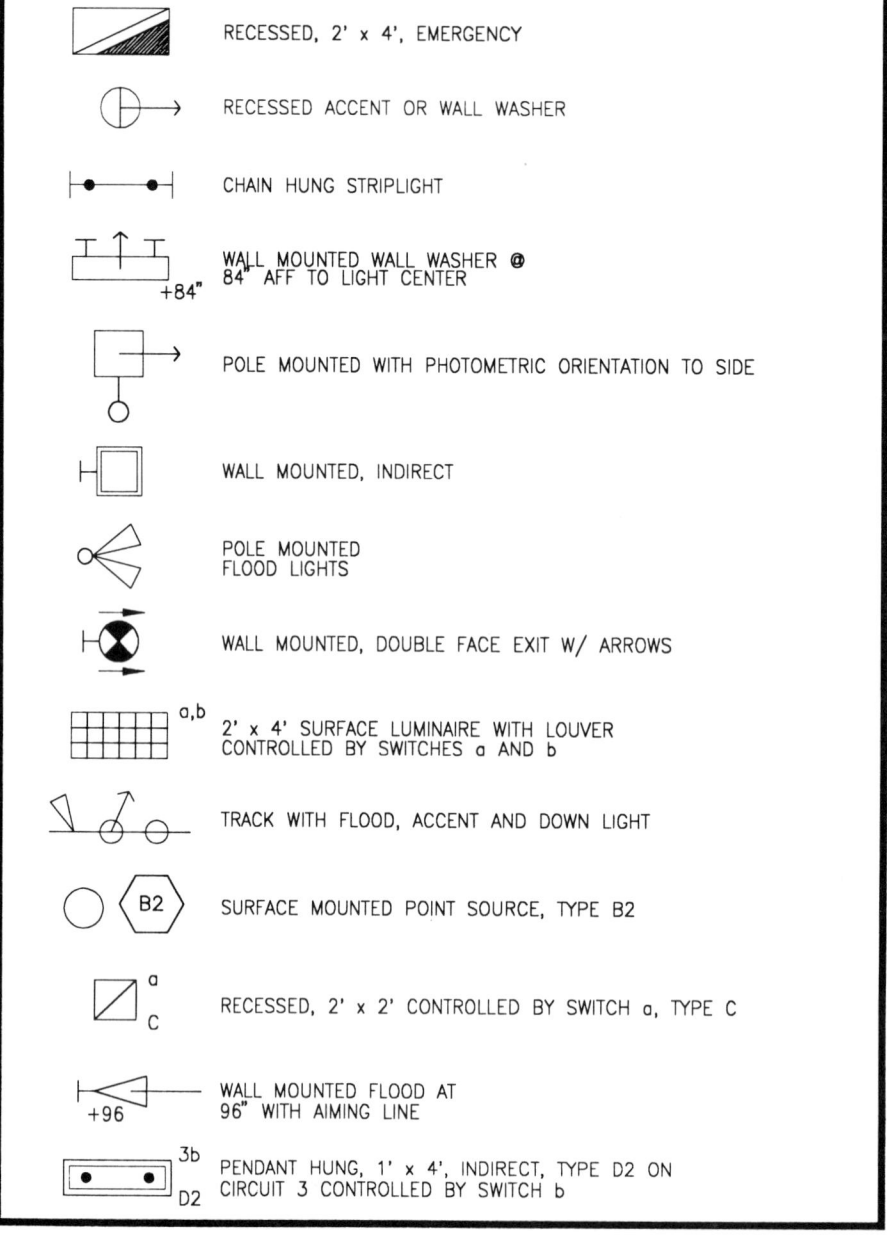

RECESSED, 2' x 4', EMERGENCY

RECESSED ACCENT OR WALL WASHER

CHAIN HUNG STRIPLIGHT

WALL MOUNTED WALL WASHER @
84" AFF TO LIGHT CENTER

POLE MOUNTED WITH PHOTOMETRIC ORIENTATION TO SIDE

WALL MOUNTED, INDIRECT

POLE MOUNTED
FLOOD LIGHTS

WALL MOUNTED, DOUBLE FACE EXIT W/ ARROWS

2' x 4' SURFACE LUMINAIRE WITH LOUVER
CONTROLLED BY SWITCHES a AND b

TRACK WITH FLOOD, ACCENT AND DOWN LIGHT

SURFACE MOUNTED POINT SOURCE, TYPE B2

RECESSED, 2' x 2' CONTROLLED BY SWITCH a, TYPE C

WALL MOUNTED FLOOD AT
96" WITH AIMING LINE

PENDANT HUNG, 1' x 4', INDIRECT, TYPE D2 ON
CIRCUIT 3 CONTROLLED BY SWITCH b

Credits

Listed below are credits for the new line art and photographs selected for this eighth edition of the IESNA's *Lighting Handbook*:

Chapter 3, Vision and Perception

Fig. 3-2, adapted from Boettner, E. A. and J. R. Walter. 1962. Transmission of the ocular media. *Invest. Ophthalmol.* 1:776.

Fig. 3-3, adapted from Coren, S. and J. S. Girgus. 1972. Density of human lens pigmentation: In vivo measures over an extended age range [Letter]. *Vision Res.* 12(2):343-346.

Fig. 3-5, adapted from Sekuler, R. and R. Blake. 1990. *Perception*. New York: McGraw-Hill, Inc.

Fig. 3-6, adapted from Ludvigh, E. and J. W. Miller. 1958. Study of visual acuity during the ocular pursuit of moving test objects, I. Introduction. *J. Opt. Soc. Am.* 48:799.

Fig. 3-7, adapted from Pierenne, M. H. 1967. *Vision and the Eye*, 2nd ed. London: Chapman and Hall, Ltd.

Fig. 3-9, adapted from Smith, V. C. and J. Pokorny. 1975. Spectral sensitivity of the foveal cone photopigments between 400 and 500 nm. *Vision Res.* 15:161.

Fig. 3-10, adapted from Hecht, S. and J. Mandelbaum. 1939. The relation between vitamin A and dark adaptation. *J. Am. Med. Assoc.* 112:1910.

Fig. 3-11, adapted from Miller, J. W. 1958. Study of visual acuity during the ocular pursuit of moving test objects, II. Effects of direction of movement, relative movement and illumination. *J. Opt. Soc. Am.* 48:803.

Fig. 3-16, adapted from Ingling, C. R. 1978. Luminance and opponent color contributions to visual detection and to temporal and spatial integration: Comment. *J. Opt. Soc. Am.* 68(8):1143.

Fig. 3-21, adapted from Ivanoff, A. 1956. About spherical aberration of the eye. *J. Opt. Soc. Am.* 46(10):901–903.

Fig. 3-22, adapted from Holladay, L. L. 1926. Fundamentals of glare and visibility. *J. Opt. Soc. Am.* 12(4):271–319.

Fig. 3-29, adapted from Rea, M. S. 1991. Technics: Solving the problem of VDT reflections. *Prog. Arch.* (October):35.

Fig. 3-32, adapted from Blackwell, H. R. 1946. Contrast thresholds of the human eye. *J. Opt. Soc. Am.* 36(11):624–643; Graham, C. H. and E. H. Kemp. 1938. Brightness discrimination as a function of the duration of the increment in intensity. *J. Gen. Physiol.* 21:635–650; Graham, C. H. and N. R. Bartlett. 1940. The relative size of stimulus and intensity in the human eye, part III. *J. Exp. Psychol.* 27:149–159; and Rea, M. S. and M. J. Ouellette. 1988. Visual performance using reaction times. *Light. Res. Tech.* 20(4)139–153.

Fig. 3-34, adapted from Baron, W. S. and G. Westheimer. 1973. Visual acuity as a function of exposure duration. *J. Opt. Soc. Am.* 63:212.

Fig. 3-35, adapted from Lythgoe, R. J. 1932. *The measurement of visual acuity*. Medical Research Council Special Report No. 173. London: H. M. Stationery Office.

Fig. 3-36, adapted from Sperling, H. G. and C. L. Jolliffe. 1965. Intensity time relationship at threshold for spectral stimuli in human vision. *J. Opt. Soc. Am.* 55:191.

Fig. 3-37, adapted from Hecht, S. and E. L. Smith. 1936. Intermittent stimulation by light, V. The relation between intensity and critical frequency for different parts of the spectrum. *J. Gen. Physiol.* 19:979.

Fig. 3-38, adapted from Kelly, D. H. 1969. Flickering patterns and lateral inhibition. *J. Opt. Soc. Am.* 59(10):1361–1370.

Fig. 3-39, adapted from Campbell, F. W. and J. G. Robson. 1968. Application of Fourier analysis to the visibility of gratings. *J. Physiol.* 197(3):551–566.

Fig. 3-40, adapted from van der Wildt, G. J. and J. P. Rijsdijk. 1979. Flicker sensitivity measured with intermittent stimuli, I. Influence of the stimulus duration on the flicker threshold. *J. Opt. Soc. Am.* 69(5):660–665.

Fig. 3-41, adapted from McCann, J. J. and J. A. Hall, Jr. 1980. Effects of average-luminance surrounds on the visibility of sine-wave gratings. *J. Opt. Soc. Am.* 70(2):212–219.

Fig. 3-42, adapted from Weston, H. C. 1945. *The relation between illumination and visual efficiency: The effect of size of work*. Prepared for Industrial Health Research Board (Great Britain) and Medical Research Council (London). London: H. M. Stationery Office.

Fig. 3-43, adapted from Rea, M. S. and M. J. Ouellette. 1991. Relative visual performance: A basis for application. *Light. Res. Tech.* 23(3):135–144.

Fig. 3-50, adapted from Boyce, P. R. 1981. *Human Factors*. New York: Macmillan.

Chapter 4, Color

Fig. 4-6, adapted from Commission Internationale de l'Eclairage. 1978. *Recommendations on uniform color spaces, color-difference equations and psychometric color terms*. CIE Publication No. 15, Supp. 2. Paris: Bureau Central de la CIE.

Fig. 4-11, adapted from Kelly, K. L. 1963. Lines of constant correlated color temperature based on MacAdam's (u, v) uniform chromaticity transformation of the CIE diagram. *J. Opt. Soc. Am.* 58(11):1528–1535.

Fig. 4-15, adapted from Brainerd, A. A. and R. A. Massey. 1942. Salvaging waste light for victory. *Illum. Eng.* 37:738.

Chapter 5, Nonvisual Effects of Radiant Energy

Fig. 5-6, adapted from Sliney, D. H. and M. Wolbarsht. 1980. *Safety with lasers and other optical sources*. New York: Plenum.

Fig. 5-12, adapted from the *New York Times* Science Section.

Fig. 5-13, adapted from Sisson, T. R. C. 1976. Visible light therapy of neonatal hyperbilirubinemia. In *Photochemical and photobiological reviews*, vol. 1, chapter 6. K. C. Smith, ed. New York: Plenum.

Fig. 5-15, adapted from Coblentz, W. W. and R. Stair. 1934. Data on the spectral erythemic reaction of the untanned human skin to ultraviolet radiation. *Bur. Stand. (U.S.) J. Res.* 12(1):13–14.

Fig. 5-21, adapted from Sager, J. C., O. W. Smith, J. L. Edwards and K. L. Cyr. 1988. Photosynthetic efficiency and phytochrome photoequilibria determination using spectral data. *Trans. ASAE* 31(6):1882–1889.

Chapter 6, Light Sources

Fig. 6-7, GE Lighting.

Fig. 6-23, Philips Lighting.

Fig. 6-29, adapted from Lowry, E. F., W. S. Frohock and G. A. Meyers. 1946. Some fluorescent lamp parameters and their effect on lamp performances. *Illum. Eng.* 41:859.

Fig. 6-36, *Specifier Reports: Power Reducers*, National Lighting Product Information Program, Lighting Research Center.

Fig. 6-45, Leviton Manufacturing Company, Incorporated.

Fig. 6-39, *Specifier Reports: Electronic Ballasts*, National Lighting Product Information Program, Lighting Research Center.

Chapter 9, Lighting Calculations

Fig. 9-10, adapted from Clark, F. 1963. Accurate maintenance factors. *Illum. Eng.* 58:124 and Clark, F. 1966. Accurate maintenance factors, part two. *Illum. Eng.* 61:37.

Chapter 15, Office Lighting

Fig. 15-3, Lighting Research Center.
Fig. 15-6, IESNA, RP-24.
Fig. 15-7, IESNA, RP-24.
Fig. 15-10, IESNA, RP-1.
Fig. 15-11, IESNA, RP-1.

Chapter 16, Educational Facilities Lighting

Fig. 16-3, Litecontrol.
Fig. 16-4, Litecontrol.
Fig. 16-5, Litecontrol.

Chapter 17, Institutions and Public Building Lighting

Fig. 17-3, Lighting Design: Hyman M. Kaplan, Belden Incorporated. Photographer: Jane Lidz.

Fig. 17-7, left and right, Genlyte.

Fig. 17-8, Litecontrol.

Fig. 17-12, Kaiser Hospital, Fresno, CA. Architects: The Ratcliff Architects and Ove Arup. Lighting design: Naomi Miller. Photographer: Jane Lidz.

Fig. 17-14, Litecontrol.

Fig. 17-15, Clovis Hospital, Fresno, CA. Architects: Anshen and Allen. Photographer: Jane Lidz.

Fig. 17-25, Public Library, Vancouver, British Columbia, Lighting design: Shail Mahanti, Mahanti Engineering, Vancouver, BC.

Fig. 17-26, Litecontrol.

Fig. 17-29, Sculpture: Alan Houser, Los Angeles County Museum of Natural History. Lighting Design: Daniel B. Howell, Los Angeles, CA. Photographer: Daniel B. Howell.

Fig. 17-32, Sculpture: Alan Houser, Los Angeles County Museum of Natural History. Lighting Design: Daniel B. Howell, Los Angeles, CA. Photographer: Daniel B. Howell.

Plate 1, IESNA RP-25.

Plate 2, Mid-American Bank, *LD + A*, October 1991. Lighting design: Mitchell Kohn, Highland Park, IL.

Plate 3, Delta Crown Room, Greater Cincinnati International Airport, *LD + A*, August 1990. Lighting design: Carrie Welker, W. L. Thompson Consulting Engineers, Inc., Atlanta, GA. Interior design: Brenda Marsh, THW Interior Design. Photographer: E. Alan Magee.

Plate 4, O'Hare Airport, pedestrian walkway, *LD + A*, September 1989. Lighting design: Sylvan R. Shemitz Associates, Inc., West Haven, CT. Photographer: Jamie Pagett, Karant & Associates.

Plate 5, Temple Emanu-El, San Francisco, CA, *LD + A*, October 1991. Lighting Design: S. Leonard Auerbach and Larry French, S. Leonard Auerbach and Associates, San Francisco, CA. Photographer: Bob Swanson.

Plate 6, Hilton Hotel, Lexington, KY, *LD + A*, August 1988. Lighting design: Chicago Design Associates, Chicago, IL.

Plate 7, Hilton Hotel, Honolulu, HI. Lighting Design: Grenald Associates, Narberth, PA.

Plate 8, Brandy Ho, San Francisco, CA. John Goldman Architects, San Francisco, CA. Photographer: Jane Lidz.

Chapter 18, Lighting for Merchandising

Fig. 18-7, *LD + A*, August 1989, Tip-Toe Shoe Store. Lighting design: Steven Brasier, Design Forum, Inc., Dayton, Ohio. Photographer: Andy Snow.

Color plate 2, Steuben Glass. Lighting design: Grenald Associates, Narberth, PA.

Color plate 3, *LD + A*, August 1988, Ralph Lauren Polo Store. Lighting design: Craig Roberts and Barbara Bouyea, Architectural Lighting Design, Inc., Dallas, TX. Photographer: Francois Halard, Jean Gabriel Kauss, Inc.

Color plate 4, *LD + A*, May 1990, Shop-Rite Supermarket. Lighting design: Barbra Barker and Linda Anderson, Off-the-Wall, Telford, PA. Photographer: Bob Hahn.

Color plates 5 and 6, *LD + A*, August 1989, 6th Street Market Place. Lighting design: Stefan Graf, Illuminart, Ypsilanti, MI. Photographer: Whitney Cox.

Color plate 7, Moorestown Mall. Lighting design: Grenald Associates, Narberth, PA.

Color plate 8, LA Entertainment. Lighting design: Grenald Associates, Narberth, PA.

Chapter 19, Residential Lighting

Fig. 19-3, Interior design: Estelle Alpert, F.A.S.I.D.. Lighting consultant: Sunny St. Pierre. Photographer: Jane Lidz.

Fig. 19-4, Interior design: Sandra Chandler. Photographer: Jane Lidz.

Fig. 19-5, Lighting design: Grenald Associates, Narberth, PA.

Fig. 19-24, Lighting Design: Julia Rezek, Lighting Design Alliance, Culver City, CA.

Fig. 19-25, Lighting Design: Grenald Associates, Narberth, PA.

Fig. 19-26, Lighting Design: Donna Bellizi and Don Elliott, South Dade Lighting, Miami, FL. Photographer: Don Elliott.

Chapter 20, Industrial Lighting

Fig. 20-5, GE Lighting.
Fig. 20-6, GE Lighting.
Fig. 20-8, GE Lighting.
Fig. 20-10, David Castle, ea Technology.
Fig. 20-13, GE Lighting.
Fig. 20-17, Mark S. Rea.
Fig. 20-23, GE Lighting.

Chapter 22, Exterior Lighting

Fig. 22-2, Clanton Engineering, Inc., Boulder, CO.

Fig. 22-3, Cincinnati City Hall, *LD + A*, April 1989. Lighting Design: Joseph Oppold, KZF Inc., Cincinnati, OH. Photographer: Jeff Friedman.

Fig. 22-4, Aerial Lift Bridge, *LD + A*, April 1989. Lighting Design: John Kennedy, GE Lighting, Cleveland, OH. Photographer: Tim Slattery, Harbor Reflections.

Fig. 22-5, Swann Memorial Fountain, *LD + A*, October 1991, Lighting Design: Donald Nardy and Stephen Nardy, Nardy Lighting Design, Ltd., Philadelphia, PA.

Fig. 22-6, CenTrust Savings Bank. Lighting Design: Douglas Leigh. Photo: GE Lighting.

Fig. 22-7, Statue of Liberty Restoration. Architects: Swanke Hayden Connell Architects, New York, NY. Associate Architects: The Office of Thierry W. Despont, New York, NY. Consultants: H. M. Brandston & Partners Inc., New York, NY. Photo: GE Lighting.

Fig. 22-8, Holiday lights, *LD + A*, March 1988. Lighting Design: Jerry Flagg, MEP Engineers, St. Louis, MO. Photographer: Lewis Portnoy, Spectra-Action Inc.

Fig. 22-9, Terminal Tower. Lighting Design: John Frier, GE Lighting, Hendersonville, NC. Photo: GE Lighting.

Fig. 22-10, Custom House Clock and Tower. *LD + A*, April 1989. Lighting Design: Lam Partners Inc., Boston, MA. Photo: Boston Edison Company.

Fig. 22-11, Mall of the Americas. *LD + A*, February 1991. Lighting Design: Ben Eglin, Miami, FL.

Fig. 22-12, Canadian War Memorial. *LD + A*, October 1991. Lighting Design: Philip Gabriel, Gabriel Design, Ottawa, Ontario, and Martin Conboy, Joseph Johannes Design, Ottawa, Ontario. Photographer: William P. McElligott.

Fig. 22-13, *LD + A*, September 1989, Lighting Design: Donna Bellizi and Don Elliott, South Dade Lighting, Miami, FL. Photographer: Don Elliott.

Fig. 22-14, GE Lighting.

Figs. 22-15 through 22-17, Clanton Engineering, Inc., Boulder, CO.

Chapter 23, Sports Lighting

Fig. 23-6, IESNA RP-6-88.

Chapter 26, Transportation Lighting

Fig. 26-7, Capital District Transportation Authority, Albany, NY.
Fig. 26-8, Capital District Transportation Authority, Albany, NY.
Fig. 26-9, Capital District Transportation Authority, Albany, NY.
Fig. 26-11, Amtrak, Washington, DC.
Fig. 26-12, Amtrak, Washington, DC.

Chapter 28, Underwater Lighting

Fig. 28-2, adapted from Duntley, S. Q. 1963. Light in the sea. *J. Opt. Soc. Am.* 53(2):214–233.

Chapter 29, Lighting for Advertising

Fig. 29-1, New York State Department of Economic Development.
Fig. 29-5, Eric Block.
Fig. 29-7, Eric Block.
Fig. 29-8, left and right, Eric Block.

Chapter 31, Lighting Controls

Fig. 31-4, Lutron Electronics Co., Inc.
Fig. 31-5, Lutron Electronics Co., Inc.
Figs. 31-11 and 31-12, *Specifier Reports: Occupancy Sensors*, National Lighting Product Information Program, Lighting Research Center.

Chapter 32, Lighting Maintenance

Figs. 32-2 through 32-9, interNational Association of Lighting Management Companies.

Chapter 33, Emergency, Safety and Security Lighting

Fig. 33-2, WHB Associates, Incorporated, Cincinnnati, Ohio.
Fig. 33-3, WHB Associates, Incorporated, Cincinnnati, Ohio.
Fig. 33-4, Photographer: Jamie Padgett, Karant & Associates, Inc.
Fig. 33-9, Avenal State Prison, *LD + A*, June 1989, Lighting Design: David G. Komonosky. Photographer: Jerry Losik.
Fig. 33-10, David Castle, ea Technology.
Fig. 33-12, Photographer: Jamie Padgett, Karant & Associates, Inc.

Index

Color temperature *Continued*
Correlated color temperature (determination of), 118, 119
Daylight lamps, 118. *See also* Daylighting
Isotemperature lines (CIE 1931), 119
Mired, 118
And perceived color, 131
Planckian distribution curves, 118, 119
Planckian locus, 118, 119
Preferred (Kruithof Effect), 98–99
Reciprocal color temperature, 118
Tungsten filament lamps, 118
Color vision
Related topics
   Color matching
   Color rendering
   Photopic region
   Psychological effects of illumination
   Retina
   Scotopic region
   Spectral luminous efficiency
   Vision, perceptual
   Vison, physiological
Chromatic contrast, 84
Color appearance (CIE models), 120
Color contrast, 120
Color discrimination (and retinal fields), 76
Colored lights, identification threshold for, 96
Defective, 108
First-order model of, 76
And luminance levels, 27–28
Mesopic region, 28
Photochromatic interval, 96
Photopic region, 9, 28
Scotopic region, 9, 27–28
Small-field tritanopia, 76
And spectral luminous efficiency, 9
Visual clarity, 127
Wavelength discrimination, 76
Colorimeters, 32. *See also* Photometry
Compensatory eye movements, 74
Contrast
Related topics
   Basic lighting calculations
   Glare
   Lighting calculations
   Task lighting
   Vision, perceptual
   Vision, physiological
Balancing for (in television lighting), 704–705
Chromatic contrast, 84
Color contrast, 120
Color schemes (contrast criteria for), 125
Contrast curves (RVP vs. trolands), 92
Contrast detection (frequency of seeing function), 86
Contrast sensitivity function, 89, 90
CRF (Contrast rendering factor), 92
Field size (and contrast sensitivity), 90
In foundries, 655
Luminance contrast, 83
In luminous signs, 840–841
Modulation contrast, 83–84
On printed material (typical calculations), 497–499
In sport and recreational area lighting, 728–729
Task contrast. *See also* Task lighting
   In educational facility lighting, 543–544
   In residential lighting, 610, 622
   vs. Visibility reference function (VL1), 86
Threshold contrast (vs. retinal illuminance), 86

Conventions and trade shows
Lighting of (general), 700
Conversion factors (tables of)
Angular measure, 949
Illuminance, 949
Luminance, 949
Power, 949
Pressure, 949
From SI units, 947
To SI units, 948
Temperature, 949
Unit prefixes, 949
Units of length, 946
Copper
In luminaires, 334
Cornea. *See* Eye, structure of
Corpuscular theory (of light)
defined, 3
Corridors, lighting of, 534
Cosine effect (in photometry), 34–35
Cotton
Standard viewing conditions (USDA), 129
CRF (Contrast rendering factor), 92
CRI (Color rendering index). *See* Color; Color rendering
Critical angle, 19
Crystalline lens (eye), 69, 70
Crystalloluminescence, 15
CSA (Canadian Standards Association)
Standard for lamp-base temperatures, 185
CU (Coefficient of Utilization). *See* Daylighting; Lighting calculations; Luminaires
Cutoff angle. *See under* Luminaires
In parabolic louvers, 528

D

Daylighting. *See also* Lighting calculations; Lighting control strategies; Lighting design process
Color matching
   Preferred daylight illumination (ISCC), 130
Daylight (availability of)
   Introduction, 359–360
   Daylight availability coefficients, 363
   Latitude and longitude (American cities), 361
   Site location, 360–361
Design evaluation
   Computer-based, 369
   Conceptual stage, 368
   During design development, 369
   Manual method, 369
   Scale models, 369
Dirt depreciation
   Sidelighting, 369
   Toplighting, 369, 374
Energy utilization (effects on), 369
Fenestration
   Atria, 371
   Bilateral lighting, 370
   Clerestory, 370
   Coefficient of utilization (sidelighting), 376–378
   Glare, 367
   Light shelves (with windows), 370
   Roof monitors, 370
   Sawtooth, 370
   Skylights, 370–371
   Staggered building sections, 370
   Unilateral sidelighting, 369

View design, 367
Windows (various configurations), 370
Illuminance, solar
   Direct normal (at sea level), 363
   On horizontal plane, 363, 366
   On vertical plane, 363
Illuminance (skylight)
   Horizontal illuminance, calculation of, 364
   Horizontal surface (clear sky), 364, 366
   Horizontal surface (partly cloudy), 364, 367
   Moon-spencer equation, 365
Illuminance (skylight)
   Clear-sky luminance distribution (Kittler, CIE), 364–365
   Cloudy/overcast-sky luminance distributions, 365
   Sky classification (sky cover method), 364
   Sky classification (sky ratio method), 363
   Vertical surface (clear sky), 365, 366
   Vertical surface (partly cloudy), 365, 366
   Zenith luminance factor, 364
Interior illuminance, calculation of
   Coefficients of utilization (sidelighting), 376–378
   Coefficients of utilization (toplighting), 374
   Computer calculation of, 372
   Light wells (efficiency factors for), 374
   Light wells (reflective loss and interreflections), 374
   Lumen method (basic), 372–373
   Room cavity ratio (toplighting), 375
   Sidelighting (lumen method, clear windows), 375–378
   Sidelighting (lumen method, diffuse windows), 378
   Toplighting, doming effect, 373–374
   Toplighting (lumen method, clear day), 373
   Toplighting (lumen method, overcast day), 375
   Well cavity ratio (toplighting), 374
Interior illuminance, measurement of
   Introduction to, 378
   Calibrated video cameras, 378
   Daylight factor (CIE), 379
   Photocell leveling, 378
   Photocell size, 378
   Sensor placement, 378
   Space contents (effects of), 378
Materials and control elements
   Diffusing materials, 371
   Directional transmitting materials, 371
   Electrically-controlled glazing, 371
   High-reflectance materials, 371
   Landscaping, 372
   Louvers, 371–372
   Reflecting elements, 372
   Shades and draperies, 371
   Specularly selective transmitting materials, 371
   Superglazings, 372
   Transmittance data, glass and plastics (table), 371
   Transparent materials, 371
Merchandising areas (interior malls), 602
In merchandising lighting, 592–593
And office lighting, 520
Photoelectric lighting control, 369
Sky conditions (measurement of), 379
Solar position
   Incident angle, 362
   Profile angle, 362
   Solar altitude, 360, 361–362
   Solar azimuth, 360, 362
   Solar declination, 361
   Solar elevation-azimuth, 362